■ THE RESOURCE FOR THE INDEPENDENT TRAVELER

"The guides are aimed not only at young budget travelers but at the indepedent traveler; a sort of streetwise cookbook for traveling alone."

—*The New York Times*

"Unbeatable; good sight-seeing advice; up-to-date info on restaurants, hotels, and inns; a commitment to money-saving travel; and a wry style that brightens nearly every page."

—*The Washington Post*

"Lighthearted and sophisticated, informative and fun to read. [Let's Go] helps the novice traveler navigate like a knowledgeable old hand."

—*Atlanta Journal-Constitution*

"A world-wise traveling companion—always ready with friendly advice and helpful hints, all sprinkled with a bit of wit."

—*The Philadelphia Inquirer*

■ THE BEST TRAVEL BARGAINS IN YOUR PRICE RANGE

"All the dirt, dirt cheap."

—*People*

"Anything you need to know about budget traveling is detailed in this book."

—*The Chicago Sun-Times*

"Let's Go follows the creed that you don't have to toss your life's savings to the wind to travel—unless you want to."

—*The Salt Lake Tribune*

■ REAL ADVICE FOR REAL EXPERIENCES

"The writers seem to have experienced every rooster-packed bus and lunar-surfaced mattress about which they write."

—*The New York Times*

"A guide should tell you what to expect from a destination. Here Let's Go shines."

—*The Chicago Tribune*

LET'S GO PUBLICATIONS

TRAVEL GUIDES

Alaska & the Pacific Northwest 2003
Australia 2003
Austria & Switzerland 2003
Britain & Ireland 2003
California 2003
Central America 8th edition
Chile 1st edition **NEW TITLE**
China 4th edition
Costa Rica 1st edition **NEW TITLE**
Eastern Europe 2003
Egypt 2nd edition
Europe 2003
France 2003
Germany 2003
Greece 2003
Hawaii 2003 **NEW TITLE**
India & Nepal 7th edition
Ireland 2003
Israel 4th edition
Italy 2003
Mexico 19th edition
Middle East 4th edition
New Zealand 6th edition
Peru, Ecuador & Bolivia 3rd edition
South Africa 5th edition
Southeast Asia 8th edition
Southwest USA 2003
Spain & Portugal 2003
Thailand 1st edition **NEW TITLE**
Turkey 5th edition
USA 2003
Western Europe 2003

CITY GUIDES

Amsterdam 2003
Barcelona 2003
Boston 2003
London 2003
New York City 2003
Paris 2003
Rome 2003
San Francisco 2003
Washington, D.C. 2003

MAP GUIDES

Amsterdam
Berlin
Boston
Chicago
Dublin
Florence
Hong Kong
London
Los Angeles
Madrid
New Orleans
New York City
Paris
Prague
Rome
San Francisco
Seattle
Sydney
Venice
Washington, D.C.

SOUTHEAST ASIA

Kate Greer Editor
Nina Jacobi Editor
Emma Nothmann Editor
Lauren Bonner Associate Editor
Jay Pendse Associate Editor

Researcher-Writers

William Lee Adams
Anthony Barker
Nick Grossman
Paul Guilianelli
Tomohiro Hamakawa
Basil Lee
Stefanie Levner
Nina Singh
Gabe Struck
Kristina Vetter
Paul Warham
Annie Wong

Yaw D.K. Osseo-Asare Map Editor
Amélie Cherlin Managing Editor
Ariel Benjamin Ergas Shwayder Typesetter

Macmillan

HELPING LET'S GO If you want to share your discoveries, suggestions, or corrections, please drop us a line. We read every piece of correspondence, whether a postcard, a 10-page email, or a coconut. Please note that mail received after May 2003 may be too late for the 2004 book, but will be kept for future editions. **Address mail to:**

Let's Go: Southeast Asia
67 Mount Auburn Street
Cambridge, MA 02138
USA

Visit Let's Go at **http://www.letsgo.com,** or send email to:

feedback@letsgo.com
Subject: "Let's Go: Southeast Asia"

In addition to the invaluable travel advice our readers share with us, many are kind enough to offer their services as researchers or editors. Unfortunately, our charter enables us to employ only currently enrolled Harvard students.

Published in Great Britain 2003 by Macmillan, an imprint of Pan Macmillan Ltd.
20 New Wharf Road, London N1 9RR
Basingstoke and Oxford
Associated companies throughout the world
www.panmacmillan.com

Published in the United States of America by St. Martin's Press.

ISBN: 1-4050-0079 1
First edition
10 9 8 7 6 5 4 3 2 1

Let's Go: Southeast Asia is written by Let's Go Publications, 67 Mount Auburn Street, Cambridge, MA 02138, USA.

ADVERTISING DISCLAIMER All advertisements appearing in Let's Go publications are sold by an independent agency not affiliated with the editorial production of the guides. Advertisers are never given preferential treatment, and the guides are researched, written, and published independent of advertising. Advertisements do not imply endorsement of products or services by Let's Go, and Let's Go does not vouch for the accuracy of information provided in advertisements.

If you are interested in purchasing advertising space in a Let's Go publication, contact: Let's Go Advertising Sales, 67 Mount Auburn St., Cambridge, MA 02138, USA.

HOW TO USE THIS BOOK

Southeast Asia is a land of tradition and flux, so be prepared to experience and enjoy both. *Let's Go* lists thousand-year-old temples that will still be around when you get there and two-year-old guest houses that will have bitten the proverbial dust before these pages go to press. Let these pages and your instinct be your guides and trust no other.

ORGANIZATION OF THIS BOOK

INTRODUCTORY MATERIAL. The first chapter, **Discover Southeast Asia,** provides an overview of travel in the region. The **suggested itineraries** give an idea of the places you shouldn't miss and how long it takes to see them. The **Essentials** section outlines practical information—bureaucratic formalities, health and safety concerns, and transport information—that you'll need both before you leave and once you're there. The new **Alternatives to Tourism** section lists opportunities to study, work, and volunteer in Southeast Asia.

COVERAGE. Each chapter covers a country, beginning with Cambodia and tracing the alphabet to Vietnam. Each chapter's **Life and Times** section outlines country-specific history, culture, and practical information. The **black tabs** in the margins—and knowing that "V" comes after "M"—will help you to navigate between chapters quickly and easily.

APPENDIX. The appendix has useful **conversions,** a **phrasebook,** a **map** to decode Southeast Asia's bizarre time zones, and a **climate** chart.

A FEW NOTES ABOUT LET'S GO FORMAT

RANKING ESTABLISHMENTS. In each section, we rank establishments, starting with our favorites. Our absolute favorites are so denoted by *Let's Go*'s highest honor, the *Let's Go* thumbs-up (■). With each accommodation and food listing, you'll find an icon indicating a price range. An explanation of the price ranges is at the start of the Essentials section in each chapter.

GRAYBOXES AND IKONBOXES. Grayboxes and **sidebars** provide wonderful cultural insights but, once in a while, are simply expressions of our bizarre sense of humor. In any case, they're usually amusing, so enjoy. **Whiteboxes,** on the other hand, provide important practical information, such as warnings (■), helpful hints and resources (■), and border crossing information (■).

OUR QUIRKS. Southeast Asia has more islands than Imelda Marcos has shoes (see p. 569). To give you island-hopping ideas, **View from Above** boxes summarize the highlights of major islands. Additionally, refer to p. 488 for a note on our coverage of Myanmar, and note that **HCMC** and **KL** are used in place of Ho Chi Minh City and Kuala Lumpur..

A NOTE TO OUR READERS The information for this book was gathered by *Let's Go* researchers from May through August of 2002. Each listing is based on one researcher's opinion, formed during his or her visit at a particular time. Those traveling at other times may have different experiences since prices, dates, hours, and conditions are always subject to change. You are urged to check the facts presented in this book beforehand to avoid inconvenience and surprises.

CONTENTS

WHO WE ARE

A NEW LET'S GO

With a sleeker look and innovative new content, we have revamped the entire series to reflect more than ever the needs and interests of the independent traveler. Here are just some of the improvements you will notice when traveling with the new *Let's Go*.

MORE PRICE OPTIONS

Still the best resource for budget travelers, *Let's Go* recognizes that everyone needs the occassional indulgence. Our "Big Splurges" indicate establishments that are actually worth those extra pennies (pulas, pesos, or pounds), and price-level symbols (❶ ❷ ❸ ❹ ❺) allow you to quickly determine whether an accommodation or restaurant will break the bank. We may have diversified, but we'll never lose our budget focus—"Hidden Deals" reveal the best-kept travel secrets.

BEYOND THE TOURIST EXPERIENCE

Our Alternatives to Tourism chapter offers ideas on immersing yourself in a new community through study, work, or volunteering.

AN INSIDER'S PERSPECTIVE

As always, every item is written and researched by our on-site writers. This year we have highlighted more viewpoints to help you gain an even more thorough understanding of the places you are visiting.

IN RECENT NEWS. *Let's Go* correspondents around the globe report back on current regional issues that may affect you as a traveler.

CONTRIBUTING WRITERS. Respected scholars and former *Let's Go* writers discuss topics on society and culture, going into greater depth than the usual guidebook summary.

THE LOCAL STORY. From the Parisian monk toting a cell phone to the Russian *babushka* confronting capitalism, *Let's Go* shares its revealing conversations with local personalities—a unique glimpse of what matters to real people.

FROM THE ROAD. Always helpful and sometimes downright hilarious, our researchers share useful insights on the typical (and atypical) travel experience.

SLIMMER SIZE

Don't be fooled by our new, smaller size. *Let's Go* is still packed with invaluable travel advice, but now it's easier to carry with a more compact design.

FORTY-THREE YEARS OF WISDOM

For over four decades *Let's Go* has provided the most up-to-date information on the hippest cafes, the most pristine beaches, and the best routes from border to border. It all started in 1960 when a few well-traveled students at Harvard University handed out a 20-page mimeographed pamphlet of their tips on budget travel to passengers on student charter flights to Europe. From humble beginnings, *Let's Go* has grown to cover six continents and *Let's Go: Europe* still reigns as the world's best-selling travel guide. This year we've beefed up our coverage of Latin America with *Let's Go: Costa Rica* and *Let's Go: Chile;* on the other side of the globe, we've added *Let's Go: Thailand* and *Let's Go: Hawaii.* Our new guides bring the total number of titles to 61, each infused with the spirit of adventure that travelers around the world have come to count on.

CHINA
Guangzhou
MYANMAR
Macau
Kowloon
HONG KONG
Mandalay
Red River
Luang
Prabang
Hanoi
Haiphong
Chiang
Mai
LAOS
Vientiane
Gulf of
Tonkin
Hainan
Island
Yangon
Mekong River
Khon
Kaen
Sukhothai
THAILAND
Hue
Da Nang
Chao Phraya
River
Nakhon
Ratchasima
Andaman
Sea
Ayutthaya
VIETNAM
Bangkok
Siem Reap
CAMBODIA
SOUTH
CHINA
SEA
Phnom Penh
Nha Trang
Ho Chi Minh City
(Saigon)
Gulf of
Thailand
Can Tho
Phuket
Banda
Aceh
Balabac Strait
Kota Bharu
Georgetown
Kota
Kinabalu
Bandar Seri
Begawan
Strait of Melaka
Medan
Kuala Lumpur
BRUNEI
DARUSSALAM
SABAH
MALAYSIA
Melaka
SINGAPORE
SARAWAK
Pulau
Nias
Kuching
SUMATRA
Riau Islands
BORNEO
Padang
KALIMANTAN
Karimata Strait
Jambi
Bangka
Makassar Strait
Palembang
Bandar
Lampung
INDO
Jakarta
Java Sea
Bandung
Surabaya
Yogyakarta
JAVA
BALI
LOMBOK
Denpasar
SUMBAWA
INDIAN OCEAN

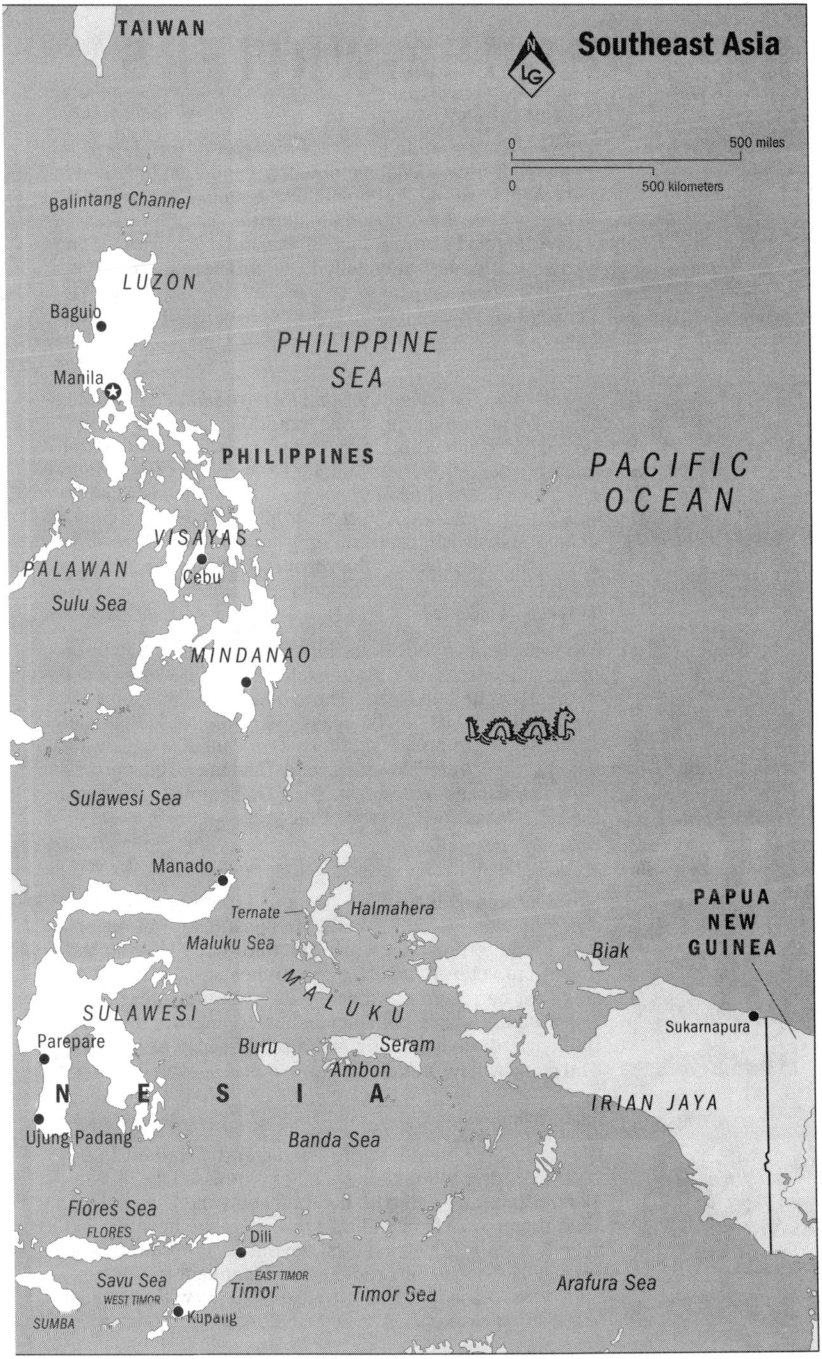
Southeast Asia
0
500 miles
0
500 kilometers
TAIWAN
Balintang Channel
LUZON
Baguio
Manila
PHILIPPINE SEA
PHILIPPINES
PACIFIC OCEAN
VISAYAS
Cebu
PALAWAN
Sulu Sea
MINDANAO
Sulawesi Sea
Manado
Ternate
Halmahera
Maluku Sea
PAPUA NEW GUINEA
Biak
MALUKU
SULAWESI
Sukarnapura
Parepare
Buru
Seram
Ambon
N E S I A
IRIAN JAYA
Ujung Padang
Banda Sea
Flores Sea
FLORES
Dili
EAST TIMOR
Savu Sea
WEST TIMOR
Timor
Timor Sea
Arafura Sea
SUMBA
Kupang

RESEARCHER-WRITERS

William Lee Adams *Sarawak, Sabah, Luzon*

William took it all in stride. A paragon of efficiency, he designed intricate hygienic directives and found method in the madness of the Philippine long-distance bus system. In his spare time, he exposed an elaborate gambling scam in Sabah, reveled in the riches of the sultan's kingdom, and parted the floods that engulfed Luzon. The unpredictability of the Malaysian postal system couldn't faze him, and William kept us amused with his anecdotes of life on the road.

Paul Guilianelli *Vietnam*

A warm-hearted adventurer and lover of *phở*, Paul scooted through Vietnam on sputtering motorbikes, turning out stellar research the whole way. A *Let's Go* star, Paul edited maps for the 2002 series, took off for Vietnam a few months later, then researched in Italy after completing his route for this book. Teaching American pop songs to guest house owners and attracting an entourage of children wherever he went, Paul charmed everyone he met (including his editors).

Tomohiro Hamakawa *Myanmar, Bangkok*

The heartthrob of the Southeast Asia office and RW Extraordinaire, Tomo left for Southeast Asia and never stopped impressing the bookteam. Though his route was long and his travel arduous, his compassion for oppressed peoples and devotion to publicizing forgotten causes were always fervent. He covered Myanmar and Thailand with appropriate graciousness and delight. *Let's Go* submitted his name for TIME Magazine's person of the year.

Stefanie Levner *Bali, Lombok, Sumbawa, Sumba, Flores*

Stef appeared suddenly and swept us off our feet. Skipping straits in single bounds, hiding in blissful A/C ATMs, and doing wildly thorough work, the nationally competitive rower and veteran *Let's Go* researcher was full of apologies—for being *ahead* of schedule—but meekness never disguised her strong opinions on how to improve the book. Diligence, thoughtfulness, and a bright sense of humor—who could ask for more? We did, and Stef delivered.

Nina Singh *Java, Bali*

Born in India, a resident of Canada, and a student in the USA, our intrepid rookie researcher impressed us all. Nina took on Java and Bali with determination and keen humor. Making her way from Jakarta to Ubud, she became fast friends with fellow travelers, devoured *gado-gado*, and pawned the occasional monkey. Independent to the core, Nina never ceased to entertain and inspire us with thorough research, wry commentary, and fabulous stories.

Gabe Struck *Laos, Cambodia*

With dedication and good humor, Gabe hopped in the back of every overloaded pickup truck, floated down the Mekong, and braved the worst roads in Southeast Asia to research Cambodia and Laos. Closed borders and an expired visa didn't stop this *Let's Go* super-vet and editor of *Let's Go: India & Nepal 2002* from trying every bush stew and cooked snake he found along the way. We can only wonder what he was muttering as he wrote his copybatches.

Kristina Vetter *The Visayas*

Kristina put her economics acumen to work uncovering the best deals under the blazing Philippine sun. Whether exploring underwater ecosystems or experimenting with the Philippine wireless network, her enthusiasm for the region was unmatched. Hopping from island to island in search of the perfect German sausage, she regaled us in the office with culinary commentary, history facts of the most obscure variety, and astute observations on Visayan urban planning.

Paul Warham *Sumatra, Sulawesi*

A fan of sushi, novels, and obscure musical references, this *Let's Go* vet and editor of *India & Nepal 2001* blazed through Sumatra and Sulawesi. A budding horticulturist, Paul was fascinated by Berastagi's cabbage statue and other Indonesian flora. Paul's penchant for witty marginalia and colorful prose always kept us giggling and wanting more. His thirst for Bintang and adventure proved inexhaustible.

Annie Wong *Singapore, Peninsular Malaysia, Southern Thailand*

Annie took Southeast Asia by storm. Employing her keen powers of observation to penetrate the veneer of Singapore, she revealed a city that likes to get down-and-dirty. Leaving the broken hearts of Malaysian men in her wake, this multilingual researcher conquered her itinerary just in time to run off and update a town or two in Southern Thailand. Her maps made our jaws drop with their cartographic precision, and her copy reminded us in the office of why we do this.

CONTRIBUTING WRITERS

Anthony Barker was a Researcher-Writer for *Let's Go: Southeast Asia 2000*. This Australia native has volunteered at clinics along the Thai-Myanmar border and studied Thai cooking with some of the country's top chefs. He plans to attend medical school in 2003.

Matthew Firestone was a Researcher-Writer for *Let's Go: Britain & Ireland 2002*. While in Thailand, he spent some time living in a Buddhist monastery. He is currently in sub-Saharan Africa researching the dietary practices of hunter-gatherer populations inhabiting the Kalahari.

Derek Glanz was the editor of *Let's Go: Spain, Portugal & Morocco 1998*. He is now a freelance journalist who recently began pursuing postgraduate studies in international relations. He has been published in *The Associated Press* and *The Miami Herald* (via AP), and served as a guest TV analyst on Colombia's *Tele-Cartagena*.

Nick Grossman was a Researcher-Writer for *Let's Go: New Zealand 1999* and editor of *Let's Go: New Zealand 2000*. Nick is now working in Bangkok for the monthly nightlife magazine *The Bangkok Metro*.

Basil Lee is currently a student at Harvard School of Design. A Researcher-Writer for *Let's Go: Thailand 2003*, Basil's coverage included East Coast and Northeast Thailand as well as Bangkok and the surrounding areas.

Graeme Wood was the editor of *Let's Go: Southeast Asia 2001* and a Researcher-Writer for *Let's Go: Southern Africa 2002* and *Let's Go: Eastern Europe 2003*. He lived in Khlong Toei, the dock district of Bangkok, where he worked for the Human Development Foundation in orphanages and hospices.

ACKNOWLEDGMENTS

SEAS THANKS. Our fabulous RWs. DK for being so cool. Amelie for rescuing us. Alex for saying what no one else would. Megha for the ice cream and encouragement. Matt for keeping things light. Gabe for stepping up. Brenda for helping out. Anne Chisholm. Brian Walsh. Adam Turner. Andrea Volfova. Bagel Friday. Midnight Snacks. And, of course, The Scooter.

KATE. My fourth-grade teacher, great aunt, and 6th-grade boyrfriend's mother all asked me to dedicate my first book to them, so in case I never get another chance, I would like thank Mrs. Dodes, Emily, and Kathy Burek.

NINA. The bookteam for making it worth it. Nina Singh for tearing it up. Matt Gibson. Alex, Amelie, DK, Megha, Anne Chisholm, and Brad Olson. Brenda for being there and for the excellent typing. Emi, also for the excellent typing. And I could not have done it without Mom, Dad, Lauren, Tim, and Anna.

EMMA. Love to my family, Dusty, Jordan, and Billy. And more thanks than I could ever articulate to Amelie, DK, the SEAS team, Alex, Blaz, the USA team, William, Kristina, the Gods of Caffeination, and The Scooter.

LAUREN. To those who loved and laughed with me this summer. Keep the faith.

JAY. To the team - for trust; ASP for purpose; Lila for words; the Déli-Cinq and Matt for jazz and a summit attempt; birds; Stef and the R-Ws for eliciting awe; small doging for brightness; some Amys for needless sweetness; the Blocks for a home; Team Australia for sparing me; a Crew that was. To Neel and my family beyond words and icons for care and patience.

DK. Thanks to the Scooter; the SEAS pod for being so good, moving at lightning speed, and keeping the laughter flowing; thanks to Masi for being an amazing sister and Meg for a great summer and saving my life from stress.

PDAs
&
Travel
(it's not what you're thinking)
LET'S GO
Let's Go City Guides
are now available for
Palm OS™ PDAs.
Download a free trial at
http://mobile.letsgo.com
Let's Go
EAT
SLEEP
SIGHTS
FUN
ESSENTIALS
LIFE & TIMES
AMSTERDAM BARCELONA BOSTON LONDON PARIS ROME NEW YORK CITY SAN FRANCISCO WASHINGTON D.C.
Palm OS is a registered trademark of Palm, Inc. Let's Go is a registered trademark of Let's Go Publications, Inc. Guidewalk is a registered trademark of Guidewalk LLC.

DISCOVER SOUTHEAST ASIA

Southeast Asia is the offspring of thousands of years of sea trade, religious conflict, colonial influence, expanding empires, political maneuvering, and continuous ethnic redefinition. Legend, mixed with scientific evidence, says that the story began when the Tai-Kadai people arrived from southern China and formed the Thai and Lao kingdoms. Indonesian Malays intermarried with Indian traders and princes to become the Khmer people, and Chinese migration added to bloodlines. Kingdoms mixed, matched, and migrated; European powers divided, conquered, and colonized; and in the wake of colonialism, nation-states formed, collapsed, and rebuilt themselves. From these shared origins, the countries of Southeast Asia—Brunei, Cambodia, Indonesia, Laos, Malaysia, Myanmar, the Philippines, Singapore, Thailand, and Vietnam—have formed distinct national identities flaunted amidst the stunning geographic and cultural diversity that has come to characterize the region. Shimmering crater lakes await the tranquil traveler, while the steamy streets of the bustling big cities challenge even the hardiest urban adventurer. Every trip to Southeast Asia is an experience that awes, frightens, challenges, educates, and spell-binds. Though little is certain in Southeast Asia, one thing is guaranteed—looking back on one of the world's most incredible regions, you'll have one heck of a story to tell.

FACTS AND FIGURES	
POPULATION: 515,600,000.	**COUNTRIES:** 10.
COUPS SINCE 1950: 42.	**SEX CHANGE OPERATIONS:** 21,473.
WATS, PAGODAS, OR TEMPLES: We stopped counting at 17,500,000.	**ISLANDS:** 25,390.
AVG. # OF WHEELS PER VEHICLE: 2.79.	**AVG. LENGTH OF THAI ISLAND PARTIES:** 31hr.
	AVG. COST OF 31HR. THAI ISLAND PARTIES: US$6.

WHEN TO GO

Southeast Asia has dry and rainy seasons which roughly correspond to high and low tourism seasons. During the low season, sights are less crowded, and fewer services are offered—however, they are offered at reduced prices. Some beaches and islands close down and fewer trekking opportunities are available.

The rainy season generally spans May to September in the north and runs later in the year the farther south you travel. For example, in Bali, the rains last from November to May. This is only a general rule. The rainy season can vary between even the west and east coasts of peninsular Malaysia. As you move closer to the equator, the weather becomes hotter and there is less variation among seasons. The weather in Southeast Asia is hot and humid; temperatures hover around 27°C (80°F) year-round everywhere except the extreme uplands of mainland Southeast Asia, where nighttime temperatures can fall to near freezing. For a rough conversion from °C to °F, multiply by two and add 30. (See the conversion chart in the **Appendix,** p. 987.)

WHAT TO DO

With ten countries and countless destinations, planning an itinerary in Southeast Asia can be as difficult as getting yaks to mate at low altitudes. Luckily for you, this section details routes, **suggested itineraries,** and must-dos to give you an idea of the country-hopping, beach-bumming, mountain-climbing, budget-living days that lie ahead of you.

BEACHES COME FIRST

Southeast Asia boasts some of the world's most inviting strips of sand. Luxury resorts have invaded famous destinations such as **Phuket,** Thailand, and **Bali,** Indonesia, while budget hideaways—bathed in the same sunlight—are still available nearly everywhere. The islands of **Ko Samet, Ko Chang, Ko Phangan,** and **Ko Tao** in Thailand; **Pulau Tioman** and the **Perhentian Islands** in Malaysia; **Pulau Nias** off Sumatra, **Kuta Beach** on Bali, and the **Gilis** off Lombok in Indonesia; and **Boracay** and **Biliran** in the Philippines should be on every self-respecting beach bummer's to-do list. In general, Thailand's beach scene is the most raucous. Ko Phangan's notorious Full Moon Party thrown every month is an all-night rave not to be missed—though it's being challenged by newcomers, Bali's legendary Kuta Beach and the Philippines' Boracay island, both increasingly infamous with faster, longer, and deeper trances into partydom. If that's exactly what you want to avoid, head to **Lovina** or **Sanur** off Bali in Indonesia or the quieter beaches on the **Vietnamese coast.**

Bali is Southeast Asia's undisputed surfing mecca. **Legundi Beach** on **Pulau Nias** is well known for its monstrous surf, and other islands in **Nusa Tenggara,** especially **Sumbawa,** have consistent breaks and minimal crowds. PADI certification courses for scuba diving are cheaper here than anywhere else. Most divers gravitate to **Ko Tao** or **Phuket** in Thailand, but the Phillipines' **Apo** and **Panglao Islands** and Sulawesi, Indonesia's **Manado** have clearer waters and more marine life.

OUT OF DOORS

Since the mid-1980s, jungle trekking and its trendy 90s cousin, "eco-tourism," have drawn many tourists to Southeast Asia. The rage began 20 years ago in **Northern Thailand,** and trips there are still high in quality and affordable. Numerous national parks offer cool, peaceful respite from the summer heat. Backpackers trek, climb, and spelunk in the parks of **Sabah** and **Sarawak. Taman Negara,** a national park in the world's oldest rainforest, offers everything from canopy walking on rickety rope bridges to week-long camping stays. **Palawan** in the Philippines has the world's longest underground river. For hikers, Southeast Asia presents peaks of varying difficulty, including **Fansipan** in northern Vietnam, **Gunung Kinabalu** in Sabah, **Gunung Agung** in Bali, **Gunung Rinjani** in Lombok, and the **Mayon** volcano and **Mt. Apo** in the Philippines. The last has an annoying habit of erupting every once in a while.

FELLOW JOURNEYERS

Love it or hate it—in every major city, backpackers huddle in their ghettos, meeting other travelers and exchanging tales, tips, and reading material. Some travelers relish the opportunity to spend weeks holed up in cheap guest houses avoiding the outside world; during the high season, grungy, scantily clad foreigners seem to outnumber the locals at haunts like: **Bangkok's Khaosan Rd., Chiang Mai, Nong Khai,** and the islands in Thailand; **Georgetown,** the **Perhentian Islands,** and **Pulau Tioman** in Malaysia; **Jogjakarta** on Java, **Ubud** and **Kuta** on Bali, the **Gilis** off Lombok, and **Bukit Tinggi** and **Lake Toba** on Sumatra, all in Indonesia; **Sabang** and **Boracay** in the Philippines; **Hồ Chí Minh City** and **Hội An** in Vietnam; and **Singapore.**

Other travelers shun contact with fellow *farang;* they prefer relatively isolated regions, which tend to see visitors more interested in exploring than in partying. Some of these include: **Northeast Thailand,** Cambodia's **Mekong River,** the **Mekong Delta** of Vietnam, Malaysia's east coast, **Flores** and **northern Sulawesi** in Indonesia, **Negros** and **Davao** in the Philippines, **southern Laos,** and all of **Myanmar.** Traveling during low season is an excellent way to dodge the crowds almost anywhere, though fewer services are available and resorts may be closed altogether.

THE LOCAL WAY

Many tourists come to the region seeking "traditional" Southeast Asian culture. At its worst, "ethnotourism" leads to human zoos such as the long-neck **Karen villages** of Northern Thailand or the so-called **"Chicken Village"** outside Đà Lạt, Vietnam; in most cases, however, travelers are welcome to observe and participate in local ceremonies and festivals. Chances to respectfully interact with indigenous cultures include: visiting **longhouses** in **Sarawak** and **Sabah;** participating in massive **funerals** in **Tana Toraja** in Sulawesi; traveling down the **Mekong** by **barge** with a Lao family; staying with a **hill-tribe village** in **Mai Chũu,** Vietnam; or living in a **Malay kampung,** a **Thai Muslim fishing community,** or an **Ifugao village** in the **Central Cordillera** of Luzon. Be sensitive and respectful of your surroundings.

ARCHITECTURAL WONDERS

Awe-inspiring temples, palaces, and wats, side-by-side with ruins of all kinds, abound in Southeast Asia. The three wonders of classical Southeast Asia are **Angkor** in Cambodia, **Bagan** in Myanmar, and **Borobudur** on Java in Indonesia. The imperial city in **Huế,** Vietnam, a microcosm of Beijing's Forbidden City, provides a fascinating counterpoint to the Indic-influenced monuments elsewhere in the region. **Luang Prabang** in Laos may be the best-preserved ancient city in the region. In Thailand, the former capitals of **Sukhothai** and **Ayutthaya** shouldn't be missed.

GOOD EATS

The unbelievable cuisine alone is worth the trip to Southeast Asia. Among the culinary highlights are the **hawker stalls** of Singapore, the **nyonya** cuisine of Penang and Melaka in Malaysia, the spicy **padang** food of Sumatra, the Vietnamese delicacies found in Huế, the hybridized dishes of European inspiration in **Ubud,**

DISCOVER

the **dim sum** of Hong Kong, and just about anything in Thailand. Eating at the vibrant **night markets** of Thailand and Malaysia, where the locals dine, is one of the truly great pleasures of traveling there. Menu headings range from pigeon and rat to squid and cobra. Abundant vegetarian options everywhere will keep the less carnivorously-inclined well-fed and content.

THE CITY SCENE

Southeast Asia's big cities are stories in themselves. Though Bangkok, Jakarta, and Manila are often portrayed as smog-ridden, choking ovens, these cities bustle with an unmatched energy, diversity, and chaos—the essence of modern-day Southeast Asia. The region's major cities gather architectural, cultural, and culinary attractions all in one place. **Hong Kong** and **Singapore** are respites from the disorder of other Southeast Asian cities; **Hanoi, Luang Prabang, Yangon, Kuching, Davao,** and **Cebu** also deserve exploration. For nightlife, **Bangkok, Hồ Chí Minh City, Kuala Lumpur, Jakarta,** and **Manila** lead the pack.

LET'S GO PICKS: SOUTHEAST ASIA

BEST GENITALIA-SHAPED ROCK: Despite stiff competition, the "grandmother and grandfather" rocks of **Ko Samui** (p. 847), in Thailand win this prize.

BEST MEMORIALS: Phnom Penh's **Tuol Sleng Genocide Museum** demands reflection, as does the **War Remnants Museum** (p. 968) in Ho Chi Minh City.

BEST REASON TO GET UP IN THE MORNING: The sunrise over **Angkor Wat** is one of the world's spectacular sights.

BEST LUNAR CYCLE: The **Full Moon Parties** (p. 845), on the beaches of Southern Thailand, or for that matter the beaches themselves, are the party centers of Southeast Asia.

BEST WAY TO SWEAT WITH THE LOCALS: Catch an impromptu soccer game in the parks of Hanoi, or indulge in the Philippines's favorite, basketball. If you fancy yourself a real athlete, try *sepak takraw* in Kuala Lumpur.

BEST PLACE TO SEE WILDLIFE: Catch the mini-dinosaurs on **Komodo Island** (p. 232) in Indonesia, on your way to **Gunung Leseur National Park.** Malaysia's **Taman Negara National Park** (p. 416) and the *babirusa* (pig-deer) of **Sulawesi** finish off the list (p. 258).

BEST PLACE TO EAT WILDLIFE: You choose: Cambodian crickets; Filipino duck embryos, ox balls, or blood soup; Vietnamese snakes and rats; Indonesian squids. What can we get you today?

BEST PLACE TO LOSE YOUR LOINS: **Bangkok**'s best hospitals have one special skill: they help Michael find the Michelle within.

BEST TRADITIONAL REMEDY: Sabang Beach (p. 597) in the Philippines, offers you the **"Feeling Shitty"** breakfast of coffee, 2 cigarettes, Coke, and ibuprofen for P70 (under US$2).

SUGGESTED ITINERARIES

THE THREE COUNTRY CIRCUIT

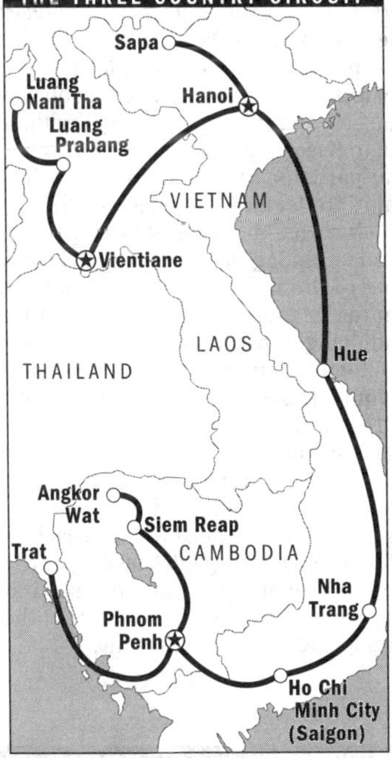

THE THREE-COUNTRY CIRCUIT (5 WEEKS)

The markets in easy-paced **Trat,** Thailand (p. 739) are a short hop from Bangkok and an ideal stop on the way to **Phnom Penh,** Cambodia (p. 69), the nation's capital and home of the poignant Killing Fields. Next, head to **Siem Reap** (p. 86), the gateway to one of the world's greatest wonders, the spectacular **Angkor Wat** (p. 90). Backtrack through Phnom Penh to bustling **Hồ Chí Minh City,** Vietnam (p. 960). Be sure to spend a few easy days on the beautiful beaches of **Nha Trang** (p. 951). History buffs rejoice in the imperial capital city of **Hue** (p. 928). The trek north finishes at **Hanoi** (p. 893), Vietnam's other major metropolis. From here, the mountains of **Sapa** (p. 915) are a must. Fly across the border to **Vientiane,** Laos (p. 327) and welcome the mellow Lao lifestyle. **Luang Prabang** (p. 336) and **Luang Nam Tha** (p. 345) are home to some of Southeast Asia's last undisturbed indigenous cultures.

FROM PAGODAS TO PATPONG: THE BEST OF THAILAND AND MYANMAR (4 WEEKS)

Begin where all good trips do, in bustling **Bangkok** (p. 683). Fly to **Yangon,** Myanmar (p. 498) and pay your respects at the Shwegadon Pagoda. Complete your Myanmar odyssey by heading up to **Mandalay** (p. 518) where cafes stand side by side with pagodas. Backtrack through Bangkok towards the north, reaching the hills of **Chiang Mai** (p. 746) where the best trekking in the region awaits you. The infamous **Golden Triangle** of Chiang Mai, **Pai** (p. 765) and **Mae Hong Son** (p. 761) bring

THE BEST OF THAILAND AND MYANMAR

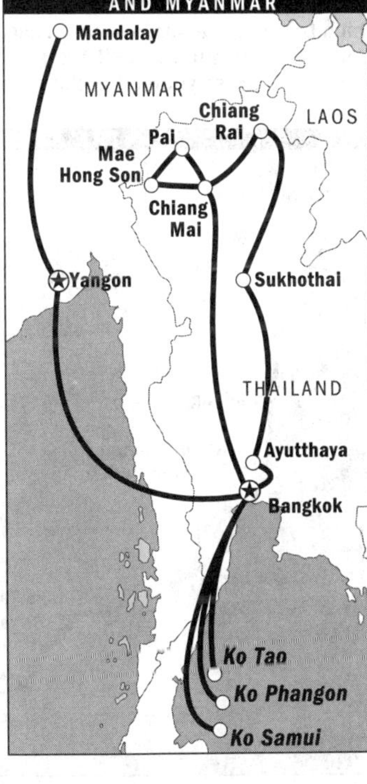

together the best of indigenous Thai culture, amazing mountain views, and respite from the sizzling Southeast Asian summer. Having conquered the triangle, move on to gentler **Chiang Rai** (p. 769) for more insights into northern culture. Head back to Bangkok via the ancient capital of **Sukhothai** (p. 790), whose ruins will remind you of the deep history of Thailand. Another former capital, **Ayutthaya** (p. 709), showcases the deep Indic influences on Thai history. Then shoot south to the **Kos** (any one will do; see **Southern Thailand,** p. 833) and reflect on your trip on the world's best beaches. Click your ruby heels, and you're back in **Bangkok,** where it all began.

ISLAND-HOPPING: HIGHLIGHTS OF INDONESIA (5 WEEKS)

Begin your explorations in Sumatra's big city, **Medan** (p. 261). Check out **Lake Toba** (p. 277), the world's largest crater lake, on your way to **Pulau Nias** (p. 284), which boasts great surf and untouched beaches. Continue to **Bukit Tinggi** (p. 291) and immerse yourself in the traditional Minangkubau culture. Head on to **Padang** (p. 296) to sample the region's famous spicy-hot cuisine. Hikers will enjoy the trails that lace **Kerinci Seblat National Park** (p. 299) on the western coast. Hop over to Java, where **Jakarta** (p. 111) awaits, but stay only as long as your lungs can take it. Continue on to **Bogor**'s (p. 126) renowned botanical gardens, and then on to bustling and intellectual **Bandung** (p. 131) via the breathtaking **Puncak Pass** (p. 130). Don't miss **Jogjakarta** (p. 139), which is one of the most popular destinations on the island—for good reason. After indulging in daytrips from here, move to Java's magnificent volcanoes at **Gunung Bromo** (p. 163). **Bali** (p. 164) offers a fantastic party scene, especially in **Kuta** (p. 175), as well as luxurious beaches. Find your own plot of sand in **Lovina** (p. 189). For more beach and less fanfare, head to **Padangbai** (p. 203) or the relaxing **Gili Islands** (p. 218). Animal-lovers must make a stop at **Komodo Island** (p. 232) to check out the archipelago's famous dragons.

THE BEST OF INDONESIA

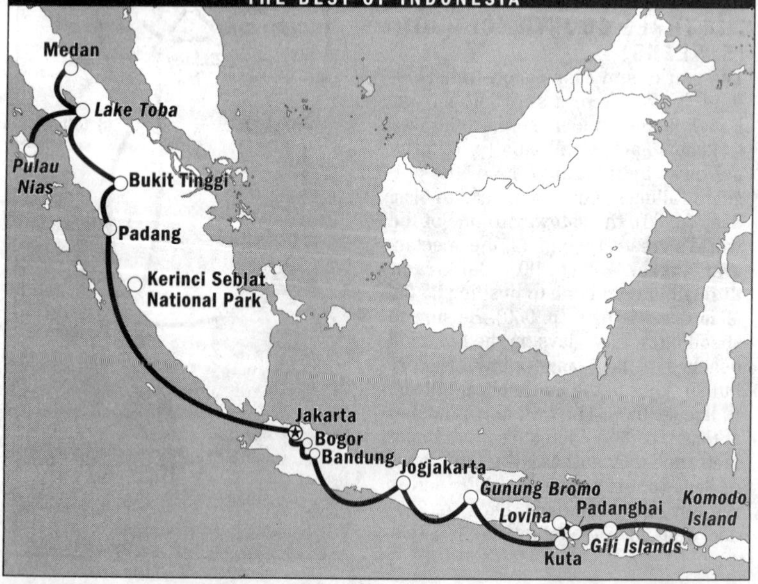

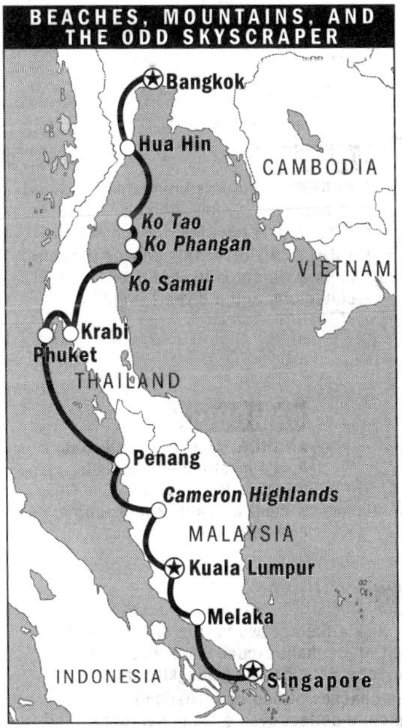

SMORGASBOARD: BEACHES, MOUNTAINS, AND THE ODD SKYSCRAPER (3 WEEKS)

Begin in **Bangkok** (p. 683) and soak up the urban chaos. Start the journey south at **Hua Hin** (p. 726) for an introduction to Thailand's pristine white sand. Now, island-hop from the diver's paradise to **Ko Tao** (p. 837) to the **Full Moon Party** on **Ko Phangan** (p. 842), and to tourist friendly **Ko Samui** (p. 847). Still craving beaches? Cut across to **Krabi** (p. 870) and **Phuket** (p. 859). On to **Penang,** Malaysia (p. 400) and its scrumptious street food. Then venture inland to the **Cameron Highlands** (p. 412) and challenge yourself with jungle hikes. **Kuala Lumpur** (p. 374) will serve as a fitting adventure for any urban guru. As a reward, plunge into Malaysian history in **Melaka** (p. 385). End your whirlwind tour of cities, beaches, mountains, and coast in **Singapore** (p. 653), the ultimate city-state.

TALES OF AMPHIBIOUS TOURISTS: THE BEST OF THE PHILIPPINES (4 WEEKS)

Stay in **Manila** (p. 559) long enough to hit the pumping nightlife and check out Intramuros, then catch your breath amidst the rice paddies in the northern hills of **Banaue** (p. 579). Linger in lazy **Sagada** (p. 578) for a while, then backtrack through Manila south to beautiful **Lake Taal** (p. 588). Next, hop over to **Mindoro Island** (p. 594) for an introduction to Filipino beach culture. After an overnight stay in **Panay** (p. 622) and a brief sun-soaking session on **Bantayan Island** (p. 609) or undiscovered **Malapascua Island** (p. 610), and world-class diving on **Moalboal** (p. 608), steam into **Cebu City** (p. 600) to appease your Bacchanalian impulses. Catch a ferry to **Bohol** (p. 610), indulge in the Chocolate Hills, and bask on the isolated beaches of **Panglao Island** (p. 614). Continue island-hopping to your finale at **Apo Island** (p. 621), where you'll find the Philippines's best-preserved marine sanctuary.

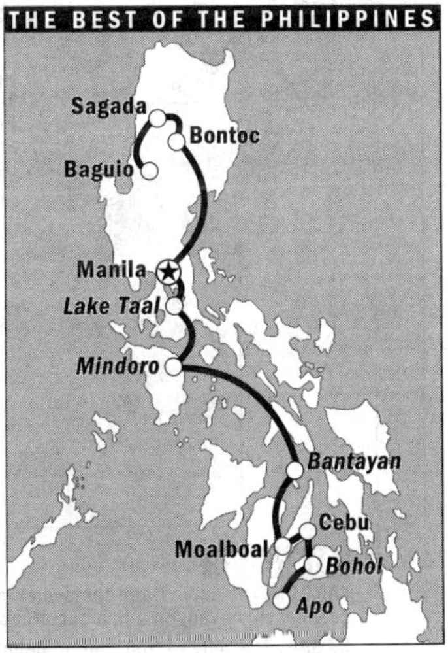

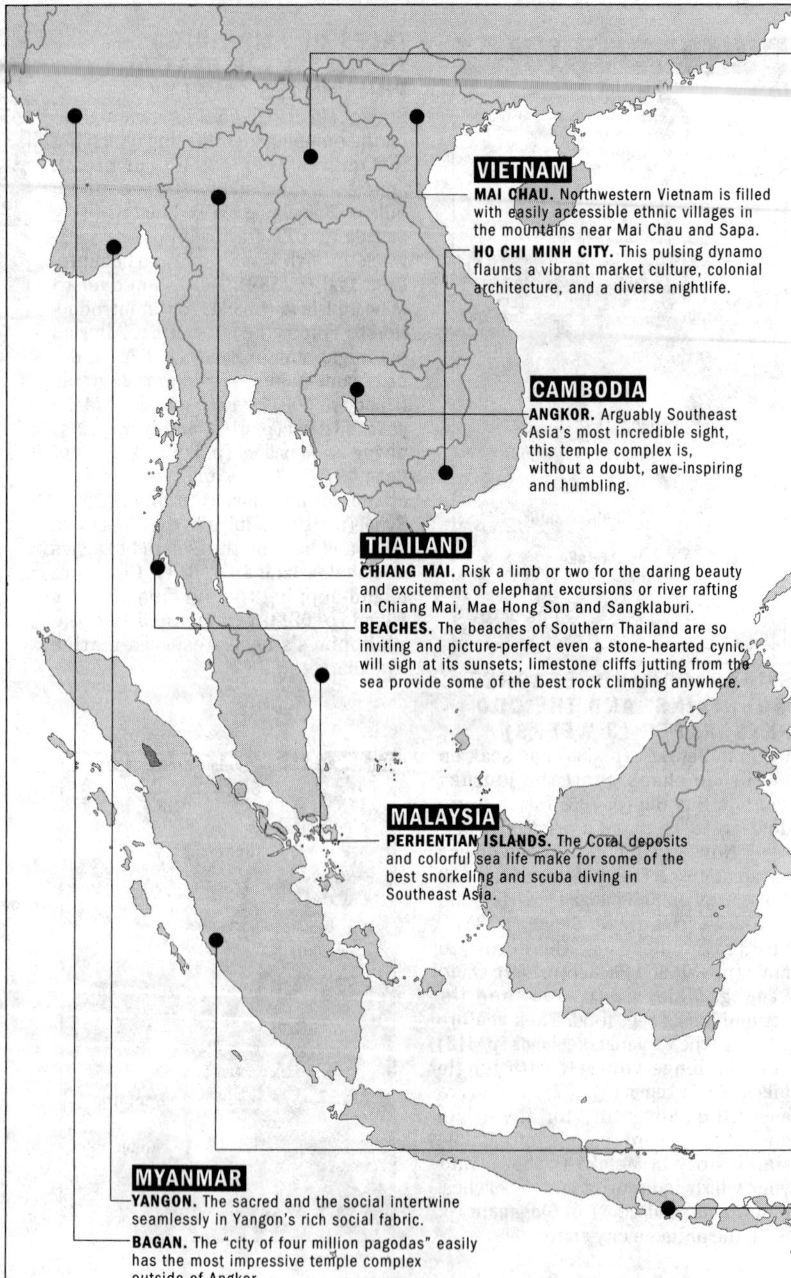
VIETNAM
MAI CHAU. Northwestern Vietnam is filled with easily accessible ethnic villages in the mountains near Mai Chau and Sapa.
HO CHI MINH CITY. This pulsing dynamo flaunts a vibrant market culture, colonial architecture, and a diverse nightlife.
CAMBODIA
ANGKOR. Arguably Southeast Asia's most incredible sight, this temple complex is, without a doubt, awe-inspiring and humbling.
THAILAND
CHIANG MAI. Risk a limb or two for the daring beauty and excitement of elephant excursions or river rafting in Chiang Mai, Mae Hong Son and Sangklaburi.
BEACHES. The beaches of Southern Thailand are so inviting and picture-perfect even a stone-hearted cynic will sigh at its sunsets; limestone cliffs jutting from the sea provide some of the best rock climbing anywhere.
MALAYSIA
PERHENTIAN ISLANDS. The Coral deposits and colorful sea life make for some of the best snorkeling and scuba diving in Southeast Asia.
MYANMAR
YANGON. The sacred and the social intertwine seamlessly in Yangon's rich social fabric.
BAGAN. The "city of four million pagodas" easily has the most impressive temple complex outside of Angkor.

Highlights of Southeast Asia

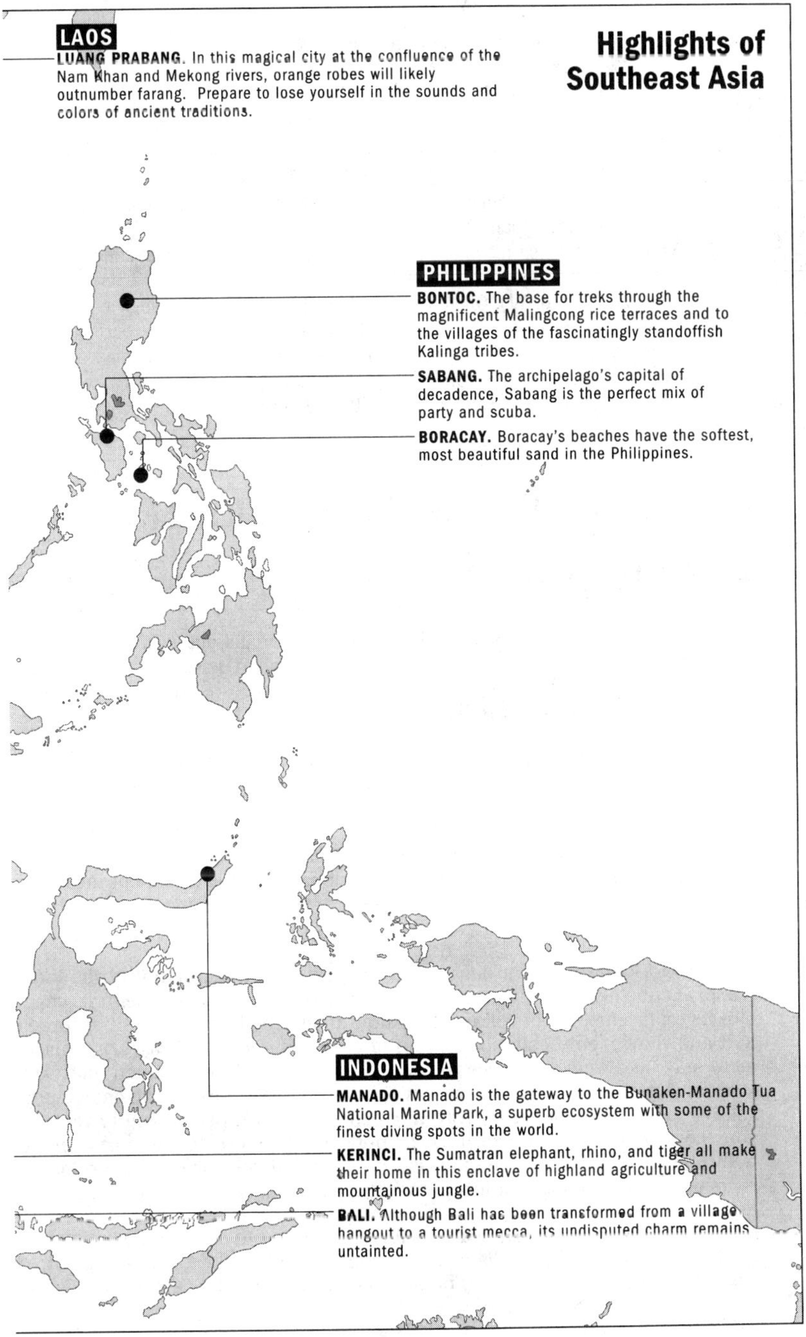

LAOS

LUANG PRABANG. In this magical city at the confluence of the Nam Khan and Mekong rivers, orange robes will likely outnumber farang. Prepare to lose yourself in the sounds and colors of ancient traditions.

PHILIPPINES

BONTOC. The base for treks through the magnificent Malingcong rice terraces and to the villages of the fascinatingly standoffish Kalinga tribes.

SABANG. The archipelago's capital of decadence, Sabang is the perfect mix of party and scuba.

BORACAY. Boracay's beaches have the softest, most beautiful sand in the Philippines.

INDONESIA

MANADO. Manado is the gateway to the Bunaken-Manado Tua National Marine Park, a superb ecosystem with some of the finest diving spots in the world.

KERINCI. The Sumatran elephant, rhino, and tiger all make their home in this enclave of highland agriculture and mountainous jungle.

BALI. Although Bali has been transformed from a village hangout to a tourist mecca, its undisputed charm remains untainted.

ESSENTIALS

SO YOU WANT TO GO TO SOUTHEAST ASIA

Passports (p. 10): Required of all travelers. Must be valid for at least 6 months after intended period of stay.

Visas (p. 11): Visa requirements vary by country. See individual countries for more information.

Special Visas (p. 11): Often required of foreigners planning to study or work in Southeast Asia.

Immunizations (p. 20): Visitors who have been in Africa or South America must have a certificate of vaccination against yellow fever.

Driving Permits (p. 36): International Driving Permits required for car rental in many countries.

DOCUMENTS & FORMALITIES

PASSPORTS

REQUIREMENTS. You need a valid passport to enter all Southeast Asian nations and to return to your home country. Most countries will require that your passport be valid for six months beyond your anticipated departure date. See individual country introductions for specifics.

PHOTOCOPIES. Be sure to photocopy the page of your passport with your photo, as well as your visas, traveler's check serial numbers, and any other important documents. Carry one set of copies in a safe place, apart from the originals, and leave another with someone at home. Consulates also recommend that you carry an expired passport or an official copy of your birth certificate separate from other documents. These additional documents can cut through a lot of bureaucracy in the event that you need to replace an important travel document.

LOST PASSPORTS. If you lose your passport, immediately notify the local police and the nearest embassy or consulate of your home government. To expedite its replacement, you will need to know all information previously recorded in it and show identification and proof of citizenship. In some cases, a replacement may take weeks to process and may only be valid for a limited time. Any visas stamped in your old passport will be irretrievably lost. In an emergency, ask for immediate temporary traveling papers that will permit you to re-enter your home country. As of April 2002, applying for American passports abroad will take longer because US embassies and consulates abroad will no longer issue passports at their location, but will have them sent from the US.

NEW PASSPORTS. All applications for new passports or renewals should be filed several weeks or months in advance of your planned departure date. Most passport offices offer emergency passport services for a hefty extra charge.

VISAS, INVITATIONS & WORK PERMITS

VISAS. Many countries in Southeast Asia require an entry visa that must be obtained in advance from a consulate abroad. For multiple entries, applying for re-entry permits may be necessary. For specific visa requirements (as of Aug. 2002), see the **Essentials** section of individual countries. Check entrance requirements at the nearest embassy for up-to-date information before departure. US citizens can take advantage of the **Center for International Business and Travel** (☎800-925-2428), which secures visas for travel to almost all countries for a variable service charge.

VISA REQUIREMENTS

	AUS	CAN	IRE	NZ	SA	UK	US
BRUNEI	N3	N3	N1	N1	Y	N1	N2
CAMBODIA	Y	Y	Y	Y	Y	Y	Y
INDONESIA	N5	N5	N5	N5	Y	N5	N5
LAOS	Y	Y	Y	Y	Y	Y	Y
MALAYSIA	N	N	N1	N	N	N	N2
MYANMAR	Y	Y	Y	Y	Y	Y	Y
PHILIPPINES	N6	N6	N6	N6	N6	N6	N6
SINGAPORE	N1	N1	N1	N1	N1	N1	N1
THAILAND	N1	N1	N1	N1	N1	N1	N1
VIETNAM	Y	Y	Y	Y	Y	Y	Y

KEY Y tourists must obtain a visa; **N** tourists do not need a visa, or do not need a visa with the following stipulations: **1** tourists can stay up to 30 days without visa; **2** tourists can stay up to 90 days without a visa; **3** tourists can stay up to 14 days without a visa; **4** tourists can stay for 6 months without a visa; **5** tourists can stay up to 60 days without a visa; **6** tourists can stay 21 days without a visa. Extensions issued within country.

SPECIAL VISAS. Entering Southeast Asia to work or study often requires a special visa that can be obtained with letters of sponsorship or invitation from businesses, organizations, or universities in Southeast Asia. Contact the embassy for specific details. For more information, see **Alternatives to Tourism,** p. 44.

IDENTIFICATION

When you travel, always carry two or more forms of identification on your person, including one photo ID. A passport and driver's license or birth certificate is usually adequate. Never carry all your forms of ID together; split them up in case of theft or loss. It is useful to bring extra passport-size photos (2 in. by 2 in.) to affix to the visas and IDs you may acquire or in case you need replacements.

STUDENT AND TEACHER IDENTIFICATION. The **International Student Identity Card** (**ISIC;** US$20) is accepted in several Southeast Asian countries for discounts on some sights and other services, like car rentals, cinemas, and upscale restaurants. Check out their discount database (www.istcnet.org/DiscountDatabase) for more information. Cardholders have access to a 24hr. emergency helpline for medical, legal, and financial emergencies. US cardholders are also eligible for insurance benefits (see **Insurance,** p. 25). Applicants must be degree-seeking students of a secondary or post-secondary school and must be at least 12 years old. The **International Teacher Identity Card (ITIC)** offers the same insurance coverage and limited discounts. For more info, contact the **International Student Travel Confederation (ISTC),** Herengracht 479, 1017 BS Amsterdam, Netherlands (☎31 20 421 28 00; fax 421 28 10; istcinfo@istc.org; www.istc.org).

YOUTH IDENTIFICATION. The International Student Travel Confederation issues a discount card to travelers who are 25 years old or under but not students. This one-year **International Youth Travel Card** (**IYTC;** formerly the **GO 25** Card) offers many of the same benefits as the ISIC and is sold in the same places (US$20).

CUSTOMS

Customs requirements vary from country to country in Southeast Asia. Upon entering you must declare certain items from abroad and pay a duty on the value of those articles if they exceed the allowance established by that country's customs service. Southeast Asian governments have harsh penalties for **drug possession and trafficking,** often considered synonymous. Note that goods and gifts purchased at **duty-free** shops abroad are not exempt from duty or sales tax at your point of return and thus must be declared as well. Additionally, several countries in Southeast Asia require official certification before cultural goods or artifacts can be taken out of the country. Such certification often takes three to five days to process; make sure you leave enough time to complete the process or your purchases cannot leave the country with you. The import of **weapons** and **pornography** is prohibited by all Southeast Asian countries. Additional country-specific customs regulations are listed below.

Cambodia: The export of antiquities, drugs, firearms, or ivory is strictly forbidden. There is no restriction on the export of local currency, but foreign nationals are restricted to a US$10,000 (cash) import limit.

Indonesia: Enforcement of Indonesia's strict customs regulations is inconsistent. Travelers carrying prescription medicines should also bring a note from a doctor. Text and videotapes in Chinese, as well as Chinese medicines, used to be prohibited, though restrictions have relaxed in recent years. Travelers with such items may still encounter problems. Consult the Indonesian embassy in your country for more information.

Laos: No antique cultural items or Buddha images may leave the country without government authorization. Silver or copper items are subject to custom duty. Travelers may encounter problems with new merchandise. Check out http://laocustoms.laopdr.net for more information.

Malaysia: There are no general restrictions on the import or export of currency, but it is illegal to leave with over RM10,000 in cash. Pornography, publications that could be offensive to the government, knives, and most broadcast receivers are prohibited. A permit is necessary to import precious stones or gold for business purposes (coins issued by the Central Bank of Malaysia and personal jewelry are permissible).

Myanmar: Non-residents can bring the equivalent of US$2000 without declaration. Jewelry, electrical goods, and cameras must be declared but are exempt from duty. Antique or archaeological souvenirs cannot be exported. Gems, jewelry, and silverware accompanied by an export-guarantee voucher from authorized gift shops may be exported.

Philippines: Visitors bringing in over US$3000 must declare the total at the Central Bank counter at customs. Drugs, coral, certain orchid species, mussels, animal parts (e.g. turtle shells), and local currency over P1000 may not leave the country. A certificate from the National Museum must accompany all antiques purchased in the country.

Singapore: Prohibited from importation are chewing gum, chewing or imitation tobacco, obscene material, "seditious and treasonable material," and toy currency. Drug possession is considered trafficking in Singapore. Also prohibited is bringing live dogs of certain breeds in Singapore—see www.gov.sg/customs.

Thailand: Travelers may bring 1 still camera with 10 rolls of film, or 1 video camera with 3 tapes; these restrictions are meant to ensure the film/equipment is for personal use only and are flexible. Firearms and pornography are prohibited. The total amount of currency taken out should not exceed the amount taken in (max. US$10,000). No authentic Buddha or Bodhisattva images, or fragments thereof, may be exported without permission from the Bangkok National Museum (☎02 224 1333) and the Department of Fine Arts; you must prove you are a practicing Buddhist or are using them for cultural or academic purposes. These rules do not apply to souvenirs. For art purchased in the country, keep receipts for customs.

Vietnam: Visitors must declare cameras, videos and camcorders, tape recorders, and all other electronic equipment upon arrival and departure. Vietnamese customs officials have recently increased the seizure of religious, political, and pornographic materials. Foreign currency (including notes, coins, and traveler's checks) in excess of US$3000 or 5,000,000 Vietnamese đồng must be declared. Antiques are not allowed out of the country without approval from the Ministry of Culture and Information. You must present your customs and immigration cards when leaving the country.

MONEY

CURRENCY & EXCHANGE

Up-to-date **exchange rates** and information on local currencies are in each country's **Essentials** section. Check the currency converter on the *Let's Go* homepage (www.letsgo.com/thumb) or a major newspaper for the latest rates. As a general rule, it's cheaper to convert money at your destination. Bring enough currency to last for the first 72 hours of a trip—banks might be closed when you arrive. Travelers from the US can get foreign currency from the comfort of home: **International Currency Express** (☎888-278-6628) delivers currency or traveler's checks overnight (US$15) or second-day (US$12) at competitive exchange rates. Smart travelers will carry US dollars even if it isn't their national currency, as many establishments in Southeast Asia prefer transactions to be in US dollars. For small transactions though, put your dollars away and use local currency. Throwing dollars around for preferential treatment is offensive and attracts thieves. If you use traveler's checks or bills, carry some in small denominations (US$50 or less), especially for times when you're forced to exchange money at disadvantageous rates.

Banks generally have the best rates outside the black market. A good rule of thumb is to go only to banks that have at most a 5% margin between their buy and sell prices. Since you lose money with each transaction, convert in large sums (unless the currency is depreciating rapidly). Freelancers on the black market often offer excellent rates, but you run the risk of being swindled or arrested.

TRAVELER'S CHECKS

Traveler's checks (**American Express** and **Visa** are the most recognized) are one of the safest and least troublesome means of carrying funds. Several agencies and banks sell them for a small commission. While traveling, keep check receipts and a record of which checks you've cashed separate from the checks themselves. Keep a copy of check numbers and leave a copy with someone at home. Never countersign checks until you're ready to cash them, and always bring your passport with you to cash them. When purchasing checks, ask about toll-free refund hotlines and the location of refund centers in the event that your checks are lost or stolen. Most Southeast Asian countries accept traveler's checks in well-traveled areas, especially at banks and hotels. They are less widely accepted in smaller towns and rural areas. Check individual city listings for more information.

American Express: In Australia, call ☎800 251 902; in New Zealand ☎0800 441 068; in the UK ☎0800 521 313; in the US and Canada ☎800-221-7282. Elsewhere, call collect to the US ☎+1 801-964-6665; www.aexp.com. Traveler's checks are available for a small fee (1-4%) at AmEx offices and banks, commission-free at AAA offices. *Cheques for Two* can be signed by either of 2 people traveling together.

Thomas Cook MasterCard: In the US and Canada ☎800-223-7373; in the UK ☎0800 62 21 01; elsewhere UK collect ☎+44 1733 31 89 50. Checks available in 13 currencies at 2% commission. Thomas Cook offices cash checks commission-free.

Visa: In the US call ☎800-227-6811; in the UK ☎0800 89 50 78; elsewhere UK collect ☎+44 20 79 37 80 91. Call for the location of their nearest office.

CREDIT CARDS

Where they are accepted, credit cards often offer superior exchange rates—up to 5% better than the rate used by banks and other currency exchange establishments. **MasterCard** and **Visa** are the most welcomed; **American Express** cards work at some ATMs, AmEx offices, and major airports. Budget travelers will find that few of the establishments they frequent will accept credit cards; you will probably have to reserve your credit card only for financial emergencies. Credit cards are also useful for **cash advances,** which allow you to withdraw local currency from associated banks and ATMs throughout Southeast Asia instantly. However, transaction fees for all credit card advances (up to US$10 per advance, plus 2-3% extra on foreign transactions after conversion) tend to make credit cards a more costly way of withdrawing cash than ATMs or traveler's checks. Be sure to check with your credit card company before you leave home to get a numerical (not alphabetical) **Personal Identification Number (PIN)** so that you are eligible for an advance.

CASH CARDS (ATMS)

Cash cards are an increasingly popular way to get money in Southeast Asia. ATMs are common in Brunei, Indonesia, Hong Kong, Malaysia, the Philippines, Singapore, and Thailand. They are rare in Cambodia, Laos, Myanmar, and Vietnam, except in large, central cities. The two major international money networks are **Cirrus** (☎800-424-7787) and **PLUS** (☎800-843-7587). Call these numbers to locate ATMs anywhere in the world, or consult http://usa.visa.com/personal/atm_locator/plus_atm.html or www.mastercard.com/cardholderservices/atm. ATMs get the same wholesale exchange rate as credit cards, but there is often a limit on the amount you can withdraw per day (around US$500), and computer networks sometimes fail. There is typically also a surcharge of US$1-5 per withdrawal.

Have your home bank issue you a four-digit PIN, the only variety accepted at some Southeast Asian ATMs. Be sure to memorize your PIN code in numeric form, since machines abroad often don't have letters on their keys.

Visa TravelMoney is a system that allows you to access money from any Visa ATM for a small fee. Deposit money before you travel, and you can withdraw up to that sum. The cards give you the same favorable exchange rate for withdrawals as a regular Visa. Check with your local bank to see if it issues TravelMoney cards (☎877-394-2247; www.usa.visa.com/personal/cards/visa_travel_money.html).

GETTING MONEY FROM HOME

AMERICAN EXPRESS. AmEx has ATMs throughout Southeast Asia, concentrated in major cities. Cardholders can withdraw cash from their checking accounts at any of AmEx's major offices and many representative offices (up to

US$1000 every 21 days; no service charge, no interest). To enroll in Express Cash, call ☎800-227-4669 in the US. The AmEx international travel assistance number is ☎800-732-1991; call from Southeast Asia for the nearest AmEx ATM. For other inquiries, in the US, Caribbean, Canada, and the Philippines, call ☎800-678-0745; the international direct number is ☎336-393-1111.

WESTERN UNION. Travelers from the US, Canada, and the UK can wire money abroad through Western Union's international money transfer services. In the US, call ☎800-325-6000; in Canada, ☎800-235-0000; in the UK, ☎0800 833 833. Money can be wired online from www.westernunion.com. The rates for sending cash are generally US$10-11 cheaper than with a credit card, and the money is usually available at the location you're sending it to within an hour.

FEDERAL EXPRESS. Some people choose to send money abroad in cash via FedEx to avoid transmission fees and taxes. In the US and Canada, ☎800-463-3339; in the UK, ☎0800 123 800; in Ireland, ☎800-535 800; in Australia, ☎13 26 10; in New Zealand, ☎0800 733 339; in South Africa, ☎021 551 7610. FedEx is reliable, but note that this method is **illegal** and somewhat risky. Also, it may take anywhere from a few days to several weeks for the package to reach you in Southeast Asia, depending on where it was sent from and where it is going.

US STATE DEPARTMENT (US CITIZENS ONLY). In dire emergencies, the US State Department will forward money to the nearest consular office, which will then disburse it for a US$15 fee. Contact the Overseas Citizens Service, Consular Affairs, Room 4811, US Department of State, Washington, D.C. 20520 (☎202-647-5225; nights, Sundays, and holidays ☎647-4000; http://travel.state.gov).

COSTS

The cost of your trip will vary considerably, depending on where you go, how you travel, and where you stay. The single biggest cost of your trip will probably be your round-trip **airfare** (see **By Plane,** p. 29). Traveling in Southeast Asia can be done on a rather small budget, spending as little as US$5 per day in some parts of the region. Before you go, spend some time calculating a reasonable per-day **budget** that will meet your needs. See the **Essentials** section for each country for a breakdown of expected daily costs in individual countries. But always keep emergency reserve funds (at least US$200) when planning how much money you'll need.

STAYING ON A BUDGET. The traveler's cost of living is very low in Southeast Asia, relative to most Western countries. This is particularly true after the recent Asian Financial Crisis of 1997. The difference between the cheapest option and the mid-range options is often only a few dollars, giving the budget traveler the option of an occasional night of luxury. Travelers looking to spend more than one night in comfort also have that option, especially in the more populated areas and beach resorts. At the moment, package tours are on the rise. Often, they offer more efficient ways to travel while still being affordable but, for many travelers, packaged tours can feel limiting. In any case, travel within Southeast Asia will certainly not drain your savings.

TIPPING & BRIBERY

Tipping is not customary in Southeast Asia. However, a general rule is: the more Western the establishment, the more likely a tip is expected. If an establishment includes a service charge in the bill tipping is not necessary. Still, most people will welcome the extra kip, riel, đồng, or baht, as the average yearly income for some in Southeast Asia is as low as US$150.

While corruption is rife in many Southeast Asian countries, as a general rule, officials are unwilling to accept bribes from foreigners, and it is unwise to initiate an under-the-table transaction. If an official demands a fee or fine that you feel may be illegal, proceed with caution. Paying the bribe might be preferable to the alternative, but keep in mind that it is also illegal. If you politely ask for a receipt, or to speak with the official's superior, you might be able to defuse the situation. As a last resort, threatening to contact your embassy may also be effective.

THE ART OF THE DEAL In Southeast Asia, bargaining is more than a pricing system. It is an art form, a crucial part of everyday social interactions, the lifeblood of every market, a riveting, exciting and skillful mind game, and, if your attitude is right, a great deal of fun. The concept of "losing face," deeply embedded in many Asian cultures, is fundamental to an understanding of bargaining. So put your cutthroat attitude aside; this game of skill is built on a foundation of mutual respect and cheeky smiles of understanding.

1. Always approach with a smile, it'll start things off on the right foot.

2. Visible interest should be inversely proportional to actual desire; covetous eyes are the cat's meow to sellers and the kiss of death to buyers. But don't confuse a calm manner of carefully calculated semi-uninterest with a look of disdain.

3. Know when to bargain. In most cases, it's clear when it's appropriate to pull out your guns. When in doubt, smile and ask tactfully whether discounts or given, or say, "Oh! Is that the best we can do?" Never bargain for prepared food.

4. Openly bargaining with several sellers simultaneously is unacceptable and usually yields higher prices. Thus, it's best to pull one person aside and settle in private.

5. To start bargaining without an intention to buy is a major *faux pas*. Agreeing on a price and declining it is the lowest of the low.

6. Cutthroat bargaining to a rock-bottom price often results in the seller's losing face. It's also worth considering that an hour of work in most Western nations yields enough money to feed a family for a week in many parts of Southeast Asia.

SAFETY & SECURITY

PERSONAL SAFETY

EXPLORING. Be careful about leaving yourself vulnerable to thieves. As pickpockets know, tourists carry a lot of cash and are not as street-savvy as locals. You can reduce your risk of getting robbed or hurt by **keeping a low profile:** the loudmouthed, camera-toting gawker looks more witless than a quietly thoughtful—but friendly—traveler. Respecting local customs (in many cases, dressing more conservatively) may placate would-be hecklers. Be open-minded and courteous; a smile goes a long way. If you show genuine interest in local languages and practices, the locals are more likely to watch your back when a mugger starts trailing you. If you are traveling by yourself, be sure someone at home knows your itinerary, and never admit that you're traveling alone.

Carry yourself with confidence and familiarize yourself with your surroundings before setting out; if you must check a map while exploring, duck into a shop. When walking at night, stick to busy, well-lit streets. Avoid dark alleyways; do not cross through parks, parking lots, or other large, deserted areas. Look for children playing, women walking in the open, and other signs of an active community. If you feel uncomfortable, leave as quickly and directly as you can, but don't allow fear of the unknown to turn you into a hermit. Careful, persistent exploration will build confidence and make your stay more rewarding.

GETTING AROUND. Renting a **motorbike** is one of the cheapest and most convenient ways to explore Southeast Asia, but you should understand the risks involved before you hop on—motor vehicle crashes are a leading cause of injury among travelers. People in different parts of Southeast Asia drive on different sides of the street, but most drive on both at once. Observing local traffic patterns and studying maps before you hit the road will help prevent accidents. Wear a helmet and drive with care to reduce the chance of serious injury. If you are using a **car,** learn local driving signals and wear a seatbelt. Not for the weak-hearted, the roads of Southeast Asia are an adventure in themselves. *Let's Go* does not recommend hitchhiking.

SELF DEFENSE. There is no sure-fire way to avoid all the threatening situations you might encounter when you travel, but a good self-defense course will help you react effectively to aggression. **Impact, Prepare, and Model Mugging** can refer you to local self-defense courses in the US (☎800-345-5425). Visit the web site at www.impactsafety.org for a list of nearby chapters. Workshops (2-3hr.) start at US$50; full courses run US$350-500. Women and men are welcome. If you find yourself in danger, remember that the best strategy is usually to run and scream "help" or "fire" in the local language. In Southeast Asia, especially, attracting attention to yourself in public could help deter any immediate threat to your safety.

TRAVEL ADVISORIES In addition to the information listed below, a comprehensive web site on terrorism is: www.terrorismanswers.com. The following government offices provide travel information and advisories by telephone, by fax, or via the web:

Australian Department of Foreign Affairs and Trade: ☎1300 555 135; faxback service 02 6261 1299; www.dfat.gov.au.

Canadian Department of Foreign Affairs and International Trade (DFAIT): In Canada and the US call ☎800-267-6788, elsewhere call ☎+1 613-944-6788; www.dfait-maeci.gc.ca. Call for their free booklet, *Bon Voyage...But.*

New Zealand Ministry of Foreign Affairs: ☎04 494 8500; fax 494 8506; www.mft.govt.nz/trav.html.

United Kingdom Foreign and Commonwealth Office: ☎020 7008 0232; fax 7008 0155; www.fco.gov.uk.

US Department of State: ☎202-647-5225, faxback service 202-647-3000; http://travel.state.gov. For *A Safe Trip Abroad,* call ☎202-512-1800.

POLITICS AND TERRORISM. Travelers to Southeast Asia should always check travel advisories and world news for the countries they will be visiting before departure. It is always helpful—and sometimes essential—to be aware of the political situation in the region; using current, proper titles for government officials and organizations is a must. Currently, one of the most prominent terrorist groups in Southeast Asia is the **Abu Sayyaf Group (ASG),** an Islamic separatist organization operating primarily in the Philippines but also in nearby parts of Malaysia and Indonesia. While ASG is responsible for kidnappings, most recent bombings and acts of violence have been committed by other groups.

COUNTRY-SPECIFIC CONCERNS

CAMBODIA. Landmines litter the country. Though de-mining operations have made significant progress, much of Cambodia remains mined, especially in rural areas. **Stay on well-traveled roads at all times.** Additionally, bandits are still at large, and corrupt police forces are always looking for extra cash. Overland travel is the most dangerous mode of transport because of raids, unofficial police "checkpoints," and road conditions.

INDONESIA. In October 2002, the US State Department issued a travel warning urging US citizens to postpone non-essential travel to Indonesia. Anti-Western violence has been increasing over the past few years; the nightclub bombings in Bali were preceded by a failed attack on the US embassy, and it is not yet known what groups are currently the most active. Radical Islamic groups have gained momentum in the country, and both separatist movements and interreligious violence threaten political and social stability. The floundering economy of the past several years has aggravated tensions. Militant groups in Surakarta have threatened to push Americans off Indonesian soil, though government forces have prevented them from acting on such threats. Foreign travelers should exercise caution: keep a low profile and avoid demonstrations. Travel is currently considered unsafe in the **Aceh Province, Central and South Sulawesi, West Timor, Central and West Kalimantan, Irian Jaya,** and **Maluku and North Maluku.** Check with your embassy for up-to-date safety information.

LAOS. Laos has a low crime rate, but travelers shouldn't let their guard down, especially as incidents of theft, burglary, and assault have risen sharply in the last year. The **Vang Vieng-Luang Prabang Rd.** is no longer a major bandit site, but some travelers feel safer avoiding it. Be especially careful in the **Golden Triangle** area near the Thai-Burmese-Lao border, which is known for its opium production. In Xieng Khouang Province, the Bolovens Plateau, and along the Ho Chi Minh Trail, unexploded ordnance is still a threat. Although several non-governmental organizations have taken up demining, some bombs remain, killing or injuring about 10 people per month. Laos has strict rules regarding **public morality.** (Remember, this is the country that outlawed karaoke in its capital city.) Bringing a Laotian into your hotel room could land you in prison.

MALAYSIA. International trafficking of **illegal drugs** is punishable by death. Very little violent crime threatens travelers; criminals stop at theft and minor cons.

MYANMAR. Ethnic clashes have made eastern Myanmar and Thai border regions dangerous in recent months, so check the news and your embassy before going to the Shan state. **Do not talk about politics**. Stay away from demonstrations, and do not engage in political conversations, no matter how harmless the topic may seem. **Political conversations put locals at risk of interrogation and arrest.** Do not photograph bridges, military installations, or anything else of economic or military importance. Officials carefully screen books and magazines at the airport. These officials may not understand English, but they are attentive to political articles, books, and pictures related to **Aung San Suu Kyi** (see p. 492).

THAILAND. Recently, northern Thailand and its border with Myanmar have been prone to violence due to the Burmese ethnic conflict. Thailand has a good safety record. Nevertheless, **scams** abound: taxi and tuk-tuk drivers, guest house operators, and fellow travelers have all been known to attempt various con games and thievery. On buses and trains and in the airport, be careful when accepting food or drink from strangers; travelers have been drugged and robbed. Most likely their friendliness is genuine, but exercise common sense. Crime committed against foreigners is usually petty thievery; violence is rare. All **narcotic drugs** in Thailand are illegal, despite what your guest house owner may tell you. Penalties for drug-related crimes can be very stiff—up to life in prison.

SINGAPORE. Singaporean law can be quite strict by most Western standards. Jay-walking is prohibited and may result in a fine. The sale (and purchase) of chewing gum is prohibited. General chewing of gum, however, is not closely monitored. Smoking in enclosed public spaces and eating or drinking on public transportation are also prohibited. The penalty for importing **illegal drugs** can be as severe as execution and will almost definitely involve a long prison sentence. Singapore is one of the safest places in the world. Women are rarely catcalled, and often walk alone after dark. Nevertheless, petty crime happens, and travelers should not surrender their street smarts.

THE PHILIPPINES. Personable Filipinos go to great lengths to give directions and point out proper jeepney routes. However, be wary of taking drinks from anyone you don't know—unsuspecting travelers have been given drinks spiked with **sedatives.** Manila seems to be a haven for such wayward pharmacists, but exercise caution everywhere. Another concern for travelers is the use of firearms by security guards protecting restaurants, banks, and clubs. Standing in front of banks and armored vehicles is unsafe, as these are often targets. Venturing unchaperoned into rarely frequented areas of the country may also make you a target for **radical separatist groups.**

VIETNAM. Never leave valuables unguarded (especially your passport); **thefts** are not uncommon within guest houses, sometimes even under the management's orchestration. Keep an eye out for con artists, pickpockets, and purse or backpack snatchers, especially prevalent in Hồ Chí Minh City. Pedicab passengers are particularly vulnerable to thieves. Avoid photographing bridges, border crossings, power stations, and military and government structures. In the past few years, minority protests have caused certain areas to be closed to travelers; check with your embassy for detailed information.

FINANCIAL SECURITY

PROTECTING YOUR VALUABLES. There are a few steps you can take to minimize the financial risk associated with traveling: First, **bring as little with you as possible.** Second, don't forget to label your luggage both inside and out. Third, buy a few combination **padlocks** to secure your belongings in hostel or train station lockers or in your pack; even twist-ties or dental floss will slow down pickpockets. Fourth, **carry as little cash as possible** and never count your money in public. Don't put a wallet with money in your backpack or back pocket. Instead, keep your traveler's checks and ATM/credit cards in a **money belt** along with your passport and ID cards. Watch out for moped riders who snatch purses and backpacks by cutting the straps. Finally, **keep a small cash reserve separate from your primary stash.** This should be about US$50 sewn into or stored in the depths of your pack, along with your traveler's check numbers and important photocopies. Be sure to photocopy both the visa page and the identification page of your passport. Leave another copy at home.

CON ARTISTS & PICKPOCKETS. **Con artists** abound in all large cities in Southeast Asia. They often work in groups; children are among the most effective. Beware of tricks designed to distract you while someone snatches your bag. **Don't ever let your passport and your bags out of your sight.** In city crowds and especially on public transportation, **pickpockets** are impressively deft. Be aware of your surroundings and look sure of yourself. Confidence is the greatest anti-theft device you have.

ESSENTIALS

ACCOMMODATIONS AND TRANSPORTATION. Never leave your belongings unattended; crime occurs in the safest-looking guest house or hotel. If you feel unsafe, look for places with a curfew or a night attendant. Most guest houses don't have lockers; consider taking a bike lock with you to secure your belongings to your bed. Be particularly careful on buses and trains. Carry your backpack in front of you where you can see it. Thieves thrive on trains; professionals wait for tourists to fall asleep and then carry off their bags. When traveling with others, sleep in alternate shifts. If you are alone, use good judgment in selecting a train compartment: never stay in an empty one, and use a lock to secure your pack to the luggage rack. Try to sleep on top bunks with your luggage stored above you or in bed with you, and keep important documents and other valuables on your person.

DRUGS & ALCOHOL

Drugs are often easily accessible in Southeast Asia and, especially in some rural communities, drug use may seem to be common and public. All drug use, however, is illegal. Buying or selling *any* type of drug may lead to anything from a prison sentence to the death penalty, especially in Malaysia, Singapore, and Cambodia. A meek "I didn't know it was illegal" will not suffice; if you break the law, your home embassies will visit you in jail and bring you candy, but they **cannot and will not do anything else** to help. Alcohol consumption varies from country to country, often reflecting the dominant religious values.

HEALTH

Common sense is the simplest prescription for good health while you travel. The heat of Southeast Asia and the foreign foods and water that may cause diarrhea make **dehydration** a major concern. Drink plenty of fluids to prevent dehydration and constipation; a supply of salt-tablets and anti-diarrheal medicine might prove useful. Sturdy, broken-in shoes and clean socks will keep your feet happy.

BEFORE YOU GO

Preparation can help minimize the likelihood of contracting a disease and maximize the chances of receiving effective health care in the event of an emergency. In your **passport,** list any allergies or medical conditions and write the names of any people you wish to be contacted in case of a medical emergency. Matching a prescription to a foreign equivalent is not always easy or possible, so carry up-to-date, legible prescriptions or a statement from your doctor with the medication's trade name, manufacturer, chemical name, and dosage. To be cautious, bring any medication you think you might need with you. Major gateway cities like Bangkok, Manila, and Jakarta will have most over-the-counter medications; stock up there before you travel out. Keep all medication with you in your carry-on luggage. For tips on packing a basic **first-aid kit**, see p. 26.

IMMUNIZATIONS & PRECAUTIONS

See the box below for a list of inoculations you might need. For recommendations on immunizations and prophylaxis, consult the CDC (see below) and check with a doctor for guidance. **Malaria** is prevalent in most of Southeast Asia. The CDC also provides information about malaria risk by country. Strains resistant to certain prophylactics are common, so ask your doctor to recommend the best preventative drug for your region of travel. While **yellow fever** is only endemic to parts of

South America and sub-Saharan Africa, many countries may deny entrance to travelers arriving from these zones without a certificate of vaccination.

INOCULATION REQUIREMENTS & RECOMMENDATIONS

The inoculations needed for travel in Southeast Asia vary with the length of your trip and the activities you plan to pursue. Visit your doctor at least 4-6 weeks prior to your departure to allow time for the shots to take effect. Be sure to keep your inoculation records with you as you travel–you may be required to show them to border officials.

Diptheria and tetanus, measles, and polio, booster doses recommended as needed.

Typhoid, strongly recommended.

Hepatitis A or immune globulin (IG), recommended.

Hepatitis B, if traveling for 6 months or more, or if exposure to blood, needle-sharing, or sexual contact is likely. Important for health care workers and those who might seek medical treatment abroad.

Japanese Encephalitis, only if you will be in rural areas for 4 weeks or more, or if there are known outbreaks in the regions you plan to visit; elevated risk usually from May to October.

Rabies, if you might be exposed to animals as you travel.

Yellow Fever, if traveling from South America or sub-Saharan Africa; certificate of vaccination may be required for entry into some countries. There is no risk in Southeast Asia.

USEFUL ORGANIZATIONS & PUBLICATIONS

The US **Centers for Disease Control and Prevention** (**CDC;** ☎877-394-8747; toll free fax 888-232-3299; www.cdc.gov/travel) maintains an international travelers' hotline and an informative web site. The CDC's booklet *Health Information for International Travel*, an annual rundown of disease, immunization, and health advice, is free online or US$25 via the Public Health Foundation (☎877-252-1200). The **United States State Department** (http://travel.state.gov) compiles consular information sheets on health, entry requirements, and other issues for most countries of the world. Government agencies of other countries offer similar services (see **Travel Advisories**, p. 17. For quick information on health and other travel warnings, call the **Overseas Citizens Services** (☎202-647-5225, toll-free hotline ☎888-401-4747), or contact a passport agency, embassy, or consulate. For information on medical evacuation services and travel insurance firms, see the US government's web site at http://travel.state.gov/medical.html or the **British Foreign and Commonwealth Office** (www.fco.gov.uk). For detailed information on travel health, including a country-by-country overview of diseases, try the **International Travel Health Guide,** by Stuart Rose, MD (US$20; www.travmed.com). For general health info, contact the **American Red Cross** (☎800-564-1234; www.redcross.org).

MEDICAL ASSISTANCE ON THE ROAD

Hospitals in Southeast Asia vary from region to region, but generally larger, centralized cities like Singapore, Bangkok, and Kuala Lumpur have high-quality facilities. Public hospitals tend be more crowded and less expensive than private hospitals, which are more likely to have English-speaking doctors, language interpreters, foreign insurance claim assistance, international emergency medical evacuation access, and embassy liaison services. For the most trusted medical care, go to Thailand or Singapore.

If you are concerned about finding medical assistance while traveling, you may wish to have special support services. The *MedPass* from **GlobalCare, Inc.** 6875 Shiloh Rd. East, Alpharetta, GA, 30005, USA (☎800-860-1111; fax 678-341-1800; www.globalems.com), provides 24hr. international medical assistance, support, and medical evacuation resources. The **International Association for Medical Assistance to Travelers** (**IAMAT;** US ☎716-754-4883, Canada ☎416-652-0137; www.iamat.org) has free membership, lists English-speaking doctors worldwide, and has detailed info on immunization requirements and sanitation. **International Security Overseas** (ISOS), 331 N Bridge Rd., Ste. 17-00 Odeon Towers, Singapore 188720 (www.internationalsos.com), provides medical services, travel insurance, and around-the-clock emergency assistance services. ISOS offers insurance for short-term and long-term travel; couples and families can purchase cheaper packages. Call ☎800-523-8930 for information or to enroll in a plan.

Those with medical conditions (such as diabetes, allergies to antibiotics, epilepsy, or heart conditions) may want to obtain a **Medic Alert** membership (first year US$35, annually thereafter US$20), which includes a stainless steel ID tag bracelet, among other benefits, including a 24hr. collect-call number. Contact the **Medic Alert Foundation,** 2323 Colorado Ave, Turlock, CA 95382, USA (☎888-633-4298, outside US ☎209-668-3333; www.medicalert.org). Diabetics can call the **American Diabetes Association** for a copy of their booklet, *The Diabetes Travel Guide* ($15, $13 for members; ☎800-342-2383).

ONCE IN SOUTHEAST ASIA

ENVIRONMENTAL HAZARDS

Heat exhaustion, characterized by **dehydration** and **salt deficiency,** can lead to fatigue, headaches, and wooziness. Prevent it by drinking plenty of fluids, eating salty foods, and avoiding dehydrating beverages (e.g. alcohol and caffeinated beverages). Adding salt or lemon juice to water also helps.

Sunburn: If you are planning to spend time near water or in the desert, bring sunscreen along. If you get burned, drink more fluids than usual and apply an aloe-based lotion.

INSECT-BORNE DISEASES

Many diseases are transmitted by insects—mainly mosquitoes. Be careful in wet or forested areas, especially while hiking and camping; wear long pants and long sleeves, tuck your pants into your socks, and sleep under a mosquito net. Use insect repellents such as DEET; consider soaking or spraying your gear with permethrin (licensed in the US for use on clothing), but be aware that permethrin can cause an allergic reaction. Natural repellents include vitamin B-12 and garlic pills. To stop the itch after being bitten, try Calamine lotion or topical cortisones like Cortaid, or take a bath with a half-cup of baking soda or oatmeal.

Malaria: Transmitted by *Anopheles* mosquitoes that bite at night. The incubation period varies from 6-8 days to several months. Symptoms include fever, chills, aches, and fatigue, followed by high fever and sweating, sometimes with vomiting and diarrhea. See a doctor for any flu-like sickness that occurs after travel in a risk area. To reduce the risk of contracting malaria, use mosquito repellent, particularly during the evenings and in forested areas, and take oral prophylactics such as **mefloquine** (sold under the name Lariam) or **doxycycline** (ask your doctor for a prescription). Be aware that these drugs can have serious side effects, including slowed heart rate and nightmares.

Dengue fever: An "urban viral infection" transmitted by *Aedes* mosquitoes, which bite during the day rather than at night. Dengue has flu-like symptoms and is often indicated by a rash 3-4 days after the onset of fever. Symptoms for the first 2-4 days include chills, high fever, headaches, swollen lymph nodes, muscle aches, and, in some instances, a pink rash on the face. If you experience these symptoms, see a doctor immediately, drink plenty of liquids, and take fever-reducing medication such as acetaminophen (Tylenol). **Never take aspirin to treat dengue fever.**

Japanese encephalitis: Most prevalent during the rainy season in rural areas. Symptoms include delirium, chills, headache, fever, vomiting, and muscle fatigue. Go to a hospital as soon as any symptoms appear. According to the CDC, there is little chance of being infected if proper precautions are taken: use mosquito repellents containing DEET and sleep under mosquito nets.

Other insect-borne diseases: Filariasis is a roundworm infestation transmitted by mosquitoes. Infection causes enlargement of extremities and has no vaccine. The **plague** is still a risk as well; early symptoms include fever, nausea, sore throat, and swollen lymph nodes. A vaccine is available for the plague; both diseases can be treated.

FOOD- & WATER-BORNE DISEASES

The **tap water** in Southeast Asia (with the exception of Singapore) is not safe, even for brushing teeth. Prevention is the best cure; be sure that your food is properly cooked and the water you drink is clean. Never drink unbottled water that you have not treated yourself. Buy bottled water, or purify your own water by bringing it to a rolling boil or treating it with **iodine tablets;** note however that some parasites such as *giardia* have exteriors that resist iodine treatment, so boiling is more reliable. Alternatively, using a high-quality **water filter** in addition to iodine treatment will prove more effective than iodine alone. Peel fruits and veggies; avoid ice cubes and anything washed in tap water, like salad. Watch out for food from markets or street vendors that may have been cooked in unhygienic conditions. Other culprits are raw shellfish, unpasteurized milk, and sauces containing raw eggs. Always wash your hands before eating or bring a quick-drying purifying liquid hand cleaner. Your bowels will thank you.

Traveler's diarrhea: A rite of passage for travelers, caused by bacteria in untreated water or uncooked foods. Symptoms include nausea, bloating, and urgency. Try quick-energy, non-sugary foods with protein and carbohydrates to keep your strength up. Over-the-counter anti-diarrheals (e.g. Immodium) should be used in moderation for temporary relief. Drink sweetened liquids, uncaffeinated soft drinks, or salted crackers to avoid dehydration. If you develop a fever or your symptoms don't go away after 4-5 days, consult a doctor. Consult a doctor immediately for treatment of diarrhea in children.

Cholera: An intestinal disease caused by a bacteria found in contaminated food. Symptoms include diarrhea, dehydration, vomiting, and muscle cramps. See a doctor immediately; if left untreated, it may be deadly. Rehydration and antibiotic treatment are crucial if you contract cholera. The 50% effective vaccine can have serious side effects.

Dysentery: Symptoms include bloody diarrhea (sometimes mixed with mucus), fever, and abdominal pain and tenderness. **Bacillary dysentery** generally only lasts a week, but is highly contagious. **Amoebic dysentery,** which develops more slowly, is a more serious disease and may cause long-term damage if left untreated. A stool test can determine which kind you have; seek medical help immediately. Dysentery can be treated with the drugs norfloxacin or ciprofloxacin (commonly known as Cipro). Consider obtaining a prescription before you leave home.

Hepatitis A: A viral infection of the liver acquired primarily through contaminated water. Symptoms include fatigue, fever, loss of appetite, nausea, dark urine, jaundice, vomiting, aches and pains, and light stools. Ask your doctor about the vaccine (Havrix or Vaqta) or an injection of immune globulin (IG; formerly called gamma globulin).

Parasites: Microbes, tapeworms, etc., that hide in unsafe water and food. **Giardiasis,** for example, is acquired by drinking untreated water from streams or lakes. Symptoms include swollen glands or lymph nodes, fever, rashes or itchiness, and digestive problems. Boil water, wear shoes, and eat only cooked food.

Schistosomiasis: A parasitic disease caused when the larvae of flatworm penetrate unbroken skin. Symptoms include an itchy localized rash, followed in 4-6 weeks by fever, fatigue, painful urination, diarrhea, loss of appetite, and night sweats. To avoid it, try not to swim in fresh water; if exposed to untreated water, rub the area vigorously with a towel and apply rubbing alcohol.

Typhoid fever: Caused by the salmonella bacteria; common in villages and rural areas. While mostly transmitted through contaminated food and water, it may also be acquired by direct contact with another person. Early symptoms include fever, headaches, fatigue, loss of appetite, constipation, and sometimes a rash on the abdomen or chest. Antibiotics can treat typhoid, but a vaccination (70-90% effective) is recommended.

OTHER INFECTIOUS DISEASES

Hepatitis B: A viral infection of the liver transmitted via bodily fluids or needle-sharing. Symptoms may not surface until years after infection. A 3-shot vaccination sequence is recommended for health-care workers, sexually active travelers, and anyone planning to seek medical treatment abroad; it must begin 6 months before traveling.

Hepatitis C: Like Hepatitis B, but the mode of transmission differs. IV drug users, those with occupational exposure to blood, hemodialysis patients, and recipients of blood transfusions are at the highest risk, but it can also spread through sexual contact or sharing items like razors and toothbrushes that may have traces of blood on them.

Rabies: Transmitted through the saliva of infected animals; fatal if untreated. By the time symptoms (thirst and muscle spasms) appear, the disease is in its terminal stage. If you are bitten, wash the wound thoroughly, seek immediate medical care, and try to have the animal located. A rabies vaccine, which consists of 3 shots given over a 21-day period, is available but is only semi-effective.

AIDS, HIV & STDS

A thriving sex and intravenous drug industry has brought **Acquired Immune Deficiency Syndrome (AIDS)** to epidemic status in parts of Southeast Asia. Over 4% of Cambodia's adult population had HIV/AIDS at the end of 1999; 66,000 died of the disease in Thailand in the same year. Condom use is uncommon in Southeast Asia, even among sex workers and their clients. Safer sexual practices have become more widespread in recent years, but not enough to combat the dramatic spread of HIV/AIDS, especially in Cambodia, Myanmar, and Thailand. For detailed information on AIDS in Southeast Asia, call the **US Centers for Disease Control**'s 24hr. hotline at ☎800-342-2437, or contact the **Joint United Nations Programme on HIV/AIDS (UNAIDS),** 20 Ave. Appia, CH-1211 Geneva 27, Switzerland (☎41 22 791 3666).

Travelers seeking pleasure in the quasi-legal bars, massage parlors, and brothels of Southeast Asia stand a good chance of bringing back unwanted viral souvenirs of their trip. The best advice is to follow all precautions concerning any sexual encounter—use a condom with spermicide, and avoid sex with strangers or with people who engage in high-risk behavior (such as IV drug use or promiscuity or unprotected sex). Many prostitutes do not know that they are infected, and even if they do, they probably won't tell their clients. Since it isn't always easy to buy condoms when traveling and Western brands tend to be more reliable, bring a supply with you. *Never* share intravenous drug, tattooing, or other needles.

Sexually transmitted diseases (STDs) such as gonorrhea, chlamydia, genital warts, syphilis, and herpes are easier to catch than HIV and can be just as serious. **Hepatitis** B and C can also be transmitted sexually (see p. 24). Though condoms may protect you from some STDs, oral or even tactile contact can lead to transmission. If you think you may have contracted an STD, see a doctor immediately.

WOMEN'S HEALTH

Women traveling in unsanitary conditions are vulnerable to **urinary tract** and **bladder infections,** common and severely uncomfortable bacterial conditions that cause a burning sensation and painful, frequent urination. Over-the-counter medicines can sometimes alleviate symptoms, but if they persist, see a doctor. The hot and humid climate of Southeast Asia also makes women especially susceptible to **vaginal yeast infections.** Wearing loose fitting trousers or a skirt and cotton underwear will help, as will over-the-counter remedies like Monistat or Gynelotrimin. Bring supplies from home if you are prone to infection, as they may be difficult to find on the road. In a pinch, some travelers use a natural alternative such as plain yogurt and lemon juice douche. Since **tampons, pads,** and reliable **contraceptive devices** are sometimes hard to find in Southeast Asia, bring supplies from home. Women using birth-control pills should bring enough to allow for possible loss or extended stays. Also bring a prescription, since forms of the pill vary considerably. **Abortion** is illegal or restricited in many countries in Southeast Asia. Even in countries where it is readily available (for as little as US$5 in some cases), it may not always be safe. Make sure you are informed about the country or countries you are visiting. Information about family planning centers can be obtained through the **International Planned Parenthood Federation,** European Regional Office, Regent's College Inner Circle, Regent's Park, London NW1 4NS, UK (☎020 7487 7900).

INSURANCE

Travel insurance generally covers four basic areas: medical or health problems, property loss, trip cancellation or interruption, and emergency evacuation. Although your regular insurance policies might extend to travel-related accidents, consider purchasing travel insurance if the cost of potential trip cancellation/interruption or emergency medical evacuation is greater than you can absorb. Prices for travel insurance purchased separately generally run about US$50 per week for full coverage, while trip cancellation/interruption may be purchased separately at a rate of about US$5.50 per US$100 of coverage.

Medical insurance (especially university policies) often covers costs incurred abroad; check with your provider. **US Medicare** does not cover foreign travel. **Canadians** are protected by their home province's health insurance plan for up to 90 days after leaving the country; check with the provincial Ministry of Health or Health Plan Headquarters for details. **Homeowners' insurance** (or your family's coverage) often covers theft during travel and loss of travel documents (passport, plane ticket, railpass, etc.) up to US$500. **ISIC** and **ITIC** (see p. 11) provide basic insurance benefits, including US$100 per day of in-hospital sickness for up to 60 days, US$3000 of accident-related medical reimbursement, and US$25,000 for emergency medical transport. Cardholders have access to a toll-free 24hr. helpline (run by the insurance provider **TravelGuard**) for medical, legal, and financial emergencies overseas (US and Canada ☎877-370-4742, elsewhere call US collect ☎1 715-345-0505). **American Express** (US ☎800-528-4800) grants most cardholders automatic car rental insurance (collision and theft, but not liability) and ground travel accident coverage of US$100,000 on flight purchases made with the card. **STA** (see p. 30) offer a range of plans that can supplement your basic coverage. Other private insurance providers in the US and Canada include: **Access America** (☎800-284-8300; www.accessamerica.com); **Berkely Group/Carefree Travel Insurance** (☎800-323-3149; www.berkely.com); **Globalcare Travel Insurance** (☎800-821-2488; www.globalcare-cocco.com); and **Travel Assistance International** (☎800-821-2828; www.travelassistance.com). Providers in the **UK** include **Columbus Direct** (☎020 7375 0011; www.columbusdirect.net). In **Australia,** try **AFTA** (☎02 9375 4955).

PACKING

PACK LIGHT. To appreciate the virtue of traveling light, pack your bag with what you think are the bare essentials, strap it on, and imagine walking uphill for three hours on hot asphalt. Now take out about half of what you packed before so you don't rue the day that you packed that hairdryer "just in case." Don't forget that you can purchase all necessary items in Southeast Asia for a fraction what they cost at home.

LUGGAGE. For travel in Southeast Asia, a sturdy **frame backpack** is unbeatable. Toting a **suitcase** or **trunk** is all right if you plan to explore from just one or two cities but a very bad idea if you're going to be moving at all. Regardless, a **daypack** (a small backpack or courier bag) is a must. Locks on the packs are a good initial deterrent, but shouldn't replace common sense. Plastic bags will keep things dry and sorted. If you use a brightly-colored fanny pack, you will get robbed.

CLOTHING. The clothes you bring should be sturdy, light, comfortable, and quick-drying. Local custom usually demands conservative dress that covers your arms and legs. Try to bring only two outfits, one to wash and one to wear. Clothing is very inexpensive in Southeast Asia, so pack light and buy what you need on the road. Essentials that you should bring with you might include a good waterproof jacket, underwear, and sturdy boots.

CONVERTERS AND ADAPTERS. Electricity in Southeast Asia is 220 volts AC, enough to fry a 110V appliance. **Americans** and **Canadians** should pick up an **adapter** and a **converter** (US$20) at a hardware store. **New Zealanders, South Africans,** and **Australians** will also need adapters, but not converters.

TOILETRIES. Most toiletries are readily available and cheap in Southeast Asia. To be safe, stock up in larger cities before going to rural areas. Contact lenses may be expensive, so bring enough pairs for your entire trip. Bring your glasses and a copy of your prescription in case you need emergency replacements.

OTHER USEFUL ITEMS. It's always a good idea to carry a **first-aid kit** including sunscreen and insect repellent. Other useful items include: an umbrella, alarm clock, moleskin (for blisters), safety pins, sunglasses, pocketknife, compass, padlock, flashlight, duct tape (for patching tears), and a moneybelt.

IMPORTANT DOCUMENTS. Don't forget your passport, traveler's checks, ATM and/or credit cards, and adequate IDs.

ACCOMMODATIONS

Choosing accommodations in Southeast Asia can sometimes be a gamble, as electricity, running water, and air-conditioning have not yet reached many rural areas. Finding inexpensive accommodations, however, never proves to be a problem. Hotels and guest houses line the streets of major cities and towns throughout Southeast Asia, many with Internet facilities and small cafes. For a few dollars, facilities can vary from a shared room with several beds to a single room with a private bath and fan. Modern and more expensive hotels can be found in highly touristed areas, allowing for a cooler and more comfortable stay.

While you should make reservations at the more expensive lodgings, finding a hotel on a day's notice is not difficult. It is not uncommon, and most often is expected, to ask to see rooms before committing to a hotel; this also allows room for bargaining. In some parts of Southeast Asia, including in all of Viet-

nam, the law requires that you leave your passport with your hotel or guest house during your stay. If you feel uncomfortable about doing this, some places will allow you to leave your customs slip from immigration.

KEEPING IN TOUCH

BY MAIL

SENDING MAIL HOME FROM SOUTHEAST ASIA

Airmail letters under 1 oz. between North America and most Southeast Asian nations cost US$1. Envelopes should be marked "air mail" or "*par avion*" to avoid having letters sent by sea. Sea or "**surface mail**" *is* an option—by far the cheapest and slowest. It takes 1-3 months to cross the Atlantic and 2-4 to cross the Pacific—appropriate for sending large items you won't need to see for a while. When ordering books and materials from abroad, always include one or two **International Reply Coupons (IRCs)**—a way of providing the postage to cover delivery. IRCs should be available at your local post office (US$1.05).

SENDING MAIL TO SOUTHEAST ASIA

Mail in Southeast Asia is unreliable. Mark envelopes "air mail" or "*par avion*" or your letter or postcard will never arrive. Expect standard mail to take 2-3 weeks to reach major cities and longer to get to rural areas. **Federal Express** (Australia ☎13 26 10; Canada and US ☎800-247-4747; New Zealand ☎0800 73 33 39; UK ☎0800 12 38 00) handles express mail services from most home countries to all Southeast Asian countries; for example, they can get a letter from New York to Vietnam in three days for US$32, and from London to Brunei in three days for UK£30.

RECEIVING MAIL IN SOUTHEAST ASIA

There are several ways to arrange pickup of letters sent to you by friends and relatives while you are abroad.

General Delivery: Mail can be sent through **Poste Restante** (the international phrase for General Delivery to almost any town with a post office), usually for no surcharge. Address *Poste Restante* letters to the recipient, with the last name underlined and in capital letters: "Anna MCLOON, Poste Restante, Bangkok, Thailand." The mail will go to a desk in the central post office, unless you specify a post office by street address or postal code. As a rule, it is best to use the largest post office in the area, as mail may be sent there regardless of what is written on the envelope. When picking up mail, bring a photo ID, preferably a passport. If the clerks insist that there is nothing for you, have them check under your first name as well. *Let's Go* lists post offices in the **Practical Information** section for each city and most towns.

American Express: If you contact them in advance, AmEx's travel offices throughout the world will act as a free mail service (the **Client Letter Service**) for cardholders, holding mail for up to 30 days and forwarding it upon request. Address the letter in the way shown above. Some offices will offer these services to non-cardholders, but you must call ahead to make sure. Check the **Practical Information** section of the countries you plan to visit; *Let's Go* lists AmEx office locations for most large cities. A complete list is available free from AmEx (US ☎800-528-4800).

BY TELEPHONE

CALLING HOME FROM SOUTHEAST ASIA

A calling card is probably your cheapest bet. Calls are billed collect or to your account. You can frequently call collect without even possessing a company's calling card just by calling their access number and following the instructions. To call home with a calling card, contact the operator for your service provider in Southeast Asia by dialing the appropriate toll-free access number (listed on the inside back cover of this book). International calling booths abound in Southeast Asia; for a small fee, some may let you receive a call as well if you ask nicely. Many hostels also have **International Direct Dial** (IDD) facilities.

Let's Go has recently partnered with **ekit.com** to provide a calling card that offers a number of services, including email and voice messaging. Before purchasing any calling card, compare rates and make sure it serves your needs (a local phone card is better for local calls). For more info, visit www.letsgo.ekit.com.

CALLING WITHIN SOUTHEAST ASIA

Details about time zones are on the inside back cover of this book. The simplest way to call within the country is to use a coin-operated phone. **Prepaid phone cards** (available at many guest houses, shops, and restaurants), which carry a certain amount of phone time depending on the card's denomination, usually save time and money in the long run. Just insert them into the phone and proceed with your call. Other prepaid phone cards come with a Personal Identification Number (PIN) and a toll-free access number. Call the access number and follow the directions on the phone to make both international and domestic calls. Purchase them in advance from major telephone companies in your country, and check to make sure that service from the company will be available in the region where you'll be traveling. Phone rates typically tend to be highest in the morning, lower in the evening, and lowest on Sunday and late at night.

BY EMAIL

Internet cafes are everywhere in Southeast Asia, even in some of the smallest towns. Many guest houses have Internet access, and some public libraries have free access. *Let's Go* lists Internet access locations in the **Practical Information** sections. It's usually difficult to forge a remote link with your home server from Southeast Asia, so take advantage of free web-based email accounts (e.g. www.hotmail.com or www.yahoo.com).

GETTING TO SOUTHEAST ASIA

BY PLANE

A little effort can save you a bundle. If your plans are flexible enough to deal with the restrictions, courier fares are the cheapest. Tickets from consolidators and standby seating are also good deals, but last-minute specials, airfare wars, and charter flights often beat them. The key is to hunt around, be patient, be flexible, and ask persistently about discounts. Students, seniors, and those under 26 should never pay full price for a ticket.

Southeast Asia regional package tickets (offered by Cathay Pacific Airlines), and round-the-world (RTW) flights are pricier but reasonable alternatives. Patching one-way flights together is the least economical way to travel.

DETAILS AND TIPS

Timing: Airfare to Southeast Asia peaks on holidays and between May and September. The cheapest times to travel are October and April. Midweek (M-Th morning) round-trip flights run US$40-50 cheaper than weekend flights, which are generally more crowded and less likely to permit frequent-flier upgrades.

Route: Round-trip flights are cheapest; "open-jaw" (arriving in and departing from different cities, e.g. New York-Hanoi, Bangkok-New York) tickets tend to be pricier. Instead, purchase a round-trip ticket to Bangkok and then a one-way flight to Hanoi upon arrival. That way you can purchase another one-way ticket from another city to Bangkok, which is very cheap. Flying into regional hubs (especially Singapore, Bangkok, and Kuala Lumpur) is usually cheaper. Regional transportation is easier to handle while in Southeast Asia, and domestic flights can usually be purchased just hours or days in advance.

Round-the-World (RTW): If Southeast Asia is only one stop on a more extensive globe-hop, consider a RTW ticket. Tickets usually include at least 5 stops and are valid for about a year; prices range US$1200-5000. Try **Northwest Airlines/KLM** (US ☎800-447-4747; www.nwa.com) or **Star Alliance,** a consortium of 13 airlines including United Airlines (US ☎800-241-6522; www.star-alliance.com).

Boarding: Confirm international flights by phone within 72hr. of departure. Most airlines require that passengers arrive at the airport 3hr. before departure. One carry-on item and 2 checked bags is the norm for non-courier flights.

BUDGET AND STUDENT TRAVEL AGENCIES

While knowledgeable agents can make your life easy and help you save, they may not spend the time to find you the lowest possible fare—they get paid on commission. Students and under-26ers holding **ISIC and IYTC cards** (see p. 11) qualify for discounts from student travel agencies. Most flights are on major airlines, but in peak season some may sell seats on less reliable chartered aircraft.

Council Travel (www.counciltravel.com). Countless US offices, including branches in Atlanta, Boston, Chicago, LA, New York, San Francisco, Seattle, and Washington D.C. Check the web site or call 800-2-COUNCIL (226-8624) for the office nearest you. Council has been bought out by STA, but, as of August 2002, their offices remain open.

STA Travel, 7890 S. Hardy Dr. Ste. 110, Tempe, AZ 85284, USA (24hr. reservations and info ☎800-781-4040; fax 480-592-0876; www.statravel.com). A student and youth travel organization with over 250 offices worldwide (check web site for a listing of all offices), including US offices in Boston, Chicago, LA, New York, San Francisco, Seattle, and Washington, D.C. Ticket booking, travel insurance, railpasses, and more. In the UK, walk-in office in Macadam Bldg., Surrey St., **London** WC2R 2LE (☎207 379 4856). In New Zealand, 229 Queen St., **Auckland** (toll free ☎0800 100 677). In Australia, Forrest Hill Chase Shopping Ctr., 270 Canterbury Rd., **Melbourne** VIC 3131 (☎03 9878 9766) or 366 Lygon St., **Carlton** VIC 3053 (☎03 9349 4344).

Travel CUTS (Canadian Universities Travel Services Limited), 187 College St., **Toronto,** ON M5T 1P7 (☎416-979-2406; fax 979-8167; www.travelcuts.com). 60 offices across Canada. Also in the UK, 295-A Regent St., **London** W1R 7YA (☎0207 255 1944 or 255 2082).

COMMERCIAL AIRLINES

The commercial airlines' lowest regular offer is the **APEX** (Advance Purchase Excursion) fare, which provides confirmed reservations and allows "open-jaw" tickets. Generally, reservations must be made seven to 21 days ahead of departure, with seven- to 14-day minimum stay and up to 90-day maximum stay restrictions. These fares carry hefty cancellation and change penalties (fees rise in summer).

Book peak season APEX fares early; by May you will have a hard time getting your desired departure date. Use **Microsoft Expedia** (http://msn.expedia.com) or **Travelocity** (www.travelocity.com) to get an idea of the lowest published fares, then use the resources outlined here to beat those fares. Low-season fares should be appreciably cheaper than high-season (June-Sept.).

AIR COURIER FLIGHTS

Light packers should consider courier flights. Couriers help transport cargo on international flights by using their checked luggage space for freight. Generally, couriers must travel with carry-ons only and deal with complex flight restrictions. Most flights are round-trip only with short fixed-length stays (usually one week) and a limit of one ticket per issue. Most of these flights operate only out of major North American gateway cities. Generally, you must be over 21 (in some cases 18). Groups such as the **Air Courier Association** (☎800-282-1202; www.aircourier.org) and the **International Association of Air Travel Couriers,** P.O. Box 980, Keystone Heights, FL 32656, USA (☎352-475-1584; www.courier.org), provide lists of opportunities and courier brokers worldwide for an annual fee. For more information, consult *Air Courier Bargains* by Kelly Monaghan (Intrepid Traveler, US$15) or the *Courier Air Travel Handbook* by Mark Field (Perpetual Press, US$13).

CHARTER FLIGHTS

Charters are flights a tour operator contracts with an airline to fly extra loads of passengers during peak season. Charter flights fly less frequently than major airlines, make refunds particularly difficult, and are almost always fully booked. Schedules and itineraries may also change or be canceled at the last moment (as late as 48 hours before the trip and without a full refund), and check-in, boarding, and baggage claim are often much slower. But these flights are usually cheaper than commercial ones. **Discount clubs** and **fare brokers** offer members savings on last-minute charter and tour deals. Study contracts closely; you don't want to end up with an unwanted overnight layover. Pay with a credit card if you can and consider traveler's insurance against trip interruption.

TICKET CONSOLIDATORS

Ticket consolidators or **"bucket shops"** buy unsold tickets in bulk from commercial airlines and sell them at discounted rates. Look in the travel section of any major newspaper, where many bucket shops place tiny ads. Call quickly, as availability is typically extremely limited. Not all bucket shops are reliable, so insist on a receipt that gives full details of restrictions, refunds, and tickets. Pay by credit card (in spite of the 2-5% fee) so you can stop payment if you never receive your tickets. For more info, see www.travel-library.com/air-travel/consolidators.html or pick up Kelly Monaghan's *Air Travel's Bargain Basement* (Intrepid Traveler, US$8).

TRAVELING FROM THE US AND CANADA. Travel Avenue (☎800-333-3335; www.travelavenue.com) rebates commercial fares from the US (5% for over US$550) and will search for cheap flights from anywhere for a fee. Other consolidators worth trying are **Interworld Travel** (☎800-468-3796 or 305-443-4929; www.interworldtravel.com), **Cheap Tickets** (☎800-652-4327; www.cheaptickets.com), **Travac** (☎800-872-8800; www.travac.com), **Internet Travel Network** (www.itn.com), **Travel Information Services** (www.tiss.com), and **TravelHUB** (www.travelhub.com). These are just suggestions to get you started; *Let's Go* does not endorse any of these agencies. Be cautious, and research companies before you hand over your credit card number.

12 minutes to defrost (medium heat).
5 minutes to book online (LA to Rome).
Save money & time on student and faculty travel at StudentUniverse.com
StudentUniverse.com
Real Travel Deals

TRAVELING FROM THE UK, AUSTRALIA, AND NEW ZEALAND. In London, the **Air Travel Advisory Bureau** (☎020 7636 5000; www.atab.co.uk) can provide names of reliable consolidators and discount flight specialists. In Australia and New Zealand, look for consolidator ads in the travel section of the *Sydney Morning Herald* and other papers.

FLIGHT PLANNING ON THE INTERNET The Internet has great travel bargains—it's fast, it's convenient, and you can spend as long as you like exploring options without driving your travel agent insane.

The **Air Traveler's Handbook** provides tips on finding cheap fares (www.cs.cmu.edu/afs/cs.cmu.edu/user/mkant/Public/Travel/airfare.html). **TravelHUB** (www.travelhub.com) is a directory of travel agents that includes a searchable database of fares from over 500 consolidators. Other sites do the legwork and compile the deals for you—try www.bestfares.com, www.onetravel.com, and www.travelzoo.com. **StudentUniverse** (www.studentuniverse.com), **STA** (www.sta-travel.com), and **Orbitz.com** provide quotes on student tickets, while **Expedia** (http://msn.expedia.com) and **Travelocity** (www.travelocity.com) offer full travel services. **Priceline** (www.priceline.com) allows you to specify a price, and obligates you to buy any ticket that meets or beats it; be prepared for odd routes. **Skyauction** (www.skyauction.com) lets you bid on both last-minute and advance-purchase tickets.

SPECIALTY CONSOLIDATORS. A limited number of travel agencies deal in unconventional arrangements of flights. Circle Pacific and Circle Asia tickets provide one-way flights to, from, and around Southeast Asia. These tickets are best for extended trips; most have flexible dates, good up to one year from commencement of travel. For itineraries more complicated than a simple round-trip, RTW and other unconventional tickets are often a better deal. Try **Air Treks** (☎877-350-0612 or 415-912-5600; www.airtreks.com) or **Ticket Planet** (☎800-799-8888; www.ticketplanet.com) and leave at least a month to book and confirm tickets.

FURTHER READING

The Worldwide Guide to Cheap Airfare, Michael McColl. Insider Publications (US$15). Out of print, check local library.

Discount Airfares: The Insider's Guide, George Hobart. Priceless Publications (US$18).

Air Traveler's Handbook, a detailed, comprehensive guide to consumer travel (www.cs.cmu.edu/afs/cs/user/mkant/Public/Travel/airfare.html).

GETTING AROUND SOUTHEAST ASIA

BETWEEN COUNTRIES

AIR. Flights between countries in Southeast Asia are inexpensive. Find the best deals on tickets in Bangkok, Singapore, Hong Kong, Kuala Lumpur, and Penang. Popular airlines include Malaysia Airlines, Singapore Airlines, Thai International, Cathay Pacific, and KLM Airlines. Booking tickets should be relatively worry-free, but travel agents can scam you. Be sure to make sure your deal is legitimate before

AIRCRAFT SAFETY The airlines of developing world nations do not always meet safety standards. The *Official Airline Guide* (www.oag.com) and many travel agencies can tell you the type and age of aircraft on a particular route. This can be especially useful in Southeast Asia, where less reliable equipment is often used for internal or short flights. The **International Airline Passengers Association** (US ☎800-821-4272, UK ☎020 8681 6555) provides region-specific safety information. The **Federal Aviation Administration** (www.faa.gov) reviews the airline authorities for countries whose airlines enter the US. **US State Department** travel advisories (☎202-647-5225; http://travel.state.gov/travel_warnings.html) sometimes involve foreign carriers, especially when terrorist bombings or hijackings may be a threat.

you buy. *Let's Go* lists reliable tourist offices and travel offices in the **Practical Information** section of large cities. In general, use common sense—don't trust agents vending tickets in coffee bars. To be sure, always reconfirm with the airlines after receiving your ticket.

BUS. Bus travel between countries can be arranged within the regions of Cambodia, Laos, and Vietnam; Myanmar, Thailand, and Malaysia. A/C buses can be very comfortable and reliable, but others offer sparse leg room and bumpy rides. Inquire about purchasing tickets, as some buses require reservations in advance, whereas others sell tickets upon departure and don't leave the station until completely full. Check visa availability before taking a bus ride; visas may not always be available at the border and must be acquired in advance in other towns. Most tourist cafes can help you with information and reservations.

BORDER CROSSINGS. Overland border crossing points represent legal points of transit between Southeast Asian countries. For detailed information on possible crossing points and requirements, refer to the **Getting There** section of individual countries. Check local news agencies and embassies to confirm which border crossing points are open.

WITHIN A COUNTRY

Southeast Asia has every type of vehicle imaginable. From buses to taxis, cyclos to trishaws, *angkot* to jeepney, if it moves on land and has wheels, you'll find detailed information in the **Local Transportation** section of each city. Car rental in Southeast Asia is not only rare, it's unreliable. If you do rent, you'll need an **International Driver's Permit (IDP)**, though documentation requirements vary. Some countries allow travelers to drive with a valid American or Canadian license. Apply for an IDP at your home country's Automobile Association. Remember that if you are driving a conventional vehicle on an unpaved road, you are almost never covered by insurance; ask about this at the rental agency.

SPECIFIC CONCERNS

WOMEN TRAVELERS

Women inevitably face some additional safety concerns, but it's easy to be adventurous without taking undue risks. If you are on your own, consider hostels which offer single rooms that lock from the inside or religious organizations with rooms for women only. Communal showers in some hotels are safer than others, but check them first. Stick to centrally located hotels and avoid walks alone at night. Always carry extra money for a phone call, bus, or taxi. **Hitchhiking** is never safe for a lone woman or even for two women traveling together. Choose train compartments occupied by women or couples; ask the conductor to put together a women-only compartment if there isn't one. Look as if you know where you're going (even when you don't) and consider approaching older women or couples for directions if you're lost or feel uncomfortable.

Generally, the less you look like a tourist, the better off you'll be. Dress conservatively, especially in rural areas. Wear shirts with sleeves and pants/skirts that fall below the knee; the more coverage the better. Trying to fit in can be effective, but dressing in the style of a different culture may cause you to be ill at ease and a conspicuous target. Wearing a **wedding band** may help prevent unwanted overtures. Some travelers report that carrying pictures of a "husband" or "children" is extremely useful to document marital status. Even a mention of a husband waiting back at the hotel may be enough to discount your unattached appearance.

Your best answer to verbal harassment is no answer at all; feigning deafness, sitting motionless, and staring straight ahead at nothing will do a world of good that reactions usually don't achieve. The extremely persistent can sometimes be dissuaded by a firm, loud, and very public "go away" in the appropriate language. Learn how to say "help" or "fire" in the local language. In Southeast Asia, making a public display is the most effective way of getting a heckler off your back. If you feel threatened, **shout** your heart out—help will instantly be on the way.

Seek out a police officer or a passerby if you are being harassed. Memorize each city's emergency numbers (listed in the **Practical Information** sections). Carry a **whistle** or an airhorn on your keychain, and don't hesitate to use it in an emergency. An **IMPACT Model Mugging** self-defense course will not only prepare you for a potential attack, but will also raise your awareness of your surroundings (see **Self Defense,** p. 17). See **Women's Health** (p. 25) for specific health concerns.

FURTHER READING

A Journey of One's Own: Uncommon Advice for the Independent Woman Traveler, Thalia Zepatos. Eighth Mountain Press (US$17).

Adventures in Good Company: The Complete Guide to Women's Tours and Outdoor Trips, Thalia Zepatos. Eighth Mountain Press (US$7).

Active Women Vacation Guide, Evelyn Kaye. Blue Panda Publications (US$18).

Gutsy Women: More Travel Tips & Wisdom for the Road, Marybeth Bond. Traveler's Tales (US$13).

TRAVELING ALONE

There are many benefits to traveling alone, including independence and greater interaction with locals. However, solo travelers are more vulnerable to harassment and street theft. Lone travelers need to be well organized and look confident at all times. Try not to stand out as a tourist and be especially careful in deserted or very crowded areas. Never admit that you're traveling alone and lie about how long you've been in the country—always say you've been there at least 3-4 weeks. Maintain regular contact with someone at home who knows your itinerary. For more tips, read *Traveling Solo* by Eleanor Berman (Globe Pequot Press, US$17) or subscribe to **Connecting: Solo Travel Network,** 689 Park Road, Unit 6, Gibsons, BC V0N 1V7, Canada (☎604-886-9099; www.cstn.org; membership US$25-35).

Alternatively, several services link solo travelers with companions who have similar travel habits and interests; for a bi-monthly newsletter for single travelers seeking a travel partner (subscription US$48), contact the **Travel Companion**

Exchange, P.O. Box 833, Amityville, NY 11701, USA (☎800-392-1256 or 631-454-0880; www.whytravelalone.com). **American International Homestays,** P.O. Box 1754, Nederland, CO 80466, USA (☎800-876-2048), has a listing of lodgings with English-speaking host families in Southeast Asia.

OLDER TRAVELERS

Travel in Southeast Asia has the potential to be particularly taxing for senior citizens. However, there may be some extra benefits to age, including greater respect from the people you encounter. The books *No Problem! Worldwise Tips for Mature Adventurers*, by Janice Kenyon (Orca Book Publishers, US$16) and *Unbelievably Good Deals and Great Adventures That You Absolutely Can't Get Unless You're Over 50*, by Joan Rattner Heilman (McGraw-Hill, US$15) are both excellent resources. A few agencies for senior group travel are:

ElderTreks, 597 Markham St., Toronto, ON M6G 2L7, Canada (☎800-741-7956; eldertreks@eldertreks.com; www.eldertreks.com). Tours offered in Cambodia, Indonesia, Laos, Malaysian Borneo, Myanmar, Thailand, and Vietnam.

Elderhostel, 11 Ave. de Lafayette, Boston, MA 02111, USA (☎877-426-8026; www.elderhostel.org). Programs at colleges, universities, and other learning centers in Cambodia, Indonesia, Laos, Malaysia, Thailand, and Vietnam (and other countries depending on season) on varied subjects lasting 1-4 weeks. Must be 55 or over (spouse can be of any age).

The Mature Traveler, 2224 Beaumont St., Ste. D, Sacramento, CA 95815, USA (☎800-460-6676). Deals and discounts for the 50+ traveler. Subscription $30.

BISEXUAL, GAY & LESBIAN TRAVELERS

The enormous range of sexualities in Southeast Asia defies easy categorization. From the *waria* communities of Indonesia to the *bakla* of the Philippines and the *kathoey* transgender communities of Thailand, the perceptive gay traveler can find a trip to Southeast Asia an enlightening experience. Although active gay communities exist in **Bangkok, Manila, Jakarta, Hong Kong, Kuala Lumpur,** and **Singapore,** Southeast Asian governments still have a rather unfavorable outlook toward homosexuality (even if laws banning homosexuality no longer exist) and rural communities may be much less accepting. Homosociality (camaraderie between members of the same sex, particularly men) is much more common than you may be accustomed to; hand-holding between two men cannot be interpreted according to typical "Western" norms. The stigma of the sex trade is such that many gay travelers find it difficult to integrate themselves into local communities. Lesbian life tends to be inaccessible to outsiders. Travelers should keep in mind that the people of Southeast Asia often disapprove of public displays of affection, be they among homosexuals or heterosexuals. *Let's Go* lists resources for gay and lesbian travelers in the **Life and Times** sections of specific countries. Listed below are contact organizations, mail-order bookstores, and publishers that offer materials addressing some specific concerns. **Out and About** (www.outandabout.com) offers a bi-weekly newsletter addressing travel concerns.

International Gay and Lesbian Travel Association, 4331 N Federal Hwy. #304, Fort Lauderdale, FL 33308, USA (☎800-448-8550 or 954-776-2626; www.iglta.com). An organization of over 1350 companies serving gay and lesbian travelers worldwide.

Gay's the Word, 66 Marchmont St., London WC1N 1AB, UK (☎44 20 7278 7654; www.gaystheword.co.uk). The largest gay and lesbian bookshop in the UK, with both fiction and non-fiction titles. Mail-order service available.

Giovanni's Room, 1145 Pine St., Philadelphia, PA 19107, USA (☎215-923-2960; www.queerbooks.com). An international lesbian/feminist and gay bookstore with mail-order service (carries many of the publications listed below).

International Lesbian and Gay Association (ILGA), 81 rue Marché-au-Charbon, B-1000 Brussels, Belgium (☎32 2 502 2471; www.ilga.org). Provides political information, such as homosexuality laws of individual countries.

FURTHER READING

Utopia-Asia (www.utopia-asia.com). The best and most comprehensive resource for the gay or lesbian traveler in Southeast Asia.

Spartacus: International Gay Guide 2002/2003. Bruno Gmunder Verlag (US$33).

Ferrari Guides' Gay Travel A to Z, Ferrari Guides' Men's Travel in Your Pocket, and *Ferrari Guides' Inn Places.* Ferrari Publications (US$16-20).

TRAVELERS WITH DISABILITIES

Southeast Asia, excluding Singapore, is ill-equipped to accommodate disabled travelers. Those with disabilities should inform airlines and hotels of their disabilities when making arrangements for travel; some time may be needed to prepare special accommodations. Hospitals cannot be relied upon to replace broken braces or prostheses; orthopedic materials, even in Bangkok, Jakarta, and Manila, are faulty at best. All public transportation is completely inaccessible. Rural areas have no sidewalks, and larger cities are packed with curbs and steps.

Attitudes toward disabled people vary. In Laos and Cambodia, where an uncommonly large part of the population consists of amputees (from land-mines and cluster-bombs), disabilities are common. Thai people with disabilities rarely come out in public. Despite this, bold travelers will find many people eager to aid them.

USEFUL ORGANIZATIONS

Mobility International USA (MIUSA), P.O. Box 10767, Eugene, OR 97440, USA (voice and TDD ☎541-343-1284; www.miusa.org). Sells *A World of Options: A Guide to International Educational Exchange, Community Service, and Travel for Persons with Disabilities* (US$35).

Moss Rehab Hospital Travel Information Service (☎215-456-9900; staff@mossresourcenet.org; www.mossresourcenet.org). An information resource center on travel-related concerns for those with disabilities.

Society for the Advancement of Travel for the Handicapped (SATH), 347 5th Ave., Ste. 610, New York, NY 10016, USA (☎212-447-7284; www.sath.org). An advocacy group that publishes free online travel information and the travel magazine *OPEN WORLD* (US$13, free for members). Annual membership US$45, students and seniors US$30.

TOUR AGENCIES

Directions Unlimited, 123 Green Ln., Bedford Hills, NY 10507, USA (☎800-533-5343). Books individual and group vacations for the physically disabled. Not an info service.

MINORITY TRAVELERS

People in Southeast Asia are largely accepting of minority travelers. However, travelers of African descent have reported stray incidents of harassment, though there have been no reports of violence. To be safe, travelers of African descent are advised not to travel alone in rural areas. In addition, ethnic Chinese in Indonesia and Malaysia have been a target of discrimination. Though violence is rare, some travelers report inferior service and stray incidents of harassment.

TRAVELERS WITH CHILDREN

Travel in Southeast Asia with children can prove a hassle. Hygienic environments and proper medical facilities are scarce. The combination of heat, mosquitoes, and dirty water might prove too much for a young child. That said, it's possible to bring children along as long as you take extra precautions and remain especially alert to potential dangers. Family vacations often require that you slow your pace and always require that you plan ahead. When deciding where to stay, call ahead to inquire about an establishment's ability to meet the special needs of children. **Be sure that your child carries some sort of ID** in case of an emergency or if he gets lost. Arrange a reunion spot in case of separation when sightseeing. International fares are usually discounted 25% for children ages two to eleven. Finding a private place for **breast-feeding** is often a problem while traveling. For more information, consult one of the following books:

Backpacking with Babies and Small Children, Goldie Silverman. Wilderness Press (US$7).

How to take Great Trips with Your Kids, Sanford Portnoy, Linda Ziedrich, and Joan Portnoy. Harvard Common Press (US$7).

Have Kid, Will Travel: 101 Survival Strategies for Vacationing With Babies and Young Children, Claire and Lucille Tristram. Andrews McMeel Publishing (US$13).

Trouble Free Travel with Children, Vicki Lansky. Book Peddlers (US$3).

DIETARY CONCERNS

Although Southeast Asian food often contains meat or uses meat bases, **vegetarian** dishes abound. For more information about traveling as a vegetarian, contact **North American Vegetarian Society,** P.O. Box 72, Dolgeville, NY 13329, USA (☎518-568-7970; www.navs-online.org), which publishes *Vegetarian Asia* ($10). While **kosher** meals are practically nonexistent, the Muslim presence in Southeast Asia makes **halal** food a large part of the cuisine, especially in the Malay-speaking world. (For more information on kosher food, see www.shamash.org/kosher.) If you are strict in your observance, consider preparing your own food. For more information, visit your local bookstore, health food store, or library, and consult *The Vegetarian Traveler: Where to Stay if You're Vegetarian, Vegan, Environmentally Sensitive*, by Jed and Susan Civic (Larson Publications, US$16).

OTHER RESOURCES

Let's Go's brief historical and cultural sketches of each country at the beginning of each chapter are no substitute for further reading and research. As a rule, the more background knowledge you can acquire before you leave, the better equipped you will be to make sense of the different cultures of Southeast Asia. Moreover, Southeast Asians are always pleased to meet foreigners who have made the effort to learn something about their heritage.

ECOLOGICALLY RESPONSIBLE TOURISM

Traveling through Southeast Asia takes visitors into ecologically sensitive areas. Avoid buying natural souvenirs such as teeth, hides, coral, butterflies, or turtle shells. Products made of animals often come at the expense of endangered species. Women may consider buying feminine hygiene products with minimal packaging. Choose glass soda bottles over marginally recyclable plastic equivalents and reuse plastic bags. Bucket showers and squat toilets are more water-efficient than their Western counterparts. To be even more water-friendly, carry a water bottle or canteen. While tap water is unsafe, purifying tablets or iodine drops save buying countless plastic water bottles.

BOOKS & PUBLISHERS

LITERATURE

Southeast Asia: An Introductory History, by Milton Osborne (1995). A basic survey of Southeast Asian history, revised and updated many times.

The Lands of Charm and Cruelty: Travels in Southeast Asia, by Stan Sesser (1994). A collection of essays originally published in the *New Yorker.*

Into the Heart of Borneo, by Redmond O'Hanlon (1987). Follows the real-life, humorous adventures of a *London Times* reviewer with poet friend, James Benton.

A Fortune-Teller Told Me: Earthbound Travels in the Far East, by Tiziano Terzani (2001). A journalist's land trek through Southeast Asia, focusing on myths, religions, and fortune-tellers.

The Chastening: Inside the Financial Crisis That Rocked the Global Financial System and Humbled the IMF, by Paul Blustein (2002). A cogent description of the Asian Financial Crisis of 1997.

TRAVEL PUBLISHERS & BOOKSTORES

Hippocrene Books, Inc., 171 Madison Ave., New York, NY 10016, USA (☎212-685-4371, orders ☎718-454-2366; www.hippocrenebooks.com). Free catalog. Publishes foreign language dictionaries and language learning guides.

Hunter Publishing, 470 W. Broadway, 2nd fl., South Boston, MA 02127, USA (☎617-269-0700; www.hunterpublishing.com). Has an extensive catalog of travel guides and diving and adventure travel books.

Rand McNally, 8255 N. Central Park, Skokie, IL 60076, USA (☎847-329-8100; www.randmcnally.com). Publishes road atlases.

Adventurous Traveler Bookstore, P.O. Box 2221, Williston, VT 05495, USA (☎800-282-3963 or 802-860-6776; www.adventuroustraveler.com).

Travel Books & Language Center, Inc., 4437 Wisconsin Ave. NW, Washington, D.C. 20016, USA (☎800-220-2665 or 202-237-1322; www.bookweb.org/bookstore/travelbks). Over 60,000 titles from around the world.

WORLD WIDE WEB

There is a wealth of information on Southeast Asia available on the World Wide Web. Recently, many regional newspapers, including the *Bangkok Post* and the *Straits Times* (Singapore), have launched online editions. Listed here are some budget travel sites to start off your surfing; other relevant web sites are listed throughout the book. Because web site turnover is high, use search engines (such as www.google.com) to strike out on your own.

THE ART OF BUDGET TRAVEL

How to See the World: www.artoftravel.com. A compendium of great travel tips, from cheap flights to self defense to interacting with local culture.

Rec. Travel Library: www.travel-library.com. A fantastic set of links for general information and personal travelogues.

Lycos: http://travel.lycos.com. General introductions to cities and regions throughout Southeast Asia, accompanied by links to applicable histories, news, and tourism sites.

INFORMATION ON SOUTHEAST ASIA

CIA World Factbook: www.odci.gov/cia/publications/factbook/index.html. Tons of vital statistics on Southeast Asia's geography, government, economy, and people.

MyTravelGuide: www.mytravelguide.com. Country overviews, with everything from history to transportation to live web cam coverage of Southeast Asia.

Geographia: www.geographia.com. Highlights, culture, and people of Indonesia, Malaysia, Myanmar, Thailand, and Vietnam.

Atevo Travel: www.atevo.com/guides/destinations. Detailed introductions, travel tips, and suggested itineraries for Cambodia, Indonesia, Malaysia, the Philippines, Singapore, Thailand, and Vietnam.

World Travel Guide: www.travel-guides.com/navigate/world.asp. Helpful practical info.

TravelPage: www.travelpage.com. Links to official tourist office sites in Southeast Asia.

PlanetRider: www.planetrider.com. A subjective list of links to the "best" web sites on the culture and tourist attractions of Hong Kong, Indonesia, Thailand, and Vietnam.

Time-Asia Now: www.time.com/time/asia. The international version of *Time Magazine* covers current events, cultural information, and technology news throughout Asia.

Cornell University Southeast Asia Program: www.einaudi.cornell.edu/southeastasia. Has links to hundreds of Southeast Asia-related sites.

Australia National University: http://coombs.anu.edu.au/WWWVL-AsianStudies.html. Maintains a fantastic "virtual library" of Asia-related materials.

AND OUR PERSONAL FAVORITE...

WWW.LETSGO.COM Our newly designed web site now features the full online content of our guides. In addition, trial versions of all nine City Guides are available for download on Palm OS™ PDAs. Our web site also contains our newsletter, links for photos and streaming video, online ordering of our titles, info about our books, and a travel forum buzzing with stories and tips.

ALTERNATIVES TO TOURISM

CAMBODIA

STUDYING ABROAD

AMERICAN PROGRAMS

Council-International Study Programs: Vietnam, Cambodia, Laos, 633 Third Avenue, 20th fl., New York, NY 10017, USA (☎800-407-8839; www.ciee.org). Introduces students to contemporary development in Indochina in a comparative framework. Based in Hanoi, but there are also extended study components in Cambodia and Laos.

Pacific Challenge, P.O. Box 3151, Eugene, OR 97401, USA (☎541-343-4124; hq@pacificchallenge.org; www.pacificchallenge.org). Experiential adventure travel program in Cambodia, Laos, Thailand, and Vietnam. US$4700 includes round-trip international flight, internal travel, program activities, accommodations, and visas.

Where There Be Dragons (☎800-982-9203; info@wherethereberagons.com). Runs youth summer programs and short trips for adults to Cambodia, Laos, Thailand, and Vietnam. Youth programs cost US$5950-6150. Adult programs cost US$3550-4500. Fee includes food, accommodations, and internal travel.

LANGUAGE SCHOOLS

Khmer School of Language, P.O. Box 1670, Phnom Penh (☎23 047 213; ksl@forum.org.kh; www.cambcomm.org.uk/ksl). Offers Khmer language programs at sites in Phnom Penh and Sihanoukville.

The Royal University of Phnom Penh, M. V. Conféderation de la Russie, Khan Tuol Kork, Phnom Penh (☎12 812 017; pitch@camnet.com.kh). Offers courses in Khmer language for foreigners.

WORKING

Australian Aid for Cambodia Fund, 345 Grimshaw St., Watsonia, Melbourne 3000, Australia (aacf@vicnet.net.au; www.vicnet.net.au/~AACF). Dedicated to bringing peace and prosperity to Cambodia through volunteer services in education, healthcare, and human resource development. Takes Australian citizens but other interested nationalities should also apply. Accommodations, meals, and a US$50-100 monthly allowance.

International Schools Services, Educational Staffing Program, P.O. Box 5910, Princeton, NJ 08543, USA (☎609-452-0990; www.iss.edu). Recruits teachers and administrators for schools in Cambodia, Indonesia, Laos, Malaysia, Myanmar, the Philippines, Singapore, Thailand, and Vietnam.

VOLUNTEERING

Doctors Without Borders, 6 E. 39th St., 8th fl., New York, NY 10016, USA (☎212-679-6800; doctors@newyork.msf.org; www.doctorswithoutborders.org). Provides emergency aid to victims of armed conflict, epidemics, and natural and man-made disasters in

Cambodia, Laos, Myanmar, the Philippines, and Thailand. Requirements for medical positions require at least two years' professional experience.

Health Volunteers Overseas, P.O. Box 65157, Washington, DC 20035, USA (☎202-296-0928; info@hvousa.org; www.hvousa.org). Sends qualified health professionals overseas to train local healthcare providers. Many sites also offer volunteers food and accommodations. Membership is required for volunteering.

Interplast, 300-B Pioneer Way, Mountain View, CA 94041, USA (☎888-467-5278 or 650-962-0123; www.interplast.org). Volunteer opportunities in Cambodia and Myanmar for medical professionals and translators to improve medical treatment.

Involvement Volunteers Association Inc., P.O. Box 218, Port Melbourne, Victoria 3207, Australia (☎03 9646 9392; ivworldwide@volunteering.org.au). Volunteer at the Sunrise Organic Farm and the Computer School and help fulfill the goal of self-sufficiency for this community of orphaned Cambodian children. Police Records Clearance and a minimum of six weeks commitment are required. Single placement fee of US$140.

Operation Smile, 6435 Tidewater Dr., Norfolk, VA 23509, USA (☎757-321-7645; dmaynard@operationsmile.org; www.operationsmile.org). Provides reconstructive surgery and related healthcare, training, and education to healthcare professionals in Cambodia, the Philippines, Thailand, and Vietnam.

Relief for Oppressed People Everywhere (ROPE), 12 Church St., Rickmansworth, Hertfordshire, WD3 1BS, UK (☎44 019 2377 1821; fax 44 019 2377 5117; rope@rope.org.uk; www.rope.org.uk/default.html). A volunteer charity that helps the poor in 85 countries, including Cambodia, Indonesia, Laos, the Philippines, Thailand, and Vietnam, with direct aid, food, education, medical help, housing, and clothing. Those helped include widows, orphans, refugees, the unemployed, and the homeless.

United Cambodian Community Development. Contact Cynthia Brooks De Martini, Center for Law and Global Justice, University of San Francisco School of Law, Ignatian Heights, CA 94117, USA (☎415-422-5922), or Linda McKinney, c/o VI, #16, St. 21, Sangkat Tonle Bassac, Khan Chamkarmon, Phnom Penh, Cambodia (☎33 932 997; 012818221@mobitel.com.kh). Help this small NGO rebuild a Cambodian community by providing small-business training and adult education with the goal of fostering small rural businesses in Kampot Province. Donation of US$100 required for one week, US$150 for two weeks, US$175 for three weeks, and US$200 for four weeks or longer. An application form is available at www.go-mad.org/uccform.htm.

United Nations Volunteers, Postfach 260 111, D-53153 Bonn, Germany (☎228 815 2000; www.unv.org). Assignments vary in length and are available in several Southeast Asian countries. Inquire for information about specific projects' language and skill requirements. Minimum monthly stipend provided.

World-Wide Opportunities on Organic Farms, P.O. Box 2675, Lewes BN7 1RB, UK (www.wwoof.org). Provides connections between volunteers and organic farms in Cambodia, Laos, Malaysia, the Philippines, Singapore, and Thailand. A minimal WWOOF membership fee is required in order to participate.

INDONESIA

STUDYING ABROAD

AMERICAN PROGRAMS

Council on International Educational Exchange (CIEE), Council ISP, 633 3rd Ave. 20th fl., New York, NY 10017, USA (☎888-268-6245 or 800-407-8839; www.ciee.org/study). Sponsors study abroad programs in Indonesia, Thailand, and Vietnam.

International Association for the Exchange of Students for Technical Experience (IAESTE), 10400 Little Patuxent Pkwy. #250, Columbia, MD 21044, USA (☎410-997-3069; www.aipt.org). Eight- to twelve-week programs in Indonesia and Thailand for college students who have done 2 years of technical study. US$25 application fee.

Naropa University, Office of International Education, 2130 Arapahoe Ave., Boulder, CO 80302, USA (fax 303-444-0410; www.naropa.edu/studyabroad). Offers semester programs in Bali, Indonesia focusing on arts and spirituality in contemporary Balinese culture. Room, board, and tuition cost US$8450 for undergrads; college credit available.

School for International Training: College Semester Abroad, Admissions, Kipling Rd., P.O. Box 676, Brattleboro, VT 05302, USA (☎800-336-1616 or 802-258-3500; www.sit.edu). Runs semester-long programs in Bali, Indonesia, and Vietnam. Programs cost roughly US$12,000. Financial aid available and US financial aid is transferable.

LANGUAGE SCHOOLS AND CULTURAL STUDY

With workshops and courses on everything from language, *batik*, meditation, and *gamelan* music to Balinese cooking and dance, the opportunities for cultural study in Indonesia are undeniably awesome. Check out Ubud's offerings on p. 184 (under **Workshops and Classes**)—there are too many to list below.

Indonesia Australia Language Foundation (www.ialf.edu), offers courses in Bahasa Indonesia, organizes group study tours, and provides individualized tuition. Homestays available. IALF offers programs in Denpasar (Jl. Kapten Agung 17, Denpasar 80232, Bali; ☎62 361 225 243; ialfbali@ialf.edu), Jakarta (Jl. Rasuna Said Kav C-6, Jakarta 12940; ☎62 21 521 3350; ialfjkt@ialf.edu), and Surabaya (Jl. Sumatera No. 49, Surabaya 60281, East Java; ☎62 31 502 6400; ialfsby@ialf.edu).

Juwita Cafe, on Tuk Tuk Peninsula on Pulau Samosir. Cooking classes are offered daily 1-4pm. See **Pulau Samosir: Food,** p. 282.

Lembaga Bahasa Colorado, Jl. Demangan Baru 33, Jogjakarta 55281 (☎62 274 562 874; www.lbcolorado.or.id). Courses in Bahasa Indonesia for all levels (1 student US$8 per hr.). Language training for business or pleasure. Homestays available.

Lucy Batik Gallery and Losmen, Sosrowijayan Wetan GT 1/94, Jogjakarta (☎513 429). Offers *batik* courses starting at 9am. Rp30,000-75,000. See **Jogjakarta: Accommodations (p. 142)** for further information and directions.

Puri Bahasa Indonesia, Dr. Unang Liesanggoro, Academic Coordinator, Puri Bahasa Indonesia, Jl. Bausasran 59, Jogjakarta 55211 (☎62 274 588 192; puriindo@indosat.net.id). Runs programs for beginning to advanced students. One-on-one or group instruction available (US$5 per hr. for 1 student; US$10 per hr. for 4 students). Homestays or accommodation at local guest houses can be arranged. Also organizes cultural activities (including batik, yoga, and wayang) and visits to local sites.

Realia Indonesian Language Training, Jl. Pandga Marta V/6, Pogung Utara, Jogjakarta 55281 (☎62 274 583 229; realia@yogya.wasantara.net.id; www.realians.net). Intensive and less intensive language training programs for up to 4 students (1 student US$10 per hr.; 4 students US$14 per hr.). Professional or social focus. Complimentary homestay can be arranged for participants in the intensive program.

Semarang 2000 Indonesian Language Center, Ms. Augustina Prasetyo, Semarang 2000, Ruko Semarang Indah E1, 12A-14, Semarang 50144, Java (☎62 24 762 0009; semarang2000@idea-snc.it). Provides instruction in Bahasa Indonesia to students of all ages (US$10 per hr.). Extra activities include lessons in batik and Indonesian cooking. Accommodations available (some meals included; US$15, with A/C US$20).

Viavia, Jl. Prawirotaman 24B, Jogjakarta (☎386 557; viavia@yogya.wasantara.net.id). Offers courses in language (Rp30,000), cooking (Rp35,000), and massage (Rp40,000). Open 8am-10pm. See **Jogjakarta, Food** (p. 144) for more information.

Wisma Bahasa, Jl. Rajawali, Gg. Nuri No. 6, Demangan Baru, Jogjakarta 55281 (☎62 274 588 409; wisba@indosat.net.id; www.wisma-bahasa.or.id). Offers courses for all proficiency levels in Indonesian, Javanese, English, and Tetun, the language of East Timor. Homestays, private tuition, cultural activities, and extensive services available. Class size varies from one student (about US$7 per hr.) to four students (about US$13 per hr.). Discounts given to students and volunteers.

WORKING

Opportunities to teach English abound in Indonesia. Check out www.teach-abroad.com for a range of options.

Global Volunteers, 375 E. Little Canada Rd., St. Paul, MN 55117, USA (☎800-487-1074 or 651-407-6100; fax 651-482-0915; e-mail@globalvolunteers.org; www.global-volunteers.org), sends volunteers of all ages to teach English in Indonesia and Vietnam. Indonesia program runs 12 days (US$1845; airfare excluded) or 19 days (US$1995). Vietnam program runs for 2-3 weeks (US$2195-2295). Student discounts.

International Schools Services, see Cambodia, p. 44.

VOLUNTEERING

ACDI/VOCA, 50 F St. NW, Ste. 1075, Washington, DC 20001, USA (☎800-929-8622 or 202-383-4961; fax 202-626-8726; volunteer@acdivoca.org; www.acdivova.org). Volunteer opportunities in Indonesia and Thailand for professionals, lasting from 2 weeks to 3 months. Volunteers provide short-term technical assistance in banking, business and cooperative planning, and agricultural production. All expenses paid.

CUSO, 500-2255 Carling Ave., Ottawa, Ontario, Canada, K2B 1A6 (☎888-434-2876 (in Canada) or 613-829-7445; fax 613-829-7446; cuso.secretariat@cuso.ca; www.cuso.org). Two-year volunteer opportunities for Canadian citizens in Indonesia, Laos, Malaysia, and Thailand. CUSO volunteers work in human rights, legal advocacy, and development. Airfare, housing, and stipend provided.

Doctors Without Borders, see Cambodia, p. 44.

Ecovolunteer, Meijersweg 29, 7553 AX Hengelo, Netherlands (☎31 74 250 8250; info@ecovolunteer.org; www.ecovolunteer.org). Volunteer opportunities with wildlife in Indonesia, Malaysia, and Thailand.

Elderhostel, Inc., 11 Avenue de Lafayette, Boston, MA 92111, USA (☎877-426-8056; fax 877-426-2166; www.elderhostel.org). Sends volunteers age 55 and over around the world to work in construction, research, teaching, and many other projects. Costs average US$100 per day plus airfare.

International Executive Service Corps, 333 Ludlow St., P.O. Box 10005, Stamford, CT 06904, USA (☎203-967-6000; fax 203-324-2531; iesc@iesc.org; www.iesc.org) sends professionals to Indonesia, the Philippines, and Thailand. Volunteers serve as consultants to businesses, government organizations, and non-profits. Assignments last from 2 weeks to 3 months; IESC can also arrange longer-term work. Major expenses paid; spouse's expenses covered if project lasts for at least a month.

Peace Brigades International, 428 8th St. SE, 2nd fl., Washington DC 20003, USA (☎202-544-3765; fax 202-544-3766; info@peacebrigades.org; www.peacebrigades.org). Volunteers work for human rights in conflict areas of Indonesia. One year minimum commitment. Costs for food, housing, and in-country travel covered by PBI.

Relief for Oppressed People Everywhere (ROPE), see Cambodia, p. 45.

United Nations Volunteers, see Cambodia, p. 45.

Voluntary Service Overseas, VSO Canada, 151 Slater St., Ste. 806, Ottawa, Ontario KIP 5H3, Canada (☎613-234-1364; fax 613-234-1444; inquiry@vsocan.com; www.vsocanada.org.). Opportunities to work in Indonesia, Laos, the Philippines, Thailand, and Vietnam on a wide range of projects. Most volunteer positions last 2 years, though some shorter-term placements are available. VSO covers expenses; stipend provided.

LAOS

STUDYING ABROAD

AMERICAN PROGRAMS

Council-International Study Programs, see Cambodia, p. 44.

Pacific Challenge, see Cambodia, p. 44.

Where There Be Dragons, see Cambodia, p. 44.

LANGUAGE SCHOOLS

CUSO (see Indonesia, p. 47) offers Lao language instruction to their volunteers in Laos.

WORKING

TEACHING ENGLISH

Panyathip Bilingual School and Thames Business School, 07/146, Singsavong Rd., Naxay Village, Vientiane, Vientiane Municipality 10000 (☎856 21 414 084). Frequently needs English teachers.

SHORT-TERM WORK

Sengsavanh, 190 Moot Banna, Vientiane, Vientiane Municipality (☎038 671 112). A local school teaching kindergarten through grade 6 and continuing education; often needs English teachers.

Spire Research and Consulting, Ltd., #09-03 Robinson Towers, 30 Robinson Road, Singapore, 048546 (☎659 686 9425; www.spireresearch.com; raysongoh@spireresearch.com). May have positions available on a project basis for consulting and market research for companies in Laos.

LONG-TERM WORK

International School Services, see Cambodia, p. 44.

The Vientiane International School (VIS), P.O. Box 3180, Vientiane (☎856 21 313 606; fax 856 21 313 008; vis@laonet.net). A private day school encompassing preschool through grade nine, mostly for the children of foreign nationals. Has occasional teaching opportunities. Contact Mr. John Ritter, Director.

VOLUNTEERING

CUSO, see Indonesia, p. 47.

Doctors Without Borders, see Cambodia, p. 44.

Relief for Oppressed People Everywhere (ROPE), see Cambodia, p. 45.

United Nations Volunteers, see Cambodia, p. 45.

Voluntary Service Overseas, see Indonesia, p. 48.

World-Wide Opportunities on Organic Farms (www.wwoof.org/wpother.html#LAOS), see Cambodia, p. 45.

MALAYSIA

STUDYING ABROAD

Association of Commonwealth Universities (ACU), 36 Gordon Sq., London WC1H OPF, UK (☎44 020 7380 6700; www.acu.ac.uk). Publishes information about Commonwealth universities including University of Brunei Darussalam, National University of Malaysia, and National University of Singapore.

AMERICAN PROGRAMS

American University, 4400 Massachusetts Avenue NW, Washington, D.C. 20016, USA (☎202-865-6000). With a branch based in Kuala Lumpur, American University provides 3-week summer programs exploring "interstate relations."

Kolej Damansara Utama, School of American Programs, KDO Petaling Jaya Jalan SS 22141 Damansara Jaya, 4700 Petaling Jaya Selangar (☎603 718 8123, ext. 308).

WORKING

TEACHING ENGLISH

ELS Language Centers in Malaysia, A-2-1 Wisma, H.B., Megan Phileo Avenue, 12 Jalan Yap Kwan Seng, 50450 Kuala Lumpur (☎603 2166 5530; www.els.edu.my). Places teachers certified to instruct Malaysians in English. Five centers, various placements.

SHORT-TERM WORK

University of Lethbridge Work-Study in Malaysia. Contact Andrea Amelinckx (E560), (☎403-329-2148; andrea.amelinckx@uleth.ca; www.uleth.ca/man-int/students/countries/malaysia.shtml). A unique program run jointly by the University of Lethbridge and the University of Victoria MBA Program, this 5-week practicum in Kuala Lumpur offers students first-hand international business experience working for a Malaysian company. Prior to their work experience, the students complete a "cross-cultural study in Malaysia." In the classroom, students study Malaysian culture, politics, and business. The program runs roughly 5 weeks and usually takes place in the spring.)

LONG-TERM WORK

International Schools Services, see Cambodia, p. 44.

Malaysia Employment Center (www.asiadragons.com/malaysia/employment/). This website serves as a employment information hub. Potential employees and employers alike can post and search for suitable matches.

VOLUNTEERING

CUSO, see Indonesia, p. 47.

Ecovolunteer, see Indonesia, p. 47.

Relief for Oppressed People Everywhere (ROPE), see Cambodia, p. 45.

Suaram, 383, 1st Fl., Jalan 5/59, Petaling Gardens, 46000 Petaling Jaya, Selangor, Malaysia (☎603 7784 3525; fax 603 7784 3526; wkpeng@pc.jaring.my, http://www.suaram.org/home.htm). An activist organization working to further human rights progress in Malaysia. Runs educational campaigns with opportunities for involvement.

World-Wide Opportunities on Organic Farms, see Cambodia, p. 45.

MYANMAR

WORKING

International Schools Services, see Cambodia, p. 44.

World-Wide Opportunities on Organic Farms, see Cambodia, p. 45.

VOLUNTEERING

Doctors Without Borders, see Cambodia, p. 44.

Free Burma Coalition (FBC), 1101 Pennsylvania Ave, SE #204 Washington, DC 20003, USA (☎202-547-5985; fax 202-544-6118; info@freeburmacoalition.org; www.freeburmacoalition.org). Modeled after the anti-apartheid movement in South Africa and working jointly with the National League for Democracy (NLD), the FBC acts as an umbrella organization, mobilizing groups around the world to promote freedom and democracy in Burma (Myanmar). The FBC's two-fold objective is to remove the totalitarian rule of the State Peace and Development Council, and to strengthen democratic forces in Burma under the leadership of Daw Aung San Suu Kyi. The FBC calls for an immediate and complete withdrawal of foreign businesses from Burma. The FBC offers a wide range of volunteer opportunities for students and professionals alike, both in Myanmar and in other countries across the globe.

Interplast, see Cambodia, p. 45.

Relief for Oppressed People Everywhere (ROPE), see Cambodia, p. 45.

THE PHILIPPINES

STUDYING ABROAD

AMERICAN PROGRAMS

International Partnership for Service Learning, 815 2nd Ave., Suite 315, New York, NY 10017, USA (☎212-986-0989; info@ipsl.org). Pursue a full range of academic studies at Manila's Trinity College, and volunteer 15 hours a week for a nearby service agency or program. Summer-, semester-, and year-long programs. Summer: US$4900. Semester: US$7200. Year-long: US$14,200. Applications are due 2 months prior to program.

Tagalog On Site, 161 Judge Juan Luna St., San Francisco Del Monte, Quezon City, Manila (☎2 371 6296; tagalog@philonline.com.ph; applications may be filled out online at http://members.aol.com/tagalogusa). Specifically designed for Filipino-American students. TOS participants spend the summer or fall semesters studying the language, history, and contemporary culture of the Philippines. Program costs US$2552.

LANGUAGE SCHOOLS

The University of the Philippines-Diliman, Kolehiyo ng Arte at Literatura, Unibersidad ng Pilipinas, Diliman, Lunsod Quezon 1101, Manila (☎2 928 7508; kal@kal.upd.edu.ph; www.upd.org.ph). Offers courses and degree programs in Filipino language and Philippine studies.

WORKING

Exotic Divers, Malapascua Island. PADI-certified instructors and dive masters can work at Exotic Divers, a dive shop on Malapascua Island (see p. 610). Check www.malapascua.net for the latest information on available positions.

International Schools Services, see Cambodia, p. 44.

Teaching Opportunities, Moalboal. Work as an English or German teacher for young children on the island of Moalboal to support your diving habit (see p. 608). Contact Jochen Hanika (planet@han-grp.de) for more information.

VOLUNTEERING

Assisi Development Foundation, Pasay City, Manila (☎2 632 1001/2; http://home.mindgate.net/tabangmindanaw). Volunteer on projects for evacuees and refugees from the war in Mindanao.

Coral Cay Conservation Ltd., 154 Clapham Park Rd., London, SW4 7DE, UK (☎171 498 6248). Volunteer with coral reef and rainforest conservation, and sustainable development projects in southern Negros (see p. 615) or in Taytay Bay, Palawan (see p. 636).

Department of Social Welfare and Development: Sagip-Kalinga Program, Manila (dswd-ncr@psdn.org.ph). Help out with advocacy for Manila's homeless.

Department of Social Welfare and Development: The Haven, Muntinlupa City, Manila (dswd-ncr@psdn.org.ph). Help out with counseling, education, legal assistance, livelihood training, and medical services for victims of abuse.

Department of Tourism: Tourism Volunteer 12 Program, Manila (☎2 525 9318; pcvcnet@info.com.ph; www.dotpcvc.gov.ph/volunteerstart.html). Promote tourism in the Philippines.

Doctors Without Borders, see Cambodia, p. 44.

Golden Acres, Quezon City, Manila (dswd-ncr@psdn.org.ph). Take care of abandoned and neglected senior citizens.

Health Volunteers Overseas, see Cambodia, p. 45.

Hope Center: Help Center for Street Kids, Makati City, Manila (☎2 893 2794; streethope@hotmail.com). Organize informal educational activities and monitor the health and nutrition of street kids in Manila.

Intercommunication Asia and Nippon: ICAN Program, Makati City, Manila (☎2 412 0980; mikisan@i-next.net; www.jca.apc.org/ican). Volunteer with their vocational training program.

International Center for Living Aquatic Resources Management, 205 Salcedo St., Legaspi Village, Makati City, Manila 1229 (☎2 818 0466, 818 9283, or 817 5255; iclarm@cgnet.com; www.cgiar.org/iclarm). Help preserve the Philippines' biodiversity and create viable policies for sustainable development of aquatic resources.

International Executive Service Corps, see Indonesia, p. 47.

International Resource Recovery and Recycling Network Foundation, 117 Copenhagen St., Green Park Village, Pasig City, National Capital Region, 1612, Palawan (☎917 204 7485; pujpujalte@hotmail.com). Help out with seminars to teach adults and children how to incorporate waste management techniques into their daily lives.

Konkokyo Art Workshop for Batang Riles and Urban Poor, Makati City, Manila (☎2 536 8565; kpacio@info.com.ph). Organize informal art education for children ages 7-16.

National Meditation Center for World Peace, Rt. 10, Box 2523, Jacksonville, TX 75766, USA (☎903-589-5706; osensei@nationalmeditation.org). Volunteer at a Philippine orphanage in Cebu City (see p. 600) and receive language and cultural training.

Operation Smile, see Cambodia, p. 45.

Relief for Oppressed People Everywhere (ROPE), see Cambodia, p. 45.

Peace Corps, Peace Corps Headquarters, 1111 20th St. NW, Washington, DC 20526, USA (☎800-424-8580; www.peacecorps.gov). Opportunities in 70 developing nations including the Philippines and Thailand. Volunteers must be US citizens ages 18+ willing to make a 2-year, 3-month commitment. A bachelor's degree is usually required.

Project Initiating Employment Through Training in Environmental Enterprises (PINE TREE), Room 3, 2nd fl., Abalos Building, Km. 6, La Trinidad, Benguet 2601 (☎74 309 3215; www.skyinet.net/~pinetree). Work with indigenous people to foster community development through environmental projects and programs.

Quezon City Jail Project, Makati City, Manila (☎2 920 5301 or 924 7722; qcjp.pahinungod@up.edu.ph; www.upd.edu.ph/~upocdil). Help with psycho-social counseling, paralegal services, and livelihood training programs for jail inmates.

United Nations Volunteers, see Cambodia, p. 45.

Voluntary Service Overseas, see Indonesia, p. 48.

World-Wide Opportunities on Organic Farms, see Cambodia, p. 45.

SINGAPORE

STUDYING ABROAD

Association of Commonwealth Universities (ACU), see Malaysia, p. 49.

National University of Singapore, Office of Admissions, University Hall Level 2, 10 Kent Ridge Crescent, Singapore 119260 (☎65 6874 1037; fax 65 6728 7570; www.nus.edu.sg). Founded in 1905, the National University of Singapore has 10 faculties and is internationally recognized, offering special programs with schools such as MIT, Johns Hopkins, Harvard, and Stanford.

WORKING

International Schools Services, see Cambodia, p. 44.

Professional Opportunities. Many major job search websites and resources will list positions available in Singapore. Virtually anyone with prior work experience or higher education may consider looking at these resources if they hope to work and live in Singapore for a longer period of time.

VOLUNTEERING

World-Wide Opportunities on Organic Farms, see Cambodia, p. 45.

THAILAND

HOMESTAYS

Center for Cultural Interchange, 17 North Second Avenue, St. Charles, IL 60174, USA (☎888-227-6231 or 630-377-2272). Offers 14-week family homestays for US$250, including room and board, for cultural exchange.

STUDYING ABROAD

Chiang Mai Thai Cookery, 1-3 Moon Muang Road, Chiang Mai 50200 (☎66 53 206 388; www.thaicookeryschool.com). Offers courses for up to 5 days in Thai cooking and fruit tasting (5 days US$100).

Lexia International, 25 South Main Street, Hanover, NH 03755, USA (☎800-775-3942 or 603-643-9898; www.lexiaintl.org). Lexia offers a progressive curriculum of language, cultural, and field study. All programs draw on cultural study in the social sciences and humanities. Lexia offers summer-, semester-, and year-long programs (US$5000-20,000).

AMERICAN PROGRAMS

Council on International Educational Exchange (CIEE), see Indonesia, p. 45.

Experiment in International Living (☎802-257-7751 or 800-345-2929; fax 802-258-3428; www.usexperiment.org). Founded in 1932, the program is run by the School for International Training: College Semester Abroad. Offers cross-cultural, educational homestays, and community work in Thailand. Programs are 5 weeks (US$2550-5000).

International Association for the Exchange of Students for Technical Experience (IAESTE), see Indonesia, p. 46.

ITTA, 3600 S. 60th Ave, Shelby, MI 49455, USA (☎231 861-0481). Thai massage classes (175 hours CEU) and travel in Thailand. $1800 includes airfare and accommodations.

Pacific Challenge, see Cambodia, p. 44.

Where There Be Dragons, see Cambodia, p. 44.

WORKING

Archaeological Institute of America, 656 Beacon St., Boston, MA 02215, USA (☎617-353-6550; www.archaeological.org). The *Archaeological Fieldwork Opportunities Bulletin* ($15.95) lists field sites in Southeast Asia, most notably in Thailand. Buy the books from Oxbow/David Brown Book Co. at www.oxbowbooks.com (☎800-791-9354).

International Schools Services, see Cambodia,p. 44 .

World-Wide Opportunities on Organic Farms, see Cambodia, p. 45.

TEACHING ENGLISH

Involvement Volunteers Association Inc., see Cambodia, p. 45.

Cross Cultural Solutions, see Volunteering, below.

Global Service Corps, see Volunteering, below.

Teaching & Projects Abroad, see Volunteering, below.

VOLUNTEERING

ACDI/VOCA, see Indonesia, p. 47.

Council on International Educational Exchange, see Indonesia, p. 45.

Cross Cultural Solutions, 47 Potter Avenue, New Rochelle, NY 10801, USA (☎800-380-4777; www.crossculturalsolutions.org). Offers programs (3-20 weeks) that focus on AIDS education and outreach, teaching English, and community work ($2000-5000).

CUSO, see Indonesia, p. 47.

Doctors Without Borders, see Cambodia, p. 44.

Ecovolunteer, see Indonesia, p. 47.

Global Service Corps, 300 Broadway #28, San Francisco, CA 94133, USA (☎415-788-3666; www.globalservicecorps.org). Offers programs and internships in education, healthcare, and environment (can be specialized) for 3-10 weeks ($2000+).

International Conservation Holidays, 36 St Mary's St., Wallingford, Oxfordshire OX10 0EU, UK (☎01491 821600; www.btcv.org/international). Runs conservation ecology trips.

International Executive Service Corps, see Indonesia, p. 47.

Operation Smile, see Cambodia, p. 45.

Peace Corps, see the Philippines, p. 51.

Population and Community Development Association, 8 Sukhumvit, Soi 12, Bangkok, 10110 (☎66 2 229 4611; www.sli.unimelb.edu.au/pda). Runs programs specializing in everything from environmental research to family planning and AIDS education.

Relief for Oppressed People Everywhere (ROPE), see Cambodia, p. 45.

Service Civil International Voluntary Service (SCI-IVS), 5474 Walnut Level Rd., Crozet, VA 22932, USA (☎/fax 206-350-6585; www.sci-ivs.org). Arranges placement in Thailand workcamps for those 21+. A special application form and previous workcamp experience is required for applicants to Southeast Asia. Registration fee US$125.

Teaching & Projects Abroad, Gerrard House, Rustington, West Sussex BN16 1AW, UK (☎440 1903 859911; www.teaching-abroad.co.uk). Projects include community action and teaching English (3 months US$2000).

United Nations Volunteers, see Cambodia, p. 45.

Voluntary Service Overseas, see Indonesia, p. 48.

World-Wide Opportunities on Organic Farms, see Cambodia, p. 45.

VIETNAM

STUDYING ABROAD

Hai Cafe, 98 Nguyễn Thái Học, Hội An (see p. 940). The cafe offers a nightly cooking class. During the one-hour class, the chef instructs students on how to make grilled fish in banana leaves, spring rolls, and squid salad. Afterwards, students chow down on their own creations in addition to Hội An specialties, white rose and fried wonton. US$5 covers enrollment and the meal.

Pacific Challenge, see Cambodia, p. 44.

AMERICAN PROGRAMS

Brockport Vietnam Program, Office of International Education, SUNY Brockport, 350 New Campus Dr., Brockport, NY 14420, USA (☎800-298-7869; overseas@brockport.edu). Study for a semester in Đà Nẵng through the State University of New York College at Brockport program. Students take courses in history, language, culture, and politics and participate in community service projects. The US$6750 program fee covers airfare.

Center for Study Abroad, CSA International, 325 Washington Ave. South #93, Kent, Washington 98032, USA (☎206-583-8191; info@centerforstudyabroad.com; www.centerforstudyabroad.com). Offers programs at Vietnam National University in Hồ Chí Minh City. Vietnamese language instruction for all levels (9-week summer programs US$1395, semester programs US$3295, airfare and housing not included).

Council on International Educational Exchange (CIEE), see Indonesia, p. 45.

International Partnership for Service Learning, see the Philippines, p. 50 .

Pacific Challenge, see Cambodia, p. 44.

School for International Training: College Semester Abroad, see Indonesia, p. 46.

Where There Be Dragons, see Cambodia, p. 44.

LANGUAGE SCHOOLS

Vietnam National University, 12 Đinh Tien Hoang, Hồ Chí Minh City (☎822 50 09). Regular and intensive Vietnamese language study during the daytime or evening, available through the Department of Vietnamese Studies and Vietnamese Language for Foreigners, University of Social Sciences and Humanities. Choose from one of six levels of study. All foreigners with a Vietnamese visa are eligible to enroll. Housing available in student dorms for those with a student visa (US$160-220 month).

WORKING

TEACHING ENGLISH

Global Volunteers, see Indonesia, p. 47.

International English Club Vietnam, 537 3 Thang 2 St., District 10, Hồ Chí Minh City. Positions teaching English at all levels; payment depends on level and previous teaching experience. Serve as a preschool English teacher for room, board, and a stipend.

ILA Vietnam, 259 Hai Ba Trung, District 3, Hồ Chí Minh City (☎820 5814). ILA Vietnam seeks experienced English teachers to provide instruction in social and business English. Salaries vary with placement.

TEFL International, 367/11-12 Yaowarat Rd, Muang, Phuket Town, Phuket 83000, Thailand, offers a 4-week intensive training course in teaching English (6-12 MA credits through the University of Washington). Course fee US$1290, with housing US$1690. After completing the course, teachers are placed in schools throughout Vietnam.

SHORT-TERM WORK

International English Club Vietnam, see Teaching English, above. Serve as a chef in Hồ Chí Minh City in exchange for board, lodging, and a modest stipend.

LONG-TERM WORK

International Schools Services, see Cambodia, p. 44.

VOLUNTEERING

Doctors Without Borders, see Cambodia, p. 44.

Global Volunteers, see Indonesia, p. 47.

Interplast, see Cambodia, p. 45.

Health Volunteers Overseas, see Cambodia, p. 45.

Operation Smile, see Cambodia, p. 45.

Peacework, 305 Washington St. SW, Blacksburg, VA 24060-4745, USA (☎540-953-1376; fax 540-552-0119; mail@peacework.org; www.peacework.org). Volunteers serve for 1 to 4 weeks in Vietnam, working on construction and repairs to schools, orphanages, and clinics (US$2000-2500, airfare included).

Relief for Oppressed People Everywhere (ROPE), see Cambodia, p. 45.

United Nations Volunteers, see Cambodia, p. 45.

Voluntary Service Overseas, see Indonesia, p. 48.

World University Service of Canada, PO Box 3000, Station C, 1414 Scott St., Ottawa, Ontario K1Y 4MB, Canada (☎613-798-7477; fax 613-798-0990; wusc@wusc.ca; www.wusc.ca). WUSC projects support local initiatives in Vietnam. Assignments typically last for 2 years. WUSC covers all expenses, including airfare. Volunteers must be citizens or residents of Canada; children of volunteers may be accepted.

CAMBODIA

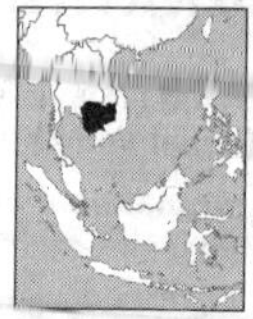

US$1 = 3815.80R (RIEL)	1000R = US$0.26
CDN$1 = 2446.62R	1000R = CDN$0.41
EURO€1 = 3746.86R	1000R = EURO€0.27
UK£1 = 5948.75R	1000R = UK£0.17
AUS$1 = 2088.21R	1000R = AUS$0.48
NZ$1 = 1791.04R	1000R = NZ$0.56
ZAR1 = 363.23R	1000R = ZAR2.75

PHONE CODE

Country code: 855. **International dialing prefix:** 00.

The story of modern Cambodia is one of the darkest in modern history. Perhaps because of the tragedy of their present, Cambodians look to their past for inspiration. It has been a thousand years since the god-kings of Angkor built their vast empire, but the Cambodians still strive to recapture a sliver of their ancestors' glory. Today the classic five-column silhouette of Angkor Wat adorns a popular brand of beer (Angkor: My Country, My Beer), and schoolgirls study the ancient art of Khmer dance, inspired by the graceful *apsaras* that adorn Angkor's walls. The veneration of the past, however, cannot hide the reality of the present. North of Phnom Penh, a once graceful temple lies in ruins, its central sanctuary pockmarked with bullet holes. Many travelers come seeking precisely this unsettling mixture of glorious and ghastly legacies. Others come on a whim and stay longer than they intended, drawn to the lazy, peaceful beach at Sihanoukville, the cheap, easy livin' in Phnom Penh, and the resilience and hospitality of people everywhere. The relative stability of recent years is a welcome change from the constant civil war since the 1970s, but no one is celebrating just yet. The Khmer Rouge may be defunct, but political corruption, violence, massive unemployment, illiteracy, and landmines are its legacies. Perhaps one day Cambodia will leave its past behind, but for now it lingers, both a comfort and a curse.

FACTS AND FIGURES

Official Name: Kingdom of Cambodia.

Government: Multi-party democracy under a constitutional monarchy.

Capital: Phnom Penh.

Land Area: 181,040 sq. km.

Geography: Borders Thailand, Laos, and Vietnam. River systems: Mekong, Bassac, Tonle Sap. Mountain ranges: Cardamom, Dangrek, Elephant.

Climate: Dry (high season) Dec.-Apr., rainy (low season) May-Nov.

Major Cities: Battambang, Siem Reap, Sihanoukville (Kompong Som).

Population: 12,491,500.

Languages: Khmer, English, French.

Religions: Buddhism (94%), Islam (5%).

Average Income Per Capita: US$260.

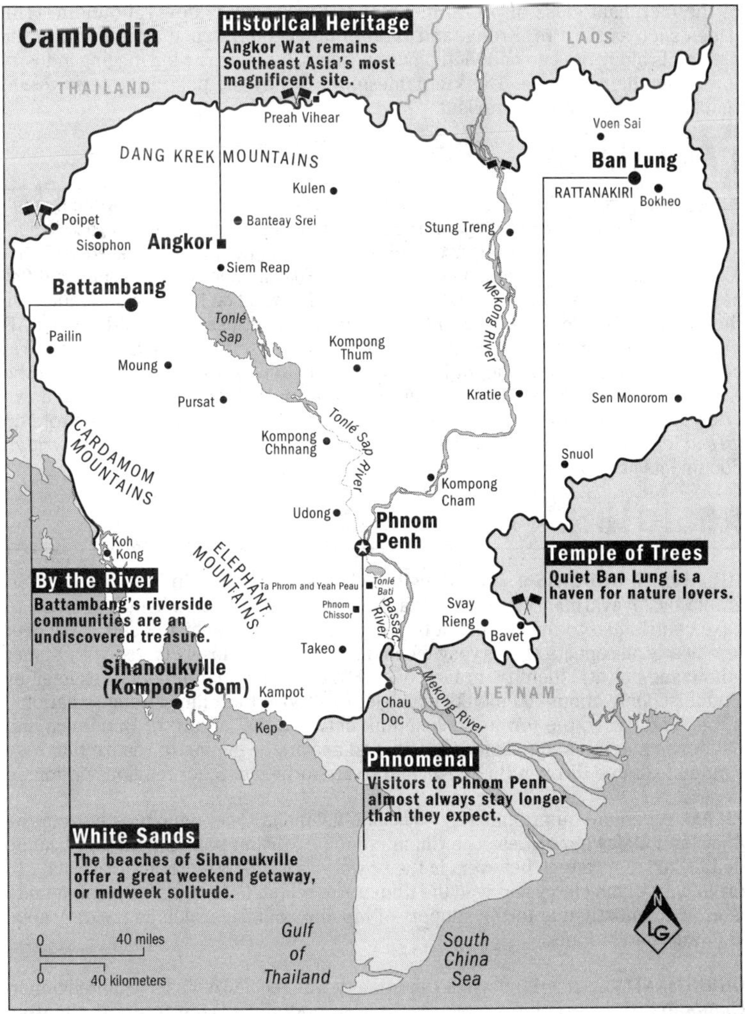

CAMBODIA

LIFE AND TIMES

DEMOGRAPHICS

Cambodia's pre-1975 population included **Khmer, Khmer Loeu** (upland Khmer hill tribes), and minority ethnic groups, including **Chinese, Vietnamese,** and **Cham** (Muslim Khmer). The Khmer Rouge genocide (see **Civil War and the Khmer Rouge,** p. 61), however, targeted minority populations, and Cambodia's population is now, consequently, almost 90% Khmer. The Chinese minority, which had been a large part of the merchant class of pre-Khmer Rouge Cambodia, is now rebounding. Hill tribes such as the Pro, Krung, and Jarai practice subsistence agriculture in the highlands along the Lao and Vietnamese borders, but the growing logging industry threatens their lifestyle. The Vietnamese, known by the pejorative term *yuon*, remain subject to virulent racism.

LANGUAGE

Although the official language of Cambodia is **Khmer,** the country is funtionally multilingual. Indigenous groups speak their own **tribal languages,** while **English** is spoken by the young, educated, urban elites and most people associated with the tourism industry. The older generation learned **French** under colonial rule, and **Chinese** is often the de facto language of business. Drawing on both Sanskrit and Pali, the Khmer language is ancient, with the earliest Khmer inscription dating from AD 612. Both Sanskrit and Khmer, however, are used in inscriptions in the Angkor Wat complex. Aside from these, only three Khmer literary works are known to be extant. Others may have survived as local folk legends that have been passed down orally from generation to generation, but since the ancient Khmer often wrote on *latina* leaves or animal skins, many works of literature as well as everyday written documents have been lost.

RELIGION

THERAVADA BUDDHISM. Introduced to Cambodia in the 12th century from Sri Lanka by Jayavarman VII, Theravada Buddhism's anti-materialism is thought to have contributed to the decline of the Angkor empire. Buddhist beliefs carry over into nearly all aspects of everyday life and have become closely linked with Khmer ethnic and cultural identity. In fact, over 90% of the population identifies itself as Buddhist. Only about 500 monks managed to survive the Khmer Rouge's national purge, and today, the formerly close link between the culture of Buddhism and nationalism is weakening. Modern Cambodians are beginning to realize that they cannot be united through Buddhism and so are turning to other religious options.

ISLAM. There are approximately 500,000 Muslims in Cambodia, mostly from the **Cham** and **Malay** minorities. The Cham combine Muslim beliefs with non-Islamic deities and are staunch believers in the power of magic. Only 20 of the original 113 prominent Cham clergy survived the Khmer Rouge, but today the Cham community is growing mostly due to the support of Muslim countries such as Saudi Arabia, Malaysia, and Indonesia.

CHRISTIANITY. Since 1990 when Christianity was recognized as a legal religion in Cambodia, the Christian population in Cambodia has risen to approximately 60,000. Even Khieu Samphan, accused of the murders of 16,000 individuals under the Khmer Rouge, has become a born-again Christian. Some missionaries worry, however, that Cambodians are becoming only **"rice-bowl Christians,"** relying on the material benefits offered by the mission's aid programs rather than being true converts.

ANIMISM. Found predominantly in remote rural areas, these beliefs encompass **local deities** as well as **ancestral spirits,** and are passed down from generation to generation through word of mouth. They form the basis of many folk arts such as traditional Khmer medicine.

HIGHLIGHTS OF CAMBODIA

CULTURAL HERITAGE. **Angkor** (p. 90) is arguably the most awe-inspiring collection of sights in Southeast Asia and reason enough to visit Cambodia. The **Tuol Sleng Genocide Museum** in Phnom Penh (p. 74) is a must-see.

HANGING OUT. Guest houses and restaurants in **Phnom Penh** (p. 69) and **Siem Reap** (p. 86) attract a fun-loving bunch. Nature-lovers will enjoy quiet **Ban Lung** (p. 84).

BEACHES. The beaches of **Sihanoukville** (p. 78), with their fine white sand, affordable guest houses, and delicious seafood, have really only been discovered by the weekending Cambodian crowd and remain largely deserted during the week.

LAND

Cambodia's land is incredibly fertile. The Tonle Sap, the largest freshwater lake in Southeast Asia, provides an abundance of fish as well as natural irrigation for the area's rice cultivation. The Tonle Sap is also the only waterway in the world in which the current flows in different directions depending on the time of year. From November until May, the water from the Tonle Sap flows as expected—into the Mekong River; however, the monsoon rains in June force the Tonle Sap to change direction, causing the lake to more than quadruple in size. The annual Water Festival (see **Holidays and Festivals (2003),** p. 65) marks this event.

HISTORY

EARLY KINGDOMS AND INDIANIZATION

Scholars base the little they know about pre-Angkorian Cambodia on Chinese travelogues and a few cryptic inscriptions. These accounts describe the **Funan Kingdom** (AD 100-500) as the first unified Cambodian polity. Trading contacts led to an **Indianization** of Khmer politics, religion, art, and literature.

THE ANGKOR PERIOD (802-1432)

IMPORTANT DATES

1113 Suryavarman II expands Khmer territory and goes on a massive wat-construction binge.	**1177** Construction binge drains national resources; Cham invade weakened Kambujadesa.	**1181** Jayavarman VII reunites Kambujadesa.	**1200** Construction on Angkor Thom begins.

Cambodia's Khmer civilization (**Kambujadesa** in inscriptions) was the mightiest kingdom in Southeast Asia during this period, drawing tribute from as far away as present-day Thailand, Myanmar, and Malaysia. **Jayavarman II** founded the Angkor state and declared himself **devaraja,** or god-king. After uniting many disparate kingdoms, he established his capital northeast of the Tonle Sap and began constructing the mammoth temple complex of **Angkor** (p. 93). Most scholars attribute Angkor's wealth to booming agriculture and a strong irrigation system, but under various monarchs, Angkor's power waxed and waned. Under **Suryavarman II,** Khmer territory expanded, and construction on Angkor Wat increased, ultimately sapping the country of strength and leaving it vulnerable to Cham invasions in 1177. In 1181, **Jayavarman VII** reunited the kingdom and instituted an ambitious public works program. Following his death, Kambujadesa suffered a slow decline, its territory steadily encroached upon by the Thai and Lao. In 1431, the Thai Ayutthaya Kingdom claimed the capital, Angkor Thom.

POST-ANGKOR COLONIALISM (1431-1945)

IMPORTANT DATES		
1594 Thais sack Angkor.	**1863** French establish a protectorate in Cambodia and kick off 90 years of colonial rule.	**1941** Playboy Prince Norodom Sihanouk comes to power as supposed "puppet king" but surprises everyone.

Some call the five centuries following the sack of Angkor a dark age of economic, political, and artistic stagnation. In the mid-15th century, the capital shifted from Angkor to **Phnom Penh,** a trade hub at the confluence of the Mekong, Tonle Sap, and Bassac Rivers, thereby increasing Cambodia's contact with the outside world. By the 19th century, Cambodia was caught between its territorially ambitious and mutually antagonistic neighbors, Vietnam and Thailand, which each invaded the country several times. Cambodia may well have been swallowed up permanently were it not for French colonists who established a protectorate there in 1863, which came at the price of heavy taxes, onerous *corvée* labor, and neglected education and social welfare. By the 1930s, an emerging educated elite in Phnom Penh responded with the first stirrings of Cambodian nationalism, recalling the pride of Angkor and Cambodia's past. Co-opted by the French, Cambodian kings were content to collaborate with colonists. Thinking they had selected a pliant puppet, the French placed **Norodom Sihanouk** on the throne in 1941. Equal parts playboy and patriot, Sihanouk surprised them all by agitating for independence.

INDEPENDENCE (1945-1970)

IMPORTANT DATES			
1945 US B-29 bomb Phnom Penh.	**1953** Pol Pot returns to Cambodia from France; Sihanouk declares Cambodian independence.	**1965** Sihanouk breaks off relations with US and allows North Vietnamese to set up bases in Cambodia.	**1970** Vietnam War leads to US invasion of Cambodia.

Cambodian independence came in stages with neither the drama nor the bloodshed of the Vietnamese war against the French. A French attempt to romanize the Khmer language outraged nationalistically inclined Khmers and catalyzed the formation of pro-independence groups, like the **Khmer Issarak** (Free Khmer) party. In 1949, the French signed a treaty granting Cambodia limited sovereignty, and complete independence followed peacefully in 1953. The next decade belonged to Sihanouk, who consolidated his autocratic domestic rule and plotted a neutral course in international affairs. Sihanouk's neutrality was thwarted as the war in South Vietnam intensified. He gave the North Vietnamese tacit permission to use Cambodia as a sanctuary and staging ground for their operations in South Vietnam. Desperate to eliminate the Viet Cong sanctuaries, US military commanders requested permission from the Nixon White House (and, some say, from Sihanouk) to begin a series of secret, devastating bombing campaigns over Cambodia, eventually invading the country outright in 1970 and planting mines that continue to haunt the country.

CIVIL WAR AND THE KHMER ROUGE (1970-1975)

IMPORTANT DATES

1970 Khmer Rouge controls most of the country.	**1975** Khmer Rouge occupy Phnom Penh; Pol Pot founds Democratic Kampuchea (DK) and declares the Year Zero.

The **Khmer People's Revolutionary Party (KPRP)** became Cambodia's revolutionary party in the 1950s, drawing its support from leftist Khmer Issarak members and Khmer students returning from study in France. In this group of students, known as the **"Paris Circle,"** was Saloth Sar, better known as **Pol Pot.** He had studied engineering in Paris but spent most of his time reading Rousseau and attending Stalinist discussion groups; however, poor grades on his exams necessitated his return to Cambodia in the early 1950s. The Marxist revolutionary movement renamed itself the **Communist Party of Kampuchea (CPK)** but was known popularly as the **Khmer Rouge.** Led by Pol Pot, the Khmer Rouge steadily expanded its influence until it had almost a quarter of the country's votes by 1970. In March 1970, Cambodia's Prime Minister, the US-backed General **Lon Nol,** deposed Sihanouk in a bloodless coup. In Sihanouk's absence, the Khmer Rouge rapidly expanded its territory until April 1975, when Pol Pot's forces marched into Phnom Penh and declared the founding of **Democratic Kampuchea (DK).** The Khmer Rouge leadership quickly implemented a program to transform Cambodia into a self-sufficient agrarian utopia, and Pol Pot, a shadowy figure whose true identity few knew, declared that the present day, **"Year Zero,"** would mark the beginning of a massive restructuring of Cambodian society.

DEMOCRATIC KAMPUCHEA (1975-1979)

IMPORTANT DATES

1975 Khmer Rouge evacuate Cambodians from cities and put them to work in the countryside.	**1975-79** Cambodian genocide engineered by Khmer Rouge kills millions.	**1978** Vietnamese invasion finally ends Khmer Rouge power.	**1979** Pro-Hanoi government installed with Hun Sen appointed prime minister.

In 1975, the Khmer Rouge ordered the evacuation of all cities, including Phnom Penh, whose two million residents fled US bombing in the countryside and were relocated to slave labor camps. The government abolished money and systematically eradicated all vestiges of pre-revolutionary society, including 5857 schools, 796 hospitals, infirmatories, and laboratories, 1968 Buddhist pagodas, and 104 mosques—not to mention the teachers, doctors, monks, and artists who worked there. Anyone suspected of being educated—as evidenced by wearing glasses or speaking a foreign language, for example—was shot or clubbed to death and then buried in a mass grave. Under the Khmer Rouge, an estimated 1.7 million people (approximately one-fifth of the 1975 population) were either murdered or perished of malnutrition and disease. Consumed by ideals of ethnic purity, the Khmer Rouge turned their loathing on the perennial Cambodian enemy, the Vietnamese, whom they blamed for the post-Angkor decline of the Khmer nation. Raids on Vietnamese border villages eventually provoked a full-scale Vietnamese invasion of Cambodia in December 1978. Two weeks later, Vietnamese forces seized Phnom Penh and instituted the **People's Republic of Kampuchea (PRK),** a pro-Hanoi regime. Pol Pot and his followers carried on their struggle from jungle strongholds along the Thai-Cambodian border, supporting themselves through timber and gem smuggling.

LANDMINES Over 25 years of civil war has left Cambodia with many sad legacies, but perhaps the worst are the 6-10 million anti-personnel mines strewn about the countryside; if you stray far from Phnom Penh, you're bound to see warning signs. Additionally, there are 500,000 tons of unexploded ordnance (UXO) that the US dropped during the Vietnam War, but which failed to explode. Injuries number between 100 and 300 each month. About half of the injured survive with amputations; one in 236 Cambodians has lost a limb due to a mine explosion. Children are disproportionately at risk, as they frequently mistake UXOs for toys. In 1996, demining groups estimated that at current rates it would take nearly 300 years to clear the fields. Generous international donations have enabled the Cambodia Mine Action Center (CMAC) to carry out demining efforts, but the group is beset with allegations of corruption and misallocation of resources. Improved technology, however, may speed up the project. In December 1997, a Japanese company introduced Mine Eye, a new landmine sensor that is able to differentiate between mines and scrap metal. If contributions continue to increase, CMAC may clear the fields within 10 or 20 years. For now, **when traveling outside touristed centers, never stray from the marked paths.**

FOREIGN INTERVENTION AND HUN SEN'S COUP (1979-1997)

IMPORTANT DATES

1980 US places embargo and recognizes Khmer Rouge as Cambodian government.	**1991** Paris Peace Accords; UNTAC tries unsuccessfully to resolve internal conflict.	**1993** Elections result in shaky coalition government.	**1994** Thousands of Khmer Rouge guerrillas surrender in response to government amnesty.	**1997** Hun Sen seizes control of government in coup.

Led by **Heng Samrin** and a young **Hun Sen** (the current Prime Minister), both former DK leaders who had defected to Vietnam, the PRK struggled to rebuild the shattered country, but the guerrilla war in the countryside hampered their efforts. The US, which recognized the Khmer Rouge as the legitimate government of Cambodia, engineered an embargo that further stifled recovery. In September 1989, the Vietnamese announced a unilateral withdrawal of their forces from Cambodia and cleared the way for the 1991 Paris Peace Accords. The UN oversaw the **United Nations Transitional Authority in Cambodia (UNTAC),** an ambitious mission to resolve the civil war and hold elections. Widely regarded as a fiasco, UNTAC failed to disarm the Khmer Rouge, which, rather than participating in the peace process, marred the elections with intimidation and violence. The May 1993 election resulted in a shaky coalition between Prince Norodom Ranariddh's **United Front for an Independent, Neutral, Peaceful, and Cooperative Cambodia (FUNCINPEC)** and Hun Sen's **Cambodia People's Party (CPP).** But the two factions were never more than uneasy partners, and the Khmer Rouge continued to wage war from border-area strongholds. Hun Sen seized sole control of the government in a July 1997 coup, and Ranariddh went into exile.

CAMBODIA TODAY

KHMER ROUGE TRIALS. Pol Pot, held under house arrest by former allies from 1997 until his death in early 1998, declared, "My conscience is clear." Many former Khmer Rouge officials struck amnesty deals with the Cambodian government in the 1990s. Yet, strides have been made to hold perpetrators of the Khmer Rouge genocide accountable. Two senior leaders, **Ta Mok** (nicknamed "The Butcher") and **Kang Kek Ieu** (known better as **Duch**), were arrested in the spring of 1999. The latter was charged with ordering the killing of over 16,000 people during his stint as Pol Pot's security chief and head of **Tuol Sleng** (codenamed **S-21**), one of Southeast Asia's largest genocidal prisons. Duch was discovered in remote western Cambodia, a born-again Christian relief worker living under the assumed name of **Hong Pin.** Former DK Head of State **Khieu Samphan** abandoned the Khmer Rouge just before its collapse and still lives freely in Pailin where he supports his family by tending ducks; he has not yet been charged with war crimes or genocide. In 2001, after prodding by the UN, US, Australia, and UK, Sihanouk approved legislation to establish a **war crimes tribunal** for those accused of genocide. Unfortunately, Sihanouk's legislation was unacceptable to the UN, and fearing that international standards of justice could not be guaranteed in the tribunal proposed by Cambodia, the UN withdrew its support altogether. In defense of Cambodia's proposal, Hun Sen asserted that if mismanaged, these trials could incite further civil war; cynics, however, note that the prime minister has a vested interest in keeping important political allies out of jail. Hun Sen is just one of several government officials with a Khmer Rouge background, but he has not yet been charged with any crimes against humanity.

FROM KILLING FIELD TO TOURISM HOTSPOT. In order to bolster its flagging tourism industry after the September 11 attacks on the United States, Cambodia is planning to convert Pol Pot's jungle hideout at **Anlong Veng** and Ta Mok's home into tourist resorts. These memorials to Cambodia's genocidal past come on the heels of the **Killing Fields,** the main execution grounds for the Khmer Rouge, and S-21, a high school that the Khmer Rouge converted into a secret interrogation center, both of which are already popular tourist sites. Due to its imminent decay, Cambodian tourism officials have recently dismantled the legendary S-21 **"skull map,"** a wall-size map of Cambodia made of the skulls of 300 prisoners executed under the Khmer Rouge; in its place, the museum has erected a Buddhist shrine. For slightly different reasons, conservation efforts have also been at work at the Angkor temple complex, making replicas of the statues and replacing the originals, which are now housed in an anonymous storage warehouse near Siem Reap. For centuries, the international stolen art market has been flooded with Khmer carvings; today, **Angkor Conservancy** is trying to force art thieves to flood this market with fakes. Discussions for a national museum in Siem Reap that would house these relics seem to be in the works.

CAMBODIAN COOKING The staples of every Cambodian meal are rice and fish. Rice can be simply steamed, fried, or made into noodles. Fish soups are common; occasionally they will also contain egg and vegetables. You'll find that lemon grass, hot peppers, ginger, and mint flavor most dishes.

Prohoc: a rite of passage for the Westerner: rotten fish is left to further ferment before it is added to rice as a paste; it has a strong flavor–strong.
Amok: fish cooked in coconut milk.
Num ansom: cylinder cake, for special celebrations.
Non kaom: sweet coconut sticky rice cake. Cambodian desserts are very sweet.
Samlaw misur: noodle soup; it's your Cambodian mother's recipe.

In Cambodia, as in the rest of Asia, natives always have tea on hand. Coffee, brought to Cambodia by the French, is quite sweet, as they add sweetened condensed milk to it. Typically, it is most polite to use chopsticks, a spoon, or your fingers to eat. As always, take cues from the locals around you.

CUSTOMS & ETIQUETTE

TABOOS. Cambodia is often considered less fervent about Buddhist doctrine than its neighbors. However, the basics still hold: don't point your feet toward people or images of the Buddha, don't touch people on the head (the head is sacred), don't lose your calm in public. Unlike in the rest of Southeast Asia, shorts and T-shirts are accepted at some temples. Also, crossing one's fingers, considered a sign of good luck in many western countries, is considered obscene in Cambodia. Similarly obscene is the use of one's left hand; always use both hands or the right one only when passing something.

PUBLIC BEHAVIOR. Always ask permission before taking someone's picture—especially monks and villagers in remote areas who may not have much exposure to westerners and their cameras. Keep your social place in mind when interacting with Cambodians; it is not polite to make eye contact with those who are older than you or socially superior to you.

BISEXUAL, GAY, AND LESBIAN TRAVELERS. There is little or no openly gay life in Cambodia. Rumors of underground communities abound, but finding them is entirely a matter of luck. Be careful and discreet; con men are known to run scams involving gay travelers.

ARTS AND RECREATION

Because of the havoc wreaked on Cambodian cultural traditions during the era of Pol Pot and the Khmer Rouge, there is a dearth of artistic professionals in Cambodia today; however, those who somehow survived are serving as catalysts for an imminent cultural renaissance.

ARCHITECTURE. The **Angkor Wat** temple complex near Siem Reap is, without a doubt, one of the most magnificent pieces of architecture in the world. According to Hindu mythology, the gods live on top of five mountains including central Mt. Meru surrounded by the cosmic ocean. The structural layout of Angkor is meant to mimic this myth with four smaller towers and one prominent one as well as a surrounding moat. The ancient Khmer also displayed their architectural prowess by devising advanced irrigational techniques that provided enough water to grow and harvest several crops of rice each year in order to support the densely populated empire. Modern Cambodian village architecture takes water into account as well; most structures are built on stilts to prevent flooding or infestation by insects and small animals during the monsoon season.

DANCE. Associated with the Royal Court for over one thousand years, Cambodian classical dance was heavily influenced by the Indian tradition. Despite the devastation of the Khmer Rouge era during which over 80% of the dance masters were killed, the classical tradition was kept alive mainly in Thai refugee camps. Cambodian dance demands the greatest precision as well as the tightest of clothes: dancers are actually sewn into their sarongs before each performance. Today, the tradition is experiencing a resurgence of sorts, and the **apsara dancer** has regained her place as one of the country's most enduring cultural icons.

FILM. Cambodia's last movie theater closed in 1998 under commercial pressure from cheap Thai videos and television soap operas. Before the Khmer Rouge banned movies—not to mention most other cultural activities—Cambodia's vibrant film industry was turning out more than 50 feature-length films per year. Today, the industry is struggling to get back on its feet. Director **Fay Sam Ang** released the myth-based film *The Snake King's Child*, a modern re-telling of the 1960s-era movie *The Snake King* in time to coincide with the lunar New Year celebrations for the Year of the Snake. Many consider Fay Sam Ang to be Cambodia's new cinematic hope.

WEAVING. Handed down from generation of women to generation of women, Khmer weaving is a tradition integral to Cambodian culture. The Khmer Rouge destroyed the mulberry trees in which the silk worms live; as a result, the tradition experienced a severe decline. Today, thanks to the efforts of several NGOs, the trees are being replanted, and Cambodian women—as well as polio and landmine victims—are being encouraged to turn to weaving as a source of income.

HOLIDAYS & FESTIVALS (2003)

DATE	NAME	DESCRIPTION
Jan. 7	Victory Day	Commemorates the fall of the Khmer Rouge in 1979.
Mar. 8	International Women's Day	Colorful parades commemorate this international holiday.
Mid-Apr. (lunar)	Bonn Chaul Chnam (Cambodian New Year's Festival)	Spans 3 days after the end of the harvest season during which Cambodians douse each other with water and clean their homes.
May 16	Visaka Buja Day	Commemorates the birth of the Buddha.
Late May (lunar)	Bonn Chroat Preah Nongkoal (Royal Ploughing Ceremony)	Commemorates the beginning of the planting season.
June 18	Queen's Birthday	Parades and a festive atmosphere mark this day.
Late Oct. (lunar)	Bonn Dak Ben & Pchum Ben	Day to remember and honor ancestors; families bring offerings of food to the local wat and prepare for the afterlife.
Oct. 30	King's Birthday	People from all over the country converge on Phnom Penh to enjoy the fireworks, parades, and festivals.
Nov. 9	Independence Day (from France)	Parade in front of Royal Palace in Phnom Penh.
Mid-Nov. (lunar)	Bonn Om Touk Water Festival	Marks the reversal of the current in the Tonle Sap. Celebration includes boat races and fireworks.
Dec. 10	UN Human Rights Day	Cambodia's recent past lends a particular poignancy to this international holiday.

ADDITIONAL RESOURCES

GENERAL HISTORY

When the War Was Over: Cambodia and the Khmer Rouge Revolution, by Elizabeth Becker (1998). A heartbreaking account of modern Cambodia, fusing together the accounts of ordinary people with an analysis of the patterns of violence and attitudes toward authority that characterizes Khmer society.

A History of Cambodia, by David Chandler (2000). An in-depth look at Cambodian political history from 1953 to 1991 from an outstanding historian.

Brother Number One: A Political Biography, by David Chandler (1999). A fascinating look into the life of one of the most reclusive and secretive Cambodian public figures.

Voices From S-21: Terror and History in Pol Pot's Secret Prison, by David Chandler (2000). A look at the psychological means by which the Khmer Rouge operated the S-21 interrogation center.

Cambodia, Pol Pot, and the United States: A Faustian Pact, by Michael Haas (1991). An exhaustive examination of the disastrous US foreign policy in Cambodia.

The Civilization of Angkor, by Charles Higham (2001). A look at Khmer civilization at its high point.

Sihanouk: Prince of Light, Prince of Darkness, by Milton E. Osborne (1994). A very human portrayal of the political career of Prince Sihanouk.

FICTION AND NON-FICTION

The Stones Cry Out: A Cambodian Childhood 1975-1980, by Molyda Szymusiak. Trans. Linda Coverdale (1999). A fascinating first-person narrative highlighting the disconnect between Khmer Rouge rhetoric and Khmer Rouge action.

Children of Cambodia's Killing Fields: Memoirs by Survivors, by Kim Depaul, Ben Kiernan, and Dith Pran, eds. (1999). A series of moving eyewitness accounts of the Khmer Rouge atrocities.

When Broken Glass Floats: Growing Up Under the Khmer Rouge, by Chanrathy Him (2000). A first-person account of the Cambodian Killing Fields, remarkable for the strength of Him's perseverance.

Cambodia: Report from a Stricken Land, by Henry Kamm (1999). An explanation of modern Cambodia's political instability as a legacy of the Khmer Rouge genocide.

Khmer Rouge End Game, by Paul Ryder Ryan (1998). A very fictional account of 6 foreigners kidnapped from Angkor Wat.

First They Killed My Father: A Daughter of Cambodia Remembers, by Loung Ung (2001). A first-person account of the Khmer Rouge told hauntingly in the present tense.

TRAVEL BOOKS

Off the Rails in Phnom Penh: Into the Dark Heart of Guns, Girls, and Ganja, by Amit Gilboa (1998). A gripping travel narrative about the legacy of 3 decades of civil strife.

The Ends of the Earth: From Togo to Turkmenistan, from Iran to Cambodia, a Journey to the Frontiers of Anarchy, by Robert Kaplan (1997). A pessimistically realistic look at what the future might have in store for us.

FILMS

The Killing Fields, dir. Roland Joffé (1984). A moving drama based on the real-life relationship between a *New York Times* reporter and his Khmer assistant, this film portrays the atrocities of the Khmer Rouge regime. One of the best war stories around.

ESSENTIALS

CAMBODIA PRICE ICONS

SYMBOL:	❶	❷	❸	❹	❺
ACCOMM.	Under US$3 Under 12,000R	US$3-7 12,000-28.000R	US$7-12 28,000-48,000R	US$12-20 48,000-80,000R	Over US$20 Over 80,000R
FOOD	Under US$2 Under 8000R	US$2-4 8000-16,000R	US$4-8 16,000-32,000R	US$8-12 32,000-48,000R	Over US$12 Over 48,000R

EMBASSIES AND CONSULATES

CAMBODIAN CONSULAR SERVICES ABROAD

Cambodia has only a limited number of diplomatic missions worldwide. If your country lacks a Cambodian embassy, try contacting the embassy geographically closest to you.

Australia: Embassy, 5 Canterbury Cres., Deakin, Canberra, ACT 2600 (☎02 6273 1259). Also accredited to **New Zealand.**

France: Embassy, 4 Rue Adolphe Yvon, 75116 Paris (☎33 1 4503 4720; fax: 33 1 4503 4740). Also recommended for citizens of **Ireland** and **the United Kingdom** (to which **no** Cambodian embassy is formally accredited).

Thailand: No. 185 Rajddamri Rd., Lumpini Patumwan, Bangkok 10330 (☎662 2 546630; fax 662 2 539859; recbkk@cscoms.com). Also recommended for citizens of **South Africa** (to which **no** Cambodian embassy is formally accredited).

US: Embassy, 4530 16th St. NW, Washington, DC 20011 (☎202-726-7742; www.embassy.org/cambodia). Also recommended for citizens of **Canada** (to which **no** Cambodian embassy is formally accredited).

CONSULAR SERVICES IN CAMBODIA

Australia: Embassy, Villa 11, Street 254, Daun Penh District, Phnom Penh (☎23 213 470).

Canada: Embassy, Street 254, Sangkat Chaktamouk, Daun Penh District, Phnom Penh (☎23 426 000). For consular services, except if in need of an emergency passport, use the Australian Embassy in Phnom Penh (see above).

UK: Embassy, #27-29, Street 75, Phnom Penh (☎23 427 124).

US: Embassy, 16, Street 228, Phnom Penh (☎23 216 436).

VISAS

All travelers must obtain visas before entering Cambodia overland. One-month visas obtained from international consulates cost US$20, and 2-month extensions cost US$45; allow three business days for processing. Thirty-day tourist visas are available at **Pochentong International Airport** in Phnom Penh (p. 69) or **Siem Reap Airport** in Siem Reap (p. 86) upon arrival for US$20. Those traveling overland from Vietnam can apply for same-day visas (US$30) in Ho Chi Minh City at the Cambodian Consulate. The Cambodian Embassy in Bangkok issues 30-day visas (1000฿, 2-days processing); many travel agencies can secure visas in one day. The Cambodian Embassy in Vientiane can also supply visas (US$20; 1-day processing). **Extensions** are available through the Immigration Office in Phnom Penh at No. 5, St. 200.

MONEY

The Cambodian **riel (r)** comes in denominations of 50, 100, 200, 500, 1000, and 10,000r notes. It's usually not necessary to exchange a lot of money because US dollars and Thai baht are accepted in most places. If you pay in either currency, you'll be given change (at a fair rate) in Cambodian riel. However, small denominations of riel are helpful for small expenses such as cab or motorcycle rides. **Tipping** is not necessary but appreciated. A tip of 2000-2500r is appropriate for moto and cyclo drivers and at cheap restaurants. Credit cards are not widely accepted. There are no **ATMs** in Cambodia.

GETTING THERE

BY PLANE. Cambodia has two **international airports:** Pochentong International Airport in Phnom Penh (p. 69) and Siem Reap Airport in Siem Reap (p. 86). The country has no national airline, but several Southeast Asian airlines such as **Silk Air, Bangkok Airways, Thai Airways, Lao Aviation,** and **Vietnam Airlines** also fly into these airports. **Air France** also flies into Phnom Penh.

BY LAND. Refer to the following table for overland border crossings in Cambodia.

BORDER CROSSINGS

LAOS. As of March 2002, the border crossing between **Stung Treng** (p. 83) in northern Cambodia and **Don Khong** in southern Laos is open to those willing to pay US$20 to cross, but is still unpredictable. Check with your embassy.

THAILAND. Boats run regularly from **Sihanoukville** (p. 78) to **Trat** (p. 739). From Siem Reap, trucks take travelers through Sisophon to the border at **Aranyaprathet/Poipet** (p. 745). The 7hr. overland route is uncomfortable and bumpy, and during the rainy season muddy roads sometimes make the route impassable.

VIETNAM. Buses and share-taxis head from Phnom Penh through **Bavet** (Svay Rieng) to **Mộc Bài** (Tây Ninh), Vietnam, from which connections can be made to Saigon. The trip to the Vietnamese border takes 4-5hr. Boats also make the trip from Phnom Penh to the Vietnamese border; from there, another boat or bus will take you to **HCMC.**

GETTING AROUND

Inexpensive daily **flights** connect cities within the country. **Boats** provide a fairly safe, enjoyable method of travel between Phnom Penh and Siem Reap and along the Mekong River. The roads in Cambodia, except for the road from Kompong Cham to Phnom Penh and the road from Phnom Penh to Sihanoukville, are terrible—pot-holed sin against one's internal organs—so take a boat wherever possible. But nonetheless, overloaded **4WD pickups** ply every road in Cambodia, and these will be your best transport option to remote areas. **Motorcycles** are ubiquitous, and although safety is suspect and helmets are rare, almost every visitor to Cambodia will find himself on the back of a motorcycle. Foreigners should avoid public transportation whenever possible; **private bus lines** run between Phnom Penh and major cities. Hiring a **shared taxi** is a smart option for border crossings; it's cheaper than flying and faster and more secure than taking a bus.

ON THE BEATEN TRACK Cambodia has the most landmines per capita of any country in the world. Though de-mining efforts continue, landmines are a serious threat, especially in rural areas. Stay on well-traveled roads at all times. Banditry has significantly decreased across the country. It is still advised never to travel alone or at night, especially in remote or rural areas.

KEEPING IN TOUCH

Cambodia's **postal service** is unreliable—**postal codes** are not used, and mail takes over two weeks to get to and from Cambodia. Phnom Penh and Siem Reap offer *Poste Restante* and **telephone** service. **Long distance calls** placed from Cambodia are costly. Incoming calls are accepted at most hotels and some communication centers. **IDD calls** can be placed from Telstra phone booths around Phnom Penh. For **Home Country Direct (HCD)** numbers from Cambodia, refer to the table on the inside back cover of this book. HCD calls can be made from phone booths with orange handsets instead of blue ones. **Internet** access is found surprisingly often, but by no means everywhere.

SOUTHERN CAMBODIA

PHNOM PENH ☎23

Phnom Penh's citizens have spent the past 21 years improvising with the left-overs from disaster. Purged of its population in April 1975, Phnom Penh sat empty for the four-year Pol Pot regime, while nearby provinces faced hard labor, famine, fear, and death. Though the city has been more stable in recent years, the past is more than a memory: many streets are still rutted and unpaved, black-outs are common, and bored policemen with acne loiter on street corners. French colonial architecture mixes with modern kitsch, and there are still plenty of guns on the streets—a relic of the chaos of the Khmer Rouge—making parts of the city dangerous at night.

INTERCITY TRANSPORTATION

BY PLANE

Most guest houses and hotels offer bus, boat, taxi, and air services to Siem Reap, Battambang, Ho Chi Minh City in Vietnam, Sihanoukville, and up the Mekong. Non-guests can also use these services.

DESTINATION	FREQUENCY	PRICE	DESTINATION	FREQUENCY	PRICE
Bangkok	daily	US$100	Siem Reap	daily	US$55
Ho Chi Minh City	daily	US$195	Singapore	daily	US$175
Kuala Lumpur	5 per week	US$192	Vientiane	4 per week	US$135

Flights to Phnom Penh arrive at **Pochentong Airport,** 3km west of the city. Airport tax US$20 on international flights, US$10 on domestic flights. Buses go to the airport from GST Express for 2000r, as do taxis (US$5). Ticketing can be done at the airport or at these offices in and around the city: **Air France,** 389 M.V. Preah Sisowath Quay (☎426 288); **Bangkok Airways,** 61A, St. 214 (☎261 707); **Lao Aviation,** 58B R.V. Samdech Preah Sihanouk (☎216 563); **Malaysia Airlines,** 172-184 M.V. Preah Monivong (☎426 688), on the second floor of the Diamond Hotel; **Phnom Penh Airways,** 209, St. 19 (☎216 487); **Silk Air,** 313 M.V. Preah Sisowath Quay (☎426 808), in the Micasa Hotel; **Thai Airways,** Regency Sq., 294 Mao Tsé Toung (☎214 359), in the Hotel Inter-Continental; **Vietnam Airlines,** 41 P. 214 (☎363 396).

BY TRAIN

! Train travel for foreigners was recently legalized, and although cheap, it remains somewhat dangerous and is not recommended, especially for those traveling alone. The **train station** is a yellow, art-deco building set back from M.V. Preah Monivong, north of M.V. Conféderation de la Russie (Pochentong Blvd.).

BY BUS

Most travelers choose to arrange their bus tickets through the guest houses. Buses depart from near the Central Market (New Market) and go to: **Kompong Cham** (3hr., 5 per day 7am-3pm, 6000r); **Sihanoukville** (4hr.; 7:30am-1:30pm; 12,000r); **Udong** (1½hr., 7am-2pm, 4500r). Pickups leave from the Central Market for: **Battambang** (6-7hr.; 5-11am; 15,000r); **Poipet** on the Thai border (9-10hr.; 5-8:30am; 40,000r);

Sem Reap (8hr.; 5-9am; 15,000r). The roads to Battambang, Poipet, and Siem Reap are notoriously bad. Capitol Guest House has a bus to **HCMC** (daily 6:45am, US$8).

BY BOAT

With Cambodia's abundance of bad roads and wide rivers, **boats** are the most expedient travel option. Most leave from the Japanese Bridge (Rt. 5). Most guest houses can arrange **express boat** service to **Kratie** (5hr; 7am; 30,000r) and **Siem Reap** (5hr., 7am, US$23). The ferries, many of which lack adequate safety equipment, can be overloaded, so it's best to travel on the roof. Boats leave from 6-7am.

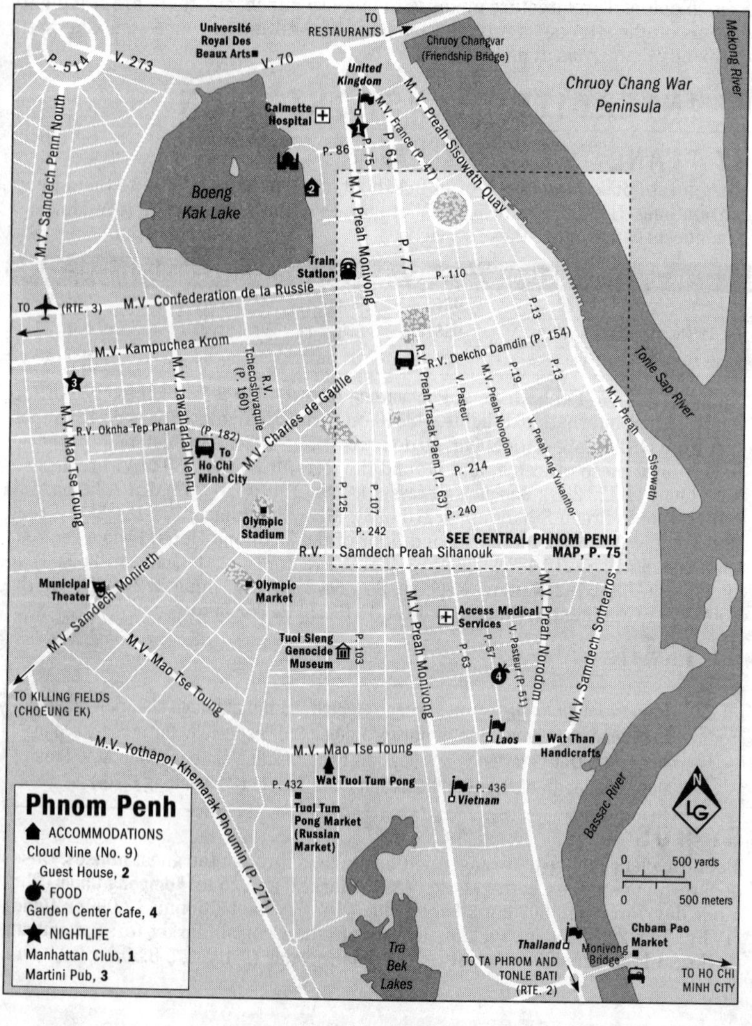

BY TAXI

Taxis can be hired on M.V. Charles de Gaulle between M.V. Preah Monivong and the New Market. Hire a taxi by the seat or by the car; a car to **Sihanoukville** costs around US$20. If you purchase just a seat (around US$3), expect to be crammed into a Toyota Corolla with six other people; buying two seats is a more comfortable option. Shared taxis to Vietnamese border at **Bavet/Mộc Bài** (US$10 per person) and **Siem Reap** (US$10 per person). Most destinations between 2-4hr. from Phnom Penh cost US$15-20 per car. Before hiring a taxi by the New Market, check with guest houses for cheaper options.

ORIENTATION

Three major north-south boulevards divide central Phnom Penh. In the east, **M.V. Preah Sisowath,** with its cafes and bars, runs alongside the **Tonle Sap** river. **M.V. Preah Norodom,** west of the river, is lined with embassies, government ministries, banks, and NGOs. One block to the east, toward the Tonle Sap, are the **National Museum, Royal Palace,** and **Silver Pagoda** complexes. The main commercial, financial, and residential thoroughfare, **M.V. Preah Monivong,** runs straight down the center of the city. Most accommodations and restaurants are between the Tonle Sap River and M.V Preah Monivong. The **New Market (Psar Thmei)** sits between M.V. Preah Monivong and Norodom just south of **M.V. Conféderation de la Russie** (called **Pochentong Blvd.** everywhere but on maps). The east-west thoroughfares are M.V. Conféderation de la Russie (Pochentong Blvd.), **R.V. Samdech Preah Sihanouk,** and **M.V. Mao Tsé Toung.** Most named streets have a number as well; both are printed on street signs.

CAMBODIA

LOCAL TRANSPORTATION

Motos and pedicabs: Motorcycle taxis (motos) and **pedicabs** go anywhere in the city for low fares (1000-2000r). Moto drivers also take passengers to sites outside of town, such as **Chœng Ek, Tonle Bati,** and **Udong.** Drivers outside expatriate and backpacker haunts speak some English. If going out alone at night, use a motorcycle driver whom you know (like the one who took you to Chœng Ek during the day). Female travelers should note that while sitting side-saddle might be customary, it is also dangerous and extremely uncomfortable on longer and less-traveled routes.

Rentals: Lucky Motorcycles, 413 M.V. Preah Monivong (☎212 788), north of the Hong Kong Hotel near Wat Koh. Motos (US$3 per day), dirtbikes (US$6), motorcycles (US$10). A passport or cash **deposit** is required. English spoken. Open daily 7am-6pm. Another option is **New New,** opposite Street 184 on Monivong. Small motorcycles (US$3-4). Larger dirtbikes (US$6-8). They require your passport as a security deposit.

PRACTICAL INFORMATION

TOURIST AND FINANCIAL SERVICES

Tourist Offices: The understaffed and underbudgeted tourist offices are useless. Speak to a guest house manager for good travel advice and bookings. Information regarding safety outside Phnom Penh should be verified at an embassy.

Tours: Diethelm Travel, 65 P. 240 (☎214 059). West of the American Embassy, it is better than most agencies. Arranges trips to Sihanoukville and Siem Reap. Also has a **branch** in the FCC building, 363 M.V. Preah Sisowath Quay. Both open M-F 11:30am-6pm, Sa 10am-1pm. **Hanuman Tourism,** 233 P. 13 (☎428 883), north of the National Museum. English spoken. Open M-Sa 7:30am-noon and 2-5:30pm.

Embassies: Australia and Canada, Villa 11, P. 254 (☎210 470 or 213 459). Consular services open M-F 8am-noon and 1:30-5pm. **Laos,** 15-17 M.V. Mao Tsé Toung (☎982 632). Visa office open M-F 8-11:30am and 2-5pm. 15-day and 1-month tourist visas US$45. 2 passport photos required. Same day processing. **Thailand,** 196 M.V. Preah Norodom (☎363 870). Visa office open M-F 9am-noon and 2-5pm. **UK,** 27-29 P. 75 (☎427 124). Consular services open M-Th 8:30-11:30am and 2-4pm, F 8:30-11:30am. Also handles concerns of **New Zealand** citizens. **US,** 16-18 P. 228 (☎216 436). Open M-F 8am-noon and 1-5pm. Consular services open M-F 9am-noon and 1-3pm. In an after-hours emergency, speak to the guard. **Vietnam,** 436 M.V. Preah Monivong (☎362 531). Visa office open M-F 8-11am and 2-4pm, Sa 8-11am. **Visa applicant must specify point of entry.** Single-entry visa US$35; double-entry US$70. 3-day processing.

Immigration Office: Opposite Pochentong Airport. Visa renewal is done here. Tourist **visas** can be extended for one month (US$30). Open M-F 8-11am and 2-5pm.

Currency Exchange: Moneychangers on the street who post their exchange rates may offer good rates, but banks are more trustworthy. **Cambodian Commercial Bank,** 26 M.V. Preah Monivong (☎425 145), on the corner of M.V. Conféderation de la Russie on the right. MC/V cash advances (2% commission; min. US$5). Open M-F 8am-3pm. **Thai Farmers Bank** (☎426 536), on M.V. Preah Monivong near the Mittapheap Hotel. MC/V cash advances. (US$10 fee; max. US$500 per day). 2% commission on traveler's checks. Open M-F 8am-3pm. **There are no ATMs in Phnom Penh.**

American Express: At **Diethelm Travel** (see **Tours,** above). No surcharge on AmEx purchases. Can issue Traveler's Cheques. Also accepts MC/V. Open M-F 7:30-11:30am and 1:30-5:30pm, Sa 7:30-11:30am.

LOCAL SERVICES

English-Language Bookstore: Monument Books, 111 Preah Norodom (☎723 020). Good selection of English books on Cambodian politics and history. Open M-Sa 8am-7pm, Su 8am-noon and 2-5pm. Visa accepted. For second-hand fiction, head to the **London Book Center,** 65 P. 240 (☎214 258).

English-Language Newspapers: The **Bangkok Post** is available most places. The **Phnom Penh Post** (3500r) publishes long stories on current events bi-monthly. Includes a map of the city. **The Cambodia Daily** (1200r) offers harder-hitting coverage of daily Cambodian, regional, and international news.

EMERGENCY AND COMMUNICATIONS

Emergency: Police ☎117. **Medical** ☎119. Free from any orange phone.

Police: Bureau des Etrangers (Office of Foreign Affairs), P. 154 (☎226 847), off V. Pasteur/P. 151. Some English spoken. Come here with complaints, but in emergencies go immediately to your embassy. Open daily 7-11am and 2-5pm.

Pharmacies: A high percentage of drugs sold in Phnom Penh have expired or are flat-out fakes. **Pharmacie de la Gare,** 81 M.V. Preah Monivong (☎426 855), on the corner of Confederation de la Russie just before the train station, is the most reliable in Phnom Penh. Some English spoken. Open M-Sa 7am-7pm, Su 7am-noon.

Hospitals: Healthcare in Cambodia is well below international standards. **AEA International/SOS Assistance,** 161 P. 51 (24hr. ☎216 911), near P. 228, specializes in emergency care and will provide evacuation to Bangkok. Australian or Khmer-French doctor on-call 24hr. Open M-F 8:30am-5pm, Sa 8am-noon. **Tropical & Travelers Medical Clinic,** 88 P. 108 (☎015 912 1000 or 012 898 981), specializes in travelers' needs. British doctor. Open M-F 8:30am-noon and 2-5pm, Sa 8am-noon.

Telephones: IDD calls can be made from Telstra phone booths at the GPO, the Ministry of Tourism, and outside many hotels on M.V. Preah Monivong. Phone cards sold at GPO and many hotels.

Internet Access: Mekong Cyber, 253 M.V. Preah Sisowath (☎012 888 788). **Friend Net,** 273 M.V. Preah Sisowath (☎216 225). Internet cafes are everywhere. Many are associated with the guest houses on Bœng Kak Lake or along the river. All US$2 per hr.

Post Office: GPO, on P. 13, at the intersection with P. 102 south of Wat Phnom. A large, yellow colonial building. Overseas calls, fax, telegram service. EMS mail available. Sells phone cards for local phone booths. *Poste Restante.* Open daily 7am-6pm.

Express Mail: DHL, 28 M.V. Preah Monivong (☎426 726), north past the intersection with Confederation de la Russie. Open M-F 8am-6pm, Sa 8am-5pm.

CAMBODIA

ACCOMMODATIONS

Guest houses (US$3-10) in Phnom Penh provide beds and a backpacker-friendly atmosphere. Hotels (US$10 and up) keep travelers cooler and cleaner, but many of them are nondescript. The best backpacker hangouts line Boeng Kak Lake, which feels a world away from the bustle of Phnom Penh. Many good hotels are along Preah Monivong. Most guest houses listed arrange visas and transportation.

Cloud Nine (No. 9) Guest House, 9 P. 93. Head toward Boeng Kak Lake on M.V. Preah Monivong, then turn left on V. Moat Chrouk (P. 86). At the end of the street, just before the mosque, turn left and walk 500m. It's on the right. Loll in hammocks on the lakeside porch with fellow backpackers. Rooms have mosquito nets. Arranges transportation to Siem Reap, Sihanoukville, and HCMC. Singles US$3; doubles US$4-6. ❷

Capital Guest House and Restaurant, 14 P. 182 (☎364 104), on the corner, 1 block off M.V. Preah Monivong. One of the longest-standing backpacker institutions in Phnom Penh. Loud neighborhood. Good English spoken. Daily bus to HCMC (US$8). Singles US$3, with bath $4; doubles US$4/$5, with A/C US$10-12. ❷

Narin Guest House No. 50, 50 P. 125 (☎213 657). Follow M.V. Preah Monivong from the city center, turn right at the Ministry of Tourism (P. 232), then left on P. 125. Good food (US$1-3) and clean rooms. Patio and balcony give guests a place to socialize. Organizes onward travel; taxis to Vietnam US$5 per person. Book rooms in advance. Singles US$3; doubles US$5, with bath US$6, with balcony US$7. ❷

The Walkabout Hotel (☎851 787), on the corner of P. 51 and P. 174. Centrally located with a security guard at the door. Offers clean rooms with bath and satellite TV. The lobby doubles as a popular bar. Doubles with fan US$6-8, with A/C US$12. ❷

Royal Guest House, 91 P. 154 (☎854 806), near the intersection with M.V. Preah Norodom. Location and wide range of room options make the few extra dollars worth it. In the heart of the city yet with quiet rooms. Arranges moto driver for US$5 per day. Singles with shared bath US$3-4. All other rooms with bath, fridge, and cable television. Singles US$8, with A/C and hot water US$10; doubles US$12. ❷

The Last Home, 47 P. 108 (☎724 917), 2 blocks west of the Old Market. Small rooms have mosquito nets, desks, and small fans. Arranges buses to Sihanoukville (12,000r), boats to Siem Reap (US$22), and transportation to the airport (taxi US$5, moto US$2) from the Internet cafe downstairs. Call ahead. Tiny room US$2; singles US$3, with bath US$4; doubles US$5, with A/C US$8. ❶

Keov Mean Guest House, 1 V. Pasteur St. (☎723 067), near P. 51 between P. 118 and P. 126. Tidy rooms within 2 blocks of the New Market. Wrap-around balconies. Rooms have fan and bath (with decent water pressure!). Rooms US$6, with A/C US$10. ❷

Paradise Hotel, 219 M.V. Preah Monivong (☎426 540), at the intersection with M.V. Charles de Gaulle. Away from the backpacker hustle and bustle, but still centrally located. Good but pricey Thai restaurant. All rooms have A/C, cable TV, phones, mini-fridges, and baths. Singles US$20; doubles US$25. ❺

FOOD

Dozens of restaurants worthy of exploration line **M.V. Preah Monivong** and **M.V. Samdech Preah Sihanouk.** Cheap and adventurous eats are at the markets. **Lucky Market Group** has two stores, one at 160 Samdech Preah Sihanouk (open daily 8am-8pm), and a large one in the Parkway Square complex, on M.V. Mao Tsé Toung, near the intersection with M.V. Preah Monivong (open M-F 9am-8:30pm, Sa-Su 9am-9pm). There's a wide selection of imported products. At 5:30pm, food stalls materialize near **Wat Koh** at the **Independence Monument.** More expensive and touristed restaurants line **M.V. Preah Sisowath,** north of the Royal Palace. Also try the restaurants over the **Chruoy Changvar** (Cambodian-Japanese Friendship Bridge), northeast of the city. Of the restaurants in this area, **Bœng Meas** (on the left) has the best food, **Heng Lay** (on the right) has the best comedy act, and **Hang Neak** (farther down the strip on the right) has great decor and entertainment. These restaurants are open from 9am-10pm. On weekends, they start filling up after 8pm.

Phnom Khiev, 138 R.V. Samdech Preah Sihanouk, on the corner of P. 63. The intimate interior (with A/C) lends a gentle ambience. Typical Cambodian dishes and some French fare. Generous, inexpensive portions US$2-6. Cocktails, *apéritifs,* wine, and imported beer served. Open daily 7am-11pm. ❷

Garden Center Cafe, 23, St. 57. Set in a lush tropical garden, this restaurant serves up a full range of Asian and Western food. Great breakfast options. Entrees US$3-6. Open Tu-Su 7am-5:30pm. ❷

Athena Restaurant, at the corner of St. 51 and 282. This place serves up excellent Greek food, although it is a bit pricey. Entrees US$5-12. ❸

Restaurant Ponlok Special Soup, 319-323 Preah Sisowath. Balcony seating overlooks the river and catches the breeze at night. Excellent Chinese and Khmer fare, especially the shrimp dishes and sour soup. Dishes US$3-8. Open daily 10am-10pm. ❷

La Terrasse, on the corner of P. 262 and P. 51, one block west of the Victory Monument, in a colonial-style building. Pricey French food. Also serves food in the secluded garden. Enjoy a *croque monsieur* (US$5). Open M-Sa 10am-6pm. ❸

"KT" Khmer-Thai Restaurant, 15 P. 49, north of Wat Phnom. Very tasty, inexpensive Khmer and Thai food. Good *tom kha gai* (spicy Thai chicken and coconut milk soup) and grilled chicken US$3. Open daily 10am-10pm. ❷

Mount Everest, 98 M.V. Samdech Preah Sihanouk, 500m west of the Independence Monument. Indian and Nepalese cuisine at very reasonable prices (entrees US$3-5). Open daily 10am-10pm. ❷

SIGHTS

Phnom Penh is better for aimless exploration than scheduled sightseeing. There are few jaw-dropping tourist attractions, but some are more profound, deserving plenty of time and attention. Chief among these are the **Tuol Sleng Genocide Museum** and the **Killing Fields** at **Chœng Ek.** Guest houses arrange motorcycle drivers for the day (US$7, more for a trip to the Killing Fields). Many government tourist attractions close on Mondays, but a gratuity may open the doors.

TUOL SLENG GENOCIDE MUSEUM. At this former high school in a residential neighborhood of Southern Phnom Penh, the Khmer Rouge imprisoned and killed over 14,000 people. Only seven survived; the rest were sent to the Killing Fields of

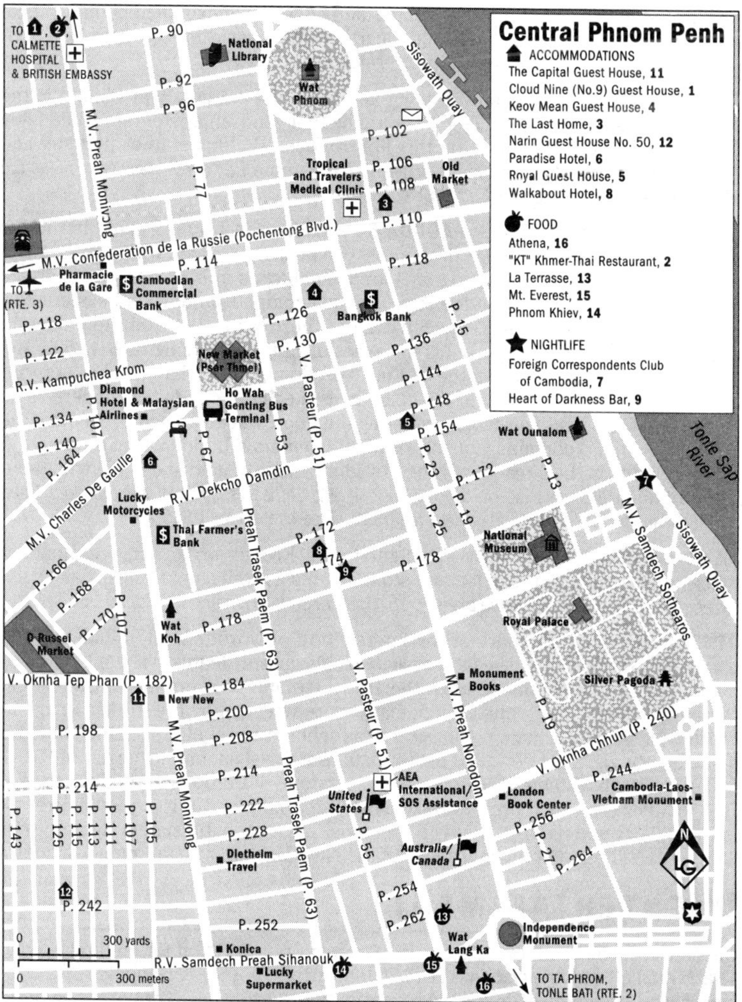

Chœng Ek. When the Vietnamese arrived in 1979, they found at Tuol Sleng a morbidly well-documented hell. The most telling memorial of the Khmer Rouge years, Tuol Sleng has been left as it was found in 1979. There are no velvet museum barricades—visitors walk freely through closet-sized detention cells and torture chambers. Many documents of torture are now displayed on the walls, including hundreds of photographs taken of each victim upon arrival. *(On P. 103. Open Tu-Sa 7:30-11am and 2-5pm. US$2. Photography permitted.)*

CHŒNG EK "KILLING FIELDS". The killing fields were the final destination for more than 40,000 victims of Pol Pot's reign of terror. Only one person survived. He was shot but didn't die and was buried. When the Vietnamese found the Killing Fields, they unearthed him, barely alive. A *stupa* was erected in 1988; a glass case inside contains 17 levels of human skulls and bones from exhumed bodies. Bits of bone and cloth still come up from the earth. *(17km south of the city. Open Tu-Su 7am-5pm, though on M a donation might open the gates. Entry US$2.)*

WAT PHNOM. With its beautiful lawn and Buddhist statues, Wat Phnom is the most sacred sight in Phnom Penh. According to legend, an aristocrat named Lady Penh founded a monastery atop this hill to house Buddha statues that she had found inside a log. *Phnom* means hill—hence, Phnom Penh. *(On a hill north of the Old Market on M.V. Preah Norodom. Entry US$1.)*

ROYAL PALACE AND SILVER PAGODA COMPLEX. The Royal Palace is closed when the royal family is home, but visitors can peek in the huge windows. English-speaking guides or English programs are available, as most of the buildings are unlabeled. Along the walls of the Silver Pagoda complex, in the southeastern corner complex, frescoes portray scenes from the *Ramayana* and the palace in ancient times. A large *stupa* holds the ashes of King Ang Duong (r. 1845-59). The pavilion beyond shelters a statue of King Norodom on horseback and a footprint of the Buddha. At the center of the complex is the **Silver Pagoda,** which derives its name from the 5000 silver blocks covering the floor. **Wat Phra Kaew** (Temple of the Emerald Buddha) contains, not surprisingly, an emerald Buddha from the 1600s. A Buddha statue in the likeness of King Norodom, made of gold and inlaid with thousands of diamonds, is also on display. *(Along M.V. Sothearos, south of Wat Ounalom. Open daily 8-11am and 2-5pm. US$3, camera fee US$2, video camera fee US$5.)*

CAMBODIA

NATIONAL MUSEUM OF ARTS. Designed by a French architect, the museum houses fine Angkorian wooden and stone figures as well as pre-Angkorian sculptures. *(North of the Royal Palace along P. 13. Open Tu-Su 8-11am and 2-5:30pm. US$2.)*

OTHER SIGHTS. In the park at the intersection of Norodom and Sihanouk, the **Liberation Monument (Cambodia-Laos-Vietnam Monument)** features a giant statue of three figures that commemorates the 1979 Vietnamese liberation of Cambodia. Phnom Penh also has wats, though many were wrecked by the Khmer Rouge in the late 1970s. The remaining ones serve as schools and shelters for the poor and disabled; they are not designed for tourists. **Wat Ounalom,** on the corner of P. 154 and M.V. Preah Sisowath Quay, is the cornerstone of Cambodian Buddhism. **Wat Tuol Tum Pong,** on the corner of M.V. Mao Tsé Toung and P.155, just before the market, has budding linguists who greet visitors with enthusiastic "hellos." **Wat Koh,** on M.V. Preah Monivong, south of the New Market, has an English school.

ENTERTAINMENT

Check the calendar of *The Cambodia Daily's* Friday edition for cultural events. The **Sovanna Phum Association,** 111 P. 360, near the Tuol Sleng Genocide Museum, performs dance and shadow-puppet shows. (☎012 846 020. Shows every 15 days. Tickets US$3.) The **Mekong Island Park,** intended as an "authentic showcase" of traditional Cambodian culture, hosts Khmer music and theater. Trips leave daily from the **Mekong Island Park Office,** 13 P. 240, at the corner of P. 19, and return at 3pm. Tickets include lunch, a visit to the zoo, an elephant ride, and a dance show. (☎016 851 1361. US$32; 4-person min.) The easiest and cheapest way to observe Khmer music and dance is to visit the **Université Royale des Beaux-Arts,** on P. 70, off M.V. Preah Monivong, north of the French Embassy. Head north on M.V. Preah Monivong and turn left at the rotary, just beyond the Thai Embassy. On the right is the university, where the faculty struggles to preserve Khmer art. Students learn the *apsara* dance, flute music, and scenes from the *Ramayana.* Unobtrusive foreigners are welcome. (Classes M-F 7-11am and Sa 8-11am.) At sundown, locals head to the decorated restaurants northeast of the city center, where cool river breezes accompany diverse menus and lively entertainment of the karaoke variety. Line-dancing Khmer and American pop-singing youngsters keep things upbeat before local comedians take the stage.

MARKETS

Phnom Penh supports more than seven markets, all of which arc food havens. Most vendors set up at 6:30am and don't leave until 5pm. Markets are best visited in the early morning. **Cobblers,** on P. 143, due west of the Tuol Sleng Genocide Museum, sell fine, custom fit, all-leather shoes and sandals (US$10-40).

New Market (Psar Thmei). The hub of Phnom Penh, this large yellow structure is often referred to as "Central Market." Large art deco structure built in the 1930s. Generally has higher prices than the other markets. Purchase up-to-date maps, Angkor guides, and Khmer phrasebooks here.

Russian Market (Tuol Tom Pong Market), between P. 163 and P. 155, south of the wat of the same name. This market wins high marks for its beautiful silk, cotton print sarongs, *krama* (the combination scarf, headdress, and bathing suit), and wide selection of cheap pirated CDs. There are many wood and stone sculptures here as well.

Old Market (Psar Char), northeast of the New Market along P. 108 and P. 15. If you want to purchase silk by the yard, this is the place. The atmosphere is less touristy and the vendors are less pushy than in the other markets.

O Russei Market, on P. 182, between M.V. Charles de Gaulle and M.V. Preah Monivong. This large market is housed in a new, indoor facility and sells electronics.

Wat Tan Handicrafts, 206a M.V. Preah Norodom, next to the Royal Air Cambodge Office. Trains students in tailoring, weaving, and carpentry as part of an effort to aid those disabled by landmines and polio. The fruits of their labor are sold at the Wat Than showroom. Items include silk pillows, clothing, and pocketbooks. Tailor-made outfits specially-ordered. Open M-Sa 7:30am-5:30pm.

CAMBODIA

NIGHTLIFE

Popular bars and cafes, such as **The Globe** and **Rising Sun,** line **Preah Sisowath.** There are many other bars near Norodom Blvd. and toward Independence Monument such as **Walkabout,** at the corner of St. 174 and 51 (open 24hr.), and **Sharky Bar,** at 126 St. 130. **Be careful at night**—tourists have been mugged.

Heart of Darkness Bar, 26 P. 51, near the corner of P. 174. Red-lit bamboo and Angkor-inspired decor, good music and ambience. The expat/backpacker bar par excellence. Inexpensive beer and mixed drinks US$1-3. Open daily 8pm-sunrise.

Foreign Correspondents Club of Cambodia (FCCC), 363 M.V. Preah Sisowath Quay (☎427 757), on the river north of the Royal Palace. Mission-style furniture on a terrace overlooking the river. Western menu, pool table. Imported beers, mixed drinks, and restaurant. A bit pricey, but great scenery. Happy hour 5-7pm. Open daily 7am-midnight.

Martini Pub, on M.V. Mao Tsé Toung, next to the giant Hotel Inter-Continental. Not so pub-like, but oddly more like an outdoor dance club out of an episode of *Star Wars*. Dancing gets going around 11pm. Open M-Th 7pm-2am, F-Sa 7pm-sunrise.

Manhattan Club, on P. 84, just east of M.V. Preah Monivong and Calmette Hospital. Part of the Holiday International Hotel. One of the best dance clubs in Phnom Penh with a high-rolling Asian clientele. Buy beer at the street stalls outside. Otherwise, it's US$6 a drink. Dancing gets going around 11pm and goes on until dawn.

DAYTRIPS FROM PHNOM PENH

UDONG

The city bus from Phnom Penh has the cheapest rate to Udong. Buses leave from the bus station at the New Market (every 45min. 6:30am-6:30pm, 4000r) for the village of Udong. From there, it is a moto ride to the temples (4000r). Capitol Travel at the Capitol Guest House in Phnom Penh offers an A/C bus to Udong daily (9am, US$5, 4-person min.). Alternatively, a moto can be chartered round-trip for US$10. Get there early, as the hill tends to simmer even when the surrounding countryside basks in a picnicker-friendly breeze.

Udong, Cambodia's capital from 1618 to 1866, sits 45km northwest of Phnom Penh. The site sees few tourists, though Phnom Penhois pour in for weekend picnics. The **twin hills of Udong** are visible from miles away; one is riddled with temples and *stupas*. From the parking lot/picnic area at the hill's base, the road on the extreme left leads to a mosque and temple, both of which suffered greatly in the civil war. From there, paths lead to countless vistas and *stupas*.

PHNOM CHISSOR

Phnom Chissor is 22km from Phnom Tamao. The turn-off is on the left beyond the school. From there, a dusty dirt track winds 6km through a small village and past lush rice fields to the foot of the hill. Hire a moto to go there (US$5 round-trip).

Phnom Chissor temple rises high above the flat plains of Takeo Province. The kings had elephants, but visitors must now walk up more than 500 steps to get there. Built in 1150 of laterite and sandstone, the temple was a regular stop on the god-king pilgrimage circuit though it was nearly destroyed by US bombers in 1973. The central sanctuary houses the original reclining Buddha statue. To protect it from thieves, the monks have concealed it behind newer images. The original can be viewed only by climbing back into the tiny sanctuary with a candle and a 500r tip. Facing east, in line with Phnom Chissor, stand two laterite gates, **Sen Thomol** and **Sen Ravang.** On the way to Phnom Chissor, the Brahman priests would bathe in Tonle Oun, the lake in front of the first gate. The original steps leading down to the gates are still visible.

ALONG RTE. 2

There are several worthwhile sights near the capital, each of which can be visited on a half-day excursion. The easiest way to reach them is by motorcycle or car. Most drivers charge tourists about US$10-15.

Ta Phrom temple is 32km south of Phnom Penh along Rte. 2. The turn-off is on the right. Look for a gate with three large Angkor-inspired towers. The first Phrom temple was constructed in the 7th century. The current one, built of laterite and sandstone in the Bayon style, is believed to have been erected during the rule of Jayavarman VII (1191-1218). Originally constructed as a Brahmanic temple, it was later reconsecrated to Buddhism. Nearby, **Yeah Peau** temple is also worth a peek. The nearby lake of **Tonle Bati** is a popular weekend retreat for urbanites. Vendors offer beer, fried chicken, cold drinks, fruit, and young coconut juice out of the shell. **Phnom Tamao** is a wildlife center and zoological preserve near Tonle Bati. Monkeys, tigers, birds, and bears are caged in the setting of lush jungles, except during the dry season (US$1).

SIHANOUKVILLE ☎034

All but destroyed during the Pol Pot years, Sihanoukville, the country's only deep-water port, was rebuilt with Soviet aid. Tourism has been on the rise in recent years, but while the number of hotels in the town has grown, the beaches remain largely deserted. Hang up the rucksack and take it easy for a couple of days—as if you hadn't been doing that already.

TRANSPORTATION

Buses: Guest houses and hotels can arrange bus tickets to **Phnom Penh.** 3 bus companies, all along V. Ekareach, go to Phnom Penh: **D.H. Cambodia,** east of the city center (7:30am, 12:30pm; 12,000r); **GST Express** (☎012 820 559), next to Chaok Sakor Hotel (3¼hr.; 4 per day 7:15am-1:30pm; 12,000r); **Ho Wah Genting Transport Co. Ltd.** (☎933 888), next to the Cambodian Commercial Bank (4hr.; 5 per day 7:10am-2pm; 12,000r). Arrive 15min. early.

Ferries: Look for signs saying "Port of Passenger Ship" at the ferry dock north of Sihanoukville, off Hun Sen Beach Dr. Take the boat to **Koh Kong** (3½-4hr., noon, US$15), where smaller boats run to the **Thai border** (10min., 100฿).

Local Transportation: Motorcycle taxis cost 1000-2500r, depending on distance. Arrange early morning transport in advance. Hire a **taxi** at the **Central Market** (Psar Loer). To **Phnom Penh** US$20-25. Night travel not recommended.

Rentals: For the bad boy in all of us, uncrowded roads make Sihanoukville an ideal place to rent **motorbikes.** Check your guest house or go to the GST and D.H. bus stations. Most places charge US$5 per day.

BORDER CROSSING: SIHANOUKVILLE/TRAT. Thirty-day Thai visas are issued at the border. Take a speedboat from the ferry dock off Hun Sen Beach Dr. to **Koh Kong** (3½hr., noon, US$15). Cross the river (5000r) and take a short moto ride to the border (3000r). Walk across the border, get your exit stamp, and enter Thailand at the border town of **Had Lek.** Take a minibus or taxi from Had Lek to **Trat** (see p. 739) where further transportation to Bangkok can be made. The border is open from 7am-5pm, but since you will probably arrive in Koh Kong in the late afternoon from Sihanoukville, do not waste time in crossing. If the border is closed when you arrive, there are accommodations in town.

ORIENTATION AND PRACTICAL INFORMATION

The town is spread thinly over hills, with long stretches of road between it and the beaches. The town's main thoroughfare is **V. Ekareach,** which runs east-west from **Victory Beach** to the city center (2km) and then elbows south to the **Golden Lion Traffic Circle** (1.5km). The main beach road, **2 Thnou St.,** follows the coast past **Independence** and **Sokha Beaches. Ochheuteal Beach** lies to the south of the Golden Lion Traffic Circle. The most popular guest houses and the main **post office** are above Victory Beach. The *Sihanoukville Visitors Guide*, published yearly and available in restaurants and hotels, includes a map. **Mekong Bank,** on V. Ekareach in the center of town, offers Visa cash advances (US$5 min.), and exchanges traveler's checks. (☎933 867. Open M-F 8am-4pm, Sa 8am-noon, Su 10am-2:30pm.) The **Central Market (Psar Loer)** is a raucous night market near the Okinawa Thmey Hotel. (Open daily 5am-6pm.) Other services include the **police** (☎833 222), on V. Ekareach at the top of the hill 1km west of city center and the **Chuen Min Hospital** (☎933 111), on V. Ekareach near the city center. **International calls** can be made at the **Camintel,** on V. Ekareach (US$3-5). There are a few Internet shops in town, including **Camintel** (open daily 7:30am-8:30pm), on V. Ekareach, but at an exorbitant US$5 per hr. The **post office** is in the building across the street from the market on 7 Makara. (Open M-F 8am-noon and 1-5pm.)

ACCOMMODATIONS AND FOOD

On Weather Station Hill above Victory Beach, **MASH & Melting Pot ❶** is characterized by its idiosyncratic charm. There is an attached restaurant, a bar, and a library of books about Cambodia and Southeast Asia. (☎012 913 714. MASH section 1-2 person US$3-4; Melting Pot section US$4-6.) **Mealy Chenda Guest House ❶,** on the bluff above Victory Beach, is a new backpacker-friendly haven with an open-air balcony and rooftop restaurant. (☎933 472. Moto rental US$4 per day. Free pickup at bus station. 3-bed dorms with shard bath US$2; singles with shared bath US$3; singles and doubles with bath US$5-6, with balcony US$7-8.) On Serendipity Beach west of Ochheuteal Beach, **Serendipity Guest House ❶** has basic accommodations in a great location to take advantage of local nightlife.

Sihanoukville has excellent seafood, especially shrimp and crab. Most guest houses sport wide selections of food but the intrepid can feast at the **night market.** Food stalls line **V. Ekareach.** (Open daily 6-11pm.) **Les Feuilles Restaurant ❹,** 400m east of the Golden Lion Traffic Circle on Kanda 1 St., serves excellent French, Western, and Khmer food. (Great *luk-lak* US$5. Open daily 7am-10pm.) **Chez Claude Restaurant ❺,** off 2 Thnou St. on a ridge high above Sokha Beach, has fantastic Asian and French cuisine and a beautiful view of the sunset over the Gulf of Thailand. (Entrees US$5-10.) **Hawaii Seaview ❸,** on South Victory Beach has excellent seafood with a great view of the beach (entrees US$2-5). Open daily 9am-late.

CAMBODIA

SIGHTS AND ENTERTAINMENT

Sihanoukville's major attraction are the many stretches of sugary sand that surround the town. A few other sights, however, are worth a look. Atop the 132m high **Sihanoukville Mountain,** the town's wat overlooks a stunning panorama of land and seascape. Head east on National Rte. 4 (toward Phnom Penh), turn right at the **Cambrew Brewery** (home of Angkor Beer; open M-Th), and follow the dirt road up the ridge. About an hour by moto outside of the town is a **waterfall** that is a popular bathing spot. Moto drivers will do the round-trip for US$4. **Angkor Arms Pub,** on V. Ekareach near the city center, is a self-proclaimed traditional British pub and a Sihanoukville institution offering beer, darts, and a restaurant. (Open daily 4pm-midnight or whenever the last person leaves.)

BEACHES

At the southeastern end of the peninsula is **Ochheuteal Beach**—long, uncrowded, and backed by some of Sihanoukville's nicest hotels. Farther west is **Independence Beach,** which has clear water and few hawkers. There is great boulder-hopping on the rocky shorelines between beaches. **Sokha Beach,** back to the east a bit, is the most popular beach. Throngs of vendors sell snacks and fresh coconuts (1000r) here, and inner tubes can be rented. **Victory Beach,** just south of the Port of Sihanoukville, has little to speak of. Get a motorbike there for 5000r.

UP THE MEKONG

KOMPONG CHAM ☎042

Although it doesn't feel like it, Kompong Cham is Cambodia's third largest city and the first major stop for travelers heading up the Mekong. With the opening of the Lao border north of Stung Treng and the recent completion of a gargantuan bridge across the Mekong, Kompong Cham has also become a transit point to the north and east of the country. Despite the fact that there is not much to see or do in the city, Kompong Cham is a pleasant provincial city, and there are certainly worse places to be stuck for one night.

TRANSPORTATION The road from Phnom Penh to Kompong Cham is in excellent condition. **Buses** leave Kompong Cham from behind the market on the same street as the Canadia Bank for **Phnom Penh** (3hr., 8 per day 7:30am-4pm, 6000r). The road to **Kratie** is horrible and there is no need to take it, since boats run to Kratie year-round. But if you're so inclined, pickups leave for Kratie from the market. Traveling north by boat is preferable. **Boats** go to **Kratie** (fast boat 3hr.; 7:30, 9am, 2pm; 20,000r; slow boat 5hr.; 6:30, 10am; 10,000r) and **Phnom Penh** (fast boat 3hr.; 9:30am; 15,000r).

CAMBODIA

ORIENTATION AND PRACTICAL INFORMATION Kompong Cham sits on the west bank of the Mekong River, 120km northeast of Phnom Penh. Fast boats from Phnom Penh and Kratie dock opposite the Mekong Hotel, on **Preah Bat Sihanouk,** the riverside road. Just south of the Mekong Hotel, Sihanouk supports a string of guest houses and intersects **Rue Pasteur,** which runs inland past the police station. Heading north from the Mekong Hotel, Sihanouk bends inland to a six-way intersection, abutting the market, also a bus stop. One block north, **Kosamak Neary Rath** runs inland through a major traffic circle to the governor's mansion.

The **tourist office,** in front of the governor's mansion on Kosamak Neary Rath, is eager to help but low on resources. (Open M-F 8-11am and 2-4pm.) **Canadia Bank** will exchange currency and cash traveler's checks (US$2 commission) but will not take credit cards. (Open M-F 8:30am-3:30pm, Sa 8:30-11am.) A **provincial market** sits next to the six-way intersection of Preah Bat Sihanouk. Here you can buy fine *kramas* (the traditional checkered scarves found everywhere around Cambodia). The **police,** on Rue Pasteur one block from the river, speak no English. The **Kompong Cham Provincial Hospital** runs a bare-bones operation on Rue Pasteur, one block from the river. The **post office** is on Khemarak Pumin, one block north of Kosamak Neary Rath. (Open M-F 7-11am and 2-5pm.) **Long distance calls** can be made from shops around the city, including some on Rue Jayavarman VII, one block north of the police station and from an international phone booth at the edge of the market. Most international calls are US$3 per min.

THE TIDES THEY ARE A CHANGING Every year between July and October, a strange natural phenomenon plays itself out between the banks of the Tonle Sap River. During these months the current of the river is reversed—the waters actually flow away from the ocean into Tonle Sap (The Great Lake). The sheer volume of the melted snows descending from the Himalayas overflows the Mekong River. The backlog turns the waters of the Tonle Sap River upon themselves. This reversal of fortune has had significant consequences in both contemporary and ancient Cambodia. During the months of the reversed current, Tonle Sap more than doubles in size, creating the world's most fertile fishing grounds. A thousand years ago, the alternating current came in handy for transporting raw material to the Angkor monument. The reversal enabled builders to float in sandstone blocks from Phnom Kulen, almost 40km away. The Tonle Sap's reversal explains why the Mekong Delta in south Vietnam rarely floods; the lake serves as a massive overflow pool, absorbing excess water that might otherwise wreak havoc on low-lying towns. Sadly, this hydraulic wonder is threatened by deforestation and damming upriver in Laos and Thailand.

ACCOMMODATIONS AND FOOD. Cheap guest houses line Preah Bat Sihanouk south of the dock. One block from the dock, on Preah Bat Sihanouk, the **Speanthmey Guest House ❶** provides the most room for your riel and the upstairs balcony offers a great view. (Singles US$3, with TV US$4; doubles with TV US$5, with A/C US$8.) The **Kim Srung Guest House ❶**, a few doors down from Speanthmey, has nice rooms, good management, and an attached restaurant. (Singles US$3; doubles US$5.) A glut of rooms in Kompong Cham means hotel-style accommodations come cheap; the **Mittapheap Hotel ❷**, across the traffic circle from Canadia Bank, has flush toilets and fans. (Rooms US$5, with A/C US$10.) Along the river, many vendors sell pots of food for 2000r, including steamed rice. More formal restaurants are scarce, but many of the nicer hotels serve decent fare. One quality eatery is **Hoa An ❶**, four blocks inland on Rue Pasteur. This local institution serves up Chinese and Khmer food with lots of beer. (Fried rice with pork sausage and egg 6500r. Large Angkor beer 5500r. Open daily 6am-8:30pm.)

SIGHTS AND NIGHTLIFE. **Wat Nokor,** an 11th-century sandstone and laterite Buddhist temple, claims top billing in Kompong Cham, which is not saying much. Many of the statues in the temple were defaced by the Khmer Rouge, and all the paintings on the walls of the scenes of the Buddha's life were painted over in black. But since then the temple has been reconstructed to its former image. The ruins contain an active temple 2km west of town. From the road to Phnom Penh, take a left at the traffic circle or hire a moto driver (US$2). **Phnom Pros** and **Phnom Sray** are 5km farther toward Phnom Penh. A moto-trip costs US$2 round-trip.

Nightlife is not one of Kompong Cham's strong points. Only **Phnom Prosh Nightclub** in the Phnom Prosh Hotel even pretends to be a spot for nighttime entertainment. If karaoke is your thing, try the open-air places that have opened up on the other side of the new bridge and are quite popular with the locals.

KRATIE

Kratie (KRA-cheh) is a pleasant town along the Mekong and is the best place in the world to see the rare Irrawaddy dolphin. For this and for the glory of the sunset over the river, Kratie is a worthy breakpoint to any journey north or south and is a destination that should not be missed.

TRANSPORTATION. The road (if you can call it that) north to Stung Treng and south to Kompong Cham is absolutely terrible. Luckily, boats go south to Kompong Cham year-round. During the dry season, however, boats rarely go north, and you may be stuck taking the road. **Pickups** leave from the market and go to **Ban Lung** (9-12hr.; 7am, noon; US$10); **Mondulkiri** (8hr.; 6, 7am; US$10); and **Stung Treng** (6-8hr.; 6, 10am; US$6). **Boats** are a much friendlier option. Boats go year-round to **Kompong Cham** (fast boat: 3hr.; 6, 10:30am; US$5; slow boat: 5hr., 5:30am, US$4) and **Phnom Penh** (4hr., 7am, US$10). During the rainy season regular boats go to Stung Treng. In the dry season slow and speed boats rarely run, but check for the availability of cargo boats to Stung Treng (2 days).

ORIENTATION AND PRACTICAL INFORMATION. Kratie dozes on the east bank of the Mekong, northeast of Kompong Cham and Phnom Penh. Navigation couldn't be easier. Kratie's two main streets run parallel to the river, **V. Preah Sura Marit** along the bank and **V. Samdech Preah Sihanouk** one block back. Streets numbered from north to south, with the town's center situated between Rue 7 and Rue 10, intersect these two roads. The **market** is on Sihanouk between Rue 8 and Rue 10, and the **post office** (open M-F 7-11am and 2-5pm) sits between the two main streets on Rue 12. The **police station** (☎971 499) is off Rue 15 near the radio

TRAVEL ON THE RIVER With the opening to foreigners of the Cambodia-Laos border at Don Khong, travel on the Cambodian Mekong has acquired a purpose other than sunbathing. Indeed, there are few better ways to start the day than atop a ferry watching the Mekong slide by. However, not all Cambodian ferries are created equal. All fast boats are Malaysian-made. **Khemara** runs the tightest ship, complete with emergency exits and plenty of leg room, as well as the flattest, most buttock-friendly roof. **Rambo** has the oldest, smallest, and creakiest fast boats. Phnom Penh's other ferry outfits fall somewhere in between. Companies alternate days and routes—ask guest house owners for details. So-called slow boats are Cambodian-made and have no need for emergency exits, as they have no windowpanes. Security and safety on slow boats is suspect; they should only be taken where fast boats fear to tread.

tower. **International phone calls** can be made from the Kodak Express MiniLab on Preah Sihanouk past Hy Heng Guest House.

ACCOMMODATIONS AND FOOD. A profusion of cheap rooms graces Preah Sihanouk near the market. **Star Guest House ❶,** on Sihanouk and Rue 10, has clean rooms and a nice atmosphere. (Singles US$2; doubles US$4; enormous double with balcony overlooking the market US$5.) **Santepheap Hotel ❷** is on Preah Sura Marit across from the docks. This classy yellow hotel has large modern rooms and great management. (Doubles with fan and bath US$5, with A/C US$10.) At **Hy Heng Guest House ❶,** just up Sihanouk from the market behind a beauty parlor, absurdly low hallways lead to bright and airy rooms. (Shared baths only. Singles US$2; doubles US$3.) **Prom Meas ❶,** on Sihanouk a block down from Star Guest House, has fully tiled rooms with desks. (Doubles US$3, with TV US$4.)

Market ❶ food is exceptionally cheap in Kratie. The standard market meal costs 1500r; most of the town shows up to partake. For a more formal setting, try the **Mekong Restaurant ❶,** on Rue 9, which has attentive service, a host of local patrons, and quality fried chicken (6000r). The the **Star Guest House Restaurant ❶** is an excellent place to have breakfast and watch the market (omelettes 2000r).

SIGHTS. The best place in Cambodia to see endangered **Irrawaddy dolphins** is 15km north of Kratie. Hundreds more survive in Laos (see p. 360). Any moto driver in town can take you to the dolphin-viewing pavilion (US$3), and a boatman will pole you out on the river for a closer look (US$2). The nearby stretch of the river is also nice for swimming, and there are small rapids as well.

BORDER CROSSING: STUNG TRENG/VEUNKHAM

While officially closed as of March 2002, the border is unofficially open, but you have to pay money to leave Cambodia and pay money again to enter Laos. You **cannot** obtain a Laos visa at the border. If you're willing to pay off corrupt border officials, you can charter a boat from Stung Treng to **Veunkham,** the border between the two countries (1hr., anytime during the day, US$20-30 for 4-person boat). You will be required to pay US$15 to leave Cambodia, and then your boat will take you across the river to Laos immigration. There you will be required to pay US$5 to enter Laos. Go back to your boat and continue on to **Don Khong** or **Don Det.**

STUNG TRENG

Stung Treng is a tiny town on the San River, just off the Mekong, that unfortunately constitutes a near-necessary overnight stop for those heading north to Laos or east to Rattanakiri. Perhaps the opening of the Lao border will spur a growth in Stung Treng's tourist attractions and infrastructure. Right now, though, one night here is plenty for most travelers.

Boat travel is the best way to get north or south from Stung Treng, but during the dry season travel by boat is not always possible. Check for availability. During the rainy season boats go to **Phnom Penh** (8-10hr., 7am, US$15) via **Kratie** (4hr., US$15) and **Kompong Cham** (3hr., US$10). Boats can be chartered any time of the day to go north to the Lao border (US$20-30 for 4-person boat). The roads are extremely shoddy around Stung Treng, especially toward Kratie. Nevertheless, 4WD **pickups** leave from in front of the dock to **Kratie** (6-8hr. of pain, around 7am, US$5). Pickups also leave for **Ban Lung** (3-4hr., around 7am, US$6), and the road is halfway decent, with only a few rough spots. **Planes** fly into the airport 6km north of town from **Phnom Penh** (45min.; M, W, F 10am; US$53). **Phnom Penh Airlines** (☎074 973 963) is open daily 7am-5pm. The only budget accommodation in town is the **Amatak Guest House ❶**, opposite the docks, where basic rooms with mosquito nets and fans go for US$3. The genial owner can help those headed to Laos. The other option is the overpriced **Sok Sombat Hotel ❷** on the northern side of the market. (Rooms with flush toilet US$6, with TV US$10, with A/C US$20.) Eating options are confined to the choose-and-chomp at the small but busy **market ❶**, one block behind the Amatak Guest House (2000r), or at the **Soup Gaot Restaurant ❶**, next to the Sekong Hotel, two blocks from the docks going away from the market, which serves excellent Khmer food (deer *lok-lak* 4000r).

CAMBODIA

BAN LUNG ☎075

Far removed from the bustle of Phnom Penh, Rattanakiri Province is defined by its countryside, dusty clay roads, and populations of fiercely independent minorities. Isolated in the mountainous northeast border with Laos and Vietnam, the people of the region have resisted lowland hegemony for centuries. Even the Khmer Rouge largely left the ethnic minorities to their own devices. Since 1986, when Ban Lung was made the provincial capital, increasing numbers of Khmer, Vietnamese, and Chinese have migrated here, but a vibrant mix of Jarai, Krung, and Tumpuon people continues to dwell in small, insular communities and farms. Ban Lung is an excellent place to explore the Cambodian countryside, and there are waterfalls, gem mines, and hill tribes all within a two-hour radius.

TRANSPORTATION The dirt strip **airfield** is 400m south of town. **President's Airlines** runs flights to **Phnom Penh** (Tu, Th, Sa 11:55am; US$55). **Phnom Penh Airlines** also runs flights to **Phnom Penh** (M, W, F; US$55). All flights must be reconfirmed, and departures can change without formal notice. **Pickups** run from the market in Ban Lung to **Kratie** (9-12hr.; leave when full, usually around 7am; US$10) via **Stung Treng** (3-4hr., US$5). Inquire at the Mountain Guest House or Ratanak Hotel (see **Accommodations and Food,** below) the night before you want to leave, and the pickup will pick you up. The stretch of road from Stung Treng to Kratie is horrible. If possible, take a **boat** from Stung Treng to **Kratie** (3-4hr., 7am, US$5).

ORIENTATION AND PRACTICAL INFORMATION The town has only one main road, so finding your way around Ban Lung isn't difficult. Heading north on the airport road brings you to the intersection with **Route 19,** Ban Lung's wide artery, which runs east-west through town and on to the Vietnamese border only 70km away. A right turn leads to town. Another right at the *naga* pillars leads past a **police station** and Ban Lung's utilitarian **market.** The road also passes the **President Airlines office** (open daily 7:30-11:30am and 1-5pm). **Phnom Penh Airlines** is to the left of the market (open daily 7:30-11:30am and 1-5pm). **Rattanakiri Provincial**

Hospital, 2km north of the airport road-Rte. 19 intersection, is not for the faint of heart. The **post office** (open daily 7:30-11am and 2-5pm) is 1km east of the *naga* pillar, next to the **telecommunications office** (☎974 006; open daily 7:30-11am and 2-5pm), which offers international service (US$3 per min.).

ACCOMMODATIONS AND FOOD Some shrewd bargaining can cause prices to plunge from March to June. The excellent **Mountain Guest House ❷** is on the airport road 400m north of Rte. 19. Plates of fruit mysteriously appear as you lounge on the veranda. (☎974 047. Large rooms with double beds, fans, and shared baths US$5.) The **Ratanak Hotel ❷,** on the same road as Mountain Guest House just past the *naga*, is also excellent, and all rooms are fully tiled with fan and private bath. (Doubles US$5.) Both owners, Mrs. Kim at the Mountain and Mr. Leng at the Ratanak, are excellent sources of information about the surrounding area and can arrange for guides, bike rental, and transportation from Ban Lung. Larger and more motel-like, the **Ban Lung Guest House ❷** is just 100m from the airport toward Rte. 19. (☎974 066. Clean rooms with private flush toilet and shower US$5, with A/C US$10.) Hidden among the vegetation, the **American Restaurant ❶,** diagonally across from Mountain Guest House, has spectacular fruit and is bound to be the highlight of any visit. (Beef *lok-lak* 4000r.) The **Ratanak Hotel ❷** has a good restaurant as well. (Khmer barbecue 15,000r, but enough for 3.)

SIGHTS There is little to see in Ban Lung proper, but there is a lot to see and do around Ban Lung. Get a map from Ratanak Hotel or Mountain Guest House. About 2km west of the airport road intersection on Rte. 19 is **Wat Phnom Suay.** At the top of Phnom Suay, 1km beyond the temple along the dirt path that runs through the temple grounds, is a large statue of the **Sleeping Buddha.** The Enlightened One's view from the top, with the jagged peaks of the Central Highlands in the distance, is magnificent, especially at sunset. **Yak Lom Lake,** a magical little crater lake, is 4km east on Rte. 19. The water is quite clear and the swimming excellent. To get there, head east on Rte. 19 past several rubber plantations. After 2km, there's a roundabout topped with statues of hill tribesmen. Take a right here, and the lake is 1.5km farther, past a hill tribe village. It makes a nice walk, if the weather cooperates. (Lake 1000r.) There is also a **museum** at Yak Lom Lake featuring exhibits on tribes in the Rattanakiri area (1000r).

DAYTRIPS FROM BAN LUNG Many travelers use Ban Lung merely as a base camp from which to see the province's attractions. The region is a patchwork of highland minorities, many of whom continue to live as they have for millennia in small, isolated communities. Indeed, during the rainy season, many villages may be largely, if not completely, deserted. At this time families head off into the forest to clear and cultivate mountain rice, their staple crop. The best way to see the countryside is to hire a motorcycle and driver in Ban Lung (US$10 per day; inquire at Mountain Guest House). The best places to see hill tribes are at **Ta Vang,** at the eastern edge of Virachay Park (51km, 2-2½hr. by motorbike), and at **Vocun Sai** (38km, 1-2hr. by motorbike), at the western edge of the park. There are **Pro, Lao,** and **Krung villages** near both places. While you can explore on your own it is best to bring a guide, for very few people speak English in the villages. The road to Ta Vang especially is quite difficult for inexperienced moto drivers. There are active gem mines within a two-hour moto-ride from Ban Lung. East on the road to Vietnam is **Bokeo,** home to several **sapphire mines,** Jarai and Lao tribe villages, and a waterfall. There are also three **waterfalls** close to Ban Lung off the main road.

FROM THE ROAD

VILLAGE-HOPPING IN RATTANAKIRI

In the early morning, I set off on a motorbike from Ban Lung with a guide to visit the hill tribes that live on the eastern edge of Virachay National Park. The only way to get to Virachay is by following a rough logging road into the jungle. By the time we arrived at the main village, I was coated in a thin layer of dust.

Ban Lung—as well as the rest of Rattanakiri Province—was left alone by the Khmer Rouge. While civil war raged throughout the rest of the country, Ban Lung remained isolated and peaceful. For the tribes who live on the outskirts of the jungle, little has changed in the past few hundred years.

At one household in a Pro settlement, my guide pointed out three wooden spears arranged in a semicircle. There was a fourth spear between them with a skull on the point and blood on the ground around it.

When I took my camera out, a man from a nearby hut shouted something angrily in the *Pro* dialect. Another man came out of the hut and explained to my guide in Khmer that their cousin was very sick, and they had sacrificed a water buffalo that morning to appease the spirits. As part of the ritual, each member of the village hacks at the animal's neck until it is almost dead. The village leader then decapitates it.

The mood in this settlement was somber, so my guide and I continued on our way. When we returned to the main village where we had started, we were greeted with exciting news.

(continued on next page)

VIRACHAY NATIONAL PARK

Rent a motorbike or hire a guide to either Ta Vang, at the eastern edge of the park, or Vocun Sai, at the western edge. There you will need to hire a ranger to take you into the forest. Rangers are generally on duty M-F, and it is best to arrive in the morning to secure one. Entrance fee US$5. Rangers charge US$10 per day. It is best to go on at least a 2-night trek into the forest, for it takes more than a full day's hike to reach the jungle. Bring bug spray, iodine pills or water purifier, and a hammock and mosquito net (Mountain Guest House, see above, will rent one for US$3).

Virachay National Park, bordering Laos and Vietnam, is still largely unexplored, and is home to dense jungle and many different kinds of birds and mammals, including elephants, tigers, gaur, and leopards. Many different hill tribes also live on the outskirts of the forest. Another option is to see the jungle by boat on the river which skirts the park. Boats can be chartered from Ta Vang to Vocun Sai (6-8hr., US$40 per boat). Inquire at the ranger station. If stuck in Ta Vang or Vocun Sai, you can stay the night for very cheap, or even free.

NORTHERN CAMBODIA

SIEM REAP ☎063

Spurred by improved safety in the region, tourism has taken off in the dusty little city of Siem Reap, which functions chiefly as a gateway to the nearby temples of Angkor. Five-star resorts and restaurants line the outskirts of town, and package tour buses are a regular sight on the way to the temples. Although Siem Reap may have the highest concentration of moto drivers in the whole country, its secluded waterfalls and isolated temples remain hidden secrets that a traveler can explore in peace.

TRANSPORTATION

The **airport** is 8km northwest of town off Rte. 6. International departure tax is US$20 and domestic is US$4. **Bangkok Airways,** 571 Rte. 6 (☎380 191; open daily 8am-4:30pm), flies to **Bangkok** (5 per day, reduced service in low season, US$158). **Siem Reap Airlines,** in the same office as Bangkok Airways, flies to **Phnom Penh** (3 per day, US$64). **Vietnam Airlines,** 108 Route 6

(☎063 964 488), flies to: **Danang** (daily, US$166); **Hanoi** (daily, US$226); **Ho Chi Minh City** (4 per day, US$104). **Minibuses** and **pickups** go to **Bangkok** (13hr., 7am, US$8) via **Poi Pot** (5-6hr., US$4); and **Phnom Penh** (7-9hr., 7am, US$8). Inquire at your guest house the night before you leave, and the bus will pick you up. If you are tired of bad roads you can take a **speedboat** to **Battambang** (4hr., 7am, US$12) and **Phnom Penh** (7hr., 7am, US$22). It is advisable to leave Siem Reap at 5:45-6am to catch the boat, because it is 18km from Siem Reap to the river and the road is bad. Any moto driver in town will take you to the temples (US$6 per day for the main temples, US$12 per day for Banteay Srei and the far temples, US$4-6 extra to see the waterfalls beyond Banteay Srei). A car and driver can be rented for the day at the tourist office (US$25).

ORIENTATION AND PRACTICAL INFORMATION

Siem Reap can be navigated by foot, but the heat and unlabeled streets make traveling by moto preferable. **Rte. 6** cuts through the north part of town, running east to the **New Market** and west to the **airport.** Those arriving by boat will follow a road heading north from Tonle Sap. The road forks into **V. Sivatha** on the left and the **West Bank River Rd.** on the right. V. Sivatha traces the west edge of town, intersecting Rte. 6 in a flurry of guest house signs. North of its intersection with Rte. 6, the West Bank River Rd. runs past the traffic circle and the Grand Hotel, and on to Angkor, 7km away. Running north-south, the **Siem Reap River** traces the eastern edge of town. The dirt road parallel to the east bank road is **V. Wat Bo,** home to several popular guest houses.

Tourist Office: ☎964 371. Opposite the Grand Hotel on the road to Angkor. Not very useful for travelers. Maps of Angkor and Siem Reap. Motorcycle with driver US$6 per day. A/C car with driver US$20-25 per day. Licensed guides US$20 per day. Open M-F 7:30-11am and 2-3pm, Sa 7:30-11am.

Currency Exchange: US dollars and Thai baht are accepted everywhere. **Cambodian Commercial Bank** (☎964 392), at the end of the Old Market across from the bridge, exchanges traveler's checks (2% commission). MC/V cash advances. US$5 flat fee, US$200 max. Open daily 9am-4pm.

Markets: New Market (Psar Leu), 1km east of town on Rte. 6. The touristy **Old Market (Psar Cha)** is at the southern end of the west bank river road.

Police: Foreigner Office (☎012 893 297), on the corner of Rte. 6 and V. Sivatha.

Pharmacies: Many located around the town center.

(continued from previous page)

Apparently a man from a nearby village had been attacked by a tiger that morning. He not only survived the attack but had also managed to kill the animal. We hopped on our motorbike and went to investigate. The tiger turned out to be a large leopard, and when we arrived in the village, its spotted pelt was drying on wooden slats. The intact skeleton lay nearby, and a woman guarded the heart, liver, and intestines, from a hungry dog.

The man who had been attacked came out of his hut to greet us. His left ear was badly mangled, and he had scratches on his arms, legs, and neck. There were deep puncture wounds on his right hand. He invited us into his hut for leopard meat and entertained us with the story.

The night before he had set traps in the forest for wild chickens. When he checked his traps that morning, he noticed that one set was broken. The leopard, which had been caught in his trap, leapt onto him from a nearby tree. He couldn't reach a stick or rock but eventually strangled the wounded animal to death with his bare hands.

He took us back outside to admire his kill. My guide expressed interest in the leopard and after some haggling, paid the man US$60 for the pelt, innards, and skeleton. With a burlap sack full of leopard parts on the front of the bike, we returned to Ban Lung.

On the ride home, I asked my guide why he had bought the leopard. He told me that he was going to make a soup from it to give him energy: bush viagra.

—Gabe Struck

Medical Services: Rustic **Siem Reap Provincial Hospital,** down the side street off V. Sivatha that veers east at Cambodian Commercial Bank; opposite the Apsara Tours branch office. Doctors on call M-F 7-11am and 2-5pm, Sa 6am-noon.

Telephones: Many guest houses offer **international** service (US$2-3 per min.). The **post office** also offers international service.

Internet Access: Internet centers are springing up everywhere. A pleasant A/C option is **E Cafe Siem Reap,** 147B V. Sivatha, opposite Cambodian Commercial Bank. US$2 per hr. Open daily 7am-9pm.

Post Office: GPO, on the west bank of the Siem Reap River 500m north of the old market. EMS mail service. *Poste Restante.* Open daily 7:30am-5pm.

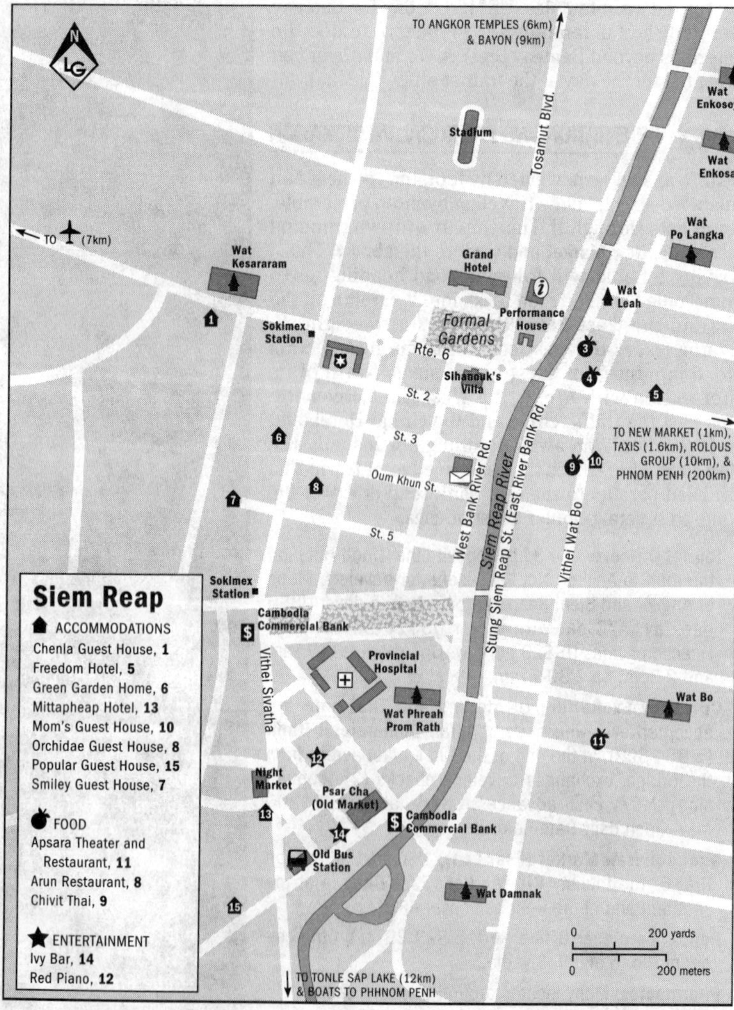

ACCOMMODATIONS

Siem Reap is teeming with places to stay, costing from US$2 to US$1900 per night. New accommodations open every month, packed with tourists heading to the Angkor temples. Make reservations in high season. Guest houses cluster near the **V. Sivatha-Rte. 6 intersection** and on **V. Wat Bo,** south of Rte. 6. Flush toilets are standard. Prices may drop up to 20% in the rainy season.

Smiley Guest House No. 019 (☎012 852 955). Coming south from Rte. 6 on V. Sivatha, turn left onto the dirt alley opposite 10 Makara High School. Very popular with backpackers. Pleasant restaurant and porch. Singles with shared bath US$2-3; doubles with bath US$5-6, with A/C $10. ❶

Popular Guest House, 33 Boboos St. (☎012 916 165). Head south from the old market along the river; it's on the right 200m after the bus station. Popular by name, popular by nature. Backpackers hang out in the leafy veranda restaurant. Singles with fan and shared bath US$2-4; doubles US$3-7, with A/C US$10. ❶

Chenla Guest House No. 260, 260 Rte. 6 (☎012 835 488), 200m west of the V. Sivatha intersection. Best rooms are in the new building. Some rooms have cable TV and fridge. Singles with shared bath and fan US$3; doubles with private bath US$6, with A/C US$10-15. ❷

Mom's Guest House, 99 V. Wat Bo (☎964 037), 30m south of intersection of Rt. 6. Very clean. Good English spoken. In the old building, rooms are functional; in the new place they're a treat. Singles with shared bath US$3-4; doubles with private bath US$6-10, with A/C US$12. ❷

Green Garden Home, 051 V. Sivatha (☎012 890 363), about 200m south of the Rte. 6 intersection; look for the blue sign. Lovely rooms with bamboo furniture and relaxing verandas all set in a flower garden. Rooms have bath, hot water, fridge, cable TV, and-fan. Doubles US$10, with A/C US$15-20. ❸

Mittapheap Hotel (☎964 375), on V. Sivatha, a few blocks from the old market. With a classy glass exterior and immaculate interior, Mittapheap is a pleasant place to stay. Restaurant attached. Rooms with A/C, TV, bath, and fridge US$15. ❹

Freedom Hotel (☎963 476), on Rte. 6 on the East Bank of the river near the Central Market. Has all the amenities of a high-range place at mid-range prices. Great restaurant. Large rooms with A/C, satellite TV (HBO), fridge, and bath US$15-20. ❹

FOOD

A small **night market** on V. Sivatha north of Cambodian Commercial Bank serves noodles for under US$1. **Food vendors ❶** also line the road to Angkor and the east bank of the river parallel to the guest house strip. For a sit-down meal, **Arun Restaurant ❸,** off East Bank River Rd. 50m north of the Rte. 6 intersection, has generous portions of Cambodian and Chinese food. (Grilled beef with tofu sauce US$4. Open daily 10am-10pm.) **Chivit Thai ❷,** 130 V. Wat Bo near a string of guest houses, has a charming open air terrace and great *pad thai* for US$2.50. (Open daily 7am-10pm.) Behind the old market, **Taj Majal ❷** has good Indian food at reasonable prices. (Entrees US$2-3.) **Apsara Restaurant and Theater ❷,** on the eastern bank a few blocks from the bridge near Wat Phreah Prom Rath, has excellent Khmer food in a beautiful setting. (Entrees US$2-5.)

MOST DANGEROUS COW IN THE EAST

Cambodia's national animal is the critically endangered kouprey *(Bos sauveli)*, a wild forest-dwelling cow. Males have frayed horns and a huge dewlap, stand 2m at the shoulder, and weigh up to 900kg. There are probably no more than 200 kouprey left in northern Cambodia, with a few spilling into northeastern Thailand, southern Laos, and central Vietnam. Thanks to human warfare, the unlucky cow has been almost impossible to study. In the late 30s, a captive kouprey calf starved to death in a Paris zoo during German occupation. Since then, a handful of 50s field notes, one grainy 1967 photograph, and a few unverified sightings have comprised the best research in the kouprey's war-torn home turf; the official UN Conservation Plan states that kouprey data is "of a very sketchy nature." Beyond its mystery and rarity, the kouprey could be profitably interbred with domestic cattle to produce disease-resistant, tropics-adapted livestock. When hiking through Rattanakiri in search of this elusive bovine, be sure to bring the proper equipment: malaria pills, a flashlight, an armed escort, de-mining equipment, and for God's sake, a decent camera.

SIGHTS

A somber **memorial** to Khmer Rouge atrocities is on the road to Angkor. Take the dirt road turn-off at the "Welcome" sign, 500m past the Grand Hotel. Follow the road to a small wat, next to the ramshackle wooden pavilion that is filled waist-deep with human skulls and bones. For those who can't get enough of Angkor architecture, **Wat Leah,** along the east bank of the river north of Arun Restaurant, has two well-preserved Angkor-period brick sanctuaries behind the modern pagoda. For a chance to watch highly skilled craftsmen create traditional Khmer wood carvings, head to the **Khmer Art of Carving Center.** Look for the sign on the left heading out of town on the road to the temples. (Open daily 7:30am-5pm.) Across the road there is also a small **stone carving workshop.** Small pieces sell for US$10-15.

NIGHTLIFE

Although nightlife in Siem Reap is picking up, it is hampered by the fact that many people get up at dawn to see the temples. The amusingly named **Angkor What?,** a block north of the Old Market on one of V. Sivatha's side streets, and the **Ivy Bar,** at the south end of the Old Market, are both youthful late-night drinking spots. **Lotus Bar,** at the north end of the market, is open **24hr.** For an expensive nightcap, try the **Elephant Bar** in the Grand Hotel d'Angkor, at the north end of the West Bank River Rd. The **Grand Hotel's Performance House,** just across the West Bank River Rd. from the hotel proper, offers a rare (and costly) chance to see traditional **Khmer dance** and **drama.** (☎963 417. Shows M, W, Sa. US$22 includes 7pm buffet dinner, 8pm performance.) You can see Khmer dancing for less money at the **Bayon II Restaurant,** on Rd. 6 on the eastern side of the river (nightly performances, US$11). The **Red Piano,** 50m northwest of the old market, is a chic restaurant/bar whose claim to fame is that it was the headquarters of the "Tomb Raider" cast and crew while they filmed at Angkor.

ANGKOR

With their unrivaled beauty and majesty, the temples of Angkor deserve their reputation as one of the great man-made wonders of the world. Begun in the 9th century, the building process lasted over 600 years, with the last of the temples being built in the late 15th century. The temples are the remains of the mighty Khmer empire that, at its height, extended its reign over most of the Malay peninsula and modern-day Cambodia, Laos, and Vietnam. The name 'Angkor' is believed to be a mispronunciation of the Khmer word *nakhon*, meaning 'city.' In the 15th century, the Khmer kings abandoned Angkor and moved their capital to the site of modern-day Phnom Penh. Angkor lay in relative obscurity until the diaries of French naturalist Henri Mouhot were published in 1864. Mouhot's description of the beautiful temples sparked international interest, drawing the droves of travelers who now come to see the rising sun break over the temple *stupas* in what the Khmer believe is the gateway between the mortal and celestial worlds.

TRANSPORTATION

If not on a package tour, most travelers stay the night in Siem Reap and hire a **motorcycle** (US$6 per day for the main temples, US$12 per day for the far temples such as Banteay Srei) or **bicycle** (US$5 per day) to see the temples. Rentals can be arranged through guest houses or at the Siem Reap Tourist Office (see p. 87) and require a passport as deposit. **Cars** with drivers can be hired for US$25 per day from hotels or the tourist office.

PRACTICAL INFORMATION

Foreigners can buy one-day (US$20), three-day (US$40), or seven-day (US$60) passes from the on-site ticket checkpoint (1 passport-sized photo required). Multi-day passes must be used on consecutive days. There is a steep US$80 fine for misusing tickets.

SAFETY CONCERNS AND TEMPLE ETIQUETTE. Keep in mind the following concerns and customs while at Angkor:

Mines: The government claims that Angkor has been de-mined, but to be safe, stay on well-trodden paths, especially at more remote temples.

Wildlife: The jungles have poisonous snakes such as small bright green *kraits*. King cobras, with enough venom to bring down a bull elephant, are rare but not unheard of—avoid dark, isolated chambers within the temples.

Preservation: Don't remove stone fragments from the temples. Government officials search all bags upon departure.

Tickets: Guards check passes at the entrances to most of the temples; it's now virtually impossible to slip in without paying.

SIGHTS

The following descriptions are arranged in the order that most travelers see the monuments. Beginning at Angkor Wat, the route proceeds clockwise on a roughly rectangular track. Angkor's magnificent ruins hold enough secret nooks and crannies for a lifetime of exploration, but with a little planning and prioritizing you can see most of the temple complex in a few days. Try to get an early start; by 11am temperatures can rise to over 39°C (100°F). Bring a map of the temple complex, a flashlight, drinking water, and extra film, or buy all these things from vendors outside the temples at inflated prices. *A Guide to Angkor*, by Dawn Rooney, sold by child vendors at Angkor Wat (US$3-6), has temple plans and is especially useful while navigating the complexities of Ta Prohm, Bayon, and Angkor Wat. If locals come up to you in one of the temples and start to give you information, they will demand US$1 at the end. Don't listen if you don't want to pay.

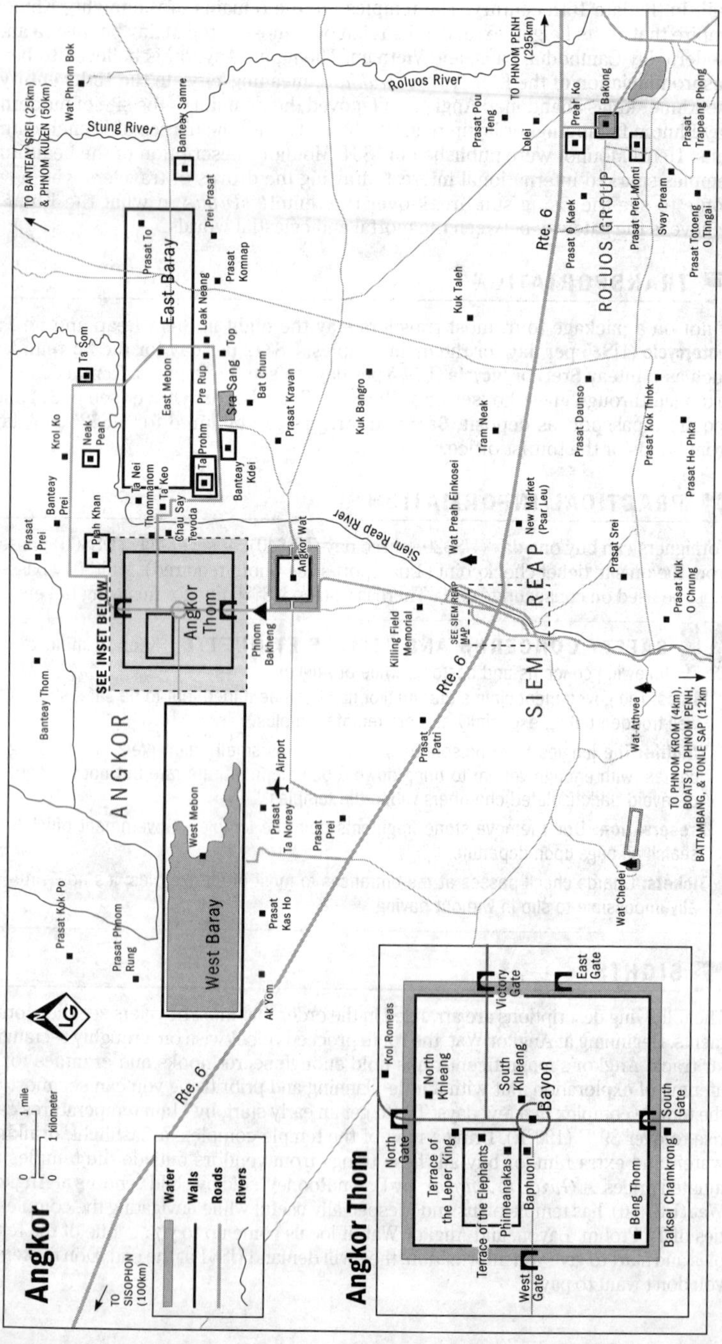
Angkor
Water
Walls
Roads
Rivers
0 1 mile
0 1 kilometer
LG
N
TO SISOPHON (100km)
Rte. 6
Prasat Kok Po
Prasat Phnom Rung
Ak Yom
West Baray
West Mebon
Prasat Kas Ho
Prasat Ta Noreay
Prasat Prei
Airport
ANGKOR
Banteay Thom
SEE INSET BELOW
Angkor Thom
Phnom Bakheng
Angkor Wat
Prasat Prei
Banteay Prei
Preah Khan
Krol Ko
Neak Pean
Ta Som
Ta Nei
Thommanom
Ta Keo
Chau Say Tevoda
Ta Prohm
Banteay Kdei
East Mebon
Pre Rup
Sra Sang
Top
Bat Chum
Prasat Kravan
Leak Neang
East Baray
Prasat To
Prasat Komnap
Prei Prasat
Banteay Samre
Wat Phnom Bok
TO BANTEAY SREI (25km) & PHNOM KULEN (50km)
Stung River
Roluos River
Siem Reap River
Killing Field Memorial
SEE SIEM REAP MAP
Prasat Patri
Wat Preah Einkosei
New Market (Psar Leu)
SIEM REAP
Kuk Bangro
Tram Neak
Kuk Taleh
Prasat Daunso
Prasat Srei
Prasat Kok Thlok
Prasat He Phka
Prasat Kuk O Chrung
Wat Athvea
Wat Chedei
TO PHNOM KROM (4km), BOATS TO PHNOM PENH, BATTAMBANG, & TONLE SAP (12km)
Lolei
Prasat Pou Teng
TO PHNOM PENH (295km)
Prasat O Kaek
Preah Ko
Bakong
ROLUOS GROUP
Prasat Prei Monti
Svay Pream
Prasat Totoeng O Thngai
Prasat Trapeang Phong
Angkor Thom
Krol Romeas
North Khleang
South Khleang
Bayon
Victory Gate
East Gate
North Gate
Terrace of the Leper King
Terrace of the Elephants
Phimeanakas
Baphuon
Beng Thom
Baksei Chamkrong
South Gate
West Gate

THE BEST OF ANGKOR

Best carvings: Angkor Wat and Banteay Srei.
Best spots to sit in quiet bliss: Banteay Kdei, Prah Khan, East Mebon, and Ta Som.
Best views: Phnom Bakheng, East Mebon, Pre Rup, and Angkor Wat.
Best "jungle" temples: Ta Prohm, Ta Som.

ANGKOR WAT. This magnificent 213m-tall laterite-and-sandstone complex was constructed during the reign of Suryavarman II (r. 1113-50). The temple faces west, the direction associated with death in Hindu cosmology, leading scholars to believe that it was constructed as a funerary temple. Designed to represent the universe in miniature, its five-tower quincunx—an arrangement that places four of the towers in a square and the fifth in its center—symbolizes the peaks of Mt. Meru used by the Hindu god Vishnu while creating the Universe. The temple contains 1200 sq. m of sandstone. Incredibly detailed stone carvings line the walls of the first-level gallery and form the largest series of reliefs in the world. Mostly depictions of scenes from Indian epics and Angkor period warfare, they are best viewed starting on the west side and proceeding counterclockwise around the structure. The first panel depicts the battle of Kuruksetra from the Hindu epic *Mahabharata.* The south wall shows a mighty military procession and a rather gruesome vision of hell. Perhaps the most famous relief in all of Angkor, *The Churning of the Sea of Milk* (see **Churn, Baby, Churn,** p. 94) adorns the eastern face of the gallery. The northern wall depicts Vishnu's victory over Bana the Demon King, a curious-looking hellion on a rhino. The second half of the gallery depicts more universe-saving battles between gods and demons. The northern panel of the west gallery depicts the battle of Lanka from the Hindu epic *Ramayana,* in which Rama and his monkey army sought to free Rama's wife Sita from the clutches of the demon Ravana (recognizable by his 10 heads and 20 arms). On the second level, the Gallery of 1000 Buddhas (of which only a few fragments remain) is on the right, and the Hall of Echoes is on the left. Temple explorers can stand in one corner of the Hall of Echoes, pound their chests like Tarzan, and feel the room thunder in response. The third level has a stunning view of the perfectly symmetrical Angkor Wat complex. Angkor Wat is best seen at sunrise or sunset; arrange with a moto driver the night before, and leave Siem Reap at 5:15-5:30am to catch the sunrise.

ANGKOR THOM. The large temple complex of Angkor Thom (literally "Great City"), constructed by Jayavarman VII (1181-1219), lies 1.5km north of Angkor Wat. Angkor Thom shares Angkor Wat's cosmological layout: a moat symbolizes the oceans, the walls are the land, and the towers represent the peaks of Mt. Meru. The remaining ruins are mainly temples, though it's believed that this city once housed many administrative buildings that didn't survive the test of time. Angkor Thom's south entrance passes through a causeway lined with 54 guardian statues of gods and demons. The Angkor Conservancy has replaced many of the original heads to prevent theft. An all-seeing, four-faced, smiling head tops the tower gates.

THE BAYON. Rising in the exact center of Angkor Thom, the Bayon was erected by Jayavarman VII and is dedicated to Buddhism. Its reliefs depict, in addition to the usual epics, scenes of everyday life in Angkorian Cambodia. The Bayon contains two sets of bas-reliefs meant to be viewed clockwise. The southern gallery contains perhaps the finest of the Bayon's bas-reliefs depicting a battle between the Khmers and Chams, while the lower tier of reliefs presents a more peaceful view of Angkorian life. The northern gallery, only some of which was completed, contains a depiction of an Angkor circus. The upper gallery contains stories from Hindu epics dotted with faces believed to represent the Bodhisattva Avalokitesvara, who selflessly delayed attaining enlightenment to aid humanity.

CHURN, BABY, CHURN An ancient Hindu legend, *The Churning of the Sea of Milk* recalls the problem-solving methods of ancient Hindu gods during the turbulent days when they were busy creating the world. Being new at world-creation, they ran into a small glitch—they lost the elixir of immortality while churning the cosmic sea. It took 1000 years before the gods and demons, in a rare joint effort—aided by Sesha, the sea snake, and Vishnu—recovered the potion. The design of Angkor's temples is based on this ancient legend. The moat represents the ocean, and the gods use Mt. Meru, represented by the tower, as their churning stick. The cosmic serpent, in a rare cameo as the good guy, selflessly offered himself as a rope to enable the gods and demons to twirl the stick and save the Universe.

BAPHUON. A few hundred meters northwest of the Bayon stands the Hindu temple of Baphuon, built by Udayadityavarman II in the late 11th century.

PHIMEANAKAS. Situated just north of Baphuon, this Hindu monument was erected by three successive kings, Rajendravarman, Jayavarman V, and Udayadityavarman I. If the monument is open, the steep climb to the top of the central sanctuary is worth the view that waits at the top. The steep laterite "stairs" are best attempted early in the day before the sun or rain set in. The west staircase has a metal rail that makes climbing slightly easier.

TERRACE OF THE ELEPHANTS. First laid out by Suryavarman I, the Terrace of the Elephants (the Royal Terrace) stretches for 300m from Baphuon to the beginning of the Terrace of the Leper King, past Phimeanakas. The bas-reliefs of near life-sized elephants seem to emerge like ghosts from the stones. Along the wall near the Terrace of the Leper King is a carving of a five-headed horse.

TERRACE OF THE LEPER KING. Another legacy of Jayavarman VII, the monument lies north of the Terrace of the Elephants. Two galleries of bas-reliefs line the terrace, while mythological creatures and *apsaras* (see **Angkor's Motley Crew,** p. 96) decorate the outer wall. The statue of the Leper King himself is a replica. The National Museum in Phnom Penh now houses the original. Some historians believe Jayavarman VII may have suffered from leprosy himself, though others believe that the statue portrays the Hindu god of death, Yama, or Kubera, the god of wealth.

PRAH KHAN. Located northwest of the Bayon outside Angkor Thom, Prah Khan is one of the largest temple complexes. It was built as a Buddhist temple by Jayavarman VII in memory of his father, and Prah Khan literally means "Sacred Sword." Some archaeologists believe that the two-story building in the northeastern corner of the compound, a location rarely used in Khmer architecture, might once have housed an Asian excalibur, left by Jayavarman VII for his descendants.

NEAK PEAN. This Buddhist temple, east of Prah Khan along the Grand Circuit access road, was also built by Jayavarman VII. Unlike any other Angkor temple, this small and charming temple is made up of five ponds that are now covered in grass. A temple stands in the exact center of what was the large, central pond. Neak Pean is said to represent Lake Anayatapa, a sacred body of water in the Himalayas. The four symmetrical ponds, one at each cardinal point, represent the earth's four rivers. A stone horse, believed to be the sacred steed *Balaha,* drags several marooned sailors toward the island sanctuary in the middle of Neak Pean.

TA SOM. Lying east of Neak Pean along the access road, Ta Som was also built by Jayavarman VII. A small, quiet temple with one sanctuary, it is unrestored and largely in ruins. A four-faced bayon (a monument distinguished by its many sculpted faces) casts its inscrutable smile over visitors as they enter from the west. Continuing to the east gate, the bayon is almost entirely in the clutches of fig tree roots, giving its smile an almost eerie feel.

EAST MEBON. Built in the 10th century by Rajendravarman II in memory of his parents, tranquil East Mebon stands southwest of Ta Som and is accessible only by boat. In the Angkor era, the temple stood in the middle of the large man-made lake *(baray)*. Impressive sculptures of elephants and lions guard each entrance.

PHNOM BAKHENG. Just north and slightly west of Angkor Wat, Phnom Bakheng was built by Yasovarman I in the late 9th century. Travelers struggle up the steep and rocky slope to enjoy a spectacular sunset and view of Angkor Wat. An elephant carriage is available to take the style-conscious and the weary to the top (US$15). Originally, 109 towers, corresponding to the animal zodiac cycle, graced the *phnom*. In January and February, a glorious sunrise directly over Angkor rewards early risers.

WEST BARAY. West of Angkor Thom, this half-filled lake is best seen from Phnom Bakheng. Believed to date from the 11th century, West Baray was built during the reign of Udayadityavarman II. A small, largely destroyed temple, **West Mebon,** stands in the center of the *baray* and is accessible by boat.

TA PROHM. West of Pre Rup and bordering Banteay Kdei, Ta Prohm was built as a Buddhist temple by Jayavarman VII in his mother's memory. This vast, crumbling temple competes with the Bayon and Angkor Wat as the most awe-inspiring of Angkor's treasures and is the most authentic "jungle" temple. Ancient trees have grown into and out of the buildings themselves, creating the visage of a "lost city." Inscriptions reveal that 79,365 people were employed in Ta Prohm's upkeep during its heyday. Early risers can witness its stunning beauty in the morning light.

PRE RUP. Five hundred meters due south of East Mebon lies Pre Rup, a Hindu temple built by Rajendravarman II in the second half of the 10th century to honor Shiva. More impressive than its contemporary East Mebon, this multi-tiered structure affords views of East Baray to the north. Two halls parallel to the laterite wall as you enter from the east are believed to have housed pilgrims who journeyed here to worship. The temple is thought to have funerary associations. The vat near the east staircase is thought to have been used at cremations.

BANTEAY KDEI. Banteay Kdei is a Buddhist temple built by Jayavarman VII, southeast of Pre Rup near the Sra Srang Reservoir. A *bayon* oversees the entrance to this unrestored temple. Lying largely in ruins, Banteay Kdei is more a spot for calm reflection than active exploration.

BANTEAY SREI. Detailed and beautiful Banteay Srei ("Citadel of Women") stands 35km northeast of the main cluster of Angkor temples. Described as the 'precious queen' by French archaeologists, Banteay Srei's construction spanned two kingships in the second half of the 10th century. Though smaller in scale than the temples at Angkor, this pinkish temple is home to many exquisite carvings that are based on Indian epics. The south library shows Ravana shaking Mt. Kailusa (east pediment). The north library depicts Indra casting down heavenly rain (east pediment) and Krishna killing his murderous uncle King Kamsa (west pediment). Unfortunately, moto drivers will charge you US$12 for the day to get to Banteay Srei and the other far temples.

ROLUOS GROUP. About 30min. by moto on the incredibly dusty Rte. 6, this collection of three temples represents the very earliest of the Angkor period and is interesting only to die-hard Angkor enthusiasts. Jayavarman II made this capital of Hariharalaya in the 9th century. All three temples were originally consecrated to Hinduism. **Lolei** (north of the other two off Rte. 6), the site of a modern Buddhist

ANGKOR'S MOTLEY CREW Several figures and objects make appearances in Angkor's carvings. *Let's Go*'s guide to who's who in Angkor:

Naga: Sanskrit for "snake." These mythical, multi-headed serpents seem to be everywhere at Angkor and often form balustrades. Possibly the most abundant motif in Southeast Asia, *naga* play a marked role in Khmer legends. It is said that the Khmer are descended from the union between a foreigner and a *naga*. According to Hindu myths, the *naga* swallowed the waters of life and were either ruptured by Indra or squeezed by Vishnu's entourage to set the waters free.

Apsara: These celestial beauties, who sprang forth during the *Churning of the Sea of Milk* (See **Churn, Baby, Churn,** p. 94), have become virtually synonymous with Khmer architecture. Their perfect, sensuous beauty was believed to have highly refined powers of seduction, and they are typically depicted facing outward with only their feet in profile. Angkor Wat *apsaras,* widely regarded as the most beautiful (and most well-endowed) nymphs of all the temples, appear individually—unlike the Bayon *apsaras* who appear in groups of three.

Vishnu: An important Hindu deity, Vishnu was widely worshiped during the height of the Angkor period. Married to Lakshmi, he is frequently portrayed with four arms and an ornamental waist sash *(sampot).* Whenever the earth is threatened by evil, he acts as its savior, assuming an *avatara* (earthly incarnation). He is seen in the bas-reliefs of Angkor Wat both in human form and as a tortoise in the *Churning of the Sea of Milk.*

Ganesha: Parvati created Ganesha, the elephant-headed Hindu god of wisdom, to guard her bath. When Parvati's husband, the powerful god Shiva, tried to gain admittance, Ganesha refused to let him pass. Shiva called upon Vishnu for help, and together they decapitated Ganesha. Rightly furious, Parvati wrought destruction on the world. Since even the mighty Shiva could not handle a women scorned, he resurrected Ganesha and placed upon his body the head of the first being he saw—an elephant.

Garuda: A late addition to Angkor's characters, this half-man, half-bird enemy of the *naga* is Vishnu's preferred means of transport.

Makara: With a face like a Chinese dragon, a body of a crocodile, and a dance costume, this demonic sea monster is often represented on lintel beams with hideous creatures, such as *naga,* coming from his mouth. Lolei, one of the Roluos temples, has a fine representation of the creature.

wat, has not been preserved very well but boasts a few beautiful lintel beams on the four brick towers of the main sanctuary. **Preah Ko** (south of Rte. 6 and north of Bakong), or "Sacred Ox," consists of a central sanctuary with six brick towers. **Bakong,** the largest and most impressive of the Roluos Group is a temple mountain representing Mt. Meru and was once the ancient capital of Hariharalaya.

KBAL SPEAN. About 10km down the road from Banteay Srei, Kbal Spean, "The Head of the Bridge," offers a free and less crowded opportunity to see riverbed *linga.* A *linga* is a symbol of the creative power of nature and is shaped like a male phallus. About 15min. up the hill lies the secluded **River of the Thousand Linga.** The stretch of riverbed before the waterfall is carved with *linga* and images of deities. The carvings bless the river's waters as they flow to the temples and fields of Angkor. Its proximity to Banteay Srei makes it practical to combine a visit to the two sites. Moto drivers will try to charge you US$4-6 extra to see Kbal Spean; bargain hard. **Stay on the path marked by red tree-trunks, as mines remain a risk.**

PHNOM KULEN. Phnom Kulen looms 50km northeast of Angkor Thom. Due to its distance from Siem Reap, the US$20 entry fee, and the presence of more impressive riverbed carvings at Kbal Spean, the trek to Phnom Kulen is not for the temple-weary. The mountain is one of Cambodia's most sacred sites and on the weekend plays host to hordes of pilgrims. They come to see the **reclining Buddha,** perched on top of a huge boulder on one of the mountain's peaks. The temple sheltering the Buddha has magnificent views over the surrounding mountains, but remember to remove your shoes before climbing the staircase. Ten meters down the hill from the river on the right is a side road leading to a **waterfall,** a popular bathing spot. The quickest way to get to Phnom Kulen is by **moto** (1½hr. each way, US$20-25 for the whole day). **Be sure you have a reliable guide before venturing off the main road; keep to well trodden paths, as mines remain a risk.**

INDONESIA

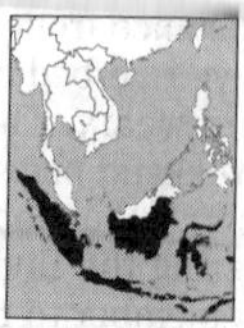

US$1 = RP8880.00 (RUPIAH)	RP1000 = US$0.11
CDN$1 = RP5568.27	RP1000 = CDN$0.18
EURO€1 = RP8680.64	RP1000 = EURO€0.12
UK£1 = RP13,823.05	RP1000 = UK£0.07
AUS$1 = RP4697.52	RP1000 = AUS$0.21
NZ$1 = RP4043.06	RP1000 = NZ$0.25
ZAR1 = RP846.52	RP1000 = ZAR1.18

PHONE CODE **Country code:** 62. **International dialing prefix:** 001, 008.

Indonesia's national motto, "*Bhinneka Tunggal Ika,*" translates to "Unity In Diversity." This simple idea has recently become the goal of political leaders, who have found that unity isn't as easy as diversity. The country is home to over 350 ethnic groups, adding cultural hodgepodge to the geographic mix of volcanoes, islands, and beaches. Achieving political unity has been most challenging; President Suharto's resignation signaled the end of the iron-fisted New Order era and the beginning of *Reformasi*, complete with student protests, strikes, and rioting. The recovering tourist industry and peaceful parliamentary elections of 1999 sparked renewed hope in divided Indonesia, although violence in East Timor, the Malukus, and Aceh Province signifies that unity remains tenuous in the wake of continuing political upheaval. Still, wary travelers can maneuver around points of instability and immerse themselves in the strongholds of Indonesia—its stunning landscapes, cultural diversity, historical legacies, and gracious people.

FACTS AND FIGURES

Official Name: Republic of Indonesia.

Government: Constitutional democracy.

Capital: Jakarta.

Land Area: 1,826,440 sq. km.

Geography: Archipelago of over 17,000 islands bordered by the Indian Ocean. Shares Borneo with Malaysia and New Guinea with Papua New Guinea.

Climate: Dry (high season) May-Oct., wet (low season) Nov.-Apr.

Major Cities: Bandung, Medan, Palembang, Semarang, Surabaya.

Population: 228,438,000.

Language: Bahasa Indonesia.

Religions: Islam 88%, Christianity 8%, Hinduism 2%, Mahayana Buddhism 1%, Taoism and other religions 1%.

Average Income Per Capita: US$570.

Major Exports: Petroleum and gas, plywood, textiles, rubber.

LIFE AND TIMES

DEMOGRAPHICS

With over 200 million people, Indonesia is the fourth most populous nation in the world. Over 75% of Indonesians live on Java and Sumatra, which together represent only a fraction of the country's total land mass. The **Javanese** and **Sundanese,** Indonesia's largest and most politically influential ethnic groups, live in Java. The

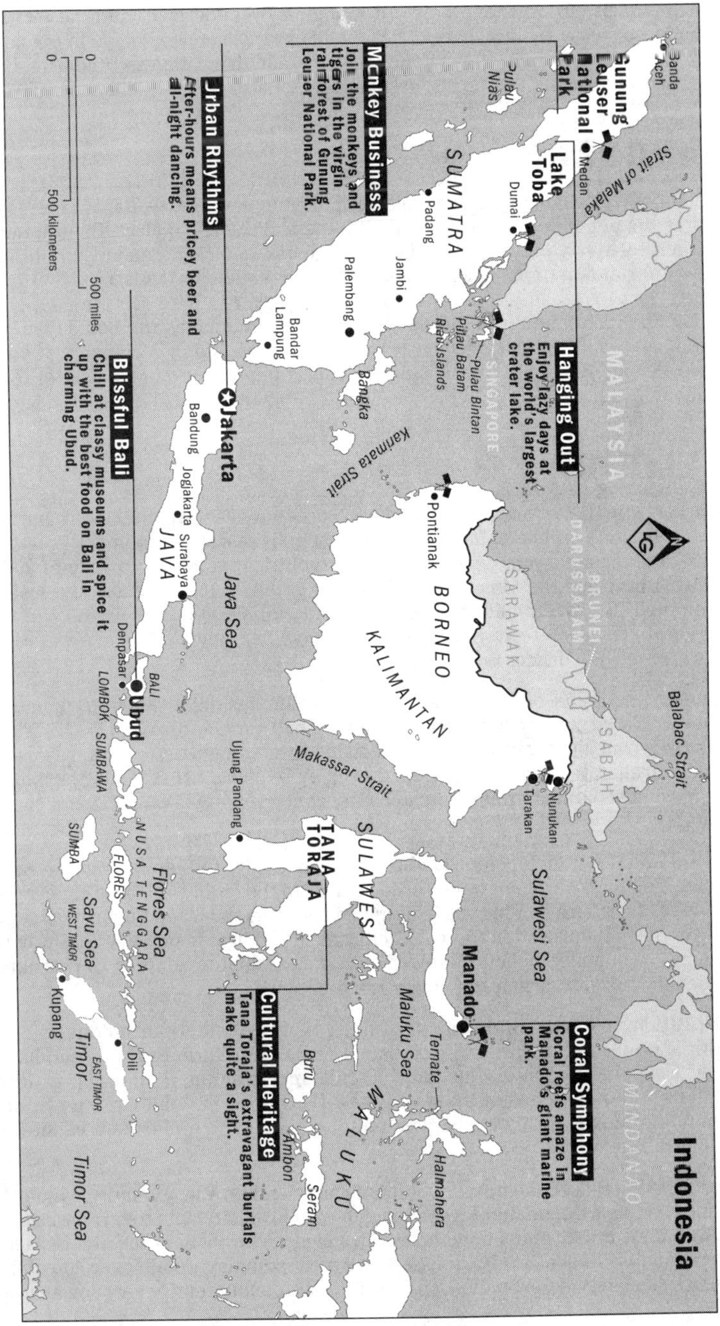
Indonesia
Gunung Leuser National Park
Monkey Business
Join the monkeys and tigers in the virgin rainforest of Gunung Leuser National Park.
Lake Toba
Hanging Out
Enjoy lazy days at the world's largest crater lake.
Jakarta
Urban Rhythms
After-hours means pricey beer and all-night dancing.
Ubud
Blissful Bali
Chill at classy museums and spice it up with the best food on Bali in charming Ubud.
TANA TORAJA
Cultural Heritage
Tana Toraja's extravagant burials make quite a sight.
Manado
Coral Symphony
Coral reefs amaze in Manado's giant marine park.
Banda Aceh
Medan
Strait of Melaka
Pulau Nias
SUMATRA
Dumai
Padang
Jambi
Palembang
Bandar Lampung
Riau Islands
Pulau Batam
Pulau Bintan
SINGAPORE
MALAYSIA
Bangka
Karimata Strait
Pontianak
BORNEO
KALIMANTAN
SARAWAK
BRUNEI DARUSSALAM
SABAH
Balabac Strait
Nunukan
Tarakan
Makassar Strait
Java Sea
Bandung
Jogjakarta
Surabaya
JAVA
Denpasar
BALI
LOMBOK
SUMBAWA
SUMBA
FLORES
NUSA TENGGARA
Flores Sea
Savu Sea
WEST TIMOR
Kupang
Dili
EAST TIMOR
Timor
Timor Sea
Ujung Pandang
SULAWESI
Sulawesi Sea
Maluku Sea
Ternate
Halmahera
MALUKU
Buru
Ambon
Seram
MINDANAO
0 500 kilometers
0 500 miles

Islamic **Bugis** (from which the word "boogieman" is derived) and the **Toraians** inhabit Sulawesi; the **Acehnese, Batak,** and **Minangkabau** people live in Sumatra. The **Balinese,** known for their flourishing arts and dedication to Hinduism, host Indonesia's most popular tourist destination.

LANGUAGE

One of over 300 languages and dialects spoken in the country, **Bahasa Indonesia** unites the population. Closely related to the Malay trade dialect, Bahasa Indonesia is relatively easy to learn; the language has no tenses, genders, or plurals. (For information on language schools, see **Alternatives to Tourism,** p. 46. If you really want to impress the locals, check out the flirting tips at www.bluep.com.au/~gerome.) Other common languages include Javanese, Sundanese, and Mandarin. Older Indonesians speak Dutch, a remnant of colonial rule, and English is becoming increasingly popular and important for tourism and business.

RELIGION

The majestic Hindu temples of Bali draw tourists, while the churches around the country attract bombers. Indonesia's diverse religions share an uneasy coexistence, and tensions sometimes escalate into outright violence. In June of 2000, conflict between the Muslim and Christian populations in **Maluku** and **Ambon** prompted the government to declare an indefinite state of emergency in the region. In the **Aceh** region of Sumatra, meanwhile, radical Islamic separatists push for independence.

ISLAM. About 85% of Indonesians practice Islam, making the country home to the world's largest Muslim population. Originally spread through trade, Islam has proved an important political force in Indonesia; much of the nationalist sentiment against the Dutch was strengthened by religious belief. Today, agitation by Muslim separatist groups threatens the country's fragile political and social stability.

CHRISTIANITY. Dutch colonizers brought Christianity to Indonesia in the early 1600s. Today, about 7% of Indonesians adhere to the faith, with large concentrations of Christians in Flores, Maluku, and Kalimantan. When Suharto came to power, his administration forced all citizens into religious practice as a way to combat Communist beliefs. Many of Indonesia's Chinese adopted Christianity, widening the cultural gap and fueling conflict.

HINDUISM. Though Hinduism was once practiced widely in Indonesia, the faith is now confined primarily to Bali. The Balinese form of Hinduism, however, has developed into something quite distinct from the Hinduism practiced in India and other areas of the world. Visit Pura Besakih, "Mother Temple," on Gunung Agung to study the largest temple complex and most sacred site of Balinese Hinduism.

BUDDHISM. Before the introduction of Islam, Sumatra was primarily Buddhist, while Hinduism dominated Java. Though few followers remain today, the strong influence of Buddhism is nonetheless still evident throughout the archipelago. For a glimpse of some of Southeast Asia's most stunning Buddhist architecture and a lesson in Buddhist philosophy, visit the Borobudur temple near Jogjakarta.

HISTORY

HINDU-BUDDHIST KINGDOMS (AD 600-1478)

IMPORTANT DATES

7th Century Indian traders introduce Buddhism, Hinduism.	**7th-12th Centuries** Shrivijaya Kingdom controls trade routes.	**8th -10th Centuries** Saliendra Kingdom expands into Indochina.	**1292-1478** Majapahit Empire leads Java's Golden Age.

Indonesian history begins with the **Shrivijaya Kingdom,** which gained power by controlling trade routes. Simultaneously, a succession of neighboring kingdoms in Central Java prospered through intensive agricultural development. At its height, the Mahayana Buddhist **Sailendra Kingdom** reconquered parts of Indochina. The **Sanjaya Kingdom** built impressive monuments during the 9th century; the temples of **Prambanan,** dedicated to the Hindu god Shiva, can still be seen today near Jogjakarta. Indonesia's last great Hindu-Buddhist kingdom, East Java's **Majapahit Empire,** unified the islands before the Dutch arrived. Its greatest rulers, **Hayam Wuruk** and **Gajah Mada,** fostered Java's Golden Age.

ISLAMIC SULTANATES (1200-1700)

IMPORTANT DATES

13th Century First Sumatran Muslim kingdom. Islamization begins.	**14th-16th Century** Islam spreads throughout the archipelago.	**16th-17th Century** Zenith of Achinese sultanate.

Arab and Indian traders introduced Islam as early as the 7th century, but Muslim communities weren't prominent in Indonesia until 600 years later when the first sultanates were established in Northern Sumatra. These soon became centralized under the state of **Aceh.** Though Islam spread as far east as Maluku and the Southern Philippines, Bali remained staunchly Hindu. During the 15th and 16th centuries, a series of sultanates arose along the coast of Java, and Islam finally penetrated inland, mixing with preexisting Hindu-Buddhist tradition. Aceh remains a Muslim stronghold today.

DUTCH COLONIALISM (1700-1927)

IMPORTANT DATES

1602 Dutch East India Company formed.	**1825-30** Locals lose Java to Dutch.	**1873-80** Achinese War. Aceh province rebels against Dutch armies.	**1900-30** Ethical Policy tries to spread European values.

The Portuguese left Indonesia with some ruins, a few street names, and about five serious Catholics. The Dutch, on the other hand, monitored by the **Dutch East India Company,** were more successful (and brutal) colonizers. Military force and exploitative diplomacy gave the Dutch a regional trade monopoly and funneled all profits away from locals. A "divide and subjugate" strategy created power imbalances among increasingly Dutch-dependent local rulers.

The Dutch East India Company went bankrupt in 1799, but the Dutch, intent on trade, stepped in to pursue what came to be known as the **Dutch East Indies.** Colonists set up an administration with compliant local rulers as middlemen. The early 20th century saw the creation of the **Ethical Policy** aimed at improving education and public health and bringing Indonesians closer to European ideals. Indonesians began organizing themselves by religious or ethnic identity and political ideology. Trade cooperatives became vehicles for political action, but internal conflicts prevented the formation of a united nationalist movement.

REVOLUTION AND INDEPENDENCE (1927-1950)

IMPORTANT DATES				
1924 Indonesian Communist Party (PKI) established.	**1927** Partai Nasional Indonesia (PNI) founded.	**1942** Brief, brutal Japanese rule.	**1945** Independence declared.	**1945-1950** Indonesian Revolution forces out the Dutch.

The stage was set for the rise of the **Partai Nasional Indonesia (PNI),** a nationalist party founded in 1927 that practiced civil disobedience and was led by charismatic **President Sukarno.** Bahasa Indonesia, the national language, was adopted in 1928 to further an ever-increasing sense of national unity.

During World War II, Japan defeated the Dutch and invaded Indonesia for its rich oil deposits. Indonesians welcomed the Japanese as they liberated them from European control, but soon discovered that incorporation into the **Greater East Asia Co-Prosperity Sphere** was a fate worse than Dutch rule. Power again changed hands as Japan's brutal 3½-year regime ended with their surrender to the Allies in 1945. Eager to take charge before the Dutch returned, Sukarno declared independence several days later. The Dutch had hoped to restore their former colonial empire, but, to their dismay, they found a mobilized and chaotic population willing to fight for the newly declared **Republik Indonesia.** The **Indonesian Revolution** (1945-50) further unified the nation against the Dutch, who, for once, quietly bowed out. The new government, however, faced raging internal disputes, especially among the **Indonesian Communist Party (PKI),** the Nationalists and their ragtag military, and an array of Islamic parties.

SUKARNO'S RULE (1950-1965)

IMPORTANT DATES		
1950-57 Sukarno's first years in power, relative politic freedom.	**1957** Sukarno introduces "Guided Democracy."	**1963** *Konfrontasi* campaign against Malaysia.

By 1950, the Dutch, embarrassed by international criticism, officially transferred sovereignty to Indonesia. Sukarno wrote the **Pancasila,** the ideological basis of the Indonesian constitution, which consisted of **Five Principles:** belief in one supreme God, humanitarianism, nationalism and national unity, social justice, and democracy. Sukarno's attempts to form a government based on representative democracy in the 1950s were the most politically free years in Indonesian history but they resulted in corruption and stagnation in a largely poor and illiterate nation.

By 1957, after economic failure and several regional rebellions, Sukarno announced his **Guided Democracy** concept, which abolished political parties and granted the president dictatorial powers. In the early 60s, matters came to a head when the masses called for "liberation" of western **New Guinea.** Under US pressure, the Dutch handed over the territory to the UN, which transferred the territory to Indonesia, with the agreement that a vote of self-determination would take place within five years. The vote never came, and the province was officially incorporated into the Indonesian Republic under the name **Irian Jaya.** To this day, conflict over the region's sovereignty persist (see **Indonesia Today,** below).

THE NEW ORDER (1965-1998)

IMPORTANT DATES		
1965 Rise of Suharto's "New Order."	**1975** East Timor annexed.	**1997-1998** Anti Suharto student protests.

Sukarno's balancing act collapsed in 1965, when he was implicated in a failed coup, supposedly perpetrated by the PKI. The coup involved the murder of six high-ranking generals and resulted in a right-wing military backlash. During the following "Year of Living Dangerously," the military slaughtered between 500,000 and one million suspected Communists. Pragmatic and mild-mannered **Major General Suharto** emerged as supreme commander, dismantling Sukarno's powers and replacing the Guided Democracy with his **New Order** government. He promptly banned the PKI and encouraged investment from the West.

Under the New Order, the next 30 years brought political stability, impressive economic growth, and major improvements in infrastructure, public health, and education—at the expense of free speech and individual human rights under military control. The suppression of independence movements by Suharto's regime resulted in the deaths of 200,000 people in East Timor and 2000 in Northern Sumatra. Newly independent **East Timor** was on the verge of forming its own government when civil war broke out. Claiming that the Timorese posed a Communist threat to the region, the Indonesian army invaded in 1975.

INDONESIA TODAY

IMPORTANT DATES

1998 Economic crisis, Suharto resigns presidency to VP Habibie.

1999 Wahid is first democratically elected president.

2001 Wahid impeached in July. VP Megawati Sukarnoputri assumes presidential responsibilities.

GOVERNMENT AND POLITICS. In March 1998, economic crisis caused by currency devaluation and stringent IMF regulations resulted in factory closings, bank liquidations, withdrawal of foreign investment, and spiraling inflation and unemployment rates. Popular opinion turned decisively against Suharto. Later that year, the military killed four student protesters in Jakarta, provoking serious outrage. Rioting, fires, and looting quickly swept cities throughout the archipelago. Meanwhile, thousands of students staged a sit-in at the House of Representatives, demanding Suharto's resignation. One by one, government ministers and high-ranking political figures stepped down, calling upon Suharto to do the same. Suharto finally resigned the presidency to Vice President **B.J. Habibie** in May 1998.

Protests subsided as Habibie, in a bid to regain confidence in the Indonesian presidency and government, released political prisoners, opened dialogue on the East Timor issue, distanced himself from Suharto, and addressed the concerns of ethnic Chinese, who had been the victims of many attacks during the riots. The most dramatic change during this so-called *reformasi* (reformation) era was an easing of censorship; political pundits now openly criticize the government. Fifty new political parties formed before the 1999 parliamentary elections, each espousing the aspirations of a different portion of Indonesian society. The **Indonesian Democratic Party (PDI),** headed by Sukarno's daughter **Megawati Sukarnoputri,** received the most votes, followed by Habibie's **GOLKAR** party.

In late 1999, **Abdurrahman Wahid** defeated front-runner Megawati in the presidential election; Megawati accepted the position of VP. Wahid's leadership over the next months, however, proved flawed. Accusations of financial scandal were leveled against the president, who responded by dismissing several top government officials. Amid confusion and intense political maneuvering, the parliament voted to impeach Wahid on July 23, 2001. Presidential responsibilities were handed over to Megawati. She now faces the immense task of holding Indonesia together amid political turmoil, ethnic and religious violence, and economic malaise.

SEPARATIST MOVEMENTS. In the months after Suharto stepped down, his enforced unity crumbled as various groups scrambled to fill the power vacuum. The most violent separatist movements erupted in **East Timor** and the **Aceh** prov-

HIGHLIGHTS OF INDONESIA

BEACHES. Despite recent troubles, **Bali**—especially **Lovina** (p. 189) and **Kuta** (p. 175)—is still home to some of the world's most beautiful beaches. Lombok's northwestern **Gili Islands** (p. 219) has smooth sands. **Manado** (p. 256), at Sulawesi's north tip, offers first-rate scuba diving. Java's **Pantai Parangtritis** (p. 147) is striking albeit not swimmable. **Pulau Nias** (p. 287) off Sumatra draws a surfer crowd.

CULTURAL HERITAGE. Jogjakarta (p. 139) is easily Java's best city. Colorful **Tana Toraja** (p. 251) in Sulawesi throws killer funerals. **Pura Besakih** (p. 193) is the mother of Balinese temples. **Bukit Tinggi** (p. 294) and **Padang** (p. 299) showcase both the artistic and culinary culture of Sumatra's Minangkabau people.

HANGING OUT. Hip **Ubud** (p. 181) on Bali has the best cafes and meditation workshops. **Malang** (p. 158) dishes out Javanese delicacies. Lombok's **Tetebatu** (p. 218), Flore's **Ende** (p. 238), and Sulawesi's **Rantepao** (p. 251) all offer cool respite from the lowland heat. **Lake Toba** (p. 279) on Sumatra is an ethereal detour.

NATURAL WONDERS. Gunung Leuser National Park (p. 275) counts whitewater rafters, trekkers, and orangutans among its denizens. Berestagi's **Karo Highlands** (p. 269) welcome hikers. Climbing **Gunung Rinjani** (p. 216) is an exhilarating challenge.

URBAN BEAT. Jakarta (p. 122) and **Bandung** (p. 131) pulse with unmatched panache.

INDONESIA

ince of Northern Sumatra. East Timor voted for independence in 1999; UN peacekeeping forces were sent in to control the resulting violence between pro-Indonesia and pro-independence factions. Under global pressure, Indonesia removed troops from East Timor and renounced claims to the territory. East Timor remained under UN administration until May 20, 2002, when the nation gained official independence and autonomy. Recently, the Indonesian government has come under criticism for its treatment of East Timorese refugees.

Wahid responded to separatist agitation in the Aceh province of Northern Sumatra by holding secret peace talks with the rebels, culminating in a truce in May of 2000. Jakarta continues to deny the region independence, but the government has granted Aceh more autonomy. There is a similar situation in **Irian Jaya,** where resentments flare over past military abuses and exploited natural resources. The province claimed independence in June 2000; the government offered autonomy and dialogue. Continuing tensions keep these areas dangerous.

ETHNIC AND RELIGIOUS VIOLENCE. Ethnic and religious violence plagues Indonesia. In **Kalimantan,** Muslim settlers have come into conflict with indigenous Dayaks and Malays. In February of 2001, 400 Muslims were massacred on the island; over 500,000 Muslims have fled in the wake of this Dayak hostility. Years of Muslim-Christian tension in **Maluku** and **Ambon** prompted the government to declare a state of emergency in the region on June 26, 2000. Church bombings throughout the country on December 24, 2000 injured over a 100 people and left 16 dead. Sectarian and ethnic strife also wrack **Lombok** and **Central and South Sulawesi.** The fragile economic situation heightens tensions all over Indonesia.

KUTA BOMBINGS. On October 12, 2002, bombs exploded at two popular nightclubs in Kuta on Bali, killing about 180—mostly Australian travelers. Foreign governments quickly advised against travel to the island; tourism in the area, already unstable as a result of post-September 11 fears, suffered even further. At press time, neither the extent of the damage nor the parties responsible were known.

CUSTOMS & ETIQUETTE

Adat, or common law, explains many Indonesian customs. *Adat,* originally rooted in religion and adapted over many years, is one of the few things that diverse Indo-

> **PLIGHT OF THE CHINESE** In the aftermath of the financial crisis that annulled 30 years of growth, Indonesia's 7 million Chinese bear an increasing burden, comprising only 3.5% of the population, they control 70% of the nation's wealth. Tycoons include Liem Sioe Liong, the Suharto family's financier, and Sofjan Wanandi, head of the Gamelan music empire. Their wealth, however, is their only security against institutionalized repression and violence. Even though most Chinese are Indonesian-born rather than first-generation immigrants, they are always reminded of their place as second-class citizens. Until recently, identity cards coded them as Chinese. Chinese-language schools and chambers of commerce, publications bearing Chinese characters, and publicly-spoken Chinese are restricted, and all Chinese must adopt indigenous Indonesian surnames and can't serve in the military.
>
> In spring 1998, anti-Chinese riots rocked Indonesia; Pamanukan, Java, Jakarta, Balung, and Ugung Pandang all have stories of blood, shattered glass, and smoky ruins. Many are convinced that the government, through incendiary statements and ambivalence, encourages anti-Chinese sentiment to deflect blame from government policies and provide a scapegoat for those frustrated by economic conditions. The violence has led to an exodus of Chinese and their billions in capital, which threatens to worsen the economy and heighten racial hatred.

nesians have in common. Though unwritten and unspoken, *adat* still remains an important code of conduct.

Friendliness is valued in Indonesia. Just keep smiling—Indonesians are known to hide negative feelings and avoid confrontation, rarely raising their voices. Indonesians also place less emphasis on punctuality than Westerners; travelers sometimes become frustrated with the country's "rubber time." Be patient, as it is considered disrespectful to show signs of annoyance.

CLOTHING. As Indonesia is a largely Islamic country, revealing clothes are inappropriate, especially if you plan to visit a mosque. Women should take special care to dress conservatively.

TABOOS. Avoid eating, passing dishes, and giving or receiving objects with the left hand, which is considered unclean. Though shaking hands is normal with introductions, never shake with the left. Indonesians regard the feet as the least sacred part of the body, so avoid pointing your feet at anyone. Conversely, don't touch anyone on the head, even young children. Pointing with a forefinger is considered impolite. To beckon someone, extend your hand with the palm down and make a scratching motion with your fingers. Finally, remember that observant Muslims do not consume pork or alcohol, while Hindus avoid beef and leather.

TABLE MANNERS. Accept hosts' offers of food and drink. Forks and spoons are the main utensils; knives are rarely used. Leave a portion of your meal on your plate to signal your satisfaction with the meal. When entering an Indonesian's house, remove your shoes if your hosts take off theirs.

BISEXUAL, GAY, AND LESBIAN TRAVELERS. Homosexuality is legal in Indonesia, but public displays of affection are not advisable for *any* couples, straight or gay. All large Indonesian cities have a substantial gay nightlife scene, but it may take some time or the advice of locals to figure out what's currently *on vogue*. Defying categories assigned by the West, Indonesia has an alternate gender, known as *waria*, which is defined as a man *(pria)* with the soul of a woman *(wanita)*. While not wholly accepted by Indonesian society, *waria* participate in a subculture of their own (see **Waria,** p. 168). Although no laws deal specifically with AIDS or HIV, affected persons may be denied entry or even quarantined under other restrictions. For more information on Indonesia's gay and lesbian scene, *waria* communities, and AIDS activism, pick up a copy of *GAYa Nusantara*, a magazine published in Surabaya. (☎593 4924. Offices at Jl. Mulyosari Timur 46, Surabaya, East Java, 60112.)

THE ARTS

ARCHITECTURE. The ancient *candi* (shrines) of central and eastern Java testify to the architectural grandeur of Indonesia. Among the achievements of the first millennium are the monuments of Borobudur and Prambanan. Over 20,000 *pura* (temples) can be found on Bali, the largest and most sacred of which is Pura Besakih on Gunung Agung. With the arrival of Islam on Java, mosques replaced temples; the *kraton* (walled palace) complexes in Jogjakarta and Surakarta exemplify the blend of Islamic and Hindu-Buddhist architectural traditions. The *pendopo*, a common structure used in Javanese households and palaces, is an open-sided pavilion with a raised floor and wooden pillars supporting a roof of beams. Every region has its distinctive *rumah adat* (traditional house), such as the western Sumatran Minang houses whose roofs resemble buffalo horns, and Batak longhouses, built with spaces for storing ancestors' bones.

BATIK AND OTHER CRAFTS. Batik, a world-renowned textile art of producing intricate patterns, often with animal motifs, is common throughout Southeast Asia. Originally done by hand, *batik tulis* is now made with a tool that holds a small amount of liquid wax and is used like a pencil to create designs on fabric. Various colored dyes are absorbed by the parts of the fabric not covered by wax. The cheaper *batik cap* is made with pre-patterned metal stamps dipped in wax and then pressed repeatedly onto fabric. *Batik* shirts are common formal dress for men; women often wear *batik* sarongs. Recently, *batik* **paintings** have become a popular art form. The best and cheapest *batik* paintings are around Jogjakarta; many galleries also give visitors a chance to make their own paintings. **Ikat** is a type of weaving in which already-dyed threads are woven into designs, while the rest of the fabric is dyed in a contrasting color. **Traditional wood-carvings,** from masks and life-size puppets to weapons and furniture, are uniquely reflective of Indonesia's many cultures. In places where Hindu culture was strongest, metalworking recreates the ancient artifacts of *moko*, bronze kettle drums, and the legendary *kris*, a ceremonial sword. For those with a hankering for gold, silver, and semi-precious stones, Indonesian artists offer inexpensive and intricate jewelry.

DANCE AND DRAMA. Indonesian dance traditions are highly developed, especially in Java and Bali. Javanese dance is meditative, deliberate, involving limber movements and contemplative pauses. Balinese dancing also requires meticulous maneuvering but is distinguished by its fast, jerky movements accompanied by the explosive Balinese *gamelan*. The most popular dances are the *Barong*, which is a battle between good and evil, and *Kecak* **(Monkey Dance),** which reenacts a scene of the Hindu epic *Ramayana* around flame torches while 100 or more men sit in concentric circles shouting and chanting in rhythm. Most modern drama has developed in Java. *Ludruk* is an all-male performance in which roles of women are humorously, if somewhat derogatorily, depicted on stage. *Kethoprak* adds a contemporary twist on classic epic stories and myths of India and Java.

MUSIC AND WAYANG. The **gamelan** orchestra, a sophisticated ensemble of gongs, metallophones, drums, vocalists, and string and wind instruments, is unique to Java and Bali. Javanese *gamelan* is trance-like, while the Balinese version is fast-paced and dramatic. *Gamelan* accompanies many events, among them dance and *wayang* (shadow puppetry). Indonesia's diverse set of popular music traditions draws upon outside influences and traditions across the islands. Lilting *kroncong* music reflects the influence of the Portuguese, while *dangdut* music shares Indian and Arabic rhythms. The Batak of North Sumatra are famed for their beautiful voices and melancholy tunes, which frequently feature unabashed sobbing by the vocalists. The ancient Javanese art of **shadow puppetry** *(wayang)* probably has its roots in ancestor worship, with the *dalang* (puppeteer) considered a conduit of spirits. Today he's highly respected for his ability to manipulate several puppets at once, to conduct the *gamelan* orchestra behind him, and to keep it going nonstop for nine hours. The stories are drawn from the *Ramayana* and *Mahabharata* Indian epics as well as indigenous stories.

HOLIDAYS & FESTIVALS (2003)

DATE	NAME	DESCRIPTION & LOCATION
Jan. 1	New Year's Day	
Feb. 12	Eid Al Adha	Celebrates Abraham's willingness to sacrifice his son.
Mar. 5	Islamic New Year	Anniversary of the day in AD 622 when Muhammad left Mecca to found a new community in Medina.
Apr. 18	Good Friday	Christian holiday.
Apr. 20	Easter	Celebrated in Flores, where Christians walk barefoot through the streets with a statue of the Virgin Mary
Apr. 23	Nyepi	Hindu New Year. After nightfall on the evening before Nyepi, Balinese parade through the streets waving torches and sounding gongs to dispel evil spirits. People spend New Year's day in meditation and prayer; the silence is thought to ward off any remaining demons.
May 14	Maulid Nabi	Prophet Muhammad's birthday
May 16	Waisak	A central Buddhist festival, celebrating the enlightenment of the Buddha. Observant Buddhists gather at the Borobudur temple near Jogjakarta.
May 29	Ascension Day	Christian holiday.
Aug. 17	Indonesian Independence Day	Celebrates Sukarno's declaration of independence in 1945.
Sept. 24	Isra' Mi'raj	Muslim celebration of the ascension of Muhammad.
Oct.27	Beginning of Ramadan	The beginning of the Muslim month of fasting and religious contemplation.
Nov. 26	Eid Al Fitr	The most important Muslim festival of the year, celebrated at the end of Ramadan with firecrackers, new clothes, and elaborate meals.
Dec. 25	Christmas Day	Christian holiday.

ADDITIONAL RESOURCES

LITERATURE

A History of Modern Indonesia Since c.1300, by MC Ricklefs (1993). A comprehensive but readable history of Indonesia, with a focus on the colonial period.

The Buru Tetralogy: This Earth of Mankind, Child of All Nations, Footsteps, and *House of Glass*, by Pramoedya Ananta Toer. Historical novels about the Indonesian national consciousness by Indonesia's most famous dissident writer. Pramoedya languished in prison and has been under house arrest since 1965.

ON THE WEB

Indonesian Homepage (http://indonesia.elga.net.id). Info on all things Indonesian.

Inside Indonesia (www.insideindonesia.org). The online version of this quarterly magazine offers information on current events.

ESSENTIALS

INDONESIA PRICE ICONS					
SYMBOL:	❶	❷	❸	❹	❺
ACCOMM.	Rp15,000 and under	Rp15,000-30,000	Rp30,000-50,000	Rp50,000-80,000	Rp80,000 and over
FOOD	Rp7000 and under	Rp7000-12,000	Rp12,000-20,000	Rp20,000-30,000	Rp30,000 and over

EMBASSIES AND CONSULATES

INDONESIAN CONSULAR SERVICES ABROAD

Australia: Embassy, 8 Darwin Ave., Yarralumla, Canberra, ACT 2600; P.O. Box 616, Kingston 2604 (☎02 6250 8600). **Consulates,** East Perth, WA (☎08 9221 5858); Darwin, NT (☎08 8941 0048); Melbourne, VIC (☎03 9525 2755); Maroubra, NSW (☎02 9344 9933); Wayville, SA (☎08 8357 8955); Brisbane, QLD (☎07 3309 0858).

Canada: Embassy, 55 Parkdale Ave., Ottawa, ON K1Y 1E5 (☎613-724-1100; www.indonesia-ottawa.org). **Consulates,** Vancouver, BC (☎604-682-8855; www.kjrivcr.org); Toronto, ON (☎416-360-4020).

New Zealand: Embassy, 70 Glen Rd., Kelburn; P.O. Box 3543, Wellington (☎04 475 8697 or 475 8698).

South Africa: Embassy, 949 Schoeman St., Arcadia, Pretoria; P.O. Box 13155, Hatfield 0028 (☎012 342 3352). **Consulate,** Cape Town (☎021 423 2321).

UK: Embassy, 38 Grosvenor Sq., London W1K 2HW (☎020 629 6966).

US: Embassy, 2020 Massachusetts Ave. NW, Washington, D.C. 20036 (☎202-775-5200). **Consulates,** New York (☎212-879-0600); Chicago (☎312-595-1777); Los Angeles (☎213-383-5126; www.kjri-la.com); San Francisco (☎415-474-9571); Houston (☎713-785-1691).

CONSULAR SERVICES IN INDONESIA

Australia: Embassy, Jl. H.R. Rasuna Said Kav. C15-16, Kuningan, Jakarta Selatan 12940 (☎62 21 2550 5555). **Consulates,** in Denpasar (p. 167) and Medan (p. 263).

Canada: Embassy, World Trade Center, 6th fl., Jl. Jend. Sudirman Kav. 29-31, Jakarta 12920; P.O. Box 8324/JKS.MP, Jakarta 12084 (☎62 021 525 0709). **Consulate,** in Surabaya (p. 156).

New Zealand: Embassy, BRI II Building, 23rd fl., Jl. Jend. Sudirman Kav. 44-46, Jakarta; P.O. Box 2439, Jakarta (☎62 21 570 9560).

South Africa: Embassy, Kedutaan Besar Afrika Selatan, Wisma GKBI, Suite 705, 7th fl., Jl. Jend. Sudirman Kav. 28, Jakarta 10210 (☎62 21 574 0660).

UK: Embassy, Jl. M.H. Thamrin No. 75, Jakarta 10310 (☎62 21 315 6264). **Consulates,** in Denpasar (p. 167), Medan (p. 261), and Surabaya (p. 156).

US: Embassy, Jl. Medan Merdeka Selatan 5, Jakarta 10110 (☎62 21 3435 9000).**Consulates,** in Denpasar (p. 167) and Surabaya (p. 156).

VISAS

For tourist stays of up to 60 days, visas aren't required for citizens of Australia, Canada, Ireland, New Zealand, the UK, and the US. Travelers must enter through specific gateway cities, but all major ports and airports are included on the list.

Multiple-entry visas are valid for one year; check with the Indonesian embassy in your home country for more information.

MONEY

The Indonesian **rupiah (Rp)** comes in denominations of Rp100, 500, 1000, 5000, 10,000, 20,000, 50,000, and 100,000, and coins come in Rp25, 50, 100, 500, and 1000. The US dollar is the most readily accepted foreign currency. Traveler's checks can be exchanged at banks, moneychangers, and some hotels. Credit cards and traveler's checks are accepted in bigger towns and tourist destinations, but if you are traveling in rural or unfrequented areas, cash is your best bet. Most major cities have **ATMs.** Bills at major hotels usually include a 10% service charge. **Tipping** is not expected, but a 5-10% tip is always appreciated. Tips for taxi and hired car drivers are not necessary, but for satisfactory taxi service a tip of Rp500-1000 is appropriate; give a bit more for a hired car. Airport **porters** should be given Rp2000 for small bags and Rp3000 for bags over 20kg.

GETTING THERE

BY PLANE. Indonesia has a number of **international airports**, including Soekarno-Hatta Airport in Jakarta (p. 112), Adi Sumarmo Airport in Surakarta (p. 147), Juanda Airport in Surabaya (p. 154), Ngurah Rai International Airport in Denpasar (p. 165), Polonia Airport in Medan (p. 261), Sam Ratulangi Airport in Manado (p. 255), and Selaparang Airport in Lombok (p. 206). **Garuda** (www.garuda-indonesia.com) runs the most flights to these airports.

BY LAND. Refer to the following table for overland border crossings in Indonesia.

BORDER CROSSINGS

MALAYSIA–SARAWAK & SABAH. You can cross from **Entikong** in West Kalimantan (near Pontianak) to **Tebedu** in Sarawak (near **Kuching,** p. 444), or from **Nunukan** in East Kalimantan to **Tawau** in Sabah.

MALAYSIA–PENINSULAR. Ferries connect Sumatra and Peninsular Malaysia via a number of routes: **Medan** (p. 261) to **Penang** (p. 400); **Dumai** to **Melaka** (p. 385); and **Pulau Batam** to **Johor Bahru** (near Singapore).

SINGAPORE. Ferries connect Singapore (p. 644) to **Pulau Bintan** in Sumatra (p. 302).

GETTING AROUND

BY PLANE. Air travel is the easiest and most comfortable way to get around Indonesia, although the economic crisis has forced many airlines to bump up fares. National carriers **Garuda** and **Merpati** (www.merpati.co.id) run to all provincial district capitals, and **Bouraq** and **Mandala** fly to more domestic destinations.

BY BOAT. Government-owned **Pelayaran Nasional Indonesia**'s (PELNI) air-conditioned ships serve all domestic main points biweekly with spartan accommodations, basic food, slow journeys, and mediocre prices. Reserve ahead. Go early to claim a mattress and floor space. Check out the useful website at www.pelni.co.id.

BY TRAIN OR BUS. Trains run in Java and parts of Sumatra; they're often slow and delayed but prove more comfortable than buses for long trips. Most locals take buses, which, like trains, are slow and unpredictable. Though buses get

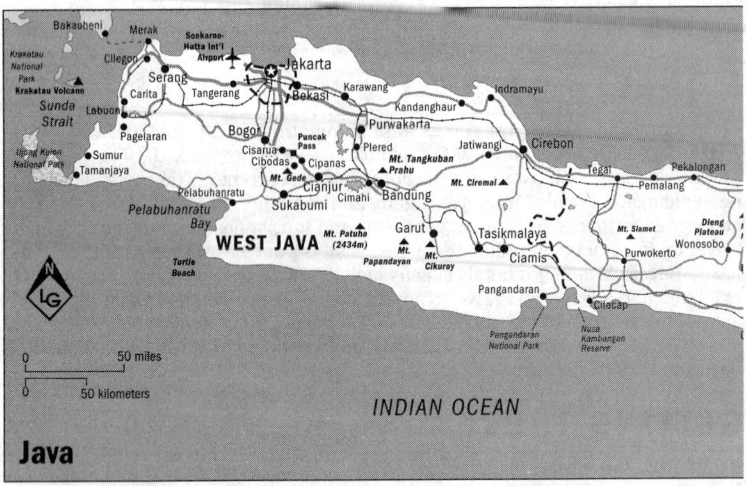

crowded, tickets are cheap. Overnight buses are usually faster, but more nerve-wracking and arrive at inconvenient hours. Combined bus/ferry tickets make island-hopping easy. Beware of pickpockets on any public transportation. Also note that buses often will not depart with fewer than five passengers, which can make travel unpredictable in rural areas.

BY CAR OR TAXI. Hired cars with driver cost Rp75,000-200,000 per day in major cities. Taxis are metered in large cities and carry five passengers on major routes—to avoid getting ripped off, make sure the driver runs the meter. If there's no meter, agree on a price before hopping in.

OTHER LOCAL TRANSPORTATION. Other forms of transport include the *andong* or *dokar* (horse-drawn cart), *angkot* or *colt* (minibus), *bajaj* (ba-JA-ee; orange motorized three-wheeler), *becak* (BAY-chuck; bicycle rickshaw), *bemo* (canopied pickup truck that runs on a regular route), *ojek* (motorcycle taxi), *oplet* or *micro-let* (a larger form of *bemo*), and *sudako* (minivans that travel a set route). Some can be hired for private use. When navigating by foot or **bicycle,** keep in mind that Jl. is an abbreviation of *jalan* (street).

KEEPING IN TOUCH

MAIL. Indonesia's postal service is not terribly reliable—**register important mail.** Check **Practical Information** listings in each town for *Poste Restante* availability. *Kantor pos* means "post office."

TELEPHONES. Most towns have Perumtel or *wartel* offices, which often also send **faxes.** Offices usually have private booths for callers; a digital display tells you how long you have been talking and how much the call costs. International calls are fairly simple, though you might have trouble using your phone card. IDD is widely available. For **Home Country Direct (HCD)** numbers from Indonesia, refer to the table on the inside back cover of this book. When calling home, remember that Indonesia falls into three separate **time zones:** west (Java and Sumatra) is seven hours ahead of GMT; central (Nusa Tenggara and Sulawesi) is eight hours ahead; and east (Maluku) is nine hours ahead. Calls to the USA cost roughly US$1 per minute.

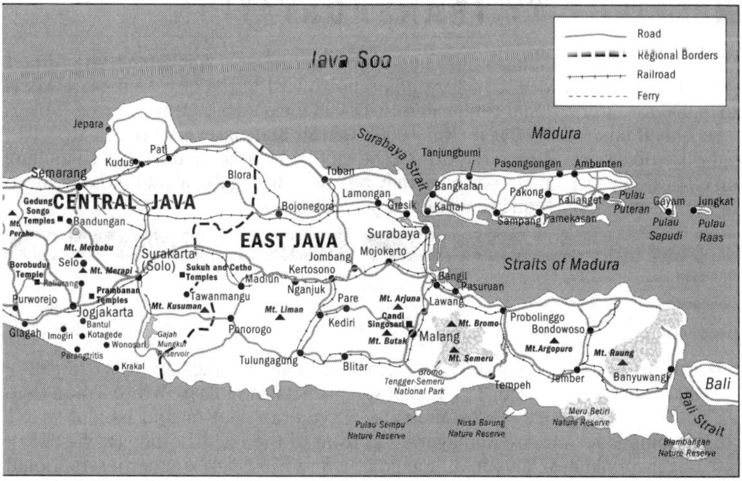

INTERNET ACCESS. You'll have no problems checking your email in big cities and major tourist destinations. Rates average around Rp3,000-5,000 per hour. In more rural areas, Internet access is harder to find and more expensive.

JAVA

Packing over 60% of Indonesia's population onto only 8% of its landmass, Java takes center stage both politically and culturally. The island's fertile volcanic soil has supported the development of sophisticated court cultures from the 7th century through the Republic's modern government. Although alone it presents an incomplete portrait of Indonesia, Java offers a wealth of ancient, colonial, and modern sites. Most travelers make a beeline from Jogjakarta to Gunung Bromo, but for those willing to step off the beaten path, Java's labyrinthine cities and mountainous landscapes are ripe for exploration.

JAKARTA ☎021

Plagued by overcrowding and political instability, Jakarta remains a city caught in transition. One of the world's most cosmopolitan cities, Jakarta is nonetheless steeped in the chaos and frenetic energy of the developing world. Corruption and economic jolts have slowed the growth of the capital of the world's fourth most populous country to a rate too slow for its swelling population of urban poor. Shiny skyscrapers sidle up next to weathered metal shacks while sleek Mercedes cut off smog-spewing *bajaj* on the streets. McDonald's meets 100% *Halal* and Dunkin' Donuts serves durian-flavored next to honey-glazed. Those willing to venture away from backpacker hangouts will witness the harsh reality of the city. Many tourists prefer other parts of the archipelago, though attractions such as the thriving harbor and exciting nightlife reward those who stick around. Travelers should be extra sensitive to potential crime. Pickpocketing is the main problem, but walking the streets late at night might be tempting fate.

INTERCITY TRANSPORTATION

BY PLANE. International and domestic flights arrive at **Soekarno-Hatta Airport** (departure/arrival info ☎550 5307), 35km northwest of the city. Departure tax is Rp75,000 for international routes and Rp11,000 for domestic travel. From the airport, **DAMRI** buses go to **Bogor** (Rp10,000), **Gambir Station** (every hr., A/C Rp8000), and other locations. A metered taxi to the city costs roughly Rp52,000 (including toll). The one-way plane fares below may be lower during the winter months. More flights are available if you are willing to pay more.

DESTINATION	FREQUENCY	PRICE	DESTINATION	FREQUENCY	PRICE
Bangkok	1 per day	US$270	**Kuala Lumpur**	1 per day	US$70
Denpasar	4 per day	Rp700,000	**Medan**	3 per day	Rp600,000
Hong Kong	1 per day	US$265	**Singapore**	1 per day	US$90

Major airlines that serve Jakarta include: **Bouraq,** Jl. Angkasa 1 (☎628 8827); **Garuda,** Jl. Merdeka Selatan 13 (☎231 1801); **Malaysian Airlines,** World Trade Center, Jl. Sudirman (☎522 9682); **Mandala,** Jl. Veteran near Mesjid Istiqlal (☎381 1107); **Merpati,** Jl. Angasa, Kemayoran, in front of the PELNI office (☎654 6789); and **Singapore Airlines/Silk Air,** Jl. Rasuda Said (☎5790 3747). Other international airlines are in the BDN Building, Jl. Thamrin 5, next to the Sari Pan Pacific Hotel, including: **American Airlines** (☎230 0033; open M-F 8am-5pm, Sa 9am-1pm); **British Airways/Qantas** (☎230 0277; open M-F 8:30am-5pm, Sa 8:30am-12:30pm); **Continental** (☎334 417; open M-F 8:30am-4:30pm, Sa 8:30am-1pm); and **Thai Airlines** (☎230 2551; open M-F 8am-5pm, Sa 8am-noon).

BY TRAIN. Trains are more comfortable and reliable than other land transport between cities. **Gambir Station** (☎384 2777), at the center of Jakarta in Merdeka Square, is a 10min. walk from Jl. Jaksa. The information counter at the station helps decode the cryptic schedule. Tickets are sold for three classes: **first-class,** or "executive," provides reclining seats, meals, and A/C; **second-class,** or "business," means smokers galore and non-reclining seats; **economy** trains have wooden benches and broken fans. First-class tickets to most destinations are sold only at Jl. Juanda 1, Narinda Building, across the street from Mesjid Istiqlal. First-class tickets to Bogor and Bandung are sold at Gambir Station. Buy other tickets at the station or for a Rp15,000 markup at travel agents. Seats can be reserved one to seven days in advance. Weekend tickets often sell out by Friday. Many trains from Gambir run through **Kota Station** in North Jakarta, where express trains to Bogor begin. All other trains (listed below) leave from Gambir Station.

DESTINATION	DURATION	FREQUENCY	PRICE
Bandung	3hr.	many	Rp30,000-45,000
Bogor	45min.	9 per day	Rp6000-8000
Jogjakarta	7-9hr.	2 per day	Rp50,000-150,000
Semarang	8hr.	4 Exec., 2 Econ. per day	Rp45,000-170,000
Solo	9hr.	2 per day	Rp18,500-185,000
Surabaya	10hr.	4 per day	Rp23,000-250,000

BY BUS. Travel agencies around Jl. Jaksa hire comfortable private buses (non-stop, usually with A/C, and far less crowded than public buses) that whisk travelers to Java's tourist destinations. Pay for public buses on board. Bus terminals are outside Jakarta and require a complicated 1-2hr. of travel by public transportation. To get to **Kali Deres Stasiun,** take bus #77 from in front of McDonald's in Sarinah (Jl. Wahid Hasyim and Jl. Thamrin). Buses (#507) go to **Pulo Gadung Terminal** from Jl. Kebon Sirih. Many buses, including #79 and 10, leave Sarinah for **Kp. Rambutan Ter-**

minal. Travel agents do not advise economy class due to heat and risk of theft. Executive class means A/C, while Super Executive provides A/C, TV and food.

DESTINATION	TIME	FREQUENCY	PRICE
		FROM KALI DERES STASIUN	
Bengkulu	30hr.	1 per day	A/C Rp160,000
Bukit Tinggi	36hr.	3 per day	A/C Rp160,000; Super Executive Rp310,000
Medan	48hr.	many 2-3pm	A/C Rp230,000; Super Executive Rp330,000
Padang	30hr.	2 per day 2-3pm	A/C Rp160,000; Super Executive Rp310,000
		FROM PULO GADUNG TERMINAL	
Denpasar	24hr.	many, 3-6pm	A/C Rp170,500; Super Executive Rp230,000
Jogjakarta	12hr.	many, 3-5pm	A/C Rp100,000
Surabaya	14hr.	many, 2-6pm	A/C Rp138,500
		FROM KP. RAMBUTAN TERMINAL	
Bandung	3-4hr.	every 20min. 6am-10pm	A/C Rp25,000
Banjar	6hr.	hourly	A/C Rp30,000
Bogor	1hr.	every 20min. 6am-10pm	A/C Rp6500

BUS SAVVY. The buses *Let's Go* lists are only suggestions; hundreds of buses are sure to go your way. Yelling out your destination or asking someone at the stop is a good way to make sure you're on the right bus. Overcharging foreigners for bus fares is common. Some bus operators will insist on high fares; others will laugh and accept the lower fare when they realize that you know their ploy. Ask another passenger to make sure you don't pay too much.

BY BOAT. The state-run **PELNI Company** on Jl. Angkasa #18, Kemayoran (sales ☎421 1921, info ☎6385 7773) has a small fleet of A/C ships that wind their way between major harbors throughout Indonesia. Those with a supply of Dramamine and a tolerance for spartan accommodations and erratic schedules can travel on them at a reasonable cost. For tickets, head to the PELNI office or pay a surcharge and buy from a travel agency on Jl. Jaksa. PELNI offers four classes: the expensive 1st and 2nd classes have toilets and TVs; 3rd and 4th don't; *wisata* class provides a bed and a locker; economy is split into seat and non-seat (read: floor) areas.

ORIENTATION

Jakarta is divided into five regions: central Jakarta and four quadrants: north, south, east, and west.

CENTRAL JAKARTA (JAKARTA DUSIT). The area revolves around **Medan Merdeka (Freedom Square),** home to **Monas,** the national monument, and **Gambir Station.** Bordering the square is the **National Museum** to the west, **Istana Merdeka** (the Presidential Palace) to the northwest, and the **Mesjid Istiqlal** to the northeast. A 10min. walk away is **Jl. Jaksa,** home to myriad budget *losmen* and eateries. Another 10min. away, **Jl. Thamrin** boasts skyscrapers, banks, shopping plazas, and international hotels. Jl. Thamrin runs north-south; at Medan Merdeka it becomes **Jl. Merdeka Barat** (Freedom Road West) and **Jl. Hayum Wuuk** farther north.

NORTH JAKARTA (TANJUNG PRIOK). The district includes **Sunda Kelapar** (the harbor), the museum-filled **old Dutch district** (Kota), the electronics-peddling **Chinatown** (Glodok), and enormous **Jaya Ancol** leisure park. To go north, hop on any bus bound for Kota Bus Terminal.

SOUTH JAKARTA. Jl. Kemang is expat-friendly, lined with expensive bars, jazz clubs, restaurants, and a disproportionate number of furniture galleries. Farther south is **Ragunan Zoo.** The heart of south Jakarta is **Block M** station, so much of the area is referred to as "Block M."

THE REST. East Jakarta is largely industrial. Closer to Block M is the huge **Taman Mini Indonesia Indah** complex. **West Jakarta** is the site of mass flower cultivation and distribution, offering little else to visitors.

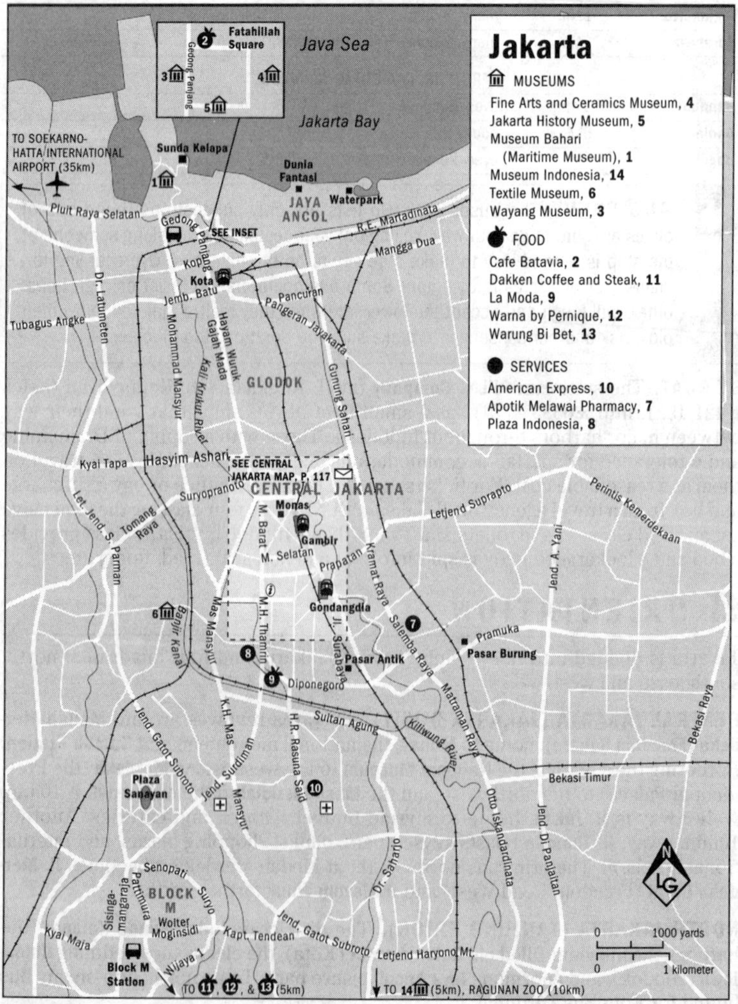

LOCAL TRANSPORTATION

There's no easy way to get around in Jakarta. A combination of patience, transportation trickery, a *Let's Go* guide, and a sense of adventure provides the quickest way to any destination.

Bajaj: Pronounced "BA-ja-ee." Rickety, smog-spewing orange three-wheelers zoom all over the city. Convenient for short trips; fix a price beforehand (Rp4000 per km).

Taxis: A/C comfort and less need for life insurance. Taxis are everywhere in Jakarta; calling for one can mean up to an hour wait. **Blue Bird Group** (☎798 9000) is by far the best, with consistent rates and safe driving. **Citra** (☎781 7233), **Silver Bird** (☎794 1234), and **Express** (☎576 1313) are decent. Get out of any taxi that does not run the meter. Rp3000 for the 1st km, Rp1300 per km after.

Buses: Run on all major roads; look for destination on windshield. Tickets sold on bus or at major stops. Ask locals to find the right route.

Microlet: Minbuses and **vans,** also known as *oplet,* run various routes. Look for destination on windshield or tell driver your destination.

Rentals: Avis, Jl. Diponegoro 25 (☎314 2900). Rp395,000-585,000 per day.

PRACTICAL INFORMATION

INDONESIA

TOURIST AND FINANCIAL SERVICES

Tourist Office: Visitor Information Center, Jl. M.H. Thamrin 9 (☎314 2067), opposite Sarinah Plaza. From Jl. Jaksa, walk south (away from Monas) to the end of the street and turn right on Jl. Wahid Hasyim. The entrance is in the Djakarta Theater building. Open unreliably M-F 9am-5pm. Another booth is in the **airport** near baggage claim, before customs. Both have free maps, brochures, shopping guides, and English-speaking help. **Information:** ☎108.

Tours: Many Jl. Jaksa establishments book bus tours and transportation. Budget travel offices on Jl. Jaksa and K.H. Wahid Hasyim cover the travel spectrum, booking seats on chartered buses to **Denpasar, Jogjakarta,** and other destinations at a small markup. **Pecto Travel,** in the BDN building, Jl. Thamrin 5 (☎230 0336), has 3-day package tours to Southeast Asian cities. Open M-F 8:30am-5pm, Sa 8:30am-noon.

Embassies and Consulates: Australia, Jl. Rasuna Said Kav. C15-16 (☎2550 5555). Take bus #P11 or #19 to Kuningan Plaza. Open M-F 7:45am-4pm. **Brunei,** 8th fl. Wisma BCA, Jl. Sudirman Kav 22-23 (☎471 2180). Open M-Th 8am-4pm. **Canada,** World Trade Center, 6th fl., Jl. Sudirman Kav. 29 (☎525 0709). Take bus for Block M and stop at Karet in front of the Meridian Hotel. Open M-Th 7:30am-4pm, F 7:30am-1pm. Visas M-F 8:30am-noon. **Laos,** Jl. Kintamani Raya C15 #33 (☎520 2673). Open M-F 8am-4pm. **Malaysia,** Jl. H.R. Rasuna Said Kav. X/6 1-3 (☎522 4947). Take bus #P11 or #66 to Jl. Prof. Dr. Satriol. Open M-Th 9am-4pm. **New Zealand** (☎570 9460), 23rd fl. BRI building, Jl. Sudirman Kav. 44-46. Open M-Th 7:30am-4pm, F 7:30am-1pm. **Philippines,** Menteng Jakarta Pusat (☎315 5118). Open M-F 8am-5pm. **Singapore,** Jl. H.R. Rasuna Said Blok X4 Kav. 2 (☎520 1489). Take bus #P11 to Mesjid. Open M-F 8:30am-5pm. Visas 8:30am-noon. **Thailand,** Jl. Imam Bonjol 74 (☎390 4054). Head 500m southwest from the traffic circle on Jl. Imam Bonjol. Open M-F 8:30am-4:30pm, consular services 8:30am-1:30pm. **UK,** Jl. M.H. Thamrin 75 (☎315 6264), near Jl. Jaksa. Open M-Th 7:45am-4pm, F 7:45am-12:45pm. **US,** Jl. Merdeka Selatan 5 (☎3435 9000). Open M-F 7:30am-4pm. **Vietnam,** Jl. Teuku Umar 25 (☎310 0357), southeast of Jl. Jaksa. Open M-F 8:30-11:30am and 1:30-4:30pm. Best time for visa applications is 9am-noon.

Currency Exchange: Airport banks offer decent rates without commission. In the city, many banks and **ATMs,** which offer slightly better rates, cluster near the Jl. Jaksa area. Traveler's checks not in US dollars can be difficult to cash, except at international banks. **BCA Bank,** Jl. Wahid Hosyim 82 (☎390 3979), cashes traveler's checks. Open M-F 8:30am-3pm. **Citibank,** Landmark Bldg., Jl. Jend Suriman 1 (☎252 9999). Hordes of **24hr. ATMs** can be found at most banks, Sarinah Plaza, and elsewhere. Some credit cards fail at certain establishments, so carry two.

American Express: Jl. Rasuna Said Blok X/1 (☎521 6111). Traveler's check services. Open M-F 8:30am-3pm.

LOCAL SERVICES

Luggage Storage: ☎550 5581. Airport Terminal D. Rp3300 per day. **Open 24hr.**

English Bookstores and Publications: Times, on the lower level of Plaza Indonesia Shopping Center beneath the Grand Hyatt on Jl. M.H. Thamrin, has British tabloids and English books. Open daily 10am-9pm. Several small book-trading posts and book-peddlers cluster along Jl. Jaksa. **The Jakarta Post** is the daily English-language newspaper. The weekly **Djakarta** magazine is half in English, half in Bahasa Indonesia and has nightlife, film, and theater listings (Rp17,500).

Pharmacies: Apotik Cerme, Jl. Wahid Hasyim 64 (☎326 207). Walk north on Jl. Jaksa and turn left; it's 100m down on the left. Open daily 8am-11:30pm. **Apotek Melawai Cabang Selemba,** Jl. Salemba Raya 57-59 (☎315 0589). **Open 24hr.** Additional pharmacies on Kebon Sirih, in the basement of Plaza Indonesia, and in Plaza Senayan.

Medical Services: Best service by doctors between 8am and 8pm. All are **open 24hr.** for emergencies. General hospitals **MMC Kuningan,** Jl. Rasuna Said Kav. C21 (☎522 5201 or 520 3435), and **RS Jakarta,** Jl. Sudirman Kav. 49 (☎573 22 41). **Ufar Madica Clinic** (☎310 2870), next to Gambir Apotik on Jl. Kebon Sirih.

INDONESIA

EMERGENCY AND COMMUNICATIONS

Emergency: Police: ☎110. **Fire:** ☎113. **Ambulance:** ☎118.

Tourist Police: ☎526 4347. Some English spoken.

Police: Jl. Sudirman 55 (☎525 0110). Another post at the corner of Jl. Wahid Hasyim and Jl. Agus Salim, near Jl. Jaksa.

Telephones: Coin (blue) and card (gray) phones on almost every street block are for local use only. For better connections, try phones in shopping centers and public buildings. **Indosat** offers **HCD** service from phones at the airport. There are several *wartel* on Jl. Jaksa. The one in the **Graha Inanta,** Jl. Jaksa 15A, offers HCD for Rp5000. **Click Internet,** Jl. Jaksa 29, has a free HCD phone. Open daily 9am-midnight.

Internet Access: Access can be found in travel agencies along Jl. Jaksa, public buildings like the Central Post Office, and, of all places, McDonald's. **Bloem Steen Hostel,** Jl. K.S. Timur I 174. Rp10,000 per hr. Open 24hr. **Click Internet** (see above) charges Rp3000 for 15min. or Rp8000 per hr. Open daily 9am-midnight. **Pinguin Internet,** 2nd fl. Sarinah Thamrin (beside Hard Rock Café). Rp8000 per hr. **Graha Inanta,** Jl. Jaksa 15A, upstairs from the travel agency. Rp10,000 per hr. Open daily 8:30am-10pm.

Post Offices: GPO, Jl. Pos 2, Pasar Baru (☎385 9889), opposite the West Indonesia Freedom Memorial, 3 buildings east of the Cathedral. Take bus #P12. *Poste Restante* at counter 43 (open M-Sa 8am-3pm). Open M-F 8am-8pm, Sa 8am-7pm, Su 8:30am-2pm. **Pt. Pos Indonesia,** on the 5th fl. of Sarinah Plaza on Jl. M.H. Thamrin (☎381 4427). Open M-Th 8am-3pm, F 8am-2pm, Sa 8am-noon. **Postal code:** 10000.

Express Mail: DHL (☎314 1708, ext. 2128), in the Djakarta Theater building, opposite Amigos bar. Open M-F 8am-4:30pm.

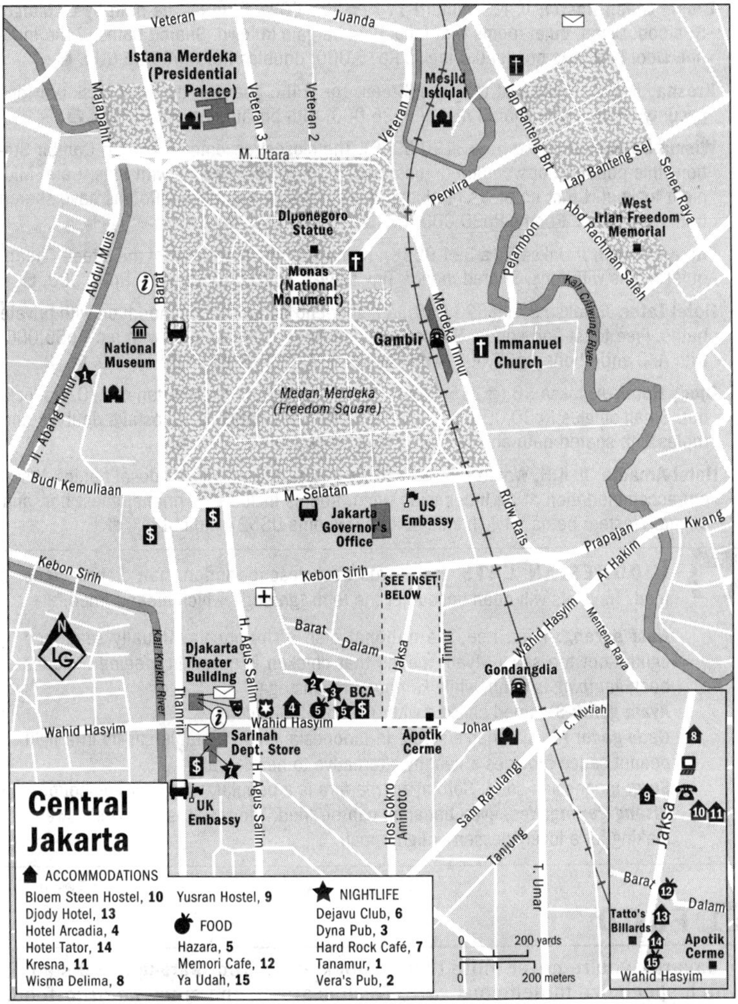

INDONESIA

ACCOMMODATIONS

Jakarta's accommodations, known locally as *losmen*, span a wide range of both prices and comfort. **Jl. Jaksa** (1km south of Gambir Station, a 15min. walk or Rp3000-3500 by *bajaj*) hosts the backpacker district. Hostel doors often close at midnight. Mosquitoes are bad, so pick up some incense coils, buy a net, or get an A/C room. It's also a good idea to bring a padlock for your door. Almost all accommodations in Jakarta have Western toilets, but eventually you'll have to get used to using a *mandi*, which involves bathing with a bucket of cold water.

Bloem Steen Hostel, Jl. K.S. Timur I 174 (☎323 002), 50m up the path by Le Margot Seafood. Clean, quiet rooms with fans. Best bargain in town. Shared baths, 24hr. Internet. Door padlocks provided. Singles Rp15,000; doubles Rp20,000-25,000. ❶

Kresna, Jl. K.S. Timur next to Bloem Steen. The 24hr. guard at the front desk provides security. Rooms with shared *mandi* Rp25,000, with private bath Rp35,000. ❷

Wisma Delima, Jl. Jaksa 5 (☎3190 5956). The closest accommodation to Gambir Station, this popular but weathered guest house offers basic rooms with fans. Cafe. Midnight lockout. Strict no drugs or alcohol policy. Books A/C buses. Rooms have shared bath downstairs. Rooms Rp30,000, with A/C Rp50,000. ❷

Yusran Hostel, Jl. Jaksa 9 (☎391 9958). Removed from the bustle of the street. Cheap, quiet rooms with fans. Shared *mandi*. Tiny singles Rp20,000; doubles Rp30,000. ❷

Hotel Tator, Jl. Jaksa 37 (☎323 940). A higher-end budget accommodation with private baths. Free toast and coffee. Singles with fan Rp45,000; doubles with fan Rp55,000, with A/C and phone Rp65,000, with hot water, A/C, and phone Rp75,000. ❸

Djody Hotel, Jl. Jaksa 35 (☎315 1404). Large range of rooms with fan or A/C. No lockout. Small singles Rp30,000; A/C doubles with bath Rp60,000; upstairs doubles and triples with shared bath and Western toilets Rp40,000-50,000. ❸

Hotel Arcadia, Jl. K.H. Wahid Hasyim 114 (☎230 0050; arcadia@indosat.net.id). Western accommodation at an Indonesian price. Rooms include TV, phone, guest bar, and private Western baths. Stylish cafe in lobby. Rooms US$27 without tax. ❺

INDONESIAN EATS Two words best describe Indonesian dishes: deep fried. Travelers will often encounter the term "*goreng,*" which means "fried."

Nasi goreng: Fried rice, the national dish of Indonesia. Usually seasoned lightly–not too spicy. *Ayam* means that chicken is mixed in, *daging* includes beef, *kambing* is lamb, while *kampung* means egg.
Ayam gulai: Steamed chicken with a coconut milk curry.
Gado-gado: A vegetarian's staple in Indonesia. This vegetable stir fry in a light peanut sauce provides a healthy alternative to heavier fare.
Soto: Indonesian soup. *Soto ayam madura* is a popular, tangy chicken soup.
Pisang goreng: Yes, even bananas can be fried. The result is not overly sweet, making for a lovely dessert or light meal.

FOOD

In Jakarta, you're never more than a block away from **warung** (food stalls), which specialize in delicious *sate*, fresh seafood, and spicy *padang* food. Ranging from little stalls to bigger areas with chairs and tables, these are your best bet for good, cheap food all over the city. The homesick can rely on international chains at one of the many malls ("plazas") in town.

Cheap backpacker restaurants cluster on **Jl. Jaksa** and one block over on **Jl. H.A. Salim.** Jl. Salim also hosts fancier restaurants, including some with A/C. Food chains pack **Jl. Wahid Hasyim** and the **Sarinah Plaza** on the corner of Jl. Hasyim and Jl. Thamrin. **Hero** and **Ramayana** supermarkets, at Sarinah and Jl. Salim 22A/B, provide the do-it-yourself option. A more upscale grocery store in the basement of Plaza Indonesia offers Western and specialty foods. Popular with expats and Indonesians alike, **Jl. Kemang Raya** hops with fancier Western bars and restaurants with higher prices. Take a cab from Jl. Jaksa (Rp20,000) or a bus from Block M.

Ya Udah, Jl. Jaksa near Jl. Wahid Hasyim, opposite Hotel Karya. Huge portions and cheap prices attract backpackers and locals alike. Good selection of German, Western, and local food. Espresso Rp4500 per pot. ❶

Memori Cafe, Jl. Jaksa 17, under the Carlsberg sign. Jam to contemporary music and rub elbows with locals and travelers while enjoying Indonesian and Western food. Often shows major sporting events on TV. Typical meal Rp8000-10,000. **Open 24hr.** ❷

Jimbani Cafe and Gallery, Jl. Kemang Raya 85 (☎719 8938). One of many "resto-galleries" in this trendy area, though this is more of a food-serving bar frequented by young Indonesians and expats. Pool table. Live music on weekends. Irish coffee Rp28,500. Cocktails Rp39,900. Happy hour 4-7pm, drinks 50% off. Open daily 11am-2am. ❸

Warna by Pernique, Jl. Kemang Selatan 101 (☎7179 3536). A real "resto-gallery." Lovely open-air courtyard caters to a higher-end crowd. Live band F-Sa 8-11pm. Expensive drinks Rp32,000-57,000. Open Su-Th 11am-11pm, F-Sa 11am-1am. ❸

Dakken Coffee and Steak, Jl. Kemang Selatan 150 (☎7883 7628), at the bottom of Jl. Kemang Raya. Less character than other places on the street, but serves exciting coffees. Avocado coffee Rp12,000. Omelettes Rp10,000. Open daily 11am-11pm. ❷

Warung Bi Bet, Jl. Kemang Raya 90A (☎718 0859), across from Jimbani. Serves coffee and local fare in a mellow *warung*-meets-indoors setting. Dishes Rp3000-10,000. Open daily 10am-10pm. ❶

La Moda, Plaza Indonesia, Grand Hyatt Hotel Jl. Thamrin. Live vocal jazz and big screen broadcasts of sporting events make this upscale restaurant comfortable. Panini sandwiches Rp22,000-36,000. Honeydew juice Rp16,000. Open daily 11am-10pm. ❹

Café Roti, Plaza Senayan 3rd fl., Jl. Asia Afrika 8. Trendy yet casual hangout. Tasty desserts. Dinner and drink Rp75,000-85,000. Open daily 11am-10pm. ❺

Hazara, Jl. Wahid Hasyim 112 (☎315 0424), next to Hotel Arcadia. Upstairs bar, pool table, the 2-for-1 happy hour before dinner, and excellent service make Hazara the expat restaurant of choice. Pricey, but the food is worth it. Entrees Rp30,000-65,000. Open daily noon-2:30pm lunch, 6-10:30pm dinner. ❺

INDONESIA

CAFES

Jakarta's cafes serve as trendy business meeting spots, but can also be a nice way to escape backpacker hangouts and read or relax in air-conditioned comfort. Plaza Senayan is the best place for cafes, but Plaza Indonesia holds its own.

The Coffee Bean & Tea Leaf, Plaza Senayan 1st fl., Jl. Asia Afrika 8 (☎572 5303). This popular meeting spot offers Western coffee shop staples at Western prices. Iced drinks Rp30,140. Muffins Rp15,000. Light lunches and breakfasts. Open daily 10am-10pm.

Tamani Café, Jl. Kemang Raya 3A (☎719 8077). This restaurant/cafe sells awesome frozen drinks, cocktails, and desserts. Try the brownies with fudge and ice cream. Drinks Rp15,000-37,000.

Phoenam, Jl. Wahid Hasyim 106 (☎314 7813). The Indonesian take on the coffee shop. Replace muffins and scones with *roti bakar* and you have Phoenam. Cheap prices go well with the A/C and cozy decor. Open daily 6:30am-10:30pm.

SIGHTS

MEDAN MERDEKA (FREEDOM SQUARE)

MESJID ISTIQLAL. Northeast of the square is the dome of Mesjid Istiqlal, the largest mosque in Southeast Asia, with a capacity of 100,000. Visitors are welcome if clothed appropriately (pants, long sleeves, and covered head). Noon prayer is

THE BIG SPLURGE

A TASTE OF HISTORY

It's hard to imagine what Jakarta, with its skyscrapers and traffic-clogged streets, was like a hundred years ago. To get a better feel for days gone by, stroll down to Cafe Batavia—you'll feel like you've stepped back into Jakarta's colonial past.

Cafe Batavia, which sits in the northwest corner of Fatahillah Square, occupies a restored colonial-era building across from the National Mus-seum. The Javan teak bar upstairs, added in 1930, has served glamorous cocktails to stylish crowds ever since—and has earned the restaurant a spot on Newsweek's "World's Best Bars" list—twice! First-time visitors should save a few minutes to study the hundreds of old photographs that cover the walls. Original antique furnishings complete the historical atmosphere.

Background swing music, slow-spinning fans, and fine cuisine draw an expat crowd to Sunday brunch. In the evenings, Cafe Batavia is a favorite hangout for Jakarta's well-heeled thirty-somethings.

The menu includes traditional Indonesian and Chinese dishes, but the house specialty remains modern Australian cuisine. The Crêpe Parmentierre with smoked salmon and caviar is a delicious luxury (Rp66,000). Beer is sold for Rp20,000, while cocktails are Rp57,000. Top off your meal with Batavia's famous homemade ice cream—if you have room. *(☎691 5531 or 691 5334; fax 692 3842. Open 24hr.)* ❺

crowded, but breathtaking. Listen for the five daily "calls to prayer" for the best times to visit. The entrance is on the north side, on Jl. Veteran. *(Free.)*

ISTANA MERDEKA (PRESIDENTIAL PALACE). Dominating the top of the square, the palace is used only for presidential functions. It makes a good snapshot while in the area, but visitors quickly move on.

MONAS. In the center of the square is Monas, Indonesia's national monument. Also known as **Sukarno's Last Erection,** this 132m monument represents the strength, freedom, and fertility of the nation, and also makes a good reference point. The base of the monument contains a diorama of Indonesia's fight for independence. *(Monument and museum open daily 8:30am-5pm, closed last M of every month. Museum and tower Rp5100, students Rp3600, children Rp2600.)*

NATIONAL MUSEUM. Across the street 300m to the west, the museum is recognizable by a small elephant statue out front. It has a vast stockpile of artifacts from all over the archipelago, ranging from Ming Dynasty pottery to models of traditional houses from the islands. *(Open Tu-Th and Su 8:30am-2:30pm, F 8:30-11:30am, Sa 8:30am-1:30pm. Free tours Tu-Th 9:30am, second Sa and last Su of every month 10:30am. Rp750, students Rp250, children Rp150.)*

TEXTILE MUSEUM. The museum displays over 300 types of fabric, including colorful *batik* sarongs, woven pieces and traditional instruments with some English descriptions. *(Jl. K.S. Tubun 4. Take a* bajaj *from Jl. Jaksa (Rp7000). Open Tu-Sa 9am-3pm, Su 9am-2pm. Rp2000, students Rp1000, children Rp600.)*

FATAHILLAH SQUARE

One kilometer northeast of Kota Station is Fatahillah Square, surrounded by Dutch period buildings where public executions were held.

JAKARTA HISTORY MUSEUM. This weathered building with teal shutters was formerly known as the Batavia Town Hall. Antique Dutch and traditional Indonesian furniture and a dozen ornate muskets are displayed. Some descriptions are in English. *(☎692 9101. Open Tu-Su 9am-3pm. Rp2000, students Rp1000, children Rp600.)*

WAYANG MUSEUM. The Dutch museum on the west side of the square houses an extensive collection of *wayang kulit* (leather) and *wayang golek* (wooden) puppets. There are puppets of modern-day bureaucrats and vignettes from revolutionary movements. Descriptions are somewhat lacking, making the displays hard to follow. *(☎629 2560. Open Tu-Su 9am-3pm. Rp2000, students Rp1000, children Rp600.)*

FINE ARTS AND CERAMICS MUSEUM. The large museum is set back on the east side of the square. Ceramics include modern *kreatif*, foreign pieces, and eerie carved tree-trunk totems. The tree in front of the building provides a welcome bit of shade. *(☎690 7062. Open Tu-Su 9am-3pm. Rp2000, students Rp1000, children Rp600.)*

OTHER SIGHTS

SUNDA KELAPA (OLD HARBOR). Northwest of Fatahillah Square, the Old Harbor features panoramic **Jl. Pasar Ikan,** which begins under a metal gate and continues past shops of all sorts to the water (see **Markets,** below). The **Museum Bahari (Maritime Museum),** on the beginning of Jl. Pasar Ilkan, is in the breezy storehouses of the Dutch East India Company, where the feel of old Batavia still lingers. The sight of old Makassar schooners sailing in the morning is truly one of the most exotic sights in Jakarta. *(☎669 3406. 20min. walk, or take a* bajaj *for Rp3000. Open Tu-Th and Su 9am-3pm, F 9am-2pm, Sa 9am-1pm. Rp2000, students 1000, children Rp600.)*

RAGUNAN ZOO. A large, green zoo where animals are kept in their natural habitats. All sorts of standard zoo animals roam here, but the most fabulous by far are the Komodo dragons, who bask like mini-dinosaurs. *(Take any bus for Ragunan. Open daily 7am-6pm. Rp3000, children under 12 Rp2000; Rp1500 extra for snake house.)*

TAMAN MINI INDONESIA INDAH. In this huge complex on the southeast corner of Jakarta, "you can see all of Indonesia in a day." The complex includes the **Museum Indonesia,** which displays traditional artwork, cultural dioramas, and flicks about Indonesia at the Imax Theater. English-speaking guides lead tours of 27 full-size provincial houses. Other areas, from the aviary to the Islamic museum, appeal to specialized interests. On crowded Sunday mornings, there are traditional dance performances. *(☎840 9210. Take bus #P11 from Sarinah, or bus #P15 from Block M, and then take a* microlet *from the Kampung Rambutan Station. Open Tu-Su 8am-5pm. Rp4000, children Rp3000, Sa-Su Rp1000 extra. Museum of Indonesia open daily 9am-4pm. Rp3000. Imax every hr. 11am-4pm. Rp6000. Rp25,000 for full-day all-access pass.)*

MARKETS

Huge malls and open-air markets are scattered throughout Jakarta and frequented by chic families. Other markets cater to the everyday man.

Pasar Ikan, in Sunda Kelapa. The fish market is a tile-roofed building on Jl. Pasar Ikan, 400m up from the Maritime Museum. Activity is almost endless, but when the catch comes in after 9pm, everything else shuts down. The fish on sale come in every shape, size, and color imaginable. Beyond the Maritime Museum, shops sell gear to prepare ships for sea—huge anchors, chains, and cables are carted from place to place.

Pasar Antik, running along Jl. Surabaya, a Rp5000 *bajaj* ride from Jl. Jaksa, is full of beautiful handicrafts from around the archipelago. Decorative items from ship wheels to ebony sculptures and ashtrays overflow from the stalls. Shopkeepers do their utmost to get you bargaining—once you've started it's expected you'll buy. Open daily 8am-6pm.

Pasar Burung, on Jl. Pramuka behind the big yellow and blue Pasar Pramuka, a Rp4000 *bajaj* ride from Jl. Jaksa. The twitter of birds slowly grows louder until millions are visible in their cages—from colorful budgies to magnificent (and outlawed) eagles. Pesky peddlers are known to hassle travelers. Open daily 6am-6pm.

Pasar Mangga Dua, on Jl. Mangga Dua, is full of electronics. Shops continue down from the top of Jl. Hayam Wuruk. **Jl. Pancuran** leads off Jl. Hayam Wuruk 300m down and through Glodok, boasting a huge **fruit market** running the length of the street. Although this market is full of deals, peddlers can be aggressive.

SHOPPING

Teenage mall culture is all the rage in Jakarta. Pricey and sterile food stalls cater to hordes of school kids while the chic-chic head straight to the designer stores.

Sarinah Department Store, on the corner of Jl. Wahid Hasyim Romald and Jl. Thamrin, a 10min. walk from Jl. Jaksa. Look for a frighteningly large inflatable Ronald McDonald. Less extravagant than some malls in town, Sarinah is the place for lesser designer clothes and Rp70,000 CDs. Supermarket downstairs. Several **24hr. ATMS** outside.

Plaza Senayan, Jl. Asia Afrika 8. Senayan has a cinema, bowling alley, and pool as well as American food chains and European couturiers. A daytime hangout for rich kids, it's best used for its recreational facilities and cafes (see **Cafes,** p. 119). Open M-F 8am-9pm, Sa-Su 8am-midnight.

Plaza Indonesia, Grand Hyatt Hotel, Jl. Thamrin. 1km up from Sarinah on the right. Much of the Hyatt's grandeur has leaked down to this 5-floor A/C mall. Piano music wafts through the air and Italian shoes sell for Rp3,000,000. A grocery store in the basement offers affordable foods and a lovely bakery. Open daily 10am-10pm.

ENTERTAINMENT

INDONESIA

At the end of the day, Jakarta has the typical big city offerings: movies, bowling, and billiards abound. Many malls offer these distractions in one stop.

CENTRAL JAKARTA. Djakarta Theater, at the corner of Jl. Wahid Hasyim and Jl. Thamrin, 10min. from Jl. Jaksa, has three screens showing last year's English movies beginning at 2pm. A similar setup runs at **Plaza Senayan,** on Jl. Asia Afrika. Plaza Senayan also boasts 30 **bowling lanes** and a big pool hall. (Bowling Rp12,000 before 4pm, Rp15,000 after. Pool Rp18,000 per hr. before 4pm, Rp24,000 after. Open daily 10am-10pm.) English movies play on the 4th floor of the plaza (Rp40,000).

NORTHERN JAKARTA. Jaya Ancol is a massive entertainment complex of Disney-like proportions. A resort facility on the coast, it's next to the mercury-laden sea, but the nearby **waterpark** has decent slides. (Open M-F 9am-4pm, Sa-Su 7am-7pm. M-F Rp15,000, Sa-Su Rp17,500.) Near the main entrance to Jaya Ancol is **Jaya Ancol Bowl.** (Rp9000 per game before 4pm, Rp13,000 after. Shoes Rp3000. Open daily 10am-1am.) **Dunia Fantasi** has a roller coaster, a ferris wheel, and other rides and games for children. (Open M-Sa 9am-4pm, Su 10am-10pm. Full pass Rp40,000.) **Sea World** aquarium boasts over 6000 aquatic animals and daily sting ray and shark feedings in the main aquarium. To get there, take bus #P64 from Kota, *microlet* #15 from Sunda Kelapa, or bus #60 up Jl. Gunung Sahar. (☎641 0080. Open M-F 9am-6pm, Sa-Su 9am-7:30pm. Feedings M-F 11am, 3:30pm; Sa-Su 11am, 2:30, 5:30pm. Rp25,000.)

NIGHTLIFE

Cheap beer flows nightly along Jl. Jaksa as live music softens the murmur of backpacker chit-chat. The dancing queen in everyone is well served by Jakarta's many nightclubs. Some establishments are rather seedy, pushing the skin trade, while others are the height of glamor.

NEAR JL. JAKSA

Hard Rock Café, Sarinah Jl. Thamrin. Locals claim it is the best Hard Rock in Southeast Asia. Although that's questionable, this club is dependable and quite popular with locals and expats alike. Beer Rp23,500-36,000. Happy hour before 8pm. Open M-Th 8:30am-10:30pm, F-Sa 8:30am-11pm, Su 8:30am-10:30pm.

Vera's Pub, Jl. Wahid Hasyim 116 (☎391 3592), 5min. from Jl. Jaksa down a side street after Dyna Pub. A Jl. Jaksa crowd. Stake out your space on the small dance floor. Beer Rp19,500. Open daily 9pm-3am.

Dyna Pub, Jl. Wahid Hasyim 116A, down the side street after Bank BCA. Quiet and cozy–somewhere between an Irish pub and old gentlemen's club. Ideal for a drink away from the backpacker droves. Bintang or Guinness Rp19,000. Open daily 11am-2am.

Dejavu Club, Jl. Wahid Hasyim 88, upstairs from Parkit Restaurant. Boasting an "artist" clientele and gentle, jazz-like music nightly. Older Indonesian family crowd. Partner dancing and a lack of heavy drinking. Beer Rp19,000. Open daily 9pm-2am.

ELSEWHERE IN JAKARTA

Jl. Hayam Wuruk in **Glodok** has a reputation for extremely large, overwhelming, and seedier clubs. The most happening places are in luxurious hotels. Cover charges and drinks aren't budget-friendly, but the clubs provide a chance to observe the top end of Jakarta's society. Taxis are the only way to get around.

Retro, on Jl. Sudirman, in the Crown Plaza Hotel. Another hangout of the rich and beautiful (and some mere mortals). Reputedly some of the best music in town–Top 40 with good lights and enough space to enjoy it. Torn trousers won't do. Cover W and F-Sa Rp50,000. Open Su-Tu and Th 10pm-1am, W 10pm-3am, F-Sa 10pm-4am.

Musro, Hotel Borobudur, Jl. Lapangan Banteng near Station Juanda. For a taste of how locals do swanky nightlife, go to Musro. Music is a mix of Top 40 and Indonesian dance. Rp100,000 cover includes all non-alcoholic drinks. Open M-F 9am-8pm, Sa 6pm-2am.

Tanamur, Jl. Abang Timur 14 (☎380 5233). Jostle with tourists, expats, and Indonesians in this club. Fast music. Beer Rp25,000. Go-go dancers M-Sa at midnight, 1, and 2am. Gay-friendly. Cover Rp30,000. Open daily 9pm-3am.

CARITA AND LABUAN ☎0253

These neighboring coastal towns, a 3hr. drive or bus ride from Jakarta, provide relief from the chaotic metropolis and make good stops on the way to Ujung Kulon National Park. Carita's beach brims with vacationing Indonesians while Labuan, a neighboring fishing town, offers a glimpse into small city Javanese life.

TRANSPORTATION

The **bus terminal** in Labuan, between the market and police station, has buses to: **Bogor** (5-6hr.; 5 per day; Rp12,000) and **Jakarta** (3-4hr.; 5am-10pm; Rp10,000). Minibuses also go to **Sumur** (2½hr.; every hr.; Rp10,000). **Becak** swarm around Labuan and are ideal for short trips. To get to Carita, hop on an **angkot** (Rp2000) or **ojek** (Rp6000) from the road or at the bus terminal.

ORIENTATION AND PRACTICAL INFORMATION

One main road goes through Labuan and Carita—the kilometer distances used in some street addresses are measured from the Labuan terminal. **Jl. Jenderal Sudirman** begins in Labuan and changes its name frequently as it runs west past the **bus terminal.** At **Pasar Labuan,** it swings right and becomes **Jl. Printis Kemerdekaan.** One kilometer farther, it bends left and crosses a bridge. Seven kilometers farther, now **Jl. Raya Carita,** it passes **Pantai Carita,** the **beach,** and a strip of densely-packed

guest houses. A 1½hr. trek through the hills behind Carita on a well-marked path leads to scenic **Curug Endang (Drum Falls Waterfall).**

Tourist Office: PHPA Office, Jl. Printis Kemerdekaan 51 (☎801 731), in Labuan. 1.5km up the road toward Carita. Insurance Rp2500. 1-week permits to Ujung Kulon and Krakatau (Rp2000). Helpful maps and information for solo travelers. Open M-Th 8am-3:30pm, F 8-11am and 1:30-3:30pm.

Tours: Black Rhino Tourist Information Service, Jl. Raya Carita Km10 (☎802 818), offers 2- to 4-day group trips to trek, dive, or surf in Ujung Kulon (minimum 2-4 people, 4 days/3 nights US$100-150) and daytrips to Krakatau (US$30-60). Lower prices for big groups. **Wanawisata,** Jl. Printis Kemerdekaan 43 (☎803 845), near Hotel Rawayana, organizes 3hr. canoe trips in the park to see jungle beasties (US$8).

Currency Exchange: Banks and moneychangers offer poor rates; ATMs in town are better. Labuan's **BRI,** Jl. Jend. Sudirman 156 (☎801 214), has a **24hr. ATM** 200m past the bus terminal from the market. Cash traveler's checks in **Cilegon** (2hr. north).

Rentals: Pricey **Marina Lippo Carita,** Jl. Raya Carita Km10, rents water sports gear.

Markets: Pasar Labuan, at the bend of Jl. Jend. Sudirman, sells ordinary wares. Stock up at **Super Bazaar Supermarket,** run by the Matahari company. Open daily 9am-9pm.

Police: Jl. Jend. Sudirman 176 (☎801 110), 50m from the bus terminal with your back to the market.

Pharmacy: Toko Obat Sumber Sehat, Jl. Jend. Sudirman 190C (☎801 153), next to Super Bazaar. Open daily 8am-8pm.

Medical Services: Clinic, Jl. Jend. Sudirman 164 (☎801 009), beside the green cross sign, 100m down from the police.

Telephones: Most **wartel** on Labuan offer **international** calls. Open daily 7am-9pm.

Post Office: GPO, Jl. Printis Kemerdekaan 40, 2km from the bus terminal in Labuan, beyond the bridge toward Carita. Open M-Th 7:30am-3pm, F 7:30-11am, Sa 7:30am-1pm. **Postal code:** 42264.

ACCOMMODATIONS

In Carita, hotels and guest houses line a 4km strip on Jl. Raya Carita, a 15min. minibus ride from the Labuan bus terminal. Weekend and holiday rates are sky-high—visit during the week if you're strapped for cash. There's not much to do in Labuan, but it's less resort-like than Carita.

CARITA

Restoran Seafood Carita Krakatau, Jl. Raya Carita Km10.3 (☎803 027). The best value in town is hidden in this roadside restaurant. Clean rooms with Western toilet and shower. Su-Th Rp30,000, F-Sa Rp40,000, holidays Rp60,000. ❸

Bandok Lucia, Jl. Raya Carita Km11 (☎801 261), farther up the road. Spacious rooms in a relaxed atmosphere. Cafe, ping-pong table, and a swimming pool. Clean doubles with fan and private *mandi* Su-Th Rp50,000, F-Sa Rp60,000, holidays Rp80,000. ❹

Yusi Inn, Jl. Raya Carita Km10 (☎801 074), next to Black Rhino Tours. Clean rooms with pleasant balconies and sitting areas offer fan-cooled respite from the beach heat. Doubles with shared *mandi* Su-Th Rp40,000, F-Sa Rp45,000, holidays Rp80,000. ❸

Pondok Pandawa, Jl. Raya Carita Km9 (☎802 139). Bamboo bungalows in the middle of the action on the beach. Doubles with private *mandi,* Western toilet, and fan Su-Th Rp50,000, F-Sa Rp70,000, holidays Rp170,000. ❹

LABUAN

Hotel Rawayana, Jl. Printis Kemerdekaan 41 (☎801 386), past the bridge toward Carita, 100m before the PHPA office. Outside town and set back from main road. Big, clean bungalows for 2 with fan, Western toilet, and *mandi* Rp30,000. ❷

Hotel Caringin, Jl. Printis Kemerdekaan 9 (☎801 388), on the way to Carita, 300m after the bridge. Friendly management. Clean doubles with *mandi* Rp30,000, with fan Rp40,000; triples with fan Rp50,000. ❷

FOOD

Labuan's *padang* restaurants and *warung* serve delicious, cheap Indonesian meals. Carita has fewer *warung* along the road but more small, inexpensive Indonesian restaurants. Check out **Rumah Makan Diminati ❷,** 50m from Black Rhino Tours, for an excellent Western, Chinese, and Indonesian menu in English. (Beef steak Rp17,500. Local fare Rp3000-8000. Open daily 6:30am-9pm.) **Maya Kantin Restaurant ❶,** right next door to Black Rhino, has Indonesian eats and an English menu. (Dishes Rp3000-8000. Open daily 6am-9pm.) For generous portions of grilled crab, squid, and fish (Rp10,000-15,000), try the woven-bamboo restaurants along the road. Particularly notable is **Rumah Makan Lancar ❸,** halfway between Labuan and Carita. Try the filling and tasty *otak-otak* (fish cakes).

INDONESIA

DAYTRIP FROM CARITA: UJUNG KULON NATIONAL PARK

The park is 4hr. southwest of Labuan. Leave your bags at your hostel, but load up on food and water before leaving—they're cheaper at the supermarket than in the park. Take a minibus to Sumur (3hr.; last bus 3pm; Rp10,000) and then an ojek *to Tamanjaya (1hr.; Rp20,000). Alternatively, 2 direct buses leave Ujung Kulon at 5:30am and return from Labuan between 11am and 1pm. Permits allow one-week access.*

The park is famous for Javan rhinos and its rich assortment of rainforest wildlife. A UNESCO World Heritage Site, it has seen major preservation efforts in the last few years. Off the coast and on the beaches, evidence of the 1883 **Krakatau explosion** and the ensuing 40m high tsunami are still visible (see **The Wrath of Krakatau,** p. 314). The spectacular secluded beaches of the south coast are still totally undeveloped. The best wildlife inhabits the least accessible areas around **Pulau Handeleum** and **Pulau Peucang.** (Rp750,000 by boat from Tamanjaya for 15 people. Smaller groups might be able to tear the fishermen away from their work for less.) A five-day hike around Ujung Kulon will give cheaper access to wildlife. A boat to Pulau Peucang can be taken from a guidepost (US$3). Consider packing snacks and lounging on one of several beautiful empty **beaches** between Sumur and Tamanjaya—they're worth the trip from Labuan.

Tickets, information, and advice on the park are available at the **PHPA office** and from locals in Labuan. Tourist agencies in Carita sell expensive package tours, but freelance guides are cheaper. There is another PHPA office in Tamanjaya, but employees there speak less English than in Labuan. (Tours Rp25,000-30,000 per person per day including food and cigarettes, Rp20,000 without.) Spiritual pilgrims hire *kuncen* who tap into the powers of the forest using special rituals (Rp50,000).

There are two accommodations in Tamanjaya. **Wisma Wisata Alam ❸** has bungalow doubles opening onto a well-manicured lawn and gorgeous sunset view. Mosquito net or coils are a must. The owner is well informed and speaks the best English in town. (Shared baths have Western toilets. Rp35,000 with breakfast.) **Penginapau Sunda Jaya ❶,** down the road, offers mosquito nets and a better value for single travelers. (Rp15,000 per person.)

In the park, camping with a mosquito net and waterproof ground cloth is feasible. Leaving Rp20,000 (more for bigger groups) for the watchman is a common courtesy best fulfilled via your guide. **Cimayang** ❶ is a favorite campground near the river. **Rangers' houses** ❷ also have rooms available (Rp20,000 or less), though many are in poor condition. One exception is on **Pulau Peucang** ❸ (doubles Rp50,000); another favorite spot is with the **lighthouse keeper.** Those stranded in Sumur can stay in the **Penginapan Citra Ayu** ❷ (Rp20,000 for clean quiet rooms).

BOGOR ☎0251

Dubbed "*Sans-Souci*" or "without worries" by the Dutch, Bogor was originally the site (chosen for its temperate climate) of capitals built by ancient Hindu-Buddhist kings. Centuries later, colonists made the town a site for weekend retreats, and the city retains a similar role today. Virtually a suburb of Jakarta, Bogor is cosmopolitan enough to satisfy a traveler's longing for creature comforts, yet small enough to provide refuge from the madness of the city. Most find it preferable to stay in Bogor and explore Jakarta rather than vice-versa. Bogor's world-renowned botanical gardens, the city's heart and soul, flourish with the nourishment of the high rainfall of West Java. Don't miss the peaceful waterfalls at Air Terjun Cilember (see **Daytrips,** p. 129) or the hot springs of nearby Puncak.

TRANSPORTATION

Trains: The **train station** (☎324 529), on Jl. Permas, is west of the Botanical Gardens off Jl. Kapten Muslihat. To get from the hostels on Jl. Palendang to the train station, take *angkot* #02 northbound and get off at the end of the road. Walk down the road to the right, turn left into the alley with *warungs* and street vendors. The station will be on your left. To **Jakarta** (economy 1hr., every 30min. 4am-9:30pm, Rp6000; executive express 30min., 9 per day until 5pm, Rp8000). Major central and east Javanese city routes go through Jakarta; ask a travel agent for these destinations.

Buses: The **terminal** is 1km southeast of the Botanical Gardens on Jl. Raya Pajajaran. To **Bandung** (economy up to 7hr., express 4hr.; Rp12,000-20,000) and **Jakarta** (Kali Deres, Tanjung Priok, and Pulo Gadung: 1½hr.; every 15min., Rp3000-5000; Kp. Rambutan: 45min., every 15min., Rp3000-5000). Buses to **Jogjakarta** and **Surabaya** go through Jakarta.

Local Transportation: Short-distance **angkot** head to the Puncak and surrounding areas from the Sukasari minibus "terminal" in South Bogor—take *angkot* #2 to the "terminal." *Angkot* swarm local roads on fixed routes at fixed rates (Rp1000), and **becak** are everywhere. Prices vary depending on weight and distance but should generally be around Rp3000 and never exceed Rp5000. Slower **delman** (pony carts) linger by gardens, but the ride is not so romantic when stuck in traffic.

ORIENTATION AND PRACTICAL INFORMATION

Bogor is built around the rectangular **Botanical Gardens,** home to many plant species and one of five Indonesian Presidential Palaces, the **Istana Bogor.** The gardens are bounded by **Jl. Ir. H. Juanda** to the west, **Jl. Otista** to the south, and **Jl. Raya Pajajaran** to the east (which leads to the **bus station**). Extending away from the palace to the west is **Jl. Kapten Muslihat,** toward **Taman Topi (Hat Park)** and the **train station.** Most guest houses lie on Jl. Raya Pajajaran and Jl. Palendang.

Tourist Offices: Jl. Palendang 35 (☎332 775). Hidden behind two white buildings. Maps and palace tours available. Open M-F 8am-4pm. **Tourist Information Center,** in Taman Topi, on Jl. Permas side. Unreliably open M-F 8am-7pm.

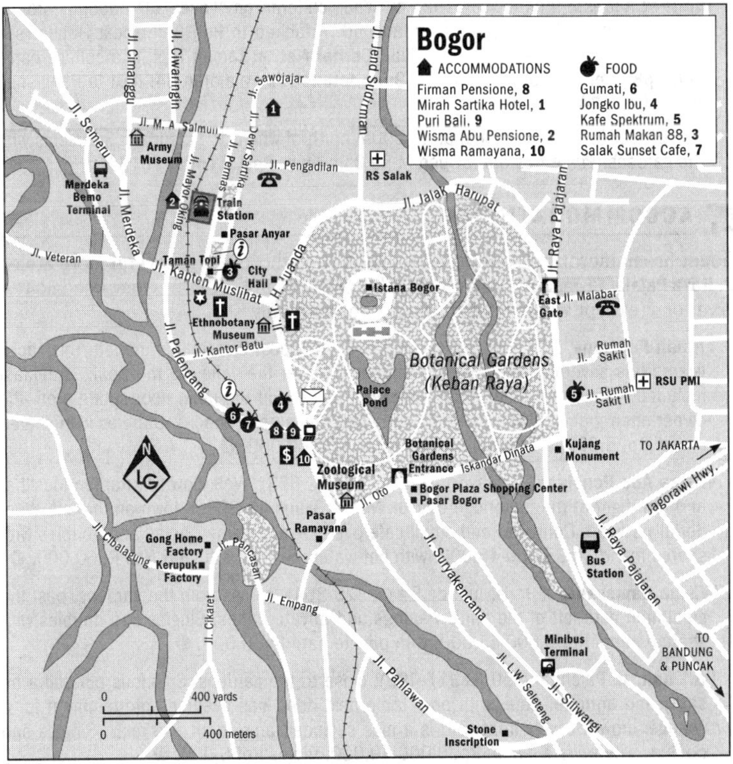

Tours: Travel Bureau Mulia Rahayu, Jl. Mayor Oking 18-20 (☎324 150). Books airplane and PELNI boat tickets. Open daily 8am-5pm. **Larasati Tours and Travel** (☎338 361), on Jl. Kapten Muslihat, in a hat-shaped building at Taman Topi, southeast of the train station. Open M-F 8am-5pm, Sa 8am-4pm, Su 9am-1pm.

Currency Exchange: Bank Bali, Jl. Kapten Muslihat 17A (☎312 990), near the railway station. **ATM.** Open M-F 8am-3pm; exchange available M-F 10am-2pm. Numerous other banks with ATMs are along Jl. Raya Pajajaran and Jl. Juanda.

Markets: Pasar Anyar, on Jl. Dewi Sartika beside Taman Topi, offers everything from *anjaman* (weaving) to *zaitun minyac* (olive oil). **Pasar Bogor,** Jl. Suryakencana 3, is near the gate to the Botanical Gardens behind **Bogor Plaza Shopping Center.**

Emergency: Police: ☎110. **Fire:** ☎113. **Ambulance:** ☎118.

Police: Jl. Kapten Muslihat 16 (☎381 360), opposite the soldier statue at Taman Topi. Open 24hr.

Medical Services: RS Salak, Jl. Jend. Sudirman 8 (☎344 609), with **pharmacy** (☎320 496) next door. **RSU PMI,** on Jl. Rumah Sakit II. Both open 24hr.

Telephones: *Wartel,* Jl. Pengadilan 14, to the left of Telkom, offers **international calls** daily 4:30am-midnight. **Wartel Exotica,** Jl. Kapten Muslihat 51, at Taman Topi. Open daily 7am-midnight.

Internet Access: Internet cafes full of schoolchildren on "Lovemail" abound. Around Rp5000 per hr. **B@linet,** Jl. Palendang 50. Attached to Puri Bali Guest House (see below). Open daily 9am-midnight. **Blue Corner Net,** at Taman Topi, is a college hangout. Rp85 per min. Open daily 9am-9pm. **Infonet,** Jl. Pajajaran 34, next to Pangrango Hotel. **Open 24hr.**

Post Office: GPO, Jl. Ir. H. Juanda 5, 200m north of where Jl. Palendang intersects with the gardens. *Poste Restante.* Open M-Sa 8am-4pm. **Postal code:** 16124.

ACCOMMODATIONS

Bogor has numerous guest houses. In addition to those listed, several more are on **Jl. Raya Pajajaran** east of the gardens. All of these listings offer free tea, need no reservations (except where noted), and accept cash only.

Firman Pensione, Jl. Palendang 48 (☎323 3246), past Puri Bali on the left. This social *wisma* has several sitting areas that look out over the valley to the peak. Breakfast included; cafe offers other meals as well. Hang out in the main floor sitting area—the owner often graces it with her delicious, free, homemade snacks. Doubles with shared *mandi* Rp25,000, with private *mandi* Rp30,000-40,000. ❷

Wisma Abu Pensione, Jl. Mayor Oking 15 (☎322 893). Walk down Jl. Kapten Muslihat and turn right at the footbridge onto Jl. Mayor Oking; it's 300m down on the left. Wonderfully serene. Courtyard and small cafe overlook a stream. Singles and doubles with shared *mandi* Rp35,000-45,000, with hot water, private bath, and A/C Rp60,000. ❸

Wisma Ramayana, Jl. Ir. H. Juanda 54 (☎320 364), across from the gardens, past the small iron gate left of the bank. *Pajungs* and private patios. Singles and doubles with shared *mandi* Rp40,000-45,000, with private bath Rp60,000. ❸

Puri Bali, Jl. Palendang 50 (☎317 498), close to the gardens. Spacious but still a bit stuffy and antique. Cafe, with pool table next door, has evening entertainment for a younger crowd. Lovely front yard is a nice secluded area to sit and relax. Singles and doubles with private *mandi* Rp30,000-40,000; triples Rp50,000. ❷

Mirah Sartika Hotel, Jl. Dewi Sartika 6A (☎312 343 or 340 387). Higher-end hotel offering clean, comfortable rooms complete with A/C, color TV, fridge, phone, and Western baths. Reservations recommended. Singles Rp110,000; doubles Rp121,000. ❺

FOOD

Warung line Jl. Dewi Sartika. Those by the railway station are seedier but make scrumptious *martabak*. **Bakeries** are in almost every supermarket and on each street corner. The **Salak Sunset Cafe ❷,** Jl. Palendang, across the train tracks, boasts a great view and a relaxed setting. Your wallet will enjoy their refreshing house drink (Sirsak juice Rp5000) and the fantastic local and foreign food. (Open M-F noon-11pm, Su 4-11pm.) For great Sundanese food, try **Jongko Ibu ❸** across from the post office, and **Mirah Sari ❷,** Jl. Merdeka 48. (Both open daily 9am-10:30pm.) Taman Topi has a slew of restaurants including **Rumah Makan 88 ❶,** which serves cheap Sudanese and Indonesian food (Rp4000-10,000). **Kafe Spektrum ❺,** Jl. Raya Pajajaran 35, in the Permata Hotel before the hospital, has nightly live music, karaoke, and Western food at Western prices. (Open daily 11am-midnight.) Come to **Gumati ❺,** Jl. Palendang 26, 150m from the gardens, for the best yet priciest view in town, and stay for a mediocre meal (oxtail Rp21,000) and a decent band. (☎313 422. Open M-F 10am-11pm, Sa-Su 10am-midnight. Bands F-Sa 7:30-10:30pm. Reservations recommended Sa-Su. Visa accepted.)

SIGHTS

Out a sprawling 87 hectares in the center of Bogor sits the stately **Istana Bogor** and the surrounding **Kebun Raya (Botanical Gardens).** Established for the Dutch governor of Indonesia, Baron Van Imhoff, as an escape from the capital, Istana Bogor housed many guests of the state and became a presidential retreat upon the country's independence in 1945. History buffs will notice Sukarno's influence in the inordinate number of statues and paintings of nude women. These women, along with his four wives, surely brightened up Sukarno's house arrest here (1967-70). Gaining admission to the grounds is a bit tricky—a consequence of Indonesian politics. Groups of 10 can visit if they request permission one week in advance, but all are welcome on national holidays.

Viewing **Kebun Raya** is simpler. The park's entrance is on the south side on Jl. Otista. Formerly part of Bogor Palace, these gardens were converted to a collection of indigenous, foreign, and exotic botanical species for educational and scientific purpose in the late 18th and early 19th centuries. Those in the mood for a soothing stroll can meander along the four recommended routes (about 1hr. each), and guides give naturalists the scoop on the thousands of unique species. (Open daily 8am-5pm. Last tickets sold at 3pm. Rp3000. Guides Rp25,000.)

Across the street from the Pasar Ramayana food market are the inanimate skeletons and stuffed animals of the **Zoological Museum,** 200m west of the entrance to the gardens. (Open daily 8am-4pm. Rp1500.) On Jl. Kantor Batu, opposite a castle-like church, is the **Ethnobotany Museum,** Jl. Ir. H. Juanda 22-24. Enter on the north side of the building to see traditional Indonesian instruments, baskets, and pottery. (Open daily 9am-3pm. Rp1500.)

Tourists can also visit the **Gong Home Factory,** Jl. Pancasan 17. A small donation of a couple thousand rupiahs is expected. Bring a pack of cigarettes to make a whole bunch of friends while enjoying the musical rhythms of metal-hammering. (Take blue *angkot* #3 from the Zoological Museum. Open Sa-Th 8am-noon and 1-4pm.) Head up the hill and turn right at the dentist sign to visit a **kerupuk factory.** The dough is kneaded, spun into cakes, dried, and dropped into hot oil. (Open daily 6am-noon and 1-4pm.) An ancient **stone inscription** *batutulis*, dating from the mid-14th century and the Pajajaran Kingdom, can be seen on Jl. Batutulis. Take *angkot* #2 10min. south of the garden, or walk (30min.).

DAYTRIPS FROM BOGOR

Buses from the main bus terminal or the Sukusari bus terminal (via green *angkot* #2) reach countless destinations in the outlying areas near Bogor. Travelers can escape to **Pelabuhanratu,** a hill-bounded coastal town to the southwest. It takes four hours by share-taxi (total Rp250,000 can be split by up to 8 people) and an indeterminate amount of time by bus (economy Rp8000; A/C Rp15,000). Unfortunately, currents render it unsafe for swimming in all but the bay area. Beaches around **Ujung Genteng** have great surfing and reasonable accommodations. Share the beaches at twilight with night-loving giant turtles. From Pelabuhanratu a bus will take you to Suradi and a *bemo* will get you to Genteng. For Rp50,000, a stay at **Mama's ❸** will keep you well-fed and happy.

To reach the seven peaceful **Air Terjun Cilember** (Cilember Waterfalls), one of the few places near Jakarta where the air doesn't smell like exhaust, take *angkot* #2 to Terminal Sukasari and then a blue #2 minibus halfway to Cisarva (Rp2500). Look for the blue gates and then catch an *ojek* (Rp2000-4000) to the entrance. The tough hike is deserted on weekdays; solo travelers might consider visiting on weekends. (Entrance fee Rp2000. Guides for less traversed routes roughly Rp5000-10,000.)

Taman Safari, in Cisarva, is more like a drive-through zoo than a safari. A swimming pool and other entertainment make this a fun half-day trip from Puncak. (☎0251 253 222. Take an *angkot* 30min. from Cilember (Rp1000); tell the driver to stop at the Safari. An *ojek* (Rp1500) will take you to the gate. Open M-F 9am-5pm, Sa-Su 8:30am-5:30pm. Tour Rp30,000, children Rp25,000. Night tours on the Taman Safari bus Sa 7-9pm.)

THE PUNCAK ☎0263

Meaning "peak" in Bahasa Indonesia, "Puncak" understates the beauty of the mountain pass connecting Jakarta and Bogor to Bandung. Tea plantations stretch for miles on either side of Rte. 2 (Jl. Raya), which winds through the towns of Cisarua and Cipanas. Enjoy the refreshing sight of lush green fields stretching for kilometers with traditional thatched huts interspersed. From here the floral Jl. Raya Cobodas branches off and leads to the Gede Pangrango National Park and the Cibodas Botanical Gardens. Terraced rice paddies and the peaks of Gunung Gede and Gunung Pangrango are visible from any patio on the hill. Beyond the park's gates, avid trekkers will find exciting wildlife, impressive waterfalls, and seemingly bottomless volcano craters on the way to the top. The view of the mountain path alone is well worth the challenging hike.

TRANSPORTATION. On weekdays, **buses** run almost every 30min. from **Jakarta, Bogor,** and **Bandung.** On the weekend, public buses are forbidden from traveling on Rte. 2 (Jl. Raya) because traffic is so heavy, though white minibuses do still make the trip from Bogor (1hr., Rp3000-5000). From Bandung, travelers can reach **Cibodas** by taking a bus to **Cianjur** and then traveling by *angkot* to Cibodas via **Cipanas** (total Rp6000-7000).

PRACTICAL INFORMATION. The **medical clinic, post office,** *wartel*, and **bank** reside on **Jl. Raya Cipanas,** the stretch of the road connecting Bogor and Bandung. A couple of kilometers from the heart of Cipanas toward Bogor, **Jl. Raya Cibodas** branches off and stretches to the parks and gardens above, where most guest houses are located.

The Cipanas **angkot station** is next to the **post office,** Jl. Raya Cipanas 109. (Open M-Th 8am-3pm, F 8-11am, Sa 8am-1pm.) Painfully slow Internet and a *wartel* are next door. (Open daily 6am-midnight.) A few hundred meters back toward the pass is **BNI Cipanas,** Jl. Raya Cipanas 167, which has a **24hr. ATM.** (☎512 022. Open M-F 8am-3pm.) BCA **ATM** (Cirrus/MC/V) is 100m toward Bandung and across the street. Next door is a general **pharmacy.** There is a **24hr. health clinic** (☎512 465) at the Jl. Raya Cibodas and Jl. Raya Cipanas intersection. **Postal code:** 43253.

ACCOMMODATIONS AND FOOD. A short *angkot* ride up Jl. Raya Cibodas leads to several well-situated accommodations, overlooking the beautiful terraced valley and a mere 10min. walk from the Botanical Gardens and Gunung Gede.

Freddy's ❷, 500m from the Cibodas gate, is the lodging of choice. This relaxed, friendly home has the only knowledgeable English-speaking guides in the area. Breakfast and tea are complimentary. (☎515 473. Doubles Rp50,000. Shared *mandi.*) Past the Cibodas Gate to the right is the **Wisma Jamur ❸,** a good option for groups of three to six, offering clean rooms with great views of the Puncak from its veranda. (Around Rp50,000 with private *mandi*, depending on size and degree of privacy.) Next door, the **Pondok Pemuda Hostel ❸,** intended for groups of four to 24, evokes memories of summer camp with its dorm-style rooms. (☎512 807. Quads Rp40,000.) Expect these hostels to be packed on weekends and holidays.

The best options for delicious, satiating eats are the guest houses above, all of which offer hot, cheap, home-cooked meals. Dozens of fruit stands and countless *warung* offering fried noodles and rice line the road leading to the garden gates, providing a quick post-trek snack for a few thousand rupiah. Several cafes inside the gardens offer somewhat more extensive menus. **Jl. Raya Cipanas** supplies fancy hotel-restaurants, sleepless *warung*, and cheap *padang* joints for spice fanatics.

SIGHTS. The walk or ride up **Jl. Raya Cibodas** is breathtaking (*angkot* Rp1000). Thanks to residents who participate in the nursery business, flowering plants and bonsai line the whole 4km stretch. The **Kebun Raya Cibodas,** an extension of the Bogor Botanical Gardens 1km beyond the Cibodas gates, is a hiking and bird-watching paradise. **Avoid crowded weekend and holiday explorations.** (Open daily 7am-6pm; last ticket sold at 4pm. Rp3000.) The gardens spread out on the lower fringe of **Gede Pangrango National Park,** a volcanic range that extends from Sumatra through Java. For Rp2500, visitors can hike roughly one hour to a mystical bat cave (guide required), three waterfalls, and a path alongside the fresh spewings of an active volcano. Another 90min. finds a hot spring, one of the least visited in all of Java—perfect for a secluded retreat. A round-trip day-hike to the summit of Gunung Gede (14km) is another option for those who start early enough. Those with a tent and sleeping bag can spend the night near the summit of **Gunung Pangrango,** a neighboring mountain. Quality maps with suggested trails and required visitor's permits are available at the Visitors Center. Though costly, guides are strongly recommended for night hiking.

The **Taman Bunga Nusantara** (National Flower Garden) has pleasant landscaping with colorful greenhouses (around Rp10,000). An *angkot* headed toward Mariwati from Cipanas will drop you at the gate. The tea-picking process can be seen at the fascinating **Gunung Mas Pabrik Teh** (Gunung Mas Tea Factory) between Bogor and Cipanas. From the gates, walk 10min. to get the factory—passing a teahouse, gift shop, and women tirelessly picking away. (Grounds open daily 8am-6pm. Rp1500. Factory open Sa-Th 8am-2pm. Rp2000, plus Rp5000 for required guide.)

INDONESIA

BANDUNG ☎022

With less pollution, a cooler climate, and extensive factory outlet shopping, Bandung often beats out Indonesia's capital as the big city of choice. Although not evident from the unpleasant backpacker ghetto, the residual European glamor and sophistication earn Bandung the title of "Paris of the East Indies." The city, West Java's capital, is home to over 50 schools and universities. With the high concentration of young people, nightlife in Bandung is more comfortable and benign than in other Javanese cities and should not be passed over.

TRANSPORTATION

Flights: Husen Sastra Negara Airport, 5km west of the city. Take a taxi from the town center (15-30min. depending on traffic; Rp20,000-40,000). Contact **Merpati,** a travel agency at the airport (☎603 47 44) and in Hotel Papandayan on Jl. Gabot Sobroto (☎730 27 37) for flight times and arrangements. Open M-F 8am-4:30pm, Sa 9am-2pm, Su 9am-1pm. Flights Tu, Th, and Sa to **Denpasar** (Rp815,000); **Lombok** (Rp 912,000); **Surabaya** (Rp530,500); **Ujung Pandang** (Rp1,199,000).

Trains: Terminal Stasiun (☎420 69 17), behind the *angkot* station on Jl. Stasiun Barat, off Jl. Kebonjati. To: **Jakarta** (3hr.; every hr. 5am-6pm; Express/Special M-F 6:30 and 9pm, F-Sa 4pm, Su and holidays 7, 8pm; Rp30,000-45,000); **Jogjakarta** (around 7hr.;

4 per day; Rp60,000-85,000); **Surabaya** (11hr.; 7am, 5, 7pm; Rp75,000-160,000). Prices depend on class (1st, 2nd) and type (standard, executive) of train.

Buses: Intercity buses go west from Leuwi Panjang Terminal and east from Terminal Cicaheum. **Leuwi Panjang Terminal** (☎522 07 68), on Jl. Sukarno-Hatta a few kilometers south of the train station. Take bus Ledeng-Leuwi Panjang or an *angkot* from *alun-alun.* To **Bogor** (3hr.; every hr. 24hr.; Rp8000-12,000) and **Jakarta** (4hr.; every hr. 24hr.; Rp25,000). **Terminal Cicaheum** (☎727 95 49), on Jl. A. Yani northeast of town center. Take bus Cicaheum-Kebon Kelapa or bus #9 Cicaheum-Leuwi Panjang from *alun-alun.* To: **Cirebon** (4hr.; every hr. 6am-6pm; Rp15,000-20,000); **Denpasar** (24hr.; 2pm; Rp132,000); **Jogjakarta** (10hr.; 6:30pm; Rp60,000); **Surabaya** (12hr.; 2pm; Rp82,000).

Local Transportation: City buses (Rp1000-1500) have north-south and east-west routes. A network of **angkot** run through city streets (Rp1000-1500) and the surrounding area. Navigation can be difficult, but locals can help. Terminals are **Station Hall** and **Kebon Kelapa** (old bus terminal). **Becak** are convenient and cheaper than elsewhere (Rp4000 gets you from Jl. Suniaraja to anyplace within 15min.). **Taxis** rarely use meters, so bargain. Share-taxi to **Pangandaran** (6hr.) Rp25,000.

INDONESIA

ORIENTATION AND PRACTICAL INFORMATION

Busy **Jl. Asia-Afrika** runs east-west passing *alun-alun,* the town center. **Jl. Otto Iskandardinata** runs north-south and ends at the Governor's Mansion, where **Jl. Merdeka** takes over as the major north-south route two blocks east. **Jl. Kebonjati** becomes **Jl. Suniaraja** in front of the train station and then runs parallel to and north of Jl. Asia-Afrika. **Jl. Braga** runs north-south by the **Museum Asia-Afrika.** Keep in mind that street signs are placed perpendicular to the streets they name.

Tourist Office: Tourist Information Center (☎420 66 44), at the northeast corner of *alun-alun*; it's the small office past the parked cars. Books tours in and around Bandung. Open M-Sa 9am-5pm. The **information counter** (☎421 66 48), at the railway station, has locked luggage storage (Rp2000 per day). Open daily 8am-5:30pm.

Tours: Sari Holiday, Jl. Naicpan 45 (☎422 07 16), 1 block northeast of the Museum Asia-Afrika. Open M-Sa 8am-4pm. **Pacto Tours and Travel,** Jl. Karapitan 87 (☎733 39 42) provides AmEx services. Open M-F 8:30am-4:30pm, Sa 8:30am-1pm.

Currency Exchange: Golden Moneychanger, Jl. Otto Iskandardinata 180 (☎423 84 38). Open M-F 9am-4:30pm, Sa 9am-1pm. Banks and ATMs are all over the city, including a **BCA ATM** at the corner of Jl. Suniaraja and Jl. Banceuy, and a full-service **Bank Bali,** Jl. Merdeka 66 (☎423 43 66). Open M-F 8am-3pm.

Markets: Pasar Baru, along Jl. Otto Iskandardinata in Chinatown. Bandung's oldest market, dating back to 1812. Textiles, shoes, fish, fruit, and a disproportionate number of bedcovers. Open daily 7am-4pm. **Pasar Ciroyom,** west of town, sells second-hand goods, food, and household products. Catch a red westward *angkot* from the train station. **Night markets** along Jl. Sudirman and Jl. Belakang Pasar are a cheap cure for midnight munchies. 2 blocks north of the train station, a flashy shopping strip on **Jeans Street (Jl. Cihampelas)** sells cheap denim products. Swanky **Plaza Bandung Indah,** Jl. Merdeka 56, features big-name foreign stores and a seven-screen cinema. Open daily 8am-6pm, Sa 9am-8pm. For *warung,* try **Pasar Malam,** off *alun-alun*'s northeast corner.

Emergency: Police: ☎110. **Ambulance:** ☎118. **Fire:** ☎113.

Police: Main Station (☎420 35 00), on Jl. Merdeka.

Pharmacy: Kimia Farma 12, Jl. Ir. H. Juanda 1 (☎420 54 21), at the intersection with Jl. Hasannudin. **Open 24hr.** Pharmacies in town are open daily 8am-8pm.

Medical Services: Hospital RS Kebonjati, Jl. Kebonjati 152 (☎601 40 58). **24hr. emergency clinic.**

Telephones: International phones at **GPO.** *Wartel* are abundant in town.

Internet Access: Ega Kineta, Jl. Braga 111 (☎420 62 91). Rp5000 per hr. Open M-Sa 8am-7pm. **Cybernet,** Jl. Gardu Jati 33. Rp5000 per hr. Open daily 10am-10pm. Although far away, the fastest and most reliable Internet cafes line Jl. Dago.

Express Mail: DHL, Jl. Asia-Afrika 81 (☎423 16 31), in the Grand Hotel Preanger. Open M-F 8am-5pm, Sa 8am-1pm.

Post Office: GPO, Jl. Asia-Afrika 49 (☎420 70 81). Enter on the side past the stands. **International phones.** *Poste Restante.* Western Union service available. Open daily 8am-8pm. **Postal code:** 40111.

ACCOMMODATIONS

Cheap accommodations line both streets near the railway station and Jl. Pangarang, two blocks south of the Museum Asia-Afrika.

By "Moritz," Luxor Permai 35 (☎420 57 88), at intersection with Jl. Belakang Pasar. A sign on the south side of Jl. Kebonjati points out the way. Comfortable, colorful, and clean. Breakfast and virtuoso guitarists included. All rooms have shared, clean, Western *mandi*. Dorms Rp16,000; singles Rp22,000; doubles Rp32,000; triples Rp43,000. ❷

Hotel Patrudissa II, Jl. Pasirkaliki 12 (☎420 26 45). Follow the "Hotel" sign down a well-lit alley. Private *mandi,* hot water, maps, and info about Bandung. Colored lights give the bland rooms character. Blue, green, or red singles and doubles Rp45,000. ❸

Hotel Surabaya, Jl. Kebonjati 71-75 (☎423 36 79). Echoey, spacious rooms are clean and comfortable. Free tea. Singles Rp25,000; doubles Rp35,000; triples Rp45,000; quads Rp50,000; deluxe Rp55,000. ❷

Le Yossie II, Jl. Belakang Pasar 112 (☎426 60 36). Bar and pool table may compromise an early trekker's shut-eye. Arranges mountain tours. Rooms lack character, but are clean. Singles Rp25,000; doubles Rp30,000; with bath Rp35,000. ❷

Le Yossie, Jl. Kebonjati 53 (☎420 54 53). Look for the pastel green shutters of the less popular older brother of Le Yossie II. One bath per floor. Singles Rp25,000; doubles Rp30,000. ❷

Wisma Nusaindah, Jl. Lodaya 95 (☎730 05 05). Walk east down Jl. Asia-Afrika and turn right onto Jl. Palasari, then left onto Jl. Lodaya. Although quite Western in appearance, popular with Indonesians—an escape from Westerners with dreads at backpacker prices. Singles with shared *mandi* and fan Rp35,000-50,000; doubles with shared *mandi* and fan Rp70,000, with TV, fan, hot water and bath Rp80,000-100,000. ❸

Asia-Afrika Conference Hotel, Jl. Asia-Afrika 112 (☎423 22 44). A standard upscale Western hotel. Delegates to the Asia-Afrika Non-Aligned Movement Conference stayed here. Check out the historical information and see which dignitary stayed in your room. Rooms have TV, A/C, bathtub, shower and an unimpressive view of the busiest street in Bandung. Singles Rp422,000; doubles Rp452,000, plus 21% tax. ❺

FOOD

Warung set up nightly on **Jl. Gardu Jati** and around the train station. From the hostels around Jl. Suniaraja, **Rumah Makan Sari Sunda** is a 7min. walk, but it's worth the trip to the suburbs of Dago to visit Kampung Daun and Dago Tea House for the fabulous views.

Kampung Daun (☎278 79 15), in the Trinity Villas Complex on Jl. Cihideung. Take an *angkot* up Jl. Setia Budi toward Lembang (15min). Transit in Parongpong onto Jl. Cihideung on the left (10min). Taxi Rp25,000-30,000. A hideaway in the beautiful hills of Dago, Bandung's suburb. Fine Sudanese and Mediterranean cuisine. *Jaipong* upon request. Reserve ahead. Entrees Rp9000-35,000. Open Tu-F 11am-midnight. ❹

Rumah Makan Sari Sunda, Jl. Jend. Sudirman 103-107. Look for the bamboo and palm tree oasis surrounded by *apoteks*. Let the calming sounds of *gamelan* music and falling water wash away stress. The mouth-watering Sudanese menu does not fall short of the atmosphere. The *ikan gurame* (smaller portion Rp23,000) and the *kelapa muda* (a coconut and syrup sipper; Rp5500) are especially good. Open daily 10am-11pm. ❹

Dago Tea House, Jl. Bukit Dago Utara. Take an *angkot* toward Dago and ask to be let out at the Dago Tea House, then ask the locals for directions. The exquisite food, thatched huts, and spectacular view make it worth the hike. Entrees Rp7000-18,000. ❸

Sindang Reret, Jl. Surapati 53 (☎250 14 74), past the running track. Performance hall restaurant provides both a great Sudanese feast (fish dishes Rp9000-18,000; rice entrees Rp3000-8000) and the only *wayang golek* show in town (Sa 7:30-10pm). Delicious *sarikaya* pudding Rp1750. Open daily 10am-11pm. ❷

INDONESIA

BANDUNG BITES Bandung offers tasty Western dishes (a rarity in Indonesia) as well as regional Indonesian specialties. With Bandung's large ethnically Chinese population, the Chinese restaurants along Jl. Gardu Jati and Jl. Sudirman serve the real thing. Your best bet for consistently excellent food remains the local Indonesian dishes:

Bakso: *Mie soto* (noodle soup) in a beef or ox broth with meat and deep fried tofu. This would be excellent on a chilly day–if such a thing existed on Java.

Bandrek: A cool and refreshing drink made with ginger, sugar, and coconut milk. *Bajigur* is the version without ginger.

Srabi: Even from *warung*, this specialty is still made the traditional way, in clay pots over low fires. Sweet coconut milk and rice flour are combined with *cokolat* (chocolate), *pisang* (bananas), coconut, or condensed milk for sweet *srabi,* with cheese and meats for the savory version.

SIGHTS

Though Bandung has a handful of interesting cultural sights, its main attractions, volcanoes and hot springs, lie outside of the city (see **Daytrips from Bandung,** p. 136). An Art Deco movement swept through this area in the 1930s (courtesy of architects Wolf Shoemacher, A.F. Aalbers, and F.W. Brinkman), leaving interesting architectural sights in its wake. Curious visitors can take free one-hour tours through the **Bandung Society for Heritage Conservation** in the Hotel Panghegar, on the fifth floor of Jl. Merdeka 2. (☎423 22 86, ext. 8554. Open M-F 10am-4pm.) Two blocks southwest is the **Gedung Merdeka,** marked by its several dozen flagpoles without flags, which houses the **Museum Asia-Afrika** at Jl. Asia-Afrika 65. The museum displays memorabilia from the 1955 Non-Aligned Movement Conference in Bandung, at which 29 African and Asian nations collectively agreed to pursue non-alignment policies during the Cold War between the US and USSR. (Open M-F 8am-noon and 1-3pm. Free.) For those in desperate need to touch a tank, visit the **Army Museum,** Jl. Lembong 38. Otherwise, the collection is small and unimpressive (☎420 33 93. Open M-Sa 8am-1pm. Donation requested.)

A. Ruchiyat's **wayang golek factory,** in a twisting alley two blocks south of the Savoy Homan Hotel off Jl. Pangarang, produces and sells *wayang golek* puppets

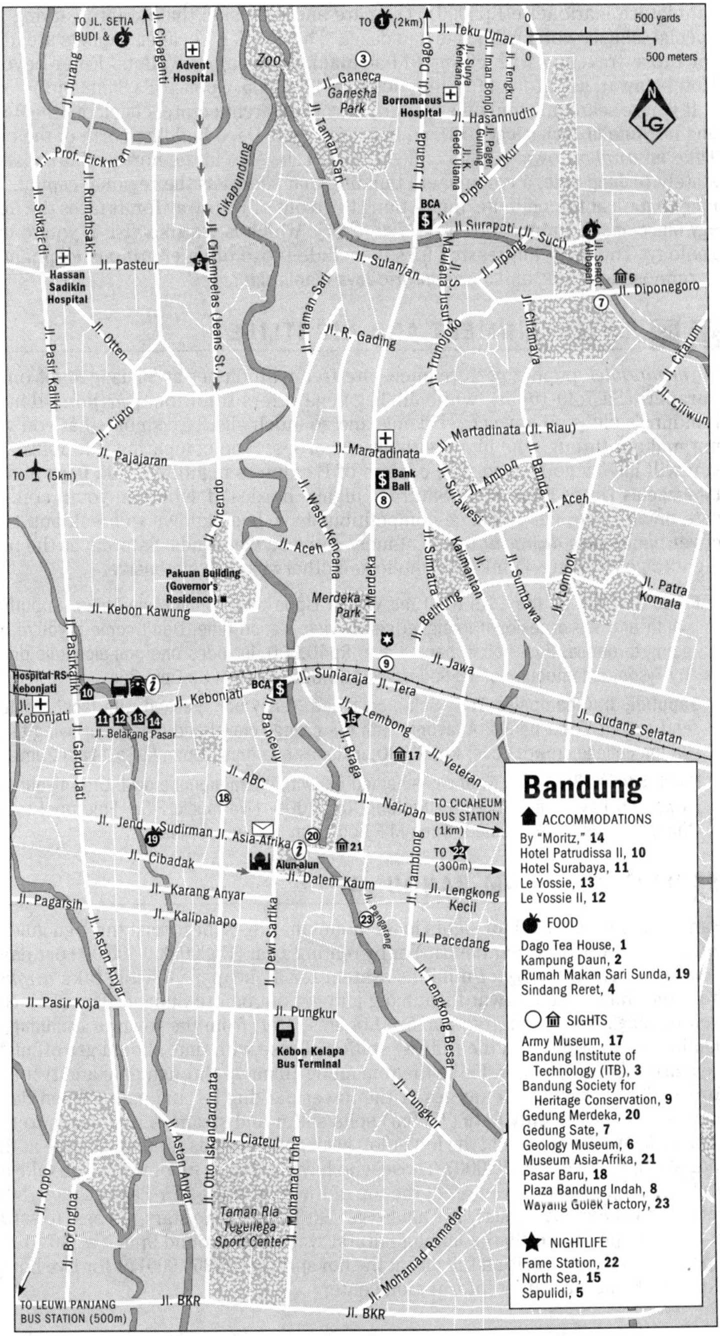
Bandung
ACCOMMODATIONS
By "Moritz," 14
Hotel Patrudissa II, 10
Hotel Surabaya, 11
Le Yossie, 13
Le Yossie II, 12
FOOD
Dago Tea House, 1
Kampung Daun, 2
Rumah Makan Sari Sunda, 19
Sindang Reret, 4
SIGHTS
Army Museum, 17
Bandung Institute of Technology (ITB), 3
Bandung Society for Heritage Conservation, 9
Gedung Merdeka, 20
Gedung Sate, 7
Geology Museum, 6
Museum Asia-Afrika, 21
Pasar Baru, 18
Plaza Bandung Indah, 8
Wayang Golek Factory, 23
NIGHTLIFE
Fame Station, 22
North Sea, 15
Sapulidi, 5
0 500 yards
0 500 meters
TO JL. SETIA BUDI & 2
TO 1 (2km)
Zoo
Jl. Teku Umar
Jl. Ganeca
Ganesha Park
Advent Hospital
Borromaeus Hospital
Jl. Hasannudin
Jl. Cipaganti
Jl. Jurang
Jl. Prof. Eickman
Jl. Rumahsaki
Jl. Sukajadi
Jl. Cikapundung
Jl. Taman Sari
Jl. Juanda (Jl. Dago)
Jl. Surapati (Jl. Suci)
Jl. Dipati Ukur
Jl. Sulanjan
Jl. Jipang
Jl. Sentot Alibasah
Jl. Diponegoro
Jl. Pasteur
Hassan Sadikin Hospital
Jl. Champelas (Jeans St.)
Jl. R. Gading
Jl. Trunojoyo
Jl. Citamaya
Jl. Citarum
Jl. Ciliwung
Jl. Otten
Jl. Pasir Kaliki
Jl. Cipto
Jl. Pajajaran
TO (5km)
Jl. Maratadinata
Jl. Martadinata (Jl. Riau)
Bank Bali
Jl. Ambon
Jl. Banda
Jl. Sulawesi
Jl. Aceh
Jl. Cicendo
Jl. Wastu Kencana
Pakuan Building (Governor's Residence)
Jl. Kebon Kawung
Merdeka Park
Jl. Merdeka
Jl. Sumatra
Jl. Kalimantan
Jl. Sumbawa
Jl. Lombok
Jl. Patra Komala
Jl. Belitung
Jl. Jawa
Hospital RS Kebonjati
Jl. Kebonjati
Jl. Pasirkaliki
BCA
Jl. Suniaraja
Jl. Tera
Jl. Belakang Pasar
Jl. Banceuy
Jl. Lembong
Jl. Braga
Jl. Veteran
Jl. Gudang Selatan
Jl. Gardu Jati
Jl. ABC
Jl. Naripan
TO CICAHEUM BUS STATION (1km)
Jl. Jend. Sudirman
Jl. Asia-Afrika
Jl. Cibadak
Alun-alun
Jl. Dalem Kaum
TO 22 (300m)
Jl. Tamblong
Jl. Lengkong Kecil
Jl. Karang Anyar
Jl. Pagarsih
Jl. Kalipahapo
Jl. Pangarang
Jl. Pacedang
Jl. Astan Anyar
Jl. Dewi Sartika
Jl. Lengkong Besar
Jl. Pasir Koja
Jl. Pungkur
Kebon Kelapa Bus Terminal
Jl. Otto Iskandardinata
Jl. Ciateul
Jl. Mohamad Toha
Taman Ria Tegellega Sport Center
Jl. Kopo
Jl. Bonglola
Jl. Mohamad Ramadan
TO LEUWI PANJANG BUS STATION (500m)
Jl. BKR

(miniature marionette Rp6000). The care and precision that go into carving the special albasia wood will leave you dazed. The smaller, cheaper puppets are ideal for those traveling with cramped backpacks and empty wallets. Enter beyond Hotel Mawar; ask around for directions. (☎420 13 35. Open M-Sa 8am-9pm.)

If you're searching for some modern European architecture, check out the **Bandung Institute of Technology (ITB),** an impressive Art Deco building north of the city. Take an *angkot* toward Dago and get off at ITB. Also in the north suburbs is the stately **Gedung Sate,** a colonial-era building that serves as the regional capital. It's nice to look at for a minute, but nothing to go out of your way for. It faces the **Geology Museum,** Jl. Diponegoro 57 (☎720 32 05), which is worth a visit if you're into geology. The most impressive fossils include those of an enormous elephant, a Tyrannosaurus Rex, and a prehistoric **Java Man's skull.**

ENTERTAINMENT AND NIGHTLIFE

Wayang golek puppet performances are free with dinner at **Sindang Reret** on Jl. Surapati (Sa 7:30-10pm), while Jl. Tegalega offers traditional *jaipong* dance. Bandung's clubs all have cover bands and so much cigarette smoke that you will not make it through the night without eye drops. Stop comparing it to Ibiza and you will have a good time. The centers of Bandung's nightlife are **Jl. Dago** and **Jl. Cihampelas (Jeans Street).** On Saturday nights, hordes of suburban youth congregate on Jl. Dago, where dance competitions have been known to break out. Live cover bands play *dangdut* music at most clubs on weekends. Saturday is the best night to go clubbing. Drinks, alcoholic and otherwise, are expensive.

Fame Station, on the 11th fl. of the Wisma Lippo tower on Jl. Asia-Afrika. Suburban youth and the occasional foreigner just having a good time. Don't come if you're not going to dance. Pool hall in back. Cover Rp40,000, includes one non-alcoholic drink. Try Tyson, a compound of 18 liquors, Rp165,000. Open M-Sa 9pm-2am.

Sapulidi, Jl. Cihampelas 107. Self-proclaimed "fancy bar" packed with local hipsters and serious cover bands. A favorite with the college crowd and older men trying to hit on the college crowd. Cover Rp30,000, includes one drink. Open M-Sa 11pm-2am.

North Sea, Jl. Braga 82. Nautically-themed bar with international crowd. Drown your sorrows and have a maritime. Bir Bintang Rp12,000. Live music F-Sa. Free pool table, though it's usually occupied. Open M-F 5pm-1am, Sa-Su noon-3am.

DAYTRIPS FROM BANDUNG

Bandung hides a wealth of sights in its mountain ridges, best seen through guided tours (about Rp75,000 per daytrip) or by renting a car (Rp200,000-300,000 per day). You can brave the *angkot*/minibus system for a cheaper viewing; take *angkot* from the train station toward Lembang and get out before Subang. Travelers can trek to **Tangkuban Prahu,** the "capsized boat" crater, from the town of **Lembang,** a 90min. *angkot* ride from the railway station. Those with time should get off at Jl. Jayagiri after one hour and hike the remaining 10km up through pine and tropical forests. The forest trail emerges at the lower parking lot and gate. (Open daily 6am-5pm.) The big gray **Ratu** (1830m) spits sulfur and steam. A path leads to the smaller **Domas Caldera** from the lower lot; get a guide for this route (available at the tourist office, Rp20,000-30,000). Those who have had their fill of vistas can take an *angkot* toward Subang. Get off at the top of the road at the "Air Panas Crater," the **hot springs** at **Sari Ater Resort,** Jl. Taman Sari 72. To see some stars, it's best to settle in the therapeutic hot baths among natural waterfalls around 9pm. (☎250 31 88. Open 24hr.) Rent a car for a full day at the hot springs (Rp250,000) or for five hours (Rp175,000) at the tourist information center.

Check out a **silk factory** in Garut at the **Candi Cangkuang Temple,** the oldest Hindu temple on West Java, dating from the 8th century. Take an *angkot* from Terminal Cicaheum, in the direction of Garut, and after one hour get out in Kadungora. It's a 4km walk or *delman* ride from there. Continue on to Garut, switch *angkots* and head to Cisurupan, a 9km hike from the crystal studded **Papandayan Volcano.** After the hike, take a soak in the **Tarogong Hot Springs** to help you relax (take *angkot* from Garut directly to Tarogong). The volcano and hot springs are worth splurging for a guided drive and hike. Tours are offered at most hostels (Rp110,000 per person from By "Moritz").

PANGANDARAN ☎0265

Though Pangandaran is known for its beach, the real attraction of this small coastal town is Green Canyon, a magnificent jade-colored river flowing between cliffs and over waterfalls. Travelers looking for black sands might be disappointed—the beach is a bit dirty and dangerous currents make it unsafe for swimming. However, nearby villages with welcoming locals and bustling home industries, coupled with lush forest and a quiet unimaginable in other parts of Java, make Pangandaran ideal for a short visit.

INDONESIA

TRANSPORTATION

Trains: No direct trains to Pangandaran. **Banjar**'s station serves all major cities. See below for information on buses to Banjar.

Buses: The **bus terminal** is 50m from main gates. To: **Bandung** (6hr.; every hr. 4-9am and noon, 3, 6, 9pm; Rp22,000. A/C chartered minibus Rp45,000); **Banjar** (1½hr.; every 10min. 4am-4pm; Rp10,000); **Bogor** (8hr.; 7am, 7pm; Rp23,000); **Jakarta** (9hr.; 5, 7, 9am and every hr. 5-9pm; Rp35,000); **Jogjakarta** (9hr.; Rp70,000); **Wonosobo** (Rp60,000). Charter minibuses available at Lotus Tours (see **Tours,** below).

Local Transportation: *Becak,* motorcycles, and bicycles rule the roads.

Rentals: Rent bicycles (Rp 20,000 per day) and mopeds (Rp 35,000 per day) from the *ojek* stand opposite the market, or from most hotels.

ORIENTATION AND PRACTICAL INFORMATION

From the bus terminal, turn left and enter the first red gates. Sign the guest book and pay a one-time cover charge of Rp3000 to enter the city. Inside the gates, a well-lit boulevard leads directly to the waves of the **west beach.** Perpendicular at the boulevard's end, mainstream **Jl. Pamugaran/Pantai Barat** stretches north-south along the shore. One kilometer south, busy **Jl. Bulak Laut** connects Jl. Pantai Barat with **Jl. Kidang Pananjung,** the town's former main road lined with cheap *losmen* and restaurants extending all the way back to the bus station.

Tours: Countless tourist information services, hotels, and restaurants sell similar package tours. One of the more popular is **Lotus Tours,** Jl. Bulak Laut 7 (☎639 635). Open daily 6am-10pm. Buses head to: **Bandung** (Rp35,000, with A/C Rp45,000); **Jakarta** (Rp35,000); **Wonosobo** (Rp50,000). A wonderful **river boat/bus trip** offers a stress-free ride to **Jogjakarta** (10hr.; Rp70,000 through an agent). Alternatively, take an early Banjar-bound bus to **Calipucang** (Rp3000), a *becak* to the harbor (Rp5000), a boat to **Cilacap** (4hr.; 6am, though known to launch late; Rp5000), a *becak* to the bus station (Rp4000), and a bus to **Jogjakarta** (6hr.; Rp25,000).

Currency Exchange: The town's greatest tourist attraction is its only **ATM,** behind the market by **Bank Negara Indonesia,** Jl. Merdeka 312 (☎639 700). **Open 24hr.** Often empty, the machine also frequently rejects cards at random—bring enough money to get to the next city. **Bank Rakyat Indonesia,** Jl. Kidang Pananjung 212 (☎639 288), by the intersection with Jl. E. Jaga Lautan. **Branch** on Jl. Merdeka behind the market. Cashes traveler's checks at reasonable rates. All banks open M-F 8am-2pm.

Markets: A narrow **main market** lies outside the entrance gates by the bus terminal. Supplier of all goods known to man. Open daily 6am-4pm; crowded on M and Th. The sadly deserted **fish market** and a mass of tourist shops are in the south, by the east beach and west beach respectively. Open daily 5am-4pm.

Emergency: Police: ☎110.

Police: Jl. Merdeka 177 (☎639 110), behind the main market and 400m to the left. Open M-Sa 7am-2pm. Police officers stationed at main gate **24hr.**

Pharmacy: Apotik Pangandaran Farma (☎639 524), in back of the main market. A 2nd pharmacy resides on Jl. Kidang Pananjung (☎639 983), 100m west of the hospital.

Medical Services: Hospital, Jl. Parapat 1 (☎639 118). Small hospital with ambulance service. **24hr. emergency care.**

Telephones: Telkom office, Jl. Kidang Pananjung 65 (☎639 333). **Open 24hr. HCD** and fax. **Adam's,** Jl. Pantai Barat 164, has **international phone** service 8am-10pm.

Post Office: Jl. Kidang Pananjung 129 (☎639 284). *Poste Restante.* Open M-Th 7:30am-3pm, F 7:30-11:30am, Sa 7:30am-1pm. **Postal code:** 49396.

INDONESIA

ACCOMMODATIONS

The town has a surplus of exceptional budget lodgings. Sundry accommodations are cluttered on the west beach road. The farther inland you go, the cheaper they get. Most places have a two-night minimum and prices decrease with length of stay. Indonesia's tourism slump has hit Pangandaran particularly hard, as it is a vacation spot for Indonesians unable to afford Bali. Prices have been driven down and many establishments have been forced to close.

Laguna Beach Bungalows (☎639 761), off Jl. Pengadilan Kebon, 2km outside the city. Laguna offers pick-up service for a price (Rp10,000 one way; call reception or ☎081 223 68806). A raft-ride or 30min. walk from the city, the most popular stay in Pangandaran offers a lip-smacking welcome drink from the full-fledged restaurant. Rooms with porches, hammocks, and a beautiful view of coconut trees and beach. Standard singles Rp35,000; doubles and triples Rp50,000-75,000. ❸

Bamboo House (☎639 419), on Jl. Baru. This popular stay offers quality bungalows far from traffic. Breakfast Rp5000. Private bath. Singles Rp20,000; standard doubles Rp30,000, with a lovely porch and jungle-themed *mandi* Rp40,000. ❷

Pondok Cocobana, Jl. Pamugaran 177, 200m north of the street to the west beach. 3-day minimum. Beautiful, spacious rooms with fan, shower, and porch. Free breakfast with stay. Singles Rp30,000; doubles Rp45,000; triples Rp60,000. ❷

Holiday Beach, Jl. Bulak Laut 50 (☎639 285). A block off the beach. Popular restaurant and tourist service. Bare rooms with fans, large beds, and private *mandi*. Singles Rp20,000; doubles Rp30,000. ❷

FOOD

Pangandaran's food scene ranges from the usual *warung* to busy cafes and seafood spots. Eateries in the old center, the southern end of Jl. Kidang Pananjung, are cheap (Rp5000-10,000 per meal) and open daily 8am-11pm. Farther north on the east beach road, the **fish market** offers the freshest food in town at low prices.

Green Garden Cafe, Jl. Kidang Pananjung 116. Next to Pondok Ibu. Seafood with a Western twist and tasty Indonesian dinner served *al fresco* (Rp6000-10,000). Very relaxed atmosphere. Open daily 5-10pm. ❷

Bunga Laut Restaurant, Jl. Bulak Laut 8-11. Opposite Lotus Tours. Savory soups (Rp5000), delightful desserts (Rp2000-4000), and sizzling seafood entrees (Rp7000-15,000). The *pisang goreng* (fried banana) with chocolate alone is worth the trip. ❷

Bamboo Cafe, on Jl. Pantai Barat beside Adam's. A popular roadside joint with a fantastic view, known to grill a mean fish (around Rp25,000). Essential fried rice Rp5000. Chicken dishes around Rp10,000. ❸

SIGHTS

Pangandaran has two major sights, **Penanjung National Park** and **Green Canyon.** Travelers can enter Penanjung National Park (Rp2000; open daily 7am-4pm) and check out black-sand beaches that promise great snorkeling (Rp60,000) and hungry monkeys. Although much of the park is technically closed, hikers can see some areas on their own or hire a guide for eco-friendly tours (Rp30,000). Expect to see limestone caves, bats with 2m wingspans, lizards, monkeys, deer, porcupines, and enormous rafflesia flowers that bloom for only four days and reek from 30m away. The Green Canyon holds a jade-colored river of reputedly holy water, which winds past sharp cliffs and through waterfalls. Majestic rock formations surround clear pools separated from the main river. Bring a swimsuit, but ask hotels about safe bathing areas or book a tour for Rp40,000. Tours include stops at **Batu Keras Beach,** ideal for beginners looking to ride waves (plastic boards Rp10,000 per hr.).

JOGJAKARTA ☎0274

If Bali is about waxed-chested surfers tanning on the beach, Jogjakarta is about long-haired travelers eagerly absorbing Java's rich cultural offerings. There are at least three full days of quality things to see and do in Jogja (as it is often called)—a city full of commission-earning locals and *becak* drivers all clamoring to "help" you through it. The abundance of cheap and excellent food and accommodations is unfortunately balanced by steep US$ entry fees to many sights. If you are here for a short time, the overpriced tours may be necessary in order to see it all, but they can easily be avoided with the excellent public transportation system. However you do it, Jogja really just must be visited.

TRANSPORTATION

Flights: The **airport** (☎566 666) is on Jl. Adisucipto, 5km from the city center. Take a taxi—by public transportation, the trip is excessively complicated, requiring 2-3 bus transfers. **Garuda** (☎522 148), in Amparukmu Hotel on Jl. Laksda Adisucipto. Open daily 5:30am-8pm. Daily flights to **Denpasar, Jakarta,** and **Mataram. Merpati** (airport office ☎512 727) is open daily 8am-4:30pm. Flies daily to **Surabaya.** Flights to **Sulawesi** start at Rp793,600 plus tax. Purchase tickets through a travel agent. Rp9000 tax is added to the flight prices listed below.

DESTINATION	FREQUENCY	PRICE
Denpasar	3 per day	economy Rp426,000; 1st class Rp574,500
Jakarta	5 per day	economy Rp456,800; 1st class Rp616,300
Mataram	1 per day	economy Rp530,700; 1st class Rp714,400
Surabaya	2 per day	economy Rp241,200

Trains: Tugu Train Station, Jl. Mangkubumi 1 (☎589 685), on Jl. Pasar Kembang. Tourist staff at the station can help demystify the schedule. Arrive 30min. early to purchase tickets. **Lempuyangan Train Station** on Jl. Lempuyangan serves economy trains only.

DESTINATION	DURATION	FREQUENCY	PRICE
Bandung	7hr.	business 2 per day, executive 3 per day	business Rp60,000; executive Rp90,000-185,000
Jakarta	7-8hr.	business 5 per day, executive 8 per day	business Rp50,000-120,000; executive Rp150,000-235,000
Malang	8hr.	1 per day	business Rp120,000; executive Rp140,000
Solo	1hr.	business 7 per day, executive 4 per day	business Rp5000-6000; executive Rp9000-23,500
Surabaya	5hr.	business 3 per day, executive 5 per day	business Rp35,000-60,000; executive Rp60,000-240,000

Buses: Umbulharjo Terminal, Jl. Veteran (☎376 013), southeast of the city. Take buses #4 and 2 from Malioboro and Prawirotaman areas, respectively. Buses (usually with evening departures) go all over Java, Sumatra, and Bali. Schedules, fares, express buses, and peace of mind available at ticket agencies on Jl. Mangkubumi, Sosrowijayan, and Prawirotaman. To: **Denpasar** (17hr.; 2:30pm; Rp125,000); **Jakarta** (9-14hr.; 4pm; Rp100,000); **Semarang** (4hr.; every hr.; Rp10,500).

Local Transportation: City buses (Rp1000) run north-south between Umbulharjo Terminal and Gadjah Mada University along Jogja's main streets. Buses are less frequent after 5pm, when unmetered **taxis** become best for longer distances. **Becak** are the best way to tour the city; agree on a price before boarding (Rp5000 per 5km is standard). **Andong,** horse-drawn carriages, cost Rp20,000 per hr. For short journeys, tell the dozens of *becak* drivers that you will *jalan-jalan* (walk).

Rentals: Fortuna Rental, Jl. Jlagran 20-21 (☎564 680), 50m to the right of Tugu Station. Bikes Rp5000 per day. Motorbikes Rp50,000-75,000 per day. Tackle mountains in a jeep (Rp150,000) or sedan (Rp350,000 with driver). Bring a passport and a credit card (MC/V). Open daily 9am-6pm.

INDONESIA

COMMISSION HUNTERS Everyone is on commission on Jogja. Random people on the street will try to direct you to hostels and "authentic" *batik* shops—hoping to collect a cut of your spending. Some might lie or invent wild stories about why your destination is closed—then conveniently redirect you. Check things out for yourself, note the times of operation listed in *Let's Go,* and stop by the incredibly helpful tourist office with multilingual staff for the real info.

ORIENTATION AND PRACTICAL INFORMATION

Jogjakarta rests at the base of **Gunung Merapi** (2911m), 603km southeast of Jakarta. The city is built around the 10-hectare fortress of the **kraton complex** and the two square fields to the south (**Alun-alun Kidul** or **Selatan**) and north (**Alun-alun Lor** or **Utara**), from which **Jl. A. Yani** runs north. As Jl. A. Yani runs through the city, it turns into **Jl. Malioboro** and becomes the main boulevard. Beyond Tugu Train Station, Malioboro becomes Jl. Mangkubumi, terminating at the **Tugu Monument.** The monument stands in the middle of the intersection of four major streets: **Jl. Mangkubumi, Diponegoro, Sangaji,** and **Sudirman,** the last of which leads east to the **airport** and eventually to Prambanan and Solo.

Tourist Office: Jl. Malioboro 16 (☎566 000), south on Malioboro past the modern Mutiara Hotel on the left. Brochures, maps, tickets, tours, and services in English, French, German, and Dutch. **International phone** service. Open M-Sa 8am-7pm.

Tourist Police: Jl. Malioboro 16 (☎566 165), at the tourist office (with the same hours).

Immigration Office: Jl. Solo Km10 (☎586 130), near the airport. Open M-Th 8am-noon, F 8-11:30am, Sa 8am-noon.

Currency Exchange: Many banks and **ATMs** in Sosrowijayan and Prawirotaman areas. Bring passport. **BNI,** across from the post office. Open M-F 8am-4pm.

American Express: In **Natour Garuda Hotel,** Jl. Malioboro 89. Open M-F 8:30am-4pm, Sa 8:30am-1pm. Also at **Pacto Tours and Travel,** Jl. Laksda Adisucipto Km8.7, in the Sheraton Hotel.

Luggage Storage: At Tugu Train Station. Rp2000-6000 for 6hr.; Rp4000-12,000 for 24hr. Counter open daily 5:30am-9:30pm.

Alternatives to Tourism: Lucy Batik Gallery and Losmen (☎513 429). Offers *batik* courses at 9am (Rp30,000-75,000). See **Accommodations,** below, for directions. **Via-via,** Jl. Prawirotaman 24B (☎386 557; viavia@yogya.wasantara.net.id). Offers courses in language (Rp30,000), cooking (Rp35,000), and massage (Rp40,000). Open daily 8am-10pm. See **Food,** below, for more information.

Emergency: Police: ☎110. **Fire:** ☎113. **Ambulance:** ☎118.

Police: Kapolresta (☎512 511), on Jl. Reksobayan. Posts throughout the city.

Pharmacy: Kimia Farma 21, Jl. Malioboro 123 (☎514 980). **Open 24hr. Apotek Ratna,** Jl. Parangtritis, near Jl. Prawirotaman (☎371 028). Open M-Sa 8am-9pm.

Medical Services: Ludira Husada Tama Hospital, Jl. Wiratama 4 (☎620 333). English-speaking doctors. **Open 24hr.**

Telephones: Wartel all over town place **international** calls (no credit cards). Try the *wartel* in the tourist office. **Telkom office,** next to Komodor Yos Sudarso Rotary, and at the **Natour Garuda Hotel,** Jl. Malioboro 89. Both are overpriced, as are the *wartel* on Jl. Sosrowijayan, and neither accepts phone cards. Pay the price or stick to email.

Internet Access: Küpi Net, on Jl. Mataram, is cheap and fast, like many other 24hr. cybercafes along Prawirotaman and Jl. Jend. Sudirman. Rp3500 per hr. Cybercafes in the backpacker community are slower and overpriced.

Post Office: Express Mail: DHL, Jl. Dr. Wahidin 58 (☎511 950). **GPO,** Jl. Senopati 2 (☎384 237), on the corner with Jl. A. Yani. *Poste Restante.* Open M-Sa 8am-8:30pm. Get stamps at Jl. Sosrowijayan 53. Open M-Th, Sa 8am-2pm, F 8am-noon. **Postal code:** 55000.

INDONESIA

ACCOMMODATIONS

Budget accommodations cluster in two main areas. In the *gangs* (alleys) that connect **Jl. Pasar Kembang** to **Jl. Sosrowijayan (Sosro),** accommodations and restaurants are plentiful and span a large cost range. This trendy, popular area is close to **Jl. Malioboro.** A 25min. walk south, **Jl. Prawirotaman** is farther from the action. Though still a tourist neighborhood, this area is nice if you're looking for more seclusion. Accommodations at the two areas are much the same. Near both, commission-earning "friends" claim to know the best places; close your ears to them.

JL. SOSROWIJAYAN

Dewi Homestay, Jl. Sosrowijayan Wetan GT 1/115 (☎516 014; dewihomestay@hotmail.com). One of the best deals in Jogja. Authentically artistic and fantastically clean. Huge rooms with private *mandi.* Singles Rp25,000; doubles Rp40,000. ❷

Bladok Losmen, Jl. Sosrowijayan 76 (☎/fax 523 832). A hit with the families hopping over from Bali, this place comes with every Western amenity. Swimming pool and one of Sosro's most popular restaurants. Standard rooms with bath Rp50,000; deluxe rooms with private balcony Rp75,000; executive rooms with hot water and refrigerator Rp95,000; VIP rooms with A/C and TV Rp145,000. ❹

Lucy Batik Gallery and Losmen (☎513 429), on Sosrowijayan Wetan GT 1/87 *(losmen)* and GT 1/94 (gallery). Walk 25m down *gang* 1 and turn right. Outside *mandi* is small and rooms are basic, but it's cheap and clean. *Batik* courses at 9am (Rp30,000-75,000). Singles Rp20,000; doubles Rp30,000; triples Rp55,000. ❷

Wisma Gembira, Jl. Sosrowijayan 35 (☎512 605). Across from Bladok Losmen, this less popular stay offers the same amenities without the good restaurant. Rooms Rp35,000, with *mandi* and A/C Rp80,000. ❸

JL. PRAWIROTAMAN

Delta, Jl. Prawirotaman II MG 111 597A (☎082 274 3177). Relaxed, with a nice courtyard and pool. Free safebox. Breakfast included. Singles Rp25,000, with *mandi* Rp45,000-70,000; doubles Rp32,500/Rp50,000-75,000. ❷

Hotel Sartika, Jl. Prawirotaman 44A (☎372 669). Need a bath? This quiet refuge has spacious rooms with fans and bathtubs! Free breakfast. Singles and doubles from Rp35,000. Rooms with tubs Rp40,000 and up. ❸

Hotel Airlangga, Jl. Prawirotaman 6-8 (☎378 044). Upscale accommodation with hot water, A/C rooms, and a swimming pool. Rooms Rp50,000-120,000. ❹

JOGJA YUMMIES As a separate sultanate within Java, Jogja has developed some truly local specialties not available anywhere else. Indonesia isn't known for its desserts, but Jl. Mataram is lined with sweet shops. Try **Tape Mataram Baru,** Jl. Mataram 191. Don't miss these Jogjan eats and treats:

Gudeg (Nasi Gudeg): Rice served in a sweet sauce of coconut, spices, and jackfruit. Often comes with egg, *tempe,* or *kercek* (cow hide).
Sambal: Indonesian hot sauce. Exported all over the island. Jogja does it best.
Geplak: These colored coconut-and-sugar bombs sit in sweet shop windows.
Wajik: Sticky rice soaked in palm sugar and coconut milk.
Yangko: Chewy, rice flour candies in mango, chocolate, and durian flavors.
Bakpia: Gelatinous squares made of sweet red and green bean paste. The least sweet, lightest of the bunch.

FOOD

On Sosrowijayan, pricey restaurants serve Western, Chinese, and—if you're lucky—even Indonesian food. For more authentic and cheaper eats, join the locals at the *warung* on the upper levels of **Pasar Beringharjo** (see **Markets,** p. 144) during the day, or on the sidewalks of **Jl. Malioboro** sitting on woven mats, playing cards, and eating *lesehan*-style at night.

FM. Resto, Jl. Sosrowijayan 54. You have a better chance of finding your long-lost Australian cousin here than anywhere else. Reason: good food, good music, incredibly friendly staff, and relaxed atmosphere. Come late to hang out with the locals. Lemon-honey juice Rp5000. Open daily 8am-3am. ❷

Rumah Makan "Es Eny," Jl. Gandekan Lor 42A. From Malioboro, head down Jl. Sosrowijayan past Bladok Losmen, and turn left. Photos on the wall of all offered Indonesian dishes–you still may not know what it is, but at least you'll know what it looks like. Cafeteria-style. Full plate Rp5000-7000. Open daily 10am-9pm. ❶

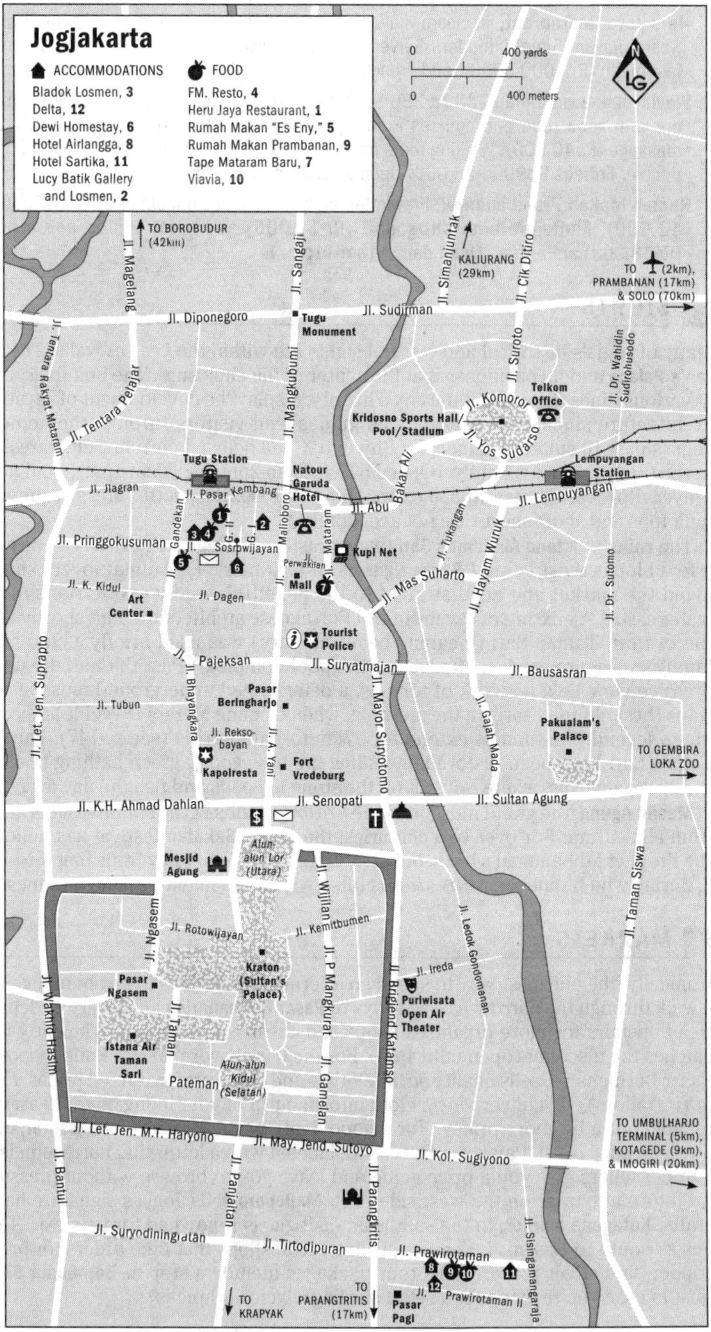
Jogjakarta
ACCOMMODATIONS
Bladok Losmen, 3
Delta, 12
Dewi Homestay, 6
Hotel Airlangga, 8
Hotel Sartika, 11
Lucy Batik Gallery and Losmen, 2
FOOD
FM. Resto, 4
Heru Jaya Restaurant, 1
Rumah Makan "Es Eny," 5
Rumah Makan Prambanan, 9
Tape Mataram Baru, 7
Viavia, 10
0 400 yards
0 400 meters
TO BOROBUDUR (42km)
KALIURANG (29km)
TO (2km), PRAMBANAN (17km) & SOLO (70km)
Jl. Magelang
Jl. Sangaji
Jl. Simanjuntak
Jl. Cik Ditiro
Jl. Diponegoro
Jl. Sudirman
Tugu Monument
Jl. Tentara Rakyat Mataram
Jl. Tentara Pelajar
Jl. Mangkubumi
Jl. Suroto
Jl. Dr. Wahidin Sudirohusodo
Jl. Komoro
Telkom Office
Kridosno Sports Hall/ Pool/Stadium
Jl. Yos Sudarso
Bakar Ali
Tugu Station
Lempuyangan Station
Jl. Jlagran
Jl. Pasar Kembang
Natour Garuda Hotel
Jl. Abu
Jl. Lempuyangan
Jl. Pringgokusuman
Jl. Gandekan
Jl. Sosrowijayan
Malioboro
Jl. Mataram
Kupi Net
Jl. Tukangan
Jl. Hayam Wuruk
Jl. Perwakilan
Mall
Jl. Mas Suharto
Jl. K. Kidul
Jl. Dagen
Art Center
Jl. Dr. Sutomo
Tourist Police
Jl. Pajeksan
Jl. Suryatmajan
Jl. Bausasran
Jl. Let. Jen. Suprapto
Jl. Bhayangkara
Pasar Beringharjo
Jl. Tubun
Jl. Mayor Suryotomo
Jl. Gajah Mada
Pakualam's Palace
Jl. Rekso-bayan
Jl. A. Yani
Kapolresta
Fort Vredeburg
TO GEMBIRA LOKA ZOO
Jl. K.H. Ahmad Dahlan
Jl. Senopati
Jl. Sultan Agung
Mesjid Agung
Alun-alun Lor (Utara)
Jl. Wijilan
Jl. Ngasem
Jl. Rotowijayan
Jl. Kemitbumen
Jl. Ledok Gondomanan
Jl. Taman Siswa
Kraton (Sultan's Palace)
Jl. P Mangkurat
Jl. Brigjend Katamso
Jl. Ireda
Pasar Ngasem
Puriwisata Open Air Theater
Jl. Wahid Hasim
Jl. Taman
Istana Air Taman Sari
Alun-alun Kidul (Selatan)
Pateman
Jl. Gamelan
Jl. Let. Jen. M.T. Haryono
Jl. May. Jend. Sutoyo
Jl. Kol. Sugiyono
TO UMBULHARJO TERMINAL (5km), KOTAGEDE (9km), & IMOGIRI (20km)
Jl. Bantul
Jl. Panjaitan
Jl. Parangtritis
Jl. Suryodiningratan
Jl. Tirtodipuran
Jl. Prawirotaman
Jl. Sisingamangaraja
Jl. Prawirotaman II
TO KRAPYAK
TO PARANGTRITIS (17km)
Pasar Pagi

INDONESIA

Heru Jaya Restaurant, Jl. Sosrowijayan GI 79 (☎515 055). Head down *gang* II off Jl. Sosrowijayan. Simple, hidden. Serves delectable dishes (Rp4500), gargantuan breakfast menu (Rp1000-5000), and French cuisine (Rp12,500). Open daily 8am-10pm. ❶

Viavia, Jl. Prawirotaman 24B (☎386 557; viavia@yogya.wasantara.net.id). Hippie hangout with good food and courses in language (Rp30,000), cooking (Rp35,000), and massage (Rp40,000). Walking tours from Rp275,000 for 2 people to Rp355,000 for 6 people. Entrees Rp9000-28,000. Open daily 8am-10pm. ❸

Rumah Makan Prambanan, Jl. Prawirotaman 14. Great cosmopolitan cuisine (Rp5000-12,000). Fantastic beef stroganoff (Rp11,000) and spicy grilled cobra meat (Rp18,000) are a treat. Open daily 11am-11pm. ❷

SIGHTS

Many of Jogja's historical and cultural sights are within the *kraton* walls. The **Sultan's Palace** and its pavilions sit at the center of the enclosure. The buildings, built at various times throughout the city's history, display the development of Javanese architecture since 1755. Multilingual guides lead visitors through the home of Jogja's past 10 sultans. Hamengku Buwono X, the beloved current Sultan, resides in the *kraton* with his family. (Open M-Th 8:30am-2pm, F 8:30am-1pm; avoid noon prayer. Rp7500. Camera Rp500 extra, video Rp1000. Respectful dress required—tank tops and short-shorts are not acceptable.)

The ruins of **Istana Air Taman Sari** (water castle and fragrant garden) can be seen a few blocks west behind **Pasar Ngasem** (a bird market). Animal lovers should avoid the market and head straight to the beautiful, wildly exotic ruins of the water castle. A mixture of Javanese and Portuguese architecture built shortly after the *kraton*, Taman Sari (meaning beautiful park) was used briefly as the royal family's pleasure garden. (Rp2000 at the pool complex.) Past the initially unimpressive view lie a network of tunnels, a deteriorated underground mosque, and ruins (best climbed early in the morning, when Gunung Merapi is visible). According to legend, the tunnels extend for 27km to Parangtritis (see p. 147). Parts of Taman Sari have been restored, including the now goopy green bathing pools of the 20 royal wives, where boys sit on the stone lily pads and fish the day away.

Mesjid Agung, the grand mosque of the *kraton*, stands at the southwest corner of Alun-alun Utara. For over two centuries, the yearly **Sekaten** festival has honored the Prophet Muhammad's birth. *Sekaten* is celebrated annually from June 7 to July 7, during which time the *alun-alun* is filled with amusement-park-style games.

MARKETS

Ironically, the cheapest way to spend an afternoon in Jogja is to go shopping. Just a walk through the narrow passageways of **Pasar Beringharjo** can be very enriching. Head upstairs for more organized shops and cheap *warung* food. The early bird catches the discount (open until 4pm). For the barter-worn, **Mirota Batik,** opposite Pasar Beringharjo, sells quality *batik* clothes and other crafts at fixed prices. *Penjahit* (tailors) will convert *batik* cloth into an outfit of your liking. **Pasar Ngasem** is reliable but a bit more pricey. For a good deal, try the turquoise **Art Center,** 20m down an alley off Jl. Pajeksan. *Batiks* are labeled with a letter that corresponds to a price; sellers give you a price guide and leave you to browse without pressure. An informal bazaar on the west side of **Jl. Malioboro** sells Jogja's signature handcrafts. **Kotagede market,** to the southeast of Jogja, is renowned for its silver. Take bus #8 south to Basen. Jl. Kemasan is lined with shops that take orders for brass, copper, and silver pieces. Most tour packages include a stop at **Borobudur Silver** (just in case you're dying for a set of sterling silver toothpicks).

ENTERTAINMENT AND NIGHTLIFE

It would be criminal to come to Jogja and not see the *Ramayana* **ballet** at the Prambanan Temples (see below). The story of Prince Rama is played out with the view of the illuminated temples behind, bats flying overhead, and if you come at the right time, the full moon rising next to the temples. (Alternating days, 7:30-9:30pm. Rp25,000-100,000.) If you cannot get to Prambanan, the condensed version is danced indoors at **Trimurti Theater.** (Tu, Th 7:30-9:30pm.) **Purawisata Open Air Theater** on Jl. Brigjen Katamso has nightly performances as well. (8-9:30pm. Rp90,000 for the ballet, combos with dinner available.) Once a religious ceremony, **wayang kulit** is now a Javanese art form. This unique theater form, in which leather shadow puppets depict the heroism of mythological ancestors, is performed at the **Sonobudoyo Archaeological Museum** on Jl. Trikora (daily 7:30-9:30pm) and in Alun-alun Selatan (every 2nd Sa of the month 9pm-5:30am). Free performances, such as classical Jogjan dance (at the Sultan's Palace, Jl. KHA Dahlan 71; Su 10:30am-noon) and *wayang golek* puppet shows with traditional *gamelan* music (M-Sa 11am-1pm), are frequent. At night, **fire-eaters** perform at the south end of Jl. Malioboro/Jl. A. Yani. Participate in a **blindfold walk** between the banyan trees at **Alun-alun Kidul,** south of the *kraton.* If you like dancing alone, head over to **Papillon,** Jl. Mayor Suryotomo 26, which was once Jogja's hottest nightclub. (☎564 343. Cover Rp15,000. Ladies' night Su-Tu, Th; gay night F. Open Su-Tu, Th 10pm-2am; W, F-Sa 10pm-3am.) A little more popular but still not exactly hopping is **Jogja-Jogja Music House** in Borobudur Plaza on Jl. Magelang. (Open daily 9pm-2am.)

INDONESIA

DAYTRIPS FROM JOGJAKARTA

BOROBUDUR. Few sights on the planet can compare to the misty sunrise over Borobudur, the world's largest Buddhist temple. Built between AD 750 and 850 during the Sailendra dynasty, Borobudur is one of the three wonders of classical Southeast Asia (along with Myanmar's Bagan and Cambodia's Angkor Wat). The temple, topped by a 40m *stupa*, consists of ten levels, symbolic of the ten stages of the Buddhist cosmic system. Along the walls, carvings depict scenes from the life of Buddha, the thousands of reincarnations and manifestations, and the final quest for truth. The three highest levels of Arupadhatu stand for the freedom from earthly bonds and represent "Karma," the highest stage of Buddhahood. Here, an exposed stone Buddha figure meditates among encapsulated neighbors. His expression of suffering communicates that life is pain because of desire, which can only be controlled by meditation. (Open daily 6am-5:15pm.)

Before facing the breathtaking climb and view, visitors often go to the **Audio Visual Center** to watch an enlightening 35min. video. (First showing 8am. Rp4000.) Many visitors try to improve their luck by reaching into any of the 432 stupas to touch the stone Buddhas' hands and navels. Use your right hand, as the left hand is considered unclean. If you're visiting in the summer, every schoolchild in Indonesia will be visiting as well, so for pictures of the temple free of the crowds, go when it opens (6am). For an awesome view, climb the hills behind the monument. **Mendut** and **Pawon,** two nearby historic temples, are sites of the actual religious ceremonies (included in tours). Devotees from as far away as China have walked across Java to attain enlightenment from Borobudur via Mendut and Pawon. *(42km northwest of Jogja, Borobudur can be reached by local buses from* ***Umbulharjo*** *(Jl. Veteran), which run to Borobudur (6am-6pm, Rp2000-6000) or Muntilan, a transfer point. Tourist offices along Jl. Sosrowijayan and Jl. Prawirotaman offer package tours. Entrance is US$7 or Rp63,000, students with valid ID US$4 or Rp34,000. Guide Rp30,000.)*

PRAMBANAN TEMPLES. Built in the 9th century during the Hindu Sanjaya dynasty, the complex consists of temples dedicated to the Hindu Trinity: Shiva the destroyer, Vishnu the protector, and Brahma the creator. The rubble littering the area is what remains of the temples destroyed by Gunung Merapi's eruption in 1006. Within the park, smaller temples, including **Candi Lumbung, Bubrah, Sewu,** and **Sojiwan,** are worth a look. Monuments to the north (**Candi Plaosan, Banyunibo, Sari, Kalasan,** and **Sambisari**) are best seen by bike or becak, but beware the gods of inflation. **Kraton Ratu Boko,** 2km south of Prambanam, offers a splendid view. Bike south along the road on the west side of the market and follow signs to the palace gate (Rp750). The Prambanan park holds Ramayana ballets in an outdoor theater during the summer; it's indoors the rest of the year (see **Entertainment,** above). (Camera pass Rp2000, video pass Rp15,000.) **Ny Muharti Guest House ❷** (☎496 103), Jl. Tampumas Ngankruk 2-3, opposite Prambanan's entrance, is an option for early-rising temple-goers. (Singles Rp25,000; doubles Rp35,000.) *(The Prambanan temples are 17km northeast of Jogja toward Solo. A direct bus runs from Umbulharjo Terminal (45min., Rp3500). On arrival, the peaks of Gunung Merapi and the main Prambanan temple should be visible. Maps are complimentary at the tourist office inside the entrance gate. Entry US$7 or Rp63,000, students US$4 or Rp34,000. To avoid the tourist scene and see more than the main temple, rent a bike (Rp5000 per day).*

WARNING Gunung Merapi killed dozens when it erupted in November 1994. In July 1998, Merapi erupted for days in a row, spewing ash over the countryside. It's now closed, although guides offer to take visitors up with assurances that it is safe. Hiking up to see live lava can be exciting, but it is extremely risky. *Let's Go* does not recommend falling into live lava.

INDONESIA

GUNUNG MERAPI AND KALIURANG. Gunung Merapi, 30km north of Jogja, rises triumphantly high above sea level and can be seen from all surrounding areas. **Vogel's,** Jl. Astamulya 76, offers recommended and reasonably priced tours. Wear layers, as temperatures increase dramatically with daybreak. Spend the night at the **hostel ❷** to avoid risky night buses. (☎895 208. Rp25,000-30,000.) For a tamer adventure, stick around **Kaliurang,** 28km north of Jogja on the slopes of Merapi. From Jogja, take a 1hr. bus ride from Umbulharjo or an *angkot* from the Terban Terminal on Jl. Simanjuntak (both Rp2000). Kaliurang offers several cheap hotels, a campground, and a youth hostel, **Vogel's ❶.** (Dorms Rp6000, 10% discount for HI members; singles Rp12,500; doubles Rp17,500-25,000.) While in the **market,** look out for Kaliurang's specialties: sweet, brown-red *tempe* or *tahu bacem* and the mild *jadah,* made from glutinous rice. To explore the town's hiking trails and nature park, head to **Hutan Wisata Kaliurang,** 1km from the youth hostel. Cool off by clambering up the observatory for a stunning view of the valley and Mt. Merapi. *(From the Umbulharjo Terminal, take a bus to Kartosuro, then to Boyolali, then to Selo. Start at 1am to reach the summit in time for sunrise, as the hike will take around 4hr.)*

IMOGIRI ROYAL CEMETERY. Imogiri Royal Cemetery, 12km south of Jogja, is the resting place for the deceased members of the Royal Houses of Jogjakarta and Surakarta, including Jogja's first sultan, Hamengku Buwono I. Imogiri is less touristed than other famous sights, and the pleasant walk affords a rare glimpse of the regard most Jogjakartans retain for members of royalty. Built in 1645 by Sultan Agung, three distinct courtyards constitute the cemetery. To the left rests the royalty of Solo, to the right, the sultans of Jogja, and at the center, the ancient Mataram kings. All visitors are expected to wear formal Javanese clothing in the tombs; after climbing the 345 steps, discard your sweaty garments and rent appropriate attire (Rp1500). Men should wear a sarong, a long-sleeved shirt, and a hat. Women can put on a sarong and *batik* halter top. The tombs are best visited with a guide, but maps are available at the dressing station. In each room, enter quietly, make a donation (Rp100 will do), and kneel by the cool marble. After paying your respects, visit the sacred burial chambers of Sultan Agung and Hamengku Buwono I. *(Buses to Imogiri leave from Umbulharjo Terminal (45min., Rp2000). Open M 10am-noon, F 1-4pm. Rp1500 for outfit.)*

PARANGTRITIS. While the harsh cliffs and clear water are inarguably beautiful, there is something a little unsatisfying about a "look, but don't touch" beach—there is no swimming or surfing allowed. However, the **meditation caves** are very well reputed. Try doing a Jogja-Imogiri-Siluk-Parangtritis route. The 35km connect Imogiri Cemetery, Kotagede silver market, and some beautiful scenery. *(27km south of Jogja. Take a public bus (Rp4500) from Umbulharjo Terminal, or a minibus from Jl. Parangtritis (Rp3000) at the southeast corner of the* kraton*. The last bus back leaves Parangtritis at 5pm. For those left stranded, dozens of guest houses ❷ (Rp20,000-50,000 per night) line the beachfront.)*

SURAKARTA (SOLO) ☎0271

Few tourists stop in Solo, but that only adds to the charm of this old-world city. Solo is about food and *batik*. The local specialty, *nasi liwet* (rice served in a mildly spicy coconut milk curry) is consistently good, and the *batik* is exported all over the world (but cheapest here). The *kratons* (palaces) are not spectacular, and there is no nightlife to speak of, but Solo is truly lovely if you want to stop in an inexpensive place where you're not constantly on a mission to see all and do all.

INDONESIA

TRANSPORTATION

Flights: Adi Sumarmo Airport (☎780 400), 10km northwest of Solo. To get to town, take a blue minibus to Kartosuro Terminal (Rp700-1000) and a bus or a taxi (Rp20,000) to Jl. Slamet Riyadi. **Garuda,** Jl. Slamet Riyadi 201 (☎630 082), in Hotel Cakra. Open M-F 7:30am-5pm, Sa-Su 9am-noon. To **Jakarta** (2 per day; 9:20am, 5:30pm; Rp460,300). **Silk Air,** Jl. Slamet Riyadi 272 (☎724 606), at Hotel Novotel, flies to **Singapore** (Tu 3:40pm, Th and Su 10:20am; US$210). Domestic airport tax Rp8000; international tax Rp30,000.

Trains: Balapan Railway Station (☎644 122), Jl. Monginsidi 112. Trains to: **Bandung** (7hr.; 8am, 9pm; Rp30,000-120,000); **Jakarta** (8-12hr.; 8pm; Rp35,000-185,000); **Jogjakarta** (1hr., 7 per day 6am-7pm, Rp4000); **Surabaya** (3hr.; 2:45, 4:30pm; Rp40,000-130,000). Bandung and Jakarta trains stop in Jogjakarta.

Buses: The **main intercity bus terminal** is **Tirtonadi,** Jl. A. Yani 262 (☎717 297), on the north side of town. Buses to: **Bandung** (11hr.; 4pm; Rp30,000-75,000); **Jakarta** (12hr.; 5, 7pm; Rp35,000-100,000); **Jogjakarta** (1½hr., every 30min., Rp3000); **Semarang** (3½hr., every 30min., Rp5000-8000); **Surabaya** (6hr.; every hr.; Rp15,000-25,000). **Gilingan Minibus Terminal,** connected to Tirtonadi, serves all major destinations. Special overnight buses must be pre-booked. Contact **Raya,** Jl. Sultan Syahir 13 (☎635 838), for buses to **Bogor** (Rp100,000) and **Jakarta** (Rp120,000); **Bandung Cepat,** Jl. Kapten Mulyadi 27 (☎653 836), for buses to **Bandung** (Rp97,500); and **Cakrawala,** Jl. Setia Budi (☎711 710), for buses to **Denpasar** (Rp120,000).

Local Transportation: The plentiful **becak** are most convenient. Metered **taxis** congregate at all major hotels. **Double-decker** and **regular buses,** the cheapest option, travel along Jl. Slamet Riyadi and Jl. Veteran (every 10min. 5am-9pm, Rp1000). Orange **minibuses** (Rp1000) run along many other routes.

ORIENTATION AND PRACTICAL INFORMATION

The city's main boulevard and bus artery, **Jl. Slamet Riyadi,** runs east-west through town. The **tourist office** is on its west side, and many restaurants and food stalls cluster on connecting streets. The **Puro Mangkunegaran Kraton** is at the northern edge. The **post** and **telephone offices** are off **Jl. Sudirman** on Jl. Slamet Riyadi's east side. Homestays are off Jl. Slamet Riyadi: to the north by **Jl. A. Dahlan,** and in the alleys between **Jl. Gatot Subroto** and **Jl. Yos Sudarso** to the south. The **Kraton Surakarta** and the bustling **batik market** are southwest, while **Tirtonadi/Gilingan Terminal** and **Balapan Train Station** are north of the city center.

Tourist Offices: Dinas Pariwisata, Jl. Slamet Riyadi 275 (☎711 435), behind the Museum Radya Pustaka on the far west end of Solo's main boulevard. Brochures, calendar of events, and a super useful booklet. Free city maps. Open M-Sa noon-4pm.

Tours: High-priced tours at agencies along Jl. Slamet Riyadi and many *losmen.* Try **Warung Baru Restaurant** on Jl. A. Dahlan.

Currency Exchange: BNI, Jl. Arifin 2 (☎645 909). Open M-F 7am-noon and 1-3pm. Numerous others are on Jl. Slamet Riyadi and the south end of Jl. Sudirman.

Markets: Pasar Klewer, near Kraton Surakarta, is an endless indoor maze of inexpensive but quality *batiks.* **Pasar Gede,** on Jl. Slamet Riyadi near the *Alun-alun,* sells fruits, vegetables, and spices. **Pasar Burung** is an outdoor aviary on the outskirts of town near Tirtonadi/Gilingan Terminal. All are open daily 8am-4pm.

INDONESIA

Emergency: Police: ☎110. **Fire:** ☎113. **Ambulance:** ☎118.

Police: Adisucipto Manahan (☎712 600) and other posts all over town.

Pharmacy: Pasar Pon, Jl. Slamet Riyadi 124 (☎645 802), and **Rapi,** Jl. Ronggowarsito 161 (☎713 067), are convenient and well stocked. The apotik at **Rumah Sakit Kasih Ibu Hospital** is **open 24hr.**

Medical Services: Rumah Sakit PKU Muhammadiyah, Jl. Ronggowarsito 130 (☎719 743). **Open 24hr. Klinik Prodia Laboratorium,** Jl. Ronggowarsito 143 (☎463 78), is a modern diagnostic clinic. Open M-F 7am-8pm, Sa 7am-5pm. MC/V.

Telephones: Telkom Office, Jl. Mayor Kusmanto 1 (☎644 606), opposite the GPO. **Open 24hr.**

Internet Access: Aloha Internet Cafe, at the Hotel Sahid Kusuma. Delightfully speedy. Rp3600 per hr. Open daily 8am-10:30pm. **NETPluzz,** Jl. Yos Sudarso 174, 500m off Jl. Slamet Riyadi. Rp4000 per hr. Open 9am-11pm.

Post Office: GPO, Jl. Sudirman 8, off the east end of Jl. Slamet Riyadi. *Poste Restante.* Open M-Sa 7am-8pm. **Postal code:** 57111.

ACCOMMODATIONS

Quality *losmen* abound near **Jl. A. Dahlan** and **Kemlayan Kidul,** connecting Jl. Gatot Subroto and Jl. Yos Sudarso. Most are scattered in nondescript alleys, but locals are more than willing to give directions.

The Westerner's Home Stay, Kemlayan Kidul 11 (☎633 106). Turn right into the first alley after Batik Keri's. Clean but basic rooms and pleasant sitting areas. Free hot tea and drinking water. Ring bell after 9:30pm. Singles Rp15,000; doubles Rp20,000. ❷

Dagdan's Home Stay, Baluwerti 02/7 42 (☎669 324), within the *kraton,* 400m past the museum entrance. Lush courtyard, meditation garden, and airy rooms. Special long-term rates. Singles Rp15,000; doubles Rp20,000. ❷

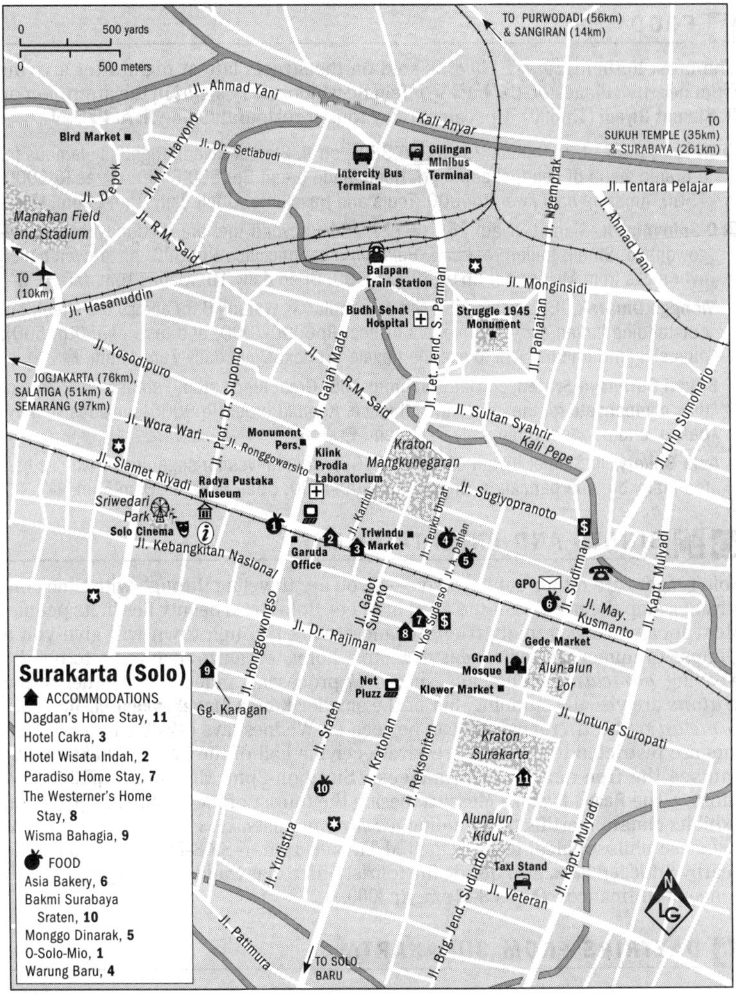

Paradiso Home Stay, Kemlayan Kidul 1/3 (☎652 960). Gorgeous Dutch building furnished with plants, pottery, and a cafe, though rooms are plain. Ring bell after 10pm. Singles Rp25,000, with *mandi* Rp30,000-50,000; doubles Rp35,000-50,000. ❷

Wisma Bahagia (Happy Home Stay), Jl. Honggowongso Gg. Karagan 12 (☎712 449). Laundry. Breakfast included. Discounts for longer stays. Rooms Rp15,000-25,000. ❷

Hotel Wisata Indah, Jl. Slamet Riyadi 173 (☎646 770). Western amenities. Standard rooms with A/C, TV, hot water, and telephone Rp110,000. ❺

Hotel Cakra, Jl. Slamet Riyadi 201 (☎458 47). Upscale hotel with a swimming pool, billiard room, and in-room satellite TV and sound system. All rooms have double beds. Standard Rp195,000; family cottage Rp712,500. AmEx/DC/MC/V. ❺

FOOD

The most authentic *nasi liwet* is sold on the streets late at night after arriving from nearby villages on the backs of female vendors. Try *srabi* in the afternoon on **Jl. Slamet Riyadi** (Rp500). Upscale, pricey tourist restaurants line **Jl. A. Dahlan.**

Warung Baru, Jl. A. Dahlan 23 (☎656 369), off Jl. Slamet Riyadi. Rightfully famous for a titanic menu of good, cheap food. Homemade bread Rp4500-6000. Pizzas Rp6000-7500. Amazing *nasi liwet* Rp4000. Tours and travel info. Open daily 7am-10pm. ❶

O-Solo-Mio, Jl. Slamet Riyadi 253 (☎727 264), beyond the intersection with Jl. Hong-gowongso. Small, Italian *restoran. Bellissimo* cappuccinos Rp8000; pizza oven-baked over rocks from Mt. Merapi Rp16,500-35,500. Open daily 10:30am-11pm. MC/V. ❹

Monggo Dinarak, Jl. A. Dahlan 22. Not as popular as Warung Baru across the street, but outstanding Indian curry and *masala* dishes (Rp6000-7000) and tasty *chai* (Rp2500), plus elegant furniture. Ask to see the travelers' book. Open daily 7am-10pm. ❶

Bakmi Surabaya Sraten, Jl. Gatot Subroto 265. Great lunch stop. Fantastic *bakmi* noodles compensate for the cafeteria ambience. *Komplit* order (Rp9000) includes *siomay, bakso,* and *pangsit*. Open daily 9am-9pm. ❷

Asia Bakery, Jl. Slamet Riyadi 68 (☎648 565). Alternatives for sugar-lovers who've had too many banana pancakes. Snacks Rp1000-4000. Open M-Sa 8:30am-5pm. ❶

INDONESIA

SIGHTS AND ENTERTAINMENT

Solo's sights are rather unimpressive—if you are traveling through with time constraints, skip them and visit the local markets. Solo's real beauty lies in its people. Most locals are extremely friendly, and a walk through town will give you a glimpse of numerous **home industries.** Most hotels organize bike tours to nearby weaving, *gamelan*, rice cracker, and *batik* processing industries. Neither of the *kratons* are visually stunning, but at the smaller **Kraton Mangkunegaran,** first-rate *gamelan* orchestra rehearsals can be seen on Wednesdays (10:30am-noon). Visitors are restricted to the unimpressive receiving hall of the **Kraton Surakarta,** but can see the free dance performances. (Su noon-2pm. Entrance Rp5000. No shorts.) The **Radya Pustaka Museum,** beside the tourist office on Jl. Slamet Riyadi, exhibits Mataram artifacts, including *wayang* puppets, *kris* daggers, and ancient Javanese philosophical texts. (Open M-Th 8am-1pm, F-Sa 8-11am. Rp1000.) The nearby **Sriwedari Park,** also beside the tourist office, has traditional *wayang orang* dance performances. (M-Sa 8-11pm. Rp3000.)

DAYTRIPS FROM SURAKARTA

SANGIRAN MUSEUM. In 1936, a Dutch paleontologist found the fossil skull of Pithecanthropus erectus **(Java Man)** in Sangiran, 15km north of Solo. The site's numerous fossils and pictures and the beautiful ojek ride up the hill are perfect for archaeology buffs. *(Take a minibus from Jl. Slamet Riyadi or Gilingan Terminal toward Purwodadi or Kalijambe and ask to get off near Sangiran (1hr.), where ojek haul visitors up the hill to the museum. To return to Solo from the ojek stand, hop on a large bus with "Berseri" printed on the front. Open M-Sa 8am-5pm. Rp1500.)*

SUKUH TEMPLE. On the slopes of Gunung Lawu 34km northeast of Solo, the Sukuh Temple is difficult to reach, but its views make the journey worthwhile. Built in the 15th century, it was one of the last Hindu temples constructed before the rise of Islam. Due to some very suggestive and descriptive reliefs, many believe that a fertility cult built the temple as a "sex education" exhibit, but the temple's resemblance to those of the Maya in Mexico and Guatemala is far more interesting and mysterious than ancient erotica. Even more difficult to reach (*ojek* is the only reliable way), **Candi Cetho,** 8km away, offers more stunning views of the tobacco and tea plantations below in addition to a larger temple complex now used exclusively for meditation. *(Catch a double-decker bus from Jl. Slamet Riyadi to Palur and then a big bus to Karang Pandan (30min.). From here, take a minibus to Sukuh (20min.). Except on market days, the minibus will drop you off at the bottom of a hill. Take an* ojek *to the temple (Rp3500) or walk 45min. to the top.)*

SEMARANG ☎024

A former Dutch city fallen from favor with tourists, the coastal capital of Semarang has few notable cultural sights and even fewer budget accommodations. Architecture buffs will appreciate the Dutch colonial buildings, but most backpackers only visit Semarang en route to more picturesque destinations nearby.

> **WARNING** Semarang can be dangerous, especially for women and solo travelers. Our coverage of Semarang was last updated in summer 2001.

TRANSPORTATION

Flights: A. Yani Airport (☎760 8735), on Jl. Siliwangi, 5km west of town. **Garuda** (☎844 9331) flies to **Jakarta** (7, 8:40am, noon, 3:20, 6:40pm; Rp386,400). **Merpati** (☎351 7137) flies to **Surabaya** (daily 6:30am and Su 1:45pm; Rp267,600).

Trains: Tawang Railway Station (☎354 4544), off Jl. Merak. Trains to **Jakarta** (6hr.; 5, 8am, 12:25, 8, 9, 11pm, midnight; Rp40,000-210,000) and **Surabaya** (3½hr.; 1:30, 3am, 3, 11:40pm; Rp14,000-130,000). **Lockers** Rp2000 per hr.

Buses: Terboyo (☎658 1924), on Jl. Terboyo. Buses to: **Jakarta** (12hr.; every hr. 4-8pm; Rp27,500, with A/C Rp45,000); **Jogjakarta** (3½hr.; every 10min. 9am-5pm; Rp15,000); **Solo** (2½hr.; every 10 min.; Rp10,000, with A/C Rp16,000); **Surabaya** (6hr.; every 10 min.; Rp25,000, with A/C Rp40,000).

Local Transportation: Semarang's orange **angkot** and large **bis kota** (city buses) have overlapping, inefficient routes. **Minibuses** head out of town and are scarce after 9pm (Rp1000). Ask a local (*not* the driver) for the *harga biasa* (usual price). Prohibited from busy streets, **becak, ojek,** and **andong** improvise through alleyways.

ORIENTATION AND PRACTICAL INFORMATION

The major transportation centers—the **airport, train station,** and **bus terminal**—form the northern edge of the city from west to east, each a few kilometers apart. The **harbor** lies to the north of the train station. The heart of the city is contained by three rotaries, linked by streets with exhaustive shopping and eating opportunities. The **Johar** complex, from which the **Pasar Johar** market stretches east, is a few blocks from the train station, southwest of the **Old Dutch District.** From Johar, **Jl. Pemuda** (which has many tourist services) runs 2km southwest to the **Tugu Muda Monument. Jl. Pandanaran** heads 1-2km eastward from Tugu Muda until **Simpang Lima** (the main square and shopping complex), from which **Jl. Gajah Mada** goes north and connects back to Jl. Pemuda. Architecture buffs should explore the Old Dutch District, **Chinatown,** the area south of the market, and the ritzy colonial-style hills of the **Candi-Kintelan district,** southwest of downtown.

Tourist Office: Kota Semarang Tourist Office, on Jl. Sriwijaya 29 (☎831 12 20). Useful maps and info. Open M-Th 7am-3pm, F 7-11am.

Currency Exchange: Banks line major streets and are usually open M-F 8am-2pm. **P.T. Supit,** Jl. Pemuda 39C (☎354 24 01), exchanges cash and checks. Open M-F 8am-4pm, Sa 8am-1pm. **BCA,** Jl. Pemuda 90-92, has a **24hr. ATM.**

Luggage Storage: At Tawang Railway Station. Lockers Rp2000 per hr.

Emergency: Police: ☎110. **Fire:** ☎113. **Ambulance:** ☎118.

Police: Central station, Jl. Dr. Sutomo 19 (☎844 4444). Open 24hr.

Pharmacy: Kimia Farma, Jl. Pemuda 135 (☎354 3646). Open 24hr.

Medical Services: Telogorejo Hospital (☎844 6444), on Jl. A. Dahlan, 1 block from Simpang Lima. Some English spoken.

Telephones: International **wartel** all over. No credit card calls. **Kopegtel,** Jl. Alun-alun Timur 2, behind GPO. Fax. **Telkom Office,** Jl. Lt. Gen. Suprapto 7. Both open 24hr.

Internet Access: Zone, 5th fl. Plaza Simpang Lima (☎831 8831). Rp6000 per hr. Open daily 10am-10pm. **Wasantara Net,** at the GPO. Rp5000 per hr. Open daily 8am-10pm.

Post Office: GPO, Jl. Pemuda 4 (☎554 563). *Poste Restante.* Open daily 8am-8pm. **Postal code:** 50000. Downtown **branch,** Jl. Imam Bardjo 3 (☎841 2135). *Poste Restante.* Open M-Th 8am-4pm, F-Sa 8am-3:30pm. **Postal code:** 50243.

INDONESIA

ACCOMMODATIONS

Hotel Blambangan, Jl. Pemuda 23 (☎541 649). Safe, immaculate, and conveniently located. Often fully booked. All rooms include private bath and morning snack. Doubles Rp27,500, with A/C Rp50,000; triples Rp36,000. ❷

Hotel Oewas Asia, Jl. Kol Sugiono 12 (☎354 2547), one block northeast of the Metro Grand Park Hotel on Jl. Pemuda. Cement floors, piercing bright lights. Not exactly cozy, but one of the cheapest places in town and close to the train station. Singles and doubles Rp25,000, with A/C 35,000, with TV and A/C Rp40,000. ❷

Hotel Natour/Dibya Puri, Jl. Pemuda 11 (☎354 7821), at the intersection with Jl. Imam Bonjol near the post office. Huge doubles, comfortable beds, and private verandas. Breakfast buffet included. Rooms with TV Rp35,000-70,000. ❸

Hotel Bojong, Jl. Pemuda 8 (☎354 6240), at the end of the short alley across Hotel Dibya Puri (south of the intersection of Jl. Pemuda and Jl. Agus Salim). Clean, basic *mandi*. Doubles Rp15,000, with fan Rp20,000 with *mandi* Rp50,000, with TV and A/C Rp75,000; Rp10,000 for extra bed. ❶

FOOD

Semarang teems with stalls and fast food chains along Jl. Pemuda and Jl. Gajah Mada's south end. **Citraland Mall** has Western and Indonesian fare at good prices. Vegetarians, however, often have to resort to *gado-gado* and *nasi goreng*. **Nusantara** ❶, Jl. Pandanaran 6 Ruko 11 & 12, near Tugu Muda, is popular for its spicy, meaty options over hot rice. (Dishes Rp1000-6000. Open 24hr.)

NEAR SEMARANG

GEDONG SONGO PARK

An ambitious hike reveals the five (of the original nine) remaining Gedong Songo Temples. Hidden on the hillside, their beauty and pleasant shade attract hikers of every level. Visit on weekdays to avoid crowded trails. Experienced hikers can head toward the peak on a trail that begins 200m before the hot spring. A stone creature stands watch among the trees and marks the path, which becomes heavily overgrown. A guide is recommended for climbing to the summit; freelance and official guides can be found at the tourist office (Rp15,000). Guides inside the gates can also show you a spectacular view of the surrounding mountains and lowlands by horseback. (Open daily 7am-5pm. Admission Rp2500.) Since the temples are a two-day trip from Jogjakarta and an exhausting daytrip from Semarang, travelers might want to stay at the cheap *losmen* in nearby Bandungan. **Sari Marin Indah ❸,** on Jl. Kauma Sari, offers doubles with hot water. (☎711 485. Rooms Rp30,000.) On the same street, **Losmen Lestari ❶** has small, damp doubles with private *mandi* (Rp7500). Gedong Songo Park is in the town of **Sumowono.** To get there, take a bus from Semarang's Terboyo Terminal for Bandungan (1½hr., Rp2000, extra for large bags), from which a 20min. *angkot* ride leads to Sumowono. From the bottom of the hill below Gedong Songo, take an *ojek* to the gates (Rp2000-3000). To reach Gedong Songo from Jogjakarta, take a bus toward Semarang (Rp5000-10,000) and ask to get off at Ambarawa (2hr.). Take a minibus to Bandungan (Rp1000). Many buses head from town to the gates. (Rp1000.)

DIENG PLATEAU

Between tourist-packed Jogjakarta and sweltering Semarang, the quiet mountain village of Dieng offers cool, clean air and a wealth of unspoiled natural and man-made sights. A 2-3hr. walk reveals the multi-colored **Telaga Warna Lake** (fed from a sulfur hot spring), mushroom and potato terraces, smoldering craters, and ancient Hindu temples. The eerie plateau of **Kawahsi Kidang** merits exploration.

The **tourist office** next to the bus terminal **stores luggage.** Minibuses go from the terminal into town. Travelers who wish to enjoy the mountain air for a little longer can stay at **Dieng Plateau ❶,** opposite the *ojek* stand. (☎92 823. Singles Rp15,000; doubles Rp20,000.) It serves food (Rp3000-7000), as do numerous *warung*. **Losmen Jawa Tengah ❷,** toward the department store on Jl. A. Yani, 150m north of the intersection with Jl. Pasman, has minimal but satisfactory rooms (Rp20,000).

Dieng Plateau is best accessed and explored by rental car (Rp300,000 per day). With the freedom of a car, you'll have the amazing chance to visit small hill villages. Alternatively, buses scurry from the town of **Wonosobo** to the highland (45min., 7am-3pm, Rp3000). Jogjakarta has direct buses to Wonosobo, but the trip from Semarang and Surakarta requires transfers at Bawen Magelang. From the Wonosobo **bus terminal** (open daily 7am-3pm), connect to **Magelang** (1½hr.; every 15min., last bus 5pm; Rp3000). Head left from where the bus drops you off and walk 1km or ride an *ojek* to the gate, where maps are available (Rp2000).

SURABAYA ☎031

As the second-largest city in Indonesia, Surabaya has six-lane streets, a formidable skyline, and five indoor shopping complexes the size of small towns. Travelers seeking an "authentic Java" may be put off by the city's restless pace, but with connections to every island in the archipelago by ferry, plane, or bus, it's an important transit city with luxuries not found in other parts of east Java.

> **WARNING** Surabaya and Semarang can be dangerous, especially for female and solo travelers. *Let's Go* includes these cities because they are important transportation hubs, but recommends avoiding these areas when possible. If you must go, be on your guard. Coverage of Surabaya and Semarang was last updated in summer 2001.

TRANSPORTATION

Flights: Juanda Airport (☎866 7513, ext. 9), 18km south of Surabaya. Taxis (Rp20,000-30,000) and DAMRI buses (Rp2500) shuttle visitors into town, leaving when full. To: **Bandar Seri Bagawan** (M, W, F; US$237, US$351 round-trip); **Denpasar** (6am, 7:20pm; Rp295,000-310,000); **Jakarta** (every 2hr. 6am-8pm; Rp457,000-625,000); **Jogjakarta** (4:20pm; Rp230,000). **Garuda** (☎534 5886; open M and Sa 9am-1pm, Tu-Th 7:30am-4:30pm, F 7:30am-5pm) and **Royal Brunei Airlines** (☎532 6407; open M-F 9am-5pm, Sa 9am-noon) are both on Jl. Basuki Rakhmat 106-128, next door to the Hyatt Regency. **Merpati,** Jl. Raya Darmo 111 (☎568 8111).

Trains: Stations are **Gubeng,** on Jl. Gubeng Masjid (☎503 3115); **Kota/Semut,** on Jl. Stasiun Kota; and **Pasar Turi** (☎534 5014), on Jl. Semarang. Trains traveling through Gubeng stop at Kota/Semut. From Gubeng, trains go to: **Bandung** (10½hr.; 7am; Rp158,800) via **Solo** (4½hr.) and **Jogjakarta** (5hr.; Rp48,500-138,500); **Banyuwangi** (5hr.; 8am, 10pm; Rp27,000-40,000); **Jakarta** (12hr.; 6pm; Rp148,500); **Malang** (1hr.; every hr.; Rp10,000). From Pasar Turi, executive trains go to **Jakarta** (12-13hr.; 6 per day 9am-9pm; Rp56,000-227,000) via **Semarang** (8hr.; Rp44,500-217,000) and **Cirebon** (10hr.; Rp44,500-217,000). Ticket offices open daily 8am-5pm.

Buses: Bungurasih/Purabaya Terminal (☎853 1701), 10km south of town. All south-bound **DAMRI** and **Patas buses** finish their routes at Bungurasih/Purabaya. Executive/deluxe buses with A/C, video, reclining seat, toilet, and food go to: **Bandung** (10hr.; 3, 3:30, 4, 4:30pm; Rp87,500); **Banyuwangi** (6hr.; every 15min.; Rp30,000); **Denpasar** (7hr.; every hr. 4-9pm; Rp55,000); **Jakarta** (11hr.; every 30min. 2-4:30pm; Rp87,500); **Malang** (1¼hr., every 10min., Rp8500); **Probolingo** (1½hr.; every 10min.; Rp10,000); **Solo/Jogjakarta** (4½-5½hr.; every hr. 10am-midnight, 12:30am; Rp24,000-28,500). Pay on the bus. Economy buses are slower, more crowded, leave when full, and charge half the price.

Ferries: The **port** is 100m from Tanjung Perak Terminal (see **Local Transportation,** below). **PELNI office,** Jl. Pahlawan 112 (☎355 9950). Open M-Th 8am-4pm, F 8-11am and 1-4pm. Purchase tickets at least 3 days in advance; cash only. To: **Bali** (Rp90,000-127,000); **Jakarta** (Rp105,000-327,000); **Ujung Pandang** (Rp119,000-374,000). Ask at the PELNI office for departure times and other destinations.

Local Transportation: Joyoboyo Terminal, on Jl. Joyoboyo by Surabaya Zoo, is the main local bus terminal. From Bungurasih Terminal, DAMRI (Rp1000) and P-1 Patas (Rp2000) **buses** run by the zoo, Tunjungan Plaza, Pasar Turi Station, the PELNI office, the GPO, and the Madura Ferry Terminal, ending at **Tanjung Perak Terminal.** Buses run 6am-9pm. There are 30 **bemo** routes, labeled alphabetically; almost half use Joyoboyo Terminal as a base. **Becak** are useful for short distances (Rp2000-3000).

Taxis: The best way to get around. If they don't turn on the meter, hop out and catch another. Rp2800 for 1st km, about Rp800 each additional km. **Taxi Citra,** Jl. Arif Rahmuin 147 (☎592 5555). **Zebra Taxi** (☎841 1111).

Rentals: Toyota Rent-A-Car, Jl. Raya Waru Km15 (☎853 0909), 2km from the airport, and Jl. Basuki Rakhmat 116 (☎546 2500). Rp275,000 per day. International Driver's Permit (see p. 36) or driver (Rp99,000 per day) required. Open daily 8am-4pm.

ORIENTATION AND PRACTICAL INFORMATION

Surabaya is a sprawling harbor city with a branching river that snakes around its more popular spots, making navigation difficult. The huge **Tunjungan Plaza** marks the intersection of **Jl. Tunjungan** and **Jl. Pemuda,** two main commercial streets. **Jl. Yos Sudarso** and Jl. Pemuda meet four blocks east around the center of town. **Gubeng Train Station** is a few blocks down at the end of Jl. Pemuda across the river,

INDONESIA

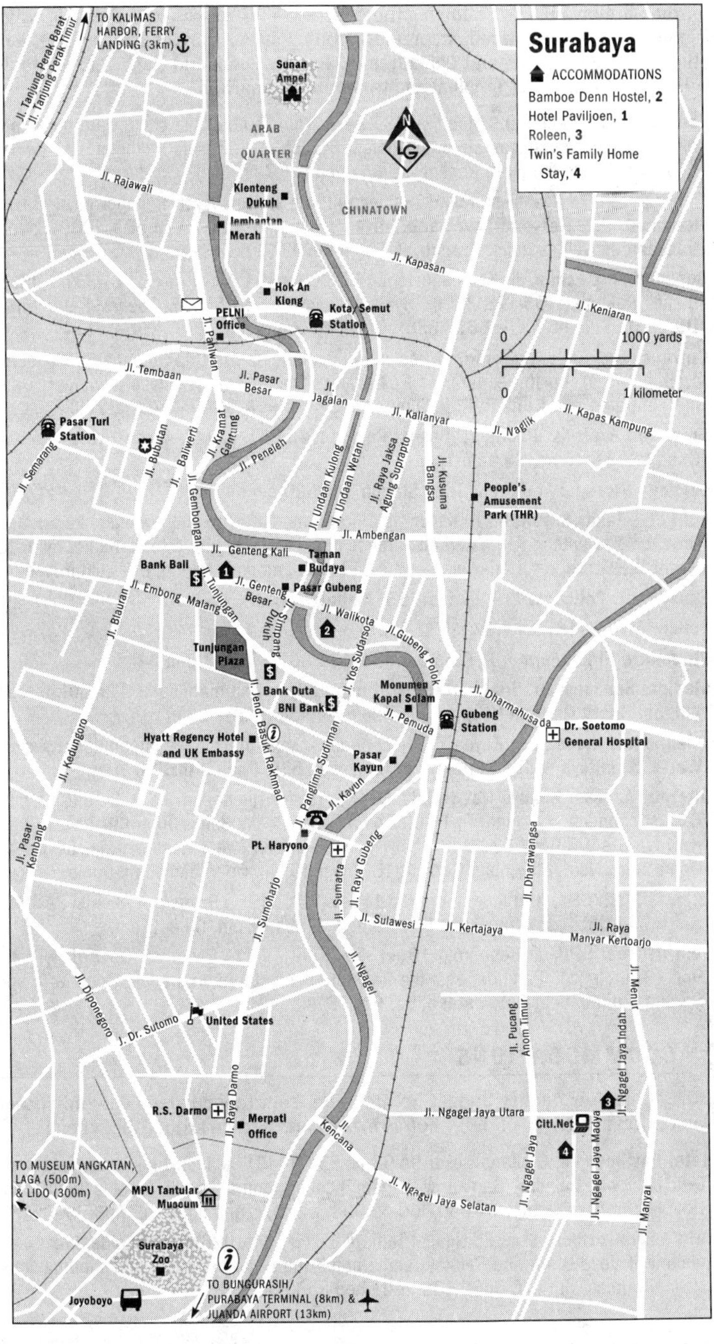
Surabaya
ACCOMMODATIONS
Bamboe Denn Hostel, 2
Hotel Paviljoen, 1
Roleen, 3
Twin's Family Home Stay, 4
0
1000 yards
0
1 kilometer
TO KALIMAS HARBOR, FERRY LANDING (3km)
Jl. Tanjung Perak Barat
Jl. Tanjung Perak Timur
Sunan Ampel
ARAB QUARTER
CHINATOWN
Jl. Rajawali
Klenteng Dukuh
Jembatan Merah
Jl. Kapasan
Hok An Kiong
Kota/Semut Station
PELNI Office
Jl. Keniaran
Jl. Pahlawan
Jl. Tembaan
Jl. Pasar Besar
Jl. Jagalan
Jl. Kalianyar
Jl. Naglik
Jl. Kapas Kampung
Pasar Turi Station
Jl. Semarang
Jl. Bubutan
Jl. Baliwerti
Jl. Kramat Gantung
Jl. Peneleh
Jl. Gemblongan
Jl. Undaan Kulong
Jl. Undaan Wetan
Jl. Raya Jaksa Agung Suprapto
Jl. Kusuma Bangsa
People's Amusement Park (THR)
Jl. Ambengan
Jl. Genteng Kali
Taman Budaya
Bank Bali
Jl. Genteng Besar
Pasar Gubeng
Jl. Embong Malang
Jl. Tunjungan
Jl. Simpang Dukuh
Jl. Walikota
Jl. Gubeng Polok
Jl. Blauran
Tunjungan Plaza
Jl. Yos Sudarso
Bank Duta
BNI Bank
Monumen Kapal Selam
Jl. Dharmahusada
Gubeng Station
Dr. Soetomo General Hospital
Jl. Pemuda
Hyatt Regency Hotel and UK Embassy
Jl. Jend. Basuki Rakhmad
Jl. Kedungdoro
Jl. Panglima Sudirman
Pasar Kayun
Jl. Kayun
Pt. Haryono
Jl. Pasar Kembang
Jl. Sumatra
Jl. Raya Gubeng
Jl. Sumoharjo
Jl. Sulawesi
Jl. Kertajaya
Jl. Raya Manyar Kertoarjo
Jl. Dharawangsa
Jl. Menur
Jl. Ngagel
Jl. Diponegoro
J. Dr. Sutomo
United States
Jl. Pucang Anom Timur
Jl. Ngagel Jaya Indah
R.S. Darmo
Jl. Raya Darmo
Merpati Office
Jl. Ngagel Jaya Utara
Citi.Net
Jl. Kencana
Jl. Ngagel Jaya
Jl. Ngagel Jaya Madya
TO MUSEUM ANGKATAN, LAGA (500m) & LIDO (300m)
MPU Tantular Museum
Jl. Ngagel Jaya Selatan
Jl. Manyar
Surabaya Zoo
Joyoboyo
TO BUNGURASIH/ PURABAYA TERMINAL (8km) & JUANDA AIRPORT (13km)

after the Surabaya Plaza. Following the river north brings you to **Jl. Peneleh,** which has some reasonably priced accommodations. Farther upriver are the **GPO, Kota Station,** the **Arab Quarter,** and **Chinatown. Jl. Tanjung Perak** and the river eventually head to the **Madura Ferry Terminal** and to Surabaya's harbor.

Tourist Office: Regional Office (☎853 1815), 7km south of the city toward the airport on Jl. Wisata Menanggal. More convenient **branch** at Jl. Basuki Rakhmat 121 (☎534 4710), opposite the Hyatt Regency. Both open M-F 7am-1pm.

Tours: Dozens of agencies around Tunjungan Plaza and the Hyatt Regency on Jl. Basuki Rakhmat. **P.T. Haryono Tours and Travel,** Jl. Sulawesi 27-29 (☎503 4000), books transport as well as tours. **Branch,** Jl. Sudirman 93 (☎532 5800).

Consulates: Canada, Jl. Kembang Jepun 38-40 (☎354 4330; fax 354 4331). **UK,** Jl. Basuki Rakhmat 106-128 3rd fl., Hyatt Regency (☎550 5500). Open M-F 9am-5pm. **US,** Jl. Dr. Sutomo 33 (☎567 6880). Open M-F 8am-4pm.

Currency Exchange: Banks with ATMs line Jl. Pemuda and Jl. Urip Sumoharjo. **Danamon** (☎534 8700), on Jl. Pemuda. AmEx Traveler's Cheques. MC/V cash advances. Open M-F 8:30am-3pm. **Bank Bali,** Jl. Tunjungan 52. **24hr. ATM** (AmEx/Cirrus/V).

American Express: Pacto, Jl. Basuki Rakhmat (☎531 1234), in the Hyatt Regency. Open M-F 9am-5pm, Sa 9am-1pm.

Luggage Storage: At Gubeng Train Station. Rp2000 per day.

Markets: Pasar Kayun, on Jl. Kayun, is a flower market lined with eateries. **Pasar Genteng,** on Jl. Genteng Kali, is an all-purpose market by day and a food market by night. **Pasar Blawuran,** on Jl. Blawuran at the end of Jl. Embong Malang, is a gold market.

Emergency: Police: ☎110. **Fire:** ☎113. **Ambulance:** ☎118.

Police: At Jl. Raden Saleh 2 (☎532 8535).

Pharmacy: Kimia Farma, Jl. Raya Darmo 2-4 (☎567 7777). **Open 24hr.**

Medical Services: Dr. Soetomo General Hospital, Jl. Dharmahusada 6 (☎502 0079). **William Booth General Hospital,** Jl. Diponegoro 34 (☎567 8917).

Telephones: Indosat, Jl. Kayun 72. HCD phones. Most malls have international **wartel. Wartel Surabaya Yudha Pratama,** Jl. Tunjungan 53k. **Open 24hr.**

Internet Access: Kokuyo Net (☎547 5848), 1st fl., Tunjungan Plaza, by the ice rink. Fastest connection around. Rp15,000 per hr. Open daily 8am-10pm. **Citi.Net,** Jl. Ngagel Jaya Utara 80 (☎502 5249), between Roleen and Twin's hostels. Rp4000 per hr. Open 24hr. Also at the main **GPO.** Rp1500 per 15min. Open daily 8am-5pm.

Express Mail: DHL, Jl. H.R. Muhammad 111 (☎734 3435). **Branch,** Jl. Basuki Rakhmat 57 (☎534 0852), by Tunjungan Plaza. Open M-F 8am-5pm, Sa 8-11am.

Post Offices: GPO, Jl. Kebonrojo 10 (☎352 2099). *Poste Restante.* Open daily 8am-9pm. **Branch** at Jl. Pemuda, past the General Soerjo statue on the left. Open M-Th and Sa 8am-2pm, F 8-11am. **Postal code:** 60175.

ACCOMMODATIONS

Surabaya has few quality budget hotels aside from those listed. The only other cheap option is a group of dingy hotels in the part of town around Jl. Peneleh.

Hotel Paviljoen, Jl. Genteng Besar 94-98 (☎534 3449), near Jl. Tunjungan. In a posh Dutch colonial building. Bargain with them if cheap rooms are full. Breakfast included. Doubles Rp40,000; triples Rp60,000-65,000, with A/C and hot water Rp85,000. ❸

Twin's Family Home Stay, Jl. Ngagel Tama A-12 (☎504 1026), on the side street connecting Jl. Jaya Utara and Selatan. Large hotel with wooden interior and winding stairwells. Doubles with A/C Rp65,000; extra bed Rp30,000. ❹

Bamboe Denn Hostel, Jl. Ketabang Kali 6A (☎534 0333), west of Jl. Yos Sudarso intersection toward the river. Cheapest beds in town. Only some rooms have locks. Bunk beds Rp5,000; singles and doubles with shared *mandi* Rp27,500. ❶

Roleen, Jl. Ngagel Jaya Indah I/18 (☎502 2619), on the corner with Jl. Ngagel Jaya Utara, south of the town center. A quiet, converted family home worth the taxi ride from the city. Rooms with A/C, bath, hot water, and TV from Rp90,000. ❺

FOOD

Most of Surabaya's restaurants aren't kind to tight budgets. Shopping malls offer an overwhelming collection of food options at better prices, but the food at the riverside restaurants along **Jl. Kayun** and at *warung* and night stalls along **Jl. Genteng Besar** is superior. **Kayun Park** is bordered by cheap eateries that serve excellent seafood. Local specialties include *ular* (fried snake). Clean, cheap **Duta Cafe ❷**, Jl. Genteng Kali, opposite Siola Department Store, serves Indonesian standards. (Open daily 7am-10pm.) **San Thauw ❸,** Jl. Raya Gubeng 64, specializes in Chinese cuisine and seafood. (Open daily 10am-4pm and 6-9pm).

SIGHTS

Surabaya's malls are worth a visit, if only to gawk at their size and enjoy soft ice cream in A/C comfort. **Tunjungan Plaza** is said to be the archipelago's largest, with an ice rink, movie theater, and stores galore. (Open daily 10am-11pm; most shops close by 9pm.) The **People's Amusement Park (THR),** behind the THR Mall, offers traditional dance and music performances. Schedules are available at the tourist office. (☎534 0956. Open Th and Sa 7pm-midnight. Rp350.) The real thrills, however, are at nearby **Taman Remaja**'s ferris wheel and mini roller coasters (Rp2000).

The **Surabaya Zoo** is Southeast Asia's largest, but animal lovers might be turned off by the unnatural, cramped living spaces and the crude spectators. From the Tunjungan area, catch a bus (15min.) south on Jl. Sudirman; ask to get off at "Kebun Binatang." (Komodo dragon feedings the 5th and 20th of every month. Open daily 7am-6pm. Rp3000. Elephant and camel rides Rp2000.)

The **Arab Quarter** and the monumental **Sunan Ampel Mosque,** the oldest mosque in East Java, can be visited in a few hours and are worth the trip for architecture buffs. The mosque was built by Sunan Ampel, one of the *wali songo*, nine Muslim holy men who initiated the spread of Islam in Java. To get there, take any *bemo* (#10 is ideal) to Jembatan Merah Terminal and then hop on a *becak* (Rp2000) or walk 15min. northeast to Sunan Ampel. Be warned that tensions are high in this area as a result of recent religious fighting—exercise caution.

NIGHTLIFE

Plenty of discotheques and karaoke bars scattered around **Tunjungan Plaza** are crowded on weekends. Surabaya's major hotels are known for their bars with nightly live music, Bintang beer at around Rp20,000, and decent vibes for a Rp40,000 cover charge. Low-key **Tavern Pub** in the Hyatt Regency, Chinese-filled **Desperado** in Sanggrila Hotel, tropical **Bongos** in the Sheraton, and the similar **Java Jimmies** in the Westin complete the hotel pub crawl. All close around 3am. You'll need to take cabs to get around, so just make sure they are metered. **Colors,** Jl. Sumatra 81, is a cozy bar/cafe crowded with hungry hip cats and kittens on the prowl. (Excellent pop bands after 9pm. Bintang Rp11,000; pitchers Rp36,000. Happy hour 7-9pm daily. Open daily 5pm-2am.) Cheap and popular on weekends, **Laga,** Jl. May Jen Sungkono 107, is one of the few "bars" that neither costs more than a hotel room nor blasts deafening dance music. (☎568 1826. Live music from 10:30pm. Cover F Rp3000, Sa Rp5000. Open M-F 6pm-1:20am, Sa 6pm-2:00am.)

MALANG ☎0341

Travelers to East Java instinctively choose Malang over sweaty Surabaya as a base from which to explore the province. The view of Mt. Bromo's lunar landscape on the horizon, seen from Malang at dusk, is truly impressive. There are few foreign tourists, but this is a hot spot for Javanese vacationers on their way to the beach.

TRANSPORTATION

Trains: Stasiun Kereta Api Kota Baru, Jl. Trunojoyo 10 (☎362 208). Visible from Tugu Monument. Trains to: **Blitar** (2hr., 5 per day 7am-6:30pm, Rp2400; express: 9am, Rp5000); **Jakarta** (12hr.; economy: 16hr., 2:30pm, Rp45,000; express: 3:20pm, Rp150,000-200,000) via **Jogjakarta** (economy: 8hr., Rp35,000; express: 6hr., Rp100,000-160,000); **Solo** (6hr.; 2:30pm; Rp35,000); **Surabaya** (2½hr., 6 per day 4:30am-5:20pm, Rp2900; express: 12:30pm, Rp5000).

Buses: Leave from Arjosari, Gadang, and Landungsari terminals. **Arjosari Terminal,** Jl. Terusan Raden Intan 1 (☎397 058), 6km north of the city by *angkot* A-G or G-A. Buses to: **Denpasar** (11hr.; every 15min.; economy Rp60,000, executive Rp80,000-100,000); **Jakarta** (18hr.; 12 per day 12:30-2:30pm; Rp120,000-160,000); **Surabaya** (2hr., every 15min., Rp3500-7500). Many express tickets are on night buses. For **Gunung Bromo,** take a bus to **Probolinggo** (2hr., Rp3500-8000) and catch a *bemo* for the final leg of the trip (1-2hr.). **Gadang Terminal,** 5km south by angkot A-G or G-A from Tugu Monument or *Alun-alun,* has **minibuses** that head toward **Bale Kambang** and other beaches to the south (1-1½hr., Rp3500). **Landungsari Terminal,** 6km northwest by *angkot* ADL from Tugu Monument, sends buses to **Selecta** (1½hr., Rp3500) via **Batu** (1hr., Rp2500).

Local Transportation: Ubiquitous **becak** can only travel on smaller roads. **Angkot** (Rp850), labeled as follows, run between terminals: **A-L** and **A-D-L,** Arjosari to Landungsari; **A-G, G-A** (**A-B-G, A-J-G,** and **A-M-G**), Arjosari past Tugu Monument and *Alun-alun* to Gadang; **L-G, G-L,** and **L-D-G,** Landungsari past *Alun-alun* to Gadang. **M-M** runs past the train station to Tugu Monument, down Jl. Majapahit to the *Alun-alun,* up Jl. Kawi, and back. *Angkot* run daily 4am-10pm.

Taxis: Can be hailed from hotels around Tugu Monument or called for pickup. Rp2000 plus Rp1200 per km. Try **Argo** (☎490 444), **Bima** (☎717 171), or **Citra** (☎490 555).

ORIENTATION AND PRACTICAL INFORMATION

Malang, 90km south of Surabaya, is bordered by volcanoes—**Gunung Butak** (2868m) to the west, **Gunung Arjuna** (3339m) to the north, and **Gunung Semeru** (3676m) and **Bromo** (2329m) to the east—and is rightly the region's hot spot. The city centers around two public spaces: the **Tugu Monument,** a traffic rotary with hotels and the **train station** to the east; and the **Alun-alun** (the town center), 500m south of Tugu Monument, near the **GPO** and the busiest shopping areas. Three **bus terminals** lie on the outer rim of the city; Arjosari, the main station to the northeast, Landungsari to the northwest, and Gadang to the south.

Tourist Offices: Bunga Wisata, Jl. Basuki Rakhmat 6H (☎323 966). Hut with limited info and overpriced tours. Open daily 9am-4pm. **Tourist Information Center,** Jl. Basuki Rakhmat 5 (☎364 052), inside Toko Oen (see **Food,** p. 161). May be more helpful—but definitely a travel agency, not an information office. Maps, brochures, travel advice, and tickets. Open daily 9am-9pm. **Branch** at the train station (☎362 208).

INDONESIA

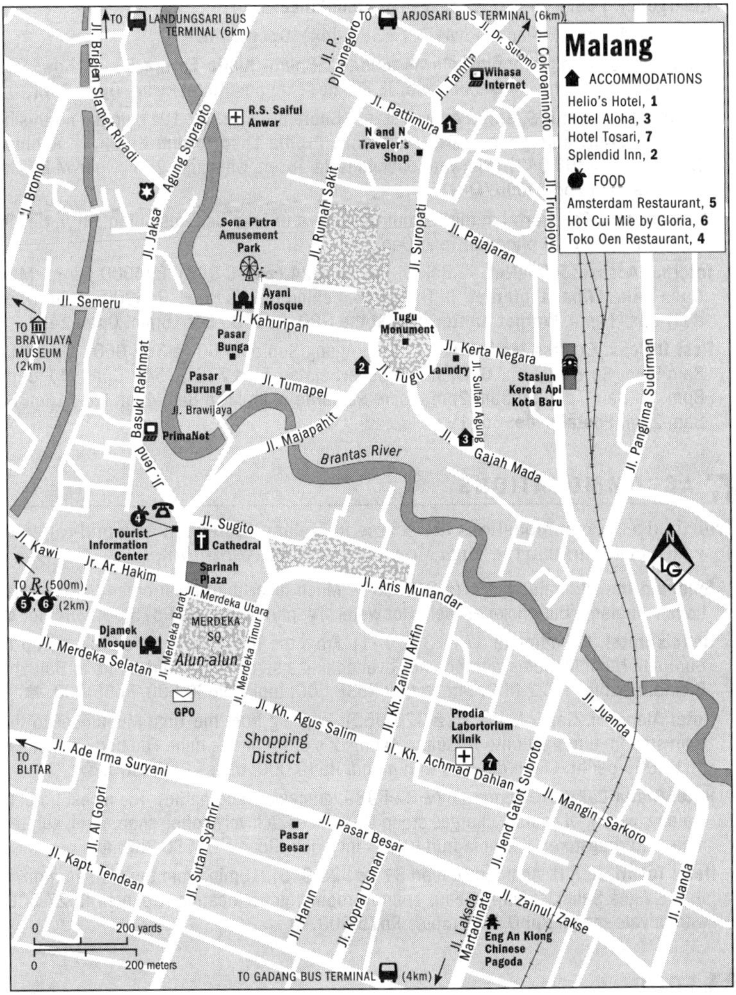

Tours: Pt. Mujur Surya, Jl. Bromo 33A (☎279 55). Books PELNI and air tickets. **N and N Traveler's Shop,** Jl. Suropati 19 (☎345 612), 50m from Helio's Hotel. Organizes tours and travel arrangements. Open daily 7am-9:30pm. All tourist offices, most hotels, and counters in Arjosari Terminal arrange tours and book express buses to major cities.

Currency Exchange: Banks are open M-F 8am-2:30pm. **Bank BCA** has a **24hr. ATM** (Cirrus/MC/V) on Jl. Basuki Rakhmat in the alley between McDonald's and Sarinah Plaza. A **moneychanger** and more ATMs are in the same building.

Luggage Storage: At the train station. Rp2000 per item. No overnight storage.

Markets: Malang is crowded with shopping. The **Alun-alun** never stops bustling with *warung* and merchants. Over the river and through Jl. Brawijaya lies the ever-chirping **Pasar Burung** and the **Pasar Bunga** (flower market). Open daily 8am-5pm.

Emergency: Police: ☎110. **Fire:** ☎113. **Ambulance:** ☎118.

Police: Polresta, Jl. Slamet Riyadi 1 (☎366 444). **Open 24hr.**

Pharmacies: In all shopping plazas along Jl. Salim. **Kimia Farma 53,** Jl. Kawi 22A (☎362 301), at the intersection with Jl. Bromo, 1km past Hotel Riche. **Open 24hr.**

Medical Services: R.S. Saiful Anwar, Jl. J.A. Suprapto 2 (☎362 101), on the north side of town. **24hr. emergency care.** Cash only. **Prodia Labortorium Klinik,** Jl. Achmad Dahlan 17 (☎366 042). With your back to Hotel Toseri, walk right 25m. Open M-F 6am-8pm, Sa 7am-2pm. AmEx/MC/V.

Telephones: 24hr. wartel at the Telkom Office next to Toko Oen Restaurant on Jl. Basuki Rakhmat. Free **HCD phone** at Toko Oen.

Internet Access: PrimaNet, Jl. Bakusi Rakhmat 24 (☎340 043). Rp4000 per hr. MTV. **Open 24hr. Wihasa Internet,** Jl. Thamrin 6, behind Helio's Hotel. Rp6000 per hr. Open daily 8am-10pm. **Warnet Kantor Pos,** at the GPO. Rp1500 per 15min. **Open 24hr.**

Post Offices: Express Mail: DHL, Jl. Jaksa Agung Suprapto 60 (☎365 060). Open M-F 8am-5pm, Sa 8am-1pm. **GPO,** Jl. Merdeka Selatan 5 (☎736 2254). Open M-F 8am-8pm, Sa 8am-7pm, Su 9am-2pm. *Poste Restante* open M-Th 8am-4pm, F 8-11am, Sa 8am-2pm. **Postal code:** 65119.

ACCOMMODATIONS

Truly budget accommodations are scarce in Malang. Hotels, mostly mid-range to upscale, cluster around the Tugu Monument and the *Alun-alun.*

Splendid Inn, Jl. Majapahit 4 (☎366 860). Much nicer than most other accommodations in Malang, but pricier as well. Hot water, TV, phone. Rooms Rp75,000 and up. ❹

Helio's Hotel, Jl. Pattimura 37 (☎362 741). From the Tugu rotary, head 2 blocks up Jl. Suropati. Humble rooms with porches overlooking a serene courtyard. Tours to Bali and Bromo. Doubles Rp22,000, with *mandi* Rp38,500; triples Rp30,500/Rp55,000. ❷

Hotel Aloha, Jl. Gajah Mada 7 (☎326 950). Walking from the Tugu Monument to the train station, turn right onto Jl. Sultan Agung; it's down on the right. Full body massages Rp15,000 per hr. Clean doubles with *mandi* Rp40,000; triples Rp50,000. ❸

Hotel Graha Cakra, Jl. Cerme 16 (☎324 989; grhcakra@indo.net.id). The nicest hotel in Malang, which, of course, charges steep US$ prices. A lovely coffee shop, pool, sun terrace, and drugstore. Welcome fruit basket included. Rooms US$80-250. ❺

Hotel Tosari, Jl. K.H. Achmad Dahlan 31 (☎326 945), 10min. from the *Alun-alun* down Jl. Kh. Agus Salim. Cheap, clean, spartan rooms; good location. Doubles Rp27,500, with private *mandi* Rp50,000; triples Rp75,000. ❷

FOOD

While in Malang, be sure to try *nasi pecel*, an east Javanese specialty of boiled vegetables with spicy peanut sauce and fried *tempe* over rice. Countless *warung* encircling the *Alun-alun* are loaded with *nasi pecel* and more. Quieter stands line Jl. Suropati and Jl. Kawi. Pricier cafes attached to hotels cook up Indonesian and Western dishes. **Hero supermarket,** inside Sarinah Plaza north of the *Alun-alun*, is a good place to stock up on food for daytrips. (Open daily 9am-9pm.)

Hot Cui Mie by Gloria, Ruko Kawi Atas 43B, beside Planet Surf 2-3km west on Jl. Kawi. *Angkot* M-M. Packed with locals. Noodle, meat, and soup masterpieces Rp4500-7000. Full juice bar cools your tongue (Rp3500-5000). Open daily 9am-9pm. ❶

Amsterdam Restaurant, Jl. Terusan Kawi 2, opposite the entrance to Taman Buah-Buahan. *Angkot* M-M. Indonesian, Western, and Chinese dishes Rp3000-20,000; steaks Rp19,000-42,500. Nightly music 8pm-midnight. Open daily 9am-midnight. ❸

Toko Oen Restaurant, Jl. Basuki Rakhmat 5, opposite McDonald's. A colonial relic serving fresh juices (Rp5000-7500) and locally produced ice cream (Rp3500-12,500). Excellent homemade pastries. Entrees Rp10,000-30,000. Open daily 8am-9pm. ❸

SIGHTS

The colorful **Eng An Kiong Chinese Pagoda,** at the intersection of Jl. Gatot Subroto and Jl. Zainul Zakse, provides a look at Chinese Buddhist, Confucian, and Taoist traditions. Intricate carvings, enormous archways, and shrines filled with homemade candles and incense add to the mystery of this place. (Open daily 6am-8:30pm. Free.) For something less peaceful, head west from Tugu Monument to the **Brawijaya Museum,** behind the welcoming tanks at Jl. Besar Ljen 25A. The two halls are covered with war photographs and battle plans. Check out Javanese military memorabilia such as stained flags, intimidating guns, and a street car named "Desoto." (Open daily 7am-5pm. Rp1000 donation expected.) The **Sena Putra Amusement Park** has dance performances. Check with the Tourist Information Center (see **Tourist Offices,** p. 158) for exact times.

DAYTRIPS FROM MALANG

CANDI SINGOSARI. Singosari Temple was built between 1268 and 1292 in honor of King Kertanagara, the last ruler of the Singosari Dynasty. The small candi has been well-restored and retains its mystique, although only one of the six interior statues remains at this location; the Dutch claimed the other patung for themselves. *(Open daily 8am-5pm. Donations accepted, usually Rp1000. From Arjosari Terminal, take a bus 12km north to Singosari (20min., Rp1000). Ask to get off at the temple.)*

BALE KAMBANG BEACH. Bale Kambang is a stretch of sea backed by dense forest. The ojek ride from Bantur to the beach is a highlight—12km of terraced fields, villages, and woods laced with scenic trails. Three offshore islands, accessible by bridges, provide spectacular views of the ocean and mainland. **Candi Bale Kambang** rests on the largest of the three, the one where visitors can spend the night. Those seeking solitude should come on weekdays. Although the sands are packed on weekends, loitering and often intoxicated young men might harass women traveling alone. There are several other beaches in the area. The white sands at **Ngliyep** are enveloped by dense jungle (take a bus from Gadang Terminal). Nearby **Tamban** has a less spectacular waterfront with more peace and quiet. **Sendang Biru**'s sweet sands offer a view of **Pulau Sempu,** a dramatic island with a 2hr. hike through the nature reserve to Segara Anak, a crystal-clear laguna fed by the ocean. *(75km south of Malang. From Malang, take any G-A angkot to Gadang Terminal. From there, bemo go south to Bantur (2hr., Rp3500), where ojek scurry to the beach (30min., Rp7500). Rare minibuses (Rp3000) make a less enjoyable trip.)*

BLITAR ☎0342

Blitar is the birthplace and final resting place of former President Sukarno (known as "Bung Karno"). Not surprisingly, Blitar has thrown its enthusiastic support behind reformist President Megawati Sukarnoputri, Sukarno's daughter. As a regional hub in the heart of East Java, Blitar exudes a relaxed atmosphere and is an ideal stopover between Solo and Malang.

TRANSPORTATION. Blitar's **train station** (☎801 940) is on Jl. Mastrip, which runs east-west on the south side of town. Trains run daily to: **Jakarta** (11-14hr.; 4, 4:30pm; economy Rp45,000) via **Cirebon; Jogjakarta** (6-7hr.; 4:30pm; economy Rp35,000); **Solo** (5-6hr.; 4, 4:30, 9pm; Rp35,000); **Surabaya** (5hr., 6 per day 5am-3:10pm, Rp4000) via **Malang** (2hr., Rp2900). *Angkot* headed south down Jl. Anggrek go to the **bus terminal** on the southern outskirts of town. Buses run to: **Denpasar** (15hr.; 2:30pm; Rp110,000); **Jakarta** (12hr.; 11:30am; Rp110,000); **Malang** (2hr., dozens per day, Rp4500); **Solo** (7hr.; every hr. 6am-1pm; Rp12,000). If arriving in Blitar from Malang, ask to be let off on the main road near the Herlingga Jaya Hotel, where *becak* (around Rp4000) greet passengers heading to the hotels near Bung Karno's grave. Otherwise, it's a long wait for an *angkot* or an expensive *becak* ride from the terminal into town and north to **Jl. Slamet Riyadi** and the tomb.

ORIENTATION AND PRACTICAL INFORMATION. One block north and parallel to **Jl. Mastrip** (home to the train station), **Jl. Merdeka** runs east-west past the **Alun-alun.** Two blocks to the west of this town center, the main boulevard intersects with **Jl. Anggrek,** which heads south to the **bus station.** Three blocks to the east, Jl. Merdeka turns into **Jl. A. Yani** as it crosses **Jl. Sudirman,** which leads to **Sukarno's tomb** in the north. The **Kantor Pos Blitar (post office),** Jl. Mastrip 87, offers slow and unreliable **Internet** (Rp3000 per 30min.). (☎801 544. Open M-Th 8am-2pm, F 8-11:30am, Sa 8am-1pm.) **BNI,** Jl. Kenonogo 7, two blocks from the post office, has a **24hr. ATM** (Cirrus/MC/V) and exchanges currency. (☎801 946. Open M-F 8am-3pm.) Farther east, the **Apotek Nirmala** pharmacy is at Jl. Seruni 45. (☎800 666. Open M-Sa 6am-10:30pm.) Continuing north and two blocks right on Jl. Merdeka is a **24hr. Telkom Office** on Jl. A. Yani 10 with **Internet** access (Rp5000 per hr.). Heading north, the **police station** is at Jl. Sudirman 32 (☎802 790).

INDONESIA

ACCOMMODATIONS AND FOOD. Finding a room around June 21 (the anniversary of Bung Karno's death) and June 6 (his birthday) is virtually impossible, but the sight of thousands of Javanese descending on Blitar might be worth the hassle. To escape the Sukarnoist hordes, consider staying at **Herlingga Jaya Hotel II ❸**, Jl. Jaksa Agung Suprapto 49 (behind the main hotel), to the northeast on the outskirts of town. A pool and karaoke bar are hidden in the back. (☎806 325. Check-out 2pm. Rooms Rp30,000, with A/C Rp50,000.) **Hotel Saptra Mandala ❷**, Jl. Slamet Riyadi 31, 150m south of Bung Karno's grave, is the city's best value. (☎801 810. Rooms Rp25,000, with TV and hot water Rp55,000; extra beds Rp8000.) **Restaurant Mandala ❶**, in the same complex, offers *nasi pecel* for Rp3000. About 150m north of the tomb at Jl. Slamet Riyadi 66, **Depot Pojok ❶** serves point-and-eat dishes such as fried chicken over rice. (Rp3000 per plate. Open daily 7am-9pm.) Dozens of hotels and eateries are scattered north of the train station, and the alleyways off Jl. Anggrek (left of the train station) have several dirt-cheap *losmen.*

SIGHTS. Sukarno wished to be buried near his family residence in Bogor, but the New Order had him interred in an unmarked grave next to his mother in his hometown of Blitar. Eight years after Sukarno's death, the Suharto regime recovered the leader, *proklamator* of Indonesian independence, and constructed a US$1 million shrine around his grave. **Makam Bung Karno,** the mausoleum complex, borrows from Balinese and Javanese architectural styles to reflect the liberator's mixed ethnicity. Beyond the massive stone entrance and within the Javanese *pendopo* pavilion, visitors gather below the elaborate ceiling. Rumor has it that Sukarno's children are trying to move his grave to Bogor to fulfill their father's wish. (Open daily 8am-5pm.) Dating back to the Majapahit period (15th century), **Candi Penataran,** East Java's largest Hindu-Buddhist temple, is worth the trip. The *candi* is 8km north of Makam Bung Karno. Take a Penataran-bound minibus from Jl. W.R. Supratman (Rp1500), 400m below Bung Karno's grave, and ask to be let off at Candi Penataran. (Open daily 7am-5pm. Donation Rp1000.)

GUNUNG BROMO ☎0335

At 2923m, dramatic Gunung Bromo is one of the most magnificent sights in Indonesia. "Bromo" refers not only to the ash-gray, semi-active crater named after the Hindu god Brahma, but also to an entire cluster of volcanoes set in an enormous crater spanning 40km, the Bromo-Semera Massif, known as Tengger. A breathtaking sunrise seen from the lookout point on Gunung Penanjaka, followed by a 5hr. hike, will give you a chance to take in the vistas. If you aren't in a hurry, the mountain air merits an extra night or two—if you don't mind the hordes of tourists.

TRANSPORTATION Gunung Bromo is 50km east of Malang. It's most commonly reached by tourist bus via the unfriendly town of **Probolinggo.** From there, take a crowded public *bemo* to **Cemorolawang** (2½hr., last bus 5pm, Rp8000), the stop for the Gunung Bromo area. Most locals will get out at the market halfway to Gunung Bromo; refuse offers for express buses and wait for the *bemo* to refill (around 10min.). For late arrivals, direct **minibuses** can be chartered from the Probolinggo bus terminal (1hr.; Rp50,000-60,000). Alternatively, Gunung Bromo can also be approached from its northern edge via the coastal town of **Pasuruan.** From Pasuruan, minibuses run to **Tosari,** where visitors can hire a jeep to the crater or take a minibus to **Penanjakan,** the premier sunrise viewpoint.

To leave, purchase bus tickets at the **Probolinggo bus terminal** or take a bus from Cemorolawang. Avoid the travel agencies in Probolinggo. Minibuses constantly run downhill to Probolinggo. From there, buses continue to **Denpasar** (8hr.; 10:30am, 12:15, 7, 8, 9pm; Rp60,000) and **Solo/Jogjakarta** (economy: 11-12hr.; 7, 8, 9pm; Rp45,000; executive: 9-10hr.; 10:30am, 8pm; Rp60,000). Alternatively, take a bus to **Panuangi** (4hr., every 30min., Rp8000), a *bemo* to **Ketapong** (45min., Rp1750), and a final bus to **Denpasar** (3½hr.; Rp10,000). **Public buses** travel to **Malang** and **Surabaya** (both 2hr., every 30min., Rp8000).

ACCOMMODATIONS AND FOOD The best deal in the Gunung Bromo area is **Yoschi ❷,** Jl. Wonokerto Km2, Ngadisari, 7km before Cemorolawang. Though it's a *bemo* ride or a steep 45min. walk from the crater, Yoschi's classy facilities, including a restaurant and morning jacket rentals, trump the competition. (☎541 018. Hot water. Doubles Rp25,000.) In Cemorolawang, on the lip of the crater, *losmen* are close together and travelers should shop around—note that *bemo* drivers often take commissions from *losmen* operators. **Hotel Lava's ❷,** beyond the entrance gate 50m up the left road, has a friendly and comfortable cafe (try the pancakes) and attracts the most tourists. (☎541 020. Doubles Rp30,000, with *mandi* and breakfast Rp85,000.) **Cemara Indah ❷** is 100m up the road to the right, where you're most likely to get dropped off. (☎541 019. Singles Rp20,000; doubles Rp25,000-30,000; deluxe rooms Rp85,000; superior deluxe Rp200,000.) Restaurants are limited to those attached to hotels. (Entrees Rp5000-15,000.) *Warung* are easy to come by on village roads (Rp1000-4000). Get your dinner early—the town shuts down after 8pm.

If you're stranded in Probolinggo, **Hotel Ratna ❸,** Jl. Sudirman 16, has pricey rooms. (☎421 597. Breakfast included. Rooms Rp35,000-75,000.) **Rumah Makan Sumber Hidup ❷,** next to Hotel Ratna at the corner at Jl. Moch Saleh 2, serves ice cream and Indonesian fare. (Dishes Rp8000-15,000. Open daily 7am-9pm).

HOLY CHICKENS! *Kadasa*, a Hindu celebration of life, attracts droves of visitors to Bromo annually, filling the *Laut Pasir* (a desert-like sea of sand in the 40km long "Tengger" crater). Around a thousand religious participants and two million interested onlookers cram under October's full moon to witness spiritual festivities of volcanic proportions: horses dance to the accompaniment of bongo-like *ketipung*, and flowers come down like rain from the main road all the way up to the lip of the crater. After the ceremonial prayer in the *Pure*, a temple in the middle of *laut pasir*, the holy *pak jai* (priest) leads participants through the night to the top of Gunung Bromo. There, the holy men throw offerings into the crater, appeasing the gods with everything from bouquets to boxes of rice to live chickens.

CLIMBING GUNUNG BROMO. Gunung Bromo and its surrounding peaks can be climbed at any point in the day, but to hike by the light of the magnificent sunrise, set your alarm clock for 3:30am. Rub your eyes and make your way to the lookout point at **Gunung Penanjaka,** which provides a premium postcard panorama at daybreak. Follow the road from Cemara Indah. Bring warm clothes to wear in layers, water, a flashlight, and hiking buddies if you're going without a guide. If you stray from the path, locals will follow your flashlight and direct you to safety for a small fee (Rp10,000 per group). Alternatively, a convoy of jeeps leaves at 4am, hauling crowds of people to Gunung Penanjaka. Purchase tickets for Rp25,000 through any Cemorolawang accommodation. After the dawn breaks, jeeps rumble back down the mountain across *Laut Pasir*, the "sea of sand," and to Gunung Bromo, where a short 15min. jaunt up the trail will take you to the caldera's edge. Expect to be surrounded by desperate men trying to rent wheezing horses—remember that the ride may be more strenuous than walking.

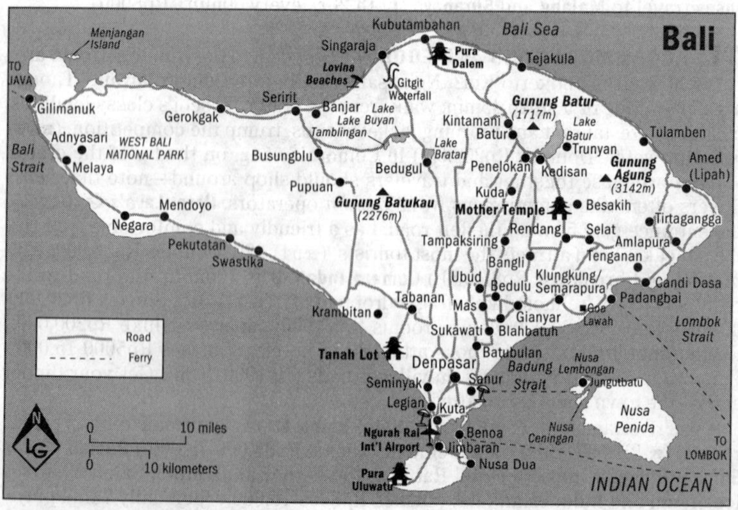

BALI

One million tourists flock to this little island (5700 sq. km) every year, seeking everything from enlightenment to drunken debauchery. Bali balances precariously between Eden and Eden after the Fall: though McDonald's has colonized Kuta, escapists can still find virgin expanse and a paradise not yet lost. You may have to share the shores and volcanoes with droves of travelers, but the white coral, black lava beaches, and gorgeous vistas are worth it. Though no part of Bali's main attractions remains untouched by tourism, the island's beauty cannot be denied.

The October 12, 2002 terrorist attack on Kuta has seriously changed the atmosphere on the island; for more information, see p. 175.

THE VIEW FROM ABOVE

Main cities: Denpasar, Kuta, Sanur, Singaraja, and Ubud.
Highlights: Enjoying dolphins in Lovina, partying in Kuta, absorbing culture in Ubud.
Something fun: Climb Gunung Agung and Gunung Batur, surf in Legian, visit the Monkey Forest.

DENPASAR ☎0361

INDONESIA

Chock full of art, markets, malls, karaoke, museums, and international cuisine, Denpasar is Bali's urban center of schmooze. Since most travelers skip over Denpasar, the city is more typically Indonesian than the rest of the island. Though the streets can be filthy, they offer a mosaic of treasures, from the literal to the metaphoric. With puppies and birds for sale and paintings and Dutch cannons to admire, the eclectic nature of Denpasar's streets should not be missed.

Due to circumstances beyond our control, the coverage of Denpasar was not updated for our 2003 edition. This information is correct as of summer 2001.

TRANSPORTATION

BY PLANE

Ngurah Rai International Airport (☎751 011, 24hr. info ext. 164) lies 30min. south of Kuta by taxi or direct shuttle. A moneychanger, baggage storage (Rp5500 per day), and **ATM** (Cirrus/MC/Plus/V) are available. The Rp75,000 international departure tax must be paid in cash; the domestic departure tax is Rp30,000. From the airport, fixed-rate taxis go to: **Denpasar** (Rp27,000-37,500); **Nusa Dua** (Rp30,000); **Sanur** (Rp30,000); and **Ubud** (Rp90,000). Cheaper public *bemo* and vehicles available for charter linger outside the airport on the main road. Beware of porters who carry your luggage without being asked and then demand large sums for their effort.

DESTINATION	FREQUENCY	PRICE	DESTINATION	FREQUENCY	PRICE
Bima	1 per day	Rp478,800	**Mataram**	5 per day	Rp233,500
Jakarta	8 per day	Rp802,200	**Singapore**	1 per day	US$255
Jogjakarta	3 per day	Rp426,000	**Sumbawa Besar**	M, W	Rp303,900
Kupang	1 per day	Rp803,300	**Ujung Pandang**	1 per day	Rp555,800

Singapore Airlines, Garuda, and **Merpati** have information desks at the airport between the domestic and international terminals, as well as main offices in Denpasar: **Garuda,** Jl. Melati 61 (☎225 245; open M-Th 7:30am-4:30pm, F 7:30am-5pm, Sa 9am-1pm); **Merpati,** Jl. Melati 51 (☎235 556; open M-F 8am-5pm, Sa-Su 9am-5pm); **Singapore Airlines,** 3rd fl., Bank Bali on Jl. Dewi Sartika (☎261 666, weekend ☎261 669; open M-F 8am-5pm, Sa 8am-1pm).

BY BUS

Overnight buses leave in mid-afternoon for Java from **Ubung Terminal** in Denpasar. Buy tickets to **Jakarta** (Rp170,500), **Jogjakarta** (Rp110,000), and **Surabaya** (Rp50,000) from tour agencies in Bali, including **Bali Buana Artha,** Jl. Diponegoro 131A, Denpasar (☎227 370), or at the terminal. A/C buses go to **Bima/Sape** on Sumbawa. **Perama,** Jl. Legian 39, Kuta (☎751 551), has daily departures to **Bima/Sape** (Rp130,000) and **Mataram** (Rp50,000). Fares include ferries. Other bus lines include **Langsung Indah, Safari Dharma Raya,** and **Simpatik,** but due to the accessibility of its offices and English-speaking staff, Perama is the most accommodating for tourists. Be vigilant on buses, as theft is common.

ISLAND-HOPPING Ferries run between **Gilimanuk** on the west tip of Bali and **Ketapang** on East Java (20min.; every 30min. 5am-9pm; Rp10,000). Ferries to **Lombok** leave from **Padangbai** (see p. 203) on Bali's east coast (4-5hr., every 1½hr., Rp9500). **Mabua Express** leaves for **Lembar** on Lombok (2½hr., 8am, US$25-30) from **Benoa Harbor** (☎721 272) in South Bali. **PELNI** ships also serve Benoa Harbor. For schedules and tickets, contact their ticket office in Benoa (☎721 377). To get to Benoa, take a taxi from Denpasar (15min.).

BY BEMO

Public *bemo*, identified by yellow license plates (government vehicles have red plates; private ones have black), are easiest to catch in the early morning and generally stop running after 9pm in Southern Bali and 6pm in the north. They can also be chartered privately. **Denpasar** is the hub of *bemo* activity for Southern Bali. Four terminals serve the island:

Batubulan, 6km northeast of Denpasar, runs *bemo* east to Bangli, Padangbai, Candi Dasa, Amlapura, and Tirtagangga and north to Ubud via Kediri and Penelokan.

Kereneng, on the east end of Denpasar off Jl. Hayam Wuruk, has connecting *bemo* to the other terminals.

Tegal, on the west end near the intersection of Jl. G. Willis and Jl. Imam Bonjol, runs *bemo* south to Kuta, Legian, Ngurah Rai Airport, Nusa Dua, Sanur, and Uluwatu.

Ubung, north of Denpasar on Jl. Cokroaminoto, handles trips to the north and west, including Bedugul, Gilimanuk, Singaraja, Tanah Lot, and points in Java.

LOCAL TRANSPORTATION

Metered taxis start at Rp3000; bargaining is usually more expensive. Taxis don't stop where *bemo* or local drivers are parked, so catch one elsewhere. The light-blue **Bali Taxi** (☎701 111) offers professional service. **Ojek** can be hired anywhere. **Dokar** (horse-drawn carts) are used in Denpasar.

TOURIST PRICE Tourists are usually charged more than locals for transportation. If you're up to the challenge, ask locals how much they pay to determine a fair price and then bargain away. Good luck.

ORIENTATION AND PRACTICAL INFORMATION

North of Denpasar, dense **Pasar Badung** lies between the two parallel east-west streets, **Jl. Hasanuddin** and **Jl. Gajah Mada,** which are connected by **Jl. Sulawesi.** Jl. Gajah Mada becomes **Jl. Surapati** to the east, which later becomes **Jl. Hayam Wuruk. Puputan Square** is east of the market, between the same streets. At one corner of the square, where Jl. Gajah Mada, **Jl. Veteran, Jl. Surapadial,** and **Jl. Udayana** meet, sits **Catur Maka statue.** The **central post office** and **Bali Government Tourist Office** are both in the **Renon District** near **Jl. Raya Puputan. Udayan University** and the massive **Duta Plaza Shopping Center** border **Jl. Diponegoro,** which heads north to the market.

Tourist Office: Dinas Pariwisata, Jl. Surapati 7 (☎234 569), near the Bali Museum. Friendly and informative. Free maps, brochures, and schedule of events. Staff helps demystify *bemo* routes. Open M-Th 7am-2pm, F 7-11am, Sa 7am-12:30pm.

Tours: Miraz Tours, Jl. Diponegoro 81 (☎246 007), books tours around Bali. Open M-Sa 8am-8pm, Su 8am-4pm.

PELNI Office: Jl. Diponegoro 165 (☎234 680). Helps with transportation and other tourist-related questions. Open daily 8am-7pm.

Consulates: Australia, Jl. Prof. Yamin 4, Renon District (☎235 092). Open M-F 8am-4pm. **US,** Jl. Hayam Wuruk 188 (☎233 605), by Hotel Sanno. Open M-F 8am-4:30pm.

Immigration Office: Jl. Niti Mandala, Renon District (☎227 828). With your back to the GPO, turn left and then left again. Visa extensions. Open M-Th 7am-2pm, F-Sa 7-11am.

Currency Exchange: Big **banks** cluster on **Jl. Gajah Mada** between Badung Market and Puputan Square. There are dozens of **ATMs;** one is at **Bank Bali,** on Jl. Diponegoro at Jl. Teuku Umar near the telephone office. **Bank Duta,** Jl. Hayam Wuruk 165 (☎226 578), has MC/V cash advances. Open M-F 8am-3pm.

Gay and Lesbian Organizations: Gaya Dewata/Citra Usadua Foundation, at Jl. Sari Gading 1, off Jl. Ratna (☎246 757). Focuses on AIDS education.

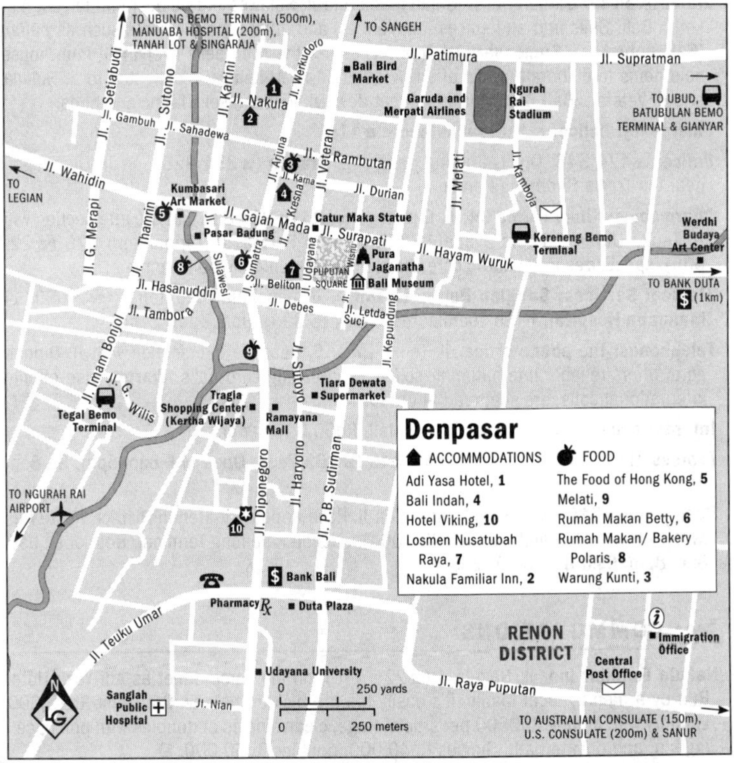

WARIA Fitra is anatomically male, but insists that she and her boyfriend, a Javanese policeman who visits her on his lunch breaks, are not gay. "He doesn't like men," Fitra insists as she brushes her long, black hair. As a teenager, she began to wear dresses and makeup. Like most *waria,* members of Indonesia's alternate gender, she believes that God gave her a female soul inside a male body. When Fitra was 13, she dressed in a female's tunic and veil, went to the mosque with her family, and confronted this belief. She sat for a few moments on the female side of the room; she couldn't sit in the male section dressed as she was. The women nearby began to shift away uneasily, making it clear they were uncomfortable in Fitra's presence. As Fitra explains it, they felt she was polluting the purity of their prayer. Fitra doesn't go to the mosque anymore. She prays alone on the red prayer mat in her room, a concrete cell in a compound filled with other Javanese immigrants hoping to strike it rich in Denpasar. The intricacies of Fitra's belief distinguish her from transvestites, hermaphrodites, homosexuals, and transsexuals. According to Fitra, she is not a "cross-dresser." She has a masculine body, but she believes that her female soul distinguishes her from homosexual men attracted to other men. She has not had nor wishes to have genital surgery. Fitra has recently updated her National Identity Card, a form of identification carried by all Indonesians. The card describes her status—once printed as male beneath her long-haired photograph—as *waria.*

Markets: Pasar Badung, at Jl. Gajah Mada and Jl. Sulawesi. The oldest and largest market in Bali. Sells fruit and spices, appliances, and ritual accoutrements such as *pajong* (Bali umbrellas). **Kumbasari Art Market,** across the river, sells everything from household items to elaborate works of art. Another on **Jl. Abimanyu** (connected to Jl. Nokula) and Jl. Veteran. **Bali Bird Market,** farther down Jl. Veteran, sells fabric and birds.

Emergency: Police: ☎110. **Ambulance:** ☎118.

Police: ☎424 346. On Jl. Gunung Sangiong. **Branch** (☎234 928), on Jl. Diponegoro near the Tragia Shopping Center.

Pharmacies: Kimia Farma 34, Jl. Diponegoro 125 (☎227 811), at the intersection with Jl. Teuku Umar. Doctors available **24hr. Bulan Farma,** Jl. Diponegoro 126 (☎227 605), specializes in pediatric care. House calls. Open daily 5am-9pm.

Medical Services: Sanglah Public Hospital, Jl. Kesehatan Selatan 1 (☎227 911). **Manuaba Hospital,** Jl. Cokroaminoto 28 (☎426 393). Both **open 24hr.**

Telephones: The **phone office,** Jl. Teuku Umar 6, near the intersection with Jl. Diponegoro, offers reliable international, collect, and calling card calls. **Wartel,** also offering international calls, are scattered about town.

Internet Access: 3rd fl. of Ramayana Mall. Rp50,000 per hr.

Express Mail: DHL, Jl. Hayam Wuruk 146 (☎262 713). Open M-F 8am-5pm, Sa 8am-1pm.

Post Offices: GPO (☎223 565), south on Jl. Raya Puputan in Renon District. *Poste Restante.* **Branch,** Jl. Kamboja 6 (☎222 004), outside Kereneng Terminal. Both open daily 8am-8pm. **Postal code:** 80235.

ACCOMMODATIONS

Nakula Familiar Inn, Jl. Nakula 4 (☎226 446), on the same street as Adi Yasa Hotel. Run by a friendly local family, it's easily the top pick in the city. Breakfast Rp15,000. Laundry with ironing Rp2500 per article. Huge, clean singles or doubles with porch, ceiling fan, and private bath. Singles Rp40,000; doubles Rp60,000. ❸

Adi Yasa Hotel, Jl. Nakula 23B (☎222 679), 50m from Nakula Familiar Inn. *Losmen*-style accommodation. Inexpensive, worn rooms with private combination *mandi* and fan. Clean and safe. Singles Rp25,000; doubles Rp40,000. ❷

Bali Indah, Jl. Kresna 11 (☎225 226). From the Catur Maka statue, the first right off Jl. Gajah Mada. A quiet hotel in noisy Denpasar, Bali Indah is near all the sights. Fewer tourists make it ideal for mingling with locals. Doubles with private *mandi* and fan Rp50,000, with A/C, TV, bath, and hot water Rp120,000. ❸

Hotel Viking, Jl. Diponegoro 120 (☎223 992). With your back to Bank Bali, turn right onto Jl. Diponegoro; it's 100m down on the left. Noisy. Free tea. Singles Rp60,000; cottages set back from road Rp70,000, with A/C Rp80,000. ❹

Losmen Nusatnbah Raya, Jl Beliton 10 (☎226 951), 2 blocks from Bali Museum on a quiet side street. Neighborly, clean outfit. Singles Rp25,000; doubles Rp35,000. ❷

FOOD

Denpasar's diverse ethnic population makes for exciting dining. You'll find *warung* and cheap eateries everywhere in town, especially along **Jl. Sumatra-Diponegoro** and at the Kereneng Terminal. A **night market** behind Pasar Badung offers *warung* dishes. (Open daily 6pm-midnight.) Another night market comes to life on Jl. Diponegoro near the **Kertha Wijaya Shopping Center. Tragia Market,** Jl. Diponegoro 98, part of the Kertha Wijaya Shopping Center, sells a large selection of fruits and vegetables. (Open daily until 10pm.) **Tiara Dewata Supermarket** is at the north end of Jl. Sudirman. Western cuisine is easy to find.

Rumah Makan Betty, Jl. Sumatra 56. 1 block east of Jl. Sulawesi. A small, low-budget cafeteria. Clean, roomy, friendly. East Javanese food and vegetarian options. Betty also gives the best directions in town. Open M-Sa 8am-9pm, Su 8am-2pm. ❷

Warung Kunti, Jl. Arjuna 37. Take 2nd right down Jl. Gajah Mada from the Catur Maka statue. A tiny mom-and-pop operation, Kunti is far from traffic and serves spicy Balinese food. Meal with rice Rp5000. Open daily 7am-2pm. ❶

Melati, Jl. Diponegoro 48. *Sate* house with English menu. Impressive array of dishes and juices. Meals and juice drinks from Rp5000. ❷

Rumah Makan/Bakery Polaris, Jl. Sulawesi 40, next to Pasar Badung. Local bakery and restaurant. Try *onde-onde* (fried dough balls in sesame seeds) or the refreshing *es kolak* (ice, banana, pineapple in bright pink coconut milk; Rp2500). Open daily 6am-8pm. ❷

The Food of Hong Kong, Jl. Gajah Mada 99 (☎434 926), next to Pasar Badung, serves up delectable and diverse Southeast Asian meals. Dishes Rp10,000-50,000. ❹

SIGHTS

BALI MUSEUM. Rebuilt in 1932 after the original collapsed in a 1917 earthquake, the museum is Denpasar's primary attraction. The building itself, with its blend of Balinese temple and palace architecture, is the finest exhibit. It also houses artifacts that provide an introduction to Balinese society and culture from the prehistoric age to today. While the museum lacks detailed labels, the courtyards are well-maintained and the rooms are informative, especially for those interested in Balinese woodcarving, weaving, and painting. *(On Jl. Mayor Wisnu east of Puputan Sq. Open Tu-F 8am-2:45pm, Sa 8am-3:15pm, Su 8am-3:45pm. Rp750, children Rp250.)*

PURA JAGANATHA. This temple, dedicated to the supreme god Sanghyang Widi, is a symbolic representation of the cosmos. A gold statue of Sanghyang Widi sits atop a tall spire. The eight gods, each clad in a symbolic color, are beneath, and under them are two dragons that balance the earth. The spire, built of white coral, is surrounded by a moat with goldfish and sacred lilies. Guides, often religion or history students, will give you a crash course on Balinese Hinduism for a few dollars. At 7pm during *purnama* (full moon) and *tilem* (dark moon), the temple becomes crowded as Balinese bring offerings and Hindu intellectuals meet for religious readings. *Wayang kulit* (shadow puppet performances) begin around 10pm during *purnama*. *(Next to the Bali Museum. Open daily 7am-6pm.)*

WERDHI BUDAYA ART CENTER. Every June and July, the **Bali Arts Festival** kicks off in Denpasar at Werdhi Budaya Art Center. The large, outdoor amphitheater and exhibition halls are a perfect home for Balinese painting. The tourist office (see **Practical Information,** p. 167) provides a schedule of events. Call ahead to find out what's on display. English-speaking guides are available—bargain with them. *(On the corner of Jl. Hayam Wuruk and Jl. Nusa Indah. ☎227 176. Open daily 8am-2pm. Rp1000.)*

PUPUTAN SQUARE. This large park, with a fountain and monument depicting a family preparing for battle, commemorates the solemn, suicidal *puputan* (final flight) of 1906, when Badung's last king, followed by family and court, refused to surrender and marched into the bullets of Dutch soldiers. Locals eat lunch and lounge around the square throughout the week. *(Opposite the Bali Museum.)*

INDONESIA

DAYTRIP FROM DENPASAR: PURA ULUWATU

Reaching Uluwatu can be challenging. Renting your own transport is the best option (motorcycle Rp30,000; taxi Rp60,000; jeep Rp70,000 per day). If you choose not to rent, it's musical bemos *for you. From Denpasar's Tegal Station, catch a* bemo *to Jimbaran, where you must catch another one to Uluwatu. (Rp10,000 is a bargain, as there are no direct* bemo *routes to the temples.) If leaving from Kuta, pick up a* bemo *from Tegal by waiting on the road heading away from the Duty Free Shop, near the gas pump on Jl. Raya Kuta. Private transport can also be hired from Kuta. The distance from Uluwatu to Kuta is bikeable if you're athletic (20km), but the roads near the temple are steep;* bemo *are your best bet once again. Returning from Uluwatu is even harder than getting there. Have an* ojek *drop you at Jimbaran, where you can catch one of the* bemo *that run sporadically until 10pm to Kuta and Denpasar. Stow your caps and sunglasses, or monkeys around the temple may snatch them and flee. Open daily 7am-6pm. Sarong and sash rental included in the Rp3000 admission.*

One of the *Sad Kahyangan*—the six most important temples in Bali—Pura Uluwatu overlooks cliffs on the southwest tip of Bukit Peninsula, the area south of Denpasar and Kuta. Thought to date back to the 11th century, Uluwatu honors the Hindu saint **Danhyang Nirartha,** who explored Bali in 1500 BC and reputedly achieved *moksa* (liberation from worldly life) at the site of this temple. Only visitors with appropriate temple clothes and offerings may enter the temple. There is no official tour, but the unofficial English-speaking guides at the entrance can be helpful and informative. Agree on a price before your tour. The Pura Uluwatu area has some of the most challenging **surfing sites** in the world. The nearby breaks of **Uluwatu, Padang Padang,** and **Bingin,** host world-class local and international surfing contests. Take an *ojek* (Rp10,000) down the descent to the beaches outside the entrance for Pura Uluwatu. Facilities range from simple *warung* to waxing and repair shops. The **Badung Tourist Information** (in Kuta, see p. 176) and surf shops have details about other surfing beaches. If passing through Jimbaran on the way back from Pura Uluwatu at dusk, go down to the bay where candlelit *warung* prepare fish, lobster, and king prawns at "tourist" prices (fish Rp50,000 per kg; crab, lobster and prawns Rp100,000 per kg). A taxi to Jimbaran Bay costs approximately Rp10,000 from Kuta, although most cafes will provide free transportation.

SANUR ☎0361

Sanur's beach is mediocre, its surf is only decent in the wet season, and the shallow reef makes swimming inconvenient. But the typical Sanur tourist doesn't care—he's too busy floating potbelly-up, sipping piña coladas from poolside bars. Sanur is Bali's first attempt at corporate development: sterile, predictable, and unexciting. Although it is essentially a mid-range resort town, it's not a hopeless cause for the budgeteer—there are a few reasonably priced accommodations of better quality than the budget rooms in Kuta, and the rupiah-conscious can entertain themselves by getting to the beach and hotel pools through A/C lobbies. All said, Sanur is a good place to crash en route to Nusa Lembongan.

TRANSPORTATION

Flights: Bali's **Ngurah Rai Airport.** To get there, take a 40min. ride by taxi or blue *bemo* (to Tegal Station), or a Perama shuttle (Rp10,000). The Bali Beach Hotel has an entire wing with international airline offices. Open M-F 8:30am-4:30pm, Sa 8am-1:30pm.

Bemo: For **Denpasar,** take a green *bemo* to **Kereneng Station** (10min., Rp2000). Blue *bemo* go south to **Tegal Station** (20min., Rp2000), where connections are available to **Kuta** and the airport. Private shuttles to destinations in Bali available from tour offices.

Boats: A **public boat** leaves from the end of Jl. Hang Tuah (daily when full, no earlier than 8am; Rp40,000) for **Nusa Lembongan.** Perama (Kuta office ☎751 551) also has daily **boat** service to Nusa Lembongan (10:30am; Rp50,000); tickets are available from the Kuta office or—on the morning of the trip only—at the kiosk in Sanur (☎287 594), at Warung Pojok on Jl. Hang Tuah, opposite the Radisson. Show up at the kiosk at 10:20am to buy tickets and meet passengers coming from Kuta.

Rentals: Wirasana, Jl. Danau Tamblingan 126 (☎288 706) and Jl. Ngurah Rai Bypass 545x (☎286 066), opposite police station. Cheap **cars** (Rp100,000 per day) and **motorcycles** (Rp60,000 per day). Cars only at Bypass store. MC/V.

ORIENTATION AND PRACTICAL INFORMATION

Sanur divides into three parallel strips. Along the beach is an almost continuous boardwalk, lined with large expensive hotels, restaurants, and watersports centers. Fifty meters inland, parallel to the boardwalk, **Jl. Danau Tamblingan** (**Jl. Tanjung Sari** at its southern end) is studded with resorts, more restaurants, boutiques, postal agents, craft shops, and tour agencies. Parallel to Jl. Danau Tamblingan 150m inland is busy **Jl. Ngurah Rai Bypass** (also known as **Bypass Rd.**), a highway whose shops and services are geared mostly to locals. The Bali Beach Hotel dominates Sanur's northern end, and the even bigger Bali Hyatt dominates the southern one. At the beach end of the northernmost cross-street is the boat service to Nusa Lembongan. **Jl. Hang Tuah** becomes **Jl. Raya Sanur** on its way to Denpasar. **Jl. Segara Ayu** becomes **Jl. Danau Buyan** as it crosses Jl. Ngurah Rai; the same happens to **Jl. Pantai Sindhu,** which becomes **Jl. Danau Tondano. Bemo** congregate at **Jl. Matasari/Jl. Suadamala** at the southern end of Jl. Danau Tamblingan.

Tourist Office: The nearest government office is in Kuta, but hotels and tour operators provide info and guided tours to anywhere in Indonesia. Private travel offices abound on Jl. Danau Tamblingan. In Bali Beach Hotel, **Barata Tours** arranges cruises to Lembongan and vicinity. Open daily 8am-9pm.

Currency Exchange: Moneychangers on Jl. Danau Tamblingan and beach boardwalk, have better rates than hotels (except for bank offices in Bali Beach Hotel), but beware of hidden commissions and shortchanging. **BNI** (☎282 590), on Jl. Danau Tamblingan next to Bali Moon, offers cash advances. Open M-F 8am-noon and 1-9pm. **24hr. ATM** (Cirrus/MC/PLUS/V). Other ATMs fairly common.

American Express: Office in the Bali Beach Hotel (☎288 449). Cardholders can buy traveler's checks. Holds letters if addressed c/o PACTO (AmEx), Hotel Bali Beach, Sanur, Denpasar. Open M-F 8:30am-4:30pm, Sa 8:30am-12:30pm.

Markets: Pasar Senggol, at the northern end of Jl. Danau Tamblingan. Open daily 5-10pm. **Alas Arum Agung Sanur,** on Jl. Danau Tamblingan, near Swastika II restaurant, is a supermarket that stocks imported food at high prices. Open daily 8am-10pm.

Emergency: Police: ☎110. **Ambulance:** ☎118.

Police: ☎288 597, on Bypass Rd. at the edge of the golf course.

Pharmacy: Pharmacy Sanur 10 (☎288 744), on Jl. Danau Buyan, opposite Hotel Tamon Sari.

Medical Services: Bali Beach Hotel has an **emergency clinic** (☎288 511; ask for the clinic). Open M-F 7am-9pm, Sa 7am-8pm, Su and holidays 10am-6pm. Doctor on duty M-Sa 8am-noon, otherwise on-call only. **Legian Medical Clinic II** (☎287 446), on Jl. Danau Tamblingan, offers **24hr.** medical service.

Telephones: Make local, collect, and cash international calls at the **Wartel** near where Jl. Segara crosses Bypass Rd. **Wartel** also on Jl. Hang Tuah—prices vary widely; it's worth shopping around. **Bali Beach Hotel** has **24hr. HCD** phone accepting credit-card calls behind the main lobby.

Internet Access: Everywhere along Jl. Danau Tamblingan and Jl. Hang Tuah. Connection speeds and rates (Rp300-500 per min.) vary.

Express Mail: Bali Prima Cargo, Jl. Danau Tamblingan 160 (☎287 360), offers DHL, FedEx, and worldwide delivery service. Open M-Sa 8am-8pm, Su 8am-5pm. Another **DHL office** on Jl. Ngurah Rai Bypass just north of its intersection with Jl. Kesari. Open M-Sa 8am-6pm. Visa.

Post Office: GPO, Jl. Danau Buyan. Send *Poste Restante* to GPO, Banjar Taman. Open M-Th 8am-2pm, F 8am-noon, Sa 8am-1pm. **Postal code:** 80228.

ACCOMMODATIONS

Most of the accommodations in Sanur are mid-range or upscale and charge prices in US dollars far from the budget range. The few places that do cater to backpackers are pricier than those in Kuta and Denpasar, but the difference in price generally translates to cleaner baths, better rooms, and bigger breakfasts.

THE LOCAL STORY

A CHEF OF TWO WORLDS

Arri grew up in Java, spent 18 months in England, and settled in Sanur to open her own restaurant. Her menu is slightly different from that of the nearby warung. Using her experience and seemingly endless skills, Arri has made Indonesian food appeal to the English and English food actually have flavor.

Q: You grew up in Bali?

A: I grew up in Java. I moved to Jakarta about 12 years [ago] when I met my Englishman in Jakarta. Then we lived together about 9 years...During that time, he brought me to England 3 times. First time with no English and then second time he asked me to work in the restaurant...I was working for 18 months but came back 3 times.

Q: Were you working in an Indonesian restaurant?

A: In his restaurant, which is Indonesian food...

Q: Did he speak Indonesian? Was he working in Java?

A: He was working with Garuda Indonesia, general manager...for the catering service.

Q: Did you learn to cook in Java?

A: Before I came to England I was helping my mother because my mother used to have a little *warung*... I knew already Indonesian food, so I gave the lessons for Indonesian food in Yorkshire.

Q: Your mom taught you to cook?

A: Yeah, she did. She is very, very good cook.

(continued on next page)

Coco's Homestay, Jl. Danau Tamblingan 42 (☎287 391). Family-run with rooms facing a lovely tropical garden. Best value in Sanur. Clean rooms with private bath, ceiling fan, and breakfast for up to 2 people Rp50,000. ❸

Risya Nanda Harry's, 19 Jl. Bumi Ayu (☎288 390). Walk south from Besakih Hotel to Jl. Bumi Ayu, then walk to the end of the street and turn left. Walk 50m more, and turn left again. It's at the end of the alley between two enclosed lots. Rooms gorgeously furnished and mosquito-netted. Call ahead for reservations. Doubles US$12. ❺

Hotel Taman Sari, Jl. Danau Buyan 37 (☎288 578). With your back to post office, turn right; it's 100m down on the left. The cheapest option. Doubles with fan Rp45,000. ❸

Yulia Art Shop, Jl. Danau Tamblingan 38 (☎288 089). Don't let the attached souvenir shop put you off: Yulia's offers fully furnished rooms in a garden setting. Private bath and fan. Breakfast included. Doubles Rp60,000. ❹

Keke's (☎287 282), on Jl. Tamblingan 100m south of Coco's and Yulia's. With the same amenities as Coco's, but pricier. Singles Rp60,000; doubles Rp75,000. ❹

FOOD

Sanur caters to the mild tastes of package tourists, so deep-fried squid and steak with fries is often as exotic as the cuisine gets. Many restaurants blend Balinese fare with Western. For cheap, tasty local grub, try a *padang* restaurant on Bypass Rd. **Warung** serving *bakso* and roast corn scatter along the northern end of the beach and at the **night market** on Jl. Danau Tamblingan's northern end.

Arri's Cafe, Jl. Pantai Sindhu 7, to the north, near the night market. English-trained Arri serves cottage pie (Rp12,000) and *rendang daging* (beef with cream, *kemiri,* ginger, *galangal,* palm sugar, and lime leaves; Rp20,000). Open daily 8am-11pm. ❹

Bali Moon, Jl. Danau Tamblingan 19. Airy, tropical restaurant with salads and Italian and Indonesian dishes. Happy hour 6-8pm; one free drink. Offers free drop-off. Pizzas (like Pizza Capriciosa) and pastas Rp27,500. Open daily 9am-11pm. ❹

Cafe Batu Timbar, Jl. Danau Tamblingan 152. What being a vegetarian is all about: delicious salads, fresh fruit juices. Also offers seafood dishes (squid in chili-tomato sauce Rp22,000). Open M-Sa 7:30am-10:30pm, Su 7:30am-3:30pm. ❸

(continued from previous page)

Q: When you were little, were you always interested in running your own restaurant?

A: Actually not. Before he asked me to go to England, he asked me to learn hair dresser, so I used to have hair dresser.

Q: Well, your hair looks very good.

A: This is wig! *(laughs)*...Before we move to Bali, I used to have 4 years my hair dresser in Jakarta, without successful. My talent is cooking...

Q: When did you decide to move to Bali?

A: When my boyfriend finished with Garuda and had no job and began working with a company in Bali...

Q: Do you prefer English food or do you prefer Indonesian food?

A: I prefer English *and* Indonesian food...

Q: You don't think English food is boring?

A: I know English food is boring, has no taste, but then I put more when I can get more taste.

Q: What's your favorite dish?

A: When I was in England, I always go out for fish and chips. Always 4 times a week, fish and chips.

Q: How long have you had this restaurant?

A: 5 years, almost 6 years...

Q: Do you [go] back to Java often?

A: For Ramadan...

Check out Arri's Cafe (see **Food,** p. 173) *for her tantalizing fusions of English and Indonesia food.*

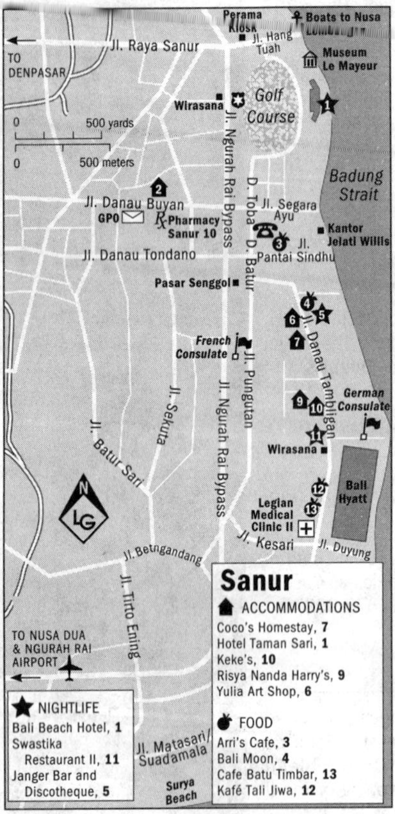

Kafé Tali Jiwa, Jl. Danau Tamblingan 148. Part of the environmentally conscious Hotel Santai. Healthy vegetarian dishes (and some non-veg.) at affordable prices (entrees Rp10,000-30,000). Popular hummus, guacamole, and homemade ice cream. Water bottle refill and **Internet access.** ❸

SIGHTS

The northern part of Sanur's coast is rocky and dark, and local wildlife like crabs, seabirds, and children flying kites dominate the scene. Farther south, on the sandy beach part of the coast, the fauna are exotic foreign species (German and Japanese sunbathers) and their parasites (countless hawkers, peddlers, massage women, and boat captains). This is an ecosystem best observed from afar. **Museum Le Mayeur,** Sanur's only non-beach related sight, has seen better days. The former home of Belgian artist Le Mayeur (who lived in Bali from 1932 to 1958) is crumbling, unswept, and filled with mostly faded paintings. Le Mayeur's work consists mostly of Impressionist portraits of Balinese women. The collection here shows little range. The museum is north of Bali Beach Hotel grounds, on the beach boardwalk, and the cheap ticket price makes it worth a quick walk-through while you wait for the boat to Nusa Lembongan, but don't go out of your way. (☎286 201. Open Tu-Th and Su 8am-2pm, F 8-11am, Sa 8am-12:30pm. Rp1000; children Rp500.)

ENTERTAINMENT AND ACTIVITIES

Sanur caters to the Elton John and John Tesh crowd, the same crowd that finds Kuta too loud and wild. **Janger Bar and Discotheque,** Jl. Danau Tamblingan 21, is a local interpretation of Western hipness. It's the largest club on the island and features four bars and a mix of Balinese (younger than in Kuta) and foreign (older than in Kuta) clientele. (☎288 88. Cover M-Th Rp25,000, W-Su Rp30,000; no cover Su-Th 9-10:30pm. Open daily 9pm-dawn.) The **Bali Beach Hotel** (☎288 511), at the north end of the beach, has dinner performances of *Ramayana* dance on Wednesdays at 7:30pm. **Swastika Restaurant II,** Jl. Danau Tamblingan 124 (☎288 573), has *Legong* dance performances on Thursday and on Sunday (both at 8:30pm). These are not full traditional shows, however, but rather half-hour excerpts. Sanur is livelier during the day. The **Kantor Jelati Willis** booth on Sanur Beach, where Jl. Segara runs into the sand, offers the most options, including traditional sailing (US$20

WHOSE SYMBOL? Upon coming to Bali for the first time, a number of tourists are shocked by the use of a familiar, threatening symbol: the swastika. Now reviled in the West, the symbol actually dates back over three millennia. Swastika is a Sanskrit sun symbol common to Hindu statues and architecture and has also been adopted by Buddhism. The four "legs" represent dynamic cyclical change. In Bali and other areas influenced by Hinduism, the swastika is a ubiquitous blessing that imbues statues and buildings with religious significance. Among their other evil deeds, Hitler and the Nazis appropriated and corrupted this symbol.

activities and trips to neighboring islands, visit the booth on the end of the boardwalk where the boats are docked. Windsurfing and snorkeling require caution, as passing motorboats have killed tourists.

NEAR SANUR: NUSA LEMBONGAN

With white sand, blue waters, and barreling waves, Nusa Lembongan is the domain of surfers who brave the three large breaks over its reef. Looking from the beach to the off-shore reefs, the major breaks (from right to left) are: **Shipwreck, Lacerations,** and **Playground.** The most reliable surf is at Shipwreck, a clean right-hand break. Almost as good as the surf is the snorkeling at **Mangrove Bay.** The cheapest way to get to Nusa Lembongan is by **public boat** from the end of Jl. Hang Tuah in Sanur. The boat leaves at 8am but requires a minimum number of people (Rp40,000). **Perama boats** leave at 10:30am. Tickets cost Rp50,000; show up at the Warung Pojok depot at 10:15am on the day of the trip. Returning boats, both public and Perama, leave around 8am from Nusa Lembongan. Coming back in the evening by public transportation is not possible. The strait between the islands is rough and the only way to navigate it is by chartering a boat. On the island, boats are readily available for rent, and guides will take you around the island for some of the best snorkeling on Bali. (Rp100,000; Rp20,000 when boat is full.) The best places for cheap food and accommodations are on the northwest corner of the island at Jungubatu Village, 500m from the boat drop-off (with the water to your back, walk left). There is little difference among the bungalows along the shore, and none of them include breakfast. **Ketut's Losmen ❹** has new, modern bungalows. (Singles Rp70,000; doubles Rp80,000.) **Ketut's Warung ❸,** past Agung's Lodge and 50m inland, has one of the cheapest options, with simple rooms with bath. (Singles Rp40,000; doubles Rp50,000.) **Agung's Lodge ❸** offers a carnival atmosphere and full amenities. (Singles Rp50,000; doubles Rp60,000.) The best place to eat is beachside at the **Mainski Inn and Restaurant ❸,** which offers fresh seafood and shows American movies at 7:30pm. (Tasty chips and bean dip Rp10,000.) The 2½hr. walk around the island is pleasant, especially at dusk. The nearby island of **Nusa Penida** has a spectacular reef for snorkeling and is also out of the way of passing motorboats. Still, it has no restaurants and only a few dilapidated accommodations on the shore. The island serves primarily as a seaweed plantation.

KUTA ☎0361

What has long been known as one of the most vibrant areas on Bali was shaken by the devastating bombings of two crowded nightspots along Jl. Legian on October 12, 2002. About 180 people were killed in the attacks, which seemed aimed specifically at Western tourists. As Kuta's economy is largely driven by tourism and its lighthearted reputation, the attacks are sure to have serious repercussions on the businesses themselves and on the livelihood of the area's residents.

As of press time, the full extent of damage caused by the terrorist attack on Jl. Legian was not known; many businesses will be forced to close, and all prices and hours are subject to change. Call ahead for up-to-date information, and check the most recent news reports to find out the current state of the region.

TRANSPORTATION

Flights: Ngurah Rai International Airport, 15min. by taxi (Rp20,000). A Perama bus also runs from Jl. Legian 39 (every hr., Rp6000). **Garuda,** Natour Kuta Beach Hotel, Jl. Pantai Kuta 1 (☎270 535). Open M-Th 7:30am-4:30pm, F 7:30am-5pm, Sa-Su 9am-1pm. Several other airlines have offices at the airport. Private tourist offices, found everywhere, offer reservation services.

Local Transportation: Bemo run from the *bemo* corner along Jl. Pantai Kuta to the beach and to **Legian** and **Seminyak.** Catch *bemo* to Denpasar's **Tegal Station** (30min.) on Jl. Tanjung Sari or from the corner of Jl. Raya Kuta/Imam Bonjol (Rp1000). Prepay the fixed-price **taxi** fares at their stand. **Perama,** Jl. Legian 39, has **buses** to destinations on **Bali, Java,** and **Lombok.**

Rentals: Cars (Rp70,000) and **motorbikes** (Rp40,000) can be rented by the day at most tour and travel agencies and hotels. You don't need an international driver's license to rent a car, but chances are you'll be asked to present one at one of the many checkpoints in the area.

INDONESIA

ORIENTATION AND PRACTICAL INFORMATION

Kilometers long but only a couple of blocks wide, the Kuta area sprawls along the beach from **Tuban** in the south to **Seminyak** in the north. Most of the action is between **Jl. Pantai Kuta** and **Jl. Legian,** the main north-south streets. They're connected by one major street, **Jl. Melasti**—technically the dividing line between the Kuta and Legian beaches—and by a labyrinth of several small *gang*, each only wide enough for one car to pass through at a time. The more traveled *gang* are **Poppies Lane I** and **Poppies Lane II** in Kuta proper. Both have cheap hotels and restaurants along their cluttered streets. The *bemo* corner is at the intersection of Jl. Legian and Pantai Kuta. Navigation in Legian has an added complication: **Jl. Pura Bagus Teruna** is also called **Jl. Werkudera,** and **Jl. Sahadewa** is also **Jl. Menuh.** There's no clear point when one becomes the other; you can walk by five buildings with a Werkudera address, then walk by five more with Pura Bagus Teruna on the door, and then discover that a couple more labeled "Werkudera" pop up.

Tourist Offices: Badung Regency Tourism Information Center, Jl. Raya Kuta 2 (☎756 175). Helpful staff gives advice about the best surfing. Free maps and copies of *Bali Plus* guide and entertaining *Hello Bali* and *Bali Travel News.* Open M-F 8am-3pm, Su 8-10am. **Mitra Praja,** Jl. Raya Kuta 1, next door to Badung RTI. More information about other destinations on Bali and Lombok.

Tours: Agencies spill out every street and alleyway. The large **PT. Amanda Legian Tour,** Jl. Bene Sari (☎754 090), has a helpful staff, offers tours and shuttle buses, and books flights for Bali, Java, and Lombok. Tanah Lot trips Rp60,000. Open daily 8am-8pm.

Immigration Office: Jl. Airport Ngurah Rai (☎751 038), Tuban. Arrive 1hr. before opening to ensure service. Open M-Th 7am-2pm, F 7-11am, Sa 7am-12:30pm.

Currency Exchange: Moneychangers and banks line **Jl. Legian** and **Jl. Pantai Kuta.** Banks generally close by 2pm weekdays and noon on Sa, and are closed on Su. **Bank Danamon,** Jl. Legian 87 (☎761 620), offers cash advances (MC/V). Open M-F 8am-3pm. **ATMs** are everywhere, including Poppies Ln. I, Poppies Ln. II, and Jl. Melasti.

Emergency: Police: ☎110. **Ambulance:** ☎118.

Police: ☎751 598. On Jl. Raya Kuta, opposite Bank Pembagnan Duta.

Pharmacy: Krisna Usada (☎758 503), next to the Legian Clinic, Jl. Benc Sari. Open daily 8am-10pm.

Medical Services: Natour Clinic (☎751 361, ext. 110), at the beach end of Jl. Pantai Kuta, next to Natour Kuta Beach Hotel. English-speaking staff. Open 24hr. **Kuta Clinic** (☎753 268), on Jl. Raya Kuta. In Legian, **Legian Medical Clinic** (☎758 503), off Jl. Legian on Gang Bene Sari, next to Century Plaza. Medi-evacuation. Open 24hr.

Telephones: International **wartel** all over, including Kuta Square Shopping Ctr. **HCD** booth in Matahari Department Store in Kuta Sq. Open daily 9:30am-10pm.

Internet Access: One Internet cafe per square centimeter. Get wired (about Rp300-500 per min.).

Post Offices: GPO (☎754 012). With your back to the Badung RTI Center, head left across Bakung Sari. Follow orange signs; it's opposite the elementary school. *Poste Restante.* Open M-Th 8am-2pm, F 8am-noon, Sa 8am-1pm. More convenient is **Ida's Postal Agent** (☎751 574), on Jl. Legian Kuta at the intersection with Poppies Ln. II. *Poste Restante.* Open M-Sa 8am-8pm. **Postal code:** 80361.

Express Mail: Perama Office, Jl. Legian 39 (☎751 551). **DHL**-authorized. Will forward **FedEx** letters, but will not send packages larger than letters.

ACCOMMODATIONS

Poppies Lane II, just meters from the surf shops and nightlife, attracts a young crowd, while **Poppies Lane I** is quieter. (Accommodations in these areas are the most likely to have been affected by the recent bombings.) Cheap beds are harder to come by in Legian; however, what does exist exudes an air of sophistication not found in Kuta proper.

Senen Beach Inn, Camplung Mas Ln. 25 (☎755 470), in an alley off Jl. Melasti. One of the cheapest options in Legian. Unusually friendly and laid-back staff help plan trips and book shuttles. Quiet garden. Restaurant. Tea fairy leaves you a fresh thermos every morning. Fan, private bath. Singles Rp30,000; doubles Rp35,000. ❷

Puri Agung (☎750 054), on Gang Bedugul. Turn onto Poppies Ln. I from Jl. Legian, and turn right at T.J.'s; it's a short way down on the right. Central location and gated entrance. Singles with fan and private bath Rp30,000; doubles Rp40,000. ❷

Suka Beach Inn (☎752 793). Turn onto Poppies Ln. II from Jl. Legian and then turn right at the Adrenalin Park sign on Jl. Bene Sari and walk 100m. Popular among

THE BIG SPLURGE

THE MACCARONI CLUB

Take a seat and let your napkin be placed on your lap for you; relax and prepare to enjoy. With low lighting and decor typical of a big-city cocktail lounge, the Maccaroni Club attracts travelers of all kinds for its authentic Italian food and extensive drink list. With a chef trained in Italy and the ocean only blocks away, the Maccaroni Club capitalizes on taste and freshness throughout the menu.

Comfy chairs covered in denim match the waiters' outfits, and fountains are scattered around the three split levels.

It does not matter if swanky cocktail lounges are not normally your scene; surfers and families alike flock here for the exquisite Balinese-flavored Italian cuisine. *Gnocchi* (Rp33,500) with pesto and pine nuts is served in portions big enough for any appetite. The house specialty, *fettuccine alla pescatore* (Rp39,000), includes amazingly fresh shrimp, calamari, and fish. Divine desserts (Rp18,000) are rich and heavenly, and a cup of Italian espresso (Rp10,000) will bring a warm close to every meal.

A dinner here, especially with cocktails (Rp15,500-50,000), could be more expensive than one night's stay in Kuta, but don't doubt it is worth it. Spoil yourself with an evening of authentic tastes and relaxing ambiance. *(Jl. Legian 52. 25min. free Internet with food or drink purchase. Open noon-midnight. MC/V.)* ❺ surfers. Free storage for boards and bags. Breakfast included. Bike (from Rp30,000 per day) and car (from Rp70,000 per day) rental. Singles with fan Rp40,000; doubles Rp50,000. ❸

Legian Beach Bungalow (☎751 087), on Jl. Padma north of Jl. Melasti. Well-kept grounds include a pool. Close to Kuta action, but secluded enough for quiet. Singles with fan Rp50,000; doubles Rp70,000. ❸

Diana House (☎751 955). Walk 1½ blocks on Poppies Ln. I from Jl. Legian toward the beach; Diana House is on the right. Carefully painted decor. Small, spotless rooms. ❸

Mahendra Beach Inn (☎752 371). From Jl. Legian take the first left off Poppies Lane II. *Losmen* with oh-so-classy blue-tile decor. Fan and private bath (extra fans available). Breakfast included. Singles from Rp35,000; doubles Rp40,000. ❸

FOOD

Kuta's tourist hordes eschew local food and instead eat at a variety of Western-style restaurants (anything from McDonald's fast food to fine European cuisine). The locals, however, will share their own cooking at the **night market** ❷. (From Jl. Pantai Kuta, walk away from the beach and take the fifth right; it's 100m down on the left.) For cheap eats, a few **warung** ❶ dot the beach boardwalk.

Ryoshi Japanese Restaurant (☎761 852), 300m from the water on Jl. Melasti. Branch at Jl. Seminyak 17 (☎731 152). Fresh sashimi melts in your mouth. White mackerel roll Rp9500. Open daily noon-midnight. MC/V. ❷

Aromas Café, on Jl. Legian, 30m south of the intersection with Jl. Melasti. More Bombay than Bali, this venue for "exotic vegetarian cuisine" will tempt even the most carnivorous. Many vegan options as well—try the avocado salad (Rp18,000). MC/V. ❹

T.J.'s (☎751 093), on Poppies Ln. I, one block from the beach. Classy, tropical atmosphere with indoor reflecting pool. The food isn't authentic Mexican but still is fresh and tasty. Enchiladas with crab meat and green chili Rp35,000. Open daily 8am-11pm. Bar open until 11:30pm. MC/V. ❺

Warung '96, Jl. Bene Sari. off Poppies Ln. II. Branch at Jl. Abimanyu 200A (☎733 800). Serves burgers and way too much J. Lo and Green Day. Join the surfers for a King Sized Burger (with beef, bacon, ham, pineapple, egg, and cheese; Rp7500). Open daily 7am-midnight. ❸

Warung Indonesia (☎759 817), on Poppies Ln. II, the first left from Jl. Legian. Fresh, quick, cheap Indonesian food. Entrees Rp6500-9000. Open daily 10am-2am. ❷

Mama's German Restaurant (☎751 805), on Jl. Legian at the intersection with Poppies Ln. II. Boasts Bintang Beer on tap (Rp30,000 per liter) as well as a stocked imported bar (Smirnoff Rp13,000; Jägermeister Rp37,000). Kitchen serves oversized bratwurst (Rp11,000). Open 24hr. Visa. ❷

ACTIVITIES

If you're a surfer, welcome home. If you aren't, now is the time to become one. While the surf is safe, the rental selection is rather poor. **Motor boats** regularly go from **Kuta Beach** to the airport reefs (Rp10,000, but don't pay full price in advance to ensure a quick pickup). Many hotels will transport surfers to beaches in **Seminyak** or **Uluwatu.** Swing by **Tubes Surf Bar and Restaurant,** on Jl. Legian between Poppies Ln. I and II, to pick up a free tide chart. (☎753 510. Open daily 10am-midnight.) Even if getting crazy barrel is not your thing, Kuta still has plenty to get you

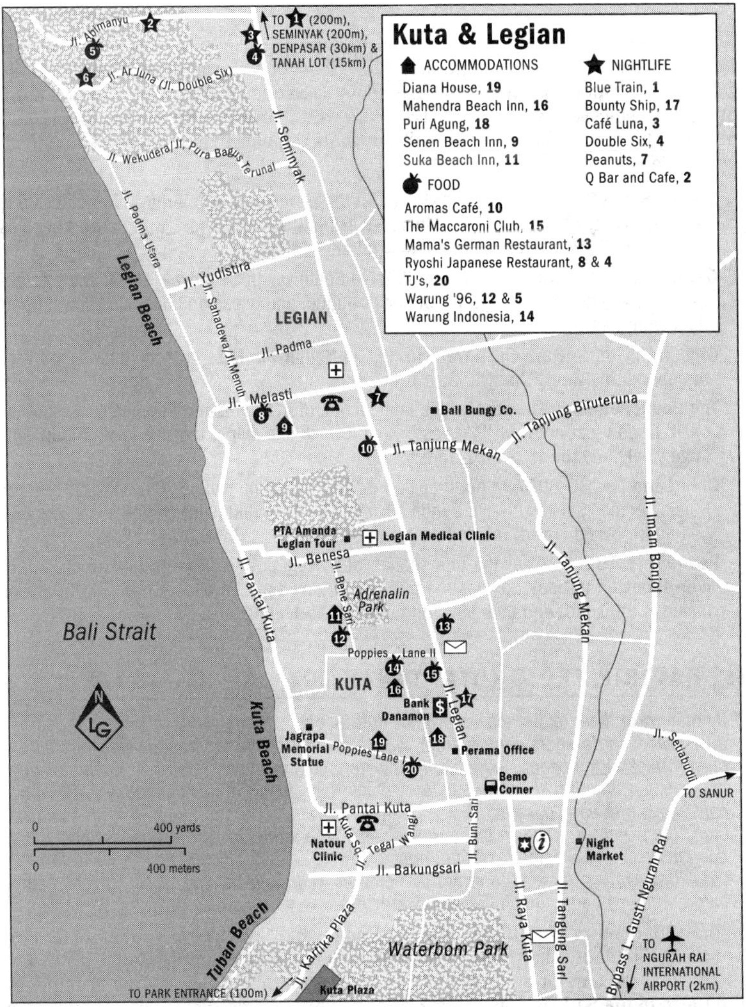

excited, including four **bungee-jumping** towers, a **waterslide park,** several **billiard halls,** and a few **arcades. Waterbom Park,** on Jl. Kartika Plaza in Tuban, a 5min. walk south from the *bemo* corner, has waterslides, a wave pool, and masseurs. (☎755 676. US$15; massage extra. Open daily 9am-6pm.) Bungee-jumping packages are available at **A.J. Hackett** (☎730 666), next to Double Six Nightclub; **Bali Bungy Co.,** on Jl. Pura Puseh (☎752 658; open daily 9am-7pm); **Adrenalin Park,** Jl. Bene Sari 69 in Legian (☎757 841; open daily noon-7pm); and **Bungee in Bali** (☎941 102), 30min. away in Glanyar. Bungee in Bali drops jumpers over a waterfall; the others do it over a pool.

NIGHTLIFE

The Sari Club, one of the most popular clubs in Kuta, was the primary target of the October 12 bombings. Other establishments were damaged as well, and the future of many businesses seems bleak. Travelers who remember Kuta's once-legendary nightlife, however, expect that it will regain its popularity if and when safety concerns abate.

Double Six (☎251 266), in north Legian, at the beach end of Jl. Arjuna. Trendy place is worth the hefty cover (Rp40,000; includes 1 drink) on weekends. Mixed crowd boogies to Euro-house/trance music. Open daily midnight-dawn.

Q Bar and Cafe, on Jl. Abimanyu off Jl. Raya Seminyak in Seminyak. Gay-friendly establishment with nightly dancing, a clothing boutique, and occasional fashion shows. Open daily 9pm-2am.

Blue Train, on Jl. Raya Seminyak No. 28, in Seminyak. Best jazz on Bali. Bands vary throughout the week. Open Tu-Su 11am-2am.

The Bounty Ship, one location at the intersection of Jl. Legian and Poppies Ln. I, another on Jl. Legian just north of Jl. Melasti. Built to look like ships, these 2 joints fill up with large weekend crowds. 2-for-1 drinks 5-7pm. Open 24hr.

Café Luna (☎730 805), in north Legian on Jl. Raya Seminyak, 100m north of Jl. Pura Bagus Teruna. Salsa with live bands (Tu and Th 10pm-midnight) or go-go dancers (Sa midnight). Mixed crowd. Drinks Rp20,000-30,000; pizza Rp18,000-32,000.

Peanuts (☎754 149), at the intersection of Jl. Legian and Jl. Melasti. Attracts a fast crowd looking to hook up. Hosts a pub crawl (May-Sept. Tu and Sa); Rp50,000 cover includes transport, entrance fees, and drop-off at the end.

DAYTRIP FROM KUTA: TANAH LOT

By motorbike, head along the coast from Kuta Beach with the water on your left. Sharp rocks necessitate short detours from the beach, but paths are easy to find and lead quickly back to the beach. Bring plenty of water and sunscreen. The journey can also be made on foot, but it takes 4½hr., so leave early (4am) to avoid the hot midday sun. If you can't leave that early but want to walk, bemo *it to Tanah Lot and then walk* back *to Kuta along the water with the sun on your back. First take a minibus to Denpasar's Tegal Station and then take a* bemo *to Ubung Terminal, then one to Kediri, and finally one to Tanah Lot (20min.). If you intend to return by* bemo *as well, then be sure to get to Tanah Lot before 4pm, as* bemo *run unpredictably after that.*

In the 15th century, the Brahman priest Danghyang Nirartha was so impressed by Tanah Lot's beauty that he convinced locals to build a temple there. If he saw today what became of it, he would probably regret his decision. This "Temple of the Earth in the Sea," is now dwarfed by the tourist infrastructure around it. Cafes and souvenir shops compete for tourists' attention, and photo-snapping tour groups swarm. To avoid the hordes, make your pilgrimage in the morning.

UBUD

☎0361

The deluge of foreigners coming to landlocked Ubud to experience "authentic" Balinese culture has gentrified the city, spawning tasteful boutiques and cafes, cozy bungalows, world-class art museums, and Bali's finest restaurants. This also means that villages and rice paddies have been less-than-genuinely "preserved" for the tourists. Despite all its pandering to outsiders, however, Ubud remains a lovely, charming city and, to a keen eye, still a Balinese one.

TRANSPORTATION

Local Transportation: Bemo congregate in front of markets and on major streets. In theory, *bemo* colors designate destinations, but this system doesn't always work. Brown *bemo* go south to **Batubulan** (40min.), where connections can be made to other cities. Orange *bemo* go to **Gianyar** (15min.), with connections to: **Amlapura** (1½hr.); **Besakih** (1½hr.); **Candi Dasa** (1½hr.); **Klungkung** (1hr.). Each ride is Rp2000. Shops and tourist centers offer **shuttle bus** services; departure times and fares are listed on storefronts. Fares vary from company to company. Destinations include: **Ngurah Rai Airport/Kuta** (1½hr.); **Candi Dasa/Padangbai** (1½hr.); **Lovina** (2½hr.); **Sanur** (1hr.). Tourist offices also rent **bicycles** (Rp20,000) and **motorcycles** (Rp30,000).

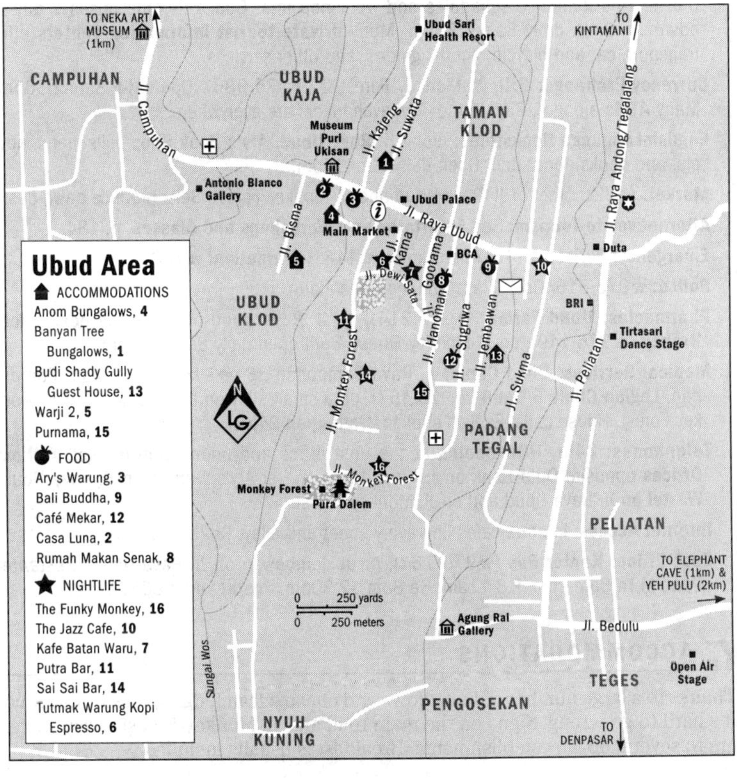

ART COLONY Bali attracts loads of Westerners—and not all of them leave. Expatriate artists are a fixture here. A tour around the Ubud galleries will acquaint you with Antonio Blanco, Walter Spies, and Arie Smit, all first-rate European artists who came into their own on Bali, then never left. Even now the island teems with artists: Perry Farrel (lead singer of Porno for Pyros) devoted an album to his Bali experience, and the spiritual depth and lush beauty of the island has made permanent visitors out of the French Buddhist photographer Jacques Guyot and the American Yogic Furniture designer Nathan Winsor.

ORIENTATION AND PRACTICAL INFORMATION

Ubud's main drag, **Jl. Raya Ubud,** runs east-west through the town's central tourist area. Most major roads are perpendicular to Jl. Raya Ubud. On the west side of town, **Jl. Monkey Forest (Jl. Warana Wana)** runs alongside the **market** to Ubud's **Monkey Forest.** There, it makes a U-turn and becomes **Jl. Hanoman,** which leads back to Jl. Raya Ubud east of the market. North of Jl. Raya Ubud, **Jl. Raya Peliatan** becomes **Jl. Raya Andong/Tegalalang,** which runs past the **police station** toward Kintamani. The market also serves as a **bemo terminal.**

Tourist Offices and Tours: Ubud Tourist Information (☎973 285), on Jl. Raya Ubud, provides performance schedules and workshop info. Books Perama buses 1 day in advance. Open daily 8am-7:30pm. Many **private tourist information centers** offer transport, car and bicycle rentals, guides, and other services.

Currency Exchange: BNI, Jl. Monkey Forest 2 (☎875 986). Open M-F 8am-2:30pm. Many **ATMs** along Jl. Raya Ubud. Moneychangers are everywhere.

English-Language Bookstores: Along **Jl. Raya Ubud. Ary's Book Shop** sells maps, novels, and books about Bali. Open daily 8am-10pm.

Market: At the corner of Jl. Raya Ubud and Jl. Monkey Forest. Sells produce dawn-dusk.

Alternatives to Tourism: See **Entertainment: Workshops and Classes,** p. 184.

Emergency: Police: ☎110. **Ambulance:** ☎118. **Information:** ☎108.

Police: ☎975 316. On Jl. Raya Andong/Tegalalang.

Pharmacies: Ubud Farma (☎974 214), on Jl. Raya Ubud opposite the post office. **Branch** (☎976 149), on Jl. Monkey Forest. Both open daily 8am-9:30pm.

Medical Services: Ubud Clinic, Jl. Raya Campuhan 36 (☎974 911), toward Campuhan. **Legian Clinic 5 Ubud** (☎976 457), on a small alley off the south end of Jl. Monkey Forest. House calls. English spoken. Both **open 24hr.**

Telephones: 24hr. HCD booths at the post office and main Ubud market. **Telkom Offices** opposite Duta Bank on Jl. Raya Ubud and at Ary's Warung on Jl. Raya Ubud. **Wartel** on Jl. Raya Ubud and on Jl. Monkey Forest.

Internet Access: Internet cafes line every street and alley. Rp250 per min.

Post Office: Kantor Pos (☎975 764), on Jl. Jembawan off Jl. Raya. *Poste Restante.* Open M-Th 8am-2pm, F 8-11am, Sa 8am-12:30pm. **Postal code:** 80571.

ACCOMMODATIONS

Thanks to a large number of bungalows and cheap, clean lodgings in central Ubud, it's hard to go wrong. Signs on the main road and Jl. Monkey Forest direct travelers to several dozen establishments. Breakfast is usually included.

Warji 2, on Jl. Bisma. Facing the tourist office, turn right and take the first left; it's 200m down. Spacious, luxurious bungalows with individual porches. Removed from the street. Screened rooms with ceiling fan and private bath with hot water. Doubles Rp50,000. ❸

Banyan Tree Bungalows, on Jl. Suwata, across from the palace. Roomy bungalows decorated in some of Ubud's finest art. Screened rooms with porch, writing desk, tea, and coffee. Singles Rp35,000; doubles Rp45,000. ❸

Anom Bungalows (☎978 491), on a small lane off Jl. Raya Ubud. Large bungalows with ceiling fans. Singles Rp20,000; doubles Rp30,000. ❷

Purnama (☎978 371), at the end of Jl. Hanoman heading toward the Monkey Forest. Clean rooms with verandas in a Balinese-style home open onto a lush garden. Tea included. Rooms Pp80,000, with private bath Rp100,000. ❹

Budi Shady Gully Guest House (☎976 027), on Jl. Jembawan. A 5min. walk from the intersection with Jl. Raya Ubud. Serene jungle views overlooking a river. Family-run and impeccably well maintained. Pricey rooms with outside bath. Doubles US$10. ❺

FOOD

Ubud lives up to its reputation for having Bali's best food. The city's international cuisine may beat out local fare for ingenuity and flavor. Trendy cafes, health food stores, and vegetarian restaurants are popular among expats—their quality and selection leave no doubt as to why. **Tino Drug Store,** on Jl. Raya Ubud near the Tourist Information Office, has a supermarket. (☎975 020. Open daily 8am-10pm.)

Casa Luna (☎977 409; www.casalunabali.com), on Jl. Raya Ubud. Serves not only the best bread in Bali, but also incredible entrees and desserts. Outdoor patio overlooks dense tropical forest. "Killer Brownie" concoction Rp9000. MC/V. ❸

Bali Buddha, on Jl. Jembawan, opposite the post office. Bright hippie colors and trendy drinks. Awesome place to sit and relax. Organic grocery, bakery. 3-level sitting area and a sandbox for the kids. Banana-date soy milkshake Rp6500. Open daily 7am-10pm. ❷

Ary's Warung, on Jl. Raya Ubud by the Tourist Information Office. Classy atmosphere and walls covered with black and white photos from Ary's backpacker days. Expensive, though the *paella* sets you back only Rp35,000. Open daily 7:30am-1am. MC/V. ❺

Cafe Mekar, Jl. Sugriwa 33. Minimal atmosphere, but cheap and hearty Indonesian food. Entrees under Rp15,000. Open daily 10am-11pm. ❷

Rumah Makan Senak, Jl. Hanoman 7. Cheap, clean, and basic, with *padang*-style sauces. Rice with tofu Rp1500, with beef Rp3500. ❶

SIGHTS

Ubud, with its classy cafes, souvenir shops, scenic boulevards, and nearby villages, is one giant sight in itself. Even so, you won't want to miss the city's rich museums or a stroll through the renowned Monkey Forest.

MONKEY FOREST. Ubud's most popular site is a miniature jungle in the middle of the city. Giant trees loom on either side of the trail, providing a habitat for about 200 monkeys. The monkeys aren't shy, so the problem isn't spotting them but keeping them from stealing your hat and sunglasses. Don't carry food—it's sure to attract some monkey business. Inside the Monkey Forest is Ubud's **Pura Dalem** ("Temple of the Dead"), flanked by statues of ogres devouring children. *(On the southern bend of Jl. Monkey Forest. Open daily 8am-5:30pm. Rp10,000.)* Paths lead from the forest to southern villages, including **Nyuhkuning,** where you will find a **woodcarving museum.**

NEKA ART MUSEUM. Set in idyllic grounds overlooking a river valley, this museum displays an extensive collection of Balinese and Bali-inspired art. One of the museum's annexes, the Arie Smit Pavilion, houses work by the Dutch expat and examples of the "Young Artist" style he established. The photography archive collection preserves photographs of Balinese ceremonies from colonial times, while its back room has a megalomaniacal tribute to the museum's founder, Suteja Neka. All paintings are labeled in English. *(Follow Jl. Raya Ubud west until it crosses the river and becomes Jl. Raya Campuhan. Then walk 1km farther until it turns right. ☎975 074. Open daily 9am-5pm. Rp10,000.)*

ANTONIO BLANCO GALLERY. The former home of the "Dali of Bali" now showcases his art. Antonio Blanco's style was eccentric, expressive, exotic, and highly erotic. The house itself is a great exhibit; the Balinese architecture is done with over-the-top pastel colors and a giant archway. *(Facing the Tourist Information Office, turn right down Jl. Raya Ubud and take the first left before the suspension bridge. ☎975 502. Open daily 8am-5pm. Rp10,000.)*

AGUNG RAI MUSEUM OF ART. Opened in 1996, ARMA holds examples of traditional styles of Balinese painting and Bali's only works of the Russian-German artist Walter Spies. An open-air stage hosts traditional dances every night at 6pm. *(On Jl. Hanoman 500m south of Jl. Monkey Forest. ☎976 659. Open daily 9am-6pm. Rp10,000.)*

INDONESIA

MUSEUM PURI LUKISAN. Built to preserve Bali's artistic heritage, the museum focuses on traditional painting styles and woodcarvings. At the center of the museum compound, a lotus pool sit in a garden, complete with elegant shrine islands. *(Opposite the Tourist Information Office. ☎975 136. Open daily 8am-4pm. Rp10,000.)*

ENTERTAINMENT

PERFORMANCES. To catch all the performances you want to see, go to the Ubud Tourist Information Center (see **Tourist Offices,** p. 182) and pick up a schedule of events as soon as you arrive in Ubud. Dance and *gamelan* are performed nightly throughout the city. Ubud's shows are well-rehearsed and elaborately staged. More natural and traditional performances are held in the surrounding area. (Shows 7pm. Tickets sold at the Tourist Information Center, tour agencies, and on the street. For shows in neighboring villages, the Tourist Information Center provides free transport.) Particularly worthwhile are the *wayang kulit* (shadow puppet shows) and the powerful *kecak* (monkey) dance, in which men beat out rhythms on their bare chests.

WORKSHOPS AND CLASSES. **Ganesha Bookstore,** on Jl. Raya Ubud, offers **gamelan lessons;** no previous musical knowledge is required. (☎963 59. Rp45,000.) **Balinese dance courses** are available at **Dewi Sekar Ayu,** Jl. Hanoman 26. With your back to Jl. Dewi Sita, turn right at the intersection with Jl. Hanoman and walk 100m. Take away a lasting memento from the **batik course** offered at the **Crackpot Gallery** on Jl. Monkey Forest. With the football field on the left, the Crackpot is 100m down. Design your own shirt or cushion cover. (☎973 411. Open daily 9am-8pm.) The **Meditation Shop,** on Jl. Monkey Forest 400m from the Monkey Forest, allows visitors to observe **meditation workshops** for free. Stop by for details or join the daily 6-7pm meditation. (☎976 206. Open daily 5-9:30pm.) **Casa Luna Restaurant** offers **Balinese cooking classes.** Sign up early for the Tuesday **market tour,** as spots are limited to eight. (M, W 10am-2pm, Tu 8am-noon. Rp100,000, includes 1 meal.) **Massages** and **skin treatments** are available at competitive prices. De-stress and rejuvenate at **Ubud Sari Health Resort,** Jl. Kajeng 35, at the end of the road. (Massages US$12 per hr.) The health food restaurant and juice bar serve high-quality dishes and drinks. (☎974 393. Open daily 8am-8pm.)

SPORTS. Although most of Ubud's draws are cultural or artistic, rafting and other adventure sport options exist for thrill-seekers. Contact **Sobek** (☎287 059), **Unda Adventures,** Jl. Raya Ubud 33 (☎977 169), or **Bali Adventure Tours** (☎751 292). You can also arrange whitewater rafting tours in the area. Daytrips include transportation and a meal (about US$60).

NIGHTLIFE

An artsy town inhabited by bohemian tourists, Ubud has a calmer nightlife than Kuta; it tends to revolve around cafes rather than bars. The coffee shops on Jl. Dewi Sata are popular—both **Tutmak Warung Kopi Espresso** (☎975 754; open daily 9am-11pm) and **Kafe Batan Waru** (☎977 528; open daily 8am-midnight) fill up after dance performances end. A few places on Jl. Monkey Forest pit American movies against Balinese dancing. For the bar-goer, the **Sai Sai Bar** plays Top 40 (M) and reggae (Th). At the **Funky Monkey,** known for its mysterious trance atmosphere, patrons sit under a black-lit, star-studded ceiling. (☎390 3729. Open daily 11am-1am.) The **Jazz Cafe** is packed nightly and plays pop, jazz, and blues. (Open daily 11am-midnight.) As the evening winds down and the night starts, crowds head to **Putra Bar.** (Open daily from 11am until the last person leaves.)

DAYTRIPS FROM UBUD

Villages and rice paddies lie within 1km of Ubud, and any road leading away from the main drag will reward the explorer with breathtaking scenery.

ON FOOT. With 2½-3½hr., you can take a decent walking tour of Ubud's surroundings. Start from the west end of Jl. Raya Ubud, circle through the picturesque landscape, and eventually get back onto Jl. Kajeng near the Ubud Sari Health Resort. With your back to Museum Puri Lukisan, walk down Jl. Raya Ubud until you come to Abangan Bungalows. Walk up the steep driveway and to the left side of the main building along a small trail that runs parallel to a stream. The trail will bear left; follow it for 30-45min. and take the first right. Take a left on the trail that leads down a small hill for a few steps and then cross the bridge on the right. Turn right

NOTES ON A BALINESE COCKFIGHT Cockfighting is still a cultural keystone in Bali. On the day of the fight, the cock-master prepares a concoction of meat and purified jackfruit–a sure mix to thicken the blood and make the cock stand strong, tall, and ready. Cockfights in Ubud are common, but they take on additional meaning on the day of *tabah rah*–literally "pouring of the blood"–a sacred event in which demons are fed sacrifices. After the *Demangku* (lay priest) gives the initial offering of rice wine, it's down to business. The masters pass their birds around to be prodded, pulled, and plucked, so spectators can evaluate the strength and ferocity of each. The owner then attaches the 10-15cm long *taji* (blade) to the cock's leg. From there, it's a winner-take-all pool between the two owners. Bets are placed in codes: the cry of "cok, cok, cok" in quick succession means 4:3 odds that the underdog will win. As the gong is struck, the cocks fly at each other in a frenzy of feathers and feet until the fatal blow is struck. The *pemsang taji* (master of the winning cock) wins the leg of the losing cock with the *taji* still attached. Hoisted up high, the winning cock lives to fight another day; the loser becomes dinner.

INDONESIA

and follow this trail the rest of the way. If you get lost, ask someone, *"Bagimana ke Jalan Kajeng?"* ("How do I get to Jl. Kajeng?") or *"Ke Ubud?"* ("To Ubud?").

ORGANIZED WALKS. It's also possible to join an organized walking tour. A guided **Herb Walk,** led by husband-and-wife team Lilir and Westi, explores native plants and medicinal herbs. (☎975 051. US$18 includes herbal teas, drinks, and snacks.) Another possibility is the **Bali Bird Walk,** offered by an Englishman, Victor Mason. (☎975 609. US$3, including walk, lunch, and bird guide.)

The road that connects Ubud to Denpasar via Batubulan links a string of **craft villages: Mas** (wood carving), **Sukawati** (wind chimes and baskets), **Celuk** (silver work), and **Batubulan** (stone carving). Sukawati is also the site of an early morning produce market. Brown *bemo* pass through these villages, offering views of artists working on open verandas. Alternatively, it's an easy downhill ride by bike (bring string to tie the bike to the *bemo* if you want a ride back).

GOA GAJAH (ELEPHANT CAVE). There never were elephants on Bali—Goa Gajah gets its name from the floppy-eared demon carved at its entrance. One section contains idols of Ganesha, the other *hingham* (phallic representation), and the Hindu trinity: Brahma, Vishnu, and Shiva. A thousand years of existence have taken their toll on Goa Gajah's carvings—many are worn. Whether it's worth the hassle of pushy souvenir hawkers is up to you. *(1km outside of Ubud on the road to Gianyar. Take a red or green* bemo *Rp3100.)*

INDONESIA

YEH PULU. For the time being, the bas-relief of Yeh Pulu is vendor-free. The walk there passes an ungentrified Balinese neighborhood and terraced rice fields. *(From Gao Gajah, walk 1km away from Ubud; the way is clearly marked by signs on the road.)*

GUNUNG KAWI. **Tampaksiring village's** Gunung Kawi is a mysterious complex of tombs surrounding a central temple. The river divides the two cliff faces, hewn from rock in the 11th century. The area left of the stone archway is thought to be the burial site of King Anak Wungsu's four concubines. Across the river are the tombs of the king and his four wives. Beside the **royal tombs** lie a courtyard and a series of caves and rock passages. Gunung Kawi is best seen in the early morning or late afternoon, when visitors can avoid hordes of tourists, sharing the grounds only with local villagers who bathe in the river. **Titra Empul,** at the north end of Tampaksiring village, is a temple near natural spring pools. The holy water is said to have therapeutic power. *(Take an orange or blue* bemo *for Gianyar and get off in Bedulu. From there, take a* bemo *or* ojek *north to Tampaksiring. If you bike, prepare for an arduous 15km ride uphill that lasts about 1hr. Each sight Rp3100. Where necessary, sarong and sash are free.)*

ANIMAL PARKS. Two animal parks were recently built in **Singapadu.** The **Bali Reptile Park (Rimba Reptil)** features reptiles from around the world, including cobras and Komodo dragons, as well as a petting zoo with huge pythons and iguanas. The conditions here are much better than in other zoos around Indonesia—the management probably fears protests by yoga-doing tofu eaters. *(☎299 344. Open daily 8:30am-6pm. Rp57,000.)* Next door is the **Bali Bird Park (Taman Burung),** home to exquisite landscaping and fantastic birds, including the endangered Bali starling. *(Catch a* bemo *toward Batubulan from Jl. Raya Ubud and tell the driver "tempat burung, di Singapadu" (the bird place in Singapadu). The trip takes 30min., and the* bemo *will probably let you off at the turn-off to Celuk. From here it's a 20min. walk to the parks. Private vans may be easier to get there or back, but bargain hard–don't pay more than 5 times what the* bemo *ride would cost. ☎299 352. Open daily 8am-7pm. Rp57,000. Combination ticket for both parks Rp103,000.)*

DEMON MANICURE Balinese belief holds that a great demon assembled his finest warriors and assaulted the gates of heaven. A fierce battle raged, and the gods triumphed over the demons. Instead of destroying them, however, the gods forced them to swear an oath of service. As a sign of submission, the demons had all but one of the claws on each of their hands shorn. Demon statues guarding temples and bridges thus have one long claw on each arm. The practice exists among Balinese people as well as Balinese demons; certain people both young and old have one long fingernail to signify that they are practitioners of white magic. It is also said that as a person grows in evil, all of his or her fingernails lengthen and turn black.

SINGARAJA ☎0362

Singaraja is Bali's second-largest city and maintains a more traditional atmosphere than Denpasar. Originally designed to be the capital of Bali and neighboring Nusa Tenggara, the once-important colonial port must settle for being capital of the Buleleng (north) region. The city has few tourist sights and little tourist infrastructure, but it does have big-city services not found elsewhere in the area.

TRANSPORTATION

Bemo leave from **Banyuasri Terminal,** on the west end of Jl. A. Yani, for **Lovina** (10min., Rp1000). **Minibuses** leave for **Denpasar** (2½hr.; Rp15,000) and **Gilimanuk** (2hr., Rp8000). **Sukasada Terminal** at south end of Singaraja has buses to: **Denpasar, Bedugul/Danau Bratan** (1hr.), and **Gitgit Waterfall** (15min.). **Penarukan Terminal,** on Jl. Surapati on the eastern side of town, has *bemo* to: **Amlapura** (2½hr.); **Kintamani** (2hr.); **Klungkung** (3hr.); **Yeh Sanih** (1¼hr.). *Bemo* shuttle between bus terminals until 6pm.

ORIENTATION AND PRACTICAL INFORMATION

Singaraja is bordered to the north by the harbor and to the south by the mountains. Most of the action revolves around the four intersections formed by two roads parallel to the harbor with two roads perpendicular to the harbor. Most of the confusion stems from the fact that, on average, these four roads have at least two names apiece. The main street, **Jl. Achmed Yani (Jl. A. Yani)/Jl. Dr. Sutomo,** runs parallel to the harbor. Farther south and inland is a parallel road named **Jl. Veteran.** Intersecting both of these roads, on the east side of town, are the two major roads that run inland from the harbor. As you walk down Jl. A. Yani with the harbor on your left, the first of these will be **Jl. Diponegoro/Jl. Pramuka/Jl. Ngurah Rai,** which is known as Jl. Diponegoro closest to the harbor and as Jl. Ngurah Rai farthest inland. As you continue on Jl. A. Yani, it will become Jl. Dr. Sutomo and the second major perpendicular road you will reach is **Jl. Imam Bonjol/Jl. Gajah Mada.** It is called Jl. Imam Bonjol closer to the harbor and Jl. Gajah Mada farther inland.

Tourist Office: Dinas Pariwisata, Jl. Veteran 23 (☎251 41), near the corner of Jl. Gajah Mada, on the southeast side. Ask for Pak Putu Tastra Wijaya and get free maps, brochures, and plenty of advice. Open M-F 7am-2pm, Sa-Su 7am-noon.

Currency Exchange: BCA Bank (☎237 66), on Jl. Dr. Sutomo, east of Jl. Diponegoro. MC/V cash advance. Exchanges traveler's checks. **24hr. ATM** (Cirrus/PLUS). Open M-F 8am-2pm.

Markets: Buleleng Market, at the corner of Jl. Veteran and Jl. Gajah Mada, sells fruit. **Pasar Anyar,** off Jl. Dr. Sutomo on the north side, sells fruit and other foods. **Tirta Dew-**

IN RECENT NEWS

CHASING THE DOLPHINS AWAY?

The unhappy relationship between tourism and the environment has a long history on Bali: one example is the destruction of Candi Dasa's beach in the mid-1970s, when its coral was dug up for cement. Today, as the huge tourist appeal for chasing dolphins for photographs continues on Bali and many other Indonesian islands, environmentalists worry that one day the dolphins too may disappear.

A.A.G. Raka Dalem, an environmental activist of Bali Greenery, sent to the June 2002 edition of *Bali Travel News* a list of precautions for boats to take to ensure dolphin safety. The article suggests avoiding changing direction, minimizing speed, and keeping a safe distance. However, fishermen and tour agencies insist that their way of pursuing dolphins is not a threat, citing innocuously narrow boats and shallow rudders. Additionally, there has been no recorded decrease in dolphin appearance since the increase in tourism. Since it is unclear who would enforce a set of rules for this industry, it seems that, for the foreseeable future, the situation will remain as it is now—with dolphin-friendly "guidelines" recommended by activists but accepted voluntarily by tour agencies or else not at all.

ata supermarket, on Jl. Pramuka near the intersection with Jl. A. Yani.

Emergency: Police: ☎110. **Ambulance:** ☎118.

Police: ☎225 10. On Jl. Pramuka, south of Jl. A. Yani, opposite Jagat Nata temple.

Pharmacies: Wijaya Kusuma Apotik, Jl. Ngurah Rai 23 (☎228 90). **Open 24hr.**

Medical Services: Singaraja Hospital (☎262 12), on Jl. Ngurah Rai, 200m south of the police station. English-speaking staff. **Open 24hr.**

Telephones: Wartel Kopegtel, Jl. Gajah Mada 154. Collect or cash **international calls. HCD** phone outside. Open 24hr. **Wartel**, Jl. A Yani 124.

Post Office: Jl. Gajah Mada 156 (☎217 88), at the intersection with Jl. A. Yani. **Internet** access Rp300 per min. *Poste Restante.* Western Union services. Open M-Sa 8am-3pm, Su 9am-1pm. **Postal code:** 81113.

ACCOMMODATIONS AND FOOD

Nearby Lovina is better promoted and more traveler-friendly, though Singaraja does have some basic accommodations. At the east end of the main strip, several *losmen* have fans, cold showers, and laundry services. **Wijaya Hotel ❷**, Jl. Sudirman 74, has the most options. (☎219 15. Basic singles with fan and shared bath Rp20,000, nicer with private *mandi* and fan Rp30,000, plush with A/C, TV, and telephone Rp70,000; doubles Rp25,000/Rp35,000/Rp75,000.) **Hotel Sentral ❸**, Jl. A. Yani 48, offers clean basic rooms without flush toilets. (☎218 96. Singles Rp35,000, with A/C and flush toilets Rp75,000; doubles Rp40,000/Rp80,000.) With your back to the post office, walk straight for 15min. Similar rooms with slightly firmer beds can be found across the road at **Losmen Duta Karya ❹**, Jl. A. Yani 59. (☎214 67. Singles and doubles with fan Rp50,000; rooms with A/C from Rp80,000.)

Jet-Z (say "Jet-Zet") **Cafe ❶**, on Jl. Seruni, 100m in from Jl. A. Yani, is a punk-rock cafe run by the drummer of the Singaraja garage-band Jet-Z. It's a great place to listen to NoFX and reminisce about Kurt Cobain while snacking on cheap Indonesian food (most items under Rp7000). For seafood, head to **Ikan Laut Warung ❷**, Jl. Gajah Mada 65, to enjoy a sampler plate with spicy fish at super-cheap prices. Hindu and Muslim **warung ❷** congregate by the harbor, to form a mini-food-market offering a wide selection of seafood dishes and fresh fruit dishes. (Open daily 9am-9pm.) With the mountains behind you, follow Jl. Diponegoro to its northern edge, then turn right and cross the bridge. Grab a cheap plate of *nasur lampur* and take it to a local vantage point, where you can watch the sunset over the harbor.

SIGHTS

Singaraja is off the well-beaten tourist track, and its sights get few outside visitors. While this means you'll often have the place all to yourself, it also means the temples of Singaraja aren't expecting you. They are poorly maintained, and few among the staff (if there is anyone around at all) speak English.

Gedong Kirtya, on Jl. Veteran next to the tourist office, holds Indonesia's largest collection of *lontor*, palm-leaf manuscripts that have been etched and then covered in charcoal to make the writing legible. It's more a depository than a museum. A better place to see *lontor* produced is the Tenganan village near Candi Dasa (see p. 200). (☎226 45. Open M-F 7am-noon.) Facing away from Gedong Kirtya, turn right down Jl. Veteran and, 60m later, left down Jl. Gajah Mada. Two hundred meters ahead on the right, the **Pura Dalem** (Temple of the Dead) displays a wall of reliefs depicting the Balinese *sorga* (heaven) and *neraka* (hell), and the earthly behavior associated with both. The intricate carvings of demons on the walls of the temple proper more than make up for the weeds in the courtyard. It can be viewed anytime. Next to Pura Dalem, wildflowers, birds, animals, and insects surround the headstones at the **Balinese Hindu Cemetery.** The cemetery's overgrown, wild-garden character is perhaps due to the fact that these graves are not final resting places. Many Balinese Hindus are buried in temporary graves until their families can afford the high cost of cremating them to allow their souls the way to reincarnation. Also on Jl. Gajah Mada, 10min. farther up, near house #97 on the left, the fascinating *tridarma* ("three truths") temple **Tempat Suci Su San Yee** (☎213 22) contains three altars, one apiece for Taoism, Buddhism, and Confucianism. Since 1985, the Chinese-style temple has served as a center for traditional healing for people of all faiths. Follow Jl. Gajah Mada another 120m and take a left to reach **Pura Agung Jagat Natha,** believed by Balinese Hindus to be more supercharged with divine spirit than any other temple on Bali. (Open daily 6am-8pm. Sarongs available to borrow.) To get to the 200-year-old **Chinese temple,** start at the tourist information office and walk to the left on Jl. Gajah Mada for 10min.; it's on the right. According to legend, this temple was impervious to shells fired by the Japanese during World War II. In April 1998, when an angry mob set fire to it, only the meeting room was destroyed; the temple stands unscathed.

INDONESIA

LOVINA ☎0362

Get it all in Lovina: multicolor sunsets, great snorkeling, superb dolphin-watching, a black lava beach, exquisite Balinese seafood, and cheap accommodations. It's a refuge for ocean-goers who want to trade in the crowded beach scene for calmer waters and relaxed Balinese hospitality. But as dollars roll in, loud nightlife and the ever-growing tourist infrastructure increasingly threaten Lovina's serenity.

TRANSPORTATION

Buses: *Bemo* run west to **Gilimanuk,** where a ferry goes to **East Java,** and east to **Singaraja,** where further connections are available to anywhere in Bali (see **Singaraja: Transportation,** p. 187). **Perama** (☎411 04), on the main road next to B.U. Warung, goes to: **Candi Dasa** (3hr.; Rp50,000); **Denpasar/Kuta** (2hr.; Rp40,000); **Gunung Batur** (2hr.; Rp20,000); **Ubud** (2½hr.; Rp40,000). For the cheapest rates but rougher, longer travel, take a *bemo* to Singaraja's **Banyuasri Terminal** and catch **public bus** connections there.

Rentals: Motorcycle (Rp10,000), **car** (Rp80,000), and **bicycle** rentals available with uniform prices. **Su-kha Rentals** (☎411 56), on Jl. Bhina Ria, rents bikes for Rp10,000 per day. Open daily 8am-10pm.

ORIENTATION AND PRACTICAL INFORMATION

"Lovina" describes an 8km stretch of beach along the Bali Sea. The main road, **Jl. Singaraja,** runs parallel to the beach and is lined with restaurants and hotels. The strip includes several villages. From east to west, they are **Pemaron, Tukadmungga Anturan** (Happy Beach), **Kalibukbuk,** and **Kaliasem** (Lovina). Tourist activity is heaviest on Kalibukbuk and Kaliasem, through which **Jl. Bhina Ria,** marked by a dolphin statue, is the main road to the beach. A smaller beach road, **Jl. Pantai Mawar,** branches from Jl. Singaraja 300m farther east. In addition, there are many smaller, unnamed beach roads lined with bungalows and restaurants. As Jl. Singaraja leaves town, it heads east to **Singaraja** (10min.) and west to the ferry point of **Gilimanuk** (2hr.) and the **Bali Barat National Park** (1¼hr.).

Tourist Office: ☎419 10. On Jl. Singaraja in Kalibukbuk between B.U. Warung and Malibu Restaurant. Diving information and directions to local sights. Open M-Sa 8am-8pm, but phones may not be answered after 2pm.

Currency Exchange: Several moneychangers along the main road offer slightly better rates than at Singaraja's banks. Most are open until 9pm. Bank BCA **24hr. ATM** on Jl. Singaraja in Kalibukuk (Cirrus/MC/PLUS/V).

Emergency: Police: ☎110. **Ambulance:** ☎118.

Police: ☎419 10. On Jl. Singaraja between Jl. Bhina Ria and Seririt.

Medical Services: Darma Bakti (☎412 11), on Jl. Singaraja, 1km to the right (with your back to the tourist office). English-speaking doctor. Open M-Sa 9am-noon and 5-7pm. Lovina has no pharmacy, but **Angosaka Mini-Market** (☎411 30), in front of Pasar Kalibukbuk on the main road, sells some medicine. Open daily 8am-10pm.

Telephones: Several **wartel** along Jl. Bhina Ria charge a small fee for international calling cards and are typically open daily 8am-midnight.

Internet Access: Internet cafes line Jl. Bhina Ria. Rp400 per min.

Post Office: GPO (☎413 92), on Jl. Singaraja. With your back to the tourist office, turn right (to the west) and walk 20min.; it's on the left. Open M-Sa 8am-2pm.

ACCOMMODATIONS

Most of Lovina's accommodations are clean and well attended. The price range comes from added amenities such as swimming pools, mosquito nets, and proximity to the beach. The region is known for its mosquitoes and for gigolos. Pick up a mosquito coil from a corner store; you're on your own with the gigolos. Expect to pay more for rooms during peak season.

Susila 2 Backpackers Hostel (☎410 80), on Jl. Bhina Ria. Best value in town. Clean with mosquito nets, table, fan, and private bath. Breakfast included. Free use of next-door Angsoka Beach Inn's swimming pool. Singles Rp40,000; doubles Rp50,000. ❸

Angsoka Beach Inn (☎410 80), on Jl. Bhina Ria. Well-kept bungalows have ceiling fans, spacious porches, and comfy beds. Swimming pool, mosquito nets, and laundry service. Singles from Rp65,000; doubles from Rp80,000. ❹

Pulesti Beach Hotel (☎410 35), 25m from the beach on the main beach road. Hard to miss; the bright facade opens onto a landscaped pool with man-made waterfalls. Singles with fan and mosquito net Rp75,000; doubles with open-air bath Rp90,000. ❹

Billibo Beach Cottages (☎413 55), opposite the post office on Lovina's western edge. Owner helps plan fun-filled days. Removed from tourist noise despite being just a few meters from the beach. Rooms with fans and screened windows from Rp75,000. ❹

Hotel Dupa (☎413 84), on the main road opposite the beach, is cheap, clean, and close to the action. The view of rice fields from upper rooms is worth the extra rupiah. Laundry service. Low rooms from Rp30,000; higher floors extra Rp10,000. ❷

Mas Bungalows (☎417 73). Facing the tourist information office, walk 1km to the right or catch a *bemo*. Take a left on Jl. Lasiana; it's on the right. Shelter from downtown means quiet evenings. Singles Rp40,000; doubles Rp50,000. ❸

FOOD

Although Western dishes are available, Lovina's premier tastebud sensations are Balinese seafood and roasted duck. Establishments offering these local specialties have signs posted on their windows; be sure to order a few hours in advance for dinner, as roasting duck takes a while.

Kakatu Bar & Restaurant (☎413 44), on Jl. Bhina Ria right before the beach, has an international menu. Mexican, Indian, Balinese, and Thai dishes go for Rp15,000-30,000. Watch your meal prepared in the open-air kitchen. Open daily 8am-11pm. ❹

Bali Bintang (☎413 59), on Jl. Bhina Ria, offers steamed duck (order 1 day in advance). Otherwise, its menu is typical Western/Indonesian (meals Rp15,000-35,000). Open daily 8am-11pm. ❹

Poco Evolution Bar (☎415 35), on Jl. Bhina Ria, has occasional live music, but otherwise plays movies or music videos while you eat. Extensive Mexican and Indonesian menu; tasty nachos Rp10,000. Open daily 8am-midnight. ❹

B.U. Warung, next door to the Perama office, is cheap and unpretentious, with scrumptious *pepes,* tuna, and lemon papaya juice. Recommendations from past visitors displayed outside in a myriad of languages. Open daily noon-9pm. ❷

Waru Bali (☎415 53), at the end of Jl. Mawar, is the place for breakfast after chasing dolphins. It lives up to the fresh-seafood potential of its location directly on the beach. Fresh fillet of the day Rp15,000-30,000, depending on size. Open daily 7am-10pm. ❸

INDONESIA

SIGHTS AND ENTERTAINMENT

Lovina's main attractions are pre-dawn boat rides to see **dolphins** and midday **snorkeling** excursions. Local fishermen offer early-morning rides past the reef for roughly Rp20,000 with hard bargaining. If the dolphins don't show (80% chance they will), the sunrise is a glorious consolation. Lovina's snorkeling is some of Bali's best, and shallow waters make it safe for beginners and children. **Scuba diving** possibilities abound. **Spice Dive** (☎415 09), on Jl. Bhina Ria, is a professional, PADI-certified outfit. Facing the tourist information office, head left 500m; it's on the left, opposite Joni's Restaurant. Spice offers full certification courses (4 days US$250), dives for beginners (US$65), and night dives. Waterskiing (Rp120,000) and parasailing (Rp89,000) are also offered. (Open daily 8am-8pm.) Fishing enthusiasts can rent boats, motorboats, traditional *sanpan* (bamboo-stabilized canoes), and other equipment on the beach. (Fishing with guide Rp20,000.)

Tiga Wasa village, a pleasant 1½hr. walk from the west edge of Lovina, makes ornate bamboo handicrafts. Follow the main road west past the post office; the turn-off is clearly marked on the left—it is then a 5km climb uphill. There are no official stores, but bamboo items are visible from the road. At the first house, a pathway to the right leads you to the **Sing Sing Waterfalls,** perfect for a dip. There are no signs, but ask and someone will help you. Although no problems have been documented, the village and waterfall are remote, so it's best to visit with a friend.

In the evening, the best place to catch a film is on top of **Mailaku Bar and Restaurant.** Seats fill up, so get there early. (Shows 6 and 8pm.) The hot, friendly bar in town is **Zigiz,** on Jl. Bhina Ria, with a full bar and live music every night. (Open daily 11am-midnight.) If you're still going strong, it's on to the **Malibu Cafe,** on the main road, for more live music, dancing, and partying until dawn.

DAYTRIPS FROM LOVINA

Though *bemo* transport to Lovina's three main excursions is both easy and cheap, many tourists still charter a car and driver in order to see all three at once. A full six-person *bemo* should cost Rp30,000.

GITGIT WATERFALL. The only thing more spectacular than the 40m high waterfall is the kilometer-long line of souvenir stalls. Local legend says that couples who swim together in the pools beneath the falls will soon separate. If you've been looking for a way out, here's your chance. *(Take a* bemo *from Sukasada Terminal in Singaraja toward Ubung Station (15min., Rp2000). At the sign to Gitgit, walk 1km along the path to the falls. Open daily 8:30am-5pm. Rp3800.)*

BANJAR BUDDHIST MONASTERY. On a forested hilltop with stunning ocean views, the monastery was damaged in the 1976 earthquake that flattened Seririt. The monks have since repaired it, and it again houses Buddha sculptures and a lotus pool. Proper dress is required and can be borrowed from the shop next door. Talking is frowned upon in monastery grounds, and a donation (albeit a small one) over and above the admission fee is expected. *(Rp3000. Catch a* bemo *from Lovina toward Seririt and get off at Dencarik Village (15min.). Grab an* ojek *or* bemo *3km to the monastery; ask the driver to go to "tempat buddha." Open daily 8am-6pm.)*

BANJAR HOT SPRINGS. Perhaps more popular than the monastery itself are the nearby hot springs. The pools, located among manicured gardens and palm trees, are often filled with tourists. *(Near the Banjar Buddhist Monastery.)*

GUNUNG AGUNG

For Balinese Hindus, Gunung Agung is the religious focus of the universe—the vantage point from which the gods observe human life in Bali and beyond. Some 3142m high and thought to be the son of the larger Mt. Semuru on Java, Gunung Agung dominates eastern Bali. An active volcano, Gunung Agung erupted most recently in 1963, killing thousands. Many believed the eruption to be a punishment for neglecting religious duty, so high priests were sent to appease the gods at Mt. Semuru. The most sacred temple complex on Bali lies on the southern slope of Gunung Agung and was untouched by the eruption as lava flowed down the other side of the mountain. It is only 6km from the village of Besakih, and once a year, in March or April, representatives from every town in Bali come to this "mother temple" for the Betara Turun Kabeh ceremony. The mountain gives the visitor a gorgeous view of the countryside and is a bit of welcome escape from the bustle of more touristed areas.

TRANSPORTATION AND PRACTICAL INFORMATION. Public **bemo** run to **Besakih** from **Klungkung** (50min., Rp3500) and **Amlapura** (1½hr., Rp4000). While the official schedule is every 30min. until the last *bemo* at 3pm, it may be necessary to flag down local *ojeks* or trucks. A common place to change *bemo* is at **Redang** between Besakih and Klungkung. Here, *bemo* can be caught to **Selat** (30min., Rp2000) and onward to Amlapura. Though most foreign visitors to the area come on package tours from Candi Dasa and Ubud, tourist facilities do exist. Below the main parking lot and beyond the ticket booth is a *dinas pariwisata*, or **tourist information bureau.** (Open daily 7am-1pm.) When this is closed, you can make do with the maps at the end of the road leading to the temples.

ACCOMMODATIONS AND FOOD. If you're climbing Gunung Agung from Besakih, it is more convenient to stay at one of the many unmarked **losmen** ❶ that line the street from the car park to the hotel. Ask any local; he or she will show you where they are. Usually the *mandi* is shared and rooms are noisy, so bargain for a cheap price. Rp15,000 is fair. **Food** ❷ may be found at the base of the temple, after the parking lot. Hit the *sate ayam* cart before dark for a cheap, filling meal. Fruit and souvenir **vendors** ❶ line the path up to the temple; try the "snakeskin" fruit, found only in Bali.

SIGHTS. Pura Besakih (The Mother Temple) is the most sacred Balinese sanctuary. The largest temple complex in Bali, consisting of nearly 30 temples, it sits 900m above sea level on the southwestern slope of Gunung Agung, affording fantastic views of southern Bali. A pantheon of Hindu gods and goddesses is worshipped at Besakih; Shiva, Brahma, and Vishnu are most important. The Shiva temple is the first and largest. A phalanx of statues protect Shiva; those on the left represent *fandwa* (good spirits), the ones on the right *krawa* (bad spirits). The three gods sit inside the temple, with Shiva in the center, Brahma on the right, and Vishnu on the left. The temple at the far right belongs to Brahma and the one at the far left belongs to Vishnu.

The temple complex is extensive, and the lack of brochures or other English-language tourist information makes hiring a local guide tempting. The same organization that supervises the Gunung Agung guides also manages those at Pura Besakih. The base price is Rp25,000, the only required fee, although the guide may want more than this as a tip or commission or as an extra *ojek* charge if you took the ride up. Decide on a price before setting out, as guides can demand outrageous sums after 5min. "tours" or a 1min. *ojek* ride to the temple, which they claim is 1km. It is important to note that the organization has a monopoly on tours of Besakih; if you bring an outside guide, you are still expected to pay the organization Rp25,000. Additionally, the central temple at Besakih is off-limits to all save for worshippers. The path around the temple's rather low outer walls gives good views of the inside, however. Another option is to pay one of the temple "caretakers" at its front gates Rp20,000 to be let in to "worship" (and take pictures). While Rp20,000 may seem like a bargain, during the requisite prayer at one of Besakih's shrines, tourists are pressured to make "offerings" of Rp50,000 or more. (Complex open daily 6am-6pm. Admission Rp7500, parking costs extra.) Besakih's great annual festival, **Bhatara Turun Kabeh** (Gods Descend Together), occurs on the full moon of the 10th lunar month *(purnama kadasa)*, in March or April. This month-long festival, during which the gods of all temples in Bali take up residence in Besakih's main shrine, attracts thousands of worshippers from all over Bali.

CLIMBING GUNUNG AGUNG. Gunung Agung is a rigorous climb, dangerous in its steeper portions, but it's an exhilarating experience for the physically fit who want a perch from which to view Bali—provided they arrive at the summit before the clouds do. Climbers should aim to reach the summit near daybreak, and definitely no later than 8am, when the mist begins to roll in. The two most popular climbs from Besakih and Selat require climbers to spend a night in the region. The one from the **Besakih** temple is a four- to six-hour, 6km ascent to the highest point on Gunung Agung; one should leave around 2am. Another route starting in **Selat** enables hikers to take transportation up to within 2km of the summit, although the

PLACATING THE DEMONS Here in Bali, misfortune is thought to be caused by demons. You'll see offerings wherever you go; these gifts are meant to placate evil spirits and keep the gift-givers from harm. Armed with woven leaf baskets filled with flowers, colored rice, chicken entrails, and incense, Balinese set out to battle with the local wild ghosts. The gifts are left on streets, on porches, in temples, around the home, on motorcycles, and even under the hoods of cars. Once the offerings are given, they are the demon's to dispose of; they often get eaten by dogs or crushed by passersby. Demons are also thought to dwell at the sites of accidents and deaths. Shrines flank the roads at the sites of fatal accidents. To avoid curses, drivers slow down and honk twice to ask permission to pass. If a Balinese is asked about this practice, they will go on about its irrationality—but add, "It's good luck!"

climb itself is steeper. For this route, one should leave around 4am. A guide is necessary as parts of the trail are hard to find; arrangements should be made at least a day in advance. The **police tourist stations** in Besakih (☎230 82) and Selat (☎241 87) have lists of **guides** in the area, or you can ask at the temple's **ticketing booth.** In Selat it's possible to shop around among different guides. **Gung Bawa Trekking** (☎243 79) is one reputable outfit. (1 person Rp100,000; decreases to Rp50,000 per person with 4 people. Guide and breakfast included. A night in Selat is required; this is Rp50,000 per person.) The guides from Besakih have been cartelized, and the standard price from there is US$50 for one person, US$75 for two, and US$100 for three. You cannot choose your guide; the cartel's members take turns on a strict system. Wear sturdy shoes and warm clothing, and bring a flashlight and something to eat. Beware of loose topsoil and falling rocks.

GUNUNG BATUR

The serene beauty of Lake Batur, which rests inside an enormous volcanic crater, masks the volcano's volatility. Gunung Batur's 1917 eruption demolished the village of Batur, killing 1400 and destroying 65,000 homes, curiously sparing only the town's temple. Believing this to be a sign of good fortune, the villagers remained in Batur until the eruption of 1926, which devastated the village again and convinced Batur residents to relocate to the outer rim. The most recent eruption occurred in 1994. The Batur region offers lavish scenery, but aggressive merchants, pricey accommodations, and mediocre food have marred many a traveler's stay here.

All listings in Gunung Batur are accurate as of summer 2001.

TRANSPORTATION. Orange **bemo** travel between **Bangli** and **Penulisan** (30min., Rp2000). To see Gunung Batur from the rim, get off at **Penelokan.** *Bemo* arriving in Gunung Batur stop in **Kintamani,** where connections run to other villages. **Taxis** and **ojek** also pick up passengers at the *bemo* stop. **Public buses** depart from Penelokan to other island destinations. Morning departures (7-9am) are most frequent. Travelers can also arrange for shuttle connections through transport agents along the main road in **Toya Bungkah** (also known as **Tirta**). **Perama** goes to: **Kuta** (3hr.; Rp30,000); **Lovina** (2½hr.; Rp20,000); **Ubud** (1½hr.; Rp20,000).

ORIENTATION AND PRACTICAL INFORMATION. The Batur area occupies Bali's northeast corner. The villages of **Penulisan, Batur, Kintamani,** and **Penelokan,** on the crater's west edge, are at the highest elevations and offer spectacular views. Of the two most frequented, **Kedisan** (on the west corner) runs boat trips across the lake, while **Toya Bungkah** (at the southern base of Batur) provides easy access to the mountains. The village of **Trunyan**, famed for its aboriginal Balinese residents, the **Bali Aga**, lies across the lake.

The **tourist office** is opposite the fork in the road at Penelokan. (Open daily 9am-3pm.) **Made "Dizzy" Darsana** (☎517 54), a guide who has been climbing Gunung Batur since he was twelve, is the best resource for tourists intent on exploring. His knowledge of the area is unsurpassed and his English is excellent. Find him at Hotel Putra Mulya. Visitors should change money elsewhere, as rates here are poor. The **post office** is on Jl. Bayung Gede in Kintamani. (Open M-Th 8am-2pm, F 8am-11pm, Sa 8am-12:30pm.)

ACCOMMODATIONS AND FOOD. If circumstances require a night on the rim, **Miranda** ❷ (☎520 22), 5km from Penelokan in Kintamani, has basic singles with *mandi* (Rp20,000) and doubles (Rp40,000). Be sure to get a room away from the main road. Toya Bungkah is the place to stay if you are climbing Batur or soaking up the view from the lake. **Arlinas Bungalows** ❸ (☎511 65), in Toya Bungkah, arranges treks up Gunung Batur. Attractive singles (from Rp30,000) and doubles (Rp40,000). **Under the Volcano I** ❸ is nestled in a peaceful garden setting. (☎511 66. Bungalows with *mandi* Rp30,000, with toilets Rp45,000.) Lakeside rooms at **Under the Volcano II** ❹, farther down the road, all have toilets (Rp65,000). **Wisma Tirtha Yatra** ❷, on the lake's edge, is the cheapest in town. Follow the main road from Penelokan and take the first right after the hot springs. (Singles Rp20,000.)

Segara Cafe ❷, opposite the boat harbor in Kedisan, prepares small but delicious fish for Rp10,000. (☎511 35. Open daily 7am-10pm.) If you are only visiting the rim, **Ramana** ❷ has simple fare and an unforgettable view. Facing the Penelokan police station at the fork in the road, turn left and walk 5min. around the corner. (Open daily 10am-5pm.) Make sure to visit a neighborhood *warung* to taste *bantal* (pillow cake): coconut, rice, and banana or peanuts wrapped in a coconut leaf.

SIGHTS. Close to Kintamani in the village of **Penulisan,** at an altitude of 1745m, stands **Pura Tegeh Kuripan,** Bali's highest temple. Built in the 9th century, the temple offers exquisite views of Gunung Batur and Bali's north coast. The temple houses *linga* statues, symbols of the god Shiva. (Open during daylight. Rp3000.)

THE BIG SPLURGE

TIRTA AYU HOTEL AND RESTAURANT

There are reasons the *rajah* decided to build his summer house in Tirtagangga: sprawling hillsides, a striking view of water, and the fresh spring pools. Though the first two of these reasons are also now available to non-royalty, unlimited access to the pools is the biggest perk of staying at Tirta Ayu. Originally the king's vacation home, it now contains several different bungalows spread over the grounds. Yet the pools are not the hotel's only royal quality: Tiled baths have marble showers where human-sized statues spout water. A full-length mirror accompanies every spacious, immaculately clean tiled room. Large comfortable beds are accompanied by night tables, a standing closet, and desk. The porches are large with comfy bamboo chairs with cushions. Statues and gardens mark paths leading along the buildings.

The restaurant overlooks the pools and garden, and an early evening meal makes for a beautiful view of these pools at dusk. Serving Indonesian specialties, the restaurant matches the kingly quality of the complex: dumplings or spring rolls Rp6000, lemon grass chicken in chili sauce with noodles Rp19,000.

At night, a lighted mosquito coil arrives at your room, though it is almost unnecessary. The nights are cool and quiet, a relaxing break from the heat of Bali's coasts. In the mornings, a large breakfast is included in the room price. *(☎216 97. Rooms, regardless of number of people, from Rp120,000.)* ❺

Tours of **Lake Batur** can be arranged from the harbor in **Kedisan.** From Kedisan, the boat goes to the **Bali Aga** village of Trunyan, **Trunyan cemetery** (both are accessible only by boat), and the hot springs at **Toya Bungkah** (US$5 to swim). The boat waits as long as you like at each stop. Standard tours last 1½-2hr. Guides are assigned and prices are fixed. (Rp196,500 for 1 person, includes admission and donation at Trunyan and the cemetery; prices go down with more people.) Beware of locals aggressively asking you for "donations."

The base of Gunung Batur is encircled by a road; the scenic walk around the base takes 4-5hr. Among the highlights is **Lucky Temple** in the northwest corner, which has miraculously survived all lava flows. After an exhausting trek up, down, and around the mountain, relax in the **Hot Springs** in Toya Bungkah. The price is steep at US$5, but worth it. (Open daily 8am-8pm.)

CLIMBING GUNUNG BATUR. A spectacular sunrise and a view of the entire Gunung Batur area is the reward for a steep, challenging climb. On a clear day you can even see Lombok's Gunung Rinjani peak. During the day, a guide is unnecessary, however, locals claim it is "illegal" to climb before sunrise without a guide. This "law" is enforced by the Komesariat Gunung Bator, the union of local guides, which harasses and threatens independent climbers. All guides must be hired through the Komesariat. (☎523 62. Rp150,000 for up to 4 people; additional Rp20,000 for breakfast and ground transportation.) Many *losmen* charge commissions that can double or triple this price. Wear warm clothes.

To climb on your own, find the yellow "Welcome to Toya Bungkah" sign at the Kedisan side of town. A dirt road next to the sign heads toward the mountain. Take this road and, when it bears right after the houses, continue following it 70m. It will then bear left; follow it. When the road reaches a temple on the right, take the narrow footpath just before the temple wall and follow it around the temple into the woods. Stick with the path for 45min. until the trees stop and the terrain turns to volcanic rock, sand, and ash. From here, there are no real "paths"—the only way to go is up. Most day-trekkers leave between 8 and 9am. If you depart much later you might be shrouded in mist before reaching the summit (2hr.).

AMLAPURA ☎0363

A sidestep from the eventful tourist locales surrounding it, Amlapura is simple in its manner but royal in its history. With just a few main streets and one night market, this city has little to offer those who intend to "hang for a few days." However, for the historically minded, the nearby royal retreats offer a unique look into the regal lifestyle of a bygone era.

TRANSPORTATION AND PRACTICAL INFORMATION. *Bemo* from the **main terminal** in the market area leave for **Denpasar** (2½hr.) via **Candi Dasa** (20min.); **Gianyar** (1½hr.); **Klungkung** (1hr.); **Singaraja** (1½hr.) via **Tirtagangga** (15min.), **Culik** (½hr.), **Tulamben** (40min.), **Yeh Sanih** (1hr.), **Selat** (1hr.), and **Besakih** (1½hr); **Padangbai** (40min.). Amlapura's main road runs north-south at the town's very east end, disguising itself with many names. From north to south: **Jl. Sultan Agung** becomes **Jl. Teuku Umar,** then **Jl. Gajah Mada,** and finally, near the Ujung Water Palace, **Jl. Bayangkara.** Jl. Gajah Mada and **Jl. Kesatrian,** which run parallel to each other, border the town center. At the south end, Jl. Kesatrian turns sharply and intersects Jl. Gajah Mada. The *bemo* and bus stop is at the south end of Jl. Kesatrian as it bends back to Jl. Gajah Mada. **BNI,** next to the *bemo* terminal on Jl. Kesatrian, changes currency and traveler's checks. (☎220 57. Open M-F 8am-4pm.) To get to the **hospital,** Jl. Ngurah Rai 40 (☎21 470, emergency ☎21 011), walk out the main street until it becomes Jl. Sultan Agung, and then turn left on Jl. R.A. Kartini and left again on

Jl. Ngurah Rai; it's on the left. Across the street from the hospital is a **pharmacy** (☎22 106). The **police station,** Jl. Bayangkara 1 (☎212 20), is near the center of town at the transition of Jl. Gajah Mada to Jl. Bayangkara. The **post office,** Jl. Gatot Subroto 29, is at the entrance to Amlapura. (☎210 10. Open M-Th 8am-2pm, F 8-11am, Sa 8am-noon.) A *wartel* sits on Jl. Gajah Mada for cash calls. (Open daily 7am-11pm.) **Postal code:** 80800.

ACCOMMODATIONS AND FOOD. Options for accommodation in Amlapura are slim—most travelers prefer to stay in resort-style Candi Dasa or in the hillsides of Tirtagangga. **Villa Amlapura ❸,** 100m downhill from the Puri Agung palace on Jl. Sultan Agung has excellent rooms including Western bath and breakfast, surrounded by late 70s, yet retro modern, designer furniture and fixtures. (☎232 46. Rooms Rp50,000.) The extremely bare **Losmen Lahar Mas ❷,** at the entrance of town, before the post office on Jl. Gatot Subroto, has basic rooms with baths. (☎213 45. Singles Rp20,000; doubles Rp30,000.) Food is largely limited to the *pasar*'s **warung ❶.** A **night market ❶** sets up next to the turn-off to Singaraja at 5pm, but usually winds down by 8pm. **Sumber Rasa ❷,** on Jl. Gajah Mada, is one of the few sit-down joints in Amlapura that serves Indonesian and Chinese food. (Most dishes under Rp10,000. Open daily 8am-8pm.)

SIGHTS. Visitors to Amlapura can stroll through what remains of the once-prosperous Karangasem kingdom. **Puri Agung,** also known as **Puri Kanginan,** the former residence of the last Karangasem *rajah* and his family, is open to the public. The palace has little labeling, but visitors can pick up a useful information sheet from the ticket window. There are no tours per se, though if you come in an organized group from Candi Dasa, the guides will walk you through the complex—and, not infrequently, one of the *rajah*'s sons, who lives in an apartment behind the palace, is on hand to cheerfully show off his childhood home. Note the evidence of Dutch artwork and furniture—the Karangasem retained power long into the 20th century because of their collaboration with the Dutch. The *puri* is north of the *pasar* along Jl. Sultan Agung. (Open daily 8am-6pm. Rp3000.) The **Ujung Water Palace** is a more modest version of what the Karangasem king built in Tirtagangga (see below). Built in 1919, it was used as a private retreat for the royal family. The 1963 eruption of Gunung Agung and the 1979 earthquake destroyed much of the palace. All that remains now are ruins jutting up through the rice paddies and water lilies. Few tourists come here; there is no formal admission. Take a blue *bemo*, from the corner of Jl. Gajah Mada and Jl. Kesatrian (10min., frequent departures, Rp500), or enjoy the passing scenery to Ujung on a *dokar*. Clamber up the surrounding hills to get a better look at the layout of the garden's pools and fountains, as well as a view of the Lombok Strait.

TIRTAGANGGA

Bali's Karangasem *rajah* built Tirtagangga in 1947 as a holiday retreat and named it after Hinduism's holiest river, the Ganges. Lying 13km northwest of Amlapura, Tirtagangga is home to multi-level ornate pools fed by a spring on the slopes of Gunung Agung. The idyllic pools offer the perfect setting in which to swim, rest, and rejuvenate yourself. (Open daily 6am-6pm. Admission to springs Rp3000, children Rp1600; privilege of swimming Rp6000, children Rp4000; still cameras Rp1500, video cameras Rp2500.) **Bemo** run between **Amlapura** (15min.) and Tirtagangga (every 20min. until 6pm); Tirtagangga is also served by **Perama shuttles:** at the entrance to the parking lot, the **Good Karma Restaurant ❷** (☎224 45) sells tickets to destinations all over the island. The main road from Tirtagangga, leading away from

Amlapura to Culik (30min.), passes some of the most picture-perfect scenery in Bali, from dense tropical forests to rugged arid mountains.

For those staying here overnight, the best value is at **Pondok Lembeh-Dukuh ❷**, three secluded bungalows on a hill. Getting there is an adventure. From the parking lot, head toward Singaraja on the main road until you come across an irrigation canal. Follow the canal through rice paddies and past houses until you reach the forest. A path there leads to a long stairway to Pondok Lembeh-Dukuh. Gorgeous views of the area more than compensate for the trek. (Breakfast included. Singles Rp30,000; doubles Rp40,000.) Cheaper accommodations can be found at **Kusuma Taya Inn ❸** (☎212 50). On the main road, with your back to the pools, turn left and climb up the stairs 300m. Standard rooms start at Rp45,000, but prices fluctuate depending on availability (breakfast included).

AMED (LIPAH)

The sleepy fishing village of Amed conjures up the Bali of 30 years ago. The village's quiet seaside air is conducive to relaxing on the warm lava-black beaches or snorkeling in the clear calm waters. Along the main road north of Amlapura/Tirtagangga, **bemo** pass the village of **Culik,** from where *bemo* run to Amed up until 11am (after that, hire an *ojek*). Change money before arriving, as there are no banks or currency exchanges. No longer inexpensive, many once-budget places in Amed have gone up-market or closed down. It is hard to find single-person accommodation for under Rp60,000. The best option is the newly merged **Amed Beach Cottages/Amed Cafe ❹.** On the main drag at the center of town, its cheaper rooms are clean and well maintained, with fan, private bath, and mosquito nets. (Doubles including breakfast Rp80,000.) Similarly priced rooms with similar amenities are 50m farther away from the center of town at **Bamboo Bali Bungalows ❹.** (Singles Rp70,000; doubles Rp90,000.) **Warung Congkang Three Brothers ❷** will cook your catch and serve it with good humor. Most menu entrees are under Rp15,000. (Open daily 8am-9pm.) The wreck of the **USAT Liberty,** torpedoed by a Japanese submarine during WWII, is at nearby **Tulamben,** and it makes both Tulamben and Amed meccas for divers. All accommodations rent diving and snorkeling equipment and normally offer dive packages. **Amed Dive Shop** comes highly recommended. (1-day, 2-dive packages US$85; introductory courses US$55. MC/V.)

INDONESIA

CANDI DASA ☎0363

Once upon a time, there was a beach at Candi Dasa. The beach attracted tourists. The tourists needed bungalows. To build the bungalows, the locals needed cement. To make cement, the coral along the coast was ripped out and ground up. Without the coral to break the tides, the beach washed away. There is no beach in Candi Dasa anymore, but there are still bungalows. Despite the lack of a beach, watersports still attract tourists to the area. In addition, Candi Dasa is the only designated resort area in eastern Bali; budget accommodation and decent restaurants abound and are scant elsewhere in the area. In turn, Candi Dasa is not as lonely for a traveler as, for example, Amlapura or Amed. The sights in Bangli, Klungkung, and Amlapura, along with the two villages of Tenganan and Trunyan, are easily accessible from Candi Dasa and make a few nights here worthwhile.

TRANSPORTATION

Local Transportation: Bemo run regularly on the main road until 6pm. With your back to the water, *bemo* going right are headed to **Amlapura** (20min., with connections to Tirtagangga and Singaraja). Those going left are headed to **Padangbai** (20min.) and **Klungkung** (40min., with connections to Gianyar, Besakih, Penelokan, Batubulan). **Per-**

ama, next to the police office at the west end of town, has daily morning bus departures to: **Denpasar/Kuta/Sanur/Airport** (Rp20,000); **Lovina/Singaraja** (3hr.; Rp50,000); **Penelokan/Kintamani** (2½hr.; Rp30,000); **Tirtagangga** (30min.; Rp20,000); **Ubud** (1½hr.; Rp15,000).

Rentals and Diving: Many accommodations and tour agencies rent **bicycles** (Rp10,000), **motor bikes** (Rp30,000), and **snorkeling equipment** (Rp15,000) by the day. **Baruna Dive** (☎411 85), at the center of Candi Dasa's main road, offers diving and snorkeling expeditions to surrounding areas.

ORIENTATION AND PRACTICAL INFORMATION

Candi Dasa is a 1km strip on Bali's east coast along the Klungkung-Amlapura Rd. With your back to the water, Klungkung is to the left (west) and Amlapura is to the right (east). Murky **Candi Dasa Lagoon** is on the seaward side of the main road at its east end; the local temple is directly across the lagoon. The waters of **Amuk Bay** border Candi Dasa on the south and hilly rice terraces to the north. From the sand, the island straight ahead is Nusa Penida (see **Near Sanur: Nusa Lembongan,** p. 175).

Tourist Offices: Besides the plethora of private tourist information centers offering tours, rentals and shuttle services, there is the official (but not very useful) **Candidasa Tourist Information Office** (☎412 04). As you're walking on the main road with the lagoon on the right, the office is one house past the end of the lagoon. Open daily 8am-noon.

Currency Exchange: Moneychangers all along the main road offer reasonable rates and take traveler's checks. Most close by 9pm. **24hr. BNI ATM** about 100m south of the lagoon on the beachside.

Emergency: Police: ☎110. **Ambulance:** ☎118.

Police: ☎416 77. At the west end of the main road, where the road runs along the bay.

Hospital: Candidasa Clinic Laboratory & Apotik (☎413 21). Traveling on the road to Padangbai, it's 100m past the turn-off to Tenganan on the left. Open M-Sa. On Sunday, the area is serviced by a doctor from Denpasar (☎0361 463 093).

Telephones: *Wartel* at the center of town on the main road. International cash calls only. Open daily 8am-11pm. **HCD** booth at Tourist Information.

Internet Access: Scattered along the main road. Rp300 per min.

Post Offices: There are several **postal agents** on the main street, including **Asri's Convenience Store.** These may take mail and sell stamps, but no more. Open until 10pm. The nearest **post office** is 20min. away in Amlapura. **Postal code:** 80851.

ACCOMMODATIONS

Budget beachside bungalows run the length of Candi Dasa, but the quieter ones cluster at either end. In the low season, it's possible to negotiate cheaper prices.

Barong Beach Inn (☎411 27). When the road bends sharply to Amlapura at the east end, go straight and take the 1st right. Best price in town. Breakfast included. Singles Rp20,000; doubles Rp25,000; beachfront rooms (nothing special) Rp40,000. ❷

Ida Home Stay (☎410 96), on the west side of the lagoon. 6 private 2-story bungalows with large rooms, modern baths, and deck chairs on private verandas. Guests include many families. Rooms available for 4 or more. Breakfast included. Doubles Rp90,000; additional persons Rp25,000. ❺

Dewi Bungalows (☎411 66, fax 411 77), bordering the eastern side of the lagoon. Private bungalows with fans around a nice garden. Laundry and massages. Breakfast included. Singles Rp50,000; doubles Rp70,000. ❸

INDONESIA

Ramu Bungalows (☎417 78). With the lagoon on the right, walk down the path toward the beach; it's on the left. Set among gardens. Quiet, well-screened rooms with fan and full bath. Laundry. Breakfast included. Singles Rp40,000; doubles Rp60,000. ❸

FOOD

For a small strip along the beach, Candi Dasa offers a surprisingly large selection of culinary delights. Cheap tourist-oriented restaurants face the street. *Warung*, only slightly cheaper, cluster at the west end of town. More expensive restaurants have superior service and atmosphere, and are worth the extra cost. Some restaurants have a double role, also serving as the source of nighttime entertainment with movies, dance floors, or live bands on weekends.

TJ's (☎41 540), across the street (to the west) from the lagoon, is on the exquisite side of food consumption with fantastically and creatively prepared daily catches (Rp30,000). Vegetarian friendly. MC/V. ❹

Raja's Bar and Restaurant, opposite Tourist Information on the main road, offers a large Western menu with burgers, pasta, and barbecue (Rp12,000-28,000). English-language movies—mainly Hollywood flicks—shown from 7:30pm. MC/V. Open daily 10am-11pm. ❸

Ciao (☎411 74), set back off the main road near Candidasa Beach Bungalows, features great Italian spaghetti, pizzas, and gelato. Entrees Rp13,000-25,000. Movies during the week at 7:30pm. On Saturdays, a band plays and a dance floor opens up below the dining area. Open daily 9am-10pm. ❸

Warung Astawa (☎413 63), on the main road at the east edge of Candi Dasa. Seafood sampler (Rp18,000) with shrimp cocktail, fish in banana leaves, and dessert. Tropical atmosphere, bamboo furniture. *Legong* dancing at 7:45pm. Open daily 7am-10pm. ❸

Warung Srijati, opposite the Ida Home Stay west of the mucky lagoon. Nicer than a real *warung*, cheaper than a real restaurant. Tasty Balinese food for under Rp10,000. Fresh fruit juice. Vegetarian-friendly. Open daily 7am-10pm. ❶

Koeno (☎420 11), 150m south of the lagoon. Tiki decor, extensive seafood menu as well as pasta and curry offerings. Entrees Rp15,500-26,000. Live band at night. Open daily 8am-10pm. ❹

DAYTRIP FROM CANDI DASA: TENGANAN AND TRUNYAN

1km south of Candi Dasa. An ojek *from Candi Dasa should cost no more than Rp5000. Walking takes a little under an hour, and is best to do in the early hours to avoid traffic. Small donation (Rp5000 is acceptable) to enter.*

The two small villages are far more quiet than Candi Dasa itself. Tenganan is an enclave of the Bali Aga, the aboriginal Balinese. Unlike those in Trunyan, the Bali Aga here do not aggressively pursue donations other than the entrance donation; in fact, while they do depend on souvenir sales for their livelihood, even the shopping here is surprisingly low-pressure. Tourists can observe the weaving of double-ikat (*geringsing*) cloth as well as the inscribing on *lontar* scrolls. The other village, Trunyan, hosts a month-long festival *(Usaba Sambah)* in May/June; tourists may view it for a donation. A very bright and lively affair, it features traditional *pandanus* fighting, in which combatants try to draw blood with spiky leaves.

KLUNGKUNG (SEMERAPURA) ☎0366

Klungkung's fame as the seat of the powerful precolonial Gelgel Kingdom makes it an important historical landmark on East Bali. The kingdom fell long ago in the bloody Battle of Klungkung, but its legacy lives on in the old palace grounds and

INDONESIA

monuments commemorating the 1908 battle. Klungkung's intriguing sights are best seen as a daytrip on the way to Candi Dasa, Besakih, or Ubud.

All listings in Klungkung are accurate as of summer 2001.

TRANSPORTATION AND PRACTICAL INFORMATION. Bemo run between 6am and 6pm to: **Amlapura** (1¼hr.) via **Padangbai** (25min.) and **Candi Dasa** (50min.); **Batubulan** (1hr.) via **Gianyar** (25min.), and **Besakih** (45min.). The yellow *bemo* at the main terminal go 1km to the city center. Officially named Semarapura, Klungkung sits 40km east of Denpasar. Klungkung's town center is small, consisting of an intersection and four streets. The central landmark is a **traffic rotary,** where the main east-west thoroughfare, **Jl. Diponegoro/Untung Surapati,** runs into north-south **Jl. Gajah Mada/Puputan.** From the rotary, the **Puputan Monument** and the old palace grounds (Island Gardens or Taman Gili) are visible. South of the rotary, the **bemo terminal** is 1km down Jl. Puputan on the right. A huge **market** is nearby. East on Jl. Diponegoro are the main commercial area and the few accommodations.

The Klungkung government **tourism office,** Jl. Untung Surapati 3 (☎214 48), lies within the Taman Gili complex. Several **banks** along Jl. Diponegoro change money and transfer cash (MC/V). **Bank BCA** (☎213 21), on Jl. Diponegoro between Jl. Puputan and Jl. Nakula, has an **ATM** (Cirrus/MC/Plus/V). The **police** (☎211 72) are on Jl. Untung Surapati to the far west, past the post office. An **apotik** is on Jl. Flamboyan on the outskirts of town (pharmacy; open M-Th 7:30am-1:30pm, F 7:30-10:30am, Sa 7:30-noon); a more central apotik is at Jl. Diponegoro (open 24hr.). A **hospital** (☎211 72) is next to the apotik on Jl Flamboyan. For English-speaking doctors, head to the 24hr. clinics in Ubud or Kuta. A **24hr. wartel** is at the corner of Jl. Diponegoro and Jl. Puputan. **HCD** booths allow collect and credit card calls. The **GPO,** on the west side of Jl. Untung Surapati, has *Poste Restante.* (☎210 10. Open M-Th 8am-2pm, F 8-11am, Sa 8am-2pm.) **Postal code**: 80700.

ACCOMMODATIONS AND FOOD. Since Klungkung can be visited as an easy daytrip, it's better to stay in Candi Dasa or Padangbai, where options are more plentiful. If you do stay overnight, there are a few budget places. To get to **Loji Ramayana Hotel ❸,** Jl. Diponegoro 152, stand at the rotary with the palace at your back and walk straight ahead on Jl. Diponegoro. (☎210 44. Doubles with *mandi* Rp30,000, with flush toilets Rp50,000.) For lower prices, cross the street to **Cahaya Pusaka Losmen ❷** (look for the "Losmen 20m" sign), where bare rooms face a small garden. (☎221 18. Singles Rp25,000; doubles Rp30,000.) The usual *warung* fare is widely available, but is best at the lively **Pasar Senggol.** (Open daily 4pm-midnight.) Two Chinese restaurants, **Sumber Rasa ❷** (☎250 97) and **Restoran Bali Indah ❷** (☎210 56), are both on Jl. Nakula. Take Jl. Diponegoro east from the rotary; Jl. Nakula is the first road on the right. (Dishes Rp6500-12,5000. Sumber Rasa open daily 7am-11pm. Restoran Indah open daily 7am-9pm.)

SIGHTS. A tour of Klungklung's sights will give the visitor an opportunity to see the influences that have shaped Bali. **Kerta Gosa,** the Court of Justice, is a pavilion in the northwest corner of the **Taman Gili complex.** The ceiling is lined with 267 painted panels that depict the story of **Bhima Swarga,** Indonesia's Dante. In his journeys, Bhima Swarga traveled through the various levels of heaven and hell to save his parents' souls. These paintings illustrate the punishment for the guilty (bottom rows) and the rewards (culminating with the birds at the top) awaiting the innocent in the afterlife. (Open daily 7am-6pm.) Also in the complex is the **Bale**

Kambang (Floating Pavilion). In dynastic times, the *bale* was the receiving area for important guests. The paintings on the inside of the roof depict the story of **King Sutasoma,** a Buddhist ruler. Many paintings show the Hindu demon **Kala** hurling weapons at Sutasoma, which transform into flowers right before hitting him. The paintings chronicle the union of Buddhism and Hinduism in Bali—the final image shows Buddha emerging from the mouth of **Naga,** a symbol of Hinduism. The paintings are all a bit faded. They do not, in content or style, break from traditional Balinese themes—if the museums in Ubud were too much for you, don't come here. The **museum** at the west edge of the Taman Gili complex was built by the Dutch, and houses fascinating photographs of the *rajah* and royal residence as well as historical artifacts. Everything is labeled in English. Across the street is the **Puputan Monument,** whose base contains labeled dioramas providing a visual crash course in Balinese history. (Open daily 7am-6pm.) One ticket into the complex includes admission to all sights (Rp2000, children Rp1000).

The fabled **Goa Lawah** (bat caves), 9km east of Klungkung on the way to Padangbai, are home to thousands of bats, and at least a thousand are visible to the visitor's eye, hanging over a makeshift temple. Snakes prey on bats in the area, giving rise to the story about a mythical serpent who dwells in the caves. The caves can only be seen from the outside, not entered. Doing so would be both sacrilegious and stupid—not only would you anger the locals, you'd be covered in bat poop in an instant. According to the Balinese, these caves extend all the way to Gunung Agung. *Bemo* heading to Padangbai pass Goa Lawah often (10min., Rp1500).

INDONESIA

BANGLI ☎0366

Although Bangli was once a strong kingdom, today it is not as developed as its neighbors. Superb night market fare, clean and uncrowded streets, a magnificent waterfall, and an important temple more than compensate for the lack of facilities.

All listings in Bangli are accurate as of summer 2001.

TRANSPORTATION AND PRACTICAL INFORMATION. Bangli is 40km north of Denpasar. The **bemo terminal,** south of the **Jl. Kusuma Yuda/Jl. Merdeka** junction, offers connections to: **Batubulan** (1hr., Rp3000); **Gianyar** (45min., Rp3000); **Kintamani** (30min., Rp2500); and **Klungkung** (30min., Rp1500). The **night market** is one block south of the *bemo* terminal along Jl. Merdeka, while the **day market** is directly opposite. Along Jl. Kusuma Yuda away from the day market are **banks,** the **hospital,** at Jl. Kusuma Yuda 27 (☎910 02), and the **post office.** The **wartel,** Jl. Merdeka 62, offers cash international calls (☎911 50; open 24hr.). The **Telkom office,** Brigen Ngurah Rai 60, offers calling card and collect calls and has HCD phones.

ACCOMMODATIONS AND FOOD. Great food and centralized accommodations make Bangli a pleasant place to spend the night. The best place in town is the **Bangli Inn ❸,** in a modern two-story building. With your back to the *bemo* terminal, turn left and then right at the roundabout; it's 200m on the right. (☎/fax 914 19. Rooms Rp50,000.) **Artha Sastra Inn ❷,** directly opposite the *bemo* terminal, was the palace of the last king of Bangli. The grandson of the last king, Agung Artha Sastra, will happily talk with guests. (☎911 79. Singles Rp25,000; doubles Rp45,000.) The cheapest option is the **Catur Adnyana ❷,** Jl. Lettu Lila 2. Take the first right after the police station; it's 1km from the *bemo* terminal as you walk south on Jl. Merdeka. (☎912 44. Rooms Rp25,000.) The **night market,** off Jl. Merdeka, starts at approximately 5pm and boasts a festive atmosphere and good cheap eats. Try *martabak mesir* (egg and onion pancake) for dinner and *martabak manis* (a chocolate and butter concoction) for dessert.

SIGHTS. Bangli's not-to-miss sight is the 11th-century **Pura Kehen** temple, with a sacred banyan tree in the courtyard. The *kulkul* is precariously high up in the banyan to call the villagers to worship. With your back turned to the *bemo* station, turn left onto Jl. Merdeka and walk 1km. When the road forks, take the right and the temple will be 200m on the left. (Rp2500. Sarong available to borrow.)

The countryside around Bangli reveals hidden wonders. The small village of **Taman Bali,** out the south end of Jl. Merdeka, offers the spectacular **Dusin Kuing waterfall.** Find an *ojek* driver who has heard of Dusin Kuing. **Demulih** is another tiny village that offers great walks and magnificent views. Behind the town lies **Bukit Demulih.** When in Demulih ask *"Dimama tangga manugu ke puncak?"* ("where are the stairs to the top?") to find the flight of 200 steps cut into the hill. To get to Demulih village, follow Jl. Kusuma Yuda out of Bangli to the west for 3km until the turn-off to Giangar appears on the left. Demulih will be the first town you pass. *Bemo* don't access this area; organize an *ojek* guide.

PADANGBAI ☎0363

Set along a crescent of narrow beach, the village is a quiet pocket of colorful outriggers, ocean-view bungalows, and cheap seafood. For many, Padangbai is no more than a busy transit point on the way to Lombok. Yet, for a modest port village, Padangbai has much to offer, including diving, snorkeling, and convenient swimmable beaches, as well as the opportunity to fish for your dinner.

TRANSPORTATION. Buses whisk travelers to destinations on Bali, Lombok, and Java. Prices include ferry fees. Tickets can be purchased along the water or at many accommodations. **Perama** (☎414 19), at Dona cafe opposite the *bemo* on the entrance road, runs several shuttles to: **Bangsal** (5½hr.; Rp30,000); **Gili Air** (7hr.); **Gili Meno** (7hr.); **Gili Trawangan** (7hr.; Rp60,000); **Kintamani** (2hr.; Rp30,000); **Kuta** (2½hr.; Rp25,000); **Mataram** (5hr.; Rp30,000); **Sanur** (2hr.; Rp25,000); **Senggigi** (5½hr.; Rp30,000); **Ubud** (1hr.; Rp15,000). Various **commercial buses** run to: **Jakarta; Jogjakarta/Surakarta; Malang; Probolinggo/Surabaya. Ferries** run continuously to **Lombok** (5hr.; every 1½hr.; Rp8500, 1st class A/C Rp17,000).

IN RECENT NEWS

RIOT2K

If you ask locals what happened in January 2000, some might say, "politics" or "religion," but most will simply look confused and say, "I don't know." The riots that swept through Lombok three years ago seem largely unexplained. Some think that Westerners were the target; others are adamant that foreigners had nothing to do with the riots. Here's what we do know:

On January 17th, 2000, during a Muslim Solidarity holiday, a group of Muslims in Ampenan began a public rally. Over the next three days, churches and two discos were burned, and a few Muslim activists were shot and killed by the police. No tourists or non-Muslims were harmed. Tourists in the greater Mataram area and Senggigi were evacuated and taken to Bali.

Locals say that the two discos that were burned down were well known for drug trafficking and prostitution, leading some to conclude that the group was after not tourists but rather the community's problems—drugs and prostitution. But this doesn't explain the burning of the churches.

The riots left many unanswered questions, including that of the visitor's safety. The marked economic harm that has resulted from this uncertainty proves to the Office of Tourism, as well as Lombok at large, that the island cannot survive without tourism. Amidst the finger pointing for lost jobs and a sore economy, one thing is sure: Lombok, with enhanced police and security, is working hard to ensure peace on the island and encourage tourists to return.

WARNING When waiting for a boat, keep your luggage with you at all times and do not let the porters take it. Some have been known to threaten to throw it overboard unless you pay a ridiculous amount (on the order of Rp100,000).

ORIENTATION AND PRACTICAL INFORMATION. Padangbai is 50km northeast of Denpasar, off the main road between Klungkung and Candi Dasa. At the end of the road entering Padangbai are the harbor gates and the overbearing ferry terminal. Facing the terminal, in the left corner closest to the water, is **Jl. Segaran.** This crosses a parking lot and runs into **Jl. Siliyuti,** which continues to head away from the port. Most of the accommodations lie off Jl. Segaran and Jl. Siliyuti. *Bemo* wait at the ferry terminal end of the entrance road. A helpful **tourist office** at the front of the ferry terminal can direct you toward the best snorkeling and beaches in the area, but has no printed information. **Snorkeling equipment** is available everywhere. **Motorcycle** (Rp30,000) and **car rentals** (Rp80,000) are available through **Hotel Puri Rai** and **Kerti Beach Inn.** To get to the **post office,** walk to the harbor gates next to the ferry, walk straight ahead, and take the first left at the **police station** (open daily 7am-11pm). The post office will be 50m ahead on the right. (Open M-Th 8am-2pm, F 8-11am, Sa 8am-12:30pm. *Poste Restante.*) A *wartel* on the street leading from the harbor gates toward the main road to Candi Dasa offers cash-only **international calls** and faxes. (Open daily 6am-12:30pm.) **Ozone Cafe** has **Internet access** (Rp300 per min.). **Moneychangers** abound on the beach boardwalk and market; most take traveler's checks. **Postal code:** 80872.

ACCOMMODATIONS AND FOOD. Several cheap accommodation options lie to the left of Jl. Siliyuti at the point where it meets Jl. Segara. **Parta ❸** is the best maintained. Rooms are worth the extra rupiah for the space, privacy, fan, and private bath. (☎41 475. Singles with fan Rp40,000; doubles Rp50,000, with hot water Rp70,000.) The **Bagus Inn ❷** has basic rooms with ceiling fans and *mandi*-style baths. (☎41 398. Breakfast included. Singles Rp25,000; doubles Rp30,000.) For a bed closer to the water, continue away from the port along Jl. Siliyuti and the beach. At **Topi Inn ❷,** try for one of the three rooms that have private *mandi.* (Singles Rp30,000; doubles Rp40,000; bungalows Rp50,000.) **Kerti Beach Inn ❸,** next to Hotel Puri Rai, has clean rooms and well-designed bungalows with an open-air lounge room and mosquito nets. (Breakfast included. Singles Rp30,000; doubles Rp50,000; bungalows Rp60,000.) **Padangbai Beach Home Stay ❹** has rooms with private bath and fan, as well as bungalows with A/C. All have springy beds and mosquito nets. (☎479 46. Breakfast included. Basic singles Rp50,000, with A/C Rp90,000; doubles Rp80,000/Rp120,000.)

Padangbai's seafood is exceptional—prawns, shark, and barracuda (see **Ooooh–Barracuda!,** below) are local specialties, served with generous amounts of garlic. The cheapest prices are found away from the water and at hotel-attached restaurants. **Kendedes Restaurant ❷** on Jl. Silayuti, has a sizeable menu of cheap, tasty Indonesian food. The second-floor seating has a good view of the ocean or, if you prefer, a better one of the graveyard. Laid-back **Ozone Cafe ❸,** before Parta, has a backpacker-friendly atmosphere, loud music, and an owner who will beat you at Scrabble. (Scrumptious pizzas from Rp15,000.) **Puri Rai Restaurant ❹,** attached to Hotel Puri Rai, is a classy tiki bar that serves seafood. On the water, **Warung Pantai Ayu ❷** is cheap. (Garlic prawns Rp15,000.)

BEACHES AND SIGHTS. Padangbai offers a surprisingly large range of water-recreation options. **Equator,** the local PADI- and CAMS-certified dive

OOOOH—BARRACUDA! Welcome to Bali, land of fresh seafood. From shark to shellfish, amazing meals from the ocean are prepared everywhere around the island; off the east coast, one specialty is barracuda. Flooding the Lombok Strait in May, these fish feed locals and tourists alike until August. Local fishermen, mostly in traditional narrow boats, catch the 1-1.5m long, 10-15kg fish. On shore, the barracuda are cleaned and gutted. Their bodies are then sliced like a loaf of French bread, into thick round fillets. A 10kg fish provides approximately 40 fillets for serving. Chefs then fire up the grill. The flaky white barracuda is dipped in a sauce of garlic, salt, pepper, and melted butter. The fillet is served with three sauces. The first is a spicy chili sauce. The second, only slightly milder, is *sambal matah,* an onion and chili sauce served cold. The final sauce is similar to the grilling sauce: finely minced garlic with butter and spices. Each sauce brings out the fish's flavor. Whichever sauce you decide on, the thick barracuda fillets, often served with rice and vegetables, make a filling meal. Prepare your cutlery and appetite, and enjoy!

Before eating barracuda, it is advisable to check that it comes from waters at low risk of ciguatera poisoning. The Lombok Strait's barracuda are not currently considered especially dangerous, but get the latest information to be safe.

INDONESIA

shop, offers dives in nearby waters (full day US$50, cash only). PADI-certified **Geko Dive** in Pandan Restaurant offers similar packages. All-inclusive diving packages to Nusa Penida cost US$70. If you can find a group of four or more divers, tagging along to snorkel is only US$10, including lunch. The best swimming option is the popular **Bias Tugel.** With your back to the ferry port, turn left at the police station. The turn-off to Bias Tugel is 50m ahead on the left before the road rises steeply. Another popular and more convenient recreation area is **Blue Lagoon,** at the opposite end of Jl. Siliyuti from the ferry-port bay. The turn-off to the Blue Lagoon is immediately after Topi Inn. The best place from which to explore the surrounding rocky coastline is **Pura Silayukti,** the temple commemorating the man who introduced the caste system to Bali. It's a 5min. walk along the sealed road from Topi Inn. When the road forks, head to the left; Pura Silayukti is the temple to the left. From high on the ridge, dirt paths lead to the shoreline, where several *pantai kecil* (little beaches) and interesting rock pools can be found. Immaculate and deserted, these beaches provide solitude and serenity.

NUSA TENGGARA

LOMBOK

Since the riots of January 2000 (see **Riot2K,** above), tourists have been wary of visiting this island; however, as its safety rating has improved, travelers seeking relief from Bali and its excessive tourism are beginning once again to flock to Lombok's serenity. The resort life of Senggigi is well known, the trek through Gunung Rinjani is more than just a touristy sleep-over, and a simple unhurried stroll through rice and tobacco paddies in Tetebatu is exquisitely calm. Meanwhile, the ever-accessible diving and snorkeling keep the adventuresome ferrying in

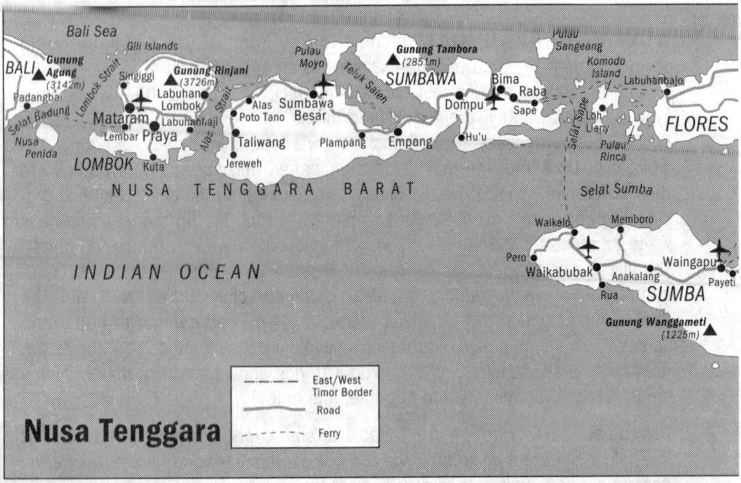

THE VIEW FROM ABOVE

The lowdown: Bali's quieter, gentler sibling.
Major towns: Greater Mataram, Senggigi, Tetebatu
Highlights: Climbing Gunung Rinjani, walking through the rice paddies of Tetebatu, riding the surf in Kuta.

GETTING TO LOMBOK

BY PLANE. Lombok's **Selaparang Airport** (☎622 987, ext. 108) marks the northern edge of Mataram, the official capital. **Taxis** have set rates and are in front of the airport (Mataram Rp9500; Senggigi Rp15,000). **Bemo** go to Ampenan (Rp1000). **Merpati** flies to: **Bima** (1¼hr.; Th, Sa; Rp475,500); **Denpasar** (30min.; 3 per day; Rp240,000); **Jakarta** (1 per day; Rp.888,000) via **Jogjakarta** (1 per day; Rp530,000); **Sumbawa Besar** (45min.; M, W, Sa; Rp248,900); **Surabaya** (M, W, Sa; Rp380,900). **Silk Air** flies to **Singapore** (Tu, F-Su; one-way US$225, round-trip US$350). International departure tax is Rp60,000; domestic departure tax is Rp8000.

BY BOAT. Ferries cross from **Lembar,** Lombok to **Padangbai,** Bali (4-5hr., every 1½hr., Rp8500), and a similar ferry system runs between **Labuhan,** Lombok and **Poto Tano,** Sumbawa (1½hr.; every hr.; Rp10,000). The **Mabua Express** (☎811 95) operates daily between Lembar and **Benoa,** Bali (2½hr., returns 5:30pm, US$25-30). Two **PELNI** ships dock at Lembar. The **KM Awu** departs once every two weeks to: **Berau; Denpasar** (Rp21,500); **Dili; Ende; Kaladahi; Kupang; Makasar; Maumere; Nunukan; Tarakan;** and **Waingapu.** The **KM Tilongkabilu** leaves every two weeks and travels to: **Bima** (Rp53,000); **Denpasar; Kumai; Labuanbajo** (Rp79,300); **Makasar; Sampit;** and **Surabaya.** Buy tickets and confirm ship arrival dates at the harbor in Lembar or at the PELNI office on Jl. Industri (☎637 212), opposite Hotel Nitour in Ampenan.

BY BUS. Buses to destinations on other islands depart Sweta Terminal, on the east side of greater Mataram (see below), around noon to: **Denpasar** (7hr.; Rp50,000); **Jakarta** (Rp175,000); **Jogjakarta** (Rp135,000); and **Surabaya** (19hr.; Rp85,000). **Langsung Indah** has the most comfortable buses, departing daily at noon and 2:30pm to: **Bima** (13hr.; Rp44,400); **Dompu** (11hr.; Rp40,500); **Sape** (15hr.; Rp47,500); and **Sumbawa Besar** (7hr.; Rp27,000). There are also buses to: **Jereveh** (Rp20,000); **Lonyuk** (Rp28,000); **Plompang** (Rp30,000); and **Taliwerg** (Rp15,000-

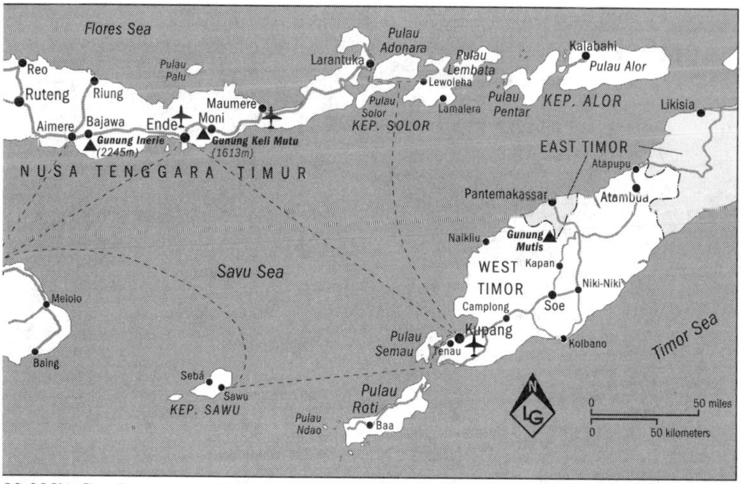

20,000). Confirm times a day in advance. Buy tickets for night buses 24hr. before departure. Long rides often include dinner.

GETTING AROUND LOMBOK

Buses departing from Sweta Terminal cost less than *bemo* and run to the same places. **Taxis** run in Greater Mataram, but aren't common outside the city. **Ojek** save time but not money. Combined, buses and **bemo** will run almost everywhere. Beware of empty *bemo*—drivers will assume that you are chartering the vehicle. **Cidomo**—horse-drawn carts with car tires and axles—ferry people around small locales. They're ubiquitous on Lombok, even in cosmopolitan Mataram. If you'd rather get yourself around, **motorcycle** rentals are everywhere, and you can rent a **car** from **Rinjani Rent Car,** on Jl. Panca Usaha in Mataram. (☎632 259. Suzuki Jimmys Rp75,000.) The following are Lombok's major terminals, in Greater Mataram:

Sweta, on the east side of Greater Mataram. Lombok's transportation hub. Serves: **Bangsal** (1½hr.); **Bayan** (20min.); **Labuhan** (2hr.); **Lembar** (1hr.); **Greater Mataram** (10min.); **Narmada** (20min.); **Praya** (1hr.).

Ampenan, north of the city's main intersection. Serves as a stop for Mataram routes from Sweta Terminal, with *bemo* running north to **Senggigi** (15min.).

Praya, in the town center. Serves the south: **Kuta** (30min.); **Sengkol** (30min.).

Narmada, in the center of town. Serves central Lombok: **Masbagik** (2hr.); **Pomotong** (1hr.); **Suranadi** (15min.); **Tetebatu** (2hr.); and points east of Greater Mataram.

GREATER MATARAM ☎0370

Home to 10% of Lombok's 2.5 million people, Greater Mataram consists of three cities—Ampenan, Mataram, and Cakranegara (Cakra for short)—along 10km of one wide street. The worst rioting in January 2000 ravaged hot and dusty Ampenan. As you browse the art and jewelry stores, you won't be able to ignore the burnt ruins of churches that serve as a sobering backdrop. As the capital of Nusa Tenggara Barat, Mataram has seen some development and investment. In the mid-90s it was busy transforming itself from sleepy provincial headquarters to a

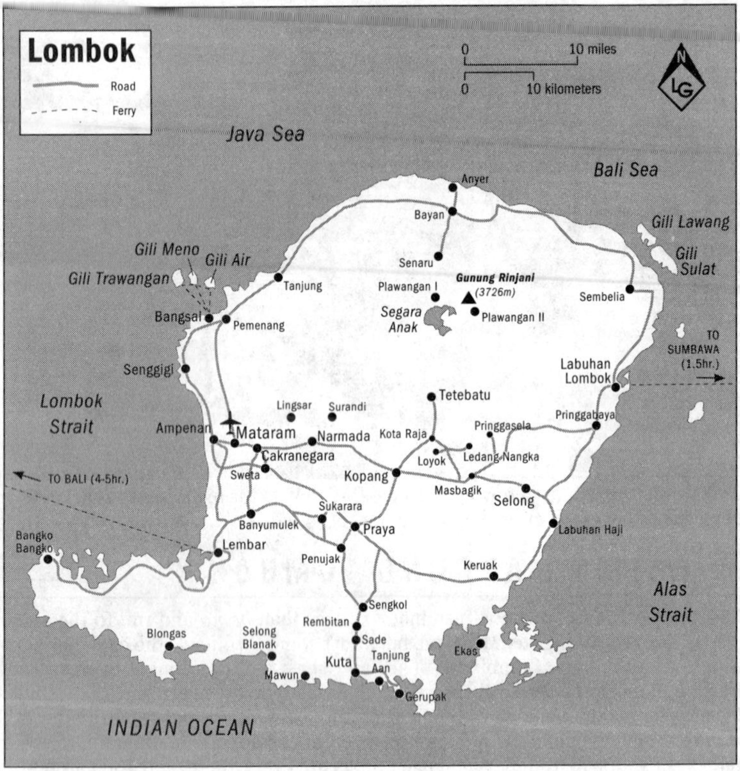

Mataram is in the process of reintroducing tourism and enlivening shopping and nightlife—although outside night markets, nightlife is, so far, nonexistent.

ORIENTATION AND PRACTICAL INFORMATION

Traffic courses through Greater Mataram on two parallel roads. *Bemo* circle between terminals at both ends. **Jl. Yos Sudarso** goes from Ampenan to Cakra, then turns into **Jl. Langko, Jl. Pejanggik,** and finally **Jl. Selaparang. Jl. Tumpang Sari** runs east-west from Cakra to Ampernan, one block south, and becomes **Jl. Panca Usaha, Jl. Pancawarga,** and finally **Jl. Pendidikan.** Giant, official-looking buildings flank the tree-lined streets of **Mataram,** the administrative center. Outside Cakra are the transportation hubs of **Sweta** and **Bertais.**

Tourist Office: Provincial Tourist Service, Jl. Singosari 2 (☎634 800), off Jl. Majapahit near central post office. Friendly staff dispenses maps and a plethora of pamphlets. Open M-Th 7am-2pm, F 7-11am, Sa 7am-12:30pm.

Tours: Perama, Jl. Pejanggik 66 (☎635 928), east of the hospital. Runs buses and cruises to Flores, Java, and Sumbawa. Many accommodations also offer tour and shuttle services.

Immigration Offices: ☎635 220. On Jl. Udayana, 300m north of Jl. Pejanggik on the way to the airport. Open M-Th 8am-2pm, F 8-11am, Sa 8am-1pm.

Currency Exchange: Moneychangers and **ATMs** abound at Ampenan's main intersection, on Jl. Pejanggik in Cakra, and opposite Sweta Terminal on Jl. Sandubaya. **BCA** (☎632 588), on Jl. Pejanggik, has a **24hr. ATM** (Cirrus/MC/PLUS/V). Open M-F 8am-2:30pm.

Emergency: Police: ☎110. **Ambulance:** ☎118.

Police: Ampenan, Jl. Langko 17 (☎633 733). **Sweta** (☎632 682), on Jl. Selaparang.

Medical Services: Rumah Sakit Umum Mataram (☎213 45), on Jl. Pejanggik, east of the Governor's office. English-speaking female doctor available in the morning. Attached **Apotik** (pharmacy; ☎637 326). MC/V. **Both open 24hr.**

Telephones: The big **Telkom office,** Jl. Langko 23 (☎634 466), has an **HCD** telephone.

Internet Access: Global Internet, in the strip mall opposite the Lombok Raya Hotel. Rp1000 per hr. Open daily 8am-8pm. **Internet places** are also scattered around the Mataram Mall area, but are more expensive (Rp200 per min.).

Express Mail: DHL, Jl. Pejanggik 20, west of the Governor's Office. Open M-F 8am-4:30pm, Sa 8am-1pm.

Post Office: GPO, on Jl. Majapahit. *Poste Restante.* Open M-Th 8am-3pm, F-Sa 8-11am. **Postal code:** 83114.

INDONESIA

ACCOMMODATIONS

Accommodations pander equally to tourists and locals. Generally comfortable and cheap, they are far from the beach and nightlife, both of which are easier to find in **Senggigi** (see p. 213). The cheapest lodgings, in Ampenan along **Jl. Koperasi,** are noisier and dustier than in Cakra.

Shanti Puri Hotel and Restaurant, Jl. Maktal 15 (☎632 649), 100m south off Jl. Pejanggik in east Cakra. Comfort exceeds price. Friendly staff, cozy restaurant. Clean rooms with fan. Singles and doubles with *mandi* Rp30,000, with toilets Rp40,000. ❸

Inap Keluagra Oka (Oka), Jl. Repatmaja 5 (☎622 406), 200m south of Jl. Pejanggik at Bank Danamon in Cakra, on a side street. Shady courtyard and *losmen*-quality rooms. Friendly staff. Breakfast included. Singles Rp20,000; doubles Rp25,000. ❷

Karthika II Hotel, Jl. Subak 6 (☎641 776), north of Jl. Pejanggik. Rooms around a bright courtyard on a surprisingly quiet side street near the heart of Cakra. Breakfast included. Singles Rp32,500, with A/C and TV Rp60,000; basic doubles Rp37,500/Rp70,000. ❸

Losmen Ayu (☎621 761), on Jl. Nursiwan, 100m south of the BCA ATM in Cakra at the corner with Jl. Panca Usaha, has clean rooms. Free unlimited tea and coffee. Singles and doubles with *mandi* Rp25,000, with toilets Rp40,000, with A/C Rp75,000. ❷

Hotel Wisata, Jl. Koperasi 19 (☎269 71), in Ampenan. A variety of rooms just secluded enough to get away from street noise. Close to antique and art shops. Singles with bath Rp35,000; doubles Rp40,000. ❸

Losmen Horas, Jl. Koperasi 62 (☎631 695). Basic and cheap. Singles Rp17,500; doubles Rp20,000. ❷

Chandra Hotel, Jl. Caturwarga 55 (☎623 979), south of the hospital. Cut down Jl. Prisaian to Jl. Caturwarga and turn right. In the heart (and heat) of Mataram. Simple, windowless rooms. Doubles Rp35,000, with A/C Rp60,000. ❸

FOOD

In Cakra, there is a variety of *warung* and numerous scrumptious night stalls. The regional specialty is spicy *sasak taliwang*, food smothered in hot chili peppers. If

THE LOCAL STORY

KING OF THE MOUNTAIN

Hardy Krüger has been like a father to the Rinjani tourist industry, helping to nurse it along as a porter in the late 80s, working as a guide with the influx of interest in the 90s, and, by 2002, organizing all treks. He is the man, as well as the man-behind-the-man, in Rinjani's present trekking organization.

Q: When did you start climbing?

A: When I was like 18 years old.

Q: Did you grow up around here?

A: No, central Lombok...my father moved here...1984, no tourists, only engineers from Jakarta climbing and my father get paid Rp2500 for 3 days. My father actually, he was the first porter here...Then [a] group [came], big group–German-Austrian–and wanted 25-30 porters.

Q: 25 porters?

A: I came along with this group and took along live chicken with the bamboo stick...4 porters just for live chicken...porter can take like 8 chickens each. And the smell...

Q: When did you start organizing treks?

A: I have to become a guide first. After 1989 I start to be a guide...When I was being porter like 38 times...I always take a book like dictionary...while I carry... I stop, open up book...writing, writing, writing... after about 2-3 years become porter but I still bring a book.

Q: How long were you a porter for then?

A: Altogether 12 years and in total 153 times.

(continued on next page)

you can't handle the heat, ask for it *"kurang pedes"* (less spicy) and ignore the snickers.

Restaurant Betawi, at the intersection of Jl. Koperasai, Jl. Saleh Sungkar, and Jl. Yos Sudarso, in a "Colonial Grand Style." Famous among expatriates, Betawi had us all worried when it closed briefly due to the 2000 riots. Thankfully, it quickly resumed offering up some lip-smacking dishes from its balcony overlooking the heart of Ampenan. Red snapper with Rico Rico (sweet tomato with chili) sauce Rp22,000. ❹

Suharti Sate House, Jl. Maktal 9 (☎ 6379 58), next to the Shanti Puri. Run by Romy Rahiem, a Mataram-renowned Indonesian master chef. Tasty *nasi goreng* (Rp5000). Open daily 9am-10pm. ❷

Kania Satu-Rumah Makan Taliwang, on Jl. Pejanggik, opposite Bank BCA in Cakra. Spicy Lombok-style food. *Ayam goreng taliwang* Rp15,000. Open daily 7am-11pm. ❸

Aroma, Jl. Palapa 12, in west Cakra, south of Jl. Pejanggik at Bank BTN. Clean, quiet, quick, and cool. Large portions of Chinese seafood. Young pigeon Rp18,000. ❸

SHOPPING

If it's modernity—escalators, bright lights, A/C, and fixed prices—you seek, then the **Mataram Mall** (formerly Glinoya Shopping Center) on Jl. Pejonggik is your place. Here you'll find clothes and electronics, and a bookstore with English, French, and German texts to boot. If you prefer a noisy rush and bargaining, then the **market** in Cakra is at the Mataram Complex farther up Jl. Pejanggik and condenses at the intersection of Jl. Pejanggik and Jl. Gede Ngurah. The market offers similar items, minus the foreign books, for cheaper prices. For art, woodcraft, jewelry, and antiques, go to **Jl. Saleh Sungkar,** in Ampenan center. One certainly worth the trip is the **Yufi Artshop,** Jl. Saleh Sungklar 22, which has brilliant and affordable pottery in all shapes and sizes. Much more art for sale can be found near the beginning of **the road to Senggigi** from Ampenan.

SIGHTS

In the small fishing village on the north side of Ampenan is **Pura Segara.** Off Jl. Yos Sudarso, the temple is still used for Hindu burial ceremonies. The front gates are locked; sometimes the gate around back is open, allowing a better look. Regardless, the surrounding fishing village warrants the trip. Pura Segara is best visited early, when the rugged foothills of Gunung Rinjani are visible. A **Chinese cemetery,** on the way to Pura Segara, is an exhibition of above-ground tombs enshrined in ornate tiles of Chinese characters and colors. Sections of the grounds have gone to seed, though, and it is not unusual for locals to graze cattle inside.

In 1894, Balinese and Western Sasaks crept to the walls of the **Mayura Water Palace,** fired on Dutch soldiers camped there, and drove them out of this former Balinese court. Deteriorating fountains, statues, and cannons are all that remain (Rp5000 entrance). Across Jl. Pejanggik from the Water Palace is **Pura Meru,** Lombok's *grande dame* of Balinese temples, with 33 shrines and three big, plain, empty pagodas. Commissioned by Anak Agung Made Karang of the Singosari Kingdom in 1772, the three pagodas honor the Hindu trinity of Brahma, Vishnu, and Shiva, and the three volcanos, Agung, Bromo, and Rinjani. Sashes are lent out for free, but the entrance fee is Rp10,000.

Museum Nusa Tenggara Barat, on Jl. Panji Tilar Negara in southeast Ampenan, displays 1239 palm-leaf Indonesian manuscripts and exhibits in English on the history, geology, and cultures of Lombok and Sumbawa. One of the curators speaks English and leads tours. (Open Tu-Su 8am-4pm. Rp1000.)

DAYTRIPS FROM GREATER MATARAM

NARMADA. On the south side of the main road in Narmada, is the **Pura Kalasa Water Palace,** a temple built into a hill and encircled by three pools. In 1805, King Ana Agun Gedengurah built the complex as a reproduction of Gunung Rinjani when he was too old to make his annual climb of the mountain. The central pool replicates Lake Segara Anak, the small pools represent the cascading hot springs near the lake, and the temple itself, built at the top of the hill, symbolizes Gunung Rinjani's peak. The water palace sated the king's lust; the Balinese monarch would watch his harems bathe in the pool from his small two-room house on the hill: one room for his wife and one for his concubine. Guides (fairly useless) will approach you near the entrance. The water palace is more popular with the locals than with tourists—it's packed on weekends. The main pool, originally for the king's use only, is now complete with starting blocks and lane markings and is used for regional and local swim meets. Locals use the lower pools for swimming and laundry, while it is believed that the higher pool's water gives eternal life if drunk. Tourists can join in the splashing for a small fee (Rp1000, Rp1000 extra to bathe). During the full

(continued from previous page)

Q: 153 times to the top?

A: 80 times only to the top. [The other times, I went only up to the rims.] Maybe my father was the first guy to climb with the customer and I'm the second...We make joke with our guides here: "Hey, Hardy, you have backpack or you have cupboard?" —"Oh, I have cupboard."

Q: Do you think tourists are wimpy climbers?

A: Yeah, yeah.

Q: Anybody go up and turn around because they don't want to go any farther?

A: Many...a few years ago, I have 3 groups: 2 English, 2 Canadian, and 2 Holland...Like 6 guys, 4 ladies, and 2 boys. The 2 Canadian ladies go 2hr. and come back down. The other 2 went from Sembalan came back after 1 night...4 come back.

Q: Is that the worst it's ever been?

A: Yeah.

Q: Do you have a family here now?

A: Yeah, together here.

Q: Have you ever hiked with them?

A: Uh, no.

Q: Are they too young now?

A: Yes...

Q: How many kids do you have?

A: I have 3, but in August 4, so you have to give me [US]$20. In August my wife [will have] another child.

Q: That's okay—just start charging more for hikes, right?

A: Yeah.

Q: So, how long do you think you are going to stay in this business?

A: Forever...

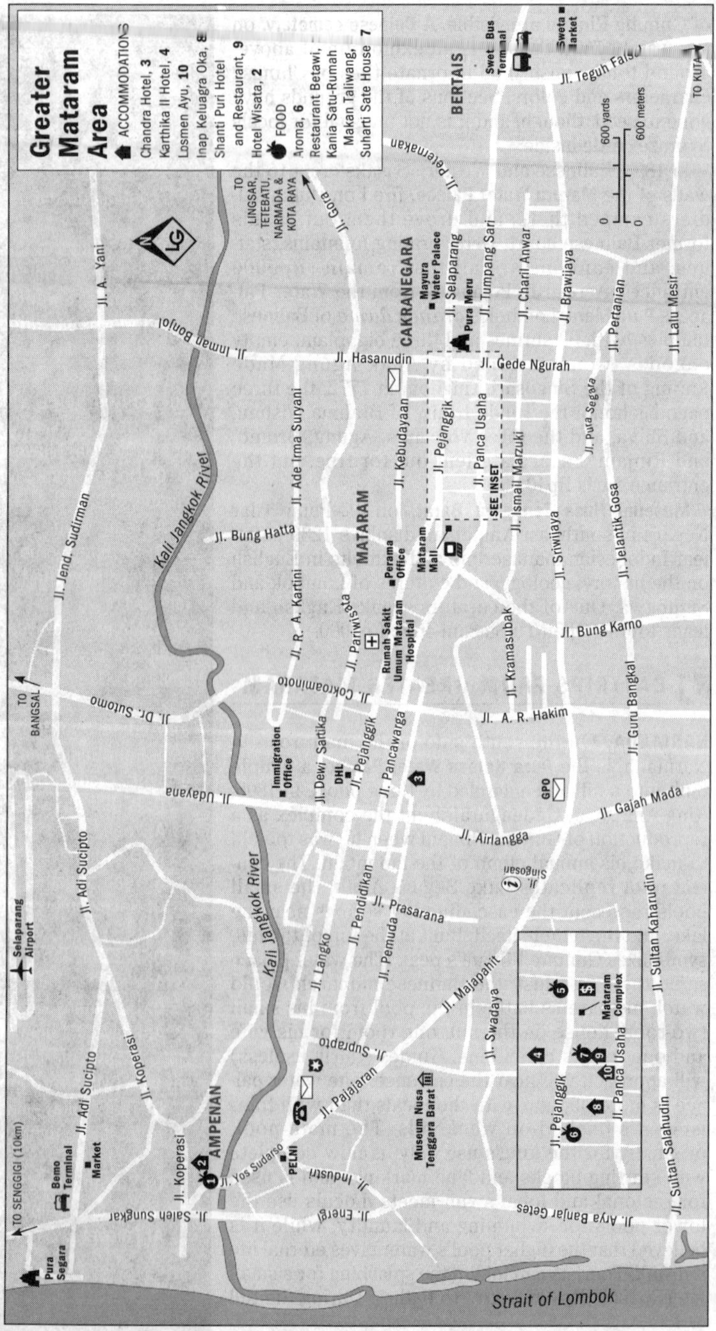
Greater Mataram Area
ACCOMMODATIONS
Chandra Hotel, 3
Karthika II Hotel, 4
Losmen Ayu, 10
Inap Keluagra Oka, 8
Shanti Puri Hotel and Restaurant, 9
Hotel Wisata, 2
FOOD
Aroma, 6
Restaurant Betawi,
Kania Satu-Rumah Makan Taliwang,
Suharti Sate House 7
TO LINGSAR, TETEBATU, NARMADA & KOTA RAYA
BERTAIS
CAKRANEGARA
MATARAM
AMPENAN
Sweta Bus Terminal
Sweta Market
Jl. Teguh Faisal
TO KUTA
600 yards
600 meters
Jl. Peternakan
Jl. Gora
Mayura Water Palace
Jl. Selaparang
Pura Meru
Jl. Tumpang Sari
Jl. Charil Anwar
Jl. Brawijaya
Jl. Pertanian
Jl. Lalu Mesir
Jl. A. Yani
Jl. Inman Bonjol
Jl. Hasanudin
Jl. Gede Ngurah
Jl. Pura Segara
Jl. Ade Irma Suryani
Jl. Kebudayaan
Jl. Pejanggik
Jl. Panca Usaha
SEE INSET
Jl. Ismail Marzuki
Jl. Jelantik Gosa
Kali Jangkok River
Jl. Jend. Sudirman
Jl. Bung Hatta
Perama Office
Mataram Mall
Jl. Sriwijaya
Jl. Bung Karno
Jl. R. A. Kartini
Jl. Pariwisata
Rumah Sakit Umum Mataram Hospital
Jl. Kramasubak
Jl. Cokroaminoto
TO BANGSAL
Jl. Dr. Sutomo
Jl. A. R. Hakim
Jl. Guru Bangkal
Immigration Office
Jl. Dewi Sartika
DHL
Jl. Pancawarga
GPO
Jl. Udayana
Jl. Airlangga
Jl. Gajah Mada
Jl. Adi Sucipto
Jl. Singosari
Jl. Pendidikan
Jl. Prasarana
Selaparang Airport
Jl. Langko
Jl. Pemuda
Jl. Majapahit
Jl. Swadaya
Jl. Sultan Kaharudin
Mataram Complex
Jl. Koperasi
Jl. Suprapto
Jl. Pajajaran
Museum Nusa Tenggara Barat
TO SENGGIGI (10km)
Bemo Terminal
Market
Jl. Yos Sudarso
PELNI
Jl. Industri
Jl. Sultan Salahudin
Pura Segara
Jl. Saleh Sungkar
Jl. Energi
Jl. Arya Banjar Getes
Strait of Lombok

moon of the 5th Balinese lunar month in December, townspeople give live ducks and other offerings to the lake in a ritual called pujawali. *(Bemo (15min., Rp1000) run from the Sweta Terminal eastward to Narmada.)*

LINGSAR. The **Pura Lingsar** temples, consisting of the Sasak **Kemaliq** and the Hindu **Pura Gaduh,** built in 1714, sit 7km northwest of Narmada (15min. from Sindu), near the village Lingsar. Both temples are simple and sparse. The complex celebrates the peaceful coexistence of Balinese and Sasaks. Annual week-long ceremonies at the start of the wet season (late Nov. or early Dec.) known as **Perang Topat (Topat War)** mark these events. As a symbol of tolerance between the two religions, Hindus and Sasaks pelt each other with ketupat (rice wrapped in coconut leaves) after giving thanks for last year's rain and asking for it to return again. A springwater **eel pool** lies within the Kemaliq section of Pura Lingsar. Eggs to feed the eels are sold at the gate. It is said that if an eel rises to eat your egg, you will have good luck. There is no fee to enter the complex, but a donation is expected for the two temples (sash provided). *(Bemo (10min., Rp1000) run to Lingsar from Narmada.)*

SENGGIGI ☎0370

With one main drag and paradise-like bungalow resorts, Senggigi is the small but hip height of nightlife and leisure on Lombok, offering everything from fine food to dancing to drag shows—and an amazing sunset over the Gilis.

ORIENTATION AND PRACTICAL INFORMATION. Only 15min. from Ampenan by *bemo* (Rp1000), Senggigi makes a nice base for exploration into north and west Lombok. Most hotels and restaurants are spread out along a 2km strip that incorporates two sandy bays.

Services, which cluster near **Pacific Supermarket,** on Jl. Raya Senggigi (☎693 005; open daily 8:30am-9:30pm), include: the **Perama Office** (☎693 007), opposite Lina's Cottages, which provides information on trips to the Gilis and Gunung Rinjani; **BNI,** next to the supermarket (☎693 546; **24hr. ATM** accepts Cirrus/MC/PLUS/V); the **police** (☎693 267), at the north end of Jl. Raya Senggigi; a **24hr. medical clinic** (☎693 210, ext. 1730), with an attached **pharmacy,** at the Senggigi Beach Hotel; a **Telekom Office,** opposite the Sheraton Hotel; a **wartel,** in Pacific Supermarket (offers cash international calls; open daily 8am-10pm); an **HCD** booth outside the supermarket; several **Internet cafes** along the main strip (all open daily around 8am-11pm; Rp250 per min.); and the **post office,** opposite the supermarket (*Poste Restante;* open M-Sa 8am-8pm, Su 8am-noon). **Postal code:** 83355.

ACCOMMODATIONS AND FOOD. Although Senggigi is resort-oriented, the lack of tourists has depressed prices considerably. Don't be afraid to bargain down from quoted prices; outside of the high season (July-Aug.) actual prices are even lower. **Lombok Coconut ❸,** at the far north end of Jl. Raya Senggigi past the Sheraton, has ocean views from the swimming pool and free evening transport into town. (☎693 195. Singles Rp35,000; doubles Rp60,000.) **Batu Bolong Hotel ❹** offers daily cleaning services, towels, and free tea all day long. Opposite the beach, it's a 10min walk below the main strip (on the same street), or a 3min. *bemo* ride. (☎693 065. Doubles Rp70,000.) **Sonya ❷,** on the main road behind Kastika Restaurant, is the cheapest place in town with warm hospitality and a delicious breakfast. (☎693 447. Singles Rp20,000; doubles Rp30,000.)

Fine international cuisine is on **Jl. Raya Senggigi ❹** (Rp20,000-30,000 per dish), but cheaper eats are scarce. Some establishments offer transportation to and from restaurants; call ahead. **Restoran Taman Senggigi ❸** (☎693 842) features a fountain with goldfish, multi-level seating, and Cajun tuna steak (Rp26,000). Its lunch sandwiches are also a good deal (Rp10,000-20,000). **Bumbu ❸,** 300m south of Pacific

Supermarket, has the best curry dishes (Rp15,000-25,000) in Senggigi. The art market in the north end is cluttered with beachside dining. **Cafe Coco Loco ❸,** next to the Sheraton Hotel end of the market, prepares an excellent *olah oluh*, a spicy Sasak dish with vegetables in coconut milk. (Entrees Rp8000-18,000.) For basic dining, four **warung ❷,** located before the bridge leading to the center of town, serve scrumptious *ikan laut* (ocean fish). The cheap **Senang Restaurant ❶,** in the supermarket complex, offers spicy *nasi pecal* for Rp6000. (Open daily 9am-9pm.)

SIGHTS AND ENTERTAINMENT. Pura Batu Bolong (Hole-in-Rock Temple), one of Lombok's most stunning Balinese temples, is within walking distance of the main strip to the south. The rocky promontory yields a gorgeous view of the ocean. It is thought that the Balinese once hurled virgins from Batu Bolong into the sea, though locals today are often not quite sure just why. A donation is expected, and sashes can be borrowed for free at the gate. Despite the increasingly grand views, tourism wanes as you go farther north, perhaps because of the simultaneously increasing hills. Much of the desolate beach is accessible from the road. *Bemo* run often along the long road as far as **Mangsit** (15min., Rp1000) until 6pm, and most rented motorbikes can manage the hills. On the way to Mangsit, buy some coconut milk from a roadside vendor, sit atop a lookout hill on the coastal road, and watch the sun drop behind the Gilis. At 10pm the to-and-fro migration between two dance clubs begins: **Club Tropicana** and **The Blue Coral,** about a half-kilometer apart on the main drag. Both offer contemporary dance music with the occasional 70s or 80s song. Sometimes, a band comes on; if you don't like it, just move on to the other club. (☎693 173. Cover Rp20,000-25,000.) **Pondok Senggigi** hosts an all-male cabaret (Sa 11pm) and **Warung Pojok,** next to Millennium Internet, titillates with an evening drag show (9pm).

INDONESIA

KUTA ☎0370

Kuta, not to be confused with Kuta on Bali, is a rock-bottom-cheap stop for surfers, beachcombers, and budget travelers in the center of Lombok's south coast. Pristine white sand clashes with a jagged, rocky shoreline in this fishing town once slated for massive tourist development. Kuta was hit hard by the economic crisis. While the villagers are friendly, the struggling populace has become desperate, and robberies are on the rise; watch your wallet and belongings carefully.

TRANSPORTATION AND PRACTICAL INFORMATION. A **Perama bus** to Kuta from Mataram costs five times more than a *bemo* but saves hours (2hr.; Rp45,000). Explore Sasak villages on the way to Kuta by taking a bus or *bemo* from **Mataram** via **Praya** (Rp2000) and **Sengkol** (Rp1500). *Bemo* from Sengkol continue on to Tanjung Aan Beach. Most tourist services, including the **police, Perama Office, moneychangers,** and the **Ocean Blue Surf Shop,** are on the beachfront road, **Jl. Raya Pantai Kuta.** The closest **hospital** is in Praya, but Kuta has a **public health clinic** 500m out of town on the road to Sengkol (doctor available M-Sa 4-6pm; attached **apotik (pharmacy) open 24hr.**). There is a *wartel* (open M-Sa 7:30am-10:30pm) and another Perama office across the intersection from Matahari Inn. **Collect** and **international calls** can be made from Wisma Segara Anak and Kuta Indah.

ACCOMMODATIONS AND FOOD. The bungalows along the beachfront are of similar quality and price. **Anda Bungalows and Restaurant ❷** provides service and care worthy of a resort, although it's best to eat elsewhere. (Singles from Rp30,000; doubles Rp35,000.) **Ketapang Cafe and Bungalow ❷,** on the corner of the beachfront and road leading inland, has a leisurely restaurant. It is clean, although the *mandi* are somewhat old. Breakfast included. (Singles Rp20,000; doubles

Rp25,000.) Farther toward Mandalika Tourist Resort, **Rinjani Agung** ❸ has a range of rooms with safes and night security. (☎654 852. Singles from Rp30,000; rooms with A/C Rp100,000.) For its landscaped gardens and the luxury of a pool, **Matahari Inn** ❹ wins the non-beach prize. (Rp60,000. MC/V.) Most accommodations in Kuta have their own restaurants, but the half-dozen waterfront **warung** ❷ are cheaper and closer to the main street's activity. **Rinjani Agung** ❸ features international dishes like Thai chicken salad (Rp10,500) and spinach and feta crepes (Rp14,000).

BEACHES AND NIGHTLIFE. Kuta's beach, **Putri Nyale,** is too rocky for swimming but great for exploring. It hosts the **Bau Nyale,** a celebration of the mating of *nyale* (seaworms), four to eight days after the second full moon of the year (in February or March). The origin of the festival stems from the story of the beautiful Princess Mandalika, who, instead of choosing one man, threw herself into the ocean where she was transformed into a *nyale* in order to be shared by everyone. The celebration marks the anniversary of her transformation. Thousands of people camp on the beach before the *nyale* make their appearance. The young eat the worms, which are supposedly powerful aphrodisiacs. The region also boasts great **surf,** and boats can be chartered to choice spots. Check the **Blue Ocean Surf Shop** for local excursions as well as trips to the breaks on Sumbawa. (☎653 911. Board rentals Rp25,000 per day.) A local favorite for surfing is **Maun Beach,** 30min. outside Kuta. (*Ojek* Rp25,000.) **Tanjungon Beach,** good for swimming and snorkeling, is 5km east of Kuta. (*Bemo* from Kuta Rp1500.) **Sartinng Beach,** completely isolated and visited most often by locals, is another swimmable white-sand beach with surrounding rock formations.

Jungle Bay, across from the Matahari Inn, sometimes has live music. If not, an eclectic selection of jazz blares through the speakers. The bar serves a parade of cocktails and Bintang draught beer (Rp10,000). Their pool is free of charge. (☎655 410. Open daily from 11am until the last person leaves.)

> **SOUTH COAST BEACHES** Due to threats against foreigners since 1998, coverage of the South Coast Beaches is not included in this edition of *Let's Go: Southeast Asia.* Check embassies for current safety information.

GUNUNG RINJANI

Magnificent Gunung Rinjani, which last erupted in 1994, rises 3726m in the center of the north coast and is Lombok's holiest site. Many local Balinese Hindus make an annual pilgrimage to the summit to toss goldfish and jewelry into Segara Anak, the crater lake, much to the delight of local fishers. Sasak Muslims believe that on the ninth day after death, spirits travel to Gunung Rinjani. By journeying to the volcano, Sasaks draw power from their ancestors. Members of both religions also believe that the waters of the lake and nearby hot springs have healing power.

TRANSPORTATION AND PRACTICAL INFORMATION. **Senaru** is the Rinjani's gateway town. Due to the popularity of treks, private tourist information centers in Senggigi and on the Gili Islands arrange transportation from there as part of package tours. Be sure your package includes return transport. Cars (Rp100,000) and *ojek* (Rp40,000) can be hired from Senggigi or Senaru. Self-fashioned expeditions cost less but require finding supplies and transportation—and you won't have a guide. *Bemo* to **Bayan** start in Mataram (3hr., Rp5000) or can be picked up on the northwest coastal road in Pemenang or Tanjung. Past Bayan, *bemo* run from Bayan to Senaru (30min., Rp1500) via **Anchak.** Transportation is possible to Anchak from **Labuhan Lombok** (2½hr., Rp7000) or **Pringgabaya.** Before coming to Senaru, the base for the trek, be prepared: there is **no wartel, post office,**

bank, hospital, or **police** in the small town. **Emy's Cafe** (see **Accommodations and Food,** below) changes **currency** and traveler's checks. Bayan has a **wartel** and **post office.**

ACCOMMODATIONS AND FOOD. All accommodations in Senaru rent equipment and provide advice for treks. **Pondok Indah ❷,** on the south end of Senaru, has fairly new rooms and a great view of the coastline and valley. The staff helps organize transport for travelers starting or completing the climb in Sembalan Lawang. (Singles Rp30,000; doubles Rp35,000.) **Segara Anak Bungalows and Restaurant ❷,** across the road from Pondok Indah, has an equally stunning view of the river valley. The rooms are plainer, though the food is tastier. (Singles Rp25,000; doubles Rp30,000.) The most convenient option is the **Bale Bayan ❸,** on the trailhead opposite the Rinjani Trek Center. (Singles Rp35,000; doubles Rp50,000.) **Emy's Cafe ❶** offers cheap food. Most trek outfitting happens here as well; they usually give hikers free tea or even lunch. (Most dishes Rp3000-8000.)

WATERFALLS. In Gunung Rinjani's picturesque foothills, Senaru itself contains the spectacular **Sindang Gile Waterfall.** The path leading to the falls appears off the main road in Senaru when the falls first come into view. A second waterfall upstream from Sindang Gile, **Tiu Kelep Waterfall,** is equally powerful and has a pool ideal for swimming. Although locals will tell you that a guide is needed to reach it, trekkers can follow the path at the bottom of the steps as they descend to Sindang Gile. The path crosses an aqueduct and fades out 500m before the waterfall at the bend in the river. From there, follow the noise and the riverbed to reach the base of the falls. A third waterfall, **Betara Lenjang,** is past the Rinjani trailhead.

CLIMBING GUNUNG RINJANI. Climbing Gunung Rinjani, one of the most exhilarating experiences on Lombok, should be tried only by those prepared for a long trek. Climbers can reach the summit from nearly all sides—Tetebatu, Saesot, or Torean. The most popular route is via Batu Koq/Senaru and Sembalan Lawang in Gunung Rinjani's northern foothills.

In January 2002, the trekking system was changed in Senaru. The government built the **Rinjani Trek Center** at the base of the trail in Senaru and set up criteria for guides. All guides brief hikers here before hitting the trail. With this new system also came the organization of trek services in Senaru, which means two things: first, trek prices are now set and it is more difficult to bargain, especially if you begin planning your trip in Senaru rather than, say, in Senggigi or the Gili Islands; second, the quality of the hiking and the safety precautions have improved. Trek prices vary depending on duration and desired amenities. All-inclusive packages (with guide, porters, three meals per day and snacks, water, and necessary equipment) cost US$20 per day for one person. The per-person price drops rapidly for larger groups; the trek will also be cheaper if you carry your own gear and food. Additionally, paths are clearly marked and it is possible to do the trek totally on your own, though this isn't recommended for groups of fewer than four people. In this case, the only fee is the Rp25,000 park entrance fee. Bring a flashlight, warm clothing (the temperature drops at night), and a bathing suit for the hot springs.

The hike up Rinjani is not easy, and those who attempt it should be in moderate shape. The most popular route is the three-day, two-night trek to the crater rims and lakeside from **Senaru.** This hike does not actually reach the top of Rinjani—for that, an extra day should be budgeted, and because the views from the summit depend heavily on the weather, many hikers feels that this fourth day is not worth it. The first night ends on the crater rim at **Base Camp V,** a 6-8hr. hike from the Trek Center. The second day starts early with a 2hr. hike after sunrise down to Lake Segara and the hot springs (2hr.), leaving gear behind at the rim. After merriment there, and lunch, it's back up to the rim again (2½hr.). When going down into the caldera, watch your step; past hikers have slipped to their deaths. The final descent to **Sembalan Lawang** is a 4-5hr. hike on the third day.

TETEBATU ☎0370

Tetebatu sits on the cusp between foothills and farmland. *Pondok* and *losmen* stand between fields of rice and tobacco in picturesque contrast to Lombok's beach attractions. Wander through the fields toward the Monkey Forest to the north, the jungle waterfalls to the east, or the natural springs to the west. If placid Tetebatu loses its charm, visit the nearby local craft villages by motorbike.

TRANSPORTATION AND PRACTICAL INFORMATION. To get to Tetebatu, catch a *bemo* to Promotong. From there, *bemo* go as far as **Kotaraja** (Rp1000), where *ojek* and *cidomo* go the extra distance to Tetebatu (Rp2000). **Perama** also makes the trip (Rp80,000 from Mataram). Tetebatu's northern and southern central areas are 1km apart. *Losmen* are in two clusters, one between Tetebatu's two centers, the other on the eastbound side road, **Jl. Waterfall.** The Monkey Forest is to the north, past Soedjones Hotel. A **Perama office** is in the **Green Orry Inn** on the south side of Jl. Waterfall from lower Tetebatu. Soedjones Hotel offers **currency exchange.** Warung Salabusa rents **motorbikes** (Rp30,000) and **cars** (Rp100,000), and the *wartel*, next door, offers cash international and collect calls. The nearest **post office** and **police station** are in Masbagik.

ACCOMMODATIONS AND FOOD. Tetebatu has high-quality accommodations south of the town center and along the eastbound road. The lack of tourists means that all prices are negotiable. **Cendrawasih Cottages ❷,** along Jl. Waterfall, has colorful Sasak-style Lumbung bungalows with back balconies. Only one of the four has a Western bath, but all are spotless and cheap. (Doubles Rp30,000.) **Pondok Tetebatu ❷,** along the main road, has bright bungalows with private *mandi*. (Singles Rp20,000-25,000; doubles Rp30,000.) Directly behind, **Merkarsari ❷** has rooms of slightly lower quality, though slightly cheaper, farther from the road. (☎22 772. Rp20,000.) **Soedjones Hotel ❸,** at the far north end of Jl. Monkey Forest, has overpriced rooms and a swimming pool. (☎62 376 22522. Bungalows with *mandi* Rp45,000; cottages with Western bath Rp50,000.) Every hotel comes with a good-quality restaurant or cafe. **Green Orry Inn's cafe ❷** serves delicious *lassis* (Rp3000-3500) and chicken curry (Rp15,000). **Harmony Cafe ❷,** on the main road, is vegetarian-friendly (vegetables with coconut milk Rp7500). **Tetebatu Cafe ❸** has billiards and an occasional band (F-Sa), and serves a small menu of cheap food (fried chicken Rp12,500). **Warung Salabuse ❸,** the other nightspot down the main road from Harmony Cafe, is also open for lunch. Nightly movies, Saturday night bands, and karaoke round out this lively cafe. (☎836 62. Entrees Rp8000-18,000.)

SIGHTS. Local hospitality makes Tetebatu a peaceful retreat. The paths around the glorious tobacco fields and terraced rice paddies merit a day of exploring. To get to the **Monkey Forest,** follow the main road north until it veers right; a dirt road marked by a park sign continues north for 4km before reaching the *hutan*. Local boys gather here to offer their services as guides. **Otak Kokok Gading (Joben Waterfall),** west of Tetebatu, is frequented by locals who believe the natural springs have healing powers. Far more impressive are the **Jeruk Manis Waterfalls,** 7km to the east of Tetebatu. To reach these falls, follow the signs along the eastbound road out of Tetebatu's southern hub to a carpark. From there it's a 30min. walk to the falls. There's a new police post at the entrance. Guides are recommended, but choose a local guide, as there are reports of non-local "guides" mugging their tourists. (Guides Rp20,000 for the falls, Rp50,000 to motorbike to all sights, including villages. Admission to Jeruk Manis Waterfalls Rp1500.)

DAYTRIPS FROM TETEBATU. Rural Lombok towns are full of textiles and craftwork. *Ojek* drivers and bungalow owners offer tourists various packages around the handicraft loop. *Bemo* and *cidomo* cover all destinations and, if you travel early, shouldn't be hard to catch. The frugal can walk to nearby villages.

The market town of **Kotaraja** is 3km south of Tetebatu. Its daily market, which carries mainly produce and petrol, is dwarfed by the massive turnouts on Wednesday and Friday. The next village, **Loyok,** is known for bamboo and rattan weaving. On its main street is a "handicraft center," but residential shops are more interesting. Visitors who ask to see weaving can get a lesson in bamboo-ring making. Five hundred meters east, in **Rungkang,** locals sell burnt-sienna pots that resemble overbaked Grecian urns. **Masbagik,** however, is the commercial center for terra-cotta pieces. East of Pomotong on the main drag, Masbagik has a market on Mondays. **Pringgasela** lies farther from Masbagik (go east toward Rempung, then veer north off the main road), but it's worth the trip to see *Sasak ikat* weaving at its finest.

The **Radiah ❷** in **Lendang Nangka** is an unorthodox way to experience central Lombok. Radiah is a teacher who leads walks through fields and teaches guests how rice is planted and harvested. Meals consist of Sasak food: *urap-urap* (veggies with young coconut and garlic), *olah olah* (veggies with coconut milk), *sayurbening* (plain boiled veggies), and *pelecing kangkung* (very spicy boiled veggies). There are two walks a day—one (from sunrise until 7:30am) to witness how Sasak farmers start their day, and another (from 4pm to sunset) to see how their day ends. Walks are free for guests, but non-guests can also tag along for Rp25,000 (includes one meal). Buses stop at Masbagik from Labuhan Lombok and Sweta. Take a *cidomo* (Rp1500) to Lendang Nangka and ask for Radiah. (Meals included. Singles Rp25,000; doubles Rp35,000; plantation room Rp45,000. If business is slow, the plantation rooms close and guests are boarded with the family.)

THE GILI ISLANDS

Gili Trawangan, Gili Air, and Gili Meno are tourist magnets, popular for their glorious blue-green reefs, white sand, and fun-loving crowds. Each island has a niche of its own: Gili Trawangan hops with an eternal party, Gili Meno is the perfect romantic getaway, and Gili Air is the best place to hide from the drunks and mushy couples. Snorkeling and diving packages are everywhere—sea life and shark sightings attract tourists. However, in addition to the harm done by rapid development, environmental changes and rising water temperatures have endangered the coral along the shore and sparked conservation efforts.

THE VIEW FROM ABOVE

The lowdown: Three islands–Gili Air, Gili Meno, and Gili Trawangan–off Lombok's northwestern coast.
Highlights: Partying at the bar shacks of Gili Trawangan, scuba diving in Gili Air's coral reefs, and finding peace and quiet on Gili Meno.

GETTING AROUND THE GILI ISLANDS

From **Mataram** (p. 207), take a **bemo** to **Pemenang** (1½hr., Rp4000), where **cidomo** go 1km to the port of **Bangsal.** Once at Bangsal, you can reach the Gilis by public, shuttle, or chartered boat. **Public boats,** the cheapest option, leave when full (at least 15 passengers and up to 2hr. wait) for Gili Air (Rp1500), Gili Meno (Rp1900), and Gili Trawangan (Rp2000). **Shuttle boats** run at 10am and 4:30pm to Gili Air

(Rp3500), Gili Meno (Rp4000), and Gili Trawangan (Rp4500) and leave for the return at 8:15am from Gili Air and Gili Meno and 8:30am from Gili Trawangan. Boats can be chartered from the Bangsal port or the islands. Prices are never fixed, but trips under 5hr. should be Rp100,000 per boat or less. **Perama** is a reputable boat operator that runs boats to the Gilis from virtually anywhere on Bali and Lombok. Direct boats leave from **Senggigi** (Rp40,000). **Island-hopping shuttles** (Rp7000 one-way) allow daytrips to other islands and leave twice daily from Gili Air (8:30am and 3pm). Other information is available at the ticket office.

GILI TRAWANGAN

Gili Trawangan, the party center of the Gilis, bustles with backpackers who come for the bars and a hip beach resort with low prices. In 1992, President Suharto marked the northwest corner of the island for massive tourist development and ordered all establishments to shut down. In July 1998, following Suharto's resignation, the people regained possession of their land. As they returned to their beachside plots, most set up stores and simple *warung* that contrast with the more upscale resorts near the landing. The island is a great place for snorkeling and scuba diving, and stretches of undeveloped beach await exploration.

The **boat landing** is at the midpoint of the eastern coast. The **Perama Office** is just south of the landing. A **medical clinic** is next door to Villa-Ombok on the south side of the main strip. There are **wartel** scattered along the strip that offer cash and collect calls. (Most open daily 8am-midnight.) **Moneychangers** line the strip and a few offer Visa advances at outrageous rates (8-10%). **Wiggis Internet,** next to the Perama Office, suffers the fewest chance disconnections. (Rp500 per min. Open daily 8:30am-11pm.) *Cidomo*, bicycles, and walking suffice for local transportation. There is **no post office.** Trawangan has more options for diving than the other Gilis. **Blue Marlin Dive Center,** with a PADI 5-star IDC rating, is one of the island's three professional dive centers (2 dives US$45.) Compare prices with **Reef Seekers** and **Dream Divers;** bargain for **snorkeling** prices around US$10.

INDONESIA

Most accommodations line a narrow strip along the eastern coast; the northern and southern ends are more secluded. Most lodgings come with electricity, fan, mosquito nets, and breakfast. In the high season, the better hotels may be booked, forcing travelers to put down a deposit while staying elsewhere for the first night. **Creatif Bungalows II ❸**, a 10min. walk north from the boat landing and just a short stroll to the best swimming area, has private hammocks in a beautiful garden. (Singles Rp30,000; doubles Rp40,000.) The cheapest option is **Mawar I Bungalows ❶,** past the southern end of the strip, with bamboo bungalows. (Singles Rp10,000; doubles Rp12,000.) For peace and quiet, head to **Pondok Santi ❷,** south of Mawar I. (Singles Rp25,000; doubles Rp40,000.) **Pondok Jessica ❸,** 100m inland from the ferry port, has well-kept cottages and fresh-water showers. (Rp40,000-60,000.) In addition to the **warung ❶** that line the beach north of the landing, many fine restaurants line the southern end of the beach strip. **Brobudur ❸** has an extensive menu including large burgers (Rp18,000) and even larger fish (Rp15,000-25,000). **Dream Divers ❹** grills fresh fish every night. (☎634 496. Entrees Rp14,000-42,000.) **Blue-Marlin Dive Center ❹** serves tasty meals on beachside tables. (Sweet and sour prawns Rp25,000.) **Villa-Ombok ❹** has delicious food that's worth the price tag (entrees Rp30,000). Try the crepes *partisia* (apple or mango and custard in a crepe drizzled with orange sauce; Rp15,500). Most of the backpacker cafes and *warung* serve the local specialty—Indonesian magic mushrooms. Be careful.

GILI AIR

Gili Air is just busy enough. It buzzes with the bustle of a tourist town yet retains a small-town air. Greener than the other Gilis, it supports coconut groves. It also has the largest permanent population of the three islands, and the local presence is felt beyond the hawkers and massage-ladies. Swimming is best in the southeastern corner of the island, but once-good snorkeling sites have deteriorated due to seaweed farming and dynamite fishing.

An obvious road traces the perimeter of the island, and a few unnamed paths cut through the village center. Most tourist services are on the beachfront. **Boats** land on the south side of the island. **Horse-carts** traverse the island constantly, but **bicycles** are the most efficient transport. The **Perama Office** (☎637 816), 100m inland from the jetty, arranges **glass-bottom boat trips** all over Lombok. Most hotels offer tickets to destinations in Bali, Lombok, and Sumbawa at similar prices. Gili Air has **no hospital, police, post office,** or **bank,** but there's a **health clinic** (*Puskesmas*) on the south side in the village, and **moneychangers** are everywhere. Hotel Gili Indah has a **wartel.** (☎636 341. Open daily 7am-10pm.) **Internet cafes** (around Rp500 per min.) are popping up all over, including at **Gili Air Santay** (see below). Several dive shops and guest houses offer **scuba-diving** trips and courses, and most bungalows rent **snorkeling** equipment. Even if you don't dive with **Reefseekers** (☎641 008), stop by to ask the staff for a tour of the **Turtle Farm.** Endangered eggs are bought from markets and hatched. The turtles are then returned to the sea.

Night owls will be grateful for the island's 24hr. electricity. Most bungalows offer rooms with mosquito nets, *mandi,* and breakfast; the variables are showers, hammocks, and location. Outside of high season (June-Sept.), it is possible to bargain down from the prices listed here. Otherwise, arrive early, as rooms are usually booked before noon. **Safari Cottages ❸,** along the south coast, has respectable bungalows on a stretch of secluded, if scruffy, beach. (Singles Rp30,000; doubles Rp45,000.) **Gili Air Santay ❸,** halfway along the eastern shore, is more expensive than others, but the cleanliness and tiled baths make it worth the extra rupiah. (Singles Rp40,000; doubles Rp50,000.) Slightly farther north on the east coast, **Coconut Cottages ❸** has a range of accommodations. (Bamboo bungalows with veranda Rp40,000-50,000.) The restaurant in **Hotel Gili Air ❹,** with beachside seating along the northern coast, is a great place to watch the sunset and chow down on pan-fried tuna (Rp27,500). Order their homemade pastas a day in advance. Next door, the **Pondok Wisata Santi ❸** features pavilions and delicious sweet-and-sour chicken (Rp15,000). **Il Pirata ❹,** in a pirate ship 100m west and inland from the landing (follow the signs), serves Italian cuisine (most entrees Rp20,000-25,000).

GILI MENO

Gili Meno is the least visited of the Gilis, making it the preferred island for a real getaway. The northern part of the island is empty, but the livelier southeast shore is entrancing. It also has the island's only decent beach. An inland **salt-water lake** can be reached by the road next to Royal Reef Hotel. There is also a **bird reserve** about 300m inland. During the low season (late Nov.-Apr.), Gili Meno operates at half speed; bungalows stay open, but restaurants usually close.

Boats arrive at the southeast shore. Most tourist facilities, including a **Perama** outpost and **moneychangers,** are near the landing. The **Blue Marlin Dive Center** offers Visa and Mastercard advances and has spotty **Internet** connections (Rp300 per min.). The **wartel,** south of the landing at the Gazebo Meno Hotel, has unreliable connections. **Royal Reef Hotel,** north of the landing, offers **phone service.** There is **no post office** or **hospital** on Meno. Generators produce the only electricity on Gili Meno; lights are switched off 10pm-midnight (or whenever the owners feel like it).

Kontiki Cottages ❹, south of the landing, has elegant, clean bungalows with Western baths. (☎632 824. Singles Rp60,000; doubles Rp80,000.) **Matahari Bungalows ❷,** 50m from the beach, is the cheapest option, with clean bungalows that have mosquito nets. The manager doesn't turn on the generator unless he has to. (Rooms

Rp25,000-35,000.) **Mallia's Child Bungalows** ❹, next door to Kontiki, tempts travelers with its beachfront location. (Bungalows with *mandi* Rp50,000-75,000.) Saleswomen hawk *gado-gado* and *nasi campur* on the beach. Most accommodations have restaurants attached. The **restaurant at Kontiki Cottages** ❷ has great beach views and cheap, tasty meals (entrees Rp10,000-15,000). The cheap **Good Heart Restaurant** ❸ is on the northwest side of the island (entrees Rp6000-30,000). Time your visit with the setting sun—but bring a flashlight for the walk back.

SUMBAWA

Hot, dry, dusty Sumbawa is rarely visited by foreigners and neglected by Jakarta. Though a fairly good road system exists, Sumbawa is still primarily a residential island, not a tourist one. The friendly residents are eager to practise their English with visitors, but otherwise keep to themselves. Surfers will appreciate Hu'u's waves—for others, however, Sumbawa is probably just dry scenery rolling by on the long bus trip from Poto Tano to Sape.

THE VIEW FROM ABOVE

The lowdown: The island that Indonesia forgot lies between Lombok and Flores.
Gateway Cities: Poto Tano, Sape.
Major Towns: Bima, Sape, Sumbawa Besar.
Highlights: Surfing Lakey's Beach in Hu'u and Taliwang's waters, stopping by the Sultan's Palace in Bima.

GETTING TO SUMBAWA

BY PLANE. Bima's airport lies 19km from town along the main road to Bima. As a major regional hub for **Merpati,** Bima offers island-hopping flights to: **Denpasar** (Tu, Th, Sa-Su; Rp528,800); **Kupang** (Th, Su; Rp720,900) via **Ruteng** (Rp284,100); **Labuhanbajo,** Flores (M, Sa; Rp223,200); **Mataram** (Th, Sa; Rp352,300). **Sumbawa Besar's airport,** on Jl. Garuda at the western edge of town, is easily reached by yellow *bemo* (Rp1000), though flights from here are less frequent than from Bima. Flights go to: **Jogjakarta; Semarang;** and **Surabaya.**

BY FERRY. Ferries run between **Labuhan Lombok** on Lombok's east coast to **Poto Tano** on Sumbawa's west coast (2hr., every hr., Rp8000). Purchase tickets at the piers. Alternatively, buy a combined ferry and A/C bus ticket (Rp27,000), which will take you directly to **Mataram** (see p. 207) on Lombok. A ferry/bus combination going in the other direction, from Mataram to Sumbawa Besar, costs Rp20,000, but buses have no A/C. Ferries also leave **Sape** for **Labuhanbajo,** Flores (8-12hr.; 8am; Rp16,000) and **Waikelo,** Sumba (M 8pm; Rp21,000).

BY BOAT. PELNI ships dock at **Bima** and at **Badas,** 5km from Sumbawa Besar. The KM *Tata Mailau* departs from both harbors every two weeks for **Denpasar, Dobo, Labuhanbajo, Larantuka, Saumlaki,** and **Tual.** The KM *Tilongkabila* leaves sporadically from Bima for **Denpasar, Kumai, Lembar, Sampit,** and **Surabaya.** The KM *Pangrango* leaves from Badas about once a week to **Ende, Labuhanbajo, Surabaya, Waingapu,** and beyond. The Bima **PELNI Office,** Jl. Pelabuhan 103, is beside the harbor. **Barito,** on Jl. Hasanudin (☎437 37), runs **express boats** from Bima to **Denpasar** (6hr.; business Rp146,000, executive Rp176,000).

SUMBAWA BESAR ☎0371

Aside from the comfort that its relative wealth affords, Sumbawa Besar has little to offer visitors. Unfortunately, this makes transportation both expensive and inconvenient. The *beraban kebo* (buffalo race) is held every Sunday for tourist edification, provided there are enough tourists to warrant one. For those with the luxury of private transport, the countryside offers some fascinating sites.

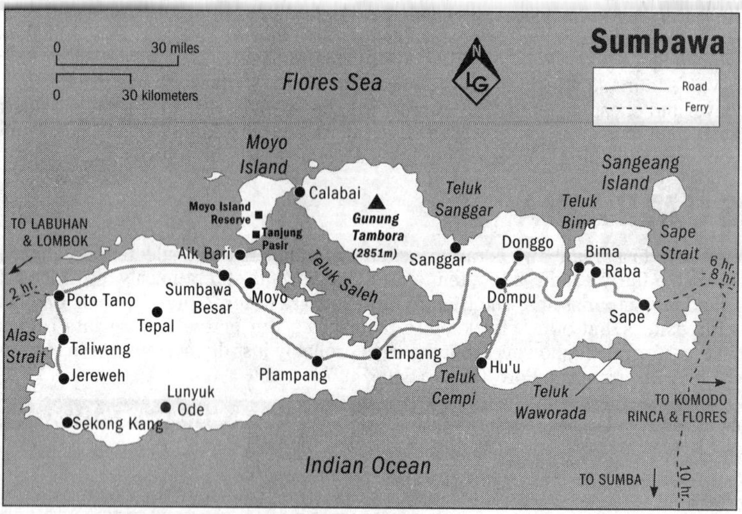

ORIENTATION AND PRACTICAL INFORMATION. All of Sumbawa Besar lies north of a river except for **Jl. Garuda,** which branches off Jl. Cendrawasin and crosses southward toward the airport. **Brangbiji Airport,** the **tourist office,** and the main **post office** are all on Jl. Garuda. The rest of the city is enclosed by **Jl. Diponegoro** (which becomes Jl. Yos Sudarso, then Jl. Setia Budi) to the north, **Jl. Hasanuddin** (which becomes Jl. Dr. Wahidin) to the south, their juncture in the west, and **Jl. Merdeka/Jl. Urip Sumoharjo** to the east. **Jl. Kartini** is lined with shops selling everything you could want. Yellow and blue *bemo* ply these streets and congregate at the *bemo* corner behind **Seketeng Market** in the northeast part of the town.

Services in Sumbawa Besar include: **Dinas Pariwisata Tourist Information,** a left turn off Jl. Garuda just past the GPO (☎237 14; open M-Th 7am-2pm, F 7am-11:30pm, Sa 7am-1:30pm); an unmarked **Perama Office,** Jl. Hasanuddin 48 (☎225 41); **BNI** (☎217 86), on Jl. Kartini, which changes traveler's checks and has a **24hr. ATM** (Cirrus/MC/PLUS/V); **police,** Jl. Hasanuddin 105 (**emergency** ☎110), at Jl. Diponegoro; **Apotik Dynasty,** Jl. Garuda 4 (☎220 33), a pharmacy, opposite the **hospital,** Jl. Garuda 5 (☎210 78; **ambulance** ☎118); **Telkom office,** Jl. Yos Sudarso 6 (☎210 00), with **Internet** access (Rp10,000 per hr.); **branch post office,** on Jl. Yos Sudarso, opposite the Telkom office, and **GPO,** Jl. Garuda 99, close to the airport and town center (*Poste Restante;* open M-Th 7:30am-5pm, F 7:30-11:30am, Sa 7:30am-1pm).

ACCOMMODATIONS AND FOOD. **Dewi Hotel ❷** has a range of rooms all coming off a comfy lounge. (☎211 70. Singles from Rp17,500; doubles Rp20,000.) **Losmen Suci ❷,** on Jl. Hasanuddin, has budget rooms as well as some new, upscale ones. (☎215 89. Singles from Rp20,000; doubles Rp25,000.) **Losmen Mekersari ❷,** on the first side street after Jl. Kamboja on Jl. Hasanuddin, has basic but clean accommodations with private *mandi.* (☎213 51. Singles Rp22,000; doubles Rp30,000.)

Although it's possible to find English menus, dining in the city often involves the "pick and pray" method of choosing dinner. Restaurants and food carts cluster along **Jl. Diponegoro. Aneka Rasa Jaya ❸,** Jl. Hasanuddin 4, is a Chinese restaurant with delicious seafood in huge portions (Rp5000-20,000). **Cirebon 2 ❶,** Jl. Kebayan 4, up the street from Hotel Tambora, has a large non-English menu. (Entrees

Rp4500-8000. Open daily 7am-10pm.) **Cirebon 1 ❶**, Cirebon 2's older sibling, is farther up Jl. Kebayan and serves cheap Indonesian food (Rp5000-7000).

SIGHTS AND ENTERTAINMENT. The old Sultan's palace, **Dalam Loka,** off Jl. Sudirman, is the city's prime attraction, though this isn't saying very much. Built at the end of the 19th century and recently restored, it's one of the largest all-wood buildings in the world. The 99 wooden pillars that adorn the palace symbolize the different representations of God. Extensive information labels explain everything—in Indonesian. Apart from the bare rooms of the palace itself, a small number of traditional artifacts are also on display. (Open Sa-Th 7am-2pm, F 7-11am; visits outside these hours can be arranged with the resident caretaker. Small donation expected.) The **Pura Agung Giri Natha** temple, next to the post office, serves a now-scant Hindu population.

Bull racing is traditionally organized before rice planting in August, but, due to recent flows of travelers through the area, races are now held whenever there are enough tourists to warrant one—but the lag was more than twelve months in 2001-2002. The Perama Office can help arrange transportation to and from these events.

NEAR SUMBAWA BESAR

Renting a car or motorbike is the best way to see sights outside Sumbawa Besar, but prices tend to be astronomical. *Bemo* and fishing boats are the next best thing.

MOYO ISLAND. A short hop from Sumbawa Besar, Moyo Island is home to a nature reserve inhabited by wild pigs, deer, and other creatures. If the US$900 per night resort on the west side of the island isn't ritzy enough, shelter is available at **Tanjung Pasir ❸** (rooms Rp40,000). Snorkeling equipment is available, though food isn't. Fishing **boats** can be hired (Rp200,000) from the nearby town of Air Bari (*ojek* from Sumbawa Besar Rp40,000). The island is renowned for diving as well as movie-star and British-royalty sightings. Most diving trips to the island originate from Lombok. For more information and maps, call the **National Forestry Office** (PHPA; ☎239 41), on Jl. Desa Nijong.

AI' BELING. Surrounded by dense forest and swimmable pools, this 50m high terrace-like waterfall is 36km southwest of Sumbawa Besar and once was the Sultan's hunting ground. On a good day you'll see monkeys, butterflies, and the occasional wild pig (*ojek* from Sumbawa Besar Rp30,000).

POTO VILLAGE. Poto Village, 12km east of Sumbawa Besar (Rp500 by *bemo*), is known for *songket* cloth, used to make sarongs and scarves laced with silver and gold. Works are not prominently displayed, but ask the first person you see for directions to local weavers. Most are happy to show their finished works as well as the process. The cloth itself is somewhat expensive (from Rp100,000).

TALIWANG. Some of the finest, least crowded waves in the Indonesian archipelago are off the west coast of Sumbawa in Taliwang, accessible by bus (3hr.; Rp17,000) from Sumbawa Besar. Moving south along the coast line, **Jelenga (Scar Reef)** is a challenging left-hand break. The surf breaks over sharp coral reefs that can mangle the careless. Beautiful Tanjung Malok has **Malok**—known as **Super Suck**—and a long sandy beach great for swimming when the water is calm. Luxurious surfing tours from Bali dock farther south at **Sekongkang (Yo-Yo's).** Most accommodations are nestled in Taliwang, but many stay in Jelenga. From Taliwang, *ojek* and *bemo* can be chartered to Jelenga, Malok, and Sekongkang.

THE LOCAL STORY

LIFE BEYOND TOURISM

Phyllis and Richard McBride aren't on the mountainous Indonesian island of Lembata simply to watch whales or soak up rays. The couple is here for 2 years to work on community development projects through the British Volunteer Services Organization (VSO), with which they have served since 1997. Phyllis, a physical therapist, and Richard, a retired professor and agricultural specialist, hail from Nova Scotia, Canada ("a terrific tourist destination, by the way," as they asked us to mention here).

LG: How is VSO different from the [American] Peace Corps?

RM: VSO started back in the 50s in Britain and...allowed people just coming out of university to go out and work in...the ex-colonies...to have that experience of development in another culture, in Africa and Asia. That carried on...getting more and more professionalism; they found they got very good results with people...who had several years' experience in their profession...Not just university people: mechanics, craftspeople...

You essentially don't work for VSO. What VSO is doing in about 40 countries, developing countries, is they are looking for employers for you...So, in our case, in this island, Lembata, there's a leprosy hospital which was requesting a physio-therapist and there was an NGO looking for an agricultural specialist. So VSO put our applications together with those two positions and said, okay, here's a match...Normally, VSO would give you about 3 choices...[but] with a couple,

(continued on next page)

HU'U ☎0373

Surf-lovers and professionals come to roast, play, and be photographed in Hu'u's aquamarine Cempi Bay before rainy-season winds dampen surfing conditions. The surrounding reefs make for great snorkeling opportunities for non-surfers—though few without boards ever make their way down here. Surfers will appreciate the easy offshore access to the successive breaks from Lakey's Beach: **Lakey's Peak, Lakey's Pipe,** and **Nanges.** For intrepid surfers, two right-hand breaks of Lakey's Beach lie to the north (**Cobblestone,** a 15min. walk) and south (**Periscope,** a 30min. walk). If you're not a professional surfer and can't tell the difference, ask anyone with a board. But be careful with your belongings at the outer breaks and do not bring valuables, as thefts have been reported.

Accommodations on **Lakey's Beach** are kilometers away from the nearest villages, so most lodgings have restaurants and general stores. **Mona Lisa Bungalows ❸,** about the fourth hotel from the northern edge of Lakey's Beach, has straw and bamboo huts with private *mandi*. (Breakfast included. Singles Rp30,000, with A/C 60,000; doubles Rp40,000/Rp75,000.) **Puma Cottages ❸** is larger with Western-style baths and a helpful staff. (Breakfast included. Laundry service. Singles Rp35,000; doubles Rp60,000.) The rooms, service, and amenities at **Hotel Aman Gati ❺** are exquisite. (☎623 031. Breakfast included. Rooms Rp140,000-210,000, with A/C and hot water Rp240,000-320,000. Extra beds Rp70,000. MC/V.) Once the low tide kills the surf, the happening **Fatma's Hand Restaurant ❸** gets lively. Come for the quiche (from Rp22,000), fresh fish (from Rp15,000), a movie, or just to hear the word "gnarly" spoken without irony.

Exchange **currency** in Bima, Dompu, or Sumbawa—rates in Hu'u are terrible. **Intan Lestari** rents **bicycles** (Rp 15,000) and **snorkeling gear** (Rp10,000). Most hotels and bungalows offer **international calls.** Fatma's Hand Restaurant provides **fax** service, transportation **bookings**, and **surfboard rental** (Rp25,000 per day). To get to Hu'u, take a bus from **Bima** (2hr., Rp5000) or **Sumbawa Besar** (4-5hr.; Rp15,000) to **Dompu,** a transit point for buses to Hu'u. In Dompu, take a *bemo* from the Northern Terminal to the city center (Rp500) and then a *cidomo* (Rp500) to the Southern Terminal. From here, pricey and sporadic transport heads to Hu'u. Accommodations such as the Hotel Aman Gati arrange transportation; call ahead and they may pick you up.

GUNUNG TAMBORA

Gunung Tambora, the rocky giant on the northern peninsula of central Sumbawa, last blew its top in 1815, a blast that resulted in a summerless 1816. Some say it was more destructive than even the eruption of Gunung Krakatau. The two-colored crater lake and far-reaching vistas are amazing rewards for those who reach the summit. The town of **Calabai** is the launching pad for the three-day ascent, but there are few trekking and transportation packages available. Transportation is easiest from Dompu (8hr.). From here, buses leave to Calabai (3 per day; 8am, noon, 4pm; Rp10,000). The time-saving but more expensive transportation option is to charter a boat from Air Bari, the port near Sumbawa Besar, to Calabai (Rp300,000). From Calabai, *bemo* go to **Prancasila,** the base point for the trek.

BIMA ☎0374

If Sumbawa Besar is mild-mannered, then Bima is its hot-blooded sibling with spice, charisma, and even a touch of bawdiness. Whether in the night market's vendors or in the *dokar* careening down its streets, Bima's energy envelopes every visitor as hundreds of bright, colored lights light up every awning, storefront, and mosque while teenagers blast music, turning downtown into a virtual discotheque. The **Sultan's Palace** (now a museum), with its impressive display of ceremonial *kris* (swords), is far more interesting than Sumbawa Besar's. (At the western end of Jl. Sumbawa. Open M-F 9am-4pm. Free, but guide tip expected.)

La'mbitu Hotel ❸ is easily the best value on Sumbawa. (☎422 22. Breakfast included. Classy rooms with bath Rp45,000, with A/C, TV, and bath Rp70,000). Next door, **Hotel Liligraha** ❷, older and more worn, gives you less for the money. (Breakfast included. Rooms Rp15,000-20,000; doubles with bath Rp50,000, with bath and fan Rp60,000.) The numerous **food carts** ❶ that line Bima's back streets and the **night market** ❶ (just south of Jl. Hasanuddin) compensate for a paucity of restaurants. Both hotels listed above have cheap, tasty **eateries** ❷ inside (most entrees at both Rp4000-12,000). In town, **Rumah Makan Anda** ❷, on Jl. Kaharnuddin before the bridge on the way to the terminal, delights with freshly baked goods and a large Chinese menu. (Limited vegetarian dishes. Entrees Rp4000-11,000. Open daily 8am-10pm.) **Ayam Goreng Pemuda** ❸, Jl. Sulawesi 12, by the night market, weighs a bit heavier on the vegetarian side. Try the vegetables in chili sauce for Rp4000. (Large fish with tomato Rp20,000. Open daily 9am-3pm and 5-10pm.)

(continued from previous page)

often there aren't as many...

VSO has a number of stages where they prepare you..."Preparing for Change"...is a 2- or 3-day session which prepares you for...how you have to adjust your profession to the needs of a third-world country, the kinds of culture-shock things you may run into, how to sorta anticipate the loneliness and what you're going to miss and how you might set up a social network when you arrive...

PM: They have courses in England more specific for your training 5 days or a week long.

RM: ...so you don't go into a community and tell them what a Canadian would do here. You ask them what they need and try and work with them rather than impose it...

PM: I have to make my own supplies because there's nothing there... I'm supposed to be working with leprosy patients, but the medications have been very successful, so there are very few...So I've branched out into any disabled people. So I've made different exercise tools for hands and I've tried to get someone to make canes from local materials like bamboo because there's nothing there at all...

RM: [As for farming,] all of the land is very steep, and according to the textbooks they shouldn't be farming at all. If they use terracing...they can farm it without a lot of erosion... The other thing is they use a lot of nitrogen-fixing plants, beans or peas...a sustainable system...[as opposed to] their old system...slash and burn. But they have adapted very quickly...And they don't use chemicals.

Buses go from **Kumbe Terminal** on Jl. Sukarno-Hatta and the **Town Bus Terminal,** across the river after Jl. Kaharnuddin, to: **Dompu** (2hr., Rp3500); **Sape** (1½hr., every 30min. 7am-4pm, Rp3000); and **Sumbawa Besar** (12hr.; Rp12,000). Bima sits between two rivers. **Jl. Terminal Baru** stretches north from the airport (south of the southern river) and becomes **Jl. Kaharnuddin,** the main street. It first intersects **Jl. Karantina/Sukarno-Hatta,** the main eastbound road that leads to **Raba,** Bima's administrative center. **Jl. Sumbawa,** which collides with the Sultan's Palace complex, runs two blocks up and parallel to Jl. Sukarno-Hatta. Along Jl. Sukarno-Hatta, Raba has a **24hr. Telkom Office** with collect calls and **Internet** (Rp12,000 per hr.); the **police** (☎430 26; **emergency** ☎110); and the **hospital,** Jl. Langsat 1 (**24hr. emergency** ☎431 42; **ambulance** ☎118). **BNI,** on Jl. Sultan Hasanuddin, has a **24hr. ATM.** (Open M-F 8am-3pm. Cirrus/MC/PLUS/V.) The **GPO** is on the eastern extension of Jl. Hasanuddin/Diponegoro at Jl. Gajah Mada. (*Poste Restante.* Open M-Sa 8am-2:30pm, Su 9am-noon.) **Postal code:** 84100.

SAPE

Sape is the port for ferries to **Labuhanbajo,** Flores (9-12hr.; 8am; economy B with hard chairs and Indonesian TV Rp13,000, economy A with soft chairs and American movies Rp20,000) and **Waikelo Somba** (14hr.; F 9pm; economy B Rp13,000, economy A Rp21,000; additional costs for: bicycles Rp5150, motorbikes Rp16,000, and cars Rp170,000). Apart from the ferry, there isn't much in Sape. *Dokar*—chariot-like vehicles jokingly called "Ben Hur"—race along the lone road from Sape to the port village of **Pelabuhan Sape,** 4km east. The **bus terminal** and **produce market** bustle on the east side, at the fringe of the farm fields 3km west of Sape. One *losmen* and the **ferry** are in Pelabuhan Sape, but most services line the main road in Sape. There are a handful of restaurants, a few *losmen*, a **police office,** a **post office,** and the **medical services** of Dr. H. Maknum, near the police station (open daily 4pm-8pm). One **wartel** stands 200m before the harbor in Pelabuhan Sape; another is on the Sape side of the bus station. (Both cash only; open daily 6am-midnight.)

INDONESIA

If you don't want take the 1hr. ride to and from Bima (Rp4000 one-way), then staying at the pier is your best bet. **Losmen Mutiara** ❸ is close to the ferry and more immediate than the 20min. buggy ride through rice fields to the other end of Sape. (Singles 20,000; doubles 35,000.) If you choose to make the trip, **Losmen Friendship** ❷ compensates for its considerable distance from the ferry landing with a helpful staff and complimentary hot beverages. (☎710 06. Rooms Rp15,000, with *mandi* Rp20,000, with *mandi* and fan Rp30,000.) Sape's small market is not a great place to scrounge for a meal and certainly not for alcohol (it is illegal in this Muslim port). The smattering of *rumah makan* offer few alternatives. At **Rumah Makan Arema** ❷, by the ferry landing, a hopping crowd enjoys cheap dishes. (Grilled prawns Rp10,500. Open daily until 10pm.) Across from Losmen Friendship, **Novita's** ❷ limited menu includes excellent grilled fish (Rp8000-15,000) and not-particularly-good Western favorites like spaghetti (Rp4500) and pizza (Rp7500).

Sape used to be the easiest point of access to **Komodo Island** (see p. 232), but this ceased to be the case when regular ferry service ended. Still, it is possible to charter a boat there from Sape. **Balai Taman Nasional Komodo,** 1km from Pelabuhan Sape, provides advice and dioramas of Komodo Island.

SUMBA

A dusty and dry island where most people live in traditional, windowless *kampung*-style homes, Sumba is as rugged and ancient a place as you'll find. Waingapu and Waikabubak are sleepy little towns where nothing seems to happen, but don't be deceived. This tropical island's tranquil appearance masks deep-seated

BAHASA INDONESIA 101 On buses on rugged, rural islands like Sumba, knowledge of Bahasa Indonesia is essential, as few people speak English. Useful phrases include *Apakah masih ada bis dari sini ke ____ hari ini?* ("Is there still a bus from here to ____ today?"), *Di mana bisa saya naik bis ke ____?* ("Where can I catch a bus to ____?"), and *Berapa ongkos dari sini ke ____?* ("How much is the fare from here to ____?"). If you hear responses like *Tidak ada lagi* or *Besok pagi* ("there are no more" or "tomorrow morning"), then ask about spending the night (*Di mana bisa saya menginap malam ini?* means "Where can I spend the night this evening?") or chartering private transport to the highway junction (*Apakah ada orang di sini yang bisa mengantar saya ke jalan raya?* means "Is there someone here who can take me to the highway?"). Be prepared to shell out rupiah for an *ojek* or private *bemo* ride.

tensions, especially between the Loli and Wewewa tribes in Western Sumba, where tribal warfare has raged sporadically since 1960. The violent streak is perpetuated every year by the island's famous ritual, the *pasola*, in which mounted horsemen with blunted spears engage in "mock" battles (often lethal). But despite the tension, visitors—whether searching for the exquisite *ikat* cloth or wandering the coastline for a perfect beach—are greeted warmly by locals.

THE VIEW FROM ABOVE

The lowdown: A rugged island still clinging to its tribal roots.
Gateway cities: Denpasar, Waikelo, Waingapu
Major towns: Waikabubak, Waingapu.
Highlights: The fantastic surf in Rua and the weaving villages near Moni.

GETTING THERE

Sumba has two **airports: Tambolaka Airport,** in the west, 42km north of Waikabubak, and **Mau Hau Airport,** in the east, 10min. outside Waingapu. **Merpati** runs flights from Tambolaka to: **Bima** (Su, Tu; Rp598,000); **Denpasar** (Su, Tu; Rp697,000); **Kupang** (W, F; Rp568,000) and also from Mau Hau to **Denpasar** (Su, W; Rp697,000) and **Kupang** (M, W; Rp483,000). (Open M-F 8am-4pm.)

A ferry runs from Waikelo in Western Sumba to **Sape** (Th, Sa; Rp21,000). Waingapu has inconsistent **ferry** service to **Ende** (W, F; Rp21,000), **Kupang,** and **Sabu.** Check the city listings for details. Waingapu also is the port for **PELNI** boats; the office is 100m from the harbor entrance. With the help of the KM *Awu*, KM *Wilis*, and KM *Pangrango*, Sumba is connected to many ports, including **Aimere, Benoa, Bima, Ende, Kupang, Labuhanbajo,** and **Surabaya.** Check the PELNI office or your hotel for schedules.

GETTING AROUND

On Sumba, **bus travel** is popular but unreliable. Buses run between **Waikabubak** and **Waingapu** (5hr.; 8-9am, noon-1pm, 3-4pm, 10pm; Rp10,000) and from these main cities to surrounding destinations (about Rp5000). The surface of the main road between Waingapu, Waikabubak, and the port in Waikelo is good, but side routes are in bad shape.

WAIKABUBAK ☎0387

Nestled in the plateaus of Western Sumba, Waikabubak is cooler and wetter than the coast. In this small town of around 25,000 people, traditional bamboo houses stand on paved streets next to sheet-metal storefronts and grandiose churches.

Beyond the town, the countryside is isolated and traditional; hunting and ritual warfare remain the local custom. The *kampung* clashed in 1992 and again in 1998, resulting in the destruction of several villages and more than 40 deaths. Even in hotels that pander to tourists, English is barely spoken, so a local guide is almost essential for those not comfortable with Bahasa Indonesia.

TRANSPORTATION. **Tambaloka Airport** is 42km north of town. Rare public buses (Rp5000) and chartered *bemo* (Rp50,000) make the trip into Waikububak. The **bus** and **bemo terminals** are on Jl. Pisang, off Jl. A. Yani. Buses leave frequently to **Waingapu** (Rp20,000) and **Waitabula** (Rp8000), and less often to **Waikelo** (Rp10,000). *Bemo* go as far as **Anakalang** to the east and **Lamboya** and **Wanokaka** to the south (all Rp5000). **Waikelo,** north of Waikabubak and the airport, runs **ferries** to **Sape** twice per week (W, F; Rp21,000; inquire at the harbor for details). **Rumah Makan Sumba Indah** (see **Accommodations and Food,** below) **rents motorcycles** (Rp30,000 per day).

ORIENTATION AND PRACTICAL INFORMATION. The city's main north-south street, **Jl. A. Yani,** has most shops and services. **Jl. Gajah Mada** runs parallel, and both cross the short east-west **Jl. Pattimura** at their southernmost points. **Jl. Pemuda** and **Jl. Adiaksa,** which becomes **Jl. Sudirman,** cut through the center of Jl. A. Yani and Jl. Gajah Mada. The northern end of Jl. A. Yani terminates at **Jl. Bhayangkara.** To the east is the road to **Waingapu;** to the north is **Tambaloka Airport.** Services in Waikabubak include: **BNI,** Jl. A. Yani 46, which changes currency and traveler's checks (☎215 40; open M-Th 8am-2pm, F 8-11am); the **police** (☎211 10, **emergency** ☎110), on Jl. Bhayangkara; **Apotik Ezri Farma,** Jl. Pattimura 12, a pharmacy (open M-Sa 8am-1pm and 5-9pm, Su 6-8:30pm); **Rumah Sakit Lende Moripa,** on Jl. Sudirman (☎210 86; **24hr. emergency care;** ambulance ☎118). The 24hr. **Telkom Office,** Jl. Pattimura 7, allows collect calls. A 24hr. **wartel** is on Jl. A. Yani. The **GPO,** Jl. Bhayangkara 1, is across the street from the police. (*Poste Restante.* Open M-Th 8am-3pm, F 8am-noon, Sa 8am-1pm.) **Postal code:** 87211.

ACCOMMODATIONS AND FOOD. Breakfast is included at listed accommodations. Most hotels organize guides and transportation (Rp30,000 per day with *ojek;* Rp50,000 by car with 2 people or more). **Hotel Manandang ❸,** Jl. Pemuda 4, has a restaurant and clean rooms with sinks. (☎211 97. Singles with shared *mandi* Rp30,000; deluxe singles with hot water, TV, phone, and fan Rp65,000; doubles Rp35,000/Rp75,000.) **Hotel Tarung Wisata ❶,** Jl. Pisang 26, near the bus and *bemo* terminals, also has clean rooms and a restaurant. (☎213 32. Small singles with shared *mandi* Rp10,000-20,000, with private bath Rp25,000; doubles Rp20,000-25,000/Rp30,000.) Culinary experiences outside hotel restaurants are limited to streetside *warung* like the ones along **Jl. A. Yani.** With an English menu, **Manandang Restaurant ❷** in Hotel Manandang is the most tourist-friendly place to eat. *Tempe goreng* (Rp6000) and *sayur asam* (sour vegetable soup; Rp6500) will satisfy vegetarians. (Open daily 6am-11pm.) **Rumah Makan Sumba Indah ❶,** on the outskirts of town leading toward the airport, specializes in Balinese cuisine. (Open M-Sa 6am-10pm.) **Rumah Makan Bali Indah ❶,** opposite the Telkom Office, serves cheap *padang* food.

DAYTRIPS FROM WAIKABUBAK. *Bemo* ride east to the numerous *kampung* and stately tombs of **Anakalang** (45min., Rp5000). **Kampung Pasunga,** along the main road, is noteworthy for its large **stone tombs,** some of which took six months to carve. Over 100 buffalo were sacrificed in the construction of the five-person tomb. Ask for directions to **Lai Tarung,** the ancestral village of the local clans. Old tombs and a ceremonial building still stand in the deserted village.

BURIED IN TRADITION While the other islands of Nusa Tenggara are slowly modernizing, Sumba stubbornly holds on to tradition. Unapologetically animist, Sumba adheres to an ancient form of ancestor worship called *Marapu*. In accordance with the roles assigned to the sexes by the "original ancestors," only males can plant rice or feed beasts, while only females can make the famous Sumba *ikat*. *Marapu* also dictates burial tradition: because ancestors are believed to influence earthly life, animals are sacrificed and monumental stone slabs are erected at the funerals of chiefs and aristocrats. Sumbans believe that the spirits appreciate the spilling of human blood, so rituals such as the *Pesola* (a "mock" cavalry battle between interior and coastal villages, which claims at least a few casualties annually) still occur and hunting trophies are still highly valued. So now you know: the long machetes worn by Sumban men are not decorations.

In the opposite direction, a trip to **Pero** in the **Kodi District** will delight visitors with beautiful scenery and sea breezes. On the west coast, the villages around Pero (including **Pronbaroro** and **Wainyapu**) are home to impressive tombs and *kampung*. People flock to Pero for the **surf** at **Pantai Radukapal,** across the river, though some enthusiasts argue that the best place to surf in Western Sumba is **Rua** in the **Lamboya District.** To reach Kodi District from the bus terminal in Waikabubak, take a bus to Waitabula (Rp2000) toward the airport and then catch a bus to Kodi (3 harrowing hours, Rp5000). You'll be dropped off in the middle of a field near a market, which comes to life on Saturdays and Wednesdays.

INDONESIA

WAINGAPU ☎0387

Waingapu offers more restaurants and accommodations than its western neighbor Waikabubak, but the dry, dusty streets that line Waingapu's coast are no match for Waikabubak's temperate highlands. *Ikat* vendors wait outside hotels, and art shops peddle collections of expensive cloth and traditional blades. The market near the central bus terminal offers the best selection of eclectic goods. Even if cloth isn't your thing, Waingapu is a good place to wait for infrequent flights and boats—just put down your luggage and rest in the east Sumba sunshine.

TRANSPORTATION. Frequent **buses** leave from the central terminal to **Melolo** (2hr., Rp5000), as well as **Baing** and **Mangili** in Southeast Sumba. Buses to **Waikabubak** (5hr.; Rp20,000) leave from the terminal outside of town, closer to the port. **PELNI,** Jl. Pelabuhan 2, is near the harbor. Check postings for the boat schedule to: **Benoa** (Rp71,000); **Ende** (Rp42,000); **Kupang** (Rp41,500); **Labuhanbajo** (Rp28,000); **Lembar** (Rp69,500); **Surabaya** (Rp109,500); **Ujung Pandang** (Rp148,000). A regular **ferry** service operates between Flores, Sabu, and West Timor; ferries go to: **Airmere** (M 7pm; Rp19,500); **Ende** (Tu, Th 10am; Rp21,000); **Kupang** (F 2pm; Rp37,000); **Sabu** (F 4pm; Rp21,500). Check at the harbor to be sure that ferries still follow this schedule, as departure times change often.

ORIENTATION AND PRACTICAL INFORMATION. Waingapu's two centers are the **port** in the north and the **bus terminal** in the south, along **Jl. Eltari,** which also hosts the **market. Jl. Yos Sudarso** loops about the north area, turning into **Jl. Hasanuddin** and **Jl. Wanggameti. Jl. A. Yani** connects the two centers.

Services in Waingapu include: **BNI,** on Jl. Ampere, which exchanges major traveler's checks and currency (☎621 46; open M-F 8am-2pm); **police** (☎629 55, **emergency** ☎110), on Jl. R. Suprapto toward the airport; **Apotik Waingapu Farma,** Jl. Wanggameti 33, a pharmacy (☎215 33; open daily 8am-1pm and 5-10pm); **Rumah Sakit Kristen Lindimara,** Jl. Prof. Dr. WZ Johanes 6 (☎610 19, ambulance ☎118);

24hr. **Telkom Office,** Jl. Cut Nya Dien 19; **wartel,** on Jl. Panjaitan in Surabaya Hotel (open daily 5am-1am); and the **GPO,** Jl. Sutomo 21 (*Poste Restante;* open M-Th 8am-2pm, F 8-11am, Sa 8am-noon). **Postal code:** 87100.

ACCOMMODATIONS AND FOOD **Hotel Merlin ❸,** around the corner from Hotel Sandal Wood on Jl. D. I. Panjaitan, is the most luxurious accommodation in town. All rooms have private showers and Western toilets. (☎613 00. Singles Rp30,000, with A/C and TV Rp45,000; doubles Rp35,000/Rp60,000.) **Hotel Sandal Wood ❷,** Jl. D. I. Panjaitan 23, practically in the bus station, has a wide selection of clean, comfortable rooms. (☎211 99. Breakfast included. Singles with shared *mandi* Rp30,000, with private bath Rp35,000-60,000; doubles Rp35,000/Rp40,000-70,000.) Cheap, excellent *rumah makan* are on almost every corner in Waingapu. **Mini Indah ❶,** on the northern end of Jl. A. Yani, has cheap, tasty *padang* entrees (Rp3000-7000 per plate).

DAYTRIPS FROM WAINGAPU: MELOLO, PAU, AND RENDE Immerse yourself in tribal culture in the **weaving villages** of southeastern Sumba. Guides are available at local hotels (Rp50,000 per day plus transportation), or you can make the 62km trip by bus from Waingapu yourself (2hr., Rp5000). The **Pau** village, a 1½hr. walk from **Melolo,** is a popular place to buy fabric and observe all the hard labor that goes into weaving *ikat* (dyed cloth) and *hikung* (fabric with woven patterns). The village also features four impressive tombs of past *rajahs. Bemo* don't go as far as Pau, but if you're coming from Waingapu, ask to be dropped off at the turn-off for Pau. Otherwise, walk toward Waingapu on the road from Melolo. Cross the bridge with the mouth of the river to your right, take the paved road to the left, and then veer right at the fork with the horse statue. The scenery on the walk is impressive. **Rende,** 7km south of Melolo, is best known for its tombs, carved intricately with animal features, and the *ikat* made for village royalty. Because of its royalty, Rende receives more tourists than Pau. The village is accessible by foot or *bemo.*

INDONESIA

FLORES

With its magnificent landscape, Flores ranks as one of Indonesia's most spectacular islands. Lush rainforests set Flores apart from barren Sumba and Sumbawa, nurtured and protected by volcanic mountains and ridges that break the passing clouds. Flores still bears the legacy of colonialism; Roman Catholicism is the faith of choice and names are often Portuguese. "Flores," in fact, is Portuguese for "flower," though the island wasn't named for its vegetation. Rather, it was so dubbed because the colonists who first circumnavigated the island believed it to be flower-shaped. Though colonialism left significant marks on Flores and its people, old habits die hard, and European influences have not supplanted traditional culture. In most remote areas, "Catholic" villages still practice traditional animistic rites and rituals along with the sacraments.

THE VIEW FROM ABOVE

The lowdown: Bali's quieter neighbor preserves the wonders of nature.
Main cities: Labuhanbajo, Ruteng, Bajawa, Ende, Maumere
Highlights: Tricolored crater lakes, sunrises over Golo Curu, the dragons of Komodo and Rinca.

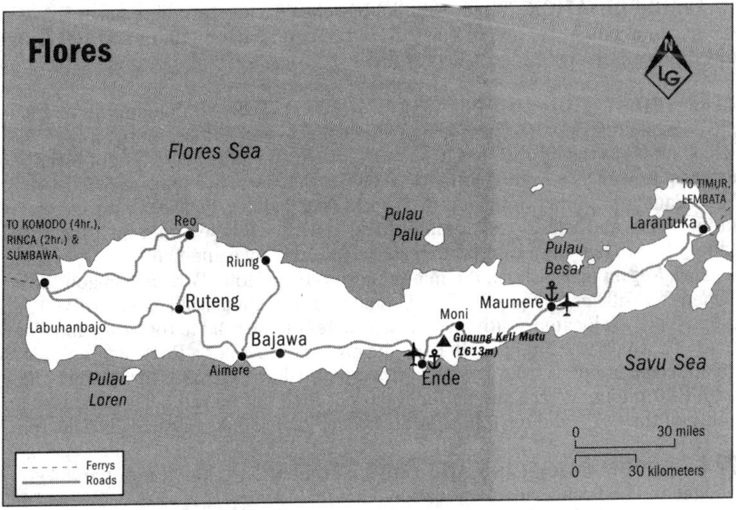

GETTING THERE

BY PLANE. An **airport** is 2km southeast of Labuhanbajo; take the road heading inland at the south end of town and turn left at the sign. **Merpati** (☎411 77) has an office on the way, as well as in Ende (see **Transportation,** p. 236) and flies a few times per week to **Denpasar** (once a week via **Bima**), **Jakarta,** and **Kupang.** Maumere's airport is a busy hub to and from Bali, with flights to **Denpasar** (3 per week; Rp883,000) and **Jakarta** (Rp921,000). Be warned that flights are frequently cancelled and, in the high season, often booked well in advance (especially the Maumere-Denpasar route). **Bajawa Airport,** 25km north of Bajawa, has flights to **Kupang** (Rp220,000).

BY BOAT. A main **ferry landing** is at the north end of Labuhanbajo. Ferries go to **Sape** (8-12hr.; W, Sa; Rp16,000). Check at the harbor to confirm the erratic ferry schedule. To get to the **PELNI office** (☎411 06), walk away from the water at the harbor, take the main road to the right, and then take the first left. Go through the intersection up the dirt road; it's 50m up on the left, cleverly disguised as a house. Check on boats to **Bali, Lombok, Sumba, Surabaya,** and **Timor** here. PELNI also has a main port in Ende, where boats depart to similar destinations. Larantuka, in the east, has a regular ferry service to **Kupang** and **Lembata.** PELNI boats also occasionally sail from Maumere. The 14hr. fast ferry, also leaving from Maumere, goes directly to **Benoa** (M; Rp275,000) before continuing on to **Surabaya** (Rp330,000).

LABUHANBAJO ☎0385

While Labuhanbajo's excellent accommodations and relaxing seaside atmosphere should make it a destination in its own right, it is still mainly a point of departure to Rinca and Komodo. Since the cancellation of regular ferry service to Komodo, most tourists book tours out of the port here. A 15min. walk will bring you to a fine stretch of sand and beach hotels; more secluded resorts lie on islands or the mainland beaches north of town.

TRANSPORTATION. While Labuhanbajo has no bus terminal, **buses** leave in the morning bound for **Ruteng** (6hr.; Rp15,000) and **Bajawa** (10hr.; Rp20,000); flag one down on the main road. Check with hotels for times and to arrange a pickup.

ORIENTATION AND PRACTICAL INFORMATION. Labuhanbajo is a simple coastal crescent stretching 1.5km. The **national parks office,** on the inland road which heads to the airport, has brochures, maps, and information about **Rinca** and **Komodo,** as well as a Komodo dragon skeleton that's worth a look. (☎410 04. Open M-Sa 7am-2pm.) Most hotels on **Jl. Sukarno/Yos Sudarso/Pelabuhan** arrange snorkeling trips and island treks. Many local tourist agencies take visitors diving (about US$75 per day). Hotels also rent out snorkeling equipment.

Bank Negara Indonesia, in the market across from Hotel Witasa, has good rates. (Open M-F 7:30am-2:30pm, Sa 7:30-11:30am.) The main **police station** (☎411 10) is inconveniently located south of the town center on the road to the **Pasar Baru** (new market), which is a 20min. walk from the center of town or a Rp1000 *bemo* ride. A **health clinic** is uphill from the main drag, near Chez Felix. A 24hr. **Telkom office,** with **HCD** phone, is past the national parks office on the right. The **GPO** is 400m south of the ferry landing. (Open M-Th 7:30am-3pm, F 7:30-11am, Sa 7:30am-1pm.)

ACCOMMODATIONS AND FOOD. Labuhanbajo has a number of good budget and mid-range accommodations that include breakfast. For seekers of solitude, beach hotels offer free transport to **bungalows ❷** on secluded beaches and islands (Rp20,000-40,000 including 3 meals). The best value in town is the **Hotel Wisata ❷,** about 1.2km south of the ferry dock on the side of the street closer to the water. All rooms have private Western bath and fan. (☎410 20. 2nd-class singles Rp25,000-30,000; doubles Rp30,000.) **Gardena Bungalows ❷,** 150m south of the ferry landing, has the best view of the sunset. (☎412 58. Singles with fan, private *mandi*, and mosquito net Rp25,000; doubles Rp30,000.) Gardena also provides free transport to its sister bungalow, **Seraya ❷,** on an isolated island an hour away. (Singles Rp20,000; doubles Rp25,000.) **Chez Felix ❷,** on Jl. Prof. Dr. Johanes, is a wonderful place to watch the street bustle without the noise. Walking south from the ferry dock, turn left at the sign (about 800m) and walk uphill another 200m. (☎410 32. Singles with shared *mandi* Rp20,000, with private *mandi* Rp25,000, with mosquito nets and flush toilets Rp40,000; doubles Rp20,000-50,000.) Simple **Hotel Matahari ❷,** 300m south of the landing, provides fans, shower and *mandi* and a view of the harbor. (☎410 83. Singles Rp25,000; doubles Rp30,000.)

The restaurants at Gardena Bungalows, Hotel Wisata, and Chez Felix have lively atmospheres and cheap prices. **Borobudur Restaurant ❸,** a couple of doors south of Gardena Bungalows, has a spectacular view and food to match. The chocolate milkshakes are an incredible treat (Rp6000), especially after a plate of sweet and sour prawns (Rp15,000). The steak, chicken, and prawn dishes at **Dewata Ayu Restaurant ❸,** also next door to Gardena, are all worth the wait (Rp20,000). Both restaurants are open until 10pm.

NEAR LABUHANBAJO: KOMODO & RINCA ISLANDS

The beautiful blue water of the coast of Flores is dotted with multiple islands, known for their reptilian inhabitants with ravenous appetites. The **Komodo dragon,** over 3m long and a hefty 50kg, is the largest of the monitor lizard family. The dragons have long claws, sharp teeth, and powerful tails. Although they're sedentary in the heat of day, they can sprint short distances and hunt with considerable prowess. Much like a snake, a Komodo can expand its chest cavity enough to swallow a goat whole. Wandering the islands alone has been forbidden since 1974, when an elderly Swiss gentleman took a walk and never

CHRISTI-ANIMISM The overwhelming presence of Christian imagery on Flores makes it something of an anomaly compared to the other Indonesian islands. But, despite that most residents of Flores are Catholic, old animist customs still persist. In Bajawa, for example, the traditional village centers honor the sky god and the earth goddess with bamboo parasols. The parasol represents the sky god, who is the protector of the earth goddess; the shadow of the bamboo on the ground symbolizes this protection. What's more, gender roles in these villages correspond to those of the gods: men are to be protectors, women are to be motivators. Still, the animism of Flores meshes surprisingly well with its professed and practiced Catholicism. For example, the traditional Ngada code of conduct includes an injunction to do unto others as you would do unto yourself—obviously reminiscent, to Christians, of Christianity's Golden Rule. Other links between the faiths have been constructed since colonial times. Villagers near Moni dress in black and speak to no one as they hike to the three lakes of Keli Mutu upon the death of a family member; the traditional belief is that spirits travel there upon death. Yet the lakes themselves are now associated with the Christian Hell, Purgatory, and Heaven. Other examples of such interconnections abound—and travelers will certainly find it rewarding to learn more about them.

came back. Though Komodo Island is perhaps better known, Rinca is equally interesting (if not more so), with savannah-like scenery and diverse wildlife, including buffalo, monkeys, deer, and the occasional cobra. The national park offices on each island lead tours in the early morning and late afternoon. (Rp6000 each for 1-2 persons, Rp2000 each for 3 or more. Entrance fee at both Rp10,000.) On Komodo, guides lead an hour-long walk to **Banu Ngulung,** a dry riverbed where the lazy dragons sunbathe. For the motivated, a hike up **Gunung Gara** (7-8km) affords magnificent views of the rugged landscape. On Rinca, the tour heads uphill toward a vista of the surroundings and then back to the port (2hr.).

SAFETY WATCH Before signing up for any overnight cruise, check the boat. Typically, boats do not have life vests or a radio, making stormy nights nerve-wracking. There have been reports of stolen money and women being molested in the middle of the night. **Women should not go alone.**

Getting to Komodo can be difficult. Since regular ferry service has been cancelled, travelers must now go through a tour agency in Labuhanbajo or charter a boat from Sape. In Labuhanbajo, the most popular tour is a two-day, one-night trip to Komodo and Rinca. Most tours include lunch both days, as well as dinner, breakfast, and a mattress on the deck. Trips block out extra time for snorkeling; make sure snorkeling gear is included or rent it before you leave. On a boat of at least 8 people, prices range Rp140,000-180,000. Alternatively, a daytrip to just one of the islands ranges Rp60,000-100,000 depending on group size, while a two-day tour is Rp100,000-130,000 (not including meals). It's also possible to visit both islands in one day, though this won't be any easier on your wallet (Rp140,000-150,000 including lunch and snacks). Extended boat trips are also available, usually including snorkeling or diving. Some leave from Labuhanbajo (diving packages start at US$50 per day), while others are booked in Lombok and make a four-day journey past Sumbawa to Komodo and Rinca, ending at Labuhanbajo (Rp350,000-500,000). Fishing boats can be chartered from Labuhanbajo or Sape (around Rp100,000; discounts for groups), though it is then necessary to spend a night at either Komodo or Rinca. Both

IN RECENT NEWS

HOLY FEAR

No one is ever fully sure of everything that happens during a riot. This is one of the things that makes riots possible: curiosity keeps people gathering, and fear of these mobs causes shops and restaurants to close. In Maumere, on July 14, 2002, the curiosity was due to one man. The local story says that this Muslim man, a member of a crew in port, damaged the wafer basket in a Catholic church. The Jakarta Post calls the man a ship's captain and alleges that he participated, blasphemously, in communion. Either way, the priest called the police and the man was arrested. End of problem, right?

Wrong. Masses of people gathered outside the prison calling for the man to be turned over to them for revenge. The scene deteriorated as rumors spread that a priest had been killed and establishments burned. When the dust finally settled, the worst offenses had been rock throwing and slight pillaging by the crowd, but given all the confusion, many closed their doors and boarded their windows, keeping them shut for days. The radio relayed out reports of the small-scale riots, recommending that tourists leave town. Many people outside Maumere refused to enter it at all.

In reality, order quickly returned. There was neither any threat to tourists nor substantial damage to the town. Tension between Muslims and Christians is not new here. Some continued calling for revenge, but others hoped for peaceful co-existence, saying that these clashes were far more numerous a decade ago.

have government-run **accommodations ❷** near the park offices. (Singles Rp20,000; doubles Rp25,000.)

RUTENG ☎0385

Although traversing Flores's circuitous interior can be arduous, persistent travelers will be rewarded with cool days in highland market towns such as Ruteng. The town is a logical stopover for travelers who prefer five hours of jarring bus travel to ten. The surrounding landscape is worth exploring, as are the nearby caves, spider web rice fields, and Manggarai villages. Hotels and locals can offer guidance and even arrange for a *caci* (traditional whip fighting) demonstration.

TRANSPORTATION AND PRACTICAL INFORMATION. Most of Ruteng is conveniently laid out in rectangles, and distances are short. The town center is up the hill around the soccer field, while most accommodations are on the far side of downtown. **Jl. A. Yani** passes the soccer field and continues to the bus depot at the eastern edge of town, which has service to **Bajawa** (5hr.; Rp10,000). Buses coming to **Labuhanbajo** (5hr.; Rp10,000) stop two blocks west of the soccer field near the market. **Merpati** is on a side street between the town and the airport. (☎211 47. Open daily 7:30am-1pm; W, Sa 4-5pm.) Hotels can arrange to have you picked up.

For exchanging currency and traveler's checks, **Bank Negara Indonesia,** on Jl. Kartini next to the Telkom office, has the best rates. (Open M-F 7:30am-12:30pm and 1:30-4:45pm, Sa 7:30-11:30am and 1:30-4:45pm.) The **police station** (☎211 10, **emergency** ☎110) is on Jl. Bhayangkara, opposite the soccer field, near the bus terminal. A **hospital** is 2km south of the town center; follow Jl. Bhayangkara uphill from the police station (**ambulance** ☎118). The **Telkom office,** Jl. Kartini 8-10, near the government offices, and the **post office,** Jl. Dewi Sartika 6, near the former king's house, are on the south side of town. (Telkom open 24hr. Post office open daily 8am-7pm). **Postal code:** 86511.

ACCOMMODATIONS AND FOOD. As the least visited of the major towns on the Trans-Flores Hwy., Ruteng offers few budget options, though it's still possible to find an affordable place to stay. **Hotel Rima ❶,** though a fair trek up to the Bajawa end of Jl. A. Yani, is an attractive building with a fine restaurant and immaculate rooms. The helpful owner arranges tours and will even drive you to the video store to rent a film to watch on the large TV. (☎221 96. Singles Rp15,000, with bath Rp25,000; doubles Rp25,000-35,000; triples Rp35,000-45,000. Breakfast included.) **Hotel Sinda ❷,** Jl. Sudarso 26 (☎211 97), has spacious rooms that open onto a lush garden. An English-speaking crowd swaps travel stories at night. The hotel's restaurant, *wartel*, and laundry service make it a convenient option. (Rooms with shared *mandi* Rp20,000, with private bath Rp30,000, with TV Rp40,000. Breakfast included.) **Wismat Agong II ❶,** on a side street northeast of the main soccer field, offers clean but basic rooms in a central location. (☎218 35. Singles Rp15,000; doubles Rp20,000.)

Dining options are rather skimpy, but the food is hearty. Smaller, independent eateries are most affordable. **Bambooden Restaurant ❷,** Jl. Motang Rua 30, serves an array of entrees starting around Rp6000, though meat dishes are more expensive. **Dunia Baru ❷,** Jl. Sudarso 10, carries the usual Chinese and Indonesian dishes (Rp6000-12,000). If you want to prepare your own meal, there is a **supermarket** on Jl. Bhayangkara near the outdoor market.

SIGHTS. Golo Curu is a godsend for the wannabe hiker in all of us—it's enough of a climb to give a good view, but doesn't take a great deal of time or preparation. Follow Jl. Motang Rua 1km north of the town center until the road crosses a bridge and immediately veers left. Follow the smaller road to the right. Travelers should stay on the paved pathway. The entire climb is a fascinating glimpse into Indonesian Catholicism; as the hill steepens, you'll see a series of Christian reliefs on the mountainside. As you ascend the hill, so does Jesus, bearing a cross, shrugging off Roman guards, and eventually rising to Heaven. That's not all—Golo Curu is crowned by a shrine to the Virgin Mary. On a clear day, you can also see the local volcano, Gunung Ranaka. Mornings and late afternoons, when the sun is reflecting off the spiderweb rice fields, are the best times to climb. The climb up is approximately 9km and takes 2hr; the descent will take you only 1½hr.

BAJAWA ☎0384

This market town of the Ngada people has weathered its transition into the modern world with grace. Although Bajawa's hotels are seldom empty, life goes on undisturbed, and nearby villages have maintained traditional homes.

TRANSPORTATION AND PRACTICAL INFORMATION. The road branching off the **Trans-Flores Hwy.** enters from the south, running into **Jl. Ahmed Yani (Jl. A. Yani),** which marks the town's southern border. **Watujaji Bus Terminal,** 3km south of town, is a Rp500 *bemo* ride away. Buses go to **Ende** (4hr.; Rp20,000) and **Ruteng** (4hr.; Rp10,000). **Bajawa Airport,** 25km north, is accessible by a Merpati shuttle (Rp5000) or chartered *bemo* (Rp20,000). **Merpati** has an office near the market. (☎210 50. Open daily 8am-1pm.)

The tiny town isn't tough to navigate. The tourist office, **Dinas Pariwisata,** is on the corner where Jl. Sukarno turns sharply to the right to become Jl. A. Yani. **Jl. Sukarno-Hatta** marks the east side of town; perpendicular to it, **Jl. Gajah Mada** runs through the center of town, past the **bemo stand.** The **market** is in the middle of town. For medical services, **Rumah Sakit Umum** (☎210 30) is on Jl. Diponegoro in the north of town. For an **ambulance,** call ☎118; in an **emergency,** call ☎110. Along Jl. Sukarno-Hatta are **Bank Rakyat Indonesia** (☎210 24; open M-F 7:30am-3:45pm, Sa 7:30-11:30am), the **Telkom office** (☎210 00; open 24hr.) with **Internet** access (Rp16,000 per hr.; available 7am-5pm), and the **post office** (open M-Th 7:30am-3pm, F 7:30-11:30am, Sa 7:30am-1pm). **Postal code:** 86415.

ACCOMMODATIONS AND FOOD. There are few good values among Bajawa's many hotels. Bargaining is worthwhile, especially in the low season. Breakfast is always included. Highland nights get cold, so make sure your hotel provides blankets. **Hotel Elizabeth ❹** is the nicest place around (but with a price to match), with bright, airy rooms and private baths. (☎212 23. Singles Rp50,000; doubles Rp60,000.) To get there, take a left from Jl. Sukarno-Hatta after the tourist office onto a gravel road; it's on the left. **Hotel Korina ❸,** on Jl. A. Yani at the southern end of town, has decent rooms with bath, blankets, and breakfast. (Book exchange. Singles Rp35,000; doubles Rp45,000.) One of the few budget places that still charges budget rates, **Hotel Dam ❶,** on a side street with the church, south of the market, has cozy rooms. (Rp12,000 per person with shared bath.)

The local specialty, **dog,** is only prepared for special occasions. Few tourists are interested in trying it, so it's left off the menu at the more touristy spots. Several *padang* joints cluster near the market. For more ambience, sample the extensive international menu at **Borobudur Garden ❶,** one block toward town from Jl. A. Yani. (Squid in chili sauce Rp15,000.) **Restaurant Carmellia ❷,** Jl. A. Yani 82, across from Hotel Korina, is acclaimed for its spring rolls and guacamole. (Entrees Rp6000-15,000.) **Restaurant Kasih Bahagia ❷,** on Jl. Gajah Mada east of the town center, serves typical Chinese favorites. (Entrees Rp5000-12,000.)

DAYTRIP FROM BAJAWA: NGADA HIGHLANDS AND WAWOMUDHA RED LAKES. Traditional **Ngada villages** dot the mountainous region around Bajawa, characterized by windowless thatched-roof houses, intricate carvings, and clusters of monoliths. Two distinctive structures can be seen in this area, evidence of the ancestor worship still practiced here: the *bhaga*, a small carved thatched-roof house, commemorates female ancestors, while the *ngadhu*, a wooden pole topped by a conical thatched roof, honors male ancestors. **Bena,** 13km south of Bajawa, is the most interesting village (Rp2500). Although it's possible to visit Bena and other villages on your own, you'll get the most for your money on a guided tour. In town, ask for the extremely knowledgeable Lukas Dua (☎864 12), who still lives in a traditional village himself. Don't miss a relaxing soak at the **superb hot springs** near **Soa,** 25km north of Bajawa. The volcanic eruption on January 7, 2001, resulted in the formation of numerous crater lakes in this area. Most have since evaporated, but four blood-red ponds known as the **Wawomudha Red Lakes** still remain. The intense color of the waters contrasts starkly with the surrounding white-gray rock and the green scenery of the hike up.

Occasional *bemo* run from Bajawa to Bena in the Ngada Highlands. Trips to the nearby volcano, crater lakes, and villages are easily arranged with a guide. Using public transport, a guide is usually Rp40,000 per person for groups of 4 or more. Private transport is required to go to Soa, bumping the price to Rp60,000 per person. Tours include lunch. It's also possible to get to Wawomudha Lakes without a guide: take a *bemo* to Ngornale (Rp1500). It's a 1hr. walk to the rim from there.

ENDE ☎038

One of Flores's more developed cities, Ende stretches along a coastline of black-sand beaches, surrounded by rolling hills and islands. As one of the main ports for Sumba and a stop on the way to the much-visited Keli Mutu, Ende is a haven for the services-starved with ATMs, bustling markets, and many of the comforts you thought you could do without.

ARRAK ATTACK Grapes may give rise to the wine of some gods, but in Nusa Tenggara, the gods like their drink a little bit stronger. Arrak, also called palm wine *(tuak putih)*, is made from the fruit of palm trees. "Wine," however, is a misnomer–arrak is distilled, giving its taste a bit more kick and making its drinker a bit more wrecked. (The joke goes: "I had two blankets last night–one of cotton, one of arrak.") The fruit, which looks like a long bean, is cut from the trees and sliced open to collect the juice. The sweet liquid is then placed in a container with the bark *(denu)* of the tree, which serves to ferment the juice and give it a bitter flavor. What results is a slightly spicy beverage with an alcohol content of about 5%. But it is rare to see the palm wine in this form–the process is usually continued to make arrak. The fermented juice is placed in a large clay pot over an open fire. The pot has a narrow mouth connected to a long bamboo tube. The vapors rise through the shoot and drip out on the other side, distilling the wine to create arrak. A fast, hot fire creates Arrak #3, which is approximately 20% alcohol, but the best arrak is kept over a slow fire for three to four days, creating Arrak #1, of 60% alcohol content. Arrak #1, an elixir for immediate inebriation, is also touted for helping to keep cholesterol low and to strengthen muscles. It is served on special occasions with honey, citrus, and egg yolk.

TRANSPORTATION

Flights: Merpati (☎213 55), on Jl. Nangka. Open M-Tu and Th-Sa 8am-1pm and 4-5pm, Su and holidays 10am-noon.

Buses: Ende has the best bus connections anywhere on Flores–at least 2 buses per day go to both ends of the Trans-Flores Hwy. **Ndao Bus Terminal** is on Jl. Mesjid, north of the city proper. Several buses per day go to: **Bajawa** (5hr.; Rp10,000); **Labuhanbajo** (10hr.; Rp27,000); **Ruteng** (8hr.; Rp20,000). **Wolowana Terminal,** east of town on Jl. A. Yani, has buses to: **Larantuka** (10hr.; Rp20,000); **Maumere** (6hr.; Rp20,000); **Moni** (2hr., Rp6000).

Ferries: PELNI, Jl. Katedral 2 (☎210 43), has info on the 2 PELNI ships that dock here, and for smaller, more frequent ferries to **Timor** (Rp31,000) and **Waingapu** (Rp22,000).

Local Transportation: *Bemo* buzz along the main streets (Rp1000). *Ojek* are quicker. Prices vary according to distance and bargaining skill.

Rentals: Hotel Ikhlas (See **Accommodations,** below) rents **cars** and **motorcycles.**

ORIENTATION AND PRACTICAL INFORMATION

Ende stretches across the neck of a peninsula, with **Ende Harbor** to the west and **Ipi Harbor** to the southeast. Most accommodations post a map on the wall. Otherwise, you can pick one up at the tourist office. In front of the Ende Harbor, the streets form rectangular blocks; **Jl. Sukarno, Jl. Kemakmuran, Jl. Pasar,** and **Jl. Yos Sudarso** run north-south, parallel to the harbor. The intersecting streets are small and mostly unnamed. Outside this grid, the city's blocks become larger and irregular. Leading directly out of the harbor is **Jl. Katedral,** which then becomes **Jl. A. Yani,** the southern border of the town. At the airport, this road turns into **Jl. Gatot** as it turns north toward the **bus station. Jl. Adi Sucipto** branches off Jl. Katedral to head to Ipi Harbor. **Jl. Sudirman** heads from its intersection with Jl. Yos Sudarso to become **Jl. Kelimutu.** Another main street, **Jl. Prof. WZ Johanes,** borders the south end of town and intersects with **Jl. Gatot Subroto.**

Tourist Office: Dinas Pariwisata, Jl. Sukarno 4 (☎213 03). Has maps and informative, colorful brochures about Ende and the surrounding sights. Free stickers.

Currency Exchange: Bank Rakyat Indonesia, Jl. Yos Sudarso 27 (☎216 15), in Dwi Putra Hotel. Exchanges currency and traveler's checks. Open M-F 8am-3pm. **BNI,** on Jl. Gatot Subroto, 200m east of the airport rotary, has a **24hr. ATM** (Cirrus/MC/PLUS/V).

Emergency: Police: ☎110. **Ambulance:** ☎118.

Police: ☎210 95. On Jl. Polisi, a few blocks up Jl. Pahlawan, on the right.

Pharmacy: Sumber Sehat, Jl. Sudirman 6 (☎216 15). Open daily 8am-1am.

Hospital: Rumah Sakit Umum (☎210 31), far from the town center on Jl. Prof. WZ Johanes.

Telephones: 24hr. Telkom office, Jl. Kelimutu 5.

Post Offices: GPO, Jl. Basuki Rahmat 15 (☎212 03), northeast of town, near the Pahjawan-El Tari intersection. (Jl. Basuki Rahmat is the continuation of Jl. El Tari.) *Poste Restante.* Open **24hr. Branch** is at Jl. Yos Sudarso 4, opposite Dwi Putra Hotel. Open M-Th 7:30am-3pm, F 7:30-11am, Sa 7:30am-1pm. **Postal code:** 86318.

INDONESIA

ACCOMMODATIONS

Ende's accommodations are cheaper and more tourist-friendly than most other places in Flores. The nicest places are east of the town center.

Dwi Putra, Jl. Yos Sudarso, next door to Bank Rakyat Indonesia. Lounge with cable TV and spacious rooms. The main attraction is the not-to-be-missed aerobics class. Laundry service and complimentary breakfast. Singles Rp40,000; doubles Rp45,000. ❸

Hotel Ikhlas (☎216 95), on Jl. A. Yani, 200m from the traffic rotary to the airport. Cheap rooms, lounge (with CNN and MTV), restaurant, and HCD phone. Basic singles Rp10,000, with bath Rp15,000-20,000; doubles Rp15,000/Rp20,000-25,000. ❶

Nurjaya Hotel, Jl. A. Yani 20 (☎212 52), closer to town center. Clean, simply furnished rooms with shared bath. Complimentary breakfast with excellent ginger coffee. Singles Rp15,000; doubles Rp25,000. ❶

FOOD

The capital's proximity to the ocean translates into good seafood. Downtown abounds with Indonesian restaurants, where window displays of delicious dishes will torture the indecisive. **Istana Bambu ❸,** Jl. Pasar 39, downtown, offers Chinese and Indonesian food. (☎214 80. Shrimp in butter sauce Rp15,000.) A rival restaurant, the other **Istana Bambu ❷,** Jl. Kemakmuran 30 (☎219 21), one block east, tempts customers with fresh sweet-and-sour squid (Rp12,500) and baked goods.

MONI

The village of Moni offers fabulous views, cool weather, hot springs, and waterfalls. Its close proximity to the base of Keli Mutu's tricolored crater lakes make this town a convenient respite en route to the nearby peaks.

Moni is 50km from Ende and 100km from Maumere. Buses run regularly from both (from Ende: 2hr., Rp6000; from Maumere: 4hr.; Rp10,000). Queasy travelers should note that the road to both cities winds along the narrow sides of jagged ravines and over antiquated bridges. The road toward **Keli Mutu** is a 15min. walk uphill on the Ende side of town. There's a **wartel** at Restaurant Kelimutu, 100m from the **police office** near the turn-off to Keli Mutu.

Arwanti Bungalows ❶, near the town center, is the best bet for groups (Rp60,000), which have two separate rooms and a sitting area. Accommodations that were once very cheap now lean toward being overpriced and dirty. Be sure to bargain—don't pay more than Rp10,000 per person or Rp20,000 with private *mandi*, including breakfast. The staff at **Wisma Kelimutu Moni ❶** is often praised for its helpfulness and honesty. **Nusa Bunga ❶,** near the east end of town, and **Daniel ❶** (in the center of the village) are both adequate for a night's sleep. (All three have singles for Rp10,000 and doubles for Rp20,000.) There are some nicer options farther away, with quiet settings, impressive vistas, and bungalow-style housing. One of the most pleasant is **Watugana Bungalows ❸,** not far uphill from the market. (Singles Rp30,000; doubles Rp40,000.) The **Arwanti Restaurant ❷,** in the Arwanti Bungalows, serves real vermicelli. People usually go to **Restaurant Kelimutu ❷,** near the turn-off to Keli Mutu, to enjoy the view rather than the food, but it's a decent spot for a simple meal. Mary, of **Mary's ❷,** can cook up a traditional dinner banquet for Rp10,000 per person if you ask her by 2pm. Bring your own drinks, as beverages can be limited and pricey (Rp15,000).

While you're here, enjoy the nightly **traditional dance performance** at the *rumah adat,* 20m off the main road, opposite the market. The bamboo dance—traditionally performed only every few years to bless children—makes it almost worth the Rp15,000 admission, though the performance is short. (Show daily at 8pm.)

DAYTRIPS FROM MONI

KELI MUTU. Moni's tourist trappings are the result of the village's proximity to Flores's grandest natural wonder—the tricolored crater lakes. The water changes color over time, owing to a geological process not fully understood. As of July 2002, the three lakes were turquoise, black, and eggplant. Previously, the middle lake was milky white; for a long time before that the lakes were maroon, blue, and white. Locals consider the pools to be the resting place of spirits, where color indicates morality; the three pools are akin to Heaven, Hell, and Purgatory. *(A truck up Keli Mutu (Rp15,000) leaves daily at 4am and stops at the park office (entrance fee Rp1000). The ride down (Rp15,000) leaves at 7am. To avoid the crowds on the truck, charter a* bemo *(Rp50,000) or walk the 13km from Moni. A shortcut* (jalan potong) *begins opposite Rumah Makan Sarty on the road to Ende, 500m from the market, and ends near the park office—it's only recommended for the descent, however, as the way up can be steep and slippery. It's possible to ascend Keli Mutu later in the day, but those who wait to climb will miss the sunrise and risk having the views obscured by a cloud cover. By road, the ascent takes 3-4hr., while the shortcut takes 2hr.)*

WEAVING VILLAGES. Central Flores is renowned for its gorgeous *ikat* weaving. Sarongs, shawls, and blankets in rich rust and orange tones are woven with elaborate patterns featuring mountains, spiders, gongs, flowers, and other motifs. The entire process, from the dyeing of the cotton to the stitching of the cloth, is done by hand. Although it's easy to find affordable, decent cloth in Moni and Ende, the villages south of **Wolowaru,** 12km east of Moni on the Maumere road, display the best work. **Jopu,** the first village, lies 5km south of Wolowaru, followed by **Wolonjita** 6km farther south. At the end of the road, a full 17km from Wolowaru, is **Nggela,** on a promontory overlooking the Savu Sea. Nggela's weaving is the best in the area; the finest pieces can sell for millions of rupiah. At any of the villages, simply ask in any house and usually a few sarongs will be brought out for display. The asking price for a high-quality sarong is usually Rp100,000, though it's often possible to end up paying half that or less. In Moni, there is a large market on Saturdays and Mondays where weavers sell their work; this is the best bet for finding good quality at the best price. Keep in mind though that the aim of haggling is to reach an acceptable price for both parties—one that recognizes the work that goes into the *ikat* cloth. *(Buses run directly from Moni to Nggela a few times every morning (Rp1500).*

Alternatively, take a bus to Wolowaru (or get off a Maumere-bound bus there; Rp4000) and walk south to Nggela. A bemo usually heads to Wolowaru in the afternoon (Rp1000). From Wolowaru, catch a bus back to Moni.)

MAUMERE ☎0382

Hit hard by the 1992 earthquake and a resulting tsunami that rocked East Flores, Maumere is slowly rebuilding itself. There's not much to occupy tourists here, and the town also sees its fair share of unrest (see **Holy Fear,** right)—most travelers stay only to catch a flight out, head west to Keli Mutu, or venture east to Larantuka, a gateway to Timor and the islands off the east coast. Those who linger stay at one of several beachside resorts east of the city and wander through the markets and surrounding villages.

TRANSPORTATION. The **airport** is 3km east of the town center. *Bemo* and taxis ask Rp10,000 for the trip, but ignore them and walk 500m to the highway, where passing *bemo* can be hailed (Rp1000). **Merpati,** Jl. Don Tomas da Silva 19, is in the center of town. (☎213 42. Open daily 8am-8pm.) Frequent **buses** heading east to **Larantuka** (4hr.; Rp10,000) leave from **Terminal Waioti,** several kilometers east of town, but you can catch them on their way out of the city. **Terminal Madawat,** a few kilometers southwest of town, is the departure point for transport headed to western destinations, including **Ende** (6hr.; Rp20,000) and **Moni** (use an Ende-bound bus, as direct *bemo* are infrequent; 4hr.; Rp10,000). The **PELNI office** (☎210 13), on Jl. Slamet Riyadi, across the west bridge at the end of town, handles ship reservations for the KM *Awu* and can point you in the right direction for fast-ferry reservations to **Bali** (14hr.; M; Rp275,000) and **Surabaya** (20hr.; M; Rp325,000).

INDONESIA

ORIENTATION AND PRACTICAL INFORMATION. Most of the town is concentrated in a wedge between the main east-west road (the **Trans-Flores Hwy.**) and the water. The downtown area centers around the **Old Market** on **Jl. A. Yani** in the west part of town. The market's west edge is formed by **Jl. Raja Centris,** which is home to most of the restaurants in Maumere. The **New Market,** on Jl. Anylik, is on the western border of the city. The **Sikka Regency tourist information office,** in the western reaches of town, has maps of Maumere. Turn left on Jl. Gajah Mada, follow Jl. A. Yani as it turns left across the river, and take the second right onto Jl. Wairklau at the sign; it's 250m up. (☎216 52. Open M-Th 7am-2pm, F 7-11am, Sa 7am-12:30pm.) The best place to change money and traveler's checks is **BNI,** Jl. Sukarno-Hatta 4, about a block south of the highway. (Open M-F 8am-3pm.) The **24hr. ATM** accepts Cirrus/MC/PLUS/V. The **police** (☎211 10, **emergency** ☎110) are at the west end of Jl. A. Yani. The new **hospital,** Rumah Sakit Umum Daerah (☎216 17, ambulance ☎118), is on Jl. Wairklau, past the tourist information office. The **pharmacy** is on Jl. Moa Toda near the **Harapan Jaya Artshop,** which has a collection of weavings and Indonesian art (artshop open M-Sa 7:15am-8pm, Su 8am-noon and 4-8pm). The **24hr. Telkom office** with **HCD** phone is opposite the police station. The **post office** is one block east of Jl. Sukarno-Hatta on the corner of the main road. *Poste Restante.* (Open M-F 8am-5pm, Sa 8am-4pm.) **Postal code:** 86100.

ACCOMMODATIONS AND FOOD. Despite a relative lack of tourists, Maumere has several decent budget spots that serve complimentary breakfasts. **Gardena Hotel ❶,** one block north of the soccer field on Jl. Patirangga, has very clean and inexpensive rooms. (Singles with bath and fan Rp15,000, with A/C Rp40,000; doubles Rp25,000-50,000.) The hotel can arrange an English-speaking guide. Call ahead for reservations. **Wini Rai Hotel ❷,** Jl. Gagah Mada 50, down the street from Terminal Madawat, 2km into the town center, is clean and welcoming with a garden and great location. (☎213 88. Singles with fan Rp25,000, with A/C Rp45,000; doubles Rp55,000-70,000.) Long-popular **Senja Wair Bubuk ❶**, Jl. Komodor Yos Sudarso 81, on the waterfront street in the east part of the town center, is a friendly place. (☎214 98. Singles Rp12,000-22,000, with A/C Rp27,500; doubles Rp17,800-30,500/Rp35,200.) Dining options are limited, though **Jl. Raja Centris** has a couple of decent places, the Chinese **Restaurant Sarinah ❷** being the best. The tourist favorite is the **Golden Fish Restaurant ❺**, on Jl. Hasanuddin as you walk toward the pier. It has fresh seafood, but at the highest prices in town (lobster Rp100,000).

In **Wairterang,** only 27km east of Maumere, travelers will find some of the best values in **beach resorts** in Indonesia. **Ankermi Bungalows ❷** sits on a secluded bay shared only with local fishermen. Guests can enjoy activities ranging from climbing the island volcano to snorkeling. Jump in one of the canoes (free at either resort) at night and observe the mesmerizing phosphorescent glow in the water. Their PADI-certified diving facility also offers **dive trips** (US$30 per dive). After working up an appetite in the sun, head to the restaurant to satisfy your cravings. The food is exceptional—try the Ankermi cake for Rp10,000. The bungalows at Ankermi are immaculate with spotless outdoor *mandi*. Electricity is only on from 6pm to 6am. (Singles Rp30,000; doubles Rp35,000; quad bungalows Rp45,000.) To get to Wairterang, take any *bemo* or bus east toward Lurantuka and ask for Ankermi (Rp2000).

NEAR MAUMERE: LARANTUKA AND BEYOND

Larantuka, a seaport 4hr. east of Maumere, is the last stop on the Trans-Flores Hwy. (almost 700km from its beginning in Labuhanbajo). The town's setting is its most attractive feature—it runs along the coast and up the slopes of volcanic **Mount Ile Mandiri.** Although the surrounding area has a few sweet spots of sand and sleepy villages, there's little of note in the town itself. Most people visit here on their way to the islands off Flores's east coast. The **Solor** and **Alor Archipelagos** offer scenic seclusion and the chance to join a whale-hunting expedition in Lamalera (on the island of **Lembata**), where hunters still use hand-thrown harpoons. Even if they don't catch a whale, the hunters will get in the water and act out the entire process. (Rp20,000-50,000 per person, depending on group and boat size.) Daily **boats** head from Larantuka to **Lewoleba** (1pm, Rp12,000), the largest city on Lembata (from where infrequent boats go to Lamalera). Less frequent boats voyage to other islands in the archipelagos and to **Kupang,** Timor. Several **buses** per day head west to **Maumere** (4hr.; Rp10,000), and a few continue farther west to **Ende** (Rp20,000). The **bus terminal** is several kilometers southwest of Larantuka, though most buses drive through town in hopes of picking up extra passengers.

Everything you need is on the waterfront boulevard or the parallel street a block uphill. Money can be changed (at horrible rates) at **BNI** (open M-F 7:30am-1:30pm) or at the main **Bank Rakyat Indonesia** (open M-F 7:30am-2:30pm, Sa 7:30-11:30am), around the corner from its branch on the main road. The **PELNI office** is on the main road in the western part of town. (Open daily 7:30am-5pm.) A **hospital** is off the main road 2km west of the town (**emergency** ☎110, ambulance ☎118).

There are only a handful of places to stay in the area. **Hotel Rulies ❷,** on the main street a bit west of what might be called downtown Lewoleba, is the most popular spot with backpackers. (☎0383 211 98. Singles with shared *mandi* Rp25,000; doubles Rp40,000.) **Hotel Tresna ❷,** next door, caters more to locals. (☎0383 210 72. Singles Rp20,000, with *mandi* Rp25,000; doubles Rp25,000-30,000.) Dining options are similarly limited. A few *rumah makan* cluster in the center of town by the monument, but **Restaurant Nirwana's ❷** Chinese food, east on the waterfront, is a better bet. (Entrees Rp7000-18,000.)

SULAWESI

Indonesia's third-largest island, Sulawesi has a population of 11 million, including the Muslim Makarese and Bugis in the south, the Minahasans in the north, and the animist-Christian Torajans in the central-south region. While major tourist spots are accessible by plane and are traveler-friendly, many of the twisty roads are damaged and the rickety smoke-filled vehicles are overcrowded. Nonetheless, travelers tend to stay longer than intended, seeing more than any guidebook could cover. For those who are up to the challenge of traveling in Sulawesi, the rewards of exquisite natural beauty and unforgettable cultural exchanges are plentiful.

SOUTH SULAWESI (SULAWESI SELATAN)

Convoluted Sulawesi seems to have as much coastline as land. Nowhere is its wealth of beachfront life as rich or textured as in the ports of South Sulawesi. North of Makassar, the peninsula becomes increasingly lush, and mountains rise dramatically from coastal plains. Farther north, Tana Toraja gives way to the labyrinthine topography of mountain valleys, offering even more natural beauty.

MAKASSAR (UJUNG PANDANG) ☎0411

Centuries after the Gowa Kingdom established Makassar as a trading *entrepot*, the site retains all the characteristics of a lively port city. Cluttered markets clatter with buyers and sellers, and waterfront bars help sailors drown their sorrows. Equally fascinating is the ethnic diversity resulting from ages of fighting over the largest city in the spice islands. Violent anti-Chinese riots in 1998 and continued tensions reveal that the racial mix is not necessarily a stable one.

TRANSPORTATION

Flights: Hasanuddin Airport, 23km from downtown. Walk 500m to the "Halte bus" hut or to the main road and flag down a *bemo* (Rp2000) to Makassar Mall. Fixed-rate taxis are available from in front of the terminal building (Rp40,000 to most hotels). From Makassar, you can fly just about anywhere within Indonesia; **Silk Air** runs 3 flights a week to **Singapore.** The best place to make ticket reservations is **Limbunan Travel Service,** 40-42 Jl. Gunung Bawakaraeng (☎315 010). Prices often much cheaper than official airline rates. Open M-Sa 8am-5pm. **Merpati,** Jl. Gunung Bawakaraeng 109 (☎442 471). **Garuda,** Jl. A.P. Pettarani 18B-C (☎423 737). **Bouraq,** Jl. Veteran 1 (☎453 139). **Mandala,** Latanet Plaza and on Jl. Cokroaminoto (info ☎323 592, reservations ☎314 880). Ask offices for exact departure times.

Buses: Panaikan Station, a 20min. drive out of town on the airport road. Serves points north and east. Take a *bemo* from Makassar Mall. The **Trans-Sulawesi Highway (Transul)** connects Makassar in the south to Manado at the northernmost tip of the island. **Public buses** to: **Mamasa** (12hr.; Rp45,000); **Parepare** (3hr.; Rp15,000); **Rantepao** (8hr.; Rp30,000-60,000); **Sengkang** (6hr.; Rp20,000-25,000).

Boats: PELNI office, Jl. Sudirman 38 (☎331 401). Buy tickets there or from a travel agent. Fares are cheaper than air tickets, but travel time is in the scale of days. Most

> **TRANS-SULAWESI TRAVEL WARNING** Sectarian violence and frequent shoot-outs mean that parts of the Trans-Sulawesi HIghway are not considered safe for non-essential travel. Tourists should avoid traveling by land across Central Sulawesi (especially the areas around Poso). Check with your embassy for the latest information and advice.

boats run on 2-week loops. Ferries to: **Bima; Denpasar; Jakarta; Kupang; Labuhanbajo; Manado; Surabaya.** Check PELNI office for times and prices. For current schedules and fares as well as online ticket reservations in English, see www.pelni.co.id.

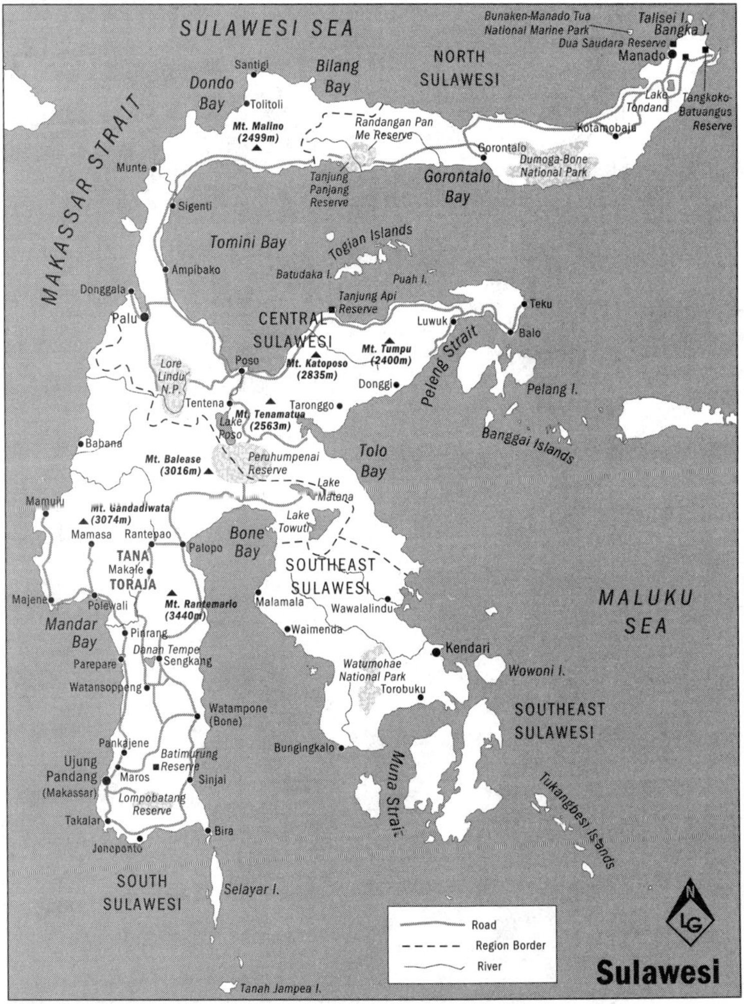

ORIENTATION AND PRACTICAL INFORMATION

Although the clamor of Makassar seems to reach as far as the **airport** some 23km to the east, the heart of the city is relatively compact and easy to navigate. **Jl. A. Yani,** the main thoroughfare, starts at the waterfront in the western edge of town. **Jl. Martadinata** runs to the north, **Jl. Ujung Pandang** (which passes **Fort Rotterdam** and morphs into **Jl. Pasar Ikan, Jl. Penghibur,** and **Jl. Rajawali**) to the south. A block inland, a gentle right turn off Jl. A. Yani leads to **Jl. Slamet Riyadi,** which becomes **Jl. Hasanuddin** and then **Jl. Cendrawasih** as it heads south out of town. Two blocks farther east, Jl. A. Yani passes the **Lampangan Karebosi** football field in the city center, changes to **Jl. Bulusarung,** and then intersects **Jl. Cokroaminoto,** a major boulevard and home

to **Makassar Mall** and the central **bemo station.** Jl. Bulusarung continues eastward to meet northbound **Jl. Andalas,** which heads to **Paotere Harbor** via **Jl. Yos Sudarso.**

Tourist Office: Government Tourist Office (☎443 355), off Jl. Sudirman by the Mandala Monument. Open M-Th 8am-3pm, F 8am-noon, Sa 8am-1pm. Staff at Legend Hostel and other hotels are more helpful.

Tours: Sena Tours, Jl. Jampea 1A (☎323 906), on the same lane as Legend Hostel.

Immigration Office: Jl. Tantura Pelajar 2 (☎315 731), in the northern part of town between Jl. Nusantara and Jl. Sulawesi near the harbor. Open M-Th 7am-2pm, F 7am-11pm, Sa 7am-1pm.

Currency Exchange: Over a dozen **banks,** several with **24hr. ATMs,** line Jl. A. Yani. Most open M-F 8am-2pm. **BNI,** Jl. Sudirman 1, at the Jl. A. Yani intersection at the top of Lampangan Karebosi, **changes cash** and traveler's checks. Open M-Th 8am-4pm, F 7:30am-4pm.

Markets: Renowned primarily for its jewelry, **Jl. Somba Opu** runs parallel to the waterfront a bit south of the fort. **Sutera Alam,** Jl. Onta Lama 47, is a silk-weaving center on a side street running east off Jl. Dr. Ratulangi.

Emergency: Police: ☎110. **Fire:** ☎113. **Ambulance:** ☎118.

Police: Jl. A. Yani 9 (☎319 277), opposite Jl. Balaikota.

Pharmacies: Apotik Kimia Farma are all over town, including **24hr. branches** at Jl. Hasanuddin 36 (☎324 442), south of Galael supermarket, and Jl. A. Yani 17-19 (☎316 722).

Medical Services: Rumah Sakit Akademis Jaury (☎317 343), on Jl. Akademis off Jl. Bulusarung. **24hr. emergency care.**

Telephones: Wartel are at Jl. Bali 71, Jl. Kajaolaliddo 2G-4, Jl. Balaikota 2, Jl. Veteran 28, and on Jl. Sulawesi and Jl. Nusantara. **HCD** phones in big hotels; try Hotel Makassar Golden.

Internet Access: Warnet Utama, Jl. A. Yani 17. Best price. Rp3600 per hr. **Surf@cybercafe,** Jl. A. Yani 2, 3rd fl., above Pizza Ria Kafe. Drinks, snacks, lightning-quick connections (Rp6000 per hr.). Open M-Th, Su 8am-11pm and F-Sa 8am-midnight.

Post Office: Jl. Slamet Riyadi 10 (☎323 180), 1 block south of Jl. A. Yani. *Poste Restante*. Open M-Sa 8am-8pm, Su 9am-4pm. **Postal code:** 90111.

ACCOMMODATIONS

Budget accommodations are not easy to find. This scarcity has resulted in the virtual monopolization of the backpacker trade by the renowned "Legend."

Legend Hostel, Jl. Jampea 5G (☎328 203), next to Yasmin Hotel, on a small side street north of Jl. A. Yani. Travel agency, cafe, sitting room, bottomless teacups, and cheap rooms. Dorms Rp15,000; singles Rp29,000-36,000; doubles Rp35,000-39,000. ❶

Richardson's Homestay, Jl. Mochtar Lufti 21 (☎320 348), 2 blocks east of Jl. Penghibur near Bundt's Orchid Garden. Comfortable, clean rooms arranged around central dining area. Shared *mandi*. Doubles with fan Rp40,000, with A/C Rp50,000. ❸

Hotel Makassar Golden, Jl. Pasar Ikan 52 (☎333 000; fax 320 951; mghupg@indosat.net.id). Right on the bay, a few minutes from the fort and Jl. A. Yani. Peaceful luxury hotel; rooms have superb views out to sea and all the perks: A/C, satellite TV, attached Western baths with hot showers. Doubles Rp240,000-390,000. ❺

Losari Beach Hotel, Jl. Penghibur 10 (☎326 002; fax 313 978). Centrally located mid-range hotel with views of the bay. All rooms come with A/C, satellite TV, hot showers, and phones. Doubles Rp300,000-450,000. ❺

FOOD

Makassar is a seafood lover's heaven. **Food carts** ❶ and seafood **warung** ❶ set up early every evening along Jl. Penghibur to make up **Pantai Losari,** named after its beachside locale. Delicious fish, crab, and squid dishes are served until well into the night, and a full meal will normally cost less than Rp10,000. If you're in the mood for a drink, grab a beer at one of Jl. Penghibur's cafes.

Istana Laut, Jl. Datumuseng 1, around the corner from Richardson's Homestay and Bundt's Orchid Garden. *The* place for tasty, fresh seafood. Fish from Rp15,000. Fried prawns Rp16,000. Crab in butter sauce Rp40,000-60,000. Open daily 9am-11pm. ❹

New Shogun Japanese Restaurant, Jl. Penghibur 2. Near the fort, on the left as you walk down Jl. Penghibur with the sea on the right. Real soy sauce, real wasabi, and real Japanese pop music. Sublime sashimi (Rp78,500) and sushi (Rp76,500) are obvious choices, but if you're thinking in yen, try the imported *shabu-shabu* (Rp79,500) too. Open daily 11:30am-3pm and 6-11pm. ❺

Warung Pak Toba, on Jl. Penghibur, right next to the fort. A series of tarpaulin-covered stalls serving outstanding seafood at unbeatable prices. Often packed. Squid, crab, fish, and chicken—all around Rp8000. Open daily 3pm-4am. ❷

Pizza Ria Kafe, Jl. A. Yani 2, on the right, just before Lampangan Karebosi. Winner of the All-Indonesia Pizza Hut Look-Alike Competition, 2002. A/C American-food wonderland. Pizzas Rp20,000-30,000. Pasta and salad bar. Call ☎336 336 for delivery. Branches at Jl. G. Latimojong 152, on the corner with Jl. Saddang, and at Jl. Boulevard Rako Ruby 12. Open daily 6:30am-11pm. ❹

Rumah Makan Maxim II, Jl. Sulawesi 78. Large A/C dining room with a TV humming to itself quietly in the corner. Chinese-style seafood. Prawns Rp20,000-35,000. Crab Rp22,500-40,000. Beef, frog, fish, and chicken also available. Open daily 10am-2:30pm and 6-11pm. ❹

SIGHTS AND NIGHTLIFE

Once called Fort Jumpandang (from which Ujung Pandang derives its name), the structure near the waterfront on Jl. Penghibur was renamed **Fort Rotterdam** after the Dutch wrested control of the area in 1669. There has been a fortification on this site since at least 1545, but most of what remains today is Dutch-built. It now houses government offices and the **La Galigo Museum.** One wing displays a collection of ethnographic exhibits from around Indonesia; a second features artifacts from various kingdoms of Southern Sulawesi. (Fort open daily 7am-6pm. Museum open Tu-Su 8am-1pm. Admission by donation.) Clustered north of the fort are several Chinese temples, including the **Temple of the Heavenly Queen,** whose front altar was reduced to rubble during anti-Chinese riots. The shrine, dedicated to the sailor-protecting goddess Tian Hou Gong, is located at the corner of Jl. Sulawesi and Jl. Serui, one block north of Jl. A. Yani. Farther up Jl. Sulawesi at Jl. Bali is the **Temple of the Dragon Apparition,** whose central altar celebrates Xian Mu, the mother of immortals. Farther north is the Javanese-style **Tomb of Diponegoro,** inside a rustic cemetery near the intersection of Jl. Diponegoro and Jl. Akademis. One of Indonesia's favorite national heroes (just count the roads named after him), Diponegoro was a beloved prince of Jogjakarta who led pro-independence forces against the Dutch during the Java War of 1825-30. For his troubles, he was exiled to Celebes (modern-day Sulawesi), where he lived in imprisonment until his death in Makassar. South of the fort off Jl. Penghibur is **Bundt's Orchid Garden (Taman Anggrek),** Jl. Mochtar Lufti 15, a pleasantly shaded yard with a stunning seashell shop. After repeating that three times, ask multilingual Clara to show you the "Golden Cowrie" and "Glory of the Sea." (☎322 572. Open daily dawn to dusk.)

Shark Café ❸, Jl. Penghibur 33, on the left as you walk down the street from the fort with the sea on your right. Cold beers and loud music make this a good spot to sit and enjoy some Bintang (large Rp15,000) at an outdoor table—as long as you don't mind a healthy dose of traffic fumes with your beer. (Open daily 6pm-midnight.) **Kareba Music Café ❸,** Jl. Penghibur 12, next door to the Losari Beach Hotel, has a pleasant beer-garden atmosphere with (mostly atrocious) live music nightly. It's a popular foreigners' hangout. (Large beer Rp16,000. Open daily 4pm-1am.)

DAYTRIPS FROM MAKASSAR

MAKASSAR BAY. Home to a collection of white-sand islands and some of the finest coral reefs in the region, Makassar Bay is ideal for aquatic exploration. Unfortunately, careless snorkeling and explosives used in dynamite fishing have nearly destroyed reefs close to shore; decent dives sites are at least 10km out. **Samalona** is the jewel of the bay, with budget bamboo huts on the beach, while the secluded island of **Kodingareng Keke** provides a quiet retreat. The ocean floor near **Kapoposang** drops dramatically and teems with sea life. In Makassar, sporting goods stores on Jl. Somba Opu sell and rent snorkeling gear. **Makassar Diving Center,** Jl. Ujung Pandang 4, 50m north of the fort, rents masks, snorkels, and fins and offers 4hr. snorkeling and island sightseeing trips (US$25), 1-day diving trips (US$50-100), or multi-day package tours (US$25-200). *(Charter boats (up to 6 people; Rp100,000 each) leave from the Tumba Kayu Bangkoa Pier, south of the intersection of Jl. Pattimura and Jl. Penghibur, for the islands of Barang Caddi (1hr.), Barang Lompo (1hr.), and Samalona (30min.). Boats to Kodingareng Keke (1hr.) and Bone Tambung (1½hr.) cost Rp200,000.)*

INDONESIA

MAROS CAVES. With over 55 caverns, the Maros Caves are a wonderland of bizarre rock formations, running streams, and prehistoric wall paintings. The most visited site is the "Prehistoric Park" at **Leang-Leang,** where two caves are decorated with paintings of babirusa (wild pig) believed to be 5000 years old. *(Take a bemo (Rp2000) or DAMRI bus (Rp3500) directly to Maros (1½hr.) and ask to be let off at the caves (gua). Bring a flashlight. Open daily 8am-6pm. Rp2500.)*

BANTIMURUNG WATERFALL. Bantimurung Falls, 1½hr. northeast of Makassar, is a park reserve surrounded by impressive cliffs that are worth the trip in themselves. The waterfalls are nothing special by Indonesian standards, but the butterfly-filled walk up the stairs to the left is delightful. A 15min. promenade up the riverbed leads to **Store Cave,** harboring a waterfall, a secluded pool, and smaller caves within. Before the main waterfall, there's a quieter walk up to **Gua Mimpi (Dream Cave),** a pitch-dark cave filled with stalactites and stalagmites and weirdly shaped rock formations. You'll have a rotten time without a flashlight. Guide hire is around Rp10,000 per person. *(Take a bemo (Rp2000) or DAMRI bus (Rp3500) from Ujung Pandang's Makassar Mall to Maros (1½hr.), then jump on a bemo (Rp1500) to Bantimurung.)*

GOWA. Along the Jeneberang River, 11km south of Ujung Padang, lie the scattered remains of the once great kingdom of Gowa, including the ruins of the fortress **Somba Opu,** the strongest of the forts that once protected Makassar. **Old Gowa,** where ancient mosques, royal tombs, and legendary coronation stones remain standing, is farther east. The sacred **Tomb of Syech Yusuf** stands in the northwest section. A religious-scholar-turned-resistance-fighter, Syech Yusuf (1626-94) purportedly brought Islam to Sri Lanka and South Africa during his Dutch-imposed exile. A road south of the tomb runs southeast to **Katangka Mosque,** Sulawesi's oldest mosque, supposedly built in 1605, shortly after Islam became Gowa's official religion. Walk 300m down the road from the mosque, make a right, and then make another to reach Gowa's kings' **Batu Pelantikan** (Coronation Stone). Beside it is the **Tomb of Hasanuddin,** the celebrated 12th king of Gowa, who waged war against the Dutch before his final defeat in 1660. *(Take a* bemo *from Makassar Mall and get off at Tangul Patompo (Rp1000). From there, boats (Rp1000) cross the river.)*

PAREPARE ☎0421

Situated between Makassar and Tana Toraja, Parepare is a major commercial port with little of the natural beauty you'll find elsewhere in Sulawesi. It's pleasant enough, with great views out to sea from the hillsides that loom above the city center, but there is little to see, and, for most tourists, this is just a transit point en route to Tana Toraja, Sengkang, Kalimantan, and Makassar.

Parepare is a major transit hub; buses run from here to most places in South Sulawesi. To: **Rantepao** (5-6hr.; several direct buses per day and frequent indirect minibuses; Rp20,000); **Sengkang** (2hr.; frequent; Rp10,000-15000); **Ujung Pandang** (3hr.; frequent; Rp15,000-20,000). Frequent buses also leave for **Polewali** (3hr.; Rp15,000), with connections to **Mamasa** (7hr.; Rp25,000). For **ferries,** contact the **PELNI Office,** Jl. Andi Cammi 96. (☎210 17. Open daily 3-11am and 1-2pm.) Boats run to many destinations, including **Balik Papan** (Rp80,000) and **Surabaya** (Rp181,000). **Bemo** run from the terminal in the town center along Jl. Pinggir Laut to points north, and down Jl. A. Yani to the bus station (Rp1000).

INDONESIA

Parepare's streets run north-south and parallel to the western waterfront. In the north, **Jl. Pinggir Laut** runs parallel to the water, with **Jl. Baso Dg. Patompo/Jl. Hasanuddin** one block inland. **Jl. Bau Massepe,** one block farther inland, is the major thoroughfare, where you'll find most of the hotels and **banks,** the **post office,** and the **Telkom office. BNI,** Jl. Veteran 41, north of the football field, changes cash and traveler's checks. (Open M-Sa 8am-3pm. **24hr. ATM.**) The **Fatima Hospital,** Jl. Ilham 3 (☎218 47), is one block up from the northeast corner of the football field between Jl. Bau Massepe and Jl. Veteran. The **Telkom office,** Jl. Bau Massepe 262, is opposite Hotel Gemini. (Open M-F 8am-5pm.) **Wartel** are at Jl. Dg. Parani 25 and Jl. Bau Massepe 306. The **post office,** Jl. Karang Burane 1, is at the intersection with Jl. Bau Massepe. (*Poste Restante.* Open M-Th 7:30am-4pm, F 7:30-11:30am, Sa 7:30am-3pm.) **Postal code:** 91100.

There are a few decent budget options in Parepare, but unless you've missed the last bus out of town, you'd do better moving on. **Hotel Pare Wisata ❹,** on Jl. Sulawesi, is probably your best bet for a good night's sleep. All rooms have A/C, showers, and Western toilets. (☎260 88; fax 277 58. Singles Rp61,500; doubles Rp75,500.) **Hotel Gandaria ❷,** Jl. Samparaja 4, is up the hill past the hospital. (☎229 71. Basic rooms with fan and *mandi* Rp15,000, with shower and Western bath Rp40,000-50,000, with A/C and color TV Rp60,000.) Another branch at Jl. Bau Massepe 395 (☎210 93) has similar rates. **Hotel Gemini ❸,** Jl. Bau Massepe 451 (☎217 54), has bare-bones rooms with twin beds, attached Western-style *mandi,* and plastic chairs for Rp25,000.

Parepare's best food is served at the various seafood **warung ❶** along the waterfront. **Sejathera ❷,** on Jl. Bau Massepe near Hotel Gemini, is a good place to stock up on water and snacks for the road. (Open daily 8am-10pm.) **Rumah Makan Padang Raya ❶,** Jl. Bau Massepe 389, just south of Hotel Gandaria, serves decent *padang*-style food. (Most dishes Rp5000-6000.)

NEAR PAREPARE: SENGKANG

A few hours from Parepare by bus or a 5hr. journey from Makassar, Sengkang is a quiet medium-sized town, a good place to pause before or after visiting Tana Toraja. Daytrips out to the floating villages of Lake Tempe or the silk-weaving centers at Sempange and Bilaugi are Sengkang's primary attractions.

Sengkang is a short boat trip (1hr.) from the shores of **Danau Tempe**. A trip out to the floating village of **Tempe** is not to be missed. Villagers are friendly and may let you visit their homes, so bring small gifts such as sweets or cigarettes. Longboats can be hired at the river (2-3hr.; Rp40,000-50,000). The best times to visit are early in the morning and just before sunset, when the bird life is most active and the light is best for photography. Trips can be organized through the Pondok Eka hotel (around Rp100,000 for 2 people). Sengkang's other main attraction is its position at the heart of Southern Sulawesi's **silk** industry. To see garment production, walk 10min. from the bus station on Jl. Kartini (which becomes Jl. Magga Amirullah) to **Toko Sumber Sutera,** Jl. Magga Amirullah 140, where you can also buy material. Hotels lead tours to the villages of **Sempange** (6km away) and **Bilaugi** (17km away) and provide a glimpse into every stage of the process, from silkworm cultivation to fabric-dyeing. Tours normally end at (surprise, surprise) a "soft-selling" silk clothing store. (Rp50,000 per person).

Buses link Sengkang to **Parepare** (2hr.; frequent; Rp10,000-15,000) and **Ujung Pandang** (5hr.; several direct buses per day; Rp15,000-25,000). For more frequent connections to Ujung Pandang, go to Parepare first. To get to **Mamasa,** go first to **Polewali** (5hr.; Rp25,000-30,000) and change there for a bus or *bemo* to Mamasa (6hr.). Central Sengkang is easy to navigate: the street with the bus station, **Jl. Kartini,** merges into **Jl. Sudirman** south of the terminal and forks at **BNI,** the bank. The **Telkom office** is at Jl. Pahlawan 6; from Jl. Sudirman, turn left at BNI and take the first left. The **post office** is north of the center on Jl. Veteran.

Pondok Eka ❷, Jl. Maluku 12, offers clean, quiet rooms with baths and breakfast. The English-speaking staff also arrange boat tours and are good guides for the area. (☎0485 212 96. Rooms Rp30,000, with A/C Rp60,000-70,000.) **Hotel Al'Salam ❷,** Jl. Emmy Saelan 8, just around the corner from Pondok Eka, is another good option, with a common sitting area/bar, a decent restaurant, and clean rooms around a central staircase. (☎212 78; fax 218 95. Singles Rp30,000-70,000; doubles Rp40,000-75,000.) Several restaurants and seafood *warung* are on Jl. Kartini and Jl. Sudirman. Close to the Pondok Eka and Hotel Al'Salam, **Tomudi ❸** is a good Chinese-run eatery with a wide-ranging menu that includes seafood. (Fried chicken Rp20,000. Open daily 7am-10pm.)

TANA TORAJA

Beautiful Tana Toraja (or "Tator") is the heart of Sulawesi's tourist trade. People from all over the world flock here by the thousands, drawn to the glorious scenery and the fascinating culture of the Torajan people. Rantepao, the regional hub, is nothing to write home about, but within easy striking distance of town—often just an hour's walk away—are the countless attractions that have helped turn "Torajaland" into one of the most popular tourist destinations in the whole of Indonesia. If the English-menu restaurants and Euro-tourists around Rantepao start to get you down, consider making the trek to Mamasa, an unforgettable three-day adventure through some of the most beautiful, untouched areas in the country.

RANTEPAO ☎0423

Rantepao is geared toward the affluent outsider. Sleek tour buses buzz past rice farmers, and "traditional houses" are touched up annually with fresh paint. Restaurants cater to European tourists with fragile digestive systems, and guides think they know exactly what you want to see. But just beyond the town limits, stretching in all directions, lies a lush green mountain paradise that remains every bit as impressive as it must have been before the tour buses arrived. Most tourists follow the same well-trodden path between the best-known cultural and natural attractions; if you're prepared to head out on your own and do a bit of exploring, you'll probably find you have the place almost to yourself.

TRANSPORTATION

Buses: Bus companies line Jl. Mappanyuki. **Limon Express** and **Litha & Co.** run frequently to **Ujung Pandang** and **Parepare.** Daily service to **Palu** (26hr.; Rp50,000) and **Ujung Pandang** (9hr.; 7:30am, 1, 6:30, 9pm; Rp30,000-60,000). Regional instability has made routes through Central Sulawesi unpredictable and potentially dangerous; keep your ears open and ask agencies and hotels for up-to-date information.

Local Transportation: Bemo run regularly between Rantepao and **Makale,** 18km south, passing many of the popular tourist sights on the way. **Becak** are also hard to miss.

Rentals: Motorcycles (Rp60,000 per day) and **bicycles** (Rp30,000 per day) available at several establishments in town, including **Holiday Tourist Service,** Jl. Mangadil 25 (☎254 68), and **Bagus Tourist Service,** Jl. Dr. Ratulangi 62, close to Wisma Maria I.

ORIENTATION AND PRACTICAL INFORMATION

Rantepao, 18km north of Makale, centers around a mercantile north-south thoroughfare, which enters from the south as **Jl. Pongtiku,** becomes **Jl. A. Yani** in the center of town, and then changes names again to become **Jl. Mappanyuki** past the large intersection with Jl. Diponegoro. Farther north, the same road (now known as **Jl. Pahlawan**) continues across the north curve of the **Sa'dan River** and leads to **Jl. Suloara,** to the left beyond the bridge. A general **market** is in the center of town, but the real market life is 1km up Jl. Diponegoro.

Tourist Office: Pusat Informasi Wisata, Jl. A. Yani 62A (☎212 77). Free maps and a listing of ceremonies. Open M-Sa 8am-2pm.

Tours: Several agencies and guide services on Jl. A. Yani/Mappanyuki. **Holiday Tourist Service,** Jl. Mangadil 25 (☎254 68), and **Bagus Tourist Service,** Jl. Dr. Ratulangi 62, both arrange guides for trips to Torajan villages and ceremonies.

Currency Exchange: BNI, Jl. A. Yani 84 (☎243 16), exchanges cash and traveler's checks. Open M-F 8am-2pm.

Bookstore: Celebes Tourist Service, Jl. Mangadil 11, has a small selection of second-hand English books for sale.

Emergency: Police: ☎110. **Ambulance:** ☎118.

Police: At the corner of Jl. A. Yani and Jl. Landorundun, close to the central market.

Pharmacy: Rayndi Farma, Jl. A. Yani 99 (☎210 13). Open M-Sa 8am-8:30pm.

Medical Services: Rumah Sakit Elim, Jl. A. Yani 68 (☎212 58), 500m out of town on the left as you head toward Makale. **Open 24hr.**

Telephones: Telkom office (☎211 08), next to the post office. Allows collect and credit-card calls from a card phone. **Open 24hr. Wartel Citra,** next to the Wisma Pasadena Hotel on Jl. Mappanyuki, is also **open 24hr.**

Post Office: Jl. A. Yani 111, opposite the bigger of the 2 Bank Rakyats. *Poste Restante.* Open M-Th 8am-2pm, F 8-11am, Sa 8am-1pm. **Postal code:** 91831.

INDONESIA

ACCOMMODATIONS

Rantepao's supply of rooms exceeds demand for much of the year. Most of the best places are on the outskirts of town, a short walk from the bustle and noise of the main road. Prices generally include a simple breakfast.

Wisma Malita, Jl. Suloara 110 (☎210 11). Go north on the main road through town and cross the Sa'dan river, then take the first left onto Jl. Suloara; it's on the right after about 700m. A quiet refuge from tourist chaos with newly renovated rooms and a small garden. Doubles with Western toilets and showers Rp35,000-40,000. ❸

Wisma Maria I, Jl. Ratulangi 23 (☎211 65). Backpacker favorite. Clean doubles with attached baths along open corridors overlooking a pleasant garden courtyard. Singles Rp25,000-50,000; doubles Rp40,000-80,000. ❷

Hotel Indra Toraja, Jl. Landorundun 63 (☎215 83; fax 215 47), at the bottom of the road, opposite the church. Mid-range hotel with A/C rooms around a courtyard and mini-jungle. Doubles with Western toilets and showers Rp100,000-150,000. ❺

Wisma Monika, Jl. Ratulangi 36 (☎212 16), a few doors down from Maria I. Friendly family-run hostel with large, clean rooms. Christian iconography on the walls and Jesus look-alikes in most of the rooms. Doubles with Western bath Rp40,000. ❸

Wisma Surya, Jl. Monginsidi 36 (☎213 12), right by the river. Good bare-bones budget option. Singles and doubles Rp25,000. ❷

TORAJAN FUNERALS The vast majority of the Torajan people embraced Christianity long ago, but the funerals that have made them famous still echo animist beliefs. Even Dutch missionaries, finding the death rites too entrenched, gave up trying to change these practices. Today, the extravagant burials last up to a week and cost millions of rupiah. Immediately after death, the body is injected with a preservative to make it last until the ceremonial burial, which takes place six months to a year later. Nobles sacrifice 24 buffalo and hundreds of pigs; people lower down the caste hierarchy might have to be happy with one or two buffalo and just one bus-load of fattened swine. The soul is meant to ride the buffalo over a huge mountain range to reach *Puka,* the afterworld. Tourists who want to see a ceremony should hire a guide and buy a gift (like a carton of *kretek* cigarettes) for the family of the deceased.

FOOD

Tourist restaurants in Rantepao reduce local specialties such as bamboo-tube-cooked meats *(pa' piong)*, black rice, and palm wine to bland fare. Small restaurants and *warung* off the main road, however, serve *pa' piong* the old-fashioned way. To eat with locals, ask around for directions to **Warung Ni'Buri ❷,** on Jl. Emmy Saelan. *Tuak* (palm wine) is cheapest in markets, but taste before you buy—it goes bad quickly. To satisfy pancake cravings, try any of the backpacker hangouts in the center of town. **Riman ❸**, Jl. Mappanyuki 115, is a popular spot on the left of the main road toward the bridge. (Roast pork Rp18,500; large beer Rp12,500. Open daily 8am-10pm.) **Mambo ❹,** opposite the Wisma Maria I, is a good place for a few beers or a quick meal. (Hamburgers Rp25,000; fried chicken Rp25,000; large Bintang Rp12,500. Open daily 6:30am-10pm.) **Mart's Café ❸,** on Jl. Ratulangi by the football field, has decent food, including tourist-friendly versions of local specialties. (*Pa' piong* Rp20,000; chicken and cheese sandwich Rp11,500.)

SIGHTS

Tana Toraja is a walker's paradise. The best time to trek is March through October, when clouds at the end of the dry season protect hikers from the harsh sun. Avoid the wet season, when roads turn into leech-infested mudslides. Guides are recommended for longer trips. Tourist attractions charge Rp10,000 entrance fees.

Many of the area's most popular sights are just a few kilometers south of Rantepao, off the main road to Makale. **Londa,** 6km from Rantepao toward Makale, is famous for its collection of *tau-tau* effigies (carved as part of Torajan burial ceremonies) and two caves filled with decaying coffins and hundreds of human skulls. Guides can help you find your way with oil lamps (Rp10,000). Braving the death-dark, bone-strewn caves without a light is not a good idea. **Lemo,** 6km farther south, has one of the most spectacular cliff-graves in all of Tana Toraja, fronted by dozens of *tau-tau* effigies. Most figures have their right hand extended, symbolically accepting offerings, and their left protecting the graves from evil spirits. Many of the carvings here are replicas financed by the government after a heist in the late 1980s. For a relaxing daytrip, catch a Makale-bound *bemo* in Rantepao and get off at the road to Lemo (Rp1000). After studying the *tau-tau,* walk north along the small paths to **Tilanga** and its swimming hole. Continue to Londa and catch a *bemo* to Rantepao. **Ke'te Kesu',** whose well-preserved *tongkonan* houses and rice barns have made it one of the most visited villages in the area, is 4km southeast of Rantepao. A path leads back from the rows of houses to a cliff gravesite packed with coffins, skulls, and *tau-tau.* Any *bemo* from Rantepao to Makale can drop you at the turn-off for Ke'te Kesu'; from there, it's a 20min. walk uphill to the village itself. Excursions into the countryside north of Rantepao take you through some of the most spectacular scenery in Sulawesi. To follow a popular route, take a *bemo* from **Terminal Bolu** north of Rantepao to **Lempo** (45min., Rp2500) and to walk uphill from there to **Batutumonga** for some stunning views out over the whole region. From here, continue uphill to the turn-off for **Pana.** Pana has a modest cliff-grave with some nearby tree-graves used for infants. A pleasant downhill walk leads to **Tikala,** where you can catch *bemo* back to Rantepao.

MAKALE

The local *bemo* network has its base in Makale, making this an important hub for daytrips. The sights to the east, at **Suaya** and nearby **Tampangallo,** can be seen in an afternoon. Although the cliff-grave at Suaya is perhaps less spectacular than the one at Lemo, the *tau-tau* are all originals and are much closer to the ground. The cave at Tampangallo is filled with skulls and coffins as well. Be sure to see the treetop **Sarapung baby graves,** 400m before the cave. Babies who die before growing teeth are placed in holes in trees and covered by woven doors, since babies are considered pure enough to be buried in the sacred trees. It is believed that by being joined with the tree, the babies continue to live on after death. Bark eventually grows over the body, creating distinct dimples. The **hot springs** at **Makula** are a few kilometers south of Sangalla. There are occasional direct *bemo* to Suaya from Makale, but it's more likely that you will have to go to **Sangalla** (30min., Rp2500) and walk from there. From the bus stop, walk uphill past the market and turn right at the sign for the school (on the right after about 5min.). It's about a 1hr. walk straight across the fields to the turn-off to Tampangallo (look for the sign), and another 20min. after that to the cliff-graves at Suaya.

Long-distance **minibuses** run to: **Bittuang** (Rp10,000); **Parepare** (Rp20,000); and **Polewali** (Rp25,000). **Jl. Nusantara,** the road south from Rantepao, passes several guest houses, the hospital, **Rumah Sakit Fatima,** and a **24hr. wartel** before reaching **Jl. Tritura,** an uphill road to the *bemo* station near the man-made lotus pond.

MAMASA

An attractive, secluded little village, Mamasa has all the natural beauty of Tana Toraja without any of the big-time crowds. Isolated by ruined roads, Mamasa offers something almost shameful to advertise: an unspoiled rural retreat surrounded by stunning scenery, enveloped by peace and quiet, and inhabited by a charming bunch of people who haven't yet grown tired of tourists in shorts pointing cameras at them.

TRANSPORTATION AND PRACTICAL INFORMATION. Cut off from the rest of the island, Mamasa straddles the **Mamasa River,** a bumpy 93km from Polewali. **Buses** head from the market to **Polewali** (5hr., daily). From there, you can continue to **Parepare** (4hr.; frequent; Rp10,000) or **Rantepao** (6hr.; at least 3 per day; Rp20,000). Buses also go from the Matana Lodge to **Makassar** (12hr.; 1 or 2 per day; Rp30,000), and there is usually at least one direct bus per day to **Rantepao** (12hr.; Rp30,000). Reserve a seat a day in advance. The closest thing to a main road in Mamasa is **Jl. A. Yani,** where you'll find Losmen Mini and Losmen Marampan, the market, several *warung,* and the **wartel.** Polewali has a **bank** with an **ATM,** but there is nowhere in Mamasa to change money; bring plenty of cash, especially if you plan to hire a guide. There is a **hospital** across the river in the northern part of town, but it's not an ideal venue for triple-bypass heart surgery.

ACCOMMODATIONS AND FOOD. Considering its size and isolation, Mamasa has a surprisingly large number of places to stay. **Matana Lodge ❷,** on a side street off Jl. A. Yani, has some of the nicest rooms around. (☎0423 23 558. Singles and doubles with bath and hot water Rp25,000-65,000.) **Losmen Mini ❷**, on Jl. A. Yani in the center of town, is the best budget option. (Clean rooms with bath Rp20,000.) **Losmen Marampan ❶**, on Jl. A. Yani, has small rooms, some with bath (Rp15,000-20,000). Don't get your hopes up for the food here. Simple noodle and rice dishes dominate most menus. Many guest houses have their own **restaurants,** and cheap *warung* dot the town selling fried chicken and *nasi goreng*.

DAYTRIPS FROM MAMASA. As long as you don't mind asking villagers for directions, guides are not necessary for day hikes in **Mamasa Valley.** For multi-day treks, you might want a guide; your hotel's staff can help you find one. Guides ask around Rp100,000 per day, though you should be able to get one for much less, especially when business is slow. There are dozens of great walks and hikes that make easy daytrips from town. Ask around at Matana Lodge or the other *losmen*—most have maps and suggestions for travelers. Martinos, at Losmen Marampan, has an amazing hand-drawn map that he may let you photocopy. A relaxing half-day trip to the northern villages of **Kole** and **Rante Buda** leads to a pool fed by **hot springs** and the oldest *banua layuk* (high house) in the area. *Bemo* head south to **Pena,** the resting grounds for 18 traditional buffalo-shaped coffins. From here, head through the traditional villages of **Pidara** and **Balla Peu** for a view of the valley from **Mussa.** Those in the mood for more culture should head west to the villages of **Tanete** and **Tai Bassi** for a look at **traditional weaving.** More ambitious trekkers can undertake **multi-day hikes** around Mamasa or head toward Tana Toraja on a three-day, 67km trek east to **Bittuang.** From there, *bemo* run to Makale and Rantepao. Finding a place to eat and sleep isn't a problem, especially at the usual stopping points (Rp30,000-40,000 per night), but pack plenty of water each day. The first day's hike is generally from Mamasa to Timbaan. (Head north past the hospital to the village of **Mama,** where the road ends and the trail begins.) Stop in **Paku** on the second day, and finish up in Bittuang on the third.

WARNING Due to sectarian violence and ethnic strife in the region, *Let's Go* has removed coverage of Central Sulawesi. Check with your embassy before traveling in this area.

NORTH SULAWESI (SULAWESI UTARA)

The smallest of the island's provinces, North Sulawesi is the most prosperous. Blessed with fertile soil fed by volcanic ash and seasonally heavy rains, the region has cashed in on coconuts and cloves. The most visible remnant of the Dutch colonial presence is the predominance of Christianity among the Minahasa people, who constitute the province's largest ethnic group. Today, most tourists come to North Sulawesi for the exquisite diving near Manado.

MANADO ☎0431

The prosperity of Manado, North Sulawesi's capital, is evident in its lively markets and Chinese and Minahasa traditions and cuisines. Thus far, the city has avoided direct ethnic conflict; during the 1998 riots, Chinese from across the archipelago sought refuge here from ethnic violence. For most tourists, Manado is the gateway to the world-class diving at Bunaken Manado Tua National Marine Park.

TRANSPORTATION

Flights: Sam Ratulangi Airport, 15km out of town. Walk left downhill to catch a *microlet* to the Paal 2 Bus Terminal in the center of town, or take a cab (Rp40,000 to most hotels). Airport tax Rp15,000 domestic, Rp75,000 international. Manado is a major air hub; there are several flights per day to most major cities in Indonesia, as well as international flights to **Singapore** (Silk Air; M, W, Sa; US$180) and **Davao, Philippines** (Bouraq; M and F; US$150). For flight bookings, try **Limbunan,** 159 Jl. Sam Ratulangi

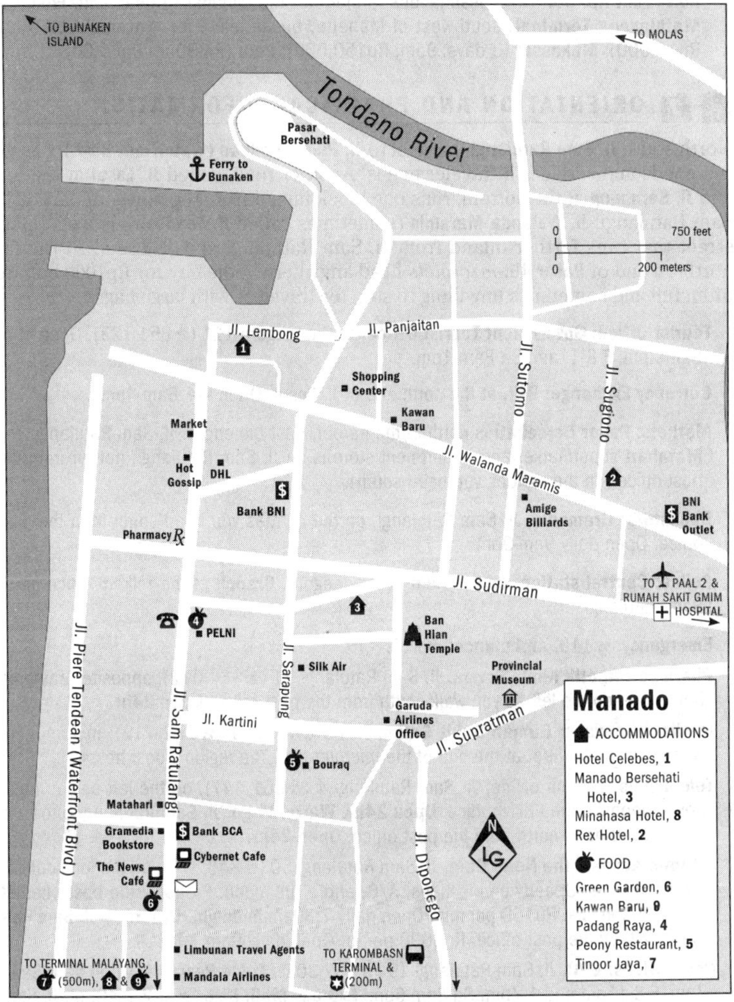

(☎857 555), an official agent for most airlines. Often has cheaper fares than the airlines themselves. **Bouraq,** Jl. Sarapung 20 (☎841 470). **Garuda,** Jl. Diponegoro 15 (☎852 154). **Mandala,** Jl. Sam Ratulangi 175 (☎859 333); **Merpati,** Jl. Martadinata 43 (☎853 213), near the Paal 2 Terminal. **Silk Air,** Jl. Sarapung 5 (☎863 744).

Ferries: PELNI boats depart from **Bitung** (see p. 259). **PELNI office,** Jl. Sam Ratulangi 7 (☎855 115). Open M-F 8am-3pm. Destinations include: **Balikpapan** (Rp214,000-724,000); **Bima; Denpasar; Makassar** (Rp350,000-1,194,500); **Surabaya; Tanjung Priok** (for **Jakarta;** Rp525,000-1,798,500); **Ternate** (Rp93,500-305,500).

Buses: Buses leave from the **Paal 2 Terminal,** east of the city, to: **Airmadidi** (30min., Rp2000); **Bitung** (1hr., every 30min. 7am-9pm, Rp2500); **Tondano** (1hr., frequent, Rp2500). From **Karombasan Station,** south of town in Wanea, buses leave for **Tomohon** (1hr., Rp2500) and destinations farther into the Minahasan heartland. From the **Malalayang Terminal,** southwest of Manado, buses leave for: **Kotamobagu** (4hr.; Rp10,000); **Makassar** (3 days; 9am; Rp150,000); **Palu** (24-30hr.; Rp60,000).

ORIENTATION AND PRACTICAL INFORMATION

North-south **Jl. Sam Ratulangi,** parallel to **Jl. Piere Tendean (Waterfront Blvd.),** has all the goods and services a traveler needs. Another road, called **Jl. Lasut** at the top and **Jl. Sarapung** at the bottom, runs one block inland from the northern part of Jl. Sam Ratulangi. **Jl. Walanda Maramis** (sometimes called **Jl. Tendean**), is a shopping street that runs farther inland from Jl. Sam Ratulangi and Jl. Lasut. At the far northern end of **Pasar 45,** *microlets* head anywhere in the city for Rp1000 but are often full and sometimes unwilling to stop for travelers with large bags.

Tourist Office: Government Tourist Office, Jl. Diponegoro 111 (☎851 723). Open M-Th 8am-2pm, F 8-11am, Sa 8am-1pm.

Currency Exchange: BNI, at the north end of Jl. Lasut. Open M-F 8am-4pm.

Markets: Pasar Bersehati is north of the harbor, past the end of Jl. Sam Ratulangi. The **Matahari** supermarket and department store is on Jl. Sam Ratulangi, not far from the post office (on the right as you head south).

Bookstore: Gramedia, Jl. Sam Ratulangi, on the right as you head south from the post office. Open daily 9am-9pm.

Police: Central station, on southern Jl. Diponegoro. **Branch** at the Telkom office on Jl. Sam Ratulangi.

Emergency: ☎110. **Ambulance:** ☎118.

Pharmacy: Apotik Kimia Farma, Jl. Sam Ratulangi 31 (☎864 012), opposite Gramedia bookstore, on the left as you walk south from the post office. **Open 24hr.**

Medical Services: Rumah Sakit Gmim, Jl. Raya Talete 1 (☎352 712), in Tomohon, 30min. from Manado, at the end of the *microlet* line. The region's best hospital.

Telephones: Telkom office, Jl. Sam Ratulangi 4 (☎861 447), on the left as you head north, opposite the PELNI office. **Open 24hr. Wartel Virgo,** Jl. Sam Ratulangi 5, on the right as you head north from the post office. **Open 24hr.**

Internet Access: The News Café, Jl. Sam Ratulangi 50 (☎846 870), on the left south of the post office. Speedy connections, A/C, and a full menu. Probably the best Internet cafe in Indonesia. Rp150 per min. Open daily 7:30am-midnight. **Cybernet,** Jl. Sam Ratulangi 23, by the post office. Rp6000 per hr. Open daily 9am-10pm.

Post Offices: GPO, Jl. Sam Ratulangi 19 (☎852 301). *Poste Restante.* Open M-Th 8am-7pm, F 8-11am and 1-7pm, Sa 8am-6pm. **Express Mail: DHL** (☎852 778), on Jl. Sam

Ratulangi between Jl. Sudirman and Jl. Walanda Maramis. Open M-F 8am-6pm. **Postal code:** 95111.

ACCOMMODATIONS

Hotel Minahasa, Jl. Sam Ratulangi 199 (☎862 559 or 862 059; fax 854 041), at the far southern end of Jl. Sam Ratulangi. Cottage-style rooms with fine views come with private Western toilets and showers. Breakfast included. Singles/doubles with fan Rp55,000/Rp75,000, with A/C Rp115,000/Rp140,000. MC/V. ❹

Hotel Celebes, Jl. Rumamhi 8A (☎870 425 or 859 069; fax 859 068), north of Jl. Sam Ratulangi, right on the port. Best location in town if you're going to Bunaken in the morning. Restaurant and travel agent. Economy rooms with shared *mandi* Rp40,000, with A/C and private bath Rp60,000, with hot water Rp100,000-120,000. ❸

Manado Bersehati Hotel, Jl. Jend. Sudirman 20 (☎855 022; fax 857 238), on a side street 1 block inland from the Jl. Sudirman and Jl. Sarapung intersection. Clean, bare rooms. Economy rooms with shared bath and fan Rp22,500; singles/doubles with private bath Rp45,000/Rp55,000; doubles with A/C Rp67,000; VIP rooms with shower, A/C, and "living room" Rp75,000-97,500. ❷

Rex Hotel, Jl. Sugiono 3 (☎851 136 or 856 650; fax 867 706). Head inland on Jl. Walanda Maramis from Jl. Sam Ratulangi and make the 4th left. Clean and affordable. Economy singles/doubles with shared *mandi* Rp22,500/Rp37,500, with A/C and private Western bath Rp60,000/Rp75,000. ❷

INDONESIA

FOOD

Minahasan cuisine features spicy specialties such as forest rat, bat, dog, and *tinutuan* (vegetable breakfast porridge). The best place to sample these delicacies is at the string of restaurants overlooking Manado near the town of **Tinoor** on the road to Tomohon. More conventional fare is available at the cheap *warung* that line the upper part of **Jl. Sam Ratulangi.**

Tinoor Jaya, Jl. Sam Ratulangi 167, close to Hotel Minahasa. Has all of Manado's specialties. There's no menu–ask for *rintek wuuk* (spicy dog), *kawaok* (fried forest rat), or *lawang pangang* (stewed bat). Most dishes around Rp6000. Open daily 1-5pm. ❶

Green Garden, on Jl. Sam Ratulangi, on the right as you head south, just past the post office. Pleasant, airy, Chinese-run place. Crab Rp7000; prawns Rp30,000; fried chicken Rp25,000-50,000. Open daily 10am-midnight; closed last Su of the month. ❹

Kawan Baru, Jl. Sam Ratulangi 212, just south of the Hotel Minahasa. Trendy youngsters' hangout. Simple Indonesian fast-food (*mie goreng* Rp10,000) and a wide range of fruit juices (*jus alpokat* Rp6000). Open daily 9am-9pm. **Branch** at Jl. Walanda Maramis 45, near the Jl. Sam Ratulangi intersection. ❷

Peony Restaurant, Jl. Sarapung 33, heading north up Jl. Sam Ratulangi, turn right just after Gramedia bookstore (opposite the Pusat Protestant Church), and take the first left; it's on the right, about 50m up. Good Chinese food in well-polished surroundings. Squid Rp23,000. Chicken in oyster sauce Rp18,000. Open daily 10am-10pm. ❸

Padang Raya, Jl. Sam Ratulangi 5, opposite the Telkom office. Good, spicy, *padang*-style food. Most dishes around Rp5000. Open daily 8:30am-10:30pm. ❶

SIGHTS AND ENTERTAINMENT

The **Provincial Museum of North Sulawesi,** at Jl. Supratman 72, contains a collection of traditional clothing, pottery, and handicrafts from North Sulawesi. (Open M-F

SULAWESI'S WILD SIDE In the 19th century, British naturalist Alfred Russel Wallace asserted that wildlife in Borneo is Asian, while Sulawesi's animal friends are Austronesian. Indeed, Sulawesi's bizarre fauna often has more in common with the creatures of Australia than with those of much closer Indonesian islands. Sulawesi's isolation from larger landmasses has resulted in a proliferation of unique species; over 60% of Sulawesi's mammals and a third of its birds are endemic. Three species are particularly celebrated on the island. Lucky travelers might catch a glimpse of the famous *babirusa* (pig deer), which has monstrous tusks that curve through the roof of its mouth. Another fearsome beast is the *anoa* (miniature buffalo), whose size belies its ferocity. Rounding out the trio is the *maleo* bird, a megapode that digs big holes in the ground with its enormous feet to bury its eggs. Unfortunately, development and poaching threaten these species with extinction.

8am-2pm. Admission by donation.) The **Ban Hian Kiong Buddhist-Confucian Temple,** on Jl. Panjaitan in the city center, serves Manado's large Chinese population. In February, two weeks after the Chinese New Year, it is home to one of Southeast Asia's largest **Toa Pa Kong Festival** celebrations.

Amigo Billiards Hall, on Jl. Walanda Maramis, is as friendly as the name suggests. (Pool Rp10,000 per hr. Open daily 9am-1am.) Word travels quickly about **Hot Gossip,** a popular bar and nightclub on Jl. Sam Ratulangi, on the left as you head north, a 5min. walk from the post office. The club is packed nightly with dancers grinding to ear-splitting disco. (Cover Rp10,000. Open 10pm-3am.)

INDONESIA

NEAR MANADO

BUNAKEN

The 753 sq. km **Bunaken-Manado Tua National Marine Park,** one of the best diving spots in the world, has turned Manado into a major stop on the backpacker circuit. There are dozens of world-class dive sites here, and many excellently run dive centers. Underwater novices can content themselves with snorkeling or take an introductory scuba course. All visitors to the park must pay an entrance fee, proceeds of which are funneled into the care of Bunaken's fragile ecosystem. Daily tickets cost Rp50,000; year-long passes are Rp150,000. From Manado, take a **boat** from behind Pasar Bersehati to **Bunaken** (1½hr.; departs roughly 2pm, returns about 7 or 8am; Rp15,000) or charter an **outrigger** (Rp50,000-100,000).

The best way to explore Bunaken is to stay at one of the dive resorts on the island itself. **Liang Beach,** 100m from the drop-off, is home to several posh dive centers and a good range of budget accommodation. Simple **cottages** ❸ with *mandi* run about Rp30,000-60,000 per person. **Papa Boa, Ibu Konda, Santika,** and **Panorama Cottages** are all good budget options. On the other side of the island, **Pangalisang Beach** has a similar range of places to stay, including **MC** ❸ (rooms Rp30,000), **Daniel's** ❸ (rooms Rp35,000), **Lorenso's Cottage** ❸ (rooms Rp30,000), and **Seabreeze** ❸ (rooms Rp40,000-60,000).

Bunaken's beaches may not be paradise, but the island's world-class dive sites more than make up for it. Turtles, tuna, and whitetip sharks frequent **Lekuan,** a superb wall dive. Schools of barracuda are often spotted in **Pangalisang,** and **Sachiko**'s spectacular density of fish and strong currents attract schools of pelagics. **Cela Cela** is an ideal site to observe reef life at night.

Sulawesi Dive Quest, on Liang Beach, is one of the island's best dive centers, with mint-condition gear and knowledgeable instructors. (☎863 023; info@sulawesi-dive-quest.com. 2 dives US$40; 5-day PADI open-water course US$340.) **Froggies** ❺ is an impressive, all-inclusive hotel and dive shop. (☎812 430; manado@divefroggies.com. 2 dives US$60; accommodation US$15-35 per person.) Other dive resorts include **Two Fishes Divers** ❹ (☎0811 432 805) and **Living Colours** ❺ (☎8124 306 063) both on Pangalisang Beach. (Two Fishes Divers: info@twofishdivers.com. US$25 per dive; PADI open-water course US$360; advanced course US$250; accommodation US$7-12 per person. Living Colours: info@livingcoloursdiving.com. US$30 per dive; PADI open-water course US$360; cottages US$20 per person).

The pricier dive centers on Manado offer better accommodations, more amenities, and easier access to shops and banks. The only downside is a 1hr. commute to the dive sites. **Nusantara Diving Center** ❺ **(NDC;** ☎863 988) is in Molas, north of Manado. (Take a *microlet* to Tuminting and then an *oplet* to Molas, or call NDC for pickup from Manado. 2 dives US$60, with accommodation US$80; PADI open-water course US$400.) Small and intimate **Murex Dive Resort** ❺**,** Jl. Sudirman 28 (☎866 280; fax 852 116; info@murexdive.com), has bungalows south of the city.

MINAHASA

The Minahasan highlands around Manado offer pleasant daytrips. Catch a bus from Manado's Karombasan Terminal south to **Tomohon** (30min., frequent departures, Rp2500). A 30min. ride east of Tomohon brings you to **Tondano,** the cultural heart of Minahasa. A few kilometers out of town toward **Airmadidi** are caves built by slave labor under the Japanese occupation during World War II. The small town of **Sawangan** (30min.) and its collection of *waruga*, traditional stone houses for the dead, rest farther north along the road to Airmadidi. *Waruga* from across Minahasa were collected here in the late 19th century, after the practice fell out of use. Another set, including a 3m tomb built to hold the remains of a local king, stands today in the town of Airmadidi. Airmadidi is on the main Manado-Bitung road (30min. from Manado); the *waruga* lot is off the road to Tondano, 500m from the Manado-Bitung road.

INDONESIA

BITUNG AND TANGKOKO

By the 1960s, Manado's port was too silted for cargo boats, and most shipping traffic moved to **Bitung** on the other side of the peninsula. The only reason to come here is to catch **PELNI ferries.** From the Paal 2 Terminal in Manado, take a bus to Bitung (1hr., frequent departures, Rp2500). **Tangkoko**'s main attraction is the **Tangkoko-Batuangus Dua Saudara National Park.** Home to the endemic *maleo* bird and the Spectral Tarsier (the world's smallest species of primate), Tangkoko supports a wealth of diverse species. To get to Tangkoko, take the Bitung bus to **Girian** (45min., Rp2000), then catch a jeep north to **Batuputih** (30min., Rp2500).

BOLAANG MONGONDOU DISTRICT

Although **Kotamobagu** is the capital of Bolaang Mongondou, the central district of North Sulawesi, most tourists find little reason to linger there. The bus from **Manado** (5hr.; 5 per day; Rp15,000) stops at a station not far from town; take a *microlet* into the main square, past the roundabout. A few buses also head west to **Gorontalo** (5hr.; Rp15,000). Buy tickets, change money, and place phone calls from the **bus agency,** left of the supermarket. From Gorontalo, an overnight ferry leaves daily for the desolate paradise of the **Togian Islands.**

DUMOGA-BONE NATIONAL PARK

With 3000 sq. km of protected land, **Dumoga-Bone National Park** (☎0434 211 08) is Sulawesi's largest wildlife preserve and the best place to see the island's range of endemic species (see **Sulawesi's Wild Side,** p. 258). Getting to the park by public

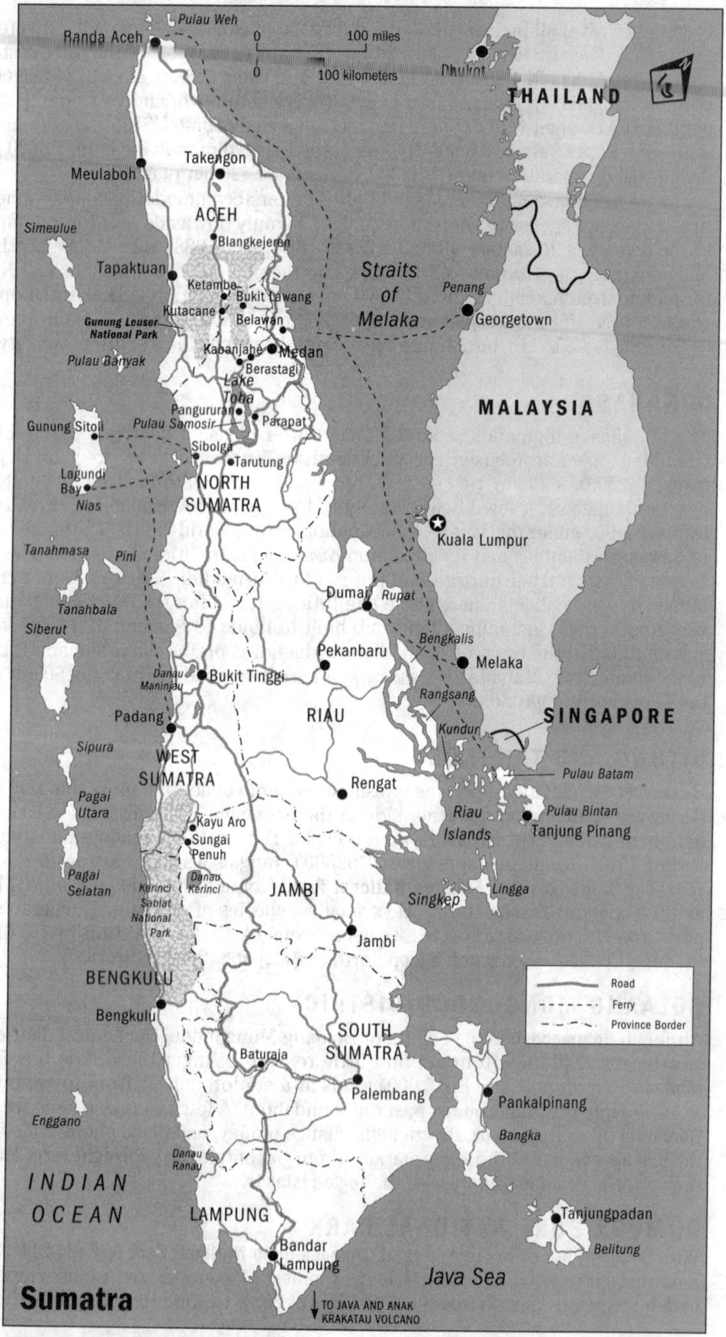
Sumatra
Pulau Weh
Banda Aceh
0
100 miles
0
100 kilometers
Phuket
THAILAND
Meulaboh
Takengon
ACEH
Simeulue
Blangkejeren
Tapaktuan
Ketambe
Bukit Lawang
Kutacane
Gunung Leuser National Park
Belawan
Straits of Melaka
Penang
Georgetown
Kabanjahe
Medan
Berastagi
Pulau Banyak
Lake Toba
Pangururan
Parapat
Pulau Samosir
Gunung Sitoli
Sibolga
Tarutung
Lagundi Bay
Nias
NORTH SUMATRA
MALAYSIA
Kuala Lumpur
Tanahmasa
Pini
Tanahbala
Siberut
Dumai
Rupat
Bengkalis
Pekanbaru
Melaka
Danau Maninjau
Bukit Tinggi
Rangsang
Padang
RIAU
SINGAPORE
Kundur
Sipura
WEST SUMATRA
Pulau Batam
Rengat
Pagai Utara
Riau Islands
Pulau Bintan
Tanjung Pinang
Kayu Aro
Sungai Penuh
Danau Kerinci
Pagai Selatan
Kerinci Sablat National Park
JAMBI
Singkep
Lingga
Jambi
BENGKULU
Bengkulu
Road
Ferry
Province Border
SOUTH SUMATRA
Baturaja
Palembang
Pankalpinang
Bangka
Enggano
Danau Ranau
INDIAN OCEAN
LAMPUNG
Tanjungpadan
Belitung
Bandar Lampung
Java Sea
TO JAVA AND ANAK KRAKATAU VOLCANO

INDONESIA

transport requires patience. From Kotamobagu's *microlet* terminal (a block from the supermarket), take a *microlet* to **Doloduo** (1hr., Rp2500). Use the word "public" to avoid paying drivers Rp30,000 for a "charter" trip. From Doloduo, catch another *microlet* (15min., Rp1000) to **Toraut,** where you'll find the park entrance, next to Wallacea Cottage. Ask Mr. Suroji for a tour (Rp35,000 for 5hr.). **Wallacea Cottage** ❸ is the park's only option for overnight stays (Rp45,000 per person).

SUMATRA

One of Indonesia's largest islands, Sumatra plays second fiddle only to Java in politics and economics. Notorious for its poor roads and fickle climate, Sumatra is no jetsetter's paradise. Many regions prove inaccessible for even the most determined, and women traveling alone may experience harassment. Still, the Medan-Padang route via Lake Toba, Nias, and Bukit Tinggi is well traveled and promises intrepid visitors a memorable experience. With hikable jungle terrain, crystalline crater lakes, and rich cultural character, Sumatra should not be overlooked by those with the desire—and stomach—for adventure.

NORTH SUMATRA

MEDAN ☎061

With a population of nearly 2 million, Medan is Sumatra's largest city by far, and the third-largest in Indonesia. It is also a major port of entry for travelers, and first impressions tend to range from disappointment to dismay. Medan is characterized by an uncompromising atmosphere of mad honking chaos, and many travelers, confronted with the smoke and grime of the traffic-choked streets, scurry straight to the safety of their hotels—emerging only to catch the first bus out of town. Behind all the fumes and noise, however, lie neighborhoods full of character, with a richness of food and architecture that reflects the diverse local population. Mosques dot the city, from the handsome Mesjid Raya to decrepit constructions weathered by the past. Colorful Hindu and Buddhist temples find their place west and east of the town center in Little India and Chinatown, neighborhoods bursting with their own tales, tongues, and tastes. If you have a secret fondness for shopping malls, McDonald's and movie theaters, Medan is a good place to get your last fix before setting off on the backpacker trail south to Lake Toba and beyond.

TRANSPORTATION

Flights: Polonia International Airport (☎456 5777), 3km south of town at the end of Jl. Imam Bonjol. Regular public transportation does not run to the airport; take a *becak* (Rp10,000) or taxi (Rp20,000) instead. Airlines accept MC/V.

Garuda, Jl. Balai Kota 2 (☎451 6400), across from the post office. Open M-F 8am-5pm, Sa 9am-1pm. Daily flights to: **Banda Aceh** (1hr.; Rp400,000); **Denpasar** (3hr.; Rp1,684,000); **Jakarta** (2hr.; Rp1,159,900).

Malaysian Airlines, Jl. Imam Bonjol 17 (☎451 9333), ground fl. of the Danau Toba Hotel. Open M-F 8:30am-4:30pm, Sa 8:30am-1:30pm. Daily flights to **Kuala Lumpur** (US$85) and **Penang** (US$85).

Merpati, Jl. Brigjen Katamso 219 (☎455 1888). Open M-F 8am-4:30 pm, Sa 9am-2pm. To: **Palembang** (Rp1,355,700); **Pekan Baru** (Rp 991,600); **Pontianak** (Rp1,170,900).

INDONESIA

Silk Air/Singapore Airlines (☎453 7744), on the lower back side of the Tiara Convention Center off Jl. Imam Bonjol. Open M-F 8am-5pm, Sa 8am-noon. To **Singapore** (US$115).

Buses: There are two main terminals and a third smaller one; *Sudako* #64 runs between them. *Sudako* can also take you from either terminal to travelers' hangouts on Jl. Sisingamangaraja. Ask around for transport to the **Mesjid Raya** (about Rp1000). Both terminals have dozens of different bus company offices—shop around for the best fares.

Amplas Terminal, 10km south of the city center at the end of Jl. Sisingamangaraja, serves most destinations south of Medan, as well as long-distance buses to Java. From the city center take any *sudako* (20min., Rp1000) marked "Amplas" running south along Jl. Sisingamangaraja; ask to get off at *"terminal."* Buses to: **Bukitinggi** (24hr.; 6 per day 8am-2pm; Rp63,000-96,000, with A/C Rp112,000); **Jakarta** (48hr.; every hr. 8am-7pm; Rp175,000-265,000, with A/C Rp300,000); **Padang** (24hr.; 6 per day 8am-2pm; Rp63,000, with A/C Rp112,000); **Parapat** (4 hr.; 5 regular buses per day, frequent minibuses 7am-midnight; Rp24,000, with A/C Rp29,000).

Pinang Baris Terminal, 12km west of the city center, with buses to Aceh and other closer destinations. Frequent *sudako* (marked *P. Baris*, 30-40min., Rp1000) run along Jl. A. Yani and Jl. Palang Merah. Destinations include: **Banda Aceh** (14hr.; 8 per day 8am-8:30pm; Rp60,000); **Berastagi** (2½hr., frequent 7am-5pm, Rp3500); **Bukit Lawang** (3½hr., frequent 7am-5pm, Rp4000).

Padang Bulan Terminal, accessible via *Sudako* #41, heading south down Jl. Sisingamangaraja past the **Mesjid Raya.** Travelers to **Kutacane** (6hr.; roughly every 2hr. 8am-5pm; Rp25,000) and connections to **Ketambe** and **Blangkejeren** might find it easier to use this smaller terminal.

Minibuses: Easier (and more expensive) than public buses are small, privately run tourist minibuses that run between Medan and major destinations throughout Sumatra. **Tobali Tour and Travel,** Jl Sisingamangaraja 79C (☎732 4471), across from and south of the mosque, runs daily buses to: **Berastagi** (11:30am; Rp28,000); **Bukit Lawang** (3 and 5pm; Rp32,000); **Lake Toba** (11:30am; Rp40,000). Reserve seats early.

Ferries: Leave from **Belawan,** 26km north of Medan. There are daily ferries to **Penang,** Malaysia (4hr.; 90 Malaysian Ringgit (RM), round-trip 160RM). Fares include transfer by bus from Medan to Belawan. Children travel half-price. **Penang Express Bahagia,** Jl. Sisingamangaraja 92A (☎732 0421) sails daily at 10am. Open M-F 8am-5pm, Sa 8am-3pm, Su 8am-1pm. **PELNI** sails to domestic ports. The main office, Jl. Kol. Sugiorno 5 (☎453 8772), is less convenient than the branch office (☎415 5777) inside Trophy Tour (see **Tours,** below), where the staff speaks English. Open M-F 8am-5pm, Sa 8am-noon. To: **Banda Aceh** (16hr.; 12 sporadic sailings per month; Rp75,000-230,000); **Jakarta** (58hr.; every other day; Rp190,000-600,000) via **Batan** (20hr.; Rp105,000-310,000).

Local Transportation: *Sudako* are rickety, multi-colored minivans that careen through the city along set routes; major stops are usually on windshields. Fares are around Rp1000. Cycle-powered *becak* and their motor-driven big brothers prowl downtown. If you don't mind a few moments of life-flashing panic, they're the fastest. Expect to pay Rp4000-8000 for a ride. The *becak* drivers that congregate opposite the Mesjid Raya typically charge much higher rates than drivers hailed elsewhere around town. **Taxis** do not have meters—bargain for a rate. Airport to downtown roughly Rp20,000.

ORIENTATION AND PRACTICAL INFORMATION

The heart of the city is made up of a few major one-way avenues with names that change several times as they ramble through the city. The main north-south road starts as **Jl. Putri Hijau** and changes to **Jl. Balai Kota** at the **Deli Plaza Shopping Center.** After passing **Merdeka Square,** it becomes **Jl. A. Yani.** South of the intersection with **Jl. Palang Merah,** it becomes **Jl. Pemuda** before changing to **Jl. Brigjen Katamso** at the next intersection and passing the **Istana Maimun** and several travel agencies. **Jl. Palang Merah,** which leads west from Jl. A. Yani (and quickly becomes **Jl. H. Z. Arifin**), passes through the **Chinese** and **Indian areas** of the city. The other important road is **Jl. Sisingamangaraja,** which roughly parallels Jl. Pemuda/Brigjen Katamso, passing the Grand Mosque, **Mesjid Raya.** Most of the budget hotels are here, and if you're arriving by boat from Penang, this is where the bus with drop you off.

Tourist Office: Provincial Tourism Office of North Sumatra, Jl. A. Yani 107 (☎453 8101). Friendly, English-speaking staff. Open M-F 7:30am-4:30pm.

Tours: Dozens of agencies line Jl. Brigjen Katamso and Jl. Sisingamangaraja. The best is **Trophy Tour,** Jl. Brigjen Katamso 33D-E (☎415 5666; www.trophytour.com). Domestic and international ferry, plane, and bus tickets. Open M-Sa 8am-5pm, Su 8am-noon.

Consulates: Australia, Jl. Kartini 32 (☎415 7810). Open M-F 8am-4:30pm. **Malaysia,** Jl. Diponegoro 43 (☎453 1342). Open M-F 8am-1pm and 2-4pm. **Singapore,** Jl. Tengku Daud 3 (☎451 3366). Open M-F 8am-12:30pm and 1:30-4:30pm. **UK,** Jl. Kaptan Pattimura 459 (☎821 0559). Open M-F 8am-noon.

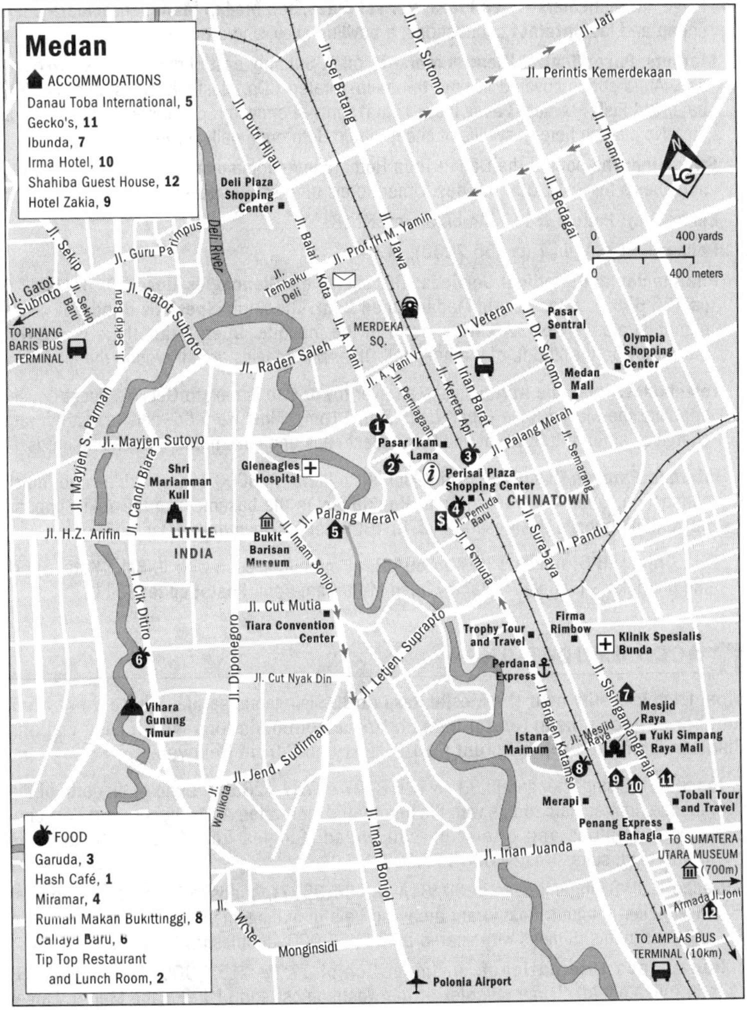

Immigration Office: Jl. Binjei 268A (☎845 2112). Several km north. Catch a DAMRI bus on Jl. A. Yani and ask to get out at "Kantor Imigrasi." Open M-F 7:30am-4pm.

Currency Exchange: Change money here—rates are often worse outside Medan. Most banks are along Jl. Pemuda/Jl. A. Yani, including **BNI,** Jl. Pemuda 12 (☎453 8166). Open M-F 8am-3pm. Many guest houses also change money. There are a number of **ATMs** around town, most are **open 24hr.** and accept international cards. Try BNI and other banks, shopping malls, and the Danau Toba Hotel on Jl. Palang Merah.

Bookstore: Gramedia, Jl. Gajah Mada 23, west of Jl. Palang Merah, has a decent selection of English books. Open M-F 9am-8:45pm, Sa-Su 9am-9:15pm. **Firma Rimbow,** Jl. Sisingamangaraja 14 (☎736 8538), also has a small number.

Shopping Centers: Several large, A/C shopping malls dominate the Medan skyline. Large movie theaters in **Deli Plaza, Perisai Plaza,** and **Medan Mall.** Perisai Plaza offers cheap and fast **Internet** connections, a bowling alley, and a disco.

Markets: Pasar Sentral (Central Market), off Jl. Sutomo, east of the Sambu *sudako* station. Amid shops covered in blue tarpaulin. Pirated CDs, plastic buckets, and live fruit bats. **Old Fish Market (Pasar Ikam Lama),** on Jl. Pernigaan, parallel to Jl. A. Yani. Quieter. No old fish here—just rolls of cheap *batik*. Both open daily dawn-dusk.

Swimming: The pool at the Danau Toba Hotel (see **Accommodations,** below) is open to non-guests for Rp11,000 per day. Other hotels offer similar deals.

Emergency: Police: ☎110. **Ambulance:** ☎118.

Police: Jl. H.Z. Arifin 7 (☎455 2000).

Pharmacies and Medical Services: The shiny new **Gleneagles Hospital,** Jl. Listrik 6 (☎456 6368), is the best in Medan. **Open 24hr.** The **Klinic Spesialis Bunda,** Jl. Sisingamangaraja 17 (☎732 1666), north of the mosque. **Open 24hr.** There is a **24hr. pharmacy** on the 2nd fl. of the hospital. Other pharmacies are all around the city.

Telephones: There are *wartel* kiosks all over town. One is next to Gecko's guest house, opposite the Mesjid Raya (open daily until 11pm). Most *wartel* owners levy a flat-rate charge of around Rp3000 per call for collect calls and calls made with calling cards.

Internet: Paragon Computer, 2nd fl. of Perisai Plaza. Rp3000 per hr. with a good, quick connection. Open daily 10am-9pm. **Hokkibear,** in the basement of the Yuki Simpang Raya Mall opposite the Mesjid Raya. Rp4000 per hr. Open daily 10am-9:45pm.

Post Office: GPO, Jl. Pos 1 (☎456 8940), at the intersection with Jl. Balai Kota, opposite Merdeka Sq. *Poste Restante.* Open M-Sa 8am-6pm. **Postal code:** 20111.

ACCOMMODATIONS

Most travelers stay near the **Mesjid Raya** on **Jl. Sisingamangaraja,** where there are a number of good, cheap (and not so cheap) accommodations within easy walking distance from the drop-off point for the "ferry bus" from Belawan.

Ibunda, Jl. Sisingamangaraja 33 (☎736 8787 or 734 1285). A 5min. walk north of the mosque. Immaculate rooms with Western baths, hot water, A/C, phones, and TV. Popular with families and often full—call ahead. Singles from Rp80,000; doubles Rp100,000; suites Rp120,000-175,000. MC/V. ❹

Gecko's, Jl. Sisingamangaraja 59/81A (☎734 3507), opposite the mosque. Popular backpacker hangout. Restaurant area and helpful management. Simple but clean and well-kept rooms. Singles with shared bath Rp25,000; doubles Rp30,000-35,000. ❷

Danau Toba International, Jl. Imam Bonjol 17 (☎415 7000; fax 453 0553; hdti@nusa.net.id). Large complex at the westernmost end of Jl. Palang Merah. Large, comfortable, A/C rooms. Swimming pool, billiard room, fitness center, restaurants, and a bar with live music. Doubles Rp169,000-214,500. ❺

Hotel Zakia (☎732 2413), on Jl. Sipiso Piso, the small lane immediately before the mosque as you head north up Jl. Sisingamangaraja (with the mosque on your left). Veteran favorite of the bare-bones backpacker crowd. 2nd fl. rooms are perfect to enjoy the *muezzin*'s 5am call to prayer. Most rooms come with Western toilet. Check-out noon. Dorms Rp8000; singles from Rp22,500; doubles Rp30,000-35,000. ❶

Irma Hotel, Jl. Tengah 1B. Just south of Mesjid Raya, around the corner from Hotel Zakia. Turn left after the cafe/restaurant on the corner. Basic but clean. Very friendly management. Doubles with shared bath Rp20,000, with private bath Rp30,000. ❷

Shahiba Guest House, Jl. Armada 1A (☎736 8528). Head south on Jl. Sisingamangaraja; at the end of Bukit Barisan Hero's Cemetery, turn right onto Jl. Armada. Simple rooms with *mandi*. Dorms Rp8000; singles Rp20,000; doubles Rp25,000-50,000. ❶

FOOD

Medan's chief culinary attraction is spicy *padang* food, the ethnic specialty of West Sumatra's Minang people. There are cheap stalls all over town. Waiters bring a number of dishes to your table—you eat and pay for what you want. In the evenings, stalls selling cheap and delicious Chinese food line **Jl. Semarang,** between Jl. Pandu and Jl. Bandung. (Open daily 6pm-midnight.) There's an excellent Chinese place north of Jl. Semarang, at the intersection of Jl. A. Yani V and Jl. Perniagaan, which serves superb stir-fry dishes for Rp15,000. (Open M-Sa 10am-9pm). A few bakeries and Indian food stalls are in the Indian quarter, near the intersection of Jl. H. Z. Arifin and Jl. Cik Ditiro. *Sate* and juice stands on Jl. Sisingamangaraja toward the Bukit Barisan Hero's Cemetery stay open late.

Miramar, Jl. Pemuda, opposite BNI. A/C Indonesian restaurant with a Costa del Sol party atmosphere. Popular with locals. "Special" chicken Rp20,000. Cuttlefish Rp5000. *Cap chai* Rp15,000. Open daily 11am-10pm. AmEx/MC/V. ❸

Garuda, Palang Merah 26, just east of Jl. Pemuda. Heading north up Jl. Pemuda, turn right before the tourist information office. Shiny-clean *padang* place with uniformed waiters. Wide selection of excellent food; dishes Rp4000-5000. Open 24hr. ❶

Hash Café, Jl. Jend A. Yani 50. The huge red Bintang beer sign is hard to miss. Dark, smoky expatriate watering hole complete with bar stools. Good steaks from Rp32,000; fried chicken Rp20,000; fried calamari Rp18,000. Draft beer Rp11,500. Open daily 11am-11pm. See **Entertainment,** below. ❹

Tip Top Restaurant and Lunch Room, Jl. A. Yani 92. North of the intersection with Jl. Palang Merah. An old Dutch-era restaurant that retains the flavor of slower-paced times. Mutton curry Rp5500. Frog legs Rp17,500. Open daily 8:30am-10:30pm. ❷

Rumah Makan Bukittinggi, Jl. Brigjen Katamso 456, opposite the Istana Maimun. Clean canteen-style place serving great pick-and-point *padang* food. Large number of chicken, mutton, and fish dishes (most around Rp5000). Open daily 7am-10pm. ❶

Cahaya Baru, Jl. Cik Ditiro 8L. Heading west along Jl. H. Z. Arifin, turn left onto Jl. Cik Ditiro. The restaurant is a 10-15min. walk south. 4-table A/C nook serves tasty curries and South Indian staples. The **Maharaja** restaurant, next door, is also good. *Alu gobi* Rp6000. Mutton curry Rp8000. *Dosas* Rp2500-17,500. Open daily 10am-10pm. ❷

SIGHTS

Medan is never going to win any prizes as a sight-seeing city. Many travelers stay here only as long as it takes to book a ticket out of town. If you aren't in a hurry to follow the crowds, however, there is enough to keep you occupied here for at least a day or two. Medan is relatively easy to navigate, and some visitors might be interested to explore a large Indonesian city little affected by foreign tourism—unlike most of the other stops along the backpacker trail through Sumatra and beyond. Apart from the real-life charm of Medan's residential neighborhoods, the city's main attraction is its **architecture.** Many of its most interesting buildings line Jl. Pemuda/Jl. A. Yani. The entire length of this street is littered with architectural relics of the colonial period, and if you can imagine away all the traffic fumes and KFC billboards, it's still possible to get a sense of what the place might have looked like back in the days when all the street signs were written in Dutch. Old-world remnants include the **Tip Top Restaurant** (see **Food,** above) and the **headquarters** of the London-Sumatera trading company (just south of Merdeka Sq.). Also worth a quick peek is the multi-colored, tumbledown **Tjong A Fie** mansion at Jl. A. Yani 105, built in a mixture of Chinese and European styles. The black domes, turquoise tiles, and soaring minarets of the **Mesjid Raya (Grand Mosque),** at Jl. Sisingamangaraja and Jl. Mesjid Raya, were built by a Dutch architect in 1908. The well-kept gardens around the mosque are a popular local hangout— people come here to chat, sleep, or play football, while the elderly pray beside the graveyard where the Sultan is buried. Non-Muslims may visit the interior of the mosque between prayer times. (Open daily dawn-dusk. Admission by donation.)

Near Mesjid Raya, where Jl. Brigjen Katamso meets Jl. Mesjid Raya, is the **Istana Maimun (Maimun Palace).** Built with tobacco money, the palace has housed the Deli Sultans since 1888. The 12th Sultan and his family still live here. The throne room is open to the public. (Open daily 8am-5pm. Admission by donation.) A Hindu temple, **Shri Mariamman Kuil,** is on Jl. H. Z. Arifin. Renovated and expanded in 1991, it turns heads with its brightly colored and ornate depictions of gods, heroes, and mythical creatures. (Open daily dawn to dusk. Free.) **Vihara Gunung Timur,** a Buddhist temple sacred to Medan's Chinese community, stands on Jl. Hang Tuah in a quiet residential suburb off Jl. Cik Ditiro. The temple is worth a visit for its impressive, cluttered interior, clouded by sweet incense and colored by flowers and fruit. (Open daily 6am-5pm. Free.) To get there, turn left onto Jl. Cik Ditiro shortly after the Hindu temple, and walk south for 20min. It's down a small lane, opposite the Methodist church. The **Museum Sumatera Utara,** Jl. H.M. Joni 51, documents the geological and cultural history of the province. An informative tour takes about 1hr. (Take any *sudako* heading south on Jl. Sisingamangaraja, or walk 1.5km from Mesjid Raya. From the south end of the Bukit Barisan Hero's Cemetery, the museum is 700m. Open Tu-Su 8am-3:30pm. Admission by donation.)

ENTERTAINMENT

Travelers in search of late-night parties featuring last year's Euro-hits and magic mushrooms will find slim pickings in Medan. But this doesn't mean that people stuck here overnight need to spend their nights watching pro-wrestling on TV. The ancient and noble pastime of drinking large amounts of beer and talking large amounts of nonsense can be indulged in all over town. For a dark, smoky atmosphere, the **Hash Café** on Jl. A. Yani (see **Food,** above) is your best bet. Mugs of draft beer go for Rp11,500. The cafe is the unofficial watering hole of the Medan branch of the **Hash House Harriers,** an Asia-wide expatriate obsession that involves weekly runs through the local countryside, followed by ritualistic boozing (see **A Drinking Club with a Running Problem,** p. 381). Visitors are welcome to join in the fun for a small entrance free. (Runs most M and Th. Ask for details of upcoming events.) Three live bands play nightly at the **Danau Toba International Hotel.** (See **Accommodations,** above. Beatles night Su. Open daily 6pm-1am.) There is also a popular **"bil-**

liard centre," where a game of 8-ball pool costs Rp2000. (Open daily 10am-1am.) The Danau Toba's **disco** was closed down at the time of press, but may have opened again by the time you read this. There is a large new **bowling alley** on the top floor of the Perisai Plaza on Jl. A. Yani. (Rp5000 per game M-F; Rp6000 Sa-Su. Open daily 11am-midnight.) Also at the top of the Perisai Plaza are a cheap **video arcade** and the **Kristal Disco,** a fun place to look silly with the locals on a Saturday night. There are **cinemas** showing English-language movies (Rp12,000) at several of Medan's shopping malls, including Perisai Plaza, Deli Plaza, and Medan Mall.

BERASTAGI ☎0628

Set against the ethereal beauty of North Sumatra's mountainous hinterland, Berastagi is a slightly scruffy hill town within easy reach of a large number of natural and cultural attractions. A number of traditional Batak Karo villages are scattered among the surrounding Karo Highlands, within daytripping distance. Using Berastagi as a base, volcano climbers can tackle steaming Gunung Sibayak or jungle-covered Gunung Sinabung. Or, visitors can take a stroll in one of the town's parks or sit in a local coffeehouse with some of the friendliest people in Sumatra.

INDONESIA

TRANSPORTATION

Most buses from Berastagi are **minibuses,** though buses from Medan occasionally pass through on their way south. The **main terminal** is in front of the market on Jl. Veteran. Buses go to: **Kutacane** (5-6hr.; every 20min. 9am-6pm; Rp18,000); **Medan** (2½hr., frequent 5am-8pm, Rp2500); **Pangururan** (5hr.; 3-4 per day 8am-1pm; Rp10,000). Buses to **Tapaktuan** (8hr.; 2 per day 7-9pm; Rp20,000) depart from a second terminal 5km out of town. (Take a *sudako* from the main terminal. Ask for Kutugadung or the PMTOH terminal. Rp500.) **Tourist buses** provide the only direct service from Berastagi to **Bukit Lawang** and **Parapat (Lake Toba).** Buy tickets at least a day ahead from **Raymond's Steak House** or **Losmen Sibayak Guest House.** Tourist buses usually only leave with 5 or more people. To **Bukit Lawang** (5hr.; 10am and 2pm; Rp45,000-50,000) and **Parapat** (6hr.; 10am and 2pm; Rp40,000-50,000).

ORIENTATION AND PRACTICAL INFORMATION

Berastagi is a small town, with a single, divided thoroughfare, **Jl. Veteran,** which forks at a 5m **war monument** at its north end. The left branch becomes **Jl. Gundaling,** which leads uphill past the **fruit market** toward **Mt. Sibayak;** the right branch leads downhill out of town, becoming the **Berastagi-Medan Hwy.** The tourist information center, post office, and *wartel* are near the monument. Most budget accommodations are on Jl. Veteran. Heading south, Jl. Veteran passes the **bus terminal** and **central market** before forking again at a large sculpture of a **cabbage** in the middle of the road. The left branch continues 11km to **Kabanjahe,** and the right branch, **Jl. Udara,** leads to **Gunung Sinabung** and the Karo village of **Lingga.**

Tourist Offices: Tourist Information Center, Jl. Gundaling 1 (☎910 84). Left of the war memorial. Offers little more than trekking maps of Gunung Sibayak and Gunung Sinabung. Arranges more arduous trekking and rafting expeditions and trips to nearby Karo villages, but at prices much higher than elsewhere. Open M-Sa 8am-6pm. The **information desk** at the Losmen Sibayak is useful, with up-to-date advice and boards advertising travelers looking to put together groups for climbing, trekking, and rafting.

Tours: Mr. Telah Bangun, an excellent **guide** who speaks English and organizes treks (US$30 per person per day, min. 4 people) in Gunung Leuser National Park, is at **Tobali Tour and Travel,** Jl. Veteran 49 (☎921 60; fax 915 13), above Raymond's Steak

House. Mr. Bangun's English students are available as guides **for free,** in exchange for a chance to practice their English. Generally available M-Sa 8am-8pm, varies Su. For plane and ferry tickets, try **P. T. Persiar Indah,** Jl. Veteran 55 (☎911 50), inside the *wartel* office as you head south from the monument. Open daily 7:30am-midnight.

Currency Exchange: BNI, Jl. Veteran 22, several blocks down from the monument, on the right as you head south. Open M-Th 8:30am-3:30pm, F 8:30am-noon and 2-3:30pm. **24hr. ATM** takes international cards.

Markets: Pasar Sentral winds along the narrow lanes around the main bus terminal on Jl. Veteran. Sells everything from live fish to rubber boots and pirated CDs. **Pasar Buah,** the fruit market, on the left of Jl. Gundaling, has Berastagi's trademark *marquisa* passion fruit among the piles. Tourist tack is also for sale. Both open daily 6am-9pm.

Pharmacy: Dharma Bakti, Jl. Veteran 49A, past the central market before the cabbage. Open daily 8:30am-8pm. A **24hr.** pharmacy is in the Public Health Center (see below).

Medical Services: Public Health Center, Jl. Veteran 34. (☎910 28). English-speaking doctors normally available in the mornings. **Open 24hr.**

Telephones: Telkom office, Jl. Perwira 1, next to the post office. Open daily 7am-midnight. International calls also available at the *wartel* office at Jl. Veteran 55, on the left as you head south from the monument. Open daily 7:30am-midnight.

Internet Access: Sporadic service at **Mikie Holiday Hotel,** 2km out of town on the main road to Medan (*Sudako* Rp700). Rp5000 per hr. Open daily 9am-4pm. The owner of the *wartel* office at Jl. Veteran 55 was expecting to offer **Internet** by August 2002.

Post Office: Jl. Veteran 4, next to the tourist office. Open M-Th, Sa 8am-2pm, F 8-11am. **Postal code:** 22156.

ACCOMMODATIONS

Berastagi has some of the finest guest houses in North Sumatra. Many double as trek and rafting organizers and travel agents.

Elshaddai Hotel and Restaurant, Jl. Veteran 65/66 (☎910 23; fax 915 13). Just north of the monument. Excellently run budget hotel. Rooftop patio with a nice view. Shared *mandi* with hot shower (Rp3000). Singles Rp10,000; doubles Rp15,000. ❶

Losmen Sibayak Guest House, Jl. Veteran 119 (☎910 95; fax 911 22). Head south from the war monument; it's 200m down on the left. Organizes trekking, rafting, and guides to local volcanoes. Hot showers Rp2000. Dorms Rp8000; simple singles/doubles with shared *mandi* Rp15,000/Rp20,000, with bath Rp25,000. ❶

Sibayak Multinational Rest House, Jl. Pendidikan 93 (☎910 31). Beautiful, quiet, secluded hotel on the grounds of an old Dutch home 2km from the war monument, on the road that leads up to Sibayak volcano. Follow directions to Gunung Sibayak (see **Hiking,** below), or take a *sudako* from the monument (Rp1000). Faultlessly clean rooms with marble floors and balconies overlooking well-kept gardens. All rooms have Western baths and hot showers. Doubles Rp35,000-50,000. ❸

Sinabung Resort Hotel, Jl. Kolam Renang, (☎914 00; fax 913 00), about 1km out of town. From the monument, walk up Jl. Gundaling past the fruit market, turn right at the sign onto Jl. Kolam Renang by the football field. The best upscale hotel in town. Immaculate rooms with satellite TV, Western baths, and hot water. Heated swimming pool, mini-golf, beauty salon, tennis courts, and health center. Doubles Rp400,000; deluxe cottages Rp550,000 and up. Discounts often available mid-week. AmEx/MC/V. ❺

Wisma Sibayak Guest House, Jl. Udara 1 (☎911 04). Head south on Jl. Veteran from the bus terminal; it's set back from the road where Jl. Udara branches right just after the cabbage sculpture. Excursions into the surrounding area. Dorms Rp8000; singles Rp10,000-15,000; doubles 25,000-40,000. Higher-end rooms have Western bath. ❶

FOOD

For such a small town, Berastagi has a surprising number of good places to eat. Most *losmen* offer extensive menus of Indonesian and Western standbys, including hearty trekkers' breakfasts. Along **Jl. Veteran,** options range from fried banana stands and *sate* stalls to shiny restaurants with window displays of mouth-watering *padang* and *batak* dishes. Jl. Veteran, between the monument and **Losmen Sibayak,** comes alive each night with cheap *warung* selling everything from fried chicken to delicious shellfish *(kerang rebus)*, most for Rp5000 or less.

Bundok Andung, Jl. Veteran 20, on the right as you walk from the post office toward BNI. Sparkling clean with simmering piles of spicy chicken, fish, and shrimp dishes. Rp15,000-20,000 for a full meal. Open daily 7am-10pm. ❸

Muslimin, Jl. Veteran 128, close to the bus terminal. Good place to meet locals, who come here every night for tasty food in an unpretentious atmosphere. Most dishes Rp5000-7000. Open daily 7am-10pm. ❶

Eropah, Jl. Veteran 60, on the right as you head south from the monument. Good Chinese food and a range of Western and Indonesian staples. Fried chicken Rp15,000. Sweet and sour pork Rp15,000. Large beer Rp10,000. Open daily 7am-9am. ❸

Raymond's, Jl. Veteran 49, on the left as you walk south from the monument. Popular foreigner's hangout with a good selection of Western and Indonesian food. Steaks Rp4000-5000. Spaghetti Rp6000-14,000. Open daily 6:30am-10pm. ❷

INDONESIA

SIGHTS AND ENTERTAINMENT

The **highland region** around Berastagi constitutes the heart of Karo Batak country, and several **Karo villages** are close enough to visit on daytrips. **Peceren,** 2km past the war monument on the road to Medan, is the closest. Traditional Karo longhouses, complete with buffalo horns and thatched roofs, stand alongside modern, concrete buildings with satellite dishes. Ask for directions to the *rumah adat* (traditional houses). Although guest house operators decry Perceren as "impure," it perhaps provides a more realistic look at contemporary Karo life than other more "traditional" settlements popular with tour groups and sightseers. It's also easy to get to the larger village of **Lingga,** where a dozen or so traditional houses are interspersed with more modern buildings (as well as the rusted shells of a number of abandoned vehicles). Thanks to its easy accessibility from Berastagi, Lingga sees more tourist traffic than other Karo Batak villages; as a result, it can feel somewhat commercialized. It may be better to visit later in the day, after most of the postcard vendors have gone home. Visitors are intercepted as they get off the bus and escorted to the "Tourist Information Center" to pay a donation (around Rp5000), after which they are free to roam and mingle as they please. To get to Lingga from Berastagi, take a *sudako* to Kabanjahe (Rp1000), then change to another minibus to Lingga (Rp1000). Other Karo villages, including **Cingkas** and **Dokan,** are slightly farther out of town. They remain slightly less "spoiled." There are hourly buses to Cingkas from Kabanjahe (Rp2500); for Dokan, take any bus from Kabanjahe bound for Siantar and ask to be let off at the turn-off for "Desa Dokan." From here, it's a 30min. walk to the village. Telah Bangun, of Tobali Tour and Travel (see **Tours,** p. 267), offers an overnight tour of **Serdang** during which you sleep and eat in a Batak longhouse. (Rp60,000. 3-person min.) The Losmen Sibayak Guest House offers a afternoon's walking tour from Berastagi through several smaller villages to Lingga. Check its office for details.

Tahura National Park, 15min. by *sudako* (Rp700) from Berastagi on the road to Medan, is home to gibbons, hornbills, and hundreds of other kinds of (mostly elusive) wildlife. You'd be quite lucky to see more than the occasional monkey, but a stroll along one of the park's marked trails is nonetheless a good way to get away from the traffic and back into the fresh air. (Open daily 8am-6pm. Rp1100.)

Back in town, **Arihta,** Jl. Veteran 36, near the splendid cabbage sculpture, is the town pool hall, where dozens of locals can be found mis-spending their youth and practicing trick shots. (Rp1000. Open daily 7am-11pm.)

HIKING

Most visitors spend their time hiking up the two spectacular volcanoes close to town. Most popular is **Gunung Sibayak** (2100m), an active volcano with clouds of sulfurous steam billowing from its peak. A well-maintained trail with concrete steps winds up the west slope to the crater. A second "jungle" trail winds up from the Berastagi-Medan Hwy., but this unmarked route is hard to follow and should not be attempted without a guide.

To reach the west route, walk north on Jl. Veteran, bearing left onto Jl. Gundaling. Turn right onto Jl. Pendidikan and follow the road past the football field. The road meanders slowly uphill through a small village, before veering right after a stretch of fields. The small bamboo shack on the left is the *pondok masuk,* where you pay your Rp1000 entrance fee. The hiking trail begins just to the left of the *pondok masuk;* take the lower path to the left of the thatched gateway. Note the sign bearing the names of the half-dozen or so unlucky tourists who came this way before but never made it home. Although a guide is not necessary for climbing the volcano via the western route, some hikers may feel safer joining up with a group. The walk uphill from here, along a pot-holed logging road through the forest, takes 2-3hr. At the summit, several steep trails lead downhill. The one on the right by the crater lake, before the radio antenna, leads down a steep flight of worn steps to the **hot springs** (Rp1000) and the village of **Semargat Gunung.** From the hot springs, regular *sudako* run back to the terminal in Berastagi (Rp2000). Maps of the route are available from the Tourist Information Office and from several of the hotels.

Gunung Sinabung (2417m), 27km west of Berastagi, makes for a much more challenging climb, requiring a good level of fitness and some previous climbing experience. Trails are rudimentary and devoid of markings. Several people have died on Sinabung over the years. Guides are available from the Losmen Sibayak guest house for Rp150,000 for a group of three. Most hikers begin at the village of Siga-ranggarang and end at Lake Kawar for a post-climb swim. Much of the hike is unspoiled jungle. The final few hundred meters cover loose rock. The ascent takes 3hr.; the earlier you begin, the better the view. On a clear day, it is possible to see the northern tip of shimmering Lake Toba, 30km to the south. Leave by 9am for the safest and most comfortable (cool on the way up, warm on top) climb.

BUKIT LAWANG ☎061

"Welcome to the jungle" is a common greeting in Bukit Lawang. But the "jungle" in this tiny town, beautifully set on the Bohorok River, is as apt a description of the tourist colony as it is of the nature that cradles it. Carved out of the rubber and cocoa plantations northwest of Medan, Bukit Lawang consists of a string of restaurants and guest houses lining the riverbank. Most people come here to visit the Bohorok Orangutan Rehabilitation Center, where the world's gentlest primates are reintroduced to their natural habitat. This is also a popular point of entry to the Gunung Leuser National Park (see p. 273), and many people get caught up in the beauty of the place, whiling away their time trekking, rafting, or tubing down the lazy river. Visitors looking for peace and quiet should avoid the weekends, when the party bus rolls in from Medan, often leaving devastation in its wake.

TRANSPORTATION

The **"bus terminal"** is the large sandy lot near the Visitors Center. Buses go to **Medan** (2½hr., every 30min. 5am-5pm, Rp5000). Tourist buses leave daily for **Berastagi** (5hr.; 8:30am; Rp45,000) and **Parapat** (10hr.; 8:30am; Rp60,000). Book at least one day in advance. Purchase tickets pretty much anywhere in town.

ORIENTATION AND PRACTICAL INFORMATION

The **Visitors Center, PHPA office,** and **tourist office** cluster near a dirt lot known as the **bus terminal.** The path leading upriver from the bus stop is **Jl. Orangutan,** lined with stalls selling blowpipes and mineral water, and (farther upriver) a dozen or so mellow bars and restaurants catering to the backpacker crowd. About 800m upriver, a gate marks the entrance to a **public campground;** the most popular guest houses are beyond the campground along the river. The **Bohorok Orangutan Center** is about 1.5km upriver from the **Visitors Center,** on the opposite bank.

Tourist Offices: PHPA Ranger Station (☎542 574), on Jl. Orangutan, opposite the bus lot. Organizes treks and nature walks. Sells permits to see orangutan feedings. Rp20,500 per person, good for 2 feedings in a day. Open daily 7am-3pm. **Bukit Lawang Visitors Center,** next door, has interesting exhibits about local wildlife. Videos screened M, W, F at 8pm. Open daily 8am-3pm. The **Tourist Information Center,** down a small path opposite the PHPA office, recruits tourists for its trekking and rafting expeditions. Open daily 7am-4pm. Most guest houses arrange these trips as well (roughly US$15 per person per day).

Currency Exchange: There are **no banks** in Bukit Lawang. Most guest houses and travel agents will change money, but often at poor rates. The **wartel** kiosk also exchanges cash and traveler's checks and stays open until midnight.

Police: Opposite the bus terminal. **Open 24hr.**

Medical Services: There is a **polyclinic** opposite the PHPA office. Open daily 8am-8pm.

Telephones: Wartel kiosk off the path to Bukit Lawang Cottages; turn left off Jl. Orangutan at the sign. International collect calls Rp3000. Open daily 6am-midnight.

Internet: Natrabu Tours and Travel, on Jl. Orangutan, opposite the Visitors Center. Also available at the **Wisma Leuser Sibayak Guest House.** Both charge Rp10,000 per 30min. and are open daily roughly 8am-9pm.

Post Offices: No post office, though several shops sell stamps. Most guest houses will mail letters for you if you're planning to be away in the jungle for a while.

ACCOMMODATIONS

Excellent accommodations line both banks for 1.5km upstream from the bus terminal. For late-night music and reggae bars, stay at one of the places close to the bus terminal in the center of the village. Places farther upriver (past the campground) are much quieter. For the cheapest sleep in town, head to the campground about 10min. upriver from the main village, on the right-hand bank as you head upstream. (Rp1000 entrance fee. Basic facilities.)

Jungle Inn (☎08 681 210 5758; thejungleinn2000@yahoo.com), 400m beyond the campground entrance gate, across the river from the Rehabilitation Center. One of the most original guest houses in the whole of Sumatra. Restaurant and a range of "jungle-themed" doubles featuring 4-poster beds, hand-carved furniture, and hammocks. Ask to see the waterfall room. Doubles with bath Rp30,000-75,000. ❷

INDONESIA

Pongo Resort (☎454 2574; dirganet@indosat.net.id), next to the Orangutan Rehabilitation Center, a 30min. walk upstream from the bus terminal. Luxury thatched huts on the river banks, surrounded by waterfalls and rainforest. A peaceful piece of paradise. Attached restaurant. Doubles (all with Western toilets and showers) Rp100,000-200,000. Prices include breakfast and orangutan feeding permits. ❺

Bukit Lawang Cottages (☎414 5061; lawang@indosat.net.id), across the river from the bus terminal. Spacious grounds right on the river—close to town but away from the crowds. Smaller bungalows with bath and 2nd-floor patio Rp15,000; bungalows with veranda Rp30,000; orangutan bungalow with "jungle" bath Rp40,000. ❷

Wisma Leuser Sibayak (☎550 576), across the river from the main "village," over one of the first bridges you reach from the bus terminal. Popular restaurant with live music and sing-alongs. Internet. Basic rooms/bungalows with bath Rp20,000-30,000. ❷

Queen Resort, a 10min. walk upstream from the bus terminal, past the campground. Away from the crowds, but within easy walking distance of pizza and cold beer. Large bamboo rooms with comfy beds and private bath go for Rp15,000-45,000. ❶

Green Paradise Backpacker and Café, a 10min. walk upriver from the bus terminal on the right. Dorm beds (Rp6000) are the cheapest in town. Basic doubles Rp15,000. ❶

FOOD

Cheap *warung* and *padang* joints are all along the river near the bus terminal. Most guest houses and hotels have their own restaurants. One of the best is the **Wisma Leuser Sibayak Resort** ❹ (see above), which serves Indonesian and Western food, often with live music. (Chicken *sate* Rp12,500. Shrimp with ginger sauce Rp13,500.) **Bamboo Pizzeria** ❸, opposite the Bukit Lawang Indah Guest House, serves excellent fresh-baked pizzas (Rp15,000-19,000) and pasta (spaghetti carbonara Rp15,000) in a classy, laid-back atmosphere. Also popular is **Lina's** ❸, a little farther upstream, with seating inside and out by the river, and a large menu of tourist and Indonesian food. (Fried squid Rp13,000. Chicken with chili Rp17,000.) Most restaurants generally stay open until at least 10pm and often much later.

SIGHTS AND ENTERTAINMENT

Most people come to Bukit Lawang in the hope of getting up close and personal with the local population of *Pongo pygmaeus abelli*, or orangutans. About 1.5km upstream from the bus terminal lies the world-famous **Orangutan Rehabilitation Center,** founded in 1973 with grants from the World Wildlife Fund and the Frankfurt Zoological Society to reintroduce illegally captured orangutans to their natural habitat. Since then, the rehabilitation project has successfully returned more than 120 animals to the rainforest. Two **daily feedings** (8-9am and 3-4pm) take place near the Rehabilitation Center, when wild and semi-wild orangutans can usually be seen feasting on bananas and swinging slowly from tree to tree. A small boat ferries visitors across the river before each feeding. Day-long **permits** (good for both feedings) can be obtained at the PHPA office (see p. 271) for Rp20,500. Visitors keen to share less orchestrated time with the primates can go on one of the **one-day treks** organized by most guest houses, or the PHPA, where guides will normally guarantee at least one sighting of the animals in the wild.

The superb **Bat Cave** is 15min. from the village center. The trail starts behind Bukit Lawang Cottages and winds through a rubber plantation before turning right to the cave. The cavern is filled with bats and leads some 600m into the hillside. A flashlight is essential. You can normally rent one (Rp3000) at the entrance, where a Rp1000 entrance fee is charged.

Bukit Lawang is a popular point of entry into the **Gunung Leuser National Park** (see below). **Treks** and expeditions can be arranged through the PHPA office, or at most guest houses. Prices are generally the same wherever you arrange your trip, and range from US$15 per person for a one-day "jungle trek" to three-day excursions to Berastagi (US$65), six-day hikes to Kutacane (US$250), and seven-day jungle expeditions (US$250). **Rafting** down the Bohorok River is another popular pastime here; one-day trekking and rafting combos cost US$25 per person.

Most guest houses at Bukit Lawang have **inner tubes** for use on the Bohorok River (Rp3000 per day). During the dry season (Feb. to June), the water level may be too low to float safely. Check with the Visitors Center first. You can also float 6km down to Bohorok village (2-3hr.). Local buses ferry the drenched back to Bukit Lawang (Rp500).

NIGHTLIFE

For a tiny, nondescript settlement in the middle of nowhere, Bukit Lawang has an impressively active nightlife—especially on weekends, when bus loads of people buzz in from Medan to party primate-style through the night. The narrow pathway along the right-hand side of the river (heading upstream from the bus terminal) is home to a number of laid-back bars, cafes, and restaurants with tourist-oriented menus (and music collections). Among the most popular are **Tony's Restaurant** and **Lina's Coffee Shop,** both serving food and drink into the wee hours. Lina's organizes a late-night "dance party" every Saturday night. Next door to Lina's is an incredibly mellow wooden **reggae shack** with dim lighting, floor cushions, and the best music collection in town.

ACEH PROVINCE

> Due to clashes between government forces and Acehnese nationalists, *Let's Go* has reduced coverage of Aceh province. Although considerable numbers of foreign tourists are now beginning to travel again to Banda Aceh, Pulau Weh, and other areas of the province, travel in Aceh is still considered dangerous. Consult your embassy before traveling here.

GUNUNG LEUSER NATIONAL PARK

The virgin rainforest enveloping the fault lines of the Alas and Kluet River Valleys constitutes the largest national park in Southeast Asia. This is perhaps the best wildlife reserve in Indonesia, stretching across more than 800,000 hectares of unspoiled wilderness and covering large parts of Northern Sumatra. The park's ecology is incredibly diverse, ranging from marshy wetlands at lower altitudes to much cooler alpine forests higher up the mountains. Gunung Leuser, for which the park is named, is Sumatra's second-highest mountain at 3119m. Most people come here to trek through the rainforest, where visitors can expect to see gibbons and orangutans, and may be lucky enough to catch a glimpse of the park's more elusive inhabitants—elephants, Sumatran rhinos, tigers, and clouded leopards. Over 300 species of birds have been identified in the park, which also supports several thousand species of plant life, including the malodorous rafflesia, the world's largest flower. The park's largest town is **Kutacane** (see p. 275), just an hour by road from **Ketambe** (see p. 276), probably the best base for treks into the jungle. Many tourists also enter the park from Bukit Lawang (see p. 270).

TREKKING

Trekking is the most popular activity in the park. Prices vary substantially: in general, the closer you are to the starting point, the cheaper the hike. Nearly every tourist office and guest house in nearby towns organizes treks. The most exorbitant treks originate in Medan. Prices include food, drink, camping equipment, necessary permits, a guide, and transport to the starting point. Most guide services can arrange transportation from the finish point to the next destination. Prices are listed in US dollars and translated to rupiah according to the daily quote. Larger groups tend to mean lower charges per person—but bear in mind that wildlife sightings are much more likely if you're in a smaller, quieter group.

Employ guides licensed with the **HPI** (the Indonesian Guide Association) whenever possible for legal, environmental, and safety reasons. Comment books of guest houses may also indicate the outstanding guides. Beware of prepackaged multiple day treks—they often involve only a few hours of hiking each day, with the rest of the time for "relaxing." Make sure your guide understands the level of intensity you are looking for. Many trekkers arrange their trips from **Bukit Lawang.** Standard HPI prices are US$15 per person for one-day treks, US$35 for two-day, and US$65 for three-day treks; group size is usually a minimum of three people.

To avoid most of the tourist traffic, consider starting from beautiful **Ketambe,** where prices tend to be lower and more open to negotiation (around Rp60,000-75,000 per person for a day's trekking). Most treks organized in Berastagi actually begin in Ketambe. As jaunts become expeditions, prices per day rise to pay for extra porters and more experienced guides. For a six-day hike from Ketambe, prices are around US$30 a day per person. Such treks include the route between Bukit Lawang and Ketambe and climbs up **Gunung Kembiri** and **Gunung Bendahara. Gunung Leuser** (3119m) and **Loser** (3404m) are best attempted from **Blangkejeren** and will take up to 10 days.

RAFTING

Rafting expeditions range from the boisterous water-park feel of the **Bohorok River** in Bukit Lawang to multiple-day adventures down the **Wampu River** near Ketambe. Rafting prices, which include all expenses, tend to be higher than trekking prices to cover multiple guides and expensive equipment. From Bukit Lawang, trips down the Wampu River average US$75 per person per day for one- to four-day jaunts. In the Kutacane area, rafting trips down the **Alas River** start in Ketambe and head toward Gelombang. The most competitive rates are with tour services in Kutacane and Ketambe. One-day floats from Ketambe to Kutacane cost Rp300,000 per person for groups of three (less per person for larger groups). Three- or four-day adventures cost US$70-85 per person. **Combined rafting/trekking** trips (3 days rafting/2 days trekking) are becoming more popular. Arrange these in Bukit Lawang, Kutacane, or Ketambe (US$130-145 in Bukit Lawang).

INDONESIA

KUTACANE ☎0629

At the heart of the stunningly beautiful Alas River Valley, Kutacane is the slightly scruffy one-street capital of the Aceh Tenggara region, a convenient stop for travelers heading north to Ketambe and Blangkejeren or south toward Berastagi. As elsewhere in Aceh, all visitors, especially women, should dress modestly, and a cursory knowledge of basic Indonesian is essential.

TRANSPORTATION AND PRACTICAL INFORMATION. Kutacane's one main road, **Jl. A. Yani,** heads north to Ketambe and Blangkejeren and south to Sidikalang and Berastagi. Buses leave from the **bus terminal,** at the north end of town on Jl. A. Yani, to: **Blangkejeren** (4hr.; every hr. 5am-2pm; Rp15,000); **Ketambe** (1hr., frequent, Rp5000); **Medan** (8hr.; every hr. 5am-8pm; Rp20,000) via **Berastagi** (6hr.; Rp16,000); and **Sidikalang** (3hr.; every hr. 8am-noon; Rp10,000). Additional buses (and minibuses) to Medan and Berastagi leave from **Terminal Terpadu,** accessible by *becak* from the main terminal (Rp1000). The staff at **Penara Rafting and Trekking Center** may be able to change money in an emergency, but you're better off bringing all the cash you'll need. The **police station,** Jl. A. Yani 108 (☎211 10), is past the bus terminal, on the road north to Ketambe on the right. **Apotik Sari** is one of several pharmacies along Jl. A. Yani. **Kutacane Public Hospital** (☎216 76) is 5km north of town on the road to Blangkejeren; if you're seriously ill, get back to Medan as quickly as possible. The **telephone office** is on Jl. A. Yani 62. (☎211 17. **Open 24hr.**) Next door is the **post office,** Jl. A. Yani 91, opposite the bus terminal. (☎213 66. Open M-Th 7:30am-3pm, F 7:30am-noon, Sa 7:30am-1pm.) **Postal code:** 24611.

ACCOMMODATIONS AND FOOD. Wisma Cut Nyal Dien ❸, Jl. Cut Nyal Dien 14, provides well-kept rooms in a pleasant family home. Head south from the bus terminal and turn right onto Jl. Rajawali opposite the Famili restaurant, after 300m. Turn left at the end of the road; the house is on the right. (☎217 36. Rooms with *mandi* Rp50,000.) On the same street (turn right instead of left at the end of Jl. Rajawali), the **Bru Dihe Hotel ❹,** Jl. Cut Nyal Dien 10, has decent doubles with attached squat toilets and *mandi*, and "deluxe" rooms with Western toilets and A/C. (☎214 44. Standard rooms Rp60,000-75,000; deluxe rooms Rp90,000.) **Wisma Pernawar ❷,** Jl. Rajawali 68, has friendly staff and clean doubles with or without squat toilets. (☎213 30. Doubles Rp20,000-35,000.) From the bus terminal, head 300m south on Jl. A. Yani, turn right on Jl. Rajawali, then left onto a side street after 30m; it's on the left. **Hotel Maroon ❷,** Jl. A. Yani II 15-17, is another good option, with clean rooms, fresh sheets, and towels. To get there, use the directions to Wisma Pernawar, but turn right onto the side street after 30m; it's on the right. (☎210 78. Doubles with bath Rp17,000-70,000.) The clean, well-kept **Rumah Makan Famili ❸,** on Jl. A. Yani, opposite Jl. Rajawala, is one of several places along Jl. A. Yani serving excellent *padang* food. (Full meal Rp10,000-15,000. Open daily 7am-midnight.)

RAFTING AND TREKKING. There is really no compelling reason to linger in Kutacane—the trekking and rafting excursions that draw travelers to the region can be arranged just as easily from Ketambe. Still, if you are in town for a while, it's worth stopping in at the **Penara Rafting and Trekking Center,** Jl. A. Yani 94, on the right as you head north toward the bus terminal, next door to the Hotel Lawe Munas. The large staff of accredited, English-speaking **HPI** guides lead treks and rafting adventures. Three-day rafting trips cost US$80 per person for groups of two (including meals, guides, camping, permits, and transportation). Five-day rafting and hiking combos start at US$95 per person (for groups of 2); For straight-up trekking expeditions, the charges start at US$65 per person for a three-day trip. Prices per person drop with larger groups. (Open daily 8am-midnight.)

INDONESIA

KETAMBE

At a natural bottleneck where mountains close in upon the rice fields of the Alas River Valley, Ketambe is one of the most scenic spots in Sumatra. Few tourists make it this far; the tranquility that disappeared from places like Bukit Lawang long ago remains here. Ketambe is an ideal spot to spend a few lazy days swimming in the river, walking through the jungle to hot springs, or sampling the bewildering array of fresh-off-the-tree fruits, including superb mangosteen, durian, and rambutan. The village is also a perfect base for rafting and trekking trips into Gunung Leuser National Park (see p. 273). Don't be surprised if you end up staying here longer than you originally planned—Ketambe is pretty close to paradise.

TRANSPORTATION AND PRACTICAL INFORMATION. Flag down a bus heading north to **Blangkejeren** (3hr.; every hr. 8am-5pm; Rp10,000) or south to **Kutacane** (1hr., every hr. 8am-6pm, Rp5000). Ketambe is a tiny village, made up of a few houses and a string of guest houses along the **Kutacane-Blangkejeren Rd.** The **Ketambe Research Station** is on the other side of the Alas River. In a pinch, you can change money at the **Pondok Wisata Guest House** (see **Accommodations and Food,** below). Purchase trekking permits (Rp4000 per day) at any of the guest houses in Ketambe. For brief wanders into the jungle from the village (paths are well marked and most guest houses have maps), you will probably be fine without a guide or a permit. For anything more ambitious than an afternoon stroll, however, you will need to take a guide (available from any guest house), who will arrange all the necessary permits for you. You *must* have a guide for any overnight trek.

INDONESIA

ACCOMMODATIONS AND FOOD. Guest houses in Ketambe arrange trekking and rafting excursions, while their kitchens cook up the only meals in town. The nicest of the guest houses that cluster along the road south of the park gate is the **Wisma Sadar Wisata ❷,** with large rooms and bungalows along the river, surrounded by gardens and rice paddies. (Doubles and bungalows with *mandi* Rp20,000.) The attached open-air restaurant features a large Western and Indonesian menu and stunning views out onto the mountains and the Alas River. Another good option is the **Pondok Wisata Guest House ❶,** across the road from the Wisma Sadar Wisata, with a wide range of rooms and lovely spacious gardens. (☎786 7051. Simple doubles with Western baths Rp7000-10,000; "luxury" doubles with hot showers Rp25,000-30,000.)

DAYTRIP FROM KETAMBE: GUNUNG LEUSER NATIONAL PARK. The **Gurah Recreation Forest** surrounding Ketambe is one of four special areas set up within the park to allow visitors to picnic, take a day hike, or stay overnight. Permits (Rp4000 per day) are needed to enter; overnight trips require a local guide. Hiking-trail maps are available at all guest houses, but not all trails are marked—it's easy to miss turn-offs without a guide. If you want to see local wildlife (gibbons, hornbills, orangutans, elephants, and even the occasional tiger), hire a guide. Prices vary according to the number of people in your group, but typical rates include: Rp350,000 per person for a 3-day trek; Rp1,300,000 per person for a 5-day hike; and Rp400,000 per person for a day's rafting. Often negotiable, rates usually include food, transport, and overnight camping. Trips can be arranged almost anywhere along "main street" in Ketambe; one excellent guide who works out of the Wisma Sadar Wisata is the implausibly named John F. Kennedy.

DANAU TOBA (LAKE TOBA)

Southeast Asia's largest freshwater lake and the largest crater lake in the world, majestic Lake Toba is Sumatra's top tourist destination, and one of the most awe-inspiring natural sights in Southeast Asia. The steep slopes that ring Toba form the rim of an ancient volcano, whose cataclysmic eruption some 75,000 years ago created the lake, and may have even triggered the last ice age. Undiscovered by the outside world until the 1850s, the area around Lake Toba is the homeland of the Batak Toba, a now predominantly Christian people whose unique language and culture still thrive today. A remarkably relaxed and laid-back place, with an abundance of excellent guest houses, bars, and restaurants sprinkled along the waterfront, Lake Toba offers breathtaking views, welcoming people, and rich cultural heritage. This is the perfect spot to kick back and take a break from traveling for a while. Be warned—Lake Toba can be a difficult place to leave behind.

TONGGING

Unspoiled and resplendent at the head of Lake Toba, Tongging is a secluded spot that not many tourists visit—a great place to get a feel for what this area must have looked like, in the days before pizza parlors and late-night bars set up shop.

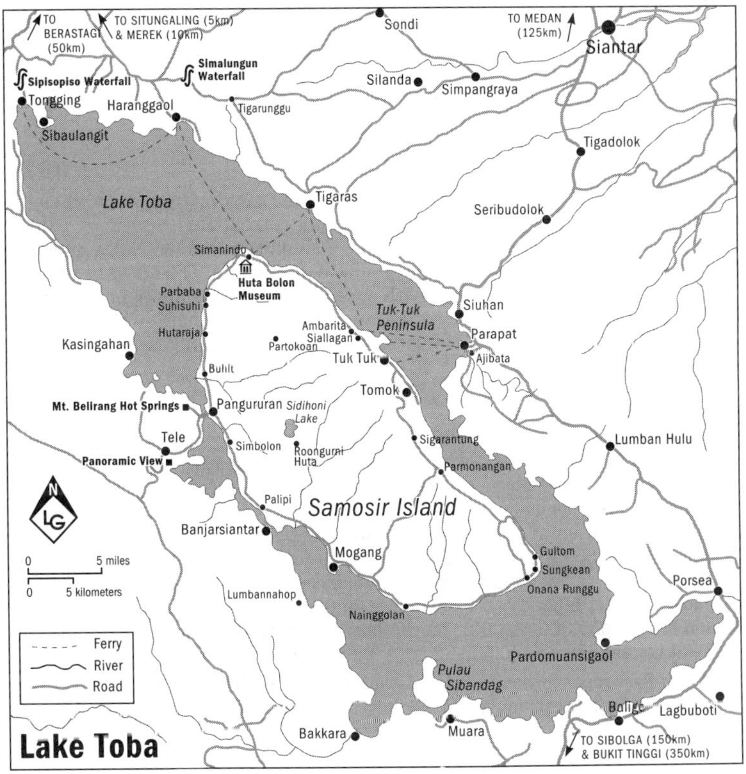

There is plenty to do around Tongging aside from admiring your reflection in the lake. **Sipisopiso and Sidompah waterfalls** are both within a 2hr. hike, with breathtaking views of Lake Toba from the top of Gunung Sipisopiso. Several nearby villages afford spectacular views **(Sibaulangit),** longhouses **(Bage),** and a monument to the Batak ancestors **(Silalahi).** Wisma Sibayak rents canoes (Rp20,000) and fishing rods (Rp5000) and will help you cook your catch.

Easily reached from Berastagi, Tongging is a good alternative to Parapat as an access point to Samosir Island, the hub of Lake Toba's tourist activity. From **Kabanjahe** (a short *sudako* ride from Berastagi), there are frequent buses to **Situngaling** (30min., Rp2000). From there, take a bus to Tongging (20min., Rp1500), or walk down the steep, winding road that leads to the lake. There are also usually four direct buses a day from Kabanjahe (1½hr., Rp2000). Buses run regularly from nearby **Merek** to **Pangururan,** on the western shore of Samosir Island (3hr., every hr. 7:30am-5pm, Rp5000). Or, hang around until Monday morning, when a market-day ferry runs from Tongging to **Haranggaol** (2½hr., M 8:30am, Rp8000). From there catch a ferry to **Ambarita** or **Tuk Tuk** on Samosir Island (4hr.; M, Th 2pm; Rp20,000).

Tongging is a tiny village with no street names or telephone numbers. The road into town winds down from the Sipisopiso Waterfall and arrives at the center of the village at the top of the lake. If you want to mail a letter, make a call, or chat it up with the police, head up the road to **Merek.** Your best source for **information** on the local area is also the town's only **guest house,** the **Wisma Sibayak ❷,** about 1.5km down the road from the bus drop-off point. (Decent sized doubles with shared *mandi* Rp20,000-25,000; bungalow-style rooms with Western bath Rp35,000.) There is also a **restaurant ❸** with a somewhat pricey, limited selection. (Fried chicken Rp15,000.) Otherwise, you'll have to catch dinner yourself, or go back to "town," where *warung* serve cheap chicken and fish meals by the harbor.

PARAPAT ☎0625

The rolling hills of Lake Toba's eastern shoreline have drawn tourists since the 1930s, when Parapat was a popular holiday retreat for the ruling Dutch. Crowds still flock here every weekend from Medan and elsewhere in Sumatra, filling the modern resorts that now dominate the skyline. The views across the lake to Samosir are hard to beat, with spectacular sunsets almost every night. For most foreign visitors, however, Parapat is little more than a transit point to Samosir, where the views are just as stunning and everything moves at a much calmer pace.

TRANSPORTATION

Buses: Public buses and private coaches depart from the terminal on Jl. Sisingamangaraja, 1km east of the police station. All buses originate in Medan and get to Parapat around midday; talk to travel agents about exact times. Minibuses booked ahead will often pick you up at your hotel. To: **Bukit Tinggi** (15hr.; 5 per day noon-8pm; Rp90,000-150,000); **Jakarta** (45hr.; 5 per day noon-5:30pm; Rp170,000-400,000); **Medan** (4hr.; 3 per day and frequent minibuses 10am-4pm; Rp25,000-40,000); **Padang** (17hr.; 5 per day noon-8pm; Rp100,000-160,000); **Sibolga** (6hr.; 11:30am and noon; Rp35,000-60,000). **Tourist buses** head to: **Berastagi** (4hr.; Rp40,000); **Bukit Lawang** (7hr.; Rp60,000-70,000); **Bukit Tinggi** (12hr.; Rp110,000).

Ferries: Passenger ferries to **Pulau Samosir** leave from Tiga Raja Pier, dropping passengers off at guest houses in Tuk Tuk (30-45min., every hr. 8:30am-7:30pm, Rp3000).

Local Transportation: *Sudako* follow streets counterclockwise (with your back to Samosir Island), from Tiga Raja Pier to the bus terminal, down Jl. Sisingamangaraja and then down Jl. Sinagara/Haranggaol back to Tiga Raja (Rp1000).

PRACTICAL INFORMATION

Jl. Sisingamangaraja, the main road, swings northwest-southeast through town, passing the **police, wartel, post office,** and **bus terminal** before rejoining the Trans-Sumatra Highway and heading south to Bukit Tinggi. **Jl. Kol. TPR Sinaga** (a.k.a. **Jl. Pulau Samosir**) branches off Jl. Sisingamangaraja at a **Welcome Gate** along the lake and follows the shore before crossing a ridge, becoming **Jl. Haranggaol** at the Natour Parapat Hotel, and leading to the **Tiga Raja Pier.** Buses usually drop backpackers off at the ferry.

Tourist Information and Tours: Use travel agents. Try **PT Dolok Silau,** Jl. Haranggaol 118 (☎415 49), near the ferry. Open daily 8am-6pm. **Branch** at Jl. Sisingamangaraja 56 (☎414 67), close to Singgalang Hotel, up the road from the police. **Andilo Nancy Travel Service** (☎415 48) has an office at the bus terminal. Open daily 6am-10pm.

Currency Exchange: Moneychangers line Jl. Haranggaol. There is a BNI **ATM** on Jl. Sisingamangaraja, but no bank. From Jl. Pulau Samosir, turn right after the gate onto Jl. Sisingamangaraja—past the police station and the mosque—and head straight uphill. It's 700m or so. **Cash advances** on credit cards are available (for a 10% commission) at the Singgalang Hotel.

Police: ☎421 10. On Jl. Sisingamangaraja next to the Welcome Gate. **Open 24hr.**

Medical Services: Parapat Public Hospital (☎413 32), on Jl. Ompu Ranjo, 800m past the bus terminal, left off Jl. Sisingamangaraja at the sign, and set back 300m on a hill.

Telephones: There are plenty of **wartel** along Jl. Haranggaol, and one **24hr.** *wartel* at Jl. Sisingamangaraja 177, across the road from the ATM, up past the gas station.

Internet: Sporadic service available at the *wartel*, Jl. Haranggaol 74. Rp300 per min. Open daily 7am-midnight.

Post Office: Jl. Sisingamangaraja 75 (☎414 88), by the Welcome Gate. *Poste Restante*. Open M-Th 7:30am-3pm, F 7:30-11:30am, Sa 7:30am-1pm. **Postal code:** 21174.

THE BIG SPLURGE

SORAKE BEACH RESORT

There's no shortage of places to stay in Sorake Beach, but one stands out from the rest. Tucked behind a grove of palm trees at the end of the beach, just a wave's length from the rows of indistinguishable wooden huts that stretch out all along the shoreline, the Sorake Beach Resort is Lagundi's only luxury hotel. In fact, it's the only real hotel of any kind for miles around.

The Sorake Beach Resort was designed as a sign of things to come, and busy teams of planners and schemers are no doubt still hoping that all of Lagundi Bay will look like this before too long, and that Nias will one day grow up to become the next Bali—which would be a shame. But so far, things haven't really taken off, and for now, any backpackers prepared to splash out the extra cash are likely to have the luxury rooms (and the priceless views) all to themselves.

Deluxe doubles start at Rp150,000 per night, which gets you a huge A/C room with a private hot shower and several sets of furniture to lounge around in. Suites start at Rp250,000, and for Rp350,000 you can be the proud overnight tenant of the magnificent presidential family suite—complete with sauna, two bedrooms, and a spacious sitting room. There's even a swimming pool, in case you get tired of all that sand and surf. *(☎211 95; fax 214 02. Major credit cards accepted; Rp750,000 minimum charge.)* ❺

ACCOMMODATIONS

Most of the cheaper hotels are on **Jl. Haranggaol** and lower **Jl. Sisingamangaraja.**

Riris Inn, Jl. Haranggaol 43 (☎413 92), 250m up Jl. Haranggaol from the harbor. Beautiful views from flowery porch. Clean doubles with Western bath Rp30,000. ❸

Singgalang Hotel, Jl. Sisingamangaraja 52 (☎412 60), 50m up from the police station on the right. Large, clean rooms with 3-4 beds off peaceful, wooden-floored corridors. All with shared *mandi.* Chinese restaurant downstairs. Rp20,000 per person. ❷

Charlie Inn (☎412 77), overlooking the market in front of the ferry landing, to the right as you face the water. Restaurant downstairs. A perfect spot for the early-morning ferry. Decent, well-kept rooms with bath Rp15,000-30,000. ❷

FOOD

There are plenty of good *padang*-style restaurants along Jl. Sisingamangaraja and Jl. Haranggaol, several serving the local specialty: fresh goldfish from the lake.

Hidangan Khas Minang, Jl. Sisingamangaraja 108, 100m up from Singgalang Hotel on the right. Clean and friendly *padang* restaurant with an English menu. Fried goldfish Rp9000. Octopus chili Rp8000. Mutton curry Rp15,000. Open daily 6am-11pm. ❷

Mitudo Cafe, Jl. Pulau Samosir, 400m past the Welcome Gate. Deck with the best views in town is perfect for a sundown drink. Guinness Rp14,000. Open daily 7am-2am. ❷

Hong Kong Restaurant, Jl. Haranggaol 9/11, near the crest of the hill. Sweet and sour pork Rp20,000. Fish hot plate Rp25,000. Open daily 7:30am-10pm. ❹

PULAU SAMOSIR

Samosir Island, larger in area than Singapore, is the focal point of North Sumatra's tourist industry—when foreign travelers wax lyrical about "Lake Toba," it's Samosir they're talking about. A bridge connects Samosir with the mainland to the west, but most travelers arrive by ferry from Parapat. Many never make it beyond the Tuk Tuk peninsula, a mellow tourist enclave of lakeside guest houses, bars, and restaurants. Those who do venture farther afield will find ancient relics of Batak culture, lush green countryside, and spectacular scenery.

TRANSPORTATION

Buses: Nearly all travelers to Samosir use the ferry to and from **Parapat,** but those who take the bus from Pangururan are rewarded with stunning views of Lake Toba's western shore. On Mondays, a market-day ferry connects **Tongging** (see p. 277) to **Haranggaol,** where another ferry runs to **Ambarita** and **Tuk Tuk** on Samosir. For regular public **buses** to elsewhere in Sumatra, you'll have to go via Parapat (or less conveniently, west across the bridge from Pangururan). Tourist agencies on the island (most in Tuk Tuk) can help arrange tickets in advance. Tourist buses go to: **Berastagi** (Rp40,000-50,000); **Bukit Lawang** (Rp60,000-70,000); **Bukit Tinggi** (Rp110,000); **Medan** (Rp40,000).

Ferries: Ferries chug along the shoreline every hr. throughout the day, stopping off to pick up passengers from their guest houses. From **Tuk Tuk** to **Parapat** (7am-6pm, Rp3000). Wave from your pier to flag one down. Also from **Tomok** (8am-7pm, Rp3000), and on market days from **Ambarita** (Tu, Th, Sa; Rp3000).

Local Transportation: Buses shuttle between **Pangururan** and **Tomok** (every hr. 6am-5pm, Rp7000) tracing the north shore via **Simanindo** (Rp5000). From Tuk Tuk, you'll have to walk to the north or south of the peninsula to catch a bus on the main road.

Rentals: Guest houses and cafes in Tuk Tuk rent **mountain bikes** (Rp20,000) and **motorcycles** (Rp40,000); usually for the day only. Bargain down later in the day.

ORIENTATION AND PRACTICAL INFORMATION

Pulau Samosir is 40km long and 20km wide. The largest town is **Pangururan,** the seat of local government, on the west shore. A single **perimeter road** circles the north half of the island, connecting Pangururan with **Tomok** on the east. At the north tip is the village of **Simanindo.** Most visitors stay on the mushroom-shaped **Tuk Tuk Peninsula,** 4km north of Tomok. The **Tuk Tuk Ring Rd.** branches off the main road to the right, 3km north of Tomok. After 2km, at the south neck of the peninsula, the shortcut to the small village of **Ambarita** branches left, and guest houses appear on the right. The narrow pavement follows Tuk Tuk's gold coast of guest houses and *warung* for 2km, joining the shortcut at the north neck and continuing to Ambarita, 3km up the coast. About 8km inland from Ambarita is the hamlet of **Partokoan,** a popular stopover point on the Ambarita-Pangururan traverse.

Tours: Agencies are everywhere in Tuk Tuk selling airline tickets and tourist bus and ferry tickets from Medan to Penang. Guest houses book tourist buses at slightly higher rates.

Currency Exchanges: Several places along the Tuk Tuk tourist trail change money, but rates are generally poor. Use the **ATM** in Parapat (see p. 279).

Bookstores: Gokhon Library, roughly halfway round the peninsular road, has a good selection of English books for rent or sale. There is another second-hand bookshop inside the **Bagus Bay** (see **Accommodations,** below).

Police: The **main station** (☎451 091) is in Ambarita, opposite a large football field, on the road from Tuk Tuk. There is a small **police post** in Tuk Tuk, near Carolina Cottages.

Medical Services: Health center (☎451 075), at the south end of the Tuk Tuk peninsula, round the corner from Carolina Cottages. Doctor speaks some English. **Open 24hr.** In an **emergency,** return to Parapat or Medan.

Telephones: There is a **wartel** (one of many) opposite Brando's Blues Bar at the north end of Tuk Tuk. Most guest houses have **international** service and free call-backs.

Internet Access: Bagus Bay, at the south end of Tuk Tuk. Rp400 per min. Open daily 8:30am-10pm. **Samosir Cottages** (for both, see **Accommodations,** below) Rp25,000 per hr. Open daily 7am-midnight. **Sibayak,** just past Tony's at the northern end of the peninsula. Rp18,000 per hr. Open daily 8am-10pm.

Post Office: Ambarita, Jl. Raya 39. Open M-Th 7:30am-3pm, F 7:30-11:30am, Sa 7:30am-1pm. **Postal code:** 22395.

ACCOMMODATIONS

As North Sumatra's premier tourist destinations, Tuk Tuk and Ambarita are full of cheap guest houses offering first-rate services. Almost all guest houses will show movies upon request. All the places listed below have views of the lake.

Bagus Bay Homestay and Restaurant (☎451 288), at the southern end of the peninsula, past Tabo cottages. One of Tuk Tuk's most popular backpacker hangouts. Movies every night, free Batak dance performances W and Sa 8:15pm. Table tennis, spacious garden, **Internet,** second-hand bookshop, and a cafe that's never empty. Dorm beds Rp7500; rooms and bungalows with bath Rp25,000-90,000. ❶

INDONESIA

Samosir Cottages (☎410 50; fax 451 170), toward the north of Tuk Tuk, a 5min. walk from Brando's Blues Bar. Not quite an upscale resort, just a well-polished budget place with a few extras—pool table, **Internet,** and hot running water. Spotless doubles with Western bath Rp15,000-25,000. Rooms with bathtub and hot water Rp35,000. ❷

Tony's Guest House (☎451 209), on the north end of the peninsula. Batak-style chalets with patios facing the lake. Cafe and TV/living room overlook the water. Sunbathing platform. Good value. Doubles with bath Rp15,000-25,000. ❷

Tabo Cottages (☎451 318; tabores@indo.net.id), on the south neck, past the Ambarita shortcut road. A cut above average, with stylish rooms, table tennis, **Internet,** vegetarian restaurant, and "wellness program." Delicious fresh-baked bread. Rooms with Western bath Rp19,000-39,000; bungalows Rp49,000-99,000. ❷

Carolina Hotel (☎415 20; fax 415 21), toward the southern end of Tuk Tuk, on a side lane that juts off the main strip just before it leads uphill to Tabo Cottages. Spacious grounds overlooking the lake. Well-appointed rooms and Batak-style villas, most with hot showers and Western toilets. Attached restaurant. Attracts a slightly more well-heeled crowd. Rooms Rp27,500-90,000. ❸

Timbul Bungalows (☎413 74), out of Tuk Tuk, along the main road north to Ambarita, 10min. by motorbike. An almost surreal quiet after Tuk Tuk; bungalows overlook the lake, with great views of Tuk Tuk and Parapat. Doubles with bath Rp15,000; larger rooms with Western toilets Rp20,000; Batak-style house with hot water Rp25,000. ❶

INDONESIA

FOOD

Most travelers eat at their guest houses, which tend to offer uninspiring menus with typical Western and Indonesian staples, but there are alternatives along the main road through Tuk Tuk. If you've been craving fresh pizza (or magic mushroom omelettes), you've come to the right place. The following are all in Tuk Tuk.

Bamboo, at the north end of the peninsula, on the right. Lovely restaurant serving tasty food accompanied by superb views over the lake. Pillows, cushions, and lots of comfy bamboo chairs. *Gado-gado* Rp8000. Pasta Rp10,000-13,000. Curries Rp8000-12,000. Large beer Rp12,000. Open daily 7am-midnight. ❷

Pizzeria Rumba, with branches in the north (past Tony's) and south (past the health clinic) of Tuk Tuk Peninsula. Rumba was the first of Tuk Tuk's countless pizzerias, and still the best. Pizza Rp19,000, extra toppings Rp1000-4000 apiece. Cheaper in the north, better in the south. Both open daily 8am-10pm. ❸

Tabo Vegetarian Restaurant and Bakery, at the cottages. Excellent fish and vegetarian food on a beautiful wooden veranda. Best are the homemade German bread (Rp2500), cake (Rp3000), and ice cream (Rp3500). Salads Rp5000-12,000. ❷

Endy's Restaurant, next to Gokhon Library, roughly halfway around the peninsular road. An excellent place to relax with a book from the lending library next door. Excellent sandwiches made with fresh brown bread. Bread Rp3000 per slice. Avocado sandwich Rp8000. Chicken sandwich Rp10,000. Open daily 9am-8pm. ❷

Juwita Cafe, toward the southern end of the peninsula, on the road that leads uphill past the health clinic. Downstairs cafe is nondescript, but the views from the hillside terrace are unbeatable. Daily cooking classes advertised (1-4pm). Coconut curries with beef Rp17,500. Fresh goldfish from the lake also available. Open daily 7am-10pm. ❸

Mafir, up the road from Juwita (see above), 50m down from the Roy's Pub sign. Wide-ranging menu and tie-dyed surroundings. Chicken *sate* Rp13,000. Curry chicken Rp13,000. Large beer Rp12,000. Fruit juices Rp5000. Open daily 7am-10pm. ❸

Rumah Makan Islam Murni, close to Carolina's, after the police post. Escape from the banana pancake crowd and remind yourself that you're in Indonesia. Airy, *padang*-style restaurant. Chicken Rp7000. Fish Rp8000. Open daily 7:30am-9:30pm. ❷

Tempo Doeloe Ruman Makan Islam, next to Brando's Blues Bar toward the north of the peninsula. Garish murals depict local scenery–and Bob Marley. Good *padang* food (beef *rendang* Rp12,500). Open daily 8am-midnight. ❸

SIGHTS

Most travelers come to spend a few lazy days chilling out and splashing in the lake, but there are also cultural attractions along the eastern shore, within 20km of Tomok. Motorcycles and bicycles are the most convenient modes of transport, but be careful: the only roads safely navigable by motorcycle are the north coast road from Tomok to Pangururan (passing through Ambarita and Simanindo) and the Tuk Tuk Ring Rd. The whole island can be circled in about seven hours, but the roads in the south are treacherous and should only be tackled in good light.

TOMOK AND AMBARITA. There are several megalithic **tomb complexes** in Tomok, 10min. by motorbike south of Tuk Tuk. Featuring moss-covered stone statues of humans and animals, they were built to hold the remains of local Batak kings, the Sidobutars, whose descendants still live in Tomok today. Signs from the main road to Tuk Tuk lead uphill through a maze of souvenir stalls to a **carved stone coffin,** guarded by stone elephants, on the right about 500m up. The nearby **Museum of King Sidobutar** was closed indefinitely when we last visited (July 2002), but may have re-opened since. The **tomb of Rajah Ompu Soribuntu Sidobutar** is farther uphill, under a *hariam* tree. More interesting and slightly less commercialized, **Siallagan village** lies 8km up the road in Ambarita, behind the post office near the town harbor. As you drive along the main road from Tuk Tuk, look for the sign on your left saying "Stone Chairs." Hidden behind a row of houses are several intricately **carved stone chairs,** about 300 years old—the site of village councils, where village chiefs arbitrated quarrels and gave out sentences. The second set of monoliths mark the site of the cannibalistic practices that made the Batak notorious following their first contact with Europeans. People found guilty of serious offenses (and enemies captured in battle) were brought here for execution. Once the poor victim's flesh had been tenderized with a stone mallet, he would be killed and cooked here—the main course at a banquet to which the whole village was invited. Cannibalism was never common practice among the Batak (it was reserved as punishment for serious offenses and as an economical way of dealing with prisoners of war), and by the early decades of the 20th century had died out completely.

SIMANINDO AND PANGURURAN. Some 20km north of Ambarita, the road reaches the village of **Simanindo,** on the north tip of the island. Here, a former chieftain's house has been converted into a **museum** full of dusty artifacts supposed to shed light on traditional Batak life. (Look for the sign on the right advertising the Huta Bolon Museum.) Daily performances of **traditional Batak dances** took place in the village until recently, but have been suspended. They may well have started up again by the time you read this; ask around in Tuk Tuk for the latest developments. Uninspiring **Pangururan** provides a base for forays into the hills on the mainland. The **Mt. Belirang Hot Springs** (Rp500) offer sulfurous comfort 4km west of town—look for signs on the main road. Although most visitors to Samosir seem to come here, the springs are unimpressive. Motorcycle enthusiasts can take a trip up **Mount Tele,** the steep ridge on the mainland. Beware of buses careening downhill. If for some reason you get stranded in Pangururan (or if you simply prefer urban grime to fresh air and fun), you can stay at **Hotel Wisata Samosir** ❶, 42 Dr.

T.B. Simatupang, next to the Telkom office on Jl. Sisingamangaraja. (☎200 50. Doubles with bath Rp10,000-18,000.) A tour of all these villages can be organized at the **Bagus Bay Guest House** (Rp50,000).

ENTERTAINMENT

Many guest houses show English movies nightly, in a cozy atmosphere with drinks. A few of the bars and restaurant along the main Tuk Tuk road stay open as long as there are customers, serving beer and tea till the wee hours to the background strum of Batak folk songs. The discos go till dawn on Saturday nights.

Brando's Blues Bar, a popular pub on the northern end of the peninsula, is a 5min. walk south from Tony's. No blues in evidence here (think U2 and Tracy Chapman), but this is a mellow, popular nightspot nonetheless—with a free pool table outside and beer (Rp14,000) and food (chicken *sate* Rp12,000) served until late. (Dance floor. Open throughout the day till 2am.) **Elios Bar,** at the southern end of Tuk Tuk, packs in the locals on Saturday nights for frantic gyrating to the pulsating beat of Indonesian house "music." (Open Sa 9pm-5am.) The nearby **Tumba Disco** is a similar affair, and is also open late on Saturday nights (closed during the week). **Roy's Pub,** down the road, is open nightly, but is often deserted during the week.

INDONESIA

HIKING ACROSS PULAU SAMOSIR

An invigorating hike across the island brings you through well-preserved Batak communities, much less impacted by tourism than those close to Tuk Tuk. The easiest and most pleasant route runs between Ambarita in the east and Pangururan in the west, and can be walked in either direction. Well-marked trails wind around coffee and tapioca plantations. It's possible to finish in one day if you start early. Alternatively, you can stay overnight in one of several villages with simple guest houses. Hikers setting out from Ambarita pass tiny **Partokoan,** which has two guest houses, **John's ❷** and **Jennie's ❷.** From Partokoan, a rocky cart path heads 9km up to the larger village of **Roongurni Huta,** where it meets the road left to Tomok (24km) and right to Pangururan (16km). The latter arrives after 6km at **Sidihoni Lake,** where **Weny Guest House ❶** puts up hikers for Rp5000 per night on the shore of the lake. The last 10km down to Pangururan offer stunning views of the steep crater walls and **Gunung Pusuk Buhit** on the western mainland.

PULAU NIAS

More than 100km west of mainland Sumatra, Pulau Nias is like nowhere else in Indonesia. Outside the two major towns, much of the interior of the island is thickly forested and remains relatively untouched by the outside world. The Niha people who inhabit the island are the proud inheritors of a unique language and culture, and Nias's rich tradition of monolithic stone sculptures and wood carving can still be seen today in dozens of villages around the island. Most visitors will pass through Gunung Sitoli, the not-so-interesting capital, on their way to the more popular southern part of the island. Many people come to Nias to surf—Sorake Beach, just a few kilometers outside Teluk Dalam, is renowned in zinc-nosed circles as home to some of the best waves in the world.

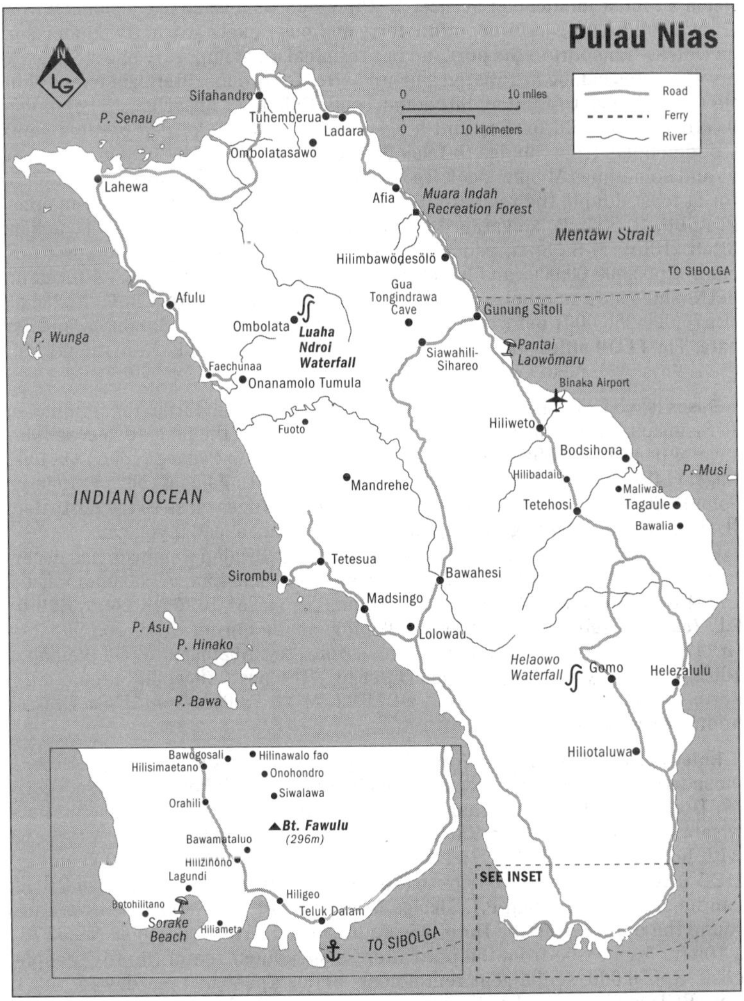

SIBOLGA

☎0631

Everything bad thing you've heard about Sibolga is true. Since this decidedly unpretty little town is the transit point to Pulau Nias, touts and aggressive hustlers swarm around the ferry and bus terminals. Happily, there is no reason why you should be stuck here for more than a couple of hours. **Scuba diving** and the **Internet** are two things you'll find in Sibolga and not on Nias.

The cheapest and safest way to buy **boat tickets** for Nias is to purchase them directly from the shipping offices. For **PT ASDP** boats to Gunung Sitoli, small branch offices at the port sell tickets right up to sailing time. If you're willing to fork out a bit of extra cash to forego the hassle of buying your own ticket,

Helen's Tourist Information Service, Jl. Diponegoro 33 (☎2542), a shack across from Mesjid Agung mosque, offers ferry and bus tickets at a hefty commission as well as transport to the port and bus terminal and temporary bag storage. As always, rates can be negotiated and are better for groups. **Overnight ferries** shuttle from Sibolga to Gunung Sitoli and Teluk Dalam. **PT Simeulue,** Jl. Pelabuhan 9, close to the old harbor and a *becak* ride from the port, operates small wooden boats from Sibolga to **Teluk Dalam** (10-12hr.; Tu, Th, Sa 8pm; return W, F, and sometimes M 8pm; deck Rp32,500). A few cabins are normally available for at least double the regular fare. (☎214 97. Office open M-Sa 8:30am-6pm.) **PT ASDP,** Jl. Sisingamangaraja 161, runs regular boats from Sibolga to **Gunung Sitoli** (10hr.; M-Sa 8pm; economy Rp19,500, A/C lounge Rp26,000, non-A/C cabin Rp55,000-60,000) and back. (☎217 52. Open M-Sa 8am-5pm.) Alternating **PELNI** ships stop in Sibolga most Saturdays and provide direct links to **Padang** (Rp75,000-250,000) before sailing on to **Jakarta, Makassar, Surabaya,** and **Ternate.** The **PELNI office,** Jl. Horas 89 (☎222 91), is a 5min. walk from the port, on the right as you head away from the sea.

INDONESIA

Buses leave from private company offices by the port and from the terminal on Jl. Sisingamangaraja in Sibolga (Rp1000 by *becak* from the pier) to: **Medan** (8hr.; several departures 7-9am and 7-9pm; Rp30,000-40,000); **Padang** (16hr.) via **Bukit Tinggi** (14hr.; 8, 9am, 3:30, 4, 8, 9pm; Rp30,000-50,000); **Parapat** (6hr.; 8, 10am, 2, 8pm; Rp30,000). Many of the bus companies have offices close to the port, along Jl. Horas and Jl. Diponegoro; buy tickets a few hours ahead if you can.

BNI, Jl. S. Parman 34, at the intersection with Jl. Brigjen Katamso, has decent exchange rates and an **ATM.** (☎227 24. Open M-Th 8am-4pm, F 7:30am-noon and 1:30-4pm.) The **police station** is at Jl. Tobing 35. (☎251 10. **Open 24hr.**) **RSU Dr. F.L. Tobing Hospital** is nearby on Jl. Tobing, at the corner of Jl. Yos Sudarso. (☎247 25. **Open 24hr.**) For **Internet** connections, try **Cyberpunk,** Jl. D.I. Panjaitan 100. (Open daily 8am-10pm. Rp6000 per hr.) The **post office,** Jl. Sutomo 40, is across from the police station. (☎221 62. M-Th 7:30am-3pm, F-Sa 7:30am-noon.) **Postal code**: 22500.

Hotel Sambas Baru ❷, Jl. Horas 100, opposite Citra Nasional Bus office, is close to the port and has decent rooms if you get stuck here overnight. (☎228 57. Doubles with fan and shared *mandi* Rp20,000.) The more upscale **Hotel Wisata Indah ❺,** Jl. Brigjen Katamso 51, has a swimming pool and A/C rooms with hot showers and TVs. (☎236 88; fax 239 88. Doubles Rp178,000 and up. MC/V.) **Scuba diving** and daytrips to the offshore island of **Pulau Pooncan Gadang** can be arranged through **P.T. Sibolga Marina Resort ❺,** whose offices are just round the corner from the Hotel Wisata Indah at Jl. Yos Sudarso 29 (☎232 78), a 10min. *becak* ride from the port. A day's speedboat rental (up to 6 people) costs Rp650,000; scuba gear rental costs about Rp260,000 per day for mask, fins, BCD, and the works. Accommodation is available on the island, though it's not cheap (rooms Rp260,000 and up).

GUNUNG SITOLI ☎0639

There's nothing particularly unique about Gunung Sitoli. Few foreign tourists come here, except to leave again on the first bus south to Teluk Dalam. For those who do decide to give Gunung Sitoli the benefit of the doubt, it's a good base for daytrips to deserted beaches and the less-touristed villages of Northern Nias, with architecture and culture distinct from what you'll find in the south.

TRANSPORTATION

Flights: Binaka Airport, 20km south of Gunung Sitoli. Regular buses run from the bus station to Binaka (30min., Rp2000). **SMAC,** Jl. Lagundi 46 (☎210 10). Open M-Sa 8am-4pm. Flights to: **Medan** (1 hr.; W 1pm, Sa noon; Rp552,500); **Padang** (1½hr.; W 8am; Rp190,600); **Pulau Batu** (30min.; W 8am; Rp83,900).

Buses: Buses south to **Teluk Dalam** leave from the **station** on Jl. Diponegoro (several departures per day, usually around 7am and 1-2pm; Rp20,000). **Private cars** to Teluk Dalam can be chartered (Rp300,000-500,000) at the bus terminal. Buses and *oplets* to the north also depart regularly.

Ferries: Leave from the harbor, 3km north of town, off the main road (Rp1000 by *oplet*, Rp5000 by *becak*). **PT ASDP,** Jl. Yos Sudarso 201, opposite the port (☎224 10). Open M-Sa 8am-4pm. Ships to **Sibolga** (10-12hr.; M-Sa 8pm; economy Rp19,500, A/C lounge Rp25,700, cabin with fan Rp80,000-140,000). Buy tickets at the dock if the office is closed. **PT Simeulue,** on Jl. Sirao opposite Hotel Gomo. Open M-Sa 8am-5pm. Also goes to **Sibolga** on smaller wooden boats (M-Sa 8pm; economy Rp16,500, "class" Rp31,000, A/C "class" Rp41,000). **PELNI,** Jl. Karet 2 (☎218 46). Open M-F 8am-noon and 1-5pm, Sa 8am-1pm. To **Padang** every other week (M 6am; Rp85,000-284,500). Weekly service may have resumed by the time you read this.

INDONESIA

ORIENTATION AND PRACTICAL INFORMATION

The main thoroughfare, **Jl. Sirao,** starts from the grassy square by the Hotel Wisata and runs west-east until it kinks south (right), crossing a bridge after 100m. Hotels cluster along Jl. Sirao—most of the action is north of the bridge. The **bus station** is on the right 200m south of the bridge (where Jl. Sirao becomes **Jl. Diponegoro**). **Jl. Lagundi** branches off Jl. Sirao to the east (toward the water), and **Jl. Gomo/Yos Sudarso** runs parallel to Jl. Sirao to the west. The **ferry port** is 3km north of town.

Tourist Office: Recently shifted to Jl. Diponegoro 268, past the bus station and 10min. by *becak* from most hotels (☎219 50). Open M-F 8am-4:15pm.

Currency Exchange: BNI, Jl. Imam Bonjol 40 (☎219 46), changes cash and traveler's checks and has an **ATM.** Walk up Jl. Hatta with the post office on your left; take the first left onto Jl. Sukarno and then your first left again. Open M-F 8am-4pm.

Police: Jl. Melati 5 (☎211 10). Signposted from Jl. Diponegoro, just before the bus station. **Open 24hr.**

Pharmacy: Apotik Mira Lina, Jl. Sirao 179 (☎217 79), on the left heading south just before the bridge. Well stocked. Open M-Sa 7am-8pm.

Medical Services: RSU Gunung Sitoli Hospital, Jl. Dr. Ciptomangunkusomo 15 (☎214 74), is 100m uphill from the grassy square. Heading up Jl. Sirao with the sea to your right, take the first left after the mosque. The best on the island. **Open 24hr.**

Post Office, Jl. Hatta 1 (☎214 40), is on the southeastern corner of the main square. *Poste Restante.* Open M-Th 8am-3pm, F 8am-noon, Sa 8am-1pm. **Postal code:** 22813.

ACCOMMODATIONS

Most establishments in Gunung Sitoli are overpriced for what they are—the cheaper rooms tend to be fairly dismal with limited facilities. This is a good place to fork out the extra cash for a better room.

Hotel Wisata, Jl. Sirao 2 (☎218 58), near the central square. The best of a bad bunch. Clean A/C rooms with private Western baths. Doubles Rp51,000. ❹

Hotel Gomo, Jl. Gomo 148-150 (☎219 26), with another entrance off Jl. Sirao. Dim, sprawling cavern of a place with rooms ranging from almost-clean twins with private squat *mandi* to A/C doubles with Western toilets. Doubles Rp25,000-40,000. ❷

Hawaii Hotel, Jl. Sirao 20 (☎210 21). Another safe bet; one of Gunung Sitoli's better-run establishments. Clean rooms with private Western toilets and *mandi*. Standard doubles Rp25,000-35,000; "VIP" rooms with A/C Rp45,000-50,000. ❷

FOOD

Restoran Bintang Terang, Jl. Sirao 10, on the right as you walk down Jl. Sirao from the main square with the sea on your left. Excellent Chinese food served from the cozy confines of a family's front room. Chow down on delicious roast pork or fish (Rp10,000) while family life goes on chaotically all around you. Open daily 6am-9pm. ❷

Rumah Makan Nasional, Jl. Sirao 87, a little farther up the road from Hotel Gomo, on the opposite side of the street. Wide range of *padang*-style food. Often packed. Expect to pay around Rp15,000 for a full meal. Open daily 6am-10pm. ❸

Rumah Makan Saiyo, Jl. Sirao 57. Good cheap *padang*-style dishes. As you eat, watch birds in a cage, fish in a tank, or fools on TV. Open daily 8am-11pm. ❷

SIGHTS

Since buses to most of the sights are irregular and unpredictable, getting around can be frustrating and time-consuming. The best way to see the sights is to hire a motorcycle guide/driver for the day. Ask at your hotel, or just hunt around for underemployed-looking men on wheels. (Around Rp100,000 per day. Bargain!)

Nearby are traditional northern **Niha villages,** whose oval houses have thatched roofs like huge straw helmets that soar up to a height of 10m. In **Siawahili-Sihare'ö,** 5km west of town, half a dozen *rumah adat* (traditional houses) line a rough pebbled pathway. (About Rp5000 by *ojek* from Gunung Sitoli.) **Muara Indah Recreation Forest,** 14km north, is made up of a lake, a beach, and a meandering estuary. (Public bus every hr. 7am-6:30pm, Rp1000-1500.) **Pantai Laowömaru,** 7km down the road to the airport, is a popular local beach (*becak* Rp5000).

Museum Pusaka Nias, Jl. Yos Sudarso 134A, halfway between Gunung Sitoli and the ferry port, has a decent collection of carved figurines, war costumes, and models of traditional Nias houses, as well as a mini-zoo containing a few sorry-looking specimens of local wildlife. The free film on Niha culture is undoubtedly the cheapest way to see the famous **stone-jumping ceremony,** where men jump over a 2m stone monument to prove their manhood and skill in war. (☎219 20. Open Tu-Sa 8am-5pm, Su 2-5pm. Rp500; extra Rp2000 to take pictures.)

SKIPPING STONES Traditionally, the most important unit of Niha culture was the village and its most important resident the king. In times of war, every village's primary defense was a 2m tall fence surrounding the community. In the heat of battle, warriors would leap over these barriers and chop off their enemies' heads before returning home to present their leader with the bloody trophies. The bearer of such highly-esteemed gifts was rewarded with a life in the lap of luxury. To be recognized as a warrior, a man had to demonstrate his aptitude by leaping over a 2m stone monument, thus indicating that he was ready for battle. Extra spice was added to the equation by the stipulation that a man could not marry until he could hurdle the stone.

TELUK DALAM AND LAGUNDI BAY ☎0630

Unexciting Teluk Dalam is the port of entry into South Nias and a transit point to the horseshoe-shaped Lagundi Bay, 12km away, known on the international surfing circuit for its perpetual waves and razor-sharp coral. For non-surfers, this is a good place to kick back and enjoy fresh fish, beautiful scenery, and trips to traditional villages. Since many surfers stick around for months at a time, there is a sense of community at Sorake Beach that ages nicely the longer you stay.

TRANSPORTATION AND PRACTICAL INFORMATION. Motorbikes are available for hire all around Sorake Beach (Rp20,000 per hr.). **Minibuses** (Rp5000) and **motorbikes** (Rp10,000) run between **Teluk Dalam** and the string of guest houses along Sorake Beach. Buses leave from the Teluk Dalam bus station for **Gunung Sitoli** (6-7hr.; around 7am and 1pm; Rp20,000-25,000). **Ferries** leave for **Sibolga** (12hr.; W, F, and sometimes M 8pm; Rp33,000). For cabin space, negotiate with the captain in advance. For tickets, contact **P.T. Simeulue,** on Jl. A. Yani in Teluk Dalam. Ships also sail for **Padang** (roughly every other week). For more details, look for the unmarked office on Jl. Diponegoro in Teluk Dalam, just up the road from the mosque and the police station. (Tickets Rp50,000, with cabin Rp75,000.)

The **police station** is next to the mosque on Jl. Diponegoro, in **Teluk Dalam.** The **post office** is at Jl. Imam Bonjol 2. (Open M-Th 8am-4pm, F 8-11am, Sa 8am-1pm.) **Postal code:** 22865.For rudimentary medical services, the **Pukesman Lagundri** is on the main road in **Lagundi village.** (☎212 02. Open daily 8am-4pm.) A road junction lies across a trestle bridge 150m west of Pukesman Lagundri. The road to Gunung Sitoli heads north, the road to **Botohilitanö Village** heads west, and the **Sorake Beach Rd.** heads south. Down Sorake Beach Rd. to the south with the bay on the left, a string of *losmen* stretches for 1km. A three-story judging tower (for surfing competitions) dominates the beach 50m south of the **wartel** office.

ACCOMMODATIONS AND FOOD. There are many cheap places to stay along the beach between the lighthouse on Lagundi Bay and the judging tower on Sorake Beach. Most of these are anonymous sea-front shacks consisting of simple bamboo-frame bedrooms with ocean views and not much else. Average rates for a double are Rp10,000-15,000 per night, often even cheaper for longer stays. Be wary of places with rates that seem absurdly low—the real money is made on food, and many *losmen* proprietors will expect you to eat on the premises. Surfers usually stay at one of the places on Sorake Beach, within a frisbee throw of the big reef waves. If you're looking for peace and quiet, head down to Lagundi Bay, where the beautiful beach with bathtub-sized ripples is often deserted. A 30min. walk away from surf and surfers is **Aman Inn ❶**, on Lagundi beach just past the lighthouse. The friendly manager is eager to please and doesn't expect you to eat in his place. (Large doubles with private *mandi* and Western toilets Rp5000-10,000.) For a place near the surf, try **Marlynto's ❶**, 150m south of the judging tower on Sorake Beach. A room with a fan, Western toilet, and spacious patio with great views will set you back Rp10,000. Another 200m south, **New Raya ❶** has quiet bungalows with private *mandi* and Western toilets for Rp10,000. The owner is friendly and helpful. Similar is **Olayama Cottages ❷** next door. (Large doubles with private *mandi* and Western toilet Rp15,000.) It's a good idea to check out different *losmen* when you arrive; it's easy to become dependent on your mama and papa (*losmen* proprietors), especially for meals. Theft is a common problem, so choose a place with locks, don't leave clothing outside, and beware of "safe deposit boxes."

Since most people dine in their *losmen*, dining options are limited. **Harus Damai ❷**, near the lighthouse on Lagundi Beach, is a simple spot serving the usual fried rice and fried noodles menu. (Open late.) The **Dolin Café ❸**, on Sorake Beach by

INDONESIA

the judging tower, is a pleasant place for a beer. (Fried chicken Rp20,000. Open daily 7am-midnight.) The real prize is the fresh local seafood, which can be bought on the beach and cooked in your *losmen*. Expect to pay about Rp5000-10,000 per person for the fish and Rp5000-10,000 for the preparation.

SIGHTS AND ENTERTAINMENT. Competition class **surf** draws wave-riders from around the world to **Sorake Beach.** The waves off Sorake (3-4m high June-Sept.) should be treated with respect—a wrong turn can send you crashing into the razor-sharp reef just below the surface. Real experts head west to the **Hinako Islands,** especially Asu, where the break is better in small surf. A chartered boat out can hold 5-6 people (Rp600,000). Several small fishing "ferries" also make the trip daily from Sirombu to Hinako and Asu Bawah (Rp2500-5000). Accommodation runs about Rp30,000 for a double on Asu, less elsewhere. Surfboards are sold, fixed, and rented along Sorake Beach (Rp10,000-15,000 per day). **Lagundi Beach** is the best place for swimming and other lazy beach-bum activities. Nighttime hangouts include **Toho Bar and Café,** on Sorake Beach Rd., a 5min. walk from the judging tower toward the main road. The mellow open-air bar serves up simple food (pizza Rp14,000; *nasi goreng* with chicken Rp10,000) and good music until around midnight. **Leletua Pub,** on Sorake Beach Rd. by Dolin Café and the judging tower, is a great place to shuffle the night away beneath Sorake's only disco ball.

DAYTRIP FROM LAGUNDI BAY: THE NIHA VILLAGES. Traditional **Niha villages** on the hillsides of Southern Nias can be visited as a daytrip from Lagundi Bay or Teluk Dalam. *Rumah adat* (traditional houses) line cobbled streets marked by carved stone benches, where villagers used to lay out their dead. In front of the chief's house in each village is a large square, where meetings are convened and **traditional dances,** including **stone-jumping,** are performed. Many of the villages are within walking distance of Lagundi Bay. Hiring a motorbike (Rp20,000 per hr.) is probably the best way of getting out to villages farther afield.

Bawamataluo, 12km from Lagundi, is the most touristed village as well as one of the most impressive. Long rows of steep-gabled *rumah adat* soar high above the village's central square, dominated by the **chief's house,** which is now a small museum of local culture. Intricate carvings mark the walls inside—one depicts a European ship complete with blazing cannons and angry-looking Dutch sailors. (Donation expected.) Take a motorcycle (Rp10,000) or a *sudako* (Rp1500) from Teluk Dalam. The smaller village of **Hiliameta** is a 45min. walk from Sorake Beach starting off the main road 1km east of Lagundi village. There is a turn-off from the main road that leads up a walkway, which turns into stone steps. **Botohilitanö** is on the hill 1km west of Sorake Beach, visible across the bay from Lagundi.

Niha war dances, featured on the back of the old Rp1000 note, are a spectacular sight. Most performances include stone-jumping, an ancient rite that involves young men launching themselves from a small stone onto a 2m high platform (see **Skipping Stones,** p. 288). Locals can arrange traditional dancing in Botohilitanö or (cheaper) Hiliameta (around Rp300,000, Rp50,000 extra for stone-jumping).

It's possible to make **day hikes** through several villages, which are linked by well-marked stone paths. A pleasant route from Orahili to Hilisimaetano passes through seven villages, including Bawamataluo. You can arrange in advance for a motorbike to pick you up at your finishing point and bring you back to the beach. Alternatively, you can stay in many villages for around Rp10,000 per night (including meals). Visit the village head *(kepala desa)* upon arrival to pay your respects. Usually he will ask for a small donation, after which you are free to wander. The deserted **Gomo village,** 40km north of Teluk Dalam, is believed to be over 2000 years old. Gomo is famous for its collection of megalithic stone chairs. Unfortunately, roads are bad, and getting to Gomo is a hassle. Budget a whole day and at least Rp150,000 for guide and bike.

CENTRAL SUMATRA

BUKIT TINGGI ☎0752

A thriving market town, Bukit Tinggi is one of the most urban of Sumatra's backpacker haunts. Its well-developed tourist infrastructure makes it ideal for exploring the countryside, where you can climb volcanoes, watch fighting buffalo, and get a glimpse of the Minangkabau people, one of the world's only surviving matrilineal societies. Bukit Tinggi is also a good base for a jaunt to the Mentawi Islands.

TRANSPORTATION

Buses: Purchase long-distance tickets from bus companies at **Aur Kuning bus terminal,** 3km southeast of Jam Gadang, or at any of the travel agencies lining Jl. A. Yani and Jl. Teuku Umar. Buses to: **Danau Maninjau** (1hr., every hr. 8am-4pm, Rp4000); **Medan** (18hr.; 5 per day 10am-7:30pm; Rp85,000-120,000); **Padang** (2-3hr., every hr. 6am-6pm, Rp8000); **Solok** (1hr.; 9, 10am; Rp6000). **Tourist buses** to **Parapat** stop at the equator and a hot spring and include a ferry to **Pulau Samosir,** though a night in Parapat is required (13hr.; several per day; Rp78,000-127,000). Also to **Jakarta** (40hr.; several per day; Rp75,000-260,000). Book at hotels and travel agents.

Ferries: To get to **Melaka,** first take a bus (12hr.; 7am, 2, 4pm; Rp35,000) or minibus (10hr.; 7:30pm; Rp55,000) to **Dumai.** From there, ferries run to **Melaka** (1¾hr.; every hr. 11am-3pm; Rp125,000). A bus to **Sibolga** (10hr.; 10am and 7pm; Rp55,000) will get you to the Nias ferries.

Local Transportation: Microlet minivans follow a roughly clockwise route up Jl. Sudirman, Jl. A. Yani, Pasar Bawah (lower market), and Aur Kuning bus terminal (Rp1000). **Dokar** (horse drawn carriages) clop around town for about Rp5000 a ride.

ORIENTATION AND PRACTICAL INFORMATION

Jam Gadang—the Dutch clock tower—and the surrounding square dominate the town center. **Pasar Atas** (upper market) is next to the square on the northeast. **Jl. A. Yani** heads roughly northwest from the square until it bends right at a four-way intersection and continues downhill under the towering footbridge past the **zoo** and the old Dutch **Fort de Kock,** into **Kampong Cina (Chinatown).** Most of the budget hotels and cafes are on Jl. A. Yani and the adjoining **Jl. Teuku Umar.** Back from the four-way intersection, **Jl. A. Karim** climbs to the southwest (with **Novotel** at its summit), and Jl. Teuku Umar (which becomes **Jl. Tengku Nan Renceh**) climbs uphill to the west, intersecting **Jl. Yos Sudarso.**

Tours: Outfits on Jl. A. Yani arrange flights, buses, taxis, and tours. Hotels and cafes along Jl. A. Yani are great place to meet guides for the local area (Rp65,000 for a day's tour) and treks up Gunung Merapi (Rp150,000 per person for overnight climb).

Currency Exchange: BNI, Perintis Kemerdekaan 15 (☎225 78), has an **ATM.** Open M-F 8am-3pm. **Branch** by the Hotel Singgalang on Jl. A. Yani. **24hr. ATM.**

English-Language Bookstores: 2 on Jl. A. Yani and 1 on Jl. Teuku Umar, which buy, sell, and trade the usual range of paperback junk.

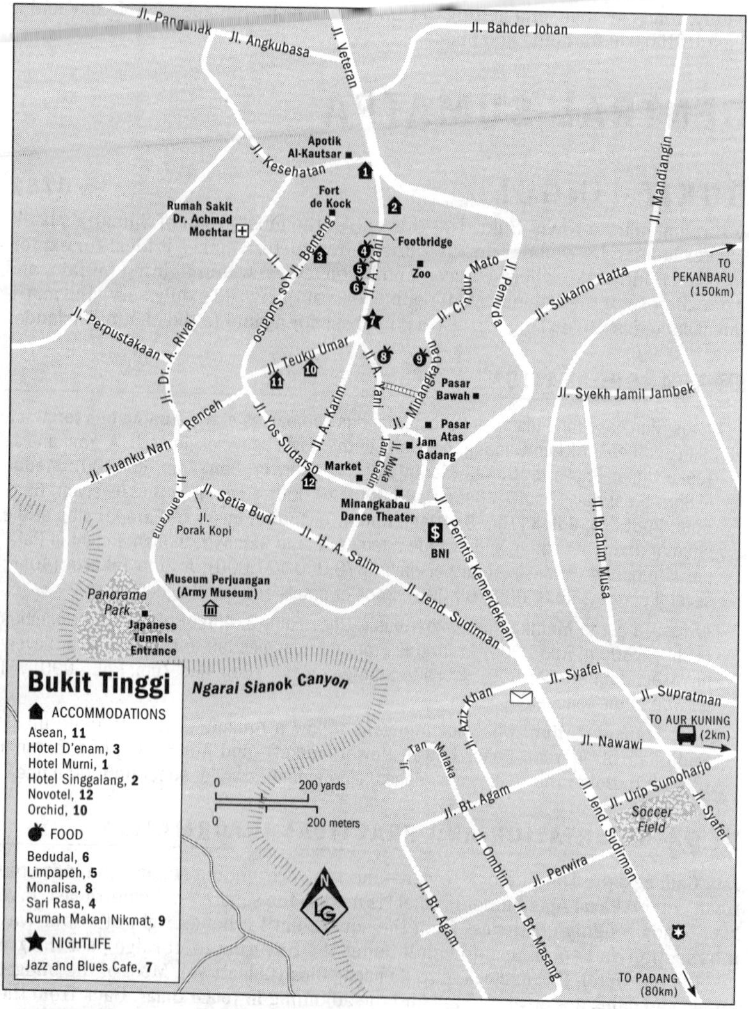

Markets: Pasar Atas (upper market) begins in the southwestern corner of the Jam Gadang square. Food stalls, magazines, and women's underwear–a happening place. **Pasar Bawah (lower market)** is a major hub for horse drawn carriages and minibuses.

Police: Jl. Sudirman 23 (☎311 10), a 10min. walk south of the post office, on the left. **Open 24hr.**

Pharmacies: Apotik Al-Kautsar, Jl. Kesehatan 17 (☎312 34), is past the bottom of Jl. A. Yani and to the left, opposite Hotel Asia. **Open 24hr.**

Medical Services: Rumah Sakit Dr. Achmad Mochtar, Jl. Dr. Rivai 1 (☎213 22). From the bottom of Jl. A. Yani, bear left onto Jl. Kesehatan. Take a left at the fork in the road; the **24hr. emergency** entrance is 100m ahead on the right.

Telephones: Wartel all over town. HCD phone in the lobby of **Novotel,** 300m southwest of Jam Gadang.

Internet: Giganet, Jl. A. Yani 96, on the right as you head downhill. Rp15,000 per hr. Open daily 9am-midnight.

Post Office: GPO, Jl. Sudirman, up the road from BNI. *Poste Restante.* Open M-Th 8am-3pm, F 8am-noon, Sa 8am-1pm. **Postal code:** 26116.

ACCOMMODATIONS

Most backpacker places are along Jl. A. Yani and Jl. Teuku Umar, up the hill.

Hotel Singgalang, Jl. A. Yani 130 (☎215 76), at the bottom of the hill on the right just after the footbridge. Popular backpacker hangout. Staff are an excellent source of information on the area and arrange tours of local sights. Clean rooms (all with shared *mandi*) around a pleasant courtyard garden. Doubles Rp20,000-25,000. ❷

Asean, Jl. Teuku Umar 13B (☎214 92), on the left as you head uphill from the junction with Jl. A. Yani. Large, well-appointed rooms, most with private baths (Western toilets and showers). Economy doubles Rp41,000; standard rooms Rp52,000-72,500. ❸

Orchid, Jl. Teuku Umar 11 (☎326 34), next to Asean Hotel. Another good mid-range budget option; pricier rooms come with TV and hot showers. Economy doubles with squat *mandi* Rp35,000; standard rooms Rp50-70,000. ❸

Novotel, Jl. Laras Datuk Bandaro (☎350 00; fax 238 00; novotel_bkt@mail.com). Close to the clock tower and the central market. The best luxury hotel in town; beautiful rooms around a large open atrium lobby. Doubles Rp320,000-370,000. ❺

Hotel D'enam, Jl. Yos Sudarso 4 (☎213 33), close to the back of the fort. Small, clean, family-run guest house on a secluded street away from the noise. Doubles with shared *mandi* Rp17,000, with private *mandi* and Western toilet Rp20,000. ❷

Hotel Murni, Jl. A. Yani 117 (☎299 84), at the bottom of the road, on the left. Helpful staff. Good, cheap option; simple twin-bedded rooms with shared *mandi* Rp15,000. ❶

INDONESIA

FOOD

Tasty, atomic-hot Minangkabau cuisine (known across the archipelago as *padang* food) dominates the menus of most local restaurants and *warung*. The cheapest meals can be had at the food stalls in **Pasar Atas** or on Jl. A. Yani itself. **Backpacker cafes** cluster at the bottom of **Jl. A. Yani** and up into **Jl. Teuku Umar,** all serving a range of Western and Indonesian favorites.

Sari Rasa, Jl. A. Yani 31, opposite BNI and next to Hotel Yany. Classy little wooden place serving excellent *padang* food as well as a range of other Indonesian, Chinese, and Western dishes. There's an English menu on display at the door, but locals eat here too. *Daging rending* Rp12,000. *Gulai ayam* Rp12,000. Open daily 8am-11pm. ❷

Bedudal, Jl. A. Yani 95/105, on the left as you head downhill. Probably the best of the backpacker restaurants/bars. Raised wooden tables and cushioned seating areas. Popular spot for an evening beer. Pizza Rp19,000; sandwiches Rp8500-14,500; steak Rp20,000-35,000; chocolate cake Rp5000. Open daily 9am-12:30am. ❹

Mona Lisa, Jl. A. Yani 58, up the hill from the bridge and left at the crossroads; it's on the left. Dark narrow corridor of a restaurant serving decent Chinese food. Sweet and sour pork Rp11,000; *cap cai* Rp8000. Open daily 7:30am-9:30pm. ❷

Rumah Makan Nikmat, Jl. Minangkabau 77, upstairs on the left as you turn onto Jl. Minangkabau from the clock square. Clean cafeteria serving good, cheap *padang*-style food. Most dishes around Rp4000. Open daily 6am-9pm. ❶

Limpapeh, Jl. A. Yani, next to the *wartel* opposite Hotel Singgalang. *Padang* restaurant serving tasty, spicy fare for around Rp10,000 a meal. Open daily 8am-9pm. ❷

WHERE WOMEN RULE West Sumatra, land of the Minangkabau people, has one of the world's only enduring matrilineal societies. In this world where women rule, property is passed from mother to daughter, and children take the mother's family name. Evidence of the persistence of this system in Minangkabau culture is their great reverence for the role of the mother–she is child-rearer, educator, and protector. Since she is seen as responsible for the family, she is honored with the responsibility of passing on her name and prosperity. The mother's eldest brother acts as the *tungganai* (manager of the clan's affairs), but Minangkabau women are quick to point out that although the men may run a business, the women own it! *Let's Go* believes that women should rule the world everywhere.

SIGHTS

Towering above Bukit Tinggi's skyline, the Minangkabau-Dutch hybrid **Jam Gadang** clock tower oversees the frenetic market. Almost nothing remains of the Dutch **Fort de Kock** at the end of Jl. Bintang except a few rusty cannons, but it's a pleasant spot for a relaxing walk. (Open daily 8am-6pm. Rp1000.) The footbridge over Jl. A. Yani, with superb views across the city to Gunung Merapi, connects Fort de Kock to the **city zoo,** where a pair of overweight and shaggy-coated orangutans are the chief exhibits. (Open daily 8am-6pm; Rp2000.) Within the zoo grounds is a small **museum** of Minangkabau culture, worth a look if only for the freakish display of deformed animals hidden at the back (Rp900). **Panorama Park** looks out across the **Ngarai Sianok Canyon,** and its clusters of *warung* afford spectacular views. Also within the park is a complex of **Japanese Tunnels,** built with forced labor during World War II, but they're nothing to write home about. (Open daily 8am-6pm. Rp1500.) Not far past the park entrance on Jl. Panorama is the **Museum Perjuangan** (Army Museum) with an old fighter plane outside. The museum contains an impressive collection of weapons dating from the struggle for independence, and a grisly exhibition of photographs of the gloriously dead. (Open daily 8am-5pm. Admission by donation.)

INDONESIA

Two volcanoes, **Gunung Singgalang** (2878m) and **Gunung Merapi** (2891m), dominate Bukit Tinggi's horizon. A guide is recommended for either 9hr. round-trip ascent; the trail may be hard to find alone. Travel companies in Bukit Tinggi leave at 11pm in order to catch the sunrise (around Rp150,000). Merapi, the more popular climb, is still active and erupted in 1974; the police will close it down if it starts smoking. The view from the summit can be spectacular.

Slightly farther afield, there are a number of traditional **Minangkabau villages,** native reserves, and a swimming lake. Public transportation can be unpredictable; either rent a motorbike or go with a tour. **Lake Singkarak** and surrounding villages can be visited in six hours on a motorbike (Rp65,000 per day). **Harau Canyon** is a pristine reserve northeast of Bukit Tinggi. Rental places can give you directions.

Pandai Sikat, a handicraft town specializing in carvings and *songket* weavings, is a popular stop on Minangkabau area tours; it's also accessible by *microlet* from the bus station (Rp1000). **Pariangan** is a village with *rumah gadang* homes; take a bus from **Aur Kuning** (1hr., every hr. 7am-6pm, Rp2000). Buses also run to **Batang Palupuh** (15min., Rp1000), a nature reserve for the rafflesia flower. Worthwhile day tours of the region can be arranged just about anywhere in town for Rp65,000 per person.

ENTERTAINMENT AND NIGHTLIFE

Nightly **Minangkabau dance performances** are held at a theater on Jl. Lenggogeni 1 (next to Hotel Jogja opposite BNI, on the lane that leads from the market and the clock tower toward Jl. Perintis Kemerdekaan). The show includes local martial arts, wedding celebrations with elaborate costumes, and the harvest celebration dance, where dancers jump and thrash around in a heap of shattered china. Purchase tickets at hotels or travel agencies, or at the door (Rp20,000). **Buffalo fighting** is also popular. Fights take place every Saturday evening, and on either Tuesday or Wednesday night (normally 5-7pm), but not always in the same place. Ask around at cafes and hotels for details and directions. (Most hotels and restaurants arrange special fight-day minibuses to ferry tourists to and from the fights. Rp25,000 per person.) Area daytrips on fight days finish with the match-up.

The **Jazz and Blues Cafe** is on Jl. A. Yani, up the road on the left from the Hotel Singgalang. With tables on the street and drawings of jazz and blues greats on the walls inside, this is a good place to have a beer or two with a mostly local crowd. (Large beer Rp14,000. Open daily 9:30am-10pm.)

NEAR BUKIT TINGGI: DANAU MANINJAU

A smaller, less touristed version of Lake Toba, Lake Maninjau is a crater lake 36km west of Bukit Tinggi. Extreme weather patterns created by the crater's micro-climate cause eerie mists, freak downpours, and dazzling sunsets. For daytrips near the lake, **bicycles** (Rp20,000) and **motorbikes** (Rp70,000) can be rented in **Maninjau village.** Painfully slow **Internet** is available at **Jack's Place** in Maninjau village, on the right as you walk along the main road toward Bayur (Rp23,000 per hr.).

A number of waterfront guest houses have sprouted north of Maninjau Village and past **Bayur,** 3km north of Maninjau. Maninjau village is more developed, with a growing number of hotels and cafes catering to the tourist crowd. Homestays in Bayur are more peaceful, separated from the main road by rice paddies. **Lili's** ❷ is the most popular of a string of similar places by the lakeside, and has rooms and bungalows for Rp20,000-30,000, as well as a decent restaurant. The great views and the unhurried air make this a wonderful place to take it easy for a few days.

Travel to Maninjau is an ordeal: the last descent from Bukit Tinggi involves 44 hairpin turns. **Buses** from Bukit Tinggi will drop you at any lakeside guest house. Alternatively, you can get off at **Lawang,** climb 2hr. uphill to **Puncak Lawang** (the highest point around the lake), and then hike 4hr. down to Bayur village. Regular **buses** run to **Bukit Tinggi** (1½hr., Rp4000). To get to **Padang** (4hr., Rp8000) you have to first go to **Lubuk Basung,** 1hr. up the road from Bayur.

HOOK 'EM HORNS The people of West Sumatra, now known as the Minangkabau, earned the moniker from their cunning victory over their enemies in battle. Realizing that they had no chance in combat, they suggested that the battle be settled by bullfight. The invaders agreed, returning with an enormous, champion bull. The clever locals brought only a tiny buffalo calf, just separated from its mother, then tied knives to its horns. The enemies snoered, sure that victory was theirs. To their surprise, the calf rushed to the bull to suckle, thereby slicing the bull open and winning the battle. In tribute to their ingenuity and to the calf, the West Sumatrans called themselves the "Minang" (Winning) "Kabau" (Buffalo), and thereafter designed their roofs and ceremonial headdresses in the shape of buffalo horns.

INDONESIA

PADANG

☎0751

The offshore islands near Padang, the southernmost stop on Northern Sumatra's backpacker ant-trail, offer excellent opportunities for beach-side frolicking. Aside from roaming the Pasar Raya, there's not much to do in the city. Padang's weather complicates any travels: the scorching sun turns anything more than a 5min. stroll into a physical endurance test, and torrential rains often wash out the views. Padang's trademark hot and spicy cuisine is famous all over the archipelago, and excellent restaurants serving local specialties can be found all over town.

TRANSPORTATION

Flights: Bandara Tabing Airport, 9km north of town. Catch *bis kota* #14 up Jl. Sudirman (Rp1000) or an *oplet* (Rp1000) up Jl. Pemuda. Taxis Rp10,000. Departure tax Rp15,000 (domestic) or Rp60,000 (international). **Merpati,** Jl. Juanda 79 (☎444 831), inside Hotel Pangerna, flies to: **Batam** (Tu, Th, Su; Rp586,000) and **Palembang** (Tu, Th, Su; Rp1,151,900). Open M-F 8am-4:30pm, Sa-Su 9am-1pm. **Garuda,** Jl. Sudirman 2 (☎301 73), in between Bank Mandisi and Bank Bukopin, flies to **Jakarta** (2 per day; Rp700,000). Open M-F 8am-4pm, Sa-Su 9am-1pm. **Mandala,** Jl. Veteran 20C (☎397 37), has the cheapest flights to **Jakarta** (daily; Rp604,000). **Silk Air** has flights to **Singapore** (3 per week).

Buses: The **terminal** is on Jl. Pemuda, west of Pasar Raya. Buy tickets from the many companies at the bus station. Each company handles 1 or 2 routes; ask around. To: **Bengkulu** (16hr.; 2pm; Rp40,000, with A/C Rp60,000); **Bukit Tinggi** (2½hr., every hr. 6am-6pm, Rp8000); **Jakarta** (30hr.; economy 1pm, Rp100,000; A/C 1pm, Rp170,000; A/C toilet 10am, Rp270,000); **Medan** (17hr.; economy 11am, Rp60,000; A/C 1pm, Rp135,000; A/C toilet 2pm, Rp135,000); **Pekanbaru** (10hr.; 8am, 7pm; Rp30,000); **Sungai Penuh** (10hr., 5pm, Rp35,000; minibuses 5hr., 9, 9:30am, 6, 6:30pm, Rp35,000; 1pm, Rp45,000).

Ferries: PELNI, Jl. Teluk Bayur 32 (☎616 24), in Teluk Bayur, near the port. The modern passenger ferries **Lambelu** and **Kambuna** dock at Padang as part of their bi-weekly travel around the archipelago. To: **Gunung Sitoli** (15hr.; Su 7am and 6pm; Rp79,500-263,000); **Jakarta** (36hr.; Tu 7am and 8pm; Rp160,500-543,500); **Sibolga** (10hr.; Su 7am and 6pm; Rp86,000-285,000); **Surabaya** (2 days; Tu 7am and 8pm; Rp283,500-969,000). These same boats sail farther east to **Sulawesi** and **Ambon,** before heading back to **Java** and **Sumatra** to begin again. There is a **PELNI** booking agent at Hotel Dipo Intertasional, Jl. Diponegoro (see **Accommodations,** below).

Local Transportation: Bis kota (big city bus) Rp1000, *oplet* Rp700-1500, depending on distance. **Pasar Raya** is a hub for buses and *oplets*.

ORIENTATION AND PRACTICAL INFORMATION

The coast runs north-south along Padang's west edge. The **bus terminal** is on the main north-south road, **Jl. Pemuda** (called **Jl. Diponegoro** south of the terminal and **Jl. Damar** and **Jl. Veteran** in the north), one block inland. The main street is **Jl. M. Yamin,** which runs west-east past the **Pasar Raya market** and the unmistakable Matahari department store. The tall Minangkabau-roofed **post office** is 300m farther down, at the intersection with **Jl. Aziz Chan/Sudirman,** after which Jl. M. Yamin continues east as **Jl. Proklamasi.**

Tourist Offices: Dinas Pariwisata, Jl. Hayam Wuruk 51 (☎341 86), at the intersection with Jl. Samudera south of Jl. Diponegoro. Open M-Th 8am-2:30pm, F 7:30-11:30am, Sa 7:30am-1pm. **Natrabu Travel,** Jl. Pemuda 29B (☎352 52), next to the Hotel Tiga Tiga, is useful for booking flights. Open daily 7am-8pm.

Immigration Office: Kantor Imigrasi Padang (☎551 13), Jl. Khatib Sulaiman, 1km north of the Telkom office. Open M-Th 8am-3pm, F 8-11:45am, Sa 8am-1pm.

Currency Exchange: BII, Jl. Sudirman 14 (☎308 11). **ATM** here and all over town. Open M-F 8am-3pm. **Moneychangers** on Jl. Pemuda offer inferior rates.

Markets: Pasar Raya, east of the bus terminal and the minibus hub. A hotspot. Tasty *warung* set up nearby every evening. Open daily 4am-7pm. The **night market** on Jl. Permindo at the west edge of the *pasar* is open until 9pm.

Police: Jl. M. Yamin 1 (☎337 24), next to the post office. **Open 24hr.**

Pharmacies: Apotik Al Azhar, Jl. Proklamasi 44A (☎359 26), 100m east of the post office, next to several other pharmacies. Open daily 8am-10pm. There is a **24hr. pharmacy** attached to the hospital (see below).

Medical Services: Rumah Sakit Dr. M. Jamil (☎810 253), on Jl. Kemerdekaan. Turn left onto Jl. Sudirman at the post office, turn right after 400m (after the BII bank). It's straight ahead at the end of the road, after around 500m. **Open 24hr.**

Telephones: Free HCD phone in the **Hotel Dipo International,** Jl. Diponegoro 13 (see **Accommodations,** below). **Open 24hr.** There is a **24hr. wartel** about halfway up Jl. M. Yamin, on the right as you head toward the post office.

Internet Access: Cyberzone, Jl. Veteran 3, slightly north of the Safari Bakery, on the opposite side of the road. Rp4000 per hr. Open daily 9am-11pm.

Post Office: Pos Besar Padang, Jl. Aziz Chan 7 (☎343 58), on the corner with Jl. M. Yamin. *Poste Restante.* Open daily 7:45am-6pm (closed F 11:30am-1:30pm). **Postal code:** 25111.

INDONESIA

ACCOMMODATIONS

Budget hotels are along **Jl. Pemuda** near the bus terminal; quieter places lie scattered about town. Stifling heat and bloodthirsty mosquitoes make this a good place to think about upgrading to an A/C room.

Rocky Plaza Hotel, Jl. Permindo 40 (☎840 888; fax 841 230), on the right as you head away from the market. Snazzy new international-standard hotel with all the perks. All rooms have A/C, satellite TV, IDD phone, and hot showers. Swimming pool, bar, and 24hr. coffee shop. If rates stay this low, this is the best mid-range deal in town. Doubles (including breakfast and tax) Rp205,000-230,000. AmEx/MC/V. ❺

Hotel Sriwijaya, Jl. Alang Lawas I 15 (☎235 77). Head right 100m east of the post office on Jl. M. Yamin/Proklamasi, down Jl. Alang Lawas I; it's on the right on a quiet back street within walking distance of the city center. Comfy lounge. Economy singles/doubles with fan and shared squat *mandi* Rp25,000/Rp35,000, with private squat *mandi* Rp40,000/Rp45,000, with A/C Rp45,000/Rp50,000. ❷

Hotel Cendrawasih, Jl. Pemuda 27 (☎228 94), next to Tiga Tiga. Simple budget rooms within spitting distance of the bus station. Economy singles/doubles with shared squat *mandi* Rp15,000/Rp25,000, with private squat *mandi* Rp25,000/Rp35,000; VIP rooms with fan, shower, and Western toilets Rp50,000. ❶

Hotel Dipo Internasional, Jl. Diponegoro 25 (☎342 61; fax 342 65), south of Jl. M. Yamin, on the right. Excellent mid-range option. All rooms have A/C with private Western toilets. In-house travel agency books buses and flights. 24hr. currency exchange and 24hr. restaurant. Singles Rp130,000-180,000; doubles 140,000-200,000, plus 21% tax. Credit cards accepted. ❺

Hotel Tiga Tiga, Jl. Pemuda 31 (☎226 23), opposite the bus terminal. Labyrinth of rooms set around a sitting area. Late-night cafe and TV. Popular with backpackers. Pricier rooms have private Western toilets. Singles Rp20,000-50,000; doubles 30,000-60,000. A newer and more upscale **branch** is farther north, at Jl. Veteran 33. ❷

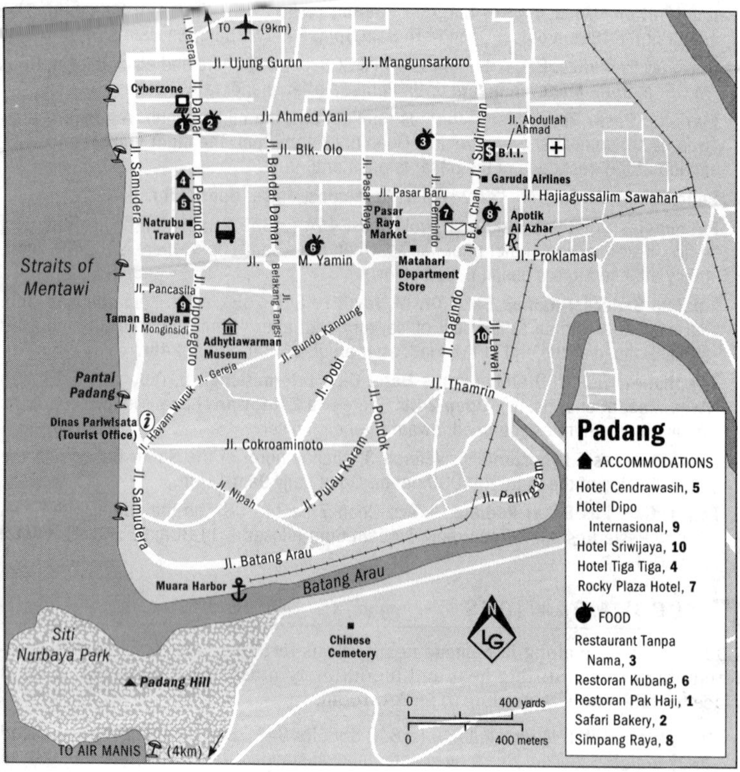

FOOD

Padang is famous all over Indonesia for its delicious spicy food. In a *padang*-style restaurant, the waiter brings you many small dishes as soon as you sit down—you only pay for what you eat. Typical dishes include dry beef *rending* and *kao ayam*, a creamy chicken curry. Lunch *warung* cluster at the bus terminal and east toward Pasar Raya. At night, Jl. M. Yamin and Jl. Permindo on the west edge of the *pasar* come to life. *Warung* with a view set up along **Pantai Padang,** where Jl. M. Yamin ends on the west edge of town, until the evening.

Simpang Raya, Jl. Aziz Chan 24, left on Jl. M. Yamin at the post office; it's on the right. A/C non-smoking restaurant serving a superb range of *padang*-style food and fresh-squeezed fruit juices. Most dishes around Rp10,000. Open daily 7am-9pm. ❷

Restaurant Tanpa Nama, Jl. Rohana Kudus 87. Head 300m north on Jl. Permindo from Pasar Raya to Jl. Rohana Kudus. Great *padang* food and fruit juices in shiny A/C diner popular with young student types. Dishes Rp5000-15,000. Open Sa-Th 8am-9pm. ❷

Restoran Kubang, Jl. M. Yamin 138, east of the bus terminal. Late-night street stall complex with fan-cooled indoor cafeteria seating attached. *Martabak* pancakes with meat and vegetables are the speciality (Rp5000); simple dishes like *sate* and fried rice also available. Open daily 2pm-midnight. ❶

Safari Bakery, Jl. Damar 50C, 500m north of the bus station on the right. Good breakfast spot. Gaggles of teeny-boppers and students flock here for the best selection of pastries (Rp2500) and cakes (Rp1600-2500) in town. Fresh coffee and excellent range of fruit juices also available. Open daily 8am-9pm. ❶

Restoran Pak Haji, Jl. Damar 67C, opposite Safari Bakery, on the left as you head north from the bus terminal. Cafeteria-style place serving cheap *martabak* (Rp5000) and *mie goreng* (Rp6000). Excellent avocado juice Rp4000. Open daily 10am-11pm. ❶

SIGHTS

The **Adhytiawarman Museum,** Jl. Diponegoro 10, presides over a fenced park with a playground, garden, and benches. The museum houses a marginally interesting exhibit of folk cultures from around West Sumatra. (Open Tu-Su 8am-3:30pm. Rp800.) Across the street at Jl. Diponegoro 19 is the **Taman Budaya (Cultural Center),** which stages outdoor dance and martial arts shows. A schedule is usually posted.

Pantai Padang extends along the western edge of town and is lined with *warung* that stay open late into the evening. The beach and water are dirty, but the view at sunset is spectacular. **Air Manis,** Padang's most famous beach, is a 2hr. hike away; from Air Manis there are great views of **Pulau Pisang Ketek** (Small Banana Island), to which you can wade during low tide. To get to Air Manis, walk south along Pantai Padang to the Arau River, where rickety canoes will ferry you across for Rp1000. On the other side, the scenic path leads past Japanese fortifications, through a Chinese cemetery, and eventually to the beach 4km down. Alternatively, *oplets* run from Pasar Raya for Rp1000. You'll have to change *oplets* at the turn-off to the beach (another Rp1000). In the opposite direction, **Pasir Jambak** (15km north of the city) is Padang's best beach for swimming. Straight out of an Indiana Jones flick, the **Jembatan Akar** (Root Bridge) in **Pulut-Pulut** spans 40m over raging rapids. The bridge is formed entirely from the interwoven roots of two giant Beringin trees on either side of the river. Usually, three buses travel daily to the village of Pulut-Pulut (2hr., Rp6000).

KERINCI SEBLAT NATIONAL PARK

Spanning four provinces and almost 15,000 sq. km, Kerinci Seblat National Park is Sumatra's hotspot for ecotourism. Designated a national park in 1982 and now an ASEAN heritage site, the park is dominated by 3805m Gunung Kerinci, Indonesia's second-highest volcano. Animal lovers come to the park in search of rare Sumatran tigers, rhinos, and elephants, as well as the mysterious *orang pendek* (short man) with the head of a man and the body of an ape, a "species" so elusive that scientists still aren't sure whether it really exists. The world's largest flower, the rafflesia, can be found here, as well as hundreds of species of birds, including the bronze-tailed peacock pheasant.

SUNGAI PENUH ☎0748

Sungai Penuh is the only town in Jambi Province that sees any kind of foreign tourism. Surrounded by beautiful scenery, this small-scale provincial capital is a convenient base for travelers wishing to explore the national park—a good place to organize climbing and trekking expeditions into the surrounding countryside.

TRANSPORTATION AND PRACTICAL INFORMATION. It's not hard to get your bearings here; Sungai Penuh is a small town with a well-defined center. South of the square, an obelisk sits at the top of **Jl. Martadinata,** the town's main road. **Jl. Agus Salini,** on the left 100m from the obelisk (away from the grass square), leads past the main **market** to the **bus terminal.** The square is flanked on the northwest by Jl. Sudirman and on the southeast and northeast by Jl. Diponegoro, which becomes Jl. Muradi north past the square. **Buses** depart from **Terminal Sungai Penuh** to: **Bengkulu** (17hr.; noon; Rp30,000-35,000); **Jambi** (11hr.; 8am and 5-8pm; Rp30,000-50,000); **Padang** (10hr.; every 2hr. 9am-8pm; Rp25,000-35,000); as well as **Bedeng Dua, Kersik Tua,** and **Pelompek** (1½hr., every 15min., Rp4000).

To get to **Kerinci National Park Headquarters,** Jl. Basuki Rahmat 11, follow Jl. Muradi 300m from the square. After the second set of concrete gateposts on either side of the road, turn left onto Jl. Basuki Rahmat; the office is at the top of the hill on the right. The office issues permits to climb Kerinci or visit Danau Gunung Tujuh (Rp15,000 per person per day) and arranges guides (Rp150,000 per day) for trekking. (☎222 50. Open M-Th 9am-2pm, F 9-11am.) **BNI,** Jl. A. Yani opposite Hotel Matahari, has an **ATM.** The **police,** Jl. Diponegoro 2, are at the far right end of the square as you approach it from Jl. Martadinata and the center of town. (☎211 70. **Open 24hr.**) A pharmacy, **Apotik Usaha Baru,** Jl. Diponegoro 4-12, is on the southeast side of the square. (☎323 583. Open daily 8am-9pm.) The **hospital,** Rumah Sakit Umum Daerah, is on Jl. Basuki Rahmat, on the left before the park office as you walk uphill. (☎118. Intensive care unit **open 24hr.**) The **Telkom office,** Jl. Imam Bonjol 2, is to the left of the obelisk as you emerge from Jl. Martadinata with the square in front of you. (Open daily 7am-1am.) The **post office** is in the far left corner of the square as you approach it from Jl. Martadinata. (Open M-Th 8am-3pm, F 8-11:30am, Sa 8am-1pm.) **Postal code:** 37114.

ACCOMMODATIONS AND FOOD. A block beyond the post office and 150m uphill on the left is **Hotel Matahari ❸,** Jl. A. Yani 25, a friendly family-run place with comfortable rooms and helpful information on the area. (☎210 61. Economy doubles with shared *mandi* Rp30,000; VIP doubles with private Western bath Rp50,000-60,000.) At the bottom left corner of the square as you approach it from Jl. Martadinata, **Hotel Aroma ❷,** Jl. Imam Bonjol 14, has a wide range of rooms and a decent restaurant. (☎211 42. Economy doubles with shared *mandi* Rp20,000, with private bath Rp30,000, with TV, hot water, and fan Rp60,000.) Just off the square on the right, the **Yani Hotel ❷,** Jl. Muradi 1 (☎214 09), has economy doubles with shared *mandi* (Rp25,000-50,000) and huge VIP rooms with full-length mirrors and boat-sized beds. **Hotel Kayu Manis ❶,** Jl. Martadinata 34, has simple rooms and a central location on the town's main road. (☎212 26. Economy rooms with shared *mandi* Rp10,000-20,000, with private bath Rp20,000-35,000.)

Warung and hole-in-the-wall establishments flourish around the square's northeast edge and continue down along Jl. Muradi. Most of the busiest places are along **Jl. Martadinata,** which brims with *nasi goreng* joints, *sate* and *martabak* vendors, and syrupy-sweet *es* (iced) goodies. **Bofet Sate Kambing ❶,** Jl. Martadinata 45, is a friendly, relaxing place to enjoy a plate of *sate* (Rp5000) or *martabak* (Rp4000) and hang out with locals. (Open daily 9am-10pm.)

SIGHTS AND ENTERTAINMENT. Mesjid Agung Pondok Tinggi, 200m from the post office on Jl. Depati Payung, was built in 1874 without a single nail. Tourists may enter. (Rp10,000 donation goes to the mosque's charity box.) The unimpressive **Semurup Hot Springs,** 9km north of town, soothes bathers. Communal *mandi* disperse hot water in the long building directly before the springs. Catch a minivan from the bus terminal; ask for "Air Panas Semurup." Most buses will drop you off at the intersection of the main road (Rp1000). From the intersection, it's a 2km walk or Rp1000 *ojek* ride; bear right at the fork after 1km and then left after another 700m. (Open M-Sa 8am-6pm, Su 6am-6pm. Rp1500.)

Traditional Kerinci dances include *Asyiek,* which contacts the spirits of dead ancestors, and *Pencak Silat,* a martial art involving swords. Music unique to the area includes *Basikie,* a complex mix of drum beats, and *Seruling Bambu,* singing with bamboo flute accompaniment. Ask about local village festivals.

KAYU ARO REGION

Dominated by Gunung Sitoli and covered with tea plantations and cinnamon groves, the beautiful Kayu Aro region is home to three towns each a short bus ride apart: Bedeng Dua, with a tea factory; Kersik Tua, 7km north and a base for mountain treks; and Pelompek, another 10km up, the starting point for hikes to Danau Gunung Tujuh. Visitors may be treated to *Kuda Kepang*, a frenetic fruit-throwing, bamboo-pounding ceremony that blends Kerinci and Javanese traditions.

TRANSPORTATION AND PRACTICAL INFORMATION. **Bedeng Dua, Kersik Tua,** and **Pelompek** are easily negotiated, one-street towns. Buses and minivans shuttle between **Kayu Aro** and **Sungai Penuh** (1-1½hr., every 15min. 6am-4pm, Rp4000), and can be flagged down for transit between the three Kayu Aro towns (Rp1000). Buses to **Padang** pass through at around 10am (5hr.; Rp25,000; reservation recommended) and 9pm (10hr.; Rp35,000). To climb Gunung Kerinci or visit Danau Gunung Tujuh, buy permits (Rp15,000 per day) at the **park headquarters** in Sungai Penuh or at the **Subandi guest house** in Kersik Tua. Each town has a **police post, health clinic,** and a local **wartel. Postal code:** 37163.

ACCOMMODATIONS AND FOOD. There are several good guest houses along the main road in Kersik Tua, all offering clean rooms, a cozy atmosphere, complimentary tea and coffee, and shared Western toilets. The most popular is **Subandi ❷**, whose owner is an excellent source of information on the local area. (Rp30,000 per person.) If you want to eat out, **Ojo Lali ❶**, across from the tiger statue, makes great *bakso* noodle soup with meatballs for Rp5000. (Open daily 7am-9pm.) Several *losmen* and restaurants dot Pelompek, but the best are found at the park, near **Sungai Jernih** village. **Losmen Mt. Solok ❷**, 150m from the PHPA hut, with bundles of sweet cinnamon downstairs, is a prime spot for hikers ready for that early climb up Danau Gunung Tujuh. (Rooms Rp15,000 per person.)

SIGHTS. The sprawling **PTP Nusantara-VI tea plantation** yields 18 tons of black tea daily, most of which is exported to Europe. (Tours 7am-5pm. Expect to be asked for a "donation" of Rp10,000-15,000.) Ensconced in dense jungle, **Danau Gunung Tujuh,** at 1996m, is the highest freshwater lake in Southeast Asia. From Pelompek, you can hike up to swim in its icy waters and marvel at the seven mountains from which the lake takes its name. A guide is helpful but not necessary for the 7km hike from Sungai Jernih village. From the end of the asphalt road at Sungai Jernih (2km east of Pelompek), a gate marks the park's entrance. Buy your permit at the **PHPA hut** (Rp15,000) and follow the path, making sure not to take the turn-off to the left at the bridge 1km up. Don't forget snacks, water, rain gear, insect repellent, and a sweater. **Telun Berasap Waterfall** cascades into a pool 50m below. From Pelompek, catch a northbound bus 4km to **Letter village** (Rp1000); the waterfall is 300m away. Guides for all activities usually charge Rp150,000 per day.

CLIMBING KERINCI. Take a guide for the two-day climb up Gunung Kerinci (about Rp150,000 per day)—as recently as 1999, an experienced Swiss climber disappeared on the mountain. The first day of hiking is not strenuous: about 6hr. through the tea plantation to the park boundary (permits Rp15,000 at the PPA hut here), then a climb up through the jungle to Camp 2, a shelter at 3000m. The final steep ascent to the summit should be done in the morning, when skies are clearest. The weather at high altitudes can be freezing and fickle (snow and hail are not unheard of), so take warm clothes and a sleeping bag (rent one in Kersik Tua for Rp10,000 per night). Also remember to bring a large supply of water, as there are no sources for replenishment along the trail.

PULAU BINTAN

Three times the size of Singapore with only a fraction of its population, the majority of Pulau Bintan remains largely undeveloped—rainforests and quiet beaches lined with palm trees dominate the landscape. The major industries are fishing and mining, while the construction of new malls and beach resorts also provides employment for island residents. The locals seem to coexist peacefully, despite the practice of Islam, Hinduism, Christianity, and Buddhism. Many travelers stay in Tanjung Pinang to access the Buddhist temples in Senggarang or Pulau Penyengat, a popular pilgrimage site for Malays. Others head to Trikora Beach to pretend they're on a deserted island. In fact, the sand on Trikora Beach is so highly desired that it's exported to Singapore's Sentosa Island. Hotel prices are steep in the posh Bintan resorts to the north, but Singaporeans come anyway, bringing their families for the weekend to fish and break some of the rules of their hometown.

THE VIEW FROM ABOVE

Main cities: Tanjung Pinang, Senggarang, Kijang, Tanjung Uban.
Highlights: Trikora Beach, Snake River, Pulau Penyenget.
Something Fun: Snorkeling at Pulau Bralas, Tanjung Pinang's water village.

TANJUNG PINANG ☎0771

Home to many services on Pulau Bintan, Tanjung Pinang is primarily a gateway city, but also boasts an intriguing water village and nearby temples. Beware of pickpockets who loiter near the harbor and often harass unsuspecting tourists. You can always seek assistance from local tourist agents, who will show you the safest areas of town and might even accompany you on your excursions.

TRANSPORTATION

Ferries: Ferry schedule and prices vary with the season. Check with travel agents around the port exit on Jl. Merdeka. To **Singapore** (1½hr.; 10 per day 7am-6:30pm; Rp100,000-120,000, round-trip Rp200,000-240,000). Exit tax to Singapore is Rp15,000. Ferries to **Jakarta** leave from the pier to the right, as you are facing Tg. Pinang (**Pt. Pelni,** 20hr., M 9am, Rp140,000; **Samudra Jaya,** 2 days, Th 5pm, Rp175,000; **ASDD Fast Ferry,** 14hr., Rp237,000 with beds). To **Pekan Baru** (8hr., daily 6:30am, Rp160,000).

Buses: The **bus terminal** is best reached by minibus (20min., Rp3500). From here, buses travel northwest to **Tanjung Uban** (every 30min. until 3am, Rp12,000).

Taxis: Bargain for fares to **Kijang** (Rp50,000 per car); **Senggarang** (Rp35,000); **Trikora Beach** (Rp85,000).

Boat Rental: To get to **Pulau Penyenget,** face away from the docks and go to the jetty on the very left. Catch a motorboat (20min., Rp20,000) or charter one if there is no group waiting to go (Rp30,000). Pick up a **motorboat** to **Senggarang** from Jl. Pelantar I by the water (Rp150,000 per 2-3hr. trip). **Pulau Batam speedboats** leave from the main pier (every hour from 7am-5pm, Rp18,000-25,000). There are two harbors in Batam, **Telaga Punggun** and **Sekupang.**

Local Transportation: Honking **minibuses** abound. Within the city Rp1300 with A/C. **Motorcycle rental** Rp150,000 per day, includes helmet, required by law. Motorcycle "taxis" go for Rp2500 per km up to 10km, when the rate goes up to Rp10,000 per km.

ORIENTATION AND PRACTICAL INFORMATION

Ferries from Singapore dock at the port in **Tanjung Pinang** or north of the island at **Bintan Resort. Pulau Penyenget** is offshore to the west. **Trikora Beach** hugs the east

coast, but is cut off from ferry ports by lack of transportation. Development will soon bring resorts to the entire northern coast of Pulau Bintan. Upon arrival at **Bandar Bintan Telani** (BBT) in Bintan Resort, take a **taxi** to the resort area (S$5-10). Getting to Tanjung Pinang is more difficult. From the drop-off point, take a minibus to the **bus terminal** and a bus onward to Tanjung Pinang (Rp12,000). In Tanjung Pinang, most travelers arrive at the main pier on the east end. Down the pier past the dock offices is **Jl. Merdeka,** which runs east-west from the arch near the pier to the fruit market. Walking through the Merdeka intersection leads to **Jl. Bintan.** Parallel and to the east is **Jl. Teuku Umar,** home to the night market. **Jl. Pos** begins opposite Jl. Bintan, close to the **post office,** and turns at the wharves. The **police station** and **bus terminal** outside of town are accessible by minibus.

Tourist Office: Riau Archipelago Tourist Office, Jl. Samudra No. 7 (☎/fax 253 73; www.indosat.id/bintan_tourist_promotions).

Currency Exchange: Bank Negara Indonesia, Jl. Teuku Umar 630 (☎214 32). Cashes traveler's checks. Open M-F 8am-6:15pm, Sa 8:30-11:30am. **Moneychangers** are near the Jl. Pos and Jl. Merdeka intersection. Open daily 8am-8pm. Many hotels will also accept Singapore dollars. **Bank Indonesia International** and **Lippo Bank,** both on Jl. Teuku Umar across from the post office, also cash traveler's checks.

Police: ☎110. At Km5 Jl. A. Yani. **Police box** at the corner of Jl. Merdeka and Jl. Ketapang. Police phone line is **24hr.**

Medical Services: Along Jl. Sudirman, in the south of the city or in the General or Navy Hospitals near the Top View Hotel. Facilities at the Navy Hospital are superior.

Telephones: Telkom office (☎281 83), on Jl. Hang Tuah. Follow the road to your right from the main pier near the large waterfront seashell statue. Long distance **24hr.**

Internet Access: Bintan Internet Cafe, on the second floor of Bintan Mall on Jl. Pos across from fruit stands. Rp5000 per 30min., Rp8000 per hr. Open 9am-5pm daily.

Post Office: On Jl. Merdeka No. 7 (☎210 71). *Poste Restante.* Located at the corner of Jl. Pos and Jl. Merdeka, 100m through the western arch on the left. Open M-Sa 8am-8pm, Su 8am-1pm. **Postal code:** 29111.

PULAU BINTAN PRICES. Since many prices in Pulau Bintan are given in Singapore dollars, the price icons below will reflect **Singapore's** price levels—not Indonesia's. Please review the price ranges for Singapore (see p. 644).

ACCOMMODATIONS

While Tanjung Pinang is lacking in cheap stays (for Indonesia, that is), it does offer a great deal of comfort—mostly at Singapore prices. If you are determined to pinch pennies, you may want to consider the budget accommodations at Trikora Beach instead. The ones in Tanjung Pinang on Jl. Bintan are not in a terrific area.

Hotel Laut Jaya, Jl. Plantar II No. 98 (☎627 71), next to the night market. View of the water village. Breakfast included. All rooms with A/C. Standard S$20; deluxe S$25. ❷

Top View Hotel, Jl. Ciptadi No. 3 (☎242 21), is a hilltop hotel with a refreshing view. Facilities include a restaurant, karaoke lounge, laundry service, and swimming pool. English-speaking staff. Breakfast included. All rooms with A/C. Reserve in advance. Standard S$32; deluxe S$42; superior S$52; S$3 more on weekends. ❷

Bintan Beach Resort, Jl. Pantai Impian No. 1 (☎236 64, fax 239 95), has a garden with starfruit groves leading to the sea. Enjoy the swimming pool, tennis court, or a drink at the **24hr.** coffee house. English spoken. All rooms have A/C and TV. Reserve in advance. Breakfast included. Standard S$46.40; deluxe S$58; sea view S$69.60 including tax. ❹

Hotel Surya, Jl. Bintan 49 (☎218 11). A hotel atmosphere with hostel prices. Its proximity to the harbor and peaceful courtyard with goldfish pond explain its popularity. Call ahead. Double with fan Rp40,000, with A/C Rp55,000, newly renovated with A/C Rp60,000. ❶

Wisma Riau Hotel, Jl. Yusuf Kahar No. 8 (☎210 23). A bit dark, but the rooms are spacious and have A/C and TV. The wide, blue-carpeted hallways invite a steady breeze. Restaurant downstairs. Breakfast included. Doubles Rp75,000-130,000; VIP rooms Rp150,000, with living rooms Rp170,000-250,000. Rates subject to 10 percent tax. ❶

FOOD

If you don't find the local chicken heart and beef lung curry appetizing, it's best to head to the **night markets** ❶, where you can choose from a variety of food vendors that cook up the fare as soon as you order. Try the one at **Bukit Cermin,** one of the highest points in the city, on top of a residential hill (Open 7pm to 1am). Another equally photogenic spot is the night market near the **water village** (open 6pm-1am). Opposite Bank Degong Negara on Jl. Teuka Umar, and on Jl. Ganbir, three blocks up Jl. Merdeka, plenty of options exist to appease taste-buds, such as Malay satay, *mie goreng* (Rp5000), and *chap chye* (cooked mixed vegetables; Rp4500). To escape the outdoor heat, try **Jawa Timur,** Jl. Raja Ali Haji No. 8, which serves Indonesian and Singaporean dishes. The staff doesn't speak English, but the whole menu is in photos so that you may point and choose from small, medium, or large servings of favorites like *ayam goreng* (fried chicken) for Rp60,000 and seafood *lumpia* (egg roll) for Rp28,000. (☎245 32. Open 10am-9pm.)

SIGHTS AND NIGHTLIFE

One of the truly amazing sights of Tanjung Pinang is the **water village** at the northern end of town, down Jl. Pasar Ikan. **Senggarang,** home of impressive 200-year-old Buddhist temples and colorful modern statues, can be reached by motorboat (20min., Rp21,000) from the fishing village on stilts at Jl. Pelantar I. Just north of Senggarang is **Snake River,** a picturesque boat ride (charter boat Rp60,000) through a curving waterway that leads to **Snake River Temple.** At night, hit the clubs on Jl. Gatot Subroto near Bintan Plaza. **Club 5** plays house music (cover Rp10,000; open Su-Th 9pm-late, F-Sa 9pm-6am), while **Singapore Discothecque** spins electronic and Indonesian hits (cover Rp5000; open Su-Th 9:30pm-2am, F-Sa 9:30pm-3am).

DAYTRIP FROM TANJUNG PINANG

PULAU PENYENGAT

Catch a motorboat (10min., Rp40,000) from the pier to the left of the middle pier when you are facing Tanjung Pinang. On Pulau Penyengat, the pier is off Jl. Pos, hidden opposite the bank. The boats drop anchor at Penyengat jetty.

Pulau Penyengat, the seat of the Riau *rajah*'s far-flung kingdom for hundreds of years, is Bintan's greatest treasure. **Mesjid Raya Sultan Riau,** a 178-year-old mosque, is just beyond the jetty. Jl. Ahmadi, to the left of this mosque, leads to the **Raja Ali Grave.** Directly past this grave is the **Tengku Bilik Building** and the **Raja Jakfar Grave,** the oldest building on the island. The **tomb of Rajah Abdurrachman** is 100m to the right, and the **island fort,** the highest point on the island, is directly behind the tomb. The path then winds through the quiet **Rajah Ali's palace,** abandoned this century. Go farther down the track to the road's end and take a right to get to the modern **Riau palace.** Pilgrims travel here to admire the royal internments of **Rajah Ali Jajai,** writer of the first Malay grammar, who received the isle as her dowry.

NEAR TANJUNG PINANG

TRIKORA

About 45km from Tanjung Pinang, Trikora is a smooth, breezy, white-sand beach. To the east of Trikora Beach, sand and snorkeling is the name of the game at **Pulau Bralas** (25-30min. by boat). Resort owners have snorkeling gear, but it's best to buy your own in town. To get to Trikora Beach, rent a taxi from Tanjung Pinang (1½-2hr.; Rp85,000). While the cheapest hotel at neighboring Bintan resorts costs S$90 on a weekday at Mana Mana, plenty of affordable beachside accommodations exist along the stretches of Trikora. For those who've ever found the term "ocean-front property" appealing, **Shady Shack Beach Resort's ❶** water-practically-under-your-feet bungalows are a dream come true. The water is clean and optimal for swimming. The friendly owner speaks fluent English. Bungalows have mosquito nets, double beds, and dipper baths. Bring your own snacks or learn to love the restaurant. (Breakfast included. Rp70,000. US$ accepted.) **Yasin's Guest House ❶** is right on the beach, though the water here is less ideal for swimming—try catching crabs at night instead. Ask to stay in bungalow #7, which is built on stilts over the water. All beds have mosquito netting. (☎267 770. Bungalow with dipper bath Rp60,000, with shower Rp100,000.) **Bukit Berbunga Cottages ❶,** recently acquired by the owner of Yasin's, offers similar bungalows at the same price. The pool table and open-air bar promise good times at night. **Trikora Beach Resort ❸,** Jl. Teluk Bakau at Km37 has no bungalows, but rooms on the second floor have patios over-looking the beach. (☎244 54. Rooms with A/C and shower S$50. Tennis court and direct beach access. Breakfast included. English spoken.)

SOUTHERN SUMATRA

BENGKULU ☎0736

Not many foreign tourists make it here, but the capital of Bengkulu Province is one of Sumatra's mellowest and most historically significant cities. Bengkulu (previously known as Bencoolen) was founded as a British trading post in 1615 and remained under British control until 1824, when the British and Dutch "rationalized" their colonial possessions and Bencoolen was exchanged for Malacca in present-day Malaysia. The fort here, still mostly intact, is one of the largest in Asia. The incredible rafflesia, the world's biggest flower, can be found in the jungle around the city. The combination of friendly people, deserted beaches, and rich colonial heritage make Bengkulu a perfect place to kick back for a couple of days.

TRANSPORTATION

Flights: Padang Kemiling Airport, 14km east of the city, is accessible via yellow *angkot* minibus (Rp2500) or taxi (Rp10,000). **Merpati,** Jl. Sudirman 246 (☎271 11), at the Hotel Samudera Dwinka. Open M-F 8am-4:30pm, Sa-Su 9am-1pm. To **Jakarta** (daily 8:40am; Rp587,900). Travel agents such as **CSH '88** (see **Tours,** below) also book flights at the same prices.

Buses: Inter-provincial buses stop at **Terminal Panorama,** 7km from town. Most companies have offices on Jl. Haryono. To: **Jakarta** (24hr.; 10am; Rp170,000-225,000); **Jogjakarta** (28hr.; 1pm; Rp250,000); **Padang** (16hr.; 1pm; Rp50,000-76,000); **Palembang** (14hr.; 1:30, 2:30pm; Rp45,000-95,000).

ORIENTATION AND PRACTICAL INFORMATION

The town's main road runs southeast-northwest, changing names from **Jl. S. Parman** to **Jl. Suprapto** at the gray BNI boat sculpture. At the **Mesjid Jamik,** it changes again to **Jl. Sudirman,** then weaves west as **Jl. A. Yani** past a square (with a tall obelisk), Fort Marlborough, and **Kampong Cina** (Chinatown). **Jl. Haryono** heads northeast from the intersection at Mesjid Jamik. The **beach** is on the southwest coast—just follow the signs for the Hotel Horison.

Tourist Office: Dinas Pariwisata, Jl. Tendean (☎212 72). Open M-Th 7:30am-2pm, F 7:30am-noon, Sa 7:30am-1pm.

Tours: G.T. Sanindo Wisata, Jl. Haryono 73 (☎275 22), next to Hotel Vista, and **CSH '88,** Jl. Suprapto 88 (☎223 85), can help you with bus and flight details. Both open M-Sa 8am-4:30pm, Su 8am-3pm.

Currency Exchange: Bank BII, Jl. Suprapto 205 (☎344 100), changes money and traveler's checks. Open M-F 8am-3pm. There are several **ATMs** along Jl. Suprapto.

Markets: Pasar Minggu extends off Jl. Suprapto onto Jl. Abidin. Well worth a wander at any time of day or night. Cruising mobile food carts sell fresh fruits and cheap *martabak*. **Pasar Baru Koto,** at the edge of Chinatown off Jl. A. Yani. If you're looking for kitchen sinks, Wellington boots, or toddler-sized English football stripes, you're going to be a happy shopper. At night, the entrance fills with food vendors.

Police: ☎221 10. Opposite the obelisk on Jl. A. Yani 1.

Pharmacies: Apotik Purnama, Jl. Suprapto 4 (☎262 86). Open daily 8am-10pm.

Medical Services: Rafflesia Hospital, Jl. Mahoni 10 (☎217 10). From Mesjid Jamik, turn left 150m after the BNI boat statue. It's another 150m on the right.

Telephones: Several **wartel** along Jl. Suprapto, most open until 10 or 11pm.

Internet: Ampera Computer Warnet, Jl. S. Parman 21, next to BNI, 100m from the boat statue. Open daily 8am-9pm. Rp5000 per hr. One of many places on Jl. S. Parman.

Post Office: GPO, Jl. R. A. Hadi 3 (☎229 51), near Ft. Marlborough. Open M-Th 8am-3pm, F 8-11am, Sa 8am-1pm. **Postal code:** 38000.

INDONESIA

ACCOMMODATIONS

Bengkulu offers the full spectrum of accommodations, from dirt-cheap *losmen* and family-run hotels to swank beach resorts.

Wisma Balai Buntar, Jl. Khadijah 122 (☎212 54). Spacious, airy place with pleasant family-run atmosphere. Large rooms with private baths, including towels, hot water, and Western toilets. Breakfast included. Singles Rp40,000; doubles Rp45,000-55,000. ❸

Hotel Vista, Jl. Haryono 67 (☎208 20). Spotless rooms open onto balconies that get glorious morning light. Doubles with shared squat *mandi* and fan Rp25,000-35,000, with A/C, TV, and breakfast Rp65,000. ❷

Permata Gading Resort, Jl. Pantai Nala 133 (☎218 55; fax 219 15). Perfect views from cottage verandas out to the beach just 50m away. Restaurant. All rooms have A/C and private Western baths. Doubles Rp80,000-85,000; breakfast and tax included. ❹

Losmen Surya, Jl. Abidin 26 (☎213 41), near Pasar Minggu. Turn left off Jl. Suprapto; it's on the left 100m up from the intersection with Jl. Haryono. A host of *warung* set up outside every evening. Frill-free market-side budget dive with more than its fair share of decrepit charm. Simple rooms with shared squat *mandi* Rp15,000-20,000. ❷

FOOD

In Bengkulu, you're never far from a refreshing *es pokat*, a creamy blend of avocado and ice. Other local specialties are *bakso*, a meatball and noodle soup, and *martabak*, a gooey sort of pancake stuffed with meat and onions. The best *martabak* are on **Jl. Sudirman** near Mesjid Jamik and on **Jl. Abidin** after 6pm (Rp5000). Restaurants and bakeries are on **Jl. Suprapto** in the center of town. **Sri Solo ❶,** Jl. Suprapto 117, offers a wide selection of Indonesian food (*gado gado* Rp4000;

grilled fish Rp5000), as well as *es pokat* for Rp2500-3000. (Open daily 8am-9:30pm.) **Roti Holland ❶**, Jl. Suprapto 124, has a wide range of pastries, most for less than Rp2000. (Open daily 8am-9pm.) **Sari Rasa ❸**, Jl. A. Yani 329B, on the right as you head toward the fort, is a pleasant Chinese-run place with first-rate seafood (fried squid Rp30,000) and chicken, beef, and frog dishes. (Open daily 7am-10pm.)

SIGHTS AND BEACHES

Bengkulu's claim to fame is the **rafflesia,** the world's largest flower, discovered here in 1818 by Sir Stamford Raffles, who later founded the British trading post at Singapore. Depictions of the flower are everywhere, but if you want to see the real thing, head to the **PHPA office,** Jl. Mahoni 11, opposite Rafflesia Hospital—they can tell you where to look. (☎216 97. Open M-Sa 7am-2pm.) Rafflesia typically bloom briefly during July and August and can be up to a meter or more across.

The **Mesjid Jamik,** an unspectacular mosque considered spectacular because it was designed by engineer-turned-president Sukarno, is in downtown Bengkulu where Jl. Sudirman and Jl. Suprapto meet. To the southeast, a 40min. walk from the center of town up Jl. S. Parman, the **Bengkulu Museum** on Jl. Musium houses a mildly interesting collection of assorted tidbits from around Bengkulu Province, including hatchets, coral, and doll houses. (☎220 98. Open Su and Tu-Th 8am-1pm, F 8-10:30am, Sa 8am-noon. Admission by donation.) North of Mesjid Jamik, at the intersection of Jl. Berlian and Jl. A. Yani, the well-preserved **Fort Marlborough** commands impressive views of the ocean. (Open daily 8am-6:30pm. Rp1000.) Completed in 1719, it's the second-oldest British fort in the East after Fort George in Madras. The hill behind Fort Marlborough is a great place to watch the sunset. Abutting the fort to the west, **Kampong Cina (Chinatown),** the oldest section of the city, suffered extensive damage during the February 1998 riots (see **Plight of the Chinese,** p. 105). Now almost completely reconstructed, Kampong Cina spreads out behind Pasar Baru Koto. The **Rumah Bung Karno,** where Sukarno lived in exile from 1938 to 1941, is south of the mosque on Jl. Suprapto, then west on Jl. Soekarno-Hatta. Now a museum, the house contains a dull collection of the president's books and clothes. For cultists only. (Open daily 8am-5pm. Rp1000.)

The 1.8km stretch of **Pantai Panjang** is usually empty except for fishermen. Large surf and sharp coral can make swimming dangerous—for a dip, try 1km south of the Horison Hotel, or just fake it and splash around in the Horison Hotel's **pool** (Rp6000 for the whole day). South of the hotel is **Pasir Putih Beach,** near Pulau Baai Harbor, 19km away. The harbor is the departure point for bi-weekly ship service to the villages of **Enggano Island.** To stay on the island, contact the *kepala desa* (village head) upon arrival—he may be able to find a bit of spare floor space for you to bed down on. The **Samudera Dwinka Hotel,** Jl. Sudirman 246 (☎216 04 or 231 28), opposite Mesjid Jamik, arranges diving and snorkeling excursions as well as boats to **Pulau Tikus** (Rat Island) for up to ten people (Rp15,000 per person).

DANAU RANAU

A popular vacation spot for Indonesians, **Danau Ranau** (Lake Ranau), flanked by hills and **Gunung Seminung** (1900m) to the south, has remained hidden from backpackers. Danau Ranau offers a retreat—not only from the noisy cities, but from activity in general. There's not much to do around the lake but row a canoe, enjoy the scenery, take a dip in the refreshing water, and lounge around with the Indonesian vacationers. To cool off from the heat, check out **Air Terjun,** a gorgeous 30m waterfall with a swimming area, a 10min. walk from Danau Ranau Cottages past Putri Gunung (Rp1000). A Rp50,000 chartered motorboat can take you 20min. across the lake to the **Gemuhak Hot Springs** (1½hr.) at the base of Seminung.

To reach this untainted splendor, travelers must endure the arduous 6-8hr. northbound transport via **Liwa** from Bandar Lampung, or a transit minibus-hopping adventure from **Baturaja** (Rp8000 direct). The place to hit is **Pusri**—get dropped off there if you can. Otherwise, take a minibus from **Simpang Sender** (20min, Rp3000). From the drop-off point, walk down 1km of steep hills to the hotels. **Buses** leave from Bandung Agung, via Simpang Sender and Pusri, for **Bandar Lampung** (7hr.; 7am, noon; Rp20,000) and **Baturaja** (3hr., twice daily, Rp8000).

Pusri has a number of hotels and bungalows, all offering scenic views of the lake. For Rp75,000, **Danau Ranau Cottages ❸** has beautiful bungalows with patios overlooking the water. (Room with *mandi* Rp40,000.) The friendly staff of the more secluded **Putri Gunung ❷,** 200m down the road, offers clean rooms with private *mandi* (Rp30,000). The cottages monopolize the restaurant business in the area.

PALEMBANG ☎0711

Sumatra's second-largest city, Palembang is an industrial powerhouse and has a long history as an important center of the mining industry. Though the city is pleasant enough, there is not much here to attract tourists, and few foreign visitors make room on their itineraries for Palembang. Recently, archaeologists have begun to find convincing evidence that this was once the capital of the powerful Srivijaya Empire, which ruled large parts of Sumatra, Java, and the Malay Peninsula for hundreds of years until its decline in the 14th century.

TRANSPORTATION

Flights: Sultan Mahmud Badaruddin II Airport, known as "Talang Betutu." Take a yellow bus up Jl. Sudirman to Km12, then switch to a gray airport *angkot* (Rp2000). A taxi runs about Rp30,000. **Garuda,** Jl. Kapten A. Rivai 35 (☎312 204), flies to **Jakarta** (1hr.; 4 per day; Rp456,800). **Merpati,** Jl. Kapten A. Rivai 6193 (☎373 366), also flies to **Jakarta** (2-3 per day; Rp424,000) and other domestic destinations.

Trains: Kertapadi train station, across the river from downtown, at the end of the yellow bus line. Trains run to **Bandar Lampung** (7hr.; 8:30, 10am, 9pm; Rp30,000-70,000).

Buses: Private bus companies line Jl. Kol. Atmo. To: **Bandar Lampung** (11am, 4, 8pm; Rp50,000-80,000); **Baturaja** (4hr.; every hr. 7am-5pm; Rp15,000); **Dumai** (noon, 2pm; Rp125,000-250,000); **Jakarta** (19hr.; several per day; Rp85,000-175,000); **Medan** (32hr.; noon-2pm; Rp185,000-250,000). Also straight through to **Bandung** (Rp100,000-160,000) and **Jogjakarta** (Rp120,000-220,000) on Java.

Ferries: Take a red Pusri-bound bus to **Bombaru** to catch a ferry to **Bantam** (10hr.; Tu, Th, Sa; Rp280,000) or **Mentok** (3hr.; 7, 8:30am, 1pm; Rp55,000).

Local Transportation: Color-coded *angkot* minibuses and larger buses run all over the city (Rp1000). The yellow bus runs from Kertapati to Ampera Bridge to Km12 on Jl. Sudirman. To call a taxi, try **Sriwijaya** (☎815 555).

ORIENTATION AND PRACTICAL INFORMATION

Palembang's main drag is **Jl. Sudirman,** which runs northwest from the **Ampera Bridge** where it passes over **Pasar Enambelas (16)** and the **Mesjid Agung** in the center of town. Sights and neighborhoods along Jl. Sudirman are indexed by their distance from the bridge in kilometers. Just before **Kamboja,** Jl. Sudirman intersects **Jl. Let. Kol. Iskandar,** where you'll find several decent budget hotels. Completing a "V" with Jl. Sudirman and Jl. Let. Kol. Iskandar, **Jl. Kolonel Atmo** is home to travel agents and bus companies. Farther up Jl. Sudirman, **Jl. Kapten A. Rivai** is lined with pricey hotels that offer an alternative to the madness of downtown Palembang. Be careful in Palembang at night, especially near Pasar 16 and the Musi River.

Tourist Office: Jl. Sultan M. Badaruddin 1 (☎358 450), at the Museum Sultan Mahmud Badaruddin, 150m before the Mesjid Agung, behind the huge concrete monument with the eagle. English-speaking staff, maps, and brochures. Open M-F 8am-3:30pm.

Tours: PT Nikita, Jl. Kol. Atmo 576D (☎368 417 or 367 543). Books plane and ferry tickets. Near bus companies. Open M-F 8am-5pm, Sa 8am-4pm, Su 9am-noon.

Currency Exchange: Bank BCA, Jl. Kapten A. Rivai 22 (☎312 244). Open M-F 7:30am-2:30pm.

Markets: The mind-boggling and chaotic **Pasar Enambelas (16)** sprawls for miles in all directions from beneath the Ampera Bridge. **Matahari International Plaza,** at Jl. Sudirman and Jl. Let. Kol. Iskandar, houses an A/C movie theater and McDonald's. **Pasar Cinde** at the intersection with the Jl. Kol. Atmo.

Police: POLDA (☎360 404), up at Km4.5 on Jl. Sudirman.

Pharmacies: Apotik Aldo, Jl. Sudirman 1269 (☎374 933). **Open 24hr.** There is also a late-night pharmacy inside the Hospital Charitas (see below).

Medical Services: Hospital Charitas, Jl. Sudirman 1054 (☎353 375), at intersection with Jl. Kapten A. Rivai. **Open 24hr.**

Telephones: Telkom office at Jl. Kapten A. Rivai 7. **Open 24hr.** There is a **24hr. wartel** on Jl. Let. Kol. Iskandar, opposite the Matahari department store.

Internet: Various places around town charge about Rp5000 per hr. Access is also available at the **post office** on Jl. Merdeka (see below). Rp4500 per hr.

Post Office: GPO, Jl. Merdeka 3 (☎352 626). Open M-Sa 8am-6pm. **Branch,** Jl. Kapten A. Rivai 63. Open M-Th 8am-2pm, F 8-11am, Sa 8am-12:30pm. **Postal code:** 30000.

ACCOMMODATIONS

The cheapest accommodations are near **Pasar 16,** but they are unsafe for tourists. Hotels on **Jl. Sudirman** are centrally located but noisy. Most travelers prefer the quieter places on **Jl. Kapten A. Rivai,** a 15min. walk or *angkot* from Jl. Sudirman. As many hotels are busy, calling ahead is a good idea.

Hotel Arjuna, Jl. Kapten A. Rivai 219 (☎356 719 or 364 761; fax 358 505). Decent mid-range option. A/C rooms with private baths (Western toilets and showers). Breakfast included. Doubles Rp72,500-133,500. ❹

Hotel Paradis, Jl. Kapten A. Rivai 58 (☎356 707 or 357 142). This old Art Deco-style hotel is starting to show its age, but still has character. All rooms come with A/C, TV, and private baths (Western toilets and showers). Doubles Rp87,120-117,475. ❺

Hotel Indayuh, Jl. Natuna 24 (☎359 453; fax 321 788), off Jl. Kapten A. Rivai, 10m after the post office. Large clean doubles, all with A/C and private Western baths. Popular with Indonesian business travelers. Doubles Rp50,000-100,000. ❸

Hotel Nusantara, Jl. Let. Kol. Iskandar 17 (☎353 306). One of several hotels on an alley off the main road. Turn right just before the sign for Pasar Raya JM. Decent (if unexciting) rooms in a central location—all with private baths, some with A/C. Rooms with fan Rp30,000, with A/C and shower Rp40,000-65,000. ❷

FOOD

Pempek, a boiled or fried concoction of seafood, egg, and flour, is the culinary specialty of Palembang, and can be found everywhere. *Martabak* and *bakso* stalls line the streets around the hotels on Jl. Let. Kol. Iskandar.

Pempek Nony 168, one of several chains with branches throughout the city—the main one is at Jl. Sudirman Km3.5. Popular place with a menu that lets you choose between *pempek, pempek,* and *pempek. Pempek telor besar* Rp4000. Open daily 7am-8pm. ❶

Mahkota Indah, Jl. Let. Kol. Iskandar 24, on the left as you walk up the road with the Matahari department store behind you. Comfortable atmosphere. Fried prawns Rp28,000; fish *sate* with rice Rp7500. Open daily 9am-9pm. ❸

Palapa Jaya, on Jl. Kapten A. Rivai, between Hotel Arjuna and Hotel Paradis. Popular, snazzy restaurant serving an excellent array of cheap *padang*-style food. Beef *rending* Rp4000; *ikan lele* (catfish) Rp4500. Open daily 9am-8:30pm. ❶

Lezat, on Jl. Kapten A. Rival. Wide array of Indonesian, Chinese, and Western dishes. Beef bowl with onions Rp15,000; salsa steak Rp14,000. Open daily 9am-8pm. ❷

Moriska Bakery, Jl. Kapten A. Rivai 55. Beyond Hotel Arjuna and Jl. Sudirman at Km3.5 953. Tasty pastries Rp1000-4000. Open daily 8am-9pm. ❶

SIGHTS

Crossing the Musi River on the Ampera Bridge, you will see the towering **Mesjid Agung mosque,** completed in 1748, on your left, and the famous **Pasar 16** on your right. The river itself can be explored with rented speedboats (Rp50,000 per hr.). During the **Srivijaya Festival** (June 16-20), the whole river is filled with traditional *bidar* racing boats. Off to the left 100m before the mosque is the **Museum Sultan Mahmud Badaruddin,** which documents the history of the Muslim sultanate Palembang Dar es Salaam, which lasted from 1659 until the Dutch turned up with muskets in 1821. (Open M-F 8am-3:30pm. Admission by donation.) Behind the mosque is **Jl. Pakih Jalaluddin,** packed with stores selling ornate wood carvings. At Jl. Sudirman Km6 is the **Museum Balaputra Dewa,** with exhibits covering the history of the city from the stone age to the Dutch age and beyond. Artifacts include several timeworn Buddhist sculptures dating back to the days when Palembang was the capital of the Srivijaya Empire, which encompassed large parts of Sumatra, Java, and the Malay Peninsula between the 7th and 14th centuries AD. (Open Tu-Su 8am-3:30pm. Rp750.) The **Punti Kayu** at Km7 is a small park and zoo, popular with kids and courting couples. (Open daily 8am-5:30pm. Rp1500.)

BANDAR LAMPUNG ☎0721

The capital of Lampung Province and a bustling transportation hub, Bandar Lampung is a convenient stop between Jakarta and the rest of Sumatra. Made up of the port city, Teluk Betung, and its hillside neighbor, Tanjung Karang, this urban region is known for its distinctive "ship cloth" tapestries and *tapis* sarongs. Its proximity to nearby attractions, including the Way Kambas Elephant Training Center and Krakatau, the infamous island-volcano whose eruption in 1883 demolished Teluk Betung, make it an ideal starting point for exploration. Every July, the people of Lampung attempt to appease the volcano gods with traditional dances and music, along with parades, races, car rallies, and a biathlon.

TRANSPORTATION

Flights: Radin Inten II Airport, 24km north of town. Take a public DAMRI bus from Rajabasa Bus Terminal (Rp1000), or a purple *angkot* bound for Teluk Betung (Rp2000). Taxis to the airport cost Rp30,000-40,000. **Merpati,** Jl. Diponegoro 189 (☎263 226), at the intersection with Jl. A. Yani, has daily flights to **Jakarta** (40min.; daily 3:30pm and M, Th, Sa 8:20am; Rp340,000). Open M-F 8am-5pm, Sa-Su 8am-1pm.

Trains: Stasium Tanjung Karang, Jl. Kotaraja 1 (☎262 854). Open prior to departures. Trains to **Palembang** (8hr.; 8:30, 9:30am, 8:30pm; Rp30,000-70,000) via **Baturaja**

Buses: Rajabasa Bus Terminal, 25min. north via light blue *microlet*. Buses to and from just about anywhere in Sumatra and Java pass through Bandar Lampung at some point. To: **Bahanheri** (for boats to Java; 2hr.; every hr. throughout the day; Rp7000-10,000); **Baturaja** (7hr.; 7am, 7pm; Rp24,000); **Bengkulu** (18hr.; noon, 5pm; Rp55,000-140,000); **Jakarta** (7hr.; many per day; Rp54,000-70,000); **Medan** (48hr.; noon, 7pm, midnight; Rp150,000-375,000); **Padang** (20hr.; 3 per day; Rp125,000-225,000); **Palembang** (12hr.; 7am, 9pm; Rp50,000). Deluxe A/C DAMRI buses to **Jakarta** leave from the train station daily in the morning (8-9am) and at night (9pm); Rp65,000-85,000. Unlike most buses passing through, these all leave from Bandar Lampung–you have a better chance of finding a seat. Reserve in advance to be sure.

Ferries: Run to Java from **Bahanheri,** 90km southeast of Bandar Lampung (roughly every hr.; Rp20,000). If you're on one of the buses to Jakarta or other places on Java, the price of the crossing is included in your ticket.

Local Transportation: Small, color-coded *angkot* zip around the city: **purple** (Tanjung Karang to Teluk Betung); **green** (Tanjung Karang to Garuntang); **red** (Kemiling to Bambu Kuning); and **blue** (Tanjung Karang to Rajabasa Bus Terminal). All Rp1000. The main station is next to the train station at the corner of Jl. Kotaraja and Jl. Raden Intan.

Taxis: All over town. For door-to-door service, try **Herodiza Taksi** (☎270 139) or **Siger Taksi** (☎771 999).

INDONESIA

ORIENTATION AND PRACTICAL INFORMATION

The bus terminal and airport are north of the city. The train station is at the end of **Jl. Kotaraja,** which intersects with **Jl. Kartini,** one of the city's main roads, in the center of **Tanjung Karang.** Jl. Kartini runs north-south and changes into **Jl. Teuku Umar** farther north and to **Jl. Monginsidi** in the south. **Jl. Diponegoro** runs from Tanjung Karang toward Teluk Betung.

Tourist Office: Jl. J. Sudirman 29 (☎261 430), can be reached via green *angkot*. Maps, brochures, and English-speaking staff. Open M-Th 8:30am-2:30pm, F 8:30-11am, Sa 8:30am-1:30pm.

Tours: Elendra Tours and Travel, Jl. Sultan Agung 32 (☎704 737), runs daytrip tours to Way Kambas (Rp275,000 per person), Way Kanan (Rp275,000 per person), and Krakatau (Rp325,000 per person). Open M-Sa 8am-4:30pm, Su 10am-1:30pm.

Currency Exchange: Banks with **ATMs** are everywhere. For currency exchange, try **BNI,** Jl. Teuku Umar 17 (☎252 145). Open M-F 8:30am-2:30pm.

Markets: Bambu Kuning Plaza, on Jl. Imam Bonjol, offers fresh mangos, American films, and everything in between. **Tanjung Karang Plaza,** a slightly glitzier version 1km down Jl. Kartini, offers McD's, cinemas, and general kitsch. **Pasar Seni,** Jl. Majapahit, features local artwork and *batik*. **Teluk Betung's Pasar Mambo** on Jl. Sultan Hasanudin is a popular spot for late-night seafood. Open daily 6pm-1am.

Police: ☎253 283. At the intersection of Jl. Kartini and Jl. Imam Bonjol. **Open 24hr.**

Medical Services: RS Dr. H. Abdul Moeloek, Jl. Dr. Rivai 6 (☎703 312), 2km down Jl. Teuku Umar in a blue *angkot*. **Open 24hr.,** as is the **pharmacy** in front.

Telephones: There are a number of **wartel** around town, including one by the **Telkom** building on Jl. Bukit Tinggi, close to the police station. Open daily 7:30am-10pm.

Internet Access: Dawiel Internet Station, Jl. Kartini 40 (☎257 893). 2min. walk down Jl. Kartini from the Tanjung Karang Plaza, with the plaza on your left. Dawiel's is on the right. A/C teeny-bopper paradise. Rp6000 per hr. Open daily 9am-10pm.

Post Office: GPO, Jl. A. Dahlan 21. Take a green *microlet.* Open M-Sa 8am-6pm. **Branch** at Jl. Kotaraja, off Jl. Kartini. Open M-Sa 8am-5pm. **Postal code:** 35111.

ACCOMMODATIONS

To get to the center of Tanjung Karang from the bus terminal, take a light blue *angkot* and ask to be dropped off at the intersection of Jl. Kartini and Jl. Kotaraja (by the rotary with the gray marble obelisk). Hotels on **Jl. Kartini** and **Jl. Raden Intan** cater to local businessmen and are generally clean and comfortable. Call ahead to make a reservation, as many hotels fill up quickly.

Lampung Inn, Jl. W. Monginsidi 178 (☎471 674), 3km south of Bambu Kuning. Head up Jl. Kartini with the plaza on your right, and follow Jl. Monginsidi downhill. Large clean doubles in a rickety house, all with fans and private squat *mandi.* Rooms Rp45,000. ❸

Marcopolo Hotel, Jl. Dr. Susilo 4 (☎262 511). Posh mid-range hotel., a short taxi ride from town center. Well-appointed rooms (A/C, attached Western bath, showers, satellite TV) have views out over the bay. Restaurant, drugstore, swimming pool, and billiard room. Standard doubles Rp118,600; deluxe rooms Rp155,900-228,700; superior rooms Rp186,300-272,250, excluding tax. All major credit cards accepted. ❺

Hotel Sahid Bandar Lampung, Jl. Yos Sudarso 294 (☎488 888; sahid@lampung.wasantara.net.id). Full-on 5-star hotel with all the little luxury perks: fountains, minibars, hot-water showers, satellite TV, swimming pool, and flushing toilets professionally "sanitized for your comfort and security." **24hr.** coffee shop and live muzak nightly 8pm-midnight. Large doubles Rp450,000-650,000, including tax. AmEx/DC/MC/V. ❺

Hotel Ria, Jl. Kartini 79 (☎266 404). From the train station, walk up Jl. Kotaraja and turn left onto Jl. Kartini; it's on the right. The cheaper end of the traveling salesman bracket. Wide range of rooms, some with bath and A/C. Doubles Rp52,500-83,500. ❹

Hotel Mini, Jl. Dwi Warna 71 (☎255 928), off Jl. Kartini, on a small alley around the corner from Hotel Ria. Simple doubles with attached (squat) bath Rp50,000. ❸

FOOD

Bakeries with names like "Roti French, London, and European" are everywhere along Jl. Kartini and Jl. Pemuda, along with standard issue *padang* restaurants.

Garuda Restaurant, Jl. Kartini 31, before Tanjung Karang Plaza. Excellent *padang*-style restaurant serves beef *rendang* (Rp10,000) and creamy avocado juice (Rp6500). A/C dining room with gurgling waterfall. Attentive service. Open daily 7am-10pm. ❷

Rumah Makan Shinta, Jl. W. Monginsidi 44B, on the right as you head downhill. Clean, Chinese-run cafeteria serves *nasi goreng* (Rp6000), *gado-gado* (Rp5000), and fried chicken (Rp28,000). Fresh fruit juices Rp5000-10,000. Open daily 9am-9pm. ❷

Kamang, on Jl. Dwi Warna, near the mosque, down a small alley just past Hotel Ria, off Jl. Kartini. An open-air cafeteria constantly enveloped by clouds of sweet-smelling *kretek* smoke. *The* place to mingle with locals and gobble down a plate of *martabak* and a cup of coffee. Yummy *padang* dishes, most Rp5000. Open daily 7am-8pm. ❶

DAYTRIPS FROM BANDAR LAMPUNG

Getting out to the sights and beaches around Bandar Lampung by public transportation can be a frustrating and time-consuming business. If all you're interested in is a short daytrip, you may be better off going on one of the expensive tours organized by travel agents (see **Tours,** p. 312). Unless your karma is so bad that you end

THE WRATH OF KRAKATAU On August 27, 1883, Krakatau exploded violently and left marks of destruction around the world. As the eruption weakened the island's foundations, water rushed into its lava interior, producing an even more terrible explosion that shot tons of debris over 20km into the air. The explosion was heard in Australia. Volcanic rocks were scattered as far as Madagascar and ash encircled the earth for three years. Giant, 40m tsunamis devastated hundreds of villages along the Sumatran and Javanese coasts; their effects were felt as far as Europe. An enormous ship buoy tossed onto shore by the tidal waves can still be seen on the south end of Jl. Monginsidi. Krakatau's peak was destroyed, and, in its place, the explosions left a crater 400m below sea level. For nearly half a century, Krakatau seemed at peace. Then in 1927, from the depths of the crater, a plume of steam unexpectedly flared up. Continued activity has already piled enough rocks and ashes together to create **Anak Krakatau** (Child of Krakatau), which now rises 150m above sea level. Seismic activity was again detected in 1979. Tension mounts as geologists ponder whether the world can take another eruption.

up on a crowded weekend outing, you'll probably find that you're one of the only people on the trip anyway. (Minimum 2 people.)

The tour to **Krakatau,** through the Hotel Beringin in **Kalianda** (see p. 314), visits **Pulau Sebesi, Sebuku,** and **Harimau,** a few of the islands dotting Lampung Bay. Alternatively, you can take a boat from **Canti,** a small town 10km from the Bakauheni port, for travel to Sebesi. Accommodations are available in Canti. **Pasir Putih,** a delightful beach with pricey hotels looking out onto **Pulau Condong,** sits southeast of Bandar Lampung—get there via the Rajabasa-Bakauheni bus.

Wild elephants are tamed at the **Way Kambas National Park and Elephant Training Center,** a 2hr. drive northeast of the city. The center also harbors a small population of Sumatran tigers and rhinos (see **Myanmar: Fauna,** p. 489). To the dismay of the tigers, camping is prohibited. Instead, travelers can stay in **bungalows ❷** (doubles Rp30,000-40,000) and play Hannibal with an elephant-powered jaunt through the jungle. The nearby **Way Kanan River** shelters 258 documented species of birds. To the west, the **Bukit Barisan** mountain range stretches along the coast, accessible by bus from Bandar Lampung, via Way Jepara. **Bukit Barisan National Park** begins at the southernmost tip at Tampang and climbs up the west coast. Travelers can explore the **Danau Menjukut** area by boat from Kota Agung to Tampang, or use the camping area near **Wonsobo.** The beaches at **Krui,** near the border with Bengkulu Province, offer decent waves for surfing. **Pugang Raharjo Archaeological Site,** which can be reached from Talang Padian, houses Buddhist-period megaliths.

KALIANDA ☎0727

Small, charming, and unspoiled, Kalianda overlooks a South Sumatran inlet, 30min. from the ferry port of Bakauheni and 1½hr. from Bandar Lampung. In addition to offering the cheapest trips to Krakatau, Kalianda is a good base for strenuous climbs through the surrounding hillside and also lies within easy reach of a number of relaxing beaches and seldom touristed hot springs.

The Sukarno-Hatta Highway passes Kalianda between Bandar Lampung and Bakauheni. Ask to be let off there (1½hr. from Bandar Lampung, Rp6000). From the main road, a Rp5000 motorcycle ride will bring you to town. Minibuses to Bakauheni run frequently (7am-3pm, Rp7000). There's **no currency exchange** or English-language **ATM** in town; bring all the rupiah you'll need. The main **police** office is at Jl. Kol. Makman Rasyid 142 (☎322 110), on the way to Pantai Laguna. The **hospital** is close by, at Jl. Lettu Rohani 14B. The attached **pharmacy** is **open**

24hr. There are several **wartel** in town, and the Telkom office on Jl. Kesuma Bangsa (on the left as you head uphill from the Beringin Hotel) is open daily 7am-11pm.

There are a couple of decent places to stay. The **Hotel Beringin ❷**, Jl. Kesuma Bangsa 55, on the town's major thoroughfare, has a pleasant family atmosphere and huge rooms. (☎322 008. Doubles, some with squat *mandi*, Rp15,000-25,000.) At the top of the hill on the same street, the **Hotel Kalianda ❸**, Jl. Kesuma Bangsa 163 (☎322 392), has shiny clean doubles with (seat) *mandi* for Rp32,000-55,000. For a bite to eat, hit up the host of food stalls and seafood restaurants all along **Jl. Kasuma Bangsa.** The scene is even more lively down at the bottom of **Jl. Veteran.**

Up the road 1.5km, **Pantai Way Urang** is a decent beach with a gorgeous view, overlooked by scenic **Gunung Rajabasa. Way Belerang Hot Springs,** 2km in the other direction, offer a pleasant soak. Both can be reached by motorbike (Rp2000). Farther afield is **Pantai Laguna Beach,** 3km up from Way Urang. Motorbikes can be rented from the Hotel Beringin for around Rp50,000 per day.

The islands of **Krakatau** mark the edge of a huge underwater crater. In ancient times, Krakatau was over 2000m high. The biggest island left after the colossal explosion of 1883 was **Rakata,** which is what tourists come to look at today. Meanwhile, the next geological generation continues to edge its way toward rock-spitting maturity, in the shape of **Anak Krakatau** (Child of Krakatau), which has been the site of increasingly violent seismic activity over the past 100 years (see **The Wrath of Krakatau,** above). Constantly growing and erupting since it appeared in 1930, this island of ash and rock entices adventurous souls to stroll around its base and peak. This can be dangerous, however, despite guides' assurances to the contrary. In 1993, Krakatau performed unexpectedly and killed two climbers.

Boats for Gunung Krakatau leave from nearby fishing villages. An overnight trip leaving at 8am from the Hotel Beringin costs Rp200,000 per person, including meals. The three- to five-hour boat ride stops at the jungle-covered "coral garden" islands of Sebuku and Sebesi for snorkeling. You then spend a night on the beach at Sertung, less than 1km away from Krakatau.

LAOS

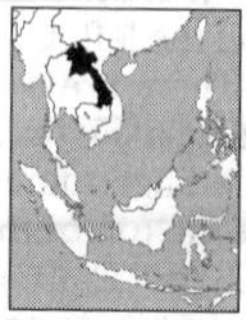

US$1 = 7562.00KIP (KIP)	1000KIP = US$0.13
CDN$1 = 4850.66KIP	1000KIP = CDN$0.21
EURO€1 = 7415.70KIP	1000KIP = EURO€0.13
UK£1 = 11,782.39KIP	1000KIP = UK£0.08
AUS$1 = 4139.94KIP	1000KIP = AUS$0.24
NZ$1 = 3550.89KIP	1000KIP = NZ$0.28
ZAR1 = 719.846KIP	1000KIP = ZAR1.39

PHONE CODE **Country code:** 856. **International dialing prefix:** 14.

There's a saying in Indochina: the Vietnamese plant the rice, the Khmer watch the rice, and the Lao listen to the rice grow. Visitors entering Laos from Vietnam, Thailand, or China are often shocked by the dramatic change in the pace of life. Undeveloped Laos is dominated by mountains and forests, and is home to more than 60 ethnic groups. Although Laos only recently opened its gates to foreigners, more and more tourists visit the "Land of a Million Elephants" each year. Whether traveling the mountainous regions near the Chinese and Burmese borders, exploring the jeweled temples of Luang Prabang, venturing into the thick jungles of the Bolovens Plateau, or kicking back in the 4000 Islands Region, visitors are often content to just sit back and listen to the rice grow.

FACTS AND FIGURES

Official Name: Lao People's Democratic Republic.

Government: Communist State.

Capital: Vientiane.

Land Area: 237,000 sq. km.

Geography: Borders Thailand, China, Myanmar, Vietnam, and Cambodia. 85% of the country is mountainous. River systems: Mekong River.

Climate: Dry (high season) Nov.-Apr., rainy (low season) May-Oct.

Major Cities: Luang Prabang, Pakse, Savannakhet.

Population: 5,635,967.

Language: Lao, French, English, hill-tribe languages.

Religion: Theravada Buddhism (60%), Animist and other (40%).

Average Income per Capita: US$290.

Major Exports: Timber, coffee, tin, textiles, electricity, opium.

LIFE AND TIMES

DEMOGRAPHICS

Traditionally, the Lao people divide into three ethnicities: the **Lao Loum,** who form more than two thirds of the current population; the **Lao Theung,** who account for nearly a quarter; and the highland **Lao Soung,** who include the **Hmong** and **Yao.** The Lao Loum, the ethnic Lao, live in the lowlands of the Mekong River. The semi-nomadic Lao Theung live in the mountains along the Lao-Vietnamese border and on the Bolovens Plateau. The Lao Soung are relatively recent newcomers to Laos

HIGHLIGHTS OF LAOS

CULTURAL HERITAGE. Serene **Luang Prabang** (p. 336) is Laos's spiritual center. The **Plain of Jars** (p. 344) is anything but ordinary. For vibrant hill-tribe culture, **Muang Sing** (p. 346) and the far north are unparalleled. Pakse's **Wat Phu** (p. 358) is the largest Angkorian temple complex outside of Cambodia.

NATURAL WONDERS. Surreal **Nam Ngum Lake** (p. 333) and **Vang Vieng's jagged cliffs** (p. 335) are within striking distance from Vientiane. The **Bolovens Plateau** (p. 359) and the **Nam Tha National Biodiversity Conservation Area** (p. 346) outside Luang Nam Tha are tops for natural beauty.

HANGING OUT. Don Det Island (p. 361), in the **4000 Islands** region (p. 360), is a great spot to put down your rucksack, string up a hammock, and relax over the Mekong.

(they arrived from China in the 19th century) and tend to be marginalized politically and economically. Some Lao Soung groups underwent diaspora as the Communist Pathet Lao came to power; some of those who stayed organized into a guerrilla army under the guidance of the United States and attempted to combat the Pathet Lao. While some conflict continued for decades, and indeed may still not be entirely over, the "secret war" was mostly a failure for the rebels, and the Communist regime responded with reprisals, especially against the Hmong.

LANGUAGE

The **Lao** language belongs to the Tai family; within this family, it is most closely related to **Thai.** The Lao speak several distinct (though mutually intelligible) **dialects.** Part of the reason that the language has never been nationally standardized is an ongoing series of politicized debates about whether to codify a more ornate version of the language, associated with tradition, Buddhism, and the aristocracy, or a more austere version, symbolic of modernity, technology, and socialism. **French** is the most common Western language in use in Laos, for the fairly obvious reason that Laos was a colony of France not so long ago. Knowledge of **English,** though, is on the rise because of Laos's participation in the Association of Southeast Asian Nations (ASEAN), of which it is the official language.

RELIGION

The Lao are generally divided into **Theravada Buddhists** and **animists,** but, for the majority of people, this distinction is hazy, as practices mix and recombine. For example, many Laotians believe in spirits *(phi)*, some of which are connected to the elements, others of which bear ill will, and thirty-two of which (the *khwan*) reside in the body to preserve and defend it, as well as various others. Offerings made to the *phi* are not seen to conflict with the anti-materialism of Buddhism and of Theravada Buddhism in particular. The Lao government's Department of Religious Affairs oversees the teachings of Buddhist monks in Laos. Unlike Cambodian Buddhist monks under the Khmer Rouge, Buddhists in Laos seem not to have been specially targeted as enemies by the Communist government. If anything, the oppression goes the other way—the monks are required to teach the compatibility of Communism with Buddhism and the non-compatibility of either with the traditional animistic practices. Similarly, they are required to use herbal or Western medicine in cases of sickness instead of the magical blessings of the old days. And, indeed, certain animistic practices seem to have disappeared entirely in the last 30 years. While this system is clearly not the conception of freedom of religion that is known in the West, many in Laos consider it a step forward for their people.

LAND

Laos is mostly forested and mountainous, with the tallest mountains located in Xieng Khouhang province. The Mekong River, more than half of which originates in Laos, comprises a large part of Laos's border with Thailand and part of the border with Cambodia. Laos is the only landlocked Southeast Asian country.

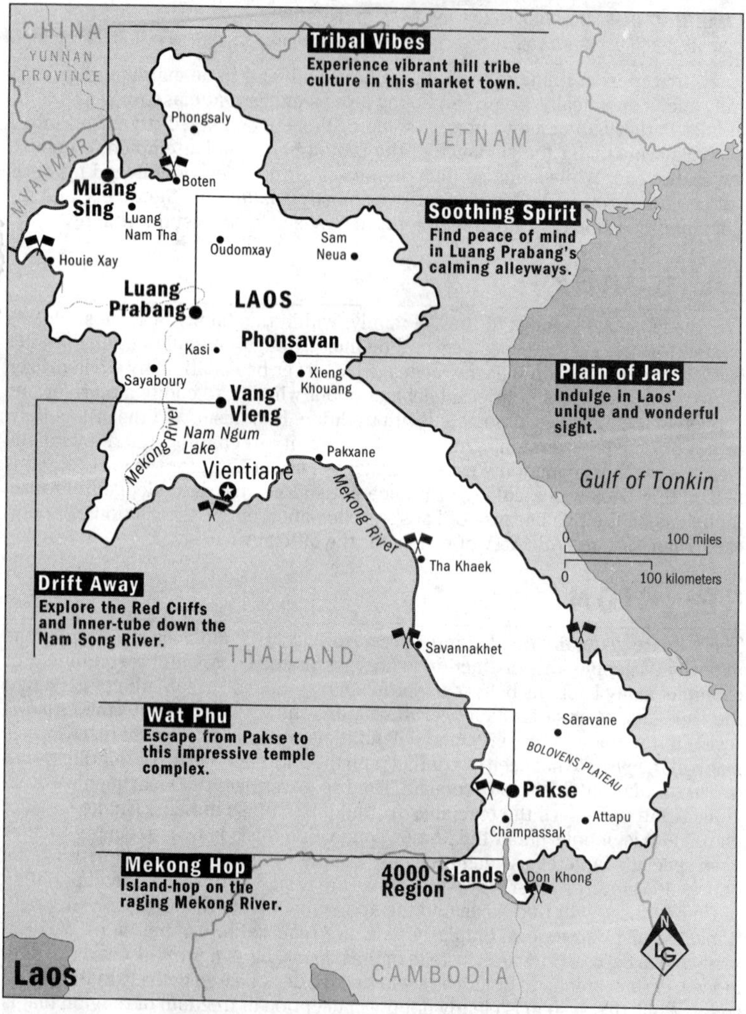

HISTORY

LANE XANG (1353-1694) AND BEFORE

IMPORTANT DATES

8th Century Tai Kadai emigrate from China.	**14th Century** Prince Fa Ngum founds Lane Xang.	**16th Century** The great King Setthathirat moves the capital from Luang Prabang to Vientiane.	**1637-1694** Lane Xang's Golden Age, which ends abruptly upon the death of King Souligna Vongsa.

According to legend, the Lao sprang from three gourds—nobility from one, peasants from another, and indigenous hill tribes from the third. The proto-Laotians of the Tai Kadai ethnic group emigrated from China in the 8th century to escape the Mongols in the mountains. The first recorded date in Lao history is 1316, when Angkor's Prince Fa Ngum was born. With Khmer aid, he united a collection of small principalities to found Lane Xang, the "Kingdom of a Million Elephants." His capital, Luang Prabang, was named after the **Pha Bang,** a golden Buddha given him by his Khmer father-in-law. The statue symbolized Lane Xang's rulers' spiritual and temporal power and the importance of Theravada Buddhism. For the next 300 years, Lane Xang prospered; at its zenith, it spanned all of north Indochina. Threatened by Burmese and Siamese invasions, **King Setthathirat** moved the capital to the more defensible Vientiane and brought the **Emerald Buddha,** the most revered Buddha in Thailand, from Lanna. Under the enlightened **King Souligna Vongsa,** Lane Xang experienced its Golden Age as its borders expanded to Yunnan to the north, Shan Myanmar to the west, Cambodia to the south, and Vietnam to the east.

INTERNAL DIVISION AND SIAMESE CONTROL (1694-1885)

IMPORTANT DATES

18th century Prolonged harassment by Vietnamese, Burmese and Thai forces.	**1791** Bangkok gains control of most of old Lane Xang.	**1805** Prince Chou Anou attempts to restore Lane Xang to Lao rule.	**1827** The Thai sack Vientiane.

Many crises after King Vongsa's death in 1694 caused Lane Xang to fragment into three weak principalities: Vientiane, Luang Prabang, and Champassak. Vietnamese warlords threatened all borders, and chaos resulted. In the 1700s, the Burmese and Thai attacked the divided kingdoms, beginning Bangkok's control over much of Laos. In 1805, **Chou Anou,** a Vientiane prince, tried to end Thai rule. In turn, Bangkok sacked Vientiane in 1827 and depopulated the area—an event that still haunts Thai-Lao relations today. By the mid-19th century, only Luang Prabang maintained a modicum of independence.

COLONIAL RULE (1885-1954)

IMPORTANT DATES

1880s The French enter Laos and arbitrarily cede the Khorat Plateau to Thailand.	**1941** Japan invades Indochina.	**1941-1945** Anti-French movements, including the Communist Pathet Lao, arise.	**1945** King Sisavangvong declares independence for Laos.

As the French consolidated their rule over Vietnam, they also assumed traditional Vietnamese interests in Laos. After establishing a protectorate over Luang Prabang, the French expanded territory in Laos through many treaties with the Thai. Blithely ignoring traditional boundaries, the French divided Laos at the Mekong, ceding all of the Khorat Plateau to Bangkok. French rule in Laos was laissez-faire;

they used the area primarily as a buffer between British interests to the west and their colonial claims in Vietnam. Health care and education were for the most part ignored. Nationalism came slowly, but the 1941 invasion of Indochina by Japan catalyzed independence movements. Several anti-French movements, including the **Lao Issara** (Free Lao) and the Communist **Pathet Lao** (Lao Nation), arose to counter French imperialism. **King Sisavangvong,** initially reluctant to break with France, was pressured to declare independence for his country in 1945 backed by Japanese support.

THE WAR YEARS (1954-80)

IMPORTANT DATES

1954, 1962 International attempts to form an independent, neutral Laos.

1965-1975 During the Second Indochina War, the US bombs Laos and supports rivals of the Communist insurgents.

1975 The Pathet Lao take Vientiane and establish the Lao PDR.

1980s Laos becomes a puppet of Vietnam.

The first attempt to establish a neutral Lao, conceived at the Geneva Conference in 1954, lasted only eight months. Another attempt in 1962 failed after the small kingdom was dragged into the Vietnam War. The North Vietnamese would accept a neutral Laos only if they could transport supplies along Laos' portion of the Ho Chi Minh Trail, while the US remained intent on shutting the trail and preventing the Pathet Lao from seizing power. The US waged a secret war in Laos, pouring aid to the right-wing government, recruiting highland minorities, and waging a destructive air campaign. From 1964 to 1972, US bombers dropped more than two billion kilograms of bombs on Laos, making it the most heavily bombed country in history. In 1975 after 30 years of division and war, the Pathet Lao marched into Vientiane and established the **Lao People's Democratic Republic (LPDR),** with the **Lao People's Revolutionary Party (LPRP)** as the sole political party. Abolishing Laos's 600-year-old monarchy, they gave leadership to **Kaysone Phomvihane.** Fear of Communists sparked a mass exodus of educated lowland Lao in the '70s and left the LPDR with very few educated bureaucrats and technicians. Hmong rebels continued to wage guerrilla wars against the LPDR. In the 1980s, Laos was a puppet state of Vietnam, with upward of 60,000 Vietnamese troops still on Lao soil.

LAOS TODAY

Corruption and economic mismanagement contribute to Laos's status as one of the world's poorest countries. The LPRP followed Hanoi's lead in 1986 by approving an economic liberalization program dubbed "New Thinking." In November 1992 after Kaysone's death, **Nouhak Phoumsavan** came to power. At the Sixth Party Congress, held in 1996, the LPRP upheld "New Thinking" but reaffirmed the state's role in the economy and its monopoly of power. Laos joined the **Association of Southeast Asian Nations (ASEAN)** in July 1997. In February 1998, the pro-reform **General Khamtay Siphandone** replaced Nouhak. Today, the Lao government remains committed to shielding the country from foreign influence. Since 1986, however, the government has made strides in decentralizing economic control and encouraging private enterprise; consequently, the average economic growth rate grew 7% from 1988 to 1996. The Asian economic crisis dealt the Lao economy a strong blow due to its close ties to Thailand. By September 1999, Lao currency had lost most of its value, and, as of mid-2002, although it has stabilized at the level it reached then—about 9000kip to US$1—the Lao government hasn't taken strong actions to try to reverse the foreign-exchange problems. Thus, Laos continues to reel from a years-past economic blow. Vientiane has earned US praise for its cooperation in the "war on drugs" (though Laos remains the world's third-largest producer of opium) and search for American MIAs. Laos receives aid as one of the world's 20 least developed nations, but the government has trouble distributing and implementing programs to help its people. Up to 80% of employed Laotians are subsistence farmers who benefit little from the country's fledgling capitalist economy.

CUSTOMS & ETIQUETTE

TABOOS. Do not point to people with your feet or place your feet on a table. Women must not touch Buddhist monks.

PUBLIC BEHAVIOR. Displays of affection or anger in public are frowned upon.

HOSPITALITY. Remove shoes before entering homes or temples. On a traditional low cushion, sit with the legs folded to one side. (Men may also sit cross-legged.) A guest is expected to accept offers of tea or fruit when visiting a home.

ARTS AND RECREATION

Influenced by Thai, Burmese, and Khmer styles, Lao art is unique and expressive, frequently inspired by Buddhist themes. Sadly, however, much of the country's artistic heritage has been lost or destroyed. While attempts at a resurgence of Lao art go on, notably in the area of cinema, the poverty and instability that lingers from a war that it theoretically never entered and that theoretically ended over 25 years ago make progress barely perceptible.

ARCHITECTURE. Buddhist temples, Laos's architectural genius, come in three chief styles. High, pointed, and layered roofs distinguish the **Vientiane style** of architecture found in the capital city. The **Luang Prabang style,** with multi-layered roofs and graceful, sweeping eaves that nearly touch the ground, is similar to that of Northern Thailand. A third temple style, **Xieng Khouang,** was irrevocably lost when American bombers razed Laos during the war. A few temples built in stone or brick with wide and sloping but layerless roofs in the Xieng style remain in Luang Prabang.

LITERATURE. Lao literature, recorded in the Lao and Tham scripts, is based on the *Jataka* tales from India and on oral traditions, and the 17th century was its golden era. The razing of Vientiane by the Thai in the early 19th century and the subsequent imposition of French as the official language under colonialism, coupled with more recent declines in the membership of monasteries and the advent of radio and television, have served to sharply curtail the Lao literary tradition.

DANCE AND DRAMA. Classical dance and drama came to Laos from India via Cambodia in the 14th century, but not until the 16th and 17th centuries was **classical theater** fully developed. The Royal Court organized dance and drama, which were accompanied by a grand orchestra of xylophones, gongs, trumpets, tambourines, violins, mandolins, and, later, chanting. **Mimic dancers** wore rich and vibrant costumes with masks and diadems. Today, the Royal Lao Ballet, who also perform a number of Lao folk dances, is the only remaining court troupe in Southeast Asia.

MUSIC. Songs and music are indispensable accompaniments to all celebrations and prominent features of everyday life. Live **mor lam** performances, involving singing jousts of Lao epic poems, occasionally take place at markets and temple fairs. The haunting, hollow sound of the **khene,** a complex bamboo reed organ that Lao musicians play at celebrations and funerals, is the center of Lao traditional music. The Hmong are renowned for their *khene* players who often perform at New Year festivals. A Lao orchestra consists of the *khene*, the **so** (a two-stringed cello), the **khouy** (a bamboo flute), and the **nang-hat** (a wooden xylophone).

FILM. Laos had a bustling film culture during the mid-20th century. During the 1960s and '70s, before Laos was equipped to process its own films, it sent them to Vietnam instead, which meant that the negatives of these films joined the comprehensive National Archiving Film Collection of Vietnam. In 1998, after over a decade of discussion and the construction of a suitable film vault in Laos, the Lao portion of this collection—1192 films—was repatriated. Lao film suffered during the Vietnam War; since the end of the war, despite efforts to revive the industry, Laos has produced only two feature-length films.

WEAVING AND HILL TRIBE ART. Young girls learn the traditional art of weaving cotton and silk with shimmering gold and silver threads (called **tdinjok**); a woman's ability to weave is considered an asset during courtship. The **pha sin** (Lao sarong), **pha baeng** (Lao shawl), and **sin** (bridal skirt with an elaborately embroidered hem), are made from these cloths. The Yao and Hmong are renowned for their excellent **silversmiths.** Both groups traditionally assessed their wealth in terms of family silver. The Hmong are the only people in Laos who make **batik,** created by dyeing fabric with resistant wax designs (see p. 106). **Appliqué** is a craft form in which cloth is layered and stitched to create a rich collage of contrasting colors, textures, and geometric shapes. Most hill tribes, such as the Akha, make beautiful appliqué.

OUTDOORS. In Laos, you can trek and visit hill tribes in the Nam Tha Biodiversity Area, outside Luang Nam Tha, or in Muang Sing. For those who want to explore a less beaten track, the remote Attapeu region in Southern Laos sees few tourists and is home to many endangered animals. **Swim** in Nam Ngum Lake and **raft** down the Nam Ngum River. For some mystery and excitement, the cliffs near Vang Vieng offer **spelunking, underground swimming, waterfalls,** and **inner-tubing** down the Nam Song River. For a more laid-back experience, go **boating** in the 4000 Islands Region and spot a rare Irrawaddy dolphin.

HOLIDAYS & FESTIVALS (2003)

Government offices and banks are closed on Lao public holidays as well as on festival days. These often coincide. Banks based in Thailand may also close on Thai holidays. Public holidays are listed below.

DATE	NAME	DESCRIPTION
Jan. 1	International New Year's Day	Celebration often includes paying visits to loved ones.
Jan. 6	Pathet Lao Day	Honors the victory of the Communist Pathet Lao in 1975.
Jan. 20	Army Day	Commemorates Lao's army, its veterans, and its casualties.
Mar. 8	Women's Day	Pays honor to women.
Mar. 22	People's Party Day	Celebrates the ruling party of Laos.
Apr. 13-15	Boun Pimai	Lao New Year
May 1	International Labour Day	Known as "May Day" in many parts of the world.
June 1	Children's Day	Pays honor to children.
Aug. 13	Lao Issara Day	Commemorates the "Free Lao," an early movement that, with the Pathet Lao, struggled for independence from France.
Aug. 23	Liberation Day	A Lao independence celebration.
Oct. 12	Freedom from France Day	Celebrates the 1953 naming of Laos as a "fully independent and sovereign" state within the French Union.
Dec. 2	National Day	Yet another Lao independence celebration—maybe the most important.

ADDITIONAL RESOURCES

GENERAL HISTORY

A History of Laos, by Martin Stuart Fox (1997). One of the few general histories of Laos. The author covers all of Lao history, emphasizing the colonial and modern periods.

The Politics of Heroin in Southeast Asia, by Alfred McCoy (1972). A fascinating account of the opium trade in Southeast Asia, focusing on America's role in opium smuggling during the Vietnam War. Since republished as *The Politics of Heroin*.

Tragedy in Paradise: A Country Doctor at War in Laos, by Charles Weldon (1999). Describes the efforts of the author and others to administer aid in Laos from 1963 to 1974, during the time of the American CIA's "secret war" there.

Indochina's Refugees: Oral Histories from Laos, Cambodia, and Vietnam, by Joanna C. Scott (1989). Tells a story of the Vietnam War from the point of view of citizens of the Indochinese countries, mostly civilians and almost half of them Lao, who chose to flee and then had to discover ways of doing so.

FICTION AND NON-FICTION

The Spirit Catches You and You Fall Down, by Anne Fadiman (1998). A carefully researched account of the tension between the traditional beliefs of a real-life Hmong family, refugees to the United States from Laos, and their Western doctors over the case of the treatment of their epileptic daughter.

The Yao: The Mien and Mun Yao in China, Vietnam, Laos, and Thailand, by Jess G. Pouret (2002). Fifteen years went into preparing this work on the many facets of the society of the various branches of this subset of the Lao Soung people.

TRAVEL BOOKS

Lao-English/English-Lao Dictionary and Phrasebook, by James Higbie (2001). The options for Lao phrasebooks are slim, but, for travelers, this is one of the most useful out there.

Stalking the Elephant Kings: In Search of Laos, by Christopher Kremmer (1998). The author describes his travels through contemporary Laos and his interviews with a wide range of Laotians as he searched for the truth about the fate of the Lao royal family, who were disappeared by the Communist Pathet Lao in 1977.

ON THE WEB

Laos News.net (www.laosnews.net). Links to Lao history and updates on daily news and current events.

Visit Laos (www.visit-laos.com). Practical tips and hotel, tour, and travel info.

ESSENTIALS

LAOS PRICE ICONS					
SYMBOL:	❶	❷	❸	❹	❺
ACCOMM.	Under US$3 Under 22,500kip	US$3-5 22,500-37,500kip	US$5-10 37,500-75,000kip	US$10-20 75,000-150,000kip	Over US$20 Over 150,000kip
FOOD	Under US$1.67 Under 12,500kip	US$1.67-2 12,500-15,000kip	US$2-4 15,000-30,000kip	US$4-6 30,000-45,000kip	Over US$6 Over 45,000kip

LAOS

EMBASSIES & CONSULATES

LAO CONSULAR SERVICES ABROAD

Laos has only a limited number of diplomatic missions worldwide. If your country has no mission from Laos, try contacting the embassy geographically closest to you. All Lao embassies will provide visa services for any foreign national.

Australia: Embassy, 1 Dalman Cres., O'Malley, Canberra, ACT 2606 (☎262 864 595; fax 262 901 910). Also accredited to **New Zealand.**

France: Embassy, 74 Avenue Raymond-Poincaré, Paris 75116 (☎33 1 4553 0298; www.laoparis.com). Also accredited to **Ireland** and the **United Kingdom.**

Thailand: Embassy, 520/502/1-3 Soi Sahakarnpramoon, Pracha Uthit Rd., Wangthonglang, Bangkok 10310, Thailand (☎662 539 6667/8; fax 662 539 6678; www.bkklaoembassy.com). Recommended for citizens of **South Africa** (to which **no** Lao embassy is formally accredited).

United States: Embassy, 2222 S St. NW, Washington, DC 20008 (☎202-332-6416; fax 202-332-4923; www.laoembassy.com). Also accredited to **Canada**.

CONSULAR SERVICES IN LAOS

Australia: Embassy, Rue Jawaharlal Nehru, Quartier Phone Xay, P.O. Box 292, Vientiane (☎856 21 413 600; fax 856 21 413 601; www.laos.embassy.gov.au).

Canada: For limited emergency consular services, contact the Australian Embassy in Vientiane (see above). Otherwise, use the Canadian Embassy in Bangkok, Thailand (see p. 681), which is also accredited to Laos.

Ireland: Use the Embassy of Ireland in Kuala Lumpur, Malaysia (see p. 370), which is also accredited to Laos.

New Zealand: For limited emergency consular services, contact the Australian Embassy in Vientiane (see above). Otherwise, use the New Zealand Embassy in Bangkok, Thailand (see p. 681), which is also accredited to Laos.

South Africa: Use the Embassy of South Africa in Bangkok, Thailand (see p. 681), which is also accredited to Laos.

United Kingdom: For limited **emergency** consular services, contact the Australian Embassy in Vientiane (see above). Otherwise, use the British Embassy in Bangkok, Thailand (see p. 682), which is also accredited to Laos.

United States: Embassy, 19 Rue Bartholonie, Vientiane (☎856 21 212 581/2/5; fax 856 21 212 584; http://usembassy.state.gov/laos/).

TOURIST INFORMATION OFFICES

Lao National Tourism Authority (LNTA) (☎856 21 212 248; mekongcenter.com) is the official tourism promotion agency of the Lao government. Perhaps marginally more useful are the private-sector **visit-laos.com** (www.visit-laos.com) and **visit-mekong.com** (www.visit-mekong.com), both run by **ETC Asia.**

VISAS

A valid passport is required to enter and leave the country, and all foreign travelers must obtain visas. Tourist visas, generally for 15 days or 30 days, are issued at **Wattay Airport** (see p. 327) in Vientiane and **Friendship Bridge** (see p. 821) at Nong Khai; bring three passport-sized photos and US$30. Visas are **no longer** available at the Chong Mek border crossing (see p. 357). Upon application, the Department of Immigration may extend an on-arrival visa for a single day, or sometimes for 15

LAOS

days if the application is made through a tour agency. If entering the country from any other international checkpoint, obtain a visa in advance. Lao consulates abroad issue 15- and 30-day tourist visas that are valid for two months. Travel agencies and Lao consulates in **Bangkok** issue visas for 300฿ (2-day processing); in **Hanoi**, US$60 (1- to 3-day processing); in **Phnom Penh,** US$45 (1-day processing);in **Saigon,** US$65 (same-day processing). Beware of fradulent visas peddled by some travel agents.

LICENSED TOURS According to the Lao Tourist Police, a group of more than 5 foreign tourists must be accompanied by a licensed tour guide, and all foreign tourists must use a licensed tour company (no unaccompanied tourism is allowed). This latter requirement has not been strongly enforced in the past.

MONEY

The Lao **kip** comes in denominations of 100, 500, 1000, 2000, and 5000 and is divided into 100 cents. Thai baht and US dollars are the most widely exchanged currencies, especially since the government devalued the kip in early 1998. Vendors in markets are eager to change US dollars and baht into kip, often at better rates than in the banks. Traveler's checks and credit cards are only accepted at major banks and businesses. It's customary to **tip** guides, but tipping in restaurants and hotels is uncommon. Feel free to **bargain** whenever a price isn't indicated.

MEDICAL EMERGENCIES

Travelers should go to Thailand for medical care, as facilities in Laos are extremely limited. The **Friendship Bridge** (see p. 821) connects Vientiane to Nong Khai, Thailand; it is open between 6am and 10pm, and in medical emergency crossing after hours is usually permitted. Ambulances from Udorn, Thailand's **AEK Udon International Hospital** (☎66 42 342 555), Nong Khai, Thailand's **Nong Kong Wattana Hospital** (☎66 18 33 4262), and Vientiane's **Setthatirat Hospital** (☎021 413 720) are pre-authorized to carry patients across.

LAOS

ACCOMMODATIONS

HOTELS. The Lao government may require hotels and guesthouses to provide information on the identity and activities of foreign guests. Moreover, hotel rooms may be searched, and phone, fax, or email communications may be monitored.

HOMESTAYS. Foreigners may not stay with Lao citizens without the prior permission of village chiefs.

GETTING THERE

BY AIR. Laos has two **international airports:** Wattay International Airport in Vientiane (see p. 327) and Luang Prabang Airport in Luang Prabang (see p. 336). **Lao Aviation** (www.laoaviation.com) runs the most international flights between major Southeast Asia gateways, but the US State Department has issued a warning (http://travel.state.gov/laos.html) regarding Lao Aviation's safety record, advising visitors to limit their use of the carrier to essential travel only. Consult your embassy for the latest safety reports. Alternatively, use **Thai Airways** or **Vietnam Airlines** for flights to Bangkok, Hanoi, and Ho Chi Minh City.

BY LAND. Refer to the following table for overland border crossings in Laos.

BY SEA. Silly rabbit, Laos is landlocked.

BORDER CROSSINGS

CAMBODIA. The border crossing between **Don Khong** in southern Laos and **Stung Treng** (p. 83) in northern Cambodia was unofficially open as of 2002. Cambodian visas are not available at the border and you may have to bribe the border guards on both sides.

CHINA. The only legal crossing is from the small town of **Boten** in northern Laos to **Mohan/Mengla** (p. 347) in southwest China.

THAILAND. There are 5 border crossings from Laos to Thailand: **Houie Xay** (p. 350) to **Chiang Khong** (p. 779); **Vientiane** (p. 327) to **Nong Khai** (p. 818); **Thakhek** to **Nakhon Phanom** (p. 818); **Savannakhet** (p. 351) to **Mukdahan** (p. 815); and **Pakse** (p. 354) to **Chong Mek** (p. 813).

VIETNAM. Travelers pass between **Savannakhet** (p. 351) in Laos and **Đà Nẵng/Huế** (p. 928) in Vietnam via **Lao Bảo** (7hr. from Savannakhet, 8hr. from Huế; p. 354). The crossing at **Điện Biên Phủ** is open to locals but not foreigners. Check with an embassy for up-to-date information. You may be denied passage, especially if your visa doesn't specify the correct points of entry and exit.

MYANMAR. It isn't currently possible to travel overland to Myanmar from Laos.

GETTING AROUND

Travel in Laos can make travel in other parts of Southeast Asia feel luxurious. Most roads are old, pot-holed, and bumpy or are just dirt tracks that become rivers of mud during the rainy season. Boat and air travel are infinitely more popular than buses and cars.

BY PLANE. During the rainy season, air travel may be the only way to reach remote areas like Luang Nam Tha. **Lao Aviation** has domestic flights that link the capital with every region of the country, but be aware that the US State Department (http://travel.state.gov/laos.html) has issued a warning regarding the carrier's safety record, especially over mountainous areas. Buy your ticket several days in advance and confirm your flight one day in advance, as some routes only run occasionally, and other forms of transportation aren't always available. Only US dollars are accepted for payment from foreigners.

BY BUS. Buses, trucks, and pickups run regularly in most provinces. Buses are cheap but take an inordinate amount of time. Overcrowded buses often stop at the driver's whim. In the north, the best way to ensure a seat is to show up around 7am; in the south, departure times vary more, and you may have to flag down a passing bus from a major junction. Thanks to fully paved roads from Vientiane to Luang Prabang and from Vientiane to Pakse, travel to the cities has become easier. But the roads north of Luang Prabang and to more remote regions like Attapeu are terrible—and nonexistent during the rainy season. While banditry used to be a danger on the northern roads, the roads have been generally safe in recent times. Night travel is still not advised, and it would still be best for travelers to inquire at their embassies about road status and safety.

BY BOAT. For centuries, boat travel was the chief means of transportation within Laos (besides elephants, of course). A jaunt down the Mekong, Nam Ou, or Nam Tha rivers remains an intriguing option; many travelers find **slow boat travel** so relaxing that they spend a good portion of their time in Laos on the water. In some areas, passenger boats have fixed prices, while in other areas, travelers need to organize a group and charter an entire vessel or bargain for a place on cargo vessels. Whatever the case, bring a sleeping bag if traveling overnight, and stock up on food and water. During the dry season, water levels drop, and boat travel may not be possible. Exact travel times depend on several variables, including the river current, amount of cargo, number of passengers, and number of stops made.

"Fast boats" (speedboats) are a different matter. These ear-splitting, leg-cramping, light-speed contraptions will (somehow) get you to your destination more quickly than slow boats but for more money and discomfort. Fast boats are especially dangerous during the dry season; ask for a helmet and life vest (which you may or may not get), and make sure your bag is securely tied to the boat, as choppy waters pitch luggage overboard. Bring earplugs.

KEEPING IN TOUCH

Mail from Laos is unreliable and slow. Postage is cheap, but many prefer to send overseas packages from Thailand. Receiving mail in Laos is possible through *Poste Restante* in Vientiane. Postal officers will inspect anything that's not a letter. The new **Lao Telecom** phone service has made international calls from Laos possible for the first time. Post offices in medium-sized towns sell US$3, US$6, and US$9 phone cards, stock English-language white pages, and invariably have a card phone outside. Cities like Luang Prabang and Vientiane have telecommunication bureaus that place calls but charge more for fewer services (no collect, credit card, or incoming calls allowed). For **Home Country Direct (HCD)** numbers from Laos, refer to the table on the inside back cover of this book. **Internet** access is found surprisingly often, but by no means everywhere.

LAOS

NORTHERN LAOS

VIENTIANE ☎21

To adventurers from a bygone era, Vientiane conjured up sepia-tinged images of an exotic colonial backwater where days melted into years and life was as sluggish as the Mekong. Today, save for a few wine shops, French expats, and baguettes, the "City of Sandalwood" has shed its colonial legacy but has not yet acquired the impersonality of a larger metropolis. For most travelers, this capital's chief appeal is its provincial feel; most linger a day or two before heading into rural Laos.

TRANSPORTATION

Flights: Wattay International Airport (☎513 200), on Luang Prabang Rd., 4km from the center of town. Taxi to downtown US$5. **Lao Air Booking Co.,** 43/1 Setthathirat Rd. (☎216 761). Open M-F 1-4:30pm, Sa 8am-noon. AmEx/V. **Lao Aviation,** 2 Pang Kham Rd. (domestic ☎212 057, international ☎212 051). Open M-F 8am-noon and 1-4:30pm, Sa 8-11:30am. MC/V. To: **Bangkok** (1 per day, US$95); **Chiang Mai** (2 per week, US$85); **Hanoi** (1 per day, US$108); **Ho Chi Minh City** (1 per week, US$168); **Houie Xay** (4 per week, US$90); **Luang Nam Tha** (5 per week, US$82); **Luang Prabang** (2 per day, US$112); **Pakse** (1 per day, US$97); **Phonsavanh** (1 per day, US$56); **Phnom Penh** (1 per day, US$140); **Savannakhet** (1 per day, US$80); **Udom Xai** (5 per week, US$72). **Thai Airways,** 27/1 Pang Kham Rd. (☎222 527). Open M-F 8:30am-noon and 1-5pm, Sa 8:30am-noon. AmEx/V. To **Bangkok** (1 per day, US$120). **Vietnam Airlines,** 63 Samsenthai Rd. (☎217 562), in Lao Plaza Hotel. Open M-Sa 8am-noon and 1:30-4:30pm. To **Hanoi** (US$110) and **Ho Chi Minh City** (US$165).

Buses: Northern Bus Terminal (☎216 507), on the corner of Mahosot and Khou Vieng Rd. To: **Friendship Bridge** (#45; 30min., every 20min. 7am-5pm, 1000kip); **Paksan** (#18; 3hr.; 7, 11am, 2pm; 6000kip); **Pakse** (#35; 13hr.; 11am, 1, 3pm; 35,000kip); **Savannakhet** (#36; 8hr.; 7:30, 10am; 25,000kip); **Tha Deua** (#14; 45min., every 20min. 7am-5pm); **Vang Vieng** (#1; 4hr.; 7, 10:30am, 1:30pm; 6000kip). Other buses leave from **Thalat Laeng** (☎413 297), accessible by *tuk-tuk* (3000kip). To: **Luang Prabang** (8hr.; 7, 8:30, 10:30am, 1, 5pm; 50,000kip); **Oudomxay** (15hr.; 6am; 60,000kip); **Phonsavanh** (10hr.; 7:30am; 60,000kip); **Xamnena** (30hr.; 7am; 80,000kip).

Boats: Boat travel to northern towns is possible, but erratic schedules, particularly during the dry season, make buses the preferred means of transport. **Speedboats** go from **Kao Liao Pier,** 3km from the city center, to **Luang Prabang** and **Pak Lay. Private boats** can also be chartered to **Luang Prabang** (10hr.; 10,000kip).

Local Transportation: Taxis congregate at the morning market on Lane Xang Ave. and in front of the Novotel on Luang Prabang Rd. (10,000-15,000kip per hr. or 200,000kip per day). To **Tha Deua** (Buddha Park) 50,000kip. **Tuk-tuk** 6000-8000kip. **Saysouly Guest House** (☎218 383), on Manthatulath Rd. 1 block west of Pang Kham Rd., rents **bicycles** (US$2 per day) and **motorbikes** (US$10 per day).

ORIENTATION AND PRACTICAL INFORMATION

The **Nam Phou Fountain,** obscured by trees on Setthathirat Rd., serves as a convenient landmark. Vientiane's three main thoroughfares are **Samsenthai Rd.,** one block north of the fountain; **Setthathirat Rd.,** one block south of the fountain; and **Lane Xang Ave.,** which runs perpendicular to the **Mekong River** until the **Anousavari Monument.** Lane Xang Ave. is home to **Talat Sao** (the morning market), the **GPO,** and most **embassies.** Most restaurants are on **Quay Fa Ngum Rd.,** which is parallel and closest to the Mekong River. The **Northern Bus Terminal** is on **Mahosot Rd.,** parallel to and one block east of Lane Xang Ave. Over toward the airport, **Khoun Boulom Rd.** runs inland from Quay Fa Ngum Rd., looping toward Talat Sao and Lane Xang Ave.

TOURIST AND FINANCIAL SERVICES

Tourist Offices: National Tourism Authority (☎212 251), on Lane Xang Ave. 300m before Anousavari Monument. Flight and bus schedules and travel info. Open M-F 8am-noon and 1-4pm. **Inter-Lao Tourism** (☎214 232), on Luang Prabang Rd. near the Novotel. Open M-F 8am-noon and 1:30-5pm, Sa 8am-noon.

Tours: Diethelm Travel (☎213 833), on Setthathirat Rd. beside the Nam Phou Fountain. Arranges transportation. Open M-F 8am-noon and 1:30-5pm, Sa 8am-noon. **Sadetour** (☎216 314), on Quay Fa Ngum Rd. near the residential palace. Laos's oldest tour company. Open M-F 8am-6pm, Sa 8am-noon.

Immigration Offices: Immigration Department (☎212 520), on Khoun Boulom Rd. before the Lane Xang Ave. intersection. 15- or 30-day visas can be extended for up to 15 days (US$2 per day). Open M-F 8am-noon and 1-4pm. Other immigration offices are at the airport and next to Mithaphrap bridge (☎812 040).

Embassies: Australia (☎413 610), on the corner of Nehru and Phone Xay Rd., near Anousavari Monument. Open M-Th 9am-noon and 1:30-5pm, F 9am-noon. Serves **UK, Canada,** and **NZ** citizens in emergencies. **Cambodia** (☎314 952), on Tha Deua Rd., 2km outside the city center. One-day visas US$20. Open M-F 7:30-11:30am and 2-5pm. **China** (☎315 103), on War Nak Rd. past Myanmar Embassy. 30-day visas US$50. Open M-F 9-11:30am. **Myanmar** (☎314 910), on Sokpaluang Rd. 500m past Wat Sokpaluang on the left. Tourist visas US$18; 3-day processing. Bring 4 photos. Open M-F 8:30am-noon and 1-4:30pm. **Thailand** (☎214 580), on Phone Keng Rd.; consular office (☎217 154), on Lane Xang Rd., 300m before the Anousavari Monu-

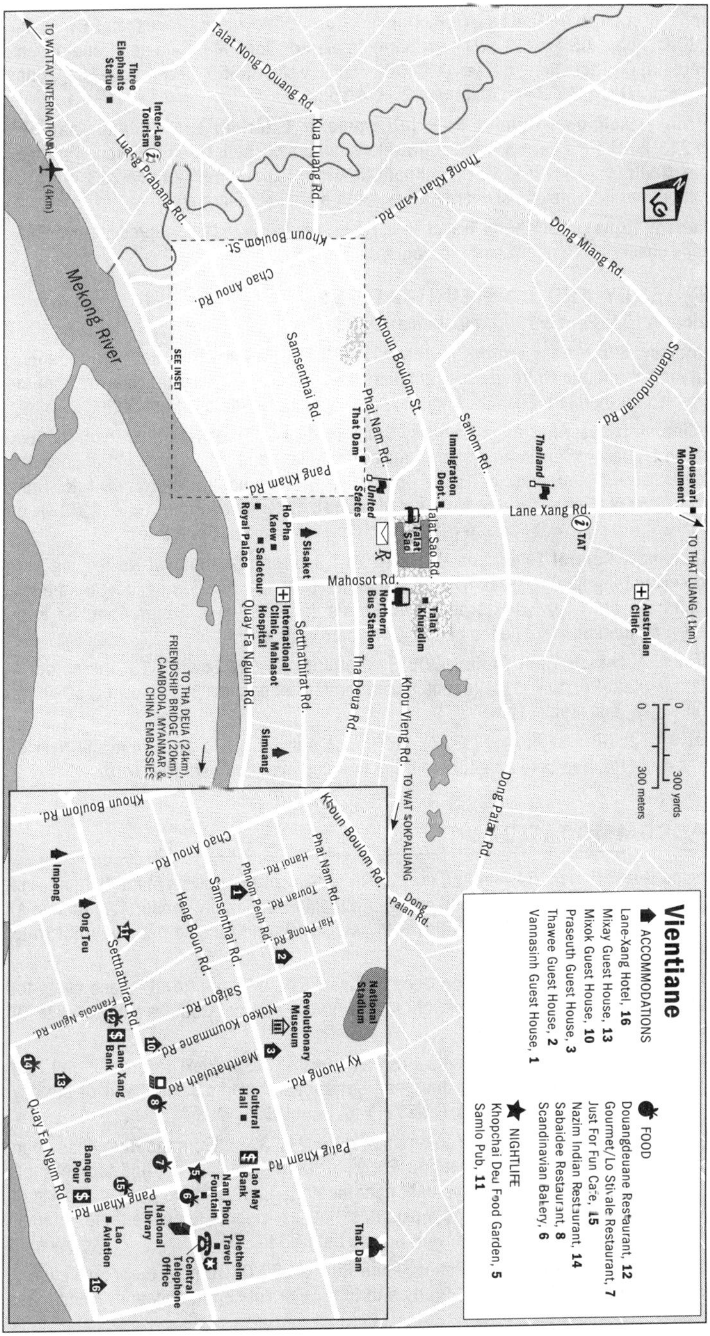
Vientiane
ACCOMMODATIONS
Lane-Xang Hotel, 16
Mixay Guest House, 13
Mixok Guest House, 10
Praseuth Guest House, 3
Thawee Guest House, 2
Vannasinh Guest House, 1
FOOD
Douangdeuane Restaurant, 12
Gourmet/Lo Stivale Restaurant, 7
Just For Fun Cafe, 15
Nazim Indian Restaurant, 14
Sabaidee Restaurant, 8
Scandinavian Bakery, 6
NIGHTLIFE
Khopchai Deu Food Garden, 5
Samlo Pub, 11
0
300 yards
0
300 meters
TO WATTAY INTERNATIONAL (4km)
Three Elephants Statue
Inter-Lao Tourism
Luang Prabang Rd.
Talat Nong Douang Rd.
Kua Luang Rd.
Thong Khan Kam Rd.
Dong Miang Rd.
Khoun Boulom St.
Chao Anou Rd.
Mekong River
SEE INSET
Samsenthai Rd.
Khoun Boulom St.
Phai Nam Rd.
That Dam
Pang Kham Rd.
United States
Sailom Rd.
Immigration Dept.
Thailand
Sidamdouan Rd.
Anousavari Monument
Lane Xang Rd.
TAT
TO THAT LUANG (1km)
Australian Clinic
Talat Sao
Talat Sao Rd.
Mahosot Rd.
Northern Bus Station
Talat Khuadim
Ho Pha Kaew
Sisaket
Royal Palace
Sadetour
International Clinic, Mahasot Hospital
Setthathirat Rd.
Quay Fa Ngum Rd.
Tha Deua Rd.
Khou Vieng Rd.
TO THA DEUA (24km), FRIENDSHIP BRIDGE (20km), CAMBODIA, MYANMAR & CHINA EMBASSIES
Simuang
TO WAT SOKPALUANG
Dong Palan Rd.
Khoun Boulom Rd.
Hanoi Rd.
Touran Rd.
Hai Phong Rd.
Phnom Penh Rd.
Impeng
Ong Teu
Heng Boun Rd.
National Stadium
Revolutionary Museum
Saigon Rd.
Francois Ngin Rd.
Lane Xang Bank
Nokeo Koummane Rd.
Manthatulath Rd.
Ky Huong Rd.
Cultural Hall
Lao May Bank
Nam Phou Fountain
Banque Pour
Lao Aviation
National Library
Diethelm Travel
Central Telephone Office
That Dam

LAOS

ment. 60-day tourist visas 300฿, transit visas 200฿; 2-day processing. Open M-F 8:30am-noon. **US** (☎212 581), on Bartholomie Rd. Open M-F 8am-noon and 1-5pm. **Vietnam,** 60 That Luang Rd. (☎413 400). Tourist visas US$55; 3-day processing. Bring 2 photos. Open M-F 8-10:30am and 2:15-4:15pm.

Currency Exchange: Banque Pour le Commerce Extérieur Lao, 1 Pang Kham Rd. (☎213 200). Visa cash advances. Traveler's checks cashed. Open M-F 8am-4pm. **Lao May Bank** (☎213 300), 39 Pang Kham Rd., and **Lane Xang Bank** (☎213 400), on Setthathirat Rd., provide similar services. Both open M-F 8am-4pm.

American Express: Diethelm Travel (see **Tours,** above) is the Lao representative. Traveler's checks (2% commission) for AmEx cardholders.

EMERGENCY AND COMMUNICATIONS

Police: ☎191. **Fire:** ☎190. **Ambulance:** ☎195.

Pharmacy: Seng Thong Osoth Pharmacy (☎213 732), on the road between the morning market and the Northern Bus Terminal, is one of many. As you move away from the river, it's on the right. Friendly, English-speaking staff. Open daily 8am-5pm.

Medical Services: Australian Embassy Clinic (☎413 603), on Nehru Rd. near the Australian Embassy. Serves Australian, British, Canadian, and NZ citizens. Initial consultation US$50. By appointment only. Open M-Th 8:30am-noon and 2-5pm, F 8:30am-noon. **International Clinic, Mahosot Hospital,** Emergency Room (☎214 023), on Mahosot Rd. past Wat Pha Kaew. Not much English spoken. **Open 24hr.**

Telephones: Central Telephone Office (☎214 977), on Setthathirat Rd. Facing Nam Phou Fountain, head 1 block right on Setthathirat Rd.; it's a yellow building on the left. Cash calls only. Fax 500kip per page. Phone cards. Open M-F 8am-4pm, Sa 8am-3:30pm. International phones also at GPO (card calls only).

Internet Access: Planet Online, 205 Setthathirat Rd. (☎218 972), at the corner of Manthatulath Rd., has many terminals and the fastest connections in town. 150kip per min. Open daily 8am-11pm.

Post Office: GPO (☎/fax 217 327), on Khou Vieng Rd. Head away from the river on Lane Xang Rd. and take a right before the morning market. *Poste Restante.*

ACCOMMODATIONS

Thawee Guest House, 64 Ban Ann (☎217 903), 2 blocks northwest of the Cultural Hall. Great guest house with energizing orange walls and wonderfully comfortable rooms; A/C rooms are a nice splurge. Singles with satellite TV and outside bath with hot water US$5; doubles US$10. ❸

Lane-Xang Hotel (☎214 102), on Quay Fa Ngum Rd., near the Royal Palace along the river. An upscale hotel with large rooms and quality service. Doubles with satellite TV, hot water, and A/C US$25. ❺

Praseuth Guest House, 312 Samsenthai Rd. (☎217 932), next to the Cultural Hall. Amicable, family-run business with small but spotless rooms in the heart of the city. Laundry. Rooms US$6-7, with A/C US$7, with bath US$8. ❸

Mixay Guest House, 39 Nokeo Koummane Rd. (☎217 023). From the Nam Phou Fountain, walk 3 blocks down Setthathirat Rd. with the river on your left and turn left onto Nokeo Koummane Rd.; it's on the right near the end. Apart from the giant snakeskin on the lobby wall, Mixay is similar to most guest houses—clean and comfortable. Internet. Doubles with shared bath US$6; with private bath US$7. ❸

Vannasinh Guest House, 051 Phnom Penh Rd. (☎222 020), near the intersection of Samsenthai Rd. with Hanoi Rd. Pretty and in a quiet yet central location. French- and

English-speaking staff manage clean, pleasant rooms. Rooms with shared bath US$8; doubles with private bath US$10, with A/C and hot water US$16. ❹

Mixok Guest House (☎251 600), on Setthathirat Rd. 2 blocks west of the Nam Phou Fountain. Small but good value rooms with dorm bunk beds. Nice balcony looks out onto the street and a temple. All rooms have shared bath. Dorms 15,000kip; singles 30,000kip, with larger bed 36,000kip; doubles 36,000kip; triples 51,000kip. ❶

FOOD

For cheap and delicious Lao food, head to one of the many eateries along the river. Most are open from dawn until late evening and serve a mix of Lao, Thai, and Western style dishes (7000-15,000kip). French bakeries and restaurants cluster near the Nam Phou Fountain.

Scandinavian Bakery, 74/1 Pang Kham Rd. beside Nam Phou Fountain. Expensive but popular. Excellent pastries (5000kip) and lunch options (10,000-18,000kip), CNN, and foreign magazines. Open daily 7am-7pm. ❷

Nazim Indian Restaurant, on Quay Fa Ngum Rd. near the François Nginn intersection. Popular Lao chain with superb food and a great view of the river. Dishes 10,000-18,000kip. Open daily 10am-11pm. ❷

Gourmet/Lo Stivale Restaurant, 44 Setthathirat Rd. Gourmet is a cafe, while Lo Stivale is a classy but expensive restaurant with authentic and utterly delicious food. Comprehensive Western menu (US$4-16 per dish). Panini US$4. Gourmet open daily 7am-8pm; Lo Stivale open daily 10am-10pm. MC/V. ❺

Douangdeuane Restaurant, on François Nginn Rd. off Setthathirat Rd. Delicious vegetarian Lao, Thai, and Vietnamese menus (entrees 8000-16,000kip) and English- and French-speaking staff. Open daily 8am-10pm. ❶

Just for Fun, 15/2 Pang Kham Rd. between the Nam Phou Fountain and Quay Fa Ngum Rd. This quirky eatery specializes in vegetarian food and sells ethnic products, clothing, etc. Most dishes US$1-2. Open M-Sa 9am-9pm. ❶

Sabaidee Restaurant, on the corner of Setthathirat Rd. and Manthatulath St. A pretty courtyard restaurant offering Lao and Western dishes. Breakfast menu. Chicken *laap* 10,000kip. Open daily 7am-10pm. ❶

SIGHTS

Several temples and some of the best-preserved colonial architecture in the city grace **Setthathirat Rd.** and **Quay Fa Ngum Rd.** Away from the city center are That Luang, the Anousavari Monument, and the steam baths of Wat Sokpaluang.

THAT LUANG. This 45m gold *stupa* is the Lao national symbol and also one of the most important religious sites in Laos. Four wats once surrounded the lotus-bud-shaped *stupa*, but only the northern and southourn wats remain. Originally built in 1566, it was restored in 1935 by the French colonial regime. Each November, That Luang hosts the **That Luang Festival,** when hundreds of monks gather to accept alms and floral gifts from the faithful. *(On That Luang Rd. 1km inland from city center. Open Tu-Su 8am-noon and 1-4pm. 1000kip donation expected.)*

HO PHRA KEO (HALL OF THE EMERALD BUDDHA). Vientiane's oldest temple has housed Buddhist sculpture and artifacts since 1970. The original temple was built in the mid-16th century by King Setthathirat to house the Emerald Buddha he brought from Chiang Mai. Razed by Thais in 1827, the wat was restored in the 1940s. *(From the Nam Phou Fountain, follow Setthathirat Rd. 100m past the Lane Xang Ave. intersection; the entrance is on the right. Open daily 8am-noon and 1-4pm. 1000kip.)*

WAT SISAKET. Built by King Anou in 1818, the temple houses 7000 Buddha statues and a sanctuary with elaborate murals. *(On the corner of Setthathirat Rd. and Lane Xang Ave. Open daily 8am-noon and 1-4pm. 1000kip.)*

WAT ONG TEU. The largest temple in the capital, Wat Ong Teu has one of the country's most prestigious Buddhist schools and a massive meditating Buddha. *(At the west end of Setthathirat Rd. at the Chao Anou Rd. intersection.)*

THAT DAM (BLACK STUPA). According to legend, a seven-headed dragon lay under the *stupa* to protect the people of Vientiane from Siamese invaders in 1828. Ever since, the *stupa* has been seen as the city's protector. *(One block north and inland of Samsenthai Rd.on Pang Kham Rd.)*

WAT SOKPALUANG. This wat offers wonderfully refreshing herbal saunas for 6000kip and rigorous 40min. massages for 15,000kip. *(1.5km southeast of the city center. Take a tuk-tuk (5000kip) or walk away from Lane Xang Ave. on Khou Vieng Rd., which runs between the morning market and the post office. The turn-off for the wat is unmarked; it is visible through the trees from the main road. Open daily late morning-8pm.)*

WAT SIMUANG. Built by King Setthathirat in 1566, this wat houses the foundation pillar of Vientiane, which, according to legend, crushed a pregnant woman, Nang Si, as it was lowered. Nang Si is revered as the guardian spirit of the city. *(On Quay Fa Ngum Rd. at the eastern end of town. Open Tu-Sa 8am-8pm.)*

ANOUSAVARI MONUMENT (VICTORY GATE). This bizarre-looking monument, at the inland end of Lane Xang Ave., is akin to a concrete mix between Paris's Arc de Triomphe (the creator's inspiration) and a wedding cake. It was built in 1969 by the government in memory of those who died during the Lao struggle for independence. When builders ran out of concrete, they completed the memorial with US cement earmarked for use in construction of Wattay International Airport. Known to some as the "vertical runway," it has an unparalleled panoramic view of town. *(At the north end of town on Lane Xang Ave. Open daily 8am-5pm. 1000kip.)*

MARKETS. Talat Sao (morning market) and **Talat Khuadim** (evening market) are two of Vientiane's main attractions. Talat Sao is in two green-roofed buildings off Lane Xang Ave., the first selling electric and silver goods, and the second selling clothes and wall-hangings. (Open daily 6am-6pm.) Talat Khuadim is the large open-air market behind the Northern Bus Terminal. **Magninom Market,** on Khou Boulom Rd., is geared more toward tourists. (Open daily 8am-9:30pm.)

ENTERTAINMENT

There is little raucous nightlife in Vientiane—bars and clubs must close by midnight. **Khopchai Deu Food Garden,** next to the Nam Phou Fountain on Setthathirat Rd., has a beautiful courtyard surrounding an aging French colonial building. Its nightly barbecues are one of Vientiane's most popular nighttime hangouts. Khopchai is busy in the afternoons as well. People sit around drinking Lao beer, listening to a looped mix tape of Radiohead, Buena Vista Social Club, and REM. Sit at the outside bar, enjoy a Lao wine cocktail (8000kip), and listen to the live band every Friday and Saturday. (Open M-Sa 9am-11:30pm, Su 5:30-11:30pm.) British **Samlo Pub,** 101 Setthathirat Rd., caters to a tourist/expat crowd. Hang out, shoot pool, or play foosball. (☎222 308. Open daily 11:30am-2pm and 5pm-midnight.)

DAYTRIPS FROM VIENTIANE

THA DEUA. Buddha sculptures are everywhere in this sculpture park built by the same self-described "half-man, half-animal" Lao monk/mystic who designed Sala Kaew Ku following the Communist victory 23 years ago. Both temples have a mix of Hindu and Buddhist themes brought to life in cement sculptures. Fat Buddhas, thin Buddhas, big Buddhas, little Buddhas, Buddha family scenes, and reclining Buddhas all make an appearance. *(Tha Deua, 24km from Vientiane, can be reached by bus from the Northern Bus Terminal (#14; 50min., every 30min. 6am-5pm, 1000kip) or tuk-tuk (45min.; 40,000kip, 1000kip for parking.) Open daily 8am-5pm. 2000kip.)*

LAO PAKO. A small eco-tourist lodge, **Lao Pako ❶** is popular with Vientiane's expatriates and lies south of Nam Ngum Lake on the Nam Ngum River, 50km from Vientiane. Austrian owner Mr. Pfabigan organizes treks, river-rafting expeditions, and village visits. The bar/restaurant is popular but expensive; bring your own food and drink if you're staying for a few days. *(☎212 981. Dorms 20,000kip; doubles 60,000kip; 2-3 person bungalows 120,000kip. Lao Pako, 50km northeast of Vientiane, can be reached by bus from the Northern Bus Terminal (#19 to Paxxap; get off at Som Sa Mai; 1½hr.; 6:30, 11am, 3pm; 2000kip). Once there, take a motorboat (25min.; 25,000kip per boat.) to Lao Pako resort.)*

NEAR VIENTIANE: NAM NGUM LAKE

Nam Ngum Lake, 90km northeast of Vientiane, is a vast reservoir formed by the damming of Nam Ngum River in the late 1970s. Today, the hydroelectric power plant supplies electricity to much of Laos and parts of Thailand. Nam Ngum's natural setting is spectacular with emerald islets, many of which were prisons and political re-education camps during the 1980s, dotting the lake. In the hurry to complete the dam, however, no one thought to harvest the surrounding forest, which was soon submerged. Ingenious Lao loggers have now developed underwater chain saws, and lumberjacks trade boots for flippers to keep the show going. Travelers seeking peace and quiet head to **Santipap Island,** the site of a dilapidated but charming **guest house ❷.** An ethereal setting, great swimming, and gorgeous sunsets compensate for the simple lodgings and sporadic electricity (rooms 30,000kip). If it's full you can sleep in hammocks outside for free. The only **restaurant ❷** on the island, to the left of the guest house, serves fresh fish (10,000-18,000kip). Boats make the trip to the island (15min.; 20,000-40,000kip per boat). To reach the lake, take a bus from Vientiane's Northern Bus Terminal (see **Transportation,** p. 327) to Ban Thalat. From there, *songthaew* and tuk-tuks run to the lake (10,000-20,000kip), passing the dam complex. To continue farther north of Nam Ngum Lake, head back to Ban Thalat and take a tuk-tuk (30min.; 10,000-20,000kip) to **Phon Hong,** or wait for a full *songthaew* (3000kip). From Phon Hong, a bus goes to **Vang Vieng** (2½hr., 9am, 3000kip), or you can take a full *songthaew*.

VANG VIENG ☎23

The small town of Vang Vieng has played various roles throughout its diverse history. During the Vietnam War, the area was a stronghold of Vang Pao's Hmong guerrillas, recruited by the US Central Intelligence Agency to fight the Pathet Lao and Vietnamese Communists. The area is now home to Hmong and Yao minority communities. More recently, the town has become overrun with backpackers drawn by the dramatic limestone cliffs dotted with spectacular caves.

TRANSPORTATION

All **buses** leave from the **bus station** next to the old airstrip on Rte. 13. Arrive at least 30min. in advance to ensure a seat on the crowded Luang Prabang buses. Buses run to **Luang Prabang** (9hr.; 9am; 40,000kip) and **Vientiane** (4-5hr.; 5:30, 6:10am, 1, 2:30pm; 8000kip). To visit **Nam Ngum Reservoir,** take a songthaew to **Phon Hong** (3hr., 8-9am, 6000kip), a tuk-tuk to **Ban Thalat** (20min.; 20,000kip), and then another tuk-tuk to the reservoir (10,000kip).

ORIENTATION AND PRACTICAL INFORMATION

Vang Vieng lies along **Rte. 13,** which runs between Vientiane and Luang Prabang. The town spans two unnamed roads that are parallel to Rte. 13 and west of the airstrip. The first one originates at the **bus station** east of town where the tuk-tuks and *songthaew* gather. One block west, the second road runs along the **Nam Song River.** At the north end of the road is the **market.** The **Vang Vieng Resort** and **Tham Chang Cave** are 2km south of the river road. Maps are available from shops all over town (3000kip). The **post office,** which sells phone cards for international calls, is on the river road next to the market. (☎511 009. Open M-F 8-11am and 2-5pm.) A **card phone** is outside. Heading away from the market is the **district hospital** (☎211 109). The **Keo** and **Aikham Pharmacies** sit opposite the hospital. (Open daily 8am-8pm.) The large, well-stocked **Kheamphone Pharmacy** is on the right on the same road heading north. (Open daily 6am-10pm.) Currency and traveler's checks can be exchanged at **Banque Pour Le Commerce Extérieur Lao** (open M-F 8:30am-3pm), on the cross-street with Wildside Bar on the corner, and also at the **Agricultural Promotion Bank** (open M-F 9am-4pm; commission US$2 on traveler's checks), on the corner of the main road near the bus station. International calls can be made from **Lao Telecom,** opposite the police station. (☎511 000. Open daily 8am-5pm.) **Bicycle rental** (5000-7000kip per day) is available from most guest houses and shops on the side road leading to the market. **Internet** access is available pretty much everywhere for roughly the same price, one place being **Planet Online,** on the same road as Banque Pour Le Commerce Extérieur Lao (250kip per min.).

LAOS

ACCOMMODATIONS AND FOOD

The growth of tourism in Vang Vieng has led to a frenzy of hotel construction. The northern end of town has most of the restaurants and nightlife activity. Across the street from the Sunset Restaurant is **Hotel Namsong ❺,** a guest house with attractive rooms and a beautiful garden. (☎511 016. Doubles with bath, hot water, and breakfast US$30.) The central **Doukkhoun 1 Guest House ❸,** 50m east of the market, has clean rooms. (☎511 032. Doubles with bath and hot water 45,000-55,000kip.) At the southern end of town, on the road that runs parallel to and east of the airstrip, the **Nana Guest House ❶** has clean, quiet rooms. (Singles 14,000kip; doubles with bath 20,000-40,000kip.) For a chance to see traditional silkworm breeding and the production of green tea and starfruit wine, head 3km north of Vang Vieng to **Mr. T's Phondindaeng Organic Farm ❷.** Spending a night in Mr. T's guest house is the ideal way to experience farm life firsthand. Guests are welcome to help with farm work. (☎511 220. Singles 30,000kip; doubles 40,000kip. If you plan to stay, write to Mr. Thanongassi Salangkoun, GPO Box 7893, Vientiane, LAO PDR. The owner prefers guests who plan on helping out to stay at least two weeks.)

The **Sunset Restaurant,** an old favorite, is 300m south of the hospital down a lane to the left off the river road and offers gorgeous views over the Nam Song River. Near the market, **Fathima Restaurant ❷** cooks up fresh *chapaati* in front of your eyes and dishes out quality Indian food. (10,000-18,000kip. Open daily 11am-9pm.) **Khamla Restaurant ❶**, 20m north of Nana Guest House, has tasty organic and vegetarian options. (Fried rice 6000kip. Open daily 7am-11:30pm.) The **Organic Farm Cafe ❶**, just north of Lao Telekom, serves produce from the Phondindaeng Organic Farm. (Starfruit wine 5000kip per glass. Open daily 8am-10:30pm.)

SIGHTS

By far the most popular activity around Vang Vieng is **inner-tubing** down Nam Song River. Shops along Luang Prabang Rd. and the river road arrange excursions 7km north of town (5000kip including tuk-tuk and tube rental). The numerous **limestone caves** in the cliffs surrounding Vang Vieng are a spelunker's dream. Apart from **Tham Chang,** which is well lit, the caves are unspoiled, beautiful, and easy to get lost in. Tour agencies line the main road. **Mr. Keo,** based across from Wildside Bar, is a reputable guide. He leads tours that include spelunking, hikes to waterfalls, subterranean swimming, and inner-tubing (1-day 40,000kip; 2-day/1-night 150,000kip). Sturdy footwear and a flashlight (sold in the market) are a must for spelunking. Many shops near the market sell maps of Vang Vieng and environs (3000kip) for those wishing to venture alone.

> **!** Many travelers explore the caves on their own and return home safely. Still, unaccompanied foreign explorers make tempting targets for rogues and bandits in more remote areas around Vang Vieng. Consider hiring a guide from one of the restaurants or guest houses on the main road; doing so reduces your chances of getting lost, hurt, or robbed.

North of town lie the largest, most spectacular caves. **Tham Xang** (Elephant Caves) are 15km north of town and accessible by tuk-tuk (20,000-30,000kip round-trip), bicycle, or foot. Take Rte. 13 north to Ban Tham Xang Village where a dirt road to the left leads to the cave. A few paddies down, villagers run an informal ferry service across the river (500kip toll), though in the dry season you may have to wade or cross a bamboo bridge. The first elephant cave rises out of the rice fields like a shark fin. Buddha images, a single footprint, and a stalactite bearing an uncanny resemblance to an elephant's head all await inside. Vang Vieng's largest cave, **Tham Nang Phomhorm** (Cave of the Fragrant-Haired Woman), is 4km past Ban Tham Xang. Take the turn-off right at the village of **Ban Patthana.** The two-level cave is 15km down this road, which passes **Ban Nam Yen,** a Yao hill tribe village 3km before the cave entrance (tuk-tuk 2500kip). It's a good idea to pay extra to get the tuk-tuk driver to wait while you explore. The most popular way to visit the caves is on one of the numerous tours (1-day tour of caves and local villages US$5) offered by guides around Vang Vieng. Some companies also offer whitewater rafting and rock-climbing trips (about US$15 per day). South of town and across the Nam Song River lies **Tham Phou Kham** (Cave of the Golden Crabs). To reach the caves, head south of town toward the river and turn right down the path next to the Sunset Restaurant. In the dry season it's possible to cross the bridge to get to the caves (1000kip toll), but in rainy season you'll need to cross by boat (2000kip). Over the bridge to the right is **Tham Chang.** Bring a flashlight. (Caves open daily 7:30-11:30am and 1-4:30pm. 4000kip.) Other highlights around Vang Vieng include ethnic villages that are best visited by bicycle. Across the river west of town are the Hmong villages of **Naxom** and **Namouang.** South of town off Rte. 13 toward Vientiane are the Yao villages of **Namone** and **Vangheua,** which offer splendid views of the surrounding mountains across paddy fields. A Hmong village of some 300 households, composed mainly of repatriated refugees from Thailand, is 13km north of Vang Vieng. The village is south of Tham Xang village, west of Nam Song River. The United Nations High Commissioner for Refugees (UNHCR) oversees their reassimilation. Ask before taking photos.

NIGHTLIFE

The nightlife scene here is small. A good way to spend an evening is to start by watching the sunset along the river and then move to one of the many restaurants along the main road that have nightly showings of bootlegged American DVDs. The bar scene centers around two establishments across the street from each other on the northern end of the main road, **Wildside Bar** and **Xayoh Downtown Bar and Restaurant,** which has a pool table. (Both open daily 10am-11pm.)

LUANG PRABANG ☎71

Luang Prabang's name is synonymous with Lane Xang, the magnificent "Kingdom of a Million Elephants" that stretched across Indochina from the 14th to the 17th century. Substitute palanquins and pachyderms for bicycles and tuk-tuks, and it really seems like the city hasn't changed much since. From Mt. Phousi in the center of town, the gold peaks of Luang Prabang's many wats shine through the palm-tree canopy, as saffron-robed monks add color to the streets below. King Setthathirat shifted the capital to Vientiane in 1556, leaving Luang Prabang in a peaceful isolation that has helped it resist the urbanization that's swept other Lao cities. It stands an ideal springboard for trips north and lazy rides down the Mekong.

TRANSPORTATION

Flights: Luang Prabang Airport (☎212 173), on Airport Rd., 5km from the town center. Tuk-tuks to Central Station on Chao Xomphou Rd. 10,000kip. Flights to: **Chiang Mai** (Th and Su, US$75); **Houie Xay** (1 per day, US$47); **Luang Nam Tha** (W and Su; US$37); **Phonsavanh** (1 per day, US$36); **Vientiane** (2-3 per day, US$56). Departure times vary, so ask at **Lao Aviation** (☎212 172), on Wisunalat Rd., near the Kitsalat Setthathirat Rd. intersection. (Open daily 8am-noon and 2-5pm.)

Buses: Northern Bus Terminal (☎252 729), 5km north of city in Ban Don. Tuk-tuks 15,000kip. Buses leave when full after 7:30am for: **Muang Ngoi** (3-4hr.; 16,000kip); **Nambak** (2½-3hr.; 16,000kip); **Oudomxay** (5hr.; 3 per day 8-11:30am; 25,000kip); **Pakmong** (2½hr.; 12,000kip). **Southern Bus Terminal** (☎252 066), south of the city off Phothisane Rd. next to the city stadium. Tuk-tuks from town center 5000kip. Buses to: **Vang Vieng** (6-7 hr.; daily 9am; 40,000kip) and **Vientiane** (10-11hr.; daily 6:30, 7:30, 9, 10, 11:30am; 50,000kip). Arrive before 8am to ensure a seat.

Boats: Book tickets for **slow boats** at the Navigation Office (☎212 237) on Souvanabalang Rd. behind the Royal Palace. Service to: **Chiang Khong,** Thailand (2-3 days; 100,000kip); **Pakbeng** (1-2 days; 52,000kip); **Pak Ou Caves** (5hr. round-trip; 100,000kip per boat); **Tha Souang** (1 day; 43,000kip). **Charter boats** for up to 20 people go to: **Muong Ngoi** (1 day, US$80); **Paklay** (2 days, US$120); **Tha Deua** (1 day, US$50); **Vientiane** (3 days, US$160-200 per boat). **Speedboats** leave when full from **Ban Don** (tuk-tuk 5000kip), 5km north of Luang Prabang; tell the driver "speedboat." Boats go to: **Houie Xay** (7hr.; 200,000kip); **Pakbeng** (3hr.; 120,000kip); **Pak Ou Caves** (20min.; 40,000kip). Speedboats can also be chartered if the water is high enough. Prices listed are per boat for at most 8 passengers, but boats for fewer passengers may cost nearly the same. To: **Muang Ngoi** (2hr., US$50); **Paklay** (4hr., US$80); **Tha Deua** (1½hr, US$30); **Vientiane** (9hr., 8300₿). For long journeys (to Houie Xay or Vientiane), arrive before 10am or you'll have to stop overnight.

Local Transportation. Fishing **boats** run across the river to and from **Ban Chiang Man** (5min., 2000kip), the gateway to **Wat Long Khoune** and **Wat Tham,** and to **Ban Chan Pottery Village** (40min.; 30,000kip round-trip). **Songthaew** run to: **Ban Hat Hien** (10min., 5000kip); **Ban Phanom Pottery Village** (15min.; 10,000kip); **Khouang Si Waterfalls** (2hr.; 90,000kip); **Pak on Caves** (90,000kip).

Rentals: Many guest houses and rental shops across the city rent **motorbikes** (US$10 per day) and **bicycles** (US$2 per day).

ORIENTATION AND PRACTICAL INFORMATION

Luang Prabang is small enough to easily navigate. The main road, running southwest to northeast from the **football stadium** to the **Nam Khan River,** is **Sisavong Rd.,** called **Phothisarath Rd.** between the football stadium and the post office. After the post office, Sisavong/Phothisarath Rd. briefly becomes **Chao Fa Ngum Rd.** and finally **Sakavongsa Rd.;** the **post office, tourist office, national museum, Wat Xieng Thong,** and the entrance to Mt. Phousi all lie along this road. Parallel to Phothisarath Rd., **Souvanabalang Rd.** runs along the Mekong River, becoming **Ounkham Rd.** to the northeast and then **Souvanna Khamphong Rd.** at the tip of the peninsula between the Nam Khan and Mekong rivers. The main cross-street, **Kitsalat Setthathirat Rd.,** runs away from the waterfront, eventually intersecting **Naneng Kham Rd.** Lao Aviation, the **police,** the Rama Hotel, and numerous restaurants sit on **Wisunalat Rd.,** which runs parallel to Naneng Kham Rd.

Tourist Office: Luang Prabang Tourism Office (☎212 487), on Wisunalat Rd. near the intersection with Chao Xan Phon Rd. Friendly if slightly clueless staff. Arranges tours to sights and ethnic villages, but guest houses do the same for less. Open M-F 8am-noon and 1-4pm.

Tours: Lane Xang Travel, 46 Phothisarath Rd. (☎212 793). Jeep tours of craft villages at high prices (US$50 per day for 3 people). Open M-F 8am-noon and 2-5pm.

Immigration Office and **Police Provincial Headquarters:** ☎212 453. On Wisunalat Rd. near the Kitsalat Setthathirat Rd. intersection. **No visa extensions.**

Currency Exchange: Lane Xang Bank, 90/8 Phothisarath Rd. (☎212 107). Exchanges currency (minimum exchange US$100; commission 3.5%) and cashes traveler's checks. Visa cash advances. Open 8:30am-3pm.

Pharmacies: Many on Kitsalat Setthathirat Rd. next to the hospital, on the Mekong side of Phothisarath Rd, although not much English spoken. Open daily 7am-7pm.

Medical Services: Luang Prabang Provincial Hospital (☎212 054), on Kitsalat Setthathirat Rd. 75m from the Wisunalat Rd. intersection. **Red Cross** (☎212 259), on Wisunalat Rd. near Wat Wisunalat. Herbal saunas (10,000kip) and aromatic massages (25,000kip). Massages 9am-9pm, steam bath 5-9pm.

Internet Access: All over town. About 200kip per minute. **Planet Online,** 1 block east of the Scandinavian Bakery on Phothisarath Rd. offers free coffee and tea and shows CNN.

Post Office: ☎212 288. At the corner of Phothisarath and Kitsalat Setthathirat Rd. *Poste Restante.* International calls US$3 per min. Cash only. Open M-F 8am-5pm.

ACCOMMODATIONS

Paphai Guest House (☎212 752), on Savang Vathana Rd. off Sisavong Rd. Charming wooden guest house with traditional decor. Centrally located with friendly English- and French-speaking staff. All rooms have shared bath. Singles US$4; doubles US$8. ❷

Pathoumphone Guest House (☎212 946), on Soukhaseum Rd. From the base of Mt. Phousi, head up the riverbank 75m; it's on the left. Small, quiet guest house overlooking the Nam Khan River. Reception in the wooden building next door. Doubles US$5, with bath US$6-12. ❸

LAOS

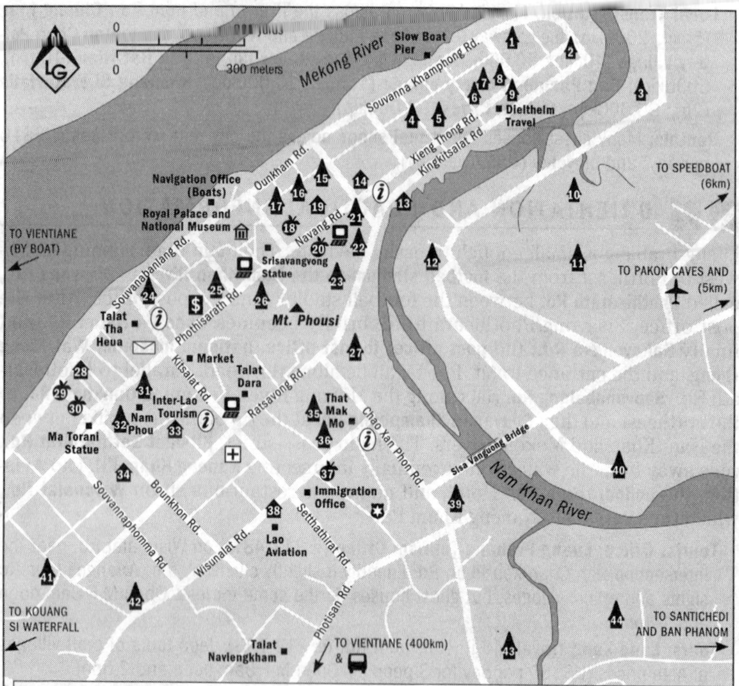

Luang Prabang

ACCOMMODATIONS
Kounsavan Guest House, **33**
Jaliya Guest House, **38**
Pathoumphone Guest House, **13**
Phounsab Guest House, **19**
Souansavahn Guest House, **34**
Paphai Guest House, **14**
Viradesa & Viradesa II Guest House, **28**

FOOD
Indochina Spirit Restaurant, **30**
Domchan Restaurant, **29**
Luang Prabang Bakery, **20**
Nazim Restaurant, **37**
Scandinavian Bakery, **18**

WATS
Aham, **35**
Aphai, **27**
Chom Phousi, **16**
Choum Kong, **17**
Ho Siang, **31**
Khili, **9**
Mai, **25**
Manorom, **42**
Munna, **39**
Nong, **4**
Pa Huak, **26**
Pa Kha, **10**
Pak Khan, **2**
Pa Nha Thiop, **43**
Pa Phai, **15**
Pha Phutthabaat, **21**
Phan Luang, **12**
Phon Sang, **11**
Phouxai, **24**
Phonsaat, **3**
Sakem, **44**
Sen, **5**
Sieng Mouane, **16**
Sop, **6**
Si Bun Heuang, **8**
Sirimungkhun, **7**
Tao Hai, **40**
Tham Phousi, **23**
Thammo, **22**
That Luang, **41**
That, **32**
Wisunnarat, **36**
Xieng Thong, **1**

Kounsavan Guest House (☎212 297), on Chaotonkham Rd., the 1st right off Kitsalat Setthathirat Rd. when heading away from the Mekong River. Like a Swiss chalet. Clean rooms with shared bath with hot water. Singles 25,000kip; doubles 35,000kip. ❸

Jaliya Guest House (☎252 154), on Wisunalat Rd., across from Lao Aviation. Spacious, spotless bungalow-style rooms behind main building. Convenience store in reception area. Singes and doubles 20,000-25,000kip; triples 30,000kip; quads 40,000kip. ❸

Phounsab Guest House, 6/7 Phothisarath Rd. (☎212 975). 1 block right of the Royal Palace. Airy, clean, friendly. Convenient location. English spoken. Rooms US$4-8. ❷

Souansavahn Guest House, 132 Boukhong Rd. (☎213 020). Spacious, clean rooms in an impersonal guest house. All rooms have hot water. Double with outside bath US$3-4, with private bath US$5; "VIP" room with A/C US$15. ❷

Viradesa Guest House, 13/2 Hoa Khoie Rd. (☎252 026). From Kitsalat Setthathirat Rd., turn left on Chao Fa Ngum Rd. and right down a lane with a "silversmith" sign; it's at the end. Basic singles US$2, with bath US$5; rooms for 3-4 people US$8. ❷

FOOD

Luang Prabang brims with good restaurants that offer traditional Lao dishes, like watercress salad, *luap kai* (spicy chicken salad), and brown sticky rice. Restaurants are located along **Sisavong** and **Wisunalat Rd.** For the best food at rock-bottom prices, head to **Talat Tha Heua.** (Open daily 6am-8pm.) In the evenings, vendors here set up on Kitsalat Setthathirat Rd. near the river. Noodle vendors and *khao jii pâté* sellers gather at **Talat Dara.** Fresh fruits and vegetables are sold at **Talat Naviengkham** on Phothisane Rd. (Open daily 6am-6pm.)

Indochina Spirit Restaurant, on Chao Fa Ngum Rd. before the Ma Torani statue. In a traditional wooden stilt house. Cushioned floor seating as well as tables. Wide selection of Lao, Thai, Western dishes. Delicious selection of *tam yam* (Lao soup), curries, and grilled dishes 15,000-25,000kip. Lao rice wine 4000kip per glass. Traditional Lao music. Open daily 10am-11pm. ❸

The Scandinavian Bakery, 52/6 Phothisarath Rd., 1 block east of the Royal Palace. Lao and Western foods. Great breakfasts (13,000-18,000kip). Open daily 7am-7pm. ❸

Luang Prabang Bakery, on Phothisarath Rd. 50m east of the Royal Palace. Superb home-baked goodies. Lao/Western menu. "Big" baguette sandwiches 12,000-15,000kip. Open daily 7am-10pm. ❷

Nazim Restaurant, 78/4 Ban Visoun, between the immigration office and Red Cross. Great Indian food and friendly service. Vegetarian options. Open daily 11am-11pm. ❸

Domchan Restaurant, on Souvanabanlang Rd. by the Mekong River. Wooden house with gorgeous sunsets. Tasty hot papaya salad. Traditional Lao dishes 10,000-15,000kip. Open daily 7am-10pm. ❷

SIGHTS

The former capital of a great Buddhist kingdom, Luang Prabang has many vestiges of its glorious past. Most notable are its many wats, which show off the Luang Prabang-style five-tier roofs that dot the city. Many of the most interesting sights line **Phothisarath Rd.,** which culminates with the magnificent Wat Xieng Thong. If you have time for only a few sights, start there and work your way up to the Royal Palace and Museum, Wat Mai, and Mt. Phousi. End the day relaxing by the Khouang Sy Waterfall or with a Lao massage at the Red Cross. Wats are locked to prevent theft, but a polite request can open them.

WAT XIENG THONG (TEMPLE OF THE GOLDEN CITY). Built by King Setthathirat in 1559, the temple is widely regarded as the *magnum opus* of Lao religious architecture, boasting elaborate golden reliefs and a mosaic of the Buddhist Tree of Life. The pagoda on the right if you enter from Sisavong Rd. houses King Sisavangvong's funeral chariot, used to transport the funerary urn to the cremation site after his death in 1959. *(On Souvanna Khampong Rd. near the Mekong River. Open daily 6am-5pm. 5000kip.)*

ROYAL PALACE AND NATIONAL MUSEUM. The Royal Palace and its contents are a highlight of many a traveler's visit to Luang Prabang. Built by King Sisavangvong in 1904, it remained the home of the royal family until the monarchy was abolished in 1975. It houses a copy of the **Pha Bang,** a golden Buddha that is Lao Buddhism's most revered image. A gift to Lane Xang's first king from the Khmer built in the 1300s, the original figure is made of 50kg of pure gold and sealed in a Vientiane bank vault. The elephant motif seen in much of the palace symbolizes the kingdoms of Luang Prabang, Champassak, and Vientiane, which were unified under Lane Xang in the 15th century. Inside the Royal Palace is the National Museum, home to a fine collection of Lao art. *(Next to Wat Mai. Museum open M-F 8-11am and 1:30-4pm. No bare thighs, upper arms, or midriffs. 10,000kip.)*

MT. PHOUSI (MARVELOUS MOUNTAIN). Despite its name, "Mt." Phousi is not very high. A leisurely climb up 329 steps takes visitors to small **Wat Chom Phousi,** whose glittering *stupa* is visible from miles away. There is no better spot to take in Luang Prabang's sunsets, but you will share the view with every tourist in town. Past the wat and up a staircase on the left, a rotund Buddha sits at the entrance of a cave. Bring a flashlight. Beyond the pavilion is a deep footprint of the Buddha. Continuing along the path down the mountain leads to an exit onto Sisavong Rd. *(Open daily 8am-9pm. 8000kip.)*

WAT MAI. It took 70 years to construct this impressive wat. It was completed in 1797 and housed the Pha Bang Buddha from 1894 to 1947. The north side of the wat is adorned with gold bas-reliefs depicting the story of *Veisantara*, Buddha's ultimate mortal reincarnation. *(Opposite Mt. Phousi. Open daily 6am-late.)*

WAT WISOUNNARATH. Built in 1523, this wat was razed by Chinese mercenaries and then rebuilt at the turn of the 19th century. The towering *sim* houses Buddhist art, overseen by the largest Buddha in the city. Stacked haphazardly along the walls are hundreds of Buddha images. Also on the temple grounds, **That Mak Mo Stupa** (aptly named the "**Melon Stupa**") was constructed in 1504 and held many Buddha statues that are now on display in the national museum. *(Open M-Sa 5am-7:30pm, Su 9-11am and 5-7:30pm.)*

OTHER SIGHTS. Wat That Luang, the final resting place of many royals, including King Sisavangvong, is another sunset-viewing spot. *(On Phalongxay Rd. south of the Ma Torani statue, which is opposite the Provincial Hall on Phalongxay Rd.)* Wacky **Wat Prabouthabat** was built in the 1950s with money from local Chinese and Vietnamese communities. *(Farther down Phalongxay Rd., opposite a Shell station. Open daily 8am-6pm. 500kip.)*

MARKETS

Luang Prabang's **markets,** although not large by Southeast Asian standards, are some of the city's most engrossing sights. **Talat Dara,** at the intersection of Kitsalat Setthathirat and Samsenthai Rd.,

FROM THE ROAD

YOUNG MONKS

I walked up to Mt. Phousi in Luang Prabang to watch the sunset over the Mekong and while the view was wonderful the place was overrun by tourists. A young novice approached me and told me that I should go see the Buddha Footprint and the Sleeping Buddha. We began to chat and he told me all about his life. His name was Kumting and he came from Pakse. He had lived in Vientiane and Hong Kong, but now studied at the monastery down the hill. He told me that being a novice was quite easy. He had to follow the 10 precepts, which were: not to kill, not to drink ("even Lao beer," he said and laughed), not to lie, not to steal, not to be greedy, to never get angry, always be generous, never talk about anyone else's faults and errors, never have pride, and most importantly, always respect the three treasures of Buddhism, the Buddha, the Dharma, and the Sangha. He also could not work in town, sit behind a monk, eat meat, or go to a brothel. He talked about life in the city, and how it was better to live here where he could grow flowers and go into the countryside. I asked him when he would become a monk, and he said one year, but added that he liked being a novice; it was easy to follow 10 precepts, but once a monk he would have to follow 220 precepts. "But," he said, "I like my temple, and every day I eat, study, and then sleep; a good life." The sun was beginning to go down so we said our goodbyes and I made ready to leave. As we parted, he said: "Maybe I will see you tomorrow, or in the next lifetime." **—Gabe Struck** sells everything imaginable. (Open daily 6am-6pm.) **Talat Tha Heua** is on Kitsalat Setthathirat Rd. near the waterfront. **Talat Naviengkham,** on Phothisane Rd., near the Kitsalat Setthathirat Rd. intersection, is the morning market. (Open daily 5:30-7:30am.) **Handicraft and textile shops** along **Phothisarath Rd.** display a wide range of products crafted from traditional woven fabrics including silks and cottons. Inspired by diverse ethnic styles and once patronized by the royal family, the industry accounts for much of Luang Prabang's trade. Embroidered fabric and off-the-rack garments, such as blue-and-black Hmong vests, are available. Bargaining is acceptable.

DAYTRIPS FROM LUANG PRABANG

KHOUANG SY WATERFALL. Numerous pools of cool, crystal water dot the slope of the hill making the waterfall a popular swimming spot for travelers despite "Do Not Swim" signs next to the pools at the base of the falls. Climb the steps cut into the clay slope to the pool at the first tier. From here you can cross the river and climb natural, water-eroded steps to the top. The view of the jungle from the top pool is amazing. But careful—the steps are steep and slippery. *(30km south of the city. Tuk-tuk (1½hr., US$10). Entrance fee 8500kip.)*

PAK OU CAVES. The two caves, **Tham Ting** (lower) and **Tham Phum** (upper), are home to hundreds of Buddha statues. The boat journey has fantastic scenery and is worth the trip in itself. Every April during **Phimai** (Lao New Year), thousands flock to the caves to pray, a tradition dating back to King Setthathirat's discovery of the caves in the 1500s. Bring a flashlight. Close to the caves is **Xang Hai Village,** famed for its *lao khao* (rice whiskey) distillation industry. Locals brew the firewater from sticky rice in oil drums along the riverbank. Traditionally, women drink the less abrasive colored whiskey, but locals are happy to provide the stonger variety to anyone who dares. *(At the confluence of the Mekong and Nam Ou Rivers, 25km upriver from Luang Prabang. Charter a boat on Souvanna Khamphong Rd., at the bank of the Mekong River (1hr., US$10 per boat, up to 6 people) or tuk-tuk (1hr., US$10, up to 6 people) to Pak Ou Village and then hire a boat to the caves (5000kip per person). Entrance 8000kip.)*

ACROSS THE RIVER. Few temples match the excellent location of **Wat Long Khoune,** a tranquil tropical garden above the Mekong. **Wat Tham** (Temple Cave) is 20m up the path from Wat Long Khoune. A passageway twists 50m underground, ending at a quartz stalactite as thick as a tree trunk. Monks guide spelunkers and point out Buddha statues and rock formations along the way. Bring a flashlight. *(To get to the other bank, hire boats(5000kip) all along the Mekong River .)*

CRAFT VILLAGES. Each of the craft villages near Luang Prabang specializes in a specific item, and workshops let visitors see the manufacturing process. **Ban Phanom,** a weaving village 4km east of the city on the banks of the Nam Khan River, is a 300-year-old Lu village which has enjoyed considerable royal patronage, and many villagers served as royal weavers and tailors. Come early before tour groups arrive. **Ban Chan,** a pottery village 45km south of Luang Prabang, is on the opposite side of the Mekong River. The entire village participates in making large *thong* (water jugs) and clay roofing tiles. Visitors can watch the entire process, from grinding clumps of clay into fine sand to throwing pots on hand-turned pottery wheels to baking the pots and tiles in large underground kilns. **Ban Xang Chang,** 7km east of Luang Prabang, is home to a traditional paper producing workshop on the village's main road. A small shop sells paper products (notebooks 8000-20,000kip). *(To get to Ban Phanom by bicycle, head away from Mt. Phousi on Vatmuenna Rd. and turn left at a large paved intersection 100m past Wat Pa Nha Thiup. After 1km take a dirt road marked by a "Luang Prabang Pre-Stress Concrete Plant" at the base of a hill with a* *pagoda on top. Follow the dirt road into Ban Phanom (tuk tuk 10,000kip). To get to Ban Chan, hire a boat (30,000kip) from Luang Prabang or Ban Chiang Man.)*

> The US government has advised its citizens to avoid Xieng Khouang Province (except for Phonsavanh town and the districts of Muang Kham and Muang Nong Haet) due to ongoing insurgent and bandit activity. Ask your embassy for up-to-date conditions before traveling here. Also note that Rte. 7, the main road to Phonsavanh from Vientiane, is periodically closed due to bad conditions. It is always closed during rainy season.

PHONSAVANH

The terrain of Xieng Khouang Province, northeast of Vientiane along the Vietnamese border, is composed of rugged mountains and beautiful rolling hills, more reminiscent of Ireland than Indochina. Its elevation ensures cool temperatures. During November and December, the mountains near the border blaze with poppy blossoms; opium, grown by the hill tribes, is the province's chief cash crop. Xieng Khouang is best known for Thong Hay Hin (Plain of Jars), an area scattered with mysterious 3000-year-old stone vessels. Xieng Khouang was one of two Lao provinces heavily bombed during the Vietnam War. B-52s damaged Xieng Khouang City so severely that after the war the provincial capital was moved from there to Phonsavanh, 36km north. The landscape is pocked with craters, and cluster bombs that litter the countryside still exact a gruesome toll in limbs and lives.

> All listings in Phonsavanh, including Plain of Jars, Xieng Khouang Province, and Muang Kham District are accurate as of November 2000.

LAOS

TRANSPORTATION

Flights: Xieng Khouang Airport, 5km from town down Rte. 4 (5000kip by tuk-tuk). To **Luang Prabang** (3 per week, US$35) and **Vientiane** (1 per day, US$44). **Lao Aviation** (☎312 177) is at the airport by the exit, a small booth on the left. Book a day before departure. Cash only (US$) for foreigners. Open daily 7am-noon and 1-4pm.

Helicopters: Inquire at the Lao Aviation booth.

Buses: Ramshackle buses and trucks leave from an empty lot on Rte. 7 adjacent to the market. Buses go to: **Ban Thatcho** (1hr.; noon, 3pm; 500kip); **Luang Prabang** (2 days; 8am; 30,000kip or more); **Muang Kham** (22km; noon, 4pm; 600kip); **Xieng Khouang** (36km, 600kip); **Vientiane** (8-10hr.; 40,000kip). Buses also run to **Vietnam** (6-7hr.; 8, 9am; 25,000-30,000kip), but make sure to check the schedule.

Local Transportation: Tuk-tuks are plentiful and go anywhere except the Plain of Jars for 4000-5000kip. To **Ban Thatcho** 120,000kip round-trip.

Rentals: Tour companies rent cars and 4WD vehicles. US$50 per day; to caves US$70; minibus seating 8 US$80. No self-drive. Check at hotels or guest houses.

ORIENTATION AND PRACTICAL INFORMATION

Three main streets—**Rte. 4, Rte. 1** (also called **Phonsavanh Rd.**), and **Rte. 7**—form three sides of a rectangle. Rte. 4 runs from the **airport** past the orphan school, **government buildings,** the **hospital,** and the construction site of a forthcoming museum to the **bank** (left) and the Phudoi Hotel (right). From there, it becomes Rte. 1, passes the town's hotels and shops, and ends with the **post office** (right) and a small unkempt park. Rte. 7 runs east-west perpendicular to Rte. 1; it makes a "T" at the **market** when it crosses Phonsavanh, and turning left onto it leads toward Vientiane. Budget hotels and guest houses line Rte. 7's east arm. South of the Phudoi Hotel, Phonsavanh Rd. veers west, passing the hospital en route to the airport. **Electricity (and therefore hot water) is only available 6-11pm.** Bring a flashlight.

Tours: The **Kong Keo Hotel** has good guides. Tours to all 3 Plains of Jars or trips to the villages and hot springs US$50 for 5-6 people. Well-run, cheap **Plain of Jars Agency Travel** (also called **Sodetour;** ☎312 403) has offices in Vientiane (☎21 216 314) and Luang Prabang (☎71 212 092). Daytrips to the Plain of Jars US$30-50 depending on size of the group. Open daily 8-11:30am and 1-5pm.

Currency Exchange: Lane Xang Bank (☎312 041), on Phonsavanh Rd. opposite Phudoi Hotel. Exchanges traveler's checks. No credit cards. Open M-Sa 8am-3:30pm.

Markets: Central market, on Rte. 7 next to the bus station and opposite the post office. Open daily 6am-6pm.

Police: Xieng Khouang Provincial Police (☎212 141), on Phonsavanh Rd., in a 2-story concrete building in the field opposite the hospital. No English spoken.

Medical Services: Xieng Khouang Provincial Hospital (☎212 240), on Phonsavanh Rd., southwest of town past the provincial hall on the right. Some English spoken.

Post Office: Post and Telegram Office (☎212 166), on the corner of Rte. 7 and Phonsavanh Rd. opposite the market. International phone cards. Direct card phone and dial using ordinary magnetic and credit cards. Up to 61,000kip can be used in the 2 booths outside post office (expect a wait).

ACCOMMODATIONS AND FOOD

Near the bus station on Rte. 7, **Phimmahaxay Guest House ❸,** is a nice airy place with satellite TV. (☎312 208. Rooms US$ 5-10 including breakfast.) **Phudoi Hotel ❷,** opposite the bank, has doubles with erratic hot water. (☎312 048. Rooms US$3-5) At **Dok Khoune Guest House ❸**, on Rte. 7 near the market, the lobby is decorated with (fake) defused bombs, and they use expended cartridges for keychains. (☎312 189. Rooms with bath and toilet 40,000-60,000kip.)

The **food market ❶** behind the post office sells produce, French bread, and prepared snack foods. (Open daily 6am-7pm.) There are **noodle stands ❶** here and across the street in the **main market ❶. Sanha Restaurant ❷,** on Rte. 7, is the town's largest and most popular. (Huge portions, large menu. Delicious steak with fries 12,000kip; most entrees 10,000-20,000kip. Open daily 6:30-9pm.) **Tuoy Restaurant ❶,** across the street by the Photo Express, serves good sweet-and-sour pork (12,000kip) and fruit shakes. (Most entrees 10,000kip. Open daily 11am-11pm.)

WARNING Areas immediately surrounding the jars are clear of mines and cluster bombs, but the rest of the countryside is not safe. Permission from the local Department of Commerce and Tourism (on Rte. 4 near the governor's office) is required to get to the official sights. Though tuk-tuk drivers will offer to take you to the Plain for cheaper prices than most package tours, it is recommended to stick to well-trodden paths and to go with an authorized guide.

SHAKY GROUND Laos is still fighting a war that ended nearly three decades ago for its primary combatants. Officially neutral, Laos allowed North Vietnamese troops on its land to start the Ho Chi Minh Trail, a conduit for supplies that eventually spelled ruin for South Vietnam and US troops. Neutrality came with a price: nearly 3 million tons of explosives dropped in a never-ending series of raids, one every eight minutes every day for nine years. Around 30% of that ordnance—only 4% of it actual mines—never exploded and is still there, experts reckon. International NGOs have tried to help, but the Lao government thinks it can do the job with locally-trained staff. Time will tell, but it's not on the Lao side. The largest building in Phonsavanh, one of the main target areas during "The War," is an orphanage with 500 residents, their parents the victims of ordnance in supposedly clear paddies. The school authorities plan to accept another 300 students soon.

DAYTRIPS FROM PHONSAVANH

THONG HAY HIN (PLAIN OF JARS)

The best way to see the plains is a day-tour of the 3 main jar sights. Tours cost US$10-30 per person depending on group size. Seen individually, sights cost 2000kip each.

The Plain of Jars consists of 3000 jars scattered in clusters on hill-tops. The largest jars are up to 3.5m high and weigh as much as three cars. They are believed to be between 2500 and 3000 years old. A theory, strengthened by the discovery of human remains in one of the jars in 1963, holds that the jars are funerary urns hewn from solid stone by ancestors of the Khamu people, who continued to place the remains of their dead in jars well into the last century. Others guess that an ancient civilization used the jars to store rice or wine; locals claim that the jars were Stone Age kegs, used to brew vats of *lao khao* for the troops of a Chinese king after their victory on the Bolovens Plateau. No one really knows, but they are a wonderful and somewhat odd sight. **Hay Hin 1,** 12km from town down Rte. 4 near the military airport, is the most impressive. Over 200 large urns cover three hill-tops in a small area marked by bomb craters. This sight includes the heaviest urn (3.7 tons) as well as a cave where locals took shelter from bombs during the Vietnam War. **Hay Hin 2** (24km) and **Hay Hin 3** (32km) are accessible from town by car, and, during the rainy season, by Russian jeeps. The jars are smaller than those of Hay Hin 1, but Hay Hin 2 boasts the longest jar (3.5m) and a sweeping view of the landscape. Hay Hin 3, reachable by foot through paddy fields and villages, is known for the Buddha statues in its jars.

XIENG KHOUANG PROVINCE

To get to Ban Thatcho, take a tuk-tuk (6000-7000kip), taxi (10,000-15,000kip), or local bus (noon, 3pm, 1000kip).

Other area highlights include the ancient capital, **Xieng Khouang City,** only 36km from Phonsavanh but difficult to access during rainy season. Despite major bombing, the city boasts two temples and a few Buddhas. Xieng Khouang is accessible by local bus. Beyond are hot springs and waterfalls, best reached by foot (with a guide to avoid bombs), and Hmong villages. **Ban Dong Dan,** near Hay Hin 2, and the larger **Ban Thatcho,** 24km from Phonsavanh, are the most visited. Xieng Khouang province, bordering Vietnam, is also home to many ethnic minorities, including the Black Tai, Khmu, and Hmong.

MUANG KHAM DISTRICT

The Phonsavanh branch of Sodetour Travel is Hmong-run and recommended by travelers. A one-day trip to Tham Phyu and Hmong villages costs 30,000kip for car, driver, and guide. Sodetour organizes three-day treks into the mountains near the Lao-Vietnamese border, where trekkers get to sleep in remote villages (40,000-80,000kip per person). More independent travelers can take a bus to Nong Haet from Phonsavanh and request to stop at the turn-off for Tham Pin (around 1500kip). The trek to the cave is difficult.

The people of Muang Kham District have put war scraps to clever use. Locals have molded bomb casings, scrap metal, and discarded shells into farmyard troughs, fences, and souvenirs. **Tham Phyu,** a cave 56km from Phonsavanh, was a civilian bomb shelter until an aircraft fired a rocket into the cave in 1968, killing all 400 people. Bone fragments are scattered around the cave. Near the caves are **Hmong villages** worth exploring. Despite the Lao government's war on drugs, these villages are interspersed with poppy fields. It is best to go with a guide.

LUANG NAM THA ☎86

Relaxed and friendly Luang Nam Tha is the principal city of Laos's most ethnically diverse region. Surrounded by luscious landscapes and home to the Nam Tha National Biodiversity Conservation area, it's a picturesque gateway to surrounding villages and also to the Chinese border crossing at Boten.

TRANSPORTATION. The **airport** is 7km south of town. The offices of **Lao Aviation** are located there. (☎312 180. Open daily 8-11:30am and 1:30-4pm.) Flights go to: **Houie Xay** (W, Su; US$43); **Luang Prabang** (M, F; US$39); **Vientiane** (Tu, Th, Sa, Su; US$82). Low-season flights may be cancelled due to low demand; check for current schedules. The Tourist Information boards at the **bus station** (☎312 164) and guest houses list up-to-date travel information. Most **buses** depart by 8:30am or when full, and they fill up quickly, so show up around 7 or 7:30am. Buses and **songthaew** depart daily from the bus station for: **Bokeo** (8hr.; 8:30am; 60,000kip); **Boten** (2hr.; every hr. 8-11am; 10,000kip); **Muang Long** (4hr.; 8:30am; 20,000kip); **Muang Sing** (2-2½hr.; every hr. 8-11am; 10,000kip); **Nalae** (3hr.; 9:30am; 30,000kip); **Oudomxay** (4-5½hr.; dry season 8:30, 9:30, 10:30, 11:30am; rainy season 8:30, 11am; 18,000kip); **Xiengkok** (4½hr.; 8:30am; 25,000kip). During the rainy season, the road to **Houie Xay** is impassable, but *songthaew* may ply the route during the dry season (8-11hr.). **Boats** vary in size and carry 4-10 people. Go to the bus landing, 7km south of Luang Nam Tha (tuk-tuk 10,000kip) the night before you wish to leave to arrange the boat. Travelers may also save money, though not time, by agreeing to let the boatman do business along the route. Boats go to **Houie Xay** (dry season 3 days, rainy season 1 day; US$75-100 per boat) via **Nalè** (2 days) and **Luang Prabang** (3 days); bring supplies. It may be quicker to hire a boat to **Pak Tha** on the Mekong (US$65-95), and then a faster boat to Houie Xay or Luang Prabang. Boats also go to **Nalè** (4hr.; 40,000-50,000kip per person).

ORIENTATION AND PRACTICAL INFORMATION. Luang Nam Tha lies along the main north-south road, Rte. 3, 217km northeast of Houie Xay and 117 km northwest of Oudomxay via Rte. 2. Boats and *songthaew* will drop you off at the **bus lot,** at the south edge of town. To get to the town center (and most guest houses), walk left out of the bus lot, passing a few hotels on your right, then take your next left and then the next right. This will bring you to Rte. 3, the main drag. The **airport** and **boat landing** on the Nam Tha River both lie off this road 7km south of town; heading north on the same road leads to **Muang Sing. Lane Xang Bank** is a few blocks down this road, and changes US dollars, Thai baht, Chinese yuan, and traveler's checks into kip. (☎312 073. Open M-F 8:30am-3:30pm and Sa 8:30-

10:30am.) **Bank for Exterior Commerce,** across from Manicham Guest House on the same road, offers Visa cash advances. (☎211 141. Open daily 8:30am-3:30pm.) Manicham Guest House **rents bicycles** (10,000kip per day). The **Telecom Office,** 100m past Lane Xang Bank, provides **international phone**/fax service. (☎312 004. Open M-F 8am-noon and 1-4pm.) Phone cards are available at the Telecom Office and various shops. The yellow **post office** (☎312 007) is opposite the Telecom Office. The bus lot, **hospital,** and **main market** are at the south edge of town. **Luang Nam Tha only has electricity from about 6:30 to 9:30pm;** guest houses have candles

ACCOMMODATIONS AND FOOD. Luang Nam Tha has many budget accommodations, most on the main road (Rte. 3) north of the bus lot, as well as a few guest houses near the bus lot. The best value is **Manicham Guest House ❶,** on the main road across the post office. The friendly staff speaks good English and offers comfortable rooms with clean, shared baths. (☎312 209. Bike rental 10,000kip per day. Curfew 10pm. Doubles with hot water when available 20,000kip, low season 15,000kip.) About 200m up the road on the left is the pricier **Darasavath Guest House ❷,** which features bungalow-style rooms and a bar/restaurant. (Rooms 25,000kip, with bath 40,000kip.) At the north end of the main road, past Kaysone Monument, is **Sing Savananh Guest House ❶,** set apart by its clean rooms and family feel. (☎211 141. Doubles 15,000kip, with bath 25,000kip.)

Many guest houses have good restaurants serving Lao and Western dishes. **Manicham Guest House's restaurant ❶** is especially popular. (Entrees 6500-10,000kip.) **Panda Restaurant ❶,** on the road parallel to Rte. 3 toward the bus lot, has excellent Chinese and Lao food. (Entrees 6000-12000kip.)

SIGHTS. The town itself offers little, but superb excursions and scenery are a few minutes away by bicycle. Keep to roads and well-trodden paths. The **Nam Tha National Biodiversity Conservation Area** is one of the best places to hike pristine forests and see hill tribes and many endangered animals. Since Nam Tha has only recently been opened to foreigners, you must go with a guide. **Wildside Eco Groups,** on Rte. 3, organizes excursions into the Nam Tha area for groups of four people. (1-day US$18 per person; 4-day US$90 per person.) These trips involve hiking, rafting down the Nam Tha River, and visiting Hmong tribe villages. One popular excursion is to **Hmong Had Yao village,** 3km down the road to Muang Sing. Head north out of town and continue past the turn-off with the bridge. The **waterfall** at Ban Nam Dee (10,000kip for tuk-tuk), 6km north of Luang Nam Tha off Rte. 3, is worth a detour. From December to March, the waterfall is the site of local paper-making. A visit to **Ban Thong Tai,** past the bridge north of town, affords views of **weaving and silk production.** Behind the Kaysone Monument, the local **museum** displays local textiles, clothing, and religious artifacts.

MUANG SING

No one knows how the tourist industry got started in this one-road hamlet on Laos's north frontier (perhaps the cloud of opium smoke obscuring Muang Sing's past had something to do with it), but tourists are, indeed, here. Nestled among small villages and rice paddies, Muang Sing is just a short walk to rural northern Laos's world of minority ethnic groups and age-old traditions.

TRANSPORTATION. Muang Sing is 58km northwest of Luang Nam Tha on a bad road (prone to mudslides in the rainy season) that continues 10km to the Chinese border. Arriving from Luang Nam Tha, the **bus** drops off passengers at Muang Sing's large **market,** on the main road. From here, **songthaew** return to Luang Nam Tha when full (2½-3½hr.; 8am-3pm; 10,000kip). *Songthaew* departure times vary;

LAOS

BORDER CROSSING: BOTEN/MOHAN

Boten village, 60km northeast of Luang Nam Tha and northwest of Oudomxay, is the only legal border crossing between Laos and China, open daily from 8am to 4:30pm. Boten has two roads: a paved road leading to the border checkpoint and a parallel dirt road with most of the town's buildings. Before the checkpoint, on the left, sits an **exchange booth** that trades Chinese yuan, US dollars, Thai baht, and kip, but no traveler's checks. (Open daily 8am-noon and 1-4pm.) Noodle shops on the dirt road have dorm-style **rooms** (5000kip per person). For those coming from China, **songthaew** leave, when full, into the early afternoon, from near the exchange booth to **Luang Nam Tha** (2hr.; 10,000kip) and **Oudomxay** (4hr.; 12,000kip). Those crossing into China must have a Chinese visa, available from the Chinese embassy in Vientiane, on hand. After the border checkpoint, you can board a tuk-tuk to Mohan, China (1-2km, 2000kip), and proceed to Mengla, the closest sizable town in China's Xishuangbanna region.

inquire at the ticket office, and be prepared to wait. **Bicycle rentals** are available from guest houses (8000-10,000kip per day).

PRACTICAL INFORMATION. Opposite the market, a branch of **Lane Xang Bank** exchanges currency. (Open M-Sa 8am-4:30pm.) Left of the bank sits a tiny **post office;** look for the "La Poste" sign. (Open M-F 7:30-11:30am and 1-4:30pm, Sa 7:30-11:30am.) With the market on your right, head up the main road through the center of town. After 200m or so the road crosses a small bridge; 200m farther down on the left is the **hospital,** a cluster of wooden buildings with blue shutters. (Open 8am-4:30pm). There is **no international phone service** in Muang Sing. **Muang Sing has electricity from 6 to 9pm.**

ACCOMMODATIONS AND FOOD. Many cheap accommodations line Muang Sing's main road. The **Viengxay Guest House ❶,** 20m to the left of the market, has friendly management and a restaurant. (Hot water when available. Singles 15,000kip; doubles 20,000kip; triples 25,000kip.) A little farther up the road on the left is the **Muang Sing Guest House ❶**, which offers small but charming double rooms for 20,000kip. Out of the way 7km north of town (tuk-tuk 2000kip), the **Adima Guest House ❸** is a great base for hikes and visits to hill tribes. Only 2km from the Chinese border, and set overlooking rice paddies amidst mountains, this guest house couldn't be more idyllic. (Restaurant. Doubles 30,000kip.) Some guest houses have restaurants. Apart from these, a few nameless **food stalls ❶,** especially around the market, offer cheap meals.

SIGHTS. For many travelers, Muang Sing's main draws are its remoteness and proximity to ethnic villages. Booths along the main road organize guided trips (up to 3 people, up to US$40 per day per group). A bike ride through the surrounding countryside is also a nice way to spend a day. Stop by the **morning market** for another chance to experience local culture. Each morning the market bustles with buyers from surrounding villages. Market activity dies down by 7:30-8am, so come early. During the rainy season, market activity may drop, as travel gets difficult.

OUDOMXAY (MOUNG XAI) ☎81

Oudomxay, 60km from China, straddles two cultures: the language is peppered with Chinese, and the televisions are tuned in to Chinese stations. Though surrounded by gentle hills and small farming villages, the town itself is unattractive with few interesting sights. Most travelers spend the night only if they have to.

BETELMANIA From Mandalay to Mindanao, few things link the disparate cultures of Southeast Asia like the chewing of betel (pronounced "beetle"). Leaves from the betel vine *(Piper betle)* are wrapped around slices of areca nut *(Areca catechu)* and powdered lime (chalk, not fruit) to form a quid. When chewed, this venerable wad produces a mouthful of blood-colored juice and a mind full of mellow vibes. Betel juice reddens the lips and stains the teeth black, a feature once considered oddly sexy throughout Southeast Asia. Since time immemorial, rulers retained betel-bearing slaves, and the betel trade made a great city out of Penang (named from the Malay word for areca nut). Beyond its role in traditional healing, betel is used in all manner of social functions, from offerings in the Thai Water Festival and exorcisms in Sarawak to Vietnamese courtships and Burmese divorces. In many languages, betel and marriage are linked concepts; in many cultures, the exchange of betel is the proper starting point for a romantic relationship and a necessity for mind-melting sex. Nobody is sure whether betel is addictive or carcinogenic, but many believe it's outmoded. The Thai government tried to outlaw it in 1945, and in the 50s the Vietnamese communists launched an aggressive campaign against this supposed *hủ tục* ("backward custom"). As Southeast Asia continues to Westernize, betel-chewing has declined, and fewer people sport the telltale ring around the mouth.

TRANSPORTATION. The **airport** is 1km outside town off the road to Pakbeng. **Lao Aviation** (☎312 047) flies to: **Houie Xay** (Tu, Sa); **Luang Prabang; Vientiane** (Tu, Th, F, Su; US$72). Buy tickets at least a day in advance from the Lao Aviation desk at the airport. Scheduled flights may be cancelled if demand is low. **Buses, trucks,** and **songthaew** leave—but only when full—from a lot near the bridge. Departures start between 8 and 9am and continue into the afternoon, going to: **Boten** (5hr.; up to 3 per day; 14,000kip); **Luang Nam Tha** (4-5hr.; 8, 11am, 2pm; 18,000kip); **Luang Prabang** (5-6hr.; 3-4 per day; 20,000kip); **Pakbeng** (7hr.; 8-9am or later; 21,500kip). To get to **Nong Khiew** take a Luang Prabang-bound bus to **Nambak** and continue from there, or catch a direct *songthaew* to Nambak (3-4hr.; several per day; 12,500kip). You can also reach Luang Prabang via **Pak Mong** (3hr.; 3-4 per day; 12,000kip), from which buses run to Luang Prabang (2-3hr.; afternoon; 17,000kip).

ORIENTATION AND PRACTICAL INFORMATION. Oudomxay lies on the intersection of **Rte. 1,** which leads east to Nambak and Nong Khiew, and **Rte. 2,** which heads north to Boten and Luang Nam Tha and south to Pakbeng. **Lane Xang Bank** (☎312 059), on the left about 400m up Rte. 1 from the intersection (open M-F 8:30am-5:30pm, Sa 8-10am), and the **Bank for Exterior Commerce,** next to the bus station (☎211 260; open M-F 8:30am-3:30pm, Sa 8:30-10:30am), **exchange currency** and traveler's checks. Other services in Oudomxay include: the **hospital,** 3km south on Rte. 1., 400m down the first road on the right after Rte. 1 becomes a dirt road (☎312 043; open M-F 8am-noon and 1-4pm); the **Telecom Office,** on Rte. 2, 100m from the main intersection away from the pagoda hill on the right, with **international phone**/fax (☎312 001; open M-F 8am-noon and 1-4pm); a box for **international calls,** opposite the Bank for Exterior Commerce; a few **Internet** shops across the bridge, all of which charge 700kip per min.; and the **post office,** next to the Telecom Office (☎312 007; open M-F 8am-noon and 1-5pm, Sa 8am-noon). **Postal code:** 0400.

ACCOMMODATIONS AND FOOD. A family feel and very friendly owners sets **Sivankham Guest House ❶,** across the bridge after the main intersection and past the gas station, apart from others. (☎312 253. Shared baths, squat toilet. Singles 15,000kip; doubles 20,000kip.) **Pholay Guest House ❷,** on Rte. 2 100m past the bridge on the right before the gas station, has clean rooms with private baths and a restaurant downstairs. (☎312 324. Doubles 30,000kip.) Up the hill from the bus station, behind the Kaysone Monument, is plain **Linda 2 Guest House ❷**, conveniently near the bus station. (☎211 242. Doubles 30,000kip.)

There are few dining options in Oudomxay. The **market ❶** offers fresh fruit and vegetables, and every morning **stalls ❶** serve baguettes with condensed milk filling (1000kip). Of Oudomxay's few restaurants, **Noisavat Restaurant ❷**, on Rte. 2 next to the post office, stands out with locals for its extensive menu and family feel. (Entrees 10,000-16,000kip. Open daily 8am-9pm.) **Sainamkor Restaurant ❷**, at the bridge on Rte. 2, takes its name from the river it overlooks. It serves substantial meals from eel to duck. (Dinners 10,000-20,000kip. Open daily 7am-9pm.)

SIGHTS AND ENTERTAINMENT To ease the pain inflicted by bumpy roads, the Red Cross operates a **herbal sauna and massage** center, behind Phon Xay Hotel down the road from Sivankham Guest House. (Sauna 10,000kip. 1hr. massage 20,000kip. ☎312 391. Open daily 4-7pm.) A **snooker hall** next to Sainamkor Restaurant has four tables. (Open daily 10am until you lose.) Apart from the large **market** (open daily 7am-7pm), in a large block off Rte. 2, which sells colorful wall-hangings and clothes, only the eye-catching **pagoda**, with a panoramic view of the town and countryside, is worth a detour. As with all the northern towns, beautiful landscapes await those who walk along the roads leading away from town.

PAKBENG

On the threshold of dense primary forest at the confluence of the Nam Beng and Mekong Rivers, tiny Pakbeng is a colorful though calm escape, relatively untouched by the tourist industry. Most travelers stay one night on their way to the Thai border or Luang Prabang and find this enough to soak in Pakbeng's ambience; others find its remoteness enticing enough to extend their visit.

> **WARNING.** All listings in Pakbeng are accurate as of November 2000.

Overlooking the Mekong between Luang Prabang to the east and Houie Xay to the northwest, one-road Pakbeng winds along Rte. 2 for 2km. **Buses, trucks,** and **songthaew** depart when full from a lot out of town (tuk-tuks leave from the pier; 4000kip to get there) for **Oudomxay** (7hr.; 8am until passengers stop showing up; 20,000kip). **Slow boats** leave for **Luang Prabang** (6-8hr.; 50,000kip) and **Houie Xay** (9-11hr.; 50,000kip). **Speedboats** depart to **Luang Prabang** (3hr.; leave 8am-4pm when full; 100,000kip) and **Houie Xay** (3hr.; leave 8am-4pm when full; 80,000kip). There is **no official currency exchange** in Pakbeng, although you can try the market 1km from the pier to the left. A **pharmacy** is on the main road to the right 500m from the pier opposite an improvised cinema. (Open daily 7am-9pm.) The **local hospital,** 1km from the pier on the right, sits opposite the **post office.** (Open M-F 8am-noon and 1-4:30pm.) Pakbeng has **no telephone office,** and has **electricity from 6 to 10pm.**

Of the dozens of guest houses near the pier, a few stand out for cleanliness and service. **Mon Savan Guest House ❶**, 300m left from the pier, has clean doubles in bamboo houses (15,000kip with net and fan). **Sarika Guest House ❶**, the large white building next to the ticket office, is pricier but larger. Its **restaurant ❷** (entrees 10,000-20,000kip) overlooks the Mekong. (Doubles with private bath 20,000kip.) A dozen restaurants cluster around the guest houses in and around town. All offer standard, though greasy, Lao rice and noodle dishes. (Open daily 6:30am-10pm.) **Pine Kham Restaurant ❷**, 200m left from the pier, and **Bounmy Restaurant ❷**, 100m farther, serve large, tasty fried rice dishes and soup (10,000-15,000kip). The **main market ❶**, 300m left from the pier, is excellent for fruits and other munchies.

HOUIE XAY

☎084

Houie Xay is a Thai border town and Laos's little link to the infamous Golden Triangle. As underappreciated as it may be, Houie Xay still provides a taste of "unsullied" Laos: children play in streets after dark, the power goes out during storms, and if you do take a walk you'll surely come across hill-tribe villages.

> **WARNING.** All listings in Houie Xay are accurate as of November 2000.

TRANSPORTATION. **Ferries** to and from **Chiang Khong** (20฿) dock right by the town center, down behind the Maniratn Hotel. They leave when full between 8:30am and 5pm, which are the official hours of the **border passport control** by the landing. It is often possible to pass customs after hours for (an unofficial) 2500kip. **Speedboats** to **Luang Prabang** (6-7hr.; 8-9am; 180,000kip) via **Pakbeng** (3-4hr.; 80,000kip) depart from a small pier 5km south of town (2000kip per person by tuk-tuk). **Slow boats** heading north and south share a landing 1.5km north of the town center. Boats don't depart on weekends. During the week, show up in the morning and hope for the best. You'll probably have to barter with the captain, but most will agree to set fares to **Luang Prabang** (48hr.; 500฿ or 100,000kip) and **Pakbeng** (5½hr.; 9, 11am; 86,000kip). Speedboats heading upriver dock north of the slow boats. During the dry season, **passenger trucks** leave from a station by the market for **Muang Sing** and **Luang Nam Tha** (up to 7hr.; leaves early; 30,000kip). **Lao Aviation** has flights (subject to weather conditions and frequently postponed during rainy season) to: **Luang Nam Tha** (1-2 per week, US$41); **Luang Prabang** (1hr., Tu, US$46); **Oudomxay** (2 per week, US$51); **Vientiane** (2-3 per week, US$88). The airstrip is 7km south of town; pay 4000kip per person for a tuk-tuk. With your back to the Maniratn Hotel, head right, then take the first left; the Lao Aviation office is 30m down on the left. (☎312 022. Open daily 8am-4pm.) **Bokeo Travel** (☎661 980 6242), off the main road by the post office, rents **jeeps** with drivers (US$100 per day).

ORIENTATION AND PRACTICAL INFORMATION. North of Luang Prabang and a few hundred meters east of Chiang Khong, Thailand, tiny Houie Xay hugs the Mekong. The main road runs north-south parallel to the river, and a small road passes shops and the customs to the pier on the Mekong. Perpendicular to the main road and opposite the pier, steps lead up the hill to a **Buddhist Temple.** Heading south, the main road also passes a **market** to the left and forks west (away from the river) toward the old French **Fort Carno,** now occupied by Lao officials. A dirt track on the way (to the left) leads uptown to the **post office.** The main road runs north-south, parallel to the river; the other road of note forks east from the main road at the north end of town, moving east (away from the river).

The **Bokeo Tourism Authority Office** has free maps. (Open M-F 9am-4pm.) To get to the **market,** head south (with your back to the river, turn right) on the main road, and then turn left at the big field with the pavilion 1.5km down; it's another 1km. The **police** hang out in a stucco house on the hill above the slow boat landing. **Lane Xang Bank** (☎312 020), opposite Aramid Guest House's (see below) back entrance, cashes traveler's checks and exchanges US dollars and Thai baht. A counter by the customs office on the Mekong provides similar services. (Open M-F 8am-3pm.) A smaller market sits at the center of town opposite the post office. **Pharmacies** dot the main road and **Bokeo Hospital** is on a back road, 1km south of the bank. The **post office** is to the left on a dirt track when you are heading south on the main road. (☎312 026. Open M-F 8am-4:30pm.) An **international card phone** is outside.

SPIES IN THE SKIES The Vietnam War made it to the living room TV of every US family, but the military missions in Laos remained covert and hushed. One of the most colorful and storied of these missions was Air America, an airline owned by the CIA and used exclusively to accomplish military objectives in Laos. The airline began in China in the early 1950s but was quickly and quietly taken over by US intelligence, which used it to ferry people discreetly around points in Asia. During the Vietnam War, Air America employed hundreds of pilots and mechanics to fly and maintain a fleet of 70 aircraft. Missions involved photo reconnaissance, airdrops, and searches-and-rescues for downed airmen. Some have alleged (notably in the 1990 film *Air America*) that the agency was also involved deeply in the Lao opium trade.

ACCOMMODATIONS AND FOOD. Most places in town are very similar, the nicest being the **Aramid Guest House ❸**, on the main road, 1km north of the border ferry. Aramid rents bicycles and has a friendly ambience and decent restaurant. (☎211 040. Doubles US$3-4) **Maniratn Hotel ❸** (☎312 040), on the main road, has doubles with private baths for US$3. **Keochampa Guest House ❸**, left from the border pier, is a comfy option with decent rooms. (☎312 035. Doubles US$3-5.) Restaurants cluster along the main road; the best restaurant is the Lao-Chinese **restaurant ❶** north of the pier (entrees 8000-15,000kip). There are two good **food stalls ❶** at the pier (soup 5000kip); the market has lunchtime **food stalls ❶**.

SOUTHERN LAOS

SAVANNAKHET ☎41

Nearly 500km south of Vientiane and on the west bank of the Mekong, Savannakhet—"Savan" to locals—is the center of Laos's most populated province. The town's charm lies in its odd mix of colonial French and modern buildings and its riverside walk. Most travelers don't stop for long en route to the Vietnamese cities of Huế and Đà Nẵng or to Wat Phu and the 4000 Islands region farther south.

TRANSPORTATION

Flights: Purchase tickets at the airport. Flights to **Pakse** (3 per week, US$46) and **Vientiane** (daily, US$63). Schedule is erratic. Buy tickets at least 1 day ahead and confirm.

Buses: The **bus station** (☎212 143) is at the intersection of Sisavangvong and Visouthat Rd., 1.5km north of the town center. Buses to **Pakse** (6-8hr.; 6:30am, 2:30pm; 20,000kip) and **Vientiane** (9hr.; several per day 6am-12:30pm; 25,000kip). Buses along the unpaved road will eventually lead you to **Vietnam: Đà Nẵng** (18-21hr.; Tu-W, F-Sa 10pm; 105,000kip); **Hanoi** (27hr., Sa 7pm, US$25); **Huế** (14hr.; M-Tu 10pm; 83,000kip). Buses also leave daily for **Lao Bảo** (6-7hr.; 6, 9am; 65,000kip), where further transportation to Vietnam is possible.

Ferries: Pier is at the immigration office, across from Simuang-Tha Heua Rd. intersection. Buy tickets at the desk downstairs to: **Mukdahan, Thailand** (15min.; M-F 9:10, 10:10, 11:30am, 1:30, 2:15pm, Sa 10:30am, 2:15, 4pm; 10,000kip). Get your exit stamp for Laos at the window, buy a ferry ticket, cross the river, and then get your entrance stamp for Thailand. Once in Mukdahan, you can catch a bus to destinations like **Bangkok** (see p. 683), or you can stay the night. (See **Mukdahan,** p. 815.) You **cannot** get a Thai visa

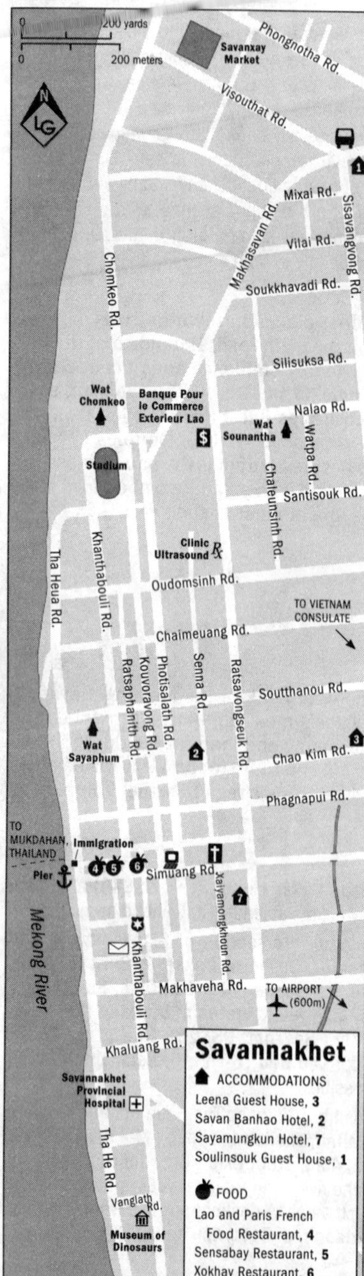

in Savannakhet or a Lao visa in Mukdahan.

Local Transportation: Tuk-tuks roam streets in large numbers 4am-10pm. Around town, don't pay more than 3000kip during daylight hours. To **That Inheng** (40min.; round-trip 20,000kip) and **That Phon** (2hr.; 40,000kip).

Rentals: Sensabay Restaurant on Simuang Rd. rents **bicycles** for 10,000kip per day with passport deposit.

PRACTICAL INFORMATION

The town's main road is **Photisalath Rd.**, north-south parallel to the river and several blocks away. **Tha Heua Rd.**, along the bank, **Khanthabouli Rd.**, a block east, and **Sisavangvong Rd.**, farther east, are also important. They are linked by east-west streets, the main one being **Oudomsinh Rd.** at the north end of town, which passes the deserted **old market** (a good landmark). **Simuang Rd.**, five blocks south, is home to the immigration pier and cheap restaurants. The **bus station** and **new market** are at Sisavangvong Rd.'s north end, and the **airport** is at the south.

Tours: Savan Travel and Tour, 644 Senna Rd. (☎/fax 212 944), in Savan Banhao Hotel. Tours are the best way to visit the Ho Chi Minh Trail near Xepon, 160km east of Savan. Car with driver US$80-100. Open M-Sa 8am-noon and 1-4pm.

Consulates: Vietnam (☎212 418), on Sisavangvong Rd. From the south end of the old market, head away from the river on Oudomsinh Rd. and take the 1st right onto Sisavangvong Rd.; it's half a block down. **Visas** for crossing at Lao Bảo US$50; bring 2 passport photos. 5-day processing (best to obtain visa from Vientiane, Thailand, or Cambodia). Open M-F 7:30-11am and 1:30-4:30pm.

Currency Exchange: Banque Pour le Commerce Extérieur Lao (☎212 261), opposite old market. American Express and Visa traveler's checks, Visa cash advances (4% commission; min. US$100). Open M-F 8:30am-3:30pm.

Markets: Savanxay market, 200m toward the river from the bus station, near the north end of Sisavangvong Rd. A sight to behold.

Police: ☎212 212. On Khanthabouli Rd., opposite the post office.

Pharmacies: Many near the old market. **Clinic Ultrasound** (☎212 711), on Ratsavongseuk Rd., near the market. Anti-malarial and Western drugs. Open daily 9am-4pm.

Medical Services: Savannakhet Provincial Hospital (☎212 131), on Khanthabouli Rd. Five blocks south of Simuang Rd. on the right. English spoken.

Internet: On Simuang Rd., at the Photisalath Rd. intersection, near the Catholic Church. Look for signs. 200kip per min. Open daily noon-9pm.

Post Office: ☎212 295. On Khanthabouli Rd. From the intersection with Simuang Rd., the post office is one block south beside the radio tower. Cash **overseas telephone** and fax service. *Poste Restante.* Open M-F 8am-5pm, Sa-Su 8am-noon. **Postal code:** 1300.

ACCOMMODATIONS

Sayamungkun Hotel ❷, 85 Ratsavongseuk Rd., one block south of the Simuang Rd. intersection, has towering ceilings, tiled floors, a large terrace, and a lovely second-floor patio. Look for the sign. (☎212 426. Doubles with bath and fan 35,000, with A/C 58,000kip.) Off Chao Kim toward the Sisavangvong intersection, **Leena Guest House ❷** has great management and lovely rooms. Look for the signs on Sisavangvong and Ratsavongseuk Rd. (Singles 30,000kip; doubles with bath 45,000-60,000kip.) The comfortable **Soulinsouk Guest House ❷** is ideally located for catching an early bus—it's opposite the Makhasavan Rd. station. (☎213 436. Doubles with bath 30,000kip.) Sometimes called the Silan Hotel, **Savan Banhao Hotel ❷** (☎212 202) has four "classes" of rooms, from tiny with shared bath (31,000kip) to decent with bath (40,000-65,000kip.) From the side of the old market nearest the Mekong, walk 1½ blocks south; it's on the right.

There aren't many decent restaurants in Savannakhet; most are on Simuang Rd. The **market ❶** boasts a large food section with *phở* (3000kip), spring rolls (1000kip each), and other Lao and Vietnamese snacks. In a Chinese-style house at the corner of Simuang Rd. and Tha Heua Rd., near the immigration office, **Lao and Paris French Food Restaurant ❶** serves popular Asian and European dishes. (Entrees 8000-15,000kip. Open daily 8am-11pm.) **Sensabay Restaurant ❶** has rice and noodle dishes as well as steaks and french fries. Take a left before the Lao and Paris Restaurant (Most entrees 10,000-17,000kip. Open daily 8am-11pm.) On Simuang Rd., past the Internet cafe, **Xokhay Restaurant ❶** serves decent Vietnamese and good Chinese fare. (Dishes 8000-15,000kip. Open daily 10am-9pm.)

SIGHTS

Wat Sayaphum, on Tha Heua Rd. north of the pier, is the Savan's only historically significant wat. The complex dates to 1896 and contains two main *sim;* the largest is a secondary school for monks decorated with murals depicting scenes from the *Ramakien.* **That Inheng,** the city's most revered shrine, is 15km north of Savan. The 25m *stupa*—built to hold the Buddha's spine—is all that remains of the ancient city of Sikhottabong. The road is poor; biking isn't advisable. Buses leave from the central station on Makhasavan Rd. every hour on the hour (6000kip). **That Phon** stands 60km south of Savannakhet on Rte. 13. with a tall, white *stupa.* It isn't awe-inspiring, but it is sacred. One of the most unusual Buddhist legends, dating from the Angkor period, explains that Buddha was in mid-sermon when nature's call came

LAOS

on strong. Exercising the prerogative of the "World-Honored One," he had a *naga* build him a toilet on the spot. That Phon's white spire now commemorates the site.

BORDER CROSSING: LAO BẢO The border town of Lao Bảo lies 200 buttock-bruising kilometers east of Savannakhet on Rte. 9, which winds around the slopes of the Annamite Mountains, on the Lao-Vietnamese border. If you opt to stay the night (or are stuck), there are simple lodgings (10,000-15,000kip). For those heading into **Vietnam,** Lao customs at Lao Bảo is a formality, though travelers must show passports and pay a US$5 fine for each day they have overstayed their visa. Vietnamese immigration requires a **visa** stamped with the right entry point (get the stamp in Vientiane, Savannakhet, or Pakse). Passing through Vietnamese customs can take up to 3hr., as officials may search bags and comb the bus for contraband. You can also bus from Savannakhet to Lao Bảo, pass through customs on foot, and then catch a motorcycle-taxi to the next town. The border opens at 8am, but since buses leave Savannakhet for Huế and Danang at 10pm, and also leave Huế and Đà Nẵng for Savannakhet at 10pm, you may be stuck in your bus at the border for the night. If you just go to the border, you can catch buses into Laos, or into Vietnam at 8am.

The Museum of Dinosaurs, on Khanthabouli Rd. near some tennis courts (head north from Hotel Santyphab on Simuang Rd.), is a surprising sight. The local archaeologist gives an interesting tour of the remains found northwest of Savan in the early 1990s. (☎212 597. Open daily 8am-noon and 4-10pm. 2000kip.)

PAKSE

☎031

Although its dirty streets and wild growth may be forbidding at first, Pakse offers a worthwhile prelude to the Emerald Triangle region, where the natural beauty of Laos reaches a crescendo of mountains, gorges, and islands. Its lively market stands out of doors as it awaits a new home—the old one burned down in 1998—and spreads colorful stalls in all directions. Pakse also boasts the largest Vietnamese population in Laos. Pakse stands in contrast to the far-flung Saravane and Attapeu provinces and to the laid-back 4000 Islands region farther south.

TRANSPORTATION

Flights: Pakse Airport, on Rte. 13, 1km west of Xedone River Bridge. To **Savannakhet** (2-3 per week, US$46) and **Vientiane** (1 per day, US$97). **Lao Aviation office** (☎212 252), before the airfield on the left, and in town, on Rd. 11 between the Banque Pour le Commerce Extérieur Lao and the pier. Both open M-F 7:30am-noon and 1-4pm, Sa 7:30am-noon.

Ferries: Ferries cross the Mekong to Ban Muang Kao (7am-6pm; 20,000kip). **Boats** to **Don Khong** (8hr.; 20,000kip) via **Champassak** (1½hr., 5000kip) leave when full from the waterfront right of the ferry pier (daily 7am-noon).

Buses: The **southbound** bus station is 8km east off Rte. 13; **northbound** buses depart from a station 10km west of town on Rte. 13. Tuk-tuks run to either for 5000kip.

Southbound Station: Buses leave daily for: **Attapeu** (4-7hr.; 7:30, 9am; 20,000kip); **Champassak** (1-2hr.; 9am, noon; 10,000kip); **Muang Khong** on the island of Don Khong (2-3hr.; 7, 9am; 12,000kip); **Pakxong** (1-2hr., every hr. 6am-noon, 8000kip); **Saravane** via **Thad Lo** (3hr.; 7, 9, 11am, 1, 2pm; 10,000kip).

Northbound Station: Buses leave daily for **Vientiane** (15-17hr.; up to 6 per day roughly 6am-12:30pm; 35,000kip) via **Savannakhet** (8hr.; 20,000kip). To get to **Vang Tao border crossing** with Thailand, charter a tuk-tuk from the central market (45min.; 10,000kip).

Local Transportation: The **tuk-tuk** hang-out is the parking area on Xedone Quay from the pier to Lao Aviation Office. Tuk-tuks will take you anywhere in town for 3000-5000kip.

ORIENTATION AND PRACTICAL INFORMATION

Pakse is confusing to navigate and the streets aren't labeled; maps are available. The **Xedone River** borders the town to the north and west. The **Mekong River** borders it to the south. **Rte. 13,** the main road, goes past the **airport** and over the Xedone at the western end of town, passes by Lankham and Phonsavanh hotels, **Lao May Bank** and the impressive Champassak Palace Hotel before leaving town at the eastern end. Most budget hotels, restaurants, and shops are along Rte. 13, around the central market, and on the Xedone. All streets are numbered: **Rd. 6, 5,** and **1** run parallel to Rte. 13, with Rd. 1 closest to the Mekong. **Rd. 8, 9, 10,** and **12** are perpendicular to Rte. 13. **Xedone Quay** (also known as **Rd. 11**) runs along the Xedone from Rte. 13 to the **ferry pier. Unhila market** is between Rd. 9 and 10; the **outdoors market** spreads its tentacles all over the center of town, making passage difficult.

Tourist Office: Lao National Tourism Authority (☎/fax 212 021), on Rd. 11 near the ferry pier. Map of Pakse 5000kip. Open M-F 8am-noon and 1-4pm.

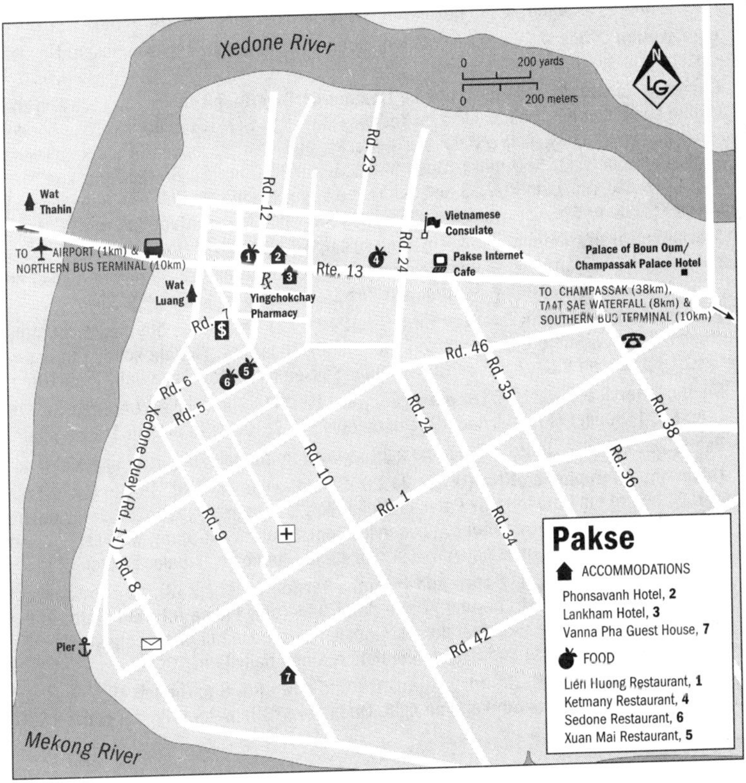

Tours: Inter-Lao Tourism, #121 Rte. 13 (☎/fax 212 226), at Champassak Palace Hotel. 4WD pickup tours of coffee plantations and waterfalls US$80-90 per day. Open M-F 8am-noon and 1-4pm, Sa 8am-noon. **Sodetour** (☎/fax 212 122), at the intersection of Rte. 13 and Rd. 24. French and English spoken. Open M-F 8am-noon and 1-4pm. **Lane Xang Travel** (☎251 467), on Rte. 13 next to Phonsavanh Hotel. Posts bus and ferry schedules and organizes tours. Open M-F 7:30am-noon and 2-5pm.

CURIOSITY KILLED THE KING In the 11th century, King Khamatha of Champassak accepted a wager to prove that he could build a temple more rapidly than his rival. Khamatha set about constructing Wat Phu, and his challenger ordered a group of women to erect Wat That Phanom (in present-day Thailand). The female engineers removed their shirts to work in the heat. When word spread that That Phanom employed a topless construction crew, the Wat Phu contractors abandoned their own site to observe the effort upstream. Wat Phu lay unfinished as That Phanom's triumphant spire was raised aloft. Khamatha, ashamed of his failure, killed himself. Heavy with guilt, the voyeuristic builders built a *stupa* for their ruined leader, which still stands not far from Wat Phu. The temple remained unfinished until Khmer King Suryavarman II completed it a century later.

Consulates: Vietnam (☎212 058), on Rd. 24 past Ketmany Restaurant on the right as you head toward Xedone River from Champassak Palace Hotel. Visas US$50. Passport and 2 photos required. 4-day processing. Open M-F 8-11am and 2-4:30pm.

Immigration Office: At the police station. Open M-F 8am-4pm. English spoken. No visa extensions—go to Vientiane.

Currency Exchange: Banque Pour Le Commerce Extérieur Lao (☎212 779), in the white concrete and glass building on Xedone Quay (Rd. 11), 150m from Xedone bridge. Exchanges currency. AmEx/V traveler's checks, and cash advances (4% commission; US$-to-kip only, US$50 min.). Open M-F 8:30am-3:30pm, Sa 8:30-10am. **Lao May Bank** (☎213 550), on Rte. 13 just before the large Honda sign (left as you head away from Xedone bridge), provides the same services. Open M-F 8:30am-3:30pm.

Markets: Pakse's morning market burned in Jan. of 1998. The current market sprawls between Rd. 10 and the Xedone River (and beyond on weekends). Another market off Rte. 13 heading toward the Southbound Bus Station sells all kinds of goods.

Pharmacies: Seng Souk Osoth, #5 Rd. 9 (☎212 272), next to the old market lot. Anti-malarial drugs. Some English spoken. Open daily 7am-5pm. **Yingchokchay Pharmacy** (☎218 139), on Rd. 12 just off Rte. 13 near Suksamlan Hotel. Open daily 7am-10pm.

Medical Services: ☎212 018, **emergency** ☎212 041. Sandwiched between Rd. 46 and Rd. 1, behind old market lot. Doctor on duty M-F 7:30-11:30am and 1:30-4:30pm.

Police: ☎212 145. On Rd. 12, on the right, away from the market past Pakse Hotel.

Telephones: Telephone office (☎/fax 212 056), at the corner of Rd. 38 and Rd. 1. Take a right before the Champassak Palace Hotel on Rte. 13, then a right on Rd. 1; it's on the right. Cash **overseas telephone,** fax service (open daily 7am-9pm), and Lao Telkom **phone cards.** Card phones outside post office and Champassak Palace Hotel.

Internet Access: T and K E-mail and Internet Service (☎212 232), next to Lankham Hotel on Rte. 13. 500kip per min. Open daily 7am-7pm. **Pakse Internet Cafe,** at the corner of Rd. 1 and Rd. 35, near the old market. Same price but faster connection. Also provides maps of Pakse and useful information. Open daily 8am-10pm.

Post Office: ☎212 199. On Rd. 8 at Rd. 1. Head down Rd. 8 to the left of the gas station next to pier; it's near the end on right. Open M-F 7:30am-9pm. **Postal code:** 1600.

LAOS

ACCOMMODATIONS AND FOOD

BORDER CROSSING: VANG TAO/CHONG MEK The **Thai** border lies 45km west of Pakse, and crossing between the two countries is quite easy. The border is open 8am-4:30pm, but note that it takes at least 45min. to get from Pakse to the border. To get to the border from Pakse go to the market near the Xedone River and charter a tuk-tuk to **Vang Tao** (45min.; 10,000-15,000kip). You will then go through Lao customs and pay US$5 for every day you outstayed your visa. Once you get your exit stamp, cross the bridge and go through Thai Immigration. From Chong Mek, *songthaew* run to **Phibun** (see **Khong Chiam,** p. 814); from here, buses head to Warin Chamrap station at **Ubon Ratchathani** (see p. 809). Buses depart from another station in Ubon, the Ubon Ratchathani bus station, to **Mukdahan** (see p. 815), from where further bus connections to **Bangkok** (see p. 683) can be made.

Lankham Hotel ❷, on Rte. 13 opposite Lao May Bank, is a modern, clean, white-and-green concrete building with a yellow sign. The staff is friendly. (☎212 125. Doubles wth bath and fan 30,000kip, with A/C 50,000kip.) **Vanna Pha Guest House ❷** has a shaded courtyard and decent rooms. From the market, go south on Rd. 9 toward the Mekong; it's 120m past the Rd. 1 intersection. (☎212 502. Doubles with fan 35,000kip, with A/C 50,000kip.) Centrally located **Phonsavanh Hotel ❶,** 294 Rte. 13 opposite the Lankham Hotel, is the town's cheapest option, but rooms are slightly dingy. (☎212 842. Singles 10,000-15,000kip; doubles 20,000kip; triples 30,000kip.)

Pakse has the largest Vietnamese population in Laos; *phở* shops are abundant. The **evening market ❶** features a pavilion that sith very cheap *kai ping*, *khao niaw*, and noodle soups. **Sedone Restaurant ❶,** #110 Rd. 5 two shops to the left of Pakse Hotel opposite the empty market lot, has great Vietnamese food and decent Lao and Thai fare. (Most dishes 6000-10,000kip. Open daily 7am-10pm.) On Rte. 13 next to Phonsavanh Hotel, **Lien Huong Restaurant ❶** serves basic Vietnamese food for 5000-8000kip. **Xuan Mai Restaurant ❶,** at the intersection of Rd. 5 and 10 opposite Pakse Hotel, serves decent Vietnamese food. (Spring rolls 5000kip. Open daily 7:30a,-10pm.) On Rte. 13 past the Honda sign, **Ketmany Restaurant ❶** serves good Lao, Vietnamese, and Western food for 8000-15,000kip.

SIGHTS

The **Palace of Boun Oum,** between the Xedone River and the bus station on Rte. 13, is one of the more bizarre landmarks in Laos. Construction of the six-story former residence of the Prince of Champassak began in 1969 and had not been completed when the Communists deposed the prince in 1975. The huge white structure presiding over the Xedone River now houses the **Champassak Palace Hotel.** Visitors can take the elevator to the top floor for a view of the Bolovens Plateau; sunsets are gorgeous. **Taat Sae Waterfall,** 8km east of town on Rte. 13, makes for a pleasant half-day trip. Large artificial pools lead to three waterfalls, two of which fall 40m. Locals bring their children to swim here. (Tuk-tuks 5000kip.) **Ban Saphay,** a weaving village 13km west of town off Rte. 13, is renowned for *ikat* silk and *mutmee* cotton. Two shops along the main road sell fabric by the meter and a few ready-made garments. The **Lao Women's Union** operates one, but the privately owned **Lao Homemade Silk Skirt Shop** carries a better selection. *Mutmee* cotton costs 10,000kip per meter, *ikat* silk 8000kip per meter. Materials are cheaper and often better from the producers in nearby homes. Take a *songthaew* from the ferry pier (30min., leaves when full, 5000kip) or a tuk-tuk (10,000kip per person).

CHAMPASSAK

The quiet little town of Champassak offers a nice stopover for travelers on their way south. It lies 38km downriver from Pakse, sandwiched between the Mekong and steep, craggy limestone hills. Its main attraction is Wat Phu, a magnificent—albeit crumbling—Khmer temple 11km south of Champassak proper.

TRANSPORTATION AND PRACTICAL INFORMATION. **Buses** leave the Southern Bus Station in Pakse 8km east of town on Rt. 13. (1hr.; 9, 11am, 2pm; 10,000kip). Tuk-tuks and *songthaew* leave from Rt. 13 (20,000-40,000kip). Champassak lies across the river from Pakse—you and your bus will be ferried across. Buses leave Champassak for **Pakse** (1-2hr., 7:30am, 8000kip). If you miss that bus, cross the river and take a tuk-tuk to Junction 30 on Rt. 13 (5km, 2000kip). From there buses come by around every hour going to Pakse. If you want to head south to **Don Khong** or **Don Det** go to the same junction and catch a bus in the opposite direction (10,000kip). Boats heading upriver to Pakse stop at the landing near the center of town (3hr.; last boat between 1 and 2pm; 10,000kip). Boats continuing downriver to **Don Khong** stop at the landing at the center of town (6-8hr.; leave around 8:30am; 20,000kip). A **bank** on the left by the pier before the traffic circle changes US dollars and Thai baht. (Open M-F 8:30am-3:30pm.)

ACCOMMODATIONS AND FOOD. Once in Champassak, the buses will continue 2km to the town center, a small traffic circle. Nearby **Dok Champa Guest House ❶** offers basic rooms with fan in little bamboo houses. (Singles 10,000kip; doubles 20,000kip.) Across the road is **Mr. Seng's Guest House ❶**, an agreeable stop overlooking the Mekong. (Singles 15,000kip; large doubles with bath 25,000kip.) For more expensive, and a bit nicer, lodgings, go to the **Sala Wat Phon Hotel and Restaurant ❹**, also near the traffic circle. (☎213 280. Singles US$10; doubles US$20.) The **Say Thong Restaurant ❶** at Mr. Seng's Guest House serves a mix of Lao and Vietnamese food (entrees 7000-12,000kip). The attached **Dok Champa Restaurant ❶** serves Lao, Vietnamese, and French food, and offers great curries, fruit salad, and many breakfast options. (Entrees 8000-15,000kip.)

SIGHTS. **Wat Phu (Hill Temple),** or rather its ruins, lie 11km south of Champassak. An ancient Khmer temple known as **Muang Kao** (Old City) constitutes one of the finest examples of Khmer art outside Cambodia. Archaeologists believe the site dates to the 500s, although construction was completed in the 12th century by Angkor's King Suryavarman II (1113-50). The temple bears stylistic similarities to Angkor Wat, and may have served as its prototype. UNESCO is planning renovations. Some of the walls are unstable; exercise caution while exploring. The temple's access road skirts a large **baray,** which, symbolizing the waters of the earth, helped to irrigate the surrounding rice fields. The causeway is now fenced off; two large rectangular galleries flank the entrance. Crowning a series of moss-covered laterite tiers is a small central **sanctuary.** Celestial nymphs guard the entrance, above which Shiva rides a three-headed elephant. A rather incongruous Buddha sits where the *linga* once did, reflecting the empire's overlapping Hindu-Buddhist influences. The temple's main gate is 8km south (downriver), along Champassak's main road. Tuk-tuks to Wat Phu run 15,000kip per person round-trip. It is also a nice bike ride to Wat Phu. Guest houses rent bicycles for 8000kip.

BORDER CROSSING: VEUNKHAM/STUNG TRENG As of March 2002, the border between Laos and Cambodia at Veunkham was officially closed, but it was "unofficially" open to travelers willing to pay the border guards for the Lao exit stamp and Cambodian entry stamp. Check in the guest houses in Don Det and Don Khong for the most up-to-date information. The border is open M-F 8am-3:30pm and all travelers must have a valid Cambodian visa which can be obtained in the embassies in Vientiane, Bangkok, Hanoi, or Ho Chi Minh City. Those willing to try crossing should take a boat from Don Khong to **Hat Xai Khun** (5000kip), or from Don Det to **Ban Nakasang** (5000kip). From there hire a tuk-tuk to **Veunkham** (15,000-20,000kip). For US$5, Lao immigration will give you an exit stamp. Walk down to the river and charter a boat to **Stung Treng,** the nearest town on the Cambodian side of the river (2hr., US$30-40 per 4-person boat). Your driver will take you across the river to Cambodian immigration and wait for you. Cambodian immigration will charge you US$15 for an entry stamp. You **cannot** obtain a visa at the border. Once you have your stamp, go back to your boat and on to Stung Treng.

THAD LO

Against the backdrop of the Bolovens Plateau, 80km northeast of Pakse and 30km from Saravane, idyllic Thad Lo sits on a bend in the Xedone River. Travelers soak their weary bodies in natural pools, visit out-of-the-way villages, or kick back in bungalows, lulled to sleep by the sound of waterfalls. Attractions in Thad Lo include hikes, which start at the waterfall (guides 10,000-15,000kip from the White House). There are tribal villages and more waterfalls within an hour's walk of the bridge. The owner of the restaurant next to Sapyasath Guest House will provide a map of a good 3hr. walk. The river above the first waterfall is a nice place to swim.

Buses run from Pakse to **Thad Lo** (2hr.; 7, 9, 11am, 1, 2pm; 10,000kip) and continue on to **Saravane.** Buses leave Saravane for **Pakse** (3hr.; 6:30, 8, 10:15am, 12:15, 1pm; 10,000kip), and stop at the main road at Thad Lo (around 7:30, 9, 11:15am, 1:15, 2pm). Make sure to arrive early to catch them. Buses drop passengers off on the road; Thad Lo village is 2km down a dirt road to the right (follow the signs). **Sapyasath Guest House ❸,** right before the bridge across from Thad Lo resort, has clean bungalows and an attached restaurant looking over the river (bungalows 45,000kip). **Saise Guest House ❸,** across the bridge, offers decent rooms with bath for 40,000kip. They also have much nicer lodging in their **Green House ❹,** on a path above the first guest house. Clean wooden rooms with a gorgeous view of the falls run 60,000-120,000kip. The best restaurant in Thad Lo is the **Sapyasath Guest House restaurant ❷,** which serves good Lao and Western fare at steep prices (entrees 15,000-20,000kip).

SARAVANE AND BOLOVENS PLATEAU

Northeast of Pakse looms the Bolovens Plateau, one of Southeast Asia's last frontiers. Laced with whitewater rivers, gorges, and valleys, the plateau is inhabited by ethnic minorities, many of whom were forced to flee their homelands in Vietnam's Central Highlands during the war. Among the larger groups are the Ngai, Suk, Katou, and Alak. Tea, coffee, fruit, and cardamom are still grown on plantations, as they have been since the days of the French. Although there is nothing to see or do in Saravane proper, it can be a good base for exploring the **Attapeu region**. This remote border area is home to many ethnic tribes, as well as tigers, gaur, Asian elephants, crocodiles, and other Lao endangered species. Travel to Attapeu is difficult and nearly impossible during the rainy season, and the region is rife with

malaria. Inquire at the Saise Guest House about hiring transport and a guide. An easier trip is to the waterfalls at **Pakxong** (1hr.; 7, 9, 11am, 1pm; 8000kip).

On the vast plateau, 113km northeast of Pakse, the provincial capital **Saravane** (or "Salavan") lies on the bank of the **Xedone River.** The road from Pakse passes the **bus station** and **airport** on the southwestern edge of town, then rings the town center. Daily **buses** and **trucks** go to: **Kongsedone** (1hr.; 10am, noon, 2pm; 10,000kip); **Pakse** (3hr.; 6:30, 8, 10:15am, 12:15, 1pm; 10,000kip); and **Sekong** (2-3hr.; 7am, 1:30pm; 8500kip). The main attraction, the **market,** is the center of town, with the **post office** and **bank** to the west and the **hospital** and football field to the north. The post office sells phone cards, and has a card phone out front. The bank exchanges US dollars and Thai baht to kip. (Open M-F 8:30am-3:30pm.) **Saise Guest House ❶,** at the northeastern corner of town near the river, has a helpful hand-drawn map of the town. (☎213 171. Dorms 20,000kip; rooms with A/C 40,000-50,000kip.) **Susai Guest House ❷,** 5min. from town, with nice views, is a bit friendlier. (Doubles with fan 25,000kip, with balcony 30,000-40,000kip.) Tuk-tuks from the bus station cost 1000kip to the market, 2000kip to Saise Guest House, and 3000kip to Susai Guest House. The **restaurant ❶** opposite Susai serves unoriginal though tasty Lao food. (Entrees 8000-15,000kip.) *Phở* shops around the market and vendors selling fresh fruit abound. Inquire at Saise about exploring the Bolovens by car (US$50-75 per day), or hire a tuk-tuk from the lot near the market (50,000-60,000kip for 5hr.).

4000 ISLANDS REGION ☎31

There are no long sandy beaches, but there are plenty of opportunities to lounge by the water. The area from Ban Munla Pamok to the Cambodian border is a tropical paradise at a point where the lazy waters of the Mekong become a raging torrent. Thousands of islets dot the branches and tributaries, earning the region its nickname. The larger, inhabited islands maintain a safe distance from mainland affairs and have a pace dictated by the cycles of the river. Don Det Island is a good place to swim the Mekong or just to kick back in a hammock over the water.

WARNING There is a risk of **dengue fever** and **malaria** in this area. Take anti-malarial drugs before coming, and bring bug spray.

TRANSPORTATION AND PRACTICAL INFORMATION. The largest island, and a good starting point for explorations, is **Don Khong.** There are several guest houses in the main village, **Muang Khong.** To get to Don Khong from Pakse, take a **boat** (8hr.; several 7am-noon; 20,000kip) or **bus** (3½hr.; 7, 9am; 12,000kip). The boat stops at **Muang Sen,** on the west side of the island. The 20min. tuk-tuk ride to Muang Khong costs up to 6000kip per person. Buses stop in **Hat Xai Khun;** take a skiff to Muang Khong (5000kip per person). Buses return to **Pakse** from Hat Xai Khun daily (3hr.; around 6:30, 9:30, 10:30am). Boats also go back to Pakse, but schedules are erratic. Ask at the pier in Muang Sen in advance. A **post/telephone office** is a few meters upriver from Don Khong's pier and can place cash-only **international calls.** (☎212 073. Open M-F 8am-noon and 1-4:30pm, Sa 8am-noon.) A **morning market** is upriver from Muang Khong pier but ends between 6 and 7am.

ACCOMMODATIONS AND FOOD. On **Don Khong,** Muang Khong has pleasant budget guest houses and many more under construction. The first, in front of the pier, is **Done Khong Guest House ❶.** The French-speaking proprietor offers basic, tidy singles (15,000kip), doubles with shared bath (20,000kip), and doubles with private bath (25,000kip). Her English-speaking son runs **Done Khong Guest House No. 2 ❶,** 200m up the road past the post office, which has a beautiful veranda overlooking rice fields. (Singles 10,000kip; doubles 20,000kip.) **Kang Khong**

Villa ❷, a large wood and concrete building with balcony and front garden, is 30m past the original Done Khong. (☎213 529. Smaller doubles 20,000kip; huge doubles with bath 25,000kip.) Every guest house rents **bicycles** for 8000kip per day.

Mr. Pon, formerly a chef in Vientiane, now operates **Pon's Restaurant ❷**, 50m upstream from Muang Khong pier. Delicious steamed fish (15,000kip) must be ordered two hours in advance. (Open daily 6am-10pm.) Mr. Pon also organizes boat tours of the islands (20,000kip per person) and trips to see the dolphins (25,000kip). Done Khong Guest House also has a good **restaurant ❶** that serves quality Vietnamese and Lao food (8000-15,000kip).

Don Det Island, 20km downriver from Don Khong, lacks Don Khong's modern facilities, but it makes up for it—the tropical haven has become the most popular destination in the 4000 Islands region. To get there, take a bus from Pakse to **Ban Nakasang** (3½hr.; 7, 9am; 12,000kip), and then a boat to Don Det Island (5000kip). To get there from Don Khong or Muang Khong, charter a **boat** (1½hr.; 10,000kip), which will drop you off at the main beach. **Khampong Bungalows ❶,** right next to the boat landing, has bungalows overlooking the river (15,000kip) and friendly owners. For slightly cheaper digs, continue walking left from the boat landing. Many bungalows line the path along the river, and most are similarly priced (10,000kip). For food, try the **Khampong Guest House restaurant ❶,** across from its bungalows, which serves tasty Lao and Western food (6000-10,000kip). The restaurant's owner, Kampai, helps arrange transport and crossing into Cambodia and gives tours to see the dolphins and waterfalls at **Don Khone Island** (25,000kip). Many other guest houses on the river path also have restaurants. If you continue to the left from the boat landing, past all the bungalows, you will reach the bridge to Don Khone Island (45min. walk from main boat landing). It costs 5000kip to cross the bridge; there are accommodations and a few restaurants on the other side.

SIGHTS. The 4000 Islands' main attractions are the waterfalls downstream from Don Khong. **Li Phi Falls,** on the southwestern tip of the island of Don Khone, are accessible by boat (20,000kip). The falls are actually rapids and are not very impressive. Don Khone shelters a 5km railroad line (now inoperative). Both sights are part of a government-owned resort. (Open daily 8am-6pm. 2000kip.) **Khone Pha Pheng (Voice of the Mekong),** the largest cascade in Southeast Asia, is farther south on the left bank, off Rte. 13. This so-called "Niagara of the Mekong" is (once again) nothing more than large rapids. Both waterfalls can be visited in a day with an early start. Guest houses and Pon's Restaurant (see **Accommodations and Food,** above) organize trips (group of 4-10 people and boat with skipper 10,000kip per person). As the final stretch of river is not navigable, travelers stop on the mainland 12km away and take a tuk-tuk to Khone Pha Pheng (whole tuk-tuk 60,000kip). This region is home to the Lao population of the endangered freshwater **Irrawaddy dolphins,** who come upriver to spawn between January and March. They can't pass the rapids, but nevertheless try each year. You might see them jumping out of the water in attempts to get to the other side. Guest houses in Don Khong or Don Det will arrange day tours to see the dolphins (see **Accommodations and Food,** above).

MALAYSIA

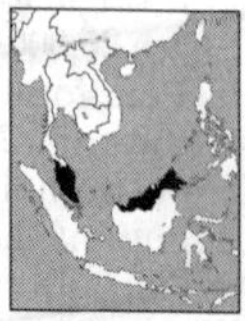

US$1 = RM3.80 (RINGGIT)
CDN$1 = RM2.44
EUR€1 = RM3.73
UK£1 = RM5.92
AUS$1 = RM2.08
NZ$1 = RM1.78
ZAR1 = RM0.36

RM1 = US$0.26
RM1 = CDN$0.41
RM1 = EUR€0.27
RM1 = UK£0.17
RM1 = AUS$0.48
RM1 = NZ$0.56
RM1 = ZAR2.77

PHONE CODE **Country code:** 60. **International dialing prefix:** 00.

Malaysians have much to be proud of—Southeast Asia's most sophisticated transportation infrastructure; clean, diverse cities; and a reasonably well-protected natural environment. For the traveler, Malaysia offers the comforts of rapid modernization as well as the grandeur of carefully preserved traditional cultures. Although the interaction between the country's Malay majority and sizable Chinese population isn't without tension, it's a credit to the Malaysians that in the wake of regional depression their society has stuck together. Malaysia's ethnic mix mingles most in the cities of the cosmopolitan west coast, while the sparsely populated east coast remains a bastion of seafaring Malay culture, but fantastic island beaches beckon eager travelers to both coasts. The eastern states of Sabah and Sarawak offer a chance to explore the wilds of Borneo, Malaysian-style, with accessible national parks, efficient tourist services, and buses that never run late.

FACTS AND FIGURES

Official Name: Malaysia.

Government: Parliamentary Democracy.

Capital: Kuala Lumpur.

Land Area: 329,758 sq. km.

Geography: Separated from the mainland by the South China Sea; borders Thailand to the north and Singapore to the south.

Climate: Tropical and humid year-round. Monsoon season in east coast Peninsular Malaysia and Sabah/Sarawak Nov.-Mar.

Major Cities: Georgetown, Kota Kinabalu, Kuala Terengganu, Kuching.

Population: 23,000,000.

Languages: Malay, Chinese, English, Tamil, indigenous languages.

Religions: Islam 59%, Buddhism 18%, Christianity 8%, Hinduism 6%.

Average Income Per Capita: US$3380.

Major Exports: Petroleum, timber, natural gas, electronic components, textiles.

LIFE AND TIMES

DEMOGRAPHICS

Malaysia's true natives are the **Orang Asli** (original people), who probably migrated to the peninsula from China some 10,000 years ago. Now, most of Malaysia's 22 million residents live on the peninsula, and the rest inhabit Sabah and Sarawak to the east. The terms "Malaysian," "Malayan," and "Malay" are distinct. "Malaysian" is a reference to a citizen of the country, "Malayan" denotes anyone from the peninsula, while "Malay" is a term for the ethnic Malay who constitute nearly 60% of the population. Almost all Malays are Muslim. Sarawak is home to the **Dayak,** Malaysia's small Christian population. **Indians** constitute the third-largest race in Malaysia, while **Chinese-Malaysians** comprise a third of the total population.

LANGUAGE

Bahasa Malay is the official language of Malaysia. Malay is taught in all schools and used in all governmental institutions such as Parliament and the courts. Malay is tied very closely to the Malaysian national identity and its cultural importance has been emphasized by the government since the founding of the Federation of Malaysia in 1957. Several different dialects of **Chinese** are spoken in Malaysia, depending on the origins of the people speaking them. The most common are Hakka, Mandarin, and Cantonese. Although **English** is recognized as Malaysia's second language, more people speak Chinese. English is much more common in the larger cities on the western coast of Peninsular Malaysia. A language of India, **Tamil** is spoken almost exclusively in Peninsular Malaysia due to the Indian population there. **Iban** is the largest language group in Sarawak, and is even spoken on some radio programs and taught in some schools. Four different dialects of **Dusun** are spoken in Sabah. Dialects of both Iban and Dusun are spoken in the Polynesian islands. Spoken on the western coast of Sabah, **Bajau** is related to but distinct from other languages of Borneo such as Sama (also known as East Coast Bajau).

RELIGION

ISLAM. Islam is the official state religion of Malaysia and is practiced by 59% of the population. Religious freedom for all faiths is guaranteed by the constitution for all but ethnic Malays, who are born Muslim by law. But Malaysia is a miracle of cultural fusion, and Muslim Malay culture has borrowed many customs from other cultural and religious traditions. Islam still exerts a conservative influence on Malay culture, and the government strongly supports Muslim values and favors ethnic Malays in housing, education, and business. Those who convert from Islam to another religion are usually fined or imprisoned for rehabilitation.

BUDDHISM. Buddhist influence was strongest before the rise of Islam in Malaysia, but due to the significant Chinese population, Buddhism still retains importance in Malaysian culture and is practiced by roughly 18% of the population. **Confucianism, Taoism,** and ancestor worship also belong to the school of Buddhism and are associated with the Chinese community. Approximately 5% of the population practices these religions.

CHRISTIANITY. Christianity is practiced by approximately 8% of Malaysia. Many Christians in Malaysia are converted Chinese. However, the publication and distribution of Malay-language Bibles is strongly disapproved of and often restricted.

HINDUISM. Malaysia's large Indian population (6% of the population) practices Hinduism. Commerce in gold and silks brought the religion to Malaysia's shores nearly one millennium before Islam, and continued trade with India reinforced Hinduism's importance to Malaysian culture.

FLORA AND FAUNA

Malaysia's plantlife alone is more than enough reason to visit this country. Malaysia has more endangered plant species than other country in the world. While all of Europe contains approximately 5000 species of plants, Malaysia alone, at a fraction of the size, boasts an estimated 12,000-15,000 plant species. The national flower is the **hibiscus** and there are over 800 species of **orchids** alone in Malaysia. Native to Sarawak, the bitahgor tree is one of three plant species that pharmaceutical companies believe may hold a cure for AIDS. Nearly 20% of Peninsular Malaysia's tree species and slightly over 20% of the tree species in Sabah and Sarawak are endangered. Thirteen species of plants have become extinct since the 1920s due to logging. Of particular note, the plantlife on **Mt. Kinabalu** (see p. 472) makes up 10% of all vascular plants in Malaysia. The **coconut palm** can grow to be 25-30m tall and is heavily harvested throughout Malaysia for its oil, as is the **oil palm.** Two other important crops in Malaysian agriculture are **rubber** and **cocoa.**

While the number of animal species in Malaysia is not as impressive as the bulk of plant species, many of the animals are just as precious. **Orangutans** and **hawksbill turtles** are just two of the endangered animals in Malaysia. There are no more than 4000 orangutans in East Malaysia, and, of endangered marine turtles, the hawksbill population is the smallest. Also native to Malaysia is the **Asian elephant** (also called the Indian elephant). The first Asain elephant equipped with satellite tracking equipment in 1995 was Mek Penawar, a female who was relocated after she raided a starfruit plantation in southern Malaysia. A few other highly endangered species are the **Malaysian sun bear,** with a population of only 600-1000 left in all of Malaysia, Myanmar, Thailand, and Sumatra (Indonesia), the **Javan rhino,** with only an estimated 150 left in Malaysia, and the **storm stork,** which may have a population of even less that 200.

HISTORY

EARLY KINGDOMS (100-1400)

As early as the first century AD, the Straits of Melaka linked China and India as traders from both countries came seeking gold. Indic influence spread throughout Malaya. Malaysia was temporarily seized by the Javanese Empire around 1080 until the Chinese, fleeing from the threatening Siamese, founded Melaka in the early 15th century. Melaka then grew quickly as a naval port and trading center for merchants from Arabia, China, Java, India, and Myanmar.

RISE OF ISLAM AND WESTERN EXPLORATION (1400-1795)

IMPORTANT DATES

15th Century Melaka converts to Islam.	**1511** Muslim loyalists flee as Portuguese invade.	**16th Century** Dutch overthrow Portuguese rule.

The 15th century saw the spread of Islam under Muslim **Muzaffar Shah,** who helped Melaka eliminate Thai vassals. By the late 15th-century reign of **Mahmud Shah,** Melaka included Peninsular Malaysia, Singapore, and parts of Thailand and northern Sumatra. The **Portuguese invasion** in 1511 marked the beginning of Malaysia's "age of exploration." Unruffled by the Portuguese presence, locals remained loyal to the Shah Dynasty and fled south to establish the state of **Johor.** The chaos following the assassination of Melaka's **Sultan Mahmud** attracted the **Bugis** and other groups from southern Sulawesi. They competed with the Sultan of Johor and the **Dutch,** who replaced the Portuguese in the 16th century.

HIGHLIGHTS OF MALAYSIA

BEACHES. **Pulau Langkawi** (p. 408) harbors budget haunts, but **Pulau Tioman** (p. 439) and the **Perhentian Islands** (p. 419) take the prize. **Similajau National Park** (p. 457) proves there's more to Borneo than jungle.

NATURAL WONDERS. **Taman Negara National Park** (p. 416) provides cool respite. Spelunk in **Niah National Park** (p. 458) or scale **Gunung Kinabalu** (p. 472), Southeast Asia's highest peak.

URBAN BEAT. Slick and never dull, **Kuala Lumpur** (p. 374) boasts capital sights, services, and after-hours elan. **Melaka** (p. 385) blends east and west both in the kitchen and on the street. **Georgetown** (p. 401) exudes the feel of a Chinese city. **Kota Bharu** (p. 424) is the heart of Malay culture. **Kuching's** (p. 444) vibrant waterfront scene and sights on the edge of the jungle are the cat's meow.

COLONIAL RULE (1795-1945)

IMPORTANT DATES

1795 British rule begins.	**1819** British claim uninhabited Singapore.	**1824** Anglo-Dutch Treaty gives Malaysia to Britain.	**1879** Treaty of Pangkor brings British residents to Malaysia.

The Dutch gave up the island of Penang to Britain in 1786, and the English acted as a stabilizing—though oppressive—force in the region. The Dutch, in turn, took control of the islands south of Singapore. The **Treaty of Pangkor of 1879** saw the import of ill-prepared English "residents" to Malaysia. By World War I, all of Peninsular Malaysia had submitted to some sort of British control, though not without resistance. Throughout the 150 years of British rule, anti-colonial sentiment grew, evidenced in the frequent popular uprisings and subsequent periods of repression that characterized the colonial period.

FORGING A NATION (1945-1957)

IMPORTANT DATES

1942-45 Japanese occupation, British desertion, and Malay nationalism.	**1946** United Malay National Organization established.	**1957** Independence: Federation of Malaysia formed.

During WWII, the Japanese moved into Malaya and returned the northern states to Thailand, hoping to exploit Malaya's resources and strategic location. The British, who had fled and left the country defenseless, returned to Malaya after the war but were unable to return the country to its former calm. In 1946, Britain's plan for refederation—which proposed that all Malayan territories except for Singapore be included in a single union—was opposed by the newly formed **United Malay National Organization (UMNO)** and the **Malay Communist Party.** But Communist hopes were soon dashed, in part due to the deportation of half a million Chinese. The government plan then shifted to unifying Malaya and guaranteeing Malay rights. In 1957, the independent **Federation of Malaya** was established.

THE TUMULTUOUS 1960S (1960-1970)

IMPORTANT DATES

1960s Government tries to enforce Islam and Malay language.	**1963** Indonesian President Sukarno declares *Konfrontasi.*	**1965** Singapore secedes.	**1969** Ethnic riots in Kuala Lumpur.

Supporting insurgency in Malaysia's eastern states and border skirmishes between Sabah/Sarawak and Kalimantan, Indonesian President **Sukarno** declared **Konfrontasi** ("confrontation") against Malaya in January 1963. With England's support, Malaya became Malaysia on September 16, 1963. This infuriated the Philippines, which held an ancient claim to Sabah. Indonesia, meanwhile, regarded Malaya's action as covert British neo-colonialism. Within Malaysia, ethnic tensions rose. The official attitude toward Singapore's predominantly Chinese population created more problems for the Malay-oriented government, which had established Islam and Bahasa Malay as its official religion and language. In 1965, Malaysia passed an amendment allowing Singapore to secede. In May 1969, **ethnic riots** erupted in Kuala Lumpur after the Malay majority party, **Alliance** (which consisted of the UMNO and the conservative Malayan Chinese Association), lost a number of seats to non-Malay-supported parties. Feeling their own culture should be adopted, at least in part, by other nationalities, the Malay forced the use of Malay language in official contexts. Malay political leaders called mass meetings but quickly lost control of the armed mobs that gathered. Ensuing riots lasted four days, leaving over 200 Chinese dead and more than 5000 homeless. Some Malays blamed the prime minister for the riots, but most blamed them on concessions to non-Malay groups rather than their own racial attitudes.

MALAY DOMINATION (1970-1999)

IMPORTANT DATES

1971 Islamic National Culture Policy established.	**1981** Mahathir elected Prime Minister, consolidates power.	**1996** First satellites launched; financial restrictions on Australia lifted.	**1999-2000** Ibrahim convicted of sodomy; receives six-year prison sentence.

Under Razak's rule, UMNO's power increased, and the country continued to promote Malay interests. Additional political alliances increased the status and political clout of Malay citizens, and economic policies were implemented to support Malay business ownership. The **Islamic National Culture Policy,** established in 1971, defined "national culture" as encompassing the indigenous traditions of the Malay people, which disregarded not only pre-Islamic Chinese and Indian influences but also those of the Orang Asli, who had populated the region thousands of years before the proto-Malay. Policy makers insisted on education in Bahasa Malay alone and provided federal support only for ethnic Malay art and literature. Though he faced allegations of human rights violations and a court's declaration that the UMNO was unconstitutional, **Mahathir Mohammed** prevailed and organized the **UMNO Baru (New UMNO).** Mahathir intertwined Western economic models with a **"Look East"** policy when seeking foreign investment and trade to pull Malaysia out of the financial crisis. Malaysia remains an active member of the **Association of Southeast Asian Nations (ASEAN).** Under Mahathir's administration, the country has become less dependent on tin and rubber resources and has moved toward industrialization. As a step toward the **Vision 2020** plan, which aims to attain developed-nation status by 2020 by improving technology, Malaysia launched its first two space satellites in August 1996. In April 1999, Ibrahim was condemned to a six-year prison sentence for allegedly interfering with police investigations into accusations of sexual misconduct. The court eventually convicted Ibrahim of sodomy, ending a controversial year-long trial. Ibrahim viewed the ordeal as a staged maneuver to halt his struggle for more liberal politics. To many human rights watchdogs worldwide, however, the trials illustrated the government's backlash against peaceful political demonstrations.

MALAYSIA TODAY

BUMIPUTRA. Though improving, Malaysia's Chinese-dominated economy suffers from income inequality. The Malay government hopes to improve the situation through the **New Economic Policy (NEP),** a state-run program dedicated to redistribute wealth to the native Malay, known as the *bumiputra* (literally "sons of the soil"). The NEP extends the *bumiputra* certain privileges to promote their economic advancement. Malaysian companies are encouraged to hire Malays over Chinese for top positions and must have at least 51% Malay shareholders, though recent economic development has loosened some of these requirements. Malays also get discounts on housing and loans. Consequently, Malays have risen economically, though critics denounce the NEP for discriminating against the Chinese. As of 1999, the Malaysian workforce was still dominated by ethnic Chinese (54%). Far fewer *bumiputra* (29%) were registered as professionals.

ECONOMIC DEVELOPMENT. The Asian Financial Crisis has since slowed Malaysia's development. Although Mahathir stopped blaming various segments of the population for the financial crisis, only recently has he accepted the gravity of the situation and decided to address it. To avoid the imposing IMF regulations, Deputy Prime Minister Anwar Ibrahim called off Mahathir's high-growth policies in December 1997 to help stabilize the ringgit and the plummeting stock market. While stagflation may continue, Ibrahim's policy changes have at least stabilized the situation. However, in the summer of 2002, Mahathir announced his intention to resign from Prime Minister on October 25, 2003.

DOWNSIDES OF DEVELOPMENT. The downside of development has been severe **environmental degradation.** Once-beautiful bus rides are now marked by hills scarred by mining, single-crop plantations, and wastelands of factories and construction sites. Environmental awareness has gained popularity, but much of it is little more than rhetoric. More recent developments include a movement by the **Parti Islam se-Malaysia (PAS)** to impose Shariah, or Islamic Law, and a simultaneous effort by Islamic fundamentalists to pass laws making it legal to cut off the hands of convicted thieves and to flog women who make unproven rape claims. Such laws were successfully passed in eastern Terengganu State in the summer of 2002, but may be overturned on account of unconstitutionality. As of April 2002, it is legal to publicly whip illegal immigrants in Malaysia.

HUMAN RIGHTS. In its quest for unity, the Malaysian government has used a heavy hand regarding freedom of expression. **Amnesty International** has criticized Malaysia for its dealings with the media, use of capital punishment, and restrictions on religion. Though the constitution provides for religious freedom, the practice of Islamic sects other than Sunni Islam is severely restricted, and religious minorities like Buddhists, Hindus, and Christians frequently face restrictions. In addition, some accuse Malaysian police of being trigger-happy; according to Mahathir, police use force appropriately to limit crime. However, this doesn't change the fact that suspected criminals under arrest face a very high death rate.

SEPTEMBER 11 AND THE WAR ON TERROR. The United States-led **War on Terror** has requested the aid of all countries that may, even unwittingly, be harboring terrorists. Fourteen suspected members of **al Qaeda,** the group responsible for the attacks, were arrested in Malaysia in April, 2002. In addition, the **Abu Sayyaf Group (ASG),** the terrorist group responsible for kidnapping several Americans in 2002, is believed to have at one time had a training ground in eastern Sabah (see **The Philippines Today,** p. 553). In the summer of 2002, Malaysia joined nine other ASEAN countries in a pledge with the United States to "prevent, disrupt and combat" global terrorism through increased sharing of information and intelligence. Malaysia's interest in this effort, like that of many other countries in Southeast Asia, is to prevent an increased US military presence in the region.

CUSTOMS AND ETIQUETTE

FROM THE HEART. As in most Muslim countries in Southeast Asia, the standard conservative codes of conduct apply. Remove shoes before entering a home or mosque, dress modestly, and use your right hand when handling food and greeting someone. Handshakes are usually suitable for both men and women, though Malays traditionally use the *salam*, a handshake in which the hands are touched to the chest to mean, "I greet you from the heart."

BISEXUAL, GAY, AND LESBIAN TRAVELERS. As a predominantly Muslim country, Malaysia is quite intolerant of homosexuality. Both Malay and visiting Muslims face flogging or imprisonment for gay or lesbian activity. Though non-Muslims are exempt from Muslim religious law, police may arrest any gay person in a public place. Discretion is advised. For more information, try **Pink Triangle,** 23 Jalan Jati Kuala Lumpur, 55100 Kuala Lampur, an organization devoted to HIV/AIDS and sexuality issues. The staff has information on GLBT venues in Kuala Lumpur and holds socials. (☎4044 4611; hotline ☎4044 9622, 4044 5455; isham@pop7jaring.my. Open M-F 10am-7pm, hotline open M-F 7:30-9:30pm.)

ARTS

ARCHITECTURE. Architecture in Malaysia is reflective not only of the historical "changing hands" of colonial rule, but also of the cultural influences in modern-day Malaysia. Buildings range from colonial-style houses to modern skyscrapers. Traditional Malay houses are common in **kampong** (villages). Such houses are built on stilts and have large windows. These features keep the houses cool and dry in the event of flooding. Also notable are the various forms of religious architecture—mosques, temples, and churches alike compete for skyline space.

DRAMA AND DANCE. Malaysian dance and drama are closely related, as exemplified by the **Ma'Yong (also Mak Yong),** a Malay dance-drama that gained prominence as a court tradition over 400 years ago. Roles are traditionally reserved for young women, except for that of the buffoon or clown. The stories are romantic dramas with nearly identical plots in which a heroic boy saves a princess from an ogre. **Malay shadow play** is an ancient and elaborate form of puppetry found across Southeast Asia. The central story is the **Ramayana,** Valmiki's epic Hindu poem, in which Rama leads an army of monkeys from India to Ceylon to rescue his wife Sita. **Malay dance** comes in many forms. Two of the most popular are the **candle dance,** in which dancers hold candles on small plates, and **silat,** an elegant dance which started as a deadly martial art. The most popular Malay dance is the **Joget,** derived from Portuguese folk dance, in which couples swirl to a lively tempo.

MUSIC. Cambodia, India, and the Middle East all influence Malay music. Among the most well-known instruments is the **rebab,** a spike fiddle. Its nasal sound leads the orchestra in the Ma'Yong. The large Arabic **gendang** drums provide the tempo for Malay drama and dance events. Popular singing styles include: **pantun,** Islamic devotionals of improvisational duets; **ghazals,** mournful Islamic love songs; and the vocal accompaniment to the powerful, percussion-heavy **dondang.**

HOLIDAYS AND FESTIVALS (2003)

DATE	NAME	LOCATION & DESCRIPTION
Jan. 1	New Year's Day	Everywhere except Johor, Keday, Kelantan, Perlis, and Terengganu
Jan. and Feb.	Thaipusam Festival	Hindu Festival, hooks and needles in flesh (see p. 385)
Feb. 1	Federal Territory Day	Federal Territory of Kuala Lumpur and Labuan
Feb. 1	Chinese New Year	Chinese–National
Mar. 5	Islamic New Year	Muslim–National (also Hari Raya Tussa)
Apr. 18	Good Friday	Christian–National
May 1	Labour Day	National
June 1-2	Dayak Festival	Sarawak
1st Sa in June	Birthday of H.M. the King	National (also Seri Paduka Baginda Yang di-Pertuan Agong)
Aug. 31	National Day	National
2nd Sa in Sept.	Birthday of Yang di-Pertua	Sarawak
Sept. 16	Malaysia Day	Sabah
Oct. 27	Start of Ramadan	Muslim–National
Dec. 25	Christmas Day	Christian–National

ADDITIONAL RESOURCES

GENERAL HISTORY

A History of Malaysia, by Barbara Watson Andaya and Leonard Andaya (2001). An in-depth look at the historical phenomena that have contributed to the formation of modern Malaysia.

LITERATURE

Joss and Gold, by Shirley Geok-lin Lim (2001). Portrays the uncertainty of newly independent Malaysia and the country's search for a definite identity.

The Malay Dilemma, by Mahathir Mohammed (1970). A controversial treatise on Malaysia's racial issues. Banned in Malaysia until Mahathir's election.

The Ordeal: My Ten Years in a Malaysian Prison, by Beatrice Saubin (1994). A personal account of time spent in a Malaysian prison for a crime she never committed.

The Lands of Charm and Cruelty: Travels in Southeast Asia, by Stan Sesser (1993). Includes an essay on logging in Sarawak originally published in *The New Yorker.*

ON THE WEB

Malaysia Tourism Promotion Board (www.interknowledge.com/malaysia). Where to go, what to see, and how to do it.

ESSENTIALS

MALAYSIA PRICE ICONS					
SYMBOL:	❶	❷	❸	❹	❺
ACCOMM.	Under US$3 Under RM12	US$3-6 RM12-24	US$6-10 RM24-40	US$10-17 RM40-68	Over US$17 Over RM68
FOOD	Under US$1 Under RM4	US$1-2 RM4-8	US$2-4 RM8-16	US$4-8 RM16-32	Over US$8 Over RM32

EMBASSIES & CONSULATES

MALAYSIAN CONSULAR SERVICES ABROAD

Australia: High Commission, 7 Perth Ave., Yarralumla, Canberra, ACT 2600 (☎02 6273 1543). **Consulate,** 67 Victoria Rd., Bellevue Hill, NSW 2023 (☎02 9327 7565).

Canada: High Commission, 60 Boteler St., Ottawa, ON K1N 8Y7 (☎613-241-5182; http://home.istar.ca/~mwottawa). **Consulate,** 1805-1111 W. Georgia St., Vancouver, BC V6C 4M3 (☎604-685-9550).

New Zealand: High Commission, 10 Washington Ave., Brooklyn, Wellington (☎04 385 2439).

South Africa: High Commission, 1007 Schoeman St., Arcadia, Pretoria 0083 (☎012 342 5990).

UK: High Commission, 45 Belgrave Sq., London SW1X 8QT (☎171 235 8033).

US: Embassy, 3516 International Court, NW, Washington, D.C. 20038 (☎202-572-9700). **Consulate,** 313 E 43rd St., New York, NY 10017 (☎212-490-2722 or 490-2723); 875 N Michigan Ave., Ste. 4101, Chicago, IL 60611 (☎312-280-9632); 350 S. Figuera St., Ste. 400, Los Angeles, CA 90071 (☎213-621-2991).

CONSULAR SERVICES IN MALAYSIA

Australia: Embassy, 6 Jl. Yap Kwan Seng, 50450 Kuala Lumpur (☎03 2146 555; fax 2141 4323; consular@australia.org.my; www.australia.org.my).

Canada: Embassy, 17th fl., Menara Tan & Tan, 207 Jl. Tun Razak, 50400 Kuala Lumpur (☎03 2718 3333; fax 2718 3399; klmpr-td@dfait-maeci.gc.ca; www.dfait-maeci.gc.ca/kualalumpur). **Consulate,** 1, Maccallum Street Ghaut, P.O. Box No. 23, 10700 Penang (☎/fax 04 262 3300; tyt@lbsb.com).

Ireland: Embassy, The Amp Walk, 218 Jl. Ampang, 50450 Kuala Lumpur (☎03 2161 2963; fax 2161 3427; ireland@po.jaring.my).

New Zealand: Embassy, 21st fl., Menara IMC, 8 Jl. Sultan Ismail, 50250 Kuala Lumpur (☎03 2078 2533; fax 2078 0387; nzhckl@po.jaring.my).

South Africa: Embassy, No. 12 Lorong Titiwangsa, Taman Tasik Titiwangsa, Setapak, 53200 Kuala Lumpur (☎03 4024 4456; fax 4024 9896; sahcpol@tm.net.my; www.afrikaselatan.com).

UK: Embassy, 185 Jl. Ampang, 50450 Ampang, Kuala Lumpur (☎03 2170 2200, emergency ☎012 322 0011; fax 03 2144 2370).

US: Embassy, 376 Jl. Tun Razak, 50400 Kuala Lumpur (☎03 2168 5000; fax 2142 2207; http://usembassymalaysia.org.my). Ask to speak to the **Consular Officer,** Sylvia D. Johnson.

TOURIST OFFICES ABROAD

Tourism Malaysia (www.tourismmalaysia.com). **Australia,** 65 York St., Sydney NSW 2000 (☎02 9299 4441); 56 William St., Perth, WA 6000 (☎09 481 0400). **Canada,** 830 Burrard St., Vancouver, BC V6Z 24K (☎604-689-8899). **South Africa,** Hutton Ct., 1st fl., CNR Jan Smuts Ave. & Summit Rd., Hyde Park, 2196 Johannesburg (☎011 327 0400). **UK,** 57 Trafalgar Sq., London WC2N 5DU (☎020 7930 7932). **US,** 120 E. 56th St., Ste. 810, New York, NY 10022 (☎212-754-1113); 818 W 7th St., Ste. 804, Los Angeles, CA 90017 (☎213-689-9702).

VISAS

American, Australian, Canadian, New Zealand, South African, and most European citizens don't need visas for stays of up to three months. Irish citizens can stay for two months without a visa, and Greek and Portuguese citizens can stay for one month. **Visa extensions** are available at immigration offices in Johor, Kuala Lumpur, and Penang, as well as at any international airport. Travelers who leave Malaysia and come back must apply for a US$10 **re-entry permit.**

MONEY

Malaysia's **ringgit (RM)** is issued in denominations of RM1, 2, 5, 10, 20, 50, 100, 500, and 1000. Each ringgit is divided into 100 **sen,** which come in coins of 1, 5, 10, 20, and 50 (there are also RM1 coins). British pounds and US dollars are the most widely accepted foreign currencies. Travelers checks are accepted at all banks, hotels, and major department stores. A 5% government tax and 10% service charge is added to most bills, making **tipping** unnecessary but appropriate for exceptional service.

GETTING THERE

BY PLANE. Malaysia's four largest **international airports** are: Bayan Lepas International Airport in Georgetown (see p. 401), Kuala Lumpur International Airport (KLIA) in Kuala Lumpur (see p. 374), Kuching International Airport in Kuching (see p. 444), and Malaysia Airport Berhad in Kota Kinabalu (see p. 466). Airports in Kota Bharu, Langkawi, Kuala Terengganu, and Kuantan also have international flights. **Malaysia Airlines** (**MAS;** www.malaysiaairlines.com.my) flies from KLIA to over 100 domestic and international locations. Kuala Lumpur, Penang, and Singapore are the major international gateways.

BY LAND. Refer to the following table for overland border crossings in Malaysia.

GETTING AROUND

BY PLANE. Malaysia's abundance of domestic airports makes plane travel between cities easy and safe. **Malaysia Airlines** monopolizes the domestic market.

BY BUS OR TRAIN. Both A/C and non-A/C **buses** run between major towns at reasonable prices. **Malayan Railways (Keretapi Tanah Melayu Berhad, KTM)** runs up and down the west coast from Alor Setar to Singapore. KTM railpasses allow unlimited travel on passenger trains in Malaysia and Singapore for 10 days (US$55, children US$28) or 30 days (US$120, children US$60). The slow but scenic **Jungle Train** connects Wakat Baru (near Kota Bharu, see p. 424) to Singapore via Jerantut. Bus travel is quick and efficient along **Hwy. 3,** a well-maintained road connecting Johor Bahru in the south to Kota Bharu in the north.

BY CAR. Fixed-rate inter-city **taxis** connect many towns and cities. Split the ride with up to three others. Local taxis are often unmetered, so agree on a price beforehand. Surcharges apply to taxis booked by phone, trips between midnight and 7am, and rides for more than two passengers. To **rent a car,** you need an **International Driver's Permit (IDP)** or a government-issued license (see p. 36). Some hotels rent cars for RM160-350. Malaysians drive on the left side of the road.

BORDER CROSSINGS

BRUNEI. From Kuala Baram in **Sarawak** (near Miri, p. 459) take the bus that stops at the border in Kuala Belait and have your passport stamped before going on into Seria and **Bandar Seri Begawan** (p. 479). Alternatively, from Lawas or Limbang (also in Sarawak), cross over to Temburong or Bangar, stopping by the immigration post near Bangar. From **Sabah,** take a ferry to **Pulau Labuan.**

INDONESIA. Buses connect Tebedu in **Sarawak** (near Kuching, p. 444) with **Entikong** (near Pontianak) in West Kalimantan. The border crossing is open daily 6am-5pm; Indonesian visas are available in Kuching. Ferries run from Tarakan/Nunukan in East Kalimantan to **Tawau** in Sabah. To reach Sumatra from Peninsular Malaysia, take a ferry from **Penang** (p. 400) to **Medan** (p. 261).

SINGAPORE. A 1056m causeway connects Singapore (p. 653) to **Johor Bahru**. Buses and trains from Malaysia run over this causeway into Woodlands town.

THAILAND. Most Western tourists can travel to Thailand from Malaysia without buying a visa before crossing borders. Obtain transit visas at the border stops instead. By ferry, you can travel from **Kuala Perlis** and **Pulau Langkawi** (p. 408) to **Satun** (p. 878); remember to stop by the immigration office at Thammalang pier to have your passport stamped. Other common crossings are (listed from Malaysia to Thailand): **Rantau Ranjang/Kota Bharu** (p. 424) to **Sungai Kolok** (p. 879) in the east and **Kangar** to **Padang Besar, Alor Setar** to **Sadao,** and **Keroh** to **Betong** in the west.

KEEPING IN TOUCH

Malaysia's **postal system** does quality work. Airmail across the globe should take one to two weeks. **Long-distance calls** are easiest from cell phones. Second-easiest are card phones, most of which offer International Direct Dialing (IDD), but you'll have to pay local charges in addition to long-distance fees. Telephone offices and convenience stores sell **phone cards.** The most convenient is the Telekom Malaysia card, except in Kuala Lumpur, where the Uniphone card is most useful. For **Home Country Direct (HCD)** numbers from Malaysia, refer to the table on the inside back cover of this book.

PENINSULAR MALAYSIA

WEST COAST

Rich with colonial history and natural beauty yet polished with a cosmopolitan veneer, peninsular Malaysia's west coast offers plenty of sights and modern amenities. With user-friendly transportation, tourist facilities, and many English speakers, the west coast may well be the best introduction to Southeast Asia. The west coast also represents Malaysia's ethnic mix well: sizable Chinese and Indian communities coexist with ethnic Malay. Although many tourists complain that industrialization has hindered local culture, it has also created many jobs and comforts.

Peninsular Malaysia
Monk Mystique
Climb the Pagoda of 10,000 Buddhas at Kek Lok Si, Malaysia's largest temple.
South China Sea
Coral Corral
Snorkel amongst the coral deposits and exotic sea life in Long Beach.
Pulau Perhentian Kecil
Pulau Langkawi
Kangar
Alor Setar
Keroh
THAILAND
Kota Bharu
Rantau Panjang
Kuala Besut
Pulau Perhentian Besar
Pulau Redang
Pulau Penang
Penang
Lake Kenering
Lake Temengor
Kuala Terengganu
Marang
Taiping
Kuala Kangsar
Ipoh
Kenyir Dam
Rantau Abang
TAMAN NEGARA NATIONAL PARK
Cameron Highlands
Pulau Pangkor
Tapah
Fraser's Hill
Jerantut
Cherating
On the DL in KL
Indulge in the wild dancing that characterizes Kuala Lumpur's popular nightlife.
Kuantan
Temerloh
Kuala Lumpur
Truly Trekking
Hike the breathtaking nine-day route to and from Gunung Tahan, Malaysia's highest peak.
Andaman Sea
Shah Alam
Lake Bera
Seramban
Pulau Tioman
Melaka
Cultural Heritage
Soak up Malaysian culture in Melaka's Chinese, Dutch, & Portuguese villages.
Mersing
Muar
Batu Pahat
Straits of Melaka
INDONESIA
Johor Bahru
SINGAPORE
0 40 miles
0 40 kilometers

MALAYSIA

KUALA LUMPUR ☎03

Seen from a distance, the skyline of Kuala Lumpur inspires awe. In the teeming urban streets, however, this quiet grandeur dissolves into the bustling activity of an efficient capital city. Kuala Lumpur displays its patriotism through "Proud to be Malaysian" songs, ubiquitous Malay flags, and the highest flagpole in Asia. A country that has been in the hands of everyone from India to Portugal, and from the Netherlands to Britain, Malaysia's multi-ethnic history is still visible: up to 7% of the population is of mixed European and Asian blood, and there is a national obsession with marriage within and between ethnic groups. And as Malaysians chant "Malaysia Boleh!" ("Malaysia Can!") at sports events, the rumblings of numerous construction projects throughout the city reiterate the same sentiment.

INTERCITY TRANSPORTATION

BY PLANE

Ultra-modern **Kuala Lumpur International Airport (KLIA;** ☎8776 4311) lies 70km southwest of the city. The most efficient way to reach KLIA by far is the new **KLIA Ekspres** (☎2267 8000), which checks in baggage at **KL CAT** (Kuala Lumpur City Air Terminal) inside KL Sentral (28min. non-stop; every 15min. 5am-1am; RM35, child RM15; wheelchair accessible). KL CAT is an official destination recognized by the International Air Transportation Association, so luggage that's checked in at KL CAT (at least 2hr. advance, please) will be loaded onto its routed flight. Take a commuter train from the KL **Sentral Railway Station** to **Nilai station** (1hr., every 15-30min. 5:54am-10:53pm, RM4.40) and connect to a KLIA-bound bus (40min., every 30min. 6:30am-10:15pm, RM2). Alternatively, take Intrakota bus #19 from Klang bus station to the Duta Hockey Stadium at **Hentian Duta** (30min., RM1.20 or 1.60) and an airport shuttle from **Hentian Duta** (☎6203 3064) to KLIA (1hr.; every 30min. 5:30am-10:15pm; RM20, child RM9). KLIA-bound buses also leave from the **Chan Sow Lin Star LRT Station** (45min.; every hr. 6:30am-9:30pm; RM14, child RM10). **KLIA Transit,** a high-speed train, leaves from KL Sentral for KLIA (37min., every 30min. 5:33am-12:03am, RM35). You can also catch the KLIA Transit at any of its three stops along the way: **Bandar Tasik Selatan** (Star LRT and Komuter Station, RM26.50), **Putrajaya-Cyberjaya** (RM6.20), or **Salak Tinggi** (RM3.20). Airport taxis (☎9223 8915) between Kuala Lumpur and KLIA charge exorbitant rates (1-1½hr.; RM60-70 to KLIA, RM70-90 from KLIA). Don't ride in a taxi without a meter.

MALAYSIA

DESTINATION	FREQUENCY	PRICE	DESTINATION	FREQUENCY	PRICE
Bangkok	2 per day	RM643	**Jakarta**	2 per day	RM683
Hanoi	4 per week	RM853	**Manila**	2 per day	RM1013
Hong Kong	2 per day	RM913	**Singapore**	10 per day	RM286

Airlines that serve Kuala Lumpur include: **Air Asia,** B-812 Kelana Sq., 17 Jl. SS7/26 Kelana Jaya (☎7809 6888); **Garuda Indonesia,** 19th fl., Citibank Bldg., 165 Jl. Ampang (☎2162 2811); **Malaysian Airlines (MAS),** MAS Bldg., Jl. Sultan Ismail (☎7846 3000); **Royal Brunei Airlines,** 2nd fl., UBN Tower, 10 Jl. P. Ramlee (☎2070 7166); **Singapore Airlines (SIA),** Wisma Singapore Airlines, 2/4 Jl. Dang Wangi (☎2692 3122); **Thai Airways,** Ste. 3001, 30th fl., Wisma Gold Hill, 67 Jl. Rajah Chulan (☎2031 2900); **Vietnam Airlines,** Wisma MPL 1st fl., Jl, Raja Chulan (☎2141 2416).

BY TRAIN

The **railway station,** known as **KL Sentral,** is in front of the National Museum, off Jl. Travers. (☎2267 1200. Open daily 6am-midnight.) Take the LRT Putra line or

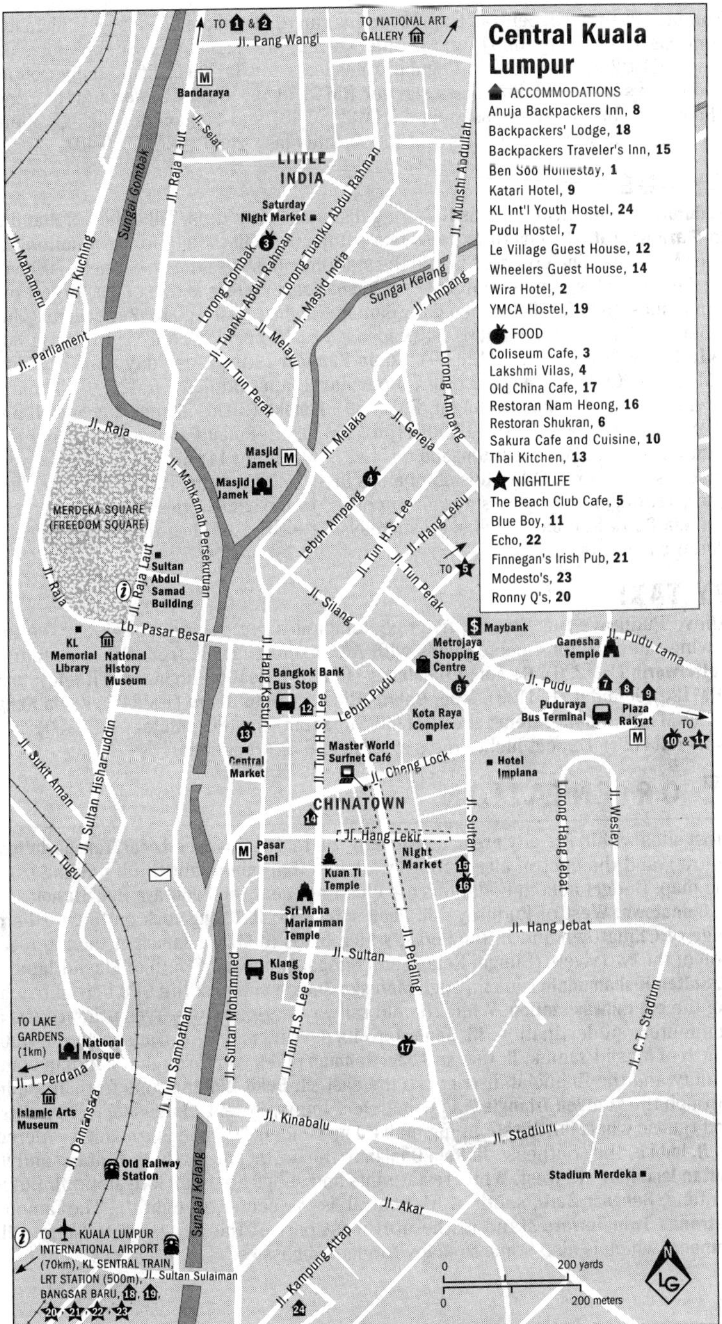
Central Kuala Lumpur
ACCOMMODATIONS
Anuja Backpackers Inn, 8
Backpackers' Lodge, 18
Backpackers Traveler's Inn, 15
Ben Soo Homestay, 1
Katari Hotel, 9
KL Int'l Youth Hostel, 24
Pudu Hostel, 7
Le Village Guest House, 12
Wheelers Guest House, 14
Wira Hotel, 2
YMCA Hostel, 19
FOOD
Coliseum Cafe, 3
Lakshmi Vilas, 4
Old China Cafe, 17
Restoran Nam Heong, 16
Restoran Shukran, 6
Sakura Cafe and Cuisine, 10
Thai Kitchen, 13
NIGHTLIFE
The Beach Club Cafe, 5
Blue Boy, 11
Echo, 22
Finnegan's Irish Pub, 21
Modesto's, 23
Ronny Q's, 20
TO 1 & 2
TO NATIONAL ART GALLERY
Jl. Pang Wangi
Bandaraya
Jl. Selat
LITTLE INDIA
Jl. Raja Laut
Sungai Gombak
Jl. Tuanku Abdul Rahman
Lorong Tuanku Abdul Rahman
Jl. Munshi Abdullah
Saturday Night Market
Lorong Gombak
Jl. Masjid India
Jl. Mahameru
Jl. Kuching
Sungai Kelang
Jl. Ampang
Jl. Melayu
Jl. Parliament
Jl. Tun Perak
Lorong Ampang
Jl. Raja
Jl. Melaka
Jl. Gereja
Masjid Jamek
Jl. Mahkamah Persekutuan
MERDEKA SQUARE (FREEDOM SQUARE)
Lebuh Ampang
Jl. Tun H.S. Lee
Jl. Hang Lekiu
TO 5
Sultan Abdul Samad Building
Jl. Silang
Lb. Pasar Besar
KL Memorial Library
National History Museum
Maybank
Metrojaya Shopping Centre
Ganesha Temple
Jl. Pudu Lama
Jl. Pudu
Jl. Hang Kasturi
Bangkok Bank Bus Stop
Lebuh Pudu
Kota Raya Complex
Puduraya Bus Terminal
Plaza Rakyat
TO 10 & 11
Jl. Sukit Aman
Jl. Sultan Hishamuddin
Central Market
Master World Surfnet Café
Jl. Cheng Lock
Hotel Impiana
CHINATOWN
Jl. Hang Lekir
Lorong Hang Jebat
Jl. Wesley
Jl. Tugu
Pasar Seni
Kuan Ti Temple
Night Market
Jl. Sultan
Sri Maha Mariamman Temple
Jl. Hang Jebat
Klang Bus Stop
Jl. Petaling
Jl. Sultan Mohammed
Jl. Tun Sambathan
TO LAKE GARDENS (1km)
National Mosque
Jl. L Perdana
Islamic Arts Museum
Jl. Damansara
Jl. C.T. Stadium
Jl. Kinabalu
Jl. Stadium
Old Railway Station
Sungai Kelang
Stadium Merdeka
Jl. Akar
TO KUALA LUMPUR INTERNATIONAL AIRPORT (70km), KL SENTRAL TRAIN, LRT STATION (500m), BANGSAR BARU, 18, 19, 20, 21, 22, 23
Jl. Sultan Sulaiman
Jl. Kampung Attap
200 yards
200 meters

Komuter train to KL Sentral. Express trains run to **Singapore** (7hr.; M-F 7:30am and 2pm, Sa-Su 11:15am; RM34) and **Jerantut** (6½hr.; M-F 8:10am, Sa-Su 6:10am; economy RM15, 2nd-class RM25). Regular trains leave for **Hat Yai** (14½hr.; daily 7:50pm; 2nd-class seat RM36, 2nd-class sleeper RM43.50-46) via **Butterworth** (11hr.; 2nd-class seat RM30, 2nd-class sleeper RM37.50-40) and **Singapore** (9hr.; 10:30pm; economy seat RM19, 2nd-class seat RM30, 2nd-class sleeper RM37.50-40).

BY BUS

Puduraya Station on Jl. Pudu is KL's long-distance bus station. Take the **LRT Star** line to **Plaza Rakyat.** Dozens of express bus companies sell tickets for destinations all over Malaysia. The counters inside the station and across the street near 7-Eleven are better for last-minute purchases. **Transnasional Express** is one of the largest bus companies. (☎2070 3300. Open daily 6am-midnight.) Buses go to: **Butterworth** (5hr., 9 per day 9am-midnight, RM20.40); **Ipoh** (3hr., 15 per day 8am-11pm, RM11.30); **Kota Bharu** (7hr., 9pm, RM26.10); **Kuala Kangsar** (4hr., 8 per day 9am-11:55pm, RM14.10); **Kuala Terengganu** (8hr., 5 per day 10am-midnight, RM25.10); **Kuantan** (4½hr., 17 per day 9am-midnight, RM14.30); **Melaka** (2½hr., 23 per day 8am-10pm, RM8); **Mersing** (5hr.; 11am, 10:30, 11pm; RM19.50); **Pulau Penang** (5hr., 7 per day 9am-midnight, RM22.80); **Singapore** (5hr.; 9:30am and 11pm; RM31.10). Express coaches cost more. Other bus companies including Eltabina, Indah Ekspres, Plusliner, Triton, and Warisan specialize in buses to the same cities mentioned above. **Hantian Putra Station,** which serves Malaysia's east coast, has the same prices as Puduraya Station.

BY TAXI

Above Puduraya Bus Station, five taxi companies serve various regions. The following rates are for 4-person cabs with A/C, excluding toll, from the taxi station: **Butterworth** (RM220); **Cameron Highlands** (RM160); **Genting Highlands** (RM45); **Ipoh** (RM120); **Jerantut** (RM100); **Johor Bahru** (RM200); **Kota Bharu** (RM240); **Kuala Kangsar** (RM140); **Kuala Terengganu** (RM240); **Kuantan** (RM120); **Melaka** (RM100); and **Muar** (RM120). Expect higher rates at night and on weekends.

ORIENTATION

Most sites within the city are accessible by the LRT trains (see **Local Transportation,** below), and the central city is more walkable that one might think judging from the map. Budget accommodations are clustered near the **Puduraya Bus Station** and in **Chinatown.** West of Puduraya, **Jl. Pudu** splits into **Jl. Cheng Lock** on the northern edge of Chinatown and **Jl. Tun Perak,** which leads to **Masjid Jamek** at the intersection of the two rivers (Sungai Kelang and Sungai Gombak). South of Masjid Jamek, **Jl. Sultan Hishamuddin** runs through **Merdeka Square** and past the **GPO** before reaching the **old railway station.** While the old railway station now serves primarily as a commuter rail destination, **KL Sentral,** to its south, is a major transportation hub. North of Masjid Jamek, **Jl. Tuanku Abdul Rahman** takes you through the Indian community and the financial district. To the east, **Jl. Bukit Bintang** runs from Jl. Pudu through the **"Golden Triangle,"** a posh area of luxury hotels, expensive restaurants, and (guess what?) more shopping malls. The Golden Triangle is roughly bordered by **Jl. Imbi** to the southeast, **Jl. Raja Chulan** to the north, and Jl. Bukit Bintang and **Jl. Sultan Ismail** to the west. While restaurants and shops are open late along Jl. Bukit Bintang, **Bangsar Baru,** south of KL Sentral, is *the* center of nightlife. The famous **Petronas Twin Towers** stand in the northeast part of the city, situated along **Jl. Ampang,** which is also home to many foreign embassies.

PIRATES! Very few of them wear eye-patches, walk on peg-legs, or have parrots named Polly, but pirates aren't just relics of dusty fantasy novels and history books. In Southeast Asia, maritime piracy is alive and kicking. In the late 1980s, when Vietnamese refugees were being repatriated, the Gulf of Thailand was particularly dangerous. Pirates, mostly Thai fishermen, attacked refugee boats and sometimes raped and murdered the passengers and kidnapped young children to sell into prostitution. Piracy in the gulf dissipated as the flow of refugees slowed. Since the 1990s, the Straits of Melaka and Singapore have become the major trouble spot. Pirates here are more sophisticated than those in Thailand. Often, they are professionals with links to organized crime and drug smuggling. They tend to target international shipping boats, which they approach with speedboats and board via grappling hooks. Some steal the ships (called "phantom ship" operations). Most tie up or kill the crew, take the money on board, then depart. Piracy is, of course, nothing new to these parts. Pirates based in the Sulu Islands and Sulawesi struck fear in the hearts of European sailors until well into the 19th century. In fact, the phrase "boogie man" comes from the Bugis, among the most dreaded sea raiders (see **Indonesia: Demographics,** p. 98). In 1992, the International Maritime Bureau established the Regional Piracy Center (RPC) in Kuala Lumpur, which coordinates the maritime law enforcement efforts of Singapore, Malaysia, and Indonesia, tracks boats in the area, and warns shippers of possible attacks. The RPC documented 229 pirate attacks in 1997, and while its efforts have successfully decreased the number of attacks in target areas like the Straits of Singapore, piracy may merely have moved offshore to the South China Sea or other channels along the vast Indonesian coast.

LOCAL TRANSPORTATION

Buses: The three local bus companies are **Intrakota, Metro,** and **Cityliner.** Fares vary by distance (RM0.70-2). Match your destination with route maps posted at bus stops and the signs visible through the front windows and ask the bus driver for the fare. Bring exact fare; change won't be provided and bills are not accepted. There are three major bus stations around town: **Klang Bus Station** (close to Central Market on Jl. Cheng Lock) has buses heading south of Kuala Lumpur, including **Petaling Jaya** and **Shah Alam; Bangkok Bank** has buses to the north **Batu Caves; Kota Raya Shopping Complex** has buses to the **Bangsar** and **Petaling Jaya** areas.

Trains: Light Rail Transit System (LRT) is Kuala Lumpur's new intra-city elevated train. **Star** has two lines, running from Sentul Timur to Ampang and Sri Petaling stations. (**Masjid Jamek** is also the only train station where the **LRT Putra** and **Star** lines connect.) **PUTRA** stops at the Petronas Twin Towers (KLCC), Chinatown (Pasar Seni), and Bangsar Baru (Bangsar), and is the line most commonly used by tourists. Trains operate M-Sa 6am-11:30pm, Su and public holidays 8am-11pm, at 5-15min. intervals. Fares RM0.75-3.60. Stored value tickets (RM20 minimum) save at least 5% on every ride. Obtain a free transit system map from a STAR or PUTRA station or the tourist office.

Taxis: Most taxis are metered. Do insist that the driver turn on his meter, as it will usually cost less than a fixed price. Bargaining with taxi drivers is mostly futile. At night, however, most cabs will have set prices. Metered cabs start at RM2 and increase by RM0.10 per 200m. Surcharges apply for trips between midnight and 6am (50%), for luggage in the trunk (RM1), and for booking by phone (RM1). To call a cab, try **Kuala Lumpur Taxi Driver's Association** (☎9221 4241), **Comfort Radio Taxi** (☎5633 0507), **City Line Cab** (☎9222 2828), or **Supercab** (☎7875 7333). All are open **24hr.**

Rentals: The convoluted layout of Kuala Lumpur is a good reason to take public transport, but if you need your own wheels, try **Avis** (☎2141 7144), **Budget** (☎2142 4693), or **Hertz** (☎2148 6433). A local or international driver's license is required.

PRACTICAL INFORMATION

TOURIST AND FINANCIAL SERVICES

Tourist Offices: Malaysian Tourism Center (MTC), 109 Jl. Ampang (☎2164 3929), after the intersection with Jl. Sultan Ismail opposite the Renaissance Hotel. Walk through the parking lot and into the white building with the red roof. A 5min. walk from Kampung Baru PUTRA station. Has a tourist police counter (24hr. ☎2163 3657), moneychanger, **ATM,** and Internet access to the tourism web site. Also offers a traditional Malaysian dance and music show (45min.; Tu, Th, Sa-Su 3pm; RM5, free for children). **Open 24hr. Tourism Malaysia,** Putra World Trade Center, level 2, 45 Jl. Tun Ismail (☎4041 1295). Take the STAR LRT to PWTC. Open M-Sa 9am-6pm. **Tourist Information Center,** at the airport, Satellite Bldg. Open daily 9am-9pm.

Tours: MSL Travel, 66 Jl. Putra (☎4042 4722), off Jl. Raja Laut, next to the Grand Central Hotel. 5min. walk from STAR PWTC station. Offers Eurotrain Explorer Pass for unlimited travel on KTM-Malayan Railway (1 week US$38, 21 days US$60) or SRT Railway of Thailand (1 week US$32, 21 days US$48). Offers airfare discounts (up to 50%) for students. Also issues **International Student Identity Cards (ISIC)** and **Teacher's Identity Cards** (RM20 including photo), as well as **Youth Travel Cards** (RM15 with photo). Open M-F 9am-5pm, Sa 9am-1pm. **Ecstasy Travel,** 28-3 Jl. 14/48A Sentul Raya, 3rd fl. (☎4042 5688; www.aseanbiz.com/my/ecstasy), off Jl. Sentul. Conducts English tours of the city, countryside, and destinations farther afield. Buses pick up at major hotels around the city. Call for latest prices and to book a tour.

Immigration Offices: Pusat Bandar Daman Sara (☎2095 5077), on Jl. Damai Selatan, near the Road Transport Dept. Block I. Same-day visa extensions RM50 per month. Open M-F 7:30am-4pm, 2nd and 4th Sa of every month 7:30am-1:15pm.

Embassies: Australia, 6 Jl. Yap Kwan Seng (☎2146 5555). Open M-F 8:30am-12:30pm and 1:30-4:30pm. **Brunei,** MBF Plaza, 172 Jl. Ampang (☎2161 2800). **Canada,** 17th fl., Menara Tan and Tan, 207 Jl. Tun Razak (☎2718 3333). Open M-Th 8am-4:30pm, F 8am-1:30pm. **Indonesia,** 233 Jl. Tun Razak (☎2145 2011). Open M-Th 8:30am-1pm and 2-4:30pm, F 8:30am-1:30pm and 2:30-4:30pm. **Ireland,** The Amp Walk, 218 Jl. Ampang, 50450 Kuala Lumpur (☎2161 2963). **Laos,** 12A Persiaran Madge, off Ampang Hilir (☎4251 1118). Open M-F 8:30am-noon and 2-5pm. **Myanmar,** 5 Taman U Thant Satu. Visas RM70; 3-day processing. Open M-F 9am-1pm. **New Zealand,** 21st fl. Menara IMC, 8 Jl. Sultan Ismail (☎2078 2533). Open M-F 8am-12:30pm and 1:30-4:30pm. **Singapore,** 209 Jl. Tun Razak (☎2161 6277). Open M-F 8:30am-5pm. **South Africa,** 12 Lorong Titiwangsa, Taman Tasik Titiwangsa (☎4024 4456). Open M-Th 8am-12:30pm, F 8am-1:15pm. **Thailand,** 206 Jl. Ampang (☎2148 8222). Open M-F 9:30am-5pm; consul open M-F 9am-12:30pm. **UK,** 185 Jl. Ampang (☎2170 2200). Open M-F 8am-12:30pm and 1:30-4:30pm. **US,** 376 Jl. Tun Razak (☎2168 5000). Open M-F 7:45am–4:30pm. **Vietnam,** 4 Persiaran Stonor (☎2148 4036). Open M-F 9am-noon and 2-4:30pm, Sa 9am-noon.

Currency Exchange: Moneychangers are on Jl. Pudu, directly across from Puduraya Bus Station, as well as in Chinatown along Jl. Tun H.S. Lee. Banks are ubiquitous–especially along Jl. Hang Kasturi, near Central Market. **MayBank,** 100 Jl. Tun Perak (☎2070 8833), close to Puduraya Station, opposite Metrojaya. Traveler's check fee RM5 plus RM0.20 per check. Open M-F 9:30am-4pm, Sa 9:30-11:30am. **24hr. ATMs.** Most ATMs accept Cirrus/MC/PLUS/V.

American Express: 18th fl. of Weld Building on corner of Raja Chulan and Jl. P. Ramlee (☎2050 0000). Mail-holding services offered. Open M-F 9am-5pm.

LOCAL SERVICES

Luggage Storage: Yakin Enterprise (☎2070 0052), on the 1st fl. toward the back of Puduraya Bus Station. RM2 per bag per day. Open daily 8am 11pm. **Matang Lockers** (☎013 343 7939), on the 2nd fl. of KL Sentral. Small bag RM3 per day, large bag RM5 per day. Open daily 7am-10:30pm.

English-Language Resources: MPH Bookstores has branches at 2 Jl. Telawi, Bangsar Baru (☎2282 7300), and the ground fl. of Mid Valley Megamall (☎2938 3812). Open daily 10am-10pm. **Kinokuniya,** 4th fl., Suria KLCC (☎2164 8133). Open daily 10am-9:30pm. Both bookstores have a wide selection of books and magazines.

Lesbian, Gay, Bisexual Organizations: Pink Triangle, 1st fl., 7C-2 Jl. Ipoh Kecil (☎4044 4611), off Jl. Raja Laut. Counseling hotline (☎4044 9622) open M-F 7:30am-9:30pm. Devoted to issues related to HIV/AIDS and sexuality. Drop-in center for drug users (M-F 10am-5pm) provides food and clinical care. Staff provides info about LGBT venues in Kuala Lumpur. Call for directions. Open M-F 9am-6pm.

EMERGENCY AND COMMUNICATIONS

Emergency: ☎999. **Fire:** ☎994.

Tourist Police: ☎2146 0522. Main office at corner of Jl. Pudu and Jl. Hang Tuah. Branch office at Puduraya Bus Terminal (☎2078 9496). **Open 24hr.**

Police: ☎2146 0522. Kuala Lumpur Police HQ, 13th fl., Jl. Hang Tuah.

Pharmacies: All around Jl. Sultan/Cheng Lock. **Guardian Pharmacy,** 123 Jl. Sultan (☎2031 4013), on the corner with Jl. Cheng Lock. Open daily 10am-10pm.

Medical Services: Kuala Lumpur General Hospital (☎2692 1044), in city's north end, on Jl. Pahang near Grand Seasons Hotel. **City Medical Center,** 415-427 Jl. Pudu (☎9221 1255), is privately run. Most doctors speak English.

Telephones: Pusat Telekom (☎2079 6025), Jl. Raja Chulan. **Perkhidmantan Biro,** at the corner of Jl. Rajah Chulan and Jl. Bukit Mahkamah. Open daily 8:30am-9pm. HCD phones, fax. Across from Puduraya Bus Terminal, **Internet Express IT Center,** 10 Jl. Pudu, 2nd fl. (☎2070 7377), has **IDD.** RM2.30-6 per min. **Open 24hr. Assisted International Calls:** ☎108. **Directory Assistance:** ☎103.

Internet Access: Internet Express IT Center, 10 Jl. Pudu, 1st fl. (☎2070 7377), across from the Puduraya Bus Terminal. RM3 per 30min., RM4 per hr., RM1 per additional 15min. Guests of Pudu Hostel (see **Accommodations,** below) receive discounts (RM3 per hr.). Overnight special RM15 10pm-6am. **Open 24hr. Master World Surfnet Cafe,** 23 Jl. Petaling, mezz. (☎2026 8618). RM2 per 15min., RM4 per 30min., RM5 per 45min., RM6 per hr. Open daily 9am-11pm.

Post Offices: GPO, 9 Jl. Sultan Hishamuddin, Dayabumi Complex (☎2274 1122). *Poste Restante.* Open M-Sa 8:30am-6pm. Closed 1st Sa of each month and public holidays. **Pos 2020** on the ground fl. is usually sufficient. **Postal code:** 50670.

ACCOMMODATIONS

CHINATOWN AREA

Pudu Hostel, 10 Jl. Pudu, 3rd fl. (☎2078 9600), opposite Puduraya Bus Terminal; look for the tall pink building. Large A/C lounge with Western food, beer, music, and movies. Convenient, comfortable, and clean rooms with fans, lockers, and hot common showers. Laundry. Reception 24hr. 4-bed dorms RM12, 2-bed dorms RM20; singles RM30; doubles RM40; triples RM40. ❶

MALAYSIA

Anuja Backpackers Inn, 28 Jl. Pudu (☎2026 6479), across the street from Puduraya Bus Terminal. Hang out on the rooftop beer garden. Cafe next door. Internet (RM2 per hr. 9am-noon and 8-11pm, RM2.50 per hr. noon-8pm). Safe at reception. Hot common showers. Laundry. Dorms with A/C RM10; singles and doubles RM10-30, with A/C RM30-40; triples RM38/RM50. ❶

Backpackers Traveler's Inn, 60 Jl. Sultan (☎2078 2473/2032 1855), 1½ blocks from Jl. Cheng Lock on the right; look for a red sign. Rooftop bar encourages partiers. Books bus tickets. Owner runs great half-day tours. Bakery downstairs. Lockers RM1. Laundry RM9. Dorms with A/C RM10; singles and doubles RM22-30, with A/C RM28-60. ❶

Wheelers Guest House, 131-133 Jl. Tun H.S. Lee (☎2070 1386), off Jl. Cheng Lock, on the right. Manager provides excellent travel advice. Laundry RM9. Dorms with A/C RM10; singles and doubles RM25, with A/C RM40, with A/C and private bath RM60; triples RM30, with A/C and private bath RM70; quads with A/C RM45. ❶

Katari Hotel, 38 Jl. Pudu (☎2031 7777; www.katari.com.my), directly opposite the Puduraya Bus Terminal. New, clean facilities. All rooms with TV and Astro Channel. Laundry and dry cleaning. Safety deposit boxes. Breakfast included. Reception 24hr. Doubles RM138-158; family rooms RM264.50 including tax and service charge. ❺

Le Village Guest House, 99 Jl. Tun H.S. Lee (☎013 355 0235). Clean and new. Cozy common area but lighting is dim. Colorfully painted pastel interior. Doubles, triples, and quads all for RM15 per person. ❷

KL SENTRAL

Backpackers' Lodge, 84 Jl. Tun Sambanthan (☎2272 3736), opposite KL Sentral. Convenient place to stay for a night, but the 20-person dorms are quite intimidating. Common showers only. Dorms RM15; singles and doubles RM40; triples RM45. ❷

YMCA Hostel, 95 Jl. Padang Belia (☎2274 1439), a 5min. walk from KL Sentral/LRT. Great facilities, comfortable rooms. Unmarried couples may not share a room. Tennis court. Hot showers. Laundry next door. Singles RM38, with A/C and private bath RM68; doubles RM50/RM78; triples RM65/RM90; quads RM75. MC/V. ❸

Kuala Lumpur International Youth Hostel (HI), 21 Jl. Kampung Attap (☎2273 6870; myha@pd.jaring.my). Turn off Jl. Attaponto Jin Manau. Clean, single-sex baths and dorms. Midnight lockout. Bookings advisable May-Aug. and Nov.-Dec. HI cards for foreigners RM30 (1 yr. membership). Dorms RM25, members RM20. MC/V. ❸

MALAYSIA

FARTHER AFIELD

Ben Soo Homestay & Travelers Service, 61B Jl. Tiong Nam, 2nd fl. (☎2691 8096; bensoohome@yahoo.com), is highly recommended. Travel tips by Ben Soo, ex-travel agent and taxi driver extraordinaire. Call ahead to reserve and arrange pick-up. Breakfast included. Singles with fan or A/C RM30; doubles with fan RM34, with A/C RM42. ❸

Wira Hotel, 123 Jl. Thamboosamy (☎4042 3333; www.wirahotel.com.my), off Jl. Putra near the PWTC LRT Station. Spacious rooms with A/C, TV, and private hot showers. Breakfast included. Laundry. Safe deposit. Singles RM85-95; doubles RM95-105; family rooms RM115. Discounts for ISIC holders, singles and doubles RM80-90. ❺

FOOD

Head to **Chinatown** for delectable delights around the clock. **Jl. Sultan** and **Jl. Hang Lekir** host an open-air carnival of steamboat restaurants, *satay* sellers, and exotic fruit juice vendors, while the **Chinatown night market** bustles on along Jl. Petaling. **Little India,** north of Chinatown around **Jl. Masjid India,** tantalizes travelers with a blend of South Indian and Malay flavors.

A DRINKING CLUB WITH A RUNNING PROBLEM In 1938, a small group of British expats founded the Hash House Harriers in Kuala Lumpur. These first inspired "Hashers," named for the unappetizing grub at the Selangor Club, married the traditional game of Paper Chase with ample alcohol. The group leader, or "hare," would blaze a tangled trail across challenging terrain, leaving behind scraps of paper and the occasional case of beer for his friends, the "hounds," to pick up. The sport was interrupted by the Japanese invasion of Malaysia during WWII, though afterward one of the Hashers was able to finagle reparation payments for some damaged mugs. During the Emergency of 1948, some hashers followed a paper path straight past a group of dangerous bandits, rushed to inform the police, and received enough bounty to buy two new cars. In the 60s, Hash House chapters sprouted up throughout Malaysia, spread to Singapore and Brunei, engulfed the rest of Southeast Asia, and subsequently exploded to over 1300 confirmed Hashes worldwide, sending their co-ed constituents over 6-8km courses with a tipsy cry of "On-on!" Though generally a safer English-style sport than, say, ferret-legging, at least one death has occurred in the history of Southeast Asian Hashing: in Myanmar, one hapless hound toppled from a waterfall. A mega-Hash celebrating the 60th anniversary of the first Hash was held in KL in October 1998. For a more trenchant and nuanced perspective on the original HHH, see www.mtiz.com/kl_hhh/home/index.html; for chapter contacts throughout the globe, see www.gthhh.com. Tally-ho and bottoms up!

Restoran Nam Heong, 56 Jl. Sultan (☎2078 5879), off Jl. Cheng Lock, next to the Backpackers Traveler's Inn, has an almost historic reputation for having the most authentic chicken rice in town (it sells out by midafternoon!). Hainanese chicken rice with cucumbers RM3.60. Kampung chicken rice RM6.70. Open daily 10am-3:30pm. ❷

Restoran Shukran, at the traffic circle off Jl. Pudu, next to Metrojaya Shopping Complex. Buzzing with activity around the clock. *Roti canai* RM0.80. Buffet of white rice and curried meats RM3-5. Great spot for city-watching at any time of the day. **Open 24hr.** ❷

Old China Cafe, 11 Jl. Balai Polis (☎2072 5915), off Jl. Petaling, preserves the feel of early 20th-century Chinese social life and serves delicious Melakan-style *nyonya* and Portuguese fare. The interior is quite dim, but the special *pie-tee* top-hat appetizers (RM3.90) and *Nyona laksa* (RM7.90) are sure to please. Expect to spend RM15-40 for a full meal. Wines available RM48-90 per bottle. Prices subject to tax and service charge. Open daily 11am-11pm. MC/V. ❹

Lakshmi Vilas, 57 Lh. Ampang (☎2078 3523), near Masjid Jamek LRT Station. Best vegetarian and South Indian cuisine in town. *Dosai* RM1; *lassi* RM2.50; set vegetarian meals RM5.50-6. *Biryani* RM6. Open daily 7:30am-8:30pm. ❷

Coliseum Cafe, 98-100 Jl. Tuanku Abdul Rahman, 3 blocks from the intersection with Jl. Perak. Old leather chairs and teak interior retain a colonial ambience. Roast chicken, veggies, and chips RM8.50; sirloin steak RM33.90. Beer RM7.50-8.50. Prices subject to tax and service charge. Open daily 10am-10pm. AmEx/MC/V. ❹

Thai Kitchen, on the mezzanine level in the Central Market. Set meals include coffee and Thai dessert for RM9.50 2:30-6:30pm. Pineapple rice RM5; *tom yum* soup RM14-23. Open daily 11:30am-9:30pm. ❹

Sakura Cafe and Cuisine, 163-169 Jl. Imbi, off Jl. Sultan Ismail. Where Malays come when they long for authentic *nyonya* food. Try the house special, *nasi lemak* (RM14.50). They also serve sirloin steak (RM34). *Chendol* (shaved ice topped with coconut syrup and colorful jellies) RM4.50. Open daily 10am-2am. ❹

SIGHTS

MERDEKA SQUARE (FREEDOM SQUARE)

Kuala Lumpur's most architecturally rich area, this expansive square was once a colonial cricket field, the site of Malaysia's independence ceremonies in 1957, and is now home to the tallest flagpole in Asia.

SULTAN ABDUL SAMAD BUILDING. Adorned with shiny copper domes and a 40m high clock tower, this stately Moorish-inspired building stretches along the eastern side of Merdeka Square. Built in 1897, it now serves as the High Court. Visitors may admire the exterior, but are not allowed inside.

NATIONAL HISTORY MUSEUM. Originally Kuala Lumpur's first bank and later used as a telecommunication base during the Japanese occupation, the museum now exhibits artifacts dating from the prehistoric period to the present. The displays are quite text-heavy and informative, though rather unexciting. *(29 Jl. Raja. ☎2694 4590. Near the southeastern edge of Merdeka Square. Open daily 9am-6pm. Free.)*

MASJID JAMEK. This mosque, built in 1909 by the same architect who designed the railway station, stands where the first settlers landed in KL. Its full splendor is best viewed from along the banks of the Kelang and Gombak Rivers. *(Follow Jl. Hang Kasturi north. Proper attire is required: long pants for everyone, long sleeves and head shawl for women. Open Sa-Th 8:30am-12:30pm and 2:30-4pm, F 8:30-11am and 2:30-4pm. Free.)*

SOUTH OF MERDEKA

NATIONAL MOSQUE (MASJID NEGARA). This white-marble mosque contrasts starkly with the Masjid Jamek across the river. Its most notable features are a 73m high minaret from which the faithful are called to prayer and a multi-fold, umbrella-like roof. The upper deck houses the main prayer hall and a reflecting pool. Visitors may borrow a robe (*jubah*) or a head scarf (*tudong*, for women) and explore. *(Enter at the intersection of Jl. Sultan Hishamuddin and Jl. Perdana. Open Sa-Th 9am-noon, 3-4pm, and 5:30-6:30pm, F 3-4 pm and 5:30-6:30pm. Free.)*

ISLAMIC ARTS MUSEUM. The building itself is testament to the elegant beauty of Islamic architecture. Inside are exhibits on the evolution of mosque architecture, complete with models of mosques from throughout Asia. Arab pottery, coins, textiles, and a collection of Qur'ans are also on display. *(On Jl. Lembah Perdana, across from the National Mosque carpark. ☎2274 2020. Open Tu-Su 10am-6pm. RM8, students RM4.)*

KUALA LUMPUR OLD RAILWAY STATION. Built by a British architect in 1900, this station is a collection of domes, minarets, and archways that house everything from a tourist office to a hostel. It is well worth a visit to admire Moorish architectural influences. KTM Komuter trains stop here. *(On Jl. Sultan Hishamuddin. Open 24hr.)*

NATIONAL MUSEUM. This museum houses the usual weapons, royal paraphernalia, and Orang Asli crafts and artifacts. Most interesting are the shadow puppet display and the natural history section, which features stuffed wildlife, including the largest crocodile ever caught. *(On Jl. Sultan Hishamuddin, 500m past the Kuala Lumpur Visitors Center. ☎2282 6255. Open daily 9am-6pm. RM2, children and senior citizens RM1.)*

LAKE GARDENS. Next to the National Museum, a pedestrian overpass leads to the Lake Gardens—91.6 hectares of greenery. The complex draws visitors with a **planetarium, orchid and hibiscus garden,** and **sculpture garden.** The most popular area is the **Taman Burung,** an outdoor aviary housing tropical birds (RM5). In the northern section of the garden, the **National Monument** is dedicated to Malaysians who died during the two World Wars and the Emergency of 1948-1960. Many people come here to jog or run, as the park provides a haven from KL's mad traffic. Rowboats, paddleboats, and surf bikes can be rented to cruise the lake. (Rowboats RM3 per hr., paddleboats RM6 per hr., surf bikes RM3 per 30min. Boathouse open M-Th 9am-12:30pm and 2-5:30pm, F 9-11:30am and 2:45-5:30pm, Sa-Su 8am-noon and 2-5:30pm) Musicians usually perform at the band shell on Sundays around 5:30pm. *(☎2698 3253. Gardens open daily 9am-5pm.)*

NEAR CHINATOWN

SRI MAHA MARIAMMAN TEMPLE. In the heart of Chinatown, this temple is the center of Kuala Lumpur's Hindu community and is known as "The Mother Temple." According to Hindu belief, Mariamman, the Mother Goddess, is wife of Lord Shiva and mother to Murga, the deity to whom the annual **Thaipusam Festival** is dedicated. The prize of the 124-year-old temple is a silver chariot. *(163 Jl. Tun H.S. Lee. From the Central Market, turn left on Jl. Cheng Lock and then right on Jl. Tun H.S. Lee. Daily* pooja *at 7:30am, 12:30, 5:30pm. Open daily until 9pm.)*

KUAN TI TEMPLE. This 114-year-old Chinese temple was restored in 1994 by the Kwong Siew Association. The temple's rooftop architecture is particularly striking. *(168 Jl. Tun H.S. Lee, across the street from Sri Maha Mariamman Temple. Incense RM1.)*

SIN SZE YA TEMPLE. Tucked in a back alley, this Chinese temple was founded in 1864—before the existence of a "Chinatown." Its patron deities are Sin Sze Ya and Si Sze Ya, who helped Kapitan Yap Ah Loy to defeat the enemies and defend Kuala Lumpur during the Civil War (1870-1873). Their two sedan chairs flank the entrance. *(113A Jl. Tun H.S. Lee. Walk through the inconspicuous gateway to the temple.)*

GANESHA TEMPLE. Thirty-two figures of the elephant-head god decorate the upper walls inside this Hindu temple. Devotees crack coconuts before entering—symbolic of purging one's sins. *(Cross Jl. Pudu from the Puduraya Bus Terminal and walk left. Turn right at 7-Eleven; the temple is near the top of the hill. Open daily 7am-9pm.)*

OTHER SIGHTS

Along with Asia's tallest flagpole, Kuala Lumpur boasts two of the tallest buildings in the world. The 88-story **Petronas Twin Towers,** in the northeast part of the city, rank as the loftiest twin towers and the fourth-tallest buildings in the world (452m). The lowest floors hold the largest mall in the country and show off Malay arts and crafts next to fancy boutiques like Escada and DKNY. Tourists are permitted to go as far as the Sky Bridge. *(Take the PUTRA LRT to KLCC. Mall open daily 10am-10pm. Sky Bridge open Tu-Su 9:30am-5:15pm. ☎2058 8181. 1300 free tickets are issued daily; the queue begins forming at 8:30am and it is recommended to get in line by 10am.)* The **Menara Kuala Lumpur,** or **KL Tower** as it is commonly called, offers a spectacular view of the city. There is a revolving restaurant at the top. *(Walk or take a taxi. ☎2020 5448. Open daily 9am-10pm. RM15, children RM9.)* The **National Art Gallery (Balai Seni Lukis Negara)** houses a diverse collection of Malaysian artwork, a sculpture garden, and a photography studio. Call ahead for updates on special contemporary art exhibitions. *(On Jl. Temerloh, off Jl. Tun Razak. ☎4025 4980. Open daily 10am-6pm. Free.)*

MARKETS

Chinatown, south of Jl. Cheng Lock and east of the Kelang River, is the liveliest place in KL. At dusk, central Jl. Petaling becomes a **pasar malam (night market).** Food stalls and open-air restaurants roll their tables onto Jl. Hang Lekir and Jl. Sultan, as do traders selling pirated movies and CDs, designer watches, handbags, and clothing. Audio CDs RM5, VCDs RM10 for 3. For other items, bargaining is the name of the game.

Central Market, on Jl. Hang Kasturi, off Jl. Cheng Lock, is an arts and crafts haven with over 150 shops selling *batik* dresses, Muslim pajamas, intricate silver jewelry, and Malay kites and masks. Free cultural performances are held here some evenings (☎2274 6542 for performance dates and times). Sarongs RM17; *kaftans* RM30; kites RM39; portraits RM50, color RM120. Open daily 10am-10pm.

Night Markets set up in different locations each night of the week. **Saturdays:** on Jl. Tuanku Abdul Rahman between Jl. Tun Perak and Jl. Dang Wangi (5-10pm); **Mondays:** section 1 in Wangsa Maju, northeast of town toward the zoo; **Tuesdays:** Seri Petaling, south toward Serembau; **Thursdays:** Jl. Kaskas in Taman Cheras; and **Fridays:** Taman Melati Gombak. The markets are difficult to reach. Ask your guest house for directions.

NIGHTLIFE

The mix of yuppies, expatriates, and rich teens means that Kuala Lumpur has many nightlife options. The life span of clubs here is typically six to 12 months. There is also a growing interest in theater and dance, and major hotels host performances. For information, call **MTC** (☎2164 3929) or **Istana Budaya** (☎4025 2525).

The Beach Club Cafe, 97 Jl. P. Ramlee (☎2166 9919), off Jl. Sultan Ismail. All-ages crowd loosens their collars to kick back under a large "hut," enjoying brick-oven pizza outside or bopping around the bar's shark tank. Try the beach party margaritas on Th, when ladies get in for free. Happy hour noon-9pm, beers RM8. Beers RM14.50. "Cover" is a first drink charge: Su-Th RM18, F-Sa RM25. Open daily noon-3am.

Orange, 1 Jl. Kia Peng (☎2141 4929). Best reached by taxi. The young, local crowd dances to the latest hip hop tunes. No cover for ladies W-Th, Sa. Cover W-Th RM20, F-Sa RM25 with drink coupons. Beer RM8. Open W-Sa 7pm-3 or 4am.

Finnegan's Irish Pub, 6 Jl. Telawi 5 (☎2284 9024), in Bangsar Baru. This Official English Premier League Bar pumps the best retro tunes and serves select beers like Kilkenny and Cream Ale. Ladies' night Th and Sa 9pm-2am, with selected drinks on the house. Beer RM18 per pint. Happy hour 5-8pm. Open Tu-Th 5pm-3am, Su-M 5pm-2am.

Modesto's, 12A Telawi 3 (☎2284 2445), in Bangsar Baru. A jeans-and-T-shirt pub with billiards, foosball, and good pizzas and pasta (RM18-25). Chill atmosphere with pop music and hip hop. Happy hour M-Sa 5-10pm and all night Su, beer RM6.50. Other times beer RM11.50. Ladies' night Tu and Th. Open Su-Th 5pm-2am, F-Sa 5pm-3am.

Ronny Q's, 32 Jl. Telawi 2 (☎2282 0722), in Bangsar Baru. A laid-back pub with TVs in every corner. Less dancing, more drinking and talking. Older crowd. Try the Goalkeeper's Delight RM11.50. Cheap beer RM9 a pint. Happy hour M-Sa 5:30-9pm and all night Su, half-price drinks. Open Su-Th 5pm-1:30am, F-Sa 5pm-2:30am.

Echo, 21 Jl. Telawi 3 (☎2284 3022), in Bangsar Baru. Each night of the week has a different sound scene: M-Tu happy hour all night with smooth acid jazz, W is ladies' night upstairs with hip hop, Th the bar is host to British net radio, spinning the latest garage, F-Sa deep house, and chill-out music on Su with happy hour all night. Beer RM12.50, jugs RM48. Open daily 5pm-3am.

Blue Boy, 54 Jl. Sultan Ismail (☎2142 1067), in a small alley off Jl. Sultan Ismail across from the 7-Eleven, behind the Regent Hotel. Mixed crowd. Karaoke 8:30-11pm and disco after 11pm with house music. Paperdolls (drag show) on a small stage Th-Su around 1:30am. Cover RM13 includes draft beer, or RM7 includes soft drink. Alcoholic drinks RM16. Open daily 8:30pm-3am.

DAYTRIPS FROM KUALA LUMPUR

BATU CAVES. The most famous attractions near KL are the Batu Caves. In January and February, hundreds of Hindu devotees from around the world descend here for the annual **Thaipusam Festival,** armed with hooks and needles with which to pierce their skin in a ritual of penance. After checking out the Hindu temple at the base, visitors can climb 272 steps to the main cave temple, where Thaipusam participants remove the *kavadis* (shrines) that are attached to the hooks and needles. A pile of last year's *kavadis* lies to the left of the final staircase inside the cave; they are removed every January or February in preparation for a new set. *(Take Intrakota bus #11D 45min. from Bangkok Bank or Central Market. ☎6189 6284. Open daily 7:30am-midnight. Donations of RM4 or more appreciated.)*

KUALA SELANGOR. Fireflies are attracted to the berembang trees that flank both sides of the river in Kampung Kuantan. Watch thousands of them flash in unison on a nocturnal boat tour along the Selangor River. The **Nature Park,** covering over 200 hectares and including a bird sanctuary, is another popular destination within Kuala Selangor. *(From Puduraya Bus Station, take Selangor Omni Bus #141 from Platform 23 (leaves every hr.). Returning to Kuala Lumpur requires chartering a taxi for RM60. Boat tours (☎3289 1439) leave from the Kampung Kuantan jetty daily 7:30-11pm, RM10. Ferries from Bukit Belimbing RM2. Seafood restaurant on the premises.)*

ROYAL SELANGOR PEWTER FACTORY. As befits the makers of the world's most famous pewter goods, this factory also has the world's largest pewter tankard. *(4 Jl. Usahawan Enam, Setapak Jaya. Take bus W12 or Intrakota #10 from the Lebuh Ampang bus stand or Intrakota #49D (30-45min.; RM0.70, with A/C RM0.90) from Central Market. ☎4022 1000. Open M-F 8:30am-4:45pm, Sa-Su 9am-4pm.)*

ORANG ASLI MUSEUM. This fascinating museum features exhibits relating to Malaysia's indigenous people. *(Take Cityliner bus #174A 45min. from Lebuh Ampang (RM2). ☎6189 2122. Open Su-Th 9am-5pm. Free.)*

NATIONAL ZOO AND AQUARIUM. This complex is home to 500 species of animals and fish. *(Intrakota bus #170 or 17 from Lh. Ampang (45min., RM1.60). ☎4108 3422. Open daily 9am-5pm. Weekdays RM7, children RM3; weekends RM9, children RM5.)*

SUNWAY LAGOON. This water theme park promises wet (and wild) fun, with giant waterslides, speed slides, twister slides, a waterfall garden, and a wave pool. *(Take bus #10 (RM1.40) from in front of Hotel Impiana at corner of Jl. Sultan and Jl. Cheng Lock. ☎5635 6000. Open M, W-Th noon-9pm, F noon-10:30pm. RM38, children RM25.)*

MELAKA ☎06

Founded around 1400 by the exiled Sumatran prince Paremaswara, Melaka succumbed to the Portuguese in 1511. The Dutch and British soon took over, dominating the city for the next four centuries. The imperial era ended when Malaysia's first Prime Minister, Tunku Abdul Rahman, proclaimed independence at Padang Pahlawan in the heart of Melaka. The many cultural layers of this historical city are best experienced by strolling through Chinatown, past the crimson hues of the Dutch square, and around the waterfront abodes of the Portuguese Settlement. Soak in Melaka's easygoing charm and let your taste buds sample *nyonya* food, an often spicy blend of Chinese and Malay cooking—full flavors that capture Melaka's rich heritage.

TRANSPORTATION

Trains: The nearest station is at **Tampin** (☎441 1034), 38km to the north. Take bus #26 from the local bus station (50min., every 15min. 6:30am-9pm, RM2.50) or take a taxi (45min.; shared RM10, charter RM40). Trains to: **KL,** where connecting trains go up the west coast to **Hat Yai** (2¼hr.; M-F 5am, 12:38, 7:54pm, Sa-Su 2:18am, 3:26pm; economy seat RM9, 2nd-class seat RM13-17, 2nd-class bunk RM20.50-23) and **Singapore** (express 5hr., regular 6½hr.; M-F 12:58, 9:34am, 4:04pm, Sa-Su 1:37pm; economy seat RM15, 2nd-class seat RM23-27, 2nd-class bunk RM30.50-33).

Buses: Express bus station, on Jl. Tun Ali. Long-distance buses run by private companies. Purchase tickets at any of the counters surrounding the station. Compare prices first, as they vary between companies. **Express Delima** (☎284 8908) goes to **KL** (2½hr.; every hr. 6am-7pm and 8:30am, 3:30pm; RM7.90) and **Singapore** via **Johor Bharu** (3hr.; every hr. 8am-6pm; RM13.80, to J.B. RM12.30). Several bus companies go to: **Alor Setar** (8hr.; 9am, 9pm; RM33-36); **Butterworth** (9hr., 6 per day, RM26-28); **Ipoh** (5hr., 5 per day, RM18-20); **Kangar** (10hr.; 9am, 9pm; RM36); **Kota Bharu** (11hr.; noon, 8pm; RM28-30); **Penang** (8hr., 4 per day, RM26-30); **Perlis** (10hr., 9am, RM38); **Seremban** (1½hr., every 30min. 7am-7pm, RM4.70); **Sungei Petani** (7hr.; 9am, 9pm; RM30-33); **Taiping** (6hr., 3 per day, RM20-28).

Taxis: Jl. Tun Ali (☎284 7163), down the street from the bus station. All cabs are shared by 4 passengers unless they are chartered. Shared cabs to: **Batu Pahet** (RM15, charter RM60); **Johor Bharu** (weekdays RM35, charter RM140; weekends RM40, charter RM160); **KL** (RM25, charter RM100); **Muar** (RM7.50, charter RM30); **Port Dickson** (RM17.50, charter RM70). These are the standard rates; bargaining will not result in lower fares. Weekend rates may be more (up to 30% higher).

Local Transportation: The town is compact enough to cover by foot, but take a break and hire a **trishaw** from Jl. Kota (RM25-30 per hr.). All local **buses** meet at the traffic circle in front of Hotel Equatorial. Bus #17 goes to the Portuguese Settlement (every 10min., RM0.50). Bus #19 heads for the zoo at Ayer Keroh (every 30min., RM1.70).

Bicycle Rentals: Muhibbah Enterprise (☎283 0631), on Jl. Munshi Abdullah in Intan Plaza Shopping Arcade. RM10 per day. Open daily 10am-6pm.

ORIENTATION AND PRACTICAL INFORMATION

The city sprawls on both sides of **Melaka River,** which winds its way southwest as it empties into the **Straits of Melaka.** The streets extending from **Lorong Hang Jebat** lead to the heart of **Chinatown.** Buddhist temples, art galleries, antique shops, and the Baba-Nyonya homes of **Old Melaka** run along **Jl. Tun Tan Cheng Lock, Jl. Hang Jebat (Jonkers Walk),** and **Jl. Tokong,** all of which are parallel to the southern coast. The bridge that extends from Jl. Hang Jebat leads to a cluster of many historical museums and sights, easily recognizable by the bright red **Christ Church** and the **Stadthuys.** South of the numerous sights and east of the **Mahkota Parade Mall** lies the gateway to backpacker heaven: **Jl. Merdeka. Taman Melaka Raya,** a series of side streets off Jl. Merdeka, offers some of the best values for budget accommodations in Malaysia. Farther east is the **Portuguese Settlement.**

Tourist Office: Melaka Tourist Information Center (☎281 4803), on Jl. Kota near bridge connecting Jl. Laksamana and Lorong Hang Jebat. Free maps. Open M-F 9am-5pm, Sa-Su 9am-4:30pm. Closed some public holidays. Sometimes closes for lunch.

Tours and Travel: The **Tourist Center** runs 45min. boat tours on Melaka River (RM8). Frequency depends on tide and demand. **NH Travel and Tours,** 209 Jl. Melaka Raya (☎281 4242), offers city tours (RM35, children RM25), plantation tours (RM40, children RM30), heritage tours (RM35, children RM25), Ayer Keroh/nature tours (RM35, children RM25), and night tours (RM55, children RM50). Open daily 9am-5pm.

Currency Exchange: MayBank, 6 Jl. Hang Tuah (☎282 2477), near the bus and taxi stations. Open M-F 9:30am-4pm, Sa 9:30-11am. Closed 1st and 3rd Sa of the month. **Branch** on 1 Jl. Melaka Raya off traffic circle. Open M-F 9am-4:30pm, Sa 9am-12:30pm. Currency exchange service stops 1hr. before closing. Both have **ATMs** (Cirrus/MC/V). **Bank Simpanan Nasional** in the Mahkota Parade Mall is open M-F 10am-5pm, Sa 10am-1pm.

English-Language Bookstore: MPH (☎283 3050), ground fl. of Mahkota Parade Mall. Open Su-Th 10:30am-9:45pm, F-Sa 10:30am-10:30pm.

Emergency: ☎999. **Fire:** ☎994.

Tourist Police: ☎285 4115. On the pedestrian mall section of Jl. Kota, opposite the Tourist Center. Open daily 8am-11pm.

Pharmacies: Guardian Pharmacy (☎282 9499), on the ground fl. of Mahkota Parade Mall. Open daily 10am-10pm.

Medical Services: Mahkota Medical Center, 3 Mahkota Melaka (☎281 4071), next to Mahkota Parade Mall. Private hospital with **24hr. emergency care.** Open M-F 9am-5pm, Sa 9am-2pm.

Telephones: Purchase **telekom cards** at any communications store, to use on the public card phones.

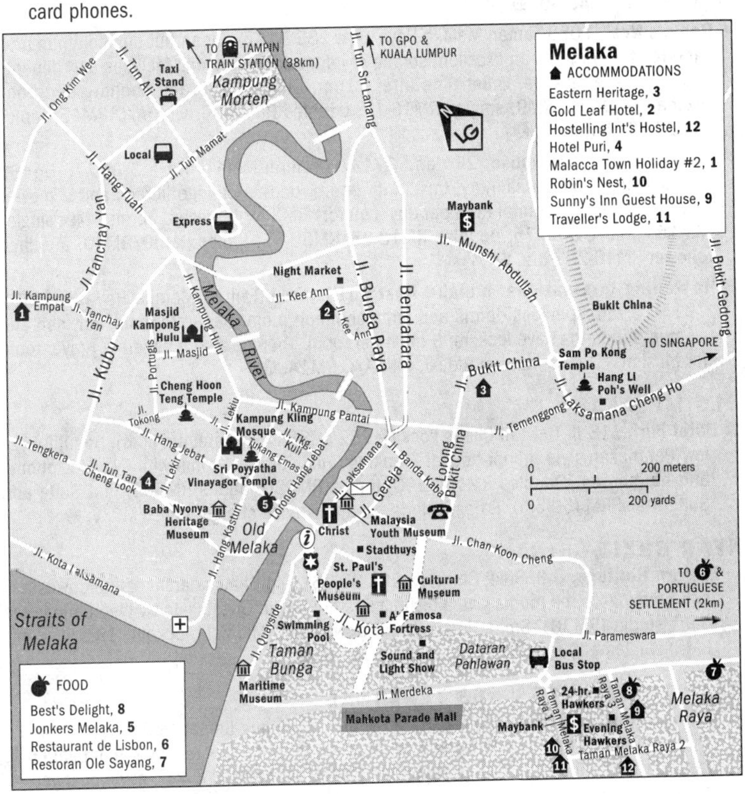

Internet Access: The **Cyber Cafe** inside **City Snooker** (☎012 608 1010), on the top fl. of Mahkota Parade Mall. RM4 per hr. Open daily 10am-2am.

Post Offices: GPO (☎283 3860), on Jl. Bukit Baru, 6km north of town center. Take bus #19 20min. from the local bus station. *Poste Restante.* Open M-Sa 8:30am-5pm. **Pos 2020** (**Postal code**: 75670. ☎284 8440), in the Youth Museum on Jl. Laksamana next to Christ Church and off south Jl. Merdaka. *Poste Restante.* Open M-Sa 8am-5pm. **Postal codes:** Old Melaka 75200; business district 75100.

ACCOMMODATIONS

Budget options cluster in the area known as **Taman Melaka Raya,** beyond Mahkota Parade Mall off Jl. Merdeka. Closer to the Express Bus Terminal, several inexpensive hotels are located near **Jl. Munshi Abdullah.** Taxis go to Taman Melaka Raya (15min., RM8) from the Express Bus Terminal.

TAMAN MELAKA RAYA

Traveller's Lodge, 214B Taman Melaka Raya 1 (☎226 5709). At night, travelers relax in the Japanese-style living room or on the new rooftop common area. Small kitchen, laundry, lockers, and a cafe downstairs. Hot showers. Clean rooms RM11; singles with fan RM16-18, with A/C RM34-35, with A/C and private bath RM43-50; doubles RM20-25/RM34-35/RM45-50. ❶

Robin's Nest, 205B Taman Melaka Raya 1 (☎282 9142). Clean but dim common area and rooms. Owner is an excellent source of information. Cooking facilities and dependable luggage storage. Quiet time after 11pm. Check-out 11am. Laundry and book exchange. Dorms RM9; singles RM16-17; doubles RM18-30, with A/C RM45; triples RM27-30/RM50-60. ❶

Sunny's Inn Guest House, 270 and 271A/B Taman Melaka Raya 3 (☎226 5446). Friendly staff, lounge, laundry, travel info board, book exchange library, and 2 movies every night. Bicycle rental RM5 per day. Laundry RM3 for 5 pieces. Dorms RM9; singles RM15, with A/C RM25; doubles RM18-25/RM30-35; triples RM30/RM40, attached shower RM10-20 extra. ❶

Hostelling International Melaka Hostel (HI), 341 Taman Melaka Raya 3 (☎282 7915). Clean, spacious dorms and large common room. Separate rooms for men and women. All dorms have lockers; 8 beds per room. There is also a separate prayer room for Muslims. Dorms with fan RM10, with A/C RM14. ❶

OLD MELAKA

Hotel Puri, 118 Jl. Tun Tan Cheng Lock (☎282 5588; www.hotelpuri.com). Beautiful yellow Peranakan-style manor house. Breakfast included. All rooms with TV, A/C, phone, and hot shower. Doubles RM110-200; triples RM230; quads RM305; Puri Suite and Suite Royal RM450-500. Rates include tax and service charge. AmEx/MC/V. ❺

NEAR BUKIT CHINA

Eastern Heritage, 8 Jl. Bukit China (☎283 30 26). Old Chinese architecture downstairs and paintings in the rooms give a distinct Eastern flavor. Guests can try their hand in the *batik* studio (RM30). Small dipping pool downstairs. Midnight lockout. 10-bed dorms RM8; singles with fan RM18; doubles RM20-30. ❶

NEAR THE EXPRESS BUS TERMINAL

Malacca Town Holiday Lodge #2, 52 A, B, C Jl. Kampung Empat (☎284 6905), in the Wine and Spirits building. Walking down Jl. Kubu from the bus terminal, turn right on Jl. Tanchay Yan and stay left on Jl. Kampung Empat as the road forks. They'll buzz you in.

Western breakfast, kitchen facilities, laundry (RM5). Singles with A/C RM25; doubles with fan RM25-30, with bath RM40; triples with bath RM50. ❸

Gold Leaf Hotel, 31 Jl. Kee Ann (☎283 6555), in the heart of Chinatown, near the night market. Caters to all types of travelers. All rooms have A/C and private bath. Doubles RM40-45; triples RM55; quads RM65. ❹

FOOD

Melaka offers a range of excellent eats, including *sate celup*, a hot-pot of spicy broth into which *sate* sticks are dipped. For a cheap meal, try the few **food stalls** ❶ in the alley between Jl. Melaka Raya 1 and 3. Hawker stalls at the corner of Jl. Melaka Raya 3 and Jl. Merdeka are open 24hr. Plenty of Chinese and Indian coffee shops line **Lorong Bukit China** and **Jl. Temenggong.**

Best's Delight, 268 Taman Melaka Raya 3 (☎281 1268). Traditional breakfast and lunch fare, such as Baba *nyonya*-style *nasi lemak* (coconut rice with fried egg, *sambal* sauce, peanuts, and dried fish; RM1.80). Coffee RM0.80-1.10. Open daily 7am-3pm. ❶

Restoran Ole Sayang, 198-199 Taman Melaka Raya (☎283 1966), on the right corner where the shops end on Jl. Merdeka. The best *nyonya* food in Melaka. *Ayam pong teh* (spicy chicken dish) RM7.50; *chap chai* (stir-fried vegetables) RM5-9. Open Th-Tu 11:30am-2:30pm and 6-9:30pm. ❸

Jonkers Melaka, 17 Jl. Hang Jebat. From the Tourist Information Center, cross the bridge and go down the road; it's 10 doors down on the left–through the gift shop. Soup and sandwich RM15; set special of 5 dishes with rice and dessert RM20; vegetarian platter RM17. Open daily 10am-5pm. ❹

Restaurant de Lisbon, Portuguese Sq. (☎284 8067). Home-cooked Portuguese fare. Baked fish with 7 spices RM20. If you dare, try the *keluak* chicken (RM10), cooked with strongly scented black *keluak* nuts. Open daily noon-midnight. ❶

SIGHTS

HISTORICAL DISTRICT

STADTHUYS ETHNOGRAPHICAL AND HISTORICAL MUSEUMS. The Stadthuys, a dark pink residence built by the Dutch in the mid-1600s for the Governor of Melaka, now displays Melakan porcelain, weaponry, and coins, as well as the boxing gloves of **Muhammad Ali.** Downstairs, an exhibit on Melaka's code of law documents corporal punishments for various offenses. If the exhibits don't satisfy you, the nightly **"Light & Sound Spectacular"** show features an informative history of Melaka. *(Opposite the Tourist Information Center. ☎284 1934. Open Sa-Th 9am-6pm, F 9am-12:15pm and 2:45-6pm. RM2, students in uniform RM0.50. English light show 8:30pm; tickets sold at Cultural Museum booth; RM10, children RM2.)*

CHRIST CHURCH. One of the most famous landmarks in Melaka, this church was built by the Dutch in 1741 to commemorate a century of colonial rule in Melaka. Check out the Dutch, Armenian, and Portuguese inscriptions, dating back to 1776, in the stone floor near the entrance. *(Between Jl. Gereja and Jl. Laksamana. ☎284 8804. Sunday service in English at 9am.)*

THE MALAYSIAN YOUTH MUSEUM. Housed in the old Melaka General Post Office, this museum celebrates and documents the activities of youth organizations in Malaysia and abroad. Inside there is also an **art gallery** showcasing works by famous Malaysian artists. *(On 430 Jl. Laksamana, next to Christ Church. ☎282 6526. Open Su-Th 9am-6pm, F 9am-12:15pm and 2:45-5pm. RM2, children RM0.50)*

RUINS OF ST. PAUL'S CHURCH AND A' FAMOSA FORTRESS. Built by a Portuguese captain grateful for his safe arrival, this church was originally dedicated to Mary and dubbed Our Lady of the Hill. The name changed to St. Paul's under Dutch rule in 1641. Before falling into ruin due to British neglect, the building served as a fortress, lighthouse, Dutch burial ground, Catholic chapel, and Protestant church. Near the altar is an open crypt that housed the body of **St. Francis Xavier,** missionary extraordinaire, for nine months before he was sent to Goa, India. *(Climb steps from Jl. Kota.)* Down the steps from St. Paul's Church and through an English cemetery, the last remnants of the **Porta de Santiago** act as a gateway to what remains of the Portuguese fortress of **A' Famosa.** The Dutch used the fort, but the British demolished it in the early 1800s to ensure that Melaka could not compete with Penang for controlling trade in the Strait of Melaka.

MUZIUM RAKYAT (PEOPLE'S MUSEUM). The "Enduring Beauty" exhibit displays the lengths that humans will go to embody beauty ideals, from male corsets and lip plates to cranium manipulations and Padong neck coils (see **The Plight of the Padong,** p. 763). *(Down Jl. Kota away from the clock tower. ☎282 6526. Repairs from fire expected to finish in spring 2003. Open Tu-Su 9am-12:15pm and 2:45-5:30pm. RM2.)*

OTHER SIGHTS. Inside a Portuguese ship, the **Maritime Museum** has three floors of ship models and exhibits on Melakan sea trade and piracy (see **Shiver Me Timbers!,** p. 377). The museum is on Jl. Quayside toward the river's mouth. *(☎283 0926. Open Sa-M and W-Th 9am-6pm, F 9am-12:15pm, 2:45-6pm. RM2, children RM0.50.)* The **Cultural Museum,** in a replica of the old sultan's palace, displays the costumes and headwear of various positions in Malay high society. *(On Jl. Parameswara, near Jl. Kota at the foot of St. Paul's Hill. ☎282 7464. Open Su-Th, Sa 9am-6pm, F 9am-12:15pm and 2:45-6pm. RM2, children RM0.50.)* Across the river is **Old Melaka,** a district of narrow, winding streets and architecturally interesting Chinese homes.

CHINATOWN

BABA NYONYA HERITAGE MUSEUM. Constructed in the 1890s as a private residence and converted into a museum in 1985, this home tells the tale of Chinese Malays. *(48-50 Jl. Tun Tan Cheng Lock. From the Tourist Information Center, cross the river and turn left on Jl. Kasturi; take the next right and it's on the right. ☎283 1273. Open daily 10am-12:30pm and 2-4:30pm. Admission and tour RM8, children RM4.)*

CHENG HOON TENG TEMPLE. The oldest functioning temple in the country (founded in 1673), the Cheng Hoon Teng Temple also served as a city hall and courthouse for Melakan Chinese during the Portuguese and Dutch control of the city. Carefully maintained by a board of trustees, the temple is still an active place of worship for Confucians, Taoists, and Buddhists. The main hall contains the altars of the Goddess of Mercy (Kwan Yin) in the center, the Guardian of Fishermen (the goddess Ma Cho Po) to the left, and the God of Justice (Kwan Ti) to the right. *(On Jl. Tokong, near the intersection with Jl. Lekiu. Obtain an English brochure from the office in the back, to the right. ☎282 9343. Open daily 7am-7pm.)*

MASJID KAMPUNG HULU. Built in 1748, Kampung Hulu is Malaysia's oldest mosque. Like Kampung Kling, Hulu has a pagoda-like minaret and a three-tiered roof, a combination of Sumatran and Chinese architectural styles. *(On the corner of Jl. Kampung Hulu and Jl. Masjid. Open Su-Th 7am-8pm.)*

KAMPUNG KLING MOSQUE. Built in 1784, Kampung Kling's construction was influenced by Sumatran, English, Greek, Portuguese, Chinese, Indian, and Moorish architectural styles. Intricately sculpted cast-iron lamps surround the outdoor pools for cleansing before prayer. *(1 block down from Cheng Hoon Teng on the opposite side of Jl. Lekiu. Open Su-Th 7am-8pm.)*

SRI POYYATHA VENAYAGER MOORTHI TEMPLE. The third holy building on the "Street of Harmony," this Hindu temple contains the shrine of Venayager, the remover of obstacles and the god of filial piety. *(Next door to Kampung Kling. Daily prayers 7, 11:30am, 6, 8:30pm.)*

BUKIT CHINA. This site housed Princess Hang Li Poh's hundreds of attendants when she came from China to marry the sultan. Now it's the largest Chinese cemetery outside of China. Many of its 12,000 tombs date back to the 12th century. At the foot of the hill are **Sam Po Kong Temple** and **Hang Li Poh**'s **well**. Legend has long held that anyone who drinks from the well will someday return to Melaka; Dutchmen and the forces of the Johor Sultanate disproved this by cruelly poisoning the well during the wars of the 1500s and 1600s. *(At the end of Jl. Temenggong, northeast of the city center. Open 24hr. Due to the isolation of the cemetery, it is advisable to visit during daylight hours and preferably with some company, particularly for female travelers.)*

FARTHER AFIELD

PORTUGUESE SETTLEMENT. Three kilometers east of historic Melaka, the Portuguese Settlement's main attractions are the seafood restaurants around the **Portuguese Square** and a look at the Portuguese houses adorned with images of both Jesus and Buddha. The **Festa San Pedro,** an extravagant festival with Portuguese dancers, singers, and beauty pageants, takes place during the weekend closest to June 29. *(Take bus #17 (RM0.50) from the roundabout near Hotel Equatorial.)*

IPOH ☎05

At the end of the 19th century, Ipoh's reputation as one of the richest mines in the world drew an influx of English, Chinese, Indian, and French fortune-hunters to the region. Within ten years, the city's size and population grew tenfold. Always on the cutting edge, Ipoh operates a "virtual" city hall (www.mbi.gov.my) and is driven by light industries, mega-malls, and fast food. Chinese-Malaysian tourists don't leave without having had a bowl of *koay teow* (which purportedly tastes different because of the limestone deposits in the water) and several cups of the local specialty, white coffee. As the capital of the state of Perak, Ipoh offers excursions to Buddhist cave temples and has nearly 25 heritage buildings in the old town.

TRANSPORTATION

Flights: Sultan Azlan Shah Airport, on Jl. Lapangan Terbang, 7km outside town. Taxi to town RM10. Airport tax RM5. **MAS,** Lot 108, Bangunan Seri Kinta, Jl. Sultan Idris Shah (airport ☎2414 4155, reservations ☎312 2459). Open M-Sa 8:30am-5:30pm. Flights to **KL** (35min., 3 per day 6:45am-7pm, RM66).

Trains: KTMB Ipoh (☎254 0481), in Majestic Ipoh Station Hotel on Jl. Panglima Bukit Gantang Wahab. To: **Hat Yai** via **Butterworth** (express 9hr.; 1:25am; 2nd-class seats RM23, 2nd class bunks RM31-33); **KL** (express 5hr.; 3:06am; 3rd-class seats RM10, 2nd-class seats RM18, 2nd-class bunks RM26-28); **Singapore** (express 8hr.; 1:55am, 11:10pm; 2nd-class RM48).

Buses: Medan Kidd Bus Terminal, on Jl. Kidd in the southwest corner of town. **Jelita Transportation** (☎241 4413) runs buses to: **Alor Setar** (4hr., 11 per day, RM15); **Melaka** (5hr., 5 per day, RM20); **Penang** (3hr., 9per day, RM12). **Kurnia Bistari** (☎012 566 1145) runs buses to: **Butterworth** (11:15am, 12:15, 6:15pm; RM9.50);

Cameron Highlands (11am, 5:30, 6:45pm; RM15). **Rhino Ekspres** (☎243 6119) runs buses to: **KL** (3hr., 25 per day, RM11.30); **Singapore** (7hr.; 9am, 8:30p; RM38). **Azra Ekspres** (☎241 8013) runs buses to **Kuala Kangsar** (50min., 11 per day, RM2.90). **Indah Ekspres** (☎255 3306) runs buses to: **Hat Yai** (7hr.; midnight, 1am; RM33); **Kota Baru** (6hr., 9:30pm, RM21.50); **Kuala Terengannu** (12hr., 8, 9:30pm, RM37); **Kuantan** (6hr.; 8:30am, 8pm; RM24.50). **Restu Interstate Ekspres** runs buses to **Lumut** (1½hr.; 1:30, 4, 6, 10pm, 1:30am; RM4.65).

Taxis: Long-distance **taxi stand,** opposite the Medan Kidd Terminal. To **KL** (RM110 per car) and **Penang** (RM100 per car). Fares have set minimum, but drivers may ask more.

Local Transportation: Twelve **local bus** (RM0.80) lines along main roads, ending at the terminal on Jl. Perhentian. **Local taxis** around town are RM4-6 (RM25 per hr.). **Radio Cab** (☎253 4188) picks up passengers within minutes of calling.

Rentals: Pacific Budget (☎1 800 883 191) and **Maju Jaya** (☎255 5510) are at the airport. Open daily 8am-5pm. Also **Hertz** (☎312 7109) and **Avis** (☎312 6586).

ORIENTATION AND PRACTICAL INFORMATION

Ipoh is 205km north of Kuala Lumpur along Rte. 1 between the capital and Penang. The **Kinta River** splits Ipoh into the western **old town** and the white buildings of the eastern **new town.** The new town scurries with business activity. The **bus** and **train stations** and the **tourist office** are in the old town. To get to the **old town,** walk to the traffic circle from the bus station, turn left on **Jl. Panglima Bukit Gantang Wahab,** and turn right onto **Jl. Sultan Iskandar** after the police station. Many **banks** lie along the northern end of **Jl. Sultan Yussuf,** while **Jl. Bandar Timah** is the heart of Chinatown. The Indian parts of town are near the **Birch Fountain** at the southern end of Jl. Sultan Yussuf and the northern end of **Jl. Bijih Timah.** The hub of new town lies between **Jl. Dato Onn Jaafar** and **Jl. Raja Ekram.**

Tourist Offices: Perak Tourist Information Center (☎241 2959), on Jl. Tun Sambanthan near the southwest corner of Padang Ipoh (the soccer field). Open M-Th 8am-noon and 2-4:30pm, F 8am-12:15pm and 2:45-4:30pm, Sa 8am-12:50pm.

Currency Exchange: Moneychangers are on Jl. Sultan Idris Shah near the central market, and in the basement of the Yik Foong Complex. Open M-F 9am-5pm. **Public Bank,** 76 Jl. Sultan Idris Shah (☎255 1068), on the corner of Jl. Laksamana. Changes traveler's checks RM5; 15sen per check. Open M-F 9:30am-4pm, Sa 9:30am-12:30pm. **ATM** open daily 7am-11pm. **HSBC,** 138 Jl. Sultan Yussuf (☎241 1022), has **24hr. ATM.**

Emergency: ☎999.

Police: ☎253 5522. On Jl. Panglima Bukit Gantang Wahab. English spoken. **24hr.**

Pharmacies: *Farmasi* are everywhere. **Guardian Pharmacy** (☎241 0673), ground fl., Ipoh Parade, Jl. Sultan Abdul Jalil. Open daily 10am-9:30pm.

Medical Services: General Hospital (☎253 3333), on Jl. Hospital, on the northeastern outskirts of town. English-speaking doctors. **24hr. emergency room.**

Telephones: Telekom Office (☎241 2825), on Jl. Sultan Idris Shah, near the eastern bank of Kinta River. Sells **international** calling cards (RM30 or RM60). Open Sa-Th 8:30am-4:15pm, F 8am-12:15pm and 2:45-4:45pm.

Internet Access: City Comp Trading (☎241 7612), in Ipoh Parade, 1st fl., on Jl. Sultan Abdul Jalil. Email RM2 per 30min., RM3 per hr. Open daily 10am-10pm.

Post Office: Ipoh GPO (☎254 6555), opposite the police, next to the train station. *Poste Restante.* Open M-Sa 8:30am-6pm. **Postal code:** 30670.

MALAYSIA

ACCOMMODATIONS

Inexpensive accommodations congregate in the new town. **Jl. Raja Musa Aziz** (Anderson Rd.) has the best options. Cheaper places line **Jl. Yang Kalsom** in the south, but numerous massage parlors lend it a seedy air.

The Majestic Station Hotel, Bangunan Stesen Koretapi, Jl. Panglima Bukit Gantang Wahab (☎255 4217), in the historic railway station. The splendor is masked a bit by neglected stairwells and hallways. "Superior" standards with shower RM63; "deluxe" with bath RM78; family rooms RM130. Reserve in advance. AmEx/DC/MC/V. ❹

Dragon and Phoenix Hotel, 23-25 Jl. Toh Puah Chah (☎253 4661). Equally close to new and old towns, near the Kinta River. All rooms with A/C, TV, phone, and private bath. Doubles RM59.80; twins RM62.10; quads RM96.50. ❹

Toyko Hotel, 159-161 Jl. Rajah Musa Aziz (☎254 2005), at the corner of Jl. Dato Onn Jaafar. Near the heart of new town. Spacious, furnished rooms and free filtered water. All rooms come with bath. Doubles and triples with fan RM30, with A/C RM40, with TV and A/C RM45; quads with A/C RM50. ❸

YMCA, 211 Jl. Rajah Musa Aziz (☎254 0809), surrounded by green parks. Take a taxi from bus or train station (RM5). Slightly far from town, but spotless rooms. Common bath a bit dingy–opt for a private room if you have the cash. Chinese restaurant. Dorms for 1-5 people RM12; singles with phone, A/C, and bath RM30; doubles from RM40. ❶

YWCA (☎242 8972), opposite the YMCA. Offers rooms for women travelers. Well-stocked kitchen and large living room. Reserve in advance. Advisable to check-in before 5pm. Singles/doubles with fan, desk, and shared bath RM35/RM45. ❸

FOOD

Find the best and biggest options at **The Food Center (Pusat Makaran Majestic),** on Jl. Dato Tahwil Azar, which serves Ipoh's signature dish *koey teow* (RM2.50; open daily 9am-11pm), and at **Pusat Penjaja Podeng Kanak (The Children's Playground),** on Jl. Raja Musa Aziz, south of Jl. Sultan Idris Shah. For Malay cuisine, look for shop names preceded by *kedai kopi*, meaning "coffee shop." While coffee is served, the name refers to a space where hawkers set up stalls. The best place for Ipoh's famous white coffee *(pak kopi)* is at the southern end of Jl. Bandar Timah, where numerous Chinese-run coffee shops serve a packed house all afternoon.

Koh-Samui Restaurant, 83-85 Jl. Rajau Ekram (☎255 6608), is in the northern part of new town, a block from Practical Internet. Upscale Thai restaurant serving *halal* food. Prices average RM10. *Tom yam* (seafood and vegetable soup) RM12-30. Other **branch** at 28 Lebuh Medan Ipoh. Open daily 11:30am-2:45pm and 6-10:30pm. MC/V. ❹

Thin Hei Vegetarian Restaurant, 25 Persiaran Greenhill (☎253 7388), in the northern part of new town. Laid-back, family atmosphere. Tofu and vegetable dishes RM5; noodle dishes RM3-6. Open daily 10:30-2:30pm and 5:30-9:30pm. ❷

Kedai Kopi Kong Heng, 75 Jl. Bandar Timah, 2 blocks below Jl. Sultan Iskandar Shah. Known for their freshly brewed white coffee. Hainanese chicken RM2.70. Fresh orange juice (in a plastic bag!) RM1.70. Open Tu-Th 7:30am-4pm. ❶

Seasons, 88 Jl. Sultan at the Syuen Hotel, features an international menu in an elegant setting. Spaghetti Carbonara RM17; burger with fries RM14; mixed fruit RM8; Guinness RM13.50. **Open 24hr.** ❸

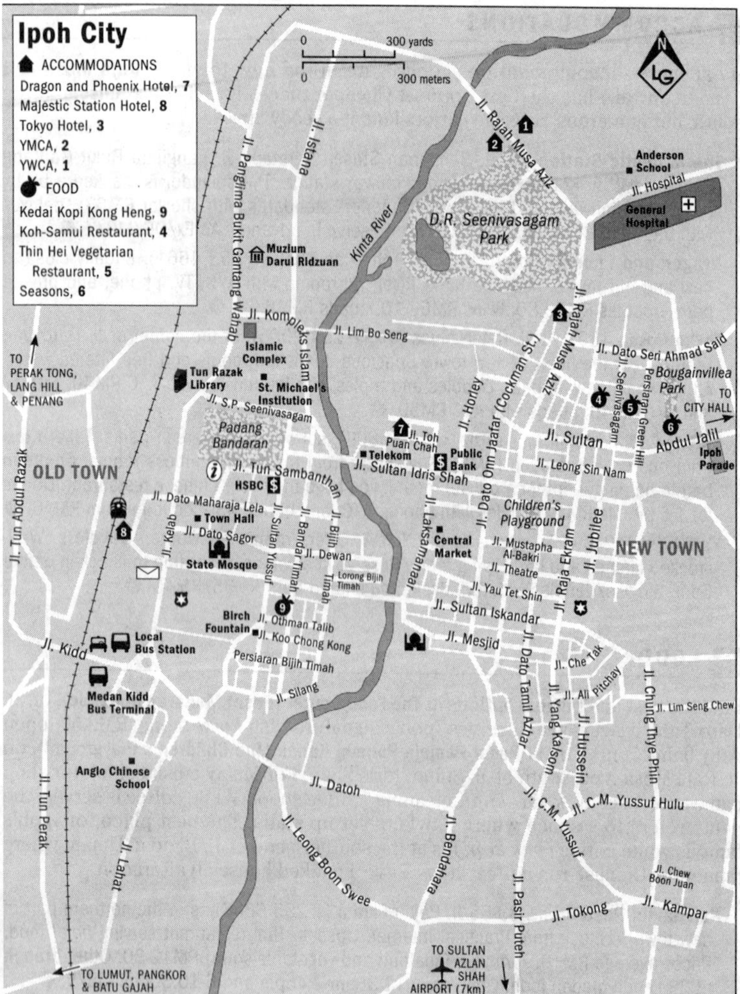

SIGHTS

Ipoh's significant sights are mostly architectural, but the cave temples on the outskirts of the city are worth a visit.

COLONIAL BUILDINGS AND PARKS. Jl. Panglima Bukit Gantang Wahab and **Jl. Kelab** have many impressive colonial buildings, including the train station and town hall. The **Ipoh Railway Station,** also designed by A. B. Hubback, rivals the one in Kuala Lumpur in grandeur. The imposing **St. Michael's Institution** was initially designed by LaSallean Brother Vernier Auguste, also the architect for the St. John's Institution in KL. **D.R. Seenivasagam Park** spans the strip between the YMCA and the traffic circle on Jl. Rajah Musa Aziz and has soccer fields, gazebos, and a Japanese garden. Smaller but more stylish, **Bougainvillea Park** which flanks Ipoh City Hall southeast of D.R. Seenivasagam Park. For detailed information on the history of Ipoh, the Perak Tourist Information Center provides heritage maps.

LIMESTONE CAVES. Limestone caves, used as Buddhist temples by Chinese immigrants, surround the city. Six kilometers north of Ipoh on the road to Kuala Kangsar is **Perak Tong,** a temple known for its paintings and endless stairwell. (Accessible by bus #141; 30min., every 30min., RM0.80. Open daily 9am-5pm.) Other cave temples are **Sam Poh Tong,** 6km south of Ipoh on the main road (RM1; open daily 8am-5pm), and **Kek Lok Tong,** near Gunung Rapat (open daily 7:30am-7pm). Sam Poh Tong is the oldest in the region, built 128 years ago; it shelters ponds brimming with fish and turtles. (Both cave temples are accessible by buses #66 or 73; 20min., every 10min. until 7:30pm, every 30min. until 10pm, RM0.90) To get to Kek Lok Tong from Sam Poh Tong, back-track to the traffic circle and make a right. Then walk for 15min. and turn right before the first traffic light, where signs will direct the way to the temple. Farther south, about 25km from Ipoh, are the impressive limestone formations of **Gunung Tempurung.** Visitors can walk through the cave along paved pathways. (☎545 8834. Accessible by taxi RM25.)

OTHER SIGHTS. The road to **Lumut,** southwest of Ipoh, passes through countryside dotted with Chinese cemeteries, open-cast mines, and small mining towns gone bust. One such town is **Papan.** Built in the 1890s, it has become a near-ghost town since the demise of the tin industry. **Kellie's Castle,** 30min. outside town, is the beautiful mansion of William Kellie Smith, a wealthy Scottish planter who died before its completion in 1926. Take a peek at the castle's empty rooms and rubble walls, fashioned in a mix of Moorish and Greco-Roman styles. (Accessible by taxi or a short ride from Gopeng on the Batu Gajah bus (RM0.60). Admission RM3, children RM1.) In the **Clearwater Century Golf Resort,** you can tour the set of *Anna and the King.* The RM15 fee includes high tea at 4pm. Northeast of Ipoh is the **Tanjung Rambutan waterfall** (accessible by the Tanjung Rambutan bus, 50min.).

LUMUT ☎05

Lumut is the gateway to **Pulau Pangkor.** Buses drop off visitors opposite the ferry terminal. Two types of ferries run from Lumut to **Pangkor:** the A/C **express** (20min.; M-F every 2hr., Sa-Su every hr. 8am-7pm; RM5) and the **local** (35min., 6:45am and every 30min. 7am-8pm, RM3), via Sungai Pinang Kecil. The **Pangkor Tourist Information Center** is in Lumut, across the street from the jetty. If you miss a ferry, don't despair—there are two decent hotels near the Lumut-Pangkor jetty. **Indah Hotel ❹,** 208 Jl. Iskandar Shah, a couple blocks from the bus station right near the beach, offers clean and spacious rooms with TV and private bath. (☎683 5064. RM60, with sea view RM80.) **Harbor View Hotel ❹,** 13 and 14 Jl. Titi Panjang, a short walk from the bus station through an alleyway, has a wider range of rooms, also by the sea. (☎683 7888. Extra bed RM10. Doubles RM50-65; quads RM80.) Malay food stalls between the two hotels serve *nasi goreng* (fried rice) well into the night. The **tourist information center,** on the other side of the gas station opposite the jetty, can answer any questions and has an assortment of brochures about other destinations in Malaysia. (Open M-F 9am-5pm, Sa 9am-1:45pm.)

PULAU PANGKOR ☎05

Despite the island's commercial success, much of Pulau Pangkor's coastline and jungle interior remain untouched. The island's 25,000 inhabitants reside mostly on the eastern coast, while travelers flock to the west coast beaches to view the vibrant sunsets, relax on white beaches, and watch black hornbills flit from tree to tree. Rustling breezes, deserted sands, and shops brimming with sacks of dried fish create the laid-back Pangkor atmosphere. Pulau Pangkor's waters reveal the diversity of its travelers; Muslim women swim fully-clothed next to bikini-clad Westerners, but all unite in an effort to relax and enjoy.

TRANSPORTATION AND PRACTICAL INFORMATION

The **Pangkor jetty** is on the island's southeastern side (the local ferry will stop first at the Sungai Pinang Jetty, where locals usually disembark). Ferries arrive frequently from Lumut (see above), the island's mainland gateway. Coming from the jetty, Pangkor's main road, which generally follows the coastline, is to the left. Heading south, the road goes past the fishing village of **Teluk Gedung** and **Kota Beland (Dutch Fort).** Off the main road is **Jl. Pasir Bogak,** which leads to the **post office, police station,** and the beaches of **Coral Beach, Pasir Bogak,** and **Teluk Nipah.**

Pink taxivans at the Pangkor jetty and by the south end of Pantai Pasir Bogak go anywhere for RM10. Taxivans line up on the main roads in Teluk Nipah and Pasir Bogak starting at 6am to shuttle passengers to the ferry. Several shops and hotels on the main road rent **motorcycles** (RM30 for 24hr.) and **bicycles** (RM15 for 12hr.). Wear a helmet and make sure rented bikes have brakes that can handle steep hills and hairpin turns. Opposite the jetty, **Maybank** changes currency and has an **ATM.** (☎685 1494. Open M-F 9:30am-4pm, Sa 9:30-11:30am.) Up the road past the post office is a **clinic** with a prescription counter and an English-speaking assistant. There is also a **24hr. sick bay.** (☎685 4048. Consultation RM2; overnight stays RM5. Clinic open 8am-4:30pm.) **JH Pharmacy,** Lot 14A Taman Desa Pangkor, is just across from the police station. (☎685 5322. Open daily 9:30am-9:30pm.) The **police** can be reached **24hr**. by telephone (☎685 1222). Downstairs from the Chuan Full Hotel, the Fisherman Cafe, 62 Main Rd., 100m left of the jetty, provides **Internet access** for RM3 per hr. (☎685 1123. Open daily 11am-10pm.) The staff at the **post office** are very helpful. (☎685 1281. Open M-F 8:30am-4:30pm, Sa 8:30am-3:30pm.)

MALAYSIA

ACCOMMODATIONS AND FOOD

Pulau Pangkor's budget accommodations cluster on two side-roads at Teluk Nipah. Travelers gather here for the beautiful sunsets and proximity to **Coral Beach** and the secluded **Monkey Bay,** and for the kayaking, fishing, and island-hopping. Prepare to bargain, as many mediocre hotels ask ridiculous prices. **Horizon Inn ❺,** on the main road in Teluk Nipah, is a well-run mini-resort with rooms overlooking the beach and a fabulous restaurant downstairs. Each room has its own porch. (☎685 3399. A/C doubles with hill view RM80, with sea view RM90. Discounts apply for stays over 2 days. Expect a 20% price increase on weekends and public holidays.) **O La La Chalets ❷,** at the end of the first lane in Teluk Nipah, has neat baths and quiet chalets, although some of the rooms have a dank ocean smell. (☎685 5112. Doubles RM40. Bike rental RM3 per hr., RM15 per 24hr. Motorbikes RM10 per hr., RM30 per 24hr.) On the same road, **Takana Juo (TJ Chalet and Restoran) ❸,** 4458 Teluk Nipah, has delicious food and comfortable rooms 50m from the beach. (☎685 4733. Singles and doubles with toilet and shower RM30; for stays over 2 nights RM20 per person and RM25 per couple.) **Nazri Nipah ❶,** at the end of the lane from Restoran Horizon in Teluk Nipah, is true backpacker grit: travelers come here for Western breakfast and the cheapest stay in town. You pay for what you get in the dorms. (☎685 2014. Dorms RM10; A-frames RM20-30; chalets with bath RM30. 4hr. trek to Pangkor Hill and drinking water RM30.)

A few stalls sell burgers and snacks at Teluk Nipah. The southern end of Pasir Bogak, 5min. from Pangkor Paradise Village Holiday Resort, has your ordinary night hawkers. Most accommodations have attached restaurants. **TJ's Restoran ❶,** at Teluk Nipah (connected to Takana Juo), is known for its Malay and Indonesian dishes. (Chicken or beef *rendang* in spicy coconut milk RM5; Western breakfast RM3-5. Open daily 8:30am-11pm.) One of Pankor's culinary specialties is fish, purchased fresh from the piers each morning. **Restoran Horizon ❸,** 4438 Teluk Nipah, the best restaurant in town, has excellent *tom yam* (spicy Thai soup RM17), Chinese-style cooked vegetables (RM5-8), and seafood dishes starting at RM8. (☎685 3388. Open Su-F noon-10pm, Sa 11am-10pm.) Across the street from Chuan Full Hotel, **Sin Nam Huan Restaurant ❸** serves tantalizing garlic butter prawns (RM16).

SIGHTS

Pulau Pangkor's best sights are its beaches and green hills. A leisurely island tour takes 45min. by motorcycle or 2hr. by bicycle. Taxivans charge RM40 to circle the island, so share the ride to offset costs. **Trekking** through the island's jungle interior makes for a good daytrip, but it is advisable to pay for a guide, as many of the trails are unmarked and overgrown. **Nazri Nipah** (see **Accommodations,** above) offers trekking trips to Pangkor Hill. **Pangkor Hill,** 371m above sea level, can be reached by an 2km trail marked with a sign reading "Hulan Simpan Sg. Pinang" on the hill's north side, near the airport. On the western side of the island between Teluk Nipah and Pasar Bogak, is the trailhead to the top of **Tortoise Hill,** as well as the **Jungle Information Center,** which provides tips on trekking through the island's interior.

For swimming and sunbathing, nice beaches on the west coast include the beautiful **Coral Beach,** north of Teluk Nipah, with a small Chinese temple at its northern end, and **Turtle Bay,** a deserted stretch of golden sand just south of Teluk Nipah, separated from the main road by waves of wild grass. There are quite a few monkeys lounging around both Turtle Bay and **Monkey Bay,** just north of Turtle Bay. Although it's often not on maps, Monkey Bay is just off the main road after the bridge from Nipah. Off Teluk Nipah's coast lies **Giam Island,** which has another small beach. Boats from Teluk Nipah motor here for RM30. You can also hire a boat to island-hop and **snorkel** for several hours (RM50). Arrange boats with **Lambaian Pulau Water Sports,** which also rents kayaks for RM10 per hour and snorkel gear for RM10 per day. (On the main road at Teluk Nipah. Open daily 8am-7pm.)

As for Pulau Pangkor's "sights," the **Fu Lin Kung Chinese Temple,** north of Pangkor town, should not be missed. From Pangkor town turn left at the first set of yellow railings and go to the end of the road. Nestled at the base of a hill surrounded by dense jungle, the temple contains pools of turtles and orange *koi* fish, a garden, statues of the 12 animals in the Chinese zodiac. About 500m north of Fu Lin Kung is a Hindu temple, **Sri Pathira Kaliamman.** To the south of Pangkor town is **Kota Beland,** a Dutch fort, built in 1680. Today the fort stands in ruins due to a number of attacks from locals and pirates.

TAIPING ☎05

Once the state of Perak's capital, proud Taiping is a city of firsts: the country's first museum, railway line, newspaper, post and telegraph office, zoo, hill station, and public garden. Downtown Taiping reveals a Chinese influence, as the city was originally settled by Chinese workers who had come from Penang to mine the rich tin-fields. It was named Taiping ("Eternal Peace") in 1874 as part of a treaty between rival Chinese secret societies that were fighting at the time for control of a water-course. For those who like long strolls among lake gardens and cool hills, Taiping is an ideal break.

THE KING OF FRUITS Among Malaysia's variety of tropical fruits is the famous (or infamous) durian. Recognizable by its spiky exterior and pungent aroma, the flesh comes in fist-sized, pulpy, yellow sacks. The texture is one-of-a-kind and the taste is indescribable, although it has been likened to the sting of fresh garlic. You'll either love it or hate it, but do give it a try. Meanwhile, higher-end hotels usually post signs forbidding the possession or consumption of durian on their premises (again, the smell!). Public consumption of durian is banned in Thailand. The finest grade is D24. Durian are sold as a whole fruit or by the kg at street vendors. They are sometimes pre-cut and pre-wrapped in plastic; insist on having a freshly cut one. A note of warning: simultaneous consumption of durian and alcohol may be **fatal** because of the chemical combination.

TRANSPORTATION

Trains: Stesyen Keretapi Taiping (☎807 5584), on Jl. Stesyen, 700m west of the downtown area near the hospital. Office open **24hr.** Trains to **Hat Yai** via **Butterworth** (7hr.; 3:20am; economy seats RM7, 2nd-class seats RM17, bunks RM24.50-27) and **KL** (8hr.; 12:36am; economy seats RM14, 2nd-class seats RM24, bunks RM31.50-34).

Buses: Stesyen Bus, at the west end of Jl. Panggong Wayang. To **Kuala Kangsar** (every 15min. 6am-9:30pm, RM2.50). **Express bus terminal** is in **Kamunting,** a 20min. bus/taxi ride from Taiping. To: **Butterworth** (every 30min. 6:30am-8:30pm, RM5) via **Alor Setar; Ipoh** (1hr., every 30min. 6:30am-8:30pm, RM3.80); **Johor Bahru** (8hr.; 9:30am, 9, 10:30pm; RM35); **KL** (4½hr., 26 per day 7:30am-11pm, RM13.30); **Penang** (1½hr.; 9, 11:30am, 4, 6:30pm; RM7.35).

Taxis: ☎808 1691. In Kamunting at express bus terminal and Taiping on Jl. Iskandar between West Jl. Kota and Jl. Panggong Wayang. From Taiping to: **Bukit Larut** (RM5); **Ipoh** (RM48, with A/C RM52); **Kamunting** (RM5); **Kuala Kangsar** (RM28).

ORIENTATION AND PRACTICAL INFORMATION

Taiping's center is set up in a grid. From south to north, the main drags (running east-west) are **Jl. Panggong Wayang, Jl. Kota, Jl. Pasar, Jl. Taming Sari, Jl. Barrack,** and **Jl. Stesyen.** To the east are the government offices, lake garden, zoo, museum, library, and the hills, including Bukit Larut. **Jl. Iskandar** is off the west end of Jl. Panggong Wayang. A warning about street names: many have two—the old, British name, and the recent, Malay name. Most maps will print the Malay names, but locals often refer to what they've known the longest.

Tourist Information: Taiping Visitor & Information Center (☎805 3245), on Jl. Kota, under the pink clock tower. Very helpful. Provides transportation info and maps. English-speaking staff helpful; ask for Annuar. Open M-F 8:30am-5:30pm, Sa 8:30am-3pm.

Currency Exchange: Bank Bumiputra Commerce (☎807 2422), on Jl. Kota, next to the pink clock tower. Open M-F 9:30am-4pm, Sa 9:30am-noon. **Maybank,** on Jl. Panggong Wayang, has **ATMs.** Open M-F 9:30am-4pm, Sa 9:30-11:30am; ATMs 6am-midnight. **HSBC** (☎807 5400), on the western end of Jl. Kota, has **24hr. ATMs.**

Emergency: ☎999.

Police: ☎808 2222. On Jl. Taming Sari, in front of the white and stately district office. Attentive and helpful. **24hr.**

Medical Service: Hospital Taiping (☎808 3333), at the west end of Jl. Taming Sari. English spoken. **24hr. emergency care.** No credit cards.

MALAYSIA

Telephones: Telekom office (☎809 9841), uptown on the far east side of Jl. Barrack. IDD/fax. Open M-F 8:45am-5pm, Sa 8:45am-1pm.

Internet Access: NTT Interactive, 16 Jl. Maharaja Lela (☎805 2933), southeast of town center, near the Lake Garden. Busy, usually with gaming students. RM1.30 per 30min., RM2.50 per hr. Open M-F noon-midnight, Sa-Su 10am-2am.

Post Office: ☎807 7555. Next to the Telekom office. *Poste Restante.* Open M-Sa 8:30am-5pm. **Postal code:** 34000.

ACCOMMODATIONS AND FOOD

Persatuan Hin Aun ❷, 218, 220, and 222 Jl. Chung Thye Phin, offers tidy guest rooms on the second floor with A/C and bath. Enter next to Chun Loong Ent. (☎808 3582. Doubles RM22; triples RM26; quads RM29.) In the heart of Taiping at 52 Market Sq., **Hotel Malaya ❸** has clean rooms with A/C, phones, and new bathrooms. From the bus station, walk down Jl. Panggong Wayang toward the Gardens and Zoo, and turn left before the film developing shop; it's 50m down. (☎807 3733. Laundry. Doubles RM30, with TV RM35; quads RM40, with TV RM45.) **Hotel Fuliyean ❺,** 14 Jl. Barrack on the corner next to the post office, has spanking new rooms with hot showers, A/C, TV, towels, and soap. (☎806 8648. Doubles RM78; triples RM88.)

The central **day market ❶** is between Jl. Taming Sari and Jl. Panggong Wayang, and the **night market ❶** is southeast of Jl. Panggong Wayang, near Jl. Maharaja Lela. (Open daily 6am-midnight.) Taiping's best food is at the huge center at **Market Square ❶** near the local bus station. Look for the large *Fajar* sign. (Open daily 6am-midnight.) *The* choice for dim sum is **Kum Loong ❷,** 45-47 Jl. Kota, east of the pink clock tower. (☎807 2649. Rice and vegetables RM 6. Open daily 5am-11pm.) **Bismillah Restaurant ❶,** 138 Jl. Taming Sari at the intersection with Jl. Lim Teong Chye, is an authentic Malay/Indian restaurant. (*Roti canai* RM0.60. Open daily 6am-9pm.) At the Legend Inn near the local bus station at 2 Jl. Long Jaafar, **Legend Cafe ❸** is perhaps the fanciest restaurant in town. (☎806 0000. US sirloin steak RM 26.50; broiled salmon RM19. Prices subject to tax and service charge.)

SIGHTS

The **Taiping Lake Gardens and Zoo,** Malaysia's first recreational garden, is one of the country's most delightful. Near the entrance is the world's smallest monkey, *pygmy marmoset,* situated next to its fellow primate *tamarins.* (Paddle boat RM10 per 30min. Zoo open daily 8am-7pm. Feeding time 10am-noon. RM4, children RM2. Tram ride around the zoo 9:30am-5:30pm; RM2, children RM1.) Malaysia's oldest hill station, **Bukit Larut,** formerly known as Maxwell's Hill, is popular for its cool temperatures, mountain greenery, and seclusion. Government-operated Land Rovers ply the route to the hill station from the base in Taiping on Jl. Air Terjun, past the northeastern end of the Lake Gardens (35min., every hr. 8am-5pm, round-trip RM5). Taxi drivers will tell you that the station base is within walking distance, but it's a 45min. walk. For an extended stay on the hill, **Larut Hill Resort ❷** (☎807 7241) runs 10-person bungalows for RM150-200, while guest rooms cost RM15. Reserve in advance. **Muzium Perak,** built in 1883, is Malaysia's first museum. One kilometer east of the town center on the left of Jl. Taming Sari, it maintains an eclectic exhibit that includes a Vietnam War-era CAC Avon Saber, exhibits of royal garb, a collection of Orang Asli tools, and a collection of animal taxidermy. It is one of the only museums that devotes so much energy to the history of the Orang Asli. There is also a *kris* collection, celebrating Malaysian and Indonesian knife-dueling. (☎807 2057. Open Sa-Th 9am-5pm, F 9am-12:15pm and 2:45-5pm. Free.)

PENANG (PULAU PINANG)

Those with illusions of a sweet little island are in for a shock. With the second-largest economy in Malaysia, Penang is more powerhouse than paradise. The island is home to a number of multinational corporations by the airport, five colleges, and Malaysia's largest Buddhist temple, as well as numerous Malaysian *kampongs* (villages) and *kongsi* (clans) scattered in the rural areas. The dense jungles contain durian, jackfruit, and nutmeg plantations, and visitors can visit the prestigious Butterfly Farm, new aquarium, botanical garden, and Forestry Museum and Arboretum. Other delights include relaxing by Batu Ferringhi's beaches, temple-hopping in Georgetown, and devouring one of Penang's culinary contributions to the world—the minty yet spicy *assam laksa*.

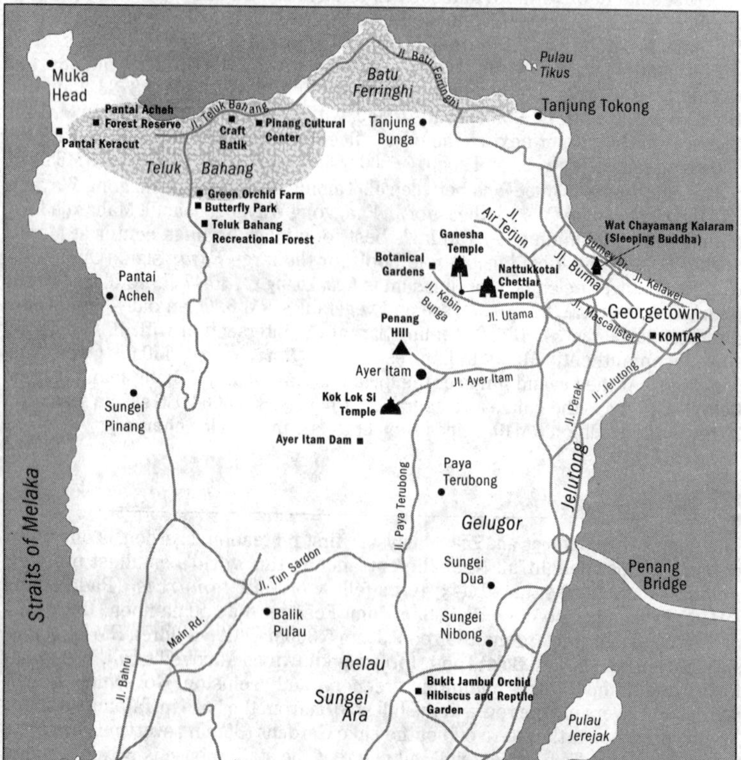

MALAYSIA

THE VIEW FROM ABOVE

The lowdown: A bustling island off the west coast with a life of its own and the most Chinese in Malaya.
Major towns: Georgetown, Batu Ferringhi, Teluk Bahang.
Highlights: Penang cuisine, lush jungles, colorful seasonal festivals, Malaysia's largest Buddhist temple.

TRANSPORTATION

Flights: Bayan Lepas International Airport (☎643 0811), 20km south of Georgetown Yellow bus #83 (every hr. 6am-10pm) and minibus #32 run between the airport and Pengkalan Weld in Georgetown. **MAS** (☎262 0011) flies to **KL** (45min., every hr., RM109) and **Medan, Indonesia** (45min., 12:55pm, RM253). **Singapore Airlines** (☎226 3201) flies to **Singapore** (1hr., 3 per day, RM295). **Thai Airlines** flies to **Bangkok** (2hr., 8am, RM499).

Trains: The **train station** (☎331 2796; www.ktmb.com.my) is below the ferry landing in Butterworth. Train schedules change bi-annually. To: **Bangkok** (21½hr., 2:20pm, 2nd-class bunks RM88-94.20) via **Hat Yai** (4½hr.; 3rd-class seats RM4, 2nd-class seats RM13); **KL** (10½hr.; 9:55pm; 3rd-class seats RM17, 2nd-class seats/bunks RM30/RM37.). Transfer to **KL** for trains to **Johor Bahru** and **Singapore.**

Buses: There are two **bus stations:** one at KOMTAR in Penang and the other below the Butterworth ferry landing. From KOMTAR, **Supercoach** buses run to: **KL** (5hr., 11 per day, RM22); **Kuantan** (8½hr., 10pm, RM35); **Singapore** via **Johor Bahru** (11hr.; 8:15, 9am, 8:30, 9:30, 10pm; RM42); **Taiping** (1hr.; 11am, 1:30, 4, 6pm; RM7.50). **Sri Maju** buses go to **Ipoh** (3hr.; 7:30, 9:30am, 2, 4:30, 7, 9pm; RM11.50). **Kurnia Bistari** buses go to **Cameron Highlands** via **Ipoh** (6hr.; 8am, 2:30pm; RM20), while their minivans go to **Hat Yai** (4hr.; 5, 8:30am, noon, 4pm; RM20). From Butterworth, **Transnasional** buses go to **KL** (5hr., 13 per day, RM20) and **Kota Bharu** (8hr.; 10am, 10, 10:30pm; RM20). **Sri Maju** buses go to **Lumut** (3hr., 7 per day, RM10.50). **Sri Jengka Ekspres** buses go to **Kuantan** (7½hr.; 8:30, 9, 10pm; RM30-35). **Kurnia Bistari** buses also go to **Cameron Highlands** via **Ipoh** and **Tapah.**

Ferries: A **24hr.** ferry runs between **Georgetown** and **Butterworth** on the mainland (every 20min., after midnight every hr.; RM0.60 to Penang, free to Butterworth).

Taxis: Long-distance taxis (☎333 4459) can be hired to: **Alor Setar** (RM200); **Cameron Highlands** (RM250); **Hat Yai** (RM220); **Ipoh** (RM120); **KL** (RM250); **Kuala Kedar** (RM200); **Lumut** (RM180); **Padang Besar** (RM150); **Taiping** (RM70).

MALAYSIA

GEORGETOWN ☎04

Georgetown is a cultural and culinary mecca, where each street has a blend of ethnic influences. Chulia St. is the main backpacker hangout and buildings here retain the character of Old Penang, but the entire city begs to be explored. On Jl. Masjid Kapitan Keling alone, there are five different religious establishments. Narrow streets and markets pulse with life late into the night, and wandering walks reveal one of Asia's most diverse architectural collections.

TRANSPORTATION

Ferries: To **Butterworth** (every 20min.; RM0.60, cars RM7). Express services to **Langkawi** and **Medan, Indonesia** run from the tourist center near the Victoria Memorial Clock Tower. **Langkawi Ferry Services** (☎966 9439) goes to **Langkawi** (2½hr.; 8am, return 5:30pm; RM35, round-trip RM60) and **Medan, Indonesia** (5hr.; 8am; RM90, round-trip RM160). **Ekspres Bahagia** (☎263 1943) also goes to: **Langkawi** (8,

8:45am; return 2:30, 5:30pm; RM35, round-trip RM60) and **Medan, Indonesia** (8am, return 10am; RM90, round-trip RM160).

Local Transportation: Buses and **Bas Mini** (minibuses) run from the *jeti* (ferry station) and KOMTAR (6am-11pm), making circular routes around the island. Fares vary by distance and bus company; tell the driver your destination to determine exact fare, and always carry loose change. *Beca* charge more for guided tours of Georgetown but are an ideal way to take in the city's atmosphere. **Yellow** buses go south while **blue** buses go north. Take **red-and-white** bus #1 or 101 to Central Penang, blue bus #93 and transit line #202 to the north shore. Both taxi and *beca* are RM20 per hr. and taxis charge 20% more at night. Lh. Chulia to the *jeti* RM5. **Taxis** from the airport are hired through a coupon system. Purchase a coupon at the Teksi counter (Georgetown RM25-30).

Rentals: A valid driver's license with photo is required for all car rentals. **Hawk** has a rental counter in the airport (☎881 3886). Manual from RM150 and auto from RM156.50. **New Bob Car Rental,** at 11 Gottlieb Rd. and at the airport (☎642 1111), also has cars from RM170.50. Rental services also provide car delivery.

ORIENTATION AND PRACTICAL INFORMATION

Penang's **ferry terminal** and a local **bus station** are on **Pengkalan Weld Quay,** along Georgetown's southeast coast. Parallel to Pengkalan Weld Quay is **Lh. Pantai (Beach St.),** the financial district, administrative buildings, **police station,** and the main **post office.** Lh. Pantai runs north to the **Victoria Memorial Clock Tower,** at the intersection with Lebuh Light. Here, **Fort Cornwallis** guards the city while boats leave from the jetty near the **Penang Tourism Centre.** Running northwest from the Penang-Butterworth ferry terminal is **Lh. Chulia.** At the western end of Lh. Chulia, **Jl. Penang** runs north to hotels and south to **KOMTAR,** the cylindrical building that dominates Penang's skyline. At KOMTAR are shopping malls, the **long-distance bus station,** and the **local** bus station. Buses run northwest from KOMTAR to Batu Ferringhi and Teluk Bahang, as well as south toward the **airport.**

Tourist Offices: Penang Tourist Center (☎261 6663), on Pesara King Edward by the clock tower. Maps and info. Open M-Th 8:30am-1pm and 2-4:30pm, Sa 8:30am-1pm. **Penang Tourist Guides Association** (☎261 4461), 3rd fl. of KOMTAR, has extremely helpful staff. Follow the signs near McDonald's. Open M-Sa 10am-6pm; closed for irregular lunch breaks. **Tourism Malaysia** (Northern Region), 10 Jl. Tun Syed Sheh Barakbah (☎262 0066), near the Penang Tourist Center. Open M-F 8am-4:30pm, Sa 8am-1pm. Closed 1st and 3rd Sa of each month.

Tours and Travel: MSL Travel, Agora Hotel, Jl. MacAlister (☎227 2655). Malay and Thai rail-passes available with ISIC. Smaller companies along Lh. Pantai and Lh. Chulia offer tours. **Newasia Tours and Travel,** 35-36 Pangkalan Weld (☎261 7933), offers plane tickets, a variety of tours, and minibuses to Thailand. Branch offices at: KOMTAR ground fl., off Jl. Ria (☎261 5558) and 27 Lh. Chulia (☎264 3930).

Consulates: Indonesia, 467 Jl. Burma (☎227 4686). Open M-F 8:30am-1pm and 2-4:30pm. **Thailand,** 1 Jl. Tuanku Abdul Rahman (☎226 8029). Open M-F 9am-noon and 2-4pm. Visa applications accepted until noon. Two-month tourist visa RM33. Accommodations also help issue visas, but it is advisable to go through a consulate.

Currency Exchange: Several moneychangers on Lh. Chulia and major banks along Lh. Pantai have good rates. **OCBC Bank,** on Lh. Pantai near Lh. Chulia, has **24hr. ATMs** (PLUS/V). Bank open M-F 9:30am-3:30pm, Sa 9:30-11:30am. **HSBC,** down the road, also has **24hr. ATM.** There are also banks with **ATMs** at KOMTAR and on Lh. Pantai.

Emergency: Police: ☎999. **Fire:** ☎994.

Tourist Police: ☎261 5522, ext. 409.

Directory Assistance: ☎103.

Pharmacies: A few large pharmacies are on Lh. Pantai. **Ego Pharmacy,** 448 Penang Rd. (☎226 4529), has a wide selection. Open M-Sa 9:30am-7:30pm. The **Guardian Pharmacy** at KOMTAR is open daily until 10pm.

Medical Service: General Hospital (☎229 3333), on Jl. Hospital. English spoken. **24hr. emergency room.** Consultation fee RM2. Performs minor surgery.

Telephones: Telekom office (☎220 9321), on Jl. Downing next to the post office. Open M-F 8:30am-4:30pm. **HCD**/fax. **IDD** from any card phone.

Internet Access: Many on Lh. Chulia. RM3 per hr. **Eighteen Internet Cafe,** 18 Lh. Cintra, off Lh. Chulia, has speedy connections. Open M-Sa 10:30am-10pm.

Post Office: GPO Penang (☎261 9222), on the corner of Lh. Downing and Pengkalan Weld. Open M-F 8:30am-6pm, Sa 8am-4pm. *Poste Restante*. **Postal code:** 10670 (for post office only).

ACCOMMODATIONS

Budget hotels are on or near Lh. Chulia. Love Lane, named for the Chinese matchmakers who once lived there, intersects the center of Lh. Chulia.

Olive Spring Hotel, 302 Lh. Chulia (☎261 4641), above Rainforest Restaurant. Lovely walls awash with Caribbean purples and blues. No skimping on cleanliness here. Lockers available. Laundry. Dorms RM8; singles with fan RM15; doubles RM22-25. ❶

SD Motel, 24 Lh. Muhtri (☎264 3743). From Lh. Chulia, take a left off Love Ln. Quiet, immaculate rooms. Singles with fan RM15; doubles with fan RM20, with A/C RM28; triples with fan RM28/RM38; 5-person rooms with A/C RM58. ❷

75 Travellers Lodge, 75 Lh. Muhtri (☎262 3378). Although it lacks character, it's popular spot for short stays. Reserve in advance. Thick mattresses. Dorms RM7; singles RM15-18; doubles RM18-22, with bath RM28-32, with A/C RM35-40. ❶

Blue Diamond Hotel, 422 Lh. Chulia (☎261 1089), 1 block before the intersection with Jl. Penang. Beer garden outside. Movies every night. Internet and motorbike rental. Dorms RM8; singles and doubles RM20-25, with bath RM25-30, with A/C RM45. ❶

Wan Hai Hotel, 35 Love Ln. (☎261 6853), on the right. Rooftop common area great for sunbathing. Beer RM5. Laundry, motorcycle (RM20 per day), bike (RM10 per day), and travel booking services. Dorms RM7; singles and doubles RM15-18; triples RM21. ❶

Cathay Hotel, 15 Leith St. (☎262 6271). Traveling buddies and couples enjoy this famous antique colonial with lofty ceilings and white sheets. Doubles with fan RM57.50; standards with A/C RM69; deluxe with A/C RM92. ❹

Hotel Noble, 36 Lg. Pasar (☎261 2372), off Jl. Masjid Kapitan Keling behind Lh. Chulia. Featured in a scene of Michelle Yeoh's film, *The Touch.* Close to the Indian part of town. Rooms all have showers inside, but common toilets. Rooms Rm18. ❷

FOOD

Streetside *nyonya* cuisine reigns supreme in Penang. The **food stall** ❶ on the corner of Lh. Cintra and Lh. Kimberley dishes out samples of Penang specials. (Open daily 6pm-1am). Another favorite is the oxtail soup at a **food stall** ❶ across from Hotel Continental on Penang Rd. The best spring rolls can be found at the **Popia Lazat Enak** ❶ stall with the tweetie bird decoration (on Gurney Dr., RM1.10 each). Malaysian **food stalls** ❶ line Lh. Tamil. Join locals for dinner at the **night market** ❶. (Call ☎263 8818 for current location.) Lh. Carnavan, between Lh. Chulia and Lh. Campbell, hosts a bustling **morning market.**

PIPIN' HOT IN PENANG

Char Kuey Teow: Flat rice noodles stir-fried with bean sprouts, seafood, and spicy sauce.

Popia: A fresh spring roll.

Top Hats: Crispy bite-size pastries filled with cooked turnips.

Ais Kacang: Shaved ice, sweet corn, sweet red beans, saso, and syrup.

Chendol: Shaved ice with green pea noodles in coconut milk and pandan syrup.

Bubur Cha Cha: Sweet coconut milk over ice with chunks of fruit and colorful rice gummies.

Hameediyah, 164A Lebuh Campbell. Terrific Indian Muslim restaurant with a selection of *Murtabak* curries. Signature Curry Kapitan dish RM3.50. Open daily noon-10pm. ❶

Oriental Seafood Cafe, 62 Jl. MacAlister (☎226 0969), near KOMTAR. Penang's best soft shell crab and baked lobster with cheese. Open daily 5:30pm-midnight. ❸

Rainforest Restaurant, 300 Lh. Chulia. Western staples like homemade health bread with fried eggs (RM3.50). Open M-Sa 8am-midnight. ❶

Green Planet, 63 Lh. Cintra (☎264 1840). Makeshift hut with photos of animals and the Orang Asli people. Scrumptious curry *devil* with lemongrass and turmeric (RM12); veggie burger RM7; chicken chop RM15. Open M-Sa noon-3pm and 7pm-midnight. ❸

The Tandoori House, 34-36 Jl. Hutton, 2 blocks north of the intersection with Penang Rd. Georgetown's finest Mughal restaurant. 19 types of *naan* and 11 types of rice. *Tandoori* *thali* with choice of meat RM14; vegetarian *naurattan qurma* RM11; homemade ice cream *kulfi payalla* RM6. Tax 15%. Open daily 11:30am-3pm and 6:30-10:30pm. ❸

Hard Life Cafe, 363 Lh. Chulia, 400m from Lh. Penang. Pool table and reggae. Beer RM6. Mostly vegetarian dishes (RM5-10). Rooms RM10, for 2 RM12. Open late. ❷

SIGHTS

All sights listed except for Wat Chayamang Kalaram, Fort Cornwallis, and the State Art Gallery are near Jl. Masjid Kapitan Keling (formerly Lh. Pitt).

WAT CHAYAMANG KALARAM. The 33m reclining Buddha at this Thai temple is Malaysia's largest, and reputedly the third largest in the world. *(Accessible by blue bus #93, 94, 102, 202, and minibus #26, 31, and 88. Off the main road to Batu Ferringhi on Lg. Burma. Open daily 8:30am-5:30pm.)* Opposite the temple is **Dhammikarama Burmese Temple,** the only Burmese temple in Malaysia, with intricately carved decorations. *(Meditation class and dharma lecture W 8-9:30pm. Open daily 8am-6pm.)*

PENANG MUSEUM AND ART GALLERY. Fantastic displays give a flavor of Penang's history and culture without the dusty aftertaste of many museum exhibits. Soundbyte displays lend insight into the city's heritage. *(On Lh. Farquar, between St. George's Church and the Cathedral of the Assumption. Open Sa-Th 9am-5pm. RM1.)*

KHOO KONGSI TEMPLE. Signs for various *kongsi*, meaning "dan house," are visible throughout the island. This one stands out for its lavish decoration and innumerable ancestral pillars, whose beauty won it the honor as a location set for *Anna and the King* in 1999. *(On Jl. Masjid Kapitan Keling, near Lh. Acheh. Go through the temple entrance; the meeting hall is on the right, and the temple is down the drive.)* Nearby, on the corner of Lh. Cannon and Lh. American, **Yap Temple** proudly displays intricately hand-carved stone pillars at its entrance. *(Open daily 8am-5pm.)*

FORT CORNWALLIS. A hankering for the imperial past might take you to Fort Cornwallis's cannons and brickwork at the northeast tip of town. Built by Captain Francis Light in 1786 as a defense against the French, Kedah, pirates, and Siam, the fort was the point at which Penang's settlement began. *(On Lh. Pantai, beyond the clock tower and tourist information. Open daily 8:30am-7pm. Last admission 6:30pm. RM1.)*

KUAN YIN TENG. Built in 1800, the temple is devoted to the Buddhist Goddess of Mercy. Devotees at Penang's oldest Chinese temple burn joss paper money for prosperity in the afterlife, with prayers for health, wealth, and longevity in a fog of sandalwood incense. Catch the temple at its liveliest during the feast days for Kuan Yin on the 19th day of the second and sixth lunar months. *(1 block from St. George's. Open daily 9am-6pm.)*

SRI MARIAMMAN TEMPLE. Lord Shiva and his consort Parvati preside over this active Hindu temple, which also shelters the Shrine of the Nine Planets. During the Thaipusam Festival in Jan. or Feb., the lavish Lord Subramanian statue is paraded from the temple. *(The back of the temple is down Jl. Masjid Kapitan Keling near the intersection with Lh. Chulia. The entrance is one block over on Lh. Queen. Open daily 8am–9pm.)*

MASJID KAPITAN KELING. A stark contrast to the frenzy of the Kuan Yin Teng, the mosque was founded in 1801 by an Indian-Muslim merchant, "Kapitan Keling." *(Across Lh. Chulia from Sri Mariamman Temple; walk down Jl. Masjid Kapitan Keling. Open daily 9am-5:30pm.)*

DAYTRIPS FROM GEORGETOWN

Kek Lok Si Temple and **Penang Hill** are accessible from the town of Ayer Itam, while the **Botanical Gardens** is a 2hr. hike from the top of Penang Hill. The **Snake Jungle,** and **Bukit Jambul Orchid, Hibiscus & Reptile Garden** are near the Penang airport.

KEK LOK SI TEMPLE. Blending Chinese, Thai, and Burmese architecture, Kek Lok Si is a must-see. Buddhist laity from all over Malaysia and Thailand flood the temple on Buddhist holidays. Remove your shoes in all sanctuaries; photographing nuns and monks is forbidden. The seven-tiered **Pagoda of 10,000 Buddhas** has six flights of stairs leading to a narrow balcony, which offers a bird's-eye view of Ayer Itam and the countryside as well as a closer look at the giant bronze statue of Kuan Yin at the top of the hill. *(Take bus #1, 85, 91, 101, 351, or minibus #84, 21. (25min.). Open daily 9am-6pm. Pagoda RM2.)*

PENANG HILL. Offering cool temperatures and wonderful views of Georgetown, the hill has a Hindu temple and an unspectacular mosque. You can stop halfway up the cable train to view the rubber plantations of old. Before going home, stop by the Ayer Itam market to try one of the best *laksa* (RM2.50) in front of the red sign. *(Take bus #1, 91, 101, 85, 351, or minibus #21 from Georgetown to Ayer Itam's Roundabout Junction, then take bus #8 (RM0.70) to the foothill. There, a train creeps up 830m Penang Hill (45min.;every 30min., every 15min. in late afternoon, M-F 6:30am-9:30pm, Sa-Su 6:30am-11:45pm; RM3, round-trip RM4). From the top, you can walk down a 3hr. jungle path. Ask for directions and watch the weather.)*

BOTANICAL GARDENS. Northwest of Georgetown, the 30-hectare Botanical Gardens are great for a stroll, jog, or picnic, but on the weekend you're likely to have the rest of Georgetown to keep you company. Admire the rhesus monkeys roaming amid the greenery, but don't feed them. During Hindu festivals, the **Ganesha Temple** on Jl. Waterfall becomes the site of many activities. Stray from the main paths to avoid crowds. *(Take bus #7 from the jeti, Lh. Chulia, or KOMTAR. Alternatively, the hike from atop Penang Hill takes approximately 2hr. Open daily 5am-8pm.)*

BUKIT JAMBUL ORCHID, HIBISCUS & REPTILE GARDEN. As the name suggests, this outdoor sight houses orchid and hibiscus plants, but the highlight is a set of giant tortoises—the elder of which is 150 years old—from the Seychelles Islands. The reptile house is a good spot for observing snakes, thought the tanks could be better maintained. *(Take yellow bus #69 or 83 to Jl. Dr. Awang at Bukit Jambul, then walk 10min. to the garden. ☎644 8863. Open daily 9:30am-6:30pm. Last entry 5:30pm. Free snake show Sa-Su 11:30am, 3:30pm. RM5, children RM2. Camera fee RM1.)*

NEAR PENANG

BATU FERRINGHI

Graced with the natural beauty that earned Penang the nickname "Pearl of the Orient," Batu Ferringhi ("Portuguese Rock") is a seafood dining mecca and local hangout. From the main road toward Teluk Bahang, look for the Coca-Cola sign with "Bayu Senja Kompleks 50m." Keep in mind that taxi drivers may badmouth certain guest houses and send you elsewhere for a commission. To avoid the hassle, ask to be dropped off at the Coca-Cola sign. Better yet, bus #93 or 202 (50m from KOMTAR) will drop you at the police station.

You can roll out of bed and onto the sand from any of the following guest houses. To get to **Baba Guest House ❷,** 52 Batu Ferringhi, turn right down this road and left at the end. Baba is the first guest house on this lane. Laundry, tickets to

Langkawi and Thailand, and motorbike rental (RM53 per day) are available. (☎881 1686. Singles RM20; doubles RM25-30, with bath and A/C RM40-50.) **Shalini's ❷**, 56 Batu Ferringhi, has clean rooms and a restaurant serving inexpensive Malay, Indian, and Chinese food. (☎881 1859. Doubles with fan RM20-30, with A/C and bath RM60. Discounts available.) **Ah Beng Guest House ❸**, offers great deals for A/C rooms. The fan rooms are simpler and more faded. (☎881 1036. Doubles RM30, with A/C, fridge, and bath RM50, triples with A/C, fridge, and bath RM60.)

Hawker stalls ❶ and waterfront **cafes ❶** are scattered amid high-class restaurants; nearly everywhere, a plate of *mee* or a bowl of *laksa* goes for RM3. For the cheapest food in town, try **Bayu Senja Corner Cafe ❶**, on the corner of Jl. Teluk Bahang and Bayu Senja, which serves Malaysian, Chinese, and Thai food. (Fried noodles RM3. Open daily 4pm-5am.) **Poker III Bayu Senja Food Court ❸**, to the right of the guest houses, is a popular beachfront dining spot offering everything from pizza (RM12-25) to Hainanese chicken rice for RM4. (Open daily noon-11pm.)

TELUK BAHANG

Known as "The End of the World" to local Malays because the road out of Georgetown once ended here, Teluk Bahang counterbalances the pressure-cooker atmosphere of Georgetown. Along the tree-lined streets, free-range roosters dodge school children, and laid-back vendors arrange piles of durian and rambutan. At the far end of town lies a *kampung nelayan* (fishing village). Rickety piers, a few weather-beaten boats, and a handful of equally weather-worn folks panning for *goleng* (tiny clams) are all that keep the *nelayan* in this *kampung*. Many travelers stay to enjoy the seafood and explore the nearby monkey beach, **Pantai Acheh Forest Preserve,** and the **Butterfly Park.** To reach Teluk Bahang from Georgetown, take blue bus #93 or 202 from the jetty, Lh. Chulia, or KOMTAR.

The **Fisherman's Village Guest House ❷**, in a turquoise house in the fishing *kampung* off the main road to the right, has basic rooms in a longhouse. Ask for one of the better rooms upstairs. (☎885 29 36. Standards with fan RM18, with A/C RM30.) Near the roundabout on the main road toward Batu Ferringhi, **Hotbay Motel ❸**, 48 Jl. Teluk Bahang, has an attentive staff and brand-new rooms; the sheets are white and clean. All rooms have two twin beds. (☎012 473 5744. Doubles with fan RM40, with A/C RM60; family rooms RM80, on weekends RM100.) For the cheapest stay in town head to **Miss Loh's Guest House ❶.** Coming from Georgetown, turn left at the traffic circle, continue 300m, and take the first right after the Telekom station; it's the first gate on the left after the bridge. (Dorms RM8-10; singles RM15-20.)

As you enter town, the main food center is before the traffic circle on Teluk Bahang. Fare is simple but tasty (RM5). The **night market ❶** by the traffic circle vends *sate, nasi kandar*, chili burgers, and local desserts. (Open daily 7:30-10:30pm.) The **morning market** on the left, beyond the public park on Jl. Teluk Bahang, sells fruits and veggies. (Open daily 6:30am-noon.) **Sun Stall ❶**, on the right side of the main road before the traffic circle, is a Malay and Indian Muslim restaurant open 24hr., serving *char koay teow* (fried flat rice noodles RM2) and banana *roti* with ice cream (RM3). **Dali Cafe ❷**, on the main road across from the gas station, serves Western and Malay meals, including a full Western breakfast for RM10. (Open daily 7am-5pm.) **Fisherman's Village Restaurant ❹**, before Fisherman's Village Guest House, serves fresh seafood. Most restaurants open for dinner at 6pm.

DAYTRIPS FROM TELUK BAHANG

Nature enthusiasts hike at the **Pantai Acheh Forest Reserve,** between Teluk Bahang and Balik Pulau. There, the **Forestry Museum and Arboretum** display the local species of rainforest trees and plants. (Open Tu-Su 9am-noon and 2:45-5pm.) The trail begins where Jl. Teluk Bahang ends, near the jetty at the fishing village. From the trailhead, walk 30min. to a campsite with a shelter near a footbridge where the trail forks. To the right, it leads to a **lighthouse;** the left branch goes to **Keracut Beach,** where there are camping facilities. Those who take the adventurous 2hr. hike to the lighthouse should bring plenty of water. The dangerous parts of the trail are marked with white squares of paper pointing out the best path. The trail leads to an empty beach, beyond which stands an out-of-date "Do Not Enter" sign. (Forest Reserve open daily 7am-7pm.) Erected in memory of the Buddhist priest and healer Chor Soo Kong, the **Snake Temple** boasts snakes that are free to wind around the temple. Every traveler in Malaysia will ask whether you went, but the 45min. bus ride is not quite worth seeing a handful of slithery reptiles unless you're dying for a photo with them. (Take yellow bus #66 or minibus #32. Open daily 7am-7pm. Donations voluntary.) From the roundabout, the road leads south 500m to the **Penang Butterfly Farm,** 830 Jl. Teluk Bahang, which breeds 120 species of butterflies. The farm also has an insect museum, a mini-zoo, and an art gallery. (☎885 12 53. Open M-F 9am-5pm, Sa-Su 9am-5:30pm. RM12.50, children RM6.25. Cameras RM1.) Up the road 5min. is the **Teluk Bahang Recreational Forest,** which boasts **camping facilities ❶** (free), a swimming pool, waterfall, and forest hiking trails. There is also a forestry **museum** near the entrance. (Open daily 7am-7pm.)

Craft Batik, 699 Mk. 2, across the main road from Mutiara Hotel, offers free tours of its factory and a gift shop showcasing traditional Malaysian crafts. (☎885 1302. Factory open daily 8am-5pm;gift shop 8:30am-5:30pm. The factory has been relocated here until renovations are complete at its permanent location, 651 Jl. Teluk Bahang.) The **Pinang Cultural Center,** 288 Teluk Bahang Rd., on the way to Batu Ferringhi, though a bit touristy, has dinner shows with award-winning performances. (☎885 1175. Open M-Sa. Cultural show 9:30am-noon, RM48. Dinner and show 7:30-10:30pm, RM 110. Cultural tour, dinner, and show 6-10pm, RM135.)

PULAU LANGKAWI

Slated to become the Phuket of Malaysia, sparsely populated Langkawi transformed from a fisherman's outpost into an efficient island resort in the early 1990s. The main attractions are eagle feeding and cave viewing, with hours and hours of relaxation to spare. Snorkelers and divers head south for daytrips to Pulau Payar to swim with black-tip sharks and schools of tropical fish.

THE VIEW FROM ABOVE

The lowdown: A well-developed island with everything from parties to sandy beaches.
Major city: Kuah.
Island Mascot: The reddish-brown eagle, for which Langkawi is named.
Beaches: Pantai Cenang, Pantai Tengah, and, the best, Pantai Tanjung Rhu.

KUAH

☎04

Kuah lays claim to *chendol* (shaved ice) hawkers, duty-free and souvenir shops, and five out of Pulau Langkawi's six traffic lights. For the most part, however, it serves as base to explore nearby beaches and the island's lush landscape.

TRANSPORTATION

Flights: Langkawi airport (☎955 1311), at Padang Matsirat, 20km from Kuah. **MAS** ground fl., Langkawi Fair Shopping Mall (☎966 6622), flies to: **Medan,** Indonesia via **Penang** (2hr., 11:35am, RM408); **Kuala Lumpur** (1hr., 5-8 per day 6:35am-9:30pm,

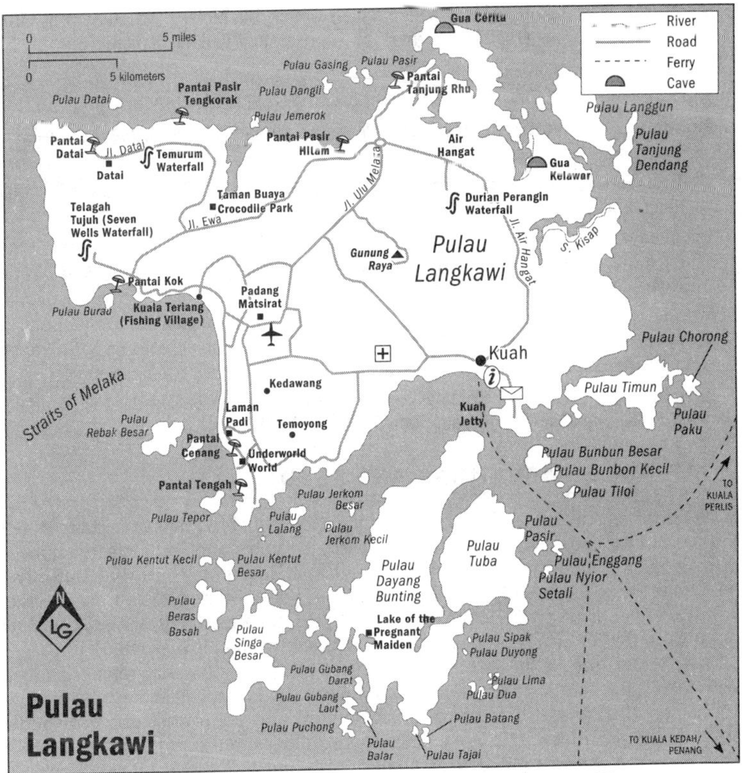

(1½hr.; Tu-Th, Sa 4:45pm; Tu, F, Su 5:10pm; Su-M, F 8:40pm; RM448).

Boats: Ferry companies have counters at the **jetty** (☎966 5889). Ferries go to: **Kuala Perlis** (45min., every 30min. 8am-7pm, RM12); **Kuala Kedah** (1¼hr., every 30min. 8am-7pm, RM15); **Penang** (2½hr.; 2, 2:30, 5:30pm; RM35, round-trip RM60); **Satun,** Thailand (1hr.; 8:30, 10am, 2, 4pm; RM18).

Taxis: Fixed-fare taxis abound. From the jetty to Kuah town (RM4) and **Pantai Cenang** (RM14), or chartered to circumnavigate the island (RM80-100).

Rentals: Major hotels and stores along Pantai Cenang rent **cars** (RM60-150 per day). **Motorcycle** (RM30-50 per day) and **bicycle** (RM3 per hr., RM10-15 per day) rentals are everywhere.

PRACTICAL INFORMATION

Tourist Office: Tourism Malaysia (☎966 7789), on Persiaran Putra. Coming from the jetty into Kuah, it's on the left. Open Sa-W 9am-5pm, Th 9am-1pm. English spoken.

Tours: Langkasia Travel and Tours (☎966 2429), at the jetty. Good prices, fishing, day or sunset cruises, snorkeling, and island-hopping tours. English spoken.

Currency Exchange: Moneychangers abound. **Bumiputra Commerce Berhat,** 1 and 3 Jl. Pandak Mayah 1 (☎966 6725), opposite the hawker stalls. **24hr. ATM** (Cirrus/MC). Open M-F 9:30am-4pm, Sa 9:30am-noon.

Markets: Pasar Malam nightly location rotates among Ulu Melaka (M), Kedawang (Tu), Kuah (W), Temoyong (Th), Air Hangat (F), Kuah (Sa), and Padang Matsirat (Su).

Emergency: ☎999.

Police: ☎966 6222. On Jl. Leboh Kisap opposite the old hospital. **24hr.**

Pharmacy: MNY Multi-Pharmacy, 102 Persiaran Mutiara (☎966 0066). Open daily 8am-11pm.

Medical Service: The **hospital** (☎966 3333) is on Bukit Tekoh, 10km toward Pantai Cenang. English-speaking doctors. **24hr. emergency care.** No credit cards.

Telephones: Telekom Office, Jl. Pandak Mayah 6 (☎966 7202), a few blocks off the main road. Sells **international** and domestic calling cards. Open Sa-W 8:30am-4:30pm, Th 8:30am-1pm. **IDD** from public phones.

Internet: Atiera Computer, Lot 3, Bangunan Arked MARA, in Kuah across from night hawkers. RM2.50 per hr. Open Sa-Th 10am-midnight, 2hr. lunch break on F. On Pantai Cenang, **AB Motel** has Internet. RM2 per 30min. Open daily 10am-midnight.

Post Office: ☎966 8690. Coming from the jetty, it's 500m before the tourist office. *Poste Restante.* Open Sa-Th 9am-5pm. **Postal code:** 07000.

ACCOMMODATIONS AND FOOD

Most travelers stay in nearby Pantai Cenang. Consequently, **Hotel Langkawi ❸,** 6-8 Persiaran Putra, down from the tourist office, is Kuah's only budget accommodation. (☎966 6248. Singles RM30, with A/C and TV RM35; doubles RM40/RM45). The new **Hotel Panggau Libau ❺,** 1592-1594 Persiaran Putra, offers a restaurant, lounge, and travel services. (☎967 2122 or 019 428 2356. Singles RM70, with A/C RM90; doubles RM80/RM100; triples RM90/RM110. Prices drop in low season.)

Despite the lure of the beaches, several of Kuah's restaurants remain packed with locals and tourists alike. For tastebud bliss, try **Prawn Village Restaurant ❷,** 7-10 Jl. Persiaran Putra, between Hotel Langkawi and the tourist office. (Noodle soup RM3. Fish fillet RM10. Open daily noon-2:30pm and 6-11pm). **Rootian Seafood Restoran ❷,** at the corner of Jl. Pandak Mayah and Jl. Pandak Mayah 6, and its neighbor, **Water Garden Hawker Center ❷,** are packed on weekends. (Open Sa-Th 5-11pm.) The **open-air hawker center ❶** lines up along Jl. Persiaran Putra with seafood. On the western end of Kuah is **Aquarium Seafood Garden ❹,** Lot 411, Kelibang, which hosts an evening Thai cultural show (F-W 8:45-9:30pm). Their own fresh seafood is cooked in an open kitchen. (☎966 8888. Open daily noon-11pm.)

SIGHTS AND BEACHES

WATER SPORTS. Pulau Langkawi is full of exquisite beaches, mountains, stone cliffs, and waterfalls. The clearest water and best **snorkeling** are at **Pulau Payar Marine Park** south of Langkawi, which has the best coral reefs off Malaysia's west coast. Full day excursions can be arranged with several travel agencies at the Kuah jetty for RM130 (includes snorkeling gear, nature guide, and ferry transport). Many hotels along Lh. Pantai Cenang arrange island-hopping tours around Pulau Beras Basah (4hr.; 9:30am, 2pm; RM45-60 not including snorkeling gear), tours of the wildlife park on Pulau Singa Besar, and a visit to the gorgeous **Lake of the Pregnant Maiden** on Pulau Dayang Bunting. Many hotels also offer water-skiing and jet-skiing. Fishing boats travel between the Kuah jetty and **Pulau Tuba** (30min., every 30min., RM3). Tuba's beach, fishing village, and bungalows are popular among backpackers and are worth a day trip. Those seeking to get away from conventional tourism can turn to Jürgen Zimmerer, a German nature guide who leads jungle treks (RM70), village excursions to a local *kampung* (RM70), and river safaris around mangrove forests (RM160). Booking is available online. (☎955 4744 or 012 484 8744; www.emmer.net/langkawi-natur/english.)

BEACHES. On the road to Datai is **Pantai Pasir Tengkorak,** a small, clean beach that gets crowded on Fridays when families come to picnic by the water. Down the road is the **Temurum waterfall.** A 10min. walk leads to the pool at its base. During the rainy season (June), the overflowing pool makes this a beautiful picnic spot; during the dry months, the waterfall is reduced to a trickle, but the beauty of the sheer cliff and surrounding trees still make the walk worthwhile. **Pantai Pasir Hitam,** a black-sand beach, is east on Rte. 113. Farther east, a road leads north from the rotary to **Pantai Tanjung Rhu,** Langkawi's most secluded beach. At low tide, walk to the neighboring beach and watch fishermen cast their nets. Tours of nearby caves in the Killem River—**Gua Cerita** and **Gua Kelawar** (the bat cave)—are available. (☎955 2745. RM40.) You can also see eagle feedings at a nearby mangrove swamp. (Feedings RM110 per person, RM250-350 per boat.)

OTHER SIGHTS. North of Pantai Cenang is **Laman Padi,** a rice-paddy-turned-museum with guided tours. (Open daily 10am-6pm. No tours on F. Free.) Small roads off Rte. 115 between Pantai Cenang and Pantai Kok wind through fields, the **Kuala Teriang fishing village,** and Padang Matsirat. By motorbike, you can follow the many small paths that lead off the main road between Padang Matsirat and Ulu Melaka to a quiet, traditional *kampung.* **Pantai Kok,** 15min. past the fishing village, was once one of the best beaches on the island, but is now merely another construction site. Its only redeeming quality is the **Anna and the King Palace** set. (Open daily 10am-7pm. RM3.50, children RM2.) Northwest of Pantai Kok is **Telaga Tujuh,** the **Seven Wells Waterfall.** While the 20min. hike is steep, a splendid view of the surrounding mountains awaits at the top. For the more adventurous, in the wet season the full hike affords spectacular views, refreshing swims in the fall's six wells (the seventh, locals say, is found only by those who get lost in the village), and close contact with monkeys. In the center of the island, a road leads off Rte. 112 to the top of **Gunung Raya,** the tallest mountain on Langkawi. Off Rte. 113 east of the traffic circle, a road leads to **Durian Perangin Waterfall,** whose large pool and thick foliage make it unique. Farther south, Rte. 113 passes a **rubber plantation.**

PANTAI CENANG

Pantai Cenang is an up-and-coming backpacker center. The easiest way to get here is by taxi from the airport (RM15) or Kuah. Family-run, backpacker-friendly **Beachview Chalets ❸,** just steps from the beach, is an unbeatable deal. (☎955 9118. Doubles and triples with A/C, bath, and breakfast RM25 person.) Beachfront **Charlie Motel ❹** has a wide variety of well-kept chalets. From Kuah, continue straight toward the beach—it's on the left near the lighthouse. (All rooms with A/C and bath. Doubles RM65; triples RM75; quads RM65-85.) **AB Motel ❸,** 1km from the intersection of Lh. Pantai Cenang and the road from Kuah, has huts on the beach. (☎955 1300. Doubles with bath and fan RM40, with A/C RM60-120.)

TJays ❸, behind the moneychanger across from Underwater World, serves Italian recipes in a romantic setting. (☎012 451 2867. Delicious thin-crust pizzas RM12-19. Open daily 1pm-late.) For early risers, there's **Breakfast Bar ❷,** a favorite for its laid-back atmosphere and low prices. (☎955 6533. Breakfast from RM4; sandwiches RM5-7; fresh fruit juices RM1.50. Open W-M 7am-2pm.) **Beach Garden Bistro and Beer Garden ❹,** on the beach 500m past AB Motel toward Pantai Kok, serves excellent but expensive international cuisine. (☎955 1363. Happy hour 4-6pm. Open daily 8am-11pm.)

The hottest spot is **Coco Jam,** at the Langkawi Village Resort in Pantai Tengah, where music blasts until the wee hours. (☎955 1511. RM15 cover includes one drink. Disco 11pm. Open daily 10pm-3am.) **Bananas Fun Pub,** in the Awana Hotel, has live music and a karaoke bar. (Beer RM10, pitcher RM34. Open daily 6pm-2am.) Check out marine life at **Underwater World,** on the left as you come from Kuah. (☎955 6100. Open daily 10am-6pm. RM18, children RM10.) The **Taman Buaya Crocodile Park,** on the road to Datai, has croc shows and a 25-foot python. (☎955 2559. Shows 11:45am, 2:15pm. Open Th-Tu 9am-6pm. RM8.)

CAMERON HIGHLANDS

Cool breezes, lush giant ferns, and fuchsia orchids await travelers at this historic retreat. Since 1885, when government surveyor William Cameron hacked away wild jungles to a "fine plateau," the Cameron Highlands have provided a sweet escape for overheated, homesick Brits and, more recently, ornithologists documenting bird species. Outside the cool jungle are vegetable and strawberry farms and vast tea plantations that supply lowlanders with their pekoe. There are three towns: Ringlet, the lowest, is primarily a farmers' hub; Brinchang, the highest, attracts locals for its weekend night market; and Tanah Rata, the main town and most expensive, offers jungle treks and the most conveniences.

TANAH RATA ☎05

In the clouds 14km north of Ringlet and 5km before Brinchang, Tanah Rata emerges with tall, mock-Tudor apartments and hotels interspersed around the main drag, which is lined with restaurants, entrances to jungle treks, and bus and taxi stands. Travelers come here for laid-back and late-night relaxation.

TRANSPORTATION

Buses: From the **bus station** (☎491 2978), halfway down the main road, **Regal Transport Co.** operates local routes to **Brinchang** (10min.) and onward to **Kampung Raja** (35min., every hr. 6:30am-6:30pm, RM0.80) and **Tapah,** a common stopover en route to the Cameron Highlands (2hr., 8 per day 8am-5:30pm, RM5). **Express buses** go to: **Ipoh** (3hr.; 8, 9am, 2:30pm; RM15); **KL** (4½hr.; 8:30, 10:30am, 1:30, 3, 4:30pm; RM13); **Penang/Butterworth** (5½hr., 8:30am and 2:30pm, RM18).

Taxis: ☎491 2355. Next to the bus station. RM18 per hr. is the lowest price. To **Brinchang** or anywhere between Tanah Rata and Brinchang RM4. Outstation taxis will go to all major cities, and even straight to KL's international airport.

ORIENTATION AND PRACTICAL INFORMATION

The town of Tanah Rata begins with a row of restaurants, hotels, and shops on both sides of the street. Two hundred meters down, the **bus station** and **Malay food stalls** signal the end of central Tanah Rata. Past the heart of town, the road leads to Bala's Holiday Chalets 1km away, and then a golf course before Brinchang.

Tourist Information: Souvenir shops sell maps (RM3). Guest houses provide detailed tourist information and free jungle trail maps. Guides and experienced trekkers at guest houses are the best source of information on trails and trekking.

Currency Exchange: HSBC, 31-32 Main Rd. (☎491 1217). Open M-F 9:30am-3:30pm, Sa 9:30-11:30am. **24hr. ATM** (Cirrus/MC/PLUS/V). **Maybank,** 69-70 Persiaran Camellia 4 (☎491 4897), by the cake house, exchanges currency. Open M-F 9:30am-4pm, Sa 9:30-11:30am. The **moneychanger** at Maybank exchanges traveler's checks (RM10 for the 1st check, RM0.15 per subsequent check). Open daily 9:30am-5:30pm.

MALAYSIA

Emergency: ☎999.

Police: ☎491 1222. Next to the hospital at the northern edge of town. **24hr.** English-speaking officers available on call.

Medical Service: Hospital (☎491 1966), on the left of the main road at the end of town. During office hours (M-F 8am-4:30pm), check in at registration room on left. **24hr. emergency care.** English spoken. No credit cards.

Telephones: No available Telekom office, but Telekom card phones all over town.

Internet Access: Pusat Computer CL, 55B, 1st fl., Persiaran Camellia 3, near Maybank. RM2.80 per hr. Open daily 9am-11pm. Most guest houses also offer Internet access.

Post Office: (☎491 10 51), on the left of the main road near Orient Hotel. Open M-Sa 8:30am-5pm. **Postal code:** 39000.

ACCOMMODATIONS

Nearly all guest houses provide attractive services, including free pickup, bus reservations, international phone service, hot water (you'll need it), kitchen facilities, book exchange, movies, food, Internet access, and tourist information.

Father's Guest House, P.O. Box 15 (☎491 2484). Perks include: 5 acres of luscious greenery; 2 dalmatians; unique Nissen-hut dorms; a volleyball court. Excellent Internet. Lower rates for longer stays. Reserve in advance. Dorms RM8; doubles RM20-30, with bath and shower RM35-80; triples RM27-55; quads RM50. ❶

Twin Pine Chalets, Jl. Mentigi 2 (☎491 2169). Follow the signs from the main road or call for pickup. Variety of rooms, with very simple attic ones for longer stays. Clean facilities. Laundry. Restaurant. Internet RM3 per hr. Attic rooms RM7.50-10. Dorms RM7; doubles RM16-30; family rooms RM40-60; rooms with bath from RM30. ❶

Daniel's Travelers Lodge, Lorong Perdah 9 (☎491 5823). The street is 1 block from the bus station. Bonfires every night. Trekking guide leads patrons into the jungle. Dorms with lockers RM6-8; singles and doubles RM16-35; triples RM24-40; quads RM32. ❶

Cameronian Inn, Jl. Mentigi 16 (☎491 1327), in a quiet area off the main road. Clean and comfortable. Trail maps, currency exchange, Internet, and motorbike rentals. Dorms RM6; singles/doubles RM18-30, with shower RM35-60; triples/quads RM30-60. ❶

Bala's Holiday Chalets, Lot 55 (☎491 1660), 2km from town (look for sign). Serene surroundings and elegant architecture. Free pickup from the bus station. Reserve ahead on weekends. Doubles RM66, RM120 on weekends; family rooms from RM120. ❺

FOOD

Delicious, inexpensive food is everywhere. Don't miss the **steamboat hot pot** offered by most restaurants. As you enter town, head for the right side of the road before the bus station for food stalls serving cheap, standard Malay and Chinese fare. The best are **Excellent Food Stall** ❶ (open daily 7am-5pm) and **Zainab San** ❶, which serves Malay food. Several good Indian and Chinese restaurants are on the left side of the road. Guest houses serve food as well.

Mayflower Restaurant, 22 Main Rd. (☎491 1793). Locals agree it's the best in town. *Tom yam* RM10; steamboat hot pots RM10-13; fried rice or noodles RM5. ❸

Restoran Bunga Suria, 66A Persiaran Camellia 3, beyond the palm trees when facing Ringlet. Runner-up on the "local favorites" list. Buffet-style banana leaf meals RM5. Many vegetarian options. Open daily 7am-10pm. ❶

The Orient Restaurant, 38 Main Rd. (☎491 1633). Great atmosphere with a collection of red lanterns and Chinese opera paraphernalia. Steamboat RM12-13. ❸

Yong Teng Cafe, Stall G15, beside the taxi stand. Pancakes with fresh highlands strawberries and ice cream RM2.50; curry noodle soup RM2.50. Open daily 7am-5pm. ❶

SIGHTS

The Highlands' best sights are agricultural. Picturesque tea plantations and terraced vegetable, strawberry, and dairy farms make a surreal "food pyramid." Check out the camouflaged leaf frogs and foot-long stick insects at the **Butterfly Park.** (Open daily 8:30am-5:30pm. RM3, children RM1.50.) Boh ("Best of Highlands") Tea Estates runs free factory tours at two locations. **Sungai Palas Boh Tea Estate,** north of Brinchang, is accessible by taxi, bus, or foot on Path #1. The cafe at larger **Boh Tea Estate** also provides stunning views of the emerald carpet of tea plants. It is 5km from Paths #9 and 9A—taxi is the best option. (Both open Tu-Su 9am-4:30pm.) **Daily countryside tours,** available at all accommodations, include a visit to the tea plantation and factory, and some combination of a Buddhist temple, strawberry garden, vegetable farm, butterfly garden, honey-bee farm, rose center, and market center. (4hr., 9am-2pm, RM15 not including admission to the rose center (RM4) and butterfly farm (RM3). Tea estates closed on M.)

Hiking is the preferred Highlands activity. Most guest houses offer trail maps and gladly answer questions about specific paths. Count on each hike being more difficult than its description, and be careful after it rains, when trails are treacherous. The mountains of **Gunung Brinchang** (2000m) and **Gunung Perdah** (1550m) have excellent panoramic views from their peaks. The hikes' level of difficulty varies widely depending on the approach taken. Path #1 to Gunung Brinchang is *very* steep. A paved road from the viewpoint leads 7km to Sungai Palas Boh Tea Estate and then another 6km to the main road. You can also climb up and arrange a car back. Path #10 goes to Gunung Jasar (1670m) before connecting with Path #12 to Gunung Perdah. Paths #3, 5, 7, and 8 lead to Gunung Peremban, with Path #8 being the steepest and most challenging. In contrast, the easiest and shortest is Path #4, a short-cut to the golf course that passes by Parit Falls before ending at Taman Sedia, which has a picnic area and trees with labels identifying their species. By far the most popular trek (highly recommended for people of average fitness level) are Paths #9 and 9A, which form a loop from Robinson Waterfall to **vegetable farms** and a **mini dairy farm** near the **Boh Tea Estate.** Path #9A is a pleasant downhill walk and the easier of the two. Budget 4-5hr. round-trip for all paths except #1, which may take a full day, and #4, which should take 1½-2hr. at most. Almost all the paths are within walking distance from Tanah Rata town. Path #1 starts from Brinchang.

BRINCHANG ☎05

A short **taxi** (RM4) or **bus** ride (RM0.80) from Tanah Rata, Brinchang is less sophisticated than Tanah Rata, but still attracts tourists for its markets. **Jl. Besar,** also known as the **Main Rd.,** loops around the central square. The car park, which becomes a **night market** on weekends and public holidays (open 4-11pm), occupies most of the square; the indoor **day market** is at the southern end. Restaurants, hotels, clinics, and shops surround the square. To its west, behind Hong Kong Hotel, is **Bandar Baru,** another looped street, with **laundry,** a **bank,** and a **drugstore.** The local **bus stop** is on Main Rd. next to the Hong Kong Hotel. (Buses stop at indefinite times; expect a 15-30min. wait.) **Public Bank** is at 41-43 Bandar Baru. (☎491 1590. Open M-F 9:30am-4pm, Sa 9:30-11:30am.) The **GPO** is on Main Rd. past the square on the left. (☎491 1016. Open M-Sa 8:30am-12:30pm and 2:30-5pm. Closed every other Sa.) **Postal code:** 39100.

Brinchang's budget accommodations are frequently booked on weekends, but discounts are usually available during the week. For backpacker camaraderie, stay in Tanah Rata (see **Tanah Rata: Accommodations,** p. 413). The **Chua Gin Hotel ❸,** 11 Main Rd., has a friendly staff and honors guests' privacy. (☎491 1801. All rooms with bath. Doubles RM35; triples RM45; quads RM55; quints RM65.) The newer branch around the corner, **The Golden Wing ❹,** has more spacious rooms. (☎491 1801. Doubles RM55; triples RM65; quads RM75.) **Hill Garden Lodge ❺,** 15-16 Jl. Besar, has immaculate rooms and a pleasant atmosphere. (☎491 2988. Doubles RM98; triples RM119; quads RM138.) Brinchang's Chinese food is good. **Malay food stalls ❶** cluster in the central square. **Shal's Curry House ❷,** 25 Main Rd., with a fish-head logo, is one of Malaysia's trendiest South Indian restaurants and serves food with a kick. Try the cheese *roti* (RM4), a *lassi* that is to die for (RM4.50), or Shal's famous apple strudel (RM5.90). (☎491 2408. Open daily 8am-10pm.)

INTERIOR PENINSULAR MALAYSIA

Malaysia's development has wrought enormous environmental harm throughout the peninsula. The protected parklands of Taman Negara, the interior's premiere attraction, sometimes seem to be the lone pristine oasis. Eco-conscious travelers still sneer at the unabashed marketing and development of this "virgin jungle paradise," but these trappings are only in the main resort—the rest remains relatively untouched, and efforts to maintain Malaysia's natural heritage deserve applause.

JERANTUT ☎09

Jerantut is largely a gateway to Taman Negara and is the best place to stock up on supplies and info about treks and other adventures.

TRANSPORTATION AND PRACTICAL INFORMATION. Taman Negara can be reached by land (1½hr.) or by water (3hr.). While the bus ride is faster, many travelers opt for the scenic boat ride at least one way. **Boats** leave for Taman Negara from **Kuala Tembeling,** 25min. outside Jerantut. To get there, take a shuttle from any of the hotels (RM4 from Hotel Sri Emas, RM5 from Green Park Rest House) or a **taxi** (RM16). NKS Hotel & Travel at Hotel Sri Emas runs **minibuses** to Kuala Tahan headquarters in Taman Negara. The Agro Tour is highly recommended. (1½hr.; 2:30, 5:30pm, or anytime for four or more people; RM15, with Agro Tour RM23.) The **bus station** is on Jl. Diwangsa. **Local buses** go to **Kuala Tembeling** (30min.; 8:15, 11am, 1:45pm; RM1.50). **Express buses** run to **Kuantan** (3½hr.; 8:30, 11am, 2:30pm; RM10.50) and **Temerloh** (1½hr., 12 per day 6am-6:30pm, RM4.20). **Express Perwira buses** depart at 8:30, 10:30am, 2:30, and 4pm for: **Klang** (4hr., RM12.65); **KL** (3hr., RM10.85); **Temerloh** (1hr., RM3.50). The station in Temerloh serves some destinations that the Jerantut station does not. The **train station** (☎266 2219) is on Jl. Stesen Keretapi. Jungle trains crawl to: **KL** (6½hr., daily 12:30am plus weekends 9:25pm, RM15-25); **Singapore** (8½hr., 9:05am, RM15-30; express 7¼hr., 2:20am, RM19-38); **Wakaf Bharu** near Kota Bharu (9hr., 12:20pm, RM12.60; express 6¼hr., 3:30am, RM18-32). Taxis go to **Kota Bharu** (RM240); **KL** (RM120); **Kuala Tahan** (RM90); **Kuantan** (RM100). Share rides to offset costs.

The two main roads are **Jl. Besar** and **Jl. Diwangsa. Bank Simpanan Nasional,** on Jl. Diwangsa, opposite the bus station, has a **24hr. ATM** (MC/PLUS/V. ☎266 5300. Open M-F 9am-4pm, Sa 9am-noon.) The **hospital** (☎266 3333) is outside the town off Jl. Besar. Turn left from the bus station onto Jl. Diwangsa and the **post office** is at the end of the street, near the intersection with Jl. Bomba. (☎266 2201. Open M-Sa 8:30am-5pm.) **Postal code:** 27000.

ACCOMMODATIONS AND FOOD. **Green Park Rest House ❶,** on Jl. Benta, 2min. from the mosque, is the most pleasant place in town. The amiable proprietor, Azam, has over 15 years experience as a tour guide. He holds nightly talks on park trails in addition to leading two tours (both 3 days and 2 nights; both RM250) geared toward more adventurous tourists. (☎266 3884. All rooms with bath. A/C dorms RM12; doubles RM30, with A/C RM45; triples RM40/RM55; quads RM50/RM65; deluxe chalets with A/C, TV, and carpet RM60-70; 5-person A/C suites RM90.) Closer to town is their newly renovated **Green Park Guesthouse ❶,** 34 Jl. Besar. Both Green Park accommodations have lounges, luggage storage, shower facilities for guests in transit, free pickup from bus or train stations, and **24hr.** check-in. (☎266 3884. Dorms RM6-8; singles RM10-12; doubles RM15-20; triples RM21-27.) In the center of town, **Sri Emas ❶,** on Jl.Besar, across from the police station, offers clean rooms at great prices. Call ahead for **24hr.** pick-up from bus and train stations. **NKS Travel** is based here and provides the usual run of park-related services. Ask for the fun and fearless Angie, the only female guide in the park. Sri Emas also offers standard amenities such as a restaurant, luggage storage, Internet, and showers for guests on the go. (☎266 4499. All A/C rooms with bath. Dorms RM7; doubles RM15, with A/C RM38, with A/C and TV RM48; triples RM21, with A/C and TV RM56; quads with A/C and TV RM64.) **Chong Heng Hotel ❶,** 24 Jl. Besar, is a cozy and quiet backpacker's place above a coffeehouse. The proprietor, Mr. Tan, is knowledgeable about Taman Negara and speaks excellent English. (☎266 3693. Dorms RM8; doubles RM15; triples RM21.)

Dine at one of the outdoor restaurants across from the market on Jl. Pasar Besar. The **night market ❶** offers the standard *kavay teow*/fried rice/*satay* standards for RM4-5. (Open Sa 4-10pm.) Look for *roti canai* stands with late-night snacks. **Restoran Al-Haj ❶,** next to Sri Emas, serves delectable Malay food like *nasi lemak* (RM0.80, with egg RM1.50) and white rice dishes—choose your own meats, fish, and vegetables for RM3-5. (☎266 2161. Open M-Sa 7:30am-10pm.)

TAMAN NEGARA NATIONAL PARK ☎09

As powerful as this 130-million-year-old rainforest seems, it is all that is left of its kind on the peninsula due to heavy deforestation. As Malaysia's first and largest national park, Taman Negara is one of the world's best-kept rainforests; yet, it is teetering on the brink of ecological disaster.

TRANSPORTATION

Taman Negara and its gateways, **Jerantut** and **Kuala Tembeling,** are accessible by **bus** from **KL** or **Kuantan,** and by **train** from **Wakaf Bharu** or **Singapore.** The park can be reached by privately arranged **bus** or **taxi,** or by **boat** on the Tembeling River. Boats to the park (3-3½hr.; 9am, 2pm; return 2-2½hr.; Sa-Th 9am, 2pm, F 9am, 2:30pm; RM19 each way) leave from the village of **Kuala Tembeling,** accessible by bus (RM1.50), minibus from hotels (RM4-5), or share-taxi (RM4 per person, RM16 per car) from Jerantut. Minibuses from Jerantut are RM15: from Hotel Sri Emas (2:30, 5:30pm) and from Nusa Camp information center at the bus station (6:30am, 4pm). Look for monkeys, lizards, water buffalo, and colorful birds on the shores. In Kuala Tembeling, fixed-price **share-taxis** (4-passenger max.) go to: **Jerantut** (RM16, with A/C RM18); **KL** (RM140); **Kuantan** (RM120). At Taman Negara, **boats** shuttle across the river for RM0.50 (7:30am-11pm). Nusa Camp runs **riverbuses** (RM30-290 per day) within the park that are cheaper than private charters. **Nusa Riverbus** routes go from Kuala Tahan to **Nusa Camp** (10am, 12:30, 3, 6pm; RM3 for registered guests, RM7 for non-guests), **Blau and Yong observation hides** (8:30am, 5:30pm; RM7), **Kuala Terengganu** (10am, 3pm; RM15, round-trip RM20), and the **cave** (9:30, 11:45am, 2:45pm; RM5, round-trip RM8).

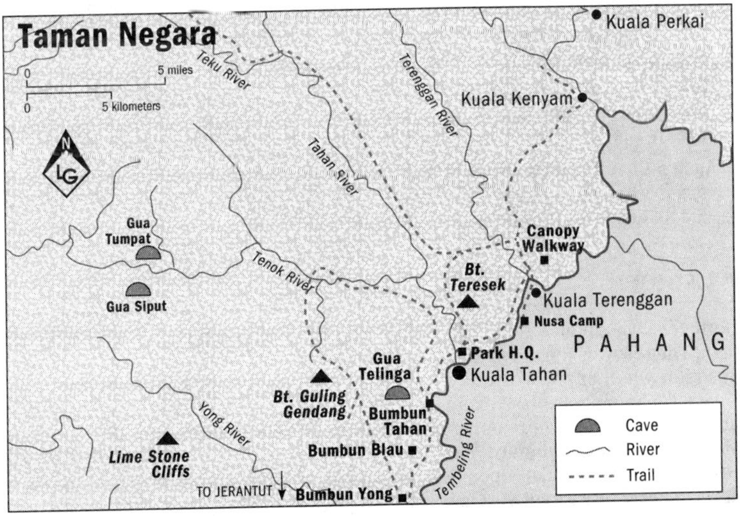

ORIENTATION AND PRACTICAL INFORMATION

Book your boat ride and accommodations at least one night in advance, especially during weekends and holidays. Hold on to your **permits** (RM1, camera RM5), as you can be fined RM50-500 if caught without one during random checks; you will also be asked to produce them when you leave. Bring extra cash; the only moneychanger is at the resort and has horrible rates. Also stock up on insect repellent and a flashlight if planning to go for a jungle or night trek.

Park headquarters, next door to a minimart, is on the left of the Tembeling River, near the park's south entrance. Across the river is the village of **Kuala Tahan** with cheaper hostels and floating restaurants. The reception area at the resort offers **telephone service** at rip-off prices. **Internet** cafes in Kuala Tahan charge about RM4 per hr. Good **maps** (RM2) with trails and points of interest are available at the Wildlife Office at the park headquarters. The resort office next to reception **rents hiking and camping gear** (tent RM20; sleeping bag RM3; jungleboots RM3). If you're undertaking a lengthy hike or are inexperienced, consider hiring one of the expensive but knowledgeable **guides** (around RM120 per day, RM600 per week). Guides specialize in different activities and areas of the park, so ask around. For the Taman Negara environs (including Kuala Tahan, Kuala Tembeling, and Jerantut) the **postal code** is 27000. Drop off mail at the resort reception desk.

ACCOMMODATIONS

For cheaper accommodations, cross the river to Kuala Tahan. It is advisable to make your own reservations rather than go through travel agencies in Jerantut.

Nusa Camp and SPKG Tours, 16 Jl. Diwangsa (☎266 2369), at Jerantut bus station. **KL Office:** Studio 2B, Arcadia Green, 1 Jl. Sultan Ismail (☎03 2070 5401). **Kuala Tembeling Office:** No. 5, Taman Negara Jetty (☎266 3043). Upriver from the Taman Negara Resort and more serene than jetty-area lodging. Rates include boat transfer between Nusa Camp and Kuala Tembeling. Campsite RM2, 2-person tent RM15; dorms RM15; A-frame chalet RM55; Malay cottages RM100; Malay house RM110. ❶

Tembeling Riverview Chalet (☎266 6766), first on the right up the stairs from the river. Has a great view of the scenic, though murky river, and a home-grown campground feel. Usually full. Dorms RM10; doubles RM45; quads RM60. ❶

Teresek View Motel (☎266 9744). Although it is a bit of a hike to get up the hill, RM10 hostel beds can't be beat. A-frames for 2 people RM40. Clean and cozy Malay houses RM 60, with A/C RM100. ❶

Agoh's Chalets (☎266 9570), farther up the embankment past Teserek View. Neat rooms with bath and newly tiled floors surrounding a garden. Dorms RM20; doubles RM40; quads RM100. ❷

FOOD

Both Nusa Camp and Taman Negara Resort have restaurants, but the prices are high. The resort is the only place in town to get a beer, though at RM18 you have to question whether it's worth it. For snacks and soft drinks, mini-markets on the Kuala Tahan side are less expensive than the one at the resort. Several eateries line the river on the shore opposite the resort. The **Family Restaurant** ❷ offers tasty Malay dishes and standard Western fare. (Burgers RM2.50; *tom yam* RM4.50; *satay* RM5 for 10 sticks. Open daily 8am-11pm.) The most romantic place to eat is at the **Rumbia Restaurant** ❸. Their *soya* sauce fish (RM20) is excellent, as are their lychee shakes (RM3). Look for the thatched roof at the end of Kuala Tahan's riverfront. (Most dishes RM5. Open daily 8am-11pm.)

OUTDOOR ACTIVITIES

Taman Negara never experienced an ice age and, as a result, is the oldest rainforest in the world. Trails are clearly marked, so it's easy to slip away in the early morning and surround yourself in the virgin jungle. The larger mammals—elephants, tigers, rhinos, leopards, and cattle—are rarer sights these days, but amazing insects, birds, and lush forest make this a forest a must-see.

CAMPING AND HIKING. The **nine-day trek** to and from **Gunung Tahan,** Peninsular Malaysia's highest peak, and the nearby four-tiered waterfall is the best way to take in the ecological riches. You must purchase food and supplies in Kuala Tahan, or hire a porter (RM600 per week, including food and water). Travelers must consult with park authorities beforehand and hire a **guide** (RM600 for 1 week, RM70 for each subsequent day). The information desk at the resort has postings from people willing to split costs. Travel agencies in Kuala Tahan organize shorter hikes, starting at two days and one night (RM200, including food, water, and shelter; minimum four people). Book with the Ombak Restaurant. Another recommended trek is the 31km **Tenor Trail** through dense jungle; ask for Nizram, the guide who is most familiar with this path. When camping on your own, pitch tents away from the river to protect against unexpected floods. The mostly uphill climb to **Bukit Teresek** (1.7km, 1hr.) offers breathtaking panoramas. Bring plenty of water.

CANOPY WALKWAY. Suspended by a web of ropes, wires, cables, and wooden planks along the treetops, the canopy walk is the longest crossing of its kind. This can be its selling point, although for those afraid of heights, it is 500m of sheer torture. The view 40m above the forest floor is tremendous; bring a camera. Authorities regularly test the safety of the walkway. It pays to go early to avoid crowds or long waits (only four people are allowed on the walkway at a time). The canopy walkway is 1.2km (25min.) from the headquarters. Set aside 30min. to 2hr. total. (Open Sa-Th 11am-3pm, F 9am-noon. RM5.)

GUA TELINGA. Also known as the "Ear Cave," this limestone cave is a tourist favorite. Look for bats and non-poisonous snakes that feed on the bats. The cave is slippery and dirty, so bring old clothes, sturdy shoes, and a flashlight. (2.6km, 1½hr. hike each way; 25min. by Nusa Riverbus).

NIGHT ADVENTURES. The rainforest really comes to life at night. Explore it on a guided night hike (RM15), 4WD safari tour (RM25), or river cruise (RM35). Hikes focus more on insects and phosphorescent fungi, while safaris attempt to track the more elusive wildlife. Be forewarned that chances of spotting wildlife around or during the full moon are slimmer, as animals are more cautious to avoid predators. Bring a flashlight. Check for times and book through the Family Restaurant.

OBSERVATION HIDES. These *bumbun*, as they are called in Malay, are elevated viewing platforms in the midst of the jungle. The platforms are enclosed with a narrow opening for viewing wildlife. Travelers are encouraged to stay overnight for increased chances of seeing animals, although it is more likely that you will just enjoy the sounds of the forest. **Bumbun Tahan** is the closest to headquarters (200m) and the most frequently visited by night trekkers. It has a great view of a salt lick to which many animals migrate. **Bumbun Blau** and **Bumbun Yong** are accessible by boat or by foot (3km and 3.9km from headquarters, respectively). Nusa Riverbus runs to Blau and Yong hides (15min. downstream and a 10min. walk; 8:30am, 5:30pm; RM7, round-trip RM10). Bring flashlights.

RIVER RAFTING AND TUBING. Ride the rapids in a "boat" or float down the river in a rubber tube for a new vantage point from which to see the forest—on your back. Expect to get wet. Book trips at the Family Restaurant at least an hour in advance. (2hr.; 10am, 3pm; RM25 per person including life jacket).

PERHENTIAN ISLANDS ☎09

One of the world's most beautiful beaches, Long Beach has brought widespread fame to the Perhentian Islands. Tourists come in search of great coral deposits, snorkeling, and scuba diving, and settle for the evening barbecues and starry nights that make up the islands' nightlife, which is limited by meager alcohol reserves. Those hoping for a taste of indigenous culture will be disappointed, as vacationers from around the world flock to the islands during tourist season. In rainy months, however, visitors find cheap hostels, fewer tourists, and great surf.

THE VIEW FROM ABOVE

The lowdown: Eastern Malaysia's northernmost island group.
Islands: Pulau Perhentian Kecil ("Little Island") and Pulau Perhentian Besar ("Big Island").
Gateway city: Kuala Besut and Tok Bali.
Beaches: On Kecil: Coral Bay, Long Beach, Mira Beach, Petani Beach, Adam and Eve beach. On Besar: Blue Lagoon, Flora Beach, Main Beach.

TRANSPORTATION

There are two embarkation points for the Perhentians—Kuala Besut and Tok Bali—which are easily accessed via Kota Bharu or Kuala Terengganu. From Kuala Besut or Tok Bali, take a boat to the islands. Tok Bali is about 20min. closer to Kota Bharu than is Kuala Besut, but boats run more frequently from Kuala Besut.

TO KUALA BESUT: From **Kota Bharu,** take a taxi to Kuala Besut (1½hr., RM28 per 4 people). Booking a taxi from a guest house (they usually arrange for a car-pool, even for non-guests) will certainly cost less than the whopping RM40 that you'll be

MALAYSIA

charged at the bus station. If you can't find other passengers to split the cost, take bus #3 to **Pasir Putih** (1hr., every 30min. 6:30am-7:30pm, RM2.80) and catch bus #96 to Kuala Besut (30min., every 30min. 6:30am-6:30pm, RM1.60). From **Kuala Terengganu,** a direct bus now heads to Kuala Besut (2½hr., 7:15am-4:30pm, RM5).

TO TOK BALI: From **Kota Bharu,** take a taxi to Tok Bali (1hr. 10min., RM24 per 4 people). Or call one of the boat services to be picked up from the bus station at **Pasir Puteh** (KB Backpackers Holiday ☎743 2125; Berjaya ☎019 962 3878).

TO THE PERHENTIANS: Boats leave for the islands from **Kuala Besut** nearly every hour or when full from around 10am to 3pm (slow boats 1½-2hr., RM20, round-trip RM40, children RM10/RM20; speed boats 30min., RM30, round-trip RM60, children RM15/RM30). From **Tok Bali,** speed boats depart at 7, 11am, and 2:30pm, while slow boats depart at 10am and 3pm (travel time and prices same as Kuala Besut). Boats bring passengers to their beach of choice on either **Besar** or **Kecil,** where motorboat taxis charge RM2 to drop passengers on shore. Returning from the Perhentians, slow boats leave at 8am and noon, and speed boats leave at 8am, noon, and 4pm. The Tourist Information Center and many guest houses in Kota Bharu and Kuala Besut sell boat tickets.

WHAT TO EXPECT Accommodations can be difficult to find during the high season (June-Aug. and public holidays). **Arrive in Kuala Besut for the 10am boat departure, or in Tok Bali for the 7am departure, as accommodations on the islands fill up quickly.** Most accommodations close from Nov.-Jan. Reservations usually aren't accepted except at more upscale resorts, and scant telephone lines make local phone calls impractical. If you don't find a bed, check with reception for free rooms the next morning at 7:30 or 11:30am, when people usually check out. It is also common for backpackers to camp on the beach in peak season. Accommodations are cheaper during the low season.

MALAYSIA

PULAU PERHENTIAN KECIL ☎09

With the constant criss-crossing of motorboats, the monotone hum of generators, and hip, young backpackers kicking back on every available plot of land, Kecil is not a mecca of serenity. But crowds aside, Long Beach is arguably Malaysia's most beautiful locale.

ORIENTATION AND PRACTICAL INFORMATION

Long Beach is on the island's east coast. Accommodations span the entire length of the beach, while tourist services run up the center. On the west coast, a 15min. walk from **Mohsin Chalets,** is quieter **Coral Bay.** A 25min. jungle trek south is **Mira Beach.** Another 20min. takes you to the southern coast and larger **Petani Beach. Perhentian Village,** on the island's southeast tip, 20min. from Petani, is home to fishermen, a **police station,** and **medical services. Motorboat taxis** line up along **Long Beach** and go to: **Coral Bay** (RM14); **D'Lagoon** (RM4); **Mira Beach** (RM12); **Perhentian Village** (RM8); **Petani Beach** (RM10); **Pulau Perhentian Besar** (RM7-15). Taxis are pricier in the evening due to rougher waves.

Tourist Office: No official tourist office, although **Turtle Shop** (☎010 983 3538), at the center of Long Beach, offers info on entertainment, transportation, and the turtle hatchery. Snorkeling trips run RM30 including equipment rental. Open daily 9am-7pm.

Currency Exchange: Both Turtle Shop and **Mama's Place** in Coral Bay change traveler's checks. Major resorts on Pulau Besar change currency at poor rates. Don't count on plastic; credit card machines at hotels are unreliable. **Bring cash from the mainland.**

Alternatives to Tourism: See **employment** under **Activities,** p. 422.

Police: ☎697 7722. In a blue building along the village beach. Open daily 8am-4pm.

Medical Services: ☎697 7680. Behind the police, across a small bridge. Basic care. English spoken. Open M W, Sa 8am-4:50pm. Go to the mainland for emergency care.

Telephones: International calls available at high rates at some accommodations. Usually RM10 per min. A **Telekom Malaysia** booth is next to the police station. For mobile phone users, the best reception is at Coral Beach.

Post Offices: Turtle Shop has stamps and better mail service than the village **post office. Postal code:** 22200.

ACCOMMODATIONS

Most accommodations on Long Beach are full throughout the tourist season (June-Aug.). Some travelers head to less-frenzied and more affordable Coral Bay or hire a boat to one of Besar's smaller beaches. Kecil offers secluded beaches.

LONG BEACH

Mohsin (☎010 333 8897) has large bungalows on the hill above the beach. Linens and towels provided. Restaurant attached. Rates in high season include dinner for 2. 24hr. electricity. All rooms with fan and bath. New dorms RM35. Low/high season doubles RM40/RM65; twins RM55/RM74; family rooms RM65/RM85. ❸

Mateheri (☎019 956 5756), in the center of the beach. Bungalows are set back in a garden with a restaurant. Laundry and safety deposit. Rates include dinner for 2. All rooms with mosquito nets and fan. Doubles RM40, with bath RM50-80. ❸

Panorama (☎010 912 2518), set back from the beach. Restaurant shows movies. High season rates include dinner. Chalets RM20/RM45, with bath RM40/RM80. ❷

Chempaka (☎010 985 7329), has a variety of standard options in a garden. All rooms have Western baths and mosquito nets. A-frames RM15/RM30; longhouses for 2 with bath and fan RM25/RM50; bungalows for 2 with bath and fan RM30/RM60. ❷

Bubu Long Beach (☎03 2078 0080), a new addition to Long Beach, caters to tourists looking for luxury. All rooms have A/C, fan, hot water, and towels. Bar and dive shop. Rooms with 2 doubles RM150; rooms with 4 bunk beds and 1 double RM250. ❺

CORAL BAY

A 10min. stroll across the island from Long Beach is Coral Bay, Kecil's second most popular beach.

Maya Beach Resort has immaculate new chalets with Western toilets surrounding a hammock garden. Doubles RM50, beachfront RM80. ❹

Rajaweli Corel Beach Resort (☎011 344 5688), at Coral Bay's north end. Balcony cafe and friendly staff make for a pleasant stay. Watersports rental and Internet. Reserve ahead. Spacious dorms RM20; A-frames RM40; cabin-style doubles with fan, A/C, and bath RM100-200; great A/C family rooms with tons of amenities RM180. MC/V. ❷

Aur Bay Chalets (☎697 7694), where the trail to Long Beach starts. Doubles with fan RM35; beautiful dark-red wooden chalets with fan and bath RM50-60. ❸

DJ Chalet (☎013 622 1906) has basic chalets in a wooded area. The cheapest lodging on the beach. Indulge in the sinful "DJ special" (chocolate banana shake RM3.50) at the restaurant. Chalets with mosquito nets and squat toilets RM25. ❸

OTHER BEACHES

From the south end of Coral Bay, a trail (follow the splotches of white paint on rocks and trees) heads for quiet **Mira Beach** (45min.) and **Petani Beach** (1-1½hr.).

Mira Beach, accessible by boat or hike from Coral Bay. Owners Suapi and Zainab create a warm family atmosphere. Hillside rooms surround the small beach. Restaurant open daily 7am-11pm. Set dinners RM10; barbecue RM15. Snorkel gear rental RM4 per hr., RM10 per day. Kayaks RM10 per hr., RM40 per day. Malay longhouses RM30-50. ❸

Petani Beach Chalets (☎019 957 1624), between Mira Beach and the village. Take a boat or hike from Coral Beach. Cozy bungalows in a garden. Restaurant fish special RM15. Snorkel gear rental. Reserve ahead. Bungalows with fan and bath RM60. ❹

Impiani Beach Resort (☎697 7346), on Petani Beach. Classy octagonal chalets with great interior. Restaurant with extensive menu. All rooms with A/C and hot-water bath. Reserve ahead. Doubles RM140, with sea view RM180. MC/V. ❺

D'Lagoon (☎010 985 7089), on the island's northeast tip, accessible by water taxi. Short hike to west coast beaches. Restaurant set dinners RM10. Gear rentals. Camping RM5, with tent RM15; dorms RM10; treehouse RM20; rooms with bath RM50. ❶

FOOD

Most accommodations have attached restaurants or *cafis*. By night, restaurants in the center of Long Beach set up barbecues with fresh seafood, chicken, and veggie options (meat, sauce, rice or fries, and fruit RM10-15). The restaurant at **Panorama** makes pizza with veggie or meat options (small RM10, large RM15). **Shake Shack** mixes up gigantic shakes for RM4 and serves mouth watering banana and chocolate pancakes for RM3.50. On Coral Bay, try the homemade cakes (RM2.50) from the **Cake Lady** in front of DJ Chalets.

ACTIVITIES

Nearby coral reef and clear waters make Kecil ideal for **snorkeling** and **diving.** Several dive shops near the beach offer PADI courses. **Turtle Bay Divers** (☎019 333 6647) is a popular shop offering two-day nitrox courses for RM450 on Long Beach, with branches at **D'Lagoon** and **Mama's Chalets** on Besar. **Sea Dragon Divers** (☎019 984 1181) is a smaller shop offering new equipment and small groups. Almost all dive shops on the islands arrange open-water courses (standardized price RM700), advanced courses (RM550), discover scuba courses (RM150), fun dives for certified divers (2 dives RM130, with own equipment RM100), and day trips to the marine park at Pulau Redang (includes 5 fun dives RM350, with own equipment RM280). MC/V accepted. All certified divers receive a discount on breakfast and lunch at the **Safety Stop Cafe** at Chempaka Chalets on Long Beach. **Snorkeling** trips can be arranged at **Turtle Shop** (see **Practical Information,** p. 420) and most accommodations (4hr., RM30; gear rental RM5-10). From June to August, places around Long Beach will advertise nighttime trips to see **turtles laying eggs** (RM25).

Lazy Buoys Shop (☎697 4806), has body boarding (RM10 per hr.) and surfing (RM20 per hr.) from November to March only. Other watersport rentals are year-round: windsurfing (RM40 per hr.), catamarans (RM50 per hr.), kayaks (RM10 per hr., RM45 per day), snorkel gear (RM10 per day), and fishing boats (4hr., RM250 including gear). **Nightlife** is limited to barbecues, card-playing, and expensive booze on Long Beach (beer RM8). Bring alcohol from the mainland or seek out Western expatriates for hidden stashes.

Long Beach is perhaps one of the easiest places in Malaysia for a foreigner to find **employment.** Expatriates can extend their travels for several months to several years by waiting tables or teaching as a dive instructor. If you speak English and another European language, there are abundant opportunities on Kecil and Besar, as the dive shops (there are over 10 on the two islands combined) are always seeking multilingual staff. Restaurants along Long Beach post "help wanted" signs for wait staff in exchange for free room and board.

PULAU PERHENTIAN BESAR ☎09

Besar, "The Big Island," languidly awaits travelers looking for more space, calm, and waves. Dive shops along the west coast attract younger travelers, while peaceful beaches lull backpackers, newlyweds, and families alike. The local way of life remains less disturbed here than on Kecil, the budding Waikiki next door.

TRANSPORTATION AND PRACTICAL INFORMATION

Most services and accommodations cluster on two chief beaches, **Main Beach** and **Flora Bay.** There is no official **tourist office,** but most guest houses and shops provide basic information. **Flora Bay** (see **Accommodations,** below) and **Kamamoto Shoppe** (see **Activities,** below) change money and make international phone calls. **Mama's Place** (see **Accommodations,** below) exchanges **traveler's checks** at poor rates and runs **boats** to: **Abdul's Chalets** (RM4); **Coral Bay** (RM10); **D'Lagoon** (RM10); **Flora Bay** (RM10); **Long Beach** (RM7); and **Perhentian Village** (RM4).

ACCOMMODATIONS

Budget accommodations are concentrated along the south and west coasts on Main Beach and Flora Bay. Upscale resorts cluster farther north.

MAIN BEACH

Coral View Island Resort (☎010 903 0943; office in Kuala Besut ☎697 4943), has comprehensive facilities and attentive service. Restaurant has set barbecue meals for RM25-48. Dive shop and snorkel rental. Internet RM30 per hr. Reservations accepted. Doubles with fan RM100, with A/C RM140-190; triples RM230/RM250-500. MC/V. ❺

Abdul's Chalet (☎697 7058), on the south end of the beach. Popular with families. Doubles RM40, with sea view RM60; quads with sea view RM80-90. ❸

New Coconut Chalet (☎697 7988), a well-oiled mini-resort. Restaurant serves Western, Thai, and local dishes. Internet RM10 per hr. Dorms with A/C RM80; doubles with fan and bath RM60-100, with A/C and bath RM100-120. ❺

Seahorse Chalet (☎019 923 8270), behind the dive shop. Cheapest on the beach. Electricity 7pm-7am. A-frames with mosquito nets and squat toilets RM10-20. ❷

FLORA BAY

Wanderer's Inn. Popular for its cheap rates, clean baths and delicious barbecue. Camping RM10 for single and RM15 for double with tent rental; A-frames RM28. ❶

Flora Bay (☎697 7266) offers a variety of well-kept rooms, a large cafe, and a friendly staff. Internet. Moneychanger. Reservations accepted. Doubles with fan RM50, with A/C RM150; triples with fan RM75; family rooms for 5 RM90. MC/V. ❺

Samudra Beach Chalet (☎697 7608), at the eastern end of Flora Bay. All rooms with fan and bath. Standard A-frames RM30; 2-person sea view bungalows RM50; 3-person bungalows RM45. ❸

Fauna Beach Chalet (☎697 7607), in the center of the beach. Pricier bungalows have ocean views. All rooms with fan and bath. Spacious doubles RM35-65; triples RM80. ❸

FOOD AND NIGHTLIFE

Nearly all hotels have attached cafes. **Seaside Cafe** ❷ at Abdul's dishes out delicious curry. (With veggies RM5.50; with beef, chicken, or seafood RM8. Open daily 7:30am-10pm.) On the Main Beach, **Kamamoto Shoppe** has a small bar where people gather until late. For the best Malay food in Flora Bay, try **Fauna Beach Cafi** ❷. (Deep fried squid, rice, soup, and fries RM7.50. Open daily 7:30am-10:30pm.) At night, hit **Wanderer's Cafe** for barbecue, and **Sea Horse Cafe** for beers.

ACTIVITIES

Like Kecil, Besar boasts fabulous **snorkeling** and **scuba diving. Kamamoto Shoppe,** on Main Beach, rents snorkel gear (mask and snorkel RM5, flippers RM5) and kayaks (RM10 per hr., RM50 per day) and hosts snorkel trips (RM20). **D'Lagoon, Shark Point,** and the water in front of **Mama's Place** are the best snorkeling sites. The best place to see sharks is at **Shark Point. Bay Watch** arranges snorkeling trips (RM20) to **Rawa Island** (RM45) and **Redang** (RM60). **Blue Lagoon,** a deserted beach on the north shore (taxi RM12 from Main Beach), is a romantic snorkeling destination. **Turtle Bay,** where many turtles lay eggs, is on Besar's northern shore. **Terumba Tiga** ("Reef Three") offers a breathtaking swim. Purportedly one of the best dive sites is **Tokong Laut,** literally the "Temple of the Sea." There are two wreck dives: a 25m ship that sank while carrying Vietnam War refugees and a 75m cargo ship that carried Indonesian sugar. Dive shops have standard scuba prices (courses last from a half-day to 4 days; fun dives for certified divers RM140, with own equipment RM110; discover scuba course RM150-200; advanced course RM550; PADI open-water certification course RM750). **Sea Horse Dive Center** (☎019 923 8270), on Main Beach, and **Scuba Ayu** (☎019 395 1463), on Flora Bay, are small shops with easy-going staffs. **Flora Bay Divers** (☎697 7266) is the best choice on Flora Bay.

EAST COAST

The fishing villages of Peninsular Malaysia's east coast offer a remarkable contrast to west-coast city life. Visitors relax on endless stretches of white beaches and observe with awe the arrival of leatherback turtles on shore. The predominantly Malay communities adhere strongly to Muslim values; keep this in mind before stripping down to your skivvies on the beach.

KOTA BHARU ☎09

Among a handful of cities in Malaysia with a majority Malay population, Kota Bharu, the capital of Kelantan State, has recently seen a revival of traditional Muslim values—separate check out-lines for men and women in supermarkets, and gender-segregated seating at movies—most of which have not lasted. If you're passing through to Thailand or the Perhentian Islands, consider staying a day or two to get a taste of true Malay.

TRANSPORTATION

Flights: Airport (☎773 7400), 9km northeast of town. Take bus #9 (RM1) into town. **MAS** (☎773 7600; 24hr. ☎1 300 88 3000), at traffic circle on Jl. Gajah Mati, flies to **KL** (1 hr., 5-7 flights daily 6:45am-10:45pm, RM158).

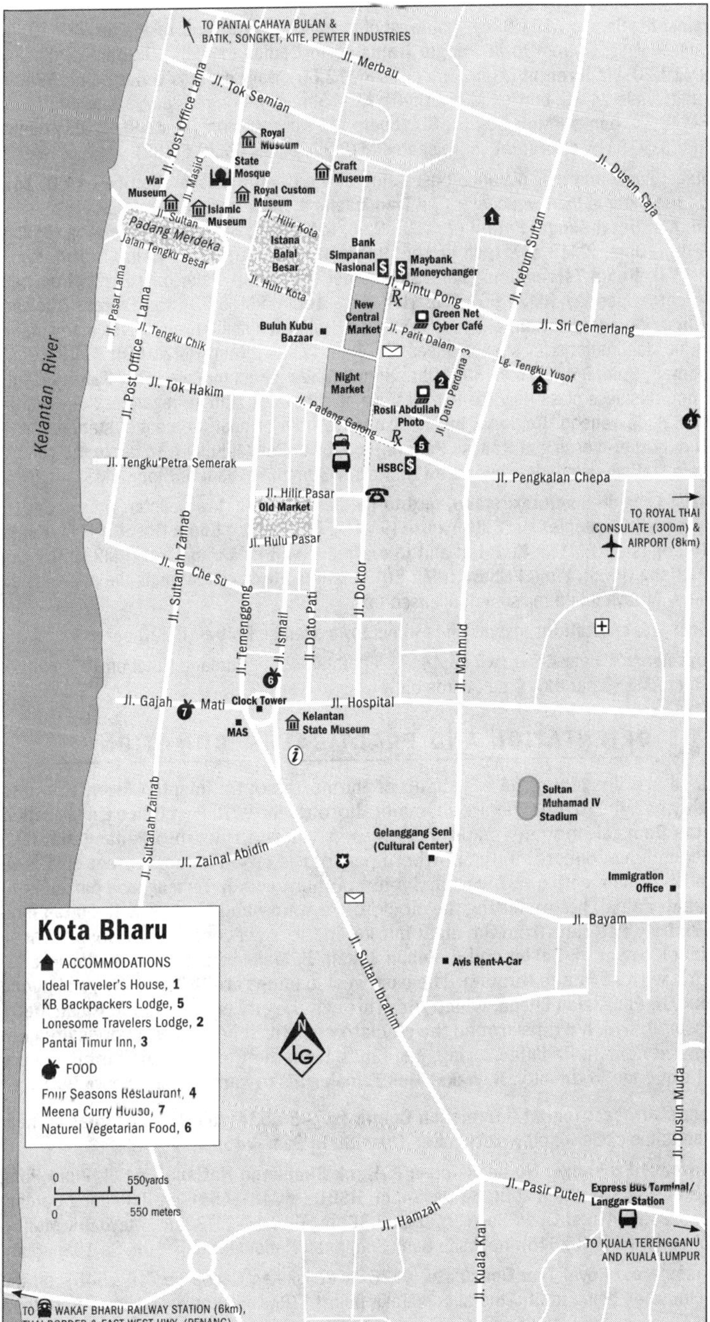
Kota Bharu
ACCOMMODATIONS
Ideal Traveler's House, 1
KB Backpackers Lodge, 5
Lonesome Travelers Lodge, 2
Pantai Timur Inn, 3
FOOD
Four Seasons Restaurant, 4
Meena Curry House, 7
Naturel Vegetarian Food, 6
TO PANTAI CAHAYA BULAN & BATIK, SONGKET, KITE, PEWTER INDUSTRIES
Jl. Merbau
Jl. Tok Semian
Jl. Post Office Lama
Royal Museum
State Mosque
Craft Museum
War Museum
Jl. Masjid
Royal Custom Museum
Islamic Museum
Jl. Sultan
Padang Merdeka
Jalan Tengku Besar
Jl. Hilir Kota
Istana Balai Besar
Jl. Hulu Kota
Bank Simpanan Nasional
Maybank Moneychanger
Jl. Pintu Pong
Jl. Dusun Raja
Jl. Kebun Sultan
New Central Market
Green Net Cyber Café
Jl. Sri Cemerlang
Buluh Kubu Bazaar
Jl. Parit Dalam
Lg. Tengku Yusof
Jl. Pasar Lama
Jl. Tengku Chik
Jl. Dato Perdana 3
Night Market
Kelantan River
Jl. Tok Hakim
Jl. Padang Garong
Rosli Abdullah Photo
HSBC
Jl. Tengku'Petra Semerak
Jl. Pengkalan Chepa
Jl. Hilir Pasar
Old Market
TO ROYAL THAI CONSULATE (300m) & AIRPORT (8km)
Jl. Hulu Pasar
Jl. Che Su
Jl. Sultanah Zainab
Jl. Temenggong
Jl. Ismail
Jl. Dato Pati
Jl. Doktor
Jl. Mahmud
Jl. Gajah Mati
Clock Tower
Jl. Hospital
MAS
Kelantan State Museum
Sultan Muhamad IV Stadium
Gelanggang Seni (Cultural Center)
Jl. Zainal Abidin
Immigration Office
Jl. Bayam
Avis Rent-A-Car
Jl. Sultan Ibrahim
Jl. Dusun Muda
Express Bus Terminal/ Langgar Station
Jl. Pasir Puteh
Jl. Hamzah
Jl. Kuala Krai
TO KUALA TERENGGANU AND KUALA LUMPUR
0 550yards
0 550 meters
TO WAKAF BHARU RAILWAY STATION (6km), THAI BORDER & EAST WEST HWY. (PENANG)

MALAYSIA

Trains: Station (☎719 6986), 7km west of town in **Wakaf Bharu.** Take a taxi (RM10) or bus #19 or 27 from town. **Jungle trains** go to **Gemas** (13½hr., 5:25am, 3rd-class RM19.20) via **Jerantut** (10hr., 3rd-class RM12.60). Daily **express trains** go to: **Gemas** (9hr.; seats 24-30, bunks RM37.50-40); **KL** (13hr.; 6:39pm, plus Sa-Su 3:50pm; seats RM28-38, bunks RM45.50-86); **Singapore** (13½hr.; 8:24pm; seats RM32-41, bunks RM48.50-51) via **Jerantut** (6hr.; seats RM18-22, bunks RM29.50-32).

Buses: Local and long-distance buses stop at the **Central Bus Station** (☎744 0114), on Jl. Doktor in the town center. The **Transnasional** office sells tickets for both stations. To: **Alor Setar-Sungai Petani** (7hr., 9:30pm, RM22.60); **Butterworth/Penang** (8½hr.; 9:30, 10pm; RM19.50); **Ipoh** (7½hr., 9:30pm, RM21.60); **Johor Bahru** (11hr., 8pm, RM34); **Kuala Terengganu** (3hr.; Su-W 6 per day, Th-Sa 7 per day; RM9); **Kuantan** (6½hr., 5 per day, RM20.50); **Temerloh** (8hr., 10pm, RM26.50). The **Express Bus Terminal/Langgar Station** (☎748 3807), on Jl. Hamzah outside town, serves many of the same destinations for similar prices. To: **Ipoh** (7½hr., 9am, RM21.60); **KL** (9-10hr.; 9am, 8, 9pm; RM26); **Melaka** (10hr., 8pm, RM32); **Singapore** via **Johor Bahru** (12hr., 8pm, business class only RM46). Reserve at either bus station, regardless of destination, 1 day ahead. **Regional buses** also leave from or near the central station to the **Thai border** crossing at **Rantau Panjang** (opposite Sungai Kolok). To get to the central train station, catch local bus #29 (1hr., every 30min. 6:45am-6:30pm, RM3).

Taxis: Long-distance taxi stand, next to the bus station in town center. Drivers depart when full (4 people) for: **Butterworth** (RM40); **KL** (RM50); **Kuala Besut** (RM7); **Kuala Terengganu** (RM16); **Kuantan** and **Cherating** (RM35); **Marang Jeti** (RM23); **Rantau Panjang** (RM5); **Wakaf Bharu** (RM2.50). Chartered taxis cost 4 times the prices listed here. Always ride a registered, licensed taxi.

Local Transportation: Trishaw rides within town average RM5-8 (RM20 per hr.).

Rentals: Avis Rent-A-Car (☎748 4457), operated out of Perdana Hotel on Jl. Mahmud. From RM150 per day. Credit cards only.

MALAYSIA

ORIENTATION AND PRACTICAL INFORMATION

Kota Bharu lies along the east bank of the north-south **Kelantan River.** Running roughly parallel to the river are six major thoroughfares. **Jl. Post Office Lama** (called **Jl. Atas Banggol** on many maps) traces the river and runs into **Padang Merdeka** (Independence Square) in the northern part of the city. The next street east is **Jl. Sultanah Zainab,** with a traffic rotary at its southern end. **Jl. Temenggong** parallels Jl. Sultanah Zainab before hitting the clock-tower rotary and becoming **Jl. Sultan Ibrahim. Jl. Dato Pati** runs from the night market in the town center to Jl. Hospital near the clock tower. **Jl. Doktor** and **Jl. Kebun Sultan/Jl. Mahmud** are next, the latter converging with Jl. Sultan Ibrahim. The east-west avenues are **Jl. Tok Hakim/Jl. Padang Garong/Jl. Pengkalan Chepa,** which runs through the city center, and **Jl. Gajah Mati/Jl. Hospital,** which wraps around the clock tower. Guest houses and hotels are concentrated near Jl. Padang Garong, just 5min. from the Central Bus Station. On the northern edge of the city, **Jl. Wakaf Mek Zainab** runs toward **Pantai Cahaya Bulan.**

Tourist Offices: Tourist Information Center (☎748 5534), on Jl. Sultan Ibrahim, near the traffic circle with the clock tower. Open Su-Th 8am-4:45pm.

Currency Exchange: No banks open F. **Bank Simpanan National,** 61 Jl. Pintu Pong (☎744 9433). Open M-Th, Sa 9am-4pm. **HSBC** (☎748 1451), on Jl. Padong Garong, has **24hr. ATMs.** Open Sa-W 9:30am-3:30pm, Th 9:30-11:30am. **Maybank Moneychanger** (☎743 2615), opposite Bank Simpanan National. Open M-Th, Sa 10am-6pm.

Consulates: Royal Thai Consulate, 4426 Jl. Pengkalan Chepa (☎748 2545), on the right when going toward the airport. Take bus #4 (RM0.50) or walk 15min. from town center. 3-month visa extensions RM33 (1-day processing); bring 3 photos. Visa office open Su-Th 9am-noon and 2-3:30pm.

Markets: New Central Market, bounded by Jl. Pintu Pong, Doktor, and Tengku Chik. Open daily 7am-7pm. **Buluh Kubu Bazaar,** next to Istana Balai Besar, and the top floor of the **Old Market,** bounded by Jl. Dato Pati and Temenggong, have fabrics and handicrafts. **Night market,** near the bus station. Open daily 6pm-late.

Emergency: ☎999. **Fire:** ☎994.

Police: ☎748 5522. On Jl. Sultan Ibrahim, between the post office and tourist office. Some English spoken.

Pharmacy: Kian Farmasi, 2981 B-C Jl. Padang Garong (☎744 1267), in the center of town opposite HSBC. Another branch on Jl. Pintu Pong. Open daily 9am-10pm.

Medical Service: Hospital (☎748 5533), at the end of Jl. Hospital. English spoken. **24hr. emergency care.**

Telephones: Telekom Malaysia (☎513 9191), on Jl. Doktor in the center of town near the Central Bus Station. Open M-Th 8:30am-5pm, Sa 8:30am-3pm. Sells RM30 and RM60 **italk cards** for domestic and international calls. Place calls at hotels or guest houses to reach international operators.

Internet Access: Green Net Cyber Cafe, 166 Jl. Parit Dalam (☎753 2015). RM1 for 15min., RM1.50 for 30min., RM2 for 1hr.

Post Office: GPO (☎748 4073), on the left side of Jl. Sultan Ibrahim, south of the clock-tower. Open Sa-Th 8:30am-5pm. **Postal code:** 15670 (for post office only).

ACCOMMODATIONS AND FOOD

Kotu Bharu has over 40 guest houses and hotels within walking distance of the town center. Do kindly remember to take your shoes off before stepping inside; it's customary in Kota Bharu. **Ideal Traveler's House ❶,** 3954 F-G Jl. Kebun Sultan, down a small road off Jl. Pintu Pong, has rooms with fans. (☎/fax 744 2246. Laundry. Breakfast RM3. Dorms RM6; doubles and triples RM20-25, with bath and balcony RM30-35.) **Lonesome Travelers Lodge ❶,** 375 Jl. Dato Perdana 3, is one of the hippest guest houses in town. The staff arrange carpools and jungle treks. To get there, walk north on Jl. Doktor past J. Padang Garong and turn right after A&W; make a left at the sign. (☎744 6637. Breakfast included. Dorms RM8; singles RM15; doubles RM20; triples RM25.) In a quieter part of town, **Pantai Timur Inn ❶,** 391 Lg. Tengku Yusuf, off Jl. Kebun Sultan, has clean A/C rooms. (☎748 3753. Internet RM7 per hr. Dorms RM15; singles RM59; doubles RM69; triples RM75; quads RM85.) **KB Backpackers Lodge ❷,** 2981-F Jl. Padang Garong, is a long-time favorite, offering tours, a book exchange, carpools, laundry, and Internet. (☎743 2125. Breakfast included. Singles and doubles RM18-25.)

Local specialties include *ayam percik* (chicken grilled on sticks) and *nasi dagang* (coconut-based rice topped with tuna). Several Chinese joints line Jl. **Kebun Sultan,** near Ideal Traveler's House. **Jl. Gajah Mati,** the road heading toward the river from the clock-tower rotary, has a handful of Indian eateries. The **night market ❶** has a dizzying assortment of food (try *murtabak*, a stuffed Indian pancake). For a sit-down culinary experience, head to **Meena Curry House ❷,** 3377-G Jl. Gajah Mati, east of Jl. Sultanah Zainab. (Vegetarian curry RM3.50; chicken curry RM5-6.50. Open daily 11am-9:30pm.) **Naturel Vegetarian Food ❶,** 2818 Jl. Ismail, near the clock-tower roundabout, has buffet-style vegetarian delights for about RM3. (☎746 1902. Open daily 7:30am-5:30pm.) For delicious Chinese *halal* food, try **Four Seasons Restaurant ❹,** 5670 B/2 & B/3 Jl. Dusun Raja. Head down Jl. Pengkalan Chepa and left onto Jl. Dusun Raja. (☎743 6666. Steamboat for 2-4 people RM58. Open daily noon-2:30pm and 6-10pm. AmEx/MC/V.)

MALAYSIA

SIGHTS

Kota Bharu's sights are within walking distance of each other but require a good day or two to explore. The **Gelanggang Seni (Cultural Center),** on Jl. Mahmud opposite the Perdana Hotel, sponsors free top-spinning, kite-flying, drum-beating, and *silat* demonstrations. From 9 to 11pm on Wednesdays and Saturdays, there are performances of *wayang kulit* (shadow-puppets), dance, and drama. (☎744 3124. Sa, M, W 3:30-5:30pm; all shows free.) **Padang Merdeka** (Independence Square) commemorates the Malay struggle against British rule. At the east end of the rectangle away from the river is the **Istana Balai Besar,** a large wooden hall built in 1844. Closer to the river to the right of the square are the **War Museum, Islamic Museum, Royal Custom Museum, Royal Museum,** and **Craft Museum. Kelantan State Museum,** next to the tourist office on Jl. Sultan Ibrahim, is worth a gawk for its cultural exhibits. (All open Sa-Th 8:30am-4:45pm. RM2, children RM1.) The **Pantai Cahaya Bulan (PCB) Beach** is pleasant and has cheap accommodations (look for homes with signs that say *tempat penginapan* or *asrama*). **Buses** leaves from the Royal Museum for PCB (#10; every 20min, last returning bus 7pm, RM1).

ACTIVITIES

If relaxing on the beach isn't enough, take a **river cruise** through the surrounding jungle. **Roselan Hanafiah,** award-winning guide, leads a half-day tour for 3-10 people through the canals and rivers of Kelantan. Check the tourist office to find Roselan. (☎748 5534. Runs 10am-1pm; RM75 per person with high tea.) Travelers on a smaller budget can cruise on a public boat and return by bus. Boats depart from **Kuala Krai,** accessible by bus #5 from the central terminal (RM3.40). Roselan can also help make reservations to stay with a family in the village, through a program called **The Kampung Experience.** Meals and transportation are included. (3-day packages RM265 per person, 2-person minimum, or RM250, 4-person minimum. 1-day workshops RM125 includes lunch.) Or, for a taste of Malaysia, try Roselan's Malay **cooking class** (RM55) taught in the comfort of his home. For more adventurous folk, KB Backpackers Lodge organizes **nature tours.** Choose among a trip to the **Jelawang Jungle,** site of the highest waterfall in Southeast Asia (RM230 for 3 days), and cave expeditions (RM99 for 1 day). Prices include meals, transportation, equipment, and in some cases insurance. There are also **city tours** or **country tours** that sample cultural sights (4-5hr., RM40, minimum 2 people). Book trips at the KB Backpackers Lodge (see **Accommodations,** above). Their web site (www.kb-backpackers.com.my) provides information on transport within Peninsular Malaysia.

PULAU REDANG ☎09

Thanks to concerted efforts of its marine park to preserve the ecosystem, Pulau Redang has the most vibrant coral and marine life in Malaysia. While visiting Pulau Redang costs a few extra ringgit compared to other destinations, given the beauty of its crystal-clear waters, its many wonderful snorkeling and diving opportunities, and its higher-quality services, it's well worth it.

THE VIEW FROM ABOVE

The lowdown: An archipelago of nine islands designated as a marine park off Malaysia's east coast.
Islands: Lima, Paku Besar, Paku Kecil, Kerengga Besar, Kerengga Kecil, Ekor Tebu, Ling, Pinang, and especially Redang.
Highlights: Snorkeling, diving, playing beach volleyball, sunbathing.

TRANSPORTATION. Everything at Pulau Redang runs on package deals, which include accommodation, food, activities, and transportation. These are available directly through resorts or through tourist agencies in Kuala Terengganu and other nearby locations (see **Pulau Perhentian Besar: Activities,** p. 422). Private resorts operate their own **boats** to Redang Island from the Merang jetty (45min.-1hr.; 9:30am, 1:30pm; RM40 one-way). Merang (not to be confused with Marang) is 30min. north of Kuala Terengganu by **taxi** (RM30) or **tourist bus** (RM10-20). **Ping Anchorage Travel and Tours,** 77A Jl. Dalo' Issacs, offers resort and camping packages and runs buses from Kuala Terengganu to the jetty. (☎626 2020. Open daily 8am-7:30pm.) Upon request, buses will pick up and drop off at the airport or bus station. For those who arrive at the jetty without reservations, many booths there also sell packages, but be warned that Redang is a popular destination for Malaysian and Singaporean tourists, so advance bookings are almost always necessary on weekends and school and public holidays.

ACCOMMODATIONS Accommodations cluster on Pasir Panjang (Long Beach) on Redang Island. Rates below always include breakfast; the phrase "with amenities" below means that rates also include boat transfer to and from the island, room with A/C, at least one guided snorkel trip for each night stayed, lunch, dinner (with BBQ options), snack, and beverages. Rental of snorkel equipment costs RM10-15. **Redang Lagoon Chalet ❺,** on the main beach, is the cheapest option and attracts a mixed crowd. (☎/fax 827 2116. Twins and doubles 2 days/1 night with amenities RM460; additional nights RM200.) At the right end of the beach is **Redang Holiday Beach Villa ❺,** which respects guests' privacy and has a NAUI dive shop. Their new hillside villa rooms have the best views on the beach. (☎624 5500; office in Kuala Terengganu ☎622 6181. Twins 2 days/1 night with amenities RM560, 3 days/2 nights with amenities RM720; triples RM720/RM990; quads RM880/RM1200; additional nights RM100-120 per person. 50% discount for children.) As the classiest lodging on Long Beach, **Coral Redang Island Resort ❺** offers an outdoor swimming pool, a poolside bar, a dive shop, and a variety of chalets. (☎626 5011; office in Kuala Terengganu ☎623 6200. Singles RM225-415, 3 days/2 nights with amenities RM680-1100, 3 days/2 nights with amenities and 4 dives RM890-1310; doubles RM610-1160/RM1060-1720/RM1480-2140; triples 3 days/2 nights with amenities RM1410-2250, 3 days/2 nights with amenities and 4 dives RM2040. Closed Nov.-Feb.) Travel agencies generally offer better prices than these. For an off-the-beaten-path alternative, **Ping Anchorage** offers a **Redang Camping Adventure ❺** in a double tent with common bath on Long Beach or Kalong Beach. Packages include snorkeling trips, all meals, and round-trip boat tickets. (☎626 2020. 2 days/1 night RM180; 3 days/2 nights RM240; additional nights RM80.)

FOOD AND ENTERTAINMENT Every resort has a restaurant, and package deals include all meals. Aside from the *mahjong*, chess, card, and dart games offered at most resorts, nightlife consists of loud music and expensive booze. A poolside **bar** at Coral Redang Island Resort sells beer (RM8) and is a quieter alternative to the karaoke bars. For information on diving and snorkeling, consult dive shops, which have maps of the best sites and experienced staff on hand. Snorkel gear rental is available everywhere (RM10-15). The **Marine Park Headquarters** at Pulau Pinang is definitely worth a visit for colorful snorkeling adventures, if not for informative exhibits on coral and marine life. (RM5, children RM2.50.) The NAUI dive shop at Redang Holiday Beach Villa (☎624 5500) has the best rates on Discover Scuba courses (RM150 for one dive), open water diver certification courses (RM750 for 5 dives), advanced diver courses (RM650 for 6 dives), and fun dives (1-4 dives RM50 each, 5-9 dives RM45 each, 10 or more dives RM40 each; regulator and BCD rental RM50 per day, wetsuit rental RM10 per day). Instructor Calin Sas (instructor #35042) emphasizes safety techniques.

KUALA TERENGGANU

☎09

Capital of the Muslim state of Terengganu, Kuala Terengganu lies beside the inlet of the Terengganu River. Until recently a large fishing village, KT, as it's commonly called, now thrives on oil and seems upstaged by the sunny beach destinations nearby. Though attractions and nightlife here are minimal, KT isn't just a gateway city to nearby Marang and Merang—its low-key seaside warrants exploration.

TRANSPORTATION

Flights: Airport (☎666 4204), 18km from town. Taxi from the airport RM20. **MAS,** 13 Jl. Sultan Omar (☎622 9279; 24hr. hotline ☎1 300 88 3000), flies to **KL** (4-5 per day, RM158). Open M-W and Sa-Su 8:30am-4:30pm, Th 8:30am-12:30pm. AmEx/MC/V.

Ferries: Pulau Duyong (Duyong Island), off the west coast, is accessible by boat from the jetty opposite the Tourist Information Center or from the jetty behind Hotel Seri Malaysia (15min., 7am-6pm, RM1).

Buses: Local buses leave from the **large bus station** (☎623 6239) at the intersection of Jl. Masjid Abidin and Jl. Syed Hussain. To: **Dungun** (every 30min., 7:30am-6pm, RM4) via **Marang** (50min., RM1.50); **Duyong** (#16 or 20; every hr. 7:40am-5:40pm, RM0.60); **Rantau Abang** (every 30min. 7:30am-6pm, RM3); **Kuala Besut** (2½hr., 7:15am-4:30pm, RM5). **Express buses** stop at the large bus station and at the **express bus station** (☎622 5335) on Jl. Sultan Zainal Abidin near the Jl. Tok Lam intersection. To: **Ipoh** and **Lumut** (12hr., 9pm, RM37); **Kota Bharu** (3hr., 5 per day 8:30am-5:30pm and Th-Sa 7:30pm, RM9); **KL** (8hr.; 9, 9:30, 10am, 9:30, 10pm; RM25, with A/C RM35); **Kuantan** (3½hr., 7 per day 9am-10pm, RM11.60); **Mersing** (6½hr., 12:30 and 10pm, RM22); **Penang** (9hr., 9pm., RM29.80); **Singapore** (9-10hr.; 9am and 8:30pm; RM30, with A/C RM42).

Taxis: From the **taxi stand** (☎622 1581) on Jl. Masjid Abidin, near the large bus station, fixed-rate taxis go to: **Kota Bharu** (RM80); **Kuala Besut** (RM60); **KL** (RM280); **Kuantan** and **Cherating** (RM100); **Marang** (RM20); **Rantau Abang** (RM35); **Merang jetty** (RM30); **Mersing** (RM180); **Taman Negara** (RM200). Passengers can split fares 4 ways. No bargaining.

Local Transportation: Trishaw rides RM3-5. **Taxis** (☎626 5150) run RM5-10 in town.

ORIENTATION AND PRACTICAL INFORMATION

Jl. Sultan Zainal Abidin runs east-west along the city's shore, on which sit the **post office, Tourist Information Center,** and **express bus terminal.** Major sights, including **Bukit Puteri** (Princess Hill), **Istana Maziah** (the Sultan's Palace) and the **Central Market,** also line the shore. Farther south along the shoreline, **Chinatown** lies near **Jl. Bandar.** The city's commercial spine, **Jl. Sultan Ismail,** runs parallel to Jl. Sultan Zainal Abidin. Its west edge begins with Hotel Seri Malaysia, while the **police station** and **immigration office** flank its eastern edge. These two streets sandwich **Jl. Dato' Isaacs.** From the city's center north to its shores, **Jl. Tok Lam** connects all three boulevards. Parallel and to the west is **Jl. Masjid Abidin;** walking from Jl. Sultan Ismail will lead to the **taxi stand** and **large bus station.** Accommodations flank the north and east sides of the mosque in the center of the city.

Tourist Office: Tourist Information Center (☎622 1553), on Jl. Sultan Zainal Abidin. Free maps and friendly staff. Open Sa-Th 9am-5pm.

Tours: Ping Anchorage, 77A Jl. Dato' Isaacs (☎626 2020). Packages to Redang Island, Lang Tengah Island, Perhentian Islands, Taman Negara, and Kenyir Lake. Open daily 8am-7:30pm.

Immigration Office: ☎622 1424. On the 1st fl. of Wisma Perseketuan Bldg., at the intersection of Jl. Pejabat and Jl. Sultan Ismail. Same-day visa extensions RM50 per month. Open Su-W 8am-12:45pm and 2-4pm, Th 8am-1pm.

Currency Exchange: Bank Bumiputra (☎622 2611), on Jl. Sultan Ismail. AmEx/MC/V/ traveler's checks. Currency exchange upstairs next to **ATM.** Open Sa-W 9:30am-4pm, Th 9:30am-12pm. **Maybank Moneychanger,** 12 Jl. Sultan Ismail (☎624 7637). Open daily 9am-5:30pm.

Laundromat: Mr. Dhoby, 18A Jl. Masjid Abidin (☎622 1671), next to Seaview Hotel. RM3.50 per kg. Ironing RM1 per item. Open daily 9am-8:30pm.

Police: ☎622 2222. On the corner of Jl. Sultan Omar and Jl. Sultan Ismail. Some English spoken. **Open 24hr.**

Pharmacy: Dew Ma, 10-D Jl. Tok Lam (☎622 0200), near the northern tip, with a large English sign. Open Sa-Th 9am-9pm.

Medical Service: General Hospital (☎623 3333), on Jl. Sultan Mahmud, south of the rotary. English-speaking doctors. Consultation fee RM2. **24hr. emergency care.**

Telephones: Telekom Malaysia (☎623 1191), on the corner of Jl. Sultan Ismail and Jl. Banggol. Sells international calling cards. Free access to international operators. Direct **international calls.** Open M-Th and Su 8:30am-4:30pm. **IDD calls** can also be made from the Telekom booth on Jl. Tok Lam near Dew Ma pharmacy using phone cards.

Internet Access: Golden Wood Internet Cafe, 59 Jl. Tok Lam (☎624 6171), near Jl. Dato' Isaacs. RM3 per hr. Open Sa-Th 10am-12:30am. **Creative Computer Communication,** No. 1-I Jl. Syed Hussain (☎956 7211), opposite bus station. RM2.50 per hr. Open daily 9am-7pm.

Post Office: ☎622 7555. On Jl. Sultan Zainal Abidin. It's 100m left of Jl. Masjid Abidin if you face the river. *Poste Restante.* Open Su-Th 8:30am-5pm. **Postal code:** 20000.

ACCOMMODATIONS AND FOOD

Ping Anchorage Traveler's Homestay ❶, 77A Jl. Dato' Isaacs near the Jl. Tok Lam intersection, caters exclusively to backpackers and offers a rooftop lounge, cafe, and travel service. From the mosque, it's on the right; the reception is through the *batik* store. (☎622 0851. Dorms RM6; singles and doubles RM12-18, with A/C and bath RM30.) Across from the palace at 18A Jl. Masjid Abidin, **Seaview Hotel ❹** has clean, spacious rooms with bath, A/C, hot showers, and TV. (☎622 1911. Reserve in advance for weekends and holidays. Doubles RM65; triples RM75; quads RM85. MC/V.) **Hotel Seri Malaysia ❹,** 1640 Jl. Hiliran, a large pink building on the western end of Jl. Sultan Ismail, has rooms facing the river and daily room service. (☎623 6454. Laundry. Breakfast included. Doubles RM80; family rooms RM130.) The only accommodation in a local village, **Awi's House ❶** is accessible by infrequent boats or by bus. Peaceful wooden rooms overlook the water. (☎624 5046. Cooking facilities. Dorms RM7; doubles RM17.)

Food stalls ❶ crowd the first floor of the bus station on Jl. Syed Hussain, and **Chinese food spots ❷** line the shores of **Pantai Batu Buruk.** Try *keropok*, a Terengganu specialty of fried ground fish with chili sauce. The **food court ❷** above the central market offers Malay dishes and a wide selection of fruits. For a good restaurant try **M.D. Curry House ❷,** 19-C Jl. Tok Lam opposite Dew Ma pharmacy. Meals come with rice, *papadam* (an Indian lentil wafer), and veggies. (☎622 0931. Chicken curry RM5.50; vegetarian meals RM4.50. Open daily 7:30am-8:30pm.) **Golden Dragon ❹,** 198 Jl. Bandar in Chinatown near the Dragon Gate. (☎622 3034. Chili *kang kong* vegetables RM10; fresh fish RM20-30. Open daily 11am-3pm and 6-9:30pm.) **Ping Anchorage Travelers Café ❷,** 77A Jl. Dato' Isaacs on the ground floor. An oasis for weary travelers hungering for Western meals and thirsting for cold beer. (☎626

2020. Four-decker club sandwich RM5.50. Open daily 7am-midnight.) **Restoran Terapung Puteri ❶** is a "floating" restaurant on Jl. Sultan Zainal Abidin opposite the Visitors Center. (☎623 5396. *Nasi lemak*—steamed coconut rice with spicy *sambal* sauce, peanuts, and anchovies RM2; *popiah*—spring rolls RM3.50. Open daily 6am-midnight.

SIGHTS AND ENTERTAINMENT

Kuala Terengganu's main tourist attractions cluster near the **Tourist Information Center.** The **central market,** on Jl. Sultan Zainal Abidin, sells handicrafts and produce. Nearby, next to the GPO, are **Istana Maziah,** the sultan's stately palace, and **Bukit Puteri,** the "hill of the princess." Climb the stairs next to the Tourist Information Center for great views over the waterfront and the remains of a fort and a lighthouse. (Open Sa-Th 9am-5pm. RM1.) Outside town, the **Muzium Negeri,** Malaysia's largest museum, features a set of Terengganu-style buildings on stilts. The main museum showcases the *batu bersurat,* an inscribed stone dated to AD 702 that states Islamic law regarding misdeeds. The complex also includes botanical gardens and an outdoor exhibit of traditional fishing boats. Bus #10 (20min., every 30min. 7:30am-6pm, RM0.70) runs between the large bus terminal and the museum. (☎622 1444. Open Sa-Th 9am-5pm. RM5.) Off the mainland, **Pulau Duyong's** locals still construct boats of all sizes with traditional techniques—without plans or diagrams. (For transportation, see **Ferries,** p. 430.) On the road south to Marang, 4.5km from KT (bus #13 or 13C; RM0.70), sits **Masjid Tengku Zaharah** (Floating Mosque), a striking white building that seems to float on the water. (Open 24hr. Best times to visit are 7am-noon and 3-4pm. Free.) Down the Ibai River from the Floating Mosque is the **Noor Arfa Craft Complex,** where visitors can witness the *batik-* and basket-making processes and browse through a large selection of souvenirs. (☎617 5700. Open Sa-Th 9am-5pm.)

MARANG ☎09

Government bulldozers have ended Marang's peaceful days as a picturesque Malay fishing village. Construction projects have devastated half the town. Breakwaters line the beach, and good food and budget accommodations are scarce. The park near the main jetty is a pleasant place to have lunch and watch the boats pass, but for most, Marang is a transit town en route to Kapas Island.

Those who stay in Marang may enjoy the **Marang River Cruise,** which stops at **Jenang,** a traditional village where craftsmen make brown sugar and mangrove roofs. (Minimum 4 people for the 4½ cruise (8am, RM100 per boat.)

Marang is 20km south of Kuala Terengganu. From KT, get to Marang via Dungun **buses** (30min., every 30min. 7:30am-6pm, RM1.50) or **share-taxi** from the Terengganu-Kuantan Hwy. (RM15 to Marang jetty, RM20 to KT). The **bus stop** is on the highway. Most people get dropped off at the four-way intersection next to the squid-and-prawn statue. The main part of town is on **Kampung Paya,** the street parallel to and east of the highway, running close to the river and beaches. North of the jetty, Kampung Paya passes shop houses and two footbridges before reaching the budget accommodations. The **police station** is on the highway before the bridge. (☎618 2222. Some English spoken. Open 24hr.) Ask for English-speaking Dr. Mohamed Reze bin Rashid at the **Klinik Kesihatan Clinic** (☎618 2216; open Sa-Th 8am-12:30pm and 2-4pm) on the highway opposite the **post office** (☎618 2215; open Su-Th 8:30am-4:30pm but closed the first Th of each month). **Postal code:** 21600.

Marang Guest House and Restaurant ❷, Lot 1367 and 1368 Kampung Paya, up the hill next to Kamal Guest House near the second footbridge, has clean rooms, and offers laundry service (RM5), massages (RM30), Internet (RM3 per hr.), and travel information. (☎/fax 618 1976. Doubles with fan and squat toilet RM15, with fan and Western bath RM25, with TV, A/C, and Western bath RM50; 5-person family rooms with A/C, TV, and Western bath RM80.) **Kamal Guest House ❷,** B283 Kg. Paya, between the two footbridges north of the jetty and market area, has a variety of nice rooms. (☎618 2181. Doubles RM15, with bath RM25; triples with bath RM35.) **Green Mango Inn ❶,** A-71 Bandar Marang, up a small hill opposite the largest tourist-boat jetty, has cozy rooms in a wooden house. (☎618 2040. Dorms RM6; singles RM10; doubles RM15.) Devour the best meals at the **food stalls ❶** opposite the market near the tourist boat agencies. **Hasnani Dinamik Bakery ❶** is on the highway near the squid-and-prawn statue intersection. (☎618 2976. Breads and pastries RM1-3. Rice and noodle dishes RM3-5. Open Sa-Th 9:30am-7pm.)

KAPAS ISLAND ☎09

Although fewer travelers have visited beautiful Kapas Island since Marang's storm of development destroyed much of the coral, many still spend time here walking through the jungle or snorkeling.

Friendly Zakaria, who runs **Suria Link** (☎019 983 9454) at the **Marang Tourist Jetty,** can help arrange diving courses, sea sport rentals, and room reservations. **Aqua-Sport Diving Service** is a PADI dive shop to the right of the jetty on Long Beach. (☎018 291 2105. Discover scuba courses RM80; 4-day open-water diver certification courses RM950; fun dives RM90 or less; kayak rental RM10 per hr.; guided jungle treks RM10; round-island boat trips RM10.)

Tourist boats to the island cost RM15-25 for a 15min. journey. Buy tickets from agents near the jetty or at guest houses. Boats leave from 9am to 6pm when there are at least 4 passengers and return from 10am to 6pm. The **jetty** is between Gua Beach and Long Beach on Kapas Island, but boatmen sometimes drop off passengers at their chalets. **Batu Payong Beach** and **Pasir Cina Beach** on the west coast are the best on the island. (Pasir Cina is a steep climb over a small cliff from Batu Payong. Rope handrails aid the journey.) **Snorkel Bay** is a half-hour jungle trek to the north coast. Rent snorkel gear from almost anywhere for RM10-15.

The Lighthouse ❶ fosters a backpacker atmosphere at the eastern end of Long Beach, with cooking facilities, a reggae bar after 7pm (beer RM9), and a hammock garden. (☎626 5544. Dorms with mosquito netting RM10; doubles with fan RM25.) The last chalet to the left of the jetty is **Kapas Garden Resort ❹,** which is run by a cheery couple who offer a 6hr. "sunset cruise" on their sailboat for RM150. (☎010 984 1686. Bar and restaurant. Internet RM5 per hr. A-frames with fan and bath RM60; chalets with fan and bath RM75.) **Tuti Puri Island Resort ❹** has beautiful Balinese-style chalets with baths. (☎624 6090. Breakfast included. Packages available. Backpacker's room RM50; doubles with fan RM70-100, with A/C RM120-180. AmEx/MC/V.) In addition, there are two **campsites ❶** on the island. (Sites RM10; tent rental RM5 per night.) The **restaurant ❸** at Tuti Puri has banana pancakes (RM7.50) and fried vegetables with garlic (RM8). Their Western- and Malay-style meals average RM8-16. (Open daily 8am-9:30pm.) Food on the island is not cheap, so bring snacks from the mainland or try the **Payung Pelancungan Café Corner ❶** to the left of the jetty. *Nasi goreng* (fried rice) and *tom yam* noodle soup run RM3.50-4, and fruit salad is RM4. (Open daily 8am-1am.)

CHERATING ☎09

On Rte. 3 lies Cherating, the town Malaysia forgot. Cherating's more attractive aspects include a windsurfing beach, cultural diversions, a few bars, and an occasional leatherback turtle. Less titillating: the omnipresent tourists.

TRANSPORTATION AND PRACTICAL INFORMATION. Cherating is 47km north of Kuantan, accessible by local bus (1hr., every hr. 8am-6pm, RM3). From **Kuala Terengganu,** take a bus from the **main bus station** (RM11.50) or a **taxi** (RM100). The beach road meets the highway at the two bus stops on the way. The west stop, closer to **Kuantan,** is near the Cherating River and marked by a "Culture Center" billboard. This stop is closer to Masnah and Mataheri Chalets. The east stop is marked by a "Residence Inn" billboard; get off here for the Moon Guest House.

The town has two main roads: the **Kuantan-Terengganu Hwy.,** which bends east-west through town, and the Y-shaped **beach road** that runs along the river and the sea. On the highway between the bus stops is the **police office** (☎581 9322). There are **no medical services** available in Cherating. Call hospitals in **Kemaman** (☎859 3333) or **Kuantan** (☎513 3333) for **24hr. emergency care.** The closest **clinic** is in **Kampung Balok,** 10km south of Cherating. The beach road is lined with restaurants, accommodations, and bars. Toward the center of the road is **Travel Post,** which provides **Internet** (RM6 per hr.), **mail service, international phone** service (RM7 per min.), and **currency exchange. Capacity Dot Com,** near the eastern end of the beach road, has travel information, Internet (RM6 per hr.), **mountain-bike rental** (RM10 per hr.), and a library. Warm and friendly Firdaus speaks flawless English and provides travel info. (☎581 9330. Open Th-Tu 10am-11pm.)

ACCOMMODATIONS AND FOOD. Guest houses pack the beach road, offering standard A-frame or small chalet-style huts. **Matahari Chalet ❸,** 100m down the road from the west bus stop, maintains solid, well-kept huts. Friendly management and a range of amenities, including an attached do-it-yourself *batik* studio (RM25-35 per piece), make Matahari one of the best abodes in the village. (☎581 9835. Doubles RM20, with fan RM25.) **Maznah Guest House ❶,** also near the west bus stop, has a cozy common area with TV and movies. (☎581 9072. Breakfast and kitchen facilities included. Internet RM5 per hr. Dorms RM12; A-frame singles with fan RM16; chalet doubles RM18, with fan RM20, with fan and bath RM25.) **The Shadow of Moon at Half Past Four ❷,** on the hillside 200m down the beach road from the east bus stop, offers a haunting atmosphere and superb bungalows. A thatched-roof bar and lounge complete this jungle setting. Ask for room #3—it's bigger. (☎581 9186. Laundry included. Singles RM16; doubles with bath and fan RM35; triples and quads with bath and fan RM55.) Roll out of bed and onto the beach at **Tanjung Inn ❸,** which has clean wooden chalets around an attractive lake toward the western end of the beach road. (☎581 9081. Breakfast included. Doubles with fan RM21, with fan and bath RM47.25, with A/C and bath RM94.50; 4-person family rooms overlooking the lake with A/C, TV, and bath RM126.)

Can't Forget Seafood ❷, on the beach road, serves superb Chinese fare. (Set meals for 2 RM16-22; sweet-and-sour chicken or squid RM6. Beer RM5. Open daily 11am-3pm and 6-11:30pm.) **Payung Cafe ❷** makes huge pizzas for RM9-13 and pasta for RM4.50-9.50. (Open daily 10:30am-2:30pm and 7-10:30pm.) **Ranting Resort ❷** has great breakfast options. (Homemade bread sandwiches RM4-6.)

SIGHTS AND ENTERTAINMENT. In front of Rhana Pippins, **Kelaut Sports** rents watersports equipment. (☎581 9658. Kayaks RM15 per hr., RM60 per day. Windsurfing RM25 per hr., RM30 with instructor. Surfboards RM15 per hr., RM60 per day. Fishing trips RM100. Snorkeling at Snake Island RM35. Firefly trip at 7:30pm RM15.) **Surfing** is best from January to March, but windsurfing is great anytime. Ibrahim and Raihman at **MAP Batik,** across the road from Maznah Guest House, offer *batik* lessons at their studio. (☎013 667 6621. Make-your-own *batik* RM35-40.) If you're in Cherating between June and September, don't miss the opportunity to see the **giant leatherback turtles** lay their eggs. The Fisheries Depart-

BANANA LEAF ETIQUETTE Those who find cutlery restrictive will enjoy banana leaf dining, common throughout Malaysia and Southeast Asia. Eating with your hands, however, doesn't mean you get to throw your manners out with the fork and knife–it's just a different set of rules.

1. Use only your right hand, as the left hand is traditionally considered unclean.
2. Using the tips of your fingers, mash toppings into your rice so that you get a little bit of everything in each bite.
3. Create a spoon with your fingers and push the food into your mouth using your thumb. Try not to look like you're eating your fingers.
4. If necessary, use your *papadam* (a crispy, round salty cracker) as a rice shovel. However, too much reliance on this will bring trouble when you run out of *papadam.*
5. If you eat something with bones, just spit 'em out.
6. Burping is acceptable only by the older generation.
7. When you're through, fold your banana leaf in half.

ment has set up a hatchery near the Club Med Beach. (Open Tu-Su.) Upon request, most lodgings will wake you if there is a sighting and take you to the beach (RM15). Two kilometers east of Cherating is the breathtaking but members-only **Club Med Beach.** Alternatively, ask guest-house managers about trails through the hills that will take you from the village beach to the promised shore. For those who want to venture to nearby villages, Firdaus at Capacity Dot Com (see **Practical Information,** above) rents mountain bikes and recommends trails through rambutan and durian plantations. The best nightspots are **Pop Inn Pub** (live cover band F-Sa; open daily 6pm-late) and **Rhana Pippins** (2-for-1 drink specials 3-11pm). Both are on the same side of the beach road.

KUANTAN ☎09

Kuantan offers little in the way of cultural attractions or remarkable cuisine, and for those coming from elsewhere on the east coast, the capital of the state of Pahang will seem either rejuvenating or overwhelmingly cosmopolitan. Surrounded by waterfalls, caves, and beaches, the town itself is home to the beautiful State Mosque, and the beaches of Teluk Chempedak are only 4km away.

TRANSPORTATION

Flights: Airport (☎538 1291), 10km west of town. Take a local bus (every hr. 7am-5pm) or a taxi (RM20). **MAS** (☎515 6030, **24hr.** ticketing ☎1 300 88 3000), on the ground floor of Wisma Persatuan Bola Sepak on Jl. Gambut, has flights to **KL** (40min., 4 per day 7:30am-10:10pm, RM112). Open M-F 8:30am-5:30pm. AmEx/DC/MC/V.

Buses: The **express bus terminal** is on Jl. Stadium. To: **Butterworth** (10hr.; 8:30, 9pm; RM35); **Jerantut** (4hr.; 10am, 1, 3pm; RM10.50); **Johor Bahru** (6hr.; 9, 10:30am, 10:30, 11pm; RM18); **Kota Bharu** (7hr., 7 per day 8am-11pm and F-Sa 1am, RM20.50); **KL** (5hr., 17 per day 12:30am-10pm, RM14); **Kuala Terengganu** (3½hr.; 9:30, 11am, noon, 1:30pm; RM11.60); **Melaka** (6hr.; 1, 8am, 2:30pm; RM16.10); **Mersing** (4hr, 9, 10:30am, 5pm; RM10.90); **Singapore** via **Johor Bahru** (7hr.; 9, 10:30am, 10:30, 11pm; RM19.40). **Luggage storage** on 2nd fl. (RM1 per day; open daily 8am-12:30am). The **local bus terminal** on Jl. Besar, 1 block toward the river from Jl. Mahkota, runs buses to **Cherating** and **Kemaman** (1hr. and 1¼hr., every 30min., RM3 and RM3.70). Buses to the **airport** leave from both terminals (every hr. 7am-5pm) but it is quite a hike to the terminals. **City buses** ply the streets at RM0.70-0.90.

MALAYSIA

Taxis: Taxis leave from the express bus terminal or **city taxi stand** on Jl. Mahkota, near the tourist office. Taxis go anywhere in town for RM5-10 and RM20 hourly. **Share-taxis** also leave from the stand. Fare per car (4-people max.) to: **Jerantut** (RM100); **Johor Bahru** (RM180); **Kota Bharu** (RM180); **KL** (RM120); **Mersing** (RM120).

ORIENTATION AND PRACTICAL INFORMATION

Kuantan lies at the crossroads of **Rte. 2** and **3.** The city sprawls in a flurry of high-rises, but the main points of interest are in the southwestern parts of town along the **Kuantan River.** The two main streets, **Jl. Besar** and **Jl. Mahkota,** run parallel along the river. The town's central landmark is the large blue and white mosque, **Masjid Negeri,** beside the town *padang* (square) on Jl. Mahkota. **Jl. Bukit Ubi** runs perpendicular to Jl. Mahkota and takes you to the **central market,** near the express bus terminal. Budget hotels lie along or near Jl. Bukit Ubi and Jl. Mahkota.

Tourist Office: (☎516 1007). On Jl. Mahkota, near the taxi station. Free maps and tour info from a friendly, English-speaking staff, notably Mustafa. Open M-Th 9am-1pm and 2-4:30pm, F 9am-12:15pm and 2:45-4:30pm, Sa 9am-1pm. Closed every other Sa.

Immigration Offices: (☎514 373), in Wisma Persekutuan. Same-day visa extensions RM100 per month. Open M-F 8am-4:30pm with varying lunch breaks, Sa 8am-1pm.

Currency Exchange: Many banks are near the intersection of Jl. Mahkota and Bank St. **HSBC,** Jl. Mahkota (☎552 4666), has **24hr. ATMs** (Cirrus/MC/Plus/V). Open M-F 9:30am-3:30pm, Sa 9:30-11:30am.

Markets: Outside the **central market,** near the express bus terminal, is a bustling **day market** selling mostly Chinese hawker food. Open daily 2-9:30pm. On Sundays, there is a market on Jl. Mahkota, opposite the town square.

Laundry: Pusat Dobi Unik, 119 Jl. Mahkota (☎516 2403), opposite the town square. Laundry priced per item; average RM6 for a small load. Extra fee for same-day service.

Emergency: ☎999.

Police: ☎513 2222, on Jl. Mahkota. **Open 24hr.**

Medical Service: Hospital Tengku Ampuan Afzan (☎513 3333), on Jl. Tanah Putih, opposite Kompleks Terantun. Head southwest on Jl. Besar, away from Teluk Chempedak; the road becomes Jl. Tanah Putih. English-speaking doctors. RM2. **Open 24hr.**

Telephones: Telekom Office (☎513 9292), next to the post office. Sells phone cards. Open M-F 8:45am-4:15pm, Sa 8:30am-12:30pm. **Cyberpoint** on Jl. Besar, 3rd fl. RM2.50 per hr. Open 9am-9pm.

Internet Access: Blue Lane Computer (☎513 1761), on the ground fl. of Kompleks Makmur next to the express bus terminal. RM2.50 per hr. Open 10am-10pm.

Post Office: Pejabat Pos Besar (☎552 1032), on Jl. Mahkota at Jl. Merdeka intersection. Turn left coming from Jl. Bukit Ubi. *Poste Restante,* at side of building, open Sa-Th 8:30am-5pm. Post office open M-Sa 8am-4:30pm. **Postal code:** 25670.

MALAYSIA

ACCOMMODATIONS AND FOOD

New Campital Hotel ❷, 55-59 Jl. Bukit Ubi, 350m from Jl. Makhota, is worth the extra ringgit. (☎513 7276. Roms RM16, with bath RM17.90, with bath and A/C RM26.) **Hotel Kristal ❸,** 2/F 59-61A Jl. Mahkota, is down from the Standard Chartered Bank across from the mosque. (☎552 6577. Doubles RM30, with TV and bath RM35; triples with shower and TV but no toilet RM45.) Near the local bus station, **Hotel Sungai Wang ❸,** 86 Jl. Besar, has tidy pink rooms with bath. (☎514 8912. Doubles RM30, with A/C RM35-37; triples RM45; quads RM50.)

Food stalls on **Jl. Mahkota** near the State Mosque on Jl. Tun Ismail are great for cheap, convenient meals. For scenic late-night eats, head to the river behind the local bus terminal. Try the steamed shredded coconut with *gula melaka* inside a short bamboo cylinder (RM0.50). **Restoran Chan Poh,** ❷52 Bukit Ubi, opposite the Snooker Bistro and a few stores down, is a great place for late-night dim sum. (Shrimp dumplings RM1.80; fried noodles RM3. Beer RM6. Open daily 6pm-midnight.) **Restoren Parvathy** ❶, 75 Jl. Bukit Ubi, has the old standbys: *dosai,roti, chapaati*, and a host of curry selections for RM0.40-4. Heading away from Jl. Mahkota, it's 7 stores past the Snooker Bistro. (Open daily 7am-10pm.) One of the finer Chinese restaurants in town, **Kum Leng Restaurant** ❶, E-897-901 Jl. Bukit Ubi, north of the roundabout, has delicious dinners for RM10-20. (☎513 4446. Sweet and sour pork RM8. Been curd RM6. Fried rice RM4.)

SIGHTS

The only noteworthy attraction is the **Masjid Negeri** (State Mosque) on Jl. Mahkota, whose blue domes are the most colorful on the peninsula. Visitors are allowed inside if they are dressed appropriately (long pants or skirt, no bare shoulders) and do not walk on the elevated areas. Admission is free, but you must ask to enter at the front desk. The best times to visit are in the morning before 11:30am and from 3-5pm in the late afternoon. The most popular attraction is **Teluk Chempedak,** 4km from town on the east-coast shore. Teluk Chempedak's sandy 2km beach is bound by rocky headlands. Walk over the bridge to do the **Denai Tebling Pelindung** (cliff walk), which leads to a secluded beach inhabited by monkeys and tiny crabs. From here, you can scramble over a cluster of rocks to venture to beaches farther north. Although the only budget accommodation recently closed, the **Kuantan Hotel** ❹ (☎568 0026), opposite the Hyatt, is comfortable. (Upper-level rooms with sea views and bathtub. Doubles with fan RM44, with A/C RM55-66; quads RM77-88.) Get to Teluk Chempedak on bus #39 from the bus stop by Masjid Negeri on Jl. Mahkota (7am-10pm, RM1).

DAYTRIPS FROM KUANTAN

For even more scenic, relaxing activities, check out several worthwhile daytrips from Kuantan. **Sungai Pandan Waterfall** is a 50m cascade with eight tiers and a large pool at the bottom. Take a bus (45min., every 30min., RM3) from the local bus station to **Felda Panching** (30km), from which it's a 3km hike to the falls along a paved road. Nearby is **Panchang Cave,** a four-million-year-old limestone cavern enclosing a statue of the "Natural Buddha" carved by water drops (RM1). Take bus #48 (toward Sungai Lembing) from the local bus station to Panching (RM3). From town, it's a 4km hike through palm-oil plantations. A taxi takes you closer to the mouth of the cave for about RM50 round-trip. Travelers are discouraged from making the trip alone due to thugs in the area. **Tasik Chini,** Malaysia's second-largest lake, is well worth a sidetrip of one or two days. The lake and its environs are a natural playground where you can fish, jog, trek, take a boat ride through twelve interconnected lakes, or absorb the serene landscape. To get there, take a taxi (RM50) or a bus to Chini Town (RM5.20), which will bring you 12km from the lake. From here you can walk, take an unlicensed taxi at exorbitant rates (RM30), or try to catch a ride, although *Let's Go* does not recommend hitchhiking. For a daytrip, taxis for RM120 take you there and back (5hr. total, price not including RM40 boat ride around lake). "Uncle" Rajan Jones runs a home stay in an Orang Asli village (RM18). There is no phone, but locals should be able to direct you.

MERSING

☎07

The bustling town of Mersing is cluttered with signs of tourists in transit—backpackers roam the sidewalks in search of food stalls, moneychangers, and short-term distractions. ATMs are rare on Tioman Island, so it is highly advisable to get some cash in advance here.

TRANSPORTATION

Buses: Express Bus Terminal in **Plaza R&R** next to the jetty. **Transnational Express** (☎799 3155) goes to: **KL** (5½hr.; 11:30am, 6:30, 10pm; RM19.50); **Kuala Terengganu** via **Cherating** (6-7hr.; noon, 10pm; RM22.10); **Kota Biaru** (10hr., 9:30pm, RM29.10); **Kuantan** (3hr.; noon, 1, 2, 10pm; RM10.60); **Singapore** via **Johor Baru** (3hr.; noon, 1:30pm; RM12.60).

Ferries: Buy boat tickets to **Pulau Tioman** in **Plaza R&R. Ferries** are the cheapest, but also slowest (2-2½hr., 5 per day 7:30am-4:30pm, RM25). **Catamaran** speed boats are a little faster (1½-2hr., 2 per day 8:30am-12:30pm depending on the tides, RM30). **Speedboats** are most efficient (1-1½hr., 2 per day 9:30am-2pm depending on tides, RM35). Don't buy round-trip tickets–they may not be honored on the return journey.

Taxis: ☎799 1393. On Jl. Sulaiman next to the local bus station. From the jetty or Plaza R&R, walk down Jl. Abu Bakar, turn right at 1st intersection and left at end of the road. Open daily 7:30am-6pm. Prices are from one taxi station to another city's taxi station.

ORIENTATION AND PRACTICAL INFORMATION

Next to the **jetty** is the blue-and-white tiled **Plaza R&R,** housing a **tourist center** and **Express Bus Terminal.** Connected to the plaza are travel agencies, restaurants, and an Internet cafe. **Jl. Abu Bakar** runs in front of the jetty and through the main part of town. Many **guest houses** and the **post office** lie along Jl. Abu Bakar within a 5min. walk of the jetty. The other major road, **Jl. Ismail,** holds **banks,** a **supermarket,** and pricier **hotels.**

MALAYSIA

Tourist Offices: Mersing Tourist Information Center (☎799 5212), on Jl. Abu Bakar. Open M-Th 2-4:30pm, F 2:45-4:30pm. English-speaking staff at **Island Connection Travel and Tours** (☎799 2535), 2 Jl. Jemaluang, at the corner opposite where Jl. Abu Bater and Jl. Ismail meet. Open M-F 9am-6pm. **Sun and Sand Holiday** (☎799 4995), at the Embassy Hotel, also has English-speaking staff.

Tours: Omar's Backpacker's Hostel (☎019 774 4268; see **Accommodations,** below) offers 1-day tours to nearby islands (RM60; includes guide, transport, lunch, and snorkeling gear; 4-12 people). **New East Coast Hotel** (☎012 762 4983) offers an **Endau River Cruise** (RM130; 4-8 people) and tours of **Gunning Berlumut** jungles, fruit farms, and rubber and tea plantations (RM150; at least 2 people).

Currency Exchange: Bank Bumiputra Malaysia Berhad, 4-5 Jl. Ismail (☎799 1600), next to Embassy Hotel. Cashes traveler's checks for RM2.15. MC/V cash advances RM4. Open M-F 9am-4:30pm, Sa 9:30am-noon. **Maybank**, on Jl. Ismail next to Parkson Supermarket. **ATM** (Cirrus/MC). Open M-F 9:30am-4pm, Sa 9:30-11:30am. **Moneychangers** line Jl. Abu Bakar. Generally open daily 9am-6pm. **Giamso Safari**, 23 Jl. Abu Bakar (☎799 2253). Licensed moneychanger inside. Open daily 8am-6pm.

Emergency: ☎999.

Police: ☎799 2222. From jetty, walk down Jl. Abu Bakar and turn left on Jl. Sultanah.

Medical Services: Hospital Daerah (☎799 3333), at end of Jl. Ismail. English spoken. **24hr.** emergency care. Open daily 8am-4:15pm.

Telephones: Card phones everywhere, especially around jetty and inside Plaza R&R. Many shops along Jl. Abu Bakar sell phone cards.

Internet: K@N Internet Café, 13 Jl. Dato Mohammad Ali (☎790 1149). Walk down Jl. Abu Bakar from the jetty and bear left at the first roundabout. The connection here is faster. A/C comfort. RM1.50 per 30min, RM3 per hr. Open daily 9:30am-11:30pm. **Mersing IT Center,** 30 Jl. Abu Bakar (☎799 6072), to the right of the jetty. RM5 per hr. Open daily 9am-6pm. **Cyberworld!,** 36 Jl. Abu Bakar (☎799 6109), next to KFC. RM1.50 per 30min., RM3 per hr. Open daily 9:30am-6:30pm and 8:30-11:30pm.

Post Office: 670 Jl. Abu Bakar (☎799 1031). Open M-Sa 8:30am-5pm. **Postal code:** 86800.

ACCOMMODATIONS AND FOOD

Embassy Hotel ❷, 2 Jl. Ismail, near the rotary by Bank Bumiputra, has good clean rooms. (☎799 3545. Doubles RM16, with bath RM28, with A/C RM40, with A/C and TV RM45; triples with bath RM30, with A/C and TV RM50; quads with A/C and TV RM60.) **New East Coast Hotel ❶,** 43A Jl. Abu Bakar, has a rooftop common area, laundry service, and Internet (RM4 per hr.). They also provide travel info and can book onward travel. (☎013 724 7081. Dorms RM10; doubles RM10; triples RM30.) Opposite the post office and 5min. from the jetty, **Omar's Backpacker's Hostel ❶,** 1D-1 Jl. Abu Bakar, has rooms with fan and shared bath as well as a simple cooking area. (☎799 5096. Dorms RM8; doubles RM20.) **Hotel Golden City ❶,** on the first floor of 23 Jl. Abu Bakar at the corner with Jl. Pasar, has dimly-lit rooms with thick mattresses. (☎799 5028. Reception 24hr. Dorms with fan RM10; doubles with shower and fan RM25, with A/C RM35.)

Food stalls ❶ at Plaza R&R sell cheap Malay food. A plate of white rice with vegetables, chicken, or fish costs RM1.50-5, while *mee goreng* is RM2. (Open daily 5:30am-8pm.) For freshly cooked food, try one of the Chinese seafood or Indian restaurants. **Restoran Ee Lo ❷,** at the roundabout where Jl. Abu Bakar and Jl. Mohammad Ali meet, cooks up special dishes such as fried wild boar meat with ginger and onion and lemon chicken both for RM6. (☎799 3050. Open daily 10am-11pm.) **Restoran Al-Arif ❶,** 44 Jl. Ismail, has excellent *roti canai* for RM0.60 and *roti telur* for RM1.20. (☎799 4518. Fried noodles/rice RM3-5. Open daily 7am-11pm.) **Restoran Halina ❶,** 53 Jl. Abu Bakar, offers a wide variety of Malaysian favorites. (☎799 7350. *Murtabak ayam* RM4. Open daily 6am-10pm.)

PULAU TIOMAN

According to legend, a magical dragon princess inhabits the island to maintain its peaceful beauty. The princess is certainly doing her job, given the island's superb beaches and clear waters that are transparent to depths of over 20m. In fact, Tioman has been rated as one of the world's top ten island destinations. There is something here for everyone, from top-notch snorkeling and diving spots to bustling resorts or secluded bays. The locals are infinitely generous and friendly. Women travelers usually feel quite comfortable sunbathing in their bikinis without fear of excessive heckling. Whether it's action or relaxation you are seeking, you might end up staying longer than expected.

TRANSPORTATION

The **airport** is in Kampung Tekek. **Berjaya Air** (☎419 1309) has daily flights to **KL** (1hr.; 11:30am, 1:50pm; RM141, children RM71) and **Singapore** (40min., 11am, RM280). Make reservations one day in advance (AmEx/MC/V).

Most travelers catch a **boat** from **Mersing** (see p. 438) to get to Pulau Tioman. Buy tickets at a travel agency for a **ferry** (2-2½hr., 5 per day 7:30am-4:30pm, RM25) or **speedboat** (1-1½hr., 2 per day 9:30am-2pm depending on tides, RM35). Ferries to Mersing leave from **Kampung Salang** (6:30am) and pick up passengers at **Kampung Air Batang** (7am) and **Kampung Tekek** (7:30-8am). Speedboats to Mersing also leave from all three piers (9:30am-noon). Ferries leave for **Singapore** from the **Berjaya Resort** (4-4½hr.; 2:30pm; RM150-170, child RM100-110; not including seaport tax or weekend surcharges; cash only). Schedules vary with the tides. Check with ticket sellers and locals. Don't buy round-trip tickets, as they may not be honored upon return. An expensive local **sea taxi,** booked at any hostel, travels between beaches (RM10-45 depending on travel distance). A daily ferry leaves from **Juara** at 3pm to: **Berjaya Resorts** (RM30); **Kampung Salang** (1hr., RM20); **Kampung Tekek** (2hr., RM25). Chartering a boat runs upward of RM200.

KAMPUNG TEKEK ☎09

Despite being Pulau Tioman's largest village, Kampung Tekek remains relatively less touristed than other destinations on the island and still manages to offer a smattering of cheap accommodations and food stalls. Kampung Tekek is an easy and welcoming place to begin your exploration of the island.

ORIENTATION AND PRACTICAL INFORMATION. The walk to Tekek from Kampung Air Batang takes 30min. A **police station** is 500m to the right of the jetty. (☎419 1167. **Open 24hr.**) The **clinic** is several doors down in a pale yellow building. (☎419 1880. Open M-Th 8am-1pm and 2-4:30pm, F 8am-12:15pm and 2:45-4:30pm, Sa 8am-1pm.) There is a RM1 charge to foreigners for medical consultation. English-speaking staff is available. For emergencies, an on-site doctor is available 24hr: ask locals to wake him. Other services are available at the **Airport Terminal Complex** across from the jetty. On the second floor is a **moneychanger** that cashes traveler's checks at poor rates—**bring cash from the mainland.** Next door is the **post office** (☎419 1145; open M-F 9am-7pm, Sa-Su 9am-5pm), which sends mail to and receives mail from Mersing three times a week. Its *Poste Restante* address is: Kampung Tekek, Pulau Tioman, 86800 K. Rompin, Pahang Darul Mamur, Malaysia. **Telekom card phones** are clustered at the jetty and near the Airport Terminal Complex; purchase phone cards at the moneychanger. An **Internet cafe** is on the second floor, inside **Featherlight.** (☎419 1609. RM5 per 30min., RM7 per hr. Open daily 9am-midnight.) Internet access is also available at **TM Mart** to the right of the jetty, close to the chalet resorts. (☎013 736 1695. The price listed is RM10 per hr., though you can bargain RM7 per hr.)

ACCOMMODATIONS AND FOOD. **Persona Island Resort ❺** has the cleanest rooms in town, but no beachfront property. All rooms have fan and A/C. Van service and discounts are available. (☎419 1213. Doubles RM90; triples RM110; sea view RM130.) Closer to the jetty, **Coral Reef Holidays ❹** has rooms facing the sea or facing a garden, where a very friendly monkey enjoys playing with the guests. Discounts are available for groups. The cafe serves Malay and Western food. (☎419 1628. Doubles RM45/RM80; triples RM50/RM60-80; larger rooms RM80/RM120-180.) **Monte Chalets ❹,** closest to the jetty, is complete luxury with bathrobes, A/C, carpeting, and hot water in all the rooms. (☎419 1648. Doubles RM60, with sea view RM80; triples RM150; family rooms RM200; VIP rooms RM250.) **Food stalls** ❶ at the Airport Terminal Complex serve *nasi lemak* (RM2.50) and fried eggs with toast (RM3.50), as well as fried rice (RM3.50) and fried noodles (RM3.50) of your choice. Two small **supermarkets** lie on the road to the right of the jetty, before you reach Sri Tioman.

ACTIVITIES AND ENTERTAINMENT. Next door to Sri Tioman and past the police station is **Tioman Dive Centre,** which offers PADI courses. (☎419 1228; www.tioman-dive-centre.com. All levels of instruction available. 2hr. intro dive course RM140, 2-day scuba dive course RM550, 4-day basic open-water course RM800, rescue diver RM850, dive master RM850+. Gear rental available. Discounts available for large groups.) Next to Cheers Souvenirs, you can **rent bicycles, motorbikes,** and **snorkel gear.** (☎419 1425. Bikes RM5 per hr., RM25 per day; motorbikes RM15 per hr., RM75 per day; mask and snorkel RM10 per day. Prices do not include deposit fees. Open daily 9am-7pm.) **Coral Reef Holidays** offers a variety of activities, from board games to frisbee to foot and body massage sessions.

KAMPUNG SALANG ☎010

Kampung Salang sits at the north tip of Tioman Island. The small, dreamy beach is delightful, but the town is crammed with travelers on their way to Coral Island and nearby dive sites.

ORIENTATION AND PRACTICAL INFORMATION. Beach and chalets stretch out on both sides of the pier. Most restaurants, shops, and budget accommodations are to the right of the jetty, while larger resorts are to the left. Exchange **currency** at most budget hotels or to the left of the jetty at **Salang Indah minimart,** which cashes traveler's checks, sells phone cards, and will let you make **international calls** (prices vary according to call destination). For **medical assistance,** most people take a sea taxi to the clinic in Kampung Tekek or seek simple first aid from one of the dive centers. The **24hr. police** office is next to B&J Diving Centre, to the left of the jetty (☎013 983 0244).

ACCOMMODATIONS AND FOOD. Half a dozen inexpensive hotels line Salang's beach and most have restaurants with Malay, Chinese, and Western dishes. **Salang Sayang (Zaid's Place)** ❹, at the southern end of the village by the beach, has clean rooms with a great view. Restaurant, library, moneychanger, Internet, and snorkel gear rental are all available here. Reserve in advance for August. (☎419

IN RECENT NEWS

PARADISE? ... OR SHOPPERS' PARADISE?

As of January 2002, Pulau Tioman has been declared the third duty-free island in Malaysia. This follows the relative success of Langkawi and Labuan as economically profitable tourist destinations after achieving duty-free status. For now, Tioman remains a fairly undeveloped place where one can find sprawling resorts alongside cheap chalets. A vast majority of the island is still jungle; transportation between villages often requires a motorbike or boat. Tioman's new status raises concerns over how to develop the island while preserving its natural beauty.

The number of visitors to Tioman has quadrupled since 1987 to over 200,000 annually. In order to handle this increased volume of tourists, the Malaysian government has planned a massive face-lift of the island—including new roads, a larger airport, and more accommodations—in conjunction with a large-scale marketing campaign. These changes reflect the hope that Tioman will eventually compete with Pulau Batam and Pulau Bintan as the destination of choice for wealthy Singapore tourists. The changes brought about by new capital flow will inevitably affect the pace and style of life on Tioman. Residents will need to set up a collaborative committee to stabilize prices and communicate local concerns to the Malaysian government.

In July of 2002, billboards advertise a cleaner Tioman by 2005. "Do not litter," they implore, but there are still soda cans strewn on the wayside.

5020. Singles RM80; doubles RM60-80; Banana Hill doubles RM75, with A/C RM100; triples with A/C and hot shower RM150; 4-person family rooms with A/C and hot shower RM180.) The fanciest resort, just to the left of the jetty, is **Salang Indah Resorts ❸,** which operates a restaurant, sea taxis, ferries, a sports center, souvenir shop, minimart, bar, and dive shop. (☎419 5015. Doubles RM35, with A/C RM90-130; triples RM50; quads with A/C RM90-150. Extra mattresses RM10. Internet RM2 per 15min.) Set back on a small hill before Zaid's Place is **Pak Long Chalet ❹,** which has basic rooms surrounding a quiet garden. (☎419 5000. Laundry RM5 per kg. Doubles RM40; triples RM50, with A/C RM150; quads with A/C RM180. Prices can be bargained down.)

Right off the jetty, **Salang Dreams Restaurant ❸** serves *nasi lemak* (RM2), chocolate pancakes (RM4), seafood fettucine (RM10), and alcoholic drinks. (☎419 5040. Open daily 8am-10:30pm.) The **Chinese Restaurant ❹** at Salang Beack Resort has an extensive menu of seafood dishes. Try the chili crab (RM15-28) or claypot Indonesian prawns (RM18-38). Vegetarian options are also available. (Open daily 8am-3pm and 6-10pm.) After 7pm, **White House Cafe ❸,** near Dive Asia, fills the air with the smell of barbecued seafood and meat (RM7-30). **Salang Indah Restaurant ❷** dishes up Chinese, Malay, Thai, and Western food. The Thai chef recommends Thai fried rice (RM4), or *laksa penang* (RM3). (Open daily 8am-10:30pm.) Nightlife stumbles on at **Four-S Cafe** with RM5-8 beers. (Open daily 6pm-1am. MC/V.)

ACTIVITIES AND ENTERTAINMENT. Near the police station, **Fishermen Dive Center** is well equipped and offers PADI courses as well as daytrips. (☎419 5014; www.fishermenscuba.com. 2 dives RM160; 3 dives RM220; 4 dives RM270; prices include equipment, food, and drink. Open daily 9am-6pm. MC/V.) Farther down, **Dive Asia** offers similar day trips and PADI courses. (☎419 5017; www.diveasia.com.my. 2 dives RM130-160; shore dives RM40-70; prices depend on if you have equipment and include lunch. Open daily 8:30am-6:30pm. AmEx/MC/V.) **Salang Indah Resorts** also has badminton courts and fishing gear at its sports center.

KAMPUNG AIR BATANG (ABC) ☎9

Kampung Air Batang is a backpacker haven buzzing with affordable accommodations, food, and souvenir shops. Life is slower-paced here; most travelers come here to relax. The beach is wider and sandier south of the jetty, while resorts to the north face a pile of warm rocks.

The **tourist information hut** is opposite the ferry landing spot, but is rarely open. Luckily, the boatman at **Zinza's Place,** to the right just off the jetty, can provide all the information you need on transportation. Diving and snorkeling expeditions are led by **B&J Diving.** (☎419 1218. Kayak rental RM15 per hr. Open daily 8:30am-6pm).

Bamboo Hill Chalets ❺, at the end of the beach left of the jetty, offers picturesque accommodations with sea views, Internet access (RM2.5 per 15min.), and international calls. All proceeds from library book rentals (RM1 per book) are donated to the local school. (☎419 1339; www.geocities.com/bamboosu. 2-person bungalows with hot showers RM70; ask about the well-equipped quad and family room. Reserve several days in advance over the Internet.) **Nazri's Place ❸** is at the southern end of the village with a small beach. (☎419 1329. Laundry priced per item. Internet RM1 per 5min. Camping RM3; doubles with fan RM25, with A/C and hot shower RM80.) **Yang Puang Chalet ❷** has rooms with brightly patterned sheets and curtains. (☎013 609 4628. Doubles RM15-20; triples RM30-35.) **Mawar Beach Chalets ❸** has a cozy restaurant in addition to standard chalets with showers. For RM35 per person, Mawar offers a daytrip to Coral Island for groups of 4 or more; reservations must be made one day in advance. (☎419 1153. Laundry RM5 per kg. Doubles RM25.) **ABC Chalets ❸** to the left of the jetty, is before Bamboo Hill Chalets. (☎419 1154. Doubles RM35-45; triples with A/C, minifridge, hot shower, large veranda, and sea view RM120. Reserve in advance.)

People flock to **Nazri's Cafe ❷**, at the south end of ABC, for excellent Malay and Western meals. For breakfast, try *roti canai* (RM1), pineapple pancakes (RM3), or the continental breakfast (RM6). Entrees cost around RM6. (Open daily 8am-10:30pm.) Nearby, the restaurant at **Mawar Beach Chalets ❷** serves similar fare that is a bit funkier. Try a Malaysian omelette with chili and onion (RM2.50) or grilled fish, garlic butter, salad, and chips for RM12. (Open daily 9am-4pm and 7-10pm.) The cheapest food on this side of the jetty is at **My Friend's Place ❶.** Many travelers stop here for a breakfast of toast and scrambled eggs (RM2.50) with coffee or tea (RM1). For a more romantic setting, **Restoran Hijau ❸**, to the left of the jetty, provides serene seaview dining atop a small hill. Hijau has steeper prices for a sophisticated dining experience. (Barbecue RM13-18; burgers RM8. ☎419 1375. Open 8am-4pm and 7pm-10:30pm.)

KAMPUNG JUARA ☎09

Kampung Juara, on the east coast of Tioman, is the hardest place to reach on the island, but those who make the trek will be rewarded with some of Pulau Tioman's best beaches.

Bushman Dive Centre, at the cafe, offers PADI courses (open water RM750, advanced diver RM600, dive master RM1200) in addition to regular dives for RM70-150. (☎419 3109; www.members.tripod.com/bushman42.)

The most scenic route to Juara is a cross-island trek through the jungle from **Kampung Tekek** (2½hr., 7km). From the jetty, turn left on the cement path and walk 500m, turning right at the sign on the paved path before the minimart. Past the mosque, the trail narrows to a thin dirt path. The halfway point is marked by what was formerly the **Jungle Cafe** (it was destroyed when a tree fell on top of it), after which there is a small waterfall and the path becomes a downhill cement walkway. Get a motorbike ride (RM15-20) up to the top (midway point) and trek back down; or from Juara, take a **sea bus** (3pm, RM25) back to Kampung Tekek. The road set back from the beach meets the **jungle trail** to Tekek south of the jetty. **Happy Market,** next to the jetty, exchanges traveler's checks and major currencies, but rates are unpredictable. **Internet** costs RM12 per hr. (☎419 3137. Open daily 7:30am-9pm.) **Ferry** and **sea bus tickets** are sold at the counter on the jetty. Rent **snorkeling equipment** at the hut next to Mini Cafe, left of the jungle trail as you come out. (RM10. Open daily 8:30am-5pm.) The Juara **clinic** is off the path to the left of the jetty (open daily 2-4:30pm).

Paradise Point ❷, to the right of the jetty, has basic two-person chalets with private bath (RM20), though the beds are on the soft side. The **restaurant ❶** serves an extensive menu (fried noodles with peanut sauce RM4) and has outdoor seating. (☎419 3145. Laundry RM4 per kg. Restaurant open daily 7am-10:30pm.) Next door is **River View Chalets ❷**, also with basic two-person rooms (RM20) and a pleasant open-air seafood **restaurant ❷** offering fried fish in *sambal* sauce for RM13.50 and *Tom Yam* noodle soup for RM5.50. (☎419 3168. Doubles with bath, fan, and mosquito net RM20.) **Juara Mutiara Resort ❸** is left of the jetty, with newly built chalets, a cafe, boat service, and a minimart. (☎419 3161. Doubles RM25; quads RM40. Group packages and daytrips available.) To reach **Rainbow Chalets ❷**, walk left of the jetty and through a football field. The beach in front has the biggest waves in Juara. (☎419 3140. Doubles RM20-25; quads RM40.) Next door, the **Bushman Cafe ❷** serves pizza (RM8-10) and homemade bread (RM3-4 for toast).

NEAR KAMPUNG JUARA

Coral Island, even more beautiful than Pulau Tioman, has reefs with abundant marine life that are perfect for snorkeling. **Salang Beach Mini Market** organizes snorkeling trips to Coral Island. (☎419 5016. 10:30am-3:30pm or 1:30-5:30pm; RM35, minimum 2 people, includes snorkel gear; RM40, minimum 4 people, includes gear and lunch. Reserve 24hr. in advance.) Many resorts and dive centers in Salang offer daytrips to Coral Island as well. **Money Bay** and **Monkey Beach** are dreamy secluded bays halfway between Kampung Salang and ABC. Follow the well-marked jungle trails going in each direction (40min. to Monkey Bay from Kampung Salang, 1½hr. to Monkey Beach from ABC). Alternatively, you can take a sea taxi to Monkey Bay from Kampung Salang (RM10). The hike is steep; bring water and look out for monkeys. If you're exhausted from the effort of lying around on the beach all day, try the **Mukut Waterfalls** at the southern tip of Tioman island. **Salang Indah Resorts** organizes a waterfall trip. (☎419 5015. RM50.) **Nazri's Place 2** in ABC also has a trip there. (☎419 1375. RM50.)

SARAWAK

Sarawak earned its name when the Sultan of Brunei handed it over to James Brooke, the first White Rajah, with the words "*Serah kapada awak*" ("I give this to you"). Though he really doesn't need the money, the sultan is probably kicking himself now—Sarawak is Malaysia's richest state and boasts nine national parks, lush jungles, secluded beaches, and giant limestone caves. The state is also home to 26 ethnic groups, including the famed Iban who live in longhouses along the Rajang River. Environmental degradation is threatening Sarawak's natural beauty and its indigenous cultures, though major conservation efforts are now underway.

MALAYSIA

KUCHING ☎082

Kuching means "cat" in Malay, and residents celebrate that appellation with gleaming feline statues. Easily the most modern city in Borneo, Kuching successfully preserves the relics of its past: Chinese temples and Muslim mosques stand in the shadow of towering skyscrapers and luxury hotels. A meticulously landscaped waterfront esplanade invites people to unwind after touring world-renowned museums or sorting through piles of handicrafts at the street markets. An ideal base from which to explore Bako National Park, the Sarawak Cultural Village, and Iban and Bidayuh longhouses, this cat bites hard and leaves visitors craving more.

TRANSPORTATION

Flights: Kuching International Airport (☎457 373), 10km south of the city. Take Sarawak Transport Company bus #12A (30min., every hr. 6am-7:20pm, RM1) or Chin Lian Long bus #8A (30min., every hr. 6am-8pm, RM0.90). Coupons for taxis (RM17.50) also available outside customs can be used on your return trip. Storage lockers RM3 per day. **MAS** (☎246 622), on Jl. Song Thian Cheok. To: **Bintulu** (RM117); **Hong Kong** (RM1167); **Kota Kinabalu** (RM228); **KL** (am flights RM197; pm flights RM262); **Miri** (RM164); **Sandakan** (RM284); **Sibu** (RM72); **Singapore** (RM286). **Royal Brunei Airlines,** 1st fl., Rugayah Building, Jl. Song Thian Cheok (☎243 344). Open M-F 8:30am-12:30pm and 1:30-5pm, Sa 8:30am-12:30pm, Su 9am-1pm. To: **Bandar Seri Begawan** (Tu, Th, Su; RM334).

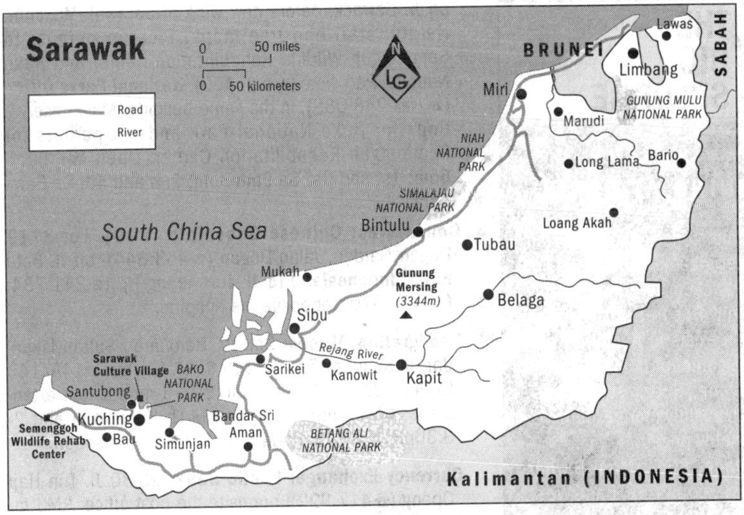

Buses: Kuching lacks a central bus terminal. Departure points depend on destination and bus company, three of which serve both Kuching and southwest Sarawak. Green-and-cream **Sarawak Transport Company** (☎242 967) buses run from the bus stop on Lh. Jawa. Blue-and-white **Chin Lian Long** (☎422 767) buses depart from Jl. Masjid, the post office, and Jl. Gambier. **Petra Jaya Transport** (☎429 418) has yellow, red, and black buses that depart from the open air market on Jl. Khoo Hun Yeang.

Long-Distance Buses: Biaramas Express, Jl. Khoo Hun Yeang (☎429 418), near Electra House, has a 24hr. office at the terminal (☎452 139). Buses depart 5 times daily (7:45, 9:45am, 1, 5, 9pm). To: **Batu Niah** (12hr., RM74); **Bintulu** (10hr., RM60); **Miri** (15hr., RM80); **Sarikei** (6hr., RM32); **Sibu** (7hr., RM40). Buses to **Pontianak, Indonesia** (7hr., RM45) depart twice daily (7:30, 11am). **Borneo Highway Express,** 63 Main Bazaar (☎413 595), and **PB Express** (☎461 277) also provide long-distance service.

Boats: Express boats depart from **Bintawa Express Wharf,** accessible by CLL buses #17 and 19 (30min., RM0.80). **Express Bahagia,** 50 Padungan Rd. (☎421 948), runs boats to **Sibu** (4hr.; 8:30am, 12:30pm; RM35, 1st-class RM45). It is advisable to arrive at the wharf 30min. prior to departure. Seats regularly sell out. **Cash only.**

ORIENTATION AND PRACTICAL INFORMATION

Kuching's city center unfolds along the southern banks of the **Sarawak River.** Its western border is **Jl. Gambier,** which becomes **Jl. Main Bazaar.** Local bus terminals, the mosque, and the waterfront promenade are in this vicinity. **Fort Margherita** stands across the river. The **central district** begins past the souvenir shops on Jl. Main Bazaar near **Tua Pek Kong Temple.** Turning right leads to **Lh. Temple** and most budget accommodations. Tourists are advised not to walk along the waterfront alone at night as this is a favorite spot for pickpockets.

Tourist Offices: Sarawak Tourism Association, Kuching Waterfront, Jl. Main Bazaar (☎240 620). Walking away from the Tua Pek Kong Temple, this octagon-shaped building is on the right. Maps, advice, and brochures available from a friendly staff. **Visitors Information Center,** Lot 31, Jl. Masjid (☎410 942). Entrance faces Padang Merdeka

THE BIG SPLURGE

FINE DINING AT DENIS'

To the health conscious, Malaysian food may feel greasy. Food stalls lining the streets seem to emanate only steam and oil. But fret not! A light, culinary oasis exists in Kuching's city center on the corner of Jl. Main Bazaar and Lh. Wayang. Better still, Denis' Place, though slightly more expensive, is still reasonably priced.

Denis' Place, 80 Jl. Main Bazaar (☎238 818), cooks up East-West fusion dishes that won't leave you feeling guilty. A fresh salad and baked potato accompany most entrees. The popular "chicken chop," a mashed chicken breast marinated in a home-made black pepper sauce and topped with caramelized onions, is well worth the RM17.90.

Of course, tortilla chips, taco meat, and salsa–the basic ingredients of nachos–are not readily available in Malaysia. Denis' creative solution? Create a "nacho" appetizer by combining sun-dried bananas, a spicy meat sauce, and yogurt (RM14.90). Among his other culinary inventions and adaptations: a delectable fresh mushroom and cheddar crepe (RM18.90) and juicy ginger and onion steak (RM16.90).

These amply-portioned dishes are served against the relaxing backdrop of local and Mediterranean art, and wooden statues compliment an intricately tiled mosaic floor. Right on the waterfront, Denis' is the perfect place to kick back and watch the world go by. Unwinding in this candle-lit café where free ice water is served in blue, chilled wine bottles may scream luxury, but don't worry. Denis' Place is worth every ringgit.

on Jl. Barrack, before new wing of Sarawak Museum. Helpful staff and free maps. Pick up permits to Semenggoh Wildlife Rehabilitation Center and Bako National Park here (see p. 450). **National Parks Office** (☎/fax 248 088), in the same building. Make reservations for Bako National Park and get permits for Semanggoh Rehabilitation Center. Open M-F 8am-6pm; 1st and 3rd Sa 9am-3pm; 2nd and 4th Sa 8am-4pm.

Consulates: Chinese Consulate (PRC), Lot 3719 Dogan Garden, Jalan Dogan (☎453 344), off Jl. Batu Kawa. **Indonesia,** 111 Jl. Tun Abang Hj. (☎241 734; fax 424 370), opposite the hospital.

Immigration Offices: 2nd fl., Bangunan Sultan Iskandar, Jl. Simpang Tiga (☎245 661). CLL bus #14A/14B to Petra Jaya (20min., RM0.50). 1-month visa extensions; RM1 filing fee. Open M-Th 8am-noon and 2-3:30pm, F 8-11am and 2-3:30pm, Sa 8am-noon.

Currency Exchange: Public Bank, 28-30 Jl. Tun Haji Openg (☎417 922), opposite the post office. RM3 for cashing first traveler's check; RM0.15 per additional check. Open M-F 9:30am-4pm, Sa 9:30-12:30am. **Standard Chartered Bank** on Jl. Padungan near Holiday Inn. **24hr. ATM.**

American Express: At **CPH Travel Agency,** 70 Jl. Padungan (☎243 708), off the intersection with Jl. Chan Chin Ann. Open M-F 8:30am-5pm, Sa 8:30am-noon.

English-Language Bookstore: Times Bookshop, 1st fl., 103 Crown Plaza Complex, Jl. Tunku Abdul Rahman (☎412 231). Proceed up escalator; the store is on your right. Open daily 10am-9:30pm. AmEx/MC/V.

Emergency: ☎999.

Police: ☎241 222. At the corner of Jl. Khoo Hun Yeang and Jl. Barrack. **Tourist Police Unit,** Kuching Waterfront, Jl. Main Bazaar (☎250 522). English spoken. The staff can help with any problem. Open daily, including public holidays, 8am-midnight.

Hospital: Sarawak General Hospital (☎257 555), on Jl. Ong Keattwi. English spoken. Taxi RM10.

Pharmacies: Apex Pharmacy, No. 125, first fl., Sarawak Plaza (☎413 605). Open daily 10am-9pm. AmEx/MC/V. **Guardian Pharmacy,** Lower Ground Floor, Riverside Plaza. Open daily 10am-9:30pm. AmEx/MC/V.

Telephones: Credit card phones at the GPO and airport. Most hotels send faxes.

Internet Access: Cyber City Cafe, 46 Block D, Taman Sri Sarawak (☎243 549). RM4 per hr. Open daily 10am-11pm. **Dotcom Cyber Cafe,** Jl. Tabuan, across from the Fata Hotel. RM4 per hr. Open daily 10am-midnight. **Waterfront Cyber Cafe,** Kuching Waterfront, Jl. Main Bazaar (☎271 176), beside the Sarawak Tourism Association. RM4.50 per hr. Prices increase on weekends. Open Th-Tu 9am-midnight.

Post Office: GPO (☎241 311), on Jl. Tun Haji Openg. *Poste Restante.* Closed 1st and 3rd Sa of the month. Open M-Sa 8am-4:30pm. **Postal code:** 93100.

ACCOMMODATIONS

B&B Inn (☎237 366), on Jl. Tabuan. Walk up Jl. Temple to rotary and veer left. Kuching's most popular backpacker inn is also its most affordable. Clean rooms and storage space (RM2). Breakfast included. Common bath. Dorms RM16; singles RM24, with A/C RM30; doubles RM32, with A/C RM38; 3-person family room RM42. ❷

Orchid Inn, 2 Jl. Green Hill (☎411 417), past Furama Lodging House. Rooms have A/C, hot water, and private bath. Laundry. Singles RM28; doubles RM35; triples RM45. ❸

Fata Hotel (☎248 111), opposite Dotcom Cyber Cafe on Jl. McDougall. Bugs biting? Hot out? It don't matta' at the Fata! A/C, TV, and a shower with bathtub. Laundry available. Cozy singles RM45; doubles from RM49; triples RM75. AmEx/MC/V. ❹

Kuching Hotel, 6 Lh. Temple (☎413 985). Across from Medan Pelita Food Court. Large rooms with fan, sink, desk and common bath. Singles RM22; doubles RM27. ❷

Diocesan Center Guest House (☎240 188), on Jl. McDougall. Enter driveway right of the Anglican cathedral parking lot and veer right at the end. Basic rooms with fan. Extremely quiet. Singles RM18-20; doubles RM23-25; apartments with A/C RM30, double occupancy RM45. Closed in late Aug. and early Sept. ❷

FOOD

Sarawak's signature dish and breakfast staple, *laksa mee*, consists of noodles cooked in a spicy curry broth laced with shredded chicken, prawns, bean curd, and bean sprouts. **Vendors** ❶ cluster in the west end of town, south of the **Jl. Gambier** terminals and opposite the Chinese temple on **Jl. Carpenter.** After breakfast, try *apam*, a sizzling pancake vendors cook before your eyes and stuff with coconut, peanut butter, and sugar. In the evening, **vendors** ❶ along the Kuching Waterfront grill up *satay* (marinated meat served on a skewer; RM0.40 per stick). The **Medan Pelita Food Court,** in the basement of the Star car com-

THE LOCAL STORY

MASTIJAH MASLEH, ORGANIZER OF "PESTA MEOWW"

LG: What goes on during Pesta Meoww?

MM: We have our live cats competition, and then we have our cat show... But then we also have human[s] dressed [as] cat[s]... and we have the imitation of the cat voice and action. Everything.

LG: What kind of competition is for the live cat?

MM: We have Siamese, local crossbreeds, all types of cats... We have the best, fancy-dressed cat. On the stage.

LG: They wear dresses?

MM: It's up to the owner how they want the cat to come out.

LG: Is there any costume that you remember very well?

MM: Yes, a few. Some putting on gowns like Lady Diana. Or Queen Margaret, that style. And then cowboy. There are all sorts of styles they have.

LG: Could you talk about the judging of the best-dressed cat?

MM: It's up to the judge... Some of the cats, they are shy. And they don't like [clothes] put on them... But some cats are very very good... They like it. Like human beings.

LG: So the cat has to be confident?

MM: Yes. I think the owner has [to] train the cat.

LG: It's about more than looks?

MM: Looks and personality itself.

LG: Is there a swimsuit competition?

MM: Oh, I would like that, but so far we don't have that. I will suggest it later on.

plon between **Lh. Temple** and **Lh. Wayang,** dishes out typical hawker food. Visit the **Top Spot Food Court** on Jl. Bukit Mata Kuching, a favorite eating place for locals, for more varied choices including claypot dishes, Malay curries, and steaks.

Zhun San Yen Vegetarian, Lot 165, Jl. Chan Chin Ann (☎230 068). Follow Jl. Tunku Abdul Rahman past Sarawak Plaza and turn left at Pizza Hut. Vegetarian heaven with over 30 dishes (RM1.40 per 100g). Savory white fungus and straw mushroom soup RM1.10. Fresh fruit juices RM2.50. Open M-Sa 7:30am-2:30pm and 5-8:30pm. ❶

Bismillah Cafe, 19 Jl. Khoo Hun Yeang (☎415 803), next to the KFC. An appetizing self-service buffet with tandoori chicken (RM2) and spicy tofu (RM2.50). Generous servings of rice and smiles. Open M-Sa 8am-5pm. ❶

Life Cafe, 108 Jl. Ewe Hai (☎411 754), close to the intersection with Lh. Wayang; look for red lanterns. The best coffee in Sarawak (RM3), light food, and delicious teas. Clay pot noodles RM4.50. Crocodile soup RM13. Open M-Sa 11am-11pm. ❷

Khatulistiwa Cafe (☎248 896), on Jl. Tunku Abdul Rahman, across from the Crowne Plaza complex. House specialty is *Sarawak laksa* served with *bee hoon* (RM8.50). Pineapple rice RM7.90. Breakfast served 24hr. AmEx/DC/MC/V. ❸

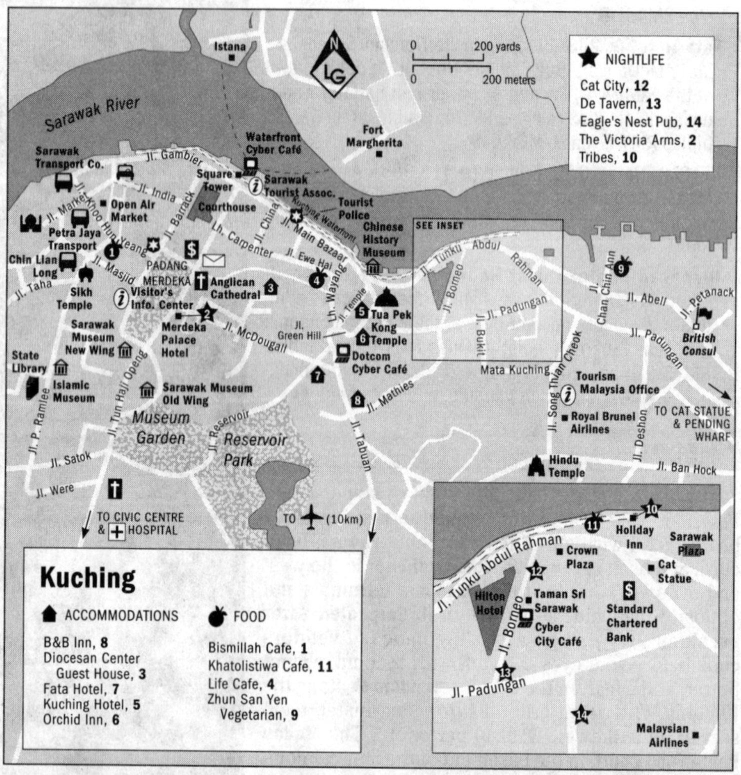

SIGHTS

Kuching's colonial architecture was spared from WWII bombing that leveled other cities on Malaysia's east coast. All the sights lie along the **Kuching Heritage Trail.** Admission to all sights is free. Along the esplanade and Jl. Main Bazaar, the **courthouse** faces the **Square Tower,** built in 1879 as a fortress and prison. Across the river are the pavilions of the **Istana,** built by Charles Brooke as a gift to his wife, and now used as the residence of Sarawak's head of state. On Jl. Tun Haji Openg is the **Round Tower,** constructed in the 1880s as a hospital and fortress. Sarawak's oldest Taoist temple, **Tua Pek Kong,** stands on Jl. Temple opposite the esplanade. The region's best **museums** are within the city center. Follow Jl. Tun Haji Openg away from the river and past the town green to get to **Sarawak Museum.** The pedestrian overpass to the new wing is visible from the road; turn left and walk to the main entrance in the old wing. The exhibits upstairs focus on Sarawak's 27 ethnic groups. The splendid grounds of the museum house an impressive **Aquarium,** the **Botanical Gardens,** and the **Heroes' Memorial,** built in honor of Malay soldiers. (Open daily 9am-6pm.) The **Sarawak Islamic Museum** showcases seven galleries of Muslim art centered about an attractive garden courtyard. (Open Sa-Th 9am-6pm.) The real treat, however, is Kuching's **Cat Museum,** in the North City Hall in the Petra Jaya district. Take Petra Jaya Transport bus #2B or 2C (RM0.80). The museum houses a tribute to "Hello Kitty" products and a mummified cat (circa 3500 BC) from ancient Egypt. The cat-crazy converge each November for **Pesta Meoww,** seven days of cat bazaars, cartoons, and competitions (see **Mastijah Masleh, Organizer of "Pesta Meoww",** p. 447). The corpse of the 1995 winner of the "Best Dressed Cat" award is even on display at the museum. (☎446 688. Open daily 9am-5pm. Free.) To get to the nearby **Timber Museum,** take Kuching Matang Transport Company bus #8 (RM0.90). The museum was established by timber companies as a response to foreign environmentalists. (Open M-Th 8:30am-4pm, F 8:30-11:30am and 2:30-4:30pm, Sa 8:30am-12:30pm.)

Across the river, **Fort Margherita,** named after Charles Brooke's wife, houses a **Police Museum.** (Open Tu-Su 10am-6pm.) Take local *sampans* (RM0.30) from the esplanade across the river and walk past the park to the road beyond. Turn right and head up the hill. At the gate, surrender your passport and pick up a pass. The **Chinese Museum,** along the esplanade opposite Tua Pek Kong Temple, traces the history of Sarawak's Chinese community. (Open M-Th, Sa-Su 9am-6pm.) The long street **market** on **Jl. Main Bazaar** offers great deals if you can survive the chaos. Bargain hard for discounts on ethnic crafts such as the popular *pua kumbu* (rugs handwoven by the Iban, RM20-180, depending on size) and elaborate beadwork and wood carvings by the Orang Ulu. The **Sunday Market,** which actually starts on Saturday afternoon, is held on Jl. Satok on the outskirts of town. The best times to go are Saturday night and Sunday morning. (Open all night.)

ENTERTAINMENT AND NIGHTLIFE

Many residents head to the **esplanade** along the Sarawak River to people-watch. *Sampan* boats (RM20-25 per hr. day or night) provide a relaxing introduction to the city as they meander past *kampungs* (Malay villages), the gold-domed **Sikh Mosque,** and picturesque mountains. And with over 30 bars in the city center, Kuching offers no excuse to go to bed early.

The Victoria Arms, Jl. Tun Abang Haji Openg (☎258 000), in the Merdeka Palace Hotel. Posh English-style pub featuring live bands each night and Kuching's most original cocktails (RM23), including the "Monkey Gland" and the "Hair of the Dog." Free drinks for ladies F-Sa 7-9pm. 2-for-1 Happy Hour daily 5-9pm. Open Su-Th 11am-2am, F-Sa 11am-3am. Cover RM25 F-Sa. AmEx/MC/V.

Eagle's Nest, No. 19 and 20, ground fl., Jl. Bukit Mata (☎234 745), behind the Top Spot Food Court. Famed for its lively bar staff. An awesome DJ pumps out R&B while locals snack on scrumptious "bamboo chicken" and down a variety of bottled wines (RM59-126). 2-for-1 happy hour daily 4-9pm on house beers (RM6). Free drinks for ladies W and F 8-10pm. Open M-Th 11am-2am, F-Sa 11am-3am. AmEx/MC/V.

Tribes, Jl. Tunku Abdul Rahman (☎423 111), at the Holiday Inn. Lavish tribal decor and performances by some of Southeast Asia's hottest groups. Hearty "elephant ribs" (300g of grilled marinated beef) RM26. "Kremlin vodka" RM18.50. Drinks are 2 for 1 daily 7-10pm. Open M-Th 7pm-1am, F-Sa 7pm-2am. AmEx/MC/V.

Cat City, Block H, Taman Sri Sarawak (☎243 699), opposite the Hilton. Nocturnal pleasure-seekers fill the pub to capacity well past 3am. Live bands complement the daily happy hour (beer RM6). Gay-friendly. Open Tu-Su 5pm-5am. AmEx/DC/MC/V.

De Tavern, Lot G21, Taman Sri Sarawak, Jl. Borneo (☎419 723), facing the Hilton parking lot. A long-established bar and an easy place to meet locals. Unbeatable happy hour 5-9pm daily and all night Sunday. Barflies can add *tuak* (rice wine, RM4 per glass) to more traditional malts like Carlsberg. Open daily 5pm-2am. AmEx/MC/V.

DAYTRIPS FROM KUCHING

SARAWAK CULTURAL VILLAGE. This award-winning "living museum" claims you can "experience Sarawak in half a day." Spread over a spectacular 17-acre site, the village highlights seven reconstructions of Bidayuh, Iban, Penan, Orang Ulu, Melanau, Malay, and Chinese dwellings. English-speaking actors and storytellers inhabit each reconstruction, interpreting traditional lifestyles while engaging in typical domestic activities. Each day ends with tribal dancing and singing in the village theater. If you arrive in July, don't miss the annual **Rainforest World Music Festival,** three days of non-stop music along the breathtaking beaches of Damai and at the Sarawak Cultural Village. Check out the web site (www.rainforestmusic-borneo.com) for exact dates.

PJ bus #2B departs from Jl. Khoo Hun Yeang for Damai and the Sarawak Cultural Village (45min., 6 per day 7:20am-7pm, RM2.70). For the return trip, PJ buses depart from the rotary in front of the village entrance (6 per day 8:20am-7pm). When the buses stop running, catch a shuttle from the Holiday Inn at Damai to Kuching (5 per day 10am-9:30pm, RM10). It is advisable to purchase an all-inclusive day package from the Holiday Inn (RM60, children RM45). Buses depart from the hotel at 9am and return in the late afternoon. *(Village open daily 9am-5pm, dances 11:30am and 4:30pm. RM45, under 12 RM22.50. For more information, check out www.sarawakculturalvillage.com.)*

SEMENGGOH WILDLIFE REHABILITATION CENTER. Sarawak's orphaned and injured animals find sanctuary at the Semenggoh Wildlife Rehabilitation Center. The center takes custody of orangutans, proboscis monkeys, and honey bears until they can survive on their own in the surrounding forest. Semi-wild orangutans halfway through rehabilitation are the main attraction. They return for free meals daily around 9am and 3pm. Arrive 30 minutes early. Gifts of fruit are appreciated. The morning feeding tends to be more populated.

STC bus #6 departs from the bus stop at the west end of the esplanade on Jl. Gambier (45min.; 7, 8:10, 10, 11, 11:30am, noon, 1:15, 2pm; RM1.50) and drops passengers off at the Forest Department nursery. From here it's a 30min. stroll to the feeding stations. Buses return from Semenggoh nursery at 7:55, 8:50, 11am, noon,

12:30, 2, 4pm. Obtain free permits at the Visitors Information Center, on Jl. Barrack in Kuching. *(Center open daily 8am-4:15pm.)*

BAKO NATIONAL PARK. Within Bako's 2700 hectares, trails squirm to cliff-lined beaches through almost every type of vegetation in Borneo—swamp forest, mangroves, and more. The rare proboscis monkey is active during early mornings and late evenings. Pick up permits while arranging advance accommodations from the Kuching's Visitors Information Center. Daytrippers can obtain a permit directly at the Bako jetty. The **park office** is over the bridge, left of the compound as you disembark; arrange a ride back with the driver. Drop by the park office to check in (RM3, cameras RM5). Hostel beds (with cooking facilities) cost RM10.50; camping spaces are RM4. A **canteen** ❶ serves up fried rice and noodles for RM3 and also offers **accommodations** ❹. (Open daily 8am-10pm. Rooms RM42; entire lodge RM84.) There's a limited selection of snacks and drinks, so **bring your own rations.** Macaques will raid dustbins in rest houses as well as steal food and unguarded bags at the canteen. Famed for sightings of proboscis monkeys, the **Lintang Trail** (5¼km., 3½hr.) is great for a day-hike. **Telok Pandan Kecil** (2½km. each way, 1½hr.) takes you to a breathtaking beach with views of Bako's renowned sea stacks. Several tour companies in downtown Kuching can arrange day and overnight trips to **local longhouses. Borneo Inbound Tours and Travel** (☎082 237 287), No. 98, 1st fl., Main Bazaar, offers a variety of trips including daytrips on the Lemanak River with a visit to an Iban longhouse (RM280), half-day trips to Land Dayak longhouses (RM100), and overnight trips (RM350-500). Home stays in Malay fishing villages can also be arranged.

PJ bus #6 departs from Jl. Khoo Hun Yeang (45min., every 40min. 6:40am-6pm, RM2.10). Return buses follow the same schedule (6:30am-5:40pm). Or take a taxi (RM30). Take buses and taxis to Kampung Bako, and charter a boat (30min., RM30, 7 person max.) to park headquarters. Low tides interfere with transport.

SIBU ☎084

In the early 20th century, Foochow immigrants from southern China settled in Sibu to escape persecution. Gradually they transformed this river town into Sarawak's second-largest city and an economic dynamo. A collection of recent public works projects entices visitors en route to Kuching, Similajau, or Niah to spend a night in Sibu for a taste of the conveniences they thought they could do without. From chic designer boutiques in the well-kept town square to indigenous handicrafts sold along freshly-paved, palm tree-lined streets, Sibu has it all.

MALAYSIA

TRANSPORTATION. The **airport** (☎307 770) is 23km outside town. Take Bus #3A from Lanang Rd. (every 30min. 6:30am-6pm, RM2) or a taxi for RM21. **MAS,** 61 Jl. Tuanku Osman, has daily flights to: **Bintulu** (RM64); **Kota Kinabalu** (RM180); **KL** (RM320); **Kuching** (RM72); **Miri** (RM112); **Sandakan** (RM218). (☎326 166. Open M-F 8:30am-4:30pm, Sa 8:30am-12:30pm.) Buy tickets at the terminal. The **Sungei Antu Express Bus Terminal** is on the outskirts of town. Take bus #2, 7, or 9 (all RM0.60) from the local bus station on Lanang Rd or a taxi for RM8. Buses run to **Bintulu** (3½hr., every hr. 6am-11:30pm, RM16.50); **Kuching** (6hr., 12 per day 6:30am-10pm, RM32); **Miri** (6½hr., every 2hr. 6am-11:30pm, RM34). **Express Bahagia** boats to **Kuching** depart from the wharf near the Chinese temple (4½hr., 11:30am, RM35-40). Boats to **Kapit** depart upriver, near the Sungei Antu Express Bus Terminal (3hr., 6am-2:30pm, RM15). Buy tickets on board.

PRACTICAL INFORMATION. The **Sarawak Visitors' Information Center,** ground fl., 32 Jl. Lintang, is helpful and offers free maps and info on Belaga, Kapit, and [illegible] (☎[illegible] 000. Open M-Th 8am-4pm, F 8am-5pm, Sa 8am-12:45pm.) **Sazhong Travel,** 4 Jl. Central, arranges air tickets and longhouse tours. A 2-day tour for 2-4 people is RM250; a 3-day tour runs from RM450. (☎336 017. Open M-F 8am-noon and 1:30-4:45pm, Sa 8am-noon and 1:30-4:15pm, Su 8:30am-noon. AmEx/MC/V.) The **Public Bank,** on Jl. Pulau in a tall white building close to the Chinese temple, cashes traveler's checks (RM3.15 for the 1st, RM0.15 per additional check). (Open M-F 9:30am-4pm, Sa 9:30am-12:30pm.) **Standard Chartered Bank** near the Visitor's Information Center has a **24hr. ATM.** The **police,** (☎322 222), are on Jl. Kampung Nyabor near the post office. **Zhunian Pharmacy,** on the 1st fl. of Wisma Sanyon, has English-speaking staff. (☎328 392. Open daily 9:30am-9pm.) **Lao King Howe Hospital,** (☎343 333), is at the west end of Jl. Pulau. To get there, take a taxi (RM10) or Sungei Merah bus #9. The **Telekom Office** is on Persiaran Brooke near the communications tower 200m from Jl. Kampung Nyabor. (☎329 292. Open M-F 8:30am-12:45pm and 2-4:45pm, Sa 8:30am-1pm.) **IDD phones** are along Jl. Tuanku Osman. There are several **Internet** cafes on the 4th fl. of Wisma Sanyon, a tall white building at the west end of town. All cost 3RM per hr. and close at 10pm. The **Civic Center** offers 30min. free Internet. (Open M-F 8am-5pm, Sa 8am-12:30pm.) The **post office** is on Jl. Kampung Nyabor. *Poste Restante.* Closed 1st and 3rd Sa each month. (☎337 700. Open M-Sa 8am-5pm.) **Postal code:** 96000.

ACCOMMODATIONS. **Hoover House ❷** is a faded white structure with blue trim on Jl. Pulau to the left of the Methodist church near the Chinese temple. All rooms have A/C, hot water, and a private bath. (☎332 491. Dorms RM15; singles RM20; doubles RM30.) More comfortable rooms with A/C, TV, and private shower with bathtub are available at **Hotel Zuhra ❹.** (☎310 711. Laundry service. Check-out 1pm. Singles and doubles RM59.) The **Sarawak Hotel ❸,** on Ramin Way near Jl. Wong Nai Siong just before the Sugar Bun Restaurant, is all smiles. Rooms all have A/C, TV, phones, and private baths. (☎333 455. Checkout noon. Singles RM35; doubles RM50.) For pure convenience, nothing beats the **River View Hotel ❸,** near the Lanang Rd. bus station and the wharf. Rooms all have A/C, private bath, and hot water. (☎325 241. Laundry service. Singles RM30; doubles RM36.)

FOOD. Chinese **kedai kopi ❶** (food stalls) line Ramin Way, Jl. Wong Nai Siang, and Jl. Morshidi Sidek. Don't leave Sibu without sampling *foochow* noodles, served in a broth of soy and oyster sauce with onions and shrimp. All *kedai kopi* serve them—ask for *kampua mee.* **Sin Yung Kiaw Cafe 98 ❶,** No. 5 Ramin Way, opposite Kee Supermarket, serves *kampua mee* for RM1.60. (Open daily 6am-10pm.) *Kong bian,* Sibu's version of a sesame bagel, is another *foochow* specialty. Pick up a freshly baked dozen at **Seng Kee Agencies** on Jl. Tinggi. **Hawker stalls ❶** line the first floor of the **SMC Market** on Jl. Channel. At the end of Jl. Market is the circular **SEDC Food Center ❶,** commonly known as "Bulatan Tanahmas," which serves *mee soto* (noodle soup with shredded chicken, RM1.50) and other *halal* Malay food. The **Pasar Malam market ❶** serves a smorgasbord of *satay,* cakes (about RM4), and steamed dumplings. **All The Best Vegetarian Restaurant ❶,** No. 39 Jl. Tuanku Osman, is on the left if you're coming from Jl. Kampong Nyabor walking toward the MAS Office. Their sweet and sour tofu (RM2.50) and fresh scallion pancakes (RM0.30) are not to be missed. (Open daily 6am-4pm and 6-10pm. Closed Th nights.) The **Mawaddah Cafe ❶,** 77 Jl. Tuanku Osman, offers hearty rice dishes like tandoori chicken for RM4. (Open daily 6am-6pm.) For truly original desserts, head to the **Idaman Cafe ❶** on the 4th floor of Wisma Sanyan. The coffee jelly cake is well worth the RM2.50. (Open daily 8:30am-7pm.)

SIGHTS. **Tua Pek Kong Temple** (Great Uncle's Temple), built in 1870, survived the fire that swallowed Sibu in 1928, only to be destroyed during WWII bombing.

MALAYSIA

The altar, however, somehow survived even this. Ask caretaker Tan Teck Chiang for the keys to climb the seven-story tower.

DAYTRIPS FROM SIBU: REJANG RIVER LONGHOUSES. Sibu is the starting point for all longhouse tours along the Rejang River. Most people arrange tours either in Sibu or Kapit, choosing from simple daytrips to strenuous week-long expeditions. Sazhong Travel (see **Practical Information,** p. 452) offers a large variety of trips and will custom design itineraries; contact Frankie Ting two weeks in advance. For those attempting a visit on their own, Kapit is a good starting point. Hang out in the coffee shops and chat with locals for advice. Permits, available for free at the Resident's Office in Kapit, are required for travel beyond Kapit.

KAPIT ☎084

A frontier town along the mighty Rejang River, Kapit serves international travelers as a jumping-off point into the surrounding jungles and the Orang Ulu and Iban longhouses. Unfortunately, most of these longhouses have become modernized, and traditional dances are saved for special holidays. Although the city itself offers little cultural enrichment, travelers with plenty of time, money, and tolerance for leeches can venture upriver to the most remote reaches of Borneo.

TRANSPORTATION

From the jetty to the right, **Express Bahagia** boats depart downriver to **Sibu** (3hr., frequent 6am-3pm, RM15 and up). Sit on the boat rooftop to see longhouses and logging sites along the way. Boats upriver depart from the jetty to the left. During the rainy season, **express boats** leave from Kapit and Sibu to **Pelagus Rapids** and **Belaga** (5-6hr., RM25); when the river is low, take a **speedboat** (2 daily before 11am, RM50-80). Longboat rentals run RM200 per day and up.

ORIENTATION AND PRACTICAL INFORMATION

Kapit stretches south of the **Rejang River. Jl. Wharf** leads from the main jetty. The New Rejang Inn is a block down on the right. Another block up at the **Public Bank,** Jl. Wharf intersects the main road, **Jl. Teo Chow Beng.** The **town square** is on the right, bounded to the east by **Jl. Tan Sit Leong** and to the west by **Jl. Kapitan Chua Leong Kee. Jl. Tiong Ung Hong** runs past the square to the west. Farther along where Jl. Teo Chow Beng intersects **Jl. Temenggong Jugah** is the **post office** and the Meligai Hotel. **Jl. Airport** is past the rotary beyond the hotel.

Currency Exchange: Public Bank, 63-64 Jl. Wharf (☎797 677), at the east end of Jl. Teo Chow Beng. Open M-F 9:30am-4pm, Sa 9:30-12:30am. Cashes traveler's checks RM2.15 for the 1st check, RM0.15 per additional (up to 5). **ATM** (Cirrus/PLUS/MC/V). **Maybank,** near Hotel Meligai. **ATM** (Cirrus/PLUS/MC/V).

Resident's Office (☎796 963). From Jl. Wharf, go past Hock Hua Bank, continue straight through a small playground and onto a road besides the Telekom. Up ahead behind a fence, the office is on the 1st fl. of a blue-trimmed building. Permits for upriver travel to Balleh and Belaga available. Open M-Th 8am-12:45pm and 2-4:15pm, F 8-11:30am and 2:30-4:45pm, Sa 8am-12:45pm.

Markets: Day Market, on Jl. Teo Chow Beng, past the town square on the right. Stalls set up between Rejang Hotel and the river on Jl. Temenggong Jugah. **Night Market,** on Jl. Penghulu Nyanggau, behind the post office.

Emergency: ☎999.

Police: ☎796 222. On east end of town, past the lake and the turn-off for Jl. Hospital.

Pharmacy: Jameo Pharmacy, 17 Jl. Tan Sit Leen (☎ 796 002). English spoken. Open M-Sa 7:30am-6:30pm, Su 7:30am-noon.

Medical: Hospital (☎ 796 333), at the east end on Jl. Hospital. English spoken.

Telephones: Kedei Telekom Kapit (☎ 796 991), on a hill opposite resident's office. Open M-F 8:30am-4:45pm, Sa 8:30am-1pm.

Internet Access: Lee Cyber Center, Lot 65, 1st fl., No. 14 Jalan Tang Sit Leong (☎ 013 820 0891), above the Wan Chew Market. RM3 per hr. Open daily 9am-11pm. **Goodtime Cyber Centre,** Lot 384, Jun Yong Moo Chai. RM3 per hr. Open daily 9am-11pm.

Post Office: (☎ 796 332), on Jl. Teo Chow Beng, west of the square. Open M-F 8am-noon and 2-5pm, Sa 8am-noon. Closed the 1st and 3rd Sa of each month. **Postal code:** 96800.

ACCOMMODATIONS AND FOOD

Many budget hotels have degenerated into brothels, but fortunately, you can still find some less seedy, affordable options. **Rejang Hotel ❷,** No. 28 Jl. Temenggong Jugah, has clean rooms with A/C and private bath. (☎ 796 709. Singles RM20; doubles RM24.) Facing Jl. Wharf at No. 104 Jl. Teo Chow Beng, **New Rejang Inn ❹** has spotless rooms with A/C, phone, and mini-fridge. (☎ 796 600. Laundry. Singles and doubles RM45.) **Hotel Meligai ❹,** at the western end of Jl. Teo Chow Beng, past the post office, is Kapit's swank option. Look for a sign that says "Meligai Kapit." All rooms have A/C, TV, phones, and carpeting. (☎ 796 611. Laundry. Singles RM65; doubles RM75.) **Greenland Inn ❹,** Lot 463-464 Jl. Teo Chow Bang, above the Sugarbun Restaurant, has rooms with hot water, A/C, TV, fridge, and complimentary coffee. (☎ 796 3888. Singles RM65; doubles RM75.)

For the cheapest eats in town, try the **food court** at the end of Jl. Tiong Ung Hong, one block uphill from the **hawker stalls** fronting the day market on Jl. Teo Chow Beng—look for the "Gelanggang Kenyalang" sign. (Open until 6pm.) A **night market** serving *halal* Malay staples sets up by the post office. Local cuisine includes *babi hutan* (wild boar) and *rusa* (venison). Yummy. (Open 7pm-midnight.) **Siong Seng Coffee Shop ❷,** No. 23 Jl. Teo Chow Beng, opposite the town square, has excellent Chinese coffee (RM0.90) and *kampua mee* for RM1.80. (☎ 796 687. Open daily 8:30am-5pm.) Opposite the day market, **Ung Tong Bakery ❶** is a popular morning stop for a cup of Milo. (Coconut-butter-raisin bun RM0.60; red bean bun RM0.40. Open daily 6:15am-5pm.) **99 Seafood Cafe ❶,** up on a hill behind Hotel Meligai and the post office, is one of the few restaurants open all afternoon and evening. (☎ 797 321. *Nasi udong* (shrimp rice) RM2.50. Open daily 1pm-midnight.)

SIGHTS AND ENTERTAINMENT

Named after the third Rajah's wife, **Fort Sylvia** was built in 1880 as a demonstration of the government's intent to end intertribal hostilities and head-hunting. The **museum,** within the Civic Center on the east edge of town, houses a fine collection of ethnic arts, handicrafts, and images of life on the Rejang. (Open M-F 9am-12:45pm and 2-4:15pm, Sa 9am-12:45pm.) Evening entertainment varies from karaoke clubs and snooker halls to the more insidious brothels staffed by Indonesian immigrants. The **Fullmoon Music Cafe** is a lively pub where locals gather for beer (RM6) and a live DJ. (☎ 797 818. Jl. Penghulu Nyangau, behind the post office. Open daily 5pm-3am.) If you hear loud drumming near Rejang Inn, children may be practicing Lion Dancing at the Chinese Temple.

DAYTRIPS FROM KAPIT: LONGHOUSES

Housing an entire Malay community, longhouses are built from ironwood and bamboo and are raised to take advantage of cooling drafts and for safety. A *tuai* (headman), who enforces strict rules to maintain harmony, traditionally presides over the longhouse community. In the past, a visit to east Malaysia was not complete without a trip to a longhouse. Guests who brought news to the isolated longhouses were welcomed with raucous parties. As these communities became more affluent, they built sturdier tin-roofed cement structures—much to the dismay of tourists. Longhouse dwellers started to resent the well-to-do foreign travelers who showed up on their doorstep expecting to be feted like a Rajah in exchange for a box of cigarettes. Needless to say, more remote areas have more traditional longhouses and less cynical residents.

Those looking for a traditional longhouse stay should try **Bareo** in eastern Sarawak or **Belaga** farther upriver from Kapit. For those short on time, pricey longhouse stays can be arranged through tour guides in Kuching and Kapit. Before you go, confirm the price, mode of transportation, and name and location of the longhouse to assure safety. **Mr. Tan Teck Chuan** at Kapit Adventure Tours, 11 Jl. Tan Sit Leong, on the western edge of the town square, is one of the area's most reputable guides. (☎796 352. P.O. Box 16, 96807 Kapit, Sarawak, Malaysia. One-day trip to Iban longhouse RM380 per person, 2-day RM650 per person.) For extensive treks into the extreme hinterlands, Chuan requests one to two months' advance notice. **Mr. Joshua M. G.,** at Regang Travel & Tours, is another experienced guide who offers daytrips (RM300) and longer treks. (☎796 600. New Regang Inn, 104 Teo Chow Beng Road, 96807 Kapit, Sarawak, Malaysia.) The best time to visit longhouses is in early June during the **Dayak Gawai** (harvest festival) celebrations that begin on June 1, but the best weather is from July to September. Bring a plastic bag for cameras, raingear, toilet paper, flashlight, sunscreen, mosquito repellent, aspirin, and basic toiletries. **Permits** from the Resident's Office are required for journeys upriver from Kapit. Most guides can help you through this simple formality.

BINTULU ☎086

Bintulu was once listed by the *Guinness Book of World Records* as the closest city in the world to an airport—the runway cut through the middle of town. Alas, Bintulu's one claim to fame is scheduled to be demolished in May 2003, when a RM350,000,000 airport will open 20km outside of the city. Beyond its convenient location halfway between Kuching and Kota Kinabalu, Bintulu offers little of interest. Still, for those awaiting connections to the sands of Similajau National Park or other more alluring destinations, attractions do exist to help pass the time.

TRANSPORTATION

Flights: Airport (☎331 958), 20km southwest of the city (when it is completed). **MAS** (☎332 898), 129 Taman Sri Dagang. Open M-F 8:30am-4:30pm, Sa 8:30am-1pm. AmEx/MC/V. Flies daily to: **Kota Kinabalu** (RM132); **Kuching** (RM122); **Miri** (RM69); **Sibu** (RM69). Airport tax RM6.

Buses: Medan Jaya Bus Terminal, on the outskirts of town. Accessible by local bus (RM0.60) or taxi (RM8) from downtown. To: **Batu Niah** (2½hr., 8 per day 6am-4:30pm, RM15); **Kuching** (5 per day 6am-5:30pm, RM60); **Miri** (3½hr., 12 per day 6am-8:30pm, RM20); **Sarikei** (6 per day 6am-5:30pm, RM28); **Sibu** (3½hr., 8 per day 6am-6pm, RM20).

Boats: Express boats leave from the waterfront daily at 8am and 1pm to **Binyo** (RM18), and at 7, 9, 10:30am, noon, and 1:30pm to: **Labang** (RM12); **Pandan** (RM9); **Sebauh** (RM8); **Tubau** (RM18).

Local Transportation: The local **bus terminal** is next to the markets on Jl. Main Bazaar/ Masjid. Buses shuttle to **Medan Jaya Bus Terminal** (20min., every 15min. 6:15am-10:15pm, RM0.60). **Taxis** congregate opposite the station and charge high fares. To **Medan Jaya** (RM8) and **Similajau National Park** (RM40).

ORIENTATION AND PRACTICAL INFORMATION

Bintulu has two parallel main streets: **Jl. Abang Galau,** which becomes **Jl. Keppel,** and **Jl. Masjid,** which becomes **Jl. Main Bazaar.** The markets, taxi station, and bus terminal are clustered around the center of **Jl. Masjid.** Beaches and parks line **Jl. Tanjung Batu,** accessible by taxi (RM10), in the city's west end.

Tourist Offices: Visitor's Information Center, 1 Jl. Tanjung Kidurong (☎332 011), on the ground floor of the **Bintulu Development Authority** (a white, cone-shaped building). Open M-F 8am-12:30pm and 2-5pm, Sa 8am-12:45pm.

Currency Exchange: Public Bank, 29-32, Jl. Sommerville (☎337 751). Cashes traveler's checks (RM1.15 for the 1st, RM0.15 per additional check). Open M-F 9am-3:30pm, Sa 9:30-11:30am. **Standard Chartered Bank,** on Jl. Keppel, down the street from the Capital Hotel, has a **24hr. ATM** (Cirrus).

Markets: The twin cones of the **day market** reach skyward along Jl. Main Bazaar. The **night market** lights up at the end of Jl. Pedada.

Emergency: ☎994.

Police: ☎311 121. On Jl. Tun Razak.

Pharmacies: L.T. Ling Pharmacy, 61 Medang Sebadoh (☎335 773), near the Plaza Hotel. Open M-Sa 8:30am-9pm, Su 8:30am-1pm.

Medical Services: Bintulu Regional Hospital (☎225 899), on the outskirts of town at the northern end of Jl. Bukit Nyabau. English-speaking staff. **24hr.** emergency care.

Telephones: Telekom office (☎319 292), on Jl. Law Gek Soon, north of the intersection with Jl. Keppel. International phone/fax. Open M-Th 8:30am-12:30pm and 2-4:15pm, F 8:30-11:30am and 2:15-4:15pm, Sa 8:30am-noon.

Post Offices: GPO (☎332 375), on Jl. Tun Razak, opposite the airport. *Poste Restante.* Open M-F 8am-4pm, Sa 8am-3pm. A reliable **courier service** (☎339 164), on Jl. Sommerville opposite Hock Hua Bank, offers good rates. Open M-F 8am-5pm, Sa 8am-1pm. Also, a **branch** is in the Medan Jaya Bus Terminal. **Postal code:** 97000.

ACCOMMODATIONS AND FOOD

Summer Inn ❸, 1st fl. 19 New Commercial Centre, behind the Plaza Hotel, has snug but spotless rooms with A/C, TV, private shower, and free bottles of water. (☎331 223. Singles and doubles RM35.) Facing the Chinese temple, at 78 Jl. Keppel, **Kemena Inn ❹** is worth the extra ringgit. The large rooms have fancy showers, carpet, and A/C. (☎331 533. Singles RM50; doubles RM55.) **City Inn ❸,** 150 Jl. Aban Galau near the Plaza Hotel, has clean A/C rooms with TV in a central location. (☎337 711. Singles and doubles RM36.)

Night markets ❶, offering an excellent selection of *sate*, grilled fish, and fruit, set up at the local bus terminal and at the former long-distance bus terminal east of Jl. Sommerville, beside the old airport runway. (Open daily 7-10pm.) An alley near the Plaza Hotel and the mini post office at the eastern end of town hosts a variety

MALAYSIA

PASS THE POTATOES, PLEASE Don't throw your manners out the window at a longhouse. The Orang Ulu, like any other people, will warm up to visitors once they are comfortable. *Let's Go* offers some basic dos and don'ts:

1. Wait for an invitation to enter a longhouse.
2. Take off your shoes before entering.
3. Dress modestly. When bathing, men should wear their underwear and women should use a sarong.
4. At meals, be sure to sample any offered food. Evenings sometimes culminate in a small celebration with *tuak* (traditional rice wine–take at least a small sip) and plenty of dancing and music. Visitors are expected to contribute, and your hosts will love it if you participate wholeheartedly, even if it means making a bit of a fool of yourself.
5. Gifts are appreciated. Bring pencils and crayons for the children, and practical clothing, such as shirts and hats, and luxuries, like foreign cigarettes, for adults. Avoid giving sweets and alcohol. It's also nice to bring some pictures of your family, postcards, coins, stamps, or a book about your home country. For instant and enduring fame, bring a Polaroid camera and lots of spare film.
6. Otherwise, basic courtesy is the rule: don't touch anything or take pictures of anyone unless properly introduced. Remember to quietly ask permission as well.

of open-air restaurants. There, **Famous Mama Cafe ❶** serves up a delicious array of meat and veggie selections, *bacadile* (veggie potato puff; RM2), freshly made *roti canai* (RM0.80), and *nasi campur* (RM2.50). **Sea View Restaurant ❶,** next to the Riverfront Inn on the east edge of the waterfront, serves fried rice or noodles for RM2.50. (Open daily 6am-10pm.) **Honey Bakery ❶,** 63 Medan Sepadu, on Jl. Abang Galau, serves a dazzling array of pastries (RM0.40-2.20). Look for the neon lights. The cheese salad roll (RM0.90) is stuffed with vegetables and delicious cheese paste. (Chili hot dog RM1.30. Open daily 7:30am-10pm.) Down the street at 97 Medan Sepadu, **Sharoa Cafe ❶** offers reasonable *halal* and Western fare. (*Sarawat laksa* RM2.50. Seafood omelette RM4. Open daily 7am-midnight.)

SIGHTS

The only zoological and botanical park in Sarawak, **Taman Tubina Bintulu** describes itself as an "animal garden." Lions, macaques, and hornbills (Malaysia's state bird) reside among the 57 hectares of unique fauna like the Borneo Giant Orchid Peacocks and crocodiles and pythons. (1 Jl. Tanjung Kidurong. ☎337 709. Open daily 8am-6pm. RM2, children RM0.50.) Down the road, the modest but scenic **Tanjung Batu Beach** is lined with the impressive children's playgrounds, gazebos, and food stalls. The **clock tower** on Jl. Abang Galau was the site of Sarawak's first state legislature, convened by Charles Brooke, the second white Rajah of Sarawak.

SIMILAJAU NATIONAL PARK

Some of Sarawak's finest beaches are 30 minutes northeast of sleepy Bintulu, nestled in Similajau National Park. Only 1.5km wide, the park encompasses 30km of sand and coastal cliffs, inlaid with exotic fauna like the pitcher plant, a carnivorous flower known as "The Assassin of the Plant World." The 9km of trails that snake through coastal forest lead to the fine sands of Turtle and Golden Beaches where turtles can be seen mating. Boats to the Kolam Sebubong pool drift through emerald water. Eager for some privacy? If you arrive during the week, you may have the entire park to yourself.

To reach park headquarters, contact **Mr. Syaidi,** who runs the park's canteen (☎010 884 18 88) and picks up guests in Bintulu for RM20. If you can't reach him, take a **taxi** from Bintulu (30min., RM40), and arrange a ride back with Mr. Syaidi (RM20). **Bus** #1322 leaves from the local bus station for Similajau (RM18); from here, it's a 1hr. (4km) walk to the park. Also negotiable is a chartered **minivan** from the park canteen to **Niah Caves** (around RM140). The **park office** (☎391 284) is down a path from the parking lot and to the right. Drop by to pick up brochures, maps, and **permits** for park entrance (RM10, cameras RM5, and video recorders RM10). The office assigns rooms and arranges transport to the mouth of **Sungai Sebubong** for trekking to **Koam Sebubong Pool.** Next door to the park office is a **Visitors Center** with a fine collection of photographs of the area's wildlife. A ranger is usually on duty, but it's best to arrive during office hours. (Open Sa-Th 8am-12:45pm and 2-4:15pm, F 8-11:30am and 2:30-4:45pm.)

Call Mr. Rahman at the **park office** (☎391 284) to reserve accommodations. The park has two identical **hostels ❶**, each with cooking facilities, communal toilets, fans, and showers. Each room sleeps four in bunk beds with sheets, blankets, and storage cubbies (RM11). Closer to park headquarters are three A/C **chalets ❹,** each with two 4-person rooms (RM63 per room; RM126 for the entire 8-bed chalet). Shaded **camping ❶** areas are nearby (RM5). A simple open-air **canteen ❶** offers staples like snacks, bottled water, fried rice (RM3), and welcome extravagances like chocolate-dipped ice cream bars (RM1-4). Dinner consists of a set menu of fresh fish and vegetable stir-fries (RM10-15). For an extended stay, it's wise to bring your own supplies. (Opens daily at 8am; usually closes at 6pm.) For a late afternoon trek, notify the canteen of your destination to ensure an evening meal.

Many visitors are content to romp in the surf and loll on the sand near the park's accommodations. Farther afield are more secluded beaches accessible only by marked forest paths. Treks range in length and difficulty. A good full-day hike goes from the park office to **Setensur Rapids** (15km, 8hr. round-trip). The trail passes through beaches and dipterocarp forests. **Turtle Beach** is an 8km hike from headquarters (permit required). There, the green turtle lays its eggs nightly. **Kolam Sebubong** is an isolated pool on the upper reaches of the Sebubong River. Arrange with the park office to hire a boat for the day (RM150). Similajau has **saltwater crocodiles.** These ferocious beasts are hard to spot and attack with lightning speed. **Do not wade across larger streams. Use boat transfers wherever possible.** Safer **coastal cruises** can be arranged through the park office.

NIAH NATIONAL PARK

Its a bird! Its a plane! No, its a flying lizard. These and other airborne creatures inhabit the extensive cave system of Niah National Park. Some visitors to these caves take away more than just photographs—licensed harvesters and illegal poachers shimmy up rickety, 30m-long bamboo poles to gather highly prized swiftlet nests, which can fetch up to RM1200 per kilogram in Chinese soup markets. Archaeologists have garnered more morbid treasures: Iron Age coffins and 40,000 year-old intact skulls were discovered in 1958. Although your visit will probably unearth no such souvenirs, Niah is a spectacle not to be missed.

Batu Niah is the gateway to Niah Park. Buses from Miri and Bintulu deposit passengers near the town jetty on the Niah River. The park is a 10min. **longboat** ride downriver (RM10 for 1-5 people, RM2 per person for more than 5) or a 2km **taxi** ride (RM10). Returning to Batu Niah is possible by boat or taxi or via a shaded concrete path along the river. **Buses** depart from Batu Niah square for **Bintulu** (2hr., 6 per day 6am-4pm, RM10) and **Miri** (2hr., every hr. 6:30am-3:30pm, RM10). Buy tickets on board. The **Park Reception Area** is a few hundred feet from the river's edge. If you don't have a reservation, pay the park entrance fee, and arrange accommodations here. (☎085 737 450. Entrance fee RM10, cameras RM5, video RM10. Open Su-Th 8am-12:30pm and 2-4:30pm, F 8-11:30am and 2:30-4:45pm, Sa 8am-12:45pm.)

FERTILE GROUND The few who examine the Niah Caves' floor will find a bizarre feast of bat dung, attracting not only cockroaches and worms but humans as well. Guano collectors have gathered bat and swiftlet feces as fertilizer for local Iban farmers since 1929. Despite the availability of chemical fertilizer, guano remains the standby in Iban societies—not only for its low price but also for its ability to prevent root-rotting disease in pepper vines. Today's harvests are nowhere near the 1950s recorded average of 476 tons per year, but professional collectors still work the cave floor. In case you were wondering, quality guano tastes salty.

The park **hostel's** ❶ wood-paneled rooms and modern baths are a bonus for those visiting Niah. Each fan-cooled dorm has four beds and a bath with hot water. If visitors are scarce, ask for a room to yourself. (Dorms RM11; 8-person chalets RM94.50.) A cheap **restaurant** ❶ on the park grounds has fried rice or noodles for RM4. (Open daily 8am-9pm.) The park has no minimart, so purchase snacks in Batu Niah.

A boat ride across the river ends at the start of the trail to **Niah Caves** (RM0.50, after 6pm RM1). Be sure to bring a flashlight, as the caves are unlit. Rent flashlights from the **museum** immediately on your right, which houses artifacts excavated from the caves. (Open daily 10am-5pm.) It's a pleasant 45min. walk from the museum through cool forest air to the caves. The sometimes slippery plank walk doesn't require a guide (RM35). The trail leads through the **Traders Cave** before arriving at the 60m by 250m mouth of the **Great Cave.** Here, in 1958, Tom Harrison and his staff from the Sarawak Museum unearthed a 40,000-year-old human skull. Excavations along the cave's left flank uncovered stone tools and other human relics. Next, the trail crosses the **Cave of Bones** and **Beunt Cave,** where bamboo poles are positioned by bird's nest collectors, and eventually leads to **Moon Cave.** It's impossible to proceed beyond this point without a flashlight, but fear not—a brief walk through the caverns leads visitors back to sunlight. The fern-covered plank walk continues to the **Painted Cave,** which originally contained coffins. The relics have since been removed for conservation, but faded paintings are faintly visible behind a locked gate. At dusk, nocturnal bats swoop out of their cave while sun-loving swiftlets return to the cave for sleep. Position yourself at the mouth of the cave to witness this dizzying aerial traffic jam. **Iban longhouses** are a 30min. walk from the main plank walk; turn left at the marked sign. Though the longhouses are not as traditional as some, the Iban, especially the English-speaking schoolchildren, still welcome visitors with traditional Dayak hospitality.

MIRI ☎085

Built by oil companies, Miri's bustling streets display new signs of wealth—the Mega Hotel prominent among them—soon to be eclipsed by even glitzier projects. But Miri is more than the booming center of Sarawak's oil industry. As a gateway to Niah National Park, Lambir Hills Rainforest, and Gunung Mulu National Park, Miri offers the wilderness-bound a final chance to enjoy some creature comforts before descending into more remote, less comfortable terrain.

TRANSPORTATION

Flights: Airport (☎615 433), west of the city limits. Taxis (RM14) and infrequent public buses run into town. **MAS office** (☎414 144), on the corner of Jl. Yu Seng. Open M-F 8:30am-4:30pm, Sa 8:30am-12:30pm. To: **Gunung Mulu National Park** (3-4 per day, RM80); **Kota Kinabalu** (5 per day 9:25am-9:10pm, RM115); **Kuching** (5 per day

FROM THE ROAD

ONE FLUSH, TWO FLUSH, NO FLUSH, YOU FLUSH

Visitors flock to Sarawak for its exotic flora and fauna. While most of this wildlife is harmless, travelers be warned! A strange and mysterious creature native to Southeast Asia lurks quietly in public parks, shopping malls, and less modern hotels. You will inevitably encounter it and are advised to be prepared.

What is it? The Sarawak species of toilet.

My first encounter with this beast occurred during a moment of urgency along a waterfront esplanade. How convenient that a public *tandas* (restroom) was set up in a small hut only a few meters away.

A male stick figure directed me to the left when I entered, and I was greeted by a smiling woman holding a glaring sign: "20 sen." Ugh. When you're a traveler, everything seems to have a price. I missed America, Land of the Free (Toilets).

I grudgingly bought my way into the bathroom and rushed to a stall. I opened the door and stared at the oddity before me.

Rather than a gleaming bowl of porcelain, I saw a bizarre metallic depression in the tiled floor. I checked the next stall just in case this was a practical joke. Alas, the toilet was identical.

Why was the floor covered in water? And *what* was that orange hose protruding from the wall?

After surveying the locals and some good ol' fashioned practice, I finally understood. As it turns out, these seemingly strange creations are

(continued on next page)

6:40am-5:00pm, RM175), **Sandakan** (2 per day, RM163); **Sibu** (3-4 per day, RM123). **Royal Brunei Airlines,** ground fl., Lot 263, Jl. South Yu Seng (☎426 322). Open M-F 8:30am-noon and 1-5:30pm, Sa 8:30am-12:30pm.

Buses: Pujut Padang Kerbau Long Distance Bus Station, several kilometers outside of downtown Miri. The #33 Shuttle Bus (every 20min., RM1) takes you to the local **bus terminal** in town. **SYKT Express** (☎439 325) and **Rejang Express** (☎435 336) are neighbors on Jl. Malay; **P.B. Express** and **Biaramas Express** are at the bus terminal. All go to **Bintulu** (3½hr., every hr. 6am-6pm, RM20). Frequent buses run to **Kuching** (RM80) and **Sibu** (RM40). **Miri-Belait Transport Co.** (☎419 129) sends buses to **Kuala Belait,** over the Brunei border (daily 7, 9, 10:30am, 1, 3:30pm; RM13). Bus changes at the border, so take all belongings off when getting your passport stamped, and hold onto your ticket. At Kuala Belait, board a purple bus outside of the immigration building and continue onward to **Seria** (B$1). Switch to a bus bound for **Bandar Seri Begawan** there (B$1). Buses in Seria stop running at 3:20pm, so leave Miri before 10:30am to avoid getting stuck in Seria for the night.

Local Transportation: Local bus station, behind Wisma Pelita on Jl. Padang. Bus #28 goes to the **airport** (every hr. 5:55am-7:10pm, RM1.50). **Taxis** (☎432 277) meet at the bus station and in front of the Fairland Inn. To: **Batu Niah** (2hr.; 9:10am, noon, 3, 4pm; RM8.50) and **Taman Selera** (#11: 5min. every 15min. 6:30am-9pm, RM0.80) depart from bus stops across Jl. Padang, opposite the Visitors Information Center.

PRACTICAL INFORMATION

The heart of the old town lies adjacent to the towering **Wisma Pelita Tunku** complex. On the southern side of the complex lie the **bus station** and **Visitors Information Center.** Most of Miri's streets are bounded by **Jl. Kingsway,** running northeast away from Wisma Pelita, and **Jl. Bendahara,** several blocks west along the edge of the **Miri River.** Jl. Bendahara leads to the bulky blue-and-white Mega Hotel. Opposite the hotel, which is now the center of the city, **Jl. Yu Seng** heads north past the **Imperial Mall Shopping Center** and the gold-domed **mosque,** where Jl. Yu Seng morphs into **Jl. Datuk Merpati. Jl. Miri Pujut** at the south end of Miri leads to the spectacular **Boulevard Shopping Center.**

Tourist Offices: Visitor's Information Center, Lot 452, Jl. Melayu (☎434 181). From Wisma Pelita, walk through the bus terminal; it's a white building in a park to the right. Staff provides maps and brochures. Reserve accommodations in Lambir, Niah, and Gunung

Mulu Parks here. Open M-F 8am-5pm, Sa 8am-12:50pm. Closed holidays.

Tours and Travels: Tropical Adventure (☎419 337), in the lobby of the Mega Hotel, organizes treks. Cash preferred. Open M-F 8:30am-5pm, Sa 8:30-12:30pm. **Transworld Travel Services,** 2nd fl., Wisma Pelita Tunku Complex (☎422 277), offers similar packages. Open M-F 8:30am-5pm, Sa 8:30am-4:30pm. AmEx/MC/V.

Immigration Offices: ☎442 105. Follow Jl. Brooke east until it becomes Jl. Sylvia and then Jl. Gartak; turn left at Jl. Persekutuan. In the pink building on the ground floor behind door 3. Free visa extensions up to 2 months. Open M-Th 8am-12:30pm and 2-4pm, F 8-11:30am and 2:30-4:15pm, Sa 8am-12:30pm.

Currency Exchange: Bank Bumiputra (☎420 371), beyond the Mega Hotel on Jl. Indica, off Jl. Bendahara. RM2.15 per check. **24hr. ATM** (Cirrus/MC/V). Open M-F 9:30am-4pm, Sa 9:30am-noon. **Bank Utama** (☎411 882) is the futuristic building on Jl. Nahoda Gampar. Open M-F 9:30am-3:30pm, Sa 9:30-11:30am.

Police: ☎433 222 ext. 204. On the corner of Jl. Kingsway and Jl. Chia Tze Chi.

Pharmacies: Guardian Farmasi, ground fl., Bintang Plaza, on the corner of Jl. Merbau and Jl. Min Pujut. Well-stocked prescription counter. Open daily 10am-10pm.

Medical Services: Hospital Umum Miri (☎420 033), on Jl. Cahaya-Lopeng, south of the city on the road to Bintulu. English spoken. **Open 24hr.**

Telephones: Telekom Office (☎421 010), next to the post office on Jl. Post, near the rear of the Imperial Mall. Open M-Th 8:30am-12:45pm and 2-4:15pm, F 8:30-11:45am and 2:30-4:15pm, Sa 8:30am-12:30pm. **IDD phones** opposite Wisma Pelita, on Jl. Padang.

Internet Access: Cyber Corner, 1st fl. Wisma Pelita. RM4 per hr. **Public library** (☎424 984) at Dewan Suarah also has access. Take Jl. Yu Seng-Datuk Merpati north and turn right on Jl. Persekutuan before the gold-domed mosque. Follow the street until it ends; the library is a glass and whitewashed, concrete creation. 10 terminals; free 30min. usage. Open Tu-F 9am-8pm, Sa 8am-8pm, Su 9am-3pm; closed holidays.

Post Office: ☎432 887. On Jl. Sylvia on the eastern edge of town. *Poste Restante.* Open M-F 8am-noon and 2-4pm, Sa 8am-12pm. Closed 1st and 3rd Sa. A **branch** is also located on the third fl. of the Boulevard Shopping Center. **Postal code:** 98000.

(continued from previous page)

quite practical. The absent bowl reduces clean-up; you won't see automated machines that cover the seats in plastic here.

While squatting will be difficult at first, rest assured that it does eventually get easier. Practice makes perfect–or just more comfortable. Plant your heels firmly on the ground for balance. If you have a backpack or large purse, place it in front of you and grasp it with your hands. The illusion of stability works wonders. And practice eliminates potentially painful leg cramps.

Back home, the next logical step involves toilet paper. In some cities in Malaysia, you'll be able to purchase it at public toilets, but at others, you are on your own. The strange hose snaking out of the wall is used for cleaning with the left hand, which is considered dirty by Muslims.

The hose explains why most Sarawak bathroom floors are completely drenched in water. Don't worry, your 20 sen usually includes soap with which to wash your hands, so the experience is as hygienic as possible. Finally, you're ready to flush. While most toilets come equipped with a flushing device, many have fallen into disuse and thus into disrepair. If this is true, a bucket will be located adjacent to the hose. Simply fill with water, and pour.

Following these simple steps will make your Sarawak toilet experience relatively painless. Unless you're willing to wait and use the facilities at a five-star hotel, bring patience, an open mind, and, if you like, some two-ply.

–William Lee Adams

ACCOMMODATIONS

Muhibba Inn, Lot 548, Jl. South Yu Seng (☎412 003), above Sin Mui Pin Restaurant. Gate locks at 2am, but someone is always on duty. Singles and doubles with private bath, A/C, and TV RM33. ❸

Tai Tong Lodging House, 1st fl., 26 Jl. Cina (☎411 498), opposite the Chinese temple. Exhibitionists will love the lack of privacy. Midnight lockout. Dorms (men-only) RM10; singles with shared bath RM28; doubles with A/C RM36, with private bath RM42. ❸

Brooke Inn, 14 Brooke Road (☎412 881). Walking away from the Miri Central Market past Yulan Plaza, it's on the right. Hot water, A/C, TV, and free storage. Singles RM40; doubles RM45; family rooms RM50. ❹

Fairland Inn, 1st fl., 21 Jl. Kingsway (☎413 981). From Wisma Pelita, it's across Jl. Kingsway, down Jl. Anatto, above Sunmay Refreshment Center on left corner. Lockout 11pm. Singles with bath and hot water RM20, with A/C RM25; doubles RM28. ❷

Silverwood Inn, 20A Jl. Bendahara (☎420 577), a few shops down from KFC. Don't let the name fool you: it's as good as gold. Phones, TVs, showers with tubs, and mini-fridges. Midnight lockout. Singles RM50; doubles RM60. AmEx/D/MC/V. ❹

FOOD

North Indian eateries line the covered promenades of the beautiful **Jade Center** on either side of **Jl. Nahkoda Gampar.** A few kilometers south of town, **Taman Selera** offers a wide range of outdoor restaurants and food stalls to suit any taste.

Bilal Restaurant (☎420 105), near Mega Hotel on Persiaran Kabor. Savory Indian cuisine. English-language menu. Tandoori chicken (RM7). Tender *rogani naan* RM2. *Lassi* RM2.50. Open daily 6am-9pm. ❷

Michael Unlimited B.B.Q. Steamboat, Lot 2406, Boulevard Commercial Centre, Jl. Miri Pujut (☎436 608). Choose your own seafood, vegetables, or noodles from an all-you-can-eat buffet and then cook them in a steamboat (RM18). Open daily 5:30-11pm. ❹

Hengyap Noodle Factory (☎412 977), on Jl. N. Yu Seng, near Standard Chartered Bank. Look for the yellow "vegetarian" sign. Vegetarian buffet with Chinese specialties. Vegetable *mee* RM2.50. Huge egg rolls RM1.50. Open daily 8am-10pm. ❶

Yi-Hah-Hai Seafood (☎413 883), on Miri Waterfront off Jl. Bendahara. Turn left after Bank Bumiputra; look for red tablecloths and orange chairs. Worth the extra ringgit. Exquisite *makan laut* (seafood) RM10-15. Open daily 9:15am-1:30am. ❸

Sin Mui Pin, 5-7 Jl. South Yu Seng (☎412 681), opposite MAS office. Popular, open-air restaurant. Venison with ginger RM10. Open daily 7am-2am. ❸

MALAYSIA

ENTERTAINMENT AND NIGHTLIFE

When the heat becomes too much, locals rush to the **public swimming pool** on Jl. Kipas. (☎411 412. RM1 for adults, children under 12 RM0.50. Open M-F 9am-9pm, Sa-S 9am-7:30pm.) The Righa and Holiday Inn hotels open their fancier, less crowded pools to the public on Sundays. Before partaking in Miri's vibrant nightlife, visitors can walk along Jl. Melayu to a roundabout, where a right turn leads to the free ferry across the Miri River. Follow the road 100m to **Long Jetty**—a perfect spot to catch Miri's pastel sunsets. Karaoke-crazed locals head to the **bowling alley** (RM4.60 per game; open daily 9am-1am) on the fourth floor of Bintang Plaza, while others enjoy the **movie theater** next door (RM8; shows every 2hr. 12:30-11pm). Across the river, catch bus #11 to **Taman Selera** (last bus 9pm), 2km south of town, for a cheap dinner from the food stalls and a stroll along the beach. Miri's hip converge at **Cheerie Berries** (☎412 128), past the Bintang Plaza Shopping Center on Jl.

Miri Pujit, for nightly live music. (Happy hour daily 9-11pm, buy-1-get-1 free. Beer RM7.) The Rihga Royal Hotel's **Rigs Fun Pub,** before Taman Selera on the right, hosts more dancing fun. (No shorts or flip-flops. Cover RM20. Beer RM14.50, RM7.25 M-Th. Open M-Sa 9pm-1:30am.) Several bars also dot **Jl. Mebau.**

GUNUNG MULU NATIONAL PARK

As Sarawak's largest park, Mulu encompasses 544 sq. km of peat swamp, heath, dipterocarp forest, moss thickets, and mountain vegetation. Over 3500 plant species and 20,000 animal species have been documented within the park. Treks include a two-day hike to the razor-sharp Pinnacles on the slopes of Gunung Api and a three-day ascent of Gunung Mulu. Perhaps most impressive, some 500km of mostly undiscovered caves lurk underground, including the world's largest cave passage, the Sarawak Chamber, which can house 18 Boeing 747s and then some. Recognized as a UNESCO World Heritage Site, Mulu is Borneo's biggest draw and one of the world's last unadulterated treasures.

TRANSPORTATION

Flights: The **airport** (☎011 205 285) is a 20min. walk from park headquarters. **MAS** runs flights from Miri to **Gunung Mulu** (2-3 daily, RM75). Reserve early or try to fly stand-by. Vans drive visitors to park headquarters (3min., RM3). **Vision Air** offers more scenic flights that travel just above and sometimes through the Pinnacles (3 per day, RM86). Arrange return transport at park headquarters the day before your departure.

Ferries: Returning to **Miri** by boat involves an entire day (and possibly night) of travel via longboat, starting with the trip to **Long Terawan.** Charter a boat (1-4 people, RM250 or RM45 per person, 5 or more people). To make the next connection, some travelers leave by 4pm the day before and arrange accommodation in longhouses in Long Terawan. Residents may let you sleep on their floor in return for a small gift or gratuity; ask at the park office. Or, leave from park headquarters by 4am and try to catch the boat to **Marudi** (express 3-4hr., 6am, RM20; speedboat 2½hr., 6am, RM22). From the Marudi jetty, take an express boat to **Kuala Baram** (3hr., 4-5 per day 7am-3pm, RM18). **Buses** from Kuala Baram go to **Miri** (45min., every 30min. 5:30am-9:30pm, RM2.50).

On Foot: After conquering the Pinnacles, you can hike from Camp 5, the Pinnacles' base camp, to the **Lubang Cina Cave** on the Terikan River. The next leg involves taking a boat, with an overnight stop at Bala Losong, to **Medamit.** Pre-arrange transportation before leaving park headquarters. It's possible to catch a taxi here into **Limbang,** with cheap sea and air connections to **Kota Kinabalu** and **Miri.** Trekking the Head-Hunters' trail requires prodigious logistical coordination; package tours are easiest.

MALAYSIA

PRACTICAL INFORMATION

Obtain all **permits** for Gunung Mulu at the park headquarters upon arrival, rendering pricey **tour operators** unnecessary unless you fancy **adventure caving.** Gunung Mulu's airport harbors the park's only **minimart,** which sells noodles, nuts, candy, and water. Trekkers to Camp 5 can avoid a trip back by stocking up here upon arrival, or better yet in Miri before arrival. Head to the **park office,** left of the boat dock, to pay park fees and for accommodations, camera and video permits and to arrange guides and transportation for adventures within the park. There are no equipment rentals at the park (try **Mulu Resort** downriver), but lockers (RM3) are available. (☎434 561. Open daily 8am-5pm.)

FROM THE ROAD

ISLANDS IN THE STREET

If the chicken tried to cross the road in Malaysian Borneo, he would be flattened by a truck, his feathers would blow away in a motorcycle's exhaust, and his body would be left to fry on the hot asphalt.

Why all the fried chicken? Because crosswalks in this region are either nonexistent or terribly misplaced.

After a long day of sweating along the black pavement, I was elated finally to come across one lone crosswalk. Small but busy roads usually lack crosswalks entirely, and major highways—regardless of how congested—are lucky to have more than one.

For a moment, it seemed that only four lanes of traffic separated me from a row of quickie marts with bottled water. But I opened my eyes and was reminded that this crosswalk, like most, was a bit of a mirage. The quickie marts were across the street—and 4km to the east! This "convenient" crossing would take me only to a wheat field with abandoned houses. Still, thirst impelled me to cross the road, and so I waited.

And I waited for a long time. It seems as though there is a mandatory 15min. waiting period before the red "don't walk" stick figure turns green. In the meantime, as I discovered, businessmen on cellular phones, children dribbling basketballs, and elderly women balancing fruit on their heads will nonchalantly step into traffic. They mount concrete islands that float in the middle of the mania. After a short wait, they simultaneously jump into the first hole in traffic, no

(continued on next page)

ACCOMMODATIONS AND FOOD

Lodgings cluster near the park's office. An 18-bed **dormitory** ❷ with cooking area and showers is the cheapest option in the park (RM15). A nicer **chalet** ❹ with A/C offers singles (RM55), 4-bed rooms (RM100), and a double-bed suite (RM240). Electricity is available until midnight. A **hostel** ❶ across the river offers a chance to mix with locals. 30m past the canteen, take a left onto a dirt path, cross a stream, and the hostel is the first building in sight. (RM10 per room.) The sole **restaurant** ❷ on the park grounds offers staples such as fried rice and noodles (RM4), set breakfasts (RM7), bottled water (RM6), and beer (RM6). Across the park entrance bridge, **Melinau Restaurant** ❸ serves large set dinners (3 courses RM15) on an open deck with loud music. **The Wildflower Coffee House** ❺ at the Royal Mulu resort serves large gourmet burgers, steak, and local favorites (RM20-46).

OUTDOOR ACTIVITIES

Gunung Mulu's numerous fees may seem high for the budget traveler, but permit fees are charged per group; cut costs significantly by joining other travelers. Permit fees for the Pinnacles and Gunung Mulu include a knowledgeable guide.

SHOW CAVES. The Show Caves are Gunung Mulu's most accessible and least strenuous attraction. All have been equipped with boardwalks and dramatic lights highlighting the rock forms and passages. Bring a flashlight, a raincoat, and a plastic bag for cameras and video recorders. **Permits** are mandatory for most visits. Standard fees per group for permits are determined by the size of the group: Deer Cave and Lang's Cave RM18 (groups of 1-5), RM20 (groups of 6-10 people); Wind Cave and Clear Water Cave RM18/RM20; Langang's Caves RM66/RM72; and Simon's Caves RM66/RM72. The **Clear Water Cave** and **Wind Cave** systems (lit 9:30am-12:30pm) were first explored 16 years ago by a Sarawak Royal Geographic Society expedition that mapped 25km of passages. Over the past decade, exploration has brought the mapped terrain to over 107km, confirming Clear Water Cave as Asia's longest. To get there, walk 4km on wooden planks, through Mook Milk Cave (flashlight required). Alternatively, charter a boat (15min., 1-4 people, RM85) up the Melanau River. The first stop is Wind Cave, up a wooden plank walk to the right of the boat dock. Clear Water Cave is a 5min. walk along the river. The path first passes through **Young Lady's Cave** and ends at a 50m chasm littered with the bones of boars who got lost in the caverns.

Beware of guano-coated handrails (see **Fertile Ground,** p. 459).

The path into **Deer Cave** hugs the base of the mountain. Deer Cave has the world's largest cave passage; at over 2km, even the shrill screeches of the two million wrinkle-lipped bats living in the cave are lost in the vast opening passage. The entrance to **Lang's Cave** is a few minutes walk from Deer Cave. A 3km boardwalk has been built from the park's office to these two caves; it makes for excellent hornbill spotting around dawn. The lush, scenic trip takes 30-45min. (Officially open daily 2:30-4:30pm, when the lights are on.) Just outside the two caves, the **bat observatory** is a good vantage point for watching the continuous stream of bats emerging from Deer Cave at 6pm (lasts about 20min.).

ADVENTURE CAVING. Guides lead the daring into Gunung Mulu's lesser-known passages to scramble over boulders, wade through subterranean rivers, and rappel into pits. **Sarawak Chambers,** the world's largest natural chamber, is the size of 16 football fields. Eight hours of round-trip romp-and-stomp through its midnight landscapes cost approximately RM88 per guide for groups of up to five people. Other destinations include the **Drunken Forest, Stone Horse Cave,** and the **Simon's Caves** system. **Lang's Cave,** which is connected to Deer Cave via a 100m external plankwalk, is well decorated with stalactites and stalagmites. Arrange expeditions through tour operators in Miri only if you need equipment (some caves require technical rope work). Park headquarters does not supply extensive caving equipment but will rent out the mandatory head-lamp and helmet for RM40 per day.

HIKING

Over five million years old, the **Pinnacles** point skyward from the upper reaches of Gunung Api. The trek begins with a scenic 2hr. longboat ride from park headquarters to **Kuala Berar.** In times of low water, you may spend more time pushing the boat than riding in it. From Kuala Berar, it's another 8km to **Camp 5,** the Pinnacles base camp, with basic lodging (claim your piece of wood floor) and cooking facilities. Bring your own food, dishes, utensils, and water bottles. The next morning, trekkers tackle the steep, slick, stone-mired hillside of Gunung Api. Although the path is only 2.4km long, you need to be fit and focused to conquer the hike. With 400m to go, climbers are greeted with ropes and ladders, some nearly vertical and others horizontally bridging 20m chasms. Hikers find this part of the climb the easiest.

(continued from previous page)

matter how small, and wade across the sea of cars to said wheat field or abandoned house.

If you're anything like I was for the first few days of my trip, you are probably still underneath the red stick figure, waiting for it to turn green. Eventually, I sucked in my stomach and fearfully waddled across a road nowhere near a crosswalk.

Attaching yourself to a group makes getting to and from the concrete islands easier. Another advantage is having other pedestrians as human shields to protect you from the threat of on-coming traffic.

That said, however, traveling in groups can make your stay on the island a bit unstable, as the laws of physics threaten even the most cohesive of groups.

The islands seem more like narrow isthmuses as SUVs, which act like urban death-machines, whistle by just a few centimeters from your face. Behind you, sporty sedans brush against your daypack.

To stop the circular spinning motion initiated by the traffic, clutch a wooden pole. Luckily, the children bouncing basketballs can often sense your all-too-visceral fear. If they offer you a hand, don't be embarrassed to take it.

Attempting to cross four lanes of Malaysian traffic all at once would be suicidal. Waiting for a group and mounting a concrete island, no matter how skinny, is definitely your safest bet.

You won't get flattened, your feathers won't fly, and I promise, there will be no fried chicken.

—William Lee Adams

The trail downhill is tricky and slippery after rain; it takes 3-5hr. to reach Camp 5. Most visitors spend another night here before returning to headquarters.

A boat to Kuala Berar, the first leg of the journey to the Pinnacles, costs RM350 for up to four people and RM85 per additional person; the permit fee is RM110 per group, which includes a guide for the three-day/two-night trek. Almost as impressive as the Pinnacles is **Larry,** Camp 5's park ranger, who makes the journey to the top a few times per week. Bring your lunch, raingear, and at least 3L of water.

Rhinos were the first to enjoy the craggy summit of **Gunung Mulu,** and the trail used by most trekkers today follows their footsteps. The journey takes four days for moderately fit travelers. Visitors to Camp 1 deal with muddy trails populated by leeches. The second day is a tough uphill battle. It takes nine leech-infested hours to reach Camp 4 (1800m). The next day, the most zealous of climbers are up before sunrise. The journey up to the wind-scarred peak involves 2hr. of climbing, some of it using thick lengths of rope to steady wobbly legs. After capturing the sunrise and a spectacular panorama all the way to the Brunei Bay, most visitors return to camp for a night before trudging back to park headquarters on day four.

SABAH

Known as the "Land Below the Winds," Sabah was once rumored to be a storehouse of gems. Although none have been found, Sabah has proven to be rich in other natural treasures. Southeast Asia's highest peak, the world's most concentrated orangutan population, and the world's largest flower are all found in a jungle teeming with wildlife and vegetation. Shopaholics feast on handicrafts at the ubiquitous markets, while the adventurous partake in the underwater paradise of Sabah's reefs. In spite of its renown for having some of the world's best diving, Sabah mainly draws those seeking to conquer the stark peak of Gunung Kinabalu.

KOTA KINABALU ☎088

Kota Kinabalu (KK) is a big-boned city where, despite the locals' best efforts, few visitors linger. But though they might not stay long, they come in hordes seeking the austere grandeur of Gunung Kinabalu. KK is also a necessary stop for sorting through travel logistics for daytrips to Kinabalu and beyond. The charming beaches of nearby Tunku Abdul Rahman Park Islands are an off-beat surf-and-turf combo where divers and sunbathers alike come seeking sun, sand, and sea. While the city itself is architecturally raw, numerous daytrips make KK worthwhile.

MALAYSIA

> **WARNING** Local con men have swindled thousands of dollars from tourists. Do not accept any invitations to learn card tricks or play card games.

TRANSPORTATION

Flights: Malaysia Airport Berhad (☎238 555), 6km from the city. From the highway outside the terminal, minibuses, Putatan Buses (RM1), and taxis (RM13.50) go to the city center. **MAS offices** are in the departure hall (☎240 632; open daily 5:30am-7pm), and in the Kompleks Karamunsing (☎239 310). MAS flies daily to: **Bandar Seri Begawan, Brunei** (RM103); **Hong Kong** (RM825); **Jakarta** (RM825); **Johor Bahru** (RM347); **Kuching** (RM228); **Manila** (RM700); **Miri** (RM104); **Sandakan** (RM95); and **Singapore** (RM584). **Singapore Airlines,** Lot 12-13, ground fl., Block C, Kompleks Kuwasa (☎255 444), flies to **Singapore** (Tu, Th; RM315). **Dragon Air,** Lot CG01-CG04, ground fl., Block C Kompleks Kuwasa (☎254 733), flies to **Hong Kong** (RM825).

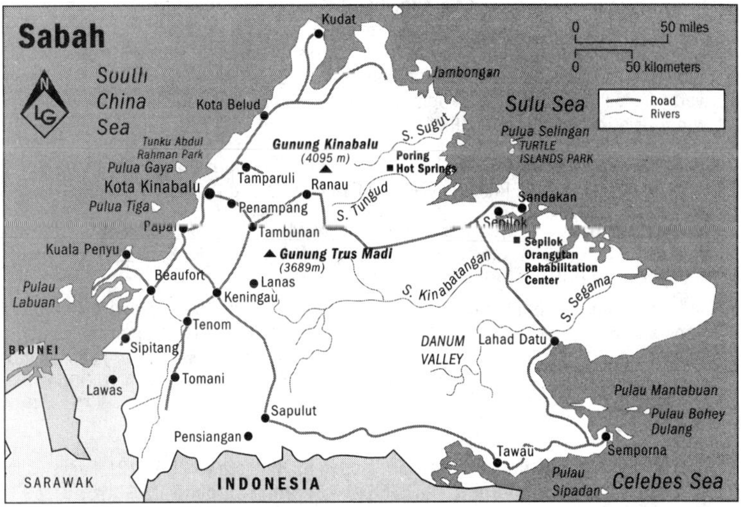

the library. Buses to **Kota Belud** (1hr., RM5) depart when full until 4pm. Buses to **Gunung Kinabalu Park** (2hr., RM6-7) and **Ranau** (2½hr., RM7-10) depart until noon. Buses to **Sandakan** (6hr., RM30) leave most frequently in the morning.

Ferries: Park boats leave from the **Harbour View Jetty** off Jl. Haji Saman to islands in **Tunku Abdul Rahman Park** (4 per day 8:30am-4:30pm, RM10 per person for groups of 4 or more). To get to **Bandar Seri Begawan, Brunei,** catch the Labuan Express ferry to **Pulau Labuan** (2½hr., 8am, RM28) and another from **Labuan** to **BSB** (1hr., 12:15pm, RM24). Purchase tickets at the jetty office (☎236 834). Open daily 7am-3pm.

Local Transportation: Local minibus terminals are opposite the post office on Jl. Tun Razak, next to the Centrepoint building. **Putatan Buses** marked "Beach" go to **Tanjung Aru Beach** (RM1). **Taxis** congregate near hotels and charge RM5-10 for intra-city hops.

ORIENTATION AND PRACTICAL INFORMATION

Completely destroyed in World War II, KK's center was rebuilt in a grid system dominated by three north-south roads. **Jl. Tun Fuad Stephens** curves along the waterfront west of the city center and houses the **Filipino Market, Pesar Besar,** and **Sabah Parks Office.** The **GPO** and **minibus terminal** are on **Jl. Tun Razak,** the city's central boulevard. The **police station, long-distance bus terminal,** and **immigration office** all line **Jl. Tunku Abdul Rahman,** which leads to the **airport, Lintas Plaza,** and **Tanjung Aru,** along the city's east edge. Other major landmarks are the Wisma Sabah, Wisma Merdeka, and Centrepoint complexes. Wisma Sabah is the L-shaped building by the Hyatt Hotel, Merdeka is down the street on Jl. Tun Razak, and Centrepoint is next to the Sinsuran neighborhood in the town's west end.

Tourist Offices: Sabah Tourism Promotion Corp., 51 Jl. Gaya (☎212 121), in the old post office. Multilingual pamphlets. Free comprehensive map. Open M-F 8am-5pm, Sa 8am-2pm. **Sabah Parks Office** (☎211 881), opposite the Filipino Market. Advice on Sabah's national parks. Open M-F 8am-1pm and 2-4:30pm, Sa 8am-12:50pm. Closed first and 3rd Sa of every month. **Tourism Malaysia** (☎211 732), opposite Sabah Tourism, ground fl., EON CMG Bldg. Open M-F 8am-4:30pm, Sa 8am-12:50pm.

Tours: Kinabalu Nature Resorts Sdn. Bhd., G15, ground fl., Wismah Sabah (☎243 029). Handles all accommodations in Gunung Kinabalu Park, Poring Hot Springs, and Tunku Abdul Rahman Park. Book at least 3 days in advance. **Borneo Divers** (☎222 226), 9th fl. Stanford College near Sabah Tourism. 5-star PADI dive center. 4-day open water course RM900, min. 2 people. Day tours to Tunku Abdul Rahman Park (RM180). Wreck dives off Pulau Labuan RM185-250 for 2 dives.

Consulates: Indonesia (☎219 110), on Jl. Kemajuan opposite Karamunsing Hotel, north of Jl. Tunku Abdul Rahman. Open M-F 8am-noon and 2-4pm.

Immigration Offices: 4th fl., Wisma Dang Bandang, Jl. H. J. Yaakob (☎280 700; visa inquiries ☎224 349). 1-month visa extensions RM6. Open M-Th 8am-12:45pm and 2-4:15pm, F 8-11:30am, Sa 8am-12:45pm.

Currency Exchange: Banks cluster by Wisma Merdeka on Jl. Tugu. **Standard Chartered Bank** and **Bank Bumiputra** have **24hr. ATMs. Maybank** (☎254 295), at the corner of Jl. Pantai and Jl. 3. Open M-F 9:30-11:30am. **Airport branch** (☎268 906) cashes traveler's checks. RM5 per transaction, RM0.15 per check. Open daily 8am-10:30pm.

Emergency: ☎999.

Police: ☎242 111, on Jl. Balai, east of town.

Pharmacies: Doses Pharmacy, Lot G 39, ground fl., KK Plaza (☎259 972). English spoken. Open daily 10am-9pm. AmEx/MC/V. **Pharmex,** ground fl., Lot 6, Block F, Kompleks Segama on Jl. Tun Razak (☎231 457). Open M-Sa 8:30am-7:30pm, Su 9:30am-1:30pm. **Syarikat Kaca Mata** (☎258 589), next door, has contact lens supplies. Open daily 8:30am-7:30pm.

Medical Services: Perdana Polyklinik (☎235 100), on Jl. Pantai. **Queen Elizabeth Hospital** (☎218 166), near State Museum. English spoken. Both **open 24hr.**

Telephones: Public phones place collect calls, and some accept Foncards. **Telekom Office,** ground fl., Block I, Jl. Ikan Juara 1, Karamunsing (☎257 676). Open M-F 8:30am-4:45pm, Sa 8:30am-1pm. **Airport branch** (☎261 261). Open daily 8am-5pm.

Internet Access: Vision De Net Cafe, Lot 91, first fl. Jl. Gaya (☎019 873 3475), near RHB Bank and Sabah Tourism. RM3 per hr., students RM2.50 per hr. Open daily 9am-2am. **PlayNet,** ground fl. Wismah Sabah. 9am-7pm RM3 per hr, 7pm-2am RM2 per hr. Open daily 9am-2am. **City Internet Cafe,** No. 1 Jl. Centre Point (☎088 255 255). RM3 per hr. Open daily 9am-2am.

Post Office: GPO, on Jl. Tun Razak (☎210 855), near Bank Negara and Kompleks Segama. *Poste Restante.* Open M-Sa 8am-5pm. Closed 1st and 3rd Sa of every month. **Postal code:** 88806.

MALAYSIA

ACCOMMODATIONS

City Park Inn, Jl. Pasar Baru 2 (☎260 607), near Kampung Air, across from Public Finance. Popular owner **Jimmy Wong** arranges daytrips, offers helpful advice, and has been known to treat his guests to dinner. This hostel-hotel hybrid has clean rooms with lockers, A/C, and private bath. Internet (RM3 per hr.) and free breakfast. Dorm RM15; singles RM45; doubles RM50. ❷

Lucy's Homestay, 1st fl., Lot 25, Lorong Dewan, Australia Place on Jl. Tun Razak (☎261 495). Common room with TV, stereo, and library. Breakfast included. Flexible curfew 11pm. Laundry. Single-sex, 12-bed dorms with shared bath RM18; doubles RM40. ❷

Trekkers Lodge, 2nd fl., Block I, Lot 5&6, Sinsuran Complex (☎252 263). Clean rooms and outgoing staff. Great deals for daytrips. Laundry (RM10 per load). Breakfast included. 4-bed dorms RM17, with A/C RM20; doubles RM37/RM43. ❷

The Jesselton Hotel, 69 Gaya St. (☎223 333; www.jaring.my/jess). In the style of "a refined English country house," this 4-star hotel offers all the modern conveniences in

each room. The lavish junior suite has a rooftop garden. Singles RM198; doubles RM228; suite RM550. AmEx/MC/V. ❺

FOOD

Affordable Malay, Indian, and Chinese restaurants dot the city. The **Kompleks Sedco**, off Jl. Laiman Diki, is an open-air food court with the feel of a family reunion gone nuts. The A/C food court in the basement of the **Centrepoint Complex** offers similar bargains and a vegetarian stall. The **Anjung Senja** esplanade past the Filipino market boasts 16 kiosks and has emerged as KK's trendiest eatery. It's one of the few places to find *ice kachang*—a dessert of iced milk, rice, red beans, and lychee. (Open daily 4pm-1am.)

Ang's, on Jl. Haji Saman, opposite Wisma Merdeka. Packed with locals. Hefty portions of Chinese seafood and meat. Sizzling Japanese bean curd RM6; BBQ prawn RM15. Open daily 11am-11pm. ❸

Port View Seafood Restaurant, on Jl. Haji Sama opposite the old customs wharf. Follow Jl. Tun Razak east out of town, 200m past Wisma Sabah; look for the blazing blue and red neon sign on the right. Scrumptious Chinese seafood. Menu priced seasonally—but never a cheap season. Fried cuttlefish with chilis RM10; lobster RM80; grilled prawn with butter sauce RM12. Open daily 10:30am-11:30pm. ❺

Restoran Sri Melaka, No. 9, Jl. Laiman Diki, Kampung Air, opposite the restaurants of Kompleks Sedco. Look for green lettering. English menu. A/C. Vegetarian options. Patrons rave about *assam* fish head (RM10). Savory *mee siam* RM4.50. Open daily 9:30am-9:30pm. ❷

Restoran Bilal, ground fl., Block B, Kompleks Segama. The best cheap North Indian food in KK. Standard buffet with rice. Curries RM2.50; *Roti canai* RM0.80; *Nasi ayam* RM3.50. Open daily 8am-7:30pm. ❶

SIGHTS AND ENTERTAINMENT

STATE MUSEUM AND ENVIRONS. KK's main cultural destination, the State Museum is a modern interpretation of traditional Rugus longhouses. Its interior has exhibits on ethnography, natural history, ceramics, and archaeology. **Kampung Warisan (Heritage Village)** is at the compound's opposite end, past the waterfall. Visitors can pose with a Murut longhouse or a traditional Bajau or Chinese farm house before continuing to the nearby **Ethno-botanic Gardens,** where plants used for ornamentation, commerce, and medicine vie for space and sunlight.

The State Museum is a 30min. walk southwest from the city center along Jl. Tunku Abdul Rahman. Walk 400m past the intersection with Jl. Kemajuan and turn left on Jl. Penampang. Through the small gate on the left, a path leads uphill to the museum. Alternatively, catch a minibus (RM0.50) from a bus stop along Jl. Tunku Abdul Rahman. *(Museum open M-Th 10am-6pm, Sa-Su and holidays 9am-6pm. RM5. Science and Technology Center open M-Th 10am-4:30pm, Sa-Su and holidays 9:30am-5pm. Heritage Village and Ethno-botanic Gardens open Sa-Th 10am-5pm.)*

TANJUNG ARU BEACH. While the warm water and soft sand make this beach ideal for relaxation, Tanjung Aru comes to life at sunset and on weekends. Hawkers sell steamed corn (RM1 per cob), peanuts, fried noodles, and chicken *satay* (RM0.40 per stick). Kampung Nalayan Restaurant in Tun Fuad Stephens Park, several kilometers east of the town center, has daily Malay and Kandazan dance performances around 7:30pm. Take a minibus bound for Luyang. *(2.5km from the museum. Take one of the buses labeled "Beach" or "Shangri-La Resort" opposite the post office.)*

OTHER SIGHTS. The **City Bird Sanctuary** on Likas Bay features an impressive lookout tower and wooden paths through a mangrove forest. Bring your binoculars to see the Great Egret and the King Fisher. *(☎246 955. Open Tu-Su 8am-6pm. Admission is free, but donations are appreciated.)* **Tun Fuad Stephens Park,** off Jl. Tun Fuad Stephens, features impressive jogging trails on which many locals train prior to hiking Mt. Kinabalu. A **waterpark** with a large slide is just inside the park's gates. Outside the park, a small **night market** serves up local favorites. *(Open daily 12:30-9pm, RM5.)* The **Poring** and **Kilan Cinemas,** at the intersection of Jl. Tunku Abdul Rahman and Jl. Laiman Diki, often show English-language movies. Most seats cost RM6-8. *(Open daily noon-midnight.)* **Asia City,** off Lh. Raya Pantai Baru across from Centrepoint, and **Lintas Plaza** are home to many karaoke bars, clubs, and discos. **Shenanigan's,** ground fl. Hyatt Hotel, next to Wisma Sabah, is a popular backpacker hangout with live music. *(No shorts or slippers. Beer from RM7.50. Cover RM15. Happy hour daily 5-9pm. Open M-Th 5pm-1am, F-Sa 5pm-2am, Su 5pm-midnight.)* The best people-watching spot is along the **Anjung Senja** esplanade, where locals sip lattes until 1am.

MARKETS

KK's market area is along the waterfront. The **Pesar Besar (big market)** lays out fresh fruit, veggies, and cheap clothing. (Open daily 8am-6pm.) Upstairs, eager foodstall owners with KK's cheapest eats shout "*Macam!*" ("Eat!"). Follow the smell of dead sea creatures to the **fish market** behind Pesar Besar. If it swims, they have it. Next door, the **Filipino Market** sells souvenirs, t-shirts, and fruit. At night, hawkers barbecue fresh fish (RM8-15). Friendly conversation and sincere smiles invariably earn travelers a discount. On Sunday mornings, **street stalls** on Jl. Gaya Browse sell everything from Chinese medicines to puppies. **Beware of pickpockets.**

DAYTRIPS FROM KOTA KINABALU

MONSOPIAD CULTURAL VILLAGE. Interested in decapitation? Head over to Monsopiad Cultural Village where former resident and famed Kadazan warrior Monsopiad is still revered over 300 years after his death. His direct descendants run the village, vividly detailing the warrior's adventures and showing off his 42 trophy heads that remain in the House of Skulls. A welcome drink of local rice wine, lessons on the blow pipe, and a taste of *hinava*—a local fresh pickle—await. The Cultural Village is several kilometers south of KK in Donggonggon. Take a taxi (RM20) or Penampang Bus from the local bus terminal in KK to the last stop in Donggonggon (RM0.80), connect to a minibus to Terawi (RM0.80), and ask to be let off at Monsopiad. *(☎ 761 336; www.monsopiad.org. Open M-F 10am-5pm. Cultural shows Sa 11am, 1pm. Guided tours 9:30, 11am, 12:30, 2, 3:30pm. RM25.)*

KOTA BELUD. Coastal Kota Belud, 75km north of KK, is a welcome diversion from KK's urban rhythms. Surrounded by rubber plantations and shaggy dipterocarp forests, Kota Belud is famous for its lively tamu (market and trade fair), one of Sabah's largest. (Open Su 6am-noon.) Historically, tamu allowed the upland Rugus and Kadazan/Dusun people to meet and trade goods with the coastal Bajau. The Bajau, Sabah's famed "cowboys of the east," wear brilliantly stitched garb on special occasions, like **Tamu Besar** in late November. The real attraction, more so than the wares, is the raucous atmosphere and bustling trade in the shaded fairgrounds.

Buses from the long-distance terminal in KK drop off passengers on the highway in the city center. Head for the pink spires and gilt dome of the city mosque and bear right down Jl. Hasbollah. The tamu grounds are a 5-10min. walk from town past the post office. **Minibuses** back to KK leave from the Esso gas station near the bookstore (1½hr.; depart when full, last bus 4pm; RM5).

NEAR KOTA KINABALU: TUNKU ABDUL RAHMAN PARK

Idyllic Tunku Abdul Rahman Park is made up of five placid islands 3-8km from KK. Park boats leave from the Harbour View Jetty to the park (9, 11am, noon, 1pm; RM14, children RM7). Admission per island is RM10, for children RM6. **Palau Gaya,** the largest island, is home to Filipino immigrants who have settled in the stilt village off the east coast. Over 20km of trails criss-cross the island through an intact **dipterocarp forest;** the trail from **park headquarters** leads through a dense mangrove thicket. Though crowded and dirty, tiny **Pulau Sapi**

(Cow Island), off Pulau Gaya's southwest coast, is also popular. **Police Beach,** once used as a police shooting range, is the most secluded, while **Manukan** and **Mamutik Beaches**—the most scenic and unfortunately the most popular—get crowded with large tour groups' barbecues. **Pulau Sulug** is the least developed and is popular with divers and snorkelers.

Camping ❶ is permitted on Pulau Sapi and Pulau Sulug (RM5 per person, under 18 RM2). Campers must obtain written permission from park headquarters and bring their own food and equipment. Four-person **chalets** ❺ are available on Manukan (RM230). Make reservations with Kinabalu Nature Resorts Sdn. Bhd. (see **Tours,** p. 468). For more information on accommodation on Mamutik, consult **Sabah Parks Office** in Komplex Sinsuran.

GUNUNG KINABALU

Gunung Kinabalu is the world's youngest non-volcanic mountain, Southeast Asia's highest peak, and Sabah's premier tourist draw. The surrounding park—larger than the nation of Singapore—stretches through four climate zones and features one of the world's richest flora collections. Feast your eyes on carnivorous plants, or treat your ailments with the medicinal flowers in the park's extravagant Botanical Garden. Whether watching the sunrise from atop Kinabalu's peak or discovering that a moving twig is actually a rare insect, visitors won't regret a trek to Sabah's most enticing attraction.

TRANSPORTATION

Regular **buses** run to **Gunung Kinabalu Park** from the long-distance terminal in KK (1½hr., first bus departs at 7:30am, RM10) and also from the smaller town of **Ranau** (RM5). **Minibuses** make the journey until noon. Flag down buses back to KK on the highway in front of the park entrance (2hr., last bus 4pm, RM10). Daily **shuttles** also make the trip (1hr., every 1½hr., RM10). Admission to **Kinabalu Park,** called a conservation fee, is RM15 (under 18 RM10). Travelers usually arrive at **park headquarters** the day before ascending the mountain. The **Visitors Center** is past the hostels before the access road loops back to the park reception. Upstairs is a small but intriguing exhibit on the park's history and wildlife. (Slide show daily 2pm, F-Su also at 7:30pm. RM2.) Learn about ecology at the **Sabah Parks Office** near the park entrance. Behind the Visitors Center is the **Mountain Garden.** Flora endemic to the park have red labels, plants used medicinally

THE BIG SPLURGE

THE EMPIRE HOTEL AND COUNTRY CLUB

Billed as "the most distinctive and exclusive property in Asia today," the Empire Hotel lives up to its reputation. After 8 years of construction and an estimated price tag of US$1.5 billion, the hotel opened its majestic doors in May 2000 to immense acclaim. Rumor had it the international hotel rating system would have to add a sixth star.

The hotel's unmatched opulence is apparent as soon as doormen open the glass and gold entry. The marble used in the intricate mosaic flooring was the last of its kind in the world; the Sultan bought out the reserve in Italy to finish the lobby.

On sunny days, light shines through the five-story atrium, refracts through glass chandeliers, and reflects off soaring towers lined with genuine gold trim. Be sure not to leave your sunglasses at home. As if the Empire needed more sumptuousness, a US$250,000 crystal camel with gold embellishments graces the hotel lobby.

The 423 rooms, suites, and villas surround guests with luxury at every corner. The deluxe rooms, the cheapest in the hotel, which start at B$500 per night, offer a private balcony with a panoramic view of the ocean, large marble bathtubs with attached phone and voicemail, and a bedside control panel for air-conditioning, lights, and automatic blinds.

The executive suites, which start at B$1000 per night, add other necessities for a life of champagne kisses and caviar dreams: gold-plated

(continued on next page)

are tagged blue, and more common species bear black tags. The garden has a beautiful selection of Kinabalu's 1200 orchid species, including the world's smallest flowering orchid, with a blossom the size of a pinhead. (Required tours 9am, noon, 3pm. RM5.)

ACCOMMODATIONS AND FOOD

Kinabalu Nature Resorts Sdn. Bhd. (www.kinabalunatureresorts.com; see **Tours,** p. 468), runs park accommodations. Make reservations one week in advance. To the right of the park entrance, the **reception office** will give you a room assignment and a map of the park with directions to accommodations. (☎088 889 077. Open daily 7am-10pm.) Many trekkers stay at **Medang Hostel** ❶ or **Menggilan Hostel** ❶. (Dorms RM12, under 18 RM6; doubles RM92; quads RM184; 5- and 6-person cabins RM230.) **Camping is not allowed.** Halfway up the mountain, the most popular dig is the **Laban Rata Rest House** ❷. (Dorms without heaters RM17; dorms with heaters, hot water, and electricity RM34; doubles with bath RM115; quads RM230.) Rooms at **Gunting Lagadan Hut, Panar Laban Hut,** and **Waras Hut** ❶ are unheated but provide cooking facilities and sleeping bags. (Dorms RM12, under 18 RM6.) The most basic accommodations (cooking facilities only) are at **Sayat Sayat Hut** ❶, a 2hr. climb up the Panar Laban rock face. Many visitors rave about Sayat's camaraderie-fostering seclusion, where groups gather in sleeping bags under the stars and chat late into the bitter cold night. Lock up food to avoid rats. (RM12, under 18 RM6.)

The **Kinabalu Balsam Canteen** ❷, below the park office, offers excellent sunset views of the mountain from its veranda. (Dishes from RM5. Open daily 6:30am-9:30pm.) Meals at **Mt. Kinabalu Restaurant** ❷, part of the Visitors Center complex, are comparable to those at canteens. (Entrees RM8. Open M-F 6:30am-10pm, Sa and holidays 6:30am-11pm.) Outside the park, **Restoran Tenompok** ❶ serves *laksa* for RM2.50 and *mee* dishes from RM4. (Open daily 9am-11pm.)

CLIMBING GUNUNG KINABALU

Arrive at park headquarters by 7am, wallet in hand. You'll need a **permit** (RM50, under 18 RM20), **accident insurance** (RM3.50), and possibly a **porter** (RM50 for the first 10kg, RM5 per additional kg). **Guides** are mandatory for climbing past Laban Rata. Groups with special interests can make requests for specific guides (fluent English speakers, plant and bird specialists, etc.) when they arrive. (Guides for 1-3 people RM60 per day, 4-6 people RM64 per day, 7-8 people

(continued from previous page)

faucets, knobs with jade trim, and 24hr. butler service. And no room at the Empire would be complete without an in-room safe. Odds are the guests here have money to store. If none of these rooms will do, there's always the Emperor's Suite: 666 sq. m of fine silk and bone china, replete with a live-in butler, private dining area, and fully stocked bar.

As of June 2002, no one besides the sultan had yet stayed in the room despite the "modest" B$30,000 per night charge. No matter how much you dish out to stay here, however, breakfast is never included.

If guests grow tired of their fax machines or big screen satellite TVs, a beautifully landscaped 11,000 sq. m saltwater pool along the beachfront and a 50m free-form pool are but steps away.

At the country club, challenge other guests to a game of bowling, take a swing on the Jack Nicklaus-designed 18-hole golf course, or enjoy the in-house cinema, which shows the latest English-language films. Leave your kids in the experienced hands of the hotel's babysitting service.

Finally, the Empire promises a "gastronomic journey to remember." Mediterranean favorites are fused with flavors of the Middle East at the Falafel Restaurant. Sizzling seafood literally served on silver platters pleases any palate at the Pantai Restaurant. And local Malay dishes are served among the alabaster-white marble columns of the Atrium Cafe. *(On the Muara-Tutong Highway, Kampong Jerudong. ☎418 888; www.empire.com.bn.)* ❺

RM70 per day.) Park officers place independent travelers in groups. Bring a change of warm clothes (temperatures can drop below freezing), gloves, hat, raingear, sunscreen, a small flashlight, comfortable shoes with traction, toilet paper, aspirin, bandages, a water bottle, and hard candy or chocolate for quick energy. Store baggage at the park office; free lockers are provided for valuables.

DAY 1. The first day takes you halfway up the mountain in 3-6hr. The trail starts at the power station, a brief bus ride (RM25) or 1hr. trek away. After a brief walk to picturesque **Carson Falls,** it's all uphill along narrow but well-maintained trails. Travelers soon arrive at the first of six rest shelters built along the trail. Over half the plants above 912m, such as the unusual **Kinabalu Balsam** with iridescent purple flowers, are unique to the park. Farther on, you'll see **pitcher plants,** whose large, liquid-filled leaves attract insects that fall and drown in the plants' digestive juices. The largest of the species holds up to two liters of fluid. Gradually, the trail gets steeper, rockier, and increasingly barren. The rare **Kinabalu Warbler** and **Mountain Blackbird** live in these landscapes. In late August and early September, the **rafflesia,** the world's largest flower, blossoms to a striking 1m in diameter. Most climbers spend the night at Laban Rata or one of the nearby huts; a hardy few trek 1.5km farther to Sayat (see **Accommodations,** above). The afternoon is spent recharging for the next day's push to the top.

DAY 2. By 3am the next day, bundled-up climbers set out with flashlights to reach the summit by sunrise. Above Laban Rata is the Panar Laban rock face, where wooden staircases become steep ladders that soon give way to shelves of bare gray granite. Ropes aid climbers up the sheerest parts. The Kadazan guides of early explorers offered sacrifices to appease the spirits of the dead at **Panar Laban** (Place of Sacrifice). The treeline stops here, and thinner air renders the rest of the climb tougher. Take it slow and steady to avoid altitude sickness. **Low's Peak,** at 4101m, rises in a gentle curve from this austere landscape of windswept granite. Tourists vie for the ideal vantage point to capture the sunrise over Borneo. The descent takes 4-8hr. Every climber is eligible to receive a certificate of achievement from the park office that makes all the effort worthwhile (RM2).

DAYTRIP FROM GUNUNG KINABALU: PORING

The sulphurous waters of Poring Hot Springs, 43km east of Kinabalu Park Headquarters are advertised as a miraculous cure for Kinabalu-weary legs. The springs (glorified bathtubs) cost RM10 for a standard tub and RM15 for a larger "deluxe" tub. Poring's isolated setting makes for a soothing visit. Hot tubs, small swimming pools, and a new seven-tiered swimming pool and waterslide are at your service for an additional fee. A brief walk past the baths leads to the **canopy walkway,** a series of suspended boardwalks 60m above the ground. Those intent on seeing wildlife eye-to-eye in the forest area can negotiate nocturnal visits for higher fees. Many trails meander through bamboo thickets and formerly bat-infested caves. A 10min. stroll to the right of the baths is **Kepungit Falls.** Another 2hr. through difficult trails, **Langanan Waterfall** drops 150m. Lepidoptera flutter at the **Butterfly Farm.**

Reserve **accommodations ❶** at Kinabalu Nature Resorts in KK on the ground fl., Wisma Sabah. (☎243 629. Dorms RM12, under 18 RM6. 4-person chalet with ceiling fan, bath, and cooking facilities RM92; 6-person chalet RM115; two 6-person chalets with A/C and a BBQ pit RM288.) The park **restaurant ❷** serves excellent meals. (Banana milkshake RM3; claypot bean curd RM9.) Several restaurants are outside the park and in the dorms there are cooking facilities. *(Canopy walkway open daily 9am-4pm. RM5, cameras RM5, video RM30. Butterfly Farm open Tu-Su 9am-4pm. RM4.)*

SANDAKAN ☎089

Grim and artless, Sandakan's grid of numbered streets and concrete blocks of shops have the charm of army barracks. Indeed, the city served as a Japanese POW camp during WWII. The splendor the city lacks, however, is made up for by its surroundings. Animal and nature lovers alike come seeking the orangutans of nearby Sepilok, the tortoises of the Turtle Islands National Park, and the wilds of the Kinabatangan River's virgin jungle.

TRANSPORTATION

Flights: Airport (☎669 969), 11km outside town. **MAS** (☎273 966), on Jl. Pelabuhan at Jl. Lebuh Dua, Sabah Bldg., 1st fl. Open M-F 8:30am-5pm, Sa 8:30am-1pm. Flights to: **Kota Kinabalu** (RM94); **Kuching** (RM300); **Miri** (RM168).

Buses: Long-distance bus terminal, on Jl. Pryer on the west edge of town. Follow Jl. Tiga out of town and turn left before the pedestrian overpass. To **Kota Kinabalu** (7½hr., regular 3 per day 6:30am-noon, RM20-25; A/C 4 per day, RM15-25; minibuses depart until 2pm, RM25) and **Ranau/Park Headquarters** (A/C 4hr., RM15-18; minibuses depart until 2pm, RM20).

Local Transportation: The **local bus terminal** sends green- and red-striped buses down **Jl. Leila** (RM0.40 to Bandar Ramai-Ramai). Blue *labuk* buses head north on **Jl. Utara** toward the **airport** (RM1.50); some buses cut the route short, so specify your destination before hopping on. Buses show how far—in kilometers (*batu*)—they go from town. *Batu* 14 runs to the **Sepilok Orangutan Rehabilitation Center** (RM1.80). **Taxis** cost RM3-5 within a few kilometers of the city center.

ORIENTATION AND PRACTICAL INFORMATION

Many of Sandakan's streets have similar names, but street signs are scarce. **Lh. Tiga** (not to be confused with **Jl. Tiga,** a cross-street at the east end of town) is the town's main thoroughfare and changes to **Jl. Leila** near the post office. South of Lh. Tiga along the waterfront is **Jl. Pryer.** At Lh. Tiga's extreme east end is the **Wisma Koo Siak Chew Bldg.,** which houses the **Sabah Park Office** and **Telekom Office.** Jl. Leila leads west to the **long-distance bus terminal, night market, post office,** and **Bandar Ramai-Ramai,** home to many restaurants, banks, and budget accommodations.

Tourist Offices: Tourist Information Office (☎229 751), across the town square from the police station on Jl. Empat. Open daily 8am-4:30pm. **Crystal Quest Tours** (☎212 711), at the Sandakan jetty near the yacht club, arranges tours. Open daily 9am-5pm.

Currency Exchange: Hong Kong Bank (☎213 122) cashes traveler's checks. First check RM2.15, each additional RM0.15. **24hr. ATM.** Open M-F 9:30am-3pm, Sa 9:30-11:30am.

Emergency: ☎999.

Police: ☎211 222. On Lh. Empat, north of town.

Pharmacies: Borneo Dispensary, 65 Lh. Tiga (☎213 981), 2 doors from KFC. English spoken. Open M-Sa 8am-5:30pm, Su 8am-12:30pm. AmEx/MC/V.

Hospital: ☎212 111. On Jl. Utara, 3km from the airport. English spoken.

Telephones: Near the long-distance bus terminal. No credit card phones. **Telekom Office,** 6th fl., Wisma Khoo Siak Chew (☎219 292), at east end of Lh. Tiga. **International phone/fax.** Open M-F 8:30am-4:45pm, Sa 8:30am-1pm.

Internet Access: Sandakan Cybercafe, Lot 305, Wisma Sandakan (☎216 150), near Hotel Sandalacan. Fast connections. RM5 per hr. Open M-Sa 9am-10pm, Su 9am-8pm.

Post Office: ☎201 501. On Jl. Leila, next to the supermarket on the outskirts of town. *Poste Restante*. Open M-Sa 8am-5pm. Closed 1st and 3rd Sa of the month. **Postal code:** 90000.

ACCOMMODATIONS

May Fair Hotel, No. 24, Block 26, 1st fl., Jl. Pryer (☎219 892), in front of the market. Newly-renovated rooms boast A/C and private bath. Laundry. 10% student discount. Singles RM36; doubles RM45. ❸

Travelers Rest Hostel, Apt. 2, Block E, 2nd fl., Bandar Ramai-Ramai (☎019 873 4289). 1 block from Jl. Leila, near MayBank Finance. Turn left at the Esso gas station. The tourist-friendly, Nelson, organizes trips to Turtle Island and Kinabatangan River (RM130). Spacious rooms with common bath. Breakfast included. Dorms RM12, with A/C RM15; rooms RM25. ❶

Rose B&B (☎232 582; rosebb@tm.net.my), opposite Travelers Rest Hostel. Clean rooms with common bath. Communal TV. Breakfast included. Dorms RM15; doubles RM25, with A/C RM38. ❷

Hotel Sandakan (☎221 122; fax 221 100; tengis@tm.net.my), on 4th Ave. next to Wisma Sandakan. Friendly service and modern rooms are worth the ringgit. Lounge with live music. Airport transportation RM15 each way. Singles RM173-287; doubles RM196-311. AmEx/MC/V. ❺

FOOD

Stingray-steak vendors compete with used-clothing stalls at Sandakan's **night market** on Jl. Tiga. (Open daily 7pm-late.) Several Indian restaurants and more market stalls line **Jl. Pryer.**

Habeeb III, on Jl. Tiga between Lh. Tiga and Lh. Empat, opposite Wisma Sandakan. Small, friendly, and with A/C. English menu. Indonesian, Malaysian, and Chinese dishes RM3-5. Open daily 8am-11pm. ❶

Supreme Garden Vegetarian Restaurant, Lots 2-3, G/F, Block 30, Bandar Ramai-Ramai, off Jl. Leila (☎213 292 or 222 993). Look for a red and gold sign. *Faux*-pork lunch specials (served M-Sa 11am-1:30pm) RM5. Stuffed bean curd RM8. Open daily 9:30am-1:45pm and 5:30-8:45pm; closed Tu evening. ❷

Kedai Minuman Shamrock, Lot 9, Block 20 (☎220 598), on the corner of Jl. Empat and Jl. Pryer. Excellent beer selection and an up-to-date jukebox. Beef chop with rice RM5. Chicken with mixed vegetable *mee* RM8. Open daily 8am-2am. ❷

Kedai Makanan King Cheong, Block 19, Lot 5A, 2 blocks from MAS office. Cheap Chinese meals and an excellent veggie selection. Owner speaks English. Wonton soup RM1.50. Dishes RM3-6. ❶

MALAYSIA

NEAR SANDAKAN

SEPILOK ORANGUTAN REHABILITATION CENTER

As the world's largest orangutan sanctuary, the center reintroduces infant orangutans taken from their mothers into the reserve. Keep in mind these rules when you visit: don't leave trash anywhere; don't smoke or carry insect repellent; don't get closer than 2m to the animals at any time; and don't attempt to feed any of the animals on the trail. Orangutans are strong, and their idea of play could put you in traction—they aren't known as "the wild man of Borneo" for nothing. They'll jump on your head, steal your camera, strip you naked (as they did to a visitor in 1992), and drop it (the camera) from the tree-tops. There are two daily feedings on platform A (10am and 3pm); arrive 30 minutes before feeding time. The **reception office** (☎215 189) is to the right of the entrance. To reach the center from Sandakan, catch a blue-and-white Sepilok "*Batu* 14" **bus** (45min., 8 per day, RM1.50) from the long-distance bus station. Buses will drop you at the turn-off to the center; from there, it's a 3km walk. (Open daily 9-11am and 2-3pm. RM10, video cameras RM10.)

Most visitors to the center stay at the **Sepilok Jungle Resort ❷** on Labuk Rd., 500m from the park entrance, which boasts an ideal location, resort-style settings, and management that falls over itself to help with trips and travel. (☎533 031. Breakfast included. Dorms RM18; doubles RM40, with A/C RM60; family rooms RM100.) Call for pickup from the main road. **Uncle Tan's ❷,** on Labuk Rd., Lot 8 Block B, SEDCO Complex/Mile 16, Gum Gum, is another great value. From Sandakan, take any bus going beyond *Batu* 16 and ask to be dropped off at Gum Gum. Uncle Tan is a local legend as a former newspaperman, an environmental activist, and a geography teacher. (☎531 917. Meals included. Rooms with mosquito nets and shared bathroom RM20. Reservations recommended.)

TURTLE ISLANDS PARK

Forty kilometers from Sandakan's coast, Turtle Islands Park is made up of three islands—**Selingaan, Gulisan,** and **Bakkungan Kecil.** It is jointly protected by the Malaysian and Philippine governments. It protects **Green** and **Hawksbill Turtles,** whose eggs and flesh are considered delicacies and have been harvested for centuries by the local Cagayan people. Egg counts dropped from 700,000 in the late 1960s to less than 250,000 in 1987. The Green Turtles prefer to lay their eggs on Selingaan from July to September, while the more elusive Hawksbills favor Gulisan from February to April. All eggs laid in Selingaan are collected each evening by park rangers and resettled at the park's turtle hatcheries. After 50-60 days, the turtles emerge and are released into the sea. It's estimated that a mere 3% survive into adulthood. Green turtles are seen year-round, and it's extremely rare for a night to pass without at least one sighting. The islands also offer opportunities to swim and **snorkel** in the Sulu Sea.

Many guest houses offer package tours. Round-trip **transportation** from Sandakan to the park costs RM100. Pricey accommodations are run by **Crystal Quest Sdn. Bhd. ❺.** Make reservations one month in advance at their office at the Sabah Parks Jetty near the yacht club in Sandakan. (☎212 711; mailing address: PO Box 848, 90709, Sandakan, Sabah, Malaysia. Doubles RM125; with shared bath, A/C, and 2 meals RM150 per person.) Crystal Quest is often booked way in advance because it sells its rooms to local tour agencies that jack up the prices.

KINABATANGAN RIVER

Sabah's largest river, the Kinabatangan supports one of the densest wildlife concentrations in the world. The proboscis monkey is the easiest animal to spot, wildly jumping through the jungle canopy as loudly as possible every morning and evening. Other treetop denizens include gibbons, macaques, and the occasional orangutan. On the ground, aardvarks, porcupines and deer meander through the trees, and civet cats are frequent night visitors to the jungle camp kitchens. And if you think you feel an earthquake, it is probably just a herd of elephants passing by.

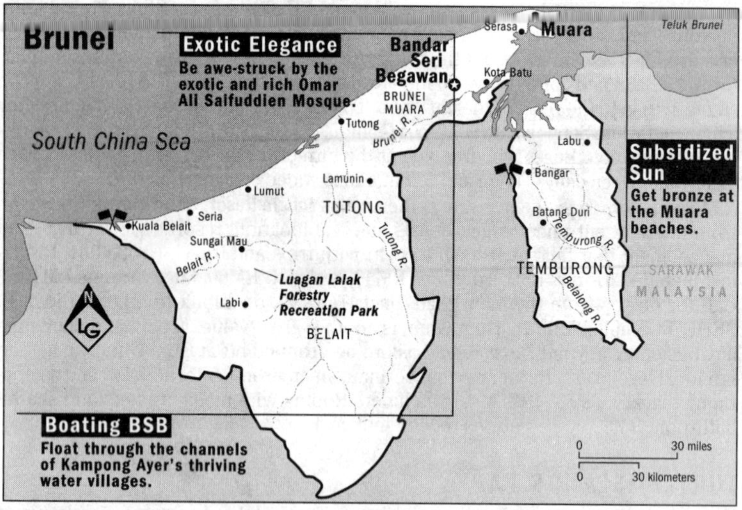

The most distinctive way to see the Kinabatangan River is on an excursion to a local jungle camp. **Jungle Sanctuary** ❷ is run by Sandakan's Travelers' Rest Hostel. The friendly staff leads free excursions for guests and prepare delicious meals. Manager Nelson takes visitors fishing on the lake, but beware of crocodiles! (Transport RM130. Meals included. Rooms RM15.)

BRUNEI DARUSSALAM

US$1 = B$1.75 (BRUNEI DOLLAR)	B$1 = US$0.57
CDN$1 = B$1.13	B$1 = CDN$0.88
EUR€1 = B$1.59	B$1 = EUR€0.63
UK£1 = B$2.54	B$1 = UK£0.39
AUS$1 = B$0.93	B$1 = AUS$1.08
NZ$1 = B$0.77	B$1 = NZ$1.30
ZAR1 = B$0.21	B$1 = ZAR4.77

Citizens of Brunei describe their ruler—His Majesty Paduka Seri Baginda Sultan Haji Hassanal Bolkiah Mu'izzaddin Waddaulah—as a man with a heart of gold. One visit to this geographically tiny yet fabulously wealthy country, and you may start taking them literally. Over the past 20 years, oil has transformed this Islamic sultanate into an impressive "Shellfare state" that offers its citizens free education and health care, no income tax, and subsidized houses, cars, and pilgrimages to Mecca. Bandar Seri Begawan, the stunning capital, has a skyline pierced with some of Asia's most lavish mosques and, courtesy of Jerudong Park Playground, Asia's tallest roller coasters. Fortunately, ostentatious buildings like the royal palace are balanced by the more humble water villages and relatively well-protected rainforest. Unfortunately, Brunei Darussalam—normally translated as "The Abode of Peace"—is more appropriately translated as "The Abode of Boredom." Nightlife is nonexistent, and the sale and consumption of liquor have been banned since 1991. Still, travelers in Borneo should check out the big things in Brunei's small package, even if they can cap off the night with only a soda.

BANDAR SERI BEGAWAN ☎02

Lavish royal monuments such as Omar Ali Saifuddien Mosque and the new Yayasan Sultan Haji Hassanal Bolkiah Mall reflect Brunei's true faiths—Islam and opulence. Shiny SUVs and beaming BMWs crowd the compact city center where banks dot every corner. Reckless speedboats snake through the city's one canal and across the Brunei River to Kampung Ayer, arguably BSB's most charming locale. There, an active water village—home to houses, restaurants, and a floating mosque—booms with life at all hours.

INTERCITY TRANSPORTATION

BY PLANE. The international airport, **Lapangan Terbang Antarabangsa,** is accessible by buses #11, 23, 24, 36, 38, and 57 from downtown BSB (B$1). A PPP taxi costs B$25. Airport departure tax is B$5 for destinations in Malaysia or Singapore (B$12 for other destinations). Airlines serving BSB include: **Garuda Indonesia,** 49-50 Jl. Sultan, Wisma Raya Building, 3rd fl. (☎235 870; open M-F 8:30am-5pm, Sa 8:30am-12:30pm); **MAS,** at 144 Jl. Pemancha (☎223 404); **Royal Brunei Airlines,** RBA Plaza, Jl. Sultan (☎242 222); and **Singapore Airlines** is at 49-50 Jl. Sultan, G/F Wisma Raya Bldg. (☎227 253). Travel agents offer cheaper airfare than the airlines.

DESTINATION	FREQUENCY	PRICE	DESTINATION	FREQUENCY	PRICE
Bangkok	3 per week	B$520	**Kuala Lumpur**	19 per week	B$441
Denpasar	2 per week	B$471	**Kuching**	3 per week	B$244
Hong Kong	3 per week	B$686	**Manila**	5 per week	B$458
Jakarta	4 per week	B$471	**Singapore**	14 per week	B$389
Kota Kinabalu	7 per week	B$81	**Surabaya**	4 per week	B$471

BY BOAT. Boats to and from **Lawas** in Sarawak and **Pulau Labuan** in Sabah (7 per day, B$15) stop at **Muara Port,** 30km east of BSB. The port is accessible by the express bus to Muara from the bus station (every 20min. 6:50am-4:50pm, B$2) or by taxi (B$25). If continuing on to **Kota Kinabalu,** purchase a ticket at **Pulau Labuan, Malaysia** (2½hr., RM28). Contact **Halim Tours & Travels,** 61 Jl. McArthur, for tickets to **Lawas** and **Kota Kinabalu.** (☎226 688. Open M-F 8am-4:30pm, Sa 8am-12pm.) Boats to **Limbang** (12 passengers, leave when full 7am-4pm, B$10) depart from the **ferry terminal** on Jl. McArthur in BSB.

BY BUS. The **bus station** in BSB is on Jl. Cator between Jl. Sultan and Sungai Kianggeh. Buses leave in the morning for **Seria** (1½hr., B$5), with connections to **Kuala Belait** (20min., every hr., B$1). At Kuala Belait, take a bus (30min., free) to the border, where buses go to **Miri, Malaysia** (45min., RM7.50). Get an early start; buses depart infrequently but post departure times in the front windows.

BORDER CROSSINGS: MALAYSIA The main overland crossing is by bus from Kuala Belait in Brunei to **Kuala Baram** (Miri) in Sarawak (p. 459). To cross into **Limbang** or **Liwas,** ferries are most convenient. Ferries connect Brunei to **Pulau Labuan** in the Malaysian province of Sabah.

ORIENTATION

A sliver of Malaysia known as Limbang divides Brunei Darussalam into two areas. To the west of Limbang are the **Belait, Tutong,** and **Brunei-Muara** regions. To the east is the **Temburong** region. BSB is in Brunei-Muara. Downtown BSB, often called "Bandar," extends south to the **Brunei River.** The **bus station** sits on **Jl. Cator** in the heart of Bandar. Jl. Cator meets **Jl. Sultan,** BSB's main street, to the west and **Jl. Sungai Kianggeh** to the east. The **canal** runs adjacent to Jl. Sungai Kianggeh. Across the canal are the **market** and **Pusat Belia.** Both Jl. Sungai Kianggeh and Jl. Sultan end at **Jl. McArthur,** which runs west along the waterfront to the **water taxi stand** and enormous **Yayasan Sultan Haji Hassanal Bolkiah Mall.** Behind the mall is the **Omar Ali Saifuddien Mosque.** Across the river is **Kampung Ayer,** the city's water village. The **Gadong** area houses the **Yaohan Shopping Mall, Kiarong Complex,** and the **Jame'Asr Hassanal Bolkiah Mosque** and borders the **Jerudong Park Playground.**

LOCAL TRANSPORTATION

Buses: Purple buses with A/C run from the **bus station** on Jl. Cator 6:30am-6pm or earlier (B$1). Express bus #33 to **Muara** B$2. Bus #11 runs most frequently, making a circular route by the **hospital, Center Point shopping district, government buildings,** and **the immigration office.** Bus #55 goes to **Jerudong Park,** #39 to the **museum,** #21 to **Kiarong Complex,** and #22 to **Jame'Asr Hassanal Bolkiah Mosque.**

Taxis: Purple Pelangi (PPP) taxis (☎394 949) wait outside major hotels and the bus station. Taxis run 6am-10pm to: **airport** (B$25); **Gadong** (B$10); **Jeradong Park** (B$25). Within town, it's B$3. It's difficult to hail cabs, so call the office instead. Booking fee B$1. **John Kwang** (☎08 731 818) is fast, reliable, and skillful.

Water taxis: Hail popular water taxis at the stand behind the Yayasan Sultan Haji Hassanal Bolkiah Mall or along the canal by the market on Jl. Sungai Kianggeh. B$0.50-3, tours B$10 per 30-60min. Fares are negotiable

PRACTICAL INFORMATION

BRUNEI

TOURIST, FINANCIAL, AND LOCAL SERVICES

Tourist Offices: Information counter at airport (☎330 142, ext. 364). **Tourist Information Center,** Jl. Elizabeth Dua, next door to the post office. Free maps and brochures. Useful *Explore Brunei* booklet at both locations. Both open daily 8am-4:30pm.

Tours: Freme Travel Service Sdn., Unit 403B, Wisma Jaya, Jl. Pemancha (☎234 280). Tours B$36-B$140 per person; inquire about min. number of people. Open M-F 8am-noon and 1:30-5pm, Sa 8am-noon. Tourism guru **Danny** (danny25174@hotmail.com) hangs out near the bus station.

Embassies: Australian High Commission, 4th fl., Teck Guan Plaza, Jl. Sultan (☎229 435). Open M-Th 8am-4:30pm, F 8am-4pm. **British High Commission,** 2nd fl., Block D, Complex Yayasan Sultan Haji Hassanal Bolkiah (☎222 231). Open M-Th 8:30am-5pm, F 8:30am-12:30pm. **Cambodia,** No. 8, Simpang 845, Kampong Tasek Meradun, Jl. Tutong BF 1520 (☎654 046). Open M-F 8:30am-5pm. **Canadian High Commission,** 5th fl., 1 Jl. McArthur (☎220 043). Open M-F 8:30am-5pm. **Laos,** No. 11 Simpang

FAST TIMES IN NEW BRUNEI In 1967, 21-year-old Hassanal Bolkiah became the Sultan of Brunei. As the country's oil and natural gas reserves were exploited in the 1970s and 80s, the sultan grew richer than Midas. His palace, the largest on the planet, tops Versailles with 1788 rooms, 500 chandeliers, 14 acres of marble, and hundreds of polo ponies in air-conditioned stables. For years, the sultan was the wealthiest person alive, until American software magnate Bill Gates stole the title. The sultan and his brother, children, wives, lovers, and advisers have blown nearly US$21.8 billion since 1987, making them the biggest spenders in history. More recently, the high-profile royal family has found itself besieged by international scandal and family turmoil. 1998 was an especially troubled year, as Prince Jefri, the sultan's youngest brother and Finance minister, led the Amedeo Development Corporation to bankruptcy at the nadir of the Asian financial crisis. Jefri was fired from the position of Finance minister, but Brunei's holdings have dropped to just a third of their peak value; the sultan brought a lawsuit against his brother, but settled when Prince Jefri agreed to give back assets he had acquired while he was Finance minister.

On the heels of the Amedeo crash, Jefri's actions were further questioned by a former Miss USA, who sued both him and the sultan for US$56 million for allegedly luring her to Brunei and pressuring her to become a sex slave. The case was dismissed because of state immunity. Jefri has since faced a multi-million-dollar civil lawsuit brought by creditors. In light of these many costly legal tangles, the prince has auctioned off thousands of his personal possessions, including hundreds of gold-plated toilet brush holders, two fire engines, and a Comanche attack helicopter simulator.

480, Jl. Kebangsaan Lama (☎345 666). **Malaysia High Commission,** No. 27 and 29, Simpang 396-39, Kampung Sungai Akar, Mukim Berakas B, Jl. Kebangsaan (☎345 652). Open M-Th, Sa 9am-noon and 3-4pm. **Myanmar,** No. 14, Simpang 212, Jl. Kampong Rimba, Gadong BE 3119 (☎450 506). Open M-F 8am-4:30pm. **Philippines,** Rooms 1 and 2, 6th fl., Badi'ah Building, Mile 1, Jl. Tutong (☎241 465). Open M-F 8:30am-12:30pm and 1:30-5:30pm, Sa 9am-noon. **Singapore High Commission,** No. 8 Simpang 74, Jl. Subok (☎262 741). Open M-F 8:30am-5pm. **Thailand,** No. 2 Simpang 52-86-16, Kampong Bunut, Jl. Tutong BF 1320 (☎653 108). Open M-F 9am-5pm. **US,** 3rd fl., Teck Guan Plaza, Jl. Sultan (☎229 670). Open M-F 8am-4:30pm. **Vietnam,** House 16, Simpang 538-37-2. Jl. Kebangsaan Lama (☎343 167). Open M-Sa 8-10am and 2-4:30pm.

Currency Exchange: Hong Kong Bank (☎242 305), at Jl. Sultan and Jl. Pemancha. Open M-F 9am-3pm, Sa 9-11am. **ATM** (Cirrus). **Standard Chartered Bank,** 51-55 Jl. Sultan (☎242 386). Unlimited exchange B$15. Open M-F 9am-3pm, Sa 9-11am.

Markets: Tamu Kianggeh Market, on the opposite side of the canal from Jl. Sungai Kianggeh. Open daily 8am-6pm. **Pasar Malam** (night market), opposite Sheraton Hotel on Jl. Tasek. Savory *satay* and good souvenirs.

EMERGENCY AND COMMUNICATIONS

Emergency: ☎993. **Fire:** ☎995. **Ambulance:** ☎991.

Police: ☎242 334. On Jl. Stoney near the intersection with Jl. Elizabeth Dua.

Pharmacies: Guardian Pharmacy, Yayasan Sultan Haji Hassanal Bolkiah Mall, ground fl. Open daily 10am-9:45pm.

Hospital: RIPAS (Rajah Isteri Pengiran Anak Saheha Hospital; ☎242 424), on Jl. Putera Al-Muhtadee Billah across Edinburgh Bridge. Take bus #11. English spoken. **Klinik Kuin Mee,** 72 Jl. Roberts (☎243 546). Open daily 7:30am-1pm and 2-5:30pm.

Telephones: Telegraph Office (☎222 323), on Jl. Sultan behind the post office. **International phone/fax.** Open daily 8am-10pm. **Directory Assistance:** ☎113.

Internet Access: LA Cybercafé, 2nd fl., Block D, Yayasan Sultan Haji Hassanal Bolkiah Mall (☎225 298). B$1 per 15min. Open M-Sa 9:30am-9:30pm, Su 10am-6pm. **Jubilee Hotel** offers Internet access daily 9am-10pm on the second floor (B$1 per hr.).

Post Office: ☎228 291. At the corner of Jl. Sultan and Jl. Elizabeth Dua. *Poste Restante.* Open M-Th and Sa 8am-4:30pm, F 8-11am and 2-4pm. **Postal code:** BS8611.

ACCOMMODATIONS

BSB's budget accommodations are rarely full; the exception is during celebrations of the sultan's birthday (July 15-31). At mid-range hotels, always ask for the "promotion" or "discount" rates, which may be 25-30% cheaper than listed prices.

Pusat Belia (☎222 900), on Jl. Sungai Kianggeh. With the canal on the right, it's to the right of the youth center building. Bring ISIC or youth hostel ID. Curfew 10:30pm. Closed for 2 weeks following the sultan's birthday. Check in early; the staff takes an endless lunch break. Curfew 10:30pm. Clean, single-sex 4-bed A/C dorm rooms with shared baths. Dorms B$10. ❶

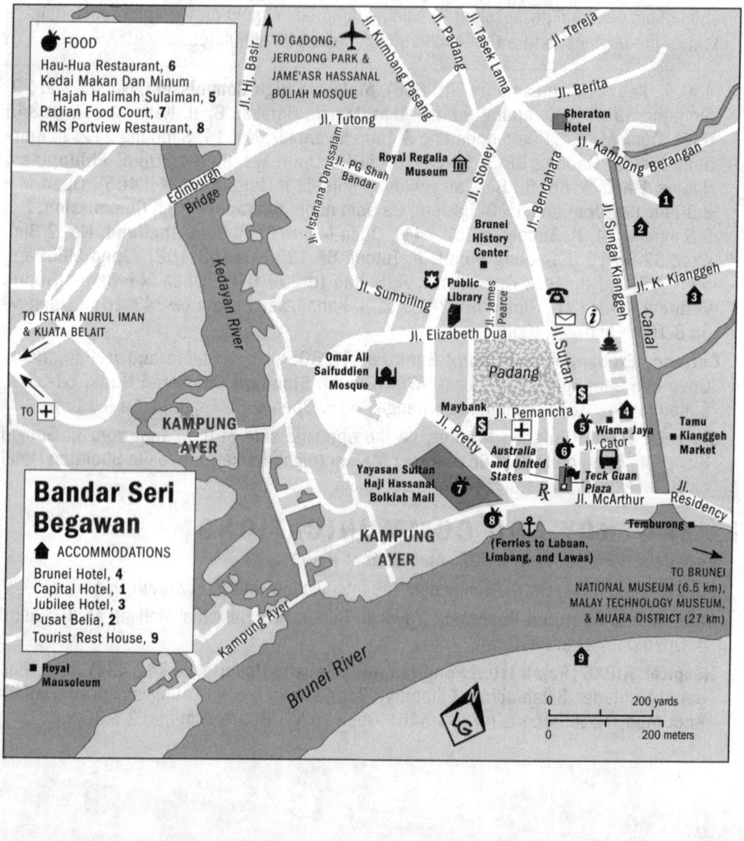

Tourist Rest House, Ketua Kampong (☎202 140), just across the river in Kampung Ayer. Take a boat from town (B$0.50) and head straight for the cream-colored building with a green roof. Clean rooms have A/C, Internet, and breakfast. Check-out noon. B$20 per person. ❷

Jubilee Hotel, Jubilee Plaza, Jl. Kampung Kianggeh (☎228 070; jubilee@brunet.bn). Turn right past the temple; it's before Pusat Belia. Offers free transport to/from the airport, Internet, cafe, and free breakfast. Singles and doubles B$70. AmEx/MC/V. ❹

Capital Hotel, No. 7, Simpang 2, Kampung Berangan (☎223 561), behind Pusat Belia. Go down Jl. Sungai Kianggeh, right on Jl. Berangan, and right onto Simpang 2. Singles B$55; doubles B$60. AmEx/MC/V. ❹

Brunei Hotel, 95 Jl. Pemancha (☎242 372), opposite the canal. Big rooms for a relatively small price. Fully stocked minibar, satellite TV, and free breakfast. Singles B$88; doubles B$99. AmEx/MC/V. ❺

FOOD

Near Pusat Belia, the **night market** ❶ behind the Chinese temple on Jl. Elizabeth Dua provides a selection of dishes and iced drinks (most items B$1). A similar **night market** ❶ sets up at the end of Jl. Sungai Kianggeh on the waterfront. (Both open daily sundown-midnight.) Pork-lovers and alcoholics be warned. As a strict Islamic state, Brunei follows a "no booze, no bacon" policy. **Kedai Makan Dan Minum Hajah Halimah Sulaiman** ❶**,** No 34 Jl. Sultan, opposite the Hong Kong Bank on Jl. Pemancha, has generous servings of the best Indian/Malay fare around. (☎234 803. *Dosai* with chicken B$3.50. Open daily 6am-9:35pm.) In Block H, Yayasan Mall, **RMS Portview Restaurant** ❸ serves up Brunei's best seafood. (☎231 465. Savory steamboats with fish, crab, vegetables, and noodles B$13 per person. Set menus B$26-30. Open daily 10am-2am. AmEx/MC/V.) On the first floor of the Yayasan Mall, **Padian Food Court** ❶ offers Malay, Indian, Indonesian, and Chinese cuisine. (Most entrees B$3-5. Fresh squid soup B$12. Open daily 9am-10pm.) **Hau-Hua Restaurant** ❶**,** No. 48 Jl. Sultan, next to Standard Chartered Bank, serves *wonton* soup for B$3 and Western breakfast for B$8. (Open daily 7am-9pm. AmEx/MC/V.)

SIGHTS

For those short on time, the best of Brunei can be seen via water taxi; ask for an hour tour (B$10-20, negotiable).

OMAR ALI SAIFUDDIEN MOSQUE. The city's most visible landmark was built in 1958 at a cost of US$500 million. Its golden dome—covered with 3.3 million pieces of Venetian glass mosaic—is only part of the grandeur. Italian marble and English stained glass dominate the interior. The replica 16th-century royal barge in its man-made lagoon occasionally hosts lively Qur'an-reading competitions. Worshipers wash before entering at the fountain on the far side. Dress conservatively and remove shoes before entering. *(On the west side of downtown; enter on Jl. Elizabeth Dua. Open Su-W 8am-noon, 1-3:30pm, and 4:30-5:30pm; F 4:30-5:30pm. Closed Th to non-Muslims.)*

KAMPUNG AYER AND ENVIRONS. Behind the mosque, **water villages** unfold along the Brunei River. This labyrinth of brightly-colored homes and restaurants sits on stilts above the water. Boardwalks link the neighborhoods of Kampung Ayer, but a less strenuous option is to explore the area by water taxi (see **Local Transportation,** p. 480). Make sure the taxi driver goes to the newest residential development at the far end, where white cookie-cutter homes stand on concrete piles, in contrast to the rickety wooden structures closer to town. While barreling around the Brunei River, check out the **Persiaran Damuan,** a landscaped park across the river on Jl. Tutong; it offers the city's best view of the **Istana Nurul Iman,** the world's largest palace and residence of the sultan. Visitors are allowed inside the palace once a year—at the end of Ramadan. Surprise: more golden domes and marble await inside this grand building.

BRUNEI MUSEUM. Modesty must not be a virtue in Brunei. His Majesty's Muslim art and artifacts, rescued from shipwrecks, exhibit the long history of wealth in the sultanate. The collection includes Qur'ans carved from sheets of gold and a shrine to the oil industry. *(6.5km east of BSB. Take bus #39 or an express bus to Muara. Open Su-Th 9:30am-5pm, F 9:30-11:30am and 2:30-5pm.)*

JAME'ASR HASSANAL BOLKIAH MOSQUE. This fancy mosque beckons worshipers, architecture enthusiasts, and tourists alike. Recently completed in commemoration of His Majesty's 25 years on the throne, Jame'Asr Hassanal Bolkiah Mosque, the largest in Brunei, trumps Omar Ali Saifuddien Mosque in every category, including gaudiness. Upon entry, remove your shoes and register at the security post. The sultan prays here on Fridays. *(In Gadong. Take bus #21 or 22. Open Su-W 8am-noon, 1-1:30pm, and 4:30-5:30pm; F 4:30-5:30pm. Closed Th to non-Muslims.*

ENTERTAINMENT

JERUDONG PARK PLAYGROUND. Even in alcohol-free Brunei, nights don't have to be tame. **Jerudong Park Playground,** the greatest attraction in BSB and, perhaps, the country, allows Bruneians and visitors alike to get high. Rides such as the **Giant Drop** and the exhilarating **Pusing Lagi** shoot passengers nearly 100m above the state-of-the-art amusement park. While airborne, guests are also privy to amazing views of the South China Sea. The less adventurous can enjoy the more mundane merry-go-round, bumper cars, and beautifully landscaped botanical gardens—all connected by a locomotive system. Each night, the spectacular "Dancing Fountain" laser show electrifies visitors with lurid lighting amidst 1216 nozzles spraying 20,000 gallons of water upward. A food court is next to the parking lot. Although the park was built in 1994 by the sultan as a gift to his people, the formerly free attraction began charging an admission fee during the 2001 season (B$1, B$4 per ride). Alternatively, visitors can purchase an unlimited pass, which includes admission and as many rides as you can stomach. (B$15, B$5 for children.) The cheapest option, which includes transportation, is to purchase an all-inclusive ticket (B$15) available from the Tourist's Information Center one day in advance. Jerudong is beyond the Bandar city limits. Take bus #55 before 5pm and arrange for a PPP cab to take you back (B$25). The manager of Pusat Belia also takes groups of four (B$10). The grounds are closed M-Tu for maintenance and open W-Su 2pm-midnight. Rides start operating at 5pm, but stop 6-8pm during Muslim prayers. The best time to go, unless you want to pray, is after 8pm.

OTHER ENTERTAINMENT. Outside BSB are a few scattered sights, all difficult to reach by public transportation. **Muara and Surasa beaches,** in Muara District, are considered Brunei's finest. Temburong District is home to **Ulu Temburong National Park, Peradayan Forest Recreational Park,** and the **Rainforest Field Studies Center (FSC)** at Kuala Belalong in Batu Apoi Forest Reserve. Travelers must go with a tour. **Freme Travel** (see **Tours,** p. 480) runs tours. (B$140, with rafting B$180; overnight tours from B$220. All require at least 2 people.)

MYANMAR

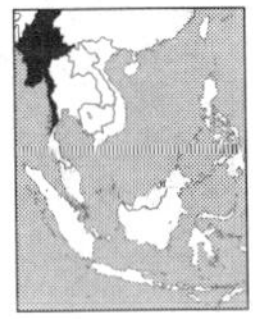

US$1 =6.39KYAT*, 750KYAT*	100KYAT = US$15.64, $0.133
CDN$1 = 4.10KYAT, 500KYAT	100KYAT = CDN$24.38, $0.2
EUR€1 = 6.27KYAT, 750KYAT	100KYAT = EUR€15.95, €0.133
UK£1 = 9.96KYAT, 1150KYAT	100KYAT - UK£10.04, £0.087
AUS$1 = 3.50KYAT, 400KYAT	100KYAT = AUS$28.57, $0.243
NZ$1 = 3.00KYAT, 350KYAT	100KYAT = NZ$33.31, $0.286
ZAR1 = 0.61KYAT, 75KYAT	100KYAT = ZAR164.32, R1.333

*Dual exchange rates reflect disparity between the pegged government rate and the market rate. The official rate is listed first, followed by the black-market rate. Rates change as much as 20% daily (see **Money,** p. 496). Only hard currencies such as those listed above are accepted for FEC conversion. Travelers should carry some amount of the above currencies when traveling to Myanmar.

PHONE CODE **Country code:** 95. **International dialing prefix:** 00.

There are two visions of Myanmar. One is of a country with glittering pagodas and a glorious past, where village life thrives undisturbed and the serenity of the country's Buddhist faith seeps into a culture of gentleness and respect. The other describes one of the poorest countries in Southeast Asia, where real incomes are lower now than they were at independence, a government represses and tortures its own people, the will of a people for democratic freedom is ruthlessly suppressed, and slave labor is the norm for public works. Both these visions grasp at some aspect of the reality of Myanmar today. Known until recently as Burma, it has been a hermit state since the 1960s and was opened up to foreign investment and tourism only in 1989—a change that many hope will be the primary agent of some movement toward reform in the country. Travelers who step down at Yangon Airport will find golden *stupas*, picturesque lakes, and unspoiled mountain scenery. Myanmar's arid central plains gave rise to some of Southeast Asia's greatest civilizations. The country's jewel, the ancient city of Bagan, is rivaled only by Angkor Wat as the most breathtaking sight in Southeast Asia. Perhaps the greatest treasure in Myanmar, however, is the grace of the Burmese people amidst the fierceness of their repression. The paradoxes of Myanmar are still alive.

FACTS AND FIGURES

Official Name: Union of Myanmar.

Government: Military rule.

Capital: Yangon.

Land Area: 676,522 sq. km.

Geography: Borders Bangladesh, India, China, Thailand, and Laos. River Systems: Ayeyarwady, Chindwin, Mekong, Sittang, Salween. Mountain Ranges: Himalayas in northern Myanmar.

Climate: Dry (high season) Oct.-May, rainy (low season) June-Sept.

Major Cities: Bago, Mandalay, Pathein.

Population: 47,700,000.

Languages: Burmese, English.

Religion: Buddhism, Islam, Christianity, Hinduism, other.

Average Income Per Capita: US$150.

Major Exports: Teak, rice, rubber, wood.

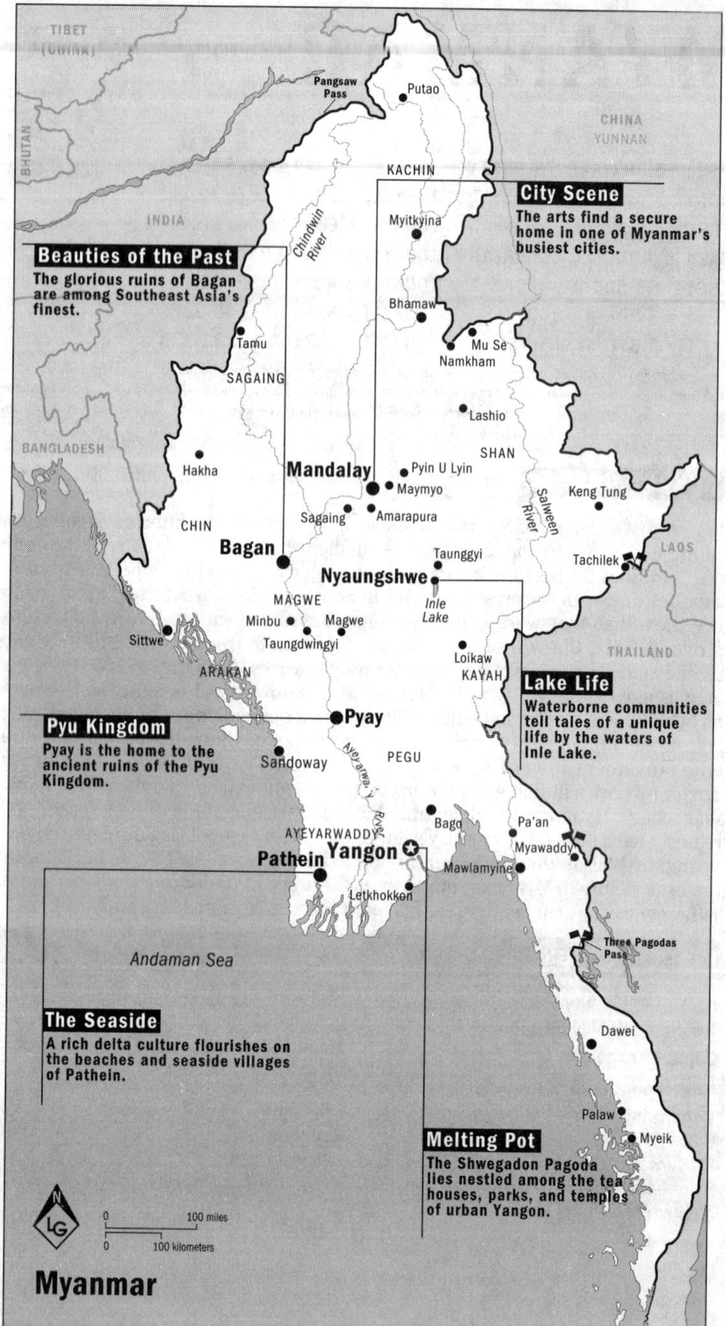
TIBET (CHINA)
Pangsaw Pass
Putao
CHINA
YUNNAN
BHUTAN
KACHIN
City Scene
The arts find a secure home in one of Myanmar's busiest cities.
INDIA
Chindwin River
Myitkyina
Beauties of the Past
The glorious ruins of Bagan are among Southeast Asia's finest.
Bhamaw
Tamu
Mu Se
Namkham
SAGAING
Lashio
BANGLADESH
SHAN
Hakha
Mandalay
Pyin U Lyin
Maymyo
Salween River
Keng Tung
Sagaing
Amarapura
CHIN
Bagan
Taunggyi
LAOS
Tachilek
Nyaungshwe
Inle Lake
MAGWE
Minbu
Magwe
Taungdwingyi
Sittwe
Loikaw
THAILAND
ARAKAN
KAYAH
Lake Life
Waterborne communities tell tales of a unique life by the waters of Inle Lake.
Pyu Kingdom
Pyay
Pyay is the home to the ancient ruins of the Pyu Kingdom.
Sandoway
Ayeyarwady River
PEGU
Bago
Pa'an
AYEYARWADDY
Yangon
Myawaddy
Pathein
Mawlamyine
Letkhokkon
Three Pagodas Pass
Andaman Sea
The Seaside
A rich delta culture flourishes on the beaches and seaside villages of Pathein.
Dawei
Palaw
Myeik
Melting Pot
The Shwegadon Pagoda lies nestled among the tea houses, parks, and temples of urban Yangon.
N
LG
0
100 miles
0
100 kilometers
Myanmar

MYANMAR

LIFE AND TIMES

DEMOGRAPHICS

Although the government officially recognizes over 135 different ethnicities, Myanmar's main ethnic groups are the **Burman** (68%), **Shan** (9%), **Karen** (7%), **Rakhine** (4%), and **Mon** (2%). It is likely that the actual percentage of the Burman population is closer to 50%; the government counts as Burman anyone who is listed as Buddhist or anyone with a Burman name, which many Burmese have adopted in order to avoid discrimination. The Shan live in the mountain ranges near the border with Thailand and have been struggling for centuries to establish an autonomous state. The Karen also have a complex relationship with the Burman majority, dating back to the times when they were drafted as cannon-fodder for the Burman armies. The last **official census** was taken in 1931, which speaks more about the central Burmese authorities than it does about the country's population. In 1994, *Asiaweek* quoted the population as 45.5 million, but a lack of reliable data makes this statistic rather nebulous. Academics today place the figure between 47 and 48 million.

LANGUAGE

The official language is **Burmese,** although ethnic minority groups often have their own dialects and languages. The Burmese script has only recently been adapted to many of the tribal languages; these previously had no written form. The precise name of the country is a subject of much contention. In 1989, the ruling military junta outlawed the name **"Burma"** in an attempt to purge the nation of its past as a British colony. After all, it was the Brits who corrupted the local word for the Burman ethnic group, *Bamar*, in order to create "Burma" in the first place; in Burmese, the nation has been referred to as **"Myanmar"** since the time of Marco Polo. Still, the "r" at the end of Myanmar is merely a linguistic construct to lengthen the last syllable; most government-run organizations leave off the "r" in favor of a more accurate romanization of the Burmese word, **"Myanma."** Most of the international press, however, refuses to acknowledge these changes as a symbolic gesture of their non-recognition of the ruling military junta.

RELIGION

THERAVADA BUDDHISM. It was not until 1044, when **King Anawratha** ascended to the throne of the Burmese Kingdom in Bagan, that Buddhism became the dominant religion in the region, brought by **Indian merchants** looking for commercial opportunities in the Ayeyarwady delta. Today, about 85% of the Burmese population practices Theravada Buddhism, but over the centuries, the religion has become laced with aspects of **animism** and **spirit worship.** As the center of the community, Buddhist temples serve educational as well as spiritual purposes. Additionally, affiliation with Buddhism often serves political ends, since the junta, infamous for its "whimsical" favoritism, tends to favor Buddhists and Buddhism.

CHRISTIANITY. A prominent 19th-century missionary to Myanmar, **Adoniram Judson** translated the Bible from Hebrew into Burmese and worked successfully to convert a large portion of the **Karen** minority group to Christianity. Based on the mystique surrounding the Karen's history and their creation myths, which many scholars believe echo Judeo-Christian stories, it has been suggested that the Karen may, in fact, be a **lost tribe of Israel.** Their Christianity has fostered an uneasy relationship between them and the Burman majority and has resulted in waves of Karen refugees flooding across the Thai border to live in refugee camps.

MYANMAR: TO GO OR NOT TO GO? The question of whether to go to Myanmar echoes the debate that once plagued travelers to South Africa under apartheid. Tourism in Myanmar undoubtedly financially supports one of the world's worst military regimes, but the reality for the people of Myanmar is not nearly so simple. In one of Southeast Asia's poorest countries, the fledgling tourist industry is, for many, the only alternative to state-sponsored slave labor. Increasingly relaxed tourist regulations mean that informed travelers can direct their money to Myanmar's people, not to its repressive government (see **Keep the Bucks Where They Belong**, p. 496). Many Burmese hope that more travelers will visit their impoverished nation and bring money with them; some also want travelers to witness the political situation and tell others about it. The Burmese government's abuses are not a new story, yet they have only recently come to the attention of the world after the country opened up to foreign investment and tourism in 1989. Many argue that responsible and informed tourism is a far more effective means to change than isolating a military government that then has no incentive to stop its abuse of power. Nonetheless, it is important to note that Burmese citizens have disappeared or been beaten severely for discussing politics with foreigners, no doubt due to an insidious network of government informants. Military intelligence interrogated a family-restaurant owner for 24hr. after he spoke with travelers who tried to visit one of Myanmar's "no-go" areas. For locals' sake, if you decide to travel to Myanmar, **avoid discussion of politics** and educate yourself about how to avoid empowering the military junta. The choice to travel to Myanmar is yours. *Let's Go* asks only that you make it an informed one.

ISLAM. Myanmar claims that Muslims enjoy freedom of worship. The veracity of this statement was somewhat undermined in mid-2002 when the international media picked up on the 18 illegal Muslim **refugees** who were seeking asylum in Malaysia, claiming that their lives in Myanmar were filled with fear of arrest and harassment. These are only the latest Muslim Burmese refugees in Malaysia; between 1991 and 1992, about 2500 Muslims fled to Malaysia from Burmese military persecution but were repatriated with the help of the **United Nations.**

NAT WORSHIP. The practice of *nat* worship still remains popular among many of the people of Myanmar. Considered the embodiment of a god, a *nat* is a traditional **animistic spirit.** The concept of the *nat* has evolved over time to designate a spirit that can hold power over a place, person, field, or experience. Most are still animistic in form, and all possess the power to wreak havoc on life. The Burmese reconcile *nat* worship with Buddhism with an easy maxim: *nat* worship tackles problems in this life, while Buddhism takes care of karma in the life to come.

FLORA AND FAUNA

Like much else in Myanmar, statistics on the country's plant and animal species are fuzzy. Some reports suggest that the flora and fauna of some regions in Myanmar have not been extensively studied since the 1800s. But with 1930km of coastline, central plains, and rugged highlands, Myanmar has extremely diverse wildlife. Unfortunately, deforestation and industrial pollution threaten these fragile ecosystems. Additionally, projects such as the **Yadana pipeline** and other governmental pipe dreams of rags-to-riches economic transformation have destroyed a great deal of rainforest and the plant and animal life within. Even in the country's national parks and wildlife preserves, which cover less than 1% of Myanmar's land area, the wildlife is protected, but the habitat is not.

FLORA. Myanmar's **teak** forests, which account for over 80% of the world's teak, are being clear-cut at a rate that far outstrips that of the Amazonian rainforest. The forests were opened to Thai loggers so that the government could earn foreign credit, but this economically motivated plan has only temporarily bumped up the country's export statistics, while the countryside is riddled with deforested areas, as fewer than 50,000 acres are replanted annually.

FAUNA. Myanmar has the most diverse population of birds in Southeast Asia, including 47 endangered birds. The **Sumatran Rhino,** the only rhino with hair on its body and the only Asian rhino with two horns, is on the brink of extinction; only a few remain, scattered throughout Myanmar, Malaysia, Thailand, and Sumatra. They live in the dense forests that are rapidly disappearing throughout the region. Also inhabiting these dense forests, the **binturong** fetches between US$1500-2000 in US exotic pet markets. Nocturnal and arboreal, the binturong is poached for its meat and for use in traditional aphrodisiacs. **Tigers** are another key ingredient in many traditional recipes; unfortunately, hunting tigers is still legal in Myanmar, which contains 40% of Southeast Asia's priority tiger habitat.

HISTORY

PREHISTORY

Five thousand years ago, the first humans settled in the **Ayeyarwady Valley.** The **Pyu** joined the upper valley around 200 BC and grew wealthy by controlling the lucrative trade route from China to India. Two centuries later, they were joined by the **Mon.** When their last major city fell to the Chinese in AD 832, the Burmese took over the Pyu River area and established the city of **Bagan** in 849.

BAGAN AND TOUNGOO DYNASTIES (1044-1776)

IMPORTANT DATES				
1044 Bagan Dynasty established under King Anawratha.	**10-12th Centuries** 3000 temples constructed.	**1287** Mongol Invasion of lower Myanmar.	**1546** Tabinshweti reunifies nation.	**1752** Toungoo Dynasty falls.

Myanmar's first unified kingdom rose under the **Bagan Dynasty,** founded in 1044 by **King Anawrahta,** who pronounced Theravada Buddhism the new state religion and expanded the kingdom. Under **King Alaungsithu,** Theravada Buddhism became increasingly dominant. Now seen as the **"classical age"** of Bagan, the dynasty saw the building of an estimated 3000 temples, 100 of which still stand. The beginning of the empire's demise was marked by the Mongol invasion of 1287 headed by **Kublai Khan.** In the 16th century, Burmese forces rose again. Declaring himself king, **Tabinshwehti** reunified Myanmar under the **Toungoo Dynasty** and established its capital at Pegu in 1546. But frequent wars with the Thai kings and the Arakanese minorities led to the fall of the Toungoo rulers in 1752. **Alaungpaya** emerged as a powerful leader against the Toungoo and gained control of Myanmar, establishing the new city of Yangon. Following Alaungpaya's death in 1760, however, border conflicts escalated to war with Siam. **King Hsinbyushin** sacked Ayutthaya in 1776 and killed the king of Siam, creating an enmity that still festers today. After the Thais recaptured Ayutthaya, the tyrranical **King Bodawpaya** spent his reign embarking on several failed attempts to re-invade Siam. His frustrations turned into religious persecution against anyone breaching Buddhist doctrine, and he strictly enforced the death penalty for smoking opium.

COLONIALISM (1777-1945)

IMPORTANT DATES

1824 First Anglo-Burmese war.	**1900-1930** British colonial rule.	**1930** Burmese Liberation movement.	**1937** New constitution adopted.	**1943** Aung San founds AFPFL.

The second Burmese invasion of the Arakan region, bordering British colonial territory in India, instilled fear in the British that Myanmar would continue to expand, finally culminating in the **Anglo-Burmese Wars** of 1824 and 1852. Britain won both wars and subsequently annexed Pegu Province, renaming it **Lower Burma.** The third Anglo-Burmese War gave Britain control over Myanmar in 1886; they renamed it "Burma" (see **Language,** p. 487) and made it a province of India with a capital at Yangon (Rangoon). During colonial occupation, Britain sought to exploit Myanmar's rich oil and mineral deposits, building fledgling industries. However, the people of Burma didn't receive many benefits from these economic boosts. The British eliminated the monarchy and separated religion and government, thereby destabilizing Burmese society. An increase in the number of Indian immigrants (already over 7% of the population) displaced local labor and caused increasing economic duress. Resentment toward Indians culminated in the violent anti-Indian riots of the **Burmese national liberation movement** in 1930 as well as the expulsion of over half a million Indians by the Burmese army during World War II. **Dr. Ba Maw** was elected Prime Minister in 1936 in the first and only election under British control. In 1937, Burma adopted a new constitution. The country's abundant natural resources and access road to China made it attractive to the **Japanese** during World War II; in March 1942, they seized Rangoon but were forced to withdraw in 1943. Meanwhile, Minister of Defense **Aung San** began a movement of organized resistance against the Japanese and planned to achieve complete independence for Burma with his **Anti-Fascist People's Freedom League (AFPFL).**

INDEPENDENCE (1945-1960)

IMPORTANT DATES

1947 Burma gains independence.	**1948** Britain recognizes the Republic of the Union of Burma.	**1950** Civil war breaks out with minority rebel armies.

After World War II, the British took over, suspended the 1937 constitution, and implemented a governor system. As the new leader of the **Council of Ministers,** Aung San expelled the Communists from the AFPFL in 1946 and began to pressure the British to free Burma completely. Aung San was slain by right-wing politician **U Saw** in July 1947, just two months before the **Burma Constituent Assembly,** under **Thakin Nu,** earned complete independence as the Republic of the Union of Burma. In opposition to the declaration, communists and other minority factions revolted, breaking the government's control over most of the country. In 1948, minority Karen groups rebelled and cut off Rangoon's river, rail, and road communication systems. At the height of the **civil war** in 1950, many nations, including Britain and India, supplied the Burmese government with weaponry and money.

THE ARMY OF SPIRITS In early 1999, two 12-year-old twins named Luther and Johnny, cigars hanging from their mouths and machine guns casually slung over their shoulders, gained international infamy for leading a fundamentalist Christian group of 200 Karen rebels, known as "God's Army." Their followers swear that the adolescent twins can't be killed by bullets or mine fields. In a Burmese army attack on their village near the Myanmar-Thailand border, the twins emerged unscathed from a cavalcade of bullets and defeated the Burmese with what many believe is an "army of spirits" that fights alongside the messiahs. In January 2000, the boys and their "army" tried to strong-arm the Thai government into opening their border to Karen refugees by taking more than 100 hostages in a Thai hospital across the border. But the Thai military raided the hospital killing nine of the gunmen (Johnny and Luther were conspicuously absent). However, the twins' "magical powers" didn't last forever—in January 2001, 17 members of "God's Army," including Luther and Johnny, surrendered to the Thai army authorities.

MILITARY RULE (1962-1995)

IMPORTANT DATES

1962 First Military Government; BSPP established.	**1962** Military crushes protests.	**1988** SLORC takes over.	**1989** "Burma" becomes "Myanmar."	**1990** SLORC throws out election results.

In March 1962, **General Ne Win,** tired of threats of secession from ethnic groups, arrested prominent leaders, revoked the 1947 constitution, and established a military government. Citizens raged at restrictions on their freedoms, and students at Rangoon University demonstrated against the regime. Acting on the indirect orders of General Ne Win, soldiers fired into the crowds and bombed the Students' Union, a Burmese nationalist symbol since 1930. Eyewitnesses reported hundreds of bodies strewn across the campus, but the official report cited only 15 deaths and 27 wounded. To protect Burma from insurgent groups, the government established **Ka Kwe Ye (KKY),** or "Home Guard," a local militia group supported with help from the area's druglords, who often bribed government drug enforcement officials to turn a blind eye to the area's thriving opium trade. After General Ne Win retired in 1972, the country sought foreign aid to combat serious economic stagnation caused by financial mismanagement and rampant corruption. By the late 1980s, resource-rich Burma had become one of the poorest nations in the world. Widespread anti-government riots erupted in Rangoon in October 1987, again accompanied by demonstrations and violent suppression by the military. By March 1988, **Aung San Suu Kyi,** daughter of the national hero Aung San, had become the driving force behind the democracy movement in Burma. One of General Ne Win's military groups, the **State Law and Order Restoration Council (SLORC),** took power and suspended the 1974 constitution, revoking the limited autonomy that had been granted to ethnic minority groups. The dictatorship, under the rule of **General Saw Maung,** changed the name of the nation from "Union of Burma" to "Union of Myanmar" in June 1989 to purge the country of colonial ghosts (see **Language,** p. 487). Aung San Suu Kyi was placed under house arrest in July 1989 for speaking openly against the government. Under the leadership of Aung San Suu Kyi, the **National League for Democracy (NLD)** won the national elections in 1990, but SLORC refused to honor the results, jailing most of the party leaders. Aung San Suu Kyi won the **Nobel Peace Prize** in 1991, though still under house arrest.

MYANMAR TODAY

INTERNATIONAL FREE BURMA ACTIVISM. Latching onto the charismatic figure of Aung San Suu Kyi and her fight for democracy in Myanmar, international **human rights activists** have turned their attention to the plight of the Burmese. Numerous organizations have sprung up to agitate for **corporate divestment** from Myanmar, to sponsor educational activities, and to lobby the governments of Western nations to put political pressure on the military junta to improve the nation's human rights records. In the early 1990s, Levi-Strauss & Co. stated explicitly that business in Myanmar meant a tacit support of the repressive military junta. One company that has topped human rights activists' blacklists is **Unocal,** a California energy company that is invested in Myanmar. EarthRights International represented a group of Burmese peasants in a case that received high publicity from coverage on ABC's *20/20* show and other media attention. These peasants claimed that Unocal was complicit in crimes against humanity allegedly committed by the Myanmar military on the construction site of the **Yadana pipeline** that stretches through Southern Myanmar and into Thailand. These accusations include forced labor, forced relocation, beatings, and rape. In a corporate responsibility discussion paper, the company actively denies these allegations. However, the 1994 ruling that the case falls within American jurisdiction sets a precedent for American companies being held responsible for their actions overseas. More than 25 American cities and states have passed divestment legislation with regards to Myanmar.

DEMOCRACY UNDER HOUSE ARREST. A hero both at home and abroad for her pro-democracy work and her leadership of the **National League for Democracy (NLD), Aung San Suu Kyi** has drifted in and out of **house arrest** since just before her party's electoral victory in 1990. Her release in 1995 was on condition that she not travel outside of Yangon; violating this restriction in 2000 landed her under house arrest for 19 months. She was unconditionally released in May 2002. Although her release was not publicized, a crowd of over 1000 gathered outside the NLD party headquarters to hear her speak. She has pledged her life-long devotion to the cause of democracy in Myanmar. However, over 1500 **political prisoners** remain behind bars for pro-democracy political agitation.

THAI-BURMESE RELATIONS. The most recent controversy between the two neighbors erupted in May 2002 when officials in Yangon accused the Thai military of firing shells over the border during a routine Thai military exercise. Myanmar claimed that Thailand's actions supported ethnic Shan rebels and closed all **border checkpoints** with Thailand immediately, stepping up anti-Thai rhetoric and requiring citizens in Yangon to fly the Burmese flag. A Burmese writer, **Ma Ta Win,** published articles in the government mouthpiece *New Light of Myanmar* that Thailand interpreted as defamation of their monarchy. Needless to say, this series of articles did little to improve the shaky relations. A subsequent Burmese military offensive against the Shan accidentally crossed into Thai territory, which further angered the Thai. Burmese aggression against minority groups in the border areas have precipitated waves of **refugees** into Thailand. By the end of 2001, Thailand was hosting 227,000 refugees, all but 700 of whom were Burmese.

DRUGS. For **United Nations International Narcotics Day** in 2002, Myanmar and Thailand incinerated a total of over US$1 billion worth of drugs—including 3000kg of **opium,** 240kg of pure **heroin** powder, and over 40 million **methamphetamines**—in a gesture to the international community that they are taking a no-nonsense attitude toward drug-smuggling in the infamous **Golden Triangle** region. But after all, Myanmar and Afghanistan control 90% of the world's opium supply and are responsible for 60% of the heroin found on US streets. Most of these poppy products are grown and produced under the auspices of infamous drug lord **Wei Hsieo-kang,** leader of the Wa State Army. But even as Myanmar's opium and heroin production is on the decline due to increased governmental pressure, drug lords have shifted their focus to methamphetamines, which are more easily produced and smuggled. Today, Myanmar produces eight times as many pills as they did two years ago.

CUSTOMS & ETIQUETTE

PUBLIC BEHAVIOR. Bamahasin chin describes an idea of an essential "Burmeseness" that encapsulates Burmese ideals of good behavior. It prizes the subtle and quiet over the loud and direct, knowledge of Buddhist scriptures, respect for elders, discretion in dress and attitudes toward the opposite sex, and the ability to speak idiomatic Burmese. It is unseemly to show too much emotion, especially in public, and loss of temper is seen as a loss of face. The **head** is considered the most spiritual part of the body. Images of the Buddha, however old, ruined, or broken, are sacred above all. The more your *bamahasin chin*, the more respect you'll get, regardless of your station or wealth.

BIXESUAL, GAY, AND LESBIAN TRAVELERS. There is virtually no acknowledgement of homosexuality in Myanmar. **Travelers should be discreet.**

ARTS AND RECREATION

ARCHITECTURE. Much of Burmese art is associated with *nat*s, deities ranging from ghosts of people to spirits of trees who wreak vengeance on those who frustrate them. The Buddha is the most important *nat*, and thus Buddhist **monasteries** and **temples** are lavishly adorned like divine palaces. **Stupas** and brick structures with bell-like apexes characterize architecture from the **Mon period.** Modern structures show an **Indian** influence, with thicker apexes that taper to the top.

DANCE & DRAMA. All-female **dance shows** feature solo performers who sing a shrill-sounding song and dance using their feet, head, and arms to create thousands of movements reminiscent of the Chinese style. Dramatic **streetside performances** are often ceremonies portraying various *nat* stories. Men dressed as women (and vice-versa) are the main performers at these shows. **Marionette theater,** or *yok-thei pwe*, which flourished in the late 18th century, has almost ceased to exist but occasionally appears at temple fairs or local festivals with a lighthearted dance and a more dramatic play.

FILM. Those **cinemas** that haven't been privatized have fallen into ruins complete with cockroaches, leaking toilets, jamming projectors, and no air-conditioning. Burmese cinemas are given a run for their money—literally—by **video parlors,** which play videos out of private homes for a fraction of the cost of a movie ticket. Myanmar's film industry has fallen into similar disrepair. Previously producing approximately 80 movies per year, Myanmar now puts out a mere dozen. One problem is a lack of the money required to import foreign film supplies.

MUSIC. The Burmese **orchestra** is dominated by its drummer, who sits within a railing enclosing 21 drums. Other instruments include a gong ensemble, bass and tenor drums, cymbals, and bamboo clappers. In larger orchestras, melody instruments such as oboes or flutes are added.

TELEVISION. An upset in relations between Myanmar and Thailand in early 2002 (see **Thai-Burmese Relations**, p. 492) and the subsequent closing of all border crossings between the two neighbors meant that Burmese television stations were unable to broadcast live coverage of the **2002 World Cup,** much to the chagrin of Burmese soccer fans.

HOLIDAYS & FESTIVALS (2003)

DATE	NAME	DESCRIPTION & LOCATION
Jan. 4	Independence Day	A 7-day fair is held in Yangon.
Jan. 10	Kachin Manao Festival	In Kachin State, the festival marks the day on which Kachin State joined the Union of Myanmar in 1948; there is also a traditional *nat* festival to ensure a good harvest that year.
Mar.	Shinbyu (Novitation) Ceremonies	Burmese Buddhists novitate their sons, accompanied by elaborate processions.
mid-Apr.	Thingyan (Water Festival)	Commemorates the Burmese New Year and is marked by throwing water on passersby to "wash away" the sins and bad memories of the year.
May	Watering the Sacred Bo Tree Festival	Held on the day of the full moon, this festival commemorates Buddha's birthday by pouring water onto the sacred Bo tree, under which he gained enlightenment.
Aug. 24-28	Taung Byone Nat Festival	Celebrated in Mandalay by spirit dances and ceremonial reenactments.
Sept.-Oct.	Phaung Daw U Kyaung Festival	20-day celebration featuring a procession in highly decorated barges.
Oct.	Thadingyut Light Festival	Celebrates Buddha's return from heaven by lighting fire balloons and paper lanterns and visiting the local pagoda.
Oct.	Kyauk-se Dummy Elephant Dance Festival	From the 14th waxing day until the full moon, life-size dummy elephants sing and dance to music in Mandalay.
late Oct.-early Nov.	Shwezigon Pagoda Festival	In Bagan, candles and fireworks are offered to the pagoda.
Nov.	Kahtein Robe-Weaving Festival	Competition in overnight robe-weaving. The robes are subsequently offered to Buddha images in local pagodas.

ADDITIONAL RESOURCES

GENERAL HISTORY

Living Silence: Burma Under the Military Rule, by Christina Fink (2001). A description of the impact of military rule on the Burmese people.

Burma in Revolt: Opium and Insurgency Since 1948, by Bertil Lintner (1994). Unravels the complex relationship between drug trade and the country's ethnic insurgencies.

FICTION AND NON-FICTION

Freedom From Fear and Other Writings, by Aung San Suu Kyi (1991). A must-read for anyone wishing to familiarize himself with the struggle to bring democracy to Myanmar. This is the work for which Aung San Suu Kyi won the Nobel Peace Prize.

The Voice of Hope, by Aung San Suu Kyi (1998). Written by a Nobel Peace Prize winner and one of the world's spiritual and political leaders, this humorous personal narrative discusses the fight for democracy in Myanmar.

Burmese Days, by George Orwell (1962). A classic. An insightful treatment of colonial Burma, drawing on Orwell's experience as a colonial official in the early 20th century.

Singing to the Dead: A Missioner's Life Among Refugees from Burma, by Victoria Armour-Hlleman (2002). The journal of a Catholic missionary working with displaced Mon refugees at an illegal camp in Thailand.

FILM

Beyond Rangoon, dir. John Boorman (1995). A poignant portrayal of the fight for democracy in Myanmar. Based on actual events, this is the movie that is largely responsible for bringing the plight of the Burmese people to the attention of the world.

TRAVEL BOOKS

The Trouser People: A Story of Burma–In the Shadow of the Empire, by Andrew Marshall (2002). An entertaining adventure that exposes the real people and organizations (including Amnesty International) of Myanmar.

ON THE WEB

Culture and History (www.soros.org/burma/CRISIS/index.htm). The Burma Briefing Book is an excellent overview of recent Burmese history, ethnic tensions, and tales of Burmese culture.

Myanmar.com (www.myanmar.com). Official government web site has information steeped in propaganda, including a link to the Ministry of Defense that publishes an online ten-volume book called "The Truth."

Free Burma (www.freeburma.org). The other side of the story, with links to pro-democracy and activists groups.

ESSENTIALS

MYANMAR PRICE ICONS					
SYMBOL:	❶	❷	❸	❹	❺
ACCOMM.	Under US$2 Under 1300kyat	US$2-5 1300-3250kyat	US$5-10 3250-6500kyat	US$10-20 6500-13,000kyat	Over US$20 Over 13,000kyat
FOOD	Under US$0.25 Under 150kyat	US$0.25-0.50 150-300kyat	US$0.50-1 300-650kyat	US$1-3 650-1950kyat	Over US$3 Over 1950kyat
Please note that currency is converted at black-market rates for the purposes of this chart.					

EMBASSIES AND CONSULATES

MYANMAR CONSULAR SERVICES ABROAD

Australia: Embassy, 22 Arkana St., Yarralumla, Canberra, ACT 2600 (☎02 73 3751 or 02 73 3811).

Canada: Embassy, 85 Range Rd., Suite 902-903, Sandringham, Ottawa, ON K1N 8J6 (☎613-232-6446).

South Africa: Embassy: 319 Murray St., Brooklyn, Pretoria 0181; mailing address: P.O. Box 12121 Queenswood 0121 (☎012 346 0451).

UK: Embassy, 19A Charles St., London W1X 8ER (☎020 7629 9531).

US: Embassy, 2300 S St. NW, Washington, D.C. 20008 (☎202-332-9044 or 332-9045/9049). **Consulate,** 10 E 77th St., New York, NY 10021 (☎212-535-1310).

CONSULAR SERVICES IN MYANMAR

Australian Embassy: 88 Strand Rd., Yangon (☎25 18 10). Open M-F 8:30am-12:30pm and 1-4pm.

South African Embassy: South African citizens are referred to the embassy in Thailand. Park Palace, 6th fl., 231 Soi Sarasin, Ratchadamri Rd., Bangkok (☎66 02 253 84 73). Open M-Th 7:45am-4:30pm, F 7:45am-3:15pm.

UK Embassy: 80 Strand Rd., Yangon (☎28 17 00). Open M-Tu, Th-F 8:30am-12:30pm and 2:30-4:30pm, W 8:30am-12:30pm. Also serves **New Zealand** citizens.

US Embassy: 581 Merchant St., Yangon (☎28 20 55). Open M-F 8am-4:30pm. Consular services open M, W 8-11am.

KEEP THE BUCKS WHERE THEY BELONG

Stupendous sights, vibrant cultures, and the friendliest people in the world aren't enough to draw more than a trickle of tourists to Myanmar each year. "Do not let your tourist dollars pay for SPDC's bullets," urge flyers in Bangkok guest houses, and socially conscious backpackers seem to listen. Many argue that visiting Myanmar may end up helping the vicious regime that controls it, but others counter that educated and responsible tourism may be an agent of change and, more importantly, may transfer valuable and scarce tourist dollars to Myanmar's impoverished citizens, who otherwise have no source of income. (See **Myanmar: To go or not to go?**, p. 488) There are simple ways to minimize your contribution to SPDC and to maximize the portion that goes to citizens who make their livelihood from the tourist industry.

Foreign Exchange Certificates (FECs): The government insists that tourists change US$250 for 250FEC, the notes that serve as a second currency in Myanmar. Doing so means giving cold, hard cash to the government. Weaseling out of the requirement was once common but is becoming more difficult because of Myanmar's dwindling foreign reserve. The best way is to arrive on a business visa, which can be obtained at Burmese embassies fairly easily with a letter of sponsorship. Not only will you be entitled to stay for several months, but you also won't have to convert your currency. Visas that indicate that you are on a package tour also exempt you. Many travelers say that a small unofficial donation at the FEC counter helps reduce the requirement.

Government-owned agencies: Government-run agencies listed in *Let's Go* are marked with a **M**. Using agencies thus marked gives money directly to the military government. Private alternatives providing the same services are always listed.

Transportation: Use only privately run transport. Don't take trains, Myanmar Tours & Travels boats, or Myanma Airways, all of which are state-owned. Look for the **M**.

Accommodation: Stay in private guest houses. Most accommodations listed in this guide are privately owned. But even private guest houses must pay for an accommodations license, so some of the money is still going to the government.

Sights: Many of Myanmar's sights carry hefty entrance fees, and it's unclear where the cash ends up. If you have an ISIC or student ID card, wave it in front of every attendant you see; some will give discounts. Ticket sellers also tend to neglect their duties very early and late in the day; if you go then, you might not have to pay at all.

TOURIST SERVICES

Myanmar Tourist Board: 36c Sisters Avenue, London SW11 5SQ (☎44 207 223 8987; www.burmaguide.net)

VISAS

Single-entry 28-day tourist visas are required of all visitors. They are issued at Myanmar's diplomatic missions abroad, the most convenient locations being Bangkok, Kuala Lumpur, and Hong Kong. Allow 1-3 days for processing. Once in Myanmar, you can usually get a **visa extension** for up to 14 days.

MONEY

The Myanmar **kyat** (pronounced "chat") comes in denominations of 1, 5, 10, 15, 45, 90, 200, 500, and 1000. Particularly in tourism industries and international trade, US dollars and their one-to-one equivalent, **Foreign Exchange Certificates (FECs)**, operate as legal tender. FECs are printed in denominations of 1, 5, 10, and 20.

The government has fixed the exchange rate at 6.7kyat to US$1, but the free market rate hovers around 750kyat, with each US dollar reaping 50kyat more than an FEC. The best places to change money at the free market rate are at officially licensed booths, guest houses, and private travel agencies. Many people will solicit you to change money on the street; not only do you stand a good chance of being cheated, but the police may also attempt to interfere. Foreigners aren't much at risk, but local changers in markets have been arrested to prevent black-market rates from soaring. Rates in larger cities like Yangon and Mandalay tend to be 10-20kyat better than in smaller towns like Kalow or Nyaungshwe, so it pays to convert before heading into the countryside. Apart from government banks and some luxury hotels and restaurants, credit cards (besides AmEx and Visa) and traveler's checks aren't readily accepted in Myanmar, so it's necessary to carry cash. Credit cards also usually incur an additional fee.

Individual travelers (called "Foreign Independent Travelers" in bureaucratic jargon) are supposedly required to exchange US$250 (£, DM, and traveler's checks also accepted) for 250FEC upon arrival at Yangon International Airport. Doing so puts cold, hard cash straight into government coffers (see **Keep the Bucks Where they Belong,** p. 496). Only FECs bought in excess of the US$250 requirement, accompanied by an official receipt, can be reconverted upon departure; anything less will have to be spent, given away, or kept as memorabilia. Since travelers need US$/FEC for accommodation expenses, train, boat, or plane tickets, and admission fees, but also need kyat for smaller purchases, a supply of both forms of currency is essential. An equal amount of US$/FEC and kyat is best. In total, budget travelers should expect to spend US$15 (or equivalent) per day.

GETTING THERE

BY PLANE. Mingaladon Airport (p. 499) in Yangon is the international gateway to Myanmar for the majority of travelers. **Air Mandalay** (www.air-mandalay.com), **M Myanma Airlines,** and **Yangon Airlines** (www.myanmars.net/ygnair) are the major international and domestic carriers.

BY LAND. Refer to the following table for overland border crossings in Myanmar.

BORDER CROSSINGS: FROM THAILAND Due to periodic fighting and fickle government regulations, the status of these border crossings changes frequently. Get an update from the nearest Burmese embassy before attempting an overland crossing. As of July 2001, foreigners could officially enter Myanmar by land from 3 points in Thailand: from **Mae Sai** (p. 774) to **Thachilek;** from **Mae Sot** (p. 797) to **Myawaddy;** and from **Sangkhlaburi** to **Phayathonzu** via the **Three Pagoda Pass** (p. 721). In the past it has also been possible to take a ferry between **Ranong** in southern Thailand and **Kawthaung.** All 3 crossings include customs and immigration checkpoints, and foreigners may be required to exchange US$250 into FECs. Depending on the level of insurgent activity, you may be confined to the immediate area near your point of entry.

GETTING AROUND

BY PLANE. Air travel is the fastest, safest, most comfortable, and most expensive means of getting around the country. Frequent connections and increasing competition on routes between major tourist destinations make flying very convenient. **M Myanmar Airways** had major accidents in 1998 and 1996. Preferable are **Yangon**

Airways and **Air Mandalay.** Air Mandalay's fares are higher than its competitors, but many travelers will pay extra for its safety and in-flight service standards. Private travel agencies charge 10-15% less than the airline offices.

BY BUS. Bus travel is the cheapest mode of transportation. The recent proliferation of private bus lines has led to improvements in comfort and convenience, though no luxury can compensate for the condition of the roads, some of the worst in Southeast Asia. Book at least one day in advance to reserve a good seat; avoid rows in the back or over the wheels. During long journeys (up to 20hr.), the bus will (thankfully) stop several times for food and bathroom breaks.

BY TRAIN. All train travel in Myanmar is state-owned and operated. **Myanma Railways** offers three classes: sleeper, upper, and normal; most travelers find the last intolerable. Fares for beds in sleeper class and reclining seats in upper-class rise considerably but remain fairly competitive internationally. The most trafficked route is the **Yangon-Bago-Thazi-Mandalay** line. An extension from Thazi to **Shwenaung (Inle Lake)** is excruciatingly slow but scenic and there is also service between Mandalay and **Bagan.**

BY BOAT. Powerful river currents render boat travel impractical for visitors on a limited tourist visa. The journey from Yangon to Pyay takes three days. The only exception is the **Inland Water Transport** boat service from Mandalay to Bagan, whcih takes 9-14hr. During the dry season, exposed sandbars have snagged boats—inquire about current conditions.

KEEPING IN TOUCH

Myanmar's **postal system** is difficult and unreliable. Sending letters is straightforward and inexpensive, but mailing parcels is a convoluted, time-consuming process—set aside at least 1½hr. Customers are requried to buy regulation boxes and tape at the post office and complete a host of customs and address forms. Packages for specific destinations are only accepted on certain days of the week. Fees amount to 900-1200kyat for a 10kg maximum limit to most parts of the world. Many locals hire private agents to handle this process. **DHL** services are available in Yangon and Mandalay.

The **telephone system** further reveals the inadequacies of Myanmar's communications infrastructure. Placing international calls can be accomplished using the expensive IDD services at government telephone offices and private telephone offices, hotels, and guest houses. (Calls to North America about US$6 per min.) Savvy planners who manage to forward itineraries and guest house numbers to acquaintances can receive calls along the way. For **Home Country Direct (HCD)** numbers from Myanmar, refer to the table on the inside back cover of this book.

LOWER MYANMAR

YANGON ရန်ကုန် ☎1

Even amid the cacophony of a packed city bus, all heads turn, all conversations stop, and all hands move gracefully to bowed foreheads at the sight of Shwedagon Pagoda. The reverence surrounding Yangon's main landmark captures the extent to which the sacred and social intertwine in the city's social fabric. As the admin-

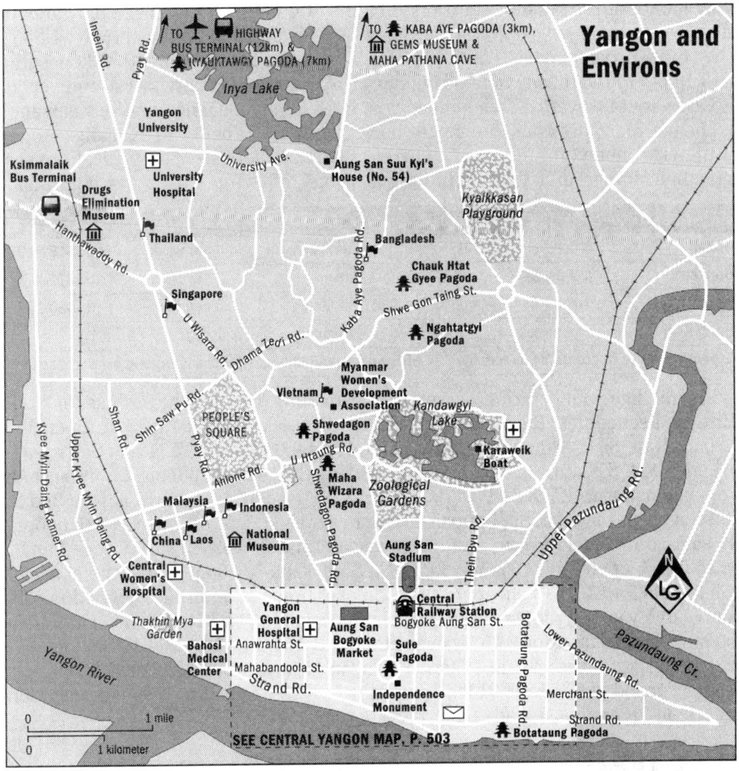

istrative, commercial, and transport hub of central Myanmar, Yangon cradles 4 million people. But while other Southeast Asian capitals have developed into modernized metropolises, Myanmar's closed-door policies have deteriorated the city's colonial glory. Dirt paths through backdrops masquerading as jungle villages abruptly give way to a sensory overload of avenues surging with *longgyi*-clad locals forced to pound the shackled pavement to eke out a living. Visitors find themselves immersed in a culture whose rigors can exhaust and whose intersections can befuddle. Just 33km from the ocean via the mighty Yangon River, Yangon is less well-known as one of the great port cities of Southeast Asia.

> **GOVERNMENT LISTINGS** Government listings are marked by a **M** symbol. Money spent at such establishments goes directly into the government's hands. For more information, see Keep the Bucks Where They Belong, p. 496.

INTERCITY TRANSPORTATION

BY PLANE

International and domestic flights arrive at **Mingaladon Airport,** 19km northwest of Yangon. There is a US$10 departure tax payable in US$ or FEC. Touts from hotels and transport services mob foreigners exiting the customs and immigration area.

Taxis monopolize transport into the city. Several companies charge flat rates to most points. **Myanmar Travel and Tours (MTT)** is high quality but pricey (US$5). They often provide maps. To avoid giving money to the government, walk past the MTT booth to the throng of taxis outside (US$2-4), but compare prices and negotiate. Beware of drivers offering the lowest fares or anyone who mentions currency exchange. Many are cons looking for naïve tourists. It is better to exchange money in the city once you find out the current black market rate. Many guest houses, including Motherlands II and White House Hotel, offer free transport for guests.

DESTINATION	FREQUENCY	PRICE	DESTINATION	FREQUENCY	PRICE
Bagan	3 per day	US$75-100	**Kuala Lumpur**	4 per week	US$185-198
Bangkok	4-9 per day	US$75-95	**Lashio**	2 per week	US$110
Heho	2-3 per day	US$75-100	**Mandalay**	6 per day	US$90-138
Hong Kong	2 per week	US$212	**Singapore**	1 per day	US$285
Expect prices to fluctuate by as much as 30-50% as demand changes for seasonal and other reasons.					

Several flights and carriers serve each destination. Contact the airlines for exact fares and schedules: **Biman Bangladesh,** 106 Pansodan Rd. (☎27 58 82; open M-F 9:30am-4pm, Sa 9:30am-1pm); **MAS,** Central Hotel, Bogyoke Aung San St. (☎24 10 07; open M-F 8:30am-12:30pm and 1:30-5:30pm, Sa 8:30am-1:30pm); **Myanma Airways International,** 123 Sule Pagoda Rd. (☎28 97 72); **Silk Air,** Sakura Tower, 2nd fl., 339 Bogyoke Aung San St., opposite Traders Hotel (☎25 52 87; open M-F 9am-5pm, Sa 9am-noon); **Thai Airways,** Sakura Tower, ground fl., 339 Bogyoke Aung San St. (☎25 54 99; open M-F 9:30am-4:30pm, Sa-Su 9:30am-12:30pm). Most travel agents sell tickets for US$5-10 cheaper than airlines. Three major airlines serve domestic routes in Myanmar: **Air Mandalay,** 146 Dhammazedi Rd. (☎53 01 44; open M-F 9am-5:30pm, Sa-Su 9am-noon); **Myanma Airways,** 104 Strand Rd. (☎27 48 74; open M-F 8:30am-3pm, Sa-Su 8:30am-1:30pm); **Yangon Airways,** MMB Tower, Level 5, 106 Upper Pansodan Rd. (☎38 31 06; open daily M-F 9am-5pm, Sa-Su 9am-noon). Contact them for exact schedules.

BY TRAIN

Yangon Central Railway Station monopolizes Kun Chan St., north of Bogyoke Aung San St., between Sule Pagoda and Pansodan Rd. Book tickets for **Myanma Railways** at the station or at the **advance booking office** on Bogyoke Aung San St. (☎25 11 81. Open daily 6am-4pm.) **Ordinary-class** tickets provide wooden seats. A bit more money will buy you a seat in an **A/C sleeper** cabin with video programming. Sleeper trains have two options: the sleeper cars or upper-class sleeper. **Sleeper cars** have A/C and audio, but the **upper-class sleeper,** a four-person cabin, has attached bath, fridge, A/C, audio, *and* video. The **foreigner ticket office** handles same-day bookings; be wary of touts whose prices reflect hefty commissions. (Open daily 9am-4pm.) The advance booking office takes upper-class and sleeper reservations three days in advance and ordinary-class reservations one day in advance. Reserving through a guest house or travel agent incurs an additional fee. Trains go to: **Mandalay** (14-15hr.; 6am, 3:15, 5, 6:30, 7:30pm; upper-class US$27-30, sleeper US$50) via **Bago** (2hr.; US$2, upper-class US$5) and **Thazi** (11-12hr.; US$12, upper-class US$32-35).

BY BUS AND LINECAR

Myanmar's buses are not nearly as comfortable as trains. Expect long, crowded rides. Companies with major long-distance routes operate from the **Highway Bus Terminal,** 18km north of Yangon, past the airport. Tickets should be purchased at branch offices at the south end of Aung San Stadium, north of the railway station or at MTT—but they only accept FEC or US$. At least seven companies go to **Mandalay** (14-15hr.; 5, 5:30pm). **Leo Express,** 23-25 Aung San Stadium (☎25 20 01; open daily 8am-8pm, 3200kyat), has a reputation for the roomiest and most punctual buses. Next door to **Rubyland Tourism Services** (See **Practical Information,** p. 502), **Hnin Thu Wai** (☎24 62 83) and **Ye Thu Aung** (☎64 21 22, ext. 96) both serve **Taunggyi (Inle Lake)** (18hr., 1pm, 2500kyat). **New Bagan Express** books tickets to **Bagan** (14hr., 3pm, 3000kyat). Both Ye Thu Aung and New Bagan Express book through Rubyland Tourism Services. Buses also serve **Pyay** (6hr., 6 per day, 800kyat).

Buses and linecars to **Kyaiktiyo** (5hr., 5 per day, 500kyat) via **Bago** (2hr., 300kyat) and buses to **Pathein** (4hr., every hr. 7am-noon, 1000kyat) leave from the **Ksimmalaik Bus Terminal** at the intersection of Hanthawaddy Rd. and Hledan St. (Taxis from downtown 1000kyat.) Buses to **Thanlyin** (1½hr., every 15min. 5:30am-6pm, 30kyat) leave from **Mahabandoola Rd.** near the corner of 37th St., in front of Nilar Win's Cold Drink and Yogurt Shop.

ORIENTATION

Flanked to the south and west by the Yangon River, the capital sprawls over 350 sq. km. In the southern part of town near the Yangon River, the **downtown** area has most accommodations, cafes, services, and markets. The area enjoys a compact grid layout, making navigation by foot feasible. In downtown, the four east-west thoroughfares are, from north to south: **Bogyoke Aung San St.,** the site of the Bogyoke Aung San Market; **Anawrahta Rd.,** home to City Hall; **Mahabandoola St.,** bisected by the **Sule Pagoda Rotary;** and **Merchant St.** The area circumscribed by Bogyoke Aung San St. and Anawrahta Rd. is the **Upper Block,** by Anawrahta and Mahabandoola St. is the **Middle Block,** and by Mahabandoola and Merchant St. is the **Lower Block. Sule Pagoda Rd.** bisects the downtown area. The short north-south streets in downtown are numbered from one to sixty; every third or sixth street also bears a proper name. **Shwedagon Pagoda** is 4km north of Yangon; **Yangon International Airport** and the **Highway Bus Terminal** are about 19km northwest.

BURMESE NUMERALS

1	2	3	4	5	6	7	8	9	0
၁	၂	၃	၄	၅	၆	၇	၈	၉	၀

Cheat Sheet for major routes: #37=၃၇ #43=၄၃ #44=၄၄ #46=၄၆ #47=၄၇ #51=၅၁

LOCAL TRANSPORTATION

Trains: A circular train line—moderately cheap and scenic, but neither comfortable nor useful—follows a route from **Yangon Central Railway Station** to **Mingaladon** (near the airport) via **Insein** to the west and **Okklapa** to the east. Five or six trains make the entire loop in each direction daily (2½hr., 6am-5pm, US$3), and numerous additional trains make shorter runs throughout the day.

Buses: Dilapidated and dirty 1970s Korean and Japanese buses provide the cheapest but most uncomfortable transportation. **As most bus numbers are labeled in Burmese, finding the right one can be challenging.** For your convenience, there's a Burmese numeral chart above. Open-air **linecars** resembling military vehicles with canvas-covered truck beds (front seat 30kyat, back seat 15kyat), **regular buses** packed to the brim (5-15kyat), and **A/C buses** (20-30kyat), which mysteriously lack A/C, ply overlapping routes. Fares vary with distance; higher linecar fares after 6pm. Routes include:

#3: Latha Rd. (in the upper block of Chinatown, 20min. west of Sule Pagoda)-Shwedagon Pagoda

#37: Sule Pagoda (leaves from the east side of Mahabandoola Park)-Shwedagon Pagoda

#10, #44 (A/C): Downtown-east side of Kaba Aye Pagoda-Maelamu Pagoda

#46: Shwedagon Pagoda-Chauk Htat Gyee Pagoda

#47: Sule Pagoda-Shwedagon Pagoda Rd.-Shwedagon Pagoda-Inya Lake (east side)

#51 (A/C): Mahabandoola Park (Mahabandoola Garden Rd.)-Inya Lake (west side)

Ferries: To go to **Letkhokkon Beach** or **Twante** or cross the **Yangon River** to the small town of **Dhala,** known for its furniture, rice, fishing, and excellent views of the port and Yangon skyline, take a steamer. Ferries leave from the jetty opposite Strand Rd. from the Port Commissioner building near Pansodan Rd. (every 10-15min. 5am-9pm).

Taxis: Four-door 1980s-style Japanese taxis provide the most convenient, albeit expensive, transport within Yangon. None have meters; settle on a price before departing. 200-400kyat within downtown. Typical fares from Sule Pagoda to: **airport** (2000kyat); **Highway Bus Terminal** (2000kyat); **Ksimmalaik Bus Terminal** (1000kyat); **Shwedagon Pagoda** (500-600kyat). Longer excursions US$25 per day.

Pedicabs (Sica): Myanmar's version of the pedicab: the passenger sits next to the pedicab driver. Though exiled from the downtown area, *sica* are easy to find and convenient for trips to the city's outskirts, including many pagodas. Short trips 200-300kyat.

PRACTICAL INFORMATION

TOURIST AND FINANCIAL SERVICES

Tourist Offices: MTT, 77-91 Sule Pagoda Rd. (☎28 39 97). State-run organization that arranges tours and travel services (planes, trains, and ferries). Free maps. Tourist **visa extensions** US$39 for up to 2 weeks. (However, the airport charges only US$3 per day for overstaying a visa, so don't get an extension if staying less than 13 days after the expiry date.) Open daily 8am-5:30pm.

Travel Agencies: Rubyland Tourism Services, 16 Aung San Stadium (☎24 50 51). One of Myanmar's most established travel companies. Adept at organizing excursions into normally restricted areas. Also arranges buses for many private companies. A reliable source for currency exchange. Open M-Sa 9:30am-4:30pm.

Embassies and Consulates: Australia, 88 Strand Rd. (☎25 18 10). Open M-F 8:30am-12:30pm and 1-4pm. **Bangladesh,** 56 Kaba Aye Pagoda Rd. (☎54 95 56). Open M-F 8:30am-12:30pm and 2-4:30pm. **China,** 1 Pyidaungzu Yeiktha Rd. (☎22 12 80). Consular services open M-F 9am-noon and 2:30-4:30pm. 30-day visa US$25-30. **India,** 545-547 Merchant St. (☎28 25 50). Consular services open M-F 9am-12:30pm. 6-month visa US$55-75. **Indonesia,** 100 Pyidaungzu Yeiktha Rd. (☎25 44 65). Open M-Th 8am-noon and 1:30-4pm, F 9am-noon. **Laos,** A-1 Diplomatic Quarters, Tawwin Rd. (☎22 24 82). Visas US$33, for US citizens US$43. Open M-F 8am-3pm. **Malaysia,** 82 Pyidaungzu Yeiktha Rd. (☎22 02 48). Open M-F 8am-3pm. **Singapore,** 326 Pyay Rd. (☎52 56 88). Open M-F 8:30am-1pm and 2-5pm. **Thailand,** 437 Pyay Rd., 8 Ward (☎51 20 18). Consular services open M-F 9-11:30am. **Vietnam,** 36 Wingaba Rd., Bahan (☎54 89 05). Visas US$50. Open M-F 8-11:30am and 1-4pm. **UK,** 80 Strand Rd. (☎28 17 00). Open M-Tu, Th-F 8:30am-12:30pm and 2:30-4:30pm, W 8:30am-12:30pm. Also serves **New Zealand** citizens. **US,** 581 Merchant St. (☎28 20 55). Open M-F 8am-4:30pm. Consular services open M and W 8-11am.

Currency Exchange: Changing money on the **black market** has become more difficult and complicated since 2000. (See **Money,** p. 496) Be careful to ignore cons on the street or at the airport who want to change your money. **Ask guest house owners** for current exchange rates. Guest house owners or **Rubyland Tourist Service,** an authorized changer (see **Travel Agencies,** above), will help you find a reliable free market rate. **Myanmar Foreign Trade Bank,** 80/86 Mahabandoola Garden Rd. (☎28 49 11), between Mahabandoola St. and Merchant St., handles AmEx/V cash advances

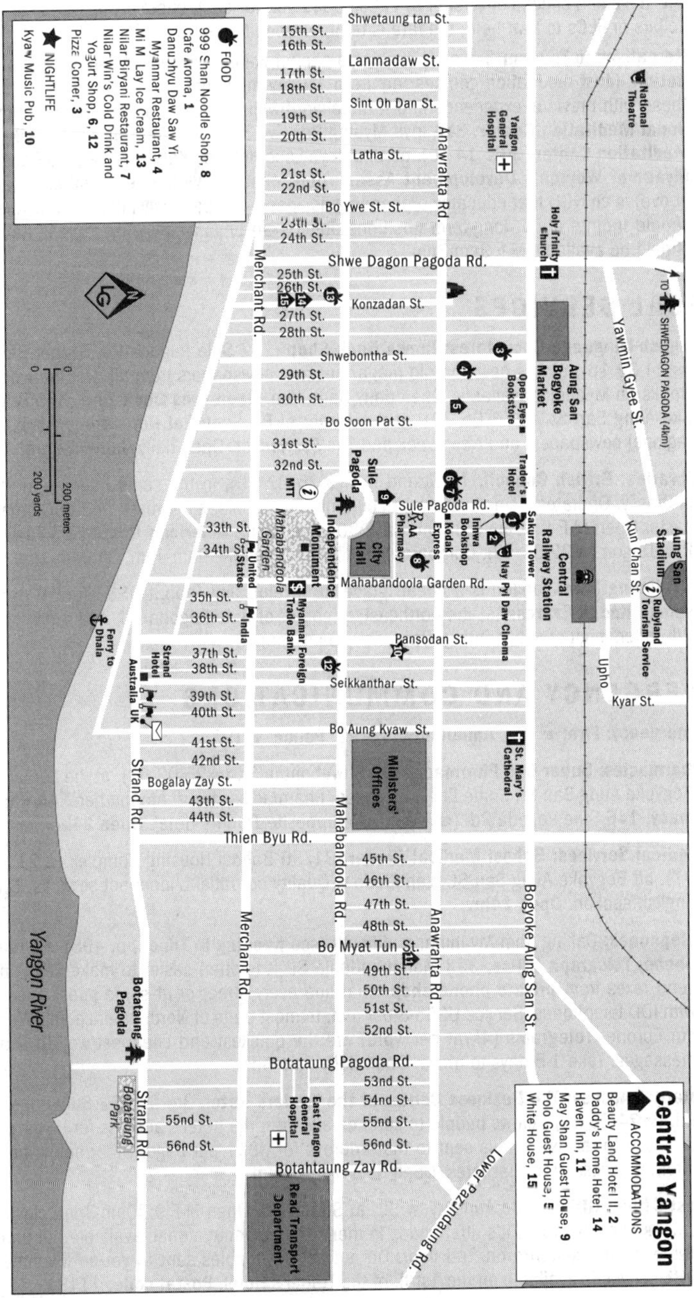
Central Yangon
ACCOMMODATIONS
Beauty Land Hotel II, 2
Daddy's Home Hotel 14
Haven Inn, 11
May Shan Guest House, 9
Polo Guest House, 5
White House, 15
FOOD
999 Shan Noodle Shop, 8
Cafe Aroma, 1
Danuphyu Daw Saw Yi
Myanmar Restaurant, 4
Mi Mi Lay Ice Cream, 13
Nilar Biryani Restaurant, 7
Nilar Win's Cold Drink and
Yogurt Shop, 6, 12
Pizza Corner, 3
NIGHTLIFE
Kyaw Music Pub, 10
0 200 meters
0 200 yards
Shwetaung tan St.
15th St.
16th St.
Lanmadaw St.
17th St.
18th St.
Sint Oh Dan St.
19th St.
20th St.
Latha St.
21st St.
22nd St.
Bo Ywe St. St.
23rd St.
24th St.
Shwe Dagon Pagoda Rd.
25th St.
26th St.
Konzadan St.
27th St.
28th St.
Shwebontha St.
29th St.
30th St.
Bo Soon Pat St.
31st St.
32nd St.
Sule Pagoda
MTT
Sule Pagoda Rd.
33rd St.
34th St.
Mahabandoola Garden
City Hall
Independence Monument
Mahabandoola Garden Rd.
35th St.
36th St.
Pansodan St.
37th St.
38th St.
Seikkanthar St.
39th St.
40th St.
Bo Aung Kyaw St.
41st St.
42nd St.
Bogalay Zay St.
43rd St.
44th St.
Thien Byu Rd.
45th St.
46th St.
47th St.
48th St.
Bo Myat Tun St.
49th St.
50th St.
51st St.
52nd St.
Botataung Pagoda Rd.
53nd St.
54nd St.
55nd St.
56nd St.
Botahtaung Zay Rd.
Merchant Rd.
Strand Rd.
Mahabandoola Rd.
Anawrahta Rd.
Bogyoke Aung San St.
Lower Pazundaung Rd.
Yawmin Gyee St.
Kun Chan St.
Upho
Kyar St.
TO SHWEDAGON PAGODA (4km)
National Theatre
Yangon General Hospital
Holy Trinity Church
Aung San Bogyoke Market
Open Eyes Bookstore
Trader's Hotel
Sakura Tower
Inwa Bookshop
Kodak Express
AA Pharmacy
Central Railway Station
Aung San Stadium
Rubyland Tourism Service
Nay Pyi Daw Cinema
Myanmar Foreign Trade Bank
United States
India
Strand Hotel
Australia
UK
Ferry to Dhala
St. Mary's Cathedral
Ministers' Offices
Botataung Pagoda
Botataung Park
East Yangon General Hospital
Road Transport Department
Yangon River

and traveler's check conversion to FECs (US$2 fee for each check). Don't change US dollars or FECs to kyat here, the rate is terrible. Open M-F 9:30am-3pm.

Alternatives to Tourism: Travelers seeking a deeper spiritual experience should try **meditation.** Most meditation courses require a 10-day minimum stay for the first retreat. Those with previous experience find it more worthwhile. Travelers recommend **International Meditation Center,** 31A Inya Myaing Rd. (☎53 15 49) and **Chan Mye Yeiktha Meditation Center** (☎66 14 79), north of Inya Lake Hotel on Kaba Aye Pagoda Rd. The **Myanmar Women's Development Association,** near the Vietnamese Embassy (see above) is an NGO that educates orphaned girls ages 5-25. Seriously interested travelers should inquire about long-term positions on-site—an English-speaking representative should be available M-F 9am-3pm.

LOCAL SERVICES

English-Language Bookstores: Innwa Book Shop, 232 Sule Pagoda Rd., Upper Block (☎24 32 16). Stocks new and old magazines and newspapers from all over the world. Books on Myanmar available. Open daily 9am-7pm. **Open Eyes Bookstore,** 365 Bogyoke Aung San St. (☎70 05 79), at the corner of Bo Soon Pat Rd., carries issues of regional newspapers and *Newsweek* and *The Economist*. Open daily 9am-6:30pm.

Libraries: British Council, 78 Strand Rd. (☎25 62 90), in the same building as the embassy. Operates a small library with current newspapers, magazines, and BBC broadcasts. Open M-F 8:30am-5:30pm, Sa 8:30am-4:30pm. **American Center,** 14 Tawwin Rd., Dagon (☎22 31 40). Comparable facilities. Open M-F 9am-4pm, Sa 9am-1pm.

Developing Film: Yangon is a cheap place to develop film (about US$3 for 36 exposures). **Kodak Express,** at the northeastern corner of Sule Pagoda Rd. and Anawrahta Rd., offers high-quality printing. Open daily 9am-7pm.

EMERGENCY AND COMMUNICATIONS

Emergency: Fire: ☎191. **Ambulance:** ☎192. **Police:** ☎199.

Pharmacies: Super One Pharmacy, 394 Shwebontha St. (☎25 02 68), at the corner of Bogyoke Aung San St. Some English spoken. Pharmacies cluster around here. **AA Pharmacy,** 146 Sule Pagoda Rd. (☎25 32 31), opposite Traders Hotel. **Open 24hr.**

Medical Services: Bahosi Medical Center, 31/36 Bahosi Housing Complex (☎21 16 97), off Bogyoke Aung San St., Lan Madaw. Quality outpatient/inpatient services. Fine English spoken. **Open 24hr.**

Telephones: Calling from Myanmar is difficult (see **Keeping in Touch,** p. 498). **Telephone/Telegraph Office,** 393 Mahabandoola St. It is often easier to make calls and send faxes from **private phone shops** that line every street or at some guest houses with IDD telephones. Service US$5-8 per min. to most parts of North America and Western Europe. **Telegrams** (4kyat per word) are the quickest and cheapest way to send messages. Take 1-5 days to arrive. Open daily 7am-8pm.

Internet Access: The Business Center at the Traders Hotel, 3rd fl., 223 Sule Pagoda Rd. (☎24 28 28). Allows people to send emails from the hotel's address for US$1 per 5KB and to receive emails sent to that address for US$1 per page. Other hotels have Internet access at similar rates. Open daily 7am-10pm.

Post Office: GPO, 80 Bo Aung Kyaw St., at Strand Rd. Open M-F 9:30am-3pm; closing time isn't set in stone. It's utter chaos in there. International airmail available but unreliable. *Poste Restante* on 2nd floor. Do not have valuables sent to you in Myanmar. **DHL** service is available on the 1st fl. of the Trader's Hotel. **Postal code:** 11181.

ACCOMMODATIONS

Budget hotels are scattered downtown, to the west of Sule Pagoda Rd. Prices drop by a few dollars in the low season (June-Sept.) and owners give discounts for longer stays. Prices usually include breakfast.

Beauty Land Hotel II, 188-192 33rd St., Upper Block (☎24 39 52). Tucked away from the busy, noisy streets, yet in a great location. The clean rooms, smiling service, and the attached restaurant well justify the couple extra dollars. Email, fax, and IDD telephone services available. Singles US$6-15, doubles US$12-20. ❸

Polo Guest House, 240 Anawrahta Rd. (☎24 12 52). Entrance on 30th St. Most likely the cheapest place with decent rooms in Yangon. Located in a lively area of downtown. Singles with fan and shared bath US$3, with A/C US$5; doubles US$5/US$7. ❷

White House, 69/71 Konzaydan St., Lower Block (☎24 07 80). All-you-can-eat breakfast buffet. Comprehensive transportation arrangements. Singles with fan and shared bath US$5, with A/C and private bath US$10; doubles US$8/US$15. ❸

May Shan Guest House (☎25 29 86), on Sule Pagoda Rd., just north of Sule Pagoda. A Chinese-run guest house with clean, comfortable rooms in a prime location. All rooms with bath, A/C, satellite TV, and refrigerator. Internet access available. Singles US$15; doubles US$20; triples US$25; family rooms US$30. ❹

Daddy's Home Hotel, 107 Konzaydan St., Lower Block (☎25 21 69). On the same block as White House. If you are desperately looking for an A/C room, those on the 6th floor may be the cheapest in town. Singles US$3, with A/C US$5; doubles with A/C US$8; superior triples with A/C, minibar, TV, and bathtub US$7. ❷

Haven Inn, 216 Bo Myat Tun St. (☎29 55 00; phyuaung@mptmail.net.mm), between Anawrahta Rd. and Mahabandoola St. Cozy and homey (only 5 rooms available) with Western- and Burmese-style breakfasts. Away from the hubbub of downtown. Free transport to and from airport with advance notice. Large, immaculate wood-floored rooms have A/C, fridge, and hot water bath. Singles US$10; doubles US$15. ❸

FOOD

Yangon's Shan, Burmese, Chinese, and Indian cuisines deliciously reflect the city's ethnic diversity. The quintessential meal includes a curry of fish, meat, or vegetables, a soup dominated by gourd or bitter greens, and a plate of steamed rice and boiled vegetables. In the evenings, downtown Yangon overflows with vendors offering snacks. Spilling out onto the streets, teahouses are also great places for cheap eats. Be sure to try a bowl of *mohinga*—Myanmar's favorite noodle snack.

RESTAURANTS

Nilar Biryani Restaurant, 203 Anawrahta Rd., between Sule Pagoda Rd. and 32nd St. Mountainous portions of superb chicken, mutton, and vegetable *biryani* (400kyat). *Chapaatis* (100kyat) are a great way to start the day. Open daily 4:30am-10pm. ❷

999 Shan Noodle Shop, 130B 34th St., between City Hall and Anawrahta Rd. Best Shan noodles in town. Great for breakfast or a light meal. Rice or wheat noodles with soup or salad dressing 250kyat; wonton soup 250kyat. Open daily 6am-7pm. ❷

Danuphyu Daw Saw Yi Myanmar Restaurant, 175/177 29th St., Upper Block. Great introduction to Burmese cuisine. Meals include soup and sides. Steamed butter beans or bamboo shoots 200kyat; meat curries 400kyat. Open daily 9am-9pm. ❸

Pizza Corner, on Shwebontha St., Upper Block, offers refreshing dosages of reasonably priced Western food for those travelers who just need a break from local fare. Margherita pizza 750kyat. Open daily 10am-9:30pm. ❹

Cafe Aroma, on Sule Pagoda Rd., Upper Block, has an expensive expat feel to it, but actually serves up delicious Western fare at a great price. Pasta 1000kyat. Cappuccino 530kyat. Open daily 7am-10pm. ❺

TEAHOUSES AND CAFES

Diamond White Cafe and Bar, on Bogyoke Aung San St., between 31st and 32nd St., next to the Central Hotel. Hip teahouse by day, popular bar by night, and, simply, *the* place to hang out. Pastries and tea 100kyat. Open daily 7am-10pm. ❶

Mi Mi Lay Ice Cream, Konzaydan St., Lower Block, near Mahabandoola St. Relive your pre-teen years and melt your worries away with two icy scoops. Several flavors 100kyat per bowl. Open daily 10am-10pm. ❶

Nilar Win's Cold Drink and Yogurt Shop, 377 Mahabandoola St., between 37th and 38th St., or on Anawratha Rd., between Sule Pagoda Rd. and 32nd St. Founded by a famous kickboxer. Avocado salad 250kyat; *lassi* 300kyat. Open daily 8am-11pm. ❷

SIGHTS

A day in the life of a sightseer: Wake up early and make a trip to **Shwedagon Pagoda** for a glimpse of praying Buddhists before crossing the street to see the **Maha Wizara Pagoda** commissioned by General Ne Win. After a morning strolling through the gardens around **Kandawgyi Lake,** stop to see the royal **Karaweik Boat.** After lunch, either visit some of the museums—National Museum, Gems Museum, or the Drugs Elimination Museum—or head downtown to the **Sule** and **Botataung Pagodas,** and catch a glimpse of the sparkling **Strand Hotel.** Cap off the day people-watching or relax with a cup of tea at one of Yangon's many teahouses.

SHWEDAGON PAGODA AND ENVIRONS

SHWEDAGON PAGODA ရွှေတိဂုံဘုရား. Visible from many points in the city, Shwedagon Pagoda is Myanmar's most sacred structure and Yangon's marquee attraction. As legend has it, two traders from Okkala (as Yangon was known 2500 years ago) traveled to India, where they met the recently enlightened Siddartha Gautama. When the travelers presented the Buddha with rice cakes and honey, he gave a sermon and gave them eight of his hairs. Upon the traders' return, King Okkalapa ordered that the hairs be enshrined in a pagoda on Singutlara Hill. Leading to the top of the hill are four stairways full of vendors selling overpriced Buddhist paraphernalia and woodcarvings. Exquisite **woodwork** and **paintings** depicting scenes from the Buddha's life adorn the stairs. Sixty-four **miniature pagodas,** four larger ones, and several lions and *manokthihas* (twin-bodied, sphinx-like creatures) surround the pagoda. Pilgrims make offerings and pour cups of water on the heads of Buddha statues at eight equally spaced planetary post shrines. In the southeast quadrant stands a *boddhi* tree, supposedly descended from the tree in India under which the Buddha gained enlightenment. As the heart and soul of religion in Myanmar, Shwedagon also serves as a sort of political icon. In 1988, the honorable **Aung San Suu Kyi** made her first public speech against the government here (see **Myanmar Today,** p. 492.) As a result, the military keeps a watchful eye on the pagoda, and government informers pay close attention to contact between locals and foreigners here. (*3km northwest of Sule Pagoda. Accessible via bus #37. Private guides near the entrance to the south staircase give tours for US$5. No sleeveless shirts or shorts. Remove shoes. Open daily 4am-9pm. US$5 about 7am-7pm.*)

DOWNTOWN YANGON

SULE PAGODA ဆူးလေဘုရား. The center of downtown Yangon, 2000-year-old Sule Pagoda provides a natural starting point for exploring the city's sights. Its Mon name, *Kyaik Athok,* means "the pagoda enshrining the sacred hair." Sure enough, the pagoda enshrines one of the Buddha's hairs that was brought by two missionaries from India. The octagonal shape architecturally delineates the eight planetary posts of the Burmese zodiac. *(On Sule Pagoda Rd. in the middle of a rotary.)*

MAHABANDOOLA PARK. Southeast from the Sule Pagoda rotary, the gardens provide a visual refuge from the surrounding city. A hotbed of student activism during the late 80s, the park now hosts sedate morning tai chi and lively afternoon chats. The **Independence Monument** rests at its center. The colonial architecture of **City Hall,** the **Supreme Court,** and the **High Court** surrounds the park. *(20kyat.)*

BOTATAUNG PAGODA ဗိုလ်တထောင်ဘုရား. Over 2000 years old, Botataung Pagoda rivals Shwedagon Pagoda in its antiquity and, like most pagodas in the country, enshrines relics of the Buddha transported from India. Its name, meaning "1000 officers," refers to the military escort these relics received upon their presentation by the king of Syriam. Allied bombing in 1943 almost completely destroyed the temple, but it has been restored, now featuring a hollow, walk-in center. Mirror-enhanced views of some relics are available, but the most sacred ones are locked below away from view. *(Along the Yangon River on Strand Rd. in the southeast part of town.)*

NORTH TO INYA LAKE

CHAUK HTAT GYEE PAGODA ကျောက်တော်ကြီးဘုရား. The selling point of this "six-story" pagoda is its enormous, 70m long reclining Buddha. With a giant 8½ carat diamond placed between its eyes, 551 smaller diamonds, and one ton of gold leaf stamped on its body, this Buddha image is worth US$18 million. Chauk Htat Gyee also lends its name to a famous **monastery,** where 600 monks study ancient Buddhist scriptures and Pali language and literature. Opposite Chauk Htat Gyee, the shorter **Ngahtatgyi Pagoda** holds a Buddha resting on the grounds of **Ashay Tawya Monastery.** Don't miss the ornate footprint highlighting the distinguishing marks of the Buddha. *(2km northeast of Shwedagon Pagoda on Shwe Gon Taing St. Accessible via bus #47. Chauk Htat Gyee Pagoda free, Ngahtatgyi US$2.)*

IN RECENT NEWS

A TICKET OUT

The Burmese have an obsession with gambling. Lottery-ticket booths are found all over the country, even in small towns without a sound telephone network.

Betting sums that are sometimes as much as their monthly salaries, people shouted and celebrated at the top of their lungs when the team on which they had bet won a match in the 2002 World Cup.

Perhaps gambling serves as a lone adrenaline rush in an otherwise peaceful, calm society. Or maybe people are buying a ticket that could potentially get them out of poverty. Whatever the reason, everyone seems to be involved.

The lottery tradition dates back to the era of King Mindon in the 1860s. Residing in the Mandalay Royal Palace, King Mindon established a lottery in which the winner would receive 12,000kyat (equivalent to 100 million kyat today) as well as a free ride around town on his royal elephant.

This system became so popular that the whole city of Mandalay supposedly became poor because everyone was funding the lottery pool.

140 years later, the tradition continues. Today, there are two different kinds of gambling: official and unofficial. The official lottery is sponsored (and acknowledged) by the government. The unofficial lottery—with better odds but smaller prizes—is far more popular.

So the next time you notice Burmese people who seem unusually busy, check the calendar—there's a good chance it's a lottery day.

KANDAWGYI LAKE. This breezy lake and its sculpted parks are a godsend amidst Yangon's urban landscape. At the eastern end is the picture-perfect **Karaweik Boat,** constructed in the 1970s as a replica of a royal barge. This 90m, nearly 2 million kg behemoth understandably doesn't actually float, but the main objective in its construction was the revival and preservation of traditional Burmese art; today, it has a restaurant featuring a titanic buffet and traditional dance performances. *(The lake can be reached from Shwedagon Pagoda via U Htaung Bo Rd. Restaurant entrance 100kyat. Dance performances US$5. Open daily 10am-10pm.)*

INYA LAKE. Despite their distance from downtown, Inya's surrounding parks and footpaths are well worth an afternoon's exploration. Bordering **Yangon University,** it is often closed, but twenty-something couples still sneak around here after sunset. Though off-limits, **Aung San Suu Kyi's house,** which doubled as her prison, is at 54 University Ave., on the lake's southeastern tip. *(4km northwest of Kandawgyi Lake.)*

OUTLYING TOWNSHIPS

NATIONAL MUSEUM အမျိုးသားပြတိုက်. Although it lacks entertaining interactive displays or high-tech attractions, travelers interested in the history and culture of Myanmar will find the National Museum educational. Topics include royal regalia, neolithic stone artifacts, clay votive tablets, and other objects from the Bagan period, as well as diverse Buddha images, cave paintings, and information on the cultures of national minorities. The big deal on the ground floor is the 180-year-old Great Lion Throne, originally used in the Mandalay Palace by the last Burmese king. *(66/74 Pyay Rd. in Dagon Township. ☎ 28 25 63. Open daily 10am-4pm. US$5.)*

GEMS MUSEUM. If you are gemstone savvy, Myanmar is the place to shop. The mining of ruby, sapphire, jade, and other stones is a significant sector of the Burmese economy. The first three floors of the Gems Museum building are saturated with jewelry shops, while the 4th floor is the actual museum, containing magnificent displays. *(66 Kaba Aye Pagoda Rd. Accessible via bus #43. Open daily 9:30am-4:30pm. US$5 to enter the 4th fl.)* Just north of the Gems Museum is **Kaba Aye Pagoda.** The first prime minister of postcolonial Burma commissioned the building of Kaba Aye Pagoda, nicknamed the "world peace" pagoda. Its five entrances correspond to the four historical Buddhas and the Buddha of the future and lead to an inner chamber sheltering a 500kg silver Buddha image. *(11km north of downtown, past Inya Lake on Kaba Aye Pagoda Rd. Accessible via bus #43.)* Adjacent to Kaba Aye Pagoda, **Maha Pathana Cave** is an enormous cave built to hold 10,000 people for the Synod, which commemorated the 2500th anniversary of the Buddha's enlightenment.

DRUGS ELIMINATION MUSEUM. The museum not only displays drugs such as opium, heroin, cocaine, ecstasy, and marijuana, but also boasts about the success of the government's anti-drug, rehabilitation, and crop substitution programs *(Hanthawaddy Rd., in San Chaung Township. Open daily 10am-4pm. US$3, with camera US$5.)*

MARKETS

Downtown Yangon is constantly abuzz with **hawkers** purveying their wares. Most of the action occurs on the main east-west streets off **Sule Pagoda Rd. Streetside shops** provide an alternative to the ever present vendors. 31st St., between Mahabandoola St. and Anawrahta Rd., sports at least a dozen paper shops, while **Konzaydan St.,** has nearly 20 wall paint stores. **Markets** are relatively few and far between in Yangon. **Bogyoke Aung San Market,** the granddaddy of them all, is on the street bearing its name west of the Central Railway Station. This massive space (indoors and out) houses a wealth of clothing and textile stores, carvings and handicrafts sellers, and **government-registered** gem and jewelry shops. The market remains fairly empty midweek, but weekends are quite busy. The result is a buyer's market; bargaining is favorable and recommended, as shopkeepers gear prices toward tourist crowds. (Open daily 9am-5pm.)

> **BUYERS BEWARE!** Buying jewelry in Myanmar essentially requires a purchase from a government shop, since exporting jewelry from the country requires an accompanying government-issued certificate. See **Keep the Bucks Where They Belong,** p. 496.

ENTERTAINMENT

Most nighttime venues in Myanmar are prostitution venues. For a night away from the skin trade, head to **Nay Pyi Daw Cinema,** on the Upper Block of Sule Pagoda Rd., which shows one recent Hollywood movie for a period of about three weeks, depending on demand. (Tickets 200-500kyat.) **Kyaw Music Pub,** in the Middle Bock of 197 Pansodan Rd., has good ambience and live music every night from 6-11pm. Food and beer are cheap, priced for locals not tourists. (Pitcher of beer 750kyat.)

DAYTRIPS FROM YANGON

THANLYIN သံလျင် **AND KYAUKTAN** ကောံ. For those in need of a breath of country air, the tiny towns of Thanlyin and Kyauktan provide a daytrip's worth of sweet refuge. **Thanlyin** was the base for Portuguese explorer Philip De Brito, who tried to establish a kingdom here in the 1600s before meeting a violent death at the hands of the Burmese. Today, Thanlyin has little more to offer than a bustling market and rustic charm. From Thanlyin's market, horsecarts make the 3km journey south to **Kyaikkhauk Pagoda,** Thanlyin's primary attraction (600kyat). Get off when you see the large pagoda staircase up the hill at the right of the road. On clear days from the top, you can see over the surrounding peanut groves and across the delta to Shwedagon Pagoda. The road in front of the pagoda continues 10km or so to **Kyauktan.** On an island in the middle of the river, **Yele Pagoda,** the highlight of the greater Yangon area, dominates the view from the village. To get to the pagoda, buy a round-trip boat ticket (30kyat) at the pavilion on the shore opposite the pagoda. Remove shoes before stepping ashore. (US$1 if someone happens to be manning the admission booth, free otherwise.) Opposite Yele Pagoda on a small hill overlooking town, the pavilion of **Kyauktauk Pagoda** is a nirvana for the heat-sensitive as it receives steady waves of cool, blustery wind. *(Thanlyin and Kyauktan, across the Bago River southeast of the capital, lie on the same bus route. Buses and linecars to Thanlyin (1½hr., every 15min. 5:30am-6pm, 30kyat) leave from Mahabandoola St., near the corner of 37th St. in front of Nilar Win's Cold Drink and Yogurt Shop. Buses that return to Yangon (2hr., every 20min. until early evening, 40-50kyat) leave from the marketplace.)*

TWANTE တွံတေး. Pottery aficionados will enjoy the village of Twante and its craft industry. **Shwesandaw Pagoda** (ရွှေဆံတော်ဘုရား) features a 76m golden *stupa* that rivals Shwedagon in antiquity, plus a small display of antique pottery and royal artifacts from the Mon and Burman kingdoms. A "wish-fulfilling" station marks a corner of the pagoda and commemorates the defeat of King Bayinnaung's uprising. *Sicas* cluster around the marketplace and peddle to the Oh Bo District or Shwesandaw Pagoda for around 100kyat. *(To get to Twante, cross the Yangon River to Dalah from the jetty on the intersection of Pansodan and Strand Rd. (every 20min. 5:20am-8:40pm, US$1) and take a linecar to Twante (1hr.; every 30min. 6am-5pm; jeep 50kyat, minibus 100kyat). A shared taxi costs 150kyat for the station-wagon trunk, 400kyat for the backseat, or 800kyat for cab.)*

MYANMAR

LETKHOKKON BEACH. Given that most travelers confine themselves to Yangon, Mandalay, Bagan, and Inle Lake, it's likely that Letkhokkon Beach will remain off the beaten path for some time. While the rainy season (June-Oct.) brings mud and fewer sunbathing opportunities, the dry season reveals the town's appeal: fresh air, powdery sand, fine views, and invigorating breezes. The water, while certainly clean enough for swimming, often looks murky because of silt discharged by the mighty delta. Although rooms the rooms are expensive (singles US$24; doubles US$36), **Letkhokkon Beach Hotel ❺** (☎247 538) was the only place to stay as of summer 2002. *(To get to Letkhokkon, cross the Yangon River to Dalah at the jetty on the intersection of Pansodan and Strand Rd. (every 20min. 5:20am-8:40pm, US$1) and then take a linecar to the beach (3hr., every 1-2hr., 300kyat). In the rainy season the only option is to hire an expensive taxi (7000kyat each way) .)*

BAGO (PEGU) ပဲခူး ☎052

There are two Bagos. The Bago at eye-level is a hot but endearing little country town with a nondescript main street and exceptionally polite residents—a place for napping through the midday heat and sipping drinks with locals at the riverside teahouse in the evenings. The Bago seen from above—from the upper reaches of the Mahazedi Pagoda or a guest house rooftop—floats in a sea of rice paddies and wilderness that stretches out of sight, peppered in every direction with gleaming pagoda spires. Come to see both—the Bago of today, provincial in scope and influence, and the Bago that exists only in legends and glittering ruins.

TRANSPORTATION

The **train station,** 250m west of the river and 100m north of the Main Rd., runs connections to **Mandalay** (14hr.; 4 per day 7:45am-10:45pm; standard US$11, upper-class US$30) and **Yangon** (2hr.; 8 per day 1:45am-7:20pm; standard US$2, upper-class US$5). The bustling **Main Rd.,** has **linecar** and **bus service** to **Yangon** (2hr.; every 15min. 6am-6pm; 200-300kyat). Many travelers stop in Bago to break up the long journey between Yangon and up-country destinations. Those wishing to continue by bus to **Mandalay** can arrange tickets at Myananda Guest House, Emperor Motel, or San Francisco Guest House for 2500kyat. Book one day in advance.

ORIENTATION AND PRACTICAL INFORMATION

A section of the **Yangon-Mandalay Hwy.** slices through the heart of Bago from southeast to northwest as **Main Rd.,** which passes some sights and the railway before reaching most of the accommodations and continuing for 200m to the river, just before the center of the town. Continuing north on Main Rd. leads to a small **clock tower** near a fork in the road. To the left, Main Rd. splits after 100m, continuing on toward Mandalay and the **Shwemawdaw Pagoda.** The right fork leads to **Myanmar Economic Bank,** which exchanges travelers checks to FECs at a 5% commission rate (☎212 97; open M-F 9:30am-3pm) and the **post office** (open M-F 9:30am-4pm). Well before the fork, **Myananda Pharmacy** is marked by a blue-and-white Burmese sign below Myananda Guest House. (Open daily 5am-9pm.)

ACCOMMODATIONS

Three guest houses and a motel vie for the patronage of budget travelers. All are near the train station. The best choice is **Emperor Motel ❷,** before the river bridge, offering excellent views and cheap, clean rooms. It's worth staying at the Emperor if for no other reason than to be under the wing of the manager, Mr. Yee, who knows virtually everyone in town. All rooms have A/C, TV, refrigerator, and hot showers. (☎230 24. Singles US$4-5, with bathtub US$12; doubles US$7-8/US$16.) If Emperor is full, try **Myananda Guest House ❸**, 10 Main Rd., which has clean rooms, provides information on Bago and Kyaiktiyo, and arranges cheap car transport. (☎222 75. Singles with A/C US$5, with bath US$7; doubles US$10/US$12.) **San Francisco Guest House ❷**, 14 Main Rd., a half-block south of the other two, has cheaper, dimmer, and older rooms and extensive travel information. Rooftop rooms afford stupendous views. (☎222 65. US$2-5.) Popular with Burmese vacationers, **Silver Snow Guest House ❸**, 527 Main Rd., before the clock tower on the other side of the bridge, offers basic rooms and fewer tourist services. (☎221 13. Rooms US$5, with bath US$8, with A/C US$15.)

FOOD AND NIGHTLIFE

A number of tourist-oriented restaurants line Main Rd. between the railroad tracks and the clock tower. For great Burmese food, try **Cho Pyone Family Restaurant ❸**, on Main Rd. before the clock tower; look for the orange "Crusher" sign. A full spread of curry, soup, and vegetable sides costs 400kyat. (Open daily 8:30am-9pm.) **Three Five Restaurant ❸**, next to the Emperor Motel, serves up a massive array of chicken, beef, prawn, and noodle dishes. For a lively after-dark atmosphere, open-air **Ngwe Pon Gyi Cafe ❷**, next to the bridge on the eastern bank of the river, serves mouth-watering pastries (50kyat) and tea. (Open daily 6am-10pm.) A number of **"Beer Stations" ❶** and **cafes ❶** fuel all-male socializing for young and old alike. Taps flow freely near the bridge and around Shwemawdaw Pagoda.

SIGHTS

Though the town's atmosphere merits a few days' stay, Bago's sights can be covered in a day or less. Energetic travelers do a walking tour of the sights (about 8km total), but the best way to soak in the town's atmosphere is by bicycle or trishaw. Rent the former at any guest house (500kyat per day); hire the latter for US$3-4 per day. **Tun Tun** at Emperor Motel offers a special deal of US$2 per day for *Let's Go* readers. He is quite knowledgeable about the town and speaks decent English. Attractions stay open daily 5am to 9pm. Most cost US$2, but paying US$6 at any sight buys a ticket to all of them. If you visit early (before 7am) or late (after 7pm) you might not be asked to pay. A morning journey to the **Shwethalyang Buddha** sheds light on Buddhist prayer rituals, while the nearby pagodas, monasteries, and **ordination hall** illustrate Buddhist history and architecture. Stop in the **market** for lunch on the way to **Shwemawdaw Pagoda** and **Hinthagone Hill**, which are best-visited in the late afternoon, when locals come to pray.

SHWEMAWDAW PAGODA. Contrary to popular belief, Yangon's Shwedagon Pagoda is not Myanmar's tallest. Monopolizing Bago's skyline at 114m, impressive Shwemawdaw Pagoda wins the title by 5m. Over 1000 years old, it was constructed to enshrine two hairs of the Buddha bequeathed to two merchant brothers. After an earthquake leveled the structure in 1930, successive reconstructions propelled it to its present height in 1953. The pagoda is a fascinating combination of modernization and tradition, and is well worth the trip. The grounds contain electric contraptions including revolving boats and bobbing serpents set amid glittery waves designed to collect projectile coin and paper money donations. *(US$2. Free after sunset. Camera fee 50kyat; video fee 200kyat. Walk 2km from Bago up Main Rd. and turn right past the clock tower at the Aung San statue.)*

SHWETHALYANG BUDDHA Debate rages over which of Bago's sights is more awe-inspiring—the massive Shwemawdaw Pagoda, or the colossal 55m by 16m Shwethalyang Buddha (reclining Buddha). Built in 994, it languished in decay until King Dhammaceti ordered its restoration in the 15th century. By 1900, it again stood in disrepair and underwent a sweeping face-lift. *(From the center of town, cross the train tracks and turn onto the right hand turn-off; it's 2km down. US$2; camera fee 50kyat; video fee 200kyat.)*

HINTHAGONE HILL. there is a smaller pagoda on Hinthagone Hill, east of Shwemawdaw Pagoda. According to legend, two *hamsa* birds perched over the water here, fulfilling a prophecy of the Buddha. Eventually, the river and surrounding delta shifted course, and that fated spot emerged as the hill's summit and the center of the Mon kingdom. The guardian of this hill and therefore of the town of Bago is a former king who was raised, according to legend, by a buffalo. His statue, with buffalo horns on its head, can be found on the right as you walk up the steps.

SEINTHALYONG BUDDHA. Not many tourists know that there is more than one giant reclining Buddha in Bago. Built in the same era as Shwethalyang—about 1000 years ago—Seinthalyong's size is shy of the former's by 8m. For many centuries, the image lacked a roof because people believed workers would be struck by lightning during its construction, but a joint effort between government officials and Seinthalyong's head monk inspired the completion of a roof just two years ago. *(Follow the road from Shwemawdaw to Hinthagone Hill for about 1km; turn right at a big pagoda sign, and walk down the road 2km to the end.)*

KALYANI SIMA (SACRED ORDINATION HALL). A wooded respite from linecars and teashops awaits at these temple grounds on the way to Swethalyang Buddha. While its present incarnation is only 48 years old, the hall stands on the site of one of the oldest structures of its kind in Myanmar. King Dhammaceti, an ardent supporter of Buddhism, sent monks to Ceylon in 1475 for re-ordination by the famed Mahavihara sect. Upon their return, he commissioned the building of Kalyani Sima, and monks consecrated the site with sand from the sacred Kalyani River. West of the ordination hall stand 10 huge stone pillars covered with inscriptions in Pali and Mon. The pillars give insight into the early history of Buddhism in Myanmar and to the role that the religion played in 15th century Bago and Ceylon. *(On the road to Shwethalyang Buddha, roughly halfway on the left.)*

MAHAZEDI PAGODA. In 1560 this pagoda enshrined a tooth of the Buddha obtained from Ceylon. Fifty years later, the relic was captured and taken north to Sagaing. Male visitors are allowed to climb to the *stupa*'s upper echelons to see Bago's finest views. In the vicinity, a handful of interesting pagodas warrant a visit for those with time. *(Continue past the front of the Shwethalyang Buddha and turn left at the "T"-intersection; it's a few hundred meters down at the end of the road. US$2.)*

KYAIKPUN PAGODA. Also constructed by the ever-building King Dhammaceti, Kyaikpun Pagoda features an unusual design of four 30m Buddhas sitting back-to-back against a pillar. *(3km southwest of Bago, off the Yangon-Mandalay Hwy. US$2.)*

MARKETS. Two blocks off Main Rd. behind Emperor Motel, Bago's day and night markets don't offer much besides raw vegetables and hygienic supplies, but the area starts moving after sunset. If the constant attention from locals gets to be too much, escape to the nearby teahouses.

DAYTRIP FROM BAGO: KYAIKTIYO PAGODA

The trek begins at a base camp in Kyaiktiyo called Kinpun, 65km east of Bago. Taxis are the best way to get to the base camp and are available at any guest house in Bago (3hr.,

US$20). While it is possible to go directly to the base camp by a combination of bus, truck, and linecar, it can be a big hassle, for service is infrequent especially during the rainy season. If you want to try anyway, go from Bago to Kyaiktho by bus (3-4hr., 400kyat), walk 5min. across town to the linecar and take that to the Kinpun base camp (30min., 50kyat). Then take a truck from the base camp to the Yathe Taung stop (1hr.; trucks depart regularly 6am-9pm, less frequently after 9pm; last truck back 4pm; 200-300kyat). You will then have to walk up a steep path to the summit (1hr.), or pay US$5 to be carried by bearers. Bring good footwear. Pagoda sight fee US$6. Buses run from the base camp to Yangon via Bago (3 per day in dry season, 1 per day in wet season). Buses also leave Kyaiktho for Yangon (4 times per day, 600kyat).

For good reason, Kyaiktiyo Pagoda is the most popular and significant religious sight in Myanmar. Tourists and pilgrims alike make the steep 13km climb to marvel at the pagoda, which is perched on a colossal golden boulder balanced on the edge of a cliff. Like most Burmese pagodas, it supposedly enshrines a Buddha relic. As the story goes, the Buddha gave a wandering monk a lock of his hair and asked him to enshrine it in a pagoda built on top of a rock resembling his head. The monk tucked away the Buddha's hair in his own hair knot for safekeeping and set out to fulfill the request. It is said that the power of the Buddha's hair alone prevents the boulder from toppling off its base. As the caretakers will demonstrate, the boulder rests upon a pivot point upon which the mount rocks back and forth.

Unless you visit the Golden Mount round trip by taxi from Bago, it is best to stay in the **accommodations** at the base camp and near the top of the mountain. Due to its ideal location, **Sea Sar Guest House ❶**, in the middle of the main road of the base camp, collects most of the visitors (Basic rooms US$1, with bath and fan US$3-5; singles with bath and A/C US$7; doubles with bath and A/C US$12.) Just a 2min. walk from Sea Sar is **Pann Myo Thu Guest House ❷**, offering cleaner rooms and hot water at the same prices as Sea Sar. (Basic rooms $2; singles with A/C and bath US$3; doubles with bath US$5, with A/C and bath US$6.) For its luxurious rooms, proximity to the Golden Mount, and beautiful views at sunrise and sunset try **Kyaikhto Hotel ❹**. (Singles US$15, with bath US$36; doubles US$24/US$44.) In the base camp, English-speaking restaurants and tea shops line the main street. Try **Myint Ta Lwin ❷** for quality Chinese food at a reasonable price.

PYAY ☎053

While most foreigners bypass Pyay on their way to Upper or Lower Myanmar, it is an important religious site for local Burmese. Shwesandaw Pagoda, in the center of town, is one of the three major pilgrimage pagodas in Myanmar. The others are Yangon's Shwedagan and Bago's Shwemawdaw. Pyay lies several kilometers from the ruins at Thayekhittaya—much older than the temples in Bagan—an ancient capital of the Pyu Kingdom, which flourished in the latter half of the first millenium AD. Pyay serves as an enjoyable one- or two-day escape from the tourist frenzy of Upper and Lower Myanmar.

TRANSPORTATION

Trains: To **Bagan** (13hr., every other day 5am, US$8) and **Yangon** (12hr., 6:50am, US$6).

Buses: To **Bagan** (9hr., 9pm, 2500kyat); **Bago** (10hr., 5:30am, 400kyat); **Mandalay** (12hr., 5pm, 1600kyat); **Ngapali Beach** (10hr., 9pm, 2500kyat); **Pathein** (10hr.; 8:30am; 2500kyat in front, 1000kyat in back). To get to **Inle Lake,** you can take a bus to Mandalay and get off at Meiktila; then switch to a bus to Taunggyi. However, *Let's Go* does not recommend this route as the Mandalay bus arrives in Meiktila in the middle of the night. A safer option is to back-track through Yangon.

ORIENTATION AND PRACTICAL INFORMATION

The **Bogyoke Aung San Statue Rotary** marks the center of town from which roads radiate in four directions. A **market** fills the path going west for about 100m before it terminates at **Strand Rd.,** which runs along the massive **Ayeyarwady River.** The road to the east is **Bogyoke St.,** which eventually leads to the **Highway Bus Terminal** (3km), a 24hr. **hospital** (2km), and **Thayekhittaya** (9km). **Kan Rd.** runs parallel to the market. It is one block north and west of the rotary. The **post office** (open M-F 9am-noon and 1-3pm) and **cinema** are both on Kan Rd. The 24hr. **telephone office,** a few blocks northwest of the post office, only allows domestic calls. The road radiating south from the rotary leads to **Shwedaung** (14km).

ACCOMMODATIONS

Compared to Bagan and Nyaungshwe, Pyay has considerably fewer guest houses, some of which specifically target Burmese visitors. All listed here include breakfast and are within a 5min. walk from the Bogyoke Aung San Statue.

Pan Ga Ba Guest House (☎212 77). Take the second left going north from Bogyoke Aung San Statue. Take your second right, and it will be on your right. Though not the newest or the cleanest, Pan Ga Ba is definitely the best deal in town with A/C and attached bath. Helpful staff will arrange transportation to, from, and within Pyay. Singles US$3; doubles US$6. ❷

Myat Lodging House (☎213 61). Take the first left going north from Bogyoke Aung San Statue, then right after the cinema. Travelers willing to splurge for A/C rooms with TV, minibar, and bath, this is your place. More basic rooms without attached bath are spacious as well. Singles US$6-12; doubles US$10-15. ❸

Aung Gabar Guest House, at the southeastern corner of the Bogyoke Aung San Statue. Shared showers have hot water; no A/C. Singles US$2-3, with attached bath US$4; doubles with or without attached bath US$6. ❷

FOOD

Numerous Burmese eateries and cafes cluster around the rotary. **San Francisco ❷,** 50m south of Hline Ayar on Strand Rd., offers Burmese and Chinese dishes at a great price and with the added bonus of A/C. The most popular restaurant is **Hline Ayar ❸,** on Strand Rd. just north of the intersection with the market path. Although main dishes (Burmese and Chinese) tend to be a bit expensive, the beautiful view of the Ayeyarwady is priceless. For a more down-to-earth dining experience, check out **Daw Khin Myint Inn ❸,** a Muslim Food Center. Heading north from the rotary, take the third right. It will be on your right 50m from the intersection. Try the *biriyani* (350kyat) or meat curry (400kyat).

SIGHTS

SHWESANDAW PAGODA. Sitting on top of a hill located just near the center of town, Shwesandaw Pagoda is one of the most sacred and popular pagodas in Myanmar and is always bustling with local visitors. Even better, there's no entrance fee (yet, at least). The top of the hill offers sweeping views of the Ayeyarwady and Pyay, as well as a beautiful sunset on a clear day.

SHWEDAUNG. For travelers staying in Pyay for more than a day, Shwedaung, a village 14km south of Pyay, offers a relaxing tour of unique pagodas. The most fascinating of the three pagodas is perhaps **Muni Pagoda,** to the right as you go through the entrance gate. Hosting miniature replicas of Kyaiktiyo's Golden Rock and Thayekhittaya's Bawbawgyi Pagoda, as well as an image which closely resembles Mandalay's Mahamuni Golden Buddha (see p. 523), this pagoda seems to be a compilation of the major religious sights in Myanmar. Here you will also find Buddha's supposed hair, molars, and canine teeth—enormous for a man of average size. But then again, legend has it that he was eight feet tall...

Shwemyetman Pagoda, just a 10min. walk from the main road, houses the bizzare bespectacled Buddha image. The practice of putting a pair of glasses on a Buddha image traces its history back to the 5th century AD. When King Duttabaung lost his eyesight after the construction of Shwemyetman, his sage prophets suggested that he donate a pair of spectacles to the image. Since then, it is believed that the bespectacled Buddha image has the special power of curing diseases or disorders of the eyes. More tourist-attraction pagodas lie 6km southwest of the village—a 1½hr. walk or a 1500kyat horsecart ride. The pagoda complex of **Shwenattaung, Maeshin,** and **Muni** stands on a hill surrounded by rice paddy fields. To the east, a Buddha image sits on top of the coiled tail and under the head of a giant snake. This memorializes the story of a giant snake giving an enlightened Buddha protection from the rain. To the right of Shwenattaung, **Maeshin Pagoda** contains a small Buddha image with many colorful gems on its body. *(Pickups to Shwedaung (30min., every 15min., 50kyat) leave from one block south of Bogyoke Aung San Statue in Pyay.)*

DAYTRIP FROM PYAY: THAYEKHITTAYA (SRI KSHETRA)

To get to Hmawza, take a taxi (3500kyat round-trip), sica *(round-trip 1500kyat), or train (30min., 3 per day, 10kyat). As usual, the trains are relatively unreliable. Linecars (50kyat) also run to Paya Gyi, but you will need to walk from there.*

Dating back to as early as the 4th century AD, the Thaekhittaya ruins are perhaps the oldest archaeological discoveries in Myanmar. This ancient capital of the Pyu Kingdom encompassed about seven square miles at the peak of its power—the boundary is still evident in the high brick walls. Places of interest include the **Old Palace Ground, Bebe Temple, Queen Beikthanoe's tomb,** and other **pagodas**, yet the most impressive is **Bawbawgyi Pagoda**—the prototype of Myanmar's ancient pagodas—audaciously rising 50m at the end of a long dirt path. Your first encounter with the ancient ruins of the Pyu Period on the way to Thayekhittaya will be the conspicuous **Paya Gyi Pagoda** on the right about 4km from Pyay. Believed to enshrine the big toenail of Buddha's right foot, Paya Gyi was one of the nine pagodas constructed by King Duttabaung between the 6th and 7th centuries AD. Another cone-shaped pagoda which King Duttabaung built is **Phayamar,** dating back to the 5th century AD. It lies just beyond the turn-off to Thayekhittaya. One of the four capitals of the ancient Pyu kingdom, Thayekhittaya is now inhabited by villagers of **Hmawza.** Near the center of Hmawza lies the **museum,** the entrance point to the ruins. Though small, it holds all of the artifacts found at the ruins that date back to between the 4th and 9th centuries AD—gold leaves with Pyu writing, bronze figures of Pyu musicians, stone funeral urns, images of Vishnu and Buddha, and ancient coins. *(You can either rent a bull-cart (1000kyat) or walk the 2-3hr. to visit the ruins. Admission US$4 for the museum and beyond. Only the most die-hard archaeological enthusiasts will find the US$4 a worthwhile investment. Some travelers sneak around the entrance to avoid paying.)*

PATHEIN

☎42

The jewel of the Ayeyarwady Delta, Pathein was once a Mon stronghold but lost its prominence under the Burmese Empire. Today, Myanmar's fourth-largest city is known for its parasol workshops, rice production, and friendly Karen, Rahkine, and Burmese population. Except for the nearby beaches, there aren't many sights, but with a relaxed pace, fascinating home industries, and some of the most hospitable people in Myanmar, Pathein is a welcome respite.

DON'T LEAVE HOME WITHOUT IT. Unlike in other towns listed in this book, entering Pathein requires passing an immigration checkpoint. Buses stop upon entering town, and valid **visas** are required for entry. If you've overstayed your visa, you'll be sent back to Yangon.

TRANSPORTATION. The **highway bus terminal** is several kilometers east of the town center. **Jeeps** run between the terminal and town (20kyat). **Buses** to **Chaungtha Beach** (3hr.; 7, 11am, 1pm; 500kyat) and **Ngwesaung Beach** (4hr., 6am) leave from Shwezedi Rd., between Merchant St. and Mingyi Rd. Buses to **Yangon** (5hr.; 4, 6, 9, 11am, 12:30, 3pm; 1000kyat) leave from the corner of Mingyi Rd. and Two Pagodas St., north of Mahabandoola Rd. Buy tickets one day in advance. The **train station,** on **Station Rd.** three blocks south of Mahabandoola Rd., offers connections to **Pyay** (13hr.; 4am, 1pm; US$7). **Trishaws** charge 50-100kyat anywhere in the city and provide the only other reliable method of transport, besides your feet.

ORIENTATION AND PRACTICAL INFORMATION. Pathein Hwy. enters Pathein from the east and becomes **Mahabandoola Rd.** as it approaches the heart of the city. A **clock tower** stands at its intersection with **Merchant Rd.,** two blocks before Mahabandoola Rd. ends at the **Pathein River** which runs north-south. **Strand Rd.** runs alongside the river, perpendicular to Mahabandoola Rd. **Shwemokhtaw Pagoda** sits at the intersection of Merchant, Strand, Mahabandoola, and Shwezedi Rd. **Myanmar Commercial Bank,** on Shwezedi Rd. opposite the pagoda, converts cash and checks to FECs at the fixed rate. (☎210 81. Open M-F 10am-2pm.) Several **pharmacies** (open daily 8am-9pm) cluster opposite the **hospital,** on the corner of Mahabandoola and Mingyi Rd. (parallel to and one block east of Merchant Rd.). The **telephone office** (open daily 7am-9pm) and **post office** (open M-F 9am-3pm) are on Mahabandoola Rd., one block west of the clock tower. **Postal Code:** 10011.

ACCOMMODATIONS AND FOOD. Only a few facilities in Pathein are authorized to house foreigners, but the best choice is the brand new **Paradise Guest House ❷,** on Zay Chaung Rd. Take a left right after crossing a small bridge as you walk away from the Shwemokhtaw Pagoda on Merchant St. Marble-tiled hallways and air-conditioned rooms make the Paradise a great value. (Restaurant attached. Singles US$4, with TV and fridge US$6; doubles US$6-10.) If Paradise is full, try the **Taan Taan Ta Hotel ❷,** 7 Merchant St., near the corner of Shwezedi Rd. (☎222 90. Singles US$3-5; doubles US$4-6.) Another option is the **Pamawady Inn ❷,** at 14A Mingyi Rd., near the corner of Shwezedi Rd. Rooms are clean, and the staff is always helpful. (☎211 65. Singles with fan US$3-10; doubles US$6-20.)

Pathein's restaurants are not accustomed to catering to tourists, so don't be surprised when restaurant owners stare at you, shocked. **Moepalay Indian Food ❸,** on Merchant St., 1½ blocks south of the traffic lights on the left side, has satisfying, spicy *biriyani* (500kyat). There is no English sign. Look or smell for the large metal bucket of *biriyani* in front of the restaurant. **Kha Kha Gyi ❸,** 68 Mingalar St., opposite the east entrance to Shwemokhtaw Pagoda, serves excellent, full spreads of Burmese food for around 400kyat. (Open daily 9am-9pm.)

SIGHTS AND ENTERTAINMENT. Shwemokhtaw Pagoda, at the intersection of Shwezedi and Merchant Rd., and the smaller Buddha figures along its perimeter create a serene spiritual scene. While not as big as its cousins in Yangon and Bago, Shwemokhtaw's sequined designs prove that size doesn't matter when it comes to beauty. **Settayaw Pagoda,** off Pathein Hwy. as you enter the city (look for statues of two old men), seems like a Disney Buddhism theme park. Warning: monstrous snakes live in the cage next to the building opposite the standing Buddha. **Twenty-Eight Pagodas,** featuring 28 images of the Buddha, deserve a look by travelers craving more splendid Buddhist abodes. One pagoda out of town that attracts tourists is **Khan Kyi Daung Pagoda,** designed after Ananda Temple in Bagan. A pickup runs once an hour, and it's about a 1hr. trip. Pathein is known for making Myanmar's most decorative parasols, and two **parasol workshops** along Shwezedi Rd. near Mingyi Rd. detail the fascinating production process. (Open daily 9am-7pm.) Guides near Shwemokhtaw help tourists find the string of family-run shops that sell the colorful umbrellas. The **Ayeyarwady Golf Club Pathein,** in the quiet neighborhood of town, offers a great break from sight-seeing. Established in 1911 during the British colonial era, its 18 holes are fairly well maintained. *(On Pathein Hwy., 3km east of the clock tower, near the Highway Bus Station. Green fee US$5; club rental 1000kyat; pull-cart 500kyat; golf cart 1000kyat; caddy 500kyat.)*

THANK GOODNESS IT'S VENUS-PIG DAY!

The Burmese astrological system is the principal base of the architecture of many pagodas. Eight planetary posts, each corresponding to a point of the compass and a day of the week, line the structure's circumference, while shrines at each post pay homage to a host of galactic and mythical entities.

DAY	DIRECTION	PLANET	GUARDIAN SPIRIT
Sunday	Northeast	Sun	Garuda
Monday	East	Moon	Tiger
Tuesday	Southeast	Mars	Lion
Wednesday am	South	Mercury	Elephant with tusks
Wednesday pm	Northwest	Rahu	Elephant without tusks
Thursday	West	Jupiter	Rat
Friday	North	Venus	Pig
Saturday	Southwest	Saturn	Dragon

A Buddhist's visit to a pagoda usually has a dual purpose: to gain brownie points by doing good deeds and to get insurance against bad luck in the future. A worshiper visits the planetary shrine linked to his birthdate to appease its guardian spirit. The ritual consists of pouring cups of water on the spirit's image (the number of cups depends on the person's age) and reciting prayers. Those especially eager to ward off impending misfortune offer eugenia sprigs, a plant associated with victory, for added protection. Rahu is the planet believed to swallow the moon during eclipses; it and Saturn are notorious as evil planets, and their planetary posts inspire anxiety and fear.

DAYTRIP FROM PATHEIN: CHAUNG THA BEACH. Ranked by most visitors as one of Myanmar's best beaches (after hard-to-reach Ngapali Beach in Rakhaine State), **Chaung Tha's** sand and surf attract visitors, both Burmese and foreign, but is dominated by locals especially during the **Water Festival** in April. When the monsoon hits, however, poor weather dampens the beach's appeal as well as spirits. Nestled in the Bay of Bengal, Chaung Tha can be reached by **bus** from Pathein (2-3hr., 500kyat; US$5 collected at the ferry).

As of July 2002, about 25 accommodations line Chaung Tha beach's main road, half of which are hotels located on the beach side and half of which are cheaper guest houses away from the beach. If you are staying in Chaung Tha overnight, you might as well pay the few extra dollars to situate yourself on a bungalow right by the beach. **Chaungtha Beach Hotel** ❸ (☎248 80, ext. 324), across from the bus station, and **Golden Beach Hotel** ❸ (☎241 26), a 5min. walk back toward Pathein from the bus station, both have more than 50 rooms ranging from economy rooms with fan (singles US$6-10), to 2-bed bungalows with satellite TV, A/C, refrigerator, hot shower, and bathtub (doubles US$30-36). A substantial 30% discount off these prices is common during the low season. The only hotel that could possibly overshadow these is the **Hotel Max** ❺ (☎249 66; maxmyanmar@mptmail.net.mm), right in the center of town. Upon the completion of its construction in December 2002, it proposes to be a world-class hotel with a swimming pool, tennis court, mini-golf course, massage parlor, beauty parlor, karaoke room, business center, convenience store, and Asian/Continental dining room. Prices will probably start around US$35 and rise steadily into the stratosphere. If you are adhering to a tighter budget, **guest houses** ❷ along the road offer singles for US$3-5. **Shwe Hein Si Guest House,** a blue building opposite the Golden Beach Hotel at the end of the pathway, has clean, cozy rooms. Fresh seafood from the Bay of Bengal is served at all the restaurants in town including **For Mon** ❹—a Chinese restaurant—at reasonable prices. Try the crab and vegetable soup (800kyat).

DAYTRIPS FROM PATHEIN. In January 2002, the government opened up the beautiful **Ngwesaung Beach** to foreigners. Because it is a "new" beach resort, the accommodation and food facilities have not been as developed as those at Chaung Tha Beach: there are five hotels and a few restaurants as of July 2002. Nestled in the Bay of Bengal and with deeper water than Chaung Tha, Ngwesaung's unspoiled conditions will definitely establish it as one of the major destinations for foreigners in the near future. *(From Chaung Tha Beach, hire a boat for US$25 round-trip, or cycle down the coast for 2-3hr. From Pathein, a 4hr. bus leaves daily at 6am.)*

UPPER MYANMAR

> **GOVERNMENT LISTINGS.** All government listings are marked with a symbol. Money spent at such establishments goes directly into the government's hands. See **Keep the Bucks Where They Belong,** p. 496.

MANDALAY မန္တလေး ☎02

Sprawling, dusty Mandalay may not exactly be eye candy, but the joy of Myanmar's second-largest city lies not in its appearance but in the cultural fabric woven into its patchwork grid of streets. The last capital of Myanmar before British rule, Mandalay retains the artistic traditions that were once the object of royal patronage, and quarters of the city still brim with performers and artisans. Daytime affords opportunities to observe local artisans, and the night brings out street performers. At the northeast and southwest corners of the city are Mandalay Hill and Mahumuni Pagoda, both of which deserve a visit, and four nearby towns provide escape from the bustle and invite travelers to linger for a few days before slipping off to a more sedate respite on Inle Lake or Bagan.

INTERCITY TRANSPORTATION

BY PLANE

Mandalay International Airport (☎347 07) is a distant 35km south of the city center. (Taxi into town 5000kyat.) **Air Mandalay** (☎274 39; open M-F 9:30am-4pm, Sa-Su 9:30am-noon), on 82nd St. between 26th and 27th St., flies to: **Bagan** (4:25pm,

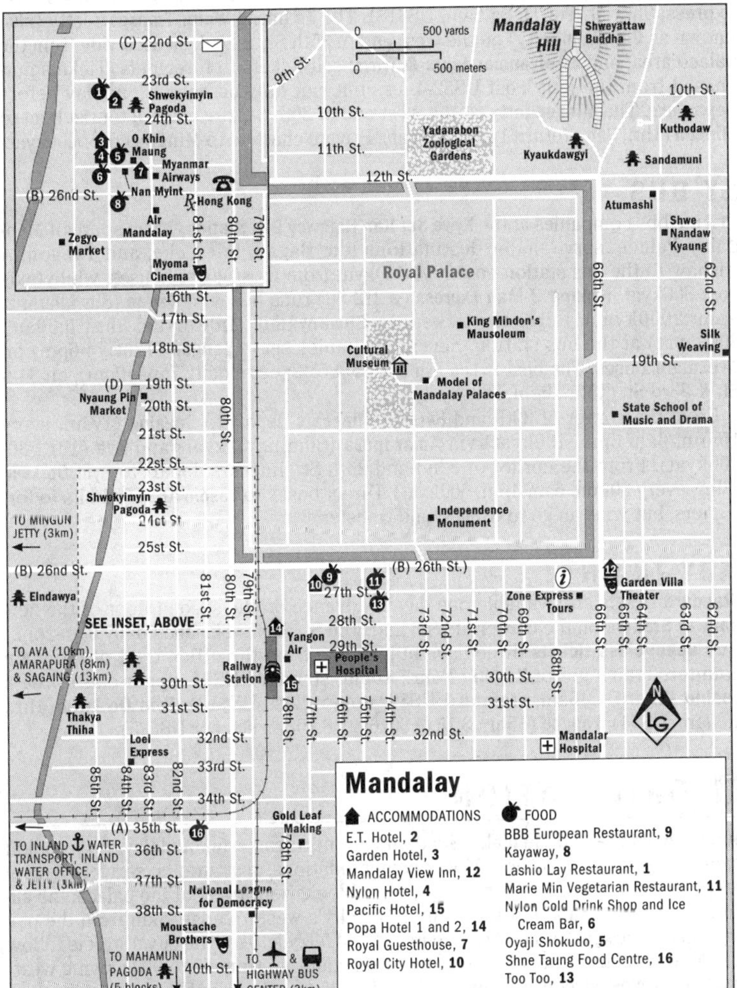

US$40); **Heho/Inle Lake** (9am, US$40); **Yangon** (1½hr., 9am, 12:20, 4:25pm; US$85). **Myanma Airways** (☎362 21; open daily 9:30am-4:30pm), on 81st St. between 25th and 26th St., flies to: **Bagan** (20min.; Sa-M, W 8am; US$40); **Baman** (30min.; M, F 8am; $50); **Heho/Inle Lake** (M 3:10pm, W 9:40am; US$35); **Tachilek** (1hr.; Tu, Sa 11:30am; $70); **Yangon** (1hr.; daily 8am, 1:30pm; US$100). Tickets bought one day in advance are only sold 9:30-10:30am. **Yangon Airways** (☎360 12; open daily 9am-5pm), on 78th St. between 29th and 30th, opposite the train station, flies to **Heho/Inle Lake** (8:50am, 12:45pm; $US32) and **Yangon** (8:50am, 5:10, 5:55pm; US$78).

BY BOAT

Boats sail to **Bagan** (regular: 14hr.; W and Su 5:30am; deck US$11, cabin US$33; express: 9hr.; M, Tu, Th-Sa 6am; US$18). The **Inland Water Transport** jetty (also known as **Gaw Wein** jetty) on the west end of 35th St., a 200kyat *sica* ride from the palace area, and **Myanmar Tours & Travel** sell tickets to foreigners. Tickets purchased from the jetty cost US$2-4 less but can only be bought one day before departure. The **Mingun** jetty, at the west end of 26th St., organizes a tourist boat to **Mingun** (1hr.; 9am, return 1pm; 500kyat). Private charters to Mingun cost 5000kyat.

BY BUS

Private bus companies at the **Kywe Ser Kan Highway Bus Station,** 10km south of Mandalay Palace, serve major destinations like Bagan, Inle Lake, and Yangon. A trishaw to the bus station costs 300-400kyat from most guest houses, while taxis cost 800kyat. **Nyaung U Man Express** (☎212 80) runs buses to **Bagan** (8hr.; 9am, 2, 9pm; 2000kyat). Purchase tickets to **Shwenyaung** (Inle Lake; 8hr., 5:30am, 3000kyat) at the bus station. Seven companies serve **Yangon** (12hr., 4-6pm) on overnight buses. The best is **Leo Express** (☎885 12; open daily 7am-10pm), on 84th St. & 33rd St. (15hr., 6pm, 2600kyat).

From the corner of 29th and 84th St., **linecars** depart to **Sagaing** (1¼hr., every 15min. 6am-6pm, 100kyat) via **Amarapura** (30min., 50kyat) and **Ava** (1hr., 30-100kyat). From the corner of 82nd and 26th St., linecars depart to **Pyin Oo Lwin** (3hr., every 30min. 6am-4pm, 500kyat). Direct buses to **Lashio** are off-limits to foreigners, but you can go to **Hsipaw,** and transfer.

BY TRAIN

Standard tickets are available one day in advance on the second floor of the new **Railway Station,** on the corner of 78th and 30th St. (☎213 85. Open daily 6am-2pm.) Buy **upper-class tickets** three days in advance from the office right of the main counter. Trains go to: **Bagan** (7½hr.; 10pm; standard US$4, upper-class US$9); **Lashio** (12hr.; 4:45am; standard US$9, upper-class US$13); **Pyin Oo Lwin** (4hr., 4:30am, US$4); **Yangon** (15hr.; 3:15, 5:30, 6:30, 8:30pm; sleeper US$35).

ORIENTATION

Mandalay Palace and **Mandalay Hill** dominate northeastern Mandalay. A 3.2sq. km moat surrounds the palace. Most accommodations, restaurants, services, travel services, and the **train station** cluster a few blocks southwest of the palace; the **airport** and **bus station** are farther south. The city's western edge, 3km from the palace, meets the **Ayeyarwady River** and its several ferry jetties. The city's streets follow a simple grid structure: north-south streets count up from 50 to 90 (moving west) while east-west streets are labeled from 1 to 45 (moving south).

LOCAL TRANSPORTATION

Unless you aren't comfortable negotiating through Mandalay's crazy traffic or it's too hot outside, go ahead and rent a bicycle. Otherwise, hire one of Mandalay's 17,000 pedicabs—trishaws or *sicas*.

Bicycles: Several guest houses and hotels rent bicycles. **O Khin Maung,** opposite the Royal Guest House, charges 500kyat per day.

Taxis: Two types of taxis are available: small **blue** taxis resemble mini linecars (500kyat per hr., US$10 per day); larger **white** taxis are typically Japanese sedans (1000kyat per hr., US$30 per day). Rates can fluctuate with the cost of petrol. Settle on a price first.

Trishaws (Sica): Hopping on a trishaw is a crucial part of the Mandalay experience. Use these pedicabs for short trips within the city, which will cost about 200kyat. Drivers charge a few thousand kyat for a day of sightseeing. Make your destination clear.

PRACTICAL INFORMATION

Tourist Office: **Myanmar Tours & Travels** (☎271 93), on 68th St. between 26th and 27th St. Myanma Airways and boat bookings. Maps 100kyat. English spoken. Open daily 8:30am-6:30pm. Guides at travel agencies and MTT US$15 per day.

Travel Agency: Zone Express Tours (☎286 02; fax 611 36; ZONE.ETT@mpt-mail.net.mm), on 27th St. between 66th and 68th St. Friendly staff will happily assist you with hiring tour cars and tour guides, accommodation, food, and intercity transportation. Airplane tickets may be several dollars cheaper here. Open daily 8am-6pm.

Currency Exchange: Most hotels and guest houses exchange US$ at fair rates. For the best rate in the city, ask around.

Emergency: Fire ☎191. **Ambulance** ☎192. **Police** ☎199.

Pharmacy: Hong Kong (☎248 04), on the corner of 26 St. and 81st St. Open daily 8am-8pm.

Medical Services: **Mandalar Hospital** (☎357 99), on 68th St., between 32nd and 33rd St. Private clinics are better. **Myat Thu Kha,** 392 80th St. (☎350 66), between 24th and 25th St. English spoken. **Open 24hr.** A smaller **clinic** (☎278 59) at 81st St., between 28th and 29th St.

Telephones: **Telephone/Telegraph Office** (☎214 44), on 26th St. between 80th and 81st St. International calls. US$5.40 per min. to call the US. Open daily 7am-9pm. **IDD** at numerous hotels cost a couple more dollars per min. Calling cards don't work. **Telegraphs** (4kyat per word) arrive in one day (M-F 7am-7pm, holidays 9am-7pm).

Internet Access: A good bet for Internet service is business centers at some of the more expensive hotels. **Sedona Hotel** (☎364 88), at the corner of 26th and 66th St. US$2 per kilobyte to send, US$1 per page to receive. Open M-F 8am-5pm. **Norotel Hotel** (☎356 38), on 10th St. at the foot of Mandalay Hill. US$3 to send to one email address. US$1 per page. **Mandalay Swan Hotel** (☎356 78), on 26th St., between 66th and 68th St. US$1.50 per page to send.

Post Office: GPO, on 22nd St. between 80th and 81st St. *Poste Restante*. Open M-Sa 9:30am-4:30pm. **Postal code:** 05071.

ACCOMMODATIONS

Mandalay's budget accommodations are west of Mandalay Palace, with the most popular ones concentrated near the intersection of 25th St. and 83rd St. Most accommodations include breakfast, bike rental, and laundry service.

Mandalay View Inn (☎611 19), on 66th St. between 26th and 27th St., across from Sedona Hotel. Convenient location at the corner of Royal Palace. Offers comfortable, quiet rooms with TV, refrigerator, phone, bath, and A/C. Breakfast included. Email service. IDD telephone service. Standard singles and doubles US$23-30, superior rooms US$30-40. Traveler's checks/AmEx/MC/V. ❺

Nylon Hotel (☎334 60; NYLON@mptmail.net.mm), at the corner of 25th and 83rd St. Pleasant staff manages cheap, and clean rooms with TV, refrigerator, phone, bath, and A/C. Bike rental and laundry service. Singles $US3-5; doubles US$6-8. ❷

E.T. Hotel (☎254 91), on 83rd St. between 23rd and 24th St. Right in the backpackers' neighborhood, E.T. has basic rooms with bath, A/C or fans, TV, and refrigerator. Singles US$5-6; doubles $8-12; triples $15. ❸

Royal Guest House, 41 25th St. (☎314 00), between 82nd and 83rd St. Personable staff and less crowded than Nylon Hotel. Cold drinks 80kyat. Singles US$3, with A/C and private bath US$4-5; doubles US$6/$8-10. ❷

Royal City Hotel, 130 27th St. (☎318 05), between 76th and 77th St. Provides the same comfort and friendliness as the Royal Guest House, but with luxury. All rooms with TV, bathtub, and A/C. IDD telephone service (US$8 per min. to US). Bicycle rental and laundry service. Singles US$13-18; doubles US$18-25. ❹

Garden Hotel, 174 83rd St. (☎276 57), between 24th and 25th St., next to Nylon Hotel. Spacious rooms with A/C, hot shower, TV, refrigerator, and telephone. Singles US$5-6; doubles US$10-15. ❸

Pacific Hotel (☎325 07), at the corner of 30th and 78th St., right in front of the railway station, offers neat rooms and a spacious lobby area. Recommended for visitors arriving on late-night trains. IDD telephone service. Restaurant attached. All rooms with TV, A/C, and bath. Singles US$20; doubles US$25. ❺

Popa Hotel 1 and 2 (☎352 31), on 78th and 30th St.; and 78th and 28th St., respectively. Conveniently located right next to the railway station. Basic rooms with TV, A/C, and mini-bath. Singles US$15; doubles US$20. ❹

FOOD

Finding a place to eat in Mandalay should be the least of your worries, as quality restaurants are everywhere, espeically in the blocks southwest of the palace. Cuisines range from Chinese, Shen, Burmese, Indian, and Thai to Western. Beer stations are scattered throughout the city, offering simple dishes and a few cold ones.

Nylon Cold Drink Shop and Ice Cream Bar (☎229 38), on the corner of 83rd St. and 25th St. Get your ice cream and milkshake fix here at local price. Divine ice cream 100kyat. Strawberry milkshake 200kyat. Open daily 7am-11pm. ❶

Kayaway, at the southeast corner of 26th and 83rd St. One of the locals' favorite *biryani* restaurants in town. Packed with people every night. At local price, the food is divine: *chapaati* (400kyat), *kima* (350kyat), *biryani* (400kyat). No beer. Open 5:30-10pm. ❸

Marie Min Vegetarian Restaurant, on 27th St., between 74th and 75th St. With refreshing drinks, veggie food, and travel info, it's an herbivore's dream come true. Shakes 130-200kyat. Guacamole with *chapaati* 275kyat. Open daily 8am-10pm. ❷

Lashio Lay Restaurant (☎385 68), 65 23rd St. between 83rd and 84th St. One of the favorite Shen restaurants among the locals. Pick your dishes from the front of the restaurant. Most meat and vegetable dishes 200-300kyat. Heapings of rice come with your food for 120kyat per person. Large bottle of beer 600kyat. Open daily 8am-10pm. ❷

BBB European Restaurant, 242 76th St. between 26th and 27th St. Don't let the name or ritzy appearance scare you away. Great, reasonably-priced Western food and wine make it popular amongst the local clientele. Burgers 500kyat. Chicken barbecue 1200kyat. Spaghetti 1300kyat. Open daily 8am-11pm. ❹

Too Too, on 27th St. between 74th and 75th St., opposite Marie Min Vegetarian Restaurant. Locals say it's the best Burmese food in the area. Succulent meat and fish curries come with side dishes of lentil and broadbean curries. Meals 500kyat, veggie-only 100kyat. Open daily 11am-8pm. ❸

Shne Taung Food Centre (☎231 27), on 35th St. between 81st and 82nd St. Live traditional music and dancing (during high season) makes it well worth a visit. Fried noodles 600kyat. Sweet and sour pork 900kyat. Beer 800kyat. Open daily 10am-10pm. ❹

Oyaji Shokudo, at the corner of 83rd St. and 25th St., across from the Garden Hotel. Offers tired travelers a place to unwind at night. All dishes at local price. Noodle soup 200kyat. Rice porridge 450kyat. Open daily 5:30pm-midnight. ❸

SIGHTS

Mandalay's historical sights are in the northeast, with the exception of Mahamuni Pagoda and the artisan quarters in the southern reaches.

MANDALAY HILL မန္တလေးတောင**.** Rising 236m above the northeastern corner of town, the seemingly endless 700-odd steps are well worth the 30min. climb. The less ambitious can use linecar service to the top (80kyat). The temples leading to the summit seem newfangled and lacking in distinction, but the Shweyattaw image, around halfway, is an exception. The towering 8m Buddha image points toward the city. This is a representation of a famous legend in which the Buddha predicted that a great Buddhist city would arise at the base of the hill, under the rule of Sandamukhi Ogress, who, being so poor, decided to cut off and donate her own breasts as a gift to Buddha. You can find an image of her toward the top of the hill. Especially at sunset or on the weekends, local teens come to practice their foreign languages with tourists. *(Open daily 6am-8pm. US$3.)*

SHWE NANDAW KYAUNG (GOLDEN PALACE MONASTERY) AND ATUMASHI (INCOMPARABLE MONASTERY). The only teak building in Mandalay to survive WWII, the architecture and ornamentation of **Shwe Nandaw Kyaung** yields one of Mandalay's most impressive sights. Originally built by King Mindon in 1878, it highlights a royal medication couch and a replica of the great Lion Throne. It used to be covered in gold, hence the name "Golden Palace Monastery." **Atumashi,** behind Shwe Nandaw Kyaung, is much less stunning. Before burning down in 1892, it was considered Mandalay's most beautiful monument, with elaborate stucco carvings, glass mosaics, fine masonry work, and a revered, diamond-encrusted Buddha image (which the British stole in 1885). The fruit of intense prison labor, the reconstructed building looks so modern that it's difficult to imagine its prior splendor. *(South of Kuthodaw Pagoda. Open daily 8:30am-5:30pm. US$5.)*

MAHAMUNI PAGODA. The "Pagoda of the Great Buddha Image" remains the holiest object in Upper Myanmar. According to legend, the Buddha brought this 3.8m bronze temple to life after embracing it seven times during a visit to the Rakhine (Arakan) State. Mahamuni was presented to Mandalay in 1784 by the Crown Prince of Amarapura, who had claimed it upon his victory over the Arakan King. Every morning around 4am, the head monk gives the image a ceremonial facial, right down to brushing its teeth. Women grind sandalwood for the ceremony in one of the side courtyards but are prohibited from entering the inner sanctuary. Male pilgrims flock daily to the podium to affix gold leaves to the Buddha. Over the years, the golden buildup has accumulated to a layer over 16cm thick. The face has reputedly expanded proportionally with this growth—stirring evidence, some say, that Mahamuni is a living entity. *Longgyi*-clad male visitors are welcome to place gold leaves on the image (*longgyi* rental 50kyat, 5 gold leaves 200kyat).

Behind the image and to the right stand **six bronze statues.** The interest here lies not so much in their artistic merit but in the statues' travels. Originating in Cambodia's Angkor Wat, the statues were moved to Ayutthaya in 1431, the Burmese Kingdom of Bago in 1564, the Arakan Kingdom in 1600, and finally to Mandalay along with the Mahamuni Pagoda in 1784. There is also a legend surrounding these bronze statues: after arriving in Mahamuni Pagoda, it was believed that they were alive as they cried at night longing for their Cambodian homeland. Many believe that rubbing the figures in a particular place cures ailments in the corresponding part of the body. The temple's atmosphere is lively. Artisans selling wood-carvings, miniature gongs, and other handicrafts crowd the walkways to the temple. Although beggars are prohibited in Myanmar by the government, you may encounter some here. *(In southern Mandalay. The main entrance is at the intersection of 82nd and 45th St. Open daily 4am-4pm. No sleeveless shirts or shorts. US$4.)*

THE ROYAL PALACE မန္တလေး နန်းတော်. Surrounded by stately walls and a formidable moat, the Royal Palace, built in the 1860s, monopolizes northern Mandalay on a 3.2 sq. km plot of land. The walls of King Mindon's teak palace and their associated guard towers are all that remain of the original structure from the WWII destructions. East of the current palace, a **scale model** of the original grounds hints at its former grandeur. A few concrete reconstructions—including the palace itself and a watchtower—make up the main tourist attractions. The palace may not be worth the steep admission; many travelers skip the palace or consciously boycott it to protest the forced labor involved in its reconstruction. The enormous moat, for example, is the result of the mass mobilization of Mandalay's citizens, who had to bring their own tools to the work site. *(Open daily 8:30am-5pm. US$5.)*

KUTHODAW PAGODA AND SANDAMUNI PAGODA. Crafted in 1857 on the model of Bagan's Shwezigon Pagoda, **Kuthodaw,** a 5min. walk east of Mandalay Hill, holds the distinction of housing the world's biggest book, a tome with all Buddhist scriptures in Pali, an ancient language which today only the monks can read. The text is inscribed on 729 stone slabs, each sheltered in masonry shrines surrounding the pagoda. One hundred meters southwest of Kuthodaw, **Sandamuni Pagoda** marks where King Mindon's younger brother, hand-picked to succeed him, was murdered in 1866 by two of the King's miffed sons. Much more interesting than the pagoda's iron Buddha are the surrounding miniature *stupas*, which shelter 1774 marble slabs containing commentaries on the Tripitaka called *Sutta Vinaya Abidhamma.* *(Open daily 6:30am-6pm. US$5; includes admission to both pagodas.)*

KYAUKDAWGYI PAGODA. Built by King Mindon from 1853 to 1878, this pagoda rests at Mandalay Hill's base opposite the main southern walkway. The Buddha statue was cut from a 3.5 million kg block of green marble; moving it from the quarry required a herculean effort of 10,000 laborers. Visitors should note that this image is unique in that unlike most other Buddha images which are coated in gold, this one bares its marble body. *(Open daily 7:30am-6pm. US$2.)*

ARTISAN WORKSHOPS. Mandalay is known as Myanmar's center of culture and art, thanks to the **artisan guilds. Marble and wood workshops** craft Buddha statues of every size in the south of the city. *(South of Mahamuni Pagoda on 84th St., between 45th and 46th St. Open daily 9am-5pm.)* The ancient art of **silk weaving** continues and can be observed in the eastern part of the city. Mandalay's silk is reputed to be Myanmar's best. *(On 19th St. between 62nd and 61st St. Open daily 7am-6pm.)* In the **Myit Pa Yup Quarter,** 200 families dedicate their energy to the production of **gold leaf,** which is used to gild *stupas* and sacred images. The labor-intensive hammering and delicate packaging processes are an eye-opening look into the effort required to make the 0.02cm thick leaves. It is well worth a stop on a bicycle or trishaw tour. *(On 36th St. between 77th and 78th St. Open daily 8am-6pm. Gold leaf 80kyat.)*

MARKETS

Equidistant from India, Bangladesh, China, and Thailand, Mandalay serves as a major shopping hub and arts center. **Handicrafts**—teak, marble, and jade carvings, lacquer ware, and metalworking abound, particularly in the south of the city around Mahamuni Pagoda. **Zegyo Market,** a three-block shopping and socializing extravaganza, provides just about everything else, including hours of people-watching. Fruit and vegetable merchants set up around midnight, and locals crowd side streets to buy produce each morning. Around midday, the inventory shifts gears: plastic and stainless steel kitchenware, *longgyi* (around 1000kyat), and bamboo weavings replace foodstuffs. The **night market** continues the selling frenzy with less practical goods like military knives, brass knuckles, and fake designer watches. (Southwest off the corner of 84th and 26th St. Open daily 5am-10pm.) **Soe Moe,** on 84th St. about a 5min. bike ride from Mahumuni Pagoda on the right side, provides an extensive selection of embroidered tapestries (US$5), teak wood carvings (US$5), puppets (US$2), and bronze buddhas (US$20).

ENTERTAINMENT

If you are in the mood for an artistic, cultural night, check out the **Mandalay Marionettes,** an entertaining traditional Burmese art form. Dating to 11th-century Bagan, Burmese puppetry adapts themes from stories of the Buddha and colorful events in Burmese mythology. Seasoned puppeteers deliver quality shows at the **Garden Villa Theater** on 66th St. between 26th and 27th St. (1hr., daily 8:30pm, US$3.) Mandalay also boasts its own **"Little Broadway."** Covering 39th to 43rd St. between 80th and 81st St., the **theater district** has 50 performance troupes, each advertised on colorful billboards. The government authorizes all but one of these troupes, to be hired to perform all night long at weddings or other festivities for 50,000kyat per day. The one exception, which has attracted international attention, is the **Moustache Brothers,** on 39th St. between 80th and 81st St. Backed by 30 years' experience, this troupe performs *a-nyeint* (see **Can't Take a Joke?**, p. 526). The performances interweave commentary, conjugal infidelity jokes, and traditional dances with elaborate costumes, culminating in a spin-off of the Demi Moore movie *Striptease.* (Shows 8:30pm. 1000kyat per person.) For a quieter evening, head to **Myoma Cinema,** at the corner of 81st and 28th St., which shows foreign films in their original language (often with Burmese subtitles) and local films without subtitles. (☎387 19. Showtimes 12:30am, 3:30, 6:30, 9:30pm. 100-600kyat.)

DAYTRIPS FROM MANDALAY

Several daytrip destinations surround Mandalay, each catering to different interests: the three ancient cities **(Amarapura, Ava,** and **Sagaing)** embody the historical and religious roots of the Burmese culture, while providing beautiful scenery. A pile of brick being the major sight, **Mingun** serves as a quick glimpse of country life. **Pyin Oo Lwin** offers nature and cooler temperatures for those who need a break from the heat of Mandalay. **Monywa** is a destination with a set of unique archaeological and religious attractions, including the monstrous reclining Buddha.

CAN'T TAKE A JOKE? *A-nyeint* theater has a long history. Burmese people flock to this synthesis of cabaret, burlesque, and vaudeville, sometimes at all-night festivals called *pwe*. From the 1960s through 1996, the Moustache Brothers in Mandalay were some of the art's most popular practitioners. A controversial incident in 1996, however, changed the lives of the Brothers forever; they have been transformed into an international symbol of political opposition against the junta and of the international movement for human rights in Myanmar much like Daw Aung San Suu Kyi. On January 4, 1996, Moustache Brother Par Par Lay and cousin U Lu Zaw were invited to the NLD's celebration of the 48th anniversary of Burmese independence, at Aung San Suu Kyi's compound, to perform before government officials and dignitaries. Par Par Lay prefaced his routine by declaring he would speak his mind, despite the threat of reprisals. In one skit, he played an imprisoned activist who refuses to die after being shot multiple times by a general. The pun hinges on the homonymy of "hit" and "right" in Burmese. In response to the general's insistence that he die after being hit, the prisoner responds, "Why should I die if I am right?" Three days after their return to Mandalay, security forces arrested dancers, musicians, comedians, and NLD attendees. After a short, undisclosed trial in Mandalay, the two comedians faced a seven-year sentence in prison, but first were held in a hard labor camp in Northern Myanmar where they were chained, tortured, and surrounded by violent criminals. Meanwhile, the remaining Moustache Brother, Lu Maw, kept the fire burning, hosting the show at home and continuing to make political jokes despite his blacklist status. Between acts and jokes, Lu Maw explained that he and his brother flipped a coin to determine who would attend the NLD celebration. The wife of Par Par Lay was also a part of the show. In 1997, 10 Hollywood comedians wrote to the government to urge that Par Par Lay and Lu Zaw be released. Then, in 1998, anti-government demonstrators in front of Myanmar's London embassy created a 6m-by-4m portrait of the comedians by applying 1.6 million thumbprints to a canvas. The portrait hangs in London's National Gallery. Such domestic courage and international support resulted in the early termination of the comedians' sentence; on July 13, 2001, they were released. Two days later, July 15, marked the first performance after the long-awaited unification of the family, during which more than 200 people filled the whole block around the theater and five government officials (whom Lu Maw refers to as KGB or military intelligence) taped the show. Having tolerated Lu Maw's political jokes for only 11 days, the government again deemed the performances subversive, and decided on July 26th, 2001, to impose strict curbs on *a-nyeint* artists, banning all-night performances, censoring advertising, and requiring comedians to submit written copies of jokes for approval. A year after the crackdown, the three comedians, ten dancers, and eight musicians continue to demonsrate their passion for entertainment and their belief in freedom. Until they attain it, however, the Moustache Brothers will not back down.

Mingun is accessible only by boat, while the others can be reached by linecar or taxi. By hiring a blue taxi (US$6-10 per day) or starting early enough on your own, you can see the three down-river towns leisurely in one day. The natural progression of sights makes it best to work your way farther away from Mandalay over the course of the day: from Amarapura to Ava to Sagaing. While finishing at U Bein's Bridge in Amarapura around dusk is ideal and picturesque, it is a delight to end the day in Sagan for views of the sunset, cities, and surrounding plains from atop the pagoda-covered splendor of Sagaing Hill. Alternately, it's possible to see Mingun by boat in the morning, return to Mandalay, catch a linecar or taxi to Sagaing in the afternoon, and visit Amarapura and Ava by linecar another day. Both Pyin Oo Lwin and Monywa require a full day. Because of its proximity to Mandalay, however, Pyin Oo Lwin in particular is a worthwhile, pleasant trip.

PYIN OO LWIN (MAIMYO)

Linecars to Pyin Oo Lwin leave from the taxi/bus station on 82nd St. between 26th and 27th St. (3hr.; departs when truck fills up; 500kyat back of pickup, 800kyat front seat). Taxis only take 1½hr. (2000kyat per person).

In the late 19th century, during British colonial rule, the British experienced the unbearable heat of the hot season in Upper Myanmar. Trying to find a resort-esque area that would relieve them from the scorching sun in Mandalay, the colonialists came upon a village situated just 70km east of Mandalay, at a cooler elevation of 1000m. This "origin" and the development of Pyin Oo Lwin explain the colonial architecture, design, and feel of the town.

The town itself does not offer many tourist sites, other than the market and the botanical garden. The **market,** right behind the central clock tower, will give you a glimpse of the locals' everyday life. The brand new, 400-acre **botanical garden** can be reached by a nice, long stroll on foot or, better yet, on a colonial horse cart. (Botanical garden open 8:30am-6pm. 1000kyat.) Out of the many waterfalls surrounding Pyin Oo Lwin, **Anisagen Falls** is a worthwhile visit, despite the hike to get there. Take a refeshing dip in the water and relax in front of a 45m waterfall after a one-hour descent down a steep slope. (Take a pickup from Pyin Oo Lwin to Anigago Junction. 50kyat, 75kyat round-trip.) You can also be dropped off at the junction on the way from Mandalay to Pyin Oo Lwin to save time on a daytrip. Biking there is also an option, as it is only 8km back to Mandalay, but the return trip is mostly uphill. (1hr. descent from the junction, 1½hr. uphill.) Either by making the daytrip an action-packed, early morning one or spending the night in town, **Peik Chin Myaing** is an interesting shrine cave to visit. In 1990, the government renovated and developed this 600m cave into a tourist attraction by adding many religious elements to it. (30km from Pyin Oo Lwin; hop on a pickup for 500kyat.)

If you decide to stay overnight, there are a few options. In the center of town is **Golden Dream Hotel ❷** (☎085 221 42), opposite the clock tower on the main street. (Singles US$3, with bath US$4.) For visitors seeking a total getaway from urban life, **Grace Hotel ❸** (☎085 212 30) is a 5min. bike ride out of town in a quiet, green neighborhood. (Bicycle 500kyat per day. Singles US$6; doubles US$10.)

MONYWA

Linecars to Monywa leave from the west end of 23rd St. (3½hrs., departs when full, 500kyat). But because the sights of interest require a bit of a drive out of Monywa, sharing a taxi with other tourists is the most convenient option (2½hr., US$30).

Unlike Pyin Oo Lwin's, Monywa's heat is known to be the worst in Myanmar, reaching 40C (104F) in the months of April and May. Despite its heat, the commercial town flourishes as a trade hub on the Chindwin River. **Shwe Zy Ghong Pagoda,** in the middle of town, majestically illuminates its big golden architecture when the lights get turned on after 7pm. Archaeological enthusiasts will find **Pho Win Taung's** Shrine Caves quite fascinating. The history of this hill, which, it's claimed, hosts more than 400,000 Buddhas, dates back to the 13th-century Inwa Dynasty. Step inside these small, serene caves (take your shoes off first!) and discover intricate wall-paintings from the 18th century. Monkey-feeding ladies follow tourists to sell monkey food for 200kyat. It's fun to challenge monkeys' food-catching coordina-

FROM THE ROAD

POLITICS AND PEOPLE

My first introduction to Myanmar, beyond a vague understanding that it's a Southeast Asian country, occurred while I was spending the semester at Oxford University—which is also the same university from which Aung San Suu Kyi received a degree.

At a meeting about clean, ethical investment in Myanmar, a video clip was played demonstrating the atrocities that the current government has inflicted upon its citizens, including the 1990 election results that were ignored to maintain the status quo (see p. 491). Amnesty International has documented cases of torture in labor camps and prisons, land confiscation, and forced displacement. The understanding that such inhumane and horrifying acts still occur in the world today utterly shocked me, and its resonance continues to echo in my mind to this day. The outrage I felt triggered a specific interest in Myanmar—the outrage about which we, in the Western world, rarely hear any news.

After pursuing the subject, I was offered a job to research Myanmar for *Let's Go*. With excitement, hesitation, and expectation, I began my stay in Myanmar.

(continued on next page)

tion, but be careful not to get the food snatched away from your hands. (First, cross the Chinwin River by ferry. Be patient; the wait can take up to a couple hours. Pho Win Taung lies a 30min. drive away, for which there is no bus. Hire a car if you took a linecar to Monywa. Entrance fee: US$2 or 600kyat.) Also of interest near Pho Win Taung is **Swreba Hill Pagoda,** which holds 19th-century Buddha images as well as giant statues of a frog and an elephant. Built on the slope of a hill, the entrance to the pagoda gives a feeling of descending into an ancient, underground city. (1km from Pho Win Taung. Entrance fee US$1.) As if to compete with Pho Win Taung in the number of Buddha images, **Thonbodday Pagoda** exhibits over 580,000 Buddhas that range from tiny ones (one inch or so in height) to larger ones that make their preserve known in the dark mystical space. The architecture of the whole complex is quite unique, with countless needle-like poles pointing upward and an unusual watchtower with a spiral staircase. (Linecars go to Thanbodday Pagoda from Monywa. Entrance fee for US$3.)

The main tourist attraction of Monywa, however, must be the monstrous 100m-long reclining Buddha embedded in the hills a few kilometers from Thanbodday Pagoda. One of the largest reclining Buddhas in the world, if not the biggest, this Buddha--**Shwe The Lakaung**--is visible from a distance, but can only be accessed by taxi. Shwe The Lakaung is surrounded by other impressive Buddha images and pagodas, including **Bodi Tatoung** with 10,000 Buddhas. (Free entry.)

Visitors who wish to stay in Monywa will find **Shwe Taung Tran Hotel and Restaurant ❸** (☎071 214 78) conveniently located opposite Shwe Zy Ghong Pagoda. All rooms with A/C and bath. (Singles US$5-9, doubles US$10-16. Restaurant: fried rice 350kyat; eggs and sausage 600kyat; beer 100kyat.)

MINGUN မင်းကွန်း

Foreign tourists are limited to 3hr. visits and required to use the daily M MTT "tourist boat" that departs from the 26th St. jetty in Mandalay (1½hr., 1hr. return; 9am, returns 1pm; 500kyat). If you want to stay longer, charter a private boat (3000kyat), but 3hr. is ample time to enjoy the town. US$3.

Once a serene village along the great Ayeyawordy River, Mingun has been turned into a government production targeting tourism. Thus, it is no surprise that Mingun's three main sights are often accompanied by hordes of children who greet tourists at the dock and hound visitors at every turn, scrapping their way through explanations of the sights in hopes of earning a few kyat. All it takes is one step off this well-beaten track, however, and the traveler is alone, free to wander Mingun's fields and hills and enjoy splendid views all the way to Mandalay and a worthwhile glimpse into Myanmar's rural life.

MINGUN PAGODA. Size mattered to King Bodawpaya, who in 1790 began construction of a 150m pagoda to dwarf the mountain range behind it. In true autocratic fashion, he mobilized 20,000 Arakanese slaves for 39 years, but the pagoda only made it to 50m before suffering damage from the 1838 earthquake. Today, the remains of the king's arrogance bear the dubious title of "largest stack of bricks in the world," and the temple carries an alternate tag, Patodawgyi Pagoda, or "Unfinished Pagoda." Brisk breezes and views extending to Mandalay make the strenuous, 174-step climb to the top more than worthwhile.

MINGUN BELL. This massive appendage to the pagoda was completed in 1790 and continues to hang as King Bodawpaya's crowning achievement. The impressive 82,000kg bell, 4m high and 5m in diameter, is the largest un-cracked bell in the world. It is customary to hit the bell three times—one each for your father, mother, and teacher—and finish with a final stroke for yourself. Thrill-seekers crawl underneath to hear its resonance from within

HSINBYUME PAGODA. North of Mingun Pagoda, Hsinbyume is humble in comparison. Built in 1816, it finds its architectural inspiration in the cosmological vision of Sulamani Pagoda atop the heavens of Mount Meru. Its seven concentric terraces symbolize the mountain ranges surrounding Meru.

OTHER SIGHTS. A good place to escape Mingun's beaten path is the horse cart track behind Hsinbyume Pagoda. After passing peanut fields and a crumbling pagoda, the trail reaches the hills that paint Mingun's backdrop. Most of the souvenir-hawking crowd disappears by the time you reach Hsinbyume Pagoda, thus allowing visitors to hike the foothills unpestered, take in excellent views of Mingun Pagoda and the river, listen to farmers singing in the fields, and make it back to Mingun in time for a quick lunch before the boat leaves.

AMARAPURA အမရပူရ

Linecars to Amarapura leave from the intersection of 29th and 84th St. From the market in Amarapura, it's easy to pick up linecar #8 onward to Ava and Sagaing or back to Mandalay (25min., every 15min. 8am-5pm, 30kyat).

(continued from previous page)

Originally, I was expecting the worst possible scenario because of two basic facts.

First, I knew that Myanmar is ruled by an oppressive military regime. Second, I knew that economically speaking, it is the poorest country in Southeast Asia with a GDP per capita of only slightly over US$130 per year.

Like so many other things, the reality of Myanmar defied my expectations.

What I have encountered here in the past few weeks are not government officials, but a people who are perhaps the most civil, peaceful, animal-loving, hardworking, content, and genuinely generous people that I have ever known. And all this in the face of incredible oppression and poverty.

Were I unaware of the political situation, I would guess that Myanmar is a peaceful, crime-free, democratic society, especially because no one speaks about politics in public.

If I didn't know the poverty level of Myanmar according to the World Bank figures, I would assume that Myanmar is more or less a self-sufficient economy endowed with natural resources because there are considerably fewer slums and beggars than in other developing countries.

In general, the political and economic situation has not decayed the good hearts of the Burmese people—though the extent to which people can tolerate and fend off these evils is uncertain.

—Tomo Hamakawa

From the late 18th century until the mid-1800s, Amarapura swapped roles with Ava several times as the Burmese capital before ultimately losing the title to Mandalay. In its heyday, one writer has contended, Amarapura stood as a "microcosm of Burmese civilization"—a center not only of wealth, fashion, and beauty but also erudition and scholarship. Apart from a few structures and four pagodas marking the original corners of the city, Amarapura —"The City of Immortals"—has nothing to show for this regal legacy. Nonetheless, the lively market, provincial atmosphere, and opportunities for leisurely people-watching on the town's famous bridge will please those seeking respite from Mandalay's clamor.

U BEIN'S BRIDGE. At the west end of town, rickety U Bein's Bridge spans much of scenic **Lake Taungthaman.** Over 1km in length, it's the longest teak bridge in the world, all the more impressive given that it's nearly 250 years old. Townspeople flock to the bridge during the rainy season to fish the shallow lake, while the dry season sees farmers tilling and harvesting paddy fields where the lake once was. Regardless of the season, however, the relationship between the people and their land is worth a look. *(Ponycarts run from the market to the bridge for 100kyat each way. During the rainy season rowboats provide an alternate route across the lake for 300kyat.)*

SILK WEAVING. With nearly every house in town weaving silk, Amarapura has emerged as one of Myanmar's premier weaving centers. Family-run silk businesses have functioned here for generations. Weaving households line the street from the market to the bridge, and many accept to visitors and will demonstrate the entire painstaking process. *(Cotton-and-silk* longgyi *US$3. Intricate silk skirts US$5.)*

OTHER SIGHTS. South of the bridge entrance lies **Mahagandayon Monastery.** The 1000 monks uphold rigorous standards in the study of Pali and meditation techniques. A visit around 10:30am will allow you to witness the monks silently eating lunch, their last meal of the day. Rising at 4am, monks meditate and study the teachings of Buddha throughout the day, interrupted only by their two meals, one at 6am and the other at 10:30am, after which they ingest nothing but fluids. On the other side of the footbridge is the dusty village of **Taungthaman.** There you'll find **Kyauktawgyi Pagoda,** constructed in 1847 using Bagan's Ananda Temple as a blueprint. It features an impressive Buddha image and evidence of British influence (frescoes portray tailcoated figures). During the rainy season, reaching the temple may require wading through knee-deep muddy water. Also of interest is the **market,** which features fresh fruits, vegetables, and bamboo weavings.

AVA (INWA) အင်းဝ

Linecars from Amarapura drop off passengers at the base of a long wooden road (trishaw 100kyat). At its opposite end is a ferry landing where boats shuttle to Ava (5min., every 30min., 10kyat; US$4 fee payable at tourist booth before crossing).

MYANMAR

Ava (commonly referred to as Inwa) lies 20km southwest of Mandalay and 7km beyond Amarapura at the junction of the Ayeyarwady and the Myitnge rivers. Thado Minbya established Ava as the capital of Burma in 1364, a position it retained until 1823—the longest streak in Burmese history. Today, disembarking on the triangular island—which has a handful of motorized vehicles, a legion of horse carts, and one backwater village in the northeast—is like stepping back in time. Let the wondrous vibe of Ava take your imagination back to when this Burmese capital was the seat of a powerful, prosperous society in Southeast Asia. The old walls of the city remain intact, guarding cultivated land, hamlets, monasteries, and pagoda ruins. Pony carts provide the best means of navigation; flurries of them await arrivals at the two dock landings. The circuit around the "hit parade" of sights—the "leaning" watchtower, King Bagyidaw's Palace, Ava Fort, Okkyaung

Monastery, and a host of pagodas—takes an hour or two and costs 1000kyat. Guides are best hired through Mandalay guest houses (US$6-10).

A lone 30m watchtower marks **King Bagyidaw's Palace,** inhabited from 1819 to 1837. Though an 1838 earthquake left the palace slanted, people are allowed to climb the reinforced stairways for a breezy panorama of the area. The nearby **Maha Aungmye Bonzan Monastery** (Okkyaung Monastery), was built in 1818 by Bagyidaw's notorious queen, Nanmadaw Me, to house her religious preceptor, Nyaunggan Sayadaw. The upper chambers are desolate and not particularly interesting, but carvings of Buddhist imagery fill the lower levels and the dark, grotto-like series of walkways used for meditating. Crumbling **Bagaya Monastery,** constructed in 1834, represents Myanmar's famous teakwood monasteries and maintains many of its original carvings despite its dilapidated present condition. Many **ruined pagodas** visible from Bagaya may prove more interesting than the monasteries.

SAGAING စစ်ကိုင်း

Linecar #8 departs for Mandalay via Ava and Amarapura until 8pm (1hr., 50kyat).

Across the Ayeyarwady River from Ava, Sagaing is the religious center of Myanmar, teeming with *stupas* and monasteries, mostly scattered near Sagaing Hill to the northeast. Sagaing is best visited late, when the hill affords sunset panoramas to the chanting of the town's 5000 monks and nuns.

SAGAING HILL. With 300 temples and pagodas, Sagaing Hill rises majestically with tremendous views of Mandalay, Ava, Amarapura, and Sagaing. The walk up the front of the hill is good exercise but offers far fewer lookouts along the way than the back staircase, which passes several pagodas. Due to the difficulty (for non-Burmese speakers) in finding the back stairs, the best route may be to head up the front and down the back before flagging down a horse cart back to the linecar drop off point. Some of Sagaing Hill's attractions include: **Padamya Zedi,** built by a monk in 1300 (perched atop one of the less-accessible peaks, Padamya Zedi requires a full day to visit); **Ohnmin Thonze** ("30 Caves"), which shelters Buddha images in a crescent-like chamber; **Ponnyashin Pagoda,** housing the Buddha's hair relics, provides splendid views; and **Tilawkaguru,** at the base of the hill, built in 1672 and displaying murals depicting the Buddha's past lives. *(The hill is 4km north of the town center; take a horse cart or trishaw (300kyat one-way) or linecar (15min.; every 20min. 7:30-11am, return until 2pm; 30-40kyat) from the bus compound outside town to the base of the mountain. Covered walkways shelter the 30min. climb. US$4.)*

KAUNGHMUDAW PAGODA. Sagaing's most renowned and biggest temple, Kaunghmudaw rests 10km outside town. In 1536, with Ceylon's Mahaceti Pagoda as his ambitious model, King Thalun of Ava built the Kaunghmudaw Pagoda, also known as **Rajamanicula,** which reputedly houses the Buddha's sacred tooth and hair relics transferred from Bagan's Mahazedi Pagoda. Some believe that its architectural signature, a 46m high white Indian-style dome, was made in the likeness of the voluptuous breast of King Thalun's queen. *(Linecars from the Sagaing bus compound outside town leave for the temple (10min., every 30min. 7:30am-4pm, 30kyat). US$3.)*

MYITTAKAN. This sacred pond is surrounded by a parapet wall. Legend has it that no autumn leaves from the tangle of nearby trees have ever dared to break its surface. *(Behind Kaunghmudaw Pagoda.)*

BAGAN (PAGAN) ပုဂံ ☎062

If Myanmar were to have a World Heritage Site nominated, it would be the 42 sq. km with over 3000 pagodas—Bagan. Bagan's early history is not completely clear, but scholars agree that its splendor prevailed for 250 years following King

Anawrahta's ascension to the throne in 1044 (see **Bagan and Toungoo Dynasties,** p. 480). Dissatisfied with the religious practices of his people, Anawrahta launched a plan to rejuvenate Theravada Buddhism that was accompanied by a flurry of temple-building. The number of pagodas is still increasing today, and the awe-inspiring sunsets in Bagan conjure up the image of rosebuds rising from a caramel sea.

GOVERNMENT LISTINGS. Government listings are marked by a symbol. Money spent at such establishments goes directly into the government's hands. For more information, see **Keep the Bucks Where They Belong,** p. 496.

TRANSPORTATION

Flights: Nyaung U Airport (☎702 06), 4km southeast of Nyaung U, off the road to Mandalay. Taxis from the airport to most destinations in Bagan 2000kyat. **Air Mandalay** (☎701 16; open M-F 9am-5:30pm), 30m up Main Rd. from Bagan-Chauk Rd., in New Bagan. Daily flights leave (8-10am) for **Thandwe** (only during high season on M, Tu, F; arr. 1pm; US$118) via **Heho/Inle Lake** (arr. 9:30am, US$59); via **Mandalay** (arr. 8:40am; US$35); via **Yangon** (arr. 11:50am, US$118). **Yangon Airways** (☎704 51; open daily 9am-4pm), in Nyaung U on Anawrahta Rd., on the right about 200m past the post office heading away from the market. Flights leave Bagan daily (8:05am) for **Thandwe** (only high season) via **Mandalay** (arr. 8:50am, US$35); via **Heho/Inle Lake** (arr. 9:35am, US$59); via **Yangon** (arr. 10:45am, US$80). **Myanma Airways** (☎701 99; open daily 9am-4pm), 150m inside Tharaba Gate in Old Bagan, flies to **Mandalay** (7:30am, US$40) and **Yangon** (Su, M, W, Sa 8:30am; US$90). Air tickets are cheaper from agents who cluster on Bagan-Nyaung U Rd., 75m south of the market area. Most open daily 8am-6pm.

Trains: The **train station** is 6km south of Nyaung U and 10km east of New Bagan off the road to Mandalay. Taxis 3000kyat. Buy tickets a day in advance at the station ticket office or the branch 200m west of the market in Nyaung U, on Bagan-Nyaung U Rd. (☎704 17; open daily 8am-8pm) or arrange through guest houses. Trains to **Mandalay** (8hr.; 7am; ordinary US$4, upper US$9) and **Yangon** (24hr.; times vary; ordinary US$15, upper US$33).

Buses: Highway Bus Center, in front of Shwezigon Pagoda on Bagan-Nyaung U Rd., in Nyaung U. Book tickets at guest houses or in person. **Nyaung U Man Express** (☎704 00) goes to **Mandalay** (8-9hr.; 4, 7, 9am; 1500kyat) and **Taunggyi** (12hr., 5am, 2000kyat). **New Bagan Express** (☎704 79) and **Popa Dagon Express** go to **Yangon** (15-16hr., 3:30pm, 2000-2300kyat).

Boats: Popular express boats to **Mandalay** depart from the Nyaung U jetty, where Bagan-Nyaung U Rd. meets the river beyond the Nyaung U market (10hr.; Tu, W, F, Sa, Su 5am; US$15). The most scenic and comfortable mode of transportation, but the schedule is unreliable. Check at least one day in advance. Buy tickets at the jetty or through guest houses.

Local Transportation: Linecars depart from the market in Nyaung U to **New Bagan** (6am-6pm; less frequent in the afternoon; 30kyat) via **Old Bagan** (60kyat). **Pony carts** provide a comfortable way to skim the sights in one day (3-person max., 3000kyat per day). **Trishaws** in Nyaung U or New Bagan make intra-town trips. **Private taxis** can be hired through most guest houses to **Inle Lake** (8hr., US$50-60), usually via **Mount Poppa** (1½hr., US$20). **Car rental** US$15 per day in the area. **Bicycles** available at guest houses (300kyat). Nicer models are worth the extra kyat.

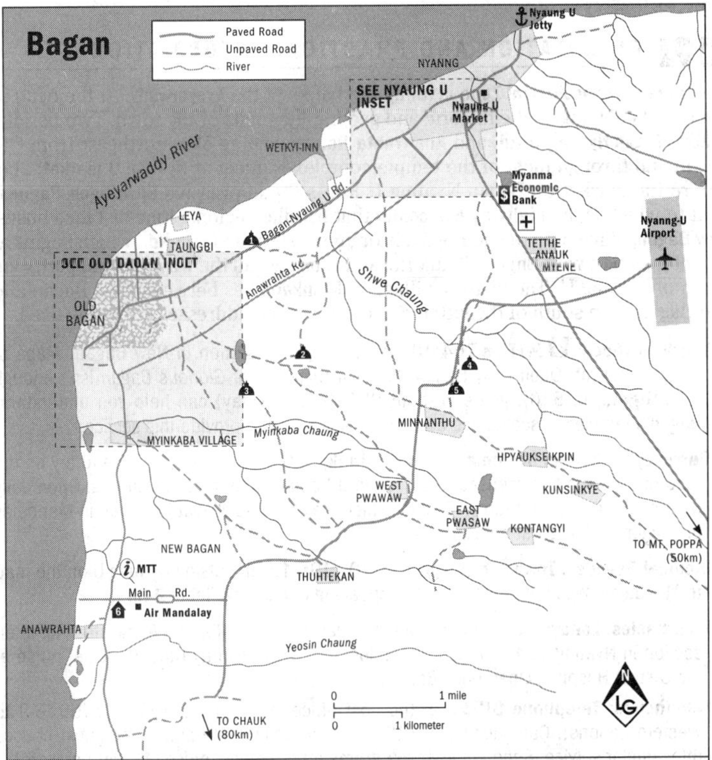

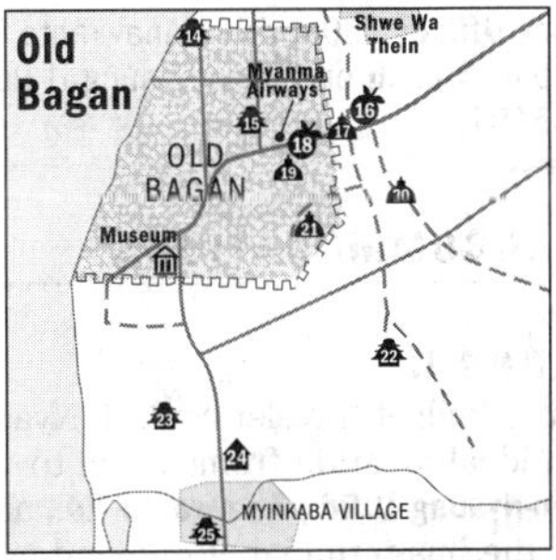

PAGODAS

Bupaya, **14**
Mahabodhi, **15**
Mingalazedi, **23**
Shwesandaw, **22**
Shwezigon, **9**

TEMPLES

Ananda, **20**
Dhammayangyi, **3**
Manuha, **25**
Nandamannya, **4**
Paya Thonezu, **5**
Pitikat Taik, **19**
Sarabha Gateway, **17**
Sulamani, **2**
Thatbyinnyu, **21**
Upali Thein, **1**

ACCOMMODATIONS

Eden Motel, **10**
New Heaven Hotel and Golden Village Inn, **13**
New Park Hotel, **12**
Phyo Guest House, **24**
Smile World Hotel, **6**

FOOD

Be Kind to Animal Vegetarian Restaurant, **18**
Pyi Wa, **11**
San Kabor Restaurant and Pub, **8**
Sarabha Restaurant, **16**
Shwe Myat Iar, **7**

ORIENTATION AND PRACTICAL INFORMATION

The **Bagan Archaeological Zone** is along the banks of the **Ayeyarwady.** At the bend in the river is **Old Bagan,** the historic and geographic focus of the town. Two parallel roads, **Bagan-Nyaung U Rd.** and **Anawrahta Rd.,** extending 5km northeast from Old Bagan and through most of the temple complexes, meet at **Nyaung U market.** 2km before the market on Bagan-Nyaung U Rd. is the impressive **Shwezigon Pagoda,** next to which is the highway **bus center** that handles regional long-distance buses. **New Bagan,** 3km south of Old Bagan, is organized around **Main Rd.,** which begins at the intersection with Bagan-Chauk Rd. and runs east all the way to the **airport,** 4km south of Nyaung U. The historic village of **Myinkaba** lies between New Bagan and Old Bagan, 1km south of the latter. Street names and addresses are rarely used.

Tourist Offices: MTT (☎704 18), near the police station in New Bagan. Maps of Bagan 200kyat. Open daily 8am-4:30pm. If *Glimpses of Glorious Bagan* isn't enough (see **Sights,** p. 536), guides (about US$15-30 per day) can help you understand Bagan's temples; it seems like every local is licensed to provide this service.

Currency Exchange: Myanma Economic Bank, 500m from the post office rotary on the road to the airport, is licensed to exchange US dollars and traveler's checks. Open daily 9am-4pm. For the best rate in Bagan, which may be 50-100kyat less than in Mandalay or Yangor, ask at guest houses and in town.

Medical Services: Township Hospital (☎702 19), 1.5km outside Nyaung U on the road to Mandalay. Western-trained, English-speaking doctors available **24hr.**

Pharmacies: Lanaynay, 50m north of the Bagan-Nyaung U Rd. and Anawratha Rd. intersection in Nyaung U. Ask a local for its location. Consult Htay Htay, the chief nurse at the District Hospital. Open daily 6am-9pm.

Telephones: Telephone Office, at the post office in Nyaung U. IDD only (US$6-9 to Western nations). Call-back service US$2. Open daily 8am-8pm. Some guest houses offer similar service. Send cheaper **telegrams** from the post office (15kyat per word).

Post Office: 750m down Anawrahta Rd. from Nyaung U market. Open daily 9:30am-4pm. **Branch** on Bagan-Nyaung U Rd in New Bagan, south of Main Rd. **Postal code:** 05191.

ACCOMMODATIONS

NYAUNG U

Bagan's budget traveler central, Nyaung U, has affordable, pleasant guest houses in an ideal location from which to visit the temples. Most guest houses are on **Bagan-Nyaung U Rd., Anawrahta Rd.,** and off a road that connects the two, running from the bus terminal at one end to near the post office at the other. All guest houses include breakfast, laundry service, bicycle rental, IDD telephone, and transportation arrangements.

New Park Hotel (☎701 22), off the road connecting Bagan-Nyaung U and Anawrahta Rd. Recently renovated and landscaped. Knowledgeable staff and clean, comfortable rooms. Rooms have A/C and hot water. Singles US$4-6; doubles US$8-12. ❷

New Heaven Hotel (☎700 61), close to New Park Hotel; follow the signs north of the highway bus center. Clean, basic rooms, and useful tourist information. All rooms include A/C and bath with hot shower. Singles US$3-5; doubles US$6-10. **Golden Village Inn** (☎700 88), behind it, is run by the same people. ❷

Taung Za Lat Hotel (☎700 84), on a road near the highway bus center that connects Bagan-Nyaung U and Anawrahta Rd. Big, comfortable rooms with A/C and hot shower. Some have TV and bathtub. Singles US$10-12; doubles US$12-15. ❹

Inn Wa Guest House (☎701 25), on Bagan-Nyaung Rd. 100m away from the market toward Old Bagan, offers basic rooms in a convenient area. Singles US$4-8; doubles US$8-15. Visa accepted. (Visa cash advances in FECs or kyat with 20% surcharge.) ❷

Yar Kinn Thar Hotel, on Anawrahta Rd., 200m from the post office. All rooms have A/C, satellite TV, bathtub, and refrigerator. Singles US$7; doubles $15-20. ❸

Eden Motel (☎700 78), on Anawrahta Rd., 15m from the market. Mid-range quality at budget prices. High season means booked rooms and a popular balcony. Small, basic A/C singles US$3-6; doubles US$10. ❷

MYINKABA VILLAGE (BETWEEN OLD BAGAN AND NEW BAGAN)

Myinkaba Village has fascinating temples and pagodas. With only two guest houses, it's removed from the travelers' scene and awash with tranquility.

Phyo Guest House (☎700 86), on Bagan-Nyaung U Rd., near a white pagoda, north of the village center. Well-furnished A/C rooms, and splendid views of cloistered *stupas* from its main sitting area. Singles US$10; doubles US$15. ❸

NEW BAGAN

The residents of this city were forcibly relocated from Old Bagan to New Bagan a decade ago. Although numerous budget accommodations line Main Rd., there is no strong incentive to stay in New Bagan over Nyaung U.

Smile World Hotel (☎701 22), 25m up Main Rd. from Bagan-Chauk Rd., on the right. Less touristy atmosphere. Offers comfortable bungalow-style rooms with A/C, front porch, and hot shower. Singles US$8; doubles US$10.

FOOD

Bagan's cuisine narrows the gap between the delicious and the mediocre, most tourist eateries serve similar Burmese, Chinese, and Italian menus. These are some suggestions to spice up the repertoire.

Sarabha Restaurant, just outside the Tharaba Gate on Bagan-Nyaung U Rd. The menu offers the same basic Burmese/Chinese dishes you find everywhere, but the taste is spectacular. Fried rice and most meat dishes 500kyat. Open daily 10am-10pm. ❸

San Kabor Restaurant and Pub, on Bagan-Nyaung U Rd. 800m from Shwezigon Pagoda. Offers the best Italian food in Nyaung U. Fettucine carbonara 1000kyat. Hawaiian pizza 1200kyat. Open daily 10am-10pm. ❹

Be Kind to Animal Vegetarian Restaurant and Cold Drinks, 30m inside Tharaba Gate, on Bagan-Nyaung U Rd. Mango lassi 125kyat. Yogurt with fruit 300kyat. Meatless Burmese meals 450kyat. Open daily 7am-10pm. ❸

Shwe Myat Tar, 50m north of the rotary where Bagan-Nyaung U Rd. and Anawrahta Rd. intersect by the market. Look for the sign at the entrance to an alley; the restaurant will be on the left 20m into the alley. Burmese food in a family atmosphere. Vegetarians should look elsewhere. Curries with side dishes 500kyat. Open daily 10am-10pm. ❸

Pyl Wa, on the road that connects Bagan-Nyaung U and Anawrahta Rd. near New Park and New Heaven Hotels. Typical Bagan food is served in an unbeatable atmosphere: candlelit, open-air tables in the shadow of a ruined temple. Free marionette show. Chinese, Burmese, and Italian food at a reasonable price with complimentary fruit salad 200-1000kyat. Open daily 7:30am-10pm. ❸

SIGHTS

Three days are enough to explore the 4000-plus ancient temples and pagodas adorning the **Bagan Plain.** The US$10 admission to the region is collected at checkpoints in the region and at the airport; presentation of the receipt is mandatory upon check-in at guest houses and hotels. This one-time fee allows access to all of the temples from around sunrise to after sunset (the larger temples close between 7 and 9pm). **Shwe Wa Thein,** about 500m northwest of Tharaba Gate, has an extensive collection of souvenir material. You can finish most of your shopping in Bagan here. (Open daily 7am-10pm. Visa accepted.)

It's also essential to talk to guest house owners, pony-cart drivers, and tour guides for insight into off-the-beaten-path destinations—valuable gems abound. Get around by **bicycle** (300kyat per day) or **horse cart** (all-day itinerary around 3000kyat). Many travelers take a one-day horse cart ride first, then strike out on their own by bicycle. A guide is useful (most US$15 per day). If you're pressed for time, be sure to see **Ananda Temple** and **Thatbyinnyu Temple** in Old Bagan, **Shwezigon Pagoda** near Nyaung U, and **Sulamani** and **Dhammayangyi Temples** between Old Bagan and New Bagan, before soaking in a red and purple sunset from atop **Shwesandaw.** If the western sky is clear, then there is nothing quite like being amidst the ancient pagodas and golden landscape. **Mingalazed Pagoda,** a popular viewpoint, offers a beautiful panoramic shot by the river. **Tayokpyi Pagoda,** lying at the eastern edge of the zone, is one of the less touristy spots, from which many of the gigantic temples can be observed. Situated right in between the two, **Shwesandaw Pagoda** is rightfully the most popular (read: crowded) viewpoint.

OLD BAGAN

Old Bagan contains many of the archaeological zone's marquee temples. The area is navigable on foot and warrants a full day of exploration.

ANANDA TEMPLE (အာနန္ဒာ). The pride of Old Bagan, Ananda represents the pinnacle of Bagan's Early Period design, with its sweeping terraces and symmetrical square Greek cross design. The 12th-century temple is commanding and awe-inspiring, with 17 *stupas* rising from its walls and exterior structure. The interior walkways feature hundreds of Buddhas staring down from their alcoves, as well as four 10m standing Buddhas (one for each reincarnation of the Buddha) in each entrance. *(East of the city walls. Camera fee 30kyat; video camera 50kyat.)*

THATBYINNYU TEMPLE (သဗ္ဗညု). This 61m two-tier temple was built in 1144 by King Alaungsithu and is the tallest structure in Bagan. Its most interesting features are its exemplary brickwork and the intricate multilevel architectural design. Tourists are no longer allowed to go to the upper terraces. *(West of Ananda.)*

BAGAN MUSEUM. The Bagan Museum complex tells the story of the cataclysmic earthquake of 1975 and features Buddha images from the 10th and 11th centuries. It's worth it only for the dedicated museum hounds. *(West of Thatbyinnyu. US$5.)*

NAMELESS TEMPLE. This tiny temple without a name is worthy of mention. Attempting to find treasure in a plaster Buddha statue, a thief performed open-heart surgery on the image. He discovered a smaller plaster Buddha whose face emerged from the chest cavity. The owners, craving the merit granted to grand figures, had simply built a larger statue over the old one. *(Opposite Bagan Museum.)*

PITAKATTAIK (LIBRARY). Legend has it that King Anawrahta built this structure in 1057 to house 30 sets of the Buddhist canon, carried by a caravan of 32 elephants from Thaton. Its design carries many similarities to a temple, with a central room surrounded by a processional hallway. The distinctive five-tier roof emerged as a later renovation at the hands of King Bodawpaya in 1783. *(North of Thatbyinnyu.)*

MAHABODHI PAGODA. This pagoda maintains spiritual ties with Bodh Gaya in India, where the Buddha attained Enlightenment under the *boddhi* tree. In the early 13th century, King Htilominlo modeled its design after the original Mahabodhi Pagoda in Bodh Gaya, accounting for its pyramidal spire and many seated Buddhas occupying niches in horizontal shelves. *(Northwest of the Pitakattaik.)*

BUPAYA PAGODA. Bupaya rests on a bank overlooking a bend of the Ayeyarwady River. It was destroyed in the 1975 earthquake, but reconstruction has restored it. The real reason to visit isn't for the temple but rather for the amazing views of the river and mountain scenery beyond. *(At the northwest corner of Bagan.)*

BETWEEN BAGAN AND NYAUNG U

SHWEZIGON PAGODA (ရွှေစည်းခုံဘုရား). According to legend, Buddha's tooth, collar bone, and frontlet relics are enshrined in this pagoda. It's said that King Anawrahta placed the frontlet relic atop a white elephant and declared that wherever the elephant knelt would be the relic's resting place; it was here that Shwezigon was built. Of all of Bagan's temples, Shwezigon is the most revered and the most frequently visited. *(5km northeast of Old Bagan, 500m before Nyaung U.)*

UPALI THEIN (ဥပါလိသိမ်). Allegedly dating back to the 13th century, Upali Thein is the only ordination hall for monks *(sima)* in the Bagan area. *(Halfway between Nyaung U and Bagan on the north side of Bagan-Nyaung U Rd.)*

NYAUNG U MARKET. Built in the latest Bagan architectural style (wood and corrugated tin), this temple enshrines nothing Buddhist whatsoever and, instead, honors the US dollar. Alcoves contain lacquerware plates and opium weights as well as dried fish and bamboo ware. While the market is not particularly awe-inspiring, a walk through the wares provides simple entertainment. *(Open daily 6am-5pm.)*

SOUTH OF THE OLD CITY: BETWEEN BAGAN AND NEW BAGAN

SHWESANDAW PAGODA (ရွှေဆံတော်ဘုရား). King Anawrahta built Shwesandaw in the late 11th century to shelter a single one of the Buddha's hairs. Archaeologists consider its design, featuring a bell-shaped dome atop five terraces, a forerunner to Shwezigon. A steep climb to the top affords a spectacular (and popular) sunset view. Also interesting is the original top felled by the 1975 earthquake, left on the pagoda's south side. *(5km west of Nyaung U on Bagan-Nyaung U Rd.)*

MANUHA TEMPLE. Manuha was named after the King of Thaton, who was exiled and imprisoned in Bagan after King Anawrahta sacked his kingdom in 1057. King Manuha sold his last possessions, even his crown jewels, to build the temple. Of interest is the claustrophobic nature of the Buddha images and temple—it's believed that the king chose to show his displeasure with imprisonment through the temple's design. *(South along the Bagan-Nyaung U Rd. in Myinkaba Village.)*

MINGALAZEDI PAGODA (မင်္ဂလာစေတီဘုရား). King Narathithapate inaugurated the construction of the "Auspicious Pagoda" in 1268 but held off completion for six years when he heard a prophecy foreseeing that it would ultimately bring his kingdom's destruction. Lo and behold, the Mongols sacked Bagan 10 years later. Due to its smooth, precise design, archaeologists consider it the last great pagoda of Bagan. *(South of Old Bagan.)*

> **FLOWER POWER** "Mountain of Flowers" is rooted in ancient legend: Bagan's King Anawrahta loved Mount Poppa's flowers so much that he sent the Indian runner Byatta to fetch bundles of them every day—from over 50km away. Between runs, Byatta fell in love with a flower-eating ogress from Poppa named Mai Wunna. Together they bore two sons, named **Shwe Phyin Gyi** and **Shwe Phyin Ngai,** or "Big Gold Pot" and "Small Gold Pot," who were wild, irreverent young men; they met their deaths for neglecting duties during the construction of the pagoda atop the mountain. After their executions, their spirits begged the king for forgiveness, and he graciously bestowed to them rights and territories to rule. By some twist of fate, the slacker sons have since become objects of worship, with Mount Poppa as the site of their veneration. Lavish festivals enlivened by transvestite *nat pwe* dancers honor them in July or August. Pilgrims follow their spirits around an ambitious circuit that includes Mount Poppa, Taungbyong (near Mandalay), and China.

SOUTHEAST OF THE OLD CITY

SULAMANI TEMPLE (စူဠာမဏိယ). King Narapatisithu built Sulamani, dubbed "Crowning Jewel" in Pali, around the turn of the 13th century. This massive, two-story structure contains a vaulted corridor encircling brickwork, each side sporting a Buddha image seated on a pedestal. Interesting wall paintings adorn many walls and ceilings, but many are believed to have been added in the 18th century.

DHAMMAYANGYI TEMPLE (ဓမ္မရံကြီး). This is one of Bagan's largest temples. Although its design, with porticos projecting from all sides of a square to form a Greek cross, follows Ananda's model, Dhammayangyi is loftier. Its unsurpassed brickwork, considered a crowning achievement of the Later Period, is airtight. As in its contemporary Sulamani, only the four porches and the outer corridors are accessible, while the interior is blocked.

MINNANTHU VILLAGE

Several temples in Minnanthu are worth a visit, and many other small temple complexes lie nearby. Few tourists come here. *(4-5km northeast of New Bagan.)*

NANDAPYINPYA TEMPLE. Built by King Kyazawa in 1248, Nandapyinpya houses the best preserved wall paintings around, depicting scenes from the life of the most recent Buddha, Gautama. A racy picture on the west wall depicts women modeling see-through clothing in provocative postures; some postulate that this picture shows the temptation of Buddha by Mara.

PAYATHONEZU TEMPLE (THREE TEMPLES). Payathonezu's unique structural design, involving a uniform trio of temples joined at the hip via narrow vaulted passages, invokes its share of curiosity. These temples also contain 11th-century wall paintings depicting Gautama Buddha's life and showing mysterious deities from outside Theravada Buddhism.

DAYTRIP FROM BAGAN: MOUNT POPPA ပုပ္ပားတောင်

Mount Poppa, 50km southeast of Bagan, is best reached by car. Guest houses and hotels in Nyaung U and New Bagan arrange transport (1½hr., US$20). Find other travelers to split costs. Alternatively, a pickup leaves daily from the Nyaung U Bus Terminal (3hr.; 8am, returns whenever truck is full; 2000kyat roundtrip).

Volcanic Mount Poppa rose to 1518m above sea level after a colossal earthquake in 442 BC, its volcanic ash transforming the barren Myingan plains below into fertile soil. Today, the mesa serves as the seat of all magical power and *nat* worship in Myanmar, adorned with *nat* shrines, monasteries, bells, and *stupas*. Mt. Poppa attracted religious attention and tourists thanks mostly to its natural wonder **Taung Kalat**—a rock tower standing about halfway up the mountain. Stunning views and cool air await those who navigate the 20min. staircase to the top. Watch your step—the staircase houses mischievous monkeys. Visitors should do as the pilgrims do to avoid offending the *nat:* be careful not to wear red or black, speak ill of others, or carry meat on the climb.

INLE LAKE REGION

NYAUNGSHWE ေညာင္ေရႊ ☎081

Idyllic Nyaungshwe rests in a fertile plain between twin corridors of rolling mountains. Visitors frazzled by the bustle of the cities or enervated by the swelter of Bagan will find relief here. Intha, Pa-O, Shan, and Burmese traditions combine to create a congenial and multifaceted culture unlike any other in Myanmar. Nyaungshwe is not merely the springboard to Inle Lake, Myanmar's most celebrated natural attraction; it's a destination in itself. With scenic treks leading to hill-tribe villages, motorboat forays on the lake, canoe paddling around the canals, and invigorating bike rides, plenty exists to delight visitors, though for many the greatest appeal is the tiny town's relaxed atmosphere.

> **GOVERNMENT LISTINGS.** Government listings are marked by a **M** symbol. Money spent at such establishments goes directly into the government's hands. For more information, see **Keep the Bucks Where They Belong,** p. 496.

TRANSPORTATION

Flights: Heho Airport lies 25km northwest (by taxi 1hr., 6000kyat). Airline offices are in **Taunggyi,** but guest houses and travel agencies arrange tickets for the same price. **Air Mandalay** flies daily to: **Mandalay** (US$45); **Yangon** (1¼hr., US$95) via **Bagan** (US$65-70). **Yangon Airways** flies daily to **Mandalay** (US$45) and **Yangon** (1¼hr., US$90). **M Myanma Airways** goes to **Mandalay** and **Yangon** (2 per week).

M Trains: The closest station is 11km away in **Shwenyaung,** from which a daily train winds its way to **Thazi** (8hr.; 8:30am; ordinary US$3, upper US$7) via **Kalaw** (3hr.; 8:30am, 10am; ordinary US$1, upper US$3). From Thazi, connections run to **Mandalay** (3hr.; 8 per day; ordinary US$3, upper US$8) and **Yangon** (9hr.; 9 per day; ordinary US$9, upper US$25, sleeper US$33). Trains are delayed in the rainy season.

Buses: Company offices are in **Taunggyi,** but guest houses and travel agencies sell tickets. Buses leave from **Shwenyaung Junction,** 11km north. **Nyaung U Man Express** runs minibuses to **Bagan** (10hr., 5:30am, 1500kyat) and buses with A/C to **Bagan** (10hr., 7pm, 2300kyat). **Honey Express, Shwe La Min,** and **Shan Maw Mye** run minibuses to **Mandalay** (9hr., 5:30am, 1500kyat). **Ye Thu Aung, Eastern State Express,** and **Taung Paw Thar** run parallel routes to **Yangon** via **Bago** on A/C, reclining-seat buses, the first two getting the nod for comfort (17-20hr., 12:30pm, 3800kyat).

Local Transportation: Linecars leave from the street one block west of the market for **Shwenyaung Junction** (every 30min., 100kyat) and **Taunggyi** (1hr., every 30min., 200kyat). From Shwenyaung Junction, connections run to **Kalaw** (3hr., every hr. 6am-2pm, 400-500kyat) via **Heho** (1hr., 200kyat) and **Aungban** (2hr.); and **Thazi** (5hr., every hr. 7am-noon, 1500kyat). Most services run daily 7am-5pm. **Taxis** can be hired at

ROUND AND ROUND Throughout the state, the Shan provinces have established a rotating market to provide villagers regular opportunities to sell their crops and buy their weekly necessities. Every fifth day, villagers trek through the Shan hills with kilos of tea leaves, jack fruits, strawberries, and cheroot (cigar) leaves on their backs or heads to market. Though there is little that tourists would want to purchase, the markets provides an insightful look into the agricultural life of the area. The bustling morning market moves according to the following schedule:

1. Kalaw (see p. 543), Shwenyaung, Kaungtaung.
2. Pindaya (see p. 545), Nyaungshwe (see p. 539), Nanpan.
3. Heho, Kyone.
4. Ywama (floating market, see p. 542), Aungban, Taunggyi (see p. 543).
5. Pin Loung, Nan Taing, Mine Thout.

most guest houses and travel agencies. To: **Bagan** (US$60); **Heho airport** (6000kyat); **Kalaw** (US$14); **Meiktila** (US$40); **Pindaya Cave** (US$20); **Shwenyaung Junction** (2500kyat); **Taunggyi** (6000kyat); **Thazi** (US$40). Guest houses and travel agencies rent **bicycles** (400kyat per day), **canoes** (400kyat per person per 3hr.), and **teak motorboats** (driver included, 5000kyat per group per day).

ORIENTATION AND PRACTICAL INFORMATION

Nyaungshwe is set in a rectangular grid and easily navigable on foot. Landmarks, rather than addresses are used for directions. Linecars from Shwenyaung Junction stop at the northwest corner of the **market,** in the north of town. Along the southern edge of the market is **Yonegyi Rd.,** home to countless **travel agencies, shops,** and **local cafes.** Yonegyi and **Phaungdawsaik Rd.** (two blocks south and recognizable by its numerous pagodas) run parallel and west to the **canal.** Most **guest houses** and **restaurants** are found east of the canal and southwest of the market. The canal (with **Canal Rd.**) forms the west edge of town and runs north-south along its length.

Tourist Office: MTT, 300m down Canal Rd. They claim to be open daily 10am-4pm, but you may not find anyone there. It's better to ask at guest houses or travel agencies.

Tours and Travel: Comet Travel Agency, 27 Yonegyi Rd., near the southeastern corner of the market. Run by friendly Nwe Ni Soe. Arranges bus, train, and air tickets and rents boats, canoes, bikes, and taxis. **Treks** US$3-5 per day, including lunch. Open daily 8am-8pm. Many others in this area provide similar services.

Currency Exchange: Guest houses offer the most reliable rates, but at 50-80kyat less than in Yangon or Mandalay. Offers on the street are generally worse.

Markets: Mingala Market, on Yonegyi Rd., sells handicrafts (including Shan handbags and wood carvings), clothes, and vegetables. Relatively tame, except when the rotating market comes (see **Round and Round,** p. 540), but foreigners can expect a hard sell. Open daily 6am-6pm except on full moons and holidays.

Emergency: ☎0 for the operator.

Medical Services: A small **hospital** is 3 blocks south of the post office. The nearest decent hospital is **Mandalar Hospital** in Taunggyi (see p. 543).

Pharmacies: Win Tin and **Zizoa,** on Yonegyi Rd., south side of market. Both open daily 6am-8pm.

Telephones: IDD available at **King Rabbit Tours** (☎229 42), 15m east of the market on Yonegyi Rd. US$7 per min. Call back service 500kyat per 8min. (plus the 1min. to call and give your number). Most guest houses do not even have regular phone lines.

Internet Access: As of July 2002, the only email service available in Nyaungshwe was at Pancake Kingdom (see **Food,** p. 541). 1500kyat per page.

Post Office: On Phaungdawpyan Rd., by Golden Express Hotel. Open M-F 9am-4:30pm.

ACCOMMODATIONS

Splendid budget guest houses and hotels offer clean, cozy rooms and reliable information on Inle Lake. Lodgings often provide free breakfast, laundry service, boat and canoe rentals, bus bookings, and taxi service.

Teakwood Guest House, 3 blocks from the canal, above Phaungdawsaik Rd. Run by a Mon-Shan couple, this popular guest house offers spacious rooms and tasty Shan cooking. Three options for breakfast: pancakes, eggs, or Shan noodles. Delicious Shan dinner is included for guests during high season. Willing to give discounts to students. Singles US$3-5; doubles US$6-10. 10 brand-new rooms with balcony will be completed by September 2002. Singles slated to be US$10-15; doubles US$20-30. ❷

Remember Inn, 80m east on the road that runs along the northern edge of the market. A 10min. walk from the canal, it's situated in a quiet block. Bountiful breakfasts, backpackers, and big bamboo bungalows with bath and hot water. Singles US$4; doubles US$6. By December 2002, 13 brand-new, bigger rooms will be completed. Singles slated to be US$8; doubles US$15. ❷

Gypsy Inn, on the Canal Rd. about 200m south from the bridge. The sounds of early morning motorboats. Its ideal location and the friendly staff—Aung Kyaw and Kyaw Soe—attract many travelers. Singles US$3-5; doubles US$6-10. ❷

View Point Hotel, on the right after crossing the bridge over the canal. For travelers who wanted to stay in one of the floating bungalows in Inle Lake but found them too expensive, View Point offers affordable, comfortable rooms built in the traditional Inle architectural style on the canal. Singles US$6-8; doubles US$10-12. ❸

Gold Star Hotel (☎216 35). Walk 3 blocks south of the market, then 2 blocks west. Gold Star is the biggest hotel in Nyaungshwe with a total of 35 rooms. Fax service available. Rooms range from bungalow-style, family-style, satellite TV- and A/C- equipped, to more basic. Singles US$10-18; doubles US$14-24. ❹

FOOD

Four Sisters Restaurant, 105 Nan Pan Quarter, at the southern end of Canal Rd. One of the finest dining experiences. Home-cooked Burmese meals. No menu: they will serve what they make that day. Pay what you feel is appropriate (except for the set-priced drinks). Open daily 6:30-9pm. Stop in early and make a reservation. They also have **accomodations ❸.** Singles US$7; doubles US$12.

Golden Kite, a couple blocks east from the market on Yonegyi Rd., serves superb pasta, growing Italian herbs in its own backyard and making fresh, homemade pasta, and using tomatoes from Inle Lake that are the best in the country. Pancakes 400kyat. Pasta dishes 1000kyat. Open daily 7:30am-9:30pm. ❹

Pancake Kingdom, toward the canal on Yonegyi Rd., is a social spot for both locals and tourists. Internet and book exchange. Mouth-watering pancakes 400kyat. Sandwiches 300kyat. Open daily 7:30am-9:30pm. ❸

Big Drum Restaurant, across the bridge at the end of Yonegyi Rd. and 50m to the left. Shan specialties in A-frame bungalows on the canal. Set meals with curry, soup, and fried potato or tomato 650kyat. Vegetable curries 250kyat. Open daily 9am-9pm. ❸

Shwe Pyi Soe Tea House, 3 blocks south from the market on the road that runs along its west side; it's just past the pagoda on the left. Rock to the latest in Myanmar pop music. Samosas 10kyat. Best tea in town 40kyat. Open daily 6am-6pm. ❶

Aroma Restaurant, 100m down Canal Rd. Set dinners (700kyat) offer all you can eat *chapaati* or rice, vegetable curry, and lentil soup. Finish the meal off with a spicy Masala Tea (300kyat). Open daily 7am-9:30pm. ❹

ENTERTAINMENT

Nyaungshwe hosts numerous makeshift **"pubs"** (cafes) after dark. Tourists stick to guest houses while locals take their pick of pubs along Yonegyi Rd. Check out **Kaung Kaung Restaurant,** on the west side of the market, for 120kyat taps of Myanmar beer. (Open daily 9am to 10pm.) Those who missed the Mandalay Marionettes might take in a show at the **Aung Traditional Puppet Show,** on Yonegyi Rd., 100m east of the market. The master puppeteer puts on excellent half-hour shows throughout the day. (500kyat per person. Open daily 9am-9pm.)

DAYTRIPS FROM NYAUNGSHWE

INLE LAKE BOAT TRIP အင်းလေးကန်

US$3, payable at the MTT office at the canal entrance.

Inle Lake, 2km down the canal from Nyaungshwe, is the showpiece of the Shan Plateau. From the lake's center, power lines, bamboo stakes, wooden homes on stilts, and the occasional palm tree punctuate the mountainous horizon. The Intha, as the lake area's residents are known, build homes on stilts over the water and succeed admirably in "living off the lake." There's little space on this lake that isn't harvested, fished, or lived on. Intha farmers tend to floating gardens that yield flowers, vegetables, and fruit (especially tomatoes) and fish from their narrow teak canoes. The Intha are also gifted weavers, carpenters, canoe-builders, and metalworkers; their workshops are very informative.

The village of **Ywama** was once an essential stop on any Inle Lake foray. Its **floating market** (see **Round and Round,** p. 540) appears in full vigor every fifth day. Recently, however, the market has been redubbed the "Souvenir Market." On official market days, it's an interesting lesson in nautical trade, but check with your guest house owner first, lest you end up being ambushed by ambitious venders with souvenir-laden canoes. The most sacred religious site in the northern Shan State, **Phaung Daw U Kyaung,** can be reached via the main boat landing in town. Though the (reconstructed) exterior architecture is impressive, the structure's contents are not. Owing to generous gold-leaf donations over the years, the Buddha images have ballooned considerably in size, rendering their original dimensions a mystery and leaving five lumps of gold in their place. Every September and October, the 20-day **Phaung Daw U Kyaung Festival** features their procession in highly decorated barges, along with hundreds of accompanying vessels, around the lake's villages. At the northern outskirts of Ywama stands the stilted **Nga Phe Kyaung,** the oldest monastery among the 268 that dot the lake's shores. The beautiful teak structure houses Bagan, Intha, Shan, and Tibetan Buddha images. For generations, the monks have trained cats to jump through hoops. Exactly how this "cat and pony show" contributes to enlightenment is open to debate.

The farther out you head on the lake, the better your chances are of escaping the souvenir scene. One good bet is **Intain,** known for its market and **Shwe Inn Tain Pagoda.** At the lake's far southern end, the villages of **Taung Doe** and **Kyauk Taing,** which have recently become accessible to foreign travelers, offer opportunities to explore stone carvings and ancient *stupas*. Because of their distance from Nyaungshwe, visiting them adds 500-1000kyat to the normal price of boat hire.

Dozens of villages to the east and west afford other exploring options. Day-hike guides are available for US$3-5 (lunch included), with higher prices for longer treks up to 25km. Fit people itching to get some exercise in should try a tiring, yet educational, full-day trek; others would enjoy a half-day trek. For a substantially more down-to-earth and personal encounter with Inle Lake monastic life, wander to the village of **Nun Te,** a 5min. walk south of Four Sisters Inn as Canal Rd. becomes a dirt path. The village contains four monasteries, **Le Bien, Pien Tha, Pai Ah Gyi,** and **Moke Thoke,** the last of which serves as home base for 17 studious monks. All welcome visitors. The ethereally gracious U Aw Bar Tha at Moke Thoke speaks excellent English and is happy to show visitors around.

TAUNGGYI

Take a pickup or taxi from Nyaungshwe (see ***Local Transportation,*** *p. 539). Pickups back to Nyaungshwe leave from just north of the market (1hr., leave when full 7am-4:30pm, 100kyat).*

The capital of Shan State, Taunggyi would feel like just another big town were it not for the frontier atmosphere of its location, nestled among the peaks of picturesque highlands at an altitude of 1430m, 28km northeast of Inle Lake. Its Shan, Burmese, Chinese, Indian, and Nepali populations, as well as its fine market, make it a stimulating daytrip from Nyaungshwe, but few travelers find reason to spend the night. Regional instability makes Taunggyi the easternmost point accessible by land in Shan State. **Bogyoke Aung San Rd.,** the main drag in Taunggyi, bisects the city as it goes uphill from north to south. Pickups from Nyaungshwe may drop passengers in a lot on the northwestern outskirts of town; from here, take another pickup to the town center (10min., 20kyat). The town's main draw is the **central market,** on Bogyoke Aung San Rd., which sells everything from handicrafts to traditional Shan dress. Taunggyi's market is less touristed but busier than Nyaungshwe's, resulting in a larger selection of goods and better bartering opportunities. The other reason travelers might visit Taunggyi is for treatment at the private **Mandalar Hospital,** 222 Bogyoke Aung San Rd. (☎227 33), near the north end of town, which has an English-speaking staff and 24hr. service. At the opposite end of town, also on Bogyoke Aung San Rd., Taunggyi's **post office** offers the most services of any in the region, while the **telephone office** next door provides the usual exorbitantly expensive IDD (US$4-8 per min.) and reasonable but unpredictable telegraph (4-15kyat per word) services. (Both open M-F 9am-4pm.) For those with time to spare, the **Shan State Museum,** south of the post office, manages to pack religious, cultural, and artistic artifacts into relatively few exhibits. (Open M-F 9:30am-3:30pm. US$2.) Affordable accommodations are at **Khemarat Hotel,** 403 Bogyoke Aung San Rd. opposite Mandalar Hospital. (☎224 64. Clean and comfortable rooms. Singles US$6-10; doubles US$12-16.)

KALAW ကလော ☎081

The sedate alpine charm of Kalaw is nothing short of paradise to travelers coming from the dusty swelter of Bagan or the frenzied sprawl of Mandalay or Yangon. The British must have thought similarly when they founded a hill station here; a colonial legacy lingers in the wide, uncluttered streets and missionary-built schools, even though most tourists do not. With jungle trekking trails and traditional villages in the surrounding hills, Kalaw serves as a base camp for hikes or the perfect place to sit back, relish the air, and take in the scenery.

TRANSPORTATION. The **train station** (booking office open daily 9am-5pm) at the southeastern corner of town only serves **Thazi** (5hr., 11:30am, US$3). Trains are often hours late in the rainy season. **Buses** originating in Taunggyi pass through Kalaw on their way to points west and south. Book tickets at numerous travel and trekking agencies near the market. Buses go to **Bagan** (7hr., 7:30am, 3000kyat); **Mandalay** (7-8hr., 7:30am, 1500kyat; 9:30pm, 2000kyat); **Yangon** (16hr., 2:30pm, 3200kyat). Two buses depart from Parami Hotel, one block west of the market, for **Taunggyi** (3hr.; 6:30, 7, 7:30am; 400kyat) via **Shwenyaung Junction** (the turn-off to Inle Lake; 2hr., 400kyat). Buy tickets one day in advance. If these buses are full, **pickups** rattle eastbound on Union Rd. (6am-4 or 5pm, 300-400kyat).

ORIENTATION AND PRACTICAL INFORMATION. Kalaw's layout is simple. **Pye Daung Su (Union) Rd.**, which runs west to Thazi and east to Taunggyi, forms the northern boundary of town. Ten parallel streets extend southward. Just before the **market, Main Rd.** bisects Union Rd. and has a large **banyan tree,** the town landmark. Travel agencies and guest houses **exchange** US dollars and FECs at free-market rates that are 50-70kyat less than what you would get in the bigger cities. On Main Rd. about halfway between Union Rd. and the banyan tree, on the market side, sits a well-stocked **pharmacy.** (☎500 08. Open daily 7am-7pm.) A private **clinic** sits on the road that runs along the southern side of the market. From Union Rd., walk down Main Rd. to the banyan tree and turn right; look for the red cross 2½ blocks down on the left. (☎501 86. Open daily 8-11am and 3-7pm.) IDD overseas calls can be made from the **Trunk Call Station** (7am-9pm) on Union Rd. near the market or the **post office,** at the west end of Union Rd opposite Natsin Rd. (☎500 57. Open daily 9am-4pm.)

Trekking agencies line Union Rd. around the market. The hillside outside Kalaw hosts several different 1- to 3-day treks. Routes focus on visits to the villages of four regional tribes. Guide fees (US$5-7 per person per day) cover food and accommodations in the villages. It pays to shop around for a guide in Kalaw; ask locals for their recommendations and try to find someone who speaks the languages of the peoples on the itinerary. Guides range from highly experienced and knowledgeable to utterly ignorant. **Sam's Trekking** (☎502 37), on Union Rd. on the north side of the market, receives raves, as does **Eddie,** owner of the Golden Kalaw Hotel. Treks to the north visit tribes that live more traditionally than those in the south, but all routes have spectacular scenery. Hiking in the rainy season, however, means slippery conditions; hiking boots are highly recommended.

ACCOMMODATIONS AND FOOD. Hotel and guest house rooms outnumber visitors, so quality is high and prices are low. **Golden Lily Guest House ❶,** at the town's west end on Nat Sin Rd., is a quiet, clean place run by a helpful family. (☎501 08. Rooms US$2 per person, with bath US$3.) **Winner Hotel ❷,** in the town center on Union Rd., has excellent rooms and satellite TV in the sitting area. (☎502 79. Basic singles US$3, with bath US$7; doubles US$10; rooms with bathtub, fridge, satellite TV, and teak decor US$20-25.) It doesn't get any cheaper—or more basic—than **Pine Land Inn ❶,** next to Winner Hotel. (☎500 20. Small, bare rooms US$2 per person, with bath US$3 per person.)

Thirigayhar (Seven Sisters) Restaurant ❹, 7 Union St., 200m west of Winner Hotel, serves delicious but expensive Burmese, Chinese, Indian, and European food ranging from sour mustard soup to vegetable spaghetti. (Dishes 700-1200kyat. Open daily 7am-10pm.) **Everest Nepali Food Center ❸,** on Aung Chan Tha St. (look for the sign near the banyan tree) offers quality Nepalese dishes. Try the dry or oily *chapaati* for 200kyat or the chicken curry for 500kyat. (Open daily 6am-9pm.) **Ye Baw Gyi ❸,** on Union Rd. at the north side of the market, is popular for Burmese curries and fried noodles. (Dishes 400-500kyat. Open daily 6am-9pm.)

DAYTRIPS FROM KALAW: PINDAYA AND SHWE U MIN. Pindaya, 1180m above sea level and 39km north of the town of **Aungban,** has crisp air, excellent scenery, and fertile farmland. The town's reputation is built on **Shwe U Min Pagoda,** or "Golden Cave Pagoda" (US$3 for admission). Stalagmites, stalactites, and 8000 Buddha images crafted in every conceivable style adorn the limestone caves. Over the years, pilgrims and adherents have donated these images to the caves, but the monument is now saturated, and trustees have put a cap on further offerings. Of the several interesting columns and images, make sure to find the "Perspiring Buddhas": scraping the "sweat" off the Buddha images is supposed to be good luck. The **rotating market** comes through town every five days (see **Round and Round,** p. 540). Pindaya is best reached from Kalaw, but public transportation is difficult, especially in the rainy season. When Pindaya hosts the market, a linecar makes the journey from Kalaw, leaving when full (1½hr.; around 6am, return around noon; 200kyat). If it's not a market day, traveling to Pindaya by public transportation is nearly impossible; it involves an overnight stay and the possibility of having to return to Kalaw via an expensive taxi ride. This situation changes frequently, so ask in Kalaw. The more stable option is to go by **taxi** (US$12-15 round-trip), which allows you to stop around Pindaya to view **handicraft centers** specializing in bamboo hats, tree bark paper, umbrellas, clay pots, and the local version of potato chips. **U Ohn Umbrella Shop** is an especially worthwhile stop.

THE PHILIPPINES

US$1 = P51.85 (PESO)	P100 = US$1.93
CDN$1 = P33.25	P100 = CDN$3.01
EUR€1 = P50.92	P100 = EUR€1.96
UK£1 = P80.84	P100 = UK£1.24
AUS$1 = P28.36	P100 = AUS$3.53
NZ$1 = P24.33	P100 = NZ$4.11
ZAR1 = P4.94	P100 = ZAR20.26

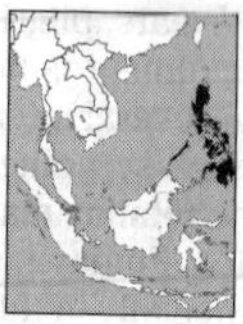

PHONE CODE **Country code:** 63. **International dialing prefix:** 00.

Possessing a history laden with Spanish and American influences, the Philippines has been permanently thrown out of sync with the rest of Southeast Asia. Described as a hodgepodge of "Malay, Madrid, and Madison Avenue," Filipino culture fosters a range of ethnicities, languages, and lifestyles among which natives have found unity and an unparalleled love for life. Their willingness to drop everything for a basketball game or a cockfighting match reflects the national philosophy of *bahala na*, roughly translated as "whatever will be, will be." At the heart of the Filipino tradition is a strong sense of community; Filipinos can't bear doing things by themselves and, above all, value family, friendliness, and personal loyalty. This cheerful attitude, along with convenient transportation, numerous English speakers, and inexpensive locales, makes the Philippines a budget traveler's paradise.

FACTS AND FIGURES

Official Name: Republic of the Philippines.

Government: Republic.

Capital: Manila.

Land Area: 300,176 sq. km.

Geography: A 7107-island archipelago stretching 1851km north-south and 1107km east-west. Divides into 4 zones: Luzon, the Visayas, Palawan, and Mindanao. Mountain ranges: Central Cordillera and Sierra Madre in Luzon. Mindanao's Mt. Apo (2954m) is the highest peak.

Climate: Tropical: Dry (high season) Nov.-Mar., and rainy (low season) Apr.-Oct.

Major Cities: Bacolod, Cagayan de Oro, Cebu, Davao, Iloilo, Zamboanga.

Population: 81,159,644.

Languages: Filipino, English.

Religions: Roman Catholic (83%), Protestant (7%), Muslim (5%), Other (5%).

Average Income Per Capita: US$1160.

Major Exports: Electronics, textiles, agricultural products.

LIFE AND TIMES

DEMOGRAPHICS

Though they inhabit over 1000 islands, Filipinos are relatively culturally homogeneous. Christian Malays, known as **Filipinos,** account for 92% of the population of the Philippines. About 8% of the Philippine population belongs to a number of ethnic and religious minorities, such as tribal groups, Muslims, ethnic Chinese, and

The Philippines
0 150 miles
0 150 kilometers
Batan Islands
Luzon Strait
Babuyan Islands
Cape Bojeador
Babuyan Channel
Cool Coral
Scuba dive at the world-famous Visayan dive sites.
Laoag
Vigan
Tabuk
LUZON
Banaue
San Fernando
South China Sea
Philippine Sea
Bolinao
100 Islands
Baguio
Dagupan
Mt. Pinatubo
San Fernando
Angeles
Polillo Islands
Olongapo
Manila
Walled Wonder
Explore the walled city of Intramuros in Manila.
Pasig
Cavite
Santa Cruz
Daet
Catanduanes Island
Batangas
Lucena
Naga
Mayon Volcano
Calapan
Marinduque
Legazpi
Mindoro
Sibuyan Sea
Romblon
Masbate
Catarman
Buguanga Island
Boracay Island
Masbate
Soft Sands
Sunbathe on Boracay's gorgeous White Beach.
Calamian Group
Kalibo
Roxas
Biliran Island
Catbalogan
Samar
Visayan Sea
El Nido
San Jose de Buenavista
Panay
Tacloban
Iloilo
VISAYAS
Ormoc
Cuyo Island
Bacolod
Leyte
Palawan Passage
Panay Gulf
La Carlota
Cebu City
Maasin
Cebu
Siargao Island
Bohol
Negros
Tagbilaran
Puerto Princesa
Sulu Sea
Paglao
Dumaguete
Siquijor
Bohol Sea
PALAWAN
Brooke's Point
Dipolog
Cagayan de Oro
Tubbaha Reef
Ozamiz
Pagadian
MINDANAO
Balabac Island
Cotabato
Davao
Hot Spot
Soak yourself in El Nido's Makin It Hot Springs.
Mt. Apo
Cagayan Sulu Island
Zamboanga
Digos
Isabela
Moro Gulf
Basilan Island
General Santos
Jolo
Jolo Island
Tawi Tawi Island
Sulu Archipelago
MALAYSIA (SABAH)
Celebes Sea
Chocolate Paradise
Trek through the stunning Chocolate Hills in Bohol.

mestizo populations (mostly Filipino-Spanish and Filipino American). The dwindling **Negrito** population, the Philippines' oldest surviving race, lives mostly in upland forests as nomadic hunters and fishermen. Similarly, the **Lumads,** a generic term for the indigenous people of various ethnic and linguistic backgrounds who inhabit Mindanao, live mainly by subsistence agriculture but are gradually being pushed farther into the hinterlands in the name of development.

LANGUAGE

Although the official languages of the Philippines are **Filipino** and **English,** over 150 different dialects and languages are spoken by groups throughout the archipelago. English is used mainly for legal, government, academic, and commercial purposes. The eight major spoken dialects are Tagalog, Cebuano, Ilocano, Hiligaynon or Ilonggo, Bicol, Waray, Pampango, and Pangasinense. Tagalog is thought to derive from *taga-ilog*, which means "people who live by the river"; it serves as the basis for the national language, Filipino, which has been heavily influenced particularly in terms of vocabulary by Sanskrit, Arabic, Chinese, English, and Spanish.

RELIGION

CATHOLICISM. The Philippines boasts that it is the only Christian nation in Asia with about 80% of the population adhering to Roman Catholicism—a legacy of Spanish missionaries. The recent scandal in the Catholic Church in America has led to a larger international discussion about sexuality and celibacy among Catholic priests. This discussion has uncovered some unpleasant aspects of Catholicism in the Philippines which may challenge the Church's prominence in the future.

ISLAM. Islam was introduced to the Philippine archipelago by Arab traders in the 14th century and has remained prevalent in the south, particularly on Mindanao. Because this area was not successfully colonized by the Spanish, the people of Mindanao have remained culturally diverse and distinct from the rest of the country, spurring demands for local autonomy and fueling separatist sentiment.

PROTESTANTISM. The American influence during the 20th century spread Protestantism throughout the Philippines, and today, about 7% of Filipinos consider themselves Protestant. During the period of American colonialism, converts to Protestantism experienced a great deal of upward social mobility at the expense of the Roman Catholics.

PHILIPPINE INDEPENDENT CHURCH. A nationalistic offshoot of Catholicism informally known as the Aglipayan Church, the Philippine Independent Church (PIC) was founded in 1902 by Gregorio Aglipay, a Roman Catholic priest who fought diligently for institutional reforms. The Aglipayan Church has recently signed a covenant with the Anglican Church.

OTHER RELIGIONS. Recently, many smaller sects have started challenging the supremacy of the Roman Catholic Church in the Philippines. There has been a proliferation of **Rizalist sects** that believe that Jose Rizal, the late 19th-century martyred nationalist leader, was the reincarnation of Christ. **Iglesia ni Kristo** is the Philippine version of Mormonism, or The Church of Jesus Christ of Latter-Day Saints, and was founded by Felix Manalo in 1914. The churches associated with Iglesia ni Kristo are architecturally distinctive and are prominent landmarks in nearly all provincial capitals and metropolitan areas.

LAND

The 7107 islands (only 1000 of which are inhabited) that make up the Philippine archipelago are composed of volcanic, rock, and coral formations. Although the country lies on the Pacific Ring of Fire, only ten of the approximately fifty volcanoes in the Philippines are known to be active; these are mostly contained within the Luzon Volcanic Arc that rings the south and west of the island. The most recent volcanic eruptions have been Mt. Pinatubo in 1991, and Mt. Mayon in 1993 and then again in 2001. However, the positive long-term effects of volcanic activity are evident throughout the Philippines in the form of fertile soil, enriched by volcanic ash and lava, that sustains unusually biologically diverse ecosystems.

HIGHLIGHTS OF THE PHILIPPINES

BEACHES. The sugar-fine sand of Boracay's **White Beach** (p. 627) lures jet-setters and backpackers alike, while **Palawan** (p. 636) draws an adventurous crowd. **Bantayan** (p. 609) and **Malapascua** (p. 610) are restful island detours en route to Cebu.

DIVING. Visayan dive sites are Southeast Asia's best: **Moalboal** (p. 608), **Panglao Island** (p. 614), and **Apo Island** (p. 621) are all on the diver's pilgrimage trail.

CULTURAL HERITAGE. Manila's walled city of **Intramuros** (p. 566), **museums** (p. 566), and **Fort San Pedro** (p. 605) simulate the drama between *conquistadores* and natives, while **Vigan's churches** (p. 585) attest to the lasting Christian influence. Indigenous Cordilleran cultures around **Banaue** (p. 579) delight budding anthropologists.

NATURAL WONDERS. Mountain air cleanses Manila-marred lungs around **Bontoc's rice terraces** (p. 576). The **Mayon Volcano** (p. 592) in Legazpi and **Mt. Kanla-on** (p. 618) near Bacolod challenge with their height and fiery tempers. Palawan's **Cabayugan River** (p. 641) offers a surreal float through the bowels of the Earth. Hikers meander through Bohol's **Chocolate Hills** (p. 613) to peek at the precious primate, the *tarsier.*

WILDLIFE

One of the ten most biologically diverse countries in the world, the Philippines are also near the top of the list of nations on the brink of environmental disaster. Despite this, the future of national parks and conservation efforts are by no means certain; ecologically-minded travelers should go to as many national parks as possible and sign the guest book to show their support for conservation projects.

ENDANGERED ANIMALS. The Philippines are home to several species of animals that are on the verge of extinction due to the destruction of their natural habitat. The **Philippine Eagle,** the largest eagle in the world, has become a symbol for Filipinos of the importance of preserving endangered habitats. Five out of the eight known species of **marine turtles** make their home in the Philippines. Hunted for their meat and leather, their eggs stolen as a purported aphrodisiac, and their nesting sites sacrificed to the gods of development, these turtles are in danger of extinction. Closer to Malaysia than to the Philippines, the sanctuary at Turtle Islands serves as one of the world's only breeding and resting grounds for the endangered marine turtle. The **Bleeding-Heart Dove** is a terrestrial pigeon that lives in forested areas of Luzon. The doves are found in public and private zoological collections all over the world, although the population in the wild has dwindled to an indeterminate number. Widely considered the most beautiful of the peacock species, the **Palawan Peacock-Pheasant** is in danger of extinction as more of its natural habitat, the coastal lowland forest of Palawan, is destroyed. The species' wild population is estimated at less than 10,000.

DANGEROUS ANIMALS. Travelers who plan to dive should watch out for dangerous marine life and stick to often-frequented dive sites. The **Salt Crocodile** is one of the world's deadliest animals. It is usually found only in remote areas, however, favoring brackish water and large river mouths, although it has also been sighted in the open ocean. The common pale blue **Banded Sea Snake** has a venom that is a deadly neurotoxin. In northern Palawan, Snake Island offers the opportunity to watch these sea snakes from a safe distance.

HISTORY

EARLY HISTORY

The original people to inhabit the area now known as the Philippines were probably immigrants of Australo-Melanesian descent—ancestors of the people known today as the Aeta. Philippine legend has it that during the early 13th century, **Ten Datus** moved to the Philippine Visayas from Sabah Province in Malaysia.

SPANISH YEARS (1521-1885)

IMPORTANT DATES		
1521 Magellan arrives; Spanish rule begins.	**1565** The Philippines becomes a Spanish colony with the capital at Manila.	**1762** The British seize Manila during Seven Year's War but promptly return it to Spain.

Ferdinand Magellan and his crew landed in the archipelago in 1521, and the Philippines were annexed as a Spanish colony in 1565, setting in motion great cultural and political transformations. For merchants moving between Canton, China, and Acupulco, Mexico, Manila served as a gateway to Asia; for the Spanish, Manila was an important commercial prize, as it increasingly became a center for international trade. The Spanish also left their religious and social imprint on the Philippines in the form of **Roman Catholicism** and the idea of a landed elite. The rural friars were left up to their own devices, and they claimed control of religious life, government, and education, creating a friarocracy, which alienated the educated Filipino elite. Known as *ilustrados*, this elite was the first driving force in the revolution to come.

REFORM MOVEMENT AND EARLY NATIONALISM (1886-1896)

IMPORTANT DATES		
1886 Jose Rizal publishes "Noli Me Tangere."	**1892** Rizal returns to the Philippines to found The Philippine League.	**1896** Rizal's execution stimulates nationalism.

Aside from a series of attempts to overthrow the friarocracy and a short-lived fling with liberalism, the Filipino expatriate community in Spain organized the **Propaganda Movement** and circulated the newspaper *La Solidaridad* (Solidarity) in both Spain and the Philippines. The most famous propagandist, **Jose Rizal,** led the fight for independence using literature as his weapon of choice; his most famous works are *Noli Me Tangere* (Touch Me Not) and *El Filibusterismo* (The Subversive). These were smuggled into the Philippines and galvanized the *ilustrados*. Returning to the Philippines in 1892 to found **The Philippine League,** an organization devoted to nonviolent reform, Rizal was arrested for revolutionary activity and executed in 1896. Budding Philippine nationalism, set in motion by Rizal, fueled the development of **Katipunan,** a radical organization dedicated to national independence through revolution and founded by **Andres Bonifacio.** Katipunan's loyalties were divided between Bonifacio and **General Emilio Aguinaldo,** who was ultimately elected to replace Bonifacio as the group's leader. After armed infighting, Bonifacio was arrested, tried, and executed on Aguinaldo's orders.

AMERICA IN THE PHILIPPINES (1896-1945)

IMPORTANT DATES

1898 US defeats Spain and buys the Philippines in giant 3-for-1 bargain.	**1910** US crushes insurrection, changes tactics, and begins cultural invasion.	**1942-45** Japanese invade Luzon and defeat US General MacArthur.

The deterioration of Spanish-American relations began with the mysterious sinking of the U.S.S. Maine off the coast of Cuba in early 1898. Shortly afterward, the US Navy under **General Dewey** attacked the Spanish fleet in Manila Bay, launching the **Spanish-American War.** Although the US had previously not expressed any desire to adopt Spain's crumbling colonial empire, they began to fear that were they to abandon the Philippines to the colonial powers, they would be forever excluded from regional trade and commerce. In the peace treaty that ended the war, the US bought the Philippines along with Guam and Puerto Rico for a bargain: US$20 million. Despite the **Philippine Insurrection** initiated by Aguinaldo, the US adopted a policy of "benevolent assimilation" toward their "little brown brothers" (so dubbed by William Taft, the first American governor of the Philippines). Education became the main means of Americanization; the emphasized literacy, a public health care system, and the development of infrastructure. Yet the involvement of the US came at a heavy cultural price. Promotion of English devalued indigenous culture, and little was done to bridge the gap between the middle class and the rural *barrios*.

INDEPENDENCE (1946-1969)

IMPORTANT DATES

1946 US grants the Philippines independence on July 4.	**1953** Suppressor of Huk Rebels, Magsaysay, elected president.	**1957** Magsaysay dies in freak plane crash.

The Japanese invaded the Philippines just ten hours after their attack on Pearl Harbor. **General MacArthur,** sent packing by the Japanese, vowed, "I shall return," and did just that in 1945, defeating the Japanese occupying forces and liberating the Philippines. The US granted their pseudo-colony independence on July 4, 1946. Elected to rehabilitate a ravaged country, **Manuel Roxas** was inaugurated as the first president of the postwar Commonwealth. World War II had fostered a poor relationship between farmers and landlords, and the landlords' attempts to collect rent often dissolved into armed conflict between members of the **Hukbalahap** peasant movement and the landlords' own armed bands. The Huks, as they were commonly known, fought against the Japanese as US-backed guerrilla forces and had expected to be embraced by the US leadership after the war. However, their communist tendencies impelled the US to provide military aid to help Defense Secretary **Ramon Magsaysay** quell the movement. Following Magsaysay's election to the presidency in 1953, he worked for land reform but died in 1957 before accomplishing his goals, and the government passed from one inept regime to another.

THE MARCOS DYNASTY (1965-1986)

IMPORTANT DATES

1965 Ferdinand Marcos elected president; wife's collection of shoes continues to grow.	**1968** NPA established; Marcos brands them communist, calls coup, and declares martial law.	**1973, 1975, 1978** Referendums rigged by Marcos "okay" the extension of martial law.	**1979** The Philippine Peso plummets in a severe economic recession.

In 1965, **Ferdinand Marcos** came to power. His wife, the former beauty queen **Imelda Marcos,** is best known for her immense shoe collection, a mere one or two thousand pairs of which are now housed in the Marikina Shoe Museum. The tale of a president-turned-dictator began benignly with widespread popularity for his aggression in tackling the problems of education, poverty, transportation, and land reform; in 1969, he became the first Philippine president to win a second term. However, claiming to root out the internal communist threat of the **New People's Army (NPA),** he declared martial law and rigged plebiscites in 1973, 1975, and 1978 that 'approved' its extension. As they became aware of the unprecedented levels of corruption in Marcos's inner circle, the Filipino public became increasingly disenchanted with the regime. In 1977, Marcos's arch rival, Senator **Benigno Aquino,** was accused on trumped-up charges of treason and murder. Upon arrival in Manila after years of exile, he was assassinated at the airport. Many suspect either First Lady Imelda Marcos or military chief **Fabian Ver** as his killer.

PEOPLE POWER (1986-1998)

IMPORTANT DATES

1968 EDSA Revolution overthrows Marcos; he escapes to Hawaii under US military escort.

1992 USS Belleau Wood leaves Subic Naval Base, ending 94 years of US military presence in the Philippines.

Aquino's assassination marked the end of Marcos's rule. **Corazon Aquino,** Benigno's widow, ran against Marcos and received overwhelming support, although Marcos had the National Assembly declare him the victor. Growing steadily more disillusioned with the regime, Marcos's Secretary of Defense **Juan Ponce Enrile** and **Fidel Ramos,** Chief of Staff of the Armed Forces, led the **EDSA Revolution,** named for the street on which local masses faced marines and tanks in support of "Cory" Aquino. The mass demonstrations forced Marcos's flight to Hawaii aboard a US Air Force plane, and international attention turned to focus on the Philippines as an example of one of the first successful pro-democracy revolutions in the developing world. President Aquino released all political prisoners of the Marcos regime and drafted a new constitution that reduced executive power. She also dealt with the continuing demands of Imelda Marcos, who was found guilty of stealing millions from the treasury. Succeeding Aquino in 1992, Fidel Ramos faced an economic crisis caused by several volcanic eruptions and the termination of the US lease on the Subic Bay naval base, a move that cost the Philippines thousands of jobs. However, Ramos successfully courted foreign investment by lifting the foreign currency restrictions and liberalizing the Philippine economy. He also sought negotiations with the terrorist group **Moro National Liberation Front** in an effort to bring peace to Mindanao.

THE PHILIPPINES TODAY

THE 1998 ELECTIONS. Though she still faced lawsuits for embezzlement and a 12-year prison sentence for corruption, **Imelda Marcos** entered the 1998 presidential race on an ironic platform: strengthening the nation's economy. She was known for her lavish spending habits during her husband's dictatorship, but Marcos claimed that her decision to run for election was motivated by the desire to see the Marcos wealth go directly to the Filipino people. However, **Joseph Estrada,** a college drop-out and popular movie star, won the election to become president on May 11, 1998. But after massive resignations from his government, the Supreme Court removed him from office in January of 2001, and he now faces a corruption trial. In his place, the court installed Vice President **Gloria Macapagal Arroyo.** The biggest challenges facing Arroyo's new administration are the swelling government budget deficit (estimated at US$2.87 billion), corruption, poverty, and high crime rates. She must also deal with increasing domestic terrorism from left-wing groups and Muslim separatists.

MILITANT SEPARATISTS AND TERRORIST GROUPS. Arroyo has linked terrorism in her country with extreme poverty and believes that effectively combating terrorism means going beyond purely military solutions. The **Abu Sayyaf Group (ASG)** is an Islamic separatist group responsible for bombings in Manila and killings and kidnappings of tourists and locals in Mindanao and Palawan. ASG leaders have admitted to having close ties with Osama bin Laden's **al Qaeda** terrorist organization. In May 2002, the US offered up to US$5 million for information leading to the arrest or conviction of the ASG leaders tied to the 2001 kidnapping of an American missionary couple, Martin and Gracia Burnham. Martin Burnham was subsequently killed during an encounter between Philippine troops and Abu Sayyaf; in a later encounter, an ASG leader, **Abu Sabaya,** was shot and went missing. Sabaya was reported to have been killed, but his body was never recovered. The **New People's Army (NPA)** is an armed wing of the Communist Party of the Philippines that seeks to overthrow the government through extended guerrilla warfare. Opposed to any US military presence, they have threatened violence to American troops participating in joint military exercises with the Philippines, as well as any other Americans who encroach on their sphere of influence in rural northern Luzon and parts of Mindanao. The **Moro Islamic Liberation Front (MILF),** another Muslim insurgent group demanding the formation of an autonomous Islamic state on the southern Philippine island of Mindanao, has racked up impressive military forces and threatens the stability of the Republic with bombings, bus hijackings, and sniper shootings. That said, these events are concentrated mainly in extremely rural areas of northern Luzon, Mindanao, and parts of Palawan; nearly two million travelers journey to the Philippines each year and have safe, enjoyable trips.

THE SECOND FRONT OF THE US WAR ON TERROR. In the wake of the **September 11, 2001** attacks on the World Trade Center in New York City, the US has stepped up its offensive against international terrorist organizations. Despite post-colonial political sensitivities, the Philippines have been the site of the largest US troop deployment after Afghanistan in the Bush administration's **War on Terror.** These troops are meant to train Filipino soldiers to fight against ASG forces on Mindanao, and to prepare Filipino defense forces for UN peacekeeping missions. Officials in Manila, however, fear a broadening of the role of US troops in the Philippines. US Defense Secretary **Donald Rumsfeld** has expressed qualms about the participation of US troops in joint jungle patrols, hinting that putting Army Special Forces at such a risk demands a valid justification and warning that such a commitment would probably bind the US to a protracted military role in Mindanao.

CUSTOMS & ETIQUETTE

TABOOS. Beckoning to someone by wiggling the index finger is considered rude; the accepted way to motion for someone to approach you is to extend your arm with the palm facing down and make a scratching motion with your fingers. Pointing is also inappropriate. Because of the national emphasis on Catholicism, it is considered impolite to swear with religious words. In general, try to avoid conversations about politics, religion, corruption, or foreign aid; Filipinos particularly enjoy discussing their families.

PUBLIC BEHAVIOR. Philippine values emphasize optimism, politeness, and respect. Extend your most kind words even to beggars with the phrase, *"Patawarin po,"* which means "Forgive me, sir." Filipinos are relatively conservative socially, so while holding hands is acceptable, any other public displays of affection (including informal physical contact) are not. Social etiquette encourages a *laissez-faire* attitude, so show up about twenty minutes later than the appointed

THE LOCAL STORY

JOHN ABUL, MANILA *BAKLA*

Homosexuality is far more open and readily accepted in the Philippines than in other parts of Southeast Asia. The bakla, as gay men are known, occupy a well-accepted niche within Philippine society and are considered arbiters of fashion, glamor, and even humor. Let's Go *sat down with clothing designer John Abul after a gay book opening in Manila to discuss the intersection of Philippine culture and sexuality:*

LG: Is homosexuality accepted in the Philippines?

JA: In so many words, yes. [Filipinos] would rather not confront reality, but [homosexuality] has been around here for ages—even before the Spanish came.

LG: Would a *bakla* be accepted in a small town?

JA: Oh, yes. They would be. If you go to the southernmost tip of this country, you'd see a parlor with a *bakla* in it...And at the northernmost part of the country...you'd see a parlor or a designer or a choreographer. Even [on] the highest mountain, you'd see a gay person here. You'd be surprised. I climb mountains, and I see them all over the place. I do, I do...within the minority groups—the indigenous groups...

LG: What about poor people and the *bakla*?

JA: The poorer families...would rather have a *bakla* kid because he's a potential money-earner....[The *bakla* could] be an entertainer in Japan or somewhere else, or perhaps

(continued on next page)

time except for business transactions. Additionally, the concept of "losing face" is prevalent in the Philippines, so be sure to allow Filipinos a way out of an awkward situation.

TABLE MANNERS. Food is an important part of most social gatherings and engagements in the Philippines. Filipinos usually eat with a fork in the right hand and a spoon in the left. Slurping soup is a sign that you enjoy the taste, but leaving something on your plate after you have finished eating indicates that you did not enjoy the meal. To get a waiter's attention in a restaurant, raise your hand and draw a square in the air. Drawing a larger air-square indicates to the waiter that you want to see a menu. Filipinos usually eat in large groups—with families or groups of friends—as everything in the Philippines is done with as many people as possible.

BISEXUAL, GAY, AND LESBIAN TRAVELERS. Homosexuality, far more readily accepted for both men and women in the Philippines than in other parts of Southeast Asia, takes a unique form in Filipino communities (see **John Abul, Manila Bakla,** p. 554). Gay men, known as *bakla*, consider themselves men with the souls of women and are attracted more to heterosexual men than other gay men. The *bakla* occupy a well-accepted niche within Philippine society, though many fear being trivialized as superficial and appearance-obsessed. Travelers to the Philippines will have no trouble finding bars, clubs, and beaches that cater to a mixed crowd.

ARTS AND RECREATION

Philippine artistic traditions have been heavily influenced by the nation's interactions with other cultures. These influences, however, have been incorporated into indigenous folk traditions in order to create what today is considered "the Philippine arts." Recently, there has been a push to bring the artistic traditions of isolated tribal-ethnic groups to light.

ARCHITECTURE. Like most of its other cultural traditions, Philippine architecture has absorbed international elements while managing to retain something distinctive. With the Spanish came European architecture of the religious and military varieties; the *Intromuros* in Manila (see p. 567) is a good example. Today, **Bobby Manosa** and the late **Leandro V. Locsin** are the major figures in the world of Philippine architecture, with designs that stress the somewhat unlikely melding of the folk and postmodern aesthetics and the 'made in the Philippines' concept.

DANCE. The quintessential **barrio dance** is the ever-popular **tinikling,** the national dance. Performers beat pairs of long bamboo sticks rhythmically against the ground and each other, as couples skip and twirl in and out of the sticks. Another dance tradition comes from the Muslim areas of the Philippines, where dances are characterized by their theatricality. In the **Langka-batuang,** men act like angry monkeys, scuttling about and nimbly climbing poles propped up by other dancers. To this day, royal princesses in the Sulu archipelago are required to learn the noble **Singkil** dance, which dramatizes a legend of the Maranao people of Mindanao.

FILM. Introduced to the Philippines in early 20th century, film has become an important medium for local artists to respond to social, political, educational, and economic conditions. The world's third largest producer of films after India and China/Hong Kong, the Philippines is one of the few nations whose domestic film industry can stand up to Hollywood in the box office; most of these local films, however, are of the sentimental or violent variety. **Yam Llaranas** and **Erik Matti** are touted as the country's most impressive young filmmakers.

LITERATURE. Though artistically hindered under Spanish rule, the Filipino *ilustrados* continued to write about their discontent with revolutionary results. When Spain exiled many of them, they began writing in Tagalog to increase their mass appeal. The period of American cultural infiltration was a low point for Philippine literature. Written in English, it merely imitated the American greats; written in Spanish, it echoed trite nationalism; and written in Tagalog, it found refuge in self-pity. The Marcos era brought little relief for the floundering literary tradition, as reading or writing "subversive" literature meant indefinite imprisonment. In recent years, however, Philippine literature seems to have begun a second renaissance.

MARTIAL ARTS. Refined over centuries into an effective fighting technique, the Philippine martial arts are highly pragmatic. Fearing its power, the Spanish colonists banned **Arnis** (also known as **Kali** or **Eskrima**), a form of Philippine martial arts. Instead of disappearing, however, it reappeared in movements incorporated into many folk dance routines. Today, Filipino martial arts schools dot the globe; in fact, many law enforcement officials all over the world are trained in Philippine martial arts because of their flexibility and effectiveness.

(continued from previous page)

even in this country, in sing-a-long bars, in beauty contests...

LG: Besides entertainment, what are some other common occupations for *bakla*?

JA: Politicians. A lot of them.

LG: What about *baklas* and the beauty industry?

JA: It's dominated by gay men. All of them are there.

LG: How does the gay life in the Philippines compare to gay life in other countries?

JA: Here, I think there's more freedom as compared to other Asian countries. We're not a Muslim country. There's no one religion for everybody. Though we're predominantly Christian, Filipinos are, by nature, tolerant.

LG: Would you be comfortable being gay in, say, Malaysia?

JA: You kidding? They'd kill me right there in the airport.

LG: You don't experience much discrimination here?

JA: Luckily, no. I guess it's how you conduct yourself. At first, they might say, "Oh, he's a *bakla*...he's gay!" But if you project yourself properly like any other person, they would take you in.

LG: Are there different types of *baklas*?

JA: Oh yes. From A to Z. The BPS—meaning "Beauty Parlor Swarthe"—they're the ones who look like they had a bad hair day. Overdone nails.

LG: How do you classify yourself?

JA: I'm regular on a daily basis, but at parties, I'm not. I did Rocky Horror Picture Show as Dr. Frankenfurter. I go in drag every now and then, just to shock people...

HOLIDAYS & FESTIVALS (2003)

DATE	NAME & LOCATION	DESCRIPTION
Jan. 9	Feast of the Black Nazarene (Manila's Quiapo District)	Mammoth procession of barefooted, white-shirted men carrying a lifesize blackwood statue of Jesus.
Jan. 18	Ati-Atihan (Kalibo)	The Philippine equivalent of Mardi Gras.
Feb. 22-25	People Power Days	Thanksgiving for the 1986 overthrow of the Marcos regime.
Apr. 17	Holy Thursday	The day of the Last Supper when Jesus washed the feet of his disciples.
Apr. 18	Good Friday	Day of mourning for the crucifiction of Jesus Christ.
Apr. 20	Easter	Commemorates Jesus's rising from the dead.
June 12	Independence Day	Military parades in major cities.
Oct. 19	Masskara Festival (Bacolod)	Masked parade.
Nov. 30	Bonifacio Day	Remembrance for the nationalist Andres Bonifacio, who launched the Philippine Revolution.
Dec. 22	Giant Lantern Festival	Lantern parade in San Fernando.
Dec. 25	Christmas Day	Commemorates the birthday of Jesus Christ.
Dec. 30	Rizal Day	Remembrance for the nationalist martyr, Jose Rizal.

ADDITIONAL RESOURCES

GENERAL HISTORY

America's Boy: A Century of Colonialism in the Philippines, by James Hamilton-Paterson (1999). Attempts to understand the scandalous reign of Ferdinand and Imelda Marcos and tell the history of the regime from the perspective of Filipinos.

Muslim Rulers and Rebels: Everyday Politics and Armed Separatism in the Southern Philippines (Comparative Studies on Muslim Societies, No. 26), by Thomas M. McKenna (1998). Places today's Muslim separatist movments in the context of Muslim-Catholic relations in the Philippines.

The Philippines: A Singular and Plural Place, by David Joel Steinberg (2000). Discusses the continuing struggle of unifying the Philippines.

Filipino Politics: Development and Decay (Politics and International Relations of Southeast Asia), by David Wurfel (1991). An in-depth look at the history of the Philippines with an emphasis on the Marcos and Aquino regimes.

FICTION AND NON-FICTION

Nelson's Run, by Peter Bacho (2002). Political and sexual satire exposing the intricacies of corruption and the effects of colonialism.

Babylon: An Anthology of Filipina and Filipina American Writers, Ed. Nick Carbo, Eileen Tabios (2000). Outstanding collection of Filipina and Filipina-American writers.

The Tesseract, by Alex Garland (1999). A thrilling tale of the streets of Manila from the author of *The Beach*.

Ghosts of Manila, by James Hamilton-Paterson (1994). A haunting exploration of Manila's post-Marcos anarchy.

Dusk: A Novel, by F. Sionil Jose (1998). A 19th-century historical novel that explores the tensions between wealth and poverty, oppression and freedom, peace and conflict.

Noli Me Tangere, by Jose Rizal (1886), translated by Ma Soledad Locson-Locsin (1997). The most famous and influential nationalist novel written under Spanish colonialism.

ESSENTIALS

PHILIPPINES PRICE ICONS					
SYMBOL:	❶	❷	❸	❹	❺
ACCOMM.	Under US$2 Under P100	US$2-4 P100-200	US$4-7.75 P200-400	US$7.75-11.50 P400-600	Over US$11.50 Over P600
FOOD	Under US$1 Under P50	US$1-2 P50-100	US$2-4 P100-200	US$4-5.75 P200-300	Over US$5.75 Over P300

EMBASSIES AND CONSULATES

PHILIPPINE CONSULAR SERVICES ABROAD

Australia: Embassy, 1 Moonah Pl., Yarralumla, Canberra, ACT 2600; mailing address: P.O. Box 3297, Manuka ACT 2603 (☎02 6273 2535; www.philembassy.au.com). **Consulates,** Sydney: (☎02 9262 7377; www.emanila.com/phconsul); Fortitude Valley (☎07 3252 8215); Nightcliff (☎08 8922 4411); Melbourne (☎03 9662 9702).

Canada: Embassy, 130 Albert St. #606, Ottawa, ON K1P 5G4 (☎613-233-1121; www.philembassyca.org). **Consulates,** Toronto (☎416-922 7181; www.philcongen-toronto.com); Vancouver (☎604-685 7645).

New Zealand: Embassy, 50 Hobson St., Thorndon; P.O. Box 12042, Wellington (☎04 472 9921).

South Africa: Embassy, 54 Nicolson St., Muckleneuk, Pretoria 0181; mailing address: P.O. Box 2560, Brooklyn Square, 0075 (☎012 346 0451 or 346 0452).

UK: Embassy, 9A Palace Green, London W8 4QE (☎020 7937 1600).

United States: Embassy, 1600 Massachusetts Ave. NW, Washington, DC 20036 (☎202-467-9300). **Consulates,** New York (☎212-764-1330); Chicago (☎312-332-6458); San Francisco (☎415-433-6666 or 433-6667); Los Angeles (☎213-639-0980).

CONSULAR SERVICES IN THE PHILIPPINES

Australian Embassy: 104 Paseo de Roxas cor. Perea St., Legaspi Village, Makati City, Manila (☎02 750-2850).

Canadian Embassy: 9th and 11th fl., Allied Bank Centre, 6754 Ayala Ave., Makati City, Manila (☎02 867-0001).

UK Embassy : 15-17th fl., LV Locsin Building, 6752 Ayala Ave., Makati City, Manila (☎02 816-7116).

United States Embassy: 1201 Roxas Blvd., Ermita 1000, Manila (☎02 523-1001).

TOURIST INFORMATION OFFICES

Philippines Department of Tourism (www.wowphilippines.com.ph/cgi-bin/dot/index2.asp). **Australia,** Tourism Information Officer, Level 1 Philippine Centre, 27-33 Wentworth Ave., Sydney NSW 2000 (☎02 9283 0711). **UK,** Embassy of the Philippines, Culture and Tourism Office, 146 Cromwell Rd., London SW7 4EF (☎020 7835 1100). **US,** Philippine Center, 556 5th Ave., New York, NY 10036 (☎212-575-7915).

VISAS

American, Australian, British, Canadian, European, and South African citizens may enter without visas and stay for 21 days. For longer stays, obtain a 59-day visa beforehand (single-entry visas US$35; multiple-entry US$50) or get an **extension** from the immigration office (P510). Extensions for longer stays require approval from the government, which can take three weeks or more.

MONEY

The Philippine **peso (P)** is divided into 100 **centavos.** In the text, the peso is denoted with "P", as in P45. Bills come in denominations of P5, 10, 20, 50, 100, 500, and 1000. Coins come in 1, 5, 10, and 25 centavos and P1, P2, and P5. Fares for taxis should be rounded up for a tip of P5-10. **ATMs** abound in most cities.

GETTING THERE

BY PLANE. The Philippines has two **international airports:** Mactan Cebu International Airport in Cebu (p. 600) and Nino Aquino International Airport in Manila (p. 559). **Philippine Airlines** (**PAL;** www.philippineair.com) operates international flights from dozens of countries.

GETTING AROUND

BY PLANE. Air travel is a godsend for island-hoppers in the Philippines. Multiple-day journeys by bus or ferry are shrunk to 1-2hr. plane rides. PAL is the national airline, but competitors include **Air Philippines** (which has some of the best student rates), **Asian Spirit, Cebu Pacific, Mindanao Express,** and **Pacific Airways.**

BY BUS AND JEEPNEY. A competitive market of bus companies runs across Luzon, with a few epic 45hr. journeys. "Ordinary" buses are hot and stuffy, while first-class and "premier" buses have A/C and more spacious seats. Jeepney (see **Jeepers Creepers,** p. 562) offer cheap, convenient transportation.

BY BOAT. Ferry travel provides a cheap but sometimes dangerous means of traversing the seas; many fatal ferry wrecks occur every year, and pirates have been a recent threat. Regulation is improving steadily, and fast, safer catamarans with radars and night-vision equipment ply many popular routes. Inter-island shipping schedules are published in daily newspapers. Journey times to the same destination vary significantly between different carriers.

KEEPING IN TOUCH

Even in some larger cities, the Philippine *Poste Restante* system is unreliable at best; use AmEx mail holding service instead. Mail usually reaches Manila from the west in 5-10 days, but it takes a few more days to snake its way through the islands. For **telephone calls,** a number of public calling offices handle domestic and international communication. The **Philippines Long Distance Telephone Company (PLDT)** is most prevalent, but **RCPI/Bayantel, Islacom,** and a few smaller companies pick up the slack in more remote areas. When using PLDT, dial 105-11 before the number. Unfortunately, not all public calling offices allow phone card calls. PLDT has phone cards which can be used for international or domestic calls, but coin-operated payphones are still commonplace. A few resort areas still lack phone service, but cell phones keep the lines of communication open for reservations. For **Home Country Direct (HCD)** numbers from the Philippines, refer to the table on the inside back cover of this book. The Philippines is **8 hours ahead of GMT. Internet** access is found surprisingly often, but by no means everywhere.

LUZON

Accounting for a third of the country's landmass and half its population, Luzon is anchored by sprawling Metro Manila to the south and extends northward along teeth-shattering rural roads. On the ride through the countryside, the Central Cordillera mountains overlook the Banaue rice terraces—the world's eighth natural wonder. Thanks to millennia of back-breaking labor by the Ifugao people, gigantic stone staircases climb skyward, carpeted with emerald puffs of rice seedlings. Leisurely treks grant glimpses of indigenous traditions, Pangasinan's Hundred Islands Park provides a taste of Philippine beaches, and nearby Baguio entertains a thriving student and artist community. While Legazpi's Mayon Volcano is the most fiery of Luzon's hotspots, the scene in Manila is doubtless the feistiest.

MANILA ☎2

In spite of a modern transit system and huge shopping malls, Manila lacks order. Chaos, in fact, seems to drive the city. The streets—in a constant jam—are filled with honking jeepneys, neighing horses, and screaming men on tricycles. Street children, dirtied from the traffic's exhaust, line the sidewalks where hagglers pitch cigarettes, fruit, and plastic dogs with bobbing heads. Policemen guard the entry to nearly every restaurant and ATM to fend off the very present threat of thieves, pickpockets, and hooligans. But somehow, despite the unmistakable poverty and pollution, Manila retains an energy that borders on exhausting. A thriving gay scene puts the "Man" in "Manila" and includes some of the world's quirkiest bars. Visitors brave enough to battle the city's heat and noise will admire the well-preserved 16th-century architecture reminiscent of Spanish colonial rule and the well-landscaped parks. For all its vices, this city leaves its guests tired and frustrated but still eager to return.

INTERCITY TRANSPORTATION

BY PLANE

Manila has separate international and domestic airports. International flights arrive at **Ninoy Aquino International Airport** (☎877 1109 for Department of Tourism, ☎877 1200 for international flight info), off Ninoy Aquino Ave. in Parañaque, 9km south of Rizal Park. Banks in the arrivals hall **change currency** at poor rates, but **ATMs** near the car rental booths offer better rates (Cirrus/MC/NYCE/V). Domestic flights arrive at **Manila Domestic Airport** (☎871 0000), off Domestic Rd. in Parañaque. The international departure tax is P550; domestic is P100.

Taxis run between NAIA and Manila Domestic Airport (P85-90). **PAL passengers** can take the **free shuttle** between terminals. Brave travelers can venture out to Ninoy Aquino Ave., where **jeepneys** and **buses** are available. Jeepneys head along Domestic Rd. to **Baclaran Market** (P4) and **Manila Domestic Airport** ("Baclaran-MIA" route, P4). To prevent pushy taxi drivers from ripping off tourists, the city has set up "coupon" taxis, which will take you into **Metro Manila** (P345). No other taxis are allowed. To get to Manila from the market, take the **Light Rail Transit** (**LRT;** P12) or a "Sucat-Hwy." or "New MIA" jeepney. Jeepneys may charge extra for large baggage. Buses bound for **Fairview, Monumento,** or **Santa Cruz** pass by Ermita and Malate Districts along Taft Ave. (P17)

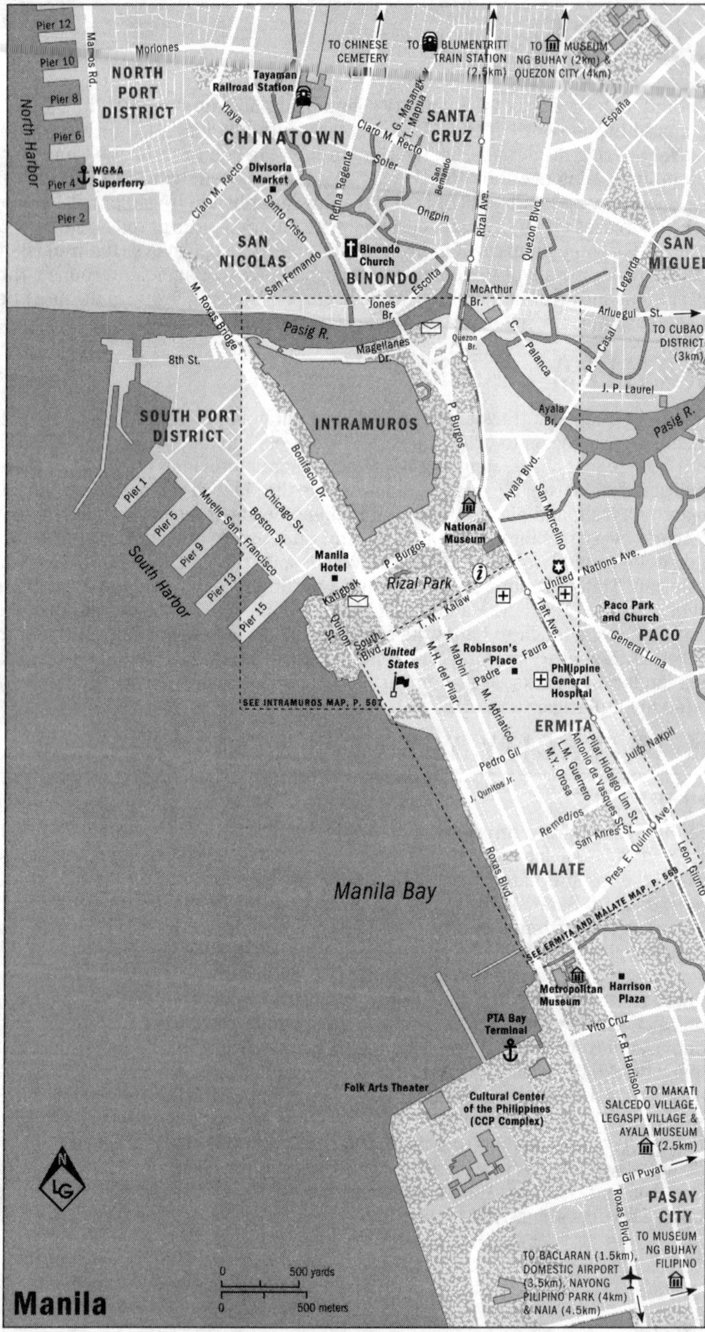
Manila
NORTH PORT DISTRICT
CHINATOWN
SANTA CRUZ
SAN NICOLAS
BINONDO
SAN MIGUEL
SOUTH PORT DISTRICT
INTRAMUROS
PACO
ERMITA
MALATE
PASAY CITY
Manila Bay
North Harbor
South Harbor
Pasig R.
Pier 12
Pier 10
Pier 8
Pier 6
Pier 4
Pier 2
Pier 1
Pier 5
Pier 9
Pier 13
Pier 15
WG&A Superferry
Tayaman Railroad Station
Divisoria Market
Binondo Church
TO CHINESE CEMETERY
TO BLUMENTRITT TRAIN STATION (2.5km)
TO MUSEUM NG BUHAY (2km) & QUEZON CITY (4km)
TO CUBAO DISTRICT (3km)
National Museum
Manila Hotel
Rizal Park
Paco Park and Church
Robinson's Place
Philippine General Hospital
United States
SEE INTRAMUROS MAP, P. 567
SEE ERMITA AND MALATE MAP, P. 569
Metropolitan Museum
Harrison Plaza
PTA Bay Terminal
Folk Arts Theater
Cultural Center of the Philippines (CCP Complex)
TO MAKATI SALCEDO VILLAGE, LEGASPI VILLAGE & AYALA MUSEUM (2.5km)
TO MUSEUM NG BUHAY FILIPINO
TO BACLARAN (1.5km), DOMESTIC AIRPORT (3.5km), NAYONG PILIPINO PARK (4km) & NAIA (4.5km)
Moriones
Marcos Rd.
Ylaya
Claro M. Recto
G. Masangkay
T. Mapua
Soler
San Bernardo
Ongpin
Rizal Ave.
Quezon Blvd.
España
Reina Regente
Santo Cristo
San Fernando
Escolta
McArthur Br.
Jones Br.
Quezon Br.
Magellanes Dr.
M. Roxas Bridge
8th St.
Legarda
Arlegui St.
C. Palanca
P. Casal
J. P. Laurel
Ayala Br.
P. Burgos
Ayala Blvd.
San Marcelino
Bonifacio Dr.
Chicago St.
Boston St.
Muelle San Francisco
United Nations Ave.
Katigbak
Quirino St.
South Blvd.
T. M. Kalaw
Taft Ave.
General Luna
A. Mabini
M.H. del Pilar
Padre Faura
M. Adriatico
Pedro Gil
J. Quintos Jr.
Antonio de Vasques St.
L.M. Guerrero
M.Y. Orosa
Pilar Hidalgo Lim St.
Julio Nakpil
Remedios
San Andres St.
Pres. E. Quirino Ave.
Leon Guinto
Roxas Blvd.
Vito Cruz
F.B. Harrison
Gil Puyat
0 500 yards
0 500 meters

DESTINATION	FREQUENCY	PRICE	DESTINATION	FREQUENCY	PRICE
Bangkok	5 per week	US$638	**Jakarta**	4 per week	US$867
Bacolod	2 per day	P2343	**Kuala Lampur**	3 per week	US$801
Cebu	13-14 per day	P1736-2183	**Legazpi**	1 per day	P1611
Ho Chi Minh City	3 per week	US$528	**Puerto Princesa**	2 per day	P2071
Hong Kong	4 per day	US$421	**Singapore**	1 per day	US$801
Iloilo	3 per day	P2342	**Tacloban**	3 per day	P2298

Most airlines have offices in the Makati Business District, though many have branches closer to Ermita and Malate. Major **international airlines** that serve Manila are: **Cathay Pacific,** 2nd fl., Tetra Global Bldg., 1616 Dr. Vasquez St., Pedro Gil, Ermita (☎848 2701); **Malaysia Airlines,** G/F, Legazpi Towers, 300, Roxas Blvd. (☎525 9404); **Philippine Airlines (PAL),** 540 P. Faura St., Cov. Adriatico St., Ermita (☎855 8888); **Royal Brunei,** 7 Saville Bldg. (☎897 3309), at the corner of Gil Puyat Ave. and Paseo de Roxas St., Makati City; **Singapore Airlines,** 138 H.V. de la Costa St., Salcedo Village, Makati City (☎810 4951); **Thai Airways,** Escolta Twin Towers, 288 Escolta St., Paco (☎243 2645). Major **domestic airlines** that serve Manila are: **Air Philippines,** 15th fl., Multinational Bank Corporation Center, 6805 Ayala Ave., Makati (☎843 7770); **Asian Spirit,** ground floor, LPL Towers, 112 Legazpi St., Legazpi Village, Makati (☎840 3811); **Cebu Pacific,** Manila Midtown Hotel, (☎636 4938), on the corner of Adriatico St. and Pedro Gil, Ermita; **PAL,** S&L Bldg., (☎521 8821, 24hr. info ☎816 6691), on Roxas Blvd., Ermita.

BY TRAIN

The **Philippine National Railway** (☎254 9772) runs between Manila and **Legaspi City** (from Tayuman Station: 8hr., daily 4pm, P179-234; from Blumentritt Station: daily 7:40pm, with A/C P234). Antiquated cars and slow speed make this government-backed operation a last resort for travelers.

BY BUS

Buses heading north leave from terminals clustered around **Epifanio de los Santos Ave. (EDSA)** in the Cubao District, accessible by a Cubao-bound jeepney or bus. Buses headed south leave from terminals along EDSA in Pasay City, best reached by LRT: EDSA Station. Call for schedules and specific prices. Major transit companies include: **Autobus** (☎743 2227), at the corner of Dimasalang and Laong-Laan St., Sampaloc; **BLTB,** 3 EDSA, Pasay City (☎833 5501); **Jam Transit** (☎831 4390), at the corner of Taft Ave. and Gil Puyat, Pasay City; **Dagupan Bus** (☎928 5639), at the corner of EDSA and New York St., Cubao, Quezon City; **Dangwa Tranco** (☎410 1991), at the corner of Aurora Blvd., and Driod St., Cubao, Quezon City; **Partas** (☎724 9820), at the corner of Aurora Blvd. and Arayat, Cubao, Quezon City; **Philippine Rabbit,** Santa Cruz Terminal (☎734 9836), at the corner of 819 Oroquieta St. and C.M. Recto; Quezon Terminal, 1240 EDSA (☎456 7659); **Philtranco** (☎833 5061), at the corner of EDSA and Apelo Cruz St., Pasay City; **Victory Liner,** Caloocan Terminal (☎361 1506), on Grays Park Ave.; Cubao Terminal, 853 Immaculate Conception Rd., (☎833 0293), along EDSA; Pasay City Terminal, 561 EDSA (☎727 4268). Bring a blanket on overnight A/C bus rides.

DESTINATION	DURATION/ FREQUENCY	PRICE	DESTINATION	DURATION/ FREQUENCY	PRICE
Baguio	6½hr., 21 per day	P187	Santa Cruz	2hr., 25 per day	P58
Banaue	9hr., 2 per day	P150	San Fernando	8hr., 24 per day	P200
Batangas City	30min., 20 per day	P70	Tagaytay	1½hr., 15 per day	P47
Legazpi	12hr., 15 per day	P270	Vigan	9hr., 20 per day	P321

JEEPERS CREEPERS Cross a jeep with a school bus, and cross that with a low-rider, and you'll have what Filipinos call a jeepney. The country's most popular form of mid-distance travel, jeepneys are built for 18 passengers but usually pack in about 25. Puffing diesel smoke, jeepney don't have set stops–flag one down, jump in the back door, and be ready to bang on the roof or yell "Ooooo!" to get off. Pay the driver through the open divider while in motion, hang on, and enjoy the ride.

BY BOAT

North Harbor District: In the North Port District along Marcos Rd., north of the Pasig River, accessible by taxi from Ermita (P65) or "North Harbor" jeepneys from Divisoria Market. **WG&A Lines,** Pier 4 and 14, North Harbor (☎528 7000) sends boats to: **Catbalogan,** Samar (25hr., M 9am, P611); **Cebu** (19-20hr.; M 7pm, Tu 3pm, Th 7pm, Su 9am; P1185); **Coron** (7-8hr., F 4pm, P800); **Davao** (2 days; M 9am, W, Sa noon; P1600); **Dumaguete** (15hr., P1185); **Iloilo** (21hr.; W and Sa 9, 10am; P1245); **Puerto Princesa** (28hr., F 4pm, P1120); **Tagbilaran** (28hr.; F and Su midnight; P1007). **Negros Navigation** (☎243 5359) offers fewer destinations at similar prices.

CCP Bay Terminal: On Roxas Blvd. in the CCP Complex in Pasay City, accessible by orange jeepneys from LRT: Vito Cruz. **Bullet Express** (☎551 0476) sends boats to **Lamao,** Bataan (55min.; 5 per day 6:20am-4:30pm; P130, students P110).

ORIENTATION

"Metro Manila" is comprised of 12 cities and five municipalities. The clogged main artery, **Epifanio de los Santos Ave. (EDSA),** traces a wide loop (24km) around the metropolis, running through **Caloocan City** and **Quezon City** in the northeast, **Makati** in the southeast, and **Pasay City** in the south. **Manila proper** sprawls along the bay, straddling the **Pasig River. Rizal Park,** also known as **Luneta,** is a widely-used landmark in the heart of the city. The heavily touristed areas of **Ermita** and **Malate** lie south of Rizal Park, bounded by **Taft Ave.** to the east and Malate Church to the south. The **Cultural Center of the Philippines (CCP)** sits south of Malate toward Pasay City. The walled city of **Intramuros** sits north of Rizal Park, extending to the Pasig River. The **Chinatown** districts of **Binondo** and **Santa Cruz** form the other bank of the Pasig River. The **LRT** above Taft Ave. runs from **Baclaran** station in the south to **Monumento** in the north. The **MRT** runs above EDSA. Affluent **Makati City** is 7km southeast. **Note:** Manila maps often use the abbreviation "cor." for "at the corner of," particularly when street numbers are absent.

LOCAL TRANSPORTATION

Taxis: An affordable and comfortable way to get around, and an ideal stepping stone for new travelers before braving the chaotic jeepney circuits. Metered A/C taxis may be reluctant to go short distances or into congested areas unless you agree to a high fixed price. Beware of taxis that charge exorbitant rates as set down in a fare-book with the deceptive title "Meters." Taxis charge a base fare of P25 plus P2 for every 200m or 1½min. wait in traffic. If drivers refuse to turn on their meters, they can be fined and, in some cases, lose their licenses. A ride from Ermita to Malate should run about P40. From Malate to Intramuros, a taxi should cost P80.

Jeepneys: The cheapest mode of transportation in town, jeepneys follow set routes all over the city (first 4km P4, P0.50 per additional km). A signboard declares destinations, and the route is detailed below the windscreen or to the side. A useful route connects the Ermita and Malate Districts to **Baclaran Market** in Pasay City to the south.

Other jeepneys run from Baclaran or LRT: Buendia (Gil Puyat Ave.) along Taft Ave. to **Quiapo, Santa Cruz,** and **Monumento** north of the Pasig River. Jeepneys marked **Project 2** and **3** head for the **Quirino District, Project 4** go to **Cubao,** and **Project 6** and **8** head to the center of **Quezon City.** The Cubao jeepney are useful for reaching several **EDSA bus terminals,** while Baclaran jeepneys cross EDSA to a cluster of **Pasay City bus terminals.** Jeepneys with the same destinations can take entirely different routes with different stops, depending on where you catch them from. Don't be afraid to ask the driver or other passengers for directions to your destination, and, as always, be aware of your surroundings and property inside a jeepney. Often overcrowded, they are primc pickpockcting locations and can be unsafe at night.

LRT and MRT (Elevated Railways): Manila's LRT is the only way to avoid hectic traffic. Trains run frequently 5am-9pm between 15 stations at 800m intervals, along a 15km route from **Monumento Station** in Caloocan City in the north to **Baclaran** in the south (30min. end to end, flat rate P12). Completed in 2001, the MRT, another elevated railway, has two lines: MRT 1 (6am-11pm, P12) and MRT 3 (6am-11:30pm, P9.50-16). MRT 1 has 18 stops along Rizal and Taft Ave. MRT 3, commonly called **Metrostar,** has 13 stops along EDSA Ave.

Other Moving Objects: Pedi-cabs, small BMX bikes with sidecars, roam Ermita and Malate's back streets (P15-30). In Binondo, Divisoria, Intramuros, and Rizal Park, **calesas** (horse-drawn carriages) cruise the city (P40 per km). Eight-seater Toyota Tamaraw FX **"mega-taxis"** threaten to surpass jeepneys as the city's most rampant vehicles (from P10). These large vehicles run along similar routes as the jeepneys and have A/C—a life-saver during Manila's severe traffic jams. **Local buses** grind along major thoroughfares, particularly Taft Ave. and EDSA (about P10 per 4km). Destinations are posted in the front windows. "Ayala" buses run along Taft Ave. to Ayala Ave. in Makati City (P14). **Tricycles** run in Caloocan City (P5 per 2min.).

PRACTICAL INFORMATION

TOURIST AND FINANCIAL SERVICES

Tourist Offices: Head Office, #106, Dept. of Tourism Bldg., Teodoro Valencia Circle, T.M. Kalaw St., Ermita (☎524 2384), at the corner of Rizal Park near the Taft Ave. and T.M. Kalaw St. intersection. LRT: UN Ave. Station. Free *Tourist Map of the Philippines plus Street Map of Manila.* **Open 24hr.** To reach **Airport Tourist Information,** take the elevator to the 4th floor. Grab a map here before tackling the city.

Travel and Tours: The Ermita and Malate areas have many travel agencies. **Swagman Travel,** 411 A. Flores St., Ermita (☎524 5816), a well-established Aussie outfit with 15 outposts all over the Philippines, organizes local tours. **Southeast Travel Corp.** (☎524 5676), at the corner of Pedro Gil and Mtt. del Pilar St., Ermita, handles air ticketing and local tours. Open M-F 8am-6pm, Sa 8am-noon. **Aqua Travel & Tours,** Ste. #201, Manila Midtown Hotel, Pedro Gil St., Ermita (☎523 1989), specializes in scuba holidays. Open daily 9am-6pm.

Embassies: Australia, 1st and 5th fl., Doña Salustiana Bldg., 104 Paseo de Roxas, Makati (☎750 2850). Open M-F 8:30am-4:30pm. **Brunei,** 11th fl., Ayala Wing, BPI Bldg., at the corner of Ayala Ave. and Paseo de Roxas St. (☎816 2836). Open M-F 8am-4pm. **Canada,** 9-11th fl., Allied Bank Center, 6754 Ayala Ave., Makati (☎867 0001). Open M-Th 9-11:30am and 1-3pm, F 9am-1pm. **Indonesia,** 185 Salcedo St., Legaspi Village, Makati (☎892 5061). Open M-F 8:30am-5pm. **Ireland,** 3rd fl., Port Royal Palace, 118 Rada St., Legaspi Village, Makati (☎819 1581). Open M-F 9am-4pm. **Laos,** 34 Lapu-Lapu St., St. Magallanes Village, Makati (☎852 5759). Open M-F 8:30am-4:30pm. **Malaysia,** 107 Tordesillas St., Salcedo Village, Makati (☎817 4581). Open M-F 9am-noon. **Myanmar,** 8/F, Xanland Center, 152 Amorsolo St.,

Legaspi Village, Makati (☎817 2373). Open M-F 9am-4:30pm. **New Zealand,** 23rd fl., Far East Bank Center, Sen. Gil Puyat Ave. near Makati Ave., Makati (☎891 5050). Open M-F 8:30am-12:30pm and 1:30-4:30pm. **Singapore,** 35th fl., Enterprise Tower 1, Ayala Corner (☎751 2345). Open M-F 8:30am-5pm. **Thailand,** 107 Rada St., Legaspi Village, Makati (☎815 4219). Open M-F 9am-5pm. **UK,** 15-17th fl., L.V. Locsin Bldg., at the corner of Ayala and Makati Ave., Makati (☎816 7116). Open M-Th 8am-4:30pm, F 8am-2pm. **US,** 1201 Roxas Blvd. (☎523 1001). Open M-F 7:30am-4:30pm. **Vietnam,** 554 Pablo Ocampo St., Malate (☎524 0364). Open M-F 8:30am- 5pm.

Immigration Office: Bureau of Immigration and Deportation, Magallanes Dr., Intramuros (☎527 3263), near Jones Bridge. Extends tourist visas to 59 days for P1570. No shorts or sandals. Open M-F 8am-noon and 1-5pm. Many travel agencies extend visas just as quickly for similar prices and shorter lines.

Currency Exchange: Ermita and Malate are rife with late-night moneychangers and **24hr. ATMs. Equitable PCI Bank,** EBC Bldg., at the corner of J. Bocobo St. and UN Ave., Ermita (☎524 9661). **Branches** throughout the city. MC/V cash advances. **24hr. ATM.** Open M-F 9am-4pm. "Traveler's check" is almost nonexistent in the Filipino moneychanger's vocabulary; bring plenty of cash.

American Express: 1810 Mabini St. (☎524 8681), at the corner with Remedios St., Malate. Mail held for free. Open M-F 8:30am-4pm, Sa 9am-noon.

LOCAL SERVICES

Bookstores: National Book Store, Robinson's Mall, Pedro Gil. St., Ermita (☎733 8265). English books, Filipiniana section, maps, and travel guides. *Metro Manila Street Map* P80. Open daily 10am-9pm. **Solidaridad Bookshop,** 531 Padre Faura St., Ermita (☎523 0870). Owned by F. Sionil "Frankie" Jose, one of the Philippines' foremost contemporary novelists. *International Herald Tribune* and *Financial Times* delivered by 5:30pm. Open M-Sa 9am-6pm.

Women's Resources: Women in Travel Club, c/o Philippine Airlines, S&L Bldg., 1500 Roxas Blvd., Manila (☎525 5420). Info on safety and discounts.

Lesbian and Gay Resources: Library Foundation, 1066 Remedios St., coordinates gay activities in the capital. Ask at **The Library Bar,** 1779 Adriatico St. (see **Entertainment: Bars and Cafes,** p. 570). **Womyn Supporting Womyn Center (WSWC),** 43-44 University of the Philippines Shopping Center, U.P. Diliman, Quezon City (☎522 2484). Lesbian info service.

EMERGENCY AND COMMUNICATIONS

Emergency: ☎166.

Police: Western District Police (☎523 8391). Smaller police **branch** on the corner of UN Ave. and San Marcelino St., east of Taft Ave.

Tourist Police: Dept. of Tourism Bldg., #112, Teodoro Valencia Circle, T.M. Kalaw St., Ermita. **24hr. Tourist Assistance Hotlines:** ☎524 1728 or 524 1660.

Pharmacies: Well-stocked **Mercury Drug** branches in every major shopping mall. Most branches open daily 7am-10pm. The **branch** in Plaza Miranda, Quiapo (☎733 2112) is open **24hr. Manila Doctors Hospital Pharmacy** (☎524 3090, see below). **Open 24hr.**

Medical Services: Manila Doctors Hospital, 667 UN Ave., Ermita (☎524 3011), opposite the Philam Bldg., is close to most accommodations. **Open 24hr.**

Telephones: Most shops and guest houses provide **local phone service** (P5 per 3min.). Prepaid PLDT **"Fonkards"** (P100-1000), available in stores throughout the city, connect local or long-distance calls from PLDT card phones. Green Eastern **card phones** line the streets of Ermita and Malate as an alternative for international calls.

Internet Access: Several Internet cafes line Pedro Gil St. in front of Robinson's Mall. P30 per hr. **Shuttle.com** on Pedro Gil St. and Adriatico St. has 20 stations for Internet and network gaming. The **Universe Cyber Cafe** (☎524 2575), on the 3rd floor of Robinson's, charges P1.50 per min. Open daily 10am-9pm.

Post Offices: GPO, Liwasang Bonifacio, Intramuros (☎527 0085). LRT: Central Station. Walk past Manila City Library and through the Quezon Blvd. underpass. It's near MacArthur Bridge on Pasig River. *Poste Restante* at Counter 218. Open M-F 7am-5pm, Sa 8am-noon. **Postal code:** 1000.

ACCOMMODATIONS

Manila can be a carbon-monoxide sauna—A/C rooms might be worth the extra pesos. Accommodations in Ermita and Malate, in the heart of Metro Manila, have the best location amidst restaurants, sights, services, and entertainment.

Malate Pensionne, 1771 Adriatico St., Malate (☎523 8304; fax 522 2389; info@mpensionne.com). Behind Starbucks. Beautiful hardwood lodgings in a superb location. Strong security precautions lend a sense of safety. Fax, Internet, airport transfer, and laundry services available. Dorms with A/C P300; super economy singles P500; doubles with A/C, TV, and private bath P1050. ❸

Pension Natividad, 1690 M.H. del Pilar St., near J. Quintos St., Malate (☎521 0524). The best-kept secret of backpackers, Natividad has clean, newly-renovated rooms at dirt-cheap prices. Same-sex dorms P200; doubles P550, with common room P650; doubles with A/C and bath P800. MC/V. ❷

UCCP Shalom Center, 1660 L.M. Guerrero St. (☎524 6242). All are welcome in this "Christian home in Manila," which offers clean rooms and heavenly service. Dorms P350; doubles with A/C and common room P1000; family room P1200. ❸

Tropical Mansion Hotel, 1242 J.C. Bocobo St., Ermita (☎521 2639). Neither tropical nor a mansion, but with murals of both. A/C in all rooms makes this urban hotel a temporary oasis from the city heat. 24hr. room service available from the Tropical Mansion Cafe next door. Singles P700; larger singles P800, with cable TV P935; family rooms with 2 twin beds, couch, and TV P1430. ❺

Bianca's Garden Hotel, 2139 Adriatico St., Malate (☎525 2846), at the south end of Adriatico St. near Quirino Ave. Bianca's may be a bit pricier but her rooms are also nicer. A beautiful house in an enclave with pool converted into a hotel. Rooms with shared bath P700, with A/C, TV, and phone P1300. ❺

Richmond Pension, 1165 Grey St. (Jaycee Way), Ermita (☎525 3864), behind Barrio Fiesta Restaurant. Some of the cheapest, most spartan dorm rooms around—only for the extremely frugal. Check-out 1pm. Dorms P160; doubles P390, with A/C P560, P50 per additional person. ❷

FOOD

Manila overflows with fast-food joints and high-quality, expensive sit-down restaurants, offering little selection in between. The **Food Plaza,** on the corner of Padre Faura and Bocobo St., Ermita, lacks the charm of street stalls but offers a wide selection of Filipino dishes such as *chicken adobo* (P35). Street stalls and canteens line **Santa Monica St.,** particularly between Adriatico and M.H. del Pilar St.

Cabalen, in Robinson's Place, 2nd fl., Ermita and Ayala Center, Quad 3, 2nd fl. Makati City, Ermita (☎911 1584). Eat *like* a pig, or just eat one at this Filipino all-you-can-eat buffet (P242, children P104). Novices dig into the *lechón* (roasted whole pig), while the truly brave go for *dinuguan* (pig blood stew). Open daily 11am-midnight. Visa. ❹

I FAN, MEAN PHILIPPINE CUISINE. Experimenting with Philippine cuisine is hit-or-miss. Taking the phrase "fusion cuisine" to a whole new level, food in the Philippines eschews the chili peppers used in other Southeast Asian cuisines for more salty and sour flavors.

Adobo: A derivative of a Spanish dish made with chicken, pork, seafood, or vegetables stewed in vinegar, soy sauce, garlic, peppercorns, and bay leaf.

Lumpia: Local spring rolls filled with vegetables and meat and served with vinegar, soy sauce, and a sweet sauce.

Sinigang: A sour soup made with tamarine leaves or unripe guavas.

Kinilaw: An unusually versatile dish that uses any meat or vegetable as a base ingredient, which is then "cooked" in a flavorful vinegar.

Lechon: A roast suckling pig served primarily on festive occasions in a sauce made of liver, vinegar, sugar, and seasonings.

Bistek: Filipinized beef steak

Halo-Halo: A fanciful creation with layers of preserved fruit, gelatin, custard, crushed ice, and ice cream.

Tuba: A local wine made with the sap of the coconut tree.

Café Adriatico, 1790 Adriatico St. (☎525 2509), on the corner of Remedios Circle. Elitism oozes from this classy eatery. Indulge in "Chocolate Eh and fruit fondue" (P225), or a mouthwatering steak (P359-599). Breakfast, including the Spanish omelette (P129), starts at midnight. Open daily 7:30am-6am. MC/V. ❺

Hap Chang Tea House, 563 Gen. Malvar St. (☎525 1635), at the intersection with Adriatico St., Malate. Draws hordes of hungry patrons at all hours to delight in oddly named cuisine. Roasted soy sauce prok head P90. Fishcake squidball noodles P80. Hong Kong soy duck P240. Open daily 10am-5am. ❸

L'Eau Vive, 1499 Paz. M. Gauzon Ave., Paco (☎563 8558). UN Ave. turns into Paz M. Gauzon Ave. 15min. east of Rizal Park. Run by nuns, "The Running Water" spreads the gospel through French cuisine. Among the sisters' favorites: ox tongue in a divine mushroom cream sauce (P340) and rabbit with vegetables (P380). Gluttony isn't a sin here. Open M-Sa 11am-3pm and 7-11pm. AmEx/MC/V. ❺

Harbor View, South Gate A, New Luneta Park (☎524 1532), across from Quirino Grandstand. Expensive, but fine oceanfront views and exquisite seafood make it easier to fork over the dough. Crab in chili sauce P120 per 100g. Expect to spend around P750 per person. Reservations recommended. Open daily 11am-midnight. AmEx/MC/V. ❺

Kamayan, 532 Padre Faura, Ermita (☎852 7674). The name means "hands," and you're encouraged to use them. Watch out for the sizzling buffalo steak (P355). *Adobo* P120. Cool your digits with the rather pricey *halo-halo* for dessert (P150). Open daily 11am-10:30pm. ❹

SIGHTS

LUNETA AND INTRAMUROS

RIZAL PARK. Also known as "Luneta," or Little Moon, Rizal Park is where all of Manila meets. Children run from 3-D dinosaurs at the children's **amusement park,** and street performers sing, dance, and play among the beautiful **Chinese and Japanese Gardens.** The Spanish executed Filipino rebels here, including national hero **Jose Rizal,** whose remains are entombed in the **Rizal Monument.** The souls of other Filipino greats rest on canvas and in clay in the **National Museum,** on P. Burgos St., in the northeast corner of the park. The collection includes painter Juan Roma's awe-inspiring *Spolarium*. *(Museum ☎527 1214. Open Tu-Su 10am-4:30pm.)*

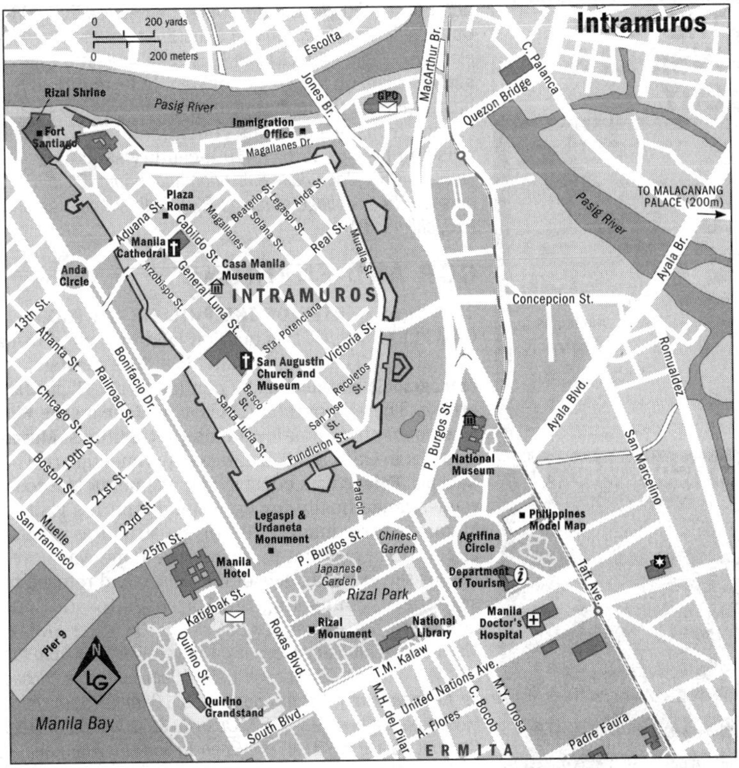

INTRAMUROS. Hundreds of years ago, the Spanish surrounded this colonial city with 4.5km of protective walls as a first line of defense. Today the area preserves the best examples of 16th-century Spanish architecture in Manila. Even the McDonald's resembles a *hacienda*. **Fort Santiago,** wedged between Bonifacio Dr. and the Pasig River on the northwest promontory of Intramuros, houses the **Rizal Shrine,** which marks the beginning of Manila's "Freedom Trail." Follow the yellow footsteps showing Rizal's final walk on the day of his execution; the **Intramuros Visitors Center (IVC)** provides maps. *(IVC ☎ 527 2961. Fort open daily 8am-6pm. P40, students and children P15. Rizal Shrine open Tu-Su 8am-5pm.)*

MANILA BAY. In May 1898, Spanish colonial rule ended suddenly when US Commodore Dewey wiped out the Spanish fleet in three hours in Manila Bay. **Manila Bay cruises** (1hr.) provide interesting lectures on the bay's history. The view of villagers living along the waters against the background of Makati's skyscrapers is a sobering reminder of the gap between Manila's rich and poor. *(Boats depart from the CCP Bay Terminal at the CCP Complex in Pasay City. ☎ 525 5698. Call for reservations.)*

OTHER SIGHTS. Strolling down Gen. Luna St. from Fort Santiago, sights pop up in every direction. **Manila Cathedral,** in Plaza Roma on Postigo St., was rebuilt in 1958 by Fernando Ocampo after being razed in WWII. With imposing high arches and heavenly blue lighting, the cathedral now hosts the weddings of Manila's rich and famous. The **Casa Manila Museum,** on the corner of Real and Gen. Luna St., is a rep-

THE INSIDER'S CITY

MALATE COCKTAIL

1. Tiny midgets with big attitudes await at the famed **Hobbit House.**
2. You won't read books at **The Library.** You will laugh alongside Manila's funniest drag queens.
3. The Flintstones have been resurrected at **Bedrock,** along with neanderthal waiters.
4. Live bands dominate **Anthropology,** where you'll hear plenty of Bob Marley and Beatles covers.
5. At **Café Adriatico,** breakfast is served at midnight, and booze is served 'round the clock.
6. Salsa anyone? **Tia Maria's** is a slice of Mexico in Malate, complete with tequilas and margaritas.
7. The **Penguin Cafe and Gallery,** a.k.a. Bohemia Revisited, attracts artists and The Misunderstood.
8. There's more to Brazil than soccer. **Cafe Rio** brings the Amazon to Malate. Latin sizzle and all.
9. Manila's best bands meet at **The Verve Bar.** Look for the neon lights.

lica of an 1850 *ilustrado* home. (*Museum ☎527 4084. Open Tu-Su 9am-6pm. Guided tours 2hr.; depart every 2hr, starting at 9am. P40, children P15.*) **San Augustin Church and Museum,** on the corner of Gen. Luna and Real St., has staggered through repeated natural disasters and foreign invasions since its construction in 1571. The museum houses 17th- to 19th-century sanctuary art. (*☎527 4061. Open daily 8am-noon and 1-6pm. Church and museum P45, college students P20, high school students P15, children P10.*)

CCP AND ENVIRONS

CULTURAL CENTER OF THE PHILIPPINES (CCP) COMPLEX. The CCP is built on land reclaimed from Manila Bay. The main building has **three theaters,** an **ethnographic museum,** and a contemporary **Filipino art exhibit.** The ethnographic **Museo ng Kalinangang Pilipino** concentrates on local cultural traditions. **Museo ng Sinig,** in GSIS Bldg., exhibits experimental art. The **Coconut Palace** was constructed at Imelda Marcos's request specifically for Pope John Paul II's visit to Manila. Approximately 70% of the structure is actually made of coconut products. The Pope was horrified by the extravagance of the palace and refused to stay there, counseling the Marcoses to put their money to better use. (*☎832 1125. On Roxas Blvd. in Malate. Take an orange jeepney with yellow stripes from the LRT: Vito Cruz. Art exhibit open Tu-Su 10am-5pm. Free. Museo ng Kalinangang Pilipino open Tu-Su 10am-6:30pm. P20. Museo ng Sinig ☎891 6161. Open Tu-Sa 10am-5pm. Free. Coconut Palace ☎831 1756. Open Tu-Su 9-11:30am and 1-4:30pm. P100 for adults, children free.*)

METROPOLITAN MUSEUM OF MANILA. Changing exhibitions feature a mix of contemporary and early 20th-century art. Save for a stunning exhibition of pre-Hispanic gold ornaments, there are few notable items in the collections. (*☎/fax 523 7855. In the Bangko Sentral ng Pilipinas Complex, on the corner of Roxas Blvd. and Vito Cruz, left of the CCP. Open M-Sa 10am-6pm. Basement open daily 10am-4:30pm. P50, students P30.*)

ON THE PERIPHERY

CHINESE CEMETERY. The Spanish, who evidently were quite territorial about their burial grounds, forced the Chinese to establish their own cemetery. Huge 3m marble mausoleums testify to the wealth and status of the Chinese businessmen buried here. On most Sundays, families come to make offerings. (*☎/fax 253 4204. Off P. Huertas St. in Tondo District. Catch the LRT to Blumentritt Station, walk a few yards up Blumentritt St., and turn left on P. Huertas St.; follow it to Aurora Blvd. to reach the cemetery. Open daily 7am-7pm. Mausoleum keepers arrange guided tours; bargain around P50-P100.*)

PACO PARK AND CHURCH. The park originally held the remains of Dr. Jose Rizal, buried here to keep him from becoming a cult figure. The plan backfired spectacularly—his body has been exhumed twice. Rows of baby-sized coffins testify to past plagues. Nevertheless, the park remains a peaceful, shady, out-of-the-way spot where naughty schoolchildren have lunch and make out daily. *(On Padre Faura St. at the San Marcelino St. intersection. Catch a Taft jeepney to the Taft-Padre Faura intersection. ☎525 5186. Open daily 8am-5pm. P5.)*

NAYONG PILIPINO PARK. Six miniature replicas of Philippine regions display a range of flora and fauna. Included on the grounds of the park are the **Philippine Museum of Ethnology,** where you can learn how to play an Ifugao nose flute, and the **Museum ng Buhay Filipino** antiques museum. Replicas of natural wonders such as the Mayon Volcano verge on being childish, but the architecture in each mini-region offers an informative crash course on the Philippines. A dance troupe performs at the Mindanao Pavilion on weekends at 2:30 and 4pm. *(Off MIA Rd. adjacent to the airport. Park open Tu-Su 7am-6pm. P40, under 12 P25. BMuseum ng Buhay Filipino ☎832 3766. Both museums open daily 8am-6pm. Free.)*

ACCOMMODATIONS	FOOD
Bianca's Garden Hotel, **11**	Cabalen, **5**
Malate Pensionne, **9**	Café Adriatico, **10**
Pension Natividad, **8**	Hap Chang Tea House, **7**
Richmond Pension, **2**	Kamayan, **4**
Tropical Mansion Hotel, **3**	L'Eau Vive, **1**
UCCP Shalom Center, **6**	

OTHER SIGHTS. The **Ayala Museum** has a superb collection of sea vessels, art exhibits, and dioramas depicting Philippine history. *(On Makati Ave., Ayala Center, opposite Shangri-La Hotel. ☎812 1191. Open Tu-Su 8am-6pm. P50, children P25. Tours P30, students P25.)* **Malacañang Palace** is the official residence of the Philippine President and a museum with rooms dedicated to past presidents. Hear a tour guide's spin on the recent overthrow of former president Joseph Estrada. *(In San Miguel, across the Pasig River from Intramuros. ☎733 3721. No shorts, slippers, singlet tops, bags, cameras, or children under 7. Open daily 9am-3pm. Guided tours M-W every 15min., Th-Su every 30-40min. P200.)* The **Marikina Shoe Museum** is an interesting gallery that traces the history of shoemaking in Manila—and yes, there is also a small selection (one or two thousand) of Imelda's shoe collection. *(Off of P. Tauzon, near the shoemart. ☎934 6784. Grab a "Yale" or "Cubao" jeepney. Open W-Sa 8am-5pm. Free.)*

ENTERTAINMENT

Manila supports several venues for cultural performances. The **Cultural Center of the Philippines,** CCP Complex, Roxas Blvd., Malate, presents concerts, ballets, dramas, and films. (☎832 3704; box office ☎832 1125, ext. 240. Open M-F 9am-5pm, Sa-Su 1-5pm. Tickets from P200.) Various plays grace the stages of the **William J. Shaw Theater,** Shangri-La Shopping Mall, 5th fl., EDSA, Mandaluyong. (☎633 4821. Box office open daily 10am-7pm.) **Intramuros Evenings** (formerly Puerto Real Evenings) feature music, dance, and madrigal singing. (☎527 3138. Shows about 6:30pm around Intramuros.)

The **Araneta Coliseum** (☎911 3101), on the corner of Gen. Roxas and Gen. Araneta Ave., stages **cockfights** in September (P100-450) and hosts **Philippine Basketball Association (PBA)** games the rest of the year. Cheer on your favorite corporate product and their sponsored players. (Game tickets from P100.)

Dragon Acupressure Center, 2nd fl., 1811 LM Guerrero St., Malate, on the road that connects J.M. Nakpil St. and Remedios Cir., offers herbal steam baths with massage for P500. (☎526 7342. Open daily noon-1am.) **Massages** from the blind are also available at Robinson's Mall. No need to be shy. Beware of "massage" offers outside massage parlors; your "masseuse" will rub down more than just sore muscles.

Movie theaters are a great place to kick back and cool off. **Robinson's Place** in Ermita and **Glorieta** in Makati boast two particularly impressive theaters. (P50, balcony seats P80. Movies run 10am-10pm.)

BARS AND CAFES

A vibrant bar and cafe scene thrives in Manila, especially on **J. Nakpil St.** and **Remedios Circle** in Malate and on **P. Burgos St.** in Makati.

The Library, 1779 A.M. Adriatico St., Malate (☎522 2484), near Remedios Circle. The country's funniest drag queens perform karaoke each night starting at 9pm to sold-out audiences. Gay patrons especially welcome, while foreigners are prime targets for (relatively painless) jokes. Thirsty for a cocktail? Try the "Blowjob" (P150). Don't worry, no one is watching. No slippers or vests. Cover P50. Open daily 7pm-4am.

Hobbit House, 1801 Mabini St., Malate (☎521 7604). Great live rock, blues, and country. "The smallest waiters in the world"–all midgets and dwarves–are ready to serve you and even pose for cheesy pictures. Gimmicks aside, one of the best bars in Manila. Food served. Beers P55. Cover P100. Open daily 6pm-2am.

Cafe Rio, 621 Remedios St., corner Maria Orosa St., Malate (☎303 7470). You may not have a Latin lover, but at this Brazilian bar, you can start with a "Dirty Man" (P195), try a "Roasted Fuck" (P145), and finish with a "Screaming Orgasm" (P195). Dance floor, live bands, and a comedian each night. Open daily 5pm-5am.

Penguin Cafe and Gallery, 604 Remedios St., off Remedios Circle, Malate (☎303 7355). Goth, Actor, Reincarnated Bohemian–you'll find them all at this artsy, well-established pub and gallery. Owner Ami dishes the dirt on every bar in Manila. Happy hour 6-9pm, 20% off beer. Open Tu-Th 6pm-1am, F-Sa noon-2pm and 7pm-3am, Su 7pm-1am.

The Verve Bar, 607 J. Nakpil St. off Adriatico St., Malate. Musically one step above the rest. Bar and DJ compete for the most innovative mixes: trip-hop, progressive house, and acid jazz. The "Adios Motherfucker," an 8-alcohol blend, will knock your socks off (P145). Open Tu-Sa 8:30pm-5am.

Bedrock, 1782 Adriatico St., Malate (☎522 7279). One of Malate's newest (and tackiest) bars. Enjoy a "stone-age cocktail" (P135-225) as waitresses dressed as cavewomen serve you. Buy-1-get-1-free happy hour daily 5-8pm. Live bands. Yabba-dabba-doo. Open M-Sa 5pm-3am. MC/V.

Anthology, 1786 Adriatico St., Malate (☎523 4975). Marilyn Monroe, Elvis, and Bob Marley stare down from the walls as customers enjoy an acoustic bar, live bands, and a wide range of vodka mixers (P85-105). Wines P120 per glass. Buy-1-get-1-free happy hour daily 5-8pm. Open M-Sa 5pm-3am. AmEx/MC/V.

Tia Maria's (☎522 0428), on the corner of Remedios and M. Ignacia St., Malate. The only bar in town with cheese enchiladas. Eight kinds of tequila (P75-100). Live bands. P300 minimum on weekends. Open Su-Th 4pm-4am, F-Sa 4pm-5am. MC/V.

Cafe Havana, 1903 M. Adriatico St., Malate (☎521 8097). Manila's only Cuban restaurant/dance club. "Limoncito" cocktail P140. Che t-shirts P250. Afro-Cuban music F-Sa 11pm. Open daily 6pm-3am.

DISCOS

Many discos are actually bars with go-go dancers, gyrating sadly. **Solution,** 369 Libertad St., in Pasay City, is cheap, cheerful, refreshingly innocent and tourist-free, with bop to pop and club classics. (☎833 1641. San Miguel P35. Happy hour M-F and Su 7-10pm. Cover M-Th and Su P30, F P50, Sa P70. Open daily 8pm-5am.) **Mars,** 2 San Lorenzo Dr., on Pasay Rd. in Makati, is glitzy and crowded with spotlights, steam, and attitude. (☎841 0088. San Miguel P100. Cover M-Th and Su P200, F-Sa P300 includes 1 drink. Open daily 9:30pm-4am.)

SHOPPING

Malls are omnipresent. **SM Megamall** in Mandaluyong offers two behemoth six-floor buildings to challenge the most ardent shopper. If shopping wears you out, take a spin on its ice-skating rink or catch a flick at the theaters. Ooh-la-la your way through upscale boutiques like DKNY and Louis Vuitton at **Shangri-La Plaza** next door. **Robinson's Place,** conveniently located in the tourist district, has two levels of restaurants and a large bowling alley. Use it as an air-conditioned shortcut from Pedro Gil to Pedro Faura.

Divisoria Market, outside Binondo, is a bargain-hunter's mecca. **Baclaran Market** in Paranaque is similar. The **Ilalim ng Tulay Market** in Quiapo hawks cheap tokens of Filipino culture, while Cubao's **Farmer's Plaza** is a collision of department stores and flea markets. In **Chinatown,** shops along Ongpin St. near Santa Cruz Church sell Chinese desserts, textiles, and herbal medicines. The heavyweight among antiques and handicraft stores is the **Silahis Center,** 744 Gen. Luna St., Intramuros (☎527 2111), near P. Burgos St.

DAYTRIPS FROM MANILA

PAGSANJAN FALLS

Pagsanjan is 5km from Santa Cruz, accessible by BLTB buses from 3 EDSA, Pasay City (every hr. 4am-7pm, P65) and JAM Transit buses leaving from Taft Ave. at Gil Puyat St., Pasay City (2hr., every 30min. 4am-10:30pm, with A/C P72).

The final scenes of Francis Ford Coppola's *Apocalypse Now* were filmed along this tropical gorge. Though more likely to see a crazed man bathing his bald head back at the guest house, tourists still pay high prices to have *banqueros* canoe them 7km upstream to the **Magdapio Falls** and shoot the rapids back down (2hr.; last trip 2hr. before sundown; standard fares for single passenger P1080, for 2-3 passengers P580 per person, plus P100-200 tip). The rapids are most active in the rainy season. At the top of the river you can float on a bamboo raft (P50 per person) to **Devil's Cavern.** Because boatmen have been known to harass tourists, it's advisable to arrange a boat through the PTA-operated **Pagsanjan Garden Resort,** Pagsanjan (☎049 808 4451), a short tricycle ride (P10) from town. Accommodations line Garcia St., which runs along the northern bank of the river.

CORREGIDOR ISLAND

The Corregidor Visitor's Information Center, Dept. of Tourism Bldg., #212, Agrifina Circle, T.M. Kalaw St., Manila (☎525 3420, ext. 329) arranges the cheapest day tours (P500). Most visitors take a package tour (P650-1690); book with Sun Cruises, CCP Bay Cruise Terminal, CCP Complex, Roxas Blvd. (☎831 8140). Tours depart at 8am from CCP Bay Cruise Terminal. Check-in 7:15am.

One of the last places to fall to the Japanese, Corregidor Island earned the unfortunate distinction of being the most bombed island of WWII. Today guides at the **Malinta Tunnel** (P150) retell the story to visitors from both sides of the conflict. The island is a can't-miss for WWII buffs, but for everybody else, the hollowed out shells of bombed buildings can become monotonous. **The Corregidor Hotel** ❹ (☎0912 304 0692) offers dorm beds (P400) and double bedrooms (P1800). Camping at the South Dock Beach or Middleside Camping Grounds costs P10 per day.

LAS PIÑAS BAMBOO ORGAN AND SARAO JEEPNEY FACTORY

Buses on Taft Ave. bound for Zapote or Cavite pass through Las Pinas. Alternatively, from LRT: Baclaran Station, catch a "Las Piñas" jeepney (20min., P4). Bamboo Organ Factory ☎826 7718. Open M-F 9pm-midnight and 2-6pm. P20, children and students P5. The jeepney factory is on Padre Diego Cerra Ave., Pulanglupa, Las Piñas, 3km south. ☎874 7885. Open M-Sa 8am-4pm.

In 1819, Friar Diego Cera became a legend among budget-oriented organ enthusiasts by building a working instrument entirely of bamboo. The **bamboo organ** of St. Joseph (San Jose) Church, in Las Piñas parish, produces a unique sound and is the centerpiece of the international **Bamboo Organ Festival** for a week each February. Kitsch-lovers will want to see the **Sarao Jeepney Factory,** where WWII jeeps have been converted into fume-spewing *objets d'art.*

BAGUIO ☎74

Sprawled amid a rugged, pine-bedecked landscape, Baguio rests 1400m above sea level. Its cooler temperatures make it the "summer capital" of the Philippines. Although popularity has put pressure on the mountain locale, highland tribes still subsist on the thriving produce market, which draws tourists looking for a taste of the Filipino way of life, as well as legions of artists and students attempting to study and protect the pre-colonial Cordilleran culture. And while cool compared to Manila, Baguio's nightlife is as hot as it gets in the rustic mountain provinces.

TRANSPORTATION

Flights: Take a taxi from Session Rd. to the **Loakan Airport** (P60). **Asian Spirit** (☎444 5413) flies daily to **Manila** (45min., P1583).

Buses: Several bus companies send out buses from different terminals in Baguio City. From the terminals on Gov. Pack Rd., near the corner of Session Rd.: **Autobus** (☎444 9056), **Byron Express** (☎442 7875), **Philippine Rabbit** (☎442 5945), **Partas** (☎444 8431), **Victory Liner** (☎442 5708). From the terminal on Rajah Soliman St., behind Baguio Central Mall: **Dangwa Tranco** and **Lizardo.** From the terminal on Otek St., **Eso-Nice Liner** (☎443 3076). Buses to:

Banaue: Autobus (8-9hr., 7:30pm, P250); Dangwa (7am, 7pm; P240); Lizardo (8-9hr.; 2:30, 7:30pm; P230).

Bontoc: Dangwa (7hr., every hr. 5-10am, P145).

Manila: Partas (midnight, 5, 6, 10am, 2pm; with A/C to Cubao District P235); Philippine Rabbit (every hr. 24hr., P225); Victory Liner (6hr.; every hr. 24hr.; with A/C to Cubao District P236, with A/C to Pasay City P250).

Sagada: Lizardo (6½hr.; every 30min. 7-9:30am, 11am; P189, students P155).

San Fernando (La Union): Eso-Nice Liner (1½hr., every 30min. 5:30am-6pm, P40).

Vigan: Partas (5hr.; 6:30, 10am, noon, 3:15, 6, 8:45pm; P154, with A/C P215); Philippine Rabbit (5hr.; every hr. until 7pm; P150, with A/C P170).

Local Transportation: Taxis start at P20 for the first 250m, P1 for each 100m thereafter. **Jeepneys** cost about P4 per trip but are slower than taxis.

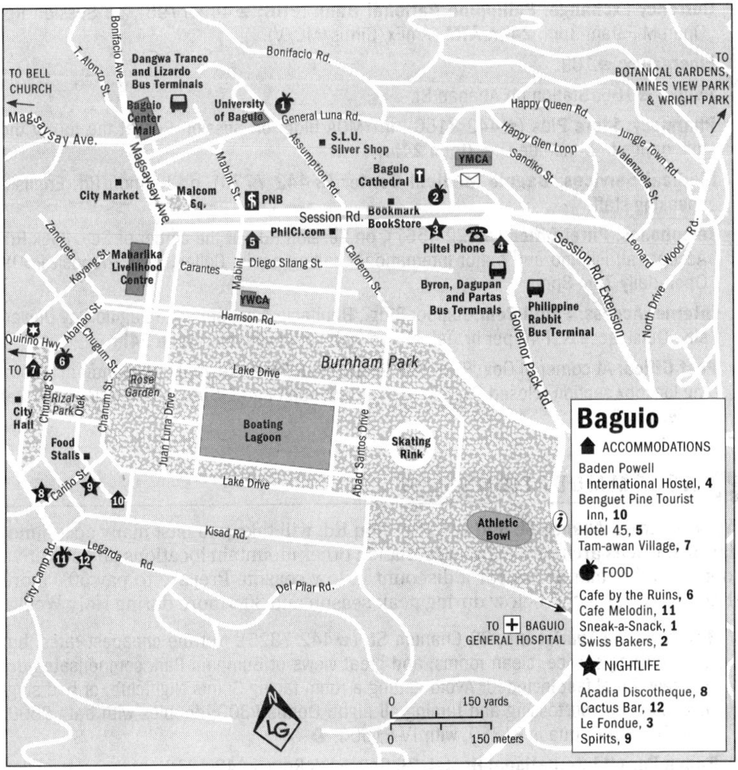

ORIENTATION AND PRACTICAL INFORMATION

Rose-colored **Baguio Cathedral** overlooks the main commercial thoroughfare, **Session Rd.,** which climbs from its intersection with **Magsaysay Ave.** to the top of a hill. Session Rd. then splits into **Leonard Wood Rd.,** which leads to the Botanical Gardens, Wright Park, and Mines View Park, and the **Session Rd. extension.** Northbound highways leading into Baguio go to **Governor (Gov.) Pack Rd.,** which borders **Burnham Park.** Half a kilometer down the road is the **Department of Tourism Complex** in front of Baguio City High School. Another kilometer down is the main **bus terminal** and a roundabout into Session Rd. Near City Hall, Rizal Park, and Malcom Sq., **Otek St.** forms an arc around the northwest end of Burnham Park. Ease your navigation by purchasing the *Baguio Road Guide*, which plots all major buildings in the city (P40) or the *Map of Baguio* by Island Viewing Publishing. A free but quite useless map is available at the **Department of Transportation (DOT).**

Tourist Office: DOT Complex (☎442 6708). 10min. down Gov. Pack Rd. from bus terminals, opposite Baguio City High School. Open daily 7am-5pm.

Travel and Tours: Swagman Travel, Swagman Attic Inn, 90 Abanao St. (☎442 5139). 3hr. city tour P850. 4-day tours to Banaue, Sagada, and Bontoc depart from the inn at 6am daily. Visa extensions P2050. Open M-Sa 8am-5pm.

Currency Exchange: Philippine National Bank (PNB; ☎442 7705), on Session Rd. Open M-F 9am-3pm. **24hr. ATM** (AmEx/Cirrus/MC/V).

Emergency: ☎169.

Police: ☎166. Station on Abanao St.

Pharmacy: Store Plus (☎442 8156), in YMCA bldg. on Session Rd., at the top of the hill, opposite Banco de Oro. **Open 24hr.**

Medical Services: Baguio Medical Center (☎442 7770), on Kennon Rd. English-speaking staff.

Telephones: Piltel Office (☎422 4567), on Session Rd., at the corner of Gov. Pack Rd. Accepts all Filipino and major international calling cards. Collect calls (deposit P50). Open daily 7am-8pm.

Internet Access: PhilCi.Com, Juniper Bldg., Bonifacio Ave., opposite Baguio City University. Quick access. P40 per hr. Telnet and web cam available. **Open 24hr.**

Post Office: At corner of Gov. Pack and Session Rd. *Poste Restante* at counter in adjoining lockbox section (closed Sa). Open M-F 8am-noon and 1-5pm, Sa 8am-noon. **Postal code:** 2600.

ACCOMMODATIONS

Walking down **Abanao St.** and onto Session Rd. will take you past many accommodations. Prices are more expensive than in other mountain locations and sensitive to seasonal demand. Ask for a discount in low season. Prepare to pay 50% more than the prices listed below during peak season and 30% more during Holy Week.

Benguet Pine Tourist Inn, 39 Chanum St. (☎442 7325). Not the cheapest rates, but the amazing service, clean rooms, and great views of Burnham Park compensate adequately. Breakfast included. Avoid getting a room facing Spirits Nightclub, or bad singers will keep you tossing and turning all night. Dorms P300; doubles with bath P800, with TV P1000; quads P1350, with TV P1500. ❸

Baden Powell International Hostel, 26 Gov. Pack Rd. (☎442 5836), at the intersection with Session Rd. Proximity to bus stations guarantees early morning honk-imposed wake-up calls. Clean and comfortable living. Dorms P300; rooms for 1-2 P900; quads P1350. 10% surcharge on credit cards. MC/V. ❸

Hotel 45, 58 Session Rd. (☎442 6634). Cheap rooms in a central location, but common toilets need a good scrub. Vampires will like the lack of windows. Beauty parlor, billiard hall, and 24hr. restaurant. Check-out 1pm. Singles P250; doubles with bath P450, with TV P750; family room P1200. ❸

Tam-awan Village (see **Sights,** below), Purok 1, Tam-awan, Pinsao Proper (☎446 2949), off Tacay Rd. on the way to La Trinidad (P35 taxi ride from Session Rd.). A slightly more expensive form of camping, the traditional Ifugao huts rise 1.5m off the ground. Toilets steps away. Singles P500; doubles P900, each extra person P200. ❹

FOOD

Fruits you won't find anywhere else in the Philippines thrive in Baguio's cool climate. Street stalls on **Shanum St.** around Burnham Park sell spit-roasted chicken, while those around **Otek St.** play the juiciest karaoke hits. For the cheapest eats around, head to the hidden **food stalls** ❶ behind the vehicle-shaped Starbus Restaurant on Assumption Rd., opposite the University of Baguia. Meals with meat, rice, vegetables, and drink (P35).

Cafe by the Ruins, 25 Chuntug St. (☎442 4010). Built from the ruins of a governor's mansion, Cafe by the Ruins is one of the best vegetarian selections in the region. Over 20 meat and non-meat selections. Freshly baked bread. Set lunches P155-230. Eggplant caviar on toast P45. Open daily 7am-10pm. MC/V. ❸

Cafe Melodin (☎442 7734), on Legarda Rd. Renews your appetite for Filipino cuisine. The all-day breakfast menu, including the cured pork *tocino* (P89), can fill you up for the rest of the day. Crispy *pata* pork (P275). Seafood rice (P190) feeds 4. Beef spare ribs P215. Open daily 6am-10pm. MC/V. ❸

Swiss Bakers (☎442 4010), on Session Rd, uphill from the steps to Baguio Cathedral. Dazzling cakes, buns, and bread—quick and delicious. Tuna turnover P22.50. Croissants P16. Cinnamon rolls P20. Open daily 7am-8pm. ❶

Sneak-a-Snack, at Gen. Luna St. and Assumption Rd., near St. Louis School. Lunch-time budget meal available on school days to entice St. Louis School children (P35). It works. Grilled cheese P15. Canton squid P28. Open daily 6:30am-6:30pm. ❶

SIGHTS

TAM-AWAN VILLAGE. Tam-awan, literally "vantage point" in the local dialect, is a gateway to the indigenous Cordilleran culture. The cluster of authentic Ifugao wood and *cogon* grass huts, dismantled from their original location and reconstructed less than an hour outside Baguio City, serves as a "living museum" and art gallery. Huts of this kind face extinction as mountain tribes switch to modern housing structures. Walk up the hill to "Batad" hut to get a glimpse of the South China Sea. Stay in the huts overnight (see **Accommodations,** above) for a true taste of the culture. *(☎446 2949. Purok 1, Tam-awan, Pinsao Proper, off Tacay Rd., on the way to La Trinidad. A P40 taxi ride from Session Rd. Open daily 9am-6pm. P20.)*

BELL TEMPLE. Bordering Trinidad Valley, the background of the Bell Temple combines Buddhist, Taoist, Confucian, and Christian beliefs. Ask a priest to tell your fortune (P4), or take a trip around the fountain of waterlilies as you ponder your existence. *(Off Magsaysay Ave. Take a jeepney (P5) from the corner of Bonifacio and Magsaysay Ave. Cameras prohibited. Open M-F 6am-5pm, Sa-Su 6am-10:30am and 1-5pm. Free.)*

ST. LOUIS UNIVERSITY MUSEUM OF ARTS AND CULTURE. Established in 1969, this museum, in the university's Msgr. Charles Vath building, conserves cultural artifacts of the Cordilleras. On display is a carabao-powered grinding machine called a *dadapilan*, normally used to squeeze juice from sugar cane but allegedly used during WWII to squeeze confessions out of prisoners. *(☎442 3043, ext. 260. Open M-Sa 7:30am-noon and 1:30-5pm. Free.)*

PARKS. Take a horse for a spin in the **Botanical Gardens, Wright Park,** and **Mines View Park**. Set routes (up to 5hr.) take you to **Mt. Santo Tomas,** the limestone peak 8km away. Behind a blockade of tourist shops, a small promontory gives a wide-angled view of Amburayan Valley and Benguet's gold and copper mines. *(The Botanical Gardens and Wright Park are on the route to Mines View Park, 4km from the city. Open daily 6am-sunset. Horses P100 per 30min.; P100 for guide.)*

MARKETS. The **City Market** on Magsaysay Ave. showcases gruesome livestock parts as well as vegetables, fruit, *ube*-flavored jam, peanut and cashew brittle, and strawberry wine. For the skilled bargainer, all will be wondrously cheap. *(Open daily 5:30am-8pm.)* Across the street is the multi-story **Maharlika Livelihood Center.** Tourists' anti-modern predilections have made the traditional garb, personal adornments, and handicrafts of the mountain tribespeople highly marketable. The **Easter Weaving Room,** on Easter Rd., on the northwest outskirts of Guisad, is the commercial counterpart to the Easter Weaving School. Watch weavers stitch clothes and tablecloths. *(☎442 4972. Open M-F 8am-5pm. Tablecloths P800-1000)*

OTHER SIGHTS. On top of a hill with a view of Session Rd., the lavender **Baguio Cathedral** is a funky church with multicolored stained glass. Less authentic than the Tam-awan Village, the **Ifugao Woodcarvers Village** churns out figurines and animals, including Buddhas, Ifugao warriors, and potency symbols for P35-150. **Asin Hot Springs** (16km northwest of Baguio) features a swimming pool surrounded by thermal springs, hanging bridges, and lush vegetation. *(Along Asin Rd. off Naguilian Rd. Take a San Luis jeepney or a taxi to Km5 for P40, or ask to be let off at the hot springs.)*

ENTERTAINMENT AND NIGHTLIFE

City Center Burnham Park, named after American urban planner Daniel Burnham, boasts an orchidarium, lake, playground, and roller-skating rink. (Roller-skating P50 per hr., roller blades P50 per hr., available 8am-midnight; boating P60 per boat, P25 per additional person, max. 5 per boat, available 8am-10pm.) The **Baguio Arts Festival,** held each November, features visual, performing, and folk arts, many of which are staged in the park. The **Modern Age Spa,** in the YMCA building on Session Rd. opposite Banco de Oro, offers shiatsu and Swedish massage (P350, with aromatherapy P450). **Reyes Salon,** near the intersection of Assumption and Session Rd., offers manicures, pedicures, and hot oil treatment starting at P50.

Cactus Club (☎442 5082), beneath the Prince Plaza Hotel, on Legarda Rd. Serves its 20-something patrons with a live band and a pulsating rock and blues mix from 10pm onward. Great whiskey sours P45. Live band 7-10pm. Open daily 5pm-2:30am.

Le Fondue (☎414 3920), on Session Rd. A lounge bar with a live band covering *la musique classique* (James Taylor, anyone?). Cozy atmosphere and happy denial of the "No Smoking" sign. Beer P40; Long Island iced tea P95. Open daily 6pm-1am.

Spirits, 34 Otek St. (☎442 6406), past the food stalls toward Cariño St. Slouch in comfy chairs, strut on the dance floor, or retire to the bar. San Miguel P90. Tu ladies night. No collarless shirts. Cover charge P120. Open daily 9pm-2am.

Acadia Discotheque (☎300 1227), on the corner of Cariño St. and Legarda Rd. Baguio's new disco geared toward the hipper-than-thou college crowd. San Miguel P70. Cover P60; M-Th 7-10pm P25. Open daily 6pm-3am.

BONTOC ☎74

Although primarily a commercial town, Bontoc retains the charm of a small village. The friendly people, inexpensive quality accommodations, and proximity to the Maligcong rice terraces attract travelers to Bontac. The opportunity to observe local Igorot culture also makes it worth a visit—you'll be walking the streets alongside tattooed members of the Kalinga tribes as well as Levi-legged locals.

TRANSPORTATION. Several companies run **buses** to nearby towns. Dangwa buses, leaving from the **bus terminal** behind the Mountain Hotel, go to **Baguio** (7hr., every hr. 6-10am, P145) and **Banaue** (signs read "Tabuk," 2½hr., 8am, P80). Rising Sun buses leave from outside City Hall to **Baguio** (every hr. 7am-1pm, P130). Von-Von buses leave from opposite the culture station going to **Banaue** (sign reads "Tabuk" or "Paracelis," 8:30am, P70). **Jeepneys** depart from beside Municipal Hall to go to **Banaue** (8:30, 9:30, 11:30am, noon, and sometimes 1pm; P80); those leaving from behind the Kodac building near Old Saints Mission Elementary School go to **Sagada** (1hr., every hr. or when full 8:30am-4:30pm, P40).

ORIENTATION AND PRACTICAL INFORMATION. Bontoc's streets are unmarked and, as far as the residents know, unnamed. **"Main St."** runs parallel to **Chico River** through the town center. Most transportation arrives at the town circle (marked by a large tree) on Main St. Adjacent to the circle and up the hill are **Rizal Plaza** and **Pines Kitchenette and Inn.** The latter gives helpful travel information, arranges guides, and sells the Bontoc-Kalinga trekking map (P10; also available at the Bontoc Museum). Main St. is intersected by five major roads. Between the circle and the first street lies **Xijen Computer School,** where you'll find **Internet access** on the second floor. (P2 per min. Open M-Sa 8am-7:30pm, occasionally Su 9am-2pm.) For cheaper rates, use computers at any of the numerous office supply stores (P50 per hr.). Opposite the second street, a road curves back up the hill past the **post office.** (*Poste Restante.* Open M-F 8am-noon and 1-5pm.) The **Philippine National Bank** exchanges currency and AmEx Traveler's Checks at no charge. (☎602 1078. Open M-F 8:30am-2:30pm.) **Bontoc General Hospital** has a **24hr. pharmacy** and emergency care. (Open M-F 8am-noon and 1-4pm, Sa 8am-noon for consultation.) **International calls** can be placed from the **Bayantel** office on Main St. (Collect calls P50. Open M-Sa 8am-noon and 2-7pm.) **Postal code:** 2616.

ACCOMMODATIONS AND FOOD. During the dry season, accommodations suffer from intermittent water supply. The road to Samoki, which runs across the river from the town circle, passes the newly furnished **Ridgebrooke Hotel, Cafe & Restaurant ❷.** Ridgebrooke offers Bontoc's brightest, cleanest, most spacious rooms and one of the few laundry services in town. (Laundry P25 per piece. Rooms P150 per person; private room P600.) **Pines Kitchenette and Inn ❶,** opposite Rizal Plaza, has large rooms and great service. (P100 per person; doubles P300, with common room P500.) Its restaurant features live bands each night starting around 6:30pm. **Eastern Star Hotel & Restaurant ❶,** near the Sagada Jeepney Station in Walter Clapp Centrum, has friendly management and sparkling private rooms. (☎0919 483 7684. Economy rooms P100; singles and doubles P300; family room with cable TV P600.)

Bluebirds Restaurant ❶, between the third and fourth streets intersecting Main St., provides large, tasty portions. Forget your pets, and try the dog (P50). For P30, the "budget meal" includes meat, rice, and vegetables. (Open daily 7am-9pm.) Next door, **Crystal's Bakery ❶** fattens patrons up with pudding bread (P2), fruit pastries (P10), and cinnamon rolls (7 for P10) fresh from the oven. (Open daily 5am-8pm.) Across Main St., the **Cable Cafe and Bar ❸** claims it is "where great singers are born." Said singers perform country and pop with live bands each night starting at 6pm. In between covers, they munch on *pusit* (squid; P130) and down beer. (Cocktails P60-120. Open daily 6am-10pm.)

SIGHTS AND ENTERTAINMENT. Before heading into the villages, check out the **Bontoc Museum,** opposite the post office, for background information. (Open daily 8am-noon and 1-5pm. P40.) Artifacts reflect the distinct cultures of the four tribes in the area. The highlight is a collection of photographs from 1908-09 that record earnest Americans trying to introduce games of tug-of-war to the males of rival villages to divert them from head-hunting. At the end of the day, there's always the **Massage Clinic,** next to the Provincial Capital Building, where blind masseurs will rub your aches away. (Whole body P140, half-body P70, foot or back P35. Open daily 7am-7pm.) After the massage, visit **Cable Cafe and Bar,** Bontoc's PG-rated version of nightlife (see **Accommodations and Food,** above).

TREKKING. You're asking for trouble if you don't hire a guide to smooth out cultural and linguistic barriers. Ask Manuela Cofulan at Pines Kitchenette to contact private guide **Francis Pa-in,** a Kalinga, highly recommended by several publications. (☎462 4225. Around P500 per day for groups of 1-5.) Treks last anywhere from one morning to three days. A typical day-hike could involve a 3hr. walk from Bontoc to the **Maligcong rice terraces,** a 2hr. trek from Maligcong to **Guina-ang,** and then a 45min. hike to the **Mainit Hot Springs,** where optimistic miners pan for gold. The return to Bontoc is a 3hr. downhill walk. **Jeepneys** leave for Maligcong from the town circle (8am, noon, 2:30, 4:30pm; P30). From the drop-off point, it's a 2km trek to the village. It is customary for trekkers to bring gifts—adults appreciate matches, while children are delighted by candy. A longer expedition might include a trip to the village of **Butbut.** From Bontoc, it's a long jeepney ride to **Basao** (P40), then a 2hr. hike up the mountain to reach Butbut. The views of Tinglayen village from along the ridge are unbeatable.

SAGADA

The chickens seem to outnumber the people on Sagada's unpaved streets. Though residents can be seen chatting on cell phones, there is still no local phone service in the area. Such seclusion is what encourages visitors to linger. Sacred burial grounds, caves, limestone formations, and heavy waterfalls prove welcome alternatives to more rice terraces. The road to Sagada is rocky, but the long and bumpy ride is punishment worth enduring to reach this quiet and spiritual town.

TRANSPORTATION AND PRACTICAL INFORMATION. The road that ascends into Sagada also serves as the town's main street. It passes **St. Theodore**'s **Hospital,** then reaches the **town center** and **Municipal Hall** about 500m down the road. Also in the town center are: the **Tourist Information Center** (open daily 7am-5pm); **Sagada Rural Bank** (open Tu-Sa 8-11:45am and 1:15-4:30pm); the **24hr. police station;** and the **post office** (*Poste Restante;* open M-F 8am-noon and 1-4:30pm). Lizardo **buses** go to **Baguio** (7hr.; every hr. 5-10am, 6:30pm; P189). **Jeepneys** to **Bontoc** leave from the market (1hr.; every 20min. 6-7am, every hr. 7:45-8:45am and 10am-noon; P25). To reach **Banaue** from Sagada, you must go through Bontoc, or hire a jeepney to take you directly (P2500). **Postal code:** 2619.

ACCOMMODATIONS AND FOOD. Masferré Inn and Restaurant ❶ (☎0918 341 6164) offers spacious, clean rooms in the center of town (P100 per person, shared bath). Laundry service is available, along with buckets of warm water (P15 per bucket; order 15min. before needed). The dining area serves decent sandwiches (ham or tuna P30) and lukewarm beer (P30). Other guest houses can be found in the town center, including the **Sagada Guest House ❶.** (9:30am check-out. Cafe open daily. P100 per person; private singles with common room P600, with hot water P800.) **Greenhouse Inn ❷** is a cozy establishment run by an endearing elderly woman. (P130 per person; private singles P200; doubles P220. Check-out 10am.) Next door, blind masseurs offer **scientific massages** for P140 per hr. To the right of the Town Hall is **Shamrock ❷,** which serves the hearty "Hangover's Anathema" (P65) breakfast of toast, eggs, and coffee as well as P110 "Shamrock meals" of soup, meat, vegetables, rice, and dessert. (☎0918 341 1912. Open daily 6am-9pm.) Down the hill from Masferré is the **Yoghurt House ❷,** highly recommended for delicious veggie fried rice (P40) and (surprise) fresh yogurt with fruit (P50). Listen to great 80s music or rent a book while you wait. (Open daily 6:30am-9pm.)

SIGHTS. The **Masferré Gallery,** about 1km down the road from St. Theodore's, displays the work of the late Eduardo Masferré, the son of a Spanish soldier who settled in the mountains at the turn of the century. His photographs of friends and neighbors have enjoyed international success. (Open daily 6am-9pm. Free.) **RJ's Souvenirs and Gift Shop,** across from the Yoghurt House, offers plenty of inexpensive trinkets to take home. (P15-100. Open daily 7am-6:30pm.)

DAMN THAT DAM! The Kalinga only recently began tolerating outsiders. A troubled relationship with the Marcos administration led to a frigid attitude toward strangers. President Marcos proposed to build a giant dam in the Chico Valley that would flood Kalinga villages and force them to relocate. The Kalinga refused offers of compensation and banded together with local Communists (the NPA) to sabotage construction. They succeeded in delaying the dam until Marcos was ousted in 1986, after which the project was scaled down. The Kalinga have continued their subversive stance since then by producing high-quality *tsonge* (Tagalog slang for marijuana), mostly exported to Boracay. They are friendlier to travelers now, but a guide is essential to help orient you to the villages.

TREKKING. The **Sagada Environmental Guides Association (SEGA)** has fixed rates; only SEGA guides can be hired at the Tourist Information Center. Typical tours include the **Sugong Hanging Coffins, Lumiang Burial Cave,** and **Sumaging Cave,** popularly known as "Big Cave." (4-5hr.; 1-4 people P300, group of 5 P350, group of 6-9 P600. Prices double after 5hr.) Another alternative is a 1-day trek including the 1800m **Mt. Ampacao** (1½hr.), **Lake Danom,** and the **Bokong Falls,** complete with a climb up the **Kiltepan Tower** to survey the rice terraces. (1-4 people P400, group of 5 P500, 6-9 P600. Guides strongly recommended for novice hikers.)

If you'd prefer not to take a tour, try exploring some of the sights on your own. Fifteen minutes past the Igorot Lodge, the road forks. The left fork, leading to Suyo Rd., passes the **Sugong Hanging Coffins,** tethered to a cliff face. Thirty minutes farther along Suyo Rd., a path leads to the Lumiang Burial Cave. Friendly signs make all of this clear. Even if you don't take a tour, it is advisable to hire a guide for Sumaging Cave, 10min. past the Burial Cave. Inside the chamber, you must wade in waist-deep water, cling to ropes, and crawl through crevices—one wrong step and you become bat food. From Bontoc Rd., a path to the right leads past St. Mary's Episcopal Church to a **cemetery** and **Calvary Hill.** To the right, the path takes you to a boulder, while another path takes you to the floor of **Echo Valley.** The path is slippery; be prepared to come back drenched in mud. These trails are unmarked, and it's easy to get lost without a guide. Hanging coffins are visible in the limestone cliff faces, accompanied by a smattering of "death chairs." In certain rituals, the deceased sits in the chair while funeral-goers perform sacrifices and songs. Fifteen minutes along the road to Bontoc, the **Matangkib Burial Cave** is at the foot of a path opposite the Rocky Valley Inn. Passing by the left of the cave leads you to the **Latang Underground River.** With a strong flashlight, you can follow the river to the Bokong Falls. If you don't want to follow the underground river, you can take the concrete steps leading up from Bontoc Rd., which wind down to the river. Cross the river, and head upstream to the falls. To visit the 40m high **Bomod-ok (Big) Waterfalls,** register with the Tourist Information Center, and obtain a guide (P500). On school days, jeepneys go to the Banga-an Elementary School from the basketball court (30min.; 8am departure, 1pm return; P15), where a trail leads to the Bomod-ok Waterfalls (1½hr. trek). On weekends and holidays, hire a jeepney for a "Special Ride" to Banga-an (P450 round-trip), or walk (2-3hr.). Follow the road to Banga-an for about an hour, turn down the steps beyond the Banga-an Elementary School, then take the path through Fidelsian village to the waterfalls.

BANAUE ☎74

Rice is king in Banaue. Generations of Ifugao farmers have constructed vast rice terraces on every mountainside in and around the city. The rugged terrain is now a spectacular gallery of geological sculptures, billed as the "Eighth Wonder of the

World" in spite of swarming tourists and tricycles that slightly spoil the terrace panoramas. The indigenous artistic tradition, marked by an outpouring of jewelry, carvings, bronze works, and textiles, enjoys immense popularity—as do the elder tribeswomen with stooped backs posing for photos. A short but often steep trek to Batad affords even more spectacular terrace views and a chance to experience local culture in a more natural, less touristed setting.

TRANSPORTATION. Most buses and jeepneys leave from the Sanafe Lodge. **Dangwa buses** run to **Baguio** (7am and 4pm, P210) and **Manila** (9hr., 4 and 4:30pm, P250). The dispatch office in Niclyn's Store at the marketplace makes reservations one day in advance from 3 to 7pm. **Autobuses** leave from near the Banaue Hotel and go to **Baguio** (5:30pm, P230) and **Manila** (5 and 5:30pm, P250). Make reservations at their office next to Tam-an village. A **KMS** bus that leaves from the top of the stairs near Cool Winds also goes to **Baguio** (9hr., 3 and 5pm, P180). Make reservations at the craft shop opposite Cool Winds. Jeepneys run to **Bontoc** (2½hr., 7am, P80).

ORIENTATION AND PRACTICAL INFORMATION. The unnamed main street starts at a parking area for **buses** and **jeepneys** surrounded by market stalls and shops. Nearby, the Town Hall houses a branch of the **post office** (☎386 4104; *Poste Restante;* open M-F 8am-noon and 1-5pm) and a desk where jeepneys and **tricycles** can be chartered. The **Tourist Information Center** is on the first floor of the Town Hall. (Open daily 8am-noon and 1-5pm.) Area maps are available at **People**'s **Inn** (P10). **RSR Merchandising** at the market **exchanges US dollars** and **traveler**'s **checks** at poor rates. From the **market,** the main street runs beside the river before it veers, crosses the river, and becomes a national road that heads back on the other side of the gully past the **Guihob Natural Pool** (4km) to the **Batad Junction** (12km). A left at the fork by the market leads uphill past the **Good News Clinic** to the Banaue Hotel overlooking **Tam-an village** (15min. walk). At the top of the drive are the **main post office** and the **Digitel telephone office** (☎386 9850; open M-F 8am-6pm). **Postal code:** 3601.

ACCOMMODATIONS AND FOOD. Hostels generally have hot water and a 10am check-out. **People**'s **Inn and Restaurant** ❷ offers serene views of the terraces, a knowledgeable staff, and a restaurant. (☎386 4014. Restaurant open daily 6am-9pm. Singles P100-150, with common room P300; doubles P200/P500; quads with common room P500.) **Uyami**'s **Green View Lodge** ❶ boasts spacious rooms with balconies but unfortunately lacks the views available at People's. (☎386 4021. Rooms with shared common room P100 per person; twins with balcony, hot shower, and private common room P400-600; quads with common room P600; family room with common room P800.) **Cozy Nook** ❷**,** opposite the Stairway Lodge, is a homey inn run by an affectionate woman and her family. (Doubles P200; triples P350; P100 extra during high season.) The most colorful rooms in Banaue can be found just outside the town center at the **Fairview Inn** ❸**.** The bright rooms have hot water, private baths, and a wrap-around terrace. (☎386 4002. Singles P300; doubles P600.) The **Banaue Hotel and Youth Hostel** ❸ is in Tam-an village. Rooms other than dorms will cost you an arm and a leg. (☎386 4087. Dorms P200, P175 for students; singles and doubles P1200. All rooms have a common room, hot shower, and pool access. Singles P2300; doubles P2800.)

Banaue has limited dining options, but a few offer delicious, reasonably priced meals. The **Las Vegas Restaurant** ❶ invites patrons to "come to where the flavor is" and delivers the finest in "Las Vegas" cuisine—whatever that means. (Quaker oats P30. Israeli salad P40. Rum and coke P30. Open daily 6am-9:15pm.) Toward the Town Hall on the left side of the main street, **Jam Cafe** ❸ serves savory entrees like pork *adobo* (P110) and chicken curry (P110) with complimentary vegetables and

OF RICE AND MEN Once you've seen one piece of rice-growing genius, you've seen them all, right? Wrong. A true rice-terrace expert knows that each terrace is different: they can be convex or concave, equiaxial or isomorphic, stone-walled or clay-packed. Though the Banaue terraces are credited by some as being 2000 years old, it is misleading to think of them as completed sculptures that have stood immutable over the centuries. The terraces are an ongoing project, requiring constant upkeep. Terraces change throughout the year. In January, they are segmented pools of water, muddy plots plowed and harrowed by farmers and their carabao. Weeks later they are transformed into lush green lawns of seedlings. By July, the terraces have started to turn yellow and brown, becoming ripe for harvest. In addition to producing high-grade rice, the terraces provide a constant source of work, worry, celebration, status, and territorial dispute for the village people who depend on them.

rice. Start the morning with the "choc'lait n' toast" (creamed hot chocolate with buttered toast; P50). (☎0917 394 5471. Open daily 6:30am-8pm.) **Cool Winds Restaurant** ❷ has a friendly staff that whips up fresh treats like fruit salad (P45). Meat-eaters and sugar addicts are welcome too. (☎386 4023. Pork dishes P75. Chocolate and cheese pancakes P35. Tomato and cucumber salad P50. Open daily 6am-9pm.)

SIGHTS AND TREKKING. The established viewpoint of the famous **Banaue rice terraces** is 4km along the road to Bontoc (round-trip tricycle to Banaue Viewpoint P100, jeepney P350). These rice terraces produce much less than those in Batad, and it is only subsidies from the United Nations that keep the land plowed and the villagers working (guide P300). Before the viewpoint, turn left onto the Hapao-Hungduan Rd. to see the **mummified couple of Hiwang,** whose final wish was to be smoked and embalmed. Their son—now a friendly, elderly man—lives off of P20 donations from visitors. While the cloth-shrouded corpses are disappointing, the son's elevated hut is worth a visit. (No photos allowed.) The **Banaue Museum** at the Banaue View Inn (on main street) holds the collection of anthropologist H. Ottley Beyer, one of the first outsiders to study Ifugao culture. (☎386 4078. Open M-Sa 8am-noon and 1-5pm. P25.) On sunny days, visitors cool off in the **Guihob Natural Pool** along the road to Batad. (Round-trip tricycle P120, jeepney P350.)

An established 2-day trek from Banaue includes the villages of Batad, Cambulo, and Pula. Cambulo, a village circumscribed by a river, has two guest houses, the **Riverside Inn** ❶ and the **Friends Inn** ❶ (both P75 per person). The treks can be difficult during the rainy season. Arrange your trip at the Banaue Viewpoint or Banaue Hotel. (1-2 people P1200 per day; 3-4 people P500 per person per day.)

BATAD

Tiny and remote, Batad is a favorite destination of travelers, who rave about the abundance of cheap rooms and some of the most phenomenal rice terraces in the Philippines. Only accessible by foot, Batad remains less touristed than Banaue and the surrounding towns. Snapshots of President Gloria Arroyo dot the walls of virtually every establishment, and with good reason: Arroyo recently promised US$10 million to revitalize Batad's prized landscape, which includes the spectacular 21m Tappia Waterfall.

TRANSPORTATION. The trek to Batad consists of a 50min. trip from Banaue to **Batad Junction,** an hour-long hike up a winding, unpaved road to the **Batad Rest**

Area, and an hour's walk down steep "stairs" and dirt paths to Batad. To reach the junction, catch the jeepney leaving from the market area outside Sanafe Lodge (10am-noon, P40). Unless you plan on spending a night in Batad, it is best to hire a round-trip tricycle (P400-500) to ensure transportation back to Banaue. Round-trip jeepneys can also be hired for P1000. Some tricycle drivers will brave the uphill road from the junction to the rest area for an extra fee (P200-300). From the rest area to Batad, there is no option but to walk. About 15min. into the hike from the junction, the "mountaineer's shortcut" veers left over the "saddle" to Batad, cutting the trek in half. The shortcut, however, is often very steep and dangerous, especially with a backpack.

ACCOMMODATIONS AND FOOD. Batad's hostels are quite similar to each other: dorm beds cost P50 everywhere, and there is no electricity—you'll need a flashlight for the outhouse. The only deviation in price occurs at **Hillside Inn ❶**, jutting out from the first hill you see entering Batad, where private singles (P100) and doubles (P200) are available in addition to P50 dorm beds. Hillside is run by the likable Orlando family, who entertain guests with board games, guitars, and village legends. They can also arrange daytrips (P15-200). Laundry service is available (P50 per kg). Farther down the path, **Simon's Inn and Restaurant ❶** is the only hostel offering views of both sides of the valley. **Pension House ❶** is closest to the rice terraces, farther downhill from Simon's and Hillside. These hostels are preferred because of their spectacular views; additional guest houses dot the village center deep in the valley, a 30min. walk away. Though they lack the vistas, village hostels afford a better chance to see Ifugao dwellings. The friendly **Foreigner's Inn ❶** on the hill is the most well established.

Even though the lack of electricity makes refrigeration impossible, Batad's cuisine is quite satisfactory. Most restaurants are found in the hostels themselves. **Terrace View Cafe and Souvenir Shop ❶** is the one exception. The shop is on your right when the valley first comes in sight. Ginger tea (P15), sauteed noodles with vegetables (P45), and garlic egg soup (P35) are all appetizing after the 2hr. trek. Handwoven bags (P25-30) and flip-flops (P35) are also available. (Open daily 6am-9:30pm.) Both **Simon's ❸** and **Hillside's ❶** restaurants serve sandwiches on *chapaati* (pita bread) and *malawach* (a flat Middle Eastern bread) for P30-60. Simon's makes a mean *pinikpikan* (chicken; P300) and delicious native coffee (P25), while Hillside is known for its more sinful treats: chocolate banana pancakes (P50), cigarettes

FROM THE ROAD

WHEELS ON THE BUS

On almost every bus I've ridden in the Philippines, the phrase "God Bless Our Trip" has been emblazoned above the driver's window. After all, only a miracle of divine intervention could keep this country's bold, borderline-reckless drivers from crashing.

For the most part, buses follow their schedules. If your bus company promises a nine-hour trip, you'll arrive in nine hours. But along the way, the driver will command slow tricycles to move through an esoteric language of honks and flashing lights. He'll then swerve around it in spite of oncoming jeepneys (overcrowded) or gasoline trucks (explosive).

Filipino buses really shine on mountain "roads," however. They have only one ambiguous lane and, inevitably, your vehicle will be forced to back up numerous times to let other vehicles pass. Don't worry, there are "barriers" on the roadsides to prevent your bus from rolling down a steep cliff.

People with a fear of heights definitely prefer to sit on the left. As your mammoth bus ascends and descends narrow roads, a view of the mountainside offers a nice alternative to the steep barrier-less cliffs on the right. Then again, signs jutting out from the mountainside—"Beware of Falling Rocks"— may not bring comfort for those averse to barrelling masses.

Be sure to board non-A/C public buses as soon as you can. After the first sixty or so seats fill up, you'll be stuck in the aisle along with twenty people and their dogs. If none of these options appeals to you, bring sedatives. And God bless.

—William Lee Adams

(P35 a pack), and 80-proof gin (P40). At both restaurants, order your dinner before 7:30pm.

THE WEST COAST

If Manila moves too fast and the mountain provinces too slow, the West Coast is just right. The beaches around San Fernando are popular with domestic tourists from Manila, but if beaches are your final goal, you would be better off heading south to Mindoro or the Visayas. Vigan's architecture, however, is second to none. Mess about on boats around the Hundred Islands National Park and unwind on the beaches around San Fernando on your way there.

SAN FERNANDO (LA UNION) ☎72

The capital of La Union Province, San Fernando emanates great civic pride. Bearing slogans declaring love for the city, tricycles buzz through the streets uncannily color-coordinated with the pastel shades of the town plaza. The crowded streets and the air reek of pollution, yet peace can be found at the spectacular Ma-cho Temple. A stretch of beach between San Fernando and Bauang to the south attracts swarms of townies on weekends but won't impress those familiar with Visayan beaches. Rougher waters to the north, at San Juan beach, support loyal surfers between November and February.

TRANSPORTATION

Partas (☎242 0465), on Quezon Ave. 100m north of P. Burgos St. intersection, runs buses to **Baguio** (2hr., sporadic daily departures 5am-8pm, with A/C P60) and **Manila** (7-8hr., 6am-12:30am, P235). **Philippine Rabbit** (☎888 2035) buses depart from the terminal off Quezon Ave. on the southernmost border of town for **Vigan** (2¾hr., every hr. 7:30am-4pm, P125) and **Laoag** (4½hr., P180). **Minibuses,** including Eso-Nice, depart from Gov. Luna St. to **Baguio** (2hr., every 15min. 5:30am-6pm, P40). For **Dagupan,** catch minibuses departing from Rizal Ave. (2hr., every 5min. 4:30am-6pm, P50). For **Alaminos,** change minibuses at Dagupan.

ORIENTATION AND PRACTICAL INFORMATION

San Fernando is 270km north of Manila, bracketed between the beaches of **Bauang** (6km) to the south and **San Juan** (10km) to the north. The town is arranged linearly, and the South China Sea makes north-south orientation easy. **Quezon Ave.** (which becomes **National Highway**) connects the beaches and the city's main road. Most accommodations lie north of the **town plaza** along Quezon Ave. The major streets running east-west include **Gen. Luna St.** (not to be confused with adjacent Gov. Luna St.), **Rizal Ave.,** and **P. Burgos St.** The sights sit on polar ends of town, with the **Ma-Cho Temple** at the northern extreme, and other sights (Freedom Park, Fil-Chinese Pagoda and the Museo de La Union) to the south. Taking Rizal Ave. west away from the hill leads to the coast.

Tourist Office: ☎888 2411. Connected to the left side of the Oasis Country Resort on National Highway. Open M-F 8am-5pm. Better maps at the **Office of the City Planner,** in the Marcos Bldg. Open M-F 7am-6pm.

Currency Exchange: Philippine National Bank (☎242 0908), on Quezon Ave., at Gov. Luna St. **24hr. ATM** (Cirrus/MC/PLUS/V). Open M-F 9am-3pm.

Bookstore: Triva (☎888 2996), on Quezon Ave. Open M-Sa 7:30am-8pm.

FROM THE ROAD

BANANAS FOR PINEAPPLES

As Daet's most important cash crop, the pineapple holds an exalted position among local fruit. Starting on June 24th, residents celebrate this fact with the annual "Daet Pineapple Festival"—five days of sporting events, fruit, and festivity. But not just any pineapple will do: only Daet's signature pineapple, the Sweet Formosa, makes the grade.

Events kick off with the *Karakanan Sa Palan* food festival. Daet's chefs face off in contests for the tastiest pineapple-and-meat platter, the most invigorating brew of pineapple wine, and the best-baked pineapple pie. Said pies are later eaten in the messy pineapple pie eating contest.

Don't worry about being a glutton. After your pineapple dinner or snack, burn those extra calories on Vinzon's Ave., as street performers dance and sing in constumes constructed entirely from pineapple shells. The dizzying dancing will leave you feeling lighter—if not light-headed.

Finally, the festival culminates with the crowning of Miss Daet Pineapple. Picking a winner isn't as easy as comparing apples and oranges, especially when the contestants are supposed to exude the qualities of a pineapple. Like the Formosa whose sweet taste pleases, contestants must have a pleasant demeanor. Like the pineapple, it is nice to have an appealing shell, but it's more important to be filled with substance. Among the victor's spoils: a parade and a crown (you can guess what it's made of). Daet admits it's mad about its fruit, just don't call them *bananas.*

—William Lee Adams

Pharmacy: Mercury Drug, on Quezon Ave., opposite Far East Bank. Open daily 6:30am-9pm.

Emergency: ☎116.

Police: ☎242 4702. North of town plaza on Quezon Ave.

Medical Services: Bethany Hospital (☎888 3671), on Widdoes St., past Union Christian College, off Gen. Luna St. toward the hill. English spoken. **Open 24hr.**

Internet Access: The NET Cafe, Quezon Ave. (☎242 2222), 30m from P. Burgos St. intersection. P30 per hr. Open M-Sa 8am-9pm, Su 1pm-7pm.

Post Office: Marcos Bldg., Rizal Ave., at the corner of P. Tavera St. (☎888 2965). *Poste Restante.* **Branch** on Mabini St., Catbangen. Open M-F 8am-6pm. **Postal code:** 2600.

ACCOMMODATIONS AND FOOD

Hotel Mikka ❺ is on Quezon Ave., next to the Partas bus terminal, 150m north of P. Burgos St. intersection toward Ma-cho Temple. The staff are particularly knowledgeable and professional, and all rooms are fully equipped with phones, A/C, and cable TV. (☎242 5737. Singles P625; doubles P750; family rooms P1250.) Also on Quezon Ave., 100m south of the town plaza, **Mandarin House Hotel ❷** is more budget-friendly. (☎888 5309. Doubles P165, with A/C and common room P435.) The **Sea & Sky Hotel and Restaurant ❺,** in Pagdaraoan, has affordable basement rooms that forego views of the South China Sea, as well as more expensive rooms with expansive vistas. All rooms include breakfast and have phones, A/C, and cable TV.

The lines are long, but the service is quick at the **Danish Baker ❶,** on Quezon Ave., past the plaza on the left. (Delicious tuna turnovers P22.50. *Pandisuelo* bread, a local favorite, P2.25. Open daily 6am-8:30pm.) The well-run **Las Villas ❺,** 2514 San Juan., 400m toward the sea from the National Highway (Quezon Ave.) in San Juan., provides fresh seafood that will melt in your mouth as you cool in the shade of the palms by the sea. The "Fisherman's Basket" feeds two for P400. It's well worth the trek out of town. If you crave fried American pigeon, head to the **Mandarin Restaurant ❸** where it costs P290. The restaurant has options for the frugal as well as the indulgent. (☎888 2424. Shrimp curry rice P80. Abalone with fresh mushroom P3600. Open daily 7am-11pm.)

SIGHTS AND ENTERTAINMENT

On the lush green hillside off Quezon Ave., 400m to the north of the town plaza, a joint group of Filipinos and Taiwanese fisherman built the **Ma-cho Temple** in gratitude for local hospitality. Ma-cho, the Taoist goddess of the sea, looks out upon the South China Sea from atop her hill; visitors can borrow her vista from the balcony, or step inside to ask her questions. A Chinese deity of the Sung dynasty, Macho is known in the Philippines as the Virgin of Caysasay. On the second week of September, the original statue of the Virgin is brought to the temple from Taal for the **Feast of Our Lady of Caysasay.** (Open daily 6am-6pm.) Beautifully landscaped gardens featuring Japanese, Chinese, and "medicinal" flora await at **La Union Botanical and Zoological Garden** (6km outside of town). Visitors with allergies should avoid the "Fragrance Garden."

Like most of San Fernando's attractions, its preeminent disco is atop a hill. The **High Altitude Disco,** on Gapuz Zig-Zag Rd., features pop/dance on Friday nights. Cover (P100) includes one beer. (☎888 2025. Open W-Sa 9pm-2am.) **Gatherings** (☎242 5737), a videoke bar in Hotel Mikka, features drunken tourists singing 80s pop from 6pm to 2am daily.

BEACHES

SAN JUAN. The rough waves make it less suitable for swimming and instead attract a cadre of surfers from November to February. Catch a jeepney (P5) bearing the signboard "Bacnotan" from the corner of Quezon and Burgos St. in San Fernando. Get off before arriving in San Juan when you see your resort's advertisement. **Las Villas ❺,** St. Jude Village, Ili Norte, is 400m from the National Highway toward the sea. Management invests fastidious pride in the food and rooms of this peaceful outpost. An eclectic group of adventurers and expatriates mingle at the bar nightly and partake in a delicious grill buffet on weekends. (☎242 3770. Doubles P1000-1200; family room P2500.) **La Union Surf Resort (Surf Camp) ❷,** 238 Urbiztondo, on the path past the Billabong Guest House rents rooms and surfboards, and is San Juan's surfer mecca. Amiable Aussie owner Brian rents surfboards and rooms. (☎242 4544. No hot water. Dorm rooms with common cooking facility P150; singles P300; bungalow P650. Surfboards P100 per hr., P300 per half-day, P500 per whole day.) The occupancy rate of **Mona Liza ❸,** in Urbiztondo, rises and falls with the height of the waves. (☎888 4892. "Budget" rooms with common room P300; doubles P400; triples P600. P50 for refrigerator.)

BAUANG. The beaches, stretching from Bacuit to Pagdalagan, are not visible from the road, but advertisements for the resorts certainly are. Take a jeepney bound for **Naguilian** or **Agoo** (P3). For travelers staying elsewhere, resorts charge a fee for use of their facilities. Farther north, the **China Sea Beach Resort ❺,** in Paringao, offers a swimming pool. (☎242 6101. Standard doubles with A/C, private common room, and breakfast P1000, "deluxe" with cable TV P1100.) Other options along the beach include the boisterous **Southern Palms Beach Resort ❺,** Arturo Balagot St., Pagdalagan. (☎242 0854. Doubles with A/C P600.) Their nightclub, **Stiletto's,** is open daily 4pm-midnight.

VIGAN ☎77

The Americans left behind McDonald's, the Japanese left behind bombed ruins, and the Spanish left behind Vigan—now a UNESCO World Heritage Site. Thankfully, the city was spared the devastation that gutted Manila's Intramuros, leaving one of the best-preserved of Spain's 16th-century colonial holdings in Asia.

TRANSPORTATION. The **Philippine Rabbit** terminal, on Gov. Reyes St., is the origin of buses to: **Baguio** (4½hr., every hr. 5am-11pm, P180); **Laoag** (1½hr., every 30min., with A/C P75); and **Manila** (8hr.; every hr. 7:30am-5pm; P284, with A/C P324). **Dominion Bus Lines** (☎722 2053), near the south end of Quezon Ave., sends buses to **Manila** (8-10 per day 4:30am-10pm, A/C P360). The **Partas** terminal (☎722 2933) is south of the public market, with buses to Cubao in **Manila** (every 30-60min. 4:45am-10:30pm, P360).

ORIENTATION AND PRACTICAL INFORMATION. Vigan lies west of the Mestizo River. Its grid-patterned streets are easily covered on foot or by horse-drawn *calesa*. **Quezon Ave.,** parallel to the river, intersects P. Burgos St. on the east side of the city's main plaza area. The main plaza area is beside Municipal Hall, which houses the **police station** (☎166). The newly restored **Mena Crisologo St.,** distinguished by its cobblestones and antique shops, runs south of Plaza Burgos near the provincial **tourist office** (open daily 8am-5pm). One block south of Burgos St., Florentino St. runs east-west and passes a branch of **Philippine National Bank,** with a **24hr. ATM.** (Cirrus/MC/PLUS/V. Open M-F 9am-3pm.) Gen. Luna St. is home to the **PT&T Telephone Office.** (☎722 2273. Open M-W 7am-8pm, Th-F 8am-8pm, Sa-Su 8am-5pm.) The **Gabriela Silang General Hospital** is on Quirino Blvd., which runs north-south on the east side of town along the river. (☎169, office ☎722 2782. **Open 24hr.** English spoken.) **Farmacia Fernandina** is on Quezon Ave., between Bonifacio and Gen. Luna St. (☎722 2470. Open daily 7am-10pm.) **Internet access** is available at **Powernet,** 32 Gov. A. Reyes St., just west of Mena Crisologo St. (☎722 1830. 1st hr. P60, P0.83 each additional min. Open daily 8am-7:30pm.) The **post office** is one block past the bank on Bonifacio St., near the corner of Gov. A. Reyes St. **Postal code**: 2700.

ACCOMMODATIONS AND FOOD. **Grandpa's Inn ❸,** 1 Bonifacio St., on the corner of Quirino Blvd., not far from the river, is an affordable way to experience old-world chic. (☎722 2118. Doubles P250, with private common room P350, with A/C P550.) **El Juliana Hotel ❹,** 5 Liberation, on the corner of Quirino Blvd., in the southeastern corner of town, recreates the Spanish villa experience. (☎722 2994. Singles and doubles with private common room, A/C, and TV P500.) The swimming pool is open to the public 7am-6pm (P35) and 6-11pm (P50). The **Vigan Hotel ❺,** at the corner of P. Burgos St. and V. Pelos Reyes, features spacious rooms. (☎722 2588. Singles with A/C and cable TV P695; doubles P850.) The comfortable **Gordion Inn ❸,** on V. Delos Reyes St., offers comfortable rooms with large beds, A/C, cable TV, private bath, and complimentary breakfast. (☎722 2526. A/C dorms P300; standard rooms P1200. MC/V.)

Street vendors ❶ along Plaza Burgos serve Spanish *empanadas*, deep-fried rice tortillas filled with local vegetables (P5) or meat and eggs (P20), and *okoy*, crispy shrimp and onion pancakes (P20), from late afternoon until early morning. **Cafe Floresita ❸,** set within attractive arches by the Ancieto Mansion, has fabulous *longganiza*. (Most dishes P40-180. Open daily 6am-9pm.) **Café Leona Restaurant & Videoke Bar ❸,** on Mena Crisologo St., is Vigan's sole outlet for Thai and Japanese entrees. The "ice tea" (P25) is actually fully frozen. (☎722 2212. Sushi P90-190. Open daily 8am-10pm.) The **8.88 Restaurant and Pool Hall ❶,** on Rizal Ave., draws a local crowd with pool tables and a variety of entrees for P40-60, from squid balls (P50) to *longsilog* (P46), a combination of egg, fried garlic rice, and *longganiza*. (☎722 2208. Open daily 8am-2am.) **Cool Spot Restaurant ❸** (☎722 2588), behind the Vigan Hotel on Quirino Blvd., is a local favorite renowned for its homemade *bagnet* (P200) and *longganiza* (P70).

SIGHTS. The legacy of the Spanish *conquistadores* is well preserved in the town's architecture, but Vigan has also been shaped by its participation in the lucrative galleon trade with Europe, Asia, and Mexico. **Rowilda's Hand Loom,** on Crisologo St. near Cordillera Inn, is reminiscent of the hand-weaving craft that once contributed to the international textile trade of colonial times. (Woven handbags P150-180. Open daily 8am-6pm.) **Pagburnayan Potteries,** on the corner of Liberation Blvd. and Rizal St., produces the stoneware *burnay* jar used by the Ilocanos to store everything from vinegar to wine. A water buffalo squashes the clay under hoof, and mammoth wood-fired kilns bake the sculpted clay. **Padre Burgos House National Museum,** 6 Burgos St., adjacent to St. Paul's Cathedral, commemorates the death of Padre Burgos, one of the most famous Chinese *mestizo* residents of Vigan, whose martyrdom in 1872 galvanized the revolutionary movement. On display, among other things, are ancient *itneg* (ovens) of the Tinggian tribe, which were recently discovered inside a bat cave in Ilocos Sur. (Open Tu-Su 8:30-11:30am and 1:30-4:30pm. P10.) **Crisologo Museum,** 23 Liberation Blvd., is another ancestral home that has evolved into a museum. This former residence of congressman, governor, and war hero Floro Crisologo contains icons and natural history exhibits. (Open daily 8:30-11:30am and 1:30-4:30pm.) **St. Paul's Metropolitan Cathedral,** the unfortunately orange-colored yet striking church on N. Segovia St., is an example of distinctive "Earthquake Baroque" architecture. Attached to it is the **Museo de San Pablo,** a religious museum with life-size Jesuses. West of the cathedral is **Plaza Salcedo,** an elevated elliptical plaza, former site of public executions, which features a 17th-century statue—the oldest in Northern Luzon.

THE PBA It seems ironic that some of the world's shortest people would play one of the world's tallest sports, let alone with the skill and intensity of the basketball players of the Philippines. Each of the Philippines Baskeball Association's ten teams, rather than representing a region, is sponsored by a corporation, so names like "San Miguel" are plastered across jerseys. Despite the league's many great successes, it has had its share of controversy. During the Marcos years, league officials were given jobs allegedly based less on their knowledge of the sport than their familial connections. Game-fixing and blue-chipping have plagued the league since its inception. Nonetheless, the talents of the players have inspired youngsters to don replica jerseys and take up the sport themselves. One of the pleasures of traveling in the Philippines is watching the PBA-hopefuls hoop it up just about anywhere, with just about anything resembling a ball and hoop.

SOUTHERN LUZON

While Manila's appeal comes mostly from man-made venues, Southern Luzon is a natural wonder. A beautiful lake fills the formerly volatile crater of Taal Volcano while layers of recently released ash cover the still active Mayon Volcano. For those seeking adventure closer to sea level, the island of Mindoro offers beaches and world-class dive sites.

LAKE TAAL REGION ☎43

Once upon a time in prehistory, the Taal Volcano was 6000m high. A massive eruption blew off the volcano's top, and a crater lake formed in the new opening. Lava rising through this lake has created an island at its center which, over thousands of years, has developed its own lake. Said to have the world's most perfect cone, the volcano affords visitors the chance to swim in crystal blue water. The town surrounding Lake Taal, however, is dreary and uncomfortable. No more than a daytrip is necessary to see the volcano and the neighboring Tagaytay Ridge.

TRANSPORTATION AND PRACTICAL INFORMATION. Lake Taal is located between the towns of **Talisay** and **Leynes. Buses** from **Batangas** and **Manila** pass through **Tanauan,** which has transportation connections to Taal. **Jeepneys** travel from the public market in Tanauan to **Talisay** (20min., 5am-7pm, P9). From there, **tricycles** (P20) can be taken toward Leynes to reach the resorts. On an alternate route, buses from Manila en route to **Nasugbu** or **Calatagan** pass **Tagaytay Ridge,** which has the best views of the volcano. To get to the lakefront from the ridge, get off the bus at **Olivares Plaza,** catch a jeepney (P5) to the top of **Ligaya Dr.,** and transfer to another jeepney down Ligaya Dr., which ends at the water (last trip 6pm, P15). Jeepneys turn left to Talisay, but you can catch a tricycle to the right if you're heading toward Leynes. Jeepneys to Tanauan depart from the corner of Laurel and Wencislao St. (3am-5pm, P10). Buses to **Batangas** and **Batangas Pier** pass along J.P. Laurel St. in Tanauan (1½hr.; P35, A/C P50). Buses also go the other way to **Manila** (1½hr.; P40, with A/C P60).

The **Tanauan Shoppers Market (TSM)** on A. Mabini St. exchanges **currency** and traveler's checks. (Open daily 7am-6pm.) The **PLDT telephone office,** on the lakefront road near the Ligaya Dr. intersection, provides international phone service. In Talisay proper, the Municipal Hall on Wencislao St. houses the **police** (☎773 0241; **emergency** ☎166) and **post office** (open M-F 8am-5pm). Farther along the street (with the lake to your right), **St. Andrew's Hospital** (☎773 0196) has a **24hr. pharmacy. Postal code:** 4220.

ACCOMMODATIONS AND FOOD. Tourists flock to the lake during summer months (Mar.-May); book well in advance. **San Roque Beach Resort ❺,** 5min. from Ligaya Dr. off Tagaytay Rd., is a labor of love for owners Lita and Leo. (☎773 0271. *Nipa* huts with common room P850; 3-bedroom guest house with living room and kitchen P4000.) **Vista Hazel's Beach Resort ❸,** down the road from San Roque and right on the beach, has a swimming pool. (☎773 0257. Cottages P400; doubles with A/C P1500.) **Buco Resort ❺,** next to the Taal Volcano Science House (see **Sights,** below), is a 5min. walk toward Leynes from San Roque. (☎773 0306. Doubles P600, with A/C P700; family room P1500.)

SIGHTS. Pick up some background knowledge on Taal and other Philippine volcanoes at the **Taal Volcano Science House,** next to the Buco Resort, halfway between Talisay and Leynes. (Open 24hr. Free.) **Taal Volcano** actually has two craters, the younger of which erupted in 1965. There are two popular ways to tackle the older crater. A boat can take you to the front of the island (30min., about P500), where a trail (by foot or horseback) leads to the lip of the old crater. Alternatively, you can pay extra for a boat to take you around the back of the island (45min., P750-1000), where islanders guide visitors into the crater to the water's edge (P300). **Resort International,** opposite Ligaya Dr. junction, and many other hotels arrange boats for daytrippers. You're free to bathe in the sulfurous waters, which are said to have medicinal value, but don't swim to the rocky outcrop in the center of the lake, and avoid areas with rising steam—the water can scald. It takes 2-4hr. to visit Taal Volcano, so go early and bring water.

DAET ☎54

Daet (pronounced Dah-et), proclaims itself "A City of Character" on its welcome sign. Beyond gas-chugging tricycles that crowd the city's main thoroughfare this character might seem elusive. The nearby coastal village of Mercedes attracts more attention, drawing in a flotilla of fishing boats for its morning fish market. The mainland beaches near Daet run the gamut from Bagasbas Beach, with its pizza parlors and videoke bars, to San Jose Beach, patronized only by the occasional picnicker or fisherman.

TRANSPORTATION. The **Philtranco** bus terminal is on F. Martinez St., off Gov. Panotes Ave. (☎571 2718), a short jeepney ride from the town center (P4). Buses depart for Pasay and Cubao in **Manila** (8-9hr.; 9-12 per day 6:30am-9:40pm; P300, with A/C P341). Buses also leave from **Superlines** bus terminal (☎721 2961), a short tricycle ride from Vinzons Ave. (P10), for Cubao in **Manila** (8-9hr.; every hr. 5:30am-9:30pm; P201, with A/C P245). **AMDG** buses depart from the **Naga City** bus terminal (2½hr., every 30-45min. 6am-5:30pm, P90). To reach **Naga City,** catch a **minivan** from the **Central Plaza Bus Terminal** in Daet, accessible by tricycle (P4).

ORIENTATION AND PRACTICAL INFORMATION. Vinzons Ave., Daet's main street, parallel to the north side of the river, is home to many hotels and restaurants. At the eastern end of Vinzons Ave., a **town plaza** rises near the cross streets of **J. Coreses, Moreno St.,** and **Pimentel Ave.** Vinzons Ave. becomes **Gov. Panotes Ave.,** which continues to **Mercedes.** J. Lukban St., across the river, leads past the **Rizal Monument** and **Freedom Park** to **Magana St.,** where the **Philippine National Bank** exchanges traveler's checks (☎571 2815; open M-F 9am-3pm). For the **police,** dial ☎166 or ☎571 2815. A **Bayantel** telephone office is on Vinzons Ave., near the J. Lukban St. intersection. (☎440 0568. Open daily 7am-7:30pm.) The **post office** is in Camambugan, a P2.50 tricycle ride from the town center. (*Poste Restante.* Open M-F 8am-noon and 1-5pm.) **Postal code:** 4600.

ACCOMMODATIONS AND FOOD. Karilagan Hotel ❷, on Moreno St. behind the elevated town plaza, is a well-established hotel with a 24hr. restaurant, piano, and beauty parlor. (☎721 2236. Singles with bath P150, with A/C P400; doubles P550; family room P800.) On Vinzons Ave. opposite the elevated town plaza, **Hotel Dolor ❸** has 24hr. room service and

THE HIDDEN DEAL

LEGAZPI TOURIST INN

Budget travelers to the Philippines often learn about the three Rs when it comes to their hotels: roaches, rodents, and rock-hard mattresses. Fortunately for the budget traveler, this "you-get-what-you-pay-for" philosophy doesn't hold at the Legazpi Tourist Inn. Conveniently located near the Pacific Mall, the Legazpi Tourist Inn has a fantastic view from the stairs of the back of Mt. Mayon.

For a P450 room, guests first scale three flights of sparkling white-tiled stairs to reach the hotel's impressive lobby. A calming waterfall runs down a glass wall into the foyer's small fountain. A few steps away, the hotel's friendly, professional staff eagerly answers questions and escorts visitors to their value-packed rooms.

In the event that nearby Mt. Mayon should erupt, guests can cool their feet on the marble-tiling in every room. Large private showers with hot water are perfect for washing off ash and come with the hotel's personalized soap.

And when hunger strikes, the hotel is also ready. A restaurant adjacent to the lobby dishes out tasty Filipino, Chinese, and Western cuisine daily from 6am to 10pm (most meals around P100).

If you crave a meal after the restaurant closes, the front desk can arrange "midnight snacks" in bed. After filling your belly, turn off the lights and switch on your A/C or fan using the convenient bedside control panel. *(☎480 6147. 3rd fl. of U & O Building, Lapu-Lapu St.)* ❹ a nightclub upstairs. (☎721 2167. Cable TV P50, Economy singles P220, with TV, A/C, hot water, and fridge P450; doubles P400/P650, with A/C and cable P850.) **Sampaguita Lodging House ❶**, on Vinzons Ave. past the town plaza near the intersection with Pimentel Ave., has a 24hr. coffeeshop. (☎571 2221. Singles P100, with toilet and bath P175, with A/C P350; doubles P200/P275/P400.) At the end of Bagasbas Beach and beside the defunct Daet airstrip, **Nautiloux Resort ❹** has food upon request and offers Swedish or shiatsu massage for P500. (☎440 036. Doubles P250, with A/C P500.)

Look for the distinctive red and yellow building on Zabala St., by Metroback off Vinzons Ave. where **Golden House ❸** (open daily 7am-10pm) serves Chinese delicacies such as sea cucumber (P200). Set meals run P70-85. For Bicol treats such as *pala tim* pork (P170) and *miki-bijon* noodles (P70), head to **Slennalo's ❷**, adjacent to the Palayok complex on Pimentel Ave. (Open daily 9am-10pm.)

SIGHTS AND ENTERTAINMENT. Four kilometers from Daet town center along J. Lukban St. (10min. tricycle ride P15), **Bagasbas Beach** is an unbroken stretch of sand, with surfing on particularly rough days. The **San Jose Beach,** near the Talisay district (15min. tricycle ride north of Daet center) makes for a relaxing beach experience. An absence of shade will probably keep any stay short. **Stroll Jazz Bar,** on the fourth floor of the Hotel Dolor Bldg. on Vinzons Ave., is better than other bars on Bagasbas Beach. (No sandals or shorts. Open daily 6pm-2am.)

As much as it is a quaint, old-fashioned fishing village, **Mercedes,** 7km from Daet up Gov. Panotes Rd., is also a successful industrial outlet. Hundreds of fishing vessels congregate here for its seafood market. The **Mercedes "Fishtival"** is held August 4-8. **Jeepneys** to Mercedes depart from the fork in Vinzons Ave. (P3). A **boat** can be hired from Mercedes to **Apuao Grande Island** (45min., up to 6 people P300) or you can wait for the local village boat (6-8am, P50, returns to Mercedes 9-10am), which departs from a spot on the Mercedes coast marked by a Caltex gas pump off Eco Ave. **Apuao Grande Island Resort ❺** offers a nine-hole golf course, scuba diving, sports, and fishing trips for guests. (☎721 1545. Facilities open daily 8am-6pm. Brutal 7am check-out. Singles and doubles with common room P600. Quads with private common room P800.)

LEGAZPI ☎52

> **!** Mt. Mayon is regarded as one of the world's most volatile volcanoes. Since 1616, it is known to have erupted at least 40 times; its most recent eruption was on June 25th, 2001. Check with the Department of Transportation in Legazpi, the local tourist office, or your embassy for updated news on safety.

Even the beautiful have to belch from time to time. Mt. Mayon, whose name derives from the local word meaning "beautiful," has been violently spewing forth ash about every 10 years since 1968. Still, adventure-seekers flock to this friendly town, leaving more burnt from the fiery local cuisine than from the volatile mountain. Legazpi also makes an ideal base for excursions into the eastern Visayas.

TRANSPORTATION

Flights: Philippine Airlines (☎245 5024) serves Legazpi with daily flights to **Manila** (9:05am, P2783). An agent is at **Hotel Victoria** (☎214 3476) on Rizal St. Open daily 8am-noon and 1:30-5pm.

Buses: There are two **bus terminals. BLTB** (☎480 8907), on Peñaranda St., past Casablanca Hotel, goes to **Ormoc** (P450) and **Tacloban** (P400). From the **Satellite Bus Terminal, Philtranco** (☎820 2794) buses depart for **Manila** (6 times daily 6am-7pm; P506, with A/C P706). **Jam** (☎480 4029) buses depart for **Manila** (2pm, P190; 5:30pm A/C P350). Local buses and **jeepneys** leave from the **Old Market terminal** on Circumferential Rd. to **Donsol** (2½hr; 15 per day, last bus 4:30pm; P47).

ORIENTATION AND PRACTICAL INFORMATION

The main commercial district, also home to most of Legazpi's budget accommodations, lies between **Albay** to the south and **Rawis** to the north. **Rizal St.** links central Legazpi with Albay and is plied by hordes of **jeepneys** (most rides P4). The **Battle of Legazpi Monument** stands in the middle of central Legazpi. To the west, **Circumferential Rd.** leads to the local bus and jeepney terminal and **Satellite Bus Terminal.** One block east (toward the bay) is **Peñaranda St.,** Legazpi's principle commercial artery. The **airport,** accessible by tricycle (P50) pr taxo (P100), is 2km northwest of town at the end of **Aquende St.,** which then becomes **Washington Dr.** The fishing quarter, known as **Victory Village,** lies along the black-sand beach south of central Legazpi, at the foot of **Kapuntaken Hill.**

The helpful **tourist office** is in Rawis, just across the bridge. (☎408 3105. Open M-F 8am-5pm.) There are a number of **banks** on Rizal St. in central Legazpi (most open M-F 9am-3pm). Many have **24hr. ATMs. Tanchuling Hospital** serves central Legazpi and is in the Imperial Court Subdivision II off of Rizal St. (☎480 6372. **Open 24hr.**) **Ago General Hospital** is in Albay, past the provincial capitol on the left. (☎481 5807. Open **24hr.**) Next door, **Mercury Drug** is on Rizal St. opposite the Bayantel office. (Open daily 6am-9pm.) The **Bayantel** office on Rizal St. at the corner of Imperial St. provides **Internet** access. (☎480 6187. Open daily 8am-5pm. P33 for collect calls.) The **PLDT office** on Rizal St. in Albay has an **IDD phone.** (☎214 3896. Open daily 7am-9pm.) **Internet** access is also available at **Joycom** on Rizal St. (☎480 4777. P30 per hr. Open daily 9am-10pm.) The **post office** is on Lapu-Lapu St. near the Legazpi Tourist Inn. (Open M-F 8am-noon and 1-5pm.) **Postal code:** 4500.

ACCOMMODATIONS

Most of Legazpi's accommodations cluster within a few blocks of the monument. The **Rex Hotel ❸** is at the corner of Peñaranda and Aguinaldo next to the church. (☎241 5290. Singles P240, with A/C P540; doubles P275/P580.) The **Xandra Hotel ❷** on Peñaranda, one block north of the Rizal intersection on the left, is the cheapest bed in town. (☎820 4808. Singles with fan and common bath P150-270, with A/C, bath, and TV P500; doubles P180-600.) Among the city's more comfortable hotels, **Hotel Victoria ❺,** near the Post Office on Rizal St., is the most reasonably priced. (☎214 3476. Videoke bar and cafe inside. Singles and doubles with A/C, cable TV, and breakfast P1200.)

FOOD AND ENTERTAINMENT

Legazpi is a great place to sample the area's signature dish, Bicol Express, a mildly vile concoction whose principle ingredient is chili peppers. **Doña Alice ❸,** in Rawis

1km north of the bridge on the left, is a pleasant establishment serving scrumptious garlic prawns (P180) and Dikolano delicacies, like *camolig*, an herbal leaf with coconut, and *pili*, an almond, honey and sugar combination. (Open daily 10am-10pm.) Closer to town, on Peñaranda just beyond the BLTB bus terminal, the **Paayahayan Beer Garden** ❸ serves delicious seafood in *nipa* huts. (Crabs in chili sauce P180. Open daily 10am-1am.) There are also a number of fast-food joints and several nondescript Chinese restaurants in central Legazpi.

For after-hours entertainment, locals hit the **Bicharra Entertainment Center** in central Legazpi, opposite the statue of Jose Rizal. Inside you'll find a movie theater (shows P30), cafes, and ice cream shops. **Bar 101** on the third floor features live bands that promise "the best of the 60s, 70s, 80s and today." (Open daily 1pm-2am.) **Club Paparazzi,** on the 4th floor of Hotel Victoria, is the city's most popular videoke bar. (☎214 3476. Consumable P100 cover. Open daily 6pm-2am.)

SIGHTS AND ACTIVITIES

During the 1814 eruption of Mt. Mayon, almost everything in the town of Cagsawa was destroyed. The eerie remains of the town church, including its forlorn belfry, can still be seen. Visitors seeking personal tours at cheaper prices should contact local tourist guru **Eddie Nolasco,** who hangs out in the lobby of the Xandra Hotel (☎820 4808) and has scaled Mt. Mayon numerous times.

CAGSAWA RUINS. Cagsawa National Museum features an exhibit about major volcanoes in the Philippines. *(Take a Guinobatan- or Camalig-bound jeepney and get off at the Cagsawa turn-off (20min., P5), marked by advertising for the Cagsawa 1814 Restaurant. It is 500m from the turn-off to the ruins. Open M-Sa 8-11am and 1-4pm. P6, students P5.)*

CAVES. The three-tiered **Hoyop-Hoyopan Caves** have crystal formations that guides insist resemble everything from the Banaue rice terraces to the Philippine eagle. Hoyop-Hoyopan literally means "blow-blow," supposedly the sound of the whispering wind at the caves' exit. Only guided tours are permitted. The **Calabidongan Caves** ("Cave of the Bats"), 3km from the Hoyop-Hoyopan Caves, are much more extensive. It takes 3hr. and a chest-deep dip in the underground river to get here. Bring a flashlight—and be prepared to get wet. *(For Hoyop-Hoyopan, take a Guinobatan-bound or Camalig jeepney to Camalig town proper (30min., last trip 8pm, P10), and find a jeepney bound for Cotmon (6am-6pm, P8), 12km away. Tell the driver to stop at the junction for the Hoyop-Hoyopan cave. It's an additional 100m to the entrance. Guided tours 45-60min.; P100. For Calabidongan, P500 for 1-2 people, each additional person P250.)*

BUSAY WATERFALLS. These seven-tiered falls in Malilipot are a godsend in the heat of the rainy season, when the water falls thick and fast. Kids play in the larger pools at each tier and dare you to stand under the pummeling waters of the highest waterfall. If you're up to it, you'll earn their deepest respect and a flash of whooping smiles. *(Take a jeepney or bus to Malilipot (35min., P15) and get off when you see the large "Busay Falls" sign. It is a 35min. walk to the falls. P5.)*

MAYON VOLCANO. In northeast Albay, Mt. Mayon peaks at 2457m. A challenging but popular climb, it's normally scaled over two days. Base camps punctuate the climb at 750m and 1500m, where climbers pitch tents for the night. The second day's trek begins at 6am and reaches the "knife edge," 2250m high, around 9:30am. Loose rocks make it risky for inexperienced mountaineers to cover the remaining 500m to the rim. Expeditions return to Legazpi by 6pm the second day. The climb is possible year-round, though March and April are ideal times. Temperatures can fall to 10-15°F on upper parts of the mountain. Guides charge P4500 for one or two climbers (each additional person P1500). The fee includes transportation, a five-person tent, rope, and food. The tourist office organizes guides (book before 5pm one day in advance). True penny-pinchers and the stamina-filled can consider attempting the peak in one day for P2500. In the third week of May, the DOT conducts the "Mayon Conquest"—a free, organized climb of the volcano. For travelers wishing to get close, but not *that* close, to the volcano, the ramshackle **Mayon Rest House** sits at 840m. To get there, take a jeepney to **Tabaco,** 26km north of Legazpi, and then transfer to a **Ligao**-bound jeepney; ask to be let off at the junction leading to the guest house—it's an 8km hike from there, unless you charter transportation.

DARAGA HILLTOP CHURCH. Established in 1773 by Franciscan missionaries as "Our Lady of the Gate," Daraga is a monumental reinterpretation of a traditional Basilican Church. Built of volcanic rock, it appears to be formed as much by geology as by human hand. *(Jeepneys (20min., P5) head west into Daraga (Locsin). Get off at the Shell station on Gen. Luna St.; walk up St. Maria St.; or take the Daraga Water District stairs next to Sarko Cafe & Bookstore. Open daily 7am-midnight.)*

OTHER SIGHTS. Visitors can take a pre-dusk stroll through **Victory Village,** an old fishing enclave incongruously appended to the characterless city. From the end of Elizondo St., pass through the entrance to the covered fish market. On the other side, the village huddles on the black-sand beach. At the far end, steps take you up **Kapuntukan Hill** for a stunning view of the volcano, the sunset, and the city. Twenty kilometers north of Legazpi is the little village of **Santa Domingo.** The town itself has little to offer but there are several decent black-sand beaches, which are fairly unimpressive by Philippine standards but are clean nonetheless. The **Mayon Spring Resort** has two swimming pools, water slides, a nice strip of beach in addition to a restaurant/bar, and well-furnished bungalows (P600 per night). They'll let you use the facilities for P50 per day. To get there, take a Santa Domingo-bound jeepney (25min., P10) and ask to be let off at the Mayon Spring Resort turn-off. The last jeepney back to Legazpi leaves at 6pm. Every October, the province-wide **Ibalong Festival** reenacts early ancestral legends interwoven with Catholic influences. Dancers and singers fill the streets performing mock battles in traditional clothes. The **Karangahan Albay Festival** in May is a celebration of abundance in thanks for a good harvest. During **Holy Week,** *banca* races are held in Bacacay, a village north of Santo Domingo. *(Accessible via jeepney from Legazpi.)*

NEAR LEGAZPI: DONSOL

The sleepy fishing village of Donsol lies 30km southeast of Legazpi in neighboring Sorsogon province. With a single phone line shared by the entire village, Donsol remained an anonymous speck on the map until the discovery of mighty whale sharks **(Rhicodon typus).** In the late 1990s, word of the *butanding* (as the sharks are locally known) spread, attracting divers and poachers alike. Local authorities promptly passed legislation banning the hunting of the sharks and, with the assistance of the United Nations Development Program, established what has become a model for ecotourism and sustainable development projects.

Prime *butanding*-watching season is December to May, though this varies from year to year. For more information, call the Bayantel phone in Donsol (☎56 411 1109), and ask for Nita Pedragoza at the Visitors Center. You will probably have to spend at least one night in Donsol. Check in at the **Visitors Center,** where officials will help you find a place to stay. There are several homestays in the village, including **Hernandez Lodging House ❸** and **Santiago Homestay ❸** (both P300 for a 3-person room). Pricier "beach resorts," **Amor Farm Beach Resort ❹** and **Woodland Beach Resort ❹** (both P500 per room), are accessible from Donsol by boat.

Donsol is accessible by local bus from Legazpi (see **Buses,** p. 591). Excursions leave at 8am and return at 5pm. It's wise to show up at the Visitors Center by about 7am to secure a spot (each boat holds six people). A "Butanding Interaction

Officer" oversees each boat and advises you on safety. (P2500 per boat, plus a P300 fee per person. Snorkeling gear P200. Scuba diving is banned.)

MINDORO

Four hours by bus from Manila, the steamy smog gives way to the salty air of Mindoro, 26km off the coast of Luzon. Teeming marine life replaces the crowds, and sizzling sand burns visitors' feet instead of hot asphalt. Exquisite reefs, excellent underwater visibility, and dazzling aquatic life make Mindoro's dive sites among the world's best. While the island's wildlife and forests continue to thrive, so does an unfortunate sex industry. Stick to the diving, and steer clear of the dives.

THE VIEW FROM ABOVE

Main towns: Batangas, Puerto Galera.
Beaches: Big Lalaguna, Sabang, Small Lalaguna, and White Beaches, all near Puerto Galera.
Something fun: Hash House Harrier runs and treks to Mt. Calavite and Mt. Halcon.

PUERTO GALERA ☎43

The beaches surrounding Puerto Galera are the destinations of choice for island-hoppers from Luzon. Sabang Beach, the most popular in the area, lays the amenities and services on thick, while other beaches are more tranquil. The harbor at Puerto Galera proper is beautiful, and accommodations await those who don't want to be on the front line of tourism development. Dive sites lie near the coast, and the interior provides numerous trekking opportunities into wilderness that has successfully resisted development.

TRANSPORTATION

Buses: The Si-Kat office on Muelle Pier sells combined ferry/bus tickets to **Manila.** Open daily 7:30am-4pm. **Si-Kat II** ferry departs from Muelle Pier and arrives at City State Tower Hotel in **Ermita** (5½hr., 9:30am, P400).

Ferries: Boats go to **Batangas** from Muelle Pier, Balatero Pier, and Sabang Beach. From **Muelle Pier: Blue Eagle** (1hr.; 7am, 1:30pm; P125) and **Si-Kat** (2hr., 9:30am, P150). From **Balatero Pier: Viva Lines'** *St. Lawrence* (2hr.; 5, 10:30am, 2:30pm; P100). From **Sabang Beach: DSL Big Bancas** outriggers (☎0912 306 5332, c/o Angelyn's Beach Resort; 1½hr.; 6, 7, 8, 11:30am; P80). "Special Ride" to Batangas in a *banca* P1500. To get to **Boracay,** take a jeepney from the R.J. Store in Puerto Galera market to **Calapan** (2hr., 5am-2:30pm, P50), then catch a bus from the wharf in Calapan to **Roxas** (3-4hr., P82). Spend the night in Roxas (a hotel is near the stone beach). In the morning, take the *Flor B* to **Boracay** (5hr.; M-Tu, Th-F 10:30am; P250). Alternatively, several **outrigger boats** leave Roxas for **Romblon Island** and **Tablas Island** north of Boracay. From Romblon Island, regular ferries cross to Tablas Island. A jeepney to **Santa Fe** on Tablas Island and a ferry across to Boracay completes the journey. An alternate route to Boracay is to travel via Batangas.

Local Transportation: Bancas to coastal destinations leave from Muelle Pier (P100-500). **Tricycles** are common but pricey (P80-150). **Jeepneys** to **Puerto Galera's** town proper congregate around **Sabang Fast Food** (15min., depart when full, 6am-5pm, P10; return approx. every hr. 6am-5pm, P10). **Tricycles** to Sabang Beach P80 (negotiable).

ORIENTATION AND PRACTICAL INFORMATION

Puerto Galera (or Población) is in **Muelle Bay** on the north coast of Mindoro, at the neck of a Y-shaped peninsula surrounded by coves and beaches. A lighthouse at **Escarcero Point** marks the easternmost tip of the peninsula. **Sabang Beach** stretches out 1-2km west along the coast. A road connects Sabang beach to Población, 5km away. A short walk west from Sabang Beach, with the sea to your right, leads around a rocky point to **Small** and **Big Lalaguna Beaches.** Small Lalaguna Beach is actually bigger than Big Lalaguna Beach—the names refer to inland lagoons, not to the beaches themselves. The west tip of the "Y" shelters ritzy and exclusive **Coco Beach.** From Población, a 7km ride west goes to **San Isidro. White Beach,** a more placid tract of sand than the eastern beaches, lines the San Isidro coast.

Tourist Office: On Muelle Pier in Población. Open M-F 8am-noon and 1-5pm. *Puerto Galera Tourist Map,* available in guest houses, the tourist office, and from travel agents, features resort listings, and transport and diving information (P70).

Travel and Tours: Island Trekking Tours, at Havanna Moon Cottage (☎0973 497 503), offers treks and kayaking. **Tarzan Trek Tours,** located at the Sunshine Coast Restaurant (see p. 597), offers beach-hopping (P800), and mountain (P1000) and waterfall (US$50) daytrips around Mindoro and Lake Taal. Ask for Naty.

Currency Exchange: Moneychangers abound on Muelle Pier in Población. Sabang Beach offers better rates than Población and Manila.

Police: ☎487 3043. Municipal Hall, H. Axalan St., opposite Puerto Galera Academy. **Open 24hr.**

Medical Services: The Puerto Galera Lying-In Clinic (☎0912 352 9531), next to the Municipal Hall, takes care of prescriptions. **Dr. Carmelita Atienza** works in Sabang down the road that turns off near Tropicana Restaurant. Open M-Sa 9am-5pm.

Telephone: IDD available at outlet next to a mini-mart and *barangay* security office in **Sabang** (☎0912 318 2840; open daily 6am-10pm). **Bayantel,** in Muelle, Población, has lowest fees for international collect calls. Open M-F 7am-8:30pm, Sa-Su 7am-6pm.

Internet Access: CJ Trading Internet Cafe (☎043 287 3062), near Nuelle Pier. P150 per hr. Open daily 8am-8pm.

Post Office: In Municipal Hall on Conception St. Open M-F 8am-5pm. **Postal code:** 5203 (Sabang).

ACCOMMODATIONS

POBLACIÓN (PUERTO GALERA PROPER)

Melxa's Greenhills Nipa Hut, E. Cobarrubias Sr. St. (☎0912 270 6248). Turn right at the crossroads 50m past Municipal Hall. Wonderfully rustic *nipa* huts with balconies. Singles and doubles with shared kitchen and common room P200; triples P250; family room with refrigerator, common room, and kitchen P1000. ❷

Coco Point Hotel & Restaurant (☎442 0109), close to busy Muelle Pier. Upstairs rooms have balcony. Restaurant open daily 6am-9pm. Doubles with common room P500; family doubles P700. ❹

SABANG BEACH

The most remarkable aspect of Sabang Beach is that there isn't much of one. Still, the most extensive selection of retaurants and dive shops make this "beach" popular among tourists.

JAA Lodge (☎0918 798 9778), west of Ed's Bar and Pool Hall, is a tropical mansion with well-equipped, comfortable rooms with balcony and couch. Doubles with TV, refrigerator, stove, and private common room. P800 in high season, P500 in low season. ❹

Villa Sabang (☎0917 562 0214), on the east edge of the beach. Currency exchange, international telephone. No-frills singles with fan P650/P700; spacious doubles with balcony hammocks, TV, and fridge P900/P800; with A/C P1200/P1000. MC/V. ❺

VIP Lodge, behind Le Bistrot restaurant (☎0917 795 9062). No-nonsense rooms with the beach's lowest rates not to mention a great owner. Flexible noon check-out. Laundry service. "Budget" doubles with cable TV, fan, and refrigerator P300; "standard" doubles with kitchen P400. MC/V. ❸

Capt'n Gregg's Dive Resort (☎/fax 0973 496 691). For the hardcore divers or the wannabes. Front and center on the beach, west of Puerto Galera Rd. 10% off with 6 dives or a dive course. Singles and doubles with common room P500/P400, with A/C and hot water P900/P800, with TV P1200/P1000. ❹

SMALL LALAGUNA BEACH

Too often overlooked, Small Lalaguna is situated between Sabang and Big Lalaguna. The lack of tourists translates to a more relaxed, more private getaway.

Nick & Sonia's Cottages (☎0917 456 7824), in the center of the beach, offers discounts for 10-day stays and has some of the nicest owners in Puerto Galera. Comfortable suites with kitchen, hot water, and TV P800/P650, with A/C P1200/P850. ❺

Laguna's Deep Blue Sea Inn (☎0917 562 0209), past Nick & Sonia's. German-owned and Filipino-operated, this international inn can arrange direct transport to and from Batangas (P1800). Doubles with refrigerator and bath P650/500, with 2 beds P850/P750, with A/C, TV and hot water P1200/P950. MC/V. ❺

BIG LALAGUNA BEACH

Big Lalaguna Beach is a 15min. walk from Sabang Beach. As you round the point between Small and Big Lalaguna Beaches, you'll traverse "Penman's Mountain Pass." A stone notes the dizzying altitude—6.7m above sea level. The near-spotless beach has crystal-clear teal waters interspersed with coral, ideal for snorkeling.

Miller's Corner (☎0919 789 2063) is as far away from Sabang as possible, with rooms on the rocks. Restaurant open daily 6am-7:30pm. *Nipa* huts with hammock P400/P350; doubles with common room P950/P750, with A/C P1100/P950. ❸

Fernando's (☎0920 600 832), at the center of the beach, has a pub upstairs. Doubles with fan and private bath P650/P500; family rooms P1000/P800. ❺

WHITE BEACH

This grainy-sand beach is a 5min. walk from San Isidoro Rd. Jeepneys run from Puerto Galera to San Isidro and vice versa (depart when full 6am-5pm, P10). A *banca* trip from Sabang costs P400-500. Nester Bhoymaranan (☎0912 316 5910) manages the beach, runs tours around Mindoro (rates negotiable), and can offer travel and accommodation advice.

White Beach Resort (☎0912 272 0774), at the eastern edge of the beach. Peak season disco and bar. International phone/fax. Great collection of books. All rooms have A/C, private bath, and hot water. Doubles with private common room P900/P600; cottages with TV, refrigerator, and kitchen P1500/P800. ❺

The Summer Connection Beach Resort (☎0912 316 5910), at the farthest, most secluded end of the beach. Lattice-work cottages with hammocks. Arranges daytreks into Mindoro's wilderness interior (P100). Reservations advised in peak season. Restaurant open daily 6am-10pm. Singles with private common room P550/P400; doubles with common room and porch P800/P500; suites P1500/P700. ❹

FOOD

SABANG BEACH

Relax Thai Restaurant (☎0917 9985 917), west of the center. Bulwark against Sabang's tendency toward "anything-but-Asian" cuisine. *Aham talay* (stir fried seafood and veggies) P280. Unusual but tasty *pad thai* P145. Open daily 10:30am-10pm. ❹

Sunshine Coast Bar & Restaurant (☎0917 339 6730). The delicious "steak and mushroom pie" won the Philippines meat pie competition (P175). "Feeling shitty" breakfast of coffee, 2 cigarettes, coke, and ibuprofen P70. Open daily 7:30am-10pm. ❹

Janelle's Fastfood (☎0918 326 9212), behind Ed's Pool and Restaurant. Good food fast. Sandwiches P30-100. Pork steak scallopini P155. Open daily 6am-3am. ❷

McRom's (☎0919 880 8899), on the southeast corner of the main street. Any of the "sizzling platters," especially "stir-fried seafood with Mcrom's peanut sauce" (P165), will satisfy the pickiest palate. Susi Q sandwich P115. Spicy tuna nuggets P80. Open daily 6am-midnight. MC/V. ❸

ELSEWHERE

Pier Pub & Pizza Restaurant, on Muelle pier, at end of the bay-side boardwalk. Sandwiches P50-100. Small pizza P135-195. Buttered shrimp P280. German *spaetale* noodles with meat sauce P150. Open daily 7am-9pm. ❸

The Point, where Small Lalaguna and Sabang Beaches meet. Catches the breeze nicely on its rocky promontory. Try the African Passage three-shooter set (P400) and get your name on a plaque. Superb steak sandwich P160. Open daily 10am-midnight. ❹

ACTIVITIES

For real seclusion, explore **Talipanan Beach** (35min. by jeepney from Muelle Pier, P20). Thirty well-established dive sites are within a 20min. boat ride from Sabang Beach. Abundant reef fish, including triggerfish, lionfish, frogfish, and scorpionfish populate the coral. A score of dive shops line the shore from Sabang to Big Lalaguna Beaches; prices are uniform. **South Sea Divers,** on Sabang Beach, stands out. Owners Sky and Paul define the word "laid-back," and divemasters Carlos and Rob will show you Sabang's nightlife. Most dive shops offer dives with equipment, boat, and guide (US$25, night dives US$32) and PADI dive courses. (☎918 865 0264. Discover course US$50; open-water course US$300; advanced open-water course US$200). Beachside stands rent snorkels and masks (P50 per day).

ENTERTAINMENT AND NIGHTLIFE

If the sun's shining, most of Sabang is on the beach or in the reefs. Only a few meters from the shore, the dive sites are tops in Luzon and among the finest in the world. When the moon comes out, however, so do the ladies of the night, and Sabang transforms into the Philippines' "Sin City." Stretch your lungs and join the **Hash House Harriers,** a beer-drinking and running club founded in 1938 in Kuala Lumpur that now has branches all over the world. Runs start from Cap'n Gregg's. (☎0912 305 0652. Su 4:30pm; P200 for first-time runners, including beer and t-shirt; P100 for repeat runners. See **A Drinking Club with a Running Problem,** p. 381.) **The Lounge** on Sabang Beach is a stylish and laid-back sports bar with soccer shirts on the walls and sports on the TV. (Happy hour 5-6pm. Open daily 9am-midnight.)

There's no shortage of **pool halls** on the beaches (P10 per game). Try **Ed's Pool and Restaurant** for excellent competition, but be wary of hustlers when betting on a game. If you need to supplement your budget, enter the peak season **pool tournament** at Le Bistrot restaurant (☎0973 861 425), on Sabang Beach, where the winner takes all (Sa 5pm, P50). If you really want to be a shark (or at least look like one), you can purchase a beautiful handmade cue (P1500).

WHOSE SIGN IS IT ANYWAY? Visitors to the Philippines may be taken aback by the blood-red flags emblazoned with "KKK" above government buildings. It's a symbol of Philippine nationalism—not any connection to the Ku Klux Klan in the United States. Here, "KKK" stands for "Kataastaasan Kagalanggalangang Katipunan ng mga Anak ng Bayan" ("Highest and Respected Society of the Sons of the People"). "Katipunan," for those challenged in the art of tongue acrobatics, was founded in 1892. Like any respectable secret society, Katipunan had passwords, blood oaths of loyalty, and color-coded masks denoting rank. Unfortunately, founder Andres Bonifacio proved a better schemer than leader, and his troops were defeated repeatedly in the revolution against the Spanish. Co-founder General Emilio Aguinaldo proved himself more capable and became president of the Katipunan. Bonifacio indignantly crowned himself king, appointed a vice-king, and was later executed for treason by President Aguinaldo (see **Reform Movement and Early Nationalism,** p. 550).

DAYTRIPS FROM PUERTO GALERA

A jeepney from the R.J. Store in Puerto Galera market goes to **Calapan** (2hr., 5am-3pm, P30). **Cockfights** in Calapan city center start at 10am on Sundays. If you're lucky, you might see one during the day in the area behind Janelle's Fastfood.

The **Tamaraw Falls** are only 30min. from Sabang Beach via jeepneys bound for **Calapan** (jeepney P25; entrance P15). Also within easy striking distance is the **Light House** on Escarcero Point, where cliffs fall away on three sides (jeepney to Sinandigan near Escarcero Point P15, "special" jeepney to the Light House P150). It's also a pleasant trek by foot. You can take longer treks into Mindoro's interior wilderness. Past White Beach, where the road thins, large tracts of rainforest have yet to be penetrated by roads. With the exception of the village 1km behind White Beach, the Mangyan tribes in the interior are unaccustomed to tourists.

A trek from White Beach to **Mt. Malisimbo** (1230m) near Ponderosa, south of White Beach, takes 3hr. Guides should be arranged from the tourist office, at Muelle pier, or via the **Summer Connection** on White Beach. **Island Trekking Tours** (☎/fax 0973 497 503; ask for Ralf) organizes treks into the interior. The **Bogdong Beach trek** leaves from Sabang beach's Sunshine Coast Restaurant. A native outrigger takes trekkers to Bogdong Beach, followed by a 2hr. trek through Mangyan valleys that ends at a lagoon with waterfalls. (Sa, W 7:30am, returns to Sabang 6pm. US$35 per person including food, additional US$17 for overnight stay. 8-person min.) If there are enough people, Island Trekking Tours or Summer Connection can arrange more extensive treks. Longer treks might include **Mt. Calavite,** where communities live on bamboo rafts at the confluence of two rivers. One-week hikes head to **Mt. Halcon,** the highest mountain in Mindoro at 2587m. **Tarzan Trek Tours** (☎0919 410 1020) arranges daytrips to Lake Taal (P900).

THE VISAYAS

After endless bus rides in the mountains of north Luzon, island-hopping brings a welcome reminder that the Philippines is, in fact, an archipelago. The ancient coral beds and volcano tips of the Visayas include six major islands: Samar and Leyte in the Eastern Visayas, Negros and Panay in the Western Visayas, and Cebu and Bohol at the heart of the chain. All of these areas have their own dialects. Amid this confusing tropical Tower of Babel, the Visayas bore witness to two unifying events in Filipino history: the spread of Catholicism in the 16th century and the wresting of the islands from Japanese oppression in the 20th. Although travelers find it hard to leave the beaches, among the loveliest in Southeast Asia, Visayan cities try their best with a generous dash of frenzied charm. From Bohol's Chocolate Hills to Mt. Kanla on Negros, inland adventures also await. Whether bounding up a hill, frolicking on a beach, or jumping into a jeepney, friendly Visayans won't hesitate to greet you with a shriek of "Hey Joe!"

CEBU

Once upon a time, Ming vases and Spanish doubloons were the currencies of choice on Cebu. Nowadays, tourist cash runs the island, and mammoth resorts serve as a testament to the new industry. The northern islands of Bantayan and Malapascua run at a slower pace, their calm broken only by the dynamite fishing that has driven divers to Pescador Island near Moalboal. For the nocturnal traveler, the nightlife in Cebu City provides evenings of endless excitement.

THE VIEW FROM ABOVE

Main cities: Cebu City, Moalboal.
Island fever: Diving off Mactan and Malapascua Islands, vegging out at deserted Bantayan Island.
Blast from the past: Discover the lingering history from Cebu City's colonial era.

CEBU CITY

☎ 32

Miguel Lopez de Legazpi anchored off the shores of Cebu in 1565, took one look at the droves of hostile natives, and aimed his galleons in the direction of friendlier shores. Two months later, the *conquistadores* returned, set Cebu ablaze, and erected the first fortified settlement in the archipelago. Modern travelers follow Legazpi's footsteps, taking off for excursions around the other islands before returning to raze Cebu in their own way. Little can prepare travelers for the energy of this "Queen City of the South," where historical and religious relics are entangled with the contemporary trappings of a major port city and transport hub. Today's visitors can expect a warmer welcome than Legazpi received, losing themselves in Cebu's first-class restaurants, vibrant nightlife, and cultural attractions.

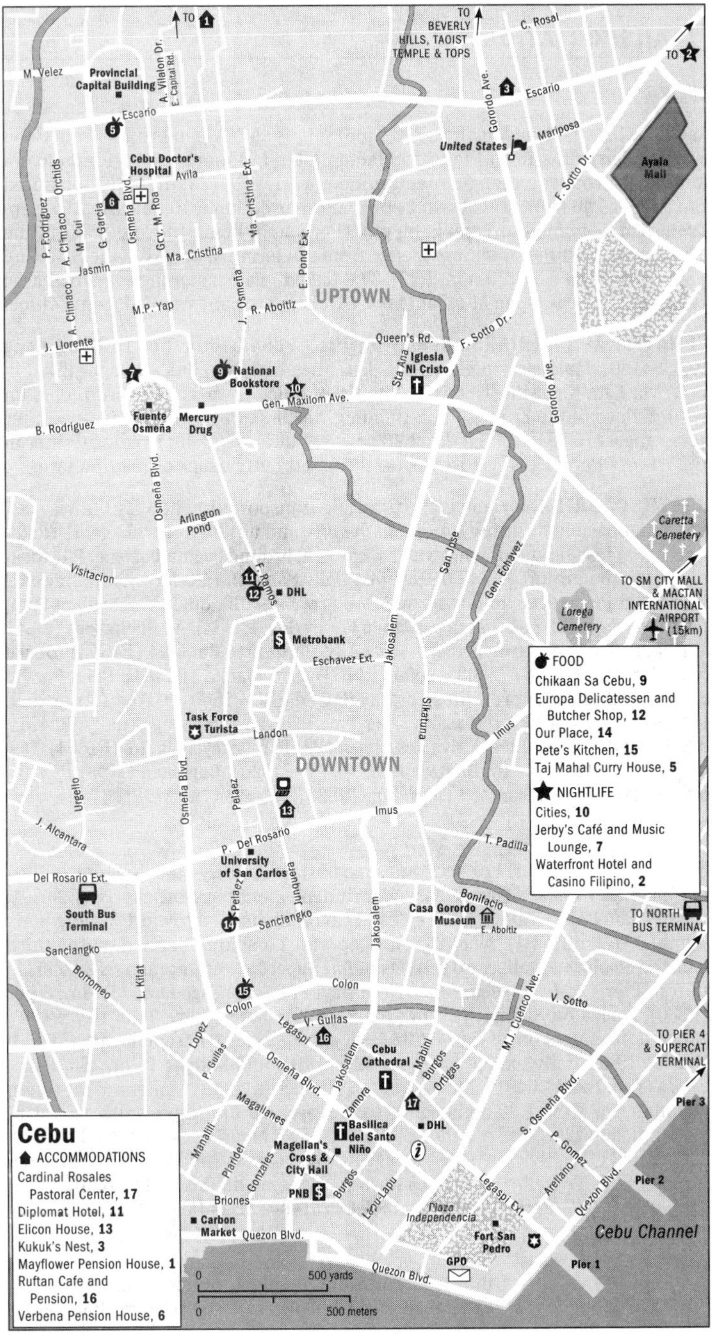
Cebu
ACCOMMODATIONS
Cardinal Rosales Pastoral Center, 17
Diplomat Hotel, 11
Elicon House, 13
Kukuk's Nest, 3
Mayflower Pension House, 1
Ruftan Cafe and Pension, 16
Verbena Pension House, 6
FOOD
Chikaan Sa Cebu, 9
Europa Delicatessen and Butcher Shop, 12
Our Place, 14
Pete's Kitchen, 15
Taj Mahal Curry House, 5
NIGHTLIFE
Cities, 10
Jerby's Café and Music Lounge, 7
Waterfront Hotel and Casino Filipino, 2
TO BEVERLY HILLS, TAOIST TEMPLE & TOPS
TO SM CITY MALL & MACTAN INTERNATIONAL AIRPORT (15km)
TO NORTH BUS TERMINAL
TO PIER 4 & SUPERCAT TERMINAL
UPTOWN
DOWNTOWN
Provincial Capital Building
Cebu Doctor's Hospital
United States
Ayala Mall
Iglesia Ni Cristo
National Bookstore
Fuente Osmeña
Mercury Drug
Caretta Cemetery
Lorega Cemetery
DHL
Metrobank
Task Force Turista
University of San Carlos
South Bus Terminal
Casa Gorordo Museum
Cebu Cathedral
Basilica del Santo Niño
Magellan's Cross & City Hall
PNB
Carbon Market
Plaza Independencia
Fort San Pedro
GPO
Cebu Channel
Pier 1
Pier 2
Pier 3
0 500 yards
0 500 meters

TRANSPORTATION

BY AIR

Mactan Cebu International Airport (☎340 2468) serves all of Cebu Island. From Cebu City, **Metro Ferry** runs from Pier 3 to Mactan Island (45min., every 15min. 6am-7:30pm, P6). From the pier on Mactan, take a tricycle (25min., P30) or a taxi (15min., about P40 from downtown Cebu). Another option is to take the 23D jeepney from S.M. City Mall to Lapu-Lapu city (P4.5) and then a tricycle (P30) to the airport. Aircon "U-hires" minibuses leave from the terminal opposite the S.M. City Mall for Lapu Lapu City (20 min, P12). The **tourist info counter** in the arrival area can help. (☎340 8229. Open M-F 8am-5pm.) Tickets are subject to a P3 airport fee.

INTERNATIONAL CARRIERS. **Cathay Pacific** (☎254 0740) flies to **Hong Kong** (daily, US$196). **Malaysia Airlines** (☎231 3887) has flights to **Kuala Lumpur** (Th, Su; US$303) via **Kota Kinabalu** (US$241). The **ticket office** is on 116 Gorordo Ave., on the second floor of the Export Bank Building. **Silkair** (☎254 0740) flies every other day to **Singapore** (US$485). The **ticket office** is in Suite 302, Cebu Holding Center in Cebu Business Park. However, travel agents can offer cheaper promotion fares.

DOMESTIC CARRIERS. Cebu is the principle transportation hub for the Visayas, making it impossible to throw a stone in the city and not hit a travel agent. Ticket booking agencies abound downtown and uptown, around **Fuente Osmeña. PAL** locations include the airport (☎340 0191, open daily 8am-5pm), S.M. City Mall (☎232 8412), and on Plaridel St. in downtown Cebu (☎254 4136, open M-F 8:30am-6pm, Sa 8:30am-noon). PAL has flights to **Manila** (7 per day, P3033). **Air Philippines** (☎341 0920; ticketing done through PAL) has daily flights to: **Bacolod** (P1553); **Davao** (P2203); **General Santos** (P2463); **Iloilo** (P1753); and **Manila** (P2463). **Cebu Pacific** (☎255 4040, at the airport), flies to: **Bacolod** (daily, P1560); **Davao** (2 per day, P2210); **Iloilo** (daily, P1763); **Manila** (7 per day, P2464); **Zamboanga** (daily, P2424). **Asian Spirit** (☎341 2555) flies daily to: **Caticlan** (P2315); **Cagayan de Oro** (P1864); **Tagbilaran** (P495). **Seair** flies to: **Bantayan** (W, F, Su; P1020); **Camiguin** (M, F; P1330); **Caticlan** (daily, P2230); **Siargao** (Tu, F, Su; P 2020); **Tacloban** (M, W, F; P1505).

BY BOAT

Ferries clutter the harbor. For schedules, go to the S.M. City Mall complex, which houses the **S.M. Traveler's Lounge** as well as independent ferry offices. (☎232 0291. Open daily 6am-8pm.) Take a jeepney from Colon St. headed toward "Colon, S.M., N. Terminal" (30min., P4). **Alboitz Express** operates a similar service on the third floor of the **Robinson Mall** at Fuente Osmeña. **SuperCat** catamarans (☎232 4511) leave from Pier 4 to **Dumaguete** (3hr., 2 per day, P500) via **Tagbilaran** (1½ hr., 3 per day, P380); **Larena** on Siquijor (2½ hr., daily, P660); **Ormoc** (2hr., 3 per day, P480). 15% student discounts on all fares. **WG&A Superferry** (☎232 0490) pulls out of Pier 6 for **Manila** (19hr.; daily except Tu, Sa; P1265-1810) and **Surigao** (5 hr., Tu, P445-810). **Trans-Asia** (☎254 6491), located on M. Cuenco Ave. by Osmeña Blvd (open daily 8am-noon, M-Sa 1:30-5pm), goes to: **Cagayan de Oro** (8hr., daily except F, P269-400); **Iloilo** (12hr., every other day, P500-750); **Maasin** (twice weekly, P230-350); **Masbate** (14hr., twice weekly, P450-810); **Tagbilaran** (2hr., M, P145-250). **Cebu Ferries** (call S.M. Traveller's Lounge) goes to: **Cagayan de Oro** (10hr., daily, P269-750); **Ormoc** (5hr.; W, F, Su; P210-550); **Tacloban** (14hr.; M, F; P290-550).

BY BUS

Northbound buses leave from **Cebu North Bus Terminal,** outside the city center along the north coast, for: **Daan Bantayan** (3½hrs., every 1½hr. 6:30am-10pm, P60);

Hagnaya (3hr., every hr. 6am-10pm, P100); and **Maya** (4hrs., every 1½hr. 6am-10pm, P65). Schedules for other destinations are available at the station. For southbound and westbound buses, walk west down Del Rosario away from Osmeña Blvd. to **Cebu South Bus Terminal.** Buses to **Moalboal** (2½hr., every 30min. 5am-6pm, P30, A/C P70) and other nearby destinations depart from here.

LOCAL TRANSPORTATION

Linking uptown and downtown (P4), **jeepneys** are the most convenient way to get around town. To venture downtown, look for jeepneys headed toward "Colon," any of the piers, "Carbon Market," or "Sto. Niño." To head back uptown, look for "Capitol Bldg.," "Escario," or "Fuente Osmeña." These routes run along Osmeña Blvd. The "Colon-SM-H. Terminal" covers S.M. City Mall complex (P4), North Bus Terminal, and Colon. The "Colon-Ayala" jeepney will take you to the Ayala Mall and the Waterfront Hotel. **Taxi** meters start at P25 and click upward in P2 increments. (From the pier area into downtown: P35. To Fuente Osmeña: P65. Across town to Beverly Hills: P85.)

ORIENTATION AND PRACTICAL INFORMATION

Halfway down the east coast, Cebu City is about 600km south of Manila. **Mactan Island,** home of Mactan Cebu International Airport, is accessible by ferry and bridge. Cebu City has two sections: downtown and uptown. Downtown sprawls along the piers to **Del Rosario.** On the seafront, **Quezon Blvd.** passes all piers, **Fort San Pedro,** and **Carbon Market. D. Jakosalem** starts at City Hall (and Magellan's Cross) and runs uptown to **Gen. Maxilom Ave. Osmeña Blvd.** runs from **Plaza Independencia** (downtown) though **Fuente Osmeña** (uptown) to **Escario. Gen. Maxilom Ave.** radiates east from Fuente Osmeña and intersects **F. Ramos, Jakosalem,** and **San Jose** on its way back to the sea and Quezon Blvd.

Tourist Office: The **main tourist office** (☎254 2811), is at the corner of Lapu-Lapu and Legaspi near Fort San Pedro. Head for glass doors midway down the block in the LDM Building. Free maps and brochures. Open M-F 8am-noon and 1-5pm. The **Airport tourist counter** (☎340 8229) is in the arrival area of Mactan International Airport. Open M-F 6am-8pm.

Travel Agencies: Swagman Travel, 301 F. Ramos (☎254 1365). Very helpful branch of this Australian-owned agency.

Consulates: US (☎231 1261), PCI Equitable Bldg., 3rd fl., on Gorordo Ave. Open M-F 8-11am.

Immigration Office: Cebu Bureau of Immigration (☎/fax 253 4339), in Mandaue City, 10km north of Cebu City. Take the 21B or 22B jeepney from S.M. City Mall to Mandaue City (20min., P4). From the Jollibee, walk past City Hall and turn right on Burgos; the office is 800m down on the right. Passport, airline ticket, visa, and patience required. Be sure to **dress neatly**—long pants and a collared shirt are appropriate. 38-day visa P2100; 59-day visa P2800. Open M-F 8am-noon and 1-5pm.

Currency Exchange: Banks, many with 24hr. **ATMs,** are all over town. **HSBC** is on the corner of Gen. Maxilom Ave. and J. Osmeña. Open M-F 9am-4pm.

English-Language Bookstore: National Bookstore (☎255 4644), down Gen. Maxilom Ave. from Fuente Osmeña; it's on the corner with J. Osmeña. Open daily 9am-8pm.

Outdoor Equipment: Hagabat (☎256 3896), on J. Osmeña, 3 blocks north of the Gen. Maxilom intersection, in the Baseline Recreation Center. Carries top-quality outdoor equipment including. Also a **branch** in the S.M. City Mall. Open M-Sa 10am-8pm.

Market: Carbon Market, on Briones and Calderon, south of the downtown area. Catch a "Carbon" jeepney (P4). Sells everything from fruit to tires.

Emergency: ☎166.

Police: Central Police Station (☎253 5636), on F. Ramos.

Tourist Police: Task Force Turista (☎254 4023), aids tourists 24hr.

Pharmacy: Mercury Drug (☎255 4187), uptown on Fuente Osmeña, at the intersection of Gen. Maxilom Ave., and Osmeña Blvd. **Open 24hr.**

Hospital: Cebu Doctor's Hospital (☎253 7511), on Osmeña Blvd. Travel up Osmeña Blvd. from Fuente Osmeña; it's on the right between Ma. Christina and J. Avila.

Telephones: Bayantel (☎255 0057) operates around Fuente Osmeña in the uptown area. Open M-F 8am-10pm, Sa-Su 8am-5pm.

Internet Access: Internet cafes have sprouted up all over town, especially on Del Rosario near the University of San Carlos and Fuente Osmeña. Expect to pay P20-40 per hr.

Post Office: Cebu Central Post Office (☎256 1696), on Quezon Blvd., south of the downtown area and opposite Fort San Pedro. *Poste Restante* available. Open M-F 8am-noon and 1-5pm. **Postal code:** 6000.

ACCOMMODATIONS

There are plenty of good budget choices downtown and uptown. Note that downtown is grimier and more chaotic and that after-dark touts pushing their "bikini bars" can get a bit oppressive; most travelers will find uptown more agreeable. To avoid the skin trade, look for hotels that don't allow visitors in their rooms.

DOWNTOWN

Elicon House (☎255 0300), on Junquera near its Del Rosario intersection and the University of San Carlos. Posh service and vibrant artwork. Cafe with room service. Laundry service. Singles P198, with A/C, bath and TV P450; doubles P288, with A/C, bath and TV P500. ❷

Ruftan Cafe and Pension, 61 Legaspi (☎256 2613). Near Basilica del Santo Niño. Backpacker haven in the heart of Cebu. Good food and travel stories. Internet P15 per hr. Wash-up P40. Doubles P165-350. "Short-time" room P100. ❷

Cardinal Rosales Pastoral Center (☎255 1269). Opposite Cebu Cathedral on Burgos. Look for "Patria de Cebu, Inc." sign. Share a dimly lit hallway with the Archbishop's office. Singles P150-200; doubles P250, with A/C P600; extra person P100. ❷

UPTOWN

Kukuk's Nest, 157 Gorordo Ave. (☎231 5180; kukus@nexus.com.ph). At Escario. Spacious, clean rooms with a Bohemian atmosphere. Excellent base to explore Cebu. Popular beer garden/restaurant open 24hr. Roast chicken P110. Diving and transportation arrangements available. Singles P200; doubles P500-560, with A/C P450. ❷

Diplomat Hotel, 90 F. Ramos (☎254 6342; fax 254 6346; diplomat@cebu.pw.net.ph). Located in a quiet area in the center of Cebu. Next door is the remarkable Europa Delicatessen and Butcher Shop (see **The Big Splurge,** p. 386). Booking service. Currency exchange. Laundry service. Room service. Caters mainly to business travelers and offers attractive, comfortable rooms with A/C, cable TV, and bath for a mere P700. ❺

Mayflower Pension House (☎255 2800; fax 255 2700; mayflower@cebu.weblinq.com), on Villalon Dr., off Escario east of the Capitol Building. TV in A/C rooms, cafe, tickets, and a library. Laundry service. Convenience store. Check-out 1pm. Singles P230-460; doubles P300-580; triples P380-720. MC/V. ❸

Verbena Pension House (☎/fax 253 3430), on G. Garcia parallel to Osmeña Blvd. Walk a block down Jasmin and turn left onto G. Garcia. Tall eucalyptus trees grow in the courtyard of this pleasant establishment. Canteen open 6:30am-7:30pm. Booking service. All rooms A/C. Singles P400; doubles P460; triples P520; quads P580. ❸

FOOD

Both swanky uptown and gritty downtown provide fine food, local and foreign. Some of the tastiest and cheapest food can be found in the food courts of Cebu's many shopping malls, including the **Robinson** complex at Fuente Osmeña and the **Ayala Center.** The mother of all food courts can be found at the **S.M. City Mall.**

DOWNTOWN

Pete's Kitchen (☎254 9910), on Pelaez. From Colon walk north; it's on the right. Local grub served up cafeteria style. *Lumpia* P25. Grilled squid P65. Fried rice P15. Takeout counter open daily 6am-8:30pm. Restaurant open daily 6:30am-10:30pm. ❶

Our Place (☎254 7196), upstairs at the corner of Pelaez and Sanciangko. Haunt of the (male) expat community. Steak P110. Spaghetti P90. Open M-Sa 10am-11pm. ❷

UPTOWN

Taj Mahal Curry House (☎254 3788), on Escario at the Osmeña Blvd. intersection. Facing the capitol, it's to the left. Tasty and cheap Indian food and lots of vegetarian entrees. Try the spinach *kofta* (P55) or the mushroom curry (P65). Also has a branch in the Ayala Center. Open M-Sa 5-11pm. ❷

Chikaan Sa Cebu (☎253 6221), on J. Osmeña. From Fuente Osmeña, go down Gen. Maxilom Ave., turn left up J. Osmeña, then left again into the shopping plaza. A worthwhile splurge, seafood menus with *adobong kangkong* (sauteed vegetables) P135. Sizzling blue marlin P150. Open daily 11am-2pm and 6-10pm. AmEx/MC/V. ❷

SIGHTS

MAGELLAN'S CROSS. Planted on April 14, 1521 by Ferdinand Magellan, **Magellan's Cross** on Magallanes marks the location where missionaries baptized the first Filipinos as Christians. Two weeks later, after Chief Lapu-Lapu killed Magellan, the expedition fled and the Spanish influence waned until Legazpi returned to raze Cebu in April 1565. Located on Osmeña Blvd. *(Admission free.)*

BASILICA DEL SANTO NIÑO. Next to **Magellan's Cross,** the **Basilica del Santo Niño** on Osmeña Blvd. displays the oldest relic in the Philippines: a figure of the Holy Child, given as a baptismal gift to Queen Juana of Spain by Magellan. Originally built as a *nipa* hut in 1575, it suffered numerous fires until it was rebuilt in 1735-37 as an example of the imported architecture of the conquering Spaniards. Religious services are held in English and Tagalog every hour from 7am-noon and at 3, 5, and 6pm. Stalls selling religious souvenirs surround the courtyard. *(Open M-Th and Sa-Su 5am-7:30pm, F 6am-6pm. Free.)*

FORT SAN PEDRO. When Legazpi began construction of **Fort San Pedro** on May 8, 1565, the days of friendly blood compacts with native chieftains were over. Swords, then crosses, became the order of the day. There isn't much left to see within the eight-foot thick walls but a few old cannons, but the view of the city from the bastion towers is good. The real perk, however, is the shaded interior garden, the most peaceful spot in downtown Cebu and frequented accordingly by young Cebuano couples. Archeology buffs might also want to take a look at the small exhibition of Ming dynasty artifacts in the **Fort San Pedro National Museum.** *(In the pier area in southern Cebu on Quezon Blvd. opposite the post office. ☎256 2284. Fort open daily 7am-11pm. Museum open Tu-Sa 8am-noon and 1-4pm. P15.)*

UNIVERSITY OF SAN CARLOS. The oldest school in the Philippines, the **University of San Carlos** on Del Rosario began as a seminary in 1595. Get a glimpse of gender inequalities of a bygone era and cranial deformation, an aesthetic pursuit to flatten the front of the skull using boards and straps, inside the **University Museum.** *(☎253 1000. Open M-Sa 8am-noon and 1:30-5:30pm. P15, students P5.)*

OTHER SIGHTS. A jaunt north to **Beverly Hills** (taxi P70-80) shows you the world of the wealthy Chinese Cebuanos. Lavish mansions surround the **Taoist Temple** high above the city. With Bohol and Mactan in the distance, this is a great place to see the sunset. The **Casa Gorordo Museum** provides an unparalleled glimpse into Cebu's late colonial past. Built in the 1860s, this beautiful Spanish colonial house was constructed without a single nail. *(35 Lopez Jaena. ☎255 5630. Open M-Sa 9am-noon and 1-5pm. P25, students P10.)*

OUTDOORS. Outdoor enthusiasts usually strike out for other islands in search of adventure. Nevertheless, there are some activities in and around Cebu to catch the traveler's attention. **Swagman Travel** (see **Practical Information,** p. 603) organizes environmental and adventure day trips, including **kayak tours** and **trekking** through Cebu's mountainous interior. The **Hagabat Outdoor Gear Shop** (see **Practical Information,** p. 603) is a meeting spot for the local hiking, climbing and diving scene. There's also a climbing gym next door. The shop frequently organizes weekend day-trips—contact Warlito "Monski" Momongan (☎253 6292).

ENTERTAINMENT

Cities (☎255 4562), on the left side of Gen. Maxilom Ave. away from Fuente Osmeña. Cover bands and zany stage acts–like dancing nuns. Beer P50-75; pitchers P250. Ladies' night Tu and Th. Cover P100. Open M-Th 7pm-1am, F-Sa 7pm-2am. MC/V.

Jerby's Cafe and Music Lounge (☎253 5401), on the north corner of Fuente Osmeña, along Osmeña Blvd, next to Dunkin' Donuts. Live bands and karaoke. San Miguel P35. Cocktails P65-90. Happy hour 6-9pm. F-Sa cover P50. Open M-Sa 10pm-2am.

Waterfront Hotel (☎232 6888). Offers intriguing after hours entertainment including the **Casino Filipino** with card tables, roulette, and slots (P100 cover), and **H_2O,** a hip bar-*cum*-nightclub that attracts a glamorous late 20s yuppie crowd. San Miguel P45. Cocktails P95. Cover P150. To get there, take a taxi (P70 from downtown) or a jeepney going to Lahug and tell the driver to drop you off at the Casino Filipino.

THE BIG SPLURGE

EUROPA DELICATESSEN AND BUTCHER SHOP

Many travelers come to Cebu for the city's cultural sights and its unique museums. Yet, the Europa Delicatessen and Butcher Shop is as much a curiosity as some of these museums. Indeed, it is a museum in its own right–a museum of imported foods.

At 90 F. Ramos, the Europa Delicatessen lies in a relatively quiet part of Cebu City–surrounded by vibrant Filipino street-life with its ubiquitous lechon stalls and pawnshops, yet somehow removed from the frenetic bustle of other areas.

On the first floor of this remarkable little shop is a traditional European butcher shop. Everyone but a German would be surprised by the numerous varieties of sausages available. Vegetarians might not appreciate the sight of hefty smoked hams hanging from the rafters, but meatlovers and Romanophiles will delight at the exhibition of Balsamic vinegars, camemberts, and Bordeaux wines.

Upstairs is a posh restaurant where even the *maitre d'* is an import from France. The menu, however, offers a greater national and cultural variety and features whatever a homesick traveler might desire–from onion rings to peanut butter and jelly sandwiches, from Aussie steaks to plum pudding and Black Forest Cake.

Whether you crave a taste of home or just want to enjoy an elegant dinner with impeccable food and service–much more affordable here than at home–your P800-1000 are well-spent at the Europa Delicatessen.

MACTAN ISLAND ☎32

Mactan is known mainly for its fine diving, though the underwater ecosystem has been hit hard by "dynamite fishing," a technique where fishermen detonate dynamite in the water to collect the fish as they float up to the surface. Other than its house reef, the island has no natural attractions. Travelers who can afford to spend $100+ per night might enjoy being pampered in one of the luxurious resorts, but anyone on a smaller budget is advised to skip the island, as similar diving with better beaches and lower prices can be found elsewhere in the Visayas.

TRANSPORTATION AND PRACTICAL INFORMATION. Just off the east coast of Cebu Island, Mactan Island is linked to Cebu City by ferry and land. A bridge connects Mactan to mainland Cebu in Mandaue, a small area of the metro sprawl 8km north of Cebu City. Mactan's capital city, **Lapu-Lapu City,** is on the northwestern coast, facing Cebu. Beaches dot the east coast. The **airport** spreads through much of the island and provides service to Cebu. **Jeepneys** leave from the S.M.City Mall in Cebu City and drop passengers at the jeepney terminal north of Lapu-Lapu City. (30-45 min., every 20 min. 4am-11pm, P5.) From Cebu City, A/C minibuses head to **Lapu-Lapu City** from the lot opposite the S.M. City Mall (25 min., P15). Metro Ferries leave Cebu City's Pier 3 for **Lapu-Lapu City** (45min., 6am-7:30pm, P10). Trips to beaches on **tricycle** require skillful negotiation (around P80). Alternatively, take a taxi from downtown Cebu directly to the beach (30min., P150). Airport services include a **tourist office** (☎340 8229, open M-F 8am-5pm); and a **post office** (open M-F 8am). **Postal code:** 6015.

ACCOMMODATIONS AND FOOD. The **Buyong Hotel and Restaurant** ❹ on Maribago Beach offers unpretentious abodes by Mactan standards. It has access to the sea but no beach. (☎492 0118. Doubles P500, with A/C P1200). The **White Sands** ❺ resort has rooms starting at US$70, but its share of Maribago Beach is unextrordinary. (☎340 5960; fax 340 5969; www.whitesands.com.ph.) Rooms at **Club Kon Tiki** ❺ (☎495 2434) start at US$30, but rates are negotiable for stays over one week and for students. Again, there is no beach, but guests can jump into the ocean from a sundeck. All these hotels have restaurants of their own. Alternatively, cheap and tasty seafood can be found at the **eateries** ❷ around the Lapu-Lapu Monument in Punta Engano (squid P100 per kg.).

SIGHTS AND DIVING. On the northeastern tip of the island in Punta Engano, the **Magellan Marker,** built in 1866, honors the explorer's death on April 27, 1521. The nearby **Lapu-Lapu Monument** commemorates the local hero (tricycle P50). Mactan's waters offer several dive sites. **Marigondon Cave** is the Philippines' largest underwater cave, recommended for advanced divers only; **Kon Tiki Reef** is suitable for all levels. The waters off Mactan are home to jet-skiing Japanese businessmen as well as snapper, tuna, and occasionally, shark. **Kon Tiki Divers,** next to the Kon Tiki Club, is a top-flight outfit. (☎495 2216; 7seas@mozcom.com. Dives US$20, nitrox dives US$28. Open-water courses US$300, advanced courses US$250. Ask Manfred about diving safaris.) The public beach at **Marigondon** offers everyone a taste of Mactan, on the rocks. A tricycle ride to Marigondon is P80 from Lapu-Lapu City and P50 from Maribago.

MOALBOAL ☎32

Sleepy Moalboal has attracted attention for its superb diving. Although ten years ago a typhoon devastated nearby reefs, alluring marine parks around uninhabited islands have remained intact. Reasonably priced diving, nearby outdoor adventures, and a laid-back, family-oriented expat community keep the huts full. Non-divers should note that there is no sand to be found here; beach bums might find Bantayan and Malapascua islands more to their liking.

TRANSPORTATION AND PRACTICAL INFORMATION. The town of Moalboal shares a peninsula with Panagsama and White Beach, 89km southwest of Cebu City on the opposite shore. Tricycle drivers make the 4km hop to **Panagsama Beach** (10min., P30). **Buses** to **Cebu** (2½hr., every 30min. 3am-8pm, P40) must be flagged down on the main drag. From Moalboal, ABC Liner buses continue south down the coast to **Bato** (2hr., P30), where rickety **ferries** make the short hop to **Tampi,** a port just a few km north of **Dumaguete.** PADI-certified dive instructors should inquire via email for **job openings** at any of the Moalboal dive shops. Travelers willing to work as English or German **teachers** for young children should inquire via email with Jochen Hanika (planet@han-grp.de). **Eve's Kiosk** has **currency exchange.** (Open daily 6:30am-9pm.) A **market** lines the left side of the road where the bus stops. The **post office** is in the municipal building at the end of the road. (Open M-F 8am-noon and 1-5pm.) There's a **telephone office** in back. (Open M-F 8am-noon and 1-8pm, Sa-Su 8am-noon and 1-5pm.) **Postal code:** 6032.

ACCOMMODATIONS AND FOOD. All accommodations are within walking distance of each other; accompanying **restaurants** ❸ serve fresh seafood for about P100-200. Ask about discounts if you dive with their shop. **Mollie's Place** ❷ is an immaculate backpacker's haven. (☎917 254 7060. Singles P100-150; doubles P200. AmEx/MC/V.) **Pacitas Beach Resort** ❸ bungalow offers private *nipa* huts. (☎919 858 2502. Call ahead Oct.-Mar. Doubles P350, with A/C P700.) **Marcosas Cottages** ❹ has gorgeous bungalows for P550. (☎474 0064.) Restaurants along the shore await hungry divers from Pescador. Feast on the Asian table BBQ (P135) while sipping a refreshingly bitter *Kalamansi* juice (P20) at the **Last Filling Station** ❸, which flanks the main path along the shore. With one of the largest menus in town including banana chocolate pancakes (P65) and *pancit canton* (P85), the **Little Corner Restaurant** ❷ (☎917 334 4096) is a little further north. European-inspired dishes such as fish in chablis sauce (P220) and elaborate crepes (P155-180) grace the tables of **Hannah's Place** ❸ at the north end of Panagsama Beach.

SIGHTS AND DIVING. Sun worshippers looking for a sandy beach will be disappointed, but bliss awaits divers. Several dive sites are accessible by a short *banca* trip. For the experienced diver, **Sunken Island** is the spot to see schools of tuna and large pelagics. The **Pescador Island Marine Park,** suitable for all divers, has vibrant coral life. **White Beach** has a coral wall that leads to a sunken airplane now piloted by turtles. Diving in Moalboal has an international feel: **Neptune Diving Adventure** (www.neptunediving.com) has a Swedish owner; **Visaya Divers** is run by a Californian expat. **Ocean Globe** is preferred by Japanese divers. **Savedra Dive Center's** (www.savedra.com) professional staff offer quality service. **Planet Action's** Jochen takes pride in finding adventure for his clients. He offers river climbing trips to **Kawasan Falls** (P900), mountain biking, canyoning, and caving expeditions in the jungles of Negros and Cebu (1-3 days US$25-120), as well as adventure tours specifically designed for kids (US$30). Prices vary little among the well-established dive centers. One dive goes for around US$20 (nitrox US$30). Open-water courses and advanced courses cost US$200-255. The **Orchid Gallery** (☎424 8058; orchidreto@rocketmail.com) in Moalboal, run by a British expat, is worth a visit.

BANTAYAN ISLAND ☎32

Just northwest of Hagnaya, Cebu, Bantayan Island is indeed magical—it's not just the locals' mystic beliefs in *aswang* (witches). Although dynamite fishing has blasted the hopes of would-be divers, it has left the beaches relatively *banca* free, a godsend for sunbathing purists. Aquanauts should head for nearby Malapascua, whose graceful thresher sharks have made it one of the Visaya's best-known dive sites. With few resorts and such potential, the island's lack of tourists is surprising, though not unwelcome for the travelers who do make it to the two main towns, Santa Fe and Bantayan.

TRANSPORTATION

Seair (☎438 5612) flies to **Cebu** (30min.; F 1:30pm, Su 3:30pm; P1005; 20% discount for students and senior citizens, 50% discount for children under 12). Bantayan is connected to Cebu by **Island Shipping Corp. ferries,** which depart from **Hagnaya** (1hr.; 4 per day 7:30am-6:30pm; P63, A/C P70-75) and land in **Santa Fe.** Buses run from Cebu City to **Hagnaya** (3hr., 6 per day, P60). When traveling from Santa Fe to **Hagnaya,** buy tickets on board (1hr., 4 per day 5:30am-2pm, P15). **Jeepneys** depart from the ferry pier to the market place in **Bantayan Town** (20min., every 20-30min. 6am-10pm, P10). The Island Shipping Corp. office in Bantayan Town is at the end of the road after City Hall. (☎352 5103. Open daily 8am-5pm.) It has service to **Cadiz** on Negros (2¼hr.; 9am; P200, tickets bought on board).

ORIENTATION AND PRACTICAL INFORMATION

Off Cebu's northwestern coast, Bantayan Island is a stepping stone to Negros and Panay. The main road connects southwestern **Bantayan Town** with southeastern **Santa Fe,** which is surrounded by beaches. For those who want to skip straight to coastal fishing communities, the road begins as **Pres. Osmeña St.** in central Bantayan Town. A trip by **dirtbike** to the northernmost community, **Madridejos,** takes 30-45min. **Nestor's Bike Rental,** on the main road in Santa Fe, rents out scooters (P150 per hr., P500 per half-day) and tricycles with a driver (P100 per hr.).

Allied Bank, on the corner of Osmeña and Escario St., cashes AmEx Traveler's Cheques. (☎352 5144. Open M-F 9am-4pm.) There are **no ATMs** on the island. The **police station** (☎352 5309) is in the town hall near the ferry pier. **Bantayan District Hospital** (☎352 5231) is 500m down the road to Santa Fe. The town hall hosts the **PLDT office** (☎198 5231; open M-Sa 8am-noon and 1-5pm) and the **post office** (open M-F 8-11:30am and 1-4pm). **Postal codes:** Bantayan Town 6052. Santa Fe 6047.

ACCOMMODATIONS AND FOOD

Santa Fe's resorts are far better than those in Bantayan, and there's no reason to stay in the latter. All resorts are a P5-10 tricycle ride from the Santa Fe pier. The decrease in tourism due to the terrorist activity in the Southern Philippines has left most resorts short on cash, so resorts give discounts for longer stays. The most comfort can be found at the intimate **Ogtong Cave Resort ❺.** (☎438 0031; travelvision@skyinet.net. Cottages with fan and bath P1440; family villas P2880-4000.) Along the main road in Santa Fe, **Budyong Beach Resort ❹** has more affordable bungalows on the nicest beach in the area. (☎438 9040. Cottages for two with fan P500, with A/C P1000.) North of the pier, Danish-managed **St. Bernard's Resort ❸** features 7 cottages and a small but pretty beach strip—a true bargain at P350-750.

Santa Fe has some very good food and, during the high seaon, a lively bar scene. **El Paso ❸,** on the 2nd floor of a cosy *nipa* hut, serves excellent Thai food (coconut soup P70, chicken *piri-piri* P170). **Little Moby Dick's** ❷ specializes in "volcano dishes," mountains of mashed potatoes with different meaty fillings (P120-140). **D'Jungle Bar** ❸ serves up German food (*Jagerschnitzel* P165, meatballs P150) and offers a dizzying assortment of alcoholic treats (P65-110).

SIGHTS AND ENTERTAINMENT

Beyond the sand and surf in Santa Fe, Bantayan's sights are slim. The nearby community often holds afternoon **cockfights** behind Little Moby Dick's. Follow the men with the roosters. **"Jungle discos"** happen spontaneously in the forest, where all ages groove to 70s classics. Ask a tricycle driver or the guest house staff for directions.

MALAPASCUA ISLAND ☎32

Off the northeastern tip of Cebu, this tiny speck captures travelers' attention as they cross from Cebu City to Boracay. Time seems to stand still on Malapascua's white beach; one might spend days reading in the shade of coconut trees, swimming in crystal-clear waters, or counting passing ships. Malapascua has become one of the Visayas' most popular dive destinations, its popularity fed by the regular appearance of thresher sharks in the channel between Cebu and Leyte.

The starting point from Cebu is Maya. **Bancas** head to **Malapascua** (10am and whenever full during the day, P50) and also ply the return journey (8am and whenever full during the day, P50). Chartered *bancas* can be hired anytime (around P500); from Santa Fe, hire one at a resort or at the pier (2hr., P1000-1500 per boat). Otherwise, take the **ferry** to **Hagnaya** (1hr., P60), a **tricycle** to **Bogo** (30min., P10), and then hop on a **bus** to **Maya** (1hr., P15). From there you can catch the scheduled trips or charter a *banca*. Certified PADI instructors and dive masters should check www.malapascua.net, **Exotic Divers'** web site, for job postings.

During low season, activity slows down, prices drop, and some establishments close. Almost all accommodations are along **Bounty Beach,** which is also the *banca* drop-off point. **Cocobana Beach Resort** ❺ has spacious waterfront and garden cottages with fan, bath, and breakfast included. Check out their floating bar. (☎0918 775 2942 or 437 1040. Waterfront P1080 high season, P960 low season; garden P780/P600.) Next door, the **Malapascua Bluewater Resort** ❹ also has beachfront cottages, "garden rooms," and small rooms. (☎0919 481 8166 or 437 1053. Beachfront P1000 high season, P800 low season; garden P800/P600; small room P500.) A little farther down Bounty Beach, **Peder Baadsmand** ❹ resort rents out small but attractive rooms with balconies and hammocks for only P550.

With specialties including crepes (P40-80), pasta (P130-185), and pizza (P140-195), **Sunsplash** ❸ (☎0919 633 3654 or 437 0982), next to the Cocobana, has great Euro-Filipino food and a floating bar to boot. Right behind it, **Ging Ging's Eatery** ❶ (☎1918 877 7765.), run by a mother and her children, serves up excellent curries (P45-60) and fresh seafood; try the squid with *pancit canton* (P45).

Several dive shops have cropped up along the beach, capitalizing on thresher-mania. Dutch-owned **Exotic Divers,** at the far end of the beach, is a well-established operation which runs daily shark-watching excursions to Monod Point.

BOHOL

In the heart of the Boholano forest, the tarsier swivels its head and leaps from tree to tree, clinging with elongated suction-cup fingers. Just north of its home, the majestic Chocolate Hills pop out of the flat landscape and offer unparalleled sunrises and sunsets. Off southwest Panglao Island, porpoises and whales slip through world-class diving reefs in the Mindanao Sea. Luckily for Bohol, tourists who come to enjoy this island have not much altered the Boholano lifestyle, which, along with its many beaches, remains undisturbed.

THE VIEW FROM ABOVE

Main towns: Carmen, Tagbilaran.
Highlights: Diving off the coast, swimming with dolphins, or just lounging on the Panglao Island beaches.
Something sweet: North of Tagbilaran, the Chocolate Hills might be your true soul food.

TAGBILARAN ☎38

The rulers of the Bohol Kingdom once used Panglao Island, off the southeastern coast of Bohol, to hide from the *Bilaan*, Muslim raiders who swept north from Mindanao. Modern-day marauders find little in Tagbilaran but telephones, Internet terminals, and ATMs. Once these are plundered, you can explore the island's inspiring interior without getting entangled in the city.

TRANSPORTATION

Flights: Tagbilaran airport, 1.5km north of the city. **Asian Spirit** (☎235 3541; www.asianspirit.com) flies to **Cebu** (8:20am daily, 2:10pm M, F, Su; P515) and **Manila** (9am daily, 2:30pm M, F, Su; P2684). Several ticketing offices on Carlos P. Garcia Ave. handle reservations. Tricycle from the airport into town P5.

Boats: The ferry pier extends from the northwest part of the city. Walking along the pier, turn right onto Gallares St. to head into town (1km). Take a tricycle to Tagbilaran center (5-10min., P4) or directly to **Alona Beach** on Panglao Island (1¼hr., P100). Ferries are operated by 4 companies with offices in the terminal (open 5am-9pm); all grant a 15% student discount. Tickets for all lines at **Alboitz Express office,** on Gallares St. next to Holy Name University. **Supercat** (☎411 4906; www.supercat.com.ph) goes to: **Cebu** (1½hr., 3 per day, P380); **Dapitan** (4hr., 10am, P680); **Dumaguete** (1½hr., 2 per day, P420); and **Larena** (3hr., 5:15pm, P545). **WG&A** (☎411 3048) departs to: **Cagayan de Oro** (4hr., Sa midnight, P370); **Dipolog** (3hr., Su 9am, P350); **Dumaguete** (2hr., W 8am, P280); and **Manila** (29hr.; M, W 10am; P1185). **Oceanjet** leaves for **Cebu** four times daily (2hr., P390). **Sulpicio Lines** departs for: **Iligan** (3hr., Th 8pm, P325) via **Dipolog** (2hr., P262); and **Manila** (27hr., M 6pm, P976). Ferries to **Siquijor** (M, W, F 7pm; P150); purchase tickets on the pier.

Buses: Dao Integrated Bus Terminal serves all of Bohol's major sights. Take a jeepney from Grupo St. or any marked "Dao" or "Int. Bus Terminal" (15-20min., P4). Buses to: **Baclayon** (15-20min., P5); **Bilar** (1½hr., P20); **Carmen** (2hr., every hr. 4am-5:30pm, P60), passing the **Chocolate Hills Complex** (6km before Carmen proper); **Loboc** (45min., P25); **Loon** (45min., P25). Buses marked "Talibon; Tubigon" follow the north-coast road to **Maribojoc** (25min., every 30min. 4am-6:30pm, P10).

Jeepneys: Leave from **Grupo St.** near Jacinto St. and from the **Cogon Public Market.** They go north to Punta Cruz in **Maribojoc** (40min., every 45min. 7am-5pm, P10) and south from **Dao Integrated Bus Terminal** to the Blood Compact site in **Bool** (5-10min., 7am-5pm, P5) on their way to **Baclayon** (20min., P5). Flag down a jeepney leaving from Boholand near the cathedral in Tagbiliran. Those marked "Panglao" head to **Doljo Beach** (45min., every hr. 7am-5pm, P15). Those marked with the number 80 or "Panglao-Tawala" pass **Alona Beach** but stop running by 4pm (P15-25).

Tricycles: P3-5 per trip in town. To **Panglao** (P100-150).

Rentals: Most hotels and pension houses can organize a rental car with driver (P1500-1800 per day).

FROM THE ROAD

ISLAND OF SPIRITS

I do not believe in ghosts, spirits, black or white magic. Growing up with the German culture's emphasis on the factual certainty of empirical science and pursuing an academic subject that attempts to determine even human irrationality as exactly as possible, I have trouble facing popular superstition without a trace of condescension on my face.

During my stay on Siquijor Island, I had the chance to take part in a ceremony to assuage angry spirits that had inflicted harm on an inhabitant of the island.

For me, this was the most interesting display of superstition I had ever encountered. Also, it was a challenge for me to take seriously the way in which the people who invited me chose to treat this life-or-death situation.

While he was building a shack on his grounds, the man for whom the ceremony was performed had carelessly picked up a few rocks that were lying around and thrown them down a slope adjacent to his house. Shortly after this incident, the man fell gravely ill and was admitted to a hospital on Negros.

The conclusion that his family drew from this unfortunate occurrence was that the rocks were inhabited by supernatural beings who had been offended by his casual disrespect when he threw them down the slope. Therefore, the supernatural spirits had taken their revenge on him by causing him to become deathly ill.

The family invited a healer to come all the way from Mindanao to Siquijor

(continued on next page)

ORIENTATION AND PRACTICAL INFORMATION

Tagbilaran, on the southwestern tip of Bohol, guards the narrow strait separating **Bohol** and **Panglao.** From the pier, **Gallares St.** follows the shore and terminates at **St. Joseph's Cathedral** and **City Hall.** In front of the cathedral, **Plaza Rizal** is bounded on the other side by **Carlos P. Garcia (CPG) Ave.,** Tagbilaran's main commercial street, on which you can find the **tourist office** (☎411 3666; open M-F 8am-8pm) opposite the **Bohol Quality** department store. Come here to book whale-watching excursions or arrange for a tour of the Chocolate Hills (guided full-day tour P1500). **Metrobank** is just down the street. (☎411 2405. Open M-F 9am-4pm.) On the opposite side of the street is **Mercury Drug Pharmacy.** (Open daily 7am-9pm.) Private **Ramiro Hospital** (☎411 3515) is on Gallares St., on the way to the pier. There are **Internet cafes** (P20-30 per hr.) all over town, especially along Lesage St., near Divine World College. The **post office** is behind the cathedral. (Open M-F 8am-noon and 1-5pm.) **Postal code:** 6300.

ACCOMMODATIONS AND FOOD

Tagbilaran has a number of cheap, forgettable budget accommodations. **Slim Pension House ❹,** on F.R. Ingles St. behind the Agora market, is the best value in town. (☎411 4858. Singles with A/C P480; doubles P620.) On CPG Ave., rooms in the friendly, tidy **Nisa's Traveler's Inn ❷** are a good value for the price. (Singles with fan P140; doubles P160, with A/C and bath P500.) The entrance is in a shopping arcade right next to the Bohol Quality Complex. The **Everglory Hotel ❸** on C. Gallares St., overlooking the pier, has decent rooms with a good view of the harbor. (☎411 3200. Singles P350, with view P400, with A/C P500.)

Seafood is the passion here, and if it's not on the pier, it's not considered fresh. With delicious kinilaw (P95) and marinated octopus (P50), **M-R Seafood ❷** occupies a prime location—on a triangle of mango trunks in front of the pier. (Open daily 6am-10pm.) The usual fast-food joints and eateries crowd the center of town. Check out the **night market ❶** next to the Bohol Quality Complex for cheap, tasty barbecues (P15-30).

DAYTRIPS FROM TAGBILARAN

THE CHOCOLATE HILLS

The Chocolate Hills are Bohol's signature attraction. The terrain is certainly unique, though whether the Hills live up to the tourist hype is questionable. Geologists believe that the 1268 coral and limestone mounds, which mysteriously materialize out of the relatively flat paddy land, have been sculped into this bizarre topography by eons of erosion.

The hills are best viewed from **Carmen,** 59km northeast of Tagbilaran. The only truly acceptable place to stay for the full dawn spectacle is on top of one of the hills themselves. The **Chocolate Hills Complex** perches atop the tallest hill 6km before Carmen; make sure the driver knows your destination. (Doubles P250-800; triples P350-800; extra person P200.) The **observation patio,** 214 steps up from the complex, is the highest point in the hills. (☎0912 856 1559. Admission P10. Open daily 6am-9pm.) Motorcyclists congregate at the turn-off to the complex and take you on a meandering tour back to Tagbilaran, stopping to see the sights along the way. (Half-day P600 for two.) Visit **Nuts Huts** (walterken@hotmail.com), 3km after Loboc on the road to Carmen; a sign on the left indicates a dirt road turn-off, and it's 750m down the road. Nuts Huts has beautiful *nipa* huts on the Loboc River surrounded by lush forest. It's a relaxed backpacker hangout and a base for adventure activities. Enjoy breathtaking views and imaginative Euro-Asian cuisine at the hilltop **restaurant ❸** (Filipino "curry" P120), or clear your head in the herbal steam sauna. Ask Walter, Chris, or Rita about mountain biking, hiking, or river swimming. (Dorm beds P165; cottages P385; larger cottages P550.)

BETWEEN TAGBILARAN AND CARMEN

A few historically significant sights are right around Tagbilaran and are worth a quick hop off the van or jeepney. Bool and Baclayan are accessible by any eastbound jeepney leaving Tagbilaran (P10). **Bool,** 3km away, boasts a small roadside memorial to the **Blood Compact Site,** where Miguel Lopez de Legazpi swore a blood oath of friendship with Chieftain Datu Sikatuna in 1565. Farther down the coastal road is the Philippines' first church, **Baclayon Church,** built in 1596. Next door, the convent houses a centuries-long accumulation of religious relics. (Open M-Sa 8:15am-noon and 1:30-5pm, Su 9:30am-noon and 1:30-4:30pm; P20.) **Maribojoc** is home to the the watchtower **Punta Cruz,** built by the Spanish in 1796. **Jeepneys** leave Tag-

(continued from previous page)

to perform a sacrifice to appease these angry rock dwellers and save the sick man.

But the ceremony was not limited merely to the man's immediate family. In fact, not only was I, a foreigner, invited, but the whole *barangay* (community) was also asked to participate in order to assist the healer's efforts with Christian prayers. Seamlessly, two spiritual worlds–one Christian, one pagan–met in this ceremony.

As part of the sacrifice, more than 10 different delicacies were put out on the site where the rocks had lain before the man had thrown them as if inviting the spirits back to their home. A roasted pig, slaughtered for the occasion, was among these savory offerings to placate the spirits.

The healer murmured words I could not understand. But at the same time, he seemed attuned to his surroundings–listening carefully as if trying to establish a dialogue with supernatural troublemakers.

The ceremony lasted about half an hour, after which the participants retired to the family home to enjoy the rest of the freshly roasted pork. Unfortunately, I had to continue my route before any news arrived about whether the sacrifice had achieved its goal of curing the man's illness.

Nonetheless, participating in this fascinating ritual made me question my usual assumptions about the ineffectiveness of superstition and magic in the face of the strength of these people's belief.

–Kristina Vetter

bilaran for Maribojoc daily, passing the tower (40min., 7am-5pm, P10).

Rajah Sikatuna National Park, south of the Chocolate Hills, covers 9000 hectares of molave forest and grasslands honeycombed with caves (P20). Among the animals inhabiting the park is the petite **tarsier,** the world's smallest primate. To get there, take a Carmen-bound bus from the Integrated Bus Terminal; get out at the market in **Bilar** (1hr., P18). From there, hire a motorcycle (P1) or pedicab (P10) to cover the few kilometers to **Camp Magsaysay.** The park is best visited with plenty of time and your own transportation, so unless you've got an obsessive interest in tarsier habitats, it is best skipped altogether. Before going, groups should contact the National Park (☎032 411 2357). *Nipa* cottages are available for rent (P100), and camping is possible (P50). The Logarita Spring-fed **swimming pool,** 2.5km from the Bilar market, is available for your bathing pleasure (P5).

The best and most humane place to view the tarsier is at the **Philippine Tarsier Breeding Center** in Carella. It is 11km west of Loboc; take a jeepney bound for **Sikatuna** (P10). The Breeding Center is 2km past Sikatuna on the right. At **Supercarp's,** you can commandeer a small *banca* (local crew included) to head upriver to a waterfall that is ideal for swimming (15min., P500). The second oldest stone church in the Philippines, **St. Peter's Church** in Loboc stands as a monument to Filipino piety. The unfinished bridge across the river is a monument to American presumptuousness. US engineers began the bridge on the assumption that locals wouldn't mind dismantling their church. They minded, and construction halted.

NEAR TAGBILARAN: PANGLAO ISLAND

With exquisite sand beaches and first-class diving, Panglao Island has much to offer travelers of every stripe; it is arguably the Visayas' best beach destination. Underwater fanatics dominate **Alona Beach,** the most developed of the island's beaches. For more seclusion, escape to **Doljo Beach.** Either way, arrange to watch the magnificent whales cavorting off Panglao's southern coast.

The well-paved central road connects Panglao in the west with Bohol and the new bridge. Most amenities can be found only in Tagbilaran. Few roads are paved, so allow for extra travel time. International calls can be made from hotels or from the **PLDT** in Panglao. (☎198 8109. Open daily 7am-10pm.) **Jeepneys** passing Alona Beach go to Panglao (15min., P4) but don't go back; return by **tricycle** (15min., P40). **Dirt bikes** are for rent along Alona Beach (P100 per hr., P600 per day).

All of the following accommodations are near each other on Alona Beach, except for the Palm Island Beach Resort on Doljo beach. Most lodgings have an attached restaurant, but exploring waterfront eateries is a tasty option. Prices rise during the high season. No shoes are allowed upstairs at **Peter's House ❸,** which has delicious pizza (P100-140) and exotic rooms in a beautiful three-story *nipa* house. (☎502 9056. Singles with fan P400; doubles P550; discounts for divers.) Down the beach, the **Alona Kew White Beach Resort ❺** has private beach facilities and cottages within a well-tended garden. (☎502 9042; kewbeach@mozcom.com; www.bohol-info.com/alonakew.html. Cottages with fan P850-1000, with A/C P1900-2200.) The cheapest option on the beach is the centrally located **Alonaville Beach Resort ❷.** (Doubles P200; cottages for two with fan P600/P500.)

For the best diving, head to **Balicasag Island,** southwest of Doljo Point. **Black Forest** is an excellent site for drift-diving, where black coral can be found. **Pamalican Island** is known as the "nesting place of manta rays," and **Doljo Beach,** on the other side of Panglao, has rich coral walls. Dive shops along **Alona Beach** go to every hot spot and offer the entire range of PADI courses. (US$34 per dive; open-water courses US$300; advanced open-water US$195-220.) Friendly **Genesis Divers** (☎502 9056), owned by Peter's House, is a notch above the rest.

Whales save their best performances for early birds, but hyperactive dolphins perform at the drop of a hat. Ask your guest house about chartering a boat. The shoreline also yields numerous locals with idle *bancas*. Organized tours leave **Bacloyan Pier** east of Tagbilaran City and cruise to **Pamalican Island.** (☎540 9279. 3-person boat P600 per person; 7-person boat P500 per person.)

NEGROS

When Spanish missionaries deemed the mountains of Negros too formidable to traverse, even for the glory of God, they split the island into two halves. Vibrant Dumaguete, a lone Protestant outpost in a sea of Catholicism and the capital of Negros Oriental, is a great base for exploring the lush jungle around Mt. Kanla-on and the untouched volcanic Apo Island. The plains of Negros Occidental, with spotless Bacolod as their capital, are known for their sugar crops, but the world-wide sugar market crash has devastated that industry. The jarring economic conditions have contributed to the rise in popularity of the communist New People's Army (NPA), an active force in the area.

THE VIEW FROM ABOVE

Major Cities: Bacolod and Dumaguete.
Nearby islands: Apo Island, Siquijor Islands.
Beaches: Head south to Apo Island for, yup, you guessed it, another great dive.
Something big: Mt. Kanla-on is the tallest peak in the Central Philippines.

BACOLOD ☎34

Bacolod is the business center of Negros Island, but the quiet little town offers plenty of attractions for tourists, too. Apart from its convenient location across the Guimaras Straight from Panay, Bacolod boasts great food and a lively bar and club scene. The city sits in the heartland of Negros's once thriving sugar industry. The island's historic wealth is preserved in the excellent Negros Museum and in the fading grandeur of the sugar baron's *haciendas* in Silay and Victorias. South of the city, Mt. Kanla-on rises dramatically from the sugar cane fields, a challenge to be taken on only by the hardiest trekkers.

TRANSPORTATION

Flights: The **airport** is south of the city, on Araneta St. Taxis to/from airport P50. To go downtown, flag down a jeepney marked "Pta. Taytay—Central Market" (P4). **PAL** (☎835 29), in the main terminal, flies to **Manila** (1hr., 3 per day, P3061). **Air Philippines** ticketing is opposite the main terminal (☎433 9211; open M-Sa 8:30am-4:30pm); the downtown office is in Victorina Arcade on Rizal St. near the plaza (☎433 9570; open M-Sa 8:30am-6pm). To **Cebu** (30min., daily, P1293) and **Manila** (1hr., daily, P2743). **Cebu Pacific**'s terminal (☎434 2052) is near Air Philippines' ticketing office; the downtown office (☎434 2020; open daily 9am-5:30pm) is on Rizal St. near the plaza. To **Cebu** (30min., daily, P1879) and **Manila** (1hr., 3 per day, P2779). All airlines offer a 20% discount to students and senior citizens. There are often additional promotions—inquire at travel agencies in town.

Buses: Ceres North Terminal, on Lopez Jaena St. near the corner of B.S. Aquino Dr. (15min. by taxi from city center, P30). To: **Cadiz** (1½hr., P34); **Cebu City** (7-8hr.; 1, 5:45, 9:30, 9:45am; P115-140) via **Toledo; Dumaguete** (8hr., 8 per day 3am-midnight, P167) via **Silay** (20min., P8); **San Carlos** (4hr., every 30min. 4am-7:30pm, P77); **Victorias** (30-40min., P10). **Public North Bus Terminal,** a few meters down Lopez Jaena St., has buses and jeepneys to **Cadiz** (1½hr., every hr. 6am-7pm, P25) and **San Carlos** (4hr., every hr. 4am-4pm, P60) via **Victorias.** Down Lopez Jaena St., at the Luzuriaga and San Sebastian St. intersection, **Public South Bus Terminal** has buses to: **Candoni** (3hr., 8 per day 4am-3pm, P56); **Canlaon** (3½hr., every hr. 4am-4pm, P60); **Dumaguete** (5hr., 6 per day 5:30am-4pm, P190); **Hinoba-an** (6hr., 12 per day 3am-10pm, P110); **Kabankalan** (2hr., 8 per day 6am-8:45pm, P58). Jeepneys leave from opposite Robinson's Mall for: **Cadiz** (P30); **Silay** (P10); **Victorias** (P12).

Ferries: All shipping lines grant a 15% discount for students, a 20% discount for senior citizens, and half-fare for ages 4-11. Passenger ferries leave from **Banago Port,** several miles north of the center of town. **Bullet Express** (☎432 0118; open daily 6am-5pm) goes to **Iloilo** (1hr.; 4-5 per day, last trip 5pm; P160). **Negros Navigation** runs to **Cagayan de Oro** (14hr., Tu 7pm, P1270) and **Manila** (18-24hr., 5 per week, P1355). The **branch office** (☎432 3627; open M-Sa 8:30am-5pm), at the corner of Rizal and Gatuslao St., sells Negros Navigation and **SeaAngels** tickets. A complimentary **shuttle** to Banago leaves 4, 3, and 2hr. before scheduled departure times from the Ceres North Terminal and the Public South Bus Terminal. **SuperCat** (main office ☎434 2350; terminal ☎441 0659) runs speedy ferries to **Iloilo** (1hr., 4 per day 6am-3:15pm, P240). Another **branch** next to Negros Navigation at 6th St. off Lacson St. Open M-F 8am-5pm, Sa 8am-noon. **WG&A** (☎435 4965) sends ferries to **Cagayan de Oro** (13hr., F 9pm, P1270) and **Manila** (21hr.; W 3:30pm, Su 2pm; P1325).

Jeepneys: Intra-city jeepney routes: "Pta. Taytay-Central Market" to **airport;** "Bata" and "Mandalagan" pass **Negros Museum** to **Robinson's Mall** (15min., P4); "Shopping" to **Ceres bus terminals;** "Libertad" to **Libertad Market.** For **Mambukal,** take a jeepney from Libertad Market (2hr., every 15min. 7am-9pm, P20).

Taxis: Fares start at P25. To the airport P50. To Banago ferry pier P50.

ORIENTATION AND PRACTICAL INFORMATION

Bacolod is on the northwestern tip of Negros Occidental. The **ferry pier** sits west of the **plaza. Lacson St.** bisects the city. Three blocks closer to the coast, **Araneta St.** begins at the plaza and continues south to the airport. Between the two, **Gatuslao St.** passes the post office and Negros Museum. **Burgos St.** intersects Lacson and Araneta St. and ends at the ferry pier. In the east, Burgos St. cuts across **Lopez Jaena St.,** which hosts the **bus terminals.**

Tourist Offices: City Tourism Office (☎434 6571), in Bacolod Plaza. Open M-F 8am-noon and 1-5pm. **Provincial Tourism Office** (☎433 2515), in the provincial government complex, north of the lagoon near the Negros Museum. Tina will help facilitate your travels. Open M-F 8am-5pm.

Budget Travel: Manna Travel Agency (☎433 9204; mannatrvl@yahoo.com), on San Juan St. near the plaza. Open M-Sa 9am-6pm.

Immigration Office: (☎433 8581), on Luzuriaga St. near San Juan. Visa extensions P2020-3000. Bring your passport. No shorts or sandals. Open M-F 8am-5pm.

Banks: BPI Bank (☎434 2751), on Araneta St. near the San Sebastian intersection. **24hr. ATM.** Accepts Cirrus/MC. Open M-F 9am-3pm.

Luggage Storage: Daytime storage at the tourist office in Bacolod Plaza.

Markets: Fruit vendors line Ballesteros, **barbecue grills** clutter Gatuslao on the corner of Hernadez and Mabini St., and the **Libertad Market** has fresh fish and produce.

Emergency: Police ☎166. **Fire** ☎161. **Ambulance** ☎166.

Police: There is a **PNP** office (☎434 8776) next to the City Tourism Bldg. in the Plaza.

Pharmacy: Mercury Drug (☎433 6604), on the corner of Araneta and Luzuriaga St. Open daily 7am-10pm.

Hospitals: Riverside Medical Center (☎433 7331), on B.S. Aquino Dr. in the northern part of the city.

Telephones: PLDT (☎433 6700), on Galo off Lacson St. Booths close at 4:30pm. Open M-F 8am-noon and 1-5pm.

Internet Access: Cyberworld, on Araneta St. near the Plaza. P30 per hr. Open daily 9am-midnight.

Post Office: (☎433 0436), on Gatuslao St. near intersection with Burgos St. *Poste Restante*. Open M-F 8am-noon and 1-5pm, Sa 8:30-11:30am. **Postal code:** 6100.

ACCOMMODATIONS

Pension Bacolod (☎433 7842), 11th St. on corner of Hilado St. This backpacker haven in a clean, quiet part of town is an excellent value. Cafe and restaurant (shrimp *sinigang* P79.50, breakfast combo P48.50). Singles P95-195, with A/C P330; doubles P155-238/P395; triples P225-290. MC/V with 10% surcharge. ❶

Business Inn, 28 S. Lacson St. (☎433 8877; fax 434 2114; businn@bed.i-next.net). Room service. Laundry service. Business center with Internet and fax. The cafe has a great all-you-can-eat breakfast buffet for P165. Hierarchical doubles range from the P790 "Junior Executive" to the P1790 "Chairman." ❺

King's Hotel (☎433 0572), on Gatuslao St. at the corner of San Sebastian. Gleaming rooms. A/C, telephone, private common room. Doubles P750. MC/V with 8% surcharge. ❺

Hotel Las Rocas (☎434 1578), on Gatuslao St. between Galo and Rizal St. near the public plaza. A bit run-down, but with a TV in every room. Doubles with fan, private common room, and bath P183-295, with A/C P350-500. ❷

FOOD

For quality and ambience, head to the **Goldenfield Commercial Complex,** which has bistros and cafes, or hit the area of **Lacson St.** between 20th and 24th St. **Cyberazia** ❷, on the corner of 22nd and Lacson St., is an Internet cafe and trendy neon bar. (Wings P70. Internet P25 per hr. Open M-Sa 9am-2am.) Nearby **Chicken House** ❶, on Lacson St. at the corner of 24th St., proves that not all chicken is created equal. Try the *pecho* (breast) or *paa* (thigh) for P45. (Open daily 10am-11pm.) The central **market** ❶ downtown offers sweet delicacies, including *piyaya* (hardened crêpe with melted sugar) and *bay ibayi* (sugar and coconut in a coconut half shell). For excellent Japanese food at bargain prices (by Western standards), try **Inaka** ❹ on Lacson St., near the 22nd St. intersection. (☎434 4045. Sushi P35-495, tempura P85. Open daily 10:30am-2pm and 6-10:30pm.)

SIGHTS AND ENTERTAINMENT

Nearly everything in the **Negros Museum,** in the Old Capitol Building, relates to the colonial sugar industry. (☎434 9505. Open M-Sa 9am-6pm. P30, students P20.) The **Old Capitol Building,** built in 1921, sprawls from Gatuslao to Lacson St. Across the street from the Negros Museum is the Negros Forest and Ecological Foundation's **Biodiversity Center.** The center is devoted to preserving what remains of Negros's indigenous flora and fauna. (Open M-Sa 10am-5pm.) The third week of October sees the celebration of the **Masskara Festival,** a melange of Mardi Gras and Rio party styles. In the Goldenfield Commercial Complex, **bars** and **karaoke joints** galore stay open daily from 9pm to 2am. **Quorum,** near the back of the complex at the Kundutel, is an enormous arena with space-tech flair. (Cover P100. Beer P35.)

DAYTRIPS FROM BACOLOD

MT. KANLA-ON NATURAL PARK

Take a jeepney from Bacolod to Mambukal (1½hr., every 30min. 7:20am-9pm, P25). The last jeepney back to Bacolod leaves Mambukal at 5pm. Guides cost around P500 per day; package deals run about P4000 for two climbers including equipment, food, and transport. To secure a permit and find accredited guides, tourists should consult the tourist office in Bacolod, or check out the Mt. Kanla-on Natural Park Bacolod Liaison Office in the Department of Environmental and Natural Resources office in the Penro Compound on Gatuslao St. near the Hall of Justice. (☎434 7769. Open M-F 8am-5pm.) Permits to explore the park and climb the volcano P300.

The tallest peak in the Central Philippines (2465m), Mt. Kanla-on offers challenge, natural beauty, and danger. Two expeditions got caught in a 1996 eruption; one British trekker and two Filipino guides died. Its unique structure consists of a small active opening on the southwestern edge of the larger collapsed caldera of the original volcano, also called the Margaja Valley. The rainy season creates a small lake inside this caldera. The surrounding rainforest is home to striking wildlife. The trails within 4km of the summit are treacherous during the rainy season (Jan.-Mar. and July-Sept.). During these months, the mountain is closed for safety and to allow for the peaceful mating of the non-human animals. The best entrance point into the park is from the **Mambukal Mountain Resort ❹,** near many hot springs and waterfalls. (☎433 8887. 2-person cottages P500; 4-person cottages P800.)

SILAY AND VICTORIAS

To either town, take a bus connecting Bacolod with Cadiz (Bacolod to Silay 20min., every 30min. 4am-7pm, P8; to Victorias 30-40min., P10) or a jeepney from opposite Robinson's Mall (P10).

Silay and Victorias are the centers of Negros's sugar industry. Silay, the "Paris of Negros," is also known for its arts and culture. Enthusiasts come for the sugar trains, and most find the "Angry Christ" rewarding, too. In Silay, hop on a jeepney at the corner of Rizal and Severino St. (10min., P4) to get to the **Hawaiian Philippines Sugar Corp.** (☎495 3200) and see the sugar trains. A letter of introduction from the Silay tourist office is recommended. The best time to visit the Sugar Corp. is in the tourist season from Oct. to May. Sandals and shorts are not allowed. *Bagasse*, a by-product of sugar production, fuels the "iron dinosaurs." The **Balay Negrenses Museum** is on Cinco de Noviembre St. near the corner of McKinley St. Attendants claim French sugar baron Yves Léopold Gaston built the house in 1898 from a single tree trunk. (☎495 4916. Open Tu-Su 10am-5pm. P30, students P10.) On National Rd., two blocks beyond the plaza on the right is the **Bernardino-Ysabel Jalandoni Ancestral House,** Silay's other museum, which documents the lifestyle of a leading sugar baron and his family. (☎495 5093. Open Tu-Su 8am-noon, 1-5pm. P20, students P10.) The **Tourism and Cultural Arts Office,** in the City Hall opposite the plaza, can point out ancestral homes and sights and give you the low-down on the **Kansilay Festival** held November 5-13. (☎495 0661. Open M-F 8am-noon and 1-5pm.)

Don't miss the **El Ideal Bakery** on the corner of National Rd. and Zulueta St. near the plaza. El Ideal satiates Silay's sweet tooth with local treats like *lumpia ubod* (fresh spring rolls) and *piaya* (sesame cakes).

The **Victorias Milling Company, Inc. (Vicmico)** is the largest sugar mill in Asia. It is accessible from the main road in Victorias by jeepney. Grab the one marked "VMC" at the corner of Osmeña and Jover St. (10min., every 30min. 5:30am-8:30pm, P3). Ask to be let off at the **Vicmico Public Relations Office** on Ossorio Rd. below the Personnel Building. Tours can be arranged at the factory and the

Church of St. Joseph the Worker, but call ahead. (☎399 3002. Open Tu-F 7am-noon and 1-4pm. Tours 30-40min.; M-F 9am and 2pm; P15, students P5.) Vicmico's real attraction is the **Church of St. Joseph the Worker** and its mural, known as the "Angry Christ," where Jesus sits in front of the hands of God, straddling a serpent-spewing skull. No miniskirts, shorts, or sleeveless shirts are allowed.

DUMAGUETE ☎35

The "City of Gentle People" guards its peace carefully. The capital of Negros Oriental, Dumaguete also serves as a haven from turbulent Mindanao to the south and the alleged witchcraft of nearby Siquijor Island. It is also a convenient springboard for exploring Siquijor or lovely Apo Island, which shelters some of the finest diving in the country. The energy of Dumaguete's student population combats the relaxed atmosphere of the beautiful waterfront in a city that has a little bit of it all.

TRANSPORTATION

Flights: To get to the **airport,** take Dumaguete North Rd. off Silliman Ave. **Air Philippines** (☎225 4266) is at the airport and the ticket outlet is in the **Honeycomb Tourist Inn** (☎225 9826). Open M-F 9am-noon and 1-4:30pm. Daily flights to **Manila** (7:30am and 2:50pm, P2493). **Cebu Pacific** (☎225 8802) also flies daily to **Manila** (3:30pm, P2094); purchase tickets at the airport or from a travel agent in town.

Buses: Dumaguete Ceres Terminal is in the south of the city across the river on Calindagan South Rd. Follow Perdices St. (tricycle P2.50). To: **Bacolod** via **Cadiz** (6hr., P110); **Kaban Kalan** (5hr., every hr. 4am-10pm, P112); **San Carlos** (7hr., every hr. 3am-11pm, P130). Buses going north stop at **Ceres Sub Terminal Northbound** near the ferry pier. Walking away from the pier, take a right up Flores St. Terminal; it's 5min. up on the right. Locals call the area **"Looc." Royal Express Bus Terminal** (☎225 2234) sends buses to **Bacolod** (5hr., 6am and 2pm, P164) via **Mabinay** (2hr., P70).

Ferries: The **pier** is at the north end of Rizal Ave. Shipping companies send representatives to pier area 1hr. before departure. There is a P15 terminal fee for all ferries. 15% student discount. **Supercat** sends daily ferries to **Cebu** (2½hr., 4:15pm, P500) via **Tagbilaran** (1½hr., P410); and **Larena** on Siquijor (45min., 7:15pm, P170). **Express** office (☎225 0735) on Ma. Christina St. behind the Metrobank Branch. Open M-Sa 8am-noon and 1-5pm. The branch office (☎225 5799) is near the pier opposite Ceres Sub Terminal in Looc. **Delta Fast Ferries** (☎225 3128) whisks passengers to **Larena** on Siquijor (45min.; 9:15am, 1:30, 4:30pm; P110). The ticket outlet is in the **Gold Label Bakeshoppe** on Perdices St. Open M-Sa 7:30am-noon and 1-7pm. **WG&A** (☎225 3538) sends ferries to **Cagayan de Oro** (6hr., F 6am, P500) and **Manila** (25hr.; W 5pm, Sa 9am; P1345). WG&A tickets can be purchased at Supercat offices. **Negros Navigation** cruises to **Manila** (24hr., Sa 5:30pm, P1295). Ferries leave from Tampi, several kilometers north of Dumaguete, for the quick hop to **Bato** on Cebu, a short ride from Moalboal (1hr., leaves when full, P50).

Local Transportation: Tricycles P3.50-5.

ORIENTATION AND PRACTICAL INFORMATION

Downtown is easily navigable by foot. **Rizal Ave.** borders the coast connecting the ferry pier in the north with roads heading inland. Silliman University sprawls north of nearby **Silliman Ave.,** which runs west from the shore. Originating at Silliman Ave., **Perdices St.** bisects the city, heads south, crosses the **Banica River,** and ends at the main bus terminals. **Dr. V. Locsin St.** intersects Perdices midway through downtown; the market, park, and post office are a few blocks south.

Tourist Office: ☎225 0549. In the city hall complex near the corner of Colon and Santa Catalina St. Open M-F 8am-noon and 1-5pm.

Budget Travel: Maganda Travel and Tours (☎225 8256), on the corner of Dr. V. Locsin and Santa Catalina St. Visa extension service, airline ticketing, and tour packages. P500 service charge over standard fares. Open M-F 8:30am-5pm, Sa 8:30am-4pm.

Immigration Office: 38 Dr. V. Locsin St., door 9, Lu Pega Bldg. (☎225 4401). Passport and visa extensions. First 59-day extension P3790; P1820 for all subsequent extensions. Open M-F 8am-noon and 1-5pm.

Currency Exchange: PCI Bank (☎225 4787), on the corner of Perdices and Legaspi St. Cashes traveler's checks. **24hr. ATM** (Cirrus/MC). Open M-F 9am-3pm.

English-Language Bookstore: The Old San Francisco Bookstore (☎225 8230), on Real St. opposite the provincial capitol. Used books, paperbacks P50-60. Open M-Sa 9:30am-7:30pm.

Emergency: ☎116 or 166. **Fire:** ☎160.

Police: Philippine National Police (☎225 1766), at the corner of Cervantes and Locsin St.

Pharmacy: Mercury Drug (☎225 0425), on Colon St. opposite the fish market. The largest of many. Open daily 6am-10pm. MC/V.

Hospitals: Holy Child Hospital (☎225 0247). On Legaspi St.

Telephones: RCPI (☎225 1733), at the corner of San Jose and Santa Catalina St. Open M-F 7am-9pm, Sa 8am-8pm.

Internet Access: Scooby's (☎422 8368), on the corner of Perdices and Silliman Ave., upstairs from the fast-food joint. 1hr. P20. Open daily 8am-11pm.

Post Offices: GPO (☎255 5877), at the corner of Santa Catalina and Pedro Teves St. *Poste Restante*. Open M-F 8am-noon and 1-5pm. **Postal code:** 6200.

ACCOMMODATIONS

All accommodations are within walking distance of the market and town plaza. Tricycle drivers make the trip with baggage from the ferry pier (P10).

Silliman University Alumni Hall Dormitory (☎225 4323). Walk north along Perdices St., which becomes Campus Drive; turn right at the first gate. Spacious A/C rooms with cable TV in the university. Dine at the university cafeteria next door. Doubles P500; quads P600. Open 6:30am-7pm. ❹

Home Quest Lodge (☎225 3327). On Silliman Ave. near the Perdices St. intersection, on the 2nd fl. Complimentary coffee 6-8am. Cable TV in lobby. Singles P177, with A/C P262; doubles with shared common room P283, with A/C P395-437. ❷

Vintage Inn (☎225 1076). On Legaspi St. opposite the public market, near the Real St. intersection. Clean rooms in a large airy building. Restaurant open daily 7am-8pm. Singles P220, with A/C P330; doubles P330, with A/C P495. ❸

Theresa's Lodge (☎225 4827). On San Juan St. between the intersections with Perdices and Maria Cristina St. Minimalist rooms with shared common room, fan, and ripped screens. Singles P140; doubles P200; triples P270. ❷

FOOD

Barbecue chicken reigns supreme in Dumaguete. There are several BBQ hotspots on Silliman Ave., and smaller evening operations set up along Rizal Blvd.

Silliman Avenue Cafe, opposite the university. This popular student hangout has scrumptious *panini* and tasty coffee concoctions (P30-110). ❷

Chin Loong, on Rizal at the corner of San Jose St. Hang out with the locals and indulge in bird's nest soup (P110) or other delicious entrees (P40-150). The ample portions of Chinese and Filipino favorites make Chin Loong's a great bargain. ❷

Don Atilano (☎225 4724), inside the hotel La Residencia. Smaller portions of strictly non-vegetarian delicacies. Try the Serrano ham (P370 per 100g) or the Angus steaks (P295 per 100g) imported from Spain and America. AmEx/MC/V. ❺

SIGHTS AND ENTERTAINMENT

Dumaguete's cleanliness makes strolls through town and seaside **Rizal Blvd.** a genuine pleasure. A block inland, **Quezon Park** is the favorite of younger Negrenses; the more mature venture to the spotless market. In the distance rises Mt. Talinas, romantically known as the Horns of Negros. **Silliman University** was the first Protestant university in the Philippines. The university's museums of ethnology and anthropology are on the corner of Silliman Ave. and Perdices St.

All nightlife inquirers will be pointed to the **Why Not Complex** (☎225 4488) on Rizal Ave., which has **Internet** access (24hr., 1hr. P70), a disco with live music (open Tu-Sa 9pm-2:30am, P50 cover), and a karaoke lounge with billiards (open daily 8pm-2am). The **Sandurot Festival,** in the third week of November, celebrates multiculturalism. After ceremonial gift giving, various costumed Negrenses parade and celebrate their *sandurot* (friendship).

NEAR DUMAGUETE

APO ISLAND

Together with Moalboal (Cebu) and Panglao Island (Bohol), Apo Island completes the trinity of world-class diving spots in the Visayas. And with its ultra-relaxed environment, seclusion, and fine accommodations, it may be the finest dive destination in the country. Secluded beaches dot the island coast, and cliffs poke through the green jungle. Fishermen inhabit a small village and tend a lighthouse with over 300 steps leading down to the water. The reefs around **Coconut Point** are suitable for divers of all levels, while the crystal-clear waters of the sanctuary give snorkelers a view of this underwater community. Barracuda swim at Coconut Point, a site perfect for drift diving. Humungous schools of jackfish are regularly spotted at **Mamsa Point.** To get to Apo, take a **jeepney** from the **Zamboangita** terminal, next to Judy's Bakeshoppe (ask a tricycle driver to bring you there for P4), and ask to be let off in **Malatapay** (40min., P13). The two accommodations can arrange a pickup by *banca* (40min., P100); otherwise, bargain hard to have local fishermen make a "special trip" (P300-1000). From Apo, you can charter a **banca** to take you to **Siquijor** (P3000-3500).

Apo is finding its way onto backpacker radar and is well within a budget traveller's grasp. At **Liberty's ❸,** bamboo rooms let in onshore breezes, and Paul, the English owner, guides divers to the Marine Sanctuary. (☎424 0888; paul@apoisland.com; www.apoisland.com. Dive with equipment US$25; PADI open-water certification US$295; advanced open-water US$245; Discover Scuba US$45. Restaurant open daily 6am-9pm. 5-bed dorms P200; doubles P500-800.) Next door, **Apo Island Beach Resort ❸** is in a secluded cove on a great beach. (☎225 5490. Extra person P200; dorms P350; hillside huts P1040, beachside P800. Restaurant open daily 6am-10pm. 1 dive US$25 with equipment; 2 dives US$48.) Several local families rent **cottages ❸** for P200-300 per night; make inquiries in the village.

BAIS

Bais, 40km north of Dumaguete, is named for a species of eel, though most people slither to Bais to see whales and dolphins in the Tañon Strait between Cebu and Negros. Buses from the **Ceres Northbound Terminal** in Dumaguete headed for **San Carlos** or **Cadiz** go via **Bais** (1½hr., every hr. 4am-6pm, P22.50). The only way to get to the whales is through the tourist office (☎541 5161), which sends out daily tour boats. (20-seater P3000; 15-seater P2500 for a daytrip including whale-watching, lunch, scuba-diving, snorkelling, and hiking.) To get to the wharf, take a pedicab (P10) or tricycle (P30) to **Capiñahan.** The best place to stay in Bais is the **Bahia Hotel ❺,** which has gorgeous views from its hilltop terrace. (☎402 8850. Doubles P850-1200.) **Elly's Place ❹,** directly on the wharf, is a breezy bamboo house on stakes. (☎402 8603. Doubles P500.) For the rocky bottom, go to **New Jacob's Eatery and Lodging House ❶,** on Mabini St. 100m from the BPI bank. (☎0919 492 9138. P100 per person. Grilled fish and rice P125.)

SIQUIJOR ISLAND

The smallest province in the Philippines, Siquijor sits 20km off of the southeastern tip of Negros Oriental, casting its own spell with its beaches, mountains, and rice fields. A fire road encircles the island, making it an excellent place to explore by motorbike—available at most accommodations. Dubbed *"Isla del Fuego"* ("Island of Fire") by Spaniards who saw strange lights in the mountains, Siquijor's name is synonymous with the black-magic shenanigans of *aswang*, witches who transform themselves into pigs. Although mysticism is not immediately visible, healers dwell in the interior mountains, especially in San Antonio north of Siquijor Town.

A handful of resorts are scattered around the island. **Casa de la Playa ❹,** 7km from Larena on **Sandugan Beach,** is a quiet retreat to calm body and soul. Its two female owners offer personalized tours of the island as well as yoga and painting classes. The excellent restaurant specializes in exotic vegetarian fare. (☎397 2291; fax 484 1170; laplaya@gmx.net. Restaurant open 6am-9pm. Laundry service. Cottages for two P550-620, with kitchen and refrigerator P720, with A/C P800; 4-person family house P1100.) Next door, **Islander's Paradise Beach Resort and Restaurant ❸** is, for a change, run by a Filipino family. Seven clean, simple cottages in a palm garden run P300-850. (☎484 1174.) Still a little farther down the beach, **Kiwi Dive Resort ❷** is the only permanent dive shop. (1 dive US$22; PADI open-water course US$290; advanced open-water US$220. Dorm beds P170; cottages P390-690.) Motorbikes can be rented at any of these places for P490 per day.

PANAY

A Goliath of an island, Panay has never matched the quick-footed and savvy tourist tendencies of its David—little Boracay off its northwest tip. Tourism officials are developing Panay's potential attractions, such as trekking in the mountains of Antique and diving off the southern coast. For now, though, the main attraction remains Kalibo's Ati-Atihan festival.

THE VIEW FROM ABOVE

Main cities: Iloilo in the south and Kalibo in the north.
Nearby islands: North of Panay, Boracay Island rivals some of the world's most beautiful tropical havens.
Tasty mangos: Guimaras Island, only a daytrip from Iloilo, is famous for its luscious mangos and beaches.

ILOILO ☎33

A century ago, Iloilo (pronounced "Eelo-Eelo") was the world's gateway to the sugar of Negros; today it is the most lively of the stopovers on Panay for travelers on their way to Boracay. The city itself is unusually livable, offering visitors a taste of its hip, cosmopolitan cool. More patient folks should consider making the short hop to Guimaras, which rewards visitors with idyllic beaches and the world's sweetest mangos.

TRANSPORTATION

Flights: Iloilo's **airport** is northwest of the city in Mandurriao. Take a "Mandurriao Iloilo" jeepney heading west on Gen. Luna (20-25min., P4); a pedicab goes the rest of the way (3min., P3). **PAL** (☎320 3030) flies to: **Davao** (daily 8am, P3390) and **General Santos** (daily 8am, P3390) both via **Cebu** (P1783); **Manila** (4 per day, P3548). **Cebu Pacific** (☎320 6889) goes to **Davao** (daily, P3295) and **Manila** (3 per day, P2498) via **Cebu** (P1790). All airlines have branch offices open daily 9:30am-6pm in the Atrium Mall at the Gen. Luna-Bonifacio intersection. Terminal fee P45.

Buses: Buses from 2 stations connect Iloilo with towns in the rest of Panay. **Ceres Bus Terminal** (☎337 0456), on Tanza St. near Ledesma St. intersection. 15% student discount. To: **Caticlan,** the gateway to **Boracay** (6hr., 6 per day, P130); **Kalibo** (4hr., every 30min. 3am-3:15pm, P120); **Roxas** (3hr., every 30min. 4:15am-5:30pm, P63). Buses to **Antique** leave from the **R. M. Panay Transport** office (☎336 8341) on Gen. Luna opposite the John B. Lacson Colleges Foundation.

Ferries: Fast ferries dock on the river after the 1st bend, near City Hall. **SuperCat** (☎336 4259) goes to **Bacolod** (1hr., 4 per day 7:30am-5pm, P240). 15% student discount. From Arrastre Pier by Fort San Pedro, **Negros Navigation** (☎336 2396) serves: **Cagayan de Oro** (14hr., Sa 4pm, P1260) and **Manila** (19hr., 5 per week, P1345). **WG&A** (☎336 2776) has similar routes but also goes to **Davao** (20hr., Su 7am, P1280) via **General Santos** (17hr., P1280). Some schedules vary, so call ahead. **Cockaliong** (W, F, Su 7pm; P500) and **Transasia** (daily 6pm, P500) liners go to **Cebu.** All shipping companies' offices are on the 3rd fl., Atrium Mall. Outriggers to **Buenavista** and **Jordan** on Guimaras island (15min., depart when full 6am-6pm, P10) leave from the pier to the right of the large ferries.

Local Transportation: Jeepneys cost P4 to most destinations. Southbound jeepneys gather at the corner of de Leon and Fuentes St. **A/C taxis** P25 plus P2 increments. **Tricycles** P5-10.

ORIENTATION AND PRACTICAL INFORMATION

The largest city on Panay, Iloilo sits on the southeastern coast across the straits from Bacolod on Negros. Iloilo covers five subdivisions and is trisected by the Iloilo and Batiano river system. The **Provincial Capitol** sits on the northern edge at the intersection of **Gen. Luna St.** and **Bonifacio Dr.,** which leads north across the river into **La Paz** and **Jaro.** Separated by a tributary, **Mandurriao** lies west of Jaro and is home to the **airport.** The main river separates **Molo,** west of the city and south of Mandurriao. Downtown revolves around the Gen. Luna St.-Bonifacio St. intersection, site of the **Atrium Mall.** From here, **jeepneys** head to the five subdivisions.

Tourist Office: ☎337 5411. On Bonifacio Dr., 2min. walk north of the capitol by the pedestrian bridge. Helpful staff. Maps. Open M-F 8am-5pm.

FROM THE ROAD

THE ATI-ATIHAN FESTIVAL

Every January, the sleepy town of Kalibo on Panay's north coast is submerged in a sea of color and passionate commotion as its inhabitants—as well as domestic and international visitors—throw all inhibition to the winds to celebrate the wildest festival of the archipelago, the Ati-Atihan Festival.

The week-long fiesta—a Filipino Mardi Gras of sorts—commemorates the 13th-century land sale of the island of Panay by the Ati chieftain Marikudo to Datu Puti, one of 12 immigrant *datus* (princes) from the island of Borneo.

The Borneans held a feast in honor of their new neighbors and blackened their faces to appear more like their guests—hence the name Ati-Atihan, or "Making Like the Atis."

Today's elaborate creations with which the different *barangays* compete for the best costume do not resemble the original Ati dress, but the ecstatic crowds ensure that all but the beautiful Miss Ati-Atihan pageant contestants wear an Ati-like smear of black soot on their faces.

The Catholic Church of course could not let such celebrations pass without imbuing them with the proper Christian spirit.

Pagan street dances are performed to make barren women bear children and businesses prosper. Seemingly incongruously, the "Pahilot" ceremony in front of an image of the Santo Niño supposedly heals pilgrims of incurable illnesses.

Thus, the traditional festival was fused with a celebration in honor of the Santo Niño (Holy Child).

Budget Travel: Panay Island Holidays (☎336 8069), at the Casa Plaza Building. Offers Boracay packages and city and Guimaras Island tours. Open M-F 8:30am-5pm, Sa 8:30-noon.

Immigration Office: Iloilo's Bureau of Immigration (☎509 9665), 2nd fl., old Customs House on Aduana St. Near intersection of J.M. Basa St. and Plaza Libertad. Extensions on visas arranged through Manila. Open M-F 8am-4:30pm.

Bank: Philippine National Bank (☎337 0481), on the corner of Gen. Luna and Valeria St. **24hr. ATM** (MC/V). Open M-F 9am-3pm.

Emergency: ☎166.

Police: ☎335 1254. On Gen. Luna St. west of the Provincial Capitol building.

Hospital: St. Paul's Hospital (☎337 2741), a 5min. walk from the Provincial Capitol building down Gen. Luna St. on the right.

Pharmacy: Mercury Drug (☎335 0037), on Iznart St. near J.M. Basa St. **Open 24hr.**

Telephones: RCPI (☎336 2220), at the corner of Iznart and Yulo St. Open M-F 7am-7pm, Sa 8am-5pm, Su 9am-2pm.

Internet Access: IPX (☎508 8678), on the 2nd fl. of the Atrium Mall, has the speediest connection in town. P35 per hr. Open daily 9am-8pm.

Post Office: ☎336 2128. In the old Customs House on Aduana St. *Poste Restante.* Open M-F 8am-noon and 1-5pm, Sa 9-11am. **Postal code:** 5000.

ACCOMMODATIONS

Family Pension House (☎335 0070), on Gen. Luna St. at the Mabini intersection. The best budget option in town. Treehouse restaurant and pool table (P10). Breakfast included. Singles P250; doubles P325, with A/C P525. ❸

Four Season Hotel (☎336 1070; fax 509 3888), at the Fuentes and Delgado St. intersection. Attractive rooms in a familial atmosphere make this hotel a great deal. Room service. Laundry service. Standard rooms P680; deluxe P980/P880. ❺

Eros Travellers Pensione (☎337 1359), on Gen. Luna St. opposite St. Paul's Hospital. Set back from the street. The cheapest A/C in town. Sterile singles P240-335; doubles P305-405; extra person P80. ❸

Castle Hotel (☎338 1022), on Bonifacio Dr., just beyond the museum. Friendly place housed in a rambling 19th-century mansion. All rooms with A/C and TV. Singles P503; doubles P592. ❹

FOOD

Iloilo prepares specialty dishes disguised with innocuous names. "Soup #5" is made from a bull's penis and testicles, and "mud soup" contains pigs' intestines soaked in blood. **Food stalls ❶** along Valeria and Gen. Luna St. offer cheap, late-night eats. For finer dining, try the **Marina ❸,** on Iloilo Diversion Rd. in Mandurriao, in an airy *nipa* pavilion on the river. (Delicious *kinilaw* P110; *adobo* P140; *lechon* P200. Open daily 9am-1am.) **Nena's Manokan ❷,** on Gen. Luna St. before the Diversion Rd. intersection, serves first-rate grilled chicken (P60) on balconies over the river. (Open daily 11am-11pm.) The **Promenade ❸** restaurant in the Days Hotel inside the Atrium Mall has themed all-you-can-eat lunch buffets for P165. (Open daily 11am-2pm.) Locals claim that Iloilo has the Visayas' best seafood—check out **Breakthrough ❸** along the water in Arevalo (villa jeepneys P4), and you'll probably agree. (Tangigue steak P151; grilled king prawns P160; green mango salad P35. Open daily 9am-10pm.)

SIGHTS AND ENTERTAINMENT

The **Museo Iloilo,** behind the capitol on Bonifacio Dr., records the history and traditions of the Western Visayas (Panay and Negros) with local art and life-size dioramas. (☎337 2986. Open daily 9am-5pm. P15, students P5.) The **Dinagyang Festival,** held during the fourth weekend of January, pays tribute to the Santo Niño (Christ Child) and the heritage of tribes with colorful street dancing. The southwest coast of Panay offers Spanish churches, including **Molo** and **San Joaquin. Miag-ao,** a church built of coral with a facade ornamented by palm trees and bananas, is a rare vernacular baroque. (Jeepneys to Miag-ao leave from the intersection of Gen. Luna St. and Bonifacio Drive; P15.)

Iloilo's student population ensures that there are plenty of nightlife options around town. For good live music, a friendly, raucous crowd, and San Miguels (P30), try the military-themed **Barracks,** on Iloilo Diversion Rd. past the S. M. City mall. (Open M-Sa 6pm-1am. No cover. Taxi P60.) **Vega,** off Gen. Luna St., is a chic restaurant/disco, which attracts a hipper-than-thou scene. (Open M-Sa 11am-4am. Cover P110, includes one drink.) There are several bars and a disco in the **Sarabia Manor** hotel complex on Gen. Luna St.

DAYTRIP FROM ILOILO: GUIMARAS ISLAND

15min. by banca *from Iloilo harbor (every hr. 5am-5:30pm, P10).*

Guimaras is famous throughout the archipelago for its mangos, said to be the country's tastiest. The island is home to a Trappist monastery whose monks produce candies and preserves from local produce. Other attractions include the **Macopo Falls** and, of course, the **Oro Verde Mango Plantation.** There are several beach resorts on **Alubihod Beach** in Nueva Valencia offering picnicking facilities as well as lodging (P300-800). Local boat owners can be hired to take you to the many outlying islands. On an idyllic islet off Lawi, the **Baras Beach Resort ❺** offers its guests an array of aquatic activities, including sailing, snorkeling, and windsurfing. (☎0917 9387 159. Cottages P750-900. Ask for Mike or Baby to arrange transportation to the island.) There is a very helpful **tourist information kiosk** on the pier in Jordan, the provincial capital. (Open daily 9am-6pm.) All of Guimaras' sights can be seen in a daytrip from Iloilo (tricycles can be hired for P200-400) or by using one of Nueva Valencia's resorts as a base. Ask at the tourist kiosk about the **International Mountain Biking Tournament,** held every year in March.

KALIBO ☎36

During the third week in January, the capital city of Aklan explodes in merriment that even Boracay can't rival when revelers smear their faces with black soot and dance about the streets in the Ati-Atihan Festival. When the last native headdress is laid to rest, Kalibo and its airport resume their appointed duty as a way-station on the well-beaten path to Caticlan and Boracay.

TRANSPORTATION

Flights: Kalibo's **airport** is a major hub for the daily traffic from Manila to Boracay. **PAL** (☎262 3263) and **Air Philippines** (☎262 4444) both fly to **Manila** (P2700). **Cebu Pacific** (☎262 5409) also serves **Manila** (P2854). PAL's office is in the terminal; the other two are across the street. From the airport parking lot, **Southwest Tours** (☎268 5100) brings tourists comfortably to **Boracay** via **Caticlan** (1½hr., P350). The cheapest option from the airport to Boracay includes a tricycle to town (P20), a Ceres liner to Caticlan jetty (P36), and then a pumpboat to Boracay itself (P20).

Buses: Ceres Bus Terminal has buses to **Iloilo** (4hr., every 30-60min. 2:30am-3:30pm, P130). **Delmabel** offers A/C vans to **Caticlan** (1hr., 7am-3:30pm, P100) and **Iloilo** (3hr., 7am-5pm, P120). **GM Liners** heads to **Roxas** (2hr., every hr. 4:30am-2:30pm, P50). Buses and jeepneys to Caticlan also depart from the corner of Roxas Ave. and Barrios St., and from the corner of Roxas and Pastrana Ave. when full (1½hr., P45).

Ferries: Ferries leave for **Manila** from Kalibo's Dumaguit port. To get there, take a jeepney from the Gonzalez St. market (45min., roughly every 30min., P15). Last jeepney from Dumaguit to Kalibo 4pm. **Negros Navigation** (☎262 4943) leaves Sa 3pm (18hr., P925). Open M-F 8am-noon and 1-4pm, Sa 8am-noon. **WG&A** (☎268 4391) takes off on Tu, Th, and Su afternoons. The schedule changes frequently, so call their office to confirm.

ORIENTATION AND PRACTICAL INFORMATION

Kalibo lies along Panay's north highway a few kilometers from the sea at the confluence of the Sooc and Aklan Rivers. **Roxas Ave.** links the city center with the Aklan Bridge. In a skewed grid south of Roxas Ave., **Burgos St., Archbishop Reyes St.,** and **XIX Martyrs St.** link the main city center with Pastrana Park. Each street terminates at **Mabini St.,** which leads from Roxas Ave. to **Maagma Ave.** Maagma Ave. eventually becomes **Quezon Ave.** heading southeast to Kalibo Airport.

Travel Agencies: Southwest Tours (☎268 5100) offers connecting bus and boat transfers to and from **Caticlan** and from Kalibo airport to **Boracay** (1½hr., P350). Open M-F 8am-noon and 1:30-5pm, Sa 8am-noon.

Banks: BPI (☎262 3504). On Martelino St. at the corner of XIX Martyrs St. Cashes AmEx Traveler's Cheques. **24hr. ATM.** Open M-F 9am-3pm.

English-Language Bookstore: Thumbelina (☎262 4017), next to the police station on XIX Martyrs St. New and used books. Open M-F 8am-5:30pm, Sa 8am-noon.

Emergency: ☎166. **Hospital:** ☎141.

Police: On XIX Martyrs St. in city center.

Hospital: Kalibo Provincial Hospital (☎268 4565), on Mabini St.

Telephone: RCPI/Bayantel (☎268 4006), at the corner of Barrios and Burgos St. Fax and calling cards. Open M-F 7am-7pm, Sa-Su 7am-4pm.

Internet: Web Center, Inc., next to Air Philippines on Roxas Ave. P50 per hr.

Post Office: GPO (☎262 3215)., in the capitol (P5 tricycle ride). *Poste Restante.* Open M-F 8am-noon and 1-5pm. **Postal code:** 5600.

ACCOMMODATIONS

Rooms are usually easy to find except during the Ati-Atihan Festival in January, when you should make reservations weeks ahead and prepare for prices to launch into the stratosphere.

La Esperanza Hotel (☎262 3989; fax 262 5858), on Osmeña Ave. This place tries to accommodate all budgets, and it does a great job. Very friendly and helpful staff. All rooms have cable TV, A/C, and bath; most have waterbeds and bathtubs. Laundry service and cafe. Dorm beds P120; pension doubles P700; standard doubles in the main building P900; deluxe triples P1300; one huge suite P2500. ❷

Garcia Legaspi Mansion, 159 Roxas Ave., 4th fl. (☎262 5588), near the corner with Barrios St. Rooms vary from comfortable to luxurious. Helpful owner runs Kalibo Tourist Association. Convenient, central location. Singles P300, with common room P350; doubles with A/C and bath P650. ❸

Beachcomber Inn (☎262 4846; fax 268 4765; bcombinn@kalibo.i-next.net), at the corner of N. Roldan and Mabini St. Marbled rooms with A/C, hot water, and TV. Internet P80 per hr. Laundry service. Economy doubles P950; 3-person standard rooms P1100; 4-person deluxe rooms P1300. ❺

Gervy's Restaurant and Lodging House (☎262 4190), on G. Pastrada St. near XIX Martyrs. Dirt cheap. Doubles P125. ❷

FOOD

Cheap eats abound in Kalibo. Basic eateries and Filipino fast-food joints encircle the plaza. **Kusina sa Kalibo** ❷ (☎262 3466), on D. Maagma St., is a pleasant beer garden serving favorites like ox tongue soup (P100) and mixed *adobo* (P80). **Niño's Ristorante and Pizzeria** ❸ (☎262 4942), on C. Laserna St., offers decent pizza for P100-140. Some of the best food in town can be found at the **Perfect Combination Bar & Restaurant** ❷ (☎268 4240) on L. Barrios St. Try the pineapple chicken (P130) or the *patatín* (P180).

BORACAY ISLAND ☎36

Filipinos all over the archipelago will ask if you've been to Boracay; if you haven't, they'll emphatically encourage a visit to the softest, most beautiful sand in the country. Boracay has fast become a flagship for the tourism industry, and resorts, restaurants, and shops are densely packed, so for tropical seclusion, look elsewhere. Boracay's raucous nightlife now approximates the hedonistic scene found on Ko Samui or Ko Phangan in Thailand. The island is not quite as budget-friendly as it was in the 1970s, when dinner meant bartering with fishermen, but affordable deals can still be found, for those willing to look hard enough.

TRANSPORTATION

Flights: Most tourists fly to **Kalibo,** the capital of Aklan, and then take a van or bus to the small town of **Caticlan,** where outriggers run to Boracay. Vans to Kalibo's airport vary by season (1½hr., 3-4 per day in low season, P120). **Southwest** (☎288 3010), south of Boat Station 1 on Boracay, runs a boat-and-bus trip to the airport (1½hr., departs 4hr. before flight departure, P200). Several airlines link Manila with Caticlan's small airport, a 15min. walk from the ferry pier (P20-30 by tricycle). The tourist center books plane tickets. **Asian Spirit** (☎288 3465) and **Seair** (☎288 7272) both fly to **Manila** (1hr., P2350-2550).

Ferries: Outriggers link Caticlan with three boat stations on White Beach and stop at the south station first (30min., every 15min. 6am-5pm, P20). In wavy conditions, the ferries dock on the southeast tip of the island; from there, it's a P20 tricycle to White Beach. Boats also run to: **Carabao,** north of Boracay (1hr., 3 per day, P20); **Roxas,** on Mindoro (6hr.; M, Th 10am; P150); **Santa Fe,** on Romblon (2hr., 9am, P100); **Tablas** (2hr., P100). Check at the tourist office on the Caticlan pier for the latest schedules and prices. **MBRS Lines** operates a ferry service to **Manila** (W, F, Su; P780).

Buses: Bus and van connections between Kalibo and Caticlan are frequent. **GM Liner** sends buses to **Iloilo** (6hr., 7:30 and 9:30am, P132). **Jeepneys** (P30) and buses (P36) run to **Kalibo,** but only some go to the **airport** (1½hr., 6am-4:30pm, P30).

Tricycles and Pedicabs: Tricycles sputter up and down the jeepney-free main road. Daytime rides P7 per person, at night P12. **Pedicabs** along White Beach P20-30.

Rentals: Mopeds can be rented everywhere. Bargain hard (half-day P600). **Mountain bike** rentals run about P50 per hr.

ORIENTATION AND PRACTICAL INFORMATION

Boracay is north of Panay between the Sulu and Sibuyan Seas. The 4km **White Beach** stretches along its west coast. Boracay's main road bisects the island vertically. **Barangay Yapak,** topped by Puka Beach, occupies the north. White Beach, in **Barangay Balabag,** has three boat stations. Accommodations are everywhere, but the southernmost **Boat Station 3** has the most shops and services. **Boat Station 2** has many restaurants and bars. **Boat Station 1** is bigger and quieter. Shady forests and rocky coves cover **Barangay Manok-Manok** in the south.

Tourist Office: DOT office (☎/fax 288 3689) is a *nipa* cottage in the Mall d'Boracay near Boat Station 2. Helpful staff. Immigration officer extends visas W 9am-3pm (P2000-3000). Open M-F 8am-noon and 1-5pm. The **Tourist Center** (☎288 3704) centralizes many helpful resources: **telecommunications services** (open daily 9am-10pm, no calling card access); **currency exchange; Internet;** safety deposit (P150 per month); activities desk (open daily 9:30am-7pm). Helpful staff. (Open 9am-6pm.)

Budget Travel: Tourist Center (see **Tourist Office,** above). Ticketing, visa extension services, and package tours. MC/V. Open M-Sa 9am-6pm. **Tribal Adventures** (☎288 3207; www.tribaladventures.com). At Sand Castle Resort south of Boat Station 1. Mountain biking, kayaking, and windsurfing. Open daily 7:30am-10pm.

Currency Exchange: Allied Bank (☎288 3048), on the main road between Boat Station 2 and 3. Open M-F 9am-4pm. Branches lie beside Boat Stations 1 and 3.

Market: Talipapa Market, north of Boat Station 3.

Emergency: Police ☎166. **Medical** ☎141.

Police: Philippine National Police (☎288 3066), between Boat Stations 2 and 3.

Medical Services: Boracay Island Emergency Hospital (☎141), on the main road; take the road next to Boracay Regency Hotel near Boat Station 2, then turn left at the main road. **Boracay Medical Clinic** (☎288 3147) is on the main road in Balabag. **Open 24hr.**

Telephones: Cruztelco phone booth near Lapu-Lapu Divers, north of Boat Station 2. **Pantelco,** north of Boat Station 2, opposite Mango Ray's. **RCPI-Bayantel** (☎/fax 288 3012), at Oro Beach Resort, Boat Station 3. Open M-Th 8am-6pm, F-Su 8am-noon and 1-5pm.

Internet Access: Tourist Center (see **Tourist Office,** above). Blazing connections P60 per hr.

Post Office: In Balabag north of Boat Station 1 on the main road. Open M-F 8am-noon and 1-4:30pm. *Poste Restante.* Tourist Center (see above) has a **postal center** (letters only) with *Poste Restante,* which they deliver from Manila every 2 days. P5 service charge per letter. Address: "PO Box 552, Manila 1099, Philippines." Open daily in high season 9am-8pm; in low season 9am-6pm.

ACCOMMODATIONS

Heading north toward Boat Station 1, the sand gets finer, and (in general) prices rise. Always bargain, and ask for discounts for extended stays.

Michelle's Bungalows (☎288 3086). A short walk north of Boat Station 3. Between Beach Life Diving and La Isla Resort; take a right and head 35m from beach. Doubles P600/P300. ❺

Trafalgar Garden Lodge (☎288 3711). From Boat Station 3, head north, turning right into the market at Beach Life. Trafalgar is 200m down on the left. Operated by a friendly British-Filipino couple, Trafalgar is one of the last truly budget accommodations on the island. Singles P200-500; doubles P300-700. ❸

Nigi Nigi Nu Noos 'e' Nu Nu Noos (☎288 3101). Between Tourist Center and Boat Station 2. Polynesian pagodas in a tropical garden. A great low season deal. Free 30min. email session per day. Cashes traveler's checks. Huts with fan P2000-3000/P1000; huts with A/C P2500-3500/P1500. MC/V. ❺

Crystal Sands (☎288 3149; fax 288 3087), a few meters south of Boat Station 2. Spacious rooms with seaview in several Italian-looking buildings. Standard doubles with TV P2950/P1475; superior doubles with fridge P3680/P1840; suites P4800/P2400. Add P1000 for Holy Week, Christmas, and Chinese New Year. ❺

Villa de Oro (☎288 5456). Simple *nipas* south of Boat Station 2. Good value in low season. Restaurant with bar. All-you-can-eat Mongolian BBQ P175. Open daily 7am-5pm. Huts P1250/P400. 5% discount for Hostelling International members. ❺

Fiesta Cottages (☎288 3818), south of Boat Station 1 near Fisheye Divers, is run by a friendly Filipina who oversees *nipas* with hammocks. Small library. Motorboat (P700) and bike (P150) rentals. Cottages with fan and common room P600/P400, with A/C P2000/P1500. ❺

FOOD

Boracay's restaurants offer travelers a break from blandness. International cuisine dots White Beach, and a few months' stay would barely exhaust the options.

Shenna's Restaurant (☎288 6120), next to Lapu-Lapu Divers. Superb inexpensive 3-course dinner combo P115. Excellent pineapple shake P50. Open daily 7am-10pm. ❸

Nigi Nigi Nu Noos 'e' Nu Nu Noos (see **Accommodations,** above). Pry the name's hidden meaning out of the owners. Unforgettable seafood cuisine P130-190. Happy hour 5-7pm. Jazz and blues Th-F. Open daily 6:30am-11pm. AmEx/MC/V with a party of five or more. ❸

Mango Ray (☎288 3371), north of Boat Station 2. Savory BBQ and international grub. 4-course meal P230. "Mango Ray Baby" mixes *kalamansi,* mango, and rum P70. Open daily 7am-1am. ❹

Sea Lovers (☎288 6139), north of Boat Station 2. Reasonable prices and snappy service. Pancit canton P75. Mango prawns P150. Open 24hr. ❸

SIGHTS AND AQUATIC ACTIVITIES

Sunset on White Beach is Boracay's premier sight. The beach is uniform, except for **Willy's Rock,** north of Boat Station 1. The north is often marvelously neglected. **Puka Beach** is isolated on the northern shore (tricycle from White Beach 30min., P30). Snorkeling tubes crisscross the water off **Ilig-Iligan Beach** to the northeast. From the beach, the **Bat Cave** is easily reached (P50). The **windsurfing beach** sits a short walk across the narrowest point of the island from White Beach. Between White Beach and the southern tip, the **Dead Forest Preserve,** really just a mosquito preserve, hardly merits attention (P20). More worthy are trails through the **southern rainforest** in *barangay* Manok-Manok. **Watersports equipment** can be rented at **Scuba World,** south of Boat Station 1. (☎288 3310. Windsurfing gear P300 per hr., with instruction P500. Kayaks P150-300 for the first hr., each additional hr. P75-150. Wakeboarding P650 per 30min. Open daily 8am-6pm.) The **Tourist Center** (see **Practical Information,** p. 429) rents water-skiing equipment (P800 per 15min.), wakeboarding equipment (P1300 per 30min.), and speedboating equipment (P2800 per hr.). Local boat owners hawk snorkeling tours (P500).

Boracay is surrounded by wall dives, channel drift dives, plunges into bat-and-snake-infested caves, and deep dives. One site ranks among the Philippines' best: **Yapak,** on the coast of Panay. At 35m, the strong currents attract pelagic fish, tuna, and whitetip sharks. On **Maniguin Island,** 48km southwest of Boracay, whitetip sharks sleep in caves. An overnight stay is recommended on Maniguin, although it can be reached in a day by boat (2hr., around US$90). To explore shallower reefs, divers head for the coral of **Crocodile Island** and the fish frenzy at **Friday's Rock.**

Dive shops litter the sands of White Beach. Shop around. Typically, dives cost US$20-25, PADI open-water courses are US$285-310, and advanced courses cost US$185-200. **Lapu-Lapu Diving Center,** next to Mango Ray north of Boat Station 2, was the first on the beach. (☎288 3302; www.lapulapu.com. Open daily 7am-8pm.) **Calypso Divers** is north of the Tourist Center and has great facilities. (☎288 3206. Open daily 8am-10pm.) **Victory Divers,** next to Nigi's and south of Boat Station 2, does regular live-aboard dive safaris to **Apo Reef** and **Busuanga,** and claim that only they know the coordinates of some magnificent wrecks within daytrip distance. (☎288 3209; info@victorydivers.com; www.victorydivers.com. Open daily 7:30am-11pm.) Arrange **horseback riding** through the Tourist Center (P500 per hr.) or go straight to **Boracay Horse Riding Stables** (☎288 3311), north of Boat Station 1.

NIGHTLIFE

At times, Boracay seems like an island that floats not only on water, but on a sea of free-flowing alcohol. White Beach is dotted by a seemingly endless parade of bars, most of which offer budget-friendly happy hour deals, ensuring that by the time the specials end, you'll be too sloshed to care. To the delight of some and the horror of others, several Boracay clubs have begun staging "full moon parties" a la Thailand's Ko Phangan. Dare to drink two or more "coconut killers" (P130) and **Barracuda,** south of Boat Station 2, will enshrine you in their Hall of Fame. (Open daily 5pm-1am.) **Beachcomber,** north of Boat Station 1, is Boracay's premier open-air disco. (Beer P40. Open daily 5pm-3am.)

LEYTE

Sipping a blood cocktail with a local chieftain and planting the first of many crosses, Ferdinand Magellan staked his claim for the glory of Spain on the tiny Leyteno island of Limasawa in 1521. Four centuries later in 1944, American General Douglas MacArthur made his triumphant return to the archipelago here. Historical significance aside, there is little of interest in Leyte to most travelers, who (unlike MacArthur) often have no desire to return, but it is a useful departure point for visits to nearby islands.

TACLOBAN ☎53

Tacloban is the geographical and historical heart of the Eastern Visayas. Choking smog, *kamikaze* jeepneys, and a lack of sights won't give travelers much cause to linger. Indeed, today's Tacloban provides the same strategic significance to travelers that it provided MacArthur—namely, a base from which to reach other islands.

THE VIEW FROM ABOVE

Major towns: Tacloban at the edge of Samar, Ormoc on the western coast.
Something different: Escape to the beach on Biliran Island, host to one of the Philippines' only hinterlands.
Natural wonders: From Tacloban, head to Sohoton Natural Bridge National Park to see nature at its best.

TRANSPORTATION

Flights: Daniel Z. Romualdez Airport (☎325 5893), 11km east of Tacloban in San Jose. Cross the airport parking lot for the cheapest jeepney into town (P5). Flights from Tacloban go to **Cebu** and **Manila. Cebu Pacific** (airport office ☎325 8486, open 5:30am-4pm; downtown office on Sen. Enage St. ☎325 7747, open 8am-5pm) offers 3 flights per day (P2864). **Philippine Airlines** (☎321 2212) has 2 flights per day (P2494). Open daily 5:30am-4:30pm. **Seair** (☎323 8805 or 321 5578) flies to **Cebu** (M, F; P1505).

Buses: To find the bus terminal, walk away from the city on Quezon Blvd. To: **Manila** (24hr.; 11 per day; P760, with A/C P852) via several destinations in **Samar** including **Allen** (6hr., 6 per day, P154); **Catbalogan** (3hr., 15 per day, P60-70); **Calbayog** (5hr., 11 per day, P100); and **San Isidro** (4hr.; 3 per day; P149, with A/C P163). San Isidro and Allen ferries run to **Matnog** on Luzon (1½hr., P71). Other destinations include: **Davao** (12hr., 2 per day, P355); **Naval** on Biliran (3-4hr., 4 per day, P100); and **Ormoc** (2hr., every 20min. 6:30am-6:30pm, P63-70). **Jeepneys** strike out for **Basey** on Samar (45min.; depart when full, last return 3pm; P10). Jeepneys also head south to **Palo** (30min., every 20min. until 7pm, P5) and **Tolosa** (1hr., P10). Yet more buses depart from the Philtranco station. To get there, take a jeepney to San José from Real St. and ask to be dropped off at the Philtranco station. These buses leave for **Cebu** (11hr.; P212, with A/C P240); **Cubao** and **Pasay** via **Manila** (24hrs.; P765, with A/C P866).

Ferries: WG&A Lines (☎321 2536) go to **Cebu** (15hr.; Tu, Sa 4pm; P210).

Local Transportation: Jeepneys cruise Magsaysay Blvd., Real St., and Veteranos St. From the jeepney stop along Quezon Blvd., cross-town fare P4. **Taxis,** ☎321 4713.

ORIENTATION AND PRACTICAL INFORMATION

Tacloban is a portal to and from Samar, across the San Juanico Straits to the northeast. The city is sandwiched between **Panalaron Bay** to the north and **Cancabato Bay** to the south. The pier, market, and bus/jeepney terminal overlook Panalaron Bay. **Magsaysay Blvd.** wraps around the northern and eastern boundaries of the peninsula, originating in the north by **Children's Park,** the **tourist office,** and Leyte's **Provincial Capitol** building, and ending in the south at **Real St.** Jeepneys blaze down southwest **Avenida Veteranos** and southeastern Real St., converging to funnel passengers southward to **Palo** or the **airport** across Cancabato Bay.

Tourist Offices: The **main office** (☎321 2048), across from the entrance to Leyte Park Resort compound on Magsaysay Blvd. Open M-F 8am-6pm.

Tours: MacArthur Landing Tours and Travel, 122 Lopez Jaena St. (☎321 5685). Off Saint Niño St. Very helpful. Open M-F 8:30am-noon and 1-5:30pm.

Currency Exchange: ATMs are available at most banks. **Philippine National Bank** (☎321 2053), at the corner of St. Niño St. and J. Romualdez St. Passport photocopy required to cash traveler's checks. **24hr. ATM** (Cirrus/MC/PLUS/V). Open M-F 9am-3pm. **PDCP Bank** (☎321 2881) is on Zamora St. Open M-F 9am-3pm.

Markets: Quezon Blvd., Torres St., and Tarcela St. Sell fruit, straw goods, and clothes.

Emergency: Police (☎166), on the Paterno Ext. **Fire** ☎911. **Ambulance** ☎325 6471. **Medical emergency** ☎321 2816.

Pharmacy: Mercury Drug (☎321 2852), on Salazar St. near the intersection with P. Zamora. Open daily 7am-10pm.

Medical Services: The **Eastern Visayas Regional Medical Center** (☎325 6471), near the gate of Children's Park on Sen. Enage St.

Telephones: Bayantel, 109 Romualdez St. (☎325 6608). Open M-F 7am-6pm.

Internet Access: Continental Internet Cafe, 170 Veteranos St. (☎321 3427). Other Internet cafes on Real and Paterno St. All P25 per hr.

Post Office: ☎321 3509. On Trece Martirez St. along the harbor. Open M-F 7am-noon and 1-5:30pm, Sa 8am-noon. **Postal code:** 6500.

ACCOMMODATIONS

LNU House (☎321 3175), at the corner of Paterno and Santa Cruz St. A laboratory for tourism students at Leyte Normal University. Balcony, TV, and tea rooms. Laundry service. All rooms have A/C and bath. TV P50. Refrigerator P50. Extra bed P120. Spacious singles P400; doubles P500; 4-bed family room P1150. ❹

Rosvenil Pensione, 302 P. Burgos St. (☎321 2676), at the corner of Real St. and P. Burgos. Turn left on P. Burgos; it's on the left before the computer college. The house-owned rooster will make you appreciate the earplugs you brought. Singles P240, with A/C P320-370; doubles P280-310, with A/C P400-450. ❸

Cecilia's Lodge, 178 Paterno St. (☎321 2815). Near Avenida Veteranos. Simple but ample rooms and an amicable owner. Singles with fan P150, with fan and private bath P180, with A/C and private bath P450; doubles with fan and private bath P550. ❷

Manabo Lodge, 191 P. Zamora St. (☎321 3727). In the heart of Tacloban, north of the intersection with Del Pilar St., past the neon blue Metrobank sign, on the left. Basic rooms with shared bathrooms are being renovated and upgraded at the time of writing. Showers P30. Singles P280; twins with private bath P450; doubles with king-size bed, A/C, bath, and TV P600. Extra person P70, folding bed P30. ❸

FOOD

Visitors can slurp a San Miguel while watching a Filipino soap opera at a **roadside barbecue** ❶ along Real St. The **fish and vegetable market** ❶ along the streets outside the bus terminal provide a great medium for the culinary artist.

Guiseppe's Restaurant (☎321 4910). On Avenida Veteranos at the corner of MH del Pilar St. This unlikely blend of Italian and Filipino cuisine is the best food in town. Steak P275. Mango shake P50. Open daily 10:30am-10:30pm. AmEx/MC/V. ❸

Join Us Cuisine (☎321 6984). On Avenida Veteranos near the intersection with Rizal Ave. A spotless venue good for sampling local cuisine like *giniling* (spicy chopped pork; P25). *Halo-halo* P35; lychee flan P12. Also serves burgers and grilled cheese sandwiches (P17). Open M-Sa 7am-8pm. ❶

Shen-Zhen Mami House (☎321 5584), on Zamora St. in the Dynasty Square Shopping Center near the MH del Pilar St. intersection. Local Chinese dishes. All entrees P35. Open daily 7:30am-7:30pm. Free downtown delivery with purchase of P50 or more. ❶

SIGHTS AND ENTERTAINMENT

The white Neoclassical facade of the **Leyte Provincial Capitol,** built in 1902, on the corner of Sen. Enage St. and Magsaysay Blvd., is architectural evidence of colonial influences. **Santo Niño Church,** at the corner of Real and Zamora St., houses the city's patron saint. In 1889, en route to a makeover in Manila, an image of the Christ child was lost overboard. Months later, natives on north Mindoro recovered the crate, which was then stolen back by impassioned residents of Tacloban. The **Santo Niño Shrine and Heritage Museum,** on Real St., founded by Imelda Marcos, displays local artists' paintings of the stations of the cross. (☎321 9775. Open M-Sa 8-11:30am and 1-4:30pm. P200. Video permit P200, camera permit P30.)

South of Tacloban, the **General Douglas MacArthur Landing Memorial** commemorates the charismatic commander's return on October 20, 1944. Take a jeepney from Avenida Veteranos to Palo via Baras (20min., last return 4:30pm, P5). Ask the driver to drop you off in front of the memorial. Hide in foxholes on nearby **Hill 522.** The **Battle of Baluarte Marker,** 52km away in Barugo, commemorates a battle between guerrillas and Japanese troops. North of the city, the **San Juanico Bridge**—the longest span of its kind in Southeast Asia—links Leyte to Samar.

DAYTRIP FROM TACLOBAN: SOHOTON

Sohoton Natural Bridge National Park is across the straits in Samar. A subterranean river snakes beneath two mountain ridges, creating the natural stone bridge for which the park is named. From Tacloban's bus terminal, take a jeepney to **Basey** (1hr., P10). Get off at Basey's Town Hall; the **Department of the Environment and Natural Resources (DENR)** is across the street. Francisco Corales Jr. arranges the necessary boat trip (1½hr., P700 per boat) and provides kerosene lamps (P50). The guide expects a tip (around P200). Boats do not go out in the rain. (☎276 1151. Open M-F 8am-5pm. Park US$2.)

Accommodations can be found at **St. Michael's Lodging House** ❷ to the left of Elsie's Bakery, next to the jeepney stop in Basey. (☎276 1003. Dorm bed P150.) Another option is the **guesthouse** ❹ in the national park. (Call DENR for reservations. Singles P300; doubles with bath P400.)

While in Basey, navigate the picturesque streets to **St. Michael's Church,** built in 1636. There are many attractions in **Western Samar:** the area around **Calbayog** is full of caves and waterfalls, while the **Samar Archaeological Museum and Research Center,** at Christ the King College in Calbayog, documents the island's history.

ORMOC ☎53

Ormoc was the stage for the decisive, if relatively unknown, World War II Battle of Ormoc Bay on November 11, 1944, which marked the beginning of the Japanese retreat from the archipelago. Today, the World War II memorial in the attractive waterfront park is frequented by families with children during the day and becomes the center of vibrant festivities at night. Cleaner and friendlier than Tacloban, this transportation hub deserves a day's stay.

TRANSPORTATION. At the bus terminal, **Philtranco** (☎255 2708) takes off for **Manila** at 5am (24hr., with A/C P890) and also at 9am and 5pm (26hr., P910). These buses stop at **Allen** (P337, with A/C P369); **Calbayog** (P203/P268); **Catbalogan** (4hr.; P201/P220); **San Isidro** (P337/P369); and **Tacloban** (2hr., P104/P114). Ferries connect San Isidro and Allen to **Matnog** on Luzon (1½hr., P71). **JD Bus Line** (☎255 2890) runs A/C vans to **Tacloban** (2hr., 4 per day 6am-8:30pm, P100); and **Naval** on Biliran (1½hr., 3 per day 6:30am-9pm, P100). **Eagle Star** (☎255 5166) and **Velmar** alternate service to **Catbalogan** (4hr.; 3, 5, 8, 9am; P124) and **Tacloban** (2½hr., every hour 3:30am-5pm, P76). **Bachelor Express** runs to **Davao** (11:30am, 11pm; P450). **SuperCat ferries** (☎255 3511; open 5am-7pm), at the end of the pier, chug to **Cebu** (2hr.; 8:30am, 1:30, 6:30pm; P480). 15% student discount with ID. **Sulpicio Lines** (☎255 2041) heads for **Cebu** (5hr., Su 11pm, P150); and **Manila** (52hr., Tu 7pm, P700). **Oceanjet** runs twice a day to **Cebu** (P430).

ORIENTATION AND PRACTICAL INFORMATION. Ormoc is in northwest Leyte, 109km across the central range from Tacloban. Tucked into the north coast of **Ormoc Bay,** the **city pier** juts directly southward. Walking out of the pier area, the bus terminal and jeepney pick-up are on the left. The first road perpendicular to the pier is **Larrazabal Blvd.,** featuring street barbecues and fresh pineapple. **Bonifacio St.** heads north, crossing Larrazabal Blvd. and **Aviles St.** Farther east, **Navarro** and **San Pedro St.** run north to south from the memorial park along the water.

Services include: the **Philippine National Bank** (☎255 4538), on Bonifacio St. with an **ATM** (open M-F 9am-3pm); a **hospital** (☎255 2475); the **police** (☎166); **Internet access** at **OrmocNet,** on Obrero St. near the Ormoc Villa Hotel (☎255 8237; P30 per hr.); **telephones** in the PLDT office, on the corner of Bonifacio and Catag St. (☎/fax 255 4737; open daily 7am-10pm); and the Cogon district **post office** (☎255 3181; open M-F 7am-noon and 1-5:30pm, Sa 8am-noon). **Postal code:** 6541.

ACCOMMODATIONS AND FOOD. On Obrero St. at the park end of Larrazabal Blvd., the **Ormoc Villa Hotel** ❺ has recently changed owners and introduced more affordable room rates (singles P1350; doubles P1600; extra person P500). The comfortable rooms, pretty garden and swimming pool (P100 for non-guests) make it worth the money. Opposite the bus terminal is the **Hotel Don Felipe** ❹ with clean, spacious rooms, a comfortable lobby and friendly staff. (☎255 2460. Singles P360, with A/C P480; doubles P420/P630; deluxe rooms in a new building P900-2400; extra person P250.)Rooms at **Eddie's Inn Lodging House** ❷ on Rizal and Aviles St. have beds and nothing else. (Singles P125; doubles P250.) **Barbecues** line the waterfront. For more formal dining, head along Larrazabal Blvd. away from the bus terminal. **Chitos Chow** ❷ serves up Chinese and Filipino dishes for P45-200. (Open daily 9am-11:30pm.) The restaurant in the **Ormoc Villa Hotel** ❷ offers Filipino specialties such as chicken pork *adobo* (P150), *halo-halo* with ice cream (P80), and pan-Asian favorites (P80-120). (Open daily 6am-11:30pm.)

SIGHTS AND ENTERTAINMENT. Magellan left behind a bridge by Larrazabal Blvd. The **Leyte Mountain Trail** snakes east 40km to Mahagnao National Park, terminating in Burauen, 66km from Tacloban. A national park since 1992, **Lake Danao** is an oasis in the heart of a wild forest. From the Ormoc bus terminal, take a jeepney (1½hr., leaves when full, P30) to the Lake Danao stop. Next walk (15min.) or take a *bangka* (5min., P5) to the Department of Environment and Natural Resources (DENR), where park ranger Quinciano Abiertas Jr. arranges *banca* trips around the lake (P40 per hr.) and treks in the forest (park entrance fee US$2; tip expected for forest treks). Camping is free. The station has showers, and huts cost P100 per person per day. **Fred's Bar,** on Jaena Lopez St. near the corner of J. Navarro St., provides a forum for the local entertainment: karaoke. The regulars sing quite well. (☎255 2953. San Miguel beer P25. Open daily 8pm-1am.) Within the Don Felipe complex, the **Swing Disco** is mainly ballroom (Tu-F 8:30pm-2am) and disco (F 11:30pm-3am, Sa 9pm-3am, Su 11:30pm-2am). Cover costs P100.

BILIRAN ISLAND

Welcome to the virtually untouched Filipino hinterland. On Biliran, water buffalo trudge through rice paddies with farmers in tow; the police chief bemoans his lack of a patrol car; and local Visayans chase *tuba* (a homemade wine concoction derived from coconut tree sap) with a quick gulp of soda. The island has managed to stay off the beaten track, but new infrastructure and a growing European-dominated tourist force may soon put Biliran on the mainstream map.

Tacloban and Ormoc are the easiest gateways to Biliran. **Eagle Star, PP Bus Lines,** and **JD Bus Lines** alternate departures to **Ormoc** (2hr., every 2-3hr. 3:30am-4:30pm, with A/C P100). The buses' arrival times to Ormoc coincide with the departure times of the **SuperCat ferries** to **Cebu** (4½hr., 4 per day, P370). There are slower ferries from Naval to Cebu: **Michael's** (8hr.; Su, Th-F 8pm; P185) and **John Carrier** (8hr.; Su, Tu, Th 9pm; P185). Eagle Star, PP Bus Lines, and JD Bus Lines also run to **Tacloban** (3hr., every 30min. 10:30am-4:30pm, P70; A/C buses 10:30am, 4:30pm; P100).

Roughly 110km northwest of Tacloban, the province of Biliran crowns the north coast of Leyte. **Biliran,** the southernmost town, is the island's chief entry point. The capital, **Naval,** lies midway up the west coast, followed by **Almeria** and **Kawayan.** A dirt road circles the island, linking **Culaba** on the northeast coast, **Caibiran** on the east coast, and **Cabucgayan** on the southeastern coast. A road skirts Caibiran volcano, connecting Naval with Caibiran and Culaba. **Maripipi Island,** a snorkeler's dream, sits off Biliran's northwest coast. **Higatangan Island** lies west of Naval.

NAVAL

Cebuano-speaking Naval stole the title of the provincial capital from its eastern Waray-Waray-speaking sister city Caibiran when Biliran became a province in 1992. The hectic activity of the **pier/bus terminal,** with its eateries and large market, emanates eastward by way of two parallel roads—**Vicentillo St.** to the north, and **P. Inocentes St.** to the south. A 15min. hike down P. Inocentes or a 5min. pedicab ride will bring you to the **Naval Institute of Technology** on the right.

The **PLDT,** on P. Inocentes St., has phone booths for domestic (P1-5 per min.) and international (P20-35 per min.) calls. (☎198 2029. Open daily 7am-10pm.) The **Philippine National Bank** is at the left end of Ballesteros St. looking toward the ocean. (No ATM. Open M-F 9am-noon and 1-3pm.) At the other end of Ballesteros St., a right on Caneja St. leads to the **police station.** From another path leading down P. Inocentes, a right on Ballesteros St. will lead to a **hospital,** 2km outside Naval. **Chapeland Pharmacy** on Casfin St. is open 24hr. Naval's pier and jeepney/bus terminal has daily departures for coastal cities and nearby islands. From the pier, walk 10-15m along P. Inocentes St. and take a right through the market to reach the **post office** (open M-F 8am-noon and 1-5pm). **Postal code:** 6543.

Enroll in night school at the **Naval Institute of Technology ❷,** or stay at their hostel for P200 (with A/C P300). The **Brigida Inn ❶** adjoins LM's Auto Supply. (Singles with fan P70; doubles with fan P160-300.) Suffer the financial consequences of A/C in the dimly lit rooms of the **Rosevic Lodging House ❹,** farther up Vicentillo St. on the left. (Singles with A/C P350; doubles P400-P500.) **Marvin's Place Seaside Inn ❺** in Atipolo is a much better value. It has a pool and access to a little beach. (P600 per room with A/C and private bath.) Hire a pedicab (20min., P5) or a motorbike driver (10min., P20) to take you to Atipolo.

Serving up Filipino dishes such as pork *adobo* (P20) and *halo-halo* (P25), as well as burgers and sandwiches (grilled cheese P20), the **Five Sisters ❶** cafe-restaurant on Inocentes St. across from the PLDT office is a great deal. Next to the CAP building at the market, **Benno's ❶** serves Filipino pork stews (P20-40) and cake (P20) in an equally relaxed setting. **Balondo Discopub** across from Brigida's Inn plays the Philippine dance charts up and down. (Open daily 7pm-2am.)

DAYTRIPS FROM NAVAL

Naval's pier and bus terminal have daily departures for coastal cities and nearby islands. The rugged highway unlocks rewards for those willing to swap sweat for seclusion. Outriggers run west to **Higatangan Island** (1hr., 11am, P25). Arrive early at the pier, as the boats fill up quickly. The only lodging option on Higatangan is the **Limpiado Tourist Inn ❹** (basic rooms with sea view P350). Higatangan's attractions include the beach and snake-infested **Ka Ventong Cave.** The snorkeling heaven of **Maripipi Island** can be reached by boat (3hr., 10am, P30). Inquire at the mayor's house for a homestay on the island. **Caibiran** is convenient for launching an expedition to **Mt. Biliran.** Surrounding villages shelter sulfur hot springs: **Caibiran Falls,** and the spring-fed **San Bernardo** pool. Jeepneys cross the island every hour (P30). Daytrippers may hire a motorcycle with driver (P400 per day). Sunsets are wonderful at secluded **Agta Beach.** Take the jeepney bound for Kawayan and tell the driver to let you off at Agta (35min., P10.) Inhabited by a hospitable family, **Agta Beach Resort ❷** has thatched huts. (P150 per person, with A/C P500 per hut.) Agta Beach faces **Dalutan Island.** The resort rents out boats to paddle to Dalutan (40min., P30). Alternatively, hire a pump boat to Dalutan (10min., P300) or **Tingkasan Bat Cave** on Tingkasan Island (10-15min., P350).

PALAWAN

Once connected to Borneo, the large, finger-shaped island of Palawan is understandably different from the rest of the Philippines. Most of the rest of the country is virtually wildlife-free, but Palawan teems with bizarre beasts ranging from the scaly anteater and Palawan bearcat to the stink badger. Instead of volcanoes, the island has limestone cliffs similar to those of China and Vietnam. Palawan takes pride in

FROM THE ROAD

THE COCKFIGHT

When I arrived in the Phillipines I was not keen on seeing a cockfight. Just the thought of the jeering spectators, waiting around a blood-stained pit for the spectacle to start, made me want to avoid the scene at all costs.

But after spending a few weeks in the country, my attitude changed. By this time I had passed through many small towns and had heard the characteristic shouts and squawks of Saturday and Sunday afternoons fights. Almost every local in these villages had a cockfight story; all were surprised that I had not attended one. I finally decided that I could not leave the Philippines without experiencing the Pinoy national obsession for myself.

On one Saturday afternoon toward the end of my trip I got my chance. I entered the bamboo cock pit with my companion, a well-known, retired government official, who drove a *jeepney* to supplement his pension and penchant for cockfight betting. The locals greeted us with good-natured cries.

Since I was with the official, they gave us the best seat in the pen. It was the last fight of the day, and as start time approached, more and more people flooded in, filling the pen beyond capacity.

The fighters, two feisty cocks with curved cutting blades protruding backwards from their left feet, were finally brought in. The proud owners circled the pen and held the cocks up for all to see, allowing the spectators to judge each cock's value and decide on how to place their bets.

(continued on next page)

its cultural preservation as well. While most of the Philippines hurtles toward modernity, it seems as though Palawan has remained frozen in time; outside Puerto Princesa, electricity and running water are rare. More than 80 tribes, untouched rainforest, and incomparably beautiful beaches earn Palawan its title: "The Last Frontier."

EW FROM ABOVE

r: Puerto Princesa.
vns: Coron, El Nido, Port Barton.
:s: Scuba diving at Tubbataha Reef or Coron's Japanese wrecks; visiting the Subterr
Park; island-hopping and snorkeling in Honda Bay or Bacuit Bay; visiting Maquinit H

PUERTO PRINCESA ☎48

The lone urban outpost in Palawan, Puerto Princesa has become environmentally conscious, ferociously fending off loggers from the wilderness and protecting its several indigenous cultures. The cleanest city in the Philippines, "Puerto" levies heavy fines on litterers. At least one night here is needed to stock up on supplies and funds, which are lacking elsewhere, but cafes, restaurants, and bustling bars often lure travelers to linger longer on the island.

TRANSPORTATION

Flights: The **airport** is 1km from the National Hwy. intersection with Rizal Ave. **PAL** (☎433 4565; open daily 8-11:30am and 1-3:30pm) is in the building to the right of the airport and flies to **Manila** (daily 10:30am, P3603). **Air Philippines,** 420 Rizal Ave. (☎433 7003; open daily 8am-5pm), flies to **Manila** (daily 11am, P2998). **Seair,** 263 Manalo Extn. (☎433 2540; open daily 8am-5pm), flies to: **Busuanga** (M, W, F 2:20pm; P2000) via **El Nido** (P1700); **Cuyo** (M, F 11:10am; P2000); **Sandoval** (W 11am, P2000) via **San Vicente** (P1700).

Ferries: The **wharf** is on the western tip of the city. Walking up the hill and to the right connects you to Rizal Ave. Tickets are sold at the wharf, but reserve a spot beforehand at the ferry offices downtown. **Negros Navigation** (☎/fax 433 7204) has an office on Roxas St. near the corner with Rizal Ave. Open M-Sa 8am-noon and 1-5pm. Ferries sail to **Manila** (22hr., M 2pm, from P1205). **WG&A** (☎433 4875) is on the right side of Rizal Ave. in the ARL building, a 5-10min. walk from the airport. Open M-F 8am-5pm. **Super ferries** sail to **Manila** (28hr.; Su 9am; from P1200, with meals P1280) via **Coron** (14hr., P925).

Local Transportation: Since public transportation is spotty when demand is low, hiring a **private vehicle** is often necessary. A jeepney-derivative costs P2500 per day. An A/C 4WD runs P5000 per day (P3000 in low

(continued from previous page)

Outside the cock pit, a designated official collected the bets, straining to to establish order amidst the jostling, shouting, money waving crowd. After all bets were placed, the owners brought the cocks close enough to peck each other's necks. This is supposed to incite their rage so that they will come out fighting.

Unfamiliar with chickens and Pinoy cockfighting culture I had trouble telling the two cocks apart. Apparently each cock has distinguishing color markers on its back, but once the fight starts the cocks lose their plumage, making identification almost impossible to the untutored eye. My companion placed a bet on the underdog, and not being able to make even an educated guess, I followed his bet.

The whistle blew, and everyone jumped up from his or her seat. The heap of blood and feathers moved too fast for my eyes to follow. Within two minutes the spectacle was over; the winner pecked upon the lifeless body of the loser. Not surprisingly, I lost on my bet. I shrugged at my loss and carried on home.

—Kristina Vetter

season) to **Sabang** and the **Underground River.** A/C vehicles to **El Nido** cost P15,000. Some agencies slap a P500-1000 overnight fee on top of a 2-day fee. All rentals come with a driver. **Go Palawan** (see **Travel Agencies,** below) rents **dirt bikes** for P800 per day.

PRACTICAL INFORMATION

Puerto Princesa sprawls from **Sabang** in the north to **Long Point** in the south. The city is on a peninsula jutting into the Sulu Sea, south of Honda Bay on the east coast. Ferries dock on the western tip, where **Rizal Ave.,** the main drag, ends. **Roxas, Burgos,** and **Valencia St.** intersect Rizal Ave. The **National Hwy.** intersects Rizal Ave. on the eastern tip of the commercial area near the **Provincial Capitol.** The only paved road outside the city center leads south to **Quezon.**

Tourist Offices: City Tourism (☎434 4211), at air and sea ports. Open daily 8am-noon and 1-5pm. More helpful is the **Provincial Tourism Office** (☎433 2968), at the corner of Rizal Ave. and the National Hwy. Excellent "Palawan Tourism Map" P50. Open M-F 8am-noon and 1-5pm. The unofficial tourist office at **Backpackers' Cafe** has a humorous and helpful "comments book" and a great wall map of Palawan. Open daily 7am-11pm. **Pat Murray,** one of Palawan's original settlers, is a walking Palawan encyclopedia. He frequents Trattoria Inn and happily offers advice.

Travel Agencies: **Go Palawan,** 353 Rizal Ave. at Trattoria Inn (☎433 4570; gopalawan@pal-onl.com). Phenomenal staff and countless brochures. Open M-Sa 9am-6pm. **Coron Tours and Travel,** 38-B R. San Juan St. at Unit 6 Bundal Business Center (☎/fax 434 2638), between the airport and the city in *barangay* San Miguel. Offers hints on getting to and exploring the northern islands. Open M-F 8am-5pm, Sa 8am-noon.

Banks: Many on Rizal Ave. near Valencia St. All banks open M-F 9am-3pm. **Bank of the Philippine Islands** has an **ATM** (Cirrus/Maestro/MC).

Bookstore: Leonar's Merrimart Bookstore has English titles. Open M-Sa 8am-7pm.

Markets: The central market is on Malvar St. between Burgos and Valencia St.

Emergency: ☎166.

Police: Police Assistance Center (☎433 9826), on Rizal Ave. near Palawan Museum.

Pharmacies: Mercury Drug (☎433 2498), on Rizal Ave. Another branch on Valencia St. Open daily 7am-10pm.

Medical Services: Adventist Hospital (☎433 2156), on San Pedro National Hwy. near the Santa Monica Rd. intersection. **Open 24hr.**

Telephones: Bayantel, 293 Rizal Ave. (☎433 4892), past the Provincial Capital. International and domestic calls. Open M-F 8am-10pm, Sa 8am-5pm.

Internet Access: Big Bad Wolf, on Valencia St. next to the market. P60 per hr. Open M-Sa 10am-10pm, Su 2-10pm. **Trattoria Inn** is the fastest. P100 per hr.

Post Office: ☎433 2556. On Burgos St. near the corner of Rizal Ave. *Poste Restante.* Open daily 8am-noon and 1-5pm. **Postal code:** 5300.

ACCOMMODATIONS

Puerto Pension, 35 Malvar St. (☎433 2969; ppension@pal-onl.com). Gorgeous, polished bamboo rooms. Restaurant with panoramic bay view. Singles P250; doubles P380, with A/C and common room P750. ❸

Trattoria Inn (☎433 2719), on P.E.O. Rd, 1km from the airport. Superb service. Laundry service. Tourist information. Doubles with A/C, cable TV, and hot water P490 (P590 double occupancy). ❹

Backpackers' Cafe, Bookshop, and Inn, 112 Valencia St., 5min. past the Palawan Museum. A fusion of cafe, bookstore, travel agency, guest house, and island-guru hangout. People stay for the company and travel advice, not the rooms. Office open daily 7am-11pm. Singles P150; doubles P220. ❷

Abelardo's Pension, 63 D. Manga St. (☎433 2049), off Burgos St. Immaculate, well-run guest house. "Clean is our best asset," boasts the convivial owner. Singles P150; twins P250, with A/C and private bath P600; add P50 for TV. ❷

FOOD

Ka Lui Restaurant (☎433 2580), on Rizal Ave., toward the airport from the city center. Easily the best restaurant in Palawan and possibly the Philippines' best seafood. Menu changes with daily catch and includes soup and a heavenly dessert fruit plate (regular P100). Open M-Sa 11am-2pm and 6-11pm. ❷

Vegetarian House, 79 Burgos St., at the corner of Manalo St. Wise sayings adorn the walls of this Buddhist eatery. "Beef steak" and other "meat" dishes that'll fool any carnivore for P50-120. Open M-Sa 9am-2pm and 4-10pm. ❶

Pho Vietnamese Restaurant (☎433 3576). A 5min. tricycle ride past the airport. Fondues P170-380. Spicy chicken with lemongrass P49. Vermicelli P44-52. Open daily W-M 9am-10pm. ❸

Cafe Arturo (☎433 4146), on the North National Hwy. in San José at the center of a mahogany plantation. Blackened prawns P200. Set menu P300-350. Open M 6-10pm, Tu-Su 11am-2pm and 6-10pm. ❹

SIGHTS

The **Kamarikutan Kape at Galeri,** on Rizal Ave. near the airport, provides an interesting glimpse at local art. The airy complex, constructed in Palawan and Ifugao styles, exhibits area artists. (☎433 5182. Open daily 8am-11pm.) The **Palawan Museum,** at the corner of Rizal Ave. and Valencia St. behind Mendoza Park, places the island in historical and cultural context. Its collection includes artifacts from the Tabon Caves, the "Cradle of Philippine Civilization." Their library contains books on Palawan. (☎433 2963. Open M-Sa 8am-noon and 1:30-5pm, Su 9-11am. P10, students P5, children P2.) At the western end of Rizal Ave., by the cathedral, a **memorial** marks where 143 US POWs were herded into a tunnel, doused with gasoline, and set on fire by Japanese captors on December 15, 1944. Eleven men survived by jumping off the cliff and swimming across the bay. Supporting the local ethno-environmental craze, **Culture Shack,** on Rizal Ave. opposite Bayantel, sells cashew wine (P80), basketry, and clothing. (Open M-Sa 8:40am-7:40pm.)

ACTIVITIES

Tubbataha Reef, 150km southeast of Puerto Princesa, is the archipelago's most sought-after dive site. Its remote location and limited accessibility (Mar.-June) make a trip to the reef difficult, but the certainty of spotting large marine life draws divers nonetheless. **Queen Anne Divers** (☎433 2719), on P.E.O. Rd., at the Trattoria Inn, operates two dive ships to Tubbataha Reef (5-7 days; US$660-900; must be booked 6 months in advance). Queen Anne also runs trips to **Busuanga** and the **Coron Islands** (which are famous for their Japanese wrecks), daytrips to reefs off the southern coast near Puerto Princesa (2-dive packages with lunch and boat US$55, with rentals US$60), and PADI courses (open-water US$300, advanced open-water US$230). **Island Divers,** 371 Rizal Ave., brings divers to southern Puerto Princesa Bay around Pete's Reef, Light House, and Table Head (2-dive daytrip US$50, with rentals US$60) and offers PADI courses for US$200-280. (☎433 5103. Open M-F 8am-5pm.)

NIGHTLIFE

Most Filipinos won't let foreigners sneak out of Puerto Princesa's numerous **karaoke joints** without wailing a song, but for a night free from the spotlight, the cozy **Tom-Tom Club** on Manalo Extn. (tomtom@pal-onl.com) leaves the music to the professionals. **Nick's Venue,** in the Admiral Hotel on Rizal Junction, is the main hotspot for Palawan's 20-something partiers. (Cover P100-150. Open daily 8pm-2am.) **Spice Bar & Disco,** on Rizal Ave., also keeps the crowd hopping until after midnight. (San Miguel P35. No cover, but P100 minimum tab. No shorts or slippers. Open M-Th 8pm-2am, F-Su 8pm-3am.)

DAYTRIPS FROM PUERTO PRINCESA

HONDA BAY. North of the city, the water is peppered with islands ideal for snorkeling, swimming, and sunbathing. Most island resorts, however, have shut down since the Abu Sayyaf terrorist group kidnapped tourists from **Areceffi Island** in 2001 (see **Militant Separatists and Terrorist Groups,** p. 553). Under drastically increased security, the bay now makes for a good daytrip. **Snake Island, Starfish Island,** and **Pandan Island** can be reached by a short *banca* trip (P800). Visitors to **Señorita Island** can check out fish and seaweed farming. *(Bancas (P250-1200) leave for Honda Bay from St. Lourdes Whart, a 30min. tricycle ride from town (P250). A tourist shack organizes bancas and snorkelling gear for P100 per day.)*

TABON CAVES. The oldest inhabited site in Southeast Asia, the caves house the 22,000-year-old Tabon man, though stone tools discovered in the 1970s prove the existence of even earlier human inhabitants. Only 14 of the 200 caves are explored and make for a great hike. *(South of Puerto Princesa in Quezon. Charing Bus Lines runs trips to Quezon leaving from the market on Malvar St. (2 buses daily, leave when full, P132). From Quezon, hire a banca to go to the caves (P500 round-trip). Bring a flashlight and hiking shoes.)*

CROCODILE FARM AND BUTTERFLY GARDEN. At the **Crocodile Farming Institute,** the freshwater Mindoro crocodile and the Indo-Pacific saltwater crocodile have multiplied from an initial population of seven to 5000 today. At the **Butterfly Garden,** on the road to the Crocodile Farm, you can view Palawan's gorgeous butterflies. (Open daily 8:30am-4:30pm. Live pupae are P20 at the giftshop.) *(To get to Irawan, hop on a "Manginisda" jeepney (15min., 6:30-7pm, P16) from the corner of Malvar and Burgos St. in Puerto Princesa, or hire a tricycle (30min., P200). Open M-Sa 9am-4pm. Tours every hr. Feedings M and Th afternoons. Butterfly Garden open daily 8:30am-4:30pm.)*

IWAHIG PRISON AND PENAL FARM. Across the bay from the city proper, brown shirt-clad prisoners work the Iwahig rice paddies, shackle-free. Iwahig is a community with basketball courts, a town center, and residential sections for the prisoners' families. When the "minimums" aren't farming, they fashion handicrafts.

Lucky travelers might convince a prisoner to sell an "Inmate—Minimum" T-shirt (P200). *(Tricycle to Penal Colony P350. Jeepneys marked "Iwahig" run from Valencia St. (30min., 2-3 per day 10am-3pm, P16). Open daily 6am-6pm.)*

PUERTO PRINCESA SUBTERRANEAN RIVER NATIONAL PARK

Between Port Barton and Puerto Princesa, the giant Puerto Princesa Subterranean River National Park lies with its gaping mouth pointed toward the South China Sea. The **Cabayugan River,** the longest underground river in the world, weaves 8.2km through a natural growth forest, home to macaques and monitor lizards, 40,000 bats, and thousands of birds. It would not be complete, however, without a natural stone statue of the Virgin Mary.

The park is best reached from **Sabang. Jeepneys** to Sabang leave from Malvar St. near the Shell station in Puerto Princesa (3hr., 7am-2am, P75). From Sabang, **motorboats** (one way P300, round-trip P500) leave from the pier where jeepneys from Puerto Princesa stop. Or you can hike along the 2hr. **Monkey Trail** that ends at the park entrance. **Boats** go to **Port Barton** (3hr., private P2500) and **El Nido** (7hr., private P5000), but prepare for a rough ride. **Jeepneys** to **Puerto Princesa** leave from the ferry pier (3hr., 3 per day 6:30am-1:30pm, P75), but they aren't very reliable. **A/C vans** offer a more comfortable ride but are just as infrequent (P400). The desperate can hire a **jeep** (P2000) or **A/C van** (P2500) from the park office.

Stop by **St. Paul's Subterranean River National Park Office** on Manalo St. near the corner with Fernandez St. in Puerto Princesa, to get **permits.** (☎433 2409. Open M-F 8am-noon and 1-5pm. General entrance P30. Cave entrance P200, children P100.) You can also grab a permit at the **Visitor's Assistance Center.** (Open daily 8am-noon and 1-5pm.) Snorkelers should rent equipment in Puerto Princesa.

Across from the pier is **Pat 'n' Let's Cottages and Seafood Restaurant ❸,** with cozy huts (P300-500) and great breakfast omelettes (P80-85). A 10min. walk down the beach with the ocean to your left ends at **Mary's Cottages ❸,** in a quiet cove with hammocks and similar amenities. (Huts with common room P300, beachfront P400.) Mary's also rents outriggers to navigate the Puyo-puyo River (P50).

PORT BARTON

Perhaps it's the very absence of phones, roads, and reliable electricity that pulls travelers in to explore, snorkel, and swim at the pristine islands off the coast of Port Barton. **Jeepneys** go to **Puerto Princesa** (5-6hr., up to 12hr. in low season due to road conditions; 8-9am; P140, private P4500). In high season, **boats** go to **El Nido** (5hr.; M, W 9:30am; Th, Su 10:30am; P1000, private P5000) and **Sabang** (3hr.; Tu, Th noon; W, Sa 12:30pm; P650, private P2000). **Rizal Ave.** hugs the coast, cradling the port's cottages. **Quezon, Mabini,** and **Ballesleros** cross Rizal Ave. toward the ocean. **The Adventist Health Care Clinic** on Bonafacio Ave., a block from Rizal Ave. between Quezon and Ballesleros Ave., provides basic care. The nearest **post office** and **phones** are in Roxas (2hr. by jeepney).

Port Barton rides the tide of tourism. During high season, the tourist swell necessitates tents, while in low season, restaurants and cottages often shut down. **Ausan's Cottages ❸** stands out for quality, cheap rooms but closes during low season. (☎433 4825. Singles P250.) **Swissippini Lodge and Resort ❺** (☎433 4757) has clean accommodations. Simple cottages for P500/P300, or cottages with a common room for P700/P500 are a good deal. **El Dorado Sunset Cottages ❸** (☎433 2110) offers similar lodgings with cottages P300-400 and a delicious seafood buffet (P225). The **Bamboo House ❷** has entrees for P60-140. (Open daily 7am-10pm.)

Port Barton's **beach** is good, if a bit crowded by *bancas*, but the bay is great for swimming; more options hide in island coves. *Bancas* island-hop for P800-1000. **Cacnipa, Exolica,** and **Albaguin islands** all have snorkeling sites, and scuba diving can be arranged through the **El Busero Inn** ($50 for 2 dives). For a freshwater experience, walk 1¼hr. inland to cascading waterfalls. Pick up a map from behind the bar at El Dorado Sunset Cottages (see above).

EL NIDO

☎48

El Nido is the frontier of travel on this "last frontier" island. Imposing limestone cliffs surround the peaceful town, sheltering tourists from tourism. It seems enchanted at dawn when the fog slowly reveals the towering islands of Bacuit Bay. A couple of hours later, turquoise waters and blinding white sands make for postcard-perfect scenery.

TRANSPORTATION. **Seair** flies to: **Manila** (M, F 3:25pm; P4400) via **Busuanga** (P2100); **Puerto Princesa** (M, W, F 9:45am; P1700). **Jeepneys** go to **Puerto Princesa** daily during high season and every 2-3 days during low season (12-14hr., P400). Alternate routes to **Puerto Princesa** include taking a **jeepney** to **Sibaltan** (2-2½hr., daily 7am, P60) where a **boat** leaves for **Taytay** (3-4hr., 9:30am, P160); from Taytay, jeepneys head to **Puerto Princesa** (8-10hr.; 2, 4pm; P190). During high season, **boats** leave for **Port Barton** (4hr., F 6am, P650) and **Sabang** (7hr.; W, Sa 7am; P850). During the low season, private boats will bring you anywhere if you pay enough.

PRACTICAL INFORMATION. **Calle Hama,** which turns into **Palmera St.,** runs along the coast; **Calle Real** runs parallel. **Rizal St.** cuts through the two and heads to the ocean. All other roads are unmarked, unnamed, and unpaved. Buy a **map** at El Nido Boutique. The **Municipal Tourism Office** (open M-F 8am-5pm) is across from the **post office** (open M-F 8am-5pm) on Calle Real. There are no banks, but **Palawan Pawnshop, El Nido Boutique and ArtCafe,** and **Lim's Store** exchange cash. The **police station** is in the Municipal Building on the corner of Calle Real. **Farmacia Comprendio** has most non-prescription drugs. (Open daily 7am-9pm.) There is also a **clinic** next to El Nido High School. (Open M-F 8am-noon and 1-5pm.) **Globe Telecom** offers **collect call** service for P60. (Open M-F 7:30am-10pm, Su 9am-10pm.)

ACCOMMODATIONS AND FOOD. Like most of Palawan, El Nido is deserted in the off season but receives large crowds of backpackers and adventurers during peak months. During low season, prices of cottages are halved and many restaurants shut down. **Lally and Abet Cottages ❸,** at the far end of the beach, is popular and quiet. (Cottages P350/P250, beachfront P900/P600, with A/C P1200/P800). Nearby, **Gloria's Beach Cottages ❸** is run by motherly Ms. Fernandez, who gives advice on El Nido and arranges island-hopping. (Cottages P400/P250.) **Dolarog Beach Resort ❸** (www.dolarog.com), a short *banca* ride from town (P350), has upscale cottages in a well-tended palm garden. Edo, the Italian owner, cooks good pastas and risottos for P150-300. Cottages run P1200-1500. A package deal includes full board and a daily boat excursion for US$60. The best breakfast in town can be found at the **El Nido Boutique and Artcafe ❸.** (Muesli P110. Yummy mixed fruit shake P55. Great travel advice included. Open daily 6:30am-8pm.) **Ric Son's ❸,** on the beachfront, has gorgeous views of Bacuit Bay and a large seafood menu. (Fish with black bean sauce P125. Open daily 6am-10pm.) **Mac-Mac Restaurant ❹,** on Calle Hama, has a large selection of German and Filipino dishes. (Excellent "Steak Hunter" with fried potatoes P250. Open daily 8am-10pm.)

SIGHTS AND ENTERTAINMENT. The islands of **Bacuit Bay** are El Nido's prime attraction. "Asia's Galapagos," these isles boast coral, three species of endangered giant turtles, and brilliant fish, all beneath rugged limestone cliffs. Among the best sights are the small lagoons of **Miniloc Island,** the secret beach of

Matinloc Island, and **Pinsail Island,** where a skeleton of a WWII Japanese soldier lies within a marble cave. **Simisu Island** offers great snorkeling. Cottages have boats that will take you wherever you want for P1200 per day. Alternatively, Judith and Tani from the **El Nido Boutique and Artcafe** (see **Food,** above) have set island-hopping trips for P300-350 per person (4-person minimum). Other tours include cliff-climbing (P120), island trekking on **Cadlao** (P300), and hiking to the **Maquinit Hot Springs** and **Nagkalit Kalit Waterfalls** (P400). All prices include lunch and are per person, with a minimum of two. **Palawan Divers** on Calle Real offers dive trips around the archipelago, but Coron Island has better diving. On most Sundays, especially holidays, **cockfights** erupt at the cockpit on Rizal Ave. The **Shipwrecked Bar,** on Palmera St., is a popular tourist hangout. (San Miguel P25. Open daily 4pm-midnight.) Locals get down at **Bom Disco,** opposite Mac-Mac Restaurant. (Cover P10. Open daily 8pm-midnight.) The bar at **Bistro El Nido** has great mixed drinks (P60-95) and relaxed live guitar music. (Open daily 8am-1am.)

CORON

Northern Palawan is a wreck-diver's Shangri-La. The waters off Coron Island and the separate town of Coron earn the curious distinction of housing the second-highest number of sunken Japanese WWII vessels after the Marianas Islands. Diving aside, the azure waters, countless islets, and gorgeous inland lakes are enough reasons to visit for one day or four.

TRANSPORTATION AND PRACTICAL INFORMATION. **Seair** flies to **Manila** (daily, P2300); and **Puerto Princesa** (P2200) via **El Nido** (M, F; P2100). **Asian Spirit** has daily flights to **Manila** (P1850). Both airlines fly out of the **YKR** airport in **Busuanga** and have offices in Coron Town. **Jeepneys** to the airport leave Coron Town 2hr. before departure time (P150). **Pacific Airways** flies to **Manila** (P1900) from the more convenient airstrip behind the Kokos Nuss Resort, but only when there is an incoming plane from Manila. Inquire directly at the airstrip office. **WG&A Superferry** (☎123 148) sails to **Manila** (14hr., Su, P925) and **Puerto Princesa** (12hr., Sa, P650). **San Nicolas Lines** also goes to **Manila** (Su-M, F; P350).

As in many small towns, roads are few and unnamed. The **National Highway** connects Coron Town only to the western side of Busuanga Island, and the town's two main streets run parallel to the highway. The "first" street is anchored by **City Hall,** which also houses the **police station** and **post office** (open M-F 8am-noon and 1-5pm). On the opposite end is the town **market** and **pier** for small boats. **Swagman Travel** (with a **Western Union** branch) lies at the intersection of the "second" street and the National Highway. The **hospital** lies 3km north along the highway, next to the Kokos Nuss Resort. **Netport,** next to Bayside Divers Lodge, has a fast Internet connection. (P50 per hr. Open daily 8am-9pm.)

ACCOMMODATIONS AND FOOD. Most of Coron's accommodations are concentrated between its two ports. **Kokos Nuss Resort ❸,** 5316 Coron, is about 1½km toward Busuanga, but its amazing service and amenities make it well worth the distance. (kokosnuss@pinoymail.com. Small cottages P300; larger cottages P500-600, with private bath P700, with A/C P800. 15% discount for singles.) **Bayside Divers Lodge ❷** has breezy rooms over the water and a very friendly staff. (Doubles P200, with bath P300-450.) A 5min. *banca* ride across from Coron Town, on Uson Island, the **Dive Link Resort ❺** has package deals starting at US$65 per person (high season) and P1500 per person (low season), including board, daily boat trips, and airport transfer. The restaurant at the **Sea Dive Center ❸** offers scrumptious seafood with changing menus depending on the day's catch (dishes P80-250).

SINGAPORE

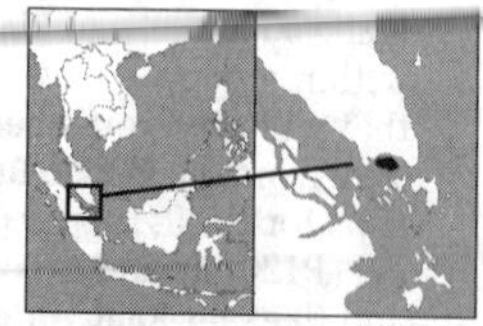

US$1 = S$1.75 (SINGAPORE DOLLAR)	S$1 = US$0.57
CDN$1 = S$1.12	S$1 = CDN$0.89
EURO€1 = S$1.72	S$1 = EURO€0.58
UK£1 = S$2.73	S$1 = UK£0.37
AUS$1 = S$0.96	S$1 = AUS$1.04
NZ$1 = S$0.82	S$1 = NZ$1.22
ZAR1 = S$0.17	S$1 = ZAR6.00

PHONE CODE **Country code:** 65. **International access code:** 001.

Singapore can be shocking after travel in other Southeast Asian nations. High-tech skyscrapers, clean streets, cutting-edge communication, and potable tap water distinguish the "Lion City" from its neighbors. But there's more to Singapore than an affinity for hygiene. Its stringent laws and extreme wealth sharply contrast with the busy, multicultural metropolis—the streets seem to march to a different urban beat. Nodding bougainvillea at the Botanical Gardens give way to ringing cash registers in downtown department stores, while sidewalks bustle with the interplay of four ethnicities and the controversy surrounding the city-state's human rights violations. Singapore is known for its harsh gum-chewing penalties, but the crab on Geylang Rd. and treks up Bukit Timah are worth restricting your behavior. Singapore is both financially and culturally rich.

FACTS AND FIGURES

Official Name: Republic of Singapore.

Government: Parliamentary Republic.

Capital: Singapore.

Land Area: 647.5 sq. km.

Geography: On the southern tip of the Malay peninsula.

Climate: Hot and humid year-round. Northeast monsoon season (Dec.-Mar.); Southwest monsoon season: (June-Sept.)

Population: 4,300,419.

Languages: Chinese (official), Malay (off. & national), Tamil (off.), English (off.)

Religions: Buddhism, Taoism, Islam, Christianity, Hinduism, Sikhism.

Average Income Per Capita: US$24,470.

Major Exports: Petroleum, machinery, electronics, minerals.

LIFE AND TIMES

DEMOGRAPHICS

Singapore's ethnic makeup is 76% **Chinese,** 15% **Malay,** and 6% **Indian,** the majority of whom are originally **Tamil** and were imported by the British as laborers. Singapore has welcomed immigrants since the 1300s. Combine the many foreign-born residents with increasing Westernization, and it's understandable why there's concern about whether Singapore can forge a strong sense of national unity. Recognizing this, the government strives to promote a vision of a unified, multicultural Singapore, free from Western influence.

LANGUAGE

Singapore's ethnic diversity is reflected in the multitude of languages spoken. Though **Malay** is the official language, virtually everyone in Singapore speaks at least one dialect of **Chinese,** Min Nan, Cantonese, Mandarin, and Hakka being the most common. Slightly over 9% of the population speaks Malay as a first language. The dialect spoken in Singapore is similar to that which is spoken in western Peninsular Malaysia. Roughly 2% of Singaporeans speak **Tamil** as a first language. A legacy of British rule, **English** is fairly common. Approximately 5% of the population speaks English as a first language, and English is the language of business and government. Its newer version in Singapore is **Singlish,** a mix of English and Chinese phrases or words. Often Singlish sounds much the same as English, but with an "a-lah" added to the end of each sentence.

RELIGION

BUDDHISM. Buddhism is practiced by 32% of the population in Singapore. Various groups from China originally established separate temples in Singapore, although those distinctions have blurred over time. Buddhism is often mixed in practice with Taoism, the second most popular religion in Singapore. Both Buddhism and Taoism are sometimes mixed with Confucianism as well.

TAOISM. A full 22% of the population is Taoist. Taoism is based on the teachings of Lao Tsu, a Chinese sage who believed in *Tao*, "the way," a system where people live in harmony with nature. It is practiced almost exclusively by the Chinese in Singapore.

ISLAM. Muslims in Singapore (15%) are often restricted by the non-denominational status of the state. In March of 2002 four Muslim girls were arrested for wearing head scarves to school, a violation of a government ban on religious symbols at schools. Most Muslims in Singapore are ethnic Malays.

CHRISTIANITY. Christianity arrived with the British and Sir Stamford Raffles (see **Raffles Hotel,** p. 663) and appears to have made a home, albeit a small one, in Singapore. Christianity is practiced by 13% of the population. Catholicism dates to the Western founding of Singapore in 1819. There are roughly 130 Catholic churches around the island. The Protestant church in Singapore, in addition to its religious impact, introduced programs such as prison counseling and anti-drug campaigns.

HINDUISM AND SIKHISM. The remaining 3% of Singapore largely practices either Hinduism or Sikhism. Hinduism and Sikhism are practiced almost exclusively by Indians. There are 24 Hindu temples in Singapore today and 16 registered Sikh organizations.

HISTORY

EARLY YEARS AND ISLAND COLONY (1300-1965)

IMPORTANT DATES

14th Century Tumasek established.	**1819** Sir Stamford Raffles docks in Singapore's harbor.	**1867** Singapore becomes British colony.	**1915** Singapore rules opium market, stifles Chinese secret societies.

The island state of Singapore, or **Tumasek** ("sea town") as it was once known, was established in the 14th century. One legend says it was founded by a Shrivijayan prince claiming relation to Alexander the Great, while another claims the island

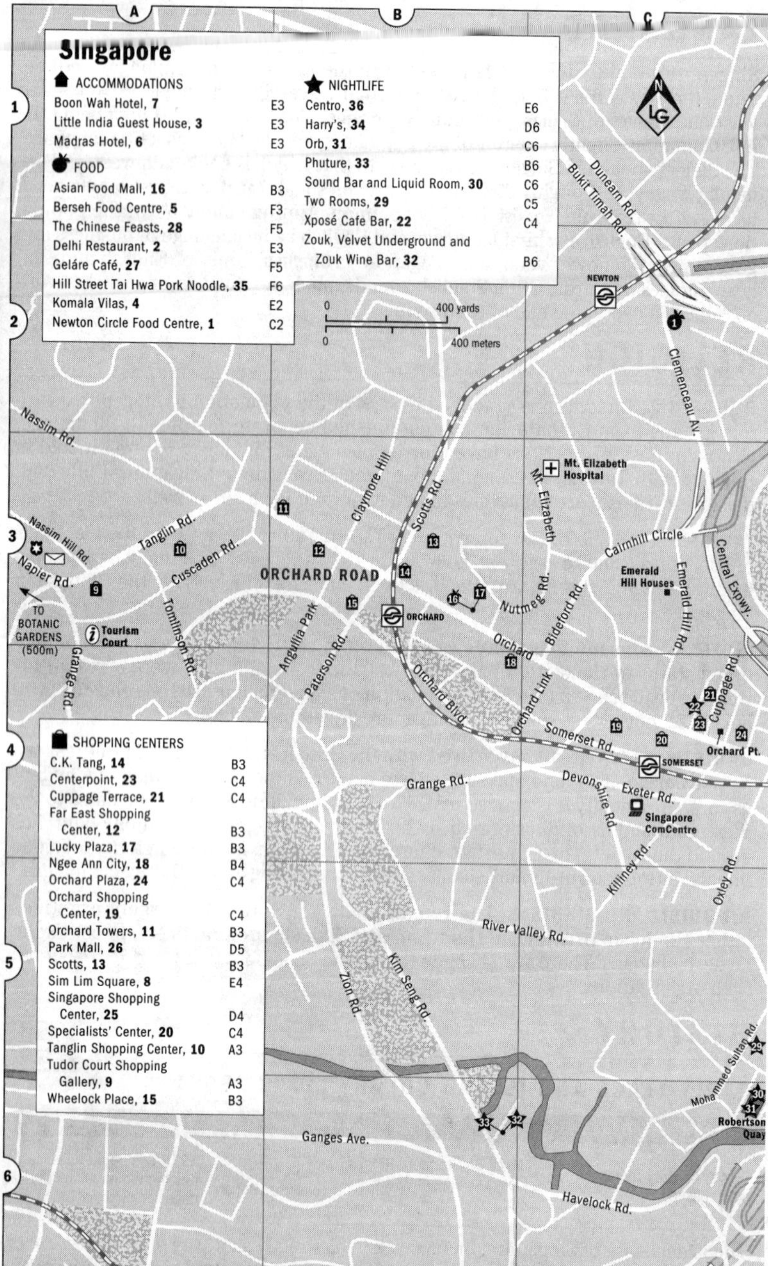
Singapore
ACCOMMODATIONS
Boon Wah Hotel, 7 E3
Little India Guest House, 3 E3
Madras Hotel, 6 E3
FOOD
Asian Food Mall, 16 B3
Berseh Food Centre, 5 F3
The Chinese Feasts, 28 F5
Delhi Restaurant, 2 E3
Geláre Café, 27 F5
Hill Street Tai Hwa Pork Noodle, 35 F6
Komala Vilas, 4 E2
Newton Circle Food Centre, 1 C2
NIGHTLIFE
Centro, 36 E6
Harry's, 34 D6
Orb, 31 C6
Phuture, 33 B6
Sound Bar and Liquid Room, 30 C6
Two Rooms, 29 C5
Xposé Cafe Bar, 22 C4
Zouk, Velvet Underground and Zouk Wine Bar, 32 B6
SHOPPING CENTERS
C.K. Tang, 14 B3
Centerpoint, 23 C4
Cuppage Terrace, 21 C4
Far East Shopping Center, 12 B3
Lucky Plaza, 17 B3
Ngee Ann City, 18 B4
Orchard Plaza, 24 C4
Orchard Shopping Center, 19 C4
Orchard Towers, 11 B3
Park Mall, 26 D5
Scotts, 13 B3
Sim Lim Square, 8 E4
Singapore Shopping Center, 25 D4
Specialists' Center, 20 C4
Tanglin Shopping Center, 10 A3
Tudor Court Shopping Gallery, 9 A3
Wheelock Place, 15 B3
0 400 yards
0 400 meters
NEWTON
Dunearn Rd.
Bukit Timah Rd.
Clemenceau Av.
Nassim Rd.
Mt. Elizabeth Hospital
Mt. Elizabeth
Scotts Rd.
Claymore Hill
Cairnhill Circle
Emerald Hill Houses
Emerald Hill Rd.
Central Expwy.
Nassim Hill Rd.
Tanglin Rd.
Cuscaden Rd.
Napier Rd.
ORCHARD ROAD
TO BOTANIC GARDENS (500m)
Tourism Court
Tomlinson Rd.
Grange Rd.
Anguilla Park
Paterson Rd.
ORCHARD
Nutmeg Rd.
Bideford Rd.
Orchard
Orchard Blvd
Orchard Link
Cuppage Rd.
Somerset Rd.
Orchard Pt.
SOMERSET
Grange Rd.
Devonshire Rd.
Exeter Rd.
Singapore ComCentre
Killiney Rd.
Oxley Rd.
River Valley Rd.
Kim Seng Rd.
Zion Rd.
Mohammed Sultan Rd.
Robertson Quay
Ganges Ave.
Havelock Rd.

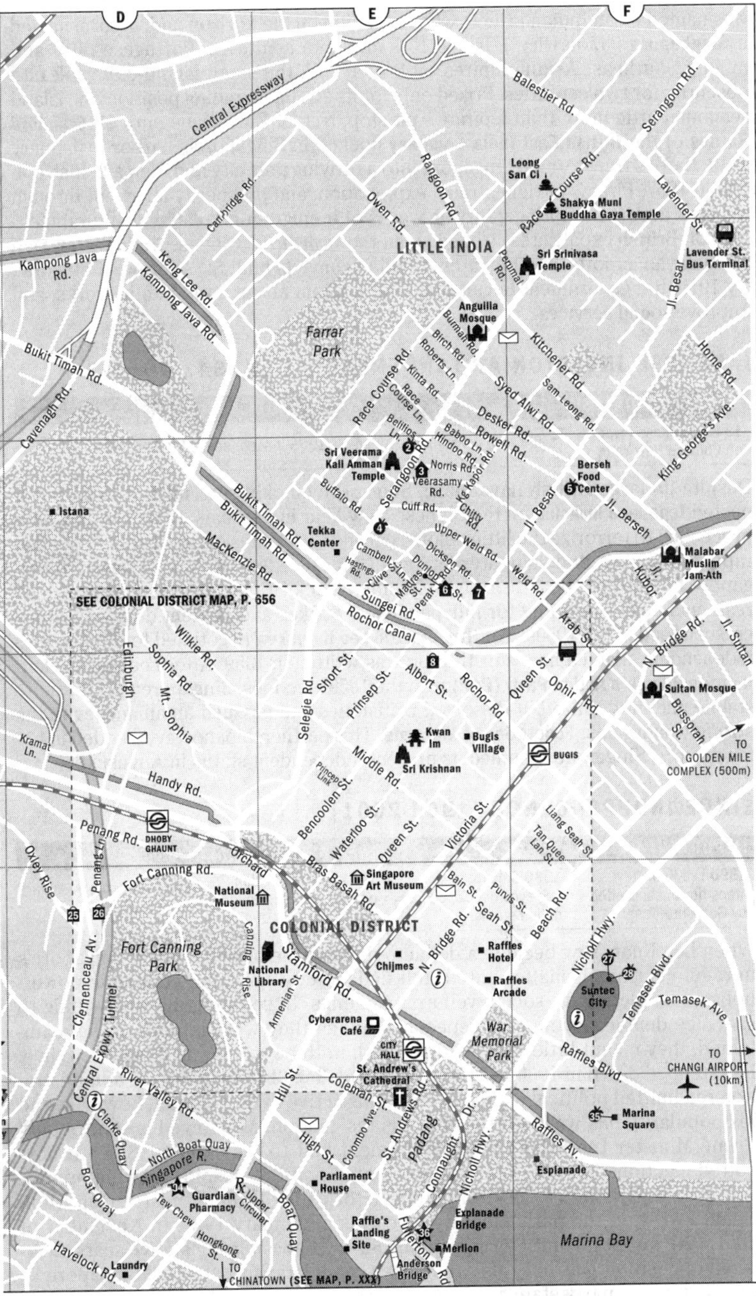
D
E
F
Central Expressway
Balestier Rd.
Serangoon Rd.
Cambridge Rd.
Owen Rd.
Rangoon Rd.
Leong San Ci
Race Course Rd.
Shakya Muni Buddha Gaya Temple
Lavender St.
Lavender St. Bus Terminal
LITTLE INDIA
Perumal Rd.
Sri Srinivasa Temple
Kampong Java Rd.
Keng Lee Rd.
Kampong Java Rd.
Jl. Besar
Farrar Park
Anguilla Mosque
Burmah Rd.
Birch Rd.
Roberts Ln.
Kitchener Rd.
Horne Rd.
Bukit Timah Rd.
Cavenagh Rd.
Race Course Rd.
Kinta Rd.
Race Course Ln.
Syed Alwi Rd.
Sam Leong Rd.
Desker Rd.
King George's Ave.
Belilios Ln.
Baboo Ln.
Hindoo Rd.
Rowell Rd.
Sri Veerama Kali Amman Temple
Norris Rd.
Kapor Rd.
Veerasamy Rd.
Berseh Food Center
Buffalo Rd.
Serangoon Rd.
Cuff Rd.
Chitty Rd.
Jl. Besar
Jl. Berseh
Istana
Bukit Timah Rd.
Bukit Timah Rd.
Tekka Center
Upper Weld Rd.
Malabar Muslim Jam-Ath
MacKenzie Rd.
Cambell Ln.
Hastings Rd
Clive St.
Dickson Rd.
Dunlop St.
Madras St.
Perak Rd.
Weld Rd.
Jl. Kubor
SEE COLONIAL DISTRICT MAP, P. 656
Sungei Rd.
Rochor Canal
Arab St.
N. Bridge Rd.
Jl. Sultan
Wilkie Rd.
Edinburgh
Sophia Rd.
Short St.
Albert St.
Rochor Rd.
Queen St.
Ophir Rd.
Sultan Mosque
Mt. Sophia
Selegie Rd.
Prinsep St.
Bussorah St.
Kramat Ln.
Kwan Im
Bugis Village
BUGIS
TO GOLDEN MILE COMPLEX (500m)
Sri Krishnan
Middle Rd.
Prinsep Link
Handy Rd.
Bencoolen St.
Waterloo St.
Victoria St.
Liang Seah St.
Tan Quee Lan St.
Penang Rd.
DHOBY GHAUT
Penang Ln.
Queen St.
Oxley Rise
Orchard
Bras Basah Rd.
Fort Canning Rd.
Singapore Art Museum
Bain St.
Purvis St.
National Museum
Seah St.
Beach Rd.
COLONIAL DISTRICT
Canning Rise
Clemenceau Av.
Fort Canning Park
Stamford Rd.
N. Bridge Rd.
Raffles Hotel
Nicholl Hwy.
Chijmes
National Library
Raffles Arcade
Suntec City
Temasek Blvd.
Armenian St.
Temasek Ave.
Central Expwy. Tunnel
Cyberarena Café
War Memorial Park
CITY HALL
Raffles Blvd.
TO CHANGI AIRPORT (10km)
St. Andrew's Cathedral
River Valley Rd.
Hill St.
Coleman St.
Marina Square
Clarke Quay
Colombo Ave.
St. Andrews Rd.
Padang
Connaught Dr.
Nicholl Hwy.
Raffles Av.
North Boat Quay
High St.
Singapore R.
Esplanade
Parliament House
Boat Quay
Guardian Pharmacy
Upper Circular
Boat Quay
Tew Chew
Explanade Bridge
Raffle's Landing Site
Fullerton Rd
Marina Bay
Merlion
Hongkong St.
Havelock Rd.
Laundry
Anderson Bridge
TO CHINATOWN (SEE MAP, P. XXX)

was named by an Indian prince, who saw a lion on the horizon and, in turn, named it **Singhapura** ("Lion City"). In the 15th and 16th centuries, Portugese raids and mighty Southeast Asian empires took their toll: the small island-city sank into obscurity for two centuries. Prized only for its strategic trading position, the island remained little more than a pirate's pit stop, free of Europeans until **Sir Stamford Raffles** of the **British East India Company** docked in Singapore's harbor in January 1819. Raffles transformed Singapore into a thriving port city and then a British colony in 1867. Piracy, intrigue, trade, exploitation, and prosperity all swept through the area during the 19th century as waves of immigration created a cultural melting pot. British expatriates strolled about the *kampung*, Chinese traders grew rich off Malayan exports, and indentured Indian convicts built St. Andrew's Cathedral. By 1915, the government began to address opium abuse, fund public works, and improve social services.

JAPANESE INVASION AND INDEPENDENCE (1941-1965)

IMPORTANT DATES

1941 Japanese invade on Chinese New Year. **1959** New constitution written. **1965** Independence for Singapore.

Despite its large British naval base, Singapore quickly surrendered to an unexpected **Japanese invasion** on the Chinese New Year in February 1941. The Japanese proceeded to terrorize the little colony, carting Europeans off to Changi Prisonand raping, pillaging, and slaughtering local Chinese. After the war, a battered Singapore fell into political disarray, welcoming back British governance, though its residents began yearning for independence. Strikes and student demonstrations crescendoed in the 1950s. For three years, **Lee Kuan Yew** negotiated for Singapore's independence, and a new constitution was written in 1959. After Lee and the left-leaning **People's Action Party (PAP)** won the 1959 elections, Singapore became more stabile and modernized. It dissolved British ties and pursued an alliance with the strongly nationalist **Federation of Malaysia.** This partnership, however, ended in bitter divorce; Singapore assumed its present independent status in August 1965.

SINCE INDEPENDENCE (1965-2001)

IMPORTANT DATES

1990 Lee Kuan Yew steps down, succeeded by Goh Chok Tong. **1996** Singapore achieves developed nation status. **1971** PAP opposition parties boycott elections in protest. **2001** PAP wins its ninth consecutive term.

When Lee Kuan Yew became a de facto dictator, he masterminded Singapore's miraculous transformation into a full-fledged city-state and economic powerhouse, complete with social-welfare trimmings. In so doing, he was willing to sacrifice democracy and free speech—though they were important, he maintained, they meant little to individuals with nothing to eat and nowhere to live. Lee stepped down in 1990 to be succeeded by **Goh Chok Tong,** whose administration readmitted political exiles. Lee remains active in the Cabinet, however, and his popularity has waned little since his resignation. Many eye his son, Deputy Prime Minister **Lee Hsien Loong,** as the next heir to the dynasty. Since it boycotted elections in 1971, PAP has dominated politics, despite growing opposition parties. In one of the first major victories for Prime Minister Goh Chok Tong, PAP won the parliamentary elections of January 1997. In November of 2001, PAP swept its ninth term, winning 82 of 84 possible legislative seats. Scattered opposition was only able to muster candidates for 29 seats. Singapore is, in effect, a one-party state.

SEMI-AUTOCRATIC WEAPONS Singapore's zeal for fining gum-chewers, litterbugs, and spitters is well-known, but the government also sponsors "harmony-imposing" initiatives. **Freedom from smut:** The Undesirable Publications Act staves off the Western cultural agendas by forbidding hundreds of magazines, books, and web sites with "controversial" sexual, political, and religious content. **Freedom from smog:** High car prices, automotive taxes, and a fantastic public transportation system are disincentives to drive. In 1998, Electronic Road Pricing (ERP), a system of taxing required debit cards on every windshield, was introduced. Those driving without a card receive a fine by mail, usually within two days. **Freedom to schmooze:** The state-sponsored Social Development Unit serves as both a matchmaking and mildly eugenic family planning service. Singapore has many matchmaking services, all of which offer mixers each year for singles in the city. Recent events include a Beverage Knowledge Class, Go-Karting, and Self-Defense for Executives. **Freedom from stench:** To eliminate the effect dirty public toilets have on the city image, the government simply didn't build them. Unfortunately, this left many bladder-full young people with nowhere to turn after a night out. Strangely enough, elevators became the latrine of choice. Many elevators in Singapore now contain **automated urine-sniffers,** which trap incontinent occupants inside until law enforcement agents arrive to levy fines.

SINGAPORE

SINGAPORE TODAY

Unlike other Asian bureaucracies, efficiency defines the Singaporean government. Technologically advanced, its overarching administration has the power to promptly establish and fund programs to improve education, cultural pursuits, and economic growth as well as fill potholes. While Singapore has not been immune to the Asian economic crisis, its robust economy, low inflation, strong commercial banks, and lack of foreign debt have shielded it from the serious economic turmoil that plagued its neighbors. Singapore's economy grew by 3.9% in the second quarter of 2002. In addition, throughout 2001 and 2002 George Yeo, the minister of trade and industry, has been working to establish a free-trade agreement with the United States. Because of their meteoric success, Singaporeans are justifiably proud of their country and refute criticisms from Western governments.

Singapore has been less affected by the United States-led **War on Terror** than its neighbors Malaysia and Indonesia. In January 2002, however, Singaporeans and Americans alike were surprised by the arrest of **al Qaeda** operatives, at least eight of whom were trained in Afghanistan. Earlier that month, 15 people intending to bomb military targets and other official buildings, including the United States Embassy, were also arrested in Singapore. In August 2002, Singapore, along with eight other ASEAN countries, entered an agreement with the United States to "prevent, disrupt, and combat" global terrorism by sharing information and intelligence. (For more information on regional terrorist activities see **The Philippines Today,** p. 552.).

CUSTOMS & ETIQUETTE

HUMAN RIGHTS. Singapore's harsh stance on drugs and crime has been internationally publicized, coming under fire from human rights groups like Amnesty International. In May 1994, 18-year-old American **Michael Fay** was flogged for spray-painting cars and throwing eggs, putting Singapore in the international spotlight. US President Clinton convinced the government to reduce Fay's caning, though laws remain the same. The government indirectly controls the press by encouraging self-censorship among journalists. Though not technically censored, newspapers critical of the government are rarely allowed into the country. In 1997, the Singaporean government began censoring the Internet, denying access to "unsuitable" web sites with references to sex, politics, or religion. Political freedom is limited by the virtual one-party system imposed by PAP. One obstacle facing potential opposition parties are restrictions on freedom of assembly and association. Jehovah's Witnesses and the Unification Church have both been banned. Still, everyday Singaporean life remains at least superficially liberal. There are small but pervasive reminders of the government's tight clamp, such as laws restricting those under 21 from watching movies with homosexual content and government posters gently encouraging procreation.

BISEXUAL, GAY, AND LESBIAN TRAVELERS. Homosexuality is illegal in Singapore. Though the laws prohibiting it are rarely enforced, Singaporean media and government have been known to treat gays harshly. Numerous clubs and hangouts, as well as a booming online community, make up a thriving gay scene (see **Adam and Steve, Darling!**, p. 669). For a complete listing of gay venues in Singapore, check out **Dragoncastle Gay Asia** web site (www.dragoncastle.net/singapore.html).

ARTS

Like other art forms in Singapore, traditional **pen and ink drawing** is influenced by older Chinese styles. Local cultural shows present traditional art, such as **Malay shadow plays, kite-flying,** and **Chinese lion dances. Chinese opera** combines high (melo)drama with elaborate costumes. Singapore's **architecture** integrates Western, Indian, Arabic, and Chinese styles, old and new. While urban renewal has destroyed many older fishing villages and bungalow-style *kampung*, conservation has saved some classic structures and neighborhoods. The Emerald Hill area, off Orchard Rd., has beautiful shophouses. Colonial architecture is predominantly found in "black and white"-style houses, like Adam Park, off Adams Rd. near the Bukit Timah intersection. Modern skyscrapers serve as constant reminders of the city's dramatic transformation. Architect **I.M. Pei**'s wizardry, including the **Gateway Building** on Beach Rd. and the **OCBC Center** on Church St., dots the landscape.

HOLIDAYS AND FESTIVALS (2003)

DATE	NAME	DESCRIPTION
Jan. 1	New Year's Day	National
Feb. 1	Chinese New Year	Chinese
Feb. 12	Hari Raya Haji	Festival of sacrifice, usually four days long
Mar. 5	Islamic New Year	Muslim
2nd M in Mar.	Commonwealth Day	National
May 1	Labour Day	National
May 15	Vesak Day	Commemorates the birth and enlightenment of Buddha
Aug. 9	National Day	National
Oct. 23	Deepavali (Diwali)	Indian–five-day festival of lights, celebrating the Ramayana
Oct. 27	Start of Ramadan	Muslim–begins month of fasting
Nov. 25	Hari Raya Puasa	Feast that marks the end of Ramadan
Dec. 25	Christmas Day	Christian

ADDITIONAL RESOURCES

LITERATURE

Fistful of Colours, by Su-Chen Christine Lim (1993). Celebrates the destinies of three women shaped by the uniqueness of Singapore's multi-ethnic society.

From Third World to First: The Singapore Story: 1965-2000, by Kuan Yew Lee (2000). With help from Henry Kissinger, Lee traces Singapore's ride (and his own) from independence to the present day.

The Singapore Puzzle, by Michael Haas (1999). Seven different writers, all of whom have suffered at the hands of the Singaporean government, examine why Singapore's democratic practices decline as its prosperity increases.

ON THE WEB

New Asia-Singapore (www.newasia-singapore.com). Choose a language and learn everything it takes to "Live it up in Singapore."

Singapore Infomap (www.sg). Endless links and information grace this page.

Singapore Tourism Board North America (www.tourismsingapore.com). Streamlines the New-Asia Singapore site specifically for US and Canadian visitors.

SINGAPORE

ESSENTIALS

SINGAPORE PRICE ICONS

SYMBOL:	❶	❷	❸	❹	❺
ACCOMM.	Under US$10 Under S$17	US$10-20 S$17-34	US$20-30 S$34-52	US$30-40 S$52-68	Over US$40 Over S$68
FOOD	Under US$3 Under S$5	US$3-7 S$5-11	US$7-13 S$11-22	US$13-20 S$22-34	Over US$20 Over S$34

EMBASSIES & CONSULATES

SINGAPORE CONSULAR SERVICES ABROAD

Check out www.embassyworld.com for easy access to many embassy web pages and to download forms. Embassies and consulates within Southeast Asia are listed in the **Practical Information** sections of individual cities.

Australia: High Commission, 17 Forster Cres., Yarralumla, ACT 2600 Canberra (☎02 6273 3944).

Canada: Consulate, 1305-999 W Hastings St., Vancouver, BC V6C 2W2 (☎604-669-5115).

New Zealand: High Commission, P.O. Box 13-140, 17 Kabul St., Khandallah, Johnsonsville, Wellington (☎04 479 2076 or 479 2077).

South Africa: High Commission, 1980 Schoeman St., Arcadia, Pretoria 0083; mailing address: Box 11809, Hatfield 0028, Pretoria (☎012 430 6035).

UK: High Commission, 9 Wilton Cres., Belgravia, London SW1X 8SP (☎020 7235 8315).

US: Embassy, 3501 International Pl. NW, Washington, DC 20008 (☎202-537-3100; www.mfa.gov.sg/washington). **Consulates,** 231 E 51st St., New York, NY 10022 (☎212-223-3331); 595 Market St., Ste. 2450, San Francisco, CA 94105. **Mission to the UN,** 231 E 51st St., New York, NY 10022 (☎212-826-0840).

CONSULAR SERVICES IN SINGAPORE

For embassies and consulates of other countries in Singapore, please see **Practical information: Embassies,** p. 658.

SINGAPORE TOURIST OFFICES ABROAD

Australia, 47 York St., Level 11, AWA Building, Sydney NSW 2000 (☎02 9290 2888).

Canada, 2 Bloor St. W, Ste. 404, Toronto, ON M4W 3E2 (☎416-363-8898; www.singapore-ca.com). Also serves New Zealand.

UK, Carrington House, 1st fl., 126-130 Regent St., London W1B 5JX (toll-free ☎080 8065 6565; ☎020 7437 0033).

US, 590 5th Ave., 12th fl., New York, NY 10036 (☎212-302-4861; www.visitsingapore.com); 2 Prudential Plaza, 180 N Stetson Ave., Ste. 2615, Chicago, IL 60601 (☎312-938-1888); 4929 Wilshire Blvd., Ste. 510, Beverly Hills, CA 90010 (☎323-677-0808).

VISAS

All travelers to Singapore must obtain a **Social Visit Pass,** issued upon arrival and valid for six months. Citizens of Ireland, Canada, South Africa, New Zealand, the US, and the UK can stay for up to 30 days. The immigration office may provide **visa extensions** for up to 90 days. For stays over three months, travelers must apply for a **Long Term Social Visit Pass** and be backed by a Singapore organization.

MONEY

The **Singapore dollar (S$)** comes in denominations of S$2, 5, 10, 20, 50, 100, 500, 1000, and 10,000, and coins come in 1, 5, 10, 20, and 50 cents and S$1. **Credit cards** are widely accepted; **ATMs** are abundant. Service charges are included, so **tipping** is uncommon. (Tipping immigration officers and other public officials is illegal.) Clubs, bars, and classy restaurants and hotels label themselves either "plus," indicating a 10% service charge, or "plus plus," indicating a 14% tax. The 3% Goods and Services Tax (GST) can be partially refunded by shopping at stores with "Tax Refund" signs. Ask for a Global Refund Cheque and present it at airport customs before departure. Unless you see a "fixed price" sign, feel free to **bargain** (it is becoming less common) in outdoor markets, at most shops in Chinatown and Little India, and on trishaw rides. For information on **currency exchange,** see p. 658.

KEEPING IN TOUCH

Singapore's postal service is probably the most reliable in Southeast Asia. Many *Poste Restante* packages actually make it to the post office. High-tech communications equipment make phone connections clear and consistent. The **international operator** number is ☎104; **directory assistance** is ☎100. For **Home Country Direct (HCD)** numbers from Singapore, refer to the table on the inside back cover.

THE CITY ☎65

INTERCITY TRANSPORTATION

BY PLANE

Changi Airport (☎1 800 542 1122, flight info ☎6542 4422), is 25min. east of the city center. A S$15 **airport tax** is usually included in your ticket price. To get downtown, take **bus** #36 (6am-midnight, S$1.50) to the **Raffles City** and **Orchard Rd.** areas, or take the **MRT** directly from the terminal (last train departs the airport at 11:18pm; S$1.40). **Taxis** run S$15-20, plus a S$3 (S$5 on weekends) airport charge and a 50% surcharge from midnight to 6am. CityCab's **Maxicab,** an A/C, wheelchair-accessible, six-seat coach, takes you to near any budget accommodation. (☎6542 8297. Every 15min. 6am-11pm from airport to city, consult shuttle desk at arrival halls of terminals 1 and 2, S$7; 8:20am-10:30pm from city to airport; S$8 in advance.)

DESTINATION	FREQUENCY	PRICE	DESTINATION	FREQUENCY	PRICE
Bangkok	5-6 per day	S$664	**Jakarta**	7 per day	S$360
Brunei	1 per day	S$431	**Kuala Lumpur**	12-14 per day	S$182
Calcutta	3 per week	S$1249	**Manila**	3 per day	S$925
Cebu	1 per day	S$1044	**Mumbai (Bombay)**	1 per week	S$1516
Hanoi	1-2 per week	S$749	**Phuket**	2 per day	S$455
Hong Kong	6-7 per day	S$680	**Yangon**	1 per day	S$858

Singapore International Airlines (SIA) is in airport terminal 2, DBS tower, 290 Orchard Rd., and SIA building, 77 Robinson Rd. #01-01. (24hr. ticketing ☎6223 8888, inquiries ☎6223 6030; www.singaporeair.com.) **Silk Air,** 8 Shenton Way #08-01 Temasek Tower, is a subsidiary of SIA. (24hr. reservations ☎6225 4488; www.silkair.net. Ticketing open M-F 8:30am-5:30pm.) Other air services are provided by: **Bangkok Airways,** airport terminal 1, #041-04F (☎6545 8481; www.bkkair.co.th); **Cathay Pacific Airways,** 10 Collyer Quay, #16-01 Ocean Building (☎6533 1333; www.cathaypacific.com); **Garuda Indonesia,** 101 Thomson Rd., #13-03 (☎6250 2888; www.indodirect.com/garunda); **Malaysia Airlines,** 190 Clemenceau Ave., #02-09/11 (reservations ☎6336 6777; www.malaysiaairlines.com.my. Open M-F 9am-6pm); **Myanmar Airways,** Singapore Station, 50 HPL House, Cuscaden Rd., #07-00 (☎6545 4733); **Philippine Airlines (PAL),** 35 Selegie Rd., #10-02 Parklane Shopping Mall (☎6336 1611; www.pal.com.ph); **Royal Brunei Airlines,** 25 Scotts Rd., #04-08 Scottswalk (☎6235 4672); **Thai Airways,** 100 Cecil St. (reservations ☎6224 9977, ticketing ☎6224 2024; www.thaiair.com); and **Vietnam Airlines,** 260 Orchard Rd., #08-08 (☎6339 3552; www.vietnamair.com.vn).

BY TRAIN

The **railway station,** 30 Keppel Rd., near Cantonment Link, is on the southern tip of the main island, 20-30min. from downtown by bus. (☎6222 5165 for 24hr. automated schedules and fares. Open daily 6am-11pm.) Buses run every 5-15min. between the station and the **Raffles Hotel** (#97, 100, 131), **Little India** (#97, 131), **Orchard Rd.** (#167), and **Chinatown** (#80). Buy tickets (8:30am-7pm). The **KTM** (☎6222 5165) has two train routes: one runs along the west coast up to **Hat Yai** (Haadyai) in Thailand; the other cuts through the middle of Malaysia and **Taman Negara National Park,** ending in **Tumpat,** the northeastern corner of Peninsular Malaysia. The Hat Yai (via Butterworth) line leaves from Kuala Lumpur. **Express**

trains with A/C go to **Kuala Lumpur** (7hr.; daily 8am, 3:05pm, Sa-Su also 10:30am; S$34) via **Tampin** (5hr., [illegible]). An overnight train runs daily to **Kuala Lumpur** (8½hr.; 10pm; seats S$19-30, bunks S$37.50-40). To go to **Taman Negara National Park,** take the Gua Musang train to **Jerantut** (8hr., 9:45am), or to **Tumpat** (13½hr.; 8:20pm; seats S$32-41, bunks S$48.50-51) via Jerantut (7½hr., seats S$19-28, bunks S$35.50-38).

SINGAPORE

BY BUS

In addition to the stations below, buses also leave from the Golden Mile Complex on Beach Rd., near Lavender St. Bus Station.

Lavender St. Bus Station: On the corner of Lavender St. and Kallang Bahru north of Little India. Take the bus from **Bugis MRT** (#145) or **Raffle Hotel** (#82) and get off at **Eminent Plaza. Hasry Express** (☎6294 9306; open M-Sa 7:45am-8pm, Su 7:45am-4pm) to: **Ipoh** (8hr.; 9:30am, 10pm; S$33); **Kuala Lumpur** (6hr., 12 buses per day, S$12); **Melaka (Malacca)** (4½hr.; 8:30, 10:30am, 2:30, 4:30pm Friday only; S$11); **Penang** (11hr., 9pm, S$38). **Transnasional Express** (☎6294 7034; open daily 8am-8pm) to: **Mersing** (4hr.; 9, 10am, 10pm; S$11.10); **Kota Bahru** (12hr., 7:30pm, S$35.10); **Kuala Lumpur** (5-6hr.; 8, 9, 11am, 4:30, 6, 10pm; S$25-30); **Kuala Terengganu** (10hr.; 9am, 8, 9pm; S$26-33); **Kuantan** (7hr.; 9, 10am, 10pm; S$16.50). **Malacca Singapore Express** (☎6293 5915) runs coaches to **Melaka** (4½hr.; 8, 9, 10, 11am, 2, 3, 4, 5pm; S$11).

Johor Bahru Bus Depot: At Queen and Arab St., a 15-20min. walk from **Bugis MRT. Singapore-Johor Express** (☎6292 8151) to **Johor Bahru** (1hr.; every 15min. 6:30am-midnight; S$2.40, purchase an extra ticket for large luggage). **Kuala Lumpur-Singapore Express** (☎6292 8254) to **Kuala Lumpur** (6hr.; 9am, 1, 5, 10pm; S$28).

Copthorne Orchid Hotel: 214 Dunearn Rd. (☎6256 5755). To **Kuala Lumpur** (5½hr., every hr. 7:30am-9:30pm, S$37) and **Melaka** (3hr.; 9am, 3:30, 9:30pm; S$12).

BY BOAT

Changi Ferry Terminal: In the northeastS, accessible by taxi. **Cruise Ferries** (☎6546 8518) sends boats to the gateway to the Peninsula's east coast, **Tanjong Belungkor** (45min.; M-Th 10am, 3, 8pm and F-Su 7:30, 10am, 3, 8pm; S$16, round-trip S$22 including seaport tax); check-in 1hr. in advance, closes 30min. before departure.

World Trade Center Ferry Terminal: At the southern tip of the island, accessible by bus from **Raffles Hotel** (#97, 131), **North Bridge Rd.** (#61, 145), and **Orchard Rd.** (#143), or **City Hall MRT** in front of St. Andrew's Cathedral (#95). **Penguin Fast Ferry** (☎6271 4866) goes to **Tanjung Balai** (2hr.; 6 per day 7:50am-6:30pm; S$26, round-trip S$37); **Tanjung Batu** (3hr.; 9:40am, 3:45pm; S$26, round-trip S$37). **Dino Shipping** (☎6270 2228) sends ferries to: **Batu Ampar** (45min.; 6 per day 9:35am-8:30pm; S$20, round-trip S$27); **Pulau Tioman** (4½hr.; 8:30am; peak-season S$106, round-trip S$174; low-season S$96, round-trip S$154); **Sekupang** (45min.; 18 per day 7:45am-8:05 pm; S$20, round-trip S$27). **Widi Express** (☎272 7540) has the most boats to **Batu Ampar** (45min.; 23 per day 8:40am-9:45pm; S$14, round-trip S$20).

ATTENTION ISLAND-HOPPERS

If you're off to Pulau Penyenget, take a ferry to Tanjung Pinang, the main city, and not to Bintan Resort. Transport from Bintan Resort to Tanjung Pinang involves a taxi and a 2hr. local bus ride.

Tanah Merah Ferry Terminal: On the southeastern corner of the island. Take MRT to Tanah Merah station and bus #35 to the last stop. Gates close 10min. before departure. **Dino Shipping** (☎6270 2228) sends ferries to **Tanjung Pinang** on Pulau Bintan (1½hr.; 3 per day 9am-5:45pm; S$30, round-trip S$40) and **Nongsapura Batam**

(45min.; every 2-2½hr. 8am-6:30pm; S$22, round-trip $29). **IndoFalcon** (☎6270 6778) sends ferries to **Sebana** (45min.-1hr.; 3 per day 9am-7pm; S$16.60, round-trip S$23.20) and **Tanjung Pinang** (1½hr.; 3 per day 10:20am-7pm; morning S$30, afternoon S$26, round-trip S$34). **Penguin Fast Ferry** (☎6271 4866), goes to **Tanjung Pinang** (1½hr.; 5 per day M-F 9:10am-6:10pm, 7 per day Sa 9:10am-6:10pm).

ORIENTATION

The city center divides into four areas. **Orchard Rd.** stretches from west to east of the city center, where it forks into **Bras Basah Rd.,** and a parallel street to the south, **Stamford Rd.** These two streets are home to the **Raffles Hotel** and **Chijmes** in the heart of the **Colonial District.** When Selengie Rd., which protrudes from the eastern end of Orchard Rd., becomes Serangoon Rd. to the north, you've reached **Little India.** South of the Singapore River, below Upper Cross and Cross St., **Chinatown's** many shops and restaurants extend as far as Cantonment Rd. The **airport** is on the eastern fringe of the city. The **railway station** is south of Chinatown.

COLONIAL DISTRICT. The extensively renovated Raffles Hotel captures the grandiose splendor of colonial Singapore, as do all the neighborhood museums. Many visitors stop by for a drink by the fountain at Chijmes, the convent-turned-shopping gallery. Backpackers flock to accommodations on North Bridge Rd., near Rochor Rd., in the Colonial District, which is gradually expanding northward. *(Take the MRT to City Hall to get to the center of the Colonial District.)*

BENCOOLEN STREET. Once a backpacker haven with a concentration of budget guest houses, Bencoolen is rumored to be slated for development into a high-wattage strip of shops and hotels. For now, it remains a land of discount stores, vacant lots, and unremarkable coffee houses. *(To reach Bencoolen St. from the airport, take the Maxicab, or take bus #36 to the YMCA on Orchard Rd.)*

ORCHARD ROAD. Shopaholics are free to roam about the street's numerous shopping centers and underground food courts. While designer boutiques are normally empty, shopping centers are usually packed with cosmopolitan consumers staying at the 5-star hotels nearby. On weeknights and weekends, the energy on Orchard Rd. reaches its peak as people come here for late-night movies and seasonal outdoor events. Bars and pubs may be hard to find, since they are either underground or at the top of shopping centers. *(Take the MRT to Orchard.)*

CHINATOWN. Chinatown stands as a testament to Singapore's pride in its newfound national heritage—Chinese-colonial shophouses have been gutted, refurbished, and repainted in lively pastels. The MRT extension has skyrocketed property values; old coffee shops have yielded to new offices and boutiques. These streets are home to Buddhist and Hindu temples, traditional Chinese medicine shops, and massage therapy centers. *(From the airport, take public bus #36 to the Stamford and North Bridge Rd. intersection, then catch #81 to Sri Mariamman Temple.)*

LITTLE INDIA. Indian immigrants used to raise cattle on land north of the Rochor Canal, using their energy to power machines for wheat grinding, sesame oil production, and pineapple preservation. As more immigrants flocked to Singapore to be construction workers in the late 19th century, Little India grew into a thriving trade center and an Indian cultural haven. Scrubbed and purified in Singaporean fashion, Little India provides a fair compromise for budget travelers—accommodations are reasonable, worthwhile sights are within easy reach, and cheap food is everywhere. Desker and Petain St. to the north host two of the three red light districts in Singapore. *(From the railway station, take public bus #97 or 131 to Little India.)*

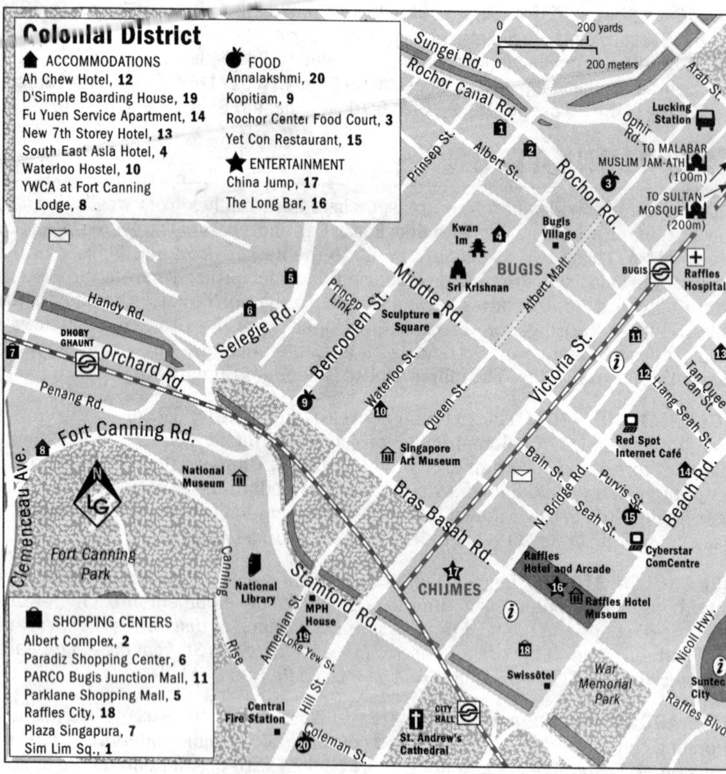

LOCAL TRANSPORTATION

Buses: SBS Transit runs local bus routes (☎1 800 287 2727; www.sbstransit.com.sg). **Trans-Island Bus Services (TIBS)** runs longer distance buses and Night Rider buses (☎1 800 482 5433; www.tibs.com.sg). **Local buses** run 6am-midnight. Striped orange-and-white-roofed stops have signs listing buses by street, frequency, and destination. **Night Rider buses** usually run 11:30pm-4:30am; bus stops have yellow NR signs and time of the last bus. NR buses charge a flat fare ($3); regular bus fares are S$0.55-1.50 depending upon distrance and payment type (cash or farecard). Ask the driver for the fare to your destination and pay the exact fare, or insert your **Farecard** (see below). **TransitLink Guide** (S$1.50), with comprehensive information on the 100+ bus routes, is sold at any bookstore.

Mass Rapid Transit (MRT): ☎1 800 336 8900; www.smrtcorp.com.sg. Two main A/C lines going east-west and north-south run 6am-midnight. First train leaves around 5:30 or 6am; last train leaves at 11:30pm. Single-trip tickets start at S$0.80 and can cost up to S$1.80 depending on distance. Stored value **Farecards** save 5-10¢ per ride (S$10 plus S$2 deposit, returned when card is returned; unused portion is refunded) and are sold at MRT stations and 7-Eleven stores. Most MRT counters (open M-F 8am-9pm, Sa 8am-6pm) also sell TransitLink Guides (S$1.50) and provide free MRT maps.

town, the Indian district **Pahurat,** and the **Hualamphong Railway Station.** Farther south is the wealthy **Silom** financial district and its less upstanding bedfellow, the **Patpong** red-light district. East of the Hualamphong Railway Station are **Siam Square**'s shopping mall and the World Trade Center. Rama I Rd. slices through, connecting Wat Phra Kaew (on its western end) with Bangkok's eastern edge and the **Sukhumvit Rd.** area, where Thais and foreigners party until the wee hours. The *Bangkok Tourist Map* (40฿) or Nancy Chandler's *Map of Bangkok* (150฿) will make all of this clearer than we ever could.

Buildings are often numbered twice in Bangkok—the first number represents the building's lot, and the second number signifies where on the lot it is. For example, 127/8-10 Sukhumvit Rd. signifies that the building is on lot 127 and occupies numbers 8-10. Minor roads that split off a main thoroughfare are called sois (alleys), although they can often be sizable roads.

LOCAL TRANSPORTATION

Maneuvering through Bangkok traffic is enough to bring out the Hyde in any Jekyll. Traffic has decreased recently, but getting from north to south is still frustrating. Taking canal boats and river taxis means less time sweating on buses and breathing exhaust. Travelers hoping to maneuver through Bangkok by public transportation will love the **Bangkok Tourist Map** (40฿), which has bus, water taxi, and Skytrain routes as well as information on sights.

BY BUS

The shiny, happy bus system, run by the Bangkok Metropolitan Transit Authority (BMTA), is extensive and cheap. Red-and-cream buses have no A/C (3.50฿); blue-and-white and yellow-and-white buses both have A/C (8-16฿). Pea-green **minibuses** (3.50฿) supposedly run the same routes as the buses but tend to stray easily. **Microbuses** cover long distances and stop only at designated places (5am-10pm, 30฿). Paying a higher price guarantees a seat and fewer stops. Buses run 5am-midnight or later. Make sure you get on the right type of bus, not just the right route number. This is a sample listing; there are many, many buses so for more options pick up a free **bus map** at any TAT office.

REGULAR BUSES WITH NO A/C (RED-AND-CREAM)

#1: Wat Pho–Yaowarat Rd. (Chinatown)–General Post Office–Oriental Hotel

THE INSIDER'S CITY

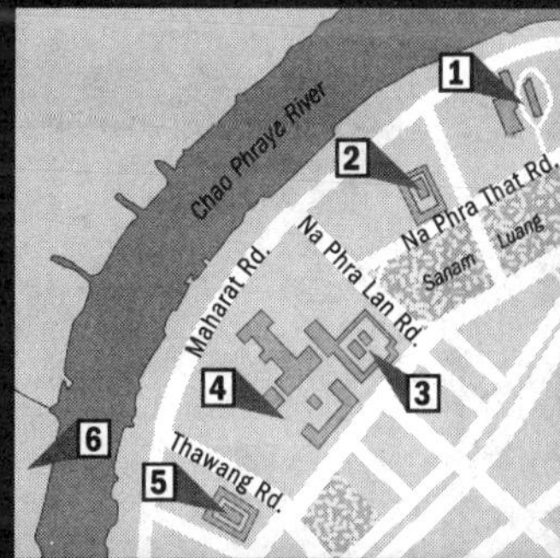

WHAT WATS?

Some of the most awe-inspiring, famous wats in Bangkok conveniently crowd around the Grand Palace, making it possible to do a cultural-religious walking tour in an afternoon. Due to the wats' proximity to Khao San Rd., there is no excuse for backpackers staying in the area to miss out on this opportunity. From Khao San Rd., head across Sanam Luang, toward the Chao Phraya River.

1. See Thailand's cultural artifacts at its biggest museum, the **National Museum** right in the Grand Palace complex.
2. Once a house, now a learning center, **Wat Mahathat** is the place to be enlightened by beauty and religious significance.
3. Buddhas overflow the premises at **Wat Phra Kaew.**
4. It's the **Grand Palace.** What can we say? Just go.
5. **Wat Pho** is the mamma of temples in Thailand—biggest and oldest.
6. For beautiful ceramic and porcelain inlays, head across the river to **Wat Arun.**

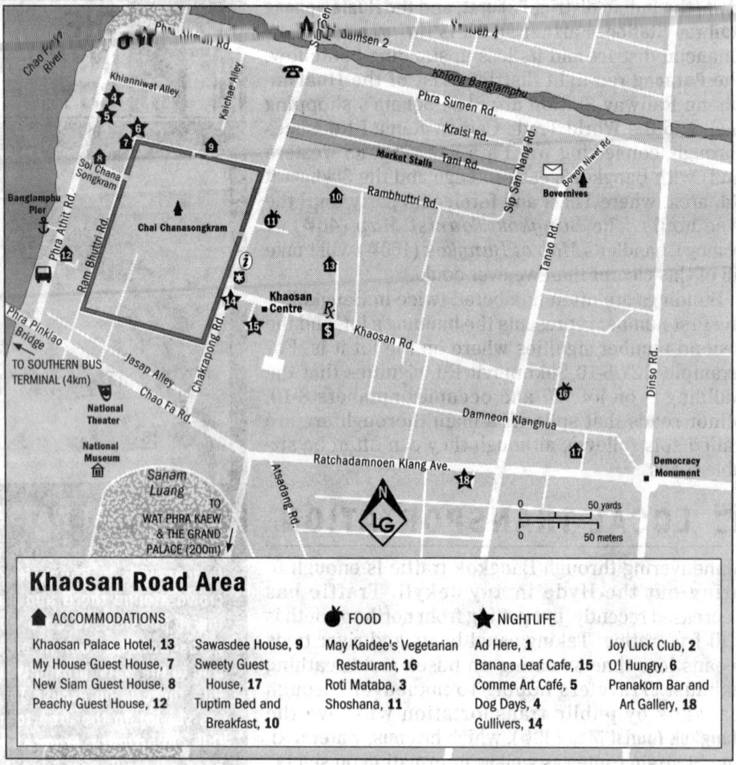

15: Banglamphu (Phra Athit Rd., Phrasumen Rd.)–Sanam Luang–Democracy Monument–Wat Saket–Siam Sq.–Ratchadamri Rd.–Lumpini Park–Silom Rd.

18 and 28: Vimarnmek Teak Museum–Dusit Zoo–Chitralada Palace–Victory Monument

25: Wat Phra Kaew–Wat Pho–Charoen Krung Rd.–Rama IV Rd. (near Hualamphong Railway Station)–Phayathai Rd.–Mahboonkrong Center–Siam Sq.–World Trade Center–Ploenchit Rd.–Sukhumvit Rd. to outer Bangkok

48: Sanam Chai Rd.–Bamrung Muang Rd.–Siam Sq.–along Sukhumvit Rd.

59: Don Muang International Airport–Victory Monument–Phahonyothin Rd.–Phetchaburi Rd.–Larnluang Rd.–Democracy Monument–Sanam Luang

70: Democracy Monument–TAT–Boxing Stadium–Dusit Zoo

72: Ratchaprarop Rd.–Si Ayutthaya Rd.–Marble Temple–Samsen Rd.–Thewet

74: Rama IV Rd. (outside Soi Ngam Duphli)–Lumpini Park–Ratchadamri Rd.–World Trade Center–Pratunam-Ratchaprarop Rd.–Victory Monument

115: Silom Rd.–Rama IV Rd.–along Rama IV Rd. until Sukhumvit Rd.

116: Sathorn Nua Rd.–along Rama IV Rd. (passes Soi Ngam Duphli)–Sathorn Tai Rd.

204: Victory Monument–Ratchaprarop Rd.–World Trade Center–Siam Sq.–Bamrung Muang Rd.

A/C BUSES (BLUE-AND-WHITE, YELLOW-AND-WHITE)

#1: Wat Pho–Charoen Krung Rd.–Rama IV Rd. (near Hualamphong Railway Station)–Phayathai Rd. (Mahboonkrong Center)–Siam Sq.–along Sukhumvit Rd.

8: Sanam Luang–Bamrung Muang Rd.–Rama I Rd.–Ploenchit Rd.–Sukhumvit Rd. to outer Bangkok

10: National Assembly (Ratchavithi Rd.)–Dusit Zoo–Chitralada Palace–Victory Monument–Phahonyothin Rd.–Don Muang International Airport

11: Khaosan Rd.–Phra Sumen Rd.–Democracy Monument (Ratchadamnoen Klang Rd.)–Phetchaburi Rd.–World Trade Center–Sukhumvit Rd.

BY TAXI, TUK-TUK, AND MOTORCYCLE TAXI

Your lungs will thank you for using Bangkok's extensive taxi system. Simple and cost-efficient, taxis are under-utilized by most travelers. Single women find taxis much safer than tuk-tuks or motorcycles.

Tuk-tuks scour the city and slither through the traffic that brings taxis to a halt. Negotiation is key: drivers may charge you twice they would a local. Skillful negotiators can get prices 30% cheaper than taxi fares.

Motorcycle taxi drivers loiter on street corners in brightly colored vests. Though faster in traffic and 10-25% cheaper than tuk-tuks, motorcycle taxis only carry a single passenger, can be dangerous for long journeys, and require calm nerves. Travelers should insist on a helmet, as police will fine non-wearers.

TOURIST SCAMMING Tuk-tuk drivers are often con artists and have been known to harass women travelers. Drivers have also been known to drive off with passenger luggage, push the skin industry, deliver passengers to expensive restaurants, or tell travelers that sights are closed and take them to jewelry and tailor shops instead. To entice *farang,* they offer tours of the city for low rates (10-20฿ per hr.), but all you'll get is a sales pitch and inflated prices. Beware of these words: *free, sexy, massage, jewelry, tailor shop, go-go* (unless of course you really want to go to a masseur, jeweler, tailor, or prostitute). Tuk-tuks aren't all bad–just be firm and make it clear that you want to go to your intended destination and nowhere else.

BY BOAT

Chao Phraya River Express ferries (6am-6pm, 3-25฿) are the best way to travel along the river and provide easy access to the Skytrain. Buy tickets at the booth at the pier or from the ticket collector on board. Specify your stop, as boats will stop only if passengers are waiting at the pier. Disembark quickly. The main stops, from north to south, are **Thewet** (for the National Library and Dusit guest houses), **Phra Athit** (for Khaosan Rd./Banglamphu), **Thonburi Railway Pier** (for Thonburi Railway Station and Royal Barges), **Chang** (for Wat Phra Kaew and Royal Palace), **Tien** (for Wat Pho), **Ratchawong** (for Chinatown and Hualumphong Railway Station), **Si Phraya** (for GPO), **Oriental** (for the Oriental Hotel and Silom), and **Sathorn** (for the Skytrain to Silom). Small brown, box-like ferries with bench seats, easily confused with river taxis, shuttle across the river to every major stop. A small sign identifies each *tha* (pier).

Klongs are small canals that zig-zag through the city's interior. Thonburi, west of Chao Praya, has an extensive network, and Bangkok proper has two useful lines. **Klong Saen Saep** links Democracy Monument near Banglamphu with the area around Siam Sq. and the World Trade Center (10min., 6-15฿). Another route links **Klong Banglamphu** and **Klong Phadung Krung Kasem.** From Tha Banglamphu, at the

THE LOCAL STORY

THE MYSTERY OF JIM THOMPSON

On Easter Sunday in 1967, Jim Thompson went for a walk and never returned. The disappearance remains unsolved. Neither credible evidence of foul play nor Thompson's body have ever turned up, leading to continued conjecture about what happened 35 years ago to the expat who single-handedly built Thailand's silk trade into a multi-million dollar industry.

Long before his disappearance gripped the public imagination, Thompson was famous, especially in Thailand. He fell in love with the country during World War II when he was training as a member of the Office of Strategic Services (OSS), the clandestine US wartime intelligence service that ultimately became the CIA. When the war ended two days before his scheduled mission, Thompson decided to stay for good.

Although he had no business experience, he was fascinated by the entrepreneurial possibilities of opening up Thailand to western visitors and exchange. At the time, Thai silk was a cottage industry on the verge of extinction. Textile manufacturing had made the time-consuming traditional methods of hand-weaving almost obsolete. Thompson, who had a keen artistic eye (he was originally an architect), became fascinated with the fabric and founded the Thai Silk Company in 1948 using only a handful of local weavers to supply his small business. Although Thompson never learned more than a few words of Thai, through his sharp sense of design, uncanny business sense, and

(continued on next page)

Chakraphong and Phrasumen Rd. intersection, you can reach Hualumphong Railway Station (15min., 6am-6pm, 6฿). Boats run every 45min. during off-peak hours and weekends and every 30min. during rush hour.

Longtail boat rentals are available at almost every pier for tourist destinations on the river and *klangs*—agree on a price before setting off. Usual rates are 400฿ for the first hour, 300฿ each additional hour.

BY SKYTRAIN

The **Skytrain (Bangkok Mass Transit System, BTS)** is an A/C delight. Incredibly useful for navigating Siam Sq., Silom, and Sukhumvit, the train has two lines that meet at Siam Sq. The **Sukhumvit Line** runs from Mo Chit next to Chatuchak Market, past the Victory Monument to Siam Sq., through Sukhumvit Rd. and terminates at On Nut, beyond the Eastern Bus Terminal. The **Silom Line** runs from the National Stadium, past Siam Sq. and Lumpini Park, and along part of Silom Rd. before terminating at Taksin Bridge. All stations have useful **maps. Fares** are based on distance (10-40฿), and ticket purchase is automated. Trip passes (10-, 15-, 30-ride) are the most cost-effective for students; flaunt that ISIC card (160-360฿, adults 500-540฿). Insert the card at the turnstile to enter the station; **hold onto it and insert it at the turnstile at your destination to leave the station.** The Skytrain operates daily 6am-midnight.

BY CAR

Travelers should avoid cars, as driving in Bangkok can be dangerous. An International Driver's Permit (see p. 36) and major credit card are required. Rental agencies include **Avis,** 2/12 Witthayu Rd. (☎255 53 00). Renting a small sedan costs 1000-1500฿ per day and insurance costs 250฿.

PRACTICAL INFORMATION

TOURIST AND FINANCIAL SERVICES

Tourist Office: TAT, 4 Ratchadamnoen Nok Rd. (☎282 1672), 500m down on the right from the 8-way intersection east of the Democracy Monument. Very helpful staff doles out **free maps** and advice. Open daily 8:30am-4:30pm.

Immigration Office: 507 Soi Suan Phlu (☎287 3101), off Sathon Tai Rd. 30-day transit visas extended for 10 days; 60-day tourist visas extended for 30 days (500฿). Open M-F 8:30am-4:30pm.

Embassies and Consulates: Australia, 37 Sathorn Tai Rd. (☎287 2680). Open M-F 8am-5pm. **Cambodia,** 185 Ratchadamri Rd. (☎254 6630). Consular services around the corner off Sarasin Rd. on first soi on left. 30-day visa; 2-day processing (1000฿). Open M-F 9-11am and 1:30-4pm. **Canada,** Abdulrahim Bldg., 15th fl., 990 Rama IV Rd. (☎636 0541). Open M-Th 7:30am-4pm, F 7:30am-1pm. **China,** 57 Ratchadaphisek Rd. (☎245 7043). Open M-F 9-11:30am and 2:30-5pm. **Indonesia,** 600 New Phetchaburi Rd. (☎252 3135). Take regular bus #2 or 11; or A/C bus #5, 11, or 12. Open M-F 8am-noon and 1-4pm. **Ireland,** 205 United Flour Mill Bldg., 11th fl., Ratchawong Rd. (☎223 0876). Open M-F 9am-noon and 1:30-4pm. **Laos,** 502/1-3 Soi Ramkhamhaeng 39 (☎539 3642). Visa 300฿; 2-day processing. Open M-F 8am-noon and 1-4pm. **Malaysia,** 33-35 Sathorn Tai Rd. (☎679 2190). Open M-F 8:30am-noon and 1-4pm. **Myanmar,** 132 Sathorn Nua Rd. (☎233 2237). Consular services on Pan Rd., off Sathorn Nua Rd., 1½ blocks from the Skytrain Surasak Station. 30-day visa 800฿ (inquire at embassy for up-to-date status of land crossings); 24hr. processing. Open M-F 8:30am-noon and 2-4:30pm. **New Zealand,** 93 Witthayu Rd. (☎254 2530). Open M-F 7:30am-noon and 1-4pm. **Singapore,** 129 Sathorn Tai Rd. (☎286 2253). Open M-F 8:30am-noon and 1-4:30pm. **South Africa,** Park Palace, 6th fl., 231 Soi Sarasin, Ratchadamri Rd. (☎253 8473). Open M-Th 7:45am-4:30pm, F 7:45am-3:15pm. **UK,** Witthayu Rd. (☎305 8333). Open M-Th 7:45am-noon and 12:45-4:30pm, F 7:45am-1:15pm. **US,** 120-122 Witthayu Rd. (☎205 4000). Consular services M-F 7am-noon and 1-4pm. **Vietnam,** 83/1 Witthayu Rd. (☎251 5836). Visa 2050฿; 2- to 3-day processing. Open M-F 8:30-11:30am and 1:30-4:30pm.

Currency Exchange: 24hr. ATMs abound. Those with "ATM" spelled in blue dots or with a purple hand holding an ATM card accept AmEx/Cirrus/MC/V. You can't throw a stone in Bangkok without hitting a bank, particularly in **Silom.**

American Express: IBM Building, 388 Phahonyothin Rd. (☎273 0033). Open M-F 8:30am-5pm. **Branch** at Sea Tours Co. Ltd, 8th fl., 128 Phayathai Plaza Bldg. (☎216 5783), on Phayathai Rd. between Phetchaburi and Si Ayutthaya Rd., next to Phayathai Skytrain station. Mail held for up to 60 days; no packages. Passport and AmEx card, check, or travel receipt needed for pickup. Open M-F 8:30am-noon and 1-5pm, Sa 8:30am-noon.

(continued from previous page)

sheer charm, he was able to expand his company into one of the country's most lucrative exporters. By exposing wealthy tourists to Thai silk, it quickly became a high-end fashion trend, and Thompson was soon filling orders for Broadway shows.

But Thompson was not simply a successful businessman. He became perhaps the most popular foreigner in Bangkok, respected for his genuine passion for the preservation of Thai arts and culture. In 1962, along a Bangkok *klong*, he restored a teak house in the traditional Thai architectural style.

The Cameron Highlands, an area of dense jungle where Thompson disappeared, provides the setting for a mystery that remains embedded in theory. The facts of that day offer essentially no clues: as his friends napped, Thompson apparently left for a walk. Did he fall down a ravine in the jungle? Was he killed by aborigines or caught in one of their animal traps? Did he take his own life?

These common explanations were generally rejected after an exhaustive search failed to turn up a single shred of evidence, not to mention his body. The failure of the search only led to more speculation. Was Thompson, the former government agent, actually on a covert mission that went awry in the Malaysian bush? Was he kidnapped by communist agents from neighboring Cambodia?

For years, private investigators turned up nothing, local seers and European psychics offered revelations, and newspapers continue to wonder, while Thailand waited for its adopted son to come home.

LOCAL SERVICES

Luggage Storage: The **airport's** the most reliable but a bit pricey (70฿ per day). Open 24hr. Also available at **Hualamphong Railway Station** for 10฿ per day. Open daily 4am-10pm. Guest houses may also offer this service, but proceed at your own risk.

English-Language Bookstores: Aporia Books, 131 Tanao Rd. (☎629 2129), opposite the end of Khaosan Rd. One of the best bookshops in Bangkok with new and used books for sale, trade, or rent. Open daily 9am-8:30pm. **Asia Books,** in the Discovery Center, Siam Sq. and Sukhumvit Rd., has an extensive collection of English books.

Local Publications: *The Bangkok Post* is an English daily, sold everywhere (20฿). Monthly *Metro* (www.bkkmetro.com) divulges the trendiest nightlife secrets (100฿).

Gay and Lesbian Resources: Anjaree (☎477 1776). Lesbian organization with monthly newsletter. *Metro* (see above) has extensive gay nightlife listings.

THAILAND

EMERGENCY AND COMMUNICATIONS

Emergency: ☎191. **Tourist Police:** ☎1155. **Ambulance:** ☎252 2171.

Tourist Police: Most useful office next to TAT, 4 Ratchadamnoen Nok Rd. (☎282 8129). All other stations will refer you here. **Branches** at 2911 Unico House Bldg., Soi Lang Suan (☎652 1721), off Ploenchit Rd. in Siam Sq., and at the corner of Khaosan and Chakraphonh Rd. English spoken. **24hr. booths** opposite Dusit Thani Hotel in Lumpini Park (☎221 6206) and at Don Muang International Airport (☎535 1641).

Pharmacies: Fortune Pharmacy (Banglamphu), in front of Khaosan Palace Hotel on Khaosan Rd. Open daily 8am-midnight. **Siam Drug** (Silom/Financial), at the cul-de-sac of Patpong 2 Rd. Open M-Sa 10am-3am, Su 3pm-3am. Many pharmacies cluster on **Sukhumvit Rd.** between Soi Nana and Soi II. Most open daily 8am-late.

Medical Services: Bamrungrad Hospital, 33 Sukhumvit Rd. Soi 3 (☎253 0250). **Open 24hr. Chulalongkorn Hospital,** 1873 Rama IV Rd. (☎252 8181). Ambulance service. The best and largest public hospital is **Siriraj Hospital** (Thonburi), 2 Pran Nok Rd. (☎411 0241). Take regular bus #19 from Sanam Luang. 24hr. ambulance. Cheapest vaccinations at **Red Cross Society's Queen Saovabha Institute** on Rama IV Rd.

Telephones: Make domestic calls at "cardphone" booths (5฿ per 3min.) and international calls at yellow "international cardphone" booths. Upper right metal button connects directly to an AT&T operator. Most post offices (see below) have **international phone** services. The **Public Telecommunication Service Center** next to GPO offers fax and telex. **Open 24hr.**

Internet Access: Try **Khaosan Rd.** and other backpacker areas. Average 40-60฿ per hr.

Post Offices: GPO (☎233 10 50), in Communications Authority of Thailand building on Charoen Krung Rd. near Soi 32. *Poste Restante*. Mail held for 2 months. Pick-up fee: 1฿ per item, 2฿ for parcels. Open M-F 8:30am-4:30pm, Sa-Su 9am-noon. **Banglamphu Office,** on Khaosan Rd.; turn left onto Bowon Niwet Rd. and walk to small square at bend in road. Open M-F 8:30am-5:30pm, Sa 9am-noon. **Overseas Telephone Office** on 2nd fl. of **Silom/Financial Office,** 113/6-7 Suriwongse Center Rd. From Silom Rd., head up Patpong Rd. to Surawong Rd. and turn left; it's a few lanes down to the left. Open M-F 8:30am-4:30pm, Sa 9am-noon. **Sukhumvit Rd. Office,** 118-122 Sukhumvit Rd. (☎251 79 72), between Soi 4 (Nana Tai) and Landmark Plaza. International calls 8am-10pm. Another at Soi 23, Sukhumvit Rd. (☎258 41 97), on the right. EMS and international calls. Open M-F 8:30am-5:30pm, Sa 9am-noon. **Postal code:** 10500; 10501 for *Poste Restante*.

ACCOMMODATIONS

BANGLAMPHU AND KO RATTANAKOSIN

Within walking distance of Wat Phra Kaew, Wat Pho, the Grand Palace, and the National Museum, this hub of royal Buddhism and ancient architecture functions as a kind of decompression chamber for international travelers and budget backpackers as they enter Thailand. The heart of the fanfare is just to the north along **Khaosan Rd.,** a dubious backpacker mecca of cheap accommodations, free-flowing *Chang* beer, and fake designer clothing. Tourist services abound, but rooms are often cramped, noisy, and full—reserve ahead by phone. About as un-Thai an experience as imaginable, "Khaosan" is laden with drunken *farang*, who haggle with Thais for overpriced goods and swap travel stories over banana pancakes.

GETTING TO BANGLAMPHU Chao Phraya River Express stop: Banglamphu Pier. Buses: Airport Bus AB2, regular bus #15, A/C bus #11.

New Siam Guest House, 21 Soi Chana Songkram (☎282 4554). On the small soi that connects the wat to the river. Though a few banana pancakes pricier than the competition, this recently renovated guest house has a comfortable feel that's worth the extra baht. Very popular and the sheets have maps of Thailand on them. Singles 200฿; doubles 245-320฿, with bath 395-450฿, with bath and A/C 550฿. ❸

My House Guest House, 37 Soi Chana Songkram (☎282 9263). From Khaosan Rd., go toward the river and across the temple grounds; it's 50m to the right. My House features a popular sitting area and proximity to cafes and bars but still maintains a relatively quiet atmosphere and clean rooms. Singles 120฿, with bath 160฿; doubles 200฿, with bath 300฿, with A/C 500฿. ❷

Peachy Guest House, 10 Phra Athit Rd. (☎281 6471). Serene garden, Internet cafe (1฿ for 2min.), and bar are bonuses to a clean and well-run guest house. 4-bed dorms 80฿; singles with shared bath 100฿; doubles 160฿, with A/C 200฿, with A/C and shower 250฿, with shower, toilet, and A/C 350฿. ❶

Tuptim Bed and Breakfast, 82 Rambhuttri Rd. (☎629 1535). From Khaosan Rd. walk to Chakrapong Rd., turn right, and right again onto Rambhuttri Rd.; it's about halfway down on the right. Bright clean rooms, smiling staff, and filling breakfasts (included) make this a fantastic bargain. A new wing with courtyard and restaurant. Singles 250฿, with A/C 499฿; doubles with A/C 550฿; new wing rooms 650฿. ❸

Sweety Guest House, 49 Ratchadamnoen Rd. (☎280 2191). Walk away from the river to the end of Khaosan Rd., cross Bowon Nivet Rd., and go 100m down the soi to the right. The cheapest stay in town. Singles 80-100฿; doubles 140-160฿, with bath 200฿, with A/C 350฿. ❶

Sawasdee House, 147 Soi Rambhuttri (☎281 8138). From Khaosan Rd., cross Chakrapong Rd. and walk down the soi along the right side of the temple wall; it's halfway down. A socialite's dream, it's practically a backpacker convention. Rooms are well kept but often full–plan ahead. Singles with fan 180฿, with balcony 250฿; twins 350฿, with A/C and bath 550฿; doubles 350฿, with A/C and bath 550฿. ❸

Khaosan Palace Hotel, 139 Khaosan Rd. (☎282 05 78), walk down the alley beneath the large green neon sign. For party animals willing to pay for comfort, the Palace is an oasis in the heart of the action. Rooms include private bath and towels. Singles with bath 280฿, with A/C, hot shower, and TV 400฿; doubles 350-580฿; triples 730฿. ❸

DUSIT AND THEWET

Just a quiet bus ride, boat jaunt, or walk from the sights of Ko Rattanakosin and Banglamphu, the guest houses behind the National Library on Thewet are some of Bangkok's best-kept secrets. Catering to those who wish to escape Khaosan Rd.'s frenetic atmosphere while retaining its affordability and accessibility, the area is quiet with little nightlife. Some taxi and tuk-tuk drivers don't even know it exists; be sure to tell them to go to Thewet, behind the National Library.

GETTING TO DUSIT Chao Phraya River Express stop: Thewet. Regular buses #16, 23, 30, 32, 33, and 72. A/C bus #5.

Shanti Lodge, 37 Si Ayutthaya, Soi 16 (☎281 2497). "The Oasis of Bangkok," Shanti has some of the best accommodations in the city. Smoking and shoes prohibited inside. Impeccably clean rooms, sparkling baths, and vegetarian restaurant. Dorms 100฿; doubles 250-280฿, with shower 400-500฿, with A/C and shower 600฿. ❶

Tavee Guest House, 83 Si Ayutthaya, Soi 14 (☎280 1447). Large common spaces with fish tanks, well-decorated rooms, and a family atmosphere. All rooms with clean shared bath. Dorms 90฿; singles 140-250฿; doubles 350฿, with A/C 450฿. ❶

Bangkok International Youth Hostel (HI), 25/2 Phitsanulok Rd. (☎281 0361), 300m from the Samsen Rd. intersection. Head south a short block from Si Ayutthaya Rd. and turn left on Phitsanulok Rd.; it's 500m on the left. Great, spacious dorm rooms. Sex-segregated. Good restaurant. Lockout. No smoking or alcohol. Very, very friendly. No reservations. HI members only; non-members can buy a year-long membership on the spot for 300฿ or 50฿ per night. Dorm-style rooms 70฿, with A/C 120฿; singles with A/C and shared bath 280฿; doubles with fan 250฿, with A/C and shared bath 350฿. ❶

THAILAND

CHINATOWN, PAHURAT, AND HUALAMPHONG

Accommodations line **Yaowarat Rd., Pahurat Rd., Chakraphet Rd.,** and **Rong Muang Rd.** Travelers staying here are either evading *farang* hordes or jumping on and off early-morning trains. Chinatown offers few budget rooms that are clean and safe. Some are rip-offs, others welcome only Asians, and many are brothels.

GETTING TO CHINATOWN, PAHURAT, AND HULAMPHONG Chao Phraya River Express stop: Ratchawong. Regular buses #1, 4, 25, and 73. A/C bus #1. Boat taxi is easy and enjoyable.

T.T. Guest House, 516-518 Soi Sawang, Si Phraya Rd. (☎236 2946). Exit Hualamphong Railway Station, take a left on enormous Rama IV Rd., turn right on Mahanakhon Rd. and take the 1st left; it's at the end of the soi. Popular in high season (reserve ahead), this family-run home has clean rooms and a friendly atmosphere. Strict midnight lockout. Dorms 100฿; singles 200฿; doubles 250฿. ❶

New Empire Hotel, 572 Yaowarat Rd. (☎234 6990), opposite the Bank of Ayudhya near the intersection with Charoen Krung Rd. and Wat Traimit. Bright, clean rooms. Singles 580-650฿; doubles 593฿; triples 750฿; deluxe rooms 650฿. ❺

SILOM ROAD

Although towering skyscrapers dominate **Silom Rd.,** the surrounding area is home to diverse neighborhoods. On **Pan Rd.,** a Burmese community lives between the Burmese Embassy and the Hindu temple. The world-famous **Patpong** red-light district explores the raunchier side of Bangkok, while the wealthy trot in and out of the Oriental Hotel. Most budget establishments are 2km from Silom Rd. along **Soi Ngam Duphli** and **Soi Si Bamphen,** off Rama IV Rd., a bus or tuk-tuk ride away.

GETTING TO SILOM RD Chao Phraya River Express: Oriental. Skytrain: Sarang Daeng. Regular buses #15, 76, 77, 115. A/C buses #2, 4, 5, 15.

Sala Thai Daily Mansion, 15 Soi Sapankoo (☎287 1436). From Rama IV Rd., walk up Soi Ngam Duphli and turn left onto Soi Si Bamphen; take the 1st soi to the left and then turn right. Quiet during low season and happenin' during high season, Sala Thai features sizable rooms with shared bath, a sitting area with cable TV, and a rooftop garden. Singles 200-300฿; doubles 300-400฿. ❸

J.M. Kennedy, 93 Pan Rd., Silom (☎635 2385), opposite the Myanma Airlines office. Walk down Silom Rd. toward the river, turn left at the Indian temple or take Skytrain to Surasak Station and walk 1½ blocks away from the river and turn left onto Pan Rd. Owner Michael dishes out Burmese and Indian food (curries with rice 30-60฿; open daily 6am-9pm) and advice on Thailand and Myanmar in 15 languages. Breakfast included. Basic but clean rooms with TV. Renovation scheduled for completion Oct. 2002. Singles 100฿; doubles 250฿, with A/C and bath 350฿. ❶

Lee Guest House 3, 13 Soi Sapankoo (☎679 7045), and **Lee Mansion 4,** 9 Soi Sapankoo (☎286 78 74), next to Sala Thai, offer clean, fan-cooled rooms at reasonable prices. Small rooms 160฿; large rooms 200฿, with bath 200฿, with A/C 350฿. ❷

THAILAND

SIAM SQUARE

In the shadow of Bangkok's ritziest malls, Siam Sq. is quieter than Khaosan and almost tout-free. Prices run high, but accommodations are a good deal for those willing to splurge a little. Proximity to the Skytrain makes much of Bangkok's nightlife and the Eastern Bus Terminal easily accessible.

GETTING TO SIAM SQUARE Skytrain: Siam Sq. Regular buses #15, 25, and 204. A/C bus #1.

The Bed and Breakfast, 36/42-43 Soi Kasem San 1 (☎215 3004). Fairly clean rooms and steel frame beds. A/C, phone, hot shower, and included breakfast. Reserve ahead Nov.-Feb. Singles 380฿; doubles 480-550฿; triples 650฿. ❹

Pranee Building, 931/12 Soi Kasem San 1 (☎216 3181). Some A/C doubles. The fan-cooled rooms make this the place if you're willing to pay extra for location but not luxury. Doubles 400฿, with hot-water bath 450฿; triples 500฿. ❹

Wendy House, 36/2 Soi Kasem 1 (☎612 3487). This popular guest house is clean and simple. Convenience sets it apart from its Kasem cousins. Laundry 50฿ per kg. Internet 65฿ per hr. Singles 350฿; doubles 400-450฿. Long-term stays offered: weekly doubles 2500฿, monthly 9000฿. ❸

SUKHUMVIT ROAD

Beneath the Skytrain, Sukhumvit Rd. is a strip of expensive pasta places, upscale chain restaurants, and massage-touting tuk-tuk drivers. Both sides of the soi are filled with Bangkok's trendiest bars. Accommodations are pricier.

GETTING TO SUKHUMVIT RD Skytrain: Nana or Asok. Regular buses #25, 38, 72, 115. A/C buses #1, 8, 11, 13.

Suk 11, 1/33 Soi 11, Sukhumvit Rd. (☎253 5927; www.suk11.com), 10m down soi on the left. A truly beautiful enclave in the heart of Bangkok's nightlife, Suk 11 is a gem with a fun vibe. Reminiscent of 1800s Thailand. Glistening clean rooms and newly tiled shared baths. All rooms (and even dorms) have A/C and are worth every baht. Dorms 250฿; singles 450฿, with bath 500฿; doubles 550฿/600฿. ❸

S.V. Guest House, 19/35-36 Soi 19, Sukhumvit Rd. (☎253 35 56), near Asok Station. Good prices, great location (close, but not too close, to the action), and quiet, furnished rooms. Reserve in high season. Singles 250฿, with A/C 300฿; doubles with A/C 350฿, with bath 400฿. ❸

FOOD

Thai cuisine is world-renowned, but no one is more obsessed with and proud of Thai food than the Thais themselves. Thus, they become visibly excited by travelers who venture out from the Thai-Western fare of *farang*-friendly restaurants to eat food like they usually do—right on the street or at no-name restaurants lining back alleys. Lose your fears and find your senses.

BANGLAMPHU AND KO RATTANAKOSIN

For good food stalls, stroll down **Soi Rambhuttri, Krai Si Rd.** (in the evening), or **Phra Chan Rd.** (during the day) opposite **Thammasat University.** The university's **cafeteria** has good street grub at cheap prices. On weekends, hawkers hang out in the area around **Sanam Luang. Khaosan Rd.** bursts with overpriced Thai and Western cuisine. One or two blocks north on **Tani Rd.** and at **Wat Chai Chanasongkram,** food stalls fry noodles and rice dishes all day and into the night.

THAILAND

May Kaidee's Vegetarian Restaurant (☎282 5702). Walk to Bowon Niwet Rd. at the end of Khaosan Rd. Take a right, a quick left, and left again down the first soi; it's 50m down. An expat favorite. Black sticky rice with coconut milk and fruit 30฿, Isaan vegetarian stir-fry 35฿. Open daily 9am-11pm. ❷

Shoshana, on Chakrapong Rd. Facing the temple at the end of Khaosan Rd., turn right and right again at the first alley. Delicious Middle Eastern cuisine such as falafel (50฿), shawarma (60฿), and salads. Plenty of vegetarian options. Open daily 11am-11pm. ❷

Roti Mataba, at the bend in Phra Athit Rd. where it becomes Phra Sumen Rd. This roadside corner is home to some of the best Muslim Thai food in the area; curry-stuffed *roti* (36฿) or beef *mataba* (25฿) are sure to satisfy. Abundant breakfast *roti* options (8-20฿). Open Tu-Su 7am-10pm. ❶

DUSIT AND THEWET

The pavement opposite the guest houses on **Si Ayutthaya Rd.** bustles with food stalls, as does the market at the end of the road by Thewet pier. Just about every Thai rice, noodle, and curry dish is available at rock-bottom prices (30-40฿).

Si Amnouai, on Si Ayutthaya Rd., at the corner with Samsen Rd., opposite the National Library. No English sign. Si Amnouai serves the same rice and noodle dishes as the stalls outside at the same prices—only indoors. Open daily 5am-late. ❷

Bangkok Youth Hostel Cafe, 25/2 Phitsanulok Rd. Mostly Thai clientele despite international flags. Menu features noodles, curries, and a few Western treats (60-130฿). Live music some nights 8-11pm. Open M-F 9am-1am, Sa-Su 10am-1am. ❸

CHINATOWN, PAHURAT, AND HUALAMPHONG

The center of **Yaowarat Rd.** is a treasure of outdoor dining; the sois that branch off it overflow with street-side culinary delights. Excellent Indian restaurants are plentiful near **Chakraphet Rd.** where it meets **Pahurat Rd.** This area requires more adventurous tastes: sharkfin soups and abalone dishes are specialties.

Royal India Restaurant, 392/1 Chakraphet Rd. (☎221 6566), near the river; look for the sign on the left as you come from Yaowarat Rd. Indian dishes of all flavors and tastes (vegetarian included) at 50-100฿. The *thali*, curry, masala, and *naan* sampler (125-165฿) saves you from making a difficult choice. Open daily 10am-10pm. ❸

White Orchid Restaurant and Coffee Shop, 409-421 Yaowarat Rd., in the White Orchid Hotel. Famed dim sum (30฿ per dish, buy 5 get 1 free) and Friday night all-you-can-eat dinner buffet (160฿) are reliably delicious. Open 24hr. for late-night snacking. ❸

Nameless Noodle Place, on Yaowarat Rd., across from the White Orchid Hotel. Popular eatery serves up a mean noodle soup (30-50฿) and simple rice dishes. Rice with braised pork rump 30฿; cold chrysanthemum juice 10฿. ❷

SILOM ROAD

Silom Rd. brims with delicious, expensive restaurants, particularly near Silom Center. Small tourist cafes set up at night on **Surawong Rd.** opposite Patpong. Look for local fare along **Convent Rd.** and inside **Soi Ngam Duphli.**

Eat Me!, 1/6 Piphat Soi 2 (☎238 0931), off Convent Rd. to the right. Creativity and food collide in this stylish, modern restaurant. Delicately prepared yet robust entrees upstairs (200-400฿). Live jazz Th-Sa 7-10pm. As luxurious as a Thai massage. Open daily 3pm-1am. AmEx/MC/V. ❺

Sphinx, 98-104 Soi 4 Silom Rd. (☎234 7249). This trendy, gay-friendly (though not exclusive) restaurant and bar serves set Thai meals (295฿) and Thai/Western dishes (80-150฿) by candlelight. The bar picks up around 11pm and doesn't let up until closing. Cocktails 125฿. Open daily 6pm-2am. AmEx/MC/V. ❹

Dick's Cafe, 894/7-8 Soi Pratoochai (☎637 0078). From Patpong cross Surawong Rd. and walk two sois to the right. This classy gay cafe and bar draws a *farang* male clientele of all ages. Thai/Western food 80-130฿. Beer from 70฿. Cocktails 140฿. ❸

Coffee and More, 990 Rama IV Rd. (☎636 1596). From Silom Rd., make a right onto Rama IV Rd., walk to the Abdulrahim Office Bldg. on your right. It's on the ground floor. One of the two places in Bangkok to offer free Internet, and if that's not reason enough, the passion fruit sorbet (40฿) is worth the trip alone. Food generally 70฿. Coffees and smoothies 30-75฿. Open M-Sa 8am-9pm. ❷

SIAM SQUARE

Siam Square is bursting with culinary flavor. In the afternoon and evening, vendors grill up juicy meats in front of the **National Stadium** on Rama I Rd., at the mouth of **Soi Kasem 1,** and along the soi weaving through Siam Sq. Sidewalk restaurants dot **Ratchaprarop Rd.** and **Soi Wattanasin** opposite the Indra Regent Hotel.

Yum Saap, 430/11-12 Siam Sq. Soi 10. Look for the yellow smiley face and the "Spicy Salad" sign. Papaya salad with seafood 35฿. Open daily 10am-8pm. ❷

Cha Cha An, 484 Siam Sq. (☎252 5038), across from the Novotel Hotel in the parking lot at the end of Soi 6. Steaming hot *yakitori* 50-200฿, finger foods, and well-portioned pieces of sushi 60-200฿. Open daily 11am-10:30pm. AmEx/MC/V. ❹

Forest Tea House, 400 Siam Sq. Soi 6 (☎251 2417), at the bottom of Siam Sq. Skytrain exit. Papaya salad, fried chicken, and sticky rice 80฿. Satisfying spicy meal and large pearl milk tea 140฿. Open daily 11am-11:30pm. ❸

Witthyakit Building Food Court. Walk through Soi 10 in Siam Sq., cross the street, and enter the basement of the tall building resembling a parking structure. Students and faculty from nearby Chulalongkorn University pack this food court for dozens of Thai dishes at 15฿ per plate. Open daily 6-11:15am and 12:45-6pm. ❶

SUKHUMVIT ROAD

If you want to burn baht for a fancy meal and get your money's worth, this is where to do it. **Soi 3/1** specializes in Middle Eastern cuisine. The usual food stalls set up on many soi at lunchtime to sell Thai dishes for 20-40฿.

Cabbages & Condoms, 10 Sukhumvit Rd., Soi 12 (☎229 4611). The brainchild of Dr. Vichit, a family planning advocate, this restaurant, bar, and handicraft shop was established in 1986 to support the Population and Community Development Association (see p. 54). Basil and chili chicken 110฿. Most dishes 80-200฿. Reserve on weekends. Open daily 11am-10pm. AmEx/V. ❸

Crepes and Co., 18/1 Sukhumvit Rd., Soi 12(☎653 3990), past Cabbages & Condoms. Every type of crepe imaginable: sweet, savory, Western, Thai—or design your own (80-250฿). *Tapas* 80-120฿. Open daily 9am-midnight. AmEx/MC/V. ❹

Moghul Room, 1/16 Sukhumvit Rd., Soi 11 (☎253 4465), down the short alley opposite "Sea Food Center." One of Bangkok's best Indian restaurants. Vegetarian dishes 80-90฿. Excellent *dosas* 130-170฿. Open daily 11am-11pm. AmEx/MC/V. ❸

SIGHTS

BANGLAMPHU AND KO RATTANAKOSIN

Ko Rattanakosin requires at least an entire day to explore fully. Because this area is compact, a walking tour is the perfect way to see the sights. Although extremely touristed, **Wat Phra Kaew** and the **Grand Palace** remain two of the most impressive sights in Bangkok. Chao Phraya River Express (Tha Chang) and buses (#1, 25, 47, 82; A/C #43, 44) stop near the compound. History and art lovers will be glued to the treasures in the nearby **National Museum.** A circuit of **monasteries** is also nearby.

WAT PHRA KAEW (TEMPLE OF THE EMERALD BUDDHA) AND THE GRAND PALACE. The Temple of the Emerald Buddha was initially the Royal Chapel of the Chakri Dynasty. Inside the main chapel building *(bot)* is the actual **Emerald Buddha,** Thailand's most sacred Buddha figure, discovered in 1434, when lightning shattered a *chedi* in Chiang Rai and an abbot found a stucco Buddha inside. The figure stayed in Lampang until 1468 before being carted off to Laos. General Chao Phraya Chakri captured Vientiane 214 years later and reclaimed the statue. In 1782, King Rama I ascended the throne, moved the capital to Bangkok, and built the Royal Chapel—Wat Phra Kaew—for the Buddha. Next door to the Temple of the Emerald Buddha is the **Grand Palace,** accessible through a gate connecting the two compounds. Inside the gate, turn right and stroll down the path past royal buildings on the left. The first is **Amarinda Vinichai Hall,** which once held court ceremonies. Next, **Chakri Mahaprasad Hall,** the residence of King Chulalongkorn, is a hybrid of European and Thai design. Today, the reception areas and central throne hall are used for royal ceremonies and are off-limits to mere mortal backpackers. Farther on, **Dusit Hall** houses a mother-of-pearl throne. The **Wat Phra Kaew Museum** is inside the Grand Palace (take a right after the gift shop). The first floor displays parts from original buildings that have been replaced. The second floor contains hundreds of Buddhas and enamel and crystal wares. *(☎222 0094, ext. 40. Free tours In English at 10, 10:30, 11am, 1:30, 2pm. Headphone audio tours 100฿ for 2hr., with guidebook and map 200฿. Admission to Wat Phra Kaew and the Grand Palace includes admission to Vimanmek Palace in Dusit and the Royal Thai Decorations and Coins Pavilion. Polite dress required: full shoes, pants, and sleeves. Shirts, long pants, and shoes are available at the entrance. Complex open daily 8:30am-3:30pm. Museum open daily 9am-3:30pm. Entrance 500฿.)*

WAT PHO (THE TEMPLE OF THE RECLINING BUDDHA). Wat Pho is the oldest, largest, and most architecturally spectacular temple in Bangkok. Its grounds are divided by Soi Chetuphon: one side is home to the monastery, while the other contains temple buildings. Wat Pho was built in the 16th century during the Ayutthaya period and expanded by King Rama I. King Rama III, built the *wiharn* that houses the Reclining Buddha, 46m in length and 15m in height. Wat Pho is also home to Thailand's first university, a monastery that taught medicine a century before Bangkok was founded. A world-famous Thai massage school is its latest achievement. *(From Wat Phra Kaew, walk around the block and take 3 left turns from entrance. ☎222 0933. Open daily 9am-5pm. 20฿.)*

WAT MAHATHAT. Previously home to King Rama I, who was an abbot before he took up military campaigning, Wat Mahathat houses a large sitting Buddha. Today, the temple is a famous center of Buddhist teaching and home to one of Thailand's two Buddhist colleges. The southern part of the complex offers English instruction in Buddhist meditation. *(Between Silpakorn University and Thammasat University on Na Phra That Rd., opposite Sanam Luang. Open daily 9am-5pm.)*

SANAM LUANG. Sanam Luang is the "national common" of Thailand. In the past, criminals were lined up and shot here. Although public executions have been discontinued, summer soccer matches and kite-fighting contests—in which the large "male" kites *(chula)* pursue the fleeing smaller "female" kites *(pukpao)*—have not. Renovation scheduled to finish by early 2003. *(On Na Phra That Rd.)*

NATIONAL MUSEUM. Southeast Asia's largest museum, it is the crown jewel of Thailand's national museum system. King Chulalongkorn (Rama V) founded the museum in 1874 to exhibit collections from the reign of his father, King Rama IV. A massive renovation promises to restore the museum to its past beauty by 2003. *(On Na Phra That Rd. past Thammasat University. ☎224 1333. Open W-Su 9am-4pm, tickets sold until 3:30pm. Free tours in English W-Th 9:30am. 40฿.)*

NATIONAL GALLERY. The gallery contains classical and contemporary Thai artwork and the National Film Archives. Rooms upstairs display paintings of scenes from epics such as *Ramayana* and classical plays. *(On Chao Fa Rd. opposite the Phra Pinklao Bridge from the National Theater. ☎282 2639. Open W-Su 9am-4pm. 30฿.)*

DEMOCRACY MONUMENT. Commemorating Thailand's transition from absolute to constitutional monarchy in the Revolution of 1932, the monument is built on the site of the bloody demonstrations of May 1992, when students and citizens protested the dictatorial rule of General Suchinda Kraprayoon. *(At the intersection of Ratchadamnoen and Dinso Rd.)*

WAT SAKET. Notable for its Golden Mount (an artificial hill topped with a gilded pagoda) soaring 80m high, this popular mount was formerly the highest point in the city. Today, its spectacular panoramic view and golden *chedi* reward those fit enough to make the trek to the top. *(On Worachak Rd. Open daily 7:30am-5:30pm. 10฿.)*

WAT SUTHAT. The wat is famous for housing Thailand's largest cast-bronze Buddha and the Sao Ching Cha (Giant Swing), the scene of several of the more curious Brahmin rituals. One featured a priest who would swing on a rope and use his teeth to catch money suspended in mid-air. Many priests lost their lives attempting this until a law prohibited the ritual. The best part of the complex is the main *wiharn* compound, with marble floors, ornate statues, and impressive murals. *(On Tithong Rd. near the Giant Swing. Open daily 9am-5pm.)*

WAT BOWONNIWET. King Rama IV spent 27 years as chief abbot and King Bhumibol Adulyadej spent his time as a monk in this less-touristed temple. The wat is home to Thailand's second Buddhist college, Mahamakut University. Drop by to admire the chapel's gorgeous ornamental borders and Chinese-style statues or observe the Western monks who live here. Be polite and discreet. *(On the corner of Phra Sawn and Bowon Nivet Rd. in Banglamphu, near Khaosan Rd. Open daily 9am-5pm.)*

IN RECENT NEWS

WHAT'S LOVE GOT TO DO WITH IT?

While most travelers are wary of catching dengue fever, "dong" fever is the more conspicuous epidemic raging through Thailand. Not-so-pretty Western men coupled with young, beautiful Thai women is a frequent sight forcing travelers to, perhaps unexpectedly, confront the questions and issues surrounding the world's oldest trade.

Prostitution has existed in Thailand since Chinese sailors arrived and started taking "minor wives" centuries ago; today, scholars estimate that 150,000-200,000 women staff brothels and street all over the country, primarily servicing Thai locals.

The industry centers in Bangkok's Patpong district, with Pattaya in the east and Phuket and Hat Yai in the south representing the largest satellites. To a lesser extent, conspicuous prostitution catering to tourists has also infiltrated Ko Samui, Chiang Mai, and Hua Hin.

However, there is hardly an area of Thailand—save the blocks surrounding the King's palace—that isn't affected by the trade. Most tourists will hear first and most frequently about the skin carnivals of Patpong and Nana Plaza in Bangkok.

The majority of Thai prostitutes come from Thailand's poorer neighborhoods in Bangkok, the Northern provinces, and most especially the northeastern region of Isaan, Thailand's most impoverished area. Women also come from Cambodia, Myanmar, and Malaysia to work in the skin trade.

(continued on next page)

DUSIT AND THEWET

The sights of Dusit and Thewet are quieter then those in the heart of the city and make for a relaxing morning or afternoon of sightseeing.

VIMANMEK PALACE. Built during the reign of King Chulalongkorn (Rama V), the palace is the largest teak mansion in the world. Held together with wooden pegs, the 72-room structure served as the king's favorite palace from 1902 to 1906. The museum in Aphisek Dusit Hall houses an impressive collection of silver jewelry, silk, and soapstone carvings. *(Entrance on the left on U Thong Nai Rd. Bus #70 stops nearby. Open daily 9:30am-4pm, last admission 3pm. Thai dancing daily 10:30am, 2pm. 50฿, students 20฿, under 5 free, free with Wat Phra Kaew and Grand Palace admission ticket. The palace can only be viewed on a tour (45min., every 30min.). Shorts and sleeveless shirts not allowed. Admission to the palace includes a visit to the museum. Open daily 10am-4pm.)*

DUSIT ZOO. Thailand's largest zoo was once part of the gardens of the Chitralada Palace. It now hosts a large collection of regional animals as well as some rare species, including white-handed gibbons and Komodo dragons. *(On the right on U Thong Nai Rd. Entrances also on Rama V and Ratchavithi Rd. Open daily 9am-6pm. 30฿, under 10 5฿.)*

WAT BENCHAMABOPHIT (MARBLE TEMPLE). The wat's symmetrical architecture and white Carrara marble walls were built in 1899 by King Chulalongkorn. The courtyard is lined with 52 bronze Buddhas that represent styles from different periods, while the garden contains sacred turtles given to the temple by worshipers. Early in the morning (6-7:30am), the monks line the streets to accept donations of food and incense. In February and May, the wat hosts Buddhist festivals and candlelight processions around the *bot*. *(On the right of Si Ayutthaya after the Ratchadamnoen Nok Rd. intersection. Take bus #72. Open daily 8am-5:30pm. 20฿.)*

OTHER SIGHTS. Past the Si Ayutthaya Rd. light, Ratchadamnoen Nok Rd. opens into Suan Amphon, site of the revered **statue of King Chulalongkorn (Rama V).** This beloved king, who ruled from 1868 to 1910, is remembered for abolishing slavery, modernizing Thai society (he introduced the first indoor bathroom), and fending off power-hungry British and French colonialists. Behind the statue and guarded by an iron fence stands the former **National Assembly** (Parliament Building). The domed building was commissioned by King Chulalongkorn in 1908 to replace his old residence. The new Royal Palace, called **Anan-**

tasamakhom, was patterned after St. Peter's Basilica in Rome. Following the 1932 coup, the palace became the National Assembly building, but the Assembly has since been moved to Dusit. Past Wat Benchamabophit and Rama V Rd. on the left is **Chitralada Palace,** the official home of the Royal Family. The walled compound is protected by a moat and specially trained soldiers. The palace is closed to the public.

CHINATOWN, PAHURAT, AND HUALAMPHONG

Chinese immigrants first settled southeast of the royal center along the Chao Phraya River in the 18th century, just after construction of the Grand Palace evicted them from Bangkok's first Chinatown. Today, this area is called **Yaowarat** (after the road that runs through Chinatown) or **Sampeng.** The neighborhood's narrow sois and vibrant street life make it worth exploring on foot, especially at night, when the area comes alive. Near Yaowarat, in an area marked by Pahurat Rd., Chakraphet Rd., lies **Pahurat District,** home of Bangkok's Indian population. Its markets are a great place to buy cheap clothing sold by Sikhs and Hindus.

WAT TRAIMIT. The only temple in this area is home to a 3m, five-ton, gold Sukhothai-style Buddha statue. When the Burmese sacked Ayutthaya, residents saved the statue by covering it with stucco. Its identity remained secret until 1955, when it slipped from a moving crane as it was being transported to Wat Traimit. The plaster cracked, the stucco was removed, and the Golden Buddha was rediscovered. *(Main entrance on Yaowarat Rd. near the Charoen Krung Rd. intersection; a smaller entrance on Traimit Rd., accessible by bus #73. ☎225 9775. Open daily 9am-5pm. 20฿.)*

SILOM ROAD

LUMPINI PARK. Lumpini Park, the largest in Bangkok, is an oasis in Bangkok's glass and steel. In the mornings, the Chinese practice *Tai Chi* while others rent paddle boats and cruise the park's lakes. *(The park is bordered by Ratchadamri, Rama IV, Sarasin, and Witthayu Rd. and is accessible from Silom by regular bus #15, 77, 115 or from Siam Sq. and Banglamphu by regular bus #15. Skytrain: Sala Daeng. Open daily 5:30am-7pm.)*

ORIENTAL HOTEL. Founded by two Danish sea captains, the Oriental is one of the world's most famous hotels. H.N. Andersen built the grand Italianate building in 1887, which still stands as the "Authors' Residence" wing of the hotel. *(48 Oriental Ave. along the Chao Phraya River. Chao Praya River Express: Tha Oriental.)*

(continued from previous page)

The Asian Financial Crisis forced more women into prostitution to feed their families. Many were sold by their own families to agents who often mislead parents to believe their daughters will work as servants.

Some women work free-lance as elite callgirls, some split earnings (rarely evenly) with their go-go bars, and an unfortunate few indentured prostitutes must work for years to pay off their "debt" to the brothel. Most work 1-2 years. Though the rate of condom use in commercial sex is up to 95%, the prostitute's risk of HIV/AIDS is still extremely high.

The chance of her marriage to a wealthy foreigner is also extremely low, despite the promises. While few marriages come out of a "working relationship," Thai-Western marriages are not uncommon. Rare is the Westerner who follows through on his promises of marrying the prostitute whom he visits.

Perhaps the most shocking aspect of the Thai skin trade is that it is not a matter of pressing debate among Thais or tourists in Thailand. A 1960 law prohibits the sex trade, but it is unenforced, full of loopholes, and punishes prostitutes more harshly than pimps, club owners, and clients.

Thais, in general, assume a bemused perspective on the subject of prostitution. Ask the average Thai woman what she thinks of a man visiting a local red-light district, and she'll most likely shrug her shoulders and comment, "What else is a single man to do?"

—Nick Grossman

SIAM SQUARE

JIM THOMPSON'S HOUSE. This elegant house was home to American Jim Thompson, who revitalized the Thai silk industry and later disappeared in Malaysia in 1967 (see sidebar, p.705-706). Actually a combination of six teak buildings, the house is home to one of Thailand's best collections of Ayutthaya- and Rattanakosin-period art. Admission includes a tour in English, during which guides discuss ingenious architectural oddities in Thai houses. *(Soi Kasem San 2, opposite the National Stadium. All Rama I Rd. buses access this site. Skytrain: National Stadium. ☎612 3744. Open daily 9am-4:30pm. Tours required; every 10min. 100฿, students 50฿.)*

CHULALONGKORN UNIVERSITY. Thailand's most prestigious academic institution is worth a visit. The buildings are an architectural representation of Thai classicism, and the bookstore contains a fine selection of English books. *(On the east and west sides of Phayathai Rd., south of Siam Sq. From MBK, cross Phayathai Rd. on the footbridge or take any bus heading south on Phayathai Rd. until you see the campus on the left.)*

SUAN PAKKAD PALACE. The palace's five traditional houses are set in an immaculate garden with plants from all over the world. Behind the garden is the Lacquer Pavilion, filled with porcelain, Buddhas, and Ban Chiang pottery. *(352 Si Ayutthaya Rd. Take regular bus #54, 73, or 204 from Siam Sq. past the Indra Regent on Ratchaprarop Rd. Get off near the corner of Ratchaprarop and Si Ayutthaya Rd. and turn down Si Ayutthaya Rd.; it's on the left. Skytrain: Phayathai. ☎245 4934. Open M-Sa 9am-4pm. 150฿, students 30฿.)*

GODDESS TUPTIM SHRINE. One of Bangkok's more arousing sights, the shrine is famous for the large numbers of phallic objects around its spirit house, brought there by couples seeking an end to their infertility. *(Near the Hilton International Hotel on Witthayu Rd. at Phetchaburi Rd.)*

SUKHUMVIT ROAD AREA

When Rama I/Ploenchit Blvd. crosses Witthaya Rd., it becomes Sukhumvit Rd., stretching southeast out of the city. The Sukhumvit Rd. area hosts trendy nightlife, upper-crust travelers, red-light districts, and great restaurants.

KAMTHIENG HOUSE. Reconstructing daily life in 19th-century Thailand, this ethnological museum is also home to the Siam Society, a cultural society supported by the royals. *(131 Soi 21 Asoke, on the left as you walk from Sukhumvit Rd. Near the Asok Skytrain station. ☎661 6470.)*

THONBURI: WEST OF THE RIVER

WAT ARUN (TEMPLE OF DAWN). Named for Aruna, the Hindu god of dawn, this wat was built in the Ayutthaya period and embellished during the reigns of Kings Rama II and III into its present Khmer-style form. The distinctive 79m *prang* is inlaid with ceramic tiles and porcelain. The best view of the wat is from the Chao Phraya River's Bangkok side in the early morning or in the evening; the top of the *prang* affords beautiful views as well. *(In Thonburi, from Wat Pho, take a right from Chetupon Rd. onto Maharat Rd. and a left at Tani Wang Rd. From an adjacent pier at the end of the road, ferries cross to the wat for 1฿. ☎465 5640. Open daily 8:30am-5:30pm. 10฿.)*

ROYAL BARGE MUSEUM. The most impressive barge in the museum is the Suphannahongsa, a 46m vessel reserved for the king when he makes his annual offering of robes to the monks during the Kathin Ceremony. *(On Arun Amarin Rd., under the bridge over Klong Bangkok Noi. Take a river taxi to Bangkok Noi pier and walk upriver, over the canal, to the museum. ☎424 0004. Open daily 8:30am-4:30pm. 80฿.)*

THAILAND

ENTERTAINMENT

NATIONAL THEATER. The National Theater, on Na Phra That Rd. past the national museum, has regular drama and dance shows. The performance program changes monthly but usually includes at least one dance-drama performance and an orchestral concert. Contact the theater for the month's schedule. *(☎224 1342. Open M-F 9am-3:30pm and 1hr. prior to performances. Tickets 30-80฿ for government-sponsored shows.)*

THAI CLASSICAL DANCE DINNERS. Many restaurants offer Thai classical dance dinners with half a dozen traditional dances in an hour-long show. Shows usually include *khon* dances from the *Ramakien* (see **Dance and Drama**, p. 679). No shorts, sandals, or tank tops are allowed. Reserve at least a day in advance. At **Ruen Thep,** Silom Village, 286 Silom Rd., in the Narai Hotel, enjoy a dance dinner in a garden of turtle pools. Performances begin at 8pm and include seven dance styles that change monthly. *(☎234 4581. Opens at 7pm; set Thai dinner at 7:30pm. Tickets 450฿. AmEx/MC/V.)*

TRADITIONAL THAI MASSAGE. Quality among massage parlors varies tremendously, and many are fronts for prostitution. Pictures of women in the window are giveaways for the latter. Ask other backpackers about their favorite masseurs. At Wat Pho, **The Traditional Massage School** (see **Wat Pho,** p. 700) offers massages for 200฿ per hr. as well as a 10-day, 30hr. course for 6000฿. (☎221 2974. Open daily 8am-5pm.) **Mr. Noi** is possibly the world's best masseur. (☎235 2148. 330฿ for 2hr. Open daily 9am-midnight.) **Winwan,** 45 Sukhumvit Rd., between Soi 1 and 3, offers excellent massages. (☎251 7467. 300฿ plus tip per 2hr. Open daily 10am-midnight.) **Marble House,** 37/18-19 Soi Surawong Plaza, one soi up Surawong Rd. from Patpong 2, has a capable, mostly Wat Pho-trained staff, including a cadre of blind masseurs, who are reputed to be the best in the business.

MUAY THAI (THAI BOXING). One of the world's more brutal sports, Muay Thai is the national pasttime (see **Muay Thai,** p. 679). For those who don't mind the actual fighting, the rituals and fervor that surround these matches are fascinating aspects of Thai culture. Muay Thai occurs daily at one of two venues. On Mondays, Wednesdays, Thursdays, and Sundays, the action's at **Ratchadamnoen Boxing Stadium** (☎281 4205), on Ratchadamnoen Nok Rd. near the TAT office. Take regular bus #70 from Sanam Luang. On Tuesdays, Fridays, or Saturdays, head for **Lumpini Boxing Stadium** (☎251 4303), on Rama IV Rd. near Lumpini Park, which stages better fights—the top card's on Friday. Fights start around 6pm; the main fight begins around 7:30pm. Take regular bus #115 from Silom Rd. Prices vary depending on the venue and are cheaper at Ratchadamnoen (about 220-240฿, ringside 880฿+).

SHOPPING

After a while in the Bangkok sun, the **Siam Sq.** and **Silom Rd.** areas begin to look like one big A/C shopping mall. Siam Sq. houses five immense shopping centers, four movie complexes, 200 restaurants, and a few discos. (Most open daily 10am-10pm.) The undisputed heavyweight of Bangkok's shopping centers, however, is **Mahboonkrong Center (MBK),** on the corner of Rama I and Phayathai Rd. in the Siam Sq. area. With seven floors of department stores, arcades, electronics, music stores, fast-food joints, and a cinema, MBK puts most Western shopping malls to shame. Connected to it by a skyway is the equally impressive **Siam Square Mall.** Spread over several soi are clothing and music stores, restaurants, movie theaters, and a hotel. MBK's main competitor, the **Zen World Trade Center,** up Ratchadamri Rd. toward Phetchaburi Rd., has the same shops as MBK but is a little less busy.

MARKETS

CHATUCHAK MARKET. This weekend market is a bargain-hunter's dream and a great example of market culture in Southeast Asia. The bustle is unmistakable and addictive as thousands of vendors sell everything from dalmatians to toucans, though the main focus is clothing and plants. Bring plenty of free time and patience to navigate the crowds. *(Skytrain: Mo Chit. Open Sa-Su 7am-6pm.)*

BANGLAMPHU MARKET. This frenzied market branches onto Chakrapong, Krai Si, and Tani Rd., but the tourist-oriented section is along Khaosan Rd. A late-afternoon/early-evening affair, the market's offerings include food, souvenirs, leather products, and fake designer clothing. Everything is overpriced, but the feel of the market itself is priceless.

OTHER MARKETS. Thewet Market is on Krung Kasem Rd. along the Chao Phraya River. The selection is not as diverse, but it's the one-stop shopping center for food or garden landscaping. *(Chao Phraya River Express: Thewet.)* A sweet and brilliant sight is **Pakklong Market,** southwest of Pahurat District over Triphet Ave. Take a river taxi to Tha Rachini. A relaxing stroll through this wholesale flower market is worth the trip. Opposite Chakraphet Rd., and east of the Pahurat Cloth Market is the **Sampaeng Lane Market.** This small alley continues for a few kilometers through the heart of Chinatown. If you need cutlery, jewelry, socks, monk's supplies, hats, or fishing equipment, this outstretched alley is the place to go. The **Pratunam Market** is a day market along Ratchaprarop Rd., opposite the Indra Hotel. Clothes are the main event here, although there is also a wide selection of knick-knacks. In the **Silom** area, vendors set up along **Patpong Soi 1** after nightfall. This is *the* place to buy overpriced fake designer watches, clothing, or soap carvings or to take in the scene as Thais tout live "shows" to elderly couples and housewives.

NIGHTLIFE

Needing little introduction, Bangkok's reputation as the epicenter of Southeast Asia's internationalism is rooted in its easy mix of traditional art and culture with the hip, connected youth who want to get down and party until dawn. Silom is the center of after-dark amusement, although Sukhumvit, Siam Sq., and Khaosan Rd. are nothing to scoff at. Silom Sois 2 and 4 are centers for gay nightlife. Places listed here are not associated with the skin trade (see **Red Light, Green Light,** p. 708).

BARS AND PUBS

Tapas, 114/7 Silom, Soi 4 (☎632 7982). Resident DJs spin chill house nightly in this "room club" bar. Outdoor seating for fresh air and people-watching. No cover downstairs. 300฿ cover upstairs. Beer 120฿. Open daily 8pm-2am.

Q Bar, 34 Sukhumvit, Soi 11 (☎252 3274). At the end of Soi 11 take a left. Posh. Dress well—you might meet someone special. Beer 160฿. Cocktails 200฿. Special parties F-Sa 400฿ cover, includes 2 free drinks. Open daily 8pm-2am.

Banana Leaf Cafe, 34/1 Khaosan Rd. (☎629 3343), 50m from Gullivers (see below). Psst—one of Bangkok's best new bars is on Khaosan Rd., and tourists haven't found it yet. Packed with Thais and just a few *farang*. Comprehensive Thai/Western menu 60-120฿. Drinks 60-140฿. Open daily 10am-2am.

Joy Luck Club, 8 Phra Sumen Rd. (☎629 4128). Artsy + moody = atmosphere. Singha 60฿. Cocktails 100฿, 800฿ for Johnny Walker black label. Open daily 5pm-1am. This junction between Phra Sumen Rd. and Phra Athit Rd. is full of other very comfortable bars like **Dog Days** and **Comme Arts Cafe.** Open daily 11am-1am.

Ad Here, 13 Samsen Rd. (☎629 2897). Right before Samsen Rd. changes into Chakrapong Rd., at the Khlong Banglamphu. Old soul, jazz, and Beatles tunes belted out by a singer with a lovely Thai-English accent. Beer 60฿. Open daily 5pm-1am.

O! Hungry, 45 Soi Chanasongkram (☎629 1412), next to My House Guest House. It is not hard to find bars serving 40฿ Chang beer, but ones like O! Hungry, which show NEW Western movies (8pm showtime) for free and serve 45฿ banana pancakes, are harder to come by. Open daily 6am-1:30am.

Pranakorn Bar and Gallery, 58/2 Soi Ratchadamnoen Klang Tai. Three floors of art, tunes, and drink. Few *farangs*. Small Singha 60฿. Open daily 11am-2am.

Shenanigans, Sivadon Bldg., 1 Convent Rd. (☎266 7160). Just off Silom Rd. near Patpong. A classy Irish pub with a 100% *farang* clientele. Well worth the extra baht, especially during happy hour (4-7:30pm) when a Jameson and Coke costs 80฿ and a large Heineken is 90฿. Guinness on tap 320฿ per pint. Open daily 11am-2am.

Telephone Pub and Restaurant, 86-88 Silom Soi 4 (☎234 3279). All orientations welcome, but caters to a gay crowd, both Thai and foreign. Signature fixture of numbered telephones at tables provides fiber-optic flirting options. Serves beer and food indoors and out. Drinks 55-125฿. Western and Thai dishes 100-190฿. Open daily 6pm-2am.

Gullivers, 3 Khaosan Rd., at the corner of Chakrapong Rd. Look for the life-size tuk-tuk hanging over the door. One of the most popular bars on Khaosan Rd. Its specialties are Western food and beer in a dark tavern atmosphere. Pool tables and a bar that won't quit until sun-up. Expect to see hordes of drunk *farangs* flocking here on the prowl for the opposite sex. Beers 60-65฿ per bottle. Open daily 11am-2am.

Radio City and **Muzzik Café,** on the south end of Patpong 1 Rd. on opposite sides of the street. After 9pm these colorful and popular bars fill with *farang* seeking either refuge from the madness outside or the nightly live music. Skip the ping-pong shows elsewhere and check out the Elvis Presley (11pm) and Tom Jones (midnight) shows. Open daily 6pm-2am. Muzzik Café stays open until the wee hours and collects much of the drunken, post-go-go bar chaos. Open daily 6pm-5am.

LIVE MUSIC

Bangkok's most rewarding nightlife centers on jazz establishments with live music and a classy Thai and foreign clientele. Off Ratchadamri Rd., **Soi Sarasin,** just north of Lumpini Rd., has restaurant/bars that play live music nightly. Bands generally start around 8pm, but things get cooking after 11pm. **Brown Sugar Jazz Pub and Restaurant,** 231/20 Sarasin Rd., opposite Lumpini Park, is regarded as one of the best in the city, with jazz bands every night that draw well-dressed patrons. (☎250 1826. Food 90-360฿. Beer 120฿. Cocktails 150฿. Happy hour 4-9pm. Open daily 11am-1am, live music 9:45pm-1am.)

CLUBS

Since Thailand is home to some of Southeast Asia's best DJs, it's no surprise that Bangkok has the largest selection of clubs in the region. In the basement of the Novotel Hotel on Soi 6, **Concept CM^2**, as in "Siam Squared," is the city's most recognized club, featuring postmodern decor and talented bartenders. (☎255 6888. Beer 140฿. Dishes 150-300฿. Officially open daily 7pm-2am, but sometimes is 10pm-2am. No shorts or sandals. 18+. Cover 100฿.) **DJ Station,** on Silom Soi 2, was awarded the title of Best Gay Disco 2001 by *Metro*, and it's no wonder. Dance to great house and techno surrounded by no-nonsense metal decor. (Cover F-Sa 200฿, includes 2 drinks; Su-Th 100฿, includes 1 drink. No shorts or sandals. 18+. Open daily 11pm-2:30am.) On Patpong 1 Rd., next to Radio City, **Lucifer** is delightfully designed to look like hell. The club certainly takes in its share of devils from the street and bars below. (Drinks 120฿. No cover. Open daily 10pm-2am.)

RED LIGHT, GREEN LIGHT Love it or loathe it, Bangkok's Red-Light District will not be denied. Thailand supports a massive sex industry, primarily for locals, but also for lonely male foreigners. Three locales—Patpong in Silom, and Nana and Soi Cowboy in Sukhumvit—are home to the densest concentration of these self-proclaimed "entertainment centers." The Sukhumvit area more prominently displays the skin industry in the higher number of go-go bars and white male-Thai female "couples" visible on the streets. You can dabble to different degrees in the sex trade. Most innocent are regular bars staffed by Thai women, whose job is to provide company and suck on drinks purchased by male customers. On the next rung up (down?) the ladder are hostess bars, which are almost exclusively for Japanese tourists. Lines of well-dressed Japanese women wait street-side to be selected and escorted by the client into their karaoke bars for food, drinks, and singing. Third are go-go bars, which feature stages for topless and/or bottomless dancing, in addition to girls for "company." Many of these go all the way, with back rooms where live trick shows or sex shows are put on throughout the night. Needless to say, additional "services" are purchased from these women (many or all of whom are heavily intoxicated with various substances) at any and all of these locations.

Let's Go does not encourage the support of these industries. Nevertheless, these activities will continue with or without curious budget travelers. Those who wish to enter go-go bars for dancing or shows should be cautious. Most of these establishments do not charge cover, and your bar tab (the only required charge, beers run 70-100฿) will be set in front of you at all times. If a woman sits with you, you will be expected to buy her drinks to consume at whatever rate she chooses. Be resolute or go to the manager if this is something you do not want. It is possible to sit and drink one beer by yourself for an hour if you so choose, although few people do. Patpong is a different situation, and stories abound amongst travelers about those who enter these sex shows under the auspices of "no cover charge" only to be prohibited from exiting before paying thousands of baht. A few of the larger clubs really have free shows, but most don't, charging 200-300฿ for a ticket to a night's worth of shows. Regardless of where you go, the only way you can really be certain is by seeking out the manager immediately upon entry and telling him what you expect of his club. He is the only one who can guarantee a "free show" and will tell you if that is not the case. If there is any uncertainty, leave immediately, as you are expected to pay for any watching. Exercise caution, do not take pictures, and be discreet.

DAYTRIPS FROM BANGKOK

Travel agencies offer pricey daytrips to attractions outside Bangkok, but these sights can be seen more cheaply independently.

NONTHABURI. Nonthaburi Province straddles the Chao Phraya River 20km north of Bangkok. The town of Nonthaburi, on the east bank, is known for its fruit and earthenware. On the west bank, in Amphoe Bangkluai, stands **Wat Chalerm Phra Kliad Wora Wihaan,** known to locals simply as Wat Chalerm. Chinese styles influence the statues around the grounds as well as the ceramics and flowering decorations. *(The best way to get to Wat Chalerm is by the Chao Phraya River Express ferry to the Nonthaburi Pier. From here, take another ferry to the west bank (1฿) and hire a motorcycle to Wat Chalerm (10฿). Open daily 9am-5pm.)*

SAMUT PRAKAN. The center of Thailand's leather industry, Samut Prakan is also home to Muang Boran and the Crocodile Farm. Muang Boran, the "Ancient City," is an open-air museum in the shape of Thailand that contains replicas of monuments and sights from around the kingdom. Highlights include the Ayutthaya-style **Saphet Prasat Palace,** the **Dusit Maha Prasat Palace,** and **Khao Phra Wihan,** which sit atop a hill affording a spectacular view. The Crocodile Farm houses the largest crocodile in captivity. At the "Crocodile Wrestling" show, trainers taunt the toothy behemoths. Other attractions include an aviary, snake pits, a dinosaur museum, and go-carts. *(Take bus #11 from the World Trade Center; the Crocodile Farm is the last stop. To reach Muang Boran from the bus stop, backtrack to the corner at the Bank of Ayudhya. Along the side street, a row of* songthaew *36 go to Muang Boran for 3฿. Muang Boran: ☎323 9253. Open daily 8am-5pm. 50฿, children 25฿. Crocodile Farm: ☎703 84 91. Crocodile shows every hr. 9-11am and 1-4pm; additional shows on weekends and holidays at noon and 5pm. Open daily 8am-6pm. 300฿, students with ID 200฿.)*

DAMNOEN SADUAK. Damnoen Saduak's **floating market,** though touristy, captures a quick snapshot of a transient canal economy. A boat tour (300฿ per hr.) is a must, but service and quality vary greatly. A ride through the actual market is included in any tour. Browse through the woodcarvings and cowboy hats, then head to the sugar farm and sample some palm flower juice or fresh-from-the-hive honey. Depicted in paintings, postcards, and picture books, the bustling scene has become the poster child for traditional Thai life. Some visitors may find the not-so-picture-perfect reality—murky waters, swarming flies, and spitting vendors—disappointing. *(Buses leave from Bangkok's southern bus terminal for Damnoen Saduak and drop off passengers in the thick of the action (every 20min. 6am-9pm; regular 30฿, with A/C 55฿). Upon arrival, visitors are approached by locals offering 1hr. boat tours for 300฿. The best time to visit is 8-10am. The market closes down at 11am weekdays, 2pm weekends. To return to Bangkok, take a yellow* songthaew *(5฿) into the center of Damnoen Saduak and wave down one of the buses.)*

CENTRAL THAILAND

Fertile Central Thailand stretches from Hua Hin in the south to Nakhon Sawan in the north and includes attractions such as the awe-inspiring ruins of Ayutthaya and the lush landscapes around Kanchanaburi, as well as the banks of the River Kwai. Southbound buses and trains wind through the beginnings of peninsular Thailand, a teaser for the sandy playgrounds farther south.

AYUTTHAYA ☎035

Entering the city of Ayutthaya is like walking into a time warp. For four centuries the city was the capital of Siam, raising 33 kings, withstanding 23 invasions by Burmese troops, and extending its rule west to Bago in Myanmar and east to Angkor in Cambodia. In 1767, however, good times turned bad when Ayutthaya was sacked by the Burmese (successfully, this time), and the capital was moved, leaving the city a mere echo of its royal past. Tuk-tuks and motorcycles weave around the massive ruins that dot Ayutthaya, and pedestrians walk by former royal palaces without so much as batting an eye. Perhaps most impressively, traffic routinely comes to a standstill as elephants bearing camera-toting tourists head from ruin to ruin. Modern Ayutthaya is loud, busy, and impersonal but comfortable with its royal past and ruins, which blend into the cityscape.

TRANSPORTATION

Trains: Ayutthaya Railway Station (☎241 54), on the mainland east of the island. Take the ferry from U Thong Rd. and walk up the street. Otherwise, it's a long walk across **Pridi Damrong Bridge** and up your first left, or a 30฿ tuk-tuk ride. Trains to: **Bangkok** (1½-2hr.; 21 per day; 15฿, rapid or express 20฿); **Chiang Mai** via **Phitsanulok** (12hr.; 4 per day; 3rd-class 296฿, 2nd-class sleeper 586฿, 1st-class 1138฿); **Saraburi** (1hr., 10 per day, 9฿); **Udon Thani** (9hr.; 3 per day; 3rd-class 145฿, 2nd-class 306฿).

Buses: The bus station at **Naresuan Rd.** sends buses to: **Bangkok** (#901; 1½hr.; every 30min. 6am-7pm; 20฿, with A/C 30฿); **Saraburi,** connecting to destinations in the northeast (#358; 2¼hr., every 30min. 6am-5pm, 27฿); **Suphanburi,** connecting with #411 to **Kanchanaburi** (#703; 1¾hr., every 30min. 6am-5pm, 17฿). The **Mainland bus terminal,** 5km east of the island (50฿ by tuk-tuk) has buses to **Chiang Mai** (9½hr.; 9 per day; 2nd-class with A/C 283฿, VIP 570฿) and **Phitsanulok** (5hr.; 9 per day; 85฿, 2nd-class with A/C 120฿, 1st-class with A/C 194฿, VIP 300฿).

Ferries: Continuous ferries to the mainland (and the train station) leave from an alley off U Thong Rd. near the intersection with Horattanachai Rd. (2฿). **Long-tailed boats** and **cruisers** can be hired at the Chantharkasem Palace pier at the island's northeast tip for a 1hr. trip around the island (500฿, with two temple stops 600฿).

Local Transportation: Tuk-tuk/songthaew hybrids wheel around the island for 30-100฿. Rent by the hour (200฿) or for a full day (700-900฿). Most guest houses rent **bicycles** (50-60฿ per day).

ORIENTATION AND PRACTICAL INFORMATION

The Ayutthaya **city center** is an island at the intersection the **Chao Phraya, Pa Sak,** and **Lopburi Rivers. U Thong Rd.** encircles the island. Intercity **buses** stop next to the **Chao Phrom Market** at the corner of **Naresuan** and **Khlong Makham Rieng Rd.,** in the island's northeastern corner. Buses from northern Thailand arrive east of the island, 5km beyond the **Pridi Damrong Bridge.** Though the wats ring the island, most tourist attractions cluster near the **Tourist Information Center (TAT)** on **Si Sanphet Rd.**

Tourist Offices: TAT (☎322 730), Si Sanphet Rd., a 5min. walk south of Wat Phra Si Sanphet. Carries timetables and large, handy maps. Open daily 9am-5pm.

Currency Exchange: Banks abound along the eastern stretch of Naresuan Rd. and the northeastern curve of U Thong Rd.; many have **24hr. ATMs. Bangkok Bank,** 20 U Thong Rd. (☎245 346/7), opposite the school near the GPO. Open M-F 8:30am-3:30pm.

Markets: Chao Phrom Market, at the corner of Naresuan and U Thong Rd. Open daily 7am-7pm.

Emergency: ☎191. **Tourist Police (Bangkok):** ☎1155. **Police:** ☎241 174.

Tourist Police (local): ☎242 352. Next to TAT on Si Sanphet Rd. Some English spoken. **Open 24hr.**

Medical Services: Phra Nakhon Si Ayutthaya Hospital, 46 U Thong Rd. (☎241 728), at the intersection of Si Sanphet and U Thong Rd. English spoken. **Open 24hr.**

Telephones: International Telephone Office, on the 2nd fl. of the GPO. Also a booth outside. Collect calls 33฿. Open daily 8am-8pm.

Internet Access: Available all over the city, especially north of the Chao Phrom Market. **9 To Nine Net,** on Bang Lan Rd. off U Thong Rd. 30฿ per hr. Open daily 9:30am-10pm. More convenient is the **nameless Internet place** next door to The Moon Cafe. 1฿ per 2min. Open daily 9am-midnight.

Post Offices: GPO, 123/11 U Thong Rd. (☎251 233), on the island's northeast corner. Open M-F 8:30am-4:30pm, Sa 9am-noon. **Postal code:** 13000.

ACCOMMODATIONS

Budget accommodations cluster in two distinct areas: off **Chikun Rd.**, across from Wat Ratburana, and north of **Naresuan Rd.**, near Chao Phrom. Room rates increase during festival season (Nov.-Dec.), and lodgings are harder to find.

PU Guest House, 20/1 Soi Thor Korsor (☎251 213). In the lane across and left of the bus terminal at Chao Phrom Market. Rooms are sunny, large, and ultra-clean. All have private toilet and shower. Plush common room with TV. Motorcycle rental 250฿ per day. Singles 150฿, with bath 200฿; doubles 200฿, with bath 250฿, with A/C 450฿. ❷

Ayutthaya Guest House, 16/2 Naresuan Rd. (☎232 658), on the soi for PU Guest House, across from the bus station. Two main buildings; the satellite one has better rooms. Rooms are large and clean. Extremely popular and occasionally full. Dorms 70฿; singles 100-120฿; doubles 180฿, with shower and toilet 350฿. ❶

Tony's Place, 12/18 Naresuan Rd. (☎252 578), north of the bus stop across from Ayutthaya Guest House. Tidy rooms. Baths have Western toilets, but some are cleaner than others. TV lounge, pool table, Internet access, outdoor drinking area, and occassional music stage. Breakfast starts at 7am; bar open until midnight. Motorcycle rental 250฿ per day. Dorms 80-100฿; doubles 180฿, with bath 250฿. ❶

Chantana Guest House, 12/22 Naresuan Rd. (☎232 300), next to Tony's Place. Ayutthaya's newest guest house is quiet, simple, and clean. After a long day sweating in wats, the A/C rooms are a godsend. All have Western toilets and shower. Worth the extra baht. Singles and doubles 250฿, with A/C and hot shower 450฿. ❸

Charlie's Guest House, on Chikun Rd. (☎232 807) opposite the entrance to Wat Ratburana. Large rooms overlooking the ruins. Seldom full, more of a last resort. Singles 160฿; doubles 200฿, with A/C 300฿. ❷

FOOD

Food stalls ❶ serving 20฿ chicken and rice are interspersed between tables of plastic guns, dried fish, and piles of fruit at Chao Phrom Market, one block east of the local bus stop. More stalls also line U Thong Rd., particularly on the eastern side of the island after the post office. Popular with locals, **Sathong River Restaurant** ❸, 4 Mu 2 U Thong Rd., has cool breezes and great views of the wat across the river. Try the *tom yum*, a hot and sour soup with prawns. (☎241 449. Open daily 10am-9:30pm.) **Siam Restaurant** ❷, on Chikun Rd., between Horattanachai and Bang Lad Rd., serves reasonably priced Thai and Vietnamese food. (☎211 070. Vietnamese beef noodle soup 60฿; green curry 100฿. Open daily 10am-11:30pm. MC/V.)

SIGHTS

Ayutthaya's crumbling ruins span several dozen kilometers; exploring all the ruins would take several days. The **Tourist Information Center** has free maps that locate and explain nearly every sight. Your best bet is to rent a motorcycle or bike from a guest house. Otherwise, tuk-tuk drivers will take you around (200฿ per hr., around 700-900฿ per day). All temples are open daily 8am-6:30pm.

ANCIENT PALACE AND WAT PHRA SI SANPHET. If you visit only one ruin, this should be it. The area was the home of the ancient Royal Palace until 1448, when a monastery was built on the grounds. As a royal monastery, Wat Phra Si Sanphet hosted important rituals and ceremonies. The site's three charred *chedis* once held the remains of the king, his father, and his brother but are now empty. *(30฿.)*

WIHAN PHRA MONGKHON BROPHIT. At 12.45m high and 9.5m wide, the 15th-century Buddha snuggled inside this wat is the largest bronze Buddha in Thailand. On display are photographs and blurbs explaining this restored Buddha's many "incarnations." *(Just south of Wat Phra Si Sanphet. Free.)*

WAT PHRARAM. Overshadowed by its more glamorous neighbors, Wat Phraram was built in 1369 by King Ramesnan to commemorate the spot where his father, King U Thong, was cremated. Dozens of broken Buddha representations sit silently around the wat's landmark *prang* (corncob-shaped *chedi*), quite likely the town's largest phallic symbol. *(Across the street from Wihan Phra Mongkhon Brophit. 30฿.)*

WAT MAHATHAT. This impressive royal monastery was founded by King Borommarachathirat in 1374 and restored several times, most recently in the 18th century. Excavations done in the 1950s uncovered relics of the Buddha hidden deep in a seven-layered reliquary in the *stupa*. With those finds safely stored at the Chao Sam Phraya National Museum, the wat's most precious attraction is a representation of the Buddha's face enshrouded in the roots of a tree. *(At the corner of Chikun Rd. and Naresuan Rd. Open daily 8am-6:30pm. 30฿.)*

WAT RATCHABURANA. Wat Mahathat's most impressive neighbor was built by King Chao Sam Phraya in 1424. Legend has it that the king's two oldest brothers coveted the throne and killed each other in a heated duel, allowing Chao Sam

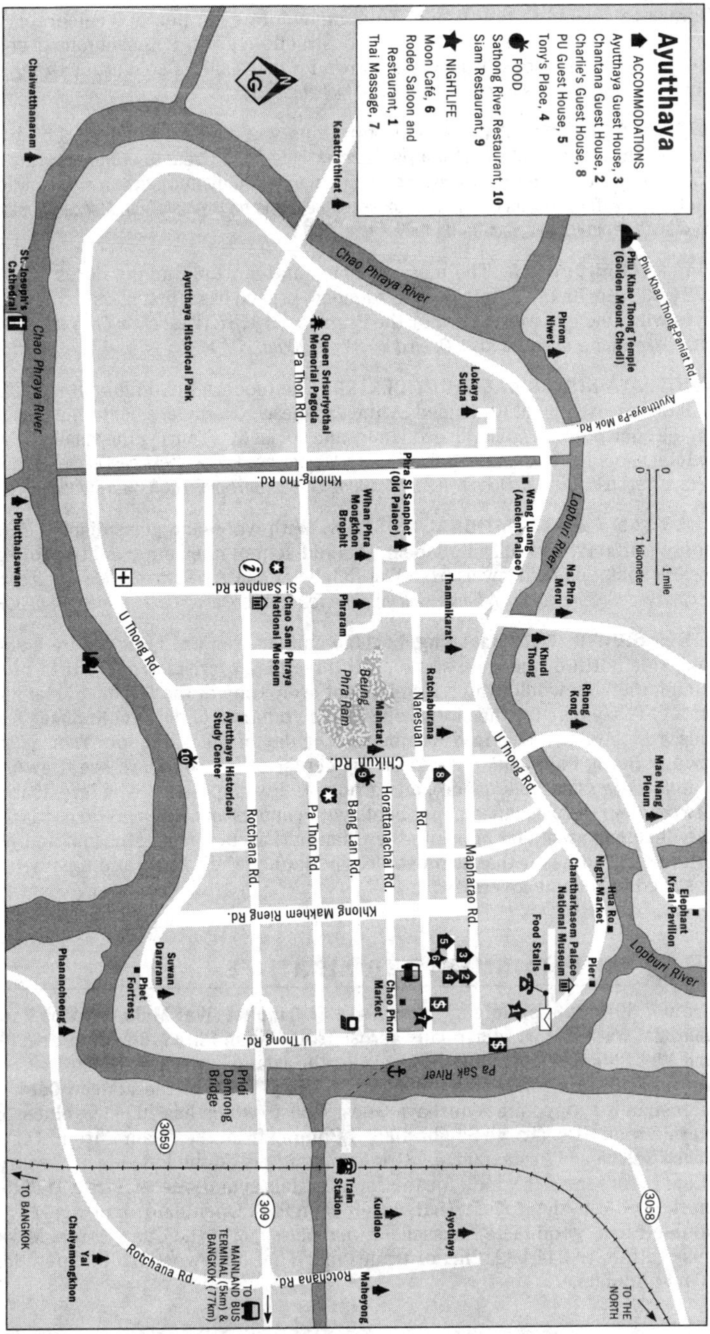
Ayutthaya
ACCOMMODATIONS
Ayutthaya Guest House, 3
Chantana Guest House, 2
Charlie's Guest House, 8
PU Guest House, 5
Tony's Place, 4
FOOD
Sathong River Restaurant, 10
Siam Restaurant, 9
NIGHTLIFE
Moon Café, 6
Rodeo Saloon and Restaurant, 1
Thai Massage, 7
0 1 mile
0 1 kilometer
Chao Phraya River
Lopburi River
Pa Sak River
Phu Khao Thong Temple (Golden Mount Chedi)
Phu Khao Thong-Paniat Rd.
Ayutthaya-Pa Mok Rd.
Khlong-Tho Rd.
Si Sanphet Rd.
U Thong Rd.
Chikun Rd.
Naresuan Rd.
Horattanachai Rd.
Bang Lan Rd.
Pa Thon Rd.
Rotchana Rd.
Mapharao Rd.
Khlong Makhem Rieng Rd.
Ayutthaya Historical Park
Phra Si Sanphet (Old Palace)
Wang Luang (Ancient Palace)
Chao Sam Phraya National Museum
Ayutthaya Historical Study Center
Chantharkasem Palace National Museum
Beung Phra Ram
Chao Phrom Market
Hua Ro Night Market
Food Stalls
Pier
Elephant Kraal Pavilion
Pridi Damrong Bridge
Train Station
Phet Fortress
St. Joseph's Cathedral
TO BANGKOK
TO THE NORTH
TO MAINLAND BUS TERMINAL (5km) & BANGKOK (77km)
3058
3059
309

THAILAND

Phraya to ascend to the throne. To commemorate (or perhaps celebrate) his brothers' deaths, the king ordered the construction of Wat Ratchaburana over the site of their cremations. This wat is known for its wealth of gold artifacts and the mural paintings in its crypt. *(North of Wat Mahathat. 30฿.)*

WAT YAI CHAIYAMONGKHON. This fabulous wat was founded in 1357 by U Thong. The giant *chedi* was built by King Naresuan the Great to commemorate the 1592 victory over the Burmese. The wat's name, Chaiyamongkhon ("Auspicious Victory"), refers to this event. *(Southeast of the island on the mainland. At least 20min. by bicycle ride from the island or a 40฿ tuk-tuk ride. 20฿.)*

WAT PHANANCHOENG. The massive brick-and-mortar Buddha dates back to 1324, 26 years before Ayutthaya was founded. Legend has it that tears formed in its eyes when the city was sacked by the Burmese in 1767. *(West of Yai Chaiyamongkhon, about 2km farther down the road. Open daily 8am-4:30pm. 20฿.)*

AYUTTHAYA HISTORICAL STUDY CENTER. The modern building houses a US$8 million research institute funded by the Japanese government, featuring displays on the ancient city's political, economic, and social life. Touring the small upstairs exhibit shouldn't take more than 45min. *(On Rotchana Rd., 2 blocks east of the Chao Sam Phraya National Museum. Open M-F 9am-4:30pm, Sa-Su 9am-5pm. 100฿, with student ID 50฿.)*

CHAO SAM PHRAYA NATIONAL MUSEUM. With wood-and-glass display cases, dusty artifacts, and missing labels, this old-school museum has little to offer except some splendid jewels from Wat Ratchaburana. *(On Rotchana Rd., near the intersection with Si Sanphet Rd. A 5min. walk from the Tourist Information Center. Open W-Su. 30฿.)*

OTHER SIGHTS. Wats Maheyong, Kudidao and smaller **Wat Ayothaya** are a short bike ride north of the train station. All three lack tourists. *(Free.)* North of the island, the king would watch his elephant army train at the **Elephant Kraal Pavilion.** Ayutthaya is also the site of one of the country's largest **Loi Krathong** festivals, which takes place in November on the day of the full moon. Thais gather around **Beung Phra Ram,** the lake in the center of the island, to see fireworks, watch *likay* (Thai folk dance), and groove to live pop music. The *loi* (floating) of *krathong* (lotus-shaped paper boats with candles and incense) takes place at the **Chantharkasem Pier** opposite the Chantharkasem Palace Museum and post office. Legend has it that two people who launch their *krathong* together are destined to become lovers.

ENTERTAINMENT AND NIGHTLIFE

From 7:30 to 9:30pm nightly, **Wat Phra Si Sanphet, Wat Mahatat, Wat Ratchaburana, Wat Phraram** (diagonally across from Wihan Phra Mongkhon Brophit), and **Wat Chiawatthanaram** (southwest of the island) are illuminated by floodlights. For more mainstream evening activity, head to the **Moon Cafe,** off Naresuan Rd., opposite Ayutthaya Guest House, which has 400 jazz, blues, and classic rock CDs. (Large Singha 100฿.) Coming from the Cham Phrom Market, **Rodeo Saloon and Restaurant,** 79/81 U Thong Rd., is on the left side of the street 200m before the GPO; look for the Jack Daniels sign. Rodeo offers a Thai take on the Old American West. (Large Heineken 95฿. Open daily 6pm-1am.) Treat yourself to a "good taste" massage at **Thai Massage,** at the Chao Phrom Market bus station. (☎244 582. 2hr. of traditional Thai bodywork 240฿. Open daily 10am-midnight.)

KANCHANABURI ☎034

The Japanese invasion during WWII immortalized the otherwise less-than-noteworthy town of Kanchanaburi and its humble River Kwai. Backpackers now use the city—once of strategic importance linking the overland route between Singapore and Rangoon—as a base for exploring the surrounding waterfalls, caves, and jungles. They return in the evenings to swap travel stories at their lively backstreet guest houses, the idyllic riverside lodgings that they share with Thai tourists from Bangkok who are glad to escape to the fresh air.

TRANSPORTATION

Trains: Kanchanaburi Train Station (☎511 285), on Saeng Chuto Rd. To **Namtok** via the **River Kwai Bridge** (2½hr.; 6:10, 10:50am, 4:30pm; 17฿) and **Bangkok** (3hr.; 7:25am, 2:50pm; 25฿). Call ☎561 052 for info on weekend trains to **Bangkok** and other destinations (2hr., Sa-Su 5pm, 28฿). Trains are convenient only for those wanting to ride across the River Kwai Bridge; head to the bus station for other destinations.

Buses: The **Kanchanaburi Bus Station** (☎511 182) is in Ban Noue Village. To: **Bangkok** (#81; 3½hr., every 15min. 4am-6:30pm, 48฿; 2nd-class with A/C, 2hr., every 20min. 3:50am-6:50pm, 62฿; 1st-class with A/C, 2hr., every 15min. 4am-7pm, 79฿) via **Nakhon Pakhon** (1½hr., 28-48฿); **Erawan National Park** (#8170; 1½hr., every 50min. 8am-5:20pm, 26฿); **Ratchaburi** with connections to **Cha Am, Hua Hin,** and **Phetchaburi** (#461; 2hr., every 15min. 5:10am-6:20pm, 36฿); **Sangkhlaburi** (#8203; 5hr.; 6, 8:40, 10:20am, noon; 84฿; VIP bus #8203; 4hr.; 9:30am, 1:30, 3:30pm; 151฿); **Suphanburi** (#411; 1½-2hr., every 20min. 5am-5:45pm, 35฿) with connections to **Ayutthaya** and **Nakhon Sawan** (last connecting bus to these destinations leaves at 5pm). A/C **vans** to **Sangkhlaburi** depart from the corner of Lak Muang Rd. and Saeng Chuto Rd. (3hr.; 7:30, 11:30am, 4:30pm; 118฿).

Local Transportation: Orange **songthaew** run up and down Saeng Chuto Rd. (5-10฿). **Samlor** cost 10-20฿ from the railway station to TAT. Motorbike taxis to guest houses from bus station 30฿. A **ferry** crosses the river (5฿) at the end of Chai Chumphol Rd.

Rentals: Bicycles available from almost all guest houses for 20-50฿ per day. **Motorbikes** on Mae Nam Kwai Rd. with passport deposit. 200฿ for 24hr.; 150฿ for 9am-5pm. Cruising motorbikes 500฿ per day. Motorcross bikes are difficult to find.

ORIENTATION AND PRACTICAL INFORMATION

Kanchanaburi is 129km from Bangkok and stretches roughly 4km from northwest to southeast along the banks of the **Kwai River,** which flows parallel to **Saeng Chuto Rd.,** the city's main drag. North of town is the famous **Kwai River Bridge;** 2km south is the **train station** and the river-side **guest house area,** where *farang* congregate. Two kilometers farther south is **Ban Noue Village,** the city's main commercial area and home to the **bus station.** West of the bus station are the **city gate, day markets,** and **river wharf area.** Because Kanchanaburi is quite spread out, consider renting a bicycle to avoid the long, dusty walks between one part of town and the other.

Tourist Office: TAT (☎/fax 511 200), on Saeng Chuto Rd., a 5min. walk south of the bus station. Friendly English-speaking staff deal out glossy leaflets. Excellent regional map (20฿ donation). Bus/train schedules. Lenso phone. Open daily 8:30am-4:30pm.

Immigration Office: ☎513 325. On Mae Nam Maeklong Rd., 4km from TAT. Follow Saeng Chuto Rd. south away from Ban Noue Village and turn right at City Hall, 1km past the GPO. 1-month visa extension 500฿, 1-day processing. Bring 1 photo and 2 copies of passport including visa and departure card. Open M-F 8:30am-noon and 1-4:30pm.

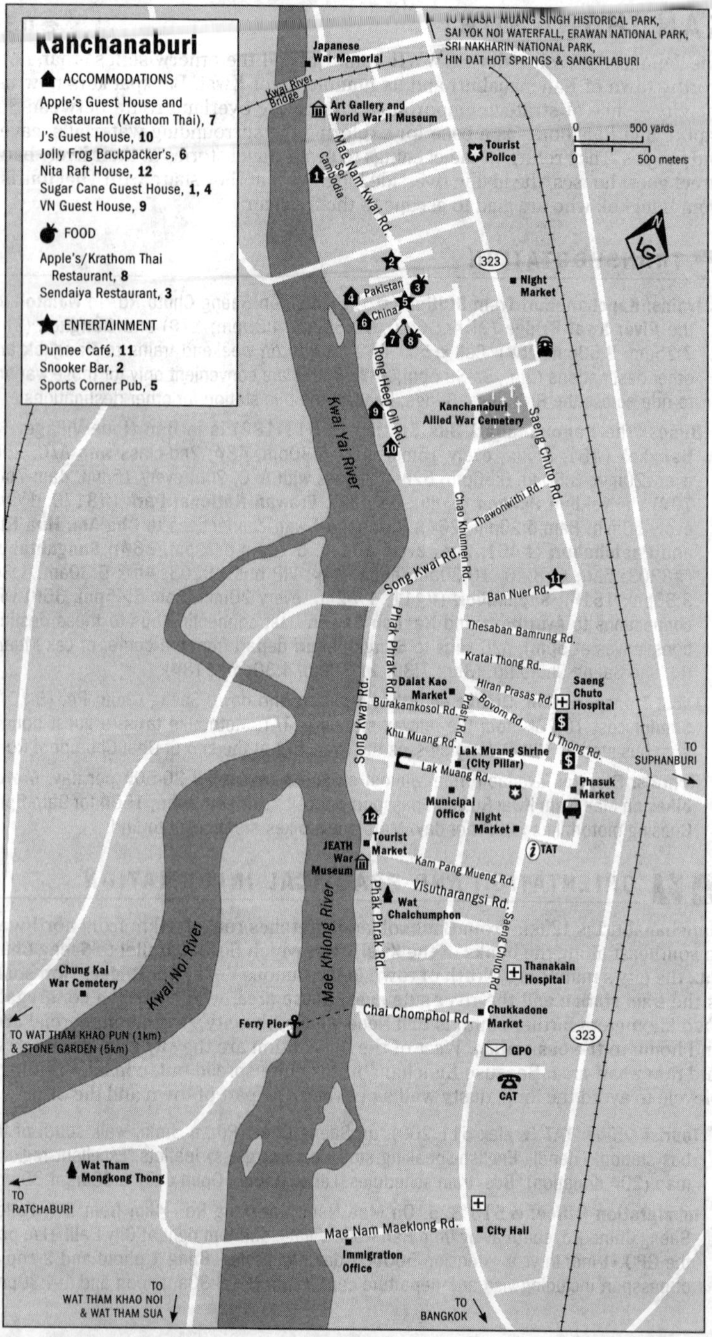
Kanchanaburi
ACCOMMODATIONS
Apple's Guest House and Restaurant (Krathom Thai), 7
J's Guest House, 10
Jolly Frog Backpacker's, 6
Nita Raft House, 12
Sugar Cane Guest House, 1, 4
VN Guest House, 9
FOOD
Apple's/Krathom Thai Restaurant, 8
Sendaiya Restaurant, 3
ENTERTAINMENT
Punnee Café, 11
Snooker Bar, 2
Sports Corner Pub, 5
TO PRASAT MUANG SINGH HISTORICAL PARK, SAI YOK NOI WATERFALL, ERAWAN NATIONAL PARK, SRI NAKHARIN NATIONAL PARK, HIN DAT HOT SPRINGS & SANGKHLABURI
Japanese War Memorial
Kwai River Bridge
Art Gallery and World War II Museum
0
500 yards
0
500 meters
Tourist Police
Mae Nam Kwai Rd.
Soi Cambodia
323
Night Market
Pakistan
China
Rong Heep Oil Rd.
Kanchanaburi Allied War Cemetery
Saeng Chuto Rd.
Kwai Yai River
Chao Khunnen Rd.
Thawonwithi Rd.
Song Kwai Rd.
Ban Nuer Rd.
Phak Phrak Rd.
Thesaban Bamrung Rd.
Kratai Thong Rd.
Hiran Prasas Rd.
Saeng Chuto Hospital
Dalat Kao Market
Burakamkosol Rd.
Prasit Rd.
Bovorn Rd.
Song Kwai Rd.
Khu Muang Rd.
U Thong Rd.
TO SUPHANBURI
Lak Muang Shrine (City Pillar)
Lak Muang Rd.
Phasuk Market
Municipal Office
Night Market
JEATH War Museum
Tourist Market
TAT
Kam Pang Mueng Rd.
Visutharangsi Rd.
Wat Chaichumphon
Saeng Chuto Rd.
Phak Phrak Rd.
Mae Khlong River
Kwai Noi River
Chung Kai War Cemetery
Thanakain Hospital
Chai Chomphol Rd.
Chukkadone Market
Ferry Pier
TO WAT THAM KHAO PUN (1km) & STONE GARDEN (5km)
323
GPO
CAT
Wat Tham Mongkong Thong
TO RATCHABURI
Mae Nam Maeklong Rd.
City Hall
Immigration Office
TO WAT THAM KHAO NOI & WAT THAM SUA
TO BANGKOK

Currency Exchange: Banks are common on the roads fanning out from the Kanchanaburi Bus Station. Several have **24hr. ATMs.** The **Punnee Cafe** can exchange money after hours (see **Alternatives to Tourism,** below).

Alternatives to Tourism: Talk to Danny at the **Punnee Cafe,** 2/15 Ban Nuer Rd. (☎513 503), just off Saeng Chuto Rd., about the possibility of working at the local private Catholic school teaching English. 1-month, 3-month, and 1-year commitments. Teachers receive room and board plus stipend. You can also contact the school directly (☎09 889 0050, ask for Orawan). The cafe doubles as an **English-language used bookstore.**

Markets: The **Dalat Kao Market,** bounded by Chao Khunnen and Burakamkosol Rd., offers fresh produce and meat. **Phasuk Market,** across from the bus station near Lak Muang Rd. in Ban Noue Village, sells clothing and accessories. Both open daily dawn-dusk. Closest **night market** to guest houses is the haphazard roadside affair just north of the train station on Saeng Chuto Rd. 10min. walk. Open daily 5-10pm.

Emergency: ☎191. **Tourist Police (Bangkok):** ☎1155.

Tourist Police (local): ☎512 795. 1.5km north of train station on Saeng Chuto Rd. on the right. English spoken. **Open 24hr.** Also 3 helpful **booths** at the foot of the Kwai River Bridge, on Song Kwai Rd. at Burakamkosol Rd., and on Mae Nam Kwai Rd. 50m past Apple's Guest House toward cemetery. Booths open daily 8:30am-6pm.

Medical Services: Saeng Chuto Hospital (☎621 129), 500m north of TAT on Saeng Chuto Rd. English spoken. **Open 24hr.** MC/V.

Telephones: Kanchanaburi Telecommunications Office, on Saeng Chuto Rd., Soi 38. Turn left at the post office; the office is 200m on the right. International calls, phone cards, and CATNET **Internet** access. 1st min. 3฿, each subsequent min. 0.50฿. 24hr. HCD phone. Open daily 8:30am-10pm.

Internet: Available all over the city, especially on Saeng Chuto Rd. south of the bus station (10฿ per hr.).

Post Office: GPO (☎511 131), on Saeng Chuto Rd., 1km south of TAT on the left. *Poste Restante.* Open M-F 8:30am-4:30pm, Sa-Su 9am-noon. **Postal code:** 71000.

ACCOMMODATIONS

Most of Kanchanaburi's best budget accommodations sit along (or in) the River Kwai in the northern part of the city, a 10min. walk from the train station or a 25min. walk from the bus station. Guest houses on Rong Heep Oil Rd. are quieter, while the ones on Mae Nam Kwai Rd. are always flooded with *farang.* All establishments listed serve Thai and Western food and help arrange tours.

VN Guest House, 44 Rong Heep Oil Rd. (☎514 082). The friendly staff welcomes a crew of easygoing backpackers who congregate on the hotel's riverside veranda late into the night. The cheaper rooms take prime position on the pontoon or next to the river. Singles 50-60฿, with bath 100฿; doubles 150฿, with A/C 250-300฿. ❶

Jolly Frog Backpacker's, 28 Soi China, Mae Nam Kwai Rd. (☎514 579). Clean, pretty rooms overlook the river. Large and extremely popular, but if you've had enough of toe rings, tank tops, and tie-dye, keep moving. Nightly guest-picked movies. Singles 70฿; doubles 150฿, on raft portion 150฿, with bath 200฿, with A/C 290฿. ❶

J's Guest House, 32/4 Rong Heep Oil Rd. (☎620 307). For those traveling on the cheap. Rooms made of flimsy plywood are set over a still inlet from the river and come with mosquito net and hammock. The same family owns the more expensive **River Guest House** next door. Singles 50฿, with bath 100฿; doubles 80฿/120฿. ❶

Nita Raft House, 27/1 Pakpraek (☎514 521). A 10min. walk from the bus station (100m north of the JEATH museum). Proximity to Song Kwai Rd.'s tourist din means floating discos rock outside until 10pm. Clean but simple rooms set on rambling connection of rafts. Singles 80฿; doubles 120฿, with Western toilet and shower 180฿. ❶

Sugar Cane Guest House in 2 locations. **22 Soi Pakistan** ❷ (☎624 520), off Mae Nam Kwai Rd., marked turn-off one block north from turn-off to Jolly Frog Backpacker's. Solid bungalows with bath around riverfront garden 150-250฿; upmarket raft house with A/C and hot shower 550฿. **7 Soi Cambodia** ❸ (☎514 988), off Mae Nam Kwai Rd., 1km farther north toward the bridge, has more room in a quieter setting. Laundry 20฿ per kg. Similarly styled bamboo bungalows 200฿; huge concrete bungalow with TV 400฿.

Apple's Guest House and Restaurant (Krathom Thai), 52 Rong Heep Oil Rd. (☎512 017), at the juncture with Mae Nam Kwai Rd. The 15 rooms, clean and popular, surround a peaceful courtyard but lack the appealing river setting. Hospitable co-owner Apple leads an excellent full-day cooking course (750฿). Free pickup from the bus and train station. Singles 200฿; doubles 150฿. ❷

THAILAND

FOOD

From May to July, be sure to try the *khanun* (jackfruit), a Thai delicacy. The **night market** ❶, north of the train station on Saeng Chuto Rd., is the most convenient spot for a nighttime snack for those staying in guest houses. If market eating is not your style, head for **Song Kwai Rd.,** where dozens of restaurants cater almost exclusively to locals. **Apple's/Krathom Thai Restaurant** ❷ (see **Accommodations,** above), offers fabulous food (dishes 30-60฿). For a Thai-style Indian dish, try chicken massaman curry (65฿). All dishes can be substituted with tofu. 50m toward the bridge on Mae Nam Kwai Rd., opposite Woi's Travel, **Sendaiya Restaurant** ❷ creates Japanese-inspired food eaten on comfy cushioned floors. (Miso soup 20฿; *gyoza* (dim sum) 60฿; *ton katsu* (fried chicken or pork) 80฿. Open daily 5pm-midnight.)

SIGHTS

Kanchanaburi's attractions are spread over 6km. To take it all in over a couple of days, rent a bicycle or motorcycle—it's infinitely faster and easier than walking and cheaper than taking taxis.

KWAI RIVER BRIDGE (DEATH RAILWAY BRIDGE). Constructed from 1941 to 1942, the original Kwai River Bridge was the Japanese army's last attempt to complete the 415km Thai-Myanmar railway line (the "Death Railway") to be used in transporting war materials to military camps in Myanmar. Roughly 16,000 POWs and 96,000 Asians died building the bridge, which was subsequently destroyed by British air raids in 1945. The bridge you see, although impressive, is a reconstruction built as a memorial to those who lost their lives. Kanchanaburi celebrates the **Kwai River Bridge Week** during the first week of December. *(3km northwest of the train station. Orange minibus #2 runs from the Focus Optic shop 2 traffic lights from TAT (10min., 6am-7pm, 6฿). Approx. 2.5km walk north of guest houses on Mae Nam Kwai Rd.)*

ART GALLERY AND WORLD WAR II MUSEUM. Luring visitors with claims of vast World War II exhibitions, the museum is actually a bizarre collection of odd, dusty exhibits. Everything from Thai stamps to dresses of former Miss Thailands are on display. *(50m toward town from the bridge. Signs imply this is the JEATH museum; do not be confused, the JEATH museum is in town. ☎512 596. Open daily 8am-6pm. 30฿.)*

JEATH WAR MUSEUM. Established in 1977 by the chief abbot of Wat Chaichumphon to honor victims of the Death Railway Bridge, JEATH (Japan, England, America/Australia, Thailand, and Holland) sits in a bamboo hut modeled after those used to house POWs. The collection of pictures, artifacts, and drawings is modest but nevertheless intriguing. *(500m south of the town gate on Phak Phraek Rd. ☎515 203. Open daily 8:30am-4:30pm. 30฿.)*

KANCHANABURI ALLIED WAR CEMETERY. The cemetery is the final resting place of 7000 Allied POWs, mostly British and Dutch, who died working on the Death Railway Bridge. Western tour groups often seem to outnumber headstones. *(2km north of the bus station on Saeng Chuto Rd., a 5min. walk from the train station. Free.)*

CHUNG KAI WAR CEMETERY. Chung Kai holds the remains of 1700 Death Railway POWs in a setting more peaceful and pleasant than its larger counterpart in town, although the tranquility is broken by the ruckus from the party boats. *(4km across the bridge at Song Kwai Rd.'s northern end. Free.)*

WATS. Wat Chaichumphon, next to JEATH, is frequented mostly by townspeople. **Wat Tham Khao Pun,** 1km beyond Chung Kai War Cemetery, has a cave full of Buddhist shrines (5-20฿ donation suggested). Four kilometers across the river, **Wat Tham Mongkon Thong,** Cave Temple of the Golden Dragon, is renowned for its "floating nun," a young woman who can lie on water without sinking (see **Floating Nun, Golden Dragon,** p. 720). Early weekend mornings are the best time to watch. Private shows are 200฿, or 10฿ per person with a minimum of 20 people to see her 10-15min. performance, which is not that impressive if you know how to swim. The temple also features a **museum** of Kanchanaburi's history. Behind the museum, dragon-shaped steps lead up the mountain and into a **limestone cave** affording views of the surrounding mountains. Motorcycle taxis make the trip for 30฿.

OTHER SIGHTS. Lak Muang Rd. is home to the **town gate** and the **city pillar shrine.** Drivers honk at the pillar to show respect to the spirit inside.

THAILAND

ENTERTAINMENT

Most *farang* stick to bars and restaurants in the area around the guest houses. The small but popular **Sports Corner Pub** at the corner of China Rd. and Mae Nam Kwai Rd., entertains Commonwealth folk with nightly showings of football, rugby, and cricket. (Open daily 9am-late.) Farther north on Mae Nam Kwai Rd. toward the bridge, **Snooker Bar** shows three recent movies per night starting at 6pm. (Large Singha 55฿. Open daily 9am-2am.) For floating dives, check out the tacky and mobile **floating discos** that cruise down the river toward the bridge from the western side of Song Kwai Rd. You'll probably have to talk your way aboard, as they're mainly for Thai tour groups. A *farang*-friendly option that's both terrestrial and away from guest houses is the **Punnee Cafe,** 2/15 Ban Nuer Rd., just off Saeng Chuto Rd. This English establishment features a used bookstore and full bar, along with the requisite fish and chips for 150฿. (☎513 503. Open daily 8am-midnight.)

DAYTRIPS FROM KANCHANABURI

Kanchanaburi makes an ideal base for exploring the dozens of waterfalls, caves, and parks that stretch all the way to Sangkhlaburi and the Thai-Myanmar border. Routes 3199 and 323 bisect the province at the northern end of Kanchanaburi and make good points of reference. Independent travelers can take public transportation but may be limited to visiting only one or two attractions per day. Most guest houses guide or arrange tours for 150-1000฿, with a minimum of 3-5 people.

ALONG ROUTE 3199

ERAWAN NATIONAL PARK. The foremost tourist destination near Kanchanaburi, **Erawan Waterfall,** features easily accessible seven-tiered cascades. The first three levels are a 5-10min. walk from the trailhead. The challenging 2.2km trail to the top (45min.-1hr.) leads past enticing clear-water swimming holes, rewarding the intrepid with more seclusion. Maps, photos, and a slide show are at the **Visitors**

FLOATING NUN, GOLDEN DRAGON For over 25 years, Wat Thum Mongkong Thong, Cave Temple of the Golden Dragon, was famous for its **"floating nun"**—a young woman who could lie on water without sinking. She was so famous that when she passed away in 1997, another woman (not actually a nun, but apparently pure enough) stepped in to fill her floating duties. The 15min. performance takes place in a miniature version of a Greek amphitheater surrounding a green pool of water. The "nun," dressed in white, but without the requisite short hair, then floats in various meditation positions.

Center, next to where the bus from Kanchanaburi stops. **Accommodations ❶** range from camping (30฿ per person; 100฿ to rent a tent) to dorms (mattresses 10฿; dorm 30฿) and bungalows (4 beds and bath 250฿ per person or 800฿ per bungalow). The **National Park Headquarters,** opposite the **Visitors Center,** handles accommodation and emergencies. *(Take public bus #8170 (1½hr.; every 50min. 8am-5:20pm, last bus back at 4pm; 26฿). Open daily 8am-4:30pm. 200฿; motorcycle 20฿; cars 30฿.)*

SRI NAKHARIN NATIONAL PARK. Sri Nakharin has more animals and fewer tourists than Erawan, but getting there demands considerable time, money, and effort. About 105km from Kanchanaburi, **Huay Mae Khamin Waterfalls'** nine tiers are best reached from **Erawan.** Only motorcross bikes and 4WD vehicles can traverse the 42km dirt road parallel to the reservoir that leads from Erawan (about 1½hr.). A romantic alternative is to charter a boat (1-2hr., up to 10 people, 1000-1500฿) from **Tha (Pier) Kraden,** 13km northeast of the Sri Nakharin Dam, 5km past Mongatet Village. The pier is accessible over dirt road from Ban Kradan, but boat options may be limited. Continue the rough journey to Sisawat if this is the case. The National Park at Huay Mae Khamin has **accommodation ❶** options from camping (30฿ per person) to bungalows with fully serviced grounds and restaurant. *(Park open daily 8am-4:30pm. 200฿ per person, children 100฿, motorbike 20฿, car 30฿.)*

ALONG ROUTE 323

HELLFIRE PASS. In their quest to complete the notorious Thai-Myanmar railway, the Japanese Imperial Army did not let a mere mountain stand in their way. Thousands of Allied POWs and oppressed Asian laborers worked for months, manually chipping away rock under grueling conditions to create the **Hellfire Pass,** so named for the ghostly campfire shadows that would dance on the mountain walls at night. Today, the pass is a trail leading down the former railway on a stunning 3km circuit around the area. The new adjoining **Hellfire Pass Memorial Museum** showcases pictures, articles, and personal stories from POWs. *(Between Sai Yok Noi and Sai Yok Yai. Take bus #8203 from Kanchanaburi and tell the attendant where you want to get off (1½hr.; every 30min. 6am-6:30pm, last bus returns at about 4:45pm; 38฿). Open daily 9am-4pm. Suggested donation 30-100฿.)*

PRASAT MUANG SINGH HISTORICAL PARK. This "City of Lions" rests along the Kwai Noi River and contains 2000-year-old artifacts and skeletal remains. Prasat Muang Singh (Tower of the City of Lions) is believed to have constituted the westernmost outpost of the Khmer empire. The Visitors Center, to the right of the main ruins, has a large park map. *(Trains (1¼hr.; leave Kanchanaburi 6:10, 10:50am, 4:35pm; return 6:20am, 1:50, 4:30pm; 10฿) come closer to the park than buses. Get off at Thakilen; from train station, walk 1km to the main road then 1km to the right. Bus #8203 stops 7km from the park; transportation for the final leg may be hard to find. Return buses are best caught before 4pm. ☎591 122. Open daily 8:30am-4:30pm. 40฿, motorcycle 20฿, car 30฿.)*

WAT LUANGTA-MAHABUA FOUNDATION. This foundation runs a tiger conservation project and wild animal rescue park. The best time to visit is in the late afternoon, when the tigers are brought out to be fed. Having been raised by the monks since birth, the tigers are very tame, but scars on the shoulders of the monks suggest that they sometimes misbehave. *(The turn-off to Wat Luangta-Mahabua is 5km toward Sangkhlaburi from the turn-off on Rte. 323 to Muang Sing Historical Park; a large billboard on the right marks the 1.5km dirt road leading to the wat's green gate entrance.)*

SAI YOK NOI WATERFALL. Although the "little" (*noi*) Sai Yok Falls are fairly large, they offer little scenery or hiking trails. Tours stop here for photographs, and that's about enough. *(60km from Kanchanaburi. Bus #8203 to Sai Yok Noi runs every 30min. 6am-6:30pm, last return 5pm; the hour-long ride costs 25฿. The waterfall is free.)*

WANG BADANG CAVE. This is for spelunkers only, not casual tourists. There are no guided tours, so those who choose to come should bring their own flashlight or rent one from the Visitors Center (20฿) for the 1½hr. round-trip. *(Turn from Rte. 323, 100m south of Sai Yok Noi, then continue 2.5km on the dirt road. Free.)*

LAWA CAVE. The electrically lit 200m cavern is the region's largest. Unfortunately, the user-friendly features don't extend to getting there. Hire a longtail boat (45min. one-way, up to 10 people 800฿) from Pak Saeng Pier, 2km southwest of Sai Yok Noi, or complete the 30min. trip on motorbike. After crossing the bridge next to Pak Saeng Pier, turn right just past the Km3 marker and follow the road to the caves. *(Open daily 6am-6pm. National Park entrance fee 200฿, children 100฿.)*

SAI YOK YAI WATERFALL AND NATIONAL PARK. Celebrated in poetry and song, the Sai Yok Yai Waterfall dribbles unimpressively, except between July and September, when it gushes unimpressively. Maps and luggage storage are available at the Visitors Center. Accommodations include **camping ❶** (30฿) and **rooms ❹** over the river (500-1000฿). *(45min. by bus from Sai Yok Noi; take any bus or* songthaew *heading north (15฿). Bus #8203 goes from Kanchanaburi every 30min. 6am-6:30pm, last return bus 4:30pm; 2hr. trip, 38฿. You'll still need to walk 3km or take a motorcycle lift (10-15฿) to the Visitors Center. Open daily 6am-6pm. 200฿, children 100฿, motorcycle 20฿, car 30฿.)*

BORDER CROSSING: THREE PAGODA PASS Anticlimactic for those with visions of border intrigue, the Three Pagoda Pass to **Phayathonzu, Myanmar,** is sporadically open to foreigners with a few caveats: prior authorization from Sangkhlaburi's immigration office is required; US$10 (450฿) gets you 2km into Myanmar, but only from 6am to 6pm; and the Burmese military requires 1 passport picture. Recent tensions between Thailand and Myanmar have resulted in frequent closures of the border crossing. Check with the Thai embassy for the most current information. *Songthaew* leaving Sangkhlaburi's bus station make the trip (30 min., every 40min. 6am-6pm, 30-35฿).

SANGKHLABURI ☎034

Unlike its neighbor Kanchanaburi, Sangkhlaburi relies mostly on its natural beauty. The few man-made attractions in town pale in comparison to the fresh air, rugged mountains, and dense jungle that envelop it. Travelers can enjoy relaxing views of Khao Laem Lake, take jungle-treks, and mingle with the Karen and Mon migrants who now call this town home. While the tiny city center offers little to visitors, its setting makes it a desirable destination.

FROM THE ROAD

WEAVING WONDERS

Wandering through the streets of Sangkhlaburi, you're bound to stumble upon a beautiful store showcasing fine handcrafted hill-tribe weavings. The store "Women for Weaving," run by the indomitable and affectionate Daisy Dwe with the help of her daughter provides the desperately poor Karen and Mon refugees with a valuable outlet for their skills.

"It didn't work for the first two years, but now we have eight weavers and eight setters," Daisy says with triumph in her voice. Her path to Sangkhlaburi is filled with tragedy and courage, perseverance and hope, but it has inextricably tied her to the plight of her fellow refugees.

"My father was an exiled Karen democratic leader. Frightened for our lives we followed him to Thailand...We were planning to apply for a visa to Australia."

However, just then, her husband came down with malaria. She and her husband had established a health care service for similarly displaced people and he most likely got sick from one of his patients. Though he was not officially recognized by the Thai government, he was so valuable to his community, as one of the few doctors, that the Thai government airlifted him to Kanchanaburi for the best medical attention. Unfortunately, he still died.

Without a husband, Daisy felt Australia would not give her a visa. "There was no way [of going]. Australia only needs doctors, not women...he was looking after so many poor people and he left me with four children."

(continued on next page)

TRANSPORTATION AND PRACTICAL INFORMATION. Public transportation from Sangkhlaburi only runs to **Kanchanaburi** (Bus #8203: 5hr; 6:45, 8:15, 10:15am, 1:15pm; 84฿; with A/C: 3½hr.; 8:45, 10:45am, 2:30pm; 150฿; A/C van: 3hr.; 6:30, 7:30, 9:30, 11:30am, 3:30pm; 118฿) and to the **Three Pagoda Pass** by **songthaew** (30min., every 40min. 6am-6pm, 30-35฿). A/C buses and minibuses from Kanchanaburi drop passengers at the market in the middle of town. Regular buses and *songthaew* arrive at the end of the street at the **bus station.** The **city center** is laid out in simple grid fashion, bordered at each end by the two turn-offs from the highway to Kanchanaburi. To get to the **wooden bridge** from the bus station, walk past the post office, and turn right at the first paved intersection.

Siam Commercial Bank, opposite the marketplace, exchanges currency but has **no ATM.** (☎595 263. Open M-F 8:30am-3:30pm.) In case of emergency, contact the **police** (☎595 300) or the **hospital** (☎595 058). To get to either, with your back to the bus station, turn left at the post office; follow the road to its end, passing the immigration office ¾ of the way down, turn right and then take the first left. The police is 50m on your right opposite the hospital. (Limited English. Both **open 24hr.**) The **immigration office** handles visa extensions and the permit to cross the Three Pagoda Pass to Myanmar. (☎595 335. 2 passport-sized photos, photocopies of the front page of your passport and Thai visa, and US$10 are required for permit. Myanmar time is 30min. behind Thailand's. Open daily 8:30am-6pm.) **Internet access** is available opposite and left of the market on the road directly across from the motorcycle taxis. (30฿ per hr. Open daily 4-10pm.) The **post office,** 25m right of the regular bus stop, has an **international telephone booth** and CAT-NET **Internet** access. (☎595 115. Open M-F 8:30am-4:30pm, Sa 9am-noon.) **Postal code:** 71240.

ACCOMMODATIONS AND FOOD. The **Burmese Inn ❶**, 52/3 Tambon Nong Loo, is 1km to the right from the bus station. Armin, Meo, and their young daughter Alissa make the clean but simple guest house feel like home. The open-air veranda offers stunning views of the bridge. Amateur astronomer Armin is a veritable walking tourist office and can arrange tailored two- and three-day jungle treks (1300-1750฿). Meo, a cooking enthusiast, runs a staggered two-day seven-dish cooking course for 500฿. (☎/fax 595 146. Motorbike rentals 200฿ per day. Singles with fan and mosquito net 80฿, with bath 120฿; doubles with fan, net, and bath 180฿; bungalow with bath 250฿; family bungalow with satellite TV 500฿.)

P. Guest House ❸, 81/2 Tumbon Nong Loo, 300m beyond the turn-off to the Burmese Inn, is a fusion of a wooden ranch and a Swiss chalet. The large rooms are immaculate, and the shared baths boast some of the cleanest squat toilets in Thailand. (☎595 061. Canoe 25฿ per hr. Motorcycle 200฿ per day. Bicycle 100฿ per day. Singles and doubles 200฿.)

Around the market, several **open-air restaurants ❶** line up unidentifiable but tasty curries in pots during the day (20฿ per plate). Otherwise, dining is primarily limited to guest houses. The **restaurant ❷** at P. Guest House can cater for large groups and has exquisite food, such as *paneng* curry (red curry with a hint of coconut milk and lime leaves; 55฿). **Burmese Inn ❷** offers a more relaxed atmosphere.

SIGHTS. Most attractions in Sangkhlaburi are a ways from the town center. Arrange **trekking trips** through P. Guest House or the Burmese Inn (see **Accommodations,** above). You can also arrange trekking trips in Kanchanaburi where more options exist. Inquire at the Kanchanaburi TAT. Those looking to take it easy might consider a **boat trip** on **Lake Khao Laem,** which features a partially submerged wat from pre-dam Sangkhlaburi. Open only to pedestrian traffic, the **longest wooden bridge in Thailand** (400m) crosses the lake and connects Sangkhlaburi to a **Mon village.** To get to **Wat Wang Wiwekaram,** walk straight uphill from the bridge to the stop sign; turn left, follow the road, and take a left at the next stop sign. The red and gold wat sits at the end of the road, opposite a **handicrafts market.**

DAYTRIPS FROM SANGKHLABURI. The border crossing to **Myanmar** is marked by three pagodas—hence the name **Three Pagoda Pass.** The small and sedate **market** displays numerous teak products and boasts some of the best prices for jade in Thailand. It is possible to daytrip into **Phayathonzu,** but travelers cannot go any farther. (See **immigration office,** above.) Due to poaching, the animals that inhabit **Thung Yai Sanctuary Park,** Thailand's largest conservation area, have moved deep into the forest. Many visitors make the trip to see **Karen villages.** Most areas are accessible only by 4WD vehicles, even during the dry season. *Songthaew* run from Sangkhlaburi to Three Pagoda Pass (30min., 6am to 6pm, 30-35฿). The clearly marked turn-off to Thung Yai Sanctuary Park and Takian Thong Waterfall is 18km from Sangkhlaburi along the road to Three Pagoda Pass. From here, it's a lonely 8km, so having your own transport is necessary. The turn-off to Three Pagoda Pass from the highway is 3km from Sanghklaburi toward Kanchanaburi.

(continued from previous page)

Daisy showed me a picture of her family. "If I'm not a strong woman, my children are in trouble. Never give up.Women must be the same as men."

She sent her children back to Burma to live with her sister so they could get an education while she set up a guest house at the Three Pagoda Pass. "Many, many people...Oh what fun we had!" she says. "I had a guide who dove in the pond, speared fish, and cooked it for my guests."

But when war broke out at the Three Pagoda Pass in 1989 between Karen and Mon groups, it was impossible to keep the business. "I've seen so many killed," she says, referring to women and children. "I'm trying to help all minorities since that time. It's a big job for one person."

After moving to Sangkhlaburi and being reunited with her children (who all attended university in Rangoon), Daisy used her English skills to become an interpreter. She worked with Aid workers at the refugee camps.

She then set up a weaving factory both to employ and benefit Burmese refugees. "So many people came to me. I am not a rich woman, but I [have saved] a little money...now I'm working for my people–I don't do this for myself...I'm looking after people through my weaving."

Open every day, **Women for Weaving** (☎595 413) is a few blocks from the Burmese Inn, on the same road. Daisy or her daughter will be delighted to answer your questions. Souvenirs start at 30฿, pencil cases 50฿, strap shoulder bags 150฿.

– Anthony Barker

PHETCHABURI ☎032

Tiny "Phetburi" is something of an oddity, but a worthwhile stop on the route from Bangkok. With no beaches to draw masses of tourists, Phetchaburi still caters predominantly to locals. Visitors enjoy a small-town atmosphere and cultural sights unspoiled by commercialism. Halfway between Bangkok and the beach getaway of Hua Hin, Phetchaburi offers a cultural welcome to Southern Thailand.

TRANSPORTATION

Trains: Phetchaburi Railway Station (☎425 211) is on the northern edge of town, a 15min. walk from the center. Head left from the station and, after 1km, take the second right on Damnernkasem Rd. To **Bangkok** (4hr., 11 per day 7:15am-10:30pm, 3rd-class 74฿) and **Hua Hin** (1hr., 13฿ plus 40-80฿ surcharge depending on the type of train) and other destinations in the south. Buses are more convenient.

Buses: A/C buses from **Bangkok** (2½hr., every 30min. 4am-8:30pm, 90฿) arrive at the intersection of Damnernkasem Rd. and Rot Fai, the road that leads to the train station. The **regular bus station,** on Phetkasem Hwy., on the eastern edge of town about 300m before the entrance to the Khao Wang cable car, has non-A/C buses to **Bangkok** (2½hr., every 20min. 5am-5pm, 70฿) and A/C buses to **Hua Hin** (1hr., frequent, 30-50฿). Finally, orange (non-A/C) buses to **Hua Hin** (1½hr., 30฿) depart frequently from Matayawong Rd., around the corner from Wat Kampaeng Laeng.

Local Transportation: Any **samlor** or **songthaew** trip within town should be 20฿, outside of town 30฿.

ORIENTATION AND PRACTICAL INFORMATION

Phetchaburi is 160km south of Bangkok. **Damnernkasem Rd.** is the city's main drag and runs parallel to the murky brown waters of the slow **Phetchaburi River.** To the north, the road curves to the left, leading to the hospital and train station. To the south, it intersects with **Ratchavidhi Rd.,** heading westward to Khao Wang Hill, and **Phongsuriya Rd.,** leading eastward to several hotels, wats, and the **Saphan Chomrut** (Chomrut Bridge) across the Phetchaburi River. Another main road is **Panichjaroen Rd.,** the first right after the bridge, with an all-purpose market.

Tourist Office: The closest tourist office is the regional **TAT office** in nearby Cha-am (☎471 005). Open daily 8:30am-4:30pm.

Currency Exchange: Siam Commercial Bank, 2 Damnernkasem Rd. (☎425 303). Halfway between the bridge and the Ratchavidhi Rd. intersection. **ATM.** Open M-F 8:30am-3:30pm.

Emergency: ☎191. **Tourist Police (Bangkok):** ☎1155.

Police: Phetchaburi Police Station (☎425 500), on Ratchavidhi Rd. close to the mountain and opposite the GPO. No English spoken.

Medical Services: Phrachomklao Hospital (☎401 125), 50m from the train station on the left. Some English spoken. No credit cards. **Open 24hr.** Farther away is the **Petcharat Hospital** (☎417 029), on Phetkasem Hwy. north of town, close to the Khao Wong cable car stop. No credit cards. **24hr.** emergency care.

Telephones: 2nd fl. of GPO. **Long-distance** and **international phone.** Fax. Open M-F 8:30am-6pm, Sa-Su 9am-5pm.

Internet Access: E-net, on Damnernkasem Rd., between Wat Mahathat and Rabieng Guest House. A/C and fast Internet connections. 30฿ per hr. Open daily 9:30am-11pm.

Post Office: GPO (☎425 146), at the corner of Ratchavidhi and Damnernkasem Rd. *Poste Restante.* Open M-F 8:30am-4:30pm, Sa-Su 9am-noon. **Postal code:** 76000.

ACCOMMODATIONS AND FOOD

Given Phetchaburi's small size and lack of tourism, there are a surprising number of high-quality budget options, most of which cluster around **Chomrut Bridge,** a few minutes from the A/C bus station or a 15-20min. walk from the railway station. **Rabieng Guest House ❷,** snuggled at the foot of the Chomrut Bridge on the west bank, diagonally across from the Chom Klao Hotel, has a young and friendly staff who keep this small guest house in tip-top shape. (☎425 707. Singles 120฿; doubles 240฿.) At 86/1 Phetchkasem Rd., a 20min. walk from the town center behind Khao Wang Hill, **Phetchkasem Hotel ❸** is a rather impersonal hotel with enormous rooms that suggest a previous life as an office building. Rooms are clean and well-maintained, and all have private bath. (☎425 581 or 410 973. Singles 350฿; doubles 450฿.) Though they show their age with peeling paint and 70s furniture, rooms at **Chom Klao Hotel ❷,** across the street and bridge from Rabieng Guest House, are large and clean. (☎425 398. Singles 120฿, with bath 160฿; doubles 200-240฿.)

There are many **food vendors ❶** on Panichjaroen Rd., the first right after crossing the bridge past Rabieng. One of Phetchaburi's specialties is a delicious egg custard (35฿), enough for two. Otherwise, the best place to eat is the **Rabieng Restaurant ❷,** at the Rabieng Guest House (see above). The extensive menu (30-70฿) offers everything under the Thai sun. From serpent heads to spicy banana blossom salads, here's the place to experiment. (Open daily 8:30am-1am.)

SIGHTS

PHRA NAKHON KHIRI HISTORICAL PARK AND NATIONAL MUSEUM. King Rama IV, tired of the heat of Central Thailand, looked south to build a new royal retreat. His search ended on the hilltops overlooking Phetchaburi, where in 1858, he built **Phra Nakhon Khiri** (or Khao Wang), an original mixture of Chinese and Western architecture, spreading across three peaks. The westernmost peak houses the **royal residence,** whose original furnishings are still on display. **Phra That Chom Phet,** a 49m tall *chedi,* sits on the middle peak. On the eastern peak is **Wat Phra Kaew,** which was constructed in the same style as Bangkok's Temple of the Emerald Buddha. The park is accessible by a cable car; your other option is the steep but short footpath from the end of Ratchavidhi Rd. In early February, the town celebrates the **Phra Nakhon Khiri Fair,** featuring local art shows and cultural performances. (*To reach the cable car, located on the opposite side of the hill town, take a* samlor *for 20฿ from the town center. Cable car runs 8:30am-5:15pm; round-trip 30฿, children 10฿. Museum open daily 9am-4pm. 40฿. Park open M-F 8:15am-5pm, Sa-Su 8:15am-5:15pm.)*

WAT KAMPHAENG LAENG. The five very impressive laterite-block structures hold Buddha images that were originally part of a 12th-century Khmer Hindu shrine. Each of the five *prangs* is thought to be dedicated to one of the five major Hindu deities. In the Ayutthaya period, the temple was reconsecrated to Buddhism, and images of Buddha now replace the Hindu sculptures within two *prangs.* Currently, the temple is the residence of **Phra Khruu Yanwitmon,** Phetchaburi's most revered monk. *(Follow Phongsuriya Rd. past Wat Yai Suwannaram and turn right on Phogarong Rd., about 500m down. The wat will be on the right after about 500m. If the front gate is locked, turn right on the road just after the wat and enter at the gate on the right.)*

THAILAND

WAT MAHATHAT WORARIHARA. With its giant white *prang* dominating the skyline, Wat Mahathat Worarihara is understandably one of the most popular religious sites in the city. Crowds are drawn by the dozens of Buddha images around the main *prang* and the striking stuccos on the *prang* pedestals. *(On Damnernkasem Rd., about a 10min. walk south of its intersection with the bridge.)*

WAT KHAO BANDAI IT. A set of steps between two elephant statues leads to several caves, which, in terms of sheer Buddha quantity, are impressive. A flashlight will help illuminate the **"Thousand Buddhas"** tucked into the crevices. *(Take the road leading west from the highway opposite the hospital past Khao Wang. The entrance is on the right side of the road at the series of 3 ornate shelters. Go through the right archway and up the short road guarded by monkeys. Motorcycle taxis from town run 40฿.)*

KHAO LUANG CAVE. This underground religious cave, about 4km north of town, is a bizarre and mildly interesting mix of Buddhist imagery, ill-tempered monkeys, and tourist gimmickry. The cave is best seen between 11am and 2pm, when sunlight illuminates the golden Buddhas and the red-tiled floor. *(The best way to get there is by taxi. Motorcycle taxis charge 40-50฿ from the town center, 100-150฿ round-trip)*

DAYTRIPS FROM PHETCHABURI

KAENG KRACHAN NATIONAL PARK. Thailand's largest national park envelops 3000 sq. km of rainforest in the western half of Phetchaburi Province. Since the park's opening in 1981, four white elephants, long considered symbols of royal prestige and good fortune, have been captured here and presented to the king. The Phetchaburi and Phanburi Rivers entice rafters, and rangers lead three-day **treks.** Inquire at the visitor station near the park entrance. To reach the park's center and the waterfalls there, get to the park by 9:30am, as the 68km road becomes one-way in the wrong direction at 10am. Car rental is 1000฿, and though *Let's Go* doesn't recommend it, hitchhiking is the preferred method of transportation among many park visitors. The alternative, spending the night at Kaeng Krachan Lake near park headquarters, gets old quickly. Four-person **bungalows ❶** are 100฿; **tents ❶** can be pitched for 10-30฿. *(To get to the park, take a dark blue* songthaew *to Tha Yong (20฿). There, switch to a Koeng Krachan* songthaew *(20฿) to park headquarters.)*

CHAO SAMRAN BEACH. Although relatively quiet, Chao Samran gets crowded on weekends, much like when the royal family basked here. *(Minibuses leave from the station on Matayawong Rd., and* songthaew *(10฿) run to the beach until 5pm.)*

HUA HIN ☎032

Long before Phuket and Pattaya were catapulted into jet-set stardom, Hua Hin ("Head Rock") catered to the Thai upper crust. King Rama VII built his summer palace here in the 1920s, and following his example, wealthy Thai families came to this long stretch of clean sand, mingling with local fishermen. Today, affluent Europeans have replaced the Thais, and towering resorts have stolen the beachfront from the fishermen. Still, seafood tantalizes the palate, the night market bustles, and the beach satisfies even the most critical beachcomber. Hua Hin may look different, but the new faces and facades only complement its aging grace.

TRANSPORTATION

Flights: Hua Hin Airport (☎522 305), on the north side of the city, is served by **Bangkok Airways.** Four flights per week (Su-M, W, F) to **Bangkok** (1hr., 7:20pm, 950฿) and **Ko Samui** (45min., 9:40am, 2080฿).

Trains: Railway Station (☎511 073), at the end of Damnernkasem Rd. A 10min. walk from the town center. Fares listed are for 3rd class on "ordinary" trains which only run a couple times per day. To: **Bangkok** (4hr., 15 per day, 54฿); **Chumphon** (4hr., 14 per day, 48฿); **Phetchaburi** (1hr., 12 per day, 34฿); **Surat Thani** (7hr., 10 per day, 73฿).

Buses: VIP bus station (☎511 654), 1st fl. of the Siripetchkasem Hotel on Srasong Rd. near Decharnuchit Rd. A/C buses to **Bangkok** (3½hr., every 40min. 3am-9pm, 120฿) via **Cha-am** (20min., 30฿). Buses heading south depart from the **regular bus station** (☎511 230), a dirt path roundabout at the end of Liab Tang Rodfai Rd., about 500m north of the railway station. To: **Bangkok** (4hr., 100฿); **Chumphon** (4hr., 4 per day, 120฿); **Phuket** (12hr., 6 per day 10am-11pm, 305-486฿); **Prachuap Khiri Khan** (1½hr., every hr. 6:30am-4pm, 50฿); **Surat Thani** (8hr.; 10am, 210฿; 11pm, 340฿).

Local Transportation: Motorcycle taxis and **samlor** go round-trip to **Khao Kai Las** and **Khao Takieb** (every 15min. 6am-7pm, 7฿). Green **songthaew** leave from the motorcycle shop at Decharnuchit Rd. and Srasong Rd. (every 15min. 6am-7pm, 7฿).

THAILAND

ORIENTATION AND PRACTICAL INFORMATION

Phetkasem Hwy. and the train tracks run parallel to the beach. Perpendicular to the tracks, **Damnernkasem Rd.** leads from the train station to the beach and forms the southern boundary of the town proper. To the north and running parallel are **Decharnuchit Rd.** and **Chomsinthu Rd.** Most hotels, restaurants, and bars cluster around **Naresdamri Rd.,** which branches off Damnernkasem Rd. close to the beach. Free maps are available at the tourist office and several restaurants and bars.

Tourist Office: Tourist Information Service Center, 114 Phetkasem Hwy. (☎532 433), on the ground floor of the municipal building, at the Damnernkasem Rd. intersection. Helpful maps. The free *Hua Hin Observer,* which provides tourist information, listings, and amusing news articles. Open daily 8:30am-4:30pm.

Currency Exchange: Banks and **exchange booths** line Naresdamri Rd. by the Hilton Hotel. **Siam Commercial Bank** (☎532 420), next to the post office. Open M-F 8:30am-3:30pm; window open Sa-Su 1-7pm.

Markets: The **night market,** on Donamuchit Rd. between Srasong Rd. and Phetkasem Hwy., has excellent Thai food.

Emergency: ☎191. **Tourist Police (Bangkok):** ☎1155.

Police: ☎511 027. On Damnernkasem Rd., 400m from the beach opposite the post office. No English spoken; go to the tourist police first. **Open 24hr.**

Medical Services: All services listed provide **24hr.** care. **San Pau Lo Hospital** (☎532 576), on Phetkasem Hwy., 400m south of the Tourist Center. Credit cards accepted. **Hua Hin Hospital** (☎520 371), 4km north of town on Phetkasem Hwy. A **Red Cross station,** next door to the municipal building, provides basic services.

Telephones: Next to the GPO. **International phone**/fax. Open daily 8am-midnight.

Internet Access: Cups & Comp, 104/1 Naeb-Khehars Rd., near corner with Decharnuchit Rd. A great ethno-cybercafe with A/C. 1฿ per min. (minimum 20฿). Open daily 9:30am-midnight.

Post Office: GPO (☎511 063), opposite the police station on Damnernkasem Rd., as soon as you turn off Phetkasem Hwy. toward the beach. *Poste Restante.* Open M-F 8:30am-4:30pm, Sa-Su and holidays 9am-noon. **Postal code:** 77110.

ACCOMMODATIONS

Most budget hotels cluster around Naresdamri Rd. and on the alleys that branch off it. While prices are similar in all hotels, style varies, so shop around. Reservations are recommended during the high season.

Pattana Guest House, 52 Naresdamri Rd. (☎513 393). Look for the sign pointing down an alley off Naresdamri Rd. 10m to the left of the pier. Serenity abounds in this enchanting, traditional 200-year-old Thai home with clean rooms and teak furnishings. No A/C. Cold water. Shared bath. Singles and doubles 350-400฿, with bath 550฿. ❸

Memory Guest House, 108 Naresdamri Rd. (☎511 816), on the ocean, about 25m to the right of the pier, on Naresdamri Rd. toward the beach. Extremely tidy and tastefully decorated. TVs 50฿. Rooms with fan 150฿; doubles 200-350฿, depending on size. Rooms with A/C 500฿, with fridge 600฿. ❷

Fulay On the Sea, 110/1 Naresdamri Rd. (☎513 145; fulayhuahin@hotmail.com), across from Memory. Breaking waves, comfortable patios, friendly staff. Rooms are simple and clean. All have private baths. Great breakfast menu 30-70฿. Rooms 250-350฿, with A/C and TV 750-1500฿, depending on size of room. ❸

Willo's Guest House, 32 Selakam Rd. (☎511 708; willo850@yahoo.co.uk). Absolutely sparkling with wooden floors, Buddhist shrine, and very comfortable rooms all with bath (if you can grab one–there are only 3). Homey feel. Internet 2฿ per min. Call ahead for reservations. Rooms 300฿. ❸

FOOD

Though Western-style restaurants are moving in, seafood reigns here. Every morning, Hua Hin's fishing fleet returns to the pier with a fresh catch. The lively **night market** ❶ is the best place to sample authentic Thai seafood. (Dishes 10-50฿. Open daily 5pm-midnight.) The **Hua Hin Brewery** ❸, next to and part of the Hilton Hotel at 33 Naresdamri Rd., offers delicious grilled filets of fresh fish with baked potato for 150฿ and seafood skewers for 180฿. (Open daily 5-10pm.) For cheap, tasty Thai food, head to the **restaurant** ❷ at the corner of Decharnuchit Rd. and Poolsuk Rd. (Noodles, fried rice, and other dishes 50-100฿. Open daily 6am-9pm.)

SIGHTS AND ENTERTAINMENT

Hua Hin's major attraction is the **Hua Hin Beach,** which rolls along for kilometers in either direction from town. The fishing pier, at the base of Chomsinthu Rd., dominates one area of the beach; the prettier part of the beach begins just past the entrance to the **Sofitel Central Hotel.** Built by Prince Purachatra, the former Director General of State Railways, it also had a brief stint in cinema as Phnom Penh's leading hotel in the film *The Killing Fields*. One of Southeast Asia's grandest five-star hotels (rooms start at 6000฿), Sofitel has beautiful grounds worthy of a stroll. Tourists on a budget can come for high tea (130฿) and meander through the topiary gardens. If you head north past the Hilton Hotel and the pier, you can see **Klai Kang Won (Far From Worries) Palace.** A royal summer residence in the 1920s, the palace now houses the ailing king, and the grounds are closed to visitors. The twin hills of **Khao Takieb** (Chopstick Hill) and **Khao Krailas,** 6km south of Hua Hin on Phetkasem Hwy., are accessible by motorbike or *songthaew* (7฿). Khao Takieb features a temple, hundreds of friendly monkeys, and an excellent view of Hua Hin. Khao Kai Las has a small lighthouse and a decent view of Hua Hin. Pine tree-lined **Suan San Beach** is farther south and has unbeatable swimming. Charter a *songthaew* or tuk-tuk (150฿). Still farther south is **Khao Tao** (Turtle Hill).

For a night away from the ubiquitous go-go, head to the **Hua Hin Brewery,** next to the Hilton Hotel, for loud live music. (Open daily 10am-2am.) **Thai Boxing Garden,** on Poolsuk Rd. between Damnernkasem and Decharnuchit Rd., has amateur and professional boxing matches nearly every weekend (9pm, 250฿).

DAYTRIPS FROM HUA HIN

TANAO SRI AND PA LA-U. The region between Hua Hin and the Burmese border has spectacular natural sights. The **Tanao Sri Range** forms the border and backdrop for the **Pa La-u Forest** in Kaeng Krachan National Park (see p. 726). Try spelunking in the three **caves** on the way to Pa La-u on Rte. 3219, 30km from Hua Hin near Nongphlab Village. At the main intersection in town, make a right onto Rte. 3301 and look for signs advertising the **Daow Lap Lae** and **Kailon** caves, which are simultaneously spectacular caves and the standard Buddha brigade. Deep in the jungle, the twin waterfalls La-u Yai and La-u Noi merge to become **Pa La-u Falls,** an 11-tier cascade. While three days are required to reach the source, trekkers can explore the first few levels in a day's hike. During high season, the park rents **tents ❶** and **bungalows ❸.** A **small eatery ❶** on the left-hand side of the road (look for a "Food & Beverages" sign) sells Thai staples (fried rice 20฿). *(Take a taxi from outside Hua Hin's Chatchai Market (up to 1200฿). A more affordable but dangerous option is to rent a motorbike (200฿) in Hua Hin and travel the 63km alone. From Hua Hin, follow local Hwy. 3218 until it meets Hwy. 3219, then follow signs. The route is well paved up to the park entrance and the scenery is inspiring. Past the checkpoint, the road turns to dirt and can be treacherous. Walk the last few kilometers to the waterfall and trailhead. It's a short hike (30min.) to the first cascade and swimming hole. Overnight trekkers should contact the Sub-Forestry Office one week in advance by writing to Kaeng Krachan National Park, Pa La Hua Hin, Prachuap Khiri Khan 77110. The office is past the checkpoint at the entrance.)*

KHAO SAM ROI YOD NATIONAL PARK. Stunning limestone hills (the "Three Hundred Peaks") rise from the surrounding sea and marshland. The park is 63km south of Hua Hin off Hwy. 4. Park **bungalows ❷** accommodate up to 20; reserve in advance (☎02 579 05 29). Insect repellent is a must for any visit. *(Take a southbound bus from Hua Hin, get off at Pranburi Market, and hire a taxi or* songthaew *to park headquarters. Park open M-F 8:30am-4:30pm.)*

EAST COAST THAILAND

Shiny new refineries, power stations, and petrochemical plants slowly give way to groves of durian and mangosteen. Off the coast of Trat, undeveloped Ko Chang and the Ko Chang National Marine Park await exploration by rainforest trekkers and beach-hunters. Farther west, Ko Samet offers convenience and beauty, while charming Ko Si Chang is overlooked by tourists. Perhaps most unfairly neglected, however, is the mainland east coast. Chanthaburi and Trat teem with mountains, jungles, waterfalls, and national parks, most of them untouched by backpackers.

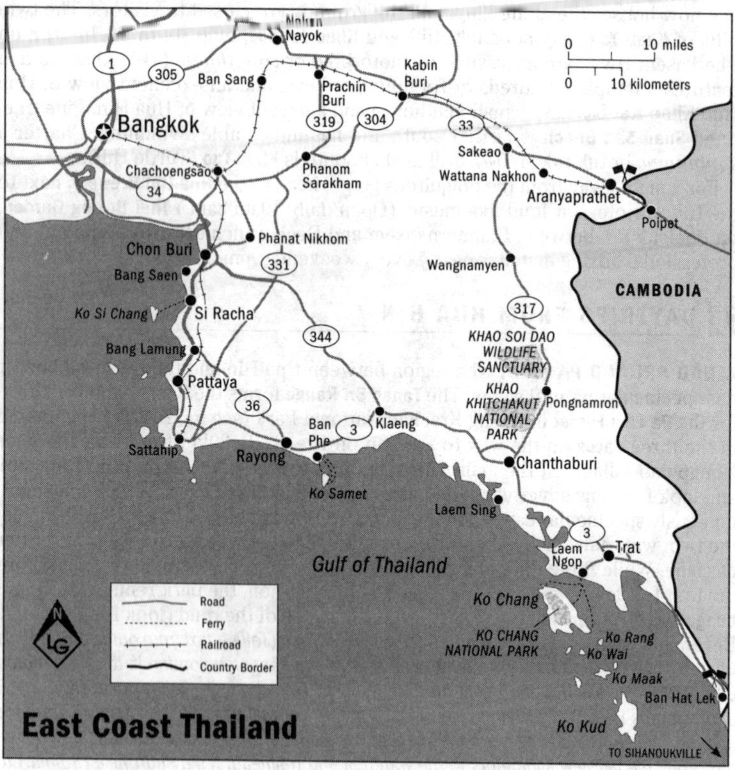

SI RACHA ☎038

Thailand may be a culinary heaven, but few towns celebrate the taste buds like Si Racha does. The maritime heritage of this fishing-village-turned-bustling-town lives on in the restaurants and foodstalls whose blinking lights beckon visitors to sample Thailand's finest and most traditional seafood. Besides its culinary appeal, the town is home to one of Thailand's best zoos. If neither seafood nor caged animals strike your fancy, make sure to arrive with enough time to catch the ferry to Ko Si Chang; there is little other reason to dawdle in Si Racha.

TRANSPORTATION AND PRACTICAL INFORMATION. All transportation operates out of the de facto **bus stop,** the **Laemthong Department Store,** a 20min. walk from the city center. **Buses** to **Bangkok** (every 20-40min. 5am-6pm; 40฿, with A/C 55฿) and **Rayong** (every 20min. 5am-10pm; 40฿/60฿) depart from **Sukhumvit Rd.,** next to the department store. To reach the **city center** and **ferry** to **Ko Si Chang,** take either a **tuk-tuk** or **motorcycle-taxi** (30฿) from the department store or walk a few blocks north on Sukhumvit Rd. and down service-laden **Surasak I Rd.**

The **Siam Commercial Bank,** on Surasak I Rd. halfway between Sukhumvit Rd. and Jermjompol Rd., exchanges traveler's checks. (Open daily 8:30am-3:30pm.) **ATMs** are available at **Bank of Ayudhya,** 50m from Jermjompol Rd., on

Si Racha Nakon Rd. 3. In an **emergency,** call ☎191. There is an infrequently staffed **police booth** at the corner of Jermjompol Rd. and Soi 10. (☎311 111. Open daily "6am-9pm.") **Phyathai General Hospital,** at 90 Si Racha Nakon Rd., is **open 24hr.** (☎770 200 or 770 208.) The second floor of the **Laemthong Department Store** has cheap **Internet access.** (25-40฿ per hr. Open M-F 11am-9pm, Sa-Su 9am-9pm.) **Internet East Co.,** 140 Si Racha Nakon Rd. 1, near Sri Racha Seafood Restaurant, has fast connections. (1฿ per min. Open daily 9am-9pm.) There is a **post office** past the park, near the road to Lo Loi at the northern end of Jermjompol Rd., a 10min. walk from the city center. (Open M-F 8:30am-4:30pm, Sa-Su 9am-noon.) **Postal code:** 20110.

ACCOMMODATIONS AND FOOD. Budget rooms hug the salty sea near the Ko Si Chang Ferry, a 20min. walk or 30฿ tuk-tuk ride from the bus stop. Literally on top of the ocean, **Siri Watana ❸** is one block north of Soi 10, opposite Si Racha Nakon Rd. Rooms are plain but clean in this 75-year-old guest house. (☎311 097. Singles 200฿; doubles 300฿.) **Samchai Hotel ❸,** at the end of Jermjompol Rd. Soi 10, near Surasak I Rd., has large rooms by the sea. (☎311 800. Rooms with fan 260฿, with A/C and TV 380฿.) The pricier **Laemthong Hotel ❺** is just through the parking lot next to the department store—you can't miss the giant neon sign on the roof of this 20-story building. Its drab apartment-style rooms are huge and well furnished. (☎322 886. Singles or doubles 900฿.)

Si Racha is famous for its **seafood**—often prepared with Si Racha sauce, a spicy red dressing appearing as ซอสศรีราชา on Thai menus. The prime location for gorging on local cuisine is on **Si Racha Nakon Rd. 3** not long after it branches off Jermjompol Rd., one block north of Soi 10. Sample fresh seafood in the **market ❶** by the clock tower at the south end of Jermjompol Rd. For a sit-down meal, head to **Khor Kav Soy ❸,** 55 Si Racha Nakon Rd. Make a right onto Si Racha Nakon Rd. from Jermjompol Rd.; head right at the fork. Enjoy succulent steamed prawns with glass noodles (180฿), with karaoke and mood lighting. (☎771 521. Most dishes 80-180฿. Open daily 4pm-1am.) Si Racha's famous fresh seafood tastes great as sushi too at **Hanamoto ❸,** 7 Si Racha Nakon Rd. Soi 8. Try the shrimp tempura for 160฿. (☎322 274. Food generally 50-180฿. Open daily 5pm-midnight.)

SIGHTS. Si Racha's main attraction is the **Si Racha Tiger Zoo,** a rather gimmicky, amusement-park-style zoo 9km east of town. Take a tuk-tuk from anywhere in the city (25min., 100฿). Take your pick from elephant, crocodile, and tiger shows or the pig-racing extravaganza. The zoo displays, on the other hand, are disappointing, featuring mostly unhappy-looking caged animals. (☎296 556. Open daily 8am-6pm. Several shows per hr. 250฿, children 150฿.) From Jermjompol Rd., **Wat Radniyomtum** is several blocks down Surasak I Rd. on the right. Near the market, Surasak Suguan leads to **Wat Mahasiracha,** on the corner of Tesaban Rd. The town's most touristed temple is **Wat Ko Loi (Floating Island Temple),** reached via a pleasant walk to the causeway at the northern end of Jermjompol Rd. The best part is just wandering around the base, where foodstalls and trinket shops create a lively atmosphere for the picnicking Thais who flock here on weekends.

KO SI CHANG ☎038

Poor Ko Si Chang is all dressed up with no place to go. A one-time tourist boom years back encouraged the residents of this 5000-person fishing village to spruce up their island with new bungalows and English signs and maps. Accordingly, Ko Si Chang remains a pretty island with good tourist services, friendly locals, and hardly a trace of commercialism. Those seeking postcard-perfect scenes should keep heading east, but for a sandy respite from Bangkok, Ko Si Chang fits the bill.

TRANSPORTATION AND PRACTICAL INFORMATION. **Ferries** depart Si Racha's main pier at the end of Jermjompol Rd., Soi 14 for **Ko Si Chang** (40min., every hr. 8am-6pm, 20฿). Boats back to **Si Racha** leave from **Ta Lang Pier** or **Ta Bon Pier** depending on the tide; ask your guest house owner to verify which you should take (every hr. 6am-6pm, 20฿). **Thai Farmers Bank,** 9-9½ Assadang Rd., between the piers, exchanges traveler's checks and has an **ATM.** (☎216 132. Open M-F 8:30am-3:30pm.) **Tiew Pai Guest House** rents **motorcycles** (170฿ for 12hr., 250฿ for 24hr.). A man named Oo rents **mountain bikes;** look for the sign at the entrance of a small soi, 75m before Tiew Pai Guest House as you come from the pier. (☎216 265. Mountain bikes 150฿.) In an **emergency,** dial ☎191, or call the **police** at ☎216 218. The **post office,** in a white building at the north end of Assadang Rd., offers **Internet access** (3฿ for first min., 1฿ for every 2min. thereafter) and has **international** and collect calls for 30฿. (☎216 227. Open M-F 8:30am-4:30pm.) **Postal code:** 20120.

ACCOMMODATIONS AND FOOD. Ko Si Chang's only budget-minded guest house is **Tiew Pai Guest House ❷**, south of Ta Lang Pier on Assadang Rd. Fortunately, it's cheap and well kept, and the owners are friendly. At night, a karaoke bar thumps to the latest Thai pop. (☎216 084. Singles with shared bath 150฿; doubles 250฿, with A/C and fridge 400฿; triples and family rooms 500-1000฿.) Pricier bungalows line the beach. The best of these is the **Sichang View Resort ❹,** opposite the Khao Khat Cliffs in the northwestern corner of the island, which offers comfortable rooms in one of the island's most beautiful settings. (☎216 210. Doubles with fan 500฿, with A/C 800฿, with hot water 900฿; add 200฿ to turn any room into a triple.) **Camping ❶** is free on the beach; bring your own supplies.

Food vendors ❶ sell noodle and rice dishes along **Assadang Rd.** Try the tasty breakfast (60฿) and entrees from typical rice dishes (25-30฿) to fish 'n' fixin's (180-200฿) at Tiew Pai Guest House's **restaurant ❸.** (Open daily 7:30am-1am.) Munch on more rice dishes (40-50฿) and fresh fish (54-220฿) at the **Sichang View Resort ❸.** Their steamed fresh grouper in black bean sauce (54฿ per 100g) is simple and satisfying. (Open daily 7am-9:30pm.)

SIGHTS. The town's main street, Assadang Rd., ends in a 163-step climb to a colorful **Chinese temple.** Four hundred steps farther up is an enshrined **Buddha footprint,** whose size makes it a good match for the **Yellow Buddha** on the island's west side. Beneath this 10m high statue are several caves accessible from the lower platform in front of the Buddha. Toward the southern end of Assadang Rd., near the two eastern beaches, are the ruins of **King Rama V's summer palace.** To get there, continue south on Assadang Rd. through the gate of the Marine Research Institute. Find **Hat Tampang,** Ko Si Chang's most swimmable beach, by taking the right branch of the road next to the gate and climbing over a steep hill. North of Hat Tampang, don't miss the **Khao Khat Cliffs,** where Rama V built a pavilion to compose poetry and enjoy the western horizon. At the bottom, a path by the Sichang View Resort leads down to the cliffs, which are best visited at sunset.

KO SAMET ☎01

Just 4hr. from Bangkok, Ko Samet is a popular vacation spot for Thais and foreigners alike. Over the last 20 years, beachside bungalows have encroached on much of the shoreline, and loud pubs and karaoke bars dominate the once still nights. Development aside, however, Ko Samet delivers, and a dip in its tranquil waters or a nap on its clean, white sand beaches will satisfy the traveler seeking good, old fashioned relaxation. Many travelers prefer Samet's low-key atmosphere to that of its rowdier and more developed island neighbors. Commercialism has not taken a strong hold on Samet's visitors or residents, so enjoy it while it lasts.

THE VIEW FROM ABOVE

The lowdown: Step 1 in your island hopping trip.
Beaches: At last count, 11.
Highlights: Snorkeling in Ao Kiu's coral reefs, hanging out at Ao Phai, camping under the stars on Ao Thian.

TRANSPORTATION

Ferries: Nuan Tip Pier and **Tarua Phe Pier** in the town of Ban Phe serve Ko Samet. Buses from Bangkok stop in front of Nuan Tip Pier, which offers service to Na Dan Pier in northern Ko Samet (40min., 20-person minimum, round-trip 100฿). To get to Nuan Tip Pier, walk through the market toward the ocean. Additional boats with a 7-passenger minimum are available during peak months to: **Ao Kiu/Ao Pakarang** (200฿); **Ao Phrao** (45min., 120฿); **Ao Wai** (50min., 200฿); **Ao Wong Duan** (45min., 120฿). If you arrive via *songthaew* from Rayong, you will be let off at Tarua Phe Pier, opposite the 7-Eleven, about 200m west of Nuan Tip Pier. Ferries here leave more regularly and go to **Ao Wong Duan** (9:30am, 1:30, 5pm; one-way 60฿) and **Na Dan Pier** (every hr. 8am-5:30pm, one-way 40฿) regardless of the number of passengers.

Buses: Ban Phe Bus Station (☎651 528), opposite Nuan Tip Pier on the mainland. Buses with A/C go to **Bangkok** (3½hr., 13 per day 4am-6:30pm, 124฿). If you're heading elsewhere, grab a *songthaew* to **Rayong** (every 15min. 6am-6pm, 20฿) and transfer to **Chanthaburi** (2½hr., every 50min. 5:50am-5:30pm, 55฿); **Khorat** (6hr.; every hr. 4:20am-9pm; 125฿, with A/C 225฿); **Nong Khai** (13hr.; 11 per day 7am-8:30pm; 241฿, with A/C 434฿); **Si Racha** (2hr., every 40min. 5:10am-6:30pm, 40฿); and other destinations. Many Ko Samet bungalows offer expensive but convenient direct service to Bangkok's **Khaosan Rd.** (around 220฿).

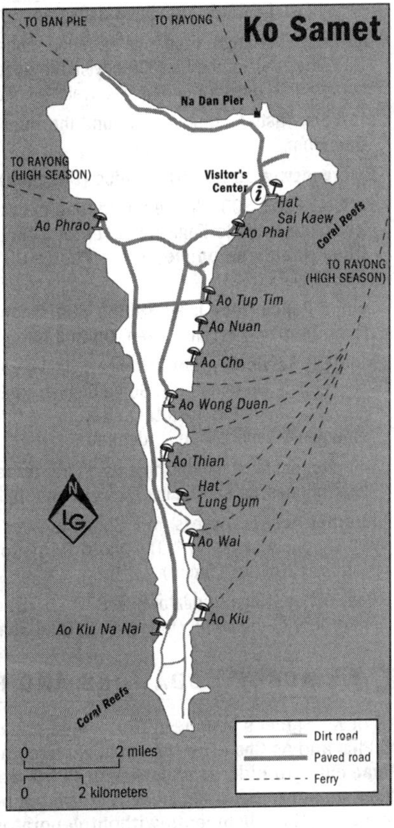

Local Transportation: Songthaew generally leave only when full. Going to more remote destinations may require you to charter the entire car–prices listed are per person, and to charter. From Na Dan Pier to: **Ao Kiu** (50฿, 400฿); **Ao Phai** (20฿, 150฿); **Ao Phrao** (30฿, 200฿); **Ao Thian** (40฿, 300฿); **Ao Tup Tim** (20฿, 150฿); **Ao Wai** (40฿, 400฿); **Ao Wong Duan** (30฿, 200฿); **Hat Sai Kaew** (10฿, 100฿). *Songthaew* returning to Na Dan Pier or offering taxi service wait at Ao Phai in front of Silver Sands Resort. The island is easily walkable once your pack is off. It's only a 500m stroll from Na Dan Pier to Hat Sai Kaew, and the walk from Ao Wong Duan to Ao Phai takes just 30min.

Rentals: Shops renting **motorbikes** cluster near Na Dan Pier and along the road to Hat Sai Kaew. 120฿ per hr., 500฿ per day with passport or 500฿ deposit.

ORIENTATION AND PRACTICAL INFORMATION

Boats disembark at **Na Dan Pier** on the island's northeastern corner. A paved road runs south to the Park Service entrance booth, where you must pay an **admission fee** to enter the island, technically a Thai national park (200฿, children under 10 100฿). Here, the path forks. Directly ahead is **Hat Sai Kaew;** the right-hand fork continues south, behind the bungalows of the eastern beaches: **Ao Cho, Ao Hin Klong, Ao Kiu, Ao Phai, Ao Nuan, Ao Thian, Ao Tup Tim, Ao Wai, Ao Wong Duan,** and **Hat Lung Dum.** To get to these beaches, bear left at the fork after Ao Phai. Head straight to go to Ko Samet's only west coast beach, **Ao Phrao.** Beach-side paths and jungle trails link all the beaches except Ao Phrao and Ao Kiu, making the island fairly walkable.

Tourist Office: Visitors Center, next to the park entrance by Hat Sai Kaew. An English-speaking man named Thawil staffs the office and can be reached **24hr.** in case of emergency (☎01 663 5055). Open daily 8am-4pm.

Currency Exchange: Exchange as much money as you think you'll need at the banks in **Ban Phe,** west of the pier. Otherwise the **post office** at Naga Bungalows offers the most comparable rates for currency, traveler's checks, or cash advances.

Markets: Tasty food stalls surround the **Nuan Tip Pier** area. 30฿ per plate. Open daily 6am-8pm.

Emergency: ☎191. **Tourist Police (Bangkok):** ☎1155.

Police: ☎651 803. On the paved road between Na Dan and Hat Sai Kaew, next to the Health Center. No English spoken. A **24hr. police box** is on the beach at Ao Wong Duan. **Mainland police** in Ban Phe (☎038 651 111). **Marine police** in Ban Phe (☎038 473 056).

Tourist Police (local): ☎038 651 669. On the mainland, a block east of the market at Nuan Tip Pier. English spoken. **Open 24hr.**

Medical Services: Health Center, halfway between Na Dan Pier and the park entry checkpoint. No telephone. Some English spoken. Open M-Sa 8:30am-4:30pm. In emergencies, phone the **hospital** in Rayong (☎038 611 104 or 038 614 708). Ko Samet's emergency services are inadequate.

Telephones: Most establishments offer **international telephone service** run through cellular phones, so service is expensive and faulty. Starts at 100฿ per min.

Internet Access: Access from Samet is like phone service–run on cellular phones and obnoxiously expensive. The **Naga Bungalows Post Office** has the cheapest rates (about 120฿ per 15min.).

Post Office: Naga Bungalows (☎353 25 75) operates a licensed makeshift **post office** next door to the hotel. Open M-F 8:10am-5pm, Sa 8:30am-1pm. **Postal code:** 21160.

ACCOMMODATIONS AND FOOD

All of Ko Samet's beaches offer some bungalow-type accommodation. In general, **Ao Phai** and **Ao Cho** offer the cheapest accommodations, while **Hat Sai Kaew** and **Ao Phrao** cater to older travelers with fatter wallets. Hat Sai Kaew, Ao Phai, and **Ao Wong Duan** are the most heavily touristed beaches; **Ao Nuan** and **Ao Kiu** the most secluded. Establishments without generators have electricity from 6pm to 6am.

Camping is available on all beaches, although your best bets are on secluded Ao Kiu, the rocks between Ao Phai and Ao Tup Tim, and the grassy knoll behind the Visitors Center near Hat Sai Kaew. The following accommodations and food options are listed by beach.

AO KIU. With glistening white sand finer than anywhere else on the island, good swimming, and the possibility for coral reef snorkeling nearby, secluded Ao Kiu is Ko Samet's best beach. A taxi from the pier will cost you a hefty 400฿, and from neighboring Ao Wai it's a 20-30min. walk along the back road. Once there, you can set up at the **Ao Kiu Coral Beach ❺,** which rules this remote roost. Bungalows are tiled, screened, and clean. Snorkeling gear rental runs 30฿ per hour. (☎01 218 6231, Ban Phe office ☎038 652 561. Rooms 600-800฿.)

AO PHRAO. Ko Samet's only western-facing beach is a white crescent of sand graced by sky-searing sunsets and the island's most luxurious accommodations. But, if you're looking for a cheap place to stay, lively backpackers, and beach frisbee, you're better off staying on the east coast. Make a right when the road forks just after the last resort. The only accommodations approximating budget, **Dome Bungalows ❺** offers clean and spacious bungalows at an almost-budget price. (☎038 651 377. Singles 1000฿, with A/C 1200฿; doubles 1200฿/1500฿.)

AO NUAN. Ascend from the main road to a small hill overlooking the rocky beach and **Nuan Bungalows ❸** below. Waves crash onto the rocks that make up a tiny beach. Woven into the single hillside behind it are clean wooden huts with mattresses on the floor and mosquito nets hanging from the ceiling—this place is like no other on the island. (Singles 250฿; doubles 400-500฿.)

HAT SAI KAEW. A 10min. walk from Na Dan Pier, Hat Sai Kaew caters mostly to European and Asian package-tour travelers and is usually packed with sarong vendors, ferries, and overweight seniors bobbing in the water. Your best bet is **Ploy Thalay Resort ❹,** halfway up the beach. The tiled rooms are tidy and come with private baths. (☎01 451 1387. Doubles 500฿, with A/C and TV 800฿.) On the southern end of the beach, the large **White Sands Resort ❹** is the only other hotel on Hat Sai Kaew approximating "budget." The dimly lit bungalows are clean but spartan. All have TV and private bath. (☎038 644 000. Rooms 500฿, with A/C 1200฿.)

THE BIG SPLURGE

RIM VIMARN RESTAURANT

Ao Phrao is Ko Samet's black-tie beach, so it's no surprise that the Rim Vimarn Restaurant in the Vimarn Resort, at the northern end of the beach, is the island's swankiest place to dine. It's impossible to miss the steep thatched roof that soars above deep-bucket wicker chairs and teak tables. Well lit and romantic, it is the local VIP vantage point for enjoying golden sunsets and palm trees turning into black silhouettes against the night sky.

Both service and food are impeccable and exquisite, complementing the surrounding natural beauty. Start with an exotic cocktail decked out with fruit slices and a fresh orchid (190฿). Follow it with succulent stir-fried prawns and cashews (220฿).

Surprisingly, the restaurant prepares Western fare as well as it does traditional Thai (and everything in between). The duckling with peaches (580฿) is deep and tangy–a good choice to mix with ocean breezes and breaking waves. As the sun finally fades out of view and the sky and sea merge into one giant mass of darkness, dessert beckons–the giant half-pineapple filled with fresh fruit and ice cream (150฿) is tops.

Although the prices are sky high, so are the views and the quality of the food, more than assuaging the aching pain of your wallet. There is another branch of the restaurant at the other end of the beach with slightly lower prices. Reservations for both can be made through the Ao Phrao Resort. *(☎01 906 5006. Open daily 7am-11pm. AmEx/MC/V.)* ❺

AO PHAI. A 5min walk from Hat Sai Kaew, Ao Phai is a backpacker haven—a more friendly and welcoming version of Bangkok's Khaosan Rd. Come here for quality, cheap lodgings with a social atmosphere and screenings of English-language flicks. Thankfully free of litter and bobbing boats, Ao Phai's waters are good for swimming, in spite of the crowds. Accommodations, while plentiful, fill up quickly. At the northern end, **Naga Bungalows ❷** is an old Ko Samet institution that still remains the most popular spot on the island. The plain bamboo bungalows sit on stilts. The **restaurant ❸** serves fresh bread, sundaes, tofu-veggie options, and more (30-250฿). Table tennis, a "Tosser's Hour" (10pm-midnight), and food available at all hours make Naga a lively nightspot. (☎01 353 2575. Huts 150฿, with fan 250฿, with A/C 700฿.) **Tok's Little Hut ❸,** south of Naga, is just as popular but slightly more upscale with wood-paneled bungalows with fans and baths. (☎038 218 1264. Bungalows 300-350฿, depending on distance from the beach.) The newer, more luxurious **Jep's ❺** features clean, bright rooms and bungalows with added luxuries like extra-large beds. Their **restaurant** is one of the best on the beach. (☎01 853 3121. Bungalows 600-800฿.) The hill-side bungalows at **Ao Phai Hut ❹** are relatively clean wooden huts. All have private baths. (☎01 353 2644. Singles 400฿; doubles 600฿, with A/C 800-1000฿.) **Sea-Breeze Bungalows ❹,** at the southern end of Ao Phai where the road branches off to Ao Phrao, has quiet bungalows with private baths and a book-exchange service (two of yours for one of theirs). (☎038 644 124. Fan bungalows 400฿; A/C rooms and bungalows 650฿.)

AO TUP TIM. This small, crescent-shaped beach is an easy 5min. walk along the coast from Ao Phai. Although it's usually less crowded than Ao Phai, it's fairly congested compared to beaches farther south. **Tubtim Resort ❹,** on the southern end of the beach, offers the best deal on accommodations. The comfortable thatch bungalows all have private baths. (☎01 218 7750. Rooms 500฿, with A/C 1200฿.)

AO CHO. Although it's far from being the most secluded or most beautiful beach on the island, Ao Cho is a quiet break from popular Ao Wong Duan next door. Budget accommodations are limited to **Wonderland Resort ❷.** (☎01 438 8409. 150฿, with bath 200฿.)

AO WONG DUAN. "Half Moon Bay" is a spacious beach filled with restaurants, bars, and tour operators. Traffic and congestion make it a noisy place to stay, and the constant roaring of jet skis and continuous ferry departures make it a less-than-ideal atmosphere for swimming or sunbathing. To get the most bang for your buck, try the red bungalows of **Samet Cabana ❹,** at the north end of the beach, which has rooms with two small beds and shared baths. (☎01 838 4853. Rooms 400฿, with bath 700฿.) **Sea Horse Bungalows ❸** has decent bungalows for a decent price. (☎01 945 9052. Bungalows with fan 200฿, with A/C and bath 500฿.)

AO THIAN AND HAT LUNG DUM. These beaches are separated by a a short stretch of rocks and are easily accessible from both Ao Wai and Ao Wong Duan. With cheap bungalows close to some of the island's best swimming and sunbathing, the Ao Thian area is a good choice for the slow-paced beach-lover. Stretching out across both beaches, **Lung Dum Hut ❸** is remote and mellow. The well-priced bungalows have private baths. Ask about their special treehouse option (200฿, long weekends 600฿). In a pinch, they may let you borrow or rent a tent. (☎01 452 9472. Singles with toilet 400฿; doubles without toilet 800฿; tent 300฿.)

AO WAI. Clear water and clean, white sand make every second of the 25min. coastal hike from Ao Wong Duan to Ao Wai worth it. You'll have to charter a taxi from the pier (400฿), but the ride itself is a real off-road journey and almost makes the high fare worth it. Targeting package tourists, **Samet Ville Resort ❺** dominates the beach with pricey rooms. The **restaurant ❹** serves Thai dishes (40-300฿). Snorkeling gear rental is 100฿ per day. (☎01 949 5394. Restaurant open daily 7:30am-9pm. Rooms with fan 900฿, with A/C 1300฿.)

SIGHTS AND ENTERTAINMENT

With coral reefs and clear waters galore, it's no wonder that Ko Samet is popular for **snorkeling.** At Ao Phrao and Ao Kiu, reef communities are a 5min. swim from shore. Ko Thalu boasts excellent **skin-diving** and a colony of fruit bats. There are now several **scuba diving** operations on the island, so it pays to shop around. **Ao Prao Divers,** based in the lobby of the Ao Prao Resort on Ao Phrao, runs a PADI-certified scuba diving school year-round. The school makes daytrips around Ko Samet and to Ko Thalu from November to May. (☎038 616 883. Two dives 2500฿; 4- to 5-day certification courses 12,000฿; specialty and more extensive dives 10-13,000฿; 3-4hr. introductory courses 2500฿. Open daily 8am-4pm.) A thirst for non-aquatic activities can be satisfied at the 14m-high **sitting Buddha** and the smaller Buddha images at his knees. A gate next to the **golden Buddha** abuts the road between Na Dan Pier and Hat Sai Kaew; follow the path to the statue.

Ko Samet remains free of Ko Phangan's drunken beachside debauchery, but it boasts a lively **nightlife** scene on Ao Phai. The bar at **Naga Bungalows,** which occasionally features a free dancing show, stays open until people go home. Nearby **Silver Sands Resort** offers a beachside bar that becomes an impromptu disco when the crowds are large enough.

THAILAND

CHANTHABURI ☎039

Chanthaburi may be the "City of the Moon," but its attraction is grounded in the fertile earth. Between May and July, the city's fruit market bulges with mouth-watering produce, and the precious stones from nearby mines are traded in the famous gem district before being distributed around the world. These, in addition to the neighboring national parks, make Chanthaburi a worthwhile visit.

TRANSPORTATION. The **bus station** on Saritidet Rd. sends buses to: **Aranyaprathet** (8hr.; 15 per day 3am-10pm; 80฿, with A/C 180฿); **Bangkok** (4hr., 27 per day, 115-148฿); **Khorat** (6hr.; every hr. 6am-10pm; 116฿, with A/C 209฿); **Mae Sot** via **Bangkok** (9am, 420฿); **Rayong** (2hr.; every 30min. 4:20am-6pm; 45฿, with A/C 55฿); **Trat** (1½hr., every hr. 6am-11:30pm, 30฿). **Taxis** go anywhere in town for 30฿.

ORIENTATION AND PRACTICAL INFORMATION. Saritidet Rd. leads downtown from the bus station and ends at **Benchamarachuthis Rd.,** by the Kasemsarn 1 Hotel. The alley to the left of the hotel leads to **Sukhaphibal Rd.,** which runs parallel to Benchamarachuthis Rd. along the river. Heading right at the Kasemsarn 1 Hotel leads to the commercial heart of town. Branching off Kasemsarn 1 to the right on **Si Rong Muan Rd.** leads to the **market.** The **gem district** is one block past Si Rong Muan Rd. on Kasemsarn 1; it is to the right down **Kwang Rd.** and left on **Si Chan Rd.** Si Chan Rd. eventually doubles back on itself.

Bangkok Bank, on Benchamarachuthis Rd. next to the post office, has a **24hr. ATM.** (☎311 495. Cirrus/MC/V. Open daily M-F 8:30am-3:30pm.) The **24hr. police booth** is at the bus station (**emergency:** ☎191; **Bangkok tourist police:** ☎1155). The **hospital** is a short 20m walk to the left of the bus station on Saritidet Rd. (English spoken. **Open 24hr.**) The **Chanthaburi Telecommunication Center** is next to the GPO on Thung Dondang Rd. near the Eastern Hotel, a 3km walk or a 30฿ taxi ride from town. (☎325 916. Open daily 7am-11pm.) **Internet access** is available all over town, especially on Tesaban 2 Rd. Another option is the 56k connection at **The Computer,** on Saritidet Rd., 40m past the bus station toward town. (☎301 140. Open daily 8am-9pm. 20฿ per hr.) The **Chantani Post Office,** more convenient than the large Chanthaburi GPO, is on Benchamarachuthis Rd. across from the Kasermsarn 1 Hotel. (☎311 013. Open M-F 8:30am-4:30pm, Sa-Su 9am-noon.) **Postal code:** 22000.

ACCOMMODATIONS AND FOOD. Accommodations of any sort are scarce in tourist-free Chanthaburi. **Kasemsarn 1 Hotel ❸,** 98 Benchamarachuthis Rd., at the intersection with Saritidet Rd., is clean and has large, comfortable rooms with desks and private baths. However, the luxury comes with traffic clamor and an impersonal atmosphere. (☎311 100. Rooms 200฿, with A/C 400฿.) The cheap and friendly **Chantra Hotel ❶,** 248 Sukhaphibal Rd., is quieter. Head down Soi Ratmaitri to the left of the Kasemsarn 1 Hotel. (☎312 310. Doubles 120฿, with bath 150฿.)

Take your grumbling stomach to Chanthaburi's immense **market ❶,** centered on the fountain one block west of Benchamarachuthis Rd. down Si Rong Muang Rd. The **seafood restaurant ❷** around the corner from the Chantra Hotel has views that are almost as impressive as the extensive menu. (Dishes generally 60฿. Open daily 10am-midnight.) **Dream Restaurant ❷,** at 22/1 Saritidet Rd, has delicious Thai salads (50-80฿). Be sure to try their specialty: milky crab spring rolls (75฿).

SIGHTS AND NIGHTLIFE. Chanthaburi's more spectacular sights are outside the city limits, but a few treasures within the town keep travelers entertained for a day or two. On weekends, shoppers head to **Si Chan Rd.,** the heart of Chanthaburi's **gem district.** Some 50-60% of the world's rubies and sapphires pass through Chanthaburi, most through this very street. The 19th-century **Cathedral of the Immaculate Conception,** across the footbridge near the southern end of Sukhaphibal Rd., was built without an architect by French soldiers, who occupied Chanthaburi from 1893 to 1905. Unfortunately, the doors to the cathedral are closed.

Chanthaburi boasts a surprisingly dynamic nightlife scene. The enormous **Diamond Pub,** on the southwestern side of town, is its epicenter. Live bands belt out Thai pop while a beautiful young crowd schmoozes and looks on. Grab a taxi from the city center for 30฿. (Soda 30฿. Singhas 80฿. Open daily 8pm to anytime between 11pm and 2:30am.)

DAYTRIPS FROM CHANTHABURI

KHAO KHITCHAKUT NATIONAL PARK. Thirty kilometers north of town on Hwy. 3249 in Khao Khitchakut National Park, the **Chanthaburi River** churns down the 13 tiers of **Nam Tok Krathing** (Krathing Falls), the park's most popular attraction. A steep, rocky trail leads up from a Buddha at the mountain's base to the highest fall. Once you've bathed in the cascades, you'll understand why 2000 Thai tourists flock to the falls every weekend. Falls #7-13 are great for swimming; butterflies swarm around #13. A small **canteen ❶** stocks basic items and prepares simple dishes. (20-25฿. Open daily 6am-6pm.) **Food stalls ❶** set up on weekends and holidays. The **Visitors Center** has information in English. **Camp ❶** on your own (free), or rent a two-person **tent** (80฿). Accommodations are limited to **bungalows ❸** (5-14 people, 200-1200฿). Call the ranger station one week in advance for weekend stays. *(Songthaew depart from the corner of Prachaniyon Rd. and Benchamarachuthis Rd., opposite Bangkok Bank, south of the post office. The songthaew (20฿) will drop you off at the 1.5km access road marked by the number 2511 and a white fleur-de-lis. The 24hr. park headquarters (☎452 074) is beyond the entrance booth. Open daily 6am-6pm. 200฿.)*

NAM TOK PHLIU NATIONAL PARK. Welcoming over 80,000 visitors a year, Nam Tok Phliu is one of Chanthaburi's best-known parks, although it's hardly the most spectacular. A trail cuts through the park linking the entrance to **Phliu Falls.** A 1km nature trail circles the falls and offers scenic views. The other falls—**Nam Tok Makok, Nam Tok Klong Nalai,** and **Nam Tok Nong**—offer more seclusion. The rest of the park's 184 sq. km of rainforest are bereft of trails. The **Park Headquarters** and **Visitors Center,** on the road leading to the Phliu Falls, has maps in English with directions to the falls as well as information on renting a **bungalow** ❺ for 800฿. *(From Chanthaburi, yellow* songthaew *(30min., 30฿) to the park leave from the north side of the market's roundabout. When leaving, take a taxi to the highway intersection (100-160฿) and wait for a passing* songthaew. *Open daily 6am-6pm. 200฿.)*

WAT KHAO SUKIM. Twenty kilometers outside Chanthaburi, Wat Khao Sukim is the pride of local Buddhists. The temple's display halls are crammed with everything from peach trees made of colored glass to furniture inlaid with mother-of-pearl; amid all these riches, wax replicas of monks sit in meditation. The roof offers panoramas of mountains, a waterfall, and fruit groves, providing a glimpse of Chanthaburi's natural beauty for those who don't have time for its parks. *(Take a taxi (400฿ round-trip), or try to catch a* songthaew *for Na Ya-am at Chanthaburi's market, get off at Sathorn, and catch a* songthaew *to the temple.* Songthaew *rarely make the trip to the temple, so a taxi may be your only hope. Open daily 6:30am-5pm.)*

TRAT ☎039

Trat is the least developed of the eastern provinces. Most of its population subsists on fishing or growing fruit. For the adventurous backpacker, oft-overlooked Trat Province teems with jungles, waterfalls, temples, and beaches. Its guest houses, markets, and plentiful transportation make it a worthy base.

TRANSPORTATION AND PRACTICAL INFORMATION. Trat is a frontier town. **A/C buses** from anywhere north or west of town stop on the east side of **Sukhumvit Rd.,** next to the cinema. Private bus companies offer A/C bus service to **Bangkok** (5hr., 157-221฿); their offices cluster around the market. **Buses** depart every 30min. 5:15am-2:30pm and once an hour until 5:30pm for **Chanthaburi** (1½hr., 22฿), where you can transfer to all other major destinations. Near the pharmacy and market, **minibuses** depart when full for **Chanthaburi** (1hr., 6am-6pm, 60฿). Blue **songthaew** heading to **Laem Ngop** (6am-6pm, 20฿) pull up one block south of the market, next to the pharmacy on Sukhumvit Rd. and leave when full. Blue **songthaew** going to **Klong Yai** (1½hr., every hr. 6am-6pm, 35฿) wait behind the market on Tat Mai Rd. Minibuses to **Klong Yai** (1½hr., every hr. 6am-6pm, 80฿) wait on Sukhumvit Rd. two blocks north of the market.

Krung Thai Bank, 59 Sukhumvit Rd., opposite the pharmacy and next to the Trat Department Store, exchanges traveler's checks and has a **24hr. ATM.** (☎520 542. 13฿ per check. Open M-F 8:30am-3:30pm.) In an **emergency,** dial ☎191 or the **police** at ☎511 239. There is no **immigration office** in Trat; the nearest one is in Laem Ngop (see below). **Trat Hospital** (☎511 040 or 520 216) is on Sukhumvit Rd., just past the traffic light at the northern end. The **Telecommunications Office,** 315 Chaimongkol Rd., has **international phones**/fax. (Open daily 7am-10pm.) There is a small **Internet** cafe in the lobby of the Trat Inn Hotel, at the corner of Sukhumvit Rd., at the southern traffic light. (☎532 119. 20฿ for the first 10min., 1฿ per additional min.) The **post office,** on Wiwatanna Rd., east of the intersection with Sukhumvit Rd., has *Poste Restante.* (Open M-F 8:30am-4:30pm, Sa-Su 9am-noon.) **Postal code:** 23000.

ACCOMMODATIONS AND FOOD. There are plenty of guest houses in Trat, and almost all of them are on **Thana Charoen Rd.** and **Lak Muang Rd.** To get there from the buses and *songthaew* stops, walk about 5min. south on Sukhumvit Rd., and take a left at the traffic light. This is Lak Muang Rd.; Thana Charoen Rd. is the next left after that. **Pop Guest House ❶,** 1/1-1/2 Thana Charoen Rd., has bright and clean bamboo bungalows and an attractive garden. (☎512 392. Breakfast 25-50฿. Singles 60-80฿; doubles 100฿.) **Windy Guest House ❶,** 64 Thana Charoen Rd., is a traditional, wooden Thai river house. To get there, take a right down the soi 25m from the Saritidet Rd. intersection. Rooms are decent and well kept. Perks include plenty of travel info and a rowboat they let guests take on the river for free. (☎523 644. Singles 80฿; doubles 100฿.) At the end of Thana Charoen Rd., **Residang Guest House ❷** is a real bargain, featuring enormous rooms with large windows that afford views of the river area. (☎530 103. Singles 80฿; doubles 120฿.)

There's no excuse for not eating in the **market ❶** on the first floor of the municipal market (soups with meat or fish 10-20฿). The **night market ❶** moves to the square two blocks north of the municipal market building behind the A/C bus terminal. (Open daily 7pm-midnight.) For a sit-down meal, a good choice is the **Sea House ❷,** at the southern traffic light on Sukhumvit Rd., which serves up a variety of drinks (large Singha 80฿) and Thai rice dishes (30-60฿) to the beat of hip Thai pop music. (Open daily 8am-1am.)

SIGHTS AND NIGHTLIFE. Most attractions lie in the province, not in the town. The travel-weary can relax with a **traditional Thai massage;** look for the sign outside a house on Thana Charoen Rd., just a few meters from the intersection with Sukhumvit Rd. (2hr. massage 200฿. Open daily 8am-8pm.) This may be just enough to loosen your limbs for the 2.3km walk to **Wat Buppharam.** Walking south on Sukhumvit Rd., turn right down the little road before the Trat Department Store and follow it out of town to reach this mildly interesting wat on a little hill. During the day, you may catch the wat's monk school in session. The walk to the temple is level; another option is to rent a bicycle from Residang Guest House.

For a bit of nightlife, head to **Jean's Cafe,** at 49 Thana Charoen Rd. Jean's serves light food and all sorts of drinks. It also sports a great collection of music. (Small Singha 40฿; ginger tea 15฿. Open daily 7am-midnight.)

DAYTRIP FROM TRAT: LAEM NGOP. A sleepy village with a chaotic pier, Laem Ngop is the place to board ferries to Ko Chang. With Trat only a short *songthaew* ride away, there is no reason to dawdle here and certainly no reason to stay the night. The last **songthaew** to **Trat** (30min., 20฿) leaves after the last boat arrives, usually around 6pm. The only other option is to take a **taxi** (150฿). For **visa extensions** (10-30 days, 500฿) and official information on visiting **Cambodia,** head for the **immigration office** (☎597 261; open M-F 8:30-noon and 1-4:30pm), on the ground floor of a white building about a 15min. stroll up the road from Laem Ngop to Trat, about 300m beyond Thai Farmers Bank. **Thai Farmers Bank,** 500m from the pier on the Trat-Laem Ngop Rd., exchanges traveler's checks. (☎597 046. 13฿ per check. Open M-F 8:30am-3:30pm.) Laem Ngop's **hospital** (☎597 040), on Trat-Laem Ngop Rd., 2km from Laem Ngop toward Trat, sells **malaria** medication (150mg doxycycline pills 2฿), which is recommended for travelers en route to Ko Chang. The **TAT** office, 50m after the bank, has a friendly staff. (☎597 255. Open daily 8:30am-4:30pm.) The **National Park Office** is a 10min. walk from the pier down the first road on the left. (☎538 100. Open 24hr.)

BORDER CROSSING: KLONG YAI/SIHANOUKVILLE To enter Cambodia, you must have a Cambodian visa. These have recently become available at the border on **Hat Lek** for 1000฿, but to be on the safe side, it is best to obtain your visa at the Cambodian embassy in **Bangkok** before leaving for Trat. The whole border-crossing process takes 9-13hr.; depending on the departure time of the boat to **Sihanoukville,** it may be necessary to spend the night. To get from Trat to **Klong Yai,** take a blue *songthaew* from behind the market (1½hr., every hr. 6am-6pm, 35฿) or a minivan from two blocks north of the market (1½hr., every hr. 6am-6pm, 80-100฿). At Klong Yai, take a taxi to **Ban Hat Lek** (30min., 20฿ per person). When you exit Thailand at the border, remember to obtain an exit stamp. After crossing the border, you can hire a taxi that crosses the newly finished bridge or take a small boat (10min., 100฿) to **Ko Kong,** where overnight accommodations can be found. A boat departs daily at 8am (sometimes earlier) for **Sihanoukville** (3½-4hr., 500-600฿). Stay the night in Sihanoukville or catch a bus to **Phnom Penh** (3½hr.; 10,000r).

KO CHANG ☎01

Ko Chang is slowly going the way of its southern cousins. A steady stream of development promises lots of tourists, piles of garbage, and resort commercialism. But, for the moment, Ko Chang is still a rough and rugged island bursting with rainforests, towering waterfalls, isolated beaches, and unexplored territory on its eastern coast. During the low season, prices are often slashed by 40%, and the beaches are almost empty. There is frequent ferry service year-round, so any time is perfect for a visit to this easternmost paradise island.

THE VIEW FROM ABOVE

Gateway: Dan Mai Pier.
Beaches: Hat Kai Bae, Hat Khlong Phrao, Hat Sai Kaow.
Something fun: Snorkeling and chartering boats to the Ko Chang National Marine Park.

TRANSPORTATION

To reach Ko Chang, take a bus to **Trat,** then a *songthaew* (every 30min. or when full 6am-6pm, 20฿) from the front of the municipal market on Sukhumvit Rd. to **Laem Ngop Pier,** and a ferry to the island. Basic one-way tourist tickets cost 50฿. The ferry lumbers to **Dan Mai Pier** on Ko Chang's northern end (1hr.). From Ko Chang, pickup truck **taxis** run frequently to the west coast beaches (30-70฿).

Ferries: Ferries between **Dan Mai Pier** and **Laem Ngop Pier** run frequently (every hr. 7am-6pm, 50฿). This is the most convenient way to get to the island, as minibuses and *songthaew* stop at this pier. However, 2 more piers, **Center Point** (10min. away by taxi) and **Ko Chang Ferry Pier** (20min. away by car) have faster service to the island (40min. from Center Point; 20min. from Ko Chang Ferry Pier). All ferries can accommodate vehicle crossings. To leave the island outside scheduled departure times, charter a **boat** from a fisherman (1000-1500฿). **Speedboats** to the mainland cost 1500฿ from Ban Rung Rang Bungalows (☎329 04 64) on Hat Sai Khaow, or 3500฿ from Sea View Resort (☎218 50 55) on Hat Kai Bae.

Local Transportation: Songthaew rule. A ride between beaches is 30-70฿. In theory, *songthaew* leave from Hat Kai Bae 1hr. before ferry departure, hit the other 2 beaches on the way up, and reach the pier just in time for departure.

Rentals: Resorts and petrol stalls along the road from Hat Sai Khaow rent **motorbikes,** ideal for exploring the east coast. 60฿ per hr.; 400-500฿ per day. Most guest houses rent as well. Contracts and insurance are uncommon.

ORIENTATION AND PRACTICAL INFORMATION

Ko Chang's interior is a trackless rainforest. There is a rudimentary road around part of the perimeter. From **Na Dan Pier** at the island's northeast end, the road goes south to the east coast, passes some waterfall trails, and ends at the village of **Sa Lak Pet.** A right turn at the pier leads down past the west coast's three beaches: **Hat Sai Kaow, Hat Khlong Phrao, Hat Kai Bae,** and **Lonely Beach.**

Tourist Office: Ko Chang National Park Headquarters (☎09 251 9244) in Than Mayom, at the midpoint of the east coast, 20km from Hat Sai Khaow. Open daily 8:30am-4:30pm. There is also a national park office in Laem Ngop.

Currency Exchange: Most bungalow operations on Hat Sai Khaow, as well as Thor's Palace Restaurant, exchange traveler's checks for a 3% commission.

Emergency: ☎191. **Tourist Police (Bangkok):** ☎1155.

Medical Services: Hospitals in Trat handle emergencies. The island's 6 clinics are in Dan Mai, Khlong Son, Sa Lak Phet, Bang Bao, Jek Bae, and Hat Khlong Phrao. All are **open 24hr.** and have radios but no phones. **Malaria testing** is available at Hat Khlong Phrao and Dan Mai 8:30am-4:30pm.

Telephones: Calls can be made at most bungalows on Hat Sai Khaow. International rates 100-150฿ per min.; 50-100฿ charge for collect calls.

Post Offices: Most bungalows mail letters and postcards. **Postal code:** 23000. (Ko Chang doesn't have its own postal code. Use Trat's, and write Ko Chang before it.)

ACCOMMODATIONS AND FOOD

Of the coast's three main beaches, **Hat Sai Khaow** is the closest to the pier and the most developed. More privacy can be had at **Hat Khlong Phrao** and **Hat Kai Bae.** Farther south, **Lonely Beach,** of full-moon-party fame and the stuff of backpacker folklore, is the most laid-back and intoxicatingly sunny. The ultimate stretch of sand is a 15min. walk through the jungle from Hat Kai Bae's southernmost cove. During the low season, guest houses slash prices and are willing to negotiate. The following accommodations and food options are listed by beach.

HAT SAI KHAOW. This white-sand beach has a bad rap. True, the beach is thin and bungalows topple on top of one another, but it is a pleasant brand of commercialism. The far ends of the strip are more sparsely settled. Affordable rooms are at **K.C. Sand Beach Resort ❸**, at the north end. (☎01 833 1010. Bungalows in high season 250-1500฿; in low season 100-150฿.) At the southernmost point, **Phlamola Cliff Resort ❺** has bamboo huts overlooking the rocky point south of Hat Sai Khaow. (☎01 863 1305. Huts 700฿ high season, 300-400฿ low season; concrete rooms with bath and A/C in the evening 1800฿/650฿.) The **White Elephant Restaurant ❷** serves the cheapest beer on the island. It's 10min. south from Hat Sai Khaow, on the right. (Large Chang 40฿; large Singha 50฿. Open daily 6am-2am.)

HAT KHLONG PHRAO. Although not the most remote, Hat Khlong Phrao is the most serene and sparsely settled of Ko Chang's three main beaches with wide expanses of sand punctuated by creeks from the interior and rock outcroppings. Each establishment has its own entrance, and only a few connect to each other by beach walks. **K.P. Bungalows ❷,** toward the center of the beach, is the favorite.

(☎01 863 7262. Rooms with 1 or 2 beds and shared baths 150-200฿, with fan 400-800฿; in low season 60-600฿.) **Magic Bungalows ❹** (☎01 861 4829) offers clean rooms with shower and fan (500฿) and with A/C (1200฿), motorbike rentals (60฿ per hr., 400฿ per day), and snorkeling trips to Ko Yauk (3hr., 200฿ per person).

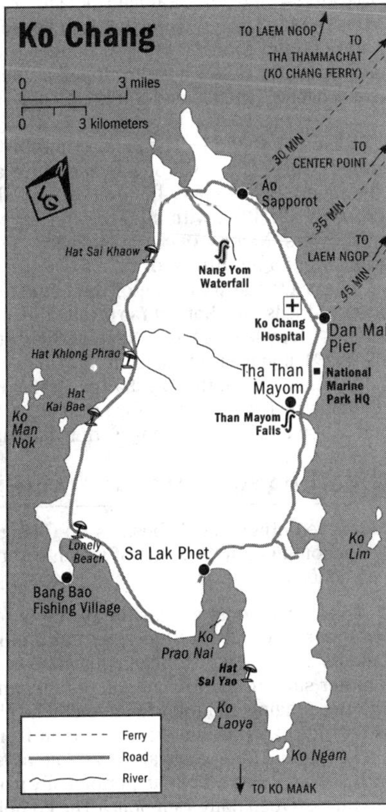

HAT KAI BAE. The most remote of the beaches, Hat Kai Bae has a fun and lively backpacker environment. It also makes a good jumping-off point for exploring the island's southern side. **Kai Bae/Comfortable Bungalows ❸** is south past graceful coconut groves. Bungalows with fans and baths (200฿ in high season, 150฿ in low season) are clean and attractive. **Kaibae Hut ❸** is the last stop before more remote southern beaches. (☎01 862 8426. Bungalows with bath and mosquito nets 200฿, with fan 300/฿500฿.) The sand-floored **restaurant ❷** serves plenty of fried Thai food, from pineapples to squid. (Dishes 60-100฿. Breakfast 40฿. Open daily 7am-10pm.) Swankier **Kai Bae Beach Bungalows ❸** and its popular attached restaurant sprawl north of Kaibae Hut. (☎01 940 9420. Rooms with fan 200฿; with toilet in low season 500฿, high season 1500฿, with A/C in high season 2000฿.) The **O_2 Bar ❷,** 15m south of Chang Park Resort, is cheery and shows Western movies in the evenings. (Breakfast 30-55฿. Most dishes 40-60฿. Open daily 11am-midnight.)

LONELY BEACH. The new road connects this once secluded beach to the rest of the world, but it remains one of the most chilled-out, tailor-made backpacker hideouts in Thailand. Take the winding road past Siam Bay Resort. The first bungalow on Lonely Beach is the **Treehouse Bungalow ❶,** at the far southern end of the beach—still cheap and very rustic. (Rooms 100-200฿.) Bungalows at the **Nature Beach Resort ❸** are of the simple bamboo variety and are very clean. (☎01 803 8933. Huts 200฿, with toilet 300฿; bigger rooms 400฿.) Across the road and up the hill is the **Jah Bar ❷.** Traditional Thai lounging pillows, hammocks, black lights, and moody music make this place a great place to chill. (☎01 916 6129. Small Singha 50฿. Cocktails 100฿. Open daily 2pm-late.)

THE WEST COAST. Mama's Very Famous Snorkel Trips (☎09 831 1059) is north of the road's end on Hat Kai Bae. A trip to Ko Yuak costs 150฿; special three-island trips leave at 9am (450฿). Fishing boats can be rented for 500฿ per hour. Snorkeling outings are designed for high-season crowds. Check out the **Seahorse Dive Shop**

(☎01 219 3844), behind Kaibae Hut. The friendly Swiss instructor offers four-day PADI courses (10,500฿) in the high season. Dives cost 1200-1500฿, including equipment and food. If you still hunger for physical and spiritual self-mastery, American Jerry Boxer has developed a unique art, which he teaches at the **Wind Eagle School of Taiji,** beyond Kai Bae Beach Bungalows (lessons 60-75฿ per hr.).

THE EAST COAST. The picturesque east coast is short on beaches but long on scenic beauty. The town of **Dan Mai** hides a path to **Khlong Nonsi Falls,** a 30min. walk inland. **Than Mayom,** 4km to the south, is home to the **National Park Headquarters** (☎039 521 122), with little to offer save a Visitors Center, free public toilets, and showers. Nearby **Than Mayom Falls,** a favorite of King Rama V, still bears his initials. Rent a motorbike or take a *songthaew* to the pier and another down the east coast. On the west side of the peninsula, jutting out from the southeastern corner of the island, **Hat Sai Yao** awaits those who will settle only for the extremely remote. A **ferry** leaves Laem Ngop at 3pm, stopping at the beach on its way to **Ko Wai** (100฿); it leaves at 8am from Ko Wai to come back (in low season 3 per week). On the other side of the bay, **Sa Lak Phet** is Ko Chang's most lively fishing village, accessible by ferry (departs for Laem Ngop 6am, returns 1pm; 70฿). You can also charter boats to the Ko Chang National Marine Park.

KO CHANG NATIONAL MARINE PARK

Forty-seven other islands besides Ko Chang make up the national park. Thirteen have accommodations, some of which cater only to package tourists; camping is free and legal anywhere.

KO MAAK. The most accessible of the outer islands, Ko Maak offers the same travel amenities as Ko Chang, but with more solitude and better beaches. The island itself is flat, with volcanic formations on the western tip that frame beaches on either side. In the low season, it is technically closed, but most guest houses will offer lodging and food to anyone who shows up. There is a **clinic** and a **police box** on the road heading into the island from the pier. Expensive bottled water, whiskey, and toilet paper are available at the **store** at the base of the pier. Just north, a casual **post office** can periodically patch through **international phone** calls at high rates. (Open daily 7am-8pm.) The complex also has a **minimart** and **bicycle** and **motorcycle rental.** Guest houses are easily accessible by trucks waiting by the pier. The farthest south is **Lazy Days ❶,** with accommodations in a relaxed party atmosphere. (Bungalows and teepees with shared bath 100฿.) At the western end, **Fantasia ❶** (open Oct.-May) has great (though fan-less) A-frame bungalows tucked back on the hill in the coconut grove, with mosquito nets, floor mattresses, and shared baths (100฿). Beachfront bungalows with private baths, beach chairs, and fans go for 250฿. Fantasia boasts the best collection of recorded music on the east coast. Up the beach, **Koh Mak Resort ❸** offers high-quality, spacious bungalows for 300-600฿. *(A ferry leaves Ko Maak from Ao Nid pier at 8am and Laem Ngop at 3pm (in high season daily, in low season on even-numbered days; 2½hr.; 210฿). Boats (15min., 50฿) go to Ko Kham twice in the morning and return around 4pm.)*

THE OUTER ISLANDS. The islands off Ko Chang's southern coast are famous for fishing, coral, rock formations, bird nests, and bat guano. You can scuba dive at **Ko Rang,** home to an abundance of coral, fish, and toothy sharks. **Ko Wai,** a less-remote version of Ko Rang, is surrounded by coral. The fishing is legendary. From Ko Maak, there is a ferry to **Ko Kham,** which features a cheap **guest house** (open Oct.-June) and more sun and solitude. **Bungalows ❶** on the islands range from 100฿ to 300฿ and package tours run 2000฿ per night. Ask at guest houses in Trat. *(To get to Ko Rang, charter a boat in Sa Lak Phet or check at Ko Chang bungalows for scuba or snorkel-*

ing tours. In high season, a ferry leaves for Ko Wai daily at 3pm from Laem Ngop, returning from Ko Wai at 8am the following morning (2hr., 120฿). A banana boat leaves year-round from the river in Trat (W, Sa 11am) for Ko Kud, returning the next morning (4½hr., 150฿). This boat often doesn't run in monsoons. In addition, a speedboat island-hopper service has started. Tickets cost 250฿.)

ARANYAPRATHET

Aranyaprathet is the border town for the Cambodia-bound. Most travelers somehow manage to avoid having to stay the night here, and local transportation schedules are arranged around that goal. Wide streets and impersonal hotels make friendly locals all Aranyaprathet has to offer.

Many travelers stay at the **Aran Garden I Hotel ❷.** Walk 500m south from the clock tower to Raduthid Rd. and then 600m east to Chitsuwarn Rd.; it's on the corner. (Bicycles 40฿ per day. Singles 150฿; doubles 200฿.) Down Raduthid Rd. one block, **Aran Garden II ❸** has much nicer, quieter rooms. (Bicycles 10฿ per hr. Singles 230฿; doubles 300฿.) Another option is the **Great Hill Hotel ❸,** 1km north of the train station. (Singles with fan 250฿, with A/C 500฿; doubles 300฿/600฿.) In the low season, many travelers crash for free on the office floor of their Siem Reap-bound tour company, which might even provide breakfast. Restaurants are dismal; it's best to enjoy noodles or rice at a street stall near the Aran Garden Hotels.

In the center of town, **Mahadthai-Suwannasorn Rd.** and **Chaoprayabodin Rd.** intersect at a wee purple clock tower. The **railway station** sits nearby at the north end of **Suwannasorn Rd. Trains** arrive from **Bangkok** at 11:40am and 7:05pm; trains depart for Bangkok at 6:30am and 1:35pm (48฿). The bus station is on the west side of town: walk three blocks straight out and one block to the right to reach the clock tower. **Buses** run to **Bangkok** (every hr., A/C 144฿). **Tuk-tuks** and **sambis** putter to hotels from the bus and train stations (20฿). At the clock tower, the **general post office** has a **Lenso** phone card machine. (Phone cards 300฿ and 500฿. Open M-F 8:30am-4:30pm.) For international calls, head to the **Telecommunications Office,** near the corner of Mahadthai and Raduthid Rd., 500m south of the clock tower. (Open M-F 8:30am-4:30pm.) The **pharmacy** is one block north of the Aran Garden I Hotel. (Open M-Sa 6:30am-7:30pm.) The border **market,** on Weruwan Rd., is colossal but caters mostly to Thais trying to look Western, sporting a dull mix of jeans, sunglasses, dresses, and other faux-Western items. (Open daily 6am-7pm.) Motorcycle rides to the market should cost 25-30฿; *tuk-tuks* run 40-50฿.

BORDER CROSSING: ARANYAPRATHET/POIPET

Travelers must obtain visas at the Cambodian embassy in Bangkok. In Aranyaprathet, touts materialize at the train and bus stations to offer trips to Siem Reap. They are helpful in navigating the chaotic bridge and boarding a public pick-up for the painful 7-8hr. ride ahead (200-350฿). Trucks leave from a station 500m on the Cambodian side on the left. Be sure to obtain an exit stamp from Thai immigration (open daily 7:30am-5:30pm) at the bridge. A tuk-tuk from anywhere in town to the bridge costs 60฿.

NORTHERN THAILAND

Northern Thailand's mountains constitute the lowest crags of the Himalayan foothills. Central Chiang Mai, formerly the capital of the prosperous Lanna Kingdom, serves as the first stop for many visitors. Throughout the region, Chinese immigrants display pictures of the Thai Royal Family in shop windows, tribal minorities

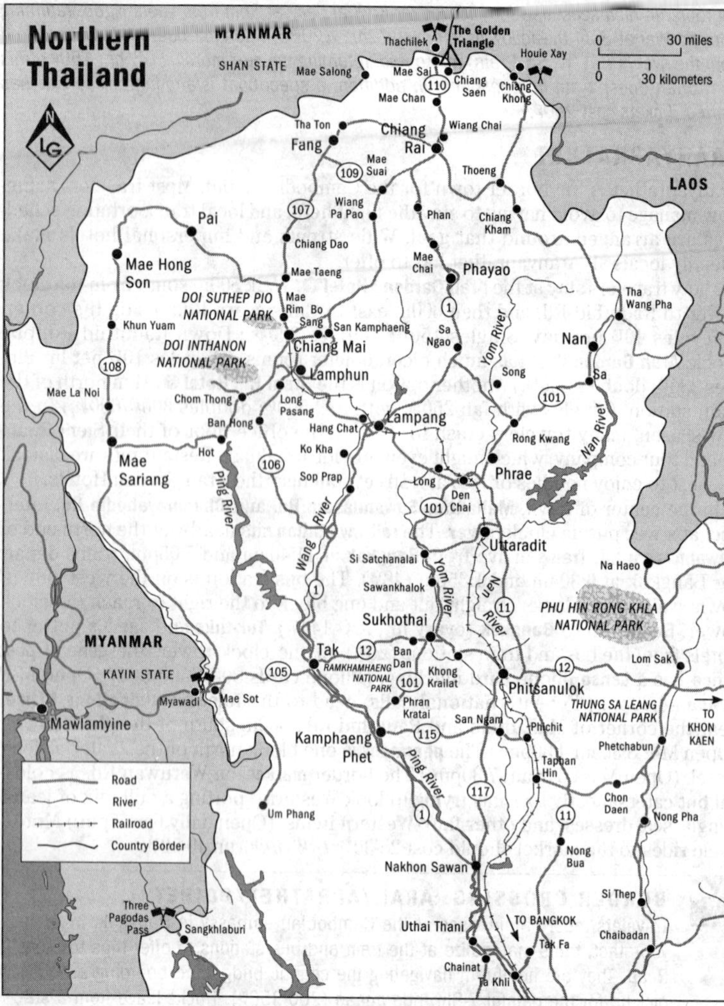

inhabit misty mountainsides, and refugee camps swell with Burmese escaping their military government—the dialect, cuisine, dance, and architecture of Northern Thailand owe much to this fusion of cultures.

CHIANG MAI ☎053

Nothing more than mice scurrying down a hole convinced King Mengrai to establish the seat of his Lanna Kingdom in Chiang Mai in 1296—an inauspicious beginning for a city that has become Thailand's second-largest in both native population and tourist crowds. Thousands of *farang*, drawn by promises of adventure and a cooler climate, clog the narrow streets of this ancient city. The increased stampede of tourists heightens concerns that both hill-tribe culture and the natural environment are quickly eroding. Nonetheless, Chiang Mai seems to have retained its cultural autonomy. The distinctive dialect, Burmese-influenced art and architecture, and an abundance of Northern culinary delicacies prove that Chiang Mai residents are not about to surrender their heritage.

INTERCITY TRANSPORTATION

BY PLANE. Chiang Mai International Airport (☎922 100) sits on Sanambin (Airport) Rd., 3km southwest of the city center. From the airport, **taxis** (☎201 307; 100฿), tuk-tuks (50฿), and *songthaew* (15-20฿) can be picked up on the main road. **Thai Airways,** 240 Phra Pokklao Rd., has branches around the city (☎211 044; open daily 8am-5pm) and flies to: **Bangkok** (11 per day 7am-9:15pm, 2275฿); **Mae Hong Son** (10am, 1, 4pm; 870฿). **Air Andaman,** at the airport (☎022 299 555), can be booked through all travel agencies and flies to: **Chiang Rai** (7:30am, 5:25pm; 925฿); **Mae Sot** (M, W, F, Su 2pm; 1085฿); **Nan** (M, W, F, Su 11:30am; 1025฿); **Phitsanulok** (Tu, Th, Sa 11:30am; 1185฿). **Bangkok Airways,** at the airport (☎281 519), flies daily to: **Bangkok** (1 per day, 2170฿) via **Sukhothai** (940฿); **Jinghong, China** (Tu, Th, Sa 3:20pm; 4540฿); **Samui** (same flight as Bangkok; 4050฿); **Xian, China** (W, Su 4:20pm, F 5pm; 10,910฿). **Lao Aviation** flies to **Vientiane, Laos** (Th, Su 1:10pm; 3360฿). Their contact in Chiang Mai is **Chiang Mai BIS Travel,** 12/1 Loi Krap Rd. (☎206 738. Open daily 8:30am-6pm.) **Air Mandalay** flies to **Mandalay, Myanmar** (Th 4:50pm, 3200฿); **Yangon, Myanmar** (Su 2:35pm, 2895฿). Contact **Charal Business,** 123 Chiang Mai-Lamphun Rd. (☎252 054. Open M-F 8:30am-6pm, Sa 8am-5pm.) **Mandarin Airlines** (☎201 268), 2nd floor at the airport, flies to **Taipei, Taiwan** (W, Th, Su 12:55pm). **Silk Air,** at the Imperial Maeping Hotel, 153 Sri Donchai Rd. (☎276 459; open M-F 8:30am-5pm, Sa-Su 8:30am-1pm), flies to **Singapore** (Tu, Su 5:30pm, F 11:20am; 7000฿). A branch of STA Travel is **Trans World Travel Service Co., Ltd.,** 259/61 Tha Pae Rd. (☎272 416), which may offer cheaper student tickets than carriers do. You'll need a student card (200฿ with passport and proof of student status). All international flights are subject to a 500฿ departure tax (cash only).

BY TRAIN. The **Chiang Mai Railway Station,** 27 Charoen Muang Rd. (☎244 795), on the eastern outskirts of the city, is accessible by *songthaew* (10-20฿) and tuk-tuk (40-50฿). Trains run daily to **Bangkok** (11-14hr.; 7 per day 6:26am-8:40pm; 3rd-class 161฿, 2nd-class sleeper 421-561฿, 2nd-class with A/C 611-681฿, 1st-class sleeper 1193฿). Most Bangkok-bound trains also stop in **Lampang** (2hr.; 3rd-class 23฿, 2nd-class 53฿) and **Phitsanulok** (6-7hr.; 3rd-class 105฿, 2nd-class 190฿). Reserve sleeper tickets well in advance; lower berths are pricier. Refunds: 80% 3 days before travel; 50% up to 1hr. after train departure; no refunds thereafter. (Ticket window open daily 6am-8pm.)

BY BUS. Tuk-tuks (30-50฿) and *songthaew* (10-20฿) shuttle between the old city and **Arcade Bus Station** (☎242 664), 3km to the northeast. **Chang Phuak Bus Station** (☎211 586), on Chang Phuak Rd., 1km north of the old city, runs buses within Chiang Mai Province.

DESTINATION, BUS#	DUR.	FREQUENCY/TIME	PRICE
ARCADE BUS STATION			
Bangkok, 18	10hr.	19 per day 6:30am-9pm	224฿, A/C II 314฿, A/C I 403฿, VIP 625฿
Chiang Rai, 166	3hr.	17 per day 6am-5:30pm	77฿, A/C 139฿
Chiang Khong, 671	6hr.	6:30, 8am, 12:30pm	121฿, A/C II 218฿, A/C I 169฿

THAILAND

DESTINATION, BUS#	DUR.	FREQUENCY/TIME	PRICE
Khon Kaen, 633 or 175	12hr.	11 per day 5am-9pm	219-243฿, A/C II 307-437฿
Khorat, 635 (Ratchasima)	12hr.	10 per day 3:30am-8:30pm	243฿, A/C 340-510฿
Lampang, 152	2hr.	every 30min. 6am-4pm	29฿
Mae Hong Son, 170	8hr.	6:30, 8, 11am, 8, 9pm	143฿, A/C 257฿
via Mae Sariang	5hr.	1:30, 3pm (Mae Sariang only)	78฿, A/C 140฿
Mae Hong Son, 612	7hr.	7, 9, 10:30am, 12:30pm	105฿, A/C 147฿
via Pai	4hr.	4pm (Pai only)	60฿
Mae Sai, 619	4hr.	8 per day 6am-5pm	95฿, A/C 171฿
Mae Sot, 672	6hr.	11am, 1:10pm	134฿, A/C 241฿
Nan, 169 or 113	6hr.	15 per day 6:15am-10:30pm	117-128฿, A/C 164-230฿
Phitsanulok, 155, 132, or 623	6hr.	11 per day 6:30am-8pm	120-140฿, A/C 184-196฿
Rayong	17hr.	8 per day 5am-6:30pm	305฿, A/C 555-645฿
via Pattaya	16hr.		285฿, A/C 605฿
Sukhothai	5hr.	13 per day 5am-8pm	122฿, A/C 171฿
Ubon Ratchathani, 587	17	6 per day 12:15-6pm	325฿, A/C 590-685฿
CHANG PHUAK BUS STATION			
Chom Thong	1¼hr.	every 20min. 6:30am-6pm	23฿
Lamphun	1hr.	every 10min. 6:20am-6pm	12฿
Tha Ton	4hr.	6 per day 6am-3:30pm	70฿
via Fang	3½hr.	every 30min. 5:30am-5:30pm	60฿

ORIENTATION

Chiang Mai's primary area of interest is within the old city and the area to its east which stretches 1.5km to the **Ping River.** A moat delineates the old city; within it, the east-west soi numbers increase as you go north. North-south **Phra Pokklao Rd.** and east-west **Ratchadamnoen Rd.** divide the square. **Moon Muang Rd.** follows the inside of the moat and intersects Ratchadamnoen Rd. at **Tha Pae Gate,** the center of backpacker activity. If Tha Pae Gate weren't closed to traffic, Ratchadamnoen Rd. would flow into **Tha Pae Rd.,** which runs east to the Ping River and **Nawarat Bridge.** Along the way, it intersects **Chang Klan Rd.,** home to the night bazaar, and **Charoen Prathet Rd.,** which flanks the Ping's west bank.

LOCAL TRANSPORTATION

Songthaew, Tuk-tuk, and Samlor: *Songthaew* 10฿ anywhere in the city, except for along special routes, to the airport or bus station, or at night. Don't pay more than 40฿. Tuk-tuks and *samlor* 20-30฿ within the old city, 40-60฿ for trips across the city, 400-500฿ per day. **Taxi** service (☎201 307) can also be arranged to Doi Suthep 300฿.

Rentals: Bicycles 30-60฿ per day. Often require a passport photocopy, a 500฿ deposit, or both. **The Chiang Mai Disabled Center,** 133/1 Ratchaphakhinai Rd., rents mountain bikes (40฿ per day). Motorbike rental shops litter the Tha Pae Gate area; all require a deposit and photocopy of passport. Motorbike rental is typically 150฿ per day, 200฿ with insurance. **Mr. Mechanic,** 4 Moon Muang Rd. Soi 5 (☎214 708), also has comprehensive insurance. Motorbike 120฿; with insurance 170฿. New bikes 150฿/200฿. Bicycle 30฿ per day; new bike with gears 60฿. **Avis,** Royal Princess Hotel, 112 Chang Klan Rd. (☎281 033), and at the airport (☎201 574). Toyota Corollas 1790฿ per day. Suzuki 4WD 1290฿ per day. Open daily 8am-5pm.

HOLD THE STUFFING Thailand is a world leader in penis-reattachment surgery, but if you're considering penile surgical augmentation, make sure your doctor is reputable and has good taste. In October 1999, the *Bangkok Post* reported that unlicensed physicians had performed 100 penis-enlargement operations by injecting mixtures of olive oil, chalk, and other substances to provide bulk and springiness. According to the always reliable *News of the Weird*, one hospital official in Chiang Mai reported having seen bits of the Bangkok telephone directory stuffed into one unsuspecting penis.

PRACTICAL INFORMATION

TOURIST AND FINANCIAL SERVICES

Tourist Office: TAT, 105/1 Chiang Mai-Lamphun Rd. (☎248 604), across from the next bridge 500m south of Nawarat Bridge. Open daily 8:30am-4:30pm.

Consulates: Australia, 165 Siri Mungkrajaru Rd. (☎225 975). Open M-F 8am-5pm. **Canada** (☎850 147), several km southeast of the old city on Chiang Mai-Lampang Rd. Consular hours M-F 9am-noon. **China** (☎200 525), on Chang Lo Rd., at Suan Prung Gate. 30-day single entry visa 1100฿; multiple-day 1650฿. 4-day processing. Visa application M-F 9-11:30am. **UK,** 198 Bamrung Rot Rd. (☎263 015). Open M-F 9-11:30am. **US,** 387 Witchayanon Rd. (☎252 629). Services for American citizens M and W 1-3:30pm. Office open M-F 8am-4pm.

Visa Services: Travel agents can organize visas for **Laos** (15-day visa: 4-day processing 750฿, 2-day processing 1050฿) and **Vietnam** (1-month visa: 4-day processing 2400฿).

Immigration Office: 97 Sanambin (Airport) Rd. (☎277 510). **Visa extensions** 500฿; 1-day processing. Bring 2 passport photos, 2 copies of passport photo page, visa, and arrival/departure card. Open M-F 8:30am-noon and 1-4:30pm.

Currency Exchange: Banks line Tha Pae Rd. **Thai Farmers Bank,** 169-171 Tha Pae Rd. (☎270 151). Open M-F 8:30am-3:30pm. **24hr. ATM** (Cirrus/MC/PLUS/V). Currency exchange booths in the night bazaar on Chang Klan Rd. Open daily until 10pm.

American Express: Sea Tours Company, 2/3 Prachasamphan Rd. (☎271 441). The only AmEx affiliate in Northern Thailand. Open M-F 8:30am-4:30pm, Sa 8:30-11:30am.

Alternatives to Tourism: Australia Center, 75/1 Moo 14, Suthep Rd. (☎810 552), on a soi after the turn-off to Wat U-Mong, provides a leaflet on working in Chiang Mai as an English teacher. **Chiang Mai Disabled Center,** 133/1 Ratchaphakhinai Rd. (☎213 941; www.infothai.com/disabled). Volunteers who can teach English or are computer literate and can make a long-term commitment are always welcome. Open daily 8am-8pm. **Rejoice Urban Development** (☎806 227; www.rejoicecharity.com). Take Suthep Rd. to Canal Rd., the next major intersection after the turn-off to the super-highway. Turn left; it's 7 bridges down on the right. Qualified nurses, doctors, social workers, and medical students, as well as those who can serve in administrative or technical positions, are welcome to volunteer for stints of 2 weeks to 2 months. Volunteers are expected to cover their own room and board. Contact the founder, Gareth, for more information. Open M-F 9am-5pm, Sa 9am-1pm.

LOCAL SERVICES

Luggage Storage: At the **train station** (☎245 363). 10฿ per day per piece for the first 5 days, 15฿ per additional day (20-day max.). Open daily 4:50am-8:45pm. At the **airport.** 30฿ per day (14-day max.). Open daily 6am-10pm. Most guest houses store luggage for free, although security can be dubious.

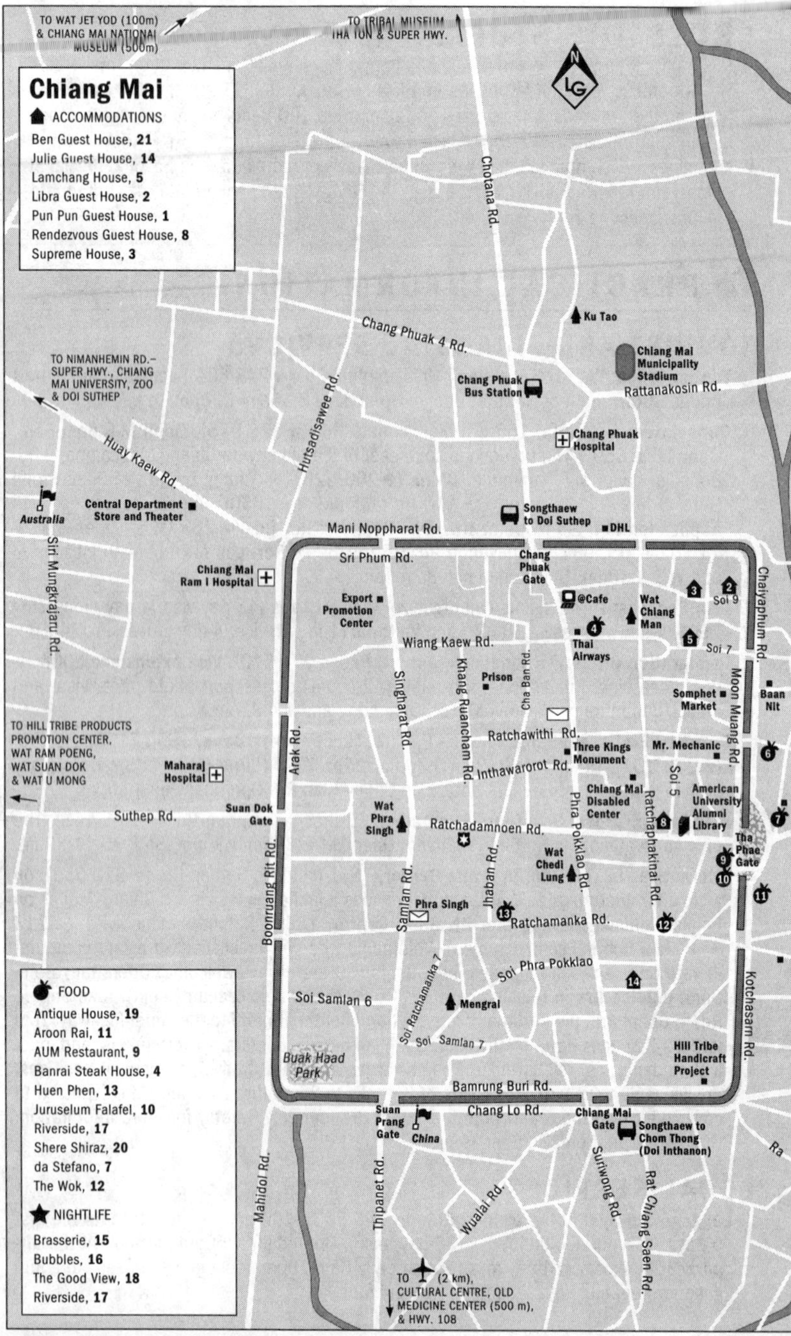
Chiang Mai
ACCOMMODATIONS
Ben Guest House, 21
Julie Guest House, 14
Lamchang House, 5
Libra Guest House, 2
Pun Pun Guest House, 1
Rendezvous Guest House, 8
Supreme House, 3
FOOD
Antique House, 19
Aroon Rai, 11
AUM Restaurant, 9
Banrai Steak House, 4
Huen Phen, 13
Juruselum Falafel, 10
Riverside, 17
Shere Shiraz, 20
da Stefano, 7
The Wok, 12
NIGHTLIFE
Brasserie, 15
Bubbles, 16
The Good View, 18
Riverside, 17
TO WAT JET YOD (100m) & CHIANG MAI NATIONAL MUSEUM (500m)
TO TRIBAL MUSEUM THA TON & SUPER HWY.
TO NIMANHEMIN RD.–SUPER HWY., CHIANG MAI UNIVERSITY, ZOO & DOI SUTHEP
TO HILL TRIBE PRODUCTS PROMOTION CENTER, WAT RAM POENG, WAT SUAN DOK & WAT U MONG
TO (2 km), CULTURAL CENTRE, OLD MEDICINE CENTER (500 m), & HWY. 108
Chotana Rd.
Ku Tao
Chang Phuak 4 Rd.
Chiang Mai Municipality Stadium
Chang Phuak Bus Station
Rattanakosin Rd.
Hutsadisawee Rd.
Huay Kaew Rd.
Chang Phuak Hospital
Australia
Central Department Store and Theater
Songthaew to Doi Suthep
DHL
Mani Noppharat Rd.
Sri Phum Rd.
Chang Phuak Gate
Siri Mungkrajaru Rd.
Chiang Mai Ram I Hospital
Export Promotion Center
@Cafe
Wat Chiang Man
Soi 9
Chaiyaphum Rd.
Thai Airways
Wiang Kaew Rd.
Soi 7
Singharat Rd.
Khang Ruancham Rd.
Cha Ban Rd.
Prison
Somphet Market
Moon Muang Rd.
Baan Nit
Ratchawithi Rd.
Three Kings Monument
Mr. Mechanic
Arak Rd.
Maharaj Hospital
Inthawarorot Rd.
Soi 5
Chiang Mai Disabled Center
American University Alumni Library
Suthep Rd.
Suan Dok Gate
Wat Phra Singh
Ratchadamnoen Rd.
Phra Pokklao Rd.
Ratchaphakinai Rd.
Tha Phae Gate
Boonruang Rit Rd.
Jhaban Rd.
Wat Chedi Lung
Samlan Rd.
Phra Singh
Ratchamanka Rd.
Soi Phra Pokklao
Soi Ratchamanka 7
Soi Samlan 6
Mengrai
Soi Samlan 7
Kotchasarn Rd.
Hill Tribe Handicraft Project
Buak Haad Park
Bamrung Buri Rd.
Chang Lo Rd.
Suan Prang Gate
China
Chiang Mai Gate
Songthaew to Chom Thong (Doi Inthanon)
Mahidol Rd.
Thipanet Rd.
Wualai Rd.
Suriwong Rd.
Rat Chiang Saen Rd.

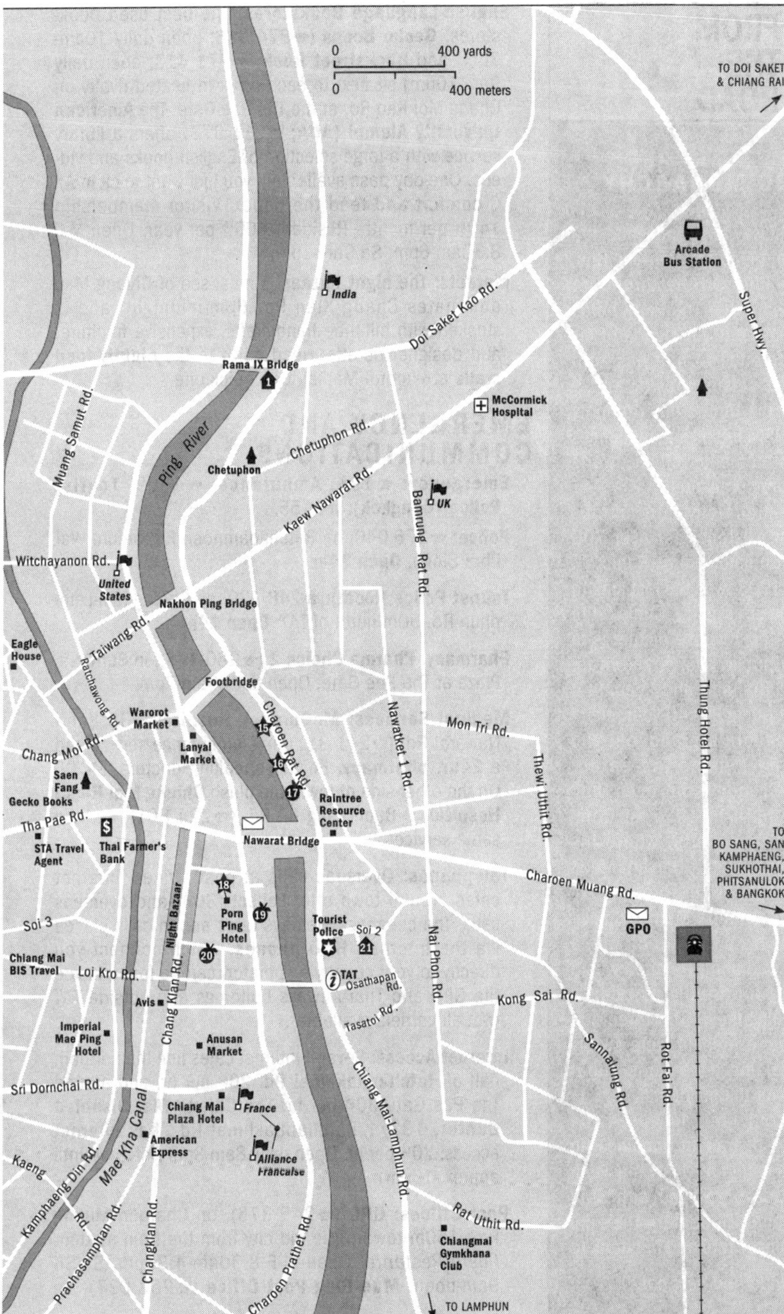
0
400 yards
0
400 meters
TO DOI SAKET & CHIANG RAI
Arcade Bus Station
Super Hwy.
India
Doi Saket Kao Rd.
Rama IX Bridge
1
McCormick Hospital
Chetuphon Rd.
Chetuphon
Ping River
Muang Samut Rd.
Kaew Nawarat Rd.
UK
Bamrung Rat Rd.
Witchayanon Rd.
United States
Nakhon Ping Bridge
Taiwang Rd.
Eagle House
Ratchawong Rd.
Footbridge
Warorot Market
Lanyai Market
Charoen Rat Rd.
15
16
17
Nawatket 1 Rd.
Mon Tri Rd.
Thewi Uthit Rd.
Thung Hotel Rd.
Chang Moi Rd.
Saen Fang
Gecko Books
Tha Pae Rd.
STA Travel Agent
Thai Farmer's Bank
Raintree Resource Center
Nawarat Bridge
TO BO SANG, SAN KAMPHAENG, SUKHOTHAI, PHITSANULOK & BANGKOK
Charoen Muang Rd.
18
Porn Ping Hotel
19
Night Bazaar
Soi 3
Tourist Police
Soi 2
21
GPO
20
Chiang Mai BIS Travel
Loi Kro Rd.
TAT
Osathapan Rd.
Nai Phon Rd.
Avis
Chang Klan Rd.
Kong Sai Rd.
Tasatoi Rd.
Sannalung Rd.
Imperial Mae Ping Hotel
Anusan Market
Rot Fai Rd.
Sri Dornchai Rd.
Chiang Mai Plaza Hotel
France
Chiang Mai-Lamphun Rd.
Mae Kha Canal
American Express
Alliance Francaise
Kaeng
Kamphaeng Din Rd.
Rat Uthit Rd.
Prachasamphan Rd.
Changklan Rd.
Charoen Prathet Rd.
Chiangmai Gymkhana Club
TO LAMPHUN

THAILAND

FROM THE ROAD

MYSTIC MONARCHY

The fastest way to get punched in a bar in Thailand is to criticize King Bhumibol Adulyadej. On the throne for nearly 60 years, the Thai king holds the dearest place in the hearts of his people. Deference to him has kept anyone from seizing power and a decree from the throne has authority greater than law: if the king denounces drugs, his statement's effect dwarfs that of anti-drug programs.

The Thai monarchy is a curious archaism, in existence for over 700 years. King Chulalongkorn (Rama V), who died in 1903, was the last king to be worshiped as a god. "Chula," the mustachioed gent whose picture is in nearly every public bus, is known for modernizing Thailand and keeping it independent during his 40-year reign.

Chulalongkorn's grandson, the present king (whose jug-eared, bespectacled mug is all over Thailand), was born in 1927 in Cambridge, Massachusetts, where his father was a student at Harvard Medical School. In 1946, his brother, 20-year-old King Ananda Mahidol, accidentally blew his own head off with a pistol in his bedroom. (Ananda was a gun fanatic, reportedly carrying a weapon at all times.) The three servants who were present were swiftly executed–raising suspicions about the specifics of the incident.

The present king accepted the crown from a distraught populace. In addition to a career as a jazz musician and composer–he played with Stan Getz and Benny Goodman–the king has been all over Thailand in efforts to

(continued on next page)

English-Language Bookstores: The best used bookstores, **Gecko Books** (☎874 066; open daily 10am-7pm) and **Backstreet Book** (☎871 413; open daily 9am-10pm) sit next to each other in heated rivalry on Chang Moi Kao Rd. at the Tha Pae Gate. The **American University Alumni (AUA;** ☎211 973) offers a library service with a large selection of English books and videos. One-day pass available if you just want to sit in A/C comfort and read the paper. Visitor membership 140฿ per month. Resident 400฿ per year. Open M-F 8:30am-6pm, Sa 9am-1pm.

Markets: The **night bazaar,** a must-see of Chiang Mai, dominates Chang Klan Rd. 6pm-midnight, and is stocked with hill-tribe handicrafts, expensive furniture, and designer rip-offs. Head north to the **nightly food stalls** at Warorot Market for a quick bite.

EMERGENCY AND COMMUNICATIONS

Emergency: ☎191. **Ambulance:** ☎1669. **Tourist Police (Bangkok):** ☎1155.

Police: ☎276 040, on Ratchadamnoen Rd. before Wat Phra Singh. **Open 24hr.**

Tourist Police (local): ☎248 130, on Chiang Mai-Lamphun Rd. 50m north of TAT. **Open 24hr.**

Pharmacy: Pharma Choice 2 (☎280 136), in Suriwong Plaza at Tha Pae Gate. Open daily 9am-7pm.

Medical Services: McCormick Hospital, 133 Kaew Nawarat Rd. (☎241 311), has ambulance service and a **24hr. pharmacy.** English-speaking doctors. MC/V. On the other side of town, the plush **Chiang Mai Ram I Hospital,** 9 Boonruang Rit Rd. (☎224 861), has the same services.

Telephones: Overseas calls at post offices. Internet cafes around town offer collect (30฿) and overseas calls. The cheapest overseas rates are on calls placed via the Internet. **HCD phones,** which connect you directly to your country's operator, can be found inside the GPO and Thai Airways buildings and outside TAT (not all carriers available).

Internet Access: Several Internet cafes line the northern half of **Ratchaphakhinai Rd.** 20฿ per hr, and around Tha Pae Gate 30฿ per hr. **The Chiang Mai Disabled Center,** 133/1 Ratchaphakhinai Rd., has Internet access. 20฿ per hr. Open daily 8am-8pm (Internet until approx. 10pm).

Post Offices: GPO (☎245 376), on Charoen Muang Rd., 150m toward the old city from the train station. *Poste Restante.* Open M-F 8:30am-4:30pm, Sa-Su 9am-noon. **Mae Ping Post Office** (☎252 037), on

Charoen Prathet Rd., just north of Nawarat Bridge. Open M-F 8:30am-4:30pm, Sa 9am-noon. **Phra Singh Post Office** (☎814 062), on Samlan Rd., south of Wat Phra Sing. Open M-F 8:30am-4:30pm, Sa 9am-noon. All 3 provide **CATNET Internet** with PIN or card. GPO and Phra Singh have **international phone**/fax. **DHL Worldwide Express,** 160/1 Mani Noppharat Rd. (☎418 501), east of the Chang Phuak Gate. Open M-F 8:30am-6pm, Sa 8:30am-5pm. **Postal code:** 50000.

ACCOMMODATIONS

Guest house signs sprout from almost every soi entrance within a 1km radius of **Tha Pae Gate.** Reservations are recommended during festival periods, during which time certain guest houses will inflate their prices. The easiest way to choose an accommodation from the multitude of options is to pick a neighborhood. Many guest houses make their money from treks. In the high season, if you don't sign up for your guest house's trek, you may be asked to sign out.

THA PAE GATE AREA

Libra Guest House, 28 Moon Muang Rd. Soi 9 (☎/fax 210 687), in the northeast corner of the old city. With its new garden setting and renovated rooms, the popular family-run establishment just keeps getting better. Consistently praised treks (3-day, 1600฿, max. 12 people). Cooking school 700฿ per day. Laundry 25฿ per kg. Free pickup from bus, train station, or airport. Check-out 10am. Reservations recommended. Dorms 50฿; doubles with bath 100฿, with bath and hot water 150฿. ❶

Rendezvous Guest House, 3/1 Ratchadamnoen Rd. Soi 5 (☎213 763), 50m left off Ratchadamnoen Rd. Superb value with bath, TV, cable, and fan in every room. Laundry service 30฿ per kg. Safety deposit box. Rooms 280฿, with A/C 380฿. ❹

Lamchang House, 24 Moon Muang Rd. Soi 7 (☎210 586). The handful of comfy bottom-floor bamboo thatch rooms are always full. All rooms with shared bath. Singles 90฿; doubles 160฿; triples 300฿. ❶

Supreme House, 44/1 Moon Muang Rd. Soi 9 (☎222 480), 100m from Libra Guest House. Helpful owner. No hassle accommodation with flexible check-out time. 4000+ multi-language books, free for guest use. Singles with hot water 100฿, with A/C 200฿; doubles 150฿/250฿; triples and quads 200฿/300฿. ❶

Julie Guest House, 7/1 Soi 5 Phra Pokklao Rd., best reached by walking down Ratchaphakhinai Rd. follow-

(continued from previous page)

connect with his people. He is also said to oversee many development projects personally.

For all its modernity, the Thai monarchy is shrouded in medieval courtesies and regulations. Speech concerning the monarchy is not free: you can be locked in prison for 15 years with impunity. In 2002, Thailand revoked the visas of two journalists for an article deemed overly critical of the monarchy. In Philadelphia, a restaurant digitally added sunglasses and a punk hairdo to a photo of the king in an advertisement. The Thai government formally protested to the United States, who said it was a private issue.

Even the Thai language is specialized for the Royal Family. The king refers to himself with an honorific "I" and people around him refer to themselves as "dust under His Majesty's feet."

The standard ways of showing disrespect go triple for Thai royalty. Dropping a 20-baht note on the ground is the equivalent of drop-kicking the king; but if you do, quickly apologize to those around you. Thai theaters play the national anthem and show fawning photos of the king before a movie. Not standing up during these ceremonies will bother fellow moviegoers. Expect to be cursed and slapped.

King Bhumibol, now 76, has minor health problems but continues to rule with broad public approval. His heir, the Crown Prince Vajiralongkorn, is in his mid-50s and on his third marriage (he dissolved the first, saying his wife played too much ping pong).

– Graeme Wood

ing the signs. Unique rooftop setting decked with hammocks. Pool table, TV, and VCR. Dorms 50฿, singles 80-90฿; doubles with hot shower 130฿; triples with hot shower 180฿. ❶

NEAR THE PING RIVER

Ben Guest House, 4/11 Chiang Mai-Lamphun Rd. Soi 2 (☎244 103). Down a soi adjacent to the tourist police. Large beds, hot showers, and fans. Laundry 40฿ per kg. Check-out 10am. Motorcycle rental 150฿, with insurance 200฿. Internet 30฿ per hr. All rooms 150฿. ❷

Pun Pun Guest House, 321 Charoen Rat Rd. (☎243 362), at Rama IX Bridge. The only budget accommodation by the river. Small restaurant/bar with cable TV and pool table. Wooden bungalows by the river 150-175฿; brick rooms with hot water and Western toilet 200-225฿. ❷

FOOD

Nowhere else in Thailand is there such a wide variety of restaurants as in Chiang Mai. The culinary highlight of Chiang Mai, however, is Northern Thai food. Dishes are served with sticky rice; traditionally diners take a small ball of sticky rice in their right hand and then a morsel of the main dish. The curries, characterized by a lack of coconut milk, are generally spicier.

Somphet Market, on Moon Muang Rd. between Soi 6 and 7, serves banana pancakes (10-15฿), fried noodles (20-40฿), and *kuaytiaw lu chin pla* (fishball noodle soup, 20฿). It's open all day, but food stalls don't get going until after 7pm. In the middle of the night bazaar, the **Galare Food Court** serves a casual dinner with nightly entertainment. In the evening, the road that runs between **Wararot Market** and **Lanyai Market** on the west bank of the Ping River north of Tha Pae Rd. is crammed with food stalls offering Chiang Mai's best. For a serious culinary experience, try a *khantoke* dinner where diners sit on the floor and use their hands to eat rice, two meat dishes, and two vegetable dishes from bowls placed on a *khantoke*, a low tray table. The **Old Chiang Mai Cultural Center,** 185/3 Wualai Rd. (☎275 097), 1.5km south of the old city, offers vegetarian and Muslim versions. State your preferences when calling ahead for the necessary reservation. The 3hr. affair, accompanied by traditional dancing, begins nightly at 7pm (270฿, transportation included).

THE OLD CITY—WITHIN THE MOAT

Huen Phen, 112 Ratchamanka Rd., west of Phra Pokklao Rd. Northern Thai dining at its finest. Locals come here for the spicy *num phrik* (chili paste with meats, 35฿). *Farang* with soft palates may prefer the curries (50-60฿). Banana flower and pork rib curry 50฿. Banana in coconut milk 15฿. Open daily 8am-3pm and 5-10pm. ❷

The Wok, 44 Ratchamanka Rd., east of Ratchaphakhinai Rd. Owners run the Chiang Mai Thai Cookery School. Impeccable "special Northern style food" includes spicy Chiang Mai sausage (60฿) and Thai-style fishcakes (60฿). Open daily 11am-10pm. ❷

Banrai Steak House, Phra Pokklao Rd. Soi 13, around the corner from Thai Airways. This Chiang Mai institution lives up to its boast as "the best steak in town." Steak and chicken barbecued in Thai marinades with veggies and baked potato 99฿. Coconut shake 20฿; sandwich 50฿; fried rice 50฿. Open daily 3pm-midnight. ❸

THA PAE GATE

Aroon Rai, 45 Kotchasarn Rd., south of Tha Pae Rd. and before Loi Kroa Rd. English menu highlights Northern specialties. Curries 40-50฿. Open daily 8:30am-10pm. ❷

da Stefano, 2/1-2 Chang Moi Kao Rd., off Tha Pae Rd. Delicious Italian food for reasonable prices. Bruschetta 30฿. Gnocchi with asparagus pesto and ricotta cheese 120฿. Spaghetti bolognese 90฿; pizza margherita 110฿. Open daily 11am-11pm.

AUM Restaurant, 65 Moon Muang Rd., just south of the Tha Pae Gate. Trendy vegetarian restaurant in a convenient locale. Soups and stir-fries with Thai sauces 40-50฿. Vietnamese spring rolls 40฿. Open daily 7am-2pm and 5-9pm.

Jurusalem Falafel, 35/3 Moon Muang Rd., near AUM Restaurant. Incredible falafel pita with hummus, tahini, and fries; 80฿. Feta salad 50฿. Open Sa-Th 9am-8pm.

NEAR THE PING RIVER

Riverside, 9-11 Charoen Rat Rd. From Nawarat Bridge, take a left on Charoen Rat Rd; it's the 1st building on the left. View from the veranda matched only by the food. Beef salad with mint leaves 60฿. Open daily 10am-1:30am.

Antique House, 71 Charoen Prathet Rd., before the turn-off to Porn Ping Tower Hotel on the opposite side of the road. Fancy the chair you're sitting on? Take it home–most of the decor in this serene, 131-year-old teak house is for sale. *Som tam* (papaya salad with seafood) 60฿. Dishes 40-150฿. Open daily 11am-midnight.

Shere Shiraz, 23-25 Charoen Prathet Rd. Soi 6, off Chang Klan Rd. down the soi south of Porn Ping Tower Hotel. Delicious South Asian restaurant serves Middle Eastern and Thai food, too. Tandoori chicken 200฿; Chicken *tikka* 100฿; Naan 15฿. 10% service charge. Open daily 10am-11pm.

SIGHTS

DOI SUTHEP AND ENVIRONS

Songthaew leave when full for Wat Phra That Doi Suthep from Chang Phuak Gate (6am-5pm, 30฿), and the Chiang Mai Zoo (6am-5pm, 30฿), continuing to Bhubing Palace (50฿) and Doi Pui, a Hmong village (80฿). Motorbikes are an option, but Huay Kaew Rd. is twisty, and the 4.5km dirt road to the Hmong village is rough. Watch for the Kruba Scrivichai Shrine, the monument to the left just before the road goes up the mountain. Kruba Scrivichai was a monk who inspired thousands of volunteers to build the road to Wat Phra That in 1934.

WAT PHRA THAT DOI SUTHEP. If you only have time to visit one of Chiang Mai's 300 wats, Wat Phra That Doi Suthep, one of Thailand's most sacred pilgrimage sights, should be it. *Phra that* refers to the Buddha's relics enshrined here, namely his incus (a teeny anvil-shaped bone in the middle ear). The sweeping survey of the city from the temple's observation deck is sublime. Upon reaching the wat, travelers have the option of ascending either via covered cable-car (round-trip 20฿) or via the 297 steps through the market tourist traps.

DOI SUTHEP PIO NATIONAL PARK. A project started in 1987 by a Chiang Mai University professor has thus far collected 2062 species of plants in the park. **Waterfalls** line Huay Kaew Rd. (Hwy. 1004), which leads up the mountain; keep an eye out for their turn-offs. The most impressive is **Namtok Monthatarn,** which lies 2km off Huay Kaew Rd. Standard national park entry fee of 200฿ applies. The **park headquarters** (☎295 117), 1km past Wat Phra That Doi Suthep, provides trail maps and accommodations. A nature trail from the park headquarters passes **Sai Yok Waterfall** (2km) and **Monthatarn Waterfall** (3km). After you reach Monthatarn Waterfall, follow the 2km access road to Huay Kaew Rd., where *songthaew* will shuttle you to Chiang Mai. **Camping** costs 10฿ per night. Two-person (200฿) and five-person (500฿) tents, and two-person (200฿) and 10-person (2000฿) **cabins** are available to rent. Reserve at least a week in advance.

OTHER SIGHTS. **Bhubing Palace,** 4km up the mountain from the wat, is the Royal Family's residence from roughly January to February. When they're not in residence, the palace and its lavish gardens are open to the public. (Open daily 8:30am-4:30pm; tickets sold until 3:30pm; 50฿.) **Doi Pui,** a Hmong Village 8km past the wat, suffers from tourist overcrowding. Doi Pui's summit (1685m), 7km up the road from Bhubing Palace, makes for a nice hike. The road splits 2km after Bhubing Palace: to the left lies Doi Bhubing Hmong Village; to the right is Doi Pui's summit.

WITHIN THE MOAT

WAT CHIANG MAN. The oldest wat in the city, Chiang Man was built in 1296 by King Mengrai. With its low-sloping roofs and intricate facade, the temple is a classic example of Northern Thai design. The *wiharn* on the right contains two Buddha images: **Phra Setangamani (Crystal Buddha),** thought to have come from Lopburi 1800 years ago, and **Phra Sila (Stone Buddha),** imported from India some 2500 years ago. *(At the north end of Ratchaphakhinai Rd. Open daily 9am-5pm.)*

WAT CHEDI LUANG. Built by King Saen Suang Ma in 1401, the temple walls hold the remains of Chiang Mai's largest *chedi*, which once spiraled 86m toward the sky before being destroyed by an earthquake in 1545. A *naga* staircase adorns the *wiharn*, which houses a **standing gold Buddha** and 32 *Jataka* story panels depicting scenes from the Buddha's life. Legend has it that Wat Chedi Luang housed the Emerald Buddha during its stay in Chiang Mai. *(From Tha Pae Gate head west on Ratchadamnoen Rd. and turn left (south) onto Phra Pokklao Rd. Opposite Yamaha music store.)*

THAILAND

WAT PHRA SINGH. This wat's chief attraction is the bronze **Phra Singh Buddha** in **Phra Wihan Lai Kam,** left and behind the main *wiharn*. The image is the focus of mid-April Songkran festivities when laymen bring sand to the wat to replace what has been dragged out by visitors during the year. *(On the western side of the old city.)*

OUTSIDE THE MOAT

WAT JED YOT. Inspired by the Mahabodhi Temple in Bodhgaya, India, King Tilokaraja built this shrine in 1455. In 1477, the eighth World Buddhist Council met here to revise the *Tripitaka* scriptures of Theravada Buddhism. The two Boddhi trees are said to be descendants of the one Gautama sat under during his enlightenment. *(On the super-highway, 1km from the Huay Kaew Rd. intersection.)*

WAT U-MONG. Another remnant of King Mengrai's building spree, this peaceful forest temple has serene footpaths that lead through the trees. Several sculptures dot the grounds, none more disturbing than the emaciated image of "Our Lord Buddha before realizing that this wasn't the path to enlightenment." *(Off Suthep Rd., on the outskirts of town. Following Suthep out of town, the turn-off is marked by a faded green sign and is the 3rd left after the super-highway. It's 2km farther down the road.)*

WAT SUAN DOK. Also known as Wat Buppharam, Wat Suan Dok was constructed by King Ku Na in 1383. Originally, the grounds served as a pleasure garden for the first kings of Chiang Mai, but later became the site of their graves. Suan Dok hosts **monk chats** (M, W, F 5-7pm); follow the signs to the building in the back. *(On Suthep Rd., after the Hill Tribe Products Promotion Center.)*

CHIANG MAI NATIONAL MUSEUM. This museum features art and artifacts from Northern Thai royalty, commoners, and hill tribes. *(☎221 308. On the super-highway, 500m past Wat Jet Yod if coming from Huay Kaew Rd. Open daily 9am-4pm. 30฿.)*

TRIBAL MUSEUM. The exhibits explore daily life, language derivation, gender roles, and costumes of various hill tribes in Northern Thailand. *(On Chotana Rd. in Ratchamangkhla Park, 4km north of Chang Phuak Gate. Follow the stadium turn-off to the left and* *turn right at the 1st sign for the park; the museum is in the middle of a lake. Tuk-tuk from Chang Phuak Gate 30-50฿. ☎210 872. Open daily 9am-4pm.)*

CHIANG MAI UNIVERSITY. Though architecturally uninspiring, the university's 725 park-like acres provide a pleasant break from the city's urban sprawl. The library is in the center of the grounds, just south of the central roundabout. *(6km northeast of the old city off Huay Kaew Rd.)*

CHIANG MAI ZOO. Everything from black bears to zebras are housed somewhere among the network of roads that are both confusing and exhausting to walk. No need to wait for feeding time—you can buy plates of hippo grub (5-10฿) to feed the animals yourself. In March 2002, the zoo announced plans to borrow two giant pandas from the Chinese government. If the project moves forward, the pandas will arrive in mid-2003. *(☎221 179. On Huay Kaew Rd. at the base of Doi Suthep, after Chiang Mai University. Open daily 8am-6pm. Last ticket sold at 5pm. 30฿, children 5฿, bicycles 1฿, motorbikes 10฿, cars 30฿.)* Next door, the **Huay Kaew Arboretum**'s rare trees provide a shady respite, or an invigorating workout if you opt for the fitness track.

THAILAND

ENTERTAINMENT

The **Galare Food Center,** 89/2 Chang Klan Rd. (☎272 067), features traditional dancing exhibitions, cross-dressing cabaret shows, and Thai boxing on a rotating schedule between two stages. The **Bar Beer Center,** on Moon Muang Rd. at the Tha Pae Gate lets you watch the So Anucha Thai Boxing School Train from 4 to 7pm. Muay Thai boxing is held every night in the same arena at 10:30pm. The Central Department Store has a **Vista Movie Theater** on the fourth floor that shows newly released movies (☎894 415; M-Th 70฿, F-Su 90฿).

SHOPPING

Chiang Mai is handicraft central. **Tha Pae Rd.** is one of the best daytime hunting grounds. The famed **night bazaar** on **Chang Klan Rd.** showcases a variety of antiques, silver jewelry, hill-tribe embroidery, Thai textiles, pottery, designer clothing knock-offs, and pirated DVDs. The **Hill Tribe Handicraft Project,** 1 Moon Muang Rd., in a brick building at the southeastern corner of the old city, sells Karen, Lisu, Akha, Lahu, Yao, and Hmong village quilts, bags, pullovers, and sculptures. (☎274 877. Open M-F 9am-4:30pm.) The better known **Hill Tribe Promotion Center,** 21/17 Suthep Rd., next to Wat Suan Dok, has a greater selection of traditional and innovative crafts. (☎277 743. Embroidered bag 280฿. Karen dress 650฿. Open daily 9am-5pm. MC/V.) Both government-run stores seek to shift tribal economies away from opium cultivation by providing alternate means of income.

NIGHTLIFE

Several wildly popular **bars** and **clubs** lie on the Ping's east bank, just north of Nawarat Bridge. The 30฿ tuk-tuk from Tha Pae Gate is well worth it. *Farang* pubs line **Moon Muang Rd.** Those immediately at Tha Pae Gate attract backpackers. There are very few outright go-go bars in Chiang Mai; "karaoke" bars fill the void.

Riverside, 9-11 Charoen Rat Rd. (☎243 239), has long been the most popular club. Two bands start rocking around 8pm. Screwdriver 110฿. Large Singha 95฿. Corona 140฿. Pitcher of beer 300฿. Open daily 10am-1:30am.

Bubbles, 46-48 Charoen Prathet Rd. (☎270 099), in the Porn Ping Tower Hotel. Chiang Mai's premier disco. Mixed gay and straight crowd. Cover 100฿ includes 1 free drink, F-Sa and holidays 200฿ includes 2 free drinks. Open daily 9pm-2am.

Brasserie, 37 Charoen Rat Rd. (☎241 665). Croonin' tunes on an intimate stage start around 9:30pm. If you're lucky, the owner Took may take a turn himself. Whiskey and soda 90฿. Large Singha 90฿. Open daily 6pm-1:30am.

The Good View, 13 Charoen Rat Rd. (☎302 764), between Riverside and Brasserie. Music is like Riverside's—only louder. Great Japanese restaurant. Large Singha 120฿. Corona 150฿. Kamikaze 150฿. Open daily 6pm-1:45am.

WELCOME TO THE JUNGLE. As of summer 1999, only 39 out of 250 trekking companies met TAT and **Northern Thailand Jungle Club** regulations, which include: stipulations that guides have at least 10 years experience and speak both English and some hill-tribe dialects; that all costs be included in the stated price; that treks have no more than 12 participants; that the company employ men from the villages they visit as porters and charge the prices set by the Northern Thailand Jungle Club. Not every company with a Jungle Club Plaque is actually a member; many have been expelled for having lawsuits brought against them. For updated information on legitimate outfits, contact the tourist police or Sangduen Chailert, the president of the Northern Thailand Jungle Club and manager of Gem Travel, 29 Charoen Prathet Rd. Soi 6 (☎272 855), which also runs treks. *Even with the stipulations set by the Northern Thailand Jungle Club and TAT, some feel that groups of 12 are far too large and have a negative impact on the hill tribes visited.*

THAILAND

TREKKING

Chiang Mai has over 200 companies itching to fulfill trekking prospects. Three-day/two-night treks (4-person min.) run 1500-1800฿ per person to the **Maeteang, Phrao, Sameong, Doi Inthanon,** or **Chiang Dao** areas. Extra days can be negotiated. These five are the only legal trekking areas around Chiang Mai. Maeteang, with its bucolic bamboo rafting, hosts the most trekkers; Chiang Dao gets the fewest because it runs along the sometimes dangerous Myanmar border. Chiang Mai's five areas encompass Akha, Lisu, Karen, Meo, Yao, and Padong villages. Pai has primarily Lisu and Karen villages; Mae Hong Son has almost exclusively Karen ones. During the low season, it's easier for solo travelers to join a trek in Chiang Mai. In Pai or Mae Hong Son, you might need to assemble your own group or you end up paying more. Some Chiang Mai-based companies also run treks to **Mae Hong Son** and **Pai.** If either of these locales tickles your fancy, it's better to hop on a bus and book from there, where a three-day trek will cost 1500-1800฿. Mae Hong Son and Pai see fewer trekkers because Pai's rivers are too low to raft in the hot season and the rivers around Mae Hong Son may become too fast to navigate in the rainy season. Mae Hong Son abuts the troubled border with Myanmar. Treks run by **Libra Guest House** and **Eagle House,** 16 Chang Mai Gao Rd. Soi 3 (☎874 126), near Somphet market, opposite the old city, consistently receive rave reviews. **Chiang Mai Green Tour and Trekking,** 29/31 Chiang Mai-Lamphun Rd. (☎247 374), donates a portion of its proceeds to a conservation program and offers nature and bird-watching tours, as well as the more conventional "ethno-tourism" variety.

DAYTRIPS FROM CHIANG MAI

LAMPHUN

Buses to Lamphun leave from the Chang Phuak Station in Chiang Mai and from just south of the footbridge near Wararot Market (1hr., every 10min. 6:20am-6pm, 12฿). Get off as the bus passes through the walled city; the Lamphun bus station is 1km outside of town.

Electric blue songthaew *leave from Chiang Mai-Lamphun Rd., south of TAT (every 20min. 5am-6pm, 15฿). Buses back to Chiang Mai depart from the front of the museum (every 30min. 6am-6pm).*

Tiny Lamphun, 26km southeast of Chiang Mai, offers a handful of worthwhile sights. The town's most exciting event of the year is the **Lum-Yai Festival** in July or August, celebrating the *lum-yai* (longan) season. **Wat Phra That Haribhunchai** is considered one of the seven most sacred temples in Thailand. The wat, Lamphun's chief landmark, sits on Inthayongyot Rd. in the town center; it's the first temple on the left after you enter the walled city from Chiang Mai. When coming from Inthayongyot Rd., you should enter from the back. There is a loosely enforced 20฿ entrance fee. A block away is the **Haribhunchai National Museum,** with a small collection of Buddhas, bells, and other bric-a-brac. With your back to the wat on Inthayongyot Rd., it's to the left. (☎511 186. Open W-Su 9am-4pm. 30฿.) With your back to Chiang Mai take a right directly after the museum onto Mukda Rd; when the road becomes Chamma Davi Rd. continue 2km to reach **Wat Chamma Davi.** The stepped-pyramid *chedi* once had a gold coating, but thieves broke it off, giving the temple its other name, Wat Ku Kat ("pagoda without top"). **Wat Phra Phut Ta Bat Tak Pah,** 20km south of Lamphun, has views that rival Doi Suthep's. Before you reach the 472-step stairway, you'll pass some of the Buddha's footprints. To get to the wat, board a light blue *songthaew* to Pasang (5฿) two blocks south of the museum, just off Inthayongyot Rd. on the left (electric blue *songthaew* to Chiang Mai also wait here). After everyone else gets off, the driver can take you the 9km to the wat for 15฿ more.

THAILAND

DOI INTHANON NATIONAL PARK

Buses from Chiang Mai leave from the Chang Phuak Station (1¼hr., every 20min. 6:30am-6pm, 23฿). Yellow songthaew *leave from Chiang Mai Gate in the morning when full (20฿). The turn-off to Hwy. 1009 and Doi Inthanon National Park lies before Chom Thong off Hwy. 108. From Chom Thong,* songthaew *head to the national park and Mae Klang Waterfall, an 8km ride up to Hwy. 1009 to the turn-off.* Songthaew *cost 10-20฿ and leave when full—which may take a while—6am-5pm. All inquiries ☎311 608. Office open M-F 8:30am-4:30pm. Park and facilities open daily 6am-6pm. Park admission 200฿. Motorbikes 20฿.*

The 188km route from Chiang Mai to Mae Sariang along Hwy. 108 is ruggedly scenic. The drama picks up 58km away near **Chom Thong,** the point of access to Doi Inthanon National Park, home to one of Thailand's highest peaks. The Thanontongchai Range, capped by Doi Inthanon (2565m), is actually a distant part of the Himalaya Mountain Range. A trip to the **summit** of Doi Inthanon costs 70฿, but the wait is bound to be long, unless you want to charter the whole truck (500฿). A summit-bound *songthaew* may leave the Mae Klang Waterfall area every 2hr.; a motorbike hired in Chiang Mai can make the trip infinitely easier. **Mae Klang Waterfall,** the park's largest waterfall, is the first stop for most visitors. It's possible to pay the national park entrance fee here, too. The 1km path above the falls leads to the Visitors Center. To get to a branch of the **Monk's College of Kamphaeng San** (Wittayalai Sung Kamphaeng San), cross the bridge just above the eating spots and take a left; after 1km there's a driveway entrance to the grounds. Just before the Visitors Center on Hwy. 1009, a 1km path leads to **Borichinda Cave.** Guided tours can be arranged at the Visitors Center, which also has information and exhibits on local animal life, notably the nocturnal pangolin. **Wachiratan Waterfall** is the next stop at the 20.8km mark. At the 31km mark is the elegant **Siriphum Waterfall.** The lane leading to it winds through the park's **Royal Project,** where hill tribes are encouraged to replace opium production with strawberry and flower cultivation. The road disappears at Doi Inthanon's summit (usually obscured by mist). The cool season (Oct.-Feb.) is the best time to visit. The average park temperature then is 12°C (50°F)—bring raingear and warm clothing, especially if you intend to hike. The park has **guest houses** ❹ (500-2000฿), **camping** ❶ (30฿), **tents** ❶ (70฿), and a **restaurant** at park headquarters just past Siriphum Falls.

MAE SARIANG ☎053

Mae Sariang, a quiet retreat from the cities, is a base for adventurers. Cross-border teak, rice, and heroin trade has fueled a building boom, and the town has prepared for an overflow of tourism from Mae Hong Son. Charming countryside, the alluring border, and superb budget accommodations await those willing to leave the beaten path connecting Chiang Mai, Pai, and Mae Hong Son.

TRANSPORTATION. The **bus terminal** (☎681 347) is on Mae Sariang Rd., 100m north of the traffic light, opposite the gas station. Buses run to **Chiang Mai** (4hr., 5 per day 7am-1am, 80฿; A/C 10:30am, 3pm, 1am, 140฿) and **Mae Hong Son** (4hr., 4 per day, 80฿; A/C 10:30am, 3pm, 1am, 140฿). **Yan Yont Tours** (☎681 532) offers VIP buses from the gas station across the street to **Bangkok** (12hr.; 4, 7pm; 420฿). **Songthaew** head to **Mae Sot** (6hr., every hr. 7:30am-12:30pm, 150฿). **Motorcross-bike rental** is just south of the gas station (200-380฿ per day).

ORIENTATION AND PRACTICAL INFORMATION. Mae Sariang is bordered by the **Yuam River** to the west and **Hwy. 108** to the east. The main roads form an "H." **Langpanit Rd.** runs parallel to the river. **Mae Sariang Rd.** is one block east, parallel to Langpanit Rd. Perpendicular **Wiangmai Rd.** stretches from the river to the highway and intersects Mae Sariang Rd. at the traffic light in the town center. **Saripol Rd.,** site of the miniature morning **market,** connects Mae Sariang and Langpanit Rd. one block south of the traffic light. A second block south of the traffic light, **Waisuksa Rd.** heads west out of town to Mae Sam Laep.

Services in Mae Sariang include: **immigration office,** 200m north of the hospital on Hwy. 108, for visa extensions (☎681 339; open M-F 8:30am-4:30pm); **Thai Farmers Bank,** on Wiangmai Rd. west of Mae Sariang Rd., has an **ATM** (Cirrus/MC/PLUS/V) and **exchanges currency** (open M-F 8:30am-3:30pm); **police** (☎681 308), on Mae Sariang Rd. 150m south of the traffic light; **government hospital** (☎681 027; **emergency** ☎191), on Hwy. 108, 200m toward Mae Hong Son from the intersection with Wiangmai Rd.; **Internet access** on Wiangmai Rd. east of the traffic light (open daily 9am-10pm; 20฿ per hr.); and **post office,** 31 Wiangmai Rd., which has an **international phone**/fax but no IDD (☎681 356; open M-F 8:30am-4:30pm, Sa-Su 9am-noon). **Postal code:** 58110.

ACCOMMODATIONS AND FOOD. For a resplendent setting, try the **Riverside Guest House** ❶, 85 Langpanit Rd., 300m north of Wiangmai Rd. From the bus station, turn right onto Mae Sariang Rd., left at the first intersection, and left again on Langpanit Rd.; it's 100m down on the right. All rooms overlook the river. (☎681 188. Check-out 11:30am. Bicycles 50฿. Motorbike 200฿. Singles with bath 80-100฿; doubles 100-180฿.) The adjacent **Riverhouse** ❹ and **Northwest Guesthouse** ❶ have an excellent range of quality lodgings. Riverhouse has the best rooms in town, with a price tag to match. (☎621 201. Internet 40฿ per hr. Rooms with fan 400฿, with A/C 600฿.) Northwest sacrifices the view for exceptionally clean rooms and modern fixtures in a cozy saloon setting. (Singles with fan 100฿; doubles 200฿).

Of all the open-air eateries along Wiangmai Rd., the popular **Renu Restaurant** ❷, 174/2 Wiangmai Rd., 50m toward the highway from the traffic light, probably has the best eats. (Most entrees 40-50฿. Open daily 6am-midnight.) The food is cheap and tasty at the **stands** ❶ that set up on Mae Sariang Rd. around the bus station in the evening. Also, many guest houses have their own restaurants.

DAYTRIPS FROM MAE SARIANG. The country around town, dotted with hill-tribe villages, is perfect for walks or bike rides. The 6km to **Pha Ma Lo** is particularly scenic. This affluent White Karen village has a charming setting and a fine temple. On the other side of town, on the road to Mae Sot, the **Big Buddha** is an intriguing sight. Those curious enough to make the trip up the hill are rewarded with a magnificent panorama of Mae Sariang. Follow Wiangmai Rd. out of town. Just before the highway, turn right onto the road to Mae Sot. It's impossible to miss the 10m Buddha. Riverhouse (see **Accommodations and Food,** above) posts a map of suggested trails and has copies at reception. Riverhouse also organizes day or overnight trekking and rafting (4-person minimum, 1500฿ per day). To explore **Mae Sam Laep,** 46km west of Mae Sariang and across the river from Myanmar., take a *songthaew*, which leaves Mae Sariang from just east of the bridge. From the center of town, walk south on Langpanit Rd. until it ends, turn right, and the bridge is 100m down. The first *songthaew* (1½hr., 50฿) leaves around 7am; others depart when full. The last comes back in the afternoon—ask your driver for a return time. If going by motorbike, you'll need a motorcross bike in the wet season—roads can be muddy and there are several creek crossings.

MAE HONG SON ☎053

The *songthaew* driver with the "Keep Mae Hong Son Small" sticker across his windshield is fighting a losing battle. Earlier this century, Mae Hong Son was used as a place of exile for criminals, and, if recent reports of opium smuggling are correct, shady dealings persist in the area. Such sinister border activities, coupled with the most picturesque scenery in Northern Thailand, have piqued the curiosity of travelers, and visitors now flock to the provincial capital.

TRANSPORTATION

Flights: Mae Hong Son Airport (☎612 057), on Nivit Pisan Rd. Turn left at the hospital at the east end of Singhanat Bumrung Rd. To **Chiang Mai** (35min.; 12:45, 3:10, 5:30pm; 870฿). **Thai Airways,** 71 Singhanat Bumrung Rd. (☎612 220). Open M-F 8am-5pm. **Air Andaman** (☎620 451), with offices at the airport, flies to **Bangkok** (1¾hr., 4 per week, 2055฿).

Buses: 33/3 Khunlum Praphat Rd. (☎611 318). To: **Chiang Mai** (7½-8½hr.; 11 per day 6am-9pm; 105-145฿, with A/C 147-261฿) via **Mae Sariang** (4hr., 4 per day 6am-9pm, 78฿; 10:30am and 9pm, with A/C 140฿) or **Pai** (3½hr., 4 per day 7am-12:30pm, 53฿; 8am, with A/C 74฿); **Pai** (4pm) via **Soppong** (2hr., 5 per day 7am-4pm, 33฿). **Yan Yont Tour** (☎611 514), south of town next to the Shell station, has an A/C bus to **Bangkok** (17hr., 3pm, 569฿).

Local Transportation: *Songthaew* leave for points north of Mae Hong Son from the day market on Punit Watana Rd. Motorcycle taxis and tuk-tuks wait at the bus station and airport (10-40฿).

Rentals: Numerous places around the traffic light rent **motorcycles. Highway,** 67/2 Khunlum Praphat Rd. (☎611 620), opposite Thai Farmers Bank, south of the lights, has "as new" motorcycles with good service facilities. 150฿ per day; passport or 500฿ and passport photocopy required for deposit. Open daily 8am-7pm. **TN tour,** 107/17 Khunlum Praphat Rd. (☎620 059), rents Suzuki 4WD.

ORIENTATION AND PRACTICAL INFORMATION

Buses stop on **Khunlum Praphat Rd.,** which is home to restaurants, trekking outfitters, and banks and runs north-south through the center of town. As you turn left out of the bus station and head south, the second intersection (with the traffic light) is **Singhanat Bumrung Rd.** Another block south, guest houses dot **Udom Chao Nithet Rd.,** which borders the lake glistening with reflections of wats and *chedis*.

Tourist Office: TAT (☎612 982), on Khunlum Praphat Rd., 200m south of traffic light, opposite post office. Open M-F 8:30am-noon and 1-4:30pm; Nov.-Jan. open daily.

Immigration Office: 11 Khunlum Praphat Rd. (☎612 106), 1km north of the bus station. 10- or 30-day visa extensions depending on visa type. 2 photos and 2 copies of passport, departure card, and visa required. 500฿. Open daily 8:30am-4:30pm.

Currency Exchange: Bangkok Bank, 68 Khunlum Praphat Rd. (☎611 275). Open M-F 8:30am-3:30pm. **24hr. ATM** (AmEx/MC/PLUS/V).

Markets: The **day market** is on Panit Watana Rd. next to Wat Hua Viang. The overpriced **night market** (Chang Kham Bazaar) on Khunlum Praphat Rd. lacks selection.

Emergency: ☎191. **Ambulance:** ☎1669. **Tourist Police (Bangkok):** ☎1155.

Police: ☎611 239. 1km south of the post office on the road to Mae Sariang.

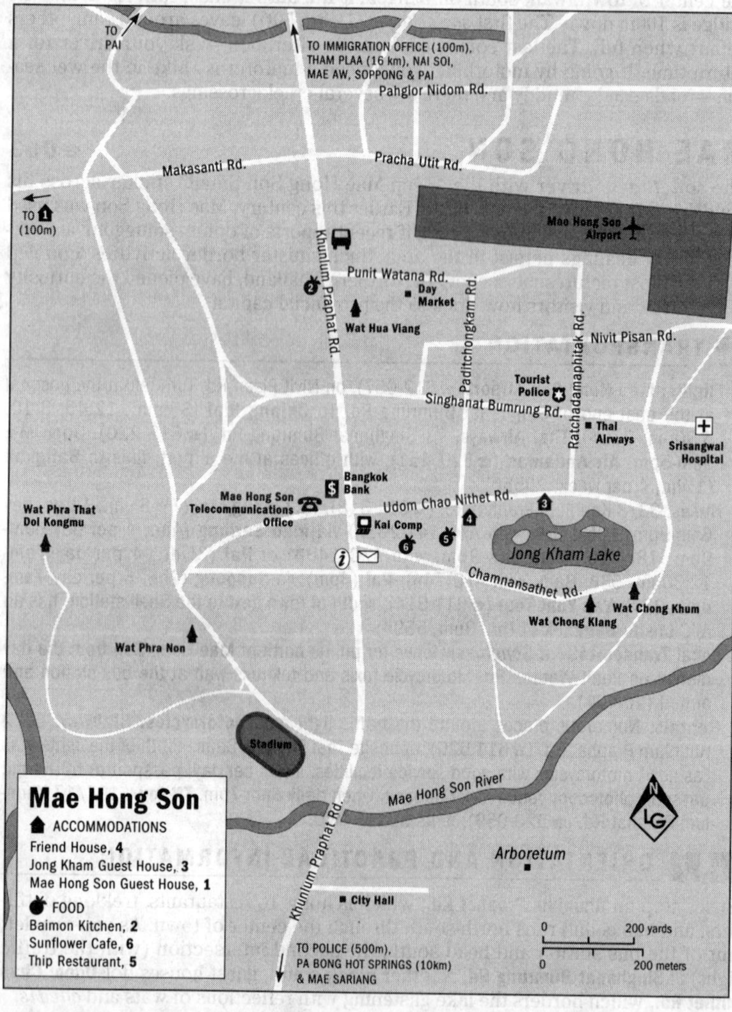

THE PLIGHT OF THE PADONG A favorite subject of Thailand's postcard photographers is the Padong tribe's "long-neck women" or "giraffe women." At the age of five, girls in this subset of the Karen hill tribe are fitted for their first heavy brass neck ring. By adulthood, the rings have compressed the woman's collarbone and ribcage so much that her neck appears stretched. Until recently, the bizarre custom had been dying out, but when the Karen began to flee Myanmar (see **Thai-Burmese Relations,** p. 676), enterprising Thais seized the Padong as a potential gold mine. The Padong "villages" in Mae Hong Son Province (Nai Soi primary among them) are creations of these entrepreneurs. There is no "authentic" village life in Nai Soi—just a refugee-camp-turned-tourist-trap.

Tourist Police (local): ☎611 812. At the corner of Rachadamphitak and Singhanat Bumrung Rd. Helpful. Maps. Open daily 9am-9pm. **24hr. emergency.**

Pharmacy: 37 Singhanat Bumrung Rd. (☎611 380). Open daily 7am-8pm.

Medical Services: Srisangwal Hospital (☎611 378), at the end of Singhanat Bamrung Rd. English-speaking doctors. **24hr. emergency care.**

Telephones: Mae Hong Son Telecommunications Office, 26 Udom Chao Nithet Rd. (☎611 711), just west of Khunlum Praphat Rd. **International phones**/fax (cash, collect, or HCD). **Lenso** phone at post office. CATNET. Open M-F 8:30am-4:30pm.

Internet Access: Cheapest (and slowest) is the CATNET Internet at the Telecommunications Office (11฿ per hr.; buy 100฿ card). Several places congregate around the traffic light. **Kai Comp,** just north of the post office. 1฿ per min. Open daily 8am-11pm.

Post Office: Mae Hong Son Post Office, 79 Khunlum Praphat Rd. (☎611 223). Open M-F 8:30am-4:30pm, Sa-Su 9am-noon. **Postal code:** 58000.

ACCOMMODATIONS

Mae Hong Son Guest House, 295 Mucksanti Rd. (☎612 510). Turn right out of the bus station and left on the 1st street; it's 500m away. Verdant garden and sleepy vibe. Doubles 150฿, with bath 300-350฿; private bungalows with bath 500฿. ❷

Friend House, 20 Paditchongkam Rd. (☎620 119). Turn left out of the bus station, 1st left after the traffic light, and then the 1st right; it's just off the intersection with Udom Chao Nithet Rd. Cleanest of the lakeside joints. Upstairs rooms have view of the lake. Laundry 30฿ per kg. Rooms 100฿, with shower 250฿. ❶

Jong Kam Guest House, 7 Udom Chao Nithet Rd. north of the lake. Turn left from the bus station, and take the 1st left after the traffic light; it's 250m down on the right. Breakfast. Laundry 30฿ per kg. 3-day/2-night walking treks to Karen village 600฿ per day. Clean rooms in main building with fans 100฿; bungalows 100฿, with bath 150฿. ❶

FOOD

Most restaurants now offer Western specialties, but the best options are still the traditional Northern Thai dishes. **Baimon Kitchen ❶,** on Khunlum Praphat Rd., opposite and south of the bus station, has an English menu. (Many different tofu dishes 10-40฿; coconut curry 20฿. Open daily 7am-11pm.) Stop by the **Sunflower Cafe ❶,** Soi 3 Khunlum Praphat Rd. near the lake, at 8am for oven-fresh bread and delicious breakfasts. To get there, face the post office, and follow the road's left fork 100m; it's on the left. The cafe also offers treks and information on the region. (Cheesecake 25฿. Papaya shake 15฿. Open daily 7:30am-11:30pm.) **Thip Restaurant ❷,** 23/11 Paditchongkam Rd., has a great view. Crispy *hoi jou* (Chinese pork sausage) 60฿; chicken with oyster sauce 30฿. Open daily 9am-10pm.)

SIGHTS AND HIKING

Wat Phra That Doi Kongmu, 474m above town, has a panoramic view of the city. Built in 1874, this Shan-influenced temple is Mae Hong Son's most important wat. Head west on Udom Chao Nithet Rd. and turn left at the end. On the right is Wat Phra Non, and the road to the hilltop vista of Wat Phra That Doi Kongmu is the right before the stadium. Nearby **Wat Phra Non** houses a 12m Burmese-style reclining Buddha and the ashes of Mae Hong Son's kings. Get there by turning left at the end of Udom Chao Nithet Rd. A jogging track circles **Jong Kham Lake.** Feed the fish (fish food 5฿) or visit the lake's south side to see the two famed wats. **Wat Chong Klang** is on the right, with Buddhist glass paintings and wooden dolls brought from Myanmar over 100 years ago. (Open daily 8am-6pm.) Next door, **Wat Chong Khum,** built in 1827, shines with gold-leafed pillars.

Mae Hong Son has some of the best trekking in Thailand. The surrounding hills support villages of Lisu, Lahu, Hmong, and Karen tribes, as well as Shan and Kuo Min Tang (KMT) zones. TAT can provide you with a list of the 28 licensed travel agents in Mae Hong Son. For those heading to the sights alone, the tourist police have the best free regional map. More detail is found in the regional map produced by the **Pai Association for Travelers** (available at some restaurants and trekking agencies; 10฿). **Sunflower Tours,** in Sunflower Cafe (see **Food,** above), offers consistently good butterfly- and bird-watching tours as well as treks featuring elephants, bamboo rafts, and visits to hill tribes. Owner La leads most outings and can tailor trips to your interests (1- to 5-day trips 600฿ per person per day; 4-person min.).

DAYTRIPS FROM MAE HONG SON

Border politics dominate Mae Hong Son Province. The Burmese Red Karen state is across the border and farther north lie various rebel camps. Trips to Myanmar from here are illegal and dangerous. Renting a motorcycle (150฿), rather than using the fickle or sometimes nonexistent public transportation, provides access to Karen, Lisu, Hmong, and Lahu hill tribe villages, Shan towns, and KMT camps.

NAI SOI (LONG-NECKED KAREN VILLAGE). Travelers can't make it as far as Mae Hong Son Province without hearing of these Burmese refugees. The women wear metal rings that crush their rib cages and collar bones down (see **The Plight of the Padong,** p. 763). Many find the zoo-like atmosphere disturbing, however, with vendors selling postcards of the women or wood carvings of their long necks. *(Take a songthaew from Mae Hong Son's day market to the Shan town (leaves when full, 30฿); then walk or hail another for the 3km to Nai Soi. Returning can be tricky; a motorbike is your best bet (250฿). For those with their own transportation, the turn-off is at the 199km road marker on the highway to Pai. Turn left at this point, and take the first left 500m down. There is a sign at this second turn-off, but it is obscured. Entrance 250฿. Open daily 6am-6pm.)*

THAM PLAA AND HIGHWAY 1095 TO PAI. Some of Thailand's most stunning, jagged scenery graces Hwy. 1095 between Mae Hong Son and Pai (111km). About 35km from Mae Hong Son and 20km before the turn-off to **Mae La Na** are two lone peaks. The **Sunnyata Forest Monastery** is nearby. Shan and Hmong villages, a waterfall, mountain panoramas, and the KMT village of **Mae Aw** are situated on a mountaintop right on the Burmese border. You need a motorbike to make it; during the muddy rainy season it's better to have a four-wheel-drive. The Fish Cave—**Tham Plaa**—waits next to the road, 16km north of Mae Hong Son. The Shan villagers who look after the fish never catch them, believing that the spirit of the mountain guards the fish from harm. As a result of their protected status, the fish grow quite large (many more than 80cm long).

Recently, a scuba-outfitted Australian camera crew penetrated the pool's depths and discovered a waterfall and an open-air cavern deep below the surface. Local lore has it that Japanese soldiers retreating from Myanmar buried treasure in such caverns. Visitors, however, are relegated to the circuitous nature trail that passes by the aquatic peep holes. *(Hop on a Pai-bound bus and signal the driver to stop at the cave. 10฿.)*

SOPPONG. If you've ever wanted to jump off a bus and frolic through the countryside (to, perhaps, a huge cave and underground river), Soppong's the place to live out your dreams. New Soppong skirts the highway where buses stop; Old Soppong dozes along the road curving from the bus station 500m toward Pai. This road follows the 9km route to the **Tham Lod** (Lod Cave). Prehistoric remains have been found among its stalagmites and stalactites. Visitors must hire a guide at the entrance to take them through the three gigantic underground caverns (100฿ for 1-4 people). A boatman will take you down the cave's river for another 100฿ per four-person raft. The best time to visit the cave is about 1½hr. before sunset. That way, the tour will conclude with the aerial display put on by swifts as they return to the cave. To get to the cave, catch a motorbike taxi (60฿) or rent your own transportation. Travelers intending only to see Tham Lod may find that the serene environs and provide an incentive to stay longer. **Jungle Guest House ❶,** 300m toward Mae Hong Son from the bus stop, has a range of rooms along with a fabulous restaurant. They also offer a **jeep** service. (☎617 099. Jeep seating five 350฿ round-trip. Motorcycle rental 150฿ per day. 10-bed dorms 70฿; rooms 80-100฿; bungalows with bath and hot shower 180-200฿.) The overlooked **Lang River Guest House ❶,** to the left before Tham Lod's parking lot, is a backpacker's dream with dorms for 70฿ and bungalows for 100-150฿. *(Buses stop in Soppong on their way between Mae Hong Son (2hr., 4 per day 10am-5:30pm, 30฿) and Pai (1½hr., 4 per day 9am-6pm, 30฿). The last bus to Chiang Mai is at 2:30pm.)*

THAILAND

PAI ☎053

An oasis halfway between Chiang Mai and Mae Hong Son, Pai attracts both artists and pilgrims who draw inspiration from the astoundingly picturesque town and surrounding area. Behind the scenes, however, a clandestine heroin and opium culture has come to the attention of local authorities, who are starting to clamp down strongly on nefarious activities in the area.

TRANSPORTATION

Buses: The **station** is on Chaisongkhram Rd. To **Chiang Mai** (4hr.; 8:30, 10:30am, noon, 2, 4pm; 60฿) and **Mae Hong Son** (4hr.; 8:30, 10:30am, noon, 2, 4pm; 48฿, with A/C 67฿) via **Soppong** (2hr., 35฿). To go to **Tha Ton,** take a Chiang Mai-bound bus to **Mae Malai** (3hr., 55฿), then take a bus to **Fang** (2½hr., every 30min. 6:30am-6pm, 45฿). Some buses continue to Tha Ton; otherwise, yellow *songthaew* make the trip from the main road in Fang (45min., 20฿). To make Tha Ton by evening, it is necessary to take the noon bus (at the latest).

Motorcycle Taxis: At the corner of Chaisongkhram and Rungsiyanon at Ban Pai. Shuttle people around town and the surrounding area. Hot springs 50฿; waterfall 60฿; Tham Lot (2hr., 300฿). Possible to arrange drop-off and pick-up.

Rentals: Many shops along Chaisongkhram Rd. rent **motorcycles.** 150฿ per day. **Aya Service,** 21 Chaisongkhram Rd. (☎699 940). Turn left out the bus station—it's 50m down. Motorcycles with insurance 180฿ per day. Open daily 7:30am-10:30pm.

ORIENTATION AND PRACTICAL INFORMATION

Pai is 136km northwest of Chiang Mai and 111km northeast of Mae Hong Son. **Hwy. 1095** cuts through town, but most traffic is channeled away from the town center, skirting the western border formed by **Ketkelang Rd.** The bus station is in the middle of the town's northern border, **Chaisongkhram Rd.,** also home to numerous Internet cafes and motorbike rental shops. As you leave the bus station, the town's main street, **Rungsiyanon Rd.,** full of restaurants and trekking outfitters, lies to your right. The **Pai River,** 400m to the left, forms the town's eastern border.

Currency Exchange: Krung Thai Bank, 90 Rungsiyanon Rd. (☎699 028). Open M-F 8:30am-3:30pm. **24hr. ATM** (Cirrus/MC/PLUS/V).

Markets: The **night market** sets up at 3pm on Rungsiyanon Rd. between Chaisongkhram and Ratchadamrong Rd.

Emergency: ☎191. **Ambulance:** ☎699 031. **Tourist Police (Bangkok):** ☎1155.

Police: 72 Rungsiyanon Rd. (☎699 217), 500m south of the bus station.

Tourist Police (local): On the road to Chiang Mai, after Ketkelang and Rungsiyanon Rd. merge.

Medical Services: Pai Hospital (☎699 031), on Chaisongkhram Rd. 500m west of the bus station. English spoken. **Open 24hr.**

Pharmacy: On Rungsiyanon Rd. between Chez Swan and the police. Open daily 6am-9pm.

Internet Access: Avu Internet Cafe, at the corner of Rungsiyanon Rd. and Ratchadamrong Rd. 1฿ per min. CATNET Internet access (11฿ per hr.) at the post office.

Post Office: 76 Ketkelang Rd. (☎699 208), on Ketkelang Rd. **International phone.** *Poste Restante.* Open M-F 8:30am-4:30pm, Sa 9am-noon. **Postal code:** 58130.

ACCOMMODATIONS

Pai Radise, 98 Moo 1 Ban Mae Yen (☎098 387 521). Turn left 50m after the 1st bridge on the way to the hot springs. The best-value bungalows in Pai are 200m on the right. Overlooks the Pai Valley rice fields and up into the hills. Rooms are new and exceptionally clean, with large baths and big, comfy beds. Best location, construction, and price combo around. Solid brick and wood lodgings 350฿. ❹

Sun Hut (☎699 730), in the small town of Mae Yen. Follow the road to the hot springs. Once you cross the 2nd bridge, Sun Hut is on your right. Teak and bamboo huts set in a beautiful garden with pond. Basic hut with towels, mosquito nets, and fan 100-120฿; average hut 120-150฿; deluxe Jupiter hut with bath 300-400฿. ❶

Blue Mountain Guest Cottages, 174 Chaisongkhram Rd. (☎699 282), 1km to the right of the bus station past the hospital. With two cats named Ham and Bacon, a dog named Mr. Falang, and a white gibbon monkey named Ooh Ooh who exchanges hugs for fruit, you're sure to make at least one new friend. Live music 10pm-2am. Rustic bungalows with mosquito nets 50-100฿; VIP rooms with bath and fan 150-200฿. ❶

FOOD

Hip cafes are in the center of town. Don't miss the baked goodies at **Homemade Muslim ❶,** at the southern end of the night market. (Delicious coconut cream pie 15฿. Chocolate croissants 10฿. Chicken potato pie 15฿.) **Chez Swan ❷,** 13 Rungsiyanon Rd., just south of the Ratchadamrong Rd. intersection, is an authentic French transplant. (Quiche Lorraine 60฿; *patate au gratin dauphinois* 55฿. Open daily 8am-late.) **All About Coffee ❷,** 100 Chaisongkhram Rd., delivers a caffeine kick along with breakfast or sandwiches throughout the day. (Pai coffee 35฿; banana coffee shake 45฿. Open daily 9am-5:30pm.) **Own Home Restaurant ❷,** 9/4 Ratchadamrong Rd., east of the intersection with Rungsiyanon Rd., serves a large variety of vegetarian options. The smoky-flavored aubergine salad (40฿) is particularly tasty. (Open daily 7:30am-11pm; kitchen closes 10pm.)

SIGHTS

Wat Phra That Mae Yen has sublime views. To get there, head east on Ratchadamrong Rd. and cross the Pai River; the 360 steps to the wat are 1km up. Some may choose to take the easier paved route. Continuing past the Mae Yen River leads to the **hot springs,** 7km from town. For a more regal experience, the local resorts (2km before the hot springs) pump the spring water to their grounds. **Natural Hot Spring Bungalows** has individual baths (40฿) or nearby **Thapai Spa Camping** has larger pools for lazing (50฿). It's possible to pitch a tent for free at the hot springs, or for 100฿ at either of the resorts. About 2km before the hot springs (5km from town), there are three **elephant schools.**

TREKKING AND RAFTING

Trekking outfitters in Pai are diversifying. Everything from hiking to rafting to elephant rides (300฿ per hr.) is available, so shop around to see what suits you. **Back Trax,** 27 Chaisongkhram Rd., leads groups around the Pai and Soppong areas, giving 15-20% of their proceeds to the villages. Owner Chao, a member of the Lahu tribe, speaks excellent English. (3 days 1500฿. Open daily 8am-8pm.) **Duang Trekking,** at Duang Guest House across the road from the bus station, offers treks that visit Karen, Lisu, and Shan villages along with several waterfalls. (2-day treks 1000฿, with rafting and elephants 1450฿; 3-day treks 1500฿, with rafting 1750฿.) Bamboo rafting is usually only possible from November to May, since Pai's rivers get rather wild in the rainy season. Whitewater rafting in rubber boats fills the void in the wet season, though by February, the water level drops too low for whitewater rafting. **Thai Adventure Rafting** (☎699 111), next to Chez Swan (see **Food,** above), and **Northern Green** (☎699 385), on Chaisongkhram Rd. next to Aya Service (see **Rentals,** p. 765), have similar adventures down the Khong and Pai rivers. By the time you've finished paddling, you're in Mae Hong Son. (2-day trips stay overnight in established campsites 1800฿; 4-person minimum.)

ENTERTAINMENT

Pai is the place to pamper your soul—**Pai Dhamma and Herbal House,** on Rungsiyanon Rd. opposite the police, has Thai massage and aromatherapy. Three- to ten-day meditation and massage courses are available, while the "Detox" course is best for those coming off Ko Phangan. (☎699 964. Meditation course with detox 1500฿ per day, includes accommodation; 3-day massage course 1000฿ per day. Note that it plans to move in the next year, so check with a tourist agency if it's not on Rungsiyanon Rd.) The town boogies nightly to blues at the renowned **BeBop,** on Chaisongkhram Rd. between Ketkelang and Rungsiyanon Rd. Show up by 9:30pm to get a seat. (Open daily 6:30pm-12:30am. Music 9-10:30pm.) **Golden Triangle Bar and Restaurant,** at the eastern end of Chaisongkhram Rd., is a more relaxed option. (Open daily 4pm-midnight.) The "free-spirited" **Tea-Room** next to BeBop has movies at 7pm. Every kind of tea except Lipton is available. The sign on the door says it all: "Open When We're Happy."

THA TON

☎053

The scenic boat trip down the Kok River to Chiang Rai is reason enough to visit idyllic and sleepy Tha Ton. Arriving from Chiang Mai before noon allows travelers to soak up the scenery over lunch, ascend the surrounding hills, and stroll among life-size Chinese, Hindu, and Buddhist figures at Wat Tha Ton—all before hopping onto a chartered longtailed boat the next morning.

TRANSPORTATION. **Rte. 1089,** which continues across the river to Mae Chan 62km away, is Tha Ton's main road. Mae Salong is 43km away, Chang Rai 92km away, and Chiang Mai 175km away. Most **buses** leave from the north side of the bridge. Those to **Chiang Mai** (4hr., 6 per day 6:25am-2:25pm, 70฿) depart from a lot 100m north of the river. Buses to **Mae Sai** (2½hr., 3pm, 35฿) stop near the police box just beyond the bus lot. For **Chiang Rai,** take a Mae Sai-bound bus to **Mae Chan** (1hr., 20฿) and wait for a connecting bus (45min., 10-15฿). Yellow *songthaew* head to **Fang** (45min., every 10min. 5:30am-3pm, 20฿) and to **Mae Salong** (1½hr., every 30min. 7:30am-4pm, 50฿) from a lot north of the bus station and around the bend. **Longtailed boats** leave from the pier on the river's south bank for **Chiang Rai** (4hr., 12:30pm, 250฿; the boat stops for 20min. in Ruammit). If you're coming from Chiang Mai, take the 6:25 or 8am bus (3-5hr., 200฿) to reach Tha Ton in time to catch the longtailed boats to Chiang Rai. Reserve a seat at the **Tha Ton Boat Office** by the pier. (☎459 427. Open daily 9am-3pm.) Chartered private craft (seats 6-8 depending on season, 1600฿ including guide) won't leave after 3pm, as the ride is dangerous in the dark.

PRACTICAL INFORMATION. There are no banks or exchange booths in Tha Ton, but **Tha Ton Tour** at Chankasem Guest House near the pier might exchange small sums. The nearest **ATM** is in Fang. A **morning market** sets up 200m south of the bridge; the fruit stand stays open all day. (Open daily 5:30-7:30am.) The closest **hospital** (☎459 036) is in Mae Ai, 7km to the south. In an emergency, call your guest house or the **Bangkok tourist police** (☎1155) for transportation. A **tourist police box** is just before the pier. (Open M-F 8:30am-4:30pm; 24hr. emergency.) There is a **pharmacy** next to the morning market. (Open daily 8am-8pm.) **ABC Amsterdam Restaurant,** next to the bus station, has **overseas calls** (60฿ per min.). **Tha Ton Internet** (1฿ per min.) is across the street from the pier on the south side of the bridge. A **post office** sits on the main road opposite the entrance to Wat Tha Ton. (Basic postcard and letter service only. Open M-F 8am-noon and 1-4:30pm.) **Postal code:** 50280.

ACCOMMODATIONS AND FOOD. Affordable **Thip's Travelers House ❶,** just south of the bridge on the main road, is run by the lovable English-speaking Mrs. Thip. (☎459 312. Restaurant open daily 7am-9pm. Laundry. Bicycle rental 80฿ per day. Singles with private cold showers 100฿; doubles 150฿.) **Apple Guest House ❶** has bungalows in two locations. To reach the more affordable ones, head south from the bridge and take the second left; it's on the right 150m down. (☎459 315. Singles 100฿; bungalows 150฿, with hot shower 250฿; triples 200฿.) **Tha Ton Garden Riverside ❸** has fabulous bungalows with Western toilets and hot showers in a manicured garden along the river. To get there, take the first left after the river; it's past the Tha Ton Chalet. While you're there, try the *tom yam* soup with shrimp for 60฿. (☎459 286. Restaurant open daily 7am-10pm. English menu. Riverside bungalows 200฿, with TV instead of view 300฿. Look for new 150฿ rooms coming soon.) Continue down the road from Tha Ton Garden Riverside to get to **Garden Home ❷.** This huge, shaded property has its own riverside beach. (☎495 325. Basic rooms with fan and cold shower 150฿, with hot water 200฿; quality and price of rooms increase as you move toward the river.)

SIGHTS AND ACTIVITIES. Wat Tha Ton dominates the hillside above Thip's Travelers House. The temple features life-size representations of figures from Hindu, Buddhist, and Chinese mythology hidden away in manmade caves, as well as fantastic views of the countryside. A visit to the two huge Buddhas is 20฿, but exploring the complex's other scenic areas costs nothing but a climb. The easiest route up the hill begins at the arch across the road from the post office. When you reach the fork in the path marked by the full-fed figure, turn left for the massive golden dragon-headed Buddha, or right for the 12m tall white Buddha.

The **Mae Kok River** originates in the mountains of Myanmar's Shan states, enters Thailand above Tha Ton, and flows 200km to meet the Mekong River in Chiang Saen. **Bamboo rafting** to Chiang Rai (a 3-day excursion) is a quiet, leisurely method of exploring villages along its banks. The Akha town of **Mae Salak** is the biggest you'll pass; it serves as a starting point for journeys south into the Wawi area, home to numerous Lahu, Lisu, Hmong, Akha, Karen, and Yao hamlets. **Phatai** is a Black Lahu village on the north bank. The large Karen village of **Ruammit,** 45min. from Chiang Rai, is a popular stop. The village has the feel of a traveling circus; you can ride elephants (400฿ per hr.), get your photo taken with a boa constrictor (10฿), and buy endless souvenirs. From there, it's another 20min. to the **Temple Cave. Tha Ton Tour** (☎373 143), before Chankasem Guest House, offers floats and treks to Chiang Rai. (2-day raft and boat trek, 1500฿ per person; 3-day Akha and Lalu village trek and boating 1800฿ per person; elephant rides and longneck village extra. Open daily 10am-8:30pm.) **Thip's Travelers House** (☎459 312) leads bamboo raft trips down the Mae Kok (3-days, 2000฿ with an elephant ride) and is conscious of ecotourism issues. All prices assume at least four participants.

THAILAND

CHIANG RAI ☎053

Chiang Rai has always played second fiddle to its southern neighbor, Chiang Mai. Besides offering stunning surrounding vistas and quality guest houses, Chiang Rai also features a night market, which stocks a wider array of tribal handicrafts than the infamous and larger Chiang Mai market, and a hill tribe museum. Basking in the poppy glow of the Golden Triangle, the city also serves as a base for one-day exploration or longer treks to villages in the mountains near the Myanmar border.

TRANSPORTATION

Flights: Chiang Rai International Airport (☎798 000), 9km out of town on Hwy. 110. To **Bangkok** (1hr.; 9:40am, 12:45, 3:50, 7:50, 9:50pm; 2645฿) and **Chiang Mai** (25min.; 8:40am, 8pm; 880฿). **Thai Airways,** 870 Phahonyothin Rd. (☎711 179), 1 block south of Teepee Bar. Open M-F 8am-noon and 1-5pm.

Buses: Chiang Rai Bus Station (☎711 224), on Prasopsuk Rd., one block east of intersection with Phahonyothin Rd., next to the night market. To: **Bangkok** (12hr., 4pm, 264฿; 2nd- and 1st-class A/C 8 per day 8am and 4:30-6:45pm, 351฿ and 370฿; VIP 7pm, 700฿; private companies 8am-7:15pm, 452฿); **Chiang Khong** (2½-3hr., every 30min. 7am-5pm, 42-54฿); **Chiang Mai** (3½hr., 6 per day 6:15am-5:30pm, 77฿; A/C 13 per day 7:30am-5pm, 139฿); **Chiang Saen** (1½-2¼hr., every 30min. 6am-6pm, 25฿); **Khon Kaen** (12hr.; 5, 9am; 239฿; 2nd-class A/C 2 and 4pm, 335฿; 1st-class A/C 6pm, 430฿) via **Phitsanulok** (6½hr.; 139฿, 2nd-class A/C 195฿, 1st-class A/C 250฿); **Lampang** (5hr., every 20min. 5:20am-3pm, 81฿); **Mae Sai** (1½hr., every 15min. 6am-6pm, 25฿); **Mae Sot** (10hr., 7:20am, 200฿; A/C 9:20am, 360฿) via **Tak** (8hr., 165฿, A/C 297฿); **Nakhon Ratchasima** (12hr., 3:30pm, 262฿; 1st-class A/C 6:15am, 1:15, 5:30pm; 472฿; VIP 7pm, 550฿) via **Phitsanulok** (6½hr.; 139฿, 2nd-class A/C 250฿,

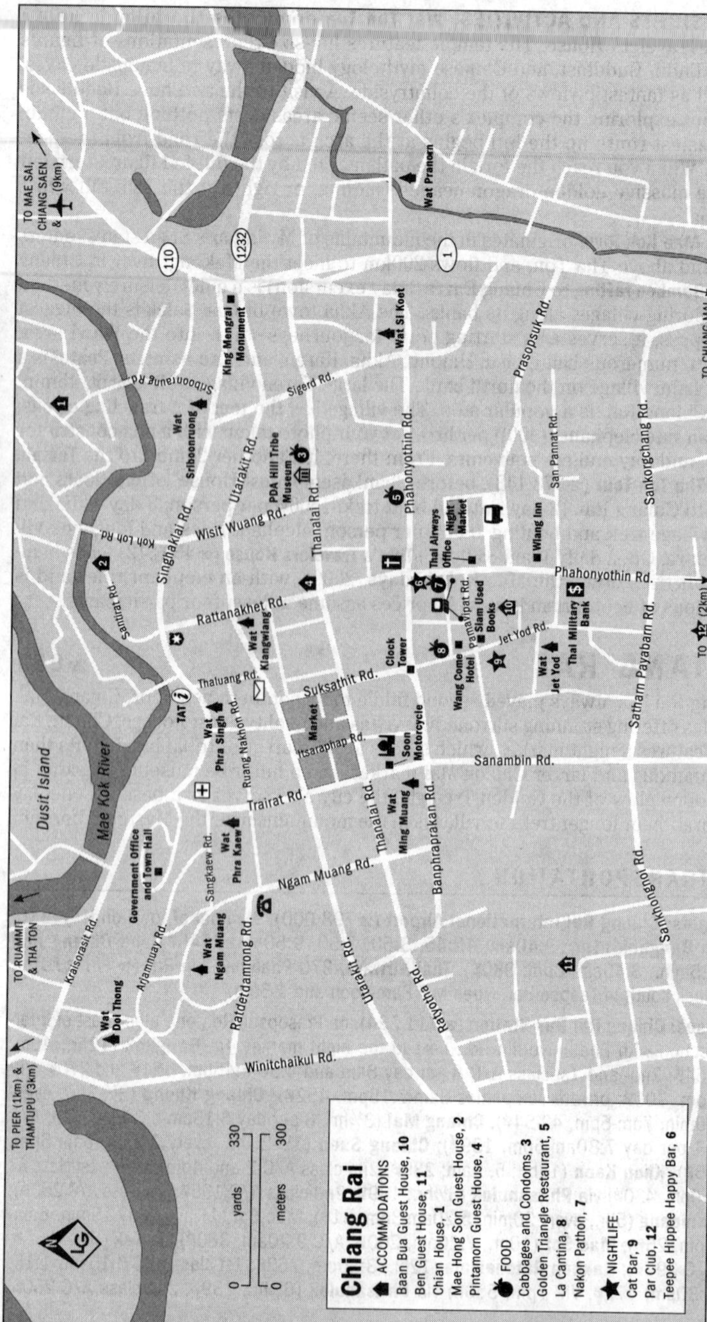
Chiang Rai
ACCOMMODATIONS
Baan Bua Guest House, 10
Ben Guest House, 11
Chian House, 1
Mae Hong Son Guest House, 2
Pintamorn Guest House, 4
FOOD
Cabbages and Condoms, 3
Golden Triangle Restaurant, 5
La Cantina, 8
Nakon Pathon, 7
NIGHTLIFE
Cat Bar, 9
Par Club, 12
Teepee Hippee Happy Bar, 6
0 yards 330
0 meters 300
TO MAE SAI, CHIANG SAEN & (9km)
TO PIER (1km) & THAMTUPU (3km)
TO RUAMMIT & THA TON
TO CHIANG MAI
TO 12 (2km)
Dusit Island
Mae Kok River
Wat Pranorn
Wat Si Koet
King Mengrai Monument
Wat Sriboonruong
PDA Hill Tribe Museum
TAT
Wat Phra Singh
Wat Klangwiang
Market
Clock Tower
Soon Motorcycle
Wat Ming Muang
Wat Phra Kaew
Government Office and Town Hall
Wat Ngam Muang
Wat Doi Thong
Wang Come Hotel
Slam Used Books
Thai Airways Office
Night Market
Wiang Inn
Wat Jet Yod
Thai Military Bank
Sriboonruang Rd.
Koh Loh Rd.
Santirat Rd.
Singhaklai Rd.
Sigerd Rd.
Utarakit Rd.
Wisit Wuang Rd.
Thanalai Rd.
Rattanakhet Rd.
Thaluang Rd.
Suksathit Rd.
Ruang Nakhon Rd.
Itsaraphap Rd.
Trairat Rd.
Sangkaew Rd.
Ngam Muang Rd.
Kraisorasit Rd.
Arjamnuay Rd.
Ratdetdamrong Rd.
Banphraprakan Rd.
Ratyotha Rd.
Winitchaikul Rd.
Sanambin Rd.
Jet Yod Rd.
Pamavipat Rd.
Phahonyothin Rd.
Prasopsuk Rd.
San Pannat Rd.
Sankorgchang Rd.
Satham Payabarn Rd.
Sankhongnoi Rd.

1st-class A/C 292฿); **Nan** (6hr., 9:30am, 95฿); **Phitsanulok** (8hr., A/C every hr. 7:30-10:30am, 214฿) via **Sukhothai** (6½hr., 190฿).

Boats: Leave from the pier (☎750 009), on the north bank of the Mae Kok river next to the Mae Fah Luang Bridge, 2km northwest of the city. To **Tha Ton** (4hr., 10:30am, 200฿) via **Ruammit** (45min., 50฿). Charter boats 1500฿ per day; maximum 6 people.

Local Transportation: Songthaew, tuk-tuk, and **samlor** cluster on Uttarakit Rd. around the market and in the evening on Phahonyothin Rd. near the night bazaar. Fares in city 10-20฿. Within 10-15km radius, *songthaew* and tuk-tuk should cost under 50฿; trips to airport up to 100฿.

Rentals: Practically every guest house rents motorcycles through **Soon Motorcycle,** 197/2 Trairat Rd. (☎714 068), which offers a convenient drop-off/pickup service from guest houses as well as free transport to the bus station. New motorbikes 200฿; secondhand 150฿. Open daily 8am-7pm.

ORIENTATION AND PRACTICAL INFORMATION

The **Mae Kok River** flows west to east, forming Chiang Rai's northern border. **Singhaklai Rd.,** site of the TAT office and guest houses, skirts the river. The northern part of town lies between Singhaklai and **Banphraprakan Rd.,** 500m south and parallel to it. The most helpful landmark, the **Haw Nariga (clock tower),** stands in the middle of Banphraprakan Rd. forming a chaotic roundabout. **Jet Yod Rd.,** chock-full of bars, leads south from there. One block east, a portion of **Phahonyothin Rd.,** with adjacent bus station and night market, runs parallel to Jet Yod Rd.

Tourist Office: TAT, 448/16 Singhaklai Rd. (☎744 674). Free maps, bus schedules, and a list of trekking outfits. English spoken. Open daily 8:30am-4:30pm.

Currency Exchange: Thai Military Bank, 897/7-8 Phahonyothin Rd. (☎715 657). Open daily 8:30am-9pm. **24hr. ATM** (AmEx/Cirrus/MC/PLUS/V). Currency exchange **booth,** on Phahonyothin Rd., next to entrance to night bazaar. Open daily 6am-10pm.

Emergency: ☎191. **Ambulance:** ☎711 366. **Tourist Police (Bangkok):** ☎1155.

Police: Chiang Rai Provincial Police Station (☎711 444), at the intersection of Rattanakhet Rd. and Singhaklai Rd. 1 block east of the TAT. **Open 24hr.**

Tourist Police (local): ☎717 779. Downstairs from the TAT. Will gladly give a "background check" on tour agencies. **Open 24hr.**

Medical Services: Overbrooke Hospital, 444/3 Singhaklai Rd. (☎711 366), 250m west of TAT. **24hr. pharmacy.** AmEx/MC/V.

Telephones: Telecommunications Office (☎776 738), on Ngam Muang Rd. at the west end of town. CATNET Internet, fax, international calls. Open M-F 8am-8pm, Sa-Su 8:30am-4:30pm. AmEx/MC/V.

Internet Access: Post@Cafe, 869/64-73 Phahonyothin Rd. (☎752 207), one block north of Pamavipat Rd. 20฿ for first hr., 0.34฿ per min. thereafter. Open daily 7:30am-9:30pm.

Post Office: 486/1 Mu 15 Uttarakit Rd. (☎711 421), 200m south of the TAT and 300m north of clock tower. HCD phone booth. *Poste Restante.* Open M-F 8:30am-4:30pm, Sa-Su and holidays 9am-noon. **Postal code:** 57000.

ACCOMMODATIONS

The best accommodations are outside the city center and worth the 20min. walk or 20฿ tuk-tuk ride. Call ahead in the high season, for the cheap rooms fill up. Guest houses can arrange motorbike rental (150-500฿), and provide luggage storage. Check-out is usually between 11 and 11:30am and all have hot water.

Mae Hong Son Guest House, 126 Singhaklai Rd. (☎ 715 367). From the TAT, head east and take the 2nd left (at the intersection with Rattanakhet Rd.). Follow the road to the far end. All rooms have fans and mosquito nets. Laundry 45฿ per kg. Trekking service. Singles 80฿; doubles 100฿; triples 150฿, with bath and western toilet 150-200฿. ❶

Chian House, 172 Sriboonraung Rd. (☎/fax 713 388). From the TAT, head east past the Rattanakhet Rd. intersection. Take the next left (onto Koh Loh Rd.), cross the bridge, and then follow signs. Perks include restaurant with cable TV and salt-water swimming pool. Laundry 25฿ per kg. Internet access and overseas calls. Family-oriented. Singles 60฿; doubles 120-250฿, with A/C 300฿; bungalows 250-300฿/350-450฿. ❶

Ben Guest House, 351/10 Sankhongnoi Rd. Soi 4 (☎ 716 775). Call ahead for a free pickup, or head west on Banphraprakan Rd. from the clock tower, turn left at the first traffic signal onto Sanambin Rd., right on Sankhongnoi Rd., right again on Soi 4, and walk to the end. Charming teak wood house with veranda and adjacent brick wing. Rooms 120฿, with bath 200฿; new wing (with carpet and A/C) 350฿. ❷

Pintamorn Guest House, 509/1 Rattanakhet Rd. (☎ 714 161). A 10min. walk on Phahonyothin Rd. from the bus station. Backpacker central. 24hr. kitchen big on Western food (cheeseburger 50฿). Cable TV, pool table, book exchange on the patio. Free luggage storage. Book ahead. Singles 80฿, with bath 150฿; doubles 100฿/180฿. ❶

Baan Bua Guest House, 879/2 Jet Yod Rd. (☎ 718 880). From the bus station turn left onto Phahonyothin, then right onto Jet Yod Rd. at Thai Military Bank. The soi off Jet Yod Rd. is 20m past the wat toward the clock tower. Spacious and immaculate rooms in a quiet backstreet location despite its close proximity to bars. All rooms have fan, western toilet, and hot water. Tiled rooms with bath 180฿; larger rooms 200฿; twins 220฿. ❸

FOOD

Chiang Rai's culinary scene is concentrated in the neighborhood bounded by Jet Yod, Banphraprakan, and Phahonyothin Rd. Menus catering to Western palates cram the entrance to the night bazaar on Phahonyothin Rd. The best food, however, lies in open-air joints unmarked by the Roman alphabet.

Nakon Pathon (no English sign), 869/25-26 Phahonyothin Rd., caters almost exclusively to the Thai working crowd. Small English menu. Unbeatable *kiaw moo dang* (barbecue pork with rice, 30฿). Noodle soups 30฿. Open daily 6am-3pm. ❷

Cabbages & Condoms, 620/25 Thanalai Rd., downstairs from the Hill Tribe Museum. C&C Chiang Rai raises money and awareness for the AIDS campaign. *Tom-yam* 60-70฿. Open daily 11am-midnight. AmEx/MC/V. ❷

Golden Triangle Restaurant, 590 Phahonyothin Rd., at Golden Triangle Inn. Thai dining with an informative English menu. Various curries, rice dishes, and noodles. Delicious *gaeng kiaw wan* (green sweet curry) 45-60฿. Open daily 7am-10pm. ❷

La Cantina, 1025/40 Jet Yod Rd. High quality Italian food in a relaxing atmosphere. 150-200฿ per person. Extensive menu of homemade pasta served with unlimited bread and butter. Pizza 90-180฿. Open daily 8am-10pm. ❹

SIGHTS AND ENTERTAINMENT

According to local lore, the *stupa* of **Wat Phra Kaew,** originally known as Wat Pa Yier, was struck by lightning in 1434 and revealed an Emerald Buddha; the temple's name changed to "Wat of the Emerald Buddha" as a result. Today, the original sits in Bangkok's Wat Phra Kaew (see p. 700), and a new image, commissioned in China and carved from Canadian jade in 1991, sits in its place. At the west end of town, walking from Trairat Rd. past Chat House, rests **Wat Ngam Muang** on top of the hill of the same name. Its *stupa* contains King Mengrai's ashes and relics.

The **PDA Hill Tribe Museum,** 620/25 Thanalai Rd., 300m east of Pintamorn Guest House, isn't nearly as informative as the one in Chiang Mai. The 25min. slide show on the region's different tribes will give you the basics although the background music proves to be distracting. (☎740 088. Open M-F 8:30am-8pm, Sa-Su 10am-8pm; closes 6pm in low season. 50฿. Slideshow 50฿.)

The most popular disco in town is the **Par Club** in the Inn Come Hotel, 172/6 Rajbamrung Rd., accessible by tuk-tuk. (☎717 850. Cover 100-150฿ includes free drink. Open daily 9pm-1am.) **Teepee Hippie Happy Bar,** 542/4 Phahonyothin Rd., just south of Banphaprakan Rd., an American West decor shop, hosts an occasional acoustic blues band (after 10pm in high season), and offers a vegetarian menu. (Open daily 11am-5pm and 6:30pm-1am.) Head to **Cat Bar,** 1013/1 Jet Yod Rd., for jamming sessions or a game of pool. (☎714 637. Small beer 50฿. Open daily noon-1am.) Next to Cat Bar on Jet Yod Rd., an endless row of bars sit next to each other, with comparable music and atmosphere. The bars on the soi linking Jet Yod Rd.'s northern end with Banphaprakan Rd. at the clock tower dismiss the pretense of karaoke and go straight to go-go.

MARKETS

The **day market ❶** takes up a whole square block, the northeastern corner of which nips at the post office on Uttarakit Rd. Lots of vegetables and fresh fruit are on the north end along Uttarakit Rd. Inside is a winding maze of, well, everything. **Food vendors ❶** move to the streets surrounding the market at night—go right there for delicious and cheap dining (before 10pm). The streets of the **night market ❶** are closed to all but pedestrian traffic making it more manageable than its southern counterpart. The market contains a massive amount of hill tribe products (including Akha ware) on the soi leading to the bus station off Phahonyothin Rd. The focal point of the courtyard is the large stage where traditional hill tribe music and Thai dancing occurs. A smaller stage lies on the soi between Phahonyothin Rd. and the bus station. (Nightly performances on both stages 8-10pm.)

TREKKING

Chiang Rai's rugged province—full of ethnic hill tribes—offers trekking routes less traveled than those around Chiang Mai. As always, trek prices should include food, transportation, and an informed guide. Typical treks run 3 days/2 nights (2-4 people around 3000฿ per person; 5-7 people around 2500฿ per person; see TAT's pamphlet), but you can do as short as a day or as long as a week. Many companies have access to horses, elephants, rafts, mountain bikes, and plain old hiking boots; mix and match your itinerary and then consider which hill tribes you'd like to visit, as they're vast and varied in the area. If you're considering a service that's not listed below, check its status with the TAT. Tours to Laos or Myanmar may be illegal, so check that with the TAT, too. **Population and Community Development Association (PDA),** 620/26 Thanalai Rd., which funds rural development, family planning, and AIDS education/treatment/prevention programs among hill tribes, offers treks and tours (see p. 54). Company treks are pricier than those run out of many guest houses. PDA also accepts volunteers for many of its health-related projects. Most of the volunteers are selected through the Bangkok office, although occasionally the Chiang Rai office will accept applications directly. Thai language skills are strongly favored. If you're interested, bring a resume and plan to wait a week. (☎/fax 740 088. 3-day/2-night trek to Lahu and Akha villages, including elephant and longtail boat rides, 3700฿ per person, min. 2 people. Daytrips to the Golden Triangle 1500฿ per person, min. 2 people. The more people, the lower the price. Maximum group size is 12.) **Ben's Guest House, Chat House, Chian House,** and **Mae Hong Son Guest House** all run flexible treks with guides who are registered with the TAT.

THAILAND

MAE SALONG ☎053

Fifty years after the Chinese Nationalists' 93rd Division fled China in the wake of the Communist victory and settled in this mountaintop village, Mae Salong maintains its Chinese identity. Chinese characters adorn doorframes, tea houses feature red-lanterns, and southern Chinese dialects are more common than Thai.

TRANSPORTATION AND PRACTICAL INFORMATION. *Songthaew* are frequent early in the morning and leave when full; you can pay the full fare (300฿) if the wait is unbearable. To get to **Chiang Rai,** take a light blue *songthaew* to **Ban Pasang** (1hr., 7am-2pm, 50฿), and then flag down a passing bus (1hr., every 30min. 6am-6pm, 20฿). Yellow *songthaew* to **Tha Ton** (1½hr., 7am-2pm, 50฿) leave from the small **day market,** 1km toward Tha Ton from the town center. The **main road** through Mae Salong stretches 2.5km and is a continuation of roads from Tha Ton (Rd. #1234) and Ban Pasang (Rd. #1130); the Khumnaipol Resort marks the Tha Ton end, the Mae Salong Resort marks the Ban Pasang end. The town center is near the guest houses and has daytime **food vendors** and a **mosque.** Starting before dawn, locals mingle at the **morning market** off the road to the Mae Salong Resort, on the road that leads directly under Shin Sane Guest House. Opposite Khumnaipol Resort is a **Thai Military Bank.** (☎765 159. Open M-F 8:30am-3:30pm. AmEx/Cirrus/MC/PLUS/V **ATM** open daily 6am-10pm.) The **police** (☎767 7109) have a booth near the Mae Salong Villa. The nearest **hospital** is in Mae Chan. **Golden Dragon Inn** has an **Internet** connection (60฿ per hr.). There are **no international phones.**

ACCOMMODATIONS AND FOOD. The family-style **Akha Mae Salong Guest House ❶,** off the main road near the mosque, has huge rooms with common bath. The owner has useful maps (10฿), sells Akha ware, and arranges horse treks for 400฿ (☎765 103. Singles and doubles 100฿; triples 150฿.) Next door, **Shin Sane Guest House ❶** has bungalows. (Singles 50฿; doubles 100฿; bungalow with western toilet 200-300฿.) **Golden Dragon ❸,** on the road between the Mae Salong Resort and Akha Guest House, has rooms with hot showers. (Singles 200฿; doubles 300฿.)

Yunnanese **noodle shops ❶** and **vendors ❶** abound (5฿ per serving). Tea shops provide a relaxing ambience; a kettle of Mae Salong tea soothes for 50฿. **Mini ❷,** 300m toward Tha Ton from Golden Dragon Inn, serves *khanom jun naam ngiaw* (Yunnanese noodle soup; 25฿), the town specialty. Ask for vegetarian options. (Beer Lao 50฿. Open daily 7am-10:30pm.) Lazy susans whirl food around at the **Sakura Restaurant ❸,** a popular Thai/Chinese restaurant in Mae Salong Resort. (Chicken with cashew nuts small 80฿, large 120฿. Open daily 7am-10pm.)

SIGHTS. For an awesome view, follow the road to the Mae Salong Resort and walk up the steps to the **pagoda.** From here, a road continues 4km through mountain scenery and finally curves back into town via the day market. Area hill tribes include **Akha, Lahu,** and **Lisu,** and in smaller numbers, **Hmong** and **Yao.** There aren't many organized trekking groups, although the intrepid can set off alone. Pick up a map at Shin Sane Guest House (10฿), but don't wander too far; in addition to hill tribe villages, pockets of Shan and KMT groups line the Burmese border. Drug trade and clashes have erupted between rival factions; ask in town about the current situation. The walk-weary can inquire about 4hr. **horseback riding treks** at Shin Sane or Akha Mae Salong guest houses (400฿ per person).

MAE SAI ☎053

One of Thailand's main links with Myanmar, Mae Sai is a bustling border town during the day, but turns into a ghost town in the evening when the border shuts down. With an established opium trade and a burgeoning gem trade stemming from a recently discovered sapphire mine in the Shan State, Mae Sai's future as a trade center looked bright—until border tensions erupted in 2001 and 2002. While the gem and antique trade from Myanmar and China is no longer what it was, it's hard to tell this from the bustle in the streets. Aside from the border intrigue, spelunkers can find impressive caves and national parks near Mae Sai's center.

TRANSPORTATION

Buses and Songthaew: Mae Sai Bus Terminal, 4km south of bridge along Phahonyothin Rd. Red *songthaew* head there every 10min. (5฿). To: **Bangkok** (14hr.; 7am, 4, 5:30pm; 481฿); **Chiang Mai** (5hr.; 6, 8, 11am, 1:45, 3:30pm; 95฿, with A/C 133-171฿); **Chiang Rai** (1½hr., every 15min. 6am-6pm, 25฿) via **Ban Pasang** (30min., 15฿), where *songthaew* go to **Mae Salong** (1hr., leave when full 7am-2pm, 50฿); **Nakhon Ratchasima** (14hr.; 5 per day 5:15am-6pm; 281฿, with A/C 590฿); **Pattaya** (14hr., 5 per day 5:15am-6pm, 530฿). South of Thai Farmers Bank, blue *songthaew* go to **Chiang Saen** (1hr., every hr. 7am-2pm, 30฿) via **Sop Ruak** (40min., 20฿).

Local Transportation: Motorcycle taxis and **samlor** smother Mae Sai. Rides within the city 10-30฿. Green *songthaew* go up and down Phahonyothin Rd. (5฿).

Rentals: Thong (☎732 815), on Silamjoi Rd. near Porm Charern Minimart, rents **motorcycles.** 150฿ per day. Passport deposit required. Open daily 8am-5pm.

ORIENTATION AND PRACTICAL INFORMATION

Hwy. 110 ends at the **border crossing** marked by the new gate. **Phahonyothin Rd.** hosts a dusty carnival of *farang*, Thais, and Burmese who browse, bargain, and beg at the street stalls. **Silamjoi Rd.** jogs along the river, heading west from the Friendship Bridge toward guest houses.

Immigration Office: ☎731 008. On Phahonyothin Rd., 2km south of bridge. 10-day visa extension 500฿; 1-month visa extension for 60-day tourist visas. Bring 2 photos and 2 photocopies of passport. Open daily 8:30am-4:30pm. For a cheaper option, see the Mae Sai/Thachilek crossing under **Border Crossings: From Thailand,** p. 497. Immigration Office at the **border** (☎733 261). Border open daily 6:30am-6:30pm. Tourists are asked to cross back by 5pm.

Currency Exchange: All along Phahonyothin Rd. **Thai Farmers Bank,** 122/1 Phahonyothin Rd. (☎640 786). Open M-F 8:30am-3:30pm. **24hr. ATM** (Cirrus/MC/V).

Markets: During the day, stalls line Phahonyothin Rd.–check out the base of the bridge for herbs, gems, teak, and flowers. 200m south, level with and opposite the police, is "ruby alley." Food stalls set up at night near the bridge.

Emergency: ☎191. **Ambulance:** ☎731 300 or 731 301. **Tourist Police (Bangkok):** ☎1155.

Police: ☎731 444. On Phahonyothin Rd. 200m south of bridge.

Tourist Police (local): ☎733 850. In a booth next to the bridge. Open daily 8am-5pm.

Pharmacy: Drugstore, south of police station. Owner speaks excellent English. Open daily 8am-8pm.

Medical Services: Mae Sai Hospital, 101 Mu 10 Pomaharat Rd. (☎751 300 or 751 301), off Phahonyothin Rd. Head 2km south. Turn right into the soi just after the overpass. Hospital is 400m down.

Telephones: Mae Sai Telecommunications Center, next to the post office. Fax. Open M-F 8:30am-4:30pm. LENSO phone at the 7-Eleven 200m south of the bridge.

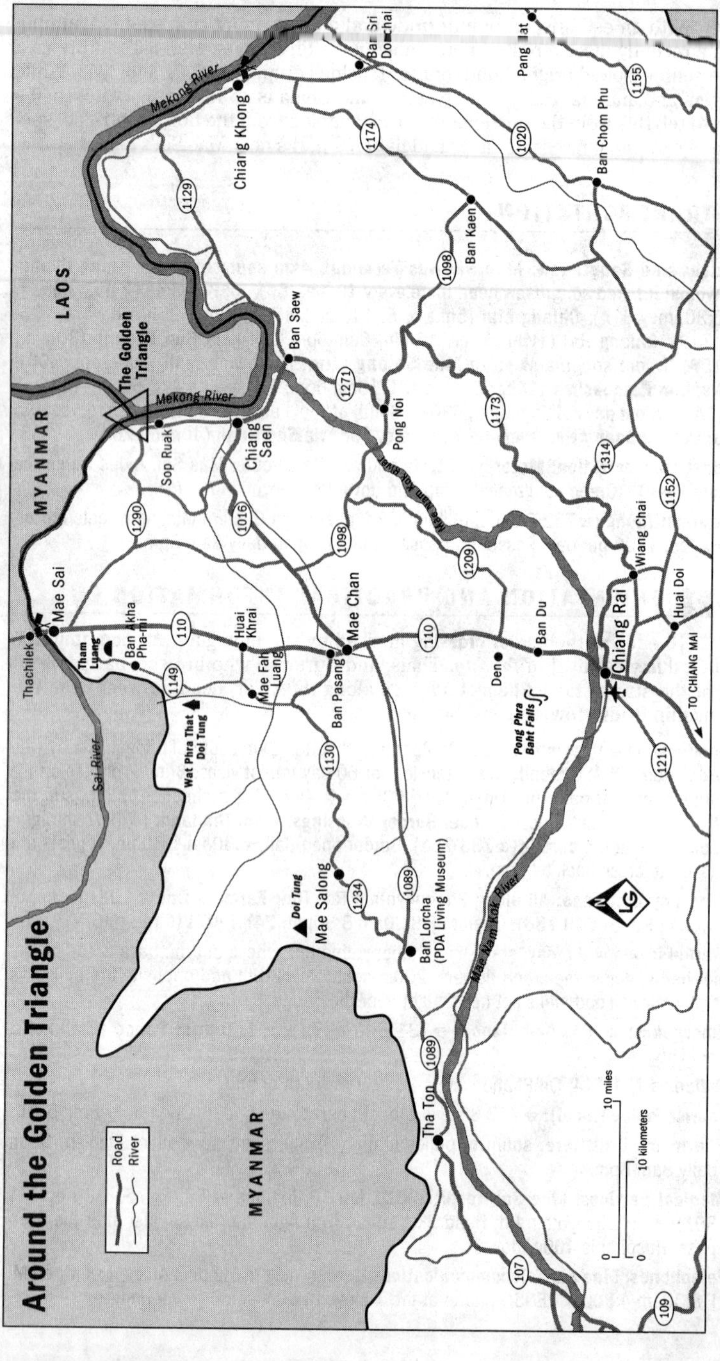
Around the Golden Triangle
Road
River
MYANMAR
LAOS
The Golden Triangle
Mekong River
Mae Nam Kok River
Sai River
Chiang Khong
Ban Sri Donchai
Pang Hat
Ban Chom Phu
Ban Kaen
Ban Saew
Pong Noi
Chiang Saen
Sop Ruak
Mae Sai
Thachilek
Tham Luang
Ban Akha Pha-mi
Huai Khrai
Mae Fah Luang
Wat Phra That Doi Tung
Mae Chan
Ban Pasang
Den
Ban Du
Pong Phra Baht Falls
Chiang Rai
Wiang Chai
Huai Doi
TO CHIANG MAI
Doi Tung
Mae Salong
Ban Lorcha (PDA Living Museum)
Tha Ton
10 miles
10 kilometers
1129
1174
1155
1020
1098
1271
1173
1314
1152
1290
1016
1209
110
1149
1130
1234
1089
1211
107
109

BORDER INTRIGUE The Golden Triangle, opium capital of the world, produces 70% of the world's heroin. In addition, the Golden Triangle's *ya ba*—a methamphetamine often coated in chocolate—has caught on with teenage users as a cheap alternative to opium and heroin. Drug money is the lifeblood of impoverished hill tribes and nearby paramilitary organizations. The drug mystique has resulted in flourishing tour companies, which fill buses with tourists eager to get a whiff of the intrigue. Trekkers with addicted guides are often convinced that opium is an integral part of tribal culture. Although a few traditional medicines of Northern Thailand use opium as a painkiller, today opium abuse is considered shameful in most communities.

Internet Access: Take the last right before the bridge, look for the sign leading to the 2nd fl. 20฿ per 30min.; 30฿ per hr. Open daily 9am-9pm.

Post Offices: Mae Sai Post and Telegraph Office, 230/40-41 Phahonyothin Rd. (☎731 402), 4km south of the bridge and despite the address, not on the main road. *Poste Restante.* Open M-F 8:30am-4:30pm, Sa-Su 9am-noon. **Postal code:** 57130.

ACCOMMODATIONS AND FOOD

Ten meters from Myanmar at the western end of Silamjoi Rd., **Mae Sai Guest House ❶** is an idyllic escape with thatch bungalows, hot water, restaurant, and laundry service. (☎732 021. Singles and doubles 100-150฿; doubles with bath 200-300฿; bungalows overhanging the water 400฿.) The owners of **King Kobra Guest House ❷,** 135/5 Silamjoi Rd., have travel info and can offer advice on motorcycle treks to northern Thailand, Myanmar, and China. (☎733 055. Singles 120฿, with bath 200฿; doubles 150-250฿; "VIP" room 350฿.) **Chad Guest House ❶,** 52/1 Soi Wiengpan off Phahonyothin Rd., 1km south of the bridge, is a quiet, cheap place run by a friendly English-speaking familiy. (☎732 054. Singles 50-100฿; doubles 100-150฿.)

The **night market ❶** along Phahonyothin Rd. has dishes on display, so a quick "point and shoot" will get you what you want. (Open daily 7-10pm.) Pamper your palate at **Jo Jo Coffee House ❷,** 233/1 Phahonyothin Rd., opposite the Thai Farmers Bank. Food tastes even better than it looks on the menu. (Bitter melon soup with white gourd on rice 35฿; banana split 40฿. Open daily 6am-5pm.) Night restaurants are limited, but **Rabieng Kaew Restaurant ❸,** 150m south on Phahonyothin Rd. of the bridge, is a good option. Their minced pork and coconut in chili paste (50฿) is a spicy treat. (Specials 80-150฿; coconut ice cream 20฿. Open daily 9am-10pm.)

DAYTRIPS FROM MAE SAI

Tham Luang National Park (Great Cave) lies 5km south of Mae Sai, 2.5km off Hwy. 110. Its caverns burrow 200m into the mountain. Other caverns, such as the **Buddha Cave** and the 7km deep **Royal Luang Cave,** are easier to explore. (Open daily 6am-6pm.) Lanterns (30฿) and maps of the area are available at the park entrance, but any extended exploration requires a flashlight and supplies. There are no guides available, but locals often wait at the park entrance and will show you around for a nominal fee. **Khun Nam Nang Non (Sleeping Lady Lagoon),** at the southern end of the park, is a popular picnic spot with locals. (Open daily 8:30am-4:30pm.) Take a green *songthaew* (10฿) to the turn-off to Khun Nam Nang Non on the west side of Hwy. 110 (approx. 7-8km). Motorcycle taxis often wait here to take visitors the remaining distance. Walking the 3 or 4km is possible. After the three-headed dragon, continue straight ahead for Khun Nam Nang Non or take the first right and then next left (about 1km) on paved roads to Tham Luang. Two more caves are inside **Wat Tham Pla,** 12km south and 3km west of Mae Sai along

Hwy. 110. *Samlor* along the highway will take you for 20฿. Fresh water surges through **Tham Plaa (Fish Cave),** also called "Monkey Cave" because of its gamboling primates. Wear boots and long pants, and feed the monkeys at your own risk. The more adventurous can explore **Tham Gu Gaeo,** rumored to lead ultimately to Myanmar. Attendants on a path to the right of the temple will take visitors to a Buddha village 2km away (50-70฿ per person). Bring a flashlight. If you are scared of cave spirits, you can buy incense and candles to dedicate to the Buddha for protection.

CHIANG SAEN ☎053

Founded by King Saen Phu in 1328 as the capital of Chiang Saen Kingdom, Chiang Saen was destroyed in 1803 by King Rama I in order to keep it from the Burmese. The district did not recover until the 1880s, when Rama V kicked out the remaining Burmese and repopulated the city with Thais. Although busloads of *farang* flock to this Golden Triangle gateway, they have not yet disrupted its sedate feel. But due to a lack of cheap accommodations many people just day-trip to the town.

TRANSPORTATION. From the river end of Phahonyothin Rd., **buses** go to: **Bangkok** (12½hr.; 3pm, 283฿; with A/C 4:20pm, 594฿); **Chiang Mai** (6hr., 8:20am, with A/C 150฿); **Chiang Rai** (1½hr., every 30min. 5:15am-5pm, 25฿) via **Mae Chan** (45min., 15฿). The booking office for Bangkok (☎650 822) is an unmarked house set back from the street near the Siam Commercial Bank. Blue **songthaew** go to **Mae Sai** (1hr., every 40min. 7am-5pm, 15฿) from across the main road. Green *songthaew* to **Chiang Khong** (2hr., 9am-3pm, 50฿) wait on Rimkhong Rd., 150m south of Phahonyothin Rd. From 8:30am to 6pm pricey longtailed **charter boats** leave from the "T" intersection for **Chiang Khong** (2hr., 1800฿ per boat) and **Sop Ruak** (40min.; 400฿ per boat, 500฿ round-trip, up to 6 people). *Samlor* wait near the river (10-20฿ to guest houses). You can rent **motorbikes** (180฿; open daily 8am-5pm) from a shop near the immigration office (see below).

PRACTICAL INFORMATION. Chiang Saen's two main roads form a "T." The top of the "T," **Rimkhong Rd.,** runs north-south along the **Mekong River,** which separates Thailand from Laos to the east. The tail of the "T" is **Phahonyothin Rd.** Route 1016 from Mae Chan bypasses the southwest end of town and continues to Chiang Khong. Following Rimkhong Rd. upstream leads to **Sop Ruak.** Chang Saen's services are scattered along Phahonyothin Rd., all within walking distance. Walking from the river on Phahonyothin Rd., the **immigration office** is at the first crossroad on the left. (☎777 118. Open M-F 8:30am-4:30pm.) A **24hr. ATM** (Cirrus/MC/PLUS/V) is at **Siam Commercial Bank,** 773 Phahonyothin Rd., which also exchanges currency. (☎777 041. Open M-F 8:30am-3:30pm.) The **police** (☎777 111) are opposite the "T" junction with Rimkhong Rd. A **pharmacy** is opposite the police (☎651 108. Open daily 8am-8pm.) **Chiang Saen Hospital** (☎777 017) lies 1km from the river. At the immigration office intersection there is **international calling** and **Internet access** (30฿ per hr.; open daily 9am-6pm). The **post office** with CATNET is 600m from the river on Phahonyothin Rd. (☎777 116. Open M-F 8:30am-4:30pm, Sa-Su 9am-noon.) **Postal code:** 57150.

ACCOMMODATIONS AND FOOD. With the river to your back, walk west on Phahonyothin Rd. and turn right before the post office. Just past a bank 100m down on the right, is **J.S. Guest House ❶,** with cozy and quiet rooms with fans and common bath—Chiang Saen's best deal. Stick to rooms in the house. (☎777 060. Rooms 100฿.) **Gin Guest House ❸,** 1.5km upstream of Rimkhong Rd., is the upmarket choice. Day hikes are pricey (2400฿ for 1-4 people) and include car and driver but not food, rafting, or elephant riding. (☎650 847. Bungalows with fan, bug nets, and hot showers 200฿; big tiled room with sitting room 300฿; family room 400฿.) **Chiang Saen Guest House ❶**, 45 Rimkhong Rd., is north of the "T" just before the wat. The owner, an avid bird-watcher, can point out the many species in the area. (Concrete singles 80฿; doubles 120฿; twins with bath and view of Mekong 150฿; triples 200฿). In the evenings, the **market ❶** on Phahonyothin Rd. is the best option for food (phat thai 20฿). Stalls congregate on **Rimkhong Rd.** 300m south of the "T." *Paw pia thawt* (spring rolls) are great. Those without tongues of steel may want to order dishes *mai champ phèt* (not spicy).

SIGHTS. **Chiang Saen National Museum** is on Phahonyothin Rd., at the entrance to the city across from the post office. The museum has impressive 15th- to 16th-century Lanna art and a well-done exposé on hill tribe cultures and costumes. (☎777 102. Open W-Su 9am-5pm. 30฿.) Next door, a 13th-century brick *chedi* dominates **Wat Chedi Luang,** the tallest Lanna Thai monument at 58m. **Wat Pasale** is outside the ancient city wall, 800m west of the river. (Open daily 8am-6pm. 30฿.) Following the road along the moat next to Wat Pasale leads to **Wat Chom Kitti,** 2km out of town. The hilltop outlook offers compelling views of Laos and the Mekong, but it is outdone by **Wat Phra That Pha-Ngao,** which includes Chiang Saen in the vista 4km southeast of town on the road to Chiang Khong. **Chiang Saen Lake,** a bird-watching site with the largest variety of water fowl in Southeast Asia, is a 7km ride southwest. The lake is off the road to Chiang Rai; the turn-off is marked.

DAYTRIP FROM CHIANG SAEN: SOP RUAK (GOLDEN TRIANGLE). Sop Ruak may be its official name, but most refer to the confluence of the Sai River and the wider Mekong where Myanmar, Laos, and Thailand meet as **Sam Liam Tongkham (Golden Triangle).** *Songthaew* bound for **Mae Sai** (45min., 25฿) and **Chiang Saen** (20min., 15฿) pass through the center of town between 7am and 2pm. Longtail **charter boats** seat up to 6 people and leave from various spots along the river to **Chiang Khong** (2hr., 1500฿) and **Chiang Saen** (50min., 400฿). Golden Triangle boat rides tour the area (400฿ for 1hr., boats accommodate up to 6 people). The few guest houses that existed have been bulldozed in anticipation of the boom expected to hit the region, now named the **Golden Quadrangle** after the addition of China, resulting in a lack of budget hotels. In the middle of town, the **House of Opium** features exhibits on the history and cultivation of opium with pipe displays, information on drug warlords, and a diorama of a drugged-out old man. (☎784 062. Open daily 7am-7pm. 20฿.) Next door, **Siam Commercial Bank** runs a **currency exchange** booth which accepts all traveler's checks and has MC/V cash advances. (☎784 191. Open daily 9am-5pm.) For a view capturing the three countries, head up the five-dragon-headed staircase next to the bank, then follow the road behind **Wat Phra That Doi Pu** up the hill to the viewpoint.

CHIANG KHONG ☎053

Chiang Khong is the archetypal border town. There are no museums, parks, or interesting shops, but several banks line the interminable main street and wait for tourists transitioning between countries and currencies. The premier attractions of Chiang Khong are rest and relaxation. Many guest houses overlook the majestic Mekong and afford alluring views of greener Laos.

TRANSPORTATION. Most **buses** leave from the market, 100m southeast of the bridge near the Esso gas station. Buses go to **Chiang Mai** (6hr., 6am, 121฿; with A/C 8am, 218฿; 11am, 169฿). The **booking office** for bus tickets to Chiang Mai (☎655 732) is between the bridge and service station. Guest houses also run a **minibus** to Chiang Mai (5hr.; 10:30am, 6pm; 220฿). Buses to **Chiang Rai** leave from the market

(3hr., 5am-5pm, 50฿). Ticket offices for private buses to **Bangkok** are scattered along the main road. **Siam-first,** in the green building opposite Thai Farmers Bank, runs the nicest buses (4pm; 491฿, VIP 573฿). **Karuhart** is opposite and toward the pier from Traveler Corner (3pm, 490฿); **99** is 20m before Bamboo Riverside Guest House (7am, 491฿; 4pm, 382฿ and VIP 760฿); **Sombat Tours** is opposite buses to Chiang Mai (☎791 644; 4pm, 491฿). Check with offices about bus departures. Tickets go quickly so buy a seat in the morning to guarantee an afternoon bus. **Songthaew** to and from **Chiang Saen** (2½hr., 7am-noon, 50฿) gather near Soi 3. **@Net.com,** in front of Bamboo Riverside Guest house, has **motorbikes** for rent (200฿ per day).

ORIENTATION AND PRACTICAL INFORMATION. Chiang Khong is 144km northeast of Chiang Rai and 55km southeast of Chiang Saen. The main drag, **Saiklang Rd.,** runs northwest to southeast, parallel to the Mekong River. Numbered soi run perpendicular to the main road—odd-numbered soi head to the river. **Soi 13** is at the southeast end near the immigration office, bridge, and day market. **Soi 1,** home to the guest houses, is a 25min. walk from the market at the northwestern end of town. Continuing northwest past Soi 1 leads to the **new pier,** then to the turn-off to **Chiang Saen** (Route 1129), and then to the **old pier,** an important landmark for travelers.

THAILAND

Traveler Corner, 17/3 Ban Wat Kaew T. Wiang opposite Ann Travel near Soi 2, has info, does bookings, and can place collect calls for 30฿. (☎655 374. Open daily 8am-9pm.) The **immigration office** is next to Soi 13; it issues Thai visa extensions for 500฿. (☎791 332. Open M-F 8:30am-noon and 1-4:30pm.) The **Thai Farmers Bank,** 20m south of Soi 7, has an **ATM.** (Cirrus/MC/PLUS/V. Open M-F 8:30am-3:30pm.) Every Friday morning, the **regional market** spills out onto the main road from the day market up to the immigration office. Saturday evening is the **night market,** on the main road around Soi 2. In an **emergency,** dial ☎191, or the **tourist police (Bangkok)** at ☎1155. Next door to the immigration office, is the **police station** (☎791 426). **Boonchai Pharmacy** is opposite Soi 7. (☎791 013. Open daily 7am-8pm.) **Chiang Khong Hospital,** 354 Moo 10, is 3km outside of town. To get there, go straight south on Hwy. 1020 toward Chiang Rai. (☎791 206. **Open 24hr.**) **Internet access** is available at **@Net.com** (see **Transportation,** above) for 40฿ per hr. Some cafes offer the **Internet** for 30฿ per hr. The **post office,** near Soi 3, has **international phones** in the compound and a Lenso phone outside. (☎791 555. Open M-F 8:30am-4:30pm, Sa-Su 9am-noon.) **Postal code:** 57140.

ACCOMMODATIONS AND FOOD. The population of *farang* in Chiang Khong rises and falls sharply with each busload. By 5pm in the high season, the town's best accommodations are at saturation point, so call ahead to reserve. The best place in town is **Bamboo Riverside Guest House ❶**, at 71 Huaviang Rd., 75m northwest of Soi 1. (☎791 621. Laundry. Dorms 70฿; singles 100฿; bungalows 150฿; doubles with bath 200-250฿.) By Soi 2, **Ban Tammila ❸** has bungalows with private showers and sells some of the funkiest hammock-tent devices you've ever seen for 1200฿. (☎/fax 791 234. Bicycle rental 150฿. Bungalows 200-400฿.) The closest place to the bus station is **River Guest House ❷.** To get there, walk toward Chiang Rai from the bridge, turn left at the Esso, then left again onto Soi 15. Turn right when you get to the river, and it's 50m ahead. For those already—or perhaps still—seeking the isolation of Laos, this is an overlooked gem. (☎791 348. Bungalows with balcony. Bungalows 150฿, with bath 200฿.)

Noodle-and-rice shops line Saiklang Rd. The **day market ❶,** south of the bridge, offers *kanon ton kanon niew* (rice flour balls with coconut filling), a tasty 5฿ morning treat The **restaurant ❷** at Bamboo Riverside Guest House has delicious food. (Pad thai 30฿. Open daily 7:30am-noon and 6-9pm.) For a mid-day meal with an excellent view, try **Ben Tammila's Restaurant's ❷** vegetarian menu. (Most entrees 25-40฿. Open daily 7am-4pm.) **Rimkhong ❷,** by the river between Soi 7 and 9, has a partially translated menu. (Green curry 50฿. Open daily 7am-11pm.)

SIGHTS. KMT Cemetery is 1km out of town on Hwy. 1129 at the top of the big hill on the left. The entrance is on a dirt road not visible from the highway. Ask at guest houses about bike rides to **Hmong villages,** though they may prove inaccessible in the rainy season (3hr., 3:30pm, 100฿ including bike and guide). In April and May, **Ban Haadkhrai** hosts the annual giant catfish competition. Lao and Thai boats alternate turns trawling the river in search of the 2.5m, 200kg beasts. To get here, head south out of town and take a left at the Esso service station with the police box in front, then walk 1km to Soi 31 and continue to the river. **Wat Haadkhrai** overlooks the pier where the fish are brought ashore.

NAN ☎054

Hidden amidst the mountains on the edge of the Lanna Kingdom, Nan developed a unique culture and history, reflected in its wat architecture. Nan was a semi-autonomous principality until 1931, and its isolation made it a haven for smugglers and the Communist rebels of the People's Liberation Army of Thailand (PLAT) during the 1960s and 1970s. Today, Nan's seclusion provokes nothing more threatening than shouts of "I love you" from children unfamiliar with *farang.*

TRANSPORTATION

Flights: Nan Airport (☎771 308), on Worawichai Rd., 4km from town center. **Thai Airways,** 34 Mahaphrom Rd. (☎710 377). Open M-F 8am-noon and 1-5pm. Flies to **Bangkok** (F 4:30pm, 2195฿) via **Phrae** (865฿). **Air Andaman** at the airport (☎711 222; open M-F 10am-2pm) or booked through Thai Airways, flies to **Bangkok** (12:50pm, 2240฿) and **Chiang Mai** (M, W, F, Su 12:30pm; 1025฿).

Buses: The **regional bus station** is on Anonta Worarittidit Rd. To: **Chiang Rai** (blue bus; 5hr., 9am, 90฿); **Phitsanulok** (5hr.; 7:45, 9:45, 11:45am, 1:45pm; 146฿) via **Uttaradit** (101฿); **Phrae** (2hr., every 45min. 5am-5pm, 47฿). Across the street is a booking office (☎710 737) for **Chiang Mai** (6-7hr.; 9 per day 7am-10:30pm; 117฿, 2nd-class A/C 164฿, 1st-class A/C 211฿) via **Lampang** (4hr.; 86฿, 2nd-class A/C 120฿, 1st-class A/C 154฿). Buses to **Bangkok** (☎710 027) depart from a station on Khao Luang Rd., 2 blocks north of Anonta Worarittidit Rd. (10-13hr.; 8 per day 8-9am and 6-7pm; 236฿, 2nd-class A/C 301฿, 1st-class A/C 387฿, VIP 600฿).

Rentals: Oversea (☎710 258), 490 Sumon Thewarat Rd. at Mahawong Rd. **Mountain bikes** 30-50฿ per day; **motorcycles** 150-180฿ per day. Open daily 8am-5:30pm.

ORIENTATION AND PRACTICAL INFORMATION

Five blocks west of the river, buses from the north arrive at the station on **Anonta Worarittidit Rd.;** this road runs roughly east-west through the center of town, perpendicular to the Nan River. A block south of Anonta Worarittidit Rd., **Mahawong Rd.** passes the **post office** and goes over the town's bridge; two blocks south, **Suriyaphong Rd.** passes the **police station, City Hall,** and many sights. Intersecting all three of these, **Sumon Thewarat Rd.**, which runs north-south through the town center, is the primary thoroughfare. A useful point of reference, the **Dhevaraj Hotel** rests on this road halfway between its intersections with Anonta Worarittidit and Mahawong Rd. Followed to its far northern end, Sumon Thewarat Rd. leads to **Worawichai Rd.** Parallel to and one block east of Sumon Thewarat Rd. is **Khao Luang Rd.** One block to the west of Sumon Thewarat lies **Mahayod Rd.,** which runs out the northern end of town via the turn-off to Pua; another block west are **Pha Kong Rd.** and its small nightly food stalls.

Tourist Office: TAT (☎751 029), in the Municipal Office, on Pha Kong Rd. at Suriyaphong Rd. Minimal English spoken. Open daily 8:30am-5:30pm.

Currency Exchange: Thai Farmers Bank, 434 Sumon Thewarat Rd. (☎710 162), has a **24hr. ATM** (Cirrus/MC/PLUS/V). Open M-F 8:30am-3:30pm.

Emergency: ☎191. **Tourist Police (Bangkok):** ☎1155.

Police: 52 Suriyaphong Rd. (☎751 681 or 751 033), opposite City Hall.

Pharmacy: 347/5 Sumon Thewarat Rd. (☎710 452), opposite Thai Farmers Bank. Open daily 8am-7pm. Another pharmacy at **Nan Provincial Hospital** (see below).

Medical Services: Nan Provincial Hospital (☎710 138), on Worawichai Rd. at the bend in Sumon Thewarat Rd. 3km north of downtown. *Songthaew* leave from the Nara department store, 1 block north of Dhevaraj Hotel (5฿). **24hr. emergency care.**

Telephone: Telecommunications Office (☎773 214), Mahayod Rd., 2km outside town 200m past turn-off to Pua. Has **international phones,** CATNET, and fax. Open M-F 8am-6pm, Sa-Su 9am-4:30pm.

Internet Access: Easy Internet, 345/8 Sumon Thewarat Rd., opposite and north of Thai Farmers Bank. 20฿ per hr. Open daily 9am-10pm, but these hours are not dependable.

Post Office: GPO, 70 Mahawong Rd. (☎710 176), west of Sumon Thewarat Rd. *Poste Restante.* Open M-F 8:30am-4:30pm, Sa-Su 9am-noon. **Postal Code:** 55000

ACCOMMODATIONS AND FOOD

PK Guest House ❶, 33/12 Premphachraj Rd., has rooms set around a pond. Walk north 1.5km on Sumon Thewarat Rd., and make a left after the school; it's down the second soi on the right. (☎751 416. Bicycle and motorbike rental 30฿/150฿. Laundry. Singles 100฿; doubles 150฿; triples 200฿; VIP 250฿.) **Nan Guest House ❷** has a great location 10min. from the bus station. Turn left onto Anonta Worarittidit Rd.; take the first right. Follow the signs 2 blocks to the back-street location. (☎771 849. Wooden-floored back house 120฿; rooms in main house 130฿.) **Amazing Guest House ❶,** 150m past the PK Guest House on the left, has spacious rooms in the family's teak house. (☎710 893. Laundry 40฿ per kg. Massage 150฿ per hr. Singles 100-120฿; doubles 160-200฿; triples 210฿; bungalows with bath 200-250฿.)

The region is known for its dog farms (and they're not breeding pets) as well as the famed **Nan River dining ❶.** In an effort to keep cool during Nan's dry and exceptionally hot season (temperatures exceed 40°C), locals sit in the Nan River up to their waists at firmly fixed tables, and then proceed to chow down on food stall fare. To get to the river dining, turn onto Nokham Rd. from Sumon Thewarat at the wat, one block north of Anonta Worarittidit Rd. A more traditional dining experience can be had at **Tanaya Kitchen ❷,** on Anonta Worarittidit Rd., one block beyond Pha Kong Rd. from the bus station on the right. (Red curry 50฿. Potato bread 10฿. Open daily 7am-8:30pm.) **Rimkaew Restaurant ❷,** on Sumon Thewarat Rd., at the bend 3km from town just before the hospital, serves mostly Thai dishes. (Most entrees 30-60฿. Open daily 10am-4pm and 7-10pm.)

SIGHTS AND MARKETS

The **Nan National Museum,** at the Suriyaphong and Pha Kong Rd. intersection, features exhibits on Nan's history and Thailand's hill tribes. (☎710 561. Open daily 9am-4pm. 30฿.) Nan's ornate, detailed wats are among the most beautiful in northern Thailand. Across the street from the museum is **Wat Phra That Chang Kham,** which houses a walking Buddha made of gold. The 400-year-old **Wat Phumin,** on Pha Kong Rd. south of the museum, holds murals depicting Lanna culture. The distinctive golden *chedi* of **Wat Phra That Chae Haeng** shines 2km beyond the Nan River bridge. Constructed nearly 700 years ago, the wat is the oldest in the region. Southwest of town, **Wat Phra That Khao Noi** offers sweeping views of the valley. The attraction at **Wat Phaya Wat** is the slightly lopsided old pagoda that parallels the bending coconut palm. Go west on Suriyaphong Rd. to Hwy. 101 and turn right after the bridge. Wat Phaya Wat is on the plain while Wat Phra That Khao Noi is 2km up the road on top of a hill. Back in town, the **Thai Payap Project** sells hill-tribe **handicrafts** from 15 villages in its showroom on Jettabut Rd. Follow the road directly opposite the Dhevaraj Hotel past the market; it's 400m down on the right. The project also arranges **homestays.** All proceeds go to community development projects in the surrounding areas. (☎772 520. Open daily 8:30am-5pm.)

A spacious **produce market** sets up on Jettabut Rd. directly opposite the Dhevaraj Hotel. Several counters serve over 20 dishes which you can point at and buy by the bag (10-15฿). Along Anonta Worarittidit Rd. next to the northern bus station is the **day market,** which is big on pineapples and really, really small turtles. The tiny **night market,** on Anonta Worarittidit Rd. outside the 7-Eleven, starts around 6pm. Cheap noodle and rice standards are 20฿. Food gets sketchier around the corner on Pha Kong Rd., but don't miss the fabulous fruit stand at the end of the stalls.

THAILAND

DAYTRIPS FROM NAN

Few travelers get a glimpse of Nan's rugged back country. Nan is now almost entirely safe—some mines remain buried in the most remote areas, but the risks are negligible, especially on roads or trails. Getting lost is actually a greater danger, as English signs are sparse. **Fhu Travel Service,** 453/4 Sumon Thewarat Rd., south of the intersection with Mahawong Rd., leads expeditions around the province. A **trek** with Mr. Fhu is the only way to visit the **Mrabi** (Phi Tong Lueng, "Spirit of the Yellow Leaves"), a tribe found only in the provinces of Nan and Phrae. Year-round **rubber rafting** on the Nan River through **Mae Charim National Park** southeast of Nan is also possible. (☎710 636. Price per person falls as group size increases. 1-day trek to Mrabi territory 1250฿ for 2 people, 700฿ for 5 or more. 3-day trek 2700฿/1500฿. 1-day rafting 2300฿/1200฿.)

DOI PHUKHA NATIONAL PARK AND ENVIRONS. Dozens of waterfalls and caves dot Doi Phukha National Park, home to Hmong and Mien tribes. (Open daily 6am-6pm. 200฿.) The **park office** (☎701 000), 25km up the road from Pua, can sometimes provide **accommodations ❶**; call the National Park Division of the Forestry Service (☎02 579 0529), in Bangkok, first to check. (Tent rental 250฿. Camping 30฿; bungalows for two 200฿, for six 1200฿.) The most easily accessed point from which to see the prized **Chomphu Phukha tree** *(Bretschneidera sinensis)* is 5km past the park office. Though not the world's only specimen (as locals tend to claim), it is still extremely rare. The slender tree blooms in February, and hordes of Thais come to see its foot-long clusters of red-veined, hibiscus-shaped flowers. Turn left off the highway and north from Ban Bor Kleua; a road leads to **Ban Sapan,** 10km away. After crossing the bridge just before the village, turn right onto a dirt road to reach the **Sapan Waterfall,** off the road to the right, marked by a red Thai sign and a smaller English one. The dry-season flow will probably leave you unimpressed, but it's worthwhile in the wet season. Take Hwy. 1080 from Nan (past an Esso station on the left) for 60km to Pua. Here, turn right just before the market (you'll have to loop back), then left 100m up the road at the English sign for the park (Hwy. 1256). The road stretches 47km over a mountain peak and through the park to Ban Bor Kleua. *Songthaew,* which leave from near Pua's market for Ban

FROM THE ROAD

POWS

Few men left the POW camps spanning between Kanchanaburi and Thanbyuzayat (Three Pagoda Pass) without coming under the care of Edward "Weary" Dunlop.

As one of the Senior Medical Officers in the region and known to the men as "King of the River," Weart inspired hope in what was a tortuous war. He was even dubbed "No. 1 Doctor" by the Japanese who heard of his miraculous surgical successes.

This soft-spoken gentleman towering at 6'4" worked tirelessly in work camps. Like his fellow POWs, he suffered from dysentery, tropical ulcers, and recurring malaria and cholera. With a tough rep from his days of playing rugby for Australia, he was just as driven to help his fellow POWs.

He was the Commanding Officer—an unprecedented appointment considering his non-combatant status. He regularly confronted Japanese Commanders about the appalling conditions of the camp. Weary ended these fiery exchanges by swearing he'd have them hanged at the end of the war.

In the wet season of 1943, Weary was instructed to force one-third of his patients to work, some 100 sick men. What came to be known as the "log sitting game" was Weary's solution. He instructed his sick patients to simply sit on the log irrespective of the Japanese orders to work and the subsequent beatings.

The result was that more POWs were put in the hospital, less able to work. His rebellion boosted morale among the men and forced the Japanese to back down and let him keep

(continued on next page)

Bor Kleua, can drop you at the park office (first *songthaew* departs between 8 and 10am, others leave infrequently throughout the day, 30฿). Orange buses speed to Pua from the bus station in Nan (1½hr., every hr. 5am-6pm, 20฿). The road to Doi Phukha is steep and windy; check brakes before departing. (*Songthaew* riders: try to remain oblivious.) Once you're at the park, there's not much to do without private transportation. It's possible to loop your way back from Ban Bor Kleua to Nan taking back routes; pick up the regional map from the TAT.

LAMPANG ☎054

Lampang dates back to the 7th-century Dvaravati period, when it played an integral role in the Lanna Kingdom of the "Million Rice Fields." Though the city may not impress you, at least one of the surrounding sights will.

TRANSPORTATION

Flights: The **airport** is on Sanambin Rd. 2km from town. **Thai Airways,** 236 Sanambin Rd. (☎217 078). Open daily 8:30am-5:30pm. To **Bangkok** (M, Sa 11:15am; 2055฿). **PB Air** at the airport (☎226 238; open daily 8am-6pm) flies to Bangkok (Su-F 9:55am, 5:10pm; 2055฿). Departure and insurance tax 105฿.

Trains: Lampang Railroad Station (☎318 648 or 217 024), on Prasanmaitri Rd. To reach the station, flag down a westbound *songthaew* (10-20฿). Trains to: **Bangkok** (10-12hr.; 6 per day; 3rd-class 146฿, 2nd-class 284฿) via **Phitsanulok** (5hr.; 3rd-class 88฿, 2nd-class 151฿) and **Ayutthaya** (9hr.; 3rd-class 135฿, 2nd-class 261฿); **Chiang Mai** (2hr.; 9 per day; 3rd-class 23฿, 2nd-class 53฿).

Buses: The **bus station** (☎227 410) is off Asia 1 Hwy., several kilometers out of town. All prices listed are with A/C. To: **Bangkok** (8hr.; 7:30am-9pm; 193฿, 2nd-class A/C 270฿, 1st-class A/C 347฿, VIP 540฿); **Chiang Mai** (2hr.; every 30min. 2am-9pm; 39฿, 2nd-class A/C 55฿, 1st-class A/C 70฿); **Chiang Rai** (5hr.; every 45min. 5am-5pm; 81฿, 2nd-class A/C 113฿); **Nan** (4hr.; 11 per day 8am-midnight; 86฿, 2nd-class A/C 120฿, 1st-class A/C 154฿); **Sukhothai** (4-5hr.; every hr. 6:30am-4:30pm; 91฿, 2nd-class A/C 127฿, 1st-class A/C 164฿) via **Phitsanulok** (4hr.; 91฿, 2nd-class A/C 153฿, 1st-class A/C 196฿).

Local Transportation: Blue **songthaew** go anywhere in town (10฿). Trips to and from the bus and train stations cost 5-10฿ more (for no good reason except that you're a captive customer). **Samlor** usually cost around 50฿.

PRACTICAL INFORMATION

Most roads radiate from the **clock-tower rotary** near the town center. **Boonyawat Rd.** heads east, passing hotels, banks, and shops. In the opposite direction, **Tah Krao Rd.** runs past the **Aswin Market. Suren Rd.**, off Tah Krao Rd., runs to the **train station. Thipchang Rd.**, a commercial avenue parallel to Boonyawat Rd. and the Wang River, lies one block north of the clock tower. The **bus station,** off **Asia 1 Hwy.**, is on **Jantsurin Rd.** 2km from the traffic circle. *Songthaew* from the bus station cut across **Phahonyothin Rd.**, a major commuter road four blocks south of the Wang River, to **Chatchai Rd.**, which terminates at the clock tower.

Tourist Office: ☎218 823. On Boonyawat Rd., just past Praisanee Rd. Set back 50m from the road. Open daily 8:30am-4:30pm.

Currency Exchange: Banks line Boonyawat Rd. **Bangkok Bank,** 36-44 Thipchang Rd. (☎228 135). **24hr. ATM** (AmEx/Cirrus/MC/PLUS/V). Open M-F 8:30am-3:30pm.

Markets: Large and lively. **Tesaban Market 1** sets up near City Hall along Rajawong Rd. 1 block toward the clock tower from Praisanee Rd.

Emergency: ☎191. **Tourist Police (Bangkok):** ☎1155.

Police: ☎221 589. On Boonyawat Rd. opposite City Hall.

Pharmacy: ☎223 869. On the corner of Boonyawat and Praisanee Rd. Open daily 8am-10pm.

Medical Services: Khelang Nakorn-Ram Hospital, 79/12 Phahonyothin Rd. (☎352 432). **Open 24hr.** AmEx/MC/V.

Telephones: Lampang Telecommunication Center, 99 Phahonyothin Rd. (☎221 700), 500m before the hospital heading to the bus station. Overseas calls, CATNET Internet, and fax. Open daily 7am-8pm. You might also try your luck at the GPO.

Internet Access: CATNET Internet access at the GPO or Lampang Telecommunications Center is the best bet (11฿ per hr.). At night, computer gamers crowd out would be 'net surfers at Lampang Telecommunications.

Post Office: GPO (☎323 497), on Thipchang Rd. Follow Boonyawat Rd. to City Hall and then turn left on Praisanee Rd. *Poste Restante.* **Lenso** telephone. Open M-F 8:30am-4:30pm, Sa-Su 9am-noon. **Postal code:** 52000.

(continued from previous page)

as many patients in the hospital as he wanted. The patients were given preferential treatment, which at the time meant protein-filled duck eggs.

When he came home to Australia after the war, he made sure the Thais who risked their lives to help the POWs were recognized. Boon Pong, a Thai trader who spearheaded an underground system of delivering the duck eggs via the Kwai River, was singled out for commendation.

Weary also came back from the war to become an internationally recognized surgeon, pioneering new techniques in thoracic cancer treatment.

Ever devoted, he returned to Asia to train other doctors in India, Vietnam, and Thailand. The Edward "Weary" Dunlop-Boon Pong Fellowship now exists to bring Thai nationals to Australia to study medicine at Melbourne University.

A companion of the Order of Australia, knighted in Britain by Her Majesty, given the Knight Grand Cross of the Most Noble Order of the Royal Crown of Thailand, made an order of the White Elephant, a fellow of the prestigious Royal College of Surgeions in London, and the recipient of honorary fellowships and doctorates, Weary died in 1993 just before turning 86.

He wished that his ashes be returned to the Hellfire Pass with the following epitaph:

"When you go home,
Tell them of us and say
We gave our tomorrow
For your today"

*– **Anthony Barker***

ACCOMMODATIONS AND FOOD

Riverside Guest House ❸, 286 Talad Gao Rd., has a relaxing veranda over the river. From the clock tower, walk along Boonyawat Rd. with the river on your left, turn left onto the soi with the sign to the guest house; it's 2 blocks down, where the soi curves. (☎227 005. Motorbike rental 200฿ per day. Doubles 250฿, riverside 250฿; twins 300฿; suites 600฿.) *The* backpacker's choice is **TT&T Guest House ❷.** It's a 30min. walk from the clock tower; go east on Boonyawat Rd. until it meets the Khelang bridge on the left. Cross the bridge and take an immediate left; it's 150m on the left. (☎225 361. Internet 40฿ per hr. Singles 120฿; doubles 160-200฿.) **9 Mituna (Gao Mituna) ❷,** 285 Boonyawat Rd. on the first block from the clock tower, has clean rooms with hot water and fan. A/C rooms have bathtubs and Western toilets. (☎222 261. Singles 143฿, with A/C 286฿; doubles 204฿/306฿.)

The Riverside Restaurant ❷ serves up strongly flavored Thai dishes in a cozy, benched patio. From the clock tower, walk to the river; it's 250m to the right. (Open daily 10am-midnight; band starts at 7:30pm.) **Chom Wang Restaurant ❷** has outdoor dining on its deck. It has no English sign but is only 50m from Riverside Guest House. (Fried chicken in banana leaves 60฿. Open daily 6pm-midnight.)

SIGHTS

Wat Phra Kaew Don Tao, in the northeastern corner of town, housed the Emerald Buddha during the reign of King Anantayot (r. 1436-68). The *wiharn* is open to visitors on Buddhist holidays only. (Wat open daily 6am-6:30pm.) Mentioning **Ban Sao Nak** ("house of many pillars") conjures up a lot of pride for the people of Lampang; the Crown Prince and Princess came to lunch here in 1977. (Open daily 10am-5pm. 30฿ admission includes soft-drink.) Despite the dry name, **Lampang Medical Plants Conservation Center** (☎350 787) is the coolest place in Lampang. It's best visited by private transport. To get there, ride west on Jamatawee Rd. over the gradual big hill, hang a right on the street across from the 7-Eleven, and turn left on the dirt road just before the bridge; it's 100m down on your left. Set in a luscious garden, this spa/research center has the remedy for whatever ails you. A practical buy is Porng Karn Yoong Tar Klai Hom (#104), an insect repellent (10-20฿). Organic shampoo is available for earthy types in the vapor rooms and is best enjoyed after the free barefoot health walk around the gardens. (Open daily 8am-8pm.)

DAYTRIPS FROM LAMPANG

THAI ELEPHANT CONSERVATION CENTER. The Thai Elephant Conservation Center is on the highway between Chiang Mai and Lampang, outside the Thung Kwian Forest. Elephants begin training here at age three and continue under one master until they are 61 years old, when they retire. The center was established to employ elephants and their mahouts in other pursuits to preserve the species given their decreasing importance in traditional labors such as logging and construction. A 30min. ride through the forest costs 400฿. (Rides daily 8am-3:30pm.) The center has a homestay program that lets you stay and work with mahouts. *(Take a Chiang Mai-bound bus; ask to be let off at the center (35min., 20฿). The showground is 2km farther on foot. ☎229 042. Shows daily 10, 11am, and weekends 1:30pm. 80฿.)*

CHAE SON (JAE SORN) NATIONAL PARK AND KEW LOM DAM. This national park boasts modern facilities and **hot springs.** The springs' main draw is not the **bubbling sulfurous pools** reaching 82°C, but rather the luxurious **private baths** (20฿; 5฿ for shower). A less private option is to plunge into the **river** where the water from the hot spring merges pleasantly with the river water. **Chae Son Waterfall,** plummeting 150m over six tiers, lies 1km farther up the road. An easy 3km nature trail along the river links the two sites. *(To get a songthaew to Chae Son Falls, 70km from Lampang, look for the dirt parking lot 100m down the soi running between Thipchang and Talad Gao Rd., one block toward the GPO from Bangkok Bank (1½hr., 50฿). Returning will be difficult. Waterfall 200฿. Camping permitted 30฿. Tent rental 180฿/250฿ for 2/3 people. 3- to 15-person bungalows for 600-3000฿ (☎229 000). Park open daily 6am-6pm.* Songthaew *to Kew Lom line up on Rob Wiang Rd., behind City Hall. Dam open daily 6am-6pm.)*

WAT PHRA THAT LAMPANG LUANG. About 18km southwest of Lampang in the town of **Ko Kha** sits Wat Phra That Lampang Luang, one of Northern Thailand's finest displays of religious architecture. Its giant *chedi* and low wooden buildings also hold Lampang's most sacred Buddha. Through the main gate, the central *wiharn* is an open-air Lanna-style structure, supported by 46 laterite columns. Constructed in 1486, the chapel houses two important Buddha images. **Phra Jao Lan Tang,** cast in 1563, is enclosed in a golden *mondop* near the rear of the temple; **Phra Jao Tan Jai** sits behind the *mondop*. Directly behind the *wiharn*, the *chedi* houses relics of the Buddha. **Wiharn Naamtaen,** to the right of the *chedi*, displays murals dating from 1501, while a 700-year-old Buddha image rests inside **Phra Phuttha Wiharn** to the left of the *chedi*. A **Buddha footprint** lies behind **Haw Phra Phutthabat,** a white building constructed in 1149. Only men can enter, whereupon they'll discover a puzzling white sheet before the indistinguishable Buddha footprint. *(*Songthaew *to Ko Kha leave from Robwiang Rd., one block west of Praisanee Rd. (20฿). It's a few kilometers farther to the temple—negotiate with a driver. If arriving with private transport from the Thai Elephant Conservation Center, there's no need to backtrack all the way to Lampang; look for signs to the wat and Ko Kha from the highway.)*

PHITSANULOK ☎055

A staging ground for Ayutthaya's campaigns against the Burmese and the station of the Third Army during Communist uprisings in the Nan hills, Phitsanulok ("Phitlok" or "Philok" to locals) retains its military tradition, hosting the annual Cobra Gold exercises between Thai and American forces. Despite its past martial prowess, the busy metropolis welcomes travelers who overnight here while taking in Phra Buddha Chinnarat, one of the world's most famous Buddha images.

TRANSPORTATION

Flights: Phitsanulok Domestic Airport (☎258 029), on Sanambin Rd. **Thai Airways,** 209/26-28 Srithammatripidok Rd. (☎242 971)—with your back to the TAT it's 50m to the right. Flies to **Bangkok** (daily 6:20am, 1:30, 8:10pm; Th-F, Su 10:05am; M, Sa 12:25pm; 1485฿) and **Lampang** (M, Sa 10am; 955฿). **Air Andaman,** booked through Thai Airways or at the airport, flies to **Chiang Mai** (Tu, Th, Sa 12:30pm; 1185฿). Open M-F 8am-5pm; open at the airport on weekends.

Trains: Phitsanulok Train Station (☎258 005), on Akatossaroth Rd. To **Bangkok** (6-7hr.; 14 per day; 3rd-class 109฿, 2nd-class 159฿) via **Ayutthaya** (5-6hr.; 9 per day; 3rd-class 98฿, 2nd-class 175฿) and **Chiang Mai** (6-8hr.; 7 per day; 3rd-class 105฿, 2nd-class 190฿).

Buses: Bo Ko So Bus Station (☎242 430), on Phitsanulok-Lomsak Rd. east of town. City bus #1 shuttles between the train and bus stations. Buses to: **Bangkok** (6hr.; 25 per day; 121฿, 2nd-class A/C 169฿, 1st-class A/C 218฿); **Chiang Mai** (6-7hr.; 26 per day; 120-140฿, A/C 168-216฿); **Chiang Rai** (6-7hr.; 20 per day; 139-153฿, A/C 195-275฿); **Khon Kaen** (5hr.; 13 per day; 137฿, 2nd-class A/C 192฿, 1st-class A/C 247฿); **Mae Sot** (A/C van 5hr., 8 per day 7am-4pm, 125฿); **Nakhon Ratchasima** (6-7hr.; 15

per day; 137-148฿, A/C 192-247฿); **Sukhothai** (1hr.; every 30min. 4:45am-6pm; 23฿, A/C 32฿); **Udon Thani** (7hr.; 9 per day; 122฿, A/C 171-220฿) via **Loei** (4hr.; 79฿, A/C 111-142฿). A/C is not available on all rides to all locations. For major destinations, buses have multiple routes; one route is often up to 1hr. quicker than another.

Local Transportation: City Bus Station, on Akatossaroth Rd., 1 block left of the train station. Buses run daily 5am-9pm. Bus #1 goes to Bo Ko So Bus Station, Wat Yai, and Naresuan University. Bus #4 goes to the airport. Regular buses 5฿, A/C 7฿.

Rentals: Lady Motor, 43/12 Baromtrilokanart Rd., 20m south of Pailyn Hotel. Motorcycles 150฿ for 9am-5pm, 200฿ for 24hr. Open M-Sa 8:30am-5:30pm.

ORIENTATION AND PRACTICAL INFORMATION

Phitsanulok lies along the east bank of the **Nan River,** 377km north of Bangkok. **Puttaboocha Rd.** runs parallel to the river. One block east is **Baromtrilokanart Rd.** The main thoroughfare, **Akatossaroth Rd.,** lies two blocks east of the river and also runs parallel to the railroad tracks. **Naresuan Rd.** shoots out from the **Phitsanulok Train Station** on Akatossaroth Rd., intersecting, through the busiest part of town, Baromtrilokanart and Puttaboocha Rd. before crossing the river. The famous **Phra Buddha Chinnarat** is at **Wat Yai** at the northern end of Puttaboocha Rd. The **Bo Ko So Bus Station** is 3km east of the wat on the other side of the train tracks.

Tourist Office: TAT, 209/7-8 Surasi Trade Center, Srithammatripidok Rd. (☎/fax 252 742). Helpful staff go out of their way to offer assistance. Open daily 8:30am-4:30pm.

Tours: Able Tours and Travel, 55/45 Srithammatripidok Rd. (☎243 851). With your back to TAT, it's 25m to the left. Books domestic and international flights. Open M-F 8am-6pm, Sa 8am-4:30pm.

Currency Exchange: Thai Farmers Bank, 144/1 Baromtrilokanart Rd. (☎241 497), at the clock tower. **24hr. ATM** (Cirrus/MC/PLUS/V). Open M-F 8:30am-3:30pm. Several **banks** are also on Naresuan Rd.

Luggage Storage: At the train station. 10฿ per piece per day. Open daily 7am-11pm.

Markets: Day market, north of the train station behind Akatossaroth Rd. **Night bazaar,** on Puttaboocha Rd., just south of the bridge. A plethora of great food stalls.

Emergency: ☎191. **Ambulance:** ☎1669. **Tourist Police (Bangkok):** ☎1155.

Police: ☎258 777. On Baromtrilokanart Rd. Walking from the train station on Naresuan Rd., turn right onto Baromtrilokanart Rd. It's 20m on the left.

Tourist Police (local): 31/15 Akatossaroth Rd. (☎245 357), 200m past back entrance to Wat Yai away from the train station. Marked as "Tourist Service Center." Some English spoken. **Open 24hr.**

Medical Services: Buddha Chinnarat Hospital (☎219 844), on the southern extension of Akatossaroth Rd. at the turn-off to TAT. (The official street address is on Srithammatripidok Rd.) **24hr. emergency room** and **pharmacy.**

Telephones: Phitsanulok Telecommunication Center (☎243 116), on Puttaboocha next to the GPO. International phone/fax. CATNET. Open daily 7am-10pm. AmEx/MC/V.

Internet Access: Speedy Net, 50m past the bridge on Naresuan Rd. heading out of town. Open daily 8am-11pm. **Skynet,** 108 Sanambin Rd. Open daily 8am-midnight. Both 30฿ per hr.

Post Office: GPO (☎258 313), on Puttaboocha Rd. 500m north of Naresuan Rd. *Poste Restante.* Open M-F 8:30am-4:30pm, Sa-Su 9am-noon. **Postal code:** 65000.

ACCOMMODATIONS AND FOOD

Phitsanulok Youth Hostel (HI) ❷ has clean rooms furnished with Thai antiques and a lush garden. From the train station, take bus #4 toward the airport, cross the train tracks, and turn right on Sanambin Rd. (☎242 060. Laundry. Dorms 120฿; singles with bath 200฿; doubles 300฿; triples 450฿.) To get to **London Hotel** ❶ from the train station, walk left to Sairuthai Rd., take a right, and it's 1½ blocks down, just past the Bridgestone tire store. (☎225 145. Singles 100฿; doubles 150฿.) **Lithai** ❷, 73/1-5 Payalithai Rd., has high-quality rooms. From the train station, walk left and take the second road to the right; it's 50m down. (☎219 626. Singles 150฿; doubles 180฿; triples 220฿; rooms with bath 200-220฿, with bath and A/C 330-440฿.)

Payalithai Road has the best and cheapest during the day. At night, the foodquake's epicenter is **the night market's northern end** (see **Markets,** above); nearly a solid kilometer of eateries begins at the Naresuan Rd. bridge. All over the city (especially the night market), **flying-vegetable restaurants** ❶ hurl *pak boong fai deng* (flaming morning glory vine) from woks to distant plates. For sit-down eats, head to **Fah-Ke-Rah** ❷, 52/6 Pra Ong Dam Rd. near the mosque. This Muslim restaurant has arguably the best food in Phitsanulok. (*Lassi* 20฿. Chicken with yellow rice 25฿; *Roti kaeng* 20฿. Open daily 6am-2pm.)

SIGHTS AND ENTERTAINMENT

Wat Phra Si Ratana Mahathat (Wat Yai), at the northern end of Puttaboocha Rd., shelters Phitsanulok's jewel. Cast in 1357, the spectacular **Phra Buddha Chinnarat** (Victorious King) is one of the world's most reproduced Buddha images. The wing of the wat that is on the left when you face Phra Buddha Chinnarat has been turned into a museum. (Museum open W-Su 9am-4pm. Wat open daily 7am-6pm. Sporadically enforced 10฿ admission. Sarongs provided free of charge to the barelegged.) The **Sgt. Maj. Thawee Folk Museum,** 26/43 Wisutkasat Rd., is doing an incredible job of trying to protect folk culture. (☎212 749. Open Tu-Su 8:30am-4:30pm. Free, but donations accepted and deserved.) Across the street, Dr. Thawee also runs the **Buranathai Buddha Image Foundry,** where you can see handcrafted bronze Buddhas, from figurines to goliaths, in different stages of creation. (☎258 715. Open daily 8am-5pm.) **Wat Chulamanee,** built in 1464, is 6km outside the city and best reached by moto-taxi (100฿).

Pubs cluster at the far northern end of **Baromtrilokanart Rd.** About the only thing **Studio 54,** at the Pailyn Hotel, has in common with its infamous New York equivalent is that it hosts the "in" crowd. (Heineken and Carlsberg 100฿. Open daily 8am-2am.) For more bar options head to the **Phitsanulok Bazaar** across the bridge on Naresuan Rd. Bars line the quadrangle around **Discovery,** a disco with live bands and the orange-haired rebellious crowd. (Open daily 9pm-1am.)

DAYTRIP FROM PHITSANULOK: PHU HIN RONG KHLA

The park is best visited during the less-crowded weekdays. Take a bus to Nakhon Thai (2hr., every hr. 6:30am-6pm, 28฿) and then a songthaew *32km to Phu Hin Rong Khla (1½hr., sporadic, 40฿). Private transportation is needed to see much of the park. To charter a* songthaew *for the day will cost 1500฿ from Phitsanulok, less from Nakhon Thai. To get there take Route 12 from Phitsanulok, and then go left onto Route 2013 to Nakhon Thai. Turn right onto Route 2331, follow signs to Nakhon Thai or National Park about 70km out on Route 12. Park headquarters open daily 8am-4pm. Park admission 200฿.*

The Thai army and the People's Liberation Army of Thailand (PLAT) clashed around Phitsanulok, on the land that this national park now encompasses. From

IN RECENT NEWS

CRAZY MEDICINE

Thailand has discovered that curbing the demand of one drug does not mean curbing drug demand.

Opium use declined dramatically in Thailand in the mid-90s because social and economic programs reduced both supply and demand. The big push worked—but only for opium. Just at that moment heroin became the world's hip drug, It was abundant, too—produced right in the Golden Triangle. Heroin became a public health nightmare since sharing hypodermic needles sped the spread of HIV/AIDS.

But heroin was only a passing fancy compared to the meteoric rise in the use of methamphetamines. Locally known as *"ya ba"* (crazy medicine), speed is Thailand's latest drug scourge. The Asian financial crisis only exacerbated the problem. *Ya ba* became the intoxicant of choice among laborers during the boom years, but its use skyrocketed among disillusioned youth after the collapse.

Ya ba is the perfect narcotic to attract young, new drug users. Heroin prices are generally out of reach for new customers (price fluctuations influence the buying behavior of new users much more than addicts). Speed also fits the pop cultural trend: it's a club drug and a cheap substitute for ecstasy. It produces temporary hyperactivity, euphoria, confidence, alertness, and tremors. Users' heart rate, temperature, breathing and blood pressure increase.

Violent behavior is common, as are

(continued on next page)

1967 to 1982, PLAT survived in the Phu Hin Rong Khla forests 123km from town near the Lao border. Recruits poured in after the clampdown on student demonstrators in Bangkok in 1976. The government then struck a decisive blow by offering amnesty to all students who joined the movement after 1976. In 1982, the area was declared a national park. The most visited sight in the park is the **flagpole,** near the old Communist headquarters. A 3.2km **nature walk** leads to the flagpole, where the Thai flag now boldly flies. The nature walk lies 2km from park headquarters along a marked and paved road. Pick up a map from the park headquarters to explore the **waterfalls** and **historical attractions** Phu Hin Rong Khla has to offer. The park headquarters also offers some **accommodations ❶.** (Tent rental 100฿. Camping 30฿; bungalows 600฿.) Those traveling with their own transport will want to explore the many **waterfalls** that lie off Route 12. The best is the three-tiered 40m drop of **Kaeng Sopha Waterfall,** 74km outside of Phitsanulok. The dry-season flow will leave you unsatisfied, but the large valley boulders entwined in trees warrant exploration. The turn-off to Kaeng Sopha Waterfall is 3km beyond the turn-off to Nakhon Thai. It's 2km from the main road to the waterfall.

SUKHOTHAI ☎055

In 1238, the Thais established the new capital of the Lanna Kingdom near the Yom River and drove the Khmer to the east. Named "Sukhothai," or "Dawn of Happiness," the city marked the birth of the first Thai nation. Sukhothai has recently joined Ayutthaya and Kanchanaburi as a sightseeing hot spot—and while Old Sukhothai is fast becoming a laterite theme park, nearby Si Satchanalai, with some of Thailand's most awe-inspiring ruins, remains untrafficked.

TRANSPORTATION

Flights: The **airport** is 26km out of town. **Bangkok Airways** (☎613 075), at the Pailyn Hotel, on the road to the old city, flies to **Bangkok** (daily 12:50pm; Su-M, W, F 4:40pm; 1500฿); **Chiang Mai** (daily 10:40am, 1040฿). 100฿ departure tax. Shuttle bus to the airport from Sukhothai Travel Service 90฿.

Buses: There is a brand new **bus station** (☎614 529) 3km out of town on Bypass Rd. White, pink, and blue *songthaew* run along Bypass Rd. into town (5฿ before 4pm). Tuk-tuks to town are a self-regulated 30฿. Buses go to: **Bangkok** (7hr.; every hr. 7:50am-11pm; 142฿, 2nd-class A/C 199฿, 1st-class A/C 256฿) via **Ayutthaya** (5hr.); **Chiang Mai** (6hr.; 12 per day 1:20am-

5pm; 122฿, A/C 171฿) via **Tak** (1hr., every hr. 7:30am-6:15pm, 31-43฿); **Chiang Rai** (6-7hr., 6:40am, 136฿; 9, 11:30am, 190฿); **Nan** (6hr., 10pm, 104฿; A/C 2:30pm, 146฿); **Phitsanulok** (1hr.; every 30min. 6:20am-8pm; 23฿, A/C 32฿). **Minibuses** to **Mae Sot** (2½hr., 7 per day 8am-4pm, 100฿) leave from a traffic triangle off Charot Withi Thong Rd., 2 blocks north of the main traffic light.

Local Transportation: Tuk-tuks 20-30฿. **Samlor** 10-20฿. At the terminal across the bridge, **trucks** run to the old city (every 20min. 6am-6pm, 10฿). A bus to **Si Satchanalai** runs from the bus station (every 30min. 7am-4:30pm, 30฿).

Rentals: Lotus Village and **Ban Thai Guest House** rent **bikes** for 20-50฿ per day. Bikes cost 20-30฿ per day at the historical park andSi Satchanalai. Most guesthouses and **Thanin Motorbikes,** 112 Charot Withi Thong (☎613 402), 20m past Thai Farmers Bank, rent motorbikes (150฿ per day; open daily 7am-8pm).

PRACTICAL INFORMATION

New Sukhothai city appears at an L-shaped bend in the Yom River. **Charot Withi Thong Rd.** and **Singhawat Rd.** run a few blocks in from the Yom's eastern bank and converge at Sukhothai's largest intersection near the bend in the "L." From there, Charot Withi Thong Rd. crosses **Praruang Bridge** and continues into the old city, intersecting **Nikorn Kasaem** and **Pravet Nakhon Rd.** along the way. Hwy. 101 bypasses the town at its northern end.

Tourist Office: The **bus information counter** deals out bus timetables. **Sukhothai Travel Service,** 327/6-7 Charot Withi Thong Rd. (☎613 075), books flights. Shuttle to the airport coincides with flights (90฿). Open daily 8am-5pm.

Bookstore: D.K. Bookstore, 41/2-3 Nikorn Kasaem Rd. (☎612 272), 100m from the bridge, has an excellent selection of **regional maps.** Open daily 7am-9pm.

Currency Exchange: Most banks change currency and traveler's checks. **Thai Farmers Bank,** 134 Charot Withi Thong Rd. (☎611 932), at the base of the bridge, has a **24hr. ATM** (Cirrus/MC/Plus/V). Open M-F 8:30am-3:30pm.

Emergency: ☎191. **Tourist Police (Bangkok):** ☎1155.

Police: 263 Nikorn Kasaem Rd. (☎613 110), 250m beyond the post office.

Medical Services: Patanavej Hospital, 89/9 Singhawat Rd. (☎621 502), 200m from the intersection of Singhawat and Charot Withi Thong Rd., on the right. Some English spoken. **Open 24hr.** Pharmacy open 24hr. Visa.

(continued from previous page)

anxiety, panic, paranoia, drowsiness, and depression. Effects on the mind may include moodiness and lack of interest in friends, sex, and food. Continued use can cause personality changes, chronic paranoia, increased blood pressure and brain damage.

The Thai Health Ministry estimates that 2.4 million of Thailand's 62 million people use the drug. In 2001, a report by the Thai Narcotics Control Board said that "Never before has any narcotic reached out to all levels of Thai society like methamphetamine does." Most users are ages 15-24, but documented addicts are as young as 5 and as old as 68.

A *ya ba* tab, which can be smoked, injected, or swallowed, can cost as little as a dollar a pill. Tabs have even become a form of currency–Bangkok taxi drivers short on baht have been known to return *ya ba* instead.

Meth is a supply-sider's dream: there's no fickle crop to deal with; labs can be quickly and easily dismantled; it is cheaply made from available ingrediemts. It only requires over-the-counter pseudoephedrine (in large supply in India and Indonesia), lithium from batteries, fertilizer, and a few other chemicals. Runners can carry as many as 200,000 tabs in a backpack across the border from Myanmar. Some 700 million tablets–more than 10 per person in Thailand–entered the country in 2001, mostly across the 1300mi. Myanmar border.

Officials believe *ya ba* use is plateauing. The Thai government is in the midst of a Southeast Asia-wide crackdown on the drug.

– Derek Glanz

Telephones: At the GPO. **International telephone,** fax, and CATNET Internet upstairs. Open M-F 8:30am-4:30pm, Sa 9am-noon.

Internet Access: Cafes line Nikorn Kasaem Rd. near the bridge. **Internet Today,** on Charot Withi Thong Rd., 100m into town from the bridge. 1฿ per min., 40฿ per hr. Open daily until midnight.

Post Office: GPO, 241 Nikorn Kasaem Rd. (☎611 645), 1km south of the bridge. *Poste Restante.* Open M-F 8:30am-4:30pm, Sa-Su 9am-noon. **Postal code:** 64000.

ACCOMMODATIONS

Sukhothai has many fine guest houses, although several of them lie near the unappealing, albeit centrally located, Yom River. Be firm about your intended destination with tuk-tuk drivers, many of whom are touts paid by guest houses. They will tell you every lie in the book about other guest houses to get their commission.

Ban Thai Guest House, 38 Pravet Nakhon Rd. (☎610 163), across the Yom River. Take a left after the bridge at Thai Farmers Bank and walk 300m. Rooms in newly renovated wooden house 120-150฿; concrete rooms or bungalows with bath 200฿. ❶

Lotus Village, 170 Ratchathanee Rd. (☎621 484), 10min. walk from Praruang Bridge. Head away from the old city and take the 1st left; it's on the left after the 4th cross-street. Rustic singles with mosquito nets in large teak houses over lotus pond. Singles 120฿; doubles 240฿, with bath 400-500฿; bungalows 400฿, with A/C 900฿. ❶

Yom River Guest House, on Kuhasuwan Rd., 150m north of Thai Farmers Bank. From here there are great views of the river and day market. Stylish upstairs rooms with shared bath 150฿. Singles and bungalows are under construction. ❷

No. 4 Guest House, 140/4 Soi Klong Maelampan, Charot Withi Thong Rd. (☎610 165). From the bridge, take the 2nd right at the buses to the old city and follow the signs (take a tuk-tuk after dark). Intimate bamboo bungalow village in tranquil field setting. Thai cooking lessons 1500฿ (150฿ per dish). Singles with bath 150฿; doubles 180฿. ❷

FOOD

Daytime food stalls congregate on the side streets west of **Charot Withi Thong Rd.;** at night, the best bet is **Ramkhamhaeng Rd.,** the first cross street on the city side of the river. Try the phat thai here; it's a point of pride for the people of Sukhothai.

Dream Cafe, 96/1 Singhawat Rd., next to Patanavej Hospital. Best restaurant in Sukhothai comes at a price, but it's worth it. Roasted eggplant and basil with shrimp 120฿. Open daily 10am-midnight. MC/V. ❸

Thai Noodles Sukhothai 2, 139 Charot Withi Thong Rd. Walk out of the city 1km; it's 300m past the school on the right at the turn-off to Ruean Thai. Look for a restaurant with fountains. The specialty is *kuaytiaw sukhothai* (noodle soup with pork, green beans, coriander, and chili; 15฿). Great phat thai 20฿. Open daily 10am-3pm. ❶

Ban Thai Restaurant, 38 Pravet Nakhon Rd., at Ban Thai Guest House. Serves great food on a nice patio. Sweet and sour pork with pineapple, papaya, and mango for 60฿. Tofu can be substituted for meat. Milk and fruit shakes 15฿. Open daily 7am-9pm. ❷

SIGHTS AND ENTERTAINMENT

Not your typical wat, **Wat Thawet**'s grounds are a three-dimensional maze of brightly colored statues that furnish more than a few morbid illustrations of the punishments awaiting those who disobey Buddhist precepts. To get there, ride away from town northeast on Charot Withi Thong Rd. Turn left onto Bypass Rd. Go over the bridge, and take the first paved right. The turn-off is 6km down the highway on your right, 700m after the major intersection with another highway. The **Sangkhalok Museum** displays hundreds of artifacts detailing the daily lives of people who inhabited the nearby ruins. It's 1.5km outside of town. Follow Singhawat Rd. out of the city as it turns into Hwy. 12 (toward Phitsanulok). Turn left at the first major intersection (Hwy. 101); it's 100m on the left. (☎614 333. Open M-F 10am-6pm, Sa-Su 10am-8pm. 250฿, 50฿ for children under 17 .)

The **Chopper Bar,** 101 Charot Withi Thong Rd., on your left walking from the river to the old city bus stop, is a nightspot for *farang* and Thais alike. (Folk music 8-10pm. Large Singha 65฿. Open daily 1pm-midnight.)

OLD SUKHOTHAI HISTORICAL PARK

Old Sukhothai Historical Park lies within the triple-layered walls of the ancient city. Outside, fragments of an old wat and *chedi* can be explored, ideally by bicycle, along any of the paths branching out from the park's four main gates. *Songthaew* from Sukhothai will enter through the Old City's East Gate and drop you at the entrance booth before Wat Mahathat. The road from Sukhothai continues to Tak cutting through the western wall of the Old City at its northern end. To reach the park, catch a *songthaew* (20min., 6am-6pm, 10฿) from the lot on the west side of the river, 300m down the road on the right. (Park open daily 6am-9pm. 40฿, bike 10฿, motorbike 20฿, car 50฿. Areas outside the North/West/South Gates are an additional 30฿ each.) If you are visiting Si Satchanalai on the same day, it is worth buying the day pass, which includes entrance to all the sites as well as the museum and kilns (150฿).

INSIDE THE OLD CITY WALL. The town centerpiece is **Wat Mahathat.** The main *chedi* is famed for its lotus shape, an architectural feature particular to the Sukhothai period. Also unusual are its several standing Buddha images in the Ceylonese style. Nearby **Wat Sri Sawai,** a south-facing Hindu shrine converted into a Buddhist temple, is the only Sukhothai ruin that doesn't face east. Its centerpiece is a set of three huge *prangs* which shoot out of the temple.

NORTH OF THE OLD CITY WALL. North of **San Luang Gate** is **Wat Phra Phai Luang.** Lying on an island encircled by a moat, the wat has a Lopburi-style *stupa* and plaster reliefs of the Buddha. There is more room to explore and fewer tourists. The wat is treasured by archaeologists for its traces of pre-Sukhothai period art. **Wat Sri Chum** sits just to the west. Its *mondop* houses the 15m tall "talking" Buddha. The tunnels as you enter the temple were escape passages for the king.

WEST OF THE OLD CITY WALL. At **Wat Mungkorn,** with its distinctively circular *chedi*, the road splits. To the left lies **Saritphong (Phra Ruang Dam),** an earthen dam 487m long and 4m wide, which today can hold up to 400,000 cubic meters of water. The water was necessary in Sukhothai's glory days to keep the moats full and the gardens green. The road to the right leads back to the main road between Sukhothai and Tak, passing the entrance to **Wat Saphan Hin,** 200m up the hill. The wat contains a towering Buddha in standing position, known as **Phra Attharot.**

EAST OF THE OLD CITY WALL. Ramkhamhaeng National Museum, left of the park's east entrance, houses an eclectic collection testifying to the city's historical and cultural legacy, including a photocopy of the stone on which King Ramkhamhaeng the Great inscribed the first Thai script. (Open daily 9am-4pm. 30฿.)

DAYTRIP FROM SUKHOTHAI: SI SATCHANALAI

67km north of Sukhothai. Take a public bus from Sukhothai bus station (every 30min. 7am-4:30pm, 30฿). Last bus returns before 5pm, from the main road. Park open daily 8:30am-4:30pm. 40฿. Kilns open daily 8am-4:30pm. 30฿.

During the 13th century, Si Satchanalai rivaled Ayutthaya in wealth and sophistication. When Ayutthaya rose to preeminence, Si Satchanalai sank into anonymity. With Sukhothai's success as a tourist attraction, the competition continues. Si Satchanalai has excellent tourist facilities, including the **Visitors Information Center,** marked by signs from the roads entering the park. Headquarters contain a model of the area and a museum detailing the history and architectural significance of the ruins. Ruins line the southwestern bank of a bend in the Yom River. After a left at the entrance (passing the ticket window), ahead on the right is **Wat Chang Lom,** the city's central wat. Across the road, **Wat Chedi Chet Thaew** combines northern, southern, and local styles. Farther on, **Wat Nang Phaya** is notable for its magnificent stucco reliefs on one wall of the *wiharn.* Upon crossing the bridge into Si Satchanalai from Hwy. 101, you'll see the central complex of the historical park to your right. To the left, where the Yom River loops back on itself are the remains of **Chaliang,** a pre-established settlement that Si Satchanalai grew to encompass. At the bend in the river 3km east of Si Satchanalai is **Wat Phra Si Rattana Mahathat,** which predates the Sukhothai period. The distinctive square *stupa* actually enshrines a smaller one. The unearthing of 200 kilns at **Ban Ko Noi,** 5km beyond the park, challenged the conceptions of ancient Siam's isolation and technological simplicity. The city's kilns produced advanced celadons (ceramics known today as *sawankhalok* or *sangkhalok*) for export to countries as far away as the Philippines. The Siam Cement Company has spent 2-3 million baht making a few of these kilns accessible to tourists. Kiln #61 is the first one you reach and has an adjacent museum. Kiln #42 and 123 (together) lie farther up the road and are covered for protection from the elements. Only one ticket is necessary to see both kiln sites.

THAILAND

TAK

☎055

All roads lead to Tak—thankfully, they also lead out. Despite its mountain views and the TAT's attempts to make it a destination in its own right, there's not much to do in town. As transportation to destinations farther west becomes more direct, more and more travelers will only see Tak from the window of their bus.

TRANSPORTATION.

The **bus station** (☎511 057), near the intersection of Hwy. 1 and 12, runs to: **Bangkok** (7hr.; 17 per day 8:45am-10:30pm; 123฿, 2nd-class A/C 190฿, 1st-class A/C 245฿); **Chiang Mai** (4hr.; approx. every hr. 8:30am-7pm; 98฿, A/C 137฿); **Sukhothai** (1½hr.; every hr. 8:30am-5:30pm; 31฿, A/C 43฿). Orange-and-white **minibuses** run to **Mae Sot** (1½hr., every 30min. 6:30am-8pm, 44฿).

ORIENTATION AND PRACTICAL INFORMATION.

Tak's four main roads run parallel on the east side of the **Mae Ping River,** which flows north to south. Closest to the river is **Kitticarjon Rd.,** then **Chompon Rd.** and its night market food stalls. Next are **Taksin Rd.** and **Mahatthai Bamruang Rd.,** lined with hotels. On the town's eastern edge runs **Hwy. 1,** which crosses **Hwy. 12** before going to Chiang Mai.

The **TAT** office, 500m west of the bus station, gives out regional maps. (☎514 341. Open daily 8:30am-4:30pm.) Other services in Tak include: **Bangkok Bank,** 683 Taksin Rd., near the Sa Nguan Thai Hotel, with a 24hr. AmEx/MC/PLUS/V **ATM** (open M-F 8:30am-3:30pm); the **police station** (☎511 354; **emergency** ☎191; Bangkok tourist police ☎1155), on Mahatthai Bamruang Rd., east of the footbridge over the river; a **pharmacy** next to Mae Ping Hotel (☎511 706; open daily 8am-8pm); **Taksin**

Hospital (☎511 025), on Hwy. 1 in the south part of town; and the **GPO,** across an athletic field and to the left of the TAT (☎511 140; open M-F 8:30am-4:30pm, Sa-Su 9am-noon), with **international calls** and CATNET on the second floor (open M-F 8:30am-4:30pm) and a **Lenso** phone outside. **Postal code:** 63000.

ACCOMMODATIONS AND FOOD. Sa Nguan Thai Hotel ❷, 6/9 Taksin Rd., one block inland from the night market, is Tak's best value. Look for the open-air sitting room and 2nd-story wood veranda 20m toward the bridge from Bangkok Bank. (☎511 153. Old wing rooms with baths 150฿; doubles with TV 220฿, with A/C 300฿; twins 340฿.) The cheap **Mae Ping Hotel ❶,** 231/4-5 Mahatthai Bamruang Rd., is another block inland from Sa Nguan Thai and 150m to the right, on the left side. (☎511 807. Singles 110฿; doubles 140฿, with A/C 200฿.) Tak doesn't have restaurants. Instead, head to **noodle shops ❶** near the police station, the **night market ❶** on Chompon Rd., or, best of all, to the **food stalls ❶,** dishing out Tak tasties near the footbridge in the park between Kitticarjon Rd. and Chompon Rd.

SIGHTS. The paved riverside path and warped suspension footbridge offer views of the mountains to the west. Continuing upstream leads to **Taksin Bridge.** Cutting east at this point, but before the TAT, is the **shrine of King Taksin** (1734-1782). **Bhumibol Dam** is the eighth-largest in the world. and its reservoir is 100 miles long.A 1½hr. bus ride (25฿) from Chompon Rd., near the night market, leads to its base; it's another 3.3km walk up to the dam's crest. **Larn Sang National Park** is 17km west of Tak on the road to Mae Sot. From where the buses drop you on the highway, it's 3km to headquarters and 5km to the **Visitors Center.** Although *Let's Go* does not recommend it, it's possible to hitch a ride to the falls. On weekends Thai tourists flood **Larn Sang Waterfall,** 150m from the visitors center, but leave the upper falls, **Pha Peung** (750m walk) and **Pha Tae** (2.2km), deserted. **Camping ❶** in the park is possible. (Camping with your own tent 30฿, with a small rented one 250฿; bungalows 200-500฿. Park open daily 6am-6pm. 200฿, children 100฿.)

MAE SOT ☎055

This little city's proximity to Myanmar (7km away) and Karen refugee camps lends a dark side to its multiculturalism: there is widespread exploitation of illegal Burmese immigrants by Thai business owners. Mae Sot's vibrant day market, where you can find "Union of Myanmar" currency, hill-tribe headdresses, pig heads, and mangos, is a sight to behold. You are as likely to meet NGO workers as you are travelers—several programs are based in the region, providing essential health care and education to the refugees and IDPs.

TRANSPORTATION

Flights: Mae Sot Airport (☎563 620), 3km west of town. Take a *songthaew* toward the Moei River Market (10฿). Daily minibus service from the airport (80฿). **Thai Airways,** 110 Prasatwithi Rd. (☎531 440), books flights with **Air Andaman.** Open daily 8am-5pm. To **Bangkok** (Su-M, W, F 3pm, Tu, Th, Sa 10am; 2065฿) and **Chiang Mai** (Su-M, W, F 3pm; 1185฿).

Buses: 5 **bus stations** in town. The station (☎532 949) for trips to and from **Bangkok** (10hr.; 10 per day 8-8:30am and 7-9:45pm; fan 172฿, 2nd-class A/C 241฿, 1st-class A/C 310฿, VIP 480฿) is 100m from Asia Rd. Ticket office open daily 9am-5pm. Orange *songthaew* to **Mae Sariang** (6hr., every hr. 6am-noon, 160฿) leave from behind the covered market area south (away from Asia Hwy.) of buses leaving for Bangkok. Orange-and-white minivans to **Tak** (1½hr., every 30min. 6am-5:30pm, 44฿) gather on the east side of the same market. A paved road leading from Intharakhiri Rd., west of the police station, will deposit you at the Mae Sariang *songthaew*. The station (☎532 331) for buses to and from **Chiang Mai** (6½hr.; 6am, 134฿; 8am, A/C 241฿) is 1 block east of the police station. To find *songthaew* to **Um Phang** (5hr., every hr. 7:30am-3:30pm, 100฿), head left with your back to the police station. Take the 1st right, and follow the street past Prasatwithi Rd. and the mosque, then take the next left–you'll see a cluster of blue *songthaew*. White vans to **Phitsanulok** (4hr., 7 per day 7am-3pm, 125฿) via **Sukhothai** (2½hr., 100฿) leave from the station south of the main market. Maps available at guest houses make this information somewhat clearer.

Local Transportation: To go to the **Moei River Market** and the **border,** catch a blue **songthaew** (10฿) opposite Thai Airways on Prasatwithi Rd. Last one returns at 6pm.

Rentals: Guest houses rent **bikes** (30฿). **Motorcycle** rental (☎532 099) is next to Bangkok Bank on Prasatwithi Rd. 160฿ per day. Open daily 8am-5:30pm.

ORIENTATION AND PRACTICAL INFORMATION

Mae Sot is 165km west of Sukhothai. **Intharakhiri Rd.,** with one-way traffic heading east, runs parallel to **Prasatwithi Rd.,** with one-way traffic heading west toward **Moei Market** and the Burmese border. Asia Hwy. bypasses town a few blocks north of these two major roads. The **police station** is on Intharakhiri Rd. in the center of town; guest houses primarily lie on the same road to the west. The **market** sprawls south of Prasatwithi Rd. near the Siam Hotel. Free maps with varying degrees of accuracy are available at guest houses. Bai Fern (see **Accommodations,** below) and the K.C.B. Snack Shop next door, provide the best.

Tours: For your wallet's sake, go to Um Phang (p. 797) yourself to book a trek. To book in Mae Sot, try TAT-approved **Mae Sot Conservation Tours,** 415/17 Tang Kim Chiang Rd. (☎544 726), 2 doors toward Prasatwithi Rd. from Pim Hut. 3 days/2 nights 5500฿, minimum 3 people. Open daily 8:30am-6pm.

Immigration Office: ☎563 003. Next to Friendship Bridge at Moei River. (For visa extension see **Border Crossing: Moei-Myawaddy,** below.) Open daily 6am-6pm.

Currency Exchange: Banks line Prasatwithi Rd. **Thai Farmers Bank,** 84/9 Prasatwithi Rd. (☎531 020), has a **24hr. ATM** (Cirrus/MC/PLUS/V). Open M-F 8:30am-3:30pm.

Markets: The **day market** is south of Prasatwithi Rd. on either side of the Siam Hotel. Remarkably large for small Mae Sot. The **gem and jade market** on Prasatwithi Rd., opposite Thai Farmers Bank, heats up by noon.

Emergency: ☎191. **Tourist Police (Bangkok):** ☎1155.

Police: ☎531 112. At intersection of Tang Kim Chiang and Intharakhiri Rd. **Open 24hr.**

Tourist Police (local): ☎533 523. Near Asia Hwy. in the vicinity of the bus station. With your back to the police station, head left, take the first left and follow it to the end; it's on the left. Minimal English. **Open 24hr.**

Medical Services: Pawo Hospital (☎544 397 or 533 912), south of town past the market, near the vans to Sukhothai. Private. Some English spoken. **Open 24hr.** MC/V. Has **24hr. pharmacy.**

Telephones: Maesot Telecommunications Office, 784 Intharakhiri Rd. (☎533 364), 10min. walk west of guest houses. Standard 33฿ for assisted collect call. Lenso phone and CATNET Internet access. Open M-F 8:30am-4:30pm.

Internet: 112/9 Prasatwithi Rd. (☎531 909), 2 doors west of Thai Airways. 20฿ per hr. Open daily 9am-8pm, but Internet access often until midnight.

Post Office: GPO (☎531 277), on Intharakhiri Rd. With back to the police station, head left; it's 150m down the road on the right. *Poste Restante.* Lenso phone. Open M-F 8:30am-4:30pm, Sa-Su 9am-noon. **Postal code:** 63110.

BORDER CROSSING: MOEI/MYAWADDY A 7km *songthaew* ride away from Mae Sot, this Thai/Myanmar border crossing is a relatively hassle-free way to extend your Thai visa. Show up at the bridge, present your passport to the Thai authorities, walk over the bridge, present your passport to be stamped and US$10 or 500฿, walk back over the bridge and receive your brand-new visa. If you intend to pay in US dollars, bring the cash with you to Mae Sot, as banks there don't have small bills and authorities are frequently out of change. If you want to see an unrealistic view of Burmese life, daytrips (return by 5pm), usually with a "guide," are permitted; keep in mind that your money will go to a government with an atrocious human rights record (see **Myanmar: To Go or Not To Go?**, p. 488).

ACCOMMODATIONS

Bai Fern Guest House, 660/2 Intharakhiri Rd. (☎533 343). With your back to the police station, it's 400m to the right. Friendly staff. All rooms with fans and shared hot-water bath. Simple singles 100฿; large but noisy doubles in teak house 150฿. ❶

Ban Thai Guest House, 740 Intharakhiri Rd. (☎531 590), 25m farther west from No. 4 Guest House. Set well off the main road, this quiet and spacious new guest house has beautifully appointed rooms with comfy mattress, sitting table, and cushioned seating. All rooms with shared bath. Dorms 50฿; singles 250฿; doubles 350฿. ❶

DK Hotel, 298/2 Intharakhiri Rd. (☎542 648), 50m east of post office. Multi-story hotel with marble floors. Large, impersonal rooms with Western toilet, hot water, and small balcony. Rooms with fan and telephone 250฿, with A/C and TV 450฿. ❸

FOOD AND NIGHTLIFE

Bai Fern Restaurant ❸ serves incredible *farang* fare. Delicious "Bai Fern delight" pizza (ham, veggies, pineapple with bacon- and cheese-stuffed crust) for 120฿. (Open daily 7am-10pm.) **Pim Hut** ❷, on Tang Kim Chiang Rd. (near the police station), serves standard Thai and *farang* entrees. (Spring rolls 50฿. Open daily 9am-10pm.) The **Crocodile Tear,** on Intharakhiri Rd. before the guest houses, has live music daily from 9pm. The 2- to 3-man band will let you join their heart-wrenching Dylan covers if you feel so inspired. (Singha 60฿. Open daily 5pm-1am.)

UM PHANG ☎055

If Um Phang's 1500m high vistas don't take your breath away, the speed of the *songthaew* on your hellish trip from Mae Sot will. Although this remote oasis is well known to Thais, who escape here on weekends and holidays to see Thee Lor Su, Thailand's most beautiful waterfall, foreigners haven't yet caught on—Um Phang welcomed fewer than 2000 *farang* trekkers last year.

TRANSPORTATION AND PRACTICAL INFORMATION. The main road from Mae Sot forks just before entering Um Phang. **Pravesphywan Rd.,** the left branch, leads into town. **Sukhomwattana Rd.,** to the right (downhill), runs parallel to Pravesphywan Rd. Note that there is not one street sign in Um Phang. The turn-off to the *songthaew* station lies halfway along Pravesphywan Rd., opposite the green-and-cream elementary education building. It's a further 200m uphill on the left. The road with the sign to Ban Pa La Tha at the backside of the wat off Sukhomwattana Rd. leads to the river and several guest houses. *Songthaew* drivers working on commission may deposit travelers on this road. The last *songth-*

aew to **Mae Sot** leaves between 2 and 3pm depending on demand; the best time to catch *songthaew* is in the morning or around noon when trekkers return. **Bikes** can be rented from Tu Ka Su Cottages, a 5min. walk farther out of town from Um Phang Hill Resort (see below), for 40฿ per day (☎561 295).

There are **no banks in** town, but other services include: the **police station** (☎561 001), on Sukhomwattana Rd., 600m into town from the fork; the **hospital** (☎561 270; **open 24hr.;** some English spoken), opposite and slightly farther uphill from the *songthaew* station; **Internet,** 50m from the end of Pravesphywan Rd. (30฿ per hr., students 20฿ per hr.; open daily 8am-9pm); and the **post office** (☎561 127), on the left before the fork as you drive into town, which also has **international telephone** service and CATNET **Internet access** (cash and collect calls only; open M-F 8:30am-noon and 1-4:30pm, Sa 9am-noon). **Postal code:** 63170.

ACCOMMODATIONS AND FOOD. **Um Phang Hill Resort ❶** offers dorms (50฿), and nice bungalows by the river (100-500฿). However, you may feel ambushed into going on a trek. Across the river, **Garden Huts ❸** (☎561 093) has basic bungalows by the river (200฿) and ones with full amenities (300฿). The **Trekker Hill Company ❶** is a big place with teak and stone shelters, mosquito nets, and toilet paper. The turn-off to Trekker Hill is down the road from Phudoi Guest House and Campsite, just before Boonchuey Camping on Pravesphywan Rd.; the accommodations are 100m up the hill on the left. (☎561 090. Laundry 5฿ per piece. Small food service available. Semi-private bungalow 100฿ per person.)

A small **morning market ❶** sets up next door at the crack of dawn to cater to your breakfast needs. **Tom's Restaurant ❶,** opposite the entrance to the wat on Pravesphywan Rd., serves plates of curries and noodles from the window selection (20฿). For a fresher feed, **Um Phang House ❶** has a small restaurant in town that whips up simple Thai dishes (chicken with cashew nuts 30฿). Facing the wat, follow the road down the right side to get to Um Phang House and the road headed to the river. Beware: restaurants close during the low season.

TREKS. There are two standard treks in the region. **Thee Lor Su,** which plummets over 400m through deep waterholes, can be visited year-round. The best viewing is in November after the wet season. At the popular **Thee Lor Lay** ("Waterfall over the Cliff"), only worth viewing May-Dec., you can raft right past the waterfall. Treks to Thee Lor Su typically last 3 days/2 nights, while Thee Lor Lay takes 2 days/1 night. Most companies have fixed prices for both treks: 3000฿ per person, which includes rafting and overnight stay in a hill-tribe village. Minimum of two people. In the dry season it is possible to view Thee Lor Su without going on a trek.

NORTHEAST THAILAND

This plateau encompasses about one-third of Thailand's total landmass and supports an equal proportion of the population. Thais call it "Isaan," meaning prosperity and vastness. Ironically, largely agrarian Isaan is one of the country's poorest regions. The United States set up air force bases in Isaan's four largest cities during the Vietnam War, and these cities remain centers of transportation, commerce, and education. For skeptics who hold that any statement containing both "Thailand" and "off the beaten path" is oxymoronic, Isaan emerges as a buried treasure.

KHAO YAI NATIONAL PARK

For travelers hoping to rescue their lungs from the fumes of Bangkok, Khao Yai National Park offers salvation. Consecrated as Thailand's first (and perhaps best) national park in 1962, this dense jungle teems with macaques, gibbons, exotic birds, and insects. The humbling 2100 sq. km of tropical rainforest are flanked by a few luxurious but aging resorts. During weekdays and in the low season, they offer discounts as delightful as the wildlife. Khao Yai can only be reached via Pak Chong, an urban strip featuring little more than basic lodging and supplies.

PAK CHONG ☎044

Approximately 1km long, Pak Chong extends on either side of the **Mitraphap (Friendship) Highway;** all its side streets are designated **Tesaban Rd.** followed by a number. The four major landmarks, starting from the side closest to Bangkok and heading toward Khorat, are the stoplight, the 7-Eleven store, the pedestrian overpass, and the Shell gas station. Giant light-blue **songthaew** leave for **Khao Yai National Park** from the highway in front of the 7-Eleven on Tesaban 19 (every 20min. 6am-3pm, every 30min. 3pm-5pm; 20฿). The **train station** (☎311 534) lies at the end of Tesaban 15 from the overpass; it's the first right after the traffic signals, 400m down the road. Trains go to **Bangkok** via **Ayutthaya** (4½hr., 11 per day, 36-262฿

with food and A/C) and **Khorat** (1hr., 6 per day, from 18฿). At the **first bus station**, beside the **Thai Farmers Bank** just after Tesaban 19, you can catch buses en route from Bangkok to **Khorat** (1½hr., every 20min. 5am-9pm, with A/C 46฿) and make connections to other destinations. An **A/C bus station** is between Tesaban 18 and the overpass, with service to **Bangkok** (3hr.; newer orange and red bus 74฿, blue bus 95฿). A **second A/C bus terminal** beneath the overpass has service to **Sukhothai** via **Phitsanulok** and **Chang** (#572; 7:10, 9:20, 10:20, 11:20am).

The **day market** starts near Tesaban 21 and extends one block uphill from the main road. (Open daily 6am-4:30pm.) The **night market,** between Tesaban 17 and 19, is the place for dinner, with row upon row of food carts. **Bank of Ayudhya** (☎311 411), centrally located between Tesaban 18 and the overpass, has a **24hr. ATM** (MC/PLUS/V), gives cash advances, and cashes traveler's checks. (Open M-F 8:30am-3:30pm.) **Thai Military Bank** is between Tesaban 19 and 21. (Open M-F 8:30am-4:30pm. 24hr. AmEx/Cirrus/MC/PLUS/V ATM.) The **post office** is on the corner of Tesaban 25. (☎311 736. Open M-F 8:30am-4:30pm.) Directly across the strip, the **Communications Authority of Thailand** places domestic and **international** phone calls. (☎311 787. Collect calls 30฿. Open M-F 8:30am-4:30pm.) Surf yourself silly at the brand-spankin'-new **Internet** between Tesaban 15 and 17. (20฿ per hr. Open daily 9am-11pm.) **Postal code:** 30130.

THAILAND

Jungle Guest House ❶, 63 Kongwaksin Rd., Soi 3, Tesaban 16 (☎313 836), is run by an amiable couple who organizes expeditions to the park. From the pedestrian overpass, head to the stoplight at Tesaban 17; take a left and, when the road forks, veer left onto Thanon Kong Vaccine Soi 1. A green and white sign announces the guest house, hiding 50m in on the right. (May be closed during low season. Dorms with fans, Western toilets, and small breakfast 70฿. Doubles 200฿, with bath 260฿.) **Khao Yai Garden Lodge ❶** is 7km out of Pak Chong on the way to the park, on the left side. A gorgeous garden weaves through a series of charming houses. A pool and waterfall are also on the grounds. (☎365 167. Singles with shared bath 100฿; doubles with private bath 500฿; suite with marble bath 1800฿.)

THE PARK

Park open daily 6am-midnight. 20฿, vehicle admission 50฿. Park headquarters and Visitors Center open daily 8am-6pm. Trail map 2฿; guide 300-500฿.

Home to one of the last wild elephant herds and some of the world's few remaining wild tigers, the park has over 40km of hiking trails through rainforest and grasslands. The waterfalls alone are worth the trek. **Nong Pak Chi Watch Tower** is the spot to spot striped tigers. Visitors officially need "approval" for tower access, but this is rarely enforced. To avoid leeches, don't trek in sandals and steer clear of salty water. It's another 12km to the park headquarters and the Visitors Center from the park entrance. If you are lucky and the phone is working that day, call ☎01 650 0164 to arrange a pickup at the entrance. **Yao Wa Chon ❶,** 1km from headquarters, has outdoor hammocks. (Hard floor-space 20฿; blanket rental at headquarters 15฿; 12-person lodges 1200฿.) **Orchard Campsite ❶,** 10km from headquarters, offers tent space for 5฿ (tent rental 80฿). To ensure weekend lodging, call ahead to the **Royal Forest Department** in Bangkok (☎02 579 7221). For a more convenient tour of the park, try **Jungle Adventure**—a 1½-day tour operated by the Jungle Guest House in Pak Chong. The tour, which incorporates Buddhist meditation caves, waterfall swims, elephant-trail treks, and a night safari, moves at a blistering pace and costs 950฿. Alternatively, three different sized buses leave the souvenir shop near the cafeteria at 7pm and 8pm for rides around the park. (Cost is split between riders: bus that seats 10, 300฿; seats 20, 450฿; seats 40, 600฿.) A free guide can also be arranged.

NAKHON RATCHASIMA (KHORAT) ☎044

Known locally as Khorat, the name of the plateau on which it rests, Nakhon Ratchasima straddles the main corridor to all other destinations in Isaan. Although it's Thailand's second-largest city, the texture of urban life found here is worlds away from the manic snarls of Bangkok. Built during the Ayutthaya period, Khorat enjoys close proximity to the silk-weaving splendor in Pak Thong Chai, the pottery manufacturers of Dan Kwian, and the ruins of Phimai and Phanom Rung.

TRANSPORTATION

Flights: Airport (☎680 086), 28km west of town. Catch a **Buriram** bus (10฿) at **Bus Terminal 2,** or a **shuttle bus** (70฿) with pickups at hotels. **Thai Airways** (☎257 211), at the corner of Suranaree and Buarong Rd. Open M-F 8:30am-4:30pm. Flies to **Bangkok** daily (8:30am, noon, 6pm; 660฿). Airport tax 30฿.

Trains: Nakhon Ratchasima Railway Station (☎242 044), on Mukkhamontri Rd. From the center of town, the station is 500m west on Mukkhamontri Rd. To **Bangkok** (5hr.; 11 per day; 3rd-class 58฿, 2nd-class 98฿, 1st-class 173฿).

Buses: Terminal 1 (☎262 899, for A/C ☎245 443), on Burin Lane. To: **Bangkok** (#21; 4hr., every 20min. 24hr., A/C with toilet 139฿); **Nakhon Sawan** (#572; 6hr.; every hr. 5am-11pm; A/C 95฿, A/C with toilet 113฿); **Pak Thong Chai** (#1303; 1½hr., every 30min. 5:30am-8:30pm, 12฿). **Terminal 2** (☎256 007), on Rte. 2 north of town beyond Takhong River; take a motorcycle or tuk-tuk (40-50฿). To: **Bangkok** (#21; 4hr., every 20min. 24hr., A/C 140฿); **Chiang Mai** (#635; 12hr.; 6 per day; 218฿, A/C 392฿); **Chiang Rai** (#651; 13hr., 4 per day, 464฿); **Nong Khai** (#22; 3½hr., every hr. 9am-3pm, 189฿) via **Khon Kaen** (2hr., 104฿) and **Udon Thani** (3hr., 162฿); **Phimai** (#1305; 1½hr., every 30min. 5am-10pm, 34฿); **Surin** (#274; 4hr., every 30min. 11:30am-4pm, 60฿); **Ubon Ratchathani** (#25; 4½hr., 6 per day 12:30-3pm, 220฿).

Local Transportation: **Samlor** and **tuk-tuks** are omnipresent. From TAT to Thao Suranaree memorial should cost no more than 60฿. City buses are just as convenient (5am-4pm; 5฿, A/C 7฿). Buses #1, 2, and 3 start on Mukkhamontri Rd. near TAT and go into the center of town. They split where Mukkhamontri forks into Phoklang Rd. (#1), Suranaree Rd. (#2), and Jomsurangyard Rd. (#3). **Songthaew** (5฿) run more frequently.

ORIENTATION AND PRACTICAL INFORMATION

Khorat stretches east-west between **Mittraphap Rd.** to the north and the Northeastern Railroad Line to the south. It is bisected by **Ratchadamnoen Rd.** and **Chumphon Rd.,** two parallel streets separated by a park. In the middle, marking the center of the city, stands the **Thao Suranaree memorial.** Khorat's western half is bounded to the south by **Mukkhamontri Rd.,** which forks into **Suranaree Rd., Phoklang Rd.,** and **Jomsurangyard Rd.** as it heads into town. These roads intersect Ratchadamnoen Rd. close to the memorial. A moat circumscribes the city's eastern half. **Chomphon Rd.,** not to be confused with Chumphon Rd., begins behind the Thao Suranaree memorial and cuts east-west through the center of the old city.

Tourist Office: TAT, 2102-2104 Mittraphap Rd. (☎213 666 or 213 030), on the western edge of town. Take bus #1, 2, or 3 heading west from the memorial; get off just before Mittraphap Rd. Cross the footbridge; it's beside Sima Thani Hotel. Open daily 8:30am-4:30pm.

Tours: Supatha Tour, 138 Chainarong Rd. (☎242 758).

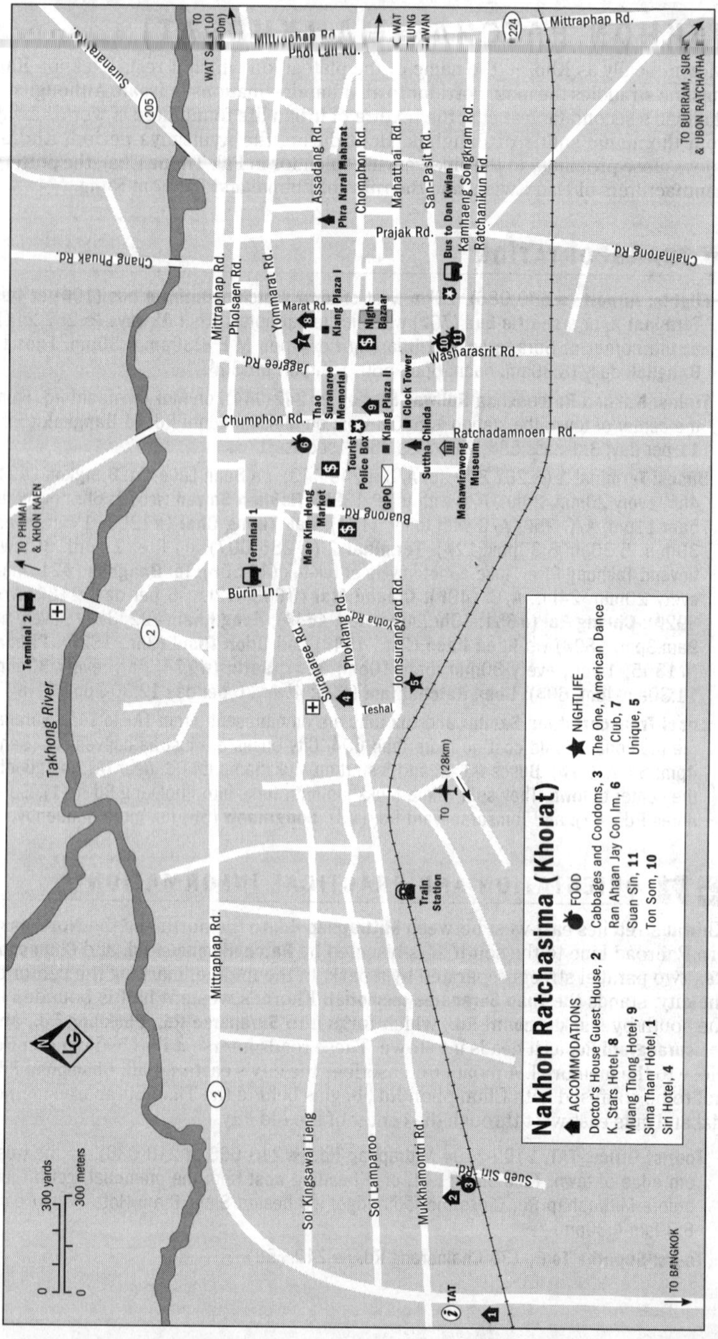
Nakhon Ratchasima (Khorat)
ACCOMMODATIONS
Doctor's House Guest House, 2
K. Stars Hotel, 8
Muang Thong Hotel, 9
Sima Thani Hotel, 1
Siri Hotel, 4
FOOD
Cabbages and Condoms, 3
Ran Ahaan Jay Con Im, 6
Suan Sin, 11
Ton Som, 10
NIGHTLIFE
The One, American Dance Club, 7
Unique, 5
0 300 yards
0 300 meters
Takhong River
Terminal 2
TO PHIMAI & KHON KAEN
TO WAT SALA LOI (200m)
TO WAT LUNG WAN
TO BURIRAM, SURIN & UBON RATCHATHANI
TO BANGKOK
TO (28km)
TAT
Mittraphap Rd.
Phol Lan Rd.
Suranarai Rd.
Chang Phuak Rd.
Chainarong Rd.
Pholsaen Rd.
Yommarat Rd.
Marat Rd.
Jaggree Rd.
Chumphon Rd.
Burin Ln.
Terminal 1
Mae Kim Heng Market
Buarong Rd.
Yotha Rd.
Phoklang Rd.
Suranaree Rd.
Jomsurangyard Rd.
Teshal
Assadang Rd.
Chomphon Rd.
Mahatthai Rd.
San-Pasit Rd.
Kamhaeng Songkram Rd.
Ratchanikun Rd.
Prajak Rd.
Phra Narai Maharat
Bus to Dan Kwian
Klang Plaza I
Night Bazaar
Thao Suranaree Memorial
Klang Plaza II
Clock Tower
Washarasrit Rd.
Tourist Police Box
GPO
Suttha Chinda
Ratchadamnoen Rd.
Mahawirawong Museum
Train Station
Soi Kingsawai Lieng
Soi Lamparoo
Mukkhamontri Rd.
Sueb Siri Rd.

Currency Exchange: Bank of Ayudhya, 168 Chomphon Rd. (☎242 388). MC/V cash advances and traveler's check exchange M-F 8:30am-3:30pm. **24hr. ATM** (Cirrus/MC/PLUS/V). Other ATMs line Chomphon Rd.

Markets: Mae Kim Heng Market, between Suranaree and Phoklang Rd. about a block beyond the city gate, bustles 24hr. The **night bazaar** fills 2 blocks of Marat Rd. between Chomphon and Mahatthai Rd. Open daily 6-10pm.

Emergency: ☎191. **Tourist Police (Bangkok):** ☎1155.

Tourist Police (local): ☎341 777. Beside the Thao Suranaree memorial.

Pharmacy: Amarin, 122 Chumphon Rd. (☎242 741), behind the memorial to the left. "Rx" on the glass doors. Adequate English. Open daily 8:30am-8:30pm. Also on the lower level of Klang Plaza II, on Jomsurangyard Rd. just off Ratchadamnoen Rd.

Medical Services: St. Mary's Hospital, 307 Mittraphap Rd./Rte. 2 (☎261 261), 50m south of Bus Terminal 2. Private hospital with excellent English-speaking staff. **Khorat Memorial Hospital,** 348 Suranaree Rd. (☎265 777). From the Thao Suranaree memorial, it's past the Sri Pattana Hotel on the right. Look for the new white building proclaiming "KMH." English spoken. Accepts Visa. **Open 24hr.**

Telephones: Communications Authority of Thailand (☎259 707), next to the post office. Overseas calls, fax, and telex. Open daily 10am-8pm.

Internet Access: Internet World (☎267 854), on the south side of Mittraphap Rd. near the corner of Ratchadamnoen Rd., halfway up the footbridge stairwell. 20฿ per hr. Open daily 10am-midnight.

Post Office: 48 Jomsurangyard Rd. (☎256 670). Facing the memorial, go right on Ratchadamnoen Rd. until Jomsurangyard Rd. Turn right and pass Klang Plaza II; it's on the right. Open M-F 8:30am-4:30pm, Sa 9am-noon. **Postal code:** 30000.

ACCOMMODATIONS

"Cheap" and "good" do not coincide here, so if you are sick of grimy squat toilets and have a few baht to spare, this is the place to splurge.

K. Stars Hotel, 191 Assadang Rd. (☎257 057). This centrally located hotel is in the thick of Khorat nightlife. All rooms are clean with A/C, shower, and Western toilets. Carpets are red red red. Singles 450฿; doubles 600฿. ❹

Doctor's Guest House, 75 Sueb Siri Rd. Soi 4 (☎255 846), on the western edge of the city near the TAT Office. Strict 10pm lockout. Laundry 5-15฿ per item. Small but clean rooms with fans 180฿. Distant location, but the best in its price range. ❸

Sima Thani Hotel (☎213 100), on Mittraphap Rd. Khorat's most luxurious hotel. With a 1300฿ price tag, one night here could afford a week's stay elsewhere. Traditional Thai dancing, pool, gym, spa, cafe. Deluxe rooms 1500฿. ❺

Muang Thong Hotel, 46 Chumphon Rd. (☎242 090). Look for the green wooden building. From the exterior it exudes an old-world Asian charm. Inside a real developing world experience awaits–only for the hardcore. Rooms 120฿, with A/C 350฿. ❷

Siri Hotel, 688-690 Phoklang Rd. (☎241 556), 350m down Phoklang Rd. after Mukkhamontri Rd. forks. Decent rooms, but pretty nasty baths. Singles with fan 120-140฿; doubles 180฿, with A/C 280฿; "special room" for 2 with TV, A/C, and fridge 380฿. ❷

FOOD

The markets are fine places to sample regional specialties, such as *sai klog* (pork sausages; 5฿) and small, coconut-stuffed pancakes (1฿). An alternative is the food court in the basement of the Klang Plaza II shopping center on Jomsurangyard Rd.

Ran Ahaan Jay Con Im, 191/2 Suranaree Rd., offers vegetarian entrees (10-20฿). Open daily 8am-midnight. ❶

Suan Sin, 163 Washarsarit Rd. Heading south on Chomphon Rd. behind Thao Suranaree memorial, take a left onto Mahatthai Rd. and then a right onto Washara Srit Rd. Open-air storefront. Isaan specialties like cow-tail soup, pig's neck noodles, and (drumroll please) bull penis salad. Dishes around 60฿. Open daily 9am-8pm. Next door is **Samram Lap,** which serves similiar food with outdoor seating at similar prices. ❷

Ton Som, 125-129 Washarsarit Rd. (☎252 275). From Chumphon Rd. take a left onto Mahatthai Rd. and a right onto Washarsarit Rd. Comfortable, A/C restaurant serving Thai and Western food, popular with tourists and locals. Spicy shrimp salad with lemongrass 85฿. Thai-topped pizza 110฿. Open daily 11am-11pm. AmEx/MC/V. ❸

Cabbages & Condoms (C&C Restaurant), 86/1 Sueb Siri Rd., just past Soi 4 and before the train tracks near Khorat Doctor's House. C&C is a nutritious meal away from the lead-laden air of Khorat. Vegetarian options 55-65฿. "Chicken in herb leaf bikinis" 65฿. Open daily 10am-10pm. ❷

SIGHTS

Khorat's handful of sights can be visited in a single afternoon. A good starting point is the **Thao Suranaree memorial.** Constructed in 1934, the memorial has been a source of inspiration for generations of Khorat citizens. **Wat Sala Loi** offers a chance to set sail for new spiritual horizons. Look for its sign on Mittraphap Rd., at the old moat's northeast corner. Sala Loi's architecturally acclaimed inner sanctuary is shaped like a Chinese ship, which symbolizes the passage of the devoted to nirvana. **Wat Phra Narai Maharat,** on Prajak Rd. between Assadang and Chomphon Rd., contains a sandstone image of the Hindu god Narayana as well as a *shiva linga* (phallus-shaped pillar). The **Mahawirawong Museum,** Khorat's branch of the National Museum, is on Ratchadamnoen Rd., two blocks toward the clock tower from the shrine. Its small collection contains artifacts from the Angkor and Ayutthaya periods. (☎242 958. Open daily 9am-noon and 1-4pm. 10฿.)

ENTERTAINMENT

The karaoke plague has reached epidemic proportions here. For temporary relief, the **Sima Thani Hotel,** next to TAT, holds outdoor performances of Isaan music and dance. (☎213 100. M-Sa 7-8pm. Free with a la carte dinner, about 250฿.) **Muay Thai** (Thai boxing) kicks off sporadically at Khorat's stadium; inquire at TAT. Khorat also has an array of movie theaters and discotheques.

WAY TO GO, MRS. MO! Embodying the spirit of Khorat like no other symbol, the **Thao Suranaree Memorial** in the town center depicts the heroic Khun Ying Mo, wife of Khorat's deputy governor who, in 1826, rallied 300 women to defend the city from Lao invaders. A 19th-century equivalent to Judith of biblical lore, Thao Suranaree persuaded the women to seduce and then murder the Laotian soldiers, thus playing a key role in the defeat of Prince Anuwong of Vientiane. Locals reverently refer to her as "Yah Mo" (Grandmother Mo), wrap the shrine in ribbons, give offerings of bananas and coconuts, and burn incense. When prayers are answered, they sing thanks or hire young women to dance in her honor. An annual Thao Suranaree Fair (March 23-April 3) draws thousands to the bronze statue over the city moat. The celebration includes a parade, folk songs and dances, and a beauty contest.

The One, American Dance Club, 191 Assadang Rd. (☎248 944), next to K. Stars Hotel. A full house of dance floors, live music, private karaoke rooms, and a cocktail lounge. Set the mood with some slow dancing (8-11pm), then get down to glittering disco (11pm-2am). 220฿ cover gets you 1 free drink. Karaoke rooms 1000฿ per night.

Unique, 1372 Jomsurangyard Rd. (☎258 540), 800m down the road from the post office, a half-block past Yotha Rd. on the left. Neon lights brag "Unique: It's Party Time." Would-be dancers are often awe-struck by the open-air terrace and 10m waterfall. When the novelty wears off, Unique is a hip dance destination. Cover 200฿, includes 1 drink. Open daily 9pm-2am.

DAYTRIPS FROM KHORAT

DAN KWIAN VILLAGE. Tiny Dan Kwian Village, 15km southeast of Khorat, has long been famous for its distinctive rust-colored pottery, cut with detailed geometric patterns. The work is beautiful but heavy and fragile. *(From Khorat, follow Chomphon Rd. behind the Thao Suranaree memorial and turn right on Chainarong Rd. At the south gate, turn left onto Kamhaeng Songkhram Rd., and walk past the vendors. On the right, you should see a small blue-striped bus (#1307; every 30min., 5฿). Indicate destination to the driver. Disembark when the small road forks into three lanes. To return, wait on the left side of the road back to Khorat. When the bus comes, gesticulate wildly.)*

PAK THONG CHAI. Pak Thong Chai is a traditional silk-producing village 32km south of Khorat. Two factories, **Matchada** (☎441 684) and **Radtree** (☎441 284), arrange tours through their facilities and allow visitors to observe the silk production cycle, from the raising of silkworms to the threading and weaving of garments. Both factories are open daily 9am-5pm. Call and arrange ahead of time as these tours are not a regular offering. *(Take bus #1303 (every 30min. 8am-4pm, 15฿) from Khorat's Bus Terminal 1.)*

PHIMAI

Since the fall of Angkor in 1432, Phimai has been transformed from an important cultural center to an idyllic satellite of Khorat. Roosters provide free wake-up calls at dawn in the shadow of Thailand's largest stone ruins, and the town's peaceful day lethargically unfolds where a great city once bustled.

TRANSPORTATION AND PRACTICAL INFORMATION. Buses to Phimai leave from Khorat's Bus Terminal 2 (#1305; Platform 41, 1½-2hr., every 30min. 5am-10pm, 34฿). They drop passengers at **New Phimai Town bus station,** in a housing development outside Phimai. Bus #1305 leaves Phimai for **Khorat** (every 30min. 4am-6pm, 34฿). Those headed to **Khon Kaen, Nong Khai,** or **Udon Thani** should get off at Talad Khae, 10km away from Phimai, and ask someone where to wait. Those heading to **Surin** should take a *songthaew* from the New Phimai bus station to Hin Dat (30min., 8am, 20฿). From here, hop on a train to Surin (2hr., 3rd-class 22฿).

At the northern end of **Chomsudasapet Rd.,** the temple is visible. Here, Chomsudasapet meets **Anantajinda Rd.,** which runs along the front of the park. Just around the corner to the left of this intersection is the **Thai Military Bank,** 222 Anantajinda Rd., which exchanges traveler's checks (☎471 334; open M-F 8:30am-3:30pm) and has an **ATM** (Cirrus/MC/V; open daily 6am-10pm). To the right of this intersection, Anantajinda Rd. passes a clock tower, which houses the **police pavilion.** To reach the **post and telegraph office,** 123 Srikeaw Rd., go left on Anantajinda Rd. at the gate to the park. **Srikaew Rd.** is the first right; the post office is 150m down on the left. (Open M-F 8:30am-4:30pm, Sa-Su 9-11am.) **Postal code:** 30110.

ACCOMMODATIONS AND FOOD. Phimai boasts two first-rate guest houses and an excellent restaurant. **Old Phimai Guest House ❶**, 214 Moo 1 Chomsudasapet Rd., 2½ blocks down Chomsudasapet from the bus terminal down a small soi to the right (look for the sign), has palatial rooms in an airy wooden house. (☎471 918. Dorms 80฿; singles 130฿, with A/C 300-350฿; doubles 160฿.) Right across the alley sits the **S&P New Phimai Guest House ❶**, 213 Moo 1 Chomsudasapet Rd. Their cosmopolitan graffiti and crotchety iguana keep boredom at bay. (☎287 275. Singles 100฿; doubles 140฿.) **Baitely Restaurant ❸**, 246/1 Chomsudasapet Rd., is a block before the soi leading to the guest houses. It doubles as an informal tourist info center. The menu features a variety of Thai dishes (30-150฿). An English menu is available. (☎471 725. Open daily 7am-midnight.)

SIGHTS. Phimai's main attractions are the stately Khmer ruins smack in the middle of town within the **Prasat Hin Phimai Historical Park.** At its zenith, the Angkor empire covered much of mainland Southeast Asia. At one time, a laterite highway linked Phimai, along with nearby Muang Tham and Phanom Rung, with the empire's magnificent capital, Angkor Thom, 225km to the south. This white sandstone temple was built in a style similar to Angkor Wat in the late 11th century, probably during the reign of Suriyavarman I. The walls of red sandstone and laterite were built over the next 150 years. On the right of the stone causeway with *naga* balustrades is a collection of faded sandstone lintels. Although the temple is Buddhist, many of the lintels depict Hindu gods and scenes from the epic *Ramayana.* (Open daily 7:30am-6pm. 40฿.) **Phimai National Museum** is north of the park, 500m down the road that runs past the eastern perimeter of the temple complex, in a large white building with a red-tiled roof. The museum includes an extensive collection of Khmer and Dvaravati art, as well as interesting anthropological exhibits documenting the social, political, and economic history of the Isaan region. (☎471 167. Open daily 9am-4pm. 40฿.) For a less cerebral diversion, **Sai Ngam,** the largest banyan tree in Thailand, stands on the banks of the Moon River 2km east of town. It's a 10min. bike ride or 40฿ motorcycle jaunt from town. Facing the park, head to the right on Anantajinda Rd. past the clock tower: stick to the main road and follow the signs. Wizened old men will read your palm for a few baht. At the center, a small pagoda houses the spirit of this 360-year-old miracle.

PHANOM RUNG AND MUANG THAM

The ancient Khmer temples of Phanom Rung and Muang Tham are the tourist magnets of lower Isaan. While transportation is not too difficult, set out early to avoid getting stranded. From **Khorat** (Bus Terminal 2) or **Surin,** catch bus #274 or 98 and get off at **Ban Ta-Ko** (2hr., 37฿), which is clearly marked as the turn-off for Phanom Rung (16km) and Muang Tham, a further 8km. If you're just going to Phanom Rung, you can catch a *songthaew* (around 30฿), but the return trip is more difficult to arrange, especially during the low season. Another option is to catch the Buriram-bound bus from **Aranyaprathet** (which starts in Chanthaburi) as early as possible. If you're seeing both Phanom Rung and Muang Tham, **motorcycle** or **pickup** drivers will take you to the temples and wait while you tour the grounds (200-300฿). To return to Surin or Khorat, get back to Ban Ta-Ko before 5pm, as buses run less frequently after that. Alternatively, book a full-day tour (380฿, 4-person minimum) to both temples at the **Old Phimai Guest House** in Phimai.

Muang Tham Temple, dating from the 10th century, is in a low valley 6km from Phanom Rung. Though fresh from an overhaul at the hands of the Thai Fine Arts Department, Muang Tham cannot match the splendor of Phanom Rung. Still, it provides a detailed picture of a Khmer temple in its present incarnation. (Open daily 7:30am-6pm. 30฿.) **Phanom Rung**, one of the largest surviving Khmer monuments, was built between the 10th and 13th centuries. Standing atop an extinct volcano 383m above sea level, the majestic temple commands dramatic vistas of the surrounding plain, broken in the southeast by the Dongrek Mountains of Cambodia. Inside the complex, three terraced platforms lead up to the "white elephant hall," a partially reconstructed stone structure on the right. The 160m promenade lined with lotus-bud-shaped pillars leads to the main complex and its stairway. The stairs that follow lead to the main temple; at the top is a second bridge and the main gallery. Once you're through the hallway of the gallery, you'll be standing in daylight on the third bridge, facing a portico of the chamber leading to the main sanctuary. The lintel above this entrance, the **Phrai Narai Lintel,** depicts a Hindu myth featuring Lord Narayana, an incarnation of Vishnu. It was stolen, resurfaced in the Art Institute of Chicago, and returned in 1988. (Open daily 6am-6pm. 40฿.)

SURIN ☎044

For one week each November, hordes of Thai and *farang* flood Surin to watch dancing, bejeweled, soccer-playing pachyderms on parade in the Surin Elephant Roundup. The other 51 weeks of the year, Surin remains a rare stop on itineraries, as most travelers press on to the Mekong River. Their loss is your gain; this town, boasting one of the most intriguing night markets around, is a jumping-off point for the many small Khmer ruins and traditional villages dotting the countryside.

TRANSPORTATION

Trains: Surin Railway Station (☎511 295), beside the elephant statue on Thornsarn Rd. Trains to **Khorat** (3hr., 11-13 per day) and **Ubon Ratchathani** (3hr., 11 per day). Many of these trains continue to **Bangkok.** Prices vary according to the type of train and seat (Bangkok 73-229฿; Khorat or Ubon 32-114฿).

Buses: Surin Bus Terminal (☎511 756), on Chit Bam Rung Rd. From the traffic circle, go 1 block east past Mr. Donut, and then 2 blocks to the left; it's on the right. Buses to: **Bangkok** (10 per day 7:30am-9pm; fan 131฿, A/C 195฿, VIP 225฿); **Chiang Mai** (15hr.; 5 per day 2:45-6:50pm; fan 255฿, A/C 455฿, VIP 525฿); **Khorat** (3½hr.; about every 30min. 4am-6pm; fan 50฿, A/C 80฿); **Pattaya** (9hr.; 8 per day 8:20am-10:15pm; fan 125฿, A/C 230฿); **Ubon Ratchathani** (4hr.; 9 per day 7:30am-9:30pm; fan 80฿, A/C 107฿).

Local Transportation: Samlor around town 20-25฿; **tuk-tuk** 30-40฿.

ORIENTATION AND PRACTICAL INFORMATION

Surin has no English street signs. The main street, **Thornsarn Rd.,** runs north-south. At its north end is the **train station,** which faces an elephant statue. Several blocks down Thornsarn Rd. from the train station is a **traffic circle.** To reach the traffic circle from the bus station, exit to the left, pass the soi with the sign for the Petchkason Hotel, and take the next right. Thornsarn Rd. is the first intersection. One block past the traffic circle on Thornsarn is the intersection with **Krung Sri Nai Rd.,** with **day** and **night markets,** the **post office, banks,** and a **hotel.**

Tourist Office: The **Surin City Hall** (☎516 075), on Lakmuang Rd., offers tourist info. Open M-F 8:30am-3:30pm. Mr. Pirom at Pirom's House (see **Accommodations,** below) is an invaluable resource.

Currency Exchange: Bangkok Bank, 252 Thornsarn Rd. (☎512 013), just past the traffic circle on the right. **24hr. ATM** (AmEx/MC/PLUS/V). Open M-F 8:30am-3:30pm.

Markets: Day and **night markets** are in the same location along Krung Sri Nai Rd. From the train station walk 1 block past the traffic circle.

Emergency: ☎191. **Tourist Police (Bangkok):** ☎1155.

Police: Surin Police Station (☎511 007), on Lakmuang Rd.

Pharmacy: Kayang Chelan Pesat, 294 Thornsarn Rd. (☎513 055). Near Krung Sri Nai Rd. Open daily 8:30am-9pm.

Medical Services: Ruam Paet, Tesaban 1 Rd. (☎513 192). In a tall building with a blue and white sign. Facing the train station at the traffic circle, turn right; it's after the 2nd stoplight on the right.

Telephones: Phone and fax available at the post office (see below) daily 7am-10pm. **International** phones (on Thornsarn Rd., 1 block from train station) require phone cards—but phone cards aren't sold in Surin.

Post Office/Telephones: Surin Post Office (☎511 009), on the corner of Thornsarn and Tesaban 1 Rd. at the traffic circle. Open M-F 8:30am-4:30pm, Sa-Su 9am-noon. **Postal code:** 32000.

ACCOMMODATIONS AND FOOD

Pirom's House ❶, 242 Krung Sri Nai Rd., is a teak wooden house—rustic in the best sense. From the traffic circle, head away from the train station on Tanasan Rd. Make a right onto Krung Sri Nai Rd.; it's 2 blocks down when the road bends a sharp left. (☎515 140. Gates lock 11pm. Dorms 70฿; singles 100฿; doubles 150฿.) From the train station, **Santhong Hotel (Nid Diew Hotel) ❷** is on the left just after the traffic circle, opposite Bangkok Bank. (☎512 009. Singles 150฿, with A/C 320฿; doubles 250-390฿.) **New Hotel ❷,** 6-8 Thornsarn Rd., is outside the train station beside the minimart. (☎511 322. Singles 160฿; doubles 280฿; A/C rooms 380-500฿.)

Surin has some of the best Isaan food around, especially at the market. **Wai Wan Restaurant ❷,** 44-46 Sanitnikhomrat Rd., has delicious *khao nam phrik goong nam sand* (rice topped with shrimp in a red curry coconut milk sauce; 40฿). From the train station, take the second left onto Sanitnikhomrat Rd.; it's on the right. (☎511 614. Open daily 8am-10pm.) **Pattee Restaurant ❹,** 40-42 Tesaban 1 Rd., is a raucous hall of a restaurant. From the traffic circle, walk west toward the KFC sign; it's on the left behind the liquor store. (☎511 682. Most dishes 80-250฿. Large seafood menu 120-180฿. Open daily noon-11pm.)

SIGHTS AND NIGHTLIFE

Surin is a pleasant place to relax and enjoy Isaan life, but there's not much in the way of "official" sights unless you're there for the annual **Elephant Roundup,** which occurs in mid-November (check with the TAT in Khorat or with Mr. Pirom for exact dates). The stars of this two-day festival honoring the national animal are the 200 pachyderms who awe audiences with feats of strength and skill. Highlights include a battle reenactment and a staged "elephant hunt" exhibiting traditional Suay techniques. The finale features a soccer match played by the agile beasts.

For those whose idea of fun involves a good beat and a dance floor, **The Sparks Music Complex** is the place. From the traffic circle, head down Tesaban Rd. toward the Mr. Donut sign. Take a left at Sirirat Rd. (the 2nd stoplight) and proceed 300m—look up high for the red sign, next to the Thong Tarin Hotel. Sparks is packed on weekends when locals gather to get their groove on. (☎514 088. Open daily 9pm-2am. Cover 70฿.)

DAYTRIPS FROM SURIN

Anyone can visit the local **silk-weaving villages,** but the communication barrier makes learning the entire silk-making process difficult. Luckily, Mr. Pirom can act as a go-between for travelers and locals (see **Pirom's House,** above); he knows the process and the people well. His tours go to places like **Ban Ta Klang,** a Suay village featuring elephants that are trained and kept as pets, **Ban Khaosinarin,** a group of traditional silk-weaving villages, and numerous Khmer ruins and temples including **Prasat Srikhoraphum,** which are similar to the ruins of Muang Tham near Phimai. To visit the villages solo, walk toward the train station on Thornsarn Rd. After the traffic circle, enter the second alley on the left. From here, trucks ferry visitors the 20km or so (approximately every hr. 7-9am).

UBON RATCHATHANI ☎045

Ubon Ratchathani (simply "Ubon" to Thais), the trading and communications hub for the northeastern corner of Thailand, attracts few travelers except during the Candle Festival in July. The festival features processions of beeswax-covered serpents, saints, and Buddhas—some candles are larger than the monks who carry them. Not far downstream, the Moon River flows into the Emerald Triangle where Laos, Cambodia, and Thailand converge in the lush jungle.

TRANSPORTATION

Flights: Ubon Ratchathani International Airport (☎263 916), on Thepyothi Rd. **Thai Airways,** 364 Chayangkun Rd. (☎313 340), 2km north of the river on the right. Open M-F 8am-4pm. Flights to **Bangkok** (3 per day, 2000฿).

Trains: Railway Station (☎321 276, advance ticketing ☎321 004), on Sathani Rd., Warin Chamrap District. Buses #2 and 6 run to the station from Upparat Rd. (5฿). Trains go to **Bangkok** (13-14hr.; 6:35, 6:55am, 1:25, 4:15, 4:50, 6:15, 7:40pm; seat with fan 95฿, seat with A/C 120-200฿, sleeper with fan 320-470฿, sleeper with A/C 450-700฿) via **Surin** (31-100฿) and **Khorat** (58-200฿).

Buses: Ubon has 6 privately run bus stations. At the far north end of town is the **Ubon Ratchathani bus station** (☎241 319); take bus #2, 3, or 11. To: **Mukdahan** (2hr.; 6:30, 7:30, 11:30am, 2, 3pm; fan 51฿, A/C 92฿) via **That Phanom** (45min.); 1st and 3rd buses continue to **Nakhon Phanom** (4hr.; fan 81฿, A/C 146฿); 2nd bus terminates in **Udon Thani** (6½hr.; fan 128฿, A/C 210฿).

Rentals: Thai Yont, 302-14 Khuanthani Rd. (☎241 242). Rental return on Upparat Rd. near Suriyat Rd. **Motorcycles** 200-300฿ per day. Open M-Sa 8am-5pm.

Local Transportation: City buses run 5am-6pm (5฿). From Upparat Rd., buses #2 and 6 run to the train station and buses #2, 3, and 11 go to the Ubon bus station. **Tuk-tuks** and **samlor** roam the streets (up to 60฿ from the Moon River to Sahamit bus station).

ORIENTATION AND PRACTICAL INFORMATION

Readily accessible by air, bus, or train, Ubon is the last stop on the northeastern branch of the national rail network. To go farther east or north, travelers must rely on the sometimes-daunting bus system. Ubon's main thoroughfare, **Upparat Rd.,** stretches north-south for 12km; at its north end it is called **Chayangkun Rd.** To the south, it crosses the **Moon River** into the **Warin Chamrap District,** where the train station is. Buses #1, 2, 3, and 6 go there from Ubon proper. North of the river, Upparat Rd. passes the riverside **market** and, two blocks up, intersects **Khuanthani Rd.** The

THE LOCAL STORY

WATER FIGHT

It's impossible to hit the streets during Songkran (Thai New Year Festival), without being hit with streams of water. Originally, water used to symbolize cleansing—to literally wash away the previous year. The more traditional aspect of the festivities is pouring scented water over the shoulders and hands of elders in a request for blessing.

Most of the time, however, you'll be dodging the masterfully aimed laser beams of water, shot from pump action pipes. If it seems somewhat dangerous, that's because it is. In 2002, three people drowned in Chiang Mai while the national death toll stood at 564, with 37,473 injuries, most from drunk driving, but also vision-impaired accidents. Some visitors gripe that the three-day festival lasts too long and complain about the unwelcome smearing of talcum powder on strangers. But most will find that they're washed away in this joyous occasion.

The traditional home of Songkran is in the villages. An exodus from the cities to family reunions in the country leads to logistical nightmares reminiscent of Heathrow on Christmas Eve.

So April 13-15 every year, families participate in cleansing and merrymaking. The first day corresponds to the last day of the Old Year; nothing impure should be brought forward. Instead it is a time to bless elders and cleanse oneself. Not even the *muangs* (Buddha images) are spared a thorough scrub; the most important ones are paraded through the streets

(continued on next page)

hospital and **museum** are here, and the **tourist office** is several blocks to the right.

Tourist Office: TAT, 264/1 Khuanthani Rd. (☎243 770), away from the river on Upparat Rd. Turn right onto Khuanthani Rd. at the National Museum; it's on the left 2 blocks down. Free, useful maps and fluent English spoken. Open daily 8:30am-4:30pm.

Tours: Siri Ratana Tours (☎245 847), on Phalorangrit Rd. With your back to the river, turn right onto Palorangit Rd.; it's 1½ blocks down on the left.

Currency Exchange: Bangkok Bank, 13 Ratchabut Rd. (☎262 453). **24hr. ATM** (AmEx/MC/PLUS/V). Open M-F 8:30am-3:30pm. Banks line Upparat Rd.

Markets: The **Riverside market** is an around-the-clock affair. As you cross the bridge into Ubon, the market is immediately to the right of Upparat Rd.

Emergency: Police ☎191. **Tourist Police (Bangkok):** ☎1155.

Tourist Police (local): ☎244 941. At the corner of Suriyat and Thepyothi Rd., near the airport. English spoken. Call here before dialing the police.

Pharmacy: Chai Wit, 87 Promathep Rd. (☎254 077). From the TAT, walk 2 blocks toward the river. Chai Wit is 1 block to the left—look for the yellow and green sign across the street. Open M-F 7am-7:30pm, Sa 7am-noon.

Medical Services: Rom Klao, 123 Upparat Rd. (☎244 658), 2 blocks down Upparat Rd. From the bridge, it's on the left before Khuanthani Rd. English spoken. **Open 24hr.**

Internet Access: The cheapest spot is on Nakhonban Rd. 100m north of Phalorangrit (☎01 447 8612). Sign reads: "Internet." 20฿ per hr. Open daily 9am-midnight.

Post Offices: GPO (☎260 465), on Phichitrangsan Rd. Walk east on Khuanthani Rd. past the TAT and turn left on Thepyothi Rd. It is 3 large blocks away from the river. *Poste Restante* behind the office. AmEx/MC/V. Open M-F 8:30am-4:30pm, Sa-Su 9am-noon. **Telephone** service available M-F 8:30am-4:30pm at a 2nd post office at 159-163 Padaeng Rd. **Lenso** phone. Phone cards sold here. The Warin Chamrap branch office, on Tahaan Rd., has same hours and also offers **Internet** access (Internet cash cards 60฿ per hr.). **Postal code:** 34000.

ACCOMMODATIONS AND FOOD

River Moon House ❷, 21 Si Saket 2 Rd., Warin Chamrap, has four teak houses set back from the road. From the train station, take the second left after the iron horse display out front. Walk 200m until the road merges into Si Saket 2 Rd.; it's across the street, 10m to the right. (☎286 093. Breakfast 50฿. Singles 120฿; room with two double beds 150฿.) Nearby, **Sri Isaan Hotel ❺,** 62 Ratchabut Rd., has clean but small rooms, though it is certainly not the miser's choice. (☎261 011. Singles 550฿; doubles 600฿.) **New Nakornhuang Hotel ❷,** 84-88 Yutthaphan Rd., a block south of TAT, has decent rooms for a decent price. (☎254 768. Singles 160฿, with A/C 270฿; doubles with fan 240฿, with TV 270฿.) Though **Suriyat Hotel ❸,** 302 Suriyat Rd., isn't much to look at from the outside, it's pristine inside. Suriyat is on the northern end of town, 30m to the right of Upparat Rd. (☎241 144. Singles 200฿, with hot water and A/C 400฿; doubles 350฿/ 450฿.)

The **market ❷,** off Promathep Rd. east of Upparat Rd. serves Isaan and Vietnamese dishes. At night, **vendors ❶** gather on Ratchabut Rd. off Khuanthani Rd., near the Ratchathani Hotel. **Chiokee Restaurant ❷,** 307 Khuanthani Rd., diagonally across from the National Museum, serves a delicious breakfast: porridge with fish for 40฿. (☎254 017. Most dishes 30-120฿. Open daily 6am-6pm.) **The Gold Fish Restaurant ❸,** 142/1-2 Khuanthani Rd., 50m east of Ratchawong Rd., is on the upscale side, serving some tasty fish dishes. (☎242 394. Steamed *cheet* fish with vegetables in *isaan* sauce 120฿. Most dishes 60-180฿. Thai menu only; owner speaks English.) For homemade vegetarian fare, head to the **Vegetarian Restaurant,** 79/ 1 Nakhonban Rd. (Meals 15-25฿. Open M-F 7am-2pm.)

SIGHTS

The **Ubon Ratchathani National Museum,** on the left side of Khuanthani Rd. immediately after turning right off Upparat Rd., documents the region's history and culture. Considered one of the country's best, this museum features a 1500-year-old bronze kettle drum from Khong Chiam, a 9th-century Dvaravati boundary stone, Khmer lintels, and local crafts. (☎255 071. Open W-Su 8am-4pm. 30฿.) **Wat Thon Sri Muang** towers above Luang Rd. opposite the kindergarten. The wat, with interior wall paintings depicting life in ancient Ubon, is over 200 years old. The July **Candle Festival** takes place in the adjacent field. Those with access to wheels can check out **Wat Ban No Muang,** northeast of town, which features a modern-style, 50m tall, three-headed elephant. Pass underneath to view a giant *wiharn* being paddled away in a large sailing vessel. Two relaxing spots on the Moon River provide diversions for locals. **Ko Hat Wat Tai** is an island surrounded by huts on stilts

(continued from previous page)

before receiving their bath at the temple. The second day is the transitional period into the New Year. Typically, sand is made into *chedis* outside temples in order to represent the sacred soil a lay person tramples upon during the year. The final day is the start of the New Year. In 2003, the year in Thailand will be 2546 (years after Lord Buddha's death).

While every day has its associated customs, if you're just looking for some good old *sanuk* ("love of life" or "fun-loving"), you'll love the water fights of Songkran. It's an unforgettable experience—like Holi in India.

Bangkok's parades are the most elaborate, while Chiang Mai appears to have been designed with Songkran in mind—the moat serves as a source of constant reloading for the patrolling pick-ups packed with would-be water assassins.

But the villages are the place to be for a more traditionally Thai Songkran experience. Fortunately, Thailand has a lot of villages, filled with water-lovin' friendly people who will share their festival with you.

If you're planning to be in any of the major cities and centers during Songrkan, book transport and accommodations early. As with every national holiday, a lack of vacancies and gross inflation of prices are the norm. Also keep in mind that all banks, museums, stores, and offices will be closed for those three days. And one last warning—don't wear anything white (it will be see-through in 10min.).

—Anthony Barker

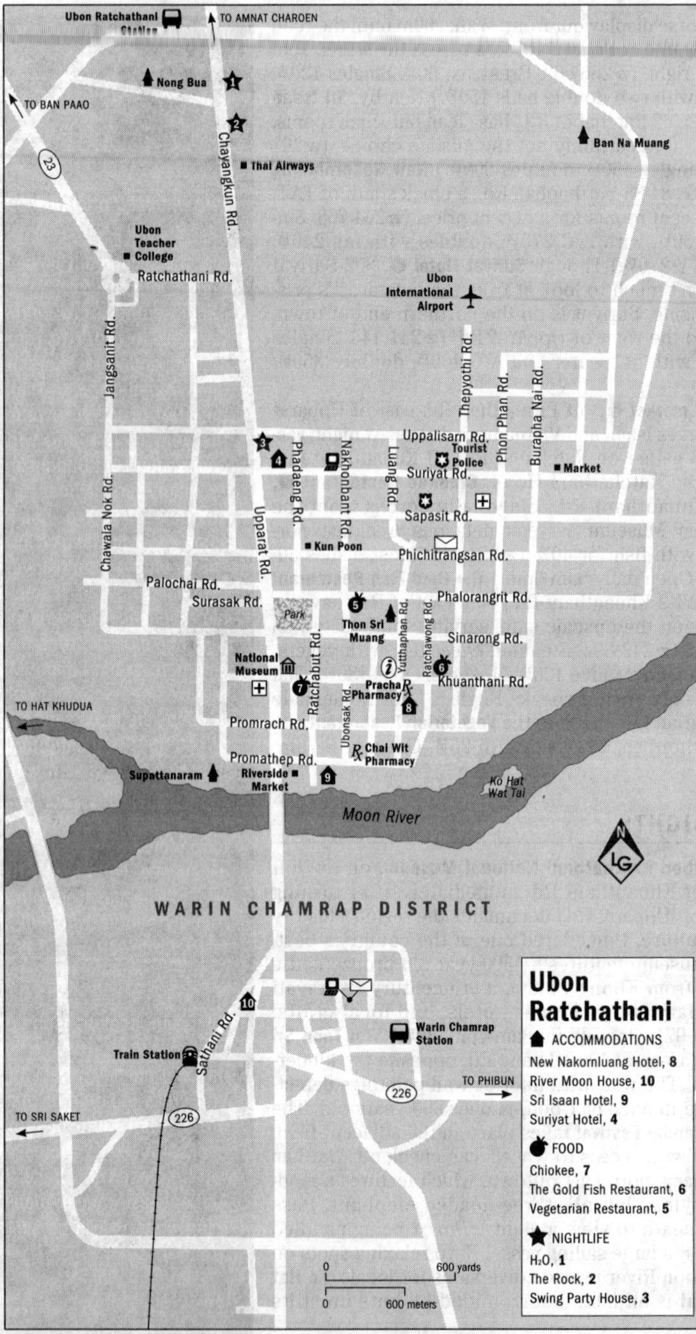
Ubon Ratchathani Station
TO AMNAT CHAROEN
Nong Bua
TO BAN PAAO
23
Chayangkun Rd.
Thai Airways
Ban Na Muang
Ubon Teacher College
Ratchathani Rd.
Ubon International Airport
Jangsanit Rd.
Thepyothi Rd.
Phon Phan Rd.
Burapha Nai Rd.
Uppalisarn Rd.
Tourist Police
Suriyat Rd.
Market
Phadaeng Rd.
Nakhonbant Rd.
Luang Rd.
Chawala Nok Rd.
Upparat Rd.
Sapasit Rd.
Kun Poon
Phichitrangsan Rd.
Palochai Rd.
Surasak Rd.
Park
Phalorangrit Rd.
Thon Sri Muang
Yutthaphan Rd.
Ratchawong Rd.
Sinarong Rd.
National Museum
Ratchabut Rd.
Khuanthani Rd.
Pracha Pharmacy
Ubonsak Rd.
TO HAT KHUDUA
Promrach Rd.
Chai Wit Pharmacy
Promathep Rd.
Supattanaram
Riverside Market
Ko Hat Wat Tai
Moon River
LG
WARIN CHAMRAP DISTRICT
Warin Chamrap Station
Train Station
Sathani Rd.
TO PHIBUN
226
TO SRI SAKET
226
0
600 yards
0
600 meters
Ubon Ratchathani
ACCOMMODATIONS
New Nakornluang Hotel, 8
River Moon House, 10
Sri Isaan Hotel, 9
Suriyat Hotel, 4
FOOD
Chiokee, 7
The Gold Fish Restaurant, 6
Vegetarian Restaurant, 5
NIGHTLIFE
H2O, 1
The Rock, 2
Swing Party House, 3

above the water. During the dry season, the island can be reached by a bamboo footbridge, but is inaccessible in the rainy season. To find it, walk east to the end of Promrach Rd., then turn right and walk down to the river bank (no entrance fee).

ENTERTAINMENT AND NIGHTLIFE

The **Nevada** multiplex, past the Ratchathani intersection on the right, shows the latest action flicks (60฿), but sadly they are all dubbed into Thai. Receive an Isaan-style traditional massage at **Traditional Pharmacy,** 369-371 Sapasit Rd., near the corner of Phadaeng Rd. (☎254 741. 100฿ per hr. Open daily 8am-6pm.) **Swing Party House,** 140/1-2 Upparat Rd., between Suriyat and Uppalisarn Rd., on the right from the river. This is the hottest bar in town. (☎265 145. Live music nightly 9:30pm. Large Singha 120฿. Open daily 7pm-1am.) In the basement of the Nevada Hotel on the northern end of Chayangkun Rd., **The Rock** is a sweaty, pumping disco. (☎280 999. Large Singha 99฿. Open daily 9pm-2am.) Housed in a metal and glass box, **H20,** 488/1 Chayangkun Rd. 100m north of the Nevada Hotel, is the epicenter of trendy. (☎280 315. Jug of Singha 140฿. Open daily 7pm-2am.)

MARKETS

Ubon is famous for its silk and *khit*-patterned cotton cloth. Two stores sell clothing made from the area's handwoven cotton. **Maybe Cotton Hut,** 124 Sinarong Rd., is near Ratchawong Rd. (☎254 932. Open daily 7:30am-9pm.) **Kun Poon,** on Phadaeng Rd. between Sapasit and Phichitrangsan Rd., offers delicately woven silks. Prices are in the 2000฿ range. (Open daily 7:30am-7pm.) Those looking for world-famous Isaan silk should try the **Women's Weaving Cooperative** in the village of **Ban Pa Ao,** 21km north of Ubon on Rte. 23. The village's traditional *mut-mee* silk is available in an array of colors and patterns. Prices begin at 650฿ per meter, and run into the thousands. The clothes, mostly women's blouses and skirts, sold in the showroom, start at 450฿. Any bus heading north from the Sayan Tour bus station passes Ban Pa Ao. (Open daily 8:30am-6:30pm.) Tell the ticket collector to drop you off there (20฿). From the main road, the cooperative is 3km east; motorcycle taxis can take you the rest of the way (20฿). To return to Ubon, flag down any bus heading south to the city, or catch a *songthaew* directly from the village (20฿).

BORDER CROSSING: CHONG MEK/VANG TAO Travelers can enter Laos at the village of Chong Mek. From the village of Vang Tao on the Lao side, it is a short ride to Pakse (p. 354). From Ubon, take a bus from the Warin Chamrap station to **Phibun** (1hr., 5am-6pm, 20฿). At the Phibun market, locals can direct you to *songthaew* heading to **Chong Mek** (1¼hr., 7am-5pm, 20฿). Travelers intending to enter Laos must first have a visa stamped with the name of the appropriate entry point (i.e. Vang Tao) from the Lao embassy in Bangkok, or from the Lao consulate in Khon Kaen. **Visas obtained in Nong Khai are not valid here.** Before crossing the border you must officially register your departure from Thailand at the **immigration office,** 30m before the fence on the right. Once in Laos, present visas to immigration, just beyond the border on the right (entry tax 50฿). From Vang Tao, *songthaew* can drive you to **Pakse** (10฿).

DAYTRIPS FROM UBON RATCHATHANI

FOREST MONASTERIES. Northeast Thailand is known for its masters of meditation. Forest wats became the home of *dudtong* (serious and ascetic) monks who keep strict vows—limiting food to one meal a day, walking as their only means of transportation, and going barefoot. **Wat Pa Nanachat Beung Wai,** a forest monastery with predominantly Western monks, is 12km west of Ubon on the way to Surin. It's a branch of the nearby **Wat Nong Pa Pong** temple, known principally for meditation teacher **Ajaan Chaa** who is renowned for his clarity, insight, and discipline. A major branch of the controversial **Santi Asok** sect resides 6km to the east of town; ask in town for details. *(Wat Pa Nanachat Beung Wai is behind a rice field off the highway to Si Saket, near Beung Wai village. Catch a Si Saket-bound bus or* songthaew *from Warin Chamrap bus terminal, and ask to get off at Wat Nanachat. Wat Nong Pa Pong temple is 10km south of Ubon and off the road to Katharalak.)*

KHAO PHRA WIHARN. A kilometer over Thailand's contested southern border, one of Thailand's best monuments is actually in Cambodia. Basking in its own gravity-defying splendor, Khao Phra Wiharn is a temple/monument complex built by the Angkor kings. The complex rises 800m up a steep grade overlooking the Cambodian plains to the south; its principal chapel is on the peak of a great cliff 600m high. A contemporary of Angkor Wat, it was built from the 10th to the 12th centuries by King Rajendravarman. Large steps lead past four pavilions and tourist markets. Although officially opened to the public in 1991, it was closed two years later because of violent hill skirmishes between the Khmer Rouge and the Cambodian government. In August 1998, it was reopened. A ripped-up helicopter is a vestige of the last government siege in 1998 that captured the mount. It lies near the first pavilion. As of April 2000, the region appears to have stabilized; however, don't stray from the well-trodden path. **The area may still contain live landmines.** During the week, the grounds are empty, and transportation requires some creativity. Catch one of the buses to Katharalak, which leave from a lot in Warin Chamrap on Upparat Rd. near the minimart (2hr., every hr. 6am-7pm, 25฿). From Katharalak, tell locals where you want to go. On weekends they will put you on a bus directly to the site, but on weekdays they will direct you to *songthaew* that go to the Poomsalon turn-off 10km north of the site (1hr., leave when full, 15฿). From there, some travelers ignore the greedy motorcycle taxis (200฿ round-trip) and try to hitch a ride from a few hundred meters south on the highway. Drivers and foreigners must cede their passports to police 3km from the park to guarantee return to Thailand. *(Park open daily 8am-5pm. 100฿.)*

KHONG CHIAM

The tranquil hamlet of Khong Chiam is 60km east of Ubon, at the confluence of the Moon and Mekong Rivers. To local youths it's "The Middle of Nowhere," but to the metropolis-weary traveler, it's a paradise where the pace of life echoes the somnolent flow of the river, and where children squeal and hide from *farang*.

Pha Taem National Park houses a 200m stretch of prehistoric rock paintings. There is little public transport, but you can get there easily with a map and rented wheels. During the high season, two or three *songthaew* may depart; inquire at Apple Guest House. Once at Pha Taem, it's a 500m walk to the paintings. **Tana Rapids National Park** is 3km south of Khong Chiam on the Moon River.

Tiny little Khong Chiam is packed with guest houses. **Mongkhon Guest House ❷,** 595 Klaewpradit Rd., 30m up from the bus station, has just been renovated. (☎01 718 31 82. Singles 150฿, with A/C 300฿.) **Apple Guest House ❷,** 267 Klaewpradit Rd., past the bank and opposite the post office, is less charming, but takes a close second place. Motorcycles are available for 150-200฿ per day. (☎351 160. Singles and doubles 150฿, with A/C 300฿.) **Khong Chiam Hotel ❷**, 355 Pakumchai Rd., offers lackluster rooms in a green concrete building. Walking away from the bus station on Klaewpradit Rd., take a right at the sign for the hotel, before the Apple Guest House. (☎351 074. Rooms with bath 150฿, with A/C 300฿.) A few good **restaurants** line Rimkhong Rd. by the river—menus and prices are similar at all of them.

Khong Chiam is shaped like a long acute triangle: its two main roads come together in a point as they jut out into the two rivers. **Klaewpradit Rd.** runs from the market and bus stop straight through the center of town, ending at a wat. Walking across the temple grounds leads to a pavilion with a view of the Moon and Mekong Rivers, joining to become the "Two-Color" River. The **post office** has an **overseas phone.** (☎351 016. Open M-F 8:30am-4:30pm, Sa-Su 9am-noon.) A **bank** exchanges some currencies. (☎351 123. Open M-F 8:30am-3:30pm.) Both are on Klaewpradit Rd. **Rimkhong Rd.** runs along the Mekong River parallel to Klaewpradit Rd. Here, a stone tablet opposite the **police station** (☎351 023) identifies Khong Chiam as the easternmost point in Thailand. **Tourist Police (Bangkok):** ☎1155. **Postal code:** 34220.

Take a bus from Ubon Ratchathani bus station to Phibun Mangsahan (platform #24, 1hr., every 30min. 5am-6pm, 28฿). From the Phibun market, take a *samlor* to the *songthaew* station on the Moon River (10฿ at most). *Songthaew* go to Khong Chiam at least once per hour (45min., 25฿). A bus runs infrequently from Ubon (platform #26; 2hr., 50฿). It takes a similar route but doesn't require a bus change. If you get stuck in Phibun, **Hotel Phibun ❸** (☎441 201) has rooms (with fan 200-250฿, with A/C 300-350฿). To get there, walk from the *songthaew* stop (with the market on the left) to the intersection, and take a right; it's ahead on the right.

MUKDAHAN ☎042

A rich history of Thai and Lao influences is evident in the golden baguettes sold at the market and the annual boat races in October enjoyed from both sides of the river. This provincial capital is easily traversed on foot and is a convenient border crossing with Savannakhet, Laos. The rest of the province is green with pristine landscapes and lush tropical forests.

TRANSPORTATION. The main **bus station,** 33 Chayang Koolurd Rd. (☎630 486) is 3km away on the side of the highway opposite the town. To walk into town, take a left out of the terminal and a right at Wiwitsurakan Rd., the first major intersection, 500m ahead. Follow this street as it merges and winds to the right. Make a left at Phitak Phanomket Rd. and walk 1km into the heart of town. Tuk-tuks to the river are 20-40฿. Buses run to: **Bangkok** (12hr.; 8, 8:30am, 4:30pm, and about every 30min. 6-7:30pm; fan 184-193฿, A/C 331-347฿, VIP 545฿) via **Khorat** (6hr.; fan 120฿, A/C 128-202฿). Prices depend on routing. There is regular service to: **Nakhon Phanom** (2½hr.; 7 per day 8:30am-5pm; fan 40฿, A/C 61฿); **That Phanom** (45min.; every 30min. 6am-6pm; fan 22฿, A/C 38฿); **Ubon Ratchathani** (2½hr.; every 30min. 6:30am-4:30pm; fan 51฿, A/C 92฿); and **Udon Thani** (4½hr.; 6 per day 9:30am-2pm; fan 82฿, A/C 148฿). With a Lao visa, you can take a **ferry** to **Savannakhet.** (Boats depart M-F 9am-3:30pm, Sa 9am-12:30pm 50฿.)

ORIENTATION AND PRACTICAL INFORMATION. The town is laid out on a grid, with streets running roughly parallel (north-south) and perpendicular (east-west) to the Mekong, the town's east border. Along the river bank is **Samron Chaikhong Rd.,** site of the **Indochina Market,** the wat, and the pier. Parallel to Samron Chaikhong, heading from the river, are **Samut Sakdarak (Mukdahan-Donton) Rd.** and **Phitak Santirat Rd.** Perpendicular to these are **Song Nang Sathit Rd.,** which runs from the pier past the Huanum Hotel to the night market, and, one road south, **Phi-**

tak Phanomket Rd., where the **post office** is. The **bus terminal** is on the main highway (Rte. 212), **Chayang Koolurd Rd.**, 3km northwest.

Thai Farmers Bank, 191 Song Nang Sathit Rd., 2 blocks up the road from the pier and one block past Huanum Hotel, has a **24hr. ATM** (MC/V) and exchanges currency. (☎611 056. Open M-F 8:30am-3:30pm except holidays.) Some officers speak English at the **police station** (☎611 333) on Phitak Phanomket Rd., between the traffic circle and Song Nang Sathit Rd. **Huan Hong Osoth Pharmacy**, at 38 Samut Sakdarak Rd., opposite Huanum Hotel, has English-speakers. (☎612 002. Open daily 6am-8pm.) The **Mukdahan International Hospital** (☎611 379) is 1km south of downtown on Samut Sakdarak Rd., past Mukdahan Hotel. **Mukdahan Post Office**, 18 Phitak Phanomket Rd., is at the traffic circle. (☎611 065. Open M-F 8:30am-4:30pm, Sa-Su 9am-noon.) The **Telekom office** (☎611 697) is downstairs. Yellow **Lenso** phones accept DC/MC/V and Access AT&T. (Open M-F 8:30am-4:30pm.) **Emergency:** ☎191. **Tourist police (Bangkok):** ☎1155. **Postal code:** 49000.

THAILAND

ACCOMMODATIONS AND FOOD. **Huanum Hotel ❷**, 36 Samut Sakdarak Rd., is on the corner of Samut Sakdarak and Song Nang Sathit Rd., 1 block from the pier. It is a sprawling labyrinth of stairs and fairly clean rooms. (☎611 137. Singles 120฿, with bath 220฿, with A/C 280฿; doubles 270฿, with A/C 350฿.) Next to Pith Bakery, **Hong Kong Hotel ❷**, 161/1 Phithak Santirat Rd., opposite the police station, provides clean rooms with firm beds and Western toilets. From the traffic circle facing the river, make a left. (☎611 143. Rooms 160฿, with A/C and TV 250฿.)

The **night market ❶** along Song Nang Sathit Rd. is especially good. Clean and well-organized stalls serve up spicy *som tam* (papaya salad) and *larb sod* (a tangy and very spicy minced pork). *Pa piya* (Vietnamese spring rolls) come *sot* (fresh) or *thawt* (fried). Many French-Lao bakeries vend breads, eclairs, and more. **Foremost Restaurant ❸** is at 74/1 Samut Sakdarak Rd. From Huanum Hotel, walk one long block past the pharmacy; it's at the next intersection. It serves the obligatory noodle soup as well as more substantial Thai and Western meals. (☎612 251. Meals 40-150฿. Open daily 7am-10pm.) The small **Mumsabai Restaurant ❷** has good clean food. Walking toward the river on Song Nang Sathit Rd., it is on the right one block before the river. (☎633 616. Fried noodles with young kale and egg 30฿. Decent vegetarian choices. Open daily 10am-10pm.)

SIGHTS. A larger-than-life golden Buddha contemplates the Mekong from **Wat Si Mongkan Tai**, on Samron Chaikhong Rd. **Chao Fa Mung Shrine**, far up Song Nang Sathit Rd., houses the city pillar. If you happen to arrive at the end of Buddhist Lent (in late fall), you'll catch boat races on the Mekong.

BORDER CROSSING: MUKDAHAN/SAVANNAKHET You **cannot** get a Lao visa in Mukdahan. Obtain one ahead of time in **Bangkok** (p. 693) or **Chiang Mai** (p. 746). From Mukdahan, you can take a **ferry** to Savannakhet (p. 351). Boats depart M-F 9am-3:30pm, Sa 9am-12:30pm (50฿).

DAYTRIP FROM MUKDAHAN: PHU PHA THEOP NATIONAL PARK. Known for its rock formations and caves, **Phu Pha Theop National Park** (pronounced poo-PAH-tayp) also boasts prehistoric rock art, stunning landscapes, wildlife, and hiking trails. The collection of huge, oddly shaped rocks at the main entrance are the chief crowd-pleasers. The undersides of many overhanging rocks are decorated with now-faded prehistoric paintings. The rangers know the area well; one speaks English. Trail maps are available from the park office at the entrance. The main 2km hike to the **Buddha Cave Waterfall** passes the rocks. Other short hikes pass through mountains and cliffs. The trails aren't always easy to follow; explore carefully. During the dry season, the falls shrink to a trickle. Rickety wooden stairs lead to the **Buddha Cave,** lined with thousands of Buddha images. The park can be reached from Mukdahan by the orange buses and *songthaew* leaving town on the Mukdahan-Dontan Rd. (Rte. 2034) past Mukdahan Hotel on the right (2 per hr. 6am-6pm, leave when full, 10-15฿). Exit at Phu Pha Theop. Drop-off is on the main road next to a large "Mukdahan National Park" sign on the left. The entrance is a 15min. walk down a small paved road on the right. (Open daily 8am-6pm.)

THAT PHANOM ☎042

That Phanom is a sleepy town overlooking the Mekong in south Nakhon Phanom Province. Wat That Phanom, the town's signature attraction, rises nearly 60m above ground, its Lao-style *chedi* glinting in the sun. The seamless fusion of the architecture is mirrored by the food, with the ready availability of Lao and Vietnamese cuisine and the famed biweekly Lao waterfront market. Given That Phanom's pleasing aesthetics, backwater pace of life, and great guest houses, it is not surprising that many enchanted travelers linger here.

TRANSPORTATION AND PRACTICAL INFORMATION. That Phanom, between Nakhon Phanom and Mukdahan, is easily reached from either town by bus or *songthaew* (20฿), which stop along **Chayangkun Rd.** (Hwy. 212) and at a small **bus station** (☎541 087) south of town. Buses leave for **Ubon Ratchathani** (3½hr.; 15 per day 7:10am-3:30pm; fan 76฿, A/C 119฿) via **Mukdahan** (1½hr.; fan 21฿, A/C 38฿) and **Udon Thani** (5hr.; 9 per day 10am-2:45pm; fan 81฿, A/C 119฿) via **Sakhon Nakhon** (1½hr.; fan 29฿, A/C 40฿). Several companies run to **Bangkok,** including **CTP Transport** (☎541 247), opposite the station (11hr.; 8am and frequently 4:30-6pm; fan 218฿, A/C 311฿). **Thaisgoon Tour,** 158 Chayangkun Rd. (☎541 288), a block from the GPO toward the wat, has daily departures to **Bangkok** (11hr.; 8am and frequently 5-7:30pm; fan 200฿, A/C 280฿, VIP 358฿) via **Khorat** (7hr.; fan 130฿, A/C 188฿, VIP 230฿). *Songthaew* to **Nakhon Phanom** (1½hr., every 10min., 20฿) leave from a stop 150m north of Thai Military Bank.

Wat That Phanom is on Chayangkun Rd. Diagonally across from the wat is **Siam Commercial Bank,** 359 Chayangkun Rd. (☎525 784. Open M-F 8:30am-3:30pm. Cirrus/MC/V **ATM.** Open 6am-11pm.) Past the bank and *songthaew* stop is the **GPO,** 322 Chayangkun Rd., which has **international phone** service. (☎541 169. Open M-F 8:30am-4:30pm, Sa-Su 9am-noon.) **That Phanom Hospital** (☎541 255) is 2km west on the highway. The **police station** (☎541 266) is in the north end of town on Phanom Phanarak Rd. **Emergency:** ☎191. **Tourist police (Bangkok):** ☎1155. **Postal code:** 48110.

ACCOMMODATIONS AND FOOD. Travelers hail **Niyana Guest House ❶,** on 288 Moo 2, Rimkhong Rd., as the best in That Phanom. From the victory arch, head to the pier and turn left onto Rimkhong. Follow the river 800m; it's on a small soi to the left. Niyana serves great food, gives Thai lessons, and rents out bicycles. (☎540 588. Dorms 60฿; singles 80฿; doubles 120฿; new bungalows facing the river 200฿, with A/C 300฿.) Another good option is **Tum Guest House ❶,** 110 Soi 14 Anvrakjaydee Rd., four soi down Rimkhong Rd. toward the town center from Niyana's. (Bike rental 40฿ per day; laundry 5-10฿ per item. Rooms 80฿.)

At **food stalls ❶** on Chayangkun Rd., 20฿ buys savory roast chicken, sticky rice, or a bowl of Vietnamese *phở*. A **floating restaurant ❷** bobs beside the pier and several terrestrial restaurants are on Phanom Phanarak Rd. A good **night market ❶** sits near the 7-Eleven and dishes up tantalizing cuisine. (Open daily until around 9pm.)

SIGHTS. Wat That Phanom is the most sacred religious structure in Isaan. Legend has it that it was built to house one of the Buddha's clavicle bones, transported from India. Topped by a 110kg gold spire, the shrine has been restored seven times. Depending on who you ask, it's between 12 and 26 centuries old. The most recent reconstruction occurred in 1978, after heavy rains in 1975 collapsed the 57m *chedi*. The temple is surrounded by a cloister housing dozens of golden Buddha images. At the beginning of February, thousands come to pay their respects during the annual 7-day **Phra That Phanom Homage Fair.** Check out the **Lao Market** near Niyana's Guest House on the far end of Rimkhong Rd. (M and Th 6am-7pm). About 15km northwest of That Phanom is the silk-weaving village of **Renu Nakhon.** Travelers can enjoy Isaan music and dance at the **Renu Nakhon Wat** on Saturdays during the winter. To get there, take any Nakhon Phanom-bound *songthaew* to the Renu Nakhon junction 8km north of town; from there, hire a tuk-tuk.

BORDER CROSSING: NAKHON PHANOM/THA KHAEK Travelers holding a Lao visa obtained in **Bangkok** or **Khon Kaen** (Nong Khai visas are invalid here) should seek an exit stamp from the **immigration office** just opposite the Indochine market on Sunthon Wichit Rd. in Nakhon Phanom (☎511 235. Open M-F 8:30am-4:30pm.) A **boat** behind the office shuttles passengers to Tha Khaek (8am-4pm, 50฿). The Lao entry tax vacillates, but currently stands at 70฿.

NONG KHAI ☎042

If Khao San Road is a noisy, spunky kid, then Nong Khai's riverfront is its calm, cool older brother. Drawn at first by the popular border crossing with Laos, travelers end up staying on to see one of Southeast Asia's best Buddhist temples—Sala Kaew Ku. The influx of foreigners mixes with Nong Khai's Lao-French influence and ornate Buddhist temples to create one of Thailand's authentic tourist towns.

TRANSPORTATION

Trains: Nong Khai Railway Station (☎411 592), on Hwy. 212, 1.5km west of town. Tuk-tuk ride from Rimkhong Rd. 50฿. Trains to **Bangkok** via **Khon Kaen** and **Udon Thani** (Rapid: 10-13hr.; 8:15am, 7:30pm; 3rd-class 143฿, 2nd-class 278฿; express: 11hr.;

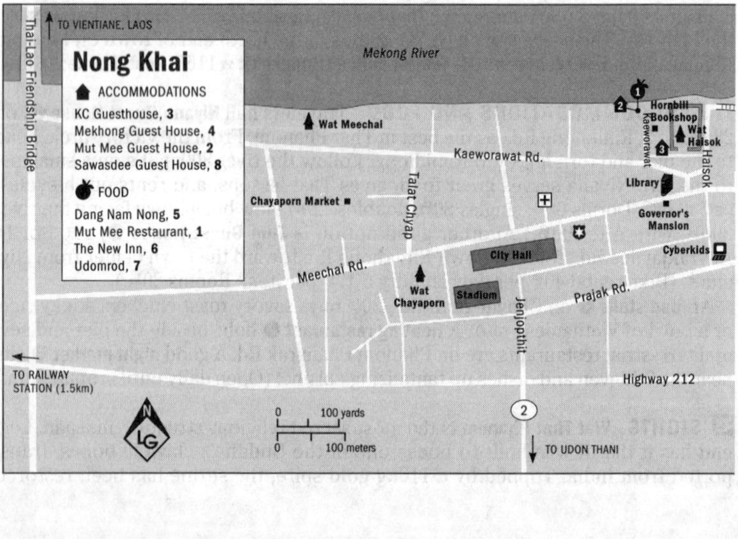

6:40pm; 3rd-class 163฿, 2nd-class 298฿) and **Khorat** (6hr., 1pm, 3rd-class 64฿). Booking office open daily 6:30-10:30am and noon-6pm.

Buses: Nong Khai Bus Terminal, on Prajak Rd. at the east end of town. To: **Bangkok** via **Khon Kaen, Khorat,** and **Udon Thani** (#23; 12hr.; every hr. 5:30am-8pm; 200฿, A/C 351฿, VIP 495฿); **Beung Kan** (#507; 3hr., every hr. 6-10:40am, 70฿); **Nakhon Phanom** (#224; 7hr., 5 per day 6:30-9:40am, 91฿); **Udon Thani** (#221; 1hr., every 30min. 5:30am-5:20pm, 21฿). Green buses go to **Loei** and **Pak Chom** (#507; 8hr., 5 per day 6am-10:40am, 84฿) via **Sangkhom** (2hr., 50฿) and **Si Chiang Mai** (1hr., 30฿), and **Rayong** (12hr.; 13 per day 6am-7:30pm; 211฿, A/C 328฿). To get to **Chiang Khan,** switch buses at **Pak Chom.**

Local Transportation: For those who just want to walk, **tuk-tuks** are abundant to the point of distraction as drivers assume all *farang* are desperately in need of their services. 20฿ for short distances, never more than 60฿.

Rentals: Bicycle rental at Mekhong Guest House (30฿ per day) and Mut Mee Guest House (39-52฿ per day). **Motorcycle rental** (200฿ per day) at **Nana Motor,** 1160 Meechai Rd. (☎411 998), opposite Chayaporn Market. Open daily 7am-5pm.

ORIENTATION AND PRACTICAL INFORMATION

Nong Khai is a major border crossing to **Vientiane, Laos**—the **Friendship Bridge** joins the two countries. In the north, Nong Khai is bordered by the **Mekong River,** while **Hwy. 212** marks the town's southern boundary. Parallel to Hwy. 212, from south to north, are **Prajak Rd., Meechai Rd.,** and **Rimkhong Rd.** The **train station,** on Hwy. 212, 2.5km west of the town center, is a bit of a hike. Taking a right out of the **bus station** and stopping at the first intersection will leave you facing north on Prajak Rd.

Currency Exchange: Bangkok Bank, 372 Soi Srisaket (☎412 675), in the ground floor office next to the ATM. Open M-F 8:30am-3:30pm. Open Sa-Su 8:30am-5pm for currency exchange only.

Markets: The **market,** along Rimkhong Rd. near the Mekong river, features a cornucopia of scented soaps, electronics, binoculars, disco balls, and, of course, massive grilled fish from China, Laos, Russia, Thailand, and Vietnam. Open daily 9am-5:30pm.

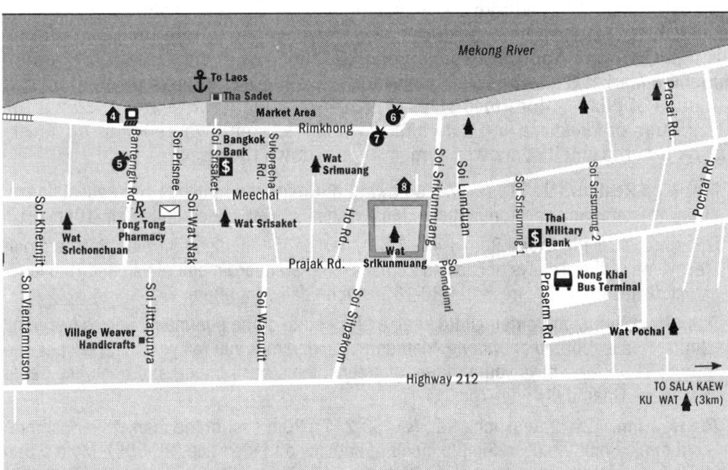

Emergency: ☎191. **Tourist Police (Bangkok):** ☎1155.

Police: ☎411 020. On Meechai Rd., facing the hospital.

Pharmacy: Tong Tong Pharmacy, 382/2 Meechai Rd. (☎411 690). Exit left from the post office; it's on the corner. Open daily 7:30am-9pm.

Medical Services: Nong Khai Hospital, 1158 Meechai Rd. (☎411 088), near City Hall and opposite the police station.

Internet Access: Cyberkids, 422 Prajak Rd., near the intersection with Haisok Rd. Best prices in town. 20฿ per hr. Open daily 8:30am-9pm.

Telephones: Lenso phones in the **GPO** and along Meechai Rd.

Post Office: GPO, 390 Meechai Rd. (☎411 521). **International phone.** *Poste Restante.* Open M-F 8:30am-4:30pm, Sa-Su 9am-noon. **Postal Code:** 43000.

THAILAND

ACCOMMODATIONS

Mut Mee Guest House, 1111/4 Kaeworawat Rd., has riverside patio, scrumptious food, loads of information, and a steady stream of talkative travelers. Clean-as-a-whistle rooms and cute-as-a-button baths. Dorms 80฿; singles 110฿; doubles 140฿, with private bath and hot water 360฿; triples 240-300฿. ❶

Sawasdee Guest House, 402 Meechai Rd. (☎412 502), 5 blocks east of post office, behind Wat Srikunmuang. This rickety wooden guest house has very clean rooms. Singles 100฿; doubles 140฿, with A/C and hot water 300฿. ❶

Mekhong Guest House, 519 Rimkhong Rd. (☎460 689), a few stores west of the immigration pier. Clean rooms upstairs, comfortable restaurant downstairs. Internet next door (30฿ per hr.). Dorms 80฿; singles 100-150฿; doubles 250฿. ❶

KC Guest House, 1018 Kaeworawat Rd. (☎09 842 8084), on the same soi that leads to Mut Mee Guest House. Basic rooms with character, almost in view of the river. Singles 100฿; doubles 150฿. ❶

FOOD

Although the anticipated tourism explosion has yet to hit with full force, eateries have already become bland and overpriced to accommodate the just-passing-through traveler. Good, inexpensive Thai food, however, can still be found. **Chayaporn Market** ❶ on the west side of town has loads of prepared eats available in clouds of chaos. More **food stalls** ❶, some offering fresh seafood, crowd the intersection of **Rimkhong** and **Haisok Rd.** Two blocks south where **Prajak Rd.** meets Haisok Rd., the smell of skewered meats wafts down the street.

Mut Mee Restaurant, 1111/4 Kaeworawat Rd. Great food matches great guest house. Thai, Western, and vegetarian menu. Most dishes 30-60฿. Open daily 8am-10pm. ❷

Udomrod, 423 Rimkhong Rd. (☎421 084), next to the immigration pier. Postcard-perfect views of the six bays of Laos and the Mekong. Standard menu of fish and Thai food. Most dishes 45-120฿; fresh fish 80-180฿. Open daily 8am-8pm. ❸

Dang Nam Nong, on Banterngit Rd., half a block north of the pharmacy. Serves one thing and serves it good: *nham nuang,* Vietnamese spring rolls you roll yourself. 50฿ per person or 155฿ for 4 buys you a platter of greens, mint, basil, meat, and fresh rice paper wrappers. Open daily 6am-7pm. ❷

The New Inn, 429/2 Rimkhong Rd., (☎460 247), 20m east of the market. Perfect for a cold drink along the river. Simple menu of noodles and fried rice (25-50฿). More a pub than a restaurant. Large beer 75฿. Cocktails 80฿. Open daily 9am-midnight. ❶

SIGHTS

SALA KAEW KU (WAT KHAEK). A few kilometers east of Nong Khai on Hwy. 212, Sala Kaew Ku, also known as Wat Khaek, is one of Thailand's most bizarre temples. Towering concrete statues of Hindu and Buddhist figures represent various levels of Buddhist cosmology: the good and the evil, the mundane and the fantastic, the innocent and the freaky—all the brainchild of a Lao mystic, **Luang Poo Boun Leya Sourirat.** Enter the giant mouth in back to learn about *samsara*, the Buddhist belief in the endless cycle of rebirth and suffering. *(15min. bike ride. Head east on Rte. 212, past "St. Paul Nong Khai School" on the right; Sala Kaew Ku is 2 turn-offs later. Grab a map for a more scenic river route. You can also arrange to have a tuk-tuk take you there and wait while you look around. The whole trip should cost 100-120฿ for the round-trip ride and an hour wait. If you have trouble communicating, Carsten at the Thasadej Café (see Food, above) can arrange it for you. Open daily 8am-5pm. 10฿.)*

VILLAGE WEAVER HANDICRAFTS. Seekers of handwoven *mut-mee* fabrics can visit Village Weaver Handicrafts, off Prajak Rd. near the Honda dealership. This 19-year-old project promotes local industry and offers lucrative work to Isaan women who are at risk of turning to brothels for their livelihood. Seamstresses tailor outfits at warp speed and ship them everywhere in the world. (*1151 Soi Jittapunya. ☎411 236. Open daily 8am-5pm, weaving demos M-F.)*

THAILAND

DAYTRIP FROM NONG KHAI: PHU PHRA BAT PARK

Catch a bus to Ban Phu (#294; 1½hr., 7:15am, 30฿) from the Nong Khai Bus Terminal. Take a left from the Ban Phu station and walk over the bridge to where songthaew (15min., every 15min., 5฿) take you to the park. From here, hike 4km to park headquarters or grab a motorcycle taxi (50฿). Leave the park by 2pm to catch the last bus.

Some 85km southwest of Nong Khai, not far from the dusty village of Ban Phu, the eerie wizardry of prehistoric hunters and gatherers lingers at Phu Phra Bat Historical Park. The park boasts a fine collection of prehistoric cave paintings and rock shelters that date back to 1500 BC. Local lore intertwines these sites with the remains of various locations. Buddhas abound in **Tham Phra (Cave of Buddha Images).** At the top of the mountain, the path yields an astounding vista of **Pha Sadet Cliff,** which has a perfect picnic area overlooking the Laotian mountains.

BORDER CROSSING: NONG KHAI/VIENTIANE 15-day Lao tourist visas are issued on the Friendship Bridge for US$30 (3 passport photos required). 30-day visas are available from the Lao embassy in Bangkok for 1100฿ (3-day processing). A tuk-tuk from Nong Khai to the bridge should cost 30-50฿. A bus shuttles people across the bridge for 10฿; once there, expect to pay a 2000kip (10฿) entry tax. On the other side, public buses run the 25km to Vientiane (30฿), or you can take a taxi (150฿).

NEAR NONG KHAI

SANGKHOM

Drowsy Sangkhom is quiet and forlorn, but its geography has stunning vistas, waterfalls, and cliffs. The surrounding jungle is dotted with caves marked on maps available at Bouy Guest House. The impressive **Than Thip Falls** are a 30min. motorbike ride west of town. Bring your bathing suit—the second tier has a swimming hole. **Than Thong Falls** are east of Sangkhom. **Wat Hin Maak Peng** is a monastery set among boulders and bamboo groves. Sangkhom sits in hills 95km west of Nong Khai. Buses go from Loei to **Sangkhom** (3½hr., every hr. 5:40-11:40am, 60฿) and **Nong Khai** (#507; 2hr., every hr. 6am-3pm, 38฿). The **police station** is 700m to the right of the guest houses facing the river. (☎441 080. **Open 24hr.**) The **post office,** 800m to the left, provides international phone service. (☎441 069. Open M-F 8:30am-4:30pm, Sa-Su 9am-noon.) **Postal code:** 43160.

The **Bouy Guest House ❶,** 60 Moo 4 Sangkhom, offers bungalows along the river. (☎441 065. Singles 80฿; doubles 100฿.) Mr. Toy, owner and chef of the guest house's **restaurant ❷,** prepares Thai and Lao specialties (jungle curry 40฿) and has tons of information—ask about boat trips. Just west is **TXK Guest House ❶,** formerly Mama's Guest House. (Free papayas and bananas. Bungalows 100฿.) TXK's **restaurant ❸** is famous for 100฿ Thai and Lao feasts. **River Huts Guest House ❶,** 80m to the right facing the river, has slow Internet access (2฿ per min.) and standard bungalows. (Singles 80฿; doubles 100฿; deluxe with bath, hot water, 2 fans 280฿.)

WAT PHU THAWK AND BUENG KHAN

Although it's one of Northeast Thailand's most spectacular sights, **Wat Phu Thawk** remains untouristed. The shrine stands on a red sandstone outcropping rising from the Nong Khai plain with each of the wat's seven levels representing a stage of enlightenment. Level five has a sanctuary built into the cliff. A skeleton encased in glass awaits your company at level six. On the opposite side of the mountain is a hermitage built on a pinnacle nestled under a boulder. Along the walkways are platforms and huts for meditation.

The sheer isolation of Wat Phu Thawk makes tackling it in one day difficult. From the **Nong Khai Bus Terminal,** take a bus to **Bueng Khan** (#224; 2hr., every hr. 6am-3pm, 45฿). From the Bueng Khan bus stop (across from the ATMs), catch a bus to **Ban Similai** (#225; 40min., 17฿). From here, get to Phu Thawk on a motorcycle (30min., 40-50฿) or jump on a tuk-tuk (100฿). Most people spend the night in Bueng Khan. Hwy. 212 becomes **Thaisamok Rd.,** with a small bus stop, clock tower, and rotary near the center of town. To reach the guest houses, turn right onto **Maesongnang Rd.** (facing the rotary) and left onto **Prasatchai Rd.** Two hotels are 100m down at the first intersection. **Santisuk Hotel ❷,** 21/2 Prasatchai Rd., is on the right. (☎491 114. Singles with TV 150฿; doubles 300฿). **Samanmit Hotel ❸,** 34/3 Prasatchai Rd., is directly across from Santisuk. (☎491 078. Doubles 300฿.)

CHIANG KHAN ☎042

Tucked behind the Mekong River, Chiang Khan is not to be missed. It offers the same stunning vistas and slow afternoons of other frontier towns, but the relative seclusion, few tourists, and spectacular guest houses make it a great rest spot.

TRANSPORTATION AND PRATICAL INFORMATION.

Pak Chom and Loei serve as Chiang Khan's connection to the world. **Songthaew** leave from Chiang Khan Rd. for **Loei** (1hr., every 30min. 5:30am-5pm, 22฿) and **Pak Chom** (1hr., every 30-60min. 6am-4pm, 20฿). From Pak Chom, **buses** run to **Nong Khai** via **Sangkhom** (#507; 4½hr. total, 2hr. to Sangkhom; last bus noon). Buses to **Bangkok** leave from Soi 9, south of the market (6pm, 176฿; A/C 8am, 6:30pm; VIP 6:30pm, 490฿).

Resting on the muddy Mekong River, Chiang Khan is in northern **Loei Province,** 50km from the provincial capital. The two main roads, parallel to each other and the river, are **Chai Khong Rd.,** closer to the water, and **Chiang Khan Rd.,** the highway through town. **Sois 1-24** connect the two roads. Services in Chiang Khan include: **immigration office,** past the hospital on the left (☎821 911; visa extensions 500฿; open M-F 8am-8pm); **police** (☎821 181; **tourist police (Bangkok):** ☎1155; **emergency:**

☎191), on a soi off Chiang Khan Rd. past the hospital; **Ruammith Osoth Pharmacy,** on Chiang Khan Rd. at Soi 9 (☎821 168; open daily 6am-9pm); **Chiang Khan Hospital** (☎821 101), on Chiang Khan Rd. past Soi 21; the **post office,** near the immigration office (☎821 011; *Poste Restante;* open M-F 8:30am-4:30pm, Sa-Su 9am-noon). **Postal code:** 42110.

ACCOMMODATIONS AND FOOD. Chiang Khan's great guest houses far outnumber sweaty *farang*. **Loogmai Guest House ❸,** 112 Chai Khong Rd., Soi 5 (☎09 210 0447), is modern and chic. White walls, abstract art, wood furniture, and concrete floors make this one of the best guest houses in Thailand. All rooms have a fan. (Small rooms 250฿; large rooms 350฿, with bath 400฿.) **Chiang Khan Guest House ❷,** 282 Chai Khong Rd. (☎821 691), has homey wooden rooms with shared Western baths. (Singles 150฿; doubles 200฿.) A wrap-around patio **restaurant ❷** serves good food (most dishes 30-60฿). **Rimkhong Guest House ❶,** 294 Chai Khong Rd., Soi 8 (☎821 125), is a fragrant wooden guest house with squat toilets. (English, French, and Thai spoken. Dorms 60฿; singles 120฿; doubles 140-250฿.)

Rabieng ❷, left of Ton Khong Guest House, churns out tasty Chinese food. (Dishes 50-80฿. Open daily 9am-11pm.) **The Look Kosana ❶,** on Soi 9 near Chai Khong Rd. opposite Phoonsavad Hotel, serves phat thai (20฿) to satisfy even the pickiest taste buds. (Open daily 6pm-midnight.) Along the river by **Kaeng Khut Khu Rapids** are a few **food stands ❶** serving a local specialty—*kung den*, tiny live shrimp that dance around your plate (around 40฿).

SIGHTS. About 3km east of town, a turn-off leads left to **Kaeng Khut Khu Rapids,** where picturesque rock piles interrupt the Mekong's seaward schlep. Follow the sign to **Wat Tha Khaek** and continue for 1km. Some guest houses and hotels provide boat transport to the rapids. *Songthaew* (10฿) and tuk-tuk (50฿ round-trip) make the trip from Chiang Khan Rd.

LOEI ☎042

A big billboard on Hwy. 201 greets visitors to Loei with, "Welcome to Loei, Land of the Sea of Mountains and Coldest in All Siam." Grammar aside, the sign captures the essence of this seldom-visited but appealing province. Those who make the trip to Loei find a perfect place to unwind after a day of exploring the countryside and national parks.

TRANSPORTATION

Buses: All buses leave from the **main bus terminal** off Maliwan Rd. Green buses go to **Nong Khai** via **Pak Chom, Sangkhom,** and **Tha Bo** (#507; every hr. 5:40-10:40am, 84฿). If you're going straight to Nong Khai, take a bus to **Udon Thani** (platform #2; every 20min. 10am-5:30pm, 55฿) and then catch a bus to Nong Khai; it's at least 3hr. faster. Buses also run to: **Bangkok** (10-11hr.; 22 per day 7am-8:30pm; 188฿, A/C 320฿); **Chiang Mai** (9hr.; 11:15am, 8:30, 9:30pm; 165฿, A/C 231฿); **Chiang Rai** (11hr.; 6:30am, 10, 10:30pm; 1st-class 374฿). Many **long-distance buses** may be full upon arrival; guarantee a seat by buying a ticket from the bus terminal counter. *Songthaew* go to **Chiang Khan** (1hr., every 30min. 5:30am-5:30pm, 20฿).

Local Transportation: Samlor and **tuk-tuk** 20-40฿. You can **rent motorbikes** (200฿ per day) at the **bike shop,** 20m north of the traffic circle at the intersection of Chum Saai and Sathon Chiang Khan Rd.

ORIENTATION AND PRACTICAL INFORMATION

Loei town is a tangled mess of streets on Loei River's western bank. **Charoen Rat Rd.** runs the length of the river, beginning in the south at the **night market.** Moving north into town on Charoen Rat Rd., you'll see the **post office** and a white suspension footbridge, followed by **Chum Saai Rd.,** which becomes **Nok Kaew Rd.** three blocks down at a busy traffic circle. Continuing up Charoen Rat Rd., Thai Udom Hotel is at the intersection with **Oua Aree Rd.** Walk a block more to reach **Ruam Jai Rd.,** a major east-west thoroughfare.

Currency Exchange: Siam Commercial Bank, 3/8 Ruam Jai Rd. (☎813 020). Open M-F 8:30am-3:30pm. Cirrus/MC/V **ATM** open daily 6am-11pm. **Bangkok Bank,** at the intersection of Oua Aree and Charoen Rat Rd., has a **24hr. ATM** (AmEx/MC/PLUS/V).

Markets: Loei has two **day/night markets.** One is at the northern end of Charoen Rat Rd., opposite the 7-Eleven. (Open daily 6-9:30pm.) The second market sets up at the southern end of Charoen Rat Rd. (Open daily 10am-9pm.)

Emergency: ☎191. **Tourist Police (Bangkok):** ☎1155.

Police: ☎811 254. On Pipat Mongkon Rd/Phipattanamongkhon Rd., the city's northern border.

Pharmacy: Bun Jung Pesat Pharmacy, 83 Charoen Rat Rd. (☎830 634), on the corner of Ruam Jai Rd. Open daily 3am-9pm.

Medical Services: Loei Provincial Hospital (☎811 541), at the intersection of Maliwan Rd. (Hwy. 201), the town's western boundary, and Nok Kaew Rd., opposite provincial offices. Some English spoken. Cash only.

Internet Access: PA Computers (☎814 761), on Charoen Rat Rd. between Chum Saai and Oua Aree Rd. 20฿ per hr. Open daily 9am-midnight.

Telephones: International calls may be placed from the **CAT** office next to the GPO.

Post Office: GPO (☎812 0222), on Charoen Rat Rd., between the footbridge and night market. Open M-F 8:30am-4:30pm, Sa-Su 9am-noon. **Postal code:** 42000.

ACCOMMODATIONS AND FOOD

King Hotel ❹, 11/9-12 Chum Saai Rd., has the cleanest rooms intown—decked out in tile, furnished with phone, TV, A/C, and hot shower. (☎811 701. Singles 380฿; doulbes 399/600฿; VIP room with fridge 1200฿.) **Thai Udom Hotel ❸,** 122/1 Charoen Rat Rd. at Oua Aree Rd., has decent clean rooms, though they are slightly run down. (☎811 763. Singles 240฿, with A/C 350฿; doubles 320/500฿; VIP rooms 600฿.) **Friendship Guest House 2 ❷,** 257/41 Charoen Rat Rd. at the southern end of the road, across from the market. There's no English sign, but medium-sized rooms (150฿ in a concrete complex are tiled and clean. (☎832 408.)

Some of the best places to eat are the **open-air restaurants ❷** in front of the movie theater just off Oua Aree Rd., opposite Thai Farmers Bank, and at the main bus terminal. A couple of **food stalls ❶** line Chum Saai Rd. where it turns into Nok Kaew Rd., just after the traffic circle. All of them serve fine noodle and rice dishes for about 30฿; the place next to the tire shop is the best. For a sit-down meal, try **Yang Kin Aeng ❸,** at the traffic circle at the intersection of Sathon Chiangkhan Rd. and Chum Saai Rd. It's a local favorite serving up heaps of Thai classics. (Open daily 5-11pm.) Another option is **Sor Ahan Thai ❷,** 32/106 Nok Kaew Rd., 2 blocks west of the traffic circle away from the river. This garden restaurant has an extensive Thai/English menu. (☎813 436. Most dishes 40-100฿. Open daily 9am-midnight.)

NIGHTLIFE

Discos and Western-style pubs line **Rhuamphattana Rd.** Walking west on Nok Kaew Rd. toward the highway, it's the first right after the traffic circle. Halfway down on the left is **Ban Muang Loei Pub,** which has live country music in Thai (small beer 50฿). Continuing down the street, you'll see two Robocop statues on your right; a large, glowing millennium falcon past the gate marks the entrance to **Robot 2029.** Thai bands play nightly at 10:30pm in a neon-lit hall.

NEAR LOEI

PHU RUA NATIONAL PARK

The majestic centerpiece of this park is a **1375m mountain.** Personal vehicles can travel to the top, where a large Buddha surveys the scene below. More low-key routes include a 2km trek to a **waterfall,** from which it's 5.5km to the peak. Pick up a map and consult park rangers before your trip. To get to the park, catch a **bus** to **Lom Sak** via **Phu Rua** (#14; 1hr., every hr. 5am-5pm, 25฿); watch for the large English sign on the right. Snacks are available at the PTT gas station opposite the bus drop-off. *Songthaew* charge an outrageous 300฿ to the park headquarters. To return to **Loei,** wait for a bus in front of the gas station (last bus 6pm). Admission to the park is 200฿. It is possible to complete the circuit in a day, but an overnight stay at the park is recommended. (**Tents ❶** 50฿; **lodging ❸** for 5-8 people 250-500฿.) Food is available daily during high season and until 6pm on weekends during low season. Large groups should contact the **National Parks Division** in Bangkok (☎02 561 4292, ext. 724). The **Song Pee Nong Bungalow ❹** (☎899 399 or 899 258) is about 0.5km away from the park entrance on the right if you are heading toward Loei. Bungalows are simple and clean with decent shared Western toilets. (Wooden bungalows 500฿; larger concrete bungalows 700฿.)

PHU KRADUNG NATIONAL PARK

The park's bell-shaped mountain inspired the name of this popular sanctuary (*kradung* means bell). Trails criss-cross the 60 sq. km plateau at the summit. The 9km hike from the mountain base to park headquarters is facilitated by bamboo stairways. Porters can tote your gear (10฿ per kg). Eager spirits can bid the Khon Kaen bus adieu at Nong Hin, the turn-off for **Ban Pha Ngarm,** a stone forest where limestone outcroppings form a natural labyrinth. Guides promise not to lose you for 100฿ per group. The 18km to Ban Pha Ngarm from the park entrance are traversed only by chartered *songthaew* (500฿). **Mountaintop lodging ❺** starts at 2000฿ per bungalow. The park is packed in high season, but closes from June to September. For more information, contact the **National Parks Division** of the Forestry Department in Bangkok (☎02 561 4292, ext. 724). **Buses** to Khon Kaen (25฿) drop you off at the Amphoe Phu Kradung Administrative Office. From here, catch a minibus (15฿) to the National Park Office where trail #9 begins. Admission is 200฿.

UDON THANI ☎042

Sheltering an almost six-digit population, Udon Thani is one the most prosperous cities in the northeast and the Isaan's chief agricultural, commercial, and transportation center. Udon Thani was the site of a US Air Force base during the Vietnam War, and the American presence can still be felt in its Western restaurants and expat community. The province also offers several worthwhile daytrips, most notably Ban Chiang's UNESCO World Heritage archaeological sites.

THAILAND

TRANSPORTATION

Flights: Udon Thani Airport (☎246 567), on Udon Thani-Loei Hwy., 5km southwest of town. Limousine bus to Nong Khai (1hr., 100฿) after all flights from Bangkok. **Thai Airways,** 60 Makkhaeng Rd. (☎243 222). Open M-F 8-11:30am and 1-4:30pm. To **Bangkok** (8:40am, 1, 7:35pm; 1785฿).

Trains: Train station (☎222 061), at the east end of Prajaksinlapacom Rd. Booking office open daily 6am-8pm. To **Bangkok** (11hr.; 9:20am, 7:30, 8:30pm; 3rd-class 155฿, 2nd-class 279฿, A/C lower bed 599฿; 1st-class 1037฿) via **Khon Kaen** (3hr.); and **Nong Khai** (1hr.; 6:15, 7:45am, 5pm; 11฿).

Buses: Bus terminal #1, near Charoensri Shopping Center at the corner of Sai Uthit and Prajaksinlapacom Rd. To: **Ban Chiang/Sakhon Nakhon** (#230; 3hr.; every 30min. 4am-7pm; 58฿, A/C 104฿); **Bangkok** (#407; 11hr., every 15min. 8:30am-11pm, 322฿) via **Khorat** (4½hr., 184฿); **Khon Kaen** (2½hr.; every 30min. 5am-6pm; 44฿, A/C 79฿); **Mukdahan** (5hr., 6 per day 5:45-11:30am, A/C 167฿); **Ubon Ratchathani** (#268; 6hr., 6 per day 7am-2pm, A/C 232฿). Northbound buses leave **bus terminal #2,** 2km northwest of town. To: **Chiang Mai** (11hr.; 7:30am, 6, 8:30pm; 228฿, A/C 410฿); **Loei** (#220; 3½hr., every 20min. 4:20am-6:10pm, 55฿); **Nong Khai** (#221; 1hr., every 1½hr. 6am-7pm, 21฿).

Local Transportation: Songthaew #23 runs between bus terminals #1 and #2 (5฿). Plenty of **samlor** (20-30฿) and **tuk-tuks** (20-50฿) run around town.

ORIENTATION AND PRACTICAL INFORMATION

Udon Thani, 562km northeast of Bangkok, lies between Khon Kaen and Nong Khai along the railroad line and **Friendship Hwy.** Navigating the city requires an eternal awareness of the landmark **Nong Prajak Reservoir,** a large park on the town's west side. **Prajaksinlapacom Rd., Posri Rd.,** and **Srisuk Rd.** run east-west through town toward the reservoir. Each road sports a traffic circle where it intersects **Udondutsadee Rd.,** the major north-south thoroughfare. Away from the reservoir, Prajaksinlapacom Rd. ends at the **train station** near **bus terminal #2.** The **airport** and **bus terminal #1** are across the reservoir, west of the town center.

Tourist Office: TAT, 16/5 Mukkhamontri Rd (☎325 406), at the edge of the reservoir. Look for the back door on Tesa Rd. Not too helpful. Open daily 8:30am-4:30pm.

Currency Exchange: Bangkok Bank, 154 Prajaksinlapacom Rd. (☎221 505). Open M-F 8:30am-3:30pm; currency exchange open daily 8:30am-5pm. **24hr. ATM.**

Markets: Ban Huay Market, at the northern end of Udondutsadee Rd., is a network of vendor-lined sois selling delicious goodies. A number of Thai dishes are cooked on the spot and put into a bag for take-away.

Emergency: ☎191. **Tourist Police (Bangkok):** ☎1155.

Police: ☎328 515. At Srisuk and Naresuan Rd.

Pharmacies: Sunsak, 194 Posri Rd. (☎222 478). Very well stocked; carries gauze and sports braces. Open daily 8am-9pm. Or try the pharmacy at **Aek Udon International Hospital** (see below). **Open 24hr.**

Medical Services: Aek Udon International Hospital, 555/5 Posri Rd. (☎341 555). One of the best hospitals in the Northeast. English-speaking doctors. Ask Peter Davison, Manager of International Services, for health advice. AmEx/MC/V.

Laundry Service: Patmoon Chai, 4/9 Pokanusom Rd. (☎244 053), 30m from Posri Rd. intersection. 15฿ per item. Open daily 6am-8pm.

Telephones: Communications Authority of Thailand, 108/2 Udondutsadee Rd. (☎222 805). North of the clock tower traffic circle before Wattananuvong Rd. **Lenso international** phone. Open daily 8am-10pm.

Internet Access: On virtually any street but Posri Rd. 15-60฿ per hr. **Click@Internet,** on Makkhaeng Rd., 40m from Posri Rd. intersection. 20฿ per hr.

Post Office: GPO (☎222 304), on Wattananuvong Rd. toward the reservoir. Open M-F 8:30am-4:30pm, Sa-Su 9am-noon. **Postal code:** 41000.

ACCOMMODATIONS AND FOOD

At the corner of Posri Rd. and Parnphrao Rd., **Chardensri Palace Hotel ❸** is the best choice in the semi-budget range. (☎242 611. Singles or doubles 300฿, with fridge and carpet 360฿; VIP 600฿.) Behind the Charoensri Shopping Complex, **Charoensri Grand Royal Hotel ❺** is Udon's most luxurious hotel complete with bar, garden, pool, and gym. (☎343 555. Breakfast included. Singles or doubles 1100฿.) **Chai Porn Hotel ❷,** 209-211 Makkhaeng Rd., is next to the Mandarin Restaurant. Rooms are well worn and baths a bit stained—the innocuous kinds. (☎222 144. Singles 150฿, with A/C 200฿; doubles 200฿/250฿.) If Chai Porn Hotel were a glitzy, pay-per-view flick, **Tang Porn Dhi Raksa Hotel ❷,** 289 Makkhaeng Rd., is a grainy home video.(☎221 032. Singles 140฿; doubles 200฿.)

About 30m east of the traffic light at Teekathananont Rd. **Steve's Bar and Restaurant ❸** is a British affair with cricket on the telly, cold Carlsbergs, and down-home pub food. (☎244 523. Fish and chips 140฿. Steaks 180-220฿. Open daily 10:30am-midnight.) **Mae Yha ❸**, 81 Ratcha Phat Sadu Rd., 4 blocks south of Posri Rd., is a multi-story cafe bursting at the seams with a giant menu and delicious desserts. Walking toward the reservoir from the fountain, take the second left; it's on the second block on the left. (9-scoop sunday 95฿. Thai, Chinese, and Western food 40-150฿. Open daily 9:59am-10:59am, sharp.) **Rabieng Pattani Restaurant ❸** is a local favorite with fabulous seafood for 85-150฿. To get there, walk toward the reservoir on Wattananuvong Rd., and make a right on Tesa Rd.; it's 400m down. (Open daily 8am-11pm.) Sample all the regional specialties at **Ban Isaan ❷**, 177 Adunyadet Rd. (Thai curries 30-40฿. Open daily 10am-7pm.)

SIGHTS AND NIGHTLIFE

About 2km northwest of town, the **Udon Sunshine Fragrant Orchid Farm** (☎242 475), 127 Nongsamrong Rd, is a botanical talent show. Mr. Pradit Kampermpoon devoted a decade of his life to developing the first scented orchid, aptly named "Miss Udon Sunshine." The next enclosure over, where *Desmodium gyrant* makes its home, is even more mind-boggling. These unremarkable-looking herbs perk up and shimmy to the vibes of music or human voice. Thanks to Mr. Kampermpoon's years spent cross-breeding, the plants respond almost instantaneously as opposed to their more lethargic wild counterparts. Some AIDS patients swear by the plants' healing powers, and sufferers of mental illness claim to show marked improvement through exposure. As if this miracle plant didn't do enough, its tea clears up skin and cures stomach ailments. The orchids thrive from September to April, while the dancing plants strut their stuff year-round. To find these living legends, take Posri Rd. past the reservoir and bear right on Phoniyom Rd. After the first stoplight, the farm is 100m ahead on the left. If you get lost, say the magic words "Udon Sunshine" to any passerby. (Open daily 6:30am-6pm. Admission 30฿, goes toward AIDS research.) **Nong Prajak Reservoir,** in the northwest section of town, is sprinkled with benches, pavilions, and footbridges. Join mothers, children, and sweethearts to feed the catfish (bag of fish chow 10฿). For a full 360° view of Udon Thani Province from the northeast's only certified **heliport,** sidle into Aek Udon Hospital and ask for Peter Davison.

Udon's nightlife is packed into a thumping section of **Teekathananont Rd.,** across from the Charoensri Grand Royal Hotel and Wattananuvong Rd. **Shaken** pumps out Euro-house with Thai lyrics to a hip crowd. **Nasa's** larger dance floor rocks with hard-core techno. The **Underground** is dark and moody. About 200m past the discos, **Mr. Tong's** outdoor bar is a great place to finish the evening. The town's expats and the locals who love them swear by **Harry's Bar,** 19/4 Banliam Bypass. Heading past the reservoir on Srisuk Rd., take a left on Pracha Ruksa Rd. and a right on Suk Rd. Tuk-tuks from the town center cost 80฿. (At all listed establishments, beers cost 60-70฿ and mixed drinks cost 100-110฿. No cover. Open nightly until 1am.)

DAYTRIPS FROM UDON THANI

BAN CHIANG. Ban Chiang, 54km east of Udon Thani, is one of Southeast Asia's most significant archaeological discoveries and was recognized as a UNESCO World Heritage Site in 1992. The story of its discovery begins in 1966, when Stephen Young, a Harvard University archaeology student, tripped over a large root. Catching himself, he found the rim of a partially unearthed pot staring him in the face. Upon closer scrutiny, he found that the entire 5m by 15m area was littered with half-buried pots. By the time excavation began in the mid-1970s, many valuable artifacts had been sold to collectors in trading centers worldwide. Since then, archaeologists have learned more about the people who lived here from 3600 to 1000 BC. The Ban Chiang people crafted cord-marked vessels and buried their deceased infants in jars. Over 100 skeletons and numerous bronze artifacts indicate that the civilization possessed knowledge of metallurgy much earlier than estimated, casting doubt on the theory that metallurgy came to Thailand from China. The **village museum** documents the unearthing of Ban Chiang. The second-floor exhibits have comprehensive captions in English. (Open daily 9:30am-4:30pm. 30฿.) At the other end of the village, **Wat Phosi Nai** displays a well-preserved burial site with intact artifacts. Exit left from the museum; the **excavation site** is 600m down on the right. *(Orange and blue* songthaew *leave from Posri Rd. to Ban Chiang (#1371; 1½hr., every 30min., 20฿). Walking south on Sai Uthit Rd., passing the bus station on your left, make a right onto Posri Rd. You will see the* songthaew *on the right side of the road opposite the small supermarket. The turn-off for Ban Chiang is on the left—but if the driver drops you off here, take a tuk-tuk for the remaining 6km (40-50฿). To return to Udon walk straight out of the museum entrance, past the two souvenir shops on the corners of the road to the end. Make a left and then a right. There are many tuk-tuks at this small market which will take you to the highway (40฿). Cross the highway–there is a bus stop diagonally across on the left; any bus going in this direction will go back to Udon. If you are lucky, a* songthaew *may leave from the museum entrance at noon and you can forgo the tuk-tuk ride.)*

ERAWAN CAVE. The gaping crevice in the cliffs that shelter the large Buddha is clearly visible from the highway. A wat at the base of the cliff marks the end of the road. To the right, a huge flight of stairs ascends the mountain. Eventually the steps branch; take the flight to the left. You can start **spelunking** at the top. A path with a panoramic view of the nearby peaks runs through the mountain to the other side. *(Erawan Cave is just off the Udon Thani-Loei Hwy. (Hwy. 210). Take a tuk-tuk along the highway until the cave becomes visible. From there, another tuk-tuk will transport you the additional 2km from the entrance to the cave.)*

THAILAND

KHON KAEN ☎043

Like other Isaan cities, Khon Kaen lacks a "big" tourist attraction. Nonetheless, its festive nightlife, open-air markets, and efficient transportation system give visitors the means to enjoy themselves. Khon Kaen University, the region's largest university (7200 students), brings a vibrant young crowd to the evening scene.

TRANSPORTATION

Flights: Khon Kaen Airport (☎346 305), 5km west of town off Maliwan Rd. **Thai Airways,** 9/9 Prachasamran Rd. (☎227 701), inside the Hotel Sofitel, flies to **Bangkok** (4 per day, 1500฿).

Trains: Khon Kaen Railway Station (☎221 112), Ruen Rom Rd. To: **Bangkok** (8hr.; 8:30, 11:20am, 9, 9:20, 10:40pm; 3rd-class 137฿, 2nd-class 289฿, A/C sleeper 559฿, 1st-class 948฿); **Khorat** (5hr., 5 per day, 38฿); **Nong Khai** (3hr.; 4, 5:30, 9:40am, 3:10pm; 35฿); **Udon Thani** (2hr., 7 per day, 25฿).

Buses: The **bus terminal** (☎237 472), on Pracha Samoson Rd., by the pedestrian overpass. Buses to: **Bangkok** (#20; 7hr., every 25min. 6:30am-9:30pm, 129฿); **Khorat** (3hr., every 30min. 5am-10am, 67฿); **Mukdahan** (4hr., every 30min. 8:10am-4:30pm, 72฿); **Ubon Ratchathani** (#282; every hr. 5:40-11:40am, 108฿); **Udon Thani** (#211 or #262; 2hr., every 20min. 7am-1pm, 3rd-class 44฿). **A/C bus terminal** (☎239 910), on Glang Muang Rd. A/C buses to: **Bangkok** (#20; 7hr., 25 per day, mornings and evenings, 302฿) via **Khorat** (3hr., 140฿); **Loei** (#319; 4hr.; 6:30, 11:30am, 4:30pm; 131฿); **Nong Khai** (#23; 3hr.; 4, 5:30am, 1, 3, 5pm; 110฿); **Ubon Ratchathani** (#268; 5hr., every 2hr. 9am-3pm, 169฿).

Local Transportation: Samlor 20-30฿, **Tuk-tuks** 20-50฿. **Songthaew** 5฿. TAT has a list of stops for all 20 *songthaew* routes. *Songthaew* #11 goes from Khon Kaen Railway Station to TAT. *Songthaew* #17 goes from TAT to the National Museum.

ORIENTATION AND PRACTICAL INFORMATION

Khon Kaen, 450km from Bangkok, is easily reached by plane, bus, or train. The main north-south streets, **Nah Muang Rd.** and **Glang Muang Rd.**, are lined with **hotels, restaurants,** and the **A/C bus terminal.** Farther south, the parallel Muangs cross **Sri Chant Rd.**, home to the best nightspots. Past Sri Chant Rd. on Glang Muang Rd. are the **post office, police station,** and **day market,** which ends at **Ruen Rom Rd.** A right turn onto Ruen Rom Rd. from Nah Muang Rd. or Glang Muang Rd. leads to the **train station.** The **regular bus terminal** and **TAT office** are on **Pracha Samoson Rd.**

Tourist Office: TAT, 15/5 Pracha Samoson Rd. (☎244 498). A brown and white building a few blocks left from the regular bus terminal. Open daily 8:30am-4:30pm.

Consulates: Laos, 171 Pracha Samoson Rd. (☎242 856). 30-day visas US$30-35 available same day if you come early. Open M-F 9am-4pm. **Vietnam,** 65/6 Chatapadung Rd. (☎241 154). 15-day visas about US$40, 2-3 working days to process. Open M-F 8-11:30am and 1:30-4:30pm. Light-blue *songthaew* #10 runs to both consulates.

Currency Exchange: Banks and ATMs on Sri Chant Rd. **Bangkok Bank,** 254 Sri Chant Rd. (☎225 144), next to Charoen Thani Princess Hotel entrance. After-hours exchange during high season. Open M-F 8:30am-7pm, Sa-Su 9am-5pm. **24hr. ATM.**

Markets: Sizable **day market** hides behind storefronts along Nah Muang and Glang Muang Rd., stretching south to Ruen Rom Rd. Popular items include *mut-mee* silks and pillows. Open daily 5am-6pm. When other shops shut down, the **night market** gets going along Ruen Rom Rd. at the south end of the day market.

Emergency: ☎191. **Tourist Police (Bangkok):** ☎1155.

Tourist Police (local): 15/5 Pracha Samoson Rd. (☎236 937), left of TAT. **Open 24hr.**

Police: ☎221 162. On Glang Muang Rd., between Chitha Khon and Sri Chant Rd.

Pharmacy: Phon Phesad, 170 Soi Kosa Hotel (☎228 260), near the Kosa Hotel. Open daily 8am-midnight.

Medical Services: Khon Kaen-Ram Hospital, 193 Sri Chant Rd. (☎336 789), on the side of the tracks away from town. English-speaking doctors. **Open 24hr.**

Telephones: Khon Kaen Telecommunications Center, 294/1 Soonratchakan Rd. (☎245 371). The real building is behind the one that faces the street.

Internet Access: Several places on Glang Muang Rd. north of Ammart Rd. 15฿ per hr. It's impossible to beat schoolchildren to the computers Su 4-7pm.

Post Office: GPO, on Glang Muang Rd., just beyond Sri Chant Rd. *Poste Restante* on ground floor. Open M-F 8:30am-4:30pm, Sa-Su 9am-noon. **CAT** next door open M-F 8:30am-4:30pm offering **international** dialing and Internet. **Postal code:** 40000.

ACCOMMODATIONS

Sansumran Hotel, 55-59 Glang Muang Rd. (☎239 611), between the giant plastic tusks. Spacious rooms with baths. Khon Kaen's best value. Singles and doubles 150-250฿. ❷

Kaen Inn, 56 Glang Muang Rd. (☎245 420), at the intersection with Ammart Rd. Standard rooms are the best value–clean, comfortable, and in an ideal location. Karaoke, restaurant, free airport transfers. Standard singles and doubles 500฿; deluxe 800฿. ❹

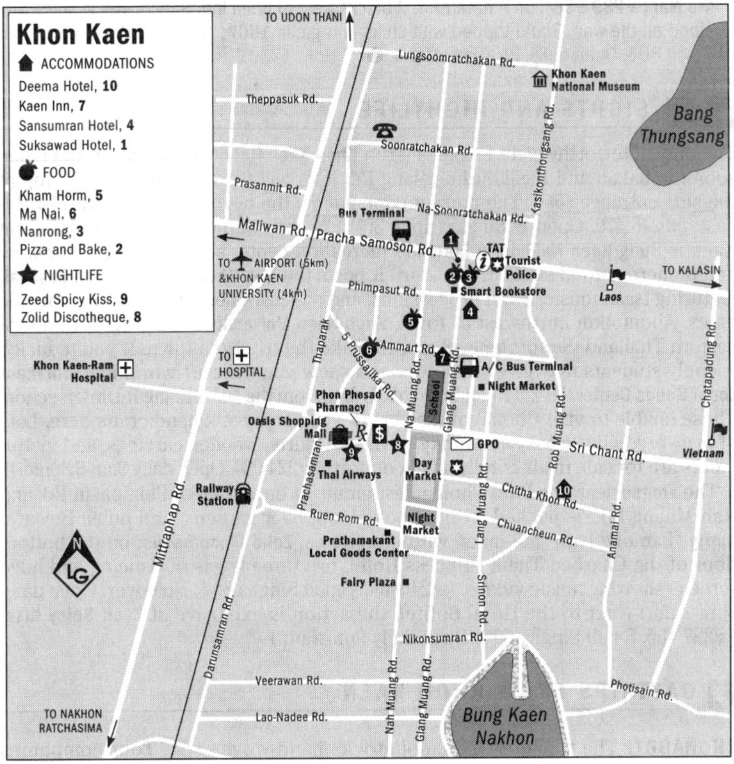

Suksawad Hotel, 2/2 Glang Muang Rd. (☎236 472), near Pracha Samoson Rd. English-speaking staff. The miser's choice in Khon Kaen. Small rooms 80฿, with toilet 100฿; double with toilet 160฿. ❶

Deema Hotel, 113 Chitha Khon Rd. (☎321 562). Very clean and comfortable, but it's a bit out of the way. Singles and doubles 200฿, with A/C 320฿. ❸

FOOD

Sidewalk **eateries** ❶ cluster on Phimpasut and Ammart Rd. Isaan meals like *sup nau mai* (shredded bamboo shoot salad) tempt hungry passersby at **night markets** on Lang Muang and Ruen Rom Rd.

Kham Horm Pub & Restaurant, 38 Nah Muang Rd. (☎243 252), between Phimpasut and Ammart Rd. BBQ outdoors and live music in the evenings. Most dishes 40-120฿; stir-fried chicken with baby corn 60฿. Open daily 10am-2am. ❷

Nanrong, on Glang Muang Rd., near the intersection with Pracha Samoson Rd. Serves a simple menu and serves it well. Curry noodles with fresh herbs and sprouts 20฿; its shock of coconut hits you like a Bangkok tuk-tuk. Open daily 8am-8pm. ❶

Pizza and Bake (☎258 883), on Glang Muang Rd. near the Suksawad Hotel. Serving Vietnamese, Thai, and Western food. *Nham nuang,* fresh spring rolls of pork meatballs, cucumbers, pineapple, banana, and fresh herbs you roll yourself are their specialty (99฿). Most dishes 50-100฿. Open daily 7:30am-11:30pm. ❷

Ma Nai (☎239 958), on Ammart Rd. 2 blocks west of Kaen Inn. Specializes in spicy Thai food all the way. Squid topped with chilis and garlic 150฿; curried seafood in coconut shell 80฿. Open daily 11:30am-10pm. ❸

SIGHTS AND NIGHTLIFE

The only noteworthy sight is the well-run **Khon Kaen National Museum,** at the Lungsoomratchakan and Kasikonthungsang Rd. intersection. Blue *songthaew* stop at the side entrance (5฿). The museum documents the history of the central Northeast. (☎246 170. Open W-Su 9am-4pm. 30฿.) In the southeastern corner of Khon Kaen is **Bung Kaen Nakhon,** a lakeside recreation center surrounded by four wats and numerous food stalls. Every April it hosts the **Dok Khoon Siang Khaen Festival,** featuring Isaan music, floral processions, and dances. Check with TAT for specific dates. About 4km northwest of town, **Khon Kaen University** is the largest in northeastern Thailand. *Songthaew* #8 and 10 make the trip from town. If you're lucky, friendly students may give you a tour and show you their art work. **Prathamakant Local Goods Center,** 79/2-3 Ruen Rom Rd., is 30m from the Nah Muang Rd. intersection. Those unable to visit Chonabot (see below) can enjoy silk handicrafts here. Lots of *mut-mee* silks, classy and funky shirts and skirts, wooden carvings, and instruments are for sale in air-conditioned comfort. (☎224 080. Open daily 9am-8:30pm.)

The **arcade** near The First Choice Restaurant, at the corner of Phimpasut Rd. and Nah Muang Rd., is packed with karaoke bars, beer gardens, and pubs. Beware: many "karaoke bars" are laden with prostitutes. **Zolid Discotheque,** on the bottom floor of the Charoen Thani Princess Hotel, has three levels of dancing and huge screens showing music videos. (☎240 400. Small Singha 80฿. No cover. Open daily 9pm-2am.) Next to the Hotel Sofitel, the action is explosive at **Zeed Spicy Kiss.** (☎227 455. Small Singha 69฿. Open daily 9pm-2am.)

DAYTRIPS FROM KHON KAEN

CHONABOT. The town of Chonabot stocks hand-woven silk. Tour companies offer expensive trips, but it's better to go on your own. There are no formal showrooms, but owners will gladly display the wares that interest you. Prices vary depending on the thickness and weight of the material. *Mut-mee* silk runs 1000฿, and *sipuen* is 250฿. *(Catch a bus to Nakhon Sawan from Khon Kaen's regular bus terminal (1hr., every hr. until 1:30pm, 35฿) and ask to be let off at Chonabot. When you disembark on the highway, face the wagon-wheel fence and police station, walk right to the first intersection, and turn left. The first silk factory is on the right before the post office. To return to Khon Kaen, walk down Phosi Sahat Rd. until it meets the highway. Wait in front of the police station for the last bus back to Khon Kaen at 5pm. Most factories open M-Sa 8am-5pm.)*

PHUWIANG. Those interested in ancient reptiles should swing by Phuwiang, home to the largest dinosaur fossils in the country. Fossils dug up from the nine quarries in the area have added weight to the theory that Tyrannosaurus rex existed first in Asia Minor before crossing the Bering Channel to North America. Don't try to take any souvenirs from the sites, as tourist literature warns, "We must not backstop wrong doings such as taking away a dinosaur fossil to be developed into an amulet of portable Buddha image." Ask TAT to photocopy its single brochure for you. *(Buses to Phuwiang leave daily from the regular bus terminal.)*

BAN KOK SA-NGA. Villagers in "King Cobra Village" have been taming deadly king cobras since 1951, using them as attention-getters for their herbal medicine businesses. Villagers stage "boxing" exhibitions: after tempting the snakes to strike, the masters skillfully sidestep death. Wear a cobra like a boa, if you dare.

(50km from Khon Kaen. From the regular bus station, take a bus to Kra Nuan (#501; every 30min., last return 6pm, 15฿) and ride a tuk-tuk to the village (30฿). Snake breeding center open to the public; 20฿.)

SOUTHERN THAILAND

One of the most famous international beach destinations, Southern Thailand has some of the world's best diving sites, thousands of kilometers of white sand beach, rock climbing, a steady nightlife, and well-developed tourist infrastructure. While this development has provided convenience, comfort, and adventure, it has also begun to overwhelm both the environment and Thai culture. In mainland towns, night markets and unjaded locals offer glimpses of Southern Thailand beyond dive shops, *farang*, cyber cafes, and bar scenes. Farther south, mosques gradually replace wats as the ethnic mix turns from Thai to Malay, and the number of tourists dwindles. For every overcrowded Ko Samui or Phuket, there are islands (especially off Trang and Satun) largely untrodden by 20฿ flip-flops.

CHUMPHON ☎077

For most travelers, Chumphon is a one-night layover en route to the tropical trinity of Ko Tao, Ko Phangan, and Ko Samui. It is also a gateway, both culturally and geographically, to the south. With quality accommodations and tourist services, Chumphon is a fine stop for refueling, regrouping, and simply relaxing. The 2km Thung Wua Laen beach makes for a good daytrip from town.

TRANSPORTATION

Trains: Chumphon Railway Station (☎511 103), at the west end of Krumluang Chumphon Rd. Luggage storage 10฿ per day. To **Bangkok** (regular: 10hr., 7am, 80฿; rapid and express trains: 7-10hr., 1:35-10:30pm, 330-370฿) and **Surat Thani** (3hr., 10 per day, rapid and express 243฿). To **Bangkok** via **Hua Hin** (4hr.; regular 49฿, rapid and express 293฿) and **Phetchaburi** (5hr.; regular 62฿, rapid and express 308฿).

Buses: Tha Tapoa Rd. Terminal (☎502 725), opposite Tha Tapoa Hotel, runs A/C and non-A/C buses to **Bangkok** (8hr., every hr. 6am-2pm and 10pm, with A/C 211฿) and **Phuket** (6hr.; 4:30am, 4:30, 10pm; with A/C 196฿). Most buses to Bangkok stop in **Hua Hin** (5hr., 126฿) and **Phetchaburi** (6hr., 160฿). Orange buses leave from across the street, next to Tha Tapao Hotel, for **Hat Yai** via **Surat Thani** (3hr.; every 30-60min. 5:30-11am, 4:30pm; 65฿, with A/C 102฿). For **Krabi,** take a bus to Chumphon Mueng Mai bus station and change there for a Krabi-bound bus.

Boats: 3 boats leave daily to **Ko Tao. Express boats** (2¼hr., 7:30am, 400฿) and **speedboats** (1¾hr., 7:30am, 400฿) leave from piers at **Hat Sai Ree,** 10km outside town. **Midnight boats** ("slow boats") leave at midnight from a different pier (6hr., 200฿). Tickets are readily available in Chumphon at tourist agencies and guest houses. Transportation to the pier is free for the faster, morning boats, or 50฿ for the midnight boats. To visit **Ko Maphraw (Coconut Island),** contact a tourist office 15 days in advance for official tours.

Rentals: Infinity Travel Service (see below) rents **motorcycles** (200฿ per day) and **cars** (1000฿ per day). The **Chumphon Cabana Resort** (☎504 442 or 501 633) rents **diving equipment.** Both open daily 9am-8pm.

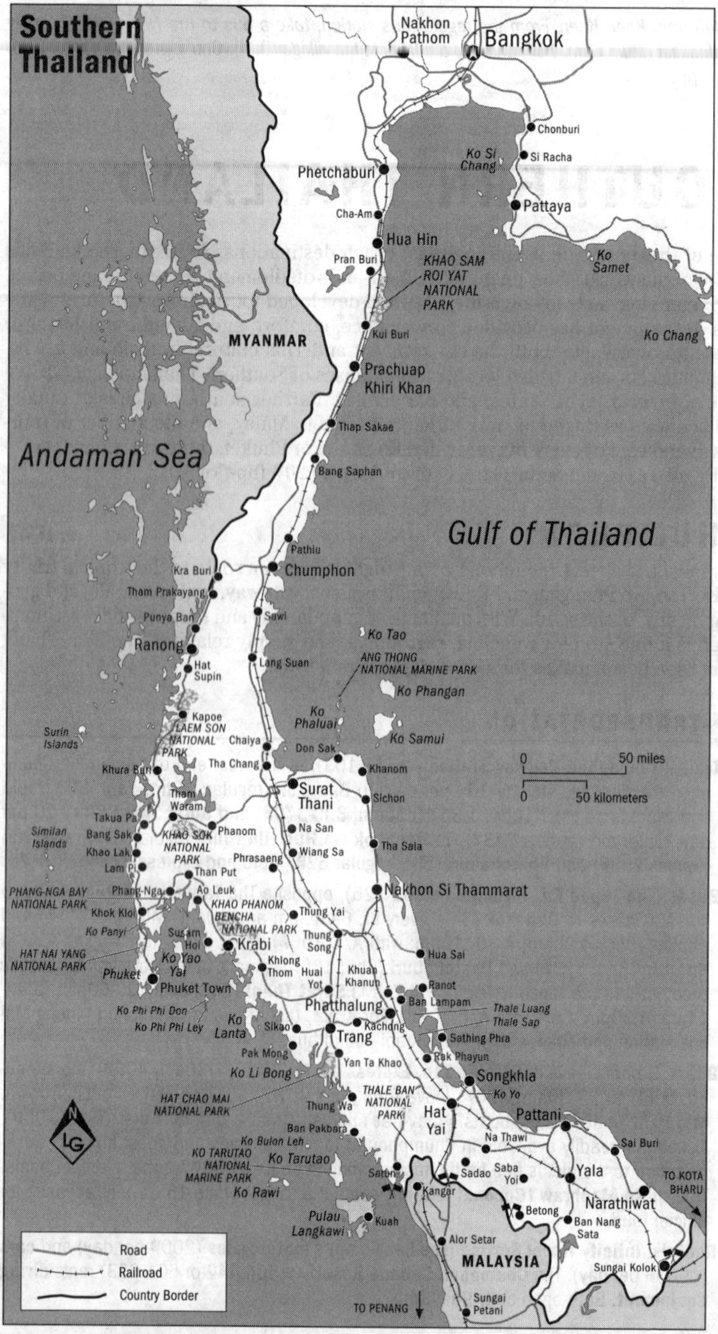
Southern Thailand
Nakhon Pathom
Bangkok
Chonburi
Si Racha
Ko Si Chang
Phetchaburi
Pattaya
Cha-Am
Hua Hin
Pran Buri
KHAO SAM ROI YAT NATIONAL PARK
Ko Samet
Kui Buri
Ko Chang
MYANMAR
Prachuap Khiri Khan
Thap Sakae
Andaman Sea
Bang Saphan
Gulf of Thailand
Pathiu
Kra Buri
Chumphon
Tham Prakayang
Punya Ban
Sawi
Ko Tao
Ranong
Hat Supin
Lang Suan
ANG THONG NATIONAL MARINE PARK
Ko Phangan
Kapoe
LAEM SON NATIONAL PARK
Ko Phaluai
Surin Islands
Ko Samui
Chaiya
Don Sak
0 50 miles
0 50 kilometers
Khura Buri
Tha Chang
Khanom
Surat Thani
Tham Waram
Sichon
Takua Pa
Similan Islands
Bang Sak
KHAO SOK NATIONAL PARK
Phanom
Na San
Khao Lak
Wiang Sa
Tha Sala
Lam Pi
Phrasaeng
Than Put
PHANG-NGA BAY NATIONAL PARK
Phang-Nga
Ao Leuk
Nakhon Si Thammarat
Khok Kloi
KHAO PHANOM BENCHA NATIONAL PARK
Thung Yai
Ko Panyi
Susam Hoi
Krabi
Thung Song
HAT NAI YANG NATIONAL PARK
Ko Yao Yai
Hua Sai
Khlong Thom
Phuket
Phuket Town
Huai Yot
Khuan Khanun
Ranot
Ban Lampam
Ko Phi Phi Don
Ko Phi Phi Ley
Phatthalung
Thale Luang
Thale Sap
Ko Lanta
Sikao
Trang
Kachong
Sathing Phra
Pak Mong
Rak Phayun
Yan Ta Khao
Ko Li Bong
Songkhla
Ko Yo
HAT CHAO MAI NATIONAL PARK
THALE BAN NATIONAL PARK
Thung Wa
Hat Yai
Pattani
Ban Pakbara
Na Thawi
Sai Buri
Ko Bulon Leh
KO TARUTAO NATIONAL MARINE PARK
Ko Tarutao
Satun
Sadao
Saba Yoi
Yala
TO KOTA BHARU
Ko Rawi
Kangar
Narathiwat
Betong
Pulau Langkawi
Kuah
Ban Nang Sata
Alor Setar
MALAYSIA
Sungai Kolok
Road
Railroad
Country Border
TO PENANG
Sungai Petani
LG

PRACTICAL INFORMATION

Chumphon's main streets roughly follow a grid system. **Krumluang Chumphon Rd.** runs east from the train station, forming the northern edge of town. The long **Poraminthra Manka Rd.** marks the southern limit; look here for the hospital, post office, and tourist office. The bus station and several travel agencies line **Tha Tapoa Rd.,** running north-south through the western part of the city. Parallel to Tha Tapoa Rd. and one block east is hotel- and eatery-studded **Sala Daeng Rd.** "V"-shaped **Pracha Uthit Rd.** straddles the city center; the day market, *songthaew* to Ko Tao-bound ferries, and Hat Thung Wua Laen are all on this road.

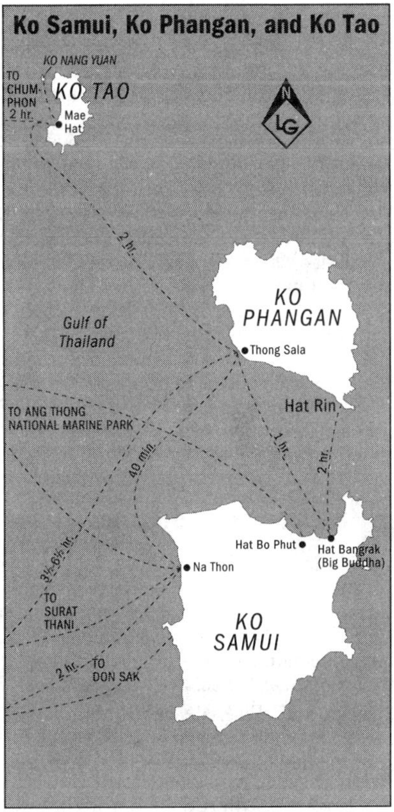

Tourist Office: Tourist Information (☎511 024, ext. 120), next to the post office. Commercial tourist agencies sell boat tickets and arrange tours on Tha Tapoa Rd., near the bus station. **Infinity Travel Services,** 68/2 Tha Tapoa Rd. (☎501 937), provides ferry tickets, advance booking for trains and buses, luggage storage, arrangements for scuba diving, and showers. Open daily 7am-11pm.

Currency Exchange: Bangkok Bank, 111/1-2 Sala Daeng Rd. (☎511 446). **24hr. ATM.** Open M-F 8:30am-3:30pm.

Markets: Day market, on Pracha Uthit Rd. Open daily 5am-5pm. **Night market,** on Krumluang Rd. between Pracha Uthit and Poraminthra Manka Rd. Open daily 6-11pm.

Emergency: ☎191. **Tourist Police (Bangkok):** ☎1155.

Police: ☎511 505. On Sala Daeng Rd., about 50m north of the intersection with Krumluang Rd. Little English spoken. **Open 24hr.**

Medical Services: Virajsilp Hospital (☎503 238), at the south end of Tha Tapoa Rd., a 5min. walk from the bus station. Great service. No credit cards. **Open 24hr.** Also has a **pharmacy.**

Telephones: Several tourist offices and guest houses such as **Infinity Travel** (see above) have **international** phone service.

Internet Access: The **Freshmart** convenience store, at the back of the Suriwong Chumphon Hotel, has a dozen computers. 30฿ per hr. (minimum 10฿). Open daily 7am-2am.

Post Office: GPO, 192 Poraminthra Manka Rd. (☎511 041), southeast of town, about 100m past the tourist office. *Poste Restante*. Open M-F 8:30am-4:30pm, Sa 9am-noon. **Postal code:** 86000.

ACCOMMODATIONS AND FOOD

Hotels and guest houses cluster near the bus station, either on Tha Tapoa Rd., Sala Daeng Rd., or in between. **Sri Chumphon Hotel ❸,** 127/22-24 Sala Daeng Rd., has spacious and comfortable rooms with luxuries like TVs, private baths, and hot water—all at unheard-of prices. (☎570 536. Singles and doubles with fan 250฿, with A/C 350฿.) Close to the bus station, **Mayazes Resthouse ❷** has cozy rooms in a delightful atmosphere. Turn left at the bus station onto Tha Tapoa Rd.; take the first right onto an alleyway. (☎504 452 or 01 607 1534; mayazes@hotmail.com. Singles 150-200฿, with A/C 280฿; doubles 250-350฿.) One of the cheapest options in town, **New Chumphon Guest House ❷** is removed from the hubbub but still close to the night market. It's 600m from the railway station, off Krumluang Rd., on a side street to the left. (☎502 900. Breakfast 60-80฿. Singles and doubles 120-160฿.)

For Chumphon's finest victuals, head to the markets. The **day market ❶** offers the renowned *gluay lep meu* (fingernail bananas) as well as the usual Thai staples. The **night market ❶** offers phat thai (20฿) and fruits. A **bakery ❶** on the corner of Sala Daeng and Pracha Uthit Rd. sells great pastries. (Open daily 6am-5pm.) Twenty meters down at the **Tiw Restaurant ❶,** brothers O and Noom serve tasty food late into the night. (Rice and curry dishes 20-40฿. Open daily noon-6am.)

THAILAND

DAYTRIPS FROM CHUMPHON

For extended excursions to explore the caves and other sights, it's best to book a tour with one of the tourist agencies such as Infinity Travel (see p. 835) or guest houses such as New Chumphon Guest House (see above). Two popular destinations are the **Rab Ro Caves** and the **Ka Po Waterfalls,** 30km from Chumphon. Prices vary depending on the number of people, but expect to pay at least 500฿. The area's premier beach, **Hat Thung Wua Laen,** is a 2km long beach that has remained relatively pristine. At the northern end of the beach, **Seabeach Bungalows ❸,** 42 Moo 8, is covered in bougainvillea. (☎560 115. Doubles with bath 300฿; bungalows with bath and fan 400฿, with A/C 600฿; quads with bath and A/C 600฿.) **Clean Wave Resort ❸,** at the midpoint of the beach, has small, tidy, hotel-like rooms. (☎560 151. Rooms 300฿, with A/C 600฿, with hot water 700฿.) Their excellent **restaurant ❷** serves Thai food for 60-100฿. **The View Restaurant ❷,** 13/2 Moo 8, has savory seafood plates (50-70฿) served by terminally upbeat young women, and new **bungalows ❹** across the road with amenities like TVs and phones. (☎560 214. Bungalows 400฿, with A/C 600-700฿, with A/C and hot water 800-900฿.) Divers or those with a bit more time may want to visit two popular islands, **Ko Ngam Yai** and **Ko Ngam Noi,** off the shores of Hat Thung Wua Laen, which are prized for their swallows' nests, coral reefs, and soaring cliffs. Chartering a boat is expensive; it's best to book with an organized tour; ask at the Chumphon Cabana Resort or their office in town. In Chumphon, yellow *songthaew* to Hat Thung Wua Laen (sometimes called Cabana Beach) leave from the market along Pracha-Uthit Rd. in front of 7-Eleven and stop at Chumphon Cabana Resort at the south end of the beach (one-way 25฿). You can also take Cabana Beach Resort's shuttle from its office on Tha Tapoa Rd. near the bus station directly to its resort on the beach. Free for Cabana's patrons. Departs around 1 and 6pm, returning at 12:30 and 5:30pm. To return to Chumphon, walk 1km to the main road and take a passing *songthaew*.

KO TAO ☎077

One of Southeast Asia's most renowned dive sites, tiny Ko Tao lures an international crowd of scuba neophytes with its cheap certification courses, as well as veterans who relish its clear gulf waters and outstanding reefs. For non-divers, the island offers superb and secluded sun-baked coves, many of which can be reached only by boat or a long hike. Despite its popularity, it remains a laid-back destination for scuba enthusiasts and backpackers alike.

THE VIEW FROM ABOVE

The lowdown: Southeast Asia's biggest dive-training site.
Gateway cities: Chumphon, Ko Phangan, Surat Thani.
Beaches: Hat Sai Ree, Ao Chalok Ban Kao, Ao Leuk, Ao Tanote, Ao Thian, Laem Taa Toh, Mae Hat.
Highlights: Fantastic snorkeling and scuba diving just about anywhere on the island.

TRANSPORTATION

Boats: Ferries leave Ko Tao from **Mae Hat** to **Chumphon** (slow boat: 5hr., 10am, 200฿; faster boat: 2-3hr.; 10:30, 11am, 3pm; 300-400฿); **Ko Phangan** (slow boat: 3hr., 9:30am, 180฿; faster boat: 1-2hr.; 9:30, 10:30am, 2, 3:30pm; 250-350฿); **Ko Samui** (slow boat: 4hr., 9:30am, 280฿; faster boat: 2-3hr.; 9:30, 10:30am, 2, 3pm; 350-

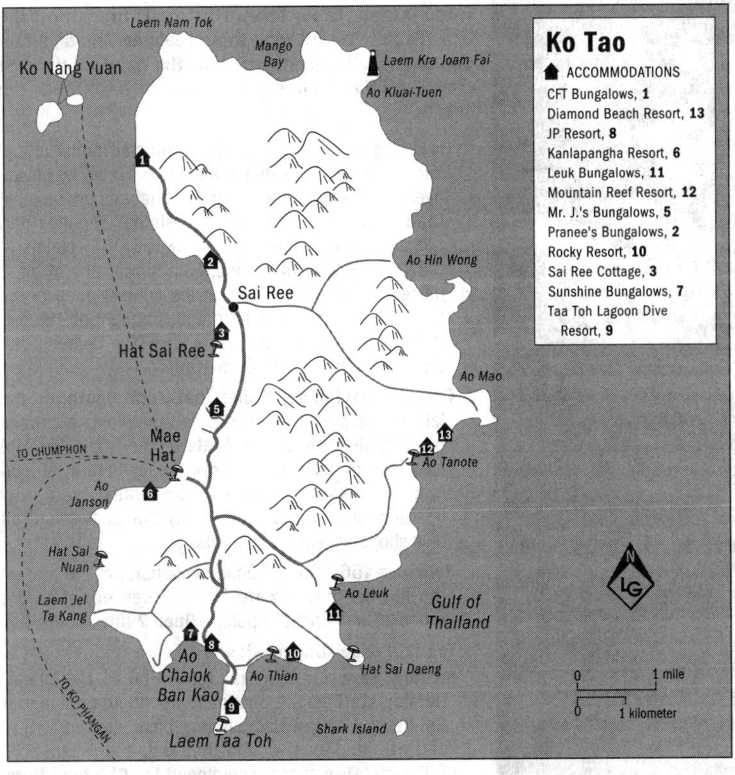

FROM THE ROAD

DEAR ABBYTTHAYA

From ramen noodle soups to beans on bread and Bay Bell cheese rounds, learning to eat cheap on the road is a rite of passage for the backpacker.

Throughout my own travels, I've consumed peanut butter and Chex mix and linguini with Heinz ketsup. When it comes to dining abroad, culinary sophistication is foregone in favor of museum admission and beer.

Travelers to Thailand are amazed by the scrumptious goodies that are as cheap as super-sizing your value meal back home. Add Thai hospitality, and you know why no one leaves.

Thais are adept at localizing foreign cuisines and finding substitutions for exotic ingredients. Unlike the stronger-spiced curries common to India, Thai curries emphasize intensity of the burn as opposed to duration. If you don't think your stomach can handle spicy food, simply smile at your waiter and politely say, *"Chan tahn pet mai dai."*

Due to the pervading influence of Theravada Buddhism, Thais shun large chunks of meat–animal cuts are usually finely shredded, laced with herbs and spices to subtly flavor a curry or soup. Instead, Thai cuisine tends to focus on the presentation of vegetables.

As a general rule, diners should order three dishes (in addition to their individual plates of steamed rice) and choose whatever they desire from the shared dishes to add to their own rice. Since grains are the cheapest part of the meal, a humble dinner guest will always eat a scoop of rice with every

(continued on next page)

550฿); **Surat Thani** (6½hr., 10:30am, 500฿; 8hr., 9pm, 400฿). For **Bangkok,** there are ferry/bus combos (9½hr., 11am, 550฿; 15hr., 3pm, 800฿).

Local Transportation: The best way to get around the island is to rent a **motorcycle,** available everywhere for 150฿ for 24hr. (passport deposit required). Otherwise, **pickup truck-taxis** go from Mae Hat to anywhere accessible by the island's few paved roads (30-60฿). **Longtail boats** may be hired to reach otherwise inaccessible bays.

PRACTICAL INFORMATION

Boats arrive at **Mae Hat** (Mother Beach), where most services and travel agencies are located. Facing the island from the pier, a paved road heads left over a small hill to **Hat Sai Ree,** Ko Tao's most popular beach and the heart of the backpacking and scuba scene (3min. by taxi or a 20min. walk). The paved road uphill from the pier eventually bends right, leading to **Ao Chalok Ban Kao,** the main southern beach, and, 500m farther, to **Ao Thian.** Dirt roads branch off the island's only paved road to **Ao Leuk; Ao Tanote,** a fantastic snorkeling destination; **Ao Hin Wong,** on the east coast; and **Hat Sai Daeng,** in the island's southeastern corner.

Travel Agencies: Ko Tao has no official tourist office; information and tickets are instead provided by private agencies lining the the pier in Mae Hat and on the main road in Hat Sai Ree. All offer similar services and prices. The omnipotent **Mr. J** (☎456 066) claims to provide any type of service. Find him at any of his 3 offices/knick-knack shops on the hill just north of the pier, a 5min. walk down the dirt path right off the pier in Mae Hat, before the Buddha View Dive Center in Hat Sai Ree. All open daily 8am-10pm.

Currency Exchange: Krung Thai Bank Booth, on the left off the pier in Mae Hat, has mainland exchange rates. While there are **no ATMs** on the island, an ATM card may be used to withdraw money here at no surcharge (passport required). Generally open daily 9:30am-noon and 1-4pm. Many bungalows and all dive shops accept credit cards.

Police: ☎456 260. A 10min. walk north of the pier on the hill heading toward Hat Sai Ree opposite the school. Some English spoken. **Open 24hr.**

Tourist Police (Bangkok): ☎1155.

Medical Services: There is **no hospital on the island. Nursing stations** are abundant around Ao Chalok, Hat Sai Ree, and Mae Hat, offering basic service for ear and eye irritations, wound dressing, and pregnancy/STD tests. Dive shops recommend the **Chintana Nurs-**

ing Unit at the top of the hill to the left, on the road to Hat Sai Ree. Open daily 8am-8pm.

Telephones: Nearly all travel agencies and bungalows offer **international** phone service. About 80฿ per min.

Internet Access: It's impossible to walk two steps without passing an Internet facility in Mae Hat or Hat Sai Ree. Prices don't vary—1฿ per min.

Post Office: ☎456 122. On the main road in Mae Hat. *Poste Restante* (very frequently utilized and reliable). Open daily 8:30am-midnight. **Postal Code:** 84280.

ACCOMMODATIONS AND FOOD

Dive agencies have bungalows that are rented almost exclusively to their clients, but there are plenty of budget places to stay if you're not here to scuba dive. Prices tend to be marginally cheaper elsewhere and the cheapest rooms run 250-300฿. Prices listed reflect high season rates; in the low season, you may be able to knock off 100-150฿. The following accommodations and food options are listed by beach.

MAE HAT. Mae Hat is the food, fuel, and ferry center of Ko Tao. The beach here is unsuitable for swimming, so there's little reason to linger upon arrival; you'll find better beaches and better vibes elsewhere on the island. Should an early morning ferry keep you on Mae Hat, budget accommodations cluster just south of the pier. Just before the Sensi Resort, the dive-oriented **Kanlapangha Resort ❷** has friendly management and cheerful bungalows, complete with hammocks. (☎456 058. Bungalows 150฿ with shared shower, otherwise 250-1000฿, depending on size and proximity to beach.) More bungalows hide north of the pier on the hill between Mae Hat and Hat Sai Ree, a 15min. walk from the pier. Jack-of-all-trades Mr. J owns several sparkling new **bungalows ❸** just behind one of his stores across from the school. (Rooms with private baths and new fixtures 300-400฿.)

Even though Mae Hat may not be the best place to stay, it's one of the better places to eat. The best place to get Western-style bread, baguettes, pastries, and sandwiches is the **Swiss Bakery ❷,** just a few steps up from the pier on the right. Try the delicious tuna sandwich for 60฿. (Open daily 6am-6:30pm.) Across the street, **La Matta ❸** not only has authentic Italian pizza and pasta (100-160฿), but authentic Italians making it too. (Open daily noon-10pm.)

HAT SAI REE. Backpackers and divers congregate in the bungalows along this 2km beach, which is Ko Tao's busiest bit of sand. Despite its popularity,

(continued from previous page)

bite of the main dish. Be careful not to leave any rice on the table, as it is commonly believed that the grains will reappear as pockmarks on the face of your future spouse.

Thai food is customarily eaten with a fork and spoon. Since the spoon is traditionally the only utensil to go in your mouth, placing a fork in your mouth is considered highly offensive. Unlike in Western culture, it is a sign of disrespect to consume the entire contents of your plate, as this reflects your inability to be satiated by a meal and your host's failure to fully provide for his guests.

If there is one thing to know about Thai culinary etiquette, it is to never use your left hand to handle food at the table. Thais have a system of personal hygiene that involves a bucket, a spigot, and the left hand. Thus, Thais also maintain a strict division of right and left, and will always reach for dishes and eat with their right hand. Children are often instructed by their parents to sit on their left hand during mealtime.

Wherever you are when your Singha-haze kicks in, indulge in the salty goodness of fried insects. Cocoons and mealworms will pop and sizzle in your mouth and ooze with oily flavor. Although many travelers have likened fried scorpions to "warm, jelly-filled toenails," surely the experience is worthwhile, even if only to immortalize the moment with a photo.

So venture beyond the phat thai, banana pancakes, and melon Fanta. Just don't forget to pass that bowl of *tom yum kung* with your right hand. *Aroy mak.*

*– **Matthew Firestone***

the beach is laid-back; candlelit dinners fade into easy-going nightlife, and by day even the palm trees are too relaxed to stand up straight. For better quality swimming, snorkeling, and sand, head elsewhere. The relatively inexpensive **Pranee's Bungalows ❸,** at the northern end of Hat Sai Ree, is a 20min. walk on the sand from the start of the beach. The accommodations are fairly standard, but the service is friendly and the clientele relaxed. (☎456 080. Bungalows 350-700฿.) A deservedly popular choice in the center of the beach is the **Sai Ree Cottage ❸,** just past Scuba Junction. Their charming wooden bungalows get points for cleanliness as does the social beachside restaurant, which boasts an extensive menu of inexpensive Thai dishes, milkshakes, and cocktails. (☎456 374 or 01 229 4952. Bungalows 250-600฿, depending on size and proximity to the beach.)

For culinary offerings, Hat Sai Ree is second only to Mae Hat. The **Lotus Restaurant ❷,** past Sai Ree Cottage at the northern end of the beach, is one of the island's few non-bungalow restaurants specializing in Thai cuisine. (Dishes 60-100฿. Open daily 6:30am-midnight.) In the evening, divers put away their gear, and sunbathers slather on aloe vera in preparation for nights passed drinking by the beach. **AC Bar,** at the south end of the beach, draws partiers from all over the island with its theme nights. Stretch out with your feet in the sand, and sip a cocktail at the **Dry Bar,** in the center of the beach. (Happy hour until 10pm. Red Bull & vodka 100฿. Open nightly until late.)

LAEM NAM TOK. The paved road continues through Hat Sai Ree to the northwestern tip of the island, the relatively developed Laem Nam Tok. There are several bungalows along this road, the most scenic of which is the **CFT Bungalow ❶,** at the end of the road. Though there's no beach, it's worth making the trip in the late evening. (Bungalows with outdoor showers 100-300฿.) To get there, take a taxi from Mae Hat (40฿) or inquire about boat transport. At the time of update in 2002, CFT Bungalow was closed due to drought (see **Water, Water Everywhere, But Not a Drop to Drink,** p. 850); confirm that it has reopened before visiting.

AO LEUK AND AO TANOTE. The two major bays on the eastern side of Ko Tao are ideal for solitude seekers and offer fantastic **snorkeling.** They can be accessed by a paved road branching off Ko Tao's main road just south of Mae Hat. It turns into a dirt road and is only recommended for experienced motorbikers. **Taxis** to both bays cost 50฿ from Mae Hat. The tiny Ao Leuk has a rocky, less-than-spectacular beach. The only accommodations in the bay are at **Leuk Bungalows ❸.** Scattered about the grounds are airy, wooden bungalows with porches. (Rooms 250-350฿. Restaurant open daily 7am-10pm.) About 2km farther north from Ao Leuk along a windy dirt road is **Ao Tanote,** which has a better beach than its smaller neighbor. Long-term vacationers recommend meals at **Mountain Reef,** a popular spot in the middle of the bay. **Diamond Beach Resort ❹,** on the northern end of the beach, is quite upscale. (☎01 958 3983. Bungalows 400-600฿.)

AO CHALOK BAN KAO. Chalok Ban Kao Bay is carved out of the island's southern end, 3km from Mae Hat (45min. by foot, 50฿ taxi ride). Unfortunately, a dense concentration of bungalows, dive shops, Internet cafes, and restaurants overwhelms the beach, meaning the bay is more convenient than scenic. Most bungalows are affiliated with dive shops, but non-divers seek refuge in the new **JP Resort ❸,** smack in the center of the beach. Its cliffside bungalows are squeaky clean with nice views of the bay and private baths. Internet (2฿ per min.) and a relaxed restaurant round out this newcomer. (☎456 099. 300-400฿.) **Sunshine Bungalows ❸** is also conveniently located but features less glamorous plywood bungalows with private baths (250฿). Behind the bungalows toward the island's main road is the well-stocked **Sunshine Mini Mart.** (Open daily 8am-11pm.)

AO THIAN. An uphill walk south from Ao Chalok leads to a fork in the dirt road. The left path leads downhill to the small but stunning Thian Bay. The bay has a white-sand beach (perhaps the island's best), ideal for both swimming and snorkeling (equipment rental 100฿, available on the beach). The only accommodations are at **Rocky Resort ❸** on the bay's eastern end, with simple bungalows, some of which include balconies right over the water. Rocky also doubles as the beach's only restaurant with decent, relatively inexpensive fare. (Bungalows 300-500฿.)

LAEM TAA TOH. This lovely cape juts into the gulf, separating Ao Chalok from Ao Thian. To get here, follow the dirt road from Ao Chalok, taking the right path leading uphill at the fork. Besides spectacular views, the cape is home to the **Taa Toh Lagoon Dive Resort ❸,** on Taa Toh Beach halfway around the cape, which has simple bungalows among the weather-beaten boulders rimming the sand. Many guests are divers-in-training at the resort's **scuba school.** (☎377 792; www.taatohdivers.com. Bungalows 300-500฿.) On the way up, stop at the romantic and atmospheric **New Heaven Restaurant ❸,** which has a delicious menu and near-celestial views of Ao Thian. (Excellent Thai dishes 60-120฿; seafood 200฿; drinks 100-120฿. Open daily 6:30pm-midnight.)

ACTIVITIES

Scuba diving is popular year-round in Ko Tao, although late September through December often brings heavy rains and choppy waters. The island also has a unique tide; September to May is high-tide season and better for snorkeling, while May to September is low-tide season and better for basking on the beach. Ko Tao has over 20 dive sites. **Chumphon Pinnacle,** where a granite tower rises 14m above the surface, is a favorite for deep dives. **Southwest Pinnacle** and **Shark Island** are known for coral and leopard sharks. **Green Rock** and **Sail Rock** on the way to Ko Phangan are known for rock "swim-throughs." Closer to Ko Tao, **Ko Nang Yuan** (see **Daytrip from Ko Tao,** below) has coral and fish in waters suitable for snorkeling.

Scuba prices are standardized, so friendliness and professionalism, not price, are the key elements for a good dive shop. Four types of classes are available. Beginners can choose from the four-day open-water certification course (7800฿) or the supervised one-day "discover scuba" dives (1600฿, with the option of additional dives for 800฿). Certified divers can hone their skills with the two-day advanced open-water course (6600฿) or tag along with any dive class on a one-day "fun dive" (one dive 800฿, 700฿ each for 2-5 dives, 600฿ each for 6-9 dives, 500฿ each for 10 or more dives). Bring your own equipment for a 15% discount. Prices include accommodations in affiliated bungalows for the duration of the course. If you choose to stay on your own in non-affiliated lodging, however, prices drop by only 150฿, which means you'll almost certainly lose money during the high season. Snorkelers can also take advantage of the dive scene by tagging along on shallower dives for around 50฿. There are plenty of dive shops from which to choose. They all have PADI certification, which requires that there be no more than eight people per instructor. The following is an abbreviated list of dive shop operations: **Asia Divers** (☎405 055; www. asiadivers-kohtao.com); **Ban's Diving Resort & Sunshine Divers** (☎456 061; www.amazingkohtao.com); **Big Blue Diving Center** (☎377 750; www.bigbluediving.com); **Buddha View Dive Resort** (☎456 074 or 01 229 4693; www.buddhaview-diving.com); **Scuba Junction** (☎456 164; www.scuba-junction.com); **Taa Toh Lagoon Dive Resort** (☎456 192; www.taatohdivers.com). The larger shops have representative offices on Mae Hat.

DAYTRIP FROM KO TAO: KO NANG YUAN

Ferries depart from Mae Hat catamaran pier (right next to the boat/ferry pier) daily at 10am, 3, and 5pm; return at 8:30am, 1, and 4pm (40฿ round-trip).

About 2km off Ko Tao's northwest coast, Ko Nang Yuan is actually three separate islets connected by a three-pronged stretch of white sand. The island's **snorkeling** is among Ko Tao's best. The steep climb up one of the islets to the **viewpoint** is well worth it. The island is best as a daytrip from Ko Tao, as its only accommodation, **Koh Nangyuan Dive Resort ❺**, is prohibitively expensive. (☎01 299 5212. Rooms 1500-3500฿.) The resort's **restaurant ❸** also has steep prices (dishes 150-200฿).

KO PHANGAN ☎077

While Ko Tao draws divers and Ko Samui caters to fat wallets, Ko Phangan remains a backpacker paradise, the island of choice for budget travelers in Southern Thailand. Ko Phangan's beaches range from unspoiled, laid-back beauties like Bottle Beach to the successfully developed, self-contained backpacker universe of Hat Rin Nok. With pirated films playing daily in restaurants and unbeatable drink specials at beachside bars, it's hard not to lose track of time on Ko Phangan, and it's even harder to leave.

THE VIEW FROM ABOVE

The lowdown: Sun-soaked beaches by day, drunken tourist-drenched beaches by night.
Gateway cities: Ko Tao/Chumphon, Ko Samui/Surat Thani.
Beaches: Hat Khuat, Hat Rin Nai, Hat Rin Nok, Thong Sala, Thong Nai Paan Yai, Thong Nai Paan Noi.
Highlights: Hat Rin Nok's full moon parties, soothing Bottle Beach, Than Sadet Historical Park's waterfalls.

TRANSPORTATION

Ferries: To get to Ko Phangan, you must go through either Ko Tao/Chumphon or Ko Samui/Surat Thani. From Ko Tao, ferries leave from Mae Hat's southern pier (5 per day 9:30am-2:30pm, 180-350฿). From Ko Samui, boats leave from Big Buddha Pier for **Hat Rin** (100฿) and from Na Thon for **Thong Sala** (9, 11am, 5:30pm; 95฿). You can also head to Ko Phangan directly from Surat Thani via the **Donsak Car Port** (10am, 1, 6pm) or the **town pier** (7:30am, 205฿; 11pm, 400฿). Ferries leaving Ko Phangan depart from Hat Rin and Thong Sala. From the pier at Hat Rin Nai, boats go to: **Ko Samui's Big Buddha Beach** (2hr.; 9:30, 11:30am, 2:30pm; 100฿); **Hat Tian** (12:40pm, 50฿); **Than Sadet** (12:40pm, 80฿); **Thong Nai Paan** (12:40pm, 100฿). From the main pier at Thong Sala, boats go to: **Chumphon** (12:30pm, 650฿); **Ko Samui's Big Buddha Beach** (1hr., noon, 115฿); **Ko Samui's Na Thon** (7am, 12:30, 4pm; 115฿; 10:30am speedboat, 200฿); **Ko Tao** (2hr.; 10, 11:30am, 12:30pm; 180-250฿); **Surat Thani** (night boat 7hr., 10pm, 400฿; express boats via Ko Samui 4hr.; 7, 11am, 12:30, 1pm; 205฿).

Local Transportation: One drawback of Ko Phangan is the cost of getting around the island. **Songthaew** (and their eager drivers) meet ferries at the pier in Thong Sala and run to the island's major beaches. To: **Ban Kai** (20-30฿); **Ban Tai** (20฿); **Chalok Lam** (50฿); **Hat Rin** (50฿); **Hat Yow** (50฿); **Thong Nai Paan** (100฿). In Hat Rin Nai, *songthaew* wait across from the police booth and go to **Thong Sala** (minimum 3 passengers, 50฿). In addition, longtail boats make trips between the major beaches.

Rentals: Motorcycles are available for rent around the pier and on the main street of Thong Sala as well as from several guest houses in Hat Rin Nai (150฿ per day with passport deposit).

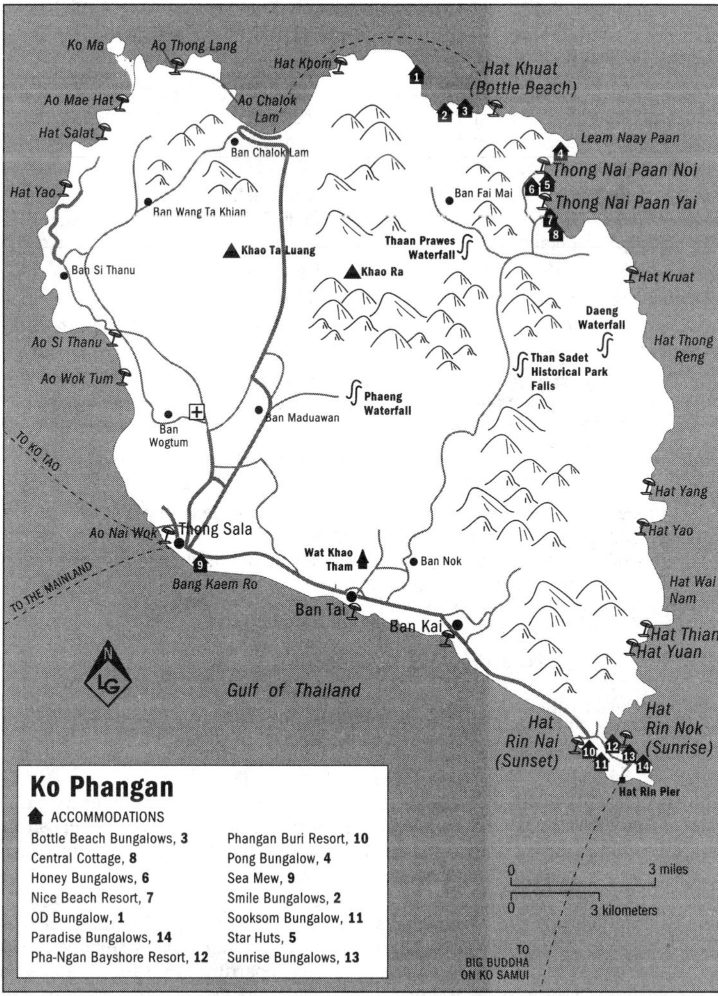

ORIENTATION AND PRACTICAL INFORMATION

While a few boats depart and dock at the Hat Rin pier, most arrive at the island's unsightly main city and port of call, **Thong Sala,** where there are many tourist services. From the Thong Sala pier, three paved roads cover most of the island; one runs 10km southeast along the coast to the party beaches of **Hat Rin,** which is split into **Hat Rin Nai** to the west and **Hat Rin Nok** to the east. Midway along this paved road, a bumpy dirt road (only for experienced motorbikers) heads to the northeastern beaches of **Thong Nai Paan Yai** and **Thong Nai Paan Noi,** and other dirt trails stretch to more remote coves. A second paved road from Thong Sala (safe for motorbikes) cuts 10km northward through the heart of the island to **Chalok Lam**

Bay, a departure point for boats heading to lovely **Hat Khuat.** The third road (alternately paved and dirt) runs a scenic course west along the coast to the less developed bays of **Hat Ao Mae Hat**.

Travel Agencies: Songserm Travel Center (☎377 096), on the left side of the main road in Thong Sala. Open daily 8:30am-5pm. The serene and helpful **Mr. Kim** (☎377 274), usually hanging around a few meters from the Thong Sala pier on the right, has encyclopedic knowledge of the island. He also books tickets.

Currency Exchange: Siam Commercial Bank, 30m from the Thong Sala pier on the left, has a **24hr. ATM.** Bank open M-F 8:30am-3:30pm. In Hat Rin, your best option is the **Siam City Bank** branch on a side street near the middle of Haadrin Rd. Exchange rates here are slightly less favorable than in Thong Sala. Open daily 9:30am-4:30pm.

Emergency: ☎191. **Tourist Police (Bangkok):** ☎1155.

Police: Main office (☎377 114), 2km north of Thong Sala on the road to Ao Chalak Lam. English spoken. **Open 24hr.**

Medical Services: Koh Pha-Ngan Hospital (☎377 034), 3km north of Thong Sala. English spoken. **Open 24hr.** In Hat Rin, private **nursing stations** provide basic medical services. For serious medical attention, take a boat to Ko Samui.

Internet Access: There are more Internet terminals per backpacker here than anywhere in the world. 1฿ per min. More expensive providers in Hat Rin (2฿ per min.).

Post Office: GPO (☎377 118), in Thong Sala. From the end of the pier, walk down the main road, take the first right, and follow the road until it ends and turn left; the post office is on the right. *Poste Restante.* In Hat Rin, a private licensed **branch** (☎375 204), on the southern road connecting Hat Rin Nok and Hat Rin Nai, functions as a tourist and telephone office. Open daily 9am-midnight. **Postal code:** 84280.

ACCOMMODATIONS AND FOOD

Most travelers to Ko Phangan head immediately to the southern coast and the beaches of Hat Rin. Those looking for more attractive, secluded beaches should head north to lovely Hat Khuat or mellow Thong Nai Paan Noi. Accommodation prices and availability rise and fall with lunar tides. The island fills to maximum capacity in the days surrounding the full moon. If you plan to be there for the party, arrive a few days early to score accommodations or be prepared to sleep on the beach. The following accommodations and food options are listed by beach.

HAT KHUAT (BOTTLE BEACH). Set against lush hills, this gorgeous and quiet beach lulls those who intend to stay for a few days into spending weeks or months instead. To get there, take a *songthaew* from Thong Sala to **Ao Chalok Lam Bay,** 10km away (20min., 100฿). The bay is the departure point for boats to **Hat Khuat** (9:30am, 3, 6pm; return 8am, 1, 5pm; 50฿.) Once on Bottle Beach, your options are limited to four bungalow operations: **Bottle Beach Bungalows 1, 2,** and **3,** and **Smile Bungalows,** all of which are owned by the same family. (You can reach all of them at ☎01 229 4762.) Bottle Beach 1 ❶, in the middle of the beach, is the cheapest, with bath-less bungalows hidden from the beach starting at 100฿. Bottle Beach 3 and **Smile Bungalows** ❸ at the far end of the beach have bungalows with private baths and hammocks starting at 250฿. All have friendly staff and similar facilities, including restaurants. **OD Bungalow** ❶, situated just above the beach on a cliff, has great views. (All rooms with squat toilets 100-150฿.)

THONG SALA. A concrete frying pan, Thong Sala is a lifeline for the island, boasting the cheapest email, most tourist services, and an aggressive barrage of *songthaew* drivers waiting at the pier. Staying here usually denotes an early ferry

SEX, DRUGS, AND LUNAR CYCLES Every month on the full moon, backpackers and 20-something tourists all over Thailand head to Ko Phangan to partake in the island's legendary lunar festivities. Originally a modest affair (first hosted by Paradise Bungalows in 1989), the party has mushroomed into a massive all-night beach rave, complete with strobe lights, imported Euro-DJs, and illicit substances galore. Some tips to survive the full moon madness:

Safety: Full moon night is a big night for theft. Keep all your valuables securely locked or in a money belt on your person.

Accommodations: If you want to have a bed in Ko Phangan the night of the full moon, arrive a few days early to secure a spot or even earlier if you want to stay on Hat Rin. Otherwise, stay on either Ko Tao or Ko Samui and take advantage of the special "Full Moon Party boats" that make round-trips to Phangan on the night of the party.

Drugs: Despite stiff penalties imposed by the Thai government, *farang* still flock to Phangan to partake in its thriving drug culture, which crescendos with the full moon. Before taking that joint or tab, be aware that Thai police, both in uniform and undercover, are out in extra numbers on full moon night. Also, an increasing number of travelers have been reportedly drugged and then robbed.

departure, an inability to find accommodation elsewhere, or a serious inertia problem, but there are some comfortable rooms close to the pier. **Sea Mew ❸,** near the waterfront and to the right heading from the pier, has a great staff. Enjoy the quirky restaurant and the cable TV. (Singles with fan 200-250฿.) The **Corner Kitchen ❷** is on the corner opposite **Poonum Pattana** and serves extensive Thai, European, and Chinese cuisine (35-60฿). Thong Sala's main drag has several decent Western-themed eateries, though all are rather pricey.

HAT RIN. Introducing Backpacker Land where your every need or fancy can be fulfilled, where the average age is 21, and the average personal savings are approaching zero. Imagine a place where you can watch the latest Hollywood hit as you check email, all the while having your back massaged to pounding techno music and chatting with your new Aussie friend with a mouthful of a 40฿ chicken sandwich. Welcome to Hat Rin Nok. *Songthaew* from Thong Sala drop off passengers on the main road, just above Hat Rin Nai. From there, it's a 5min. walk to the beach or a 10min. walk to Hat Rin Nok's quieter twin, Hat Rin Nai. The two beaches are connected by several dusty roads, all of which intersect Haadrin Rd., the area's main artery, which runs parallel to the beach.

Hat Rin Nok: Accommodations-wise, Hat Rin Nok brims with over-priced and flimsy bungalows along its beachfront road. It's worthwhile to shop around. Beyond a gate at the northern end of this road is **Pha-Ngan Bayshore Resort ❸,** a well-maintained set of bungalows reaching from the beach to the *songthaew* drop-off. (Basic bungalows with fan and shared bath 200฿, with A/C and private bath 500฿.) Toward the center of the beach, things get louder and more crowded, especially at night. **Sunrise Bungalows ❸,** in the middle of the beach, has breezy bamboo cottages with large beds. (☎375 145. Bungalows 250฿, with bath 300฿.) At the opposite end from Pha-Ngan Bayshore is **Paradise Bungalows ❸,** the proud host of the first Full Moon Party in 1989. While the bungalows have balconies and are a bit removed from all the action, they are basic. (☎375 245. Bungalows 200-250฿.) Restaurants, representing half a dozen nationalities, line Haadrin Rd. (which connects the southern ends of both Hat Rin beaches) and the small dirt alleys stemming from it. **Mr. Chicken ❷** is something of a landmark and local meeting place. It has chicken sandwiches (40฿) that will make you forget about phat thai. Around the corner is **Niras Beach Kitchen and Bakery ❷,** which caters to health spa types and sweet tooths. (Chocolate croissant 40฿. Hummus sandwich 50฿. Kitchen open daily 8am-10pm. Bakery open 24hr.) Across the street is **Bao's Kitchen ❶**, which offers decent tofu-based vegetarian food. (☎375 166. Vegetable curries 40฿. Pumpkin soup with coconut milk 40฿. Open daily 8:30am-10:30pm.)

Hat Rin Nai: The strip of muddy sand at Hat Nai is hardly attractive, but the beach does have its perks—a good selection of bungalows, pretty sunsets, and a great location. There are a number of basic accommodations, restaurants, and ticket agencies along the ragged main drag. Beachside budget bungalows lie at the northern end of the beach, a 15min. walk from the Hat Rin Pier and past a rocky outcropping. **Sooksom Bungalow ❷**, just past the rocky outcropping, has simple, wooden huts and a vegetarian-friendly restaurant. (☎375 230. Bungalows 150฿, with bath 300-350฿.) Next door, **Phangan Buri Resort ❸** has concrete bungalows and tiled patios that are more expensive, but cleaner and prettier. (☎375 330. Bungalows 300-800฿.)

THONG NAI PAAN NOI AND THONG NAI PAAN YAI. With sparkling water and a relaxed atmosphere, these twin beaches offer ample reward for those who endure the hour-long *songthaew* ride from Thong Sala or the boat ride from Hat Rin. *Songthaew* stop first at Thong Nai Paan Noi, the more populated of the two and favored among backpackers. This bay is known for its long stretch of cheap and rustic bungalows. Near the *songthaew* drop-off, the popular **Star Huts ❷** is the largest operator on the beach and teems with long-term guests. (☎299 005. Bungalows 150-200฿, with bath 300-400฿.) Younger backpackers frequent **Honey Bungalows ❸**, behind Star Huts away from the beach. (Bungalows 250฿.) At the northern end of the beach, a 15min. walk from the *songthaew* drop-off, **Pong Bungalow ❷** is deservedly popular for its lively bar. (Bungalows 150-180฿, with bath 250-300฿.)

Thong Nai Paan Yai to the south is longer, less populated, and has calm waters suitable for swimming and snorkeling. Ask the *songthaew* driver to let you off here or make the 20min. walk across the small promontory from Thong Nai Paan Noi. At the end of the road to Thong Nai Paan's easternmost point, **Nice Beach Resort ❹** has bright, white-washed rooms with mosquito nets, high ceilings, and private baths. (☎238 542. Bungalows 200-1600฿, depending on season and A/C.) Three bungalow operations cluster toward the middle of the beach. **Central Cottage ❸** provides simple, but comfortable, thatched bungalows and a restaurant. (☎299 059. Bungalows 350-400฿.)

SIGHTS AND NIGHTLIFE

After full moons and beaches, **waterfalls** are Ko Phangan's major attractions. The most famous stretches of river run through **Than Sadet Historical Park,** a good daytrip from the beach. Kings Rama V, VII, and IX all walked along its bathtub-sized waterfalls and cascades, leaving their initials as seals of inspection. Longtail boats from Hat Rin (50฿) drop off passengers at the mouth of the river. From here, you can make the 2.5km trek to the park by following the parallel road north. **The Sanctuary** is a backpacker's spa that comes highly recommended by Ko Phangan's long-term vacationers. It is noted for its seclusion, clean facilities, and attentive staff. Many are happy to pay 60฿ for a dorm bed and splurge on yoga classes (150฿), oil massages (400฿), and 10-day fasts. The location is only accessible by longtail boat; from Hat Rin; it costs 50฿. (Singles and doubles with bath 200-1000฿.)

All of Hat Rin Nok's nightlife takes place right on the beach itself with open-air bars facing the ocean where you can lounge or dance on the beach. **Drop-In Bar** plays Top 40 dance music. The most popular spot these days is the **Cactus Club,** which creates an outdoor ambience with its fleet of oil lamps, and hip, bottle-spinning bartenders. Both offer nightly drink deals or happy hours worth checking out.

The moon party (see **Sex, Drugs, and Lunar Cycles,** p. 845) is the stuff of legends. Each month under the full moon, thousands gather on this strip of sand. Bodies gyrate to the latest imported mixes, minds dance to the beat of illicit substances, and stomachs and bladders empty themselves gratefully into the ocean. Even when the moon isn't full, don't come here for a quiet beach. Hat Rin Nok is loud, brash, and proud of it.

KO SAMUI ☎077

Thailand's third-largest island has come a long way since its "discovery" by backpackers in the 1970s. Ko Samui ("Coconut Island") is Thailand's biggest exporter of coconuts, the major source of income for its 40,000 occupants. Thousands of travelers, and increasingly more packaged-tour visitors, rush to Ko Samui's beaches, which run the gamut from loud, shop-crammed Chaweng and Hat Lamai to quiet, tropical enclaves like Hat Bo Phut and Hat Choeng Mon. Those looking for a range of entertainment, swimming, and sunbathing options will not be disappointed; those looking for a deserted island most certainly will be.

THE VIEW FROM ABOVE

The lowdown: An island of extremes: from McDonald's to the jungle.
Gateway city: Surat Thani.
Beaches: Chaweng's beach, Ao Thongsai, Ao Yai Noi, Hat Bangrak (Big Buddha Beach), Hat Choeng Mon, Hat Lamai, Hat Mae Nam, Laem Thongson, Na Thon.

THAILAND

TRANSPORTATION

Flights: Samui Airport is between Hat Chaweng and Big Buddha Beach (Hat Bangrak). **Bangkok Airways,** in Chaweng (☎422 2234 or 422 5129, at the airport ☎245 6018), flies daily to: **Bangkok** (every hr. 6:30am-7:30pm, 3450฿); **Phuket** (9:50, 10:10am, 3:10pm; 1820฿); **Singapore** (8am, 4690฿). Book tickets at Bangkok Airways or other tourist services on the island.

Trains and buses: Most travel agents can book joint boat/train or boat/bus tickets to the mainland. Prices vary slightly from agent to agent. Tickets to **Bangkok** (16hr.; A/C bus 280฿, sleeper train 700฿) and **Kuala Lumpur, Malaysia** (22hr., A/C bus 800฿).

Boats: There are 3 piers in Ko Samui. The main pier in **Na Thon** is dominated by **Songserm Travel Center,** which runs boats to: **Chumphon** (6½hr., 11am, 745฿); **Ko Tao** (2½hr.; 9, 11am; 345฿); **Krabi** (7hr., 2pm, 250฿); **Surat Thani** (3hr., 2pm, 150฿; night boat 7hr., 9pm, 150฿); Ko Phangan's **Thong Sala** (45min.; 9, 11am, 5pm; 115฿). **Seatran** sends express boats from Na Thon to **Donsak Pier,** 60km away from **Surat Thani** (2hr. plus 1hr. by bus, 3 per day, 250฿). A slow, but cheaper **car ferry** also runs between Na Thon and **Donsak Pier** (5hr., 120฿). The **Raja Car Ferry** runs between a pier 10km south of Na Thon and Donsak Pier. The pier at the **Big Buddha Beach** has direct service to **Hat Rin** on **Ko Phangan** (2hr.; 10:30am, 1, 4pm; 100฿).

Local Transportation: The cheapest and most convenient way to explore the island is to rent a **motorcycle** (see **Rentals,** below). Clearly labeled **songthaew** congregate near the pier and circle the island frequently 5am-6pm. From Na Thon to: **Hat Bangrak** (30฿); **Hat Bo Phut** (20฿); **Hat Chaweng** (40฿); **Hat Lamai** (40฿). There are official fares, but actual rates tend to be higher. Speedy **motorcycle taxis** also circle the island, providing a faster but more expensive alternative to *songthaew*. From Na Thon to: **Hat Bo Phut** (150฿); **Hat Chaweng** (200฿); **Hat Mae Nam** (100฿).

Rentals: Motorcycles 150฿ per day; **jeeps** 800฿ per day, with insurance 1000-2000฿. Rental places abound all over the island. Officially, there is a 300฿ fine for not wearing a helmet while on a motorcycle, but no one seems to care.

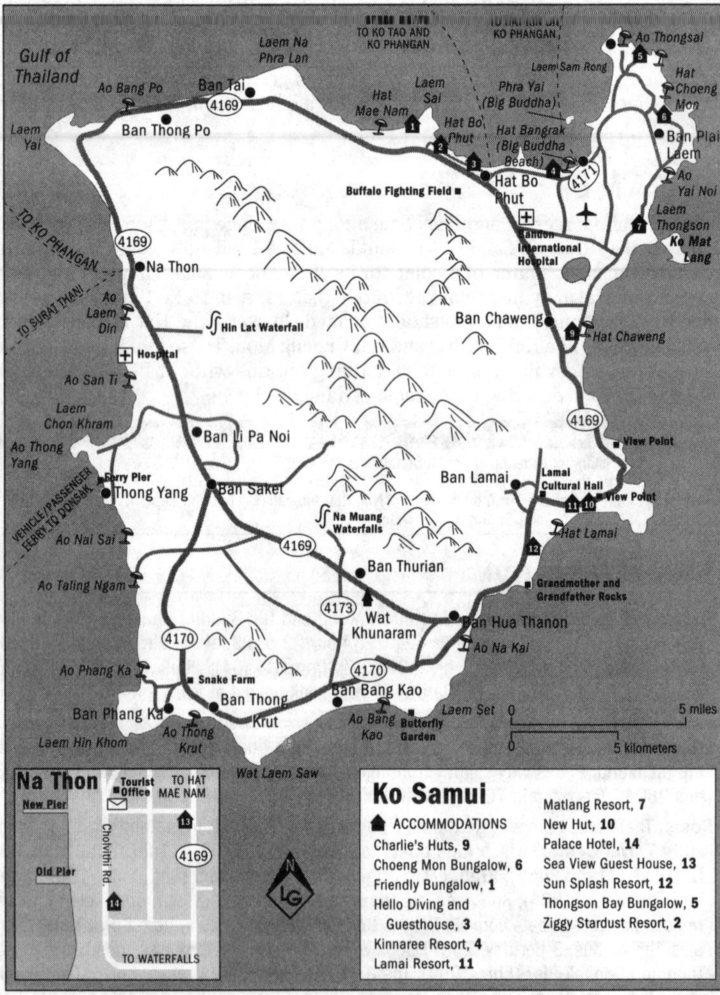

ORIENTATION AND PRACTICAL INFORMATION

Oval-shaped Ko Samui is encircled by **Rte. 4169,** making getting around fairly easy but somewhat time-consuming. The island's main transportation hub and service center, **Na Thon,** lies on the west coast. From here, Rte. 4169 runs to **Hat Mae Nam** on the northern coast and cuts down the east coast to **Hat Chaweng,** the island's most celebrated beach, and to **Hat Lamai,** Hat Chaweng's smaller and more budget-oriented sibling. **Rte. 4171,** enveloping the island's northeastern peninsula, branches off Rte. 4169 just past Hat Mae Nam and reconnects with it in Chaweng. It passes through **Hat Bo Phut** (Fisherman's Village), **Hat Bangrak** (Big Buddha Beach), and the smaller beaches of **Hat Choeng Mon, Ao Thongsai,** and **Ao Yai Noi.** In general, Na Thon, Hat Chaweng, and Hat Lamai are the liveliest areas and offer the most services, while Hat Mae Nam, Hat Bo Phut, and Hat Choeng Mon are quiet and more relaxed.

Tourist Office: TAT (☎/fax 420 504 or 420 7202; tatsamui@samart.co.th), on Na Thon Rd. in Na Thon. With your back to the pier, turn left and follow the signs to a cluster of new buildings behind the post office. Helpful, English-speaking staff provides a wide range of maps of the island and environs. Open daily 8:30am-noon and 1-4:30pm.

Travel Agencies: Hundreds of establishments all over Na Thon, Hat Chaweng, and Hat Lamai sell boat/bus/train ticket combinations and arrange Ang Thon Marine Park tours (from 550฿), fishing trips, and elephant treks. In Na Thon, agencies line Na Thon Rd. near the pier. **Songserm Travel Center** (☎420 157, 236 489, or 236 490), directly opposite the pier in Na Thon, operates most of the ferries (daily 5am-5pm).

Immigration Office: (☎421 069), 2km south of Na Thon at the intersection of Rte. 4167 and Rte. 4172. Visa extensions 555฿. Open M-F 8:30am-noon and 1-4:30pm.

Currency Exchange: Dozens of banks offering currency exchange at good rates, credit card advances, and **ATMs** line the main roads of Na Thon, Hat Chaweng, and Hat Lamai. Generally open M-F 8:30am-3:30pm.

Markets: The market on **Thaweerat Pakdee Rd.** in Na Thon has fresh produce.

Emergency: ☎191. **Tourist Police (Bangkok):** ☎1155.

Tourist Police (local): ☎421 281. On Na Thon Rd. in Na Thon, 400m south of the pier. English spoken. **Open 24hr.**

Police: ☎421 095. On Thaweerat Pakdee Rd. in Na Thon. Other beaches have smaller offices or booths: Hat Chaweng (☎422 067), Hat Lamai (☎424 068), Hat Mae Nam (☎425 070), and Hat Bo Phut (☎425 071). **Open 24hr.**

Medical Services: The island has three main hospitals: **Bandon International Hospital** in Hat Bo Phut (☎425 382); **Government Hospital** in Na Thon (☎421 230); the private **Samui International Hospital** in Hat Chaweng (☎422 272). Smaller **nursing stations** can be found in Na Thon, Hat Chaweng, and Hat Lamai. English-speaking staff. Credit cards accepted. **Open 24hr.**

Telephones: GPO, 2nd fl. **International** calls, fax, and cheap Internet. Open daily 7am-10pm. Travel agencies around the island offer pricier international phone service.

Internet Access: Cheapest access at the **GPO's Telephone Office** at GPO (30฿ per hr.) Travel agencies in Hat Chaweng and Hat Lamai provide pricier access (1฿ per min.).

Post Offices: GPO (☎421 130), on Na Thon Rd., 50m left of the pier parking lot. *Poste Restante.* Open M-F 8:30am-4:30pm, Sa-Su 9am-noon. Licensed, private **branches** along Rte. 4169. **Postal code:** 84140.

ACCOMMODATIONS AND FOOD

Although Ko Samui caters to well-off tourists rather than to backpackers, cheap beds may be found at all of the island's beaches. The following accommodations and food options are listed by beach.

NA THON. Na Thon is Ko Samui's waiting room for visitors killing time until the next ferry. Cheaper communications and souvenirs make it a nice place to spend a rainy afternoon, but unless you have an early ferry to catch or the last *songthaew* has skipped town, there's no reason to spend the night. **Palace Hotel ❹,** 152 Cholvithi Rd., 100m on the right as you exit the pier, has spacious, comfortable rooms with sea views and a very hotel-like feel. (☎421 079. Doubles 400฿, with A/C and TV 550฿; twins 450฿/650฿; triples with A/C 800฿.) **Sea View Guest House ❸,** 67/15 Thaweerat Pakdee Rd., opposite the Shell gas station, has modest-sized rooms with showers and peeling paint. Regrettably, the hotel has no sea view. (☎420 298. Doubles with shower 200-400฿, with bath 300฿, with A/C 400฿.) On the waterfront, food carts sell fruit, meat-on-sticks, noodles, and sandwiches. Popular **Ruangthong Bakery ❷**, opposite the pier, serves breads, pastries, and Thai dishes for 20-100฿. It's a great place to grab a quick meal, cup of coffee, or snack before the ferry ride. (Open daily 6:30am-7pm.)

HAT MAE NAM. With its narrow strip of sand, the Mae Nam beach, stretching for 4km along the northern coast of Ko Samui, is probably the island's least spectacular beach. Thanks to its secluded feel, Mae Nam draws those looking for tranquility and long-termers tired of the hustle and bustle of the island's more popular beaches. Cheap bungalows here are interchangeable; shop around for a resort that suits you. Close to Hat Bo Phut, the popular **Friendly Bungalow ❸** has standard beachside huts with baths and mosquito nets. (☎425 484. Laundry service. 3-night minimum. Small huts 300฿ per day, large huts 400฿.)

HAT BO PHUT. The charming Bo Phut, or Fisherman's Village, offers a pleasant combination of white sand, quiet atmosphere, selection of seafood restaurants, and trendy shops. Though developed, Bo Phut is noticeably less commercial than other areas of island. Its friendly locals and traditional architecture create an ambience that reminds you that you are, indeed, still in Thailand. **Hello Diving and Guesthouse ❶**, a few meters from the pier, boasts cheap dorm beds in a smartly restored wooden house and doubles as a dive shop offering excursions to Ko Tao's dive sites. Those enrolled in their diving classes stay free in the dorms. (☎66 77 427 608; warren@hello-diving.com; www.hello-diving.com. Dorms with fan 100฿, with A/C 150฿.) The old-time favorite **Ziggy Stardust Resort ❹**, farther down the road, has beautiful, spacious rooms with old carved wooden furniture, beds, and clean full baths. The beachfront bar/restaurant features fabulous homemade yogurt. (☎425 173. Bar/restaurant open daily 7:30am-10pm. Small doubles with fan 400฿; large doubles with fan 800฿, with A/C 1000฿.) Of all the area's seafood restaurants, try the **Summer Night Restaurant ❸**, in the heart of Bo Phut village. (Breakfast 80-110฿; seafood 40฿ per 100g; Thai dishes 60-120฿. Open daily 7:30am-11:30pm.)

HAT BANGRAK (BIG BUDDHA BEACH). Big Buddha Beach lies in the north of Samui's northeastern peninsula, along Rte. 4171. Bungalows abound in

IN RECENT NEWS

WATER, WATER EVERYWHERE, BUT NOT A DROP TO DRINK

After a jaunt in central and northeastern Thailand, I was ready to hit the beaches on the southern kos. But travelers and Thais in Bangkok said there's no water.

Southern and east coast Thailand, particularly the heavily touristed kos, have had a water shortage since the beginning of 2002. While there's plenty of salt water (an ocean-full, actually), the fresh water reserves are dwindling.

Because tourism is such a booming industry, all the fresh water resources are allocated to guest houses and hotels. In Ko Samui the drought has been so significant that hotels have had to import water from the mainland; other guest houses have simply closed, unable to afford the substantial costs.

Some guest houses have limited water usage, but most hotels refuse to do so for fear of losing business. In fact, guests at the high-end hotels are largely clueless about the shortage. It is the goal of these island establishments to keep the water flowing as freely as Singha beer.

Unfortunately, at backpacker bungalows, the problem is slightly more apparent. I endured the salty showers on Ko Tao, but farmers and fishermen have suffered much worse. Unable to afford to pump their own water, they are reliant upon the Thai government, who has prioritized the profits of tourism over its local workers and environmentalism.

—Nick Grossman

this lively area, but the rocky, boat-filled beach is not good for swimming. **Kinnaree Resort ❹,** close to the Big Buddha pier and across from the primary school, is a villa with flower gardens, cooing doves, and beach views. (☎245 111. Motorbike rental. Singles and doubles 400฿, with hot shower and A/C 800฿.)

NORTHEASTERN PENINSULA: LAEM THONGSON, AO THONGSAI, HAT CHOENG MON, AO YAI NOI The northeastern cape wraps around some of the island's best views and most delightfully secluded coves. Beaches are down dirt roads off the mountain highway connecting northern Hat Chaweng to Rte. 4171 and are most easily accessed by motorbike. Solitude-seekers should follow the signs 2km down to **Thongson Bay Bungalow ❸,** on the tip of the promontory. The beach here, with a view of Ko Phangan, is rocky and scenic but not particularly suitable for swimming. (☎01 891 4640. Bungalows with bath 250-500฿, on the beach 1000฿.) North of Ao Yai Noi, bordering Ao Thongsai, and 4km north of Hat Chaweng, Hat Choeng Mon's serene beaches make it worth visiting, especially if crowds annoy you. **Choeng Mon Bungalow ❸** has modern, well-maintained, concrete bungalows with baths and a quiet, sandy beach. (☎425 372. In high season, singles and doubles 300฿, with A/C and hot water 450-1200฿, with satellite TV from 650฿ minimum.)

HAT CHAWENG The biggest and brashest of Ko Samui's beaches, Hat Chaweng roars 5km over the eastern coast. As the sunbathing and party capital of the island, the beach is a loud, happy enclave of superb sand, clean waters, cheap booze, and loud music. Hat Chaweng's main road, **Chaweng Rd.,** is parallel to the beach and connected to Rte. 4169 via three access roads; most services can be found there. Budget accommodations in Hat Chaweng are scarce and fill up quickly. By far the best option for those on a budget is **Charlie's Huts ❸,** in the middle of the beach near the turn-off for the lagoon, which caters almost exclusively to backpackers. The wooden bungalows have thatched roofs, bamboo walls, and mosquito netting. (☎230 283. Doubles 200฿, with bath and closer to the beach 300฿.) Old-timer **Matlang Resort ❸,** 1541 Chaweng Rd., in North Chaweng by the end of the cape, is a quiet hideaway from the main drag. The beach here gets a little too shallow for quality swimming at low tide but is more picturesque than anywhere else on Chaweng. (☎/fax 422 172. Singles and doubles with bath and fan 300-370฿, with A/C 800฿ in high season, 650฿ in low season.) Budget accommodations on Chaweng may be scarce, but budget food is not. Inexpensive **food stalls ❶** cramming the road by the Green Mango serve pizzas, sandwiches, and Thai favorites. **The Deck Restaurant ❸,** before the Green Mango as you approach from Na Thon, has great food (including vegan and vegetarian options), music, and three levels of cushions to enjoy it all on. (☎230 898. 3-course breakfast 99฿; 5-course dinner 175฿; Thai dishes 60-80฿; sandwiches 70฿. Open daily 8am-2am.)

HAT LAMAI. Hat Lamai is second to Hat Chaweng in terms of nightlife and beauty, but has a more family-friendly environment, good body surfing, and fewer crowds. Most tourist services can be found in South Lamai on the road running parallel to the beach, while the best budget accommodations are in North Lamai, some distance from the thick of things. **New Hut ❷,** the unofficial backpacker center, is the best and cheapest. (☎230 439. Bungalows 150฿, with bath 200-250฿.) Just to the south, **Lamai Resort ❸** has more expensive, sturdier bungalows. (Bungalows with bath 200-450฿.) Though more centrally located, South Lamai has fewer budget options. The friendly Italian owners of the **Sun Splash Resort ❹,** next to the Utopia Resort, keep their rooms in good shape. All bungalows have baths. (☎418 021. Bungalows with fan 400-500฿, with A/C 900-1000฿.) Most bungalows serve standard meals until 10pm. Street food abounds. The **Will Wait Bakery,** in the center of Lamai Beach Rd., serves Thai and Western favorites. (Open daily 7:30am-10:30pm.) The **market ❶** at Ban Hua Thanon sells fruit and munchies. (Open daily until sunset.)

SIGHTS

Ko Samui has a few sights and cultural attractions to keep you entertained if you get too sun-burned. Most are off Rte. 4169; you'll have to take a taxi or walk. Travel agencies also offer one-day tours of the island for around 1000฿.

WAT KHUNARAM. Rather sensational as far as wats go, this temple, off Rte. 4169 in the island's southeast corner, is known for a **mummified monk** who died in 1973 but somehow evaded decomposition via complex pre-death meditation.

THE BIG BUDDHA IMAGE (PHRA YAI). Ko Samui's most prominent landmark, the golden "Big Buddha" is off Rte. 4171 on Ko Fan Mountain on the island's northeast corner. Overlooking Samui Island from its location near Hat Bangrak, the 15m statue was built in 1972 as a place for both islanders and *farang* to worship.

SAMUI BUTTERFLY GARDEN. One of Samui's most popular non-beach attractions, the Butterfly Garden maintains over 24 species of southern Thai butterflies in addition to less spectacular (and less popular) species of insects. *(Off Rte. 4170, opposite Central Samui Village. ☎424 020. Open daily 8:30am-5:30pm. 120฿, children 60฿.)*

WATERFALLS. Ko Samui boasts several waterfalls scattered around the interior of the island. Two-tiered **Hin Lat Waterfall,** 3km south of Na Thon, is the most accessible though not the most beautiful. The two **Na Muang Waterfalls,** 11km south of Na Thon, are more impressive though they require a hike through the mountainous heart of the island. *(Difficult to reach without a motorbike. Taxis from Na Thon can drop you off at the foot of the waterfalls, and many travel agencies offer waterfall and trekking trips.)*

GRANDMOTHER AND GRANDFATHER ROCKS (HIN TA AND HIN YAI). According to an old Samui legend, an elderly couple was en route to the mainland to procure a wife for their son when a fierce storm pummeled the ship and killed the two seafarers. Their bodies washed ashore, and their respective genitals somehow petrified in the shapes of "Grandfather Rock" and "Grandmother Rock," a set of unusual, and slightly distasteful, natural formations. *(On South Lamai Beach.)*

SAMUI SNAKE FARM. This gimmicky complex, on Rte. 4170 in the island's southeast corner, features snakes indigenous to Samui. The snake farmers also offer potentially exciting but absurd events like centipede and scorpion fighting shows. *(☎423 247. Shows daily 11am and 2pm. Open M-F 8:30am-4pm, Sa-Su 8:30am-noon. 150฿.)*

THE SAMUI AQUARIUM. Thailand's only privately owned aquarium features fish native to the Gulf of Thailand as well as sharks and turtles. The adjacent tiger farm houses several displaced Bengal tigers. *(Off Rte. 4170, south of Lamai Beach near Ban Han and the Butterfly Garden. ☎424 017. Open daily 9am-6pm. 250฿.)*

BAN LAMAI CULTURAL CENTER. Located where Rte. 4169 takes a sharp right turn at Kilometer 20, Lamai Cultural Hall's museum holds a small but interesting collection of phonographs, pottery, and weaponry. *(Open daily 6am-6pm. Free.)*

NIGHTLIFE

With dozens of pubs and go-go bars, Hat Chaweng is Samui's nightlife capital. The mega-pub **Green Mango** is a massive complex of six bars that draws a raging, young drink-and-dance crowd. The mood picks up at around 11pm and doesn't die until 4am. (Beers 80-100฿. Cocktails 120-150฿. Red Bull & vodka 130฿. Champagnes 800-2000฿. Open daily from 8pm.) The area around the Green Mango overflows with smaller but uninspired bars. The popular **Reggae Pub** attracts an older, more mellow crowd. More like an entertainment center than a "pub," it comes complete with a tacky souvenir shop. To get there, follow the signs to the boxing stadium across the lagoon. Hat Lamai has fewer nighttime options than Hat Chaweng, but bars and strip joints are popping up by the dozen. **Bauhaus Pub, Bistro and Disco,** south of the go-go bar area, is *the* hot spot for Lamai's young and restless. The Saturday Gin and Vodka party offers half-price cocktails. Foam party takes over on Friday nights. (Most drinks 30-100฿. M-Tu and Th buy-one-get-one-free. Open daily 6pm-2am.)

DAYTRIP FROM KO SAMUI: ANG THONG MARINE PARK

The only way to visit the marine park is on a tour through one of Ko Samui's travel agencies. Songserm (see ***Travel Agencies,*** *p. 849) sends boats from Na Thon's pier (8:30am, return around 5pm; 550฿ including lunch). If you have the money, a more worthwhile kayaking option (1800฿) allows you to explore the craggy island inlets.*

Made infamous as the setting for Alex Garland's *The Beach*, Ang Thong Marine National Park is a breathtaking collection of over 40 limestone islands 60km north of Ko Samui. Among the islands are **Ko Mae Ko** (Mother Island), popular for saltwater lake **Thalay Nai** (Lake Crater); **Ko Sam Sao** (Tripod Island), famous for its huge rock arch and fantastic snorkeling; and **Ko Wua Talap** (Sleeping Cow Island), home to the **park office. Ko Lak** and similar limestone formations tower 400m above the water. Dolphins dance in the water around the longtail boats that sail near **Ko Thai Plao.** The waters at **Hat Chan Charat** (Moonlight Beach) are as good for diving as Ko Tao's. Visit the park on your own by arranging transportation with the tour ferry operator. If you the end up staying on the island, the park office rents several modest **bungalows** ❺ for 1000฿; **camping** ❶ is free.

SURAT THANI ☎077

Most travelers know Surat Thani only as a stopover en route farther south or as a point of departure for Ko Samui and Ko Phangan. The increasing prevalence of joint bus, train, and boat tickets means that only a few stay here for more than a quick stroll or snack. Overnight visitors, however, are able to indulge in the vibrant and colorful local night market.

TRANSPORTATION

Flights: Airport (☎253 500), 30km outside of town. **Thai Airways,** 3/27-8 Karoonrat Rd. (☎441 137), flies daily to **Bangkok** (noon and 7pm, 2400฿).

Trains: Railway station (☎311 213), in Phun Phin, 13km from Surat Thani. Orange buses run constantly between the local bus terminal (Talaat Kaset 1) in town and the station; catch them anywhere on Talaat Mai Rd. (every 5min., 10฿). Listed fares are for both 3rd- and 2nd-class tickets where they are available; otherwise, they are 3rd-class. Trains to: **Bangkok** (11hr.; 10 per day 10:25am-midnight; 147฿, 508฿); **Butterworth, Malaysia** (11hr., 2:50am, 2nd-class 800฿); **Chumphon** (3hr.; 10 per day 10:25am-midnight; 78฿, 178฿); **Hat Yai** (6hr.; 5 per day 9:20am-1:20am; 120฿, 306฿); **Sungai Kolok** (10hr.; 1:20, 3, 4am; 231฿); **Trang** (5hr.; 6, 8am; 115฿).

Buses: Bus travel in and out of Surat Thani is somewhat complicated. There are 3 bus stations, one for local and provincial travel known as **Talaat Kaset 1;** another one, across the street, for longer routes known as **Talaat Kaset 2;** and a **new station,** just outside of town by the train station, with **Bangkok** buses. Talaat Kaset 1 serves **Chumphon** (80฿) and **Surat Thani Province** with frequent buses to the railway station. Talaat Kaset 2 (☎272 341), behind Thai Tani Hotel next to the market, has regular orange

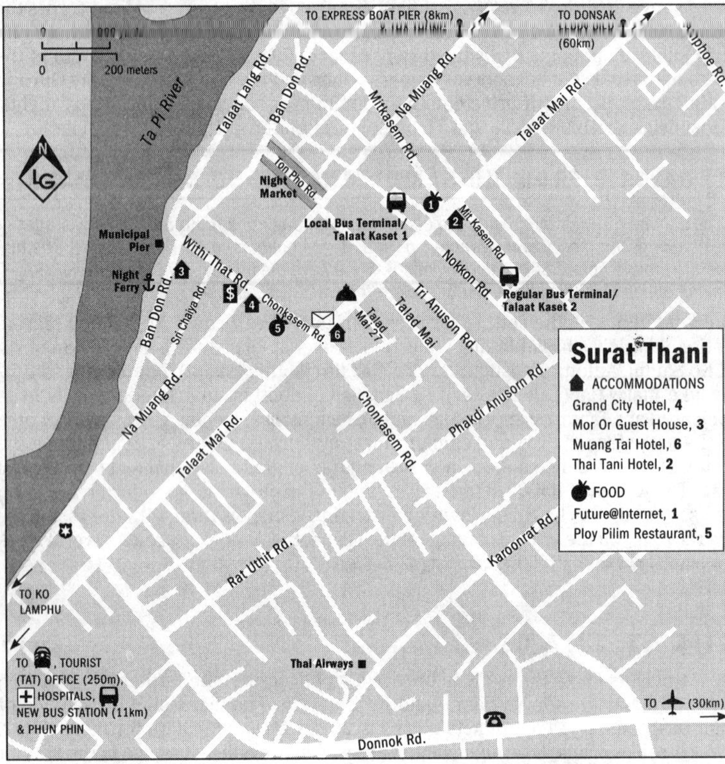

buses departing for **Hat Yai** (5hr., 120฿); **Krabi** (4hr., 80฿); **Phang-Nga** (3½hr., 60฿); **Phuket** (5hr., 100฿), as well as other southern destinations (roughly every 30min. 6am-5pm). Tour and travel agencies will try to lure you to **private buses,** which cost 50-100฿ more than public buses but take significantly less time. Private minibuses to: **Hat Yai** (5hr.; every hr. 6:30am-5pm; 150฿, minibus 180฿); **Krabi** (3hr.; every hr. 6:30am-5:30pm; 120฿, minibus 150฿); **Penang, Malaysia** (6hr., every hr. 6am-5pm, minibus 450฿); **Phuket** (3hr.; 8am-5pm; 130฿, minibus 250฿).

Boats: Ferries depart from several points outside town. **Songserm Travel Center** operates a **daily express boat** that leaves from the pier 8km outside of town to **Ko Phangan** (4hr., 7:30am, 250฿) and **Ko Samui** (3hr.; 7:30, 8am, 2pm; 150฿); ticket includes transportation to the pier. The same company operates a **night boat** which sets off from the Surat Thani pier at 11pm for: **Ko Phangan** (6hr., 200฿); **Ko Samui** (6hr., 150฿); **Ko Tao** (7hr., 400฿). **Samui Tours** offers buses (1hr.; 7 per day 6:15am-4:30pm; 45฿, with A/C 65฿) to the Donsak Car Port, about 60km from Surat Thani, where **Raja Car Ferry** goes to **Ko Phangan** (5hr., 120฿) and **Ko Samui** (2hr., every 2hr. 6am-6pm, 55฿). The new company **Seatran** also leaves from Donsak for **Ko Samui** (ferry 2hr.; 7am, 12:30pm; 250฿; bus service included; the 7am boat continues on to **Ko Phangan**). Buying from an agent will cost an added 50-100฿ surcharge.

Local Transportation: Few tourists stray from the bus-train-ferry station triangle, which is well served by the railway station bus.

ORIENTATION AND PRACTICAL INFORMATION

Trains arrive at **Phun Phin Railway Station,** 13km from Surat Thani. Phun Phin and Surat Thani are connected by the busy and noisy **Talaat Mai Rd.,** which enters Surat Thani from the southwest and passes the **tourist, police,** and **post offices.** Local buses leave from two separate **markets,** each just a block off Talaat Mai Rd., near the center of town. Ferries depart from the town pier on **Ban Don Rd.,** which runs along the banks of the mighty **Ta Pi River** and from piers outside town.

Tourist Office: TAT, 5 Talaat Mai Rd. (☎288 817). A 20min. walk on Talaat Mai Rd. from the town center; it's best to jump on an orange local bus heading to the train station. Friendly staff, good info, and maps. English spoken. Open daily 8:30am-4:30pm.

Travel Agencies: Agencies touting everything from daytrips to bus and train tickets abound near the pier and on Talaat Mai Rd. between two markets.

Currency Exchange: Surat Thani's exchange rates are better than those on the islands. Banks with **24hr. ATMs** line Na Muang Rd. Usually open M-F 8:30am-3:30pm. **Bangkok Bank,** 195-7 Na Muang Rd. (☎281 298), has a booth in front. Open daily 8:30am-5pm.

Markets: Talaat Kaset 1 and **2,** near the bus stations. The fabulous and popular **night market** sprawls on a single street (Ton Pho Rd.) between Na Muang Rd. and Talaat Lang Rd. From the bus stations, head toward the river.

Emergency: ☎191. **Tourist Police (Bangkok):** ☎1155.

Police: 188 Na Muang Rd. (☎272 095). Little English spoken. **Open 24hr.**

Hospitals: Surat Thani Provincial Hospital (☎284 700), 1km past TAT on Talaat Mai Rd., on the way to privately-run **Phun Phin Taksin Hospital** (☎273 239). Both have English-speaking staff. Credit cards accepted. **Open 24hr.**

Telephones: Surat Thani Telecommunication Center (☎283 050), on Donnok Rd., 2km from most hotels. Walk down Talaat Mai Rd. toward the TAT from the intersection with Chonkasem Rd. and turn left onto Donnok Rd.; it's 20min. down on the left under the radio tower. HCD. Open daily 8am-10pm.

Internet Access: Cheap Internet is available at **Welcome Internet,** by the Muang Tai Hotel on Chonkasem Rd. 20฿ per hr. Open daily 9am-midnight. Expensive Internet access (2฿ per min.) available around the pier area.

Post Offices: GPO (☎272 013), near the corner of Talaat Mai Rd. and Chonkasem Rd. *Poste Restante.* Open M-F 8:30am-4:30pm, Sa-Su 9am-noon. **Postal code:** 84000.

ACCOMMODATIONS

Surat Thani has several good hotels with relatively low prices, though it lacks a quality backpacker option. Ignore touts trying to push you onto a tuk-tuk; unless you're arriving by train or at the new bus station, it's just a short walk.

Muang Tai Hotel, 390-2 Talaat Mai Rd. (☎273 586), at the intersection with Chonkasem Rd. The best option in town, though some rooms capture a lot of street noise from the busy intersection. Rooms are average-sized but come with creature comforts such as tables, cushy chairs, and private baths. Cheerful staff. Singles with fan 240฿, with A/C 360฿; doubles 260฿/390฿; doubles with hot water and A/C 420฿. ❸

Thai Tani Hotel, 442/306-308 Talaat Kaset 2 (☎272 977), off Talaat Mai Rd. between the two markets, right in the thick of things. Reception on 3rd fl. Clean and popular. Rooms include private bath. Singles 240฿, with A/C 320฿; twin beds 260-380฿. ❸

Grand City Hotel, 428/6-10 Na Muang Rd. (☎272 560), at the corner of Chonkasem Rd. Clean rooms with standard amenities in a prime location. Singles and doubles 200฿, with A/C and hot water 350฿; twin beds with fan 250฿, with A/C 500฿. ❸

Mor Or Guest House, 136-8 Ban Don Rd. (☎210 268), across from the pier. Right on the waterfront and cheap, it's popular among backpackers because. However, the rooms are extremely basic and sauna-like with mattresses that induce *rigor mortis*. Common showers and toilets. Internet 2฿ per min. Cafe/restaurant. Singles and doubles 150฿. ❷

FOOD

The **night market** is almost reason enough to spend the night in Surat Thani and is perhaps its most memorable aspect. With a vast variety of vendors offering a tremendous range of snacks, sweets, and meals, the market seems to draw everyone in town. From crunchy bugs to duck eggs to enormous oysters to oil-drenched crepes, this is the place to sample Thai cuisine. **Talaat Kaset 1** and **Talaat Kaset 2** both have stalls and buffets displaying curries, meats, and vegetables ladled over rice. **Future@Internet ❶,** across from the Thai Tani Hotel, has a reasonably priced menu of mostly 30฿ items. (*Tom yam* 35฿. Open daily 8am-9:30pm.) For a variety of Thai dishes and seafood, try the **Ploy Pilim Restaurant ❷,** 100 Chonkasem Rd., 30m behind the post office on the bottom floor of the Tapee Hotel. (Standard dishes 40-60฿; specialties 60฿ and way up. Open daily 7:30am-11pm.)

SIGHTS

While the town itself has no true sights, you can visit most of the areas around Surat Thani via *songthaew*. Large **oysters** are bred around the Kadaeh and Ta Tong Rivers. If you're interested in how they're raised and harvested, catch a bus to **Kanchanadit** (15km from Surat Thani) and hire a longtail boat (100-150฿), or contact **Kiang Lay Oyster Farm** (☎255 288) for information. For more active distractions, observe primate pedagogy at the **Monkey Training College,** where monkeys learn to do tricks like collect gigantic coconuts from the river and bring them to their trainer. (☎227 351. 1-3 people 300฿, 4-10 people 700฿.) To go on your own, catch a *songthaew* (10฿) on Talaat Mai Rd. on the Phanthip Co. side of the street. Ask to be let off at *Rong Rian Sawn Ling*. Take a motorcycle taxi the rest of the way (20฿) or hike the 2km.

DAYTRIP FROM SURAT THANI: CHAIYA

The most direct way to get to Chaiya is to take a Chumphon-bound bus from Surat Thani's local market bus station, get off at Suan Mokkha, and catch a north-bound songthaew *to Wat Phra That (1½hr. total). From there, it's a 15min. walk to Chaiya town and the Surat* songthaew. *Another option is to leave from Phang-Nga (see below). You can also catch a songthaew from Surat Thani all the way to Chaiya town (1½hr., 25-30฿) and arrange the short transport to the wats from there. The first option is more direct.*

If the cultural vacuum of the islands has you yearning for a more historical experience, the town of Chaiya, 40km north of Surat Thani, while lacking splendor, may fulfill your needs. Once a powerful and important city-state in the southern Gulf Coast, Chaiya boasts several temples, museums, and ruins including one of the more revered Buddhist sights in the south. **Wat Phra Borommathat,** known as Wat Phra That, is a 1200-year-old pagoda housing relics and surrounded by 174 Buddha images. Unlike most Thai temples, this one is consecrated to Mahayana Buddhism, the religion of the ancient Sumatran Srivijaya Empire. The elaborate stone *chedi* is considered a masterful example of Srivijaya art. Next door, the small but interesting **National Museum** houses engaging artifacts dating from Chaiya's heyday. (☎431 090. Open W-Su 9am-4pm. 30฿.) Situated in a forest along Hwy. 41, **Wat Suan Mokkha Phalaram** (Suan Mok) is more a working monastery than a tourist attraction. Established by one of Thailand's most famous monks, the area contains few modern buildings since it was structured to return Buddhist practice and teaching to a more traditional and serene setting (i.e. the woods), while at the same time incorporating modern influences and design. As if to combat the indulgent lifestyles of nearby islands, Suan Mok urges restraint in all its attendees, discouraging vices like cigarette smoking and mosquito slapping. Anyone can attend **meditation retreats** (☎431 552; 1200฿ covers food, accommodations, and expenses for the 12-day retreat) held by resident monks. Retreats start on the last day of each month and run to the 11th day of the following month. It's not possible or necessary to reserve a spot; you need only show up a few days before the end the month.

NEAR SURAT THANI: KHAO SOK NATIONAL PARK

Nestled in the mountain ridge separating the eastern and western coasts of peninsular Thailand, splendid Khao Sok National Park is one of the more worthwhile interior escapes in southern Thailand. A relic of the country's topological past, the 160 million-year-old rain forest (some date it as old as 380 million years) covers roughly 650 sq. km, mostly comprised of jungle-covered foothills and protruding limestone formations. Its unique geography and generous rainfall allow it to sustain a remarkable ecosystem, home to hundreds of wildlife species. The park's jewel is doubtless the native flora, which includes dozens of species of orchids and ferns. Most spectacular is the *Bua Phut*, a lotus flower that can grow up to 80cm. The **park headquarters** near the entrance dispenses trail maps and arranges guided hikes to some of the waterfalls and caves. The headquarters also offers a **camping area** (pitch your own) and **bungalows.** Just outside of the park are fun tree-house-style accommodations which are popular among backpackers. **Art's Riverview Jungle Lodge** or **Bamboo House** are both quality choices. Park admission is 200฿ for three days. For more information on the park's facilities, call ☎299 150. Many Surat Thani travel agencies and private guest houses that cluster near the park's entrance arrange excursions into the park. Otherwise, take a Phuket- or Takuapa-bound orange public bus from Surat Thani's southern market (every 30min. 6am-5pm) and direct the driver to Khao Sok, roughly 60km (1½hr.) away.

PHANG-NGA ☎076

While Phang-Nga Province is rich in natural beauty and cultural attractions, its capital, the small mainland town of Phang-Nga, has not been so blessed. Hot, sticky, and devoid of any worthwhile sights, the city has only two mentionable assets: a friendly population and proximity to some of the most spectacular scenery on the Thai-Malay Peninsula. Still, with less tourist traffic and cheaper tour services, Phang-Nga attracts budget travelers who spend a night or two here before heading out to explore the wonders of the bay and province areas.

TRANSPORTATION AND PRACTICAL INFORMATION. The bus station is on **Phetkasem Hwy.** near the center of town. **Buses** run to: **Bangkok** (13hr.; 5pm, 357฿; with A/C 2, 4:30pm; 441฿); **Hat Yai** (6hr., every hr. 8am-2pm, with A/C 220฿); **Ko Samui** (6hr., 9:30 and 11:30am, with A/C and ferry 240฿); **Krabi** (1½hr.; every 30min. 7:30am-8pm; 35-40฿, with A/C 59฿); **Phuket** (1½hr.; every hr. 9am-9pm; 50฿, with A/C 65฿); **Surat Thani** (2½hr.; 5 per day 9:30am-5pm, 60฿; with A/C 9:30am, 11pm; 130฿); and **Trang** (4½hr., every hr. 7:30am-8:30pm, with A/C 139฿). Blue

songthaew run along the highway from the bus station to points around town (10-15฿) and the pier (20฿). **Motorcycle taxis** cost about 20฿ around town.

The unregistered **travel agencies** near the bus station provide most tourist services. These agencies are less professional than those offering tours from Phuket and Krabi but are also about 200-400฿ cheaper (day tours 250-550฿; overnight tours to Phang-Nga Bay 550-750฿). **Sayan Tour,** next to the bus terminal, is one of the more established tour operators. (☎430 348. Open daily 6am-8pm.) Other services include: **Thai Farmers Bank,** 126 Phetkasem Hwy., across the street from the bus station, with a **24hr. ATM** (open M-F 8:30am-3:30pm); a **police station,** 193 Borirakbamrung Rd. (☎412 075), 500m to the left of the bus station; **Phang-Nga General Hospital,** 436 Phetkasem Hwy., 2km to the left of the bus station (☎412 034; **open 24hr.;** English spoken; no credit cards); and a **post office** on Phetkasem Hwy. (☎412 171; open M-F 8:30am-4:30pm, Sa-Su 9am-noon) with *Poste Restante* and **international phone** (open daily 8:30am-4:30pm). In an **emergency,** dial ☎191; for **Bangkok tourist police** dial ☎1155. **Postal code:** 82000.

ACCOMMODATIONS AND FOOD. Centrally located and antiseptically clean, **Phang-Nga Guest House ❸** is on Phetkasem Hwy., to the right of the bus station near Krug Thai Bank. The new rooms and common baths are spotless. (☎411 358. Continental breakfast 50฿. Singles with fan 220฿, with A/C 350฿; doubles with fan 250฿, with bath and A/C 400฿.) **Thawisuk Hotel ❷,** 79 Phetkasem Hwy. is in a seemingly ancient building. The hallways aren't great, but the rooms are cozy with the extra bonus of wooden floors. (☎412 100. No A/C. Singles 150฿; doubles 200฿.)

Phang-Nga has several good dining options near the bus station. The best restaurant around, **Duang Seafood ❷,** 122 Phetkasem Hwy., next to Thai Farmers Bank and opposite the night market, serves shrimp fried rice and hot-and-sour seafood soup. (Dishes 50-100฿. Open daily 9am-10:30pm.) **Bismilla ❷,** 247 Phetkasem Hwy., on the same side of the street as the bus station, is a Muslim restaurant with wonderful *roti*, curries, and Thai soups—especially lemon. (Open daily 7am-11pm.) The **day market ❶,** off Phetkasem Hwy., to the right of the bus station, sells fruit from 4am to 6pm. The **night market ❶** sets up near the post office on Phetkasem Hwy. and along Riverside Rim Kong Rd. (Open daily 4:30pm-midnight.)

DAYTRIPS FROM PHANG-NGA: PHANG-NGA BAY NATIONAL PARK. Travelers don't come to see Phang-Nga Town; they come to see Phang-Nga Province. With its majestic limestone formations and stunning Phang-Nga Bay, the province offers the rugged beauty missing from built-up tourist resorts like Phuket and Krabi. Unfortunately, travelers without a car or boat find the province highly inaccessible. Rather than attempt to go it alone, join one of the day tours or overnight stays offered by many travel agencies (from Phang-Nga 200-500฿; from Phuket 450-650฿). The real attraction, **Phang-Nga Bay National Park** stretches over 400 sq. km, encompassing more than 120 postcard-perfect limestone islands. Use the old maxim: see as it is, leave as it was. Most tourists make a beeline to the park's twin jewels, beautiful **Ko Khao Ping Gan** and its satellite, **Ko Tapu,** better known as "James Bond Island"—the 1974 Bond flick, *The Man With The Golden Gun*, was filmed here. While the image of the thin limestone rock that is Ko Tapu (literally, "Nail Island") slicing into the bay is quite striking, be prepared to throw elbows at shell-vendors and tourists to stake a prime photo-taking spot. While larger boats visit from Krabi and Phuket, the most common tours from Phang-Nga are on longtail boats. **Sayan Tour** offers half-day (200฿), full-day (500฿), and overnight trips, which include a memorable stay at **Ko Panyi** (extra 250฿). The latter option, whether tacked on after the half-day or full-day tour, is highly recommended (see below). A final option for touring the bay is by kayak. This pricey option (roughly 2000฿) allows you to fully explore the hidden lagoons and wildlife without the deafening buzz of the longtail motor.

NEAR PHANG-NGA

KO PANYI AND THE MUSLIM FISHING VILLAGE. Though technically part of the Phang-Nga Bay National Park, Ko Panyi is worth a separate visit. About 250 years ago, Muslim fishermen from Indonesia settled on the island, constructing homes and businesses on stilts jutting into the water. Almost three centuries later, the Muslim Fishing Village is alive and well, though nowadays it seems to cater more to tourists than to fish. Other than the prominent town **mosque,** there's not much to see in the village (besides a gorgeous sunset and sunrise); the real fascination is ambling down the rickety, suspended streets to watch the town inhabitants—some 200 of them in all—go about their daily chores in the most unusual of settings. Overnight stays are recommended, as the village assumes a different character after daytrippers return to the mainland. It's possible to arrange a room with the locals or book an overnight stay through a travel agency for 500-650฿.

WAT SUWANNAKUHA. A popular stop for most tourist groups, this pleasant Buddhist temple, known by locals as Wat Tham, consists of several caves, the largest of which measures 40m long and houses an impressive 15m long reclining Buddha. The temple (and its resident monkeys) are best visited late in the afternoon when the tourist buses have returned to Phuket, leaving the temple relatively undisturbed. *(8km outside Phang-Nga, off Phang-Nga Koke Kloy Rd. 10฿.)*

PHUKET ☎076

A tropical playground of international stature, Phuket (FOO-ket) is best compared to other Eden-cum-tourist-meccas. Thailand's biggest island in the Andaman Sea and its most wealthy province, Phuket draws tourists looking for anything but a cultural or solitary experience. Most visitors arrive by plane and are swiftly shepherded into air-conditioned taxis, which deposit them at five-star luxury resorts. Here they frolic and play for a week or two, safely avoiding almost everything having to do with, God forbid, Thailand. Consequently, for the budget traveler, Phuket can be an over-touristed experience. Backpackers relax on beaches like Hat Kamala and Hat Karon by day and revel with randy Romeos cruising the discos in nightlife hub Hat Patong by night. The mantra is simple: give up your dreams of idyllic seclusion for a few nights, soak up a raucous good time with fellow vacationing tourists, and, in your own way, make the most of the "Jewel of the South."

THE VIEW FROM ABOVE

The lowdown: Thailand's biggest and most-touristed island.
Gateway city: Phuket Town.
Beaches: Ao Bang Tao, Ao Chalong, Hat Kamala, Hat Karon, Hat Kata, Hat Nai Yang, Hat Patong, Hat Rawai, Hat Surin.
Highlights: Snorkeling and diving around Hat Karon and Hat Kata, Hat Surin, legendary nightlife hub Hat Patong, and Phuket Town's Vegetarian Festival (early Oct.).

TRANSPORTATION

Flights: Phuket International Airport, 28km outside of Phuket Town on Rte. 4026. **Taxi** from airport to Phuket Town 300฿. **Bangkok Airways,** 158/2-3 Yao Warat Rd. (☎225 033; open daily 8am-5pm), and **Thai Airways,** 78/1 Ranong Rd. (☎211 195; open daily 8am-5pm), across from the local bus station, run most domestic and international flights. To: **Bangkok** (every hr. 8am-8pm, 2730฿); **Hat Yai** (12:50pm, 1100฿); **Ko Samui** (50min.; daily 11:15am, 4:20pm; 11,870฿; M, W, F, Su 11:10am; 1480฿); **Kuala Lumpur, Malaysia** (daily, 3730฿); **Penang, Malaysia** (Tu, F, Su 12:30pm; 2230฿); **Singapore** (4 per day, 6085฿).

Buses: Intercity bus station (☎211 480), off Phang-Nga Rd. in eastern Phuket Town, behind a shopping plaza. TAT office has a good, free bus schedule. A/C and non-A/C buses to: **Bangkok** (14hr., 19 per day 6am-7pm, 278-755฿); **Hat Yai** (7hr., 12 per day, 150-270฿); **Khao Sok National Park** (7:30, 9am); **Krabi** (4hr., 22 per day, 65-117฿); **Phang-Nga** (2½hr., 5 per day 10:10am-4:30pm, 36฿); **Surat Thani** (5hr., 14 per day, 104-180฿); **Trang** (6hr., 20 per day 6am-6:30pm, 105-189฿).

Boats: Boats to **Ko Phi Phi** depart from Tonsai Bay (9am, 2:30pm; 350-450฿), the deep-sea port on the southeast coast. Tickets are cheaper in Ko Phi Phi—buy your return ticket there. A tuk-tuk to the pier costs 50฿.

Local Transportation: Local bus station on Ranong Rd. in Phuket Town, near the market. Labeled **songthaew** (every 30min. 7am-5pm) to: **Hat Kamala** (25฿); **Hat Karon** (20฿); **Hat Kata** (20฿); **Hat Patong** (15฿); **Hat Rawai** (20฿); **Hat Nai Yang** (30฿); **Hat Surin** (20฿). **Tuk-tuk** to: **Hat Kamala** (250฿); **Hat Kata** (150฿); **Hat Nai Yang** (300฿); **Hat Patong** (15฿); **Hat Rawai** (100฿); **Hat Surin** (250฿). Within Phuket Town, tuk-tuks charge 10-20฿; rates are negotiable to other points on the island and go up after 5pm. **Metered taxis** cost 30฿ for the first 2km and 4฿ for each additional km.

Rentals: Motorcycles (150-200฿ per day) and **jeeps** (600-1000฿ per day) are available for rent all over the island. All vehicles are uninsured, and accident rates for foreigners are alarmingly high. **TAT does not recommend renting a motorcycle.** Helmets are required now for drivers, but amazingly, not even offered to backseat passengers.

THAILAND

ORIENTATION

Phuket is connected to the mainland by **Rte. 402,** the island's main north-south artery. Bordering the Andaman Sea, the west coast is lined with beaches. The northern beaches, especially **Hat Kamala, Hat Surin,** and **Sing Cape** are quieter and prettier, while south of Kamala, party central **Hat Patong** has a sensory overload of tacky bars, cabaret shows, and gimmicky tourist stalls. Farther south are the gentle duo of **Hat Karon** and **Hat Kata,** while a few smaller, less attractive beaches fringe the island's southwestern tip. Phuket's eastern coast is filled with mangroves, prawn farms, and bobbing boats. **Phuket Town,** the island's lifeline, is on the island's southeastern corner.

PRACTICAL INFORMATION

Tourist Office: TAT, 73-75 Phuket Rd. (☎212 213), in Phuket Town, northwest of the clock tower and hidden among furniture stores. Open daily 8:30am-4:30pm.

Travel Agencies: Tour operators are a dime a dozen in Hat Karon, Hat Kata, Hat Patong, and Phuket Town. Most can arrange tours to Phang-Nga Bay and nearby islands (450-650฿) and bus or ferry transportation to Krabi and Ko Phi Phi. The agency in the **On On Hotel** (see **Accommodations,** below) is reportedly one of the cheapest.

Currency Exchange: In Phuket Town, a slew of banks are on Phang-Nga Rd. in front of the On On Hotel, and several more are one block down on Ratsada Rd. **Thai Farmers Bank,** 14 Phang-Nga Rd. (☎216 928). Open daily 8:30am-5pm. **24hr. ATM.**

Medical Services: Phuket has some of Thailand's finest hospitals outside Bangkok. **Bangkok Phuket Hospital,** 21 Hong Yok-H-Thit Rd. (☎254 421), on the northwest side of Phuket Town. **Phuket International Hospital,** 44 Chalerm Prakiat Rd. (☎249 400), on the way to the airport. Credit cards accepted. English spoken. Both **open 24hr.**

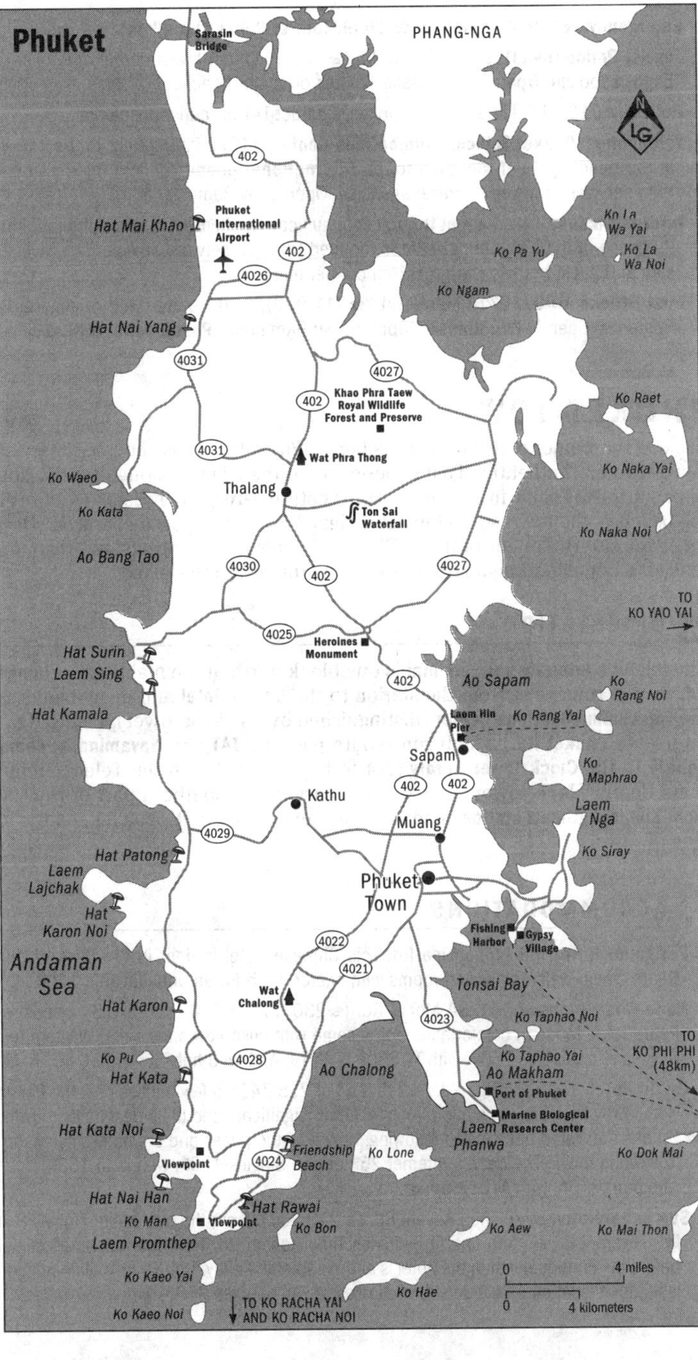
Phuket
Sarasin Bridge
PHANG-NGA
402
Phuket International Airport
Hat Mai Khao
402
4026
Ko La Wa Yai
Ko Pa Yu
Ko La Wa Noi
Ko Ngam
Hat Nai Yang
4031
4027
Khao Phra Taew Royal Wildlife Forest and Preserve
402
Ko Raet
4031
Wat Phra Thong
Ko Naka Yai
Ko Waeo
Thalang
Ton Sai Waterfall
Ko Kata
Ko Naka Noi
Ao Bang Tao
4030
402
4027
TO KO YAO YAI
4025
Heroines Monument
Hat Surin
Laem Sing
402
Ao Sapam
Ko Rang Noi
Hat Kamala
Laem Hin Pier
Ko Rang Yai
Sapam
Ko Maphrao
402
402
Kathu
Laem Nga
4029
Muang
Ko Siray
Hat Patong
Laem Lajchak
Phuket Town
Hat Karon Noi
Fishing Harbor
Gypsy Village
4022
Andaman Sea
4021
Wat Chalong
Tonsai Bay
Hat Karon
4023
Ko Taphao Noi
Ko Pu
4028
Ko Taphao Yai
TO KO PHI PHI (48km)
Ao Chalong
Ao Makham
Hat Kata
Port of Phuket
Marine Biological Research Center
Laem Phanwa
Hat Kata Noi
Friendship Beach
4024
Ko Lone
Ko Dok Mai
Viewpoint
Hat Nai Han
Hat Rawai
Ko Man
Viewpoint
Ko Bon
Ko Aew
Ko Mai Thon
Laem Promthep
Ko Kaeo Yai
0
4 miles
Ko Hae
0
4 kilometers
Ko Kaeo Noi
TO KO RACHA YAI AND KO RACHA NOI

THAILAND

Emergency: ☎199. **Ambulance:** ☎ 1699. **Tourist Police (Bangkok):** ☎1155.

Tourist Police (local): 81-83 Satun Rd. (☎225 361), northwest corner of Phuket Town. English spoken. **Open 24hr.** Smaller booths on major beaches.

Police: ☎212 115. Little English spoken. Contact TAT or tourist police first.

Telephones: Phuket Telecommunications Center, 112/2 Phang-Nga Rd. (☎216 861), in the building under the radio tower. **International phone**/fax and Internet. Cheaper than services provided by travel agencies. Open daily 8am-midnight.

Internet Access: Cheapest at the Telecommunications Center (see **Telephones,** above). Purchase of a 100฿ Internet card is required to begin service. 30฿ per hr. Travel agencies and guest houses charge 1-2฿ more per min.

Post Offices: GPO, 12/16 Montri Rd. (☎211 020), on the corner with Talang Rd. *Poste Restante.* Open M-F 8:30am-4:30pm, Sa-Su 9am-noon. **Postal code:** 83000.

PHUKET TOWN ☎076

Lacking the glamor of its beachside siblings, Phuket Town is about as close as you can get to an "authentic" Thai experience on the island. Though tourist dollars have started to trickle in as more *farang* venture here from the island's more alluring beaches, the town still retains its original Sino-Portuguese character. Despite its scant entertainment options, Phuket Town's budget hotels and restaurants make it a popular springboard for exploring the rest of the island.

ORIENTATION

The island's **intercity bus terminal** is one block north of the main road, **Phang-Nga Rd.,** which runs west from the station to the **On On Hotel** and many banks. Past the **Telecommunications Center** (distinguished by its clock tower), Phang-Nga Rd. intersects **Phuket Rd.,** which runs south past the **TAT** and **Navamindra Memorial Square** to the **Clock Tower Rotary** (not to be confused with the Telecommunications Center clock tower), a main landmark in the southern part of town. The **local bus/songthaew station** is adjacent to the market on **Ranong Rd.,** on the west side of town.

ACCOMMODATIONS

Pengmen Hotel, 69 Phang-Nga Rd. This Chinese hotel is right in the thick of things. Rents clean, well-maintained rooms with shared bath for an unbelievable 120฿. ❶

Nana Chart Mansion, 41/34 Montri Rd. (☎230 041 or 230 041, ext. 3), opposite the Pearl Hotel. Modern, comfortable rooms come with crisp new sheets and Western toilets. Singles and doubles 250฿, with TV 300฿, with TV, A/C, and hot shower 350-450฿. ❸

On On Hotel, 19 Phang-Nga Rd. (☎211 154 or 225 741), a few houses past the Pengmen Hotel away from the bus station. Architecturally significant and the oldest hotel in town, On On has a devoted backpacker following, drawn by the prices and the hotel's cameo in the Hollywood movie *The Beach.* Internet 25฿ per hr. Singles 120฿, with bath 180฿; doubles with bath 250฿, with A/C 360฿. ❷

Suk Sabai Hotel, 82/9 Thep Kasatri Rd. (☎212 287). From the bus station, follow Phuket Rd. several blocks north until it becomes Thep Kasatri Rd. Turn onto the small alley just before the Ford dealership; the hotel is at the end of the alley. Suk Sabai's main advantage is its quiet location on a side street. Singles 180฿; doubles 250฿. ❸

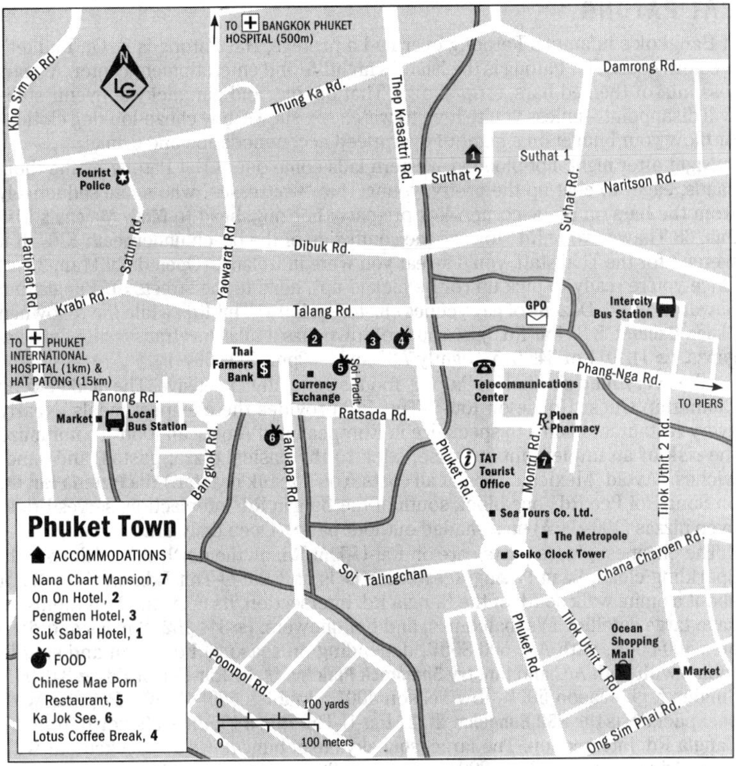

FOOD

Phuket is famous for its culinary delights, including *tao sor* (Chinese crepes) and *kanohm jin Phuket* (breakfast noodles in spicy curry). The daily **market** ❶ on Ranong Rd. sells aisle upon aisle of tropical fruit and seafood. The **night market** ❶ is at the junction of Tilok Uthit 1 and Ong Sim Phai Rd. A good *farang* place to grab a Western breakfast or a sandwich is **Lotus Coffee Break** ❶, at the corner of Phang-Nga and Phuket Rd. (Thai dishes 25-35฿; shakes 20-25฿; sandwiches 20-30฿. Open daily 7:30am-9:30pm.) The expensive but excellent **Ka Jok See** ❹, 26 Takuapa Rd., is several shops south of the Ratsada Rd. intersection, hidden by plants. The staff treats you like royalty. Thai dishes run 80-380฿. Try the *tom yum* or *goong-sarong* for 150฿ each. (Reservations recommended. Open Tu-Su 6-11pm.) The **Chinese Mae Porn Restaurant** ❸, on Phang-Nga Rd. across from the Pengmen Hotel, is deservedly popular among travelers and Thais alike for its scrumptious dishes and neighborly atmosphere. Portions are on the skimpy side, but taste compensates. (Various seafood dishes or chicken with cashew nuts 60-100฿. Open daily 8:30am-10pm.)

> **BEACH WARNING** Phuket is known for dangerous, sometimes fatal, ocean currents during the rainy season. Exercise caution in the water, especially at high tide. If you're caught in a current, signal distress by waving one arm (wave two arms for serious distress).

THAILAND

HAT PATONG

If Bangkok's infamous Patpong ever had a protege, Hat Patong is it. On Phuket's western coast, Hat Patong is the island's nightlife and entertainment center. A tasteless mix of themed bars, strip shows, Thai boxing, and gimmicky souvenir stalls will disappoint—unless you're here to watch sex shows, buy cheap-looking clothes, or blow your budget on a night of overpriced accommodation and drinks.

Night after night, hot-blooded Western lads come out in Hat Patong by the thousands, eager to chat up the pretty, young Thai "waitresses" who smile seductively from the bars on every corner. For pre-party boozing, head to **Molly Malone's Irish Pub,** 68 Thaweewong Rd., toward the south side of the beach underneath KFC. If it weren't for the Thai staff, you'd swear you were in Ireland. (Open daily 11am-2am.) Once you're ready to pick up (or be picked up), head to the streets off Bangla and Sawatdirak Rd. Dozens of gay venues cluster on Rat-U-Thit Rd., while the renowned **Simon Cabaret,** 8 Sirirat Rd., just south of town, has a hilarious transvestite extravaganza. (☎342 011 or 342 015. Nightly 7:30 and 9:30pm. 500-600฿.)

Like everything else in Hat Patong, food is generally expensive. The **market ❶** by Chanathip Guest House on Rat-U-Thit Rd. provides the cheapest meals. Nearly every restaurant claims to specialize in European and American food. To minimize the risk of an unpleasant surprise, stick to the basics: pizza, pastas, and sandwiches. (Avoid "Mexican" food at all costs. You'll thank us later.) **The Pizzeria Hut ❸,** on Song Roi Pee Rd., one block south of the Bangla Rd. intersection, serves brick-oven pizzas (100-200฿) on a shaded outdoor patio. (Open daily 11am-11pm.)

The cheapest places to stay are on Rat-U-Thit Rd. on the north side of the beach. Sparkling clean, **Baan Patong Guesthouse ❹** is at 3 Rat-U-Thit Rd., on a small soi about a 5min. walk south of the Bangla Rd. intersection. Its cozy, modern rooms all have large satellite TVs, balconies, and hot showers. (☎344 152. Singles and doubles 400-600฿, with A/C 600-850฿, depending on season.) For clean and simple rooms with both A/C and fan, try **Shamrock Park Inn ❹,** 31 Rat-U-Thit Rd. (☎340 991. Singles high season 500฿, low season 400฿; doubles 600฿/450฿.) Popular with backpackers is the **PS2 Bungalow ❺,** 21 Rat-U-Thit Rd., a 15min. walk north from the Bangla Rd. intersection. The large, squeaky-clean bungalows are decked out with micro-fridges. (☎342 207 or 290 032; www.ps2bungalows.com. Singles and doubles 600-900฿ in high season, 400-600฿ in low season, with A/C and TV 900-1500฿.)

HAT KARON AND HAT KATA

Popular with backpackers and package tourists alike, the beaches of Hat Karon and Hat Kata have the best balance of lively nightlife, plentiful dining options, and sweet sand, and they are blissfully free of the go-go bars that dominate Hat Patong. Though they can get crowded, especially around Hat Kata's Club Med Beach, Hat Karon and Hat Kata are nonetheless pleasant getaways.

For those with the cash, Hat Karon and Hat Kata offer some of the world's best **snorkeling** and **diving** around the Similan and Racha Islands. Head to PADI-certified **Siam Dive n' Sail,** 68/14 Patak Road, Moo 2, behind Club Med near the Jiva Resort. They specialize in live-aboard diving trips, which is all the rage in Phuket now. Four-day trips to Similan and Surin start at 20,000฿ per person, seven-day trips to Myanmar (Burma) start at 57,000฿, and daytrips start at 2000-3100฿ per person. Gear rental costs 700฿ per day. All trips include transportation from your hotel, tanks and weights, and most meals and drinks. (☎330 967; info@siamdivers.com; www.siamdivers.com. Open M-Sa 11am-8pm. MC/V.) **Hat Kata Center**'s bar scene offers rowdy excitement after a long day in the sun, while **Dino Park Mini-Golf** provides more innocent fun. (Golf open daily 10am-midnight. 240฿, children 180฿.)

Hat Karon and Hat Kata are actually three separate beaches. To the north, luxury resorts dot the 3km of Hat Karon. To the south, a hilly, rocky cape separates Hat

Karon from Hat Kata. Here, budget restaurants and hotels cluster around **Taina Rd.,** which winds inland from the beachside **Patak Rd.** Hat Kata itself is split into the beaches of **Hat Kata** and **Hat Kata Noi.** While Hat Kata is monopolized by **Club Med,** Hat Kata Noi to the south is the most solitary beach of the three.

Backpacker Land spreads off the beach along Taina Rd. on the cape separating Hat Karon from Hat Kata. One of the best budget hotels is the Scandinavian-themed **Little Mermaid Guest House ❹,** on Taina Rd., near the highway intersection and opposite the PTT gas station. The four-story multicolored building has rooms with hot water, phones, and optional fridges and TVs (50฿ extra each). Two restaurants, three bars, a pool table, a swimming pool, and Internet access (2฿ per min.) are provided for general use. (☎330 730; fax 330 733; mermaid@phuket.ksc.co.th; www.littlemermaidphuket.net. Low season: rooms with fan 265฿, with A/C 365฿; bungalows with A/C 850฿. High season: rooms 365฿/500฿/590฿. Discounts for long-term stays.) A bit closer to the beach, the family-run **Rose Inn ❹,** 114/24 Moo 4 Taina Rd., has simple, clean rooms. The staff speaks little English. (☎330 582; fax 330 591. Singles and doubles 400฿, with A/C 650฿.) Another option is the **Lucky Guest House ❸,** 110/44 Moo 4 Taina Rd., a few meters away from the Rose Inn. It's clean and empty during the off-season. (☎330 572. Singles and doubles with bath 250-450฿.) Both Hat Karon and Hat Kata have a good selection of inexpensive restaurants on Taipan Rd. **The Kwong Seafood Shop ❷** is a no-frills, no-nonsense place to get a good, fast bite to eat. (Chicken and beef dishes 50-70฿. Seafood dishes 200฿. Open daily 9am-midnight.) At the **Dive Cafe ❸,** 111/25-26 Taina Rd., about one block from the water on the left, divers and beach-goers devour the house specialty, *kai manao* (lemon chicken), for 120฿. (Open daily 9am-11pm.)

THAILAND

HAT SURIN, AO BANG TAO, AND HAT NAI YANG

Once known to harbor the most beautiful and undeveloped beaches on Phuket, the island's northwestern shore has exploded with luxury resorts over the past decade. **Hat Surin** is no exception, though there are some cheaper guest houses closer to the highway. **Tiw-Too Guest House ❹,** 13/11 Srisoonthorn Rd., a 10min. walk from the beach, has exceptionally clean rooms, TVs, refrigerators, and sweet owners—it's easy to feel at home here. (☎270 240. Singles with A/C 400-700฿.) On the southern end of Surin Beach, **Diver's Place** is a beachfront pub with a friendly expat crowd. Diver, who's saved over 90 people over the years, is a good person to ask about the surf. (Beers 60฿.)

If you bring your own food, a towel, and a book, attractive **Ao Bang Tao** makes a decent daytrip, especially between May and July, before the heavy rains hit, but after the crowds have skedaddled. Ao Bang Tao is dominated by two resorts that monopolize access to the water. Squeezed between the two beaches on the road from Surin to Ao Bang Tao, **Bangtao Lagoon Bungalows ❺,** 72/3 Moo 3 T. Cherngtalay, has compact, comfortable huts with a blue patina and marble floors. The bungalows range from standard to deluxe suites. Ask the bus driver from Phuket Town to drop you off here or you may never find it. (☎324 260; fax 324 168; http://phuket-bangtaolagoon.com. Standard bungalows 400฿ low season, 680฿ high season; superior bungalows 600฿/1150฿. Extra bed 200฿.)

The national park of **Hat Nai Yang,** 13km of coconut and rubber trees on the northeastern tip of the island, has kept private developers at bay, although condominium vultures still stalk the park boundaries. In the rainy season, Hat Nai Yang has Phuket's most dangerous riptides. The **Visitors Office** is near the entrance. (☎327 407 or 328 226. Open daily 8:30am-4:30pm.) It's possible to rent **tents ❶** (small sleeps 2-4, 100฿; large sleeps 5-8, 200฿). **Park bungalows ❸** on the beach are popular among Thai vacationers (300-600฿).

HAT KAMALA

Escape to quiet **Hat Kamala** on the way to Hat Surin from Phuket Town (*songthaew* 20฿). There are no luxury hotels and the beaches are decent. To get to the spotless rooms of **Malinee House ❺**, 74/7 Moo 3, follow the beach road from the south end of the beach until it curves inland; the restaurant/guest house is on the right. An Internet cafe is below. (☎324 094 or 271 355. Singles and doubles in high season 650฿, with A/C 950฿; in low season 350฿/500฿. Cable TV 100฿ extra.)

HAT RAWAI AND AO CHALONG

Squashed into the southeastern tip of Phuket Island, **Hat Rawai** caters mostly to locals. The beach's narrow strip of sand and muddy water render it quite unappealing; try its more attractive neighbor **Hat Nai Han.** Both slow down during rainy season. At Hat Rawai, **Pornmae Bungalows ❸**, 58/1 Wiset Rd., inside the hair salon opposite the central part of the beach, has simple rooms with fridges. (☎/fax 381 300. Singles and doubles 300-400฿.) Pleasant **Ao Chalong,** north of Hat Rawai on the island's southeastern side, is the largest bay on Phuket. It's a good place to stay if you want to learn more about the active Andaman Sea yachting culture. A good place to meet other sailors is **Friendship Beach ❺**, 27/1 Soi Mittraphap, about 2km north of Hat Rawai toward Phuket Town on the southern side of the bay, across from the Phuket Shell Museum. Friendly and relaxed, it has bungalows, a restaurant, Sunday jam sessions, a pool table, cable TV, and Internet (1฿ per min.). The kitchen serves good Thai and Western food. (☎381 281; fax 381 424. Spanish omelette 100฿. Bungalows 600฿ high season, 350฿ low season.)

SIMILAN ISLANDS ☎076

While the southern Thailand backpacker superhighway swallows up other islands, Ko Similan, a national park consisting of nine small islands, remains the original beauty of the Andaman Sea. Relative inaccessibility and higher expenses have preserved Ko Similan above and below water. Its outstanding underwater visibility and coral gardens filled with abundant marine life make the Similan Archipelago one of the world's best deep-water dive sites. If time and budget are not an issue, Ko Similan is worth the trip (at least November through April, when it's open).

November through February, sea turtles lay eggs on the beach at **Ko Hu Yong.** To explore the underwater in depth, you'll need to shell out money for a tour. **Khao Lak** on the mainland is the launching point for many of these tours. A typical dive lasts four nights and three days and includes 10 dives (10,000-20,000฿). If you're not interested in diving, there's superb **snorkeling** and **hiking** (with fantastic views) and, well, whatever else one fancies to do in a timeless paradise.

The nine islands 60km off the west coast of Phang-Nga are numbered from north to south. The second-largest island, **Ko Miang,** is where boats dock and the only island that allows overnighters. It's also the site of the **Visitors Center, park headquarters,** and the area's only drinking water. Boat trips between the islands are irregular and cost 250฿ per person. It's best to contact the **Similan National Park Office** (☎411 913) at Thap Lamu pier with any questions about transportation and practicalities. There's a 40฿ admission fee to the park, collected at Ko Miang upon arrival. The park is closed from May until November due to rough seas. Services on the Similan Islands are more than limited—they're non-existent. Think messages in bottles, shells, roots, and sticks. There are three reasonable ways to access the Similan Islands, either from Ban Thap Lamu pier (3hr., 8am, 2100฿) closest to Phang-Nga Town, by boat from Amphoe Khuru Buri pier (3hr.) farther north, or from Phuket (1½hr., 8am, 700฿). **Met Sine Tours** (☎443 276), at Ban Thap Lamu, is the most reliable booking agent. In Phuket, contact Songserm Travel Center (☎076 222 570). Rough seas might result in cancellation or a sickening journey.

Ko Miang has the only accommodations, a campground offering both **tents** ❷ (150฿) and **bungalows** ❺ (600฿ for four beds). There's a small fee for those who bring their own tent. Elsewhere in the Similan Islands, camping is prohibited, as are campfires. If you're not camping out, it's absolutely necessary to book in advance through the park office (see above). Ko Miang also has the area's only restaurant, a rather over-priced affair. You're better off bringing your own grub.

KO PHI PHI DON ☎075

The secret is out. Beautiful Ko Phi Phi Don—once an untouristed island dotted with swaying palms, shimmering turquoise waters, and isolated spits of sand—is now *the* destination for backpackers in southern Thailand. Paradoxically, it was the filming of *The Beach,* which depicted a secluded beach paradise on nearby Ko Phi Phi Ley that helped transform the once ignored island into a hub of backpacker activity. Instead of the peace and solace promised by the film, travelers will find street after street of restaurants, travel agencies, and guest houses. The inland is now strewn with garbage, fish-filled fringes of coral are being destroyed, and the buzz of longtail boats never ceases. As a result, islanders and the government are currently debating the virtues of shutting down Ko Phi Phi Don for an entire year. Whatever its fate, for now, only Ko Phangan can match Ko Phi Phi Don in terms of balancing island entertainment and island ambience. Yes, the beaches are beautiful, but none of them is *The Beach.* It's too late for that.

THAILAND

THE VIEW FROM ABOVE

The lowdown: Isolated island turned backpacker hotspot.
Gateway city: Ko Lanta, Krabi, or Phuket.
Beaches: Ao Lo Dalam, Ao Thon Sai, Hat Hin Kohn, Laem Him, Ma Prao, Hat Yao.
Highlights: Diving off Bamboo Island and Mosquito Island, and visiting Ko Phi Phi Ley.

TRANSPORTATION

To get to Ko Phi Phi Don, go through either **Ko Lanta, Krabi,** or **Phuket.** Ferries depart regularly from Ko Phi Phi to the above destinations, except during the low season, when ferry service may be irregular as rough seas can make travel dangerous. From **Ton Sai Pier,** boats head to: **Ko Lanta** (2hr.; 11:30am, 2pm; 200฿); **Krabi** (1½hr.; 9am, 1:30pm; 200฿); **Phuket** (1½hr.; 9am, 2:30pm; 250฿). Boats to **Ko Phi Phi Ley** depart from the pier or can be hired independently from Ao Thon Sai travel agencies. Hire **longtail boats** for more remote beaches.

ORIENTATION AND PRACTICAL INFORMATION

Shaped like a lop-sided dumbbell, Ko Phi Phi is small, without roads, and devoid of vehicular traffic. It's easy to walk the entire island, save the parts that consist of high cliffs. The main port is pretty **Ao Thon Sai Bay,** nestled in the narrow part of the island, where travelers come to check email, shop, eat, make travel plans and party until morning. On the other side of the island, beautiful **Ao Lo Dalam** has several bungalows. Smaller, less developed beaches ring the island's outer peninsulas, the most popular of which is **Hat Yao (Long Beach),** east of Ao Thon Sai. The more rugged interior affords stellar views of the bays and surrounding islands.

Travel Agencies: The **TAT** office in Krabi serves Ko Phi Phi (see p. 870). Ao Thon Sai **travel agencies** arrange trips to Ko Phi Phi Ley and boat/train/bus combos to Bangkok and Malaysia. **Maya Tour & Travel** (☎612 403), in Ao Thon Sai, is helpful and offers many tours. From the pier, take a right; it's 20m on the right.

Currency Exchange: For best rates, get cash before heading to Ko Phi Phi. The **Siam Commercial Bank** in Ao Thon Sai exchanges cash and gives credit card advances. Open daily 9:30am-7:30pm. Travel agents have poor rates.

Emergency: ☎191. **Tourist Police (Bangkok):** ☎1155.

Tourist Police (local): Off the pier in Ao Thon Sai. Provides some tourist information. English spoken. Erratic hours. **Police booth** past the Chao Khao Lodge in Ao Thon Sai.

Medical Services: Pi Pi Hospital (☎622 151), in Ao Thon Sai, to the left of the pier. Basic medical services. Some English spoken. Open daily 8:30am-noon and 1-4:30pm.

Telephones: Private travel agencies in Ao Thon Sai offer expensive connections. Unless it's an emergency, wait until you get back onto the mainland.

Internet Access: All over Ao Thon Sai. Type quickly–it's expensive. 3฿ per min.

THAILAND

ACCOMMODATIONS

Ko Phi Phi's bungalows are plentiful but fluctuate in price and quality between high and low seasons. Generally, the island is more expensive than its neighbors, but rooms are cheaper around the pier and isolated beaches. The following accommodations are listed by beach.

AO LO DALAM AND AO THON SAI. The best place for thrifty travelers is Ao Thon Sai's pier area, where loads of fly-by-night travel agencies offer cheap accommodations. The bungalows are far from the beach but conveniently located to shops and restaurants. **Chong Khao Lodge ❸**, between the pier and Ao Lo Dalam Bay, is not highly recommended, but it's one of the cheapest places on the island—hence, a backpacker favorite. Plain plywood bungalows have crusty squat toilets and spigots are scattered amidst litter and clucking chickens. (Singles 200฿; doubles 300-400฿.) **Charlie Beach Resort ❺** has clean bungalows on a beachfront property. It has a lively **restaurant ❷** attached. Bungalows in the back are a bit noisier (600-1000฿). Across from Ao Thon Sai, Ao Lo Dalam's handsome crescent-shaped bay is good for swimming and sunbathing.

HAT HIN KOHN AND LAEM HIM. Just southeast of Ao Thon Sai, a path by a rocky hill leads to flat Hat Hin Kohn, a long stretch of sand generously sprinkled with bungalows. **Andaman Guest House ❺** has rows of new rooms that are plain but fairly clean. (Singles and doubles 500-600฿.) The staff are eager to attract backpackers to the similarly named but more professional **Andaman Resort ❺** at the end of the beach. Clean, white bungalows occupy a quiet spot by the island's sole primary school. (Singles and doubles 850฿.) Heading right from the pier next to the coast takes you along a paved walkway and around a small promontory known as Laem Him (still part of Ao Thon Sai). Two bungalow operations, inland from the path after the mosque, are great values. **Gypsy 1 ❸**, about 100m from the shore, has clean and basic bungalows with baths at rock-bottom prices by Phi Phi standards. (☎01 229 1674. Bungalows 350-600฿ depending on season.)

MA PRAO AND HAT YAO (LONG BEACH). The best option in the area is actually just before Long Beach on a lush promontory called Ma Prao. The aptly named **Ma Prao Bungalows ❸** has charming wood and bamboo huts secluded against the hill and only a stone's throw from the water. The restaurant has excellent ambience, music, drink, and food. (☎622 486. Basic bungalows 300฿, with amenities up to 800฿.) Just over the hill, past Ma Prao, is Hat Yao, known commonly as Long Beach. It has Ko Phi Phi's best sand and swimming, but staying here can be problematic for late-night partiers. It's possible to walk here from Ao

Thon Sai by continuing past Hat Kin Kohn through some rocky jungle, but the 30-45min. walk is a bit tedious. Longtail boats (40฿) from Ao Thon Sai's pier are more convenient. The most wallet-friendly accommodation is the friendly, expat-run **Long Beach Resort ❷.** It little more than four walls surrounding a bed, but at least it's with a smile. (☎612 217. Singles and doubles 150-350฿.)

FOOD AND NIGHTLIFE

Ko Phi Phi contains an outstanding range of international cuisine as a result of its healthy expat population, many of whom have started businesses on the island. The cream of the crop is **Cosmo Resto ❸,** an Italian restaurant with exceptional handmade pasta. Run by an Italian expat, the restaurant is only open for dinner and closes on random days of the week for preparation. When it's open, the tiny, unassuming place is one of Thailand's best restaurants. (No phone. Open for dinner roughly 5 days per week.) The **Lemongrass Restaurant ❷,** off the main drag in Ao Thon Sai, is one of the only places to get good Thai food. (Rice dishes 60฿; curries 70-80฿. Open daily 9am-11pm.) There are plenty of pancake stalls, bakeries, and excellent seafood restaurants in Ao Thon Sai. Take your pick.

By night, Ao Thon Sai transforms into a surprising hotbed of nightlife activity. **Jordan's Irish Bar** denies anything Irish in favor of any music that will make *farang* wave their hands in the air and dance like they just don't care. The self-explanatory **Rolling Stoned Bar** blasts chill music and good times until sunrise. The similarly themed **Reggae Bar** has a large dance floor and a Thai boxing ring featuring nightly matches (starting around 10pm). **Carlito's Bar,** on the walkway toward Long Beach, has live entertainment. Look for drink specials at all of the above bars.

WATER SPORTS

Ko Phi Phi's waters are so clear you almost don't need to bother with a mask to check out the marine life. **Bamboo Island** and **Mosquito Island** are famous dive sites. There are many dive shops and tour agents eager—extremely eager—to serve you. Dive courses here generally cost 10,000฿ for a PADI certification course (far more expensive than in Ko Tao). **Visa Diving Center** is one of the best. In addition to diving, snorkeling is also outstanding and far cheaper (usually 500฿ for a daytrip with lunch and gear included). **Maya Tour & Travel** (see **Travel Agenices,** p. 867) runs quality half- and full-day tours.

DAYTRIP FROM KO PHI PHI: KO PHI PHI LEY

Struggling to cope with the post-Hollywood tourist demand, the island has become the battleground between corporate filmmakers and environmental groups, which claim that the island's delicate environment has been irreversibly damaged by the planting of coconut palms and beach digging that occurred during filming of *The Beach.* Politics aside, the real reason to visit the island is for the natural beauty that made it such a spectacular backdrop in the first place. Getting to Ko Phi Phi Ley from Ko Phi Phi Don usually involves some sort of organized tour. Plenty of Ao Thon Sai agencies arrange daytrips to the island, but individual longtail boat tours around the island cost less. While the limestone cliffs that practically enclose white-sand Ao Maya make it stunning, the row of longtails and wandering tourists mean that it hardly lives up to expectations created by images from the film. Ao Maya and Ko Phi Phi Ley are really just more stops on any snorkeling or day tour from Ko Phi Phi Don and are nothing to get too excited about.

KRABI

☎075

The word is out about Krabi, in particular about the nearby beaches of Hat Rai Lay and Ao Nang. The town of Krabi is little more than a necessary transit point, but it has a mellow vibe all its own, and the emergence of excellent budget accommodations more than redeems overnight stays.

THE VIEW FROM ABOVE

The lowdown: The new budget hotspot.
Gateway cities: Ko Lanta, Phuket Town, Trang.
Beaches: Hat Phra Nang, Hat Rai Lay, Ao Nang.
Highlights: Rai Lay's limestone cliffs, Phra Nang's Princess Cave.

TRANSPORTATION

Buses: The **bus station** (☎611 804) is 5km outside town. Red *songthaew* run between the bus station and town (every 15min., 7฿). Buses to: **Bangkok** (12hr., 4 per day 7am-7pm, 486-710฿); **Hat Yai** (5hr., every hr. 9am-3:20pm, 173฿); **Phuket** (5hr., every hr. 9am-5pm, 117฿); **Satun** (5hr., 11am and 1pm, A/C 175฿); **Surat Thani** (4½hr., every hr. 9:30am-1:30pm, 80฿; A/C 3½hr.; 7, 8, 9, 11:40am, 1pm; 120฿); **Trang** (2½hr., every 2hr. 9am-5pm, 90฿). Private travel agents operate **A/C minivans** to various towns in Thailand and Malaysia.

Ferries: Longtail boats leave from **Chao Fah Pier** on Kongka Rd. for **Hat Rai Lay** (30min., 8am-5pm, 70฿). From the same pier, **express boats** go to **Ko Lanta** (2½hr.; 10:30am, 1:30pm; 200฿) and **Ko Phi Phi** (1½hr.; 10:30am, 2:30pm; 200฿). Service is irregular during low season. Tourist offices have up-to-date boat schedules.

Local Transportation: Songthaew waiting opposite the City Hotel by the market go to **Ao Nang** (20฿, 30฿ after 6pm); the **Shell Cemetery** (16-20฿); **Wat Tham Sua** (20฿); and other places near Krabi.

ORIENTATION AND PRACTICAL INFORMATION

Central Krabi is easily navigable by foot. **Utarakit Rd.,** the city's main street, runs parallel to the **Krabi River** and is home to communications and tourist services. Parallel and one block over, **Maharat Rd.** has shops and cheap eateries. Boats to Hat Rai Lay, Ko Phi Phi, and Ko Lanta leave from **Chao Fah Pier** on **Kongka Rd.,** which branches off Utarakit Rd. and runs along the river.

Tourist Offices: TAT (☎612 740), on Utarakit Rd. Good maps. Open daily 8:30am-4:30pm.

Tours: For a small town, Krabi has an obscene number of travel agencies. For boat tickets, go to **PP Family** on Chao Fah Pier (☎612 463). Open daily 7:30am-9pm.

Currency Exchange: Several banks line Utarakit Rd including **Bangkok Bank,** 147 Utarakit. Open M-F 8:30am-3:30pm.

Markets: A large market sets up across from the City Hotel on Sukhon Rd.

Emergency: ☎191. **Tourist Police (Bangkok):** ☎1155.

Police: ☎637 208. 500m past the post office. Little English spoken.

Medical Services: The **Town Hospital** (☎611 227), on Utarakit Rd., 2km from town. Some English spoken. No credit cards. **Open 24hr.**

Internet Access: All along Utarakit Rd. in cafes and guest houses. 1฿ per min.

Post Office: 190 Utarakit Rd. (☎611 497), on top of the hill on the left. *Poste Restante.* Open M-F 8:30am-4:30pm, Sa 9am-noon. **Postal code:** 81000.

ACCOMMODATIONS

Krabi has a good selection of budget accommodations, most of which lie one block from the pier along **Utarakit Rd.** Prices below represent high season rates; in the low season rates may be 100-200฿ cheaper.

Chan-Cha-Lay Guest House, 55 Utarakit Rd. (☎620 952), on the slope uphill. The recently opened guest house is already one of the hippest digs in town, with ultra-clean, bright rooms with showers. Popular restaurant and super-friendly staff. Laundry. Internet. Singles and doubles 200฿; twins 250฿. Reservations recommended. ❸

Grand Tower Hotel, 9 Chao Fah Rd. (☎621 456), at the intersection with Utarakit Rd. Multi-storied, it's not your typical guest house, but it's popular with those waiting for the next ferry. Plain, cheap rooms with double mattresses. International phones, Internet, and fax. Singles and doubles 150฿, with bath 300฿, with A/C 500฿; twins with bath 400฿, with A/C 700฿. ❷

City Hotel, 15/2-3 Sukhon Rd. (☎621 280), between Utarakit and Maharat Rd. in the heart of downtown. Off the main backpacker drag. Spacious, well-furnished rooms, all with cable TV and phone. Singles and doubles with fan 400฿, with A/C 550-650฿. ❹

Siboya Guest House, 69 Utarakit Rd. (☎623 561). Modestly sized, cheap rooms are cozy with funky, fresh decor. Singles and doubles 120-150฿. ❷

THAILAND

FOOD

There are two **night markets** ❶, one opposite the City Hotel (until 9pm) and one by the pier. Several *farang*-friendly restaurants and cheap food stalls cluster on **Kongka Rd.,** just north of the pier. For a memorable experience, try **Ruenmai Thai** ❷ on Maharat Rd., 2km from town past the hospital (motorcycle taxi 30฿). This huge outdoor restaurant has tables amidst jungle-like vegetation. For 60฿, try the blissful coconut cream prawn soup with *pak mieng* or edible ferns with fish. (Open daily 10am-10pm.) **Kwan Restaurant** ❷, 30 Kongkha Rd., serves affordable Thai and Western meals and shakes. (Open daily 7:30am-5pm, until 9pm in high season.) Hang out with locals at the **Muslim Restaurant** ❶, 110 Praksa-Uthit Rd., a morning meeting spot for *roti* (10฿) and coffee (10฿).

SIGHTS

Krabi's most impressive sight is **Wat Tham Sua,** 8km outside town. A working monastery of monks, nuns, and tourists, the wat is best known for its **Tiger Cave.** Legend has it that a large tiger once lived here, and its footsteps adorn the wat's entrance (donation requested). Outside, stairs by the rear of the monastery lead 30-45min. up the mountain to a pair of **Buddha's footprints.** *Songthaew* (15min., 10฿) from the Sukhon Rd. market drop you off at an access road 2km from the wat. Otherwise, walk or take a motorcycle taxi (5min., 10฿) to the entrance.

NEAR KRABI

The beaches near Krabi are some of Thailand's most popular, so if you're planning on staying at Ao Nang or Hat Rai Lay, it's best to bypass Krabi and head straight for the sand. A regional festival in November celebrates the coming of a prosperous tourist season. Still, a supreme mellowness prevails.

HAT RAI LAY AND HAT PHRA NANG ☎075

With spectacular limestone cliffs dropping onto sand beaches and luminous, turquoise waters, Hat Rai Lay has become a haven for both climbers and beach lovers. It has developed into a climbing mecca, especially for beginners; climbing schools are opening all over the beach. For those who prefer their feet on the ground, Hat Rai Lay also offers hiking trails, a mellow nightlife, and pretty beaches, while Hat Phra Nang's caves provide hours of exploring.

The Rai Lay beaches and environs have become the rock climbing capital of Southeast Asia. Prices are the same everywhere. **Krabi Rock Climbing,** on Hat Rai Lay East is well-known for its friendly staff. (☎676 0642. Half-day course 800฿, 1-day course 1800฿, 3-day course 5000฿.) **Hot Rock Climbing** (☎01 677 3727), next to CoCo Restaurant on Hat Rai Lay East, is also popular. Adventures closer to sea level await you on Hat Phra Nang. Extending past the water, stalagmites protect **Princess Cave,** which can be explored with a flashlight. About halfway down the dirt path to Hat Phra Nang from Hat Rai Lay East, another dirt path leads to a few mountain viewpoints and a lagoon best visited at high tide. Closer to Hat Rai Lay East beach, a hidden path leads to the popular **Diamond Cave,** whose walls sparkle with the precious stones. Nights on Hat Rai Lay bring together opposite tourist factions: beach bums and hard-core climbing/hiking/diving types. Everyone achieves equal party status under the moon, relaxing at **Yaya's Bar, Last Bar,** or the **beachfront,** where fire dancers sometimes light up the beach to pulsing music.

Hat Rai Lay is actually two beaches, **Hat Rai Lay East** and **Hat Rai Lay West.** The only way to get to Hat Rai Lay is by **longtail boat** docking at Hat Rai Lay East from Ao Nang (50฿) or Krabi (70฿). This side of the peninsula has a few accommodations, climbing schools, mangrove trees, and Hat Rai Lay East and **Hat Phra Nang.** To get to Hat Phra Nang from Hat Rai Lay East, with your back to the boats, turn left and walk to the end of the beach; a dirt path to your right snakes to the limestone cliffs and crystal waters of Hat Phra Nang.

Finding good deals on Hat Rai Lay can be quite difficult; the prices listed reflect high season (Nov.-May) rates. **Ya-Ya Bungalow** (☎622 593), the most popular among budget travelers, has the best off-beach location and a lively restaurant. On the northern end of Hat Rai Lay East, **Viewpoint Bungalow ❹** has clean, modern bungalows and the only Internet access on the beach. (☎622 588. Singles with bath 400฿; doubles with bath 500-800฿.) **Diamond Bungalow ❸** has the cheapest accommodations on the island. (Singles and doubles 350฿, with bath 500฿, with fan 700฿, with A/C 900-1200฿.) Hat Rai Lay West has upscale accommodations. **Rai Lay Village Resort ❺** has fancy, posh bungalows with nicer baths and landscaping. (☎622 578. Bungalows 1200-2500฿.) After a hard day of climbing, many travelers flock to **CoCo Restaurant ❷** on the northern part of Hat Rai Lay East for tasty Thai dishes, including chicken wrapped in steamed leaves (60฿). **Cholay Pancakes ❶,** in a booth outside Ya-Ya Bungalow, serves delicious *roti* for 15-30฿. (Open daily 9am-midnight.)

AO NANG

Ao Nang's accessibility by car gives it a completely different atmosphere from either secluded Rai Lay or Phang-Nga. With brightly colored shops and beachfront hotels, it has a holiday feel. The bustle dies out past the Phra Nang Inn. From here, you can walk down a dirt road into forested seclusion. Alternatively, rent a bike and escape through the surrounding rice paddies and villages. On the road that runs past the beach, there are **moneychangers,** a **minimarket,** restaurants, and **tour offices.** For **police,** dial ☎611 222 (**emergency** ☎191, **Bangkok tourist police** ☎1155). White **songthaew** from Krabi leave from Pattana Rd. opposite the New Hotel (every 15min. or when full, 20฿) to ply the route to Ao Nang and Hat Noppharat Thara. **Sea Canoe Krabi** (☎612 740), near Gift's Bungalows, offers half-day (500-800฿) and full-day (800-1200฿) self-paddled trips along the coast and rental equipment. A guided trip, including meals, fruit, and water costs 1200-1600฿. Rent **mountain bikes** (30฿ per hr.) at **Ao Nang Adventure Travel and Tour** on the corner before the main shops coming from Krabi. Ask for a map. **Nosy Parker's Elephant Trekking and River Camp** (☎637 464) offers elephant treks (700฿) and half-day tours (1600฿).

Blue Bayou ❸, in the quiet outskirts of town, has kayak rentals (200฿ per 2hr.) and a volleyball court. The **restaurant ❸** serves Thai and Western cuisine. (☎637 148. Single and double bungalows in high season with fan 350-500฿, with A/C 750฿; in low season 200-400฿/500฿.) If you happen to hit Ao Nang in the low season, fabulous rates abound. One such steal is **For You House ❺,** 245/11-12 Moo 2, which has hotel-style rooms with A/C, minibar, satellite TV, and hot showers. Get off the *songthaew* at Henry's Collection, and walk behind it. (☎637. High season 600฿, low season 300฿.) Other cheap places are in the same soi as For You. The ideally situated **Poda Restaurant ❸,** in Felix Phra Nang Inn, in the circular building, is an alternative to bungalow basics. The green curry soup with shrimp is exceptional. (Open daily 7am-10pm.) **Azzurra Ristorante-Pizzeria ❸** cooks homemade pasta, fresh bread, and focaccia for 80฿. (Open daily 7am-11pm.)

THAILAND

KHLONG THOM

The **Khao Nawe Choochee Lowland Forest** is one of the last remaining forests of its kind in Thailand. Among the 290-plus bird species that nest in the forest is *Pitta gurneyi*, a brightly colored, ground-dwelling bird of which only 150 remain. The **Thung Tieo Nature Trail,** a 2.7km path, eases through some of Thailand's most lush and undisturbed slices of nature. Bring your swimming gear and hop into the natural pool or hot spring for relaxation. To get to the trail, motorbike from Krabi or take a *songthaew* to **Khlong Thom. Mr. Koyou** at the **Krabi Bird Club,** 24 Phetkasem Rd., will haul tourists around in his pickup truck (300฿). Contact him by calling the park's tourist office (☎622 124); TAT officials can also track him down. If hiring a motorcycle taxi from Khlong Thom (100฿), arrange return transport.

KO LANTA YAI

Ko Lanta Yai is an up-and-coming island on the backpacker trail. Because the island's industry has yet to be completely shelved in favor of tourism, there's a local flavor here that is lacking in tourist hotspots like Ko Samui. But it's not a rugged or particularly undeveloped island, with boats stopping regularly from Krabi at Ko Lanta Yai's **Ban Sala Dan Pier** (2½hr.; 10:30am, 1:30pm, return 8am; 150฿) at the northern tip of the island. Boats also leave from Ko Phi Phi for Ko Lanta (1½hr., 10am-1pm, 150฿). Otherwise, minivans depart year-round from Krabi and connect via ferry to Ko Lanta (2hr.; 11am, 1, 4pm; 150฿). **Ban Sala Dan** is the island's largest town, with plenty of tour operators, a police booth, a post office, Internet cafes, banks, a health center, and other conveniences.

Around the corner from Ban Sala Dan is Ko Lanta Yai's main sandy drag, **Hat Klong Dao,** a 2km beach sprinkled with quality resorts. **Golden Bay Cottages ❺** offers comfortable, spacious accommodations. (High season cottages with fan 800฿, with A/C 1500฿; in low season 100฿/300-600฿.) Klong Dao has decent corals at its north end. There are eight other beaches on the island, including the beautiful **Nin** and **Kanthiang** beaches for scenery and **Hin** beach for snorkeling. There is excellent **diving** and **snorkeling** at the offshore islands. In the interior of Ko Lanta Yai, there are a few outstanding daytrips, most notably the **Tham Mai Ka** caves. You can also see waterfalls and go on elephant treks. Two hours by boat from Krabi, Ko Lanta is actually closer to Trang. Low season makes the island a ghost town, ideal for those seeking cheap solitude. **Klong Dao Beach** and **Long Beach** are the main beaches in the north; **Kantiang Bay** and **Klong Jak Bay** greet travelers headed south.

TRANG

☎075

Trang has been riding the highway (Hwy. 4, that is) of prosperity for 30 years. Though the provincial capital itself is hardly worth writing home about, the surrounding areas are full of national-park beaches and a formidable collection of small islands, all undisturbed by the brazen bandits of large-scale development. Off the usual circuit, Trang is for travelers seeking relief from *farang*-heavy traffic and a chance to explore undeveloped areas.

TRANSPORTATION

Flights: Trang Airport (☎210 804), on Trang-Palian Rd., 7km south of the city. Take Trang Travel's airport vans (30฿) or a tuk-tuk (50฿) into town. **Thai Airways,** 199/2 Visetkul Rd. (☎218 066). Turn right at the clock tower onto Visetkul Rd.; it's several blocks down on the left, just past Soi 5. Open daily 8am-noon and 1-4:30pm. Daily flights to **Bangkok** (9:15pm, additional flights F-Su 6pm; 2575฿).

Trains: Railway station (☎218 012), at the west end of Phraram 6 Rd. Fares listed are 2nd-class express. Trains to: **Bangkok** (16hr.; sleeper 2:30, 5:20pm; 970฿) via **Chumphon** (7hr., 571฿) and **Surat Thani** (5hr., 201฿).

Buses: Bus station (☎215 718), on Huay Yod Rd., north of downtown. Check with TAT for buses that leave from other parts of city. Buses to: **Bangkok** (10hr., 4:30pm, 565฿); **minibuses** to **Hat Yai** (every 30min. 6am-6pm; 70฿, with A/C 99฿); **Krabi** (2hr., every hr. 7am-6pm, 90฿); **Phang-Nga** (4hr., every hr. 7am-6pm, 139฿); **Phuket** (5hr., every hr. 7am-6pm, 189฿); **Satun** (3hr.; 1:30, 3:30pm; 101฿); **Surat Thani** (3hr., every hr. 9:30am-5pm, 125฿; leaves from train station).

Local Transportation: Tuk-tuks within the city run 15฿. **Taxis** (15฿) and **minivans** (10฿) leave when full from different parts of town (every 20min. 5am-7pm). For vans to **Kantang Pier,** go down Phraram 6 Rd. by the train station, and turn right on Kantang Rd.; vans line up on the right (15-20฿). Vans to **Hat Tao Mai, Hat Yong Ling,** and **Hat Pakmeng** leave from Tha Klang Rd., also by the train station (every hr. 7am-5pm, 50฿).

ORIENTATION AND PRACTICAL INFORMATION

Buses arrive at the **bus station** near the intersection of **Ploenpitak Rd.** and **Huay Yod Rd.,** a 20min. walk north of town or 5min. by motorcycle taxi or tuk-tuk (both 20฿). The **railway station** sits at the west end of **Phraram 6 Rd.,** a large hotel-lined avenue with the **TAT office,** landmark **clock tower,** and most other tourist services, including banks, Internet cafes, and travel agencies. North of Phraram 6 Rd., **Ratchadamnoen Rd.** (which becomes **Pattalung Rd.**) winds roughly parallel to the main day market and connects to Phraram 6 Rd. by Kantang Rd. to the west and Visetkul Rd. to the east by the clock tower.

Tourist Office: TAT (☎/fax 215 580), next to the Trang Hotel on Phraram 6 Rd. Very helpful staff and free maps. Open daily 8am-5pm. Private travel agencies offering organized tours and transport line Phraram 6 Rd.

Currency Exchange: Bangkok Bank, 2 Phraram 6 Rd. (☎218 203), 1 block from the train station on the right. **24hr. ATM.** Open M-F 8:30am-3:30pm.

Markets: A **night market** is outside the Diamond Department Store near the train station; another, bigger one is at the intersection of Visetkul and Phraram 6 Rd.

Emergency: ☎191. **Tourist Police (Bangkok):** ☎1155.

Police: 6 Pattalung Rd. (☎211 311). Some English spoken. **Open 24hr.**

Medical Services: Wattanapat Hospital, 247 Pattalung Rd. (☎218 585), at the intersection with Ploenpitak Rd., northeast of clock tower. **Open 24hr.**

Internet Access: All over Phraram 6 Rd. 30฿ per hr.

Post Offices: GPO (☎218 521), at the bend on Jermpanya Rd., which branches north from Phraram 6 Rd. 20min. walk from train station. *Poste Restante.* **International phones.** Open M-F 8:30am-3:30pm. **Branch** on Phraram 6 Rd., 1 block from train station. Open M-F 8:30am-4:30pm, Sa-Su 9am-noon. **Postal code:** 92000.

ACCOMMODATIONS AND FOOD

Trang's first guest house, **Yamawa Bed and Breakfast ❸,** 94 Visetkul Rd., has ten carefully decorated rooms. A rooftop bar is under construction, but there are TVs, reading rooms, a terrace, Internet, and a massage parlor. (☎75 216 617; www.trang-yamawa.com. 200฿ per person.) Five blocks from the train station on the left, **Koh Teng Hotel ❸** has recently added ten reasonably priced rooms complete with satellite TV. (☎218 148. Singles and doubles 180฿.) **Queen Hotel ❸** has standard, clean rooms. (☎218 229; fax 210 415. Singles 180฿, with A/C 280฿.)

Trang's cuisine has a distinct Chinese flavor. The town has two **night markets ❶,** a smaller one next to Diamond Department Store by the train station, and a larger one down Visetkul Rd. from the Phraram 6 Rd. intersection. (Both open daily 6-10pm.) There's also an expansive **day market ❷** by the train station with fresh produce. Nearby, **Sin O Cha ❷** has good service and reasonably priced breakfasts, pastries, and delicious cuisine. **Kao Tom Pui ❸,** 111 Tarad Rd., halfway up Phraram Rd from the train station, on the right, is an open restaurant with excellent Thai fare. (Open daily 5pm-5am.)

ENTERTAINMENT

Trang's nightlife doesn't rival that of Phuket or Ko Phi Phi but offers a different kind of fun—the type you'll still remember the next morning. In the morning on Phraram 6 Rd., traders sell colorful **fighting fish.** Makeshift **cockfighting** arenas set up below stilt houses, and **bullfights** are staged once or twice a year (tickets from 100฿). Direct tuk-tuk drivers to Sanam Wuah Chon (10฿) near the bullfight field. The Trang Chamber of Commerce organizes events, like the **Cake Festival** (Aug.) and **Barbecue Festival** (Sept.), which promote Trang's famed dessert and pork.

NEAR TRANG

Trang's surrounding areas offer a bevy of attractions, from caves to natural ocean-side Edens, most of them overlooked by travelers making a beeline from Surat Thani to Ko Phi Phi, Phuket, or Malaysia. Expect few travelers in even relatively populated places like **Ko Mook** and **Pakmeng** and only a smattering of locals on isolated **Hat Yong Ling.** Most towns are accessible from Trang by minivans, which depart from various points around town. **Boats** to islands near Pakmeng, such as **Ko Hai** and Ko Mook, leave from **Pakmeng Pier** (100-300฿). Boats to **Ko Sukorn** leave from the pier at Tasae Cape in southern Trang Province.

HAT YONG LING. Hat Yong Ling National Park has two coves sheltered by wild orchid-covered rocky mountains. Trek through a lush patch of tropical forest and a bat cave to reach one of the best sand-and-sea combos around. Spelunkers should bring flashlights. Minibuses (50฿) leave every hour or when full from the station by the beach. Hat Yong Ling's **National Park Office** also accommodates its distant neighbor **Hat Jao Mai.** (☎210 099. Open M-F 9am-5pm.)

HAT PAKMENG. Busier Hat Pakmeng is the only mainland beach with a significant commercial presence. This beach is long but shallow, though several picturesque limestone formations dot the horizon. Minivans (45min., every hr., 50฿) from Trang will take you to the beach on the popular **Pakmeng Resort ❹**, farther south, which has tidy bungalows and private baths. (☎210 321. Singles and doubles 400฿, with A/C 750-800฿.) To return to **Trang,** flag down a white van from the main road (roughly every hr.).

KO MOOK. Easily accessible from Pakmeng Pier, Ko Mook is the most popular choice among European budgeteers, and with four resorts, it's the most developed of the Trang Province islands. There is also a large Muslim community in the area. **Emerald Cave,** so named for its tinted waters, is a spectacular sight. To reach the cliff-surrounded lagoon at the center, visitors must swim. The lovelier and cheaper western side of the island boasts a sweet white-sand beach. Of the island's four resorts, **Had Farung Bungalows ❸** is the least expensive (bungalows 200฿, with bath 300฿), and **Sawatdee Resort ❸** has a highly recommended restaurant (bungalows 300฿). To get to Ko Mook, take a minivan to **Pakmeng Pier** (1hr., 50฿) and hop on a boat to the island (1hr.; 11am; 400฿, alone 600฿).

KO HAI (KO NGAI). With white-sand beaches and three pricey resorts, teardrop-shaped Ko Hai (sometimes spelled "Ko Ngai") is a true tropical paradise and an excellent dive and snorkeling spot. **Koh Ngai Villa ❹** has the cheapest rooms and arranges transport to and from the island. (☎210 496. Bungalows with fan 400-700฿, depending on season.) More upscale **Koh Ngai Resort ❺** has a diving center. (☎210 317. Bungalows 600-780฿.)

KO KRADAN. Although it's beautifully pristine, Ko Kradan, under the protection of the **Hat Jao Mai National Park,** contains only one high-end resort, which does not do justice to the island. At **Ko Kradan Paradise Beach ❺,** they know you're a hostage, so the food is as expensive as the rooms; bring your own from the mainland. (☎211 391. Bungalows from 600฿.)

HAT YAI ☎074

Crowded and noisy Hat Yai is southern Thailand's transportation, commerce, and prostitution center. Shopping conquers all in this metropolitan arena, since almost everything—pirated Robbie Williams CDs, pet fish, women—is cheaper here than in Singapore or Malaysia. Despite the cosmopolitan veneer, it is a snorkeling hotspot. Travelers would do well to bypass the town, although there are quality accommodations if a stay is essential.

TRANSPORTATION

Flights: Airport (☎251 007), 13km west of Hat Yai. **Thai Airways,** 166/4 Niphat Uthit 2 Rd. (☎233 433). Open M-Sa 8am-5pm, Su 9am-4pm. Flights to: **Bangkok** (1½hr., 6 per day, 2885฿); **Kuala Lampur, Malaysia** (2hr.; F, Su 2:25pm; 9890฿); **Phuket** (45min., 11:15am, 1180฿); **Singapore** (2½hr., 1:10pm, 5760฿).

Trains: Railway station (☎243 705), at the west end of Thamnoon Vithi Rd. Trains to: **Bangkok** (16hr.; 5 per day 2:45-6:10pm; 3rd-class 275฿, sleeper 730-1200฿); **Butterworth, Malaysia** (5½hr., 7:40am, 233฿); **Sungai Kolok** (3½-4½hr.; 4 per day 6:30am-12:15pm; 3rd-class 60฿, 1st-class 159฿); **Surat Thani** (4-5hr., 5 per day, 215฿).

Buses: Bus station (☎232 404), on Ranchanawanit Rd., in the southeast corner of town. Buses also stop at the market on Phetkasem Rd. 10-15min. after scheduled departure time. Tuk-tuk from town to terminal 10฿. Buses to: **Bangkok** (14hr., 9 per day 7am-7pm, 535-830฿); **Chumphon** (9-10hr.; 7:15, 8:15, 9:30, 10:30am, noon; 162-280฿); **Krabi** (5hr., 11am, 173฿); **Padang Besar, Malaysia** (1½hr., every 10min.

5:45am-7:20pm, 26-36฿); **Phuket** (7hr., 13 per day 5:30am-9:30pm, 150-420฿); **Satun** (2hr., every 15min. 5:20am-5:40pm, 36-65฿); **Sungai Kolok** (4hr., 1:30pm, 148฿); **Surat Thani** (5½hr., 10 per day 5:20am-3pm, 103-160฿).

Local Transportation: Tuk-tuks (10฿ inside town; 20฿ outside) and **motorcycle taxis** (20฿) crisscross downtown.

ORIENTATION AND PRACTICAL INFORMATION

Most travelers arrive at the train station on the west side of town at the intersection of **Rathakarn Rd.** and **Thamnoon Vithi Rd.,** one of the main commercial thoroughfares. Cheap guest houses and tourist services cluster near the train station. Buses enter the city on **Phetkasem Rd.** and drop passengers off in the market area north of downtown. Central Hat Yai is organized by a grid system, marked by **Suphasarnrangsan, Prachathipat,** and Thamnoon Vithi Rd., running eastward from the train station; **Niphat Uthit 1, 2,** and **3 Rd.** intersect them from north to south.

Tourist Office: TAT, 1/1 Soi 2, Niphat Uthit 3 Rd. (☎243 747). Head south on Niphat Uthit 3 Rd. for 15-20min; it's on the left behind the police station. Enthusiastic staff, timetables, and free maps. Open daily 8:30am-4:30pm.

Tours: Ubiquitous on the Niphat Uthit roads. **Cathay Tour,** 93/1 Niphat Uthit 2 Rd. (☎234 535), in the same building as the Cathay Guest House. Specializes in transportation to major Thai and Malaysian tourist destinations. Open daily 7am-8pm.

Immigration Office: ☎233 760. On Phetkasem Rd., west of the train tracks, next to the police station. Open M-F 8:30am-4:30pm.

Currency Exchange: There are banks on every block. **Bangkok Bank,** 39 Niphat Uthit 2 Rd. (☎235 330), near Suphasarnrangsan Rd. Open daily 8:30am-3:30pm.

Markets: Morning market on Niphat Uthit 3 Rd by the clock tower. **Day** and **night markets** between Montri 1 and 2 Rd., off Rathakarn Rd., north of the station.

Emergency: ☎191. **Tourist Police (Bangkok):** ☎1155.

Tourist Police (local): ☎246 733. On Sripoovanart Rd. near its intersection with Niphat Uthit 1 Rd. English spoken. **Open 24hr.**

Pharmacies: Santi Bheasaj, 129/12 Niphat Uthit 3 Rd. (☎246 537).

Medical Services: Hat Yai Public Hospital (☎230 8001), on Rathakarn Rd. The back of the hospital faces the GPO. English spoken. **Open 24hr.** Also **Songkhla Nakarind Hospital** (☎212 070), on Karnchanavanid Rd.

Telephones: Telecommunication Center, 490/1 Phetkasem Rd. (☎231 080), east of the rotary. Open daily 8am-midnight.

Internet Access: Plentiful and cheap in the area near the train station. 20฿ per hr.

Post Offices: GPO (☎243 013), at the corner of Niphat Songkraw 1 Rd. and Soi 4, 500m north of the rotary. *Poste Restante.* **International phone** upstairs. Open M-F 8:30am-4:30pm, Sa-Su 9am-noon. **Postal code:** 90110.

ACCOMMODATIONS AND FOOD

Many of the cheapest hotels in Hat Yai offer sleazy services, often under the guise of "ancient Thai massage." A few blocks from the train station at the corner of Niphat Uthit 2 Rd. and Thamnoon Vithi Rd., **Cathay Guest House** ❶ is reminiscent of a university hostel. (☎243 815. 4-bed dorms 90฿; singles 160฿; doubles 200฿; triples 250฿.) With over 75 rooms, **Kings Hotel** ❹ is remarkably well kept. Rooms come with standard amenities such as TV, A/C, and shower. (☎261 700. Singles 390฿; doubles 490฿; triples 590฿.) Five minutes from the train station, **Ladda Guest**

THAILAND

House ❶, 13-15 Thamnoon Vithi Rd., has a friendly staff who make up for the peeling paint. (☎220 233. Singles 200฿, with A/C 360฿; twins 240฿.)

Muslim and Chinese influences are apparent in Hat Yai's dim sum restaurants and *roti* shops. Near Cathay Guest House on Thamnoon Vithi Rd. is **Shangrila ❶**, respected for its dim sum. (Open daily 6am-3pm.) **Food vendors ❶** set up day and night in the Niphat Uthit Rd. area and near the plaza market and cinema on Phetkasem Rd. For local flavor, try *khanom bueng* (crepes with shredded coconut). **T.S. Vegetarian ❶**, 16 Prachathipat Rd., across from Central Department Store, lets you pick three cooked veggies for your rice. (Dishes 20฿. Open daily 7am-8pm.)

ENTERTAINMENT

Your credit card may collapse from exhaustion on **Phetkasem Rd.** For cheaper, more structured entertainment, check out **Post Laser Disc,** 82-83 Thamnoon Vithi Rd., about two blocks past Niphat Uthit 3 Rd. opposite Indra Hotel. There's live music nightly and a daily happy hour 4-9pm with great drink deals. (☎232 027. 30฿ cover charge for a table upstairs. Schedule on sandwich board outside. Open daily 9am-2am.) **Thai Boxing Stadium** hosts matches one or two weekends a month. (Around 180฿. Tuk-tuk to stadium 20-30฿.) **Bullfights** are staged on most weekend days. A 35m by 15m reclining Buddha rests in **Wat Hat Yai Nai,** 7km west of Hat Yai. (Open daily 8am-5pm; tuk-tuk to wat 10฿ minimum.)

SATUN ☎074

Satun is best known to travelers entering Thailand from Malaysia or passing through Ko Tarutao, the national park off the coast. Since Ko Tarutao is only open from October to May, Satun has little for tourists during the other half of the year. Backpackers sometimes stick around to enjoy Satun's friendly small-town atmosphere, but the town itself has little more than a few open-air bars.

At its southern end, **Satunthanee Rd.** forms a "T" intersection with **Samanthapradit Rd.** South on Satunthanee Rd. before the mosque, **Burivanich Rd.** splits to the right toward the **immigration office.** (☎711 080. Open M-F 8:30am-4:30pm.) Across the road, the **Thai Military Bank** and **Bangkok Bank** both have **24hr. ATMs** (AmEx/Cirrus/MC/V). The **police** are on the corner of Yarttrasawaddee and Satunthanee Rd. (☎711 025. **Emergency:** ☎191. **Open 24hr.**) **Pon Phasaj Pharmacy,** 62 Burivanich Rd., is near the police box. (Open M-Sa 7am-9pm.) **Satun Hospital,** 55/1 Hatthakumsuksa Rd., is on the corner of Yarttrasawaddee Rd. (☎732 460. English spoken. **Open 24hr.**) Overseas calls can be made from the **Telecom Office,** 7 Satun Thanee Rd., at the base of the red tower. (Open M-F 8:30am-4:30pm.) Just east of the intersection of Satunthanee and Samanthapradit Rd. is the **post office.** (*Poste Restante.* Open M-F 8:30am-4:30pm. **Postal code:** 91000.) **Satun Travel and Ferry Service,** 45/8-9 Satunthanee Rd., arranges tours and travel. (☎711 453. Open daily 8am-5pm.)

Non-A/C **orange buses** leave from the school on Satunthanee Rd. for **Hat Yai** (2hr., every hr., 50฿) and from Sulakanukul, Burivanich, or Satunthanee Rd. for **Trang** (3hr., every 30min. 6:30am-5pm, 70฿). For A/C comfort to **Hat Yai,** take a **minivan** from the 7-Eleven on Satunthanee Rd. It also stops across from the Wangmai Hotel, in front of the open-air market (2hr., every 30min. or when full 6am-5pm, 150฿). A daily **ferry** service runs from Tamalang Pier to **Pulau Langkawi** (45min.; 9:30am, 1:30, 4pm; 180฿). In high season, **boats** run from Pak Bara Pier, north of Satun, to **Ko Lipe** (departs 10:30am, returns 3pm; round-trip 440฿) and **Ko Tarutao** (departs 10am, returns 3pm; round-trip 300฿).

The central **Satultanee Hotel ❷,** 90 Satunthanee Rd., has bright rooms with private baths. (Singles with fan 210฿, with A/C 370฿.) Satun's other budget accommodation is the **Rain Tong Hotel ❷,** 4 Samanthapradit Rd. From the Satunthanee

Rd. intersection, turn onto Samanthapradit Rd. and walk toward the river; it's on the left. The old rooms are plain and clean. (☎711 036. Singles and doubles 140฿.)

Satun's Muslim majority sets the tone for the local cuisine. Several breakfast *roti* places serve patrons throughout the day. Both the extensive **day market ❶** on Satunthanee Rd. and the **night market ❶** on Tammango Uthit Rd. whip up cheap meals. (Duck noodle soup 20฿. Both open daily 5pm-midnight.) For a spicy nirvana, ask locals to point you to **Sri Trang ❷,** 127 Satunthanee Rd., which has served curry and rice dishes for as long as anyone can remember. (Open daily 4-9pm.)

KO TARUTAO NATIONAL MARINE PARK

Once a pirate outpost and then an island prison, Ko Tarutao National Marine Park is an archipelago of 51 spectacular islands in the Andaman Sea. Previously only forest department officials lived on mainland Ko Tarutao, but in the summer of 2002, CBS filmed its fifth season of *Survivor* here, bringing intense publicity to this relatively untouched wilderness. Ko Tarutao is open from November to May. The park's main island is **Ko Tarutao,** 56km from Langkawi Island, a major point of entry into Malaysia. The largest of the park islands, covering 151 sq. km, Ko Tarutao was a labor camp for political prisoners during the 1940s. The **park office** (☎729 002) is at the northern tip of Tarutao on Ao Phante Melaka, near the pier and is only open during peak season. The **pier** in Pak Bara (☎074 783 485) provides tourist information only during peak season. The beaches along the west coast provide the best **campsites ❶** (about 10฿ per night). Bring your own tent. Otherwise, Tarutao provides **park housing ❸.** (4-bed rooms 280฿; bungalows with two bedrooms and two baths 400฿; larger cottages with two bedrooms and one bath 600฿.) Make reservations in advance with the National Park Division of the **Royal Forest Department** in Bangkok (☎02 579 0529) or in Pak Bara (☎781 285) before departure.

Ko Tarutao's beaches sprawl on its coral-filled west coast, while farther inland, waterfalls, mountains, caves, and wildlife attract adventurous travelers. From October to January, **sea turtles** paddle ashore to deposit eggs on **Ko Khai** (Egg Island), 15km southwest of Ko Tarutao. A popular way to explore the island is the 2hr. **hiking trail** from Ao Phante Melaka to Ao Talo Wao; it extends south for another 3hr. to Ao Talo U-Dang. For more information on Ko Tarutao, contact **Adang Sea Tour** (☎781 268) in Pak Bara. To get to Ko Tarutao from **Satun,** take a **songthaew** to **La-Ngu,** 60km from Satun (30฿). Here, *songthaew* and **taxis** go to **Pak Bara Pier** (12฿), from which **boats** leave daily for Ko Tarutao (10:30am, 3pm; return 9:30am; round-trip 300฿). Otherwise, charter your own **longtail boat** from the Tarutao pier (from 500฿). From **Hat Yai,** board a **bus** to La-Ngu or go straight to Pak Bara by minivan (2½hr., every 30min. 7am-5pm, 34฿).

SUNGAI KOLOK ☎073

Sungai Kolok is a raucous border town through which Malaysians smuggle booze. Most travelers go straight to the train station without staying at the hotels. Ban Taba, a small town 5km south of Tak Bai, is the preferred border-crossing point. Ferries from Ban Taba (where border hours are the same) to Malaysia cost 15฿.

The **border crossing** (see below) is at the end of **Asia 18 Rd.,** a broad avenue running parallel to the train tracks. Heading north, the **Tourist Information Center** (☎612 126) is in a building right after passport control. (☎612 008. **Bangkok tourist police:** ☎1155. **Open 24hr.**) **Motorcycle taxis** wait just past the TAT (around town 20฿ or RM2). Opposite the train station, **Charoenkhet Rd.** runs perpendicular to Asia 18 Rd. into the heart of Sungai Kolok. The **police station** (☎611 070) is here, opposite the **Narathiwat Immigration Office,** 70 Charoenkhet Rd. (☎611 231; open M-F 8:30am-4:30pm), and **Thai Farmer's Bank,** 1/6 Vorakamin Rd. (☎611 578; **24hr. ATM;** open M-F 8:30am-3:30pm). For **Internet,** try **CS Internet,** 2-4-6-8 Charoenkhet Rd. (☎615 444.

30฿ per hr.) The **post office** is on On Prachawiwat Rd. (☎611 141. *Poste Restante.* Open M-F 8:00am-4:30pm, Sa-Su 9am-noon.) **Postal code:** 96120.

From the **railway station** (☎614 060), on Asia 18 Rd. on the right, trains leave for: **Bangkok** (28hr./21hr.; 11:55am/2:05pm; seats 220-497฿, beds 557-1493฿) via **Chumphon** (12hr./8hr., 150-334฿); **Hat Yai** (3½hr., 82-176฿); and **Surat Thani** (8-9hr., 126-279฿). **Thai Airways,** at 53 Soi 1, Charoenkhet Rd. (☎612 132), arranges transport to **Narathiwat Airport** (8am, 140฿), with daily flights to **Bangkok** (3hr., 10:40am, 2950฿) via **Phuket** (1hr., 1155฿). The **bus office,** 95 Vorakamin Rd. (☎612 045), is six blocks from the intersection with Charoenkhet Rd. **Buses** run to **Bangkok** (19hr.; with A/C 8, 11:30am, 12:30pm; 546-1090฿) via **Surat Thani** (9-10hr., 277฿). Buses also run from here to **Phuket** (11hr.; 6, 8am, 5:30pm; 432฿) via **Trang** (7hr., 261฿) and **Krabi** (9hr., 335฿). Private **A/C minivans** (☎614 350) leave from the office opposite the railway station on Asia 18 Rd. one block west from the intersection with Charoenkhet Rd. for **Hat Yai** (4hr., every hr. 6am-5pm, 150฿).

There is no reason to spend a night in Sungai Kolok unless transportation forces you. **Savoy Hotel ❷,** 34 Charoenkhet Rd., has a Chinese **restaurant ❷.** Its rooms have fans and bearable baths. (☎611 093. Singles with bath 150฿; doubles with bath 170฿. Reception and restaurant both open daily 6am-midnight.) Sungai Kolok's daily **market ❶** spreads out behind Asia 18 Rd. before the sun gets out of bed. At night, **food vendors ❶** along Shern Maroar Rd. sell local specialties. Those who want to sit while they eat can try the vendors along Vorakamin Rd., starting at the Thai Farmers Bank (fried vegetables on rice 20-25฿). **Siam Restaurant ❸,** 2-4 Shern Maroar Rd., cooks up several extravagantly garnished seafood dishes for 50-150฿. (☎611 360. Open daily 10am-3pm and 5-9pm.)

BORDER CROSSING: SUNGAI KOLOK/RANTAU PANJANG

The Thailand/Malaysia border, on Asia 18 Rd. near the Sungai Kolok River, is open daily from 5am to 9pm Thai time (1hr. behind Malaysian time). Those crossing over into Malaysia can take a share-taxi (RM5 per person; price doubles after dark) or bus #29 (RM2.70, every hr. until 6:15pm) from Rantau Panjang to Kota Bharu. Transportation on both sides of the border is most abundant in the morning. Before you cross, go to Thai Farmers Bank to exchange any leftover baht for Malaysian ringgit. Most banks in Kota Bharu are closed on Fridays.

VIETNAM

US$1 = 15,323.00Đ (ĐONG)
CDN$1 = 9604.19Đ
EURO€1 = 15,069.40Đ
UK£1 = 23,983.56Đ
AUS$1 = 8106.63Đ
NZ$1 = 7014.10Đ
ZAR1 = 1459.68Đ

10,000Đ = US$0.65
10,000Đ = CDN$1.04
10,000Đ = EURO€0.66
10,000Đ = UK£0.42
10,000Đ = AUS$1.23
10,000Đ = NZ$1.43
10,000Đ = ZAR6.85

PHONE CODE **Country code:** 84. **International dialing prefix:** 00.

Whether drifting along the slow-moving Mekong or battling the rush of motorbikes in Hanoi, travelers are surrounded by Vietnam's hardworking and friendly people. Vietnam prides itself on its unique heritage and strong survival instinct; after centuries of invasion and forcible influence by the Chinese, French, and Japanese, Vietnamese culture is anything but simple. Vietnamese soil has hosted over a dozen wars. The country's history of struggle against imperialism and desire for independence has created a culture distinct from that of its Southeast Asian neighbors—the nuances can be hard for visitors to grasp. Tourist cafes whisk travelers around on sputtering minibuses, usually providing only spoon-fed doses of local color. A truer taste of contemporary Vietnam hides in alleyway eateries, *bia hơi* stalls, and amid the plastic furniture of streetside cafes. Few experiences rival the spontaneous smile and wave inviting one in for a glass of Bia Hanoi (a local beer) or the sound of the busy street markets coming to life.

FACTS AND FIGURES

Official Name: Socialist Republic of Vietnam.

Government: One-party rule by the Vietnamese Communist Party.

Capital: Hanoi.

Land Area: 329,560 sq. km.

Geography: Borders China, Laos, and Cambodia.

Climate: Rainy (low season) May-Oct., dry (high season) Nov.-Apr.

Official Language: Vietnamese.

Population: 79,939,000.

Major Cities: Đà N{ng, H· Chí Minh City.

Religion: Mahayana Buddhism, Hoa Hao, Cao Đài, Catholicism, Taoism, Islam.

Average Income Per Capita: US$390.

Major Exports: Crude oil, rice, coffee, rubber, tea, garments, shoes.

LIFE AND TIMES

DEMOGRAPHICS

Ethnic Vietnamese (also called **Kinh**) constitute 90% of the population. The **Chinese** (Hoa), concentrated in the urban south, are the largest minority. **Chàm, Khmer,** and other **hill tribes** (generally darker-skinned than Vietnamese) inhabit the northern and central regions. The Vietnam War's death tolls dramatically shifted the country's demographics. Today, over 60% of the population is under the age of 25.

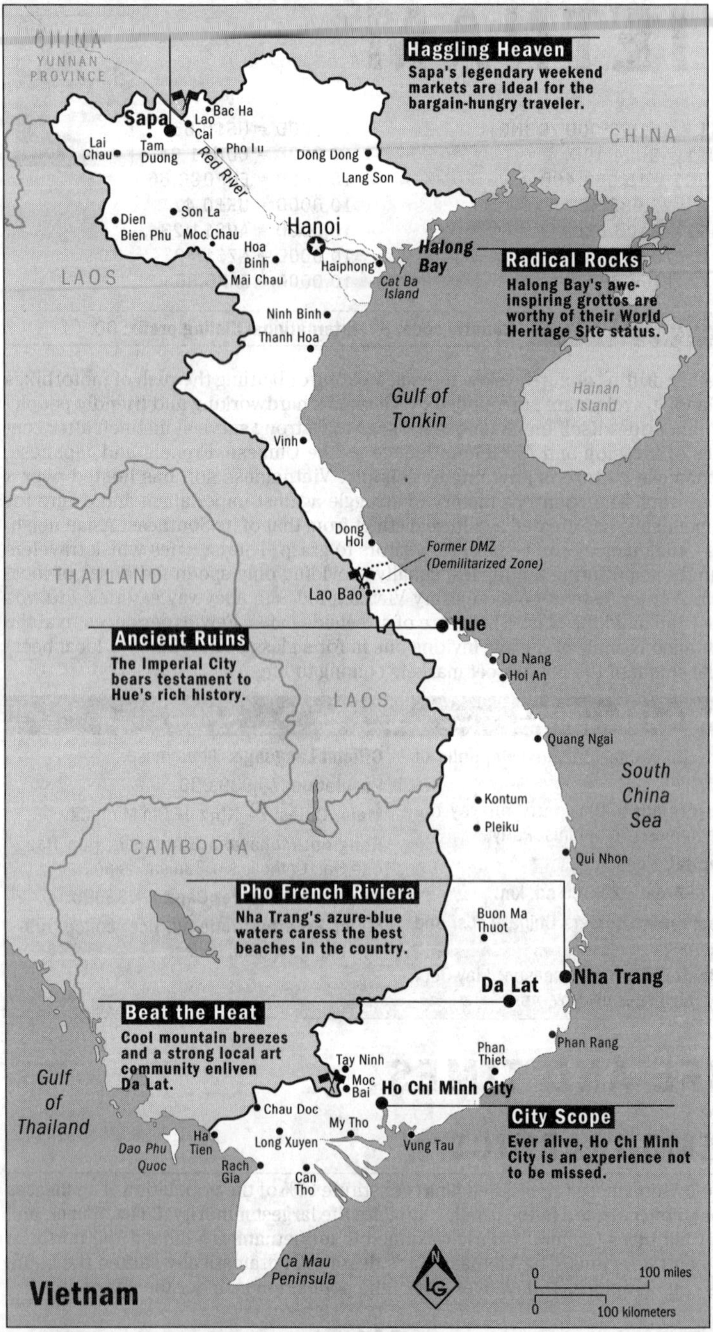
CHINA
YUNNAN PROVINCE
Haggling Heaven
Sapa's legendary weekend markets are ideal for the bargain-hungry traveler.
Sapa
Lao Cai
Bac Ha
Lai Chau
Tam Duong
Pho Lu
Red River
Dong Dong
Lang Son
CHINA
Dien Bien Phu
Son La
Moc Chau
Hanoi
Hoa Binh
Mai Chau
Haiphong
Cat Ba Island
Halong Bay
Radical Rocks
Halong Bay's awe-inspiring grottos are worthy of their World Heritage Site status.
LAOS
Ninh Binh
Thanh Hoa
Gulf of Tonkin
Hainan Island
Vinh
Dong Hoi
Former DMZ (Demilitarized Zone)
THAILAND
Lao Bao
Hue
Ancient Ruins
The Imperial City bears testament to Hue's rich history.
Da Nang
Hoi An
LAOS
Quang Ngai
South China Sea
Kontum
Pleiku
CAMBODIA
Qui Nhon
Pho French Riviera
Nha Trang's azure-blue waters caress the best beaches in the country.
Buon Ma Thuot
Nha Trang
Da Lat
Beat the Heat
Cool mountain breezes and a strong local art community enliven Da Lat.
Phan Rang
Phan Thiet
Tay Ninh
Moc Bai
Ho Chi Minh City
Gulf of Thailand
Chau Doc
City Scope
Ever alive, Ho Chi Minh City is an experience not to be missed.
My Tho
Ha Tien
Long Xuyen
Vung Tau
Dao Phu Quoc
Rach Gia
Can Tho
Ca Mau Peninsula
N
LG
0
100 miles
0
100 kilometers
Vietnam

VIETNAM

LANGUAGE

Vietnamese, the official language, is spoken throughout the country. Other common tongues include Chinese, English, French, Russian, Khmer, and tribal languages such as Mon-Khmer and Malayo-Polynesian. Though students of English were often arrested during the 1980s as part of a government effort to discourage people from leaving the country, English is becoming increasingly popular and important for business today. For most of history, Vietnamese was written using traditional Chinese characters. In the 17th century, however, Catholic missionaries developed a Latin-based orthography called *quốc ngữ* to help spread their beliefs. The system stuck; all Vietnamese is written in *quốc ngữ* today. For helpful Vietnamese phrases, see the **Appendix,** p. 987.

RELIGION

Several major religions and philosophies have influenced Vietnam, from Taoism and Buddhism to Christianity; Islam and Hinduism have played a lesser role. Confucianism, which acted more as a code of morality than a religious faith, proved an important force in shaping the Vietnamese social system. Two distinctly Vietnamese religions, Cao Đài and Hoa Hao, have developed in the country. The majority of Vietnamese identify themselves as Buddhist, while about 7% are Catholic. With the unification of the country in 1975, Communist leaders began to repress religious activity. In 1997, however, religion received official government sanction.

BUDDHISM. The major religion in Vietnam remains Mahayana Buddhism; Zen is the predominant sect. While followers of Theravada Buddhism seek nirvana, Mahayana Buddhists strive to become a *bodhisattva*—one who perfects himself through virtue but remains in the world to guide others. Travelers interested in important Buddhist sights in Vietnam can visit the Perfume Pagoda (p. 906).

CAO ĐÀI. Based on the premise that all religions stem from the same spiritual truths, Cao Đài attempts to synthesize these fundamental principles into one doctrine. Founded in 1926, the religion revolves around love, justice, peace, spiritual liberation, and belief in a supreme being—symbolized by a single, omniscient eye. Followers do not seek to convert others, but rather to promote tolerance among religions. Cao Đài has two branches; those who practice **esoterism** seek self-purification through meditation and contemplation, while those who follow **exoterism** attempt to practice good, show kindness, and avoid evil in everyday living. See p. 970 for more history. Interested travelers can visit the central Cao Đài temple near Hồ Chí Minh City (see p. 970).

HOA HAO. A practical form of Buddhism founded by Prophet Huynh Phu So in 1939, Hoa Hao emphasizes simplicity, gratitude, and self-improvement. Primarily concentrated in the Mekong Delta region, followers of this sect have become an important religious and political force in the country.

TAOISM. The ancient religion of Taoism, which emphasizes simplicity and contemplation, has been incorporated into Vietnamese culture primarily as mysticism. The concept of the participation of man in the universal order is central to the Taoist doctrine.

HISTORY

CHINESE OCCUPATION AND THE LÝ-TRẦN PERIOD (111 BC-AD 1400)

IMPORTANT DATES

111 BC Chinese armies capture Nam Việt.	**AD 939** Đại Việt established.	**1009** Lý Thái Tổ establishes the Lý Dynasty.	**13th-14th Centuries** Chinese Ming Dynasty gains further control, attacks Vietnamese culture.

Much of Vietnam's early history revolves around the struggle with Chinese forces over territorial control. The Chinese began their quest to acquire Vietnamese land in the 2nd century BC, when Han armies captured Nam Việt. Power shifted back and forth until AD 939, when Ngô Quyền defeated the Chinese army and founded the independent state of **Đại Việt.** Đại Việt was ruled by the **Lý Dynasty,** founded in 1009 by Lý Thái Tổ; the Trần Dynasty also held power (1225-1400). During the 12th century, however, Chinese forces once again gained a foothold in Vietnamese territory. As Chinese leaders gained power, they enslaved the Vietnamese and began attempts to eradicate their culture.

THE LÊ DYNASTY (1428-1776) AND THE TÂY SƠN REBELLION (1788-1802)

IMPORTANT DATES

1428 Lê Dynasty defeats Ming, establishes Confucian state.	**1460-97** Đai Việt expands under Lê Thánh Tông.	**18th Century** Nguyễn Huệ unites all of Đai Việt.	**1790** Nguyễn Anh comes to power and brings back Chinese influences.

In 1428, **Lê Lợi,** an aristocrat, and **Nguyễn Trãi,** a brilliant military strategist, drove out the Chinese and founded the Lê Dynasty, which instituted a highly centralized state founded upon Confucian principles (see **Hoàn Kiếm Lake,** p. 902). Modern-day Vietnam was briefly unified under Đại Việt when **Nguyễn Huệ** and his brothers capitalized on widespread peasant discontent to spark the **Tây Sơn Rebellion.** After crushing a Chinese army dispatched to prop up the last of the Lê Dynasty rulers, Nguyễn Huệ declared himself emperor. However, Confucian values were reinstated soon afterward when **Nguyễn Anh** took over the throne.

CONTACT WITH THE WEST AND COLONIALISM (1857–1925)

IMPORTANT DATES

1857 French ships sail into Vietnam.	**1867-80** French gain control of Mekong Delta and then entire country.	**19th Century** French landlords exploit Vietnamese.

The first Westerners to visit Vietnam were the **Portuguese,** who established a trading center at Faifo (Hội An). Missionaries and Jesuits, never far behind, began proselytizing in Northern and Central Vietnam. Among them was Alexander de Rhodes, a Portuguese priest who devised a system of transliterating the Vietnamese language into Latin characters, an early version of today's *quốc ngữ* (national language) script (see **Language,** p. 883). The Portuguese presence didn't last long, and the West left Vietnam relatively undisturbed for almost 300 years. **France**'s interest in Indochina lay in trade, natural resources, and a chance to compete with Britain's rapidly expanding Asian empire. In 1857, Napoleon III decided to colonize Vietnam; by 1867 the French had seized the entire Mekong Delta region. By the mid-1880s, the French had control of the whole country as well as Laos and Cambodia, though only the Mekong Delta region was an official colony.

The French *mission civilisatrice*, as they euphemistically dubbed their colonial endeavor, was anything but civil. Landless tenancy skyrocketed in the south as ownership became concentrated in the hands of wealthy landlords. In Northern and Central Vietnam, the French forced peasants to work on rubber plantations. Apologists for the colonial regime claimed that the French had made great strides in the areas of medicine and education. Some experts, however, say that reforms were largely cosmetic. Only one doctor was available for every 50,000 Vietnamese, and literacy rates actually declined during the colonial period—only an estimated 10% of all school-age children received an education.

NATIONALISM AND REVOLUTIONARY MOVEMENT (1920-45)

IMPORTANT DATES			
1920s Resistance movements grow.	**1930** Hồ Chí Minh establishes Indochinese Communist Party.	**1941** Vietnam Independence League formed.	**1941** Japanese annex Indochina, place Vietnamese government in charge.

By the 1920s, a new generation of young Vietnamese assumed control of a rising nationalist movement. In 1930, **Hồ Chí Minh** founded the **Indochinese Communist Party (ICP),** which helped instigate a series of violent uprisings in the central provinces of Nghệ An and Hà Tĩnh; both were brutally suppressed by the French. In the early 40s, the Communists shifted from a platform of class struggle to a more moderate approach that emphasized independence; the **Vietnam Independence League (Việt Minh)** was established in 1941. That same year, the Japanese gained permission to occupy Indochina militarily, hastily deposing the French and placing an ill-prepared Vietnamese government in charge.

THE FIRST INDOCHINA WAR AND ITS AFTERMATH (1946-65)

IMPORTANT DATES				
1944 Việt Minh leads August Revolution.	**1945-46** Vietnam gains independence. First Indochina War begins.	**1954** French defeated at Điện Biên Phủ. Geneva Accords, division of Vietnam.	**Late 1950s** Ngô Đình Diệm rules South Vietnam.	**Early 1960s** US involvement increases as North Vietnam allies with USSR. Diệm assassinated in 1963.

Power struggles began with the largely peaceful August Revolution, in which the Việt Minh forces occupied most of the country. The culmination of the Việt Minh anti-colonial movement occurred on September 2, 1945, when Hồ Chí Minh read Vietnam's **Declaration of Independence** in Hanoi's Ba Đình Square (see p. 903). The French were not content to watch their empire slip away, however, and in October drove the Việt Minh out of South Vietnam. After a year of failed negotiations, the First Indochina War officially began. In the spring of 1954, after a bloody eight-year struggle, Việt Minh forces defeated the French at **Điện Biên Phủ,** an isolated valley in the northwest. Humiliated, the French agreed to begin a peace process.

At the Geneva Accords in July of 1954, both sides agreed to an interim compromise and partitioned Vietnam along the 17th Parallel. Plans were drawn up calling for national elections to reunify the country two years after the treaty. In the meantime, the Communists gained control of the north while a coalition of non-Communists came to power in the south. The **Republic of Vietnam (RVN)** in the south became an American client-state ruled by the dictatorial Catholic Ngô Đình Diệm, who refused to hold the elections agreed upon at the Geneva Convention. In fall 1963, Diệm's own generals assassinated him; General Nguyễn Văn Thiệu seized power. The **Democratic Republic of Vietnam (DRV)** in the north sought to build a socialist state, carrying out a disastrous land reform campaign in the late 1950s.

HIGHLIGHTS OF VIETNAM

CULTURAL HERITAGE. Hanoi (p. 893) is a 1000-year-old city steeped in history and tradition. Hill tribe cultures are the chief attractions of **Mai Châu** (p. 922) and **Sapa** (p. 915) in the northwest. The **Perfume Pagoda** (p. 906) ranks as one of the region's most unique shrines. Gentle **Huế** (p. 928) stewards an array of palaces and tombs. **Hội An**'s (p. 939) ornate Chinese architecture is some of the best-preserved in Southeast Asia.

URBAN BEAT. Hồ Chí Minh City (p. 960) flaunts a vibrant market culture, colonial architecture, and extravagant nightlife.

BEACHES. Nha Trang (p. 951), "the Vietnamese Riviera," features infamous pleasure cruises and fine food. **Phú Quốc Island** (p. 984) remains tourist-free...for now.

NATURAL WONDERS. Treks in the northwest around **Sapa** (p. 915) or the rugged **Central Highlands** (p. 947) rival the best that Thailand has to offer. **Hạ Long Bay's** (p. 911) cool green waters and over 3000 islets capture a calm beauty.

HANGING OUT. Đà Lạt (p. 955) boasts cool vibes, an eclectic avant-garde scene, and friendly locals. The livin' is easy on the Mekong in **Cần Thơ'** (p. 974) and **Châu Đốc** (p. 978). Remote **Hà Tiên** (p. 982) is likely the most mellow town on earth.

Hanoi maintained good relations with both the USSR and China, receiving military and economic aid from both.

In the early 1960s, things began to heat up as the north gave support to the popular **National Liberation Front of South Vietnam (NLF)**—guerrilla forces in the south. The NLF was modeled on the Việt Minh, with front organizations accommodating women, students, and peasants. The fighting arm of the NLF, known as the Việt Cộng (pejorative slang meaning Vietnamese Communist), with military aid from the north's DRV, marched down the Hồ Chí Minh Trail through Laos and Cambodia into Southern Vietnam. The anti-Communist US, alarmed at the accelerated wave of Việt Cộng violence, began to increase its presence in the south.

THE SECOND INDOCHINA WAR (1965-75)

IMPORTANT DATES

1965 US officially enters Second Indochina War, bombs the north.	**1968** NLF forces launch Tet Offensive.	**1972** Christmas bombings.	**1973** Paris Peace Accords finally end war.	**1975** North Vietnamese enter Saigon, form Socialist Republic of Vietnam.

Known in Vietnam as the "American War," the Second Indochina War marked the pinnacle of destruction and violence on Vietnamese soil. The US officially entered the war in 1965, when President Lyndon Johnson approved regular bombings of North Vietnam and deployed American troops to the south. By 1968, half a million US troops were fighting in South Vietnam. During the first part of 1968, NLF forces launched the **Tet Offensive,** attacking more than 100 cities and military bases over the course of the Vietnamese New Year (early February). Although a military defeat, the bloody offensive was a propaganda victory for Hanoi and fueled American dissatisfaction with the war. The US stepped up bombing campaigns against the north, culminating in the 1972 **Christmas bombings,** an attempt to force the Vietnamese to come to the negotiating table. Without popular support to sustain the conflict, the US terminated active participation in the war with the **1973 Paris Peace Accords.** On April 30, 1975, North Vietnamese tanks rolled into Saigon and reunited the country under Communist rule. At the Hanoi Citadel, travelers can see the tank that crashed through the gates of the presidential palace (see p. 903).

THE SOCIALIST REPUBLIC OF VIETNAM (1975-98)

IMPORTANT DATES

1976 War continues: conflict with the Khmer Rouge.	**1979** Foreign relations weaken after a brief war with China.	**1986** "Renewal" reforms sweep the country.	**1990** Vietnamese forces leave Cambodia.	**1995** Relations with US normalized; Vietnam joins ASEAN.

The decade following the end of the war was one of the darkest in modern Vietnamese history. More than a seventh of the population had been wounded or killed in the war; millions were left homeless. Immediately after the **Socialist Republic of Vietnam (SRV)** was established, the country began a protracted war with the Khmer Rouge in Cambodia. Worsening relations with Beijing climaxed in a brief but destructive border war with China in 1979. South Vietnam's agricultural production declined precipitously. In the north, conditions approached famine.

In 1986, at the historic **8th Party Congress,** the Communist Party approved sweeping economic reforms, dubbed **Đổi Mới (Renewal).** Frightened by events in the former Soviet Union and by the Tiananmen Square pro-democracy uprising in China, the Vietnamese Politburo sought to grant the Vietnamese economic freedom while maintaining a tight grip on political power. Since Đổi Mới, Hanoi has pursued a foreign policy aimed at reintegrating the country into regional and global affairs. Vietnam's withdrawal from Cambodia in 1990 cleared the way for better relations with its Southeast Asian neighbors. On July 11, 1995, Vietnam normalized relations with the US and joined the Association of Southeast Asian Nations (ASEAN) 17 days later.

VIETNAM TODAY

Vietnam stands at a crossroads. While the first 10 years of Đổi Mới have brought impressive results, talk of "the next Asian Tiger" now appears to have been premature. The government has been reluctant to push economic reforms too far, especially in the wake of the region's recent economic crisis. While the January 1998 Politburo reshuffle brought two pro-reform officials to power—President **Trần Đức Lương** and Prime Minister **Phan Văn Khải**—conservative elements within the Politburo (led by the military) have succeeded in keeping reforms in check. A series of demonstrations in Thái Bình and Đồng Nai provinces over local government corruption prompted President Lương to call for the elimination of "immoral and incapable officials." The response is part of a nationwide effort to reduce corruption, rife within the government and businesses.

In November 2000, US President Bill Clinton visited Hanoi, the first trip a US president has made to a reunified Vietnam. The US began crafting new relations with its former adversary when President Clinton lifted the trade embargo from Vietnam in 1994. Two years later, the US embassy in Hanoi reopened, and diplomatic relations slowly resumed. Even with other foreign investors taking interest in Vietnam, the average income remains only about US$1 a day.

Large-scale prisoner absolution in 1998—including the early release of Professor Doan Viet Hoat, a prominent pro-democracy demonstrator—was another step toward human rights protection in Vietnam. However, the same laws under which Doan Viêt Hoat and other peaceful political protestors were arrested still exist. Open letters to the Politburo calling for political reform have also been tacitly tolerated. Some human rights groups have aligned themselves with Buddhism, calling to help the people, the country, and education. However, in creating a better Vietnam, such groups remain intent on keeping out foreign powers, mimicking a long history of similar struggle with foreign counterparts. Many human rights activists in Vietnam currently push for democracy.

CUSTOMS & ETIQUETTE

In Vietnam, a smile goes a mile. Be polite, courteous, and patient—if you expect promptness, you will probably be disappointed. If you must criticize, try to find a way to express your complaint as a joke. Displays of anger are frowned upon.

A LITTLE RESPECT. As a gesture of respect, take off your hat and bow your head slightly when addressing elders or monks. Remove your shoes before entering a temple; when invited into someone's home, note whether your host takes off his shoes, then do the same.

TABOOS. The feet are regarded as the least holy part of the body; don't point the bottoms of your feet at any person or Buddhist image, as this is considered rude. Conversely, Vietnamese regard the head as the most sacred part of the body; never touch a person's head, even a small child's.

TABLE MANNERS. Chopsticks sticking out of a rice bowl are thought to resemble the incense burned for the dead. Never leave your chopsticks in this position, as it is considered a negative omen. Dog lovers should avoid *thit cho* (dog meat). Vietnamese puppies are man's best lunch, not man's best friend.

GIFTS. Give or receive objects with both hands. Wrap gifts in lucky green or red paper; black and white are considered inauspicious.

FAMILY MATTERS. The Vietnamese value family tremendously; in conversation with locals, be attentive to family details.

BISEXUAL, GAY, AND LESBIAN TRAVELERS. Homosexuality is not openly discussed in Vietnam, though major cities like Hồ Chí Minh City and Hanoi have a small but growing gay nightlife. The importance of procreation in Vietnamese society, however, means that most gay men remain closeted, so the gay community stays underground. Public displays of romantic affection are frowned upon for both heterosexuals and homosexuals. *The Men of Vietnam*, by Douglas Thompson, is the first comprehensive account of Vietnamese gay subculture. Utopia-Asia (www.utopia-asia.com) also offers tips for gay travelers in Vietnam.

ARTS

ART. Pre-modern Vietnamese art was a reflection of traditional Chinese styles. During the colonial period, painting was heavily influenced by French impressionism, and a generation of Vietnamese artists was trained at the Indochina College of Art. Following independence, art in the Democratic Republic of Vietnam mirrored Soviet Socialist realism. Today, Vietnam's artistic scene is centered in Hanoi, but traditional **folk art** (including weaving, musical instrument construction, and wood figure carving) is found in all regions. The Hindu kingdom of Champa produced many sculptures, some examples of which are at the Chàm Museum in Đà Nẵng (see **Sights**, p. 938).

DANCE AND DRAMA. Vietnam has many traditional musical genres, especially **folk music** and **theater/opera,** that remain popular today. Folk songs *(dân ca)* originated in the countryside and were sung at festivals and in the fields. One common style, the *quan họ* tradition of Bắc Ninh Province north of Hanoi, was sung in a call and response fashion between young men and women as an important element in courtship. **Musical theater** is also characterized by regional variation. Most famous in the north is *hát chèo*, which combines singing, acting, and dancing.

Today, traditional music troupes sometimes stage performances in Hanoi theaters. More popular in Central and Southern Vietnam are *hát tuồng* and *cải lương* (reformed opera). *Tuồng* was influenced by Chinese opera in plot, costumes, and instrumentation, while *cải lương* combines elements of *tuồng* with Western musical traditions. A third popular genre, *múa rối nước* (water puppetry), originated in the north. Wooden puppets cavort across the surface of a shallow pool, acting out fairy tales. Puppeteers, standing knee-deep in water behind a screen, manipulate the puppets with rods. Witness this exquisite art form in Hanoi (see **Entertainment,** p. 905).

LITERATURE. Literature is Vietnam's most treasured legacy of the pre-modern period. Early literature was written in classical Chinese and the *nôm* demotic script. During the 17th and 18th centuries, one of Vietnam's greatest *nôm* writers, poet **Hồ Xuân Hương,** was famous for her innuendo-laden poems about the lives of court women. **Nguyễn Du** is recognized as Vietnam's greatest writer, based on *Truyện Kiều (Tale of Kieu)*, an epic in verse about the tragic life of an aristocratic woman. Vietnamese of all ages and social classes can recite passages from the epic. When the French occupied Vietnam, they sought to curtail Chinese influence by banning Chinese and instituting the *quốc ngữ* script. Literature written in the vernacular flourished by the 1920s and 30s and played a significant role in the nationalist struggle by highlighting the injustices of the colonial regime.

HOLIDAYS & FESTIVALS (2003)

Government offices and businesses are closed on public holidays.

DATE	NAME & LOCATION	DESCRIPTION
Jan. 1	Western New Year's Day	
Feb. 1-3	Tet	Vietnamese and Chinese New Year, taking place during the first week of the new lunar calendar. The most important Vietnamese celebration of the year.
Feb. 3	Anniversary of the Founding Day of the Communist Party of Vietnam	
Mar. 8	Hai Ba Trung Day	Commemorates the Trung sisters, who led a rebellion against Chinese rulers in AD 40; the 6th day of the 2nd lunar month.
Apr. 6	Thanh Minh	Vietnamese All Soul's day; the 5th day of the 3rd lunar month. Families gather to worship the dead.
Apr. 30	Liberation of South Vietnam and Saigon	Celebrates the reunification of Vietnam.
May 1	International Labour Day	
May 19	Ho Chi Minh's Birthday	
May 28	Celebration of the Buddha	
Aug. 12	Trung Nguyen, also called Ram Trang Bay	The day of Wandering Souls and Hungry Ghosts; the 15th day of the 7th lunar month. People lay out food in temples and burn paper money. A day of forgiveness.
Sept. 2	National Day	
Sept. 3	President Ho's Anniversary	
Oct. 10	Mid-Autumn Festival	The 15th day of the 9th lunar month. This celebration is dedicated to children, who parade through the streets carrying paper lanterns.
Oct. 23	Confucius's Birthday	The 28th day of the 9th lunar month.
Dec. 25	Christmas Day	Not a government holiday; only celebrated by Christians.

ADDITIONAL RESOURCES

HISTORY, FICTION, AND NONFICTION

A Bright, Shining Lie: John Paul Vann and America in Vietnam, by Neil Sheehan (1988). Winner of the National Book Award. A scathing indictment of America's involvement in Vietnam by a correspondent who covered the war.

The Sorrow of War, by Bảo Ninh (1994). A moving novel about love and war in the North; a must-read for anyone familiar with American Vietnam War literature. Written by a North Vietnamese veteran.

Vietnam: A History, by Stanley Karnow (1983). A straightforward modern Vietnamese history, focusing on the Second Indochina War. Winner of the Pulitzer Prize.

ON THE WEB

Vietnam News (www.vietnamnews.net). Updated daily, this comprehensive website has the scoop on current events. Also includes links to information on history and culture.

Nam Viet (www.namviet.net). A great source of information on anything from current events to traditional art and Vietnamese recipes.

ESSENTIALS

VIETNAM PRICE ICONS					
SYMBOL:	❶	❷	❸	❹	❺
ACCOMM.	Under US$4 Under 64,000Đ	US$4-8 64,000-128,000Đ	US$8-15 128,000-240,000Đ	US$15-25 240,000-400,000Đ	Over US$25 Over 400,000Đ
FOOD	Under US$0.75 Under 10,000Đ	US$0.75-2 10,000-30,000Đ	US$2-4 30,000-60,000Đ	US$4-7 60,000-105,000Đ	Over US$7 Over 105,000Đ

EMBASSIES AND CONSULATES

VIETNAMESE CONSULAR SERVICES ABROAD

Australia: Embassy, 6 Timbarra Cres., O'Malley, ACT 2606 (☎02 6286 6059). **Consulate,** Double Bay, NSW (☎02 9327 2539).

Canada: Embassy, 470 Wilbrod St., Ottawa, ON K1N 6M8 (☎613-236-0772).

South Africa: Embassy, 955 Arcadia St., Arcadia, Pretoria 0083 (☎012 430 7378).

UK: Embassy, 12-14 Victoria Rd., London W8 5RD (☎020 7937 3222).

US: Embassy, 1233 20th St. NW #400, Washington, D.C. 20036 (☎202-861-0737; www.vietnamembassy-usa.org). **Consulate,** San Francisco, CA (☎415-922-1577).

CONSULAR SERVICES IN VIETNAM

Australia: Embassy, 8 Đạo Tan St., Ba Đinh District, Hanoi (☎84 4 831 7755). See p. 897. **Consulate,** Hồ Chí Minh City (☎ 84 8 829 6035). See p. 964.

Canada: Embassy, 31 Hùng Vương, Hanoi (☎84 4 823 5500). See p. 897. **Consulate,** Hồ Chí Minh City (☎ 84 8 824 5025). See p. 964.

New Zealand: Embassy, 32 Hàng Bài, Hanoi (☎84 4 824 1481). See p. 897. **Consulate,** Hồ Chí Minh City (☎84 8 822 6908). See p. 964.

UK: Embassy, Central Building, 31 Hai Bà Trưng St., Hanoi (☎84 4 825 2510). See p. 897. **Consulate,** Hồ Chí Minh City (☎84 8 829 8433). See p. 964.

US: Embassy, 7 Láng Hạ St., Ba Đinh District, Hanoi (☎84 4 772 1500). See p. 897. **Consulate,** Hồ Chí Minh City (☎84 8 822 9433). See p. 964.

VISAS

All travelers must obtain a one-month single-entry tourist visa at any Vietnamese consulate or embassy. Visas for longer time periods are available; a three-month, multiple-entry visa costs US$150. One-week **extensions** can be arranged by tour agencies or hotels. Travelers can enter and depart from any international airport or port; see the box on overland border crossings below.

MONEY

The Vietnamese **đồng (Đ)** comes in denominations of 100; 200; 500; 1000; 2000; 5000; 10,000; 20,000; 50,000; and 100,000Đ. US dollars are widely accepted in accommodations and restaurants in larger towns, where prices are frequently quoted in dollars. However, for other expenses, paying in đồng allows more room to bargain. *Let's Go* lists prices according to the currency cited by the establishments. Many establishments list prices in US$ but accept đồng as well. Credit cards are generally accepted in major cities, especially at expensive restaurants, hotels, and travel agencies. Banks regularly give credit card cash advances in dollars. **Tipping** is not necessary but is appreciated and occasionally expected at some touristy establishments. At expensive restaurants and hotels, a 10% service charge is added. **Bargaining** should always be done in đồng.

GETTING THERE

BY PLANE. Vietnam has three **international airports:** Nội Bài International Airport in Hanoi (p. 893), Tân Sơn Nhất International Airport in Hồ Chí Minh City (p. 960), and Đà Nẵng International Airport in Đà Nẵng (see p. 935). **Don't lose your baggage claim tickets**—you won't be allowed to take your luggage without them. **Vietnam Airlines** (www.vietnamair.com.vn) runs the most flights to these airports.

BY LAND. Refer to the table below for overland border crossings to Vietnam.

BORDER CROSSINGS On your visa application, be sure to specify the correct point of entry and exit.

LAOS. There is a crossing open from **Đà Nẵng/Huế** (p. 928) through **Lao Bảo** to **Savannakhet** (p. 351). The crossing at **Điện Biên Phủ** is only open to locals.

CHINA. Borders are open from **Đồng Đăng,** near Lạng Sơn (p. 913), to **Pingxiang** (Guangxi Province) and from **Lào Cai** (p. 914) to **Hekou** (Yunnan province).

CAMBODIA. The border at **Mộc Bài** (p. 962) provides a cheap way to get between Vietnam and Cambodia.

VIETNAM

GETTING AROUND

BY PLANE. If you can afford it, travel by plane is the fastest and most comfortable way to get from one end of the country to the other. **Vietnam Airlines** has extensive domestic connections from hubs in Hồ Chí Minh City and Hanoi.

BY TRAIN. Trains exist in Vietnam, but solely for the joy of existing. They move slowly and require patience. Tracks that once extended throughout the country were destroyed during the Vietnam War. Passengers should retain their tickets, lest they be charged a fee upon disembarking. A journey on the "**Unification Express**" from Hanoi to HCMC or vice versa is a scenic way to visit most of Vietnam's major cities and offers much more contact with local culture than travel by tourist minibus.

BY BUS. Vietnam's public bus system is the cheapest way to travel off the beaten path. Buses go everywhere, and foreign faces are rare. To avoid getting stuck with ridiculous "tourist prices," try to learn numbers and phrases for "how much is it to..." and "no, it is..." (See **Appendix,** p. 988.) Buses are not for the impatient, faint of heart, or claustrophobic. Expect to be packed in with bikes, fruits, vegetables, and sweating commuters. The rides tend to be exciting, loud, dusty, and tiring. Tourist buses may be worth the extra đồng, as they drop you off in the middle of town, while public buses deposit you at the outskirts.

BY MINIBUS. Many backpackers use minibuses operated by budget travel cafes based in Hồ Chí Minh City and Hanoi. Minibuses, which cost a bit more than public buses, reduce the headaches of public transportation. The downside is that they limit your contact with locals as well as the places you can visit, since many of the destinations *Let's Go* lists lie off the well-trodden minibus path.

> **SCAMS** In any major city, you'll likely be surrounded by *cyclo* and motorbike drivers. They'll attempt to bring you to a hotel that is paying them a commission instead of wherever it is that you want to go. Be adamant about your intended accommodation and quoted price. It's a good idea to write down your destination (with accent marks) and the fare before you negotiate.

BY BICYCLE OR MOTORCYCLE. Despite safety risks, traveling by motorbike is a good alternative for getting from city to city without the hassle of public transportation. Travelers can flag down motos (called *"xe ôm,"* literally "hugging bike," because the passenger hugs the driver to stay on) for intercity travel. Bicycles are readily available for rent, but helmets aren't; bring your own if you plan on doing some serious cycling. Vietnamese drivers tend to be much more attuned to cyclists than drivers in the West; nonetheless, be sure to ride defensively, signal clearly, and avoid highways.

BY CYCLO. Ubiquitous three-wheeled bicycle rickshaws ply the streets. Passengers sit in front while the driver pedals behind. As most drivers can't speak English, a map or written address will prove helpful to communicate your destination. Agree on a fare in advance.

KEEPING IN TOUCH

The Vietnamese **postal service** is reliable when letters are sent to or from major cities, although letters to most Western countries can take anywhere from 10 days to three weeks to arrive. All overseas packages must be processed through customs before they can be received. **Poste Restante** is available in Đà Lạt, Đà Nẵng, Hanoi, Hồ Chí Minh City, and Nha Trang, but isn't always reliable.

Long-distance calls placed from Vietnam can cost an arm and a leg. Make international calls at the local post office. **International phone cards,** such as those issued by AT&T and MCI, can be used for no fee, but rarely work. **Credit card calls** are available in Hanoi and Hồ Chí Minh City. For **HCD** numbers from Vietnam, refer to the table on the inside back cover of this book.

If you're feeling dismayed at the exorbitant cost of phone calls, take comfort in the fact that you can check your email regularly. **Internet access** is available in most tourist destinations. Average prices hover around 100 đồng per minute, though Internet service may cost twice that in Nha Trang and Hội An. Log on in Hanoi for the best rates in the country.

NORTHERN VIETNAM

Vietnamese civilization came of age in the northern half of the country over two millennia before civilization flourished in the south. Due to Chinese influence, northern Vietnamese maintain Confucian reserve and a dedicated work ethic. They are further affected by the legacy of over 40 years of socialism and 30 years of war. In addition to the contrast with unfettered capitalism in the south, the ethnic diversity in the northwest in particular lends the region its distinct flavors. As the north's population elevates itself out of hardship and poverty, the region's sights are becoming more popular with foreign visitors. Using Hanoi as a base, travelers can make excursions east to the coast, north to the mountains, or south to the Red River Delta.

HANOI (HÀ NỘI) ☎4

The idea of Hanoi evokes images of a stern, austere bastion of Vietnamese communism, ravaged by war and closed to the world. Visitors to the capital, however, will be surprised to find themselves in one of Southeast Asia's most charming cities. With its Chinese architecture, majestic French colonial buildings, and tree-lined lanes, this ancient city of lakes extends a reserved but genuine friendliness—the essence of the North Vietnamese. Less cosmopolitan than Hồ Chí Minh City, Hanoi is kinder and gentler than its southern rival. Fewer skyscrapers tower overhead and less traffic clogs the streets. However, the almost overnight transformation of the infamous "Hanoi Hilton" prison into the Hanoi Tower Commercial Center is surely an omen for things to come. Hammers and sickles still adorn the cityscape, but the Doi Moi "Renovation" policies are slowly taking effect.

INTERCITY TRANSPORTATION

BY PLANE

Flights into Hanoi land at **Nội Bài International Airport,** 35km north of the city. There's a 25,000Đ domestic departure tax and a US$12 tax for international flights.

> **!** Keep your baggage tags or you won't be allowed to claim your bags. **Keep your stamped immigration card with your passport at all times;** you'll need it to leave the country.

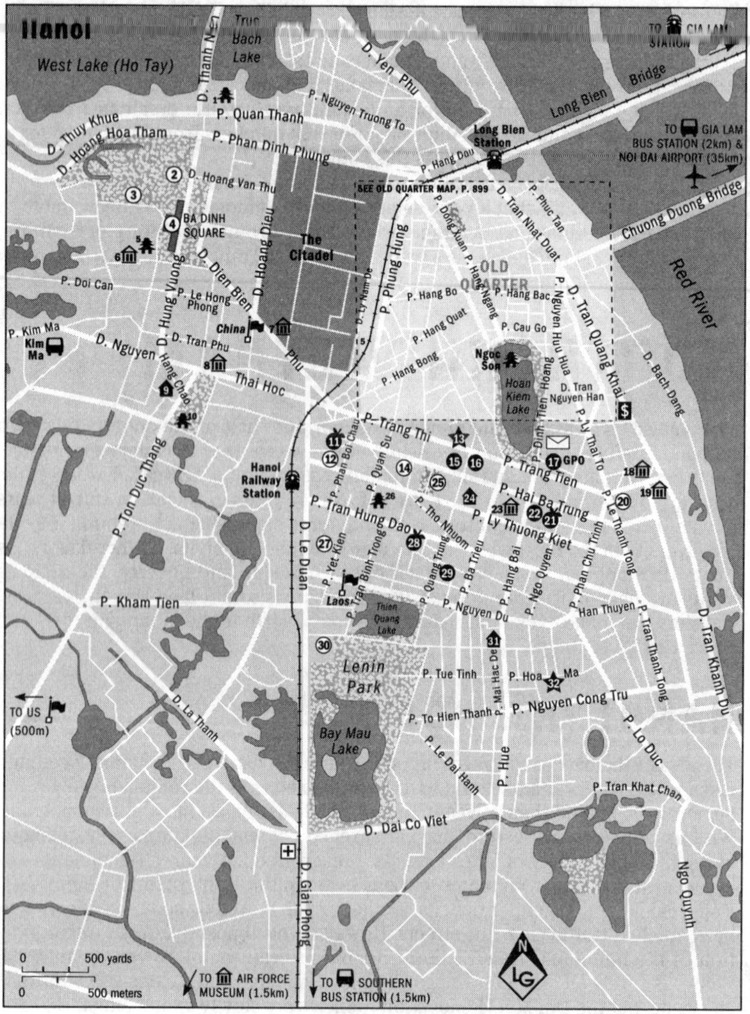

Hanoi

ACCOMMODATIONS
- Lotus Guest House, **24**
- Trang An Hotel, **9**
- Polonez Hotel, **31**

SERVICES
- Foreign Book Center, **17**
- International SOS Hanoi Clinic and UK Embassy, **22**
- National Library, **15**
- Vietnam Airlines Office, **16**

NIGHTLIFE
- Apocalypse Now, **32**
- New Century Night Club, **13**

FOOD
- Al Fresco's Cafe, Bar and Grille, **21**
- Com Chay Nang Tam Vegetarian Restaurant, **28**
- Indochine Restaurant, **11**

SIGHTS
- 19/12 Market, **25**
- Alliance Francaise, **27**
- Army Museum, **7**
- Fansland, **12**
- Museum of Fine Arts, **8**
- Hoa Lo Prison/Hanoi Towers, **14**
- Ho Chi Minh Mausoleum, **4**
- History Museum, **19**
- Ho Chi Minh Museum, **6**
- Ho Chi Minh's Stilted House, **3**
- National Circus, **30**
- One Pillar Pagoda, **5**
- Opera House, **20**
- Presidential Palace, **2**
- Quan Su Pagoda, **26**
- Quan Thanh Pagoda, **1**
- Revolutionary Museum, **18**
- Temple of Literature/Royal College, **10**
- Women's Museum, **23**

The white Nội Bài Transport Co-op booth right outside the airport runs **taxis** to (US$10) and from (US$7.50) town. Most travelers split the fare with one or two others, so ask around. **Minibuses** run US$2 (20,000Đ if you purchase tickets on board), though they're mostly reserved for locals. Where you get dropped off depends on the whim of your latest friend, the hotel commission hound. The more disinterested you seem in your choice of hostel, the more likely it is that you will get a better value. **Vietnam Airlines minibuses** also run between the airport and city every hour (40min., US$2), stopping at the Vietnam Airlines office on Quang Trưng. To head back to the airport, call ☎886 56 15 to arrange for pick up.

DESTINATION	FREQUENCY	PRICE	DESTINATION	FREQUENCY	PRICE
Bangkok	3 per day	US$180	**Kuala Lumpur**	2 per day	US$260
Đà Nẵng	3 per day	US$65	**Manila**	1 per day	US$280
Hồ Chí Minh City	10 per day	US$122	**Nha Trang**	1 per day	US$95
Hong Kong	2 per day	US$277	**Singapore**	1 per day	US$325
Huế	2 per day	US$65	**Vientiane**	2 per day	US$101

Several airlines operate domestic and international flights from Hanoi: **Cathay Pacific Airways,** 49 Hai Bà Trưng (☎826 72 98); **China Airlines,** 18 Trần Hưng Đạo (☎824 26 88); **Lao Aviation,** 269 Kim Ma (☎846 48 73); **Malaysia Airlines,** 15 Ngô Quyền (☎826 88 20); **Pacific Airlines,** 100 Lê Duẩn (☎733 21 62); **Singapore Airlines,** 17 Ngô Quyền (☎826 88 88); **Thai Airways,** 44B Lý Thường Kiệt (☎826 68 93); and **Vietnam Airlines,** 1 Quang Trưng, at the intersection with Trang Thi (☎825 08 88; open M-F 7am-6:30pm, Sa-Su 8-11:30am and 1:30-5pm).

VIETNAM

BY TRAIN

Trains are the safest, most comfortable mode of domestic transport in Vietnam.

Hanoi Railway Station (Ga Hà Nội), 120 Lê Duẩn (☎825 39 49), at the west end of Trần Hưng Đạo, a 10min. cyclo ride from the city center (5000-10,000Đ). Travelers arriving in Hanoi from Lang Son, Lào Cai, and southern Vietnam disembark here. Purchase tickets for points south from the special booking window for foreigners in the main building (open daily 7am-12:30am and 1-8:45pm). A booth beside the tourist window exchanges foreign currency. Buy tickets for Haiphong, Lang Son, and Lào Cai at another booth near Gate 5 (open daily 7am-12:30pm and 1-7pm). For special events like the Saturday market in Sapa, buy tickets several days in advance. **Save your ticket** or you will be forced to pay again upon arrival. Fares vary by speed. Prices listed reflect the full range of comfort from hard seats to soft sleepers. To: **Đà Nẵng** (15-19hr., 239,000-367,000Đ); **Haiphong** (2hr.; 6:15, 9:30am; 22,000Đ); **Hồ Chí Minh City** (32-41hr., 494,000-758,000Đ); **Huế** (12-16hr., 206,000-316,000Đ); **Nha Trang** (24-32hr., 449,000-689,000Đ); **Ninh Bình** (2½-3hr., 24,000-47,000Đ); **Sapa** via **Lào Cai** (9hr.; 6:05am, 9:30pm; 62,000-121,000Đ); **Vinh** (5-7hr., 92,000-140,000Đ).

Other Departure Points: On the opposite side of the tracks from the main station (accessible via Trần Quý Cáp), daily trains run to **Lạng Sơn** (7¼hr., 10pm; 9hr., 5:40am; 78,000Đ). Trains to **Haiphong** (2hr., 22,000Đ) leave from **Long Biên Station** near Đồng Xuân Market (2hr.; 9:38am, 5:45pm; 22,000Đ). Trains also leave from **Gia Lâm Station** across the Red River (near the **Gia Lâm** bus station) to: **Haiphong** (12:40, 3:35pm; 19,000Đ); **Lạng Sơn** (6hr.; 6:07am, 2:15pm; 26,000Đ); **Lào Cai** (6:35am, 1:15, 10:17pm; 54,000-61,000Đ).

BY BUS

Using public buses requires patience for overcrowded, jostling rides that leave only when full, regardless of quoted departure time. In true Vietnamese style, the prices below are approximations. Always try to buy your ticket at the station; on board, the collector may demand an inflated fare.

Gia Lâm Bus Station: 2km across the Red River on the left. To: **Haiphong** (2¼hr.; roughly every hr. 6am-4:30pm; 25,000Đ); **Hạ Long City** (3hr.; 6am-3pm; 35,000Đ); **Lạng Sơn** (5hr.; every hr. from 7am; 35,000Đ). Moto to the station 10,000Đ. Minibuses to **Haiphong** (35,000Đ) can also be caught on Trần Quang Khải at Long Biên Station, in the shadow of the Long Biên Railway Bridge over the Red River.

Southern Bus Station (Bến Xe Nam Hà Nội): On Đường Giải Phóng, the extension of Lê Duẩn, 5km south of the train station. For all destinations south of Hanoi. To **Điện Biên Phủ** (16-20hr.; 4, 8am, 1pm; 100,000Đ); **HCMC** (1-2 days; 10am-3pm; 185,000Đ); **Ninh Bình** (2½hr.; every 2hr.; 20,000Đ).

Kim Mã Bus Station: On Nguyễn Thái Học. To **Lào Cai** (20hr.; 5am; 70,000Đ) and **Sơn La** (8hr.; 5:30am; 55,000Đ). To get to **Mai Châu,** head toward Sơn La and ask to get off at **Tòng Đâu.**

Tourist buses: More comfortable and reliable, albeit more expensive. An established bus line departs daily at 6:30pm from **Sinh Cafe,** 18 Lương Văn Can (☎828 75 72) to: **Dong Ha** (13½hr., US$10); **Huế** (15¼hr., US$10) via **Ninh Bình** (2¼hr., US$4); **Quang Bình** (11hr., US$9); **Vinh** (6¼hr., US$8). A popular **open ticket** to **HCMC** (US$23) via **Đà Nẵng, Đà Lạt, Hội An,** and **Nha Trang** lets you get off at any of these towns and then jump back on the bus to the next destination southward at your leisure.

ORIENTATION

Hanoi divides into seven districts (quận): **Hoàn Kiếm** (the **Old Quarter**), **Hai Bà Trưng** to the south, **Ba Đình** and **Đống Đa** to the west, **Cầu Giấy** and **Thanh Xuân** to the far southwest, and **Tây Hồ** to the north. Most streets in Vietnam are called "đường," though Hanoi still uses the word "phố" and, in the Old Quarter, "hàng." Downtown Hanoi is small but disorganized; a good map is helpful. Large color maps (10,000-25,000Đ) are available from guest houses, bookstores, the international post office, and hawkers around **Hoàn Kiếm Lake,** the heart of central Hanoi. A backpacker's heaven of shops, cafes, and hotels, Hoàn Kiếm is the oldest and most interesting district. The one-way **Đường Lê Duẩn** leads south to **Bẩy Mẫu Lake** in the more residential Hai Bà Trưng district, and west (down Khâm Tiên) to Đống Đa's pagodas and small lakes. Farther north, up Đường Hùng Vương, the Ba Đình district hosts the **Hồ Chí Minh Mausoleum** and **Temple of Literature.**

LOCAL TRANSPORTATION

Bicycles (Xe Đạp) and Motorcycles (Xe Máy): In spite of Hanoi's hectic and challenging traffic, driving a motorcycle is a convenience that many think is worth the woe. Most hotels, guest houses, and rental shops in the Old Quarter, north of Hoàn Kiếm Lake, rent **motorcycles** (US$5-9 per day). Be prepared to fork over 1000-2000Đ each time you park your motorbike. **Cường's Motorbike Adventure,** 40 Lương Ngọc Quyên (☎826 65 86), is the most reliable Minsk dealer in Hanoi. Cường rents a Minsk, helmet, saddlebags, repair manual, tools, and a map for US$6 a day. If you're looking for a bike with post-WWII engineering, check out the rental shops on **Hàng Bạc** (US$3-5). **Bicycles** are less glamorous but sufficient for getting around town. Rent them from most accommodations or rental shops for 10,000-15,000Đ per day.

Cyclos and Motorcycle Taxis (Xe Ôm): Abundant and cheap three-wheeled **cyclos** (pedicabs) are the bastard children of rickshaws, tricycles, and bicycles. Banned from most major thoroughfares, but a must for any traveler, with chatty drivers and winding routes. Agree on a price beforehand (10,000-15,000Đ per hr.); ask hotel employees for a ballpark figure if you're unsure about a reasonable fare. Hire **motorcycle taxis** for longer rides (2000-3000Đ per km, 10,000Đ around town).

Taxis: Everywhere in Hanoi. Lines form outside the Vietnam Airlines office, the train station, and major hotels. **Hanoi Taxi** (☎853 52 52) or **Huong Lua Taxi** (☎825 25 25) will pick you up curbside (7000Đ per km). Insist that the driver use the meter. **Airport Taxi** (☎873 33 33) runs to and from the airport (40,000Đ). Renting **cars** is uncommon but an option. **Especen,** 22 Tràng Thi (☎826 68 56). Price includes driver and depends on type of vehicle and destination. 2 days to Mai Châu US$75. Open daily 9am-5pm.

PRACTICAL INFORMATION

TOURIST AND FINANCIAL SERVICES

Tours: Tourist cafes organize cheap package tours, which provide a hassle-free way to see Northern Vietnam. Services and prices vary slightly, but quality can vary considerably. Standard packages include: **Hạ Long Bay** (1 night US$18-35, 2 nights including **Cát Bà Island** US$28-53); **Hoa Lư-Tam Cốc** (daytrip US$15-20); **Mai Châu** (1 night US$20-25); **Perfume Pagoda** (daytrip US$9-16); **Sapa** (3 nights including **Bắc Hà** US$30-70). Established tourist cafes include: **Green Bamboo Cafe,** 24 Đường Thành (☎828 65 04); **Queen Cafe,** 50 Hàng Be, 13 and 65 Hàng Bạc (☎826 08 60); **TF Handspan Cafe,** 116 Hàng Bạc (☎828 19 96), branch at 18 Bảo Khánh (☎828 99 31). Most tourist cafes also arrange **visas** to China (1 month US$25-30) and Laos (1 month US$60) and 30-day Vietnam **visa extensions** (US$25-35).

Embassies: Australia, 8 Đạo Tan (☎831 77 55), behind Hanoi-Daewoo Hotel. Open M-F 8:30am-5pm. **Cambodia,** 71 Trần Hưng Đạo (☎942 12 49). Visa US$20, 1-day processing. Bring a photo. Open M-F 8-11:30am and 2-4:30pm. **Canada,** 31 Hùng Vương (☎823 55 00). Open M-F 8am-noon and 1-4:30pm. **China,** 46 Hoàng Diệu (☎845 37 36). For visas, go to the consulate (☎823 55 69) on Trần Phú. Visa US$30, 4-day processing; US$47, 2-day processing. Bring 2 photos. Open M-F 8:30-11am. **Indonesia,** 50 Ngô Quyền (☎825 33 53). **Laos,** 22 Trần Bình Trọng (☎942 45 76). Visa US$60, 1-day processing. Bring a photo. Open M-F 8-11:30am and 1-4pm. **Malaysia,** Fortuna Hotel, GB Lang Ha (☎831 34 00). Open M-F 8am-4:30pm. **Myanmar,** Block A3 Vạn Phúc (☎845 33 69). Open M-F 8:30am-noon and 1:30-5pm. **New Zealand,** 32 Hàng Bài (☎824 1481). Open M-F 8:30am-noon and 1-5pm. **Philippines,** 27B Trần Hưng Đạo (☎943 79 48). **Singapore,** 41-43 Trần Phú (☎823 39 66). **Thailand,** 63-65 Hoàng Diệu (☎823 50 92). Open M-F 8:30am-noon and 1:30-5pm. **UK,** 31 Hai Bà Trưng (☎825 25 10). Open daily 8:30am-4:30pm. Visa applications 8:30-11:30am only. **US,** 7 Láng Hạ (☎831 45 90). Open daily 8am-noon and 1-5pm. Visa services to Cambodia, Laos, and Thailand also available in tourist cafes.

Currency Exchange: Vietcombank Building (☎824 08 80), on the corner of Trân Quang Khải and Le Lai. Best exchange rates in Hanoi. Open M-F 8-11:30am and 1-3:30pm, Sa 9am-3pm for currency exchange. **ANZ Bank,** 14 Lê Thái Tổ (☎825 81 90), on the west bank of Hoàn Kiếm Lake. Hanoi's only **24hr. ATM.** Bank open M-F 8:30am-4pm. Both banks exchange and issue traveler's checks and offer MC/V cash advances. For currency exchange with half the hassle, change your đong to dollars at a **gold shop,** and then, armed with those dollars, head to the bank to get traveler's checks if you need them. The shop at 5 Hàng Trong has an authorized Vietcombank exchange bureau.

LOCAL SERVICES

Local Publications: The Guide, published monthly with the *Vietnam Economic Times,* provides useful information on events, hotels, shops, and local services (10,000Đ). **Hanoi Pathfinder** has a similar monthly listing with a map, although it only lists businesses that advertise. Available free at most Western restaurants and guest houses.

English-Language Bookstores: The Bookworm, 15A Ngo Van So (☎943 72 26). 1 block south of Tran Hung Dao. Hanoi's only English language bookshop with a second-hand section. Buys paperbacks. Open Th-Su 10am-7pm. **Foreign Book Center,** 44 Tràng Tiền, 2nd fl. (☎826 03 13, ext. 228). Chinese, English, French, Korean, Japanese, Lao, and Russian books. Open M-F 8am-9pm, Sa-Su 8am-10pm. **Thâng Long Bookshop,** 55 Tráng Tiền (☎825 70 43), has paperbacks and phrasebooks. Open daily 8am-7pm.

Library: National Library of Vietnam (Thư Viện Quốc Gia) (☎825 53 97). Enter across from 39 Hai Bà Trưng. A limited mix of English magazines on the 2nd fl. Dress modestly. Open daily 8am-6pm.

EMERGENCY AND COMMUNICATIONS

Emergency: ☎115. **Police:** ☎113.

Police: Hoàn Kiếm District Headquarters, 2 Lê Thái Tổ (☎825 41 08), on the northwest corner of Hoàn Kiếm Lake. Don't expect knights in shining armor.

Pharmacy: A strip of pharmacies lines Quán Sú near the intersection with Tràng Thi southwest of Hoàn Kiếm Lake. The **24hr. pharmacy** at 14 Phu Doan (☎825 59 34) is small but well stocked.

Medical Services: International SOS Clinic, 31 Hai Bà Trưng (☎934 06 66). From south of Hoàn Kiếm Lake, walk 1 block down Bà Triệu. Large office signpost. **24hr. emergency care.** US$65 per consultation, $55 for dental, $15 for vaccine. Medivac service available. **Hanoi French Hospital,** 1 Phuong Mai (☎570 07 40). Expat doctors provide **24hr.** emergency care. US$25-30 per consultation. **Hanoi Family Medical Practice,** 1A Van Phuc 109-112 Kim Ma (☎843 07 48, emergency 09 040 19 19).

Telephones: Telephone office, 75B Đinh Tiên Hoàng (☎825 52 36), next to the international post office. International calls 33,000Đ per min. Fax and AT&T/MCI card calls are free but don't always work. Open in summer daily 6am-10pm; in winter 6am-9:30pm. **Branch office,** 66 Lương Văn Can (☎826 29 99). Open daily 6am-9pm. **Information** ☎1080. **Directory** ☎1080. **International Operator (collect calls)** ☎110. Only available from post office. Travelers often have a hard time getting through.

Internet Access: Most cyber cafes, especially those concentrated near Hàng Bạc, offer Internet access for 50Đ per min.

Post Offices: International Post Office, 6 Đinh Tiên Hoàng, on the corner with Đinh Le, is a large Stalinist-looking building east of Hoàn Kiếm Lake. *Poste Restante.* Open in summer daily 7am-9pm; in winter daily 7am-8:30pm.

Express Mail: FedEx, 6 Đinh Le (☎826 49 25). **DHL,** 778 Làng (☎775 39 99). English spoken.

ACCOMMODATIONS

Most tourists stay in the **Old Quarter.** Plan ahead during the high season when the best hotels are packed. Most accommodations charge by the room, not by the number of people—get cozy and get cheap. In case you've forgotten that you're in a communist bureaucracy, your hotel owner will request your passport and papers so he can register you with the local police.

THE OLD QUARTER (HOÀN KIẾM)

Hàng Bè and **Hàng Bạc** streets are still the center of the backpacking universe in Hanoi, while the streets to the north and west offer better and quieter alternatives.

Anh Đào Hotel, 37 Ma May (☎828 19 94; anhdao@camellia-hotels.com). 31 spotless wooden rooms run by a professional team. 30min. free Internet each day. Includes all-you-can-eat breakfast buffet (7-10am). All rooms have A/C and satellite TV. Doubles US$10-15, superior US$17, deluxe with free laundry service US$23-25. MC/V. ❸

Green Hotel, 50 Quán Sú (☎824 97 38). All rooms include breakfast and satellite TV. Clean, comfortable doubles US$8-18. ❷

Van Xuan 11, 46 Lương Ngọc Quyến (☎825 69 48), above the Á Đông Restaurant, 30m from the intersection with Ta Hiện. Cheap, quiet rooms. Restaurant serves cheap, tasty local cuisine. Singles with A/C and TV US$6; doubles with TV and A/C US$7-8. ❷

Prince II Hotel, 24 Quán Sú (☎828 94 65). Rooms with bathtub, desk, and a pleasant balcony if you're lucky. Small breakfast included. Doubles US$18-20. MC/V. ❶

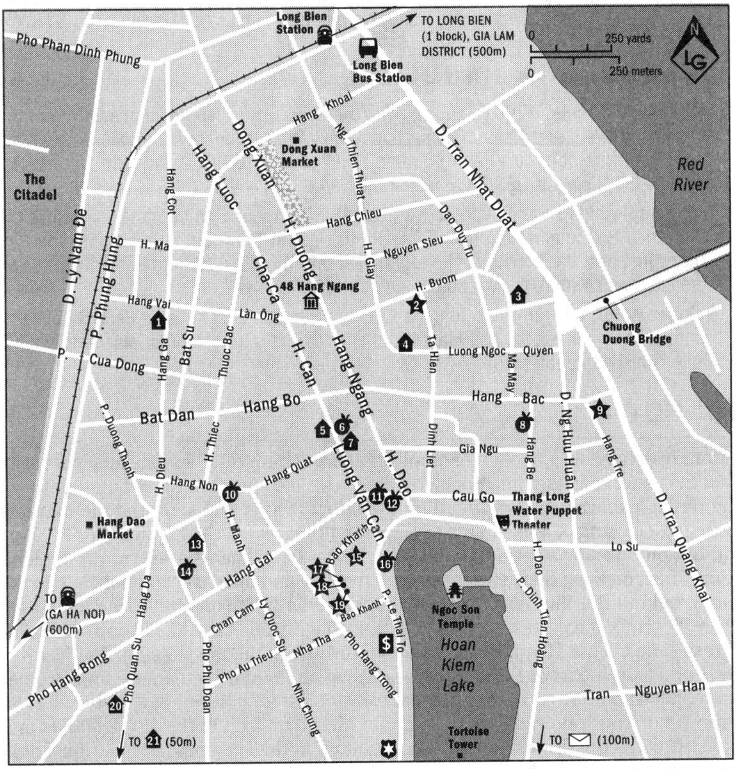

Hanoi Old Quarter

ACCOMMODATIONS
- Anh Dao Hotel, **3**
- Green Hotel, **21**
- Manh Dung Internet Guest House, **13**
- Phu Hoa Hotel Guest House, **5**
- Prince II Hotel, **20**
- Thanh An Hotel, **1**
- Van Xuan 11, **4**
- Youth Hotel, **7**

NIGHTLIFE
- Dong Khoi, **19**
- Le Maquis Bar, **2**
- Funky Monkey Bar, **15**
- Golden Cock Bar, **17**
- Highway 4, **9**
- Polite Pub, **18**

FOOD
- Cafe Giang, **12**
- Cyclo Bar and Restaurant, **14**
- Little Hanoi, **11**
- Pho Chua Ngot, **6**
- Tandoor Restaurant, **8**
- Thuy Ta Cafe, **16**
- Nha Hang Dac Kim, **10**

Thanh An Hotel, 46 Hàng Ga (☎826 71 91), in the northwest part of the Old Quarter. Rooms are immaculate, though the ones in the rear can be a bit dark. Doubles with A/C and satellite TV US$8-20. ❸

Youth Hotel, 33 Lương Văn Can (☎828 58 22). Centrally located; 50m to Hoàn Kiếm Lake. Popular with younger crowds. Internet 200Đ per min. in a buzzing backpacker cafe. Connected to Sinh Cafe for tour booking. Dorms US$3; doubles US$7-20. ❶

Phú Hoa Hotel Guest House, 16 Lương Văn Can (☎828 51 73). Good budget option in the center of town. Singles that moonlight as bike storage with external bath US$4; doubles with A/C US$5-7. ❶

Mạnh Đung Internet Guest House, 2 Tam Thường St. (☎826 72 01), down a small alley off Hàng Bông near Hàng Đa Market. Organizes tours. Friendly feel in an English-speaking household. Cozy rooms with private bath. Doubles US$6, with A/C US$8. ❷

ELSEWHERE IN HANOI

Lotus Guest House, 42V Lý Thường Kiệt (☎/fax 826 86 42). Walking south from the lake on Bà Triệu, turn right at intersection with Lý Thường Kiệt; it's 2 blocks down on the right. Idiosyncratic, cozy, and popular. Food (5000-25,000Đ), laundry, and tours. Dorms US$4; singles US$6-8; doubles with fan US$8, with A/C US$10-15. ❷

Tràng An Hotel, 46 Hàng Cháo (☎/fax 823 28 37). About 1km from the lake, cross the Điện Biên Phủ intersection from Tràng Thi to Nguyễn Thái Học, turn left onto Tôn Đức Thắng just past the Temple of Literature, then take the 1st right onto Hàng Cháo; it's on the left. Twins with A/C, TV, and private bath US$8-10. ❸

Polonez Hotel, 6A Trấn Nhan Tong (☎822 57 15), 1km east of Lenin Park. Satellite TV with extensive channels. Breakfast included; dartboard in restaurant also free. Beautifully furnished doubles US$25-35. ❺

FOOD

Culinary delights in Hanoi cater to all palates and budgets. Backpackers can easily find the usual spaghetti and pancake fare in the Old Quarter, but the most rewarding dining experiences are found on the street. Street stalls around the markets dish up delectable staples like *phở* (noodles) or *cōm* (rice) and plenty of vegetarian options. Vendors set up all day long in the **Dong Xuan Market,** north of Hoàn Kiếm Lake, on **Hãng Bong** street between the lake and main train station, and in the block behind the Vietnam Airlines office at **Trấn Binh Trong** and **Trần Hùng Đạo.** Over 30 seafood eateries beckon your patronage along **Thuy Khue** south of **Ho Tay** (West Lake). It's a 10min. walk directly north from the mausoleum. **Phồ Mai Hac De,** in the south part of the city, serves cheap, authentic Vietnamese food. To get there, head south from Hoàn Kiếm Lake on Bà Triệu for seven blocks, turn left on Trấn Nhan Tong and right on Mai Hac De. Gorge on fruit at the **19/12 Market** and cool off with cool drinks *Bia hơi* shops set up in the evening on Phan Chu Trinh, three blocks south of the Opera House.

Cafe Giang, 7 Hàng Gai. Open since 1945, this is a famous coffee shop among locals, and for good reason. The unique egg coffee (*nâu trung sữa nóng;* 3000Đ), a shot of espresso with sugar and a beaten egg, is an absolute can't-miss. Open daily 6am-noon and 3-9:30pm. ❶

Nhà Hàng Đắc Kim, Số 1 Hàng Mành. Heaping servings of *bún chả,* grilled pork over cold rice noodles, keep locals coming back for more. Comes with crab rolls (16,000Đ). Open daily 7am-7pm. ❷

A MINI-KEG A DAY... Though most *bia hơi* (draft beer) stands fall short of Munich beer gardens, the enthusiasm with which the Vietnamese quaff their beer rivals that of malt-drinkers anywhere in the world. Every morning, beer is delivered fresh in mini-keg beer bombs. There are no added preservatives which reduces the chances of hangovers should you imbibe too liberally. Be warned: though *bia hơi*'s alcohol content is low, its cheap price and light taste make it easy to toss back a few liters, which could spell trouble. However, it's tastier than the other national favorite, *mua loi* (rice vodka), which will send you rolling under the table without ceremony. The Vietnamese celebrate their traditional booze with plenty of drinking games. If you're playing "50/50," they'll make you drink half the beer that's in your glass. *"Tram Phan Tram"* means "bottoms up," the global slogan for draining your cup. Almost every city or region also has its own local brew: in Hanoi, try Bia Hanoi or Halida; in Huế, drink Hú Đá; in HCMC, don't miss 333 or Bia Saigon. Haiphong brews Bia Haiphong, and even tiny Sơn La brews its own Bia Son Dong. Locals everywhere insist their beer is Vietnam's best—but we all know that the true answer lies in careful research. To find a good beer stall, look for peanut shells on the floor or a crowd. You'll find that good *bia hơi* is a social equalizer: doctors and lawyers swig elbow-to-elbow with cyclo drivers and shoeshine boys. Get to your stall early and grab a handful of peanuts or dried squid. As they say, *Tram Phan Tram* and let the night begin.

Phở Chua Ngọt, 29 Lương Văn Can. A brightly lit local dive that serves only two specialties: sweet and sour noodles (10,000Đ per bowl) and fried dumplings (5000Đ). Open daily 9am-9pm or later. ❶

Cyclo Bar and Restaurant, 38 Duòng Thành. Duòng Thành intersects Hàng Gai as it becomes Hàng Bông; the restaurant is 100m down on the left. Good variety of Vietnamese and Western food. Local brew and Heineken available. Cyclo chairs and a nice garden add to the ambience. Set lunch menu 50,000Đ. *A la carte* 45,000-75,000Đ. Open daily 9am-11pm. ❸

Cơm Chay Nàng Tấm Vegetarian Restaurant, 79A Trần Hưng Đạo, between Quang Trưng and Quán Sứ intersections. Buddhist eatery. Come early for lunch, since it gets crowded. Most entrees 30,000-50,000Đ. Open daily 11am-1:30pm and 5-10pm. The same menu is served at a smaller location in the heart of the Old Quarter at 79 Hàng Bạc. ❸

Al Fresco's Cafe, Bar and Grille, 23L Hai Bà Trưng, 2 blocks south of the main GPO. Big portions of pizza and buffalo wings. A local expat hangout. Its claim to fame: since 1996, 39 tons of ribs have been sold here. An annual rib-eating contest is held in Nov. Entrees US$4.50-11. Open daily 9am-11pm. ❺

Indochine Vietnamese Restaurant, 16 Nam Ngư. High quality local specialties with impeccable service. The house spring rolls have achieved crispy fried yet un-oily perfection. Entrees start at US$3. Open daily 11:30am-2pm and 5-10pm. ❹

Thuỷ Ta Cafe, 1 Lê Thái Tổ. The tasty French cakes, Italian ice creams, and Vietnamese coffee are a bit pricey, but terrace tables overlooking the Ngoc Sơn Temple make it worth the extra đong. Desserts 5000-55,000Đ. Open daily 6am-11pm. ❸

Little Hanoi, 21 Hàng Gai, a block from the lake. A favorite meeting point for Westerners. Quiche, shakes, and a good selection of dessert cakes run 10,000-40,000Đ. Open daily 7:30am-11:30pm. ❷

Tandoor Restaurant, 24 Hàng Bè. From Đinh Tiên Hoàng on the eastern shore of Hoàn Kiếm Lake, walk up Hàng Dầu, which becomes Hàng Bè; it's on the left past the intersection with Gia Ngư. Delicious *naan* and good vegetarian selections. Set lunch 52,000Đ. Sa buffet 11:30am-2:30pm, 70,000Đ. Open daily 11am-2:15pm and 6-10:30pm. ❸

SIGHTS

Concentrated in Hoàn Kiếm and Ba Đình, most of Hanoi's sights can be reached by foot or bicycle. Hanoi has a fascinating mixture of old and new, juxtaposing traditional Vietnamese and French colonial designs with 1930s Art Deco, 1970s communist looks, and modern skyscrapers, each style symbolizing a different epoch in Vietnam's troubled history.

HOÀN KIẾM DISTRICT

OLD QUARTER. North of Hoàn Kiếm Lake and west of the Hanoi Citadel, this labyrinthine neighborhood stretches to Long Biên Bridge, which was continually bombed and repaired during the war. Many streets *(hàng)* take their names from the goods sold there. **Hàng Bạc** (Silver St.) is lined with gold and silver shops, and **Hàng Thiếc** (Tin St.) is home to metalworkers. Since merchants used to be taxed by the length of their storefronts, a typical house is 3m wide and 50-60m long. After hitting the shops, check out the museum at **48 Hàng Ngang,** where Hồ Chí Minh drafted the Declaration of Independence in 1945. *(Open daily 8-11am and 1-4:30pm. Free.)* The winding **Nguyễn Quang Bịch** hosts a mix of typical Old Quarter and 1900s French-style houses painted bright yellow and green. Though the Old Quarter is well touristed, foreigners are still viewed with (polite) bewilderment.

HOÀN KIẾM LAKE (HỒ HOÀN KIẾM). The lake takes its name from a 15th-century legend of a magic turtle who loaned a sacred sword to Lê Lợi, the nobleman who led the Vietnamese against the invading Ming army. Paddling in the lake following the victory, the newly crowned emperor encountered the turtle, who demanded the sword back. The **Tortoise Tower** on a tiny island in the lake's center commemorates the event. Several mammoth turtles still live in the lake and occasionally surface, an event that locals believe is a sign of the impending death of one of the country's leaders. Travelers can enjoy a relaxing stroll here, though persistent kids sell postcards and T-shirts on the north side of the lake.

NGỌC SƠN TEMPLE (ĐỀN NGỌC SƠN). Generations have added more and more frills to this shrine since its construction during the Trần Dynasty (1225-1400). Last renovated in 1865, this Chinese-style temple is located on a wooded island in Hoàm Kiêm lake and is dedicated primarily to Văn Xương, the god of literature. Thirteenth-century hero Trần Hưng Đạo and the physician La To are also honored. The entrance to the temple is through **Tam Quan** (Three Passage) gate on the northeast shore on Đinh Tiên Hoàng. Behind the **Hall of the Cult,** the sanctuary to **Văn Xương** offers a beautiful view of the lake. *(Open daily 8am-6pm. 12,000Đ.)*

HỎA LÒ PRISON. Nicknamed the "Hanoi Hilton," Hỏa Lò Prison held Vietnamese revolutionaries under French rule and American POWs during the Vietnam War. The imposing **Hanoi Towers,** which hold offices, a five-star hotel, and a shopping center, now occupy most of the site. A portion of the old prison, preserved on Phố Hỏa Lò off Hai Bà Trưng just before the skyscraper, is now a small, worthwhile **museum.** *(A few blocks past the intersection of Quang Trưng and Hai Bà Trưng, walking away from the lake. Open daily 8-11:30am and 1-4:30pm. 5000Đ.)*

QUÁN SỨ PAGODA (CHÙA QUÁN SỨ). The official center of Buddhism in Hanoi, this site served as a guest house for visiting Buddhist ambassadors. The structure as it stands today was completed in 1942. Inside are several depictions of the Buddha. Be extremely respectful in dress and manners. *(73 Quán Sứ, a block south of the prison between Lý Thường Kiệt and Trần Hưng Đạo. Open Nov.-Mar. Tu-Su 6am-9:30pm; Apr.-Oct. Tu-Su 5:30am-9:30pm.)*

OTHER SIGHTS. The French-built **Opera House (Nhà Hát Lớn),** constructed in 1911, majestically stands guard over the main traffic circle facing east over Pho Trang Tiên and remains one of the country's best examples of colonial architecture (see **Entertainment,** p. 905). Both the **Revolutionary Museum (Bảo Tàng Cách Mạng)** and the **History Museum (Bảo Tàng Lịch Sử)** are just a short walk behind the Opera House. The former is a visual lesson in Communist historiography that retells the history of Vietnam's struggle against foreign aggression. *(216 Trần Quang Khải. Open Tu-Su 8-11:45am and 1:30-4:15pm. 10,000Đ.)* At the latter, don't miss the Đông Sơn bronze drums and ceramics or the Khmer and Champa artifacts. *(Across Pho Trang Tiên from Revolutionary Museum. Open Tu-Su 8-11:30am and 1:30-4:30pm. Admission 15,000Đ, with camera 30,000Đ.)* The **Women's Museum,** 36 Lý Thường Kiêt, details the role of women in Vietnamese history and culture. *(Open Tu-Su 8am-4pm. 10,000Đ.)*

BA ĐÌNH DISTRICT

The area around **Ba Đình Square,** site of Hồ Chí Minh's delivery of Vietnam's Declaration of Independence in 1945, contains the principal sights west of Hoàn Kiếm Lake. The most convenient route to get here is via Điện Biên Phủ. Along the way is a small park with a massive **statue of Lenin.**

HANOI CITADEL. Inside its gates is the **Army Museum (Bảo Tàng Quân Đội),** which details the exploits of the People's Army of Vietnam. Highlights include a light-and-sound diorama of Điện Biên Phủ Valley and the tank that crashed through the gates of the Presidential Palace in Saigon in April 1975. Next door is the 31m **Hanoi Flag Staff,** built in 1812 under the Nguyễn Dynasty. *(Museum: 28A Điện Biên Phủ, across from Lenin. Open Tu-Th, Sa-Su 8-11:30am and 1-4:30pm. 10,000Đ, cameras 2000Đ.)*

HỒ CHÍ MINH MAUSOLEUM (LÂNG HỒ CHÍ MINH). Poor Hồ Chí Minh couldn't escape his well-preserved fate despite his wish to be cremated. Completed in 1975, the granite structure serves as a receiving stand for officials and party leaders and continues the Communist tradition of building glass sarcophagi to attract pilgrims. *(Up Điện Biên Phủ, away from the Army Museum, west of the lake. Open Apr.-Oct. Tu-Th 7:30-10:30am, Sa-Su 7:30-11am; Nov.-Mar. Tu-Th 8-11am, Sa-Su 8-11:30am. Closed briefly every Nov. for the make-up artist, eh, embalmer to touch up a bit. Free. Be certain to wear respectable attire—no shorts, short skirts, or tank tops. No bags or cameras allowed; stash them at the visitors entrance at the south end of the square.)*

PRESIDENTIAL PALACE AND HỒ CHÍ MINH'S STILTED HOUSE. The former residence of the Governor General of French Indochina, the **presidential palace** has served as a state guest house since 1954, when the Việt Minh defeated the French. Hồ Chí Minh believed the building should belong to the people and chose to live in an **electrician's hut** on the grounds. His personal area in the hut remains as he left it. In 1958, he moved into a simple **stilted house** near a carp pond, which remained his residence until 1969. The home was built for Uncle Hồ near the Presidential Palace so he would feel more "with the people." The house overlooks the carp pond where Uncle Hồ used to summon the fish for feeding by clapping. Living proof of Pavlovian conditioning, the fish still respond to clapping tourists. *(North of the mausoleum. Open daily 8-11:30am and Tu-Th, Sa-Su 2-4pm. 5000Đ buys a guided tour of palace, electrician's hut, and stilted house.)*

HỒ CHÍ MINH MUSEUM (BẢO TÀNG HỒ CHÍ MINH). If you visit one museum in Hanoi, this should be it. It chronicles the life and times of the leader through a series of bizarre displays that blend Socialist Realism and postmodernism. Musicians in the concert hall play traditional Vietnamese music. *(From the mausoleum, head south on Hùng Vương and make the first right. Museum is 200m straight ahead. Open Tu-Th, Sa-Su 8-11am and 1:30-4pm. 5000Đ.)*

ONE PILLAR PAGODA (CHÙA MỘT CỘT). One of the few structures remaining from old Thâng Long, the pagoda is dedicated to Quan Âm, the goddess of mercy. Emperor Lý Thánh Tông built the pagoda after dreaming that the goddess, sitting on a lotus flower, gave him a boy. Soon after, a son was born to him. The pagoda was thus built to resemble a lotus plant. The French destroyed the pagoda on their way out of Hanoi in 1954, but the government has since rebuilt it. *(Between the mausoleum and Hồ Chí Minh Museum. Wear respectful attire. Open daily 6-11:30am and 2-6:30pm.)*

TEMPLE OF LITERATURE (VÂN MIẾU)/ROYAL COLLEGE (QUỐC TỬ GIÁM). To enter, head to the south entrance of the Four Pillars, allegedly built in 1070 during the reign of Emperor Lý Thánh Tông to honor scholars and literary men. Dedicated to Khổng Tử (Confucius), the college was founded to educate the children of court Mandarins. The succession of open courts is established by a series of gates, symbolic of the academic experience. The first set is the Gates of Talent and Virtue. The next set heading north leads to one of the 82 Tortoise Stelae, on which the names of 1306 successful examination candidates are inscribed. Next come the Gate of Synthesis and the sanctuary, housing statues of Confucius and his four greatest disciples. *(At the intersection of Tôn Đức Thắng and Nguyễn Thái Học, 2km west of Hoàn Kiếm Lake. Enter off Quốc Tử Giám. Open daily 7:30am-5:30pm. 2000Đ.)*

VIETNAM

OTHER SIGHTS. **West Lake (Hồ Tây)** is 500 hectares of green-brown water north of the mausoleum. **Đường Thánh Niên,** between West Lake and Trúc Bạch Lake, is a venue for fruit and drink vendors and a hangout spot for young lovers at sunset. A statue on the shore commemorates the site where an American fighter plane, piloted by future US Senator John McCain, was gunned down during the Vietnam War. For a scenic walk from West Lake to the Old Quarter, take tree-lined **Phố Phan Đình Phùng,** which runs parallel to the north wall of the citadel. At the intersection of Phố Quán Thánh and Đường Thánh Niên is **Quán Thánh Pagoda (Đền Quán Thánh),** built by Emperor Lý Thái Tổ during the 11th century. *(Open daily 8am-5:30pm. 2000Đ.)* On a bit of land jutting into West Lake near the north end of Đường Thanh Niên is **Trần Quốc Pagoda (Chùa Trần Quốc),** built during the Lê dynasty. Spend a relaxing day at **Lenin Park (Công Viên Lenin),** the largest in Hanoi, 1km south of the train station on Lê Duẩn. *(Enter off Tràn Nhân. 2000Đ.)* To get to the **Air Force Museum,** go 1km farther south from Lenin Park on Lê Duẩn, take a right on Trường Chinh, and walk down another kilometer; the museum is on the left. *(Open Tu-Sa 8-11am and 1-4:30pm. 10,000Đ.)* The **Museum of Fine Arts (Bảo Tàng Mỹ Thuật),** across from the Temple of Literature, features premodern and modern art. *(66 Nguyễn Thái Học. Open Tu-Su 9:15am-5pm. 10,000Đ.)*

MARKETS

In the olden days, each of the Old Quarter's 36 streets had its own specialty trade. **Hàng Dầu** specializes in cheap shoes (many of them exported to Europe) while its continuation, **Hàng Bê,** makes funeral stones. Best known are the silk shops on **Hàng Gai** and **Lương Vàn Can,** which sell ready-made and tailored clothing of varying quality. **Hàng Quạt** peddles colorful funeral flags and religious objects; **Hàng Mã** sells paper products, including votive candles burned for ancestors; **Lãn Ông** exudes the sweet scent of medicinal herbs; and **Hàng Đào** sells clothing. **Chợ Đồng**

Xuân (Dong Xuan Market) is in the northern part of the Old Quarter, off the extension of Hàng Đào. **Chợ Hôm** (Hôm Market), on Phố Huế, the extension of Hàng Bài, burgeons six blocks south of Hoàn Kiếm Lake. (Open daily 6:30am-7pm.) **19/12 Market** takes up the block between Hai Bà Trưng and Lý Thường Kiệt, west of Quang Trưng. Produce at the entrance tends to be more expensive than at the stands within. (Open daily 6am-6pm.)

ENTERTAINMENT

A definite must-see is the **Thăng Long Water Puppet Theatre,** 57B Đinh Tiên Hoàng, up the street two blocks north of the GPO on Hoàn Kiếm Lake. The troupe has performed in folk art festivals worldwide. (☎824 51 17. Shows nightly at 6:30, 8:15, 9pm. 45min.-1hr. Tickets 20,000-40,000Đ.) To rub shoulders with well-heeled Hanoians, try the **Hanoi Opera House,** 1 Pho Trang Tiên, also home to the **Vietnam National Symphony Orchestra.** The architecture and primly manicured courtyards alone are worth the 80,000-150,000Đ tickets. Call the **Vietnam Opera & Ballet Theater,** 18 Nui Truc (☎869 45 63), for additional cultural events. **August Cinema,** 45 Hàng Bai (☎825 39 11), and **Fansland,** 84 Lỷ Thủờng Kiĩt (☎942 44 84), next to the Saigon Hotel, show Western films regularly (12,000-20,000Đ). French films are shown most nights (except Monday) at the **Alliance Francaise,** 42 Yet Kein (☎942 29 70), near the train station. To see amazing human contortions by pubescent boys and girls (if that's your thing), spend an evening at the **Vietnam National Circus** in Lenin Park. Animal lovers should steer clear. (☎822 02 77. Shows W-Su 8pm.)

NIGHTLIFE

New Century Night Club, 10 Trang Thi St. (☎928 52 85). Disco of the moment. Young local hipsters grooving to Euro-techno. 40,000Đ ticket includes one drink. 20,000Đ before 9pm. Open daily 7pm-2am.

Highway 4, 5 Hàng Tre (☎926 06 39). Laid-back restaurant/bar specializes in traditional "medicinal" liquor from the northwest hill tribes. Bartender will help match a liquor to your ailment. Doses run 5000-25,000Đ.

Funky Monkey Bar, 15B Hàng Hành (☎928 61 13). Self-advertised as having "cool muzik," but you be the judge. Beer 15,000-20,000Đ. Happy hour 5-8pm.

Le Maquis Bar, 2A Ta Hiềm St. (☎828 25 98). From Hoàn Kiếm Lake, go north on Hàng Dàu; take a right on Hàng Buom and the 1st right on Ta Hiềm. A tiny grotto-like bar with metal chairs, this place is known as the home of the Minsk Club. Open daily 5pm-2am.

Apocalypse Now, 5C Hòa Mã (☎971 27 83). Caters to the well-to-do of all nationalities and ages and the "working girls" who like them. Army motif. Music ranges from Britney Spears to the B-52s. Beer 25,000Đ. Open daily 7:30pm-4am. Best after 11pm.

Golden Cock Bar, 5A Bảo Khánh (☎825 04 99). Commonly referred to as the GC, Hanoi's only gay bar is also one of the most comfortable drinking holes for all persuasions, which explains its large straight male (local and foreign) following. Happy hour 5-11pm. Open daily 5pm-whenever.

Đông Khôi, 7 Bảo Khánh (☎828 98 81). In the same neighborhood as the GC and Polite Pub. At 20,000Đ per hr., you can drink, relax, and think about the music that isn't blasting in your ear. Beer 10,000-13,000Đ. Open 24hr.

Polite Pub, 5 Bảo Khánh (☎825 09 59). Right next to the GC, this bar exudes heterosexuality, albeit politely. Frequented by expatriates for after-hour drinks. Darts, pool table, and sports on TV. Happy hour 5-8pm. Open daily 4pm-whenever.

DAYTRIP FROM HANOI: CHÙA HƯƠNG

Set in lush rice paddies studded with jagged limestone karsts like the ones found in Hạ Long Bay, Chùa Hương, the Perfume Pagoda, is a center of Buddhism in Vietnam. The shrine derives its name from the huge grotto in the Hương Tích Mountains (Mountain of the Fragrant Traces) in which it resides. Though the Perfume Pagoda itself is disappointing, the complex of temples at the bottom of the mountain, known as **Thiên Trù Pagodas,** is serene and beautiful. The pagoda area, where over 100 temples once stood, was destroyed during the French war. Though it was partly rebuilt in 1968, only seven temples remain today. For one month after the Lunar New Year, thousands of Buddhist pilgrims flock to the temple during the **Perfume Pagoda Festival** (Lễ Hội Chùa Hương). To avoid shuffling shoulder to shoulder for two hours up the mountain, check out the pagoda Monday to Wednesday during this month. A typical tour to the Perfume Pagoda from Hanoi includes road transport, a boat ride, and the 3-4km hike to the main temple. Alternatively, travelers can take a public bus to Hà Đông (30min, 5000-7000Đ) and catch another bus to Yên Vô village, or rent a motorbike for the day in Hanoi (US$4-6). (US$9-16 includes transport, lunch, and admission.)

VIETNAM

HAIPHONG (HẢI PHÒNG) ☎31

A quiet city of wide, shady avenues and crumbling colonial buildings, Haiphong offers little to travelers on their way to Cát Bà Island and Hạ Long Bay. Built by the French in the early 1900s, it is meant to imitate the landscape of quiet towns in the south of France. However, it has a darker history. Because of its key role as a conduit for Soviet aid to Northern Vietnam during the Vietnam War, Haiphong suffered severe US bombing and, at times, it seems like it has yet to recover. Fledgling industries have changed the face of the Haiphong that the French imagined, making it an industrial center that drives most travelers toward the beaches and parks of nearby Cát Bà Island. Remnants of the city's old pace still remain in its food-laden alleyways, away from the inevitable forces of change.

TRANSPORTATION

Flights: Cát Bi Airport (☎728 209), 7km southwest of the town center. Take a taxi (50,000Đ), motorcycle taxi (US$5), or cyclo (15,000-20,000Đ) from the town center. **Vietnam Airlines,** 30 Trần Phú (☎921 137; open M-Sa 8-11:30am and 1:30-6pm) offers flights to **HCMC,** direct (1hr.; W-F 2pm; 1,800,000Đ), or via **Hanoi** (2hr.; Tu, Sa 3pm; 1,800,000Đ).

Trains: Haiphong Railway Station, 75 Lương Khánh Thiện (☎846 433), at the end of Phạm Ngũ Lão. Trains to **Hanoi Central Station** (2hr.; 1 per day 6:10pm; hard seat 20,000Đ, soft seat 25,000Đ) and **Hanoi Long Bien Station** (2hr.; 6:10am, 8:20, 2:45pm; same prices).

Buses: Tam Bạc Bus Station, opposite the steel market. Buses to **Hanoi's Kim Ma Station** (2-3hr.; every 15min. 5:30am-7pm, every 30min. after 7pm; 25,000Đ). Buses also go to **Hạ Long City** (2¾hr.; 6am-4pm; 50,000Đ).

Ferries: Pier on Bến Bính Rd. on the Cấm River. From the west end of Điện Biên Phủ, head north toward the port. Competing companies typically run a morning slow boat and hydrofoil as well as early afternoon slow boats to Cát Bà. Exact times vary, prices don't. To **Cát Bà** (slow boat: 2-3hr.; 70,000Đ; hydrofoil: 45min.-1hr.; 90,000Đ). To **Hạ Long City** (Hòn Gai) (slow boat 3hr.; 6:30am-2:30pm; 60,000Đ). In the summer boats fill up so purchase tickets one day in advance to guarantee a seat.

Local Transportation: Cyclos should get you anywhere in the city for 5000-10,000Đ. **Haiphong Taxi** (☎822 991) charges 6000Đ per km; ask the driver to use the meter.

ORIENTATION AND PRACTICAL INFORMATION

On the Red River Delta 103km east of Hanoi on **Hwy. 5,** Haiphong has a compactly populated center flanked by industrial zones. After crossing the **Lạc Long Bridge,** Hwy. 5 becomes **Điện Biên Phủ,** Haiphong's main drag, and runs past many hotels. A block east of the Lac Long Bridge, Điện Biên Phủ intersects **Hoàng Văn Thụ,** the second-largest street in town. **Trần Hưng Đạo, Trần Phú,** and **Lương Khánh Thiện** run diagonally between Điện Biên Phủ and Hoàng Văn Thụ. This area, called "Center" is home to the **train station,** a park, and **Tam Bạc Lake.** From the **Municipal Theater**, at the intersection of Trần Hưng Đạo and Hoàng Văn Thụ, **Quang Trưng** runs along Tam Bạc Lake before ending at the **Tam Bạc bus station** and **steel market.**

Tourist Office: Haiphong Tourist Company, 57 Điện Biên Phủ (☎745 432), in the Thắng Nam Hotel. Open M-Sa 7-11:30am and 2-5pm. **Branch office,** 15 Lê Đại Hành (☎822 516), next to Hotel du Commerce at Điện Biên Phủ intersection.

Currency Exchange: Vietcombank, 11 Hoàng Diệu (☎842 658). Heading east on Điện Biên Phủ, turn left onto Minh Khai; it's at the end on the left. Open M-F 7:30-11:30am and 1:30-4pm. **No ATM.**

Emergency: Police: ☎113. **Ambulance:** ☎115.

Pharmacy: Hoang Le Pharmacy, 63 Điện Biên Phủ (☎841 605). Well-stocked. Open M-Sa 8am-7pm, Su 8am-2pm.

Medical Services: Việt-Tiệp Friendship Hospital, 1 Nhà Thương (☎700 436).

Telephones: Inside the GPO. International phone/fax. Open daily 6:30am-9pm.

Internet: A few cyber cafes have cropped up near 80 Điện Biên Phủ (50Đ per min.).

Post Office: GPO, 5 Nguyễn Tri Phương (☎842 563), at intersection with Hoàng Văn Thụ. *Poste Restante.* Open daily 6:30am-9pm. **DHL** inside GPO.

ACCOMMODATIONS AND FOOD

Most hotels are on **Điện Biên Phủ,** and rooms are pricey. For better options, move on to **Cát Bà Island** (see p. 909). **Thắng Nam Hotel ❸,** 55-57 Điện Biên Phủ, has rooms with TV, A/C, phone, and balcony. (☎842 820. Rooms US$11-17.) **Điện Biên Hotel ❶,** 135 Điện Biên Phủ, is a decaying colonial mansion with bare-bones rooms and smelly shared bathrooms. (Rooms US$4-5, with hot water US$8.) **Bến Bính Hotel ❹,** 6 Đúong Bến Bính, 100m east of the ferry dock, has standard rooms in a convenient location. (☎842 260. Doubles with bath and A/C US$15-25.)

Food stalls ❶ crowd the corner of Điện Biên Phủ and Minh Khai, and Trần Hưng Đạo. The **Ga Market** on Lương Khánh Thiện is known for giant seafood dishes. For a classier dinning experience, try the restaurants on Hoàng Văn Thụ between Điện Biên Phủ and Trần Hưng Đạo. **Quang Minh Hotel Restaurant ❹,** 20 Minh Khai, halfway down the block from the intersection with Điện Biên Phủ, serves a variety of Vietnamese and Western dishes for 30,000-100,000Đ. (Open daily 6am-8pm.)

VIETNAM

SIGHTS

MUNICIPAL THEATER (CITY SQUARE THEATER). The recently-renovated Municipal Theater is proof of Hanoi's French architectural influence. It was built using materials imported from France in the style of the Hanoi Opera House. The square in front of the theater was the site of a bloody four-day standoff between French forces and Việt-Minh revolutionaries in November 1946. *(At the intersection of Quang Trưng/Trần Hưng Đạo and Hoàng Văn Thụ. Ticket prices vary.)*

NGHÈ TEMPLE. The colorful temple and its large courtyard commemorate Lê Chân, a leader of the Trung sisters' insurrection against the Chinese before she founded An Biên Village, Haiphong's predecessor. The Vietnamese celebrate Lê Chân's birth and death at the temple on the eighth day of the second lunar month and the twenty-fifth day of the twelfth lunar month, respectively. Special offerings are made at the shrine. Check out the ornate, bronze sedan chair housed to the right of the entrance. *(55 Lê Chân. Best reached by cyclo. Open daily 6am-9pm.)*

DƯ HÀNG PAGODA. Dư Hàng Pagoda on Chùa Hàng is a beautiful Chinese-style garden with a multitude of little inner courtyards. Built during the Trần dynasty (1225-1400), the pagoda was restored earlier this century. The monks can be callous to visitors because of the families who come here to discuss their problems at the two meeting-houses in the temple. *(Open daily 5-11:30am and 1:30-6pm.)*

ĐỒ SƠN BEACH. The beach attracts tourists from all over Vietnam and is cleaned regularly in a government-led effort to boost the local economy. Đồ Sơn also boasts Vietnam's lone (foreigners-only) casino. *(22km southeast of Haiphong. Motorcycle taxi (30,000Đ) is best. Buses depart to Đồ Sơn daily from Haiphong's bus stations when full. To reach the beach and casino make a right at the ocean and continue 4km.)*

OTHER SIGHTS. Pagoda-like **Flower Stalls,** built in 1944, dot the squares near Tam Bạc Lake with vibrant colors. Farther west, hawker shops flank **Quang Trưng** and its side streets. At the end of Quang Trưng by the bus station, on the site of old rice markets, is the modern behemoth known as **Chợ Sắt (Steel Market).** History buffs should stop by the **Hàng Kênh Communal House** (Đình Hàng Kênh), 1.5km south, just off Hàng Kênh on Nguyễn Cong Tru. Remnants of imperial Vietnam adorn all objects and surfaces within this Chinese-style compound. On an altar stands a statue of Ngô Quyền, the liberator and king. *(Open M-Sa 8am-5pm. 10,000Đ.)* Also check out the **Navy Museum,** 38 Điện Biên Phủ, which contains some poignant remnants of the city's battles with foreigners. *(Open Tu-Su 8am-5pm. 10,000Đ.)*

NIGHTLIFE

Despite being a port city, Haiphong has a pretty quiet nightlife. Relaxing cafes at night include **Dilman,** 84 Điện Biên Phủ (juices 3000Đ, beer 10,000Đ), and **Dat Cang,** 28 Quang Trưng, near the theater (cocktails 35,000Đ). Good bars include **Maxim's,** 51B Điện Biên Phủ, which has live music until late every night plus cocktails (30,000-40,000Đ). Other happening places are the plush **Piano Bar** inside the Hữu Nghị Hotel, 60 Điện Biên Phủ (☎823 314), which has a great view and live strings and piano music nightly, and nearby **Biện Goi Disco,** 31 Điện Biên Phủ, the only place to dance in town. (Cover 20,000-40,000Đ. Open daily 8am-2am.)

VIETNAM

CÁT BÀ ISLAND

Home of **Cát Bà Island National Park,** 50km east of Haiphong, the island is the site of a recent tourist boom, as backpackers and Vietnamese vacationers have descended on its 350 sq. km. The island is an impressive array of limestone mountains overgrown with jungle and ringed by fine sand beaches, but is also fertile enough to support rice, maize, and lychee plantations. Guides and locals are quick to point out that Cát Bà is not just a larger version of Hạ Long Bay. Despite the horde of tourists, especially in July and August, Cát Bà is the ideal place to go on rigorous hikes, boat excursions into Hạ Long Bay, or simply to relax on the beach.

TRANSPORTATION AND PRACTICAL INFORMATION. This little paradise is most easily reached via a cafe tour from Hanoi. Independent travelers can take a ferry from Haiphong (see **Transportation,** p. 906). **Ferries** run to **Hạ Long** (4hr.; May-Aug. 1 per day 5:45am; 80,000Đ) and **Haiphong** (slow boat: 3hr.; daily 5:45am, 1pm; 70,000Đ; hydrofoil: 1hr.; daily 3pm; 90,000Đ). Otherwise, hitch onto a tour (US$6-10). Public **buses** run from Cát Bà town to the National Park entrance. Bus drivers assume any foreigners to be part of an organized tour and usually don't charge anything. The official fare starts from 500Đ. Alternatively, hire a **motorcycle** (US$8 per day) or charter a **boat** (US$15 for 4hr.).

The main ferry dock at Cát Bà town is the center of the island's universe. The **GPO**—with **telephone** booths—is directly across the street. (Open M-F 7am-10pm, Sa-Su 9:30am-9pm.) Hotels line the main drag for about 400m to either side. With your back to the harbor, the closest swimming beach is 200m to your right, while the highway to the National Park is on your left. **Väng Bac,** a pharmacy that doubles as a **foreign exchange** counter, is 500m down this road on the way to the National Park. (☎888 308. Open daily 9am-11pm.)

ACCOMMODATIONS AND FOOD. Since the introduction of electricity in 1998, hotels and restaurants have sprung up like mushrooms. Most line Cát Bà's main drag and offer similar services including tours of the island and the bay, rooms with A/C and sea views, and motorbike and boat rentals. Expect to pay US$5 more during the high season (May-Aug.), if you can find a room at all. The

Quang Đuc Family Hotel ❸, directly across from the dock, has a professional English-speaking tour service. (☎888 231. Balcony rooms US$10.) About 300m toward the National Park, **Giang Son Hotel ❷** sits opposite the fishing dock and has great rates on clean, comfortable rooms (US$5-10). The brand-spanking-new **Princes Hotel ❸** towers 200m from the water on the Nui Ngoc closest to Cat Co Beach. (Unsullied doubles US$10-12.)

> **BOOK AHEAD** In the high season call from Hanoi or Haiphong to book ahead or try the tourist cafes; some hotels have permanent contracts with tourist cafes like Sinh and Queens Cafe and refuse service to walk-ins.

Since most visitors eat inferior hotel food as part of their deal, restaurants have fewer foreigners than most tourist sites. The restaurants sell good seafood and the local specialty, crab. **Hữu Dũng Restaurant ❸**, 100m past the Princes Hotel, and **Hoang Y Restaurant ❸**, on the waterfront strip past the Quang Đuc Family Hotel, both serve tasty seafood dishes (25,000-50,000Đ).

SIGHTS. In order to visit the island at your own pace, rent a motorbike with a driver (US$5-6) from a hotel or restaurant. Otherwise, join up with a tour and ride around in their minibus (US$5-6). Apart from the bay itself, Cát Bà's main attraction is its lush **National Park**, 17km from the pier. (15,000-25,000Đ depending on length of trek. Guides US$3-6 per day.) The park hosts a botanical garden, fields of lychee trees, and around 120 animal species. It's an ideal place to go on short hikes (2hr. up a very steep hill) or more demanding hikes (5-6hr. up six hills). While camping is not possible, there are a few guest rooms in the visitor's center near the park entrance (US$8). Just off the road 1km before the park entrance is **Trung Trang Cave.** During the summer guides are available on site; in the winter arrange a tour at the national park entrance (15,000Đ). The "army hospital cave," **Hoang Sòn,** used by North Vietnamese during the war is 4km before Trung Trang.

VIETNAM

Another 15km past the park, surrounded by fields, lies the town of **Phu Long.** The town proper is bland, and the cave that lies 2km upriver, with its cement paths and neon overhead lights, would make a true spelunker scoff. (Open daily 8am-7pm. 15,000Đ.) **Boats** can also be hired at the end of the main drag (40,000Đ). Boat owners offer tours of the coastline. Check with hotels for other half- or full-day tours.

If any movement at all sounds unappealing, loll in the warm water at **Cat Co Beach,** accessible via the road over the hill at the edge of Cát Bà town (toll 7000Đ). To escape Cat Co's crowds, sneak up the stairs at the back or follow the red and white scaffolding walkway to **Cat Tien Beach** (a.k.a. Cat Co II). A tiny **guest house ❸** right on the beach offers rooms with double beds, electricity, and fans (US$12). Another popular option is **Monkey Island** (45min. from Cát Bà by boat, toll 7000Đ). Most backpackers organize afternoon trips themselves so ask around. (40,000-50,000Đ per person for a 4hr. trip for a group of 15.)

NIGHTLIFE. Nightlife can be found on the main drag that runs along the water. Beer and refreshment stalls on the dock have outdoor seatings and an almost Riviera-like ambience. Toward the park, past Hoang Y Restaurant, is the best bar in town, the Vietnamese-Kiwi owned **Flightless Bird Cafe** (☎888 517), which has darts, movies, and a book exchange. The two discotheques, perched on the hill behind the GPO, are refreshingly devoid of prostitution. Follow the neon signs for **Cát Bà Night Club** (☎888 789) and next-door **Sóng Xanh Disco** (☎888 637; no cover; Tiger beer only 10,000Đ) Try them if you ever wondered how Public Enemy can blend with Canto-pop in a remix that features Celine Dion.

HẠ LONG BAY (VỊNH HẠ LONG) ☎33

With its 1968 limestone islands and 23 grottoes, this marvel of nature is now protected by UNESCO. According to legend, Hạ Long ("Dragon Descending") Bay was formed when a dragon spat out divine pearls that formed a barrier against an invading Chinese fleet. Once the enemy had been turned back, the dragon settled in the bay and its scales converted into rocky islets. At first glance, Hạ Long City is an impersonal town full of identical minihotels, outrageous prices, and pushy locals. But the reality of Vietnam today is one of places like Hạ Long City, where a drive for development and a liberalizing economy are redefining Vietnamese society. In the past decade, local authorities have furthered regional investment in hotels and recreation facilities, making Hạ Long City into a top tourist getaway for northern Vietnamese and southern Chinese. The bay is most effectively and inexpensively reached by tour from Hanoi. It's also possible to skip Hạ Long City altogether and explore the bay from Cát Bà Island via Haiphong.

TRANSPORTATION

Buses depart from Bãi Cháy Bus Station, 600m south of the Hòn Gai Ferry on Hạ Long Rd. Destinations include: **Hanoi** (3-4hr.; every 20-30min. 4:50am-5pm; 35,000Đ); **HCMC** (W, Th, Su 7:30am; 225,000Đ); **Mong Cai** (3hr.; every 30min. 6am-5pm; 35,000Đ); and **Vinh** (7-8hr.; 6:30am; 55,000Đ). **Minibuses** leave from across the street and can be flagged down along Hạ Long Rd. Catch one to **Haiphong** (2½hr.; 6am-5pm; 18,000Đ) or **Hanoi** (4hr.; 6am-5pm; from 80,000Đ). **Ferries** leave from Bãi Cháy to **Hòn Gai** (every 10min. until 10pm, then every 30min.; 500Đ). The Hòn Gai pier (Bến Tàu Hòn Gai), 1.5km down Lê Thánh Tông from the pier, at the end of the road to the right at the first small traffic circle, has ferries to **Cát Bà Island** (2½hr.; Sa-Su 7am; 70,000Đ) and **Haiphong** (2½hr.; 6, 8:30, 11am, 4pm; 60,000Đ). A better option is to take the **Tourist Hydrofoil.** It runs to Cát Bà (daily 7:30am-8:10am, return 4:15pm-4:55pm; 90,000Đ) and to the Chinese border town of **Mong Cai** (3hr., 8am and 11pm, US$12).

VIETNAM

ORIENTATION AND PRACTICAL INFORMATION

Bãi Cháy and **Hòn Gai** are the west and east halves of **Hạ Long City** which lies 165km east of Hanoi and 55km northeast of Haiphong. Tourist-oriented Bãi Cháy is across a strait from the more industrial Hòn Gai. **Hạ Long,** the main road in Bãi Cháy, runs northeast, along the bay front and terminates at the ferry to Hòn Gai. From the **tourist boat pier,** the center of Bãi Cháy is 2km east. The **Royal Amusement Park** is between Hạ Long Rd. and the bay, extending 1km between the tourist pier and the town center. Restaurant Row and the GPO crowd the Vườn Đào intersection with Hạ Long Rd. continuing 1km farther northeast to the bus station and local ferry. All chartered boats to the grottoes leave from the tourist boat piers. **Hạ Long Tourist Company,** at the tourist pier, organizes 4hr. boat trips (US$22-27) and gives useful information. (☎846 272. Open M-Sa 7:30-11:30am and 1-5pm.) **Commercial Bank of Quảng Ninh,** on Hạ Long Rd. down the road from the tourist pier, changes major currencies and traveler's checks. (☎825 297. Open M-F 8-11am and 1-5pm.) The main branch is in Hòn Gai 1.5km east down Lệ Thánh Tông at the first major traffic circle. (☎628 692. Open M-F 8-11am and 1-5pm.) In **emergencies,** call ☎825 486. **Quảng Ninh Provincial Hospital,** 651 Lê Thánh Tông, is 1km beyond the Hòn Gai GPO on the road that forks to the right. The director of the hospital, Mr. Hanh, speaks English. (☎825 494. US$50 per visit.) **Internet access** can be found at **Emotion Cyber Cafe** (☎847 354; 400Đ per min.) and various tourist agencies. The **Hạ**

Long City Post Office, at Vườn Đào intersection, has **telephones;** you must purchase a phone card (100,000Đ) first. (☎840 201. Open daily 6:30am-9:30pm.)

ACCOMMODATIONS AND FOOD

To catch a sight like no other, veer off to the left from the GPO and walk 400m up the hill on Vườn Đào. **Minihotels** line this street with a vengeance—over 75 on this small hill alone. All ask US$8-15 depending on amenities that include two beds, hot showers, and A/C. Enjoy making your choice. **Khách San Vân Anh ❷,** across from the ferry dock, is at the top of 100 steps with a commanding view of the bay. From the public bus station, turn left and follow the sign 50m away. (☎847 618. Singles 100,000Đ; doubles 120,000Đ.) **Hong Minh Hotel ❷** has clean rooms in a great location. Facing the GPO, walk 100m along the water on Hạ Long Rd. (☎846 264. Doubles Oct.-Apr. US$10, with view US$12; May-Sept. US$14/US$18.) **Hưởng Trầm Hotel ❷** is a comfortable minihotel overlooking the bay; the local military police have a hand in running it. Facing the GPO, take the right fork (Hạ Long Rd.). Take the first left, a dirt path leading up the bluff, 200m from the GPO. (☎846 365. Doubles 100,000-120,000Đ.)

Seafood is the specialty in Hạ Long Bay, but it doesn't come cheaply. **Restaurant Row** around the GPO is the culinary epicenter for tourists. Live lobster, crabs, fish, and clams await customers in water tanks outside each eatery. (Seafood entrees 30,000-180,000Đ.) In this lot, **Phướng Oanh ❸** (☎846 145) is recommended for its cheap prices. The farther you walk away from the row, the cheaper the food. **Cafe Halong ❹** (☎847 780), near the bus station, has a more extensive English menu. A small **market ❶** hides in the shadows of the hotels. From the GPO head up Vườn Đào; the first road branching right peters out at the market.

VIETNAM

SIGHTS

Travelers from all over come to explore beautiful Hạ Long Bay. Of the 1500 plus limestone grottoes protruding from the sea, over 150 caves have been identified so far, and at least 50 of them are blessed with multi-colored illumination for the benefit of tourists. Private boats are necessary to explore the obscure grottoes, because packaged boat tours only stop at a select few. The favorite stop is the **Heavenly Palace Grotto** and the **Dau Go Grotto** (grotto of the Wooden Stakes). The former is so named because of the varying shape of mineral formations that resemble a den of heavenly creatures, while legend has it that the latter hid shipbuilding wood for the Vietnamese during their conflicts with the Chinese at the turn of the millennium. As the most visited cave, their splendor is compromised by the Disney-esque neon lighting and concrete paths. Another site is the **Virgin Grotto,** named for a stalagmite figure that resembles a young maiden pining after her lost love. All grottoes require the purchase of tickets (10,000-20,000Đ, included if you are booked on a boat tour from Hanoi or Hạ Long City).

The easiest way to see Hạ Long Bay is via a tour booked in Hanoi. The most popular agencies are **TF Hanspan,** 116 Pho Hang Bạc (☎828 1996), and its sister organization **Kangaroo Cafe,** 18 Pho Bao Khánh (☎828 9931). Three-day trips, including Cát Bà, cost US$50-60 (all inclusive). Cheaper tours are run by **Queen and Sinh Cafes** (see **By Bus,** p. 895). Tours are also available on-site; fear not, the touts will find you. (4hr. trip, US$20-40 depending on boat size, comfort, and time on the water.) Groups can charter boats at the **Bãi Cháy Tourist Wharf.** All tours include a US$2 surcharge for foreigners. Tours from Cát Bà Island are possible, though these tend to focus less on exploring caves than swimming in coves.

ENTERTAINMENT AND NIGHTLIFE

In the daytime, travelers can rent jet skis on the beachfront (US$15 per 15 min.), parasailing gear (US$100 per hr.), and a variety of aquatic paraphernalia. At night, the same area boasts **Oh La La Bar** with assorted live music (from Tchaïkovsky to the Titanic theme song) played in bamboo-decorated bliss. (Beer from 15,000Đ. Open daily 3-11pm.) Nearby **Disco 2000** blasts the latest Chinese pop. (US$5 includes one drink. Half-priced drinks and no cover for ladies M-Th. Open daily 4pm-midnight.) The waterfront **Royal Amusement Park** with jet skis, fake sand, and carnival games in the daytime turns into food stalls, live music and fancy pubs at night. The young (or young at heart), kitsch-friendly, and anthropologically-astute traveler should not miss this place. All others should keep an open mind, get ear plugs at night, and quit whining. One ticket to the gated portion of the park buys access to orchid gardens, a museum, an art-gallery, and traditional dance, water-puppet, and cockfighting performances. (Open daily 2-11pm. 100,000Đ.)

LẠNG SƠN ☎25

During the last 2000 years, the pass at Lạng Sơn has seen many uninvited crossings by Chinese armies. In 1979, Chinese troops razed Lạng Sơn as part of Deng Xiaoping's effort to "teach the Vietnamese a lesson." Ironically, Lạng Sơn's sole attraction now is Đồng Đăng, one of three legal places in Vietnam to enter China. Travelers should follow the lead of the many big-rig trucks—just pass on through.

BORDER CROSSING: ĐONG ĐANG/PINGXIANG. North of Lạng Sơn at the northern terminus of Rte. 1 lies the tiny border town of Đồng Đăng. The border is past 2 checkpoints, 3km beyond Đồng Đăng at the Hữu Nghị (Friendship) Crossing. To enter China here, your **visa** must have a Đồng Đăng **exit stamp.** Tourist cafes in Hanoi can procure Chinese visas (US$34) and can change the exit stamp on Vietnamese visas (US$30). At **Pingxiang,** in Guangxi Province, there are rail and bus connections to Nanning. Travelers have found Chinese customs here low-key, quick, and easy.

TRANSPORTATION AND PRACTICAL INFORMATION. Buses drop people at the **Ngộ Quyền bus station,** left off Trần Đăng Ninh, 2km north of the Lê Lợi intersection—unless they have to transfer buses en route from Hanoi, in which case they terminate at the **Lạng Sơn Bus Station** off **Lê Lợi** on Ngộ Quyền, 1km east of the intersection with Trần Đăng Ninh. Buses run from Ngộ Quyền Bus Station to **Đồng Đăng** on the border (20-30min.; 8am; 20,000Đ). Buses from Lạng Sợn Bus Station leave for **Hanoi** (3½-4½hr.; 6am-1pm, leave when full; 35,000Đ). **Minibuses** to **Hanoi** (4hr.; 50,000-80,000Đ for foreigners) ply the streets. Smaller minibuses run to the border (20min.; up to 50,000Đ). **Taxis** are for hire in front of the Kim Sơn Hotel off **Đường Minh Khai** (20,000-30,000Đ). **Trains** from Lạng Sơn Station (☎873 452), at the end of Lê Lợi, leave for **Hanoi** (5-6hr.; 2, 6am; 25,000Đ hard seat, 32,000Đ soft seat). Tickets for the M1 train to **Beijing, China** leave from Đồng Đăng Train Station (Tu and F 6:30pm) and should be booked in Hanoi.

Lạng Sơn is 130km north of Hanoi on Rte. 1. The town's main drag, **Trần Đăng Ninh,** heads north to Đồng Đăng. In the southern part of town, **Đường Lê Lợi** branches east from Trần Đăng Ninh, passes the **post office,** and ends at the **train station.** 100m south of the intersection, Trần Đăng Ninh crosses a **river** and continues to **Đầu Tư Bank,** 2 Hoàng Văn Thụ, which exchanges currency but not traveler's checks. (☎870 033. Open daily 7am-11:30pm.) There is a **pharmacy** on the road that branches left off Trần Đăng Ninh, 30m north of the Lê Lợi intersection. This road

VIETNAM

continues through a six-way intersection to the **hospital**, west of town. The **GPO**, 40 Lê Lợi, 100m from the Trần Đăng Ninh intersection, has an **international telephone.** (☎870 047. Open daily 6am-10pm.)

ACCOMMODATIONS AND FOOD. Khăch San Xuân Lộc ❷, 68 Trần Đăng Ninh, offers bright, clean rooms near the center of town. (☎870 992. Doubles US$7-10.) Around the corner, the **Ngọc Mai Hotel ❸**, 25 Lê Lợi, drives a harder bargain but has equally comfortable lodgings. (☎871 837. Doubles US$12.) For rustic charm closer to China, the **Kỳ Lừa Hotel ❷**, 208 Trần Đăng Ninh, delivers. (☎870 020. Doubles and triples with bathtub, TV, and phone 120,000Đ.)

In the evenings a large **market** sets up on Lê Lợi and spills down along the riverside; Trần Đăng Ninh and Lê Lợi host the usual **phở' shops** (full meals 10,000-20,000Đ). Providing a bit of a break from the routine, **Vân Anh Restaurant ❷**, on Lê Lợi 100m past the post office on the right as you come from Trần Đăng Ninh, serves everything from civet to rabbit, at reasonable prices. (Most entrees under 30,000Đ. Open daily 7am-11pm.) Also good and affordable is the **Minh Quang Restaurant ❷**, 45 Ngộ Quyền, serving excellent beef dishes (15,000-20,000Đ).

SIGHTS. A motorcycle taxi can take travelers to the mountains 2-3km west of town to the **Tam Thanh Cave** (transport 5000Đ) and **Nhị Thanh Cave** (transport 10,000Đ). An opening at the cave's rear displays the surrounding countryside and mountains—a fine photo-op. (Open daily 7am-7pm. 10,000Đ each.)

VIETNAM

NORTHWEST VIETNAM

The remote Hoàng Liên Sơn Mountains of northwest Vietnam present some of the most challenging—and rewarding—travel opportunities in mainland Southeast Asia. The physical beauty of the region is breathtaking, and the ethnic diversity of the highland population is reminiscent of northern Laos, with whom the peoples of this region share close cultural and linguistic bonds. Travel is arduous when navigating windy roads with constant ascent and descent, but the government is making an effort to improve some of the nastier sections. Travelers with limited time can get a taste of the region with a trip to highly touristed Sapa or Mai Châu. Otherwise, those braving the entire circuit of Mai Châu, Sơn La, Điện Biên Phủ, Lai Châu, Sapa, and Bắc Hà will get more than kitschy embroideries and encounters with prepubescent tourist-hound veterans. The loop can be done by public bus, by motorbike (highly recommended), or for the masochistic, by bicycle.

LÀO CAI ☎20

Lào Cai is one of two border crossings into Yunnan Province, China, and the chief point of access to Sapa and Bắc Hà. Despite blossoming trade between China and Vietnam, Lào Cai is really just a boring little town. Most travelers hardly pause before speeding north into China, south to Hanoi, or directly into the mountains.

Most travelers arrive in Lào Cai by **train** from Hanoi or China. Train ticket stubs are collected at the gate on arrival; don't lose them. Trains run to **Hanoi** (10hr.; 10:20am, 6:45, 8:20pm; 55,000Đ hard seat, 121,000Đ soft sleeper). Plenty of transfer options await at the Lào Cai train station to take you to guest houses in Sapa. Some guest houses have **minibuses** (35,000Đ per person); you are not obliged to stay at the assigned address, only to look. An official from Hanoi Tourism also has a makeshift desk selling 30,000Đ Sapa bus tickets redeemable at most private vans outside the station. Purchase directly from drivers outside, however, and you'll

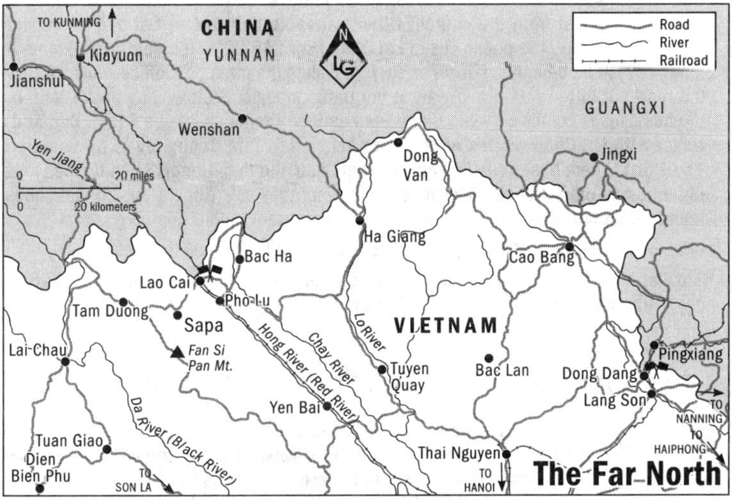

likely pay only 25,000Đ. **Tickets cheaper than 25,000Đ are likely to be fraudulent.** Other modes of Sapa-bound transport include **motorcycle taxis** (2hr. on bumpy road; 50,000Đ), **taxis** (150,000Đ or less), or **public buses** at the bus station (2hr.; around 6, 9am, 1, 4pm; 25,000Đ), though buying a ticket from the counter may prove difficult. **Buses** also depart to: **Bắc Hà** (2-3hr.; 35,000Đ); **Hanoi** (10-12hr.; 104,000Đ); and **Lai Châu** (8hr.; 6:30am; 60,000Đ).

Lào Cai suffers from poor urban planning; the three locations tourists frequent are inconveniently far apart. The **Lào Cai train station** lies 2km south of the **customs building** (open daily 7:30am-4pm). Both the train station and customs office house **currency exchange** offices (US dollars, Đong, Chinese yuan accepted; open daily 7am-4pm). The **bus station** sits between the train and customs, but on the other side of the river. Motorcycle taxis run from one end to the other for 5000-10,000Đ. There are hotels clustered around the customs building, along with eateries and a post office. The **Sông Hông Guest House ❷** is your best bet; it has all the amenities in a clean environment. (☎830 004. Doubles 80,000-120,000Đ.)

SAPA ☎20

The hills around Sapa are alive—with the sound of tourists and the vendors who love them. Once a remote hill station, Sapa is now the premier spot for weekend package tours. The famed Saturday market has become a spectacle, where everyone becomes a caricature for others in an amusing arena of mutual—and communal—bewilderment. For that reason, more visitors choose to come mid-week to see Sapa's true idyllic beauty. The communities of Sapa have little other than a history of deprivation and an intense pride—something travelers should remember before losing their patience in front of a persistent hawker.

TRANSPORTATION

Buses: Tourist minibuses to **Lào Cai** leave from the large square in front of the church (1½hr.; every hr. from 6am; 25,000Đ). Buy tickets at the post office or in any of the tourist cafes a day in advance. **Public buses** (2hr.; 7:30am, 3:30pm; 30,000Đ), as well as **jeeps, sedans,** and **minibuses** (2hr.; leave when full, no more than 30,000Đ) leave for Lào Cai from the church. Other transportation to Lào Cai can be secured through your hotel. The public bus to **Lai Châu** (8hr.; 45,000Đ for Vietnamese, more for foreigners) must be flagged down on Hwy. 4. Facing the main post office, walk left down the road out of town 1km and wait at the traffic triangle. Start waiting at 7:30am, but the bus usually comes between 8 and 9am and may come as late as 11am. **Demand a ticket with Lai Châu written on it.** Buses also run to **Tam Đuong** (every hr. 6am-2pm; 15,000Đ), where buses can be caught to Lai Châu and then Hanoi. Since the bus to Lai Châu has no official price, travelers can pay what they ask. Bring a trusted Vietnamese friend (often from the guest house) to purchase a ticket before boarding.

Local Transportation: Motos (at the church) can usually take you to hotels.

Rentals: Many hotels rent **minsks,** old Russian motorcycles (US$1 per hr., US$6 per day), and **jeeps** with drivers (from US$30 per day).

ORIENTATION AND PRACTICAL INFORMATION

The Sapa Church faces a soccer field and park at the town's center. From the church, it takes 10-15min. to reach anywhere in town. Facing the church, the **GPO** is one block to your left, with the **Friendly Cafe** just across the park. A stairway 100m to the right of the church leads down to the **market** and the **main street.** Tourist services cluster on the main street before the road heads out of town. The other road that winds down the valley (toward Càt Càt Village) runs perpendicular to the mainstreet and originates at the fruit and vegetable end of the market.

Tours: Friendly Cafe in the Prince (Hoàng Tư) Hotel offers treks around Sapa (1-day trek, US$7-18 depending on group size), as well as trips up **Fan Si Pan Mountain** (3 days, US$30-65). They have another office in the Royal Hotel on the main street. **Sapa Trekking Tours** (☎871 021), down the main street from the market on the right, offers similar services, while across the street, Hung, manager of a branch of Hanoi's **Green Bamboo Cafe** (☎871 556), serves travelers well.

Currency Exchange: The bank won't change currency. Most guest houses change US dollars and traveler's checks at high rates (5-7% commission).

Hospital: ☎871 237. 1km down the road, from the GPO toward Lao Cai.

Telephones: Cash calls available at the GPO. US$2.35 per min.

Internet Access: Available at most hotels and guest houses for 500Đ per min.

Post Offices: GPO (☎871 292). Facing the church, go left on the road leading back to Lào Cai. *Poste Restante*. Open daily 7am-9:30pm. Another **branch** (☎871 247) is on the main street below the market.

ACCOMMODATIONS

Most rooms in Sapa run on both a seasonal and weekly price schedule. During the weekend in high season (May-July for Vietnamese tourists, July-Oct. for foreigners), hotels charge what they want. On the off days, however, it's a buyers market: bargain hard.

Twilight Guest House (☎871 601), 150m down the road toward Càt Càt Village from the market (vegetable section). New hotel offers sparkling rooms with astounding views at cheap prices. First floor room without view US$3, with view US$4-10. ❶

Càt Càt Guest House (☎871 387), opposite the Twilight Guest House. If you crave wild parties and hordes of beer-guzzling backpackers, the perennial favorite Càt Càt is for you. Great tourist info. Rooms US$4-15. ❷

Minh Quang Hotel (☎871 449), past the Auberge (see below), 250m toward the main street's remote end. New, bright, palatial-looking building away from tourist fanfare...for now. Rooms with views of Fan Si Pan, still awaiting their first scratches, US$7. ❷

Phoenix Guest House (☎871 515), 50m closer to town from Minh Quang. Unobstructed view of Fan Si Pan. Rooms US$7, with a view and balcony US$10-15. ❷

Queen Hotel (☎871 301), on the main road around the bend below the market, next to Auberge. Ask for Room 403 or 503 for a deluxe experience. Fastest Internet in town (500Đ per min.). Rooms with hot water US$8-15. ❸

Cầu Mây Guest House (☎871 293). From the market head up the main road until it terminates and then go left. Away from usual tourist hangouts. Rooms are sparse though hot water and satellite TV are guaranteed to work. Rooms US$7 or 100,000Đ. ❷

Auberge Dang Trung Hotel (☎871 243). From the market head down the main street and follow the bend 200m down. An old-time favorite in a stylish French villa. Relax by the bonsai garden. French- and English-speaking staff. Internet access. Same rates all year. Rooms US$6-28. ❷

FOOD AND NIGHTLIFE

Local culinary delights aim to please all. **Stalls** ❶ in the market and around town serve *phở*, rice dishes, and grilled corn. Sapa Wine, though neither wine nor a product of Sapa, is the choice spirit for chilly evenings.

Mimosa Restaurant, on the left side of the main street down from the market; a sign points up a stairway to the restaurant. Favorite tourist spot in a secluded setting. Excellent lemon grass frog legs. Open daily 7am-11pm. ❷

Nhà Nghỉ Đức Tú, facing the church, walk 150m to the right past the stairs to the market; restaurant is two doors past Huy Hoang Guest House. Stuff yourself on local fare for 15,000Đ. Open daily 7am-11pm. ❷

Auberge Dang Trung Restaurant, in the Auberge Hotel, has terrace seating with fine views. Slightly pricier, but worth it. Can put together a vegetarian plate (25,000Đ). Banana shake 5000Đ. Open daily 7am-10pm. ❷

Camellia Restaurant, across the market, on the right before Càt Càt Guest House. Chicken curry 24,000Đ. Excellent beef dishes 20,000Đ. Open daily 6am-midnight. ❷

Chapa Cafe, 50m from Auberge. Typical backpacker's stable: muesli, pancakes, etc. Full dinner menu as well. Open daily 7am-11pm. ❶

Green Bamboo Bar, in the Green Bamboo Hotel, down the main street past the Auberge. Tourists crowd in at 8:30pm F-Sa to watch local Hmong perform traditional music. The direct relationship between inebriation and loosening purse strings is not lost on the little Hmong salesgirls also in attendance. Beer 8000-15,000Đ. ❶

SIGHTS

Fan Si Pan Mountain (3143m), across the valley, is Vietnam's highest peak and a popular expedition for those willing to brave its deceptively steep slopes. A competent guide and provisions are necessary for the three- to five-day trip to the summit and back. All guest houses can arrange tours complete with sleeping bags, tents, rain gear, guide, and porter. Expect to pay at least US$40 per person from a reputable source, such as the Green Bamboo, Friendly Cafe, or Càt Càt. **Thác Bac**

Waterfall, 7km from Sapa on the road to Lai Châu, with its 500m drop and staircase to the top, is also worth a photo, though maybe not for the 5000Đ fee. Instead, walk, or better yet ride a motorbike, for a few more kilometers and experience the breathtaking **Tram Ton Pass** on the route to Lai Châu.

MARKETS

Sapa's main attraction is its **market.** On Saturday afternoons and Sunday mornings, mountain tribal groups come to sell their goods—colorful shirts, musical instruments, and silver jewelry—to travelers. The market began as a "Love Market" by the Daos, where friends from near and far villages came to meet, sing, impress, and entertain each other. Unfortunately, with tourists filming their every move, the event ceased. If you see the "Love Market" advertised now, it's for the fleeting kind you have to pay for. For weekday visitors, there are still plenty of trinket sellers. The second floor of **Chợ Sa Pa,** the town market, is their gathering spot.

DAYTRIPS FROM SAPA

Shorter hikes through ethnic villages, past waterfalls and green rice fields, rival Fan Si Pan and transcend Sapa's commercialism. Though it's possible to hike solo, guides are available for US$8-10. The round-trip to three villages around Sapa takes 4-8hr., and makes for a relaxing and pleasant walk. From Sapa, head out of town past the Auberge Restaurant. Pay the 5000Đ "entrance fee." About 7km into the hike, a bridge appears far below the road. After a series of waterfalls and just behind a Hmong homestead, a steep trail leads downhill toward the river and across a footbridge to the Hmong village of **Lao Chai.** From here, the river downstream leads to the Giay village of **Ta Van,** just past a second bridge, 4km away. It's possible to spend the night in Ta Van for 40,000-50,000Đ. If you're planning on doing this, bring along enough food for the trek because meals in the village can't be guaranteed. Backtrack across this bridge to return to the main road. From here, it's about 2hr. back to town or 1½hr. on to the Dao village of **Giang Ta Chai.** The village is across the river on the left at the fork. Prehistoric etchings adorn rocks along the road. The path crosses a small waterfall on the way. To get to more villages from another direction, cross the market, head downhill past Càt Càt Guest House, and follow the path northwest along the valley (5000Đ entrance fee). You'll see a French villa built in the 1930s, that is now a center for wildlife protection. About 10min. farther, a small path splits off to the left. The main path leads to the Hmong village of **Sin Chai** after 5km. The left path leads to **Càt Càt,** another Hmong village, less than 1km away. Deeper in the valley is an old hydroelectric power station and **Càt Càt Waterfall,** which is visible from town.

BẮC HÀ ☎20

Bắc Hà, 100km northeast of Sapa, recently came into the crosshairs of Hanoi's tourist cafes, which tout it as an "alternative to Sapa." Once a mountain hamlet of hill-tribe traders and old wooden homes, the village is changing fast. Since few travelers attempt to visit on their own, from Monday through Saturday Bắc Hà really does become an "alternative" for those wishing to encounter north Vietnam's ethnic minorities and mountain scenery free from the tourism industry.

Bắc Hà's **Sunday market** (open 7am-2pm) is still genuine: Hmong come from all around to buy clothes and accessories. The market is also known for its food stalls, which serve cheap dishes. English-speaking guides, fluent in some of the hill-tribe languages, can be hired at the Sao Mai Hotel to lead one- or multi-day treks through nearby minority villages, markets, and mountains (US$20 per day to stay overnight in the villages, all-inclusive). Some popular destinations include **Coc Ly,** 50km away, which has a **waterfall (Thác Coc Ly)** and a large **suspension bridge (Cầu Treo Coo Ly)** built over the Chay River by local hill tribes, and the **Saturday morning market** in another town, **Can Cau,** 18km away. Ask whether the Si Ma Cai Market, 10km past Can Cau, is open to foreigners.

Bắc Hà has one main road which splits into three near the north side of town. The right fork, as you head away from Hanoi or Lào Cai, leads to the **bus station** and the rear entrance to the **market.** Buses run to **Lào Cai** (2-3hr.; 6am, 12:30pm; 20,000Đ), and **Pho Lu** (1hr.; 7, 11:30am; 10,000Đ), where buses or trains can be caught to Hanoi. The middle fork heads out of town toward the nearest minority villages and on to Can Cau. The left fork runs past the **Sao Mai Hotel** and the **hospital** (☎880 263). The **post office** is on the right side of the main road 150m prior to the three-way fork. (☎880 280. Open daily 7am-8pm.) A road cuts right just past the post office and heads to the front of the **market.** A **pharmacy** is 60m uphill from the post office on the right. (☎880 365. Open daily 8am-noon and 1:30-5pm.)

The largest and most modern accommodation by far is **Sao Mai Hotel ❸,** 150m along the road that branches to the left. Most rooms have great views of the surrounding peaks. The **restaurant ❷** and bar (entrees 10,000-20000Đ) are connected to Hanoi's Sinh Cafe and in addition to running tours can arrange transportation to Sapa or Hanoi. (☎880 288. Doubles with TV, fridge, and hot water US$12-25, prices slashed 30% during the week.) The **Dang Khoa Hotel ❷,** on the main road on the left 75m up from the post office, is a solid option. (☎880 290. Singles US$5-8; doubles US$10-15, highly bargainable.) **Anh Đuong Hotel ❶** shows its age a bit, but is near the market. (☎880 329. Basic doubles with hot water 60,000Đ.) Bắc Hà is renowned for its small plums *(quả mận)*, a definite must-try. Locals dip them in salt and eat them when they are still green and bitter. **Xuân Về ❶,** opposite the Sao Mai Hotel (omelette 8000Đ, spring rolls 10,000Đ; open daily 6am-11pm), and **Tan Thành Restaurant ❷,** between the post office and the market (☎880 575; *cóm* dishes 10,000-15,000Đ), have English menus.

VIETNAM

LAI CHÂU AND TAM ĐUONG ☎23

The landscapes between Sapa and Điện Biên Phủ, a succession of majestic mountains, ethnic villages, and gorgeous rice fields, are superb. The relatively long distance, however (300km), forces the traveler to stop in two insignificant and unappealing towns: Lai Châu and Tam Đuong (Phuong Tho). **Buses** leave from a lot marked by a sign labeled "Bến Xe Thị Xã Lai Châu" 3km toward Điện Biên Phủ from Lai Châu proper. To: **Hanoi** (18-30hr.; 6am; 90,000Đ) via **Điện Biên Phủ** (5-6hr.; every hr.; 30,000Đ); and **Lào Cai** (10-14hr.; 6am; 45,000Đ) via **Sapa** (8-11hr.; 45,000Đ). The Lai Châu **GPO,** at the far end of town toward Sapa, has *Poste Restante* and international phones. (☎852 301. Open daily 7am-9pm.)

The most popular accommodation is town is the **Lan Anh Hotel ❸.** Coming from Điện Biên Phủ, turn left 3km after the bus station and follow the signs. Free bananas and rooms with all-wood interiors set this place apart. (☎852 370. Singles and doubles US$8-15.) The cheapest of the town's hotels is **Nâm Lay Hotel ❶,** at the far end of town toward Sapa. Look for the stairs climbing the mountainside on your right. (☎852 346. Large cell block with shared bath 40,000Đ; nicer doubles with fan 80,000Đ.) **Song Da Hotel ❸,** on the main road near the town center, offers decent rooms and an owner keen on practicing his English. (☎852 527. Doubles with fan US$8, with A/C US$12.) The Lan Anh boasts a **restaurant ❸** that serves a set menu lunch (30,000-50,000Đ), as well as standard fare for dinner.

The small town of **Tam Đuong,** where many buses also stop, lies 100km down the road and 90km before Sapa. The bus station is on the main street, to the right if you're coming from Điện Biên Phủ, off the side street across from the Tam Đuong

Hotel. **Buses** run to: **Điện Biên Phủ** (4-6hr.; 6, 11am, 40,000Đ) via **Lai Châu; Hanoi** (12-14hr; 5am; 100,000Đ); and **Sapa** (2hr.; 6, 7, 11am; 25,000Đ) via **Lào Cai.**

Tam Đuong has two nice hotels offering similar rooms for the same price. **Tam Đuong Hotel ❸,** on the left off the main street, is modern. (☎875 288. Doubles 150,000Đ.) **Phuong Thanh Mini-hotel ❸,** on both sides of the street farther down toward Sapa, has comfortable rooms and gorgeous views of the valley. (☎875 235. Doubles 150,000Đ.) Prices can be lowered by telling one hotel that the other is offering a better rate. **Phuong Thanh Restaurant ❷,** opposite Tam Đuong Hotel, serves good food for 10,000-20,000Đ.

ĐIỆN BIÊN PHỦ ☎23

Điện Biên Phủ, an ugly but historically significant town, is easy to miss. Off the backpacker ant-trail, it holds a sacred place in the lore of the Vietnamese Revolution. As the site of the French defeat in 1954 at the hands of Hồ Chí Minh's Việt Minh, Điện Biên Phủ remains one of the best-known symbols in Vietnam of the collapse of European colonialism. The town is adjusting to its newfound role as capital of Lai Châu Province. Only time will tell whether authorities will usher in a second wave of Western invaders into the valley by opening the border to Laos 30km west of town. In the meantime, the tanks and bunkers scattered through the corn fields make a stop here worthwhile for military history buffs.

VIETNAM

TRANSPORTATION. The **airstrip** runs parallel to Hwy. 12 and the **terminal** is on the left, 1km north of the bus station on the road to Lai Châu. Flights go to **Hanoi** (Sa-Tu, Th 12:10, 2:10pm; 635,000Đ) and **HCMC** via Hanoi (1,800,000Đ). Buy tickets at the **Vietnam Airlines office** in the airport hotel on Phuong Thành Binh, left off the main street, between the bus station and the Mường Thanh intersection on Hwy. 12. (☎824 692. Open daily 7:30-10am and 2-4pm.) **Buses** run to: **Hanoi** (20-30hr.; 4:30, 8:30, 10:30am; 95,000Đ) via **Sơn La** and **Tong Dau (Mai Chău)**; **Lai Châu** (5-6hr.; every hr. 6-11am and 1:30pm; 25,000Đ+ for tourists); **Sơn La** (6-7hr.; 4:45am, noon; 38,000Đ for tourists). Buy tickets before boarding.

ORIENTATION AND PRACTICAL INFORMATION. Over 450km northwest of Hanoi and 34km from the Lao border, Điện Biên Phủ is in the **Mường Thành Valley.** The **bus station** is west of town on **Highway 12,** which continues northwest to Lai Châu. As Hwy. 12 heads east from the bus station, it bridges the **Nam Yum River** after 300m and intersects **Dường Mường Thành,** the town's main street. A right at this intersection leads toward the rest of town and on to Laos (34km), the hospital, post office, Điện Biên Phủ Museum, and most of the military sights. The **Bank for Investment and Development of Vietnam,** 3 Dường Mường Thành, halfway to the post office, exchanges foreign cash. (☎825 774. Open M-F 7-11am and 2-5pm.) A **hospital** (☎825 463) is on Hoang Van Thai, left off the main street between A1 Hill and the Vietnamese cemetery. From the bridge, turn left onto Mường Thành and the **Ngọc Ánh pharmacy** is up 75m on the right. (☎825 335. Open daily 6:30-11am and 1:30-7pm.) The **GPO** is just past the bank on the right. It has *Poste Restante* and an **international telephone office.** (☎825 833. Open daily 7am-9:15pm.)

ACCOMMODATIONS AND FOOD. Opposite the bus station, the **Mǎy Hồng Hotel ❷** offers the best value in town. (☎826 300. Singles and doubles with baths 100,000Đ; spacious doubles 120,000Đ.) The nicest hotel in town is off the main road from Sơn La before the bridge: **Mường Thành Hotel ❷,** 25 Phuong Him Lam, has a swimming pool, ping-pong, massage parlor, and large rooms. (☎826 719. Cozy, wood-finished doubles with fan US$7, doubles with A/C and bath US$12-20.)

Cheaper, the **Binh Long Hotel ❸**, on Mường Thành 200m north of the Hwy. 12 intersection, has tidy rooms with hot showers. (☎824 345. Doubles with A/C US$10.)

Rice and *phở* can be bought along **Mường Thành; stalls ❶** past the GPO offer a wider selection of eats, and **Bế Văn Đàn**, the second street on the right after the bridge, has little restaurants serving dog (*cho*) meat. The **market ❷** next to the bridge features a wide selection of produce. Three restaurants are worth mentioning: **Ngoc Mai ❷** (☎825 932), on Hoang Van No, across a retention pond from the GPO, serves excellent spring rolls and entrees (8000-15,000Đ). **Ăn Uống ❷**, in the Mường Thành Hotel, has Western, Vietnamese, and traditional minority Thai dishes on the menu (entrees 20,000-30,000Đ). **Lien Tuoi Restaurant ❷**, on Hoang Van Thai near the hospital, serves quality Vietnamese dishes for 15,000-30,000Đ. To get there, follow the left branch of Hoang Van Thai. It's 200m down on the right.

SIGHTS. Điện Biên Phủ's main draw is its history. For travelers who come to Điện Biên Phủ by bus, it is not difficult to imagine why the French reckoned the valley too remote to be threatened by the Việt Minh. The key to the Việt Minh victory was their sly plan to drag artillery to the ridges ringing Điện Biên Phủ Valley. On May 6, 1954, the French lowered the *tricouleur* and hoisted another flag—the white one. A day later, negotiations began in Geneva. Điện Biên Phủ is now a memorial to the Vietnamese victory. For a battle primer, head to the **museum**, the large yellow building across from the cemetery. (Open M-Sa 9am-4:30pm. 5000Đ.) Opposite the museum, 60m toward Hwy. 12, is **A1 Hill**, scene of the fiercest fighting of the campaign. (Open daily 9am-5pm. 5000Đ.) A large Vietnamese cemetery opposite the museum, next to Al Hill, has become a popular pilgrimage destination for Vietnamese tourists, more so than for foreign ones. (Open daily 7am-7pm.) From the hill, head 500m back toward town and turn left onto Bế Văn Đàn, which crosses a small bridge to the battlefield after 50m. After the bridge, turn left; 50m up the road on the right lies **Colonel Christian de Castries' command bunker.** (Open M-Sa 8-10:30am and 2-4:30pm. 5000Đ.) Ask to be let into the **French cemetery** (Nghæa Trang Pháp) up the road. The roads in this area are littered with the remains of (genuine) French mortars and tanks in fields of red roses.

VIETNAM

SO'N LA ☎22

Travelers who don't know where to look may feel their experience in Sơn La resembles that of the political prisoners incarcerated here by the French: surrounded by natural beauty, but trapped in an uninteresting town. Like the revolutionaries who escaped in 1936, there's hope for you, too. Sơn La is surrounded by Black Thài hill tribes, whose villages offer an adventuresome side to this small town, and there are caves and hot springs within easy reach.

TRANSPORTATION AND PRACTICAL INFORMATION. Sơn La is 320km west of Hanoi and two-thirds of the way from the capital to Điện Biên Phủ on **Route 6. Nguyễn Luong Bâng,** which becomes **Điện Biên,** intersects with **Trường Chinh Rd.,** which runs south to Hanoi, to form the center of Sơn La. Approaching from Mai Chau or Hanoi, a left off of Trường Chinh on to Điện Biên will lead across a small bridge. Stay straight on Điện Biên to head toward Điện Biên Phủ and Lai Châu or turn right on Tô Hiệu Rd. which passes the GPO before continuing out of town as Rt. 12. The bus station is 7km outside of town on Rt. 6 toward Mai Châu. From the bus station, **buses** and **minibuses** leave for **Điện Biên Phủ** (6-7hr.; 4am, noon; 39,000Đ) and **Hanoi** (8-10hr.; every hr. 4am-noon; 63,000Đ). Occasional buses plying the Hanoi-Điện Biên Phủ route can be hailed as they cross the bridge. Buses also run to **Lai Châu** (6hr.; every hr. from 5am; 60,000Đ), but must be flagged down. The largest **pharmacy** in town is **Nha Thuốc Trấn Minh Sáu,** 37Đ Điện Biên, just across the bridge. (☎852 005. Open daily 6:30am-10pm.) The **hospital** (☎852 325) is 2.5km down Tô Hiệu on the right. A large **market** sits 1km down from the Trường Chinh/Nguyễn Luong Bâng intersection off Trường Chinh, and sells fresh fruit, meat, and vegetables as well as clothes and all kinds of goods. (Open daily 6am-6pm.) The **GPO,** 200m down Tô Hiệu, has an **international telephone office.** (☎852 421. Open daily 6:30am-9pm.)

ACCOMMODATIONS AND FOOD. A popular choice is the **Union Hotel ❸** (Nhà Khách Công Đoàn), 200m off Tô Hiệu on Dương 26/4. The turn-off for the hotel is 300m past the GPO and marked by a blue sign. The staff speaks English and provides a free guidebook for guests. (☎852 804. Doubles with fan US$10, with A/C US$15-25.) **Hoa Hong Hotel ❷,** 39 Road 3/2, take the first right off Hwy 6/ Trường Chinh Rd. after the marker indicating 2km to the town center. The hotel will be on your right at the first rotary intersection. The hulking building houses clean rooms, an English-speaking receptionist, and large glass-walled hallways that look onto the surrounding mountains. (☎854 301. Doubles with bath and A/C US$7-9.) A more bureaucratic option is the **People's Committee Guest House ❸,** 400m up Điện Biên from the bridge. (☎852 080. All rooms US$15.)

For a local specialty, head 500m up Điện Biên from the bridge; as the road curves past the Tô Hiệu Monument, look for a sign on the left reading **Thịt Dê ❷.** The name means "goat meat," which the cook will whip up in a kebab for 25,000Đ. (Open daily 10am-8pm.) **Long Phuong Restaurant ❷,** 6 Nguyễn Luong Bâng, just off the intersection with Trường Chinh, serves local specialties from the forests (pheasant, rabbit, and quail) for 10,000-20,000Đ. **Tiệm Ăn Restaurant ❸,** 158 Tô Hiệu, on the right just before the GPO from the bridge, has an English menu. (Entrees 30,000-60,000Đ. Open daily 7am-8pm.) The local brew, Bia Sơn Dương, is on tap all over town. Though less tasty than Bia Hanoi, it has some kick to it and will make up for the lack of nightlife in town.

SIGHTS. The **French prison** (Nhà Tù Cũ Của Pháp) is a monument to French oppression of the Việt Minh in the 1930s and 1940s. To get to the prison, head toward Điện Biên Phủ on Điện Biên for 500m. Along the way, **Tô Hiệu Monument** stands on the left, dedicated to the favorite son of Sơn La. Roughly 75m beyond the monument, take the first right on Khâu Cả and follow it to the top. The museum is the yellow building on the right before the radio tower. The entrance to the prison is down a path to the right. Ask the museum attendant to open the exhibit inside the prison. The left wing of the reconstructed prison building has a photo-exhibit of the prison's history, and the main yellow building—where the guards used to stay—now hosts a **cultural museum** containing some artifacts of local ethnic minorities and a photo history of the prison. (Monument and museum open daily 7-11:30am and 1:30-5pm. 10,000Đ.) Ask at the Công Đoàn Guest House to hire a guide to visit the **hill-tribe villages** around Sơn La. The **Tam Tong Caves** are 3km toward Điện Biên Phủ on Hwy. 12. A local guide costs 10,000Đ at the caves. If visiting alone, make sure to take a flash-light. A motorcycle costs 20,000Đ to the **hot springs** (Suối Nước Nóng), 7km south of town. The springs are worth the detour only in the winter, when their temperature reaches 25C°.

MAI CHÂU ☎18

Surrounded by steep mountains, tiny Mai Châu is a slow-paced paradise of rice paddies. Just outside town, Bản Làc, one of the many Thài ethnic minority villages scattered throughout the valley, allows visitors to step into Thài life by spending nights in stilt-houses, eating home-cooked meals, and observing rural Thài and

Vietnamese culture. Many stay a few days to explore the hills and villages and to get a true taste of the White Thài lifestyle.

TRANSPORTATION AND PRACTICAL INFORMATION. Mai Châu is 140km west of Hanoi and 6km from Tòng Đậu, which lies on Rte. 6 roughly halfway to Sơn La. The entire town stretches along 1.5km of Rte. 15A, from the **post office** at the end of town closest to Tòng Đậu, to the **Mai Châu Guest House** at the opposite end of town. About halfway between the two is the **market** and, on the other side of the street, the **bus station.** There are daily buses to **Hòa Bình** (2-3hr.; 6am, noon; 20,000Đ), from which travelers can catch buses to **Hanoi** (2-3hr.; 6:30, 7:30am; 30,000-40,000Đ). **Motorcycle taxis** gather near the market. Take one to **Tòng Đậu** (6000-10,000Đ) to reach buses traveling to **Sơn La** or **Hanoi.** Locals can tell you when to expect buses (as early as 6:30am). There is **no formal currency exchange** in Mai Châu, but some residents will change dollars into đồng. A **pharmacy** is on the main road 100m past the market toward Mai Châu Guest House. (☎867 129. Open daily 7am-4pm.) Another 200m in the same direction on the main road is a **hospital.** (☎867 244. Open daily 7-11am and 1:30-5:30pm; in winter 7:30-11:30am and 1-5pm.) The **post office** is 500m from the market toward Tòng Đậu, and has **international telephone** and fax but no calling card access. (☎867 100. Open daily 7am-9pm.)

ACCOMMODATIONS AND FOOD. Mai Châu's accommodations are its primary attraction. Tourists are permitted to stay in the White Thai village of **Bản Lác ❶,** 1km past Mai Châu (take the road branching to the right). A majority of the traditional stilt houses now serve as guest houses, and for 50,000Đ visitors can sleep on a mat on the floor in the main room; mosquito nets are provided. The fee includes breakfast but for 20,000Đ Bản Lác families also serve up a filling traditional dinner. The nicest views are available from the **guest house ❶** at the entrance of the village (☎867 255), which contains a modern bathroom and shower and charges the same price as families. For standard accommodations the **Mai Châu Guest House ❷,** a modern building by the lake at the end of town farthest from Tòng Đậu, has large rooms and a balcony with views of surrounding rice paddies. (☎867 262. Singles and doubles 70,000-100,000Đ.)

Other options for food are the **phở' shops** in Mai Châu proper and the market that sells fresh fruit, vegetables, and meat in the morning. Heading toward the post office from the market, the *phở'* shop ❶ at the bend in the road before the bridge, on the right as you head toward the post office, has an English-speaking proprietor. (*Phở'* 5000Đ. Open daily 7am-9pm.)

SIGHTS. The area around Mai Châu is teeming with Thài, Hmong, and Mường villages, as well as thrilling scenery. Dayhikes down any of the roads that branch out from town are the best means of exploration. More extensive treks require a guide and are best booked through a tourist cafe in Hanoi. A stay in **Bản Lác** is a staple of these tours (US$30 for a 2-day/1-night trip booked in Hanoi). Past Mai Châu heading toward Sơn La, **La Linh** and **Yen Chau** are two excellent villages to visit. The area around **Mộc Châu** on the way to Sơn La is one of the most densely populated in the northwest. Mainly inhabited by Thài and Hmong people, it offers beautiful hilly landscapes, waterfalls, and hot springs. Though an insignificant town in itself, Mộc Châu—with its three hotels and two guest houses—can be used as a convenient base to explore the surrounding countryside. The **Hang Dơ'í Cave,** 400m past the center of Mộc Châu on the right as you head toward Sơn La, is an excellent pit stop. Stretch your legs climbing the 240 stairs to the impressive cavern. (Open daily 8am-6pm. Bargain toward 2000Đ.)

NINH BÌNH ☎30

Someday travelers will wise up and notice that Ninh Bình is more than just a place to stop for breakfast on the way to Hanoi from Huè or vice versa. Dramatic scenery, historic intrigues, religious pilgrimage sites, and an endangered animal sanctuary all within 50km of town constitute a region that deserves to be explored. Poverty-stricken Ninh Bình town itself is a forgettable collection of concrete buildings, but it has some of the best accommodations in Vietnam. Intense (and hilarious) rivalry among the few choices has kept prices reasonable and quality high.

TRANSPORTATION

The **bus station** is on **Lê Đại Hành** opposite the bridge. **Buses** leave for: **Hanoi** (2½-3hr.; 12 per day 6:40am-3:30pm; 14,000-16,000Đ); **HCMC** (45hr.; 6:15am; 179,000Đ); **Haiphong** (6hr.; 5:45am; 20,000Đ); and **Kim Sơn** (Phát Diệm Church; 50min., 13 per day 5:30am-5pm, 4500Đ; return from Kim Sơn 4pm). Additional buses can be flagged down anywhere along **Trần Hùng Đạo** (prices are at least double for foreigners). An easier option are **tourist buses** to **Hanoi** (US$3) and **Huế** (US$5) which run daily at 7am. Seats can be booked at any hotel (see below), but the best seats are usually taken since these are part of open tour tickets. The **train station** lies at the end of Đường Hoàng Hoa Thám. Walk up the street from the station to **Lê Đại Hành,** turn left, and walk 100m or so to reach the bridge. Trains go north to **Hanoi** (2-3½hr.; 8 per day at all hours; 24,000-47,000Đ), and south to **Vinh** (3½-4½hr.; 60,000-130,000Đ), followed by **Huế** (12½-15hr.; 8 per day; 125,000-241,000Đ), and continuing on to **HCMC** (30-40hr.; 347,000-672,000Đ). Buy tickets to the south several days in advance, preferably in Hanoi. Tickets to Hanoi can be purchased in Ninh Bình a day ahead. Time and prices are posted on a bulletin outside the main entrance.

ORIENTATION AND PRACTICAL INFORMATION

Ninh Bình lies 93km south of Hanoi on Highway 1A. Most of the town lies along the highway **(Đường Trần Hưng Đạo). Đường Lê Đại Hành,** the town's second main street, leads to Hồ Chí Minh City and runs parallel to **Trần Hưng Đạo** along a narrow river until the two intersect at a **bridge** at the south end of town. Near the bridge, **Đường Hải Thượng Lãn Ông** intersects Trần Hưng Đạo next to the radio tower at the west edge of town. Just south of the radio tower Lý Tự Trọng heads west from Trần Hưng Đạo and terminates in front of the **hospital** (☎871 030). The **telephone office** (with fax) is inside the **GPO,** which is two buildings to the right of the radio tower and near the bridge, on Trần Hưng Đạo; look for the red Bưu Điện sign. (☎871 104. Open M-F 6am-10pm, Sa-Su 7am-9pm; in winter open daily 6:30am-9:30pm.) The **pharmacy** is a few doors north of the GPO on Trần Hưng Đạo. Hotels will exchange đồng for dollars, but to exchange traveler's checks or obtain a cash advance, head up Trần Hưng Đạo past the Star Hotel. On the right is the brand new **Industrial and Commercial Bank of Vietnam,** 1 Lương Văn Tuý, in a large yellow building. (☎872 675. Open M-Sa 7-11am and 1-4:30pm.) There is one cyber cafe in town, **50 263 Trần Hưng Đạo,** between the bank and the Star Hotel (200Đ per min.).

ACCOMODATIONS AND FOOD

The best value in town is the **Queen Hotel ❶,** 21 Hoang Hoa Tham, 150m directly outside the station. It's also the home of superstar guide Luong, who organizes tours throughout Vietnam. (☎871 874; fax 871 200. Spotless comfortable rooms US$3-15.) Mr. De at **Thuy Anh Hotel ❸,** 55 Truong Han Sieu, off Trân Hưng Đạo in the center of town, leads the quality hotel rat-race. Full tourist service includes full-day tour US$14, motorbike rental US$5, and Internet 500Đ per min. (A/C doubles with bath from US$10-25. A few outside toilet tiny rooms US$7.) **Thanh Thuy's Guest House ❶**, 128 Lê Hồng Phong, can definitely give Thuy Anh a run for its money. The German- and English-speaking owners have clean singles with fan for US$3-8 and A/C doubles for US$10. (☎871 811. Sturdy Japanese mountain bikes 13,000Đ per day, Chinese models 8000Đ. Internet 400Đ per min.) The tree-shaded street in front of Queen Hotel to the train station has good **phơ'** and **còm** shops. For famed local **miện lúón,** or eel in vermicelli noodle soup, go to the intersection of Trân Hưng Đạo and Van Glang, near the Thuy Anh Hotel (10,000Đ).

SIGHTS

TAM CỐC. Ninh Bình's rice fields become otherworldly in the Tam Cốc ("three caves") area. The mountains have earned the area the nickname "Hạ Long Bay without water," a moniker borne out by the limestone karst which dominate the landscape. Four-person bamboo skiffs float to and through the caves, past spectacular cliffs, tiny farming communities, graveyards, and intricate rock formations. The awe-inspiring beauty is occasionally interrupted by local entrepreneurs pitching their embroidery to the captive, water-borne audience. Visitors can leave the boat at Thành boat stop and, after a short walk, explore the 13th-century **Thai Vi Temple.** *(From Ninh Bình head 4km south on Hwy. 1. Turn right at the Tam Cốc turn-off, cross a short bridge, and follow the wide, dirt road 5km to the boats. A booth sells tickets (open daily 6am-5pm; 55,000Đ) for the 3hr. floating tour.)*

BÍCH ĐỘNG PAGODAS. Dating back to 1428, three pagodas called the Bích Động Pagodas perch at varying heights on the mountainside. A stairway leads past these beautiful temple buildings, through a grotto, and yields fantastic views of the cliffs and surrounding farmlands. They are especially beautiful during harvest season in June, when the fields resemble a yellow sea. It's possible to enter the pagodas from the rear via a torchlight boat trip through the low-hanging cave followed by a short climb over the front side of the mountain. To reach the pagodas, continue past Tam Cốc for 2km until the road terminates in a small square in front of the pagodas. For the backdoor entrance, backtrack 50m and take a right on the narrow path. Follow this for another 100m around the mountain until you see the boats and the cave entrance. *(Open daily 7am-5pm. 30,000Đ gets you in either way.)*

HANG MÚA. Hang Múa, Ninh Bình's newest attraction, lies on the way to Hoa Lư from Tam Cốc. Five hundred steps ascend past billowing, multi-colored flags, and painted concrete animals to a breathtaking vista 200m above the paddies at the mountain's summit. An unimproved access road prohibits tour buses from gaining access... for now. Don't forget your camera, or your inhaler. From Tam Cốc head back toward Hwy. 1. After 2km turn left at the Hang Múa Tourist Center sign. The turn-off is marked by a large tree. Drive until you see the white staircase winding up the side of Hang Múa Mountain (about 2km). *(Entrance fee 20,000Đ.)*

HOA LƯ. Hoa Lư, the capital of Đại Cồ Việt, the first independent Việt state following the millennium of Chinese rule, lies 12km north of town in a valley ringed with volcanic peaks. It was chosen for its geographic location, virtually impregnable to attack, and served as the capital from AD 938 until **Lý Công Uẩn,** founder of the Lý dynasty, moved the capital to Thăng Long (modern-day Hanoi) in 1011. Nothing remains of the citadel. Two temples dating from the 17th century commemorate **Đinh Bộ Lĩnh** (Đinh Tiên Hoàng), the first Vietnamese king to declare himself emperor, and **Lê Hoàn,** founder of the short-lived early Lê dynasty. The site is still used for occasional village and religious festivities, which explains the perfectly manicured lotus pond and burning of incense as tribute. Hoa Lư can be reached

VIETNAM

from Hang Múa 8km farther down the road, through some spectacular karst landscapes. From Ninh Bình head north on Hwy. 1 for 6km, then take a left and continue 6km farther. *(Open daily 7am-6pm. 30,000Đ for foreigners accesses both temples and the mountain stairway.)*

PHÁT DIỆM CATHEDRAL. The center of Vietnamese Catholicism is the Phát Diệm Cathedral, one of the 30 or so churches in this area once colonized by French Jesuits. Built from 1875 to 1899 by Vietnamese **Father Sáu,** it was nearly destroyed in 1972 by American bombs, but was quickly repaired. The edifice blends Chinese (pagodas on the rooftops and bell-tower, Buddhist lotuses carved on the walls of the Stone Chapel) and Western (neo-Romanesque columns and rectangular structure) styles. Thousands of Vietnamese Catholics visit every year from Ninh Bình diocese (140,000 Catholics) and elsewhere. The church is 29km southeast of Ninh Bình. From Trần Hưng Đạo head east over the river, past the bus station, and over the railroad tracks. Once in Phát Diệm (a.k.a. Kim Sơn) look for a sign reading "Nhà Thờ Phát Diệm" with an arrow pointing right. The church is 300m farther. It is also accessible by public bus from Ninh Bình to Kim Sơn. Mass is held daily at 5am and 5:30pm though curious onlookers—more Vietnamese than foreigners—should come at visiting hours only. *(Open daily 7:30-11:30am and 2:30-5pm.)*

CÚC PHƯƠNG NATIONAL PARK. Nature-lovers may escape to the Cúc Phương National Park, 45km north of town. The park is an excellent daytrip, offering hikes and wildlife. The **Endangered Primate Rescue Center** provides a much appreciated antidote to caged bears in **Chó Ninh Bình.** This is a research, not tourist, facility. Some travel agencies can make discreet arrangements. Ask around. The park can be reached by motorbike, but the most convenient way to get there is with an organized tour from Ninh Bình or Hanoi for about US$15 per day. *(Open daily 7am-5pm.)*

VINH

☎038

Historically a poor region, Nghệ An province, and its capital Vinh, hosted the first Communist rebellion, the Xô Viết Nghệ Tĩnh uprisings. Today this unappealing highway town attracts die-hard tourists who come to see the birthplace of Hồ Chí Minh. Accommodations and food leave much to be desired, but those searching for an unromanticized glimpse of poor industrial Vietnam will find it in Vinh.

TRANSPORTATION AND PRACTICAL INFORMATION. Vinh is equidistant from Hanoi and Huế. Hwy. 1, suffering from an identity crisis, rolls in from the north becoming **Lê Lợi,** then **Quang Trưng** (near the bus station) before breaking east near the market as **Trần Phú.** Finally, the highway kinks southeast toward Huế as **Le Duan. Vietnam Airlines** flies to **Ban Me Thuot** (3½hr., 1,200,000Đ) via **Đà Nẵng** (1hr.; M, W, Sa 12:10pm; 685,000Đ) and **Hồ Chí Minh City** (5hr., 1,640,000Đ). The booking office is in the Huu Nghi Hotel, 74 Lê Lợi near the intersection with Phan Boi Chàn. The **bus station** (☎844 127), on Lê Lợi, sends early risers to **Đà Nẵng** (10hr.; 5am; 63,000Đ); **Hai Phong** (7½hr.; 5:30, 6am, 2:30pm; 53,500Đ); **Hanoi** (6hr.; every hr. 5-10am; 40,000Đ); **HCMC** (5am; 199,000Đ); **Huế** (10hr.; 5am; 48,500Đ). The **train station** (☎824 924) is northwest of the bus station. To get there, turn left from the bus station on Lê Lợi and make another left on Phan Boi Chàn. The station is 1km from the intersection. Trains head daily to: **Hanoi** (4½-6½hr.; 67,000-140,000Đ); **HCMC** (27-33hr.; 329,000, soft seat 694,000Đ); **Huế** (7-9hr.; soft seat 82,000-155,000Đ). Cash-starved foreigners should hit the **Vietcombank,** 9 Nguyễn Sỹ Sách, off Lê Lợi. (☎842 304. V/MC advance. Open M-Sa 7:30-11:30am and 1:30-4:30pm.) A **market** looms near the town center at the intersection of Quang Trưng and Trần Phú. The **post office** has temporarily set up on Hồ Tung Mau around the corner from its 2 Nguyễn Thị Minh Khai building, which is undergoing renovations. (☎833 711. Open daily 6:30am-9:30pm.)

ACCOMMODATIONS AND FOOD. **Phú Nguyên Hải Hotel and Restaurant ❸**, 81 Lê Lợi, is a gaudy pink building conveniently located next to the bus station. Don't miss the rooftop **restaurant ❷**. No meal without stewed eel and banana (20,000Đ) could be complete (☎848 429; ctpnh@h.n.vnn.vn. Fully equipped. A/C doubles US$15, but can be bargained down). A few doors down is the **Hồng Ngọc Hotel 1 ❸**, 99 Lê Lợi. Front rooms, sparkling tile floors, and wall-sized windows are reported to lie behind its current renovations. (A/C doubles from US$10.) Across the highway is **Hồng Ngoc 2 ❸**, a more cabin-like arrangement hidden behind a restaurant. All rooms have A/C, TV, and fridges. The accompanying **restaurant ❷** serves up exotic dishes along with old standbys. A filling plate of *cổm ga* costs 15,000Đ. (Singles US$10; doubles US$12.) For a bed and not much else, drop your pack at **Bong Sen Hotel ❶**, 39 Quang Trưng. (☎844 397. Cells with fans US$4-7.)

SIGHTS. Party members from across the country pay homage to Hồ Chí Minh at his maternal and paternal villages, known collectively as **Làng Sen** or **Làng Kim Liên (Lotus Village).** Hồ spent his formative years (ages 5-10) in a modest thatched house. The attached museum pays tribute to the leader and his cause, displaying his personal artifacts. (Open M-Sa 6:30-11am and 2-5pm. Free.) The family altar of laureate **Nguyễn Du,** author of the *Tale of Kieu*, is also near Vinh, 13km south of town. All above sites exude a forced grandeur in shabbily maintained environments. Due to a dearth of visitors, exotic foreigners sometimes become the most interesting display, particularly those with children. Taxi hire for a full day trip from hotels start at US$20 per day. The undeveloped **Cửa Lò** beaches, some of the most pristine sand north of Nha Trang, are about 17km from Vinh, though price inflation is worse than in similar resort towns.

VIETNAM

NEAR VINH: PHONG NHA CAVES

The Phong Nha Caves are one of Central Vietnam's most interesting natural land formations, or at least the tourism authorities think so. The attraction consists of large caverns—illuminated with Christmas lights—through which visitors float on boats. A visit to the caves is best launched from **Đồng Hới,** 50km southeast of the caves (70km north of the DMZ). Hwy. 1 parts the small but spread-out town, first under the alias Quang Trưng in the south, and later as Lý Thường Kiệt at its intersection with Trần Hưng Đạo, the major east-west street. The **tourist office,** adjacent to the reception at the **Đồng Hới Hotel,** 50 Quang Trưng, has information, tickets, and rentals provided by excellent English-speakers. (☎822 160. Open daily 7-11am and 1:30-4:30pm. Moto with driver 120,000Đ; 4-person rental cars 400,000Đ. Entrance 25,000Đ. Boat into caves 1-10 people 60,000Đ; 11-15 people 75,000Đ; 16-20 people 90,000Đ.) There are English-speaking guides at Phong Nha Tourist Center, 7km from the cave entrance. Huế tourist agencies also offer tours to the caves and the main sights of the DMZ (2 days; includes bus, accommodation, meals, guide, and a boat through the cave; 390,000Đ).

There is no interprovince bus station in **Đồng Hới,** but buses rumbling through on Hwy. 1 can be flagged down to **Hanoi** (70,000Đ) and **Huế** (25,000Đ). The **train station** lies 3km west of town. Trains depart for **Hanoi** (9-13hr.; 9 per day; 120,000-280,000Đ); **HCMC** (23-30hr.; 9 per day; 250,000-500,000Đ); **Huế** (3hr.; 9 per day; 35,000-125,000Đ). Exchange currency at **Vietinde Bank,** 3 Nguyễn Trãi St. (Open M-F 7-11:30am and 1:30-4pm.) Nguyễn Trãi St., a small road off Quang Trưng and next to a bridge, is marked by a sign for the Nha Khach Hotel. The **Đồng Hới Hotel ❶**, 50 Quang Trưng, has lackluster fan-cooled chambers and pricey A/C rooms.

(Singles 60,000Đ; doubles with A/C and TV 150,000Đ.) Clean A/C rooms at the **Mỹ Ngọc Travel Hotel ❸,** 5 Lý Thường Kiệt, opposite the post office, are prone to price reductions. (☎822 074. All rooms 150,000Đ.) Search the market area on Me Suot near the river, 300m east of the drive-through monument on Quang Trưng, for a decent bite.

CENTRAL VIETNAM

Nowhere is the tragedy of modern Vietnamese history more palpable than in the provinces north of Huế. The most intense fighting of the Vietnam War occurred in Central Vietnam, but today the region offers some of the most exciting travel in Southeast Asia. Along the coast, the imperial city at Huế and the historic old town at Hội An are two of Vietnam's most arresting sights. The beaches of Nha Trang and Phan Thiết are easily the best in the country, and no trip is complete without a few days in cool, misty Đà Lạt. Independent travel here isn't easy, but with stamina and flexibility, it can be the highlight of a trip to Vietnam.

HUẾ ☎54

As Vietnam's spiritual, artistic, and cultural center, Huế has an incredible concentration of sights and ruins. In the 19th century, under the rule of the Nguyễn Dynasty, Huế reached preeminence as the seat of Vietnam's first united court. Home rule was short-lived, however, as French ships blockaded and prepared to attack the city in 1833. Recognizing the might of the French, the emperor relented, and Vietnam became a French protectorate. Though the colonial administration tried to protect Huế's treasures and preserve its historic integrity, it eventually became a combat zone during the war with the US. During the 1968 Tet Offensive, the Citadel was captured by both sides as fighting raged in the Imperial City.

TRANSPORTATION

Flights: Phú Bài Airport, 15km south of the city off Hwy. 1. **Taxis** (75,000-100,000Đ) and Vietnam Airlines airport **buses** (30,000Đ) run between the airport and city center. **Vietnam Airlines,** 7 Nguyễn Tri Phương St. (☎824 709), in Thuận Hóa Hotel. Open M-Sa 7-11am and 1:30-4:30pm, Su 7:30-11am and 2-4:30pm. To **Hanoi** and **HCMC** (both 970,000Đ).

Trains: Huế Railway Station (☎822 175), at the southwest end of Lê Lợi over the small bridge that spans the canal. Trains to: **Đà Nẵng** (3hr.; 6am, 1pm; 32,000Đ); **Hanoi** (13-16hr.; 8 per day; 150,000-316,000Đ); **HCMC** (20-25hr.; 7 per day; 225,000-471,000Đ) via **Nha Trang** (15-17hr.; 223,000-681,000Đ). Purchase tickets early.

Buses: Most hotels book minibuses to: **Đà Nẵng** (3hr.; 8am, 1pm; US$3); **Hanoi** (16hr., 6pm, US$7); **HCMC** (20hr., 2:30pm, US$15); **Hội An** (4hr.; 8am, 1pm; US$3); **Nha Trang** (16hr., 2:30pm, US$8); **Lao Bảo** (4hr., 6am, US$11); **Savannakhet, Laos** (6, 9pm; US$15). Huế has three bus stations:

An Hòa Bus Station (☎822 716), outside the Citadel at the northwest corner off Hwy. 1, 2km from town center. Buses go north to: **Đồng Hới** (5hr.; 5, 6am; 25,000Đ); **Hanoi** (24hr.; 6am; 80,000Đ); **Khe Sanh** (5½hr.; 5am; 40,000Đ); **Vinh** (11hr.; 6am; 70,000Đ). To get to **Lao Bảo,** catch a bus to **Đông Ha** (5-10am) and transfer to a bus bound for the Laotian border.

Phía Nam Bus Station (☎823 817), on Hùng Vương, 2.5km southeast of the Perfume River. Primarily serves southern destinations. Buses to: **Buôn Ma Thuột** (18hr.; 6am; 78,000Đ); **Đà Lạt** (20hr.; 5am; 100,000Đ); **Đà Nẵng** (3hr.; every 50min. 5am-3:30pm; 20,000Đ); **HCMC** (30hr.; 6am; 118,500Đ).

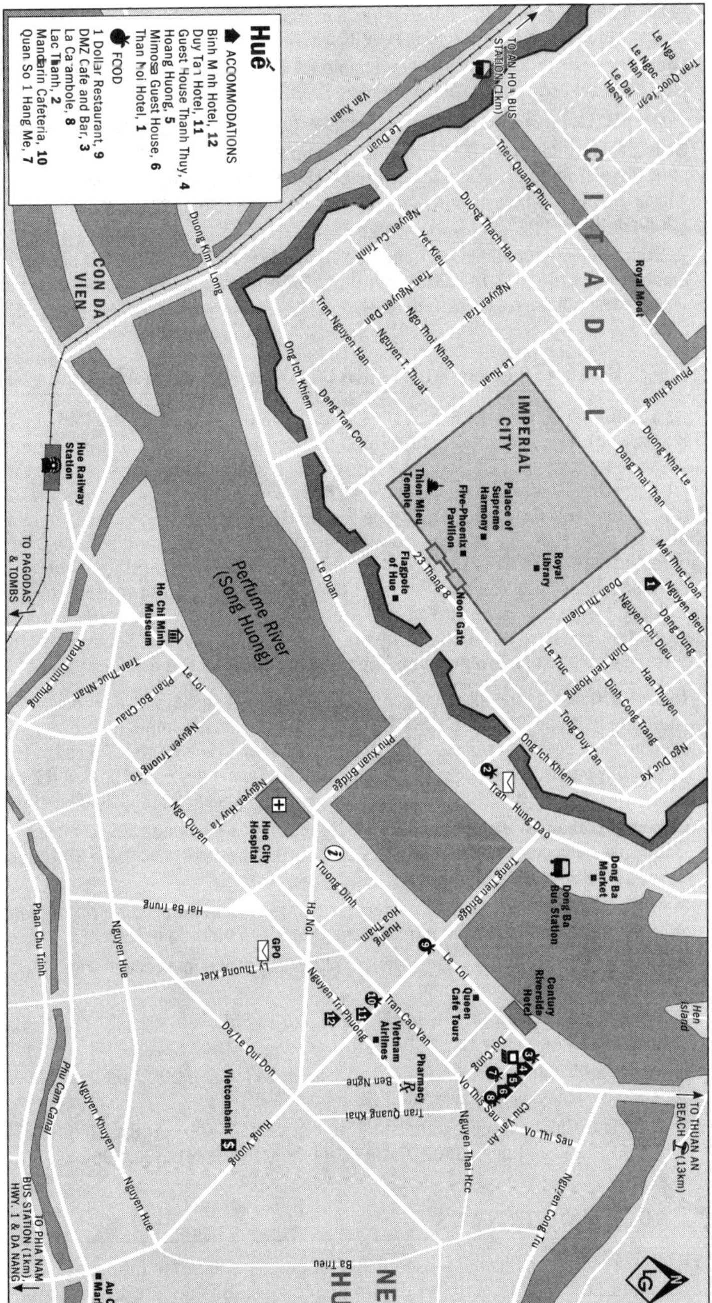
Huế
ACCOMMODATIONS
Duy Tan Hotel, 11
Guest House Thanh Thuy, 4
Hoang Huong, 5
FOOD
1 Dollar Restaurant, 9
DMZ Cafe and Bar, 3
Lac Thanh, 2
Quan So 1 Hang Me, 7
CITADEL
IMPERIAL CITY
Palace of Supreme Harmony
Five-Phoenix Pavilion
Royal Library
Thien Mieu Temple
Flagpole of Hue
Ngon Gate
Royal Moat
Perfume River (Song Huong)
CON DA VIEN
Hue Railway Station
TO PAGODAS & TOMBS
Ho Chi Minh Museum
Hue City Hospital
Phu Xuan Bridge
Trang Tien Bridge
Dong Ba Market
Dong Ba Bus Station
Century Riverside Hotel
Hen Island
Queen Cafe Tours
Vietnam Airlines
Pharmacy
GPO
Vietcombank
TO THUAN AN BEACH (13km)
TO PHIA NAM BUS STATION (1km), HWY. 1 & DA NANG
Au Cuu Market
NEW HUE
Phu Cam Canal
Le Duan
Le Loi
Tran Hung Dao
Hung Vuong
Ba Trieu
Ly Thuong Kiet
Hai Ba Trung
Nguyen Hue
Phan Chu Trinh
Ha Noi
Truong Dinh
Ngo Quyen
Doi Cung
Vo Thi Sau
Chu Van An
Ben Nghe
Tran Quang Khai
Nguyen Thai Hoc
Nguyen Cong Tru
Nguyen Tri Phuong
Tran Cao Van
Hoang Hoa Tham
Da/Le Qui Don
Nguyen Khuyen
Dinh Tien Hoang
Doan Thi Diem
Mai Thuc Loan
Ong Ich Khiem
23 Thang 8
Le Huan
Nguyen Trai
Thach Han
Trieu Quang Phuc
Duong Nhat Le
Dang Thai Than
Van Xuan
Duong Kim Long
Tran Nguyen Han
Dang Tran Con
Nguyen Chi Dieu
Han Thuyen
Dinh Cong Trang
Tong Duy Tan
Le Truc
Nguyen Bieu
Dang Dung
Ngo Duc Ke
Phan Dinh Phung
Tran Thuc Nhan
Phan Boi Chau
Nguyen Truong To
Nguyen Huy Tu
Yet Kieu
Ngo Thoi Nham
Nguyen Cu Trinh
Phung Hung
Le Ngoc Han
Le Dai Hanh
Le Nga
Tran Quoc Toan

Đông Ba Bus Station (☎833 055), on Trần Hưng Đạo, on the Citadel side of the Perfume River. Buses to **Thuận An Beach** (20min., every 30min. 7am-3pm, 8000Đ).

Local Transportation: Cyclos swarm around the city. 10,000Đ per ride. Bargain. **Motos** are often cheaper. 3000-7000Đ per ride; 10,000-15,000Đ per hr.

Taxis: ATC Taxi (☎833 333). Unmetered rides to almost anywhere. Agree on a price.

Boats: Tourist Boat Pier, 7 Lê Lợi. 1-day tour up Perfume River to **Thiên Mụ Pagoda** and the **Royal Tombs** or to **Thuận An Beach** (8am-5pm, 10-person boat US$10). The acclaimed **Folk Songs of Huế** boat tour and performance leaves every night (1½hr.; 7, 8:30pm; US$4 or US$20 for 10 people).

Rentals: Hotels and outfits on Hùng Vương rent **bicycles** (7000-8000Đ per day) and **motorcycles** (50,000-110,000Đ per day). **DMZ Tours** (see **Tourist Offices,** below) rents **cars** with drivers (US$35 per day).

ORIENTATION AND PRACTICAL INFORMATION

Over 16km inland from the South China Sea, Huế is bisected by the **Perfume River (Sông Hương).** The ancient **Citadel,** which fails to keep armies of tourists from penetrating to the Imperial City and the Royal Palace of the Nguyễn Dynasty within, is on the northwest bank. The **Flagpole of Huế,** which marks the front gate of the Royal Palace and the Imperial City, is inside the Citadel. Across the river on the southeast side, **New Huế** is home to most hotels, restaurants, and services. On the Citadel side, **Lê Duẩn/Trần Hưng Đạo** runs between the river and the Citadel wall. On the southeast bank of the Perfume River, **Lê Lợi,** the main tourist strip, runs parallel to the water. **Hùng Vương,** the other major tourist drag, starts at the **Tràng Tiền Bridge,** crosses Lê Lợi, and heads southeast to **Hwy. 1.** Farther upstream (southwest), **Phú Xuân Bridge** spans the river between Lê Lợi and Lê Duẩn.

Tourist Offices: Nearly all tour agencies offer identical services (1-day tours US$7-8; half-day Perfume River tour US$2). The smaller agencies frequently offer cheaper prices. Most guest houses also book tours. **DMZ Tour Office Center,** 26 Lê Lợi (☎825 242). Day on the Perfume River with lunch US$20. Open daily 6am-10pm. **A II Z Queen Cafe,** 38D Lê Lợi (☎833 897). Same tours, cheaper prices. Open daily 6am-10pm.

Currency Exchange: Vietcombank, 78 Hùng Vương (☎846 058). 3% commission on MC/V cash advances. Cashes traveler's checks (US$2.50 per check). **No ATM.** Open M-F 7:30-11:30am and 1:30-4:30pm.

Market: Đông Ba Market, Huế's largest, sprawls on the Citadel side of the Perfume River at the far northeast end of Trần Hưng Đạo. Open daily 6am-7:30pm.

Pharmacy: Khánh Duy, 37 Bến Nghé (☎832 079), at the intersection with Nguyễn Tri Phương. Open daily noon-11pm.

Medical Services: Huế City Hospital, 16 Lê Lợi (☎822 325, ext. 2247). Emergency entrance on Nguyèn Huy Tá.

Internet: MQV Computer, 6A Phạm Ngũ Lão (☎847 052). 200Đ per min. Generally **open 24hr.** Many places have 100Đ per min. rates.

Post Office: Mini-post offices abound in tourist centers. **GPO,** 14B Lý Thường Kiệt, 1 block southwest of Húng Vương. *Poste Restante.* Open daily 6:30am-9pm.

ACCOMMODATIONS

The alley at 46 Lê Lợi has a dense cluster of quality accommodations. Elsewhere, bargain until the quality matches the price. Most establishments arrange tours.

Hoàng Hương, 46/2 Lê Lợi (☎828 509), down a small alley off Vo This Sau. Cheap and friendly. Dorms US$3; doubles with fan US$4-6, with A/C US$7-10. ❶

Mimosa Guest House, 46/6 Lê Lợi (☎828 068), in the alley. Friendly owner and lovely, quiet rooms. Breakfast on the terrace (US$1). Doubles US$5-6, with A/C US$8-10. ❷

Guest House Thanh Thủy, 46/4 Lê Lợi (☎824 585). Front rooms have quiet balconies overlooking the alley. Discounts for long stays. Rooms US$5-7. ❷

Duy Tan Hotel, 12 Hùng Vương (☎825 001), is a monster building behind the Mandarin Cafeteria. Soft beds in clean, white rooms. Rooms with A/C US$8-10, with satellite TV US$12-15, with minibar US$15-18. ❷

Binh Minh Hotel, 36/12 Nguyễn Tri Phương (☎825 526). Big rooms with satellite TV. Rooms US$8-10, with balcony and breakfast US$12-15, with decor US$20-30. ❷

Thàn Nội Hotel, 3 Dang Dung (☎522 478), next to the Forbidden City in the old town. A worthy upscale choice with ornate Chinese furniture. Small outdoor swimming pool is heaven on a hot day. Room US$15-25. ❸

FOOD

Huế's food is arguably the best in Vietnam. Scores of touristy eateries on **Hùng Vương** and **Lê Lợi** entice patrons with greasy dishes. Venture farther for more authentic victuals. Try *bánh nam* (shrimp and pork with sticky rice in a banana leaf), *nem lựi* (grilled pork and greens in rice paper with peanut sauce), or *bánh khoái*, usually called the "Huế pancake" on menus.

1 Dollar Restaurant, 30 Lê Lợi, in the fancy Saigon Morin Hotel. Classy ambience, a picture menu, and a simple pricing scheme. Nightly buffet inside a lovely courtyard 70,000Đ. All dishes US$1 or 17,000Đ after tax. Open daily 10am-10pm. ❷

Lạc Thạnh, 6A Đinh Tiên Hoàng, outside the Citadel's easternmost gate by the river. Famous for the deaf and mute owner who takes orders by hand signal. Sizable serving of *nem lựi* 12,000Đ. Open daily 7am-11pm. ❷

Mandarin Cafeteria, 12 Hùng Vương. A veritable Huế institution for backpackers. Owner Mr. Cuu is an amateur photographer. Books Sinh Café tours. Exquisite rice dishes 10,000Đ. Open daily 6am-10pm. ❶

30 Bèn Nghè, across from Binh Minh II Hotel. Head here for a break from the grease and for delicious fresh juices and desserts (1500-3000Đ). ❶

La Carambole, 19 Phạm Ngu Lão. Decent European and Vietnamese fare. Bamboo decor and uniformed hostesses. Entrees 20,000-50,000Đ. Open daily 7am-11pm. ❸

Quán Sô 1 Hàng Me, 8 Phạm Ngu Lão. Authentic Huế specialties hidden away amid the tourist carnival. Sample the region's culinary delights with the *bánh* sampler 20,000Đ. Open daily 10:30am-7pm. ❷

DMZ Café and Bar, 44 Lê Lợi. An unpretentious hangout with free pool, cheap beer, and a lively crowd by 11pm. Beer 8000-15,000Đ. Opens 2:30pm–late. ❷

SIGHTS

The ancient Citadel, Imperial City, and Royal Tombs dominate the tourist landscape of Huế. All are pricey; only some are worth it. Pay admission in đong to avoid higher rates.

THE CITADEL

Emperor Gia Long, founder of the Nguyễn Dynasty, began building the Citadel in 1805. **Emperor Minh Mạng** completed the structure by reinforcing the wall with

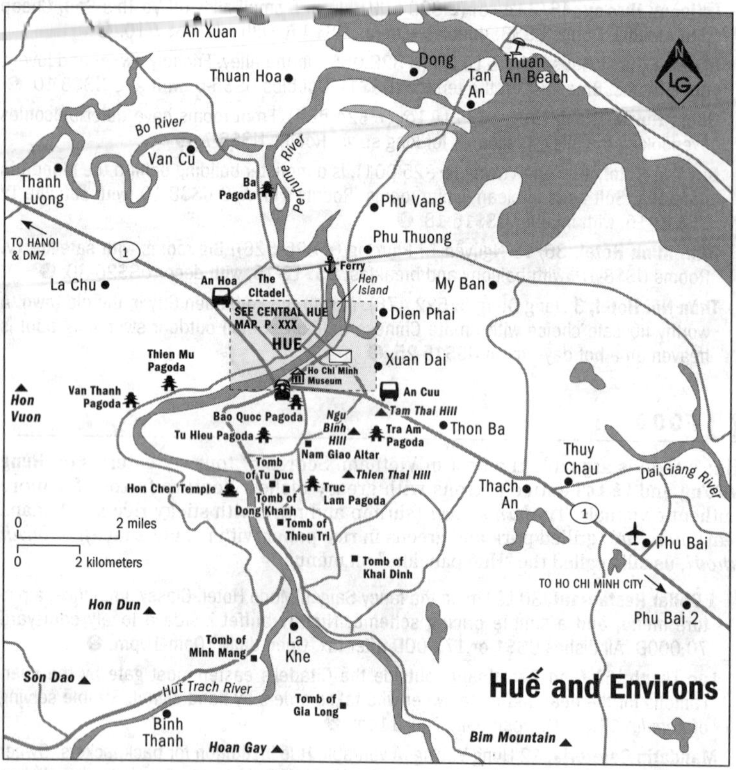

brick and expanding the moat to its current size of 4m deep and 23m wide. Today, the massive square has a 10km perimeter, four gates on its front side along the Perfume River, and two more on each of the other three sides. Within the Citadel lie the remnants of the **Imperial City**.

FLAGPOLE OF HUẾ AND PAVILION OF EDICTS. The 47m **Flagpole of Huế** stands between the central front gates just inside the Citadel. The tallest pole in Vietnam, it has been rebuilt several times since its construction in 1807. The **Pavilion of Edicts** was built in 1810. The square was used by Emperor Gia Long to announce the successful national exam candidates and declare important edicts. *(Just off Hwy. 1, opposite the pole and outside the Citadel. Both sights free.)*

IMPERIAL CITY. The red and saffron **Noon Gate (Ngọ Môn),** the grand entrance to the Imperial City, is opposite the flagpole. The city was modeled on the much larger Forbidden City of Beijing's Qing Dynasty. Built in 1833, the **Five-Phoenix Pavilion,** which sits at the gate, served as a viewing platform from which the emperor could observe ceremonies. Behind it, the **Palace of Supreme Harmony** once housed the emperor's throne. The different heights of the courts in front of the throne corresponded to the status of the mandarins (the court's intellectual elite), with military leaders on the right and civil leaders on the left. The **Forbidden Purple City,** the formerly walled-in residence of the royal family, is in line with the Imperial City and Citadel. Elaborate inscriptions explain what was here before it was heavily bombed. The **Royal Library,** on the right side as you face north, is one of the few structures still intact. West of the city are the **residences** of the Queen Mother and Great Queen Mother. In the west corner of the Imperial City is **Thiên Miếu Temple,** dedicated to Gia Long and his successors. The **Nine Dynastic Urns** by the temple represent members of the dynasty. These structures are undergoing extensive renovations with funds from UNESCO, which has declared Huế a World Heritage Site. *(Imperial City open daily 6:30am-5:30pm. 55,000Đ. English-speaking tour guides price negotiable; hire them in the office to the left of the entrance.)*

ROYAL TOMBS

Huế is home to the tombs of seven emperors of the Nguyễn Dynasty. Designed by the rulers themselves, each tomb represents the expressive spirit of the emperor as well as the architecture of the time; most are a mix of Vietnamese and French styles. A few kilometers southwest of the city center, the tombs are accessible by motorcycle or bike. Most visitors, however, opt for a US$2 dragon boat trip, which, though charming, throws all sorts of sales pitches at tourists. For some tombs the additional motorbike ride from the river may cost upwards of 50,000Đ. Poorly marked roads connect most of the sights. The locals are usually helpful in pointing confused tourists in the right direction. *(Tombs open daily 6am-sunset.)*

TOMB OF TỰ ĐỨC AND ROYAL ARENA. The tomb of Tự Đức, whose indecisive rule was one of the factors causing the Nguyễn's quick capitulation to the French, is the tomb to see if time or budget are tight. *(Once on Bùi Thị Xuân, backtrack toward the train station 300m to a dirt road heading off to the right. Follow this for 2km, then take 2nd left. 55,000Đ.)* Nearby, the Royal Arena was built in 1830 to stage duels between elephants and tigers. *(From Lê Lợi, head west toward the train station. Across the small bridge, turn right on Bùi Thị Xuân, continue for 3km, and start asking locals for directions to Hô Quyên. They'll point you to a small alleyway off the left side of Bùi Thi Xuân.)*

TOMBS OF ĐỒNG KHÁNH AND THIỆU TRI. The less-visited tomb of Đồng Khánh dedicated to the late emperor, contains portraits of many of his nine wives as well as one of himself. *(500m from the tomb of Tự Đức. 22,000Đ.)* One kilometer down the gravel track is the tomb of Thiệu Trị. *(22,000Đ.)*

TOMB OF MINH MANG AND TEMPLE OF MINH LẦU. Built from 1841 to 1843, Minh Mạng's tomb has the greatest architectural balance and poise of all Huế's tombs. Three sets of stairs lead to a steel pavilion that bears Minh Mạng's eulogy, composed by Thiệu Trị. Three large courtyards sit at the bottom of the pavilion. *(From Thiệu Trị take a left on the paved road and continue for 2km. The river and the slim ferryboats will appear on your right. Round-trip crossing with moto 20,000-30,000Đ. Bargain. Take a left after crossing and Minh Mạng is 1km farther on your left.)* The Minh Lầu Temple houses an altar to the king's prosperity and longevity. Over a stone bridge is the tomb proper; look for a dirt mound. *(Opposite the courtyards at the tomb of Minh Mạng. 55,000Đ.)*

TOMBS OF GIA LONG AND KHẢI ĐINH. Gia Long's tomb was built from 1814 to 1820; this rarely visited mausoleum has a courtyard surrounded by a lotus pond. *(Several kilometers from the tomb of Minh Mạng. Follow the access road southeast through Minh Mạng Village to a tributary of the Perfume River. Cross the river on a ferry for 10,000Đ round-trip, then take the dirt path to the tomb.)* After 11 years of construction, the tomb of Khải Định was finally completed in 1931. The last of the tombs to be built, it shows European architectural influence. At the top, a large altar houses a gilded statue of Khải Định, making it the only tomb with a visual representation of the emperor. *(From Gia Long, head toward the ferry dock and backtrack across the Perfume River. Turn right at the top of the bluff and left after 200m. Khải Định is 1km down the road on the right. 55,000Đ.)*

NAM GIAO ALTAR AND BĂO QUỐC PAGODA. The Nam Giao Altar is a giant open-air monument where the Nguyễn emperors performed Confucian rituals. Its three levels represent Heaven, Earth, and Man. *(From the tomb of Khải Định, head north up the access road until it ends near the altar.)* Before returning, stop at the **Bảo Quốc Pagoda.** Built in 1670, this pagoda sits atop stairs in a quiet sanctuary. Its altar is flanked by classrooms where monks have taught for 50 years. *(Walking toward the city center, head north on Phan Bội Châu, take a left on Điện Biên Phủ and a left just before the train tracks.)*

OTHER SIGHTS

THIÊN MỤ PAGODA. On a high hill overlooking the Perfume River, this pagoda is dedicated to a legendary 16th-century woman who declared that a time of great prosperity would come if a Buddhist pagoda were built on the site. Lord Nguyễn Hoàng heard her decree and constructed the pagoda in 1601. Past the seven-story pagoda is an active monastery. The first monk to immolate himself publicly in Saigon during Ngô Đình Diệm's presidency came from this temple. His car is on display. Monks chant periodically in the well-manicured wooden temple behind the golden Buddha statue; tourists stream through constantly at a decidedly less spiritual pace. *(3km southwest of the Citadel. An easy and enjoyable riverside bike ride. Head west on Lê Duẩn and continue across the train tracks on Kim Long.)*

DAYTRIPS FROM HUÊ

THUẬN AN BEACH

Head northeast on Lê Lợi/Thuận An until it branches off the Perfume River, 3km north of the post office. The road follows a stream 10km to the beach, past the Huda Beer Factory. Take a motorbike (1hr.; park it before the road ends as parking there costs an exorbitant 6000Đ), hop on a boat from the pier (1½hr., US$10), or flag down a bus (7am-3pm, 8000Đ) from the station in Đông Hà near the market by the east corner of the Citadel.

Thuận An Beach, 13km from Huế, is the perfect place to kick back between long days of sightseeing. The beach is empty on weekdays but receives a flood of visitors on the weekends. Thuận An's floating restaurant serves basic dishes and rents umbrella-shelters for beachgoers—agree on a price beforehand.

THE DEMILITARIZED ZONE (DMZ)

Touring solo requires at least 2 days, a good motorcycle, and an excellent map. Although you can find guides in Đồng Hới and Đông Hà (halfway to Đồng Hới from Huế), the easiest and most reliable way to tour is from Huế. DMZ Tours and other agencies offer US$9-11 tours that include breakfast and A/C transport. Tours leave at 6am and return at 7pm.

ON THE BEATEN TRACK As per the guidelines of the Geneva Accords of 1954, Vietnam was divided at the 17th parallel that runs through the DMZ. **Live mines and undetonated shells still litter the area.** Be careful and stick to well-established paths.

HIỀN LƯƠNG BRIDGE AND VĨNH MỘC TUNNELS. The Bến Hải River follows the 17th parallel. Spanning the river 59km north of Huế, **Hiền Lương Bridge** was one of the first targets destroyed by the US. North of the river, winding roads lead to the Vĩnh Mộc Tunnels, the DMZ's most interesting sight. Built in 1966, Vĩnh Mộc offers more breathing room than the Củ Chi tunnels in Tây Ninh (see p. 970), has walkways 1.5m tall and 1.2m wide, a maternity ward, and a deep freshwater spring.

ĐÔNG HÀ AND FARTHER WEST. Đông Hà is 22km south of the 17th parallel. On Hwy. 1 (called Lê Duẩn here), the **bus station** runs public buses to **Đà Nẵng** (4½hr.; 8am; 50,000Đ) and **Huế** (2hr.; every 30min. 7am-6pm; 30,000Đ). Next door, the **Quảng Tri Tourist Company** operates from the **Đông Hà Hotel ❷**. (Tourist office ☎053 852 927. Guide with car US$15-20 per day. Open M-Sa 7-11am and 1:30-5pm. Hotel ☎053 852 292. All rooms with shared bath. Singles US$6, with A/C US$8; doubles US$8-10.) From Đông Hà, Rte. 9 runs 60km west to Laos and was one of the principal highways the Americans used for artillery and troop transport. About 15km west on the highway is **Cam Lộ,** where a road heads north to both **Con Thien Firebase,** the site of a fierce 1968 battle that served as a diversion for the Tet Offensive, and **Trường Sơn National Cemetery,** a memorial to the tens of thousands of soldiers who died on the Hồ Chí Minh Trail. Five kilometers west of Cam Lộ, an unpaved road turns left off Rte. 9 to the old US base at **Camp Carroll.** The **rockpile,** which stands another 7km west on Rte. 9, was thought by US Marines to be an unassailable helicopter landing pad until it was stormed by Việt Minh commandos. The **Khe Sanh Combat Base** is 10km from the bridge toward Khe Sanh. Amazingly, many of these military intrigues are little more than wild weeds and arable land. While there are still some landmines strewn about, most tourists will need some help from guides to reconstruct the past.

ĐÀ NẴNG ☎511

In the 19th century, Đà Nẵng replaced nearby Hội An as Central Vietnam's principal port. The city received steady foreign traffic, albeit largely unwanted, first in the form of French colonialists and then in the form of the US Marines, who splashed ashore in 1965. Today, the tables have turned—while thousands of tourists flock to Hội An, Đà Nẵng is content to carry on with business as usual, easily accommodating the few backpackers who swing through. Although the city doesn't beckon to the average traveler, it does provide: beer and snack stalls line the riverside, while ice cream parlors, pagodas, and churches dot the city and its environs. The Chàm Museum is the best of its kind in the country.

TRANSPORTATION

Flights: Đà Nẵng International Airport (☎827 286), 4km west of town. **Vietnam Airlines,** 35 Trần Phú (☎811 111). Open daily 7:30-11am and 1:30-5:30pm. Flights to: **Bangkok** (Tu, Th, Sa 11:10am; US$170); **Buôn Ma Thuột** (M, W, Sa 2:10pm; F 10:10am; 550,000Đ); **Hanoi** (3 per day; 975,000Đ); **HCMC** (4 per day; 975,000Đ); **Nha Trang** (daily 10:15am; 575,000Đ); **Pleiku** (M, W, Sa-Su 10:15am; 545,000Đ); **Vinh** (M, W, Sa 10:20am; 700,000Đ).

Trains: Đà Nẵng Railway Station (Ga Đà Nẵng), 4 Hải Phòng (☎823 810). To **Hanoi** (15-22hr.; 6:30am-9pm; 246,000-639,000Đ) and **HCMC** (17-23hr.; 5:30am-8pm; 284,000-740,000Đ). Ticket office open daily 6am-5pm.

Buses: Full-sized public buses make the trip to **Hội An** from well-marked stops all over town; there's one outside the Đà Nẵng Cathedral (20,000Đ). **A/C tourist minibuses** can be booked at most hotels to: **Hanoi** (1 day, 2pm, US$10); **HCMC** (24hr., 5:30am, US$17); **Hội An** (1hr.; 7, 9am, 2pm; US$3); **Huế** (3hr.; 7, 9am, 2pm; US$3); **Nha Trang** (10-12hr., 5:30am, US$7); **Savannakhet, Laos** (6, 9pm; US$18). There are 2 formal bus stations in Đà Nẵng:

Interprovince bus station, 33 Điện Biên Phủ (☎821 265), 2km west of town. Buses to: **Đà Lạt** (19hr.; 4am; 107,000Đ); **Hanoi** (1 day; 5, 6-9am; 87,000Đ); **HCMC** (24hr.; 5:30-9:30am;

104,000Đ); **Huế** (3hr.; every 30min. 6am-4pm; 22,000Đ); **Nha Trang** (13hr.; 5am; 57,000Đ); **Qui Nhơn** (9hr.; 4:30-9:20am; 32,000Đ); **Savannakhet, Laos** (19hr.; 8pm; 300,000Đ).

Intraprovince bus station, 29 Điện Biên Phủ (☎823 715), next to the interprovince bus station. Sends tiny buses to **Hội An** (10,000Đ).

Local Transportation: Motorbike and **cyclo** drivers will gladly take you to: the **airport** (8000Đ); the **bus station** (7000Đ); **China Beach** (30,000Đ); **Marble Mountains** (30,000Đ). Metered **taxis** to the airport 30,000Đ.

Rentals: Most hotels rent **motorcycles** (US$5 per day) and **bicycles** (15,000Đ per day).

ORIENTATION AND PRACTICAL INFORMATION

Almost at the center of Vietnam, 750km south of Hanoi and 990km north of HCMC, Đà Nẵng is bounded in the east by the **Hàn River** and in the north by **Đà Nẵng Bay. Bạch Đằng,** the main boulevard, runs north along the river's west bank. One block inland, **Trần Phú** runs south, and three blocks inland, **Lê Lo'i/Phan Chu Trinh** is the major north-south artery. These three streets are intersected by **Điện Biên Phủ/Lý Thái Tổ/Hùng Vư'ơng,** the busy east-west road that branches off Hwy. 1 and bisects the city. A few blocks north, **Lê Duẩn** ends in a bridge across the river. The city's southern boundary, **Nguyễn Văn Trỗi,** runs east over the Hàn River and toward the Marble Mountains, China Beach, and Hội An.

Tourist Office: Most hotels offer basic tour services. **An Phu Tourist,** 147 Lê Lợi (☎818 366), has the best reputation. Mr. An speaks excellent English.

Consulates: Laos, 16 Trần Quý Cáp (☎821 208). Issues tourist visas to cross the border at Lao Bảo; 1-day processing. Open M-F 8-11:30am and 2-4:30pm.

Currency Exchange: Vietcombank, 140 Lê Lợi (☎823 503). Cashes traveler's checks and gives credit card cash advances. No ATM. Open M-Sa 7:30-11am and 1-4pm.

Markets: Chợ' Hàn is on the river by Hùng Vương and Trần Phú. Open daily 6am-8pm. **Chợ' Cồn** hulks near Hùng Vương and Ông Ích Khiêm. Open daily 6:30am-6:30pm.

Pharmacies: 45 Quang Trưng. Open daily 7am-4:30pm.

Police: 1 Nguyễn Thị Minh Khai (☎828 371).

Medical Services: Central Đà Nẵng Hospital, 124 Hải Phòng (☎ 821 118), 1 block north of Lê Duẩn. Has a Foreign Relations Affairs Office affiliated with AEA International.

Internet Access: Avoid solitary terminals. Find a multi-computer center (80Đ per min).

Post Offices: GPO, 60 Bạch Đằng, north of the Hùng Vương intersection. **Foreign Services Post Office,** 64 Bạch Đằng (☎821 327). **International phone**/fax. *Poste Restante.* Open daily 6am-10pm.

VIETNAM

ACCOMMODATIONS

Budget travelers usually bypass Đà Nẵng, so cheap beds are spread out and difficult to reach with a backpack. This may be the place to splurge for a pricier room.

Thuận An Mini Hotel, 14 Bạch Đằng (☎820 527), at the northern end. Truly budget. Doubles with fan US$5, with hot water US$7, with telephone and A/C US$10-15. ❷

Binh Dương Hotel, 30-32 Trần Phú (☎821 930). Exceedingly friendly owner. All rooms with A/C and satellite TV. Standard doubles US$15; immaculate, apartment-style rooms with carpeting, matching decor, and breakfast US$25-30 for two. ❹

Hoa Sen (Lotus) Hotel, 123 Hùng Vương (☎824 505). Sparkling clean rooms in a bustling spot not far from Chợ' Cồn Market. Breakfast included. Big doubles US$15-25. ❹

Royal Hotel, 17 Quang Trưng (☎823 295). Higher-end hotel features in-house bar, restaurant, and fitness area. Adjoining **VIP club** (see **Nightlife,** below) assures convenient brews and beats. Standard rooms US$30; suites US$50. ❺

FOOD AND NIGHTLIFE

Most food options are pretty bare-bones. For after-dinner treats, however, Đà Nẵng residents have gone ice cream crazy. **Ice cream parlors** cluster near the Đà Nẵng Cathedral on Trần Phú and Quang Trưng. Evening strolls along the river on Bạch Đằng are peaceful and pleasant as long as you don't mind rats milling about. **VIP Club,** 17 Quang Trưng, is the nightclub where small—but loud—hip young locals shake it alongside aging foreigners aspiring to be hip young locals. (☎823 295. Beer 25,000Đ. Open daily 8pm-2am.)

Miền Trung, 9 Bạch Đằng. Riverfront views. Popular for local weddings. Entrees 20,000-50,000Đ. Open daily 7:30am-9:30pm. ❷

Christie's, 112 Trần Phú, just north of the market. An expatriate haunt with English book exchange and **Internet** (800Đ per min.). Prices are inversely proportional to the amount of food. Pizza 50,000-80,000Đ. Open daily 9:30am-10pm. ❹

Linh Café, 22/04 Đong Da (☎820 401). A true backpacker eatery. Serves pancakes and provides tours and rental info. Breakfast 12,000Đ. Open daily 6:30am-midnight. ❷

SIGHTS

The small but celebrated **Chàm Museum,** 2 Tieu La, on the south end of town past where Trần Phú and Bạch Đằng merge, is the premier exhibit of Chàm sculpture. The open-air galleries showcase sandstone sculptures dating from the 4th to the 16th centuries, organized by their recovery location, including Mỹ Sơn. (☎821 951. Open daily 7am-5pm. 20,000Đ.) The Theravada Buddhist **Tam Bảo Pagoda,** 323 Phan Chu Trinh, lies southwest of the Chàm Museum. Built in 1953, this towering combination of French, Chinese, and Chàm architectural styles has five tiers which represent the steps to heaven. The light pink **Đà Nẵng Cathedral,** 156 Trần Phú, is a more grandiose house of worship. Called the "rooster cathedral" for its steeple-top weathercock, the cathedral was built in 1923 to serve the French Catholic community. (Open to visitors daily 8-10am and 2-5pm. Mass M-Sa 5am and 5pm, Su 5:15, 7:30am, 3:30, 5pm.) Đà Nẵng's **Cao Đài Temple,** 63 Hải Phòng, is farther north opposite the Central Hospital. Built in 1956, the temple serves 10,000 locals, sports the all-seeing eye, and is the largest such temple outside Tây Ninh. (Services daily 5:30, 11am, 5:30, and 11pm.)

VIETNAM

DAYTRIPS FROM ĐÀ NẴNG

MARBLE MOUNTAINS (NGŨ HÀNH SƠN). The Marble Mountains are named after the five fundamental elements: the popular **Water Mountain (Ngon Thủy Sơn),** the thin Metal Mountain, the subtle Wood Mountain, the double-peaked Fire Mountain, and the Earth Mountain. Limestone and marble quarries cluster around the foot of Water Mountain, with grand temples, eerie grottoes, and idols hewn from the rock. In the 1960s, the mountain served as a base for the NLF. From the entrance closest to the beach, stairs lead past a white Buddha to the towering **Linh Ứng Pagoda.** The **Tàng Chôn Cave,** in the back, contains a shrine flanked by a Chàm sculpture and a square stone platform on which, according to legend, fairies and gods played checkers. Moving on up, the "Simply Stunning Sea View," **Vọng Hải Đài,** really isn't so stunning. For a grander panorama of China Beach from the mountain's highest accessible point, ascend **Động Vân Thông,** the "Way to Heaven." Back on the path, the **Tam Thái Pagoda** sports some beautiful bas reliefs and sits in front of the unspectacular **Linh Nham Cave.** To the pagoda's right, a stone representation of Quan Am—a buddha and Vietnam's patron saint—is carved from **Oa Nghiêm Cave,** but the best sight lies behind it: the light that penetrates the **Huyền Không Cave** through overgrown holes above. Four warrior statues at the cavern's entrance, dating from Minh Mạng's time, protect it from evil spirits. Near the left stairwell, a path leads past two small pagodas to **Vọng Giang Đài,** the perfect place to take in the "Five-Mountain View." *(17km north of Hội An and 12km south of Đà Nẵng. Motos and cyclos make the trip for 30,000Đ. All tourist buses stop here for an hour. Open daily 7am-6pm. 10,000Đ.)*

CHINA BEACH. Famous for its role as a landing spot for US troops during the Vietnam war, China Beach makes a great daytrip from Đà Nẵng or Hội An. You'll find few foreigners here and even fewer Vietnamese, though the **Non Nước Resort Hotel ❸** complex hopes to lure another wave of invaders. (☎836 216. Doubles US$10-12.) Just a hop, skip, and jump away, the clean, wide, white beach stretches to both horizons. *(East of the Marble Mountains. Motos and cyclos charge 30,000Đ.)*

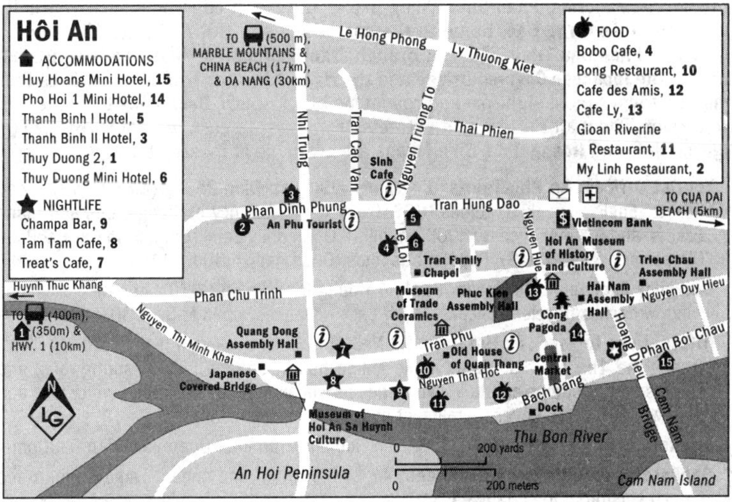

HỘI AN ☎51

From the 16th to the 19th centuries, Hội An (known to Europeans as "Faifo") was a bustling port frequented by Chinese, Japanese, and European merchants. As the river began to silt up in the 19th century, the French chose nearby Đà Nẵng, with its superior port, as the next commercial center. Hội An remained a backwater town until the tourism floodgates swung open with a vengeance. Merchants' mansions, ornate Chinese assembly halls, and laid-back charm—as well as over 100 quality tailor shops—win travelers' hearts. A government-sponsored celebration every month on the full and new moon closes the town center to motorized traffic, letting pedestrians meander amid thousands of glowing multicolored lanterns.

TRANSPORTATION

Buses: Public bus station, 84 Huỳnh Thúc Kháng (☎861 284), 400m west of town. Tiny open-air trucks (2hr.; every hr. 5am-4pm; 10,000Đ) and full-size red and white buses run to **Đà Nẵng** via **Marble Mountain** or **China Beach** (1hr.; every hr. 5:30am-5:30pm; 20,000Đ) from less than 1km northwest of town at the intersection of Nhị Trưng and Lê Hồng Phong. For **Nha Trang** and **Quảng Ngãi,** head to Hwy. 1, about 10km away, and flag down a bus. **Tourist minibuses** are available at any hotel to: **Đà Nẵng** (1hr.; 2, 8am; US$3); **Huế** (3hr.; 2, 8am; US$3); **Nha Trang** (10hr.; 6am, 8pm; US$7-12).

Rentals: Most hotels and travel agencies rent **cars** with drivers (from US$20 per day), **motorbikes** (US$5 per day including petrol), and **bicycles** (4000-7000Đ per day). Freelance operations are at the east end of Trần Phú and across the Cẩm Nam Bridge.

ORIENTATION AND PRACTICAL INFORMATION

Hội An is 25km south of Đà Nẵng and 102km north of Quảng Ngãi. Most public buses drop passengers at the side of **Hwy. 1;** from here, it's a 10km, 10,000Đ motorbike ride east to Hội An via **Huỳnh Thúc Kháng.** Just before town, the street breaks into three branches. **Phan Đình Phung** marks the north edge of town, eventually becoming **Trần Hưng Đạo,** home to the **post office** and Hội An Hotel. The middle branch is **Phan Chu Trinh.** The last branch, **Nguyễn Thị Minh Khai,** heads southeast toward the **Japanese Covered Bridge** and the river. After the bridge it becomes **Trần Phú,** the town's most sight-packed road. One block south, **Bạch Đằng** hugs the Thu Bon River. The major north-south streets, from west to east, are **Nhị Trưng, Lê Lợi, Nguyễn Huệ,** and **Hoàng Diệu.** Small **maps** are available at most hotels.

Tourist Offices: An Phu Tourist Company, 29 Phan Đình Phung (☎862 643). Open tickets, English-speaking guides (US$10 per day), currency exchange, bus and plane tickets, and Internet access (200Đ per min.). Open daily 6am-10pm. **Sinh Cafe,** 2 Phan Đình Phung (☎863 948). Popular bus tours. Open daily 5:30am-11pm.

Currency Exchange: Vietincom Bank, 4 Hoàng Diệu (☎862 675). Currency exchange window cashes traveler's checks. MC/V cash advances. Open M-Sa 7:30am-7pm.

Alternatives to Tourism: Hai Cafe, 98 Nguyễn Thái Học, offers a nightly cooking class. During the 1hr. class students make grilled fish in banana leaves, spring rolls, and squid salad. Students eat their own dishes as well as Hội An specialties, white rose and fried wonton. US$5 covers enrollment and the following meal.

Markets: Near the intersection of Nguyễn Huệ and Trần Phú. Open daily 6am-7:30pm.

Bookstore: Foreign Book Exchange, 48 Lê Lợi. Good and cheap. Large German and French sections. Open daily 9am-10pm.

Police: 8 Hoàng Diệu (☎861 204).

Pharmacy: 65 Lê Lợi (☎862 470), close to the water. Open daily 7am-10pm.

Medical Services: Local **hospital,** 4 Trần Hưng Đạo (☎861 218), across from the GPO.

Internet Access: Outlets proliferating by the day. 200Đ per min. **Banana Split Cafe** and **Thùy Dương I Hotel** are the fastest. Or try one of Hội An's "cyber-tailor shops"!

Post Office: GPO, 4B Trần Hưng Đạo (☎861 480). **International phone calls.** *Poste Restante.* Open daily 6am-10pm.

ACCOMMODATIONS

The high volume of tourists inflates hotel prices. The prices below reflect peak months (July-Aug. and Dec.-Feb.). In off season, bargaining can cut the price. The newer, larger hotels on Huynh Thúc Kháng just west of town offer the best value.

Thùy Dương 2, 68 Huynh Thúc Kháng (☎861 394), between the bus station and the Cao Đai Pagoda on the western outskirts of town. Thùy Dương Mini Hotel's quieter sibling. Spacious, clean rooms. Singles US$8-12; doubles US$10-14. ❸

Thùy Dương Mini Hotel, 11 Lê Lợi (☎861 574). On a happening strip. Tourist services galore in the lobby. Windowless doubles US$8-12. ❸

Huy Hoàng Mini Hotel, 73 Phan Bội Châu (☎861 453). Spotless waterfront property with French architecture and superb service invokes the romance of yesteryear. Singles and doubles US$12-18, with river view US$30-35. ❸

Phố Hội 1 Mini Hotel, 7/2 Trần Phú (☎861 633), in the alley. As good a choice as any for "cheap livin'," Hội An-style. Bare but clean with A/C, full bath, hot water, and balconies. Singles US$8; doubles US$12-18. ❷

Thanh Binh I Hotel, 11 Lê Lợi (☎861 740). More affordable but cramped. Singles US$8; doubles US$10, with balcony and A/C US$15. ❷

Thanh Binh II (☎863 715), at the corner of Nhị Trưng and Phan Đình Phung. Upscale rooms at decent prices–if you can avoid the tailor shop on the second floor. For those more interested in threads than beds, smaller rooms start at US$15. Large, beautiful doubles top out at US$30. ❹

FOOD

Hội An's local culinary specialties are its true attractions. Try *cao lầu,* thick rich noodles in a tasty soup, or white roses, steamed shrimp in rice paper. Only two families in town have the recipe for the secret noodle dough in *hoành thánh,* fried wonton. For dessert, try *bánh ít,* sugary rice and beans in a banana leaf.

Bong Restaurant, 59 Lê Lợi. Reputed among locals to offer the finest *cao lầu* in Hội An (5000Đ, with free tea as well). ❶

Bobo Cafe, 18 Lê Lợi, facing Thùy Dương Mini Hotel. A long-time favorite among backpackers. Vegetarian versions of local specialties. ❶

Cafe Ly, 22 Nguyễn Huệ. Excellent *cao lầu* (8000Đ), white roses (12,000Đ), and fried wonton (17,000Đ) are among Mrs. Ly and Belgian hubby René's top offerings. Open daily 8am-11pm. ❷

Cafe des Amis, 11 Bạch Đằng, on the river near the market. 14 splendid dishes, seafood or vegetarian, US$3. Open daily 8am-11:30pm. ❸

Gioan Riverine Restaurant, 78A Bạch Đằng. Pleasant riverfront location. Generous portions of seafood delicacies. Fixed price menu 30,000-50,000Đ. ❸

Restaurant My Linh, 59 Phan Đình Phung. This family-run eatery will make you feel right at home. Western and Vietnamese entrees, plus Hội An specialties (6000-20,000Đ). ❷

SIGHTS

Hội An's official sights hold less interest for most travelers than the town's narrow streets. The most beautiful sights demand an **entry ticket** (50,000Đ), available 7am-6pm at **Hội An Tourist Offices:** 12 Phan Chu Trinh (☎862 715); 5 Hoàng Diệu (☎861 114); 37 Trần Phú (☎862 118); 78 Lê Lợi (☎861 982); and 19 Nhị Trưng (☎861 984). Each ticket provides access to the Japanese Covered Bridge or the Công Pagoda, your choice of one old house, one assembly hall, one museum, and one additional sight. Government **tour guides** have a sweeping knowledge of local history (free for groups over 8; 50,000Đ per 2hr. tour for smaller groups).

OLD HOUSES

TRẦN FAMILY CHAPEL. Devoted to ancestor worship, the 200-year-old Trần Family Chapel incorporates Chinese, Japanese, and Vietnamese design into its roof beams and woodwork. The 10th generation of the Trần Family, who live next door, explain their heritage and serve refreshments to guests. On the family altar rests a group of boxes, each one containing a small personal object from a patriarch and a wooden tablet listing his accomplishments. In the garden behind the sanctuary, a newborn baby's umbilical cord and placenta were buried as a token of family remembrance. *(At the corner of Lê Lợi and Phan Chu Trinh. Open daily 7am-6pm.)*

TRƯƠNG FAMILY CHAPEL. For a less polished (but free) house of ancestor worship, head to the Trương Family Chapel. First constructed in 1840 and rebuilt in 1897, this edifice honors a family that came from Fukien, China, 10 generations ago. The central altar honors the family's first three generations, the left altar honors generations four through six, and the right altar awaits those next in line. The best time to visit is after 5pm when guide Trương Tri is home. *(69/1 Phan Chu Trinh.)*

OTHER HOUSES. The 200-year-old **Old House of Phùng Hưng** shelters eight people of the 8th generation. *(4 Nguyễn Thị Minh Khai, just west of the Japanese Covered Bridge. Open daily 7am-6pm.)* The **Old House of Tấn Ký** boasts an illustrious commercial history, a trap door, and memorabilia. *(101 Nguyễn Thái Học. Open daily 8am-5pm.)* Built by a Chinese captain in the 18th century, the **Old House of Quân Thắng** is said to be the oldest in Hội An. The house's 7th-generation owner, Diệp Bảo Hùng, encourages guests to come after 6pm, when entrance is free. *(77 Trần Phú. Open daily 7am-9pm.)*

ASSEMBLY HALLS

When Chinese merchants came to Hội An centuries ago, they formed congregations *(bang)* according to native region. The halls follow similar patterns and purposes: four open chambers surround a courtyard, providing an ornate environment for meeting peers, worshiping gods, and honoring ancestors.

PHÚC KIẾN ASSEMBLY HALL. Hội An's oldest, largest, most colorful, and most complex structure, this hall was first constructed in 1697 by Fukienese immigrants who later rebuilt the hall in 1757. Past the pink columns of the Red Phoenix Gate, look down to see the symbol for longevity surrounded by the five bats of happiness. The first courtyard contains stonework and a statue called "Carp Contemplating the Moon." Above the inner archway, five bats frame the phrase "The goddess will give her fellow man favor." This goddess is Thánh Mẫu, Holy Mother, Protectress of Sailors, and Goddess of the Sea. Just inside the main building, a mural depicts Thánh Mẫu preparing to rescue a ship from a wipeout-caliber wave. The main altar pays tribute to the congregation's ancestors; a smaller one to the right honors the God of Prosperity. *(46 Trần Phú. Open daily 7am-6pm.)*

QUẢNG DONG ASSEMBLY HALL. This hall serves the families of Cantonese merchants who arrived during the 17th century, built the hall in the 18th century, renovated it in 1885, and built the courtyard's colorful dragon fountain 20 years ago. A large bas-relief mural at the entrance depicts a red-faced Quan Công, a military hero from the 3rd century whose morality was high enough to earn him deification. The main sanctuary houses a 3D image of Quan Công with the Goddess of Mercy and God of Prosperity on either side. *(176 Trần Phú. Open daily 6am-6pm.)*

TRIỀU CHÂU ASSEMBLY HALL. Intricate wood carvings lure visitors to this 150-year-old hall. Inside the sanctuary, a first-century Han emperor sits surrounded by tiny figures carved and painted on wooden panels. *(157 Nguyễn Duy Hiệu, the east extension of Trần Phú. Open daily 6am-6pm. Free, despite what the entrance ticket says.)*

HẢI NAM ASSEMBLY HALL. For a glimpse of amazing woodwork, go to the Hải Nam Assembly Hall. This congregation came from the island of Hainan near the coast of North Vietnam. In 1851, 108 of their merchant sailors were wrongfully killed by local mandarins, who in turn were executed by the emperor. The assembly hall was built in the sailors' memory. *(10 Trần Phú. Open daily 6am-5pm.)*

MUSEUMS

MUSEUM OF TRADE CERAMICS. The front room introduces Western visitors to the maritime global network through rather boring displays, including a map of ocean routes, a model of a trading ship, and a 17th-century Japanese painting of Faifo. More engaging exhibits on modern-day architectural preservation efforts, along with a section of Hội An's signature yin and yang roof tiles, await in the back room. *(80 Trần Phú. Open daily 7am-5:30pm.)*

HÔI AN MUSEUM OF HISTORY AND CULTURE. This 300-year-old museum (which used to be a Quan Âm Pagoda) provides a decent overview of the town's history. Today, its secular displays trace local civilization through the early Sa Huỳnh culture, Champa Empire, and Đại Việt era. *(7 Nguyễn Huệ, around the corner from and connected to the Công Pagoda. Open daily 7am-6pm.)*

MUSEUM OF HÔI AN SA HUỲNH CULTURE. This museum displays remnants of the Sa Huỳnh civilization, first unearthed around Hội An in 1993. Like Oc Eo in the south and Đông Sơn in the north, the details of this prehistoric, pre-Champa culture remain elusive. There's a war and revolution museum upstairs. *(159 Trần Phú, opposite the Quảng Dông Assembly Hall. Open daily 6am-6pm.)*

OTHER SIGHTS

JAPANESE COVERED BRIDGE. The pink Japanese Covered Bridge, Hội An's most famous symbol, is known locally as Chùa Cầu ("Pagoda Bridge"). Japanese traders built it in the early 17th century. The stone piles were meant to be driven into the heart of a monster, whose pesky tail supposedly caused earthquakes in Japan.

CÔNG PAGODA. The Công Pagoda honors Quan Công, a general of the Han Dynasty during the 2nd and 3rd centuries. The 350-year-old temple has the distinction of housing the largest statue of a god in Hội An. *(24 Trần Phú. Opens into the Museum of History and Culture. Open daily 7am-5:30pm.)*

NIGHTLIFE

For those bent on liver destruction, rice whiskey (see **A Mini-keg a Day,** p. 901) flows on the corner of Lê Lợi and Trần Phú until 4am most nights; most other bars are packed until 2am, with "happy hour" lasting from 4 to 9pm.

Treat's Cafe, 158 Trần Phú. In an elegant two-story building. Mostly Western crowd alternates between drinking cheap beer (10,000Đ, 6000Đ during happy hour), shooting pool/darts, and bantering with pesky but charming sales kids. Open daily until 1am.

Tam Tam Cafe, 110 Nguyễn Thái Học, 1 block toward the river from Trần Phú. The early evening is quiet as diners enjoy pricey Western cuisine (Australian steaks US$9). The French owners start coaxing the raucous crowd out at 1am. A bottle of Larue drops from 18,000Đ to 10,000Đ in happy hour. Homemade ice cream is worth a try (18,000Đ).

Champa Bar, 75 Nguyễn Thái Học. Calmer than its larger neighbors. Big drinks, Western music, and 2 pool tables. Doubles as a traditional art performance center with sporadic folk music and dancing shows. Tall Larue beer 13,000Đ. Open daily 4pm-midnight.

SHOPPING

In a region renowned for its tailors and dressmakers, Hội An's *couture* scene shines. While those oblivious to quality can find US$20 suits, a good suit should cost about US$40, a shirt US$6, and a pair of silk pajamas US$10—all made within a day according to the shopper's specifications. Shops are concentrated on Lê Lợi. Most have old fashion magazines and pattern books to aid the designing process. The **cloth market,** on Trần Phú near Hóang Dieu, is also worth a look, though seamstresses there tend to be more aggressive. Most tailoring places offer great value and quality, but talk to the dressmakers, look at their previous work, and ask other customers' opinions. The trilingual (English, French, and Vietnamese) seamstress at unassuming **Ngọc Huệ,** 61 Phan Đình Phùng, does excellent work at reasonable prices. Another solid option is **Thu Thủy,** 60 Lê Loi. Architecture lovers should ask to see its showroom in the back, which has exquisite handcarved wood beams. While linings might cost extra, double-stitching, which prevents fraying, should not. Also remember that you can take off the extra inch; you can't add one. "Chinese silk," "Japanese silk," and "Vietnamese silk" mean different things to different people, but when all's said and done, real silk burns in a flame, while synthetics melt away. Ask for a small sample and test the fabric yourself with a lighter.

DAYTRIPS FROM HỘI AN

CUA DAI BEACH. Although Cua Dai Beach today may be quiet and relaxed (and free), for up to 10 years after liberation, this served as the departure point for many fleeing refugee "boat people" embarking upon the 10-day passage to the Philippines. In town on Bạch Đằng, boat tours depart from near the market between 7am and 10pm. Independent operators charge 30,000Đ per hour; Hội An Tourist's tours (see p. 941) are more expensive but better planned. Stops are made along the way at three handicraft villages: the **Ceramics Village (Làng Gốm), "Carpenter's Village" (Làng Mộc),** and **Carpet Village (Lang Chieu).** *(5km east of town on Trần Hưng Đạo.)*

MỸ SƠN. A newly minted UNESCO World Heritage Site, the ruins at Mỹ Sơn were once the major religious center of the ancient Champa Kingdom. The earliest artifacts from the ruins date from the 4th century, though more permanent temples were not built until the 7th century. From the 7th to the 13th centuries, over 70 towers were built. Today, the ruins are organized into groups A-H. The path from the entrance leads directly to the B-C-D group, of which the C1 *kalan* (main tower) is most prominent. The broad, rectangular D1 and D2 were once *mandapas* (meditation chambers) for the Bs and Cs, respectively. Now they house a motley assortment of sculpture—the best have been moved to Đà Nẵng's Chàm Museum (see p. 938). US bombing reduced the A1 tower, once the most spectacular testament to Chàm artistry, to a sad perimeter of stone. Despite the alphabetized grouping, there is little written description at the sights. A visit to the Chàm Museum beforehand will lend a context to this important pilgrimage site. *(50km west of Hội An. Minibus tours allow 2hr. at the ruins (8am, return by 2pm). Smaller tourist offices put you on the same buses for less (US$1-5). To beat the crowds, hire a motorbike driver (US$5-6 round-trip) or get detailed directions and head out early. Ruins open daily 6:30am-4:30pm. Visitors must purchase a 50,000Đ ticket, take a brief bus ride around a hill, and proceed 300m on foot. English-speaking guides cost an extra 30,000Đ (up to 4 people) or 50,000Đ (5 or more), but are rarely available on the spot.)*

QUẢNG NGÃI ☎55

An unremarkable provincial capital between Hội An and Qui Nhơn, Quảng Ngãi is the launching spot for visits to the remains of Sơn Mỹ Village, site of the Mỹ Lai Massacre. Though differing only in scale and circumstance from countless other events in the war, the massacre has come to symbolize the inhumanity of the conflict. The area's sobering history is a lesson in humility for visitors from the West.

TRANSPORTATION. The **bus station,** 26 Lê Thánh Tôn (☎822 895), 100m east of the Central Hotel runs service to: **Buôn Ma Thuột** (13hr.; 5:30am; 62,000Đ); **Đà Lạt** (16hr.; 3am; 74,000Đ); **HCMC** (24hr.; 8am; 100,000Đ); **Hội An/Đà Nẵng** (3-4hr.; approx. every hr. 5-8am; 18,000Đ); **Kontum** (11hr.; 5am; 43,000Đ); **Nha Trang** (9hr.; 5am; 49,000Đ); **Pleiku** (10hr.; 5am; 37,000Đ); **Qui Nhơn** (4hr.; 5am-noon; 19,000Đ). Flagging buses in front of the **Petro-Song Tra Hotel** on the north side of town, as they pass on the new Hwy. 1 bypass, is also an option. The **train station** (Ga Quảng Ngãi; ☎820 272) is 3km west of town at the end of Nguyễn Chanh. Trains go to all major stops in either direction on the **Reunification Express,** including **Hanoi** (24-35hr.; hard seat 230,000Đ, soft sleeper 460,000Đ) and **HCMC** (20-30hr.; hard seat 145,000Đ, soft sleeper 295,000Đ).

ORIENTATION AND PRACTICAL INFORMATION. Quảng Ngãi is 180km north of Qui Nhơn, 102km south of Hội An, and 117km south of Đà Nẵng. Hwy. 1 used to run north-south through town as **Quảng Trung.** Most of Quảng Ngãi's services are on **Hùng Vương,** which cuts east-west across Quảng Trung, 2km north of the bus station. **Quảng Ngãi Tourist Company** (Công Ty Du lịch Quảng Ngãi), 310 Quảng Trung, is 100m from Hùng Vương. (☎829 829. Open M-Sa 7-11am and 1:30-5pm.) The **Foreign Currency Transaction Department,** 89 Hùng Vương, cashes traveler's checks. (☎822 626. Open M-Sa 7-11:30am and 1:30-4:30pm.) A large **market,** 30 Nguyễn Nghiêm, is east of Quảng Trung. (Open daily 6am-8pm.) The **hospital** is 2km west of Quảng Trung on Hùng Vương. (☎822 888. Some English spoken.) The **post office,** 80 Phan Đình Phùng at Hùng Vương, has **international phones.** (☎822 930. Open daily 6:30am-9pm.) **Internet** is at 282-284 Quảng Trung (100Đ per min).

ACCOMMODATIONS AND FOOD. Đồng Hưng Hotel ❷, 497 Quảng Trung, 500m south of Hùng Vương, has clean rooms and a chatty staff. (☎821 704. Doubles US$5-8, with A/C and hot water US$10, with tub and fridge US$13.) **Kim Thanh Hotel ❷,** 19 Hùng Vương, is your best bet for clean baths and a friendly, English-speaking staff. (☎823 471. Small singles US$5; doubles with A/C US$12.) **Petro-Song Tra Hotel ❺,** 2 Quảng Trung at the Hwy. 1 bridge, offers three-star amenities and service at upscale prices. (☎822 665. Singles US$25-55; doubles $30-75.) If you're feeling the munchies, head for **Bông Hồng ❶,** 243 Nguyễn Nghiêm, where *cơm gà* (a local chicken and rice concoction) with soup is 8000Đ. (Open daily 7am-11pm.) **Mimosa Com Vietnam ❷,** 21 Hùng Vương, serves superb grilled beef for 18,000Đ on *Titanic* tablecloths. (Open daily 6am-6pm.)

SIGHTS. Quảng Ngãi's most arresting sights lie along the road to Sơn Mỹ, beginning 1km north of Hùng Vương, over the bridge and to the east. Just past the sign that marks the turn-off, a dirt road runs up the top of **Triên An Hill.** American, Australian, and South Korean soldiers were based here during the Vietnam War. A monument to **Huỳnh Thúc Kháng,** an important figure in the anti-colonial movement, overlooks the area below. Colorful **Triên An Pagoda** stands nearby.

The **Sơn Mỹ Memorial,** site of the 1968 **Mỹ Lai Massacre,** sits amid peaceful rice fields 8km farther east along the road. Only one of the surrounding hamlets is called Mỹ Lai, but the US armed forces used this name to refer to all four hamlets of Sơn Mỹ village. On the morning of March 16, 1968, Charlie Company, devastated by losses it had incurred from an enemy it hadn't been able to distinguish from civilians, swept through the area, killing everyone in sight. Within four hours, they had murdered 504 villagers, many of them children and elders. The world didn't learn the truth until 18 months later. After lengthy investigations, just one low-ranking officer, Lieutenant William Calley, was court-martialed—and later granted a pardon from President Nixon. The memorial to Sơn Mỹ's victims was established in 1976 at the site of the gruesome massacre.

The worthwhile **museum** has an inscription over the entrance, loosely translated as, "Always remember the hating heart of the US invaders." Inside, photographs and personal belongings of the victims are displayed, with a list of all 504 victims' names and ages. Outside the museum, signs point out trees riddled with bullet holes from the massacre. (Open daily 7am-5pm. 10,000Đ.)

Biển Khé Ky An, a small, picturesque beach, is 11km beyond Sơn Mỹ. The road to the beach (which passes several shrimp farms) can be quite rough and windy. It's best undertaken on a moto. Most motos are stationed outside the swanky Petro-Song Tra Hotel. Round-trip rides with waiting time start at 60,000Đ.

QUI NHƠN ☎56

This charmless seaport town is the capital of Bình Định Province, but its current decrepit state masks a once glorious past. In the 18th century, the Tây Sơn brothers led the great Tây Sơn Rebellion, ending two centuries of division between the North and South. This region, the Tây Sơn District, was also home to two of Vietnam's greatest poets, **Hàn Mạc Tử** (1912-1940) and **Xuân Diệu** (1916-1985). While contemporary Qui Nhon has little to show for its history, rampant road construction and economic redevelopment indicate that locals have their sights firmly set on the future. In the meantime, travelers settle for gray hotels and satisfying sands.

TRANSPORTATION. Any A/C tourist bus originating in Hội An or Nha Trang will drop passengers off on Hwy. 1, 10 km west of Qui Nhơn. To get to the city center, pick from the smorgasbord of motorized vehicles that hover around the junction (3000-15,000Đ). The **airport** is 34km out of town. **Vietnam Airlines,** the large blue building near the corner of Nguyễn Tat Thanh and Nguyễn Thai Hoc (☎823 125; open daily 7-11:30am and 1:30-5pm), flies to **HCMC** (W-M; 670,000Đ). For **trains,** ignore the cargo transport station at Qui Nhơn and head to **Ga Diêu Trì** (☎833 255), 10km outside the city (15,000Đ by motorcycle taxi). Tickets and schedules are at **Ga Qui Nhơn** on Lý Thường Kiệt across from **Quảng Trung Park**. (☎822 036. Open daily 7am-4:30pm.) Trains go to: **Đà Nẵng** (6hr.; 8:20am; 87,000-129,000Đ); **Hanoi** (22hr.; 8:20am; 246,000-484,000Đ); **HCMC** (12½hr.; 5:45pm; 138,000-282,000Đ); **Huế** (8½hr.; 8:20am; 117,000-172,000Đ); and **Nha Trang** (4½hr.; 5:45pm; 69,000-101,000Đ). The **bus station,** 2km west of **Quảng Trung Park** on Tây Sơn, runs buses to: **Buôn Ma Thuột** (9hr.; 43,000Đ); **HCMC** (15hr.; 78,000Đ); **Huế** (11hr.; 6am; 48,000Đ) via **Đà Nẵng; Nha Trang** (6hr.; 28,000Đ); **Pleiku** (4hr.; 20,000Đ). All of these buses depart between 5 and 8am. For more frequent journeys on crowded buses, go to Hwy. 1, 10km west of town, and flag away.

ORIENTATION AND PRACTICAL INFORMATION. Qui Nhơn is on a triangular peninsula 220km north of Nha Trang, 210km south of Quảng Ngãi, 150km east of Pleiku, and 12km east of Hwy. 1. **Hwy. 19** runs east into town as **Trần Hưng Đạo** from its intersection with Hwy. 1, eventually reaching **Quảng Trung Park.** From here **Phan Bội Châu** runs east, **Lê Hồng Phong** heads southeast, and **Lý Thường Kiệt** curves southwest, passing the airstrip-turned-boulevard **Nguyễn Tat Thanh.** The other end of this street ends at **Nguyễn Huệ,** which runs parallel to the beachfront.

Services include: **Bình Định General Hospital** (☎822 330), 106 Nguyễn Huệ; **Tram Y Tế Pharmacy,** 61 Trần Phu, (☎824 143); **Vietcombank,** 152 Lê Lợi (☎822 408; open M-F 7-11am and 1-4pm, Sa 8am-noon); **market,** 1 Tháng 4 between Phan Bội Châu and Tăng Bạt Hổ; **police,** 247 Lê Hồng Phong (☎822 491); **Internet,** 245 Lê Hồng Phong. (☎823 055; 100Đ per min.); and the **GPO,** 197 Phan Bội Châu, with **international phones** (☎821 441; open daily 6:30am-9:30pm).

ACCOMMODATIONS AND FOOD. Accommodations tend to be uninspiring but chock-full of services. **Movies Hotel ❸,** 296 Phan Bội Châu, overlooks the central park and has clean, modern rooms. (☎822 876. Doubles with satellite TV US$9-15.) **Quy Nhon Hotel ❺,** 8 Nguyễn Hué, across the street from the public beach, offers carpeted, wood-paneled rooms at bargainable prices. (☎892-401. Doubles with all the trimmings US$25-60. Breakfast included.)

Away from the city center and beach, a large bowl of spicy rice soup with meat *(cháo)* and a tall glass of sugarcane juice or ice milk costs 5000Đ—check out the corner of Phan Bội Châu and Mai Xuan Thương, two blocks from the water. **Quê Hương 2 ❷,** 185 Lê Hồng Phong, is good, clean fun. ("Browned-rolling froggy" 15,000Đ. Open daily 8am-9pm.) **Thu Hông ❸,** 189 Tăng Bạt Hổ, is another solid choice that whips up a truly fine do-it-yourself hot pot with squid for 40,000Đ. (Open daily 8am-10pm.)

SIGHTS. Qui Nhơn's **public beach** is busy and interesting. Standing in front of the Qui Nhon Hotel, the **Xiem Riep-Ratanakiri Zoo** is on the left at 2B Nguyễn

Hué. To the right, a 5km walk to the end Nguyễn Hué leads to the base of **Hàn Mạc Tủ Mountain.** The tomb and shrine of one of Vietnam's most revered poets, Hàn Mạc Tủ, rest halfway up the mountain (2000Đ). Continue past Hàn Mạc Tủ and climb among the smooth rocks that lend **Egg Beach** its name. At the unusual, well-kept **Leper Hospital,** patients live with their families and work in the small community. The hospital is on the other side of the mountain accessible from the highway that heads south out of town from the Tay Son-Nguyễn Hué rotary (3000Đ entry fee). The **Long Khánh Pagoda** is downtown on Trần Cao Vân, between Phan Bội Châu and Tăng Bạt Hổ. A huge teal Buddha greets visitors from atop a lotus; the main golden Buddha sits indoors with a *bodhi* tree behind him. (Open daily 6am-9pm.)

DAYTRIP FROM QUI NHON: BÌNH ĐỊNH. Bình Định is the birthplace of revered poet **Xuân Diệu.** A museum has been set up in the village of Túng Giản (approximately 23km north) at the late great's former home. (Open daily 7:30-11am.) **Hồ Núi Một** (Lake First Mountain) and the dam that created it are off Hwy. 19, 30km west of town; look for the small sign and head south. Surrounded by hills, the tranquil lake is perfect for contemplation or romance. Boatmen will ferry a four-seat boat to a waterfall upriver (US$10). **Tháp Bánh Ít,** the Cake Towers, sit on a hill near the crossroads of Hwy. 1 and Hwy. 19, 19km from town. Once a sizeable Chàm temple complex, these 11th-century ruins now sit amid arid scrub.

CENTRAL HIGHLANDS

Most foreigners, if they're familiar with the Central Highlands at all, heard about them 30 years ago when the region saw some of the bloodiest combat of the Vietnam War. Today, veterans return on remembrance tours, but the region's beauty and native cultures are its main attractions. Of Vietnam's **54 minorities,** many make their homes here: Mnong and Edeh reside near Buôn Ma Thuột, while the Bahnar, Jarai, and Sodang live around Pleiku and Kontum. Coffee and rubber plantations mingle with forests amid a backdrop of rounded mountains, peaceful lakes, and few tourists. As most attractions are far from the region's principal towns and many require expensive guides, solo backpackers find budget travel near-impossible. Groups can split guide fees.

INTERCITY TRANSPORTATION

Two main routes lead into the highlands from **Highway 1** on the coast. **Highway 26** begins 30km north of Nha Trang and leads to **Buôn Ma Thuột,** capital of **Daklak Province. Highway 19** starts near Qui Nhơn and leads to **Pleiku,** capital of **Gialai Province.** Highland cities are connected by **Highway 14,** which spans almost 200km from Buôn Ma Thuột north to Pleiku and an additional 50km up to **Kontum,** capital of **Kontum Province.** Until other highways are improved, these remain the only viable arteries. You can't get directly from Buôn Ma Thuột to Đà Lạt by car or bus, and you have to backtrack through Pleiku to go from Kontum to the coast.

PLEIKU ☎59

Come in a group, bring wads of cash, or consider pushing on to more budget-friendly locales. Even more than its northern and southern neighbors, Pleiku is a lousy locale for cheap travel. In-town attractions are nonexistent and hill-tribe villages are distant. Most budgeteers don't hang around for long.

TRANSPORTATION. The **airport** (☎825 097) is 7km east of town off Lê Lợi. The **Vietnam Airlines office** is at 55 Quang Trưng. (☎824 680. Open daily 7:00-11am and 1:30-5:30pm.) Flights go to: **Hanoi** (M, W-Th, Sa 8:25am; 770,000Đ) via **Đà Nẵng** (270,000Đ); **HCMC** (M, W-Th, Sa 11:50am, Su 8:30am; 400,000Đ). The **Gia Lai bus station** (☎824 117) is 1km east of town where Hùng Vương meets Hwy. 1. The following foreigner rates are based on listed Vietnamese prices. Buses go to: **Buôn Ma Thuột** (4hr.; 6:30am; 62,000Đ); **Đà Nẵng** (14hr.; 6:30, 7, 7:30am; 147,000Đ); **Hanoi** (45hr.; 6:30-9am; 134,000Đ); **HCMC** (13hr.; 6am-6pm; 180,000Đ); **Huế** (16hr.; 6:30am; 180,000Đ); **Quảng Ngãi** (9hr.; 6:15, 7, 7:45am; 100,000Đ); **Qui Nho'n** (4hr.; every hr. 7am-5pm; 57,000Đ). Minibuses (1hr.; 20,000Đ) and motorcycles (1hr.; 25,000Đ) leave all day for **Kontum** from Lê Lợi, opposite the Pleiku Hotel.

ORIENTATION AND PRACTICAL INFORMATION. Pleiku is 48km south of Kontum, 168km west of Qui Nhơn, and 190km north of Buôn Ma Thuột. **Hùng Vương** leads to Pleiku from the bus station; **Lê Lợi** and **Trần Hưng Đạo** branch off to the right, crossing Quang Trưng before meeting at the northeast corner of town.

Gialai Tourist, 215 Hùng Vương, at Lê Lợi, organizes tours and distributes **maps.** (☎872 406. Open M-Sa 7-11am and 1:30-4:30pm.) **Vietcombank,** 12 Trần Hưng Đạo, one block from the GPO, cashes traveler's checks and issues credit card cash advances. (☎828 593. Open M-Sa 7-11am and 1-4:30pm.) For **police,** contact the **immigration office,** on the west end of Trần Phú. (☎69 180. Open M-Sa 7:30-11am and 1:30-5pm.) The **hospital** is at 64 Trần Hưng Đạo. (☎824 125. English spoken.) The **GPO** and its **international phones** are at the corner of Trần Hưng Đạo and Hùng Vương. (☎824 129. Open daily 6am-10pm.)

ACCOMMODATIONS AND FOOD. **Thanh Lịch Hotel ❷,** 86 Nguyễn Văn Trỗi, off Quang Trưng, offers good value and fine service. (☎824 674. Singles with fan and hot water US$7; doubles US$10; rooms with A/C US$17.) Rooms at the **Pleiku Hotel ❸,** 124 Lê Lợi, are spacious and soulless, with hot water and satellite TV. (☎824 628. Doubles US$11; larger rooms with refrigerator US$26-37.) **Húng Long ❷,** 44 Trần Húng Đạo, is full of tourists and locals scarfing up Vietnamese tasties. (Cuttlefish pressed with lotus root 18,000Đ. Open daily 7am-10pm.)

SIGHTS. The Jarai village **Pleiful,** 38km north of Pleiku, is famed for its gravesite wood carvings. About 35km east of town on the way to Qui Nhơn, a small track on the left leads to **Dektu,** a Bahnar village of 200. Unlike most Bahnar communities, this one never converted to Catholicism. When someone dies, the family kills a buffalo and erects a *rong*-shaped grave. The family pays its respects every month by placing food and wine into a hole over the buried body. A moto and guide to both sights cost US$32.

KONTUM ☎60

Kontum province borders Cambodia and Laos, a location that gave it considerable strategic significance during the Vietnam War. In 1972, despite US and South Vietnamese boasts to the contrary, DRV forces of North Vietnam (see **The First Indochina War and Its Aftermath,** p. 885) captured the South Vietnamese base at nearby Đak Tô. Today, Kontum provides some of the region's most stunning scenery.

TRANSPORTATION AND PRACTICAL INFORMATION. Kontum is 48km north of Pleiku, 228km north of Buôn Ma Thuột, and 216km northwest of Qui Nhơn. The streets form a grid. **Highway 14** rolls north from Pleiku, passing over a small bridge and becoming **Phan Đình Phùng. Lê Hồng Phong** and **Trần Phú** are the other major north-south roads. **Nguyễn Huệ** runs eastward along the Dakbla River at the bottom end of town, paralleled to the north by **Trần Hưng Đạo, Phan Chu Trinh,** and **Bà Triệu.**

The interprovince **bus station** is 2km north of the town center on Phan Đình Phùng. The ticket office won't serve foreigners; the bus driver is the man to talk to. The following are local prices—use them as a base for your bargaining. Buses go to: **Buôn Ma Thuột** (6hr.; 7am; 26,000Đ); **Đà Nẵng** (14hr.; 6:30am; 56,000Đ); **HCMC** (14hr.; 7am; 69,000Đ); **Huế** (17hr.; 7am; 73,000Đ); **Qui Nho'n** (6hr.; 7am; 25,000Đ); **Quảng Ngãi** (11hr.; 7am; 40,000Đ). Minibuses leave all day for **Pleiku** (1hr., 8000Đ).

Kontum Tourist handles tours, permits, and transportation from its Dakbla Hotel office at 2 Phan Đình Phùng. (☎861 626. Free maps. Guide and driver to Đak Tô US$15. Open daily 7-11am and 1-5pm.) **Vietindebank,** 1 Trần Phú at Nguyễn Huệ, handles **currency exchange.** (☎862 164. Open M-Sa 7-11am and 1-4:30pm.) The **market** is at the corner of Trần Hưng Đạo and Lê Hồng Phong. (Open daily 5am-7pm.) The **police** (**emergency** ☎862 459) are at 90 Phan Chu Trinh. The **hospital** (☎862 572) is at 224 Bà Triệu. The **GPO,** under the giant radio tower, at Lê Hồng Phong and Bà Triệu, offers fax and **international phones.** (☎862 361. Open daily 7am-9pm.)

ACCOMMODATIONS AND FOOD. The **Dakbla Hotel II ❸** is tucked away inside the administrative-looking building at 163 Nguyễn Huệ. Its new rooms include satellite TV and spotless baths. (☎863 335. US$11, with hot water and A/C US$16.) At **Phòng Ngủ Bình Dân ❶,** 43 Lê Hồng Phong (☎862 706), barren doubles are 60,000Đ. **Food stalls ❶,** serving fruit shakes and rice dishes (7000Đ), line **Lê Hồng Phong** toward the market. **Quán Ăn Dakbla ❷,** 168 Nguyễn Huệ, near Dakbla Hotel, is adorned with etchings and weapons. The sauteed frog (*ếch xào;* 30,000Đ) isn't on the English menu, but should be.

SIGHTS. A **rong house,** a traditional communal hall with a towering thatched roof, stands on the east side of town, at the intersection of Nguyễn Huệ and Lữ Tự Trọng. Next door, the **Montagnard Church** combines Catholic symbolism with local artistry. (Open daily 5am-6pm. Daily mass 5am; Su 5, 6, 7am.) Unlike the highland cities, many of Kontum's **Bahnar villages** lie close to town.

In town, a **Vietnam War-era airstrip** (for civilian aircraft) stretches to the horizon off Bà Triệu. During the early morning, this lengthy strip of asphalt entertains Kontum youth and provides picturesque sunrises and sunsets. The rambling, colonial-style **Kontum Diocese Seminary** crouches behind wire fencing and orchards at 56 Trần Hưng Đạo. It was closed by the Vietnamese government following the war but is now open to the public. (Open daily 7-11am and 2-5pm.)

Continuing east on Nguyễn Huệ, you pass through heavily populated **Kon Klor.** The road then butts into Đạo Duy Tu. Two right turns will put you on Trần Húng Đạo, 600m from a suspension bridge over the Kon Klor River: across the bridge is **Kon Klor 2.** Take the first left, then the first right, to reach a winding dirt road which leads to a dammed **lake** at the bottom of a series of small hills. Local hill tribes work and paddle here.

DAYTRIP FROM KONTUM: ĐAK TÔ. Đak Tô, 40km north of Kontum on Hwy. 14, was a strategic region during the Vietnam War, valued for its proximity to the Lao and Cambodian borders. **Skull Hill,** the site of a clash between Northern DRV and Southern RVN forces in the spring of 1972, stands on the road to Đak Tô, 17km from Kontum. By overtaking the hill, the Communists severed the land route to Kontum. The location of the bloody attack is marked by a concrete shrine and three piles of stones where locals burn incense. A right turn after the post office in the village of Đak Tô leads to a Chinese-made anti-aircraft gun, a Russian-made DRV tank, and remnants of a US reconnaissance helicopter. Atop a plateau, 1km left and beyond the monument at the center of Đak Tô, was the site of a **South Viet-**

namese/US base. A large facade marks the spot, bearing the heading, *"Di Tích Lịch Sử Chiến Thắng Đak Tô-Tân Cảnh"* ("Site of the Đak Tô-Tân Cảnh Victory"). On April 24, 1972, following a five-hour barrage and assault, DRV forces wrested control of the Đak Tô base from the South Vietnamese army and their US advisors. The remains of a **US airbase** (Phượng Hoàng) are farther down the road, 4.5km from town on the left. **Pak Đri,** a Sedang minority village accessible by a hanging bridge, is a few kilometers down the road.

BUÔN MA THUỘT ☎50

This capital of the Đak Lak region was developed in 1899 by the French colonial Companie d'Agriculture d'Asie for the production of coffee and rubber, which grow well in the fertile red soil. On March 10, 1975, tank treads were planted here as the North Vietnamese Army swept through Buôn Ma Thuột (BMT), signaling the inception of their Hồ Chí Minh campaign and the beginning of the end for the South Vietnamese Army. Today in BMT, rubber is still stripped, coffee still grows, and the first tank to arrive on "Liberation Day" sits at the town's center. Those visitors not impressed by the best coffee in Vietnam linger only long enough to visit the local villages and natural attractions.

TRANSPORTATION. Buôn Ma Thuột Airport (☎862 248) is 13km northeast of town via Hwy. 14. The **Vietnam Airlines Booking Office** is at 67 Nguyễn Tất Thành (☎855 055), just before the bus station. Flights go to: **Hanoi** (M, W, F-Sa 8:05am; 975,000Đ) via **Đà Nẵng** (545,000Đ); and **HCMC** (M-W, F-Sa 4:15pm, Th 8:14am; 635,000). Reserve early. Buses leave the station at 71 Nguyễn Tất Thành (☎852 603) for: **Đà Lạt** (6hr.; 6am; 56,000Đ); **Đà Nẵng** (19hr.; 11am, noon, 8pm; 80,000Đ); **HCMC** (9hr.; frequent; 91,000Đ); **Huế** (25hr.; 6am; 70,000Đ); **Kontum** (7hr.; 6am; 35,000Đ); **Lak** (2hr.; leave when full; 10,000Đ); **Nha Trang** (5hr.; 6am; 28,000Đ); **Pleiku** (4hr.; 6am; 28,000Đ); **Quảng Ngãi** (16hr.; 6am; 48,000Đ); **Qui Nho'n** (11hr.; 6am; 34,000Đ). Travel time often varies seasonally. **Motorbike rentals** can be arranged by most hotels (50,000Đ per day). Moto drivers ask 15,000Đ per hour.

ORIENTATION AND PRACTICAL INFORMATION. Buôn Ma Thuột is 190km south of Pleiku, 180km northwest of Nha Trang, and 350km northeast of HCMC. The big tank is a navigational godsend. The turret, in its current position, could easily fire shots down Nguyễn Tất Thành (Hwy. 14) toward the bus station, 2km away. The back left corner of the tank points down Nơ Trang Long, which runs west past the market. Heading from the tank down this street, the first three rights, cutting through the heart of BMT, are Hai Bà Trưng, Lý Thướng Kiệt, and Y Jŭt.

Daklaktourist, 3 Phan Chu Trinh, the green house next to the Thang Loi Hotel by the tank's front left corner, has info on tours and hill tribes. (☎852 108. Cars to Lak Lake US$50; guide US$15 per day; **maps** 15,000Đ. Open daily 7-11am and 1:30-5pm.) **Vietcombank,** 6 Trấn Hung Dao on the corner of Le Thánh Tông, exchanges travelers' checks and offers MC and V advances. (☎855 037. Open M-Sa 7:30-11am and 1:30-4:30pm.) The **Đak Lak General Hospital** is at 2 Mai Hắc Đế (☎852 662), by way of Lê Duẩn (Độc Lập). The **GPO,** 4 Lê Duẩn, 150m south of the tank, has fax and **international phones.** (☎852 612. Open daily 7am-9pm.)

ACCOMMODATIONS AND FOOD. Government-run hotels are woefully overpriced; bargain vigorously. The private **White Horse Hotel ❸,** 54 Hai Bà Trung, rents remarkable rooms with satellite TV, hygienic hot-water bath, and A/C. (☎853 963. Singles US$26; doubles US$36; highly negotiable.) **Huy Hoàng Hotel ❶,** 30 Lý Thương Kiệt, offers clean rooms at backpacker prices. Great value for Buôn Ma

Thuột. (☎858 020. Singles US$4; doubles US$6-12.) **Khách Sạn San Bay Buôn Ma Thuột** (Buôn Ma Thuột Airport Hotel) ❷, 67 Nguyễn Tất Thành, above the booking office, offers laundry service (3000-5000Đ per item) and cheap rooms. (☎856 266. Singles with A/C, TV, fridge, and hot water US$8; doubles US$12.)

Be sure to sample Vietnam's finest *ca phe* brews at any one of the ubiquitous cafes. Tasty *nem nướng* **stalls** ❶ line Lý Thương Kiệt near the Huy Hoàng Hotel (8000Đ). Alternatively, head to the market, which spills out from the intersection of Quang Trang and Điện Biên Phủ. For a filling meal, try **Bò Né Bốn Triệu** ❷, 33 Hai Bà Trưng. Ask for *bò né* (10,000Đ), the breakfast specialty: eggs, beef, scallions, and a pork-ball on a sizzling cow-shaped plate. (Open daily 6am-10pm.)

SIGHTS. The immaculate Edeh village of **Buôn Akŏ Dhong,** just beyond the end of Trần Nhận Duật amid 50 acres of lucrative coffee fields, offers a conveniently close view of village life, even though it's the most affluent neighborhood in town. Two small museums highlight local hill-tribe culture and explain the history of the tank. The **Revolutionary Museum (Bảo Tàng Cách Mạng),** 1 Lê Duẩn, houses Hồ Chí Minh paraphernalia and a presentation on the liberation of BMT, along with a comic attempt at displaying indigenous wildlife. (☎852 527. Both museums open M-Sa 7:30-11:30am and 2-5pm. 10,000Đ.) The **Museum of National Cultures (Bảo Tàng Văn Hóa Dân Tộc),** 4 Nguyễn Du (☎850 426), on the corner of Lê Duẩn, in the former Bảo Đại Palace, houses a cross-section of tools, instruments, weapons, and traditional dresses.

The **Dray Sap Falls,** 29km southwest of town, make for a wild daytrip. A path descends into rainforest, complete with strangler figs, pungent flowers, and hanging vines. Lower Dray Sap (Dray Sap I) are the first falls you see. When the water level is low, a river crossing leads to the higher falls referred to by locals as *Gia Long.*(Open daily dawn-dusk. 5000Đ.) At **Yokdon National Park** (☎050 789 149), 37km northwest of town by way of **Phan Boi Chau,** elephants replace Soviet trucks as the chief mode of transport (2-3 people US$30 per hr.). The 60,000 hectares between Cambodia and the Serepok river constitute Vietnam's largest wildlife preserve. **Accommodations** ❸ are available (doubles with fan US$10). **Ban Đon,** a small hill-tribe village (a mix of Jarai, Mnong, and Edeh), 4km beyond the park, boasts a long history of elephant-taming. The tomb of **Khonsonuk,** a legendary elephant-snatcher, stands nearby. One-day treks around the lake and the surrounding countryside can be arranged (1-5 people US$10). **Lak Lake,** 56km south of Buôn Ma Thuӱt, is accessible by a straight shot along Hwy. 27. A Mnong community lives by the water, growing rice and raising livestock beneath elevated longhouses. Visitors enjoy touring by elephant (1hr., 2 people US$30, in a special longhouse US$5 per person). The memorable aspects of Lak Lake—children playing soccer, boats on the water, description-defying dawns and dusks—are free.

NHA TRANG ☎58

Nha Trang is Vietnam's oasis. With high green hills falling away to white sand and turquoise waters, the "Vietnamese Riviera" has yet to turn into holiday-resort hell. Budget accommodations, street-side *phở* stalls, and inexpensive snorkeling and diving opportunities still abound in the "City of the Blue Sea."

TRANSPORTATION

Flights: Nha Trang Airport (☎823 798), 1km south of town, off Trần Phú. Book tickets at **Vietnam Airlines,** 91 Nguyễn Thiện Thuật (☎826 768), 2 blocks up from the beach's south end. Open daily 7:30-11am and 2-4:30pm. To: **Đà Nẵng** (Sa-Tu, Th 2pm; 550,000Đ); **Hanoi** (daily 10am; 1,450,000Đ); **HCMC** (3 per day; 650,000Đ).

VIETNAM

Trains: Train station (Ga Nha Trang), 17 Thái Nguyên. Open daily 7-11am and 2-4:00pm. To **HCMC** (7-10hr., frequent, 86,000-166,000Đ). Northbound trains leave 5 times per day for: **Đà Nẵng** (9-12hr.; 113,000-220,000Đ); **Hanoi** (25-34hr.; 326,000-632,000Đ); **Huế** (12-16hr.; 136,000-263,000Đ).

Buses: Provincial bus station at **Nội Tỉnh Station,** 2 Tháng 4. Most travelers use **Liên Tỉnh Station,** 58 23 Tháng 10 (☎822 397), 250m west of the Long Sơn Pagoda. Buses to: **Buôn Ma Thuột** (4-6hr.; 4 per day; 36,000Đ); **Đà Lạt** (5hr.; frequent; 40,000Đ); **Đà Nẵng** (14hr.; 1 per day; 56,000Đ); **HCMC** (10hr.; 7 per day 5:30am-8pm; 65,000Đ) via **Phan Thiết** (5hr.; 45,000Đ); **Huế** (15hr.; 5am; 68,000Đ); **Pleiku** (7hr.; Tu, Sa; 54,000Đ); **Quảng Ngãi** (8hr.; 1 per day; 43,000Đ); **Qui Nhơn** (6hr.; 1 per day; 33,000Đ). A "no tickets to foreigners" policy means you have to negotiate with the driver himself. Faster private **minibuses** leave from many hotels. To: **Đà Lạt** (US$5); **Hội An** (US$8); **HCMC** (US$8).

Rentals: Most hotels rent **motorcycles** (US$3-6 per day) and **bicycles** (8000-10,000Đ per day).

ORIENTATION AND PRACTICAL INFORMATION

Nha Trang lies 450km northeast of HCMC and 175km northeast of Đà Lạt. Two-lane **Trần Phú** runs north-south along the length of the 6km beach. **Hùng Vương,** a block inland, becomes **Trần Hưng Đạo** and then **Pasteur** on its way northward. **Lê Thánh Tôn** shoots northwest from Trần Phú's **memorial tower,** hits a six-way intersection, and becomes **Thái Nguyên,** which continues west as **23 Tháng 10** past the **train station** and **bus station.** Near the northern end of Trần Phú, **Yersin** heads inland toward another six-way hub; from here, **Quang Trưng** runs north and continues out of town as **2 Tháng 4. Lê Lợi** runs west from Trần Phú's north end to the town **market.**

Travel Agencies: Agents line Biêt Thú and Trần Hùng Đạo. **Sinh Cafe,** 10 Biêt Thú (☎811 981), handles "open-tour" bus ticketing (see **Open Tour Buses,** p. 962). **Hanh Cafe,** 5A Trần Hùng Đạo (☎829 015). Both open daily 6am-10pm.

Currency Exchange: Vietcombank, 17 Quang Trưng (☎824 093). MC/V cash advances. No ATM. Open M-F 7:30-11am and 1:30-4pm. Most hotels and tourist offices exchange cash and traveler's checks at punishing rates.

Markets: Chợ Đàm, west of the post office (take Lê Lợi) at the end of Trưng Nư. Known for its dried squid. Central gazebo sells tourist-oriented handicrafts.

Emergency: ☎115.

Pharmacy: Nhà Thuốc Tây, 42 L Thánh Tôn (☎825 753). Open daily 6am-10pm.

Medical Services: Khánh Hòa General Hospital, 94 Yersin St. (☎822 168), at the intersection with Quang Trưng. Some English and French spoken. **Open 24hr.**

Internet Access: At most tourist agencies. 100Đ per min. Some places away from the beach (and the tourists) charge 3000Đ per hr.

Post Offices: GPO, 4 Lê Lợi (☎829 657). *Poste Restante.* No collect or card calls for foreigners. Open daily 6:30 am-10pm.

ACCOMMODATIONS

Mini-hotels line **Trần Phú.** Quality and services improve as you move inland.

Đông Phương 1, 103 Nguyễn Thiện Thuật (☎825 986), just south of Biên Thú. Spacious lobby and top-floor terrace complement large, clean rooms. Recently expanded. Single with shared bath US$4-6; rooms with bath US$6-20. ❶

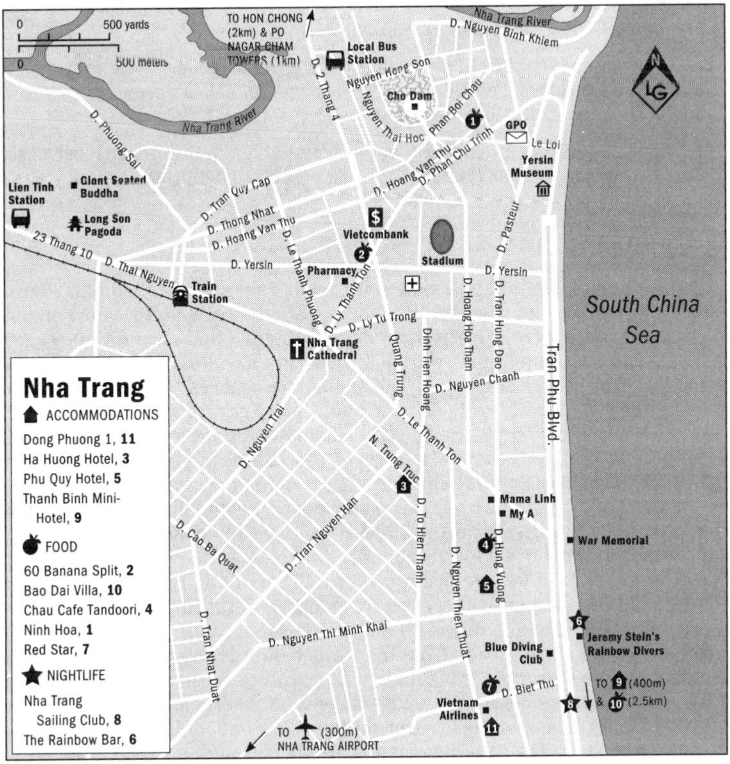

Thanh Binh Mini-Hotel, 84 Trần Phú (☎825 203), on the south end of the beach. Small family-run guest house. Clean rooms. TV. Doubles US$8, with A/C US$10. ❷

Hà Hư'o'ng Hotel, 26 Nguyễn Trưng Trực (☎512 069), off Tô Hiến Thánh, 2 blocks south of Lê Thánh Tôn. Large, airy hotel recently refurbished and renamed. Slightly removed from the beach. Doubles with TV and phone US$8, with A/C US$10. ❷

Phú Quý Hotel, 54 Hùng Vương (☎810 609), near the intersection with Nguyễn Thị Minh Khai, 1 block from the beach. Rooftop terrace. Rooms US$8-25. ❸

FOOD

Nem nướng, grilled pork and vegetables rolled into rice paper and dipped in fish sauce, is a regional specialty not to be missed. A *nem nướng* district sits near Đàm Market around Lê Lợi. Beach vendors sell everything from chewing gum to lobsters. Don't worry—they'll find you.

Red Star, 14B Biêt Thú, next to Sinh Cafe. Table-top grill-it-yourself dishes 20,000Đ. Open daily 8am-midnight. ❷

Chau Café Tandoori, 42 Hùng Vương, between Lê Thánh Tôn and Nguyễn Thị Minh Khai. Indian food and a whole lot more. Free wine, rum, vodka, fruit salad, and 10min. of Internet with your meal. Book exchange. Entrees 18,000-32,000Đ. ❷

Ninh Hòa, 16A Lãn Ông, past the east end of Hoàng Văn Thụ. Large servings of delicious *nem nướng* 8000Đ. Open daily 7am-11pm. ❶

Bảo Đại Villa (☎590 147), at the southern end of Trần Phú. Affordable restaurant in unaffordable holiday resort with a magnificent view of Cau Da harbor. Dishes from 30,000Đ. Reservations recommended. ❸

60 Banana Split, 60 Lê Thánh Tôn, at the intersection with Quang Trưng and Yersin. Cheap, delicious ice cream (3000Đ) and shakes (5000-10,000Đ). ❶

SIGHTS AND SAND

The city's most splendid attraction is its **public beach.** Ample sand and azure water run the length of town, with plenty of beach chairs and roving vendors offering everything from fresh mangos and English books to oil massages. Cushions and beach umbrellas start at 10,000Đ per day. For a more remote seaside experience, pedal north on 2 Tháng 4 to the beaches of **Hòn Chồng.** After crossing the two harbor bridges, turn right onto Nguyễn Đình Chiểu and left before the fishery university. Besides its beach, Hòn Chồng's most striking sight is the yellow boulders that form part of the shore. (Open daily 6am-6pm. 3000Đ.) The **Long So'n Pagoda,** Nha Trang's postcard picture of choice, stands at the west end of Yersin. The pagoda is dedicated to the Buddhists who gave their lives protesting the US-supported Diệm regime. Its renowned 9m high hilltop white **Buddha statue** overlooks a commanding view of the city. The **Po Nagar Chàm Towers,** or **Tháp Bà,** are just north of the Xóm Bóng Bridge and south of Hòn Chồng. The temple is a fascinating example of the appropriation of one faith's deity (the Hindu goddess Po-negar) by Mahayana Buddhists. From the entrance, a brief ascent leads from the former *mandapa* (meditation hall) to the towers. A sculpture of Shiva marks the entrance to the north tower. Buddhists place offerings before Po-negar's image and the *linga* in the smaller towers. (Open daily 6am-6pm. 4000Đ; free during Tet.) South of Lê Lợi on Trần Phú, the yellow Pasteur Institute houses the **Yersin Museum.** Alexandre Yersin, a Swiss-born French doctor remains one of the most revered Europeans in Vietnam. Artifacts include the microscope he used to discover the black plague bacillus. (Open M-Sa 8-11am and 2-4:30pm. 25,000Đ.)

VIETNAM

ENTERTAINMENT

Boat tours (US$7) are big business in Nha Trang. The famous cigarette-toting diva **Mama Hanh,** who used to run boat tours, is currently on a government-mandated hiatus from the business. Nevertheless, her raucous spirit endures tours that bear her name. After being picked up at 9am, touring several islands, snorkeling, gorging on seafood and fruit, and testing the "floating bar," satiated travelers are brought home by 5pm. Life preservers become increasingly handy as intoxication is the norm by late afternoon. Buy tickets at the main office, 44 L Thánh Tôn (☎821 309). Similar tours are offered by **Mỹ Á,** 10 Hùng Vương (☎826 195), and **Mama Linh,** 01 Húng Vương (☎826 693).

Jeremy Stein's Rainbow Divers, 55 Trần Phú (☎829 946), in the booth adjacent to the Rainbow Bar, is Vietnam's only PADI-certified 5-star dive center and offers four-day open-water courses for US$200-250 and two dive daytrips for US$40-45. The **Blue Diving Club,** 66 Trần Phú, at the Vina Hotel Resort, has several diving and snorkeling options. (☎825 390. 2 dives US$40; PADI open-water course US$250.)

NIGHTLIFE

Outside HCMC, it's difficult to find a city that hits the taps as hard as Nha Trang. Unfortunately, the criminal elements also target foreigners as hard as they do in HCMC. Bars may be less safe for women than for men, and safe, comfortable spaces for gays and lesbians are still nonexistent. Foreigners mingle on the beach late into the night; locals favor inland *bia hơi* joints. **Nha Trang Sailing Club,** 72 Trần Phú, is laid-back by day and increasingly crowded at night. (☎826 528. Cocktails 45,000-100,000Đ. Bia Sai Gon 18,000Đ. Big bottle of Tiger 25,000Đ. Open daily from noon until the last person stumbles home.)

The Rainbow Bar, 55 Trần Phú, north of the sailing club under the ferris wheel. Similar to other clubs along the beach, but more intimate. Also home to **Jeremy Stein's Rainbow Divers.** Beer 18,000Đ. Cocktails 18,000-70,000Đ. Happy hour 8:30-10:30pm. Open daily until 3am or later.

ĐÀ LẠT ☎63

Forget everything you know about Vietnam—Đà Lạt is different. The mountainous city's flourishing artistic community, easygoing atmosphere, and the "Da Lat Eiffel" have led it to be named "Le Petit Paris." Doctor/adventurer Alexandre Yersin was smitten by the alpine climate during a 1892 highland expedition. Following his suggestion to build a city, the French displaced ethnic Vietnamese communities and established Đà Lạt in the early 1910s. Đà Lạt's appeal hasn't been limited to Frenchmen; the "Honeymoon City" also has a proud history of domestic tourism, and, for once, Vietnamese couples outnumber the backpacker hordes.

TRANSPORTATION

Flights: Đức Trọng Airport, 30km south of the city. **Vietnam Airlines** booking office in Hotel Hàng Khôi, 40 Hồ Tùng Mậu (☎822 895). Daily flights via **HCMC** (40min.; 3:10pm; 430,000Đ) to: **Đà Nẵng** (950,000Đ); **Hanoi** (2,230,000Đ); **Huế** (1,380,000Đ).

Buses: Tourist minibuses, booked and boarded at any hotel, go to **Nha Trang** via **Phan Rang** (6hr., 7:30am, US$5) and **HCMC** (7hr., 7:30am, US$7). **Public bus station** (☎822 077), 3 Tháng 4. Doesn't sell tickets to foreigners, but you can wait outside, hop aboard, and bargain. Local buses to: **Buôn Ma Thuột** (10hr.; 1 per day; 63,000Đ); **Đà Nẵng** (15hr.; 1 per day; 105,000Đ); **HCMC** (6hr.; frequent; 50,000Đ); **Huế** (26hr.; 1 per day; 120,000Đ); **Nha Trang** (7hr.; 3 per day; 32,000Đ) via **Phan Rang** (3hr.; 21,000Đ); **Quảng Ngãi** (8½hr.; 3 per day; 86,000Đ).

Rentals: Motorbike (US$4-8 per day) and **bicycle** (20,000Đ per day) rentals are cheapest at hotels.

ORIENTATION AND PRACTICAL INFORMATION

The capital of Lâm Đồng Province, Đà Lạt is 300km north of HCMC on **Hwy. 20.** The **market area,** just west of **Lake Xuân Hương,** forms the town center. To the left of the market, steps lead up to **Hòa Bình Square,** dominated by the 3/4 Cinema. **Trương Công Định** leads from the cinema into **Phan Đình Phùng,** which runs roughly north-south; most of Đà Lạt's hotels and restaurants line these roads. **Trần Phú** runs east-west along the south side of town, from which **3 Tháng 4** runs out of the city.

Tours: Dalat Holidays (☎829 4[illegible]), at the corner of Trương Công Định and Phan Đình Phùng. Outdoor adventure tours. Sturdy mountain bikes for rent. Open daily 7:30am-8:30pm. See **Outdoors,** p. 957.

Currency Exchange: Incombank, 46 Hòa Bình (☎824 929). Traveler's checks cashed. MC/V advances. Open M-Sa 7-11:30am and 1-4:30pm.

Markets: Chợ' Đà Lạt, in the town center. The market converts into a cheap food stall and bargain heaven. Open daily 4am-1am.

Emergency: ☎115. **Police:** ☎113. **Fire:** ☎114.

Police: 19 Trần Phú (☎822 468).

Hospital: Bệnh Vien Tinh LD, 4 Phan Ngọc Thạch (☎827 550). Emergency room **open 24hr.**

Pharmacy: Ladopan, 34 Khu Haa Bình (☎822 570). Open daily 7am-10pm.

Internet Access: Việt Hưng Internet Cafe, 7 Nguyễn Chí Thành, toward the lake from the bank. 150Đ per min. Open daily 8am-midnight. Simpler operations charge 100Đ per min.

Post Office: GPO, 14-16 Trần Phú (☎822 586), under the Đà Lạt Eiffel. Fax/telex/**international phone calls.** *Poste Restante.* Open daily 6:30am-9pm. **Branch** at 178 Phan Đing Phùng. Open daily 7am-9pm.

ACCOMMODATIONS

Many hotels in Đà Lạt have restrictions on housing foreign guests, which explains the "available to foreigners" sign on some of them. But establishments long frequented by budget travelers are clean, affordable, and invariably friendly.

Dreams Hotel & Internet Service, 151 Phan Đinh Phùng (☎833 778). Outstanding value. Free breakfast and Internet service (7-10pm) with stay. Nicely furnished rooms in a central location. Singles US$7; doubles US$10. ❷

Như My Minihotel, 3 Bùi Thị Xuân (☎827 069), across from 20 Bùi Thi Xuân. French- and English-speaking owners eager to serve foreign tourists. Tell 'em *Let's Go* sent you. Spotless rooms. Singles US$5; doubles US$10; triples US$12. ❷

Hòa Bình (Peace) Hotel I and II, 64 Trương Công Định (☎822 787) and 67 Trương Công Định (☎822 982). Former is impersonal while latter is smaller and family-run. Singles US$5; doubles US$7; triples US$9. Peace I has truly budget top-floor singles for US$2-3. ❶

Lâm Sơn Hotel, 5 Hải Thượng (☎822 362). From Hòa Bình Square, head down 3 Tháng 2, take a right onto Hài Thượng; it's uphill on the left. High wooden ceilings, pink stucco, and an eager staff. Doubles US$8, with TV US$10, with balcony US$15. ❸

FOOD

Đà Lạt's alpine environs supply cartloads of fruits and vegetables and an array of forest critters from deer to porcupine. The cheapest eats are in the **market** ❶ area, close to the steps, where a bowl of *hủ tiếu* soup and all-you-can-drink hot tea costs 5000Đ. Particularly noteworthy *cơm* and *phở* shacks nestle together on the west side of **Phan Đinh Phùng,** just past the intersection with Trương Công Dinh.

Đông Á Restaurant, 82 Phan Đình Phùng, between the Hòa Bình and Cao Nguyên Hotels. Wild beasts (35,000-50,000Đ) fill the menu; Western tourists fill the booths. *Cơm* dishes 8000-14,000Đ. Open daily 9am-10pm. ❷

Stop 'N' Go, 2A Lữ Tự Trọng. Walk length of Phan Bội Châu away from cinema area; take hairpin left turn; it's uphill on the right. A cafe and art gallery owned by local poet/artist/ex-mayor Duy Việt. Croissant 4000Đ. Coffee 6000Đ. Open daily 7am-7:30pm. ❶

Bành Bèo, 20A Nguyễn Chí Thành. Heading from the cinema, it's past the bank. Named after its speciality: rice cakes with pork rinds, sprinkled with shrimp powder (3000Đ). Open daily 6am-6pm. ❶

Larry's Bar, 12 Trần Phú. In the basement of the Sofitel Dalat Palace. A pricey bar and cafe modeled after a golf course club house. Soft jazz, western fare, and two-for-one happy hour (5-7pm daily) draw in all seven of the Đã Lạt area expats on Fridays. ❹

SIGHTS

Linh So'n Pagoda, Đà Lạt's oldest, lies between the north ends of Phan Đình Phùng and Nguyễn Văn Trỗi, a short walk from the market area. Inside the central sanctum is a uniquely human *Thích Ca* (Gautama Buddha). Vien Nhu, an elder monk at the pagoda, speaks good English and is happy to explain Mahayana Buddhism's basic tenets. (Open daily 7am-6pm.) Man-made **Lake Xuân Hương** curves away from the downtown center. At its northeast corner, Đà Lạt's magnificent **Flower Garden** grows at the intersection of Bà Huyện Thành Quan and Phù Đổng Thiên Vương. (Open daily 7am-6pm. 4000Đ.) Đà Lạt's historic **train station,** 1 Nguyễn Trãi, is east of the lake. You can ride one of the old trains 8km to the village of **Trại Mát** (30 min.; 7:30, 9am, 2, and 3:30pm; 70,000Đ). There, the **Linh Phước Pagoda,** 120 Tự Phước (☎825 410), features a colorful dragon around the courtyard fountain. (Pagoda open daily 6am-7pm; train station closes at 5pm.)

The **Governor General's Residence,** 12 Trần Hưng Đạo, is surrounded by European gardens. (☎822 092. Open daily 7am-4:30pm. 10,000Đ.) The **Palace of Emperor Bảo Đại (Dinh III)** is 2km southwest of Lake Xuân Hương, on Triệu Việt Vương at the end of Lê Hồng Phong. The royal family lived here from the building's completion in 1938, even after playboy Bảo Đại's 1945 abdication under Việt Minh pressure. (Open daily 7:30am-5:30pm. 5000Đ.)

The **Hang Nga Tree House Hotel** (also called **Cobweb Mansion** and **Crazy House**), sitting in riotous splendor at 3 Huỳnh Thúc Kháng near Lê Hồng Phong, is both art and accommodation (US$19-80). Two enormous concrete trees tower over a fanciful sculpture garden. The trees contain nine nature-themed chambers. The building was sculpted by local architect Hang Nga, daughter of former president Trơng Chinh. (☎822 070. Tours 5000Đ.) Just north of Crazy House at 2 Thiệm Mỹ is **Lâm Tỳ Ny Pagoda.** Here, **Viễn Thức,** popularly known as the Crazy Monk, has established a tranquil one-man art gallery. Viễn Thức may let you take a peek at his collection, which includes over 100,000 pieces. Inside the **Nhà Thờ' Chính Tòa Đà Lạt** (Đà Lạt Cathedral), on Trần Phú near the post office, an intricate series of stained-glass windows will entrance even non-believers. (Daily mass 5:15am, 5:15pm; Su mass 5:15, 7, 8:30am, 4, and 6pm.)

OUTDOORS

Dalat Holidays has teamed with the American **Phat Tire Ventures,** 73 Trương Công Định (☎829 422), to offer the most advanced adventure tourism packages in Vietnam. Climb and ride with the support of state-of-the-art equipment. Ride on half- and full-day mountain biking tours, including a one-way ride to Phan Rang on the coast. Twenty percent of all profits go to hill tribe education projects.

DAYTRIPS FROM ĐÀ LẠT

WATERFALLS. Đà Lạt's waterfalls are popular with domestic tourists. The overwhelming stench has earned **Cam Ly Falls,** 5km west of town, the moniker "Toilet Falls." *(Open daily 7am-6pm. 4000Đ.)* **Prenn Falls,** 11km south on Hwy. 20, is a much more scenic tourist trap. *(Open daily 6am-6pm. 6000Đ.)* **Đa Tanla Falls,** 5km south of town, is surprisingly pristine. *(Open daily 6am-5pm. 5000Đ.)* More remote cascades to the south on Hwy. 20 include **Lien Khuong Falls** (30km), **Gougah Falls** (40km), and **Pongour Falls** (55km). All falls but Pongour dry up during the winter months. Honeymooners and hikers may want to enter the **Thung Lũng Tình Yêu** (Valley of Love), 6km north of the city, featuring rolling hills, views of Lang Bian Mountain, swarms of tourists, and the nationally famous "Đà Lạt Cowboys," whose American cowboy get-ups complete the tourist-trap atmosphere. *(Open daily 6am-6pm. 5000Đ.)*

TUYEN LAM LAKE AND TRUC LAM MEDITATION PAGODA. The artificial lake 5km south of town hosts a variety of outdoor activities. Boat across the lake to ride the elephants (120,000Đ per hr.) and taste the local "wine." The serene Truc Lam Pagoda complex overlooks the lake. No t-shirts, shorts, or sandals please. *(Turn off just north of Đa Tanla Falls.)*

K'LONG VILLAGE. The K'ho, Chil, Ma, Lat, and Churu highland minorities live and work around Đà Lạt. **K'long Village** (Chicken Village), has received much tourist attention. However, the colorful shops seem only weakly connected to the actual village, where the 700 impoverished K'ho residents wear worn Western clothes. Aside from the giant concrete chicken, there's nothing very funny about this place, founded in 1975 as a permanent home for K'ho nomads. *(18km south of town.)*

LANG BIAN MOUNTAIN. The symbol of the Lang Bian highland region, the mountain overshadows the touristed Lat village. For permit-free frolicking, consider Lake Dankia and Ankroet Falls, 20km north of town behind Lang Bian. *(12km north of Đà Lạt. Dalat tourist guide US$12. Entry fee 5000Đ.)*

VIETNAM

PHAN THIẾT AND MŨI NÈ BEACHES ☎62

Four hours northeast of Hồ Chí Minh City on Hwy. 1, Phan Thiết has slumbered as a tourist destination while Vũng Tàu captures the weekend crowd. Surrounding Bình Thuận Province is home to a stunning set of landscapes, including the scenic, uncrowded beaches of Mũi Nè. In town, paths line the banks of the Cà Ty River's green waters, making the city a pleasant stop on a central Vietnam itinerary.

TRANSPORTATION AND PRACTICAL INFORMATION. Phan Thiết is 198km northeast of Hồ Chí Minh City, 247km south of Đà Lạt, and 250km southwest of Nha Trang. Many of the tourist buses headed to Nha Trang will drop you off at the highway (4hr., US$3-4), a short moto ride from the town center (5000Đ). A **bus station** on Trần Hưng Đạo, northeast of town, offers frequent service to **HCMC** (4hr.; 31,000Đ), and rare service to **Đà Lạt** (8hr.; 27,500Đ) and **Nha Trang** (approximately 6hr.; 30,000Đ). Buses run more frequently to **Phan Rang** (3hr.; 16,500Đ), where transfers can be made to Đà Lạt or Nha Trang.

Trần Hưng Đạo, Phan Thiết's main drag, runs from the direction of HCMC northeast toward Nha Trang, crossing the southernmost of three bridges spanning the **Cà Ty River.** Just west of town, **Trần Phú** branches north off Trần Hưng Đạo and heads into town, passing the market (where it is part of a seven-street intersection) and crosses the river at the north bridge. **Võ Thị Sáu** fronts the Nha Trang side of the river, while Trưng Trắc does the same on the HCMC bank. From the middle bridge, Thủ Khoa Huân heads east toward Mũi Nè.

A friendly **tourist office**, Công Ty Du lịch Bình Thuận, 82 Trưng Trắc, lies near the southernmost bridge. (☎821 394. Maps 10,000Đ. Motorcycle rental 10,000Đ per hr. Open M-Sa 8-11:30am and 2-5pm.) **Vietincom Bank** is across the river (as you head toward Nha Trang), at the intersection of Trần Hưng Đạo and Nguyễn Tất Thành. (☎828 078. Cashes traveler's checks. MC/V advances. Open daily 7-11am and 1:30-4:30pm.) Access to the town's **market** is at the seven-street junction. **Pharmacie Hồng Hưng,** 240 Trần Hưng Đạo, has an English-speaking proprietor. (☎821 501. Open daily 6am-9pm.) The **general hospital** (☎823 939) is across the river, 1km northwest of town on Hải Thượng Lãn Ông. The **post office,** 2 Nguyễn Văn Cừ, opposite the market, at the seven-street intersection, has an **international phone.** (☎821 921. Open daily 6am-9:30pm.)

ACCOMMODATIONS AND FOOD. Those sojourning in Phan Thiết for the scenery should head east to Mũi Nè (for accommodations, see **Mũi Nè Beaches,** below). Travelers in transit will find cheap options on **Trần Hưng Đao** near the bus station. Beachside and close to town, the **Cong Doan Hotel ❷,** 314 Võ Thị Sáu, has a great location and fan-cooled rooms. (☎821 395. Triples 100,000-150,000Đ.) Generic, benign US$7 rooms can be had at most of the look-alike mini-hotels on Trần Hưng Đao. Exceptional service and an English-to-Vietnamese computer translation program lift **Nhã Nghỉ 145 ❷,** 145 Trần Hung Đao, above the crowd. (Clean singles with fan US$7, with A/C US$9.) **Nhà Trọ Hồng Ngọc ❶** is notable among cheaper options for its keenness on lodging foreigners. (Small fan room with clean shared Western bath 50,000Đ.)

Lẩu Bò Hồng ❷, 94 Trần Hưng Đao, serves *lẩubò*, a mix-your-own beef soup with tangy dipping sauce, to crowds of locals (70,000Đ feeds 4). **Nam Thạnh Lầu ❸,** 50 Nguyễn Thị Minh Khai, facing the small park before the center bridge, teems with seafood delights. (Grilled shrimp 30,000Đ. Open daily 6:30am-9pm.)

SIGHTS. **Chùa Ông** (Ông Pagoda), on the north end of Trần Phú, is composed of two smaller temples, Chùa Ông (Grandfather's) on the right and Chùa Bà (Grandmother's) on the left. (Open daily 7am-6pm.)

A large pink **statue of Hồ Chí Minh** keeps vigilant watch over town (north of Chùa Ông, at the west end of the river park, on Trần Phú). Hồ Chí Minh, then known as Nguyễn Tất Thành, taught at the Đức Thành school in Phan Thiết in 1911. The **Hồ Chí Minh Museum,** in an ornate building fronting the statue, chronicles his time in Phan Thiết as well as his later years. (☎821 276. Open Tu-Su 7:30-11:30am and 1:30-4:30pm.) Nguyễn Tất Thành supposedly spent his days reading and teaching in the **garden** across the street. (Open daily 7-11am and 1-5pm.)

Though unremarkable compared to the beaches farther from town, the **local beach,** northeast of the river (Nha Trang side), between Nguyễn Tất Thành and Võ Thị Sáu, does provide respectable sand for local beach bathers.

MŨI NÈ BEACHES. Most of the out-of-town sights are northeast along Thủ Khoa Huñn. Moto drivers in Phan Thiết will putter to the road's end and back for 70,000Đ. You can also rent a motorbike from any of the hotels for US$5 per day. Above-ground graves mark the cemeteries that dot the sandy bluff just outside of town. Two **Chàm towers** stand atop rolling hills 7km east of town. Continuing northeast, the road returns to the sea, coming upon **Địa Ông,** 9km from town. Once the site of a rock carved to resemble Địa Ông (Genie of the Earth), it has been replaced by a small Buddhist shrine. The beach at this spot is a mix of sand, rock, and, at times, crashing surf. Those seeking untrammeled beach access will find tranquility and a pricey menu at **Vườn Nhỏ** (Small Garden) **❷,** 11km northeast of Phan Thiết. The compound is run by a Vietnamese-Swiss couple. (☎847 012. Breakfast included. US$7 per room.) Stop by one of the roadside stands to pick up

VIETNAM

a bottle of *nước mắm*—this translucent fish sauce here is reputedly some of the best in Vietnam. **Suối Tiên** (Fairy Stream) cuts through the sand dunes 18km east of Phan Thiết. A pleasant stroll along the small path lining the 2km of stream gives a taste of the dunes. Pause just west of the village of Mũi Nè to survey the hundreds of primary-colored fishing boasts crowding the harbor. Head past the town to **Khu Du Lich Ganh ❷**, at the capes' end. The center's bungalows are simple but clean. (2 people 90,000Đ.)

SOUTHERN VIETNAM

Approaching the region from the north, rocky outcroppings and jagged hills grind to a halt and smooth into rivers and plains. Distinct in geography and personality from the northern and central regions, Southern Vietnam speeds forward on the momentum of governmental reform. The price gap closes, Việt Cộng pith helmets are replaced by baseball caps, and when people speak of "The City" (Thành Phố), they mean Hồ Chí Minh. For the land-weary, waterways replace asphalt and gravel, leading to floating markets and distant fields. Whether in a small Delta village, on a distant tropical island, or in the nation's largest city, travelers will find the Southern Vietnamese open and welcoming.

HỒ CHÍ MINH CITY (HCMC) ☎8

After their tanks stormed the Independence Palace on April 30, 1975, ending 30 years of continuous warfare, the North Vietnamese renamed Saigon after their socialist hero Hồ Chí Minh. The city had been the center of Vietnamese capitalism for some 350 years. The French transformed Saigon from a dank citadel to a thriving port with broad boulevards and monumental hotels. During the Vietnam War, Saigon worked and played while South Vietnam burned. After a depressing flirtation with socialism, Hồ Chí Minh City (HCMC) today races with the speed of the thousands of Honda Dreams that zip down its roads. However, this emerging capitalism hasn't overtaken the city—the Saigonese care more about good times than profits, and no one parties as hard as they do. Removed neighborhoods hide amazing temples, makeshift markets, and charming guest houses, all welcome respites from the city's dizzying pulse. Hồ Chí Minh might be turning in his tomb, but the locals aren't fazed—after all, everyone calls it Saigon anyway.

INTERCITY TRANSPORTATION

BY PLANE

International flights arrive at **Tân Sơn Nhất International Airport** (☎844 63 21), 4km north of the city center. **Taxis** (US$4-6) and **motos** (US$2-3) run into the city. The international departure tax is US$10; domestic is 20,000Đ. Note that flight prices are likely to change.

DESTINATION	FREQUENCY	PRICE	DESTINATION	FREQUENCY	PRICE
Bangkok	6 per day	US$200	**Kuala Lumpur**	9 per day	US$225
Đà Lạt	1 per day	US$29	**Manila**	4 per day	US$275
Đa Nẵng	3-5 per day	US$63	**Nha Trang**	2-3 per day	US$42
Hai Phòng	1 per day (Tu-Sa)	US$120	**Phu Quoc Island**	1 per day	US$45

DESTINATION	FREQUENCY	PRICE	DESTINATION	FREQUENCY	PRICE
Hanoi	8-13 per day	US$120	**Phnom Penh**	1 per day	US$338
Hong Kong	9 per day	US$450	**Qui Nho'n**	1 per day	US$45
Huế	2 per day	US$63	**Singapore**	5 per day	US$300

Major airlines that serve HCMC are: **Lao Aviation,** 181 Hai Ba Trung in District 3 (☎09 190 26 51; open M-F 8:30-11:30am and 2:30-4:30pm); **MAS,** 132-134 Đồng Khởi, in the Continental Hotel (☎829 25 29; open M-F 9am-noon and 1:30-5pm, Sa 9am-noon); **Singapore Airlines,** 29 Lê Duẩn, in the Saigon Tower (☎823 15 88; open M-F 8am-4pm, Sa 8am-noon); **Thai Airlines,** 65 Nguyễn Du (☎829 28 09; open M-F 8am 4:30pm, Sa 8am-noon); and **Vietnam Airlines,** 116 Nguyễn Hue, next to City Hall (☎832 03 20; open M-Sa 7:30am-6pm, Su 8:30am-noon).

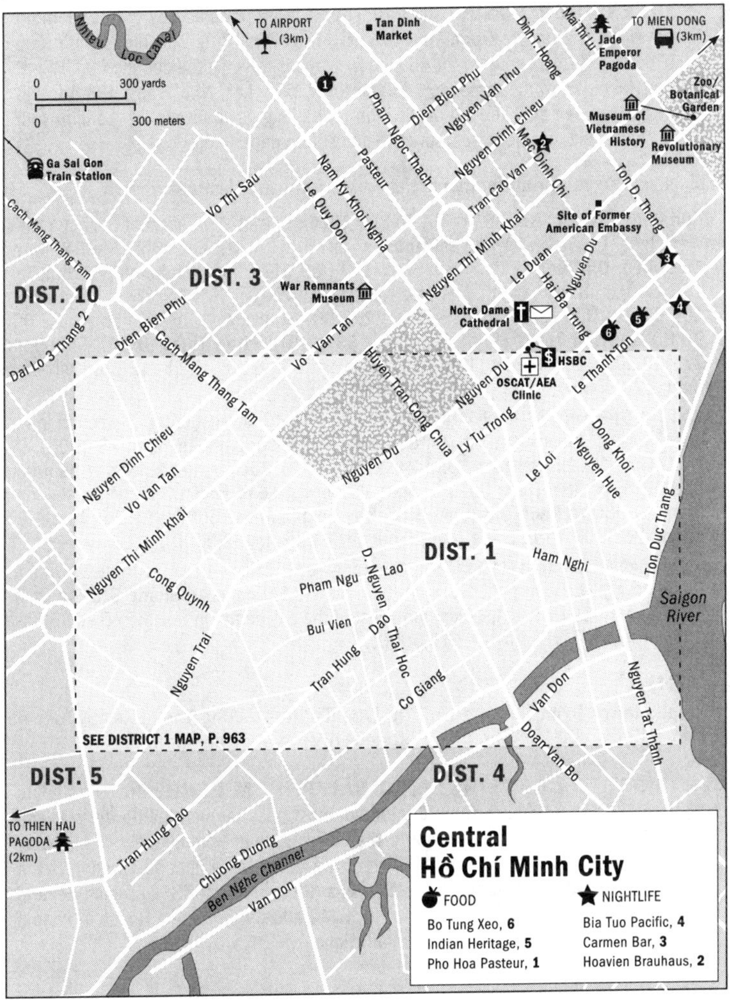

BY TRAIN

The railway station, **Ga Sài Gòn,** is on 1 Nguyễn Thông (☎843 65 28), off Cách Mạng Tháng Tám in District 3. Guest houses and travel agencies assist with bookings. Purchase tickets at the **Vietnam Railway Union,** 136 Ham Nghi (open daily 8-11:30am and 1:30-4pm), or from the **Saigon Railway Tourist Services Co.,** 275C Pham Ngữ Lão (☎836 76 40; open daily 7:30am-4:30pm). Tickets may also be purchased at counters #4, 5, and 7-11 in the train station. An **express train** departs nightly at 9pm for **Hanoi** (32hr.; 9pm; 258,000-796,000Đ) via: **Nha Trang** (7hr.; 62,000-190,000); **Đà Nẵng** (16½hr.; 146,000-447,000Đ); **Huế** (19½hr.; 161,000-495,000Đ).

BY BUS

OPEN TOUR BUSES. The easiest and most popular way to see Vietnam over land is on the **Open Tour Buses** run by Sinh Cafe and Kim's Cafe (see **Tours,** p. 964). Large 24- or 45-seat A/C buses traverse the country from HCMC to Hanoi, allowing passengers to stop over in **Đà Lạt, Nha Trang, Hội An,** and **Huế.** You can stay in each destination for as long as you wish; just confirm your ticket at the local representative the day before departure.

HCMC has four major **bus stations** that serve domestic destinations.

Miền Đông Station: (☎898 40 56). In Bình Thạnh district, 4km north of District 1 off Xô Việt Nghệ Tinh. **Buses** and **minibuses** go north to: **Đà Lạt** (6hr.; 6am-evening; 46,000Đ); **Dá Nẵng** (24hr.; 5am-5pm; 102,000-117,000Đ); **Haiphong** (52hr.; 6am; 193,500Đ); **Hanoi** (48hr.; 10am, 4pm; 182,000Đ); **Hôi An** (24hr.; 5am-5pm; 101,000Đ); **Huế** (27hr.; 5am-noon; 112,500Đ); **Kontum** (14hr.; 6am-6pm; 82,000-95,000Đ); **Nha Trang** (9hr.; 6am-6pm; 63,000Đ); **Phan Thiết** (3⅓hr.; 5am-5pm.; 22,000-30,000Đ); **Pleiku** (12hr.; 6am-6pm; 74,000-85,000Đ); **Vũng Tàu** (2hr.; 5am-6pm; 22,000Đ).

Miền Tây Station: 137 Hung Vương (☎751 05 24), 12km west of the city center in Bình Chánh District. Buses go south to: **Bến Tre** (2hr.; 8 per day 6am-4pm; 13,000Đ); **Cần Thơ'** (4hr.; 10 per day 5am-6pm; 24,000Đ); **Châu Đốc** (6hr.; 14 per day 5am-8pm; 38,500Đ); **Hà Tiên** (8hr.; 5am, 3, 5pm; 49,000Đ); **Long Xuyên** (4hr.; 7 per day 5am-8pm; 32,000Đ); **Rạch Giá** (6hr.; 8 per day 5am-8pm; 38,500Đ); **Sa Đéc** (3hr.; 7, 9, 11am; 20,500Đ); **Sóc Trăng** (6hr.; 8 per day 5am-8pm; 32,000Đ).

Other stations: Chợ' Lớ'n Station, 86 Trang Tử, 2 blocks north of Bình Tây Market. Buses to **Mỹ Tho** (2hr.; every 30min. 5am-6pm; 11,000Đ). **An Súong Station,** Ngã 4 An Súong (☎ 891 87 97), 16km northwest of the city center in Hóc Môn District. Buses to **Tây Nihn** (1½hr; 4am-7pm; 18,500Đ).

BY BOAT

Hydrofoils leave from the pier on Tôn Đức Thắng to **Vũng Tàu** (1¼hr., 8 per day 6:15am-4:45pm, US$10). The ticket office is open daily 7am-8pm.

BORDER CROSSING: MOC BÀI/PHNOM PENH. Travelers going from HCMC to Phnom Penh, Cambodia, must pass through the border crossing at Mộc Bài. Public bus service to the crossing point is frequently disrupted by poor road conditions on both sides of the border. The cheapest option is the **Sinh Cafe-Capitol Guest House tour bus** (9hr., 8:45am, US$6), which departs from Sinh Café (see **Tours,** below) in HCMC and Capitol Guest House in Phnom Penh (see **Phnom Penh: Accommodations,** p. 73).

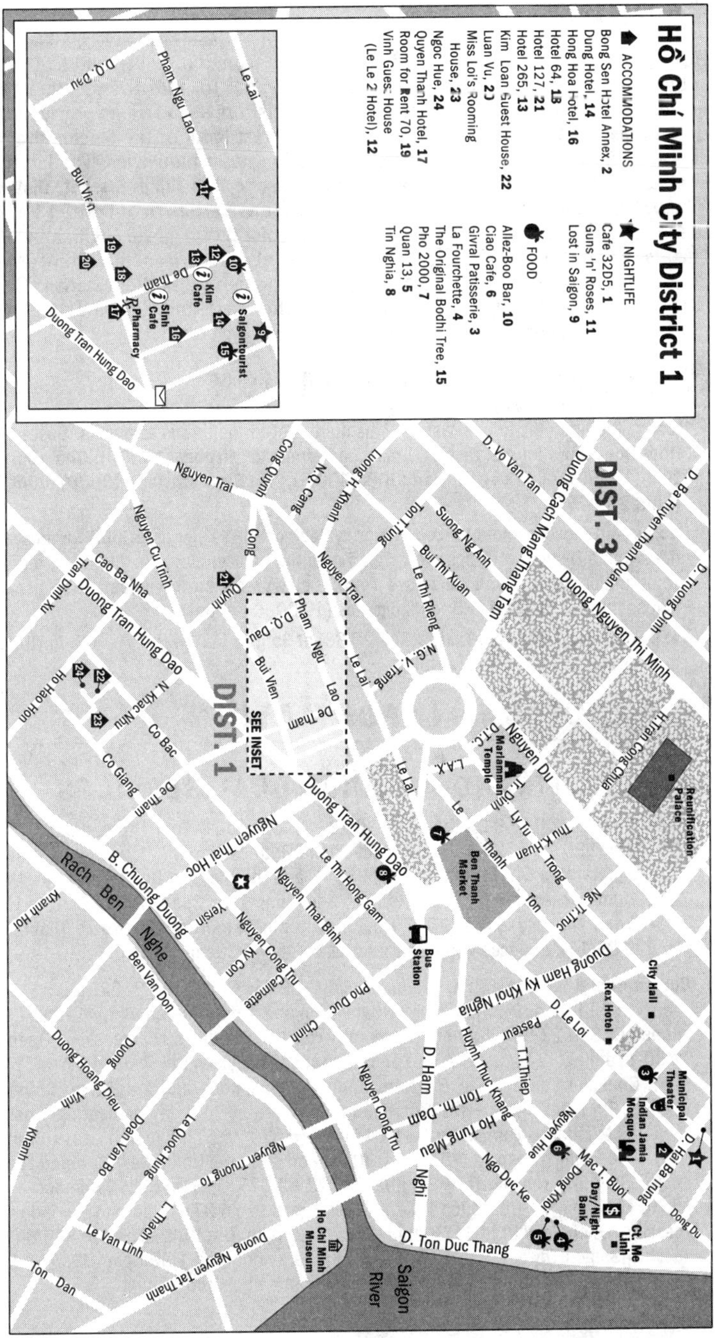
Hồ Chí Minh City District 1
ACCOMMODATIONS
Bong Sen Hotel Annex, 2
Dung Hotel, 14
Hong Hoa Hotel, 16
Hotel 64, 18
Hotel 127, 21
Hotel 265, 13
Kim Loan Guest House, 22
Luan Vu, 20
Miss Loi's Rooming House, 23
Ngoc Hue, 24
Quyen Thanh Hotel, 17
Room for Rent 70, 19
Vinh Guest House (Le Le 2 Hotel), 12
NIGHTLIFE
Cafe 32D5, 1
Guns 'n' Roses, 11
Lost in Saigon, 9
FOOD
Allez-Boo Bar, 10
Ciao Cafe, 6
Givral Patisserie, 3
La Fourchette, 4
The Original Bodhi Tree, 15
Pho 2000, 7
Quan 13, 5
Tin Nghia, 8
DIST. 3
DIST. 1
SEE INSET
Reunification Palace
Mariamman Temple
Ben Thanh Market
Bus Station
City Hall
Rex Hotel
Municipal Theater
Indian Jamia Mosque
Day/Night Bank
Ho Chi Minh Museum
Saigon River
Rach Ben Nghe
Saigontourist
Kim Cafe
Sinh Cafe
Pharmacy
Duong Cach Mang Thang Tam
Duong Nguyen Thi Minh
Duong Tran Hung Dao
Duong Ham Ky Khoi Nghia
D. Ton Duc Thang
Duong Nguyen Tat Thanh
Pham Ngu Lao
De Tham
Bui Vien
Le Lai
Nguyen Trai
Nguyen Du
D. Le Loi
Pasteur
Nguyen Hue
Dong Khoi

ORIENTATION

HCMC is carved into 12 numbered districts, five named districts, and five named suburban districts. Districts are preceded by a "Q" for *quận*, and some street names are preceded by a "Đ" for *đường*. Most visitors spend the majority of their time in **District 1** (Quận một), which hugs the west bank of the **Saigon River** and contains the city's burgeoning commercial and tourist industries. The latter are concentrated on **Phạm Ngũ Lão,** which runs east to **Bến Thành Market. District 4** (Quận bốn), home to several museums and pagodas, lies south of District 1 across the Bến Nghé Canal. **District 5** (Quận năm), **District 6** (Quận sáu), which includes **Chinatown** and numerous pagodas, and **Chợ' Lớ'n** (also known as Chợ Bình Tây), are directly west of District 1. **District 3** (Quận ba), home to the **train station** (Ga Sài Gòn), is bound by Nguyễn Thị Minh Khai in the north and Hai Bà Trưng in the northwest. The **airport** lies far northwest in the **Tân Bình District.**

LOCAL TRANSPORTATION

Buses: The limited city bus system is useful to get to major bus terminals. Buses leave from Ben Thãnh Market (every 15min. 5am-7pm) to: **airport** (1000Đ); **Chỗ' Lờ'n Station** (1000Đ); **Miện Tây Station** (3000-4000Đ); **Tại Binh Station** (1000Đ); **Vũng Tàu** (2hr.; 25,000Đ).

Cyclos and Motorcycles: Moto-taxis or **cyclos** cost US$1 per hr, 5000Đ for most short rides within District 1. Cyclos are banned near the palace, along Saigon River, and from some major streets. **Sinh Cafe** (see **Tours,** below) rents **motorcycles** (US$5 per day). Across the street, **Hotel 265** rents bicycles (10,000Đ per day).

Taxi: For pick-up, call **Vina Taxi** (☎842 28 88) or **Saigon Taxi** (☎842 42 42). Anything up to 2km will set you back 12,000Đ.

PRACTICAL INFORMATION

TOURIST, FINANCIAL, AND LOCAL SERVICES

Tours: Sinh Cafe, 246-8 Đề Thám (☎836 73 38). Open daily 7am-11pm. **Kim Cafe,** 270 Đề Thám (836 98 59). Open daily 7am-10pm. Both cafes run A/C bus tours to the **Củ Chi Tunnels, Cao Đài Temple** (1 day, US$4), and the **Mekong Delta** (1-4 days, US$7-45). Airline tickets, visas, heaps of info, and **Open Tour Buses** from HCMC to Hanoi (see **Open Tour Buses,** p. 962). Government-run **Saigontourist,** 49 Le Thánh Tông (☎829 89 14), arranges visa extensions. Open daily 7:30am-6:30pm.

Consulates: Australia, 5th fl. Landmark Bldg., 5B Tôn Đức Thắng (☎829 60 35, emergency ☎090 82 469). Open M-F 8:30am-noon and 1-5pm. **Cambodia,** 41 Phùng Khắc Khoan (☎829 27 51). 1-month single-entry visa US$30; one-day processing. Open M-F 7:30-11am and 2-5pm, Sa 7:30-11am. **Canada,** 61 Nguyễn Du, Suite 1002 (☎824 50 25). Consular services M-F 8-10am. Open M-F 8am-noon and 1-4:30pm. **China,** 39 Nguyễn Thị Minh Khai (☎829 24 57). 1-month visa; 1- to 4-day processing. Consular services M-F 8am-11am. **Laos,** 93 Pasteur St. (☎829 76 67). 2-month visas US$50; 1-day processing. Open M-F 8:30-11:30am and 2:30-4:30pm. **New Zealand,** 5th fl. YOCO Bldg., 41 Nguyễn Thị Minh Khai (☎822 69 07). Open M-F 8:30am-noon and 1-5pm. **Thailand,** 77 Trần Quốc Thảo, District 3 (☎836 76 37). 2-month visa; 2-day processing. Open daily 8:30-11:30am and 1:30-4:30pm. **UK,** 25 Lê Duẩn (☎829 84 33), next to Saigon Tower building. Open M-F 8:30am-noon and 1:30-5pm. **US,** 4 Lê Duẩn St., District 1 (24hr. ☎822 94 33). Open M-F 8am-noon and 1-5pm.

Currency Exchange: Gold shops have the best rates. Travel agencies are the most popular but offer lower rates. Count your money on the premises. **HSBC,** 235 Đồng Khởi (☎829 22 88). MC/V cash advances. **24hr. ATM.** Open M-Th 8:30am-4:30pm, F 8:30am-5pm. **ANZ Night and Day Bank,** 11 Cong Trường Mê Linh, behind the Dao Monument. **24hr. ATM.**

English-Language Bookstore: Lệ Duẩn, 2A Lệ Duẩn (☎823 45 42), near the US consulate. Diverse selection of new and used books and dictionaries. Open daily 8am-9pm. **Bookstore,** 251 Đề Thám (☎ 837 21 12), sells used books in English, French, and Japanese as well as new and used travel guides. Open daily 8:30am-11pm.

EMERGENCY AND COMMUNICATIONS

Emergency: ☎115. **Police:** ☎113. **Fire:** ☎114.

Police: District 1 Police Office, 73 Yersin St. (☎829 76 43). Open 7:30am-4:30pm.

Pharmacy: Corner of Đề Thám and Búi Viện. Open daily 9am-8pm.

Medical Services: OSCAT/AEA International Clinic, 65 Nguyễn Du (☎829 85 20), inside the Han Nam office building west of intersection with Đồng Khởi. English, French, German, Russian, Chinese, Korean, and Japanese spoken. Consultations US$55-65. **Open 24hr.** AmEx/MC/V.

Telephones: Murderously expensive international calls at upper-end hotels and at GPO. **Directory assistance** ☎**1080.**

Internet Access: Cheapest access on Búi Viện. 100Đ per min. Rates change frequently, so check the posted signs.

Post Offices: GPO, 2 Công Xã Paris, next to the Notre Dame Cathedral. Open M-Sa 6am-10pm. International calling card and collect calls. *Poste Restante.* **Branch,** 227 Phạm Ngũ Laõ. Open daily 7am-11pm.

ACCOMMODATIONS

The cheapest rooms in HCMC are in District 1 on **Phạm Ngũ Lão,** a block south on **Bùi Viện,** and on **Đe Thám,** the road that connects them. For more peace and quiet, head to **Cộ Giang,** two blocks south of Trần Hung Dao. **Chợ' Lớ'n** has some budget spots, but the area is better known for its brothels and thieves. Upscale neighborhoods have some classier digs in houses posting *"phòng thue"* (room for rent).

AROUND PHAM NGU LÃO

Hotel 64, 64 Bùi Viện (☎836 50 73). A great value. Warm, communal atmosphere. Free breakfast and dinner; endless supply of complimentary tea, coffee, and bananas. Rooms with fan US$10, with A/C US$12, with A/C, satellite TV, and minibar US$18. All rooms US$2 cheaper in the low season. ❸

Hong Hoa Hotel, 185/28 Phạm Ngũ Lão (☎836 19 15), on a side street off Phạm Ngũ Lao by a mini-mart—all the action without the noise. Motorbikes US$5 per day; bicycles US$1 per day. Free 2hr. Internet for guests. Satellite TV. Rooms $12-16. MC/V. ❸

Room for Rent 70, 70 Bùi Viện (☎836 95 69), near the intersection with Đề Thám. Clean and simple rooms are pretty in pink paint. Breakfast, dinner, coffee, tea, and bananas all included in the price of a room. Rooms with fan US$8, with A/C US$10, with A/C and cable TV US$15. Owner's son has opened a newer, quieter clone, **Luan Vu,** across the street at 35/2 Bùi Viện (☎837 71 85). ❷

Vinh Guest House (Le Le 2 Hotel), 269 Đề Thám (☎836 85 85), across the street from Kim's Cafe. Spacious, clean rooms complemented by great service. Private bath, minibar, and TV. Rooms with fan US$7-8, with A/C US$10-15. Rooms US$2 cheaper during low season. MC/V. ❷

Quyen Thanh Hotel, 212 Đề Thám (☎836 85 70), at the intersection with Bùi Viện. Five stories of rooms with terraces perfect for people-watching. With 24hr. security, the gift shop downstairs poses more threat to your money belt than do neighborhood crooks. Rooms with a fan US$8, with A/C US$10. AmEX/MC/V. ❷

Hotel 265, 265 Đề Thám (☎836 75 12). Regular rooms are nothing to write home about, but 4-bed dorms are a good value for those on a tight budget. Rent a bicycle (10,000Đ per day) or moto (US$3.50-4 per day). Dorms with fan US$3; singles with fan US$7, with A/C US$9; doubles US$8-10. ❶

Dung Hotel, 185/6 Phạm Ngũ Lão (☎836 10 67), down an alley marked by a mini-mart, 30m from the intersection with Nguyễn Thái Học. Ideal location just off the main strip. Don't fault it for its name—it's pronounced "yoom." Rooms with fan US$7, with A/C US$15. A/C rooms run US$2 cheaper in low season. MC/V. ❷

ELSEWHERE IN DISTRICT 1

Miss Lợi's Rooming House, 178/20 Cô Giang (☎836 79 73), down an alley between Cô Bắc and Cô Giang, one of the first guest houses in Saigon. Patio area, TV room, and pool table create a great social atmosphere. Good for long-term stays. Breakfast included. Relax with a massage (60,000Đ per hr.). Singles with fan US$7, with A/C US$8; doubles with fan US$8, with bath US$10. ❷

Ngọc Huệ, 171/22 Cô Bắc (☎836 00 89), down the alley from Miss Lợi's. The 26 average-sized rooms have minifridges, desks, and fabulous roof-top terraces. Internet 200Đ per min. Motorbike rental US$5 per day. Bicycles 10,000Đ per day. Breakfast and family-style Su dinner included. Tourist visa extensions. Singles with fan US$6, with A/C US$8; doubles US$8/10. ❷

Hotel 127, 127 Công Quynh (☎836 87 61). Prettier but less successful than its older sibling Hotel 64. Same friendly staff and same free breakfasts, dinners, coffee, and bananas included. Singles with fan US$12, with A/C US$14; doubles US$18-20. ❸

Kim Loan Guest House, 171 Cô Bắc (☎836 83 51), in the alley with Miss Lợi's and Ngọc Huệ. Clean rooms with big windows. Internet 200Đ per min. Breakfast included. Singles with fan US$6, with A/C US$9. ❷

Bong Sen Hotel Annex, 61-63 Hai Bà Tru'ng (☎829 42 02), downtown near the intersection with Lê Lợi. A step up from the guest houses around Phạm Ngũ Lão, the Annex offers hotel comforts at a reasonable price. First-floor office area features computers and a variety of newspapers. Economy singles US$25; doubles US$30; suites US$45-50. ❺

FOOD

Pull up a plastic stool—the true taste of Saigon is found on the streets. Market stalls, sidewalk stands, and *cơm bình dân* eateries provide meager ambience, but the food is unbeatable (*phở* soups 5000-7000Đ, beer 8000Đ, *cơm* dishes 9000Đ). Along **Phạm Ngũ Lão** and **Đề Thám,** tourist cafes serve decent food—banana pancakes, pizza, salads—to a mostly Western crowd. The best of the lot are **Kim's Cafe** and **Sinh Cafe,** both on Đề Thám. Some slightly more expensive restaurants occupy side streets off Đong Khởi, between the Continental Hotel and the river.

AROUND PHAM NGU LÃO

Phở 2000, 1-3 Phan Chu Trinh (☎821 25 38), at the intersection with the Ben Thành Market. Introducing *phở*—21st-century style. The brainchild of Vietnamese-American businessmen, this place is modern, clean, and hi-tech. Fruit shakes 6000-10,000Đ. Northern-style *phở* prepared without MSG or sugar 14,000Đ. Open daily 6am-2am. ❷

The Original Bodhi Tree, 175/4 Phạm Ngũ Lão (☎837 19 10), in an alley marked by a Kodak shop—it's the first Bodhi Tree restaurant on the right. Vegetarian food good enough to tempt the most avid carnivores. Great breakfasts 5000-8000Đ. Appetizers 6000-9000Đ. Entrees 6000-20,000Đ. Open daily 7am-11pm. ❷

Allez-Boo, 187 Phạm Ngũ Lão, (☎837 25 05) at the intersection with Đề Thám. While it's known for its late-night rowdiness, daytime diners can enjoy quality dishes in a tranquil atmosphere. The most popular bar in the backpacker ghetto. Beer 10,000-35,000Đ. Cocktails 30,000-45,000Đ. Entrees 25,000-40,000Đ. Open daily 7am-2am. ❸

Tín Nghĩa, 9 Trần Hưng Đạo (☎821 25 38), at the Phạm Ngũ Lão intersection opposite BP Station. Simple vegetarian menu, standard Vietnamese decor. Picky eaters are in luck—accommodating owners speak good English. Dishes 6000-10,000Đ. Open daily 7am-2pm and 4-9pm. ❶

IT'S A DOG-EAT-DOG WORLD. Hồ Chí Minh City has whole markets devoted to selling live animals. A menagerie of caged puppies, birds, mice, roosters, and fish unfolds between Lê Hồng Phong and Vinh Vien at the southeastern edge of District 10. Commonly called "the Pet Market" (Chợ Bán Chim Thú), it's the place to go to get a new best friend—or if you change your mind, just dinner. Though it boasts a large selection of leashes and doggie treats, most of the cute canines won't ever need them.

ELSEWHERE IN HCMC

Bò Túng Xẻo, 31 Lý Tự Trọng (☎825 13 30), 150m east of intersection with Hai Bà Trung. Just mention the name and moto drivers know where to go. Popular with Vietnamese and tourists alike, who crowd over 100 tables to dine on everything from grilled beef (35,000Đ) to fried scorpion (30,000Đ). Open daily 10am-10pm. ❸

Phở Hoà Pasteur, 260C Pasteur Rd., in District 3 opposite the Pasteur Institute. Long regarded as the best *phở* in the city. Bowl of chicken or beef *phở* 13,000-15,000Đ. Open daily 6am-midnight. ❷

Indian Heritage, 12 Thái Văn Lung (☎823 46 87), at the intersection with Lê Thánh Tôn. Quality Indian food in Vietnam! Who knew? Free delivery in District 1. Vegetarian entrees 30,000-40,000Đ, meat entrees 40,000-65,000Đ. Open M-F noon-2pm and 5-10:30pm. ❸

La Fourchette, 9 Ngô Đức Kế (☎829 81 43), off Đong Khởi. Favorite of French expats who add authenticity to bistro decor. Pricey, but treat yourself! Appetizers 60,000-130,000Đ. Entrees 80,000-155,000Đ. Desserts 35,000-55,000Đ. Cheeses 50,000Đ. Open daily noon-3pm and 7-10pm. ❺

Ciao Cafe, 72 Nguyễn Huệ (☎825 12 03). A cheery, Italian cafe in the Đong Khởi area. Extensive menu, great for those nights when you just can't eat another bowl of *phở*. Italian *gelato* 25,000-57,000Đ. Pizzas 38,000-60,000Đ. Open daily 7am-11:30pm. ❸

Quán 13, 13 Ngô Đức Kế, near the intersection with Đong Khởi, near the Trận Hưng Đao Monument. Solid Vietnamese cuisine. 10 delicious spring rolls for 18,000Đ. Appetizers 18,000-47,000Đ. Entrees 24,000-75,000Đ. Open daily 7am-11:30pm. ❸

Givral Patisserie, 2A Lê Lợi (☎824 27 50), at the intersection with Đồng Khởi, opposite the Continental Hotel. Try the all-you-can-eat dessert buffet (M-F 2-5:30pm; 30,000Đ). Mouthwatering pastries 5000-8000Đ. Open daily 6am-10:30pm. AmEx/MC/V. ❶

SIGHTS

Most of HCMC's major sights can be seen in one or two days. Major historical sights are concentrated in District 1; popular pagodas are in **District 5 (Chợ Lớn).** It is possible to cover all the sights by following a path starting at the zoo in the northeast and ending at Chợ Lớn in the southwest. The pagodas generally stay open later than historical sites and museums.

WAR REMNANTS MUSEUM. Formerly known as the American War Crimes Museum, this six-room museum exhibits vivid, sometimes gruesome war memorabilia, including photographs of the My Lai Massacre and bottled fetuses deformed by Agent Orange. Don't skip an engrossing exhibit on war photographers who died in the line of duty. *(28 Võ Văn Tần, District 3, 1 block north of the palace. ☎ 930 63 25. Open daily 7:30-11:45am and 1:30-4:45pm. 10,000Đ.)*

REUNIFICATION PALACE. This former residence of South Vietnam's presidents has a complex and violent history. The French built the palace in 1868 as a home for the Governor General of Indochina. The US-backed Ngô Đình Diệm assumed residence in 1954, changing its name from Reunification Palace to Independence Palace. In 1962, Diệm's own troops tried to assassinate him but destroyed the palace instead. A new mansion was completed in 1966, only to be bombed again in 1975 by a disloyal Vietnamese Air Force pilot. Once-rebuilt, twice-bombed, and thrice-christened, today's Reunification Palace remains frozen in its 1975 state. (Note the entertainment room on the 3rd floor. Groovy.) Multilingual guides lead tourists through ornate but run-down chambers and underground war rooms, concluding with a rooftop view of the city and an unintelligible film. *(Entrance on Nam Kỳ Khởi Nghĩa a few blocks west of the cathedral. Open daily 7:30am-11am and 1-4pm. 15,000Đ.)*

HỒ CHÍ MINH MUSEUM. To learn more about Vietnam's famous leader, check out this commemorative museum, which features a collage portrait of Hồ Chí Minh made with Vietnamese stamps. Afterwards, relax with an excellent view of the Saigon River and city center from the accompanying gardens. *(1 Nguyễn Tất Thành, across the Bến Nghè Canal. Open Tu-Th 7:30-11:30am and 1:30-4:30pm, F 1:30-4:30pm, Sa-Su 1:30-9pm. Free music performances daily at 8am and 2:30pm.)*

OTHER SIGHTS. Highlights of the **Museum of Vietnamese History** include ancient Hindu sculptures from the Mekong region and a room dedicated to comparative Buddha images. A must-see for Southeast Asian art connoisseurs; for everyone else, it's optional. *(2 Nguyễn Bỉnh Khiêm, next to the zoo. Open M-Sa 8-11am and 1:30-4:30pm, Su 8:30am-4pm. 10,000Đ.)* The **Revolutionary Museum** documents the liberation of the South. The murals, displays, and photographs make it a big hit with children. *(2 Lê Duẩn. Open Tu-F, Su 8-10am and 2-4pm.)* A **monument** at 29 Lê Duẩn commemorates the site of the pre-1975 US embassy, which was torn down in 1998.

ZOO AND BOTANICAL GARDEN. Founded in 1864, these gardens are Vietnam's largest. Once inside, stroll past the blaring children's rides into the well-manicured gardens, complete with several species of cacti, orchids, and bonsai trees. The zoo facilities house over 100 species including many native to Vietnam. Just inside the main entrance, turn right to see the **Temple of King Hùng,** the mythical ruler worshipped as the father of ancient Vietnam. *(Entrance at the corner of Nguyễn Bỉnh Khiêm and Lê Duẩn. Concerts Sa-Su 8-10pm. Both open 7am-9pm. Adults 8000Đ, children 6-10 years 4000Đ; concerts 12,000Đ.)*

ARCHITECTURAL SIGHTS. Surrounded by an area filled with pre-liberation opulence, an ironically juxtaposed statue of Uncle Hồ (Chí Minh) overlooks the lush boulevard of Nguyển Huệ near its intersection with Lệ Lọi. To his right, the **Rex Hotel** served as an American business center throughout the 1960s and boasts a panoramic view of the city from its **Rooftop Garden.** Next door, the yellow colonial-style **City Hall** (not open to foreigners) faces Nguyễn Huệ and hides a pretty garden inside. The simple pink and white **Municipal Theater,** stands at the end of Lê Lợi, near Hai Bà Trung. Graham Greene fans will want to visit the **Continental Hotel,** the setting of his novel *A Quiet American*, next to the Municipal Theater.

RELIGIOUS SIGHTS. If time constraints only allow you to visit one of HCMC's pagodas, the **Jade Emperor Pagoda** should be it. A wide terrace leads past a turtle-filled pond into the main sanctuary. Behind the Buddhist images is an area devoted to Taoist deities, centered on Ngọc Hoàng, the Jade Emperor and father of all kings. *(73 Mai Thị Lưu, at the northern end of District 1. Open daily 6am-6pm.)* The stunning **Thiên Hậu Pagoda** is named for the goddess of the sea. Its rich ornamentation includes wooden carvings from China and gilded statues of King Hậu. Peer through the haze from the burning incense spirals at the intricate woodwork above the interior courtyards. *(710 Nguyễn Trãi, District 5. Open daily 6am-5:30pm.)* Built in 1880, the picturesque **Notre Dame Cathedral** is a twin-spired miniature of its Parisian sister. *(On a paved square near the intersection of Lê Duẩn and Đồng Khởi. Open M-F 7-11am and 3-4pm; mass 5:30am and 5pm, Su mass every 2hr. 5:30am-6:30pm, 9am mass in French.)* Built in 1935, the **Indian Jamia Muslim Mosque** conducts services for a practicing Muslim community of Chàm, Vietnamese, and Indian followers. *(66 Đông Du, 1 block south of the Lê Lợi. Open daily sunrise-sunset. Proper attire required.)* The **Mariamman Hindu Temple** (Black Lady Temple) has an unassuming entrance that opens into a surprisingly tacky interior. Envision a traditional Hindu temple crossed with an 80s rockstar mansion. From 1975 to 1989, the communist government used this building to store rice, but the temple's religious function has since resumed. *(45 Trương Định, southwest of the Reunification Palace. Open daily 7am-7pm.)*

NIGHTLIFE

Locals rave about HCMC's legendary nightlife, and backpackers who venture beyond District 1 will wholeheartedly agree. Downtown, **Nguyễn Huệ** and **Đồng Khởi** jump with nightly activity. The intersection of **Nguyễn Thiện Thuột** and **Nguyễn Đình Chiểu** in District 3 is a cruising strip where locals and travelers munch on cheap food and sip plastic cups of *bia hơi* into the wee hours. Near De Tham, **Phạm Ngũ Lão** also hosts several popular Western bars.

Hoaviện Brauhaus, 28 Mac Dính Chi (☎829 05 85). Longing for some Pilsner Urquell after one too many mugs of *bia hơi*? The only place serving the classic Czech brew is also Vietnam's only microbrewery. Copper brewing equipment and a wooden-accented interior complete the 19th-century *brauhaus* motif. Tour the place with the brew master or watch European *futbol* while pounding the local brew. Beer 10,000-25,000Đ.

Allez-Boo Bar, see **Food,** p. 966.

Lost in Saigon, 169 Phạm Ngũ Lão. Another popular spot with the 20-something foreign crowd. Drink 5 "Lost Bowls" (1 bowl for 4 people 75,000Đ) and get your picture on the "Wall of Lost Souls." Drink ten and get a free map and a taxi ride home. Beer 12,000-16,000Đ. Cocktails 40,000-55,0000Đ. Open daily 6pm-6am.

Guns 'n' Roses, 207 Phạm Ngũ Lão. Axel would be proud—nothing but G'n'R all night long. More *Use Your Illusion II* than *The Spaghetti Incident*, thankfully. Beer 13,000-36,000Đ. Cocktails 20,000-50,000Đ. Open daily 6pm-6am.

Cafe 32D5, 74/2 Hai Bà Trung, behind the Municipal Center. Pleasant cafe by day, a lean, mean, party-generating machine by night. Coffees 15,000-28,000Đ. Beer 28,000Đ. Cocktails 39,000-49,000Đ. Open daily 7:30am-2am.

Bia Tươ' Pacific, 15 Lê Thánh Tôn, a block from the intersection with Tôn Đức Thắng. Cheaper beer (3500Đ) a cut above *bia hơi* makes this a great place to start off the night. Large open-air restaurant also serves decent seafood and meat hot pots (40,000-80,000Đ). Open daily 9am-10pm.

Carmen Bar, 8 I Tự Trọng (☎829 76 99), near the intersection with Tôn Đức Thắng. Duck into a candle-lit corner table and sip cocktails to soft flamenco beats. Live music nightly 9-11:45pm. Beer 32,000-65,000Đ. Cocktails 53,000-65,000Đ. Open daily 4pm-2am.

VIETNAM

DAYTRIPS FROM HCMC

CỦ CHI TUNNELS

Tourist cafes set up cheap, easy trips to the tunnels. Daytrips to the tunnels depart from Sinh Cafe and Kim Cafe (8:30am, return 2pm; tunnel entrance fee US$5 or 65,000Đ). Visitors can climb down into the actual tunnels for 30-150m, depending on their degree of claustrophobia. Wear breathable clothing and shoes with good traction.

Few sights capture the tenacity and ingenuity of the Vietnamese guerrillas better than the Củ Chi Tunnels. The Việt Minh constructed the first tunnels during the war against the French in the 1940s. During the 1960s, the National Liberation Front (NLF; Việt Cộng) greatly expanded the tunnel network—at one point, the network of underground passageways stretched from Củ Chi to the Cambodian border. The tunnels were a base for commando raids and infiltrations into HCMC and enabled the NLF to surprise the increasingly frustrated American forces with wily defense maneuvers. The area around Củ Chi, known as the "Iron Triangle," is one of the most bombed pieces of real estate on earth. Tourists can contribute their own *matériel* by firing an M16 or AK47 at the National Defense Sports Shooting Range ($1 per bullet). Collect your souvenir bullet casing on your way out.

CAO ĐÀI TEMPLE

Tourist cafes in Đề Thám offer combined one-day tours to the temple and Củ Chi Tunnels (8:30am, return 7pm; US$4, tunnel entrance fee US$9).

The gaudy, expansive main temple, centerpiece of the Cao Đài Holy See Complex, reflects a religion not known for its artistic subtlety. Under the ever-watchful eye, (see **Here's Looking at Chieu,** below) white-robed congregationers usher visitors to an observation balcony, which provides a bird's-eye view of the prayer ceremony (6am, noon, 6pm, and midnight). Many travelers feel it is not worth the long trek to this temple, situated near the capital of Tây Ninh Province, 100km from HCMC.

NAM CÁT TIÊN NATIONAL PARK

Off Hwy. 20, approximately 150km from HCMC. A bus from Sinh Cafe leaves at 7:30am (3hr., 15,000Đ). Ask to be dropped off at Talai. From here, moto drivers cover the final 25km to a river ferry crossing (40,000Đ). After picking up an entrance permit at the ranger station, take the ferry across the river to the park headquarters (☎061 791 228 for more information).

Nam Cát Tiên National Park functions as a research center where rangers collect information on wildlife, including elephants, tigers, bears, and rhinos. **Jeeps**

HERE'S LOOKING AT CHIEU In 1919 on Phu Quoc Island, a huge, bright, disembodied eye floated before Ngo Van Chieu as he lay in his hammock. The eye, a divine sign that initiated a series of heart-to-heart talks between God and Ngo, became the symbol of Caodaism, the hybrid religion that Ngo founded from his communications with the Cao Dai (High Palace). In his first chats with the colonial bureaucrat and occult enthusiast Chieu, God expressed deep frustration that humanity had been ignoring his prophets. Over the years, he said, he had sent–to name only a few–Jesus, Gautama, Victor Hugo, Joan of Arc, Louis Pasteur, Shakespeare, René Descartes, Lenin, and Lao Tse as agents of the gospel. Frustrated with discord and rivalry among religions, God chose Chieu to act as a prophet for a rainbow coalition, including Buddhism, Taoism, Confucianism, Islam, Hinduism, and Christianity. Caodaism stresses love for one another and the belief that God resides within each of us; its saints include persons who have guided, inspired, and instilled ideals of truth and beauty in others. The new faith has spread quickly and now includes three million adherents, most of whom worship in the 300 temples found in Southern Vietnam.

(60,000-150,000Đ per day) are the most popular means of transport. Hikers have the driver drop them off in the park, arrange a pickup time, and head into the forest. The lack of marked trails make guides (100,000Đ per day) worthwhile.

For **overnight stays** ❷, head to park headquarters for a bed (rooms with fans 80,000Đ, with A/C 100,000Đ). For a unique experience, **camp** ❶ on a sand dune along the banks of the Mekong River tributaries that ring the park (5000Đ per person; tents 20,000Đ). The **canteen** ❷ in the park headquarters sells meals (breakfast 7000Đ, lunch and dinner 20,000-25,000Đ), canned food, and drinks.

VŨNG TÀU ☎64

For over a century, Saigonese have flocked to Vũng Tàu to escape the daily grind of their urban existence. Today, the scope has been widened to include Hanoi schoolteachers and beach-hungry Mekong Delta families. Few foreigners mean that the beachgoing tourist is greeted with curiosity and warmth. Vũng Tàu's beaches are its raison d'être. **Bãi Đầu** lies in an alcove northwest of town, **Bãi Tru'ó'c** hosts a stretch of sand west of the city center, rocky **Bãi Dú'a** hugs the southwest coast, and **Bãi Sau,** a long pristine expanse of beach, lies to the east.

Buses arrive at **Vũng Tàu Station,** 50 Nam Kỳ Khởi Nghĩa (☎859 727), and go to **HCMC** (2½hr., every hr. 5am-5pm, 25,000Đ) and **Mỹ Tho** (4am, 25,000Đ). Most guest houses rent **bicycles** (10,000-20,000Đ per day) and **motorcycles** (US$5-7). Sinh Cafe in HCMC runs a bus to Vũng Tàu as well (7:30am, returns 6:30pm; US$8).

Chợ' Mớ'i, the largest market in town, is on Nam Kỳ Khởi Nghĩa, north of the bus station. (Open daily 5am-5pm.) For all money matters, try **Vietcombank,** 27-29 Trần Hưng Đạo. (☎852 309. MC/V cash advances. Open M-F 7-11:30am and 1:30-4pm; no transactions Th afternoon.) **Lê Lợ'i Hospital,** 22 Lê Lợi (☎832 667), operates a small clinic. **Internet access** is in the center of town at **Dich Vu Internet,** 32 Bacu. (500Đ per min. Open daily 8-11am and 2-9pm.) The **post office,** 45 Lê Hồng Phong, dominates the Xô Viết Nghệ Tĩnh intersection. (24hr. international phones/fax, telegram, FedEx, and DHL. Open daily 6:30-8:30pm.)

Accommodations tend to be expensive. A strip of *nhà trọ* (guest houses) on **Thùy Vân** offers easy access to Vũng Tàu's most popular beach, Bãi Sau, though most guest houses cater solely to Vietnamese. A hearty exception is **145A Thùy Vân** ❷. (☎853 481. Western breakfast US$1. Singles with bath US$5, with A/C US$10.) **Bimexico** ❸, on Thùy Vân at the north end of Bãi Sau, offers rustic A-frames. (☎859 916. 130,000Đ, with A/C 170,000Đ.) **Restaurant Solid** ❹, 22 Hạ Long, offers pricier seafood overlooking the South China Sea. (☎510 512. Seafood entrees 20,000-180,000Đ. Open M-F 10am-8:30pm, Sa-Su 8:30am-10pm.) **Cửu Long** ❷, 57 Thùy Vân next to Bãi Sau, serves flavorful fare. (☎854 018. Fried rice with chicken 15,000Đ. Open daily 6am-11pm.)

VIETNAM

MEKONG DELTA

What the rest of the world calls the Mekong Delta, the Vietnamese call *đồng bằng sông Cửu Long* (River of the Nine-Headed Dragon), a reference to the Mekong River's nine principal tributaries. As the river fans out on its final push to the sea, it forms dozens of tributaries and canals, flattening the landscape and sustaining a vibrant waterfront culture. Agriculture dominates the region's lifestyle and creates a more leisurely pace than nearby Hồ Chí Minh City—a characteristic of which delta residents are proud. Inhabitants of the region also take pride in its status as the world's third largest rice exporter. Relatively new to the region, the Vietnamese began large-scale immigration to the Mekong in the early 19th century, displacing many ethnic Khmers. With a close proximity to Cambodia and a history of dislike and distrust between the two countries, ethnic tension still exists. However, travelers still enjoy the calm pace of life on the river, the diligent yet slow character of the small fishing villages, and some of the area's best beaches.

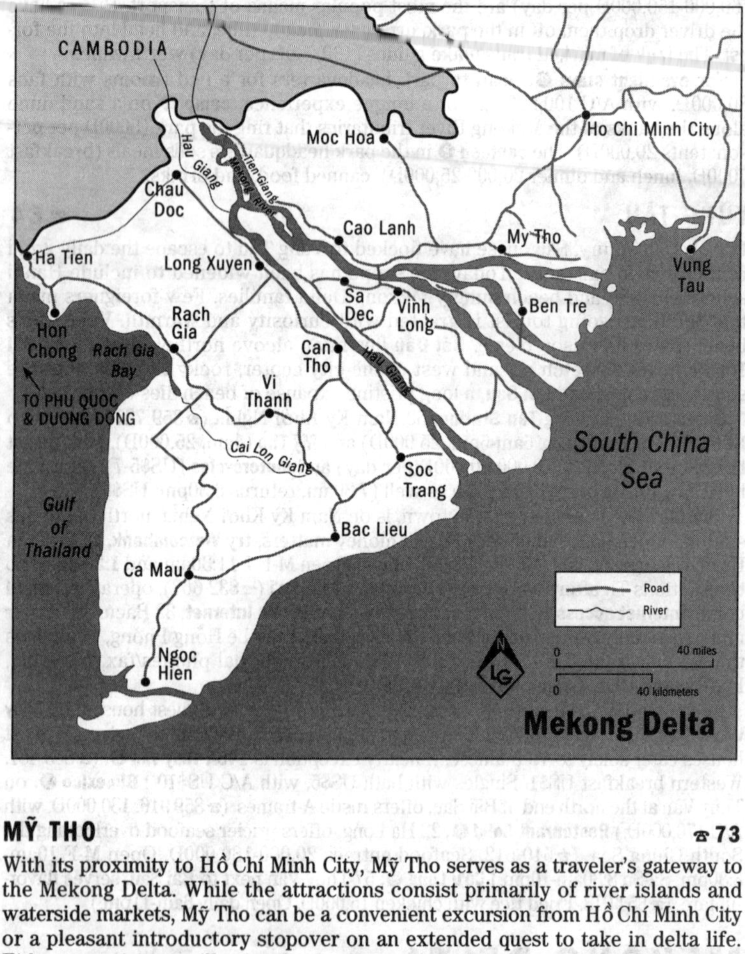

VIETNAM

MỸ THO ☎73

With its proximity to Hồ Chí Minh City, Mỹ Tho serves as a traveler's gateway to the Mekong Delta. While the attractions consist primarily of river islands and waterside markets, Mỹ Tho can be a convenient excursion from Hồ Chí Minh City or a pleasant introductory stopover on an extended quest to take in delta life. Either way, visitors will enjoy the small-town feel of these streets within a river.

TRANSPORTATION AND PRACTICAL INFORMATION. Mỹ Tho, 70km south of HCMC, is the capital of Tiền Giang Province. The **bus station** (☎875 274) lies on **Âp Bắc St.,** which runs into town from the northwest (10,000Đ to town). Most buses depart between 4-8am, although buses to Hồ Chí Minh City and Căn Thó run frequently from morning until early evening. **Buses** to: **Cần Thơ'** (3hr.; 5am; 14,500Đ); **Châu Đốc** (6hr.; 6am; 28,000Đ); **HCMC** (1½hr., every 30min., 9000Đ). **Tây Ninh** and **Vũng Tàu** are best reached from HCMC. Ask about buses to **Long Xuyên** and **Sa Đéc,** as they often need to be boarded at someplace other than the bus station. **Nam Kỳ Khởi Nghĩa,** a north-south thoroughfare, intersects Âp Bắc St., running to the Tiền River. A left turn at the end of Nam Kỳ Khởi Nghĩa is **Đuong 30/4,** becoming **Trưng Trắc** after a 90° turn at a big statue, which leads along the Bao Dinh River, past restaurants, hotels, and the **market.**

BULLS AND BEARS ON BOATS Most tourists visit the floating markets of the Mekong Delta, but few take time to see the true dynamo of the delta economy: the floating stock market. In a hard-to-find canal south of Mỹ Tho known to the tourist industry as "Dau," the market features over 3000 local companies (such as Fong's Noodle Stand and Greasy Machine Parts by Vin) traded by short Asian men in red and yellow ties, starched shirts, and small boats. The market is open daily from 4am to 11am; hire a guide at the Mỹ Tho pier to explain the frantic gesticulations and the way the brokers' lips seem to continue moving long after they've finished yelling. Perhaps with a long enough stay, you too could join in the trades.

Services in Mỹ Tho include: **Tiền Giang Tourist Office,** 8 Đuong 30/4, which operates **boat tours** (☎873 477; 2-5hr. Up to three people, 2hr., US$20; 3hr. US$32; extra charges for additional persons and longer tours. Open daily 7:30am-5pm); a bank, **Ngân Hàng Công Thương Việt Nam,** 15B Nam Kỳ Khởi Nghĩa (☎873 026, open M-Sa 7:15 -11am and 1:30-4:30pm, MC/V cash advances); **Mỹ Tho Commercial Service Center,** at the corner of Lê Lợi and Lê Đại Hành, is a large indoor market (open daily 7am-7pm); **Internet** access is available at **Dich Vu Internet** (☎883 993), 80 Nam Kỳ Khởi Nghĩa (open sporadically throughout the day 7am--8pm, 500Đ per min.); **General Hospital,** 2 Hùng Vương (☎872 359 or 872 360, **24hr.** service); and the **GPO,** 59 Đuong 30/4 (☎873 214, **fax** and **international telephones,** open daily 6am-9pm).

ACCOMMODATIONS AND FOOD. The few tourist hotels sit on Đuong 30/4 facing the river. The cheapest option is at the end of Đuong 30/4, **Huớng Du'o'ng Hotel ❶,** 33 Tru'ng Trắc, which has decent rooms for its price. (☎872 011. Triple with fan and bathroom 60,000Đ.) **Chu'o'ng Du'o'ng Hotel ❹,** 10 Đuong 30/4, across from the post office, dominates the southern river bank. Opened in 1999, it offers beautiful rooms and a large restaurant. (☎870 875. All rooms with A/C, TV, fridge, bath, and telephone. Doubles US$20, with living room US$30.) **Rạng Đông Hotel ❷,** 25 Đuong 30/4, has rooms equipped with TV, A/C, and bath. (☎874 400. 2-3 person rooms 100,000Đ, with hot water, fridge, telephone, and living room 150,000Đ.) **Công Đoàn Hotel ❷,** 61 Đuong 30/4, next to the post office, has clean rooms and outdoor terraces. All rooms have private bath. (☎874 324. Doubles with fan, TC, and telephone 100,000Đ; doubles with A/C, fridge, telephone, and hot water 150,000Đ.)

Mỹ Tho's famous noodle soup, *Hủ tiếu Mỹ Tho* is cooked up in small food stalls all over town. **Thuân Kiều ❶,** 47 Nam Ky Khởi Nghia, two blocks from the river, is popular with town residents for its friendly atmosphere. (*Hủ tiếu Mỹ Tho* with *longans* for dessert 8000Đ. Open daily 7am-9pm.) **Chí Thành Quăn ❷,** 279 Tét Maù Thân, a short walk inland from Đuong 30/4, is recommended for its good food and clean, bright interior. (Fried noodles with beef 15,000Đ. Open daily 9am-10pm.)

SIGHTS. **Boat tours** to the nearby islands typically include a visit to canals, fruit orchards, bee farms, a coconut candy factory, and the **Temple of the Coconut Monk** on Phoenix Island. The temple was home to the French-educated Coconut Monk who preached a fusion of Buddhism and Christianity and ate nothing but coconuts for three years. Boat trips during sunset or after dark should make a stop by a riverbank near the temple where fireflies flood the trees, giving the effect of twinkling Christmas trees. Boat operators cluster on the tourist pier at the intersection of Đuong 30/4 and Lê Lợi (2-5 hr., US$3-4 per hr.) Trips run by the tourist office are reasonably priced for groups (see **Transportation and Practical Information,** above). About 1km east of town over the Nguyễn Trãi Bridge (off Trưng Trắc) stands **Vĩnh Tràng Pagoda,** a large temple surrounded by fountains, gardens, and knick knacks for sale. (Open daily Apr.-July 7am-9pm; daily Aug.-Mar. 7, 11am and 1-7pm.) Tucked away in the village behind the temple, there is a **rice noodle factory,** as well as a household that sells **rice wine.** Ask locals or moto drivers for directions.

The **Đồng Tâm Snake Farm (Trại Rắn Đống Tam)** sits 7km west of Mỹ Tho, past the **Foster's/BGI Beer Plant.** Motorcycle drivers will round-trip it for 20,000Đ. Here, caged cobras are milked for their venom, which is used in a snake-bite antidote and pain-killing ointments. In addition, bears, monkeys, and birds are on display in an archaic **zoo.** (Open daily 7am-5pm. 15,000Đ.)

DAYTRIPS FROM MỸ THO. For people who want to experience another town in the Mekong Delta yet do not have the time to journey beyond Cần Thơ, **Sa Đéc** is an ideal town for a relaxing stroll. Sa Đéc's main attractions are its gardens on the outskirts of town, the **Flower Village,** Làng Hoa. The gardens are in full bloom Nov.-Dec. but may not be worth the trip during the rest of the year. A lack of reasonably priced accommodation makes it a better option for a quick daytrip. The Flower Village is a pleasant 30min. walk north of town on the river's eastern bank. From the metal bridge off Hùng Vương, turn left and continue for 2km along the bank until you get to the phone box and the bridge over the tributary; then turn right. **Vườ̀ng Hồng Tư Tôn (Tư Tôn's Garden),** one of the area's lushest gardens, lies within the village. (☎861 685. Open early morning to late evening.) The garden is one of the nurseries that form the life-bestowing phloem of the region's decorative flower industry. In the town of Sa Đéc itself, there are several pagodas that may be worth a look.

VIETNAM

Ask at the bus station in Mỹ Tho about buses to Sa Đéc, as they often have to be combined with a short motorbike ride. From HCMC, Sa Đéc is a four-hour bus ride (3 per day, 17,5000Đ), or can be arranged in combination with a tour from most guest houses. Foreigners are prohibited from most budget hotels. If you're planing to stay the night, an affordable option is **Sa Đéc Hotel ❷,** 108/5A Hùng Vu'ờ̀ng, at the end of the road. (☎67 861 430. Rooms with fan, telephone, and 2 beds US$8, with 4 beds US$14; A/C suites with 2 beds, TV, fridge, telephone, and living room US$18.) Close by, **Thuỹ ❷,** 439 Hùng Vu'ờ̀ng, has both breakfast and lunch/dinner menus. (☎67 861 644. Delicious grilled fish 15,000Đ. Open daily 7am-9pm.)

CẦN THƠ ☎71

Cosmopolitan without the noise or grime, Cần Thơ (pop. 400,000) is the capital of Cần Thơ Province, the unofficial capital of the delta region, and the most popular destination in the delta. The city is best experienced from its most vital perspective—the water. Travelers hire boats to visit floating markets or bob through tiny canals bordering quiet villages, rice paddies, and fruit orchards.

TRANSPORTATION

Buses: The **bus station** (☎821 462) is northwest of town on Nguyễn Trãi. Daily buses to: **Châu Đốc** (3hr.; continuously 6am-5pm; 13,800Đ); **Hà Tiên** (8hr.; 3:40, 4:20am; 22,500Đ); **HCMC** (3½hr.; 5am-6pm; 24,500Đ); **Long Xuyên** (2hr., every hr. 6am-4:30pm, 8000Đ); **Mỹ Tho** (2hr.; 10am; 14,500Đ); **Rạch Giá** (4hr.; every 45min. 3am-4pm; 14,000Đ); **Sóc Trăng** (1½hr., every 30min. 4:30am-5pm, 8000Đ). Buses to **Vũng Tàu** don't run every day; it is best reached from HCMC.

Minibuses: ☎829 476. Run at all hours from near the Hậu Giang ferry crossing, about 3km northeast of the city on Trần Phú. To: **HCMC** (35,000Đ; hotel pick up possible); **Vũng Tàu** (50,000Đ); **Mỹ Tho** (25,000Đ).

Rentals: Motorcycles available from most hotels (US$5-7 per day).

ORIENTATION AND PRACTICAL INFORMATION

Cần Thơ is 140km southwest of HCMC, at the confluence of the Hậu Giang and Cần Thơ Rivers. **Nguyễn Trãi,** 1km from the bus station, leads into the city and curves to form **Hòa Bình,** the city's main thoroughfare. East toward the Hậu Giang River are parallel streets **Đồng Khởi** and **Phan Đình Phùng,** and along the riverbank **Hai Bà Trưng** passes restaurants and a silver statue of Hồ Chí Minh before ending at the market. **Châu Văn Liêm** links Hai Bà Trưng with Hòa Bình. Budget hotels lie along **Châu Văn Liêm,** between **Phan Đình Phùng** and **Đồng Khởi.**

Tourist Office: Cần Thơ Tourist, 20 Hai Bà Trưng (☎821 852). Sells poster-size maps (6000Đ). 3hr. guided boat tour for group of 5-20 US$20. Open daily 7-11am and 1-4:30pm.

Currency Exchange: Vietcombank, 7 Hòa Bình (☎820 445). Exchanges traveler's checks. Gives MC/V cash advances (3% fee). Open M-F 7:30-10:45am and 1-4:30pm.

Markets: The newly installed market lies north of Nguyễn Trãi.

Emergency: ☎115. **Police:** ☎113. **Fire:** ☎114.

Medical Services: Cần Thơ General Hospital, 4 Châu Văn Liêm (☎821 288), on corner of Hòa Bình. **Pharmacy** at front entrance. Open daily 7-11am and 1-5pm.

Internet Access: Many servers in town. **Dich Vu Internet,** 67 Phan Đình Phùng, next to Hậu Giang B Hotel, is in the center of town. 100Đ per min. Open daily 8am-10pm.

Post Office: 2 Hòa Bình (☎820 077). **International phones** and fax. Open daily 6am-8pm.

ACCOMMODATIONS

Hotels cluster along **Hai Bà Trưng** south of the Hồ Chí Minh statue, along **Châu Văn Liêm,** and on smaller **Ngô Đức Kế,** one block south of Châu Văn Liêm. Use caution when hiring transport to hotels from the bus station or the ferry port. Moto drivers operate with hotels who pay them commission for bringing in business. To subsidize this commission, the hotel inflates prices. Choose a hotel in advance and be firm when telling the driver where to go.

Hien Guest House, 118/10 Phan Đình Phùng (☎812 718; hien_gh@yahoo.com), south of Ngô Đức Kế. English-speaking owners treat guests like long-lost family. Only 5 cozy rooms with fans and shared bath US$4, with A/C US$8. ❶

Hậu Giang B Hotel, 27 Châu Văn Liêm (☎821 950). Not to be confused with the more upscale Hậu Giang Hotel. Spacious doubles with hot water and fan US$10, with A/C US$15. ❸

Phan Trung, 9 Lê Thánh Tôn (☎824 477), one block from the riverbank. Central, convenient location. Doubles with fan 50,000Đ, with fan and bath 70,000Đ, with A/C 110,000-150,000Đ. ❶

Hotel 31, 31 Ngô Đức Kế St. (☎825 287). The restaurant downstairs, a local favorite, is a big draw. 10 comfortable rooms with fan and bath US$5, with A/C US$8. ❷

NK02 Hotel, 5 Hai Bà Trưng (☎811 619). A new building with a superb view of the river from its luxurious rooms. Massive attached restaurant with plenty of variety. Double rooms with A/C, TV, and phone US$15, with fridge and living room US$23. ❹

FOOD

Students munch on local delicacies along **Đề Thám,** east of Hòa Bình. Cheap restaurants line **Nam Kỳ Khởi Nghĩa** east of Điện Biên Phủ. Bakeries are on the north end

VIETNAM

of Đồng Khởi before its intersection with Hòa Bình. Hai Bà Trưng's riverside chowhouses bask in the glow of neon billboards. Popular with travelers, the **stall** ❶ at 49 Nam Kỳ Khởi Nghĩa serves baguettes with assorted fillings.

THE BEST WAYS TO FILL UP IN THE MEKONG DELTA.

Hủ tiếu Mỹ Tho: Mỹ Tho is famous for its delicious noodle soup.

Lẩu: A specialty seafood soup native to Cần Thơ.

Canh chua: Another of Cần Thơ's special soups—this time with sour fish.

The best phở in the Mekong: Arguably at Cần Thơ's Tiệm Cơm Nam Đô.

Bò khô: A local favorite in Châu Đốc, dried beef.

Tôm chiên bột: A shrimp dish often made in Hà Tiên at Tiệm Cơm Hương Biển.

Nước nắm: An Thới, on Phú Quốc (see **p. 984**), is famed for this fish sauce.

Phở Oanh, 98 Ly Tú Trong. The 10min. walk from town center is well worth it. Fast service and divine *phở*. Open daily 6am-11pm, but often open later. ❶

Lò Bánh Sài Gòn, 15 Đồng Khởi, near the intersection with Hòa Bình. Pastries vie for attention in front of this standout bakery. *Bơ đường* (butter sugar) 2000Đ. Oversized eclairs 2000Đ. Open daily 5am-10pm. ❶

Tiệm Cơm Nam Đô, at the northeast intersection of Đai Lô Hòa Dình and Châu Văn Liệm. Spacious restaurant is a local favorite. Food cooked outside, eaten inside. Crispy fried shrimp 15,000Đ. Frog with rice and noodles 20,000Đ. Open daily 10am-10pm. ❷

Thien Hoa Restaurant, 26 Hai Bà Trưng, a great location for an after-dinner stroll along the river. Try a bite of stir-fried snake (40,000Đ). Open daily 9am-2pm and 5-11pm. ❸

SIGHTS

A trip through the tiny canals that spiderweb through Cần Thơ is a highlight of the area. A typical tour includes fruit tasting and a visit to a **floating market.** The four main floating markets lie progressively farther from Cần Thơ. **Cái Răng** (7km, 3-4hr. round-trip) lies under a nearby bridge; **Phong Điền** (18km, 4-5hr. round-trip) sits in a four-river confluence; **Trà Ôn**'s five-river market (20km, 6hr. round-trip) is the most popular with foreigners; and **Phụng Hiệp** (33km, 8hr. round-trip) always bustles (open daily 4-11am). Independent boats line Hai Bà Trưng's riverside at dawn to help you catch the sublime sunrise (20,000Đ per hr.).

Cần Thơ's wide, clean boulevards, back alleys, and manicured riverfront are well suited to aimless strolling. The **Muniransyarama Pagoda,** 36 Hòa Bình, is a Theravada Buddhist temple patronized by Cần Thơ's Khmer population. Khmers come here to pray, offer food to the monks, and listen to the resident 80-year-old master. Some of the monks speak English and enjoy talking with tourists. (Open daily 6am-10:30pm.) The **Hồ Chí Minh Museum (Bảo Tàng Hồ Chí Minh),** 6 Hòa Bình, is the large white structure next to the post office. (☎822 173. Open Tu and Th-Sa 8-11am and 2-4pm, Su 8-11am and 7-9pm.) The **Ninth Military Section Museum** is next door. Each of the 12 provinces has its own gallery commemorating local victories. All displays are in Vietnamese.

NIGHTLIFE

Cần Thơ has more options for nightlife than its delta neighbors, but the variety falls short of what you find in Hồ Chí Minh City. For a drink among locals, head to one of the restaurants in town, offering traditional *bia hơi* and karaoke. **Cửa Hàng Bia Sài Gòn,** 78 Nguyễn Trãi, under the Công Ty Liên Doanh Bia Saigon sign, is Cần Thơ's "Labor Bar." Locals will wave you in; smiles will bid you adieu. (*Bia hơi*

4500Đ per liter; gentler drinks only slightly more expensive. Open daily 8am-10pm.) **Golf Discotheque Club,** 2 Hai Bà Trưng, and **Bên Thãnh Club,** on Trân Van Kheó St., are busy with teenagers and adults alike dancing the night away. (Cover depends on night. Open daily 8pm-midnight.)

DAYTRIPS FROM CẦN THƠ

VƯỜN CÒ (GARDEN OF THE STORKS)

The journey is treacherous but can be painless and enjoyable when booked as a tour. Visit the tourist office or ask your guest house owner for more information. On your own, the easiest method is to catch a bus for Long Xuyên (10,000Đ) and ask to be let off at Băng Lăng Bridge in Thốt Nốt Village. From there you can either make the 30min. walk to the garden (after the bridge, go down the alley on the left) or hire a boat from 200m back toward Cần Thơ (30,000Đ round-trip per boat). Another option is to hire a moto for about 50,000Đ round-trip from Cần Thơ.

Some 45km northwest of Cần Thơ, in a dense jungle 2km off the main road, hides Vườn Cò (Garden of the Storks), a breeding ground for thousands of *cò trắng* (white storks) and *cò cộc* (short storks). Storks interact freely with visitors and with locals, who sometimes climb the trees to capture the stork chicks with 6m long poles. The best time to visit the garden is in the afternoon, when the male storks return from gathering food, but there is always some activity.

VIETNAM

SÓC TRÂNG

Buses run from Cần Thơ to Sóc Trăng (1½hr., every 30min., 8000Đ). Buses go back to Cần Thơ as well as to HCMC throughout the day (30,000Đ). Moto from Cần Thơ US$10.

On the way to temple-crazy Sóc Trăng, 62km southeast of Cần Thơ, be sure to stop at the small town of **Phung Hiêp,** which is known for its snakes. Live snakes are sold on the streets as cooking ingredients, while dead ones sit in rice wine bottles, adding medicinal effects to the alcoholic drink. With a predominantly Khmer population and a Chinese minority, Sóc Trăng offers an interesting mix of Cambodian and Chinese Buddhism. **Buu Son Tu,** commonly known as **Chua Dat Set (Clay Pagoda),** sits about 1km east of the Sóc Trăng River and the town center on Đ. Mậu Thân 68. The indoor menagerie includes life-size clay statues of lions, tigers, and elephants. Several of the dozens of Buddha figures are adorned with carnival-style flashing lights. A pair of candles, originally 2.5m tall, have been burning for 32 years now—ever since the founder Ngô Kim Tong died—and will run out of wax in 2005 or so. Ngô Kim Giang, the resident monk, is fluent in French and eagerly entertains his visitors. **Im Som Rong Pagoda,** east of the Clay Pagoda and to the left down a dirt road, is an open-air temple with a large Buddha on center stage. **Chùa Dơi,** the aptly-named **Bat Pagoda,** awaits 4km west of town down a dirt road off Đ. Lê Hồng Phong. Thousands of fruit bats, with wing spans of up to 1.5m, hang in the surrounding trees by day and pillage local orchards by night. They're most active around 6pm. The site also features a collection of rare five-toed pigs. Farmers bring such animals to the temple, since locals say that it's unlucky to eat them. **Chùa Khleang Pagoda,** in the center of town, houses a huge golden Buddha which is visited by Khmer people. Across the street there is even a **Khmer Museum** that can be seen in 10min. (Open M-F 7am-4:30pm. Free.)

Local accommodations include **Phong Lan II ❷,** 133 Nguyễn Chí Thanh. (☎821 757. Doubles with A/C US$7, with A/C, TV, fridge, and telephone US$14-16.)

LONG XUYÊN ☎76

While not the most magnetic of delta destinations, this cheerful town with friendly inhabitants admirably serves as a daytrip from Cần Thơ or a transit point. The Hậu Giang River and Long Xuyên's gargantuan market are major attractions.

TRANSPORTATION. The **bus station,** 144 Trần Hưng Đạo (☎841 125), has daily buses to: **Cần Thơ** (1½hr.; bus 9000Đ, minibus 12,000Đ); **Châu Đốc** (1½hr.; 10,000Đ; ask your hotel proprietor where to catch it); **Hà Tiên** (3½hr.; 22,000Đ); **HCMC** (4½hr.; bus 32,000Đ, minibus 40,000Đ); **Rạch Giá** (bus 10,500Đ; minibus 14,000Đ). Buses to **HCMC** also wait before crossing the Hậu Giang at a stop near the ferry at the east end of Lý Thái Tổ. **Minibuses** go from the Bình Khánh bus station, 3km north of the town center, to **Châu Đốc** (2hr., 6400Đ). The long-distance **ferry terminal** (☎854 846) is on the small road to the right of the Duy Tân Bridge at the northern end of Hai Bà Trưng.

ORIENTATION AND PRACTICAL INFORMATION. From the bus station, **Trần Hưng Đạo** runs 1km north past a traffic circle to reach the **Catholic church,** a useful landmark. **Nguyễn Huệ** leads east from the church to the Hậu Giang River. **Hai Bà Trưng** intersects Nguyễn Huệ on its way north to the Duy Tân Bridge. One block east from the church, **Hùng Vương** runs south, passing the **Vietcombank,** 1 Hùng Vương, which offers **traveler's check exchange** and MC/V **cash advances**—this is the last town that offers these services as you head south into the Mekong Delta. (☎841 813. Open M-F 7:30-11am and 1:30-4:30pm.) **Internet** access is across from the church on Nguyễn Huệ (3000Đ per hr.). A **pharmacy** is at 34-36 Ngô Gia Tự, near the intersection with Lương Văn Cư. (☎841 558. Open M-F 7am-5pm, Sa 7am-noon.) There is a **post office,** 106 Trần Hưng Đạo, north from the church (hire a moto) that has **international phone** and fax. (☎841 755. Open daily 6am-10pm.)

ACCOMMODATIONS AND FOOD. The **Thái Bình 2 Hotel ❷,** 4 Nguyễn Huệ, has affordable and comfortable rooms. (☎847 078. Doubles with fan 70,000Đ, with A/C 120,000Đ.) **An Giang Hotel ❷,** 40 Hai Bà Trưng, also offers clean rooms at a reasonable price. (☎841 297. Singles with fan 66,000Đ; doubles with fan, telephone, and hot water 88,000Đ.) **Đông Xuyên Hotel ❹,** 9 W'ơng Văn Cù St., is perhaps the most decadent hotel in the Mekong Delta, with facilities including a sauna, hot tub, massage, currency exchange, and Vietnam Airlines booking. (☎942 260. Standard US$20; suite US$30. MC/V.) There are several cheap restaurants along **Nguyễn Trãi** between the traffic circle and the intersection with Hai Bà Trưng. One of the best eateries, **Hồng Phát ❸,** 242/4 Lương Văn Cư, is just off Nguyễn Trãi. (Open daily 8am-10pm.) The market at the end of Nguyễn Huệ has numerous **food stalls ❶.**

SIGHTS. Long Xuyên's most exciting sight is the busy **riverside market,** which spans several blocks north and south of Nguyễn Huệ, at the eastern end of the river; trading continues around the clock. A few large barns are devoted to clothing and raw textiles. For those with a spiritual bent, Long Xuyên's **Catholic church** offers peace, but not quiet, as it lies at the confluence of three main roads. Its thin walls do little to block the noise of traffic. (Mass M-Sa 4:30am and 6pm, Su 5am, 4, and 6pm; children's baptisms 7am. Open to visitors 4am-6pm. Ask the guard at the gate to unlock the doors.) For a tour of Long Xuyên's **river-home community,** small boats for hire are at the landing on the end of Nguyễn Huệ (20,000Đ).

CHÂU ĐỐC ☎76

Twenty years ago, this remote border town fell victim to Khmer Rouge terror tactics. Today, the shrine to Lady Buddha at nearby Sam Mountain has made Châu Đốc a famous pilgrimage site, to which people come from as far away as Hong

Kong and Taiwan, especially on Buddha's birthday (in late April). Boat trips on the Hậu Giang, attractive colonial style architecture, and a bustling riverside market beckon travelers back to the charming town center. Those few who stick around long enough always feel right at home. Don't miss a chance to daytrip to Tuc Dup Hill and Ba Chuc, two of the area's highlights.

TRANSPORTATION. The **bus station** is 2km southeast of town at the intersection of Hwy. 91 and Lê Lợi. Buses leave for: **Cần Thơ** (3hr.; bus 15,000Đ, minibus 30,000Đ); **Hà Tiên** (5hr.; 8:30, 11:30am, 1pm; 30,000Đ); **HCMC** (9-11hr.; every hr.; 38,000Đ); **Long Xuyên** (1hr., 8000Đ); **Mỹ Tho** (6hr.; 25,500Đ); **Rạch Giá** (3½hr.; 8:30, 11:30am; 20,000Đ). **Buses** to **HCMC** also depart from 387 Lê Lợi (6hr.; every hr. 4am-11pm; 50,000Đ.) **Ferries** depart from the pier at the west end of the market, near the intersection of Thượng Đăng Lễ and Trần Hưng Đạo. A boat heads to **Hà Tiên** (4hr.; 1pm; 80,000Đ); inquire at 86 Trần Hưng Đạo, 500m west of the market. **Moto** drivers also ply the bumpy dirt track to Hà Tiên (3hr.; 100,000Đ).

ORIENTATION AND PRACTICAL INFORMATION. Châu Đốc is 7km southeast of the Cambodian border. The town's grid-like street layout makes navigating relatively easy. **Đường Lê Lợi/Gia Long/Trần Hưng Đạo** runs the length of town along the shore. East of the market it becomes Lê Lợi, in the market Gia Long, and west of the market Trần Hưng Đạo. **Bạch Đằng, Nguyễn Hứu Cảnh,** and **Chi Lăng** are the central arteries, beginning at the river and continuing southwest to the public park and a temple. Central Châu Đốc is dominated by the **market,** spreading from Nguyễn Hữu Cảnh in the east to Thượng Đăng Lễ in the west, and south from the river to Phan Văn Vàng. The **MHB,** 54 Nguyễn Văn Thoại, exchanges cash but not traveler's checks. Châu Đốc has **no ATM** or cash advances. (Open M-F 7am-4:39pm.) A **pharmacy,** 3B Lê Lợi, lies a block east of the market. (☎866 769. Open daily 7am-9:30pm.) The **General Provincial Hospital,** 5 Lê Lợi, has English-speaking staff. (☎867 184. Open daily 5-7am, 10:30am-2pm, and 4-10pm.) **Internet** is available at **Quôc Thaní,** 16/2 Đuòng Nui Sam. (100Đ per min. Open daily 7:30am-10pm.) The **GPO,** 73 Lê Lợi, at the intersection with Nguyễn Hữu Cảnh just east of the market, has **international phones.** (☎866 191. Open daily 6am-10pm.)

ACCOMMODATIONS AND FOOD. The newest addition to the Châu Đốc hotel scene is **Mekong Guest House ❶,** Đuòng Lên Tao Ngô, Sam Mountain, 5km from Châu Đốc. This is possibly the best guest house in the entire Mekong Delta, with squeaky clean rooms, a lounge to watch DVDs, hammocks to read in, and Internet. The charming owner, Terry, can provide you with all the information you want. (☎861 870; mekongguesthouse@yahoo.com. Dorms US$3; doubles with A/C US$6.) If Mekong Guest House is full, there are options in downtown Châu Đốc. **Hotel Vĩnh Phước ❷,** 12-14 Quang Trưng, just off Bạch Đằng near the market, has comfortable rooms. (☎866 242. Singles with fan 80,000Đ; doubles with A/C 120,000Đ, with balcony 160,000Đ.) Slightly more upscale **Hàng Châu II ❷,** 10 Nguyễn Văn Thoại, offers some luxuries. (☎868 891. All rooms with telephone, fridge, and TV. Doubles with fan 120,000Đ, with A/C 170,000Đ.)

Makeshift restaurants lie at the entrance to the market at Chi Lăng and Bạch Đằng. They serve up *bò khô* (dry beef), a local specialty. If eating in a large tent doesn't catch your fancy, consider **Bày Bông,** 22 Thượng Đăng Lễ, which cooks up mouth-watering beefsteak with rice for 23,000D. (Open daily 7:30am-10pm.)

SIGHTS. About 5km southwest of town stands **Sam Mountain** (Núi Sam), the top of which offers panoramic views of endless rice fields (when it's not flooded) and of Cambodia. Sam Mountain is also the region's prime pilgrimage site, featuring the **Temple of Bà Chúa Xứ** ("Lady Ruling the Region"). Inside, the Lady's image

VIETNAM

BORDER CROSSING: TO CAMBODIA Those travelling in the Mekong Delta region can cross to Cambodia by boat from **Châu Đốc** (2hr., 1 per day) to the border village **Vinh Xuong** and on to **Neak Luong** (1½hr.). From Neak Luong, it's a short bus trip to **Phnom Penh** (1½hr.). Alternatively, a new road crossing will open up in September 2002. A US$5 bus (3hr.) will go to Phnom Penh via **Tinh Bien,** a border village just 20km from Châu Đốc. Ask at Mekong Guest House (see above) for more information. The trip can be arranged only through **Saigontourist** (see **Tour and Travel Agencies,** p. 964) in HCMC and costs US$15. **Cambodian visas** must be obtained in HCMC, although Tinh Bien will have this service in the near future (see **Opening New Doors Between Vietnam and Cambodia,** p. 985).

has received throngs of devotees and tourists since the early 19th century. The temple overflows with visitors at the end of the fourth lunar month (around April 26), when the faithful come to thank *Bà* for the gifts of the last year or pray for better luck in the year to come. On the other side of the road, the **Tây An Pagoda** sits at the foot of the mountain. The **tomb of Thoại Ngọc Hầu,** a retainer of Emperor Gia Long, is next door. The **Châu Phu Temple,** opposite the post office within the market on the east edge, is dedicated to local hero Nguyễn Hữu Cảnh, who vanquished the Khmers almost 300 years ago. This colorful *đình* (meeting house) contains a stairwell of central images, flanked by ornate wooden columns. (Open daily 7am-7pm.) Across the street, at the wooden jetty, hire a rowboat to explore the Hậu Giang River (30,000Đ per hr.). Highlights include **floating houses** with self-contained **fish farms,** the local **fish sauce factory,** the Cambodian border area, and the Muslim **Chàm communities,** famous for their weaving.

DAYTRIPS. **Tuc Dup Hill** and **Ba Chuc** are best reached on a motorcycle. Tuc Dup Hill lies about 45km to the southwest of Châu Đốc and 11km from Tri Ton. Coming from Châu Đốc, enter Tri Ton and take a right at the intersection with the sign to Tuc Dup Hill. To get to Ba Chuc from Tuc Dup Hill, backtrack about 1km from that intersection toward Châu Đốc and hang a left at the Tri Ton bus station. Ba Chuc village is about 12km away from there.

Also known as the Two Million Dollar Hill, **Tuc Dup Hill** is situated deep in the Mekong Delta near the Cambodian border. This hill is the site where Vietnamese soldiers withstood the force of the US military against odds of 3-to-20 between 1968 and 1976. The US military, although superior in technology and training, failed to invade the hill after spending two million dollars on firepower. Visitors are free to wander through natural tunnels, over huge boulders, and into hidden caves which served as meeting rooms, hospitals, living quarters, and command headquarters. Visitors who have some connection to the Vietnam War, particularly from an American perspective, may find it interesting to catch a glimpse of how the Vietnamese lived. Adorable children will likely guide you through the labyrinth and take you back to their parents' cafe—a small tip for the children is suggested. (Entrance fee 10,000Đ for two people and a motorcycle.) There are accommodations around the entrance to Tuc Dup, but you'll be better off in Châu Đốc.

If Tuc Dup Hill embodies perserverance in wartime, **Ba Chuc**'s "Skullbone Monument" conveys war's sheer horror. In a matter of days, from April 12 to April 30, 1978, the infamous **Khmer Rouge** invaded this village just 7km from the Cambodian border, massacring the 3157 residents. Only two people, one man and one woman, both of whom are alive today, survived the atrocity. This devastating event in world history is commemorated by a glass case enclosing dozens of skulls. The skulls, ranging from infants' to adults', are neatly stacked and face outwards, toward visitors. A nearby building contains horrifying pictures of the torture and slaughter of 1978. Be emotionally prepared for them. Next to the building is **Philai Pagoda,** better known as **Blood Pagoda.** Both Vietnamese and Cambodian residents of Ba Chuc hid in this pagoda during the massacre of 1978, hoping to escape the Khmer Rouge. They were found and mercilessly killed. Traces of blood still remain inside on the walls. (Entrance fee 3000Đ for two people and a motorcycle.)

RẠCH GIÁ ☎77

Travelers in Rạch Giá are en route to Phú Quốc Island, Hon Chong Beach, or Hà Tiên. People who stay on in this busy city and are able to avoid the seedier side will enjoy the friendly locals, colorful waterways, and delicious seafood.

TRANSPORTATION. The **airport** in Rạch Sơi has flights to **HCMC** (5 per week; 695,000Đ) and **Dương Đông** (5 per week; 450,000Đ); check with Vietnam Airlines (HCMC ☎823 08 96; www.vietnamairlines.com) for departure times. The **Rạch Sơi Station** (☎864 086) is 7km south on Nguyễn Trung Trực. Buses run to: **Cần Thơ** (3hr.; every hr.; 17,000Đ); **Châu Đốc** (5hr.; 30,000Đ); **HCMC** (6hr.; every hr.; 53,000Đ); and **Long Xuyên** (3hr.; 15,000Đ). Evening **minibuses** to **HCMC** (5hr.; 10, 11pm; 55,000Đ) leave from stand 10 on Mâu Thân (☎862 261). The **Provincial Bus Station** (☎862 274), on the corner of Đại Lội and Mâu, has buses to **Hòn Chông** (3hr.; 10,000Đ) and **Hà Tiên** (10,000Đ). The **ferry** to **Phú Quốc Island** (6-8hr.; 66,000Đ) leaves between 9 and 10am, from the pier at the end of Nguyễn Công Trứ. Tickets go on sale at 3pm the day before, but you can take the chance of purchasing one by 7:30am on the day of departure.

VIETNAM

ORIENTATION AND PRACTICAL INFORMATION. Rạch Giá straddles two branches of the Mekong River 250km from HCMC and 80km from Cần Thơ. Busy **Nguyễn Trung Trực** runs northwest, crosses the first tributary (becoming **Lê Lợi**), and ends in front of the statue. With your back to the statue, **Duy Tân** runs to your left; head left on Duy Tân, and the first right will be **Ly Tự Trọng.** Two blocks farther east, **Trần Phú** also crosses both tributaries, changing names both times (becoming **Đại Lộ** to the northwest and **Ngô Quyền** to the southeast). From the GPO, **Nguyễn Công Trứ** runs southward along the northwestern tributary to the ferry pier. Heading northwest on Đại Lộ, the second road to the right after the bridge is **Mâu Thân,** a busy thoroughfare that heads toward Hà Tiên. Services in Rạch Giá include: **Kiên Giang Tourist,** 12 Ly Tự Trọng, opposite Thanh Bình Hotel (☎862 081; map of the city, province, and Hà Tiến 10,000Đ; open M-Sa 7am-5pm); the **GPO,** 2 Tu Duc (☎862 551; open daily 6:30am-10pm; **international phones**); the **Vietcombank,** 1 Huỳnh Mẫn Đạt, next door to the GPO (☎863 178; open M-F 7-11am and 1-4pm); the **General Hospital,** 46 Lê Lợi (☎863 325), before the bridge (on the south side of the island), on the right; and many **pharmacies** around the city center (open daily 6am-6pm). **Internet** access is available at the **Children's Palace,** an amusement park on Nguyễn Công Trứ. (100Đ per min. Open daily 7am-9pm.)

ACCOMMODATIONS AND FOOD. The conspicuous "*khách san*" ("hotel") signs dominate the budget scene. Most are in the city center and charge 50,000-70,000Đ for a double with fan, and up to 120,000Đ for A/C. **Binh Minh ❷,** 44 Phạm Hồng Thái, has clean, bright rooms. (☎862 154. Doubles with fan and bath 90,000Đ, with A/C and bath 120,000Đ; triples 150,000Đ.) Down the road, **Tô Châu Hotel ❷,** 16 Lê Lợi, near the Nguyễn Trung Trực statue, offers blissful A/C. (☎863 718. Doubles with bath 120,000-140,000Đ; triples with bath 150,000Đ.) **Nhà Trọ Kim Ngân ❶,** 36 Võ Thị Sáu, is a clean and friendly guest house that provides great value for money. To get there from the town center, follow Trần Phú, turn right onto

Trần Quốc Tuấn, then right onto Võ Thị Sáu. (☎863 118. Singles with fan 30,000Đ; doubles with fan 50,000Đ, with fan and bath 70,000Đ.) Those hoping to save money should head to the *nhà tro* (guest house) area near the pier. Be aware that this option is not for the faint-hearted, nor the very tall, as low ceilings could pose discomfort. **Xuñ't Ha'i ❶,** under the Hem 38 sign has an English-speaking staff. (☎863 942. Doubles with bath 30,000Đ.) Up the road, **Nha Tro Xuñn Mai ❶** has cheaper rooms and cleaner baths, but no English is spoken. (☎868 437. Singles with bath 20,000Đ; doubles with bath 30,000Đ.) There are not many restaurant options in Rạch Giá. Cheap *cỏm* food stalls line Nguyễn Trung Trực. **Trường Cafe ❶,** 181 Trần Phú, is a simple, popular cafe with food cooked out front and eaten inside. (Pork ribs and rice run 8000Đ. Open daily 6am-6pm.)

SIGHTS. Rạch Giá has few sights of interest for the visitor—the list consists of just two temples. **Nguyễn Trung Trực Temple** is in the town center on Nguyễn Công Trứ facing the canal, 500m from the post office. Its namesake is a local hero, who led a daring raid in the 1860s against the French warship *Esperance.* He was later captured and executed. (Open daily 6am-9pm.) Outside, machete-wielding women chop up plant parts for the **traditional medicine clinic.** An array of dried stems and leaves covers every sun-exposed surface in sight. Surrounded by lush gardens, **Phật Lớn Pagoda (Chùa Phật Lớn),** 2km north of the post office on Quang Trưng, is a Theravada Buddhist temple that serves Rạch Giá's Cambodian population. A beautiful series of paintings that chronicle the Buddha's life encircle the sanctuary. (Open daily 4am-5:30pm.)

HÀ TIÊN ☎77

Tucked into the far southwest corner of Vietnam, picturesque Hà Tiên is sweet relief at the end of a delta tour. This small coastal town is surrounded by gorgeous turquoise water and thriving farmland irrigated by Mekong tributaries fanning out into the sea. Hà Tiên fell into Vietnamese hands in 1708 when Mạc Cửu, a Chinese governor appointed by the Khmer, shifted his allegiance to the Nguyễn Lords in Huế. Tensions ignited when the Khmer Rouge massacred 130 villagers in 1978. Stability has since returned to the region, and the ethnically mixed population draws a peaceful livelihood from fishing and farming.

TRANSPORTATION. The **bus station** (☎852 560) is southeast of town, across the Tô Châu River. Buses run daily to: **Cần Thơ** (4hr.; 30,000Đ); **HCMC** (8hr.; 8am, 8pm; 49,000Đ); **Long Xuyên** (3hr.; 6am, 10pm; 28,000Đ); **Rạch Giá** (3½hr.; frequently; 15,000Đ). The 100km, 4hr. trip to **Châu Đốc** necessitates hiring a moto driver (usually US$12-15). From the bus station, a pontoon bridge (toll with bike 500Đ, with moto 1000Đ) leads to Hà Tiên's busiest thoroughfare, **Trần Hầu,** which runs parallel to the river and west into town past accommodations, cafes, restaurants, and the **market** (open daily 5am-7pm). **Ferries** to **Phú Quốc Island** are limited to Vietnamese only; foreigners must depart from **Rạch Giá** (see p. 981) or **Bà Hòn,** the latter of which can be reached by bus (7000Đ) or moto. The ferry supposedly leaves at 9am, but get there early because it leaves when full (5hr.; 60,000-100,000Đ).

ORIENTATION AND PRACTICAL INFORMATION. Hà Tiên is 338km from HCMC, 90km from Rạch Giá, and 7km from the Cambodian border. Hà Tiên's main road, **Trần Hầu,** runs west from the pontoon bridge through the market, terminating at the intersection with **Phương Thành,** which runs north to the Cambodian border.

Kiên Giang Tourist offers Western Union money transfers and is in the Đông Hồ Hotel; after crossing the bridge into town, it's across the street. **BIDV Bank,** 15A Chi Lang St., has currency exchange service. (Open M-F 7:30am-4:30pm.) There are several **pharmacies** on Trần Hầu in the market vicinity. (Open daily roughly 6am-

10pm.) To get to the **police** station, go right after the bridge and left on Tô Châu. The **General Hospital** is at the far (north) end of Bạch Đằng, at the intersection with Mạc Cửu. The **post office** is on Tô Châu St., one block north from the bridge. (☎852 190. Fax and **international phone**. Open daily 6:30am-9pm.) **Minh Nguyen,** across from the post office, has **Internet.** (500Đ per min. Open daily 7am-10pm.)

ACCOMMODATIONS AND FOOD. Hà Tiên is popular in the dry season, with swarms of minibuses invading this serene spot which only recently acquired daytime electricity. The **Hải Vân Hotel ❷,** 646A Đ. Lam Sơn, one block off Trần Hầu, has very comfortable rooms and an accommodating staff. (☎852 872. All rooms have hot shower and satellite TV. Doubles with fan 70,000Đ, with A/C 120,000-150,000Đ.) **Đông Hồ Hotel ❷,** across the bridge on Trần Hầu, has a great, albeit noisy location. (☎852 141. Doubles with fan and bath 70,000Đ, with A/C, hot water, TV, and fridge 120,000Đ; 4-person dorms 120,000Đ/150,000Đ.) **Thanh Xuân Room for Rent ❶,** 952A Bạch Đằng, on the road just west of the bridge, is a clean guest house that doubles as a barber shop. (☎852 318. Singles with fan 50,000Đ; doubles 60,000Đ, with A/C 100,000Đ.)

Cheap cafes selling *hủ tiếu* soup, *phở*, and rice dishes line Trần Hầu along the sea side. However, most workers don't speak English. You'll have to mime your order to try *cơm sườn heo nướng* (grilled pork with rice; 6000Đ), or *cơm tôm* (cooked shrimp with rice; 7000Đ). **Tiệm Cơm Hương Biển,** 974 Tô Châo St., specializes in shrimp dishes called *tôm chiên bột*. (Open daily 6am-8pm.) One block over on Bạch Đằng, **Quán Cóm Phó Tiní,** has cheap meat dishes (5000Đ).

SIGHTS. Some of the most pleasant sightseeing in Hà Tiên can be done by bike. The **tomb of Mạc Cửu,** erected by Emperor Gia Long in 1809, is 2km northwest of the town center. To reach Mạc Cửu, head away from town on Phương Thành, past the church and turn left down the dirt path, and left again at its end. The pagoda's entrance is 50m down on the right. Turning right on the initial dirt path leads to **Phú Dung Pagoda,** another small temple. About 4km north of town on Phương Thành, a wide, tree-covered shaft of gray rock thrusts skyward. This is the entrance to **Thạch Động (Stone Cave),** marked by a roadside gray fist in memory of 130 Vietnamese slaughtered by the Khmer Rouge in 1978. From the temple, there are stunning views of geometrically arranged rice fields, nearby Cambodia, and the Gulf of Thailand. (1000Đ. Open daily until dusk.) **Bãi Mũi Nai (Deer's Nose Beach),** a strip of black sand flanked by thickly forested hills and a strip of snake stands, is popular with locals and their inner tubes (1500Đ). To reach the beach, continue down the road past Thạch Động, take the first left, and continue 3km; an entrance is on the right. Stunning views of the area abound, though the water is a bit murky. In the mid-1990s, many Vietnamese embarked on boats here with hopes of escaping the war-ridden country and reaching places like Thailand or Australia. Hà Tiên also boasts some in-town attractions. The region is known for its **tortoise shell** *(đồi mồi)* carvings. Visitors might also catch wind of Hà Tiên's famous **four-headed coconut tree** (Dùa Bốn Ngon) on **Lâm Văn Quang.** To find it, follow Trần Hầu west until it almost turns back on itself. Head toward the church, turning left onto Lâm Văn Quang. The tree is in a yard on the right, 300m down the road.

DAYTRIPS FROM HÀ TIÊN: BEACHES AT HÒN CHONG. Twenty kilometers southeast of Hà Tiên (65km northwest of Rạch Giá), a feeder road branches off at the town of Bà Hòn, leading 15km southward to **Hòn Chong.** This peninsula harbors the most seductive beaches in the delta. The shore stretches east several kilometers before ending inside a crowded and touristy park called **Hòn Phụ Tử (Father and Son Islet).** Entry to the park is a meager 1000Đ. Beaches on the road before the park are just as inviting. Moto drivers will do a day-long round-trip from

Hà Tiên for 80,000Đ. As a resort village, Hòn Chông lacks cheap guest houses, although the medium-range accommodations are of high quality. Driving from Hà Tiên or Bà Hòn, you will first come across **Green Hill Hotel ❸,** which offers clean rooms on a beach-surveying bluff. (☎854 369. Restaurant attached. Doubles with bath, hot water, fridge, TV, and fan US$10, with A/C US$15; huge luxury rooms with bathtub US$20.) About 0.5km from Green Hill Hotel, toward the beach park, **Milan Hotel ❷** has new, clean rooms as well as a restaurant, karaoke, and pool table. (☎759 044. Doubles with fan, TV, hot water, and fridge 120,000Đ, with A/C 150,000Đ.) About 400m before the park entrance **Hòn Trẹm ❸** boasts luxury beachfront cabins. (☎854 331. Doubles with bath, A/C, fridge, and satellite TV 140,000Đ.)

Cheap *cơm bình dân* (6000-8000Đ) is at several stands around the park. Inside the park, rows of souvenir stands pave the way to **Chùa Hang (Cave Pagoda),** a temple built into caves on the adjacent hillside. Islands of fluted gray stone lie offshore, including the double crags of **Hòn Phụ Tử,** said to resemble a father and son awaiting a faraway mother. At the far end of the beach, boat tours go for 5000Đ, and kayaks rent for 10,000Đ per 15min. For a bite to eat in the park, head to **Hồng Ngọc,** which is on the right when heading toward the temple. The enthusiastic owner is fluent in French. A nice restaurant in town, other than the ones in the hotels, **Tan Phat Restaurant ❸** is built over the water and has an extensive seafood menu in English. (About 1.5km from Green Hill Hotel back toward Bà Hòn.)

VIETNAM

PHÚ QUỐC ISLAND

Phú Quốc Island, closer to Cambodia than Vietnam, has been claimed and reclaimed by the Thai, Khmer, and Vietnamese throughout its history. Now, the island is claimed by Star Cruise Lines and an ever-increasing number of resorts. With major development schemes planned, such as hydroelectric power and paved roads, the commercialization of this island will only grow. For now, there are still hidden coves and secluded and dramatic landscapes for every solitude-seeker, but the island's idyllic air is dissipating fast—get it while you still can.

THE VIEW FROM ABOVE

Gateway cities: Dương Đông, the island's largest urban spread, to the west, and An Thới, to the south.
Beaches: Bãi Tam (Long Beach), Bãi Dan, Han Yen, and Bãi Sao.
Highlights: Trying the world-renowned fish sauce. You know you love it.

TRANSPORTATION. **Vietnam Airlines** (☎846 086) flies to **HCMC** from Dương Đông (8:20am; 685,000Đ) and to **Rạch Sới** (M-Tu, Th-Sa 8:20am; 450,000Đ). Purchase tickets at least 5 days in advance. Three ferries leave daily from Phú Quốc to the mainland: from An Thới to **Rạch Giá** (6-8hr.; 9am; 66,000Đ); from Hàm Ninh to **Bà Hòn** (5hr.; 10am; 80,000-100,000Đ); from Cầu Sáu to **Bà Hòn** (4hr.; 9am; 80,000-100,000Đ). A 45min., 30,000Đ moto ride goes the rest of the distance from An Thới to Dương Đông.

ORIENTATION. Phú Quốc Island (48km long, and 12km wide in the middle) is at its northwest tip just 7km from Cambodia. The major points of entry are by ferry from Rạch Giá to **An Thới** on the island's southern tip, and by plane from HCMC or Rạch Sới to **Dương Đông** in the west. Dương Đông is the largest town on the island, and most travelers stay nearby. A series of sandy paths connect the smaller villages in the mountainous east and the flatter west. Dương Đông is in central Phú Quốc on its west coast, 28km north of An Thới.

DƯƠNG ĐÔNG ☎77

With the start of weekly visits from the behemoth Star Cruise Lines boats, life in Dương Đông has assumed a seven-day periodicity. Every Saturday at 12:30pm, the entire town turns to the harbor to greet its tanned, relaxed, and above all moneyed guests with open arms and sticky fingers. The other six days of the week, the new, nearby, and very posh Saigon-Phú Quốc Resort seems an anomaly, and the town goes quietly about its coastal existence.

TRANSPORTATION AND PRACTICAL INFORMATION. The town's major road begins before the airport and heads west into town where it crosses **Nguyễn Trung Trực** bridge, ending where it intersects with **Bạch Dằng,** which runs to the coast. Two blocks up from the intersection, **30 Tháng 4** leads eastward out of town, along the Dương Đâng River, passing the post office and the hospital. **Buses** run once a day between An Thới and Dương Đông. The bus from An Thới to **Dương Đông** leaves soon after the ferry from Rạch Giá arrives (around 4pm), and the bus from Dương Đông to **An Thới** leaves at 7am from near the post office. The **market** is on the embankment next to the Nguyễn Trung Trực bridge. (Open daily 5am-6pm.) A **pharmacy** is on Nguyễn Trung Trực, 50m away from the market, toward the airport (☎848 121. Open daily 7am-9pm.) The **hospital** (☎846 074) is 1km from town. Currently, the cheapest **Internet** access is at Dịch Vụ Vi Tính, Húng Vương, and Khu Phô's. (1000Đ per min. Open daily 7am-5pm.) The **post office** has fax and **international** calling services. (☎846 040. Open daily 7am-9pm.)

ACCOMMODATIONS AND FOOD. Travelers usually stay on the beach near Dương Đông, although inland options are either brimming with amenities or are much cheaper. The **Tropicana Resort ❸,** 2km from the town center, is a bit pricier than other options, but the luxurious bungalows are worth it. The shaded beachside bar and restaurant chairs are open to all. (☎847 127. Internet 2000Đ per min. 2-person rooms US$15; 2-person bungalows US$25-35.) The cheapest option along the beach is brand-new **Nam Phương ❷,** just 1km south of town, before Tropicana. Although not much English is spoken, the family-run business provides good service. (☎846 319. Doubles with fan US$6; bungalows with A/C US$20.) Most hotels are in Dương Đông. **Hương Toáh ❶,** on Nguyễn Thái Bình, the first road to the right from the airport, heading out of town, has secure, clean doubles in a quiet atmosphere, but no English spoken. (☎846 792. Without bath 40,000Đ, with bath 60,000Đ.) **Hotel Mini Hồng Hạnh ❶,** opposite the airport, has a beautiful courtyard and rooms with fridge, TV, and private bath. (☎846 187. Rooms with fan 80,000Đ, with A/C 180,000Đ. Bikes 30,000Đ per day; moto rentals 100,000Đ.)

IN RECENT NEWS

OPENING NEW DOORS BETWEEN VIETNAM AND CAMBODIA

Travel in Southeast Asia, particularly in Southern Vietnam and Cambodia, will change drastically in the near future with the establishment of one building: an immigration office in Tinh Bien (Vietnam). Just 20km from Châu Đốc, Tinh Bien will be the first border crossing on land in the Mekong Delta and will serve as the second border crossing in all of the Mekong Delta after Vinh Xuong.

The opening of Tinh Bien as a border crossing—it does not yet have an official name—in September 2002 will not only provide more itinerary options for travelers from HCMC to Cambodia via the Mekong Delta, but will also permit a quick 3hr. bus ride from the Vietnamese border, Châu Đốc, and Phnom Penh, currently being arranged by Châu Đốc's Mekong Guest House. More importantly, the overland border crossing will create new traffic flow between the Mekong Delta and Southern Cambodia's Sihanoukville. Otherwise, Southern Cambodia can be reached only through Phnom Penh (except for the boat to and from Trat in Eastern Thailand).

The most significant change will take place when the Tinh Bien immigration office starts to offer tourist visas on the spot for entry into both countries. Currently, visas must be applied for in HCMC and Phnom Penh prior to crossing. The new service will undoubtedly put smiles on the faces of itinerary-less wanderers who head in whatever direction the wind blows, wherever the sun shines.

For delicious seafood head to **Lê Giang ❷**, 289 Khu Phô Trần Hưng. Try the baked fish with rice (20,000Đ). (Open daily 5am-10pm.) **An Thu ❷**, 100m on the right heading away from the airport toward Nguyễn Trung Trực bridge in Dương Đông, features seafood goodies for 10,000Đ. (Open daily 6am-10pm.) To find **Tươi Thăm ❶**, turn right on the dirt road after the post office, the street with the beach-side hotels. Tasty meals are served steaming hot for under 10,000Đ.

BEACHES. Phú Quốc Island boasts a stunning landscape, and largely, an empty one. Most beaches are accessible by sandy paths removed from main roads, so you can claim a patch of sand for yourself. You can hire a moto driver and set a return time, or hire your own moto for about 100,000Đ per day from most hotels. **Bãi Tam (Long Beach)** stretches from Dương Đông to An Thới on the west coast, offering kilometers of convenient access. A short trip east of Dương Đông through pepper groves leads to the local bathing area of choice, **Suối Đá Bán,** a river with a series of waterfalls and clear freshwater. Access to the northwest and north parts of the island opened up to foreigners two years ago, offering views of lush forests and a mountain peak in Cambodia. The east coast of Phú Quốc Island houses coves and inlets and the island's most renowned beaches. Directly east of Dương Đông is **Hàm Ninh**, a small seaside town with a rocky stretch of coast that is home to tide pools and magnificent *ốc* (seashells). Farther south, **Bãi Sao** has gorgeous turquoise water and white-sand beaches. Foreigners and Vietnamese alike gravitate to this natural beauty and enjoy fresh seafood at the few restaurants that line the beach. (To get to Bãi Sao, take a moto there in the morning and arrange for pick up in the afternoon for about 8000Đ. To drive there on your own, head south to An Thới from Dương Đông and hang a left at the top of the hill after the sign that marks 5km to An Thới. It's a bumpy 5min. ride to heaven.) **Hòn Thóm** is an island off Phú Quốc's south coast, which has great scuba diving and snorkeling sites. (Boats can be hired at Tropicana Hotel in Dương Đông or An Thới.)

APPENDIX

COUNTRY CODES

Australia	61	Myanmar	95
Brunei	673	New Zealand	64
Cambodia	855	Philippines	63
Canada	1	Singapore	65
Indonesia	62	South Africa	27
Ireland	353	Thailand	66
Laos	856	United Kingdom	44
Malaysia	60	United States	1

MEASUREMENTS

1 meter (m) = 1.09 yards (yd.)	1 yard = 0.92m
1 meter (m) = 3.28 feet (ft.)	1 foot = 0.305m
1 kilometer (km) = 0.625 miles (mi.)	1 mile = 1.6km
1 kilogram (kg) = 2.2 pounds (lb.)	1 pound = 0.45kg

LANGUAGES

Languages in Southeast Asia are without exception extremely different from English. Even gifted learners won't be able to pick up more than the barest rudiments of Thai during a short trip, although the rewards of making an effort—however small—to learn local languages are great.

PRONUNCIATION KEY

TONES: Thai, Lao, Burmese and Vietnamese are tonal languages; word meanings are partially determined by intonation and pitch. Five tones in Thai and Lao are neutral, low, high, falling, rising (the phrasebook doesn't distinguish between high- and low-falling tones in Lao); these tones are distinguished in the phrasebook by diacritical markings over the vowels to which they apply. Neutral tones (unmarked) are spoken in a level voice in the middle of the speaker's vocal range. Low (marked thus over the letter "a": à) and high (á) tones are spoken in level pitch from the bottom and top of the speaker's range, respectively. Falling tones (â) begin high and end low, as in the English pronunciation of "Hey!" Rising tones (ä) begin low and end high, as in the English interrogative "What?" Six Vietnamese tones are neutral, high (á), low (à), stopped (ă), rising-falling (ã), broken (ạ).

VOWELS: Vowels are very roughly pronounced as in English, except the "eu" sound in Thai and Lao, which represents the vowel sound in the French "bleu."

CONSONANTS: Consonants are pronounced (very roughly) as in English. Exceptions: in Bahasa Indonesia and Bahasa Malayu, "c" is pronounced "ch" as in "cherry." In Vietnamese, "d" is pronounced "z" as in "Zulu" in North, or "y" as in "yankee" in South, while "đ" and "Đ" are pronounced "d" as in "delta." "X" and "x" are pronounced "s" as in "sierra"; "s" and "S" pronounced "sh" as in "shovel"; "ph" pronounced "f" as in "foxtrot." "Th" is usually pronounced as in "tango."

ENGLISH	THAI//LAO	BURMESE
one	neung // neung	ti
two	säwng // säwng	hni
three	sähm // sähm	thoun
four	sèe // see	le
five	hâh // hâh	nga
six	hòk // hók	chau
seven	jèt // jét	khun ni
eight	pàet // pâet	shi
nine	gâo // kâo	ko
ten	sìp // síp	tahse
eleven	sìp-èt // síp-ét	she
twelve	sìp-säwng // síp-säwng	seh-hni
twenty	yêe-sìp // sáo	hna se
thirty	sähm-sìp // sähm-síp	thoun ze
forty	sèe-sìp // see-síp	lei ze
fifty	hâh-sìp // häh-síp	nga ze
one hundred	róy // hâwy	taya
one thousand	pun // pán	taya fahse
hello	sàwatdee // sábài-dèe	mingala ba
good-bye	sawàtdee // pai jao	thwabi
yes / no	<n/a> / mâi // ya / baw	hou ke / hin in
thank you	khàwp khun // khâwp jài	kye zui tin ba de
excuse me	khäw tôht // khäw thôt	(m) khin mya, (f) shin
How are you?	ben yahng ngai // sábài-dèe baw	nei kaun ye la
fine/well.	sabai-dee // sábài-dee	nei kaun ba de
Help!	chûay dûay // suay dae	lai kya ba oun
doctor	mäw // mäw	hsaya wun
police	tham ruat // tham ploh	ye sa khan
hospital	rohng paiahban // hóhng mäw	hsei youn
toilet	sûam // sûam	ein tha
Where is . . . ?	. . . yòo têe näi // . . . yôo säi	. . . bema shi th a le
to the right	khwä meu // lîaw khwaa	nya be cho
to the left	saí meu // lîaw sâai	be be cho
straight ahead	throng bai // pai seu seu	te da thwai
How much?	tâo rài // tao dài	da be lan le
bus	rót meh // lót meh	ba saka
train	rót fai // lot duan	mi ya tha
plane	krêuang bin // héua bìn	lei yin byan
car	rót yon // lot	twei
restaurant	ráhn ah-hän // lán ah-han	sa than hsain
guest house	bâhn pák // häw hap khäek	e yei tha
market	thah làt // thah làt	zei
bank	tanahkhan // thanáhkháhn	ban
post office	praisanee // pài-sá-née	sa dai
yesterday	mêua wahn née // mêu wáhn nêe	manei ga
today	wan née // mêu nêe	dinei
tomorrow	prûng née // mêu eun	ne hpan

APPENDIX

KHMER	VIETNAMESE	MALAY/INDONESIAN
mouy	một	satu
pee	hai	dua
bei	ba	tiga
boun	bốn	empat
bram	năm	lima
bram-mouy	sáu	eman
bram-pee	bảy	tujuh
bram-bei	tám	delapan
bram-boun	chín	sembilan
duop	mười	sepuluh
duop-mouy	mười m t	sebelas
duop-pee	mười hai	duabelas
maphei	hai mươi	duapuluh
samseb	ba mươi	tigapuluh
sairseb	bốn mươi	empatpuluh
hahseb	năm mươi	limapuluh
mouy-rouy	một trăm	seratus
mouy-paun	một ngàn	seribu
suas dei	Chào ông (to males) Chào bà (to females)	selamat siang (good afternoon)
lia soon hao-i	Chào ông/Chào bà	selamat tinggal (to one staying)/ selamat jalan (to one going)
baht (males), chaat (females) / te	Dạ / Không	ya / tidak
aw kohn	Cám ơn	terima kasih
sohm toh	Xin lỗi	ma'af
niak sohk sabah-ay tay	ần/aẩ	Apa kabar?
khnyohm sohk sabah-ay	ần/aẩ	baik
juay khnyohm pawng	Cứu với	Tolong!
kroo paet	bác sĩ	dokter
po'leez	cảnh sát	polisi
mun'ti peyt	bệnh viện	rumah sakit
bawng-kohn	buồng tắm	kamar kecil
. . . neuv ai nah	ở đâu	Di mana . . . ?
bawt chweng	rẽ trái	ke kanan
bawt sdam	rẽ phải	ke kiri
teuv trawng	đi thẳng	terus menerus
nee tlay pohnmahn	Giá bao nhiêu	Berapa?
lahn chnual	xe buýt	bas (Mal.)/bis (Ind.)
roht plirng	xe lửa	kereta api
yohn haw	máy bay	kapal terbang
laht	xe ô tô	mobil
restoorahn	tiệm ăn	rumah makan
oh-tail	nhà khách	wisma
psah	chợ	pasar
thniakia	ngân hàng	bank
praisuhnee	bưu điện	pejebat pos (Mal.) kantor pos (Ind.)
m'sool mein	hôm qua	kemarin
thngay nee	hôm nay	hari ini
thngay saik	ngày mai	besok

APPENDIX

CLIMATE

High and low tourist seasons roughly correspond with rainy and dry seasons in Southeast Asia. There is no uniform seasonal pattern for the region; see the **Facts and Figures** section in each chapter for country-specific variations. Keep in mind that the monsoon is rarely an impediment for travel in the region, except for in rural Laos and Cambodia. Generally, rainfall peaks from May to September north of Singapore (including the Philippines), and between December to March south and east of Singapore (including Indonesia). To roughly convert Celsius to Fahrenheit, double the Celsius and add 30.

Temperature and Precipitation by City

City	January			April			July			October		
	High (F/C)	Low (F/C)	Rain (in)	High (F/C)	Low (F/C)	Rain (in)	High (F/C)	Low (F/C)	Rain (in)	High (F/C)	Low (F/C)	Rain (in)
Bali	90/32	76/25	13.9	91/33	76/24	3.5	87/31	74/23	2.1	90/32	76/24	3.6
Bangkok	91/33	71/22	0.4	96/36	80/27	2.4	92/33	78/26	5.7	91/33	78/25	7.2
Bandar Seri Begawan	87/30	74/23	11.7	88/31	77/25	6.9	90/32	77/25	8.8	88/31	76/24	11.9
Hanoi	70/21	54/13	0.9	79/26	68/20	4.0	90/32	82/28	10.2	85/29	74/23	5.9
Hong Kong	68/20	59/15	1.2	79/26	71/22	5.6	90/32	82/28	14.4	85/29	76/25	4.8
Jakarta	90/32	75/24	13.1	93/34	75/24	8.3	93/34	72/22	3.4	95/35	74/23	6.3
Kuala Lumpur	91/33	74/23	6.5	93/34	76/24	10.6	92/33	74/24	5.2	91/33	75/24	10.3
Manila	88/31	71/22	0.7	96/35	76/24	1.0	91/33	77/25	17.7	90/32	76/24	7.2
Phnom Penh	74/23	62/17	0.2	84/29	75/24	3.3	82/28	77/25	10.5	80/27	74/23	3.4
Phuket	90/32	73/23	1.8	93/34	77/25	6.1	88/31	78/25	10.2	88/31	76/24	14.3
Singapore	87/30	77/25	6.5	91/33	79/26	10.6	89/32	80/27	5.2	89/32	79/26	10.3
Vientiane	82/28	58/15	0.4	91/33	74/23	3.6	88/31	78/25	9.9	88/31	70/21	3.4
Yangon	91/33	67/19	3.5	101/38	78/25	3.6	87/30	78/25	3.5	90/32	79/26	2.9

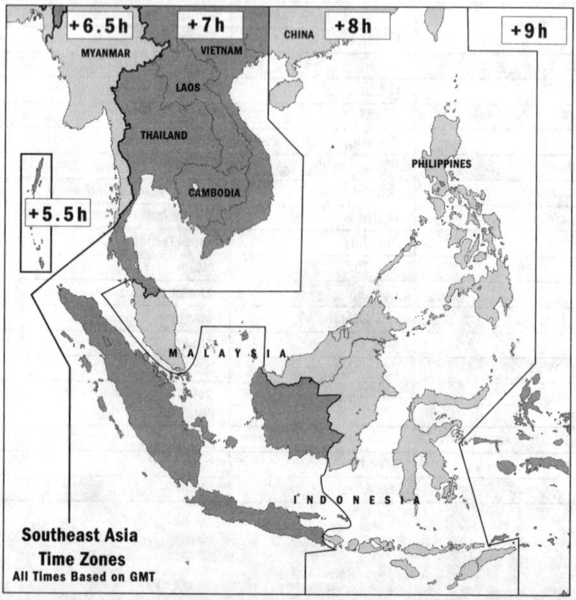

APPENDIX

Check this out!
EXPERIENCE THE ASIA MOST TRAVELLERS MISS OUT ON
- AT A PRICE YOU CAN AFFORD!
INTREPID
MAX GROUP SIZE OF 12
EXPERIENCED LEADERS
LOCAL TRANSPORT
ACCOMMODATION IN GUESTHOUSES, HOMESTAYS & TRIBAL VILLAGES
INTREPID RUNS OVER 170 TRIPS IN 18 COUNTRIES!
CENTRAL ASIA
SOUTH EAST ASIA
CHINA
INDIA
NEPAL
INDOCHINA
EGYPT
BRITISH AIRWAYS
Tourism for Tomorrow
Highly Commended 2001
www.intrepidtravel.com
Order your brochure now - you could win a trip!

INDEX

A

B

C

D

INDEX

INDEX

I

J

K

INDEX

INDEX

INDEX

INDEX

INDEX

INDEX

WHO WE ARE

A NEW LET'S GO

With a sleeker look and innovative new content, we have revamped the entire series to reflect more than ever the needs and interests of the independent traveler. Here are just some of the improvements you will notice when traveling with the new *Let's Go*.

MORE PRICE OPTIONS

Still the best resource for budget travelers, *Let's Go* recognizes that everyone needs the occassional indulgence. Our "Big Splurges" indicate establishments that are actually worth those extra pennies (pulas, pesos, or pounds), and price-level symbols (❶ ❷ ❸ ❹ ❺) allow you to quickly determine whether an accommodation or restaurant will break the bank. We may have diversified, but we'll never lose our budget focus—"Hidden Deals" reveal the best-kept travel secrets.

BEYOND THE TOURIST EXPERIENCE

Our Alternatives to Tourism chapter offers ideas on immersing yourself in a new community through study, work, or volunteering.

AN INSIDER'S PERSPECTIVE

As always, every item is written and researched by our on-site writers. This year we have highlighted more viewpoints to help you gain an even more thorough understanding of the places you are visiting.

IN RECENT NEWS. *Let's Go* correspondents around the globe report back on current regional issues that may affect you as a traveler.

CONTRIBUTING WRITERS. Respected scholars and former *Let's Go* writers discuss topics on society and culture, going into greater depth than the usual guidebook summary.

THE LOCAL STORY. From the Parisian monk toting a cell phone to the Russian *babushka* confronting capitalism, *Let's Go* shares its revealing conversations with local personalities—a unique glimpse of what matters to real people.

FROM THE ROAD. Always helpful and sometimes downright hilarious, our researchers share useful insights on the typical (and atypical) travel experience.

SLIMMER SIZE

Don't be fooled by our new, smaller size. *Let's Go* is still packed with invaluable travel advice, but now it's easier to carry with a more compact design.

FORTY-THREE YEARS OF WISDOM

For over four decades *Let's Go* has provided the most up-to-date information on the hippest cafes, the most pristine beaches, and the best routes from border to border. It all started in 1960 when a few well-traveled students at Harvard University handed out a 20-page mimeographed pamphlet of their tips on budget travel to passengers on student charter flights to Europe. From humble beginnings, *Let's Go* has grown to cover six continents and *Let's Go: Europe* still reigns as the world's best-selling travel guide. This year we've beefed up our coverage of Latin America with *Let's Go: Costa Rica* and *Let's Go: Chile;* on the other side of the globe, we've added *Let's Go: Thailand* and *Let's Go: Hawaii*. Our new guides bring the total number of titles to 61, each infused with the spirit of adventure that travelers around the world have come to count on.

Book your air, hotel, and transportation all in one place.
Hotel or hostel? Cruise or canoe? Car? Plane? Camel? Wherever you're going, visit Yahoo! Travel and get total control over your arrangements. Even choose your seat assignment. So. One hump or two? travel.yahoo.com
powered by hp
YAHOO!
Travel
DO YOU YAHOO!?

MAP INDEX

MAP LEGEND

- Hospital
- Police
- Post Office
- Tourist Office
- Bank
- Embassy/Consulate
- Site or Point of Interest
- Telephone Office
- Theater
- Library
- Pharmacy
- Airport
- Taxi Stand
- Minibus Taxi
- Bus Station
- Train Station
- METRO STATION
- Ferry Landing
- Church
- Mosque
- Wat
- Hindu Temple
- Buddhist Temple
- Pagoda
- Museum
- Hotel/Hostel
- Food & Drink
- Shopping
- Nightlife
- Internet Café
- Mountain
- Cave
- Pedestrian Zone
- Park
- Beach
- Water

The Let's Go compass always points NORTH.